Financial & Managerial Accounting

8th edition

INFORMATION FOR DECISIONS

John J. Wild

University of Wisconsin at Madison

Ken W. Shaw

University of Missouri at Columbia

Mc
Graw
Hill
Education

To my students and family, especially Kimberly, Jonathan, Stephanie, and Trevor.
To my wife Linda and children Erin, Emily, and Jacob.

FINANCIAL AND MANAGERIAL ACCOUNTING: INFORMATION FOR DECISIONS, EIGHTH EDITION

Published by McGraw-Hill Education, 2 Penn Plaza, New York, NY 10121. Copyright ©2019 by McGraw-Hill Education. All rights reserved. Printed in the United States of America. Previous editions ©2018, 2016, and 2013. No part of this publication may be reproduced or distributed in any form or by any means, or stored in a database or retrieval system, without the prior written consent of McGraw-Hill Education, including, but not limited to, in any network or other electronic storage or transmission, or broadcast for distance learning.

Some ancillaries, including electronic and print components, may not be available to customers outside the United States.

This book is printed on acid-free paper.

1 2 3 4 5 6 7 8 9 LWI 21 20 19 18

ISBN 978-1-260-24785-5 (bound edition)
MHID 1-260-24785-6 (bound edition)
ISBN 978-1-260-41719-7 (loose-leaf edition)
MHID 1-260-41719-0 (loose-leaf edition)

Executive Portfolio Manager: *Steve Schuetz*
Product Developers: *Michael McCormick, Christina Sanders*
Marketing Manager: *Michelle Williams*
Content Project Managers: *Lori Koetters, Brian Nacik*
Buyer: *Sandy Ludovissy*
Design: *Debra Kubiak*
Content Licensing Specialist: *Melissa Homer*
Cover Image: *Runner: ©Maridav/Shutterstock; Statistics icons: ©A-spring/Shutterstock;*
   Background image: ©Vector work/Shutterstock
Compositor: *Aptara®, Inc.*

All credits appearing on page or at the end of the book are considered to be an extension of the copyright page.

Library of Congress Cataloging-in-Publication Data
Names: Wild, John J., author. | Shaw, Ken W., author.
Title: Financial and managerial accounting : information for decisions / John
   J. Wild, University of Wisconsin at Madison, Ken W. Shaw, University of
   Missouri at Columbia.
Description: 8th Edition. | Dubuque, IA : McGraw-Hill Education, [2018] |
   Revised edition of Financial and managerial accounting, [2018] | Includes
   bibliographical references and index.
Identifiers: LCCN 2018035310| ISBN 9781260247855 (alk. paper) | ISBN
   1260247856 (alk. paper)
Subjects: LCSH: Accounting. | Managerial accounting.
Classification: LCC HF5636 .W674b 2018 | DDC 658.15/11—dc23 LC record available at https://lccn.loc.gov/2018035310

The Internet addresses listed in the text were accurate at the time of publication. The inclusion of a website does not indicate an endorsement by the authors or McGraw-Hill Education, and McGraw-Hill Education does not guarantee the accuracy of the information presented at these sites.

mheducation.com/highered

About the Authors

Courtesy of John J. Wild

JOHN J. WILD is a distinguished professor of accounting at the University of Wisconsin at Madison. He previously held appointments at Michigan State University and the University of Manchester in England. He received his BBA, MS, and PhD from the University of Wisconsin.

John teaches accounting courses at both the undergraduate and graduate levels. He has received numerous teaching honors, including the Mabel W. Chipman Excellence-in-Teaching Award and the departmental Excellence-in-Teaching Award, and he is a two-time recipient of the Teaching Excellence Award from business graduates at the University of Wisconsin. He also received the Beta Alpha Psi and Roland F. Salmonson Excellence-in-Teaching Award from Michigan State University. John has received several research honors, is a past KPMG Peat Marwick National Fellow, and is a recipient of fellowships from the American Accounting Association and the Ernst and Young Foundation.

John is an active member of the American Accounting Association and its sections. He has served on several committees of these organizations, including the Outstanding Accounting Educator Award, Wildman Award, National Program Advisory, Publications, and Research Committees. John is author of *Financial Accounting, Managerial Accounting, Fundamental Accounting Principles,* and *College Accounting,* all published by McGraw-Hill Education.

John's research articles on accounting and analysis appear in *The Accounting Review; Journal of Accounting Research; Journal of Accounting and Economics; Contemporary Accounting Research; Journal of Accounting, Auditing and Finance; Journal of Accounting and Public Policy; Accounting Horizons;* and other journals. He is past associate editor of *Contemporary Accounting Research* and has served on several editorial boards including *The Accounting Review* and the *Journal of Accounting and Public Policy.*

In his leisure time, John enjoys hiking, sports, boating, travel, people, and spending time with family and friends.

Courtesy of Ken W. Shaw

KEN W. SHAW is an associate professor of accounting and the KPMG/Joseph A. Silvoso Distinguished Professor of Accounting at the University of Missouri. He previously was on the faculty at the University of Maryland at College Park. He has also taught in international programs at the University of Bergamo (Italy) and the University of Alicante (Spain). He received an accounting degree from Bradley University and an MBA and PhD from the University of Wisconsin. He is a Certified Public Accountant with work experience in public accounting.

Ken teaches accounting at the undergraduate and graduate levels. He has received numerous School of Accountancy, College of Business, and university-level teaching awards. He was voted the "Most Influential Professor" by four School of Accountancy graduating classes and is a two-time recipient of the O'Brien Excellence in Teaching Award. He is the advisor to his school's chapter of the Association of Certified Fraud Examiners.

Ken is an active member of the American Accounting Association and its sections. He has served on many committees of these organizations and presented his research papers at national and regional meetings. Ken's research appears in the *Journal of Accounting Research; The Accounting Review; Contemporary Accounting Research; Journal of Financial and Quantitative Analysis; Journal of the American Taxation Association; Strategic Management Journal; Journal of Accounting, Auditing, and Finance; Journal of Financial Research;* and other journals. He has served on the editorial boards of *Issues in Accounting Education; Journal of Business Research;* and *Research in Accounting Regulation.* Ken is co-author of *Fundamental Accounting Principles, Managerial Accounting,* and *College Accounting,* all published by McGraw-Hill Education.

In his leisure time, Ken enjoys tennis, cycling, music, and coaching his children's sports teams.

Author Letter   Using Learning Science and Data Analytics

We use data to make decisions and maximize performance. Like the runner on the cover who uses data to track her progress, we used student performance data to identify content areas that can be made more direct, concise, and systematic.

Learning science reveals that students do not read large chunks of text, so we streamlined this edition to present it in a more focused, succinct, blocked format to improve student learning and retention. Our new edition delivers the same content in 112 fewer pages. Visual aids and numerous videos offer additional learning aids. New summary Cheat Sheets conclude each chapter to visually reinforce key concepts and procedures.

Our new edition has over 1,500 videos to engage students and improve outcomes:

- **Concept Overview Videos**—cover each chapter's learning objectives with multimedia presentations that include Knowledge Checks to engage students and assess comprehension.
- **Need-to-Know Demos**—walk-through demonstrations of key procedures and analysis to ensure success with assignments and tests.
- **Guided Examples (Hints)**—step-by-step walk-through of assignments that mimic Quick Studies, Exercises, and General Ledger.

Difference Makers in Teaching . . .

Learning Science

Learning analytics show that students learn better when material is broken into "blocks" of content. Each chapter opens with a visual preview. Learning objective numbers highlight the location of related content. Each "block" of content concludes with a Need-to-Know (NTK) to aid and reinforce student learning. Visual aids and concise, bullet-point discussions further help students learn.

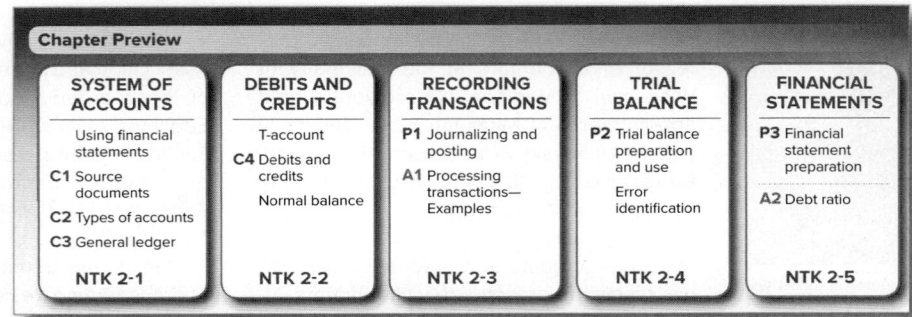

Chapter Preview

SYSTEM OF ACCOUNTS	DEBITS AND CREDITS	RECORDING TRANSACTIONS	TRIAL BALANCE	FINANCIAL STATEMENTS
Using financial statements	T-account	**P1** Journalizing and posting	**P2** Trial balance preparation and use	**P3** Financial statement preparation
C1 Source documents	**C4** Debits and credits	**A1** Processing transactions—Examples	Error identification	**A2** Debt ratio
C2 Types of accounts	Normal balance			
C3 General ledger				
NTK 2-1	**NTK 2-2**	**NTK 2-3**	**NTK 2-4**	**NTK 2-5**

Sales Discounts, Returns, and Allowances—Adjusting Entries   Revenue recognition rules require sales to be reported at the amount expected to be received. This means that period-end adjusting entries are commonly made for

- Expected sales discounts.
- Expected returns and allowances (revenue side).
- Expected returns and allowances (cost side).

These three adjustments produce three new accounts: Allowance for Sales Discounts, Sales Refund Payable, and Inventory Returns Estimated. Appendix 4B covers these accounts and the adjusting entries.

New Revenue Recognition

- Wild uses the popular gross method for merchandising transactions (net method is covered in an appendix). The gross method is widely used in practice and best for student success.
- Adjusting entries for new revenue recognition rules are included in an appendix. Assignments are clearly marked and separated. Wild is GAAP compliant.

Up-to-Date

This book reflects changes in accounting for revenue recognition, investments, leases, and extraordinary items. It is important that students learn GAAP accounting.

Less Is More

Wild has markedly fewer pages than competing books covering the same material.
- The text is to the point and uses visuals to aid student learning.
- Bullet-point discussions and active writing aid learning.
- The 8th edition has 112 fewer pages than the 7th edition—a 10% reduction!

Visual Learning

- Learning analytics tell us today's students do not read large blocks of text. Wild has adapted to student needs by having informative visual aids throughout. Many visuals and exhibits are new to this edition.

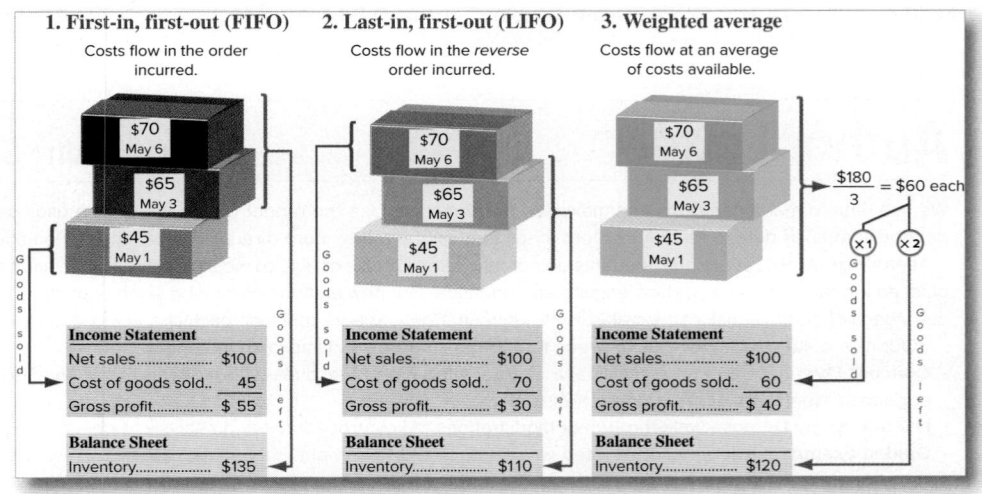

Videos

- A growing number of students now learn accounting online. **Wild offers over 1,500 videos** designed to increase student engagement and improve outcomes.

- Hundreds of hint videos or Guided Examples provide a narrated, animated, step-by-step walk-through of select exercises similar to those assigned. These short presentations, which can be turned on or off by instructors, provide reinforcement when students need it most. (Exercise PowerPoints are available for instructors.)

- Concept Overview Videos cover each chapter's learning objectives with narrated, animated presentations that frequently assess comprehension. Wild's concept overview presentations cover learning objectives broken down into over 700 videos.

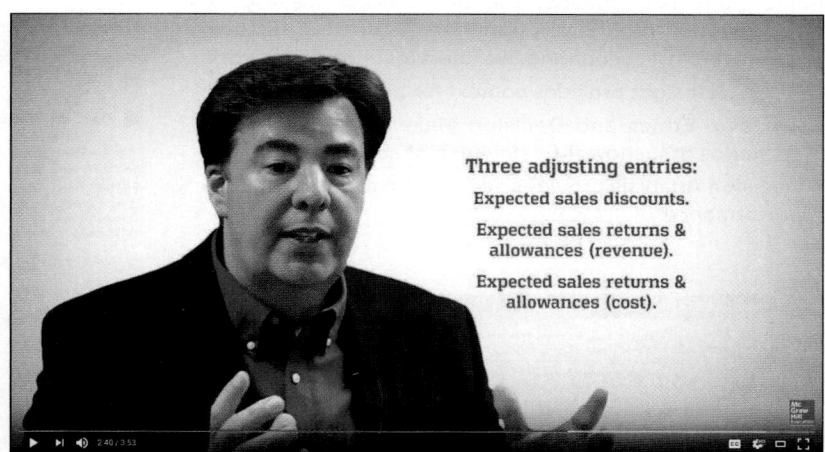

Need-to-Know Demos

Need-to-Know demonstrations are located at key junctures in each chapter. These demonstrations pose questions about the material just presented—content that students "need to know" to learn accounting. Accompanying solutions walk students through key procedures and analysis necessary to be successful with homework and test materials.

Need-to-Know demonstrations are supplemented with narrated, animated, step-by-step walk-through videos led by an instructor and available via **Connect**.

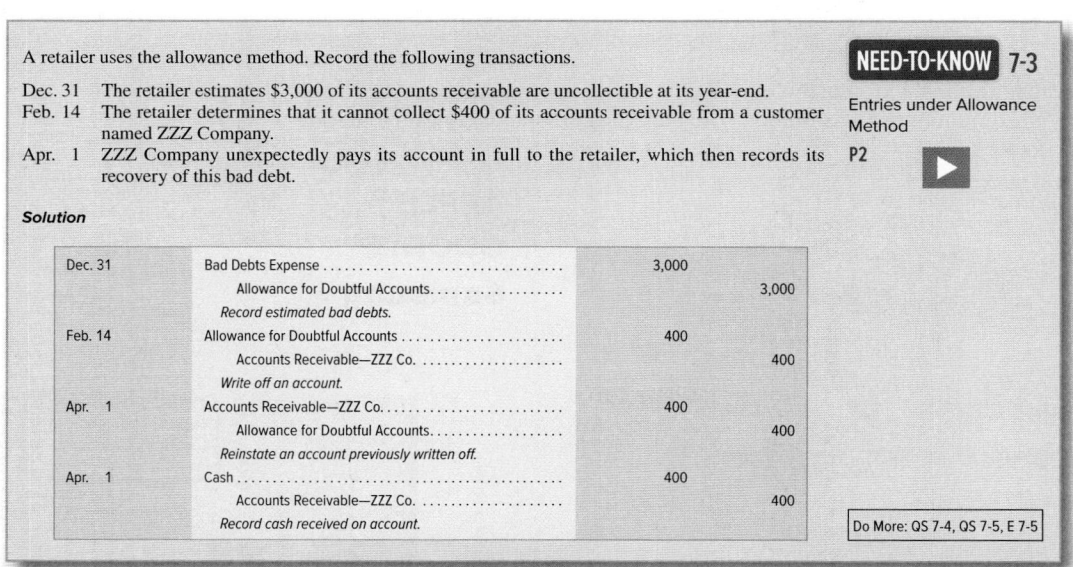

Comprehensive Need-to-Know Comprehensive Need-to-Knows are problems that draw on material from the entire chapter. They include a complete solution, allowing students to review the entire problem-solving process and achieve success.

Difference Makers in Teaching . . .

Driving Decisions

Whether we prepare, analyze, or apply accounting information, one skill remains essential: decision making. To help develop good decision-making habits and to show the relevance of accounting, we use a learning framework.

- **Decision Insight** provides context for business decisions.
- **Decision Ethics** and **Decision Maker** are role-playing scenarios that show the relevance of accounting.
- **Decision Analysis** provides key tools to assess company performance.

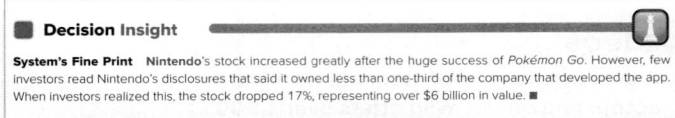

Decision Insight

System's Fine Print Nintendo's stock increased greatly after the huge success of *Pokémon Go*. However, few investors read Nintendo's disclosures that said it owned less than one-third of the company that developed the app. When investors realized this, the stock dropped 17%, representing over $6 billion in value. ■

Decision Ethics

Payables Manager As a new accounts payable manager, you are being trained by the outgoing manager. She explains that the system prepares checks for amounts net of favorable cash discounts, and the checks are dated the last day of the discount period. She tells you that checks are not mailed until five days later, adding that "the company gets free use of cash for an extra five days, and our department looks better." Do you continue this policy? ■ *Answer: One point of view is that the late payment policy is unethical. A deliberate plan to make late payments means the company lies when it pretends to make payment within the discount period. Another view is that the late payment policy is acceptable. Some believe attempts to take discounts through late payments are accepted as "price negotiation."*

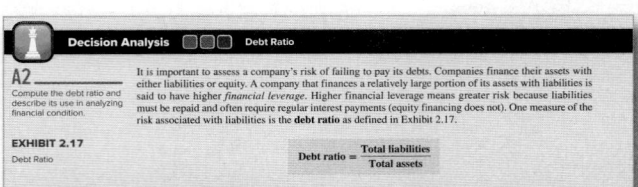

Decision Analysis ▢▢▢ **Debt Ratio**

A2
Compute the debt ratio and describe its use in analyzing financial condition.

It is important to assess a company's risk of failing to pay its debts. Companies finance their assets with either liabilities or equity. A company that finances a relatively large portion of its assets with liabilities is said to have higher *financial leverage*. Higher financial leverage means greater risk because liabilities must be repaid and often require regular interest payments (equity financing does not). One measure of the risk associated with liabilities is the **debt ratio** as defined in Exhibit 2.17.

EXHIBIT 2.17
Debt Ratio

$$\text{Debt ratio} = \frac{\text{Total liabilities}}{\text{Total assets}}$$

Decision Maker

Entrepreneur You open a wholesale business selling entertainment equipment to retail outlets. Most of your customers want to buy on credit. How can you use the balance sheets of customers to decide which ones to extend credit to? ■ *Answer: We use the accounting equation (Assets = Liabilities + Equity) to identify risky customers to whom we would not want to extend credit. A balance sheet provides amounts for each of these key components. The lower a customer's equity is relative to liabilities, the less likely you would be to extend credit. A low equity means the business already has many creditor claims to it.*

Accounting Analytics

New to this edition, Accounting Analysis assignments have students evaluate the most current financial statements from Apple, Google, and Samsung. Students compute key metrics and compare performance between companies and industry.

These assignments are auto-gradable in Connect and are included after Problem Set B in the text.

AA 7-2 Comparative figures for Apple and Google follow.

COMPARATIVE ANALYSIS

A1 P2

APPLE
GOOGLE

$ millions	Apple			Google		
	Current Year	One Year Prior	Two Years Prior	Current Year	One Year Prior	Two Years Prior
Accounts receivable, net ..	$ 17,874	$ 15,754	$ 16,849	$ 18,336	$14,137	$11,556
Net sales	229,234	215,639	233,715	110,855	90,272	74,989

Required

1. Compute the accounts receivable turnover for (*a*) Apple and (*b*) Google for each of the two most recent years using the data shown.
2. Compute how many days, *on average*, it takes to collect receivables for the two most recent years for (*a*) Apple and (*b*) Google.
3. Which company more quickly collects its accounts receivable in the current year?

Hint: Average collection period equals 365 divided by the accounts receivable turnover.

Keep It Real

Research shows that students learn best when using current data from real companies. Wild uses the most current data from real companies for assignments, examples, and analysis in the text. See Chapter 13 for use of real data.

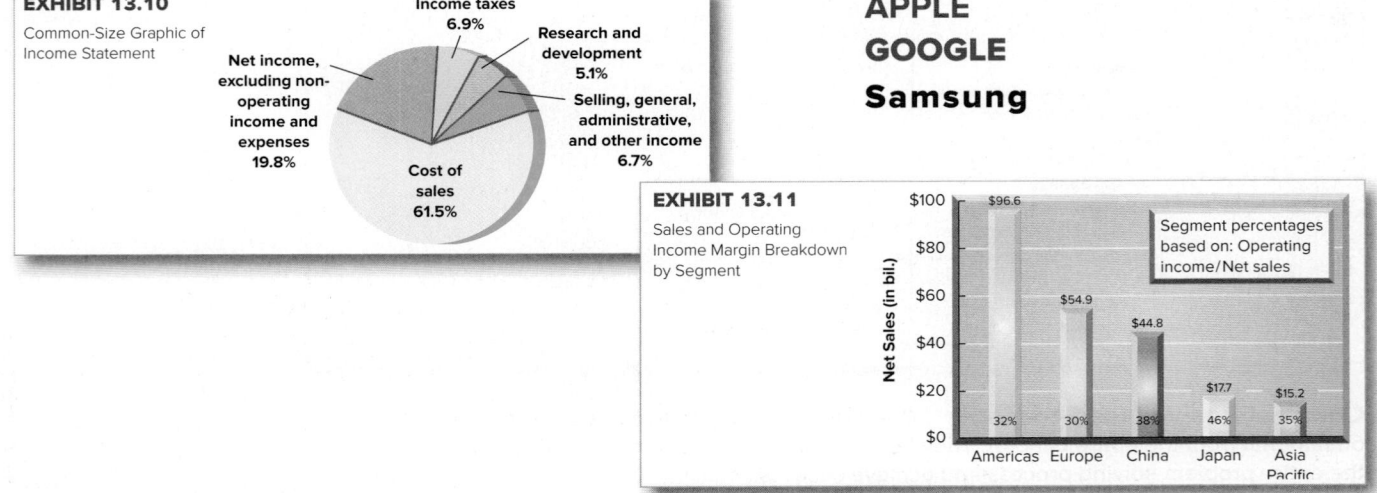

EXHIBIT 13.10

Common-Size Graphic of Income Statement

Income taxes 6.9%
Research and development 5.1%
Net income, excluding non-operating income and expenses 19.8%
Selling, general, administrative, and other income 6.7%
Cost of sales 61.5%

APPLE
GOOGLE
Samsung

EXHIBIT 13.11

Sales and Operating Income Margin Breakdown by Segment

Segment percentages based on: Operating income/Net sales

Net Sales (in bil.)

	Americas	Europe	China	Japan	Asia Pacific
	$96.6	$54.9	$44.8	$17.7	$15.2
	32%	30%	38%	46%	35%

Cheat Sheets

New to this edition, Cheat Sheets are provided at the end of each chapter. Cheat Sheets are roughly one page in length and include key procedures, concepts, journal entries, and formulas.

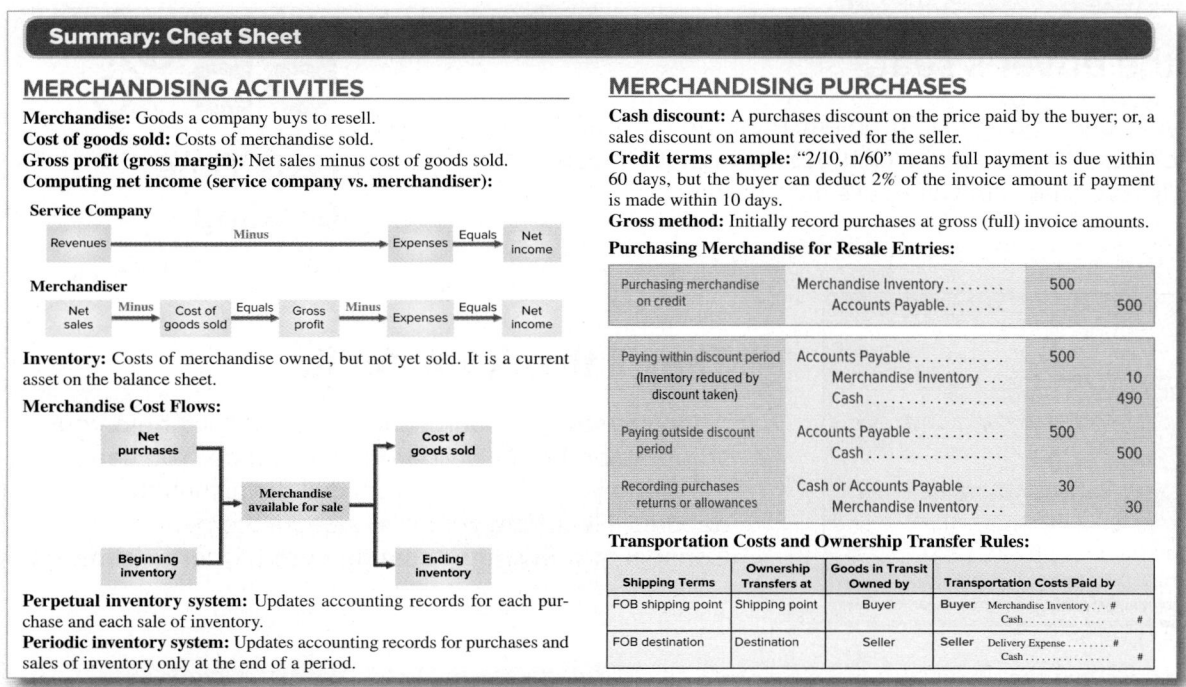

Summary: Cheat Sheet

MERCHANDISING ACTIVITIES

Merchandise: Goods a company buys to resell.
Cost of goods sold: Costs of merchandise sold.
Gross profit (gross margin): Net sales minus cost of goods sold.
Computing net income (service company vs. merchandiser):

Service Company

Revenues — Minus → Expenses — Equals → Net income

Merchandiser

Net sales — Minus → Cost of goods sold — Equals → Gross profit — Minus → Expenses — Equals → Net income

Inventory: Costs of merchandise owned, but not yet sold. It is a current asset on the balance sheet.

Merchandise Cost Flows:

Net purchases → Merchandise available for sale → Cost of goods sold
Beginning inventory → Merchandise available for sale → Ending inventory

Perpetual inventory system: Updates accounting records for each purchase and each sale of inventory.
Periodic inventory system: Updates accounting records for purchases and sales of inventory only at the end of a period.

MERCHANDISING PURCHASES

Cash discount: A purchases discount on the price paid by the buyer; or, a sales discount on amount received for the seller.
Credit terms example: "2/10, n/60" means full payment is due within 60 days, but the buyer can deduct 2% of the invoice amount if payment is made within 10 days.
Gross method: Initially record purchases at gross (full) invoice amounts.

Purchasing Merchandise for Resale Entries:

| Purchasing merchandise on credit | Merchandise Inventory........ | 500 | |
| | Accounts Payable........ | | 500 |

Paying within discount period (Inventory reduced by discount taken)	Accounts Payable............	500	
	Merchandise Inventory ...		10
	Cash.................		490

| Paying outside discount period | Accounts Payable............ | 500 | |
| | Cash................. | | 500 |

| Recording purchases returns or allowances | Cash or Accounts Payable..... | 30 | |
| | Merchandise Inventory ... | | 30 |

Transportation Costs and Ownership Transfer Rules:

Shipping Terms	Ownership Transfers at	Goods in Transit Owned by	Transportation Costs Paid by
FOB shipping point	Shipping point	Buyer	Buyer — Merchandise Inventory ... # Cash............... #
FOB destination	Destination	Seller	Seller — Delivery Expense........ # Cash................ #

Doing What's Right

Companies increasingly issue sustainability reports, and accountants are being asked to prepare, analyze, and audit them. Wild includes brief sections in the managerial chapters. This material focuses on the importance of sustainability within the context of accounting, including standards from the Sustainability Accounting Standards Board (SASB). Sustainability assignments cover chapter material with a social responsibility twist.

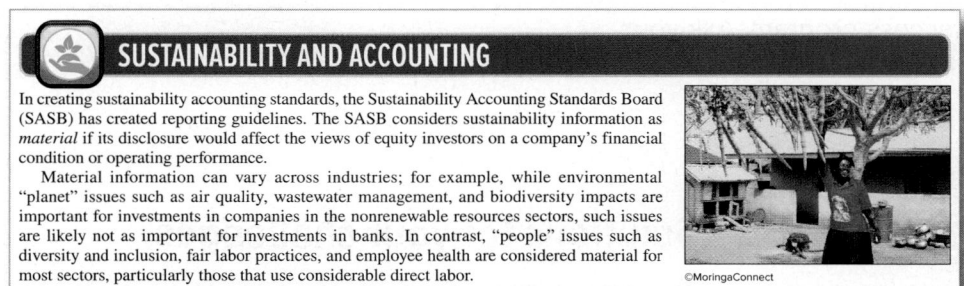

SUSTAINABILITY AND ACCOUNTING

In creating sustainability accounting standards, the Sustainability Accounting Standards Board (SASB) has created reporting guidelines. The SASB considers sustainability information as *material* if its disclosure would affect the views of equity investors on a company's financial condition or operating performance.

Material information can vary across industries; for example, while environmental "planet" issues such as air quality, wastewater management, and biodiversity impacts are important for investments in companies in the nonrenewable resources sectors, such issues are likely not as important for investments in banks. In contrast, "people" issues such as diversity and inclusion, fair labor practices, and employee health are considered material for most sectors, particularly those that use considerable direct labor.

©MoringaConnect

QS 21-22
Sustainability and standard costs

P1

MM Co. uses corrugated cardboard to ship its product to customers. Management believes it has found a more efficient way to package its products and use less cardboard. This new approach will reduce shipping costs from $10.00 per shipment to $9.25 per shipment. (1) If the company forecasts 1,200 shipments this year, what amount of total direct materials costs would appear on the shipping department's flexible budget? (2) How much is this sustainability improvement predicted to save in direct materials costs for this coming year?

![McGraw Hill Education] **connect**® | Students—study more efficiently, retain more and achieve better outcomes. Instructors—focus on what you love—teaching.

SUCCESSFUL SEMESTERS INCLUDE CONNECT

FOR INSTRUCTORS

You're in the driver's seat.

Want to build your own course? No problem. Prefer to use our turnkey, prebuilt course? Easy. Want to make changes throughout the semester? Sure. And you'll save time with Connect's auto-grading too.

65%
Less Time Grading

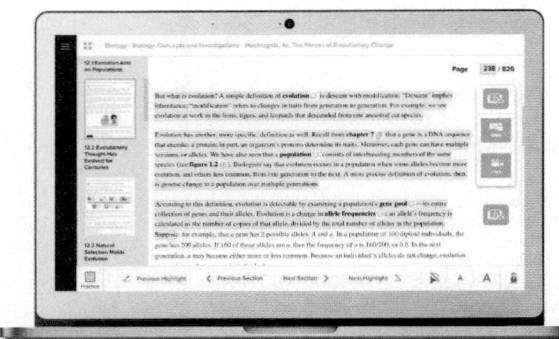

They'll thank you for it.

Adaptive study resources like SmartBook® help your students be better prepared in less time. You can transform your class time from dull definitions to dynamic debates. Hear from your peers about the benefits of Connect at **www.mheducation.com/highered/connect**

Make it simple, make it affordable.

Connect makes it easy with seamless integration using any of the major Learning Management Systems—Blackboard®, Canvas, and D2L, among others—to let you organize your course in one convenient location. Give your students access to digital materials at a discount with our inclusive access program. Ask your McGraw-Hill representative for more information.

©Hill Street Studios/Tobin Rogers/Blend Images LLC

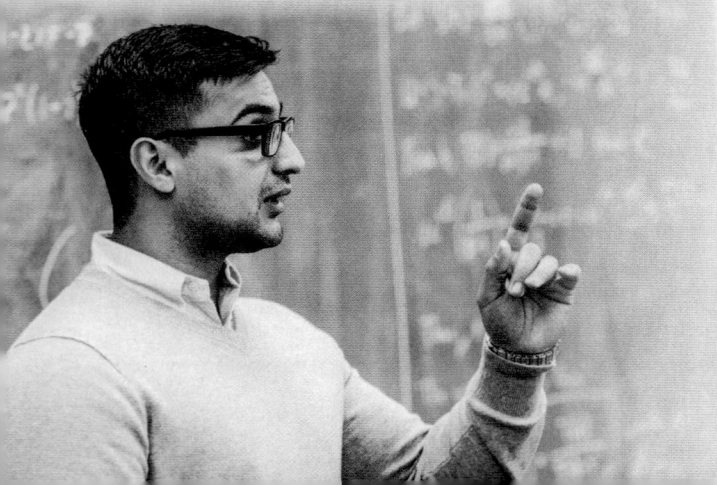

Solutions for your challenges.

A product isn't a solution. Real solutions are affordable, reliable, and come with training and ongoing support when you need it and how you want it. Our Customer Experience Group can also help you troubleshoot tech problems—although Connect's 99% uptime means you might not need to call them. See for yourself at **status.mheducation.com**

Effective, efficient studying.

Connect helps you be more productive with your study time and get better grades using tools like SmartBook, which highlights key concepts and creates a personalized study plan. Connect sets you up for success, so you walk into class with confidence and walk out with better grades.

©Shutterstock/wavebreakmedia

> " I really liked this app—it made it easy to study when you don't have your text-book in front of you. "
>
> - Jordan Cunningham, Eastern Washington University

Study anytime, anywhere.

Download the free ReadAnywhere app and access your online eBook when it's convenient, even if you're offline. And since the app automatically syncs with your eBook in Connect, all of your notes are available every time you open it. Find out more at **www.mheducation.com/readanywhere**

No surprises.

The Connect Calendar and Reports tools keep you on track with the work you need to get done and your assignment scores. Life gets busy; Connect tools help you keep learning through it all.

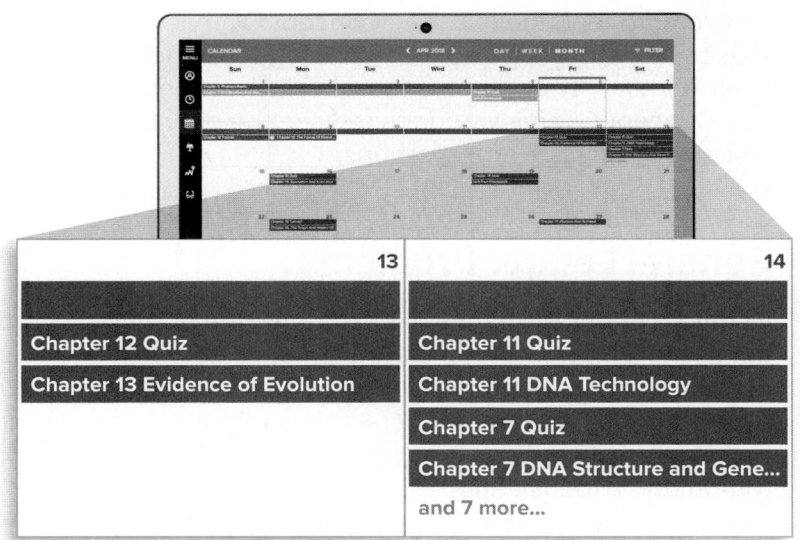

13	14
Chapter 12 Quiz	Chapter 11 Quiz
Chapter 13 Evidence of Evolution	Chapter 11 DNA Technology
	Chapter 7 Quiz
	Chapter 7 DNA Structure and Gene...
	and 7 more...

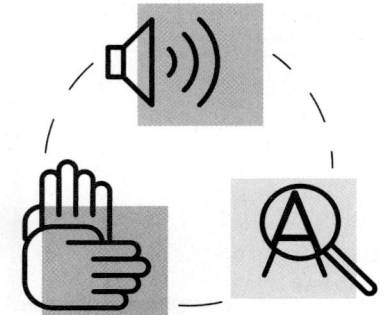

Learning for everyone.

McGraw-Hill works directly with Accessibility Services Departments and faculty to meet the learning needs of all students. Please contact your Accessibility Services office and ask them to email accessibility@mheducation.com, or visit **www.mheducation.com/accessibility** for more information.

SUPERIOR ASSIGNMENTS

Connect helps students learn more efficiently by providing feedback and practice material when they need it, where they need it. Connect grades homework automatically and gives immediate feedback.

- Wild has auto-gradable and algorithmic assignments; most focus on one learning objective and are targeted at introductory students.
- 90% of Wild's Quick Study, Exercise, and Problem Set A assignments are available in Connect with algorithmic options.
- Over 210 assignments new to this edition—all available in Connect with algorithmic options. Nearly all are Quick Studies (brief exercises) and Exercises.

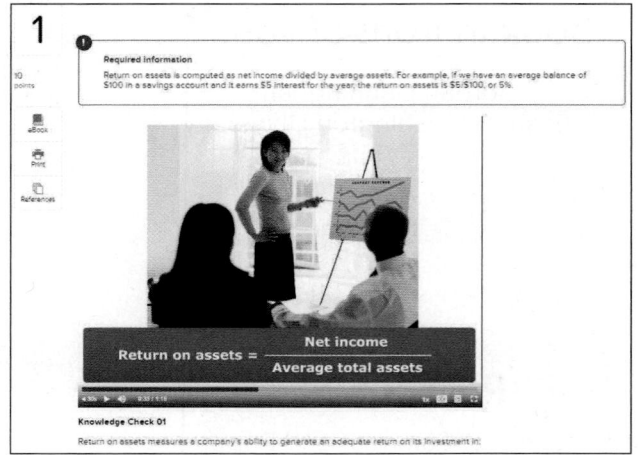

NEW! Concept Overview Videos

Concept Overview Videos teach each chapter's learning objectives through an engaging multimedia presentation. These learning tools enhance the text through video, audio, and checkpoint questions that can be graded—ensuring students complete and comprehend the material. Concept Overview Videos harness the power of technology to appeal to all learning styles and are ideal in all class formats. The Concept Overview Videos replace the previous edition's Interactive Presentations.

General Ledger Problems

General Ledger Problems offer students the ability to record financial transactions and see how these transactions flow into financial statements. Easy minimal-scroll navigation, instant "Check My Work" feedback, and fully integrated hyperlinking across tabs show how inputted data affect each stage of the accounting process. General Ledger Problems expose students to general ledger software similar to that in practice, without the expense and hassle of downloading additional software. Algorithmic versions are available. **All are auto-gradable.**

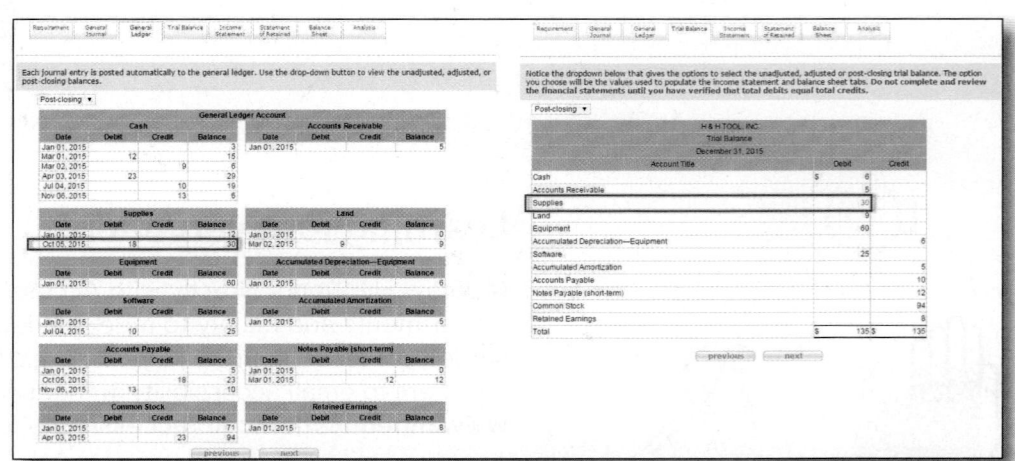

NEW! Applying Excel

Applying Excel enables students to work select chapter problems or examples in Excel. These problems are assignable in Connect and give students instant feedback as they work through the problems in Excel. Accompanying Excel videos teach students how to use Excel and the primary functions needed to complete the assignment. Short assessments can be assigned to test student comprehension of key Excel skills.

Excel Simulations

Simulated Excel Questions, assignable within Connect, allow students to practice their Excel skills—such as basic formulas and formatting—within the context of accounting. These questions feature animated, narrated Help and Show Me tutorials (when enabled), as well as automatic feedback and grading for both students and professors. These questions differ from Applying Excel in that students work in a simulated version of Excel. *Downloading the Excel application is **not** required to complete Simulated Excel Questions.*

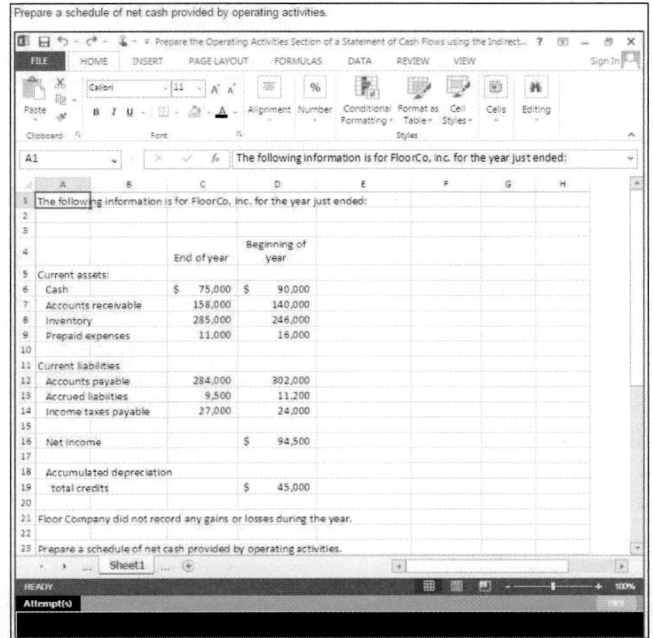

Guided Examples

The **Guided Examples** (*Hints*) in Connect provide a narrated, animated, step-by-step walk-through of most Quick Studies, Exercises, and General Ledger Problems similar to those assigned. These short presentations can be turned on or off by instructors and provide reinforcement when students need it most.

Exercise Presentations

Animated PowerPoints, created from text assignments, enable instructors to be fully prepared for in-class demonstrations. Instructors also can use these with Tegrity (in Connect) to record online lectures.

Content Revisions Enhance Learning

Instructors and students guided this edition's revisions. Revisions include

- New **Cheat Sheets** at each chapter-end visually reinforce key chapter concepts.
- More concise text covering the same content. New 8th edition has 112 fewer pages than 7th edition.
- Over 210 new assignments—all available in Connect with algorithmic options.
- Gross method is used for merchandising transactions, reflecting practice—adjusting entries for new revenue recognition rules are set in an appendix.
- Revised Investments chapter for the new standard.

- New **Accounting Analysis** assignments—all available in Connect—using real-world data from **Apple**, **Google**, and **Samsung**.
- Many new and revised **General Ledger** and **Excel** assignments.
- New assignments that focus on financial statement preparation.
- Updated videos for each learning objective in new **Concept Overview Video** format.
- Many new **Need-to-Know (NTK)** demos and accompanying videos to reinforce learning.

Chapter 1
Updated opener—**Apple** and entrepreneurial assignment.
Updated salary info for accountants.
Revised business entity section along with adding LLC.
Updated section on FASB objectives and accounting constraints.
New layout for introducing the expanded accounting equation.
New layout for introducing financial statements.
Updated **Apple** numbers for NTK 1-5.
New Cheat Sheet reinforces chapter content.
Updated return on assets analysis using **Nike** and **Under Armour**.
Added a new Exercise assignment and Quick Study assignment.
Added new analysis assignments: Company Analysis, Comparative Analysis, and Global Analysis.

Chapter 2
NEW opener—**Fitbit** and entrepreneurial assignment.
New visual for process to get from transactions to financial statements.
New layout on four types of accounts that determine equity.
Improved presentation of "Double-Entry System" section.
Updated **Apple** data for NTK 2-4.
Updated debt ratio analysis using **Costco** and **Walmart**.
New Cheat Sheet reinforces chapter content.
Added four new Quick Studies.
Added three new Exercises.
Added new analysis assignments: Company Analysis, Comparative Analysis, and Global Analysis.

Chapter 3
NEW opener—**Snapchat** and entrepreneurial assignment.
Revised learning objectives and chapter preview—each type of adjusting entry is assigned its own learning objective.
Updated "Recognizing Revenues and Expenses" section.
New streamlined "Framework for Adjustments" section.
Enhanced Exhibit 3.12 on summary of adjustments.
Enhanced Exhibit 3.19 on steps of accounting cycle with images.
Streamlined section on classified balance sheet.
Updated profit margin analysis using **Visa** and **Mastercard**.
Updated current ratio analysis using **Costco** and **Walmart**.
Improved layouts for Exhibits 3A.1 through 3A.5.
New Cheat Sheet reinforces chapter content.
Added three new Quick Studies.
Added two new Exercises.
Added new analysis assignments: Company Analysis, Comparative Analysis, and Global Analysis.

Chapter 4
NEW opener—**Build-A-Bear** and entrepreneurial assignment.
Updated introduction for servicers vs. merchandisers using **Liberty Tax** and **Nordstrom**.
Revised NTK 4-1 covers basics of merchandising.
Reorganized "Purchases" section to aid learning.
New Decision Insight on growing number of returns for businesses.
Enhanced entries on payment of purchases within discount period vs. after discount period.
Improved discussion of entries for sales with discounts vs. sales without discounts.
Color-coded Exhibit 4.12 highlights different merchandising transactions.
Updated acid-test ratio and gross margin analysis using **Nike** and **Under Armour**.
Appendix 4B explains adjusting entries for future sales discounts, returns, and allowances.
Appendix 4C covers the net method.
Appendix 4D moved to online only.
New Cheat Sheet reinforces chapter content.
Added three new Quick Studies.
Added four new Exercises.
Added new analysis assignments: Company Analysis, Comparative Analysis, and Global Analysis.

Chapter 5
NEW opener—**Shake Shack** and entrepreneurial assignment.
New Ethical Risk on the alleged fraud of **Homex**.
Simplified introduction to inventory costing.
Shortened explanation for specific identification.
Enhanced layout to explain effects of inventory errors across years.
Updated inventory turnover and days' sales in inventory analysis using **Costco** and **Walmart**.
Added colored arrow lines to Exhibits 5A.3 and 5A.4 to show cost flows from purchases to sales.
New Cheat Sheet reinforces chapter content.
Added one new Quick Study.
Added two new Exercises.
Added new analysis assignments: Company Analysis, Comparative Analysis, and Global Analysis.

Chapter 6
NEW opener—**Care.com** and entrepreneurial assignment.
New COSO framework to guide internal control, including COSO cube.
New discussion of internal control failure at **Amazon** that cost customers $150 million.
Simplified bank statement for learning.
Revised "Bank Reconciliation" section to separate bank balance adjustments and book balance adjustments.

New summary image on adjustments for bank balance and for book balance.
Removed collection expenses and NSF fees—most are immaterial and covered in advanced courses.
Updated days' sales uncollected analysis using **Starbucks** and **Jack in the Box**.
New Cheat Sheet reinforces chapter content.
Added three new Quick Studies.
Added eight new Exercises.
Added new analysis assignments: Company Analysis, Comparative Analysis, and Global Analysis.

Chapter 7
NEW opener—**Facebook** and entrepreneurial assignment.
Updated company data in Exhibit 7.1.
Streamlined direct write-off method.
Enhanced Exhibit 7.6 showing allowances set aside for future bad debts along with journal entries.
New calendar graphic added as learning aid with Exhibit 7.12.
New Excel demo to compute maturity dates.
Updated accounts receivable analysis using **Visa** and **Mastercard**.
New Cheat Sheet reinforces chapter content.
Added five new Quick Studies.
Added one new Exercise.
Added new analysis assignments: Company Analysis, Comparative Analysis, and Global Analysis.

Chapter 8
NEW opener—**New Glarus Brewery** and entrepreneurial assignment.
Updated company data in Exhibit 8.1.
Added entry with Exhibit 8.3 and Exhibit 8.4.
Simplified "Partial-Year Depreciation" section.
Added margin table to Exhibit 8.14 as a learning aid.
New Decision Insight box on extraordinary repairs to **SpaceX**'s reusable orbital rocket.
New simple introduction to finance leases and operating leases for the new standard.
Updated asset turnover analysis using **Starbucks** and **Jack in the Box**.
Simplified Appendix 8A by postponing exchanges without commercial substance to advanced courses.
New Cheat Sheet reinforces chapter content.
Added two new Quick Studies.
Added one new Exercise.
Added two new Problems.
Added new analysis assignments: Company Analysis, Comparative Analysis, and Global Analysis.

Chapter 9
NEW opener—**Pandora** and entrepreneurial assignment.
Updated data in Exhibit 9.2.
Streamlined "Short-Term Notes Payable" section.
Simplified explanation of FICA taxes.

Updated payroll tax rates and explanations.
Revised NTK 9-4.
New W-4 form added to Appendix 9A.
New Cheat Sheet reinforces chapter content.
Added two new Quick Studies.
Added four new Exercises.
Added new analysis assignments: Company Analysis, Comparative Analysis, and Global Analysis.

Chapter 10
NEW opener—**e.l.f. Cosmetics** and entrepreneurial assignment.
Updated **IBM** bond quote data.
Simplified numbers in Exhibit 10.7.
Simplified Exhibit 10.10 on premium bonds.
Simplified numbers in Exhibit 10.11.
Bond pricing moved to Appendix 10A.
Simplified Exhibit 10.12 for teaching the note amortization schedule.
Updated debt-to-equity analysis using **Nike** and **Under Armour**.
New Excel computations for bond pricing in Appendix 10A.
Simplified numbers in Exhibits 10B.1 and 10B.2.
Revised Appendix 10C for new standard on finance leases and operating leases.
New Cheat Sheet reinforces chapter content.
Added five new Quick Studies.
Added four new Exercises.
Added four new Problems.
Added new analysis assignments: Company Analysis, Comparative Analysis, and Global Analysis.

Chapter 11
NEW opener—**Yelp** and entrepreneurial assignment.
New Decision Insight on bots investing in stocks based on erroneous news.
New **AT&T** stock quote explanation.
New graphic visually depicting cash dividend dates.
New table summarizing differences between small stock dividends, large stock dividends, and stock splits.
Updated **Apple** statement of equity in Exhibit 11.10.
Updated PE ratio and dividend yield using **Amazon**, **Altria**, **Visa**, and **Mastercard**.
Simplified book value per share explanation and computations.
New Cheat Sheet reinforces chapter content.
Added six new Quick Studies.
Added four new Exercises.
Added new analysis assignments: Company Analysis, Comparative Analysis, and Global Analysis.

Chapter 12
NEW opener—**Vera Bradley** and entrepreneurial assignment.
Slightly revised infographics on cash flows from operating, investing, and financing.
Streamlined sections on analyzing the cash account and noncash accounts.

New presentation to aid learning of indirect adjustments to income.
Simplified T-accounts to reconstruct cash flows.
New box on **Tesla**'s cash outflows and growing market value.
Simplified reconstruction entries to help compute cash flows.
Updated cash flow on total assets analysis using **Nike** and **Under Armour**.
New Cheat Sheet reinforces chapter content.
Added ten new Quick Studies.
Added four new Exercises.
Added new analysis assignments: Company Analysis, Comparative Analysis, and Global Analysis.

Chapter 13

Updated opener—**Morgan Stanley** and entrepreneurial assignment.
Updated data for all analyses of **Apple** using horizontal, vertical, and ratio analysis.
Updated comparative analysis using **Google** and **Samsung**.
Streamlined section on ratio analysis.
Streamlined the "Analysis Reporting" section.
Shortened Appendix 13A.
New Cheat Sheet reinforces chapter content.
Added eight new Quick Studies.
Added two new Exercises.
Added new analysis assignments: Company Analysis, Comparative Analysis, and Global Analysis.

Chapter 14

NEW opener—**MoringaConnect** and entrepreneurial assignment.
Added discussion on role of managerial accounting for nonaccounting and nonbusiness majors.
New margin exhibit showing product and period cost flows.
Added equation boxes for total manufacturing costs and cost of goods manufactured.
Added lists of common selling and administrative expenses.
Updated and edited several exhibits for clarity.
New Cheat Sheet reinforces chapter content.
Added new analysis assignments: Company Analysis, Comparative Analysis, and Global Analysis.

Chapter 15

NEW opener—**HoopSwagg** and entrepreneurial assignment.
Revised discussions of manufacturing costs and link between job cost sheets and general ledger.
Added graphic linking job cost sheets and general ledger accounts.
Enhanced exhibit of 4-step overhead process.
Added formula for computing applied overhead.
New short discussion of cost-plus pricing.
Added margin T-accounts and calculations for clarity.

New Cheat Sheet reinforces chapter content.
Added one new Quick Study.
Added new analysis assignments: Company Analysis, Comparative Analysis, and Global Analysis.

Chapter 16

NEW opener—**Azucar Ice Cream** and entrepreneurial assignment.
Revised discussion comparing process and job order costing systems.
Added cost flow graphic.
New margin graphic illustrating EUP.
Revised discussion of weighted-average versus FIFO method of process costing.
Revised discussion of using the process cost summary.
New graphic on FIFO goods flow.
Added margin T-accounts and calculations for clarity.
New Cheat Sheet reinforces chapter content.
Added one new Exercise.
Added new analysis assignments: Company Analysis, Comparative Analysis, and Global Analysis.

Chapter 17

NEW opener—**Sycamore Brewing** and entrepreneurial assignment.
New graphic showing activities for service businesses.
Added examples to discussion of ABC for service businesses.
New Cheat Sheet reinforces chapter content.
Added one new Discussion Question.
Added one new Quick Study.
Added new analysis assignments: Company Analysis, Comparative Analysis, and Global Analysis.

Chapter 18

NEW opener—**Ellis Island Tropical Tea** and entrepreneurial assignment.
Added margin graphs of fixed, variable, and mixed costs.
New Excel steps to create a line chart.
Moved details of creating scatter plot to Appendix 18A, with Excel steps.
Revised discussion of scatter plots.
Moved details of creating a CVP chart to Appendix 18C, with Excel steps.
New Cheat Sheet reinforces chapter content.
Added one new Exercise.
Added new analysis assignments: Company Analysis, Comparative Analysis, and Global Analysis.

Chapter 19

NEW opener—**Lantern Inn B&B** and entrepreneurial assignment.
New Cheat Sheet reinforces chapter content.
Added new analysis assignments: Company Analysis, Comparative Analysis, and Global Analysis.

Chapter 20

NEW opener—**Misfit Juicery** and entrepreneurial assignment.

Added T-accounts and steps to exhibit margins.
Added numbered steps to several exhibits.
Expanded discussion of cost of goods sold budgeting.
New exhibit for calculation of cash paid for interest.
Expanded discussion with bulleted list on use of a master budget.
New Cheat Sheet reinforces chapter content.
Added one new Quick Study.
Added one new Exercise.
New assignment on CMA exam budgeting coverage.
Added new analysis assignments: Company Analysis, Comparative Analysis, and Global Analysis.

Chapter 21

NEW opener—**Away** and entrepreneurial assignment.
Added graph to flexible budget exhibit.
Revised discussion of flexible budget.
New exhibit and discussion of computing total cost variance.
Edited discussion of direct materials cost variance.
Edited discussion of evaluating labor variances.
Edited discussion of overhead variance reports.
New exhibit for summary of variances.
New Cheat Sheet reinforces chapter content.
Added two new Exercises.
Added new analysis assignments: Company Analysis, Comparative Analysis, and Global Analysis.

Chapter 22

NEW opener—**Jibu** and entrepreneurial assignment.
Updated **Walt Disney** ROI example.
New Decision Analysis on cash conversion cycle.
New Cheat Sheet reinforces chapter content.
Added two new Quick Studies.
Added two new Exercises.
Added new analysis assignments: Company Analysis, Comparative Analysis, and Global Analysis.

Chapter 23

NEW opener—**Solugen** and entrepreneurial assignment.
Organized decision scenarios into three types: production, capacity, and pricing.
Expanded discussion of product pricing.
Added other pricing methods: value-based, auction-based, and dynamic.
New Decision Insight on blockchain technology.
New Decision Analysis on time and materials pricing of services.
New Cheat Sheet reinforces chapter content.
Added four new Quick Studies.
Added one new Exercise.

Added new analysis assignments: Company Analysis, Comparative Analysis, and Global Analysis.

Chapter 24

NEW opener—**Fellow Robots** and entrepreneurial assignment.
Added example of investment in robotics.
New discussion of postaudit of investment decisions.
New Cheat Sheet reinforces chapter content.
Added two new Exercises.
Added new analysis assignments: Company Analysis, Comparative Analysis, and Global Analysis.

Appendix A

New financial statements for **Apple**, **Google**, and **Samsung**.

Appendix B

New Decision Maker on postponed retail pricing.
Continued Excel demos for PV and FV of lump sums.
Continued Excel demos for PV and FV of annuities.

Appendix C

New learning objective P4 for new category of stock investments.
Revised and simplified Exhibit C.2 for new standard on investments.
Reorganized text to first explain debt securities and then stock securities.
Revised trading and available-for-sale securities to cover only debt securities given the new standard.
New section on stock investments with insignificant influence.
New Exhibit C.6 to describe accounting for equity securities by ownership level.
Updated component-returns analysis using **Costco** and **Walmart**.
New Cheat Sheet reinforces chapter content.
Added three new Quick Studies.
Added four new Exercises.
Added two new Problems.
Added new analysis assignments: Company Analysis, Comparative Analysis, and Global Analysis.

Appendix D

NEW appendix on lean principles and accounting.
Describes lean business principles.
Measures production efficiency.
Illustrates how to account for product costs using lean accounting.
New: 13 Discussion Questions, 14 Quick Studies, 14 Exercises, and 3 Problems.

Acknowledgments

John J. Wild, Ken W. Shaw, and McGraw-Hill Education recognize the following instructors for their valuable feedback and involvement in the development of *Financial and Managerial Accounting.* We are thankful for their suggestions, counsel, and encouragement.

Darlene Adkins, University of Tennessee–Martin

Peter Aghimien, Indiana University South Bend

Janice Akao, Butler Community College

Nathan Akins, Chattahoochee Technical College

John Alpers, Tennessee Wesleyan University

Sekhar Anantharaman, Indiana University of Pennsylvania

Karen Andrews, Lewis-Clark State College

Chandra D. Arthur, Cuyahoga Community College

Steven Ault, Montana State University

Victoria Badura, Metropolitan Community College

Felicia Baldwin, City College of Chicago

Reb Beatty, Anne Arundel Community College

Robert Beebe, Morrisville State College

George Henry Bernard, Seminole State College of Florida

Cynthia Bird, Tidewater Community College, Virginia Beach

Pascal Bizarro, Bowling Green State University

Amy Bohrer, Tidewater Community College, Virginia Beach

John Bosco, North Shore Community College

Nicholas Bosco, Suffolk County Community College

Jerold K. Braun, Daytona State College

Doug Brown, Forsyth Technical Community College

Tracy L. Bundy, University of Louisiana at Lafayette

Marci Butterfield, University of Utah

Ann Capion, Scott Community College

Amy Cardillo, Metropolitan State University of Denver

Anne Cardozo, Broward College

Crystal Carlson-Myer, Indian River State College

Julie Chasse, Des Moines Area Community College

Patricia Chow, Grossmont College

Maria Coclin, Community College of Rhode Island

Michael Cohen, Lewis-Clark State College

Jerilyn Collins, Herzing University

Scott Collins, Penn State University, University Park

William Conner, Tidewater Community College

Erin Cornelsen, University of South Dakota

Mariah Dar, John Tyler Community College

Nichole Dauenhauer, Lakeland Community College

Donna DeMilia, Grand Canyon University

Tiffany DeRoy, University of South Alabama

Susan Dickey, Motlow State Community College

Erin Dischler, Milwaukee Area Technical College–West Allis

Holly Dixon, State College of Florida

Vicky Dominguez, College of Southern Nevada

David Doyon, Southern New Hampshire University

Chester Drake, Central Texas College

Christopher Eller, Appalachian State University

Cynthia Elliott, Southwest Tennessee Community College–Macon

Kim Everett, East Carolina University

Corinne Frad, Eastern Iowa Community College

Krystal Gabel, Southeast Community College

Harry Gallatin, Indiana State University

Rena Galloway, State Fair Community College

Rick Gaumer, University of Wisconsin–Green Bay

Tammy Gerszewski, University of North Dakota

Pradeep Ghimire, Rappahannock Community College

Marc Giullian, Montana State University, Bozeman

Nelson Gomez, Miami Dade College–Kendall

Robert Goodwin, University of Tampa

Steve G. Green, U.S. Air Force Academy

Darryl Greene, Muskegon Community College

Lisa Hadley, Southwest Tennessee Community College–Macon

Penny Hahn, KCTCS Henderson Community College

Yoon Han, Bemidji State University

Becky Hancock, El Paso Community College

Amie Haun, University of Tennessee–Chattanooga

Michelle Hays, Kalamazoo Valley Community College

Rhonda Henderson, Olive Harvey College

Lora Hines, John A. Logan College

Rob Hochschild, Ivy Tech Community College of Indiana–South Bend

John Hoover, Volunteer State Community College

Roberta Humphrey, Southeast Missouri State University

Carley Hunzeker, Metro Community College, Elkhorn

Kay Jackson, Tarrant County College South

Elizabeth Jennison, Saddleback College

Mary Jepperson, Saint John's University

Vicki Jobst, Benedictine University

Odessa Jordan, Calhoun Community College

Susan Juckett, Victoria College

Amanda Kaari, Central Georgia Technical College

Ramadevi Kannan, Owens Community College

Jan Klaus, University of North Texas

Aaron P. Knape, The University of New Orleans

Cedric Knott, Henry Ford Community College

Robin Knowles, Texas A&M International University

Kimberly Kochanny, Central Piedmont Community College

Sergey Komissarov, University of Wisconsin–La Crosse

Stephanie Lareau Kroeger, Ocean County College

Joseph Krupka, Lander University

Tara Laken, Joliet Junior College

Suzanne Lay, Colorado Mesa University

Brian Lazarus, Baltimore City Community College

Kevin Leifer, Long Island University, CW Post Campus

Harold Levine, Los Angeles Valley College

Yuebing Liu, University of Tampa

Philip Lee Little, Coastal Carolina University

Delores Loedel, Miracosta College

Rebecca Lohmann, Southeast Missouri State University

Ming Lu, Santa Monica Community College

Annette C. Maddox, Georgia Highlands College

Natasha Maddox, KCTCS Maysville Community and Technical College

Rich Mandau, Piedmont Technical College

Robert Maxwell, College of the Canyons

Karen McCarron, Georgia Gwinnett College

Michael McDonald, College of Southern Nevada

Gwendolyn McFadden-Wade, North Carolina A&T University

Allison McLeod, University of North Texas

Kate McNeil, Johnson County Community College

Jane Medling, Saddleback College

Heidi H. Meier, Cleveland State University

Tammy Metzke, Milwaukee Area Technical College

Jeanine Metzler, Northampton Community College

Michelle Meyer, Joliet Junior College

Pam Meyer, University of Louisiana at Lafayette

Deanne Michaelson, Pellissippi State Community College

Susan Miller, County College of Morris

Carmen Morgan, Oregon Tech

Karen Satterfield Mozingo, Pitt Community College

Haris Mujahid, South Seattle College

Andrea Murowski, Brookdale Community College

Jaclynn Myers, Sinclair Community College

Micki Nickla, Ivy Tech Community College of Indiana–Gary

Dan O'Brien, Madison College–Truax

Jamie O'Brien, South Dakota State University

Grace Odediran, Union County College

Ashley Parker, Grand Canyon University

Pamela Parker, NOVA Community College Alexandria

Margaret Parrish, John Tyler Community College

Reed Peoples, Austin Community College

Rachel Pernia, Essex County College

Brandis Phillips, North Carolina A&T University

Debbie Porter, Tidewater Community College–Virginia Beach

M. Jeff Quinlan, Madison Area Technical College

James E. Racic, Lakeland Community College

Ronald de Ramon, Rockland Community College

Robert J. Rankin, Texas A&M University–Commerce

Robert Rebman, Benedictine University

Jenny Resnick, Santa Monica Community College

DeAnn Ricketts, York Technical College

Renee Rigoni, Monroe Community College

Kevin Rosenberg, Southeastern Community College

David Rosser, University of Texas at Arlington

Michael J. Rusek, Eastern Gateway Community College

Alfredo Salas, El Paso Community College

Carolyn Satz, Tidewater Community College–Chesapeake

Kathy Saxton, Bryant & Stratton College

Wilson Seda, Lehman College–CUNY
Perry Sellers, Lonestar College–North Harris
James Shimko, Ferris State University
Philip Slater, Forsyth Technical Community College
Clayton Smith, Columbia College Chicago
Patricia Smith, DePaul University
Jane Stam, Onondaga Community College
Natalie Strouse, Notre Dame College
Erica Teague-Friend, Gwinnett Technical College
Louis Terrero, Lehman College
Geoff Tickell, Indiana University of Pennsylvania
Judith A. Toland, Bucks County Community College
Debra Touhey, Ocean County College
Jim Ulmer, Angelina College
Bob Urell, Irvine Valley College
Kevin Veneskey, Ivy Tech Community College

Teresa Walker, North Carolina A&T University
Terri Walsh, Seminole State College of Florida
Eric Weinstein, Suffolk County Community College, Brentwood
Andy Welchel, Greenville Technical College
Joe Welker, College of Western Idaho
Jean Wells, Howard University
Denise White, Austin Community College
Jonathan M. Wild, Oklahoma State University
Kenneth Wise, Wilkes Community College
Shondra Woessner, Holyoke Community College
Mindy Wolfe, Arizona State University
Jan Workman, East Carolina University
Lori Zaher, Bucks County Community College
Jessie Zetnick, Texas Woman's University
Laurence Zuckerman, Fulton-Montgomery Community College

Many talented educators and professionals have worked hard to create the materials for this product, and for their efforts, we're grateful. **We extend a special thank you to our contributing and technology supplement authors,** who have worked so diligently to support this product.

Contributing Author, Connect Content, General Ledger Problems, and **Exercise PowerPoints:** Kathleen O'Donnell, *Onondaga Community College*

Text and Supplements Accuracy Checkers: Dave Krug, *Johnson County Community College;* Mark McCarthy, *East Carolina University;* Kate McNeil, *Johnson County Community College;* Wanda Wong, *Chabot College;* and Beth Kobylarz

Test Bank Authors and Accuracy Checkers: Melodi Bunting, *Madison College;* Brian Schmoldt, *Madison College;* M. Jeff Quinlan, *Madison College;* and Teri Zuccaro, *Clarke University*

LearnSmart Author, Concept Overview Videos, PowerPoint Presentations, and **Instructor Resource Manual:** April Mohr, *Jefferson Community and Technical College, SW*

Special recognition extends to the entire team at McGraw-Hill Education: Tim Vertovec, Steve Schuetz, Natalie King, Michelle Williams, Julie Wolfe, Michele Janicek, Christina Sanders, Michael McCormick, Lori Koetters, Xin Lin, Kevin Moran, Debra Kubiak, Brian Nacik, and Daryl Horrocks. We could not have published this new edition without your efforts.

John J. Wild   *Ken W. Shaw*

Brief Contents

Contents

Financial & Managerial Accounting

1 Accounting in Business

Chapter Preview

ACCOUNTING USES	ETHICS AND ACCOUNTING	TRANSACTION ANALYSIS	FINANCIAL STATEMENTS
C1 Purpose of accounting	**C3** Ethics	**A1** Accounting equation and its components	**P2** Income statement
C2 Accounting information users	**C4** Generally accepted accounting principles	Expanded accounting equation	Statement of retained earnings
Opportunities in accounting	Conceptual framework	**P1** Transaction analysis—Illustrated	Balance sheet
			Statement of cash flows
			A2 Financial analysis
NTK 1-1	**NTK 1-2**	**NTK 1-3, 1-4**	**NTK 1-5**

Chapter Preview is organized by "blocks" of key content and learning objectives followed by *Need-to-Know (NTK)* guided video examples

Learning Objectives are classified as conceptual, analytical, or procedural

Learning Objectives

CONCEPTUAL

C1 Explain the purpose and importance of accounting.

C2 Identify users and uses of, and opportunities in, accounting.

C3 Explain why ethics are crucial to accounting.

C4 Explain generally accepted accounting principles and define and apply several accounting principles.

C5 *Appendix 1B*—Identify and describe the three major activities of organizations.

ANALYTICAL

A1 Define and interpret the accounting equation and each of its components.

A2 Compute and interpret return on assets.

A3 *Appendix 1A*—Explain the relation between return and risk.

PROCEDURAL

P1 Analyze business transactions using the accounting equation.

P2 Identify and prepare basic financial statements and explain how they interrelate.

Big Apple

"We ran the business . . . with just a few hundred bucks"—**STEVE WOZNIAK**

CUPERTINO, CA—"When I designed the Apple stuff," says Steve Wozniak, "I never thought in my life I would have enough money to fly to Hawaii or make a down payment on a house." But some dreams do come true. Woz, along with Steve Jobs and Ron Wayne, founded **Apple** (**Apple.com**) when Woz was 25 and Jobs was 21.

The young entrepreneurs faced challenges, including how to read and interpret accounting data. They also needed to finance the company, which they did by selling Woz's HP calculator and Jobs's Volkswagen van. The $1,300 raised helped them purchase the equipment Woz used to build the first Apple computer.

In setting up their company, the owners chose between a partnership and a corporation. They decided on a partnership that included Ron as a third partner with 10% ownership. Days later, Ron withdrew when he considered the unlimited liability of a partnership. He sold his 10% share to Woz and Jobs for $800. Within nine months, Woz and Jobs converted Apple to a corporation.

As Apple grew, Woz and Jobs had to learn more accounting, along with details of preparing and interpreting financial statements. Important questions involving transaction analysis and financial reporting arose, and the owners took care to do things

©Miguel Medina/AFP/Getty Images

right. "Everything we did," asserts Woz, "we were setting the tone for the world."

Woz and Jobs focused their accounting system to provide information for Apple's business decisions. Today, Woz believes that Apple is key to the language of technology, just as accounting is the language of business. In retrospect, Woz says, "Every dream I have ever had in life has come true ten times over."

Sources: *Apple website,* January 2019; *Woz.org,* January 2019; *Apple 2016 Sustainability Report,* April 2016; *Greenbiz,* October 2014; *iWoz: From Computer Geek to Cult Icon,* W.W. Norton & Co., 2006; *Founders at Work,* Apress, 2007

IMPORTANCE OF ACCOUNTING

Why is accounting so popular on campus? Why are there so many openings for accounting jobs? Why is accounting so important to companies? The answer is that we live in an information age in which accounting information impacts us all.

Accounting is an information and measurement system that identifies, records, and communicates an organization's business activities. Exhibit 1.1 shows these accounting functions.

C1

Explain the purpose and importance of accounting.

Identifying	Recording	Communicating
Select transactions and events	Input, measure, and log	Prepare, analyze, and interpret
Examples are **Apple's** sale of iPhones and **TicketMaster's** receipt of ticket money.	Examples are dated logs of transactions measured in dollars.	Examples are reports that we analyze and interpret.

EXHIBIT 1.1

Accounting Functions

Our most common contact with accounting is through credit checks, checking accounts, tax forms, and payroll. These experiences focus on **recordkeeping,** or **bookkeeping,** which is the recording of transactions and events. This is just one part of accounting. Accounting also includes analysis and interpretation of information.

Technology plays a major role in accounting. Technology reduces the time, effort, and cost of recordkeeping while improving accuracy. As technology makes more information available, the demand for accounting knowledge increases. Consulting, planning, and other financial services are closely linked to accounting.

Users of Accounting Information

C2

Identify users and uses of, and opportunities in, accounting.

Accounting is called the *language of business* because it communicates data that help people make better decisions. People using accounting information are divided into two groups: *external users* and *internal users*. **Financial accounting** focuses on the needs of external users, and **managerial accounting** focuses on the needs of internal users.

External Users
External users of accounting information do *not* directly run the organization and have limited access to its accounting information. These users get accounting information from general-purpose financial statements. Following is a partial list of external users and decisions they make with accounting information.

- *Lenders* (creditors) loan money or other resources to an organization. Banks, savings and loans, and mortgage companies are lenders. Lenders use information to assess if an organization will repay its loans.
- *Shareholders* (*investors*) are the owners of a corporation. They use accounting reports to decide whether to buy, hold, or sell stock.
- *Boards of directors* oversee organizations. Directors use accounting information to evaluate the performance of executive management.
- *External* (independent) *auditors* examine financial statements to verify that they are prepared according to generally accepted accounting principles.
- *Nonmanagerial* and *nonexecutive employees* and *labor unions* use external information to bargain for better wages.
- *Regulators* have legal authority over certain activities of organizations. For example, the Internal Revenue Service (IRS) requires accounting reports for computing taxes.
- *Voters* and *government officials* use information to evaluate government performance.
- *Contributors* to nonprofits use information to evaluate the use and impact of donations.
- *Suppliers* use information to analyze a customer before extending credit.
- *Customers* use financial reports to assess the stability of potential suppliers.

Internal Users
Internal users of accounting information directly manage the organization. Internal reports are designed for the unique needs of managerial or executive employees, such as the chief executive officer (CEO). Following is a partial list of internal users and decisions they make with accounting information.

- *Purchasing managers* need to know what, when, and how much to purchase.
- *Human resource managers* need information about employees' payroll, benefits, and performance.
- *Production managers* use information to monitor costs and ensure quality.
- *Distribution managers* need reports for timely and accurate delivery of products and services.
- *Marketing managers* use reports to target consumers, set prices, and monitor consumer needs.
- *Service managers* use reports to provide better service to customers.
- *Research and development managers* use information on projected costs and revenues of innovations.

Opportunities in Accounting

Accounting has four areas of opportunities: financial, managerial, taxation, and accounting-related. Exhibit 1.2 lists selected opportunities in each area.

Opportunities in Accounting

EXHIBIT 1.2

Accounting Opportunities

Financial	Managerial	Taxation	Accounting-related
• Preparation	• General accounting	• Preparation	• Lenders
• Analysis	• Cost accounting	• Planning	• Consultants
• External auditing	• Budgeting	• Regulatory	• Analysts
• Regulatory	• Internal auditing	• Investigations	• Traders
• Consulting	• Consulting	• Consulting	• Directors
• Planning	• Controller	• Enforcement	• Underwriters
• Criminal investigation	• Treasurer	• Legal services	• Planners
	• Strategy	• Estate plans	• Appraisers

Accounting-related (continued):
• FBI investigators
• Market researchers
• Systems designers
• Merger services
• Business valuation
• Forensic accounting
• Litigation support
• Entrepreneurs

Point: The largest accounting firms are **EY, KPMG, PwC,** and **Deloitte.**

Point: Higher education yields higher pay:

Master's degree	$73,738
Bachelor's degree	56,665
Associate's degree	39,771
High school degree	30,627
No high school degree	20,241

Exhibit 1.3 shows that the majority of opportunities are in *private accounting,* which are employees working for businesses. *Public accounting* involves accounting services such as auditing and taxation. Opportunities also exist in government and not-for-profit agencies, including business regulation and law enforcement.

Accounting specialists are highly regarded, and their professional standing is often denoted by a certificate. Certified public accountants (CPAs) must meet education and experience requirements, pass an exam, and be ethical. Many accounting specialists hold certificates in addition to or instead of the CPA. Two of the most common are the certificate in management accounting (CMA) and the certified internal auditor (CIA). Employers also look for specialists with designations such as certified bookkeeper (CB), certified payroll professional (CPP), certified fraud examiner (CFE), and certified forensic accountant (CrFA).

Accounting specialists are in demand. Exhibit 1.4 reports average annual salaries for several accounting positions. Salaries vary based on location, company size, and other factors.

EXHIBIT 1.3

Accounting Jobs by Area

Private accounting 54%
Government and not-for-profit 22%
Public accounting 24%

EXHIBIT 1.4

Accounting Salaries

Public Accounting	Salary
Partner	$245,000
Manager (6–8 years)	112,000
Senior (3–5 years)	90,000
Junior (0–2 years)	62,500

Private Accounting	Salary
CFO	$290,000
Controller/Treasurer	180,000
Manager (6–8 years)	98,500
Senior (3–5 years)	81,500
Junior (0–2 years)	58,000

Recordkeeping	Salary
Full-charge bookkeeper	$60,500
Accounts manager	58,000
Payroll manager	59,500
Accounting clerk (0–2 years)	39,500

NEED-TO-KNOWs *highlight key procedures and concepts in learning accounting; instructional audio/video recordings accompany each one*

Identify the following users of accounting information as either an (a) external or (b) internal user.

NEED-TO-KNOW 1-1

1. ____ Regulator
2. ____ CEO
3. ____ Shareholder
4. ____ Marketing manager
5. ____ Executive employee
6. ____ External auditor
7. ____ Production manager
8. ____ Nonexecutive employee
9. ____ Bank lender

Accounting Users

C1   C2

Solution

1. a **2.** b **3.** a **4.** b **5.** b **6.** a **7.** b **8.** a **9.** a.

Do More: QS 1-1, QS 1-2, E 1-1, E 1-2, E 1-3

FUNDAMENTALS OF ACCOUNTING

C3_____

Explain why ethics are crucial to accounting.

Point: A *Code of Conduct* is available at **AICPA.org**.

Ethics—A Key Concept

For information to be useful, it must be trusted. This demands ethics in accounting. **Ethics** are beliefs that separate right from wrong. They are accepted standards of good and bad behavior.

Accountants face ethical choices as they prepare financial reports. These choices can affect the salaries and bonuses paid to workers. They even can affect the success of products and services. Misleading information can lead to a bad decision that harms workers and the business. There is an old saying: *Good ethics are good business.* Exhibit 1.5 gives a three-step process for making ethical decisions.

EXHIBIT 1.5

Ethical Decision Making

1. Identify ethical concerns	2. Analyze options	3. Make ethical decision
Use ethics to recognize an ethical concern.	Consider all consequences.	Choose best option after weighing all consequences.

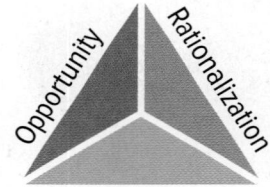

Fraud Triangle: Ethics under Attack   The fraud triangle shows that *three* factors push a person to commit fraud.

- **Opportunity**. A person must be able to commit fraud with a low risk of getting caught.
- **Pressure**, or incentive. A person must feel pressure or have incentive to commit fraud.
- **Rationalization**, or attitude. A person justifies fraud or does not see its criminal nature.

The key to stopping fraud is to focus on prevention. It is less expensive and more effective to prevent fraud from happening than it is to detect it.

To help prevent fraud, companies set up internal controls. **Internal controls** are procedures to protect assets, ensure reliable accounting, promote efficiency, and uphold company policies. Examples are good records, physical controls (locks), and independent reviews.

Point: SOX requires a business that sells stock to disclose a code of ethics for its executives.

Point: An **audit** examines whether financial statements are prepared using GAAP.

Enforcing Ethics

In response to major accounting scandals, like those at **Enron** and **WorldCom**, Congress passed the **Sarbanes-Oxley Act,** also called *SOX,* to help stop financial abuses. SOX requires documentation and verification of internal controls and emphasizes effective internal controls. Management must issue a report stating that internal controls are effective. **Auditors** verify the effectiveness of internal controls. Ignoring SOX can lead to penalties and criminal prosecution of executives. CEOs and CFOs who knowingly sign off on bogus accounting reports risk millions of dollars in fines and years in prison.

Dodd-Frank Wall Street Reform and Consumer Protection Act, or *Dodd-Frank,* has two important provisions.

- *Clawback* Mandates recovery (clawback) of excessive pay.
- *Whistleblower* SEC pays whistleblowers 10% to 30% of sanctions exceeding $1 million.

Ethical Risk boxes highlight ethical issues from practice.

Ethical Risk

Ethics Pay   The $100 million mark in total payments made by the SEC to whistleblowers was recently surpassed. Since the SEC began awarding whistleblowers a percentage of money from sanctions, over 14,000 tips have been reported. Many of the tips come from accountants. ∎

Generally Accepted Accounting Principles

Financial accounting is governed by concepts and rules known as **generally accepted accounting principles (GAAP)**. GAAP wants information to have *relevance* and *faithful representation*. Relevant information affects decisions of users. Faithful representation means information accurately reflects the business results.

The **Financial Accounting Standards Board (FASB)** is given the task of setting GAAP from the **Securities and Exchange Commission (SEC)**. The SEC is a U.S. government agency that oversees proper use of GAAP by companies that sell stock and debt to the public.

International Standards   Our global economy demands comparability in accounting reports. The **International Accounting Standards Board (IASB)** issues **International Financial Reporting Standards (IFRS)** that identify preferred accounting practices. These standards are similar to, but sometimes different from, U.S. GAAP. The FASB and IASB are working to reduce differences between U.S. GAAP and IFRS.

C4 _____

Explain generally accepted accounting principles and define and apply several accounting principles.

Point: CPAs who audit financial statements must disclose if they do not comply with GAAP.

Conceptual Framework

The FASB **conceptual framework** in Exhibit 1.6 consists of the following.

- **Objectives**—to provide information useful to investors, creditors, and others.
- **Qualitative characteristics**—to require information that has *relevance* and *faithful representation*.
- **Elements**—to define items in financial statements.
- **Recognition and measurement**—to set criteria for an item to be recognized as an element; and how to measure it.

EXHIBIT 1.6

Conceptual Framework

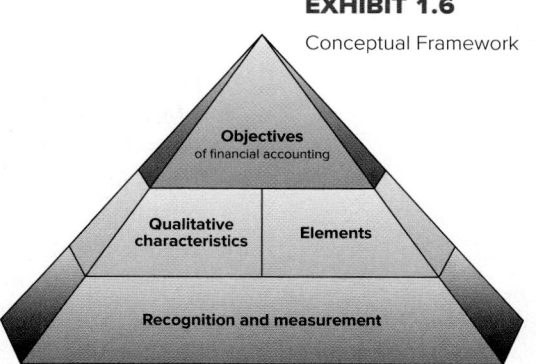

Principles, Assumptions, and Constraint   There are two types of accounting principles (and assumptions). *General principles* are the assumptions, concepts, and guidelines for preparing financial statements; these are shown in purple font in Exhibit 1.7, along with key assumptions in red font. *Specific principles* are detailed rules used in reporting business transactions and events; they are described as we encounter them.

EXHIBIT 1.7

Building Blocks for GAAP

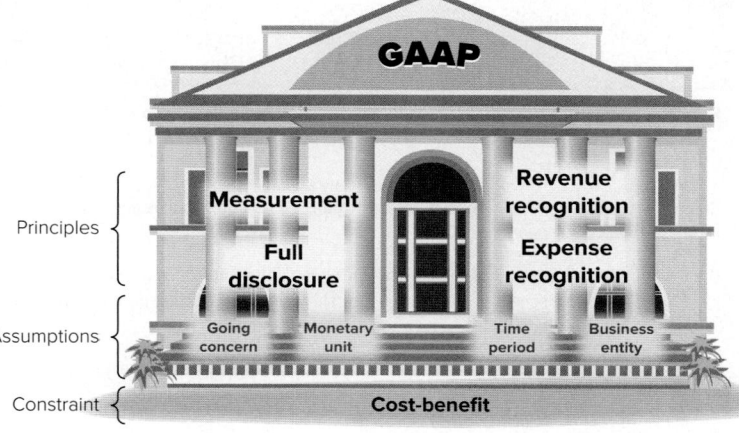

Accounting Principles   There are four general principles.

- **Measurement principle (cost principle)** Accounting information is based on actual cost. Cost is measured on a cash or equal-to-cash basis. This means if cash is given for a service, its cost is measured by the cash paid. If something besides cash is exchanged (such as a car traded for a truck), cost is measured as the cash value of what is given up or received. Information based on cost is considered objective. *Objectivity* means that information is supported by independent, unbiased evidence. Later chapters cover adjustments to market and introduce *fair value*.

- **Revenue recognition principle** Revenue is recognized (1) when goods or services are provided to customers and (2) at the amount expected to be received from the customer. Revenue (sales) is the amount received from selling products and services. The amount received is usually in cash, but it also can be a customer's promise to pay at a future date, called credit sales. (To *recognize* means to record it.)

Point: A company pays $500 for equipment. The cost principle requires it be recorded at $500. It makes no difference if the owner thinks this equipment is worth $700.

Example: A lawn service bills a customer $800 on June 1 for two months of mowing (June and July). The customer pays the bill on July 1. When is revenue recorded? *Answer:* It is recorded over time as it is earned; record $400 revenue for June and $400 for July.

Example: Credit cards are used to pay $200 in gas for a lawn service during June and July. The cards are paid in August. When is expense recorded? *Answer:* If revenue is earned over time, record $100 expense in June and $100 in July.

- **Expense recognition principle (matching principle)** A company records the expenses it incurred to generate the revenue reported. An example is rent costs of office space.
- **Full disclosure principle** A company reports the details behind financial statements that would impact users' decisions. Those disclosures are often in footnotes to the statements.

©Shane Roper/CSM/REX/Shutterstock

Decision Insight

Measurement and Recognition   Revenues for the **Seattle Seahawks**, **Atlanta Falcons**, **Green Bay Packers**, and other professional football teams include ticket sales, television broadcasts, concessions, and advertising. Revenues from ticket sales are earned when the NFL team plays each game. Advance ticket sales are not revenues; instead, they are a liability until the NFL team plays the game for which the ticket was sold. At that point, the liability is removed and revenues are reported. ∎

Accounting Assumptions   There are four accounting assumptions.

- **Going-concern assumption** Accounting information presumes that the business will continue operating instead of being closed or sold. This means, for example, that property is reported at cost instead of liquidation value.
- **Monetary unit assumption** Transactions and events are expressed in monetary, or money, units. Examples of monetary units are the U.S. dollar and the Mexican peso.
- **Time period assumption** The life of a company can be divided into time periods, such as months and years, and useful reports can be prepared for those periods.
- **Business entity assumption** A business is accounted for separately from other business entities and its owner. Exhibit 1.8 describes four common business entities.

EXHIBIT 1.8

Attributes of Businesses

	Sole Proprietorship	Partnership	Corporation	Limited Liability Company (LLC)
Number of owners	1 owner; easy to set up.	2 or more, called *partners;* easy to set up.	1 or more, called *stockholders;* can get many investors by selling **stock** or **shares** of corporate ownership.*	1 or more, called *members*.
Business taxation	No additional business income tax.	No additional business income tax.	Additional corporate income tax.	No additional business income tax.
Owner liability	Unlimited liability. Owner is personally liable for proprietorship debts.	Unlimited liability. Partners are jointly liable for partnership debts.	Limited liability. Owners, called **stockholders (or shareholders)**, are not liable for corporate acts and debts.	Limited liability. Owners, called **members**, are not personally liable for LLC debts.
Legal entity	*Not* a separate legal entity.	*Not* a separate legal entity.	A separate entity with the same rights and responsibilities as a person.	A separate entity with the same rights and responsibilities as a person.
Business life	Business ends with owner death or choice.	Business ends with a partner death or choice.	Indefinite.	Indefinite.

*When a corporation issues only one class of stock, it is called **common stock** (or *capital stock*).

Point: Proprietorships, partnerships, and LLCs are managed by their owners. In a corporation, the owners (shareholders) elect a board of directors who hire managers to run the business.

Accounting Constraint   The **cost-benefit constraint,** or **cost constraint,** says that information disclosed by an entity must have benefits to the user that are greater than the costs of providing it. *Materiality,* or the ability of information to influence decisions, is also sometimes mentioned as a constraint. *Conservatism* and *industry practices* are sometimes listed as well.

Decision Ethics boxes are role-playing exercises that stress ethics in accounting

■ **Decision Ethics**

Entrepreneur   You and a friend develop a new design for ice skates that improves speed. You plan to form a business to manufacture and sell the skates. You and your friend want to minimize taxes, but your big concern is potential lawsuits from customers who might be injured on these skates. What form of organization do you set up? ■ *Answer:* You should probably form an LLC. An LLC helps protect *personal* property from lawsuits directed at the business. Also, an LLC is not subject to an additional business income tax. You also must examine the ethical and social aspects of starting a business where injuries are expected.

Point: Double taxation means that (1) the corporation income is taxed and (2) any dividends to owners are taxed as part of the owners' personal income.

Part 1: Identify each of the following terms/phrases as either an accounting (a) principle, (b) assumption, or (c) constraint.

1. ____ Cost-benefit
2. ____ Measurement
3. ____ Business entity
4. ____ Going-concern
5. ____ Full disclosure
6. ____ Time period
7. ____ Expense recognition
8. ____ Revenue recognition

NEED-TO-KNOW 1-2

Accounting Guidance

C3   C4

Solution

1. c   **2.** a   **3.** b   **4.** b   **5.** a   **6.** b   **7.** a   **8.** a

Part 2: Complete the following table with either a *yes* or a *no* regarding the attributes of a partnership, corporation, and LLC.

Attribute Present	Partnership	Corporation	LLC
Business taxed	a. ____	e. ____	i. ____
Limited liability	b. ____	f. ____	j. ____
Legal entity.	c. ____	g. ____	k. ____
Unlimited life	d. ____	h. ____	l. ____

Solution

a. no   **b.** no   **c.** no   **d.** no   **e.** yes   **f.** yes   **g.** yes   **h.** yes   **i.** no   **j.** yes   **k.** yes   **l.** yes

Do More: QS 1-3, QS 1-4, QS 1-5, QS 1-6, E 1-4, E 1-5, E 1-6, E 1-7

BUSINESS TRANSACTIONS AND ACCOUNTING

Accounting shows two basic aspects of a company: what it owns and what it owes. *Assets* are resources a company owns or controls. The claims on a company's assets—what it owes—are separated into owner (equity) and nonowner (liability) claims. Together, liabilities and equity are the source of funds to acquire assets.

A1

Define and interpret the accounting equation and each of its components.

Assets   Assets are resources a company owns or controls. These resources are expected to yield future benefits. Examples are web servers for an online services company, musical instruments for a rock band, and land for a vegetable grower. Assets include cash, supplies, equipment, land, and accounts receivable. A *receivable* is an asset that promises a future inflow of resources. A company that provides a service or product on credit has an account receivable from that customer.

Point: "On credit" and "on account" mean cash is paid at a future date.

Liabilities   Liabilities are creditors' claims on assets. These claims are obligations to provide assets, products, or services to others. A *payable* is a liability that promises a future outflow of resources. Examples are wages payable to workers, accounts payable to suppliers, notes (loans) payable to banks, and taxes payable.

Equity   Equity is the owner's claim on assets and is equal to assets minus liabilities. Equity is also called *net assets* or *residual equity*.

Accounting Equation

The relation of assets, liabilities, and equity is shown in the following **accounting equation.**
The accounting equation applies to all transactions and events, to all companies and organizations, and to all points in time.

$$\textbf{Assets = Liabilities + Equity}$$

Point: This equation can be rearranged. Example: Assets − Liabilities = Equity

We can break down equity to get the **expanded accounting equation.**

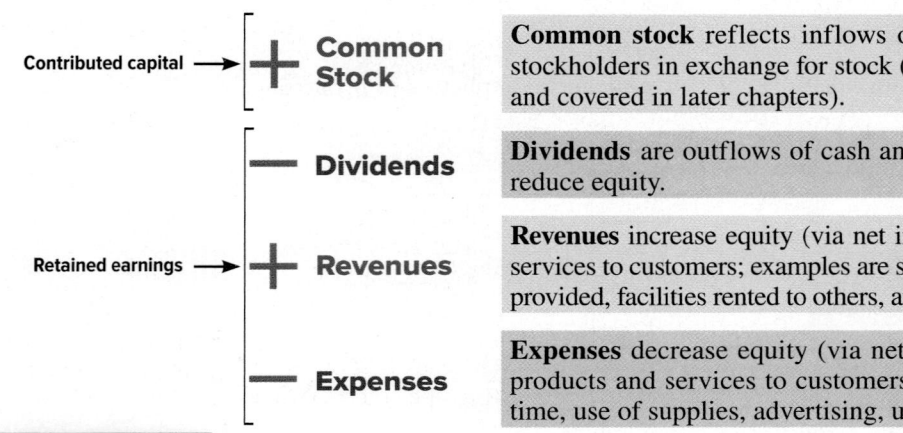

$$\text{Equity}$$
$$\textbf{Assets = Liabilities + Contributed Capital \quad + \quad Retained Earnings}$$
$$\textbf{= Liabilities + Common Stock − Dividends + Revenues − Expenses}$$

We see that equity increases from **owner investments,** called *stock issuances,* and from revenues. It decreases from dividends and from expenses. Equity consists of four parts.

Contributed capital ➞

+ Common Stock — **Common stock** reflects inflows of cash and other net assets from stockholders in exchange for stock (stock is part of contributed capital and covered in later chapters).

— Dividends — **Dividends** are outflows of cash and other assets to stockholders that reduce equity.

Retained earnings ➞

+ Revenues — **Revenues** increase equity (via net income) from sales of products and services to customers; examples are sales of products, consulting services provided, facilities rented to others, and commissions from services.

— Expenses — **Expenses** decrease equity (via net income) from costs of providing products and services to customers; examples are costs of employee time, use of supplies, advertising, utilities, and insurance fees.

©Greg Epperson/Shutterstock

■ Decision Insight ♟

Big Data   The SEC keeps an online database called **EDGAR** (**sec.gov/edgar**) that has accounting information for thousands of companies, such as **Columbia Sportswear**, that issue stock to the public. The annual report filing for most publicly traded U.S. companies is known as Form 10-K, and the quarterly filing is Form 10-Q. Information services such as **Finance.Yahoo.com** offer online data and analysis. ■

NEED-TO-KNOW 1-3

Accounting Equation

A1 ▶

Part 1: Use the *accounting equation* to compute the missing financial statement amounts.

Company	Assets	Liabilities	Equity
Bose	$150	$ 30	$ (a)
Vogue	$ (b)	$100	$300

Solution

a. $120   **b.** $400

Part 2: Use the *expanded accounting equation* to compute the missing financial statement amounts.

Company	Assets	Liabilities	Common Stock	Dividends	Revenues	Expenses
Tesla	$200	$ 80	$100	$5	$ (a)	$40
YouTube	$400	$160	$220	$ (b)	$ 120	$90

Do More: QS 1-7, QS 1-8, E 1-8, E 1-9

Solution

a. $65   **b.** $10

Transaction Analysis

Business activities are described in terms of transactions and events. **External transactions** are exchanges of value between two entities, which cause changes in the accounting equation. An example is the sale of the *AppleCare Protection Plan* by **Apple**. **Internal transactions** are exchanges within an entity, which may or may not affect the accounting equation. An example is **Target**'s use of its supplies, which are reported as expenses when used. **Events** are happenings that affect the accounting equation *and* are reliably measured. They include business events such as changes in the market value of certain assets and liabilities and natural events such as fires that destroy assets and create losses.

This section uses the accounting equation to analyze 11 transactions and events of FastForward, a start-up consulting (service) business, in its first month of operations. Remember that after each transaction and event, assets *always* equal liabilities plus equity.

Transaction 1: Investment by Owner   On December 1, Chas Taylor forms a consulting business named FastForward and set up as a corporation. FastForward evaluates the performance of footwear and accessories. Taylor owns and manages the business, which will publish online reviews and consult with clubs, athletes, and others who purchase **Nike** and **Adidas** products.

Taylor invests $30,000 cash in the new company and deposits the cash in a bank account opened under the name of FastForward. After this transaction, cash (an asset) and stockholders' equity each equals $30,000. Equity is increased by the owner's investment (stock issuance), which is included in the column titled Common Stock. The effect of this transaction on FastForward is shown in the accounting equation as follows (we label the equity entries).

P1

Analyze business transactions using the accounting equation.

FASTForward

Real company names are in bold magenta

	Assets	=	Liabilities	+	Equity
	Cash	=			Common Stock
(1)	+$30,000	=			+$30,000 Owner investment

Transaction 2: Purchase Supplies for Cash   FastForward uses $2,500 of its cash to buy supplies of Nike and Adidas footwear for performance testing over the next few months. This transaction is an exchange of cash, an asset, for another kind of asset, supplies. It simply changes the form of assets from cash to supplies. The decrease in cash is exactly equal to the increase in supplies. The supplies of footwear are assets because of the expected future benefits from the test results of their performance.

	Assets			=	Liabilities	+	Equity
	Cash	+	Supplies	=			Common Stock
Old Bal.	$30,000			=			$30,000
(2)	−2,500	+	$2,500				
New Bal.	$27,500	+	$2,500	=			$30,000
		$30,000				$30,000	

Transaction 3: Purchase Equipment for Cash   FastForward spends $26,000 to acquire equipment for testing footwear. Like Transaction 2, Transaction 3 is an exchange of one asset, cash, for another asset, equipment. The equipment is an asset because of its expected future benefits from testing footwear. This purchase changes the makeup of assets but does not change the asset total. The accounting equation remains in balance.

	Assets					=	Liabilities	+	Equity
	Cash	+	Supplies	+	Equipment	=			Common Stock
Old Bal.	$27,500	+	$2,500			=			$30,000
(3)	−26,000			+	$26,000				
New Bal.	$ 1,500	+	$2,500	+	$ 26,000	=			$30,000
		$30,000						$30,000	

Transaction 4: Purchase Supplies on Credit

Taylor decides more supplies of footwear and accessories are needed. These additional supplies cost $7,100, but FastForward has only $1,500 in cash. Taylor arranges to purchase them on credit from CalTech Supply Company. Thus, FastForward acquires supplies in exchange for a promise to pay for them later. This purchase increases assets by $7,100 in supplies, and liabilities (called *accounts payable* to CalTech Supply) increase by the same amount.

	Assets				=	Liabilities	+	Equity
	Cash	+	Supplies	+	Equipment	=	Accounts Payable	+	Common Stock
Old Bal.	$1,500	+	$2,500	+	$26,000	=			$30,000
(4)		+	7,100				+$7,100		
New Bal.	$1,500	+	$9,600	+	$26,000	=	$ 7,100	+	$30,000
			$37,100					$37,100	

Transaction 5: Provide Services for Cash

FastForward plans to earn revenues by selling online ad space and consulting with clients about footwear and accessories. It earns net income only if its revenues are greater than its expenses. In its first job, FastForward provides consulting services and immediately collects $4,200 cash. The accounting equation reflects this increase in cash of $4,200 and in equity of $4,200. This increase in equity is shown in the far right column under Revenues because the cash received is earned by providing consulting services.

	Assets				=	Liabilities	+	Equity		
	Cash	+	Supplies	+	Equipment	=	Accounts Payable	+	Common Stock	+	Revenues
Old Bal.	$1,500	+	$9,600	+	$26,000	=	$7,100	+	$30,000		
(5)	+4,200									+	$4,200 Consulting
New Bal.	$5,700	+	$9,600	+	$26,000	=	$7,100	+	$30,000	+	$ 4,200
			$41,300						$41,300		

Transactions 6 and 7: Payment of Expenses in Cash

FastForward pays $1,000 to rent its facilities. Paying this amount allows FastForward to occupy the space for the month of December. The rental payment is shown in the following accounting equation as Transaction 6. FastForward also pays the biweekly $700 salary of the company's only employee. This is shown in the accounting equation as Transaction 7. Both Transactions 6 and 7 are December expenses for FastForward. The costs of both rent and salary are expenses, not assets, because their benefits are used in December (they have no future benefits after December). The accounting equation shows that both transactions reduce cash and equity. The far right column shows these decreases as Expenses.

Increases in expenses yield decreases in equity.

	Assets				=	Liabilities	+	Equity				
	Cash	+	Supplies	+	Equipment	=	Accounts Payable	+	Common Stock	+	Revenues	−	Expenses
Old Bal.	$5,700	+	$9,600	+	$26,000	=	$7,100	+	$30,000	+	$4,200		
(6)	−1,000											−	$1,000 Rent
Bal.	4,700	+	9,600	+	26,000	=	7,100	+	30,000	+	4,200	−	1,000
(7)	− 700											−	700 Salaries
New Bal.	$4,000	+	$9,600	+	$26,000	=	$7,100	+	$30,000	+	$4,200	−	$ 1,700
			$39,600						$39,600				

Transaction 8: Provide Services and Facilities for Credit

FastForward provides consulting services of $1,600 and rents its test facilities for an additional $300 to Adidas on credit. Adidas is billed for the $1,900 total. This transaction creates a new asset, called *accounts receivable,* from Adidas. Accounts receivable is increased instead of cash because the payment has not yet been received. Equity is increased from the two revenue components shown in the Revenues column of the accounting equation.

Point: Transaction 8, like 5, records revenue when work is performed, not necessarily when cash is received.

	Cash	+	Accounts Receivable	+	Supplies	+	Equipment	=	Accounts Payable	+	Common Stock	+	Revenues	−	Expenses
							Assets	=	*Liabilities*	+			*Equity*		
Old Bal.	$4,000			+	$9,600	+	$26,000	=	$7,100	+	$30,000	+	$4,200	−	$1,700
(8)		+	$1,900									+	1,600 Consulting		
												+	300 Rental		
New Bal.	$4,000	+	$ 1,900	+	$9,600	+	$26,000	=	$7,100	+	$30,000	+	$6,100	−	$1,700

$41,500 $41,500

Transaction 9: Receipt of Cash from Accounts Receivable

The client in Transaction 8 (Adidas) pays $1,900 to FastForward 10 days after it is billed for consulting services. This Transaction 9 does not change the total amount of assets and does not affect liabilities or equity. It converts the receivable (an asset) to cash (another asset). It does not create new revenue. Revenue was recognized when FastForward performed the services in Transaction 8, not when the cash is collected.

Point: Transaction 9 involved no added client work, so no added revenue is recorded.

Point: Receipt of cash is not always a revenue.

	Cash	+	Accounts Receivable	+	Supplies	+	Equipment	=	Accounts Payable	+	Common Stock	+	Revenues	−	Expenses
							Assets	=	*Liabilities*	+			*Equity*		
Old Bal.	$4,000	+	$1,900	+	$9,600	+	$26,000	=	$7,100	+	$30,000	+	$6,100	−	$1,700
(9)	+1,900	−	1,900												
New Bal.	$5,900	+	$ 0	+	$9,600	+	$26,000	=	$7,100	+	$30,000	+	$6,100	−	$1,700

$41,500 $41,500

Transaction 10: Payment of Accounts Payable

FastForward pays CalTech Supply $900 cash as partial payment for its earlier $7,100 purchase of supplies (Transaction 4), leaving $6,200 unpaid. This transaction decreases FastForward's cash by $900 and decreases its liability to CalTech Supply by $900. Equity does not change. This event does not create an expense even though cash flows out of FastForward (instead the expense is recorded when FastForward uses these supplies).

	Cash	+	Accounts Receivable	+	Supplies	+	Equipment	=	Accounts Payable	+	Common Stock	+	Revenues	−	Expenses
							Assets	=	*Liabilities*	+			*Equity*		
Old Bal.	$5,900	+	$ 0	+	$9,600	+	$26,000	=	$7,100	+	$30,000	+	$6,100	−	$1,700
(10)	−900								−900						
New Bal.	$5,000	+	$ 0	+	$9,600	+	$26,000	=	$6,200	+	$30,000	+	$6,100	−	$1,700

$40,600 $40,600

Transaction 11: Payment of Cash Dividend   FastForward declares and pays a

Increases in dividends yield decreases in equity.

$200 cash dividend to its owner (the sole shareholder). Dividends (decreases in equity) are not reported as expenses because they do not help earn revenue. Because dividends are not expenses, they are not used in computing net income.

	Assets				=	Liabilities	+			Equity			
	Cash	+ Accounts Receivable	+ Supplies	+ Equipment	=	Accounts Payable	+ Common Stock	− Dividends	+ Revenues	− Expenses
Old Bal.	$5,000	+ $ 0	+ $9,600	+ $26,000	=	$6,200	+ $30,000		+ $6,100	− $1,700
(11)	− 200							− $200 Dividends		
New Bal.	$4,800	+ $ 0	+ $9,600	+ $26,000	=	$6,200	+ $30,000	− $200	+ $6,100	− $1,700
		$40,400						$40,400		

EXHIBIT 1.9

Summary of Transactions Using the Accounting Equation

Summary of Transactions

Exhibit 1.9 shows the effects of these 11 transactions of FastForward using the accounting equation. Assets equal liabilities plus equity after each transaction.

	Assets				=	Liabilities	+		Equity		
	Cash	+ Accounts Receivable	+ Supplies	+ Equipment	=	Accounts Payable	+ Common Stock	− Dividends	+ Revenues	− Expenses
(1)	$30,000				=		$30,000			
(2)	− 2,500		+ $2,500							
Bal.	27,500		+ 2,500		=		30,000			
(3)	−26,000			+ $26,000						
Bal.	1,500		+ 2,500	+ 26,000	=		30,000			
(4)			+ 7,100		=	+$7,100				
Bal.	1,500		+ 9,600	+ 26,000	=	7,100	+ 30,000			
(5)	+ 4,200								+ $4,200	
Bal.	5,700		+ 9,600	+ 26,000	=	7,100	+ 30,000		+ 4,200	
(6)	− 1,000									− $1,000
Bal.	4,700		+ 9,600	+ 26,000	=	7,100	+ 30,000		+ 4,200	− 1,000
(7)	− 700									− 700
Bal.	4,000		+ 9,600	+ 26,000	=	7,100	+ 30,000		+ 4,200	− 1,700
(8)		+ $1,900							+ 1,600	
									+ 300	
Bal.	4,000	+ 1,900	+ 9,600	+ 26,000	=	7,100	+ 30,000		6,100	− 1,700
(9)	+ 1,900	− 1,900								
Bal.	5,900	+ 0	+ 9,600	+ 26,000	=	7,100	+ 30,000		+ 6,100	− 1,700
(10)	− 900					− 900				
Bal.	5,000	+ 0	+ 9,600	+ 26,000	=	6,200	+ 30,000		+ 6,100	− 1,700
(11)	− 200							− $200		
Bal.	$ 4,800	+ $ 0	+ $ 9,600	+ $ 26,000	=	$ 6,200	+ $ 30,000	− $ 200	+ $6,100	− $ 1,700

Assume Tata Company began operations on January 1 and completed the following transactions during its first month of operations. Arrange the following asset, liability, and equity titles in a table like Exhibit 1.9: Cash; Accounts Receivable; Equipment; Accounts Payable; Common Stock; Dividends; Revenues; and Expenses.

Jan. 1   Jamsetji Tata invested $4,000 cash in Tata Company in exchange for its common stock.
        5   The company purchased $2,000 of equipment on credit.
      14   The company provided $540 of services for a client on credit.
      21   The company paid $250 cash for an employee's salary.

Solution

	Assets				=	Liabilities	+			Equity				
	Cash	+	Accounts Receivable	+	Equipment	=	Accounts Payable	+	Common Stock	−	Dividends	+	Revenues	−	Expenses
Jan. 1	$4,000					=			$4,000						
Jan. 5				+	$2,000		+$2,000								
Bal.	4,000			+	2,000	=	2,000	+	4,000						
Jan. 14		+	$540									+	$540		
Bal.	4,000	+	540	+	2,000	=	2,000	+	4,000			+	540		
Jan. 21	−250													−	$250
Bal.	3,750	+	540	+	2,000	=	2,000	+	4,000			+	540	−	250

$6,290 $6,290

COMMUNICATING WITH USERS

Financial statements are prepared in the order below using the 11 transactions of FastForward. (These statements are *unadjusted*—we explain this in Chapters 2 and 3.) The four financial statements and their purposes follow.

P2

Identify and prepare basic financial statements and explain how they interrelate.

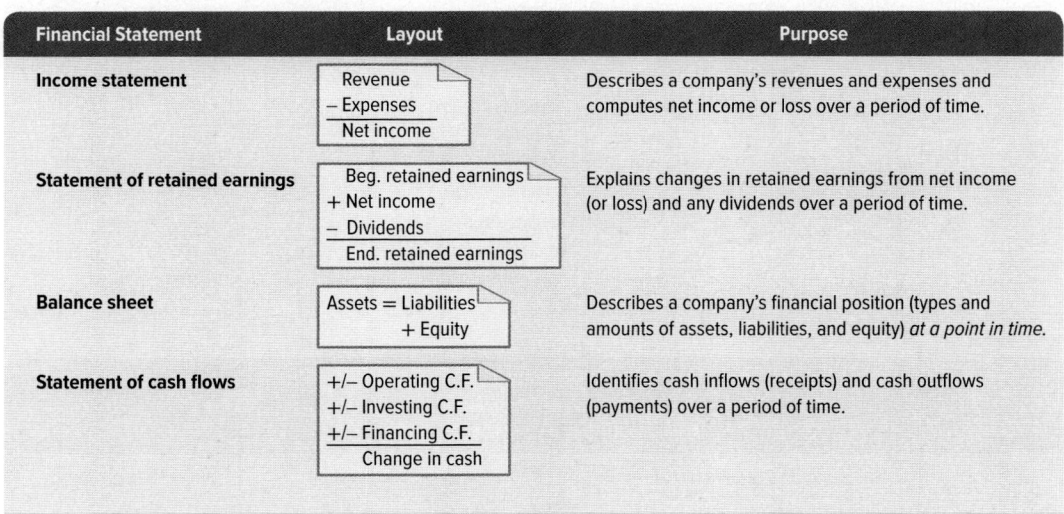

Financial Statement	Layout	Purpose
Income statement	Revenue − Expenses Net income	Describes a company's revenues and expenses and computes net income or loss over a period of time.
Statement of retained earnings	Beg. retained earnings + Net income − Dividends End. retained earnings	Explains changes in retained earnings from net income (or loss) and any dividends over a period of time.
Balance sheet	Assets = Liabilities + Equity	Describes a company's financial position (types and amounts of assets, liabilities, and equity) *at a point in time.*
Statement of cash flows	+/− Operating C.F. +/− Investing C.F. +/− Financing C.F. Change in cash	Identifies cash inflows (receipts) and cash outflows (payments) over a period of time.

Income Statement

FastForward's income statement for December is shown at the top of Exhibit 1.10. Information about revenues and expenses is taken from the Equity columns of Exhibit 1.9. Revenues are reported first on the income statement. They include consulting revenues of $5,800 from Transactions 5 and 8 and rental revenue of $300 from Transaction 8. Expenses are reported after revenues. Rent and salary expenses are from Transactions 6 and 7. Expenses are the costs to generate the revenues reported. **Net income** occurs when revenues exceed expenses. A **net loss** occurs when expenses exceed revenues. Net income (or loss) is shown at the bottom of the statement and is the amount reported in December. Stockholders' investments and dividends are *not* part of income.

*Key **terms** are in bold and defined again in the* **glossary**

Point: Net income is sometimes called *earnings* or *profit.*

EXHIBIT 1.10

Financial Statements and
Their Links

Point: A statement's heading identifies the company, the statement
title, and the date or time period.

Point: Arrow lines show how the
statements are linked.
① Net income is used to
compute retained earnings.
② Retained earnings is used to
prepare the balance sheet.
③ Cash from the balance sheet is
used to reconcile the statement
of cash flows.

Point: The income statement, the
statement of retained earnings,
and the statement of cash flows
are prepared for a *period* of time.
The balance sheet is prepared as
of a *point* in time.

Point: A single ruled line means
an addition or subtraction. Final
totals are double underlined.
Negative amounts may or may
not be in parentheses.

FASTFORWARD
Income Statement
For Month Ended December 31, 2019

Revenues		
Consulting revenue ($4,200 + $1,600)	$ 5,800	
Rental revenue	300	
Total revenues		$ 6,100
Expenses		
Rent expense	1,000	
Salaries expense	700	
Total expenses		1,700
Net income		$ 4,400

FASTFORWARD
Statement of Retained Earnings
For Month Ended December 31, 2019

Retained earnings, December 1, 2019		$ 0
Plus: Net income		**4,400**
		4,400
Less: Dividends		200
Retained earnings, December 31, 2019		$ 4,200

①

FASTFORWARD
Balance Sheet
December 31, 2019

Assets		Liabilities	
Cash	$ 4,800	Accounts payable	$ 6,200
Supplies	9,600	Total liabilities	6,200
Equipment	26,000	**Equity**	
		Common stock	30,000
		Retained earnings	4,200
		Total equity	34,200
Total assets	$40,400	Total liabilities and equity	$ 40,400

②

FASTFORWARD
Statement of Cash Flows
For Month Ended December 31, 2019

Cash flows from operating activities		
Cash received from clients ($4,200 + $1,900)	$ 6,100	
Cash paid for expenses ($2,500 + $900 + $1,000 + $700). . . .	(5,100)	
Net cash provided by operating activities		$ 1,000
Cash flows from investing activities		
Cash paid for equipment	(26,000)	
Net cash used by investing activities		(26,000)
Cash flows from financing activities		
Cash investments from shareholders	30,000	
Cash dividends to shareholders	(200)	
Net cash provided by financing activities		29,800
Net increase in cash		$ 4,800
Cash balance, December 1, 2019		0
Cash balance, December 31, 2019		$ 4,800

③

Statement of Retained Earnings

The statement of retained earnings reports how retained earnings changes over the reporting period. This statement shows beginning retained earnings, events that increase it (net income), and events that decrease it (dividends and net loss). Ending retained earnings is computed in this statement and is carried over and reported on the balance sheet. FastForward's statement of retained earnings is the second report in Exhibit 1.10. The beginning balance is measured as of the start of business on December 1. It is zero because FastForward did not exist before then. An existing business reports a beginning balance equal to the prior period's ending balance (such as from November 30). FastForward's statement shows the $4,400 of net income for the period, which links the income statement to the statement of retained earnings (see line ①). The statement also reports the $200 cash dividend and FastForward's end-of-period retained earnings balance.

©Pavel1964/Shutterstock

Balance Sheet

FastForward's balance sheet is the third report in Exhibit 1.10. This statement shows FastForward's financial position at the end of business day on December 31. The left side of the balance sheet lists FastForward's assets: cash, supplies, and equipment. The upper right side of the balance sheet shows that FastForward owes $6,200 to creditors. Any other liabilities (such as a bank loan) would be listed here. The equity balance is $34,200. Line ② shows the link between the ending balance of the statement of retained earnings and the retained earnings balance on the balance sheet. (This presentation of the balance sheet is called the *account form:* assets on the left and liabilities and equity on the right. Another presentation is the *report form:* assets on top, followed by liabilities and then equity at the bottom. Both are acceptable.) As always, the accounting equation balances: Assets of $40,400 = Liabilities of $6,200 + Equity of $34,200.

Statement of Cash Flows

FastForward's statement of cash flows is the final report in Exhibit 1.10. The first section reports cash flows from *operating activities*. It shows the $6,100 cash received from clients and the $5,100 cash paid for supplies, rent, and employee salaries. Outflows are in parentheses to denote subtraction. Net cash provided by operating activities for December is $1,000. The second section reports *investing activities,* which involve buying and selling assets such as land and equipment that are held for *long-term use* (typically more than one year). The only investing activity is the $26,000 purchase of equipment. The third section shows cash flows from *financing activities,* which include *long-term* borrowing and repaying of cash from lenders and the cash investments from, and dividends to, stockholders. FastForward reports $30,000 from the owner's initial investment and a $200 cash dividend. The net cash effect of all financing transactions is a $29,800 cash inflow. The final part of the statement shows an increased cash balance of $4,800. The ending balance is also $4,800 as it started with no cash—see line ③.

Point: Payment for supplies is an operating activity because supplies are expected to be used up in short-term operations (typically less than one year).

Point: Investing activities refer to long-term asset investments by the company, *not* to owner investments.

Prepare the (a) income statement, (b) statement of retained earnings, and (c) balance sheet for **Apple** using the following *condensed* data from its fiscal year ended September 30, 2017 ($ in millions).

NEED-TO-KNOW 1-5

Financial Statements

P2

APPLE

Accounts payable	$ 49,049	Revenues	$229,234
Other liabilities	192,223	Investments and other assets	303,373
Cost of sales	141,048	Land and equipment (net)	33,783
Cash	20,289	Selling, general, and other expenses	39,835
Common stock	35,867	Accounts receivable	17,874
Retained earnings, Sep. 24, 2016	96,998	Net income	48,351
Dividends	47,169	Retained earnings, Sep. 30, 2017	98,180

Solution ($ in millions)

APPLE
Income Statement
For Fiscal Year Ended September 30, 2017

Revenues		$229,234
Expenses		
Cost of sales	$141,048	
Selling, general, and other expenses	39,835	
Total expenses		180,883
Net income		**$ 48,351**

APPLE
Statement of Retained Earnings
For Fiscal Year Ended September 30, 2017

Retained earnings, Sep. 24, 2016	$ 96,998
Plus: Net income	**48,351**
	145,349
Less: Dividends	47,169
Retained earnings, Sep. 30, 2017	**$ 98,180**

APPLE
Balance Sheet
September 30, 2017

Assets		Liabilities	
Cash	$ 20,289	Accounts payable	$ 49,049
Accounts receivable	17,874	Other liabilities	192,223
Land and equipment (net)	33,783	Total liabilities	241,272
Investments and other assets	303,373	**Equity**	
		Common stock	35,867
		Retained earnings	**98,180**
		Total equity	134,047
Total assets	$375,319	Total liabilities and equity	$375,319

Do More: QS 1-12, QS 1-13,
QS 1-14, E 1-15, E 1-16,
E 1-17

---

*Decision Analysis (a section at the end of each chapter) covers ratios for decision making using real
company data. Instructors can skip this section and cover all ratios in Chapter 13*

Decision Analysis ▢▢▢   Return on Assets

A2

Compute and interpret
return on assets.

We organize financial statement analysis into four areas: (1) liquidity and efficiency, (2) solvency,
(3) profitability, and (4) market prospects—Chapter 13 has a ratio listing with definitions and groupings
by area. When analyzing ratios, we use a company's prior-year ratios and competitor ratios to identify
good, bad, or average performance.

This chapter presents a profitability measure: return on assets. Return on assets is useful in evaluating
management, analyzing and forecasting profits, and planning activities. **Return on assets (ROA),** also
called *return on investment (ROI)*, is defined in Exhibit 1.11.

EXHIBIT 1.11

Return on Assets

$$\text{Return on assets} = \frac{\text{Net income}}{\text{Average total assets}}$$

Net income is from the annual income statement, and average total assets is computed by adding the beginning and ending amounts for that same period and dividing by 2. **Nike** reports total net income of $4,240
million for the current year. At the beginning of the current year its total assets are $21,396 million, and at
the end of the current year they total $23,259 million. Nike's return on assets for the current year is:

$$\text{Return on assets} = \frac{\$4,240 \text{ million}}{(\$21,396 \text{ million} + \$23,259 \text{ million})/2} = 19.0\%$$

Is a 19.0% return on assets good or bad for Nike? To help answer this question, we compare (benchmark) Nike's return with its prior performance and the return of its competitor, **Under Armour** (see Exhibit 1.12). Nike shows a stable pattern of good returns that reflects effective use of assets. Nike has outperformed Under Armour in each of the last three years. Its management performed well based on Nike's return on assets.

Return on Assets	Current Year	1 Year Ago	2 Years Ago
Nike.	19.0%	17.5%	16.3%
Under Armour	7.9	9.4	11.4

EXHIBIT 1.12

Nike and Under Armour Returns

Decision Analysis ends with a role-playing scenario to show the usefulness of ratios

■ Decision Maker

Business Owner   You own a winter ski resort that earns a 21% return on its assets. An opportunity to purchase a winter ski equipment manufacturer is offered to you. This manufacturer earns a 14% return on its assets. The industry return for competitors of this manufacturer is 9%. Do you purchase this manufacturer? ■ *Answer:* The 14% return on assets for the manufacturer exceeds the 9% industry return. This is positive for a potential purchase. Also, this purchase is an opportunity to spread your risk over two businesses. Still, you should hesitate to purchase a business whose 14% return is lower than your current 21% return. You might better direct efforts to increase investment in your resort if it can earn more than the 14% alternative.

Comprehensive Need-to-Know is a review of key chapter content; the Planning the Solution section offers strategies in solving it

After several months of planning, Jasmine Worthy started a haircutting business called Expressions. The following events occurred during its first month of business.

NEED-TO-KNOW 1-6

COMPREHENSIVE

Transaction Analysis, Statement Preparation, and Return on Assets

a. Aug.	1	Worthy invested $3,000 cash and $15,000 of equipment in Expressions in exchange for its common stock.
b.	2	Expressions paid $600 cash for furniture for the shop.
c.	3	Expressions paid $500 cash to rent space in a strip mall for August.
d.	4	Purchased $1,200 of equipment on credit for the shop (recorded as accounts payable).
e.	15	Expressions opened for business on August 5. Cash received from haircutting services in the first week and a half of business (ended August 15) was $825.
f.	16	Expressions provided $100 of haircutting services on credit.
g.	17	Expressions received a $100 check for services previously rendered on credit.
h.	18	Expressions paid $125 cash to an assistant for hours worked for the grand opening.
i.	31	Cash received from services provided during the second half of August was $930.
j.	31	Expressions paid $400 cash toward the accounts payable entered into on August 4.
k.	31	Expressions paid a $900 cash dividend to Worthy (sole shareholder).

Required

1. Arrange the following asset, liability, and equity titles in a table similar to the one in Exhibit 1.9: Cash; Accounts Receivable; Furniture; Store Equipment; Accounts Payable; Common Stock; Dividends; Revenues; and Expenses. Show the effects of each transaction using the accounting equation.
2. Prepare an income statement for August.
3. Prepare a statement of retained earnings for August.
4. Prepare a balance sheet as of August 31.
5. Prepare a statement of cash flows for August.
6. Determine the return on assets ratio for August.

PLANNING THE SOLUTION

- Set up a table like Exhibit 1.9 with the appropriate columns for accounts.
- Analyze each transaction and show its effects as increases or decreases in the appropriate columns. Be sure the accounting equation remains in balance after each transaction.
- Prepare the income statement, and identify revenues and expenses. List those items on the statement, compute the difference, and label the result as *net income* or *net loss*.
- Use information in the Equity columns to prepare the statement of retained earnings.
- Use information in the last row of the transactions table to prepare the balance sheet.
- Prepare the statement of cash flows; include all events listed in the Cash column of the transactions table. Classify each cash flow as operating, investing, or financing.
- Calculate return on assets by dividing net income by average assets.

SOLUTION

1.

	Cash	+	Accounts Receivable	+	Furniture	+	Store Equipment	=	Accounts Payable	+	Common Stock	−	Dividends	+	Revenues	−	Expenses
	Assets							=	**Liabilities**	+			**Equity**				
a.	$3,000						$15,000				$18,000						
b.	− 600			+	$600												
Bal.	2,400			+	600	+	15,000	=			18,000						
c.	− 500															−	$500
Bal.	1,900			+	600	+	15,000	=			18,000					−	500
d.						+	1,200		+$1,200								
Bal.	1,900			+	600	+	16,200	=	1,200	+	18,000					−	500
e.	+ 825													+	$ 825		
Bal.	2,725			+	600	+	16,200	=	1,200	+	18,000			+	825	−	500
f.		+	$100											+	100		
Bal.	2,725	+	100	+	600	+	16,200	=	1,200	+	18,000			+	925	−	500
g.	+ 100	−	100														
Bal.	2,825	+	0	+	600	+	16,200	=	1,200	+	18,000			+	925	−	500
h.	− 125															−	125
Bal.	2,700	+	0	+	600	+	16,200	=	1,200	+	18,000			+	925	−	625
i.	+ 930													+	930		
Bal.	3,630	+	0	+	600	+	16,200	=	1,200	+	18,000			+	1,855	−	625
j.	− 400								− 400								
Bal.	3,230	+	0	+	600	+	16,200	=	800	+	18,000			+	1,855	−	625
k.	− 900											−	$900				
Bal.	$ 2,330	+	0	+	$ 600	+	$ 16,200	=	$ 800	+	$ 18,000	−	$ 900	+	$1,855	−	$625

2.

EXPRESSIONS
Income Statement
For Month Ended August 31

Revenues		
Haircutting services revenue		$ 1,855
Expenses		
Rent expense	$ 500	
Wages expense	125	
Total expenses		625
Net income		$ 1,230

3.

EXPRESSIONS
Statement of Retained Earnings
For Month Ended August 31

Retained earnings, August 1*.............		$ 0
Plus: Net income		1,230
		1,230
Less: Dividends		900
Retained earnings, August 31		$ 330

*If Expressions had existed before August 1, the beginning retained earnings balance would equal the prior period's ending balance.

[continued on next page]

4.

EXPRESSIONS
Balance Sheet
August 31

Assets		Liabilities	
Cash	$ 2,330	Accounts payable	$ 800
Furniture	600	**Equity**	
Store equipment	16,200	Common stock	18,000
		Retained earnings	330
		Total equity	18,330
Total assets	$19,130	Total liabilities and equity	$19,130

5.

EXPRESSIONS
Statement of Cash Flows
For Month Ended August 31

Cash flows from operating activities		
Cash received from customers	$1,855	
Cash paid for expenditures ($500 + $125 + $400)	(1,025)	
Net cash provided by operating activities		$ 830
Cash flows from investing activities		
Cash paid for furniture		(600)
Cash flows from financing activities		
Cash investments from shareholders	3,000	
Cash dividends to shareholders	(900)	
Net cash provided by financing activities		2,100
Net increase in cash		$2,330
Cash balance, August 1		0
Cash balance, August 31		$2,330

6. $$\text{Return on assets} = \frac{\text{Net income}}{\text{Average assets}} = \frac{\$1,230}{(\$18,000^* + \$19,130)/2} = \frac{\$1,230}{\$18,565} = \underline{\underline{6.63\%}}$$

*Uses the initial $18,000 investment as the beginning balance for the *start-up period only*.

Return and Risk

1A

A3

Explain the relation between return and risk.

This appendix covers return and risk analysis.

Net income is often linked to **return.** Return on assets (ROA) is stated in ratio form as income divided by assets invested. For example, banks report return from a savings account in the form of an interest return such as 2%. We also could invest in a company's stock, or even start our own business. How do we decide among these options? The answer depends on our trade-off between return and risk.

Risk is the uncertainty about the return we will earn. All business investments involve risk, but some investments involve more risk than others. The lower the risk of an investment, the lower is our expected return. The reason that savings accounts pay such a low return is the low risk of not being repaid with interest (the government guarantees most savings accounts). If we buy a share of **eBay** or any other company, we might get a large return. However, we have no guarantee of any return; there is even the risk of loss.

Exhibit 1A.1 shows recent returns for 10-year bonds with different risks. *Bonds* are written promises by organizations to repay amounts loaned with interest. U.S. Treasury bonds have a low expected return, but they also have low risk because they are backed by the U.S. government. High-risk corporate bonds have a much larger potential return but have much higher risk.

The trade-off between return and risk is a normal part of business. Higher risk implies higher, but riskier, expected returns. To help us make better decisions, we use accounting information to assess both return and risk.

EXHIBIT 1A.1

Average Returns for Bonds with Different Risks

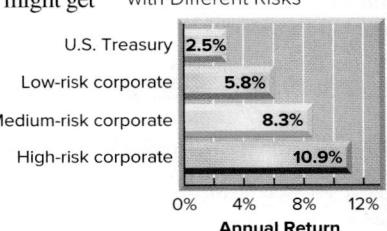

APPENDIX

1B

Business Activities

C5

Identify and describe the three major activities of organizations.

Point: Investing (assets) and financing (liabilities plus equity) totals are *always* equal.

EXHIBIT 1B.1

Activities of Organizations

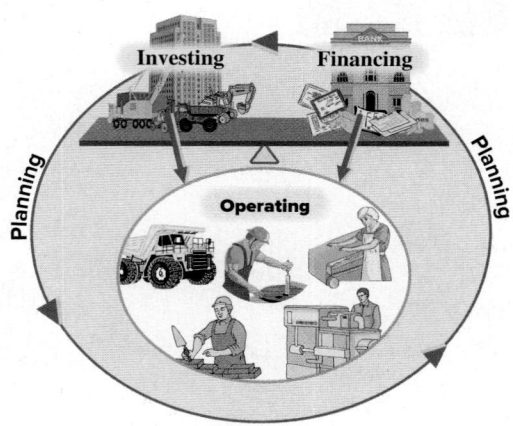

This appendix explains how the accounting equation is linked to business activities. There are three major types of business activities: financing, investing, and operating. Each of these requires planning. *Planning* is defining an organization's ideas, goals, and actions.

Financing *Financing activities* provide the resources organizations use to pay for assets such as land, buildings, and equipment. The two sources of financing are owner and nonowner. *Owner financing* refers to resources contributed by the owner along with any income the owner leaves in the organization. *Nonowner* (or *creditor*) *financing* refers to resources loaned by creditors (lenders).

Investing *Investing activities* are the acquiring and disposing of assets that an organization uses to buy and sell its products or services. Some organizations require land and factories to operate. Others need only an office. Invested amounts are referred to as *assets*. Creditor and owner financing hold claims on assets. Creditors' claims are called *liabilities,* and the owner's claim is called *equity*. This yields the *accounting equation:* Assets = Liabilities + Equity.

Operating *Operating activities* involve using resources to research, develop, purchase, produce, distribute, and market products and services. Sales and revenues are the inflow of assets from selling products and services. Costs and expenses are the outflow of assets to support operating activities.

Exhibit 1B.1 summarizes business activities. Planning is part of each activity and gives them meaning and focus. Investing (assets) and financing (liabilities and equity) are opposite each other because they always are equal. Operating activities are below to show that they are the result of investing and financing.

Summary: Cheat Sheet

ACCOUNTING USES

External users: Do not directly run the organization and have limited access to its accounting information. Examples are lenders, shareholders, boards of directors, external auditors, nonexecutive employees, labor unions, regulators, voters, donors, suppliers, and customers.
Internal users: Directly manage organization operations. Examples are the CEO and other executives, research and development managers, purchasing managers, production managers, and other managerial-level employees.
Private accounting: Accounting employees working for businesses.
Public accounting: Offering audit, tax, and accounting services to others.

ETHICS AND ACCOUNTING

Fraud triangle: Factors that push a person to commit fraud.

- **Opportunity:** Must be able to commit fraud with a low risk of getting caught.
- **Pressure,** or incentive: Must feel pressure or have incentive to commit fraud.
- **Rationalization,** or attitude: Justifies fraud or does not see its criminal nature.

Common business entities:

	Sole Proprietorship	Partnership
Number of owners	1 owner; easy to set up.	2 or more, called *partners;* easy to set up.
Business taxation	No additional business income tax.	No additional business income tax.
Owner liability	Unlimited liability. Owner is personally liable for proprietorship debts.	Unlimited liability. Partners are jointly liable for partnership debts.
Legal entity	*Not* a separate legal entity.	*Not* a separate legal entity.
Business life	Business ends with owner death or choice.	Business ends with a partner death or choice.

	Corporation	Limited Liability Company (LLC)
Number of owners	1 or more, called *stockholders;* can get many investors by selling **stock** or **shares** of corporate ownership.	1 or more, called *members*.
Business taxation	Additional corporate income tax.	No additional business income tax.
Owner liability	Limited liability. Owners, called **stockholders** (or **shareholders**), are not liable for corporate acts and debts.	Limited liability. Owners, called **members**, are not personally liable for LLC debts.
Legal entity	A separate entity with the same rights and responsibilities as a person.	A separate entity with the same rights and responsibilities as a person.
Business life	Indefinite.	Indefinite.

SYSTEM OF ACCOUNTS

Assets: Resources a company owns or controls that are expected to yield future benefits.
Liabilities: Creditors' claims on assets. These are obligations to provide assets, products, or services to others.
Equity: Shareholders' claim on assets. It consists of:

+ Common Stock	**Common stock** reflects inflows of cash and other net assets from stockholders in exchange for stock.
— Dividends	**Dividends** are outflows of cash and other assets to stockholders that reduce equity.
+ Revenues	**Revenues** increase equity (via net income) from sales of products and services to customers; examples are sales of products, consulting services provided, facilities rented to others, and commissions from services.
— Expenses	**Expenses** decrease equity (via net income) from costs of providing products and services to customers; examples are costs of employee time, use of supplies, advertising, utilities, and insurance fees.

TRANSACTION ANALYSIS

Accounting equation: Applies to all transactions and events, to all companies and organizations, and to all points in time.

$$\text{Assets} = \text{Liabilities} + \text{Equity}$$

Summary of transactions:

	Cash	+ Accounts Receivable	+ Supplies	+ Equipment	= Accounts Payable	+ Common Stock	− Dividends	+ Revenues	− Expenses
(1)	$30,000				=	$30,000			
(2)	− 2,500		+ $2,500						
Bal.	27,500		+ 2,500		=	30,000			
(3)	−26,000			+ $26,000					
Bal.	1,500		+ 2,500	+ 26,000		30,000			
(4)			+ 7,100		= +$7,100				
Bal.	1,500		+ 9,600	+ 26,000	= 7,100	+ 30,000			
(5)	+ 4,200							+ $4,200	
Bal.	5,700		+ 9,600	+ 26,000	= 7,100	+ 30,000		+ 4,200	
(6)	− 1,000								− $1,000
Bal.	4,700		+ 9,600	+ 26,000	= 7,100	+ 30,000		+ 4,200	− 1,000
(7)	− 700								− 700
Bal.	4,000		+ 9,600	+ 26,000	= 7,100	+ 30,000		+ 4,200	− 1,700
(8)		+ $1,900						+ 1,600	
								+ 300	
Bal.	4,000 +	1,900	+ 9,600	+ 26,000	= 7,100	+ 30,000		6,100	− 1,700
(9)	+ 1,900 −	1,900							
Bal.	5,900 +	0	+ 9,600	+ 26,000	= 7,100	+ 30,000		+ 6,100	− 1,700
(10)	− 900				− 900				
Bal.	5,000 +	0	+ 9,600	+ 26,000	= 6,200	+ 30,000		+ 6,100	− 1,700
(11)	− 200						− $200		
Bal.	$ 4,800 +	$ 0	+ $9,600	+ $ 26,000	= $ 6,200	+ $ 30,000	− $ 200	+ $6,100	− $ 1,700

Transaction 1: Investment by owner
Transaction 2: Purchase supplies for cash
Transaction 3: Purchase equipment for cash
Transaction 4: Purchase supplies on credit
Transaction 5: Provide services for cash
Transactions 6 and 7: Payment of expenses in cash
Transaction 8: Provide services and facilities for credit
Transaction 9: Receipt of cash from accounts receivable
Transaction 10: Payment of accounts payable
Transaction 11: Payment of cash dividends

FINANCIAL STATEMENTS

Financial Statement	Layout	Purpose
Income statement	Revenue − Expenses Net income	Describes a company's revenues and expenses and computes net income or loss over a period of time.
Statement of retained earnings	Beg. retained earnings + Net income − Dividends End. retained earnings	Explains changes in retained earnings from net income (or loss) and any dividends over a period of time.
Balance sheet	Assets = Liabilities + Equity	Describes a company's financial position (types and amounts of assets, liabilities, and equity) *at a point in time.*
Statement of cash flows	+/− Operating C.F. +/− Investing C.F. +/− Financing C.F. Change in cash	Identifies cash inflows (receipts) and cash outflows (payments) over a period of time.

A list of key terms concludes each chapter (a complete glossary is also available)

Key Terms

Accounting (3)
Accounting equation (10)
Assets (9)
Audit (6)
Auditors (6)
Balance sheet (15)
Bookkeeping (3)
Business entity assumption (8)
Common stock (8, 10)
Conceptual framework (7)
Contributed capital (10)
Corporation (8)
Cost-benefit constraint (8)
Cost constraint (8)
Cost principle (7)
Dividends (10)
Dodd-Frank Wall Street Reform and Consumer Protection Act (6)
Double taxation (9)
Equity (9)
Ethics (6)
Events (11)
Expanded accounting equation (10)
Expense recognition principle (8)

Expenses (10)
External transactions (11)
External users (4)
Financial accounting (4)
Financial Accounting Standards Board (FASB) (7)
Full disclosure principle (8)
Generally accepted accounting principles (GAAP) (7)
Going-concern assumption (8)
Income statement (15)
Internal controls (6)
Internal transactions (11)
Internal users (4)
International Accounting Standards Board (IASB) (7)
International Financial Reporting Standards (IFRS) (7)
Liabilities (9)
Limited liability company (LLC) (8)
Managerial accounting (4)
Matching principle (8)
Measurement principle (7)
Members (8)

Monetary unit assumption (8)
Net income (15)
Net loss (15)
Owner investments (10)
Partnership (8)
Proprietorship (8)
Recordkeeping (3)
Retained earnings (10)
Return (21)
Return on assets (ROA) (18)
Revenue recognition principle (7)
Revenues (10)
Risk (21)
Sarbanes-Oxley Act (SOX) (6)
Securities and Exchange Commission (SEC) (7)
Shareholders (8)
Shares (8)
Sole proprietorship (8)
Statement of cash flows (15)
Statement of retained earnings (15)
Stock (8)
Stockholders (8)
Time period assumption (8)

Multiple Choice Quiz

1. A building is offered for sale at $500,000 but is currently assessed at $400,000. The purchaser of the building believes the building is worth $475,000, but ultimately purchases the building for $450,000. The purchaser records the building at:

a. $50,000.
b. $400,000.
c. $450,000.
d. $475,000.
e. $500,000.

2. On December 30 of the current year, **KPMG** signs a $150,000 contract to provide accounting services to one of its clients in *the next year*. KPMG has a December 31 year-end. Which accounting principle or assumption requires KPMG to record the accounting services revenue from this client in *the next year* and not in the current year?

   a. Business entity assumption

   b. Revenue recognition principle

   c. Monetary unit assumption

   d. Cost principle

   e. Going-concern assumption

3. If the assets of a company increase by $100,000 during the year and its liabilities increase by $35,000 during the same year, then the change in equity of the company during the year must have been:

   a. An increase of $135,000.   **d.** An increase of $65,000.

   b. A decrease of $135,000.   **e.** An increase of $100,000.

   c. A decrease of $65,000.

4. **Brunswick** borrows $50,000 cash from Third National Bank. How does this transaction affect the accounting equation for Brunswick?

   a. Assets increase by $50,000; liabilities increase by $50,000; no effect on equity.

   b. Assets increase by $50,000; no effect on liabilities; equity increases by $50,000.

   c. Assets increase by $50,000; liabilities decrease by $50,000; no effect on equity.

   d. No effect on assets; liabilities increase by $50,000; equity increases by $50,000.

   e. No effect on assets; liabilities increase by $50,000; equity decreases by $50,000.

5. **Geek Squad** performs services for a customer and bills the customer for $500. How would Geek Squad record this transaction?

   a. Accounts receivable increase by $500; revenues increase by $500.

   b. Cash increases by $500; revenues increase by $500.

   c. Accounts receivable increase by $500; revenues decrease by $500.

   d. Accounts receivable increase by $500; accounts payable increase by $500.

   e. Accounts payable increase by $500; revenues increase by $500.

ANSWERS TO MULTIPLE CHOICE QUIZ

1. c; $450,000 is the actual cost incurred.

2. b; revenue is recorded when services are provided.

3. d;

Assets	=	Liabilities	+	Equity
+$100,000	=	+$35,000	+	?

Change in equity = $100,000 − $35,000 = $65,000

4. a

5. a

A(B) *Superscript letter A or B denotes assignments based on Appendix 1A or 1B.*

🔲 Icon denotes assignments that involve decision making.

Discussion Questions

1. What is the purpose of accounting in society?

2. Technology is increasingly used to process accounting data. Why then must we study and understand accounting?

3. 🔲 Identify four kinds of external users and describe how they use accounting information.

4. 🔲 What are at least three questions business owners and managers might be able to answer by looking at accounting information?

5. Identify three actual businesses that offer services and three actual businesses that offer products.

6. 🔲 Describe the internal role of accounting for organizations.

7. Identify three types of services typically offered by accounting professionals.

8. 🔲 What type of accounting information might be useful to the marketing managers of a business?

9. Why is accounting described as a service activity?

10. What are some accounting-related professions?

11. How do ethics rules affect auditors' choice of clients?

12. What work do tax accounting professionals perform in addition to preparing tax returns?

13. What does the concept of *objectivity* imply for information reported in financial statements?

14. A business reports its own office stationery on the balance sheet at its $400 cost, although it cannot be sold for more than $10 as scrap paper. Which accounting principle and/or assumption justifies this treatment?

15. Why is the revenue recognition principle needed? What does it demand?

16. Describe the four basic forms of business organization and their key attributes.

17. Define (*a*) *assets,* (*b*) *liabilities,* (*c*) *equity,* and (*d*) *net assets.*

18. What events or transactions change equity?

19. Identify the two main categories of accounting principles.

20. What do accountants mean by the term *revenue*?

21. Define *net income* and explain its computation.

22. Identify the four basic financial statements of a business.

23. 🔲 What information is reported in an income statement?

24. Give two examples of expenses a business might incur.

25. What is the purpose of the statement of retained earnings?

26. 🔲 What information is reported in a balance sheet?

27. The statement of cash flows reports on what major activities?

28. 🔲 Define and explain return on assets.

29.A 🔲 Define return and risk. Discuss the trade-off between them.

30.B Describe the three major business activities in organizations.

31.B Explain why investing (assets) and financing (liabilities and equity) totals are always equal.

32. Refer to **Google**'s financial statements in **GOOGLE** Appendix A near the end of the text. To what level of significance are dollar amounts rounded? What time period does its income statement cover?

33. 🔲 Access the SEC EDGAR database (**SEC.gov**) and retrieve **Apple**'s 2017 10-K **APPLE** (filed November 3, 2017). Identify its auditor. What responsibility does its independent auditor claim regarding Apple's financial statements?

Connect reproduces assignments online, in static or algorithmic mode, which allows instructors to monitor, promote, and assess student learning. It can be used for practice, homework, or exams

ᵐᶜGraw Hill Education connect·

Quick Study exercises offer a brief check of key points.

Choose the term or phrase below that best completes each statement.

a. Accounting **c.** Recording **e.** Governmental **g.** Language of business

b. Identifying **d.** Communicating **f.** Technology **h.** Recordkeeping (bookkeeping)

1. _____ reduces the time, effort, and cost of recordkeeping while improving clerical accuracy.

2. _____ requires that we input, measure, and log transactions and events.

3. _____ is the recording of transactions and events, either manually or electronically.

QUICK STUDY

QS 1-1
Understanding accounting
C1

Identify the following users as either external users (E) or internal users (I).

_____ **a.** Customers   _____ **e.** Managers   _____ **i.** Controllers

_____ **b.** Suppliers   _____ **f.** District attorney   _____ **j.** FBI and IRS

_____ **c.** External auditors   _____ **g.** Shareholders   _____ **k.** Consumer group

_____ **d.** Business press   _____ **h.** Lenders   _____ **l.** Directors

QS 1-2
Identifying accounting users
C2

The fraud triangle asserts that the following *three* factors must exist for a person to commit fraud.

A. Opportunity **B.** Pressure **C.** Rationalization

Identify the fraud risk factor (A, B, or C) in each of the following situations.

_____ **1.** The business has no cameras or security devices at its warehouse.

_____ **2.** Managers are expected to grow business or be fired.

_____ **3.** A worker sees other employees regularly take inventory for personal use.

_____ **4.** No one matches the cash in the register to receipts when shifts end.

_____ **5.** Officers are told to show rising income or risk layoffs.

_____ **6.** A worker feels that fellow employees are not honest.

QS 1-3
Identifying ethical risks
C3 ▲

This icon highlights ethics-related assignments

Identify each of the following terms or phrases as an accounting (*a*) principle, (*b*) assumption, or (*c*) constraint.

_____ **1.** Full disclosure   _____ **3.** Going-concern

_____ **2.** Time period   _____ **4.** Revenue recognition

QS 1-4
Identifying principles, assumptions, and constraints C4

Complete the following table with either a *yes* or *no* regarding the attributes of a proprietorship, partnership, corporation, and limited liability company (LLC).

QS 1-5
Identifying attributes of businesses
C4

Attribute Present	Proprietorship	Partnership	Corporation	LLC
1. Business taxed	____	____	____	____
2. Limited liability	____	____	____	____
3. Legal entity	____	____	____	____

QS 1-6

Identifying accounting
principles and assumptions

C4

Identify the letter for the principle or assumption from *A* through *F* in the blank space next to each numbered situation that it best explains or justifies.

A. General accounting principle
B. Measurement (cost) principle
C. Business entity assumption

D. Revenue recognition principle
E. Expense recognition (matching) principle
F. Going-concern assumption

_____ **1.** In December of this year, Chavez Landscaping received a customer's order and cash prepayment to install sod at a house that would not be ready for installation until March of *next year*. Chavez should record the revenue from the customer order in March of *next year*, not in December of this year.

_____ **2.** If $51,000 cash is paid to buy land, the land is reported on the buyer's balance sheet at $51,000.

_____ **3.** Mike Derr owns both Sailing Passions and Dockside Digs. In preparing financial statements for Dockside Digs, Mike makes sure that the expense transactions of Sailing Passions are kept separate from Dockside Digs's transactions and financial statements.

QS 1-7

Applying the accounting
equation   A1

a. Total assets of Charter Company equal $700,000 and its equity is $420,000. What is the amount of its liabilities?

b. Total assets of Martin Marine equal $500,000 and its liabilities and equity amounts are equal to each other. What is the amount of its liabilities? What is the amount of its equity?

This icon highlights assignments that enhance decision-making skills

---

QS 1-8

Applying the accounting
equation

A1

1. Use the accounting equation to compute the missing financial statement amounts (*a*), (*b*), and (*c*).

	A	B		C		D
1	**Company**	**Assets**	**=**	**Liabilities**	**+**	**Equity**
2	1	$ 75,000		$ (a)		$ 40,000
3	2	(b)		25,000		70,000
4	3	85,000		20,000		(c)

2. Use the expanded accounting equation to compute the missing financial statement amounts (*a*) and (*b*).

	A	B	C	D	E	F	G
1				**Common**			
2	**Company**	**Assets**	**Liabilities**	**Stock**	**Dividends**	**Revenues**	**Expenses**
3	1	$ 40,000	$ 16,000	$ 20,000	$ 0	(a)	$ 8,000
4	2	$ 80,000	$ 32,000	$ 44,000	(b)	$ 24,000	$ 18,000

QS 1-9

Identifying and computing
assets, liabilities, and equity

A1 **GOOGLE**

Use **Google**'s December 31, 2017, financial statements, in Appendix A near the end of the text, to answer the following.

a. Identify the amounts (in $ millions) of its 2017 (1) assets, (2) liabilities, and (3) equity.

b. Using amounts from part *a*, verify that Assets = Liabilities + Equity.

QS 1-10

Identifying effects of
transactions using
accounting equation—
Revenues and Expenses

P1

Create the following table similar to the one in Exhibit 1.9.

Assets		=	Liabilities	+			Equity			
Cash	+	Accounts Receivable	=	Accounts Payable	+	Common Stock	−	Dividends	+	Revenues	−	Expenses

Then use additions and subtractions to show the dollar effects of each transaction on individual items of the accounting equation (identify each revenue and expense type, such as commissions revenue or rent expense).

a. The company completed consulting work for a client and immediately collected $5,500 cash earned.

b. The company completed commission work for a client and sent a bill for $4,000 to be received within 30 days.

c. The company paid an assistant $1,400 cash as wages for the period.

d. The company collected $1,000 cash as a partial payment for the amount owed by the client in transaction *b*.

e. The company paid $700 cash for this period's cleaning services.

Create the following table similar to the one in Exhibit 1.9.

Assets				=	Liabilities	+		Equity			
Cash +	Supplies +	Equipment +	Land	=	Accounts Payable	+	Common − Stock	Dividends	+	Revenues −	Expenses

QS 1-11
Identifying effects of transactions using accounting equation—Assets and Liabilities
P1

Then use additions and subtractions to show the dollar effects of each transaction on individual items of the accounting equation.

a. The owner invested $15,000 cash in the company in exchange for its common stock.

b. The company purchased supplies for $500 cash.

c. The owner invested $10,000 of equipment in the company in exchange for more common stock.

d. The company purchased $200 of additional supplies on credit.

e. The company purchased land for $9,000 cash.

Indicate in which financial statement each item would most likely appear: income statement (I), balance sheet (B), or statement of cash flows (CF).

_____ **a.** Assets

_____ **b.** Cash from operating activities

_____ **c.** Equipment

_____ **d.** Expenses

_____ **e.** Liabilities

_____ **f.** Net decrease (or increase) in cash

_____ **g.** Revenues

_____ **h.** Total liabilities and equity

QS 1-12
Identifying items with financial statements
P2

Classify each of the following items as revenues (R), expenses (EX), or dividends (D).

_____ **1.** Cost of sales

_____ **2.** Service revenue

_____ **3.** Wages expense

_____ **4.** Cash dividends

_____ **5.** Rent expense

_____ **6.** Rental revenue

_____ **7.** Insurance expense

_____ **8.** Consulting revenue

QS 1-13
Identifying income and equity accounts
P2

Classify each of the following items as assets (A), liabilities (L), or equity (EQ).

_____ **1.** Land

_____ **2.** Common stock

_____ **3.** Equipment

_____ **4.** Accounts payable

_____ **5.** Accounts receivable

_____ **6.** Supplies

QS 1-14
Identifying assets, liabilities, and equity P2

On December 31, Hawkin's records show the following accounts. Use this information to prepare a December income statement for Hawkin.

Equipment	$3,000	Accounts receivable	$ 600	Wages expense	$8,000
Cash	2,400	Services revenue	16,000	Utilities expense	700
Rent expense	1,500	Accounts payable	6,000		

QS 1-15
Preparing an income statement
P2

In a recent year's financial statements, **Home Depot** reported the following results. Compute and interpret Home Depot's return on assets (assume competitors average an 11.0% return on assets).

Sales	$95 billion	Net income	$8 billion	Average total assets	$42 billion

QS 1-16
Computing and interpreting return on assets
A2

Use **Samsung**'s December 31, 2017, financial statements in Appendix A near the end of the text to answer the following.

a. Identify the amounts (in millions of Korean won) of Samsung's 2017 (1) assets, (2) liabilities, and (3) equity.

b. Using amounts from part *a*, verify that Assets = Liabilities + Equity.

QS 1-17
Identifying and computing assets, liabilities, and equity
A1
Samsung

*Most **Exercises** and **Quick Study** assignments are supported with Guided Examples ("Hints") in Connect using different numbers; an instructor can choose whether to make them available to students*

connect

EXERCISES

Exercise 1-1
Classifying activities reflected in the accounting system   **C1**

Classify the following activities as part of the identifying (I), recording (R), or communicating (C) aspects of accounting.

_____ **1.** Analyzing and interpreting reports.   _____ **5.** Preparing financial statements.
_____ **2.** Presenting financial information.   _____ **6.** Acquiring knowledge of revenue transactions.
_____ **3.** Keeping a log of service costs.   _____ **7.** Observing transactions and events.
_____ **4.** Measuring the costs of a product.   _____ **8.** Registering cash sales of products sold.

Exercise 1-2
Identifying accounting users and uses

C2

Part A. Identify the following questions as most likely to be asked by an internal (I) or an external (E) user of accounting information.

_____ **1.** Which inventory items are out of stock?
_____ **2.** Should we make a five-year loan to that business?
_____ **3.** What are the costs of our product's ingredients?
_____ **4.** Should we buy, hold, or sell a company's stock?
_____ **5.** Should we spend additional money for redesign of our product?
_____ **6.** Which firm reports the highest sales and income?
_____ **7.** What are the costs of our service to customers?

Part B. Identify the following users as either an internal (I) or an external (E) user.

_____ **1.** Research and development executive   _____ **5.** Distribution manager
_____ **2.** Human resources executive   _____ **6.** Creditor
_____ **3.** Politician   _____ **7.** Production supervisor
_____ **4.** Shareholder   _____ **8.** Purchasing manager

Exercise 1-3
Describing accounting responsibilities

C2

Many accounting professionals work in one of the following three areas.

A. Financial accounting   **B.** Managerial accounting   **C.** Tax accounting

Identify the area of accounting that is most involved in each of the following responsibilities.

_____ **1.** Internal auditing   _____ **5.** Enforcing tax laws
_____ **2.** External auditing   _____ **6.** Planning transactions to minimize taxes
_____ **3.** Cost accounting   _____ **7.** Preparing external financial statements
_____ **4.** Budgeting   _____ **8.** Analyzing external financial reports

---

Exercise 1-4
Learning the language of business

C1   C2   C3

Match each of the numbered descriptions *1* through *5* with the term or phrase it best reflects. Indicate your answer by writing the letter *A* through *H* for the term or phrase in the blank provided.

A. Audit   **C.** Ethics   **E.** SEC   **G.** Net income
B. GAAP   **D.** FASB   **F.** Public accountants   **H.** IASB

_____ **1.** An assessment of whether financial statements follow GAAP.
_____ **2.** Amount a business earns in excess of all expenses and costs associated with its sales and revenues.
_____ **3.** A group that sets accounting principles in the United States.
_____ **4.** Accounting professionals who provide services to many clients.
_____ **5.** Principles that determine whether an action is right or wrong.

Exercise 1-5
Identifying ethical terminology

C3

Match each of the numbered descriptions *1* through *7* with the term or phrase it best reflects. Indicate your answer by writing the letter *A* through *G* for the term or phrase in the blank provided.

A. Ethics   **D.** Internal controls   **F.** Audit
B. Fraud triangle   **E.** Sarbanes-Oxley Act   **G.** Dodd-Frank Act
C. Prevention

_____ **1.** Requires the SEC to pay whistleblowers.
_____ **2.** Examines whether financial statements are prepared using GAAP; it does not ensure absolute accuracy of the statements.

_____ **3.** Requires documentation and verification of internal controls and increases emphasis on internal control effectiveness.

_____ **4.** Procedures set up to protect company property and equipment, ensure reliable accounting, promote efficiency, and encourage adherence to policies.

_____ **5.** A less expensive and more effective means to stop fraud.

_____ **6.** Three factors push a person to commit fraud: opportunity, pressure, and rationalization.

_____ **7.** Beliefs that distinguish right from wrong.

The following describe several different business organizations. Determine whether each description best refers to a sole proprietorship (SP), partnership (P), corporation (C), or limited liability company (LLC).

_____ **a.** Micah and Nancy own Financial Services, which pays a business income tax. Micah and Nancy do not have personal responsibility for the debts of Financial Services.

_____ **b.** Riley and Kay own Speedy Packages, a courier service. Both are personally liable for the debts of the business.

_____ **c.** IBC Services does not have separate legal existence apart from the one person who owns it.

_____ **d.** Trent Company is owned by Trent Malone, who is personally liable for the company's debts.

_____ **e.** Ownership of Zander Company is divided into 1,000 shares of stock. The company pays a business income tax.

_____ **f.** Physio Products does not pay income taxes and has one owner. The owner has unlimited liability for business debt.

_____ **g.** AJ Company pays a business income tax and has two owners.

_____ **h.** Jeffy Auto is a separate legal entity from its owner, but it does not pay a business income tax.

Exercise 1-6
Distinguishing business organizations
C4

Enter the letter _A_ through _H_ for the principle or assumption in the blank space next to each numbered description that it best reflects.

A. General accounting principle
B. Measurement (cost) principle
C. Business entity assumption
D. Revenue recognition principle

E. Specific accounting principle
F. Expense recognition (matching) principle
G. Going-concern assumption
H. Full disclosure principle

_____ **1.** A company reports details behind financial statements that would impact users' decisions.

_____ **2.** Financial statements reflect the assumption that the business continues operating.

_____ **3.** A company records the expenses incurred to generate the revenues reported.

_____ **4.** Concepts, assumptions, and guidelines for preparing financial statements.

_____ **5.** Each business is accounted for separately from its owner or owners.

_____ **6.** Revenue is recorded when products and services are delivered.

_____ **7.** Detailed rules used in reporting events and transactions.

_____ **8.** Information is based on actual costs incurred in transactions.

Exercise 1-7
Identifying accounting principles and assumptions
C4

Determine the missing amount from each of the separate situations _a_, _b_, and _c_ below.

	A		B		C
1	**Assets**	**=**	**Liabilities**	**+**	**Equity**
2	$ _(a)_		$ 20,000		$ 45,000
3	100,000		34,000		_(b)_
4	154,000		_(c)_		40,000

Exercise 1-8
Using the accounting equation
A1

Answer the following questions. _Hint:_ Use the accounting equation.

a. At the beginning of the year, Addison Company's assets are $300,000 and its equity is $100,000. During the year, assets increase $80,000 and liabilities increase $50,000. What is the equity at year-end?

b. Office Store Co. has assets equal to $123,000 and liabilities equal to $47,000 at year-end. What is the equity for Office Store Co. at year-end?

c. At the beginning of the year, Quaker Company's liabilities equal $70,000. During the year, assets increase by $60,000, and at year-end assets equal $190,000. Liabilities decrease $5,000 during the year. What are the beginning and ending amounts of equity?

Exercise 1-9
Using the accounting equation
A1

Check (c) Beg. equity, $60,000

Exercise 1-10
Analysis using the accounting equation

P1

Zen began a new consulting firm on January 5. Following is a financial summary, including balances, for each of the company's first five transactions (using the accounting equation form).

		Assets					=	Liabilities	+		Equity	
Transaction	Cash	+	Accounts Receivable	+	Office Supplies	+	Office Furniture	=	Accounts Payable	+	Common Stock	+	Revenues
___ 1.	$40,000	+	$ 0	+	$ 0	+	$ 0	=	$ 0	+	$40,000	+	$ 0
___ 2.	38,000	+	0	+	3,000	+	0	=	1,000	+	40,000	+	0
___ 3.	30,000	+	0	+	3,000	+	8,000	=	1,000	+	40,000	+	0
___ 4.	30,000	+	6,000	+	3,000	+	8,000	=	1,000	+	40,000	+	6,000
___ 5.	31,000	+	6,000	+	3,000	+	8,000	=	1,000	+	40,000	+	7,000

Identify the explanation from *a* through *j* below that best describes each transaction *1* through *5* above and enter it in the blank space in front of each numbered transaction.

a. The company purchased office furniture for $8,000 cash.
b. The company received $40,000 cash from a bank loan.
c. The owner invested $1,000 cash in the business in exchange for its common stock.
d. The owner invested $40,000 cash in the business in exchange for its common stock.
e. The company purchased office supplies for $3,000 by paying $2,000 cash and putting $1,000 on credit.
f. The company billed a customer $6,000 for services provided.
g. The company purchased office furniture worth $8,000 on credit.
h. The company provided services for $1,000 cash.
i. The company sold office supplies for $3,000 and received $2,000 cash and $1,000 on credit.
j. The company provided services for $6,000 cash.

Exercise 1-11
Identifying effects of transactions on the accounting equation

P1

The following table shows the effects of transactions *1* through *5* on the assets, liabilities, and equity of Mulan's Boutique.

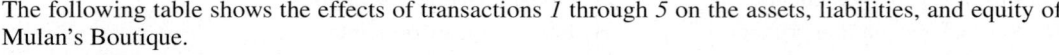

	Cash	+	Accounts Receivable	+	Office Supplies	+	Land	=	Accounts Payable	+	Common Stock	+	Revenues
	$ 21,000	+	$ 0	+	$3,000	+	$19,000	=	$ 0	+	$43,000	+	$ 0
___ 1.	− 4,000					+	4,000						
___ 2.				+	1,000				+1,000				
___ 3.		+	1,900									+	1,900
___ 4.	− 1,000								− 1,000				
___ 5.	+ 1,900	−	1,900										
	$ 17,900	+	$ 0	+	$4,000	+	$23,000	=	$ 0	+	$43,000	+	$1,900

Identify the explanation from *a* through *j* below that best describes each transaction *1* through *5* and enter it in the blank space in front of each numbered transaction.

a. The company purchased $1,000 of office supplies on credit.
b. The company collected $1,900 cash from an account receivable.
c. The company sold land for $4,000 cash.
d. The company paid $1,000 cash in dividends to shareholders.
e. The company purchased office supplies for $1,000 cash.
f. The company purchased land for $4,000 cash.
g. The company billed a client $1,900 for services provided.
h. The company paid $1,000 cash toward an account payable.
i. The owner invested $1,900 cash in the business in exchange for its common stock.
j. The company sold office supplies for $1,900 on credit.

For each transaction *a* through *f*, identify its impact on the accounting equation (select from *1* through *5* below).

_____ **a.** The company pays cash toward an account payable.

_____ **b.** The company purchases equipment on credit.

_____ **c.** The owner invests cash in the business in exchange for its common stock.

_____ **d.** The company pays cash dividends to shareholders.

_____ **e.** The company purchases supplies for cash.

_____ **f.** The company provides services for cash.

1. Decreases an asset and decreases equity.

2. Increases an asset and increases a liability.

3. Decreases an asset and decreases a liability.

4. Increases an asset and decreases an asset.

5. Increases an asset and increases equity.

Exercise 1-12
Identifying effects of transactions on the accounting equation

P1

Ming Chen began a professional practice on June 1 and plans to prepare financial statements at the end of each month. During June, Ming Chen (the owner) completed these transactions.

a. Owner invested $60,000 cash in the company along with equipment that had a $15,000 market value in exchange for its common stock.

b. The company paid $1,500 cash for rent of office space for the month.

c. The company purchased $10,000 of additional equipment on credit (payment due within 30 days).

d. The company completed work for a client and immediately collected the $2,500 cash earned.

e. The company completed work for a client and sent a bill for $8,000 to be received within 30 days.

f. The company purchased additional equipment for $6,000 cash.

g. The company paid an assistant $3,000 cash as wages for the month.

h. The company collected $5,000 cash as a partial payment for the amount owed by the client in transaction *e*.

i. The company paid $10,000 cash to settle the liability created in transaction *c*.

j. The company paid $1,000 cash in dividends to the owner (sole shareholder).

Exercise 1-13
Identifying effects of transactions using the accounting equation

P1

Required

Create the following table similar to the one in Exhibit 1.9.

Assets			=	Liabilities	+	Equity				
Cash +	Accounts Receivable	+ Equipment	=	Accounts Payable	+ Common Stock	−	Dividends	+ Revenues	− Expenses

Then use additions and subtractions to show the dollar effects of the transactions on individual items of the accounting equation. Show new balances after each transaction.

Check   Ending balances: Cash, $46,000; Expenses, $4,500

Swiss Group reports net income of $40,000 for 2019. At the beginning of 2019, Swiss Group had $200,000 in assets. By the end of 2019, assets had grown to $300,000. What is Swiss Group's 2019 return on assets? How would you assess its performance if competitors average an 11% return on assets?

Exercise 1-14
Analyzing return on assets

A2

On October 1, Ebony Ernst organized Ernst Consulting; on October 3, the owner contributed $84,000 in assets in exchange for its common stock to launch the business. On October 31, the company's records show the following items and amounts. Use this information to prepare an October income statement for the business.

Exercise 1-15
Preparing an income statement

P2

Cash..........................	$11,360	Cash dividends	$ 2,000
Accounts receivable............	14,000	Consulting revenue..................	14,000
Office supplies	3,250	Rent expense........................	3,550
Land.........................	46,000	Salaries expense....................	7,000
Office equipment	18,000	Telephone expense...................	760
Accounts payable..............	8,500	Miscellaneous expenses..............	580
Common stock	84,000		

Check   Net income, $2,110

Use the information in Exercise 1-15 to prepare an October statement of retained earnings for Ernst Consulting.

Exercise 1-16
Preparing a statement of retained earnings   P2

Exercise 1-17
Preparing a balance
sheet   **P2**

Use the information in Exercise 1-15 to prepare an October 31 balance sheet for Ernst Consulting. *Hint:* The solution to Exercise 1-16 can help.

Exercise 1-18
Preparing a statement of
cash flows

P2

Use the information in Exercise 1-15 to prepare an October 31 statement of cash flows for Ernst Consulting. Assume the following additional information.

a. The owner's initial investment consists of $38,000 cash and $46,000 in land in exchange for its common stock.

b. The company's $18,000 equipment purchase is paid in cash.

c. The accounts payable balance of $8,500 consists of the $3,250 office supplies purchase and $5,250 in employee salaries yet to be paid.

Check   Net increase in cash, $11,360

d. The company's rent, telephone, and miscellaneous expenses are paid in cash.

e. No cash has been collected on the $14,000 consulting fees earned.

Exercise 1-19
Identifying sections of the
statement of cash flows

P2

Indicate the section (O, I, or F) where transactions *1* through *8* would appear on the statement of cash flows.

O. Cash flows from operating activity   **F.** Cash flows from financing activity

I. Cash flows from investing activity

_____ **1.** Cash purchase of equipment   _____ **5.** Cash paid on account payable to supplier

_____ **2.** Cash paid for dividends   _____ **6.** Cash received from clients

_____ **3.** Cash paid for advertising   _____ **7.** Cash paid for rent

_____ **4.** Cash paid for wages   _____ **8.** Cash investment from shareholders

Exercise 1-20
Preparing an income
statement for a company

P2

Ford Motor Company, one of the world's largest automakers, reports the following income statement accounts for the year ended December 31 ($ in millions). Use this information to prepare Ford's income statement for the year ended December 31.

Selling and administrative costs	$ 12,196	Revenues................................	$151,800
Cost of sales	126,584	Other expenses...........................	8,413

Exercise 1-21ᴮ
Identifying business
activities

C5

Match each transaction *a* through *e* to one of the following activities of an organization: financing activity (F), investing activity (I), or operating activity (O).

_____ **a.** An owner contributes cash to the business in exchange for its common stock.

_____ **b.** An organization borrows money from a bank.

_____ **c.** An organization advertises a new product.

_____ **d.** An organization sells some of its land.

_____ **e.** An organization purchases equipment.

Exercise 1-22
Preparing an income
statement for a company

P2

BMW Group, one of Europe's largest manufacturers, reports the following income statement accounts for the year ended December 31 (euros in millions). Use this information to prepare BMW's income statement for the year ended December 31.

Revenues................................	€75,350	Selling and administrative costs	€6,139
Cost of sales	60,946	Other expenses	4,988

Exercise 1-23
Using the accounting
equation

A1

*This icon highlights
sustainability-related
assignments*

Answer the following questions. *Hint:* Use the accounting equation.

a. On January 1, Lumia Company's liabilities are $60,000 and its equity is $40,000. On January 3, Lumia purchases and installs solar panel assets costing $10,000. For the panels, Lumia pays $4,000 cash and promises to pay the remaining $6,000 in six months. What is the total of Lumia's assets after the solar panel purchase?

b. On March 1, ABX Company's assets are $100,000 and its liabilities are $30,000. On March 5, ABX is fined $15,000 for failing emission standards. ABX immediately pays the fine in cash. After the fine is paid, what is the amount of equity for ABX?

c. On August 1, Lola Company's assets are $30,000 and its liabilities are $10,000. On August 4, Lola issues a sustainability report following SASB guidelines. Investors react positively to this report. On August 5, a new investor contributes $3,000 cash and $7,000 in equipment in exchange for ownership in Lola. After the investment, what is the amount of equity for Lola?

Problem Set B, *located at the end of* **Problem Set A,** *is provided for each*
problem to reinforce the learning process

🅜 **connect**

Identify how each of the following separate transactions *1* through *10* affects financial statements. For increases, place a "+" *and* the dollar amount in the column or columns. For decreases, place a "−" *and* the dollar amount in the column or columns. Some cells may contain both an increase (+) and a decrease (−) along with dollar amounts. The first transaction is completed as an example.

Required

a. For the balance sheet, identify how each transaction affects total assets, total liabilities, and total equity. For the income statement, identify how each transaction affects net income.

b. For the statement of cash flows, identify how each transaction affects cash flows from operating activities, cash flows from investing activities, and cash flows from financing activities.

PROBLEM SET A

Problem 1-1A
Identifying effects of transactions on financial statements

A1   P1

| | | a. | | | | b. | | |
| | | Balance Sheet | | | Income Statement | Statement of Cash Flows | | |
	Transaction	Total Assets	Total Liab.	Total Equity	Net Income	Operating Activities	Investing Activities	Financing Activities
1	Owner invests $900 cash in business in exchange for stock	+900		+900				+900
2	Receives $700 cash for services provided							
3	Pays $500 cash for employee wages							
4	Buys $100 of equipment on credit							
5	Purchases $200 of supplies on credit							
6	Buys equipment for $300 cash							
7	Pays $200 on accounts payable							
8	Provides $400 services on credit							
9	Pays $50 cash in dividends							
10	Collects $400 cash on accounts receivable							

The following financial statement information is from five separate companies.

Problem 1-2A
Computing missing information using accounting knowledge

A1   P1

	Company A	Company B	Company C	Company D	Company E
December 31, 2018					
Assets............................	$55,000	$34,000	$24,000	$60,000	$119,000
Liabilities.........................	24,500	21,500	9,000	40,000	?
December 31, 2019					
Assets............................	58,000	40,000	?	85,000	113,000
Liabilities.........................	?	26,500	29,000	24,000	70,000
During year 2019					
Stock issuances	6,000	1,400	9,750	?	6,500
Net income (loss)	8,500	?	8,000	14,000	20,000
Cash dividends....................	3,500	2,000	5,875	0	11,000

Required

1. Answer the following questions about Company A.
   a. What is the amount of equity on December 31, 2018?
   b. What is the amount of equity on December 31, 2019?
   c. What is the amount of liabilities on December 31, 2019?
2. Answer the following questions about Company B.
   a. What is the amount of equity on December 31, 2018?
   b. What is the amount of equity on December 31, 2019?
   c. What is net income for year 2019?

[continued on next page]

Check   (1*b*) $41,500

(2*c*) $1,600

(3) $55,875

3. Compute the amount of assets for Company C on December 31, 2019.

4. Compute the amount of stock issuances for Company D during year 2019.

5. Compute the amount of liabilities for Company E on December 31, 2018.

Problem 1-3A
Preparing an income statement
P2

As of December 31, 2019, Armani Company's financial records show the following items and amounts.

Cash.	$10,000	Retained earnings, Dec. 31, 2019.	$ 5,000
Accounts receivable	9,000	Dividends	13,000
Supplies.	7,000	Consulting revenue	33,000
Equipment.	4,000	Rental revenue	22,000
Accounts payable	11,000	Salaries expense.	20,000
Common stock	14,000	Rent expense	12,000
Retained earnings, Dec. 31, 2018.	3,000	Selling and administrative expenses.	8,000

Required

Check Net income, $15,000

Prepare the 2019 year-end income statement for Armani Company.

Problem 1-4A
Preparing a statement of retained earnings **P2**

Use the information in Problem 1-3A to prepare a year-end statement of retained earnings for Armani Company.

Problem 1-5A
Preparing a balance sheet
P2

Use the information in Problem 1-3A to prepare a year-end balance sheet for Armani Company.

Problem 1-6A
Preparing a statement of cash flows
P2

Following is selected financial information of Kia Company for the year ended December 31, 2019.

Cash used by investing activities.	$(2,000)	Cash from operating activities.	$6,000
Net increase in cash.	1,200	Cash, December 31, 2018.	2,300
Cash used by financing activities.	(2,800)		

Required

Check Cash balance, Dec. 31, 2019, $3,500

Prepare the 2019 year-end statement of cash flows for Kia Company.

Problem 1-7A
Analyzing transactions and preparing financial statements
P1 P2

Gabi Gram started The Gram Co., a new business that began operations on May 1. The Gram Co. completed the following transactions during its first month of operations.

May 1 G. Gram invested $40,000 cash in the company in exchange for its common stock.
    1 The company rented a furnished office and paid $2,200 cash for May's rent.
    3 The company purchased $1,890 of office equipment on credit.
    5 The company paid $750 cash for this month's cleaning services.
    8 The company provided consulting services for a client and immediately collected $5,400 cash.
   12 The company provided $2,500 of consulting services for a client on credit.
   15 The company paid $750 cash for an assistant's salary for the first half of this month.
   20 The company received $2,500 cash payment for the services provided on May 12.
   22 The company provided $3,200 of consulting services on credit.
   25 The company received $3,200 cash payment for the services provided on May 22.
   26 The company paid $1,890 cash for the office equipment purchased on May 3.
   27 The company purchased $80 of office equipment on credit.
   28 The company paid $750 cash for an assistant's salary for the second half of this month.
   30 The company paid $300 cash for this month's telephone bill.
   30 The company paid $280 cash for this month's utilities.
   31 The company paid $1,400 cash in dividends to the owner (sole shareholder).

Required

Check (1) Ending balances: Cash, $42,780; Expenses, $5,030

1. Create the following table similar to the one in Exhibit 1.9.

		Assets			=	Liabilities	+			Equity			
Date	Cash	+	Accounts Receivable	+	Office Equipment	=	Accounts Payable	+	Common Stock	−	Dividends	+	Revenues	−	Expenses

Enter the effects of each transaction on the accounts of the accounting equation by recording dollar increases and decreases in the appropriate columns. Do not determine new account balances after each transaction. Determine the final total for each account and verify that the equation is in balance.

2. Prepare the income statement and the statement of retained earnings for the month of May, and the balance sheet as of May 31.

(2) Net income, $6,070; Total assets, $44,750

3. Prepare the statement of cash flows for the month of May.

Lita Lopez started Biz Consulting, a new business, and completed the following transactions during its first year of operations.

Problem 1-8A
Analyzing effects of transactions
A1 P1

a. Lita Lopez invested $70,000 cash and office equipment valued at $10,000 in the company in exchange for its common stock.

b. The company purchased an office suite for $40,000 cash.

c. The company purchased office equipment for $15,000 cash.

d. The company purchased $1,200 of office supplies and $1,700 of office equipment on credit.

e. The company paid a local newspaper $500 cash for printing an announcement of the office's opening.

f. The company completed a financial plan for a client and billed that client $2,800 for the service.

g. The company designed a financial plan for another client and immediately collected a $4,000 cash fee.

h. The company paid $3,275 cash in dividends to the owner (sole shareholder).

i. The company received $1,800 cash as partial payment from the client described in transaction *f*.

j. The company made a partial payment of $700 cash on the equipment purchased in transaction *d*.

k. The company paid $1,800 cash for the office secretary's wages for this period.

Required

Check (1) Ending balances: Cash, $14,525; Expenses, $2,300; Accounts Payable, $2,200

1. Create the following table similar to the one in Exhibit 1.9.

	Assets							=	Liabilities	+			Equity			
Cash	+	Accounts Receivable	+	Office Supplies	+	Office Equipment	+	Office Suite	=	Accounts Payable	+	Common Stock	−	Dividends	+	Revenues	−	Expenses

Use additions and subtractions within the table to show the dollar effects of each transaction on individual items of the accounting equation. Show new balances after each transaction.

2. Determine the company's net income.

(2) Net income, $4,500

Sanyu Sony started a new business and completed these transactions during December.

Problem 1-9A
Analyzing transactions and preparing financial statements
C4 P1 P2

Dec. 1 Sanyu Sony transferred $65,000 cash from a personal savings account to a checking account in the name of Sony Electric in exchange for its common stock.

2 The company rented office space and paid $1,000 cash for the December rent.

3 The company purchased $13,000 of electrical equipment by paying $4,800 cash and agreeing to pay the $8,200 balance in 30 days.

5 The company purchased office supplies by paying $800 cash.

6 The company completed electrical work and immediately collected $1,200 cash for these services.

8 The company purchased $2,530 of office equipment on credit.

15 The company completed electrical work on credit in the amount of $5,000.

18 The company purchased $350 of office supplies on credit.

20 The company paid $2,530 cash for the office equipment purchased on December 8.

24 The company billed a client $900 for electrical work completed; the balance is due in 30 days.

28 The company received $5,000 cash for the work completed on December 15.

29 The company paid the assistant's salary of $1,400 cash for this month.

30 The company paid $540 cash for this month's utility bill.

31 The company paid $950 cash in dividends to the owner (sole shareholder).

Required

1. Create the following table similar to the one in Exhibit 1.9.

			Assets					=	Liabilities	+			Equity			
Date	Cash	+	Accounts Receivable	+	Office Supplies	+	Office Equipment	+	Electrical Equipment	=	Accounts Payable	+	Common Stock	−	Dividends	+	Revenues	−	Expenses

Use additions and subtractions within the table to show the dollar effects of each transaction on individual items of the accounting equation. Show new balances after each transaction.

2. Prepare the income statement and the statement of retained earnings for the current month, and the balance sheet as of the end of the month.

3. Prepare the statement of cash flows for the current month.

Analysis Component

4. Assume that the owner investment transaction on December 1 was $49,000 cash instead of $65,000 and that Sony Electric obtained another $16,000 in cash by borrowing it from a bank. Compute the dollar effect of this change on the month-end amounts for (*a*) total assets, (*b*) total liabilities, and (*c*) total equity.

Problem 1-10A
Determining expenses,
liabilities, equity, and return
on assets

A1   A2

Kyzera manufactures, markets, and sells cellular telephones. The average total assets for Kyzera is $250,000. In its most recent year, Kyzera reported net income of $65,000 on revenues of $475,000.

Required

1. What is Kyzera's return on assets?

2. Does return on assets seem satisfactory for Kyzera given that its competitors average a 12% return on assets?

3. What are total expenses for Kyzera in its most recent year?

4. What is the average total amount of liabilities plus equity for Kyzera?

Problem 1-11A
Computing and interpreting
return on assets

A2

Coca-Cola and **PepsiCo** both produce and market beverages that are direct competitors. Key financial figures for these businesses for a recent year follow.

Key Figures ($ millions)	Coca-Cola	PepsiCo
Sales	$46,542	$66,504
Net income	8,634	6,462
Average assets	76,448	70,518

Required

1. Compute return on assets for (*a*) Coca-Cola and (*b*) PepsiCo.

2. Which company is more successful in its total amount of sales to consumers?

3. Which company is more successful in returning net income from its assets invested?

Analysis Component

4. Write a one-paragraph memorandum explaining which company you would invest your money in and why. (Limit your explanation to the information provided.)

Problem 1-12A^A
Identifying risk and return

A3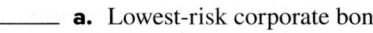

All business decisions involve aspects of risk and return. Rank order the following investment activities from *1* through *4*, where "1" is most risky and "4" is least risky.

     _____ **a.** Lowest-risk corporate bond   _____ **c.** Company stock in a start-up

     _____ **b.** Medium-risk corporate bond   _____ **d.** U.S. government Treasury bond

---

Problem 1-13A^B
Describing business
activities

C5

A start-up company often engages in the following transactions during its first year of operations. Classify those transactions in one of the three major categories of an organization's business activities.

F. Financing   **I.** Investing   **O.** Operating

    _____ **1.** Shareholders investing in business   _____ **5.** Purchasing equipment

    _____ **2.** Purchasing a building   _____ **6.** Selling and distributing products

    _____ **3.** Purchasing land   _____ **7.** Paying for advertising

    _____ **4.** Borrowing cash from a bank   _____ **8.** Paying employee wages

An organization undertakes various activities in pursuit of business success. Identify an organization's three major business activities, and describe each activity.

Problem 1-14A[B]
Describing business
activities   **C5**

Identify how each of the following separate transactions *1* through *10* affects financial statements. For increases, place a "+" *and* the dollar amount in the column or columns. For decreases, place a "−" *and* the dollar amount in the column or columns. Some cells may contain both an increase (+) and a decrease (−) along with dollar amounts. The first transaction is completed as an example.

PROBLEM SET B

Problem 1-1B
Identifying effects of
transactions on financial
statements

A1   P1

Required

a. For the balance sheet, identify how each transaction affects total assets, total liabilities, and total equity. For the income statement, identify how each transaction affects net income.

b. For the statement of cash flows, identify how each transaction affects cash flows from operating activities, cash flows from investing activities, and cash flows from financing activities.

| | | a. | | | | b. | | |
| | | Balance Sheet | | | Income Statement | Statement of Cash Flows | | |
	Transaction	Total Assets	Total Liab.	Total Equity	Net Income	Operating Activities	Investing Activities	Financing Activities
1	Owner invests $800 cash in business in exchange for stock	+800		+800				+800
2	Purchases $100 of supplies on credit							
3	Buys equipment for $400 cash							
4	Provides services for $900 cash							
5	Pays $400 cash for rent incurred							
6	Buys $200 of equipment on credit							
7	Pays $300 cash for wages incurred							
8	Pays $50 cash in dividends							
9	Provides $600 services on credit							
10	Collects $600 cash on accounts receivable							

The following financial statement information is from five separate companies.

Problem 1-2B
Computing missing
information using
accounting knowledge

A1   P1

	Company V	Company W	Company X	Company Y	Company Z
December 31, 2018					
Assets	$54,000	$ 80,000	$141,500	$92,500	$144,000
Liabilities.	25,000	60,000	68,500	51,500	?
December 31, 2019					
Assets	59,000	100,000	186,500	?	170,000
Liabilities.	36,000	?	65,800	42,000	42,000
During year 2019					
Stock issuances	5,000	20,000	?	48,100	60,000
Net income (or loss)	?	40,000	18,500	24,000	32,000
Cash dividends	5,500	2,000	0	20,000	8,000

Required

1. Answer the following questions about Company V.

   a. What is the amount of equity on December 31, 2018?

   b. What is the amount of equity on December 31, 2019?

   c. What is the net income or loss for the year 2019?

[continued on next page]

Check   (1*b*) $23,000

2. Answer the following questions about Company W.

   a. What is the amount of equity on December 31, 2018?

   b. What is the amount of equity on December 31, 2019?

(2c) $22,000

   c. What is the amount of liabilities on December 31, 2019?

3. Compute the amount of stock issuances for Company X during 2019.

(4) $135,100

4. Compute the amount of assets for Company Y on December 31, 2019.

5. Compute the amount of liabilities for Company Z on December 31, 2018.

Problem 1-3B

Preparing an income statement

P2

As of December 31, 2019, Audi Company's financial records show the following items and amounts.

Cash.	$2,000	Retained earnings, Dec. 31, 2019.	$1,300
Accounts receivable	1,800	Dividends	2,600
Supplies.	1,200	Consulting revenue	6,600
Equipment.	1,000	Rental revenue	4,400
Accounts payable	3,600	Salaries expense.	4,000
Common stock	1,100	Rent expense	2,400
Retained earnings, Dec. 31, 2018.	900	Selling and administrative expenses.	1,600

Required

Check Net income, $3,000

Prepare the 2019 year-end income statement for Audi Company.

Problem 1-4B

Preparing a statement of retained earnings **P2**

Use the information in Problem 1-3B to prepare a year-end statement of retained earnings for Audi Company.

Problem 1-5B

Preparing a balance sheet **P2**

Use the information in Problem 1-3B to prepare a year-end balance sheet for Audi Company.

Problem 1-6B

Preparing a statement of cash flows

P2

Selected financial information of Banji Company for the year ended December 31, 2019, follows.

Cash from investing activities	$1,600	Cash used by operating activities	$(3,000)
Net increase in cash	400	Cash, December 31, 2018.	1,300
Cash from financing activities	1,800		

Required

Prepare the 2019 year-end statement of cash flows for Banji Company.

Problem 1-7B

Analyzing transactions and preparing financial statements

P1 P2

Nina Niko launched a new business, Niko's Maintenance Co., that began operations on June 1. The following transactions were completed by the company during that first month.

June	1	Nina Niko invested $130,000 cash in the company in exchange for its common stock.
	2	The company rented a furnished office and paid $6,000 cash for June's rent.
	4	The company purchased $2,400 of equipment on credit.
	6	The company paid $1,150 cash for this month's advertising of the opening of the business.
	8	The company completed maintenance services for a customer and immediately collected $850 cash.
	14	The company completed $7,500 of maintenance services for City Center on credit.
	16	The company paid $800 cash for an assistant's salary for the first half of the month.
	20	The company received $7,500 cash payment for services completed for City Center on June 14.
	21	The company completed $7,900 of maintenance services for Paula's Beauty Shop on credit.
	24	The company completed $675 of maintenance services for Build-It Coop on credit.
	25	The company received $7,900 cash payment from Paula's Beauty Shop for the work completed on June 21.
	26	The company made payment of $2,400 cash for equipment purchased on June 4.
	28	The company paid $800 cash for an assistant's salary for the second half of this month.
	29	The company paid $4,000 cash in dividends to the owner (sole shareholder).
	30	The company paid $150 cash for this month's telephone bill.
	30	The company paid $890 cash for this month's utilities.

Required

1. Create the following table similar to the one in Exhibit 1.9.

	Assets				=	Liabilities	+			Equity			
Date	Cash	+	Accounts Receivable	+	Equipment	=	Accounts Payable	+	Common Stock	−	Dividends	+	Revenues	−	Expenses

Enter the effects of each transaction on the accounts of the accounting equation by recording dollar increases and decreases in the appropriate columns. Do not determine new account balances after each transaction. Determine the final total for each account and verify that the equation is in balance.

2. Prepare the income statement and the statement of retained earnings for the month of June, and the balance sheet as of June 30.

3. Prepare the statement of cash flows for the month of June.

Check (1) Ending balances: Cash, $130,060; Expenses, $9,790

(2) Net income, $7,135; Total assets, $133,135

Neva Nadal started a new business, Nadal Computing, and completed the following transactions during its first year of operations.

a. Neva Nadal invested $90,000 cash and office equipment valued at $10,000 in the company in exchange for its common stock.

b. The company purchased an office suite for $50,000 cash.

c. The company purchased office equipment for $25,000 cash.

d. The company purchased $1,200 of office supplies and $1,700 of office equipment on credit.

e. The company paid a local newspaper $750 cash for printing an announcement of the office's opening.

f. The company completed a financial plan for a client and billed that client $2,800 for the service.

g. The company designed a financial plan for another client and immediately collected a $4,000 cash fee.

h. The company paid $11,500 cash in dividends to the owner (sole shareholder).

i. The company received $1,800 cash from the client described in transaction *f*.

j. The company made a payment of $700 cash on the equipment purchased in transaction *d*.

k. The company paid $2,500 cash for the office secretary's wages.

Problem 1-8B
Analyzing effects of transactions

A1 P1

Required

1. Create the following table similar to the one in Exhibit 1.9.

Check (1) Ending balances: Cash, $5,350; Expenses, $3,250; Accounts Payable, $2,200

	Assets								=	Liabilities	+			Equity			
Cash	+	Accounts Receivable	+	Office Supplies	+	Office Equipment	+	Office Suite	=	Accounts Payable	+	Common Stock	−	Dividends	+	Revenues	−	Expenses

Use additions and subtractions within the table to show the dollar effects of each transaction on individual items of the accounting equation. Show new balances after each transaction.

2. Determine the company's net income.

(2) Net income, $3,550

Rivera Roofing Company, owned by Reyna Rivera, began operations in July and completed these transactions during that first month of operations.

July	1	Reyna Rivera invested $80,000 cash in the company in exchange for its common stock.
	2	The company rented office space and paid $700 cash for the July rent.
	3	The company purchased roofing equipment for $5,000 by paying $1,000 cash and agreeing to pay the $4,000 balance in 30 days.
	6	The company purchased office supplies for $600 cash.
	8	The company completed work for a customer and immediately collected $7,600 cash for the work.
	10	The company purchased $2,300 of office equipment on credit.
	15	The company completed work for a customer on credit in the amount of $8,200.
	17	The company purchased $3,100 of office supplies on credit.
	23	The company paid $2,300 cash for the office equipment purchased on July 10.
	25	The company billed a customer $5,000 for work completed; the balance is due in 30 days.
	28	The company received $8,200 cash for the work completed on July 15.
	30	The company paid an assistant's salary of $1,560 cash for this month.
	31	The company paid $295 cash for this month's utility bill.
	31	The company paid $1,800 cash in dividends to the owner (sole shareholder).

Problem 1-9B
Analyzing transactions and preparing financial statements

C4 P1 P2

Required

1. Create the following table similar to the one in Exhibit 1.9.

			Assets					=	Liabilities	+			Equity			
Date	Cash	+	Accounts Receivable	+	Office Supplies	+	Office Equipment	+	Roofing Equipment	=	Accounts Payable	+	Common Stock	− Dividends + Revenues − Expenses

Check   (1) Ending balances: Cash, $87,545; Accounts Payable, $7,100

(2) Net income, $18,245; Total assets, $103,545

Use additions and subtractions within the table to show the dollar effects of each transaction on individual items of the accounting equation. Show new balances after each transaction.

2. Prepare the income statement and the statement of retained earnings for the month of July, and the balance sheet as of July 31.

3. Prepare the statement of cash flows for the month of July.

Analysis Component

4. Assume that the $5,000 purchase of roofing equipment on July 3 was financed from an owner investment of another $5,000 cash in the business in exchange for more common stock (instead of the purchase conditions described in the transaction above). Compute the dollar effect of this change on the month-end amounts for (*a*) total assets, (*b*) total liabilities, and (*c*) total equity.

Problem 1-10B
Determining expenses, liabilities, equity, and return on assets

A1   A2

Ski-Doo Company manufactures, markets, and sells snowmobiles and snowmobile equipment and accessories. The average total assets for Ski-Doo is $3,000,000. In its most recent year, Ski-Doo reported net income of $201,000 on revenues of $1,400,000.

Required

1. What is Ski-Doo Company's return on assets?

2. Does return on assets seem satisfactory for Ski-Doo given that its competitors average a 9.5% return on assets?

Check   (3) $1,199,000

(4) $3,000,000

3. What are the total expenses for Ski-Doo Company in its most recent year?

4. What is the average total amount of liabilities plus equity for Ski-Doo Company?

Problem 1-11B
Computing and interpreting return on assets

A2

AT&T and **Verizon** produce and market telecommunications products and are competitors. Key financial figures for these businesses for a recent year follow.

Key Figures ($ millions)	AT&T	Verizon
Sales	$126,723	$110,875
Net income	4,184	10,198
Average assets	269,868	225,233

Required

Check   (1*a*) 1.6%; (1*b*) 4.5%

1. Compute return on assets for (*a*) AT&T and (*b*) Verizon.

2. Which company is more successful in the total amount of sales to consumers?

3. Which company is more successful in returning net income from its assets invested?

Analysis Component

4. Write a one-paragraph memorandum explaining which company you would invest your money in and why. (Limit your explanation to the information provided.)

Problem 1-12B[A]
Identifying risk and return

A3

All business decisions involve aspects of risk and return. Rank order the following investment activities from *1* through *4*, where "1" reflects the highest expected return and "4" the lowest expected return.

_____ **a.** Low-risk corporate bond   _____ **c.** Money stored in a fireproof vault

_____ **b.** Stock of a successful company   _____ **d.** U.S. Treasury bond

---

Problem 1-13B[B]
Describing business activities

C5

A start-up company often engages in the following activities during its first year of operations. Classify each of the following activities into one of the three major activities of an organization.

F. Financing   **I.** Investing   **O.** Operating

_____ **1.** Providing client services   _____ **5.** Supervising workers

_____ **2.** Obtaining a bank loan   _____ **6.** Shareholders investing in business

_____ **3.** Purchasing machinery   _____ **7.** Renting office space

_____ **4.** Research for its products   _____ **8.** Paying utilities expenses

Identify in outline format the three major business activities of an organization. For each of these activities, identify at least two specific transactions or events normally undertaken by the business's owners or its managers.

Problem 1-14B[B]
Describing business
activities C5

Serial Problem starts here and continues throughout the text

SERIAL PROBLEM
Business Solutions

C4 P1

SP 1 On October 1, 2019, Santana Rey launched a computer services company, **Business Solutions**, that is organized as a corporation and provides consulting services, computer system installations, and custom program development.

Required

Create a table like the one in Exhibit 1.9 using the following headings for columns: Cash; Accounts Receivable; Computer Supplies; Computer System; Office Equipment; Accounts Payable; Common Stock; Dividends; Revenues; and Expenses. Then use additions and subtractions within the table to show the dollar effects for each of the following October transactions for Business Solutions on the individual items of the accounting equation. Show new balances after each transaction.

Oct. 1 S. Rey invested $45,000 cash, a $20,000 computer system, and $8,000 of office equipment in the company in exchange for its common stock.
3 The company purchased $1,420 of computer supplies on credit from Harris Office Products.
6 The company billed Easy Leasing $4,800 for services performed in installing a new web server.
8 The company paid $1,420 cash for the computer supplies purchased from Harris Office Products on October 3.
10 The company hired Lyn Addie as a part-time assistant for $125 per day, as needed.
12 The company billed Easy Leasing another $1,400 for services performed.
15 The company received $4,800 cash from Easy Leasing as partial payment toward its account.
17 The company paid $805 cash to repair computer equipment damaged when moving it.
20 The company paid $1,728 cash for advertisements published in the local newspaper.
22 The company received $1,400 cash from Easy Leasing toward its account.
28 The company billed IFM Company $5,208 for services performed.
31 The company paid $875 cash for Lyn Addie's wages for seven days of work this month.
31 The company paid $3,600 cash in dividends to the owner (sole shareholder).

©Alexander Image/Shutterstock

Check Ending balances:
Cash, $42,772; Revenues,
$11,408; Expenses, $3,408

Accounting professionals apply many technology tools to aid them in their everyday tasks and decision making. The **General Ledger** tool in Connect automates several of the procedural steps in the accounting cycle so the accounting professional can focus on the impacts of each transaction on the full set of financial statements. Chapter 2 is the first chapter to use this tool in helping students see the advantages of technology and, in particular, the power of the General Ledger tool in accounting practice, including financial analysis and "what-if" scenarios.

**GENERAL
LEDGER
PROBLEM**

Accounting Analysis (AA) is a section aimed to refine company analysis, comparative analysis, and global analysis skills; Accounting Analysis assignments are available in Connect.

Accounting Analysis

AA 1-1 Key financial figures for **Apple**'s two most recent fiscal years follow.

$ millions	Current Year	Prior Year
Liabilities + Equity	$375,319	$321,686
Net income	48,351	45,687
Revenues.	229,234	215,639

**COMPANY
ANALYSIS**

A1 A2

APPLE

Required

1. What is the total amount of assets invested in Apple in the current year?
2. What is Apple's return on assets for the current year?
3. How much are total expenses for Apple for the current year?
4. Is Apple's current-year return on assets better or worse than competitors' average of 10% return?

COMPARATIVE ANALYSIS

A1   A2

APPLE

GOOGLE

Note: Reference to **Google** throughout the text refers to **Alphabet Inc.,** as Google is a wholly owned subsidiary of Alphabet.

AA 1-2   Key comparative figures ($ millions) for both **Apple** and **Google** follow.

Key Figures	Apple		Google	
	Current Year	Prior Year	Current Year	Prior Year
Liabilities + Equity	$375,319	$321,686	$197,295	$167,497
Net income	48,351	45,687	12,662	19,478
Revenues.................	229,234	215,639	110,855	90,272

Required

1. What is the total amount of assets invested for the current year in (*a*) Apple and (*b*) Google?
2. What is the current-year return on assets for (*a*) Apple and (*b*) Google?
3. How much are current-year expenses for (*a*) Apple and (*b*) Google?
4. Is the current-year return on assets better than the 10% return of competitors for (*a*) Apple and (*b*) Google?
5. Relying only on return on assets, would we invest in Google or Apple?

GLOBAL ANALYSIS

A1   A2

Samsung

APPLE

GOOGLE

AA 1-3   **Samsung** is a leading global manufacturer that competes with **Apple** and **Google**. Key financial figures for Samsung follow.

Korean Won & USD in millions	Samsung*		Apple	Google
	Current Year	Prior Year	Current Year	Current Year
Average assets	₩281,963,207	₩252,176,923	$348,503	$182,396
Net income	42,186,747	22,726,092	48,351	12,662
Revenues..............	239,575,376	201,866,745	229,234	110,855

*Figures prepared in accordance with International Financial Reporting Standards as adopted by the Republic of Korea.

Required

1. What is the return on assets for Samsung in the (*a*) current year and (*b*) prior year?
2. Does Samsung's return on assets exhibit a favorable or unfavorable change?
3. Is Samsung's current-year return on assets better or worse than that for (*a*) Apple and (*b*) Google?

Beyond the Numbers (BTN) is a special problem section aimed to refine communication, conceptual, analysis, and research skills. It includes many activities helpful in developing an active learning environment.

Beyond the Numbers

ETHICS CHALLENGE

C3   C4

BTN 1-1   Tana Thorne works in a public accounting firm and hopes to eventually be a partner. The management of Allnet Company invites Thorne to prepare a bid to audit Allnet's financial statements. In discussing the audit fee, Allnet's management suggests a fee range in which the amount depends on the reported profit of Allnet. The higher its profit, the higher will be the audit fee paid to Thorne's firm.

Required

1. Identify the parties potentially affected by this audit and the fee plan proposed.
2. What are the ethical factors in this situation? Explain.
3. Would you recommend that Thorne accept this audit fee arrangement? Why or why not?
4. Describe some ethical considerations guiding your recommendation.

COMMUNICATING IN PRACTICE

C2   C4

APPLE

BTN 1-2   Refer to this chapter's opening feature about **Apple**. Assume that the owners, sometime during their first five years of business, desire to expand their computer product services to meet business demand regarding computing services. They eventually decide to meet with their banker to discuss a loan to allow Apple to expand and offer computing services.

Required

1. Prepare a half-page report outlining the information you would request from the owners if you were the loan officer.
2. Indicate whether the information you request and your loan decision are affected by the form of business organization for Apple.

BTN 1-3   Visit the EDGAR database at SEC.gov. Access the Form 10-K report of **Rocky Mountain Chocolate Factory** (ticker: RMCF) filed on May 23, 2017, covering its 2017 fiscal year.

TAKING IT TO THE NET

A2

Required

1. Item 6 of the 10-K report provides comparative financial highlights of RMCF for the years 2013–2017. Describe the revenue trend for RMCF over this five-year period.
2. Has RMCF been profitable (see net income) over this five-year period? Support your answer.

BTN 1-4   Teamwork is important in today's business world. Successful teams schedule convenient meetings, maintain regular communications, and cooperate with and support their members. This assignment aims to establish support/learning teams, initiate discussions, and set meeting times.

TEAMWORK IN ACTION

C1

Required

1. Form teams and open a team discussion to determine a regular time and place for your team to meet between each scheduled class meeting. Notify your instructor via a memorandum or e-mail message as to when and where your team will hold regularly scheduled meetings.
2. Develop a list of telephone numbers, LinkedIn pages, and/or e-mail addresses of your teammates.

BTN 1-5   Refer to this chapter's opening feature about **Apple**. Assume that the owners decide to open a new company with an innovative mobile app devoted to microblogging for accountants and those learning accounting. This new company will be called **AccountApp**.

ENTREPRENEURIAL DECISION

A1   A2

APPLE

Required

1. AccountApp obtains a $500,000 loan and the two owners contribute $250,000 in total from their own savings in exchange for ownership of the new company.
   a. What is the new company's total amount of liabilities plus equity?
   b. What is the new company's total amount of assets?
2. If the new company earns $80,250 in net income in the first year of operation, compute its return on assets (assume average assets equal $750,000). Assess its performance if competitors average a 10% return.

Check   (2) 10.7%

BTN 1-6   You are to interview a local business owner. (This can be a friend or relative.) Opening lines of communication with members of the business community can provide personal benefits of business networking. If you do not know the owner, you should call ahead to introduce yourself and explain your position as a student and your assignment requirements. You should request a 30-minute appointment for a face-to-face or phone interview to discuss the form of organization and operations of the business. Be prepared to make a good impression.

HITTING THE ROAD

C4

Required

1. Identify and describe the main operating activities and the form of organization for this business.
2. Determine and explain why the owner(s) chose this particular form of organization.
3. Identify any special advantages and/or disadvantages the owner(s) experiences in operating with this form of business organization.

2 Accounting for Business Transactions

Chapter Preview

SYSTEM OF ACCOUNTS

Using financial statements

C1 Source documents

C2 Types of accounts

C3 General ledger

NTK 2-1

DEBITS AND CREDITS

T-account

C4 Debits and credits

Normal balance

NTK 2-2

RECORDING TRANSACTIONS

P1 Journalizing and posting

A1 Processing transactions— Examples

NTK 2-3

TRIAL BALANCE

P2 Trial balance preparation and use

Error identification

NTK 2-4

FINANCIAL STATEMENTS

P3 Financial statement preparation

A2 Debt ratio

NTK 2-5

Learning Objectives

CONCEPTUAL

C1 Explain the steps in processing transactions and the role of source documents.

C2 Describe an account and its use in recording transactions.

C3 Describe a ledger and a chart of accounts.

C4 Define *debits* and *credits* and explain double-entry accounting.

ANALYTICAL

A1 Analyze the impact of transactions on accounts and financial statements.

A2 Compute the debt ratio and describe its use in analyzing financial condition.

PROCEDURAL

P1 Record transactions in a journal and post entries to a ledger.

P2 Prepare and explain the use of a trial balance.

P3 Prepare financial statements from business transactions.

Have a Fit

©Daniel Boczarski/Stringer/Fitbit/Getty Images

"I'm always confident"—**JAMES PARK**

SAN FRANCISCO—James Park and Eric Friedman created a wooden box with a circuit board inside. James recalls that to fix an antenna, he "literally took a piece of foam and put it on the circuit board." Their device could be used to track fitness activity, such as steps taken. The device James and Eric built would later be known as a **Fitbit** (**Fitbit.com**).

As Fitbit grew, the co-founders struggled to track sales and expenses. "It was pretty challenging," recalls James. "I would just try to use the weekend to see if I could catch up." James and Eric knew that having reliable accounting data would help "manage the ups and downs of running a company."

To address this concern, the co-founders took action. They set up recordkeeping processes, transaction analysis, control procedures, and financial statement reporting. "You need to see the data," insists James.

With accounting data, James says he "can uncover insights that weren't possible or very practical before . . . and enable the discovery of new insights and trends."

Eric offers the following advice to aspiring entrepreneurs unsure of how to unlock the potential of accounting data: "Get your hands dirty and do it yourself. You learn more that way."

Sources: *Fitbit website,* January 2019; *Wareable.com,* September 2016; *Business Wire,* November 2015; *Fortune,* July 2015; *Marketing Land,* March 2015; *Fast Company,* March 2014

BASIS OF FINANCIAL STATEMENTS

Business transactions and events are the starting points of financial statements. The process to go from transactions and events to financial statements includes the following.

- Identify each transaction and event from source documents.
- Analyze each transaction and event using the accounting equation.
- Record relevant transactions and events in a journal.
- Post journal information to ledger accounts.
- Prepare and analyze the trial balance and financial statements.

C1_____

Explain the steps in processing transactions and the role of source documents.

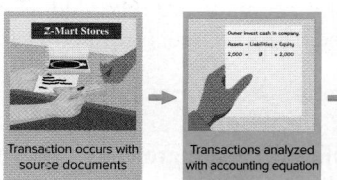 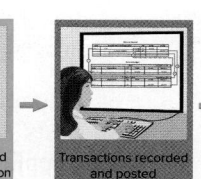 

| Transaction occurs with source documents | Transactions analyzed with accounting equation | Transactions recorded and posted | Transactions reported in financial statements |

Source Documents

Source documents identify and describe transactions and events entering the accounting system. They can be in hard copy or electronic form. Examples are sales receipts, checks, purchase orders, bills from suppliers, payroll records, and bank statements. For example, cash registers record each sale on a tape or electronic file. This record is a source document for recording sales in the accounting system. Source documents are objective and reliable evidence about transactions and events and their amounts.

Point: Accounting records also are called *accounting books* or *the books.*

The "Account" Underlying Financial Statements

An **account** is a record of increases and decreases in a specific asset, liability, equity, revenue, or expense. The **general ledger,** or simply **ledger,** is a record of all accounts used by a company. The ledger is often in electronic form. While most companies' ledgers have similar accounts, a company often uses one or more unique accounts to match its type of operations. An ***unclassified balance sheet*** broadly groups accounts into assets, liabilities, and equity. Exhibit 2.1 shows common asset, liability, and equity accounts.

C2_____

Describe an account and its use in recording transactions.

Asset Accounts   Assets are resources owned or controlled by a company. Resources have expected future benefits. Most accounting systems include (at a minimum) separate accounts for the assets described here.

Cash   A *Cash* account shows a company's cash balance. All increases and decreases in cash are recorded in the Cash account. It includes money and any funds that a bank accepts for deposit (coins, checks, money orders, and checking account balances).

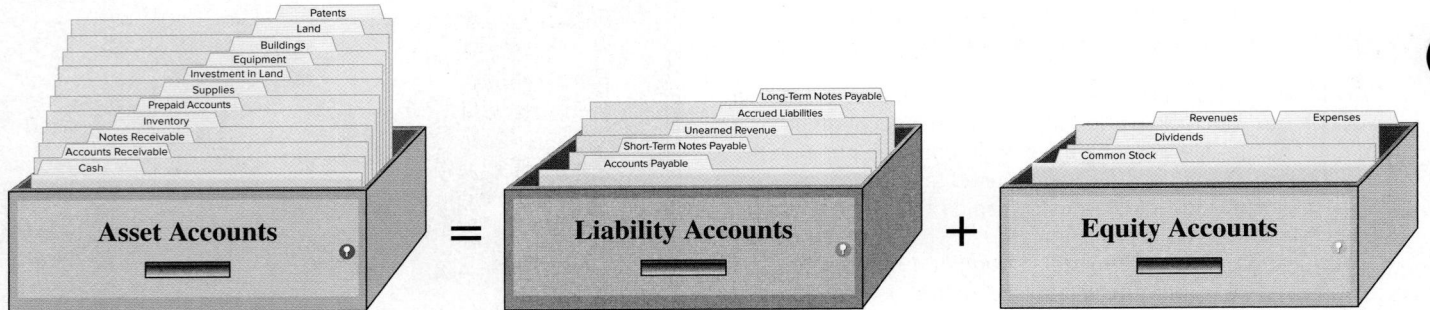

EXHIBIT 2.1

Accounts Organized by the Accounting Equation

Point: Customers and others who owe a company are **debtors.**

Point: A note receivable is different than an account receivable because it comes from a *formal contract called a promissory note.* A note receivable usually requires interest, whereas an account receivable does not.

Point: At the beginning of the term, a prepaid college parking pass is an asset that allows a student to park on campus. Benefits of the parking pass expire as the term progresses. At term-end, prepaid parking (asset) equals zero as it has been entirely recorded as parking expense.

Point: Some assets are called *intangible* because they do not have physical existence. **Coca-Cola** reports billions in intangible assets.

©Rob Kim/Getty Images

Accounts Receivable *Accounts receivable* are held by a seller and are promises of payment from customers to sellers. Accounts receivable are increased by *credit sales* or *sales on account* (or *on credit*). They are decreased by customer payments. We record all increases and decreases in receivables in the Accounts Receivable account. When there are multiple customers, separate records are kept for each, titled Accounts Receivable—'Customer Name'.

Note Receivable A *note receivable,* or promissory note, is a written promise of another entity to pay a specific sum of money on a specified future date to the holder of the note; the holder has an asset recorded in a Note (or Notes) Receivable account.

Prepaid Accounts *Prepaid accounts* (or *prepaid expenses*) are assets from prepayments of future expenses (expenses expected to be incurred in future accounting periods). When the expenses are later incurred, the amounts in prepaid accounts are transferred to expense accounts. Common examples of prepaid accounts are prepaid insurance, prepaid rent, and prepaid services. Prepaid accounts expire with the passage of time (such as with rent) or through use (such as with prepaid meal plans). When financial statements are prepared, (1) all expired and used prepaid accounts are recorded as expenses and (2) all unexpired and unused prepaid accounts are recorded as assets (reflecting future benefits). Chapter 3 covers prepaid accounts in detail.

Supplies Accounts *Supplies* are assets until they are used. When they are used up, their costs are reported as expenses. Unused supplies are recorded in a Supplies asset account. Supplies often are grouped by purpose—for example, office supplies and store supplies. *Office supplies* include paper and pens. *Store supplies* include packaging and cleaning materials.

Equipment Accounts *Equipment* is an asset. When equipment is used and wears down, its cost is gradually reported as an expense (called *depreciation*). Equipment often is grouped by its purpose—for example, office equipment and store equipment. *Office equipment* includes computers and desks. The *Store Equipment* account includes counters and cash registers.

Buildings Accounts *Buildings* such as stores, offices, warehouses, and factories are assets because they provide expected future benefits. When a building is used and wears down, its cost is reported as an expense (called *depreciation*). When several buildings are owned, separate accounts are sometimes kept for each of them.

Land The cost of *land* is recorded in a Land account. The cost of buildings located on the land is separately recorded in building accounts.

Decision Insight

Women Entrepreneurs Sara Blakely (in photo), the billionaire entrepreneur/owner of **SPANX**, has promised to donate half of her wealth to charity. The Center for Women's Business Research reports the following for women-owned businesses.

- They total more than 11 million and employ nearly 20 million workers.
- They generate $2.5 trillion in annual sales and tend to embrace technology.
- They are philanthropic—70% of owners volunteer at least once per month. ∎

Liability Accounts   Liabilities are obligations to transfer assets or provide products or services to others. They are claims (by creditors) against assets. **Creditors** are individuals and organizations that have rights to receive payments from a company. Common liability accounts are described here.

Accounts Payable   *Accounts payable* are promises to pay later. Payables can come from purchases of merchandise-for-resale, supplies, equipment, and services. We record all increases and decreases in payables in the Accounts Payable account. When there are multiple suppliers, separate records are kept for each, titled Accounts Payable—'Supplier Name'.

Point: Accounts payable also are called *trade payables*.

Note Payable   A *note payable* is a written promissory note to pay a future amount. It is recorded as either a short-term note payable or a long-term note payable, depending on when it must be repaid. We explain short- and long-term classification in the next two chapters.

Point: A note payable is different than an account payable because it comes from a *formal contract called a promissory note* and requires interest.

Unearned Revenue Accounts   **Unearned revenue** is a liability that is settled in the future when a company delivers its products or services. When customers pay in advance for products or services (before revenue is earned), the seller records this receipt as unearned revenue. Examples of unearned revenue include magazine subscriptions collected in advance by a publisher, rent collected in advance by a landlord, and season ticket sales by sports teams. The seller would record these in liability accounts such as Unearned Subscriptions and Unearned Rent. When products and services are later delivered, the earned portion of the unearned revenue is transferred to revenue accounts such as Subscription Fees Revenue and Rent Revenue.[1]

Point: Two words that almost always identify liability accounts: "payable," meaning liabilities that must be paid, and "unearned," meaning liabilities that must be fulfilled.

Accrued Liabilities   *Accrued liabilities* are amounts owed that are not yet paid. Examples are wages payable, taxes payable, and interest payable. These often are recorded in separate liability accounts by the same title. If they are not a large amount, one or more ledger accounts can be added and reported as a single amount on the balance sheet. (Financial statements often report totals of several ledger accounts.)

■ **Decision Insight** ━━

Unearned Revenue   The **Dallas Cowboys**, **Atlanta Falcons**, **New England Patriots**, and most NFL teams have over $100 million in advance ticket sales in *Unearned Revenue*. When a team plays its home games, it settles this liability to its ticket holders and then transfers the amount earned to *Ticket Revenue*. Teams in other major sports such as the National Women's Soccer League and the Women's National Basketball Association also have unearned revenue. ■

©Mike Zarrilli/Getty Images

Equity Accounts   The owner's claim on a company's assets is called *equity, stockholders' equity,* or *shareholders' equity.* Equity is the owner's *residual interest* in the assets of a business after subtracting liabilities. Equity is impacted by four types of accounts.

$$\text{Equity} \ = \ \text{Common stock} \ - \ \text{Dividends} \ + \ \text{Revenues} \ - \ \text{Expenses}$$

We show this in Exhibit 2.2 by expanding the accounting equation. We also organize assets and liabilities into subgroups that have similar attributes. An important subgroup for both assets and liabilities is the *current* items. Current items are expected to be either collected or owed within the next year. The next chapter explains this. At this point, know that a ***classified balance sheet*** groups accounts into classifications (such as land and buildings into Plant Assets) *and* it reports current assets before noncurrent assets and current liabilities before noncurrent liabilities.

---

[1]In practice, account titles vary. Subscription Fees Revenue is sometimes called Subscription Fees, Subscription Fees Earned, or Earned Subscription Fees. Rent Revenue is sometimes called Rent Earned, Rental Revenue, or Earned Rent Revenue. Titles can differ even within the same industry. Product sales are called *net sales* at **Apple**, *revenues* at **Google**, and *revenue* at **Samsung**. *Revenues* or *fees* is commonly used with service businesses, and *net sales* or *sales* is used with product businesses.

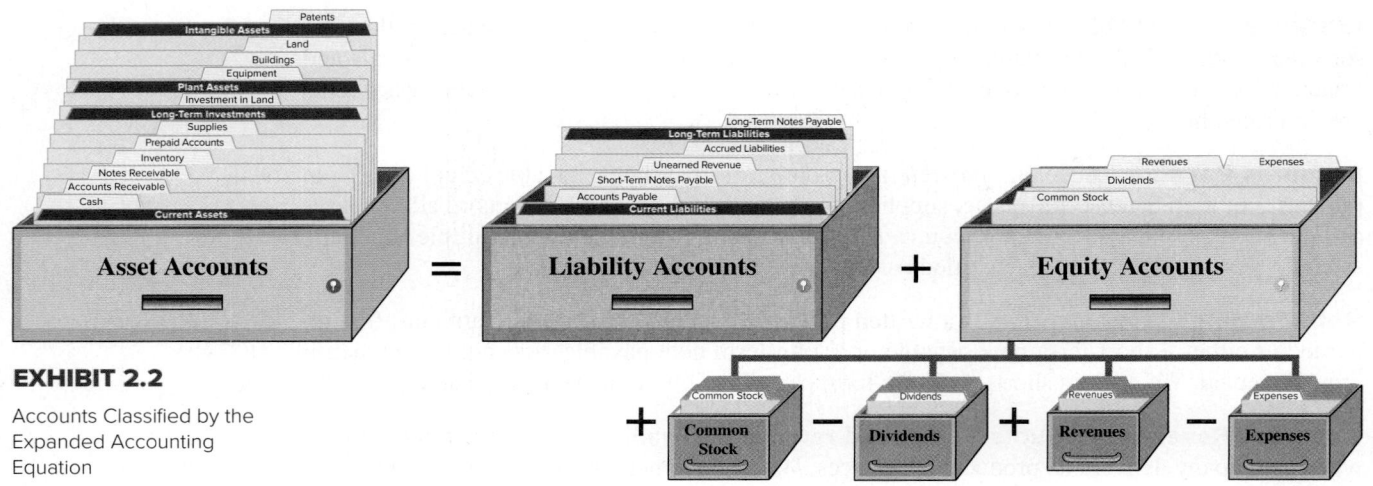

EXHIBIT 2.2

Accounts Classified by the Expanded Accounting Equation

Owner Investments   When an owner invests in a company, it increases both assets and equity. The increase to equity is recorded in the account titled **Common Stock**. Owner investments are not revenues of the business.

Point: Dividends account can be viewed as a *contra equity* account because it reduces the normal balance of equity.

Owner Distributions   When a corporation distributes assets to its owners, it decreases both company assets and total equity. The decrease to equity is recorded in an account titled **Dividends**. Dividends are not expenses of the business; they are simply the opposite of owner investments.

Revenue Accounts   Amounts received from sales of products and services to customers are recorded in revenue accounts, which increase equity. Examples of revenue accounts are Sales, Commissions Earned, Professional Fees Earned, Rent Revenue, and Interest Revenue. **Revenues always increase equity.**

Expense Accounts   Amounts used for costs of providing products and services are recorded in expense accounts, which decrease equity. Examples of expense accounts are Advertising Expense, Salaries Expense, Rent Expense, Utilities Expense, and Insurance Expense. **Expenses always decrease equity.** A variety of revenues and expenses are in the *chart of accounts* at the end of this book. (Different companies use different account titles to describe the same thing. For example, some use Interest Revenue instead of Interest Earned.)

■ **Decision Insight**

Sporting Accounts   The **Cleveland Cavaliers**, **Boston Celtics**, **Golden State Warriors**, and other NBA teams have revenue accounts that include Ticket Sales, Broadcast Fees, and Advertising Revenues. Expense accounts include Player Salaries, NBA Franchise Costs, and Promotional Costs. ■

C3_____

Describe a ledger and a chart of accounts.

EXHIBIT 2.3

Typical Chart of Accounts for a Smaller Business

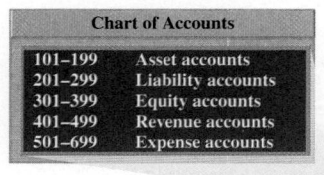

Chart of Accounts	
101–199	Asset accounts
201–299	Liability accounts
301–399	Equity accounts
401–499	Revenue accounts
501–699	Expense accounts

Ledger and Chart of Accounts

The collection of all accounts and their balances is called a *ledger* (or *general ledger*). A company's size and diversity of operations affect the number of accounts needed. A small company can have as few as 20 accounts; a large company can require thousands. The **chart of accounts** is a list of all ledger accounts and has an identification number assigned to each account. Exhibit 2.3 shows a common numbering system of accounts for a smaller business.

These account numbers have a three-digit code that is useful in recordkeeping. In this example, the first digit of asset accounts is a 1, the first digit of liability accounts is a 2, and so on. The second and third digits relate to the accounts' subcategories. Exhibit 2.4 shows a partial chart of accounts for FastForward.

EXHIBIT 2.4

Partial Chart of Accounts for FastForward

Chart of Accounts					
Assets	**Liabilities**	**Equity**			

Assets	Liabilities	Equity			
101 Cash	201 Accounts payable		**Revenues**		**Expenses**
106 Accounts receivable	236 Unearned consulting	307 Common stock	403 Consulting revenue	622 Salaries expense	
126 Supplies	revenue	318 Retained earnings	406 Rental revenue	637 Insurance expense	
128 Prepaid insurance		319 Dividends		640 Rent expense	
167 Equipment				652 Supplies expense	
				690 Utilities expense	

Classify each of the following accounts as either an asset (A), liability (L), or equity (EQ) account.

_____ **1.** Prepaid Rent   _____ **5.** Accounts Receivable   _____ **9.** Land

_____ **2.** Common Stock   _____ **6.** Equipment   _____ **10.** Prepaid Insurance

_____ **3.** Note Receivable   _____ **7.** Interest Payable   _____ **11.** Wages Payable

_____ **4.** Accounts Payable   _____ **8.** Unearned Revenue   _____ **12.** Rent Payable

Solution

1. A   **2.** EQ   **3.** A   **4.** L   **5.** A   **6.** A   **7.** L   **8.** L   **9.** A   **10.** A   **11.** L   **12.** L

NEED-TO-KNOW 2-1

Classifying Accounts

C1   C2   C3

Do More: QS 2-2, QS 2-3

DOUBLE-ENTRY ACCOUNTING

Debits and Credits

A **T-account** represents a ledger account and is used to show the effects of transactions. Its name comes from its shape like the letter **T**. The layout of a T-account is shown in Exhibit 2.5.

The left side of an account is called the **debit** side, or *Dr.* The right side is called the **credit** side, or *Cr.* To enter amounts on the left side of an account is to *debit* the account. To enter amounts on the right side is to *credit* the account. The term *debit* or *credit,* by itself, does not mean increase or decrease. Whether a debit or a credit is an increase or decrease depends on the account.

Account Title	
(Left side)	(Right side)
Debit	*Credit*

The difference between total debits and total credits for an account, including any beginning balance, is the **account balance.** When total debits exceed total credits, the account has a *debit balance*. It has a *credit balance* when total credits exceed total debits. When total debits equal total credits, the account has a *zero balance*.

Double-Entry System

Double-entry accounting demands the accounting equation remain in balance, which means that for each transaction:

- **At least two accounts are involved, with at least one debit and one credit.**
- **Total amount debited must equal total amount credited.**

This means total debits must equal total credits for all entries, and total debit account balances in the ledger must equal total credit account balances. The system for recording debits and credits follows the accounting equation—see Exhibit 2.6.

C4 _____

Define *debits* and *credits* and explain double-entry accounting.

EXHIBIT 2.5

The T-Account

Point: *Dr.* and *Cr.* come from 18th-century English where terms *debitor* and *creditor* were used instead of *debit* and *credit. Dr.* and *Cr.* use the first and last letters of these terms, just as we still do for Saint (St.) and Doctor (Dr.).

"Total debits equal total credits for each entry."

EXHIBIT 2.6

Debits and Credits in the Accounting Equation

Point: *Debit* and *credit* are accounting directions for left and right.

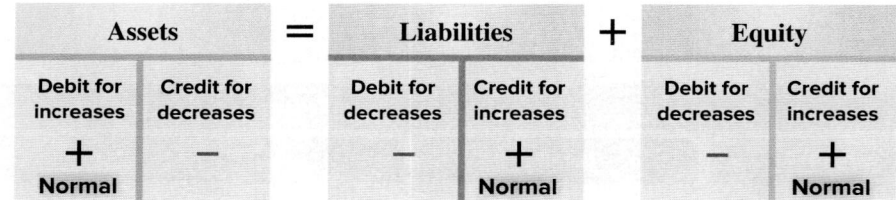

Assets		=	Liabilities		+	Equity	
Debit for increases	**Credit for decreases**		**Debit for decreases**	**Credit for increases**		**Debit for decreases**	**Credit for increases**
+	**−**		**−**	**+**		**−**	**+**
Normal				**Normal**			**Normal**

Net increases or decreases on one side have equal net effects on the other side.   For example, a net increase in assets must include an equal net increase on the liabilities and equity side. Some transactions affect only one side of the equation, such as acquiring a land asset by giving up a cash asset, but their net effect on this one side is zero.

Point: Assets are on the left-hand side of the equation and thus increase on the left. Liabilities and equity are on the right-hand side of the equation and thus increase on the right.

The left side is the *normal balance* side for assets; the right side is the *normal balance* side for liabilities and equity.   This matches their layout in the accounting equation, where assets are on the left side and liabilities and equity are on the right.

Equity increases from revenues and owner investments (stock issuances), and it decreases from expenses and dividends.   We see this by expanding the accounting equation to include debits and credits in double-entry form, as shown in Exhibit 2.7.

EXHIBIT 2.7

Debit and Credit Effects for Component Accounts

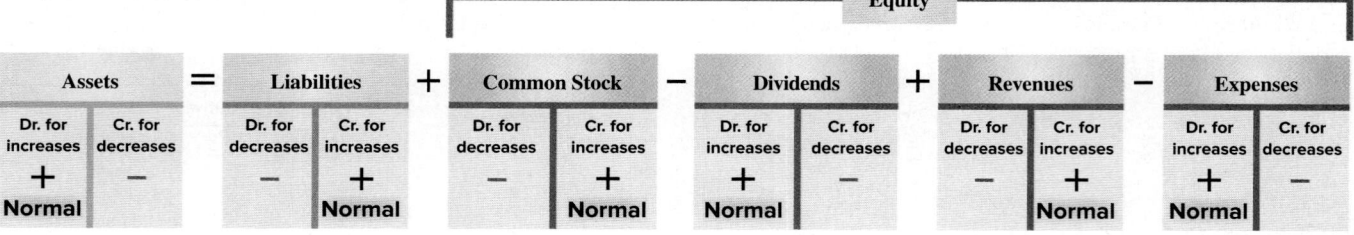

				Equity						
Assets	=	**Liabilities**	+	**Common Stock**	−	**Dividends**	+	**Revenues**	−	**Expenses**
Dr. for increases / **Cr. for decreases**		**Dr. for decreases** / **Cr. for increases**		**Dr. for decreases** / **Cr. for increases**		**Dr. for increases** / **Cr. for decreases**		**Dr. for decreases** / **Cr. for increases**		**Dr. for increases** / **Cr. for decreases**
+ / **−**		**−** / **+**		**−** / **+**		**+** / **−**		**−** / **+**		**+** / **−**
Normal		**Normal**		**Normal**		**Normal**		**Normal**		**Normal**

Increases (credits) to common stock and revenues *increase* equity; increases (debits) to dividends and expenses *decrease* equity.   The normal balance of each account is the side where *increases* are recorded.

Point: DrEAD means debit (**Dr**) is the normal balance side for **E**xpense, **A**sset, and **D**ividend accounts; credit the others.

The T-account for FastForward's Cash account, reflecting its first 11 transactions (from Exhibit 1.9), is shown in Exhibit 2.8. The total increases (debits) in its Cash account are $36,100, and the total decreases (credits) are $31,300. Total debits exceed total credits by $4,800, resulting in its ending debit balance of $4,800.

EXHIBIT 2.8

Computing the Balance for a T-Account

Cash				
Receive investment by owner for stock	30,000	Purchase of supplies	2,500	
Consulting services revenue earned	4,200	Purchase of equipment	26,000	
Collection of account receivable	1,900	Payment of rent	1,000	
		Payment of salary	700	
		Payment of account payable	900	
		Payment of cash dividend	200	
Balance	4,800			

36,100

31,300

36,100 − 31,300

Point: The ending balance is on the side with the larger dollar amount. Also, a plus (+) and minus (−) are *not* used in a T-account.

NEED-TO-KNOW **2-2**

Normal Account Balance

C4

Do More: QS 2-4, QS 2-5, QS 2-7, E 2-4

Identify the normal balance (debit [Dr] or credit [Cr]) for each of the following accounts.

_____ **1.** Prepaid Rent   _____ **5.** Accounts Receivable   _____ **9.** Land

_____ **2.** Common Stock   _____ **6.** Equipment   _____ **10.** Prepaid Insurance

_____ **3.** Note Receivable   _____ **7.** Interest Payable   _____ **11.** Dividends

_____ **4.** Accounts Payable   _____ **8.** Unearned Revenue   _____ **12.** Utilities Expense

Solution

1. Dr.   **2.** Cr.   **3.** Dr.   **4.** Cr.   **5.** Dr.   **6.** Dr.   **7.** Cr.   **8.** Cr.   **9.** Dr.   **10.** Dr.   **11.** Dr.   **12.** Dr.

ANALYZING AND PROCESSING TRANSACTIONS

This section explains the analyzing, recording, and posting of transactions.

Journalizing and Posting Transactions

The four steps of processing transactions are shown in Exhibit 2.9. Steps 1 and 2—transaction analysis and the accounting equation—already were covered. This section focuses on steps 3 and 4. Step 3 is to record each transaction chronologically in a journal. A **journal** is a complete record of each transaction in one place. It also shows debits and credits for each transaction. Recording transactions in a journal is called **journalizing.** Step 4 is to transfer (or *post*) entries from the journal to the ledger. Transferring journal entry information to the ledger is called **posting.**

P1

Record transactions in a journal and post entries to a ledger.

EXHIBIT 2.9

Steps in Processing Transactions

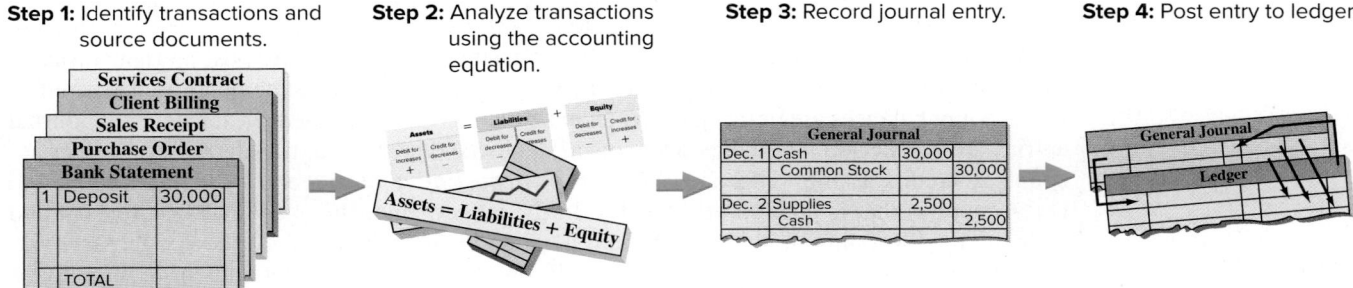

Step 1: Identify transactions and source documents.

Step 2: Analyze transactions using the accounting equation.

Step 3: Record journal entry.

Step 4: Post entry to ledger.

Journalizing Transactions
Journalizing transactions requires an understanding of a journal. While companies can use various journals, every company uses a **general journal.** It can be used to record any transaction. Exhibit 2.10 shows how the first two transactions of FastForward are recorded in a general journal.

To record entries in a general journal, apply these steps; refer to Exhibit 2.10.

General Journal

Date	Account Titles and Explanation	PR	Debit	Credit
2019 ⓐ Dec. 1	ⓑ Cash		30,000	
	ⓒ Common Stock			30,000
	Receive investment by owner. ⓓ			
Dec. 2	Supplies		2,500	
	Cash			2,500
	Purchase supplies for cash.			

ⓐ Date the transaction: Enter the year at the top of the first column and the month and day on the first line of each journal entry.

ⓑ Enter titles of accounts debited and then enter amounts in the Debit column on the same line. Account titles are taken from the chart of accounts and are aligned with the left margin of the Account Titles and Explanation column.

ⓒ Enter titles of accounts credited and then enter amounts in the Credit column on the same line. Account titles are from the chart of accounts and are indented from the left margin of the Account Titles and Explanation column to separate them from debited accounts.

ⓓ Enter a brief explanation of the transaction on the line below the entry (it often references a source document). This explanation is indented about half as far as the credited account titles to avoid confusing it with accounts, and it is italicized.

EXHIBIT 2.10

Partial General Journal for FastForward

Point: There are no exact rules for a journal entry explanation—it should be short yet describe why an entry is made.

A blank line is left between each journal entry for clarity. When a transaction is first recorded, the **posting reference (PR) column** is left blank (in a manual system). Later, when posting entries to the ledger, the identification numbers of the individual ledger accounts are entered in the PR column.

Balance Column Account
T-accounts are simple and show how the accounting process works. However, actual accounting systems need more structure and therefore use a different formatting of T-accounts, called **balance column accounts,** shown in Exhibit 2.11.

General Ledger					
Cash					**Account No. 101**
Date	**Explanation**	**PR**	**Debit**	**Credit**	**Balance**
2019					
Dec. 1		G1	30,000		30,000
Dec. 2		G1		2,500	27,500
Dec. 3		G1		26,000	1,500
Dec. 10		G1	4,200		5,700

EXHIBIT 2.11

Cash Account in Balance Column Format

Point: Explanations are included in ledger accounts only for unusual transactions or events.

The balance column account format is similar to a T-account in having columns for debits and credits. It is different in including transaction date and explanation columns. It also has a column with the balance of the account after each entry is recorded. FastForward's Cash account in Exhibit 2.11 is debited on December 1 for the $30,000 owner investment, yielding a $30,000 debit balance. The account is credited on December 2 for $2,500, yielding a $27,500 debit balance. On December 3, it is credited for $26,000, and its debit balance is reduced to $1,500. The Cash account is debited for $4,200 on December 10, and its debit balance increases to $5,700; and so on.

The heading of the Balance column does not show whether it is a debit or credit balance. Instead, an account is assumed to have a *normal balance*. Unusual events can sometimes temporarily create an abnormal balance. An *abnormal balance* is a balance on the side where decreases are recorded. For example, a customer might mistakenly overpay a bill. This gives that customer's account receivable an abnormal (credit) balance. An abnormal balance often is identified by setting it in brackets or entering it in red. A zero balance is shown by writing zero or a dash in the Balance column.

Posting Journal Entries Step 4 of processing transactions is to post journal entries to ledger accounts. All entries are posted to the ledger before financial statements are prepared so that account balances are up-to-date. When entries are posted to the ledger, the debits in journal entries are transferred into ledger accounts as debits, and credits are transferred into ledger accounts as credits. Exhibit 2.12 shows *four parts to **posting** a journal entry*. Ⓐ Identify the ledger account(s) that is debited in the entry. In the ledger, enter the entry date, the journal and page in its PR column, the debit amount, and the new balance of the ledger account. (*G* shows it came from the general journal.) Ⓑ Enter the ledger account number in the PR column of the journal. Parts Ⓒ and Ⓓ repeat the first two steps for credit entries and amounts. The posting process creates a link between the ledger and the journal entry. This link is a useful cross-reference for tracing an amount from one record to another.

Point: Posting is automatic with accounting software.

Point: The fundamental concepts of a manual system are identical to those of a computerized information system.

EXHIBIT 2.12

Posting an Entry to the Ledger

Key:

Ⓐ Identify debit account in ledger: enter date, journal page, amount, and balance (red line).

Ⓑ Enter the debit account number from the ledger in the PR column of the journal (blue line).

Ⓒ Identify credit account in ledger: enter date, journal page, amount, and balance (gold line).

Ⓓ Enter the credit account number from the ledger in the PR column of the journal (green line).

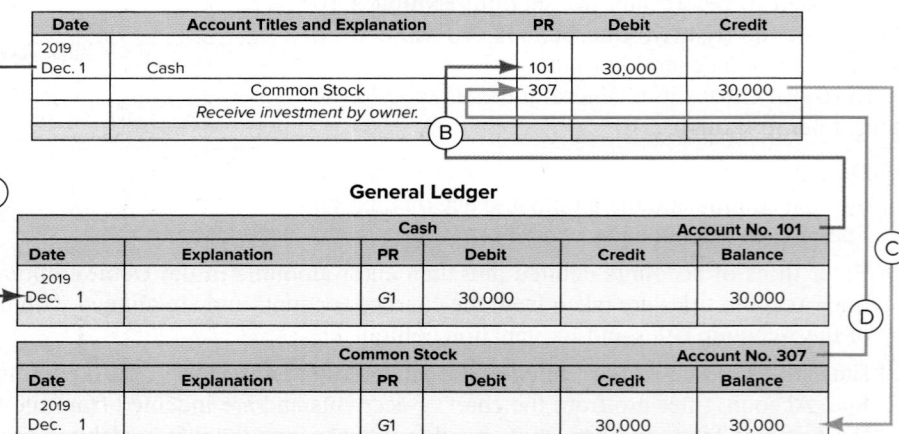

Processing Transactions—An Example

A1 _____

Analyze the impact of transactions on accounts and financial statements.

We use FastForward to show how double-entry accounting is used in analyzing and processing transactions. Analysis of each transaction follows the four steps of Exhibit 2.9.

Step 1 Identify the transaction and any source documents.

Step 2 Analyze the transaction using the accounting equation.

Step 3 Record the transaction in journal entry form applying double-entry accounting.

Step 4 Post the entry (for simplicity, we use T-accounts to represent ledger accounts).

Study each transaction before moving to the next. The first 11 transactions are from Chapter 1, and we analyze five additional December transactions of FastForward (numbered 12 through 16).

Point: In Need-to-Know 2-5, we show how to use balance column accounts for the ledger.

*FAST*Forward

1. Receive Investment by Owner

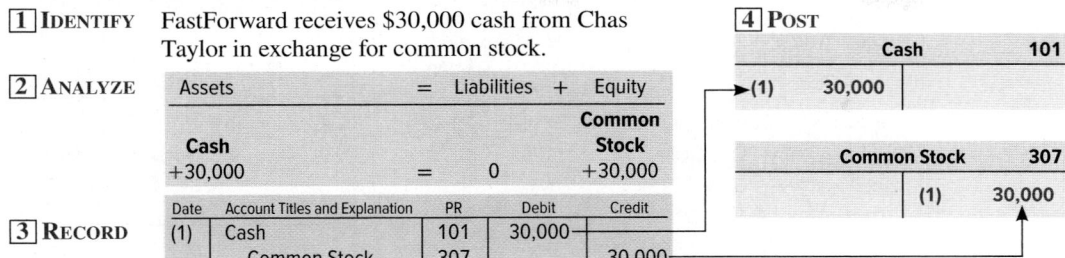

1 IDENTIFY FastForward receives $30,000 cash from Chas Taylor in exchange for common stock.

2 ANALYZE

Assets	=	Liabilities	+	Equity
Cash				**Common Stock**
+30,000	=	0		+30,000

3 RECORD

Date	Account Titles and Explanation	PR	Debit	Credit
(1)	Cash	101	30,000	
	Common Stock	307		30,000

4 POST

Cash		101
(1)	30,000	

Common Stock		307
	(1)	30,000

2. Purchase Supplies for Cash

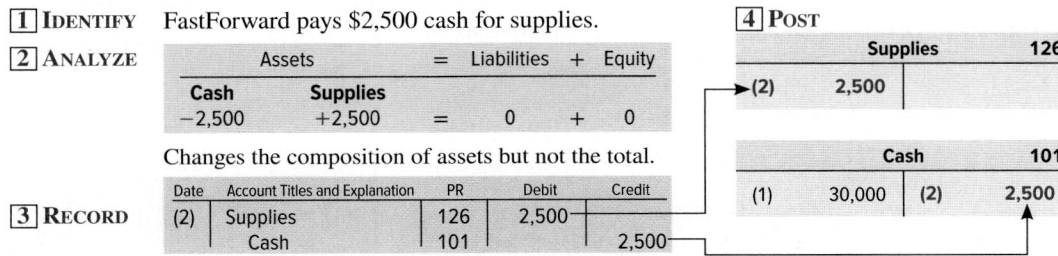

1 IDENTIFY FastForward pays $2,500 cash for supplies.

2 ANALYZE

Assets		=	Liabilities	+	Equity
Cash	**Supplies**				
−2,500	+2,500	=	0	+	0

Changes the composition of assets but not the total.

3 RECORD

Date	Account Titles and Explanation	PR	Debit	Credit
(2)	Supplies	126	2,500	
	Cash	101		2,500

4 POST

Supplies		126
(2)	2,500	

Cash			101
(1)	30,000	(2)	2,500

3. Purchase Equipment for Cash

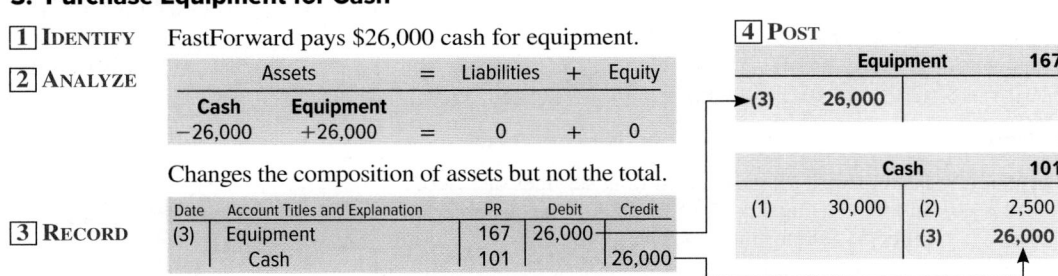

1 IDENTIFY FastForward pays $26,000 cash for equipment.

2 ANALYZE

Assets		=	Liabilities	+	Equity
Cash	**Equipment**				
−26,000	+26,000	=	0	+	0

Changes the composition of assets but not the total.

3 RECORD

Date	Account Titles and Explanation	PR	Debit	Credit
(3)	Equipment	167	26,000	
	Cash	101		26,000

4 POST

Equipment		167
(3)	26,000	

Cash			101
(1)	30,000	(2)	2,500
		(3)	26,000

4. Purchase Supplies on Credit

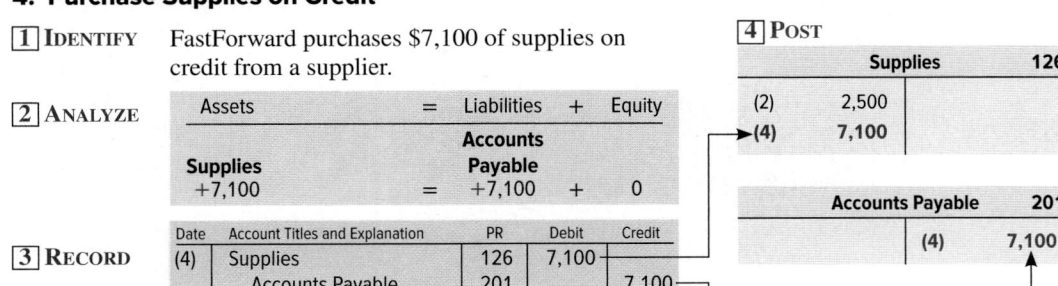

1 IDENTIFY FastForward purchases $7,100 of supplies on credit from a supplier.

2 ANALYZE

Assets	=	Liabilities	+	Equity
		Accounts Payable		
Supplies				
+7,100	=	+7,100	+	0

3 RECORD

Date	Account Titles and Explanation	PR	Debit	Credit
(4)	Supplies	126	7,100	
	Accounts Payable	201		7,100

4 POST

Supplies		126
(2)	2,500	
(4)	7,100	

Accounts Payable		201
	(4)	7,100

5. Provide Services for Cash

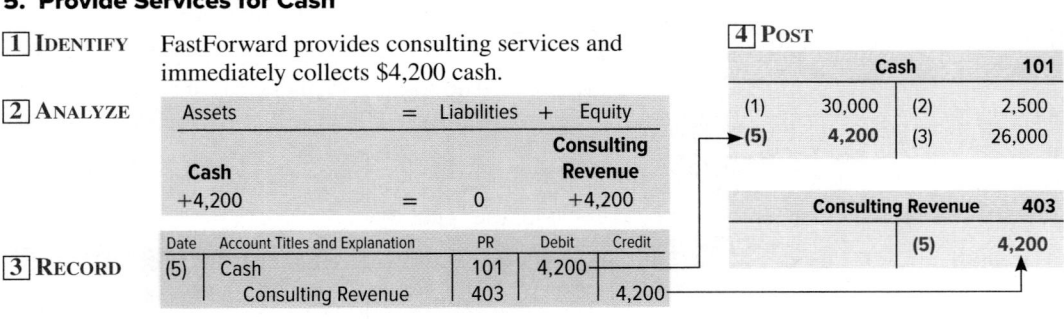

1 IDENTIFY FastForward provides consulting services and immediately collects $4,200 cash.

2 ANALYZE

Assets	=	Liabilities	+	Equity
				Consulting Revenue
Cash				
+4,200	=	0		+4,200

3 RECORD

Date	Account Titles and Explanation	PR	Debit	Credit
(5)	Cash	101	4,200	
	Consulting Revenue	403		4,200

4 POST

Cash			101
(1)	30,000	(2)	2,500
(5)	4,200	(3)	26,000

Consulting Revenue		403
	(5)	4,200

©Adie Bush/Getty Images

6. Payment of Expense in Cash

1 IDENTIFY FastForward pays $1,000 cash for December rent.

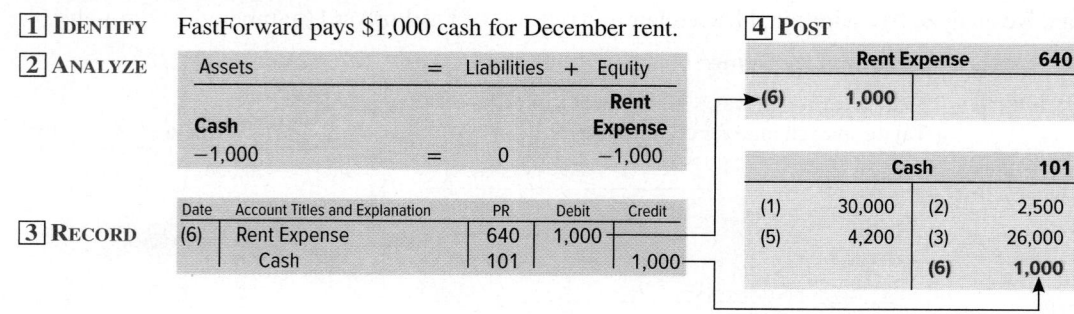

7. Payment of Expense in Cash

Point: *Salary* usually refers to compensation of a fixed amount for a given time period. *Wages* is compensation based on time worked.

1 IDENTIFY FastForward pays $700 cash for employee salary.

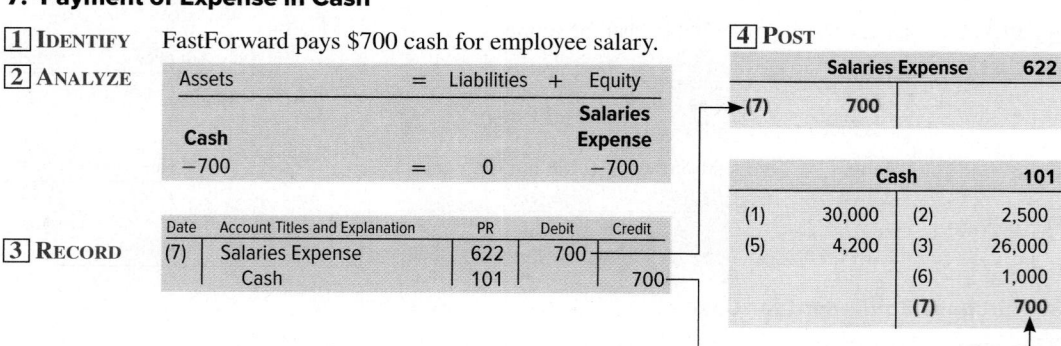

8. Provide Consulting and Rental Services on Credit

Point: The *revenue recognition principle* requires revenue to be recognized when the company provides products and services to a customer. This is not necessarily the same time that the customer pays.

Point: Transaction 8 is a **compound journal entry**, which is an entry that affects three or more accounts. The rule that total debits equal total credits continues.

1 IDENTIFY FastForward provides consulting services of $1,600 and rents its test facilities for $300. The customer is billed $1,900 for these services.

9. Receipt of Cash on Account

1 IDENTIFY FastForward receives $1,900 cash from the customer billed in Transaction 8.

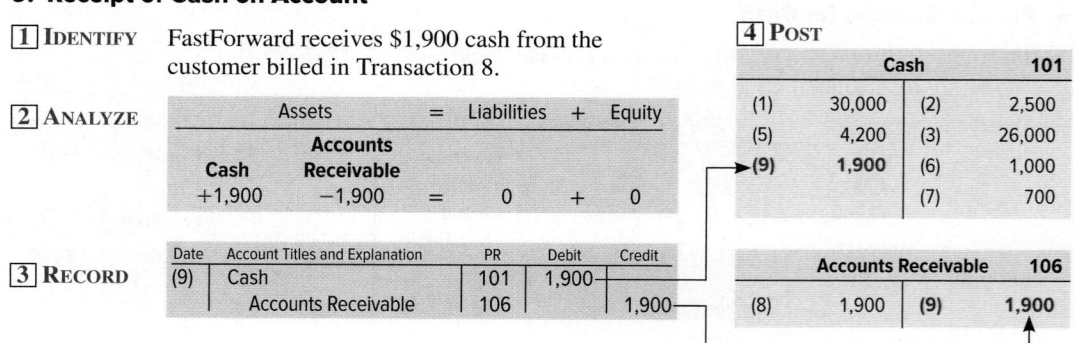

10. Partial Payment of Accounts Payable

1 IDENTIFY   FastForward pays CalTech Supply $900 cash toward the payable of Transaction 4.

2 ANALYZE

Assets	=	Liabilities	+	Equity
Cash		**Accounts Payable**		
−900	=	−900	+	0

3 RECORD

Date	Account Titles and Explanation	PR	Debit	Credit
(10)	Accounts Payable	201	900	
	Cash	101		900

4 POST

Accounts Payable			201
(10)	900	(4)	7,100

Cash			101
(1)	30,000	(2)	2,500
(5)	4,200	(3)	26,000
(9)	1,900	(6)	1,000
		(7)	700
		(10)	**900**

11. Payment of Cash Dividend

1 IDENTIFY   FastForward pays a $200 cash dividend.

2 ANALYZE

Assets	=	Liabilities	+	Equity
Cash				**Dividends**
−200	=	0		−200

3 RECORD

Date	Account Titles and Explanation	PR	Debit	Credit
(11)	Dividends	319	200	
	Cash	101		200

4 POST

Dividends			319
(11)	200		

Cash			101
(1)	30,000	(2)	2,500
(5)	4,200	(3)	26,000
(9)	1,900	(6)	1,000
		(7)	700
		(10)	900
		(11)	**200**

Point: Dividends always decrease equity.

12. Receipt of Cash for Future Services

1 IDENTIFY   FastForward receives $3,000 cash in advance of providing consulting services to a customer.

2 ANALYZE

Assets	=	Liabilities	+	Equity
		Unearned		
Cash		**Consulting Revenue**		
+3,000	=	+3,000	+	0

Accepting $3,000 cash requires FastForward to perform future services and is a liability. No revenue is recorded until services are provided.

3 RECORD

Date	Account Titles and Explanation	PR	Debit	Credit
(12)	Cash	101	3,000	
	Unearned Consulting			
	Revenue	236		3,000

4 POST

Cash			101
(1)	30,000	(2)	2,500
(5)	4,200	(3)	26,000
(9)	1,900	(6)	1,000
(12)	**3,000**	(7)	700
		(10)	900
		(11)	200

Unearned Consulting Revenue			236
		(12)	**3,000**

Point: "Unearned" accounts are liabilities that must be fulfilled.

13. Pay Cash for Future Insurance Coverage

1 IDENTIFY   FastForward pays $2,400 cash (insurance premium) for a 24-month insurance policy. Coverage begins on December 1.

2 ANALYZE

Assets		=	Liabilities	+	Equity
	Prepaid				
Cash	**Insurance**				
−2,400	+2,400	=	0	+	0

Changes the composition of assets from cash to prepaid insurance. Expense is recorded as insurance coverage expires.

3 RECORD

Date	Account Titles and Explanation	PR	Debit	Credit
(13)	Prepaid Insurance	128	2,400	
	Cash	101		2,400

4 POST

Prepaid Insurance			128
(13)	2,400		

Cash			101
(1)	30,000	(2)	2,500
(5)	4,200	(3)	26,000
(9)	1,900	(6)	1,000
(12)	3,000	(7)	700
		(10)	900
		(11)	200
		(13)	**2,400**

14. Purchase Supplies for Cash

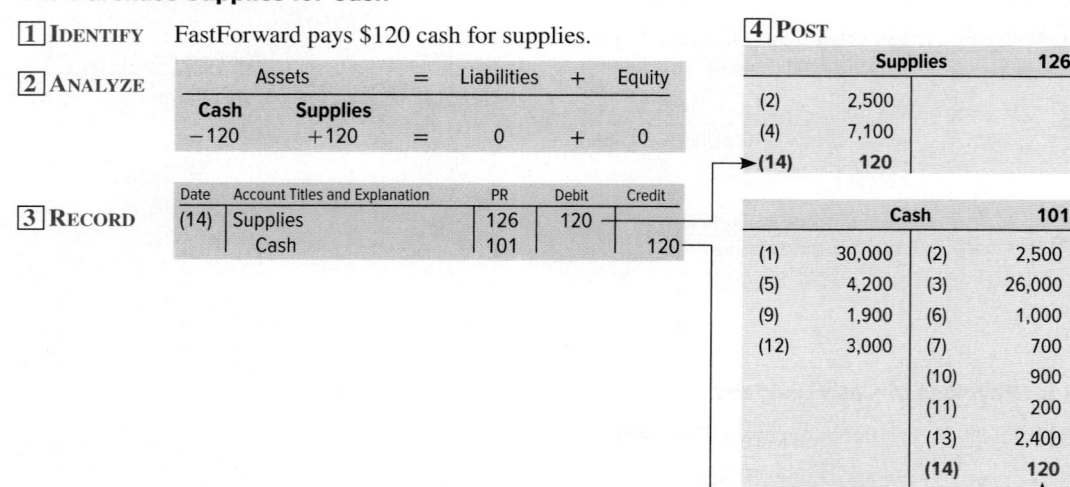

1 IDENTIFY   FastForward pays $120 cash for supplies.

2 ANALYZE

Assets		=	Liabilities	+	Equity
Cash	**Supplies**				
−120	+120	=	0	+	0

3 RECORD

Date	Account Titles and Explanation	PR	Debit	Credit
(14)	Supplies	126	120	
	Cash	101		120

4 POST

Supplies		126
(2)	2,500	
(4)	7,100	
(14)	**120**	

Cash		101
(1)	30,000	(2)	2,500
(5)	4,200	(3)	26,000
(9)	1,900	(6)	1,000
(12)	3,000	(7)	700
		(10)	900
		(11)	200
		(13)	2,400
		(14)	**120**

Point: Luca Pacioli, a 15th-century monk and famous mathematician, was the first to devise double-entry accounting.

15. Payment of Expense in Cash

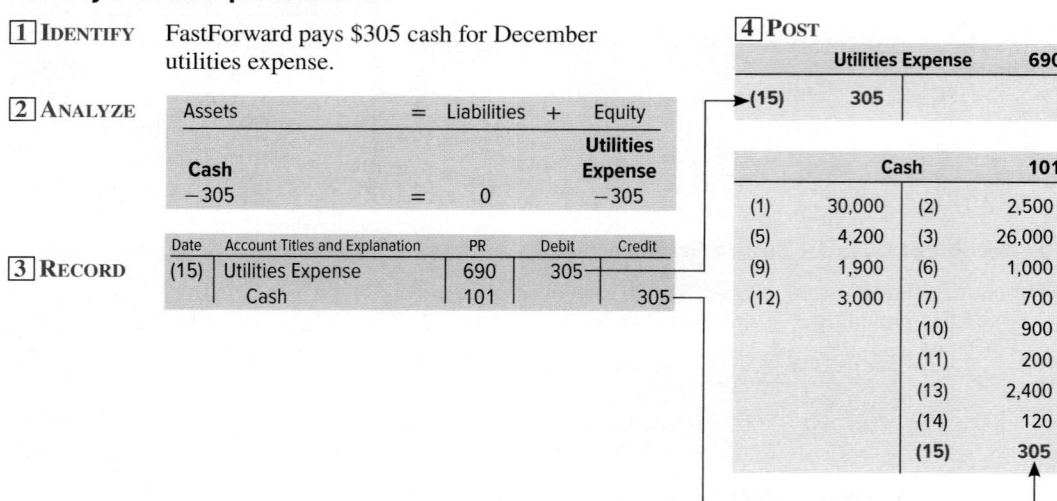

1 IDENTIFY   FastForward pays $305 cash for December utilities expense.

2 ANALYZE

Assets	=	Liabilities	+	Equity
				Utilities
Cash				**Expense**
−305	=	0		−305

3 RECORD

Date	Account Titles and Explanation	PR	Debit	Credit
(15)	Utilities Expense	690	305	
	Cash	101		305

4 POST

Utilities Expense		690
(15)	**305**	

Cash		101
(1)	30,000	(2)	2,500
(5)	4,200	(3)	26,000
(9)	1,900	(6)	1,000
(12)	3,000	(7)	700
		(10)	900
		(11)	200
		(13)	2,400
		(14)	120
		(15)	**305**

16. Payment of Expense in Cash

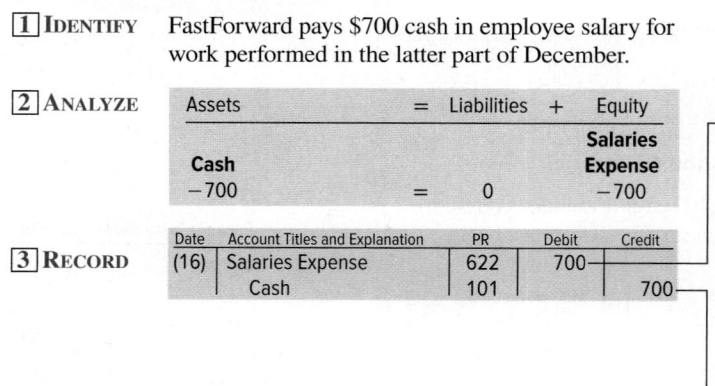

1 IDENTIFY   FastForward pays $700 cash in employee salary for work performed in the latter part of December.

2 ANALYZE

Assets	=	Liabilities	+	Equity
				Salaries
Cash				**Expense**
−700	=	0		−700

3 RECORD

Date	Account Titles and Explanation	PR	Debit	Credit
(16)	Salaries Expense	622	700	
	Cash	101		700

4 POST

Salaries Expense		622
(7)	700	
(16)	**700**	

Cash		101
(1)	30,000	(2)	2,500
(5)	4,200	(3)	26,000
(9)	1,900	(6)	1,000
(12)	3,000	(7)	700
		(10)	900
		(11)	200
		(13)	2,400
		(14)	120
		(15)	305
		(16)	**700**

Summarizing Transactions in a Ledger

Exhibit 2.13 shows the ledger accounts (in T-account form) of FastForward after all 16 transactions are recorded and posted and the balances computed. The accounts are grouped into three columns following the accounting equation: assets, liabilities, and equity.

- Totals for the three columns obey the accounting equation:
  Assets equal **$42,395** ($4,275 + $0 + $9,720 + $2,400 + $26,000).
  Liabilities equal **$9,200** ($6,200 + $3,000).
  Equity equals **$33,195** ($30,000 − $200 + $5,800 + $300 − $1,400 − $1,000 − $305).
  The accounting equation: $42,395 = $9,200 + $33,195.
- Common stock, dividends, revenue, and expense accounts reflect transactions that change equity.
- Revenue and expense account balances are reported in the income statement.

Debit and Credit Rules

Accounts	Increase (normal bal.)	Decrease
Asset	Debit	Credit
Liability...........	Credit	Debit
Common Stock	Credit	Debit
Dividends.........	Debit	Credit
Revenue	Credit	Debit
Expense	Debit	Credit

EXHIBIT 2.13

FAST Forward

Ledger for FastForward (in T-Account Form)

General Ledger

Assets	=	Liabilities	+	Equity

Cash   101

(1)	30,000	(2)	2,500
(5)	4,200	(3)	26,000
(9)	1,900	(6)	1,000
(12)	3,000	(7)	700
		(10)	900
		(11)	200
		(13)	2,400
		(14)	120
		(15)	305
		(16)	700
Balance	4,275		

Accounts Receivable   106

(8)	1,900	(9)	1,900
Balance	0		

Supplies   126

(2)	2,500	
(4)	7,100	
(14)	120	
Balance	9,720	

Prepaid Insurance   128

(13)	2,400	

Equipment   167

(3)	26,000	

Accounts Payable   201

(10)	900	(4)	7,100
		Balance	6,200

Unearned Consulting Revenue   236

	(12)	3,000

Common Stock   307

	(1)	30,000

Dividends   319

(11)	200	

Consulting Revenue   403

	(5)	4,200
	(8)	1,600
	Balance	5,800

Rental Revenue   406

	(8)	300

Salaries Expense   622

(7)	700	
(16)	700	
Balance	1,400	

Rent Expense   640

(6)	1,000	

Utilities Expense   690

(15)	305	

Accounts in this white area are on the income statement.

$42,395	=	$9,200	+	$33,195

 **2-3**

Recording Transactions

P1   A1

Assume Tata Company began operations on January 1 and completed the following transactions during its first month of operations. For each transaction, (a) analyze the transaction using the accounting equation, (b) record the transaction in journal entry form, and (c) post the entry using T-accounts to represent ledger accounts. Tata Company has the following (partial) chart of accounts—account numbers in parentheses: Cash (101); Accounts Receivable (106); Equipment (167); Accounts Payable (201); Common Stock (307); Dividends (319); Services Revenue (403); and Wages Expense (601).

Jan. 1 Jamsetji Tata invested $4,000 cash in the Tata Company in exchange for common stock.
      5 Tata Company purchased $2,000 of equipment on credit.
     14 Tata Company provided $540 of services for a client on credit.

Solution

Jan. 1 Receive Investment by Owner

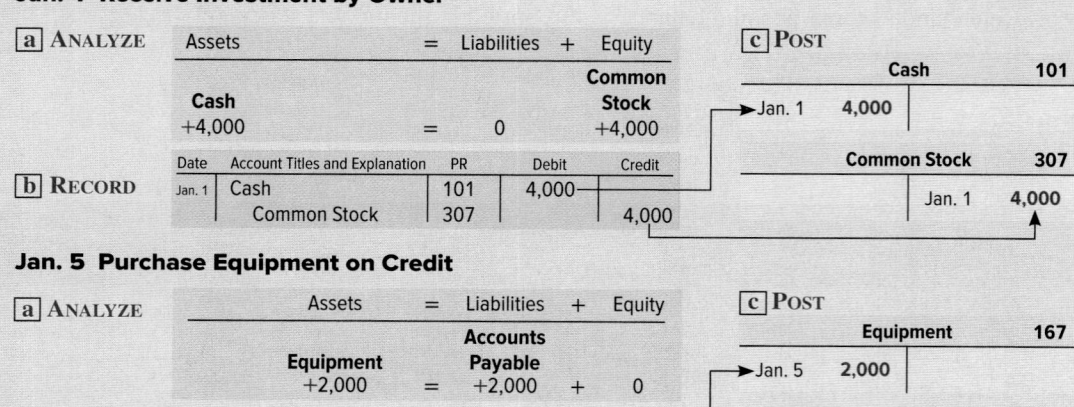

Jan. 5 Purchase Equipment on Credit

Jan. 14 Provide Services on Credit

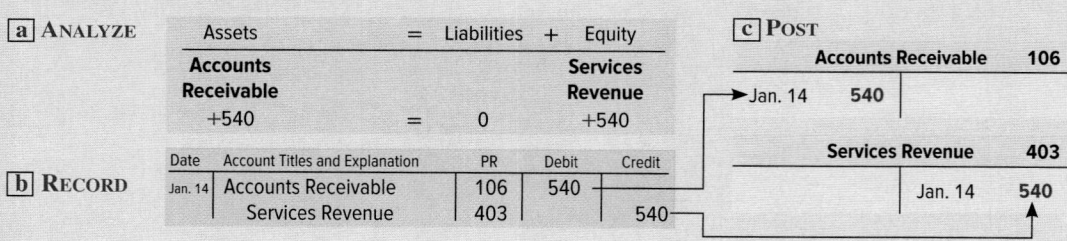

Do More: QS 2-6, E 2-7, E 2-9, E 2-11, E 2-12

TRIAL BALANCE

P2

Prepare and explain the use of a trial balance.

A **trial balance** is a list of all ledger accounts and their balances at a point in time. Exhibit 2.14 shows the trial balance for FastForward after its 16 entries are posted to the ledger. (This is an *unadjusted* trial balance. Chapter 3 explains adjustments.)

Preparing a Trial Balance

Preparing a trial balance has three steps.

1. List each account title and its amount (from the ledger) in the trial balance. If an account has a zero balance, list it with a zero in its normal balance column (or omit it).
2. Compute the total of debit balances and the total of credit balances.
3. Verify (*prove*) total debit balances equal total credit balances.

The total of debit balances equals the total of credit balances for the trial balance in Exhibit 2.14. Equality of these two totals does not guarantee that no errors were made. For example, the column totals will be equal when a debit or credit of a correct amount is made to a wrong account. Another error not identified with a trial balance is when equal debits and credits of an incorrect amount are entered.

EXHIBIT 2.14

Trial Balance (Unadjusted)

FASTFORWARD Trial Balance December 31, 2019		
	Debit	**Credit**
Cash.	$ 4,275	
Accounts receivable	0	
Supplies.	9,720	
Prepaid insurance.	2,400	
Equipment.	26,000	
Accounts payable		$ 6,200
Unearned consulting revenue . . .		3,000
Common stock		30,000
Dividends	200	
Consulting revenue		5,800
Rental revenue		300
Salaries expense.	1,400	
Rent expense	1,000	
Utilities expense.	305	
Totals.	$45,300	$45,300

Point: A trial balance is *not* a financial statement but a tool for checking equality of debits and credits in the ledger.

Searching for Errors   If the trial balance does not balance (when its columns are not equal), the error(s) must be found and corrected. An efficient way to search for an error is to check the journalizing, posting, and trial balance preparation in *reverse order.* Step 1 is to verify that the trial balance columns are correctly added. If step 1 does not find the error, step 2 is to verify that account balances are accurately entered from the ledger. Step 3 is to see whether a debit (or credit) balance is mistakenly listed in the trial balance as a credit (or debit). A clue to this error is when the difference between total debits and total credits equals twice the amount of the incorrect account balance. Step 4 is to recompute each account balance in the ledger. Step 5 is to verify that each journal entry is properly posted. Step 6 is to verify that the original journal entry has equal debits and credits. At this point, the errors should be uncovered.

Example: If a credit to Unearned Revenue was incorrectly posted to the Revenue ledger account, would the ledger still balance? *Answer:* The ledger would balance, but liabilities would be understated, equity would be overstated, and income would be overstated.

Ethical Risk

Accounting Quality   Recording valid and accurate transactions enhances the quality of financial statements. Roughly 30% of employees in IT report observing misconduct such as falsifying accounting data. They also report increased incidences of such misconduct in recent years. Source: KPMG. ◾

Financial Statements Prepared from Trial Balance

P3

Prepare financial statements from business transactions.

Financial Statements across Time   How financial statements are linked in time is shown in Exhibit 2.15. A balance sheet reports an organization's financial position at a *point in time.* The income statement, statement of retained earnings, and statement of cash flows report financial performance over a *period of time.* The three statements in the middle column of Exhibit 2.15 explain how financial position changes from the beginning to the end of a reporting period.

EXHIBIT 2.15

Links between Financial Statements across Time

A one-year (annual) reporting period is common, as are semiannual, quarterly, and monthly periods. The one-year reporting period is called the *accounting,* or *fiscal, year.* Businesses whose accounting year begins on January 1 and ends on December 31 are called *calendar-year* companies.

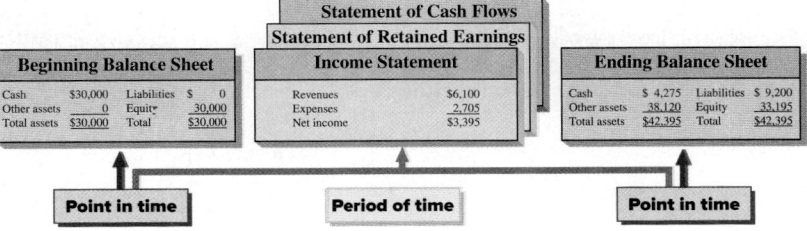

Financial Statement Preparation   This section shows how to prepare *financial statements* from the trial balance. (These are *unadjusted statements.* Chapter 3 explains adjustments.) We prepare these statements in the following order.

❶ Income Statement   An income statement reports revenues earned minus expenses incurred over a period of time. FastForward's income statement for December is shown at the top right side of Exhibit 2.16. Information about revenues and expenses is taken from the trial balance on the left side. Net income of $3,395 is the *bottom line* for the income statement. Owner investments and dividends are *not* part of income.

❷ Statement of Retained Earnings   The statement of retained earnings reports how retained earnings changes over the reporting period. FastForward's statement of retained earnings is the second report in Exhibit 2.16. It shows the $3,395 of net income, the $200 dividend, and the $3,195 end-of-period balance. (The beginning balance in the statement of retained earnings is rarely zero, except in the first period of operations. The beginning balance in January 2020 is $3,195, which is December 2019's ending balance.)

❸ Balance Sheet   The balance sheet reports the financial position of a company at a point in time. FastForward's balance sheet is the third report in Exhibit 2.16. This statement shows financial condition at the close of business on December 31. The left side of the balance

EXHIBIT 2.16

Financial Statements Prepared from Trial Balance

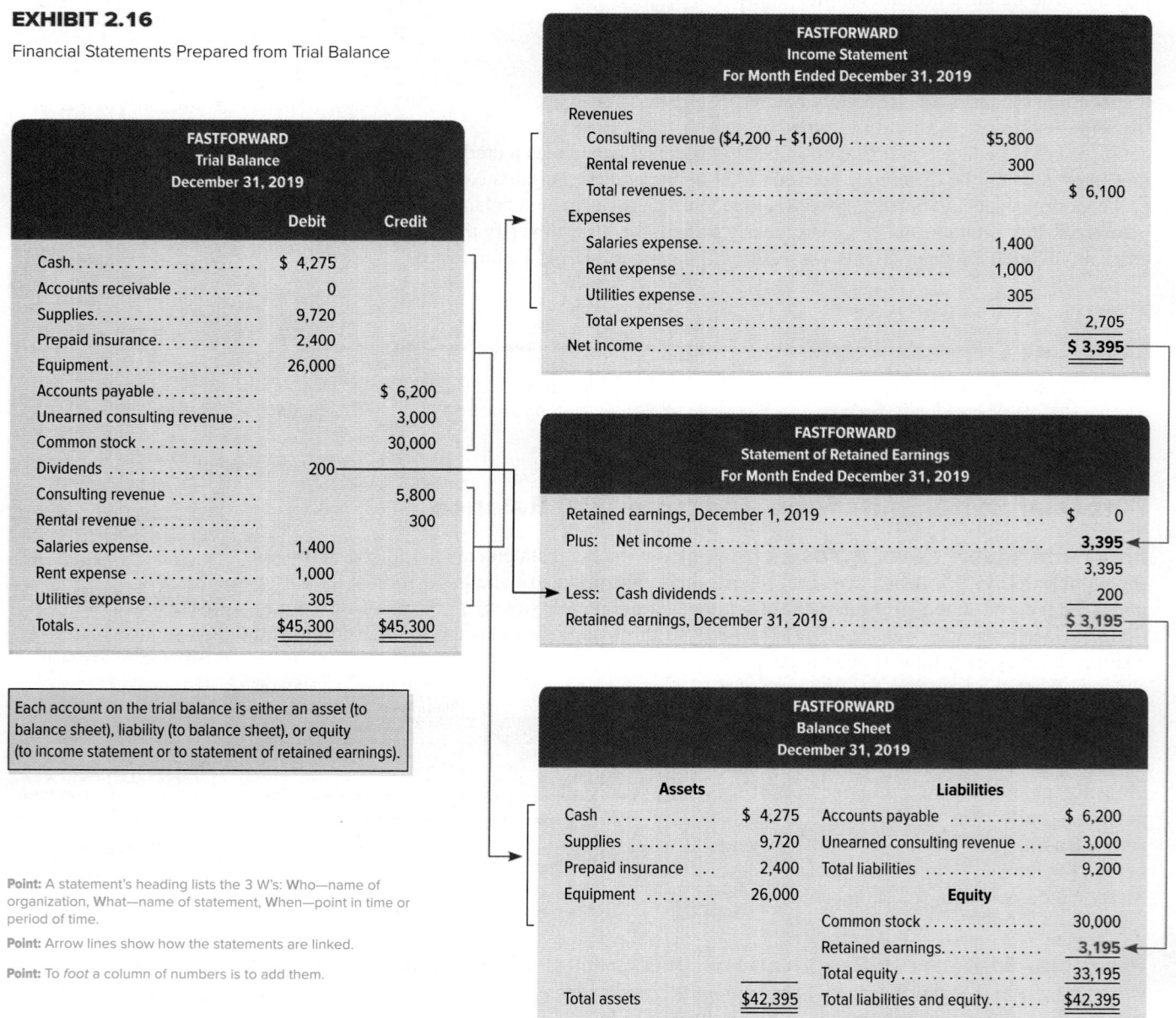

Each account on the trial balance is either an asset (to balance sheet), liability (to balance sheet), or equity (to income statement or to statement of retained earnings).

sheet lists its assets: cash, supplies, prepaid insurance, and equipment. The liabilities section of the balance sheet shows that it owes $6,200 to creditors and $3,000 in services to customers who paid in advance. The equity section shows an ending balance of $33,195. Note the link between the ending balance of the statement of retained earnings and the retained earnings balance. (This presentation of the balance sheet is called the *account form:* assets on the left and liabilities and equity on the right. Another presentation is the *report form:* assets on top, followed by liabilities and then equity. Either presentation is acceptable.)

Presentation Issues   Dollar signs are not used in journals and ledgers. They do appear in financial statements and other reports such as trial balances. We usually put dollar signs beside only the first and last numbers in a column. **Apple**'s financial statements in Appendix A show this. Companies commonly round amounts in reports to the nearest dollar, or even to a higher level. Apple, like many large companies, rounds its financial statement amounts to the nearest million. This decision is based on the impact of rounding for users' decisions.

■ Decision Maker

Entrepreneur   You open a wholesale business selling entertainment equipment to retail outlets. Most of your customers want to buy on credit. How can you use the balance sheets of customers to decide which ones to extend credit to? ■   *Answer:* We use the accounting equation (Assets = Liabilities + Equity) to identify risky customers to whom we would not want to extend credit. A balance sheet provides amounts for each of these key components. The lower a customer's equity is relative to liabilities, the less likely you would be to extend credit. A low equity means the business already has many creditor claims to it.

Prepare a trial balance for **Apple** using the following condensed data from its recent fiscal year ended September 30 ($ in millions).

NEED-TO-KNOW 2-4

Preparing Trial Balance

P2

APPLE

Common stock	$ 35,867	Dividends	$ 47,169
Accounts payable	49,049	Investments and other assets	303,373
Other liabilities	192,223	Land and equipment	33,783
Cost of sales (and other expenses)	141,048	Selling and other expense	39,835
Cash	20,289	Accounts receivable	17,874
Revenues	229,234	Retained earnings, beginning fiscal year	96,998

Solution ($ in millions)

APPLE Trial Balance September 30	Debit	Credit
Cash	$ 20,289	
Accounts receivable	17,874	
Land and equipment	33,783	
Investments and other assets	303,373	
Accounts payable		$ 49,049
Other liabilities		192,223
Common stock		35,867
Retained earnings, beginning fiscal year		96,998
Dividends	47,169	
Revenues		229,234
Cost of sales (and other expenses)	141,048	
Selling and other expense	39,835	
Totals	$603,371	$603,371

Do More: E 2-8, E 2-10

 **Decision Analysis**    **Debt Ratio**

A2 _____
Compute the debt ratio and describe its use in analyzing financial condition.

It is important to assess a company's risk of failing to pay its debts. Companies finance their assets with either liabilities or equity. A company that finances a relatively large portion of its assets with liabilities is said to have higher *financial leverage*. Higher financial leverage means greater risk because liabilities must be repaid and often require regular interest payments (equity financing does not). One measure of the risk associated with liabilities is the **debt ratio** as defined in Exhibit 2.17.

EXHIBIT 2.17

Debt Ratio

$$\text{Debt ratio} = \frac{\text{Total liabilities}}{\text{Total assets}}$$

Costco's total liabilities, total assets, and debt ratio for the past three years are shown in Exhibit 2.18. Costco's debt ratio ranges from a low of 0.63 to a high of 0.70. Its ratio exceeds Walmart's in each of the last three years, suggesting a higher than average risk from financial leverage. So, is financial leverage good or bad for Costco? The answer: If Costco is making more money with this debt than it is paying the lenders, then it is successfully borrowing money to make more money. A company's use of debt can turn unprofitable quickly if its return from that money drops below the rate it is paying lenders.

EXHIBIT 2.18

Computation and Analysis of Debt Ratio

Company	($ millions)	Current Year	1 Year Ago	2 Years Ago
Costco	Total liabilities........................	$25,268	$20,831	$22,174
	Total assets...........................	$36,347	$33,163	$33,017
	Debt ratio............................	0.70	0.63	0.67
Walmart	Debt ratio	0.59	0.58	0.58

 Decision Maker

Investor   You consider buying stock in **Converse**. As part of your analysis, you compute the company's debt ratio for 2017, 2018, and 2019 as 0.35, 0.74, and 0.94, respectively. Based on the debt ratio, is Converse a low-risk investment? Has the risk of buying Converse stock changed over this period? (The industry debt ratio averages 0.40.) ■   *Answer:* The debt ratio suggests that Converse's stock is of higher risk than normal and that this risk is rising. The average industry ratio of 0.40 supports this conclusion. The 2019 debt ratio for Converse is twice the industry norm. Also, a debt ratio approaching 1.0 indicates little to no equity.

NEED-TO-KNOW **2-5**

COMPREHENSIVE

Journalizing and Posting Transactions, Statement Preparation, and Debt Ratio

This problem extends Need-to-Know 1-6 from Chapter 1: Jasmine Worthy started a haircutting business called Expressions. The following events occurred during its first month.

Aug. 1   Worthy invested $3,000 cash and $15,000 of equipment in Expressions in exchange for common stock.
   2   Expressions paid $600 cash for furniture for the shop.
   3   Expressions paid $500 cash to rent space in a strip mall for August.
   4   Expressions purchased $1,200 of equipment on credit for the shop (recorded as accounts payable).
  15   Expressions opened for business on August 5. Cash received from haircutting services in the first week and a half of business (ended August 15) was $825.
  16   Expressions provided $100 of haircutting services on account.
  17   Expressions received a $100 check for services previously rendered on account.
  18   Expressions paid $125 to an assistant for hours worked for the grand opening.
  31   Cash received from services provided during the second half of August was $930.
  31   Expressions paid $400 cash toward the account payable entered into on August 4.
  31   Expressions paid a $900 cash dividend to Worthy (sole shareholder).

Required

1. Open the following ledger accounts in balance column format (account numbers are in parentheses): Cash (101); Accounts Receivable (102); Furniture (161); Store Equipment (165); Accounts Payable (201); Common Stock (307); Dividends (319); Haircutting Services Revenue (403); Wages Expense (623); and Rent Expense (640). Prepare general journal entries for the transactions.

2. Post the journal entries from part 1 to the ledger accounts.

3. Prepare a trial balance as of August 31.

4. Prepare an income statement for August.

5. Prepare a statement of retained earnings for August.

6. Prepare a balance sheet as of August 31.

7. Determine the debt ratio as of August 31.

Extended Analysis

8. In the coming months, Expressions will have a greater variety of business transactions. Identify which accounts are debited and which are credited for the following transactions. *Hint:* We must use some accounts not opened in part 1.

   a. Purchase supplies with cash.

   b. Pay cash for future insurance coverage.

   c. Receive cash for services to be provided in the future.

   d. Purchase supplies on account.

PLANNING THE SOLUTION

- Analyze each transaction and use the debit and credit rules to prepare a journal entry for each.
- Post each debit and each credit from journal entries to their ledger accounts and cross-reference each amount in the posting reference (PR) columns of the journal and ledger.
- Calculate each account balance and list the accounts with their balances on a trial balance.
- Verify that total debits in the trial balance equal total credits.
- To prepare the income statement, identify revenues and expenses. List those items on the statement, compute the difference, and label the result as *net income* or *net loss*.
- Use information in the ledger to prepare the statement of retained earnings.
- Use information in the ledger to prepare the balance sheet.
- Calculate the debt ratio by dividing total liabilities by total assets.
- Analyze the future transactions to identify the accounts affected and apply debit and credit rules.

SOLUTION

1. General journal entries.

	General Journal			
Date	**Account Titles and Explanation**	**PR**	**Debit**	**Credit**
Aug. 1	Cash	101	3,000	
	Store Equipment..	165	15,000	
	Common Stock	307		18,000
	Owner's investment in exchange for stock.			
2	Furniture...	161	600	
	Cash...	101		600
	Purchased furniture for cash.			
3	Rent Expense	640	500	
	Cash...	101		500
	Paid rent for August.			
4	Store Equipment..	165	1,200	
	Accounts Payable	201		1,200
	Purchased additional equipment on credit.			
15	Cash	101	825	
	Haircutting Services Revenue...........................	403		825
	Cash receipts from first half of August.			

[continued on next page]

[continued from previous page]

16	Accounts Receivable	102	100	
	Haircutting Services Revenue............................	403		100
	Record revenue for services provided on account.			
17	Cash	101	100	
	Accounts Receivable.................................	102		100
	Record cash received as payment on account.			
18	Wages Expense	623	125	
	Cash...	101		125
	Paid wages to assistant.			
31	Cash	101	930	
	Haircutting Services Revenue............................	403		930
	Cash receipts from second half of August.			
31	Accounts Payable..	201	400	
	Cash...	101		400
	Paid cash toward accounts payable.			
31	Dividends	319	900	
	Cash...	101		900
	Paid a cash dividend.			

2. Post journal entries from part 1 to the ledger accounts (in balance column format).

General Ledger

Cash   **Account No. 101**

Date	PR	Debit	Credit	Balance
Aug. 1	G1	3,000		3,000
2	G1		600	2,400
3	G1		500	1,900
15	G1	825		2,725
17	G1	100		2,825
18	G1		125	2,700
31	G1	930		3,630
31	G1		400	3,230
31	G1		900	2,330

Accounts Receivable   **Account No. 102**

Date	PR	Debit	Credit	Balance
Aug. 16	G1	100		100
17	G1		100	0

Furniture   **Account No. 161**

Date	PR	Debit	Credit	Balance
Aug. 2	G1	600		600

Store Equipment   **Account No. 165**

Date	PR	Debit	Credit	Balance
Aug. 1	G1	15,000		15,000
4	G1	1,200		16,200

Accounts Payable   **Account No. 201**

Date	PR	Debit	Credit	Balance
Aug. 4	G1		1,200	1,200
31	G1	400		800

Common Stock   **Account No. 307**

Date	PR	Debit	Credit	Balance
Aug. 1	G1		18,000	18,000

Dividends   **Account No. 319**

Date	PR	Debit	Credit	Balance
Aug. 31	G1	900		900

Haircutting Services Revenue   **Account No. 403**

Date	PR	Debit	Credit	Balance
Aug. 15	G1		825	825
16	G1		100	925
31	G1		930	1,855

Wages Expense   **Account No. 623**

Date	PR	Debit	Credit	Balance
Aug. 18	G1	125		125

Rent Expense   **Account No. 640**

Date	PR	Debit	Credit	Balance
Aug. 3	G1	500		500

3. Prepare a trial balance from the ledger—see how it feeds the financial statements.

EXPRESSIONS
Trial Balance
August 31

	Debit	Credit
Cash.	$ 2,330	
Accounts receivable	0	
Furniture	600	
Store equipment	16,200	
Accounts payable		$ 800
Common stock		18,000
Dividends.	900	
Haircutting services revenue		1,855
Wages expense.	125	
Rent expense	500	
Totals	$20,655	$20,655

4.

EXPRESSIONS
Income Statement
For Month Ended August 31

Revenues		
Haircutting services revenue		$1,855
Operating expenses		
Rent expense	$500	
Wages expense.	125	
Total operating expenses.		625
Net income		$1,230

5.

EXPRESSIONS
Statement of Retained Earnings
For Month Ended August 31

Retained earnings, August 1		$ 0
Plus: Net income		1,230
		1,230
Less: Cash dividends.		900
Retained earnings, August 31		$ 330

6.

EXPRESSIONS
Balance Sheet
August 31

Assets		Liabilities	
Cash	$ 2,330	Accounts payable	$ 800
Furniture	600	**Equity**	
Store equipment.	16,200	Common stock	18,000
		Retained earnings	330
		Total equity	18,330
Total assets.	$19,130	Total liabilities and equity	$19,130

7. Debt ratio $= \dfrac{\text{Total liabilities}}{\text{Total assets}} = \dfrac{\$800}{\$19,130} = \mathbf{4.18\%}$

8a. Supplies *debited*
    Cash *credited*

8c. Cash *debited*
    Unearned Services Revenue *credited*

8b. Prepaid Insurance *debited*
    Cash *credited*

8d. Supplies *debited*
    Accounts Payable *credited*

Summary: Cheat Sheet

SYSTEM OF ACCOUNTS

Asset Accounts

Cash: A company's cash balance.

Accounts receivable: Held by a seller; promises of payment from customers to sellers. Accounts receivable are increased by credit sales; often phrased as sales *on account* or *on credit*.

Note receivable: Held by a lender; a borrower's written promise to pay the lender a specific sum of money on a specified future date.

Prepaid accounts (or expenses): Assets that arise from prepayment of future expenses. Examples are prepaid insurance and prepaid rent.

More assets: Supplies, equipment, buildings, and land.

Liability Accounts

Accounts payable: Held by a buyer; a buyer's promise to pay a seller later for goods or services received. More generally, payables arise from purchases of merchandise for resale, supplies, services, and other items.

Note payable: Held by a borrower; a written promissory note to pay a future amount at a future date.

Unearned revenue: A liability to be settled in the future when a company delivers its products or services. When a customer pays in advance for products or services (before revenue is earned), the seller records this receipt as unearned revenue.

Accrued liabilities: Amounts owed that are not yet paid. Examples are wages payable, taxes payable, and interest payable.

Equity Accounts

Common stock: When an owner invests in a company in exchange for stock, the company increases both assets and equity.

Dividends: When a company pays dividends, it decreases both company assets and total equity.

Revenue: Amounts received from sales of products and services to customers. Revenue increases equity.

Expenses: Costs of providing products and services. Expenses decrease equity.

DEBITS AND CREDITS

The left side of an account is called the **debit** side, or Dr.
The right side is called the **credit** side, or Cr.

Double-entry accounting transaction rules:
- At least two accounts are involved, with at least one debit and one credit.
- Total amount debited must equal total amount credited.

Debits and credits in accounting equation:

Assets	=	Liabilities	+	Common Stock		Dividends	+	Revenues		Expenses
Dr. for increases / Cr. for decreases		Dr. for decreases / Cr. for increases		Dr. for decreases / Cr. for increases		Dr. for increases / Cr. for decreases		Dr. for decreases / Cr. for increases		Dr. for increases / Cr. for decreases
+ Normal / **−**		**−** / **+** Normal		**−** / **+** Normal		**+** Normal / **−**		**−** / **+** Normal		**+** Normal / **−**

Net increases or decreases on one side have equal net effects on the other side.
Left side is the normal balance side for assets.
Right side is the normal balance side for liabilities and equity.

RECORDING TRANSACTIONS

Receive owner investment for stock:

Date	Account Titles and Explanation	PR	Debit	Credit
(1)	Cash	101	30,000	
	Common Stock	307		30,000

Purchase supplies for cash:

Date	Account Titles and Explanation	PR	Debit	Credit
(2)	Supplies	126	2,500	
	Cash	101		2,500

Purchase equipment for cash:

Date	Account Titles and Explanation	PR	Debit	Credit
(3)	Equipment	167	26,000	
	Cash	101		26,000

Purchase supplies on credit:

Date	Account Titles and Explanation	PR	Debit	Credit
(4)	Supplies	126	7,100	
	Accounts Payable	201		7,100

Provide services for cash:

Date	Account Titles and Explanation	PR	Debit	Credit
(5)	Cash	101	4,200	
	Consulting Revenue	403		4,200

Payment of expenses in cash:

Date	Account Titles and Explanation	PR	Debit	Credit
(6)	Rent Expense	640	1,000	
	Cash	101		1,000

Date	Account Titles and Explanation	PR	Debit	Credit
(7)	Salaries Expense	622	700	
	Cash	101		700

Date	Account Titles and Explanation	PR	Debit	Credit
(15)	Utilities Expense	690	305	
	Cash	101		305

Provide consulting and rental services on credit:

Date	Account Titles and Explanation	PR	Debit	Credit
(8)	Accounts Receivable	106	1,900	
	Consulting Revenue	403		1,600
	Rental Revenue	406		300

Receipt of cash on account:

Date	Account Titles and Explanation	PR	Debit	Credit
(9)	Cash	101	1,900	
	Accounts Receivable	106		1,900

Partial payment of accounts payable:

Date	Account Titles and Explanation	PR	Debit	Credit
(10)	Accounts Payable	201	900	
	Cash	101		900

Payment of cash dividend:

Date	Account Titles and Explanation	PR	Debit	Credit
(11)	Dividends	319	200	
	Cash	101		200

Receipt of cash for future services:

Date	Account Titles and Explanation	PR	Debit	Credit
(12)	Cash	101	3,000	
	Unearned Consulting Revenue	236		3,000

Pay cash for future insurance coverage:

Date	Account Titles and Explanation	PR	Debit	Credit
(13)	Prepaid Insurance	128	2,400	
	Cash	101		2,400

FINANCIAL STATEMENTS

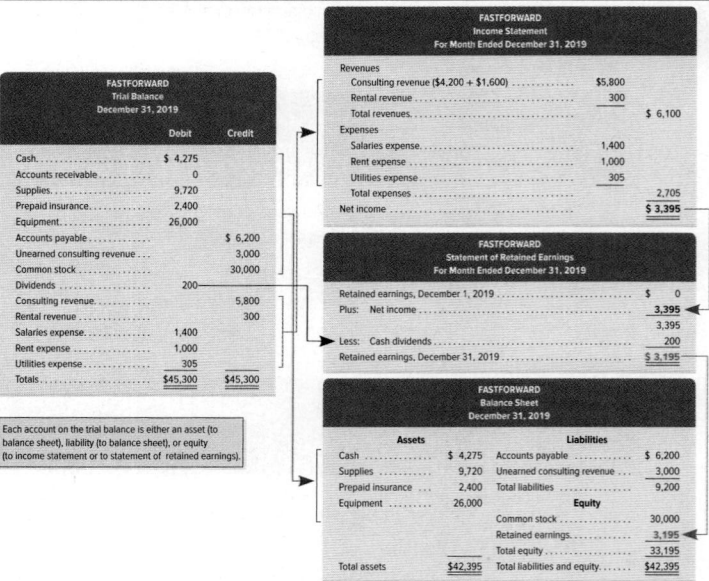

FASTFORWARD
Trial Balance
December 31, 2019

	Debit	Credit
Cash	$ 4,275	
Accounts receivable	0	
Supplies	9,720	
Prepaid insurance	2,400	
Equipment	26,000	
Accounts payable		$ 6,200
Unearned consulting revenue		3,000
Common stock		30,000
Dividends	200	
Consulting revenue		5,800
Rental revenue		300
Salaries expense	1,400	
Rent expense	1,000	
Utilities expense	305	
Totals	$45,300	$45,300

Each account on the trial balance is either an asset (to balance sheet), liability (to balance sheet), or equity (to income statement or to statement of retained earnings).

FASTFORWARD
Income Statement
For Month Ended December 31, 2019

Revenues		
Consulting revenue ($4,200 + $1,600)	$5,800	
Rental revenue	300	
Total revenues		$ 6,100
Expenses		
Salaries expense	1,400	
Rent expense	1,000	
Utilities expense	305	
Total expenses		2,705
Net income		$ 3,395

FASTFORWARD
Statement of Retained Earnings
For Month Ended December 31, 2019

Retained earnings, December 1, 2019	$ 0
Plus: Net income	3,395
	3,395
Less: Cash dividends	200
Retained earnings, December 31, 2019	$ 3,195

FASTFORWARD
Balance Sheet
December 31, 2019

Assets		Liabilities	
Cash	$ 4,275	Accounts payable	$ 6,200
Supplies	9,720	Unearned consulting revenue	3,000
Prepaid insurance	2,400	Total liabilities	9,200
Equipment	26,000	**Equity**	
		Common stock	30,000
		Retained earnings	3,195
		Total equity	33,195
Total assets	$42,395	Total liabilities and equity	$42,395

Key Terms

Multiple Choice Quiz

1. Amalia Company received its utility bill for the current period of $700 and immediately paid it. Its journal entry to record this transaction includes a
   a. Credit to Utility Expense for $700.
   b. Debit to Utility Expense for $700.
   c. Debit to Accounts Payable for $700.
   d. Debit to Cash for $700.
   e. Credit to Accounts Receivable for $700.

2. On May 1, Mattingly Lawn Service collected $2,500 cash from a customer in advance of five months of lawn service. Mattingly's journal entry to record this transaction includes a
   a. Credit to Unearned Lawn Service Fees for $2,500.
   b. Debit to Lawn Service Fees Earned for $2,500.
   c. Credit to Cash for $2,500.
   d. Debit to Unearned Lawn Service Fees for $2,500.
   e. Credit to Accounts Payable for $2,500.

3. Liang Shue contributed $250,000 cash and land worth $500,000 to open his new business, Shue Consulting. Which of the following journal entries does Shue Consulting make to record this transaction?

a. Cash Assets	750,000	
Common Stock		750,000
b. Common Stock	750,000	
Assets.		750,000

c. Cash	250,000	
Land.	500,000	
Common Stock		750,000
d. Common Stock	750,000	
Cash.		250,000
Land.		500,000

4. A trial balance prepared at year-end shows total credits exceed total debits by $765. This discrepancy could have been caused by
   a. An error in the general journal where a $765 increase in Accounts Payable was recorded as a $765 decrease in Accounts Payable.
   b. The ledger balance for Accounts Payable of $7,650 being entered in the trial balance as $765.
   c. A general journal error where a $765 increase in Accounts Receivable was recorded as a $765 increase in Cash.
   d. The ledger balance of $850 in Accounts Receivable was entered in the trial balance as $85.
   e. An error in recording a $765 increase in Cash as a credit.

5. Bonaventure Company has total assets of $1,000,000, liabilities of $400,000, and equity of $600,000. What is its debt ratio (rounded to a whole percent)?
   a. 250%   **c.** 67%   **e.** 40%
   b. 167%   **d.** 150%

ANSWERS TO MULTIPLE CHOICE QUIZ

1. b; debit Utility Expense for $700, and credit Cash for $700.
2. a; debit Cash for $2,500 and credit Unearned Lawn Service Fees for $2,500.
3. c; debit Cash for $250,000, debit Land for $500,000, and credit Common Stock for $750,000.

4. d
5. e; Debt ratio = $400,000/$1,000,000 = 40%

Icon denotes assignments that involve decision making.

Discussion Questions

1. Provide the names of two (*a*) asset accounts, (*b*) liability accounts, and (*c*) equity accounts.
2. What is the difference between a note payable and an account payable?
3. Discuss the steps in processing business transactions.
4. What kinds of transactions can be recorded in a general journal?
5. Are debits or credits typically listed first in general journal entries? Are the debits or the credits indented?
6. Should a transaction be recorded first in a journal or the ledger? Why?
7. If assets are valuable resources and asset accounts have debit balances, why do expense accounts also have debit balances?
8. Why does the recordkeeper prepare a trial balance?

9. If an incorrect amount is journalized and posted to the accounts, how should the error be corrected?
10. Identify the four financial statements of a business.
11. What information is reported in a balance sheet?
12. What information is reported in an income statement?
13. Why does the user of an income statement need to know the time period that it covers?
14. Define (*a*) *assets,* (*b*) *liabilities,* and (*c*) *equity.*
15. Which financial statement is sometimes called the *statement of financial position?*
16. Review the **Apple** balance sheet in Appendix A. Identify three accounts on its balance sheet that carry debit balances and three accounts on its balance sheet that carry credit balances.   **APPLE**

17. Review the **Google** balance sheet in **GOOGLE** Appendix A. Identify an asset with the word *receivable* in its account title and a liability with the word *payable* in its account title.

18. Review the **Samsung** balance sheet in Appendix A. Identify three current liabilities and three noncurrent liabilities in its balance sheet. **Samsung**

---

connect

QUICK STUDY

QS 2-1
Identifying source documents   **C1**

Identify the items from the following list that are likely to serve as source documents.

a. Sales receipt	**d.** Prepaid insurance account	**g.** Income statement
b. Trial balance	**e.** Invoice from supplier	**h.** Bank statement
c. Balance sheet	**f.** Company revenue account	**i.** Telephone bill

---

QS 2-2
Identifying financial statement accounts
C2

Classify each of the following accounts as an asset (A), liability (L), or equity (EQ) account.

a. Cash	**d.** Prepaid Insurance	**g.** Accounts Payable
b. Prepaid Rent	**e.** Office Equipment	**h.** Unearned Rent Revenue
c. Office Supplies	**f.** Common Stock	**i.** Dividends

QS 2-3
Reading a chart of accounts
C3

A chart of accounts is a list of all ledger accounts and an identification number for each. One example of a chart of accounts is near the end of the book on pages CA and CA-1. Using that chart, identify the following accounts as either an asset (A), liability (L), equity (EQ), revenue (R), or expense (E) account, along with its identification number.

a. Advertising Expense	**d.** Machinery	**g.** Notes Payable
b. Rent Revenue	**e.** Accounts Payable	**h.** Common Stock
c. Rent Receivable	**f.** Furniture	**i.** Utilities Expense

QS 2-4
Identifying normal balance
C4

Identify the normal balance (debit or credit) for each of the following accounts.

a. Fees Earned (Revenues)	**d.** Wages Expense	**g.** Wages Payable
b. Office Supplies	**e.** Accounts Receivable	**h.** Building
c. Dividends	**f.** Prepaid Rent	**i.** Common Stock

QS 2-5
Linking debit or credit with normal balance
C4

Indicate whether a debit or credit *decreases* the normal balance of each of the following accounts.

a. Interest Payable	**e.** Common Stock	**i.** Dividends
b. Service Revenue	**f.** Prepaid Insurance	**j.** Unearned Revenue
c. Salaries Expense	**g.** Buildings	**k.** Accounts Payable
d. Accounts Receivable	**h.** Interest Revenue	**l.** Land

QS 2-6
Analyzing transactions and preparing journal entries
P1

For each transaction, (1) analyze the transaction using the accounting equation, (2) record the transaction in journal entry form, and (3) post the entry using T-accounts to represent ledger accounts. Use the following (partial) chart of accounts—account numbers in parentheses: Cash (101); Accounts Receivable (106); Office Supplies (124); Trucks (153); Equipment (167); Accounts Payable (201); Unearned Landscaping Revenue (236); Common Stock (307); Dividends (319); Landscaping Revenue (403); Wages Expense (601), and Landscaping Expense (696).

a. On May 15, DeShawn Tyler opens a landscaping company called Elegant Lawns by investing $7,000 in cash along with equipment having a $3,000 value in exchange for common stock.

b. On May 21, Elegant Lawns purchases office supplies on credit for $500.

c. On May 25, Elegant Lawns receives $4,000 cash for performing landscaping services.

d. On May 30, Elegant Lawns receives $1,000 cash in advance of providing landscaping services to a customer.

QS 2-7
Analyzing debit or credit by account
A1

Identify whether a debit or credit results in the indicated change for each of the following accounts.

a. To increase Land	**f.** To decrease Prepaid Rent
b. To decrease Cash	**g.** To increase Notes Payable
c. To increase Fees Earned (Revenues)	**h.** To decrease Accounts Receivable
d. To increase Salaries Expense	**i.** To increase Common Stock
e. To decrease Unearned Revenue	**j.** To increase Store Equipment

A trial balance has total debits of $20,000 and total credits of $24,500. Which one of the following errors would create this imbalance? Explain.

a. A $2,250 debit to Utilities Expense in a journal entry was incorrectly posted to the ledger as a $2,250 credit, leaving the Utilities Expense account with a $3,000 debit balance.

b. A $4,500 debit to Salaries Expense in a journal entry was incorrectly posted to the ledger as a $4,500 credit, leaving the Salaries Expense account with a $750 debit balance.

c. A $2,250 credit to Consulting Fees Earned (Revenues) in a journal entry was incorrectly posted to the ledger as a $2,250 debit, leaving the Consulting Fees Earned account with a $6,300 credit balance.

d. A $2,250 debit posting to Accounts Receivable was posted mistakenly to Land.

e. A $4,500 debit posting to Equipment was posted mistakenly to Cash.

f. An entry debiting Cash and crediting Accounts Payable for $4,500 was mistakenly not posted.

QS 2-8
Identifying a posting error

P2

Indicate the financial statement on which each of the following items appears. Use *I* for income statement, *E* for statement of retained earnings, and *B* for balance sheet.

a. Services Revenue	**e.** Equipment	**i.** Dividends
b. Interest Payable	**f.** Prepaid Insurance	**j.** Office Supplies
c. Accounts Receivable	**g.** Buildings	**k.** Interest Expense
d. Salaries Expense	**h.** Rental Revenue	**l.** Insurance Expense

QS 2-9
Classifying accounts in financial statements

P3

Determine the ending balance of each of the following T-accounts.

QS 2-10
Computing T-account balance

C4

a.

Cash	
100	50
300	60
20	

b.

Accounts Payable	
2,000	8,000
2,700	

c.

Supplies	
10,000	3,800
1,100	

d.

Accounts Receivable	
600	150
	150
	150
	100

e.

Wages Payable	
	700
700	

f.

Cash	
11,000	4,500
800	6,000
100	1,300

Prepare general journal entries for the following transactions of Green Energy Company. Use the following (partial) chart of accounts: Cash; Accounts Receivable; Supplies; Accounts Payable; Consulting Revenue; and Utilities Expense.

May 1   The company billed a customer $2,000 in consulting revenue for sustainable proposals.
   3   The company purchased $300 of energy-efficient supplies on credit.
   9   The company collected $500 cash as partial payment of the May 1 consulting revenue.
   20   The company paid $300 cash toward the payable for energy-efficient supplies.
   31   The company paid $100 cash for May's renewable energy utilities.

QS 2-11
Preparing journal entries

P1

Liu Zhang operates Lawson Consulting, which began operations on June 1. On June 30, the company's records show the following selected accounts and amounts for the month of June. Prepare a June income statement for the business.

Cash	$5,000	Accounts payable	$ 3,000	Service revenue	$12,000
Accounts receivable	4,500	Common stock	10,500	Rent expense	2,000
Equipment	6,500	Dividends	1,500	Wages expense	6,000

QS 2-12
Preparing an income statement

P3

Use the information in QS 2-12 to prepare a June statement of retained earnings for Lawson Consulting. The Retained Earnings account balance at June 1 was $0. *Hint:* Net income for June is $4,000.

QS 2-13
Preparing a statement of retained earnings **P3**

QS 2-14 Preparing a balance sheet **P3**	Use the information in QS 2-12 and QS 2-13 to prepare a June 30 balance sheet for Lawson Consulting. *Hint:* The ending Retained Earnings account balance as of June 30 is $2,500.
QS 2-15 Computing and using the debt ratio **A2**	In a recent year's financial statements, **Home Depot** reported the following: Total liabilities = $38,633 million and Total assets = $42,966 million. Compute and interpret Home Depot's debt ratio (assume competitors average a 60.0% debt ratio).

🔲 connect

EXERCISES

Exercise 2-1 Steps in analyzing and recording transactions **C1**	Order the following steps in the accounting process that focus on analyzing and recording transactions. _____ **a.** Prepare and analyze the trial balance. _____ **b.** Analyze each transaction from source documents. _____ **c.** Record relevant transactions in a journal. _____ **d.** Post journal information to ledger accounts.
Exercise 2-2 Identifying and classifying accounts **C2**	Enter the number for the item that best completes each of the descriptions below. **1.** Asset **2.** Equity **3.** Account **4.** Liability **5.** Three **a.** Balance sheet accounts are arranged into _____ general categories. **b.** Common Stock and Dividends are examples of _____ accounts. **c.** Accounts Payable and Note Payable are examples of _____ accounts. **d.** Accounts Receivable, Prepaid Accounts, Supplies, and Land are examples of _____ accounts. **e.** A(n) _____ is a record of increases and decreases in a specific asset, liability, equity, revenue, or expense item.
Exercise 2-3 Identifying a ledger and chart of accounts **C3**	Enter the number for the item that best completes each of the descriptions below. **1.** Chart **2.** General ledger **3.** Journal **4.** Account **5.** Source document **a.** A(n) _____ of accounts is a list of all accounts a company uses, not including account balances. **b.** The _____ is a record containing all accounts used by a company, including account balances. **c.** A(n) _____ describes transactions entering an accounting system, such as a purchase order. **d.** Increases and decreases in a specific asset, liability, equity, revenue, or expense are recorded in a(n) _____. **e.** A(n) _____ has a complete record of every transaction recorded.
Exercise 2-4 Identifying type and normal balances of accounts **C4**	For each of the following, (1) identify the type of account as an asset, liability, equity, revenue, or expense; (2) identify the normal balance of the account; and (3) enter *debit* (*Dr.*) or *credit* (*Cr.*) to identify the kind of entry that would increase the account balance. **a.** Land **e.** Accounts Receivable **i.** Fees Earned **b.** Cash **f.** Dividends **j.** Equipment **c.** Legal Expense **g.** License Fee Revenue **k.** Notes Payable **d.** Prepaid Insurance **h.** Unearned Revenue **l.** Common Stock
Exercise 2-5 Analyzing effects of a compound entry **A1**	Groro Co. bills a client $62,000 for services provided and agrees to accept the following three items in full payment: (1) $10,000 cash, (2) equipment worth $80,000, and (3) to assume responsibility for a $28,000 note payable related to the equipment. For this transaction, (*a*) analyze the transaction using the accounting equation, (*b*) record the transaction in journal entry form, and (*c*) post the entry using T-accounts to represent ledger accounts. Use the following (partial) chart of accounts—account numbers in parentheses: Cash (101); Supplies (124); Equipment (167); Accounts Payable (201); Note Payable (245); Common Stock (307); and Revenue (404).
Exercise 2-6 Analyzing account entries and balances **A1**	Use the information in each of the following separate cases to calculate the unknown amount. **a.** Corentine Co. had $152,000 of accounts payable on September 30 and $132,500 on October 31. Total purchases on account during October were $281,000. Determine how much cash was paid on accounts payable during October. **b.** On September 30, Valerian Co. had a $102,500 balance in Accounts Receivable. During October, the company collected $102,890 from its credit customers. The October 31 balance in Accounts Receivable was $89,000. Determine the amount of sales on account that occurred in October.

[continued on next page]

c. During October, Alameda Company had $102,500 of cash receipts and $103,150 of cash disbursements. The October 31 Cash balance was $18,600. Determine how much cash the company had at the close of business on September 30.

Prepare general journal entries for the following transactions of a new company called Pose-for-Pics. Use the following (partial) chart of accounts: Cash; Office Supplies; Prepaid Insurance; Photography Equipment; Common Stock; Photography Fees Earned; and Utilities Expense.

Aug. 1 Madison Harris, the owner, invested $6,500 cash and $33,500 of photography equipment in the company in exchange for common stock.
 2 The company paid $2,100 cash for an insurance policy covering the next 24 months.
 5 The company purchased office supplies for $880 cash.
 20 The company received $3,331 cash in photography fees earned.
 31 The company paid $675 cash for August utilities.

Exercise 2-7
Preparing general journal entries

P1

Use the information in Exercise 2-7 to prepare a trial balance for Pose-for-Pics. Begin by opening these T-accounts: Cash; Office Supplies; Prepaid Insurance; Photography Equipment; Common Stock; Photography Fees Earned; and Utilities Expense. Then, (1) post the general journal entries to these T-accounts (which will serve as the ledger) and (2) prepare the August 31 trial balance.

Exercise 2-8
Preparing T-accounts (ledger) and a trial balance **P2**

Prepare general journal entries to record the transactions below for Spade Company by using the following accounts: Cash; Accounts Receivable; Office Supplies; Office Equipment; Accounts Payable; Common Stock; Dividends; Fees Earned; and Rent Expense. Use the letters beside each transaction to identify entries. After recording the transactions, post them to T-accounts, which serve as the general ledger for this assignment. Determine the ending balance of each T-account.

a. Kacy Spade, owner, invested $100,750 cash in the company in exchange for common stock.
b. The company purchased office supplies for $1,250 cash.
c. The company purchased $10,050 of office equipment on credit.
d. The company received $15,500 cash as fees for services provided to a customer.
e. The company paid $10,050 cash to settle the payable for the office equipment purchased in transaction c.
f. The company billed a customer $2,700 as fees for services provided.
g. The company paid $1,225 cash for the monthly rent.
h. The company collected $1,125 cash as partial payment for the account receivable created in transaction f.
i. The company paid a $10,000 cash dividend to the owner (sole shareholder).

Exercise 2-9
Recording effects of transactions in T-accounts

A1

Check Cash ending balance, $94,850

After recording the transactions of Exercise 2-9 in T-accounts and calculating the balance of each account, prepare a trial balance. Use May 31 as its report date.

Exercise 2-10
Preparing a trial balance **P2**

---

1. Prepare general journal entries for the following transactions of Valdez Services.
 a. The company paid $2,000 cash for payment on a 6-month-old account payable for office supplies.
 b. The company paid $1,200 cash for the just completed two-week salary of the receptionist.
 c. The company paid $39,000 cash for equipment purchased.
 d. The company paid $800 cash for this month's utilities.
 e. The company paid a $4,500 cash dividend to the owner (sole shareholder).
2. Transactions a, c, and e did not result in an expense. Match each transaction (a, c, and e) with one of the following reasons for not recording an expense.
 _____ This transaction is a distribution of cash to the owner. Even though equity decreased, that decrease did not occur in the process of providing goods or services to customers.
 _____ This transaction decreased cash in settlement of a previously existing liability (equity did not change). Supplies expense is recorded when assets are used, not necessarily when cash is paid.
 _____ This transaction involves the purchase of an asset. The form of the company's assets changed, but total assets did not (and neither did equity).

Exercise 2-11
Analyzing and journalizing transactions involving cash payments

P1

Exercise 2-12

Analyzing and journalizing transactions involving receipt of cash

P1

1. Prepare general journal entries for the following transactions of Valdez Services.
   a. Brina Valdez invested $20,000 cash in the company in exchange for common stock.
   b. The company provided services to a client and immediately received $900 cash.
   c. The company received $10,000 cash from a client in payment for services to be provided next year.
   d. The company received $3,500 cash from a client in partial payment of accounts receivable.
   e. The company borrowed $5,000 cash from the bank by signing a note payable.
2. Transactions *a, c, d,* and *e* did not yield revenue. Match each transaction (*a, c, d,* and *e*) with one of the following reasons for not recording revenue.
   _____ This transaction changed the form of an asset from a receivable to cash. Total assets were not increased (revenue was recognized when the services were originally provided).
   _____ This transaction brought in cash (increased assets), and it also increased a liability by the same amount (represented by the signing of a note to repay the amount).
   _____ This transaction brought in cash, but this is an owner investment.
   _____ This transaction brought in cash, but it created a liability to provide services to the client in the next year.

Exercise 2-13

Entering transactions into T-accounts

A1

Fill in each of the following T-accounts for Belle Co.'s seven transactions listed here. The T-accounts represent Belle Co.'s general ledger. Code each entry with transaction number *1* through *7* (in order) for reference.

1. D. Belle created a new business and invested $6,000 cash, $7,600 of equipment, and $12,000 in web servers in exchange for common stock.
2. The company paid $4,800 cash in advance for prepaid insurance coverage.
3. The company purchased $900 of supplies on account.
4. The company paid $800 cash for selling expenses.
5. The company received $4,500 cash for services provided.
6. The company paid $900 cash toward accounts payable.
7. The company paid $3,400 cash for equipment.

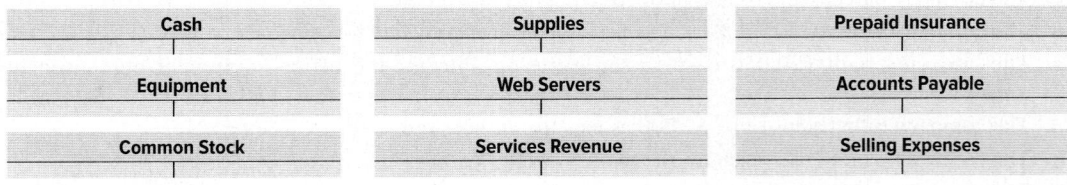

Cash	Supplies	Prepaid Insurance

Equipment	Web Servers	Accounts Payable

Common Stock	Services Revenue	Selling Expenses

Exercise 2-14

Preparing general journal entries　**P1**

Use information from Exercise 2-13 to prepare the general journal entries for Belle Co.'s first seven transactions.

Exercise 2-15

Computing net income

A1

A corporation had the following assets and liabilities at the beginning and end of this year.

	Assets	Liabilities
Beginning of the year............	$ 60,000	$20,000
End of the year	105,000	36,000

Determine net income or net loss for the business during the year for each of the following *separate* cases.
a. Owner made no investments in the business, and no dividends were paid during the year.
b. Owner made no investments in the business, but dividends were $1,250 cash per month.
c. No dividends were paid during the year, but the owner did invest an additional $55,000 cash in exchange for common stock.
d. Dividends were $1,250 cash per month, and the owner invested an additional $35,000 cash in exchange for common stock.

Exercise 2-16

Preparing an income statement　**C3　P3**

Carmen Camry operates a consulting firm called Help Today, which began operations on August 1. On August 31, the company's records show the following selected accounts and amounts for the month of August. Use this information to prepare an August income statement for the business.

Cash $25,360	Accounts payable........... $ 10,500	Salaries expense $5,600
Accounts receivable...... 22,360	Common stock 102,000	Telephone expense 860
Office supplies 5,250	Dividends 6,000	Miscellaneous expenses 520
Land 44,000	Consulting fees earned 27,000	
Office equipment 20,000	Rent expense 9,550	

Check Net income, $10,470

Use the information in Exercise 2-16 to prepare an August statement of retained earnings for Help Today. The Retained Earnings account balance at August 1 was $0. *Hint:* Net income for August is $10,470.

Exercise 2-17
Preparing a statement of retained earnings **P3**

Use the information in Exercise 2-16 to prepare an August 31 balance sheet for Help Today. *Hint:* The ending Retained Earnings account balance as of August 31 is $4,470.

Exercise 2-18
Preparing a balance sheet **P3**

Compute the missing amount for each of the following separate companies in columns B through E.

Exercise 2-19
Analyzing changes in a company's equity

P3

	A	B	C	D	E
1		CBS	ABC	CNN	NBC
2	Equity, beginning of year	$ 0	$ 0	$ 0	$ 0
3	Owner investments during the year	110,000	?	87,000	210,000
4	Dividends during the year	?	(47,000)	(10,000)	(55,000)
5	Net income (loss) for the year	22,000	90,000	(4,000)	?
6	Equity, end of year	104,000	85,000	?	110,000

Posting errors are identified in the following table. In column (1), enter the amount of the difference between the two trial balance columns (debit and credit) due to the error. In column (2), identify the trial balance column (debit or credit) with the larger amount if they are not equal. In column (3), identify the account(s) affected by the error. In column (4), indicate the amount by which the account(s) in column (3) is under- or overstated. Item (a) is completed as an example.

Exercise 2-20
Identifying effects of posting errors on the trial balance **A1   P2**

	Description of Posting Error	(1) Difference between Debit and Credit Columns	(2) Column with the Larger Total	(3) Identify Account(s) Incorrectly Stated	(4) Amount That Account(s) Is Over- or Understated
a.	$3,600 debit to Rent Expense is posted as a $1,340 debit.	$2,260	Credit	Rent Expense	Rent Expense understated $2,260
b.	$6,500 credit to Cash is posted twice as two credits to Cash.				
c.	$10,900 debit to the Dividends account is debited to Common Stock.				
d.	$2,050 debit to Prepaid Insurance is posted as a debit to Insurance Expense.				
e.	$38,000 debit to Machinery is posted as a debit to Accounts Payable.				
f.	$5,850 credit to Services Revenue is posted as a $585 credit.				
g.	$1,390 debit to Store Supplies is not posted.				

You are told the column totals in a trial balance are not equal. After careful analysis, you discover only one error. Specifically, a correctly journalized credit purchase of an automobile for $18,950 is posted from the journal to the ledger with an $18,950 debit to Automobiles and another $18,950 debit to Accounts Payable. The Automobiles account has a debit balance of $37,100 on the trial balance. (1) Answer each of the following questions and (2) compute the dollar amount of any misstatement for parts *a* through *d*.

Exercise 2-21
Analyzing a trial balance error

P1   P2

a. Is the Debit column total of the trial balance overstated, understated, or correctly stated?

b. Is the Credit column total of the trial balance overstated, understated, or correctly stated?

c. Is the Automobiles account balance overstated, understated, or correctly stated in the trial balance?

d. Is the Accounts Payable account balance overstated, understated, or correctly stated in the trial balance?

e. If the Debit column total of the trial balance is $200,000 before correcting the error, what is the total of the Credit column before correction?

Exercise 2-22
Calculating and interpreting
the debt ratio

A2

Company	Expenses	Total Assets	Net Income	Total Liabilities
DreamWorks	$22,000	$ 40,000	$19,000	$ 30,000
Pixar	67,000	150,000	27,000	147,000
Universal	12,000	68,000	5,000	17,000

a. Compute the debt ratio for each of the three companies.

b. Which company has the most financial leverage?

Exercise 2-23
Preparing journal entries

P1

Prepare general journal entries for the following transactions of Sustain Company. Use the following (partial) chart of accounts: Cash; Prepaid Insurance; Accounts Receivable; Furniture; Accounts Payable; Unearned Revenue; Fees Earned; and Common Stock.

June 1   T. James, owner, invested $11,000 cash in Sustain Company in exchange for common stock.

    2   The company purchased $4,000 of furniture made from reclaimed wood on credit.

    3   The company paid $600 cash for a 12-month insurance policy on the reclaimed furniture.

    4   The company billed a customer $3,000 in fees earned from preparing a sustainability report.

   12   The company paid $4,000 cash toward the payable from the June 2 furniture purchase.

   20   The company collected $3,000 cash for fees billed on June 4.

   21   T. James invested an additional $10,000 cash in Sustain Company in exchange for common stock.

   30   The company received $5,000 cash in advance of providing sustainability services to a customer.

PROBLEM SET A

Karla Tanner opened a web consulting business called Linkworks and completed the following transactions in its first month of operations.

Problem 2-1A
Preparing and posting
journal entries; preparing a
trial balance

C3   C4   A1   P1   P2

Apr. 1   Tanner invested $80,000 cash along with office equipment valued at $26,000 in the company in exchange for common stock.

    2   The company prepaid $9,000 cash for 12 months' rent for office space. *Hint:* Debit Prepaid Rent for $9,000.

    3   The company made credit purchases for $8,000 in office equipment and $3,600 in office supplies. Payment is due within 10 days.

    6   The company completed services for a client and immediately received $4,000 cash.

    9   The company completed a $6,000 project for a client, who must pay within 30 days.

   13   The company paid $11,600 cash to settle the account payable created on April 3.

   19   The company paid $2,400 cash for the premium on a 12-month insurance policy. *Hint:* Debit Prepaid Insurance for $2,400.

   22   The company received $4,400 cash as partial payment for the work completed on April 9.

   25   The company completed work for another client for $2,890 on credit.

   28   The company paid a $5,500 cash dividend.

   29   The company purchased $600 of additional office supplies on credit.

   30   The company paid $435 cash for this month's utility bill.

Required

1. Prepare general journal entries to record these transactions (use account titles listed in part 2).

Check (2) Ending
balances: Cash, $59,465;
Accounts Receivable, $4,490;
Accounts Payable, $600

2. Open the following ledger accounts—their account numbers are in parentheses (use the balance column format): Cash (101); Accounts Receivable (106); Office Supplies (124); Prepaid Insurance (128); Prepaid Rent (131); Office Equipment (163); Accounts Payable (201); Common Stock (307); Dividends (319); Services Revenue (403); and Utilities Expense (690). Post journal entries from part 1 to the ledger accounts and enter the balance after each posting.

(3) Total debits, $119,490

3. Prepare a trial balance as of April 30.

Problem 2-2A
Preparing and posting
journal entries; preparing a
trial balance

C3   C4   A1   P1   P2

Aracel Engineering completed the following transactions in the month of June.

a. Jenna Aracel, the owner, invested $100,000 cash, office equipment with a value of $5,000, and $60,000 of drafting equipment to launch the company in exchange for common stock.

b. The company purchased land worth $49,000 for an office by paying $6,300 cash and signing a long-term note payable for $42,700.

c. The company purchased a portable building with $55,000 cash and moved it onto the land acquired in *b*.

d. The company paid $3,000 cash for the premium on an 18-month insurance policy.

e. The company completed and delivered a set of plans for a client and collected $6,200 cash.

f. The company purchased $20,000 of additional drafting equipment by paying $9,500 cash and signing a long-term note payable for $10,500.

g. The company completed $14,000 of engineering services for a client. This amount is to be received in 30 days.

h. The company purchased $1,150 of additional office equipment on credit.

i. The company completed engineering services for $22,000 on credit.

j. The company received a bill for rent of equipment that was used on a recently completed job. The $1,333 rent cost must be paid within 30 days.

k. The company collected $7,000 cash in partial payment from the client described in transaction *g*.

l. The company paid $1,200 cash for wages to a drafting assistant.

m. The company paid $1,150 cash to settle the account payable created in transaction *h*.

n. The company paid $925 cash for minor maintenance of its drafting equipment.

o. The company paid a $9,480 cash dividend.

p. The company paid $1,200 cash for wages to a drafting assistant.

q. The company paid $2,500 cash for advertisements on the web during June.

Required

1. Prepare general journal entries to record these transactions (use the account titles listed in part 2).

2. Open the following ledger accounts—their account numbers are in parentheses (use the balance column format): Cash (101); Accounts Receivable (106); Prepaid Insurance (108); Office Equipment (163); Drafting Equipment (164); Building (170); Land (172); Accounts Payable (201); Notes Payable (250); Common Stock (307); Dividends (319); Engineering Fees Earned (402); Wages Expense (601); Equipment Rental Expense (602); Advertising Expense (603); and Repairs Expense (604). Post the journal entries from part 1 to the accounts and enter the balance after each posting.

3. Prepare a trial balance as of the end of June.

> **Check** (2) Ending balances: Cash, $22,945; Accounts Receivable, $29,000; Accounts Payable, $1,333
>
> (3) Trial balance totals, $261,733

Denzel Brooks opened a web consulting business called Venture Consultants and completed the following transactions in March.

> **Problem 2-3A**
> Preparing and posting journal entries; preparing a trial balance
>
> C3 C4 A1 P1 P2

Mar. 1 Brooks invested $150,000 cash along with $22,000 in office equipment in the company in exchange for common stock.

  2 The company prepaid $6,000 cash for six months' rent for an office. *Hint:* Debit Prepaid Rent for $6,000.

  3 The company made credit purchases of office equipment for $3,000 and office supplies for $1,200. Payment is due within 10 days.

  6 The company completed services for a client and immediately received $4,000 cash.

  9 The company completed a $7,500 project for a client, who must pay within 30 days.

  12 The company paid $4,200 cash to settle the account payable created on March 3.

  19 The company paid $5,000 cash for the premium on a 12-month insurance policy. *Hint:* Debit Prepaid Insurance for $5,000.

  22 The company received $3,500 cash as partial payment for the work completed on March 9.

  25 The company completed work for another client for $3,820 on credit.

  29 The company paid a $5,100 cash dividend.

  30 The company purchased $600 of additional office supplies on credit.

  31 The company paid $500 cash for this month's utility bill.

Required

1. Prepare general journal entries to record these transactions (use the account titles listed in part 2).

2. Open the following ledger accounts—their account numbers are in parentheses (use the balance column format): Cash (101); Accounts Receivable (106); Office Supplies (124); Prepaid Insurance (128); Prepaid Rent (131); Office Equipment (163); Accounts Payable (201); Common Stock (307); Dividends (319); Services Revenue (403); and Utilities Expense (690). Post the journal entries from part 1 to the ledger accounts and enter the balance after each posting.

3. Prepare a trial balance as of the end of March.

> **Check** (2) Ending balances: Cash, $136,700; Accounts Receivable, $7,820; Accounts Payable, $600
>
> (3) Total debits, $187,920

Business transactions completed by Hannah Venedict during the month of September are as follows.

> **Problem 2-4A**
> Recording transactions; posting to ledger; preparing a trial balance
>
> C3 A1 P1 P2

a. Venedict invested $60,000 cash along with office equipment valued at $25,000 in a new business named HV Consulting in exchange for common stock.

b. The company purchased land valued at $40,000 and a building valued at $160,000. The purchase is paid with $30,000 cash and a long-term note payable for $170,000.

c. The company purchased $2,000 of office supplies on credit.

[continued on next page]

[continued from previous page]

d. Venedict invested her personal automobile in the company in exchange for more common stock. The automobile has a value of $16,500 and is to be used exclusively in the business.

e. The company purchased $5,600 of additional office equipment on credit.

f. The company paid $1,800 cash salary to an assistant.

g. The company provided services to a client and collected $8,000 cash.

h. The company paid $635 cash for this month's utilities.

i. The company paid $2,000 cash to settle the account payable created in transaction *c*.

j. The company purchased $20,300 of new office equipment by paying $20,300 cash.

k. The company completed $6,250 of services for a client, who must pay within 30 days.

l. The company paid $1,800 cash salary to an assistant.

m. The company received $4,000 cash in partial payment on the receivable created in transaction *k*.

n. The company paid a $2,800 cash dividend.

Required

1. Prepare general journal entries to record these transactions (use account titles listed in part 2).

2. Open the following ledger accounts—their account numbers are in parentheses (use the balance column format): Cash (101); Accounts Receivable (106); Office Supplies (108); Office Equipment (163); Automobiles (164); Building (170); Land (172); Accounts Payable (201); Notes Payable (250); Common Stock (307); Dividends (319); Fees Earned (402); Salaries Expense (601); and Utilities Expense (602). Post the journal entries from part 1 to the ledger accounts and enter the balance after each posting.

3. Prepare a trial balance as of the end of September.

Check   (2) Ending balances: Cash, $12,665; Office Equipment, $50,900

(3) Trial balance totals, $291,350

Problem 2-5A

Computing net income from equity analysis, preparing a balance sheet, and computing the debt ratio

C2   A1   A2   P3

The accounting records of Nettle Distribution show the following assets and liabilities as of December 31, 2018 and 2019.

December 31	2018	2019	December 31	2018	2019
Cash	$ 64,300	$ 15,640	Building......................	$ 0	$80,000
Accounts receivable............	26,240	19,100	Land	0	60,000
Office supplies	3,160	1,960	Accounts payable..............	3,500	33,500
Office equipment	44,000	44,000	Note payable	0	40,000
Trucks	148,000	157,000			

Required

1. Prepare balance sheets for the business as of December 31, 2018 and 2019. *Hint:* Report only total equity on the balance sheet and remember that total equity equals the difference between assets and liabilities.

2. Compute net income for 2019 by comparing total equity amounts for these two years and using the following information: During 2019, the owner invested $35,000 additional cash in the business (in exchange for common stock) and the company paid a $19,000 cash dividend.

3. Compute the 2019 year-end debt ratio (in percent and rounded to one decimal).

Check   (2) Net income, $6,000

(3) Debt ratio, 19.5%

Problem 2-6A

Analyzing account balances and reconstructing transactions

C1   C3   A1   P2

Yi Min started an engineering firm called Min Engineering. He began operations and completed seven transactions in May, which included his initial investment of $18,000 cash. After those seven transactions, the ledger included the following accounts with normal balances.

Cash	$37,600	Office equipment	$12,900	Dividends	$ 3,370
Office supplies	890	Accounts payable.......	12,900	Engineering fees earned	36,000
Prepaid insurance.......	4,600	Common stock	18,000	Rent expense	7,540

Required

1. Prepare a trial balance for this business as of the end of May.

2. The following seven transactions produced the account balances shown above.

a. Y. Min invested S18,000 cash in the business in exchange for common stock.

b. Paid $7,540 cash for monthly rent expense for May.

c. Paid $4,600 cash in advance for the annual insurance premium beginning the next period.

Check   (1) Trial balance totals, $66,900

(2) Ending Cash balance, $37,600

d. Purchased office supplies for $890 cash.

e. Purchased $12,900 of office equipment on credit (with accounts payable).

f. Received $36,000 cash for engineering services provided in May.

g. The company paid a $3,370 cash dividend.

Prepare a Cash T-account, enter the cash effects (if any) of each transaction, and compute the ending Cash balance. Code each entry in the T-account with one of the transaction codes *a* through *g*.

Angela Lopez owns and manages a consulting firm called Metrix, which began operations on March 1. On March 31, Metrix shows the following selected accounts and amounts for the month of March.

Problem 2-7A

Preparing an income statement, statement of retained earnings, and balance sheet

P3

Equipment.	$ 4,000	Accounts receivable.	$ 3,500	Prepaid insurance.	$1,000
Salaries expense	3,000	Common stock	11,600	Accounts payable.	1,300
Consulting revenue	12,000	Dividends	2,000	Note receivable	2,500
Cash	8,000	Office supplies	1,500	Rent expense	2,000
Utilities expense.	200	Rental revenue	500	Unearned revenue	300
Note payable	2,400	Advertising expense.	400		

Required

1. Prepare a March income statement for the business.

2. Prepare a March statement of retained earnings. The Retained Earnings account balance at March 1 was $0, and the owner invested $11,600 cash in the company on March 2 in exchange for common stock.

3. Prepare a March 31 balance sheet. *Hint:* Use the Retained Earnings account balance calculated in part 2.

Humble Management Services opened for business and completed these transactions in September.

PROBLEM SET B

Problem 2-1B

Preparing and posting journal entries; preparing a trial balance

C3 C4 A1 P1 P2

Sep. 1 Henry Humble, the owner, invested $38,000 cash along with office equipment valued at $15,000 in the company in exchange for common stock.

2 The company prepaid $9,000 cash for 12 months' rent for office space. *Hint:* Debit Prepaid Rent for $9,000.

4 The company made credit purchases for $8,000 in office equipment and $2,400 in office supplies. Payment is due within 10 days.

8 The company completed work for a client and immediately received $3,280 cash.

12 The company completed a $15,400 project for a client, who must pay within 30 days.

13 The company paid $10,400 cash to settle the payable created on September 4.

19 The company paid $1,900 cash for the premium on an 18-month insurance policy. *Hint:* Debit Prepaid Insurance for $1,900.

22 The company received $7,700 cash as partial payment for the work completed on September 12.

24 The company completed work for another client for $2,100 on credit.

28 The company paid a $5,300 cash dividend.

29 The company purchased $550 of additional office supplies on credit.

30 The company paid $860 cash for this month's utility bill.

Required

1. Prepare general journal entries to record these transactions (use account titles listed in part 2).

2. Open the following ledger accounts—their account numbers are in parentheses (use the balance column format): Cash (101); Accounts Receivable (106); Office Supplies (124); Prepaid Insurance (128); Prepaid Rent (131); Office Equipment (163); Accounts Payable (201); Common Stock (307); Dividends (319); Services Revenue (401); and Utilities Expense (690). Post journal entries from part 1 to the ledger accounts and enter the balance after each posting.

3. Prepare a trial balance as of the end of September.

Check (2) Ending balances: Cash, $21,520; Accounts Receivable, $9,800; Accounts Payable, $550

(3) Total debits, $74,330

At the beginning of April, Bernadette Grechus launched a custom computer solutions company called Softworks. The company had the following transactions during April.

Problem 2-2B

Preparing and posting journal entries; preparing a trial balance

C3 C4 A1 P1 P2

a. Bernadette Grechus invested $65,000 cash, office equipment with a value of $5,750, and $30,000 of computer equipment in the company in exchange for common stock.

b. The company purchased land worth $22,000 for an office by paying $5,000 cash and signing a long-term note payable for $17,000.

[continued on next page]

[continued from previous page]

c. The company purchased a portable building with $34,500 cash and moved it onto the land acquired in *b*.

d. The company paid $5,000 cash for the premium on a two-year insurance policy.

e. The company provided services to a client and immediately collected $4,600 cash.

f. The company purchased $4,500 of additional computer equipment by paying $800 cash and signing a long-term note payable for $3,700.

g. The company completed $4,250 of services for a client. This amount is to be received within 30 days.

h. The company purchased $950 of additional office equipment on credit.

i. The company completed client services for $10,200 on credit.

j. The company received a bill for rent of a computer testing device that was used on a recently completed job. The $580 rent cost must be paid within 30 days.

k. The company collected $5,100 cash in partial payment from the client described in transaction *i*.

l. The company paid $1,800 cash for wages to an assistant.

m. The company paid $950 cash to settle the payable created in transaction *h*.

n. The company paid $608 cash for minor maintenance of the company's computer equipment.

o. The company paid a $6,230 cash dividend.

p. The company paid $1,800 cash for wages to an assistant.

q. The company paid $750 cash for advertisements on the web during April.

Required

1. Prepare general journal entries to record these transactions (use account titles listed in part 2).

2. Open the following ledger accounts—their account numbers are in parentheses (use the balance column format): Cash (101); Accounts Receivable (106); Prepaid Insurance (108); Office Equipment (163); Computer Equipment (164); Building (170); Land (172); Accounts Payable (201); Notes Payable (250); Common Stock (307); Dividends (319); Fees Earned (402); Wages Expense (601); Computer Rental Expense (602); Advertising Expense (603); and Repairs Expense (604). Post the journal entries from part 1 to the accounts and enter the balance after each posting.

3. Prepare a trial balance as of the end of April.

Check   (2) Ending balances: Cash, $17,262; Accounts Receivable, $9,350; Accounts Payable, $580

(3) Trial balance totals, $141,080

Problem 2-3B
Preparing and posting journal entries; preparing a trial balance

C3   C4   A1   P1   P2

Zucker Management Services opened for business and completed these transactions in November.

Nov. 1   Matt Zucker, the owner, invested $30,000 cash along with $15,000 of office equipment in the company in exchange for common stock.

2   The company prepaid $4,500 cash for six months' rent for an office. *Hint:* Debit Prepaid Rent for $4,500.

4   The company made credit purchases of office equipment for $2,500 and of office supplies for $600. Payment is due within 10 days.

8   The company completed work for a client and immediately received $3,400 cash.

12   The company completed a $10,200 project for a client, who must pay within 30 days.

13   The company paid $3,100 cash to settle the payable created on November 4.

19   The company paid $1,800 cash for the premium on a 24-month insurance policy.

22   The company received $5,200 cash as partial payment for the work completed on November 12.

24   The company completed work for another client for $1,750 on credit.

28   The company paid a $5,300 cash dividend.

29   The company purchased $249 of additional office supplies on credit.

30   The company paid $831 cash for this month's utility bill.

Required

1. Prepare general journal entries to record these transactions (use account titles listed in part 2).

2. Open the following ledger accounts—their account numbers are in parentheses (use the balance column format): Cash (101); Accounts Receivable (106); Office Supplies (124); Prepaid Insurance (128); Prepaid Rent (131); Office Equipment (163); Accounts Payable (201); Common Stock (307); Dividends (319); Services Revenue (403); and Utilities Expense (690). Post the journal entries from part 1 to the ledger accounts and enter the balance after each posting.

3. Prepare a trial balance as of the end of November.

Check   (2) Ending balances: Cash, $23,069; Accounts Receivable, $6,750; Accounts Payable, $249

(3) Total debits, $60,599

Nuncio Consulting completed the following transactions during June.

Problem 2-4B

Recording transactions; posting to ledger; preparing a trial balance

C3   A1   P1   P2

a. Armand Nuncio, the owner, invested $35,000 cash along with office equipment valued at $11,000 in the new company in exchange for common stock.

b. The company purchased land valued at $7,500 and a building valued at $40,000. The purchase is paid with $15,000 cash and a long-term note payable for $32,500.

c. The company purchased $500 of office supplies on credit.

d. A. Nuncio invested his personal automobile in the company in exchange for more common stock. The automobile has a value of $8,000 and is to be used exclusively in the business.

e. The company purchased $1,200 of additional office equipment on credit.

f. The company paid $1,000 cash salary to an assistant.

g. The company provided services to a client and collected $3,200 cash.

h. The company paid $540 cash for this month's utilities.

i. The company paid $500 cash to settle the payable created in transaction *c*.

j. The company purchased $3,400 of new office equipment by paying $3,400 cash.

k. The company completed $4,200 of services for a client, who must pay within 30 days.

l. The company paid $1,000 cash salary to an assistant.

m. The company received $2,200 cash in partial payment on the receivable created in transaction *k*.

n. The company paid a $1,100 cash dividend.

Required

1. Prepare general journal entries to record these transactions (use account titles listed in part 2).

2. Open the following ledger accounts—their account numbers are in parentheses (use the balance column format): Cash (101); Accounts Receivable (106); Office Supplies (108); Office Equipment (163); Automobiles (164); Building (170); Land (172); Accounts Payable (201); Notes Payable (250); Common Stock (307); Dividends (319); Fees Earned (402); Salaries Expense (601); and Utilities Expense (602). Post the journal entries from part 1 to the ledger accounts and enter the balance after each posting.

Check   (2) Ending balances: Cash, $17,860; Office Equipment, $15,600

3. Prepare a trial balance as of the end of June.

(3) Trial balance totals, $95,100

The accounting records of Tama Co. show the following assets and liabilities as of December 31, 2018 and 2019.

Problem 2-5B

Computing net income from equity analysis, preparing a balance sheet, and computing the debt ratio

C2   A1   A2   P3

December 31	2018	2019	December 31	2018	2019
Cash	$30,000	$ 5,000	Building	$ 0	$250,000
Accounts receivable	35,000	25,000	Land	0	50,000
Office supplies	8,000	13,500	Accounts payable	4,000	12,000
Office equipment	40,000	40,000	Note payable	0	250,000
Machinery	28,000	28,500			

Required

1. Prepare balance sheets for the business as of December 31, 2018 and 2019. *Hint:* Report only total equity on the balance sheet and remember that total equity equals the difference between assets and liabilities.

2. Compute net income for 2019 by comparing total equity amounts for these two years and using the following information: During 2019, the owner invested $5,000 additional cash in the business (in exchange for common stock) and the company paid a $3,000 cash dividend.

Check   (2) Net income, $11,000

3. Compute the December 31, 2019, debt ratio (in percent and rounded to one decimal).

(3) Debt ratio, 63.6%

Roshaun Gould started a web consulting firm called Gould Solutions. He began operations and completed seven transactions in April that resulted in the following accounts, which all have normal balances.

Problem 2-6B

Analyzing account balances and reconstructing transactions

C1   C3   A1   P2

Cash	$20,000	Office equipment	$12,250	Dividends	$ 5,200
Office supplies	750	Accounts payable	12,250	Consulting fees earned	20,400
Prepaid rent	1,800	Common stock	15,000	Miscellaneous expenses	7,650

Required

1. Prepare a trial balance for this business as of the end of April.

2. The following seven transactions produced the account balances shown above.

    a. Gould invested $15,000 cash in the business in exchange for common stock.

    b. Paid $1,800 cash in advance for next month's rent expense.

    c. Paid $7,650 cash for miscellaneous expenses.

    d. Purchased office supplies for $750 cash.

    e. Purchased $12,250 of office equipment on credit (with accounts payable).

    f. Received $20,400 cash for consulting services provided in April.

    g. The company paid a $5,200 cash dividend.

    Prepare a Cash T-account, enter the cash effects (if any) of each transaction, and compute the ending Cash balance. Code each entry in the T-account with one of the transaction codes *a* through *g*.

Problem 2-7B
Preparing an income
statement, statement of
retained earnings, and
balance sheet

P3

Victoria Rivera owns and manages a consulting firm called Prisek, which began operations on July 1. On July 31, the company's records show the following selected accounts and amounts for the month of July.

Equipment	$12,000	Accounts receivable	$10,500	Prepaid insurance	$3,000
Salaries expense	9,000	Common stock	34,800	Accounts payable	3,900
Consulting revenue	36,000	Dividends	6,000	Note receivable	7,500
Cash	24,000	Office supplies	4,500	Rent expense	6,000
Utilities expense	600	Rental revenue	1,500	Unearned revenue	900
Note payable	7,200	Advertising expense	1,200		

Required

1. Prepare a July income statement for the business.

2. Prepare a July statement of retained earnings. The Retained Earnings account balance at July 1 was $0, and the owner invested $34,800 cash in the company on July 2 in exchange for common stock.

3. Prepare a July 31 balance sheet. *Hint:* Use the Retained Earnings account balance calculated in part 2.

SERIAL PROBLEM
Business Solutions

A1   P1   P2

©Alexander Image/Shutterstock

This serial problem started in Chapter 1 and continues through most of the chapters. If the Chapter 1 segment was not completed, the problem can begin at this point.

SP 2   On October 1, 2019, Santana Rey launched a computer services company called **Business Solutions**, which provides consulting services, computer system installations, and custom program development. Rey adopts the calendar year for reporting purposes and expects to prepare the company's first set of financial statements on December 31, 2019. The company's initial chart of accounts follows.

Account	No.	Account	No.
Cash	101	Common Stock	307
Accounts Receivable	106	Dividends	319
Computer Supplies	126	Computer Services Revenue	403
Prepaid Insurance	128	Wages Expense	623
Prepaid Rent	131	Advertising Expense	655
Office Equipment	163	Mileage Expense	676
Computer Equipment	167	Miscellaneous Expenses	677
Accounts Payable	201	Repairs Expense—Computer	684

Required

1. Prepare journal entries to record each of the following transactions for Business Solutions.

Oct. 1   S. Rey invested $45,000 cash, a $20,000 computer system, and $8,000 of office equipment in the company in exchange for common stock.

     2   The company paid $3,300 cash for four months' rent. *Hint:* Debit Prepaid Rent for $3,300.

     3   The company purchased $1,420 of computer supplies on credit from Harris Office Products.

     5   The company paid $2,220 cash for one year's premium on a property and liability insurance policy. *Hint:* Debit Prepaid Insurance for $2,220.

     6   The company billed Easy Leasing $4,800 for services performed in installing a new web server.

8   The company paid $1,420 cash for the computer supplies purchased from Harris Office Products on October 3.

10   The company hired Lyn Addie as a part-time assistant.

12   The company billed Easy Leasing another $1,400 for services performed.

15   The company received $4,800 cash from Easy Leasing as partial payment on its account.

17   The company paid $805 cash to repair computer equipment that was damaged when moving it.

20   The company paid $1,728 cash for advertisements published in the local newspaper.

22   The company received $1,400 cash from Easy Leasing on its account.

28   The company billed IFM Company $5,208 for services performed.

31   The company paid $875 cash for Lyn Addie's wages for seven days' work.

31   The company paid a $3,600 cash dividend.

Nov. 1   The company reimbursed S. Rey in cash for business automobile mileage allowance (Rey logged 1,000 miles at $0.32 per mile).

2   The company received $4,633 cash from Liu Corporation for computer services performed.

5   The company purchased computer supplies for $1,125 cash from Harris Office Products.

8   The company billed Gomez Co. $5,668 for services performed.

13   The company agreed to perform future services for Alex's Engineering Co. No work has yet been performed.

18   The company received $2,208 cash from IFM Company as partial payment of the October 28 bill.

22   The company paid $250 cash for miscellaneous expenses. *Hint:* Debit Miscellaneous Expenses for $250.

24   The company completed work and sent a bill for $3,950 to Alex's Engineering Co.

25   The company sent another bill to IFM Company for the past-due amount of $3,000.

28   The company reimbursed S. Rey in cash for business automobile mileage (1,200 miles at $0.32 per mile).

30   The company paid $1,750 cash for Lyn Addie's wages for 14 days' work.

30   The company paid a $2,000 cash dividend.

2. Open ledger accounts (in balance column format) and post the journal entries from part 1 to them.

3. Prepare a trial balance as of the end of November.

Check   (2) Cash, Nov. 30 bal., $38,264

(3) Trial bal. totals, $98,659

Using transactions from the following assignments along with the **General Ledger** tool, prepare journal entries for each transaction and identify the financial statement impact of each entry. The financial statements are automatically generated based on the journal entries recorded.

GENERAL LEDGER PROBLEM

GL 2-1 Transactions from the FastForward illustration in this chapter

GL 2-2 Based on Exercise 2-9

GL 2-3 Based on Exercise 2-12

GL 2-4 Based on Problem 2-1A

Using transactions from the following assignments, record journal entries, create financial statements, and assess the impact of each transaction on financial statements.

GL 2-5 Based on Problem 2-2A   **GL 2-7** Based on Problem 2-4A

GL 2-6 Based on Problem 2-3A   **GL 2-8** Based on the Serial Problem SP 2

Accounting Analysis

AA 2-1   Refer to **Apple**'s financial statements in Appendix A for the following questions.

Required

1. What amount of total liabilities does Apple report for each of the fiscal years ended (*a*) September 30, 2017, and (*b*) September 24, 2016?

2. What amount of total assets does it report for each of the fiscal years ended (*a*) September 30, 2017, and (*b*) September 24, 2016?

3. Compute its debt ratio for each of the fiscal years ended (*a*) September 30, 2017, and (*b*) September 24, 2016. (Report ratio in percent and round it to one decimal.)

4. In which fiscal year did it employ more financial leverage: September 30, 2017, or September 24, 2016? Explain.

COMPANY ANALYSIS

A1   A2

APPLE

COMPARATIVE ANALYSIS

A1　A2　

APPLE

GOOGLE

AA 2-2　Key comparative figures for **Apple** and **Google** follow.

$ millions	Apple Current Year	Apple Prior Year	Google Current Year	Google Prior Year
Total liabilities	$241,272	$193,437	$ 44,793	$ 28,461
Total assets	375,319	321,686	197,295	167,497

1. What is the debt ratio for Apple in the current year and for the prior year?

2. What is the debt ratio for Google in the current year and for the prior year?

3. Which of the two companies has the higher degree of financial leverage in the current year?

GLOBAL ANALYSIS

A2　

APPLE

GOOGLE

Samsung

AA 2-3　Key comparative figures for **Apple**, **Google**, and **Samsung** follow.

In millions	Samsung Current Year	Samsung Prior Year	Apple Current Year	Google Current Year
Total liabilities	₩ 87,260,662	₩ 69,211,291	$241,272	$ 44,793
Total assets	301,752,090	262,174,324	375,319	197,295

Required

1. Compute Samsung's debt ratio for the current year and prior year.

2. Is Samsung on a trend toward increased or decreased financial leverage?

3. Looking at the current-year debt ratio, is Samsung a more risky or less risky investment than (*a*) Apple and (*b*) Google?

Beyond the Numbers

ETHICS CHALLENGE

C1　

BTN 2-1　Assume that you are a cashier and your manager requires that you immediately enter each sale when it occurs. Recently, lunch hour traffic has increased and the assistant manager asks you to avoid delays by taking customers' cash and making change without entering sales. The assistant manager says she will add up cash and enter sales after lunch. She says that, in this way, customers will be happy and the register record will always match the cash amount when the manager arrives at three o'clock.

　　The advantages to the process proposed by the assistant manager include improved customer service, fewer delays, and less work for you. The disadvantage is that the assistant manager could steal cash by simply recording less sales than the cash received and then pocketing the excess cash. You decide to reject her suggestion without the manager's approval and to confront her on the ethics of her suggestion.

Required

Propose and evaluate two other courses of action you might consider, and explain why.

COMMUNICATING IN PRACTICE

C1　C2　A1　P3　

BTN 2-2　Lila Corentine is an aspiring entrepreneur and your friend. She is having difficulty understanding the purposes of financial statements and how they fit together across time.

Required

Write a one-page memorandum to Corentine explaining the purposes of the four financial statements and how they are linked across time.

TAKING IT TO THE NET

A1　　

BTN 2-3　Access EDGAR online (**SEC.gov**) and locate the 2016 10-K report of **Amazon.com** (ticker: AMZN) filed on February 10, 2017. Review its financial statements reported for years ended 2016, 2015, and 2014 to answer the following questions.

Required

1. What are the amounts of Amazon's net income or net loss reported for each of these three years?

2. Do Amazon's operating activities provide cash or use cash for each of these three years? *Hint:* See the statement of cash flows.

3. If Amazon has 2016 net income of $2,371 million and 2016 operating cash flows of $16,443 million, how is it possible that its cash balance at December 31, 2016, increases by only $3,444 million relative to its balance at December 31, 2015?

BTN 2-4 The expanded accounting equation consists of assets, liabilities, common stock, dividends, revenues, and expenses. It can be used to reveal insights into changes in a company's financial position.

TEAMWORK IN ACTION

C1   C2   C4   A1

Required

1. Form *learning teams* of six (or more) members. Each team member must select one of the six components, and each team must have at least one expert on each component: (*a*) assets, (*b*) liabilities, (*c*) common stock, (*d*) dividends, (*e*) revenues, and (*f*) expenses.

2. Form *expert teams* of individuals who selected the same component in part 1. Expert teams are to draft a report that each expert will present to his or her learning team addressing the following:

   a. Identify for its component the (i) increase and decrease side of the account and (ii) normal balance side of the account.

   b. Describe a transaction, with amounts, that increases its component.

   c. Using the transaction and amounts in (*b*), verify the equality of the accounting equation and then explain any effects on the income statement and statement of cash flows.

   d. Describe a transaction, with amounts, that decreases its component.

   e. Using the transaction and amounts in (*d*), verify the equality of the accounting equation and then explain any effects on the income statement and statement of cash flows.

3. Each expert should return to his/her learning team. In rotation, each member presents his/her expert team's report to the learning team. Team discussion is encouraged.

BTN 2-5 Assume that James Park and Eric Friedman of **Fitbit** plan on expanding their business to accommodate more product lines. They are considering financing expansion in one of two ways: (1) contributing more of their own funds to the business or (2) borrowing the funds from a bank.

ENTREPRENEURIAL DECISION

A1   A2   P3

Required

Identify at least two issues that James and Eric should consider when trying to decide on the method for financing their expansion.

BTN 2-6 Angel Martin is a young entrepreneur who operates Martin Music Services, offering singing lessons and instruction on musical instruments. Martin wishes to expand but needs a $30,000 loan. The bank requests that Martin prepare a balance sheet and key financial ratios. Martin has not kept formal records but is able to provide the following accounts and their amounts as of December 31.

ENTREPRENEURIAL DECISION

A1   A2   P3

Cash	$ 3,600	Accounts receivable	$ 9,600	Prepaid insurance	$ 1,500
Prepaid rent	9,400	Store supplies	6,600	Equipment	50,000
Accounts payable	2,200	Unearned lesson fees	15,600	Total equity*	62,900
Annual net income	40,000				

*The total equity amount reflects all owner investments, dividends, revenues, and expenses as of December 31.

Required

1. Prepare a balance sheet as of December 31 for Martin Music Services. (Report only the total equity amount on the balance sheet.)

2. Compute Martin's debt ratio and its return on assets (the latter ratio is defined in Chapter 1). Assume average assets equal its ending balance.

3. Do you believe the prospects of a $30,000 bank loan are good? Why or why not?

BTN 2-7 Obtain a recent copy of the most prominent newspaper distributed in your area. Research the classified section and prepare a report answering the following questions (attach relevant printouts to your report). Alternatively, you may want to search the web for the required information. One suitable website is **CareerOneStop** (**CareerOneStop.org**). For documentation, print copies of websites accessed.

HITTING THE ROAD

C1

1. Identify the number of listings for accounting positions and the various accounting job titles.

2. Identify the number of listings for other job titles, with examples, that require or prefer accounting knowledge/experience but are not specifically accounting positions.

3. Specify the salary range for the accounting and accounting-related positions if provided.

4. Indicate the job that appeals most to you, the reason for its appeal, and its requirements.

3 Adjusting Accounts for Financial Statements

Chapter Preview

DEFERRAL OF EXPENSE	DEFERRAL OF REVENUE	ACCRUED EXPENSE	ACCRUED REVENUE	REPORTING	CLASSIFICATION AND ANALYSIS
C1 Timing Accrual vs. cash 3-Step process **P1** Framework Examples	**P2** Framework Examples	**P3** Framework Examples	**P4** Framework Examples Summary	**P5** Adjusted trial balance **P6** Financial statements **P7** Closing process **P8** Post-closing trial balance	**C2** Accounting cycle **C3** Classified balance sheet **A1** Profit margin **A2** Current ratio
NTK 3-1	**NTK 3-2**	**NTK 3-3**	**NTK 3-4**	**NTK 3-5, 6**	**NTK 3-7**

Learning Objectives

CONCEPTUAL

C1 Explain the importance of periodic reporting and the role of accrual accounting.

C2 Identify steps in the accounting cycle.

C3 Explain and prepare a classified balance sheet.

ANALYTICAL

A1 Compute profit margin and describe its use in analyzing company performance.

A2 Compute the current ratio and describe what it reveals about a company's financial condition.

PROCEDURAL

P1 Prepare adjusting entries for deferral of expenses.

P2 Prepare adjusting entries for deferral of revenues.

P3 Prepare adjusting entries for accrued expenses.

P4 Prepare adjusting entries for accrued revenues.

P5 Explain and prepare an adjusted trial balance.

P6 Prepare financial statements from an adjusted trial balance.

P7 Describe and prepare closing entries.

P8 Explain and prepare a post-closing trial balance.

P9 *Appendix 3A*—Explain the alternatives in accounting for prepaids.

P10 *Appendix 3B*—Prepare a work sheet and explain its usefulness.

P11 *Appendix 3C*—Prepare reversing entries and explain their purpose.

Snap!

©J. Emilio Flores/Corbis/Getty Images

"Creativity creates value"—**EVAN SPIEGEL**

VENICE, CA—Evan Spiegel met his future co-founder Bobby Murphy in college. "We weren't cool," recalls Bobby, "so we tried to build things to be cool!" One of their cool projects was an app that could send messages that disappeared after a few seconds. This app would later be called **Snapchat** (**Snapchat.com**).

The first headquarters of Snapchat was the home of Evan's dad. However, within a matter of months, their app had over a million users.

As Snapchat grew, Evan and Bobby knew an effective accounting system was key to attracting investors. "One of the things I did underestimate," admits Evan, "was how much more important communication becomes [when seeking investors]."

Investors wanted to know revenues, costs, assets, and liabilities for Snapchat. "You really need to explain . . . how your business works," insists Evan.

To communicate "the Snap story," the entrepreneurs learned how to defer and accrue revenues and expenses and to prepare financial statements for investors. This included learning the accounting cycle. With accounting reports in hand, Evan and Bobby were able to secure additional financing. Exclaims Evan: "That was the greatest feeling of all time!"

Sources: *Snapchat website,* January 2019; *Vanity Fair,* October 2017; *LA Times,* March 2017; *Forbes,* January 2014

TIMING AND REPORTING

The Accounting Period

The value of information is linked to its timeliness. Useful information must reach decision makers frequently. To provide timely information, accounting systems prepare reports at regular intervals. The **time period assumption** presumes that an organization's activities can be divided into specific time periods such as a month, a three-month quarter, a six-month interval, or a year. Exhibit 3.1 shows various **accounting,** or *reporting,* **periods.** Most organizations use a year as their primary accounting period. Reports covering a one-year period are known as **annual financial statements.** Many organizations also prepare **interim financial statements** covering one, three, or six months of activity.

C1

Explain the importance of periodic reporting and the role of accrual accounting.

"Apple announces annual income of . . ."

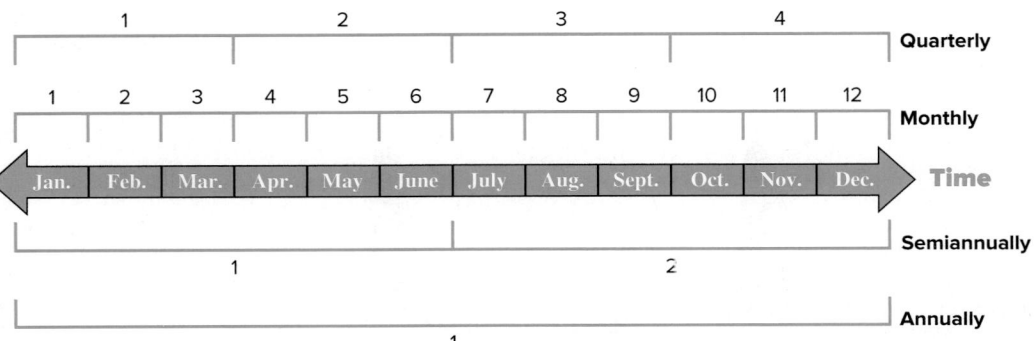

EXHIBIT 3.1

Accounting Periods

The annual reporting period is not always a calendar year ending on December 31. An organization can use a **fiscal year** consisting of any 12 consecutive months or 52 weeks. For example, **Gap**'s fiscal year consistently ends the final week of January or the first week of February each year.

©Vixit/Shutterstock

Companies with little seasonal variation in sales often use the calendar year as their fiscal year. **Facebook** uses calendar-year reporting. Companies that have seasonal variations in sales often use a **natural business year** end, which is when sales are at their lowest level for the year. The natural business year for retailers such as **Target** and **Dick's Sporting Goods** ends around January 31, after the holidays.

Accrual Basis versus Cash Basis

After external transactions and events are recorded, several accounts require adjustments before their balances appear in financial statements. This is needed because internal transactions and events are not yet recorded.

- **Accrual basis accounting** records revenues when services and products are delivered and records expenses when incurred (matched with revenues).
- **Cash basis accounting** records revenues when cash is received and records expenses when cash is paid. Cash basis income is cash receipts minus cash payments.

Most agree that accrual accounting better reflects business performance than cash basis accounting. Accrual accounting also increases the *comparability* of financial statements from period to period.

Accrual Basis   To compare these two systems, let's consider FastForward's Prepaid Insurance account. FastForward paid $2,400 for 24 months of insurance coverage that began on December 1, 2019. Accrual accounting requires that $100 of insurance expense be reported each month, from December 2019 through November 2021. (This means expenses are $100 in 2019, $1,200 in 2020, and $1,100 in 2021.) Exhibit 3.2 shows this allocation of insurance cost across the three years. Any unexpired premium is reported as a Prepaid Insurance asset on the accrual basis balance sheet.

EXHIBIT 3.2

Accrual Accounting for Allocating Prepaid Insurance to Expense

 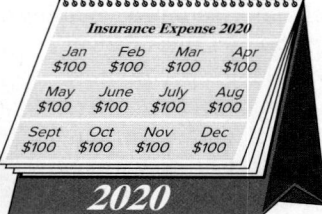 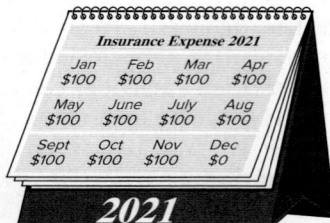

Point: Annual income statements for Exhibit 3.2 follow:

Accrual Basis	2019		2020		2021	
Revenues.......	$	#	$	#	$	#
Insurance exp....	$100		$1,200		$1,100	

EXHIBIT 3.3

Cash Accounting for Allocating Prepaid Insurance to Expense

Cash Basis   A *cash basis* income statement for December 2019 reports insurance expense of $2,400, as shown in Exhibit 3.3. The cash basis income statements for years 2020 and 2021 report no insurance expense. The cash basis balance sheet never reports a prepaid insurance asset because it is immediately expensed. Also, cash basis income for 2019–2021 does not match the cost of insurance with the insurance benefits received for those years and months.

 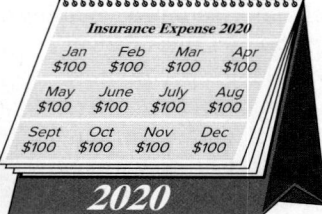 

Point: Annual income statements for Exhibit 3.3 follow:

Cash Basis	2019		2020	2021
Revenues.......	$	#	$#	$#
Insurance exp. ...	$2,400		$0	$0

Recognizing Revenues and Expenses

We divide a company's activities into time periods, but not all activities are complete when financial statements are prepared. Thus, adjustments are required to get proper account balances.

We use two principles in the adjusting process: revenue recognition and expense recognition.

- **Revenue recognition principle** requires that revenue be recorded when goods or services are provided to customers and at an amount expected to be received from customers. Adjustments ensure revenue is recognized (reported) in the time period when those services and products are provided.

- **Expense recognition** (or matching) **principle** requires that expenses be recorded in the same accounting period as the revenues that are recognized as a result of those expenses.

Point: Recording revenue early overstates current-period income; recording it late understates current-period income.

Point: Recording expense early understates current-period income; recording it late overstates current-period income.

Ethical Risk

Clawbacks from Accounting Fraud   Former executives at **Saba Software**, a cloud-based talent management system, were charged with accounting fraud by the SEC for falsifying revenue to boost income. This alleged overstatement of income led to a payback of millions of dollars to the company by the former CEO and former CFO. See SEC release 2015–28. ∎

©Marco Marchi/Getty Images

Framework for Adjustments

Four types of adjustments exist for transactions and events that extend over more than one period.

⟨ **Deferral of expense** ⟩   ⟨ **Deferral of revenue** ⟩   ⟨ **Accrued expense** ⟩   ⟨ **Accrued revenue** ⟩

Adjustments are made using a 3-step process, as shown in Exhibit 3.4.

EXHIBIT 3.4

Three-Step Process for Adjusting Entries

> **Step 1:**   Determine what the current account balance *equals*.
>
> **Step 2:**   Determine what the current account balance *should equal*.
>
> **Step 3:**   Record an adjusting entry to get from step 1 to step 2.

Each **adjusting entry** made at the end of an accounting period reflects a transaction or event that is not yet recorded. An adjusting entry affects one or more income statement accounts *and* one or more balance sheet accounts (but never the Cash account).

DEFERRAL OF EXPENSE

Prepaid expenses, or *deferred expenses,* are assets *paid for* in advance of receiving their benefits. When these assets are used, those advance payments become expenses.

P1

Prepare adjusting entries for deferral of expenses.

Framework   Adjusting entries for prepaid expenses increase expenses and decrease assets, as shown in the T-accounts of Exhibit 3.5. This adjustment shows the using up of prepaid expenses. To demonstrate accounting for prepaid expenses, we look at prepaid insurance, supplies, and depreciation. In each case we decrease an asset (balance sheet) account and increase an expense (income statement) account.

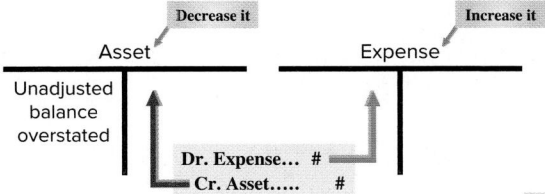

EXHIBIT 3.5

Adjusting for Prepaid Expenses (decrease an asset and record an expense)

Prepaid Insurance

Prepaid insurance expires with time. We use our three-step process.

Step 1:   We determine that the current balance of FastForward's prepaid insurance is equal to its $2,400 payment for 24 months of insurance benefits that began on December 1, 2019.

Step 2:   As time passes, the benefits of the insurance gradually expire and a portion of the Prepaid Insurance asset becomes expense. For instance, one month's insurance coverage expires by December 31, 2019. This expense is $100, or 1/24 of $2,400, which leaves $2,300.

Insurance		
Dec. 1	Pay insurance premium and record asset	
	Prepaid Insurance.......	2,400
	Cash........................	2,400
	Two-Year Insurance Policy Total cost is $2,400 Monthly cost is $100	
Dec. 31	Coverage expires and record expense	

Step 3: The adjusting entry to record this expense and reduce the asset, along with T-account postings, follows.

Assets = Liabilities + Equity
−100   −100

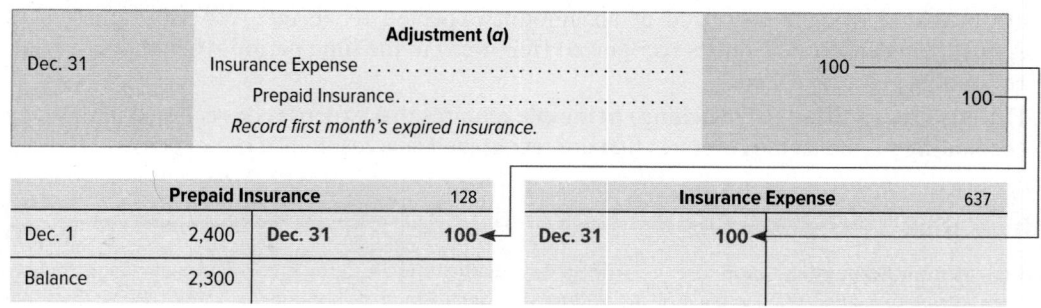

Adjustment (a)		
Dec. 31	Insurance Expense	100
	Prepaid Insurance...............................	100
	Record first month's expired insurance.	

Prepaid Insurance			128		Insurance Expense		637
Dec. 1	2,400	Dec. 31	100	Dec. 31	100		
Balance	2,300						

Explanation   After adjusting and posting, the $100 balance in Insurance Expense and the $2,300 balance in Prepaid Insurance are ready for reporting in financial statements. *Not* making the adjustment on or before December 31 would

- Understate expenses by $100 for the December income statement.
- Overstate prepaid insurance (assets) by $100 in the December 31 balance sheet.

The following highlights the adjustment for prepaid insurance.

Before Adjustment	Adjustment	After Adjustment
Prepaid Insurance = $2,400	**Deduct $100 from Prepaid Insurance** **Add $100 to Insurance Expense**	**Prepaid Insurance = $2,300**
Reports $2,400 policy for 24 months' coverage.	Record current month's $100 insurance expense and $100 reduction in prepaid.	Reports $2,300 in coverage for remaining 23 months.

Supplies

We count supplies at period-end and make an adjusting entry.

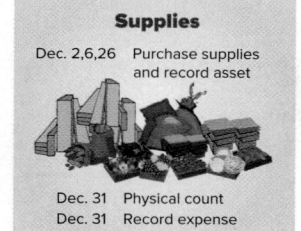

Supplies

Dec. 2,6,26   Purchase supplies
and record asset

Dec. 31   Physical count
Dec. 31   Record expense

Step 1:   FastForward purchased $9,720 of supplies in December, some of which were used during that same month. When financial statements are prepared at December 31, the cost of supplies used during December is expensed.

Step 2:   When FastForward computes (physically counts) its remaining unused supplies at December 31, it finds $8,670 of supplies remaining of the $9,720 total supplies. The $1,050 difference between these two amounts is December's supplies expense.

Step 3:   The adjusting entry to record this expense and reduce the Supplies asset account, along with T-account postings, follows.

Assets = Liabilities + Equity
−1,050   −1,050

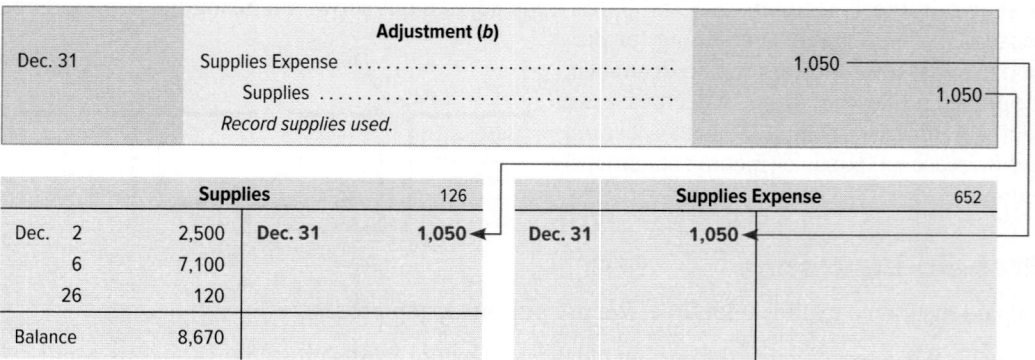

Adjustment (b)		
Dec. 31	Supplies Expense	1,050
	Supplies	1,050
	Record supplies used.	

Supplies			126		Supplies Expense		652
Dec. 2	2,500	Dec. 31	1,050	Dec. 31	1,050		
6	7,100						
26	120						
Balance	8,670						

Explanation   The balance of the Supplies account is $8,670 after posting—equaling the cost of the remaining supplies. *Not* making the adjustment on or before December 31 would

- Understate expenses by $1,050 for the December income statement.
- Overstate supplies by $1,050 in the December 31 balance sheet.

The following highlights the adjustment for supplies.

Before Adjustment	Adjustment	After Adjustment
Supplies = $9,720	**Deduct $1,050 from Supplies** **Add $1,050 to Supplies Expense**	**Supplies = $8,670**
Reports $9,720 in supplies.	Record $1,050 in supplies used and $1,050 as supplies expense.	Reports $8,670 in supplies.

Other Prepaid Expenses

Other prepaid expenses, such as Prepaid Rent and Prepaid Advertising, are accounted for exactly as insurance and supplies are.

Some prepaid expenses are both paid for *and* fully used up within a single period. One example is when a company pays monthly rent on the first day of each month. In this case, we record the cash paid with a debit to Rent Expense instead of an asset account.

■ Decision Maker

Investor A publisher signs an Olympic skier to write a book. The company pays the skier $500,000 to sign plus future book royalties. A note to the company's financial statements says that "prepaid expenses include $500,000 in author signing fees to be matched against future expected sales." How does this affect your analysis? ■ *Answer:* Prepaid expenses are assets paid for in advance of receiving their benefits—they are expensed as they are used up. As an investor, you are concerned about the risk of future book sales. The riskier the likelihood of future book sales is, the more likely your analysis is to treat the $500,000, or a portion of it, as an expense, not a prepaid expense (asset).

©Don Hammond/Design Pics

Depreciation

A special category of prepaid expenses is **plant assets,** which are long-term tangible assets used to produce and sell products and services. Plant assets provide benefits for more than one period. Examples of plant assets are buildings, machines, vehicles, and fixtures. All plant assets (excluding land) eventually wear out or become less useful. The costs of plant assets are gradually reported as expenses in the income statement over the assets' useful lives (benefit periods). **Depreciation** is the allocation of the costs of these assets over their expected useful lives. Depreciation expense is recorded with an adjusting entry similar to that for other prepaid expenses.

Point: Plant assets are also called *Plant & Equipment* or *Property, Plant & Equipment (PP&E).*

Point: Depreciation does not necessarily measure decline in market value.

Point: An asset's expected value at the end of its useful life is called *salvage value.*

Step 1: FastForward purchased equipment for $26,000 in early December to use in earning revenue. This equipment's cost must be depreciated.

Step 2: The equipment is expected to have a useful life (benefit period) of five years and to be worth about $8,000 at the end of five years. This means the *net* cost of this equipment over its useful life is $18,000 ($26,000 − $8,000). FastForward depreciates it using **straight-line depreciation,** which allocates equal amounts of the asset's net cost to depreciation during its useful life. Dividing the $18,000 net cost by the 60 months (5 years) in the asset's useful life gives a monthly cost of $300 ($18,000/60).

Step 3: The adjusting entry to record monthly depreciation expense, along with T-account postings, follows.

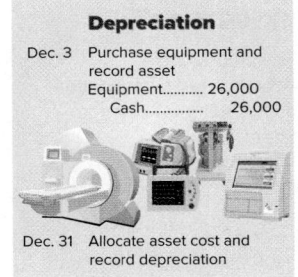

Depreciation

Dec. 3 Purchase equipment and record asset
Equipment........... 26,000
Cash................ 26,000

Dec. 31 Allocate asset cost and record depreciation

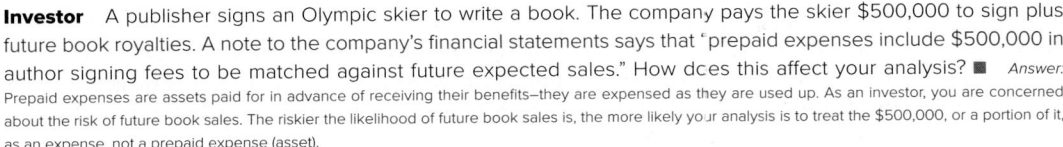

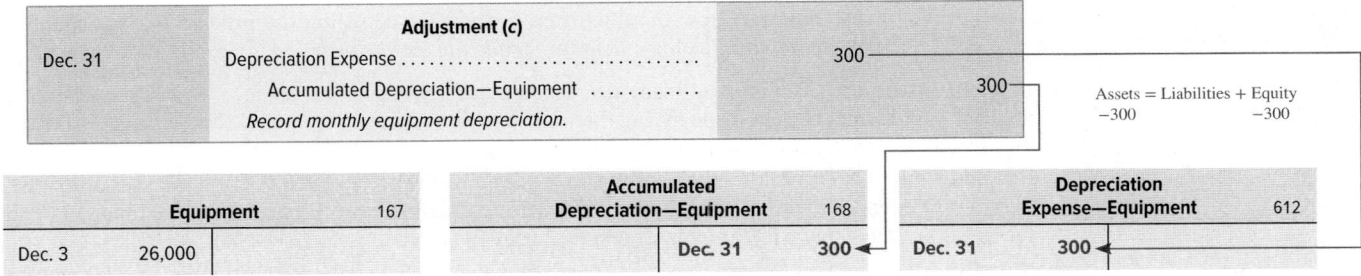

Adjustment (c)		
Dec. 31	Depreciation Expense	300
	Accumulated Depreciation—Equipment	300
	Record monthly equipment depreciation.	

Assets = Liabilities + Equity
−300 −300

Equipment		167
Dec. 3	26,000	

Accumulated Depreciation—Equipment		168
	Dec. 31	300

Depreciation Expense—Equipment		612
Dec. 31	300	

Explanation After posting the adjustment, the Equipment account ($26,000) minus its Accumulated Depreciation ($300) account equals the $25,700 net cost. The $300 balance in the

Depreciation Expense account is reported in the December income statement. *Not* making the adjustment at December 31 would

- Understate expenses by $300 for the December income statement.
- Overstate assets by $300 in the December 31 balance sheet.

The following highlights the adjustment for depreciation.

Before Adjustment	Adjustment	After Adjustment
Equipment, net = $26,000	Deduct $300 from Equipment, net Add $300 to Depreciation Expense	Equipment, net = $25,700
Reports $26,000 in equipment.	Record $300 in depreciation and $300 as accumulated depreciation.	Reports $25,700 in equipment, net of accumulated depreciation.

Point: Accumulated Depreciation has a normal credit balance; it decreases the asset's reported value.

Accumulated Depreciation is a separate contra account. A **contra account** is an account linked with another account, it has an opposite normal balance, and it is reported as a subtraction from that other account's balance. FastForward's contra account of Accumulated Depreciation—Equipment is subtracted from the Equipment account in the balance sheet.

The Accumulated Depreciation contra account includes total depreciation expense for all prior periods for which the asset was used. To demonstrate, on February 28, 2020, after three months of adjusting entries, the Equipment and Accumulated Depreciation accounts appear as in Exhibit 3.6. The $900 balance in the Accumulated Depreciation account is subtracted from its related $26,000 asset cost. The difference ($25,100) between these two balances is called **book value,** or *net amount,* which is the asset's costs minus its accumulated depreciation.

Point: The net cost of equipment is also called *depreciable basis.*

EXHIBIT 3.6

Accounts after Three Months of Depreciation Adjustments

Equipment		167
Dec. 3	26,000	

Accumulated Depreciation—Equipment		168
	Dec. 31	300
	Jan. 31	300
	Feb. 28	300
	Balance	**900**

These account balances are reported in the assets section of the February 28 balance sheet in Exhibit 3.7. This presentation shows the full cost of assets and accumulated depreciation.

EXHIBIT 3.7

Equipment and Accumulated Depreciation on February 28 Balance Sheet

Assets (at February 28, 2020)		
Cash		$_____
⋮		
Equipment	$26,000	
Less accumulated depreciation	900	25,100
Total Assets		$_____

← Commonly titled *Equipment, net*

NEED-TO-KNOW **3-1**

Prepaid Expenses

P1

For each separate case below, follow the three-step process for adjusting the prepaid asset account at December 31. *Assume no other adjusting entries are made during the year.*

1. **Prepaid Insurance.** The Prepaid Insurance account has a $5,000 debit balance to start the year, and no insurance payments were made during the year. A review of insurance policies shows that $1,000 of unexpired insurance remains at its December 31 year-end.

2. **Prepaid Rent.** On October 1 of the current year, the company prepaid $12,000 for one year of rent for facilities being occupied from that day forward. The company debited Prepaid Rent and credited Cash for $12,000. December 31 year-end statements must be prepared.

3. **Supplies.** The Supplies account has a $1,000 debit balance to start the year. Supplies of $2,000 were purchased during the current year and debited to the Supplies account. A December 31 physical count shows $500 of supplies remaining.

4. Accumulated Depreciation. The company has only one fixed asset (equipment) that it purchased at the start of this year. That asset had cost $38,000, had an estimated life of 10 years, and is expected to be valued at $8,000 at the end of the 10-year life. December 31 year-end statements must be prepared.

Solution

1. Step 1: Prepaid Insurance equals $5,000 (before adjustment)
Step 2: Prepaid Insurance should equal $1,000 (the unexpired part)
Step 3: Adjusting entry to get from step 1 to step 2

Dec. 31	Insurance Expense...	4,000	
	Prepaid Insurance..		4,000
	Record expired insurance coverage ($5,000 − $1,000).		

2. Step 1: Prepaid Rent equals $12,000 (before adjustment)
Step 2: Prepaid Rent should equal $9,000 (the unexpired part)*
Step 3: Adjusting entry to get from step 1 to step 2

Dec. 31	Rent Expense	3,000	
	Prepaid Rent		3,000
	Record expired prepaid rent. *$12,000 − $3,000 = $9,000, where $3,000 is from: ($12,000/12 months) × 3 months		

3. Step 1: Supplies equal $3,000 (from $1,000 + $2,000; before adjustment)
Step 2: Supplies should equal $500 (what's left)
Step 3: Adjusting entry to get from step 1 to step 2*

Dec. 31	Supplies Expense..	2,500	
	Supplies...		2,500
	*Record supplies used. *$1,000 + $2,000 purchased − $ **2,500** supplies used = $500 remaining*		

4. Step 1: Accumulated Depreciation equals $0 (before adjustment)
Step 2: Accumulated Depreciation should equal $3,000 (after current-period depreciation of $3,000)*
Step 3: Adjusting entry to get from step 1 to step 2

Dec. 31	Depreciation Expense—Equipment..................................	3,000	
	Accumulated Depreciation—Equipment.............................		3,000
	Record depreciation for period. *($38,000 − $8,000)/10 years		

> **Do More: QS 3-5, QS 3-6, QS 3-7, QS 3-8, QS 3-9**

DEFERRAL OF REVENUE

Unearned revenue is cash received in advance of providing products and services. Unearned revenues, or *deferred revenues,* are liabilities. When cash is accepted, an obligation to provide products or services is accepted.

P2

Prepare adjusting entries for deferral of revenues.

Framework As products or services are provided, the liability decreases and the unearned revenues become *earned* revenues. Adjusting entries for unearned revenue decrease the unearned revenue (balance sheet) account and increase the revenue (income statement) account, as shown in Exhibit 3.8.

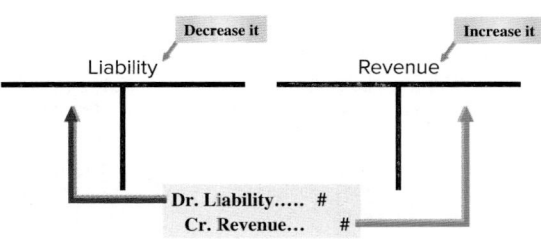

EXHIBIT 3.8

Adjusting for Unearned Revenues (decrease a liability and record revenue)

Point: To *defer* is to postpone. We postpone reporting amounts received as revenues until the product or service is provided.

Unearned revenues are common in sporting and concert events. When the **Boston Celtics** receive cash from advance ticket sales, they record it in an unearned revenue account called *Deferred Game Revenues.* The Celtics record revenue as games are played.

Unearned Consulting Revenue

FastForward has unearned revenues. The company agreed on December 26 to provide consulting services to a client for 60 days for a fixed fee of $3,000.

Step 1: On December 26, the client paid the 60-day fee in advance, covering the period December 27 to February 24. The entry to record the cash received in advance is

Assets = Liabilities + Equity
+3,000   +3,000

Dec. 26	Cash	3,000	
	Unearned Consulting Revenue		3,000
	Received advance payment for services over the next 60 days.		

Unearned Revenues

Dec. 26   Cash received in advance and record liability

Thanks for cash in advance. I'll work now through Feb. 24

Dec. 31   Provided 5 days of services and record revenue

This advance payment increases cash and creates a liability to do consulting work over the next 60 days (5 days this year and 55 days next year).

Step 2: As time passes, FastForward earns this payment through consulting. By December 31, it has provided five days' service and earned 5/60 of the $3,000 unearned revenue. This amounts to $250 ($3,000 × 5/60). The *revenue recognition principle* requires that $250 of unearned revenue be reported as revenue on the December income statement.

Step 3: The adjusting entry to reduce the liability account and recognize earned revenue, along with T-account postings, follows.

Assets = Liabilities + Equity
−250   +250

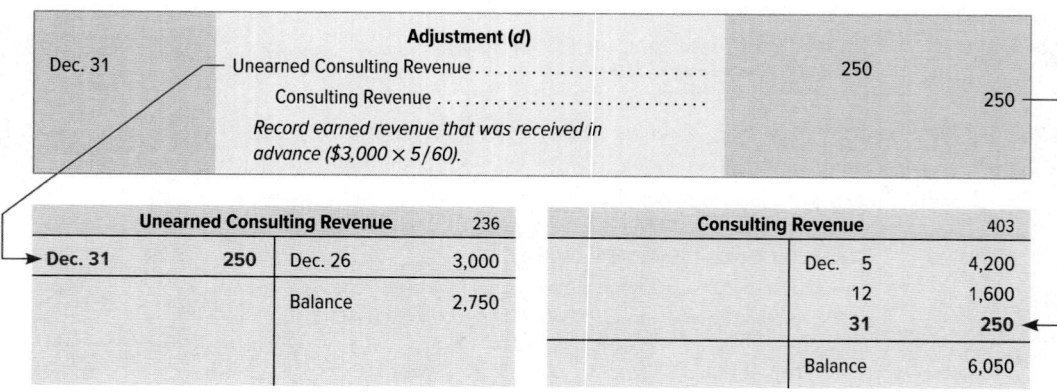

	Adjustment (d)		
Dec. 31	Unearned Consulting Revenue	250	
	Consulting Revenue		250
	Record earned revenue that was received in advance ($3,000 × 5/60).		

Unearned Consulting Revenue			236
Dec. 31	250	Dec. 26	3,000
		Balance	2,750

Consulting Revenue			403
		Dec. 5	4,200
		12	1,600
		31	250
		Balance	6,050

Explanation   The adjusting entry transfers $250 from unearned revenue (a liability account) to a revenue account. *Not* making the adjustment

- Understates revenue by $250 in the December income statement.
- Overstates unearned revenue by $250 on the December 31 balance sheet.

The following highlights the adjustment for unearned revenue.

Before Adjustment	Adjustment	After Adjustment
Unearned Consulting Revenue = $3,000	**Deduct $250 from Unearned Consulting Revenue** **Add $250 to Consulting Revenue**	**Unearned Consulting Revenue = $2,750**
Reports $3,000 in unearned revenue for consulting services promised for 60 days ($50 per day).	Record 5 days of earned consulting revenue, which is 5/60 of unearned amount.	Reports $2,750 in unearned revenue for consulting services owed over next 55 days (55 days × $50 = $2,750).

For each separate case below, follow the three-step process for adjusting the unearned revenue liability account at December 31. *Assume no other adjusting entries are made during the year.*

a. Unearned Rent Revenue. The company collected $24,000 rent in advance on September 1, debiting Cash and crediting Unearned Rent Revenue. The tenant was paying 12 months' rent in advance and moved in on September 1.

b. Unearned Services Revenue. The company charges $100 per month to spray a house for insects. A customer paid $600 on November 1 in advance for six treatments, which was recorded with a debit to Cash and a credit to Unearned Services Revenue. At year-end, the company has applied two treatments for the customer.

Solution

a. Step 1: Unearned Rent Revenue equals $24,000 (before adjustment)
Step 2: Unearned Rent Revenue should equal $16,000 (current-period earned revenue is $8,000*)
Step 3: Adjusting entry to get from step 1 to step 2

Dec. 31	Unearned Rent Revenue........................	8,000	
	Rent Revenue		8,000
	Record earned portion of rent received in advance.		
	*($24,000/12 months) × 4 months' rental usage		

b. Step 1: Unearned Services Revenue equals $600 (before adjustment)
Step 2: Unearned Services Revenue should equal $400 (current-period earned revenue is $200*)
Step 3: Adjusting entry to get from step 1 to step 2

Dec. 31	Unearned Services Revenue......................	200	
	Services Revenue		200
	Record earned portion of revenue received in advance.		
	*$100 × 2 treatments = Services revenue		

Do More: QS 3-10, QS 3-11

ACCRUED EXPENSE

Accrued expenses are costs that are incurred in a period that are both unpaid and unrecorded. Accrued expenses are reported on the income statement for the period when incurred.

Framework   Adjusting entries for recording accrued expenses increase the expense (income statement) account and increase a liability (balance sheet) account, as shown in Exhibit 3.9. This adjustment recognizes expenses incurred in a period but not yet paid. Common examples of accrued expenses are salaries, interest, rent, and taxes. We use salaries and interest to show how to adjust accounts for accrued expenses.

P3

Prepare adjusting entries for accrued expenses.

EXHIBIT 3.9

Adjusting for Accrued Expenses (increase a liability and record an expense)

Point: Accrued expenses are also called *accrued liabilities.*

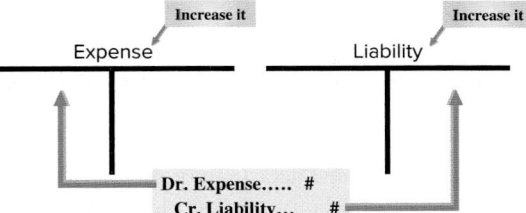

Accrued Salaries Expense

FastForward's employee earns $70 per day, or $350 for a five-day workweek beginning on Monday and ending on Friday.

Step 1:   Its employee is paid every two weeks on Friday. On December 12 and 26, the wages are paid, recorded in the journal, and posted to the ledger.

Step 2:   The calendar in Exhibit 3.10 shows three working days after the December 26 payday (29, 30, and 31). This means the employee has earned three days' salary by the close of business on Wednesday, December 31, yet this salary cost has not been paid or recorded. FastForward must report the added expense and liability for unpaid salary from December 29, 30, and 31.

EXHIBIT 3.10

Salary Accrual and Paydays

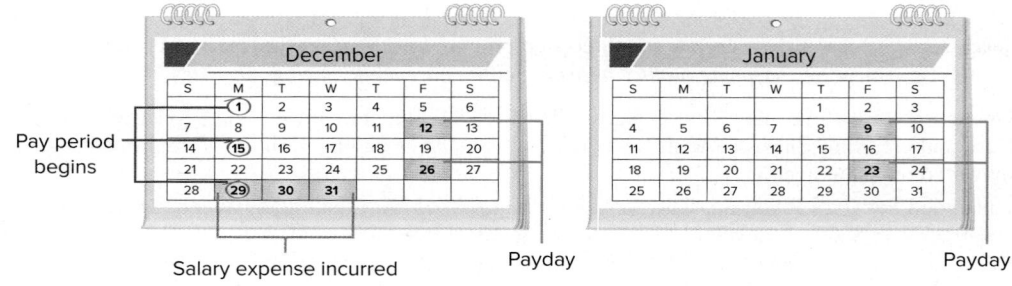

Step 3:   The adjusting entry for accrued salaries, along with T-account postings, follows.

Assets = Liabilities + Equity
  +210   −210

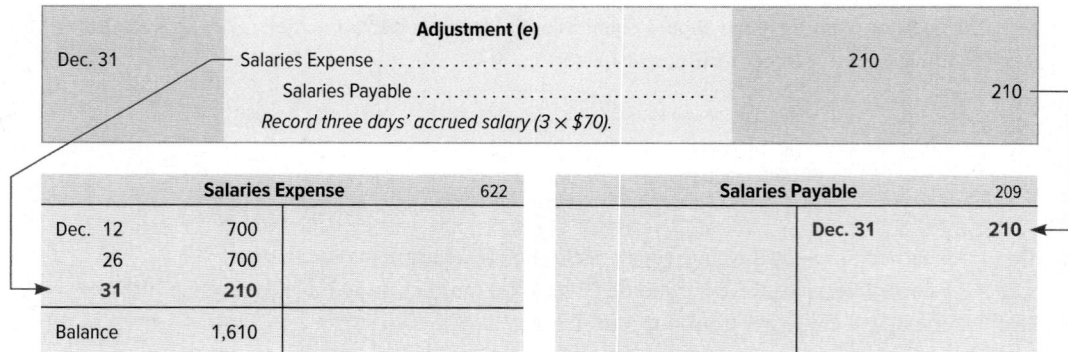

	Adjustment (e)	
Dec. 31	Salaries Expense	210
	Salaries Payable	210
	Record three days' accrued salary (3 × $70).	

	Salaries Expense			Salaries Payable	
		622			209
Dec. 12	700			Dec. 31	210
26	700				
31	210				
Balance	1,610				

Explanation   Salaries expense of $1,610 is reported on the December income statement, and $210 of salaries payable (liability) is reported in the balance sheet. *Not* making the adjustment

- Understates salaries expense by $210 in the December income statement.
- Understates salaries payable by $210 on the December 31 balance sheet.

The following highlights the adjustment for salaries incurred.

Before Adjustment	Adjustment	After Adjustment
Salaries Payable = $0	**Add $210 to Salaries Payable** **Add $210 to Salaries Expense**	**Salaries Payable = $210**
Reports $0 from employee salaries incurred but not yet paid in cash.	Record 3 days' salaries owed, but not yet paid, at $70 per day.	Reports $210 salaries payable to employee but not yet paid.

Accrued Interest Expense

©Plus One Pix/Alamy Stock Photo

Point: Interest computations use a 360-day year, called the *bankers' rule*.

Companies accrue interest expense on notes payable (loans) and other long-term liabilities at the end of a period. Interest expense is incurred as time passes. Unless interest is paid on the last day of an accounting period, we need to adjust for interest expense incurred but not yet paid. This means we must accrue interest cost from the most recent payment date up to the end of the period. The formula for computing accrued interest is

Principal amount owed × Annual interest rate × Fraction of year since last payment

If a company has a $6,000 loan from a bank at 5% annual interest, then 30 days' accrued interest expense is $25—computed as $6,000 × 0.05 × 30/360. The adjusting entry debits Interest Expense for $25 and credits Interest Payable for $25.

Future Cash Payment of Accrued Expenses

Accrued expenses at the end of one accounting period result in *cash payment* in a *future period(s)*. Recall that FastForward recorded accrued salaries of $210. On January 9, the first payday of the next period, the following entry settles the accrued liability (salaries payable) and records salaries expense for seven days of work in January.

Jan. 9	Salaries Payable (3 days at $70 per day)	210	
	Salaries Expense (7 days at $70 per day)	490	
	Cash		700
	Paid two weeks' salary including three days accrued.		

Assets = Liabilities + Equity
−700   −210   −490

The $210 debit is the payment of the liability for the three days' salary accrued on December 31. The $490 debit records the salary for January's first seven working days (including the New Year's Day holiday) as an expense of the new accounting period. The $700 credit records the total amount of cash paid to the employee.

For each separate case below, follow the three-step process for adjusting the accrued expense account at December 31. *Assume no other adjusting entries are made during the year.*

a. Salaries Payable. At year-end, salaries expense of $5,000 has been incurred by the company but is not yet paid to employees.

b. Interest Payable. At its December 31 year-end, the company holds a mortgage payable that has incurred $1,000 in annual interest that is neither recorded nor paid. The company intends to pay the interest on January 3 of the next year.

NEED-TO-KNOW 3-3

Accrued Expenses

P3

Solution

a. Step 1: Salaries Payable equals $0 (before adjustment)
Step 2: Salaries Payable should equal $5,000 (not yet recorded)
Step 3: Adjusting entry to get from step 1 to step 2

Dec. 31	Salaries Expense	5,000	
	Salaries Payable		5,000
	Record employee salaries earned but not yet paid.		

b. Step 1: Interest Payable equals $0 (before adjustment)
Step 2: Interest Payable should equal $1,000 (not yet recorded)
Step 3: Adjusting entry to get from step 1 to step 2

Dec. 31	Interest Expense	1,000	
	Interest Payable		1,000
	Record interest incurred but not yet paid.		

Do More: QS 3-12, QS 3-13

ACCRUED REVENUE

Accrued revenues are revenues earned in a period that are both unrecorded and not yet received in cash (or other assets). An example is a technician who bills customers after the job is done. If one-third of a job is complete by the end of a period, then the technician must record one-third of the expected billing as revenue in that period—even though there is no billing or collection.

P4

Prepare adjusting entries for accrued revenues.

Framework The adjusting entries for accrued revenues increase a revenue (income statement) account and increase an asset (balance sheet) account, as shown in Exhibit 3.11. Accrued revenues usually come from services, products, interest, and rent. We use service fees and interest to show how to adjust for accrued revenues.

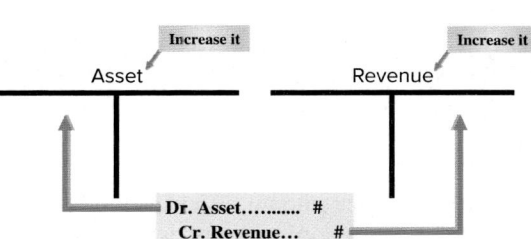

EXHIBIT 3.11

Adjusting for Accrued Revenues (increase an asset and record revenue)

Point: Accrued revenues are also called *accrued assets.*

Accrued Services Revenue

Accrued revenues are recorded when adjusting entries are made at the end of the accounting period. These accrued revenues are earned but unrecorded because either the buyer has not yet paid or the seller has not yet billed the buyer. FastForward provides an example.

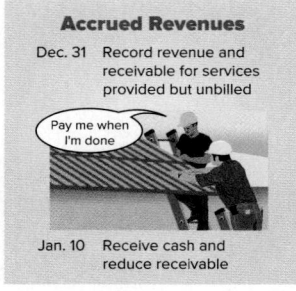

Accrued Revenues

Dec. 31   Record revenue and receivable for services provided but unbilled

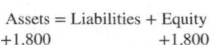

Pay me when I'm done

Jan. 10   Receive cash and reduce receivable

Step 1:   In the second week of December, FastForward agreed to provide 30 days of consulting services to a fitness club for a fixed fee of $2,700 (or $90 per day). FastForward will provide services from December 12 through January 10, or 30 days of service. The club agrees to pay FastForward $2,700 on January 10 when the service is complete.

Step 2:   At December 31, 20 days of services have already been provided. Because the contracted services have not yet been entirely provided, FastForward has neither billed the club nor recorded the services already provided. Still, FastForward has earned two-thirds of the 30-day fee, or $1,800 ($2,700 × 20/30). The *revenue recognition principle* requires FastForward to report the $1,800 on the December income statement. The balance sheet reports that the club owes FastForward $1,800.

Step 3:   The adjusting entry for accrued services, along with T-account postings, follows.

Assets = Liabilities + Equity
+1,800   +1,800

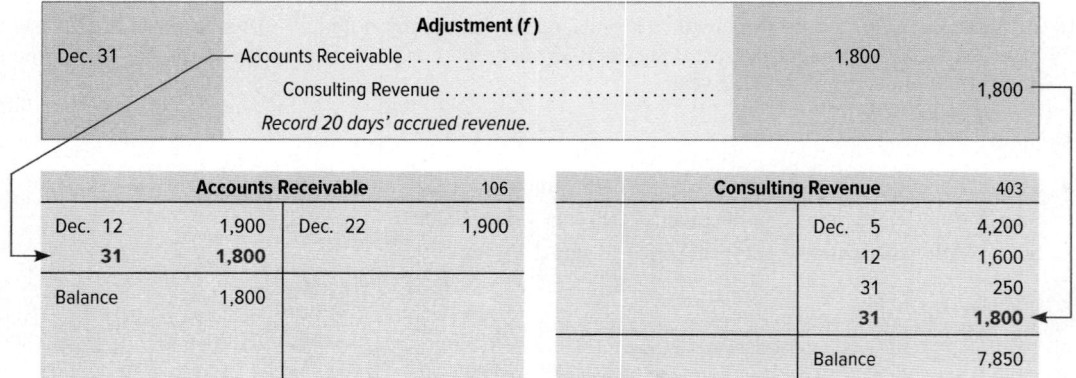

	Adjustment (*f*)	
Dec. 31	Accounts Receivable	1,800
	Consulting Revenue	1,800
	Record 20 days' accrued revenue.	

Accounts Receivable			106
Dec. 12	1,900	Dec. 22	1,900
31	**1,800**		
Balance	1,800		

Consulting Revenue		403
Dec. 5		4,200
12		1,600
31		250
31		**1,800**
Balance		7,850

Example: What is the adjusting entry if the 30-day consulting period began on December 22? *Answer:* One-third of the fee is earned:
Accounts Receivable 900
  Consulting Revenue   900

Explanation   Accounts receivable are reported on the balance sheet at $1,800, and the $7,850 total of consulting revenue is reported on the income statement. *Not* making the adjustment

- Understates consulting revenue by $1,800 in the December income statement.
- Understates accounts receivable by $1,800 on the December 31 balance sheet.

The following highlights the adjustment for accrued revenue.

Before Adjustment	Adjustment	After Adjustment
Accounts Receivable = $0	Add $1,800 to Accounts Receivable Add $1,800 to Consulting Revenue	Accounts Receivable = $1,800
Reports $0 from revenue earned but not yet received in cash.	Record 20 days of earned revenue, which is 20/30 of total contract.	Reports $1,800 in accounts receivable from services provided.

Accrued Interest Revenue

If a company is holding notes receivable that produce interest revenue, we must adjust the accounts to record any earned and yet uncollected interest revenue. The adjusting entry is similar to the one for accruing services revenue. Specifically, debit Interest Receivable (asset) and credit Interest Revenue.

Future Cash Receipt of Accrued Revenues

Accrued revenues at the end of one accounting period result in *cash receipts* in a *future period(s)*. Recall that FastForward made an adjusting entry for $1,800 to record 20 days' accrued revenue earned from its consulting contract. When FastForward receives $2,700 cash on January 10 for the entire contract amount, it makes the following entry to remove the accrued asset (accounts receivable) and record revenue earned in January. The $2,700 debit is the cash received. The $1,800 credit is the removal of the receivable, and the $900 credit is revenue earned in January.

Jan. 10	Cash	2,700	
	Accounts Receivable (20 days at $90 per day)		1,800
	Consulting Revenue (10 days at $90 per day)		900
	Received cash for accrued asset and recorded earned		
	consulting revenue for January.		

Assets = Liabilities + Equity
+2,700   +900
−1,800

 **Decision Maker**

Loan Officer   The owner of a home theater store applies for a business loan. The store's financial statements reveal large increases in current-year revenues and income. Increases are due to a promotion that let consumers buy now and pay nothing until January 1 of next year. The store recorded these sales as accrued revenue. Does your analysis raise any concerns? ■   *Answer:* While increased revenues and income are fine, your concern is with collectibility of these promotional sales. If the store sold products to customers with poor records of paying bills, then collectibility of these sales is low. Your analysis must assess this possibility and estimate losses.

©Yin Yang/Getty Images

For each separate case below, follow the three-step process for adjusting the accrued revenue account at December 31. *Assume no other adjusting entries are made during the year.*

a. Accounts Receivable. At year-end, the company has completed services of $1,000 for a client, but the client has not yet been billed for those services.

b. Interest Receivable.   At year-end, the company has earned, but not yet recorded, $500 of interest earned from its investments in government bonds.

NEED-TO-KNOW 3-4

Accrued Revenues

P4

Solution

a. Step 1: Accounts Receivable equals $0 (before adjustment)
Step 2: Accounts Receivable should equal $1,000 (not yet recorded)
Step 3: Adjusting entry to get from step 1 to step 2

Dec. 31	Accounts Receivable	1,000	
	Services Revenue		1,000
	Record services revenue earned but not yet received.		

b. Step 1: Interest Receivable equals $0 (before adjustment)
Step 2: Interest Receivable should equal $500 (not yet recorded)
Step 3: Adjusting entry to get from step 1 to step 2

Dec. 31	Interest Receivable	500	
	Interest Revenue		500
	Record interest earned but not yet received.		

Do More: QS 3-3, QS 3-14

Links to Financial Statements

Exhibit 3.12 summarizes the four adjustments. Each adjusting entry affects one or more income statement (revenue or expense) accounts *and* one or more balance sheet (asset or liability) accounts, but never the Cash account.

EXHIBIT 3.12

Summary of Adjustments and Financial Statement Links

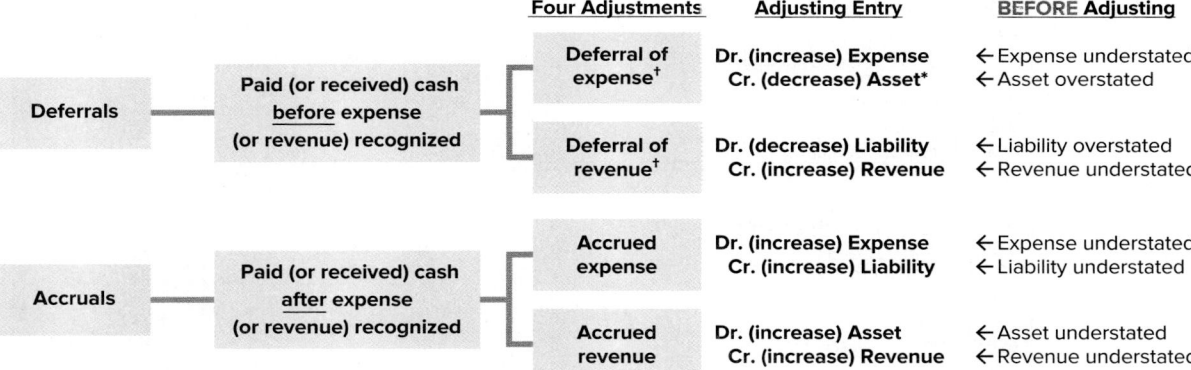

Four Adjustments		Adjusting Entry	BEFORE Adjusting
Deferrals	Paid (or received) cash **before** expense (or revenue) recognized	**Deferral of expense†**	Dr. (increase) Expense / Cr. (decrease) Asset*	← Expense understated / ← Asset overstated
		Deferral of revenue†	Dr. (decrease) Liability / Cr. (increase) Revenue	← Liability overstated / ← Revenue understated
Accruals	Paid (or received) cash **after** expense (or revenue) recognized	**Accrued expense**	Dr. (increase) Expense / Cr. (increase) Liability	← Expense understated / ← Liability understated
		Accrued revenue	Dr. (increase) Asset / Cr. (increase) Revenue	← Asset understated / ← Revenue understated

*For depreciation, the credit is to Accumulated Depreciation (contra asset).
†Exhibit assumes that deferred expenses are initially recorded as assets and that deferred revenues are initially recorded as liabilities.

Information for some adjustments is not available until after the period-end. This means that some adjusting and closing entries are recorded later than, but dated as of, the last day of the period. One example is a company that receives a December utility bill on January 10. When it receives the bill, the company records the expense and the payable as of December 31. The income statement and balance sheet include these adjustments even though amounts were not known at period-end.

■ Decision Ethics

Financial Officer   At year-end, the president instructs you, the financial officer, not to record accrued expenses until next year because they will not be paid until then. The president also directs you to record in current-year sales a recent purchase order from a customer that requires merchandise to be delivered two weeks after the year-end. Your company would report a net income instead of a net loss if you follow these instructions. What do you do? ■ *Answer:* Omitting accrued expenses and recognizing revenue early mislead financial statement users. One action is to explain to the president what is required. If the president persists, you might talk to lawyers and any auditors involved.

TRIAL BALANCE AND FINANCIAL STATEMENTS

P5

Explain and prepare an adjusted trial balance.

Adjusted Trial Balance

An **unadjusted trial balance** is a list of accounts and balances *before* adjustments are recorded. An **adjusted trial balance** is a list of accounts and balances *after* adjusting entries have been recorded and posted to the ledger.

Exhibit 3.13 shows both the unadjusted and the adjusted trial balances for FastForward at December 31, 2019. The order of accounts in the trial balance usually matches the order in the chart of accounts. Several new accounts usually arise from adjusting entries.

Each adjustment (see middle columns) has a letter that links it to an adjusting entry explained earlier. Each amount in the Adjusted Trial Balance columns is computed by taking that account's amount from the Unadjusted Trial Balance columns and adding or subtracting any adjustment(s). To demonstrate, Supplies has a $9,720 Dr. balance in the unadjusted columns. Subtracting the $1,050 Cr. amount shown in the Adjustments columns equals an adjusted $8,670 Dr. balance for Supplies. An account can have more than one adjustment, such as for Consulting Revenue. Also, some accounts might not require adjustment for this period, such as Accounts Payable.

EXHIBIT 3.13

Unadjusted and Adjusted Trial Balances

*FAST**Forward**

Acct. No.	Account Title	Unadjusted Trial Balance Dr.	Unadjusted Trial Balance Cr.	Adjustments Dr.	Adjustments Cr.	Adjusted Trial Balance Dr.	Adjusted Trial Balance Cr.
		FASTFORWARD Trial Balances December 31, 2019					
101	Cash	$ 4,275				$ 4,275	
106	Accounts receivable	0		*(f)* $1,800		1,800	
126	Supplies	9,720			*(b)* $1,050	8,670	
128	Prepaid insurance	2,400			*(a)* 100	2,300	
167	Equipment	26,000				26,000	
168	Accumulated depreciation—Equip.		$ 0		*(c)* 300		$ 300
201	Accounts payable		6,200				6,200
209	Salaries payable		0		*(e)* 210		210
236	Unearned consulting revenue		3,000	*(d)* 250			2,750
307	Common stock		30,000				30,000
318	Retained earnings		0				0
319	Dividends	200				200	
403	Consulting revenue		5,800		*(d)* 250		7,850
					(f) 1,800		
406	Rental revenue		300				300
612	Depreciation expense—Equip.	0		*(c)* 300		300	
622	Salaries expense	1,400		*(e)* 210		1,610	
637	Insurance expense	0		*(a)* 100		100	
640	Rent expense	1,000				1,000	
652	Supplies expense	0		*(b)* 1,050		1,050	
690	Utilities expense	305				305	
	Totals	$45,300	$45,300	$3,710	$3,710	$47,610	$47,610

Preparing Financial Statements

We can prepare financial statements directly from information in the *adjusted* trial balance. Exhibit 3.14 shows how revenue and expense balances are transferred from the adjusted trial balance to the income statement (red lines). The net income and dividends amounts are then used to prepare the statement of retained earnings (black lines). Asset and liability balances are

P6

Prepare financial statements from an adjusted trial balance.

EXHIBIT 3.14

Preparing Financial Statements (Adjusted Trial Balance from Exhibit 3.13)

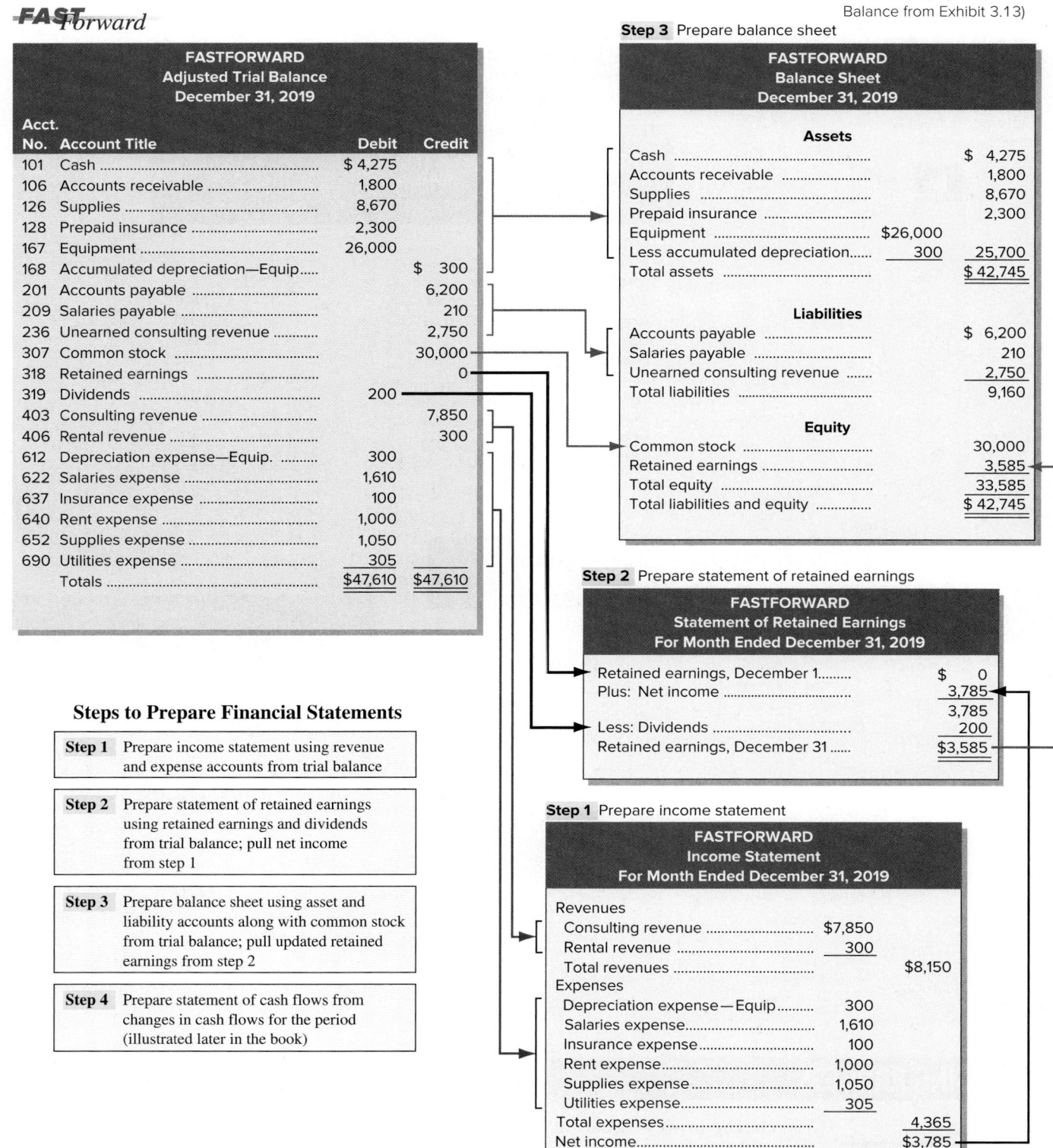

Steps to Prepare Financial Statements

Step 1	Prepare income statement using revenue and expense accounts from trial balance
Step 2	Prepare statement of retained earnings using retained earnings and dividends from trial balance; pull net income from step 1
Step 3	Prepare balance sheet using asset and liability accounts along with common stock from trial balance; pull updated retained earnings from step 2
Step 4	Prepare statement of cash flows from changes in cash flows for the period (illustrated later in the book)

then transferred to the balance sheet (blue lines). The ending retained earnings is computed in the statement of retained earnings and transferred to the balance sheet (green line).

We prepare financial statements in the following order: (1) income statement, (2) statement of retained earnings, and (3) balance sheet. This order makes sense because the balance sheet uses information from the statement of retained earnings, which in turn uses information from the income statement. The statement of cash flows is usually the final statement prepared.

Point: Each trial balance amount is used in only *one* financial statement.

NEED-TO-KNOW 3-5

Preparing Financial Statements from a Trial Balance

P6

Use the following adjusted trial balance of Magic Company to prepare its December 31 year-end (1) income statement, (2) statement of retained earnings, and (3) balance sheet (unclassified). The Retained Earnings account balance was $45,000 on December 31 of the *prior year*.

MAGIC COMPANY
Adjusted Trial Balance
December 31

Account Title	Debit	Credit
Cash	$ 13,000	
Accounts receivable	17,000	
Land	85,000	
Accounts payable		$ 12,000
Long-term notes payable		33,000
Common stock		30,000
Retained earnings		45,000
Dividends	20,000	
Fees earned		79,000
Salaries expense	56,000	
Office supplies expense	8,000	
Totals	$199,000	$199,000

Solution

Step 1

MAGIC COMPANY
Income Statement
For Year Ended December 31

Fees earned		$79,000
Expenses		
Salaries expense	$56,000	
Office supplies expense	8,000	
Total expenses		64,000
Net income		$15,000

Step 2

MAGIC COMPANY
Statement of Retained Earnings
For Year Ended December 31

Retained earnings, December 31 prior year-end	$45,000
Add: Net income	15,000
	60,000
Less: Dividends	20,000
Retained earnings, December 31 current year-end	$40,000

Step 3

MAGIC COMPANY
Balance Sheet
December 31

Assets	
Cash	$ 13,000
Accounts receivable	17,000
Land	85,000
Total assets	$115,000

Liabilities	
Accounts payable	$ 12,000
Long-term notes payable	33,000
Total liabilities	45,000

Equity	
Common stock	30,000
Retained earnings	40,000
Total equity	70,000
Total liabilities and equity	$115,000

Do More: QS 3-22, E 3-8, P 3-4

CLOSING PROCESS

P7

Describe and prepare closing entries.

The **closing process** occurs at the end of an accounting period *after* financial statements are completed. In the closing process we (1) identify accounts for closing, (2) record and post the closing entries, and (3) prepare a post-closing trial balance. The closing process has two purposes. First, it resets revenue, expense, and dividends account balances to zero at the end of each period (which updates the Retained Earnings account for inclusion on the balance sheet). This is done so that these accounts can properly measure income and dividends for the next period. Second, it helps summarize a period's revenues and expenses. This section explains the closing process.

Temporary and Permanent Accounts

Temporary accounts relate to one accounting period. They include all income statement accounts, the dividends account, and the **Income Summary** account. They are temporary because the accounts are opened at the beginning of a period, used to record transactions and events for that period, and then closed at the end of the period. **The closing process applies only to temporary accounts.**

Temporary Accounts (closed at period-end)	Permanent Accounts (not closed at period-end)
Revenues Expenses Dividends Income Summary	Assets Liabilities Common Stock Retained Earnings

Permanent accounts report on activities related to one or more future accounting periods. They include asset, liability, and equity accounts (all balance sheet accounts). **Permanent accounts are not closed each period and carry their ending balance into future periods.**

Recording Closing Entries

Closing entries transfer the end-of-period balances in revenue, expense, and dividends accounts to the permanent Retained Earnings account. Closing entries are necessary at the end of each period after financial statements are prepared because

- Revenue, expense, and dividends accounts must begin each period with zero balances.
- Retained Earnings must reflect prior periods' revenues, expenses, and dividends.

Point: If **Apple** did not make closing entries, prior-year revenue from iPhone sales would be included with current-year revenue.

An income statement reports revenues and expenses for a *specific accounting period*. Dividends are also for a specific accounting period. Because revenue, expense, and dividends accounts record information separately for each period, they must start each period with zero balances.

Exhibit 3.15 uses the adjusted account balances of FastForward (from the Adjusted Trial Balance columns of Exhibit 3.14 or from the left side of Exhibit 3.16) to show the four steps to close its temporary accounts.

①② To close revenue and expense accounts, we transfer their balances to Income Summary. **Income Summary is a temporary account only used for the closing process** that contains a credit for total revenues (and gains) and a debit for total expenses (and losses).

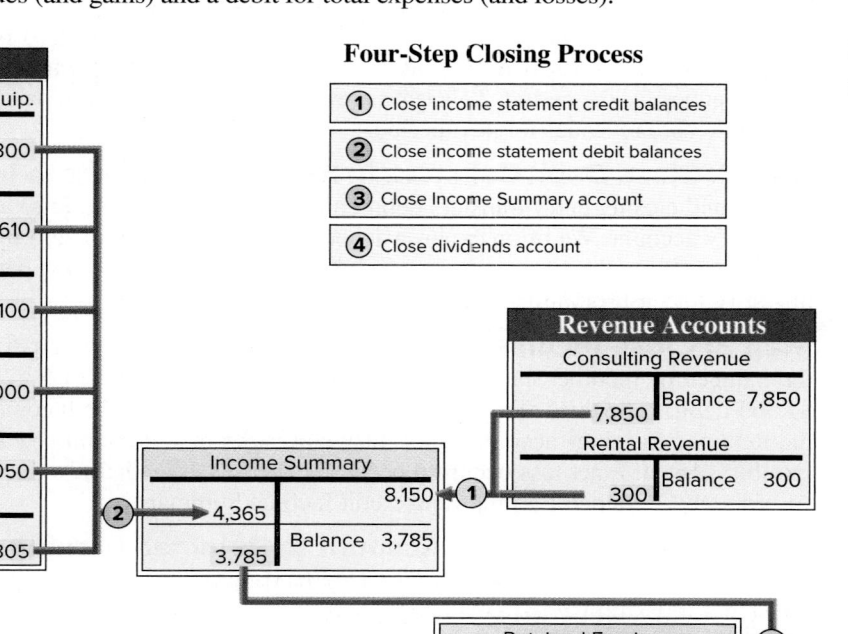

EXHIBIT 3.15

Four-Step Closing Process

Point: Retained Earnings is the only *permanent account* in Exhibit 3.15—meaning it is not closed, but it does have Income Summary closed to it.

③ The Income Summary balance, which equals net income or net loss, is transferred to the Retained Earnings account.

④ The Dividends account balance is transferred to the Retained Earnings account. After closing entries are posted, the revenue, expense, dividends, and Income Summary accounts have zero balances and are said to be *closed* or *cleared*.

Exhibit 3.16 shows the four closing journal entries to apply the closing process of Exhibit 3.15.

EXHIBIT 3.16

Preparing Closing Entries

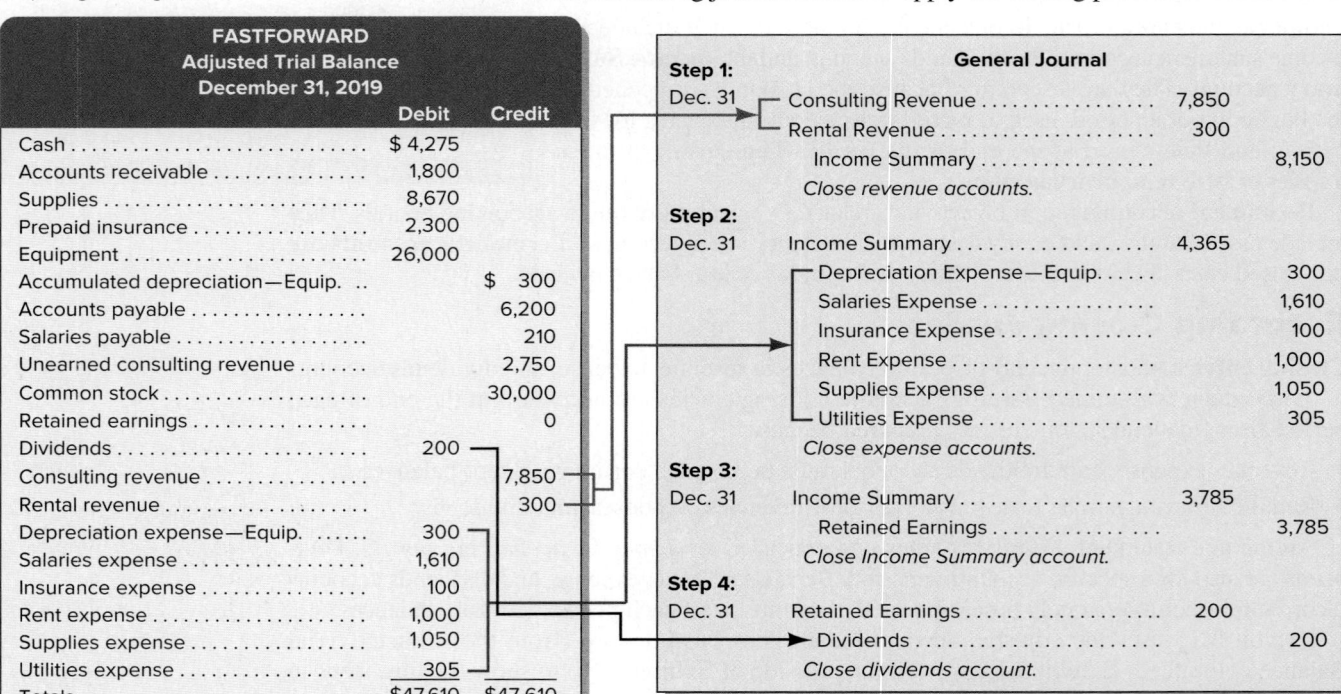

Step 1: Close Credit Balances in Revenue Accounts to Income Summary

The first closing entry transfers credit balances in revenue (and gain) accounts to the Income Summary account. We bring accounts with credit balances to zero by debiting them. For FastForward, this is step 1 in Exhibit 3.16. The $8,150 credit entry to Income Summary equals total revenues for the period. This leaves revenue accounts with zero balances, and they are now ready to record revenues for next period.

Step 2: Close Debit Balances in Expense Accounts to Income Summary

The second closing entry transfers debit balances in expense (and loss) accounts to the Income Summary account. We bring expense accounts' debit balances to zero by crediting them. With a balance of zero, these accounts are ready to record expenses for next period. This second closing entry for FastForward is step 2 in Exhibit 3.16.

Step 3: Close Income Summary to Retained Earnings

After steps 1 and 2, the balance of Income Summary equals December net income of $3,785 ($8,150 credit less $4,365 debit). The third closing entry transfers the balance of the Income Summary account to the Retained Earnings account. This entry closes the Income Summary account—see step 3 in Exhibit 3.16. (If a net loss occurred because expenses exceeded revenues, the third entry is reversed: debit Retained Earnings and credit Income Summary.)

Step 4: Close Dividends Account to Retained Earnings

The fourth closing entry transfers any debit balance in the Dividends account to the Retained Earnings account—see step 4 in Exhibit 3.16. This entry gives the Dividends account a zero balance, and the account is now ready to record next period's dividends.

Exhibit 3.17 shows the entire ledger of FastForward as of December 31 *after* adjusting and closing entries are posted. The temporary accounts (revenues, expenses, and dividends) have ending balances equal to zero.

EXHIBIT 3.17

General Ledger after the Closing Process for FastForward

Asset Accounts

Cash					Acct. No. 101
Date	Explan.	PR	Debit	Credit	Balance
2019					
Dec. 1	(1)	G1	30,000		30,000
2	(2)	G1		2,500	27,500
3	(3)	G1		26,000	1,500
5	(5)	G1	4,200		5,700
6	(13)	G1		2,400	3,300
12	(6)	G1		1,000	2,300
12	(7)	G1		700	1,600
22	(9)	G1	1,900		3,500
24	(10)	G1		900	2,600
24	(11)	G1		200	2,400
26	(12)	G1	3,000		5,400
26	(14)	G1		120	5,280
26	(15)	G1		305	4,975
26	(16)	G1		700	**4,275**

Accounts Receivable					Acct. No. 106
Date	Explan.	PR	Debit	Credit	Balance
2019					
Dec. 12	(8)	G1	1,900		1,900
22	(9)	G1		1,900	0
31	Adj.(f)	G1	1,300		1,800

Supplies					Acct. No. 126
Date	Explan.	PR	Debit	Credit	Balance
2019					
Dec. 2	(2)	G1	2,500		2,500
6	(4)	G1	7,100		9,600
26	(14)	G1	120		9,720
31	Adj.(b)	G1		1,050	8,670

Prepaid Insurance					Acct. No. 128
Date	Explan.	PR	Debit	Credit	Balance
2019					
Dec. 6	(13)	G1	2,400		2,400
31	Adj.(a)	G1		100	2,300

Equipment					Acct. No. 167
Date	Explan.	PR	Debit	Credit	Balance
2019					
Dec. 3	(3)	G1	26,000		**26,000**

Accumulated Depreciation— Equipment					Acct. No. 168
Date	Explan.	PR	Debit	Credit	Balance
2019					
Dec. 31	Adj.(c)	G1		300	300

Liability and Equity Accounts

Accounts Payable					Acct. No. 201
Date	Explan.	PR	Debit	Credit	Balance
2019					
Dec. 6	(4)	G1		7,100	7,100
24	(10)	G1	900		**6,200**

Salaries Payable					Acct. No. 209
Date	Explan.	PR	Debit	Credit	Balance
2019					
Dec. 31	Adj.(e)	G1		210	210

Unearned Consulting Revenue					Acct. No. 236
Date	Explan.	PR	Debit	Credit	Balance
2019					
Dec. 26	(12)	G1		3,000	3,000
31	Adj.(d)	G1	250		2,750

Common Stock					Acct. No. 307
Date	Explan.	PR	Debit	Credit	Balance
2019					
Dec. 1	(1)	G1		30,000	30,000

Retained Earnings					Acct. No. 318
Date	Explan.	PR	Debit	Credit	Balance
2019					
Dec. 31	Clos.(3)	G1		3,785	3,785
31	Clos.(4)	G1	200		3,585

Dividends					Acct. No. 319
Date	Explan.	PR	Debit	Credit	Balance
2019					
Dec. 24	(11)	G1	200		200
31	Clos.(4)	G1		200	0

Revenue and Expense Accounts (Including Income Summary)

Consulting Revenue					Acct. No. 403
Date	Explan.	PR	Debit	Credit	Balance
2019					
Dec. 5	(5)	G1		4,200	4,200
12	(8)	G1		1,600	5,800
31	Adj.(d)	G1		250	6,050
31	Adj.(f)	G1		1,800	7,850
31	Clos.(1)	G1	7,850		0

Rental Revenue					Acct. No. 406
Date	Explan.	PR	Debit	Credit	Balance
2019					
Dec. 12	(8)	G1		300	**300**
31	Clos.(1)	G1	300		0

Depreciation Expense— Equipment					Acct. No. 612
Date	Explan.	PR	Debit	Credit	Balance
2019					
Dec. 31	Adj.(c)	G1	300		300
31	Clos.(2)	G1		300	0

Salaries Expense					Acct. No. 622
Date	Explan.	PR	Debit	Credit	Balance
2019					
Dec. 12	(7)	G1	700		700
26	(16)	G1	700		1,400
31	Adj.(e)	G1	210		1,610
31	Clos.(2)	G1		1,610	0

Insurance Expense					Acct. No. 637
Date	Explan.	PR	Debit	Credit	Balance
2019					
Dec. 31	Adj.(a)	G1	100		100
31	Clos.(2)	G1		100	0

Rent Expense					Acct. No. 640
Date	Explan.	PR	Debit	Credit	Balance
2019					
Dec. 12	(6)	G1	1,000		**1,000**
31	Clos.(2)	G1		1,000	0

Supplies Expense					Acct. No. 652
Date	Explan.	PR	Debit	Credit	Balance
2019					
Dec. 31	Adj.(b)	G1	1,050		1,050
31	Clos.(2)	G1		1,050	0

Utilities Expense					Acct. No. 690
Date	Explan.	PR	Debit	Credit	Balance
2019					
Dec. 26	(15)	G1	305		**305**
31	Clos.(2)	G1		305	0

Income Summary					Acct. No. 901
Date	Explan.	PR	Debit	Credit	Balance
2019					
Dec. 31	Clos.(1)	G1		8,150	8,150
31	Clos.(2)	G1	4,365		3,785
31	Clos.(3)	G1	3,785		0

Post-Closing Trial Balance

P8

Explain and prepare a post-closing trial balance.

A **post-closing trial balance** is a list of permanent accounts and their balances after all closing entries. It lists the balances for all accounts not closed. A post-closing trial balance verifies that (1) total debits equal total credits for permanent accounts and (2) all temporary accounts have zero balances. FastForward's post-closing trial balance is in Exhibit 3.18 and often is the last step in the accounting process.

EXHIBIT 3.18

Post-Closing Trial Balance

FASTFORWARD Post-Closing Trial Balance December 31, 2019		
	Debit	**Credit**
Cash	$ 4,275	
Accounts receivable	1,800	
Supplies	8,670	
Prepaid insurance	2,300	
Equipment	26,000	
Accumulated depreciation—Equipment		$ 300
Accounts payable		6,200
Salaries payable		210
Unearned consulting revenue		2,750
Common stock		30,000
Retained earnings		3,585
Totals	$43,045	$43,045

Point: Only balance sheet (permanent) accounts are on a post-closing trial balance.

©IM_photo/Shutterstock

■ **Decision Maker**

Staff Accountant   A friend shows you the post-closing trial balance she is working on. You review the statement and see a line item for rent expense. How do you know that an error exists? ■   *Answer:* This error is apparent in a post-closing trial balance because Rent Expense is a temporary account. Post-closing trial balances only contain permanent accounts.

NEED-TO-KNOW 3-6

Closing Entries

P7

Do More: QS 3-18, E 3-9, E 3-10

Use the adjusted trial balance solution for Magic Company from Need-to-Know 3-5 to prepare its closing entries—the accounts are also listed here for convenience.

Cash	$13,000 Dr.		Retained earnings	$45,000 Cr.
Accounts receivable	17,000 Dr.		Dividends	20,000 Dr.
Land	85,000 Dr.		Fees earned	79,000 Cr.
Accounts payable	12,000 Cr.		Salaries expense	56,000 Dr.
Long-term notes payable	33,000 Cr.		Office supplies expense	8,000 Dr.
Common stock	30,000 Cr.			

Solution

Dec. 31	Fees Earned	79,000	
	Income Summary		79,000
	Close revenue account.		
Dec. 31	Income Summary	64,000	
	Salaries Expense		56,000
	Office Supplies Expense		8,000
	Close expense accounts.		

Dec. 31	Income Summary	15,000	
	Retained Earnings		15,000
	Close Income Summary.		
Dec. 31	Retained Earnings	20,000	
	Dividends		20,000
	Close Dividends account.		

ACCOUNTING CYCLE

C2

Identify steps in the accounting cycle.

The **accounting cycle** is the steps in preparing financial statements. It is called a *cycle* because the steps are repeated each reporting period. Exhibit 3.19 shows the 10 steps in the cycle. Steps 1 through 3 occur regularly as a company enters into transactions. Steps 4 through 9 are done at the end of a period. *Reversing entries* in step 10 are optional and are explained in Appendix 3C.

EXHIBIT 3.19

Steps in the Accounting Cycle*

Accounting Cycle

1. Analyze transactions

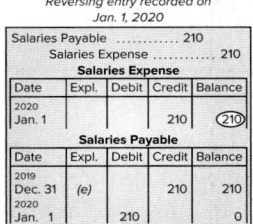

	Assets				=	Liabilities	+	Equity
	Cash	+	Supplies	+	Equipment	=	Accounts Payable	+	Common Stock
Old Bal.	$1,500	+	$2,500	+	$26,000	=		+	$30,000
(4)		+	7,100			=	+$7,100		
New Bal.	$1,500	+	$9,600	+	$26,000	=	$7,100	+	$30,000

2. Journalize

Date	Account Titles and Explanation	PR	Debit	Credit
(4)	Supplies	126	7,100	
	Accounts Payable	201		7,100

3. Post

General Ledger

Supplies	126		Accounts Payable	201
(2) 2,500				(4) 7,100
(4) 7,100				

4. Prepare unadjusted trial balance

FASTFORWARD
Trial Balance
December 31, 2019

	Debit	Credit
Cash	$ 4,275	
Accounts receivable	0	
Supplies	9,720	
Prepaid insurance	2,400	
Equipment	26,000	
Accounts payable		$6,200
Unearned consulting revenue		3,000

5. Adjust and post accounts

Adjustment (b)

Dec. 31	Supplies Expense	1,050	
	Supplies		1,050
	Record supplies used.		

Supplies Expense	652		Supplies	126
Dec. 31 1,050		Dec. 2 2,500	Dec. 31 1,050
		6 7,100	
		26 120	
		Balance 8,670	

6. Prepare adjusted trial balance

FASTFORWARD
Trial Balances
December 31, 2019

Acct. No.	Account Title	Unadjusted Trial Balance Dr.	Unadjusted Trial Balance Cr.	Adjustments Dr.	Adjustments Cr.	Adjusted Trial Balance Dr.	Adjusted Trial Balance Cr.
101	Cash	$ 4,275				$ 4,275	
106	Accounts receivable	0		(f) $1,800		1,800	
126	Supplies	9,720			(b) $1,050	8,670	
128	Prepaid insurance	2,400			(a) 100	2,300	
167	Equipment	26,000				26,000	
168	Accumulated depreciation—Equip.		$ 0		(c) 300		$ 300
201	Accounts payable		6,200				6,200
209	Salaries payable		0		(e) 210		210

7. Prepare financial statements

FASTFORWARD
Statement of Retained Earnings
For Month Ended December 31, 2019

Retained earnings, December 1	$ 0
Plus:	

FASTFORWARD
Income Statement
For Month Ended December 31, 2019

Revenues	
Consulting revenue	$7,850

FASTFORWARD
Balance Sheet
December 31, 2019

Assets	
Cash	$ 4,275
Accounts receivable	1,800
Supplies	8,670
Prepaid insurance	2,300

8. Close accounts

General Journal

Step 1:			
Dec. 31	Consulting Revenue	7,850	
	Rental Revenue	300	
	Income Summary		8,150
	Close revenue accounts.		
Step 2:			
Dec. 31	Income Summary	4,365	
	Depreciation Expense—Equip.		300
	Salaries Expense		1,610
	Insurance Expense		100
	Rent Expense		1,000
	Supplies Expense		1,050
	Utilities Expense		305
	Close expense accounts.		

9. Prepare post-closing trial balance

FASTFORWARD
Post-Closing Trial Balance
December 31, 2019

	Debit	Credit
Cash	$ 4,275	
Accounts receivable	1,800	
Supplies	8,670	
Prepaid insurance	2,300	
Equipment	26,000	
Accumulated depreciation—Equipment		$ 300
Accounts payable		6,200

10. Reverse and post (optional)

Reversing entry recorded on Jan. 1, 2020

Salaries Payable	210	
Salaries Expense		210

Salaries Expense

Date	Expl.	Debit	Credit	Balance
2020 Jan. 1			210	(210)

Salaries Payable

Date	Expl.	Debit	Credit	Balance
2019 Dec. 31	(e)		210	210
2020 Jan. 1		210		0

Explanations

1. Analyze transactions	Analyze transactions to prepare for journalizing.
2. Journalize	Record accounts, including debits and credits, in a journal.
3. Post	Transfer debits and credits from the journal to the ledger.
4. Prepare unadjusted trial balance	Summarize unadjusted ledger accounts and amounts.
5. Adjust and post	Record adjustments to bring account balances up to date; journalize and post adjustments.
6. Prepare adjusted trial balance	Summarize adjusted ledger accounts and amounts.
7. Prepare financial statements	Use adjusted trial balance to prepare financial statements.
8. Close accounts	Journalize and post entries to close temporary accounts.
9. Prepare post-closing trial balance	Test clerical accuracy of the closing procedures.
10. Reverse and post (optional step)	Reverse certain adjustments in the next period—optional step; see Appendix 3C.

* Steps 4, 6, and 9 can be done on a work sheet. A work sheet is useful in planning adjustments, but adjustments (step 5) must always be journalized and posted. Steps 3, 4, 6, and 9 are automatic with a computerized system.

CLASSIFIED BALANCE SHEET

This section describes a classified balance sheet. An **unclassified balance sheet** broadly groups accounts into assets, liabilities, and equity. One example is FastForward's balance sheet in Exhibit 3.14. A **classified balance sheet** organizes assets and liabilities into subgroups.

C3

Explain and prepare a classified balance sheet.

Classification Structure

A classified balance sheet typically contains the categories in Exhibit 3.20 (there is no required layout). An important classification is the separation between current and noncurrent for both

EXHIBIT 3.20

Typical Categories in a
Classified Balance Sheet

Assets	Liabilities and Equity
Current assets	Current liabilities
Noncurrent assets	Noncurrent liabilities
Long-term investments	Equity
Plant assets	
Intangible assets	

assets and liabilities. Current items are expected to come due (either collected or owed) within one year or the company's operating cycle, whichever is longer. The **operating cycle** is the time span from when *cash is used* to acquire goods and services until *cash is received* from the sale of goods and services. Most operating cycles are less than one year, which means most companies use a one-year period to classify current and noncurrent items. To make it easy, assume an operating cycle of one year, unless we say otherwise.

A balance sheet lists current assets before noncurrent assets and current liabilities before noncurrent liabilities. Current assets and current liabilities are listed in order of how quickly they will be converted to, or paid in, cash.

Classification Categories

The balance sheet for Snowboarding Components in Exhibit 3.21 shows the typical categories. Its assets are classified as either current or noncurrent. Its noncurrent assets include three main categories: long-term investments, plant assets, and intangible assets. Its liabilities are classified as either current or long-term. Not all companies use the same categories. **Jarden**, a producer of snowboards, reported a balance sheet with five asset classes: current assets; property, plant, and equipment; goodwill; intangibles; and other assets.

©Sean Sullivan/Getty Images

Point: Current is also called *short-term*, and noncurrent is also called *long-term*.

Current Assets **Current assets** are cash and other resources that are expected to be sold, collected, or used within one year or the company's operating cycle, whichever is longer. Examples are cash, short-term investments, accounts receivable, short-term notes receivable, goods for sale (called *merchandise* or *inventory*), and prepaid expenses.

Long-Term Investments **Long-term** (or *noncurrent*) **investments** include notes receivable and investments in stocks and bonds when they are expected to be held for more than the longer of one year or the operating cycle. Land held for future expansion is a long-term investment because it is *not* used in operations.

EXHIBIT 3.21

Example of a Classified
Balance Sheet

SNOWBOARDING COMPONENTS
Balance Sheet
January 31, 2019

Assets

Current assets
Cash	$ 6,500	
Short-term investments	2,100	
Accounts receivable, net	4,400	
Merchandise inventory	27,500	
Prepaid expenses	2,400	
Total current assets		$ 42,900

Long-term investments
Notes receivable (due in three years)	1,500	
Investments in stocks and bonds	18,000	
Land held for future expansion	48,000	
Total long-term investments		67,500

Plant assets
Equipment and buildings	203,200	
Less accumulated depreciation	53,000	
Equipment and buildings, net		150,200
Land		73,200
Total plant assets		223,400
Intangible assets		10,000
Total assets		$343,800

Liabilities

Current liabilities
Accounts payable	$15,300	
Wages payable	3,200	
Notes payable (due within one year)	3,000	
Current portion of long-term liabilities	7,500	
Total current liabilities		$ 29,000
Long-term liabilities (net of current portion)		150,000
Total liabilities		179,000

Equity
Common stock	50,000
Retained earnings	114,800
Total equity	164,800
Total liabilities and equity	$343,800

Plant Assets
Plant Assets   Plant assets are tangible assets that are both *long-lived* and *used to produce or sell products and services*. Examples are equipment, machinery, buildings, and land that are used to produce or sell products and services.

Point: Plant assets are also called *fixed assets; property, plant and equipment (PP&E);* or *long-lived assets.*

Intangible Assets
Intangible assets are long-term assets that benefit business operations but lack physical form. Examples are patents, trademarks, copyrights, franchises, and goodwill. Their value comes from the privileges or rights granted to or held by the owner.

©Johannes Simon/Getty Images

Current Liabilities
Current liabilities are liabilities due to be paid or settled within one year or the operating cycle, whichever is longer. They usually are settled by paying out cash. Current liabilities include accounts payable, notes payable, wages payable, taxes payable, interest payable, and unearned revenues. Also, any portion of a long-term liability due to be paid within one year or the operating cycle, whichever is longer, is a current liability. Unearned revenues are current liabilities when products or services are to be provided within one year or the operating cycle, whichever is longer.

Long-Term Liabilities
Long-term liabilities are liabilities *not* due within one year or the operating cycle, whichever is longer. Notes payable, mortgages payable, bonds payable, and lease obligations are common long-term liabilities. If a company has both short- and long-term items in each of these categories, they are commonly separated into two accounts in the ledger.

Equity
Equity is the owner's claim on assets. For a corporation, this claim is reported in the equity section as common stock and retained earnings.

Point: Only assets and liabilities (not equity) are classified as current or noncurrent.

NEED-TO-KNOW 3-7

Use the following account balances for Magic Company from Need-To-Know 3-5 to prepare its classified balance sheet as of December 31.

Classified Balance Sheet
C3

Cash	$13,000 Dr.	Retained earnings	$40,000 Cr.
Accounts receivable	17,000 Dr.	Dividends	20,000 Dr.
Land	85,000 Dr.	Fees earned	79,000 Cr.
Accounts payable	12,000 Cr.	Salaries expense	56,000 Dr.
Long-term notes payable	33,000 Cr.	Office supplies expense	8,000 Dr.
Common stock	30,000 Cr.		

Solution

MAGIC COMPANY
Balance Sheet
December 31

Assets		Liabilities	
Current assets		**Current liabilities**	
Cash	$ 13,000	Accounts payable	$ 12,000
Accounts receivable	17,000	Total current liabilities	12,000
Total current assets	30,000	Long-term notes payable	33,000
Plant assets		Total liabilities	45,000
Land	85,000	**Equity**	
Total plant assets	85,000	Common stock	30,000
		Retained earnings	40,000
		Total equity	70,000
Total assets	$115,000	Total liabilities and equity	$115,000

Do More: QS 3-21, QS 3-23, E 3-12, P 3-7

Decision Analysis   Profit Margin and Current Ratio

Profit Margin

A useful measure of a company's operating results is the ratio of its net income to net sales. This ratio is called **profit margin,** or *return on sales,* and is computed as in Exhibit 3.22. This ratio shows the percent of profit in each dollar of sales.

$$\text{Profit margin} = \frac{\text{Net income}}{\text{Net sales}}$$

EXHIBIT 3.22

Profit Margin

A1

Compute profit margin and describe its use in analyzing company performance.

Visa's profit margins are shown in Exhibit 3.23. Visa's profit margin is superior to **Mastercard**'s in each of the last three years. For Mastercard to improve its profit margin, it must either reduce expenses or increase revenues at a relatively greater amount than expenses.

EXHIBIT 3.23

Computation and Analysis using Profit Margin

Company	Figure ($ millions)	Current Year	1 Year Ago	2 Years Ago
Visa	Net income	$ 6,699	$ 5,991	$ 6,328
	Net sales	$18,358	$15,082	$13,880
	Profit margin	**36%**	**40%**	**46%**
Mastercard	Profit margin	31%	38%	39%

■ Decision Maker

CFO   Your health care equipment company consistently reports a 9% profit margin, which is similar to that of competitors. The treasurer argues that profit margin can be increased to 20% if the company cuts marketing expenses. Do you cut those expenses? ■   *Answer:* Cutting those expenses increases profit margin in the short run. However, over the long run, cutting such expenses can hurt current and future sales. You must explain that the company can cut the "fat" (expenses that do not create sales) but should be careful if cutting those that create sales.

Current Ratio

An important use of financial statements is to help assess a company's ability to pay its debts in the near future. Such analysis affects decisions by suppliers when allowing a company to buy on credit. It also affects decisions by creditors when lending money to a company, including loan terms such as interest rate and due date. The **current ratio** is one measure of a company's ability to pay its short-term obligations. It is defined in Exhibit 3.24.

A2

Compute the current ratio and describe what it reveals about a company's financial condition.

$$\text{Current ratio} = \frac{\text{Current assets}}{\text{Current liabilities}}$$

EXHIBIT 3.24

Current Ratio

Costco's current ratio for each of the last three years is in Exhibit 3.25. A current ratio of over 1.0 means that current obligations can be covered with current assets. For the recent two years, Costco's current ratio was slightly below 1.0. This means Costco could face challenges in covering current liabilities. Although Costco has a better ratio than **Walmart** in each of the last three years, management must continue to monitor current assets and liabilities.

EXHIBIT 3.25

Computation and Analysis using Current Ratio

Company	Figure ($ millions)	Current Year	1 Year Ago	2 Years Ago
Costco	Current assets.	$17,317	$15,218	$16,779
	Current liabilities	$17,495	$15,575	$16,539
	Current ratio	**0.99**	**0.98**	**1.01**
Walmart	Current ratio	0.86	0.93	0.97

©sgpage902/Getty Images

■ Decision Maker

Analyst   You are analyzing a dirt bike company's ability to meet upcoming loan payments. You compute its current ratio as 1.2. You find that a major portion of accounts receivable is due from one client who has not made any payments in the past 12 months. Removing this receivable from current assets lowers the current ratio to 0.7. What do you conclude? ■   *Answer:* A current ratio of 1.2 suggests that current assets are sufficient to cover current liabilities. Removing the past-due receivable reduces the current ratio to 0.7. You conclude that the company will have difficulty meeting its loan payments.

The following information relates to Fanning's Electronics on December 31, 2019. The company, which uses the calendar year as its annual reporting period, initially records prepaid and unearned items in balance sheet accounts (assets and liabilities, respectively).

a. The company's weekly payroll is $8,750, paid each Friday for a five-day workweek. Assume December 31, 2019, falls on a Monday, but the employees will not be paid their wages until Friday, January 4, 2020.

b. Eighteen months earlier, on July 1, 2018, the company purchased equipment that cost $20,000. Its useful life is predicted to be five years, at which time the equipment is expected to be worthless (zero salvage value).

c. On October 1, 2019, the company agreed to work on a new housing development. The company is paid $120,000 on October 1 in advance of future installation of similar alarm systems in 24 new homes. That amount was credited to the Unearned Services Revenue account. Between October 1 and December 31, work on 20 homes was completed.

d. On September 1, 2019, the company purchased a 12-month insurance policy for $1,800. The transaction was recorded with an $1,800 debit to Prepaid Insurance.

e. On December 29, 2019, the company completed a $7,000 service that has not been billed or recorded as of December 31, 2019.

NEED-TO-KNOW 3-8

COMPREHENSIVE 1

Preparing Year-End
Accounting Adjustments

Required

1. Prepare any necessary adjusting entries on December 31, 2019, in relation to transactions and events *a* through *e*.

2. Prepare T-accounts for the accounts affected by adjusting entries, and post the adjusting entries. Determine the adjusted balances for the Unearned Revenue and the Prepaid Insurance accounts.

3. Complete the following table and determine the amounts and effects of your adjusting entries on the year 2019 income statement and the December 31, 2019, balance sheet. Use up (down) arrows to indicate an increase (decrease) in the Effect columns.

Entry	Amount in the Entry	Effect on Net Income	Effect on Total Assets	Effect on Total Liabilities	Effect on Total Equity

PLANNING THE SOLUTION

- Analyze each situation to determine which accounts need to be updated with an adjustment.
- Calculate the amount of each adjustment and prepare the necessary journal entries.
- Show the amount of each adjustment in the designated accounts, determine the adjusted balance, and identify the balance sheet classification of the account.
- Determine each entry's effect on net income for the year and on total assets, total liabilities, and total equity at the end of the year.

SOLUTION

1. Adjusting journal entries.

(a) Dec. 31	Wages Expense	1,750	
	Wages Payable		1,750
	Accrue wages for last day of year ($8,750 × 1/5).		
(b) Dec. 31	Depreciation Expense—Equipment	4,000	
	Accumulated Depreciation—Equipment		4,000
	Record depreciation expense for year *($20,000/5 years = $4,000 per year).*		
(c) Dec. 31	Unearned Services Revenue	100,000	
	Services Revenue		100,000
	Record revenue earned ($120,000 × 20/24).		
(d) Dec. 31	Insurance Expense	600	
	Prepaid Insurance.		600
	Adjust for expired portion of insurance ($1,800 × 4/12).		
(e) Dec. 31	Accounts Receivable	7,000	
	Services Revenue		7,000
	Record services revenue earned.		

2. T-accounts for adjusting journal entries *a* through *e*.

Accounts Receivable		Wages Payable		Wages Expense	
(e) 7,000			(a) 1,750	(a) 1,750	

Prepaid Insurance		Unearned Services Revenue		Insurance Expense	
Unadj. Bal. 1,800			Unadj. Bal. 120,000	(d) 600	
	(d) 600	(c) 100,000			
Adj. Bal. 1,200			Adj. Bal. 20,000		

Accumulated Depreciation—Equipment		Services Revenue		Depreciation Expense—Equipment	
	(b) 4,000		(c) 100,000	(b) 4,000	
			(e) 7,000		
			Adj. Bal. 107,000		

3. Financial statement effects of adjusting journal entries.

Entry	Amount in the Entry	Effect on Net Income	Effect on Total Assets	Effect on Total Liabilities	Effect on Total Equity
a	$ 1,750	$ 1,750 ↓	No effect	$ 1,750 ↑	$ 1,750 ↓
b	4,000	4,000 ↓	$4,000 ↓	No effect	4,000 ↓
c	100,000	100,000 ↑	No effect	$100,000 ↓	100,000 ↑
d	600	600 ↓	$ 600 ↓	No effect	600 ↓
e	7,000	7,000 ↑	$7,000 ↑	No effect	7,000 ↑

NEED-TO-KNOW 3-9

COMPREHENSIVE 2

Preparing Financial
Statements from
Adjusted Account
Balances

Use the following year-end adjusted trial balance to answer questions 1–3.

CHOI COMPANY Adjusted Trial Balance December 31		
	Debit	Credit
Cash	$ 3,050	
Accounts receivable	400	
Prepaid insurance	910	
Equipment	217,200	
Accumulated depreciation—Equipment		$ 29,100
Interest payable		4,480
Unearned rent		460
Long-term notes payable		150,000
Common stock		10,000
Retained earnings		30,340
Dividends	21,000	
Rent earned		57,500
Wages expense	25,000	
Utilities expense	1,900	
Insurance expense	3,450	
Depreciation expense—Equipment	5,970	
Interest expense	3,000	
Totals	$281,880	$281,880

1. Prepare the annual income statement from the adjusted trial balance of Choi Company.

Answer:

CHOI COMPANY		
Income Statement		
For Year Ended December 31		
Revenues		
Rent earned		$57,500
Expenses		
Wages expense	$25,000	
Utilities expense	1,900	
Insurance expense	3,450	
Depreciation expense—Equipment	5,970	
Interest expense	3,000	
Total expenses		39,320
Net income		$18,180

2. Prepare a statement of retained earnings from the adjusted trial balance of Choi Company.

Answer:

CHOI COMPANY	
Statement of Retained Earnings	
For Year Ended December 31	
Retained earnings, December 31 prior year-end	$30,340
Plus: Net income	18,180
	48,520
Less: Dividends	21,000
Retained earnings, December 31 current year-end	$27,520

3. Prepare a balance sheet (unclassified) from the adjusted trial balance of Choi Company.

Answer:

CHOI COMPANY		
Balance Sheet		
December 31		
Assets		
Cash		$ 3,050
Accounts receivable		400
Prepaid insurance		910
Equipment	$217,200	
Less accumulated depreciation.	29,100	188,100
Total assets		$192,460
Liabilities		
Interest payable		$ 4,480
Unearned rent		460
Long-term notes payable		150,000
Total liabilities		154,940
Equity		
Common stock		10,000
Retained earnings.		27,520
Total equity		37,520
Total liabilities and equity.		$192,460

APPENDIX

Alternative Accounting for Prepayments   **3A**

This appendix explains alternative accounting for deferred expenses and deferred revenues.

RECORDING PREPAYMENT OF EXPENSES <u>IN EXPENSE ACCOUNTS</u>

P9 _____

Explain the alternatives in accounting for prepaids.

An alternative method is to record *all* prepaid expenses with debits to expense accounts. If any prepaids remain unused or unexpired at the end of an accounting period, then adjusting entries transfer the cost of the unused portions from expense accounts to prepaid expense (asset) accounts. The financial statements are identical under either method, but the adjusting entries are different. To demonstrate the differences between these two methods, let's look at FastForward's cash payment on December 1 for 24 months of insurance coverage beginning on December 1. FastForward recorded that payment with a debit to an asset account, but it could have recorded a debit to an expense account. These alternatives are shown in Exhibit 3A.1.

Payment Recorded as Asset		
Dec. 1	Prepaid Insurance	2,400	
	Cash.		2,400

Payment Recorded as Expense		
Dec. 1	Insurance Expense	2,400	
	Cash		2,400

EXHIBIT 3A.1

Alternative Initial Entries for Prepaid Expenses

At the end of its accounting period on December 31, insurance protection for one month has expired. This means $100 ($2,400/24) of insurance coverage expired and is an expense for December. The adjusting entry depends on how the original payment was recorded. This is shown in Exhibit 3A.2.

EXHIBIT 3A.2

Adjusting Entry for Prepaid Expenses for the Two Alternatives

Payment Recorded as Asset		
Dec. 31 Insurance Expense	100	
Prepaid Insurance		100

Payment Recorded as Expense		
Dec. 31 Prepaid Insurance	2,300	
Insurance Expense ..		2,300

When these entries are posted, we see in Exhibit 3A.3 that the two methods give identical results.

EXHIBIT 3A.3

Account Balances under Two Alternatives for Recording Prepaid Expenses

Payment Recorded as Asset			
Prepaid Insurance			128
Dec. 1	2,400	Dec. 31	100
Balance	2,300		

| **Insurance Expense** | | | 637 |
| Dec. 31 | 100 | | |

Payment Recorded as Expense			
Prepaid Insurance			128
Dec. 31	2,300		

Insurance Expense			637
Dec. 1	2,400	Dec. 31	2,300
Balance	100		

RECORDING PREPAYMENT OF REVENUES IN REVENUE ACCOUNTS

An alternative method is to record *all* unearned revenues with credits to revenue accounts. If any revenues are unearned at the end of an accounting period, then adjusting entries transfer the unearned portions from revenue accounts to unearned revenue (liability) accounts. The adjusting entries are different for these two alternatives, but the financial statements are identical. To demonstrate the differences between these two methods, let's look at FastForward's December 26 receipt of $3,000 for consulting services covering the period December 27 to February 24. FastForward recorded this transaction with a credit to a liability account. The alternative is to record it with a credit to a revenue account, as shown in Exhibit 3A.4.

EXHIBIT 3A.4

Alternative Initial Entries for Unearned Revenues

Receipt Recorded as Liability		
Dec. 26 Cash	3,000	
Unearned Consulting Revenue ...		3,000

Receipt Recorded as Revenue		
Dec. 26 Cash	3,000	
Consulting Revenue ..		3,000

By the end of its accounting period on December 31, FastForward has earned $250 of this revenue. This means $250 of the liability has been satisfied. Depending on how the initial receipt is recorded, the adjusting entry is as shown in Exhibit 3A.5.

EXHIBIT 3A.5

Adjusting Entry for Unearned Revenues for the Two Alternatives

Receipt Recorded as Liability		
Dec. 31 Unearned Consulting Revenue .	250	
Consulting Revenue		250

Receipt Recorded as Revenue		
Dec. 31 Consulting Revenue	2,750	
Unearned Consulting Revenue ..		2,750

After adjusting entries are posted, the two alternatives give identical results, as shown in Exhibit 3A.6.

EXHIBIT 3A.6

Account Balances under Two Alternatives for Recording Unearned Revenues

Receipt Recorded as Liability			
Unearned Consulting Revenue			236
Dec. 31	250	Dec. 26	3,000
		Balance	2,750

| **Consulting Revenue** | | | 403 |
| | | Dec. 31 | 250 |

Receipt Recorded as Revenue			
Unearned Consulting Revenue			236
		Dec. 31	2,750

Consulting Revenue			403
Dec. 31	2,750	Dec. 26	3,000
		Balance	250

Work Sheet as a Tool

3B

Benefits of a Work Sheet (Spreadsheet)   A **work sheet** is a document that is used internally by companies to help with adjusting and closing accounts and with preparing financial statements. It is an internal accounting aid and is not a substitute for journals, ledgers, or financial statements. A work sheet

P10
Prepare a work sheet and explain its usefulness.

- Helps in preparing financial statements.
- Reduces the risk of errors when working with many accounts and adjustments.
- Links accounts and adjustments to financial statements.
- Shows the effects of proposed or "what-if" transactions.

Use of a Work Sheet   When a work sheet is used to prepare financial statements, it is constructed at the end of a period before the adjusting process. The complete work sheet includes a list of the accounts, their balances and adjustments, and their sorting into financial statement columns. It provides two columns each for the unadjusted trial balance, the adjustments, the adjusted trial balance, the income statement, and the balance sheet. To describe and interpret the work sheet, we use the information from FastForward. Preparing the work sheet has five steps.

1 Step 1. Enter Unadjusted Trial Balance

Refer to Exhibit 3B.1—green section. The first step in preparing a work sheet is to list the title of every account and its account number that appears on its financial statements. This includes all accounts in the ledger plus any new ones from adjusting entries. The unadjusted balance for each account is then entered in the correct Debit or Credit column of the Unadjusted Trial Balance columns. The totals of these two columns must be equal. The light green section of Exhibit 3B.1 shows FastForward's work sheet after completing this first step (dark green rows show accounts that arise because of the adjustments). Sometimes an account can require more than one adjustment, such as for Consulting Revenue. The additional adjustment can be added to a blank line below (as in Exhibit 3B.1), squeezed on one line, or combined into one adjustment amount.

FASTForward

2 Step 2. Enter Adjustments

Exhibit 3B.1—yellow section. The second step is to enter adjustments in the Adjustments columns. The adjustments shown are the same ones shown in Exhibit 3.13. An identifying letter links the debit and credit of each adjustment. This is called *keying* the adjustments. After preparing a work sheet, **adjustments must still be entered in the journal and posted to the ledger.** The Adjustments columns provide the information for adjusting entries in the journal.

3 Step 3. Prepare Adjusted Trial Balance

Exhibit 3B.1—blue section. The adjusted trial balance is prepared by combining the adjustments with the unadjusted balances for each account. As an example, the Prepaid Insurance account has a $2,400 debit balance in the Unadjusted Trial Balance columns. This $2,400 debit is combined with the $100 credit in the Adjustments columns to give Prepaid Insurance a $2,300 debit in the Adjusted Trial Balance columns. The totals of the Adjusted Trial Balance columns confirm debits and credits are equal.

4 Step 4. Sort Adjusted Trial Balance Amounts to Financial Statements

Exhibit 3B.1—orange section. This step involves sorting account balances from the adjusted trial balance to their proper financial statement columns. Expenses go to the Income Statement Debit column and revenues to the Income Statement Credit column. Assets and dividends go to the Balance Sheet Debit column. Liabilities, retained earnings, and common stock go to the Balance Sheet Credit column.

5 Step 5. Total Statement Columns, Compute Income or Loss, and Balance Columns

Exhibit 3B.1—purple section. Each financial statement column (from step 4) is totaled. The difference between the Debit and Credit column totals of the Income Statement columns is net income or net loss. This occurs because revenues are entered in the Credit column and expenses in the Debit column. If the Credit total exceeds the Debit total, there is net income. If the Debit total exceeds the Credit total, there is a net loss. For FastForward, the Credit total exceeds the Debit total, giving a $3,785 net income.

EXHIBIT 3B.1

Work Sheet with Five-Step Process for Completion

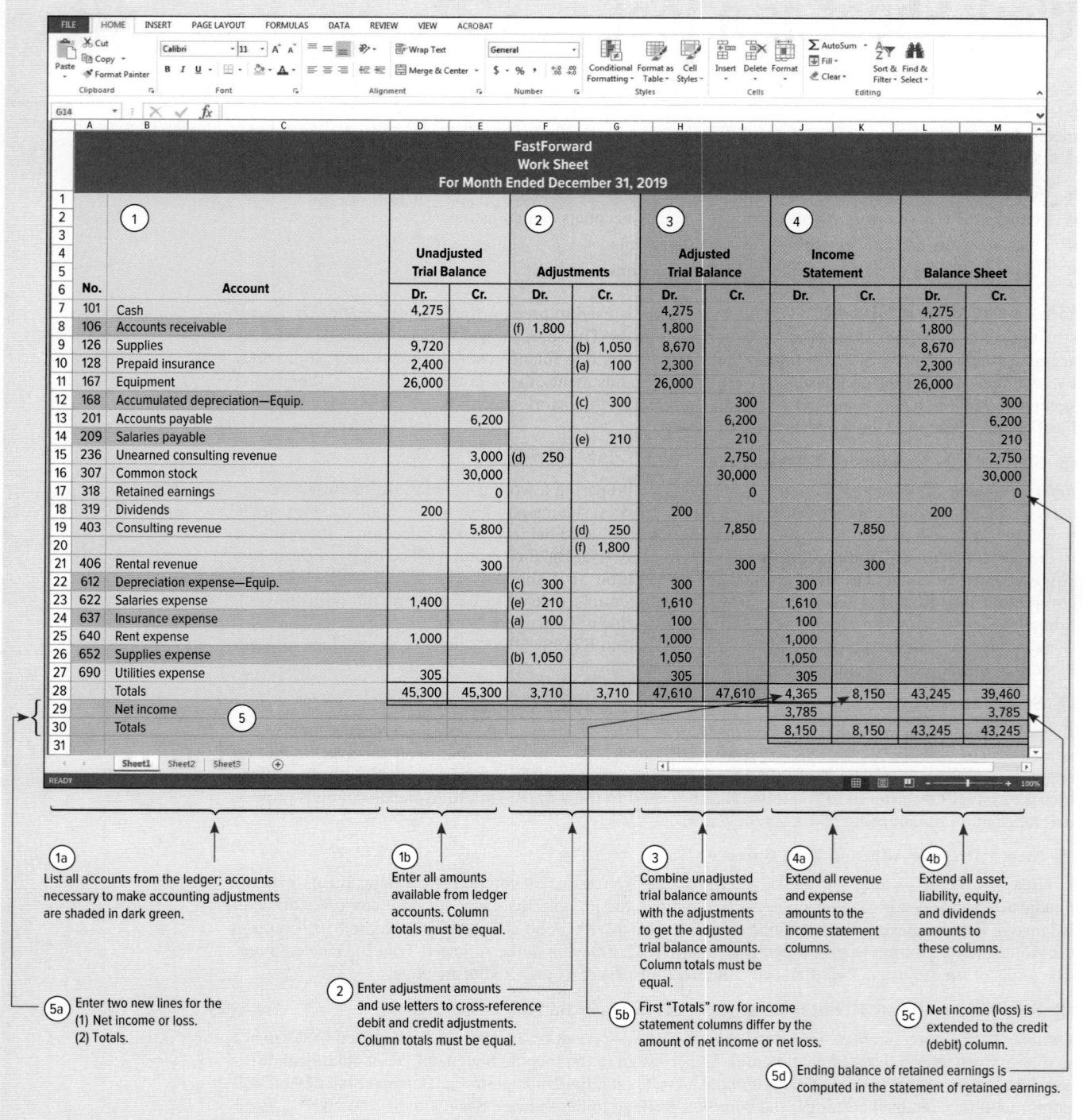

FastForward
Work Sheet
For Month Ended December 31, 2019

No.	Account	Unadjusted Trial Balance Dr.	Cr.	Adjustments Dr.	Cr.	Adjusted Trial Balance Dr.	Cr.	Income Statement Dr.	Cr.	Balance Sheet Dr.	Cr.
101	Cash	4,275				4,275				4,275	
106	Accounts receivable			(f) 1,800		1,800				1,800	
126	Supplies	9,720			(b) 1,050	8,670				8,670	
128	Prepaid insurance	2,400			(a) 100	2,300				2,300	
167	Equipment	26,000				26,000				26,000	
168	Accumulated depreciation—Equip.				(c) 300		300				300
201	Accounts payable		6,200				6,200				6,200
209	Salaries payable				(e) 210		210				210
236	Unearned consulting revenue		3,000	(d) 250			2,750				2,750
307	Common stock		30,000				30,000				30,000
318	Retained earnings		0				0				0
319	Dividends	200				200				200	
403	Consulting revenue		5,800		(d) 250		7,850		7,850		
					(f) 1,800						
406	Rental revenue		300				300		300		
612	Depreciation expense—Equip.			(c) 300		300		300			
622	Salaries expense	1,400		(e) 210		1,610		1,610			
637	Insurance expense			(a) 100		100		100			
640	Rent expense	1,000				1,000		1,000			
652	Supplies expense			(b) 1,050		1,050		1,050			
690	Utilities expense	305				305		305			
	Totals	45,300	45,300	3,710	3,710	47,610	47,610	4,365	8,150	43,245	39,460
	Net income							3,785			3,785
	Totals							8,150	8,150	43,245	43,245

Circled numbers: ① ② ③ ④ ⑤

1a List all accounts from the ledger; accounts necessary to make accounting adjustments are shaded in dark green.

1b Enter all amounts available from ledger accounts. Column totals must be equal.

3 Combine unadjusted trial balance amounts with the adjustments to get the adjusted trial balance amounts. Column totals must be equal.

4a Extend all revenue and expense amounts to the income statement columns.

4b Extend all asset, liability, equity, and dividends amounts to these columns.

2 Enter adjustment amounts and use letters to cross-reference debit and credit adjustments. Column totals must be equal.

5a Enter two new lines for the (1) Net income or loss. (2) Totals.

5b First "Totals" row for income statement columns differ by the amount of net income or net loss.

5c Net income (loss) is extended to the credit (debit) column.

5d Ending balance of retained earnings is computed in the statement of retained earnings.

A work sheet organizes information used to prepare adjusting entries, financial statements, and closing entries.

The net income from the Income Statement columns is then entered in the Balance Sheet Credit column. Adding net income to the last Credit column means that it is to be added to retained earnings. If a loss occurs, it is added to the Debit column. This means that it is to be subtracted from retained earnings. **The ending balance of retained earnings does not appear in the last two columns as a single amount, but it is computed in the statement of retained earnings** using these account balances. When net income or net loss is added to the proper Balance Sheet column, the totals of the last two columns must balance. If they do not, one or more errors have occurred.

Work Sheet Applications and Analysis   A work sheet does not substitute for financial statements. It is a tool we use to help prepare financial statements. FastForward's financial statements are shown in Exhibit 3.14. Its income statement amounts are taken from the Income Statement columns of the work sheet. Amounts for its balance sheet and its statement of retained earnings are taken from the Balance Sheet columns of the work sheet.

Work sheets are also useful in analyzing the effects of proposed, or what-if, transactions. This is done by entering financial statement amounts in the Unadjusted (what-if) columns. Proposed transactions are then entered in the Adjustments columns. We then compute "adjusted" amounts from these proposed transactions. The extended amounts in the financial statement columns produce **pro forma financial statements** because they show the statements *as if* the proposed transactions had occurred.

Reversing Entries

3C

P11_____

Prepare reversing entries and explain their purpose.

Reversing entries are optional. They are recorded in response to accrued assets and accrued liabilities that were created by adjusting entries at the end of a reporting period. Reversing entries simplify recordkeeping. Exhibit 3C.1 shows an example of FastForward's reversing entries. The top of the exhibit shows the adjusting entry FastForward recorded on December 31 for its employee's earned but unpaid salary. The entry recorded three days' salary of $210, which increased December's total salary expense to $1,610. The entry also recognized a liability of $210. The expense is reported on December's income statement. The expense account is then closed. The ledger on January 1, 2020, shows a $210 liability and a zero balance in the Salaries Expense account. At this point, the choice is made between using or not using reversing entries.

Accounting *without* Reversing Entries   The path down the left side of Exhibit 3C.1 is described in the chapter. To summarize, when the next payday occurs on January 9, we record payment with a compound entry that debits both the expense and liability accounts and credits Cash. Posting that entry creates a $490 balance in the expense account and reduces the liability account balance to zero because the payable has been settled.

Accounting *with* Reversing Entries   The right side of Exhibit 3C.1 shows reversing entries. A reversing entry is the exact opposite of an adjusting entry. For FastForward, the Salaries Payable liability account is debited for $210, meaning that this account now has a zero balance after the entry is posted on January 1. The Salaries Payable account temporarily understates the liability, but this is not a problem because financial statements are not prepared before the liability is settled on January 9. The credit to the Salaries Expense account is unusual because it gives the account an *abnormal credit balance*. We highlight an abnormal balance by circling it. Because of the reversing entry, the January 9 entry to record payment debits the Salaries Expense account and credits Cash for the full $700 paid. It is the same as all other entries made to record 10 days' salary for the employee. We see that after the payment entry is posted, the Salaries Expense account has a $490 balance that reflects seven days' salary of $70 per day (see the lower right side of Exhibit 3C.1). The zero balance in the Salaries Payable account is now correct. The lower section of Exhibit 3C.1 shows that the expense and liability accounts have exactly the same balances whether reversing entries are used or not.

Point: Adjusting entries that create new asset or liability accounts likely require reversing.

EXHIBIT 3C.1

Reversing Entries for an
Accrued Expense

Accrue salaries expense on December 31, 2019

Salaries Expense 210
    Salaries Payable 210

Salaries Expense

Date	Expl.	Debit	Credit	Balance
2019				
Dec. 12	(7)	700		700
26	(16)	700		1,400
31	(e)	210		1,610

Salaries Payable

Date	Expl.	Debit	Credit	Balance
2019				
Dec. 31	(e)		210	210

WITHOUT Reversing Entries	— OR —	**WITH Reversing Entries**
No reversing entry recorded on Jan. 1, 2020		*Reversing entry recorded on Jan. 1, 2020*

WITHOUT Reversing Entries

NO ENTRY

Salaries Expense

Date	Expl.	Debit	Credit	Balance
2020				

Salaries Payable

Date	Expl.	Debit	Credit	Balance
2019				
Dec. 31	(e)		210	210
2020				

WITH Reversing Entries

Salaries Payable 210
    Salaries Expense 210

Salaries Expense*

Date	Expl.	Debit	Credit	Balance
2020				
Jan. 1			210	(210)

Salaries Payable

Date	Expl.	Debit	Credit	Balance
2019				
Dec. 31	(e)		210	210
2020				
Jan. 1		210		0

Pay the accrued and current salaries on January 9, the first payday in 2020

WITHOUT Reversing Entries

Salaries Expense 490
Salaries Payable 210
    Cash 700

Salaries Expense

Date	Expl.	Debit	Credit	Balance
2020				
Jan. 9		490		**490**

Salaries Payable

Date	Expl.	Debit	Credit	Balance
2019				
Dec. 31	(e)		210	210
2020				
Jan. 9		210		0

WITH Reversing Entries

Salaries Expense 700
    Cash 700

Salaries Expense*

Date	Expl.	Debit	Credit	Balance
2020				
Jan. 1			210	(210)
Jan. 9		700		**490**

Salaries Payable

Date	Expl.	Debit	Credit	Balance
2019				
Dec. 31	(e)		210	210
2020				
Jan. 1		210		0

Under both approaches, the expense and liability accounts have
identical balances after the cash payment on January 9.

Salaries Expense $490
Salaries Payable .... $ 0

*Circled numbers in the *Balance* column indicate abnormal balances.

Summary: Cheat Sheet

DEFERRAL OF EXPENSE

Prepaid expenses: Assets paid for in advance of receiving their benefits.
When these assets are used, the advance payments become expenses.

Prepaid insurance expires:

Insurance Expense	100	
Prepaid Insurance		100

Supplies are used up:

Supplies Expense	1,050	
Supplies		1,050

Accumulated depreciation: A separate contra account. A **contra account**
is an account linked with another account. It has an opposite normal balance and is a subtraction from that other account's balance.

Depreciation of assets:

Depreciation Expense	300	
Accumulated Depreciation—Equipment		300

DEFERRAL OF REVENUE

Unearned revenue: Cash received in advance of providing products and services. When cash is accepted, the company has a liability to provide products or services.

Record unearned revenue (cash received in advance):

Cash	3,000	
Unearned Consulting Revenue................		3,000

Reduce unearned revenue (products or services are provided):

Unearned Consulting Revenue	250	
Consulting Revenue		250

ACCRUED EXPENSE

Accrued expenses: Costs incurred in a period that are both unpaid and unrecorded. They are reported on the income statement for the period when incurred.

Salaries expense owed but not yet paid:

Salaries Expense	210	
Salaries Payable		210

Accrued interest formula:

Principal amount owed × Annual interest rate × Fraction of year since last payment

Payment of accrued expenses:

Salaries Payable (3 days at $70 per day)	210	
Salaries Expense (7 days at $70 per day)	490	
Cash		700

ACCRUED REVENUE

Accrued revenues: Revenues earned in a period that are both unrecorded and not yet received in cash.

Revenue earned but not received in cash:

Accounts Receivable	1,800	
Consulting Revenue		1,800

Receipt of accrued revenue:

Cash	2,700	
Accounts Receivable (20 days at $90 per day) ...		1,800
Consulting Revenue (10 days at $90 per day) ...		900

REPORTING AND ANALYSIS

Unadjusted trial balance: A list of ledger accounts and balances *before* adjustments are recorded.
Adjusted trial balance: A list of accounts and balances *after* adjusting entries have been recorded and posted to the ledger.

Preparing financial statements from adjusted trial balance:

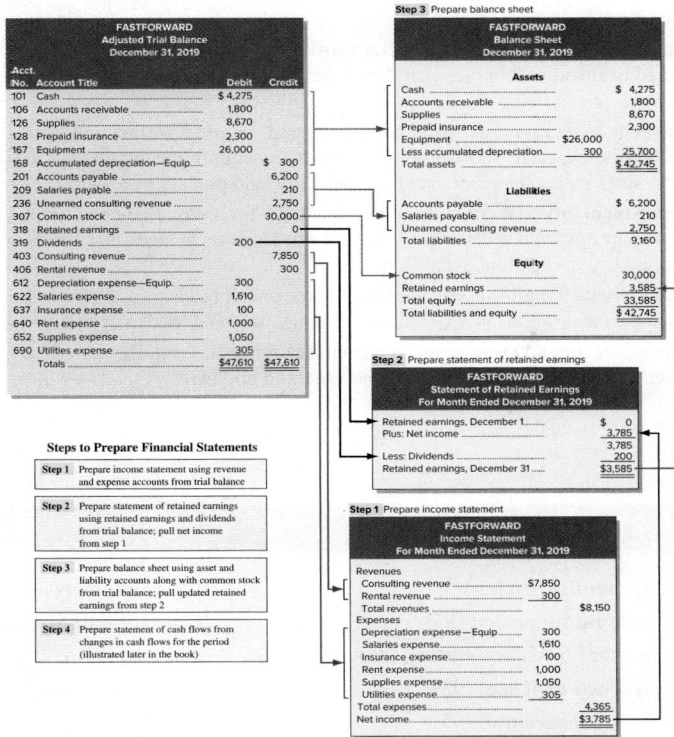

Steps to Prepare Financial Statements

Step 1	Prepare income statement using revenue and expense accounts from trial balance
Step 2	Prepare statement of retained earnings using retained earnings and dividends from trial balance; pull net income from step 1
Step 3	Prepare balance sheet using asset and liability accounts along with common stock from trial balance; pull updated retained earnings from step 2
Step 4	Prepare statement of cash flows from changes in cash flows for the period (illustrated later in the book)

CLOSING PROCESS

Closing process: Occurs at period-end after financial statements have been prepared. Resets revenue, expense, and dividends balances to zero.

Temporary accounts: Closed at period-end. They consist of revenue, expense, dividends, and Income Summary.

Permanent accounts: *Not* closed at period-end. They consist of asset, liability, common stock, and retained earnings (all balance sheet accounts).

Income Summary: A temporary account only used for the closing process that has a credit for total revenues and a debit for total expenses.

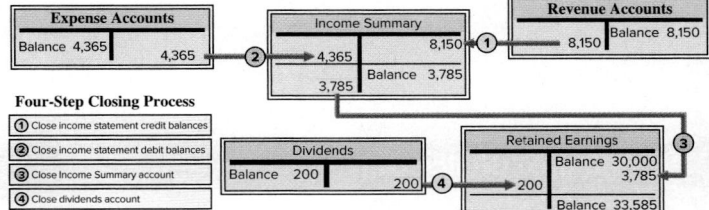

Closing Process Journal Entries by Step

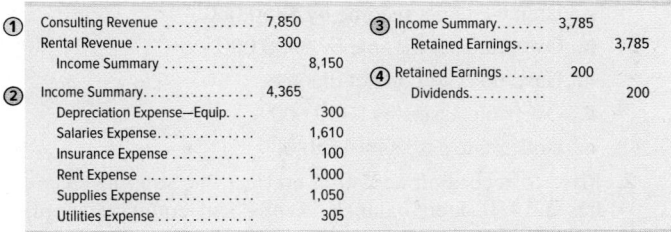

Post-closing trial balance: A list of permanent accounts (assets, liabilities, equity) and their balances after all closing entries.

CLASSIFIED BALANCE SHEET

Classified balance sheet: Organizes assets and liabilities into meaningful subgroups.

Current vs. long-term classification: Current items are to be collected or owed within one year. Long-term items are expected after one year.

Current assets: Assets to be sold, collected, or used within one year. Examples are cash, short-term investments, accounts receivable, short-term notes receivable, merchandise, inventory, and prepaid expenses.

Long-term investments: Assets to be held for more than one year. Examples are notes receivable, long-term investments in stock and bonds, and land held for future expansion.

Plant assets: Tangible assets used to produce or sell products and services. Examples are equipment, machinery, buildings, and land used in operations.

Intangible assets: Long-term assets that lack physical form. Examples are patents, trademarks, copyrights, franchises, and goodwill.

Current liabilities: Liabilities to be paid or settled within one year. Examples are accounts payable, wages payable, taxes payable, interest payable, unearned revenues, and current portions of notes or long-term debt.

Long-term liabilities: Liabilities not due within one year. Examples are notes payable, mortgages payable, bonds payable, and lease obligations.

Equity: The owner's claim on assets. For a corporation, this is common stock and retained earnings.

Common Layout of Classified Balance Sheet

Assets	Liabilities and Equity
Current assets	Current liabilities
Noncurrent assets	Noncurrent liabilities
Long-term investments	
Plant assets	Equity
Intangible assets	

Key Terms

Accounting cycle (104)

Accounting period (85)

Accrual basis accounting (86)

Accrued expenses (93)

Accrued revenues (95)

Accumulated depreciation (90)

Adjusted trial balance (98)

Adjusting entry (87)

Annual financial statements (85)

Book value (90)

Cash basis accounting (86)

Classified balance sheet (105)

Closing entries (101)

Closing process (100)

Contra account (90)

Current assets (106)

Current liabilities (107)

Current ratio (108)

Depreciation (89)

Expense recognition (or matching) principle (87)

Fiscal year (85)

Income Summary (101)

Intangible assets (107)

Interim financial statements (85)

Long-term investments (106)

Long-term liabilities (107)

Natural business year (86)

Operating cycle (106)

Permanent accounts (101)

Plant assets (89)

Post-closing trial balance (104)

Prepaid expenses (87)

Pro forma financial statements (115)

Profit margin (108)

Revenue recognition principle (87)

Reversing entries (115)

Straight-line depreciation (89)

Temporary accounts (101)

Time period assumption (85)

Unadjusted trial balance (98)

Unclassified balance sheet (105)

Unearned revenue (91)

Work sheet (113)

Multiple Choice Quiz

1. A company forgot to record accrued and unpaid employee wages of $350,000 at period-end. This oversight would
   a. Understate net income by $350,000.
   b. Overstate net income by $350,000.
   c. Have no effect on net income.
   d. Overstate assets by $350,000.
   e. Understate assets by $350,000.

2. Prior to recording adjusting entries, the Supplies account has a $450 debit balance. A physical count of supplies shows $125 of unused supplies still available. The required adjusting entry is

   a. Debit Supplies $125; credit Supplies Expense $125.
   b. Debit Supplies $325; credit Supplies Expense $325.
   c. Debit Supplies Expense $325; credit Supplies $325.
   d. Debit Supplies Expense $325; credit Supplies $125.
   e. Debit Supplies Expense $125; credit Supplies $125.

3. On May 1 of the current year, a two-year insurance policy was purchased for $24,000 with coverage to begin immediately. What is the amount of insurance expense that appears on the company's income statement for the current year ended December 31?

   a. $4,000   c. $12,000   e. $24,000
   b. $8,000   d. $20,000

4. On November 1, Stockton Co. receives $3,600 cash from Hans Co. for consulting services to be provided evenly over the period November 1 to April 30—at which time Stockton credits $3,600 to Unearned Consulting Fees. The adjusting entry on December 31 (Stockton's year-end) would include a

  a. Debit to Unearned Consulting Fees for $1,200.

  b. Debit to Unearned Consulting Fees for $2,400.

  c. Credit to Consulting Fees Earned for $2,400.

  d. Debit to Consulting Fees Earned for $1,200.

  e. Credit to Cash for $3,600.

ANSWERS TO MULTIPLE CHOICE QUIZ

  1. b; the forgotten adjusting entry is: *dr.* Wages Expense, *cr.* Wages Payable.

  2. c; Supplies used = $450 − $125 = $325

  3. b; Insurance expense = $24,000 × (8/24) = $8,000; adjusting entry is: *dr.* Insurance Expense for $8,000, *cr.* Prepaid Insurance for $8,000.

5. The following information is available for a company before closing the accounts. After all of the closing entries are made, what will be the balance in the Retained Earnings account?

| Total revenues .. | $300,000 | Retained earnings ... | $100,000 |
| Total expenses .. | 195,000 | Dividends .... | 45,000 |

  a. $360,000   **d.** $150,000

  b. $250,000   **e.** $60,000

  c. $160,000

  4. a; Consulting fees earned = $3,600 × (2/6) = $1,200; adjusting entry is: *dr.* Unearned Consulting Fees for $1,200, *cr.* Consulting Fees Earned for $1,200.

  5. c; $100,000 + $300,000 − $195,000 − $45,000

A(B,C) *Superscript letter A, B, or C denotes assignments based on Appendix 3A, 3B, or 3C.*

🏺 Icon denotes assignments that involve decision making.

Discussion Questions

1. What is the difference between the cash basis and the accrual basis of accounting?

2. 🏺 Why is the accrual basis of accounting generally preferred over the cash basis?

3. What type of business is most likely to select a fiscal year that corresponds to its natural business year instead of the calendar year?

4. What is a prepaid expense and where is it reported in the financial statements?

5. 🏺 What contra account is used when recording and reporting the effects of depreciation? Why is it used?

6. What is an accrued revenue? Give an example.

7. What are the steps in recording closing entries?

8. What is the purpose of the Income Summary account?

9. 🏺 Explain whether an error has occurred if a post-closing trial balance includes a Depreciation Expense account.

10. What is a company's operating cycle?

11. What classes of assets and liabilities are shown on a typical classified balance sheet?

12. How is unearned revenue classified on the balance sheet?

13.ᴬ If a company initially records prepaid expenses with debits to expense accounts, what type of account is debited in the adjusting entries for those prepaid expenses?

14.ᶜ If a company recorded accrued salaries expense of $500 at the end of its fiscal year, what reversing entry could be made? When would it be made?

15. 🏺 Refer to **Apple**'s most recent balance sheet in Appendix A. What five main noncurrent asset categories are used on its classified balance sheet?   **APPLE**

16. 🏺 Refer to **Google**'s most recent balance sheet in Appendix A. Identify the six accounts listed as current liabilities.   **GOOGLE**

17. 🏺 Review **Google**'s balance sheet in Appendix A. Identify the amount for property and equipment. What adjusting entry is necessary (no numbers required) for this account when preparing financial statements?   **GOOGLE**

18. 🏺 Refer to **Samsung**'s financial statements in Appendix A. What journal entry was likely recorded as of December 31, 2017, to close its Income Summary account?   **Samsung**

🅜 **connect**

Choose from the following list of terms and phrases to best complete the statements below.

  a. Fiscal year   **c.** Accrual basis accounting   **e.** Cash basis accounting

  b. Timeliness   **d.** Annual financial statements   **f.** Time period assumption

1. _____ presumes that an organization's activities can be divided into specific time periods.

2. Financial reports covering a one-year period are known as _____.

3. A(n) _____ consists of any 12 consecutive months.

4. _____ records revenues when services are provided and records expenses when incurred.

5. The value of information is often linked to its _____.

QUICK STUDY

QS 3-1
Periodic reporting
C1

QS 3-2
Computing accrual and cash income

C1

In its first year of operations, Roma Company reports the following.

- Earned revenues of $45,000 ($37,000 cash received from customers).
- Incurred expenses of $25,500 ($20,250 cash paid toward them).
- Prepaid $6,750 cash for costs that will not be expensed until next year.

Compute Roma's first-year net income under the cash basis *and* the accrual basis of accounting.

QS 3-3
Identifying accounting adjustments

P1 P2 P3 P4

Classify the following adjusting entries as involving prepaid expenses (PE), unearned revenues (UR), accrued expenses (AE), or accrued revenues (AR).

_____ **a.** To record revenue earned that was previously received as cash in advance.

_____ **b.** To record wages expense incurred but not yet paid (nor recorded).

_____ **c.** To record revenue earned but not yet billed (nor recorded).

_____ **d.** To record expiration of prepaid insurance.

_____ **e.** To record annual depreciation expense.

QS 3-4
Concepts of adjusting entries

P1 P2 P3 P4

During the year, a company recorded prepayments of expenses in asset accounts and cash receipts of unearned revenues in liability accounts. At the end of its annual accounting period, the company must make three adjusting entries.

(1) Accrue salaries expense. . . . . Dr. ___ Cr. ___

(2) Adjust the Unearned Services Revenue account to recognize earned revenue. . . . . . . Dr. ___ Cr. ___

(3) Record services revenue earned for which cash will be received the following period. . . Dr. ___ Cr. ___

For each of the adjusting entries (1), (2), and (3), indicate the account to be debited and the account to be credited—from *a* through *i* below.

a. Prepaid Insurance **d.** Unearned Services Revenue **g.** Accounts Receivable

b. Cash **e.** Salaries Expense **h.** Accounts Payable

c. Salaries Payable **f.** Services Revenue **i.** Depreciation Expense

---

QS 3-5
Prepaid (deferred) expenses adjustments

P1

For each separate case below, follow the three-step process for adjusting the prepaid asset account at December 31. Step 1: Determine what the current account balance equals. Step 2: Determine what the current account balance should equal. Step 3: Record the December 31 adjusting entry to get from step 1 to step 2. *Assume no other adjusting entries are made during the year.*

a. Prepaid Insurance. The Prepaid Insurance account has a $4,700 debit balance to start the year. A review of insurance policies shows that $900 of unexpired insurance remains at year-end.

b. Prepaid Insurance. The Prepaid Insurance account has a $5,890 debit balance at the start of the year. A review of insurance policies shows $1,040 of insurance has expired by year-end.

c. Prepaid Rent. On September 1 of the current year, the company prepaid $24,000 for two years of rent for facilities being occupied that day. The company debited Prepaid Rent and credited Cash for $24,000.

QS 3-6
Prepaid (deferred) expenses adjustments

P1

For each separate case below, follow the three-step process for adjusting the Supplies asset account at December 31. Step 1: Determine what the current account balance equals. Step 2: Determine what the current account balance should equal. Step 3: Record the December 31 adjusting entry to get from step 1 to step 2. *Assume no other adjusting entries are made during the year.*

a. Supplies. The Supplies account has a $300 debit balance to start the year. No supplies were purchased during the current year. A December 31 physical count shows $110 of supplies remaining.

b. Supplies. The Supplies account has an $800 debit balance to start the year. Supplies of $2,100 were purchased during the current year and debited to the Supplies account. A December 31 physical count shows $650 of supplies remaining.

c. Supplies. The Supplies account has a $4,000 debit balance to start the year. During the current year, supplies of $9,400 were purchased and debited to the Supplies account. The inventory of supplies available at December 31 totaled $2,660.

QS 3-7
Adjusting prepaid (deferred) expenses

P1

For each separate case, record the necessary adjusting entry.

a. On July 1, Lopez Company paid $1,200 for six months of insurance coverage. No adjustments have been made to the Prepaid Insurance account, and it is now December 31. Prepare the year-end adjusting entry to reflect expiration of the insurance as of December 31.

b. Zim Company has a Supplies account balance of $5,000 at the beginning of the year. During the year, it purchases $2,000 of supplies. As of December 31, a physical count of supplies shows $800 of supplies available. Prepare the adjusting journal entry to correctly report the balance of the Supplies account and the Supplies Expense account as of December 31.

For each separate case below, follow the three-step process for adjusting the Accumulated Depreciation account at December 31. Step 1: Determine what the current account balance equals. Step 2: Determine what the current account balance should equal. Step 3: Record the December 31 adjusting entry to get from step 1 to step 2. *Assume no other adjusting entries are made during the year.*

QS 3-8
Accumulated depreciation adjustments
P1

a. Accumulated Depreciation. The Krug Company's Accumulated Depreciation account has a $13,500 balance to start the year. A review of depreciation schedules reveals that $14,600 of depreciation expense must be recorded for the year.

b. Accumulated Depreciation. The company has only one fixed asset (truck) that it purchased at the start of this year. That asset had cost $44,000, had an estimated life of five years, and is expected to have zero value at the end of the five years.

c. Accumulated Depreciation. The company has only one fixed asset (equipment) that it purchased at the start of this year. That asset had cost $32,000, had an estimated life of seven years, and is expected to be valued at $4,000 at the end of the seven years.

For each separate case, record an adjusting entry (if necessary).

QS 3-9
Adjusting for depreciation
P1

a. Barga Company purchases $20,000 of equipment on January 1. The equipment is expected to last five years and be worth $2,000 at the end of that time. Prepare the entry to record one year's depreciation expense of $3,600 for the equipment as of December 31.

b. Welch Company purchases $10,000 of land on January 1. The land is expected to last forever. What depreciation adjustment, if any, should be made with respect to the Land account as of December 31?

For each separate case below, follow the three-step process for adjusting the unearned revenue liability account at December 31. Step 1: Determine what the current account balance equals. Step 2: Determine what the current account balance should equal. Step 3: Record the December 31 adjusting entry to get from step 1 to step 2. *Assume no other adjusting entries are made during the year.*

QS 3-10
Unearned (deferred) revenues adjustments
P2

a. Unearned Rent Revenue. The Krug Company collected $6,000 rent in advance on November 1, debiting Cash and crediting Unearned Rent Revenue. The tenant was paying 12 months' rent in advance and occupancy began November 1.

b. Unearned Services Revenue. The company charges $75 per insect treatment. A customer paid $300 on October 1 in advance for four treatments, which was recorded with a debit to Cash and a credit to Unearned Services Revenue. At year-end, the company has applied three treatments for the customer.

c. Unearned Rent Revenue. On September 1, a client paid the company $24,000 cash for six months of rent in advance (the client leased a building and took occupancy immediately). The company recorded the cash as Unearned Rent Revenue.

For each separate case, record the necessary adjusting entry.

QS 3-11
Adjusting for unearned (deferred) revenues
P2

a. Tao Co. receives $10,000 cash in advance for four months of evenly planned legal services beginning on October 1. Tao records it by debiting Cash and crediting Unearned Revenue both for $10,000. It is now December 31, and Tao has provided legal services as planned. What adjusting entry should Tao make to account for the work performed from October 1 through December 31?

b. Caden started a new publication called *Contest News*. Its subscribers pay $24 to receive 12 monthly issues. With every new subscriber, Caden debits Cash and credits Unearned Subscription Revenue for the amounts received. The company has 100 new subscribers as of July 1. It sends *Contest News* to each of these subscribers every month from July through December. Assuming no changes in subscribers, prepare the year-end journal entry that Caden must make as of December 31 to adjust the Subscription Revenue account and the Unearned Subscription Revenue account.

For each separate case below, follow the three-step process for adjusting the accrued expense account at December 31. Step 1: Determine what the current account balance equals. Step 2: Determine what the current account balance should equal. Step 3: Record the December 31 adjusting entry to get from step 1 to step 2. *Assume no other adjusting entries are made during the year.*

QS 3-12
Accrued expenses adjustments
P3

a. Salaries Payable. At year-end, salaries expense of $15,500 has been incurred by the company but is not yet paid to employees.

[continued on next page]

b. Interest Payable. At its December 31 year-end, the company owes $250 of interest on a line-of-credit loan. That interest will not be paid until sometime in January of the next year.

c. Interest Payable. At its December 31 year-end, the company holds a mortgage payable that has incurred $875 in annual interest that is neither recorded nor paid. The company intends to pay the interest on January 7 of the next year.

QS 3-13
Accruing salaries
P3

Molly Mocha employs one college student every summer in her coffee shop. The student works the five weekdays and is paid on the following Monday. (For example, a student who works Monday through Friday, June 1 through June 5, is paid for that work on Monday, June 8.) The coffee shop adjusts its books *monthly,* if needed, to show salaries earned but unpaid at month-end. The student works the last week of July, which is Monday, July 28, through Friday, August 1. If the student earns $100 per day, what adjusting entry must the coffee shop make on July 31 to correctly record accrued salaries expense for July?

QS 3-14
Accrued revenues
adjustments
P4

For each separate case below, follow the three-step process for adjusting the accrued revenue account at December 31. Step 1: Determine what the current account balance equals. Step 2: Determine what the current account balance should equal. Step 3: Record the December 31 adjusting entry to get from step 1 to step 2. *Assume no other adjusting entries are made during the year.*

a. Accounts Receivable. At year-end, the L. Cole Company has completed services of $19,000 for a client, but the client has not yet been billed for those services.

b. Interest Receivable. At year-end, the company has earned, but not yet recorded, $390 of interest earned from its investments in government bonds.

c. Accounts Receivable. A painting company bills customers when jobs are complete. The work for one job is now complete. The customer has not yet been billed for the $1,300 of work.

QS 3-15
Recording and analyzing
adjusting entries
P1   P2   P3   P4

Adjusting entries affect at least one balance sheet account and at least one income statement account. For the entries below, identify the account to be debited and the account to be credited from the following accounts: Cash; Accounts Receivable; Prepaid Insurance; Equipment; Accumulated Depreciation; Wages Payable; Unearned Revenue; Revenue; Wages Expense; Insurance Expense; and Depreciation Expense. Indicate which of the accounts is the income statement account and which is the balance sheet account.

a. Entry to record revenue earned that was previously received as cash in advance.

b. Entry to record wage expenses incurred but not yet paid (nor recorded).

c. Entry to record revenue earned but not yet billed (nor recorded).

d. Entry to record expiration of prepaid insurance.

e. Entry to record annual depreciation expense.

QS 3-16
Determining effects of
adjusting entries
P1   P3

In making adjusting entries at the end of its accounting period, Chao Consulting mistakenly forgot to record:

1. $3,200 of insurance coverage that had expired (this $3,200 cost had been initially debited to the Prepaid Insurance account).

2. $2,000 of accrued salaries expense.

As a result of these two oversights, the financial statements for the reporting period will [choose one]:

a. Understate assets by $3,200.   **c.** Understate net income by $2,000.

b. Understate expenses by $5,200.   **d.** Overstate liabilities by $2,000.

QS 3-17
Preparing an adjusted
trial balance
P5

Following are unadjusted balances along with year-end adjustments for Quinlan Company. Complete the adjusted trial balance by entering the adjusted balance for each of the following accounts.

No.	Account Title	Unadjusted Trial Balance		Adjustments		Adjusted Trial Balance	
		Dr.	Cr.	Dr.	Cr.	Dr.	Cr.
101	Cash	$8,000					
106	Accounts receivable	2,000		$4,000			
126	Supplies	4,500			$2,500		
209	Salaries payable		$ 0		400		
307	Common stock		3,000				
318	Retained earnings		6,000				
403	Consulting revenue		11,000		4,000		
622	Salaries expense	5,500		400			
652	Supplies expense	0		2,500			

QS 3-18
Preparing closing entries
from the ledger   **P7**

The ledger of Mai Company includes the following accounts with normal balances as of December 31: Common Stock $9,000; Dividends $800; Services Revenue $13,000; Wages Expense $8,400; and Rent Expense $1,600. Prepare its December 31 closing entries.

Identify which of the following accounts would be included in a post-closing trial balance.

_____ **a.** Accounts Receivable   _____ **c.** Goodwill   _____ **e.** Income Tax Expense

_____ **b.** Salaries Expense   _____ **d.** Land   _____ **f.** Salaries Payable

QS 3-19
Identifying post-closing
accounts   **P8**

List the following steps of the accounting cycle in their proper order.

_____ **a.** Posting the journal entries.   _____ **f.** Preparing the financial statements.

_____ **b.** Journalizing and posting adjusting entries.   _____ **g.** Preparing the unadjusted trial balance.

_____ **c.** Preparing the adjusted trial balance.   _____ **h.** Journalizing transactions and events.

_____ **d.** Journalizing and posting closing entries.   _____ **i.** Preparing the post-closing trial balance.

_____ **e.** Analyzing transactions and events.

QS 3-20
Identifying the accounting
cycle
C2

The following are common categories on a classified balance sheet.

A. Current assets   **C.** Plant assets   **E.** Current liabilities

B. Long-term investments   **D.** Intangible assets   **F.** Long-term liabilities

For each of the following items, select the letter that identifies the balance sheet category where the item typically would best appear.

_____ **1.** Land held for future expansion   _____ **5.** Accounts payable

_____ **2.** Notes payable (due in five years)   _____ **6.** Store equipment

_____ **3.** Accounts receivable   _____ **7.** Wages payable

_____ **4.** Trademarks   _____ **8.** Cash

QS 3-21
Classifying balance sheet
items
C3

Use the following adjusted trial balance of Sierra Company to prepare its (1) income statement and (2) statement of retained earnings for the year ended December 31. The Retained Earnings account balance was $5,500 on December 31 of the *prior year*.

Adjusted Trial Balance	Debit	Credit
Cash	$ 5,000	
Prepaid insurance	500	
Notes receivable (due in 5 years)	4,000	
Buildings	20,000	
Accumulated depreciation—Buildings		$12,000
Accounts payable		2,500
Notes payable (due in 3 years)		3,000
Common stock		5,000
Retained earnings		5,500
Dividends	1,000	
Consulting revenue		9,500
Wages expense	3,500	
Depreciation expense—Buildings	2,000	
Insurance expense	1,500	
Totals	$37,500	$37,500

QS 3-22
Preparing financial
statements
P6

Use the information in the adjusted trial balance reported in QS 3-22 to prepare Sierra Company's *classified* balance sheet as of December 31.

QS 3-23
Preparing a classified
balance sheet   **C3**

Damita Company reported net income of $48,025 and net sales of $425,000 for the current year. Calculate the company's profit margin and interpret the result. Assume that its competitors earn an average profit margin of 15%.

QS 3-24
Analyzing profit margin

A1

Compute Chavez Company's current ratio using the following information.

Accounts receivable	$18,000	Long-term notes payable	$21,000
Accounts payable	11,000	Office supplies	2,800
Buildings	45,000	Prepaid insurance	3,560
Cash	7,000	Unearned services revenue	3,000

QS 3-25
Identifying current accounts
and computing the current
ratio

A2

QS 3-26ᴬ

Preparing adjusting entries

P9

Garcia Company had the following selected transactions during the year. (A partial chart of accounts follows: Cash; Accounts Receivable; Prepaid Insurance; Wages Payable; Unearned Revenue; Revenue; Wages Expense; Insurance Expense; Depreciation Expense.)

Jan. 1   The company paid $6,000 cash for 12 months of insurance coverage beginning immediately.

Aug. 1   The company received $2,400 cash in advance for 6 months of contracted services beginning on August 1 and ending on January 31.

Dec. 31   The company prepared any necessary year-end adjusting entries related to insurance coverage and services performed.

a. Record journal entries for these transactions assuming Garcia follows the usual practice of recording a prepayment of an expense in an asset account *and* recording a prepayment of revenue received in a liability account.

b. Record journal entries for these transactions assuming Garcia follows the alternative practice of recording a prepayment of an expense in an expense account *and* recording a prepayment of revenue received in a revenue account.

QS 3-27ᴮ

Extending accounts in a work sheet **P10**

The Adjusted Trial Balance columns of a 10-column work sheet for Planta Company follow. Complete the work sheet by extending the account balances into the appropriate financial statement columns and by entering the amount of net income for the reporting period.

No.	Account Title	Unadjusted Trial Balance Dr.	Cr.	Adjustments Dr.	Cr.	Adjusted Trial Balance Dr.	Cr.	Income Statement Dr.	Cr.	Balance Sheet Dr.	Cr.
101	Cash					$ 7,000					
106	Accounts receivable					27,200					
153	Trucks					42,000					
154	Accumulated depreciation—Trucks						$ 17,500				
183	Land					32,000					
201	Accounts payable						15,000				
209	Salaries payable						4,200				
233	Unearned fees						3,600				
307	Common stock						20,000				
318	Retained earnings						45,500				
319	Dividends					15,400					
401	Plumbing fees earned						84,000				
611	Depreciation expense—Trucks					6,500					
622	Salaries expense					38,000					
640	Rent expense					13,000					
677	Miscellaneous expenses					8,700					
	Totals					$189,800	$189,800				
	Net income										
	Totals										

Check Net income, $17,800

QS 3-28ᶜ

Reversing entries

P11

On December 31, Yates Co. prepared an adjusting entry for $12,000 of earned but unrecorded consulting revenue. On January 16, Yates received $26,700 cash as payment in full for consulting work it provided that began on December 18 and ended on January 16. The company uses reversing entries.

a. Prepare the December 31 adjusting entry.   **c.** Prepare the January 16 cash receipt entry.

b. Prepare the January 1 reversing entry.

connect

EXERCISES

Exercise 3-1

Preparing adjusting entries

P1   P2   P3

Prepare adjusting journal entries for the year ended (date of) December 31 for each of these separate situations. Entries can draw from the following partial chart of accounts: Cash; Accounts Receivable; Supplies; Prepaid Insurance; Prepaid Rent; Equipment; Accumulated Depreciation—Equipment; Wages Payable; Unearned Revenue; Revenue; Wages Expense; Supplies Expense; Insurance Expense; Rent Expense; and Depreciation Expense—Equipment.

a. Depreciation on the company's equipment for the year is computed to be $18,000.

b. The Prepaid Insurance account had a $6,000 debit balance at December 31 before adjusting for the costs of any expired coverage. An analysis of the company's insurance policies showed that $1,100 of unexpired insurance coverage remains.

Check (c) Dr. Supplies Expense, $3,880

c. The Supplies account had a $700 debit balance at the beginning of the year; and $3,480 of supplies were purchased during the year. The December 31 physical count showed $300 of supplies available.

d. Two-thirds of the work related to $15,000 of cash received in advance was performed this period.

e. The Prepaid Rent account had a $6,800 debit balance at December 31 before adjusting for the costs of expired prepaid rent. An analysis of the rental agreement showed that $5,800 of prepaid rent had expired.   (e) Dr. Rent Expense, $5,800

f. Wage expenses of $3,200 have been incurred but are not paid as of December 31.

Pablo Management has five employees, each of whom earns $250 per day. They are paid on Fridays for work completed Monday through Friday of the same week. Near year-end, the five employees worked Monday, December 31, and Wednesday through Friday, January 2, 3, and 4. New Year's Day (January 1) was an unpaid holiday.

Exercise 3-2
Adjusting and paying accrued wages
P3

a. Prepare the year-end adjusting entry for wages expense.

b. Prepare the journal entry to record payment of the employees' wages on Friday, January 4.

The following three *separate* situations require adjusting journal entries to prepare financial statements as of April 30. For each situation, present both:

Exercise 3-3
Adjusting and paying accrued expenses
P3

- The April 30 adjusting entry.
- The subsequent entry during May to record payment of the accrued expenses.

Entries can draw from the following partial chart of accounts: Cash; Accounts Receivable; Salaries Payable; Interest Payable; Legal Services Payable; Unearned Revenue; Revenue; Salaries Expense; Interest Expense; Legal Services Expense; and Depreciation Expense.

a. On April 1, the company hired an attorney for a flat monthly fee of $3,500. Payment for April legal services was made by the company on May 12.

b. As of April 30, $3,000 of interest expense has accrued on a note payable. The full interest payment of $9,000 on the note is due on May 20.   **Check** (b) May 20, Dr. Interest Expense, $6,000

c. Total weekly salaries expense for all employees is $10,000. This amount is paid at the end of the day on Friday of each five-day workweek. April 30 falls on a Tuesday, which means that the employees had worked two days since the last payday. The next payday is May 3.

For each of the following separate cases, prepare adjusting entries required of financial statements for the year ended (date of) December 31. Entries can draw from the following partial chart of accounts: Cash; Interest Receivable; Supplies; Prepaid Insurance; Equipment; Accumulated Depreciation—Equipment; Wages Payable; Interest Payable; Unearned Revenue; Interest Revenue; Wages Expense; Supplies Expense; Insurance Expense; Interest Expense; and Depreciation Expense—Equipment.

Exercise 3-4
Preparing adjusting entries
P1   P3   P4

a. Wages of $8,000 are earned by workers but not paid as of December 31.

b. Depreciation on the company's equipment for the year is $18,000.

c. The Supplies account had a $240 debit balance at the beginning of the year. During the year, $5,200 of supplies are purchased. A physical count of supplies at December 31 shows $440 of supplies available.

d. The Prepaid Insurance account had a $4,000 balance at the beginning of the year. An analysis of insurance policies shows that $1,200 of unexpired insurance benefits remain at December 31.   **Check** (d) Dr. Insurance Expense, $2,800

e. The company has earned (but not recorded) $1,050 of interest revenue for the year ended December 31. The interest payment will be received 10 days after the year-end on January 10.   (e) Cr. Interest Revenue, $1,050

f. The company has a bank loan and has incurred (but not recorded) interest expense of $2,500 for the year ended December 31. The company will pay the interest five days after the year-end on January 5.

Prepare year-end adjusting journal entries for M&R Company as of December 31 for each of the following separate cases. Entries can draw from the following partial chart of accounts: Cash; Accounts Receivable; Interest Receivable; Equipment; Wages Payable; Salary Payable; Interest Payable; Lawn Services Payable; Unearned Revenue; Revenue; Interest Revenue; Wages Expense; Salary Expense; Supplies Expense; Lawn Services Expense; and Interest Expense.

Exercise 3-5
Preparing adjusting entries—accrued revenues and expenses
P3   P4

a. M&R Company provided $2,000 in services to customers in December, which are not yet recorded. Those customers are expected to pay the company in January following the company's year-end.

b. Wage expenses of $1,000 have been incurred but are not paid as of December 31.

c. M&R Company has a $5,000 bank loan and has incurred (but not recorded) 8% interest expense of $400 for the year ended December 31. The company will pay the $400 interest in cash on January 2 following the company's year-end.

d. M&R Company hired a firm that provided lawn services during December for $500. M&R will pay for December lawn services on January 15 following the company's year-end.

e. M&R Company has earned $200 in interest revenue from investments for the year ended December 31. The interest revenue will be received on January 15 following the company's year-end.

f. Salary expenses of $900 have been earned by supervisors but not paid as of December 31.

Exercise 3-6

Preparing adjusting entries

P1   P2   P3   P4

For each of the following separate cases, prepare the required December 31 year-end adjusting entries. Entries can draw from this partial chart of accounts: Interest Receivable; Prepaid Insurance; Accumulated Depreciation—Equipment; Wages Payable; Unearned Revenue; Consulting Revenue; Interest Revenue; Wages Expense; Insurance Expense; Interest Expense; and Depreciation Expense—Equipment.

a. Depreciation on the company's wind turbine equipment for the year is $5,000.

b. The Prepaid Insurance account for the solar panels had a $2,000 debit balance at December 31 before adjusting for the costs of any expired coverage. Analysis of prepaid insurance shows that $600 of unexpired insurance coverage remains at year-end.

c. The company received $3,000 cash in advance for sustainability consulting work. As of December 31, one-third of the sustainability consulting work had been performed.

d. As of December 31, $1,200 in wages expense for the organic produce workers has been incurred but not yet paid.

e. As of December 31, the company has earned, but not yet recorded, $400 of interest revenue from investments in socially responsible bonds. The interest revenue is expected to be received on January 12.

Exercise 3-7

Analyzing and preparing adjusting entries

P5

Following are two income statements for Alexis Co. for the year ended December 31. The left number column is prepared before adjusting entries are recorded, and the right column is prepared after adjusting entries. Analyze the statements and prepare the seven adjusting entries *a* through *g* that likely were recorded. *Hint:* The entry for *a* refers to fees that have been earned but not yet billed. None of the entries involve cash.

Income Statements For Year Ended December 31			
	Unadjusted	Adjustments	Adjusted
Revenues			
Fees earned	$18,000	a.	$25,000
Commissions earned	36,500		36,500
Total revenues	54,500		61,500
Expenses			
Depreciation expense—Computers	0	b.	1,600
Depreciation expense—Office furniture	0	c.	1,850
Salaries expense	13,500	d.	15,750
Insurance expense	0	e.	1,400
Rent expense	3,800		3,800
Office supplies expense	0	f.	580
Advertising expense	2,500		2,500
Utilities expense	1,245	g.	1,335
Total expenses	21,045		28,815
Net income	$33,455		$32,685

Exercise 3-8

Preparing financial statements from a trial balance

P6

Following are the accounts and balances (in random order) from the adjusted trial balance of Stark Company. Prepare the (1) income statement and (2) statement of retained earnings for the year ended December 31 and (3) balance sheet at December 31. The Retained Earnings account balance was $14,800 on December 31 of the *prior year*.

Notes payable.	$11,000	Accumulated depreciation—Buildings	$15,000
Prepaid insurance	2,500	Accounts receivable	4,000
Interest expense	500	Utilities expense	1,300
Accounts payable	1,500	Interest payable	100
Wages payable	400	Unearned revenue	800
Cash	10,000	Supplies expense	200
Wages expense	7,500	Buildings	40,000
Insurance expense	1,800	Dividends	3,000
Common stock	10,000	Depreciation expense—Buildings	2,000
Retained earnings	14,800	Supplies.	800
Services revenue	20,000		

Following are **Nintendo**'s revenue and expense accounts for a recent March 31 fiscal year-end (yen in millions). Prepare the company's closing entries for (1) its revenues and (2) its expenses.

Exercise 3-9
Preparing closing entries

P7

Net sales..........................	¥504,459	Advertising expense	¥ 46,636
Cost of sales	283,494	Other expense, net	157,811

The following adjusted trial balance contains the accounts and year-end balances of Cruz Company as of December 31. (1) Prepare the December 31 closing entries for Cruz Company. Assume the account number for Income Summary is 901. (2) Prepare the December 31 post-closing trial balance for Cruz Company. *Note:* The Retained Earnings account balance was $37,600 on December 31 of the *prior year.*

Exercise 3-10
Preparing closing entries and a post-closing trial balance

P7   P8

No.	Account Title	Debit	Credit
101	Cash.......................................	$19,000	
126	Supplies....................................	13,000	
128	Prepaid insurance...........................	3,000	
167	Equipment..................................	24,000	
168	Accumulated depreciation—Equipment		$ 7,500
307	Common stock		10,000
318	Retained earnings.............................		37,600
319	Dividends...................................	7,000	
404	Services revenue		44,000
612	Depreciation expense—Equipment.................	3,000	
622	Salaries expense..............................	22,000	
637	Insurance expense	2,500	
640	Rent expense	3,400	
652	Supplies expense	2,200	
	Totals.....................................	$99,100	$99,100

Use the following adjusted year-end trial balance at December 31 of Wilson Trucking Company to prepare the (1) income statement and (2) statement of retained earnings for the year ended December 31. The Retained Earnings account balance was $155,000 at December 31 of the *prior year.*

Exercise 3-11
Preparing financial statements   **P6**

Account Title	Debit	Credit
Cash.......................................	$ 8,000	
Accounts receivable..........................	17,500	
Office supplies	3,000	
Trucks	172,000	
Accumulated depreciation—Trucks..............		$ 36,000
Land.......................................	85,000	
Accounts payable............................		12,000
Interest payable		4,000
Long-term notes payable......................		58,000
Common stock		15,000
Retained earnings............................		155,000
Dividends	20,000	
Trucking fees earned		130,000
Depreciation expense—Trucks	23,500	
Salaries expense.............................	61,000	
Office supplies expense.......................	8,000	
Repairs expense—Trucks......................	12,000	
Totals.....................................	$410,000	$410,000

Exercise 3-12
Preparing a classified
balance sheet **C3**

Use the information in the adjusted trial balance reported in Exercise 3-11 to prepare Wilson Trucking Company's *classified* balance sheet as of December 31.

Exercise 3-13
Computing and interpreting
profit margin

A1

Use the following information to compute profit margin for each separate company *a* through *e*. Which of the five companies is the most profitable according to the profit margin ratio? Interpret the profit margin ratio for company *c*.

	Net Income	Net Sales			Net Income	Net Sales
a.	$ 4,361	$ 44,500		d.	$65,646	$1,458,800
b.	97,706	398,800		e.	80,132	435,500
c.	111,281	257,000				

Exercise 3-14
Computing and analyzing
the current ratio

A2

Calculate the current ratio for each of the following companies (round the ratio to two decimals). Identify the company with the strongest liquidity position. (These companies are competitors in the same industry.)

	Current Assets	Current Liabilities
Edison	$ 79,040	$ 32,000
MAXT...........	104,880	76,000
Chatter	45,080	49,000
TRU	85,680	81,600
Gleeson.........	61,000	100,000

Exercise 3-15ᴬ
Adjusting for prepaids
recorded as expenses and
unearned revenues
recorded as revenues

P9

Ricardo Construction began operations on December 1. In setting up its accounting procedures, the company decided to debit expense accounts when it prepays its expenses and to credit revenue accounts when customers pay for services in advance. Prepare journal entries for items *a* through *d* and the adjusting entries as of its December 31 period-end for items *e* through *g*. Entries can draw from the following partial chart of accounts: Cash; Accounts Receivable; Interest Receivable; Supplies; Prepaid Insurance; Unearned Remodeling Fees; Remodeling Fees Earned; Supplies Expense; Insurance Expense; and Interest Expense.

a. Supplies are purchased on December 1 for $2,000 cash.

b. The company prepaid its insurance premiums for $1,540 cash on December 2.

c. On December 15, the company receives an advance payment of $13,000 cash from a customer for remodeling work.

d. On December 28, the company receives $3,700 cash from another customer for remodeling work to be performed in January.

e. A physical count on December 31 indicates that the company has $1,840 of supplies available.

Check *(f)* Cr. Insurance
Expense, $1,200

f. An analysis of insurance policies in effect on December 31 shows that $340 of insurance coverage had expired.

(g) Dr. Remodeling Fees
Earned, $11,130

g. As of December 31, only one remodeling project has been worked on and completed. The $5,570 fee for this project had been received in advance and recorded as remodeling fees earned.

Exercise 3-16ᴮ
Preparing unadjusted and
adjusted trial balances,
including the adjustments

P10

The following data are taken from the unadjusted trial balance of the Westcott Company at December 31. Each account carries a normal balance. Set up a 10-column work sheet to answer the requirements.

Accounts Payable...................	$ 6	Prepaid Insurance......	$18	Retained Earnings............	$32
Accounts Receivable	12	Revenue..............	75	Dividends..................	6
Accumulated Depreciation—Equip.......	15	Salaries Expense.......	18	Unearned Revenue	12
Cash	21	Supplies..............	24	Utilities Expense	12
Equipment	39	Common Stock	10		

1. Enter the accounts in proper order and enter their balances in the correct Debit or Credit column of the Unadjusted Trial Balance columns of the 10-column work sheet.

[continued on next page]

2. Use the following adjustment information to complete the Adjustments columns of the work sheet from part 1.

a. Depreciation on equipment, $3   **d.** Supplies available at December 31, $15

b. Accrued salaries, $6   **e.** Expired insurance, $15

c. The $12 of unearned revenue has been earned

3. Extend the balances in the Adjusted Trial Balance columns of the work sheet to the proper financial statement columns. Compute totals for those columns, including net income.

The following two events occurred for Trey Co. on October 31, the end of its fiscal year.

a. Trey rents a building from its owner for $2,800 per month. By a prearrangement, the company delayed paying October's rent until November 5. On this date, the company paid the rent for both October and November.

b. Trey rents space in a building it owns to a tenant for $850 per month. By prearrangement, the tenant delayed paying the October rent until November 8. On this date, the tenant paid the rent for both October and November.

Exercise 3-17ᶜ
Preparing reversing entries

P11

Required

1. Prepare adjusting entries that the company must record for these events as of October 31.

2. Assuming Trey does *not* use reversing entries, prepare journal entries to record Trey's payment of rent on November 5 and the collection of the tenant's rent on November 8.

3. Assuming that the company uses reversing entries, prepare reversing entries on November 1 and the journal entries to record Trey's payment of rent on November 5 and the collection of the tenant's rent on November 8.

⬛ connect

For journal entries *1* through *12,* enter the letter of the explanation that most closely describes it in the space beside each entry. You can use letters more than once.

A. To record receipt of unearned revenue.

B. To record this period's earning of prior unearned revenue.

C. To record payment of an accrued expense.

D. To record receipt of an accrued revenue.

E. To record an accrued expense.

F. To record an accrued revenue.

G. To record this period's use of a prepaid expense.

H. To record payment of a prepaid expense.

I. To record this period's depreciation expense.

PROBLEM SET A

Problem 3-1A
Identifying adjusting entries with explanations

P1   P2   P3   P4

_____	1.	Interest Expense	1,000		_____	7.	Salaries Expense	6,000
		Interest Payable		1,000			Salaries Payable		6,000
_____	2.	Depreciation Expense	4,000		_____	8.	Interest Receivable	5,000
		Accumulated Depreciation		4,000			Interest Revenue		5,000
_____	3.	Unearned Professional Fees	3,000		_____	9.	Cash	9,000
		Professional Fees Earned		3,000			Accounts Receivable (from consulting)		9,000
_____	4.	Insurance Expense	4,200		_____	10.	Cash	7,500
		Prepaid Insurance		4,200			Unearned Professional Fees		7,500
_____	5.	Salaries Payable	1,400		_____	11.	Cash	2,000
		Cash		1,400			Interest Receivable		2,000
_____	6.	Prepaid Rent	4,500		_____	12.	Rent Expense	2,000
		Cash		4,500			Prepaid Rent		2,000

Arnez Company's annual accounting period ends on December 31, 2019. The following information concerns the adjusting entries to be recorded as of that date. Entries can draw from the following partial chart of accounts: Cash; Rent Receivable; Office Supplies; Prepaid Insurance; Building; Accumulated Depreciation—Building; Salaries Payable; Unearned Rent; Rent Earned; Salaries Expense; Office Supplies Expense; Insurance Expense; and Depreciation Expense—Building.

Problem 3-2A
Preparing adjusting and subsequent journal entries

P1   P2   P3   P4

[continued on next page]

a. The Office Supplies account started the year with a $4,000 balance. During 2019, the company purchased supplies for $13,400, which was added to the Office Supplies account. The inventory of supplies available at December 31, 2019, totaled $2,554.

b. An analysis of the company's insurance policies provided the following facts. The total premium for each policy was paid in full (for all months) at the purchase date, and the Prepaid Insurance account was debited for the full cost. (Year-end adjusting entries for Prepaid Insurance were properly recorded in all prior years.)

Policy	Date of Purchase	Months of Coverage	Cost
A	April 1, 2017	24	$14,400
B	April 1, 2018	36	12,960
C	August 1, 2019	12	2,400

c. The company has 15 employees, who earn a total of $1,960 in salaries each working day. They are paid each Monday for their work in the five-day workweek ending on the previous Friday. Assume that December 31, 2019, is a Tuesday, and all 15 employees worked the first two days of that week. Because New Year's Day is a paid holiday, they will be paid salaries for five full days on Monday, January 6, 2020.

d. The company purchased a building on January 1, 2019. It cost $960,000 and is expected to have a $45,000 salvage value at the end of its predicted 30-year life. Annual depreciation is $30,500.

e. Since the company is not large enough to occupy the entire building it owns, it rented space to a tenant at $3,000 per month, starting on November 1, 2019. The rent was paid on time on November 1, and the amount received was credited to the Rent Earned account. However, the tenant has not paid the December rent. The company has worked out an agreement with the tenant, who has promised to pay both December and January rent in full on January 15. The tenant has agreed not to fall behind again.

f. On November 1, the company rented space to another tenant for $2,800 per month. The tenant paid five months' rent in advance on that date. The payment was recorded with a credit to the Unearned Rent account.

Check (1b) Dr. Insurance
Expense, $7,120
(1d) Dr. Depreciation
Expense, $30,500

Required

1. Use the information to prepare adjusting entries as of December 31, 2019.

2. Prepare journal entries to record the first subsequent cash transaction in 2020 for parts *c* and *e*.

Problem 3-3A
Preparing adjusting entries,
adjusted trial balance, and
financial statements

P1 P2 P3 P4 P5 P6

Wells Technical Institute (WTI), a school owned by Tristana Wells, provides training to individuals who pay tuition directly to the school. WTI also offers training to groups in off-site locations. Its unadjusted trial balance as of December 31 follows, along with descriptions of items *a* through *h* that require adjusting entries on December 31.

Additional Information

a. An analysis of WTI's insurance policies shows that $2,400 of coverage has expired.

b. An inventory count shows that teaching supplies costing $2,800 are available at year-end.

c. Annual depreciation on the equipment is $13,200.

d. Annual depreciation on the professional library is $7,200.

e. On September 1, WTI agreed to do five courses for a client for $2,500 each. Two courses will start immediately and finish before the end of the year. Three courses will not begin until next year. The client paid $12,500 cash in advance for all five courses on September 1, and WTI credited Unearned Training Fees.

f. On October 15, WTI agreed to teach a four-month class (beginning immediately) for an executive with payment due at the end of the class. At December 31, $7,500 of the tuition has been earned by WTI.

g. WTI's two employees are paid weekly. As of the end of the year, two days' salaries have accrued at the rate of $100 per day for each employee.

h. The balance in the Prepaid Rent account represents rent for December.

WELLS TECHNICAL INSTITUTE Unadjusted Trial Balance December 31	Debit	Credit
Cash	$ 34,000	
Accounts receivable	0	
Teaching supplies	8,000	
Prepaid insurance	12,000	
Prepaid rent	3,000	
Professional library	35,000	
Accumulated depreciation—Professional library		$ 10,000
Equipment	80,000	
Accumulated depreciation—Equipment		15,000
Accounts payable		26,000
Salaries payable		0
Unearned training fees		12,500
Common stock		10,000
Retained earnings		80,000
Dividends	50,000	
Tuition fees earned		123,900
Training fees earned		40,000
Depreciation expense—Professional library	0	
Depreciation expense—Equipment	0	
Salaries expense	50,000	
Insurance expense	0	
Rent expense	33,000	
Teaching supplies expense	0	
Advertising expense	6,000	
Utilities expense	6,400	
Totals	$317,400	$317,400

Required

1. Prepare T-accounts (representing the ledger) with balances from the unadjusted trial balance.
2. Prepare the necessary adjusting journal entries for items *a* through *h* and post them to the T-accounts. Assume that adjusting entries are made only at year-end.
3. Update balances in the T-accounts for the adjusting entries and prepare an adjusted trial balance.
4. Prepare Wells Technical Institute's income statement and statement of retained earnings for the year and prepare its balance sheet as of December 31. The Retained Earnings account balance was $80,000 on December 31 of the *prior year*.

Check (2e) Cr. Training Fees Earned, $5,000
(2f) Cr. Tuition Fees Earned, $7,500
(3) Adj. trial balance totals, $345,700
(4) Net income, $49,600

The adjusted trial balance for Chiara Company as of December 31 follows.

Problem 3-4A
Preparing financial statements from the adjusted trial balance

P6

	Debit	Credit
Cash	$ 30,000	
Accounts receivable	52,000	
Interest receivable	18,000	
Notes receivable (due in 90 days)	168,000	
Office supplies	16,000	
Automobiles	168,000	
Accumulated depreciation—Automobiles		$ 50,000
Equipment	138,000	
Accumulated depreciation—Equipment		18,000
Land	78,000	
Accounts payable		96,000
Interest payable		20,000
Salaries payable		19,000
Unearned fees		30,000
Long-term notes payable		138,000
Common stock		20,000
Retained earnings		235,800
Dividends	46,000	

[continued on next page]

[continued from previous page]

Fees earned		484,000
Interest earned		24,000
Depreciation expense—Automobiles	26,000	
Depreciation expense—Equipment	18,000	
Salaries expense	188,000	
Wages expense	40,000	
Interest expense	32,000	
Office supplies expense	34,000	
Advertising expense	58,000	
Repairs expense—Automobiles	24,800	
Totals	$1,134,800	$1,134,800

Required

Check Total assets, $600,000

Use the information in the adjusted trial balance to prepare (*a*) the income statement for the year ended December 31; (*b*) the statement of retained earnings for the year ended December 31 [*Note:* Retained Earnings at December 31 of the *prior year* was $235,800]; and (*c*) the balance sheet as of December 31.

Problem 3-5A

Applying the accounting cycle

P1 P2 P3 P4 P5 P6 P7 P8

On April 1, Jiro Nozomi created a new travel agency, Adventure Travel. The following transactions occurred during the company's first month.

Apr.	1	Nozomi invested $30,000 cash and computer equipment worth $20,000 in the company in exchange for common stock.
	2	The company rented furnished office space by paying $1,800 cash for the first month's (April) rent.
	3	The company purchased $1,000 of office supplies for cash.
	10	The company paid $2,400 cash for the premium on a 12-month insurance policy. Coverage begins on April 11.
	14	The company paid $1,600 cash for two weeks' salaries earned by employees.
	24	The company collected $8,000 cash for commissions earned.
	28	The company paid $1,600 cash for two weeks' salaries earned by employees.
	29	The company paid $350 cash for minor repairs to the company's computer.
	30	The company paid $750 cash for this month's telephone bill.
	30	The company paid $1,500 cash in dividends.

The company's chart of accounts follows.

101	Cash	307	Common Stock	640	Rent Expense
106	Accounts Receivable	318	Retained Earnings	650	Office Supplies Expense
124	Office Supplies	319	Dividends	684	Repairs Expense
128	Prepaid Insurance	405	Commissions Earned	688	Telephone Expense
167	Computer Equipment	612	Depreciation Expense—Computer Equip.	901	Income Summary
168	Accumulated Depreciation—Computer Equip.	622	Salaries Expense		
209	Salaries Payable	637	Insurance Expense		

Required

1. Use the balance column format to set up each ledger account listed in its chart of accounts.

2. Prepare journal entries to record the transactions for April and post them to the ledger accounts. The company records prepaid and unearned items in balance sheet accounts.

Check (3) Unadj. trial balance totals, $58,000

3. Prepare an unadjusted trial balance as of April 30.

4. Use the following information to journalize and post adjusting entries for the month:

(4*a*) Dr. Insurance Expense, $133

   a. Prepaid insurance of $133 has expired this month.

   b. At the end of the month, $600 of office supplies are still available.

   c. This month's depreciation on the computer equipment is $500.

   d. Employees earned $420 of unpaid and unrecorded salaries as of month-end.

   e. The company earned $1,750 of commissions that are not yet billed at month-end.

(5) Net income, $2,197; Total assets, $51,117

5. Prepare the adjusted trial balance as of April 30. Prepare the income statement and the statement of retained earnings for the month of April and the balance sheet at April 30.

6. Prepare journal entries to close the temporary accounts and post these entries to the ledger.

(7) P-C trial balance totals, $51,617

7. Prepare a post-closing trial balance.

The adjusted trial balance for Tybalt Construction as of December 31, 2019, follows. O. Tybalt invested $5,000 cash in the business in exchange for common stock during year 2019. The December 31, 2018, credit balance of the Retained Earnings account was $121,400.

Problem 3-6A
Preparing closing entries and financial statements

P6   P7

No.	Account Title	Debit	Credit
	Adjusted Trial Balance		
	December 31, 2019		
101	Cash	$ 5,000	
104	Short-term investments	23,000	
126	Supplies	8,100	
128	Prepaid insurance	7,000	
167	Equipment.....................................	40,000	
168	Accumulated depreciation—Equipment		$ 20,000
173	Building.......................................	150,000	
174	Accumulated depreciation—Building		50,000
183	Land	55,000	
201	Accounts payable..............................		16,500
203	Interest payable		2,500
208	Rent payable..................................		3,500
210	Wages payable................................		2,500
213	Property taxes payable		900
233	Unearned professional fees.....................		7,500
244	Current portion of long-term note payable...........		7,000
251	Long-term notes payable.......................		60,000
307	Common stock		5,000
318	Retained earnings		121,400
319	Dividends	13,000	
401	Professional fees earned.......................		97,000
406	Rent earned		14,000
407	Dividends earned.............................		2,000
409	Interest earned...............................		2,100
606	Depreciation expense—Building.................	11,000	
612	Depreciation expense—Equipment...............	6,000	
623	Wages expense	32,000	
633	Interest expense..............................	5,100	
637	Insurance expense............................	10,000	
640	Rent expense	13,400	
652	Supplies expense.............................	7,400	
682	Postage expense	4,200	
683	Property taxes expense........................	5,000	
684	Repairs expense..............................	8,900	
688	Telephone expense	3,200	
690	Utilities expense..............................	4,600	
	Totals.......................................	$411,900	$411,900

Required

1. Prepare the income statement and the statement of retained earnings for calendar-year 2019 and the classified balance sheet at December 31, 2019.

2. Prepare the necessary closing entries at December 31, 2019.

Check (1) Total assets (12/31/2019), $218,100; Net income, $4,300

In the blank space beside each numbered balance sheet item, enter the letter of its balance sheet classification. If the item should not appear on the balance sheet, enter a Z in the blank.

A. Current assets
B. Long-term investments
C. Plant assets
D. Intangible assets
E. Current liabilities
F. Long-term liabilities
G. Equity

Problem 3-7A
Determining balance sheet classifications

C3

_____ **1.** Long-term investment in stock
_____ **2.** Depreciation expense—Building
_____ **3.** Prepaid rent (2 months of rent)
_____ **4.** Interest receivable
_____ **5.** Taxes payable (due in 5 weeks)
_____ **6.** Automobiles
_____ **7.** Notes payable (due in 3 years)
_____ **8.** Accounts payable
_____ **9.** Cash
_____ **10.** Common stock

_____ **11.** Unearned services revenue
_____ **12.** Accumulated depreciation—Trucks
_____ **13.** Prepaid insurance (expires in 5 months)
_____ **14.** Buildings
_____ **15.** Store supplies
_____ **16.** Office equipment
_____ **17.** Land (used in operations)
_____ **18.** Repairs expense
_____ **19.** Office supplies
_____ **20.** Current portion of long-term note payable

PROBLEM SET B

Problem 3-1B

Identifying adjusting entries with explanations

P1   P2   P3   P4

For each of the following journal entries *1* through *12,* enter the letter of the explanation that most closely describes it in the space beside each entry. You can use letters more than once.

A. To record payment of a prepaid expense.
B. To record this period's use of a prepaid expense.
C. To record this period's depreciation expense.
D. To record receipt of unearned revenue.
E. To record this period's earning of prior unearned revenue.

F. To record an accrued expense.
G. To record payment of an accrued expense.
H. To record an accrued revenue.
I. To record receipt of accrued revenue.

_____	1.	Interest Receivable	3,500
		Interest Revenue	3,500
_____	2.	Salaries Payable	9,000
		Cash	9,000
_____	3.	Depreciation Expense	8,000
		Accumulated Depreciation ..	8,000
_____	4.	Cash	9,000
		Unearned Professional Fees .	9,000
_____	5.	Insurance Expense	4,000
		Prepaid Insurance	4,000
_____	6.	Interest Expense	5,000
		Interest Payable	5,000

_____	7.	Cash	1,500
		Accounts Receivable (from services)	1,500
_____	8.	Salaries Expense	7,000
		Salaries Payable	7,000
_____	9.	Cash	1,000
		Interest Receivable	1,000
_____	10.	Prepaid Rent	3,000
		Cash	3,000
_____	11.	Rent Expense	7,500
		Prepaid Rent	7,500
_____	12.	Unearned Professional Fees	6,000
		Professional Fees Earned	6,000

Problem 3-2B

Preparing adjusting and subsequent journal entries

P1   P2   P3   P4

Natsu Company's annual accounting period ends on October 31, 2019. The following information concerns the adjusting entries that need to be recorded as of that date. Entries can draw from the following partial chart of accounts: Cash; Rent Receivable; Office Supplies; Prepaid Insurance; Building; Accumulated Depreciation—Building; Salaries Payable; Unearned Rent; Rent Earned; Salaries Expense; Office Supplies Expense; Insurance Expense; and Depreciation Expense—Building.

a. The Office Supplies account started the fiscal year with a $600 balance. During the fiscal year, the company purchased supplies for $4,570, which was added to the Office Supplies account. The supplies available at October 31, 2019, totaled $800.

b. An analysis of the company's insurance policies provided the following facts. The total premium for each policy was paid in full (for all months) at the purchase date, and the Prepaid Insurance account was debited for the full cost. (Year-end adjusting entries for Prepaid Insurance were properly recorded in all prior fiscal years.)

Policy	Date of Purchase	Months of Coverage	Cost
A	April 1, 2018	24	$6,000
B	April 1, 2019	36	7,200
C	August 1, 2019	12	1,320

c. The company has four employees, who earn a total of $1,000 for each workday. They are paid each Monday for their work in the five-day workweek ending on the previous Friday. Assume that October 31, 2019, is a Monday, and all four employees worked the first day of that week. They will be paid salaries for five full days on Monday, November 7, 2019.

d. The company purchased a building on November 1, 2016, that cost $175,000 and is expected to have a $40,000 salvage value at the end of its predicted 25-year life. Annual depreciation is $5,400.

e. Because the company does not occupy the entire building it owns, it rented space to a tenant at $1,000 per month, starting on September 1, 2019. The rent was paid on time on September 1, and the amount received was credited to the Rent Earned account. However, the October rent has not been paid. The company has worked out an agreement with the tenant, who has promised to pay both October and November rent in full on November 15. The tenant has agreed not to fall behind again.

f. On September 1, the company rented space to another tenant for $725 per month. The tenant paid five months' rent in advance on that date. The payment was recorded with a credit to the Unearned Rent account.

Check   (1*b*) Dr. Insurance Expense, $4,730
(1*d*) Dr. Depreciation Expense, $5,400

Required

1. Use the information to prepare adjusting entries as of October 31, 2019.

2. Prepare journal entries to record the first subsequent cash transaction in November 2019 for parts *c* and *e*.

Following is the unadjusted trial balance for Alonzo Institute as of December 31. The Institute provides one-on-one training to individuals who pay tuition directly to the business and offers extension training to groups in off-site locations. Shown after the trial balance are items *a* through *h* that require adjusting entries as of December 31.

Problem 3-3B
Preparing adjusting entries, adjusted trial balance, and financial statements

P1 P2 P3 P4 P5 P6

ALONZO INSTITUTE Unadjusted Trial Balance December 31	Debit	Credit
Cash	$ 60,000	
Accounts receivable	0	
Teaching supplies	70,000	
Prepaid insurance	19,000	
Prepaid rent	3,800	
Professional library	12,000	
Accumulated depreciation—Professional library		$ 2,500
Equipment	40,000	
Accumulated depreciation—Equipment		20,000
Accounts payable		11,200
Salaries payable		0
Unearned training fees		28,600
Common stock		11,000
Retained earnings		60,500
Dividends	20,000	
Tuition fees earned		129,200
Training fees earned		68,000
Depreciation expense—Professional library	0	
Depreciation expense—Equipment	0	
Salaries expense	44,200	
Insurance expense	0	
Rent expense	29,600	
Teaching supplies expense	0	
Advertising expense	19,000	
Utilities expense	13,400	
Totals	$331,000	$331,000

Additional Information

a. An analysis of the Institute's insurance policies shows that $9,500 of coverage has expired.

b. An inventory count shows that teaching supplies costing $20,000 are available at year-end.

c. Annual depreciation on the equipment is $5,000.

d. Annual depreciation on the professional library is $2,400.

e. On November 1, the Institute agreed to do a special two-month course (starting immediately) for a client. The contract calls for a $14,300 monthly fee, and the client paid the two months' fees in advance. When the cash was received, the Unearned Training Fees account was credited.

f. On October 15, the Institute agreed to teach a four-month class (beginning immediately) to an executive with payment due at the end of the class. At December 31, $5,750 of the tuition has been earned by the Institute.

g. The Institute's only employee is paid weekly. As of the end of the year, three days' salaries have accrued at the rate of $150 per day.

h. The balance in the Prepaid Rent account represents rent for December.

Required

1. Prepare T-accounts (representing the ledger) with balances from the unadjusted trial balance.

2. Prepare the necessary adjusting journal entries for items *a* through *h*, and post them to the T-accounts. Assume that adjusting entries are made only at year-end.

3. Update balances in the T-accounts for the adjusting entries and prepare an adjusted trial balance.

4. Prepare the company's income statement and statement of retained earnings for the year, and prepare its balance sheet as of December 31. The Retained Earnings account balance was $60,500 on December 31 of the *prior year*.

Check   (2e) Cr. Training Fees Earned, $28,600
(2f) Cr. Tuition Fees Earned, $5,750
(3) Adj. trial balance totals, $344,600
(4) Net income, $54,200

Problem 3-4B

Preparing financial statements from adjusted trial balance

P6

The adjusted trial balance for Speedy Courier as of December 31 follows.

	Debit	Credit
Cash	$ 58,000	
Accounts receivable	120,000	
Interest receivable	7,000	
Notes receivable (due in 90 days)	210,000	
Office supplies	22,000	
Trucks	134,000	
Accumulated depreciation—Trucks		$ 58,000
Equipment	270,000	
Accumulated depreciation—Equipment		200,000
Land	100,000	
Accounts payable		134,000
Interest payable		20,000
Salaries payable		28,000
Unearned delivery fees		120,000
Long-term notes payable		200,000
Common stock		15,000
Retained earnings		110,000
Dividends	50,000	
Delivery fees earned		611,800
Interest earned		34,000
Depreciation expense—Trucks	29,000	
Depreciation expense—Equipment	48,000	
Salaries expense	74,000	
Wages expense	300,000	
Interest expense	15,000	
Office supplies expense	31,000	
Advertising expense	27,200	
Repairs expense—Trucks	35,600	
Totals	$1,530,800	$1,530,800

Required

Check Total assets, $663,000

Use the information in the adjusted trial balance to prepare (*a*) the income statement for the year ended December 31; (*b*) the statement of retained earnings for the year ended December 31 [*Note:* Retained Earnings at Dec. 31 of the *prior year* was $110,000]; and (*c*) the balance sheet as of December 31.

Problem 3-5B

Applying the accounting cycle

P1 P2 P3 P4 P5 P6 P7 P8

On July 1, Lula Plume created a new self-storage business, Safe Storage Co. The following transactions occurred during the company's first month.

July   1   Plume invested $30,000 cash and buildings worth $150,000 in the company in exchange for common stock.

     2   The company rented equipment by paying $2,000 cash for the first month's (July) rent.

     5   The company purchased $2,400 of office supplies for cash.

    10   The company paid $7,200 cash for the premium on a 12-month insurance policy. Coverage begins on July 11.

    14   The company paid an employee $1,000 cash for two weeks' salary earned.

    24   The company collected $9,800 cash for storage fees from customers.

    28   The company paid $1,000 cash for two weeks' salary earned by an employee.

    29   The company paid $950 cash for minor repairs to a leaking roof.

    30   The company paid $400 cash for this month's telephone bill.

    31   The company paid $2,000 cash in dividends.

The company's chart of accounts follows.

101	Cash	307	Common Stock	640	Rent Expense
106	Accounts Receivable	318	Retained Earnings	650	Office Supplies Expense
124	Office Supplies	319	Dividends	684	Repairs Expense
128	Prepaid Insurance	401	Storage Fees Earned	688	Telephone Expense
173	Buildings	606	Depreciation Expense—Buildings	901	Income Summary
174	Accumulated Depreciation—Buildings	622	Salaries Expense		
209	Salaries Payable	637	Insurance Expense		

Required

1. Use the balance column format to set up each ledger account listed in its chart of accounts.

2. Prepare journal entries to record the transactions for July and post them to the ledger accounts. Record prepaid and unearned items in balance sheet accounts.

3. Prepare an unadjusted trial balance as of July 31.

4. Use the following information to journalize and post adjusting entries for the month:

   a. Prepaid insurance of $400 has expired this month.

   b. At the end of the month, $1,525 of office supplies are still available.

   c. This month's depreciation on the buildings is $1,500.

   d. An employee earned $100 of unpaid and unrecorded salary as of month-end.

   e. The company earned $1,150 of storage fees that are not yet billed at month-end.

5. Prepare the adjusted trial balance as of July 31. Prepare the income statement and the statement of retained earnings for the month of July and the balance sheet at July 31.

6. Prepare journal entries to close the temporary accounts and post these entries to the ledger.

7. Prepare a post-closing trial balance.

Check   (3) Unadj. trial balance totals, $189,800

(4*a*) Dr. Insurance Expense, $400

(5) Net income, $2,725; Total assets, $180,825

(7) P-C trial balance totals, $182,325

The adjusted trial balance for Anara Co. as of December 31, 2019, follows. P. Anara invested $40,000 cash in the business in exchange for common stock during year 2019. The December 31, 2018, credit balance of the Retained Earnings account was $52,800.

Problem 3-6B
Preparing closing entries and financial statements

P6   P7

No.	Account Title	Debit	Credit
	Adjusted Trial Balance **December 31, 2019**		
101	Cash	$ 7,400	
104	Short-term investments	11,200	
126	Supplies	4,600	
128	Prepaid insurance	1,000	
167	Equipment....................................	24,000	
168	Accumulated depreciation—Equipment		$ 4,000
173	Building......................................	100,000	
174	Accumulated depreciation—Building		10,000
183	Land	30,500	
201	Accounts payable.............................		3,500
203	Interest payable		1,750
208	Rent payable.................................		400
210	Wages payable...............................		1,280
213	Property taxes payable		3,330
233	Unearned professional fees....................		750
244	Current portion of long-term notes payable.........		8,400
251	Long-term notes payable......................		31,600
307	Common stock...............................		40,000
318	Retained earnings		52,800
319	Dividends	8,000	
401	Professional fees earned......................		59,600
406	Rent earned		4,500
407	Dividends earned.............................		1,000
409	Interest earned...............................		1,320
606	Depreciation expense—Building.................	2,000	
612	Depreciation expense—Equipment...............	1,000	
623	Wages expense	18,500	
633	Interest expense.............................	1,550	
637	Insurance expense...........................	1,525	
640	Rent expense	3,600	
652	Supplies expense............................	1,000	
682	Postage expense	410	
683	Property taxes expense.......................	4,825	
684	Repairs expense.............................	679	
688	Telephone expense	521	
690	Utilities expense.............................	1,920	
	Totals......................................	$224,230	$224,230

Required

1. Prepare the income statement and the statement of retained earnings for calendar-year 2019 and the classified balance sheet at December 31, 2019.

2. Prepare the necessary closing entries at December 31, 2019.

Problem 3-7B
Determining balance sheet classifications

C3

In the blank space beside each numbered balance sheet item, enter the letter of its balance sheet classification. If the item should not appear on the balance sheet, enter a Z in the blank.

A. Current assets   **D.** Intangible assets   **F.** Long-term liabilities

B. Long-term investments   **E.** Current liabilities   **G.** Equity

C. Plant assets

_____ **1.** Commissions earned

_____ **2.** Interest receivable

_____ **3.** Long-term investment in stock

_____ **4.** Prepaid insurance (4 months of rent)

_____ **5.** Machinery

_____ **6.** Notes payable (due in 15 years)

_____ **7.** Copyrights

_____ **8.** Current portion of long-term
note payable

_____ **9.** Accumulated depreciation—Trucks

_____ **10.** Office equipment

_____ **11.** Rent receivable

_____ **12.** Salaries payable

_____ **13.** Income taxes payable
(due in 11 weeks)

_____ **14.** Common stock

_____ **15.** Office supplies

_____ **16.** Interest payable

_____ **17.** Rent revenue

_____ **18.** Notes receivable (due in 120 days)

_____ **19.** Land (used in operations)

_____ **20.** Depreciation expense—Trucks

SERIAL PROBLEM
Business Solutions

P1 P2 P3 P4 P5 P6 P7 P8

©Alexander Image/Shutterstock

This serial problem began in Chapter 1 and continues through most of the book. If previous chapter segments were not completed, the serial problem can begin at this point.

SP 3 After the success of the company's first two months, Santana Rey continues to operate **Business Solutions**. (Transactions for the first two months are described in the Chapter 2 serial problem.) The November 30, 2019, unadjusted trial balance of Business Solutions (reflecting its transactions for October and November of 2019) follows.

No.	Account Title	Debit	Credit
101	Cash	$38,264	
106	Accounts receivable.....................................	12,618	
126	Computer supplies	2,545	
128	Prepaid insurance..	2,220	
131	Prepaid rent	3,300	
163	Office equipment	8,000	
164	Accumulated depreciation—Office equipment................		$ 0
167	Computer equipment	20,000	
168	Accumulated depreciation—Computer equipment		0
201	Accounts payable		0
210	Wages payable		0
236	Unearned computer services revenue		0
307	Common stock		73,000
318	Retained earnings..		0
319	Dividends	5,600	
403	Computer services revenue		25,659
612	Depreciation expense—Office equipment	0	
613	Depreciation expense—Computer equipment	0	
623	Wages expense	2,625	
637	Insurance expense	0	
640	Rent expense	0	
652	Computer supplies expense	0	
655	Advertising expense.....................................	1,728	
676	Mileage expense	704	
677	Miscellaneous expenses	250	
684	Repairs expense—Computer	805	
	Totals	$98,659	$98,659

Business Solutions had the following transactions and events in December 2019.

Dec. 2 Paid $1,025 cash to Hillside Mall for Business Solutions's share of mall advertising costs.
  3 Paid $500 cash for minor repairs to the company's computer.
  4 Received $3,950 cash from Alex's Engineering Co. for the receivable from November.
  10 Paid cash to Lyn Addie for six days of work at the rate of $125 per day.
  14 Notified by Alex's Engineering Co. that Business Solutions's bid of $7,000 on a proposed project has been accepted. Alex's paid a $1,500 cash advance to Business Solutions.
  15 Purchased $1,100 of computer supplies on credit from Harris Office Products.
  16 Sent a reminder to Gomez Co. to pay the fee for services recorded on November 8.
  20 Completed a project for Liu Corporation and received $5,625 cash.
22–26 Took the week off for the holidays.
  28 Received $3,000 cash from Gomez Co. on its receivable.
  29 Reimbursed S. Rey for business automobile mileage (600 miles at $0.32 per mile).
  31 The company paid $1,500 cash in dividends.

The following additional facts are collected for use in making adjusting entries prior to preparing financial statements for the company's first three months.

a. The December 31 inventory count of computer supplies shows $580 still available.

b. Three months have expired since the 12-month insurance premium was paid in advance.

c. As of December 31, Lyn Addie has not been paid for four days of work at $125 per day.

d. The computer system, acquired on October 1, is expected to have a four-year life with no salvage value.

e. The office equipment, acquired on October 1, is expected to have a five-year life with no salvage value.

f. Three of the four months' prepaid rent have expired.

Required

1. Prepare journal entries to record each of the December transactions and events for Business Solutions. Post those entries to the accounts in the ledger.

2. Prepare adjusting entries to reflect *a* through *f*. Post those entries to the accounts in the ledger.

3. Prepare an adjusted trial balance as of December 31, 2019.

4. Prepare an income statement for the three months ended December 31, 2019.

5. Prepare a statement of retained earnings for the three months ended December 31, 2019.

6. Prepare a balance sheet as of December 31, 2019.

7. Record and post the necessary closing entries as of December 31, 2019.

8. Prepare a post-closing trial balance as of December 31, 2019.

Check (3) Adjusted trial balance totals, $109,034

(6) Total assets, $83,460

(8) Post-closing trial balance totals, $85,110

The **General Ledger** tool in Connect allows students to immediately see the financial statements as of a specific date. Each of the following questions begins with an unadjusted trial balance. Using transactions from the following assignment, prepare the necessary adjustments and determine the impact each adjustment has on net income. The financial statements are automatically populated.

GENERAL LEDGER PROBLEM

GL 3-1 Based on the FastForward illustration in this chapter

Using transactions from the following assignments, prepare the necessary adjustments, create the financial statements, and determine the impact each adjustment has on net income.

GL 3-2 Based on Problem 3-3A   **GL 3-4** Extension of Problem 2-2A

GL 3-3 Extension of Problem 2-1A   **GL 3-5** Based on Serial Problem SP 3

Accounting Analysis

AA 3-1 Use **Apple**'s financial statements in Appendix A to answer the following.

1. Compute Apple's profit margin for fiscal years ended (*a*) September 30, 2017, and (*b*) September 24, 2016.

2. Is the change in Apple's profit margin favorable or unfavorable?

3. In 2017, did Apple's profit margin outperform or underperform the industry (assumed) average of 12%?

4. For the fiscal year ended September 30, 2017, what is the balance of its Income Summary account before it is closed?

COMPANY ANALYSIS

A1   P7

APPLE

COMPARATIVE ANALYSIS

A1   A2

APPLE
GOOGLE

AA 3-2   Key figures for the recent two years of both **Apple** and **Google** follow.

$ millions	Apple		Google	
	Current Year	Prior Year	Current Year	Prior Year
Net income................	$ 48,351	$ 45,687	$ 12,662	$ 19,478
Net sales	229,234	215,639	110,855	90,272
Current assets.............	128,645	106,869	124,308	105,408
Current liabilities..........	100,814	79,006	24,183	16,756

Required

1. Compute profit margins for (*a*) Apple and (*b*) Google for the two years of data reported above.
2. In the current year, which company is more successful on the basis of profit margin?
3. Compute current ratios for (*a*) Apple and (*b*) Google for the two years reported above.
4. In the current year, which company has the better ability to pay short-term obligations according to the current ratio?

GLOBAL ANALYSIS

A1

Samsung
APPLE
GOOGLE

AA 3-3   Key comparative figures for **Samsung**, **Apple**, and **Google** follow.

In millions	Samsung	Apple	Google
Net income	₩ 42,186,747	$ 48,351	$ 12,662
Net sales	239,575,376	229,234	110,855

Required

1. Compute profit margin for Samsung, Apple, and Google.
2. Which company has the highest profit margin?

Beyond the Numbers

ETHICS CHALLENGE

P4   P6

BTN 3-1   On January 20, 2019, Tamira Nelson, the accountant for Picton Enterprises, is feeling pressure to complete the annual financial statements. The company president has said he needs up-to-date financial statements to share with the bank on January 21 at a dinner meeting that has been called to discuss Picton's obtaining loan financing for a special building project. Tamira knows that she will not be able to gather all the needed information in the next 24 hours to prepare the entire set of adjusting entries. Those entries must be posted before the financial statements accurately portray the company's performance and financial position for the fiscal period ended December 31, 2018. Tamira ultimately decides to estimate several expense accruals at the last minute. When deciding on estimates for the expenses, she uses low estimates because she does not want to make the financial statements look worse than they are. Tamira finishes the financial statements before the deadline and gives them to the president without mentioning that several account balances are estimates that she provided.

Required

1. Identify several courses of action that Tamira could have taken instead of the one she took.
2. If you were in Tamira's situation, what would you have done? Briefly justify your response.

COMMUNICATING IN PRACTICE

P7   P8

BTN 3-2   One of your classmates states that a company's books should be ongoing and therefore not closed until that business is terminated. Write a half-page memo to this classmate explaining the concept of the closing process by drawing analogies between (1) a scoreboard for an athletic event and the revenue and expense accounts of a business or (2) a sports team's record book and the retained earnings account. *Hint:* Think about what would happen if the scoreboard were not cleared before the start of a new game.

BTN 3-3   Access EDGAR online (<u>SEC.gov</u>) and locate the 10-K report of **The Gap, Inc.** (ticker: GPS), filed on March 20, 2017. Review its financial statements reported for the year ended January 28, 2017, to answer the following questions.

TAKING IT TO THE NET

A1

Required

1. What are Gap's main brands?
2. When is Gap's fiscal year-end?
3. What is Gap's net sales for the period ended January 28, 2017?
4. What is Gap's net income for the period ended January 28, 2017?
5. Compute Gap's profit margin for the year ended January 28, 2017.
6. Do you believe Gap's decision to use a year-end of late January or early February relates to its natural business year? Explain.

BTN 3-4   Four types of adjustments are described in the chapter: (1) prepaid expenses, (2) unearned revenues, (3) accrued expenses, and (4) accrued revenues.

TEAMWORK IN ACTION

P1   P2   P3   P4

Required

1. Form *learning teams* of four (or more) members. Each team member must select one of the four adjustments as an area of expertise (each team must have at least one expert in each area).
2. Form *expert teams* from the individuals who have selected the same area of expertise. Expert teams are to discuss and write a report that each expert will present to his or her learning team addressing the following:
   a. Description of the adjustment and why it's necessary.
   b. Example of a transaction or event, with dates and amounts, that requires adjustment.
   c. Adjusting entry(ies) for the example in requirement *b*.
   d. Status of the affected account(s) before and after the adjustment in requirement *c*.
   e. Effects on financial statements of not making the adjustment.
3. Each expert should return to his or her learning team. In rotation, each member should present his or her expert team's report to the learning team. Team discussion is encouraged.

BTN 3-5   Review this chapter's opening feature involving Evan and Bobby and **Snapchat**.

ENTREPRENEURIAL DECISION

C3   P7

1. Explain how a classified balance sheet can help Evan and Bobby know what bills are due when and whether they have the resources to pay those bills.
2. Why is it important for Evan and Bobby to match costs and revenues in a specific time period? How do closing entries help them in this regard?
3. What objectives are met when Evan and Bobby apply closing procedures each fiscal year-end?

BTN 3-6   Select a company that you can visit in person or interview on the telephone. Call ahead to the company to arrange a time when you can interview an employee (preferably an accountant) who helps prepare the annual financial statements. Inquire about the following aspects of its *accounting cycle:*

HITTING THE ROAD

C1   C2

1. Does the company prepare interim financial statements? What time period(s) is used for interim statements?
2. Does the company use the cash or accrual basis of accounting?
3. Does the company use a work sheet in preparing financial statements? Why or why not?
4. Does the company use a spreadsheet program? If so, which software program is used?
5. How long does it take after the end of its reporting period to complete annual statements?

4 Accounting for Merchandising Operations

Learning Objectives

CONCEPTUAL

C1 Describe merchandising activities and identify income components for a merchandising company.

C2 Identify and explain the inventory asset and cost flows of a merchandising company.

ANALYTICAL

A1 Compute the acid-test ratio and explain its use to assess liquidity.

A2 Compute the gross margin ratio and explain its use to assess profitability.

PROCEDURAL

P1 Analyze and record transactions for merchandise purchases using a perpetual system.

P2 Analyze and record transactions for merchandise sales using a perpetual system.

P3 Prepare adjustments and close accounts for a merchandising company.

P4 Define and prepare multiple-step and single-step income statements.

P5 *Appendix 4A*—Record and compare merchandising transactions using both periodic and perpetual inventory systems.

P6 *Appendix 4B*—Prepare adjustments for discounts, returns, and allowances per revenue recognition rules.

P7 *Appendix 4C*—Record and compare merchandising transactions using the gross method and net method.

Bear Up

"Understand what matters"—**Maxine Clark**

ST. LOUIS—"When I graduated from college," explains Maxine Clark, "I felt the retail world had lost its spark. I wanted to be more creative." Maxine was determined to start a business that would be different. Then she went shopping with the young daughter of a friend. "When we couldn't find anything new, Katie picked up a Beanie Baby and said we could make one," recalls Maxine. "Her words gave me the idea to create a company that would allow people to create their own customized stuffed animals." **Build-A-Bear Workshop (BuildaBear.com)** was born!

"I did some research and began putting together a plan," says Maxine. The Build-A-Bear Workshops were an instant success.

As her company grew, Maxine says accounting data on her merchandising operations fell short. "We can't give up!" was her view. In response, Maxine set up an accounting system to measure, track, summarize, and report on merchandising transactions, especially purchases.

Maxine computerized the accounting system, prepared monthly financial statements per store, developed annual budgets, and tracked all bank accounts and payables.

Build-A-Bear's successful use of accounting data has made Maxine a self-made woman. She insists, however, it is not about

©Monty Brinton/CBS/Getty Images

the financial rewards. "We're a family business," explains Maxine. "It's important to set an example for children by being a company that does good things and cares about the well-being of others."

Sources: *Build-A-Bear website,* January 2019; *Fortune,* March 2012; *LEADERS,* April 2011; *CSRwire,* August 2008

MERCHANDISING ACTIVITIES

Previous chapters covered accounting for service companies. A merchandising company's activities differ from those of a service company. **Merchandise** refers to products, also called *goods,* that a company buys to resell. A **merchandiser** earns net income by buying and selling merchandise. Merchandisers are wholesalers or retailers. A **wholesaler** buys products from manufacturers and sells them to retailers. A **retailer** buys products from manufacturers or wholesalers and sells them to consumers.

C1

Describe merchandising activities and identify income components for a merchandising company.

Reporting Income for a Merchandiser

Net income for a merchandiser equals revenues from selling merchandise minus both the cost of merchandise sold and other expenses—see Exhibit 4.1. Revenue from selling merchandise is called *sales,* and the expense of buying and preparing merchandise is called **cost of goods sold.** (Some service companies use the term *sales* instead of revenues; cost of goods sold is also called *cost of sales*.)

Point: **SuperValu** and **SYSCO** are wholesalers. **Target** and **Walmart** are retailers.

Service Company

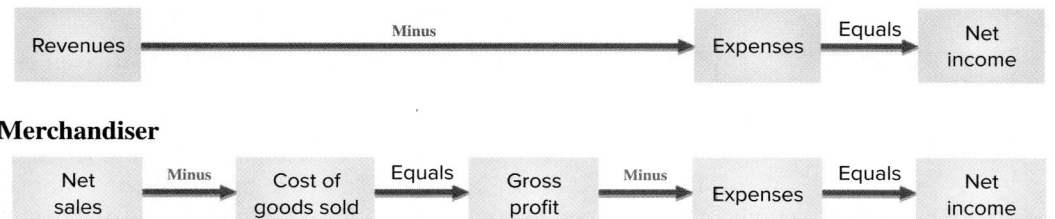

Merchandiser

EXHIBIT 4.1

Computing Income for a Merchandising Company versus a Service Company

The income statements for a service company, **Liberty Tax**, and for a merchandiser, **Nordstrom**, are in Exhibit 4.2. We see that the merchandiser, Nordstrom, reports cost of goods sold, which is not reported by the service company. The merchandiser also reports **gross profit,** or **gross margin,** which is net sales minus cost of goods sold.

EXHIBIT 4.2

Income Statement for a Service Company and a Merchandising Company

Service Company	
LIBERTY TAX **Income Statement ($ millions)**	
Revenues.............................	$174
Expenses.............................	162
Net income	$ 12

Merchandising Company	
NORDSTROM INC. **Income Statement ($ millions)**	
Net sales............................	$14,757
Cost of goods sold	9,440
Gross profit	5,317
Expenses............................	4,963
Net income	$ 354

C2
Identify and explain the inventory asset and cost flows of a merchandising company.

Reporting Inventory for a Merchandiser

A merchandiser's balance sheet has a current asset called *merchandise inventory,* an item not on a service company's balance sheet. **Merchandise inventory,** or simply **inventory,** refers to products that a company owns and intends to sell. Inventory cost includes the cost to buy the goods, ship them to the store, and make them ready for sale.

EXHIBIT 4.3

Merchandiser's Operating Cycle

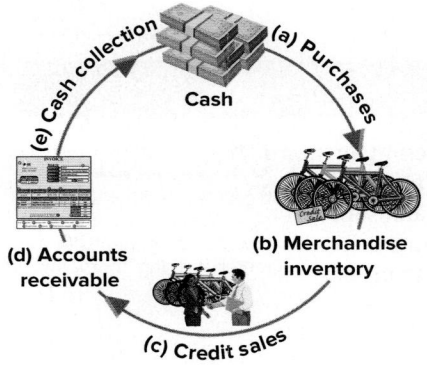

(a) Purchases
Cash
(e) Cash collection
(d) Accounts receivable
(b) Merchandise inventory
(c) Credit sales

Operating Cycle for a Merchandiser

Exhibit 4.3 shows an operating cycle for a merchandiser with credit sales. The cycle moves from (*a*) cash purchases of merchandise to (*b*) inventory for sale to (*c*) credit sales to (*d*) accounts receivable to (*e*) receipt of cash. The length of an operating cycle differs across the types of businesses. Department stores often have operating cycles of two to five months. Operating cycles for grocery stores are usually from two to eight weeks. Companies try to keep their operating cycles short because assets tied up in inventory and receivables are not productive. Cash sales shorten operating cycles.

Inventory Systems

Exhibit 4.4 shows that a company's merchandise available for sale consists of what it begins with (beginning inventory) and what it purchases (net purchases). The merchandise available for sale is either sold (cost of goods sold) or kept for future sales (ending inventory).

Companies account for inventory in one of two ways: *perpetual system* or *periodic system.*

- **Perpetual inventory system** updates accounting records for *each* purchase and *each* sale of inventory.
- **Periodic inventory system** updates accounting records for purchases and sales of inventory *only at the end of a period.*

EXHIBIT 4.4

Merchandiser's Cost Flow for a Single Time Period

Merchandise Inventory		
Beg. inventory	#	
Net purchases	#	
Merchandise avail. for sale	#	
		COGS #
End. inventory	#	

Point: Merchandise avail. for sale:
MAS = EI + COGS,
which can be rewritten as MAS − EI = COGS, or MAS − COGS = EI.

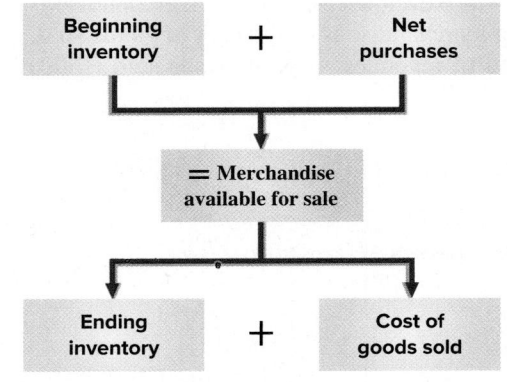

Beginning inventory + Net purchases

= **Merchandise available for sale**

Ending inventory + Cost of goods sold

Technology has dramatically increased the use of the perpetual system. It gives managers immediate access to information on sales and inventory levels, which allows them to strategically react and increase profit. (Some companies use a *hybrid* system where the perpetual system is used for tracking units available and the periodic system is used to compute cost of sales.)

Use the following information (in random order) from a merchandising company and from a service company to complete the requirements. *Hint:* Not all information may be necessary for the solutions.

SaveCo Merchandiser			
Supplies............	$ 10	Expenses.......	$ 20
Beginning inventory ...	100	Net purchases ...	80
Ending inventory......	50	Net sales	190

Hi-Tech Services			
Expenses.....	$170	Prepaid rent........	$25
Revenues.....	200	Accounts payable ...	35
Cash.........	10	Supplies...........	65

1. For the merchandiser only, compute (a) goods available for sale, (b) cost of goods sold, and (c) gross profit.

2. Compute net income for each company.

Solution

1. a. Computation of goods available for sale (SaveCo).

b. Computation of cost of goods sold (SaveCo).

c. Computation of gross profit (SaveCo).

Beginning inventory..........	$100
Plus: Net purchases..........	80
Goods available for sale	$180 →

Beginning inventory..........	$100
Plus: Net purchases..........	80
Goods available for sale	180
Less: Ending inventory........	50
Cost of goods sold...........	$130 —

Net sales..................	$190
Less: Cost of goods	
→ sold (from part b)........	130
Gross profit...............	$ 60

2. Computation of net income for each company.

SaveCo Merchandiser	
Net sales.....................................	$190
Less: Cost of goods sold (from part 1b)..........	130
Gross profit.................................	60
Less: Expenses...............................	20
Net income	$ 40

Hi-Tech Services	
Revenues......................	$200
Less: Expenses..................	170
Net income	$ 30

Do More: QS 4-3, E 4-1, E 4-2

ACCOUNTING FOR MERCHANDISE PURCHASES

This section explains how we record purchases under different purchase terms.

Purchases <u>without</u> Cash Discounts

Z-Mart records a $500 cash purchase of merchandise on November 2 as follows.

Nov. 2	Merchandise Inventory	500	
	Cash...		500
	Purchased goods for cash.		

If these goods are instead *purchased on credit,* and no discounts are offered for early payment, Z-Mart makes the same entry except that Accounts Payable is credited instead of Cash.

■ **Decision Insight** ══

Trade Discounts   When a manufacturer or wholesaler prepares a catalog of items for sale, each item has a **list price,** or *catalog price.* However, an item's *selling price* equals list price minus a percent called a **trade discount.** A wholesaler buying in large quantities gets a larger discount than a retailer buying in small quantities. A buyer records the net amount of list price minus trade discount. If a supplier of Z-Mart lists an item at $625 and gives Z-Mart a 20% trade discount, Z-Mart's purchase price is $500, computed as $625 − (20% × $625). ■

Purchases <u>with</u> Cash Discounts

The purchase of goods on credit requires credit terms. **Credit terms** include the amounts and timing of payments from a buyer to a seller. To demonstrate, when sellers require payment within 10 days after the end of the month (**EOM**) of the invoice date, credit terms are "n/10

P1_____

Analyze and record transactions for merchandise purchases using a perpetual system.

Assets = Liabilities + Equity
+500
−500

Point: Costs recorded in Merchandise Inventory are called *inventoriable costs.*

Point: Trade discounts are not journalized; purchases are recorded based on the invoice amount.

EOM." When sellers require payment within 30 days after the invoice date, credit terms are "n/30," meaning *net 30 days*.

Credit Terms   Exhibit 4.5 explains credit terms. The amount of time allowed before full payment is due is the **credit period.** Sellers can grant a **cash discount** to encourage buyers to pay earlier. A buyer views a cash discount as a **purchases discount.** A seller views a cash discount as a **sales discount.** Any cash discounts are described on the invoice. For example, credit terms of "2/10, n/60" mean that full payment is due within a 60-day credit period, but the buyer can deduct 2% of the invoice amount if payment is made within 10 days of the invoice date. This reduced payment is only for the **discount period.**

EXHIBIT 4.5

Credit Terms

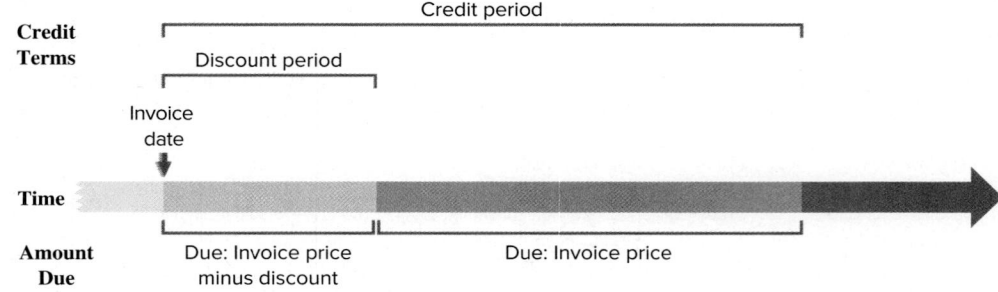

Invoice   On November 2, Z-Mart purchases $500 of merchandise **on credit** with terms of 2/10, n/30. The invoice for this purchase is shown in Exhibit 4.6. This is a purchase invoice for Z-Mart (buyer) and a sales invoice for Trex (seller). The amount recorded for merchandise inventory includes its purchase cost, shipping fees, taxes, and any other costs necessary to make it ready for sale.

EXHIBIT 4.6

Invoice

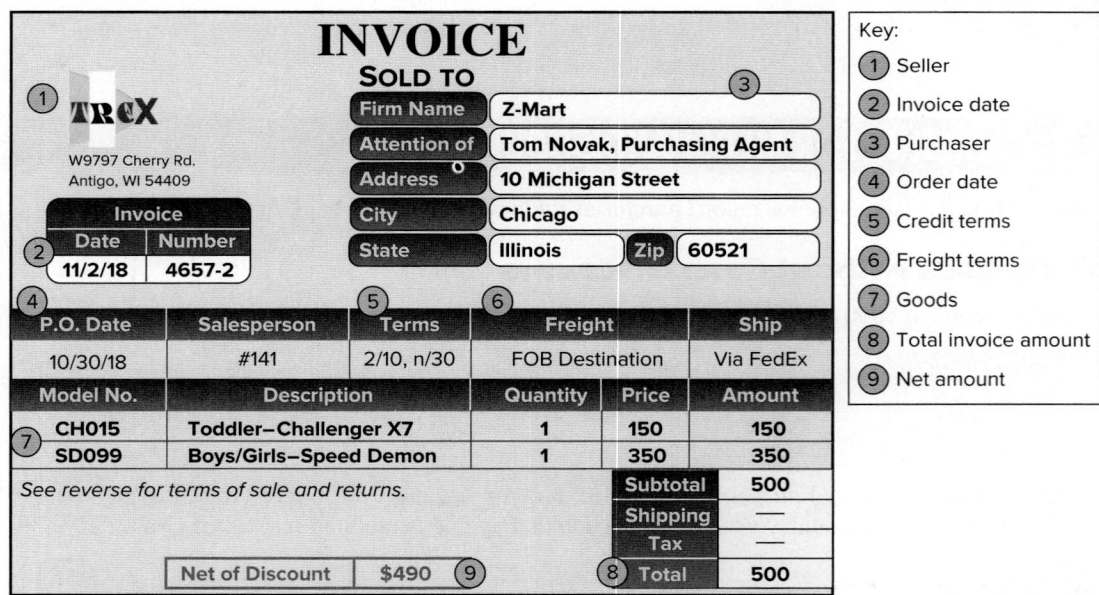

Point: The invoice date sets the discount and credit periods.

Gross Method   Z-Mart purchases $500 of merchandise on credit terms of 2/10, n/30. The November 2 invoice offers a 2% discount if paid within 10 days; if not, Z-Mart must pay the full amount within 30 days. The buyer has two options.

- Pay within discount period (Nov. 2 through Nov. 12):   Due = $490.
  or
- Pay after discount period (Nov. 13 through Dec. 2):   Due = $500.

The $490 equals the $500 invoice minus $10 discount (computed as $500 × 2%).

On the purchase date, we do not know if payment will occur within the discount period. The **gross method** records the purchase at its *gross* (full) invoice amount. For Z-Mart, the purchase of $500 of merchandise with terms of 2/10, n/30 is recorded at $500. *The gross method is used here because it is (1) used more in practice, (2) easier to apply, and (3) less costly.*

Purchases on Credit
Z-Mart's entry to record the November 2 purchase of $500 of merchandise on credit follows. (For recording, it can help to add the name to the payable, such as Accounts Payable—Trex.)

(*a*) Nov. 2	Merchandise Inventory	500	
	Accounts Payable		500
	Purchased goods, terms 2/10, n/30.		

Assets = Liabilities + Equity
+500   +500

Point: Appendix 4A repeats journal entries *a* through *g* using the periodic system.

Payment within Discount Period
Good cash management means that invoices are not paid until the last day of the discount or credit period. This is because the buyer can use that money until payment is required. If Z-Mart pays the amount due on (or before) November 12, the entry is

(*b1*) Nov. 12	Accounts Payable...............................	500	
	Merchandise Inventory..........................		10
	Cash*...		490*
	*Paid for goods within discount period. *$500 × (100% − 2%)*		

Assets = Liabilities + Equity
−490   −500
− 10

The Merchandise Inventory account equals the $490 net cost of purchases after these entries, and the Accounts Payable account has a zero balance.

Accounts Payable				Merchandise Inventory				Cash		
		Nov. 2	500	Nov. 2	500					
Nov. 12	500					Nov. 12	10	Nov. 12	490	
		Bal.	0	Bal.	490					

Payment after Discount Period
If the invoice is paid *after* November 12, the discount is lost. If Z-Mart pays the gross (full) amount due on December 2 (the n/30 due date), the entry is

(*b2*) Dec. 2	Accounts Payable.................................	500	
	Cash...		500
	Paid for goods outside discount period.		

Assets = Liabilities + Equity
−500   −500

Purchases with Returns and Allowances

Purchases returns are merchandise a buyer purchases but then returns. *Purchases allowances* refer to a seller granting a price reduction (allowance) to a buyer of defective or unacceptable merchandise.

Purchases Allowances
On November 5, Z-Mart (buyer) agrees to a $30 allowance from Trex for defective merchandise (assume allowance is $30 whether paid within the discount period or not). Z-Mart's entry to update Merchandise Inventory and record the allowance follows. Z-Mart's allowance for defective merchandise reduces its account payable to the seller. If cash is refunded, Cash is debited instead of Accounts Payable.

(*c1*) Nov. 5	Accounts Payable.................................	30	
	Merchandise Inventory..........................		30
	Allowance for defective goods.		

Point: When a buyer returns or takes an allowance on merchandise, the buyer issues a **debit memorandum**. This informs the seller of a debit made to the seller's account payable in the buyer's records.

Assets = Liabilities + Equity
−30   −30

Purchases Returns
Returns of inventory are recorded at the amount charged for that inventory. On June 1, Z-Mart purchases $250 of merchandise with terms 2/10, n/60—see entries below. On June 3, Z-Mart returns $50 of those goods. When Z-Mart pays on June 11, it

Point: Credit terms apply to both partial and full payments.

takes the 2% discount only on the $200 remaining balance ($250 − $50). When goods are re-turned, a buyer takes a discount on only the remaining balance. This means the discount is $4 (computed as $200 × 2%) and the cash payment is $196 (computed as $200 − $4).

Assets = Liabilities + Equity
+250   +250

Assets = Liabilities + Equity
−50   −50

Assets = Liabilities + Equity
−196   −200
−   4

June 1	Merchandise Inventory	250	
	Accounts Payable		250
	Purchased goods, terms 2/10, n/60.		
(c2) June 3	Accounts Payable.	50	
	Merchandise Inventory.		50
	Returned goods to seller.		
June 11	Accounts Payable.	200	
	Merchandise Inventory.		4
	Cash.		196
	Paid for $200 of goods less $4 discount.		

These T-accounts show the final $196 in inventory, the zero balance in Accounts Payable, and the $196 cash payment.

Example: If on June 20, Z-Mart returns all goods paid for on June 11, the entry is
Cash 196
   Merchandise Inventory . . .   196

Accounts Payable			Merchandise Inventory			Cash	
	Jun. 1	250	Jun. 1	250			
Jun. 3	50				Jun. 3	50	
Jun. 11	200				Jun. 11	4	Jun. 11 **196**
	Bal.	0	Bal.	**196**			

©Michael DeYoung/Blend Images

■ **Decision Insight**

What's Your Policy? Return policies are a competitive advantage for businesses. **REI** offers a 1-year return policy on nearly every product it sells. **Amazon** picks up returned items at your door. On the other hand, some stores like **Best Buy** allow only 14 days to return products. ■

Purchases and Transportation Costs

The buyer and seller must agree on who is responsible for paying freight (shipping) costs and who has the risk of loss during transit. This is the same as asking at what point ownership trans-fers from the seller to the buyer. The point of transfer is called the **FOB** (*free on board*) point. Exhibit 4.7 covers two alternative points of transfer.

1. *FOB shipping point* means the buyer accepts ownership when the goods depart the seller's place of business. The buyer pays shipping costs and has the risk of loss in transit. The goods are part of the buyer's inventory when they are in transit because ownership has transferred to the buyer. **1-800-Flowers.com**, a floral merchandiser, uses FOB shipping point.

2. *FOB destination* means ownership of goods transfers to the buyer when the goods arrive at the buyer's place of business. The seller pays shipping charges and has the risk of loss in transit. The seller does not record revenue until the goods arrive at the destination.

EXHIBIT 4.7

Ownership Transfer and Transportation Costs

Point: When the party not respon-sible for shipping pays shipping cost, it either bills the other party responsible or adjusts its account payable or account receivable with the other party. Freight pay-ments are *not* applied in comput-ing discounts.

Seller   Buyer

Shipping point   Goods in transit   Destination

Shipping Terms	**Ownership Transfers at**	**Goods in Transit Owned by**	**Transportation Costs Paid by**	
FOB shipping point	Shipping point	Buyer	**Buyer**	Merchandise Inventory . . . # Cash . . . . #
FOB destination	Destination	Seller	**Seller**	Delivery Expense . . . . # Cash . . . . #

When a buyer is responsible for paying transportation costs, the payment is made to a carrier or directly to the seller. The cost principle requires that transportation costs of a buyer (often called *transportation-in* or *freight-in*) be part of the cost of merchandise inventory. Z-Mart's entry to record a $75 freight charge from **UPS** for merchandise purchased FOB shipping point is

Point: If we place an order online and receive free shipping, we have terms FOB destination.

(d) Nov. 24	Merchandise Inventory	75	
	Cash..		75
	Paid freight costs on goods.		

Assets = Liabilities + Equity
+75
−75

When a seller is responsible for paying shipping costs, it records these costs in a Delivery Expense account. Delivery expense, also called *transportation-out* or *freight-out,* is reported as a selling expense in the seller's income statement.

Point: INcoming freight costs are charged to INventory. When inventory EXits, freight costs are charged to EXpense.

Itemized Costs of Purchases

In summary, purchases are recorded as debits to Merchandise Inventory (or Inventory). Purchases discounts, returns, and allowances are credited to (subtracted from) Merchandise Inventory. Transportation-in is debited (added) to Merchandise Inventory. Z-Mart's itemized costs of merchandise purchases for the year are in Exhibit 4.8.

The accounting system described here does not provide separate records (accounts) for total purchases, total purchases discounts, total purchases returns and allowances, and total transportation-in. Many companies collect this information in supplementary records to evaluate these costs. **Supplementary records,** or *supplemental records,* refer to information outside the usual ledger accounts.

Itemized Costs of Merchandise Purchases	
Invoice cost of merchandise purchases	$ 235,800
Less: Purchases discounts received	(4,200)
Purchases returns and allowances.........	(1,500)
Add: Costs of transportation-in	2,300
Total net cost of merchandise purchases	**$232,400**

EXHIBIT 4.8

Itemized Costs of Merchandise Purchases

Point: Some companies have separate accounts for purchases discounts, returns and allowances, and transportation-in. These accounts are then transferred to Merchandise Inventory at period-end. This is a *hybrid system* of perpetual and periodic. That is, Merchandise Inventory is updated on a perpetual basis but only for purchases and cost of goods sold.

Decision Ethics

Payables Manager As a new accounts payable manager, you are being trained by the outgoing manager. She explains that the system prepares checks for amounts net of favorable cash discounts, and the checks are dated the last day of the discount period. She tells you that checks are not mailed until five days later, adding that "the company gets free use of cash for an extra five days, and our department looks better." Do you continue this policy? ■ *Answer:* One point of view is that the late payment policy is unethical. A deliberate plan to make late payments means the company lies when it pretends to make payment within the discount period. Another view is that the late payment policy is acceptable. Some believe attempts to take discounts through late payments are accepted as "price negotiation."

Prepare journal entries to record each of the following purchases transactions of a merchandising company. Assume a perpetual inventory system using the gross method for recording purchases.

NEED-TO-KNOW 4-2

Merchandise Purchases

P1

Oct. 1 Purchased $1,000 of goods. Terms of the sale are 4/10, n/30, and FOB shipping point; the invoice is dated October 1.

3 Paid $30 cash for freight charges from UPS for the October 1 purchase.

7 Returned $50 of the $1,000 of goods from the October 1 purchase and received full credit.

11 Paid the amount due from the October 1 purchase (less the return on October 7).

31 *Assume the October 11 payment was never made.* Instead, payment of the amount due, less the return on October 7, occurred on October 31.

Solution

Oct. 1	Merchandise Inventory	1,000	
	Accounts Payable		1,000
	Purchased goods, terms 4/10, n/30.		
Oct. 3	Merchandise Inventory	30	
	Cash..		30
	Paid freight on purchases FOB shipping point.		

[continued on next page]

[continued from previous page]

Oct. 7	Accounts Payable...	50	
	Merchandise Inventory.............................		50
	Returned goods.		
Oct. 11	Accounts Payable...	950	
	Merchandise Inventory*............................		38
	Cash†...		912
	Paid for goods within discount period.		
	*$950 × 4% †$950 − ($950 × 4%)		
Oct. 31	Accounts Payable‡..	950	
	Cash...		950
	Paid for goods outside discount period. ‡$1,000 − $50		

Do More: QS 4-5, QS 4-6,
QS 4-7, E 4-3, E 4-5

ACCOUNTING FOR MERCHANDISE SALES

P2

Analyze and record transactions for merchandise sales using a perpetual system.

Merchandising companies must account for sales, sales discounts, sales returns and allowances, and cost of goods sold. Z-Mart has these items in its gross profit computation—see Exhibit 4.9. This shows that customers paid $314,700 for merchandise that cost Z-Mart $230,400, yielding a gross profit of $84,300.

EXHIBIT 4.9

Gross Profit Computation

Computation of Gross Profit	
Net sales (net of discounts, returns, and allowances)	$314,700
Cost of goods sold	230,400
Gross profit	**$ 84,300**

The perpetual accounting system requires that **each sales transaction for a merchandiser, whether for cash or on credit, has** *two entries:* **one for revenue and one for cost.**

1. **Revenue received (and asset increased) from the customer.**
2. **Cost of goods sold incurred (and asset decreased) to the customer.**

Sales without Cash Discounts

Revenue Side: Inflow of Assets   Z-Mart sold $1,000 of merchandise on credit terms n/60 on November 12. The revenue part of this transaction is recorded as follows. This entry shows an increase in Z-Mart's assets in the form of accounts receivable. It also shows the increase in revenue (Sales). If the sale is for cash, debit Cash instead of Accounts Receivable.

Assets = Liabilities + Equity
+1,000   +1,000

Nov. 12	Accounts Receivable	1,000	
	Sales		1,000
	Sold goods on credit.		

Point: Gross profit on Nov. 12 sale:

Net sales	$1,000
Cost of goods sold.	300
Gross profit	$ 700

Assets = Liabilities + Equity
−300   −300

Cost Side: Outflow of Assets   The cost side of each sale requires that Merchandise Inventory decrease by that item's cost. The cost of the merchandise Z-Mart sold on November 12 is $300, and the entry to record the cost part of this transaction follows.

Nov. 12	Cost of Goods Sold	300	
	Merchandise Inventory..........................		300
	Record cost of Nov. 12 sale.		

▦ Decision Insight

Future Demands Large merchandising companies, such as **Amazon**, bombard suppliers with demands. These include discounts for bar coding and technology support systems and fines for shipping errors. Merchandisers' goals are to reduce inventories, shorten lead times, and eliminate errors. Colleges offer programs in supply chain management and logistics to train future employees to help merchandisers meet such goals. ∎

©Polaris/Newscom

Sales with Cash Discounts

Offering discounts on credit sales benefits a seller through earlier cash receipts and reduced collection efforts. We use the *gross method,* which records sales at the full amount and records sales discounts if, and when, they are taken. The gross method requires a period-end adjusting entry to estimate future sales discounts. (The **net method** records sales at the net amount, which assumes all discounts are taken. This method requires an adjusting entry to estimate future discounts lost. See Appendix 4C.)

Sales on Credit Z-Mart makes a credit sale for $1,000 on November 12 with terms of 2/10, n/45 (cost of the merchandise sold is $300). The entries to record this sale follow.

Nov. 12	Accounts Receivable	1,000	
	Sales		1,000
	Sold goods, terms 2/10, n/45.		
Nov. 12	Cost of Goods Sold	300	
	Merchandise Inventory.		300
	Record cost of Nov. 12 sale.		

Assets = Liabilities + Equity
+1,000   +1,000

Assets = Liabilities + Equity
−300   −300

Buyer Pays within Discount Period One option is for the buyer to pay $980 within the 10-day discount period ending November 22. The $20 sales discount is computed as $1,000 × 2%. If the customer pays on (or before) November 22, Z-Mart records the cash receipt as follows. **Sales Discounts** is a **contra revenue account,** meaning the Sales Discounts account is subtracted from the Sales account when computing net sales. The Sales Discounts account has a *normal debit balance* because it is subtracted from Sales, which has a normal credit balance.

Point: Net sales is the amount received from the customer.

Sales.	$1,000
Sales discounts	(20)
Net sales	$ 980

Nov. 22	Cash*	980	
	Sales Discounts	20	
	Accounts Receivable.		1,000
	Received payment on Nov. 12 sale less discount.		
	*$1,000 − ($1,000 × 2%)		

Assets = Liabilities + Equity
+ 980   −20
−1,000

Buyer Pays after Discount Period The customer's second option is to wait 45 days until December 27 (or at least until after the discount period) and then pay $1,000. Z-Mart records that cash receipt as

Dec. 27	Cash	1,000	
	Accounts Receivable.		1,000
	Received payment on Nov. 12 sale after discount period.		

Assets = Liabilities + Equity
+1,000
−1,000

Sales with Returns and Allowances

If a customer is unhappy with a purchase, many sellers allow the customer to either return the merchandise for a full refund (*sales return*) or keep the merchandise along with a partial refund (*sales allowance*). Most sellers can reliably estimate returns and allowances (abbreviated *R&A*).

Buyer Returns Goods—Revenue Side When a buyer returns goods, it impacts the seller's revenue *and* cost sides. When a return occurs, the seller debits **Sales Returns and**

Allowances, a **contra revenue account** to Sales. Assume that a customer returns merchandise on November 26 that sold for $15 and cost $9; the revenue-side returns entry is

Assets = Liabilities + Equity
−15   −15

(e1) Nov. 26	Sales Returns and Allowances	15	
	Cash...		15
	Goods returned from Nov. 12 sale.		

Buyer Returns Goods—Cost Side   When a return occurs, the seller must reduce the cost of sales. Continuing the example where the returned items sold for $15 and cost $9, the cost-side entry depends on whether the goods are defective.

Returned Goods Not Defective.   If the merchandise returned is not defective and can be resold, there is a cost-side entry. The seller adds the cost of the returned goods back to inventory and reduces cost of goods sold as follows. This entry reverses the cost-side entry of November 12 for only $9 of goods returned.

Assets = Liabilities + Equity
+9   +9

(e2) Nov. 26	Merchandise Inventory	9	
	Cost of Goods Sold..............................		9
	Returned goods are added back to inventory.		

Returned Goods Are Defective.   If the merchandise returned is defective, the returned inventory is recorded at its estimated value, not its cost. The following entry assumes the returned goods costing $9 are defective and are worth $2.

Assets = Liabilities + Equity
+2   −7
+9

Nov. 26	Merchandise Inventory	2	
	Loss from Defective Merchandise......................	7	
	Cost of Goods Sold..............................		9
	Returned defective goods to inventory and record loss.		

Buyer Granted Allowances   If a buyer is not satisfied with the goods, the seller might offer a price reduction for the buyer to keep the goods. There is no cost-side entry in this case as the inventory is not returned. On the revenue side, the seller debits Sales Returns and Allowances and credits Cash or Accounts Receivable depending on what's agreed. Assume that $40 of merchandise previously sold is defective. The seller gives a price reduction and credits the buyer's accounts receivable for $10. The seller records this allowance as follows.

Assets = Liabilities + Equity
−10   −10

(f) Nov. 24	Sales Returns and Allowances	10	
	Accounts Receivable.............................		10
	Sales allowance granted.		

Point: When a seller accepts returns or grants an allowance, the seller issues a **credit memorandum**. This informs the buyer of a credit made to the buyer's account in the seller's records.

If the seller has already collected cash for the sale, the seller could give the price reduction in cash. For example, instead of crediting the buyer's Accounts Receivable in the entry above, the seller can credit Cash for $10.

NEED-TO-KNOW 4-3

Merchandise Sales

P2

Prepare journal entries to record each of the following sales transactions of a merchandising company. Assume a perpetual inventory system and use of the gross method (beginning inventory equals $9,000).

June 1   Sold 50 units of merchandise to a customer for $150 per unit under credit terms of 2/10, n/30, FOB shipping point, and the invoice is dated June 1. The 50 units of merchandise had cost $100 per unit.

7   The customer returns 2 units purchased on June 1 because those units did not fit its needs. The seller restores those units to its inventory (as they are not defective) and credits Accounts Receivable from the customer.

11   The seller receives the balance due from the June 1 sale to the customer less returns and allowances.

14   The customer discovers that 10 units have minor damage but keeps them because the seller sends a $50 cash payment allowance to compensate.

Solution

June 1	Accounts Receivable	7,500	
	Sales		7,500
	Sold goods. 50 units × $150		
June 1	Cost of Goods Sold	5,000	
	Merchandise Inventory.		5,000
	Cost of sale. 50 units × $100		
June 7	Sales Returns and Allowances	300	
	Accounts Receivable.		300
	Returns accepted. 2 units × $150		
June 7	Merchandise Inventory	200	
	Cost of Goods Sold.		200
	Returns added to inventory. 2 units × $100		
June 11	Cash	7,056	
	Sales Discounts*	144	
	Accounts Receivable		7,200
	Received payment. *($7,500 − $300) × 2%		
June 14	Sales Returns and Allowances	50	
	Cash.		50
	Recorded allowance on goods.		

> **Do More:** QS 4-8, E 4-4, E 4-6, E 4-7

ADJUSTING AND CLOSING FOR MERCHANDISERS

Exhibit 4.10 shows the flow of merchandising costs during a period and where these costs are reported at period-end. Specifically, beginning inventory plus the net cost of purchases is the merchandise available for sale. As inventory is sold, its cost is recorded in cost of goods sold on the income statement; what remains is ending inventory on the balance sheet. A period's ending inventory is the next period's beginning inventory.

EXHIBIT 4.10

Merchandising Cost Flow in the Accounting Cycle

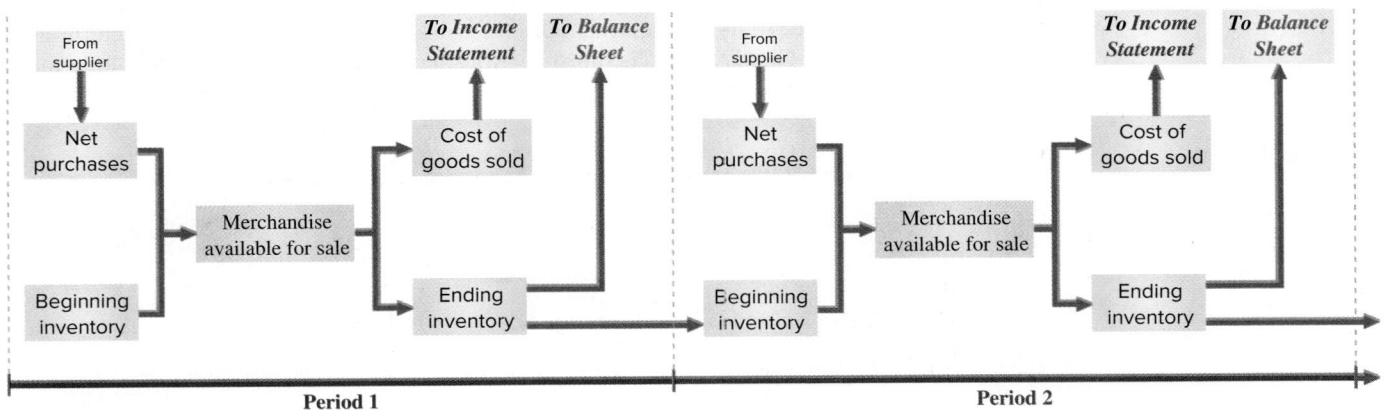

Adjusting Entries for Merchandisers

Each of the steps in the accounting cycle described in the prior chapter applies to a merchandiser. We expand upon three steps of the accounting cycle for a merchandiser—adjustments, statement preparation, and closing.

P3

Prepare adjustments and close accounts for a merchandising company.

Inventory Shrinkage—Adjusting Entry   A merchandiser using a *perpetual* inventory system makes an adjustment to Merchandise Inventory for any loss of merchandise, including theft and deterioration. **Shrinkage** is the loss of inventory, and it is computed by comparing a physical count of inventory with recorded amounts.

Z-Mart's Merchandise Inventory account at the end of the year has a balance of $21,250, but a physical count shows only $21,000 of inventory exists. The adjusting entry to record this $250 shrinkage is

Assets = Liabilities + Equity
−250   −250

Dec. 31	Cost of Goods Sold	250	
	Merchandise Inventory..........................		250
	Adjust for $250 shrinkage.		

Sales Discounts, Returns, and Allowances—Adjusting Entries

Revenue recognition rules require sales to be reported at the amount expected to be received. This means that period-end adjusting entries are commonly made for

- Expected sales discounts.
- Expected returns and allowances (revenue side).
- Expected returns and allowances (cost side).

These three adjustments produce three new accounts: Allowance for Sales Discounts, Sales Refund Payable, and Inventory Returns Estimated. Appendix 4B covers these accounts and the adjusting entries.

Preparing Financial Statements

The financial statements of a merchandiser are similar to those for a service company described in prior chapters. The income statement mainly differs by the addition of *cost of goods sold* and *gross profit*. Net sales is affected by discounts, returns and allowances, and some additional expenses such as delivery expense and loss from defective merchandise. The balance sheet differs by the addition of *merchandise inventory* as part of current assets. (Appendix 4B explains *inventory returns estimated* as part of current assets and *sales refund payable* as part of current liabilities.) The statement of retained earnings is unchanged.

Closing Entries for Merchandisers

Closing entries are similar for service companies and merchandising companies. The difference is that we close some new temporary accounts that come from merchandising activities. Z-Mart has temporary accounts unique to merchandisers: Sales (of goods), Sales Discounts, Sales Returns and Allowances, and Cost of Goods Sold. The third and fourth closing entries are identical for a merchandiser and a service company. The differences are in **red** in the closing entries of Exhibit 4.11.

EXHIBIT 4.11

Closing Entries for a Merchandiser

Step 1: Close Credit Balances in Temporary Accounts to Income Summary.

Dec. 31	Sales	321,000	
	Income Summary		321,000
	Close credit balances in temporary accounts.		

Step 2: Close Debit Balances in Temporary Accounts to Income Summary.

Dec. 31	Income Summary....................................	308,100	
	Sales Discounts...............................		4,300
	Sales Returns and Allowances		2,000
	Cost of Goods Sold		230,400
	Depreciation Expense..........................		3,700
	Salaries Expense		43,800
	Insurance Expense		600
	Rent Expense		9,000
	Supplies Expense		3,000
	Advertising Expense		11,300
	Close debit balances in temporary accounts.		

Step 3: Close Income Summary.

| Dec. 31 | Income Summary...... | 12,900 | |
| | Retained Earnings.. | | 12,900 |

Step 4: Close Dividends.

| Dec. 31 | Retained Earnings .... | 4,000 | |
| | Dividends........... | | 4,000 |

Sales, having a normal credit balance, is debited in step 1. Sales Discounts, Sales Returns and Allowances, and Cost of Goods Sold, having normal debit balances, are credited in step 2.

Summary of Merchandising Entries

Exhibit 4.12 summarizes the adjusting and closing entries of a merchandiser (using a perpetual inventory system).

EXHIBIT 4.12

Summary of Key Merchandising Entries (using perpetual system and gross method)

	Merchandising Transactions	Merchandising Entries	Dr.	Cr.
Purchases	Purchasing merchandise for resale.	Merchandise Inventory..................... Cash or Accounts Payable..............	#	#
	Paying freight costs on purchases; FOB shipping point.	Merchandise Inventory..................... Cash.......................................	#	#

	Paying within discount period.	Accounts Payable..........................
		    Merchandise Inventory.................
		    Cash.......................................
			#	#
				#

	Paying outside discount period.	Accounts Payable.......................... Cash.......................................	#	#
	Recording purchases returns or allowances.	Cash or Accounts Payable................. Merchandise Inventory..................	#	#

Sales	Selling merchandise.	Cash or Accounts Receivable..............
		    Sales.....................................
		Cost of Goods Sold.........................
		    Merchandise Inventory.................
			#
			
			#
				#
				
				#

	Receiving payment within discount period.	Cash....................................... Sales Discounts............................ Accounts Receivable..................	# #	#
	Receiving payment outside discount period.	Cash....................................... Accounts Receivable..................	#	#

	Receiving sales returns of nondefective inventory.	Sales Returns and Allowances..............
		    Cash or Accounts Receivable...........
		Merchandise Inventory......................
		    Cost of Goods Sold....................
			#
			
			#
				#
				
				#

	Recognizing sales allowances.	Sales Returns and Allowances.............. Cash or Accounts Receivable...........	#	#
	Paying freight costs on sales; FOB destination.	Delivery Expense........................... Cash.......................................	#	#

	Merchandising Events	Adjusting and Closing Entries	Dr.	Cr.
Adjusting	Adjustment for shrinkage (occurs when recorded amount larger than physical inventory).	Cost of Goods Sold......................... Merchandise Inventory.................	#	#
	Period-end adjustment for expected sales discounts.*	Sales Discounts............................ Allowance for Sales Discounts...........	#	#

	Period-end adjustment for expected returns—both revenue side and cost side.*	Sales Returns and Allowances..............
		    Sales Refund Payable..................
		Inventory Returns Estimated...............
		    Cost of Goods Sold....................
			#
			
			#
				#
				
				#

Closing	Closing temporary accounts with credit balances.	Sales...................................... Income Summary......................	#	#

	Closing temporary accounts with debit balances.	Income Summary...........................
		    Sales Returns and Allowances...........
		    Sales Discounts......................
		    Cost of Goods Sold....................
		    Delivery Expense......................
		    "Other Expenses".....................
			#	
				#
				#
				#
				#
				#

Merchandise Inventory

Beginning inventory	
Purchases	Pur. returns
Freight-in (FOB shp pt)	Pur. allowances
	Pur. discounts
	Shrinkage
Goods avail. for sale	
Customer returns	COGS
Ending inventory	

*Period-end adjustments depend on unadjusted balances, which can reverse the debit and credit in the adjusting entries shown; these three entries are covered in Appendix 4B.

NEED-TO-KNOW 4-4

Recording Shrinkage
and Closing Entries

P3

A merchandising company's ledger on May 31, its fiscal year-end, includes the following accounts that have normal balances (it uses the perpetual inventory system). A physical count of its May 31 year-end inventory reveals that the cost of the merchandise inventory still available is $656. (a) Prepare the entry to record any inventory shrinkage. (b) Prepare the four closing entries as of May 31.

Merchandise inventory	$ 756	Sales	$4,300	Depreciation expense.........	$400
Common stock...........	1,000	Sales discounts	50	Salaries expense.............	600
Retained earnings	1,300	Other operating expenses	300	Sales returns and allowances...	250
Dividends	150	Cost of goods sold	2,100		

Solution

a.	May 31	Cost of Goods Sold	100	
		Merchandise Inventory............................		100
		Adjust for shrinkage ($756 − $656).		
b.	May 31	Sales.......................................	4,300	
		Income Summary		4,300
		Close temporary accounts with credit balances.		
	May 31	Income Summary......................................	3,800	
		Sales Discounts.....................................		50
		Sales Returns and Allowances.....................		250
		Cost of Goods Sold*		2,200
		Depreciation Expense..........................		400
		Salaries Expense.................................		600
		Other Operating Expenses.......................		300
		Close temporary accounts with debit balances.		
		*$2,100 (Unadj. bal.) + $100 (Shrinkage)		
	May 31	Income Summary......................................	500	
		Retained Earnings................................		500
		Close Income Summary account.		
	May 31	Retained Earnings	150	
		Dividends		150
		Close Dividends account.		

Do More: QS 4-9, QS 4-10,
E 4-10, E 4-12, P 4-4

MORE ON FINANCIAL STATEMENT FORMATS

P4

Define and prepare
multiple-step and single-
step income statements.

This section covers two income statement formats: multiple-step and single-step. The classified balance sheet of a merchandiser also is covered.

Multiple-Step Income Statement

A **multiple-step income statement** details net sales and expenses and reports subtotals for various types of items. Exhibit 4.13 shows a multiple-step income statement. The statement has three main parts: (1) *gross profit,* which is net sales minus cost of goods sold; (2) *income from operations,* which is gross profit minus operating expenses; and (3) *net income,* which is income from operations plus or minus nonoperating items.

Operating expenses are separated into two sections. **Selling expenses** are the expenses of advertising merchandise, making sales, and delivering goods to customers. **General and administrative expenses** support a company's overall operations and include expenses related to accounting, human resources, and finance. Expenses are allocated between sections when they contribute to more than one. Z-Mart allocates rent expense of $9,000 from its store building between two sections: $8,100 to selling expense and $900 to general and administrative expenses.

Nonoperating activities consist of other expenses, revenues, losses, and gains that are unrelated to a company's operations. *Other revenues and gains* commonly include interest revenue, dividend revenue, rent revenue, and gains from asset disposals. *Other expenses and losses* commonly include interest expense, losses from asset disposals, and casualty losses. When there are no reportable nonoperating activities, its income from operations is simply labeled *net income.*

Example: Sometimes interest revenue and interest expense are netted and reported on the income statement as *Interest, net.*

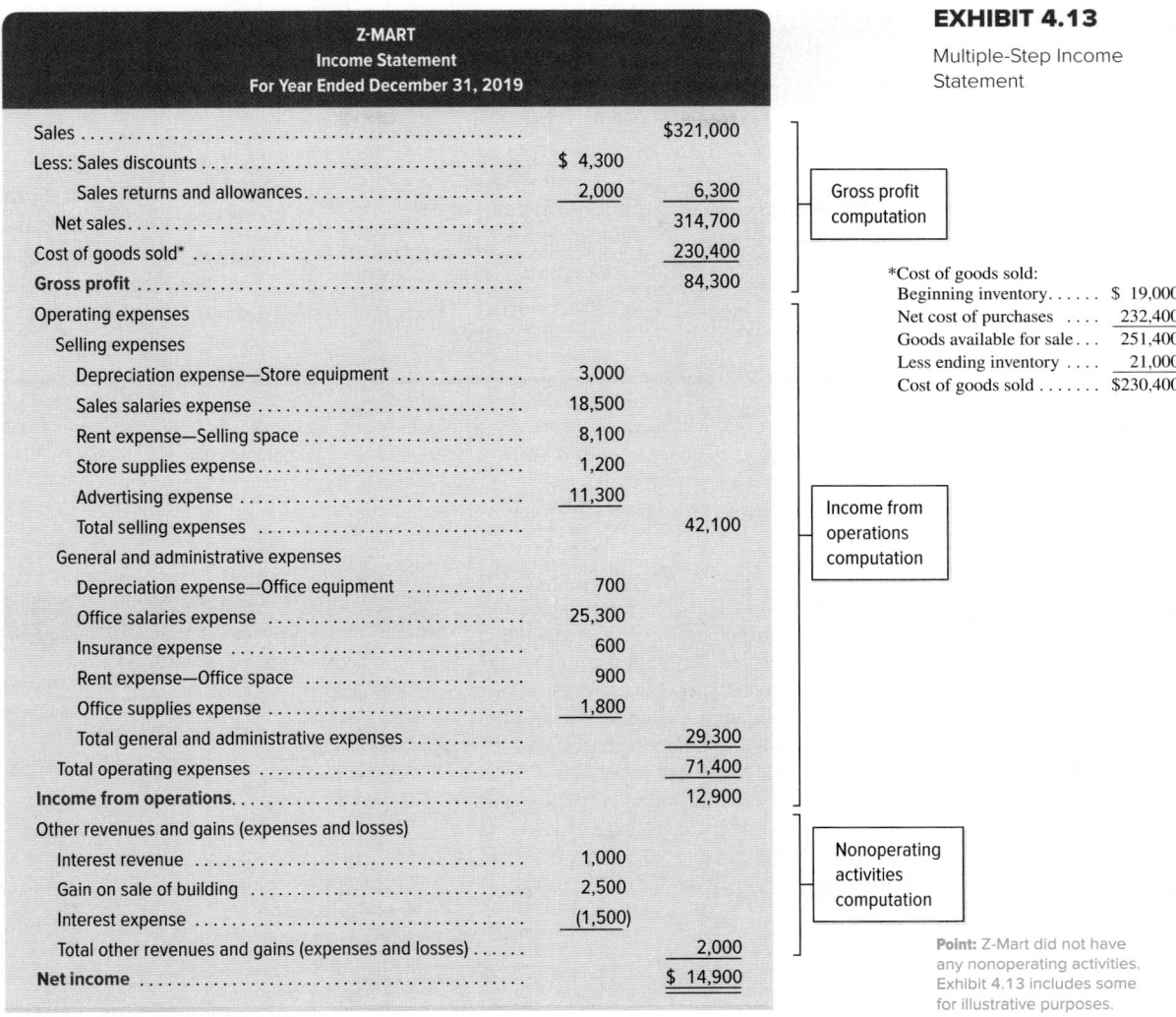

EXHIBIT 4.13

Multiple-Step Income Statement

Z-MART
Income Statement
For Year Ended December 31, 2019

Sales		$321,000
Less: Sales discounts	$ 4,300	
Sales returns and allowances	2,000	6,300
Net sales		314,700
Cost of goods sold*		230,400
Gross profit		84,300
Operating expenses		
Selling expenses		
Depreciation expense—Store equipment	3,000	
Sales salaries expense	18,500	
Rent expense—Selling space	8,100	
Store supplies expense	1,200	
Advertising expense	11,300	
Total selling expenses		42,100
General and administrative expenses		
Depreciation expense—Office equipment	700	
Office salaries expense	25,300	
Insurance expense	600	
Rent expense—Office space	900	
Office supplies expense	1,800	
Total general and administrative expenses		29,300
Total operating expenses		71,400
Income from operations		12,900
Other revenues and gains (expenses and losses)		
Interest revenue	1,000	
Gain on sale of building	2,500	
Interest expense	(1,500)	
Total other revenues and gains (expenses and losses)		2,000
Net income		$ 14,900

Gross profit computation

*Cost of goods sold:
Beginning inventory...... $ 19,000
Net cost of purchases 232,400
Goods available for sale... 251,400
Less ending inventory 21,000
Cost of goods sold $230,400

Income from operations computation

Nonoperating activities computation

Point: Z-Mart did not have any nonoperating activities. Exhibit 4.13 includes some for illustrative purposes.

Single-Step Income Statement

A **single-step income statement** is shown in Exhibit 4.14. It lists cost of goods sold as another expense and shows only one subtotal for total expenses. Expenses are grouped into few, if any, categories. Many companies use formats that combine features of both single- and multiple-step statements. Management chooses the format that best informs users.

EXHIBIT 4.14

Single-Step Income Statement

Z-MART
Income Statement
For Year Ended December 31, 2019

Revenues		
Net sales		$314,700
Interest revenue		1,000
Gain on sale of building		2,500
Total revenues		318,200
Expenses		
Cost of goods sold	$230,400	
Selling expenses	42,100	
General and administrative expenses	29,300	
Interest expense	1,500	
Total expenses		303,300
Net income		$ 14,900

Point: Net income is identical under the single-step and multiple-step formats.

EXHIBIT 4.15

Classified Balance Sheet
(partial) of a Merchandiser

Z-MART Balance Sheet (partial) December 31, 2019	
Current assets	
Cash	$ 8,200
Accounts receivable	11,200
Merchandise inventory	**21,000**
Office supplies	550
Store supplies.................	250
Prepaid insurance..............	300
Total current assets	$41,500

Classified Balance Sheet

The classified balance sheet reports merchandise inventory as a current asset, usually after accounts receivable, according to how quickly they can be converted to cash. Inventory is converted less quickly to cash than accounts receivable because inventory first must be sold before cash can be received. Exhibit 4.15 shows the current asset section of Z-Mart's classified balance sheet (other sections are similar to the previous chapter).

Ethical Risk

Shenanigans   Accurate invoices are important to both sellers and buyers. Merchandisers use invoices to make sure they receive full payment for products provided. To achieve this, controls are set up. Still, failures occur. A survey reports that 30% of employees in sales and marketing witnessed false or misleading invoices sent to customers. Another 29% observed employees violating contract terms with customers (KPMG). ∎

NEED-TO-KNOW 4-5

Multiple- and Single-Step Income Statements

P4

Taret's adjusted trial balance on April 30, its fiscal year-end, is shown here (accounts in random order). (a) Prepare a multiple-step income statement that begins with gross sales and includes separate categories for net sales, cost of goods sold, selling expenses, and general and administrative expenses. (b) Prepare a single-step income statement that begins with net sales and includes these expense categories: cost of goods sold, selling expenses, and general and administrative expenses.

Adjusted Trial Balance	Debit	Credit
Merchandise inventory....................	$ 800	
Other (noninventory) assets...............	2,600	
Total liabilities........................		$ 500
Common stock		400
Retained earnings.......................		1,700
Dividends	300	
Sales		9,500
Sales discounts........................	260	
Sales returns and allowances	240	
Cost of goods sold	6,500	
Sales salaries expense..................	450	
Rent expense—Selling space.............	400	
Store supplies expense	30	
Advertising expense	20	
Office salaries expense	420	
Rent expense—Office space	72	
Office supplies expense	8	
Totals................................	$12,100	$12,100

Solution

a. Multiple-step income statement.

TARET Income Statement For Year Ended April 30		
Sales..		$9,500
Less: Sales discounts	$260	
Sales returns and allowances...................	240	500
Net sales		9,000
Cost of goods sold		6,500
Gross profit		2,500
Operating expenses		
Selling expenses		
Sales salaries expense........................	450	
Rent expense—Selling space....................	400	
Store supplies expense	30	
Advertising expense..........................	20	
Total selling expenses........................		900
General and administrative expenses		
Office salaries expense	420	
Rent expense—Office space	72	
Office supplies expense	8	
Total general and administrative expenses		500
Total operating expenses		1,400
Net income.....................................		$1,100

b. Single-step income statement.

TARET Income Statement For Year Ended April 30		
Net sales		$9,000
Expenses		
Cost of goods sold	$6,500	
Selling expenses............................	900	
General and administrative expenses...........	500	
Total expenses		7,900
Net income.....................................		$1,100

Do More: QS 4-11, E 4-11, E 4-15, P 4-3

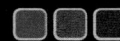

Acid-Test Ratio

A1

One measure of a merchandiser's ability to pay its current liabilities (referred to as its *liquidity*) is the acid-test ratio. The **acid-test ratio,** also called *quick ratio,* is defined as *quick assets* (cash, short-term investments, and current receivables) divided by current liabilities—see Exhibit 4.16. It differs from the current ratio by excluding less liquid current assets such as inventory and prepaid expenses that take longer to be converted to cash.

Compute the acid-test ratio and explain its use to assess liquidity.

EXHIBIT 4.16

Acid-Test (Quick) Ratio

$$\text{Acid-test ratio} = \frac{\text{Cash and cash equivalents} + \text{Short-term investments} + \text{Current receivables}}{\text{Current liabilities}}$$

Exhibit 4.17 shows both the acid-test and current ratios of **Nike** and **Under Armour** for three recent years. Nike's acid-test ratio implies that it has enough quick assets to cover current liabilities. It is also on par with its competitor, Under Armour. Nike's current ratio suggests it has more than enough current assets to cover current liabilities. Analysts might argue that Nike could invest some current assets in more productive assets. An acid-test ratio less than 1.0 means that current liabilities exceed quick assets. A rule of thumb is that the acid-test ratio should have a value near, or higher than, 1.0. Less than 1.0 raises liquidity concerns unless a company can get enough cash from sales or if liabilities are not due until late in the next period.

EXHIBIT 4.17

Acid-Test and Current Ratios for two competitors

Company	$ millions	Current Year	1 Year Ago	2 Years Ago
Nike	Total quick assets	$ 9,856	$ 8,698	$ 9,282
	Total current assets	$16,061	$15,025	$15,587
	Total current liabilities	$ 5,474	$ 5,358	$ 6,332
	Acid-test ratio................	1.8	1.6	1.5
	Current ratio.................	2.9	2.8	2.5
Under Armour	Acid-test ratio	0.9	1.3	1.2
	Current ratio	2.2	2.9	3.1

■ Decision Maker

Supplier A retailer requests to purchase supplies on credit from your company. You have no prior experience with this retailer. The retailer's current ratio is 2.1, its acid-test ratio is 0.5, and inventory makes up most of its current assets. Do you extend credit? ■ *Answer:* A current ratio of 2.1 suggests sufficient current assets to cover current liabilities. An acid-test ratio of 0.5 suggests, however, that quick assets can cover only about one-half of current liabilities. The retailer depends on money from sales of inventory to pay current liabilities. If sales decline, the likelihood that this retailer will default on its payments increases. You probably do not extend credit.

Point: Successful use of a just-in-time inventory system can narrow the gap between the acid-test ratio and the current ratio.

Gross Margin Ratio

A2

Without enough gross profit, a merchandiser can fail. The gross margin ratio helps understand this link. It differs from the profit margin ratio in that it excludes all costs except cost of goods sold. The **gross margin ratio** (or *gross profit ratio*) is defined as *gross margin* (net sales minus cost of goods sold) divided by net sales—see Exhibit 4.18.

Compute the gross margin ratio and explain its use to assess profitability.

EXHIBIT 4.18

Gross Margin Ratio

$$\text{Gross margin ratio} = \frac{\text{Net sales} - \text{Cost of goods sold}}{\text{Net sales}}$$

Exhibit 4.19 shows the gross margin ratio of **Nike** for three recent years. For Nike, each $1 of sales in the current year yielded about 44.6¢ in gross margin to cover all expenses and still produce a net income. This 44.6¢ margin is down from 46.2¢ in the prior year. This decrease is unfavorable.

EXHIBIT 4.19

Nike's Gross Margin Ratio

$ millions	Current Year	1 Year Ago	2 Years Ago
Gross margin......................................	$15,312	$14,971	$14,067
Net sales..	$34,350	$32,376	$30,601
Gross margin ratio	**44.6%**	**46.2%**	**46.0%**

■ Decision Maker

NEED-TO-KNOW 4-6

COMPREHENSIVE 1

Single- and Multiple-Step Income Statements, Closing Entries, and Analysis Using Acid-Test and Gross Margin

Use the following adjusted trial balance and additional information to complete the requirements.

KC ANTIQUES
Adjusted Trial Balance
December 31

	Debit	Credit
Cash.	$ 7,000	
Accounts receivable	13,000	
Merchandise inventory (ending)	60,000	
Store supplies	1,500	
Equipment	45,600	
Accumulated depreciation—Equipment		$ 16,600
Accounts payable		9,000
Salaries payable		2,000
Common stock		20,000
Retained earnings.		59,000
Dividends	10,000	
Sales		343,250
Sales discounts.	5,000	
Sales returns and allowances	6,000	
Cost of goods sold	159,900	
Depreciation expense—Store equipment	4,100	
Depreciation expense—Office equipment	1,600	
Sales salaries expense	30,000	
Office salaries expense	34,000	
Insurance expense	11,000	
Rent expense—Selling space.	16,800	
Rent expense—Office space	7,200	
Store supplies expense	5,750	
Advertising expense	31,400	
Totals	$449,850	$449,850

KC Antiques's *supplementary records* for the year reveal the following itemized costs for merchandising activities.

Invoice cost of merchandise purchases	$150,000	Purchases returns and allowances	$2,700
Purchases discounts received	2,500	Cost of transportation-in	5,000

Required

1. Use the supplementary records to compute the total cost of merchandise purchases for the year.

2. Prepare a multiple-step income statement for the year. (Beginning inventory was $70,100.)

3. Prepare a single-step income statement for the year.

4. Prepare closing entries for KC Antiques at December 31.

5. Compute the acid-test ratio and the gross margin ratio. Explain the meaning of each ratio and interpret them for KC Antiques.

PLANNING THE SOLUTION

- Compute the total cost of merchandise purchases for the year.
- To prepare the multiple-step statement, first compute net sales. Then, to compute cost of goods sold, add the net cost of merchandise purchases for the year to beginning inventory and subtract the cost of ending inventory. Subtract cost of goods sold from net sales to get gross profit. Then classify expenses as selling expenses or general and administrative expenses.
- To prepare the single-step income statement, begin with net sales Then list and subtract the expenses.
- The first closing entry debits all temporary accounts with credit balances and opens the Income Summary account. The second closing entry credits all temporary accounts with debit balances. The third entry closes the Income Summary account to the Retained Earnings account, and the fourth entry closes the Dividends account to the Retained Earnings account.
- Identify the quick assets on the adjusted trial balance. Compute the acid-test ratio by dividing quick assets by current liabilities. Compute the gross margin ratio by dividing gross profit by net sales.

SOLUTION

1.

Invoice cost of merchandise purchases	$150,000
Less: Purchases discounts received	2,500
Purchases returns and allowances	2,700
Add: Cost of transportation-in	5,000
Total cost of merchandise purchases	$149,800

2. Multiple-step income statement.

KC ANTIQUES
Income Statement
For Year Ended December 31

Sales		$343,250
Less: Sales discounts	$ 5,000	
Sales returns and allowances	6,000	11,000
Net sales....................................		332,250
Cost of goods sold*		159,900
Gross profit		172,350
Expenses		
Selling expenses		
Depreciation expense—Store equipment	4,100	
Sales salaries expense	30,000	
Rent expense—Selling space	16,800	
Store supplies expense	5,750	
Advertising expense	31,400	
Total selling expenses....................		88,050
General and administrative expenses		
Depreciation expense—Office equipment.....	1,600	
Office salaries expense...................	34,000	
Insurance expense	11,000	
Rent expense—Office space...............	7,200	
Total general and administrative expenses		53,800
Total operating expenses		141,850
Net income		$ 30,500

Tax expense for a corporation appears immediately before Net income in its own category.

3. Single-step income statement.

KC ANTIQUES
Income Statement
For Year Ended December 31

Net sales................................		$332,250
Expenses		
Cost of goods sold...................	$159,900	
Selling expenses	88,050	
General and administrative expenses ...	53,800	
Total expenses		301,750
Net income		$ 30,500

*Cost of goods sold also can be directly computed:

Beginning merchandise inventory	$ 70,100
Total cost of merchandise purchases (from part 1)	149,800
Goods available for sale	219,900
Ending merchandise inventory	60,000
Cost of goods sold	$159,900

4.

Dec. 31	Sales	343,250	
	Income Summary		343,250
	Close credit balances in temporary accounts.		
Dec. 31	Income Summary	312,750	
	Sales Discounts		5,000
	Sales Returns and Allowances		6,000
	Cost of Goods Sold		159,900
	Depreciation Expense—Store Equipment		4,100
	Depreciation Expense—Office Equipment		1,600
	Sales Salaries Expense		30,000
	Office Salaries Expense		34,000
	Insurance Expense		11,000
	Rent Expense—Selling Space.....................		16,800
	Rent Expense—Office Space		7,200
	Store Supplies Expense		5,750
	Advertising Expense		31,400
	Close debit balances in temporary accounts.		
Dec. 31	Income Summary..................................	30,500	
	Retained Earnings..............................		30,500
	Close Income Summary account.		
Dec. 31	Retained Earnings	10,000	
	Dividends		10,000
	Close Dividends account.		

5. Acid-test ratio = (Cash and equivalents + Short-term investments + Current receivables)/ Current liabilities

= (Cash + Accounts receivable)/(Accounts payable + Salaries payable)

= ($7,000 + $13,000)/($9,000 + $2,000) = $20,000/$11,000 = 1.82

Gross margin ratio = Gross profit/Net sales = $172,350/$332,250 = 0.52 (or 52%)

KC Antiques has a healthy acid-test ratio of 1.82. This means it has $1.82 in liquid assets to satisfy each $1.00 in current liabilities. The gross margin of 0.52 shows that KC Antiques spends 48¢ ($1.00 − $0.52) of every dollar of net sales on the costs of acquiring the merchandise it sells. This leaves 52¢ of every dollar of net sales to cover other expenses incurred in the business and to provide a net profit.

NEED-TO-KNOW 4-7

COMPREHENSIVE 2

Recording Merchandising Transactions—Both Seller and Buyer

Prepare journal entries for the following transactions for both the seller (BMX) and buyer (Sanuk).

May 4   BMX sold $1,500 of merchandise on account to Sanuk, terms FOB shipping point, n/45, invoice dated May 4. The cost of the merchandise was $900.

6   Sanuk paid transportation charges of $30 on the May 4 purchase from BMX.

8   BMX sold $1,000 of merchandise on account to Sanuk, terms FOB destination, n/15, invoice dated May 8. The cost of the merchandise was $700. This sale permitted returns for 30 days.

10   BMX paid transportation costs of $50 for delivery of merchandise sold to Sanuk on May 8.

16   BMX issued Sanuk a $200 credit memorandum for merchandise returned. The merchandise was purchased by Sanuk on account on May 8. The cost of the merchandise returned was $140.

18   BMX received payment from Sanuk for the May 8 purchase.

21   BMX sold $2,400 of merchandise on account to Sanuk, terms FOB shipping point, 2/10, n/EOM. The cost of the merchandise was $1,440. This sale permitted returns for 90 days.

31   BMX received payment from Sanuk for the May 21 purchase, less discount.

Solution

	BMX (Seller)				Sanuk (Buyer)		
May 4	Accounts Receivable—Sanuk	1,500			Merchandise Inventory	1,500	
	Sales		1,500		Accounts Payable—BMX		1,500
	Cost of Goods Sold	900					
	Merchandise Inventory		900				
6	No entry.				Merchandise Inventory	30	
					Cash		30
8	Accounts Receivable—Sanuk	1,000			Merchandise Inventory	1,000	
	Sales		1,000		Accounts Payable—BMX		1,000
	Cost of Goods Sold	700					
	Merchandise Inventory		700				
10	Delivery Expense	50			No entry.		
	Cash		50				
16	Sales Returns & Allowances	200			Accounts Payable—BMX	200	
	Accounts Receivable—Sanuk		200		Merchandise Inventory		200
	Merchandise Inventory	140					
	Cost of Goods Sold		140				
18	Cash	800			Accounts Payable—BMX	800	
	Accounts Receivable—Sanuk		800		Cash		800
21	Accounts Receivable—Sanuk	2,400			Merchandise Inventory	2,400	
	Sales		2,400		Accounts Payable—BMX		2,400
	Cost of Goods Sold	1,440					
	Merchandise Inventory		1,440				
31	Cash	2,352			Accounts Payable—BMX	2,400	
	Sales Discounts	48			Merchandise Inventory		48
	Accounts Receivable—Sanuk		2,400		Cash		2,352

APPENDIX

Periodic Inventory System

4A

A periodic inventory system requires updating the inventory account only at the *end of a period*. During the period, the Merchandise Inventory balance remains unchanged and cost of merchandise is recorded in a temporary *Purchases* account. When a company sells merchandise, it records revenue ***but not the cost of the goods sold.*** At the end of the period, it takes a *physical count of inventory* to get ending inventory. The cost of goods sold is then computed as cost of merchandise available for sale minus ending inventory.

Recording Merchandise Purchases
Under a periodic system, the purchases, purchases returns and allowances, purchases discounts, and transportation-in transactions are recorded in separate temporary accounts. At period-end, each of these temporary accounts is closed, which updates the Merchandise Inventory account. To demonstrate, journal entries under the periodic inventory system are shown for the most common transactions (codes *a* through *d* link these transactions to those in the chapter). For comparison, perpetual system journal entries are shown to the right of each periodic entry. Differences are highlighted.

P5

Record and compare merchandising transactions using both periodic and perpetual inventory systems.

Credit Purchases with Cash Discounts   The periodic system uses a temporary **Purchases** account that accumulates the cost of all purchase transactions during each period. The Purchases account has a normal debit balance, as it increases the cost of merchandise available for sale. Z-Mart's November 2 entry to record the purchase of merchandise for $500 on credit with terms of 2/10, n/30 is

(a)	Periodic				Perpetual		
	Purchases	500			Merchandise Inventory	500	
	Accounts Payable		500		Accounts Payable		500

Payment of Purchases   The periodic system uses a temporary **Purchases Discounts** account that accumulates discounts taken during the period. If payment for transaction *a* is made *within the discount period,* the entry is

(b1)

Periodic		
Accounts Payable	500	
Purchases Discounts*.....		10
Cash		490
*$500 × 2%		

Perpetual		
Accounts Payable	500	
Merchandise Inventory*.......		10
Cash		490
*$500 × 2%		

If payment for transaction *a* is made *after the discount period expires,* the entry is

(b2)

Periodic		
Accounts Payable	500	
Cash		500

Perpetual		
Accounts Payable	500	
Cash		500

Purchases Allowances   The buyer and seller agree to a $30 purchases allowance for defective goods (whether paid within the discount period or not). In the periodic system, the temporary **Purchases Returns and Allowances** account accumulates the cost of all returns and allowances during a period. The buyer records the $30 allowance as

Point: Purchases Discounts <u>and</u> Purchases Returns and Allowances are contra purchases accounts *and* have normal credit balances, as they both decrease the cost of merchandise available for sale.

(c1)

Periodic		
Accounts Payable	30	
Purchases Returns and Allowances		30

Perpetual		
Accounts Payable	30	
Merchandise Inventory		30

Purchases Returns   The buyer returns $50 of merchandise within the discount period. The entry is

(c2)

Periodic		
Accounts Payable	50	
Purchases Returns and Allowances		50

Perpetual		
Accounts Payable	50	
Merchandise Inventory		50

Transportation-In   The buyer paid a $75 freight charge to transport goods with terms FOB destination. In the periodic system, this cost is recorded in a temporary **Transportation-In** account, which has a normal debit balance as it increases the cost of merchandise available for sale.

(d)

Periodic		
Transportation-In	75	
Cash.................		75

Perpetual		
Merchandise Inventory	75	
Cash		75

Recording Merchandise *Sales*
Journal entries under the periodic system are shown for the most common transactions (codes *e* through *h* link these transactions to those in the chapter). Perpetual system entries are shown to the right of each periodic entry. Differences are highlighted.

Credit Sales and Receipt of Payments   Both the periodic and perpetual systems record sales entries similarly, using the gross method. The same holds for entries related to payment of receivables from sales both during and after the discount period. However, under the periodic system, the cost of goods sold is *not* recorded at the time of each sale (whereas it is under the perpetual system). The entry to record $1,000 in credit sales (costing $300) is

Periodic		
Accounts Receivable..........	1,000	
Sales		1,000
No cost-side entry		

Perpetual		
Accounts Receivable..............	1,000	
Sales		1,000
Cost of Goods Sold	300	
Merchandise Inventory		300

Returns Received by Seller A customer returned merchandise for a cash refund. The goods sell for $15 and cost $9. (*Recall:* The periodic system records only the revenue effect, not the cost effect, for sales transactions.) The entry for the seller to take back the return is

	Periodic				Perpetual		
(e1)	Sales Returns and Allowances	15			Sales Returns and Allowances......	15	
	Cash		15		Cash.......................		15
(e2)					Merchandise Inventory	9	
	No entry				Cost of Goods Sold		9

Allowances Granted by Seller The seller gives a price reduction and credits the buyer's accounts receivable for $10. The entry is identical under the periodic and perpetual systems. The seller records this allowance as

	Periodic				Perpetual		
(f)	Sales Returns and Allowances	10			Sales Returns and Allowances......	10	
	Accounts Receivable		10		Accounts Receivable.........		10

Recording Adjusting Entries

Shrinkage—Adjusting Entry Adjusting (and closing) entries for the two systems are in Exhibit 4A.1. The $250 shrinkage is only recorded under the perpetual system—see entry *z* in Exhibit 4A.1. Shrinkage in cost of goods is unknown using a periodic system because inventory is not continually updated and therefore cannot be compared to the physical count.

	Periodic				Perpetual		
	Adjusting Entries				**Adjusting Entries**		
(z)	None				Cost of Goods Sold	250	
					Merchandise Inventory		250
(g)	Sales Discounts................	50			Sales Discounts	50	
	Allowance for Sales Discounts		50		Allowance for Sales Discounts ..		50
(h1)	Sales Returns and Allowances	900			Sales Returns and Allowances.....	900	
	Sales Refund Payable.......		900		Sales Refund Payable		900
(h2)	Inventory Returns Estimated......	300			Inventory Returns Estimated	300	
	Purchases................		300		Cost of Goods Sold		300

Entries in gray are covered in Appendix 4B. Entries in gray are covered in Appendix 4B.

EXHIBIT 4A.1

Comparison of Adjusting and Closing Entries—Periodic and Perpetual

	Periodic				Perpetual		
	Closing Entries				**Closing Entries**		
(1)	Sales	321,000			Sales	321,000	
	Merchandise Inventory (ending)	**21,000**					
	Purchases Discounts	**4,200**					
	Purchases Returns and Allowances	**1,500**					
	Income Summary.........		347,700		Income Summary		321,000
(2)	Income Summary	334,800			Income Summary	308,100	
	Sales Discounts		4,300		Sales Discounts		4,300
	Sales Returns and Allowances		2,000		Sales Returns and Allowances ..		2,000
	Merch. Inven. (beginning)...		**19,000**				
	Purchases		**235,800**		Cost of Goods Sold		230,400
	Transportation-In		**2,300**				
	Depreciation Expense		3,700		Depreciation Expense		3,700
	Salaries Expense		43,800		Salaries Expense		43,800
	Insurance Expense		600		Insurance Expense		600
	Rent Expense		9,000		Rent Expense		9,000
	Supplies Expense		3,000		Supplies Expense		3,000
	Advertising Expense		11,300		Advertising Expense		11,300
(3)	Income Summary	12,900			Income Summary	12,900	
	Retained Earnings		12,900		Retained Earnings...........		12,900
(4)	Retained Earnings	4,000			Retained Earnings	4,000	
	Dividends		4,000		Dividends.................		4,000

Expected Sales Discounts—Adjusting Entry   Both the periodic and perpetual methods make a period-end adjusting entry under the gross method to estimate the $50 sales discounts arising from current-period sales that are likely to be taken in future periods. Z-Mart made the period-end adjusting entry *g* in Exhibit 4A.1 for expected sales discounts.

Expected Returns and Allowances—Adjusting Entry   Both the periodic and perpetual inventory systems estimate returns and allowances arising from current-period sales that will occur in future periods. The adjusting entry for both systems is identical for the sales side, but slightly different for the cost side. The period-end entries *h1* and *h2* in Exhibit 4A.1 are used to record the updates to expected sales refunds of $900 and the cost side of $300. Under both systems, the seller sets up a **Sales Refund Payable** account, which is a current liability reflecting the amount expected to be refunded to customers, and an **Inventory Returns Estimated** account, which is a current asset reflecting the inventory estimated to be returned.

Recording Closing Entries   Periodic and perpetual inventory systems have slight differences in closing entries. The period-end Merchandise Inventory balance (unadjusted) is $19,000 under the periodic system. Because the periodic system does not update the Merchandise Inventory balance during the period, the $19,000 amount is the beginning inventory. A physical count of inventory taken at the end of the period reveals $21,000 of merchandise available. The adjusting and closing entries for the two systems are in Exhibit 4A.1. Recording the periodic inventory balance is a two-step process. The ending inventory balance of $21,000 is entered by debiting the inventory account in the first closing entry. The beginning inventory balance of $19,000 is deleted by crediting the inventory account in the second closing entry.[1]

By updating Merchandise Inventory and closing Purchases, Purchases Discounts, Purchases Returns and Allowances, and Transportation-In, the periodic system transfers the cost of sales amount to Income Summary. Review the periodic side of Exhibit 4A.1 and see that the **red** items affect Income Summary as follows.

Credit to Income Summary in the first closing entry includes amounts from	
Merchandise inventory (ending)	$ 21,000
Purchases discounts	4,200
Purchases returns and allowances	1,500
Debit to Income Summary in the second closing entry includes amounts from	
Merchandise inventory (beginning)	(19,000)
Purchases	(235,800)
Transportation-in	(2,300)
Net effect on Income Summary (net debit = cost of goods sold)	**$(230,400)**

This $230,400 effect on Income Summary is the cost of goods sold amount (which is equal to cost of goods sold reported in a perpetual inventory system). The periodic system transfers cost of goods sold to the Income Summary account but without using a Cost of Goods Sold account. Also, the periodic system does not separately measure shrinkage. Instead, it computes cost of goods available for sale, subtracts the cost of ending inventory, and defines the difference as cost of goods sold, which includes shrinkage.

Calculation of Cost of Goods Sold	
Beginning inventory	$ 19,000
Net cost of purchases	232,400
Cost of goods available for sale	251,400
Less ending inventory	21,000
Cost of goods sold	$230,400

Preparing Financial Statements   The financial statements of a merchandiser using the periodic system are similar to those for a service company described in prior chapters. The income statement mainly differs by the inclusion of *cost of goods sold* and *gross profit*—of course, net sales is affected by discounts, returns, and allowances. The cost of goods sold section under the periodic system follows. The balance sheet mainly differs by the inclusion of *merchandise inventory,* inventory returns estimated, allowance for sales discounts, and sales refund payable. *Visit the Additional Student Resource section of the Connect ebook to view sample chart of accounts for periodic and perpetual systems.*

---

[1]This approach is called the *closing entry method.* An alternative approach, referred to as the *adjusting entry method,* would not make any entries to Merchandise Inventory in the closing entries of Exhibit 4A.1, but instead would make two adjusting entries. Using Z-Mart data, the two adjusting entries would be (1) Dr. Income Summary and Cr. Merchandise Inventory for $19,000 each and (2) Dr. Merchandise Inventory and Cr. Income Summary for $21,000 each. The first entry removes the beginning balance of Merchandise Inventory, and the second entry records the actual ending balance.

Adjusting Entries under New Revenue Recognition Rules

4B

Expected Sales Discounts—Adjusting Entry

P6

Prepare adjustments for discounts, returns, and allowances per revenue recognition rules.

New revenue recognition rules require sales to be reported at the amount expected to be received. This means that a period-end adjusting entry is made to estimate sales discounts for current-period sales that are expected to be taken in future periods. To demonstrate, assume Z-Mart has the following unadjusted balances.

Accounts Receivable	$11,250	Allowance for Sales Discounts	$0

Of the $11,250 of receivables, $2,500 of them are within the 2% discount period for which we expect buyers to take $50 in future-period discounts (computed as $2,500 × 2%) arising from this period's sales. The adjusting entry for the $50 update to Allowance for Sales Discounts is

(g) Dec. 31	Sales Discounts	50	
	Allowance for Sales Discounts		50
	Adjustment for future discounts.		

Assets = Liabilities + Equity
−50   −50

Allow. for Sales Discounts

Beg. bal.	0
Req. adj.	50
Est. bal.	50

Allowance for Sales Discounts is a **contra asset account** and is reported on the balance sheet as a reduction to the Accounts Receivable asset account. The Allowance for Sales Discounts account has a *normal credit balance* because it reduces Accounts Receivable, which has a normal debit balance. This adjusting entry results in both accounts receivable and sales being reported at expected amounts.*

Balance Sheet—partial			**Income Statement—partial**	
Accounts receivable	$11,250		Sales	$321,000
Less allowance for sales discounts	50		Less sales discounts, returns & allowances	6,300
Accounts receivable, net	$11,200		Net sales	$314,700

*__Next Period Adjustment__ The Allowance for Sales Discounts balance remains unchanged during a period except for the period-end adjusting entry. At next period-end, assume that Z-Mart computes an $80 balance for the Allowance for Sales Discounts. Using our three-step adjusting process we get:
Step 1: Current bal. is $50 credit in Allowance for Sales Discounts.
Step 2: Current bal. should be $80 credit in Allowance for Sales Discounts.
Step 3: Record entry to get from step 1 to step 2.   Sales Discounts   30
                                                                    Allowance for Sales Discounts.   30

Expected Returns and Allowances—Adjusting Entries

To avoid overstatement of sales and cost of sales, sellers estimate sales returns and allowances in the period of the sale. Estimating returns and allowances requires companies to maintain the following two balance sheet accounts that are set up with adjusting entries. Two adjusting entries are made: one for the revenue side *and* one for the cost side.

Current Asset→Inventory Returns Estimated	**Current Liability**→Sales Refund Payable

Revenue Side for Expected R&A   When returns and allowances are expected, a seller sets up a **Sales Refund Payable** account, which is **a current liability showing the amount expected to be refunded to customers.** Assume that on December 31 the company estimates future sales refunds to be $1,200. Assume also that the *unadjusted balance* in Sales Refund Payable is a $300 credit. The adjusting entry for the $900 update to Sales Refund Payable follows. The Sales Refund Payable account is updated only during the adjusting entry process. Its balance remains unchanged during the period when actual returns and allowances are recorded.

(h1) Dec. 31	Sales Returns and Allowances	900	
	Sales Refund Payable		900
	*Expected refund of sales.**		

Assets = Liabilities + Equity
          +900   −900

Sales Refund Payable

Beg. bal.	300
Req. adj.	900
Est. bal.	1,200

*This entry uses our three-step adjusting process:
Step 1: Current bal. is $300 credit for Sales Refund Payable.
Step 2: Current bal. should be $1,200 credit for Sales Refund Payable.
Step 3: Record entry to get from step 1 to step 2.

Cost Side for Expected R&A   On the cost side, some inventory is expected to be returned, which means that cost of goods sold recorded at the time of sale is overstated due to expected returns. A seller sets up an **Inventory Returns Estimated** account, which is **a current asset showing the inventory estimated to be returned.** Extending the example above, assume that the company estimates future inventory returns to be $500 (which is the cost side of the $1,200 expected returns and allowances above). Assume also that the (beginning) *unadjusted balance* in Inventory Returns Estimated is a $200 debit. The adjusting entry for the $300 update to expected returns follows. The Inventory Returns Estimated account is updated only during the adjusting entry process. Its balance remains unchanged during the period when actual returns and allowances are recorded.

Point: If estimates of returns and allowances prove too high or too low, we adjust future estimates accordingly.

Assets = Liabilities + Equity
+300   +300

Inventory Returns Est.		
Beg. bal.	200	
Req. adj.	300	
Est. bal.	500	

(h2) Dec. 31	Inventory Returns Estimated	300	
	Cost of Goods Sold		300
	Expected return of inventory. *		

*This entry uses our three-step adjusting process:
Step 1: Current bal. is $200 debit for Inventory Returns Estimated.
Step 2: Current bal. should be $500 debit for Inventory Returns Estimated.
Step 3: Record entry to get from step 1 to step 2.

NEED-TO-KNOW 4-8

Estimating Discounts, Returns, and Allowances

P6

At the current year-end, a company shows the following unadjusted balances for selected accounts.

Allowance for Sales Discounts	$ 75 credit	Sales Discounts	$1,850 debit
Sales Refund Payable	800 credit	Sales Returns and Allowances	4,825 debit
Inventory Returns Estimated	450 debit	Cost of Goods Sold	9,875 debit

a. After an analysis of future sales discounts, the company estimates that the Allowance for Sales Discounts account should have a $275 credit balance. Prepare the current year-end adjusting journal entry for future sales discounts.

b. After an analysis of future sales returns and allowances, the company estimates that the Sales Refund Payable account should have an $870 credit balance (revenue side).

c. After an analysis of future inventory returns, the company estimates that the Inventory Returns Estimated account should have a $500 debit balance (cost side).

Solution

Dec. 31	Sales Discounts	200	
	Allowance for Sales Discounts		200
	Adjustment for future discounts. $275 Cr. − $75 Cr.		
Dec. 31	Sales Returns and Allowances	70	
	Sales Refund Payable		70
	Adjustment for future sales refund. $870 Cr. − $800 Cr.		
Dec. 31	Inventory Returns Estimated	50	
	Cost of Goods Sold		50
	Adjustment for future inventory returns. $500 Dr. − $450 Dr.		

Do More: QS 4-19, QS 4-20, E 4-20, E 4-21, E 4-22

APPENDIX

4C   Net Method for Merchandising

P7_____

Record and compare merchandising transactions using the gross method and net method.

The **net method** records an invoice at its *net* amount (net of any cash discount). The **gross method,** covered earlier in the chapter, initially records an invoice at its gross (full) amount. This appendix records merchandising transactions using the net method. Differences with the gross method are highlighted.

When invoices are recorded at *net* amounts, any cash discounts are deducted from the balance of the Merchandise Inventory account when initially recorded. **This assumes that all cash discounts will be taken.** If any discounts are later lost, they are recorded in a **Discounts Lost** expense account reported on the income statement.

Perpetual Inventory System

PURCHASES—Perpetual A company purchases merchandise on November 2 at a $500 invoice price ($490 net) with terms of 2/10, n/30. Its November 2 entries under the gross and net methods are

Gross Method—Perpetual			Net Method—Perpetual		
Merchandise Inventory........	500		Merchandise Inventory...........	490	
Accounts Payable........		500	Accounts Payable...........		490

If the invoice is paid on (or before) November 12 within the discount period, it records

Gross Method—Perpetual			Net Method—Perpetual		
Accounts Payable	500		Accounts Payable	490	
Merchandise Inventory ...		10			
Cash		490	Cash		490

If the invoice is paid *after the discount period,* it records

Gross Method—Perpetual			Net Method—Perpetual		
Accounts Payable	500		Accounts Payable	490	
			Discounts Lost*	10	
Cash		500	Cash		500

*For simplicity, we record Discounts Lost on the *payment date.*

SALES—Perpetual A company sells merchandise on November 2 at a $500 invoice price ($490 net) with terms of 2/10, n/30. The goods cost $200. Its November 2 entries are

Gross Method—Perpetual			Net Method—Perpetual		
Accounts Receivable..........	500		Accounts Receivable..............	490	
Sales.................		500	Sales.....................		490

Gross Method—Perpetual			Net Method—Perpetual		
Cost of Goods Sold	200		Cost of Goods Sold	200	
Merchandise Inventory ...		200	Merchandise Inventory		200

If cash is received on (or before) November 12 within the discount period, it records

Gross Method—Perpetual			Net Method—Perpetual		
Cash......................	490		Cash...........................	490	
Sales Discounts..............	10				
Accounts Receivable		500	Accounts Receivable		490

If cash is received *after the discount period,* it records

Gross Method—Perpetual			Net Method—Perpetual		
Cash......................	500		Cash...........................	500	
			Interest Revenue		10
Accounts Receivable		500	Accounts Receivable		490

Periodic Inventory System

PURCHASES—Periodic Under the periodic system, the balance of the Merchandise Inventory account remains unchanged during the period and is updated at period-end. During the period, three accounts are used to record purchases of inventory: Purchases; Purchases Discounts; and Purchases Returns and Allowances. *The entries below are identical to the perpetual system except that Merchandise Inventory is substituted for each of the three purchases accounts.*

To demonstrate, we apply the periodic system to purchases transactions. On November 2, a buyer purchases goods ($500 gross; $490 net) with terms of 2/10, n/30. Its November 2 entries under the gross and net methods are

Gross Method—Periodic			Net Method—Periodic		
Purchases	500		Purchases	490	
Accounts Payable........		500	Accounts Payable...........		490

If the invoice is paid on (or before) November 12 within the discount period, it records

Gross Method—Periodic		
Accounts Payable	500	
Purchases Discounts		10
Cash		490

Net Method—Periodic		
Accounts Payable	490	
Cash		490

If the invoice is paid *after the discount period,* it records

Gross Method—Periodic		
Accounts Payable	500	
Cash		500

Net Method—Periodic		
Accounts Payable	490	
Discounts Lost	10	
Cash		500

SALES—Periodic   For sales transactions, the **perpetual and periodic entries are identical except that under the periodic system the cost-side entries are *not* made at the time of each sale nor for any subsequent returns.** Instead, the cost of goods sold is computed at period-end based on a physical count of inventory. This entry is shown in Exhibit 4A.1.

APPENDIX

4D   Work Sheet—Perpetual System

This appendix along with assignments is available online.

Summary: Cheat Sheet

MERCHANDISING ACTIVITIES

Merchandise: Goods a company buys to resell.
Cost of goods sold: Costs of merchandise sold.
Gross profit (gross margin): Net sales minus cost of goods sold.
Computing net income (service company vs. merchandiser):

Service Company

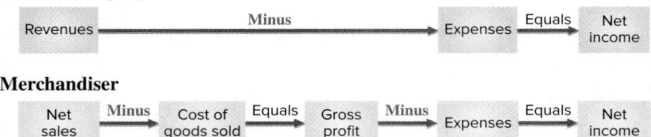

Merchandiser

Inventory: Costs of merchandise owned, but not yet sold. It is a current asset on the balance sheet.

Merchandise Cost Flows:

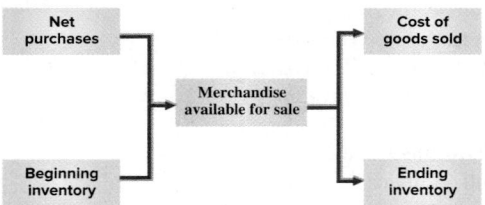

Perpetual inventory system: Updates accounting records for each purchase and each sale of inventory.
Periodic inventory system: Updates accounting records for purchases and sales of inventory only at the end of a period.

MERCHANDISING PURCHASES

Cash discount: A purchases discount on the price paid by the buyer; or, a sales discount on amount received for the seller.
Credit terms example: "2/10, n/60" means full payment is due within 60 days, but the buyer can deduct 2% of the invoice amount if payment is made within 10 days.
Gross method: Initially record purchases at gross (full) invoice amounts.

Purchasing Merchandise for Resale Entries:

Purchasing merchandise on credit	Merchandise Inventory	500	
	Accounts Payable		500

Paying within discount period (Inventory reduced by discount taken)	Accounts Payable	500	
	Merchandise Inventory . . .		10
	Cash		490

Paying outside discount period	Accounts Payable	500	
	Cash		500

Recording purchases returns or allowances	Cash or Accounts Payable	30	
	Merchandise Inventory . . .		30

Transportation Costs and Ownership Transfer Rules:

Shipping Terms	Ownership Transfers at	Goods in Transit Owned by	Transportation Costs Paid by		
FOB shipping point	Shipping point	Buyer	**Buyer**	Merchandise Inventory . . . #	
				Cash	#
FOB destination	Destination	Seller	**Seller**	Delivery Expense . . . . #	
				Cash	#

MERCHANDISING SALES

Selling merchandise on credit	Accounts Receivable.	1,000	
	Sales		1,000
	Cost of Goods Sold	300	
	Merchandise Inventory		300
Receiving payment within discount period	Cash.	980	
	Sales Discounts.	20	
	Accounts Receivable		1,000

Receiving payment outside discount period	Cash.	1,000	
	Accounts Receivable		1,000

Sales Discounts: A contra revenue account, meaning Sales Discounts is subtracted from Sales when computing net sales.

Customer Merchandise Returns Entries:

Receiving sales returns of nondefective inventory	Sales Returns and Allowances. .	15	
	Cash or Accounts Receivable		15
	Merchandise Inventory.	9	
	Cost of Goods Sold.		9

If goods are defective, Inventory is debited for estimated value. A loss is recorded for the difference between cost of merchandise and estimated value.

Receiving sales returns of defective inventory	Merchandise Inventory	2	
	Loss from Defective Merchandise. . .	7	
	Cost of Goods Sold		9

Sales allowance: A price reduction agreed to with the buyer if they are unsatisfied with the goods.

Recognizing sales allowances	Sales Returns and Allowances. .	10	
	Cash or Accounts Receivable		10

MERCHANDISER REPORTING

Inventory shrinkage: An adjusting entry to account for the loss of inventory due to theft or deterioration. It is computed by comparing a physical count of inventory with recorded amounts.

Adjustment for shrinkage (occurs when recorded amount larger than physical inventory)	Cost of Goods Sold.	250	
	Merchandise Inventory		250

Closing Entries: Differences between merchandisers and service companies in red.

Step 1: Close Credit Balances in Temporary Accounts to Income Summary	Sales.	321,000	
	Income Summary.		321,000

Step 2: Close Debit Balances in Temporary Accounts to Income Summary	Income Summary	308,100	
	Sales Discounts		4,300
	Sales Returns and Allowances. .		2,000
	Cost of Goods Sold.		230,400
	Other Expenses		71,400

Steps 3 and 4: Same entries as those for service companies.

Multiple-step income statement: Three parts: (1) gross profit; (2) income from operations, which is gross profit minus operating expenses; and (3) net income, which is income from operations plus or minus nonoperating items.

Operating expenses: Separated into selling expenses and general & administrative expenses.

Selling expenses: Expenses of advertising merchandise, making sales, and delivering goods to customers.

General & administrative expenses: Expenses that support a company's overall operations, including accounting and human resources.

Nonoperating activities: Consist of expenses, revenues, losses, and gains that are unrelated to a company's main operations.

Multiple-Step Income Statement Example

Sales			$321,000
Less: Sales discounts	$4,300		
Sales returns and allowances.	2,000		6,300
Net sales.			314,700
Cost of goods sold			230,400
Gross profit			84,300
Operating Expenses			
Selling expenses[†]			
General and administrative expenses[†]			
Total operating expenses			71,400
Income from operations			12,900
Total other revenues and gains (expenses and losses)			2,000
Net income			$ 14,900

[†]Must list all individual expenses and amounts—see Exhibit 4.13 (not done here for brevity).

Single-Step Income Statement Example

Revenues	
Total revenues*	$318,200
Expenses	
Total expenses*	303,300
Net income	$ 14,900

*Must list all individual items and amounts—see Exhibit 4.14 (not done here for brevity).

Key Terms

Acid-test ratio (159)	**Discounts Lost** (168)	**Inventory Returns Estimated** (166)
Allowance for Sales Discounts (167)	**EOM** (145)	**List price** (145)
Cash discount (146)	**FOB** (148)	**Merchandise** (143)
Cost of goods sold (143)	**General and administrative expenses** (156)	**Merchandise inventory** (144)
Credit memorandum (152)	**Gross margin** (144)	**Merchandiser** (143)
Credit period (146)	**Gross margin ratio** (159)	**Multiple-step income statement** (156)
Credit terms (145)	**Gross method** (147, 168)	**Net method** (151, 168)
Debit memorandum (147)	**Gross profit** (144)	**Periodic inventory system** (144)
Discount period (146)	**Inventory** (144)	**Perpetual inventory system** (144)

Purchases discount (146)
Retailer (143)
Sales discount (146)
Sales Refund Payable (166)

Sales Returns and Allowances (151)
Selling expenses (156)
Shrinkage (153)
Single-step income statement (157)

Supplementary records (149)
Trade discount (145)
Wholesaler (143)

Multiple Choice Quiz

1. A company has $550,000 in net sales and $193,000 in gross profit. This means its cost of goods sold equals
   a. $743,000.   c. $357,000.   e. $(193,000).
   b. $550,000.   d. $193,000.

2. A company purchased $4,500 of merchandise on May 1 with terms of 2/10, n/30. On May 6, it returned $250 of that merchandise. On May 8, it paid the balance owed for merchandise, taking any discount it is entitled to. The cash paid on May 8 is
   a. $4,500.   c. $4,160.   e. $4,410.
   b. $4,250.   d. $4,165.

3. A company has cash sales of $75,000, credit sales of $320,000, sales returns and allowances of $13,700, and sales discounts of $6,000. Its net sales equal

   a. $395,000.   c. $300,300.   e. $414,700.
   b. $375,300.   d. $339,700.

4. A company's quick assets are $37,500, its current assets are $80,000, and its current liabilities are $50,000. Its acid-test ratio equals
   a. 1.600.   c. 0.625.   e. 0.469.
   b. 0.750.   d. 1.333.

5. A company's net sales are $675,000, its cost of goods sold is $459,000, and its net income is $74,250. Its gross margin ratio equals
   a. 32%.   c. 47%.   e. 34%.
   b. 68%.   d. 11%.

ANSWERS TO MULTIPLE CHOICE QUIZ

1. c; Gross profit = $550,000 − $193,000 = $357,000
2. d; ($4,500 − $250) × (100% − 2%) = $4,165
3. b; Net sales = $75,000 + $320,000 − $13,700 − $6,000 = $375,300

4. b; Acid-test ratio = $37,500/$50,000 = 0.75
5. a; Gross margin ratio = ($675,000 − $459,000)/$675,000 = 32%

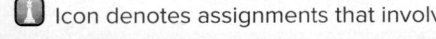

$^{A(B,C)}$ *Superscript letter A, B, or C denotes assignments based on Appendix 4A, 4B, or 4C.*

🔲 Icon denotes assignments that involve decision making.

Discussion Questions

1. What items appear in financial statements of merchandising companies but not in the statements of service companies?

2. In comparing the accounts of a merchandising company with those of a service company, what additional accounts would the merchandising company likely use, assuming it employs a perpetual inventory system?

3. 🔲 Explain how a business can earn a positive gross profit on its sales and still have a net loss.

4. 🔲 Why do companies offer a cash discount?

5. How does a company that uses a perpetual inventory system determine the amount of inventory shrinkage?

6. Distinguish between cash discounts and trade discounts for purchases. Is the amount of a trade discount on purchased merchandise recorded in the accounts?

7. What is the difference between a sales discount and a purchases discount?

8. 🔲 Why would a company's manager be concerned about the quantity of its purchases returns if its suppliers allow unlimited returns?

9. Does the sender (maker) of a debit memorandum record a debit or a credit in the recipient's account? What entry (debit or credit) does the recipient record?

10. What is the difference between the single-step and multiple-step income statement formats?

11. 🔲 Refer to **Apple**'s balance sheet and income statement in Appendix A. What does the company title its inventory account? Does the company present a detailed calculation of its cost of goods sold? **APPLE**

12. Refer to **Google**'s income statement in Appendix A. What title does it use for cost of goods sold? **GOOGLE**

13. Refer to **Samsung**'s income statement in Appendix A. What does Samsung title its cost of goods sold account? **Samsung**

14. Refer to **Samsung**'s income statement in Appendix A. Does its income statement report a gross profit figure? If yes, what is the amount? **Samsung**

15. 🔲 Buyers negotiate purchase contracts with suppliers. What type of shipping terms should a buyer attempt to negotiate to minimize freight-in costs?

connect

Enter the letter for each term in the blank space beside the definition that it most closely matches.

A. Sales discount
B. Credit period
C. Discount period

D. FOB destination
E. FOB shipping point
F. Gross profit

G. Merchandise inventory
H. Purchases discount

———— **1.** Goods a company owns and expects to sell to its customers

———— **2.** Time period that can pass before a customer's full payment is due.

———— **3.** Seller's description of a cash discount granted to buyers in return for early payment.

———— **4.** Ownership of goods is transferred when the seller delivers goods to the carrier.

———— **5.** Purchaser's description of a cash discount received from a supplier of goods.

———— **6.** Difference between net sales and the cost of goods sold.

———— **7.** Time period in which a cash discount is available.

———— **8.** Ownership of goods is transferred when delivered to the buyer's place of business.

QUICK STUDY

QS 4-1
Applying merchandising terms

C1   P1

Costs of $5,000 were incurred to acquire goods and make them ready for sale. The goods were shipped to the buyer (FOB shipping point) for a cost of $200. Additional necessary costs of $400 were incurred to acquire the goods. No other incentives or discounts were available. What is the buyer's total cost of merchandise inventory?

a. $5,000   **b.** $5,200   **c.** $5,400   **d.** $5,600

QS 4-2
Identifying inventory costs
C2

Use the following information (in random order) from a merchandising company and from a service company. *Hint:* Not all information may be necessary for the solutions.

a. For the merchandiser only, compute (1) goods available for sale, (2) cost of goods sold, and (3) gross profit.

b. Compute net income for each company.

QS 4-3
Merchandise accounts and computations
C2

Kleiner Merchandising Company			
Accumulated depreciation...	$ 700	Expenses........	$1,450
Beginning inventory........	5,000	Net purchases....	3,900
Ending inventory..........	1,700	Net sales	9,500

Krug Service Company			
Expenses............	$12,500	Prepaid rent	$ 800
Revenues...........	14,000	Accounts payable	200
Cash...............	700	Equipment	1,300

Compute the amount to be paid for each of the four separate invoices assuming that all invoices are paid *within* the discount period.

Merchandise (gross)	Terms	Merchandise (gross)	Terms
a. $5,000	2/10, n/60	**c.** $75,000	1/10, n/30
b. $20,000	1/15, EOM	**d.** $10,000	3/15, n/45

QS 4-4
Computing net invoice amounts
P1

Prepare journal entries to record each of the following transactions of a merchandising company. The company uses a perpetual inventory system and the gross method.

Nov. 5   Purchased 600 units of product at a cost of $10 per unit. Terms of the sale are 2/10, n/60; the invoice is dated November 5.
        7   Returned 25 defective units from the November 5 purchase and received full credit.
       15   Paid the amount due from the November 5 purchase, minus the return on November 7.

QS 4-5
Recording purchases, returns, and discounts taken
P1

Prepare journal entries to record each of the following transactions. The company records purchases using the gross method and a perpetual inventory system.

Aug. 1   Purchased merchandise with an invoice price of $60,000 and credit terms of 3/10, n/30.
       11   Paid supplier the amount owed from the August 1 purchase.

QS 4-6
Recording purchases and discounts taken
P1

Prepare journal entries to record each of the following transactions. The company records purchases using the gross method and a perpetual inventory system.

Sep. 15   Purchased merchandise with an invoice price of $35,000 and credit terms of 2/5, n/15.
       29   Paid supplier the amount owed on the September 15 purchase.

QS 4-7
Recording purchases and discounts missed
P1

QS 4-8
Recording sales, returns, and discounts taken
P2

Prepare journal entries to record each of the following sales transactions of a merchandising company. The company uses a perpetual inventory system and the gross method.

Apr. 1   Sold merchandise for $3,000, with credit terms n/30; invoice dated April 1. The cost of the merchandise is $1,800.
      4   The customer in the April 1 sale returned $300 of merchandise for full credit. The merchandise, which had cost $180, is returned to inventory.
      8   Sold merchandise for $1,000, with credit terms of 1/10, n/30; invoice dated April 8. Cost of the merchandise is $700.
     11   Received payment for the amount due from the April 1 sale less the return on April 4.

QS 4-9
Accounting for shrinkage—perpetual system
P3

Nix'It Company's ledger on July 31, its fiscal year-end, includes the following selected accounts that have normal balances (Nix'It uses the perpetual inventory system).

Merchandise inventory	$ 37,800	Sales returns and allowances	$ 6,500
Retained earnings	115,300	Cost of goods sold	105,000
Dividends	7,000	Depreciation expense	10,300
Sales	160,200	Salaries expense	32,500
Sales discounts	4,700	Miscellaneous expenses	5,000

A physical count of its July 31 year-end inventory discloses that the cost of the merchandise inventory still available is $35,900. Prepare the entry to record any inventory shrinkage.

QS 4-10
Closing entries   **P3**

Refer to QS 4-9 and prepare journal entries to close the balances in temporary revenue and expense accounts. Remember to consider the entry for shrinkage from QS 4-9.

QS 4-11
Multiple-step income statement
P4

For each item below, indicate whether the statement describes a multiple-step income statement or a single-step income statement.

  a. Multiple-step income statement   **b.** Single-step income statement

_____ **1.** Commonly reports detailed computations of net sales and other costs and expenses.
_____ **2.** Statement limited to two main categories (revenues and expenses).
_____ **3.** Reports gross profit on a separate line.
_____ **4.** Separates income from operations from the other revenues and gains.

QS 4-12
Preparing a multiple-step income statement
P4

Save-the-Earth Co. reports the following income statement accounts for the year ended December 31. Prepare a multiple-step income statement that includes separate categories for net sales, cost of goods sold, selling expenses, and general and administrative expenses. Categorize the following accounts as selling expenses: Sales Staff Salaries and Advertising Expense. Categorize the remaining expenses as general and administrative.

Sales discounts.....................	$ 750	Office supplies expense..............	$ 500
Office salaries expense	2,000	Cost of goods sold	9,000
Rent expense—Office space	1,500	Sales	20,000
Advertising expense................	500	Insurance expense..................	1,000
Sales returns and allowances	250	Sales staff salaries	2,500

QS 4-13
Preparing a classified balance sheet for a merchandiser
P4

Clear Water Co. reports the following balance sheet accounts as of December 31. Prepare a classified balance sheet.

Buildings	$25,000	Notes payable (due in 7 years)	$30,000
Accounts receivable..............	2,000	Office supplies	1,000
Land............................	11,000	Common stock	10,000
Merchandise inventory............	7,000	Retained earnings	6,000
Accounts payable.................	5,000	Wages payable......................	3,000
Cash...........................	8,000		

Use the following information on current assets and current liabilities to compute and interpret the acid-test ratio. Explain what the acid-test ratio of a company measures.

Cash	$1,490	Prepaid expenses	$ 700
Accounts receivable	2,800	Accounts payable	5,750
Inventory	6,000	Other current liabilities	850

QS 4-14
Computing and interpreting acid-test ratio

A1

Compute net sales, gross profit, and the gross margin ratio for each of the four separate companies. Interpret the gross margin ratio for Carrier.

	Carrier	Lennox	Trane	York
Sales	$150,000	$550,000	$38,700	$255,700
Sales discounts	5,000	17,500	600	4,800
Sales returns and allowances	20,000	6,000	5,100	900
Cost of goods sold	79,750	329,589	24,453	126,500

QS 4-15
Computing and analyzing gross margin ratio

A2

Identify whether each description best applies to a periodic or a perpetual inventory system.

_____ **a.** Updates the inventory account only at period-end.
_____ **b.** Requires an adjusting entry to record inventory shrinkage.
_____ **c.** Returns immediately affect the account balance of Merchandise Inventory.
_____ **d.** Records cost of goods sold each time a sales transaction occurs.
_____ **e.** Provides more timely information to managers.

QS 4-16[A]
Contrasting periodic and perpetual systems

P5

Refer to QS 4-5 and prepare journal entries to record each of the merchandising transactions assuming that the company records purchases using the *gross* method and a *periodic* inventory system.

QS 4-17[A]
Recording purchases, returns, and discounts—periodic & gross methods **P5**

Refer to QS 4-8 and prepare journal entries to record each of the merchandising transactions assuming that the company records purchases using the *gross* method and a *periodic* inventory system.

QS 4-18[A]
Recording sales, returns, and discounts—periodic & gross methods **P5**

ProBuilder has the following June 30 fiscal-year-end unadjusted balances: Allowance for Sales Discounts, $0; and Accounts Receivable, $10,000. Of the $10,000 of receivables, $2,000 are within a 3% discount period, meaning that it expects buyers to take $60 in future discounts arising from this period's sales.

a. Prepare the June 30 fiscal-year-end adjusting journal entry for future sales discounts.
b. Assume the same facts above *and* that there is a $10 fiscal-year-end unadjusted credit balance in the Allowance for Sales Discounts. Prepare the June 30 fiscal-year-end adjusting journal entry for future sales discounts.

QS 4-19[B]
Recording estimates of future discounts

P6

ProBuilder reports merchandise sales of $50,000 and cost of merchandise sales of $20,000 in its first year of operations ending June 30. It makes fiscal-year-end adjusting entries for estimated future returns and allowances equal to 2% of sales, or $1,000, and 2% of cost of sales, or $400.

a. Prepare the June 30 fiscal-year-end adjusting journal entry for future returns and allowances related to sales.
b. Prepare the June 30 fiscal-year-end adjusting journal entry for future returns and allowances related to cost of sales.

QS 4-20[B]
Recording estimates of future returns

P6

Refer to QS 4-5 and prepare journal entries to record each of the merchandising transactions assuming that the company records purchases using the *net* method and a *perpetual* inventory system.

QS 4-21[C]
Recording purchases, returns, and discounts—net & perpetual methods **P7**

Refer to QS 4-8 and prepare journal entries to record each of the merchandising transactions assuming that the company records purchases using the *net* method and a *perpetual* inventory system.

QS 4-22[C]
Recording sales, returns, and discounts—net & perpetual methods **P7**

QS 4-23
Sales transactions

P2

Prepare journal entries to record each of the following sales transactions of EcoMart Merchandising. EcoMart uses a *perpetual* inventory system and the *gross* method.

Oct. 1   Sold fair trade merchandise for $1,500, with credit terms n/30, invoice dated October 1. The cost of the merchandise is $900.

6   The customer in the October 1 sale returned $150 of fair trade merchandise for full credit. The merchandise, which had cost $90, is returned to inventory.

9   Sold recycled leather merchandise for $700, with credit terms of 1/10, n/30, invoice dated October 9. Cost of the merchandise is $450.

11   Received payment for the amount due from the October 1 sale less the return on October 6.

EXERCISES

Fill in the blanks in the following separate income statements *a* through *e*. Identify any negative amount by putting it in parentheses.

Exercise 4-1
Computing revenues,
expenses, and income

C1   C2

	a	b	c	d	e
Sales	$62,000	$43,500	$46,000	$?	$25,600
Cost of goods sold					
Merchandise inventory (beginning).	8,000	17,050	7,500	8,000	4,560
Total cost of merchandise purchases	38,000	?	?	32,000	6,600
Merchandise inventory (ending)	?	(3,000)	(9,000)	(6,600)	?
Cost of goods sold	34,050	16,000	?	?	7,000
Gross profit	?	?	3,750	45,600	?
Expenses	10,000	10,650	12,150	3,600	6,000
Net income (loss)	$?	$16,850	$ (8,400)	$42,000	$?

Exercise 4-2
Operating cycle for
merchandiser

C2

The operating cycle of a merchandiser with credit sales includes the following five activities. Starting with merchandise acquisition, identify the chronological order of these five activities.

_____ **a.** Prepare merchandise for sale.   _____ **d.** Purchase merchandise.

_____ **b.** Collect cash from customers on account.   _____ **e.** Monitor and service accounts receivable.

_____ **c.** Make credit sales to customers.

Exercise 4-3
Recording purchases,
purchases returns, and
purchases allowances

P1

Check Apr. 28, Cr. Cash,
$7,920

Prepare journal entries to record the following transactions for a retail store. The company uses a perpetual inventory system and the gross method.

Apr. 2   Purchased $4,600 of merchandise from Lyon Company with credit terms of 2/15, n/60, invoice dated April 2, and FOB shipping point.

3   Paid $300 cash for shipping charges on the April 2 purchase.

4   Returned to Lyon Company unacceptable merchandise that had an invoice price of $600.

17   Sent a check to Lyon Company for the April 2 purchase, net of the discount and the returned merchandise.

18   Purchased $8,500 of merchandise from Frist Corp. with credit terms of 1/10, n/30, invoice dated April 18, and FOB destination.

21   After negotiations over scuffed merchandise, received from Frist a $500 allowance toward the $8,500 owed on the April 18 purchase.

28   Sent check to Frist paying for the April 18 purchase, net of the allowance and the discount.

Exercise 4-4
Recording sales, sales
returns, and sales
allowances

P2

Allied Merchandisers was organized on May 1. Macy Co. is a major customer (buyer) of Allied (seller) products. Prepare journal entries to record the following transactions for Allied assuming it uses a perpetual inventory system and the gross method.

May 3   Allied made its first and only purchase of inventory for the period on May 3 for 2,000 units at a price of $10 cash per unit (for a total cost of $20,000).

5   Allied sold 1,500 of the units in inventory for $14 per unit (invoice total: $21,000) to Macy Co. under credit terms 2/10, n/60. The goods cost Allied $15,000.

7   Macy returns 125 units because they did not fit the customer's needs (invoice amount: $1,750). Allied restores the units, which cost $1,250, to its inventory.

8   Macy discovers that 200 units are scuffed but are still of use and, therefore, keeps the units. Allied gives a price reduction (allowance) and credits Macy's accounts receivable for $300 to compensate for the damage.

15   Allied receives payment from Macy for the amount owed on the May 5 purchase; payment is net of returns, allowances, and any cash discount.

Refer to Exercise 4-4 and prepare journal entries for Macy Co. to record each of the May transactions. Macy is a retailer that uses the gross method and a perpetual inventory system; it purchases these units for resale.

Exercise 4-5
Recording purchases, purchases returns, and purchases allowances   **P1**

Santa Fe Retailing purchased merchandise "as is" (with no returns) from Mesa Wholesalers with credit terms of 3/10, n/60 and an invoice price of $24,000. The merchandise had cost Mesa $16,000. Assume that both buyer and seller use a perpetual inventory system and the gross method.

1. Prepare entries that the *buyer* records for the (*a*) purchase, (*b*) cash payment *within* the discount period, and (*c*) cash payment *after* the discount period.
2. Prepare entries that the *seller* records for the (*a*) sale, (*b*) cash collection *within* the discount period, and (*c*) cash collection *after* the discount period.

Exercise 4-6
Recording sales, purchases, and cash discounts—buyer *and* seller

P1   **P2**

Sydney Retailing (buyer) and Troy Wholesalers (seller) enter into the following transactions. Both Sydney and Troy use a perpetual inventory system and the gross method.

May 11   Sydney accepts delivery of $40,000 of merchandise it purchases for resale from Troy: invoice dated May 11, terms 3/10, n/90, FOB shipping point. The goods cost Troy $30,000. Sydney pays $345 cash to Express Shipping for delivery charges on the merchandise.
   12   Sydney returns $1,400 of the $40,000 of goods to Troy, who receives them the same day and restores them to its inventory. The returned goods had cost Troy $1,050.
   20   Sydney pays Troy for the amount owed. Troy receives the cash immediately.

1. Prepare journal entries that Sydney Retailing (buyer) records for these three transactions.
2. Prepare journal entries that Troy Wholesalers (seller) records for these three transactions.

Exercise 4-7
Recording sales, purchases, shipping, and returns—buyer *and* seller

P1   **P2**

Check   (1) May 20, Cr. Cash, $37,442

The following summarizes Tesla's merchandising activities for the year. Set up T-accounts for Merchandise Inventory and for Cost of Goods Sold. Enter each line item into one of the two T-accounts and compute the T-account balances.

Exercise 4-8
Inventory and cost of sales transactions in T-accounts

P1   **P2**

Cost of merchandise sold to customers	$196,000
Merchandise inventory, beginning-year	25,000
Cost of merchandise purchases, gross amount	192,500
Shrinkage on merchandise as of year-end	800
Cost of transportation-in for merchandise purchases	2,900
Cost of merchandise returned by customers and restored to inventory	2,100
Discounts received from suppliers on merchandise purchases	1,700
Returns to and allowances from suppliers on merchandise purchases	4,000

Check   Ending Merch. Inventory, $20,000

Prepare journal entries for the following merchandising transactions of Dollar Store assuming it uses a perpetual inventory system and the gross method.

Exercise 4-9
Recording purchases, sales, returns, and shipping

P1   **P2**

Nov. 1   Dollar Store purchases merchandise for $1,500 on terms of 2/5, n/30, FOB shipping point, invoice dated November 1.
   5   Dollar Store pays cash for the November 1 purchase.
   7   Dollar Store discovers and returns $200 of defective merchandise purchased on November 1, and paid for on November 5, for a cash refund.
   10   Dollar Store pays $90 cash for transportation costs for the November 1 purchase.
   13   Dollar Store sells merchandise for $1,600 with terms n/30. The cost of the merchandise is $800.
   16   Merchandise is returned to the Dollar Store from the November 13 transaction. The returned items are priced at $160 and cost $80; the items were not damaged and were returned to inventory.

The following list includes selected permanent accounts and all of the temporary accounts from the December 31 unadjusted trial balance of Emiko Co., a business owned by Kumi Emiko. Use these account balances along with the additional information to journalize (*a*) adjusting entries and (*b*) closing entries. Emiko Co. uses a perpetual inventory system.

Exercise 4-10
Preparing adjusting and closing entries for a merchandiser

P3

	Debit	Credit		Debit	Credit
Merchandise inventory	$30,000		Cost of goods sold	$212,000	
Prepaid selling expenses	5,600		Sales salaries expense	48,000	
Dividends	33,000		Utilities expense	15,000	
Sales		$529,000	Selling expenses	36,000	
Sales returns and allowances	17,500		Administrative expenses	105,000	
Sales discounts	5,000				

[continued on next page]

Additional Information

Check   Dr. $84,500 to close
Income Summary

Accrued and unpaid sales salaries amount to $1,700. Prepaid selling expenses of $3,000 have expired. A physical count of year-end merchandise inventory is taken to determine shrinkage and shows $28,700 of goods still available.

Exercise 4-11

Computing net sales for multiple-step income statement

P4

A company reports the following sales-related information. Compute and prepare the net sales portion only of this company's multiple-step income statement.

Sales, gross	$200,000		Sales returns and allowances............	$16,000
Sales discounts	4,000		Sales salaries expense	10,000

Exercise 4-12

Impacts of inventory error on key accounts

P3

A retailer completed a physical count of ending merchandise inventory. When counting inventory, employees did not include $3,000 of incoming goods shipped by a supplier on December 31 under FOB shipping point. These goods had been recorded in Merchandise Inventory, but *they were not included in the physical count because they were in transit.* This means shrinkage was incorrectly overstated by $3,000.

    Compute the amount of overstatement or understatement for each of the following amounts for this period.

a. Ending inventory   **b.** Total assets   **c.** Net income   **d.** Total equity

---

Exercise 4-13

Physical count error and profits   **A2**

Refer to the information in Exercise 4-12 and indicate whether the failure to include in-transit inventory as part of the physical count results in an overstatement, understatement, or no effect on the following ratios.

a. Gross margin ratio   **b.** Profit margin ratio   **c.** Acid-test ratio   **d.** Current ratio

---

Exercise 4-14

Computing and analyzing acid-test and current ratios

A1

Compute the current ratio and acid-test ratio for each of the following separate cases. (Round ratios to two decimals.) Which company is in the best position to meet short-term obligations? Explain.

	Camaro	GTO	Torino
Cash...........................	$2,000	$ 110	$1,000
Short-term investments	50	0	580
Current receivables	350	470	700
Inventory.......................	2,600	2,420	4,230
Prepaid expenses................	200	500	900
Total current assets	$5,200	$3,500	$7,410
Current liabilities.................	$2,000	$1,000	$3,800

Exercise 4-15

Preparing a multiple-step income statement

P4

Fit-for-Life Foods reports the following income statement accounts for the year ended December 31. Prepare a multiple-step income statement that includes separate categories for net sales; cost of goods sold; selling expenses; general and administrative expenses; and other revenues, gains, expenses, and losses. Categorize the following accounts as selling expenses: Sales Staff Wages, Rent Expense—Selling Space, TV Advertising Expense, and Sales Commission Expense. Categorize the remaining expenses as general and administrative.

Gain on sale of equipment............	$ 6,250		Depreciation expense—Office copier...........	$ 500
Office supplies expense..............	700		Sales discounts	16,000
Insurance expense..................	1,300		Sales returns and allowances.................	4,000
Sales	220,000		TV advertising expense......................	2,000
Office salaries expense	32,500		Interest revenue	750
Rent expense—Selling space..........	10,000		Cost of goods sold..........................	90,000
Sales staff wages	23,000		Sales commission expense...................	13,000

Exercise 4-16

Preparing a classified balance sheet for a merchandiser

P4

Adams Co. reports the following balance sheet accounts as of December 31. Prepare a classified balance sheet.

Salaries payable	$ 6,000		Retained earnings	$50,000
Buildings..........................	55,000		Notes payable (due in 9 years)................	30,000
Prepaid rent	7,000		Office supplies.............................	2,000
Merchandise inventory...............	14,000		Land......................................	22,000
Accounts payable...................	10,000		Accumulated depreciation—Building...........	5,000
Prepaid insurance..................	3,000		Mortgages payable (due in 5 years)...........	12,000
Accounts receivable.................	4,000		Cash......................................	16,000
Common stock	10,000			

Refer to Exercise 4-3 and prepare journal entries to record each of the merchandising transactions assuming that the buyer uses the *periodic inventory system* and the *gross method*.

Exercise 4-17ᴬ
Recording purchases, returns, and allowances—periodic **P5**

Refer to Exercise 4-6 and prepare journal entries to record each of the merchandising transactions assuming that the *periodic inventory system* and the *gross method* are used by both the buyer and the seller.

Exercise 4-18ᴬ
Recording sales, purchases, and discounts: buyer and seller—periodic **P5**

Refer to Exercise 4-7 and prepare journal entries to record each of the merchandising transactions assuming that the *periodic inventory system* and the *gross method* are used by both the buyer and the seller.

Exercise 4-19ᴬ
Recording sales, purchases, shipping, and returns: buyer and seller—periodic **P5**

Med Labs has the following December 31 year-end unadjusted balances: Allowance for Sales Discounts, $0; and Accounts Receivable, $5,000. Of the $5,000 of receivables, $1,000 are within a 2% discount period, meaning that it expects buyers to take $20 in future-period discounts arising from this period's sales.

a. Prepare the December 31 year-end adjusting journal entry for future sales discounts.

b. Assume the same facts above *and* that there is a $5 year-end unadjusted credit balance in Allowance for Sales Discounts. Prepare the December 31 year-end adjusting journal entry for future sales discounts.

c. Is Allowance for Sales Discounts a contra asset or a contra liability account?

Exercise 4-20ᴮ
Recording estimates of future discounts
P6

Chico Company allows its customers to return merchandise within 30 days of purchase.

• At December 31, the end of its first year of operations, Chico estimates future-period merchandise returns of $60,000 (cost of $22,500) related to its current-year sales.

• A few days later, on January 3, a customer returns merchandise with a selling price of $2,000 for a cash refund; the returned merchandise cost $750 and is returned to inventory as it is not defective.

a. Prepare the December 31 year-end adjusting journal entry for estimated future sales returns and allowances (revenue side).

b. Prepare the December 31 year-end adjusting journal entry for estimated future inventory returns and allowances (cost side).

c. Prepare the January 3 journal entries to record the merchandise returned.

Exercise 4-21ᴮ
Recording estimates of future returns
P6

Lopez Company reports unadjusted first-year merchandise sales of $100,000 and cost of merchandise sales of $30,000.

a. Compute gross profit (using the unadjusted numbers above).

b. The company expects future returns and allowances equal to 5% of sales and 5% of cost of sales.

   1. Prepare the year-end adjusting entry to record the sales expected to be refunded.

   2. Prepare the year-end adjusting entry to record the cost side of sales returns and allowances.

   3. Recompute gross profit using the adjusted numbers from parts 1 and 2.

c. Is Sales Refund Payable an asset, liability, or equity account?

d. Is Inventory Returns Estimated an asset, liability, or equity account?

Exercise 4-22ᴮ
Recording estimates of future returns
P6

Refer to Exercise 4-7 and prepare journal entries to record each of the merchandising transactions assuming that the *perpetual inventory system* and the *net method* are used by both the buyer and the seller.

Exercise 4-23ᶜ
Recording sales, purchases, shipping, and returns: buyer and seller—perpetual and net method **P7**

Piere Imports uses the perpetual system in accounting for merchandise inventory and had the following transactions during the month of October. Prepare entries to record these transactions assuming that Piere Imports records invoices (*a*) at gross amounts and (*b*) at net amounts.

Oct. 2   Purchased merchandise at a $3,000 price ($2,940 net), invoice dated October 2, terms 2/10, n/30.
     10   Returned $500 ($490 net) of merchandise purchased on October 2 and debited its account payable for that amount.
     17   Purchased merchandise at a $5,400 price ($5,292 net), invoice dated October 17, terms 2/10, n/30.
     27   Paid for the merchandise purchased on October 17, less the discount.
     31   Paid for the merchandise purchased on October 2.

Exercise 4-24ᶜ
Recording purchases, sales, returns, and discounts: buyer and seller—perpetual and both net & gross methods
P7

Exercise 4-25

Purchasing transactions

P1

Prepare journal entries to record the following transactions of Recycled Fashion retail store. Recycled Fashion uses a perpetual inventory system and the gross method.

Mar. 3   Purchased $1,150 of merchandise made from recycled material from GreenWorld Company with credit terms of 2/15, n/60, invoice dated March 3, and FOB shipping point.
      4   Paid $75 cash for shipping charges on the March 3 purchase.
      5   Returned to GreenWorld unacceptable merchandise that had an invoice price of $150.
     18   Paid GreenWorld for the March 3 purchase, net of the discount and the returned merchandise.
     19   Purchased $425 of fair trade merchandise from PeopleFirst Corp. with credit terms of 1/10, n/30, invoice dated March 19, and FOB destination.
     21   After negotiations, received from PeopleFirst a $25 allowance (for scuffed merchandise) toward the $425 owed on the March 19 purchase.
     29   Sent check to PeopleFirst paying for the March 19 purchase, net of the allowance and the discount.

PROBLEM SET A

Problem 4-1A

Preparing journal entries for merchandising activities—perpetual system

P1 P2

Prepare journal entries to record the following merchandising transactions of Cabela's, which uses the perpetual inventory system and the gross method. *Hint:* It will help to identify each receivable and payable; for example, record the purchase on July 1 in Accounts Payable—Boden.

July 1   Purchased merchandise from Boden Company for $6,000 under credit terms of 1/15, n/30, FOB shipping point, invoice dated July 1.
      2   Sold merchandise to Creek Co. for $900 under credit terms of 2/10, n/60, FOB shipping point, invoice dated July 2. The merchandise had cost $500.
      3   Paid $125 cash for freight charges on the purchase of July 1.
      8   Sold merchandise that had cost $1,300 for $1,700 cash.
      9   Purchased merchandise from Leight Co. for $2,200 under credit terms of 2/15, n/60, FOB destination, invoice dated July 9.

Check   July 12, Dr. Cash, $882

July 16, Cr. Cash, $5,940

     11   Returned $200 of merchandise purchased on July 9 from Leight Co. and debited its account payable for that amount.
     12   Received the balance due from Creek Co. for the invoice dated July 2, net of the discount.
     16   Paid the balance due to Boden Company within the discount period.
     19   Sold merchandise that cost $800 to Art Co. for $1,200 under credit terms of 2/15, n/60, FOB shipping point, invoice dated July 19.
     21   Gave a price reduction (allowance) of $100 to Art Co. for merchandise sold on July 19 and credited Art's accounts receivable for that amount.

July 24, Cr. Cash, $1,960
July 30, Dr. Cash, $1,078

     24   Paid Leight Co. the balance due, net of discount.
     30   Received the balance due from Art Co. for the invoice dated July 19, net of discount.
     31   Sold merchandise that cost $4,800 to Creek Co. for $7,000 under credit terms of 2/10, n/60, FOB shipping point, invoice dated July 31.

Problem 4-2A

Preparing journal entries for merchandising activities—perpetual system

P1 P2

Prepare journal entries to record the following merchandising transactions of Lowe's, which uses the perpetual inventory system and the gross method. *Hint:* It will help to identify each receivable and payable; for example, record the purchase on August 1 in Accounts Payable—Aron.

Aug. 1   Purchased merchandise from Aron Company for $7,500 under credit terms of 1/10, n/30, FOB destination, invoice dated August 1.
      5   Sold merchandise to Baird Corp. for $5,200 under credit terms of 2/10, n/60, FOB destination, invoice dated August 5. The merchandise had cost $4,000.
      8   Purchased merchandise from Waters Corporation for $5,400 under credit terms of 1/10, n/45, FOB shipping point, invoice dated August 8.

Check   Aug. 9, Dr. Delivery Expense, $125

      9   Paid $125 cash for shipping charges related to the August 5 sale to Baird Corp.
     10   Baird returned merchandise from the August 5 sale that had cost Lowe's $400 and was sold for $600. The merchandise was restored to inventory.
     12   After negotiations with Waters Corporation concerning problems with the purchases on August 8, Lowe's received a price reduction from Waters of $400 off the $5,400 of goods purchased. Lowe's debited accounts payable for $400.
     14   At Aron's request, Lowe's paid $200 cash for freight charges on the August 1 purchase, reducing the amount owed (accounts payable) to Aron.
     15   Received balance due from Baird Corp. for the August 5 sale less the return on August 10.

Aug. 18, Cr. Cash, $4,950

     18   Paid the amount due Waters Corporation for the August 8 purchase less the price allowance from August 12.

[continued on next page]

19   Sold merchandise to Tux Co. for $4,800 under credit terms of n/10, FOB shipping point, invoice dated August 19. The merchandise had cost $2,400.

22   Tux requested a price reduction on the August 19 sale because the merchandise did not meet specifications. Lowe's gave a price reduction (allowance) of $500 to Tux and credited Tux's accounts receivable for that amount.

29   Received Tux's cash payment for the amount due from the August 19 sale less the price allowance from August 22.   Aug. 29, Dr. Cash, $4,300

30   Paid Aron Company the amount due from the August 1 purchase.

Valley Company's adjusted trial balance on August 31, its fiscal year-end, follows. It categorizes the following accounts as selling expenses: Sales Salaries Expense, Rent Expense—Selling Space, Store Supplies Expense, and Advertising Expense. It categorizes the remaining expenses as general and administrative.

Problem 4-3A
Computing merchandising amounts and formatting income statements

C2   P4

	Debit	Credit
Merchandise inventory (ending)	$ 41,000	
Other (noninventory) assets	130,400	
Total liabilities.		$ 25,000
Common stock		10,000
Retained earnings.		94,550
Dividends	8,000	
Sales		225,600
Sales discounts.	2,250	
Sales returns and allowances	12,000	
Cost of goods sold	74,500	
Sales salaries expense.	32,000	
Rent expense—Selling space.	8,000	
Store supplies expense	1,500	
Advertising expense.	13,000	
Office salaries expense	28,500	
Rent expense—Office space	3,600	
Office supplies expense.	400	
Totals.	$355,150	$355,150

Beginning merchandise inventory was $25,400. Supplementary records of merchandising activities for the year ended August 31 reveal the following itemized costs.

Invoice cost of merchandise purchases	$92,000	Purchases returns and allowances.	$ 4,500
Purchases discounts received	2,000	Costs of transportation-in	4,600

Required

1. Compute the company's net sales for the year.

2. Compute the company's total cost of merchandise purchased for the year.   **Check** (2) $90,100

3. Prepare a multiple-step income statement that includes separate categories for net sales, cost of goods sold, selling expenses, and general and administrative expenses.   (3) Gross profit, $136,850; Net income, $49,850

4. Prepare a single-step income statement that includes these expense categories: cost of goods sold, selling expenses, and general and administrative expenses.   (4) Total expenses, $161,500

Use the data for Valley Company in Problem 4-3A to complete the following requirement.

Problem 4-4A
Preparing closing entries and interpreting information about discounts and returns   C2   P3

Required

Prepare closing entries as of August 31 (the perpetual inventory system is used).

The following unadjusted trial balance is prepared at fiscal year-end for Nelson Company. Nelson Company uses a perpetual inventory system. It categorizes the following accounts as selling expenses: Depreciation Expense—Store Equipment, Sales Salaries Expense, Rent Expense—Selling Space, Store Supplies Expense, and Advertising Expense. It categorizes the remaining expenses as general and administrative.

Problem 4-5A
Preparing adjusting entries and income statements; computing gross margin, acid-test, and current ratios

A1   A2   P3   P4

NELSON COMPANY		
Unadjusted Trial Balance		
January 31		
	Debit	Credit
Cash	$ 1,000	
Merchandise inventory	12,500	
Store supplies	5,800	
Prepaid insurance	2,400	
Store equipment	42,900	
Accumulated depreciation—Store equipment		$ 15,250
Accounts payable		10,000
Common stock		5,000
Retained earnings		27,000
Dividends	2,200	
Sales		111,950
Sales discounts	2,000	
Sales returns and allowances	2,200	
Cost of goods sold	38,400	
Depreciation expense—Store equipment	0	
Sales salaries expense	17,500	
Office salaries expense	17,500	
Insurance expense	0	
Rent expense—Selling space	7,500	
Rent expense—Office space	7,500	
Store supplies expense	0	
Advertising expense	9,800	
Totals	$169,200	$169,200

Required

1. Prepare adjusting journal entries to reflect each of the following:
   a. Store supplies still available at fiscal year-end amount to $1,750.
   b. Expired insurance, an administrative expense, is $1,400 for the fiscal year.
   c. Depreciation expense on store equipment, a selling expense, is $1,525 for the fiscal year.
   d. To estimate shrinkage, a physical count of ending merchandise inventory is taken. It shows $10,900 of inventory is still available at fiscal year-end.

Check (2) Gross profit, $67,750

2. Prepare a multiple-step income statement for the year ended January 31 that begins with gross sales and includes separate categories for net sales, cost of goods sold, selling expenses, and general and administrative expenses.

(3) Total expenses, $106,775; Net income, $975

3. Prepare a single-step income statement for the year ended January 31.

4. Compute the current ratio, acid-test ratio, and gross margin ratio as of January 31. (Round ratios to two decimals.)

PROBLEM SET B

Problem 4-1B

Preparing journal entries for merchandising activities—perpetual system

P1   P2

Check   May 14, Dr. Cash, $10,780
May 17, Cr. Cash, $9,900

Prepare journal entries to record the following merchandising transactions of IKEA, which uses the perpetual inventory system and gross method. *Hint:* It will help to identify each receivable and payable; for example, record the purchase on May 2 in Accounts Payable—Havel.

May   2   Purchased merchandise from Havel Co. for $10,000 under credit terms of 1/15, n/30, FOB shipping point, invoice dated May 2.
      4   Sold merchandise to Rath Co. for $11,000 under credit terms of 2/10, n/60, FOB shipping point, invoice dated May 4. The merchandise had cost $5,600.
      5   Paid $250 cash for freight charges on the purchase of May 2.
      9   Sold merchandise that had cost $2,000 for $2,500 cash.
     10   Purchased merchandise from Duke Co. for $3,650 under credit terms of 2/15, n/60, FOB destination, invoice dated May 10.
     12   Returned $650 of merchandise purchased on May 10 from Duke Co. and debited its account payable for that amount.
     14   Received the balance due from Rath Co. for the invoice dated May 4, net of the discount.
     17   Paid the balance due to Havel Co. within the discount period.

[continued on next page]

20   Sold merchandise that cost $1,450 to Tamer Co. for $2,800 under credit terms of 2/15, n/60, FOB shipping point, invoice dated May 20.

22   Gave a price reduction (allowance) of $300 to Tamer Co. for merchandise sold on May 20 and credited Tamer's accounts receivable for that amount.

25   Paid Duke Co. the balance due, net of the discount.

30   Received the balance due from Tamer Co. for the invoice dated May 20, net of discount and allowance.   May 30, Dr. Cash, $2,450

31   Sold merchandise that cost $3,600 to Rath Co. for $7,200 under credit terms of 2/10, n/60, FOB shipping point, invoice dated May 31.

Prepare journal entries to record the following merchandising transactions of Menards, which applies the perpetual inventory system and gross method. *Hint:* It will help to identify each receivable and payable; for example, record the purchase on July 3 in Accounts Payable—OLB.

Problem 4-2B
Preparing journal entries for merchandising activities—perpetual system

P1   P2

July   3   Purchased merchandise from OLB Corp. for $15,000 under credit terms of 1/10, n/30, FOB destination, invoice dated July 3.

7   Sold merchandise to Brill Co. for $11,500 under credit terms of 2/10, n/60, FOB destination, invoice dated July 7. The merchandise had cost $7,750.

10   Purchased merchandise from Rupert Co. for $14,200 under credit terms of 1/10, n/45, FOB shipping point, invoice dated July 10.

11   Paid $300 cash for shipping charges related to the July 7 sale to Brill Co.

12   Brill returned merchandise from the July 7 sale that had cost Menards $1,450 and been sold for $2,000. The merchandise was restored to inventory.

14   After negotiations with Rupert Co. concerning problems with the merchandise purchased on July 10, Menards received a price reduction from Rupert of $1,200. Menards debited accounts payable for $1,200.

15   At OLB's request, Menards paid $200 cash for freight charges on the July 3 purchase, reducing the amount owed (accounts payable) to OLB.

17   Received balance due from Brill Co. for the July 7 sale less the return on July 12.   **Check**   July 17, Dr. Cash, $9,310

20   Paid the amount due Rupert Co. for the July 10 purchase less the price reduction granted on July 14.

21   Sold merchandise to Brown for $11,000 under credit terms of 1/10, n/30, FOB shipping point, invoice dated July 21. The merchandise had cost $7,000.

24   Brown requested a price reduction on the July 21 sale because the merchandise did not meet specifications. Menards gave a price reduction (allowance) of $1,000 to Brown and credited Brown's accounts receivable for that amount.

30   Received Brown's cash payment for the amount due from the July 21 sale less the price allowance from July 24.   July 30, Dr. Cash, $9,900

31   Paid OLB Corp. the amount due from the July 3 purchase.   July 31, Cr. Cash, $14,800

Barkley Company's adjusted trial balance on March 31, its fiscal year-end, follows. It categorizes the following accounts as selling expenses: Sales Salaries Expense, Rent Expense—Selling Space, Store Supplies Expense, and Advertising Expense. It categorizes the remaining expenses as general and administrative.

Problem 4-3B
Computing merchandising amounts and formatting income statements

C1   C2   P4

	Debit	Credit
Merchandise inventory (ending)	$ 56,500	
Other (noninventory) assets..............	202,600	
Total liabilities.........................		$ 42,500
Common stock		10,000
Retained earnings......................		154,425
Dividends	3,000	
Sales		332,650
Sales discounts.......................	5,875	
Sales returns and allowances	20,000	
Cost of goods sold	115,600	
Sales salaries expense.................	44,500	
Rent expense—Selling space............	16,000	
Store supplies expense	3,850	
Advertising expense....................	26,000	
Office salaries expense	40,750	
Rent expense—Office space	3,800	
Office supplies expense................	1,100	
Totals...............................	$539,575	$539,575

Beginning merchandise inventory was $37,500. Supplementary records of merchandising activities for the year ended March 31 reveal the following itemized costs.

Invoice cost of merchandise purchases	$138,500	Purchases returns and allowances.	$6,700
Purchases discounts received	2,950	Costs of transportation-in	5,750

Required

1. Compute the company's net sales for the year.

Check   (2) $134,600

(3) Gross profit, $191,175;
Net income, $55,175

(4) Total expenses, $251,600

2. Compute the company's total cost of merchandise purchased for the year.

3. Prepare a multiple-step income statement that includes separate categories for net sales, cost of goods sold, selling expenses, and general and administrative expenses.

4. Prepare a single-step income statement that includes these expense categories: cost of goods sold, selling expenses, and general and administrative expenses.

Problem 4-4B

Preparing closing entries
and interpreting information
about discounts and
returns   C2   P3

Use the data for Barkley Company in Problem 4-3B to complete the following requirement.

Required

Prepare closing entries as of March 31 (the perpetual inventory system is used).

Problem 4-5B

Preparing adjusting entries
and income statements;
computing gross margin,
acid-test, and current ratios

P3   P4   A1   A2

The following unadjusted trial balance is prepared at fiscal year-end for Foster Products Company. Foster Products Company uses a perpetual inventory system. It categorizes the following accounts as selling expenses: Depreciation Expense—Store Equipment, Sales Salaries Expense, Rent Expense—Selling Space, Store Supplies Expense, and Advertising Expense. It categorizes the remaining expenses as general and administrative.

FOSTER PRODUCTS COMPANY Unadjusted Trial Balance October 31	Debit	Credit
Cash	$ 7,400	
Merchandise inventory	24,000	
Store supplies	9,700	
Prepaid insurance	6,600	
Store equipment	81,800	
Accumulated depreciation—Store equipment		$ 32,000
Accounts payable		18,000
Common stock		3,000
Retained earnings		40,000
Dividends	2,000	
Sales		227,100
Sales discounts	1,000	
Sales returns and allowances	5,000	
Cost of goods sold	75,800	
Depreciation expense—Store equipment	0	
Sales salaries expense	31,500	
Office salaries expense	31,500	
Insurance expense	0	
Rent expense—Selling space	13,000	
Rent expense—Office space	13,000	
Store supplies expense	0	
Advertising expense	17,800	
Totals	$320,100	$320,100

Required

1. Prepare adjusting journal entries to reflect each of the following:
   a. Store supplies still available at fiscal year-end amount to $3,700.
   b. Expired insurance, an administrative expense, is $2,800 for the fiscal year.

[continued on next page]

    c. Depreciation expense on store equipment, a selling expense, is $3,000 for the fiscal year.

    d. To estimate shrinkage, a physical count of ending merchandise inventory is taken. It shows $21,300 of inventory is still available at fiscal year-end.

2. Prepare a multiple-step income statement for the year ended October 31 that begins with gross sales and includes separate categories for net sales, cost of goods sold, selling expenses, and general and administrative expenses.

3. Prepare a single-step income statement for the year ended October 31.

4. Compute the current ratio, acid-test ratio, and gross margin ratio as of October 31. (Round ratios to two decimals.)

Check (2) Gross profit, $142,600

(3) Total expenses, $197,100; Net income, $24,000

This serial problem began in Chapter 1 and continues through most of the book. If previous chapter segments were not completed, the serial problem can begin at this point.

SERIAL PROBLEM
Business Solutions

P1   P2   P3   P4

SP 4 Santana Rey created **Business Solutions** on October 1, 2019. The company has been successful, and its list of customers has grown. To accommodate the growth, the accounting system is modified to set up separate accounts for each customer. The following chart of accounts includes the account number used for each account and any balance as of December 31, 2019. Santana Rey decided to add a fourth digit with a decimal point to the 106 account number that had been used for the single Accounts Receivable account. This change allows the company to continue using the existing chart of accounts.

No.	Account Title	Dr.	Cr.
101	Cash	$48,372	
106.1	Alex's Engineering Co.	0	
106.2	Wildcat Services	0	
106.3	Easy Leasing	0	
106.4	IFM Co.	3,000	
106.5	Liu Corp.	0	
106.6	Gomez Co.	2,668	
106.7	Delta Co.	0	
106.8	KC, Inc.	0	
106.9	Dream, Inc.	0	
119	Merchandise inventory	0	
126	Computer supplies	580	
128	Prepaid insurance	1,665	
131	Prepaid rent	825	
163	Office equipment	8,000	
164	Accumulated depreciation—Office equipment		$ 400
167	Computer equipment	20,000	
168	Accumulated depreciation—Computer equipment		1,250
201	Accounts payable		1,100

No.	Account Title	Dr.	Cr.
210	Wages payable		$ 500
236	Unearned computer services revenue		1,500
307	Common stock		73,000
318	Retained earnings.....................		7,360
319	Dividends	$0	
403	Computer services revenue		0
413	Sales		0
414	Sales returns and allowances	0	
415	Sales discounts	0	
502	Cost of goods sold	0	
612	Depreciation expense—Office equipment	0	
613	Depreciation expense—Computer equipment	0	
623	Wages expense	0	
637	Insurance expense	0	
640	Rent expense	0	
652	Computer supplies expense	0	
655	Advertising expense	0	
676	Mileage expense	0	
677	Miscellaneous expenses	0	
684	Repairs expense—Computer	0	

In response to requests from customers, S. Rey will begin selling computer software. The company will extend credit terms of 1/10, n/30, FOB shipping point, to all customers who purchase this merchandise. However, no cash discount is available on consulting fees. Additional accounts (Nos. 119, 413, 414, 415, and 502) are added to its general ledger to accommodate the company's new merchandising activities. Its transactions for January through March follow.

Jan. 4 The company paid cash to Lyn Addie for five days' work at the rate of $125 per day. Four of the five days relate to wages payable that were accrued in the prior year.

     5 Santana Rey invested an additional $25,000 cash in the company in exchange for more common stock.

     7 The company purchased $5,800 of merchandise from Kansas Corp. with terms of 1/10, n/30, FOB shipping point, invoice dated January 7.

     9 The company received $2,668 cash from Gomez Co. as full payment on its account.

   11 The company completed a five-day project for Alex's Engineering Co. and billed it $5,500, which is the total price of $7,000 less the advance payment of $1,500. The company debited Unearned Computer Services Revenue for $1,500.

©Alexander Image/Shutterstock

13   The company sold merchandise with a retail value of $5,200 and a cost of $3,560 to Liu Corp., invoice dated January 13.

15   The company paid $600 cash for freight charges on the merchandise purchased on January 7.

16   The company received $4,000 cash from Delta Co. for computer services provided.

17   The company paid Kansas Corp. for the invoice dated January 7, net of the discount.

20   The company gave a price reduction (allowance) of $500 to Liu Corp. and credited Liu's accounts receivable for that amount.

22   The company received the balance due from Liu Corp., net of the discount and the allowance.

24   The company returned defective merchandise to Kansas Corp. and accepted a credit against future purchases (debited accounts payable). The defective merchandise invoice cost, net of the discount, was $496.

26   The company purchased $9,000 of merchandise from Kansas Corp. with terms of 1/10, n/30, FOB destination, invoice dated January 26.

26   The company sold merchandise with a $4,640 cost for $5,800 on credit to KC, Inc., invoice dated January 26.

31   The company paid cash to Lyn Addie for 10 days' work at $125 per day.

Feb. 1   The company paid $2,475 cash to Hillside Mall for another three months' rent in advance.

3   The company paid Kansas Corp. for the balance due, net of the cash discount, less the $496 credit from merchandise returned on January 24.

5   The company paid $600 cash to Facebook for an advertisement to appear on February 5 only.

11   The company received the balance due from Alex's Engineering Co. for fees billed on January 11.

15   The company paid a $4,800 cash dividend.

23   The company sold merchandise with a $2,660 cost for $3,220 on credit to Delta Co., invoice dated February 23.

26   The company paid cash to Lyn Addie for eight days' work at $125 per day.

27   The company reimbursed Santana Rey $192 cash for business automobile mileage. The company recorded the reimbursement as "Mileage Expense."

Mar. 8   The company purchased $2,730 of computer supplies from Harris Office Products on credit with terms of n/30, FOB destination, invoice dated March 8.

9   The company received the balance due from Delta Co. for merchandise sold on February 23.

11   The company paid $960 cash for minor repairs to the company's computer.

16   The company received $5,260 cash from Dream, Inc., for computing services provided.

19   The company paid the full amount due of $3,830 to Harris Office Products, consisting of amounts created on December 15 (of $1,100) and March 8.

24   The company billed Easy Leasing for $9,047 of computing services provided.

25   The company sold merchandise with a $2,002 cost for $2,800 on credit to Wildcat Services, invoice dated March 25.

30   The company sold merchandise with a $1,048 cost for $2,220 on credit to IFM Company, invoice dated March 30.

31   The company reimbursed Santana Rey $128 cash for business automobile mileage. The company recorded the reimbursement as "Mileage Expense."

The following additional facts are available for preparing adjustments on March 31 prior to financial statement preparation.

a. The March 31 amount of computer supplies still available totals $2,005.

b. Prepaid insurance coverage of $555 expired during this three-month period.

c. Lyn Addie has not been paid for seven days of work at the rate of $125 per day.

d. Prepaid rent of $2,475 expired during this three-month period.

e. Depreciation on the computer equipment for January 1 through March 31 is $1,250.

f. Depreciation on the office equipment for January 1 through March 31 is $400.

g. The March 31 amount of merchandise inventory still available totals $704.

Required

1. Prepare journal entries to record each of the January through March transactions.

2. Post the journal entries in part 1 to the accounts in the company's general ledger. *Note:* Begin with the ledger's post-closing adjusted balances as of December 31, 2019.

3. Prepare a 6-column work sheet (similar to the one shown in Exhibit 3.13) that includes the unadjusted trial balance, the March 31 adjustments (*a*) through (*g*), and the adjusted trial balance. Do not prepare closing entries and do not journalize the adjustments or post them to the ledger.

Check (2) Ending balances at March 31: Cash, $68,057; Sales, $19,240
(3) Unadj. TB totals, $151,557; Adj. TB totals, $154,082

[continued on next page]

4. Prepare an income statement (from the adjusted trial balance in part 3) for the three months ended March 31, 2020. (*a*) Use a single-step format. List all expenses without differentiating between selling expenses and general and administrative expenses. (*b*) Use a multiple-step format that begins with gross sales (service revenues plus gross product sales) and includes separate categories for net sales, cost of goods sold, selling expenses, and general and administrative expenses. Categorize the following accounts as selling expenses: Wages Expense, Mileage Expense, and Advertising Expense. Categorize the remaining expenses as general and administrative.

(4) Net income, $18,833

5. Prepare a statement of retained earnings (from the adjusted trial balance in part 3) for the three months ended March 31, 2020.

6. Prepare a classified balance sheet (from the adjusted trial balance) as of March 31, 2020.

(6) Total assets, $120,268

The **General Ledger** tool in *Connect* automates several of the procedural steps in the accounting cycle so that the accounting professional can focus on the impacts of each transaction on the various financial reports. The following General Ledger questions highlight the operating cycle of a merchandising company. In each case, the trial balance is automatically updated from the journal entries recorded.

GENERAL LEDGER PROBLEM

GL 4-1   Based on Problem 4-1A

GL 4-2   Based on Problem 4-2A

GL 4-3   Based on Problem 4-5A

Accounting Analysis

AA 4-1   Refer to **Apple**'s financial statements in Appendix A to answer the following.

Required

1. Assume that the amounts reported for inventories and cost of sales reflect items purchased in a form ready for resale. Compute the net cost of goods purchased for the year ended September 30, 2017.

2. Compute the current ratio and acid-test ratio as of September 30, 2017, and September 24, 2016.

3. Does Apple's 2017 current ratio outperform or underperform the (assumed) industry average of 1.5?

4. Does Apple's 2017 acid-test ratio outperform or underperform the (assumed) industry average of 1.0?

COMPANY ANALYSIS

A1

APPLE

AA 4-2   Key comparative figures for **Apple** and **Google** follow.

COMPARATIVE ANALYSIS

A2

APPLE
GOOGLE

$ millions	Apple		Google	
	Current Year	Prior Year	Current Year	Prior Year
Net sales	$229,234	$215,639	$110,855	$90,272
Cost of sales	141,048	131,376	45,583	35,138

Required

1. Compute the amount of gross margin and the gross margin ratio for the two years shown for each of these companies.

2. Which company earns more in gross margin for each dollar of net sales for the current year?

3. Do (*a*) Apple's and (*b*) Google's current-year gross margins underperform or outperform the industry (assumed) average of 35.0%?

4. Are (*a*) Apple's and (*b*) Google's current-year gross margins on a favorable or unfavorable trend?

AA 4-3   Key comparative figures for **Samsung**, **Apple**, and **Google** follow.

GLOBAL ANALYSIS

A2   P4

APPLE
GOOGLE
Samsung

In millions	Net Sales	Cost of Sales
Samsung	₩239,575,376	₩129,290,661
Apple	$ 229,234	$ 141,048
Google	$ 110,855	$ 45,583

Required

1. Compute the gross margin ratio for each of the three companies.

2. Is Samsung's gross margin ratio better or worse than (*a*) Apple's ratio? (*b*) Google's?

3. Do (*a*) Apple, (*b*) Google, and (*c*) Samsung use single-step or multiple-step income statements?

Beyond the Numbers

ETHICS CHALLENGE

C1   P2

BTN 4-1   Amy Martin is a student who plans to attend approximately four professional events a year at her college. Each event necessitates a financial outlay of $100 to $200 for a new suit and accessories. After incurring a major hit to her savings for the first event, Amy developed a different approach. She buys the suit on credit the week before the event, wears it to the event, and returns it the next week to the store for a full refund on her charge card.

Required

1. Comment on the ethics exhibited by Amy and possible consequences of her actions.

2. How does the merchandising company account for the suits that Amy returns?

COMMUNICATING IN PRACTICE

C2   P3   P5

BTN 4-2   You are the financial officer for Music Plus, a retailer that sells goods for home entertainment needs. The business owner, Vic Velakturi, recently reviewed the annual financial statements you prepared and sent you an e-mail stating that he thinks you overstated net income. He explains that although he has invested a great deal in security, he is sure shoplifting and other forms of inventory shrinkage have occurred, but he does not see any deduction for shrinkage on the income statement. The store uses a per-petual inventory system.

Required

Prepare a brief memorandum that responds to the owner's concerns.

TAKING IT TO THE NET

C1   A2

BTN 4-3   Access the SEC's EDGAR database (**SEC.gov**) and obtain the March 21, 2017, filing of its fiscal 2017 10-K report (for year ended January 28, 2017) for **J. Crew Group, Inc.** (ticker: JCG).

Required

Prepare a table that reports the gross margin ratios for J. Crew using the revenues and cost of goods sold data from J. Crew's income statement for each of its most recent three years. Analyze and comment on the trend in its gross margin ratio.

TEAMWORK IN ACTION

C1   C2

BTN 4-4   Official Brands's general ledger and supplementary records at the end of its current period reveal the following.

Sales, gross	$600,000	Merchandise inventory (beginning of period)	$ 98,000
Sales returns & allowances	20,000	Invoice cost of merchandise purchases	360,000
Sales discounts	13,000	Purchases discounts received	9,000
Cost of transportation-in	22,000	Purchases returns and allowances	11,000
Operating expenses	50,000	Merchandise inventory (end of period)	84,000

Required

1. *Each* member of the team is to assume responsibility for computing *one* of the following items. You are not to duplicate your teammates' work. Get any necessary amounts to compute your item from the appropriate teammate. Each member is to explain his or her computation to the team in preparation for reporting to the class.

Point: In teams of four, assign the same student *a* and *e*. Rotate teams for reporting on a different computation and the analysis in step 3.

    a. Net sales   **d.** Gross profit

    b. Total cost of merchandise purchases   **e.** Net income

    c. Cost of goods sold

2. Check your net income with the instructor. If correct, proceed to step 3.

3. Assume that a physical inventory count finds that actual ending inventory is $76,000. Discuss how this affects previously computed amounts in step 1.

BTN 4-5 Refer to the opening feature about **Build-A-Bear Workshop** and its founder Maxine Clark. Assume the business reports current annual sales at approximately $1 million and prepares the following income statement.

BUILD-A-BEAR WORKSHOP Income Statement For Year Ended January 31, 2018	
Net sales	$1,000,000
Cost of sales	610,000
Expenses (other than cost of sales)	200,000
Net income	$ 190,000

Assume the business sells to individuals and retailers, ranging from small shops to large chains. Assume that they currently offer credit terms of 1/15, n/60, and ship FOB destination. To improve their cash flow, they are considering changing credit terms to 3/10, n/30. In addition, they propose to change shipping terms to FOB shipping point. They expect that the increase in discount rate will increase net sales by 9%, but the gross margin ratio (and ratio of cost of sales divided by net sales) is expected to remain unchanged. They also expect that delivery expenses will be zero under this proposal; thus, expenses other than cost of sales are expected to increase only 6%.

Required

1. Prepare a forecasted income statement for the year ended January 31, 2019, based on the proposal.
2. Based on the forecasted income statement alone (from your part 1 solution), do you recommend that the business implement the new sales policies? Explain.
3. What else should the business consider before deciding whether to implement the new policies? Explain.

BTN 4-6 Arrange an interview (in person or by phone) with the manager of a retail shop in a mall or in the downtown area of your community. Explain to the manager that you are a student studying merchandising activities and the accounting for sales returns and sales allowances. Ask the manager what the store policy is regarding returns. Also find out if sales allowances are ever negotiated with customers. Inquire whether management perceives that customers are abusing return policies and what actions management takes to counter potential abuses. Be prepared to discuss your findings in class.

5 Inventories and Cost of Sales

Chapter Preview

INVENTORY BASICS

C1 Determining inventory items

C2 Determining inventory costs

Control of inventory

Physical count

NTK 5-1

INVENTORY COSTING

P1 Cost flow assumptions:

Specific identification

First-in, first-out

Last-in, first-out

Weighted average

A1 Effects on financial statements

NTK 5-2

INVENTORY VALUATION, ERRORS, AND ANALYSIS

P2 Lower of cost or market

A2 Effects of inventory errors

A3 Inventory management

P3 *Appendix:* Periodic system

P4 *Appendix:* Inventory estimation

NTK 5-3, 5-4

Learning Objectives

CONCEPTUAL

C1 Identify the items making up merchandise inventory.

C2 Identify the costs of merchandise inventory.

ANALYTICAL

A1 Analyze the effects of inventory methods for both financial and tax reporting.

A2 Analyze the effects of inventory errors on current and future financial statements.

A3 Assess inventory management using both inventory turnover and days' sales in inventory.

PROCEDURAL

P1 Compute inventory in a perpetual system using the methods of specific identification, FIFO, LIFO, and weighted average.

P2 Compute the lower of cost or market amount of inventory.

P3 *Appendix 5A*—Compute inventory in a periodic system using the methods of specific identification, FIFO, LIFO, and weighted average.

P4 *Appendix 5B*—Apply both the retail inventory and gross profit methods to estimate inventory.

Shake It Up

"Show guests you care"—**DANNY MEYER**

NEW YORK—Danny Meyer opened his first **Shake Shack** (**ShakeShack.com**) restaurant in Madison Square Park. The first Shake Shack was a hot dog stand! While much has changed since the first Shack, Danny's commitment to high-quality ingredients has not.

"We call it fine-casual," explains Danny. "Shake Shack . . . is proving that people don't want to go backwards in terms of how their food was sourced, how it was cooked."

Managing this "modern-day roadside burger stand" was not easy. Danny's Shack grew from "$5,000 worth of hamburgers" to "$30,000-plus" of hamburgers per day. Danny needed an accounting system to track everything.

"The thinking back then was, to have a successful restaurant, the owner had to be there 24/7," says Danny. To expand Shake Shack, that had to change. Danny put in an inventory system for each of his Shacks. "Great companies," insists Danny, "figured [inventory] out."

To ensure fresh sourced ingredients were available at the Shacks, Danny set up an inventory tracking system. He prepared and read inventory reports and applied inventory management tools. His inventory system tracks all transactions, and he regularly reviews accounting data in making key decisions.

"You need to get your ducks in a line," asserts Danny. This means that Shake Shack must successfully manage its inventory, even as growth continues.

©Monica Schipper/NYCWFF/Getty Images

To be successful, Danny insists that "the numbers add up." Once your financial house is in order, explains Danny, "you need to take more risk." He adds, "The best start-ups are businesses that find a unique way to solve problems for people—sometimes problems that people didn't even know they had."

Sources: *Shake Shack website,* January 2019; *Fool.com,* December 2016; *Eater.com,* September 2016; *Inc.com,* May 2015

INVENTORY BASICS

Determining Inventory Items

Merchandise inventory includes all goods that a company owns and holds for sale. This is true regardless of where the goods are located when inventory is counted. Special attention is directed at goods in transit, goods on consignment, and goods that are damaged or obsolete.

C1_____
Identify the items making up merchandise inventory.

Goods in Transit   Does a buyer's inventory include goods in transit from a supplier? If ownership has passed to the buyer, the goods are included in the buyer's inventory. We determine this by reviewing shipping terms.

- FOB shipping point—goods are included in buyer's inventory once they are shipped.
- FOB destination—goods are included in buyer's inventory after arrival at their destination.

Goods on Consignment   Goods on consignment are goods shipped by the owner, called the **consignor,** to another party, the **consignee.** A consignee sells goods for the owner. The consignor owns the consigned goods and reports them in its inventory. For example, **Upper Deck** pays sports celebrities such as Russell Wilson of the Seattle Seahawks to sign memorabilia, which are offered to card shops on consignment. Upper Deck, the consignor, reports these items in its inventory until sold. The consignee *never* reports consigned goods in inventory.

Goods Damaged or Obsolete   Damaged, obsolete (out-of-date), and deteriorated goods are not reported in inventory if they cannot be sold. If these goods can be sold at a lower price, they are included in inventory at **net realizable value.** Net realizable value is sales price minus the cost of making the sale. A loss is recorded when the damage or obsolescence occurs.

©Aleksandar Georgiev/Getty Images

Ethical Risk

Eyes in the Sky   One of the largest builders, **Homex**, was accused of faking the construction and sale of 100,000 homes. How were they caught? When the SEC used satellite imagery to confirm the existence of homes, they found nothing but bare soil. SEC 2017-60 ■

Determining Inventory Costs

C2

Identify the costs of merchandise inventory.

Merchandise inventory includes costs to bring an item to a salable condition and location. Inventory costs include invoice cost minus any discount, plus any other costs. Other costs include shipping, storage, import duties, and insurance. The *expense recognition principle* says that inventory costs are expensed as cost of goods sold when inventory is sold.

Internal Controls and Taking a Physical Count

Events can cause the Inventory account balance to be different than the actual inventory available. Such events include theft, loss, damage, and errors. Thus, nearly all companies take a *physical count of inventory* at least once each year. This physical count is used to adjust the Inventory account balance to the actual inventory available.

Fraud: Auditors observe employees as they count inventory. Auditors also take their own count to ensure accuracy.

■ Decision Insight

In Control   A company applies internal controls when taking a physical count of inventory that usually include the following to minimize fraud and to increase reliability.

- *Prenumbered inventory tickets* are distributed to *counters*—each ticket must be accounted for.
- Counters of inventory are assigned and do not include those responsible for inventory.
- Counters confirm the existence, amount, and condition of inventory.
- A second count is taken by a different counter.
- A manager confirms all inventories are ticketed once, and only once. ■

Point: The Inventory account has *subsidiary ledgers* that contain a separate record (units and costs) for each separate product.

NEED-TO-KNOW 5-1

Inventory Items and Costs

C1   C2

Do More: QS 5-1, QS 5-2, QS 5-23, E 5-1, E 5-2

1. A master carver of wooden birds operates her business out of a garage. At the end of the current period, the carver has 17 units (carvings) in her garage, 3 of which were damaged by water and cannot be sold. She also has another 5 units in her truck, ready to deliver per a customer order, terms FOB destination, and another 11 units out on consignment at retail stores. How many units does she include in the business's period-end inventory?

2. A distributor of artistic iron-based fixtures acquires a piece for $1,000, terms FOB shipping point. Additional costs in obtaining it and offering it for sale include $150 for transportation-in, $300 for import duties, $100 for insurance during shipment, $200 for advertising, a $50 voluntary gratuity to the delivery person, $75 for enhanced store lighting, and $250 for sales staff salaries. For computing inventory, what cost is assigned to this artistic piece?

Solutions

1.

Units in ending inventory	
Units in storage.	17 units
Less damaged (unsalable) units.	(3)
Plus units in transit	5
Plus units on consignment	11
Total units in ending inventory	30 units

2.

Merchandise cost	$1,000
Plus:	
Transportation-in	150
Import duties	300
Insurance	100
Total inventory cost.	$1,550

INVENTORY COSTING UNDER A PERPETUAL SYSTEM

When identical items are purchased at different costs, we must decide which amounts to record in cost of goods sold and which amounts remain in inventory. Four methods are used to assign costs to inventory and to cost of goods sold: (1) specific identification; (2) first-in, first-out (FIFO); (3) last-in, first-out (LIFO); and (4) weighted average. Exhibit 5.1 shows the frequency in use of these methods.

Each method has a pattern for how costs flow through inventory. The cost flow assumption does not have to match the actual physical flow of goods. For example, **Kroger**'s grocery chain sells food first-in, first-out, meaning they sell the oldest food in inventory first. However, Kroger can use last-in, first-out to assign costs to food sold. With the exception of specific identification, the **physical flow and cost flow do not have to be the same.**

EXHIBIT 5.1

Frequency in Use of Inventory Methods

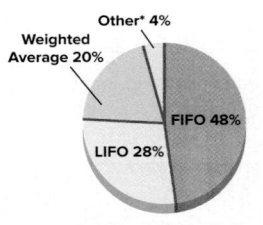

*Includes specific identification.

Inventory Cost Flow Assumptions

To show inventory cost flow assumptions, assume that three identical units are purchased separately at the following three dates and costs: May 1 at $45, May 3 at $65, and May 6 at $70. One unit is then sold on May 7 for $100. Exhibit 5.2 shows the flow of costs to either cost of goods sold on the income statement or inventory reported on the balance sheet for FIFO, LIFO, and weighted average.

Point: Cost of goods sold is abbreviated COGS.

EXHIBIT 5.2

Cost Flow Assumptions

1. First-in, first-out (FIFO)
Costs flow in the order incurred.

| $70 May 6 |
| $65 May 3 |
| $45 May 1 |

Goods sold / Goods left

Income Statement

Net sales..................	$100
Cost of goods sold..	45
Gross profit..............	$ 55

Balance Sheet

| Inventory.................. | $135 |

2. Last-in, first-out (LIFO)
Costs flow in the *reverse* order incurred.

| $70 May 6 |
| $65 May 3 |
| $45 May 1 |

Goods sold / Goods left

Income Statement

Net sales..................	$100
Cost of goods sold..	70
Gross profit..............	$ 30

Balance Sheet

| Inventory.................. | $110 |

3. Weighted average
Costs flow at an average of costs available.

| $70 May 6 |
| $65 May 3 |
| $45 May 1 |

$\frac{\$180}{3} = \$60$ each

×1   ×2

Goods sold / Goods left

Income Statement

Net sales..................	$100
Cost of goods sold..	60
Gross profit..............	$ 40

Balance Sheet

| Inventory.................. | $120 |

(1) *FIFO assumes costs flow in the order incurred.* The unit purchased on May 1 for $45 is the earliest cost incurred—it is sent to cost of goods sold on the income statement first. The remaining two units ($65 and $70) are reported in inventory on the balance sheet.

(2) *LIFO assumes costs flow in the reverse order incurred.* The unit purchased on May 6 for $70 is the most recent cost incurred—it is sent to cost of goods sold on the income statement. The remaining two units ($45 and $65) are reported in inventory on the balance sheet.

(3) *Weighted average assumes costs flow at an average of the costs available.* The units available at the May 7 sale average $60 in cost, computed as ($45 + $65 + $70)/3. One unit's $60 average cost is sent to cost of goods sold on the income statement. The remaining two units' average costs are reported in inventory at $120 on the balance sheet.

Cost flow assumptions impact gross profit and inventory numbers. Exhibit 5.2 shows that gross profit ranges from $30 to $55 due to the cost flow assumption.

Point: Recall inventory cost flow.

Beginning inventory **+** Net purchases

= Merchandise available for sale

Ending inventory **+** Cost of goods sold

The following sections on inventory costing use the *perpetual system*. Appendix 5A uses the periodic system. An instructor can choose to cover either one or both systems. If the perpetual system is skipped, then read Appendix 5A and return to the "Valuing Inventory at LCM and the Effects of Inventory Errors" section.

EXHIBIT 5.3

Purchases and Sales of Goods

©Michael DeYoung/Blend Images

Inventory Costing Illustration

This section demonstrates inventory costing methods. We use information from Trekking, a sporting goods store. Among its products, Trekking sells one type of mountain bike whose sales are directed at resorts that provide inexpensive bikes for guest use. We use Trekking's data from August. Its mountain bike (unit) inventory at the beginning of August and its purchases and sales during August are in Exhibit 5.3. It ends August with 12 bikes in inventory.

Date	Activity	Units Acquired at Cost	Units Sold at Retail	Unit Inventory
Aug. 1	Beginning inventory.......	10 units @ $ 91 = $ 910		10 units
Aug. 3	Purchases..............	15 units @ $106 = $ 1,590		25 units
Aug. 14	Sales..................		20 units @ $130	5 units
Aug. 17	Purchases..............	20 units @ $115 = $ 2,300		25 units
Aug. 28	Purchases..............	10 units @ $119 = $ 1,190		35 units
Aug. 30	Sales..................		23 units @ $150	**12 units**
	Totals	**55 units** **$5,990**	**43 units**	

Units available for sale   Goods available for sale   Units sold   Units left

Trekking uses the **perpetual inventory system**, which means that its Merchandise Inventory account is updated for each purchase and sale of inventory. (Appendix 5A describes the assignment of costs to inventory using a periodic system.) Regardless of what inventory method is used, cost of goods available for sale must be allocated between cost of goods sold and ending inventory.

Specific Identification

When each item in inventory can be matched with a specific purchase and invoice, we can use **specific identification** or **SI** to assign costs. We also need sales records that identify exactly which items were sold and when. Trekking's internal documents show the following specific unit sales.

August 14   Sold 8 bikes costing $91 each and 12 bikes costing $106 each. Total cost = $2,000.
August 30   Sold 2 bikes costing $91 each, 3 bikes costing $106 each, 15 bikes costing $115 each, and 3 bikes costing $119 each. Total cost = $2,582.

Exhibit 5.4 begins with the $5,990 in total units available for sale. For the 20 units sold on August 14, the total cost of sales is $2,000. Next, for the 23 units sold on August 30, the total cost of sales is $2,582. The total cost of sales for the period is $4,582. We then subtract this $4,582 in cost of goods sold from the $5,990 in cost of goods available to get $1,408 in ending inventory.

EXHIBIT 5.4

Specific Identification Computations

Total cost of 55 units available for sale (from Exhibit 5.3)		$ 5,990
Cost of goods sold		
Aug. 14 (8 @ $91) + (12 @ $106)...	$2,000	
Aug. 30 (2 @ $91) + (3 @ $106) + (15 @ $115) + (3 @ $119).................	2,582	**4,582**
Ending inventory		**$1,408**

Trekking's cost of goods sold reported on the income statement is **$4,582**, and ending inventory reported on the balance sheet is **$1,408**. The following graphic shows this flow of costs.

Merchandise Inventory (SI)

Aug. 1	910			
Aug. 3	1,590			
			Aug. 14	2,000
Aug. 17	2,300			
Aug. 28	1,190			
			Aug. 30	2,582
Aug. 31	1,408			

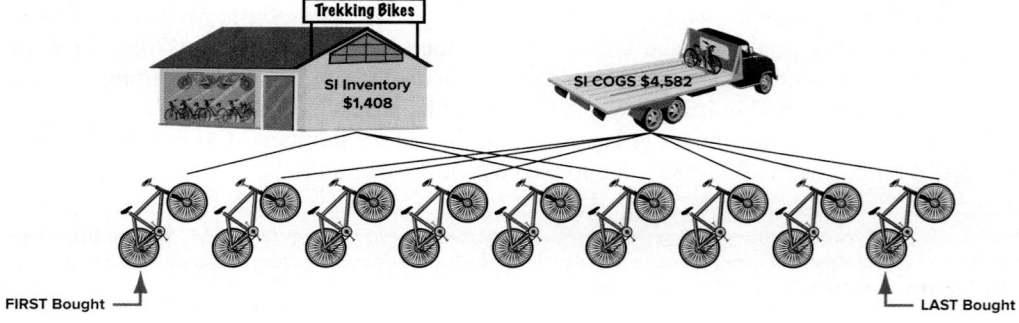

First-In, First-Out

First-in, first-out (FIFO) assumes that inventory items are sold in the order acquired. When sales occur, the costs of the earliest units acquired are charged to cost of goods sold. This leaves the costs from the most recent purchases in ending inventory.

Exhibit 5.5 starts with beginning inventory of 10 bikes at $91 each.

August 3	Purchased 15 bikes costing $106 each for $1,590. Inventory now consists of 10 bikes at $91 each and 15 bikes at $106 each, for a total of $2,500.
August 14	Sold 20 bikes—applying FIFO, the first 10 sold cost $91 each and the next 10 sold cost $106 each, for a total cost of $1,970. This leaves 5 bikes costing $106 each, or $530, in inventory.
August 17	Purchased 20 bikes costing $115 each, and on August 28, purchased another 10 bikes costing $119 each, for a total of 35 bikes costing $4,020 in inventory.
August 30	Sold 23 bikes—applying FIFO, the first 5 bikes sold cost $106 each and the next 18 sold cost $115 each, for a total of $2,600. This leaves 12 bikes costing $1,420 in ending inventory.

Point: "Goods Purchased" column is identical for all methods.

EXHIBIT 5.5

FIFO Computations—
Perpetual System

Date	Goods Purchased	Cost of Goods Sold	Inventory Balance
Aug. 1	Beginning balance		10 @ $ 91 = $ 910
Aug. 3	15 @ $106 = $1,590		10 @ $ 91 15 @ $106 } = $ 2,500
Aug. 14		10 @ $ 91 = $ 910 10 @ $106 = $1,060 } = **$1,970**	5 @ $106 = $ 530
Aug. 17	20 @ $115 = $2,300		5 @ $106 20 @ $115 } = $ 2,830
Aug. 28	10 @ $119 = $1,190		5 @ $106 20 @ $115 } = $ 4,020 10 @ $119
Aug. 30		5 @ $106 = $ 530 18 @ $115 = $2,070 } = **$2,600**	2 @ $115 10 @ $119 } = **$1,420**
		$4,570	

Merchandise Inventory (FIFO)

Aug. 1	910		
Aug. 3	1,590		
		Aug. 14	1,970
Aug. 17	2,300		
Aug. 28	1,190		
		Aug. 30	2,600
Aug. 31	1,420		

Trekking's cost of goods sold reported on its income statement is **$4,570** ($1,970 + $2,600), and its ending inventory reported on the balance sheet is **$1,420.**

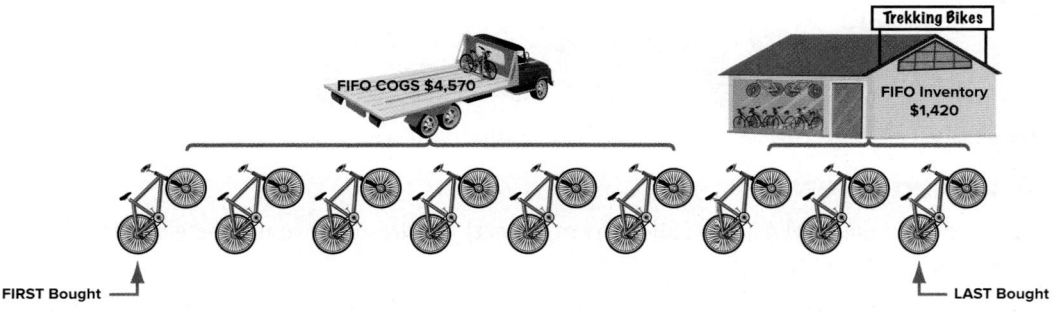

FIFO COGS $4,570   Trekking Bikes   FIFO Inventory $1,420

FIRST Bought   LAST Bought

Last-In, First-Out

Last-in, first-out (LIFO) assumes that the most recent purchases are sold first. These more recent costs are charged to the goods sold, and the costs of the earliest purchases are assigned to inventory.

Point: By assigning costs from the most recent purchases to cost of goods sold, LIFO comes closest to matching current costs of goods sold with revenues.

Exhibit 5.6 starts with beginning inventory of 10 bikes at $91 each.

August 3   Purchased 15 bikes costing $106 each for $1,590. Inventory now consists of 10 bikes at $91 each and 15 bikes at $106 each, for a total of $2,500.

August 14   Sold 20 bikes—applying LIFO, the first 15 sold are from the most recent purchase costing $106 each, and the next 5 sold are from the next most recent purchase costing $91 each, for a total of $2,045. This leaves 5 bikes costing $91 each, or $455, in inventory.

August 17   Purchased 20 bikes costing $115 each, and on August 28, purchased another 10 bikes costing $119 each, for a total of 35 bikes costing $3,945 in inventory.

August 30   Sold 23 bikes—applying LIFO, the first 10 bikes sold are from the most recent purchase costing $119 each, and the next 13 sold are from the next most recent purchase costing $115 each, for a total of $2,685. This leaves 12 bikes costing $1,260 in ending inventory.

EXHIBIT 5.6

LIFO Computations—
Perpetual System

Date	Goods Purchased	Cost of Goods Sold	Inventory Balance
Aug. 1	Beginning balance		10 @ $ 91 = $ 910
Aug. 3	15 @ $106 = $1,590		10 @ $ 91 ⎫ 15 @ $106 ⎬ = $ 2,500
Aug. 14		15 @ $106 = $1,590 ⎫ 5 @ $ 91 = $ 455 ⎬ = **$2,045**	5 @ $ 91 = $ 455
Aug. 17	20 @ $115 = $2,300		5 @ $ 91 ⎫ 20 @ $115 ⎬ = $ 2,755
Aug. 28	10 @ $119 = $1,190		5 @ $ 91 ⎫ 20 @ $115 ⎬ = $ 3,945 10 @ $119 ⎭
Aug. 30		10 @ $119 = $1,190 ⎫ 13 @ $115 = $1,495 ⎬ = **$2,685** **$4,730**	5 @ $ 91 ⎫ 7 @ $115 ⎬ = **$1,260**

Merchandise Inventory (LIFO)

Aug. 1	910		
Aug. 3	1,590		
		Aug. 14	2,045
Aug. 17	2,300		
Aug. 28	1,190		
		Aug. 30	2,685
Aug. 31	1,260		

Trekking's cost of goods sold reported on the income statement is **$4,730** ($2,045 + $2,685), and its ending inventory reported on the balance sheet is **$1,260**.

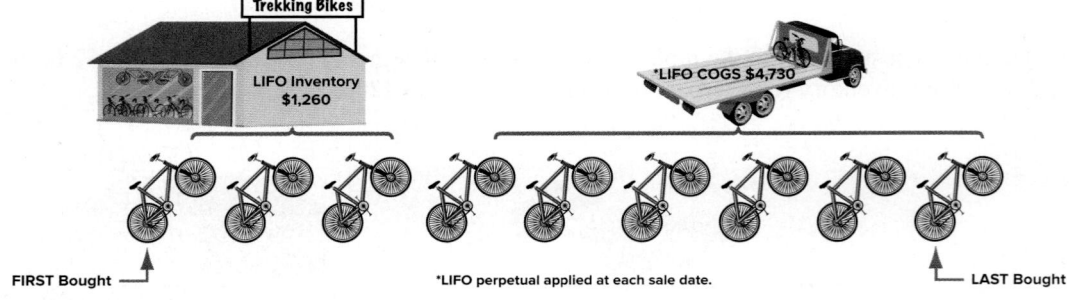

FIRST Bought   *LIFO perpetual applied at each sale date.   LAST Bought

Weighted Average

Weighted average or **WA** (also called **average cost**) requires that we use the weighted average cost per unit of inventory at the time of each sale.

$$\text{Weighted average cost per unit at time of each sale} = \frac{\text{Cost of goods available for sale (at each sale)}}{\text{Number of units available for sale (at each sale)}}$$

Exhibit 5.7 starts with beginning inventory of 10 bikes at $91 each.

August 3   Purchased 15 bikes costing $106 each for $1,590. Inventory now consists of 10 bikes at $91 each and 15 bikes at $106 each, for a total of $2,500. The average cost per bike for that inventory is $100, computed as $2,500/(10 bikes + 15 bikes).

August 14 Sold 20 bikes—applying WA, the 20 sold are assigned the $100 average cost, for a total of $2,000. This leaves 5 bikes with an average cost of $100 each, or $500, in inventory.

August 17 Purchased 20 bikes costing $2,300, and on August 28, purchased another 10 bikes costing $1,190, for a total of 35 bikes costing $3,990 in inventory at August 28. The average cost per bike for the August 28 inventory is $114, computed as $3,990/35 bikes.

August 30 Sold 23 bikes—applying WA, the 23 sold are assigned the $114 average cost, for a total of $2,622. This leaves 12 bikes costing $1,368 in ending inventory.

EXHIBIT 5.7

Weighted Average Computations—Perpetual System

Date	Goods Purchased	Cost of Goods Sold	Inventory Balance
Aug. 1	Beginning balance		10 @ $ 91 = $ 910 (10 @ $ 91 per unit)
Aug. 3	15 @ $106 = $1,590		10 @ $ 91 } 15 @ $106 } = $2,500 (25 @ $100 per unit)[a]
Aug. 14		20 @ $100 = **$2,000**	5 @ $100 = $ 500 (5 @ $100 per unit)[b]
Aug. 17	20 @ $115 = $2,300		5 @ $100 } 20 @ $115 } = $2,800 (25 @ $112 per unit)[c]
Aug. 28	10 @ $119 = $1,190		25 @ $112 } 10 @ $119 } = $3,990 (35 @ $114 per unit)[d]
Aug. 30		23 @ $114 = **$2,622**	12 @ $114 = **$1,368** (12 @ $114 per unit)[e]
		$4,622	

[a]$100 per unit = ($2,500 inventory balance ÷ 25 units in inventory).   [d]$114 per unit = ($3,990 inventory balance ÷ 35 units in inventory).
[b]$100 per unit = ($500 inventory balance ÷ 5 units in inventory).   [e]$114 per unit = ($1,368 inventory balance ÷ 12 units in inventory).
[c]$112 per unit = ($2,800 inventory balance ÷ 25 units in inventory).

Merchandise Inventory (WA)

Aug. 1	910		
Aug. 3	1,590		
		Aug. 14	2,000
Aug. 17	2,300		
Aug. 28	1,190		
		Aug. 30	2,622
Aug. 31	1,368		

Trekking's cost of goods sold reported on the income statement is **$4,622** ($2,000 + $2,622), and its ending inventory reported on the balance sheet is **$1,368**.

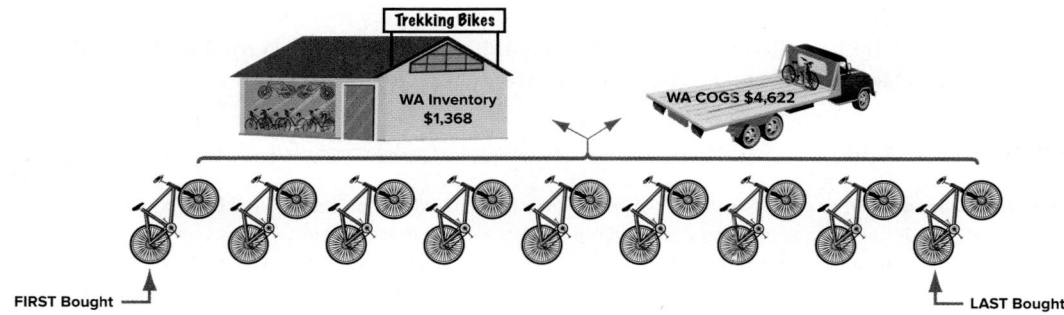

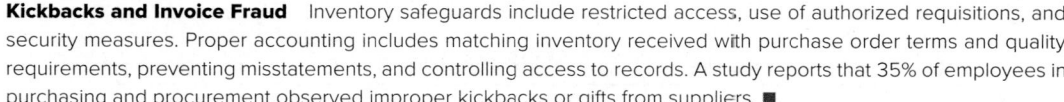

Point: WA perpetual applied at each sale date.

Ethical Risk

Kickbacks and Invoice Fraud   Inventory safeguards include restricted access, use of authorized requisitions, and security measures. Proper accounting includes matching inventory received with purchase order terms and quality requirements, preventing misstatements, and controlling access to records. A study reports that 35% of employees in purchasing and procurement observed improper kickbacks or gifts from suppliers. ∎

Financial Statement Effects of Costing Methods

When purchase prices do not change, each inventory costing method assigns the same cost amounts to inventory and to cost of goods sold. When purchase prices are different, the methods assign different cost amounts. We show these differences in Exhibit 5.8 using Trekking's data.

A1

Analyze the effects of inventory methods for both financial and tax reporting.

Rising Costs   When purchase costs *regularly rise,* as in Trekking's case, the following occurs.

* FIFO reports the lowest cost of goods sold—yielding the highest gross profit and net income.
* LIFO reports the highest cost of goods sold—yielding the lowest gross profit and net income.
* Weighted average yields results between FIFO and LIFO.

EXHIBIT 5.8

Financial Statement
Effects of Inventory
Costing Methods

Trekking Company For Month Ended August 31	Specific Identification	FIFO	LIFO	Weighted Average
Income Statement				
Sales.................................	$ 6,050	$ 6,050	$ 6,050	$ 6,050
Cost of goods sold..................	4,582	4,570	4,730	4,622
Gross profit	1,468	1,480	1,320	1,428
Expenses	450	450	450	450
Income before taxes	1,018	1,030	870	978
Income tax expense (30%)	305	309	261	293
Net income	$ 713	$ 721	$ 609	$ 685
Balance Sheet				
Inventory...........................	$1,408	$1,420	$1,260	$1,368

Falling Costs   When costs *regularly decline,* the reverse occurs for FIFO and LIFO.

- FIFO gives the highest cost of goods sold—yielding the lowest gross profit and income.
- LIFO gives the lowest cost of goods sold—yielding the highest gross profit and income.

Method Advantages   Each method offers advantages.

- FIFO—inventory on the balance sheet approximates its current cost; it also follows the actual flow of goods for most businesses.
- LIFO—cost of goods sold on the income statement approximates its current cost; it also better matches current costs with revenues.
- Weighted average—smooths out erratic changes in costs.
- Specific identification—matches the costs of items with the revenues they generate.

Point: LIFO inventory is often less than the inventory's replacement cost because LIFO inventory is valued using the oldest inventory purchase costs.

Tax Effects of Costing Methods

Inventory costs affect net income and have potential tax effects. Exhibit 5.8 shows that Trekking gains a temporary tax advantage by using LIFO because it has less income to be taxed. Many companies use LIFO for this reason. The IRS requires that when LIFO is used for tax reporting, it also must be used for financial reporting—called *LIFO conformity rule*.

■ **Decision Ethics**

Inventory Manager   Your compensation as inventory manager includes a bonus plan based on gross profit. Your superior asks your opinion on changing the inventory costing method from FIFO to LIFO. As costs are expected to continue to rise, your superior predicts that LIFO would match higher current costs against sales, thereby lowering taxable income (and gross profit). What do you recommend? ■   *Answer:* It seems your company can save (or at least postpone) taxes by switching to LIFO, but the switch is likely to reduce bonus money that you believe you have earned and deserve. Your best decision is to tell your superior about the tax savings with LIFO. You should discuss your bonus plan and how this is likely to hurt you unfairly.

 5-2

Perpetual SI, FIFO, LIFO, and WA

P1

A company reported the following December purchase and sales data for its only product.

Date	Activities	Units Acquired at Cost	Units Sold at Retail
Dec. 1	Beginning inventory	5 units @ $3.00 = $ 15.00	
Dec. 8	Purchase	10 units @ $4.50 = 45.00	
Dec. 9	Sales.........................		8 units @ $7.00
Dec. 19	Purchase	13 units @ $5.00 = 65.00	
Dec. 24	Sales.........................		18 units @ $8.00
Dec. 30	Purchase	8 units @ $5.30 = 42.40	
Totals	....	36 units $167.40	26 units

The company uses a *perpetual inventory system.* Determine the cost assigned to ending inventory and to cost of goods sold using (a) specific identification, (b) FIFO, (c) LIFO, and (d) weighted average. (Round per unit costs and inventory amounts to cents.)

For specific identification, ending inventory consists of 10 units, where 8 are from the December 30 purchase and 2 are from the December 8 purchase. Specific unit sales follow.

Dec. 9   Sold 2 units costing $3.00 each and 6 units costing $4.50 each. Total cost = $33.00.

Dec. 24   Sold 3 units costing $3.00 each, 2 units costing $4.50 each, and 13 units costing $5.00 each. Total cost = $83.00.

Solutions

a. Specific identification: Ending inventory—eight units from December 30 purchase and two units from December 8 purchase.

Specific Identification	Ending Inventory	Cost of Goods Sold
(8 × $5.30) + (2 × $4.50)	$51.40	
(5 × $3.00) + (8 × $4.50) + (13 × $5.00) + (0 × $5.30)		
or $167.40 [Total Goods Available] − $51.40 [Ending Inventory].		$116.00

Merchandise Inventory (SI)

Beg. inventory	15.00			
Dec. 8	45.00			
			Dec. 9	33.00
Dec. 19	65.00			
			Dec. 24	83.00
Dec. 30	42.40			
End. inventory	51.40			

b. FIFO—Perpetual.

Date	Goods Purchased	Cost of Goods Sold	Inventory Balance
12/1			5 @ $3.00 = $15.00
12/8	10 @ $4.50		5 @ $3.00 ⎫ = $60.00 10 @ $4.50 ⎭
12/9		5 @ $3.00 ⎫ = $ 28.50 3 @ $4.50 ⎭	7 @ $4.50 = $31.50
12/19	13 @ $5.00		7 @ $4.50 ⎫ = $96.50 13 @ $5.00 ⎭
12/24		7 @ $4.50 ⎫ = $ 86.50 11 @ $5.00 ⎭	2 @ $5.00 = $10.00
12/30	8 @ $5.30		2 @ $5.00 ⎫ = $52.40 8 @ $5.30 ⎭
		$115.00	

Merchandise Inventory (FIFO)

Beg. inventory	15.00			
Dec. 8	45.00			
			Dec. 9	28.50
Dec. 19	65.00			
			Dec. 24	86.50
Dec. 30	42.40			
End. inventory	52.40			

OR "short-cut" FIFO—Perpetual.

FIFO	Ending Inventory	Cost of Goods Sold
(8 × $5.30) + (2 × $5.00)	$52.40	
(5 × $3.00) + (10 × $4.50) + (11 × $5.00)		
or $167.40 [Total Goods Available] − $52.40 [Ending Inventory].		$115.00

c. LIFO—Perpetual.

Date	Goods Purchased	Cost of Goods Sold	Inventory Balance
12/1			5 @ $3.00 = $15.00
12/8	10 @ $4.50		5 @ $3.00 ⎫ = $60.00 10 @ $4.50 ⎭
12/9		8 @ $4.50 = $ 36.00	5 @ $3.00 ⎫ = $24.00 2 @ $4.50 ⎭
12/19	13 @ $5.00		5 @ $3.00 ⎫ 2 @ $4.50 ⎬ = $89.00 13 @ $5.00 ⎭
12/24		13 @ $5.00 ⎫ 2 @ $4.50 ⎬ = $ 83.00 3 @ $3.00 ⎭	2 @ $3.00 = $ 6.00
12/30	8 @ $5.30		2 @ $3.00 ⎫ = $48.40 8 @ $5.30 ⎭
		$119.00	

Merchandise Inventory (LIFO)

Beg. inventory	15.00			
Dec. 8	45.00			
			Dec. 9	36.00
Dec. 19	65.00			
			Dec. 24	83.00
Dec. 30	42.40			
End. inventory	48.40			

d. Weighted Average—Perpetual.

Date	Goods Purchased	Cost of Goods Sold	Inventory Balance
12/1			5 @ $3.00 = $15.00 (5 @ $3.00 per unit)
12/8	10 @ $4.50		5 @ $3.00 ⎱ = $60.00 10 @ $4.50 ⎰
			($60.00/15 units = $4.00 avg. cost)
12/9		8 @ $4.00 = $ 32.00	7 @ $4.00 = $28.00 (7 @ $4.00 per unit)
12/19	13 @ $5.00		7 @ $4.00 ⎱ = $93.00 13 @ $5.00 ⎰
			($93.00/20 units = $4.65 avg. cost)
12/24		18 @ $4.65 = $ 83.70	2 @ $4.65 = $ 9.30 (2 @ $4.65 per unit)
12/30	8 @ $5.30		2 @ $4.65 ⎱ = $51.70 8 @ $5.30 ⎰
		$115.70	($51.70/10 units = $5.17 avg. cost)

Merchandise Inventory (WA)

Beg. inventory	15.00		
Dec. 8	45.00		
		Dec. 9	32.00
Dec. 19	65.00		
		Dec. 24	83.70
Dec. 30	42.40		
End. inventory	51.70		

Do More: QS 5-3, QS 5-4, QS 5-5, QS 5-6, QS 5-10, QS 5-11, QS 5-12, E 5-3

VALUING INVENTORY AT LCM AND THE EFFECTS OF INVENTORY ERRORS

This section covers how market value and inventory errors impact financial statements.

Lower of Cost or Market

P2

Compute the lower of cost or market amount of inventory.

After companies apply one of four costing methods (FIFO, LIFO, weighted average, or specific identification), inventory is reviewed to ensure it is reported at the **lower of cost or market (LCM).**

Computing the Lower of Cost or Market   *Market* in the term *LCM* is *replacement cost* for LIFO, but *net realizable value* for the other three methods—advanced courses cover specifics. A decline in market value means a loss of value in inventory. When market value is lower than cost of inventory, a loss is recorded. When market value is higher than cost of inventory, no adjustment is made.

Point: LCM applied to each individual item always yields the lowest inventory.

LCM is applied in one of three ways: (1) to each individual item separately, (2) to major categories of items, or (3) to the whole of inventory. With the increasing use of technology and inventory tracking, companies increasingly apply LCM to each individual item separately. Accordingly, we show that method only; advanced courses cover other methods. To demonstrate LCM, we apply it to the ending inventory of a motorsports retailer in Exhibit 5.9.

EXHIBIT 5.9

Lower of Cost or Market Computations

$140,000 is the lower of $170,000 or $140,000.

The amount of $190,000 is lower than the $220,000 recorded cost.

Inventory Items	Units	Per Unit Cost	Per Unit Market	Total Cost	Total Market	LCM Applied to Items
Roadster.............	20	$8,500	$7,000	$170,000	$140,000	$ 140,000
Sprint	10	5,000	6,000	50,000	60,000	50,000
Totals				$220,000		$190,000

For Roadster, $140,000 is the lower of the $170,000 cost and the $140,000 market. For Sprint, $50,000 is the lower of the $50,000 cost and the $60,000 market. This yields a $190,000 reported inventory, computed from $140,000 for Roadster plus $50,000 for Sprint.

Recording the Lower of Cost or Market   Inventory is adjusted downward when total "LCM applied to items" is less than total cost of inventory. To demonstrate, if LCM is applied in Exhibit 5.9, the Merchandise Inventory account must be adjusted from the $220,000 recorded cost down to the $190,000 LCM amount as follows.

Cost of Goods Sold.............................	30,000	
Merchandise Inventory		30,000
Adjust inventory cost to market.		

A company has the following products in its ending inventory, along with cost and market values. (a) Compute the lower of cost or market for its inventory when applied *separately to each product*. (b) If the market amount is less than the recorded cost of the inventory, then record the December 31 LCM adjustment to the Merchandise Inventory account.

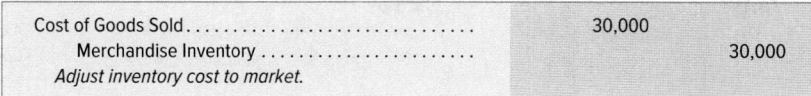

NEED-TO-KNOW 5-3

LCM Method

P2

	Units	Cost per Unit	Market per Unit
Road bikes	5	$1,000	$800
Mountain bikes...........	4	500	600
Town bikes	10	400	450

Solution

a.

Inventory Items	Units	Cost per Unit	Market per Unit	Total Cost	Total Market	LCM Items
Road bikes	5	$1,000	$800	$ 5,000	$4,000	$ 4,000
Mountain bikes...............	4	500	600	2,000	2,400	2,000
Town bikes	10	400	450	4,000	4,500	4,000
Totals.......................				$11,000		$ 10,000
LCM applied to each product....						$10,000

b.

Dec. 31	Cost of Goods Sold	1,000	
	Merchandise Inventory................................		1,000
	Adjust inventory cost to market ($11,000 − $10,000).		

Do More: QS 5-19, E 5-10

Financial Statement Effects of Inventory Errors

An inventory error causes misstatements in cost of goods sold, gross profit, net income, current assets, and equity. It also causes misstatements in the next period's statements because ending inventory of one period is the beginning inventory of the next. As we consider financial statement effects, we recall the following *inventory relation*.

A2

Analyze the effects of inventory errors on current and future financial statements.

Beginning inventory	+	Net purchases	−	Ending inventory	=	Cost of goods sold

Income Statement Effects   Exhibit 5.10 shows the effects of inventory errors in the current and next period's income statements.

- **Row 1, Year 1.** Understating ending inventory overstates cost of goods sold. This is because we subtract a smaller ending inventory in computing cost of goods sold. A higher cost of goods sold yields a lower income.
- **Row 1, Year 2.** Understated ending inventory for Year 1 becomes an understated beginning inventory for Year 2. If beginning inventory is understated, cost of goods sold is understated (because we are starting with a smaller amount). A lower cost of goods sold yields a higher income.
- **Row 2, Year 1.** Overstating ending inventory understates cost of goods sold. A lower cost of goods sold yields a higher income.
- **Row 2, Year 2.** Overstated ending inventory for Year 1 becomes an overstated beginning inventory for Year 2. If beginning inventory is overstated, cost of goods sold is overstated. A higher cost of goods sold yields a lower income.

EXHIBIT 5.10

Effects of Inventory Errors on the Income Statement

		Year 1		Year 2	
Ending Inventory		**Cost of Goods Sold**	**Net Income**	**Cost of Goods Sold**	**Net Income**
Understated ↓		Overstated ↑	Understated ↓	Understated ↓	Overstated ↑
Overstated ↑		Understated ↓	Overstated ↑	Overstated ↑	Understated ↓

Inventory Error Example
Consider an inventory error for a company with $100,000 in sales for each of Year 1, Year 2, and Year 3. If this company has a steady $20,000 inventory level and makes $60,000 in purchases in each year, its cost of goods sold is $60,000 and its gross profit is $40,000.

Year 1 Understated Inventory: Year 1 Impact   Assume the company makes an error in computing its Year 1 ending inventory and reports $16,000 instead of the correct amount of $20,000. The effects of this error are in Exhibit 5.11. The $4,000 understatement of Year 1 ending inventory causes a $4,000 overstatement in Year 1 cost of goods sold and a $4,000 understatement in both gross profit and net income for Year 1.

EXHIBIT 5.11

Effects of Inventory Errors on Three Periods' Income Statements

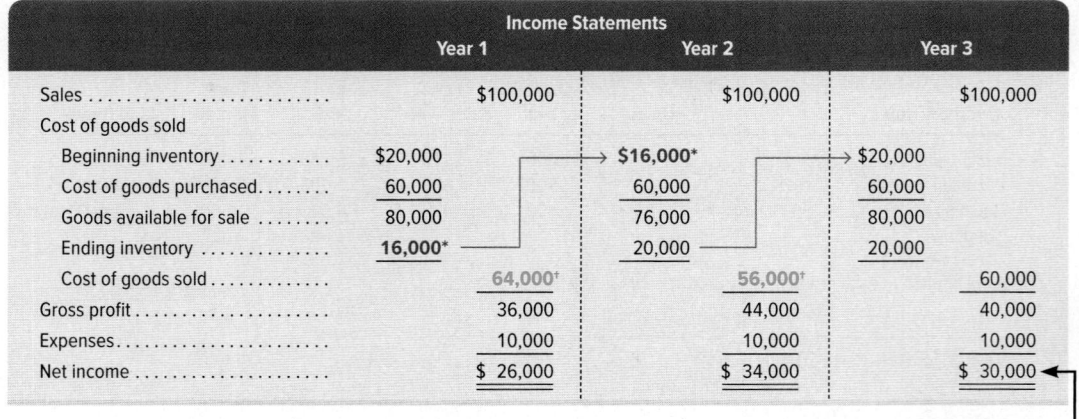

	Income Statements		
	Year 1	Year 2	Year 3
Sales	$100,000	$100,000	$100,000
Cost of goods sold			
Beginning inventory...........	$20,000	→ $16,000*	→ $20,000
Cost of goods purchased........	60,000	60,000	60,000
Goods available for sale	80,000	76,000	80,000
Ending inventory	**16,000***	20,000	20,000
Cost of goods sold	64,000†	56,000†	60,000
Gross profit	36,000	44,000	40,000
Expenses......................	10,000	10,000	10,000
Net income	$ 26,000	$ 34,000	$ 30,000

*Correct amount is $20,000.   †Correct amount is $60,000.   Correct income is $30,000 for each year.

Example: If Year 1 ending inventory in Exhibit 5.11 is overstated by $3,000, cost of goods sold is understated by $3,000 in Year 1 and overstated by $3,000 in Year 2. Net income is overstated in Year 1 and understated in Year 2. Assets and equity are overstated in Year 1.

Year 1 Understated Inventory: Year 2 Impact   The Year 1 understated ending inventory becomes the Year 2 understated beginning inventory. This error causes an understatement in Year 2 cost of goods sold and a $4,000 overstatement in both gross profit and net income for Year 2.

Year 1 Understated Inventory: Year 3 Impact   The Year 1 ending inventory error affects only that period and the next. It does not affect Year 3 results or any period thereafter.

Balance Sheet Effects
Understating ending inventory understates both current and total assets. An understatement in ending inventory also yields an understatement in equity because of the understatement in net income. Exhibit 5.12 shows the effects of inventory errors on the current period's balance sheet amounts.

EXHIBIT 5.12

Effects of Inventory Errors on Current Period's Balance Sheet

Ending Inventory	**Assets**	**Equity**
Understated ↓	Understated ↓	Understated ↓
Overstated ↑	Overstated ↑	Overstated ↑

NEED-TO-KNOW 5-4

Effects of Inventory Errors

A2

A company had $10,000 of sales, and it purchased merchandise costing $7,000 in each of Year 1, Year 2, and Year 3. It also maintained a $2,000 physical inventory from the beginning to the end of that three-year period. In accounting for inventory, it made an error at the end of Year 1 that caused its Year 1 ending inventory to appear on its statements as $1,600 rather than the correct $2,000. (a) Determine the correct amount of the company's gross profit in each of Year 1, Year 2, and Year 3. (b) Prepare comparative income statements as in Exhibit 5.11 to show the effect of this error on the company's cost of goods sold and gross profit for each of Year 1, Year 2, and Year 3.

Solution

a. Correct gross profit = $10,000 − $7,000 = $3,000 (for each year).

b. Cost of goods sold and gross profit figures follow.

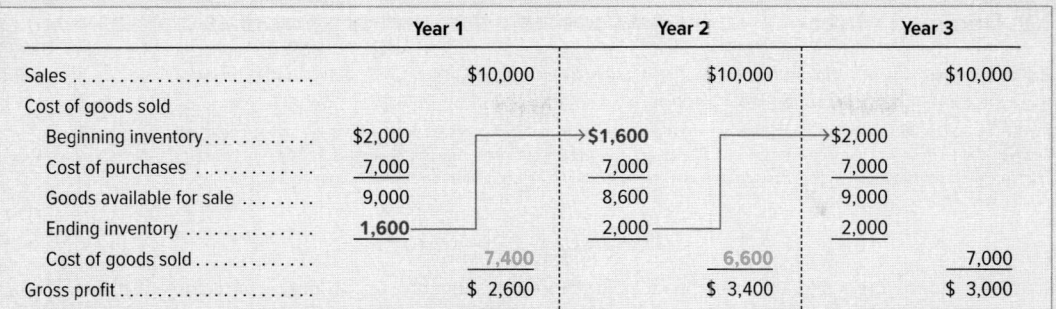

	Year 1	Year 2	Year 3
Sales	$10,000	$10,000	$10,000
Cost of goods sold			
Beginning inventory.	$2,000	→$1,600	→$2,000
Cost of purchases	7,000	7,000	7,000
Goods available for sale	9,000	8,600	9,000
Ending inventory	1,600	2,000	2,000
Cost of goods sold	7,400	6,600	7,000
Gross profit	$ 2,600	$ 3,400	$ 3,000

Combined income for the 3 years is $9,000 ($2,600 + $3,400 + $3,000), which is correct, meaning the inventory error is "self-correcting" (even though individual years' inventory amounts are in error).

Do More: QS 5-20, E 5-12

Inventory Turnover and Days' Sales in Inventory      **Decision Analysis**

Inventory Turnover

Inventory turnover, also called *merchandise inventory turnover,* is defined in Exhibit 5.13. Inventory turnover tells how many *times* a company turns over (sells) its inventory in a period. It is used to assess whether management is doing a good job controlling the amount of inventory. A low ratio means the company may have more inventory than it needs. A very high ratio means inventory might be too low. This can cause lost sales if customers must back-order merchandise. Inventory turnover has no simple rule except to say *a high ratio is preferable if inventory is adequate to meet demand*.

A3

Assess inventory management using both inventory turnover and days' sales in inventory.

EXHIBIT 5.13

Inventory Turnover

$$\text{Inventory turnover} = \frac{\text{Cost of goods sold}}{\text{Average inventory}}$$

Days' Sales in Inventory

Days' sales in inventory is a ratio that shows how much inventory is available in terms of the number of days' sales. It can be interpreted as the number of days one can sell from existing inventory if no new items are purchased. This ratio reveals the buffer against out-of-stock inventory and is useful in evaluating how quickly inventory is being sold. It is defined in Exhibit 5.14. Days' sales in inventory uses *ending* inventory, whereas inventory turnover uses *average* inventory.

Point: Low inventory turnover can reveal obsolescence.

Point: Inventory turnover is higher and days' sales in inventory is lower for industries such as foods.

EXHIBIT 5.14

Days' Sales in Inventory

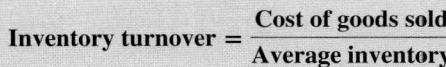

$$\text{Days' sales in inventory} = \frac{\text{Ending inventory}}{\text{Cost of goods sold}} \times 365$$

Analysis of Inventory Management

Merchandisers must plan and control inventory purchases and sales. **Costco's** inventory at the end of the current year was $9,834 million. This inventory was 57% of its current assets and 27% of its total assets. We apply the analysis tools in this section to Costco and **Walmart,** as shown in Exhibit 5.15.

EXHIBIT 5.15

Inventory Turnover and Days' Sales in Inventory for Costco and Walmart

Company	Figure ($ millions)	Current Year	1 Year Ago	2 Years Ago
Costco	Cost of goods sold	$111,882	$102,901	$101,065
	Ending inventory.	$ 9,834	$ 8,969	$ 8,908
	Inventory turnover	**11.9** times	**11.5** times	**11.6** times
	Days' sales in inventory	**32.1** days	**31.8** days	**32.2** days
Walmart	Inventory turnover	8.3 times	8.1 times	8.1 times
	Days' sales in inventory	43.5 days	45.0 days	45.1 days

Costco's current year inventory turnover of 11.9 times means that it turns over its inventory 11.9 times per year. Costco's inventory turnover exceeded Walmart's turnover in each of the last three years. This is a positive for Costco, as we prefer inventory turnover to be high provided inventory is not out of stock and the company is not losing customers. Days' sales in inventory of 32.1 days means that Costco is carrying 32.1 days of sales in inventory. This inventory buffer seems sufficient. As long as Costco is not at risk of running out of stock, it prefers its assets not be tied up in inventory.

Point: Take care when comparing turnover ratios across companies that use different costing methods (such as FIFO and LIFO).

Decision Maker ━━━

Entrepreneur   Your retail store has an inventory turnover of 5.0 and a days' sales in inventory of 73 days. The indus-try norm for inventory turnover is 4.4 and for days' sales in inventory is 74 days. What is your assessment of inventory management? ■   *Answer:* Your inventory turnover is higher than the norm, whereas days' sales in inventory approximates the norm. Because your turnover is already 14% better than average, you should probably direct attention to days' sales in inventory. You should see if you can reduce the level of inventory while maintaining service to customers. Given your higher turnover, you should be able to hold less inventory.

NEED-TO-KNOW 5-5

COMPREHENSIVE 1

Perpetual Method: Computing Inventory Using LIFO, FIFO, WA, and SI; Financial Statement Impacts; and Inventory Errors

Craig Company buys and sells one product. Its beginning inventory, purchases, and sales during calendar-year 2019 follow.

Date	Activity	Units Acquired at Cost		Units Sold at Retail	Unit Inventory
Jan. 1	Beg. inventory...........	400 units @ $14 = $ 5,600			400 units
Jan. 15	Sale...................			200 units @ $30	200 units
Mar. 10	Purchase..............	200 units @ $15 = $ 3,000			400 units
Apr. 1	Sale...................			200 units @ $30	200 units
May 9	Purchase..............	300 units @ $16 = $ 4,800			500 units
Sep. 22	Purchase..............	250 units @ $20 = $ 5,000			750 units
Nov. 1	Sale...................			300 units @ $35	450 units
Nov. 28	Purchase..............	100 units @ $21 = $ 2,100			550 units
	Totals.................	1,250 units $20,500		700 units	

Additional tracking data for specific identification: (1) January 15 sale—200 units @ $14, **(2)** April 1 sale—200 units @ $15, and **(3)** November 1 sale—200 units @ $14 and 100 units @ $20.

Required

1. Compute the cost of goods available for sale.

2. Apply the four methods of inventory costing (FIFO, LIFO, weighted average, and specific identification) to compute ending inventory and cost of goods sold under each method using the *perpetual system*.

3. Compute gross profit earned by the company for each of the four costing methods in part 2. Also, report the inventory amount reported on the balance sheet for each of the four methods.

4. In preparing financial statements for year 2019, the financial officer was instructed to use FIFO but failed to do so and instead computed cost of goods sold according to LIFO, which led to a $1,400 over-statement in cost of goods sold from using LIFO. Determine the impact on year 2019's income from the error. Also determine the effect of this error on year 2020's income. Assume no income taxes.

5. Management wants a report that shows how changing from FIFO to another method would change net income. Prepare a table showing (1) the cost of goods sold amount under each of the four methods, (2) the amount by which each cost of goods sold total is different from the FIFO cost of goods sold, and (3) the effect on net income if another method is used instead of FIFO.

PLANNING THE SOLUTION

- Compute cost of goods available for sale by multiplying the units of beginning inventory and each purchase by their unit costs to determine the total cost of goods available for sale.

- Prepare a perpetual FIFO table starting with beginning inventory and showing how inventory changes after each purchase and after each sale (see Exhibit 5.5).

- Prepare a perpetual LIFO table starting with beginning inventory and showing how inventory changes after each purchase and after each sale (see Exhibit 5.6).

- Make a table of purchases and sales recalculating the average cost of inventory prior to each sale to arrive at the weighted average cost of ending inventory. Total the average costs associated with each sale to determine cost of goods sold (see Exhibit 5.7).

- Prepare a table showing the computation of cost of goods sold and ending inventory using the specific identification method (see Exhibit 5.4).

- Compare the year-end 2019 inventory amounts under FIFO and LIFO to determine the misstatement of year 2019 income that results from using LIFO. The errors for years 2019 and 2020 are equal in amount but opposite in effect.

- Create a table showing cost of goods sold under each method and how net income would differ from FIFO net income if an alternate method were adopted.

SOLUTION

1. Cost of goods available for sale (this amount is the same for all methods).

Date		Units	Unit Cost	Cost
Jan.	1	Beg. inventory............	400	$14	$ 5,600
Mar.	10	Purchase.................	200	15	3,000
May	9	Purchase.................	300	16	4,800
Sep.	22	Purchase.................	250	20	5,000
Nov.	28	Purchase.................	100	21	2,100
	Total goods available for sale	1,250		$20,500

2a. FIFO **perpetual** method.

Date	Goods Purchased	Cost of Goods Sold	Inventory Balance
Jan. 1	Beginning balance		400 @ $14 = $ 5,600
Jan. 15		200 @ $14 = $2,800	200 @ $14 = $ 2,800
Mar. 10	200 @ $15 = $3,000		200 @ $14 200 @ $15 } = $ 5,800
Apr. 1		200 @ $14 = $2,800	200 @ $15 = $ 3,000
May 9	300 @ $16 = $4,800		200 @ $15 300 @ $16 } = $ 7,800
Sep. 22	250 @ $20 = $5,000		200 @ $15 300 @ $16 250 @ $20 } = $ 12,800
Nov. 1		200 @ $15 = $3,000 100 @ $16 = $1,600	200 @ $16 250 @ $20 } = $ 8,200
Nov. 28	100 @ $21 = $2,100		200 @ $16 250 @ $20 100 @ $21 } = $10,300
Total cost of goods sold		**$10,200**	

Note: **In a classroom situation,** once we compute cost of goods available for sale, we can compute the amount for either cost of goods sold or ending inventory—it is a matter of preference. **In practice,** the costs of items sold are identified as sales are made and immediately transferred from the Inventory account to the Cost of Goods Sold account. The previous solution showing the line-by-line approach illustrates actual application in practice. The following alternate solutions illustrate that, once the concepts are understood, other solution approaches are available. Although this is only shown for FIFO, it could be shown for all methods.

Alternate Methods to Compute FIFO Perpetual Numbers

[FIFO Alternate No. 1: Computing ending inventory first]

Cost of goods available for sale (from part 1).....		$ 20,500
Ending inventory*		
Nov. 28 Purchase (100 @ $21)...........	$2,100	
Sep. 22 Purchase (250 @ $20)..........	5,000	
May 9 Purchase (200 @ $16)..........	3,200	
Ending inventory...........................		**10,300**
Cost of goods sold		**$10,200**

[FIFO Alternate No. 2: Computing cost of goods sold first]

Cost of goods available for sale (from part 1)........		$ 20,500
Cost of goods sold		
Jan. 15 Sold (200 @ $14)	$2,800	
Apr. 1 Sold (200 @ $14)	2,800	
Nov. 1 Sold (200 @ $15 and 100 @ $16)....	4,600	10,200
Ending inventory.............................		**$10,300**

*FIFO assumes that the earlier costs are the first to flow out; thus, we determine ending inventory by assigning the most recent costs to the remaining items.

2b. LIFO **perpetual** method.

Date	Goods Purchased	Cost of Goods Sold	Inventory Balance
Jan. 1	Beginning balance		400 @ $14 = $ 5,600
Jan. 15		200 @ $14 = $2,800	200 @ $14 = $ 2,800
Mar. 10	200 @ $15 = $3,000		200 @ $14 200 @ $15 } = $ 5,800
Apr. 1		200 @ $15 = $3,000	200 @ $14 = $ 2,800
May 9	300 @ $16 = $4,800		200 @ $14 300 @ $16 } = $ 7,600
Sep. 22	250 @ $20 = $5,000		200 @ $14 300 @ $16 250 @ $20 } = $12,600
Nov. 1		250 @ $20 = $5,000 50 @ $16 = $ 800	200 @ $14 250 @ $16 } = $ 6,800
Nov. 28	100 @ $21 = $2,100		200 @ $14 250 @ $16 100 @ $21 } = $ 8,900
Total cost of goods sold		**$11,600**	

2c. Weighted average **perpetual** method.

Date	Goods Purchased	Cost of Goods Sold	Inventory Balance
Jan. 1	Beginning balance		400 @ $14.00 = $ 5,600 ($5,600/400 units = $14.00 avg. cost)
Jan. 15		200 @ $14.00 = $ 2,800	200 @ $14.00 = $ 2,800
Mar. 10	200 @ $15.00 = $3,000		200 @ $14.00 200 @ $15.00 } = $ 5,800 ($5,800/400 units = $14.50 avg. cost)
Apr. 1		200 @ $14.50 = $ 2,900	200 @ $14.50 = $ 2,900
May 9	300 @ $16.00 = $4,800		200 @ $14.50 300 @ $16.00 } = $ 7,700 ($7,700/500 units = $15.40 avg. cost)
Sep. 22	250 @ $20.00 = $5,000		500 @ $15.40 250 @ $20.00 } = $ 12,700 ($12,700/750 units = $16.93[†] avg. cost)
Nov. 1		300 @ $16.93 = $ 5,079	450 @ $16.93 = $ 7,618.50
Nov. 28	100 @ $21.00 = $2,100		450 @ $16.93 100 @ $21.00 } = $9,718.50 ($9,718.50/550 units = $17.67 avg. cost)
Total cost of goods sold*		**$10,779**	

*Cost of goods sold ($10,779) plus ending inventory ($9,718.50) is $2.50 less than the cost of goods available for sale ($20,500) due to rounding.

[†]Rounded to 2 decimal places.

2d. Specific identification method.

Cost of goods available for sale (from part 1)...............		$ 20,500
Ending inventory*		
May 9 Purchase (300 @ $16).....................	$4,800	
Sep. 22 Purchase (150 @ $20).....................	3,000	
Nov. 28 Purchase (100 @ $21).....................	2,100	
Ending inventory.....................................		9,900
Cost of goods sold		$10,600

*The additional tracking data provided are used to identify the items in ending inventory.

3.

	FIFO	LIFO	Weighted Average	Specific Identification
Income Statement				
Sales*	$ 22,500	$22,500	$ 22,500	$22,500
Cost of goods sold	10,200	11,600	10,779	10,600
Gross profit....................	$ 12,300	$10,900	$ 11,721	$11,900
Balance Sheet				
Inventory	$10,300	$ 8,900	$9,718.50	$ 9,900

*Sales = (200 units × $30) + (200 units × $30) + (300 units × $35) = $22,500

4. Mistakenly using LIFO when FIFO should have been used overstates cost of goods sold in year 2019 by $1,400, which is the difference between the FIFO and LIFO amounts of ending inventory. It understates income in 2019 by $1,400. In year 2020, income is overstated by $1,400 because of the understatement in beginning inventory.

5. Analysis of the effects of alternative inventory methods.

	Cost of Goods Sold	Difference from FIFO Cost of Goods Sold	Effect on Net Income If Adopted Instead of FIFO
FIFO........................	$10,200	—	—
LIFO........................	11,600	+$1,400	$1,400 lower
Weighted average	10,779	+ 579	579 lower
Specific identification..........	10,600	+ 400	400 lower

Craig Company buys and sells one product. Its beginning inventory, purchases, and sales during calendar-year 2019 follow.

NEED-TO-KNOW 5-6

COMPREHENSIVE 2

Periodic Method: Computing Inventory Using LIFO, FIFO, WA, and SI; Financial Statement Impacts; and Inventory Errors

Date	Activity	Units Acquired at Cost	Units Sold at Retail	Unit Inventory
Jan. 1	Beg. inventory...........	400 units @ $14 = $ 5,600		400 units
Jan. 15	Sale		200 units @ $30	200 units
Mar. 10	Purchase...............	200 units @ $15 = $ 3,000		400 units
Apr. 1	Sale		200 units @ $30	200 units
May 9	Purchase...............	300 units @ $16 = $ 4,800		500 units
Sep. 22	Purchase...............	250 units @ $20 = $ 5,000		750 units
Nov. 1	Sale		300 units @ $35	450 units
Nov. 28	Purchase...............	100 units @ $21 = $ 2,100		550 units
Totals.................		1,250 units $20,500	700 units	

Additional tracking data for specific identification: (1) January 15 sale—200 units @ $14, **(2)** April 1 sale—200 units @ $15, and **(3)** November 1 sale—200 units @ $14 and 100 units @ $20.

Required

1. Compute the cost of goods available for sale.

2. Apply the four methods of inventory costing (FIFO, LIFO, weighted average, and specific identification) to compute ending inventory and cost of goods sold under each method using the *periodic system*.

3. Compute gross profit earned by the company for each of the four costing methods in part 2. Also, report the inventory amount reported on the balance sheet for each of the four methods.

4. In preparing financial statements for year 2019, the financial officer was instructed to use FIFO but failed to do so and instead computed cost of goods sold according to LIFO. Determine the impact of the error on year 2019's income. Also determine the effect of this error on year 2020's income. Assume no income taxes.

PLANNING THE SOLUTION

- Compute cost of goods available for sale by multiplying the units of beginning inventory and each purchase by their unit costs to determine the total cost of goods available for sale.
- Prepare a periodic FIFO computation starting with cost of units available and subtracting FIFO ending inventory amounts to obtain FIFO cost of goods sold (see Exhibit 5A.3).
- Prepare a periodic LIFO computation starting with cost of units available and subtracting LIFO ending inventory amounts to obtain LIFO cost of goods sold (see Exhibit 5A.4).
- Compute weighted average ending inventory and cost of goods sold using the three-step process illustrated in Exhibits 5A.5a and 5A.5b.
- Prepare a table showing the computation of cost of goods sold and ending inventory using the specific identification method (see Exhibit 5A.2).
- Compare the year-end 2019 inventory amounts under FIFO and LIFO to determine the misstatement of year 2019 income that results from using LIFO. The errors for years 2019 and 2020 are equal in amount but opposite in effect.

SOLUTION

1. Cost of goods available for sale (this amount is the same for all methods).

Date		Units	Unit Cost	Cost
Jan. 1	Beg. inventory.............	400	$14	$ 5,600
Mar. 10	Purchase.................	200	15	3,000
May 9	Purchase.................	300	16	4,800
Sep. 22	Purchase.................	250	20	5,000
Nov. 28	Purchase.................	100	21	2,100
Total goods available for sale		1,250		$20,500

2a. FIFO **periodic** method.

Cost of goods available for sale (from part 1)....			$ 20,500
Ending inventory*			
Nov. 28	Purchase (100 @ $21).........	$2,100	
Sep. 22	Purchase (250 @ $20).........	5,000	
May 9	Purchase (200 @ $16).........	3,200	
Ending inventory.........................			10,300
Cost of goods sold			$10,200

*FIFO assumes that the earlier costs are the first to flow out; thus, we determine ending inventory by assigning the most recent costs to the remaining items.

2b. LIFO **periodic** method.

Cost of goods available for sale (from part 1)....			$ 20,500
Ending inventory†			
Jan. 1	Beg. inventory (400 @ $14) ...	$5,600	
Mar. 10	Purchase (150 @ $15)........	2,250	
Ending inventory..........................			7,850
Cost of goods sold			$12,650

†LIFO assumes that the most recent (newest) costs are the first to flow out; thus, we determine ending inventory by assigning the earliest (oldest) costs to the remaining items.

2c. Weighted average **periodic** method.

Step 1:	400 units @ $14 = $ 5,600
	200 units @ $15 = 3,000
	300 units @ $16 = 4,800
	250 units @ $20 = 5,000
	100 units @ $21 = 2,100
	1,250 units **$20,500**

Step 2: $20,500/1,250 units = **$16.40** weighted average cost per unit

Step 3: Total cost of 1,250 units available for sale .... $ 20,500
Less **ending inventory** priced on a weighted average
cost basis: 550 units at $16.40 each **9,020**
Cost of goods sold (700 units at $16.40 each)........ **$11,480**

2d. Specific identification method.

Cost of goods available for sale (from part 1)...		$ 20,500
Ending inventory*		
May 9	Purchase (300 @ $16).......	$4,800
Sep. 22	Purchase (150 @ $20).......	3,000
Nov. 28	Purchase (100 @ $21).......	2,100
Ending inventory.........................		**9,900**
Cost of goods sold		**$10,600**

*The additional tracking data provided are used to identify the items in ending inventory.

3.

	FIFO	LIFO	Weighted Average	Specific Identification
Income Statement				
Sales*	$ 22,500	$22,500	$ 22,500	$22,500
Cost of goods sold	10,200	12,650	11,480	10,600
Gross profit.....................	$ 12,300	$ 9,850	$ 11,020	$11,900
Balance Sheet				
Inventory	$10,300	$ 7,850	$ 9,020	$ 9,900

*Sales = (200 units × $30) + (200 units × $30) + (300 units × $35) = $22,500

4. Mistakenly using LIFO, when FIFO should have been used, overstates cost of goods sold in year 2019 by $2,450, which is the difference between the FIFO and LIFO amounts of ending inventory. It understates income in 2019 by $2,450. In year 2020, income is overstated by $2,450 because of the understatement in beginning inventory.

Inventory Costing under a Periodic System   5A

P3

Compute inventory in a periodic system using the methods of specific identification, FIFO, LIFO, and weighted average.

This section demonstrates inventory costing methods. We use information from Trekking, a sporting goods store. Among its many products, Trekking sells one type of mountain bike whose sales are directed at resorts that provide inexpensive bikes for guest use. We use Trekking's data from August. Its mountain bike (unit) inventory at the beginning of August and its purchases and sales during August are shown in Exhibit 5A.1. It ends August with 12 bikes remaining in inventory.

EXHIBIT 5A.1

Purchases and Sales of Goods

Date	Activity	Units Acquired at Cost	Units Sold at Retail	Unit Inventory
Aug. 1	Beginning inventory.......	10 units @ $ 91 = $ 910		10 units
Aug. 3	Purchases...............	15 units @ $106 = $ 1,590		25 units
Aug. 14	Sales...................		20 units @ $130	5 units
Aug. 17	Purchases...............	20 units @ $115 = $ 2,300		25 units
Aug. 28	Purchases...............	10 units @ $119 = $ 1,190		35 units
Aug. 30	Sales...................		23 units @ $150	12 units
	Totals	55 units $5,990	43 units	
		Units available for sale Goods available for sale	Units sold	Units left

Trekking uses the periodic inventory system, which means that its Merchandise Inventory account is updated at the end of each period (monthly for Trekking) to reflect purchases and sales. Regardless of what inventory method is used, cost of goods available for sale must be allocated between cost of goods sold and ending inventory. (Many companies use the periodic system for tracking costs [not so much for sales]. Reasons include the use of standard costs by some companies and dollar-value LIFO by others. Also, the methods of specific identification and FIFO, used by a majority of companies, give the same result under the periodic and the perpetual systems.)

Specific Identification

When each item in inventory can be matched with a specific purchase and invoice, we can use **specific identification** or **SI** to assign costs. We also need sales records that identify exactly which items were sold and when. Trekking's internal documents show the following specific unit sales.

August 14   Sold 8 bikes costing $91 each and 12 bikes costing $106 each. Total cost = $2,000.
August 30   Sold 2 bikes costing $91 each, 3 bikes costing $106 each, 15 bikes costing $115 each, and 3 bikes costing $119 each. Total cost = $2,582.

Exhibit 5A.2 begins with the $5,990 in total units available for sale. For the 20 units sold on August 14, the total cost of sales is $2,000. Next, for the 23 units sold on August 30, the total cost of sales is $2,582. The total cost of sales for the period is $4,582. We then subtract this $4,582 in cost of goods sold from the $5,990 in cost of goods available to get $1,408 in ending inventory.

EXHIBIT 5A.2

Specific Identification Computations

Total cost of 55 units available for sale (from Exhibit 5A.1)........................		$ 5,990
Cost of goods sold		
Aug. 14 (8 @ $91) + (12 @ $106)...	$2,000	
Aug. 30 (2 @ $91) + (3 @ $106) + (15 @ $115) + (3 @ $119).................	2,582	4,582
Ending inventory		$1,408

Point: Specific identification is common for custom-made inventory. Examples include jewelers and fashion designers.

Trekking's cost of goods sold reported on the income statement is **$4,582**, and ending inventory reported on the balance sheet is **$1,408**. The following graphic shows these cost flows.

Point: SI yields identical results under both periodic and perpetual.

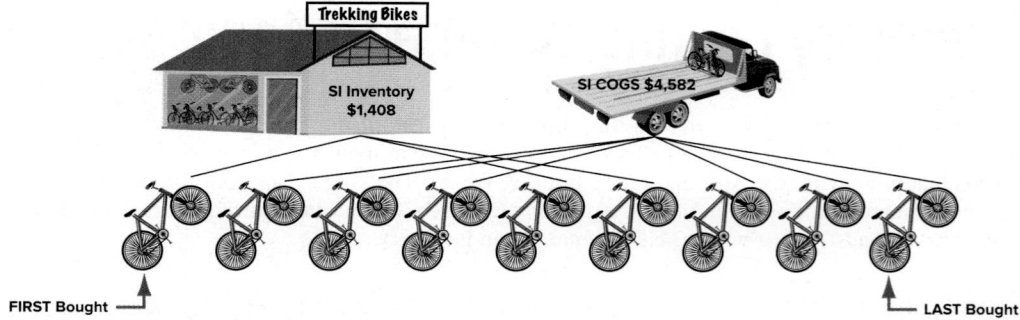

First-In, First-Out

First-in, first-out (FIFO) assumes that inventory items are sold in the order acquired. When sales occur, the costs of the earliest units acquired are charged to cost of goods sold. This leaves the costs from the most recent purchases in ending inventory.

Exhibit 5A.3 starts with $5,990 in total units available for sale. Applying FIFO, the 12 units in ending inventory are reported at the cost of the most recent 12 purchases. Reviewing purchases in reverse order, we assign costs to the 12 bikes in ending inventory as follows: $119 cost to 10 bikes and $115 cost to 2 bikes. This yields $1,420 in ending inventory. We subtract this $1,420 in ending inventory from $5,990 in cost of goods available to get $4,570 in cost of goods sold.

Point: For FIFO, COGS and ending inventory are the same for periodic and perpetual.

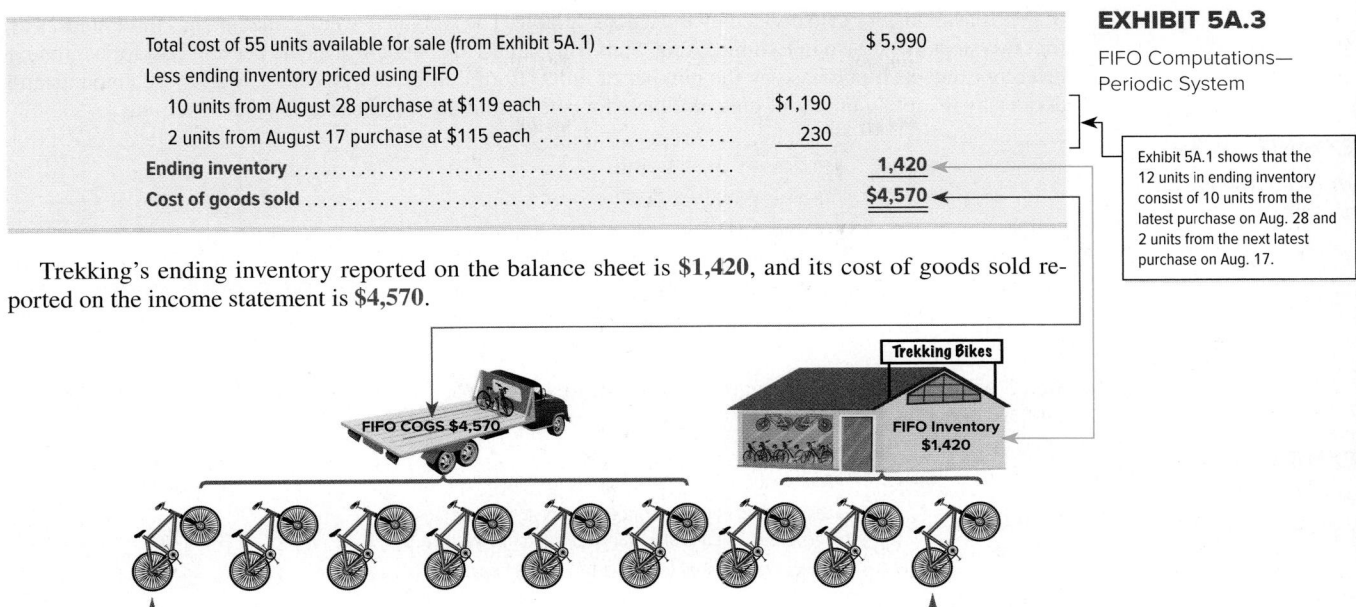

EXHIBIT 5A.3

FIFO Computations—
Periodic System

Total cost of 55 units available for sale (from Exhibit 5A.1)		$ 5,990
Less ending inventory priced using FIFO		
10 units from August 28 purchase at $119 each	$1,190	
2 units from August 17 purchase at $115 each	230	
Ending inventory		1,420
Cost of goods sold		$4,570

Exhibit 5A.1 shows that the 12 units in ending inventory consist of 10 units from the latest purchase on Aug. 28 and 2 units from the next latest purchase on Aug. 17.

Trekking's ending inventory reported on the balance sheet is **$1,420**, and its cost of goods sold reported on the income statement is **$4,570**.

Last-In, First-Out

Last-in, first-out (LIFO) assumes that the most recent purchases are sold first. These more recent costs are charged to goods sold, and the costs of the earliest purchases are assigned to inventory.

Exhibit 5A.4 starts with $5,990 in total units available for sale. Applying LIFO, the 12 units in ending inventory are reported at the cost of the earliest 12 purchases. Reviewing the earliest purchases in order, we assign costs to the 12 bikes in ending inventory as follows: $91 cost to 10 bikes and $106 cost to 2 bikes. This yields $1,122 in ending inventory. We subtract this $1,122 in ending inventory from $5,990 in cost of goods available to get $4,868 in cost of goods sold.

Point: By assigning costs from the most recent purchases to cost of goods sold, LIFO comes closest to matching current costs of goods sold with revenues.

EXHIBIT 5A.4

LIFO Computations—
Periodic System

Total cost of 55 units available for sale (from Exhibit 5A.1)...............		$ 5,990
Less ending inventory priced using LIFO		
10 units in beginning inventory at $91 each	$910	
2 units from August 3 purchase at $106 each......................	212	
Ending inventory..		1,122
Cost of goods sold		$4,868

Exhibit 5A.1 shows that the 12 units in ending inventory consist of 10 units from the earliest purchase (beg. inv.) and 2 units from the next earliest purchase on Aug. 3.

Trekking's ending inventory reported on the balance sheet is **$1,122**, and its cost of goods sold reported on the income statement is **$4,868**.

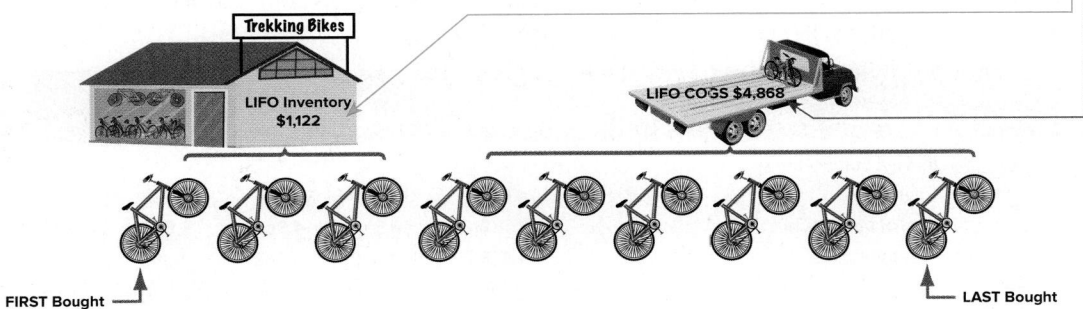

Weighted Average

Weighted average or **WA** (also called **average cost**) requires that we use the average cost per unit of inventory at the end of the period. Weighted average cost per unit equals the cost of goods available for sale divided by the units available. The weighted average method has three steps. The first two steps are shown in Exhibit 5A.5a. Step 1 in Exhibit 5A.5a multiplies the per unit cost for beginning inventory and each purchase by the number of units (from Exhibit 5A.1). Step 2 adds these amounts and divides by the total number of units available for sale to find the weighted average cost per unit.

EXHIBIT 5A.5a

Weighted Average Cost per Unit

Step 1:	10 units @ $ 91 =	$ 910
	15 units @ $106 =	1,590
	20 units @ $115 =	2,300
	10 units @ $119 =	1,190
	55	$5,990
Step 2:	$5,990/55 units = **$108.91** weighted average cost per unit	

Step 3 uses the weighted average cost per unit to assign costs to ending inventory and to cost of goods sold, as shown in Exhibit 5A.5b.

EXHIBIT 5A.5b

Weighted Average Computations—Periodic

Step 3: Total cost of 55 units available for sale (from Exhibit 5A.1)	$ 5,990
Less **ending inventory** priced on a weighted average cost basis: 12 units at $108.91 each (from Exhibit 5A.5a)	1,307
Cost of goods sold (43 units at $108.91 each).	**$4,683**

Trekking's ending inventory reported on the balance sheet is **$1,307**, and its cost of goods sold reported on the income statement is **$4,683**.

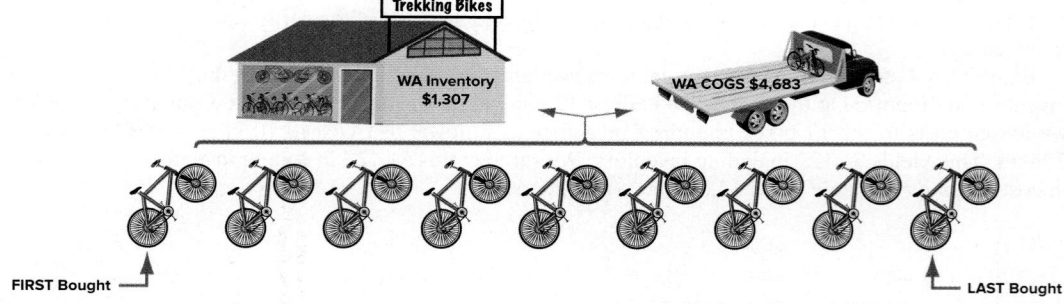

Financial Statement Effects of Costing Methods   When purchase prices do not change, each inventory costing method assigns the same cost amounts to inventory and to cost of goods sold. When purchase prices are different, the methods assign different cost amounts. We show these differences in Exhibit 5A.6 using Trekking's data.

Rising Costs   When purchase costs *regularly rise,* as in Trekking's case, the following occurs.

- FIFO reports the lowest cost of goods sold—yielding the highest gross profit and net income.
- LIFO reports the highest cost of goods sold—yielding the lowest gross profit and net income.
- Weighted average yields results between FIFO and LIFO.

EXHIBIT 5A.6

Financial Statement Effects of Inventory Costing Methods

Trekking Company For Month Ended August 31	Specific Identification	FIFO	LIFO	Weighted Average
Income Statement				
Sales.	$ 6,050	$ 6,050	$ 6,050	$ 6,050
Cost of goods sold.	4,582	4,570	4,868	4,683
Gross profit	1,468	1,480	1,182	1,367
Expenses	450	450	450	450
Income before taxes	1,018	1,030	732	917
Income tax expense (30%)	305	309	220	275
Net income	$ 713	$ 721	$ 512	$ 642
Balance Sheet				
Inventory.	$1,408	$1,420	$1,122	$1,307

Falling Costs When costs *regularly decline,* the reverse occurs for FIFO and LIFO. FIFO gives the highest cost of goods sold—yielding the lowest gross profit and income. LIFO gives the lowest cost of goods sold—yielding the highest gross profit and income.

Method Advantages Each method offers advantages.

- FIFO—inventory on the balance sheet approximates its current cost; it also follows the actual flow of goods for most businesses.
- LIFO—cost of goods sold on the income statement approximates its current cost; it also better matches current costs with revenues.
- Weighted average—smooths out erratic changes in costs.
- Specific identification—matches the costs of items with the revenues they generate.

Point: LIFO inventory is often less than the inventory's replacement cost because LIFO inventory is valued using the oldest inventory purchase costs.

A company reported the following December purchases and sales data for its only product.

NEED-TO-KNOW 5-7

Periodic SI, FIFO, LIFO, and WA

P3

Date	Activities	Units Acquired at Cost	Units Sold at Retail
Dec. 1	Beginning inventory	5 units @ $3.00 = $ 15.00	
Dec. 8	Purchase	10 units @ $4.50 = 45.00	
Dec. 9	Sales..........................		8 units @ $7.00
Dec. 19	Purchase	13 units @ $5.00 = 65.00	
Dec. 24	Sales..........................		18 units @ $8.00
Dec. 30	Purchase	8 units @ $5.30 = 42.40	
Totals	....	36 units $167.40	26 units

The company uses a *periodic inventory system.* Determine the cost assigned to ending inventory and to cost of goods sold using (a) specific identification, (b) FIFO, (c) LIFO, and (d) weighted average. (Round per unit costs and inventory amounts to cents.) For specific identification, ending inventory consists of 10 units, where 8 are from the December 30 purchase and 2 are from the December 8 purchase.

Solutions

a. Specific identification: Ending inventory—eight units from December 30 purchase and two units from December 8 purchase.

Specific Identification	Ending Inventory	Cost of Goods Sold
(8 × $5.30) + (2 × $4.50)	$51.40	
(5 × $3.00) + (8 × $4.50) + (13 × $5.00) + (0 × $5.30)		
or $167.40 [Total Goods Available] − $51.40 [Ending Inventory].................		$116.00

b. FIFO—Periodic.

FIFO	Ending Inventory	Cost of Goods Sold
(8 × $5.30) + (2 × $5.00)	$52.40	
(5 × $3.00) + (10 × $4.50) + (11 × $5.00)		
or $167.40 [Total Goods Available] − $52.40 [Ending Inventory].................		$115.00

c. LIFO—Periodic.

LIFO	Ending Inventory	Cost of Goods Sold
(5 × $3.00) + (5 × $4.50)	$37.50	
(8 × $5.30) + (13 × $5.00) + (5 × $4.50)		
or $167.40 [Total Goods Available] − $37.50 [Ending Inventory].................		$129.90

d. WA—Periodic.

WA	Ending Inventory	Cost of Goods Sold
10 × $4.65 (computed from $167.40/36)	$46.50	
26 × $4.65 (computed from $167.40/36)		
or $167.40 [Total Goods Available] − $46.50 [Ending Inventory].		$120.90

Do More: QS 5-7, QS 5-8, QS 5-9, QS 5-14, QS 5-15, QS 5-16, QS 5-17, E 5-5

APPENDIX

5B   Inventory Estimation Methods

P4

Apply both the retail inventory and gross profit methods to estimate inventory.

Inventory sometimes is estimated for two reasons. First, companies often report **interim financial statements** (financial statements prepared for periods of less than one year), but they only annually take a physical count of inventory. Second, companies may require an inventory estimate if some casualty such as fire or flood makes taking a physical count impossible. Estimates are usually only required for companies that use the periodic system. Companies using a perpetual system would presumably have updated inventory data.

This appendix describes two methods to estimate inventory.

Retail Inventory Method   To avoid the time-consuming process of taking a physical inventory, some companies use the **retail inventory method** to estimate cost of goods sold and ending inventory.

The retail inventory method uses a three-step process to estimate ending inventory. We need to know the amount of inventory a company had at the beginning of the period in both *cost* and *retail* amounts. We already explained how to compute the cost of inventory. The *retail amount of inventory* is measured using selling prices of inventory items. We also need to know the net amount of goods purchased (minus returns, allowances, and discounts) in the period, both at cost and at retail. The amount of net sales at retail also is needed. The process is shown in Exhibit 5B.1.

The reasoning behind the retail inventory method is that if we can get a good estimate of the cost-to-retail ratio, we can multiply ending inventory at retail by this ratio to estimate ending inventory at cost. Exhibit 5B.2 shows how these steps are applied to estimate ending inventory. First, we find that $100,000 of goods (at retail selling prices) were available for sale. A total of $70,000 of these

EXHIBIT 5B.1

Retail Inventory Method of Inventory Estimation

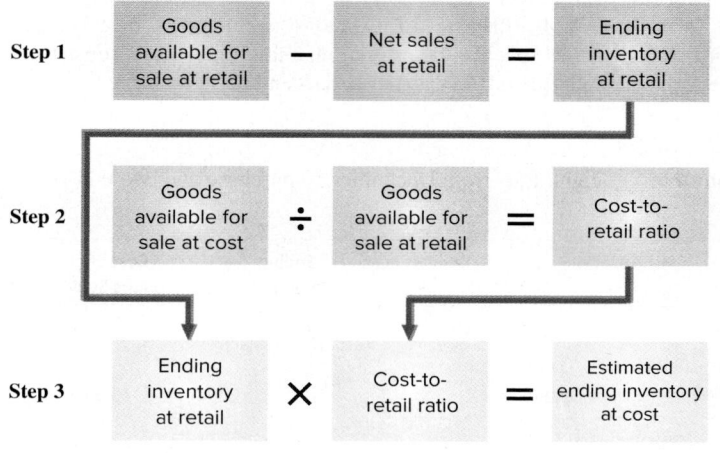

EXHIBIT 5B.2

Estimated Inventory Using the Retail Inventory Method

		At Cost	At Retail
Goods available for sale			
	Beginning inventory	$ 20,500	$ 34,500
	Cost of goods purchased	39,500	65,500
	Goods available for sale	60,000	100,000
Step 1:	Deduct net sales at retail		70,000
	Ending inventory at retail		$ 30,000
Step 2:	Cost-to-retail ratio: ($60,000 ÷ $100,000) = 60%		
Step 3:	Estimated ending inventory at cost ($30,000 × 60%)	$18,000	

goods were sold, leaving $30,000 (retail value) of merchandise in ending inventory. Second, the cost of these goods is 60% of the $100,000 retail value. Third, because cost for these goods is 60% of retail, the estimated cost of ending inventory is $18,000.

Gross Profit Method   The **gross profit method** estimates the cost of ending inventory by applying the gross profit ratio to net sales (at retail). This type of estimate often is used when inventory is destroyed, lost, or stolen. This method uses the historical relation between cost of goods sold and net sales to estimate the proportion of cost of goods sold making up current sales. This cost of goods sold estimate is then subtracted from cost of goods available for sale to estimate the ending inventory at cost. These two steps are shown in Exhibit 5B.3.

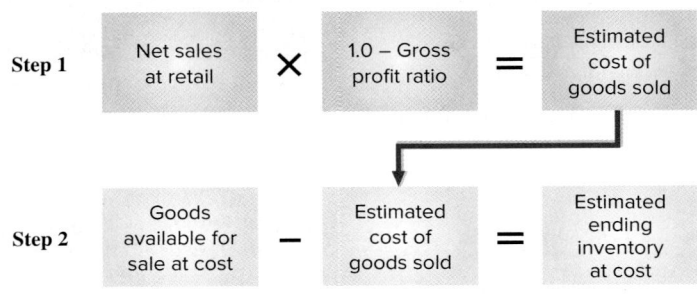

EXHIBIT 5B.3

Gross Profit Method of Inventory Estimation

To demonstrate, assume that a company's inventory is destroyed by fire in March. When the fire occurs, the company's accounts show the following balances for January through March: Net Sales, $30,000; Beginning Inventory, $12,000 (at January 1); and Cost of Goods Purchased, $20,500. If this company's gross profit ratio is 30%, then 30% of each net sales dollar is gross profit and 70% is cost of goods sold. We show in Exhibit 5B.4 how this 70% is used to estimate lost inventory of $11,500.

EXHIBIT 5B.4

Estimated Inventory Using the Gross Profit Method

Goods available for sale		
Beginning inventory, January 1	$12,000	
Cost of goods purchased	20,500	
Goods available for sale (at cost)...........................	32,500	
Net sales at retail..		$30,000 ⌐
Step 1: **Estimated cost of goods sold ($30,000 × 70%)**	**(21,000)** ⟵ × 0.70 ⌐
Step 2: **Estimated March inventory at cost**	**$11,500**

NEED-TO-KNOW 5-8

Using the retail method and the following data, estimate the cost of ending inventory.

	Cost	Retail
Beginning inventory	$324,000	$530,000
Cost of goods purchased	195,000	335,000
Net sales		320,000

Retail Inventory Estimation

P4

Solution

Estimated ending inventory (at cost) is $327,000. It is computed as follows.

Step 1:   ($530,000 + $335,000) − $320,000 = $545,000

Step 2: $\dfrac{\$324,000 + \$195,000}{\$530,000 + \$335,000} = 60\%$

Step 3: $545,000 × 60\% = \underline{\$327,000}$

Do More: QS 5-22, E 5-16, E 5-17, P 5-9

Summary: Cheat Sheet

INVENTORY BASICS

FOB shipping point: Goods are included in buyer's inventory once they are shipped.

FOB destination: Goods are included in buyer's inventory after arrival at their destination.

Consignee: Never reports consigned goods in inventory; stays in consignor's inventory until sold.

Merchandise inventory: Includes any *necessary* costs to make an item ready for sale. Examples—shipping, storage, import fees, and insurance.

INVENTORY COSTING

FIFO: Earliest units purchased are the first to be reported as cost of goods sold.

LIFO: Latest units purchased are the first to be reported as cost of goods sold.

Weighted average: The weighted average cost per unit (formula below) of inventory at the time of each sale is reported as cost of goods sold.

$$\frac{\text{Cost of goods available for sale (at each sale)}}{\text{Number of units available for sale (at each sale)}}$$

Specific identification: Each unit is assigned a cost, and when that unit is sold, its cost is reported as cost of goods sold.

Cost Flow Assumptions Example

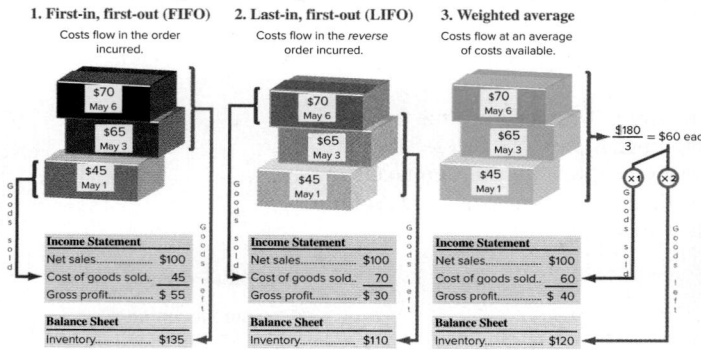

1. First-in, first-out (FIFO)   Costs flow in the order incurred.
2. Last-in, first-out (LIFO)   Costs flow in the *reverse* order incurred.
3. Weighted average   Costs flow at an average of costs available.

Financial Statement Effects

Rising Costs—FIFO reports lowest cost of goods sold and highest net income. LIFO reports highest cost of goods sold and lowest income. Weighted average reports results in between LIFO and FIFO.

Falling Costs—FIFO reports highest cost of goods sold and lowest net income. LIFO reports lowest cost of goods sold and highest income.

INVENTORY VALUATION, ERRORS, & ANALYSIS

Lower of cost or market (LCM): When market value of inventory is lower than its cost, a loss is recorded. When market value is higher than cost of inventory, no adjustment is made.

LCM Example (applied to individual items separately)

Inventory Items	Units	Per Unit Cost	Per Unit Market	Total Cost	Total Market	LCM Applied to Items
Roadster	20	$8,500	$7,000	$170,000	$140,000	$ 140,000
Sprint	10	5,000	6,000	50,000	60,000	50,000
Totals				$220,000		$190,000

Roadster: $140,000 is the lower of the $170,000 cost and $140,000 market.
Sprint: $50,000 is the lower of the $50,000 cost and $60,000 market.
LCM: Results in a $190,000 reported inventory.

LCM Journal Entry: To get from $220,000 reported inventory to the $190,000 LCM inventory, make the following entry.

Cost of Goods Sold..........................	30,000	
Merchandise Inventory		30,000

Effects of Overstated or Understated Inventory for Income Statement

	Year 1			Year 2	
Ending Inventory	Cost of Goods Sold	Net Income		Cost of Goods Sold	Net Income
Understated ▼	Overstated ▲		Understated ▼	Understated ▼	Overstated ▲
Overstated ▲	Understated ▼		Overstated ▲	Overstated ▲	Understated ▼

Effects of Overstated or Understated Inventory for Balance Sheet

Ending Inventory	Assets	Equity
Understated ▼	Understated ▼	Understated ▼
Overstated ▲	Overstated ▲	Overstated ▲

Multiple Choice Quiz

Use the following information from Marvel Company for the month of July to answer questions 1 through 4.

July 1	Beginning inventory............	75 units @ $25 each
July 3	Purchase.....................	348 units @ $27 each
July 8	Sale.........................	300 units
July 15	Purchase.....................	257 units @ $28 each
July 23	Sale.........................	275 units

1. **Perpetual:** Assume that Marvel uses a *perpetual* FIFO inventory system. What is the dollar value of its ending inventory?
   a. $2,940   c. $2,625   e. $2,705
   b. $2,685   d. $2,852

2. **Perpetual:** Assume that Marvel uses a *perpetual* LIFO inventory system. What is the dollar value of its ending inventory?
   a. $2,940   c. $2,625   e. $2,705
   b. $2,685   d. $2,852

3. Perpetual and Periodic: Assume that Marvel uses a specific identification inventory system. Its ending inventory consists of 20 units from beginning inventory, 40 units from the July 3 purchase, and 45 units from the July 15 purchase. What is the dollar value of its ending inventory?

a. $2,940   c. $2,625   e. $2,840

b. $2,685   d. $2,852

4.ᴬ Periodic: Assume that Marvel uses a *periodic* FIFO inventory system. What is the dollar value of its ending inventory?

a. $2,940   c. $2,625   e. $2,705

b. $2,685   d. $2,852

5.ᴬ Periodic: A company reports the following beginning inventory and purchases, and it ends the period with 30 units in inventory.

Beginning inventory.........	100 units at $10 cost per unit
Purchase 1	40 units at $12 cost per unit
Purchase 2	20 units at $14 cost per unit

i) Compute ending inventory using the FIFO *periodic* system.

a. $400   b. $1,460   c. $1,360   d. $300

ii) Compute cost of goods sold using the LIFO *periodic* system.

a. $400   b. $1,460   c. $1,360   d. $300

6. A company has cost of goods sold of $85,000 and ending inventory of $18,000. Its days' sales in inventory equals

a. 49.32 days.   c. 4.72 days.   e. 1,723.61 days.

b. 0.21 day.   d. 77.29 days.

ANSWERS TO MULTIPLE CHOICE QUIZ

1. a; FIFO perpetual

Date	Goods Purchased	Cost of Goods Sold	Inventory Balance
July 1			75 units @ $25 = $ 1,875
July 3	348 units @ $27 = $9,396		75 units @ $25 ⎫ 348 units @ $27 ⎬ = $11,271
July 8		75 units @ $25 ⎫ 225 units @ $27 ⎬ = $ 7,950	123 units @ $27 = $ 3,321
July 15	257 units @ $28 = $7,196		123 units @ $27 ⎫ 257 units @ $28 ⎬ = $10,517
July 23		123 units @ $27 ⎫ 152 units @ $28 ⎬ = $ 7,577	105 units @ $28 = **$2,940**
		$15,527	

2. b; LIFO perpetual

Date	Goods Purchased	Cost of Goods Sold	Inventory Balance
July 1			75 units @ $25 = $ 1,875
July 3	348 units @ $27 = $9,396		75 units @ $25 ⎫ 348 units @ $27 ⎬ = $11,271
July 8		300 units @ $27 = $ 8,100	75 units @ $25 ⎫ 48 units @ $27 ⎬ = $ 3,171
July 15	257 units @ $28 = $7,196		75 units @ $25 ⎫ 48 units @ $27 ⎬ = $10,367 257 units @ $28 ⎭
July 23		257 units @ $28 ⎫ 18 units @ $27 ⎬ = $ 7,682	75 units @ $25 ⎫ 30 units @ $27 ⎬ = **$ 2,685**
		$15,782	

3. e; Specific identification (perpetual and periodic are identical for specific identification)—Ending inventory computation follows.

20 units @ $25	$ 500
40 units @ $27	1,080
45 units @ $28	1,260
105 units	$2,840

4. a; FIFO periodic. Ending inventory computation: 105 units @ $28 each = $2,940. (*Hint:* FIFO periodic inventory computation is identical to the FIFO perpetual inventory computation.)

5. i) a; FIFO periodic inventory = (20 × $14) + (10 × $12)
= $400

ii) b; LIFO periodic cost of goods sold = (20 × $14) + (40 × $12)
+ (70 × $10) = $1,460

6. d; Days' sales in inventory = (Ending inventory/Cost of goods sold)
× 365 = ($18,000/$85,000) × 365
= 77.29 days

A(B) *Superscript letter A or B denotes assignments based on Appendix 5A or 5B.*

Icon denotes assignments that involve decision making.

Discussion Questions

1. Describe how costs flow from inventory to cost of goods sold for the following methods: (*a*) FIFO and (*b*) LIFO.

2. Where is the amount of merchandise inventory disclosed in the financial statements?

3. If costs are declining, will the LIFO or FIFO method of inventory valuation yield the lower cost of goods sold? Why?

4. If inventory errors are said to correct themselves, why are accounting users concerned when such errors are made?

5. Explain the following statement: "Inventory errors correct themselves."

6. What is the meaning of *market* as it is used in determining the lower of cost or market for inventory?

7. What factors contribute to (or cause) inventory shrinkage?

8.ᴮ When preparing interim financial statements, what two methods can companies utilize to estimate cost of goods sold and ending inventory?

9. Refer to **Apple**'s financial statements in Appendix A. On September 30, 2017, what **APPLE** percent of current assets is represented by inventory?

10. Refer to **Apple**'s financial statements in Appendix A and compute its cost of goods **APPLE** available for sale for the year ended September 30, 2017.

11. Refer to **Samsung**'s financial statements in Appendix A. Compute its cost of goods **Samsung** available for sale for the year ended December 31, 2017.

12. Refer to **Samsung**'s financial statements in Appendix A. What percent of its cur- **Samsung** rent assets is inventory as of December 31, 2017 and 2016?

---

connect

QUICK STUDY

QS 5-1
Inventory ownership
C1

Homestead Crafts, a distributor of handmade gifts, operates out of owner Emma Finn's house. At the end of the current period, Emma looks over her inventory and finds that she has

- 1,300 units (products) in her basement, 20 of which were damaged by water and cannot be sold.
- 350 units in her van, ready to deliver per a customer order, terms FOB destination.
- 80 units out on consignment to a friend who owns a retail store.

How many units should Emma include in her company's period-end inventory?

QS 5-2
Inventory costs
C2

A car dealer acquires a used car for $14,000, with terms FOB shipping point. Compute total inventory costs assigned to the used car if additional costs include

- $250 for transportation-in.
- $300 for shipping insurance.
- $900 for car import duties.

- $150 for advertising.
- $1,250 for sales staff salaries.
- $180 for trimming shrubs.

QS 5-3
Computing goods available for sale   **P1**

Wattan Company reports beginning inventory of 10 units at $60 each. Every week for four weeks it purchases an additional 10 units at respective costs of $61, $62, $65, and $70 per unit for weeks 1 through 4. Compute the cost of goods available for sale and the units available for sale for this four-week period. Assume that no sales occur during those four weeks.

QS 5-4
Perpetual: Inventory costing with FIFO

P1

A company reports the following beginning inventory and two purchases for the month of January. On January 26, the company sells 350 units. Ending inventory at January 31 totals 150 units.

	Units	Unit Cost
Beginning inventory on January 1.............	320	$3.00
Purchase on January 9......................	80	3.20
Purchase on January 25....................	100	3.34

Required

Assume the perpetual inventory system is used. Determine the costs assigned to ending inventory when costs are assigned based on the FIFO method. (Round per unit costs and inventory amounts to cents.)

Refer to the information in QS 5-4 and assume the perpetual inventory system is used. Determine the costs assigned to ending inventory when costs are assigned based on LIFO. (Round per unit costs and inventory amounts to cents.)

QS 5-5
Perpetual: Inventory costing with LIFO   **P1**

Refer to the information in QS 5-4 and assume the perpetual inventory system is used. Determine the costs assigned to ending inventory when costs are assigned based on the weighted average method. (Round per unit costs and inventory amounts to cents.)

QS 5-6
Perpetual: Inventory costing with weighted average   **P1**

Refer to the information in QS 5-4 and assume the periodic inventory system is used. Determine the costs assigned to ending inventory when costs are assigned based on the FIFO method. (Round per unit costs and inventory amounts to cents.)

QS 5-7[A]
Periodic: Inventory costing with FIFO   **P3**

Refer to the information in QS 5-4 and assume the periodic inventory system is used. Determine the costs assigned to ending inventory when costs are assigned based on the LIFO method. (Round per unit costs and inventory amounts to cents.)

QS 5-8[A]
Periodic: Inventory costing with LIFO   **P3**

Refer to the information in QS 5-4 and assume the periodic inventory system is used. Determine the costs assigned to ending inventory when costs are assigned based on the weighted average method. (Round per unit costs and inventory amounts to cents.)

QS 5-9[A]
Periodic: Inventory costing with weighted average   **P3**

Trey Monson starts a merchandising business on December 1 and enters into the following three inventory purchases. Also, on December 15, Monson sells 15 units for $20 each.

QS 5-10
Perpetual: Assigning costs with FIFO

P1

Purchases on December 7......	10 units @ $ 6.00 cost
Purchases on December 14.....	20 units @ $12.00 cost
Purchases on December 21.....	15 units @ $14.00 cost

Required

Monson uses a perpetual inventory system. Determine the costs assigned to the December 31 ending inventory based on the FIFO method. (Round per unit costs and inventory amounts to cents.)

Refer to the information in QS 5-10 and assume the perpetual inventory system is used. Determine the costs assigned to ending inventory when costs are assigned based on the LIFO method. (Round per unit costs and inventory amounts to cents.)

QS 5-11
Perpetual: Inventory costing with LIFO   **P1**

Refer to the information in QS 5-10 and assume the perpetual inventory system is used. Determine the costs assigned to ending inventory when costs are assigned based on the weighted average method. (Round per unit costs and inventory amounts to cents.)

QS 5-12
Perpetual: Inventory costing with weighted average   **P1**

Refer to the information in QS 5-10 and assume the perpetual inventory system is used. Determine the costs assigned to ending inventory when costs are assigned based on specific identification. Of the units sold, eight are from the December 7 purchase and seven are from the December 14 purchase. (Round per unit costs and inventory amounts to cents.)

QS 5-13
Perpetual: Inventory costing with specific identification   **P1**

Refer to the information in QS 5-10 and assume the periodic inventory system is used. Determine the costs assigned to ending inventory when costs are assigned based on the FIFO method. (Round per unit costs and inventory amounts to cents.)

QS 5-14[A]
Periodic: Inventory costing with FIFO   **P3**

Refer to the information in QS 5-10 and assume the periodic inventory system is used. Determine the costs assigned to ending inventory when costs are assigned based on the LIFO method. (Round per unit costs and inventory amounts to cents.)

QS 5-15[A]
Periodic: Inventory costing with LIFO   **P3**

QS 5-16^A
Periodic: Inventory costing with weighted average   **P3**

Refer to the information in QS 5-10 and assume the periodic inventory system is used. Determine the costs assigned to ending inventory when costs are assigned based on the weighted average method. (Round per unit costs and inventory amounts to cents.)

QS 5-17^A
Periodic: Inventory costing with specific identification   **P3**

Refer to the information in QS 5-10 and assume the periodic inventory system is used. Determine the costs assigned to ending inventory when costs are assigned based on specific identification. Of the units sold, eight are from the December 7 purchase and seven are from the December 14 purchase. (Round per unit costs and inventory amounts to cents.)

QS 5-18
Contrasting inventory costing methods

A1

Identify the inventory costing method (SI, FIFO, LIFO, or WA) best described by each of the following separate statements. Assume a period of increasing costs.

_____ **1.** Results in the highest cost of goods sold.
_____ **2.** Yields the highest net income.
_____ **3.** Has the lowest tax expense because of reporting the lowest net income.
_____ **4.** Better matches current costs with revenues.
_____ **5.** Precisely matches the costs of items with the revenues they generate.

QS 5-19
Applying LCM to inventories

P2

Ames Trading Co. has the following products in its ending inventory. Compute lower of cost or market for inventory applied separately to each product.

Product	Quantity	Cost per Unit	Market per Unit
Mountain bikes	11	$600	$550
Skateboards	13	350	425
Gliders	26	800	700

QS 5-20
Inventory errors

A2

In taking a physical inventory at the end of Year 1, Grant Company forgot to count certain units and understated ending inventory by $10,000. Determine how this error affects each of the following.

a. Year 1 cost of goods sold   **c.** Year 2 cost of goods sold
b. Year 1 net income   **d.** Year 2 net income

QS 5-21
Analyzing inventory   **A3**

Endor Company begins the year with $140,000 of goods in inventory. At year-end, the amount in inventory has increased to $180,000. Cost of goods sold for the year is $1,200,000. Compute Endor's inventory turnover and days' sales in inventory. Assume there are 365 days in the year.

QS 5-22^B
Estimating inventories—gross profit method

P4

Confucius Bookstore's inventory is destroyed by a fire on September 5. The following data for the current year are available from the accounting records. Estimate the cost of the inventory destroyed.

Beginning inventory, Jan. 1	$190,000
Jan. 1 through Sept. 5 purchases (net)	$352,000
Jan. 1 through Sept. 5 sales (net)	$685,000
Current year's estimated gross profit rate	44%

QS 5-23
Inventory costs

C2

A solar panel dealer acquires a used panel for $9,000, with terms FOB shipping point. Compute total inventory costs assigned to the used panel if additional costs include

• $1,500 for sales staff salaries.
• $280 for transportation-in by train.
• $110 for online advertising.

• $135 for shipping insurance.
• $550 for used panel restoration.
• $300 for lawn care.

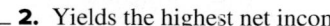

EXERCISES

Exercise 5-1
Inventory ownership   **C1**

1. At year-end, Barr Co. had shipped $12,500 of merchandise FOB destination to Lee Co. Which company should include the $12,500 of merchandise in transit as part of its year-end inventory?

2. Parris Company has shipped $20,000 of goods to Harlow Co., and Harlow Co. has arranged to sell the goods for Parris. Identify the consignor and the consignee. Which company should include any unsold goods as part of its inventory?

Walberg Associates, antique dealers, purchased goods for $75,000. Terms of the purchase were FOB shipping point, and the cost of transporting the goods to Walberg Associates's warehouse was $2,400. Walberg Associates insured the shipment at a cost of $300. Prior to putting the goods up for sale, they cleaned and refurbished them at a cost of $980. Determine the cost of inventory.

Exercise 5-2
Inventory costs
C2

Laker Company reported the following January purchases and sales data for its only product.

Exercise 5-3
Perpetual: Inventory costing methods
P1

Date	Activities	Units Acquired at Cost	Units Sold at Retail
Jan. 1	Beginning inventory	140 units @ $6.00 = $ 840	
Jan. 10	Sales........................		100 units @ $15
Jan. 20	Purchase	60 units @ $5.00 = 300	
Jan. 25	Sales........................		80 units @ $15
Jan. 30	Purchase	180 units @ $4.50 = 810	
	Totals	380 units $1,950	180 units

Required

The company uses a perpetual inventory system. Determine the cost assigned to ending inventory and to cost of goods sold using (*a*) specific identification, (*b*) weighted average, (*c*) FIFO, and (*d*) LIFO. (Round per unit costs and inventory amounts to cents.) For specific identification, ending inventory consists of 200 units, where 180 are from the January 30 purchase, 5 are from the January 20 purchase, and 15 are from beginning inventory.

Check Ending inventory:
LIFO, $930; WA, $918

Use the data in Exercise 5-3 to prepare comparative income statements for the month of January for Laker Company similar to those shown in Exhibit 5.8 for the four inventory methods. Assume expenses are $1,250 and the applicable income tax rate is 40%. (Round amounts to cents.)

1. Which method yields the highest net income?
2. Does net income using weighted average fall above, between, or below that using FIFO and LIFO?
3. If costs were rising instead of falling, which method would yield the highest net income?

Exercise 5-4
Perpetual: Income effects of inventory methods
A1

Refer to the information in Exercise 5-3 and assume the periodic inventory system is used. Determine the costs assigned to ending inventory and to cost of goods sold using (*a*) specific identification, (*b*) weighted average, (*c*) FIFO, and (*d*) LIFO. (Round per unit costs and inventory amounts to cents.) For specific identification, ending inventory consists of 200 units, where 180 are from the January 30 purchase, 5 are from the January 20 purchase, and 15 are from beginning inventory.

Exercise 5-5[A]
Periodic: Inventory costing
P3

Use the data and results from Exercise 5-5 to prepare comparative income statements for the month of January for the company similar to those shown in Exhibit 5.8 for the four inventory methods. Assume expenses are $1,250 and the applicable income tax rate is 40%. (Round amounts to cents.)

Exercise 5-6[A]
Periodic: Income effects of inventory methods
P3   A1

Required

1. Which method yields the highest net income?
2. Does net income using weighted average fall above, between, or below that using FIFO and LIFO?
3. If costs were rising instead of falling, which method would yield the highest net income?

Hemming Co. reported the following current-year purchases and sales for its only product.

Exercise 5-7
Perpetual: Inventory costing methods—FIFO and LIFO
P1

Date	Activities	Units Acquired at Cost	Units Sold at Retail
Jan. 1	Beginning inventory...........	200 units @ $10 = $ 2 000	
Jan. 10	Sales........................		150 units @ $40
Mar. 14	Purchase	350 units @ $15 = 5 250	
Mar. 15	Sales........................		300 units @ $40
July 30	Purchase	450 units @ $20 = 9 000	
Oct. 5	Sales........................		430 units @ $40
Oct. 26	Purchase	100 units @ $25 = 2,500	
	Totals	1,100 units $18,750	880 units

Required

Hemming uses a perpetual inventory system. Determine the costs assigned to ending inventory and to cost of goods sold using (*a*) FIFO and (*b*) LIFO. (*c*) Compute the gross margin for each method. (Round amounts to cents.)

Exercise 5-8
Specific identification   **P1**

Refer to the information in Exercise 5-7. Ending inventory consists of 45 units from the March 14 purchase, 75 units from the July 30 purchase, and all 100 units from the October 26 purchase. Using the specific identification method, compute (*a*) the cost of goods sold and (*b*) the gross profit. (Round amounts to cents.)

Exercise 5-9ᴬ
Periodic: Inventory
costing   **P3**

Refer to the information in Exercise 5-7 and assume the periodic inventory system is used. Determine the costs assigned to ending inventory and to cost of goods sold using (*a*) FIFO and (*b*) LIFO. (*c*) Compute the gross margin for each method.

Exercise 5-10
Lower of cost or market
P2

Martinez Company's ending inventory includes the following items. Compute the lower of cost or market for ending inventory applied separately to each product.

Product	Units	Cost per Unit	Market per Unit
Helmets..........	24	$50	$54
Bats.............	17	78	72
Shoes...........	38	95	91
Uniforms	42	36	36

Exercise 5-11
Comparing LIFO numbers
to FIFO numbers; ratio
analysis
A1   A3

Cruz Company uses LIFO for inventory costing and reports the following financial data. It also recomputed inventory and cost of goods sold using FIFO for comparison purposes.

	Year 2	Year 1
LIFO inventory.......................	$160	$110
LIFO cost of goods sold	740	680
FIFO inventory.......................	240	110
FIFO cost of goods sold	660	645
Current assets (using LIFO)	220	180
Current assets (using FIFO).............	300	180
Current liabilities.....................	200	170

1. Compute its current ratio, inventory turnover, and days' sales in inventory for Year 2 using (*a*) LIFO numbers and (*b*) FIFO numbers. (Round answers to one decimal.)
2. Comment on and interpret the results of part 1.

Exercise 5-12
Analyzing inventory
errors
A2

Vibrant Company had $850,000 of sales in each of Year 1, Year 2, and Year 3, and it purchased merchandise costing $500,000 in each of those years. It also maintained a $250,000 physical inventory from the beginning to the end of that three-year period. In accounting for inventory, it made an error at the end of Year 1 that caused its Year 1 ending inventory to appear on its statements as $230,000 rather than the correct $250,000.

1. Determine the correct amount of the company's gross profit in each of Year 1, Year 2, and Year 3.
2. Prepare comparative income statements as in Exhibit 5.11 to show the effect of this error on the company's cost of goods sold and gross profit for each of Year 1, Year 2, and Year 3.

Exercise 5-13
Inventory turnover and
days' sales in inventory
A3

Use the following information for Palmer Co. to compute inventory turnover for Year 3 and Year 2, and its days' sales in inventory at December 31, Year 3 and Year 2. (Round answers to one decimal.) Comment on Palmer's efficiency in using its assets to increase sales from Year 2 to Year 3.

	Year 3	Year 2	Year 1
Cost of goods sold	$643,825	$426,650	$391,300
Ending inventory..............	97,400	87,750	92,500

Lopez Company reported the following current-year data for its only product. The company uses a periodic inventory system, and its ending inventory consists of 150 units—50 from each of the last three purchases. Determine the cost assigned to ending inventory and to cost of goods sold using (*a*) specific identification, (*b*) weighted average, (*c*) FIFO, and (*d*) LIFO. (Round per unit costs and inventory amounts to cents.) (*e*) Which method yields the highest net income?

Exercise 5-14[A]
Periodic: Cost flow assumptions
P3

Jan.	1	Beginning inventory	96 units @ $2.00 = $ 192
Mar.	7	Purchase	220 units @ $2.25 = 495
July	28	Purchase	544 units @ $2.50 = 1,360
Oct.	3	Purchase	480 units @ $2.80 = 1,344
Dec.	19	Purchase	160 units @ $2.90 = 464
		Totals	1,500 units $3,855

Check   Inventory; LIFO, $313.50; FIFO, $435.00

Flora's Gifts reported the following current-month data for its only product. The company uses a periodic inventory system, and its ending inventory consists of 60 units—50 units from the January 6 purchase and 10 units from the January 25 purchase. Determine the cost assigned to ending inventory and to cost of goods sold using (*a*) specific identification, (*b*) weighted average, (*c*) FIFO, and (*d*) LIFO. (Round per unit costs and inventory amounts to cents.) (*e*) Which method yields the lowest net income?

Exercise 5-15[A]
Periodic: Cost flow assumptions
P3

Jan.	1	Beginning inventory	138 units @ $3.00 = $ 414
Jan.	6	Purchase	300 units @ $2.80 = 840
Jan.	17	Purchase	540 units @ $2.30 = 1,242
Jan.	25	Purchase	22 units @ $2.00 = 44
		Totals	1,000 units $2,540

Check   Inventory: LIFO, $180.00; FIFO, $131.40

Dakota Company had net sales (at retail) of $260,000. The following additional information is available from its records. Use the retail inventory method to estimate Dakota's year-end inventory at cost.

Exercise 5-16[B]
Estimating ending inventory—retail method
P4

	At Cost	At Retail
Beginning inventory	$ 63,800	$128,400
Cost of goods purchased	115,060	196,800

Check   End. inventory at cost, $35,860

On January 1, JKR Shop had $225,000 of beginning inventory at cost. In the first quarter of the year, it purchased $795,000 of merchandise, returned $11,550, and paid freight charges of $18,800 on purchased merchandise, terms FOB shipping point. The company's gross profit averages 30%, and the store had $1,000,000 of net sales (at retail) in the first quarter of the year.

Use the gross profit method to estimate its cost of inventory at the end of the first quarter.

Exercise 5-17[B]
Estimating ending inventory—gross profit method   P4

Tree Seedlings has the following current-year purchases and sales for its only product.

Exercise 5-18
Perpetual inventory costing
P1

Date		Activities	Units Acquired at Cost	Units Sold at Retail
Jan.	1	Beginning inventory...........	40 units @ $2 = $ 80	
Jan.	3	Sales........................		30 units @ $8
Feb.	14	Purchase....................	70 units @ $3 = $210	
Feb.	15	Sales........................		60 units @ $8
June	30	Purchase....................	90 units @ $4 = $360	
Nov.	6	Sales........................		86 units @ $8
Nov.	19	Purchase....................	20 units @ $5 = $100	
		Totals	220 units $750	176 units

Required

The company uses a perpetual inventory system. Determine the costs assigned to ending inventory and to cost of goods sold using (*a*) FIFO and (*b*) LIFO. (*c*) Compute the gross margin for each method.

Exercise 5-19ᴬ
Periodic inventory costing

P3

Refer to the information in Exercise 5-18 and assume the periodic inventory system is used. Determine the costs assigned to ending inventory and to cost of goods sold using (*a*) FIFO and (*b*) LIFO. (*c*) Compute the gross margin for each method.

PROBLEM SET A

Problem 5-1A
Perpetual: Alternative cost flows

P1

Warnerwoods Company uses a perpetual inventory system. It entered into the following purchases and sales transactions for March. (For specific identification, the March 9 sale consisted of 80 units from beginning inventory and 340 units from the March 5 purchase; the March 29 sale consisted of 40 units from the March 18 purchase and 120 units from the March 25 purchase.)

Date	Activities	Units Acquired at Cost	Units Sold at Retail
Mar. 1	Beginning inventory.............	100 units @ $50.00 per unit	
Mar. 5	Purchase.....................	400 units @ $55.00 per unit	
Mar. 9	Sales		420 units @ $85.00 per unit
Mar. 18	Purchase.....................	120 units @ $60.00 per unit	
Mar. 25	Purchase.....................	200 units @ $62.00 per unit	
Mar. 29	Sales		160 units @ $95.00 per unit
	Totals........................	820 units	580 units

Required

1. Compute cost of goods available for sale and the number of units available for sale.
2. Compute the number of units in ending inventory.
3. Compute the cost assigned to ending inventory using (*a*) FIFO, (*b*) LIFO, (*c*) weighted average, and (*d*) specific identification. (Round all amounts to cents.)
4. Compute gross profit earned by the company for each of the four costing methods in part 3.

Check   (3) Ending inventory: FIFO, $14,800; LIFO, $13,680; WA, $14,352
(4) LIFO gross profit, $17,980

Problem 5-2Aᴬ
Periodic: Alternative cost flows

P3

Refer to the information in Problem 5-1A and assume the periodic inventory system is used.

Required

1. Compute cost of goods available for sale and the number of units available for sale.
2. Compute the number of units in ending inventory.
3. Compute the cost assigned to ending inventory using (*a*) FIFO, (*b*) LIFO, (*c*) weighted average, and (*d*) specific identification. (Round all amounts to cents.)
4. Compute gross profit earned by the company for each of the four costing methods in part 3.

Problem 5-3A
Perpetual: Alternative cost flows

P1

Montoure Company uses a perpetual inventory system. It entered into the following calendar-year purchases and sales transactions. (For specific identification, units sold consist of 600 units from beginning inventory, 300 from the February 10 purchase, 200 from the March 13 purchase, 50 from the August 21 purchase, and 250 from the September 5 purchase.)

Date	Activities	Units Acquired at Cost	Units Sold at Retail
Jan. 1	Beginning inventory.............	600 units @ $45.00 per unit	
Feb. 10	Purchase.....................	400 units @ $42.00 per unit	
Mar. 13	Purchase.....................	200 units @ $27.00 per unit	
Mar. 15	Sales		800 units @ $75.00 per unit
Aug. 21	Purchase.....................	100 units @ $50.00 per unit	
Sep. 5	Purchase.....................	500 units @ $46.00 per unit	
Sep. 10	Sales		600 units @ $75.00 per unit
	Totals........................	1,800 units	1,400 units

Required

1. Compute cost of goods available for sale and the number of units available for sale.
2. Compute the number of units in ending inventory.
3. Compute the cost assigned to ending inventory using (*a*) FIFO, (*b*) LIFO, (*c*) weighted average, and (*d*) specific identification. (Round all amounts to cents.)
4. Compute gross profit earned by the company for each of the four costing methods in part 3.

Check   (3) Ending inventory: FIFO, $18,400; LIFO, $18,000; WA, $17,760
(4) LIFO gross profit, $45,800

Analysis Component

5. The company's manager earns a bonus based on a percent of gross profit. Which method of inventory costing produces the highest bonus for the manager?

Refer to the information in Problem 5-3A and assume the periodic inventory system is used.

Problem 5-4A^A
Periodic: Alternative cost flows

P3

Required

1. Compute cost of goods available for sale and the number of units available for sale.
2. Compute the number of units in ending inventory.
3. Compute the cost assigned to ending inventory using (*a*) FIFO, (*b*) LIFO, (*c*) weighted average, and (*d*) specific identification. (Round all amounts to cents.)
4. Compute gross profit earned by the company for each of the four costing methods in part 3.

Analysis Component

5. The company's manager earns a bonus based on a percentage of gross profit. Which method of inventory costing produces the highest bonus for the manager?

A physical inventory of Liverpool Company taken at December 31 reveals the following.

Problem 5-5A
Lower of cost or market

P2

Item	Units	Cost per Unit	Market per Unit
Car audio equipment			
Speakers	345	$ 90	$ 98
Stereos	260	111	100
Amplifiers	326	86	95
Subwoofers	204	52	41
Security equipment			
Alarms	480	150	125
Locks	291	93	84
Cameras	212	310	322
Binocular equipment			
Tripods	185	70	84
Stabilizers	170	97	105

Required

1. Compute the lower of cost or market for the inventory applied separately to each item.
2. If the market amount is less than the recorded cost of the inventory, then record the LCM adjustment to the Merchandise Inventory account.

Check   (1) $273,054

Navajo Company's financial statements show the following. The company recently discovered that in making physical counts of inventory, it had made the following errors: Year 1 ending inventory is understated by $56,000 and Year 2 ending inventory is overstated by $20,000.

Problem 5-6A
Analysis of inventory errors

A2

For Year Ended December 31		Year 1	Year 2	Year 3
(*a*)	Cost of goods sold	$ 615,000	$ 957,000	$ 780,000
(*b*)	Net income	230,000	285,000	241,000
(*c*)	Total current assets	1,255,000	1,365,000	1,200,000
(*d*)	Total equity	1,387,000	1,530,000	1,242,000

Required

1. For each key financial statement figure—(a), (b), (c), and (d) above—prepare a table similar to the following to show the adjustments necessary to correct the reported amounts.

Figure: _____	Year 1	Year 2	Year 3
Reported amount			
Adjustments for: Year 1 error.................			
Year 2 error.................			
Corrected amount			

Check (1) Corrected net income: Year 1, $286,000; Year 2, $209,000; Year 3, $261,000

2. What is the total error in combined net income for the three-year period resulting from the inventory errors? Explain.

Problem 5-7A^A
Periodic: Alternative cost flows   **P3**

Seminole Co. began the year with 23,000 units of product in its January 1 inventory costing $15 each. It made four purchases of its product during the year as follows. The company uses a periodic inventory system. On December 31, a physical count reveals that 40,000 units of its product remain in inventory.

Mar. 7	30,000 units @ $18.00 each	Aug. 1	23,000 units @ $25.00 each
May 25	39,000 units @ $20.00 each	Nov. 10	35,000 units @ $26.00 each

Required

Check (2) Cost of goods sold: FIFO, $2,115,000; LIFO, $2,499,000; WA, $2,310,000

1. Compute the number and total cost of the units available for sale during the year.
2. Compute the amounts assigned to ending inventory and the cost of goods sold using (a) FIFO, (b) LIFO, and (c) weighted average. (Round all amounts to cents.)

Problem 5-8A^A
Periodic: Income comparisons and cost flows
A1   P3

QP Corp. sold 4,000 units of its product at $50 per unit during the year and incurred operating expenses of $5 per unit in selling the units. It began the year with 700 units in inventory and made successive purchases of its product as follows.

Jan. 1	Beginning inventory............	700 units @ $18.00 per unit
Feb. 20	Purchase	1,700 units @ $19.00 per unit
May 16	Purchase	800 units @ $20.00 per unit
Oct. 3	Purchase	500 units @ $21.00 per unit
Dec. 11	Purchase	2,300 units @ $22.00 per unit
	Total	6,000 units

Required

Check (1) Net income: FIFO, $61,200; LIFO, $57,180; WA, $59,196

1. Prepare comparative income statements similar to Exhibit 5.8 for the three inventory costing methods of FIFO, LIFO, and weighted average. (Round all amounts to cents.) Include a detailed cost of goods sold section as part of each statement. The company uses a periodic inventory system, and its income tax rate is 40%.
2. How would the financial results from using the three alternative inventory costing methods change if the company had been experiencing *declining* costs in its purchases of inventory?
3. What advantages and disadvantages are offered by using (a) LIFO and (b) FIFO? Assume the continuing trend of *increasing* costs.

Problem 5-9A^B
Retail inventory method
P4

The records of Alaska Company provide the following information for the year ended December 31.

	At Cost	At Retail
Beginning inventory, January 1	$ 469,010	$ 928,950
Cost of goods purchased	3,376,050	6,381,050
Sales		5,595,800
Sales returns.........................		42,800

Required

Check (1) Inventory, $924,182 cost
(2) Inventory shortage at cost, $36,873

1. Use the retail inventory method to estimate the company's year-end inventory at cost.
2. A year-end physical inventory at retail prices yields a total inventory of $1,686,900. Prepare a calculation showing the company's loss from shrinkage at cost and at retail.

Wayward Company wants to prepare interim financial statements for the first quarter. The company wishes to avoid making a physical count of inventory. Wayward's gross profit rate averages 34%. The following information for the first quarter is available from its records.

Problem 5-10A[B]
Gross profit method   **P4**

Beginning inventory, January 1	$ 302,580
Cost of goods purchased	941,040
Sales	1,211,160
Sales returns	8,410

Required

Use the gross profit method to estimate the company's first-quarter ending inventory.

Check   Estimated ending inventory, $449,805

Ming Company uses a perpetual inventory system. It entered into the following purchases and sales transactions for April. (For specific identification, the April 9 sale consisted of 8 units from beginning inventory and 27 units from the April 6 purchase; the April 30 sale consisted of 12 units from beginning inventory, 3 units from the April 6 purchase, and 10 units from the April 25 purchase.)

PROBLEM SET B

Problem 5-1B
Perpetual: Alternative cost flows

P1

Date	Activities	Units Acquired at Cost	Units Sold at Retail
Apr. 1	Beginning inventory	20 units @ $3,000.00 per unit	
Apr. 6	Purchase	30 units @ $3,500.00 per unit	
Apr. 9	Sales		35 units @ $12,000.00 per unit
Apr. 17	Purchase	5 units @ $4,500.00 per unit	
Apr. 25	Purchase	10 units @ $4,800.00 per unit	
Apr. 30	Sales		25 units @ $14,000.00 per unit
	Total.	65 units	60 units

Required

1. Compute cost of goods available for sale and the number of units available for sale.
2. Compute the number of units in ending inventory.
3. Compute the cost assigned to ending inventory using (*a*) FIFO, (*b*) LIFO, (*c*) weighted average, and (*d*) specific identification. (Round all amounts to cents.)
4. Compute gross profit earned by the company for each of the four costing methods in part 3.

Check   (3) Ending inventory: FIFO, $24,000; LIFO, $15,000; WA, $20,000
(4) LIFO gross profit, $549,500

Refer to the information in Problem 5-1B and assume the periodic inventory system is used.

Problem 5-2B[A]
Periodic: Alternative cost flows

P3

Required

1. Compute cost of goods available for sale and the number of units available for sale.
2. Compute the number of units in ending inventory.
3. Compute the cost assigned to ending inventory using (*a*) FIFO, (*b*) LIFO, (*c*) weighted average, and (*d*) specific identification. (Round all amounts to cents.)
4. Compute gross profit earned by the company for each of the four costing methods in part 3.

Aloha Company uses a perpetual inventory system. It entered into the following calendar-year purchases and sales transactions. (For specific identification, the May 9 sale consisted of 80 units from beginning inventory and 100 units from the May 6 purchase; the May 30 sale consisted of 200 units from the May 6 purchase and 100 units from the May 25 purchase.)

Problem 5-3B
Perpetual: Alternative cost flows

P1

Date	Activities	Units Acquired at Cost	Units Sold at Retail
May 1	Beginning inventory	150 units @ $300.00 per unit	
May 6	Purchase	350 units @ $350.00 per unit	
May 9	Sales		180 units @ $1,200.00 per unit
May 17	Purchase	80 units @ $450.00 per unit	
May 25	Purchase	100 units @ $458.00 per unit	
May 30	Sales		300 units @ $1,400.00 per unit
	Total.	680 units	480 units

Required

1. Compute cost of goods available for sale and the number of units available for sale.

2. Compute the number of units in ending inventory.

Check   (3) Ending inventory:
FIFO, $88,800; LIFO,
$62,500; WA, $75,600
(4) LIFO gross profit, $449,200

3. Compute the cost assigned to ending inventory using (*a*) FIFO, (*b*) LIFO, (*c*) weighted average, and (*d*) specific identification. (Round all amounts to cents.)

4. Compute gross profit earned by the company for each of the four costing methods in part 3.

Analysis Component

5. If the company's manager earns a bonus based on a percent of gross profit, which method of inventory costing will the manager likely prefer?

Problem 5-4B[A]

Periodic: Alternative
cost flows

P3

Refer to the information in Problem 5-3B and assume the periodic inventory system is used.

Required

1. Compute cost of goods available for sale and the number of units available for sale.

2. Compute the number of units in ending inventory.

3. Compute the cost assigned to ending inventory using (*a*) FIFO, (*b*) LIFO, (*c*) weighted average, and (*d*) specific identification. (Round all amounts to cents.)

4. Compute gross profit earned by the company for each of the four costing methods in part 3.

Analysis Component

5. If the company's manager earns a bonus based on a percentage of gross profit, which method of inventory costing will the manager likely prefer?

Problem 5-5B

Lower of cost or market

P2

A physical inventory of Office Necessities Company taken at December 31 reveals the following.

Item	Units	Cost per Unit	Market per Unit
Office furniture			
Desks	536	$261	$305
Chairs	395	227	256
Mats	687	49	43
Bookshelves	421	93	82
Filing cabinets			
Two-drawer	114	81	70
Four-drawer	298	135	122
Lateral	75	104	118
Office equipment			
Projectors	370	168	200
Copiers	475	317	288
Phones	302	125	117

Required

Check   (1) $580,054

1. Compute the lower of cost or market for the inventory applied separately to each item.

2. If the market amount is less than the recorded cost of the inventory, then record the LCM adjustment to the Merchandise Inventory account.

Problem 5-6B

Analysis of inventory errors

A2

Hallam Company's financial statements show the following. The company recently discovered that in making physical counts of inventory, it had made the following errors: Year 1 ending inventory is overstated by $18,000 and Year 2 ending inventory is understated by $26,000.

For Year Ended December 31		Year 1	Year 2	Year 3
(*a*)	Cost of goods sold	$207,200	$213,800	$197,030
(*b*)	Net income	175,800	212,270	184,910
(*c*)	Total current assets.	276,000	277,500	272,950
(*d*)	Total equity	314,000	315,000	346,000

Required

1. For each key financial statement figure—(*a*), (*b*), (*c*), and (*d*) above—prepare a table similar to the following to show the adjustments necessary to correct the reported amounts.

Figure: _____	Year 1	Year 2	Year 3
Reported amount	_____	_____	_____
Adjustments for: Year 1 error.................	_____	_____	_____
Year 2 error.................	_____	_____	_____
Corrected amount	_____	_____	_____

Check (1) Corrected net income: Year 1, $157,800; Year 2, $256,270; Year 3, $158,910

2. What is the total error in combined net income for the three-year period resulting from the inventory errors? Explain.

Seneca Co. began the year with 6,500 units of product in its January 1 inventory costing $35 each. It made four purchases of its product during the year as follows. The company uses a periodic inventory system. On December 31, a physical count reveals that 8,500 units of its product remain in inventory.

Problem 5-7B[A]
Periodic: Alternative cost flows
P3

Jan. 4	11,500 units @ $33 each	July 9	11,000 units @ $29 each
May 18	13,400 units @ $32 each	Nov. 21	7,600 units @ $27 each

Required

1. Compute the number and total cost of the units available for sale during the year.
2. Compute the amounts assigned to ending inventory and the cost of goods sold using (*a*) FIFO, (*b*) LIFO, and (*c*) weighted average. (Round all amounts to cents.)

Check (2) Cost of goods sold: FIFO, $1,328,700; LIFO, $1,266,500; WA, $1,294,800

Shepard Company sold 4,000 units of its product at $100 per unit during the year and incurred operating expenses of $15 per unit in selling the units. It began the year with 840 units in inventory and made successive purchases of its product as follows.

Problem 5-8B[A]
Periodic: Income comparisons and cost flows
A1 P3

Jan. 1	Beginning inventory	840 units @ $58 per unit
Apr. 2	Purchase	600 units @ $59 per unit
June 14	Purchase	1,205 units @ $61 per unit
Aug. 29	Purchase	700 units @ $64 per unit
Nov. 18	Purchase	1,655 units @ $65 per unit
	Total	5,000 units

Required

1. Prepare comparative income statements similar to Exhibit 5.8 for the three inventory costing methods of FIFO, LIFO, and weighted average. (Round all amounts to cents.) Include a detailed cost of goods sold section as part of each statement. The company uses a periodic inventory system, and its income tax rate is 40%.
2. How would the financial results from using the three alternative inventory costing methods change if the company had been experiencing decreasing prices in its purchases of inventory?
3. What advantages and disadvantages are offered by using (*a*) LIFO and (*b*) FIFO? Assume the continuing trend of increasing costs.

Check (1) Net income: LIFO, $52,896; FIFO, $57,000; WA, $55,200

The records of Macklin Co. provide the following information for the year ended December 31.

Problem 5-9B[B]
Retail inventory method
P4

	At Cost	At Retail
Beginning inventory, January 1	$ 90,022	$115,610
Cost of goods purchased	502,250	761,830
Sales		782,300
Sales returns.........................		3,460

Required

1. Use the retail inventory method to estimate the company's year-end inventory.
2. A year-end physical inventory at retail prices yields a total inventory of $80,450. Prepare a calculation showing the company's loss from shrinkage at cost and at retail.

Check (1) Inventory, $66,555 cost
(2) Inventory shortage at cost, $12,251.25

Problem 5-10B^B
Gross profit method
P4

Otingo Equipment Co. wants to prepare interim financial statements for the first quarter. The company wishes to avoid making a physical count of inventory. Otingo's gross profit rate averages 35%. The following information for the first quarter is available from its records.

Beginning inventory, January 1	$ 802,880
Cost of goods purchased	2,209,636
Sales	3,760,260
Sales returns	79,300

Check   Est. ending
inventory, $619,892

Required

Use the gross profit method to estimate the company's first-quarter ending inventory.

SERIAL PROBLEM
Business Solutions

A3   P2

This serial problem began in Chapter 1 and continues through most of the book. If previous chapter segments were not completed, the serial problem can begin at this point.

SP 5
Part A

Santana Rey of **Business Solutions** is evaluating her inventory to determine whether it must be adjusted based on lower of cost or market rules. Business Solutions has three different types of software in its inventory, and the following information is available for each.

©Alexander Image/Shutterstock

Inventory Items	Units	Cost per Unit	Market per Unit
Office productivity	3	$ 76	$ 74
Desktop publishing.	2	103	100
Accounting	3	90	96

Required

Compute the lower of cost or market for ending inventory assuming Rey applies the lower of cost or market rule to each product in inventory. Must Rey adjust the reported inventory value? Explain.

Part B

Selected accounts and balances for the three months ended March 31, 2020, for Business Solutions follow.

Beginning inventory, January 1	$ 0
Cost of goods sold	14,052
Ending inventory, March 31	704

Required

1. Compute inventory turnover and days' sales in inventory for the three months ended March 31, 2020.
2. Assess the company's performance if competitors average 15 times for inventory turnover and 25 days for days' sales in inventory.

Accounting Analysis

COMPANY ANALYSIS

C2   A3

APPLE

AA 5-1   Use **Apple**'s financial statements in Appendix A to answer the following.

Required

1. What amount of inventories did Apple report as a current asset (*a*) on September 30, 2017? (*b*) On September 24, 2016?
2. Inventories make up what percent of total assets (*a*) on September 30, 2017? (*b*) On September 24, 2016?
3. Assuming Apple has enough inventory to meet demand, does Apple prefer inventory to be a lower or higher percentage of total assets?
4. Compute (*a*) inventory turnover for fiscal year ended September 30, 2017, and (*b*) days' sales in inventory as of September 30, 2017.

AA 5-2   Comparative figures for **Apple** and **Google** follow.

	Apple			Google		
$ millions	Current Year	One Year Prior	Two Years Prior	Current Year	One Year Prior	Two Years Prior
Inventory..............	$ 4,855	$ 2,132	$ 2,349	$ 749	$ 268	$ 491
Cost of sales	141,048	131,376	140,089	45,583	35,138	28,164

Required

1. Compute inventory turnover for each company for the most recent two years shown.
2. Compute days' sales in inventory for each company for the three years shown.
3. In the current year, does (*a*) Apple's and (*b*) Google's inventory turnover underperform or outperform the industry (assumed) average of 15?

AA 5-3   Key figures for **Samsung** follow.

₩ millions	Current Year	One Year Prior	Two Years Prior
Inventory..............	₩ 24,983,355	₩ 18,353,503	₩ 18,811,794
Cost of sales	129,290,661	120,277,715	123,482,118

Required

1. Compute Samsung's (*a*) inventory turnover and (*b*) days' sales in inventory for the most recent two years.
2. Is Samsung's inventory turnover on a favorable or unfavorable trend?
3. In the current year, does Samsung's inventory turnover underperform or outperform the industry (assumed) average of 15?

Beyond the Numbers

BTN 5-1   Golf Challenge Corp. is a retail sports store carrying golf apparel and equipment. The store is at the end of its second year of operation and is struggling. A major problem is that its cost of inventory has continually increased in the past two years. In the first year of operations, the store assigned inventory costs using LIFO. A loan agreement the store has with its bank, its prime source of financing, requires the store to maintain a certain profit margin and current ratio. The store's owner is currently looking over Golf Challenge's preliminary financial statements for its second year. The numbers are not favorable. The only way the store can meet the financial ratios agreed on with the bank is to change from LIFO to FIFO. The store originally decided on LIFO because of its tax advantages. The owner recalculates ending inventory using FIFO and submits those numbers and statements to the loan officer for the required bank review. The owner thankfully reflects on the available latitude in choosing the inventory costing method.

Required

1. How does Golf Challenge's use of FIFO improve its net profit margin and current ratio?
2. Is the action by Golf Challenge's owner ethical? Explain.

BTN 5-2   You are a financial adviser with a client in the wholesale produce business that just completed its first year of operations. Due to weather conditions, the cost of acquiring produce to resell has escalated during the latter part of this period. Your client, Javonte Gish, mentions that because her business sells perishable goods, she has striven to maintain a FIFO flow of goods. Although sales are good, the increasing cost of inventory has put the business in a tight cash position. Gish has expressed concern regarding the ability of the business to meet income tax obligations.

Required

Prepare a memorandum that identifies, explains, and justifies the inventory method you recommend that Ms. Gish adopt.

TAKING IT TO THE NET

A3

APPLE

BTN 5-3   Access the September 30, 2017, 10-K report for **Apple, Inc.** (ticker: AAPL), filed on November 3, 2017, from the EDGAR filings at **SEC.gov**.

Required

1. What products are manufactured by Apple?
2. What inventory method does Apple use? *Hint:* See Note 1 to its financial statements.
3. Compute its gross margin and gross margin ratio for the 2017 fiscal year. Comment on your computations—assume an industry average of 40% for the gross margin ratio.
4. Compute its inventory turnover and days' sales in inventory for the year ended September 30, 2017. Comment on your computations—assume an industry average of 15 for inventory turnover and 9 for days' sales in inventory.

TEAMWORK IN ACTION

A1   P1

Point: Step 1 allows four choices or areas for expertise. Larger teams will have some duplication of choice, but the specific identification method should not be duplicated.

BTN 5-4   Each team member has the responsibility to become an expert on an inventory method. This expertise will be used to facilitate teammates' understanding of the concepts relevant to that method.

1. Each learning team member should select an area for expertise by choosing one of the following inventory methods: specific identification, LIFO, FIFO, or weighted average.
2. Form expert teams made up of students who have selected the same area of expertise. The instructor will identify where each expert team will meet.
3. Using the following data, each expert team must collaborate to develop a presentation that illustrates the relevant concepts and procedures for its inventory method. Each team member must write the presentation in a format that can be shown to the learning team.

Data

The company uses a *perpetual* inventory system. It had the following beginning inventory and current-year purchases of its product.

Jan.	1	Beginning inventory	50 units @ $100 = $ 5,000
Jan.	14	Purchase	150 units @ $120 = 18,000
Apr.	30	Purchase	200 units @ $150 = 30,000
Sep.	26	Purchase	300 units @ $200 = 60,000

The company transacted sales on the following dates at a $350 per unit sales price.

Jan.	10	30 units.	specific cost: 30 @ $100
Feb.	15	100 units.	specific cost: 100 @ $120
Oct.	5	350 units.	specific cost: 100 @ $150 and 250 @ $200

Concepts and Procedures to Illustrate in Expert Presentation

a. Identify and compute the costs to assign to the units sold. (Round per unit costs to three decimals.)
b. Identify and compute the costs to assign to the units in ending inventory. (Round inventory balances to the dollar.)
c. How likely is it that this inventory costing method will reflect the actual physical flow of goods? How relevant is that factor in determining whether this is an acceptable method to use?
d. What is the impact of this method versus others in determining net income and income taxes?
e. How closely does the ending inventory amount reflect replacement cost?

4. Re-form learning teams. In rotation, each expert is to present to the team the presentation developed in part 3. Experts are to encourage and respond to questions.

ENTREPRENEURIAL DECISION

A3

BTN 5-5   Review the chapter's opening feature highlighting Danny Meyer and **Shake Shack**. Assume that the business consistently maintains an inventory level of $30,000, meaning that its average and ending inventory levels are the same. Also assume its annual cost of sales is $120,000. To cut costs, the business proposes to slash inventory to a constant level of $15,000 with no impact on cost of sales. The business plans to work with suppliers to get quicker deliveries and to order smaller quantities more often.

Required

1. Compute the company's inventory turnover and its days' sales in inventory under (*a*) current conditions and (*b*) proposed conditions.
2. Evaluate and comment on the merits of the proposal given your analysis for part 1. Identify any concerns you might have about the proposal.

BTN 5-6 Visit four retail stores with another classmate. In each store, identify whether the store uses a bar coding system to help manage its inventory. Try to find at least one store that does not use bar coding. If a store does not use bar coding, ask the store's manager or clerk whether he or she knows which type of inventory method the store employs. Create a table that shows columns for the name of store visited, type of merchandise sold, use or nonuse of bar coding, and the inventory method used if bar coding is not employed. You also might inquire as to what the store's inventory turnover is and how often physical inventory is taken.

HITTING THE ROAD

C1   C2

6 Cash, Fraud, and Internal Control

Chapter Preview

FRAUD AND INTERNAL CONTROL

C1 Purpose and principles of controls

Technology and controls

Limitations of controls

NTK 6-1

CONTROL OF CASH

C2 Definition and reporting of cash

P1 Control of cash receipts and cash payments

NTK 6-2

TOOLS OF CONTROL AND ANALYSIS

P2 Control of petty cash

P3 Bank reconciliation as a control tool

A1 Assessing liquidity

NTK 6-3, 6-4

Learning Objectives

CONCEPTUAL

C1 Define internal control and identify its purpose and principles.

C2 Define cash and cash equivalents and explain how to report them.

ANALYTICAL

A1 Compute the days' sales uncollected ratio and use it to assess liquidity.

PROCEDURAL

P1 Apply internal control to cash receipts and payments.

P2 Explain and record petty cash fund transactions.

P3 Prepare a bank reconciliation.

P4 *Appendix 6A*—Describe use of documentation and verification to control cash payments.

Taking Care of Business

"Take the risks"—**SHEILA MARCELO**

WALTHAM, MA—Sheila Marcelo was in college when her first child was born. "We had to scramble for child care throughout our college years," recalls Sheila. "It was harder than it should have been."

The struggle to find child care led Sheila to start **Care.com** (**Care.com**). Care.com matches caregivers with families online.

A key part of Care.com's business is its internal control systems. Sheila explains that controls are important to Care.com's future, to the integrity of its systems, and to the trust of its members. Her controls extend to monitoring transactions and safeguarding its assets and members.

Sheila insists that controls raise productivity, cut expenses, reduce fraud, and enhance the member experience. "People fear finance [and accounting] courses," admits Sheila. "[But] if you want to be an entrepreneur," declares Sheila, "don't underestimate the value of skills learned in those classes."

Sheila offers two suggestions for pursuing a business. First, "don't worry about how you're being perceived . . . about fitting into the mold." Second, "to grow in leadership, you have to be a

©Jin Lee/Bloomberg/Getty Images

narcissist." Adds Sheila, "Focus on yourself, understand yourself, take time for yourself. It will make you a better leader."

Sources: *Care.com website,* January 2019; *EAK,* October 2016; *Business Insider,* March 2014; *Boston Globe,* August 2014; *Bloomberg,* September 2012

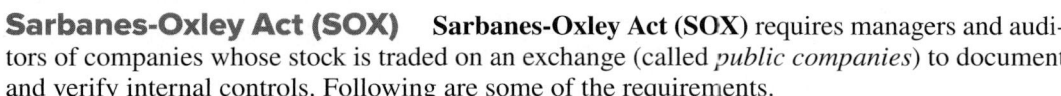

FRAUD AND INTERNAL CONTROL

Purpose of Internal Control

Managers or owners of small businesses often control the entire operation. They know if the business is actually receiving the assets and services it paid for. Most companies, however, cannot maintain personal supervision and must rely on internal controls.

C1 _____
Define internal control and identify its purpose and principles.

Internal Control System

Managers use an internal control system to monitor and control business activities. An **internal control system** is policies and procedures used to

- Protect assets.
- Ensure reliable accounting.
- Promote efficient operations.
- Uphold company policies.

Managers use internal control systems to prevent avoidable losses, plan operations, and monitor company and employee performance. For example, internal controls for **UnitedHealth Group** protect patient records and privacy.

©Wright Studio/Shutterstock

Sarbanes-Oxley Act (SOX)

Sarbanes-Oxley Act (SOX) requires managers and auditors of companies whose stock is traded on an exchange (called *public companies*) to document and verify internal controls. Following are some of the requirements.

- The company must have effective internal controls.
- Auditors must evaluate internal controls.
- Violators receive harsh penalties—up to 25 years in prison with fines.
- Auditors' work is overseen by the *Public Company Accounting Oversight Board* (PCAOB).

Committee of Sponsoring Organizations (COSO)

Committee of Sponsoring Organizations (COSO) lists five ingredients of internal control that add to the quality of accounting information.

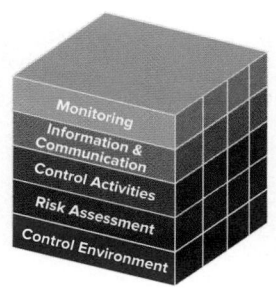

- **Control environment**—company structure, ethics, and integrity for internal control.
- **Risk assessment**—identify, analyze, and manage risk factors.
- **Control activities**—policies and procedures to reduce risk of loss.
- **Information & communication**—reports to internal and external parties.
- **Monitoring**—regular review of internal control effectiveness.

Principles of Internal Control

Internal control varies from company to company, but internal control principles apply to all companies. The **principles of internal control** are to

1. Establish responsibilities.
2. Maintain adequate records.
3. Insure assets and bond key employees.
4. Separate recordkeeping from custody of assets.
5. Divide responsibility for related transactions.
6. Apply technological controls.
7. Perform regular and independent reviews.

A control system is only as strong as its weakest link

Point: Many companies have a mandatory vacation policy for employees who handle cash. When another employee must cover for the one on vacation, it is more difficult to hide cash frauds.

Establish Responsibilities   Responsibility for a task should be clearly established and assigned to one person. When a problem occurs in a company where responsibility is not established, determining who is at fault is difficult. For example, if two salesclerks share the same cash register and cash is missing, neither clerk can be held accountable. To prevent this problem, a company can use separate cash drawers for each clerk.

Maintain Adequate Records   Good recordkeeping helps protect assets and helps managers monitor company activities. When there are detailed records of equipment, for example, items are unlikely to be lost or stolen without detection. Similarly, transactions are less likely to be entered in wrong accounts if a chart of accounts is used. Preprinted forms are also part of good internal control. When sales slips are properly designed, employees can record information efficiently with fewer errors. When sales slips are prenumbered, each slip is the responsibility of one salesperson, preventing the salesperson from stealing cash by making a sale and destroying the sales slip. Computerized point-of-sale systems achieve the same control results.

Courtesy of Commercial Collection Agency Association of the Commercial Law League of America

Point: ACFE estimates that employee fraud costs more than $150,000 per incident.

Insure Assets and Bond Key Employees   Assets should be insured against losses, and employees handling lots of cash and easily transferable assets should be bonded. An employee is *bonded* when a company purchases an insurance policy, or a bond, against theft by that employee. Bonding discourages theft because bonded employees know the bonding company will pursue reported theft.

Separate Recordkeeping from Custody of Assets   A person who controls or has access to an asset must not have access to that asset's accounting records. This principle reduces the risk of theft or waste of an asset because the person with control over it knows that another person keeps its records. Also, a recordkeeper who does not have access to the asset has no reason to falsify records. This means that to steal an asset and hide the theft from the records, two or more people must *collude*—or agree in secret to commit the fraud.

Divide Responsibility for Related Transactions   Responsibility for a transaction should be divided between two or more individuals or departments. This ensures the work of one person acts as a check on the other to prevent fraud and errors. This principle, called *separation of duties,* does not mean duplication of work. For example, when a company orders inventory, the task should be split among several employees. One employee submits a request to purchase inventory, a second employee approves the request, a third employee makes the payment, and a fourth employee records the transaction.

Apply Technological Controls   Cash registers, time clocks, and ID scanners are examples of devices that can improve internal control. A cash register with a locked-in tape or electronic file makes a record of each cash sale. A time clock records the exact hours worked by an employee. ID scanners limit access to authorized individuals.

Perform Regular and Independent Reviews   Regular reviews of internal controls help ensure that procedures are followed. These reviews are preferably done by auditors not directly involved in the activities. Auditors evaluate the efficiency and effectiveness of internal controls. Many companies pay for audits by independent auditors. These auditors test the company's financial records and evaluate the effectiveness of internal controls.

 Decision Maker ═══════════════════════════════════════

Entrepreneur   As owner of a start-up surfboard company, you hire a systems analyst. The analyst sees that your company employs only two workers. She says that as owner you must serve as a compensating control. What does the analyst mean? ■   *Answer:* Transaction authorization, recording, and asset custody are ideally handled by three employees. Many small businesses do not employ three workers. In such cases, an owner must make sure that the lack of separation of duties does not result in fraud.

©EpicStockMedia/iStockphoto/
Getty Images

Technology, Fraud, and Internal Control

Principles of internal control are relevant no matter what the technological state of the accounting system, from manual to fully automated. Technology allows us quicker access to information and improves managers' abilities to monitor and control business activities. This section describes technological impacts we must be alert to.

Reduced Processing Errors   Technology reduces, but does not eliminate, errors in processing information. Less human involvement can cause data entry errors to go undiscovered. Also, errors in software can produce consistent but inaccurate processing of transactions.

Point: Internal control failure reduces confidence in financial statements.

More Extensive Testing of Records   When accounting records are kept manually, only small samples of data are usually checked for accuracy. When data are accessible using technology, large samples or even the entire database can be tested quickly.

New Evidence of Processing   Technology makes it possible to record additional transaction details not possible with manual systems. For example, a system can record who made the entry, the date and time, the source of the entry, and so on. This means that internal control depends more on the design and operation of the information system and less on the analysis of its resulting documents.

Point: To assess a company's internal controls, review the auditor's report, management report on controls (if available), management discussion and analysis, and financial press.

Separation of Duties   A company with few employees risks losing separation of duties. For example, the person who designs the information system should not operate it. The company also must separate control over programs and files from the activities related to cash receipts and payments. For example, a computer operator should not control check-writing activities.

Increased E-Commerce   **Amazon** and **eBay** are examples of successful e-commerce companies. All e-commerce transactions involve at least three risks: (1) credit card number theft, (2) computer viruses, and (3) impersonation or identity theft. Companies use technological internal controls to combat these risks.

 Decision Insight ═══════════════════════════════════════

Butterfingers   Internal control failures can cost a company and its customers millions. Amazon learned the hard way when its web services failed. This failure led hundreds of websites to slow down. Reports say this failure cost companies in the S&P 500 index $150 million. The culprit? A typo in Amazon's code. ■

Limitations of Internal Control

Internal controls have limitations from (1) human error or fraud and (2) the cost-benefit principle.
   Human error occurs from carelessness, misjudgment, or confusion. *Human fraud* is intentionally defeating internal controls, such as management override, for personal gain. Human fraud is driven by the *triple threat* of fraud.

- **Opportunity**—internal control weaknesses in a business.
- **Pressure**—financial, family, and societal stresses to succeed.
- **Rationalization**—employees justifying fraudulent behavior.

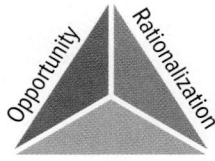

Opportunity

Rationalization

Financial Pressure

The *cost-benefit principle* says that the costs of internal controls must not exceed their benefits. Analysis of costs and benefits considers all factors, including morale. For example, most companies have a legal right to read employees' e-mails but rarely do unless there is evidence of potential harm.

Hacker's Guide to Cyberspace

Pharming Viruses attached to e-mails and websites monitor keystrokes; when you sign on to financial websites, it steals your passwords.

Phishing Hackers send e-mails to you posing as banks; you are asked for information using fake websites where they steal your passwords and personal data.

Wi-Phishing Cybercrooks set up wireless networks hoping you will use them to connect to the web; passwords and data are stolen when you connect.

Bot-Networking Hackers send out spam and viruses from your PC.

Typo-Squatting Hackers set up websites with addresses similar to legit businesses; when you make a typo and hit their sites, they infect your PC.

NEED-TO-KNOW 6-1

Internal Controls

C1

Do More: QS 6-1, E 6-1, E 6-2, E 6-3, P 6-1

Identify each of the following as a (a) purpose of an internal control system, (b) principle of internal control, or (c) limitation of internal control.

_____ **1.** Protect assets
_____ **2.** Establish responsibilities
_____ **3.** Human error
_____ **4.** Maintain adequate records
_____ **5.** Apply technological controls
_____ **6.** Ensure reliable accounting
_____ **7.** Insure assets and bond key employees
_____ **8.** Human fraud
_____ **9.** Separate recordkeeping from custody of assets
_____ **10.** Divide responsibility for related transactions
_____ **11.** Cost-benefit principle
_____ **12.** Promote efficient operations
_____ **13.** Perform regular and independent reviews
_____ **14.** Uphold company policies

Solution

1. a   **2.** b   **3.** c   **4.** b   **5.** b   **6.** a   **7.** b   **8.** c   **9.** b   **10.** b   **11.** c   **12.** a   **13.** b   **14.** a

---

CONTROL OF CASH

C2

Define cash and cash equivalents and explain how to report them.

Cash is easily hidden and moved. Internal controls protect cash and meet three guidelines.

1. Handling cash is separate from recordkeeping of cash.
2. Cash receipts are promptly deposited in a bank.
3. Cash payments are made by check or electronic funds transfer (EFT).

The first guideline applies separation of duties to minimize errors and fraud. When duties are separated, two or more people must collude to steal cash and hide this action. The second guideline uses immediate deposits of all cash receipts to produce an independent record of the cash received. It also reduces the chance of cash theft (or loss). The third guideline uses payments by check to develop an independent record of cash payments. It also reduces the risk of cash theft (or loss).

Cash, Cash Equivalents, and Liquidity

Liquidity refers to a company's ability to pay for its current liabilities. Cash and similar assets are called **liquid assets** because they can be readily used to pay for liabilities.

Cash includes currency, coins, and deposits in bank accounts. Cash also includes items that can be deposited in these accounts such as customer checks, cashier's checks, certified checks, and money orders. **Cash equivalents** are short-term, highly liquid investment assets meeting two criteria: (1) readily convertible to a known cash amount and (2) close enough to their due date so that their market value will not greatly change. Only investments within three months of their due date usually meet these criteria. Cash equivalents are short-term investments such as U.S. Treasury bills. Most companies combine cash equivalents with cash on the balance sheet.

Point: The most liquid assets are usually reported first on a balance sheet; the least liquid assets are reported last.

Point: Companies invest idle cash in cash equivalents to increase income.

Cash Management

A common reason companies fail is inability to manage cash. Companies must plan both cash receipts and cash payments. Goals of cash management are to

1. Plan cash receipts to meet cash payments when due.
2. Keep a minimum level of cash necessary to operate.

The *treasurer* is responsible for cash management. Effective cash management involves applying the following cash management strategies.

- **Encourage collection of receivables.** The quicker customers and others pay the company, the quicker it can use the money. Some companies offer discounts for quicker payments.
- **Delay payment of liabilities.** The more delayed a company is in paying others, the more time it has to use the money. Companies regularly wait to pay bills until the last day allowed.
- **Keep only necessary assets.** Acquiring expensive and rarely used assets can cause cash shortages. Some companies lease warehouses or rent equipment to avoid large up-front payments.
- **Plan expenditures.** Companies must look at seasonal and business cycles to plan expenditures when money is available.
- **Invest excess cash.** Excess cash earns no return and should be invested in productive assets like factories. Excess cash from seasonal cycles can be placed in a short-term investment for interest.

Control of Cash Receipts

Internal control of cash receipts ensures that cash received is properly recorded and deposited. Cash receipts arise from transactions such as cash sales, collections of customer accounts, receipts of interest, bank loans, sales of assets, and owner investments. This section explains internal control over two types of cash receipts: over-the-counter and by mail.

P1_____

Apply internal control to cash receipts and payments.

Over-the-Counter Cash Receipts

Over-the-counter cash sales should be recorded on a cash register after each sale, and customers should get a receipt. Cash registers should hold a permanent, locked-in record of each transaction. The register is often linked with the accounting system. Less advanced registers record each transaction on a paper tape or electronic file locked inside the register.

Custody over cash should be separate from recordkeeping. The clerk who has access to cash in the register should not have access to its record. At the end of the clerk's work period, the clerk should count the cash in the register, record the amount, and turn over the cash and record to the company cashier. The cashier, like the clerk, has access to the cash but should not have access to accounting records (or the register tape or file). A third employee, often a supervisor, compares the record of total register transactions with the cash receipts reported by the cashier. This record is used for a journal entry recording over-the-counter cash receipts. The third employee has access to the records for cash but not to the actual cash. The clerk and the cashier have access to cash but not to the accounting

Point: Many businesses have signs that read: If you receive no receipt, your purchase is free! This helps ensure that clerks ring up all transactions on registers.

records. None of them can make a mistake or steal cash without the difference being noticed (see the following diagram).

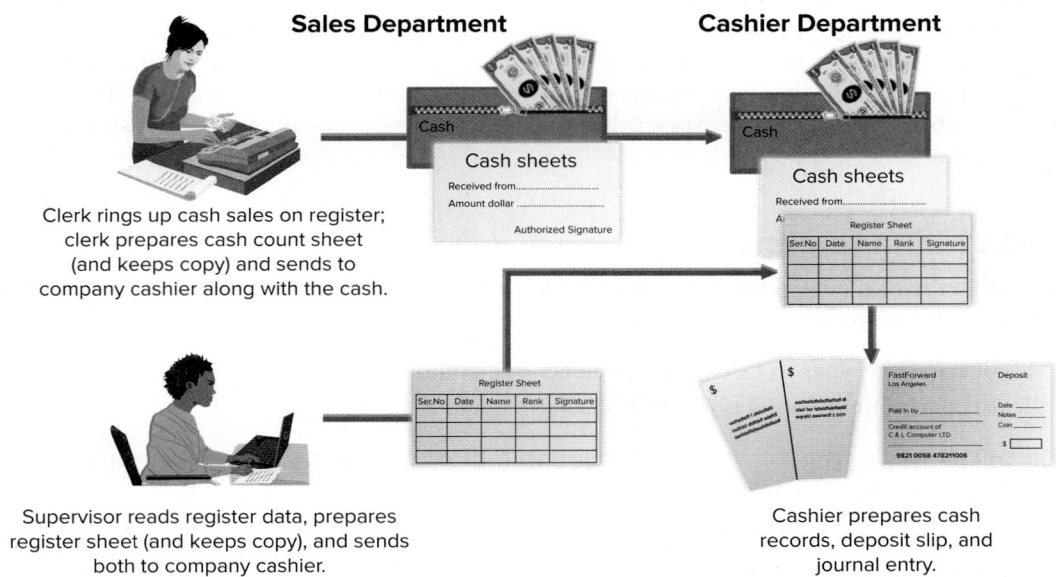

Sales Department   **Cashier Department**

Clerk rings up cash sales on register; clerk prepares cash count sheet (and keeps copy) and sends to company cashier along with the cash.

Supervisor reads register data, prepares register sheet (and keeps copy), and sends both to company cashier.

Cashier prepares cash records, deposit slip, and journal entry.

Cash Over and Short

One or more customers can be given too much or too little change. This means that at the end of a work period, the cash in a cash register might not equal the record of cash receipts. This difference is reported in the **Cash Over and Short** account, also called *Cash Short and Over,* which is an income statement account recording the income effects of cash overages and cash shortages. If a cash register's record shows $550 but the count of cash in the register is $555, the entry to record cash sales and its overage is

Assets = Liabilities + Equity
+555   + 5
               +550

Cash...	555	
Cash Over and Short..............................		5
Sales..		550
Record cash sales and a cash overage.		

Alternatively, if a cash register's record shows $625 but the count of cash in the register is $621, the entry to record cash sales and its shortage is

Assets = Liabilities + Equity
+621   − 4
               +625

Cash...	621	
Cash Over and Short.................................	4	
Sales..		625
Record cash sales and a cash shortage.		

Because customers are more likely to dispute being shortchanged than being given too much change, the Cash Over and Short account usually has a debit balance. A debit balance reflects an expense. It is reported on the income statement as part of selling, general, and administrative expenses. (Because the amount is usually small, it is often reported as part of *miscellaneous expenses*—or as part of *miscellaneous revenues* if it has a credit balance.)

Cash Receipts by Mail

Two people are assigned the task of opening the mail. In this case, theft of cash receipts by mail requires collusion between these two employees. The person(s) opening the mail enters a list (in triplicate) of money received. This list has each sender's name, the amount, and an explanation of why the money was sent. The first copy is sent with the money to the cashier. A second copy is sent to the recordkeeper. A third copy is kept by the person(s) who opened the mail. The cashier deposits the money in a bank, and the recordkeeper records the amounts received.

This process is good internal control because the bank's record of cash deposited must agree with the records from each of the three. If the mail person(s) does not report all receipts correctly, customers will question their account balances. If the cashier does not deposit all the cash, the bank balance does not agree with the recordkeeper's cash balance. The recordkeeper does not have access to cash and has no opportunity to steal cash. This system makes errors and fraud highly unlikely. The exception is employee collusion.

■ Decision Insight

Cash Register Insight   **Walmart** uses a network of information links with its point-of-sale cash registers to coordinate sales, purchases, and distribution. Its stores ring up tens of thousands of separate sales on heavy days. By using cash register information, the company can fix pricing mistakes quickly and capitalize on sales trends. ■

©Amble Design/Shutterstock

Control of Cash Payments

Control of cash payments is important as most large thefts occur from payment of fictitious invoices. One key to controlling cash payments is to require all payments to be made by check. The only exception is small payments made from petty cash. Another key is to deny access to accounting records to anyone other than the owner who has the authority to sign checks. A small-business owner often signs checks and knows that the items being paid for are actually received. Large businesses cannot maintain personal supervision and must rely on internal controls described here, including the voucher system and petty cash system.

Cash Budget   Projected cash receipts and cash payments are summarized in a *cash budget*. If there is enough cash for operations, companies wish to minimize the cash they hold because of its risk of theft and its low return versus other assets.

Voucher System of Control   A **voucher system** is a set of procedures and approvals designed to control cash payments and the acceptance of liabilities that consist of

- Verifying, approving, and recording liabilities for cash payment.
- Issuing checks for payment of verified, approved, and recorded liabilities.

A voucher system's control over cash payments begins when a company incurs a liability that will result in cash payment. The system only allows authorized departments and individuals to incur liabilities and limits the type of liabilities. In a large retail store, for example, only a purchasing department is authorized to incur liabilities for inventory. Purchasing, receiving, and paying for merchandise are divided among several departments (or individuals). These departments include the one requesting the purchase, the purchasing department, the receiving department, and the accounting department.

To coordinate and control responsibilities of these departments, a company uses several different business documents. Exhibit 6.1 shows how documents are accumulated in a **voucher,** which is an internal document (or file) used to collect information to control cash payments and to ensure that a transaction is properly recorded. This specific example begins with a *purchase requisition* and ends with issuing a *check*.

Point: A purchase requisition is a request to purchase merchandise.

A voucher system should be applied to all payments (except those using petty cash). When a company receives a monthly telephone bill, it should review the charges, prepare a voucher (file), and insert the bill. This transaction is then recorded. If the amount is due, a check is issued. If not, the voucher is filed for payment on its due date. Without records, an employee could collude with a supplier to get more than one payment, payment for excessive amounts, or payment for goods and services not received. A voucher system helps prevent such frauds.

Ethical Risk

Cash Fraud   The Association of Certified Fraud Examiners (ACFE) reports that 87% of fraud is from asset theft. Of those asset thefts, a few stand out—in both frequency and median loss. Namely, cash is most frequently stolen through billing (22%) and theft (20%), followed by expense reimbursements (14%), skimming (12%), check tampering (11%), and payroll (9%). Interestingly, the average loss per incident is greatest for check tampering ($158,000) and billing ($100,000). *Source:* "Report to the Nations," ACFE. ■

EXHIBIT 6.1

Document Flow in
a Voucher System

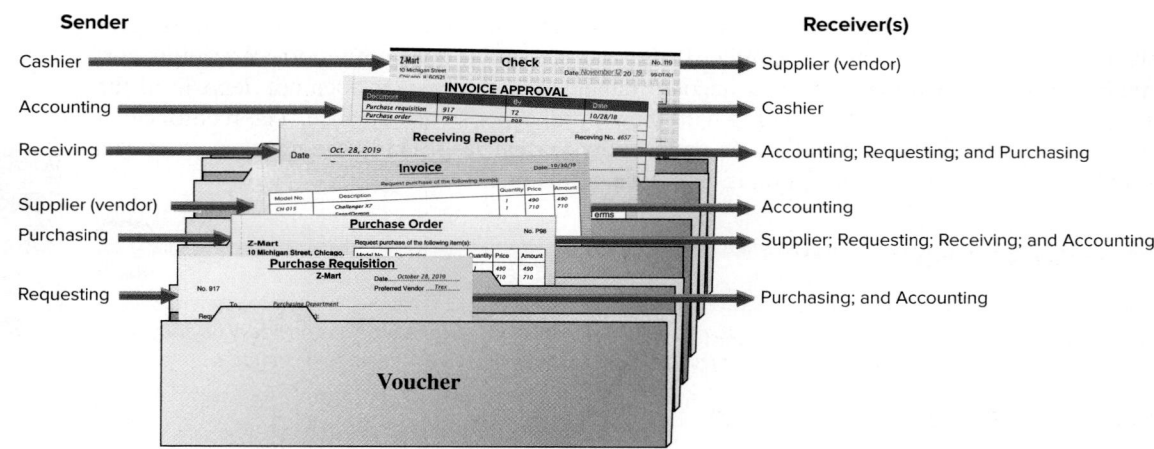

Sender		Receiver(s)
Cashier		Supplier (vendor)
Accounting		Cashier
Receiving		Accounting; Requesting; and Purchasing
Supplier (vendor)		Accounting
Purchasing		Supplier; Requesting; Receiving; and Accounting
Requesting		Purchasing; and Accounting

NEED-TO-KNOW 6-2

Control of Cash Receipts
and Payments

P1   C2

Which of the following statements are true regarding the control of cash receipts and cash payments?

_____ **1.** Over-the-counter cash sales should be recorded on a cash register after each sale.

_____ **2.** Custody over cash should be separate from the recordkeeping of cash.

_____ **3.** For control of cash receipts that arrive through the mail, two people should be present for opening that mail.

_____ **4.** One key to controlling cash payments is to require that no expenditures be made by check; instead, all expenditures should be made from petty cash.

_____ **5.** A voucher system of control should be applied only to purchases of inventory and never to other expenditures.

Do More: QS 6-2, QS 6-4,
QS 6-5, E 6-4, E 6-5, E 6-6,
E 6-7

Solution

1. True   **2.** True   **3.** True   **4.** False   **5.** False

---

P2 _____

Explain and record petty
cash fund transactions.

Petty Cash System of Control
To avoid writing checks for small amounts, a company sets up a **petty cash** system. *Petty cash payments* are small payments for items such as shipping fees, minor repairs, and low-cost supplies.

Operating a Petty Cash Fund   A petty cash fund requires estimating the amount of small payments to be made during a short period such as a week or month. A check is then drawn by the company cashier for an amount slightly in excess of this estimate. The check is cashed and given to an employee called the *petty cashier* or *petty cash custodian*. The petty cashier keeps this cash safe, makes payments from the fund, and keeps records of it in a secure *petty cashbox*.

EXHIBIT 6.2

Petty Cash Receipt

Z-Mart No. 9
PETTY CASH RECEIPT
For _Office supplies used_
Date _November 15, 2019_
Charge to _Office Supplies Exp._
Amount _$4.75_
Approved by _Jeb Gull_
Received by _Dk Fll_

When a cash payment is made, the person receiving payment signs a prenumbered *petty cash receipt,* also called *petty cash ticket*—see Exhibit 6.2. The petty cash receipt is then placed in the petty cashbox with the remaining money. Under this system, the total of all receipts plus the remaining cash equals the total fund amount. A $100 petty cash fund, for example, contains any combination of cash and petty cash receipts that totals $100 (examples are $80 cash plus $20 in receipts, or $10 cash plus $90 in receipts).

The petty cash fund is reimbursed when it is nearing zero and at the end of an accounting period. The petty cashier sorts the paid receipts by the type of expense or account and then totals the receipts. The petty cashier gives all paid receipts to the company cashier, who stamps all receipts *paid* so they cannot be reused, files them for recordkeeping, and gives the petty cashier a check. When this check is cashed and the money placed in the cashbox, the total money in the cashbox is restored to its original amount. The fund is now ready for a new cycle of petty cash payments.

Point: Companies use surprise
petty cash counts for verification.

Illustrating a Petty Cash Fund Assume Z-Mart sets up a petty cash fund on November 1. A $75 check is drawn, cashed, and the proceeds given to the petty cashier. The entry to record the setup of this petty cash fund is

Nov. 1	Petty Cash	75	
	Cash		75
	Establish a petty cash fund.		

Assets = Liabilities + Equity
+75
−75

After the petty cash fund is established, the Petty Cash account is not debited or credited again unless the amount of the fund is changed.

Next, assume that Z-Mart's petty cashier makes several November payments from petty cash. On November 27, after making a $46.50 cash payment for tile cleaning, only $3.70 cash remains in the fund. The petty cashier then summarizes and totals the petty cash receipts as shown in Exhibit 6.3.

Petty Cash Payments Report	
Miscellaneous Expense	
Nov. 27 Tile cleaning	$ 46.50
Merchandise Inventory (transportation-in)	
Nov. 5 Transport of merchandise purchased	15.05
Delivery Expense	
Nov. 18 Customer's package delivered	5.00
Office Supplies Expense	
Nov. 15 Purchase of office supplies immediately used	4.75
Total	**$71.30**

EXHIBIT 6.3

Petty Cash Payments Report

Point: This report also can include receipt number and names of those who approved and received cash payment (see Need-to-Know 6-3).

The petty cash payments report and all receipts are given to the company cashier in exchange for a $71.30 check to reimburse the fund. The petty cashier cashes the check and puts the $71.30 cash in the petty cashbox. The company records this reimbursement as follows. A petty cash fund is usually reimbursed at the end of an accounting period so that expenses are recorded in the proper period, even if the fund is not low on money.

Nov. 27	Miscellaneous Expenses....................................	46.50	
	Merchandise Inventory.....................................	15.05	
	Delivery Expense...	5.00	
	Office Supplies Expense	4.75	
	Cash*...		71.30
	Reimburse petty cash. *$75 fund bal. − $3.70 cash remaining.		

Assets = Liabilities + Equity
−71.30   −46.50
+15.05   − 5.00
               − 4.75

Increasing or Decreasing a Petty Cash Fund A decision to increase or decrease a petty cash fund is often made when reimbursing it. Assume Z-Mart decides to *increase* its petty cash fund from $75 to $100 on November 27 when it reimburses the fund. The entries required are to (1) reimburse the fund as usual (see the preceding November 27 entry) and (2) increase the fund amount as follows.

Nov. 27	Petty Cash	25	
	Cash		25
	Increase petty cash fund from $75 to $100.		

Instead, if it *decreases* the petty cash fund from $75 to $55 on November 27, the entry is

Nov. 27	Cash...	20	
	Petty Cash...		20
	Decrease petty cash fund from $75 to $55.		

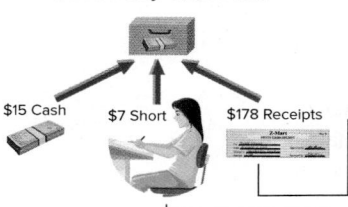

Summary of Petty Cash Accounting

Event	Petty Cash	Cash	Expenses
Set up fund	Dr.	Cr.	—
Reimburse fund.	—	Cr.	Dr.
Increase fund	Dr.	Cr.	—
Decrease fund.	Cr.	Dr.	—

$200 Petty Cash Fund

$15 Cash $7 Short $178 Receipts

Cash Over and Short

Sometimes a petty cashier fails to get a receipt for payment or overpays for the amount due. When this occurs and the fund is later reimbursed, the petty cash payments report plus the cash remaining will not equal the fund balance. This mistake causes the fund to be *short*. This shortage is recorded as an expense in the reimbursing entry with a debit to the Cash Over and Short account. (An *overage* in the petty cash fund is recorded with a credit to Cash Over and Short in the reimbursing entry.)

Following is the June 1 entry to reimburse a $200 petty cash fund when its payments report shows $178 in miscellaneous expenses and only $15 cash remains.

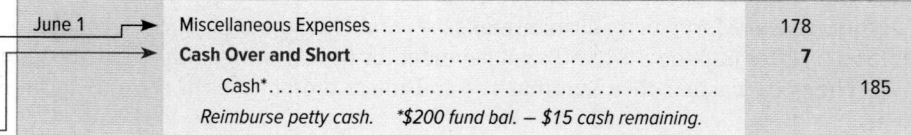

June 1	Miscellaneous Expenses.....................................	178	
	Cash Over and Short.......................................	7	
	Cash*...		185
	*Reimburse petty cash. *$200 fund bal. − $15 cash remaining.*		

Ethical Risk

Get Clued In   There are clues to fraudulent activities. Clues from accounting include (1) an increase in customer refunds—could be fake, (2) missing documents—could be used for fraud, (3) differences between bank deposits and cash receipts—could be cash embezzled, and (4) delayed recording—could reflect fraudulent records. Clues from employees include (1) lifestyle change—could be embezzlement, (2) too close with suppliers—could signal fraudulent transactions, and (3) refusal to leave job, even for vacations—could conceal fraudulent activities. ■

NEED-TO-KNOW 6-3

Petty Cash System

P2

Bacardi Company established a $150 petty cash fund with Eminem as the petty cashier. When the fund balance reached $19 cash, Eminem prepared a petty cash payments report, which follows.

Petty Cash Payments Report				
Receipt No.	Account Charged		Approved by	Received by
12	Delivery Expense	$ 29	Eminem	A. Smirnoff
13	Merchandise Inventory	18	Eminem	J. Daniels
15	(Omitted)......................	32	Eminem	C. Carlsberg
16	Miscellaneous Expense	41	(Omitted)	J. Walker
	Total	$120		

Required

1. Identify four internal control weaknesses from the petty cash payments report.
2. Prepare general journal entries to record
   a. Establishment of the petty cash fund.
   b. Reimbursement of the fund. (Assume for this part only that petty cash Receipt No. 15 was issued for miscellaneous expenses.)
3. What is the Petty Cash account balance immediately before reimbursement? After reimbursement?

Solution

1. Four internal control weaknesses that are apparent from the payments report include
   a. Petty cash Receipt No. 14 is missing. This raises questions about the petty cashier's management of the fund.
   b. The $19 cash balance means that $131 has been withdrawn ($150 − $19 = $131). However, the total amount of the petty cash receipts is only $120 ($29 + $18 + $32 + $41). The fund is $11 short of cash ($131 − $120 = $11). Management should investigate.
   c. The petty cashier (Eminem) did not sign petty cash Receipt No. 16. This could have been a mistake on his part or he might not have authorized the payment.
   d. Petty cash Receipt No. 15 does not say which account to charge. Management should check with C. Carlsberg and the petty cashier (Eminem) about the transaction. Without further information, debit Miscellaneous Expense.

2. Petty cash general journal entries.

a. Entry to establish the petty cash fund.

b. Entry to reimburse the fund.

Petty Cash.	150	
Cash.		150

Delivery Expense	29	
Merchandise Inventory	18	
Miscellaneous Expense ($41 + $32)	73	
Cash Over and Short	11	
Cash ($150 fund bal. − $19 cash rem.)		131

3. The Petty Cash account balance *always* equals its fund balance, in this case $150. This account balance does not change unless the fund is increased or decreased.

> Do More: QS 6-6, E 6-8, E 6-9, E 6-10, P 6-2, P 6-3

BANKING ACTIVITIES AS CONTROLS

Basic Bank Services

Banks safeguard cash and provide detailed records of cash transactions. They provide services and documents that help control cash, which is the focus of this section.

Bank Account, Deposit, and Check   A *bank account* is used to deposit money for safekeeping and helps control withdrawals. Persons authorized to write checks on the account must sign a **signature card,** which the bank uses to verify signatures.

Each bank deposit has a **deposit ticket,** which lists items such as currency, coins, and checks deposited along with amounts. The bank gives the customer a receipt as proof of the deposit. Exhibit 6.4 shows a deposit ticket.

Point: Firms often have multiple bank accounts for different needs and for specific transactions such as payroll.

EXHIBIT 6.4

Deposit Ticket

To withdraw money, the depositor can use a **check,** which is a document telling the bank to pay a specified amount to a designated recipient. A check involves three parties: a *maker* who signs the check, a *payee* who is the recipient, and a *bank* (or *payer*) on which the check is drawn. The bank provides the depositor the checks. Exhibit 6.5 shows one type of check. It has an optional *remittance advice* explaining the payment. The *memo* line is used for an explanation.

Electronic Funds Transfer   **Electronic funds transfer (EFT)** is the electronic transfer of cash from one party to another. Companies are increasingly using EFT because of its convenience and low cost. Payroll, rent, utilities, insurance, and interest payments are usually done by EFT. The bank statement lists cash withdrawals by EFT with the checks and other deductions. Cash receipts by EFT are listed with deposits and other additions.

EXHIBIT 6.5

Check with Remittance
Advice

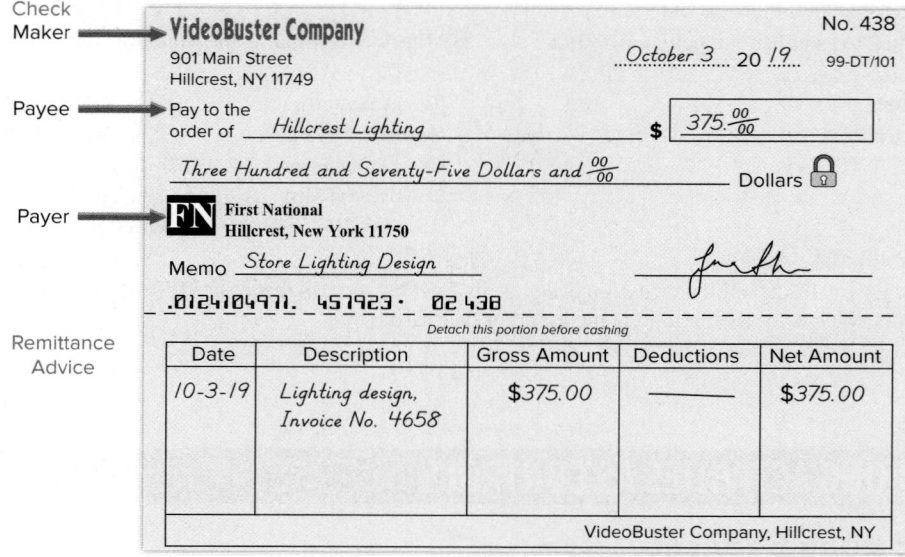

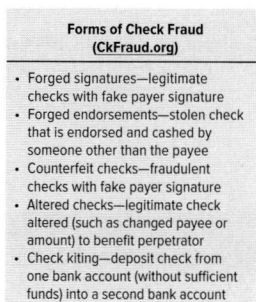

Forms of Check Fraud
(CkFraud.org)

- Forged signatures—legitimate checks with fake payer signature
- Forged endorsements—stolen check that is endorsed and cashed by someone other than the payee
- Counterfeit checks—fraudulent checks with fake payer signature
- Altered checks—legitimate check altered (such as changed payee or amount) to benefit perpetrator
- Check kiting—deposit check from one bank account (without sufficient funds) into a second bank account

Bank Statement

Point: Good control is to send a copy of the bank statement directly to a party without access to cash or recordkeeping.

Usually once a month, the bank sends a **bank statement** showing the account activity. Different banks use different formats for their bank statements, but all of them include the following.

1. Beginning-of-period account balance.
2. Checks and other debits decreasing the account during the period.
3. Deposits and other credits increasing the account during the period.
4. End-of-period account balance.

Exhibit 6.6 shows one type of bank statement. Part Ⓐ of Exhibit 6.6 summarizes changes in the account. Ⓑ lists paid checks along with other debits. Ⓒ lists deposits and credits to the account.

   Canceled checks are checks the bank has paid and deducted from the customer's account. We say such checks *cleared the bank*. Other usual deductions on a bank statement include (1) bank

EXHIBIT 6.6

Bank Statement

Bank's Liability to VideoBuster		
	Sep. 30 bal.	1,610
	CRs	1,163
DRs 723		
	Oct. 31 bal.	2,050

Point: Debit memos (DM) from the bank produce credits on the depositor's books. Credit memos (CM) from the bank produce debits on the depositor's books.

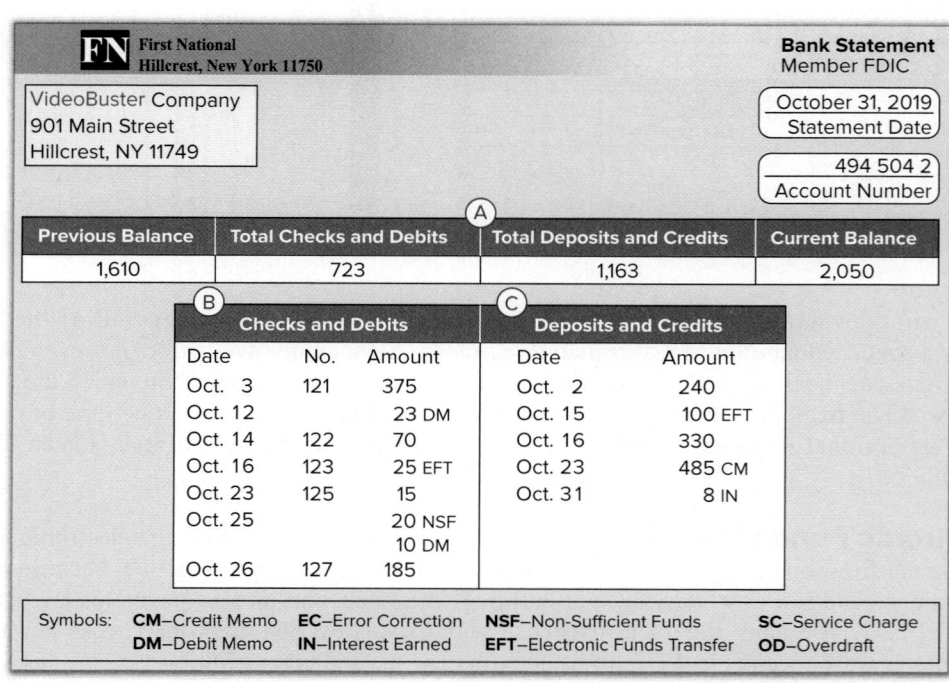

service fees, (2) checks deposited that are uncollectible, (3) corrections of previous errors, (4) withdrawals through automated teller machines (ATMs), and (5) payments arranged in advance by a depositor. A **debit memorandum** notifies a depositor of a deduction.

Increases to the depositor's account include amounts the bank collects on behalf of the depositor and the corrections of previous errors. A **credit memorandum** notifies the depositor of all increases. Banks that pay interest on checking accounts credit interest earned to the depositor's account each period. In Exhibit 6.6, the bank credits $8 of interest to the account.

Bank Reconciliation

The balance of a checking account on the bank statement rarely equals the depositor's book balance (from its records). This is due to information that one party has that the other does not. We must therefore verify the accuracy of both the depositor's records and the bank's records. To do this, we prepare a **bank reconciliation** to explain differences between the checking account balance in the depositor's records and the balance on the bank statement. The following explains bank and book adjustments.

Bank Balance Adjustments

+ **Deposits in transit** (or **outstanding deposits**). **Deposits in transit** are deposits made and recorded in the depositor's books but not yet listed on the bank statement. For example, companies can make deposits (in the night depository) after the bank is closed. If such a deposit occurred on a bank statement date, it would not appear on this period's statement. The bank would record such a deposit on the next business day, and it would appear on the next period's bank statement. Deposits mailed to the bank near the end of a period also can be in transit and not listed on the bank statement.

− **Outstanding checks. Outstanding checks** are checks written by the depositor, subtracted on the depositor's books, and sent to the payees but not yet turned in for payment at the bank statement date.

± **Bank errors.** Any errors made by the bank are accounted for in the reconciliation. To find errors, we (a) compare deposits on the bank statement with deposits in the accounting records and (b) compare canceled checks on the bank statement with checks recorded in the accounting records.

Book Balance Adjustments

+ **Interest earned and unrecorded cash receipts.** Banks sometimes collect notes for depositors. Banks also receive electronic funds transfers to the depositor's account. When a bank collects an item, it is added to the depositor's account, less any service fee. The bank statement also includes any interest earned.

− **Bank fees and NSF checks.** A company sometimes deposits another party's check that is uncollectible. This check is called a *nonsufficient funds (NSF)* check. The bank initially credits (increases) the depositor's account for the check. When the check is uncollectible, the bank debits (reduces) the depositor's account for that check. The bank may charge the depositor a fee for processing an uncollectible check. Other bank charges include printing new checks and service fees.

± **Book errors.** Any errors made by the depositor in the company books are accounted for in the reconciliation. To find errors, we use the same procedures described in the "Bank errors" section above.

Adjustments Summary   Following is a summary of bank and book adjustments. Each of these items has already been recorded by either the bank or the company, but not both.

Bank Balance Adjustments	Book Balance Adjustments
Add deposits in transit.	Add interest earned and unrecorded cash receipts.
Subtract outstanding checks.	Subtract bank fees and NSF checks.
Add or subtract corrections of bank errors.	Add or subtract corrections of book errors.

Point: Your checking account is a liability from the bank's perspective (but an asset from yours). When you make a deposit, they "credit your account." Credits increase the bank's liability to you. When you write a check or use your debit card, the bank decreases its liability to you; they "debit your account." Debits decrease the bank's liability to you.

P3_____

Prepare a bank reconciliation.

Point: *Books* refer to accounting records.

Point: The person preparing the bank reconciliation should not be responsible for processing cash receipts, managing checks, or maintaining cash records.

Point: Businesses with few employees often allow recordkeepers to both write checks and keep the general ledger. If this is done, the owner must do the bank reconciliation.

Bank Reconciliation Demonstration   In preparing the bank reconciliation, refer to Exhibit 6.7 and steps ❶ through ❽.

❶ Enter VideoBuster's bank balance of $2,050 taken from the bank statement.

❷ Add any unrecorded deposits and bank errors that understate the bank balance to the bank balance. VideoBuster's $145 deposit in the bank's night depository on October 31 is not listed on its bank statement.

❸ Subtract any outstanding checks and bank errors that overstate the bank balance from the bank balance. VideoBuster's comparison of canceled checks with its books shows two checks outstanding: No. 124 for $150 and No. 126 for $200.

❹ Compute the *adjusted bank balance*.

❺ Enter VideoBuster's cash account book balance of $1,405 taken from its accounting records.

❻ Add any unrecorded cash receipts, interest earned, and errors understating the book balance to the book balance. VideoBuster's bank statement shows the bank collected a note receivable and increased VideoBuster's account for $485. The bank statement also shows $8 for interest earned that was not yet recorded on the books.

❼ Subtract any unrecorded bank fees, NSF checks, and errors overstating the book balance from the book balance. Deductions on VideoBuster's bank statement that are not yet recorded include (a) a $23 charge for check printing and (b) an NSF check for $30. (The NSF check is dated October 16 and was in the book balance.)

❽ Compute the *adjusted book balance*.

Verify that the two adjusted balances from steps 4 and 8 are equal (reconciled).

Point: Outstanding checks are identified by comparing canceled checks on the bank statement with checks recorded. This includes identifying any outstanding checks listed on the *previous* period's bank reconciliation that are not included in the canceled checks on this period's bank statement.

EXHIBIT 6.7

Bank Reconciliation

	VIDEOBUSTER					
	Bank Reconciliation					
	October 31, 2019					
① Bank statement balance			$ 2,050	⑤ Book balance.		$ 1,405
② Add				⑥ Add		
Deposit of Oct. 31 in transit			145	Collected note	$485	
			2,195	Interest earned	8	493
③ Deduct						1,898
Outstanding checks				⑦ Deduct		
No. 124.	$150			Check printing charge	23	
No. 126.	200	350		NSF check	30	53
④ **Adjusted bank balance**			**$1,845**	⑧ **Adjusted book balance**		**$1,845**

Balances are equal (reconciled)

Adjusting Entries from a Bank Reconciliation   A bank reconciliation often finds unrecorded items that need recording by the company. In VideoBuster's reconciliation, the adjusted balance of $1,845 is the correct balance as of October 31. But the company's accounting records show a $1,405 balance. We make adjusting entries so that the book balance equals the adjusted balance. **Only items impacting the *book balance* need entries.** Exhibit 6.7 shows that four entries are required.

Collection of Note   The first entry is to record collection of a note receivable by the bank.

Assets = Liabilities + Equity
+485
−485

Oct. 31	Cash	485	
	Notes Receivable		485
	Record note collected by bank.		

Interest Earned   The second entry records interest earned.

Assets = Liabilities + Equity
+8   +8

Oct. 31	Cash	8	
	Interest Revenue.		8
	Record interest earned in checking account.		

Check Printing   The third entry records expenses for the check printing charge.

Oct. 31	Miscellaneous Expenses............................	23	
	Cash..		23
	Check printing charge.		

Assets = Liabilities + Equity
−23   −23

NSF Check   The fourth entry records the NSF check that is returned as uncollectible. The check was from T. Woods in payment of his account. The bank deducted $30 total from VideoBuster's account. This means the entry must reverse the effects of the original entry when the check was received.

Point: The company will try to collect the $30 from the customer.

Oct. 31	Accounts Receivable—T. Woods........................	30	
	Cash..		30
	Charge Woods's account for $30 NSF check.		

Assets = Liabilities + Equity
+30
−30

After these four entries are recorded, the book balance of cash is adjusted to the correct amount of $1,845 (the adjusted book balance). The Cash T-account to the side shows the computation, where entries match the steps in Exhibit 6.7.

Point: Need-to-Know 6-4 shows an adjusting entry for an error correction.

Cash			
Unadj. bal.	1,405		
⑥	485	⑦	23
⑥	8	⑦	30
Adj. bal.	1,845		

Ethical Risk ➤

Cause for Alarm   The Association of Certified Fraud Examiners (ACFE) reports that the primary factor contributing to fraud is the lack of internal controls (30%), followed by the override of existing controls (19%), lack of management review (18%), poor tone at the top (10%), and lack of competent oversight (8%). These findings highlight the importance of internal controls over cash. *Source:* "Report to the Nations," ACFE. ∎

©Redpixel.pl/Shutterstock

The following information is available to reconcile Gucci's book balance of cash with its bank statement cash balance as of December 31.

NEED-TO-KNOW 6-4

Bank Reconciliation

P3

a. The December 31 cash balance according to the accounting records is $1,610, and the bank statement cash balance for that date is $1,900.

b. Gucci's December 31 daily cash receipts of $800 were placed in the bank's night depository on December 31 but do not appear on the December 31 bank statement.

c. Gucci's comparison of canceled checks with its books shows three checks outstanding: No. 6242 for $200, No. 6273 for $400, and No. 6282 for $100.

d. When the December checks are compared with entries in the accounting records, it is found that Check No. 6267 had been correctly drawn (taken from the bank) for $340 to pay for office supplies but was erroneously entered in the accounting records as $430.

e. The bank statement shows the bank collected a note receivable and increased Gucci's account for $470. Gucci had not recorded this transaction before receiving the statement.

f. The bank statement included an NSF check for $150 received from Prada Inc. in payment of its account. It also included a $20 charge for check printing. Gucci had not recorded these transactions before receiving the statement.

Required

1. Prepare the bank reconciliation for this company as of December 31.

2. Prepare the journal entries to make Gucci's book balance of cash equal to the reconciled cash balance as of December 31.

No. 2024...............	4,810		Recording error (No. 2025) ...	120	
No. 2026...............	5,000	9,810	Service charge	40	1,260
Adjusted bank balance		**$46,020**	**Adjusted book balance**........		**$46,020**

Solutions

Required Adjusting Entries for Jamboree

Nov. 30	Cash	30,000	
	Notes Receivable		30,000
	Record collection of note.		
Nov. 30	Cash	900	
	Interest Revenue................		900
	Record collection of revenue.		
Nov. 30	Accounts Receivable—M. Welch	1,100	
	Cash..........................		1,100
	Reinstate account due from an NSF check.		

Nov. 30	Rent Expense	120	
	Cash...........................		120
	Correct recording error on Check No. 2025.		
Nov. 30	Miscellaneous Expenses	40	
	Cash...........................		40
	Record bank service charges.		

APPENDIX

6A   Documentation and Verification

P4

Describe use of documentation and verification to control cash payments.

This appendix covers the documents of a voucher system of control.

Purchase Requisition   Department managers are usually not allowed to place orders directly with suppliers for control purposes. Instead, a department manager must inform the purchasing department of its needs by preparing and signing a **purchase requisition,** which lists the merchandise requested to be purchased—see Exhibit 6A.1. Two copies of the purchase requisition are sent to the purchasing department, which then sends one copy to the accounting department. When the accounting department receives a purchase requisition, it creates and maintains a voucher for this transaction. The requesting department keeps a third copy.

EXHIBIT 6A.1

Purchase Requisition

Z-Mart			
PURCHASE REQUISITION			No. 917

From _Sporting Goods Department_   **Date** _October 28, 2019_
To _Purchasing Department_   **Preferred Vendor** _Trex_

Request purchase of the following item(s):

MODEL NO.	DESCRIPTION	QUANTITY
CH 015	Toddler—Challenger X7	1
SD 099	Boys/Girls—Speed Demon	1

Reason for Request _Replenish inventory_
Approval for Request _J.Z._

For Purchasing Department use only: Order Date _10-30-19_   P.O. No. _P98_

Purchase Order   A **purchase order** is a document the purchasing department uses to place an order with a **vendor** (seller or supplier). A purchase order authorizes a vendor to ship merchandise at the stated price and terms—see Exhibit 6A.2. When the purchasing department receives a purchase requisition, it prepares at least five copies of a purchase order. The copies are distributed as follows: *copy 1* to the vendor as a purchase request to ship merchandise; *copy 2,* along with a copy of the purchase requisition, to the accounting department, where it is entered in the voucher and used in approving payment of the invoice; *copy 3* to the requesting department to inform its manager of the purchase; *copy 4* to the receiving department without order quantity so it can compare with goods received and provide an independent count of goods received; and *copy 5* kept on file by the purchasing department.

Point: This appendix shows one example of a common voucher system design, but *not* the only design.

Invoice   An **invoice** is an itemized statement of goods prepared by the vendor listing the customer's name, items sold, sales prices, and terms of sale. An invoice is also a bill sent to the buyer from the supplier. From the vendor's point of view, it is a *sales invoice.* The buyer, or **vendee,** treats it as a *purchase*

uncollected for the current year. Starbucks took less time to collect its receivables. The less time money is tied up in receivables, the better.

Decision Maker

Sales Representative   The sales staff are told to help reduce days' sales uncollected for cash management purposes. What can you, a salesperson, do to reduce days' sales uncollected? ■   *Answer:* A salesperson can (1) push cash sales over credit, (2) identify customers most delayed in their payments and require earlier payments or cash sales, and (3) eliminate credit sales to customers that never pay.

Prepare a bank reconciliation for Jamboree Enterprises for the month ended November 30. The following information is available as of November 30.

NEED-TO-KNOW 6-5

COMPREHENSIVE

Preparing Bank Reconciliation and Adjusting Entries

a. On November 30, the company's book balance of cash is $16,380, but its bank statement shows a $38,520 balance.

b. Checks No. 2024 for $4,810 and No. 2026 for $5,000 are outstanding.

c. In comparing the canceled checks on the bank statement with the entries in the accounting records, it is found that Check No. 2025 in payment of rent is correctly drawn (taken from the bank) for $1,000 but is erroneously entered in the accounting records as $880.

d. The November 30 deposit of $17,150 was placed in the night depository after banking hours on that date, and this amount does not appear on the bank statement.

e. In reviewing the bank statement, a check written by Jumbo Enterprises in the amount of $160 was erroneously drawn against Jamboree's account.

f. The bank statement says that the bank collected a $30,000 note and $900 of interest was earned. These transactions were not recorded by Jamboree prior to receiving the statement.

g. The bank statement lists a $1,100 NSF check received from a customer, Marilyn Welch. Jamboree had not recorded the return of this check before receiving the statement.

h. Bank service charges for November total $40. These charges were not recorded by Jamboree before receiving the statement.

PLANNING THE SOLUTION

- Set up a bank reconciliation (as in Exhibit 6.7).
- Examine each item *a* through *h* to determine whether it affects the book or the bank balance and whether it should be added or subtracted.
- After all items are analyzed, complete the reconciliation and arrive at a reconciled balance between the bank side and the book side.
- For each reconciling item on the book side, prepare an adjusting entry. Additions to the book side require an adjusting entry that debits Cash. Deductions on the book side require an adjusting entry that credits Cash.

SOLUTION

JAMBOREE ENTERPRISES Bank Reconciliation November 30					
Bank statement balance.......		$ 38,520	Book balance		$ 16,380
Add			Add		
Deposit of Nov. 30	$17,150		Collection of note...........	$30,000	
Bank error (Jumbo)	160	17,310	Interest earned.............	900	30,900
		55,830			47,280
Deduct			Deduct		
Outstanding checks			NSF check (M. Welch)........	1,100	
No. 2024................	4,810		Recording error (No. 2025) ...	120	
No. 2026................	5,000	9,810	Service charge	40	1,260
Adjusted bank balance		**$46,020**	**Adjusted book balance**........		**$46,020**

Required Adjusting Entries for Jamboree

Nov. 30	Cash	30,000	
	Notes Receivable		30,000
	Record collection of note.		
Nov. 30	Cash	900	
	Interest Revenue.................		900
	Record collection of revenue.		
Nov. 30	Accounts Receivable—M. Welch	1,100	
	Cash...........................		1,100
	Reinstate account due from an NSF check.		

Nov. 30	Rent Expense	120	
	Cash...........................		120
	Correct recording error on Check No. 2025.		
Nov. 30	Miscellaneous Expenses	40	
	Cash...........................		40
	Record bank service charges.		

6A   Documentation and Verification

P4

Describe use of documentation and verification to control cash payments.

This appendix covers the documents of a voucher system of control.

Purchase Requisition   Department managers are usually not allowed to place orders directly with suppliers for control purposes. Instead, a department manager must inform the purchasing department of its needs by preparing and signing a **purchase requisition,** which lists the merchandise requested to be purchased—see Exhibit 6A.1. Two copies of the purchase requisition are sent to the purchasing department, which then sends one copy to the accounting department. When the accounting department receives a purchase requisition, it creates and maintains a voucher for this transaction. The requesting department keeps a third copy.

EXHIBIT 6A.1

Purchase Requisition

Z-Mart

PURCHASE REQUISITION   No. 917

From   *Sporting Goods Department*
To   *Purchasing Department*

Date   *October 28, 2019*
Preferred Vendor   *Trex*

Request purchase of the following item(s):

MODEL NO.	DESCRIPTION	QUANTITY
CH 015	Toddler—Challenger X7	1
SD 099	Boys/Girls—Speed Demon	1

Reason for Request   *Replenish inventory*
Approval for Request   *T.Z.*

For Purchasing Department use only: Order Date   *10-30-19*   P.O. No.   *P98*

Purchase Order   A **purchase order** is a document the purchasing department uses to place an order with a **vendor** (seller or supplier). A purchase order authorizes a vendor to ship merchandise at the stated price and terms—see Exhibit 6A.2. When the purchasing department receives a purchase requisition, it prepares at least five copies of a purchase order. The copies are distributed as follows: *copy 1* to the vendor as a purchase request to ship merchandise; *copy 2,* along with a copy of the purchase requisition, to the accounting department, where it is entered in the voucher and used in approving payment of the invoice; *copy 3* to the requesting department to inform its manager of the purchase; *copy 4* to the receiving department without order quantity so it can compare with goods received and provide an independent count of goods received; and *copy 5* kept on file by the purchasing department.

Point: This appendix shows one example of a common voucher system design, but *not* the only design.

Invoice   An **invoice** is an itemized statement of goods prepared by the vendor listing the customer's name, items sold, sales prices, and terms of sale. An invoice is also a bill sent to the buyer from the supplier. From the vendor's point of view, it is a *sales invoice.* The buyer, or **vendee,** treats it as a *purchase*

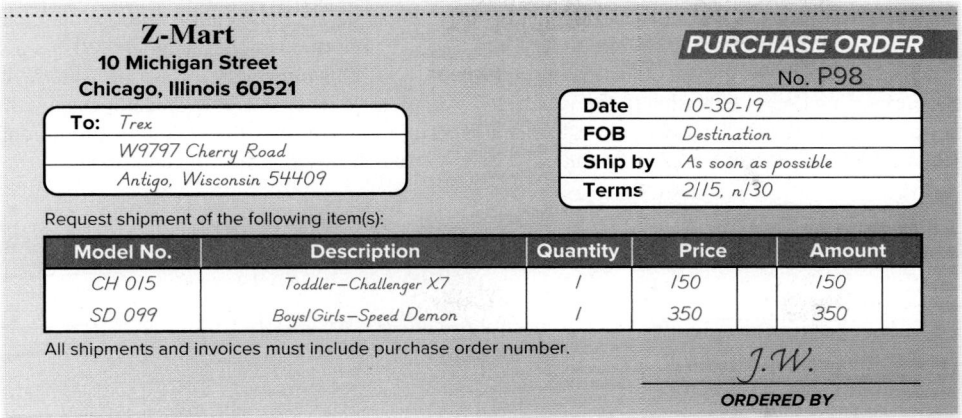

EXHIBIT 6A.2

Purchase Order

Point: Shipping terms and credit terms are shown on the purchase order.

invoice. The invoice is sent to the buyer's accounting department, where it is placed in the voucher. (Refer back to Exhibit 4.6, which shows Z-Mart's purchase invoice.)

Receiving Report

Many companies have a receiving department to receive all merchandise and purchased assets. When each shipment arrives, this receiving department counts the goods and checks them for damage and agreement with the purchase order. It then prepares four or more copies of a **receiving report,** which is used within the company to notify that ordered goods have been received and to describe the quantities and condition of the goods. One copy is sent to accounting and placed in the voucher. Copies also are sent to the requesting department and the purchasing department to notify them that the goods have arrived. The receiving department keeps a copy in its files.

Invoice Approval

When a receiving report arrives, the accounting department should have copies of the following documents in the voucher: purchase requisition, purchase order, and invoice. With the information in these documents, the accounting department can record the purchase and approve its payment. In approving an invoice for payment, it checks and compares information across all documents. To verify this information and to ensure that no step is missing, it often uses an **invoice approval,** also called *check authorization*—see Exhibit 6A.3. An invoice approval is a checklist of steps necessary for approving an invoice for recording and payment. It is a separate document either filed in the voucher or preprinted (or stamped) on the voucher.

INVOICE APPROVAL				
DOCUMENT			**BY**	**DATE**
Purchase requisition		917	TZ	10-28-19
Purchase order		P98	JW	10-30-19
Receiving report		R85	SK	11-03-19
Invoice:		4657		11-12-19
Price			JK	11-12-19
Calculations			JK	11-12-19
Terms			JK	11-12-19
Approved for payment			BC	

EXHIBIT 6A.3

Invoice Approval

As each step in the checklist is approved, the person initials the invoice approval and records the current date. Final approval means the following steps have occurred.

1. **Requisition check:** Items on invoice are requested per purchase requisition.
2. **Purchase order check:** Items on invoice are ordered per purchase order.
3. **Receiving report check:** Items on invoice are received per receiving report.
4. **Invoice check: Price:** Invoice prices are as agreed with the vendor.
   Calculations: Invoice has no mathematical errors.
   Terms: Terms are as agreed with the vendor.

Point: Recording a purchase is initiated by an invoice approval, not an invoice. An invoice approval verifies that the amount is consistent with that requested, ordered, and received. This controls and verifies purchases and related liabilities.

Point: Auditors, when auditing inventory, check a sampling of purchases by reviewing the purchase order, receiving report, and invoice.

Voucher

Once an invoice has been checked and approved, the voucher is complete. A complete voucher is a record summarizing a transaction. Once the voucher certifies a transaction, it authorizes recording an obligation. A voucher also contains approval for paying the obligation on an appropriate date.

Completion of a voucher usually requires a person to enter certain information on both the inside and outside of the voucher. Typical information required on the inside of a voucher is on the left-hand side of Exhibit 6A.4, and that for the outside is on the right-hand side. This information is taken from the invoice and the supporting documents filed in the voucher. A complete voucher is sent to an authorized individual (often called an *auditor*). This person performs a final review, approves the accounts and amounts for debiting (called the *accounting distribution*), and authorizes recording of the voucher.

EXHIBIT 6A.4

A Voucher

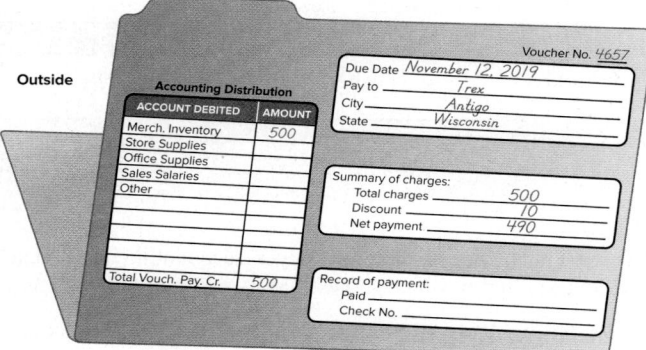

After a voucher is approved and recorded (in a journal called a **voucher register**), it is filed by its due date. A check is then sent on the payment date from the cashier, the voucher is marked "paid," and the voucher is sent to the accounting department and recorded (in a journal called the **check register**). The person issuing checks relies on the approved voucher and its signed supporting documents as proof that an obligation has been incurred and must be paid. The purchase requisition and purchase order confirm the purchase was authorized. The receiving report shows that items have been received, and the invoice approval form verifies that the invoice has been checked for errors. There is little chance for error and even less chance for fraud without collusion unless all the documents and signatures are forged.

Summary: Cheat Sheet

FRAUD AND INTERNAL CONTROL

Principles of Internal Control

Establish responsibilities: Responsibility for a task should be assigned to one person. If responsibility is not established, determining who is at fault is difficult.

Maintain adequate records: Good recordkeeping helps protect assets and helps managers monitor company activities.

Insure assets and bond key employees: Assets should be insured, and employees handling cash and easily transferable assets should be bonded.

Separate recordkeeping from custody of assets: An employee who has access to an asset must not have access to that asset's accounting records.

Divide responsibility for related transactions: Responsibility for a transaction should be divided between two or more individuals or departments. One person's work is a check on the others to prevent errors. This is *not* duplication of work.

Apply technological controls: Use technology such as ID scanners to protect assets and improve control.

Perform regular and independent reviews: Regular reviews of internal controls should be performed by outside reviewers, preferably auditors.

CONTROL OF CASH

Cash account: Includes currency, coins, checks, and deposits in bank accounts.

Cash equivalents: Short-term, liquid investment assets meeting two criteria: (1) convertible to a known cash amount and (2) close to their due date, usually within 3 months. An example is a U.S. Treasury bill.

Cash management strategies: (a) Encourage early collection of receivables, (b) delay payment of liabilities, (c) keep only necessary assets, (d) plan expenditures, and (e) invest excess cash.

Over-the-Counter Cash Receipt Control Procedures

- Sales are recorded on a cash register after each sale, and customers are given a receipt.
- Cash registers hold a locked-in record of each transaction and often are linked with the accounting system.
- Custody over cash is separate from recordkeeping. The clerk who has access to cash in the register cannot access accounting records. The recordkeeper cannot access the cash.

Cash Over and Short Journal Entries

If cash received is *more* than recorded cash sales:

Cash	555	
Cash Over and Short		5
Sales......................................		550

If cash received is *less* than recorded cash sales:

Cash	621	
Cash Over and Short	4	
Sales......................................		625

Cash Receipts by Mail Control Procedures

- Two people are tasked with opening mail. Theft of cash would require collusion between these two employees.
- A list (in triplicate) is kept of each sender's name, the amount, and an explanation of why money was sent. The first copy is sent with the money to the cashier. A second copy is sent to the recordkeeper. The employees who opened the mail keep the third copy. The cashier deposits the money in a bank, and the recordkeeper records amounts received.
- No employee has access to both accounting records and cash.

Cash Payment Control Procedures

- Require all payments to be made by check or EFT. The only exception is small payments made from petty cash.
- Deny access to records to employees who can sign checks (other than the owner).

Voucher system: Set of procedures to control cash payments. Applied to all payments.

TOOLS OF CONTROL AND ANALYSIS

Petty cash: System of control used for small payments.

Entry to set up a petty cash fund:

Petty Cash	75	
Cash		75

Reimburse and record expenses for petty cash:

Miscellaneous Expenses	46.50	
Merchandise Inventory	15.05	
Delivery Expense	5.00	
Office Supplies Expense	4.75	
Cash		71.30

Increasing a petty cash fund (after reimbursement):

Petty Cash	25	
Cash		25

Decreasing a petty cash fund (after reimbursement):

Cash	20	
Petty Cash		20

Petty cash fund has unexplained shortage:

Miscellaneous Expenses	178	
Cash Over and Short	7	
Cash		185

Canceled checks: Checks the bank has paid and deducted from the customer's account.

Bank reconciliation adjustments:

Bank Balance Adjustments	Book Balance Adjustments
Add deposits in transit.	Add interest earned and unrecorded cash receipts.
Subtract outstanding checks.	Subtract bank fees and NSF checks.
Add or subtract corrections of bank errors.	Add or subtract corrections of book errors.

Adjusting Entries from Bank Reconciliation—Examples

Collection of note:

Cash	485	
Notes Receivable		485

Interest earned:

Cash	8	
Interest Revenue		8

Bank fees:

Miscellaneous Expenses	23	
Cash		23

NSF checks:

Accounts receivable–Name	30	
Cash		30

Key Terms

Bank reconciliation (247)
Bank statement (246)
Canceled checks (246)
Cash (239)
Cash equivalents (239)
Cash Over and Short (240)
Check (245)
Check register (254)
Committee of Sponsoring Organizations (COSO) (235)
Credit memorandum (247)
Days' sales uncollected (250)

Debit memorandum (247)
Deposit ticket (245)
Deposits in transit (247)
Electronic funds transfer (EFT) (245)
Internal control system (235)
Invoice (252)
Invoice approval (253)
Liquid assets (238)
Liquidity (238)
Outstanding checks (247)
Petty cash (242)
Principles of internal control (236)

Purchase order (252)
Purchase requisition (252)
Receiving report (253)
Sarbanes-Oxley Act (SOX) (235)
Signature card (245)
Vendee (252)
Vendor (252)
Voucher (241)
Voucher register (254)
Voucher system (241)

Multiple Choice Quiz

1. The following information is available for Hapley Co.
- November 30 bank statement shows a $1,895 balance.
- The general ledger shows a $1,742 balance at November 30.
- A $795 deposit placed in the bank's night depository on November 30 does not appear on the November 30 bank statement.
- Outstanding checks amount to $638 at November 30.
- A customer's $320 note was collected by the bank and deposited in Hapley's account in November.

- A bank service charge of $10 is deducted by the bank and appears on the November 30 bank statement.

How will the customer's note appear on Hapley's November 30 bank reconciliation?
- **a.** $320 appears as an addition to the book balance of cash.
- **b.** $320 appears as a deduction from the book balance of cash.
- **c.** $320 appears as an addition to the bank balance of cash.
- **d.** $320 appears as a deduction from the bank balance of cash.
- **e.** $335 appears as an addition to the bank balance of cash.

2. Using the information from question 1, what is the reconciled balance on Hapley's November 30 bank reconciliation?

   a. $2,052   **c.** $1,742   **e.** $1,184

   b. $1,895   **d.** $2,201

3. A company needs to replenish its $500 petty cash fund. Its petty cashbox has $75 cash and petty cash receipts of $420. The journal entry to replenish the fund includes

   a. A debit to Cash for $75.

   b. A credit to Cash for $75.

   c. A credit to Petty Cash for $420.

   d. A credit to Cash Over and Short for $5.

   e. A debit to Cash Over and Short for $5.

4. A company had net sales of $84,000 and accounts receivable of $6,720. Its days' sales uncollected is

   a. 3.2 days.   **c.** 230.0 days.   **e.** 12.5 days.

   b. 18.4 days.   **d.** 29.2 days.

ANSWERS TO MULTIPLE CHOICE QUIZ

1. a; recognizes cash collection of note by bank.

2. a; the bank reconciliation follows.

Bank Reconciliation November 30			
Balance per bank statement....	$1,895	Balance per books........	$1,742
Add: Deposit in transit.........	795	Add: Note collected.......	320
Deduct: Outstanding checks....	(638)	Deduct: Service charge....	(10)
Reconciled balance...........	$2,052	Reconciled balance.......	$2,052

3. e; The entry follows.

Debits to expenses (or assets)	420	
Cash Over and Short..................	5	
Cash		425

4. d; ($6,720/$84,000) × 365 = <u>29.2 days</u>

---

^A *Superscript letter A denotes assignments based on Appendix 6A.*

 Icon denotes assignments that involve decision making.

Discussion Questions

1. List the seven broad principles of internal control.

2. Internal control procedures are important in every business, but at what stage in the development of a business do they become especially critical?

3. Why should responsibility for related transactions be divided among different departments or individuals?

4. Why should the person who keeps the records of an asset not be the person responsible for its custody?

5. When a store purchases merchandise, why are individual departments not allowed to directly deal with suppliers?

6. What are the limitations of internal controls?

7. Which of the following assets—inventory, building, accounts receivable, or cash—is most liquid? Which is least liquid?

8. What is a petty cash receipt? Who should sign it?

9. Why should cash receipts be deposited on the day of receipt?

10. **Apple**'s statement of cash flows in Appendix A describes changes in cash and cash equivalents **APPLE** for the year ended September 30, 2017. What total amount is provided (used) by investing activities? What amount is provided (used) by financing activities?

11. Refer to **Google**'s financial statements in Appendix A. Identify Google's net earnings (income) for the year ended December 31, 2017. Is its net earnings equal to the change in cash and cash equivalents for the year? Explain the difference between net earnings and the change in cash and cash equivalents. **GOOGLE**

12. Refer to **Samsung**'s balance sheet in Appendix A. How does its cash (titled "Cash and cash equivalents") compare with its other current assets (in both amount and percent) as of December 31, 2017? Compare and assess its cash at December 31, 2017, with its cash at December 31, 2016. **Samsung**

13. **Samsung**'s statement of cash flows in Appendix A reports the change in cash and equivalents for the year ended December 31, 2017. Identify the cash generated (or used) by operating activities, by investing activities, and by financing activities. **Samsung**

---

connect

QUICK STUDY

QS 6-1
Internal control objectives

C1

Indicate which statements are true and which are false.

_____ **1.** Separation of recordkeeping for assets from the custody over assets helps reduce fraud.

_____ **2.** The primary objective of internal control procedures is to safeguard the business against theft from government agencies.

_____ **3.** Internal control procedures should be designed to protect assets from waste and theft.

_____ **4.** Separating the responsibility for a transaction between two or more individuals or departments will not help prevent someone from creating a fictitious invoice and paying the money to himself.

COSO lists five components of internal control: control environment, risk assessment, control activities, information and communication, and monitoring. Indicate the COSO component that matches with each of the following internal control activities.

____ **a.** Independent review of controls   ____ **c.** Reporting of control effectiveness

____ **b.** Executives' strong ethics   ____ **d.** Analyses of fraud risk factors

QS 6-2
COSO internal control components
C1

Choose from the following list of terms and phrases to best complete the following statements.

  a. Cash   **c.** Outstanding check   **e.** Cash over and short

  b. Cash equivalents   **d.** Liquidity   **f.** Voucher system

____ **1.** The _____ category includes currency, coins, and deposits in bank accounts.

____ **2.** The term _____ refers to a company's ability to pay for its current liabilities.

____ **3.** The _____ category includes short-term, highly liquid investment assets that are readily convertible to a known cash amount and sufficiently close to their due dates so that their market value will not greatly change.

QS 6-3
Cash and equivalents
C2

Identify each of the following statements as either true or false.

____ **a.** A guideline for safeguarding cash is that all cash receipts be deposited monthly or yearly.

____ **b.** A voucher system of control is a control system exclusively for cash receipts.

____ **c.** A guideline for safeguarding cash is to separate the duties of those who have custody of cash from those who keep cash records.

____ **d.** Separation of duties eliminates the possibility of collusion to steal an asset and hide the theft from the records.

QS 6-4
Internal control for cash
P1

Record the journal entry for Sales and for Cash Over and Short for each of the following separate situations.

a. The cash register's record shows $420 of cash sales, but the count of cash in the register is $430.

b. The cash register's record shows $980 of cash sales, but the count of cash in the register is $972.

QS 6-5
Cash Over and Short
P1

---

1. Brooks Agency set up a petty cash fund for $150. At the end of the current period, the fund contained $28 and had the following receipts: entertainment, $70; postage, $30; and printing, $22. Prepare journal entries to record (*a*) establishment of the fund and (*b*) reimbursement of the fund at the end of the current period.

2. Identify the two events from the following that cause a Petty Cash account to be credited in a journal entry.

    ____ **a.** Fund amount is being reduced.   ____ **c.** Fund is being eliminated.

    ____ **b.** Fund amount is being increased.   ____ **d.** Fund is being established.

QS 6-6
Petty cash accounting
P2

For *a* through *g*, indicate whether its amount (1) affects the bank or book side of a bank reconciliation, (2) is an addition or a subtraction in a bank reconciliation, and (3) requires an adjusting journal entry.

	Bank or Book Side	Add or Subtract	Adj. Entry or Not
a. Interest on cash balance...............	_____	_____	_____
b. Bank service charges	_____	_____	_____
c. Minimum balance bank fee	_____	_____	_____
d. Outstanding checks	_____	_____	_____
e. Collection of note by bank	_____	_____	_____
f. NSF checks	_____	_____	_____
g. Outstanding deposits	_____	_____	_____

QS 6-7
Bank reconciliation
P3

Nolan Company's Cash account shows a $22,352 debit balance and its bank statement shows $21,332 on deposit at the close of business on June 30. Prepare a bank reconciliation using the following information.

a. Outstanding checks as of June 30 total $3,713.

b. The June 30 bank statement lists $41 in bank service charges; the company has not yet recorded the cost of these services.

QS 6-8
Bank reconciliation
P3

[continued on next page]

c. In reviewing the bank statement, a $90 check written by the company was mistakenly recorded in the company's books as $99.

d. June 30 cash receipts of $4,724 were placed in the bank's night depository after banking hours and were not recorded on the June 30 bank statement.

e. The bank statement included a $23 credit for interest earned on the company's cash in the bank. The company has not yet recorded interest earned.

QS 6-9
Bank reconciliation

P3

Organic Food Co.'s Cash account shows a $5,500 debit balance and its bank statement shows $5,160 on deposit at the close of business on August 31. Prepare a bank reconciliation using the following information.

a. August 31 cash receipts of $1,240 were placed in the bank's night depository after banking hours and were not recorded on the August 31 bank statement.

b. The bank statement shows a $120 NSF check from a customer; the company has not yet recorded this NSF check.

c. Outstanding checks as of August 31 total $1,120.

d. In reviewing the bank statement, an $80 check written by Organic Fruits was mistakenly drawn against Organic Food's account.

e. The August 31 bank statement lists $20 in bank service charges; the company has not yet recorded the cost of these services.

QS 6-10
Days' sales uncollected

A1

The following annual account balances are from Armour Sports at December 31.

	Year 2	Year 1
Accounts receivable.	$ 100,000	$ 85,000
Net sales	2,500,000	2,000,000

a. What is the change in the number of days' sales uncollected between Year 1 and Year 2? (Round the number of days to one decimal.)

b. From the analysis in part *a*, is the company's collection of receivables improving?

QS 6-11^A
Documents in a voucher
system   **P4**

Management uses a voucher system to help control and monitor cash payments. Which one or more of the four documents listed below are prepared as part of a voucher system of control?

_____ **a.** Purchase order   _____ **b.** Outstanding check   _____ **c.** Invoice   _____ **d.** Voucher

---

■ connect

EXERCISES

Exercise 6-1
Analyzing internal control

C1

Identify the internal control principle that was violated in each of the following separate situations.

a. The recordkeeper left town after the owner discovered a large sum of money had disappeared. An audit found that the recordkeeper had written and signed several checks made payable to his fiancée and recorded the checks as salaries expense.

b. An employee was put in charge of handling cash. That employee later stole cash from the business. The company incurred an *uninsured* loss of $184,000.

c. There is $500 in cash missing from a cash register drawer. Three salesclerks shared the cash register drawer, so the owner cannot determine who is at fault.

Exercise 6-2
Applying internal control
principles

C1

Whole Fruits Market took the following actions to improve internal controls. For each of the following actions, identify the internal control principle the company followed.

a. Prohibit the recordkeeper from having control over cash.

b. Purchased an insurance (bonding) policy against losses from theft by a cashier.

c. Each cashier is designated a specific cash drawer and is solely responsible for cash in that drawer.

d. Detailed records of inventory are kept to ensure items lost or stolen do not go unnoticed.

e. Digital time clocks are used to register which employees are at work at what times.

f. External auditors are regularly hired to evaluate internal controls.

Determine whether each procedure described below is an internal control strength or weakness; then identify the internal control principle violated or followed for each procedure.

1. The same employee requests, records, and makes payment for purchases of inventory.

2. The company saves money by having employees involved in operations perform the only review of internal controls.

3. Time is saved by not updating records for use of supplies.

4. The recordkeeper is not allowed to write checks or initiate EFTs.

5. Each salesclerk is in charge of her own cash drawer.

Exercise 6-3
Internal control strengths and weaknesses
C1

Determine whether each policy below is good or bad cash management; then identify the cash management strategy violated or followed for each policy.

1. Bills are paid as soon as they are received.

2. Cash receipts and cash payments are regularly planned and reviewed.

3. Excess cash is put in checking accounts, earning no interest income.

4. Customers are regularly allowed to pay after due dates without concern.

5. Rarely used equipment is rented rather than purchased.

Exercise 6-4
Cash management strategies
C2

Specter Co. combines cash and cash equivalents on the balance sheet. Using the following information, determine the amount reported on the year-end balance sheet for cash and cash equivalents.

- $3,000 cash deposit in checking account.
- $20,000 bond investment due in 20 years.
- $5,000 U.S. Treasury bill due in 1 month.
- $200, 3-year loan to an employee.
- $1,000 of currency and coins.
- $500 of accounts receivable.

Exercise 6-5
Cash and cash equivalents
C2

Determine whether each cash receipts procedure is an internal control strength or weakness.

1. If a salesclerk makes an error in recording a cash sale, she can access the register's electronic record to correct the transaction.

2. All sales transactions, even those for less than $1, are recorded on a cash register.

3. Two employees are tasked with opening mail that contains cash receipts.

4. One of the two employees tasked with opening mail is also the recordkeeper for the business.

5. The supervisor has access to both cash and the accounting records.

6. Receipts are given to customers only for sales that are above $20.

Exercise 6-6
Control of cash receipts
P1

Determine whether each cash payment procedure is an internal control strength or weakness.

1. A voucher system is used for all payments of liabilities.

2. The owner of a small business has authority to write and sign checks.

3. When the owner is out of town, the recordkeeper is in charge of signing checks.

4. To save time, all departments are allowed to incur liabilities.

5. Payments over $100 are made by check.

6. Requesting and receiving merchandise are handled by the same department.

Exercise 6-7
Voucher system and control of cash payments
P1

Waupaca Company establishes a $350 petty cash fund on September 9. On September 30, the fund shows $104 in cash along with receipts for the following expenditures: transportation-in, $40; postage expenses, $123; and miscellaneous expenses, $80. The petty cashier could not account for a $3 shortage in the fund.

The company uses the perpetual system in accounting for merchandise inventory. Prepare (1) the September 9 entry to establish the fund, (2) the September 30 entry to reimburse the fund, and (3) an October 1 entry to increase the fund to $400.

Exercise 6-8
Petty cash fund with a shortage **P2**

Check (2) Cr. Cash, $246 and (3) Cr. Cash, $50

EcoMart establishes a $1,050 petty cash fund on May 2. On May 30, the fund shows $326 in cash along with receipts for the following expenditures: transportation-in, $120; postage expenses, $369; and miscellaneous expenses, $240. The petty cashier could not account for a $5 overage in the fund. The company uses the perpetual system in accounting for merchandise inventory.

Prepare the (1) May 2 entry to establish the fund, (2) May 30 entry to reimburse the fund [*Hint:* Credit Cash Over and Short for $5 and credit Cash for $724], and (3) June 1 entry to increase the fund to $1,200.

Exercise 6-9
Petty cash fund with an overage

P2

Exercise 6-10

Petty cash fund accounting

P2

Check   (3) Cr. Cash, $162 & $250

Palmona Co. establishes a $200 petty cash fund on January 1. On January 8, the fund shows $38 in cash along with receipts for the following expenditures: postage, $74; transportation-in, $29; delivery expenses, $16; and miscellaneous expenses, $43.

Palmona uses the perpetual system in accounting for merchandise inventory. Prepare journal entries to (1) establish the fund on January 1, (2) reimburse it on January 8, and (3) both reimburse the fund and increase it to $450 on January 8, assuming no entry in part 2. *Hint:* Make two separate entries for part 3.

Exercise 6-11

Bank reconciliation and adjusting entries

P3

Prepare a table with the following headings for a monthly bank reconciliation dated September 30.

Item	Bank Balance	Book Balance		Shown or Not Shown on Reconciliation
	Add or Subtract	Add or Subtract	Dr. or Cr.	Shown or Not Shown

Indicate whether each item should be added to or deducted from the book or bank balance and whether it should or should not appear on the September 30 reconciliation. For items that add or deduct from the book balance column, place a *Dr.* or *Cr.* after the "Add" or "Deduct" to show the accounting impact on Cash.

1. NSF check from a customer is shown on the bank statement but not yet recorded by the company.
2. Interest earned on the September cash balance in the bank is not yet recorded by the company.
3. Deposit made on September 5 and processed by the bank on September 6.
4. Checks written by another depositor but mistakenly charged against this company's account.
5. Bank service charge for September is not yet recorded by the company.
6. Checks outstanding on August 31 that cleared the bank in September.
7. Check written against the company's account and cleared by the bank; erroneously not recorded by the company's recordkeeper.
8. A note receivable is collected by the bank for the company, but it is not yet recorded by the company.
9. Checks written and mailed to payees on October 2.
10. Checks written by the company and mailed to payees on September 30.
11. Night deposit made on September 30 after the bank closed.
12. Bank fees for check printing are not yet recorded by the company.

Exercise 6-12

Bank reconciliation

P3

Del Gato Clinic's Cash account shows an $11,589 debit balance and its bank statement shows $10,555 on deposit at the close of business on June 30. Prepare its bank reconciliation using the following information.

a. Outstanding checks as of June 30 total $1,829.
b. The June 30 bank statement lists a $16 bank service charge.
c. Check No. 919, listed with the canceled checks, was correctly drawn for $467 in payment of a utility bill on June 15. Del Gato Clinic mistakenly recorded it with a debit to Utilities Expense and a credit to Cash in the amount of $476.
d. The June 30 cash receipts of $2,856 were placed in the bank's night depository after banking hours and were not recorded on the June 30 bank statement.

Check   Reconciled bal., $11,582

Exercise 6-13

Adjusting entries from bank reconciliation   **P3**

Prepare the adjusting journal entries that Del Gato Clinic must record as a result of preparing the bank reconciliation in Exercise 6-12.

Exercise 6-14

Bank reconciliation

P3

Wright Company's Cash account shows a $27,500 debit balance and its bank statement shows $25,800 on deposit at the close of business on May 31. Prepare its bank reconciliation using the following information.

a. The May 31 bank statement lists $100 in bank service charges; the company has not yet recorded the cost of these services.
b. Outstanding checks as of May 31 total $5,600.
c. May 31 cash receipts of $6,200 were placed in the bank's night depository after banking hours and were not recorded on the May 31 bank statement.
d. In reviewing the bank statement, a $400 check written by Smith Company was mistakenly drawn against Wright's account.
e. The bank statement shows a $600 NSF check from a customer; the company has not yet recorded this NSF check.

Check   Reconciled bal., $26,800

Barga Co.'s net sales for Year 1 and Year 2 are $730,000 and $1,095,000, respectively. Its year-end balances of accounts receivable follow: Year 1, $65,000; and Year 2, $123,000.

a. Compute its days' sales uncollected at the end of each year. Round the number of days to one decimal.

b. Did days' sales uncollected improve or worsen in Year 2 versus Year 1?

Exercise 6-15

Liquid assets and accounts receivable **A1**

Match each document in a voucher system with its description.

Document	Description
1. Purchase requisition	___ **A.** An itemized statement of goods prepared by the vendor listing the customer's name, items sold, sales prices, and terms of sale.
2. Purchase order	
3. Invoice	___ **B.** An internal file used to store documents and information to control cash payments and to ensure that a transaction is properly authorized and recorded.
4. Receiving report	
5. Invoice approval	___ **C.** A document used to place an order with a vendor that authorizes the vendor to ship ordered merchandise at the stated price and terms.
6. Voucher	

___ **D.** A checklist of steps necessary for the approval of an invoice for recording and payment; also known as a check authorization.

___ **E.** A document used by department managers to inform the purchasing department to place an order with a vendor.

___ **F.** A document used to notify the appropriate persons that ordered goods have arrived, including a description of the quantities and condition of goods.

Exercise 6-16^A

Documents in a voucher system

P4

---

connect

Following are five separate cases involving internal control issues.

a. Chi Han receives all incoming customer cash receipts for her employer and posts the customer payments to their respective accounts.

b. At Tico Company, Julia and Trevor alternate lunch hours. Julia is the petty cash custodian, but if someone needs petty cash when she is at lunch, Trevor fills in as custodian.

c. Nori Nozumi posts all patient charges and payments at the Hopeville Medical Clinic. Each night Nori backs up the computerized accounting system but does not password lock her computer.

d. Ben Shales prides himself on hiring quality workers who require little supervision. As office manager, Ben gives his employees full discretion over their tasks and for years has seen no reason to perform independent reviews of their work.

e. Carla Farah's manager has told her to reduce costs. Carla decides to raise the deductible on the plant's property insurance from $5,000 to $10,000. This cuts the property insurance premium in half. In a related move, she decides that bonding the plant's employees is a waste of money because the company has not experienced any losses due to employee theft. Carla saves the entire amount of the bonding insurance premium by dropping the bonding insurance.

Required

1. For each case, identify the principle(s) of internal control that is violated.

2. Recommend what should be done to adhere to principles of internal control in each case.

PROBLEM SET A

Problem 6-1A

Analyzing internal control

C1

Kiona Co. set up a petty cash fund for payments of small amounts. The following transactions involving the petty cash fund occurred in May (the last month of the company's fiscal year).

May 1 Prepared a company check for $300 to establish the petty cash fund.

    15 Prepared a company check to replenish the fund for the following expenditures made since May 1.
        a. Paid $88 for janitorial expenses.
        b. Paid $53.68 for miscellaneous expenses.
        c. Paid postage expenses of $53.50.
        d. Paid $47.15 to Facebook for advertising expense.
        e. Counted $62.15 remaining in the petty cashbox.

    16 Prepared a company check for $200 to increase the fund to $500.

[continued on next page]

Problem 6-2A

Establishing, reimbursing, and adjusting petty cash

P2

31   The petty cashier reports that $288.20 cash remains in the fund. A company check is drawn to replenish the fund for the following expenditures made since May 15.

 f. Paid postage expenses of $147.36.

 g. Reimbursed the office manager for mileage expense, $23.50.

 h. Paid $34.75 in delivery expense for products to a customer, terms FOB destination.

31   The company decides that the May 16 increase in the fund was too large. It reduces the fund by $100, leaving a total of $400.

Required

Check Cr. to Cash: May 15, $237.85; May 16, $200.00

Prepare journal entries to establish the fund on May 1, to replenish it on May 15 and on May 31, and to reflect any increase or decrease in the fund balance on May 16 and May 31.

Problem 6-3A

Establishing, reimbursing, and increasing petty cash

P2

Nakashima Gallery had the following petty cash transactions in February of the current year. Nakashima uses the perpetual system to account for merchandise inventory.

Feb. 2 Wrote a $400 check to establish a petty cash fund.

   5 Purchased paper for the copier for $14.15 that is immediately used.

   9 Paid $32.50 shipping charges (transportation-in) on merchandise purchased for resale, terms FOB shipping point. These costs are added to merchandise inventory.

  12 Paid $7.95 postage to deliver a contract to a client.

  14 Reimbursed Adina Sharon, the manager, $68 for mileage on her car.

  20 Purchased office paper for $67.77 that is immediately used.

  23 Paid a courier $20 to deliver merchandise sold to a customer, terms FOB destination.

  25 Paid $13.10 shipping charges (transportation-in) on merchandise purchased for resale, terms FOB shipping point. These costs are added to merchandise inventory.

  27 Paid $54 for postage expenses.

  28 The fund had $120.42 remaining in the petty cashbox. Sorted the petty cash receipts by accounts affected and exchanged them for a check to reimburse the fund for expenditures.

  28 The petty cash fund amount is increased by $100 to a total of $500.

Required

1. Prepare the journal entry to establish the petty cash fund.

2. Prepare a petty cash payments report for February with these categories: delivery expense, mileage expense, postage expense, merchandise inventory (for transportation-in), and office supplies expense.

Check Cash credit: (3*a*) $279.58; (3*b*) $100.00

3. Prepare the journal entries for part 2 to both (*a*) reimburse and (*b*) increase the fund amount.

Problem 6-4A

Preparing a bank reconciliation and recording adjustments

P3

The following information is available to reconcile Branch Company's book balance of cash with its bank statement cash balance as of July 31.

a. On July 31, the company's Cash account has a $27,497 debit balance, but its July bank statement shows a $27,233 cash balance.

b. Check No. 3031 for $1,482, Check No. 3065 for $382, and Check No. 3069 for $2,281 are outstanding checks as of July 31.

c. Check No. 3056 for July rent expense was correctly written and drawn for $1,270 but was erroneously entered in the accounting records as $1,250.

d. The July bank statement shows the bank collected $7,955 cash on a note for Branch. Branch had not recorded this event before receiving the statement.

e. The bank statement shows an $805 NSF check. The check had been received from a customer, Evan Shaw. Branch has not yet recorded this check as NSF.

f. The July statement shows a $25 bank service charge. It has not yet been recorded in miscellaneous expenses because no previous notification had been received.

g. Branch's July 31 daily cash receipts of $11,514 were placed in the bank's night depository on that date but do not appear on the July 31 bank statement.

Required

Check (1) Reconciled balance, $34,602; (2) Cr. Notes Receivable, $8,000

1. Prepare the bank reconciliation for this company as of July 31.

2. Prepare the journal entries necessary to make the company's book balance of cash equal to the reconciled cash balance as of July 31.

Chavez Company most recently reconciled its bank statement and book balances of cash on August 31 and it reported two checks outstanding, No. 5888 for $1,028 and No. 5893 for $494. Check No. 5893 was still outstanding as of September 30. The following information is available for its September 30 reconciliation.

Problem 6-5A
Preparing a bank reconciliation and recording adjustments

P3

From the September 30 Bank Statement

PREVIOUS BALANCE	TOTAL CHECKS AND DEBITS	TOTAL DEPOSITS AND CREDITS	CURRENT BALANCE
16,800	9,617	11,270	18,453

CHECKS AND DEBITS			DEPOSITS AND CREDITS	
Date	No.	Amount	Date	Amount
Sep. 3	5888	1,028	Sep. 5	1,103
Sep. 4	5902	719	Sep. 12	2,226
Sep. 7	5901	1,824	Sep. 21	4,093
Sep. 17		600 NSF	Sep. 25	2,351
Sep. 20	5905	937	Sep. 30	12 IN
Sep. 22	5903	399	Sep. 30	1,485 CM
Sep. 22	5904	2,090		
Sep. 28	5907	213		
Sep. 29	5909	1,807		

From Chavez Company's Accounting Records

Cash Receipts Deposited			Cash Payments	
Date		Cash Debit	Check No.	Cash Credit
Sep.	5	1,103	5901	1,824
	12	2,226	5902	719
	21	4,093	5903	399
	25	2,351	5904	2,060
	30	1,682	5905	937
		11,455	5906	982
			5907	213
			5908	388
			5909	1,807
				9,329

Cash						Acct. No. 101
Date		Explanation	PR	Debit	Credit	Balance
Aug.	31	Balance				15,278
Sep.	30	Total receipts	R12	11,455		26,733
	30	Total payments	D23		9,329	17,404

Additional Information (*a*) Check No. 5904 is correctly drawn for $2,090 to pay for computer equipment; however, the recordkeeper misread the amount and entered it in the accounting records with a debit to Computer Equipment and a credit to Cash of $2,060. (*b*) The NSF check shown in the statement was originally received from a customer, S. Nilson, in payment of her account. Its return has not yet been recorded by the company. (*c*) The credit memorandum (CM) is from the collection of a $1,485 note for Chavez Company by the bank. The collection is not yet recorded.

Required

1. Prepare the September 30 bank reconciliation for this company.
2. Prepare journal entries to adjust the book balance of cash to the reconciled balance.

Check (1) Reconciled balance, $18,271; (2) Cr. Notes Receivable, $1,485

Following are five separate cases involving internal control issues.

a. Tywin Company keeps very poor records of its equipment. Instead, the company asserts its employees are honest and would never steal from the company.

b. Marker Theater has a computerized order-taking system for its tickets. The system is backed up once a year.

c. Sutton Company has two employees handling acquisitions of inventory. One employee places purchase orders and pays vendors. The second employee receives the merchandise.

PROBLEM SET B

Problem 6-1B
Analyzing internal control

C1

d. The owner of Super Pharmacy uses a check software/printer to prepare checks, making it difficult for anyone to alter the amount of a check. The check software/printer, which is not password protected, is on the owner's desk in an office that contains company checks and is normally unlocked.

e. To ensure the company retreat would not be cut, the manager of Lavina Company decided to save money by canceling the external audit of internal controls.

Required

1. For each case, identify the principle(s) of internal control that is violated.

2. Recommend what should be done to adhere to principles of internal control in each case.

Problem 6-2B
Establishing, reimbursing, and adjusting petty cash

P2

Moya Co. establishes a petty cash fund for payments of small amounts. The following transactions involving the petty cash fund occurred in January (the last month of the company's fiscal year).

Jan. 3   A company check for $150 is written and made payable to the petty cashier to establish the petty cash fund.

  14   A company check is written to replenish the fund for the following expenditures made since January 3.
  a.   Purchased office supplies for $14.29 that are immediately used.
  b.   Paid $19.60 COD shipping charges on merchandise purchased for resale, terms FOB shipping point. Moya uses the perpetual system to account for inventory.
  c.   Paid $38.57 to All-Tech for repairs expense to a computer.
  d.   Paid $12.82 for items classified as miscellaneous expenses.
  e.   Counted $62.28 remaining in the petty cashbox.

  15   Prepared a company check for $50 to increase the fund to $200.

  31   The petty cashier reports that $17.35 remains in the fund. A company check is written to replenish the fund for the following expenditures made since January 14.
  f.   Paid $50 to *The Smart Shopper* in advertising expense for January's newsletter.
  g.   Paid $48.19 for postage expenses.
  h.   Paid $78 to Smooth Delivery for delivery expense of merchandise, terms FOB destination.

  31   The company decides that the January 15 increase in the fund was too little. It increases the fund by another $50.

Required

Check Cr. to Cash:
Jan. 14, $87.72;
Jan. 31 (total), $232.65

Prepare journal entries (in dollars and cents) to establish the fund on January 3, to replenish it on January 14 and January 31, and to reflect any increase or decrease in the fund balance on January 15 and 31.

Problem 6-3B
Establishing, reimbursing, and increasing petty cash

P2

Blues Music Center had the following petty cash transactions in March of the current year. Blues uses the perpetual system to account for merchandise inventory.

Mar. 5   Wrote a $250 check to establish a petty cash fund.

   6   Paid $12.50 shipping charges (transportation-in) on merchandise purchased for resale, terms FOB shipping point. These costs are added to merchandise inventory.

  11   Paid $10.75 in delivery expense on merchandise sold to a customer, terms FOB destination.

  12   Purchased office file folders for $14.13 that are immediately used.

  14   Reimbursed Bob Geldof, the manager, $11.65 for office supplies purchased and used.

  18   Purchased office printer paper for $20.54 that is immediately used.

  27   Paid $45.10 shipping charges (transportation-in) on merchandise purchased for resale, terms FOB shipping point. These costs are added to merchandise inventory.

  28   Paid postage expense of $18.

  30   Reimbursed Geldof $56.80 for mileage expense.

  31   Cash of $61.53 remained in the fund. Sorted the petty cash receipts by accounts affected and exchanged them for a check to reimburse the fund for expenditures.

  31   The petty cash fund amount is increased by $50 to a total of $300.

Required

1. Prepare the journal entry to establish the petty cash fund.

Check (2) Total expenses,
$189.47
(3*a* & 3*b*) Total Cr. to Cash,
$238.47

2. Prepare a petty cash payments report for March with these categories: delivery expense, mileage expense, postage expense, merchandise inventory (for transportation-in), and office supplies expense.

3. Prepare the journal entries for part 2 to both (*a*) reimburse and (*b*) increase the fund amount.

The following information is available to reconcile Severino Co.'s book balance of cash with its bank statement cash balance as of December 31.

a. The December 31 cash balance according to the accounting records is $32,878.30, and the bank statement cash balance for that date is $46,822.40.

b. Check No. 1242 for $410.40, Check No. 1273 for $4,589.30, and Check No. 1282 for $400 are outstanding checks as of December 31.

c. Check No. 1267 had been correctly drawn for $3,456 to pay for office supplies but was erroneously entered in the accounting records as $3,465.

d. The bank statement shows a $762.50 NSF check received from a customer, Titus Industries, in payment of its account. The statement also shows a $99 bank fee in miscellaneous expenses for check printing. Severino had not yet recorded these transactions.

e. The bank statement shows that the bank collected $18,980 cash on a note receivable for the company. Severino did not record this transaction before receiving the statement.

f. Severino's December 31 daily cash receipts of $9,583.10 were placed in the bank's night depository on that date but do not appear on the December 31 bank statement.

Required

1. Prepare the bank reconciliation for this company as of December 31.

2. Prepare the journal entries necessary to make the company's book balance of cash equal to the reconciled cash balance as of December 31.

Problem 6-4B
Preparing a bank reconciliation and recording adjustments

P3

Check (1) Reconciled balance, $51,005.80; (2) Cr. Notes Receivable, $18,980.00

Shamara Systems most recently reconciled its bank balance on April 30 and reported two checks outstanding at that time, No. 1771 for $781 and No. 1780 for $1,425.90. Check No. 1780 was still outstanding as of May 31. The following information is available for its May 31 reconciliation.

Problem 6-5B
Preparing a bank reconciliation and recording adjustments

P3

From the May 31 Bank Statement

PREVIOUS BALANCE	TOTAL CHECKS AND DEBITS	TOTAL DEPOSITS AND CREDITS	CURRENT BALANCE
18,290.70	13,094.80	16,566.80	21,762.70

CHECKS AND DEBITS			DEPOSITS AND CREDITS	
Date	No.	Amount	Date	Amount
May 1	1771	781.00	May 4	2,438.00
May 2	1783	382.50	May 14	2,898.00
May 4	1782	1,285.50	May 22	1,801.80
May 11	1784	1,449.60	May 25	7,350.00 CM
May 18		431.80 NSF	May 26	2,079.00
May 25	1787	8,032.50		
May 26	1785	63.90		
May 29	1788	654.00		
May 31		14.00 SC		

From Shamara Systems's Accounting Records

Cash Receipts Deposited		Cash Payments	
Date	Cash Debit	Check No.	Cash Credit
May 4	2,438.00	1782	1,285.50
14	2,898.00	1783	382.50
22	1,801.80	1784	1,449.60
26	2,079.00	1785	63.90
31	2,727.30	1786	353.10
	11,944.10	1787	8,032.50
		1788	644.00
		1789	639.50
			12,850.60

Cash						Acct. No. 101
Date		Explanation	PR	Debit	Credit	Balance
Apr.	30	Balance				16,083.80
May	31	Total receipts	R7	11,944.10		28,027.90
	31	Total payments	D8		12,850.60	15,177.30

[continued on next page]

Additional Information (*a*) Check No. 1788 is correctly drawn for $654 to pay for May utilities; however, the recordkeeper misread the amount and entered it in the accounting records with a debit to Utilities Expense and a credit to Cash for $644. The bank paid and deducted the correct amount. (*b*) The NSF check shown in the statement was originally received from a customer, W. Sox, in payment of her account. The company has not yet recorded its return. (*c*) The credit memorandum (CM) is from a $7,350 note that the bank collected for the company. The collection has not yet been recorded.

Required

Check   (1) Reconciled
balance, $22,071.50; (2) Cr.
Notes Receivable, $7,350.00

1. Prepare the May 31 bank reconciliation for Shamara Systems.

2. Prepare journal entries to adjust the book balance of cash to the reconciled balance.

SERIAL PROBLEM
Business Solutions

P3

©Alexander Image/Shutterstock

This serial problem began in Chapter 1 and continues through most of the book. If previous chapter segments were not completed, the serial problem can begin at this point.

SP 6   Santana Rey receives the March bank statement for **Business Solutions** on April 11, 2020. The March 31 bank statement shows an ending cash balance of $67,566. The general ledger Cash account, No. 101, shows an ending cash balance per books of $68,057 as of March 31 (prior to any reconciliation). A comparison of the bank statement with the general ledger Cash account, No. 101, reveals the following.

a. The bank erroneously cleared a $500 check against the company account in March that S. Rey did not issue. The check was actually issued by Business Systems.

b. On March 25, the bank statement lists a $50 charge for a safety deposit box. Santana has not yet recorded this expense.

c. On March 26, the bank statement lists a $102 charge for printed checks that Business Solutions ordered from the bank. Santana has not yet recorded this expense.

d. On March 31, the bank statement lists $33 interest earned on Business Solutions's checking account for the month of March. Santana has not yet recorded this revenue.

e. S. Rey notices that the check she issued for $128 on March 31, 2020, has not yet cleared the bank.

f. S. Rey verifies that all deposits made in March do appear on the March bank statement.

Required

Check   (1) Adj. bank bal.,
$67,938

1. Prepare a bank reconciliation for Business Solutions for the month ended March 31, 2020.

2. Prepare any necessary adjusting entries. Use Miscellaneous Expenses, No. 677, for any bank charges. Use Interest Revenue, No. 404, for any interest earned on the checking account for March.

**GENERAL
LEDGER
PROBLEM**

connect

The **General Ledger** tool in Connect automates several of the procedural steps in the accounting cycle so that the financial professional can focus on the impacts of each transaction on the various financial reports.

GL 6-1   General Ledger assignment GL 6-1, based on Problem 6-2A, focuses on transactions related to the petty cash fund and highlights the impact each transaction has on net income, if any. Prepare the journal entries related to the petty cash fund and assess the impact of each transaction on the company's net income, if any.

Accounting Analysis

**COMPANY
ANALYSIS**

C2   A1

APPLE

AA 6-1   Use **Apple**'s financial statements in Appendix A to answer the following.

1. Identify the total amount of cash and cash equivalents for fiscal years ended (*a*) September 30, 2017, and (*b*) September 24, 2016.

2. Compute cash and cash equivalents as a percent (rounded to one decimal) of total current assets, total current liabilities, total shareholders' equity, and total assets at fiscal year-end for both 2017 and 2016.

3. Compute the percent change (rounded to one decimal) between the beginning and ending year amounts of cash and cash equivalents for fiscal years ended (*a*) September 30, 2017, and (*b*) September 24, 2016.

4. Compute the days' sales uncollected (rounded to one decimal) as of (*a*) September 30, 2017, and (*b*) September 24, 2016.

5. Does Apple's collection of receivables show a favorable or unfavorable change?

AA 6-2   Key comparative figures for **Apple** and **Google** follow.

COMPARATIVE ANALYSIS

A1

APPLE
GOOGLE

$ millions	Apple		Google	
	Current Year	Prior Year	Current Year	Prior Year
Accounts receivable	$ 17,874	$ 15,754	$ 18,336	$14,137
Net sales	229,234	215,639	110,855	90,272

Required

1. Compute days' sales uncollected (rounded to one decimal) for (*a*) Apple and (*b*) Google for the current and prior years.

2. Which company had more success collecting receivables?

AA 6-3   Key figures for **Samsung** follow.

GLOBAL ANALYSIS

C2   A1

Samsung

₩ millions	Current Year	Prior Year
Cash.........................	₩ 30,545,130	₩ 32,111,442
Accounts receivable	31,804,956	27,800,408
Current assets.................	146,982,464	141,429,704
Total assets	301,752,090	262,174,324
Current liabilities..............	67,175,114	54,704,095
Shareholders' equity	214,491,428	192,963,033
Net sales.....................	239,575,376	201,866,745

Required

1. Compute cash and cash equivalents as a percent (rounded to one decimal) of total current assets, total assets, total current liabilities, and total shareholders' equity for both years.

2. Compute the percentage change (rounded to one decimal) between the current year and prior year cash balances.

3. Compute the days' sales uncollected (rounded to one decimal) at the end of both the (*a*) current year and (*b*) prior year.

4. Does Samsung's collection of receivables show a favorable or unfavorable change?

Beyond the Numbers

BTN 6-1   Harriet Knox, Ralph Patton, and Marcia Diamond work for a family physician, Dr. Gwen Conrad, who is in private practice. Dr. Conrad is knowledgeable about office management practices and has segregated the cash receipt duties as follows. Knox opens the mail and prepares a triplicate list of money received. She sends one copy of the list to Patton, the cashier, who deposits the receipts daily in the bank. Diamond, the recordkeeper, receives a copy of the list and posts payments to patients' accounts. About once a month the office clerks have an expensive lunch they pay for as follows. First, Patton

ETHICS CHALLENGE

C1

endorses a patient's check in Dr. Conrad's name and cashes it at the bank. Knox then destroys the remittance advice accompanying the check. Finally, Diamond posts payment to the customer's account as a miscellaneous credit. The three justify their actions by their relatively low pay and knowledge that Dr. Conrad will likely never miss the money.

Required

1. Who is the best person in Dr. Conrad's office to reconcile the bank statement?
2. Would a bank reconciliation uncover this office fraud?
3. What are some procedures to detect this type of fraud?
4. Suggest additional internal controls that Dr. Conrad could implement.

COMMUNICATING IN PRACTICE

P4

BTN 6-2   Assume you are a business consultant. The owner of a company sends you an e-mail expressing concern that the company is not taking advantage of its discounts offered by vendors. The company currently uses the gross method of recording purchases. The owner is considering a review of all invoices and payments from the previous period. Due to the volume of purchases, however, the owner recognizes that this is time-consuming and costly. The owner *seeks your advice about monitoring purchase discounts* in the future. Provide a response in memorandum form. *Hint:* It will help to review the recording of purchase discounts in Appendix 4C.

TAKING IT TO THE NET

C1   P1

BTN 6-3   Visit the Association of Certified Fraud Examiners website and open the "2016 Report to the Nations" (**s3-us-west-2.amazonaws.com/acfepublic/2016-report-to-the-nations.pdf**). Read the two-page Executive Summary and fill in the following blanks.

1. The median loss for all cases in our study was _____, with _____ of cases causing losses of $1 million or more.
2. The typical organization loses _____ of revenues in a given year as a result of fraud.
3. The median duration—the amount of time from when the fraud commenced until it was detected—for the fraud cases reported to us was _____.
4. Asset misappropriation was by far the most common form of occupational fraud, occurring in more than _____ of cases, but causing the smallest median loss of _____.
5. Financial statement fraud was on the other end of the spectrum, occurring in less than 10% of cases but causing a median loss of _____. Corruption cases fell in the middle, with _____ of cases and a median loss of _____.
6. The most common detection method in our study was _____ (39.1% of cases).
7. Approximately _____ of the cases reported to us targeted privately held or publicly owned companies. These for-profit organizations suffered the largest median losses among the types of organizations analyzed, at _____ and _____, respectively.

TEAMWORK IN ACTION

C1

BTN 6-4   Organize the class into teams. Each team must prepare a list of 10 internal controls a consumer could observe in a typical retail department store. When called upon, the team's spokesperson must be prepared to share controls identified by the team that have not been shared by another team's spokesperson.

BTN 6-5   Review the opening feature of this chapter that highlights Sheila Marcelo and her company **Care.com**. Her company plans to open a kiosk in the Ferry Building in San Francisco to sell Care.com shirts, hats, and other merchandise. Other retail outlets and expansion plans may be in the works.

ENTREPRENEURIAL DECISION

C1   P1

Required

1. List the seven principles of internal control and explain how a retail outlet might implement each of the principles in its store.
2. Do you believe that a retail outlet will need to add controls to the business as it expands? Explain.

BTN 6-6   Visit an area of your college that serves the student community with either products or services. Some examples are food services, libraries, and bookstores. Identify and describe between four and eight internal controls being implemented.

HITTING THE ROAD

C1

7 Accounting for Receivables

Learning Objectives

CONCEPTUAL

C1 Describe accounts receivable and how they occur and are recorded.

C2 Describe a note receivable, the computation of its maturity date, and the recording of its existence.

C3 Explain how receivables can be converted to cash before maturity.

ANALYTICAL

A1 Compute accounts receivable turnover and use it to help assess financial condition.

PROCEDURAL

P1 Apply the direct write-off method to accounts receivable.

P2 Apply the allowance method to accounts receivable.

P3 Estimate uncollectibles based on sales and accounts receivable.

P4 Record the honoring and dishonoring of a note and adjustments for interest.

At Face Value

"Taking initiative pays off"—**SHERYL SANDBERG**

MENLO PARK, CA—Many know the story of how Mark Zuckerberg started **Facebook** (**Facebook.com**) in his college dorm room. How Facebook went from a "cool website" to a profitable company is less well known.

It began at a Christmas party when Sheryl Sandberg met Mark. "We talked for probably an hour by the door," recalls Mark. After much convincing, Sheryl joined Facebook as its chief operating officer.

Sheryl began by reviewing Facebook's financial statements and was alarmed by the lack of revenue and receivables. "There was this open question," explains Sheryl. "Could we make money . . . ever?" She organized a meeting where ideas such as charging a subscription fee and inserting ads were proposed.

As we now know, Facebook committed to an ad-focused model. The strategy was a huge success, and revenues and receivables soared. Sheryl then moved to her next challenge: managing accounts receivable.

Sheryl and Mark saw that decisions on credit sales and extending credit were impacting income. To combat risk of loss, credit is extended to customers who make timely payments.

©Kim White/Bloomberg/Getty Images

Sheryl and Mark also look at cash inflow patterns to estimate uncollectibles and minimize bad debts.

Sheryl enjoys Facebook's success, but her passion is "mission-based." She explains: "I believe strongly in what Facebook's doing. That's why I get up and go to work every day."

Sources: *Facebook website,* January 2019; *BSR.org,* April 2016; *McKinsey,* April 2013; *New Yorker,* July 2011

VALUING ACCOUNTS RECEIVABLE

A *receivable* is an amount due from another party. The two most common receivables are accounts receivable and notes receivable. Other receivables include interest receivable, rent receivable, tax refund receivable, and receivables from employees.

Accounts receivable are amounts due from customers for credit sales. Exhibit 7.1 shows amounts of receivables and their percent of total assets for some well-known companies.

C1

Describe accounts receivable and how they occur and are recorded.

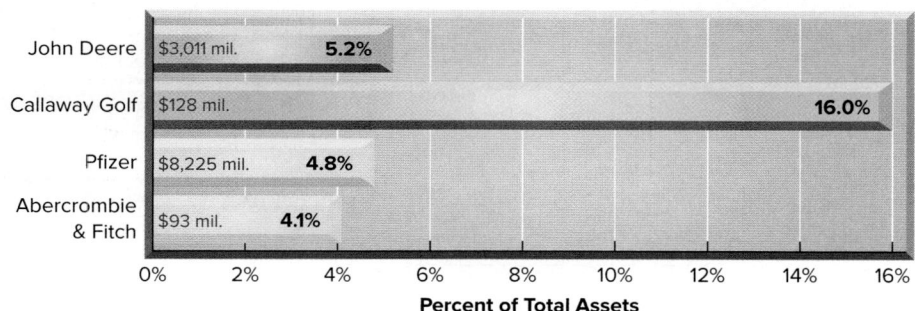

EXHIBIT 7.1

Accounts Receivable for Selected Companies

Sales on Credit   Credit sales are recorded by increasing (debiting) Accounts Receivable. The general ledger has a single Accounts Receivable account (called a *control* account). A company uses a separate account for each customer to track how much that customer purchases, has already paid, and still owes. A supplementary record has a separate account for each customer and is called the *accounts receivable ledger* (or *accounts receivable subsidiary ledger*).

Exhibit 7.2 shows the relation between the Accounts Receivable account in the general ledger and its customer accounts in the accounts receivable ledger for TechCom, a small wholesaler. TechCom's accounts receivable reports a $3,000 ending balance for June 30. TechCom has two credit customers: CompStore and RDA Electronics. Its *schedule of accounts receivable* shows that the $3,000 balance of the Accounts Receivable account in the general ledger equals the total of its two customers' balances in the accounts receivable ledger.

EXHIBIT 7.2

General Ledger and the Accounts Receivable Ledger (before July 1 transactions)

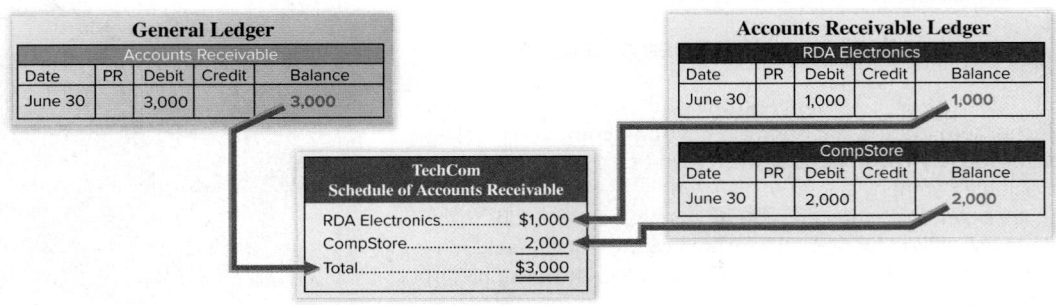

To see how to record accounts receivable from credit sales, we look at two transactions between TechCom and its credit customers—see Exhibit 7.3. The first is a credit sale of $950 to CompStore. The second is a collection of $720 from RDA Electronics from a prior credit sale.

EXHIBIT 7.3

Accounts Receivable Transactions

Assets = Liabilities + Equity
+950   +950

Assets = Liabilities + Equity
+720
−720

July 1	Accounts Receivable—CompStore	950	
	Sales		950
	*Record credit sales.**		
July 1	Cash	720	
	Accounts Receivable—RDA Electronics.............		720
	Record collection of credit sales.		

*We omit the entry to Dr. Cost of Sales and Cr. Inventory to focus on sales and receivables; no sales returns and allowances are expected.

Exhibit 7.4 shows the general ledger and the accounts receivable ledger after recording the two July 1 transactions. The general ledger shows the effects of the sale, the collection, and the resulting balance of $3,230. These transactions are also shown in the individual customer accounts: RDA Electronics's ending balance is $280 and CompStore's ending balance is $2,950. The $3,230 total of customer accounts equals the balance of the Accounts Receivable account in the general ledger.

EXHIBIT 7.4

General Ledger and the Accounts Receivable Ledger (after July 1 transactions)

General Ledger

Accounts Receivable

Date	PR	Debit	Credit	Balance
June 30		3,000		3,000
July 1		950		3,950
July 1			720	**3,230**

Accounts Receivable Ledger

RDA Electronics

Date	PR	Debit	Credit	Balance
June 30		1,000		1,000
July 1			720	**280**

CompStore

Date	PR	Debit	Credit	Balance
June 30		2,000		2,000
July 1		950		**2,950**

TechCom
Schedule of Accounts Receivable

RDA Electronics.................. $ 280
CompStore.......................... 2,950
Total................................ $3,230

Sales on Store Credit Cards

Like TechCom, many large retailers such as **Home Depot** sell on credit. Many also have their own credit cards to grant credit to approved customers and to earn interest on any balance past due. The entries in this case are the same as those for TechCom except for added interest revenue as follows.

Assets = Liabilities + Equity
+1,000   +1,000

Assets = Liabilities + Equity
+15   +15

Nov. 1	Accounts Receivable	1,000	
	Sales		1,000
	Record sales on store credit card.		
Dec. 31	Accounts Receivable	15	
	Interest Revenue.....................................		15
	Interest of $15 earned on store card sales past due.		

Sales on Bank Credit Cards

Most companies allow customers to pay using bank (or third-party) credit cards, such as **Visa**, **Mastercard**, or **American Express**, and debit cards. Sellers allow customers to use credit cards and debit cards for several reasons. First, the seller does not have to decide who gets credit and how much. Second, the seller avoids the risk of customers not paying (this risk is transferred to the card company). Third, the seller typically receives cash from the card company sooner than had it granted credit directly to customers. Fourth, more credit options for customers can lead to more sales.

©Science Photo Library/Image Source

The seller pays a fee when a card is used by the customer, often ranging from 1% to 5% of card sales. This fee reduces the cash received by the seller. If TechCom has $100 of credit card sales with a 4% fee, the entry follows. Some sellers report Credit Card Expense in the income statement as a discount subtracted from sales to get net sales. Other sellers report it as a selling expense or an administrative expense. In this text, we report credit card expense as a selling expense.

Point: JCPenney reported third-party credit card costs exceeding $10 million.

July 15	Cash	96	
	Credit Card Expense	4	
	Sales		100
	*Record credit card sales less a 4% credit card expense.**		

Assets = Liabilities + Equity
+96   +100
                        −4

*We omit the entry to Dr. Cost of Sales and Cr. Inventory to focus on credit card expense.

■ Decision Insight

Credit or Debit? A credit card is authorization by the card company of a line of credit for the buyer—hence, the term *credit card*. A buyer's debit card purchase reduces the buyer's Cash account balance at the card company, which is often a bank. Because the buyer's Cash account balance is a liability (with a credit balance) for the card company to the buyer, the card company would debit that account for a buyer's purchase—hence, the term *debit card*. ■

Sales on Installment

Many companies allow their credit customers to make periodic payments over several months. For example, **Harley-Davidson** reports more than $2 billion in installment receivables. The seller reports such assets as *installment accounts* (or *finance*) *receivable*, which are amounts owed by customers from credit sales for which payment is required in periodic amounts. Most installment receivables require interest payments, and they can be either current or noncurrent assets depending on the time of repayment.

©PhotoAlto

■ Decision Maker

Entrepreneur As a small retailer, you are considering allowing customers to use credit cards. Until now, your store accepted only cash. What analysis do you use to decide? ■ *Answer:* This analysis must weigh benefits versus costs. The main benefit is the potential to increase sales by attracting customers who prefer credit cards. The main cost is the fee charged by the credit card company. We must estimate the expected increase in sales from allowing credit cards and then subtract (1) normal costs and expenses and (2) card fees from the expected sales increase. If analysis shows an increase in profit, the store should probably accept credit cards.

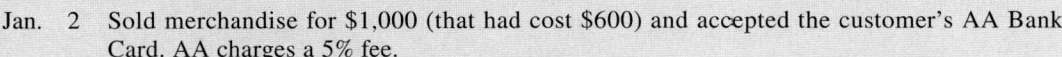

A small retailer accepts credit cards and has its own store credit card. Prepare journal entries to record the following transactions for the retailer. (The retailer uses the perpetual inventory system.)

Jan. 2 Sold merchandise for $1,000 (that had cost $600) and accepted the customer's AA Bank Card. AA charges a 5% fee.

6 Sold merchandise for $400 (that had cost $300) and accepted the customer's VIZA Card. VIZA charges a 3% fee.

31 Recognized the $75 interest revenue earned on its store credit card for January.

NEED-TO-KNOW 7-1

Credit Card Sales

C1

Solution

Jan. 2	Cash	950	
	Credit Card Expense*......................................	50	
	Sales		1,000
	*Record credit card sales less 5% fee. *($1,000 × 0.05)*		
Jan. 2	Cost of Goods Sold	600	
	Merchandise Inventory..........................		600
	Record cost of sales.		
Jan. 6	Cash	388	
	Credit Card Expense†......................................	12	
	Sales		400
	Record credit card sales less 3% fee. †($400 × 0.03)		
Jan. 6	Cost of Goods Sold	300	
	Merchandise Inventory..........................		300
	Record cost of sales.		
Jan. 31	Accounts Receivable	75	
	Interest Revenue..............................		75
	Record interest earned from store credit card.		

Do More: QS 7-1, E 7-2, E 7-3

DIRECT WRITE-OFF METHOD

P1

Apply the direct write-off method to accounts receivable.

When a company directly grants credit to customers, it expects some customers will not pay what they promised. The accounts of these customers are *uncollectible accounts,* or **bad debts.** Uncollectible accounts are an expense of selling on credit. Why do companies sell on credit if they expect uncollectible accounts? The answer is that companies believe that granting credit will increase total sales enough to offset bad debts. Companies use two methods for uncollectible accounts: (1) direct write-off method and (2) allowance method.

Recording and Writing Off Bad Debts   The **direct write-off method** records the loss from an uncollectible account receivable when it is determined to be uncollectible. No attempt is made to predict bad debts expense. If TechCom determines on January 23 that it cannot collect $520 owed by its customer J. Kent, it records the loss as follows. The debit in this entry charges the uncollectible amount directly to the current period's Bad Debts Expense account. The credit removes its balance from the Accounts Receivable account.

Point: Managers realize that some credit sales will be uncollectible, but which credit sales is unknown.

Assets = Liabilities + Equity
−520   −520

Jan. 23	Bad Debts Expense	520	
	Accounts Receivable—J. Kent		520
	Write off an uncollectible account.		

Recovering a Bad Debt   Sometimes an account written off is later collected. If the account of J. Kent that was written off directly to Bad Debts Expense is later collected in full, then we record two entries.

Point: Recovery of a bad debt always requires two journal entries.

Assets = Liabilities + Equity
+520   +520

Mar. 11	Accounts Receivable—J. Kent..........................	520	
	Bad Debts Expense.............................		520
	Reinstate account previously written off.		

Assets = Liabilities + Equity
+520
−520

Mar. 11	Cash	520	
	Accounts Receivable—J. Kent		520
	Record full payment of account.		

Assessing the Direct Write-Off Method   Many publicly traded companies and thousands of privately held companies use the direct write-off method; they include

Rand Medical Billing, Gateway Distributors, First Industrial Realty, New Frontier Energy, Globalink, Solar3D, and **Sub Surface Waste Management**. The following disclosure by **Pharma-Bio Serv** is the usual justification: Bad debts are mainly accounted for using the direct write-off method . . . this method approximates that of the allowance method.

Companies weigh at least two concepts when considering use of the direct write-off method. (1) Expense recognition requires expenses be reported in the same period as the sales they helped produce. The direct write-off method usually does *not* best match sales and expenses because bad debts expense is not recorded until an account becomes uncollectible, which often occurs in a period after the credit sale. (2) The materiality constraint permits use of the direct write-off method when its results are similar to using the allowance method. Otherwise, companies must use the allowance method.

Direct write-off method

Advantages:
- Simple
- No estimates needed

Disadvantages:
- Receivables and income temporarily overstated
- Bad debts expense often not matched with sales

A retailer uses the direct write-off method. Record the following transactions.

Feb. 14   The retailer determines that it cannot collect $400 of its accounts receivable from a customer named ZZZ Company.

Apr. 1   ZZZ Company unexpectedly pays its account in full to the retailer, which then records its recovery of this bad debt.

Solution

Feb. 14	Bad Debts Expense	400	
	Accounts Receivable—ZZZ Co.		400
	Write off an account.		
Apr. 1	Accounts Receivable—ZZZ Co.	400	
	Bad Debts Expense...............................		400
	Reinstate an account previously written off.		
Apr. 1	Cash	400	
	Accounts Receivable—ZZZ Co.		400
	Record cash received on account.		

NEED-TO-KNOW 7-2

Entries under Direct Write-Off Method

P1

Do More: QS 7-2, QS 7-3, E 7-4

ALLOWANCE METHOD

The **allowance method** for bad debts matches the *estimated* loss from uncollectible accounts receivable against the sales they helped produce. We use estimated losses because when sales occur, sellers do not know which customers will not pay. This means that at the end of each period, the allowance method requires an estimate of the total bad debts expected from that period's sales. This method has two advantages over the direct write-off method: (1) It records estimated bad debts expense in the period when the related sales are recorded and (2) it reports accounts receivable on the balance sheet at the estimated amount to be collected.

P2 _____

Apply the allowance method to accounts receivable.

Recording Bad Debts Expense   The allowance method estimates bad debts expense at the end of each accounting period and records it with an adjusting entry. TechCom had credit sales of $300,000 in its first year of operations. At the end of the first year, $20,000 of credit sales were uncollected. Based on the experience of similar businesses, TechCom estimates that $1,500 of its accounts receivable is uncollectible and makes the following adjusting entry.

Method	Bad Debts Expense Recorded . . .
Direct write-off. . .	*In future,* when accounts are uncollectible.
Allowance.	*Currently,* using estimated uncollectibles.

Dec. 31	Bad Debts Expense	1,500	
	Allowance for Doubtful Accounts..................		1,500
	Record estimated bad debts.		

Assets = Liabilities + Equity
−1,500   −1,500

Allowance method

Advantages:
- Receivables fairly stated
- Bad debts expense matched with sales
- Writing off bad debt does not affect net receivables or income

Disadvantages:
- Estimates needed

The estimated Bad Debts Expense of $1,500 is reported on the income statement (as either a selling expense or an administrative expense). The **Allowance for Doubtful Accounts** is a contra asset account. TechCom's account balances for Accounts Receivable and the Allowance for Doubtful Accounts follow.

Accounts Receivable				Allowance for Doubtful Accounts		
Dec. 31	20,000				Dec. 31	1,500

The Allowance for Doubtful Accounts credit balance of $1,500 reduces accounts receivable to its **realizable value,** which is the amount expected to be received. Although credit customers owe $20,000 to TechCom, only $18,500 is expected from customers. (TechCom still bills its customers for $20,000.) In the balance sheet, the Allowance for Doubtful Accounts is subtracted from Accounts Receivable and is often reported as follows.

Current assets		
Accounts receivable...	$20,000	
Less allowance for doubtful accounts.......................	1,500	$18,500

Sometimes the Allowance for Doubtful Accounts is not reported separately as follows.

Current assets	
Accounts receivable (net of $1,500 doubtful accounts)..........	$18,500

Writing Off a Bad Debt

When specific accounts become uncollectible, they are written off against the Allowance for Doubtful Accounts. TechCom decides that J. Kent's $520 account is uncollectible and makes the following entry to write it off.

Assets = Liabilities + Equity
+520
−520

Jan. 23	Allowance for Doubtful Accounts	520	
	Accounts Receivable—J. Kent		520
	Write off an uncollectible account.		

Point: Bad Debts Expense is not debited in the write-off because it was recorded in the period when sales occurred.

This entry removes $520 from the Accounts Receivable account (and the subsidiary ledger). The general ledger accounts appear as follows.

Accounts Receivable				Allowance for Doubtful Accounts			
Dec. 31	20,000					Dec. 31	1,500
		Jan. 23	520	Jan. 23	520		

Point: In posting a write-off, the Explanation column shows the reason for this credit so it is not misinterpreted as payment in full.

The write-off does *not* affect the realizable value of accounts receivable; see Exhibit 7.5. Neither total assets nor net income is affected by the write-off of a specific account. Instead, both assets and net income are affected in the period when bad debts expense is predicted and recorded with an adjusting entry.

EXHIBIT 7.5

Realizable Value before and after Write-Off of a Bad Debt

	Before Write-Off	After Write-Off
Accounts receivable	$ 20,000	$ 19,480
Less allowance for doubtful accounts	1,500	980
Realizable value of accounts receivable	**$18,500**	**$18,500**

Exhibit 7.6 portrays the allowance method. It shows the creation of the allowance for future write-offs—adding to a cookie jar. It also shows the decrease of the allowance through write-offs—taking cookies from the jar.

EXHIBIT 7.6

Increases and Decreases to the Allowance for Doubtful Accounts

Increase Allowance

Bad Debts Expense... #
    Allow. for Doubtful Accts... #

Adjusting entries add to allowance for doubtful accounts.

Allowance for doubtful accounts

Decrease Allowance

Write-offs

Allow. for Doubtful Accts... #
    Accts Receivable—J.Kent... #

Allowance for doubtful accounts

Bad debt write-offs subtract from allowance for doubtful accounts.

Recovering a Bad Debt   If an account that was written off is later collected, two entries are made. The first is to reverse the write-off and reinstate the customer's account. The second is to record the collection of the reinstated account. If on March 11 Kent pays in full his account previously written off, the entries are

Mar. 11	Accounts Receivable—J. Kent..........................	520	
	Allowance for Doubtful Accounts...................		520
	Reinstate account previously written off.		
Mar. 11	Cash...	520	
	Accounts Receivable—J. Kent		520
	Record full payment of account.		

Assets = Liabilities + Equity
+520
−520

Assets = Liabilities + Equity
+520
−520

Kent paid the entire amount previously written off, but sometimes a customer pays only a portion. If we believe this customer will later pay in full, we return the entire amount owed to accounts receivable (in the first entry only). If we expect no further collection, we return only the amount paid.

A retailer uses the allowance method. Record the following transactions.

Dec. 31   The retailer estimates $3,000 of its accounts receivable are uncollectible at its year-end.
Feb. 14   The retailer determines that it cannot collect $400 of its accounts receivable from a customer named ZZZ Company.
Apr. 1   ZZZ Company unexpectedly pays its account in full to the retailer, which then records its recovery of this bad debt.

NEED-TO-KNOW 7-3

Entries under Allowance Method

P2

Solution

Dec. 31	Bad Debts Expense	3,000	
	Allowance for Doubtful Accounts...................		3,000
	Record estimated bad debts.		
Feb. 14	Allowance for Doubtful Accounts	400	
	Accounts Receivable—ZZZ Co.		400
	Write off an account.		
Apr. 1	Accounts Receivable—ZZZ Co........................	400	
	Allowance for Doubtful Accounts..................		400
	Reinstate an account previously written off.		
Apr. 1	Cash..	400	
	Accounts Receivable—ZZZ Co.		400
	Record cash received on account.		

Do More: QS 7-4, QS 7-5, E 7-5

ESTIMATING BAD DEBTS

P3 _____

Estimate uncollectibles based on sales and accounts receivable.

Point: Focus on *credit* sales because cash sales do not produce bad debts.

Bad debts expense is estimated under the allowance method. This section covers methods for estimating bad debts expense.

Percent of Sales Method

The *percent of sales method,* or *income statement method,* assumes that a percent of credit sales for the period is uncollectible. For example, Musicland has credit sales of $400,000 in 2019. Musicland estimates 0.6% of credit sales to be uncollectible. This means Musicland expects $2,400 of bad debts expense from its sales ($400,000 × 0.006) and makes the following adjusting entry.

Assets = Liabilities + Equity
−2,400   −2,400

Dec. 31*	Bad Debts Expense	2,400	
	Allowance for Doubtful Accounts.		2,400
	Record estimated bad debts.		

Bad Debts Expense	
Unadj. bal.	0
Adj. (% sales)	**2,400**
Est. bal.	2,400

*The adjusting entry applies our three-step adjusting entry process:
Step 1: Current balance for Bad Debts Expense <u>is</u> $0 debit (as the expense account was closed in prior period).
Step 2: Current balance for Bad Debts Expense <u>should be</u> $2,400 debit.
Step 3: Record entry to get from step 1 to step 2.

Point: When using the *percent of sales method* for estimating uncollectibles, and because the "Unadj. bal." in Bad Debts Expense is always $0, the adjusting entry amount always equals the % of sales.

Allowance for Doubtful Accounts, a balance sheet account, is not closed at period end. Unless a company is in its first period of operations, its Allowance for Doubtful Accounts balance rarely equals the Bad Debts Expense balance. (When computing bad debts expense as a percent of sales, managers monitor and adjust the percent so it is not too high or too low.)

Percent of Receivables Method

The *percent of accounts receivable method,* also called a *balance sheet method,* assumes that a percent of a company's receivables is uncollectible. This percent is based on experience and economic trends. Total receivables is multiplied by this percent to get the estimated uncollectible amount as reported in the balance sheet as Allowance for Doubtful Accounts.

Assume Musicland has $50,000 of accounts receivable on December 31, 2019. It estimates 5% of its receivables is uncollectible. This means that *after* the adjusting entry is posted, we want the Allowance for Doubtful Accounts to show a $2,500 credit balance (5% of $50,000). Musicland's beginning balance is $2,200 on December 31, 2018—see Exhibit 7.7.

EXHIBIT 7.7

Allowance for Doubtful Accounts after Bad Debts Adjusting Entry

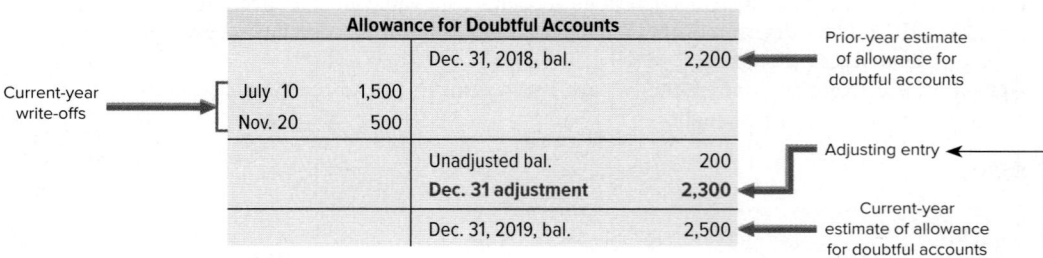

During 2019, accounts of customers are written off on July 10 and November 20. The account has a $200 credit balance *before* the December 31, 2019, adjustment. The adjusting entry to give the allowance account the estimated $2,500 balance is

Assets = Liabilities + Equity
−2,300   −2,300

Dec. 31*	Bad Debts Expense	2,300	
	Allowance for Doubtful Accounts.		2,300
	Record estimated bad debts.		

*The adjusting entry applies our three-step adjusting entry process:
Step 1: Current balance for Allowance account <u>is</u> $200 credit.
Step 2: Current balance for Allowance account <u>should be</u> $2,500 credit.
Step 3: Record entry to get from step 1 to step 2.

■ **Decision Insight**

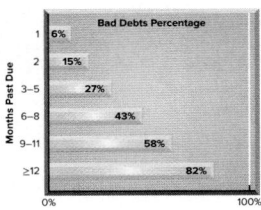

For the Ages   Unlike wine, accounts receivable do not improve with age. The longer a receivable is past due, the less likely it is to be collected. An *aging schedule* uses this knowledge to estimate bad debts. The chart here is from a survey that reported estimates of bad debts for receivables grouped by how long they were past their due dates. Each company sets its own estimates based on its customers and its customers' payment patterns. ■

Aging of Receivables Method

The **aging of accounts receivable** method, also called a *balance sheet method,* is applied like the percent of receivables method except that several percentages are used (versus one) to estimate the allowance. Each receivable is classified by how long it is past its due date. Then estimates of uncollectible amounts are made assuming that the longer an amount is past due, the more likely it is uncollectible. After the amounts are classified (or aged), experience is used to estimate the percent of each uncollectible class. These percents are multiplied by the amounts in each class to get the estimated balance of the Allowance for Doubtful Accounts. An example schedule is shown in Exhibit 7.8.

Exhibit 7.8 lists each customer's balance assigned to one of five classes based on its days past due. The amounts in each class are totaled and multiplied by the estimated percent of uncollectible accounts for each class.

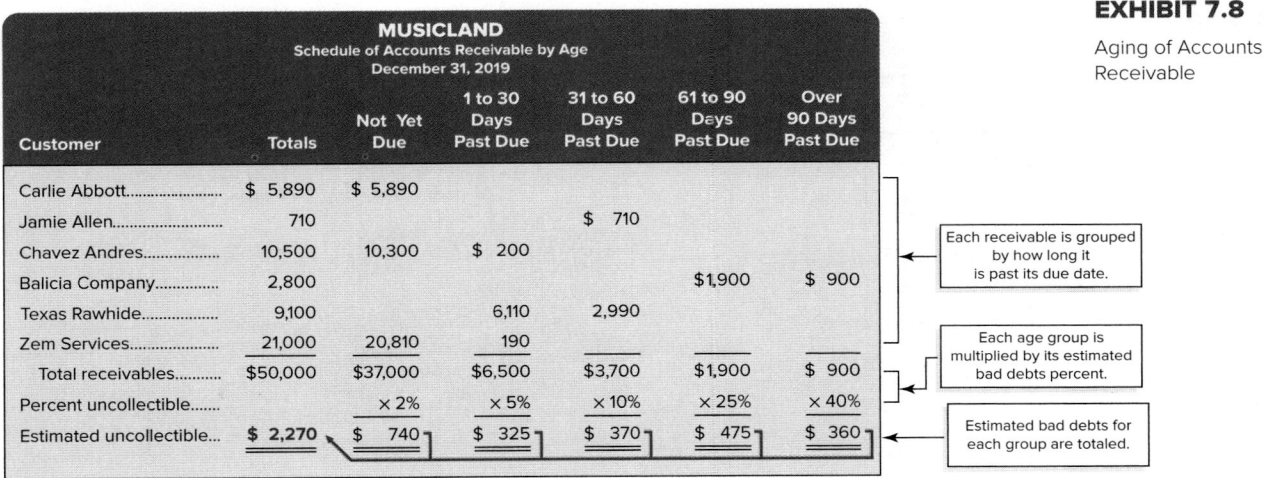

EXHIBIT 7.8

Aging of Accounts Receivable

To explain, Musicland has $3,700 in accounts receivable that are 31 to 60 days past due. Management estimates 10% of the amounts in this class are uncollectible, or a total of $370 ($3,700 × 10%). Similar analysis is done for each class. The final total of $2,270 ($740 + $325 + $370 + $475 + $360) shown in the first column is the estimated balance for the Allowance for Doubtful Accounts. Exhibit 7.9 shows that because the allowance account has an unadjusted

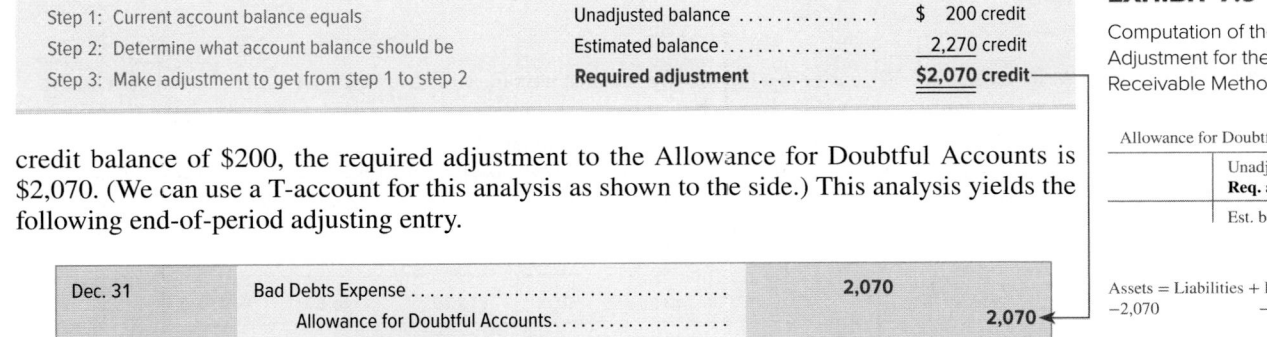

EXHIBIT 7.9

Computation of the Required Adjustment for the Accounts Receivable Method

credit balance of $200, the required adjustment to the Allowance for Doubtful Accounts is $2,070. (We can use a T-account for this analysis as shown to the side.) This analysis yields the following end-of-period adjusting entry.

Allowance for Doubtful Accounts		
Unadj. bal. 500		
	Req. adj.	2,770
	Est. bal.	2,270

Assets = Liabilities + Equity
−2,770   −2,770

EXHIBIT 7.10

Methods to Estimate Bad Debts under the Allowance Method

Unadjusted Debit Balance in the Allowance Account   If the allowance account had an unadjusted *debit* balance of $500 (instead of the $200 credit balance), its required adjustment is computed as follows. (A T-account can be used for this analysis as shown to the side.)

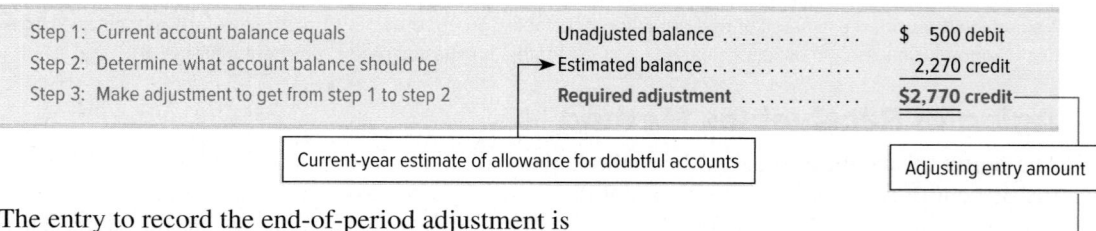

Step 1: Current account balance equals → Unadjusted balance .... $ 500 debit
Step 2: Determine what account balance should be → Estimated balance................. 2,270 credit
Step 3: Make adjustment to get from step 1 to step 2 → **Required adjustment** .... **$2,770 credit**

Current-year estimate of allowance for doubtful accounts

Adjusting entry amount

The entry to record the end-of-period adjustment is

Dec. 31	Bad Debts Expense	2,770	
	Allowance for Doubtful Accounts...................		2,770
	Record estimated bad debts.		

Estimating Bad Debts—Summary of Methods   Exhibit 7.10 summarizes the three estimation methods. The aging of accounts receivable method focuses on specific accounts and is usually the most reliable of the estimation methods.

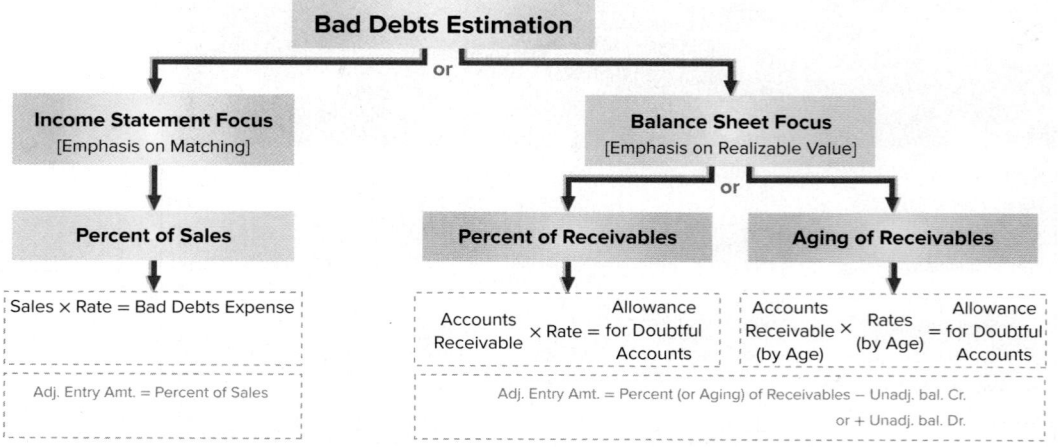

Bad Debts Estimation

Income Statement Focus [Emphasis on Matching]

Percent of Sales

Sales × Rate = Bad Debts Expense

Adj. Entry Amt. = Percent of Sales

Balance Sheet Focus [Emphasis on Realizable Value]

Percent of Receivables

Accounts Receivable × Rate = Allowance for Doubtful Accounts

Aging of Receivables

Accounts Receivable (by Age) × Rates (by Age) = Allowance for Doubtful Accounts

Adj. Entry Amt. = Percent (or Aging) of Receivables − Unadj. bal. Cr. or + Unadj. bal. Dr.

■ Decision Maker

©kali9/Getty Images

Labor Union   One week prior to labor contract negotiations, financial statements are released showing no income growth. A 10% growth was predicted. Your analysis finds that the company increased its allowance for uncollectibles from 1.5% to 4.5% of receivables. Without this change, income would show a 9% growth. Does this analysis impact negotiations? ■   *Answer:* Yes, this information is likely to impact negotiations. The obvious question is why the company greatly increased this allowance. The large increase means a substantial increase in bad debts expense and a decrease in earnings. This change (coming prior to labor negotiations) also raises concerns because it reduces labor's bargaining power. We want to ask management for documentation justifying this increase.

 **NEED-TO-KNOW 7-4**

Estimating Bad Debts

P3

At its December 31 year-end, a company estimates uncollectible accounts using the allowance method.
1. It prepared the following aging of receivables analysis. (a) Estimate the balance of the Allowance for Doubtful Accounts using the aging of accounts receivable method. (b) Prepare the adjusting entry to record bad debts expense using the estimate from part *a*. Assume the unadjusted balance in the Allowance for Doubtful Accounts is a $10 debit.

| | Total | Days Past Due | | | | |
		0	1 to 30	31 to 60	61 to 90	Over 90
Accounts receivable	$2,600	$2,000	$300	$80	$100	$120
Percent uncollectible		1%	2%	5%	7%	10%

2. Refer to the data in part 1. (a) Estimate the balance of the Allowance for Doubtful Accounts assuming the company uses 2% of total accounts receivable to estimate uncollectibles instead of the aging of receivables method in part 1. (b) Prepare the adjusting entry to record bad debts expense using the estimate from part 2*a*. Assume the unadjusted balance in the Allowance for Doubtful Accounts is a $4 credit.

3. Refer to the data in part 1. (a) Estimate the balance of the uncollectibles assuming the company uses 0.5% of annual credit sales (annual credit sales were $10,000). (b) Prepare the adjusting entry to record bad debts expense using the estimate from part 3*a*. Assume the unadjusted balance in the Allowance for Doubtful Accounts is a $4 credit.

Solutions

1a. Computation of the estimated balance of the allowance for uncollectibles.

Not due	$2,000 × 0.01 =	$20
1 to 30	300 × 0.02 =	6
31 to 60	80 × 0.05 =	4
61 to 90	100 × 0.07 =	7
Over 90	120 × 0.10 =	12
		$49 credit

Do More: QS 7-7, QS 7-8, QS 7-9, E 7-6, E 7-7, E 7-8, E 7-9, E 7-10, E 7-11

1b.

Dec. 31	Bad Debts Expense	59	
	Allowance for Doubtful Accounts		59
	*Record estimated bad debts.**		

Allowance for Doubtful Accounts

Unadj. Dec. 31	10		
		Adj. Dec. 31	59
		Est. bal. Dec. 31	49

Step 1: Current account balance equals	*Unadjusted balance	$10 debit
Step 2: Determine what account balance should be	Estimated balance	49 credit
Step 3: Make adjustment to get from step 1 to step 2	Required adjustment	$59 credit

2a. Computation of the estimated balance of the allowance for uncollectibles.

$2,600 × 0.02 = $52 credit

2b.

Dec. 31	Bad Debts Expense	48	
	Allowance for Doubtful Accounts		48
	*Record estimated bad debts.**		

Allowance for Doubtful Accounts

		Unadj. Dec. 31	4
		Adj. Dec. 31	48
		Est. bal. Dec. 31	52

Step 1: Current account balance equals	*Unadjusted balance	$ 4 credit
Step 2: Determine what account balance should be	Estimated balance	52 credit
Step 3: Make adjustment to get from step 1 to step 2	Required adjustment	$48 credit

3a. Computation of the estimated balance of the bad debts expense.

$10,000 × 0.005 = $50 credit

3b.

Dec. 31	Bad Debts Expense	50	
	Allowance for Doubtful Accounts		50
	Record estimated bad debts.		

Bad Debts Expense

Unadj. Dec. 31	0	
Adj. Dec. 31	50	
Est. bal. Dec. 31	50	

NOTES RECEIVABLE

A **promissory note** is a written promise to pay a specified amount, usually with interest, either on demand or at a stated future date. Promissory notes are used in many transactions, including paying for products and services and lending and borrowing money. Sellers sometimes ask for a note to replace an account receivable when a customer requests more time to pay a past-due account. Sellers prefer notes when the credit period is long and when the receivable is for a large amount. If a lawsuit is needed to collect from a customer, a note is the customer's written promise to pay the debt, its amount, and its terms.

C2

Describe a note receivable, the computation of its maturity date, and the recording of its existence.

Exhibit 7.11 shows a promissory note dated July 10, 2019. For this note, Julia Browne promises to pay TechCom or to its order a specified amount ($1,000), called the **principal of a note,** at a stated future date (October 8, 2019). As the one who signed the note and promised to pay it, Browne is the **maker of the note.** As the person to whom the note is payable, TechCom is the **payee of the note.** To Browne, the note is a liability called a *note payable.* To TechCom, the same note is an asset called a *note receivable.* This note's interest rate is 12%, as written on the note. **Interest** is the charge for using the money until its due date. To a borrower, interest is an expense. To a lender, it is revenue.

EXHIBIT 7.11

Promissory Note

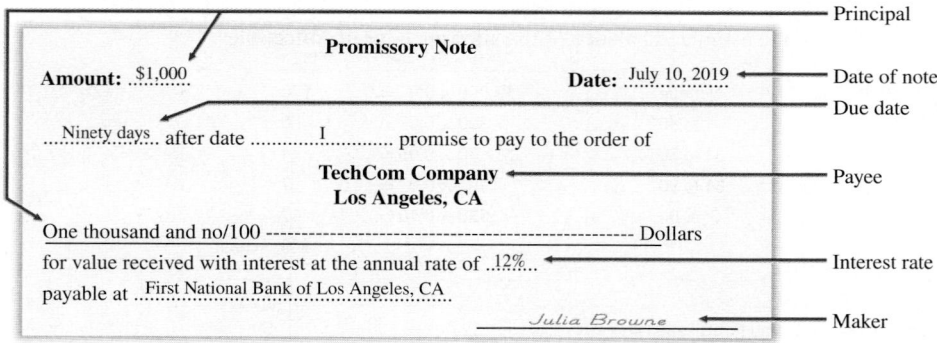

Computing Maturity and Interest

This section covers a note's maturity date, period covered, and interest computation.

Maturity Date and Period   The **maturity date of a note** is the day the note (principal and interest) must be repaid. The *period* of a note is the time from the note's (contract) date to its maturity date. Many notes mature in less than a full year, and the period they cover is often expressed in days. As an example, a five-day note dated June 15 matures and is due on June 20. A 90-day note dated July 10 matures on October 8. This count is shown in Exhibit 7.12. The period of a note is sometimes expressed in months or years. When months are used, the note is payable in the month of its maturity on the *same day of the month* as its original date. A nine-month note dated July 10, for example, is payable on April 10. The same rule applies when years are used.

Point: When counting days, omit the day a note is issued, but count the due date.

EXHIBIT 7.12

Maturity Date Computation

Days in July.	31
Minus the date of the note.	10
Days remaining in July	21 ← July 11–31
Add days in August.	31 ← Aug. 1–31
Add days in September	30 ← Sep. 1–30
Days to equal 90 days, or **maturity date of October 8**.	8 ← Oct. 1–8
Period of the note in days	90

Point: Excel for maturity date.

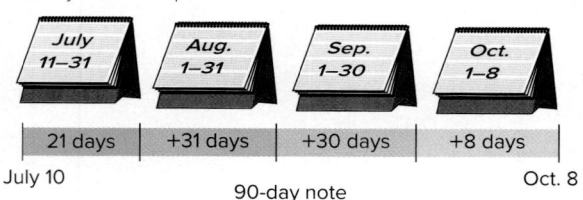

Interest Computation   *Interest* is the cost of borrowing money for the borrower and the profit from lending money for the lender. Unless otherwise stated, the rate of interest on a note is the rate charged for the use of principal for one year (*annual rate*). The formula for computing interest on a note is in Exhibit 7.13.

EXHIBIT 7.13

Computation of Interest Formula

Principal of the note	×	Annual interest rate	×	Time expressed in fraction of year	=	Interest

To simplify interest computations, a year is commonly treated as having 360 days (called the *banker's rule* and widely used in business transactions). **We treat a year as having 360 days**

for interest computations in examples and assignments. Using the promissory note in Exhibit 7.11, where we have a 90-day, 12%, $1,000 note, the total interest follows.

$$\$1,000 \times 12\% \times \frac{90}{360} = \$1,000 \times 0.12 \times 0.25 = \$30$$

Point: If the *banker's rule* is <u>not</u> used, interest is **$29.589041**. The *banker's rule* yields $30, which is easier to account for than $29.589041.

Point: *Maturity value* of a note equals principal plus interest earned.

Recording Notes Receivable

Notes receivable are usually recorded in a single Notes Receivable account to simplify record-keeping. To show how we record receipt of a note, we use the $1,000, 90-day, 12% promissory note in Exhibit 7.11. TechCom received this note at the time of a product sale to Julia Browne. This is recorded as

July 10*	Notes Receivable...	1,000	
	Sales		1,000
	Sold goods in exchange for a 90-day, 12% note.		

Assets = Liabilities + Equity
+1,000   +1,000

*We omit the entry to Dr. Cost of Sales and Cr. Inventory to focus on sales and receivables.

When a seller accepts a note from an overdue customer to grant a time extension on a past-due account receivable, it often will collect part of the past-due balance in cash. Assume that TechCom agreed to accept $232 in cash along with a $600, 60-day, 15% note from Jo Cook to settle her $832 past-due account. TechCom makes the following entry.

Oct. 5	Cash	232	
	Notes Receivable...	600	
	Accounts Receivable—J. Cook....................		832
	Received cash and note to settle account.		

Assets = Liabilities + Equity
+232
+600
−832

Valuing and Settling Notes

Recording an Honored Note
The principal and interest of a note are due on its maturity date. The maker of the note usually *honors* the note and pays it in full. When J. Cook pays the note above on its due date, TechCom records it as follows. Interest revenue, or *interest earned,* is reported on the income statement.

P4

Record the honoring and dishonoring of a note and adjustments for interest.

Dec. 4	Cash	615	
	Notes Receivable		600
	Interest Revenue................................		15
	Collect note with interest of $600 × 15% × 60/360.		

Assets = Liabilities + Equity
+615   +15
−600

Recording a Dishonored Note
When a note's maker does not pay at maturity, the note is *dishonored*. Dishonoring a note does not mean the maker no longer has to pay. The payee still tries to collect. How do companies report this? The balance of the Notes Receivable account should only include notes that have not matured. When a note is dishonored, we remove the amount of this note from Notes Receivable and charge it back to an account receivable from its maker. Assume that J. Cook dishonors the note at maturity. The following records the dishonoring of the note.

Dec. 4	Accounts Receivable—J. Cook	615	
	Interest Revenue...............................		15
	Notes Receivable		600
	Charge account of J. Cook for a dishonored note and interest of $600 × 15% × 60/360.		

Assets = Liabilities + Equity
+615   +15
−600

Charging a dishonored note to accounts receivable does two things. First, it removes the note from the Notes Receivable account and records the dishonored note in the maker's account. Second, if the maker of the dishonored note asks for credit in the future, his or her account will show the dishonored note.

Recording End-of-Period Interest Adjustment

When notes receivable are outstanding at period-end, any accrued interest is recorded. Assume on December 16 TechCom accepts a $3,000, 60-day, 12% note from a customer. When TechCom's accounting period ends on December 31, $15 of interest has accrued on this note ($3,000 × 12% × 15/360). The following adjusting entry records this revenue.

Assets = Liabilities + Equity
+15   +15

Dec. 31	Interest Receivable	15	
	Interest Revenue...............................		15
	Record accrued interest earned.		

Interest revenue is on the income statement, and interest receivable is on the balance sheet as a current asset. When the December 16 note is collected on February 14, TechCom's entry to record the cash receipt is

Assets = Liabilities + Equity
+3,060   +45
−15
−3,000

Feb. 14	Cash	3,060	
	Interest Revenue...............................		45
	Interest Receivable............................		15
	Notes Receivable		3,000
	Received payment of note and its interest.		

Total interest on the 60-day note is $60 ($3,000 × 12% × 60/360). The $15 credit to Interest Receivable is the collection of interest accrued from the December 31 entry. The $45 interest revenue is from holding the note from January 1 to February 14.

NEED-TO-KNOW 7-5

Honoring and
Dishonoring Notes

C2 P4

Ace Company purchases $1,400 of merchandise from Zitco on December 16. Zitco accepts Ace's $1,400, 90-day, 12% note as payment. Zitco's accounting period ends on December 31.

a. Prepare entries for Zitco on December 16 and December 31.

b. Prepare Zitco's March 16 entry if Ace dishonors the note.

c. Instead of the facts in part *b*, prepare Zitco's March 16 entry if Ace honors the note.

d. Assume the facts in part *b* (Ace dishonors the note). Then, on March 31, Zitco writes off the receivable from Ace Company. Prepare that write-off entry assuming that Zitco uses the allowance method.

Solution

a.

Dec. 16	Note Receivable—Ace.............................	1,400	
	Sales		1,400
Dec. 31	Interest Receivable	7	
	Interest Revenue ($1,400 × 12% × 15/360)......		7

b.

Mar. 16	Accounts Receivable—Ace	1,442	
	Interest Revenue ($1,400 × 12% × 75/360)......		35
	Interest Receivable............................		7
	Notes Receivable—Ace		1,400

c.

Mar. 16	Cash	1,442	
	Interest Revenue...............................		35
	Interest Receivable............................		7
	Notes Receivable—Ace		1,400

d.

Mar. 31	Allowance for Doubtful Accounts	1,442	
	Accounts Receivable—Ace....................		1,442

Do More: QS 7-10, QS 7-11,
QS 7-12, QS 7-13, E 7-12,
E 7-13, E 7-14, E 7-15

Disposal of Receivables

Companies convert receivables to cash before they are due if they need cash or do not want to deal with collecting receivables. This is usually done by (1) selling them or (2) using them as security for a loan.

C3

Explain how receivables can be converted to cash before maturity.

Selling Receivables

A company can sell its receivables to a finance company or bank. The buyer, called a *factor,* acquires ownership of the receivables and receives cash when they come due. The seller is charged a *factoring fee*. By incurring a factoring fee, the seller gets cash earlier and can pass the risk of bad debts to the factor. The seller also avoids costs of billing and accounting for receivables. If TechCom sells $20,000 of its accounts receivable and is charged a 4% factoring fee, it records this sale as follows.

Point: A seller of receivables always receives less cash than the amount of receivables sold due to factoring fees.

Aug. 15	Cash	19,200	
	Factoring Fee Expense	800	
	Accounts Receivable............................		20,000
	Sold accounts receivable for cash less 4% fee.		

Assets = Liabilities + Equity
+19,200   −800
−20,000

Pledging Receivables

A company can borrow money by *pledging* its receivables as security for the loan. If the borrower defaults on (does not pay) the loan, the lender is paid from the cash receipts of the receivables. The borrower discloses pledging receivables in financial statement footnotes. If TechCom borrows $35,000 and pledges its receivables as security, it records

Aug. 20	Cash	35,000	
	Notes Payable................................		35,000
	Borrow with a note secured by pledging receivables.		

Assets = Liabilities + Equity
+35,000 +35,000

▪ Decision Maker

Analyst/Auditor   You are reviewing accounts receivable. Over the past five years, the allowance account as a percentage of gross accounts receivable shows a steady downward trend. What does this finding suggest? ▪ *Answer:* The downward trend means the company is reducing the relative amount charged to bad debts expense each year. This could be to increase net income. Alternatively, collections may have improved and fewer bad debts are justified.

©Rawpixel.com/Shutterstock

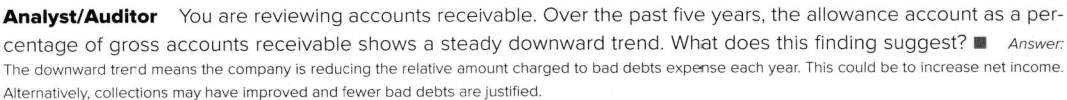 

Accounts Receivable Turnover ▢▢▢ **Decision Analysis**

Accounts receivable turnover helps assess the quality and liquidity of receivables. *Quality* of receivables is the likelihood of collection without loss. *Liquidity* of receivables is the speed of collection. **Accounts receivable turnover** measures how often, on average, receivables are collected during the period and is defined in Exhibit 7.14.

$$\text{Accounts receivable turnover} = \frac{\text{Net sales}}{\text{Average accounts receivable, net}}$$

EXHIBIT 7.14

Accounts Receivable Turnover

The denominator is the *average* accounts receivable, net balance, computed as (Beginning balance + Ending balance) ÷ 2. TechCom has an accounts receivable turnover of 5.1. This means its average accounts receivable balance is converted into cash 5.1 times during the period, which is pictured here.

A1

Compute accounts receivable turnover and use it to help assess financial condition.

5.1 times per year

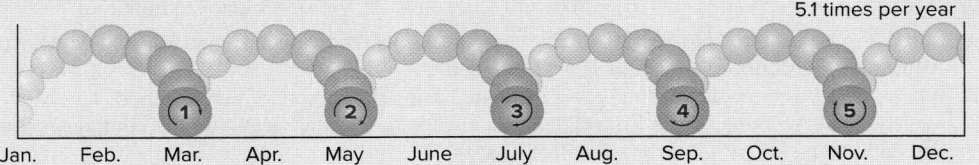

Accounts receivable turnover shows how well management is doing in granting credit to customers. A high turnover suggests that management should consider using less strict credit terms to increase sales. A low turnover suggests management should consider more strict credit terms and more aggressive collection efforts to avoid having assets tied up in accounts receivable.

Exhibit 7.15 shows accounts receivable turnover for **Visa** and **Mastercard**.

EXHIBIT 7.15

Analysis Using Accounts
Receivable Turnover

Company	Figure ($ millions)	Current Year	1 Year Ago	2 Years Ago
Visa	Net sales..............................	$18,358	$15,082	$13,880
	Average accounts receivable, net...........	$ 1,087	$ 944	$ 835
	Accounts receivable turnover.............	**16.9**	**16.0**	**16.6**
Mastercard	Net sales..............................	$12,497	$10,776	$ 9,667
	Average accounts receivable, net...........	$ 1,693	$ 1,248	$ 1,094
	Accounts receivable turnover.............	**7.4**	**8.6**	**8.8**

Visa's current year turnover is 16.9, computed as $18,358/$1,087 ($ millions). This means that Visa's average accounts receivable balance was converted into cash 16.9 times in the current year. Its turnover slightly increased in the current year (16.9) compared with one year ago (16.0). Visa's turnover also exceeds that for Mastercard in each of these three years. Both Visa and Mastercard seem to be doing an adequate job of managing receivables.

■ **Decision** Maker ━━━━━━━━━━━━━━━━━━━━━━━

Family Physician   Your medical practice is barely profitable, so you hire an analyst. The analyst says, *"Accounts receivable turnover is too low. Tighter credit policies are recommended along with discontinuing service to those most delayed in payments."* What actions do you take? ■   *Answer:* Both suggestions are probably financially wise recommendations, but we may be troubled by eliminating services to those less able to pay. One alternative is to follow the recommendations but start a care program directed at patients less able to pay for services. This allows you to continue services to patients less able to pay and to discontinue services to patients able but unwilling to pay.

NEED-TO-KNOW **7-6**

COMPREHENSIVE

Recording Accounts
and Notes Receivable
Transactions; Estimating
Bad Debts

Clayco Company completes the following transactions during the year.

July 14 Writes off a $750 account receivable arising from a sale to Briggs Company that dates to 10 months ago. (Clayco Company uses the allowance method.)

    30 Clayco Company receives a $1,000, 90-day, 10% note in exchange for merchandise sold to Sumrell Company (the merchandise cost $600).

Aug. 15 Receives $2,000 cash plus a $10,000 note from JT Co. in exchange for merchandise that sells for $12,000 (its cost is $8,000). The note is dated August 15, bears 12% interest, and matures in 120 days.

Nov. 1 Completes a $200 credit card sale with a 4% fee (the cost of sales is $150). The cash is transferred immediately from the credit card company.

     3 Sumrell Company refuses to pay the note that was due to Clayco Company on October 28. Prepare the journal entry to charge the dishonored note plus accrued interest to Sumrell Company's accounts receivable.

     5 Completes a $500 credit card sale with a 5% fee (the cost of sales is $300). The cash is transferred immediately from the credit card company.

    15 Receives the full amount of $750 from Briggs Company that was previously written off on July 14. Record the bad debts recovery.

Dec. 13 Receives payment of principal plus interest from JT for the August 15 note.

Required

1. Prepare Clayco Company's journal entries to record these transactions.

2. Prepare a year-end adjusting journal entry as of December 31 for each separate situation.

  a. Bad debts are estimated to be $20,400 by aging accounts receivable. The unadjusted balance of the Allowance for Doubtful Accounts is a $1,000 debit.

  b. Alternatively, assume that bad debts are estimated using the percent of sales method. The Allowance for Doubtful Accounts had a $1,000 debit balance before adjustment, and the company estimates bad debts to be 1% of its credit sales of $2,000,000.

PLANNING THE SOLUTION

● Examine each transaction to determine the accounts affected, and then record the entries.

● For the year-end adjustment, record the bad debts expense for the two approaches.

SOLUTION

1.

July 14	Allowance for Doubtful Accounts	750	
	Accounts Receivable—Briggs Co.		750
	Wrote off an uncollectible account.		
July 30	Notes Receivable—Sumrell Co.	1,000	
	Sales		1,000
	Sold merchandise for a 90-day, 10% note.		
July 30	Cost of Goods Sold	600	
	Merchandise Inventory.		600
	Record the cost of July 30 sale.		
Aug. 15	Cash	2,000	
	Notes Receivable—JT Co.	10,000	
	Sales		12,000
	Sold merchandise for $2,000 cash and $10,000 note.		
Aug. 15	Cost of Goods Sold	8,000	
	Merchandise Inventory.		8,000
	Record the cost of Aug. 15 sale.		
Nov. 1	Cash	192	
	Credit Card Expense	8	
	Sales		200
	Record credit card sale less a 4% credit card expense.		
Nov. 1	Cost of Goods Sold	150	
	Merchandise Inventory.		150
	Record the cost of Nov. 1 sale.		

Nov. 3	Accounts Receivable—Sumrell Co.	1,025	
	Interest Revenue.		25
	Notes Receivable—Sumrell Co.		1,000
	Charge account of Sumrell Co. for a $1,000 dishonored note and interest of $1,000 × 10% × 90/360.		
Nov. 5	Cash	475	
	Credit Card Expense	25	
	Sales		500
	Record credit card sale less a 5% credit card expense.		
Nov. 5	Cost of Goods Sold	300	
	Merchandise Inventory.		300
	Record the cost of Nov. 5 sale.		
Nov. 15	Accounts Receivable—Briggs Co.	750	
	Allowance for Doubtful Accounts. . . .		750
	Reinstate account of Briggs Co. previously written off.		
Nov. 15	Cash	750	
	Accounts Receivable—Briggs Co.		750
	Cash received in full payment of account.		
Dec. 13	Cash	10,400	
	Interest Revenue.		400
	Note Receivable—JT Co.		10,000
	Collect note with interest of $10,000 × 12% × 120/360.		

2a. Aging of accounts receivable method.

Dec. 31	Bad Debts Expense	21,400	
	Allowance for Doubtful Accounts.		21,400
	Adjust allowance account from a $1,000 debit balance to a $20,400 credit balance.		

2b. Percent of sales method. (For the income statement approach, which requires estimating bad debts as a percent of sales or credit sales, the Allowance for Doubtful Accounts balance is *not* considered when making the adjusting entry.)

Dec. 31	Bad Debts Expense	20,000	
	Allowance for Doubtful Accounts.		20,000
	Record bad debts expense as 1% × $2,000,000 of credit sales.		

Summary: Cheat Sheet

VALUING RECEIVABLES

Accounts Receivable: Amounts due from customers for credit sales.

Credit sales and later collection:

Accounts Receivable—CompStore	950	
Sales.		950
Cash	720	
Accounts Receivable—RDA Electronics		720

Store credit card interest revenue:

Accounts Receivable	15	
Interest Revenue		15

Sales using bank credit card:

Cash	96	
Credit Card Expense.	4	
Sales.		100

DIRECT WRITE-OFF METHOD

Direct write-off method: Record bad debt expense when an account is determined to be uncollectible.

Writing off a bad debt under *direct method*:

| Bad Debts Expense .... | 520 | |
| Accounts Receivable—J. Kent.................. | | 520 |

Bad debt later recovered under *direct method*:

Accounts Receivable—J. Kent	520	
Bad Debts Expense.........................		520
Cash	520	
Accounts Receivable—J. Kent..................		520

ALLOWANCE METHOD

Allowance method: Matches estimated loss from uncollectible accounts receivable against the sales they helped produce.

Estimating bad debts:

| Bad Debts Expense .... | 1,500 | |
| Allowance for Doubtful Accounts .... | | 1,500 |

Allowance for Doubtful Accounts: A contra asset account that reduces accounts receivable.

Writing off a bad debt under *allowance method*:

| Allowance for Doubtful Accounts .... | 520 | |
| Accounts Receivable—J. Kent.................. | | 520 |

Bad debt is later recovered under *allowance method*:

Accounts Receivable—J. Kent	520	
Allowance for Doubtful Accounts		520
Cash	520	
Accounts Receivable—J. Kent..................		520

ESTIMATING BAD DEBTS

When using the allowance method, we often use one of the following methods to estimate bad debts.

- **Percent of sales:** Uses a percent of credit sales for the period to estimate bad debts.
- **Percent of accounts receivable:** Uses a percent of accounts receivable to estimate bad debts.
- **Aging of accounts receivable:** Applies several percentages to accounts receivable to estimate bad debts.

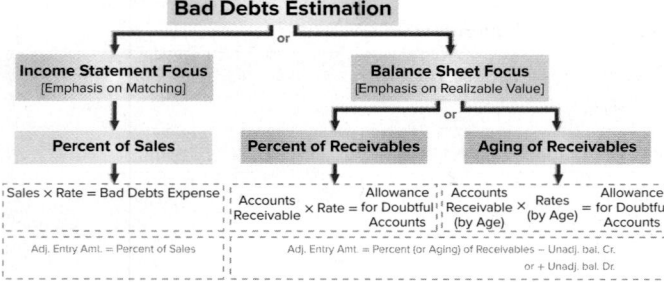

NOTES RECEIVABLE

Note receivable: A promise to pay a specified amount of money at a future date.
Principal of a note: Amount promised to be repaid.
Maturity date: Day the note must be repaid.

Interest formula (year assumed to have 360 days):

| Principal of the note | × | Annual interest rate | × | Time expressed in fraction of year | = | Interest |

Note receivable from sales:

| Notes Receivable .... | 1,000 | |
| Sales.. | | 1,000 |

Note receivable and cash in exchange for accounts receivable:

Cash	232	
Notes Receivable	600	
Accounts Receivable—J. Cook		832

Note is *honored;* cash received in full (with interest):

Cash	615	
Notes Receivable............................		600
Interest Revenue		15

Note is *dishonored;* receivable and interest recorded:

Accounts Receivable—J. Cook.....................	615	
Interest Revenue		15
Notes Receivable............................		600

Accrue interest on note receivable:

| Interest Receivable.............................. | 15 | |
| Interest Revenue .... | | 15 |

Note is *honored;* when note term runs over two periods:

Cash	3,060	
Interest Revenue		45
Interest Receivable		15
Notes Receivable............................		3,000

Factoring (selling) receivables: Accounts receivable are sold to a bank and the seller is charged a *factoring fee*.

Sale of receivables for cash with a charged factor fee:

Cash	19,200	
Factoring Fee Expense..........................	800	
Accounts Receivable.........................		20,000

Pledging of receivables: Borrowing money by *pledging* receivables as security for a loan. Borrower discloses pledging in notes to financial statement.

Key Terms

Accounts receivable (271)
Accounts receivable turnover (285)
Aging of accounts receivable (279)
Allowance for Doubtful Accounts (276)
Allowance method (275)

Bad debts (274)
Direct write-off method (274)
Interest (282)
Maker of the note (282)
Maturity date of a note (282)

Payee of the note (282)
Principal of a note (282)
Promissory note (or note) (281)
Realizable value (276)

Multiple Choice Quiz

1. A company's Accounts Receivable balance at its December 31 year-end is $125,650, and its Allowance for Doubtful Accounts has a credit balance of $328 before year-end adjustment. Its net sales are $572,300. It estimates that 4% of outstanding accounts receivable are uncollectible. What amount of bad debts expense is recorded at December 31?
   a. $5,354   c. $5,026   e. $34,338
   b. $328   d. $4,698

2. A company's Accounts Receivable balance at its December 31 year-end is $489,300, and its Allowance for Doubtful Accounts has a debit balance of $554 before year-end adjustment. Its net sales are $1,300,000. It estimates that 6% of outstanding accounts receivable are uncollectible. What amount of bad debts expense is recorded at December 31?
   a. $29,912   c. $78,000   e. $554
   b. $28,804   d. $29,358

3. Total interest to be earned on a $7,500, 5%, 90-day note is
   a. $93.75.   c. $1,125.00.   e. $125.00.
   b. $375.00.   d. $31.25.

4. A company receives a $9,000, 8%, 60-day note. The maturity value of the note is
   a. $120.   c. $9,120.   e. $9,720.
   b. $9,000.   d. $720.

5. A company has net sales of $489,600 and average accounts receivable of $40,800. What is its accounts receivable turnover?
   a. 0.08   c. 1,341.00   e. 111.78
   b. 30.41   d. 12.00

ANSWERS TO MULTIPLE CHOICE QUIZ

1. d; Desired balance in Allowance for Doubtful Accounts = $ 5,026 cr.
   ($125,650 × 0.04)
   Current balance in Allowance for Doubtful Accounts =   (328) cr.
   Bad debts expense to be recorded   = $ 4,698

2. a; Desired balance in Allowance for Doubtful Accounts = $ 29,358 cr.
   ($489,300 × 0.06)
   Current balance in Allowance for Doubtful Accounts =   554 dr.
   Bad debts expense to be recorded   = $29,912

3. a; $7,500 × 0.05 × 90/360 = $93.75

4. c; Principal amount $9,000
   Interest accrued . . . .   120 ($9,000 × 0.08 × 60/360)
   Maturity value $9,120

5. d; $489,600/$40,800 = 12

🅘 Icon denotes assignments that involve decision making.

Discussion Questions

1. 🅘 How do sellers benefit from allowing their customers to use credit cards?

2. 🅘 Why does the direct write-off method of accounting for bad debts usually fail to match revenues and expenses?

3. Explain the accounting constraint of materiality.

4. Why might a business prefer a note receivable to an account receivable?

5. Explain why writing off a bad debt against the Allowance for Doubtful Accounts does not reduce the estimated realizable value of a company's accounts receivable.

6. 🅘 Why does the Bad Debts Expense account usually not have the same adjusted balance as the Allowance for Doubtful Accounts?

7. 🅘 Refer to the financial statements and notes of **Apple** in Appendix A. In its presentation of **APPLE** accounts receivable on the balance sheet, how does it title accounts receivable? What does it report for its allowance as of September 30, 2017?

8. 🅘 Refer to the balance sheet of **Google** in Appendix A. Does it use the direct write-off **GOOGLE**

method or allowance method in accounting for its accounts receivable? What is the realizable value of its receivables balance as of December 31, 2017?

9. Refer to the financial statements of Samsung in Appendix A. What is the **Samsung** amount of Samsung's accounts receivable, titled as

"Trade receivables," on its December 31, 2017, balance sheet?

10. Refer to the December 31, 2017, financial statements of Samsung in Appendix A. **Samsung** Does Samsung report its accounts receivable, titled as "Trade receivables," as a current or noncurrent asset?

connect

QUICK STUDY

QS 7-1
Credit card sales
C1

Prepare journal entries for the following credit card sales transactions (the company uses the perpetual inventory system).

1. Sold $20,000 of merchandise, which cost $15,000, on Mastercard credit cards. Mastercard charges a 5% fee.
2. Sold $5,000 of merchandise, which cost $3,000, on an assortment of bank credit cards. These cards charge a 4% fee.

QS 7-2
Direct write-off method
P1

Solstice Company determines on October 1 that it cannot collect $50,000 of its accounts receivable from its customer, P. Moore. Apply the direct write-off method to record this loss as of October 1.

QS 7-3
Recovering a bad debt
P1

Solstice Company determines on October 1 that it cannot collect $50,000 of its accounts receivable from its customer, P. Moore. It uses the direct write-off method to record this loss as of October 1. On October 30, P. Moore unexpectedly pays his account in full to Solstice Company. Record Solstice's entries for recovery of this bad debt.

QS 7-4
Distinguishing between allowance method and direct write-off method
P1   P2

Indicate whether each statement best describes the allowance (A) method or the direct write-off (DW) method.

_____ 1. Does not predict bad debts expense.

_____ 2. Accounts receivable on the balance sheet is reported at net realizable value.

_____ 3. The write-off of a specific account does not affect net income.

_____ 4. When an account is written off, the debit is to Bad Debts Expense.

_____ 5. Usually does *not* best match sales and expenses because bad debts expense is not recorded until an account becomes uncollectible, which usually occurs in a period after the credit sale.

_____ 6. Estimates bad debts expense related to the sales recorded in that period.

QS 7-5
Allowance method for bad debts
P2

Gomez Corp. uses the allowance method to account for uncollectibles. On January 31, it wrote off an $800 account of a customer, C. Green. On March 9, it receives a $300 payment from Green.

1. Prepare the journal entry for January 31.
2. Prepare the journal entries for March 9; assume no additional money is expected from Green.

QS 7-6
Reporting allowance for doubtful accounts
P2

On December 31 of Swift Co.'s first year, $50,000 of accounts receivable is not yet collected. Swift estimates that $2,000 of its accounts receivable is uncollectible and recorded the year-end adjusting entry.

1. Compute the realizable value of accounts receivable reported on Swift's year-end balance sheet.
2. On January 1 of Swift's second year, it writes off a customer's account for $300. Compute the realizable value of accounts receivable on January 1 after the write-off.

QS 7-7
Percent of accounts receivable method
P3

Warner Company's year-end unadjusted trial balance shows accounts receivable of $99,000, allowance for doubtful accounts of $600 (credit), and sales of $280,000. Uncollectibles are estimated to be 1.5% of accounts receivable.

1. Prepare the December 31 year-end adjusting entry for uncollectibles.
2. What amount would have been used in the year-end adjusting entry if the allowance account had a year-end unadjusted debit balance of $300?

Warner Company's year-end unadjusted trial balance shows accounts receivable of $99,000, allowance for doubtful accounts of $600 (credit), and sales of $140,000. Uncollectibles are estimated to be 1% of sales. Prepare the December 31 year-end adjusting entry for uncollectibles.

QS 7-8
Percent of sales method
P3

Net Zero Products, a wholesaler of sustainable raw materials, prepares the following aging of receivables analysis. (1) Estimate the balance of the Allowance for Doubtful Accounts using the aging of accounts receivable method. (2) Prepare the adjusting entry to record bad debts expense assuming the unadjusted balance in the Allowance for Doubtful Accounts is a $1,000 credit.

QS 7-9
Aging of receivables method
P3

				Days Past Due		
	Total	0	1 to 30	31 to 60	61 to 90	Over 90
Accounts receivable...........	$115,200	$80,000	$18,000	$7,200	$4,000	$6,000
Percent uncollectible		1%	3%	5%	8%	11%

Determine the maturity date and compute interest for each note.

QS 7-10
Computing note interest and maturity date
C2

Note	Contract Date	Principal	Interest Rate	Period of Note (Term)
1............	March 1	$10,000	6%	60 days
2............	May 15	15,000	8	90 days
3............	October 20	8,000	4	45 days

On August 2, Jun Co. receives a $6,000, 90-day, 12% note from customer Ryan Albany as payment on his $6,000 account receivable. (1) Compute the maturity date for this note. (2) Prepare Jun's journal entry for August 2.

QS 7-11
Note receivable
C2

On August 2, Jun Co. receives a $6,000, 90-day, 12% note from customer Ryan Albany as payment on his $6,000 account receivable. Prepare Jun's journal entry assuming the note is honored by the customer on October 31 of that same year.

QS 7-12
Note receivable honored
P4

On December 1, Daw Co. accepts a $10,000, 45-day, 6% note from a customer. (1) Prepare the year-end adjusting entry to record accrued interest revenue on December 31. (2) Prepare the entry required on the note's maturity date assuming it is honored.

QS 7-13
Note receivable interest and maturity   **P4**

Record the sale by Balus Company of $125,000 in accounts receivable on May 1. Balus is charged a 2.5% factoring fee.

QS 7-14
Factoring receivables   **C3**

Selected accounts from Fair Trader Co.'s adjusted trial balance for the year ended December 31 follow. Prepare its income statement.

QS 7-15
Preparing an income statement
P2   P4   C3

Factoring fees	$ 300	Interest revenue.......................	$ 3,000
Insurance expense......................	4,000	Salaries expense	22,000
Sales...................................	50,000	Supplies expense......................	200
Rent expense	15,000	Bad debt expense	1,000

Selected accounts from Bennett Co.'s adjusted trial balance for the year ended December 31 follow. Prepare a classified balance sheet. *Note:* Allowance for doubtful accounts is subtracted from accounts receivable on the company's balance sheet.

QS 7-16
Preparing a balance sheet
P2   P4   C3

Prepaid rent	$ 1,000	Accounts payable......................	$2,500
Accounts receivable.....................	10,000	Allowance for doubtful accounts..........	500
Cash	12,000	Notes payable (due in 10 years)	6,000
Total equity............................	18,000	Notes receivable (due in 4 years)	4,000

QS 7-17

Accounts receivable turnover

A1

The following data are for Ruggers Company. Compute and interpret its accounts receivable turnover for the current year (competitors average a turnover of 7.5).

	Current Year	1 Year Ago
Accounts receivable, net	$153,400	$138,500
Net sales	861,105	910,600

EXERCISES

Exercise 7-1

Accounts receivable subsidiary ledger; schedule of accounts receivable

C1

Vail Company recorded the following transactions during November.

Nov.	5	Accounts Receivable—Ski Shop	4,615	
		Sales		4,615
	10	Accounts Receivable—Welcome Enterprises	1,350	
		Sales		1,350
	13	Accounts Receivable—Zia Natara.	832	
		Sales		832
	21	Sales Returns and Allowances	209	
		Accounts Receivable—Zia Natara		209
	30	Accounts Receivable—Ski Shop	2,713	
		Sales		2,713

1. Open a general ledger having T-accounts for Accounts Receivable, Sales, and Sales Returns and Allowances. Also open an accounts receivable subsidiary ledger having a T-account for each of its three customers. Post these entries to both the general ledger and the accounts receivable ledger.

Check Accounts Receivable ending balance, $9,301

2. Prepare a schedule of accounts receivable (see Exhibit 7.4) and compare its total with the balance of the Accounts Receivable controlling account as of November 30.

Exercise 7-2

Accounting for credit card sales

C1

Levine Company uses the perpetual inventory system. Prepare journal entries to record the following credit card transactions of Levine Company.

Apr. 8   Sold merchandise for $8,400 (that had cost $6,000) and accepted the customer's Suntrust Bank Card. Suntrust charges a 4% fee.
     12   Sold merchandise for $5,600 (that had cost $3,500) and accepted the customer's Continental Card. Continental charges a 2.5% fee.

Exercise 7-3

Sales on store credit card

C1

Z-Mart uses the perpetual inventory system and has its own credit card. Z-Mart charges a per-month interest fee for any unpaid balance on its store credit card at each month-end.

Apr. 30   Z-Mart sold merchandise for $1,000 (that had cost $650) and accepted the customer's Z-Mart store credit card.
May 31   Z-Mart recorded $4 of interest earned from its store credit card as of this month-end.

Exercise 7-4

Direct write-off method

P1

Dexter Company uses the direct write-off method. Prepare journal entries to record the following transactions.

Mar. 11   Dexter determines that it cannot collect $45,000 of its accounts receivable from Leer Co.
     29   Leer Co. unexpectedly pays its account in full to Dexter Company. Dexter records its recovery of this bad debt.

Exercise 7-5

Writing off receivables

P2

On January 1, Wei Company begins the accounting period with a $30,000 credit balance in Allowance for Doubtful Accounts.

a. On February 1, the company determined that $6,800 in customer accounts was uncollectible; specifically, $900 for Oakley Co. and $5,900 for Brookes Co. Prepare the journal entry to write off those two accounts.

b. On June 5, the company unexpectedly received a $900 payment on a customer account, Oakley Company, that had previously been written off in part *a*. Prepare the entries to reinstate the account and record the cash received.

At year-end (December 31), Chan Company estimates its bad debts as 1% of its annual credit sales of $487,500. Chan records its bad debts expense for that estimate. On the following February 1, Chan decides that the $580 account of P. Park is uncollectible and writes it off as a bad debt. On June 5, Park unexpectedly pays the amount previously written off.

Prepare Chan's journal entries to record the transactions of December 31, February 1, and June 5.

Exercise 7-6
Percent of sales method; write-off
P3

Mazie Supply Co. uses the percent of accounts receivable method. On December 31, it has outstanding accounts receivable of $55,000, and it estimates that 2% will be uncollectible.

Prepare the year-end adjusting entry to record bad debts expense under the assumption that the Allowance for Doubtful Accounts has (*a*) a $415 credit balance before the adjustment and (*b*) a $291 debit balance before the adjustment.

Exercise 7-7
Percent of accounts receivable method
P3

Daley Company prepared the following aging of receivables analysis at December 31.

Exercise 7-8
Aging of receivables method
P3

			Days Past Due			
	Total	0	1 to 30	31 to 60	61 to 90	Over 90
Accounts receivable............	$570,000	$396,000	$90,000	$36,000	$18,000	$30,000
Percent uncollectible		1%	2%	5%	7%	10%

a. Estimate the balance of the Allowance for Doubtful Accounts using aging of accounts receivable.

b. Prepare the adjusting entry to record bad debts expense using the estimate from part *a*. Assume the unadjusted balance in the Allowance for Doubtful Accounts is a $3,600 credit.

c. Prepare the adjusting entry to record bad debts expense using the estimate from part *a*. Assume the unadjusted balance in the Allowance for Doubtful Accounts is a $100 debit.

Refer to the information in Exercise 7-8 to complete the following requirements.

a. Estimate the balance of the Allowance for Doubtful Accounts assuming the company uses 4.5% of total accounts receivable to estimate uncollectibles, instead of the aging of receivables method.

b. Prepare the adjusting entry to record bad debts expense using the estimate from part *a*. Assume the unadjusted balance in the Allowance for Doubtful Accounts is a $12,000 credit.

c. Prepare the adjusting entry to record bad debts expense using the estimate from part *a*. Assume the unadjusted balance in the Allowance for Doubtful Accounts is a $1,000 debit.

Exercise 7-9
Percent of receivables method
P3

Following is a list of credit customers along with their amounts owed and the days past due at December 31. Following that list are five classifications of accounts receivable and estimated bad debts percent for each class.

1. Create an aging of accounts receivable schedule similar to Exhibit 7.8 and calculate the estimated balance for the Allowance for Doubtful Accounts.

2. Assuming an unadjusted credit balance of $100, record the required adjustment to the Allowance for Doubtful Accounts.

Exercise 7-10
Aging of receivables schedule
P3

Customer	Accounts Receivable	Days Past Due
BCC Company	$4,000	12
Lannister Co.	1,000	0
Mike Properties	5,000	107
Ted Reeves	500	72
Jen Steffens	2,000	35

Days Past Due	0	1 to 30	31 to 60	61 to 90	Over 90
Percent uncollectible	1%	3%	5%	8%	12%

At December 31, Folgeys Coffee Company reports the following results for its calendar year.

Exercise 7-11
Estimating bad debts
P3

Cash sales.........................	$900,000	Credit sales	$300,000

Its year-end unadjusted trial balance includes the following items.

Accounts receivable	$125,000 debit	Allowance for doubtful accounts	$5,000 debit

Check   Dr. Bad Debts
Expense: (1) $9,000

1. Prepare the adjusting entry to record bad debts expense assuming uncollectibles are estimated to be 3% of credit sales.

2. Prepare the adjusting entry to record bad debts expense assuming uncollectibles are estimated to be 1% of total sales.

(3) $12,500

3. Prepare the adjusting entry to record bad debts expense assuming uncollectibles are estimated to be 6% of year-end accounts receivable.

Exercise 7-12

Notes receivable transactions   **C2**

Check   Dec. 31, Cr. Interest Revenue, $38

Prepare journal entries for the following transactions of Danica Company.

Dec. 13   Accepted a $9,500, 45-day, 8% note in granting Miranda Lee a time extension on her past-due account receivable.

    31   Prepared an adjusting entry to record the accrued interest on the Lee note.

Exercise 7-13

Notes receivable transactions   **P4**

Check   Jan. 27, Dr. Cash, $9,595

June 1, Dr. Cash, $5,125

Refer to the information in Exercise 7-12 and prepare the journal entries for the *following year* for Danica Company.

Jan. 27   Received Lee's payment for principal and interest on the note dated December 13.

Mar. 3   Accepted a $5,000, 10%, 90-day note in granting a time extension on the past-due account receivable of Tomas Company.

    17   Accepted a $2,000, 30-day, 9% note in granting H. Cheng a time extension on his past-due account receivable.

Apr. 16   Cheng dishonored his note.

May 1   Wrote off the Cheng account against the Allowance for Doubtful Accounts.

June 1   Received the Tomas payment for principal and interest on the note dated March 3.

Exercise 7-14

Honoring a note

P4

Prepare journal entries to record transactions for Vitalo Company.

Nov. 1   Accepted a $6,000, 180-day, 8% note from Kelly White in granting a time extension on her past-due account receivable.

Dec. 31   Adjusted the year-end accounts for the accrued interest earned on the White note.

Apr. 30   White honored her note when presented for payment.

Exercise 7-15

Dishonoring a note

P4

Prepare journal entries to record the following transactions of Ridge Company.

Mar. 21   Accepted a $9,500, 180-day, 8% note from Tamara Jackson in granting a time extension on her past-due account receivable.

Sep. 17   Jackson dishonored her note.

Dec. 31   After trying several times to collect, Ridge Company wrote off Jackson's account against the Allowance for Doubtful Accounts.

Exercise 7-16

Selling and pledging accounts receivable

C3

On November 30, Petrov Co. has $128,700 of accounts receivable and uses the perpetual inventory system. (1) Prepare journal entries to record the following transactions. (2) Which transaction would most likely require a note to the financial statements?

Dec. 4   Sold $7,245 of merchandise (that had cost $5,000) to customers on credit, terms n/30.

    9   Sold $20,000 of accounts receivable to Main Bank. Main charges a 4% factoring fee.

    17   Received $5,859 cash from customers in payment on their accounts.

    27   Borrowed $10,000 cash from Main Bank, pledging $12,500 of accounts receivable as security for the loan.

Exercise 7-17

Accounts receivable turnover

A1

The following information is from the annual financial statements of Raheem Company. (1) Compute its accounts receivable turnover for Year 2 and Year 3. (2) Assuming its competitor has a turnover of 11, is Raheem performing better or worse at collecting receivables than its competitor?

	Year 3	Year 2	Year 1
Net sales	$405,140	$335,280	$388,000
Accounts receivable, net (year-end)	44,800	41,400	34,800

≡ connect

Mayfair Co. completed the following transactions and uses a perpetual inventory system.

June 4 Sold $650 of merchandise on credit (that had cost $400) to Natara Morris, terms n/15.
  5 Sold $6,900 of merchandise (that had cost $4,200) to customers who used their Zisa cards. Zisa charges a 3% fee.
  6 Sold $5,850 of merchandise (that had cost $3,800) to customers who used their Access cards. Access charges a 2% fee.
  8 Sold $4,350 of merchandise (that had cost $2,900) to customers who used their Access cards. Access charges a 2% fee.
  13 Wrote off the account of Abigail McKee against the Allowance for Doubtful Accounts. The $429 balance in McKee's account was from a credit sale last year.
  18 Received Morris's check in full payment for the June 4 purchase.

Required

Prepare journal entries to record the preceding transactions and events.

PROBLEM SET A

Problem 7-1A
Sales on account and credit card sales
C1

Check June 18, Dr. Cash, $650

At December 31, Hawke Company reports the following results for its calendar year.

| Cash sales. . . . . | $1,905,000 | Credit sales . . . . | $5,682,000 |

In addition, its unadjusted trial balance includes the following items.

| Accounts receivable. . . . . | $1,270,100 debit | Allowance for doubtful accounts . . . . . | $16,580 debit |

Required

1. Prepare the adjusting entry to record bad debts under each separate assumption.
   a. Bad debts are estimated to be 1.5% of credit sales.
   b. Bad debts are estimated to be 1% of total sales.
   c. An aging analysis estimates that 5% of year-end accounts receivable are uncollectible.
2. Show how Accounts Receivable and the Allowance for Doubtful Accounts appear on its December 31 balance sheet given the facts in part 1*a*.
3. Show how Accounts Receivable and the Allowance for Doubtful Accounts appear on its December 31 balance sheet given the facts in part 1*c*.

Problem 7-2A
Estimating and reporting bad debts
P2 P3

Check Bad Debts Expense: (1*a*) $85,230, (1*c*) $80,085

On December 31, Jarden Co.'s Allowance for Doubtful Accounts has an unadjusted credit balance of $14,500. Jarden prepares a schedule of its December 31 accounts receivable by age.

Problem 7-3A
Aging accounts receivable and accounting for bad debts
P2 P3

	A	B	C
1	**Accounts**	**Age of**	**Expected Percent**
2	**Receivable**	**Accounts Receivable**	**Uncollectible**
3	$830,000	Not yet due	1.25%
4	254,000	1 to 30 days past due	2.00
5	86,000	31 to 60 days past due	6.50
6	38,000	61 to 90 days past due	32.75
7	12,000	Over 90 days past due	68.00

Required

1. Compute the required balance of the Allowance for Doubtful Accounts at December 31 using an aging of accounts receivable.
2. Prepare the adjusting entry to record bad debts expense at December 31.

Analysis Component

3. On June 30 of the next year, Jarden concludes that a customer's $4,750 receivable is uncollectible and the account is written off. Does this write-off directly affect Jarden's net income?

Check (2) Dr. Bad Debts Expense, $27,150

Problem 7-4A
Accounts receivable
transactions and bad debts
adjustments

C1   P2   P3

Liang Company began operations in Year 1. During its first two years, the company completed a number of transactions involving sales on credit, accounts receivable collections, and bad debts. These transactions are summarized as follows.

Year 1

a. Sold $1,345,434 of merchandise (that had cost $975,000) on credit, terms n/30.

b. Wrote off $18,300 of uncollectible accounts receivable.

c. Received $669,200 cash in payment of accounts receivable.

Check (*d*) Dr. Bad Debts
Expense, $28,169

d. In adjusting the accounts on December 31, the company estimated that 1.5% of accounts receivable would be uncollectible.

Year 2

e. Sold $1,525,634 of merchandise on credit (that had cost $1,250,000), terms n/30.

f. Wrote off $27,800 of uncollectible accounts receivable.

g. Received $1,204,600 cash in payment of accounts receivable.

(*h*) Dr. Bad Debts Expense,
$32,199

h. In adjusting the accounts on December 31, the company estimated that 1.5% of accounts receivable would be uncollectible.

Required

Prepare journal entries to record Liang's summarized transactions and its year-end adjustments to record bad debts expense. (The company uses the perpetual inventory system, and it applies the allowance method for its accounts receivable. Round to the nearest dollar.)

Problem 7-5A
Analyzing and journalizing
notes receivable
transactions

C2   C3   P4

The following transactions are from Ohlm Company.

Year 1

Dec. 16   Accepted a $10,800, 60-day, 8% note in granting Danny Todd a time extension on his past-due account receivable.

       31   Made an adjusting entry to record the accrued interest on the Todd note.

Year 2

Check Feb. 14, Cr. Interest
Revenue, $108

Feb. 14   Received Todd's payment of principal and interest on the note dated December 16.

Mar. 2   Accepted a $6,100, 8%, 90-day note in granting a time extension on the past-due account receivable from Midnight Co.

       17   Accepted a $2,400, 30-day, 7% note in granting Ava Privet a time extension on her past-due account receivable.

Apr. 16   Privet dishonored her note.

May 31, Cr. Interest Revenue,
$122

May 31   Midnight Co. dishonored its note.

Aug. 7   Accepted a $7,440, 90-day, 10% note in granting a time extension on the past-due account receivable of Mulan Co.

Sep. 3   Accepted a $2,100, 60-day, 10% note in granting Noah Carson a time extension on his past-due account receivable.

Nov. 2, Cr. Interest Revenue,
$35

Nov. 2   Received payment of principal plus interest from Carson for the September 3 note.

Nov. 5   Received payment of principal plus interest from Mulan for the August 7 note.

Dec. 1   Wrote off the Privet account against the Allowance for Doubtful Accounts.

Required

1. Prepare journal entries to record these transactions and events.

Analysis Component

2. If Ohlm pledged its receivables as security for a loan from the bank, where on the financial statements does it disclose this pledge of receivables?

Archer Co. completed the following transactions and uses a perpetual inventory system.

Aug. 4 Sold $3,700 of merchandise on credit (that had cost $2,000) to McKenzie Carpenter, terms n/10.
   10 Sold $5,200 of merchandise (that had cost $2,800) to customers who used their Commerce Bank credit cards. Commerce charges a 3% fee.
   11 Sold $1,250 of merchandise (that had cost $900) to customers who used their Goldman cards. Goldman charges a 2% fee.
   14 Received Carpenter's check in full payment for the August 4 purchase.
   15 Sold $3,250 of merchandise (that had cost $1,758) to customers who used their Goldman cards. Goldman charges a 2% fee.
   22 Wrote off the account of Craw Co. against the Allowance for Doubtful Accounts. The $498 balance in Craw Co.'s account was from a credit sale last year.

Required

Prepare journal entries to record the preceding transactions and events.

PROBLEM SET B

Problem 7-1B
Sales on account and credit card sales C1

Check Aug. 14, Dr. Cash, $3,700

At December 31, Ingleton Company reports the following results for the year.

| Cash sales................. | $1,025,000 | Credit sales .. .. | $1,342,000 |

In addition, its unadjusted trial balance includes the following items.

| Accounts receivable........... | $575,000 debit | Allowance for doubtful accounts ..... | $7,500 credit |

Required

1. Prepare the adjusting entry to record bad debts under each separate assumption.
   a. Bad debts are estimated to be 2.5% of credit sales.
   b. Bad debts are estimated to be 1.5% of total sales.
   c. An aging analysis estimates that 6% of year-end accounts receivable are uncollectible.
2. Show how Accounts Receivable and the Allowance for Doubtful Accounts appear on its December 31 balance sheet given the facts in part 1a.
3. Show how Accounts Receivable and the Allowance for Doubtful Accounts appear on its December 31 balance sheet given the facts in part 1c.

Problem 7-2B
Estimating and reporting bad debts

P2 P3

Check Dr. Bad Debts Expense: (1b) $35,505, (1c) $27,000

At December 31, Hovak Co.'s Allowance for Doubtful Accounts has an unadjusted debit balance of $3,400. Hovak prepares a schedule of its December 31 accounts receivable by age.

Problem 7-3B
Aging accounts receivable and accounting for bad debts

P2 P3

	A	B	C
1	**Accounts Receivable**	**Age of Accounts Receivable**	**Expected Percent Uncollectible**
2			
3	$396,400	Not yet due	2.0%
4	277,800	1 to 30 days past due	4.0
5	48,000	31 to 60 days past due	8.5
6	6,600	61 to 90 days past due	39.0
7	2,800	Over 90 days past due	82.0

Required

1. Compute the required balance of the Allowance for Doubtful Accounts at December 31 using an aging of accounts receivable.
2. Prepare the adjusting entry to record bad debts expense at December 31.

Analysis Component

3. On July 31 of the following year, Hovak concludes that a customer's $3,455 receivable is uncollectible and the account is written off. Does this write-off directly affect Hovak's net income?

Check (2) Dr. Bad Debts Expense, $31,390

Problem 7-4B
Accounts receivable
transactions and bad debts
adjustments

C1   P2   P3

Check   (*d*) Dr. Bad Debts
Expense, $11,287

(*h*) Dr. Bad Debts Expense,
$9,773

Sherman Co. began operations in Year 1. During its first two years, the company completed several transactions involving sales on credit, accounts receivable collections, and bad debts. These transactions are
summarized as follows.

Year 1

a. Sold $685,350 of merchandise on credit (that had cost $500,000), terms n/30.
b. Received $482,300 cash in payment of accounts receivable.
c. Wrote off $9,350 of uncollectible accounts receivable.
d. In adjusting the accounts on December 31, the company estimated that 1% of accounts receivable
would be uncollectible.

Year 2

e. Sold $870,220 of merchandise on credit (that had cost $650,000), terms n/30.
f. Received $990,800 cash in payment of accounts receivable.
g. Wrote off $11,090 of uncollectible accounts receivable.
h. In adjusting the accounts on December 31, the company estimated that 1% of accounts receivable
would be uncollectible.

Required

Prepare journal entries to record Sherman's summarized transactions and its year-end adjusting entries to
record bad debts expense. (The company uses the perpetual inventory system, and it applies the allowance
method for its accounts receivable.)

Problem 7-5B
Analyzing and journalizing
notes receivable
transactions

C2   C3   P4

Check   Jan. 30, Cr. Interest
Revenue, $32

Apr. 30, Cr. Interest Revenue,
$124

Sep. 19, Cr. Interest Revenue,
$190

The following transactions are from Springer Company.

Year 1

Nov. 1	Accepted a $4,800, 90-day, 8% note in granting Steve Julian a time extension on his past-due account receivable.
Dec. 31	Made an adjusting entry to record the accrued interest on the Julian note.

Year 2

Jan. 30	Received Julian's payment for principal and interest on the note dated November 1.
Feb. 28	Accepted a $12,600, 30-day, 8% note in granting a time extension on the past-due account receivable from King Co.
Mar. 1	Accepted a $6,200, 60-day, 12% note in granting Myron Shelley a time extension on his past-due account receivable.
30	The King Co. dishonored its note.
Apr. 30	Received payment of principal plus interest from M. Shelley for the March 1 note.
June 15	Accepted a $2,000, 72-day, 8% note in granting a time extension on the past-due account receivable of Ryder Solon.
21	Accepted a $9,500, 90-day, 8% note in granting J. Felton a time extension on his past-due account receivable.
Aug. 26	Received payment of principal plus interest from R. Solon for the June 15 note.
Sep. 19	Received payment of principal plus interest from J. Felton for the June 21 note.
Nov. 30	Wrote off King's account against the Allowance for Doubtful Accounts.

Required

1. Prepare journal entries to record these transactions and events.

Analysis Component

2. If Springer pledged its receivables as security for a loan from the bank, where on the financial statements does it disclose this pledge of receivables?

SERIAL PROBLEM
Business Solutions

P1   P2

*This serial problem began in Chapter 1 and continues through most of the book. If previous chapter seg-
ments were not completed, the serial problem can begin at this point.*

SP 7   Santana Rey, owner of **Business Solutions**, realizes that she needs to begin accounting for bad
debts expense. Assume that Business Solutions has total revenues of $44,000 during the first three months
of 2020 and that the Accounts Receivable balance on March 31, 2020, is $22,867.

Required

1. Prepare the adjusting entry to record bad debts expense on March 31, 2020, under each separate assumption. There is a zero unadjusted balance in the Allowance for Doubtful Accounts at March 31.

   a. Bad debts are estimated to be 1% of total revenues.

   b. Bad debts are estimated to be 2% of accounts receivable. (Round to the dollar.)

2. Assume that Business Solutions's Accounts Receivable balance at June 30, 2020, is $20,250 and that one account of $100 has been written off against the Allowance for Doubtful Accounts since March 31, 2020. If Rey uses the method in part 1b, what adjusting journal entry is made to recognize bad debts expense on June 30, 2020?

3. Should Rey consider adopting the direct write-off method of accounting for bad debts expense rather than one of the allowance methods considered in part 1? Explain.

©Alexander Image/Shutterstock

Check   (2) Dr. Bad Debts Expense, $48

The **General Ledger** tool in Connect automates several of the procedural steps in accounting so that the financial professional can focus on the impacts of each transaction on various financial reports and performance measures.

GL 7-1   General Ledger assignment GL 7-1, based on Problem 7-5A, focuses on transactions related to accounts and notes receivable and highlights the impact each transaction has on interest revenue.

GENERAL LEDGER PROBLEM

Accounting Analysis

AA 7-1   Use **Apple**'s financial statements in Appendix A to answer the following.

1. What is the amount of Apple's accounts receivable as of September 30, 2017?
2. Compute Apple's accounts receivable turnover as of September 30, 2017.
3. How long does it take, *on average,* for the company to collect receivables for the fiscal year ended September 30, 2017?
4. Apple's most liquid assets include (*a*) cash and cash equivalents, (*b*) short-term marketable securities, (*c*) accounts receivable, and (*d*) inventory. Compute the percentage that these liquid assets (in total) make up of current liabilities as of September 30, 2017, and as of September 24, 2016.
5. Did Apple's liquid assets as a percentage of current liabilities improve or worsen as of its fiscal 2017 year-end compared to its fiscal 2016 year-end?

COMPANY ANALYSIS

A1

APPLE

AA 7-2   Comparative figures for **Apple** and **Google** follow.

$ millions	Apple			Google		
	Current Year	One Year Prior	Two Years Prior	Current Year	One Year Prior	Two Years Prior
Accounts receivable, net ..	$ 17,874	$ 15,754	$ 16,849	$ 18,336	$14,137	$11,556
Net sales	229,234	215,639	233,715	110,855	90,272	74,989

COMPARATIVE ANALYSIS

A1   P2

APPLE GOOGLE

Required

1. Compute the accounts receivable turnover for (*a*) Apple and (*b*) Google for each of the two most recent years using the data shown.
2. Compute how many days, *on average,* it takes to collect receivables for the two most recent years for (*a*) Apple and (*b*) Google.
3. Which company more quickly collects its accounts receivable in the current year?

Hint: Average collection period equals 365 divided by the accounts receivable turnover.

GLOBAL ANALYSIS

C1 A1

Samsung

AA 7-3   Key figures for **Samsung** follow.

₩ millions	Current Year	One Year Prior	Two Years Prior
Accounts receivable, net	₩ 27,695,995	₩ 24,279,211	₩ 25,168,026
Sales	239,575,376	201,866,745	200,653,482

1. Compute its accounts receivable turnover for the current year.
2. How long does it take on average for Samsung to collect receivables in the current year?
3. In the current year, does Samsung's accounts receivable turnover underperform or outperform the industry (assumed) average of 7?

Beyond the Numbers

ETHICS CHALLENGE

P2 P3

BTN 7-1   Anton Blair is the manager of a medium-size company. A few years ago, Blair persuaded the owner to base a part of his compensation on the net income the company earns each year. Each December he estimates year-end financial figures in anticipation of the bonus he will receive. If the bonus is not as high as he would like, he offers several recommendations to the accountant for year-end adjustments. One of his favorite recommendations is for the controller to reduce the estimate of doubtful accounts.

Required

1. What effect does lowering the estimate for doubtful accounts have on the income statement and balance sheet?
2. Do you believe Blair's recommendation to adjust the allowance for doubtful accounts is within his rights as manager, or do you believe this action is an ethics violation? Justify your response.
3. What type of internal control(s) might be useful for this company in overseeing the manager's recommendations for accounting changes?

COMMUNICATING IN PRACTICE

P2 P3

BTN 7-2   As the accountant for Pure-Air Distributing, you attend a sales managers' meeting devoted to a discussion of credit policies. At the meeting, you report that bad debts expense is estimated to be $59,000 and accounts receivable at year-end amount to $1,750,000 less a $43,000 allowance for doubtful accounts. Sid Omar, a sales manager, expresses confusion over why bad debts expense and the allowance for doubtful accounts are different amounts. Write a one-page memorandum to him explaining why a difference in bad debts expense and the allowance for doubtful accounts is not unusual. The company estimates bad debts expense as 2% of sales.

TAKING IT TO THE NET

C1 P3

BTN 7-3   Access **eBay**'s February 6, 2017, filing of its 10-K report for the year ended December 31, 2016, at **SEC.gov**.

Required

1. What is the amount of eBay's net accounts receivable at December 31, 2016, and at December 31, 2015?
2. "Financial Statement Schedule II" of its 10-K report lists eBay's allowance for doubtful accounts (including authorized credits). For the two years ended December 31, 2016 and 2015, identify its allowance for doubtful accounts (including authorized credits), and then compute it as a percent of gross accounts receivable.
3. Do you believe that these percentages are reasonable based on what you know about eBay? Explain.

TEAMWORK IN ACTION

P2 P3

BTN 7-4   Each member of a team is to participate in estimating uncollectibles using the aging schedule and percents shown in Problem 7-3A. The division of labor is up to the team. Your goal is to accurately complete this task as soon as possible. After estimating uncollectibles, check your estimate with the instructor. If the estimate is correct, the team then should prepare the adjusting entry and the presentation of accounts receivable (net) for the December 31 year-end balance sheet.

BTN 7-5 Sheryl Sandberg and Mark Zuckerberg of **Facebook** are introduced in the chapter's opening feature. Assume that they are considering two options.

Plan A. Facebook would begin selling access to a premium version of its website. The new online customers would use their credit cards. The company has the capability of selling the premium service with no additional investment in hardware or software. Annual credit sales are expected to increase by $250,000.

  Costs associated with Plan A: Additional wages related to these new sales are $135,500; credit card fees will be 4.75% of sales; and additional recordkeeping costs will be 6% of sales. Premium service sales will reduce advertising revenues for Facebook by $8,750 annually because some customers will now only use the premium service.

Plan B. The company would begin selling Facebook merchandise. It would make additional annual credit sales of $500,000.

  Costs associated with Plan B: Cost of these new sales is $375,000; additional recordkeeping and shipping costs will be 4% of sales; and uncollectible accounts will be 6.2% of sales.

Required

1. Compute the additional annual net income or loss expected under (*a*) Plan A and (*b*) Plan B.
2. Should the company pursue either plan? Discuss both the financial and nonfinancial factors relevant to this decision.

Check (1*b*) Additional net income, $74,000

BTN 7-6 Many commercials include comments similar to the following: "We accept **VISA**" or "We do not accept **American Express**." Conduct your own research by contacting at least five companies via interviews, phone calls, or the Internet to determine the reason(s) companies discriminate in their use of credit cards. Collect information on the fees charged by the different cards for the companies contacted. (The instructor can assign this as a team activity.)

8 Accounting for Long-Term Assets

Learning Objectives

CONCEPTUAL

C1 Compute the cost of plant assets.

C2 Explain depreciation for partial years and changes in estimates.

C3 Distinguish between revenue and capital expenditures, and account for them.

ANALYTICAL

A1 Compute total asset turnover and apply it to analyze a company's use of assets.

PROCEDURAL

P1 Compute and record depreciation using the straight-line, units-of-production, and declining-balance methods.

P2 Account for asset disposal through discarding or selling an asset.

P3 Account for natural resource assets and their depletion.

P4 Account for intangible assets.

P5 *Appendix 8A*—Account for asset exchanges.

Crafting the Dream

"Strive to surpass yourself"—**DEB CAREY**

NEW GLARUS, WI—Deb Carey told her husband Dan, "I could start a brewery and you could work for me." A few days later, she recalls, "We were bidding on equipment from a brew pub." Dan reminded her, "But we don't have any money." Deb declared, "I'm going to sell the house!" Soon, she says, **New Glarus Brewing** (**NewGlarusBrewing.com**) was up and running.

"In that first year," explains Deb, "we had no money, and we were working from 5 a.m. to midnight." Deb focused on the business. She stresses that long-term assets in the brewery such as brew houses, packaging lines, and fermentation cellars are expensive but key to success. Financing that equipment, buildings, and other assets, she says, is not easy.

A constant challenge for Deb and Dan is maintaining the right kind and amount of assets to meet business demands and be profitable. "Machinery cannot be divorced from the process," insists Dan. "You have to work with the strengths and weaknesses of your machinery."

Deb explains that success depends on monitoring and controlling the types and costs of long-term assets. Each of her tangible and intangible assets commands Deb's attention. She accounts for, manages, and focuses on recovering all costs of those acquisitions.

©Casper Hedberg/Bloomberg/Getty Images

Their company is on a roll—employing nearly 150 workers, offering unique products such as Spotted Cow, and generating over 250,000 barrels. Adds Deb, running a company "is like having a big family."

Sources: *New Glarus Brewing website*, January 2019; *Wisconsin State Journal*, July 2011; *NBC 26 Green Bay*, February 2018; *Daily Dose*, October 2017

Section 1—Plant Assets

Plant assets are tangible assets used in a company's operations that have a useful life of more than one accounting period. Plant assets are also called *plant and equipment; property, plant and equipment (PP&E);* or *fixed assets.* Exhibit 8.1 shows plant assets as a percentage of total assets for several companies.

EXHIBIT 8.1

Plant Assets of Selected Companies

Plant assets are set apart from other assets by two important features. First, *plant assets are used in operations.* A computer purchased to resell is reported on the balance sheet as inventory. If the same computer is used in operations, it is a plant asset. Another example is land held for expansion, which is reported as a long-term investment. Instead, if this land holds a factory used in operations, the land is a plant asset.

McDonald's	$21,258 mil.	69%
Boston Beer	$408 mil.	66%
Walmart	$114,178 mil.	57%
eBay	$1,516 mil.	6%

0%   20%   40%   60%   80%

As a Percentage of Total Assets

The second important feature is that *plant assets have useful lives extending over more than one accounting period.* This makes plant assets different from current assets such as supplies that are normally used up within one period.

Point: *Capital-intensive* refers to companies with large amounts of plant assets.

Exhibit 8.2 shows four issues in accounting for plant assets: (1) computing the costs of plant assets, (2) allocating the costs of plant assets, (3) accounting for subsequent expenditures to plant assets, and (4) recording the disposal of plant assets. The following sections discuss these issues.

EXHIBIT 8.2

Issues in Accounting for Plant Assets

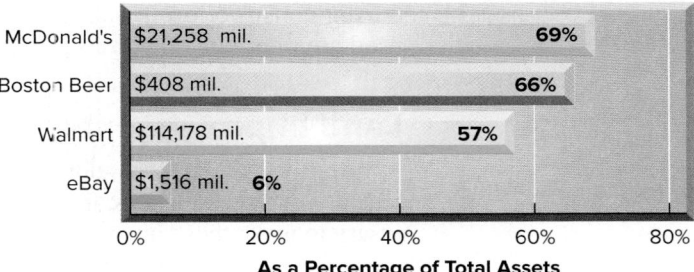

Decline in asset book value over its useful life

Acquisition	**Use**	**Disposal**
1. Compute cost.	2. Allocate cost to periods benefited.	4. Record disposal.
	3. Account for subsequent expenditures.	

COST DETERMINATION

C1_____
Compute the cost of plant assets.

Plant assets are recorded at cost when acquired. **Cost** includes all expenditures necessary to get an asset in place and ready for use. The cost of a machine, for example, includes its invoice cost minus any discount, plus necessary shipping, assembling, installing, and testing costs. Examples are the costs of building a base for a machine, installing electrical hookups, and testing the asset before using it in operations.

To be recorded as part of the cost of a plant asset, an expenditure must be normal, reasonable, and necessary in preparing it for its intended use. If an asset is damaged during unpacking, the repairs are not added to its cost. Instead, they are charged to an expense account. Costs to modify or customize a new plant asset are added to the asset's cost. This section explains how to determine the cost of plant assets for its four major classes.

Machinery and Equipment

The costs of machinery and equipment consist of all costs normal and necessary to purchase them and prepare them for their intended use. These include the purchase price, taxes, transportation charges, insurance while in transit, and the installing, assembling, and testing of the machinery and equipment.

Buildings

©Syda Productions/Shutterstock

A Building account consists of the costs of purchasing or constructing a building that is used in operations. A purchased building's costs include its purchase price, taxes, title fees, and lawyer fees. Its costs also include all expenditures to ready it for its intended use, including necessary repairs or renovations. When a company constructs a building or any plant asset for its own use, its costs include materials and labor plus indirect overhead cost. Overhead includes heat, lighting, power, and depreciation on machinery used to construct the asset. Costs of construction also include design fees, building permits, and insurance during construction. However, costs such as insurance to cover the asset *after* it is being used are operating expenses.

Land Improvements

Point: Entry for cash purchase of land improvements:
Land Improvements. . . . .   #
  Cash. . . . .   #

Land improvements are additions to land and have limited useful lives. Examples are parking lots, driveways, walkways, fences, and lighting systems. Land improvements include costs necessary to make those improvements ready for their intended use.

Land

Land is the earth's surface and has an indefinite (unlimited) life. Land includes costs necessary to make it ready for its intended use. When land is purchased for a building site, its cost includes the total amount paid for the land, including real estate commissions, title insurance fees, legal fees, and any accrued property taxes paid by the purchaser. Payments for surveying, clearing, grading, and draining also are included in the cost of land. Other costs include government assessments, whether incurred at the time of purchase or later, for items such as public roads, sewers, and sidewalks. These assessments are included because they permanently add to the land's value (and are not depreciated as they are not the company's responsibility). Land purchased as a building site can include unwanted structures. The cost of removing those structures, less amounts recovered through sale of salvaged materials, is charged to the Land account.

Assume **Starbucks** paid $167,000 cash to acquire land for a coffee shop. This land had an old service garage that was removed at a net cost of $13,000 ($15,000 in costs less $2,000 proceeds from salvaged materials). Additional closing costs total $10,000, consisting of brokerage fees ($8,000), legal fees ($1,500), and title costs ($500). The cost of this land to Starbucks is $190,000 and is computed as shown in Exhibit 8.3.

Cash price of land.....................	$ 167,000
Net cost of garage removal	13,000
Closing costs........................	10,000
Cost of land	**$190,000**

Entry for cash purchase of land:

Land......................	190,000	
Cash		190,000
Record purchase of land.		

EXHIBIT 8.3

Computing and Recording Cost of Land

Lump-Sum Purchase

Plant assets sometimes are purchased as a group in a single transaction for a lump-sum price. This transaction is called a *lump-sum purchase,* or *group, bulk,* or *basket purchase.* When this occurs, we allocate the cost to the assets acquired based on their *relative market* (or *appraised*) *values.* Assume **CarMax** paid $90,000 cash to acquire a group of items consisting of a building appraised at $60,000 and land appraised at $40,000. The $90,000 cost is allocated based on appraised values as shown in Exhibit 8.4. The entry to record the lump-sum purchase also is shown in Exhibit 8.4.

	Appraised Value	Percent of Total	Apportioned Cost
Building...	$ 60,000	60% ($60,000/$100,000)	**$54,000** ($90,000 × 60%)
Land	40,000	40 ($40,000/$100,000)	36,000 ($90,000 × 40%)
Totals	$100,000	100%	$ 90,000

Entry for lump-sum cash purchase:

Building..............	54,000	
Land	36,000	
Cash...........		90,000
Record costs of plant assets.		

EXHIBIT 8.4

Computing and Recording Costs in a Lump-Sum Purchase

Compute the recorded cost of a new machine given the following payments related to its purchase: gross purchase price, $700,000; sales tax, $49,000; purchase discount taken, $21,000; freight cost—terms FOB shipping point, $3,500; normal assembly costs, $3,000; cost of necessary machine platform, $2,500; and cost of parts used in maintaining machine, $4,200.

NEED-TO-KNOW 8-1

Cost Determination

C1 ▶

Do More: QS 8-1, QS 8-2, E 8-1, E 8-2, E 8-3

Solution

$737,000 = $700,000 + $49,000 − $21,000 + $3,500 + $3,000 + $2,500

DEPRECIATION

Depreciation is the process of allocating the cost of a plant asset to expense while it is in use. Depreciation does not measure the decline in the asset's market value or its physical deterioration. This section covers computing depreciation.

Factors in Computing Depreciation

Factors that determine depreciation are (1) cost, (2) salvage value, and (3) useful life.

Cost   The cost of a plant asset consists of all necessary and reasonable expenditures to acquire it and to prepare it for its intended use.

Salvage Value   The **salvage value,** also called *residual value* or *scrap value,* is an estimate of the asset's value at the end of its useful life. This is the amount the owner expects to receive from disposing of the asset at the end of its useful life. If the asset is expected to be traded in on a new asset, its salvage value is the expected trade-in value.

Useful Life   The **useful life** of a plant asset is the length of time it is used in a company's operations. Useful life, or *service life,* might not be as long as the asset's total productive life. For example, the productive life of a computer can be eight years or more. Some companies, however, trade in old computers for new ones every two years. In this case, these computers

P1_____

Compute and record depreciation using the straight-line, units-of-production, and declining-balance methods.

Point: If we expect disposal costs, the salvage value equals the expected amount from disposal less any disposal costs.

Point: Useful life and salvage value are estimates.

have a two-year useful life. The useful life of a plant asset is impacted by inadequacy and obsolescence. **Inadequacy** is the inability of a plant asset to meet its demands. **Obsolescence** is the process of becoming outdated and no longer used.

©Fuse/Getty Images

■ Decision Insight

Sweet Life   The useful life of plant assets is different for each company. **Hershey Foods** and **Tootsie Roll** are competitors and apply similar manufacturing processes, but their equipment's life expectancies are different. Hershey depreciates equipment over 3 to 15 years, but Tootsie Roll depreciates them over 5 to 20 years. Such differences impact financial statements. ■

Depreciation Methods

Depreciation methods are used to allocate a plant asset's cost over its useful life. The most frequently used method is the straight-line method. The units-of-production and double-declining methods are also commonly used. We explain all three methods. Computations in this section use information about a machine used by **Reebok** and **Adidas** to inspect athletic shoes before packaging. Data for this machine are in Exhibit 8.5.

EXHIBIT 8.5

Data for Inspection Machine

Cost..................	$10,000	Useful life:	
Salvage value..........	1,000	Accounting periods........	5 years
Depreciable cost.......	$ 9,000	Units inspected...........	36,000 shoes

Straight-Line Method   **Straight-line depreciation** charges the same amount to each period of the asset's useful life. A two-step process is used. We first compute the *depreciable cost* of the asset, also called *cost to be depreciated*. It is computed as asset total cost minus salvage value. Second, depreciable cost is divided by the number of accounting periods in the asset's useful life. The computation for the inspection machine is in Exhibit 8.6.

EXHIBIT 8.6

Straight-Line Depreciation
Formula and Example

Point: Excel for SLN.

	A	B
1	Cost	$10,000
2	Salvage	$1,000
3	Life	5
4	SLN depr.	

=SLN(B1,B2,B3) = $1,800

$$\frac{\text{Cost} - \text{Salvage value}}{\text{Useful life in periods}} = \frac{\$10,000 - \$1,000}{5\text{ years}} = \$1,800 \text{ per year}$$

If this machine is purchased on December 31, 2018, and used during its predicted useful life of five years, the straight-line method allocates equal depreciation to each of the years 2019 through 2023. We make the following adjusting entry at the end of each of the five years to record straight-line depreciation.

Assets = Liabilities + Equity
−1,800   −1,800

Dec. 31	Depreciation Expense	1,800	
	Accumulated Depreciation—Machinery		1,800
	Record annual depreciation.		

The $1,800 Depreciation Expense is reported on the income statement. The $1,800 **Accumulated Depreciation is a contra asset account to the Machinery account on the balance sheet.** The left graph in Exhibit 8.7 shows the $1,800 per year expense reported in each of the five years. The right graph shows the Machinery account balance (net) on each of the six December 31 balance sheets.

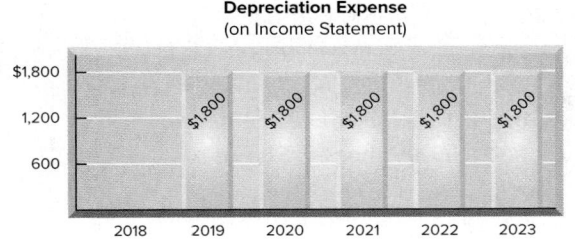

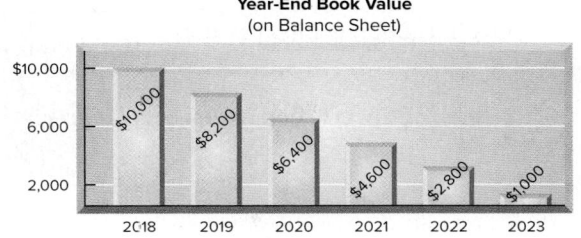

EXHIBIT 8.7

Financial Statement Effects of Straight-Line Depreciation

The net balance sheet amount is the **asset book value,** or *book value,* and is computed as the asset's total cost minus accumulated depreciation. For example, at the end of Year 2 (December 31, 2020), its book value is $6,400, which is $10,000 minus $3,600 (2 years × $1,800), and is reported in the balance sheet as follows.

Book value = Cost − Accumulated depreciation

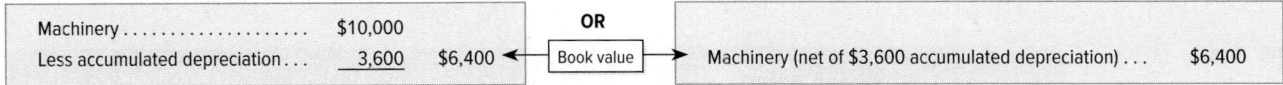

| Machinery.................... | $10,000 | | | | |
| Less accumulated depreciation... | 3,600 | $6,400 ← | Book value | → Machinery (net of $3,600 accumulated depreciation) ... | $6,400 |

OR

We also can compute the *straight-line depreciation rate,* which is 100% divided by the number of periods in the asset's useful life. For the inspection machine, this rate is 20% (100% ÷ 5 years, or 20% per period). We use this rate, along with other information, to compute the machine's *straight-line depreciation schedule* shown in Exhibit 8.8. This exhibit shows (1) straight-line depreciation is the same each period, (2) accumulated depreciation is the total of current and prior periods' depreciation expense, and (3) book value declines each period until it equals salvage value.

Point: Once an asset's book value equals its salvage value, depreciation stops.

Example: If salvage value of the machine is $2,500, what is the annual depreciation? *Answer:* ($10,000 − $2,500)/ 5 years = $1,500 per year

EXHIBIT 8.8

Straight-Line Depreciation Schedule

| | Depreciation for the Period | | | End of Period | |
Annual Period	Depreciable Cost*	Depreciation Rate	Depreciation Expense	Accumulated Depreciation	Book Value†
2018	—	—	—	—	$10,000
2019	$9,000	20%	$1,800	$1,800	8,200
2020	9,000	20	1,800	3,600	6,400
2021	9,000	20	1,800	5,400	4,600
2022	9,000	20	1,800	7,200	2,800
2023	9,000	20	1,800	9,000	1,000 ◄
			$9,000 ◄		

Salvage value is not depreciated.

$10,000 cost − $1,000 salvage

*$10,000 − $1,000.   †Book value is total cost minus accumulated depreciation.

Units-of-Production Method

The use of some plant assets varies greatly from one period to the next. For example, a builder might use a piece of equipment for a month and then not use it again for several months. When equipment use varies from period to period, the units-of-production depreciation method can better match expenses with revenues. **Units-of-production depreciation** charges a varying amount for each period depending on an asset's *usage.*

A two-step process is used. We first compute *depreciation per unit* as the asset's total cost minus salvage value and then divide by the total units expected to be produced during its useful life. Units of production can be expressed in product or other units such as hours used or miles driven. The second step is to compute depreciation for the period by multiplying the units produced in the period by the depreciation per unit. The computation for the machine described in Exhibit 8.5 is in Exhibit 8.9. *Note:* 7,000 shoes are inspected and sold in its first year.

EXHIBIT 8.9

Units-of-Production Depreciation Formula and Example

$$\text{Step 1} \quad \text{Depreciation per unit} = \frac{\text{Cost} - \text{Salvage value}}{\text{Total units of production}} = \frac{\$10,000 - \$1,000}{36,000 \text{ shoes}} = \$0.25 \text{ per shoe}$$

$$\text{Step 2} \quad \text{Depreciation expense} = \text{Depreciation per unit} \times \text{Units produced in period}$$
$$\$0.25 \text{ per shoe} \times 7,000 \text{ shoes} = \$1,750$$

Example: Refer to Exhibit 8.10. If the number of shoes inspected in 2023 is 5,500, what is depreciation for 2023? *Answer:* $1,250 (never depreciate below salvage value)

Using data on the number of units inspected (shoes produced) by the machine, we compute the *units-of-production depreciation schedule* in Exhibit 8.10. For example, depreciation for the first year is $1,750 (7,000 shoes at $0.25 per shoe). Depreciation for the second year is $2,000 (8,000 shoes at $0.25 per shoe). Exhibit 8.10 shows (1) depreciation expense depends on unit output, (2) accumulated depreciation is the total of current and prior periods' depreciation expense, and (3) book value declines each period until it equals salvage value.

EXHIBIT 8.10

Units-of-Production Depreciation Schedule

Annual Period	Depreciation for the Period			End of Period	
	Number of Units	Depreciation per Unit	Depreciation Expense	Accumulated Depreciation	Book Value
2018	—	—	—	—	$10,000
2019	7,000	$0.25	**$1,750**	$1,750	8,250
2020	8,000	0.25	**2,000**	3,750	6,250
2021	9,000	0.25	**2,250**	6,000	4,000
2022	7,000	0.25	**1,750**	7,750	2,250
2023	5,000	0.25	**1,250**	9,000	**1,000**
	36,000 units	$10,000 cost − $1,000 salvage	**$9,000**	Salvage value is not depreciated.	

$$\text{SL rate} = \frac{100\%}{\text{Useful life}}$$

$$\text{DDB rate} = \frac{200\%}{\text{Useful life}}$$

Point: Excel for DDB.

	A	B
1	Cost	$10,000
2	Salvage	$1,000
3	Life	5
4	DDB depr.	
5	1	
6	2	
7	etc.	

=DDB(B1,B2,B3,A5) = $4,000
=DDB(B1,B2,B3,A6) = $2,400

Declining-Balance Method An **accelerated depreciation method** has more depreciation in the early years and less depreciation in later years. The most common accelerated method is the **declining-balance method,** which uses a depreciation rate that is a multiple of the straight-line rate. A common depreciation rate is double the straight-line rate. This is called *double-declining-balance (DDB)*. This is done in three steps.

1. Compute the asset's straight-line depreciation rate.
2. Double the straight-line rate.
3. Compute depreciation by multiplying this rate by the asset's beginning-period book value.

Let's return to the machine in Exhibit 8.5 and use double-declining-balance to compute depreciation. Exhibit 8.11 shows the first-year depreciation computation. The three steps are (1) divide 100% by five years to get the straight-line rate of 20%, or 1/5, per year; (2) double this 20% rate to get the declining-balance rate of 40%, or 2/5, per year; and (3) compute depreciation as 40%, or 2/5, multiplied by the beginning-period book value.

EXHIBIT 8.11

Double-Declining-Balance Depreciation Formula*

Step 1 Straight-line rate = 100% ÷ Useful life = 100% ÷ 5 years = 20%

Step 2 Double-declining-balance rate = 2 × Straight-line rate = 2 × 20% = 40%

Step 3 Depreciation expense = Double-declining-balance rate × Beginning-period book value
40% × $10,000 = $4,000 (for 2019)

*In simple form: DDB depreciation = (2 × Beginning-period book value)/Useful life.

The *double-declining-balance depreciation schedule* is in Exhibit 8.12. The schedule follows the formula except for year 2023, when depreciation is $296. This $296 is not equal to 40% × $1,296, or $518.40. If we had used the $518.40 for depreciation in 2023, the ending book value would equal $777.60, which is less than the $1,000 salvage value. Instead, the $296 is computed as $1,296 book value minus $1,000 salvage value (for the year when DDB depreciation cuts into salvage value).

Example: What is the DDB depreciation in year 2022 if salvage value is $2,000? *Answer:* $2,160 − $2,000 = $160

EXHIBIT 8.12

Double-Declining-Balance Depreciation Schedule

Annual Period	Depreciation for the Period			End of Period	
	Beginning-of-Period Book Value	Depreciation Rate	Depreciation Expense	Accumulated Depreciation	Book Value
2018	—	—	—	—	$10,000
2019	$10,000	40%	$4,000	$4,000	6,000
2020	6,000	40	2,400	6,400	3,600
2021	3,600	40	1,440	7,840	2,160
2022	2,160	40	864	8,704	1,296
2023	1,296	40	296*	9,000	**1,000**
			$9,000		

Salvage value is not depreciated.

$10,000 cost − $1,000 salvage

*Year 2023 depreciation is $1,296 − $1,000 = $296 (never depreciate book value below salvage value).

Comparing Depreciation Methods Exhibit 8.13 shows depreciation for each year under the three methods. While depreciation per period differs, total depreciation of $9,000 is the same over the useful life.

Period	Straight-Line	Units-of-Production	Double-Declining-Balance
2019	$1,800	$1,750	$4,000
2020	1,800	2,000	2,400
2021	1,800	2,250	1,440
2022	1,800	1,750	864
2023	1,800	1,250	296
Totals	$9,000	$9,000	$9,000

EXHIBIT 8.13

Depreciation Expense for the Different Methods

Most Popular Methods

Straight-line, 85%

Units-of-production, 5%

Declining-balance, 4%

Accelerated and other, 6%

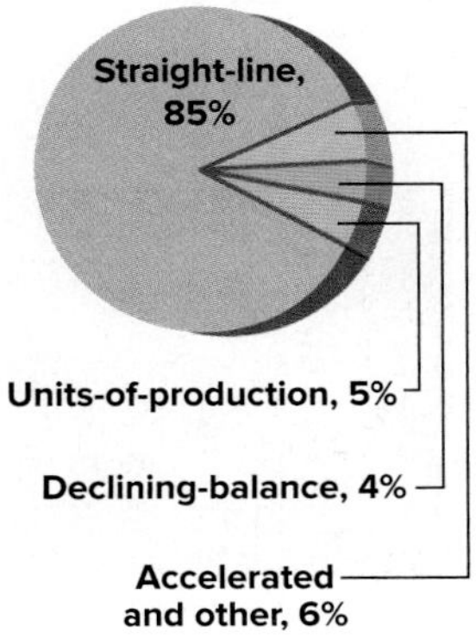

Depreciation for Tax Reporting Many companies use accelerated depreciation in computing taxable income. Reporting higher depreciation expense in the early years of an asset's life reduces the company's taxable income in those years and increases it in later years. The goal is to *postpone* its tax payments. The U.S. tax law has rules for depreciating assets. These rules include the **Modified Accelerated Cost Recovery System (MACRS),** which allows straight-line depreciation for some assets but requires accelerated depreciation for most kinds of assets. MACRS is *not* acceptable for financial reporting because it does not consider an asset's useful life or salvage value.

Partial-Year Depreciation

When an asset is purchased or sold at a time other than the beginning or end of an accounting period, depreciation is recorded for part of that period.

C2

Explain depreciation for partial years and changes in estimates.

Mid-Period Asset Purchase Assume that the machine in Exhibit 8.5 is purchased and placed in service on October 1, 2018, and the annual accounting period ends on December 31. Because this machine is used for three months in 2018, the calendar-year income statement reports depreciation for those three months. Using straight-line depreciation, we compute three months' depreciation of $450 as follows.

$$\frac{\$10,000 - \$1,000}{5 \text{ years}} \times \frac{3}{12} = \$450$$

Mid-Period Asset Sale   Assume that the machine above is sold on June 1, 2023. Depreciation is recorded in 2023 for the period January 1 through June 1 as follows.

$$\frac{\$10{,}000 - \$1{,}000}{5 \text{ years}} \times \frac{5}{12} = \$750$$

Change in Estimates

Depreciation is based on estimates of salvage value and useful life. If our estimate of an asset's useful life and/or salvage value changes, what should we do? The answer is to use the new estimate to compute depreciation for current and future periods. Revising an estimate of the useful life or salvage value of a plant asset is called a **change in an accounting estimate** and only affects current and future financial statements. We do not go back and restate (change) prior years' statements. This applies to all depreciation methods.

Let's return to the machine in Exhibit 8.8 using straight-line depreciation. At the beginning of this asset's third year, its book value is $6,400. Assume that at the beginning of its third year, the estimated number of years remaining in its useful life changes from three to four years *and* its estimate of salvage value changes from $1,000 to $400. Depreciation for each of the four remaining years is computed as in Exhibit 8.14.

Annual Period	Original Depreciation	Revised Depreciation
2018	—	—
2019	$1,800	$1,800
2020	1,800	1,800
2021	1,800	1,500
2022	1,800	1,500
2023	1,800	1,500
2024		1,500
	$9,000	$9,600

EXHIBIT 8.14

Computing Revised Straight-Line Depreciation

$$\frac{\text{Book value} - \text{Revised salvage value}}{\text{Revised remaining useful life}} = \frac{\$6{,}400 - \$400}{4 \text{ years}} = \$1{,}500 \text{ per year}$$

Reporting Depreciation

Some companies, such as **O'Reilly Auto**, report both the cost and accumulated depreciation of plant assets on the balance sheet. **Apple** and many other companies show plant assets on one line with the net amount of cost minus accumulated depreciation. When this is done, accumulated depreciation is disclosed in a note—see Appendix A for Apple.

Impairment   When there is a *permanent decline* in the fair value of an asset relative to its book value, the company writes down the asset to this fair value. This is called an asset **impairment.** Assume equipment has a book value of $800 and a fair (market) value of $750, *and* this $50 decline in value meets the impairment test (details are in advanced courses). The impairment entry is

Impairment Loss...	50	
Accumulated Depreciation—Equipment		50
Record impairment of equipment.		

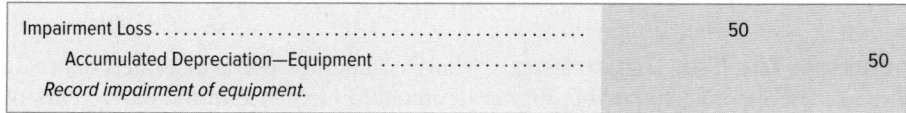

■ Decision Ethics

Controller   You are the controller for a struggling wingsuit company. Depreciation is its largest expense. Competitors depreciate equipment over three years. The company president tells you to revise useful lives of equipment from three to six years. What should you do? ■   *Answer:* The president's instructions may be an honest and reasonable prediction of the future. However, you might confront the president if you believe the aim is only to increase income.

©Cultura Creative/Alamy Stock Photo

NEED-TO-KNOW **8-2**

Depreciation Computations

C2   P1

Part 1. A machine costing $22,000 with a five-year life and an estimated $2,000 salvage value is installed on January 1. The manager estimates the machine will produce 1,000 units of product during its life. It actually produces the following units: 200 in Year 1, 400 in Year 2, 300 in Year 3, 80 in Year 4, and 30 in Year 5. The total units produced by the end of Year 5 exceed the original estimate—this difference was not predicted. (The machine must not be depreciated below its estimated salvage value.) Compute depreciation expense for each year and total depreciation for all years combined under straight-line, units-of-production, and double-declining-balance.

Part 2. In early January, a company acquires equipment for $3,800. The company estimates this equipment has a useful life of three years and a salvage value of $200. On January 1 of the third year, the company changes its estimates to a total four-year useful life and zero salvage value. Using the straight-line method, what is depreciation expense for the third year?

Solution—Part 1

Year	Straight-Line[a]	Units-of-Production[b]	Double-Declining-Balance[c]
1..............	$ 4,000	$ 4,000	$ 8,800
2..............	4,000	8,000	5,280
3..............	4,000	6,000	3,168
4..............	4,000	1,600	1,901
5..............	4,000	400	851
Totals..........	$20,000	$20,000	$20,000

[a]Straight-line: Cost per year = ($22,000 − $2,000)/5 years = $4,000 per year

[b]Units-of-production: Cost per unit = ($22,000 − $2,000)/1,000 units = $20 per unit

Year	Units	Depreciation per Unit	Depreciation	Accum. Deprec.	Book Value
1.................	200	$20	$ 4,000	$ 4,000	$18,000
2.................	400	20	8,000	12,000	10,000
3.................	300	20	6,000	18,000	4,000
4.................	80	20	1,600	19,600	2,400
5.................	30	20	400*	20,000*	2,000
Total..............			$20,000		

*30 × $20 = $600; however, $600 would make accumulated depreciation exceed the $20,000 total
depreciable cost. This means we take only enough depreciation in Year 5, or $400, to decrease book value
to the asset's $2,000 salvage value (never lower).

[c]Double-declining-balance: (100%/5) × 2 = 40% depreciation rate

Year	Beginning Book Value	Annual Depreciation (40% of book value)	Accumulated Depreciation at Year-End	Ending Book Value ($22,000 cost less accumulated depreciation)
1........	$22,000	$ 8,800	$ 8,800	$13,200
2........	13,200	5,280	14,080	7,920
3........	7,920	3,168	17,248	4,752
4........	4,752	1,901*	19,149	2,851
5........	2,851	851†	20,000	2,000
Total.....		$20,000		

*Rounded to the nearest dollar.
†Set depreciation in Year 5 to reduce book value to the $2,000 salvage value; namely, instead of $1,140
($2,851 × 40%), we use the maximum of $851 ($2,851 − $2,000).

Solution—Part 2

($3,800 − $200)/3 years = $1,200 (original depreciation per year)

$1,200 × 2 years = $2,400 (accumulated depreciation at date of change in estimate)

($3,800 − $2,400)/2 years = **$700** (revised depreciation)

> Do More: QS 8-3
> through QS 8-8, E 8-4
> through E 8-13

ADDITIONAL EXPENDITURES

Plant assets require maintenance, repairs, and improvements. We must decide whether to
expense or capitalize these expenditures (to capitalize is to increase the asset account).

C3

Distinguish between
revenue and capital
expenditures, and
account for them.

   Revenue expenditures, also called *income statement expenditures,* are costs that do not
materially increase the plant asset's life or capabilities. They are recorded as expenses on the
current-period income statement.

   Capital expenditures, also called *balance sheet expenditures,* are costs of plant assets that
provide benefits for longer than the current period. They increase the asset on the balance sheet.

Ordinary Repairs

Ordinary repairs are expenditures to keep an asset in good operating condition. Ordinary repairs do not extend an asset's useful life or increase its productivity beyond original expectations. Examples are normal costs of cleaning, lubricating, changing oil, and replacing small parts of a machine. Ordinary repairs are *revenue expenditures.* This means their costs are reported as expenses on the current-period income statement. Following this rule, **Brunswick** reports that "maintenance and repair costs are expensed as incurred." If Brunswick's current-year repair costs are $9,500, it makes the following entry.

Assets = Liabilities + Equity
−9,500   −9,500

Dec. 31	Repairs Expense......................................	9,500	
	Cash...		9,500
	Record ordinary repairs of equipment.		

Betterments and Extraordinary Repairs

Betterments and extraordinary repairs are *capital expenditures.*

Additional Expenditures	Examples	Expense Timing	Entry	
Ordinary repairs	• Cleaning • Lubricating • Adjusting • Repainting	Expensed currently	Repairs Expense..... Cash.............	# #
Betterments and extraordinary repairs	• Replacing main parts • Major asset expansions	Expensed in future	Asset (such as Equip.) Cash.............	# #

Example: Assume a firm owns a web server. Identify each cost as a revenue or capital expenditure: (1) purchase price, (2) necessary wiring, (3) platform for operation, (4) circuits to increase capacity, (5) monthly cleaning, (6) repair of a faulty switch, and (7) replacement of a worn fan. *Answer:* Capital expenditures: 1, 2, 3, 4; Revenue expenditures: 5, 6, 7.

Betterments (Improvements) **Betterments,** or *improvements,* are expenditures that make a plant asset more efficient or productive. A betterment often involves adding a component to an asset or replacing an old component with a better one and does not always increase useful life. An example is replacing manual controls on a machine with automatic controls. One special type of betterment is an *addition,* such as adding a new dock to a warehouse. Because a betterment benefits future periods, it is debited to the asset account as a capital expenditure. The new book value (less salvage value) is then depreciated over the asset's remaining useful life. Assume a company pays $8,000 for a machine with an eight-year useful life and no salvage value. After three years and $3,000 of depreciation, it adds an automated control system to the machine at a cost of $1,800. The cost of the betterment is added to the Machinery account with the following entry.

Assets = Liabilities + Equity
+1,800
−1,800

Jan. 2	Machinery..	1,800	
	Cash...		1,800
	Record installation of automated system.		

Point: Both extraordinary repairs and betterments require revising future depreciation.

After this entry, the remaining cost to be depreciated is $6,800, computed as $8,000 − $3,000 + $1,800. Depreciation for the remaining five years is $1,360 per year, computed as $6,800/5 years.

Extraordinary Repairs (Replacements) **Extraordinary repairs** are expenditures that extend the asset's useful life beyond its original estimate. Their costs are debited to the asset account.

Source: NASA/Tony Gray and Kevin O'Connell

■ **Decision Insight**

To the Moon and Back **SpaceX** made history when it relaunched a used Falcon 9 rocket. This was the first time an orbital rocket was launched into space a second time. SpaceX made extraordinary repairs to the rocket to make this relaunch possible. However, these repairs were considerably less costly than building a new rocket for tens of millions of dollars. ■

DISPOSALS OF PLANT ASSETS

Disposal of plant assets occurs in one of three ways: discarding, sale, or exchange. Discarding and selling are covered here; Appendix 8A covers exchanges. The steps for disposing plant assets are in Exhibit 8.15.

1. Record depreciation up to the date of disposal—this also updates Accumulated Depreciation.
2. Record the removal of the disposed asset's account balances—including its accumuated depreciation.
3. Record any cash (and/or other assets) received or paid in the disposal.
4. Record any gain or loss—equal to the value of any assets received minus the disposed asset's book value.

EXHIBIT 8.15

Accounting for Disposals
of Plant Assets

Discarding Plant Assets

P2_____

Account for asset disposal
through discarding or
selling an asset.

A plant asset is *discarded* when it is no longer useful to the company and it has no market value.
Assume that a machine costing $9,000 with accumulated depreciation of $9,000 is discarded.
When accumulated depreciation equals the asset's cost, it is said to be *fully depreciated* (zero
book value). The entry to record the discarding of this asset is

June 5	Accumulated Depreciation—Machinery	9,000	
	Machinery.....................................		9,000
	Discarding of fully depreciated machinery.		

Assets = Liabilities + Equity
+9,000
−9,000

This entry reflects all four steps of Exhibit 8.15. Step 1 is unnecessary because the machine is
fully depreciated. Step 2 is reflected in the debit to Accumulated Depreciation and credit to
Machinery. Because no other asset is involved, step 3 is irrelevant. Finally, because book value
is zero and no other asset is involved, no gain or loss is recorded in step 4.

How do we account for discarding an asset that is not fully depreciated or one whose depreciation is not up-to-date? To answer this, consider equipment costing $8,000 with accumulated
depreciation of $6,000 on December 31 of the prior fiscal year-end. This equipment is being
depreciated by $1,000 per year using the straight-line method over eight years with zero salvage.
On July 1 of the current year it is discarded. Step 1 is to bring depreciation up-to-date.

Point: Recording depreciation
expense up-to-date gives an
up-to-date book value for
determining gain or loss.

July 1	Depreciation Expense	500	
	Accumulated Depreciation—Equipment............		500
	Record 6 months' depreciation ($1,000 × 6/12).		

Assets = Liabilities + Equity
−500   −500

Steps 2 through 4 of Exhibit 8.15 are reflected in the second (and final) entry.

July 1	Accumulated Depreciation—Equipment.................	6,500	
	Loss on Disposal of Equipment.......................	1,500	
	Equipment.....................................		8,000
	Discard equipment with a $1,500 book value.		

Assets = Liabilities + Equity
+6,500   −1,500
−8,000

This loss is computed by comparing the equipment's $1,500 book value ($8,000 − $6,000 −
$500) with the zero net cash proceeds. The loss is reported in the Other Expenses and Losses
section of the income statement. Discarding an asset can sometimes require a cash payment that
would increase the loss.

Selling Plant Assets

To demonstrate selling plant assets, consider BTO's March 31 sale of equipment that cost
$16,000 and has accumulated depreciation of $12,000 at December 31 of the prior year-
end. Annual depreciation on this equipment is $4,000 using straight-line. Step 1 of this sale
is to record depreciation expense and update accumulated depreciation to March 31 of the
current year.

Mar. 31	Depreciation Expense	1,000	
	Accumulated Depreciation—Equipment............		1,000
	Record 3 months' depreciation ($4,000 × 3/12).		

Assets = Liabilities + Equity
−1,000   −1,000

Steps 2 through 4 need one final entry that depends on the amount received from the sale. We cover three different possibilities.

Sale price = Book value ┄ → No gain or loss

Sale at Book Value
If BTO receives $3,000 cash, an amount equal to the equipment's book value as of March 31 (book value = $16,000 − $12,000 − $1,000), no gain or loss is recorded. The entry is

Assets = Liabilities + Equity
+3,000
+13,000
−16,000

Mar. 31	Cash...	3,000	
	Accumulated Depreciation—Equipment	13,000	
	Equipment		16,000
	Record sale of equipment for no gain or loss.		

Sale price > Book value ┄ → Gain

Sale above Book Value
If BTO receives $7,000, an amount that is $4,000 above the equipment's $3,000 book value as of March 31, a gain is recorded. The entry is

Assets = Liabilities + Equity
+7,000   +4,000
+13,000
−16,000

Mar. 31	Cash...	7,000	
	Accumulated Depreciation—Equipment	13,000	
	Gain on Disposal of Equipment....................		4,000
	Equipment		16,000
	Record sale of equipment for a $4,000 gain.		

Sale price < Book value ┄ → Loss

Sale below Book Value
If BTO receives $2,500, an amount that is $500 below the equipment's $3,000 book value as of March 31, a loss is recorded. The entry is

Assets = Liabilities + Equity
+2,500   −500
+13,000
−16,000

Mar. 31	Cash...	2,500	
	Loss on Disposal of Equipment	500	
	Accumulated Depreciation—Equipment	13,000	
	Equipment		16,000
	Record sale of equipment for a $500 loss.		

 **NEED-TO-KNOW 8-3**

Additional Expenditures and Asset Disposals

C3 P2

Part 1. A company pays $1,000 for equipment expected to last four years and have a $200 salvage value. Prepare journal entries to record the following costs related to the equipment.

a. During the second year of the equipment's life, $400 cash is paid for a new component expected to materially increase the equipment's productivity.

b. During the third year, $250 cash is paid for normal repairs necessary to keep the equipment in good working order.

c. During the fourth year, $500 is paid for repairs expected to increase the useful life of the equipment from four to five years.

Part 2. A company owns a machine that cost $500 and has accumulated depreciation of $400. Prepare the entry to record the disposal of the machine on January 2 in each separate situation.

a. The company disposed of the machine, receiving nothing in return.

b. The company sold the machine for $80 cash.

c. The company sold the machine for $100 cash.

d. The company sold the machine for $110 cash.

Solution—Part 1

a.

Year 2	Equipment	400	
	Cash...		400
	Record betterment.		

b.

Year 3	Repairs Expense	250	
	Cash...		250
	Record ordinary repairs.		

c.

Year 4	Equipment	500	
	Cash......................................		500
	Record extraordinary repairs.		

Do More: QS 8-9, QS 8-10,
E 8-14, E 8-15, E 8-16,
E 8-17

Solution—Part 2   (*Note:* Book value of machine = $500 − $400 = <u>$100</u>)

a. Disposed of at no value.

Jan. 2	Loss on Disposal of Machine............	100	
	Accumulated Depreciation—Machine.....	400	
	Machine........................		500
	Record disposal of machine.		

b. Sold for $80 cash.

Jan. 2	Cash	80	
	Loss on Sale of Machine	20	
	Accumulated Depreciation—Machine.....	400	
	Machine........................		500
	Record sale of machine below book value.		

c. Sold for $100 cash.

Jan. 2	Cash	100	
	Accumulated Depreciation—Machine.....	400	
	Machine........................		500
	Record sale of machine at book value.		

d. Sold for $110 cash.

Jan. 2	Cash	110	
	Accumulated Depreciation—Machine.....	400	
	Gain on Sale of Machine...........		10
	Machine........................		500
	Record sale of machine above book value.		

Section 2—Natural Resources

Natural resources are assets that are physically consumed when used. Examples are standing timber, mineral deposits, and oil and gas fields. These assets are soon-to-be inventories of raw materials after cutting, mining, or pumping. Until that conversion happens, they are reported as noncurrent assets under either plant assets or their own category using titles such as *Timberlands, Mineral deposits,* or *Oil reserves.*

P3

Account for natural resource assets and their depletion.

Cost Determination and Depletion

Natural resources are recorded at cost, which includes all expenditures necessary to acquire the resource and prepare it for use. **Depletion** is the process of allocating the cost of a natural resource to the period when it is consumed. Natural resources are reported on the balance sheet at cost minus *accumulated depletion.* The depletion expense per period is usually based on units extracted from cutting, mining, or pumping. This is similar to units-of-production depreciation.

To demonstrate, consider a mineral deposit with an estimated 250,000 tons of available ore. It is purchased for $500,000, and we expect zero salvage value. The depletion charge per ton of ore mined is $2, computed as $500,000 ÷ 250,000 tons. If 85,000 tons are mined and sold in the first year, the depletion charge for that year is $170,000. These computations are in Exhibit 8.16.

EXHIBIT 8.16

Depletion Formula and Example

Step 1 $\text{Depletion per unit} = \dfrac{\text{Cost} - \text{Salvage value}}{\text{Total units of capacity}} = \dfrac{\$500,000 - \$0}{250,000 \text{ tons}} = \$2 \text{ per ton}$

Step 2 $\text{Depletion expense} = \text{Depletion per unit} \times \text{Units extracted and sold in period}$
$$= \$2 \times 85,000 = \$170,000$$

Depletion expense for the first year is recorded as follows.

Dec. 31	Depletion Expense—Mineral Deposit....................	170,000	
	Accumulated Depletion—Mineral Deposit...........		170,000
	Record depletion of the mineral deposit.		

Assets = Liabilities + Equity
−170,000   −170,000

The period-end balance sheet reports the mineral deposit as shown in Exhibit 8.17.

EXHIBIT 8.17

Balance Sheet Presentation of Natural Resources

Mineral deposit	$500,000	
Less accumulated depletion	**170,000**	$330,000

Because all 85,000 tons of the mined ore are sold during the year, the entire $170,000 of depletion is reported on the income statement. If some of the ore remains unsold at year-end, the depletion related to the unsold ore is carried forward on the balance sheet and reported as Ore Inventory, a current asset. Altering our example, assume that of the 85,000 tons mined the first year, only 70,000 tons are sold. We record depletion of $140,000 (70,000 tons × $2 depletion per unit) and the remaining ore inventory of $30,000 (15,000 tons × $2 depletion per unit) as follows.

Assets = Liabilities + Equity
−170,000   −140,000
+30,000

Dec. 31	Depletion Expense—Mineral Deposit	140,000	
	Ore Inventory	30,000	
	Accumulated Depletion—Mineral Deposit		170,000
	Record depletion and inventory of mineral deposit.		

Plant Assets Tied into Extracting

Mining, cutting, or pumping natural resources requires machinery, equipment, and buildings. When the usefulness of these plant assets is directly related to the depletion of a natural resource, their costs are depreciated using the units-of-production method in proportion to the depletion of the natural resource. For example, if a machine is permanently installed in a mine and 10% of the ore is mined and sold in the period, then 10% of the machine's cost (minus any salvage value) is depreciated. The same procedure is used when a machine is abandoned once resources are extracted. If the machine will be used at another site when extraction is complete, it is depreciated over its own useful life.

©GIRODJL/Shutterstock

Ethical Risk

Lost Cause   Long-term assets must be safeguarded against theft, misuse, and damage. Controls include use of security tags, monitoring of rights infringements, and approvals of asset disposals. A study reports that 43% of employees in operations and services witnessed the wasting, mismanaging, or abusing of assets in the past year (KPMG). ∎

NEED-TO-KNOW 8-4

Depletion Accounting

P3

A company acquires a zinc mine at a cost of $750,000 on January 1. At that same time, it incurs additional costs of $100,000 to access the mine, which is estimated to hold 200,000 tons of zinc. The estimated value of the land after the zinc is removed is $50,000.

1. Prepare the January 1 entry(ies) to record the cost of the zinc mine.

2. Prepare the December 31 year-end adjusting entry if 50,000 tons of zinc are mined, but only 40,000 tons are sold the first year.

Solution

1.

Jan. 1	Zinc Mine	850,000	
	Cash...		850,000
	Record cost of zinc mine.		

2. Depletion per unit = ($750,000 + $100,000 − $50,000)/200,000 tons = $4.00 per ton

Dec. 31	Depletion Expense—Zinc Mine	160,000	
	Zinc Inventory	40,000	
	Accumulated Depletion—Zinc Mine.............		200,000
	Record depletion of zinc mine (50,000 × $4.00).		

Do More: QS 8-11, E 8-18, P 8-7

Section 3—Intangible Assets

Intangible assets are nonphysical assets used in operations that give companies long-term rights or competitive advantages. Examples are patents, copyrights, licenses, leaseholds, franchises, and trademarks. Lack of physical substance does not always mean an intangible asset. For example, notes and accounts receivable lack physical substance but are not intangibles. This section covers common types of intangible assets.

P4

Account for intangible assets.

Cost Determination and Amortization

An intangible asset is recorded at cost when purchased. Intangibles can have limited lives or indefinite lives. If an intangible has a **limited life,** its cost is expensed over its estimated useful life using **amortization.** If an intangible asset has an **indefinite life**—meaning that no legal, competitive, economic, or other factors limit its useful life—it is not amortized. (If an intangible with an indefinite life is later judged to have a limited life, it is amortized over that limited life.)

Amortization of intangible assets is similar to depreciation. However, only the straight-line method is used for amortizing intangibles *unless* the company can show that another method is preferred. Amortization is recorded in a contra account, Accumulated Amortization. The acquisition cost of intangible assets is disclosed along with the accumulated amortization. The disposal of an intangible asset involves removing its book value, recording any other asset(s) received or given up, and recognizing any gain or loss for the difference.

Many intangibles have limited lives due to laws, contracts, or other reasons. Examples are patents, copyrights, and leaseholds. The cost of intangible assets is amortized over the periods expected to benefit from their use, but this period cannot be longer than the assets' legal existence. Other intangibles such as trademarks and trade names have indefinite lives and are not amortized. An intangible asset that is not amortized is tested annually for **impairment**—if necessary, an impairment loss is recorded. (Details are in advanced courses.)

Intangible assets are often in a separate section of the balance sheet immediately after plant assets. For example, **Nike** follows this approach in reporting nearly $300 million of intangible assets in its balance sheet, plus $140 million in goodwill. Companies usually disclose their amortization periods for intangibles. The remainder of our discussion focuses on accounting for specific types of intangible assets.

©Michael DeYoung/Blend Images

Types of Intangibles

Patents   The federal government grants patents to encourage the invention of new technology and processes. A **patent** is an exclusive right granted to its owner to manufacture and sell a patented item or to use a process for 20 years. When patent rights are purchased, the cost to acquire the rights is debited to an account called Patents. If the owner engages in lawsuits to successfully defend a patent, the cost of lawsuits is debited to the Patents account; if the defense is unsuccessful, the book value of the patent is expensed. However, the costs of research and development leading to a new patent are expensed when incurred.

A patent's cost is amortized over its estimated useful life (not to exceed 20 years). If we purchase a patent costing $25,000 with a useful life of 10 years, we make the following adjusting entry at the end of each of the 10 years to amortize one-tenth of its cost. The $2,500 debit to Amortization Expense is on the income statement as a cost of the patented product or service. The Accumulated Amortization—Patents account is a contra asset account to Patents.

Dec. 31	Amortization Expense—Patents	2,500	
	Accumulated Amortization—Patents		2,500
	Amortize patent costs over its useful life.		

Assets = Liabilities + Equity
−2,500   −2,500

Copyrights

Copyrights   A **copyright** gives its owner the exclusive right to publish and sell a musical, literary, or artistic work during the life of the creator plus 70 years, although the useful life of most copyrights is much shorter. The costs of a copyright are amortized over its useful life. The only identifiable cost of many copyrights is the fee paid to the Copyright Office. Identifiable costs of a copyright are capitalized (recorded in an asset account) and amortized by debiting an account called Amortization Expense—Copyrights.

Franchises and Licenses   **Franchises** and **licenses** are rights that a company or government grants an entity to sell a product or service under specified conditions. Many organizations grant franchise and license rights—**Anytime Fitness, Firehouse Subs,** and **Major League Baseball** are just a few examples. The costs of franchises and licenses are debited to a Franchises and Licenses asset account and are amortized over the life of the agreement. If an agreement is for an indefinite time, those costs are not amortized.

Point: McDonald's "golden arches" are one of the world's most valuable trademarks, yet this asset is not on McDonald's balance sheet.

Trademarks and Trade Names   A **trademark** or **trade (brand) name** is a symbol, name, phrase, or jingle identified with a company, product, or service. Examples are Nike Swoosh, Big Mac, Coca-Cola, and Corvette. Ownership and exclusive right to use a trademark or trade name often are granted to the company that used it first. Ownership is best established by registering a trademark or trade name with the government's Patent Office. The cost of developing, maintaining, or enhancing the value of a trademark or trade name (such as advertising) is charged to expense when incurred. If a trademark or trade name is purchased, however, its cost is debited to an asset account and then amortized over its expected life. If the company plans to renew indefinitely its right to the trademark or trade name, the cost is not amortized.

Point: Amortization of goodwill is different for financial accounting and tax accounting. The IRS requires the amortization of goodwill over 15 years.

Example: Assume goodwill has a book value of $500, an implied fair value of $475, *and* this $25 decline in value meets the impairment test. The impairment entry is
Impairment Loss 25
  Goodwill 25

Goodwill   **Goodwill** is the amount by which a company's value exceeds the value of its individual assets and liabilities. This implies that the company as a whole has certain valuable attributes not measured in assets and liabilities. These can include superior management, skilled workforce, good supplier or customer relations, quality products or services, good location, or other competitive advantages.

  Goodwill is only recorded when an entire company or business segment is purchased. Purchased goodwill is computed as purchase price of the company minus the market value of net assets (excluding goodwill). **Google** paid $1.19 billion to acquire **YouTube**; about $1.13 of the $1.19 billion was for goodwill. Goodwill is recorded as an asset, and it is *not* amortized. Instead, goodwill is annually tested for impairment. (Details are in advanced courses.)

Right-of-Use Asset (Lease)   Property is rented under a contract called a **lease.** The property's owner, called the **lessor,** grants the lease. The one who secures the right to possess and use the property is called the **lessee.** A **leasehold** is the rights the lessor grants to the lessee under the terms of the lease.

Lease or Buy   Some advantages of leasing an asset versus buying it are that

- Little or no up-front payment is normally required (making it more affordable).
- Lease terms often allow exchanges to trade up on leased assets (reducing obsolescence).

Point: At lease start:
Right-of-Use Asset .... #
  Lease Liability .... #
    At each period-end:
Amortization Expense .... #
  Acc Amor—RoU Asset... #

Lease Accounting   For noncurrent leases, the lessee records a "Right-of-Use Asset" and "Lease Liability" equal to the value of lease payments. At each period-end, the lessee records amortization with a debit to Amortization Expense and a credit to Accumulated Amortization—Right-of-Use Asset.

Point: A Leasehold account implies existence of future benefits that the lessee controls because of a prepayment. It also meets the definition of an asset.

Leasehold Improvements   A lessee sometimes pays for improvements to the leased property such as partitions, painting, and storefronts. These improvements are called **leasehold improvements,** and the lessee debits these costs to a Leasehold Improvements account. The lessee amortizes these costs over the life of the lease or the life of the improvements, whichever is shorter. The amortization entry *debits* Amortization Expense—Leasehold Improvements and *credits* Accumulated Amortization—Leasehold Improvements.

Other Intangibles

There are other types of intangible assets such as software, non-compete covenants, customer lists, and so forth. Accounting for them is the same as for other intangibles.

Research and Development

Research and development costs are expenditures to discover new products, new processes, or knowledge. Creating patents, copyrights, and innovative products and services requires research and development costs. **The costs of research and development are expensed when incurred** because it is difficult to predict the future benefits from research and development. GAAP does **not** include them as intangible assets.

■ **Decision Insight**

Free Mickey   The Walt Disney Company successfully lobbied Congress to extend copyright protection from the life of the creator plus 50 years to the life of the creator plus 70 years. This extension allows the company to protect its characters for 20 additional years before the right to use them enters the public domain. Mickey Mouse is now protected by copyright law until 2023. The law is officially termed the Copyright Term Extension Act (CTEA), but it is also known as the Mickey Mouse Protection Act. ■

©Yoshikazu Tsuno/AFP/Getty Images

NEED-TO-KNOW 8-5

Accounting for Intangibles

P4 ▶

Part 1. A publisher purchases the copyright on a book for $1,000 on January 1 of this year. The copyright lasts five more years. The company plans to sell prints for seven years. Prepare entries to record the purchase of the copyright on January 1 and its annual amortization on December 31.

Part 2. On January 3 of this year, a retailer pays $9,000 to modernize its store. Improvements include lighting, partitions, and a sound system. These improvements are estimated to yield benefits for five years. The retailer leases its store and has three years remaining on its lease. Prepare the entry to record (a) the cost of modernization and (b) amortization at the end of this year.

Part 3. On January 6 of this year, a company pays $6,000 for a patent with a remaining 12-year legal life to produce a supplement expected to be marketable for 3 years. Prepare entries to record its acquisition and the December 31 amortization entry.

Solution—Part 1

Jan. 1	Copyright...	1,000	
	Cash		1,000
	Record purchase of copyright.		
Dec. 31	Amortization Expense—Copyright	200	
	Accumulated Amortization—Copyright....................		200
	Record amortization of copyright ($1,000/5 years).		

Solution—Part 2

a.

Jan. 3	Leasehold Improvements.....................................	9,000	
	Cash		9,000
	Record leasehold improvements.		

b.

Dec. 31	Amortization Expense—Leasehold Improvements	3,000	
	Accumulated Amortization—Leasehold Improvements		3,000
	*Record amortization of leasehold over remaining lease life.**		

*Amortization = $9,000/3-year lease term = $3,000 per year.

Solution—Part 3

Jan. 6	Patents...	6,000	
	Cash		6,000
	Record purchase of patent.		
Dec. 31	Amortization Expense*	2,000	
	Accumulated Amortization—Patents......................		2,000
	*Record amortization of patent. *$6,000/3 years = $2,000*		

Do More: QS 8-12, QS 8-13, E 8-19, E 8-20

 Decision Analysis 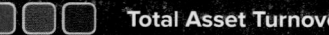   **Total Asset Turnover**

One important measure of a company's ability to use its assets efficiently and effectively is **total asset turnover,** defined in Exhibit 8.18.

EXHIBIT 8.18

Total Asset Turnover

$$\text{Total asset turnover} = \frac{\text{Net sales}}{\text{Average total assets}}$$

A1

Compute total asset turn-over and apply it to analyze a company's use of assets.

Net sales is net amounts earned from the sale of products and services. Average total assets is (Current period-end total assets + Prior period-end total assets)/2. A higher total asset turnover means a company is generating more net sales for each dollar of assets. Management is evaluated on efficient and effective use of total assets by looking at total asset turnover.

Let's look at total asset turnover in Exhibit 8.19 for two competing companies: **Starbucks** and **Jack in the Box**.

EXHIBIT 8.19

Analysis Using Total Asset Turnover

Company	Figure ($ millions)	Current Year	1 Year Ago	2 Years Ago
Starbucks	Net sales............................	$22,387	$21,316	$19,163
	Average total assets....................	$14,339	$13,364	$11,585
	Total asset turnover	1.56	1.60	1.65
Jack in the Box	Net sales............................	$1,554	$1,599	$1,540
	Average total assets....................	$1,289	$1,326	$1,287
	Total asset turnover	1.21	1.21	1.20

To show how we use total asset turnover, let's look at Starbucks. We express Starbucks's use of assets in generating net sales by saying "it turned its assets over 1.56 times during the current year." This means that each $1.00 of assets produced $1.56 of net sales.

Is a total asset turnover of 1.56 good or bad? All companies want a high total asset turnover. Interpreting the total asset turnover requires an understanding of company operations. Some operations are capital-intensive, meaning that a relatively large amount is invested in plant assets to generate sales. This results in a lower total asset turnover. Other companies' operations are labor-intensive, meaning that they generate sales using people instead of assets. In that case, we expect a higher total asset turnover.

Starbucks's turnover is higher than that for Jack in the Box. However, Starbucks's total asset turnover decreased over the last three years. To maintain a strong total asset turnover, Starbucks must grow sales at a rate equal to, or higher than, its total asset growth.

■ Decision Maker

Environmentalist   A paper manufacturer claims it cannot afford more environmental controls. It points to its low total asset turnover of 1.9 and argues that it cannot compete with companies whose total asset turnover is much higher. Examples cited are food stores (5.5) and auto dealers (3.8). How do you respond? ■   *Answer:* The paper manufacturer's comparison of its total asset turnover with food stores and auto dealers is misdirected. You need to collect data from competitors in the paper industry to show that a 1.9 total asset turnover is about the norm for this industry.

On July 1, 2018, Tulsa Company pays $600,000 to acquire a fully equipped factory. The purchase includes the following assets and information.

Asset	Appraised Value	Salvage Value	Useful Life	Depreciation Method
Land..........................	$160,000			Not depreciated
Land improvements	80,000	$ 0	10 years	Straight-line
Building.........................	320,000	100,000	10 years	Double-declining-balance
Machinery	240,000	20,000	10,000 units	Units-of-production
Total...........................	$800,000			

NEED-TO-KNOW 8-6

COMPREHENSIVE

Acquisition, Cost Allocation, and Disposal of Tangible and Intangible Assets

Required

1. Allocate the total $600,000 purchase cost among the separate assets.

2. Compute the 2018 (six months) and 2019 depreciation expense for each asset, and compute the company's total depreciation expense for both years. The machinery produced 700 units in 2018 and 1,800 units in 2019.

3. On the last day of calendar-year 2020, Tulsa discarded equipment that had been on its books for five years. The equipment's original cost was $12,000 (estimated life of five years) and its salvage value was $2,000. No depreciation had been recorded for the fifth year when the disposal occurred. Journalize the fifth year of depreciation (straight-line method) and the asset's disposal.

4. At the beginning of year 2020, Tulsa purchased a patent for $100,000 cash. The company estimated the patent's useful life to be 10 years. Journalize the patent acquisition and its amortization for the year 2020.

5. Late in the year 2020, Tulsa acquired an ore deposit for $600,000 cash. It added roads and built mine shafts for an additional cost of $80,000. Salvage value of the mine is estimated to be $20,000. The company estimated 330,000 tons of available ore. In year 2020, Tulsa mined and sold 10,000 tons of ore. Journalize the mine's acquisition and its first year's depletion.

6.[A] (This question applies to this chapter's Appendix coverage.) On the first day of 2020, Tulsa exchanged the machinery that was acquired on July 1, 2018, along with $5,000 cash for machinery with a $210,000 market value. Journalize the exchange of these assets assuming the exchange has commercial substance. (Refer to background information in parts 1 and 2.)

PLANNING THE SOLUTION

- Complete a three-column table showing the following amounts for each asset: appraised value, percent of total value, and apportioned cost.

- Using allocated costs, compute depreciation for 2018 (only one-half year) and 2019 (full year) for each asset. Summarize those computations in a table showing total depreciation for each year.

- Depreciation must be recorded up-to-date before discarding an asset. Calculate and record depreciation expense for the fifth year using the straight-line method. Record the loss on the disposal as well as the removal of the discarded asset and its accumulated depreciation.

- Record the patent (an intangible asset) at its purchase price. Use straight-line amortization over its useful life to calculate amortization expense.

- Record the ore deposit (a natural resource asset) at its cost, including any added costs to ready the mine for use. Calculate depletion per ton using the depletion formula. Multiply the depletion per ton by the amount of tons mined and sold to calculate depletion expense for the year.

- Gains and losses on asset exchanges that have commercial substance are recognized. Make a journal entry to add the acquired machinery and remove the old machinery, along with its accumulated depreciation, and to record the cash given in the exchange.

SOLUTION

1. Allocation of the total cost of $600,000 among the separate assets.

Asset	Appraised Value	Percent of Total Value	Apportioned Cost
Land........................	$160,000	20%	**$120,000** ($600,000 × 20%)
Land improvements	80,000	10	**60,000** ($600,000 × 10%)
Building....................	320,000	40	**240,000** ($600,000 × 40%)
Machinery..................	240,000	30	**180,000** ($600,000 × 30%)
Total.......................	$800,000	100%	$ 600,000

2. Depreciation for each asset. (Land is not depreciated.)

Land Improvements

Cost..	$ 60,000
Salvage value..	0
Depreciable cost	$ 60,000
Useful life..	10 years
Annual depreciation expense ($60,000/10 years)	$ 6,000
2018 depreciation ($6,000 × 6/12)..........................	**$ 3,000**
2019 depreciation	**$ 6,000**

Building

Straight-line rate = 100%/10 years = 10%

Double-declining-balance rate = 10% × 2 = 20%

2018 depreciation ($240,000 × 20% × 6/12)	**$ 24,000**
2019 depreciation [($240,000 − $24,000) × 20%].	**$ 43,200**

Machinery

Cost..	$180,000
Salvage value..	20,000
Depreciable cost	$160,000
Total expected units of production	10,000 units
Depreciation per unit ($160,000/10,000 units)	$ 16
2018 depreciation ($16 × 700 units)	**$ 11,200**
2019 depreciation ($16 × 1,800 units)	**$ 28,800**

Total depreciation expense for each year.

	2018	2019
Land improvements	$ 3,000	$ 6,000
Building......................	24,000	43,200
Machinery....................	11,200	28,800
Total........................	$38,200	$78,000

3. Record the depreciation up-to-date on the discarded asset.

Depreciation Expense—Equipment	2,000	
Accumulated Depreciation—Equipment.................................		2,000
Record depreciation on date of disposal: ($12,000 − $2,000)/5.		

Record the removal of the discarded asset and its loss on disposal.

Accumulated Depreciation—Equipment	10,000	
Loss on Disposal of Equipment..	2,000	
Equipment..		12,000
Record the discarding of equipment with a $2,000 book value.		

4.

Patent..	100,000	
Cash		100,000
Record patent acquisition.		

Amortization Expense—Patent...	10,000	
Accumulated Amortization—Patent....................................		10,000
Record amortization expense: $100,000/10 years = $10,000.		

5.

Ore Deposit...	680,000	
Cash..		680,000
Record ore deposit acquisition and its related costs.		

Depletion Expense—Ore Deposit...	20,000	
Accumulated Depletion—Ore Deposit...............................		20,000
Record depletion expense: ($680,000 − $20,000)/330,000 tons = $2 per ton.		
10,000 tons mined and sold × $2 = $20,000 depletion.		

6.ᴬ Record the asset exchange: The book value on the exchange date is $180,000 (cost) − $40,000 (accumulated depreciation). The book value of the machinery given up in the exchange ($140,000) plus the $5,000 cash paid is less than the $210,000 value of the machine acquired. The entry to record this exchange of assets that has commercial substance and recognizes the $65,000 gain ($210,000 − $140,000 − $5,000) is

Machinery (new)..	210,000	
Accumulated Depreciation—Machinery (old)...............................	40,000	
Machinery (old)...		180,000
Cash..		5,000
Gain on Exchange of Assets.....................................		65,000
Record exchange with commercial substance of old equipment		
plus cash for new equipment.		

Exchanging Plant Assets

8A

P5
Account for asset exchanges.

Many plant assets such as machinery, automobiles, and equipment are exchanged for newer assets. In a typical exchange of plant assets, a *trade-in allowance* is received on the old asset and the balance is paid in cash. Accounting for the exchange of assets depends on whether the transaction has *commercial substance*. An exchange has commercial substance if the company's future cash flows change as a result of the exchange of one asset for another asset. If an asset exchange has commercial substance, a gain or loss is recorded based on the difference between the book value of the asset(s) given up and the market value of the asset(s) received. Because most exchanges have commercial substance, we cover gains and losses for only that situation. Advanced courses cover exchanges without commercial substance.

Exchange with Commercial Substance: A Loss A company acquires $42,000 in new equipment. In exchange, the company pays $33,000 cash and trades in old equipment. The old equipment originally cost $36,000 and has accumulated depreciation of $20,000, which implies a $16,000 book value at the time of exchange. This exchange has commercial substance and the old equipment has a trade-in allowance of $9,000. This exchange yields a loss as computed in the middle (Loss) columns of Exhibit 8A.1; the loss is computed as Asset received − Assets given = $42,000 − $49,000 = $(7,000). We also can compute the loss as Trade-in allowance − Book value of assets given = $9,000 − $16,000 = $(7,000).

EXHIBIT 8A.1

Computing Gain or Loss on Asset Exchange with Commercial Substance

Asset Exchange Has Commercial Substance	Loss		Gain	
Market value of asset received............................		$42,000		$42,000
Book value of assets given:				
Equipment ($36,000 − $20,000).........................	$16,000		$16,000	
Cash..	33,000	49,000	23,000	39,000
Gain (loss) on exchange................................		**$(7,000)**		**$ 3,000**

The entry to record this asset exchange and the loss follows.

Assets = Liabilities + Equity
+42,000   −7,000
+20,000
−36,000
−33,000

Jan. 3	Equipment (**new**)	42,000	
	Loss on Exchange of Assets	7,000	
	Accumulated Depreciation—Equipment (**old**)	20,000	
	Equipment (**old**)		36,000
	Cash...		33,000
	Record exchange (with commercial substance) of		
	old equipment and cash for new equipment.		

Point: "New" and "old" equipment are for illustration only. Both the debit and credit are to the same Equipment account.

Exchange with Commercial Substance: A Gain   Let's assume the same facts as in the preceding asset exchange *except that the company pays $23,000 cash, not $33,000, with the trade-in.* This exchange has commercial substance and the old equipment has a trade-in allowance of $19,000. This exchange yields a gain as computed in the right-most (Gain) columns of Exhibit 8A.1; the gain is computed as Asset received − Assets given = $42,000 − $39,000 = $3,000. We also can compute the gain as Trade-in allowance − Book value of assets given = $19,000 − $16,000 = $3,000. The entry to record this asset exchange and the gain follows.

Assets = Liabilities + Equity
+42,000   +3,000
+20,000
−36,000
−23,000

Jan. 3	Equipment (**new**)	42,000	
	Accumulated Depreciation—Equipment (**old**)	20,000	
	Equipment (**old**)		36,000
	Cash...		23,000
	Gain on Exchange of Assets......................		3,000
	Record exchange (with commercial substance)		
	of old equipment and cash for new equipment.		

NEED-TO-KNOW 8-7

Asset Exchange

P5

▶

A company acquires $45,000 in new web servers. In exchange, the company trades in old web servers along with a cash payment. The old servers originally cost $30,000 and had accumulated depreciation of $23,400 at the time of the trade. Prepare entries to record the trade under two different assumptions where (a) the exchange has commercial substance and the old servers have a trade-in allowance of $3,000 and (b) the exchange has commercial substance and the old servers have a trade-in allowance of $7,000.

Solution

a.

	Equipment (new)	45,000	
	Loss on Exchange of Assets	3,600	
	Accumulated Depreciation—Equipment (old)	23,400	
	Equipment (old)		30,000
	Cash ($45,000 − $3,000)		42,000

b.

	Equipment (new)	45,000	
	Accumulated Depreciation—Equipment (old)	23,400	
	Equipment (old)		30,000
	Cash ($45,000 − $7,000)		38,000
	Gain on Exchange of Assets.......................		400

Do More: QS 8-16, E 8-23, E 8-24

Summary: Cheat Sheet

PLANT ASSETS

Cost of plant assets: Normal, reasonable, and necessary costs in preparing an asset for its intended use. If an asset is damaged during unpacking, the repairs are not added to its cost. Instead, they are charged to an expense account.

Machinery and equipment: Cost includes purchase price, taxes, transportation, insurance while in transit, installation, assembly, and testing.
Building: A purchased building's costs include its purchase price, real estate fees, taxes, title fees, and attorney fees. A constructed building's costs include construction costs and insurance during construction, but not insurance after it is completed.

Land improvements: Additions to land that have limited useful lives. Examples are parking lots, driveways, and lights.

Land: Has an indefinite (unlimited) life and costs include real estate commissions, clearing, grading, and draining.

Lump-sum purchase: Plant assets purchased as a group for a single lump-sum price. We allocate the cost to the assets acquired based on their relative market (or appraised) values.

	Appraised Value	Percent of Total	Apportioned Cost
Building...	$ 60,000	60% ($60,000/$100,000)	$54,000 ($90,000 × 60%)
Land	40,000	40 ($40,000/$100,000)	36,000 ($90,000 × 40%)
Totals.....	$100,000	100%	$ 90,000

Entry for lump-sum cash purchase:

Building..............	54,000	
Land	36,000	
Cash.............		90,000
Record costs of plant assets.		

Depreciation: Process of allocating the cost of a plant asset to expense while it is in use.

Salvage value: Estimate of the asset's value at the end of its useful life.

Useful life: Length of time a plant asset is to be used in operations.

Record depreciation expense:

Depreciation Expense	1,800	
Accumulated Depreciation—"Asset Type".......		1,800

Straight-line depreciation: Charges the same amount of depreciation expense in each period of the asset's useful life.

Straight-line depreciation formula:

$$\text{Depreciation expense} = \frac{\text{Cost} - \text{Salvage value}}{\text{Useful life in periods}}$$

Asset book value (or book value): Computed as the asset's total cost minus accumulated depreciation.

Units-of-production depreciation: Charges a varying amount for each period depending on an asset's usage.

Units-of-production formula:

Step 1 $\text{Depreciation per unit} = \dfrac{\text{Cost} - \text{Salvage value}}{\text{Total units of production}}$

Step 2 Depreciation expense = Depreciation per unit × Units produced in period

Double-declining-balance depreciation: Charges more depreciation in early years and less depreciation in later years.

Double-declining-balance formula:

Step 1 Straight-line rate = 100% ÷ Useful life

Step 2 Double-declining-balance rate = 2 × Straight-line rate

Step 3 Depreciation expense = Double-declining-balance rate × Beginning-period book value

Change in an accounting estimate: For plant assets, it is changing the estimate of useful life or salvage value. It only affects current and future depreciation expense. Do not go back and change prior years' depreciation.

Straight-line depreciation after change in accounting estimate:

$$\frac{\text{Book value} - \text{Revised salvage value}}{\text{Revised remaining useful life}}$$

Impairment: Permanent decline in the fair value of an asset relative to its book value.

Impairment Loss..............................	50	
Accumulated Depreciation—Equipment		50

Ordinary repairs (revenue expenditure): Expenditures to keep an asset in good operating condition. They do not increase useful life or productivity. Include cleaning, changing oil, and minor repairs.

Repairs Expense..............................	9,500	
Cash.....................................		9,500

Betterments (capital expenditure): Expenditures to make a plant asset more efficient or productive. Include upgrading components and adding additions onto plant assets.

Extraordinary repairs (capital expenditure): Expenditures that extend the asset's useful life beyond its original estimate.

Betterments and extraordinary repairs: These expenditures are "capitalized" by adding their costs to the plant asset.

"Plant Asset"...................................	1,800	
Cash.......................................		1,800

Before discarding, selling, or exchanging a plant asset: Must record depreciation up to that date.

Depreciation Expense	500	
Accumulated Depreciation—Equipment		500

Discarding *fully* depreciated asset:

Accumulated Depreciation—Machinery	9,000	
Machinery		9,000

Discarding *partially* depreciated asset: Loss is the book value (Cost − Accumulated depreciation) of the asset when discarded.

Accumulated Depreciation—Equipment.............	6,500	
Loss on Disposal of Equipment	1,500	
Equipment		8,000

Sale of asset at book value: If sale price = book value, no gain or loss.

Cash	3,000	
Accumulated Depreciation—Equipment.............	13,000	
Equipment		16,000

Sale of asset *above* book value: If sale price > book value → gain.

Cash	7,000	
Accumulated Depreciation—Equipment.............	13,000	
Gain on Disposal of Equipment................		4,000
Equipment		16,000

Sale of asset *below* book value: If sale price < book value → loss.

Cash	2,500	
Loss on Disposal of Equipment	500	
Accumulated Depreciation—Equipment.............	13,000	
Equipment		16,000

NATURAL RESOURCES

Natural resources: Assets that are physically consumed when used. Examples are standing timber, mineral deposits, and oil and gas fields.

Depletion: Process of allocating the cost of a natural resource.

Depletion formula:

Step 1 $\text{Depletion per unit} = \dfrac{\text{Cost} - \text{Salvage value}}{\text{Total units of capacity}}$

Step 2 Depletion expense = Depletion per unit × Units extracted and sold in period

Depletion expense (when *all* units extracted are sold):

Depletion Expense—Mineral Deposit	170,000	
Accumulated Depletion—Mineral Deposit.......		170,000

Depletion expense (when *not all* units extracted are sold):

Depletion Expense—Mineral Deposit	140,000	
Ore Inventory	30,000	
Accumulated Depletion—Mineral Deposit.......		170,000

INTANGIBLE ASSETS

Intangible assets: Nonphysical assets (used in operations) that give companies long-term rights, privileges, or competitive advantages.

Amortization: Intangible assets with limited useful lives require amortization. It is similar to depreciation and uses the shorter of the legal life or useful life of the intangible for straight-line amortization.

Amortization Expense—Patents....................	2,500	
Accumulated Amortization—Patents		2,500

Patent: Exclusive right to manufacture and sell a patented item or to use a process for 20 years.

Copyright: Exclusive right to publish and sell a musical, literary, or artistic work during the life of the creator plus 70 years.

Franchises or licenses: Rights to sell a product or service under specified conditions.

Trademark or trade (brand) name: A symbol, name, phrase, or jingle identified with a company, product, or service.

Goodwill: Amount by which a company's value exceeds the value of its individual assets and liabilities (net assets). Goodwill is only recorded when an entire company or business segment is purchased. Not amortized, but tested for impairment.

Right-of-use asset (lease): Rights the lessor grants to the lessee under terms of the lease.

Leasehold improvements: Improvements to a leased (rented) property such as partitions, painting, and storefronts. The lessee amortizes these costs over the life of the lease or the life of the improvements, whichever is shorter.

Key Terms

Accelerated depreciation method (308)

Amortization (317)

Asset book value (307)

Betterments (312)

Capital expenditures (311)

Change in an accounting estimate (310)

Copyright (318)

Cost (304)

Declining-balance method (308)

Depletion (315)

Depreciation (305)

Extraordinary repairs (312)

Franchises (318)

Goodwill (318)

Impairment (310, 317)

Inadequacy (306)

Indefinite life (317)

Intangible assets (317)

Land improvements (304)

Lease (318)

Leasehold (318)

Leasehold improvements (318)

Lessee (318)

Lessor (318)

Licenses (318)

Limited life (317)

Modified Accelerated Cost Recovery System (MACRS) (309)

Natural resources (315)

Obsolescence (306)

Ordinary repairs (312)

Patent (317)

Plant assets (303)

Research and development costs (319)

Revenue expenditures (311)

Salvage value (305)

Straight-line depreciation (306)

Total asset turnover (320)

Trademark or trade (brand) name (318)

Units-of-production depreciation (307)

Useful life (305)

Multiple Choice Quiz

1. A company paid $326,000 for property that included land, land improvements, and a building. The land was appraised at $175,000, the land improvements were appraised at $70,000, and the building was appraised at $105,000. What is the allocation of costs to the three assets?

  a. Land, $150,000; Land Improvements, $60,000; Building, $90,000

  b. Land, $163,000; Land Improvements, $65,200; Building, $97,800

  c. Land, $150,000; Land Improvements, $61,600; Building, $92,400

  d. Land, $159,000; Land Improvements, $65,200; Building, $95,400

  e. Land, $175,000; Land Improvements, $70,000; Building, $105,000

2. A company purchased a truck for $35,000 on January 1, 2019. The truck is estimated to have a useful life of four years and a salvage value of $1,000. Assuming that the company uses straight-line depreciation, what is depreciation expense for the year ended December 31, 2020?

  a. $8,750   **c.** $8,500   **e.** $25,500

  b. $17,500   **d.** $17,000

3. A company purchased machinery for $10,800,000 on January 1, 2019. The machinery has a useful life of 10 years and an estimated salvage value of $800,000. What is depreciation expense for the year ended December 31, 2020, assuming that the double-declining-balance method is used?

  a. $2,160,000   **c.** $1,728,000   **e.** $1,600,000

  b. $3,888,000   **d.** $2,000,000

4. A company sold a machine that originally cost $250,000 for $120,000 when accumulated depreciation on the machine was $100,000. The gain or loss recorded on the sale of this machine is

  a. $0 gain or loss.   **d.** $30,000 gain.

  b. $120,000 gain.   **e.** $150,000 loss.

  c. $30,000 loss.

5. A company had average total assets of $500,000, gross sales of $575,000, and net sales of $550,000. The company's total asset turnover is

  a. 1.15.   **d.** 0.87.

  b. 1.10.   **e.** 1.05.

  c. 0.91.

ANSWERS TO MULTIPLE CHOICE QUIZ

1. b;

	Appraisal Value	%	Total Cost	Allocated
Land.............	$175,000	50%	$326,000	$163,000
Land improvements ..	70,000	20	326,000	65,200
Building...........	105,000	30	326,000	97,800
Totals.............	$350,000			$326,000

4. c;

Cost of machine	$250,000
Accumulated depreciation...........	100,000
Book value	150,000
Cash received.....................	120,000
Loss on sale	$ 30,000

5. b; $550,000/$500,000 = 1.10

2. c; ($35,000 − $1,000)/4 years = $8,500 per year

3. c; 2019: $10,800,000 × (2 × 10%) = $2,160,000
2020: ($10,800,000 − $2,160,000) × (2 × 10%) = $1,728,000

[A] *Superscript letter A denotes assignments based on Appendix 8A.*

[I] Icon denotes assignments that involve decision making.

Discussion Questions

1. [I] What characteristics of a plant asset make it different from other assets?

2. What is the general rule for cost inclusion for plant assets?

3. What is different between land and land improvements?

4. Why is the cost of a lump-sum purchase allocated to the individual assets acquired?

5. [I] Does the balance in the Accumulated Depreciation— Machinery account represent funds to replace the machinery when it wears out? If not, what does it represent?

6. Why is the Modified Accelerated Cost Recovery System not generally accepted for financial accounting purposes?

7. What is the difference between ordinary repairs and extraordinary repairs? How should each be recorded?

8. [I] Identify events that might lead to disposal of a plant asset.

9. What is the process of allocating the cost of natural resources to expense as they are used?

10. Is the declining-balance method an acceptable way to compute depletion of natural resources? Explain.

11. What are the characteristics of an intangible asset?

12. What general procedures are applied in accounting for the acquisition and potential cost allocation of intangible assets?

13. [I] When do we know that a company has goodwill? When can goodwill appear in a company's balance sheet?

14. [I] Assume that a company buys another business and pays for its goodwill. If the company plans to incur costs each year to maintain the value of the goodwill, must it also amortize this goodwill?

15. [I] How is total asset turnover computed? Why would a financial statement user be interested in total asset turnover?

16. On its recent balance sheet in Appendix A, **APPLE** Apple lists its plant assets as "Property, plant and equipment, net." What does "net" mean in this title?

17. Refer to **Google**'s recent balance sheet in **GOOGLE** Appendix A. What is the book value of its total net property, plant, and equipment assets at December 31, 2017?

18. [I] Refer to **Samsung**'s balance sheet in **Samsung** Appendix A. What does it title its plant assets? What is the book value of its plant assets at December 31, 2017?

19. Refer to **Samsung**'s December 31, 2017, **Samsung** balance sheet in Appendix A. What long-term assets discussed in this chapter are reported by the company?

20. Identify the main difference between (*a*) plant assets and current assets, (*b*) plant assets and inventory, and (*c*) plant assets and long-term investments.

■ connect

Kegler Bowling buys scorekeeping equipment with an invoice cost of $190,000. The electrical work required for the installation costs $20,000. Additional costs are $4,000 for delivery and $13,700 for sales tax. During the installation, the equipment was damaged and the cost of repair was $1,850.

What is the total recorded cost of the scorekeeping equipment?

QUICK STUDY

QS 8-1

Cost of plant assets

C1

QS 8-2
Assigning costs to
plant assets
C1

Listed below are costs (or discounts) to purchase or construct new plant assets. (1) Indicate whether the costs should be *expensed* or *capitalized* (meaning they are included in the cost of the plant assets on the balance sheet). (2) For costs that should be capitalized, indicate in which category of plant assets (Equipment, Building, or Land) the related costs should be recorded on the balance sheet.

Expensed or Capitalized	Asset Category	
_____	_____	**1.** Wages paid to train employees to use new equipment.
_____	_____	**2.** Invoice cost paid for new equipment.
_____	_____	**3.** Early payment discount taken on the purchase of new equipment.
_____	_____	**4.** Realtor commissions incurred on land purchased.
_____	_____	**5.** Property taxes on land incurred after it was purchased.
_____	_____	**6.** Costs of oil for the truck used to deliver new equipment.
_____	_____	**7.** Costs to lay foundation for a new building.
_____	_____	**8.** Insurance on a new building during its construction.

QS 8-3
Straight-line depreciation
P1

On January 1, the Matthews Band pays $65,800 for sound equipment. The band estimates it will use this equipment for four years and perform 200 concerts. It estimates that after four years it can sell the equipment for $2,000. During the first year, the band performs 45 concerts.
Compute the first-year depreciation using the straight-line method.

QS 8-4
Units-of-production
depreciation   P1

On January 1, the Matthews Band pays $65,800 for sound equipment. The band estimates it will use this equipment for four years and perform 200 concerts. It estimates that after four years it can sell the equipment for $2,000. During the first year, the band performs 45 concerts.
Compute the first-year depreciation using the units-of-production method.

QS 8-5
Double-declining-balance
method   P1

A building is acquired on January 1 at a cost of $830,000 with an estimated useful life of eight years and salvage value of $75,000. Compute depreciation expense for the first three years using the double-declining-balance method.

QS 8-6
Straight-line, partial-year
depreciation   C2

On October 1, Organic Farming purchases wind turbines for $140,000. The wind turbines are expected to last six years, have a salvage value of $20,000, and be depreciated using the straight-line method.
1. Compute depreciation expense for the last three months of the first year.
2. Compute depreciation expense for the second year.

QS 8-7
Computing revised
depreciation
C2

On January 1, the Matthews Band pays $65,800 for sound equipment. The band estimates it will use this equipment for four years and after four years it can sell the equipment for $2,000. Matthews Band uses straight-line depreciation but realizes at the start of the second year that this equipment will last only a total of three years. The salvage value is not changed.
Compute the revised depreciation for both the second and third years.

QS 8-8
Recording plant asset
impairment   C2

Equipment has a book value of $16,000 and a fair value of $14,750. The decline in value meets the impairment test. Prepare the entry to record this $1,250 impairment.

QS 8-9
Revenue and capital
expenditures
C3

1. Classify the following as either a revenue expenditure (RE) or a capital expenditure (CE).
   _____ **a.** Paid $40,000 cash to replace a motor on equipment that extends its useful life by four years.
   _____ **b.** Paid $200 cash per truck for the cost of their annual tune-ups.
   _____ **c.** Paid $175 for the monthly cost of replacement filters on an air-conditioning system.
   _____ **d.** Completed an addition to a building for $225,000 cash.
2. Prepare the journal entries to record the four transactions from part 1.

QS 8-10
Disposal of assets   P2

Garcia Co. owns equipment that cost $76,800, with accumulated depreciation of $40,800. Record the sale of the equipment under the following three separate cases assuming Garcia sells the equipment for (1) $47,000 cash, (2) $36,000 cash, and (3) $31,000 cash.

Perez Company acquires an ore mine at a cost of $1,400,000. It incurs additional costs of $400,000 to access the mine, which is estimated to hold 1,000,000 tons of ore. The estimated value of the land after the ore is removed is $200,000.

1. Prepare the entry(ies) to record the cost of the ore mine.
2. Prepare the year-end adjusting entry if 180,000 tons of ore are mined and sold the first year.

QS 8-11
Natural resources and depletion
P3

Identify the following as intangible assets (IA), natural resources (NR), or some other asset (O).

____ **a.** Oil well	____ **d.** Gold mine	____ **g.** Franchise
____ **b.** Trademark	____ **e.** Building	____ **h.** Coal mine
____ **c.** Leasehold	____ **f.** Copyright	____ **i.** Salt mine

QS 8-12
Classifying assets
P3   P4

On January 1 of this year, Diaz Boutique pays $105,000 to modernize its store. Improvements include new floors, ceilings, wiring, and wall coverings. These improvements are estimated to yield benefits for 10 years. Diaz leases (does not own) its store and has eight years remaining on the lease. Prepare the entry to record (1) the cost of modernization and (2) amortization at the end of this current year.

QS 8-13
Intangible assets and amortization   **P4**

Selected accounts from Westeros Co.'s adjusted trial balance for the year ended December 31 follow. Prepare its income statement.

Sales	$30,000	Depreciation expense	$ 5,000
Repairs expense	500	Salaries expense	10,000
Depletion expense	4,000	Amortization expense	2,000

QS 8-14
Preparing an income statement
P1   P3   P4

Aneko Company reports the following: net sales of $14,800 for Year 2 and $13,990 for Year 1; end-of-year total assets of $19,100 for Year 2 and $17,900 for Year 1. (1) Compute total asset turnover for Year 2. (2) Aneko's competitor has a turnover of 2.0. Is Aneko performing better or worse than its competitor based on total asset turnover?

QS 8-15
Computing total asset turnover   **A1**

Caleb Co. owns a machine that had cost $42,400 with accumulated depreciation of $18,400. Caleb exchanges the machine for a newer model that has a market value of $52,000.

1. Record the exchange assuming Caleb paid $30,000 cash and the exchange has commercial substance.
2. Record the exchange assuming Caleb paid $22,000 cash and the exchange has commercial substance.

QS 8-16[A]
Asset exchange
P5

---

connect

Rizio Co. purchases a machine for $12,500, terms 2/10, n/60, FOB shipping point. Rizio paid within the discount period and took the $250 discount. Transportation costs of $360 were paid by Rizio. The machine required mounting and power connections costing $895. Another $475 is paid to assemble the machine, and $40 of materials are used to get it into operation. During installation, the machine was damaged and $180 worth of repairs were made. Compute the cost recorded for this machine.

EXERCISES

Exercise 8-1
Cost of plant assets
C1

Cala Manufacturing purchases land for $390,000 as part of its plans to build a new plant. The company pays $33,500 to tear down an old building on the lot and $47,000 to fill and level the lot. It also pays construction costs of $1,452,200 for the new building and $87,800 for lighting and paving a parking area. Prepare a single journal entry to record these costs incurred by Cala, all of which are paid in cash.

Exercise 8-2
Recording costs of assets
C1

Rodriguez Company pays $395,380 for real estate with land, land improvements, and a building. Land is appraised at $157,040; land improvements are appraised at $58,890; and the building is appraised at $176,670. Allocate the total cost among the three assets and prepare the journal entry to record the purchase.

Exercise 8-3
Lump-sum purchase of plant assets   **C1**

Ramirez Company installs a computerized manufacturing machine in its factory at the beginning of the year at a cost of $43,500. The machine's useful life is estimated at 10 years, or 385,000 units of product, with a $5,000 salvage value. During its second year, the machine produces 32,500 units of product. Determine the machine's second-year depreciation under the straight-line method.

Exercise 8-4
Straight-line depreciation
P1

Exercise 8-5
Units-of-production
depreciation **P1**

Ramirez Company installs a computerized manufacturing machine in its factory at the beginning of the year at a cost of $43,500. The machine's useful life is estimated at 10 years, or 385,000 units of product, with a $5,000 salvage value. During its second year, the machine produces 32,500 units of product. Determine the machine's second-year depreciation using the units-of-production method.

Exercise 8-6
Double-declining-balance
depreciation **P1**

Ramirez Company installs a computerized manufacturing machine in its factory at the beginning of the year at a cost of $43,500. The machine's useful life is estimated at 10 years, or 385,000 units of product, with a $5,000 salvage value. During its second year, the machine produces 32,500 units of product. Determine the machine's second-year depreciation using the double-declining-balance method.

Exercise 8-7
Straight-line depreciation
P1

NewTech purchases computer equipment for $154,000 to use in operating activities for the next four years. It estimates the equipment's salvage value at $25,000. Prepare a table showing depreciation and book value for each of the four years assuming straight-line depreciation.

Exercise 8-8
Double-declining-balance
depreciation **P1**

NewTech purchases computer equipment for $154,000 to use in operating activities for the next four years. It estimates the equipment's salvage value at $25,000. Prepare a table showing depreciation and book value for each of the four years assuming double-declining-balance depreciation.

Exercise 8-9
Straight-line depreciation
and income effects

P1

Tory Enterprises pays $238,400 for equipment that will last five years and have a $43,600 salvage value. By using the equipment in its operations for five years, the company expects to earn $88,500 annually, after deducting all expenses except depreciation. Prepare a table showing income before depreciation, depreciation expense, and net (pretax) income for each year and for the total five-year period, assuming straight-line depreciation is used.

Exercise 8-10
Double-declining-balance
depreciation **P1**

Check   Year 3 NI, $54,170

Tory Enterprises pays $238,400 for equipment that will last five years and have a $43,600 salvage value. By using the equipment in its operations for five years, the company expects to earn $88,500 annually, after deducting all expenses except depreciation. Prepare a table showing income before depreciation, depreciation expense, and net (pretax) income for each year and for the total five-year period, assuming double-declining-balance depreciation is used.

Exercise 8-11
Straight-line, partial-year
depreciation **C2**

On April 1, Cyclone Co. purchases a trencher for $280,000. The machine is expected to last five years and have a salvage value of $40,000. Compute depreciation expense at December 31 for both the first year and second year assuming the company uses the straight-line method.

Exercise 8-12
Double-declining-
balance, partial-year
depreciation **C2**

On April 1, Cyclone Co. purchases a trencher for $280,000. The machine is expected to last five years and have a salvage value of $40,000. Compute depreciation expense at December 31 for both the first year and second year assuming the company uses the double-declining-balance method.

Exercise 8-13
Revising depreciation
C2

Check   (2) $3,710

Apex Fitness Club uses straight-line depreciation for a machine costing $23,860, with an estimated four-year life and a $2,400 salvage value. At the beginning of the third year, Apex determines that the machine has three more years of remaining useful life, after which it will have an estimated $2,000 salvage value. Compute (1) the machine's book value at the end of its second year and (2) the amount of depreciation for each of the final three years given the revised estimates.

Exercise 8-14
Ordinary repairs,
extraordinary repairs,
and betterments
C3

Oki Company pays $264,000 for equipment expected to last four years and have a $29,000 salvage value. Prepare journal entries to record the following costs related to the equipment.

1. Paid $22,000 cash for a new component that increased the equipment's productivity.
2. Paid $6,250 cash for minor repairs necessary to keep the equipment working well.
3. Paid $14,870 cash for significant repairs to increase the useful life of the equipment from four to seven years.

Martinez Company owns a building that appears on its prior year-end balance sheet at its original $572,000 cost less $429,000 accumulated depreciation. The building is depreciated on a straight-line basis assuming a 20-year life and no salvage value. During the first week in January of the current calendar year, major structural repairs are completed on the building at a $68,350 cost. The repairs extend its useful life for 5 years beyond the 20 years originally estimated.

1. Determine the building's age (plant asset age) as of the prior year-end balance sheet date.
2. Prepare the entry to record the cost of the structural repairs that are paid in cash.
3. Determine the book value of the building immediately after the repairs are recorded.
4. Prepare the entry to record the current calendar year's depreciation.

Exercise 8-15
Extraordinary repairs; plant asset age

C3

Check (3) $211,350

Diaz Company owns a machine that cost $250,000 and has accumulated depreciation of $182,000. Prepare the entry to record the disposal of the machine on January 1 in each separate situation.

1. The machine needed extensive repairs and was not worth repairing. Diaz disposed of the machine, receiving nothing in return.
2. Diaz sold the machine for $35,000 cash.
3. Diaz sold the machine for $68,000 cash.
4. Diaz sold the machine for $80,000 cash.

Exercise 8-16
Disposal of assets

P2

Rayya Co. purchases a machine for $105,000 on January 1, 2019. Straight-line depreciation is taken each year for four years assuming a seven-year life and no salvage value. The machine is sold on July 1, 2023, during its fifth year of service. Prepare entries to record the partial year's depreciation on July 1, 2023, and to record the sale under each separate situation.

1. The machine is sold for $45,500 cash.   2. The machine is sold for $25,000 cash.

Exercise 8-17
Partial-year depreciation; disposal of plant asset

P2

Montana Mining Co. pays $3,721,000 for an ore deposit containing 1,525,000 tons. The company installs machinery in the mine costing $213,500. Both the ore and machinery will have no salvage value after the ore is completely mined. Montana mines and sells 166,200 tons of ore during the year. Prepare the year-end entries to record both the ore deposit depletion and the mining machinery depreciation. Mining machinery depreciation should be in proportion to the mine's depletion.

Exercise 8-18
Depletion of natural resources

P3

Milano Gallery purchases the copyright on a painting for $418,000 on January 1. The copyright is good for 10 more years, after which the copyright will expire and anyone can make prints. The company plans to sell prints for 11 years. Prepare entries to record the purchase of the copyright on January 1 and its annual amortization on December 31.

Exercise 8-19
Amortization of intangible assets   P4

Robinson Company purchased Franklin Company at a price of $2,500,000. The fair market value of the net assets purchased equals $1,800,000.

1. What is the amount of goodwill that Robinson records at the purchase date?
2. Does Robinson amortize goodwill at year-end for financial reporting purposes? If so, over how many years is it amortized?
3. Robinson believes that its employees provide superior customer service, and through their efforts, Robinson believes it has created $900,000 of goodwill. Should Robinson Company record this goodwill?

Exercise 8-20
Goodwill

P4

Selected accounts from Gregor Co.'s adjusted trial balance for the year ended December 31 follow. Prepare a classified balance sheet.

Exercise 8-21
Preparing a balance sheet

P1   P3   P4

Total equity	$50,000	Accounts payable...	$ 2,000
Patents	4,000	Accumulated depreciation—Equipment	13,000
Cash	6,000	Notes payable (due in 9 years)	11,000
Land	30,000	Goodwill	5,000
Equipment	20,000	Accumulated depletion—Silver mine	3,000
Silver mine	15,000	Accumulated amortization—Patents	1,000

Lok Co. reports net sales of $5,856,480 for Year 2 and $8,679,690 for Year 3. End-of-year balances for total assets are Year 1, $1,686,000; Year 2, $1,800,000; and Year 3, $1,982,000. (*a*) Compute Lok's total asset turnover for Year 2 and Year 3. (*b*) Lok's competitor has a turnover of 3.0. Is Lok performing better or worse than its competitor on the basis of total asset turnover?

Exercise 8-22
Evaluating efficient use of assets   A1

Exercise 8-23ᴬ

Exchanging assets

P5

Check (2) $14,500

Gilly Construction trades in an old tractor for a new tractor, receiving a $29,000 trade-in allowance and paying the remaining $83,000 in cash. The old tractor had cost $96,000 and had accumulated depreciation of $52,500. Answer the following questions assuming the exchange has commercial substance.

1. What is the book value of the old tractor at the time of exchange?
2. What is the loss on this asset exchange?
3. What amount should be recorded (debited) in the asset account for the new tractor?

Exercise 8-24ᴬ

Recording plant asset disposals

P5

Check (3) Dr. Loss on Exchange, $4,375

On January 2, Bering Co. disposes of a machine costing $44,000 with accumulated depreciation of $24,625. Prepare the entries to record the disposal under each separate situation.

1. The machine is sold for $18,250 cash.
2. The machine is traded in for a new machine having a $60,200 cash price. A $25,000 trade-in allowance is received, and the balance is paid in cash. Assume the asset exchange has commercial substance.
3. The machine is traded in for a new machine having a $60,200 cash price. A $15,000 trade-in allowance is received, and the balance is paid in cash. Assume the asset exchange has commercial substance.

PROBLEM SET A

Problem 8-1A

Plant asset costs; depreciation methods

C1   P1

Check (2) $30,000

(3) $10,800

Timberly Construction makes a lump-sum purchase of several assets on January 1 at a total cash price of $900,000. The estimated market values of the purchased assets are building, $508,800; land, $297,600; land improvements, $28,800; and four vehicles, $124,800.

Required

1. Allocate the lump-sum purchase price to the separate assets purchased. Prepare the journal entry to record the purchase.
2. Compute the first-year depreciation expense on the building using the straight-line method, assuming a 15-year life and a $27,000 salvage value.
3. Compute the first-year depreciation expense on the land improvements assuming a five-year life and double-declining-balance depreciation.

Analysis Component

4. Compared to straight-line depreciation, does accelerated depreciation result in payment of less total taxes over the asset's life?

Problem 8-2A

Depreciation methods

P1

A machine costing $257,500 with a four-year life and an estimated $20,000 salvage value is installed in Luther Company's factory on January 1. The factory manager estimates the machine will produce 475,000 units of product during its life. It actually produces the following units: 220,000 in Year 1, 124,600 in Year 2, 121,800 in Year 3, and 15,200 in Year 4. The total number of units produced by the end of Year 4 exceeds the original estimate—this difference was not predicted. *Note:* The machine cannot be depreciated below its estimated salvage value.

Required

Prepare a table with the following column headings and compute depreciation for each year (and total depreciation of all years combined) for the machine under each depreciation method.

Check Year 4: units-of-production depreciation, $4,300; DDB depreciation, $12,187

Year	Straight-Line	Units-of-Production	Double-Declining-Balance

Problem 8-3A

Asset cost allocation; straight-line depreciation

C1   P1

On January 1, Mitzu Co. pays a lump-sum amount of $2,600,000 for land, Building 1, Building 2, and Land Improvements 1. Building 1 has no value and will be demolished. Building 2 will be an office and is appraised at $644,000, with a useful life of 20 years and a $60,000 salvage value. Land Improvements 1 is valued at $420,000 and is expected to last another 12 years with no salvage value. The land is valued at $1,736,000. The company also incurs the following additional costs.

Cost to demolish Building 1	$ 328,400	Cost of additional land grading	$175,400
Cost to construct Building 3, having a useful life of 25 years and a $392,000 salvage value. . . .	2,202,000	Cost of new Land Improvements 2, having a 20-year useful life and no salvage value	164,000

Required

1. Prepare a table with the following column headings: Land, Building 2, Building 3, Land Improvements 1, and Land Improvements 2. Allocate the costs incurred by Mitzu to the appropriate columns and total each column.

2. Prepare a single journal entry to record all the incurred costs assuming they are paid in cash on January 1.

3. Using the straight-line method, prepare the December 31 adjusting entries to record depreciation for the first year these assets were in use.

Check (1) Land costs, $2,115,800; Building 2 costs, $598,000

(3) Depr.—Land Improv. 1 and 2, $32,500 and $8,200

Champion Contractors completed the following transactions involving equipment.

Year 1

Jan. 1   Paid $287,600 cash plus $11,500 in sales tax and $1,500 in transportation (FOB shipping point) for a new loader. The loader is estimated to have a four-year life and a $20,600 salvage value. Loader costs are recorded in the Equipment account.
   3   Paid $4,800 to install air-conditioning in the loader to enable operations under harsher conditions. This increased the estimated salvage value of the loader by another $1,400.
Dec. 31   Recorded annual straight-line depreciation on the loader.

Year 2

Jan. 1   Paid $5,400 to overhaul the loader's engine, which increased the loader's estimated useful life by two years.
Feb. 17   Paid $820 for minor repairs to the loader after the operator backed it into a tree.
Dec. 31   Recorded annual straight-line depreciation on the loader.

Required

Prepare journal entries to record these transactions and events.

Problem 8-4A
Computing and revising depreciation; revenue and capital expenditures
C1   C2   C3

Check Dec. 31, Year 1: Dr. Depr. Expense—Equip., $70,850

Dec. 31, Year 2: Dr. Depr. Expense—Equip., $43,590

Yoshi Company completed the following transactions and events involving its delivery trucks.

Year 1

Jan. 1   Paid $20,515 cash plus $1,485 in sales tax for a new delivery truck estimated to have a five-year life and a $2,000 salvage value. Delivery truck costs are recorded in the Trucks account.
Dec. 31   Recorded annual straight-line depreciation on the truck.

Year 2

Dec. 31   The truck's estimated useful life was changed from five to four years, and the estimated salvage value was increased to $2,400. Recorded annual straight-line depreciation on the truck.

Year 3

Dec. 31   Recorded annual straight-line depreciation on the truck.
   31   Sold the truck for $5,300 cash.

Required

Prepare journal entries to record these transactions and events.

Problem 8-5A
Computing and revising depreciation; selling plant assets
C2   P1   P2

Check Dec. 31, Year 2: Dr. Depr. Expense—Trucks, $5,200

Dec. 31, Year 3: Dr. Loss on Disposal of Trucks, $2,300

Onslow Co. purchased a used machine for $178,000 cash on January 2. On January 3, Onslow paid $2,840 to wire electricity to the machine and an additional $1,160 to secure it in place. The machine will be used for six years and have a $14,000 salvage value. Straight-line depreciation is used. On December 31, at the end of its fifth year in operations, it is disposed of.

Required

1. Prepare journal entries to record the machine's purchase and the costs to ready it for use. Cash is paid for all costs incurred.

2. Prepare journal entries to record depreciation of the machine at December 31 of (a) its first year of operations and (b) the year of its disposal.

3. Prepare journal entries to record the machine's disposal under each separate situation: (a) it is sold for $15,000 cash; (b) it is sold for $50,000 cash; and (c) it is destroyed in a fire and the insurance company pays $30,000 cash to settle the loss claim.

Problem 8-6A
Disposal of plant assets
C1   P1   P2

Check (2b) Depr. Exp., $28,000

(3c) Dr. Loss from Fire, $12,000

Problem 8-7A
Natural resources
P3

On July 23 of the current year, Dakota Mining Co. pays $4,715,000 for land estimated to contain 5,125,000 tons of recoverable ore. It installs and pays for machinery costing $410,000 on July 25. The company removes and sells 480,000 tons of ore during its first five months of operations ending on December 31. Depreciation of the machinery is in proportion to the mine's depletion as the machinery will be abandoned after the ore is mined.

Required

Check (c) Depletion, $441,600
(d) Depreciation, $38,400

Prepare entries to record (a) the purchase of the land, (b) the cost and installation of machinery, (c) the first five months' depletion assuming the land has a net salvage value of zero after the ore is mined, and (d) the first five months' depreciation on the machinery.

Analysis Component

(e) If the machine will be used at another site when extraction is complete, how would we depreciate this machine?

Problem 8-8A
Right-of-use lease asset
P4

On January 1, Falk Company signed a contract to lease space in a building for three years. The current value of the three lease payments is $270,000.

Required

Prepare entries for Falk to record (a) the lease asset and obligation at January 1 and (b) the $90,000 straight-line amortization at December 31 of the first year.

PROBLEM SET B

Problem 8-1B
Plant asset costs; depreciation methods
C1   P1

Check (2) $65,000

(3) $50,400

Nagy Company makes a lump-sum purchase of several assets on January 1 at a total cash price of $1,800,000. The estimated market values of the purchased assets are building, $890,000; land, $427,200; land improvements, $249,200; and five trucks, $213,600.

Required

1. Allocate the lump-sum purchase price to the separate assets purchased. Prepare the journal entry to record the purchase.
2. Compute the first-year depreciation expense on the building using the straight-line method, assuming a 12-year life and a $120,000 salvage value.
3. Compute the first-year depreciation expense on the land improvements assuming a 10-year life and double-declining-balance depreciation.

Analysis Component

4. Compared to straight-line depreciation, does accelerated depreciation result in payment of less total taxes over the asset's life?

Problem 8-2B
Depreciation methods
P1

On January 1, Manning Co. purchases and installs a new machine costing $324,000 with a five-year life and an estimated $30,000 salvage value. Management estimates the machine will produce 1,470,000 units of product during its life. Actual production of units is as follows: 355,600 in Year 1, 320,400 in Year 2, 317,000 in Year 3, 343,600 in Year 4, and 138,500 in Year 5. The total number of units produced by the end of Year 5 exceeds the original estimate—this difference was not predicted. *Note:* The machine cannot be depreciated below its estimated salvage value.

Required

Prepare a table with the following column headings and compute depreciation for each year (and total depreciation of all years combined) for the machine under each depreciation method.

Check DDB Depreciation, Year 3, $46,656; U-of-P Depreciation, Year 4, $68,720

Year	Straight-Line	Units-of-Production	Double-Declining-Balance

Problem 8-3B
Asset cost allocation; straight-line depreciation
C1   P1

On January 1, ProTech Co. pays a lump-sum amount of $1,550,000 for land, Building A, Building B, and Land Improvements B. Building A has no value and will be demolished. Building B will be an office and is appraised at $482,800, with a useful life of 15 years and a $99,500 salvage value. Land Improvements B is valued at $142,000 and is expected to last another five years with no salvage value. The land is valued at $795,200. The company also incurs the following additional costs.

Cost to demolish Building A	$ 122,000		Cost of additional land grading	$174,500
Cost to construct Building C, having a useful life . . of 20 years and a $258,000 salvage value	1,458,000		Cost of new Land Improvements C, having a 10-year useful life and no salvage value	103,500

Required

1. Prepare a table with the following column headings: Land, Building B, Building C, Land Improvements B, and Land Improvements C. Allocate the costs incurred by ProTech to the appropriate columns and total each column.

2. Prepare a single journal entry to record all incurred costs assuming they are paid in cash on January 1.

3. Using the straight-line method, prepare the December 31 adjusting entries to record depreciation for the first year these assets were in use.

Check (1) Land costs, $1,164,500; Building B costs, $527,000

(3) Depr.—Land Improv. B and C, $31,000 and $10,350

Mercury Delivery Service completed the following transactions involving equipment.

Problem 8-4B
Computing and revising depreciation; revenue and capital expenditures

C1   C2   C3

Year 1

Jan.   1   Paid $25,860 cash plus $1,810 in sales tax for a new delivery van that was estimated to have a five-year life and a $3,670 salvage value. Van costs are recorded in the Equipment account.

      3   Paid $1,850 to install sorting racks in the van for more accurate and quicker delivery of packages. This increases the estimated salvage value of the van by another $230.

Dec. 31   Recorded annual straight-line depreciation on the van.

Check Dec. 31, Year 1: Dr. Depr. Expense—Equip., $5,124

Year 2

Jan.   1   Paid $2,064 to overhaul the van's engine, which increased the van's useful life by two years.

May 10   Paid $800 for minor repairs to the van after the driver backed it into a loading dock.

Dec. 31   Recorded annual straight-line depreciation on the van.

Dec. 31, Year 2: Dr. Depr. Expense—Equip., $3,760

Required

Prepare journal entries to record these transactions and events.

York Instruments completed the following transactions and events involving its machinery.

Problem 8-5B
Computing and revising depreciation; selling plant assets

C2   P1   P2

Year 1

Jan.   1   Paid $107,800 cash plus $6,470 in sales tax for a new machine. The machine is estimated to have a six-year life and a $9,720 salvage value.

Dec. 31   Recorded annual straight-line depreciation on the machinery.

Year 2

Dec. 31   The machine's estimated useful life was changed from six to four years, and the estimated salvage value was increased to $14,345. Recorded annual straight-line depreciation on the machinery.

Check Dec. 31, Year 2: Dr. Depr. Expense— Machinery, $27,500

Year 3

Dec. 31   Recorded annual straight-line depreciation on the machinery.

      31   Sold the machine for $25,240 cash.

Dec. 31, Year 3: Dr. Loss on Disposal of Machinery, $16,605

Required

Prepare journal entries to record these transactions and events.

On January 1, Walker purchased a used machine for $150,000. On January 4, Walker paid $3,510 to wire electricity to the machine and an additional $4,600 to secure it in place. The machine will be used for seven years and have an $18,110 salvage value. Straight-line depreciation is used. On December 31, at the end of its sixth year of use, the machine is disposed of.

Problem 8-6B
Disposal of plant assets

C1   P1   P2

Required

1. Prepare journal entries to record the machine's purchase and the costs to ready it for use. Cash is paid for all costs incurred.

2. Prepare journal entries to record depreciation of the machine at December 31 of (*a*) its first year of operations and (*b*) the year of its disposal.

3. Prepare journal entries to record the machine's disposal under each separate situation: (*a*) it is sold for $28,000 cash; (*b*) it is sold for $52,000 cash; and (*c*) it is destroyed in a fire and the insurance company pays $25,000 cash to settle the loss claim.

Check (2*b*) Depr. Exp., $20,000

(3*c*) Dr. Loss from Fire, $13,110

Problem 8-7B
Natural resources

P3

On February 19 of the current year, Quartzite Co. pays $5,400,000 for land estimated to contain 4 million tons of recoverable ore. It installs and pays for machinery costing $400,000 on March 21. The company removes and sells 254,000 tons of ore during its first nine months of operations ending on December 31. Depreciation of the machinery is in proportion to the mine's depletion as the machinery will be abandoned after the ore is mined.

Required

Check (c) Depletion, $342,900
(d) Depreciation, $25,400

Prepare entries to record (a) the purchase of the land, (b) the cost and installation of the machinery, (c) the first nine months' depletion assuming the land has a net salvage value of zero after the ore is mined, and (d) the first nine months' depreciation on the machinery.

Analysis Component

(e) If the machine will be used at another site when extraction is complete, how would we depreciate this machine?

Problem 8-8B
Right-of-use lease asset

P4

On January 1, Mason Co. entered into a three-year lease on a building. The current value of the three lease payments is $60,000.

Required

Prepare entries for Mason to record (a) the lease asset and obligation at January 1 and (b) the $20,000 straight-line amortization at December 31 of the first year.

SERIAL PROBLEM
Business Solutions

A1   P1

This serial problem began in Chapter 1 and continues through most of the book. If previous chapter segments were not completed, the serial problem can begin at this point.

SP 8   Selected ledger account balances for **Business Solutions** follow.

	For Three Months Ended December 31, 2019	For Three Months Ended March 31, 2020
Office equipment	$ 8,000	$ 8,000
Accumulated depreciation—Office equipment	400	800
Computer equipment	20,000	20,000
Accumulated depreciation—Computer equipment.....	1,250	2,500
Total revenue	31,284	44,000
Total assets	83,460	120,268

Check (3) Three-month (annual) turnover = 0.43 (1.73 annual)

Required

1. Assume that Business Solutions does not acquire additional office equipment or computer equipment in 2020. Compute amounts for *the year ended* December 31, 2020, for Depreciation Expense—Office Equipment and for Depreciation Expense—Computer Equipment (assume use of the straight-line method).
2. Given the assumptions in part 1, what is the book value of both the office equipment and the computer equipment as of December 31, 2020?
3. Compute the three-month total asset turnover for Business Solutions as of March 31, 2020. Use total revenue for the numerator and average the December 31, 2019, total assets and the March 31, 2020, total assets for the denominator. Interpret its total asset turnover if competitors average 2.5 for annual periods. (Round turnover to two decimals.)

Accounting Analysis

COMPANY ANALYSIS

A1

APPLE

AA 8-1   Refer to **Apple**'s financial statements in Appendix A to answer the following.

1. What percent of the original cost of Apple's Property, Plant and Equipment account remains to be depreciated as of (a) September 30, 2017, and (b) September 24, 2016? Assume these assets have no salvage value and the entire account is depreciable. *Hint:* Accumulated Depreciation is listed under "Property, Plant and Equipment" in the notes to Apple's financial statements in Appendix A.

2. Much research and development is needed to create the next iPhone. Does Apple capitalize and amortize research and development costs over the life of the product, or are research and development costs expensed as incurred?

3. Compute Apple's total asset turnover for the year ended (a) September 30, 2017, and (b) September 24, 2016. Assume total assets at September 26, 2015, are $290,345 ($ millions).

4. Using the results in part 3, is the change in Apple's asset turnover favorable or unfavorable?

AA 8-2 Comparative figures for **Apple** and **Google** follow.

	Apple			Google		
$ millions	Current Year	One Year Prior	Two Years Prior	Current Year	One Year Prior	Two Years Prior
Total assets............	$375,319	$321,686	$290,345	$197,295	$167,497	$147,461
Net sales.............	229,234	215,639	233,715	110,855	90,272	74,989

Required

1. Compute total asset turnover for the most recent two years for Apple and Google using the data shown.

2. In the current year, which company is more efficient in generating net sales given total assets?

3. Does each company's asset turnover underperform or outperform the industry (assumed) asset turnover of 0.5 for (a) Apple and (b) Google?

AA 8-3 Comparative figures for **Samsung, Apple,** and **Google** follow.

	Samsung			Apple		Google	
In millions	Current Year	Prior Year	Two Years Prior	Current Year	Prior Year	Current Year	Prior Year
Total assets...	₩301,752,090	₩262,174,324	₩242,179,521	$375,319	$321,686	$197,295	$167,497
Net sales.....	239,575,376	201,866,745	200,653,482	229,234	215,639	110,855	90,272

Required

1. Compute total asset turnover for the most recent two years for Samsung using the data shown.

2. Is the change in Samsung's asset turnover favorable or unfavorable?

3. For the current year, is Samsung's asset turnover better or worse than the asset turnover for (a) Apple and (b) Google?

Beyond the Numbers

BTN 8-1 Flo Choi owns a small business and manages its accounting. Her company just finished a year in which a large amount of borrowed funds was invested in a new building addition as well as in equipment and fixture additions. Choi's banker requires her to submit semiannual financial statements so he can monitor the financial health of her business. He has warned her that if profit margins erode, he might raise the interest rate on the borrowed funds to reflect the increased loan risk from the bank's point of view. Choi knows profit margin is likely to decline this year. As she prepares year-end adjusting entries, she decides to apply the following depreciation rule: All asset additions are considered to be in use on the first day of the following month. (The previous rule assumed assets are in use on the first day of the month nearest to the purchase date.)

Required

1. Identify decisions that managers like Choi must make in applying depreciation methods.
2. Is Choi's rule an ethical violation, or is it a legitimate decision in computing depreciation?
3. How will Choi's new depreciation rule affect the profit margin of her business?

COMMUNICATING IN PRACTICE

A1

BTN 8-2   Teams are to select an industry, and each team member is to select a different company in that industry. Each team member is to acquire the financial statements (Form 10-K) of the company selected—see the company's website or the SEC's EDGAR database (**SEC.gov**). Use the financial statements to compute total asset turnover. Communicate with teammates via a meeting, e-mail, or telephone to discuss the meaning of this ratio, how different companies compare to each other, and the industry norm. The team must prepare a one-page report that describes the ratios for each company and identifies the conclusions reached during the team's discussion.

TAKING IT TO THE NET

P4

BTN 8-3   Access the **Yahoo!** (renamed as Altaba, ticker: AABA) 10-K report for the year ended December 31, 2016, filed on March 1, 2017, at **SEC.gov**.

Required

1. What amount of goodwill is reported on Yahoo!'s balance sheet? What percentage of total assets does its goodwill represent? Is goodwill a major asset for Yahoo!? Explain.
2. Compute the change in goodwill from December 31, 2015, to December 31, 2016. Comment on the change in goodwill over this period.
3. Locate Note 6 to its financial statements. What are the three categories of intangible assets that Yahoo! reports at December 31, 2016? What proportion of total assets do the intangibles represent?
4. What does Yahoo! indicate is the life of "Tradenames, trademarks, and domain names" according to its Note 6?

TEAMWORK IN ACTION

P1

Point: This activity can follow an overview of each method. Step 1 allows for three areas of expertise. Larger teams will have some duplication of areas, but the straight-line choice should not be duplicated. Expert teams can use the book and consult with the instructor.

BTN 8-4   Each team member is to become an expert on one depreciation method to facilitate teammates' understanding of that method. Follow these procedures:

a. Each team member is to select an area of expertise from one of the following depreciation methods: straight-line, units-of-production, or double-declining-balance.
b. Expert teams are to be formed from those who have selected the same area of expertise. The instructor will identify the location where each expert team meets.
c. Using the following data, expert teams are to collaborate and develop a presentation answering the requirements. Expert team members must write the presentation in a format they can show to their learning teams.

Data and Requirements On January 8, 2017, Whitewater Riders purchases a van to transport rafters back to the point of departure at the conclusion of the rafting adventures they operate. The cost of the van is $44,000. It has an estimated salvage value of $2,000 and is expected to be used for four years and driven 60,000 miles. The van is driven 12,000 miles in 2017; 18,000 miles in 2018; 21,000 in 2019; and 10,000 in 2020.

1. Compute the annual depreciation expense for each year of the van's estimated useful life.
2. Explain when and how annual depreciation is recorded.
3. Explain the impact on income of this depreciation method versus others over the van's life.
4. Identify the van's book value for each year of its life and illustrate the reporting of this amount for any one year.

d. Re-form original learning teams. In rotation, experts are to present to their teams the results from part c. Experts are to encourage and respond to questions.

BTN 8-5   Review the chapter's opening feature involving Deb and Dan Carey and their company, **New Glarus Brewing Company**. Assume that the company currently has net sales of $8,000,000 and that it is planning an expansion that will increase net sales by $4,000,000. To accomplish this expansion, the company must increase its average total assets from $2,500,000 to $3,000,000.

ENTREPRENEURIAL DECISION

A1

Required

1. Compute the company's total asset turnover under (*a*) current conditions and (*b*) proposed conditions.
2. Evaluate and comment on the merits of the proposal given the analysis in part 1. Identify any concerns we would express about the proposal.

BTN 8-6   Team up with one or more classmates for this activity. Identify companies in your community or area that must account for at least one of the following assets: natural resource, patent, lease, leasehold improvement, copyright, trademark, or goodwill. You might find a company that has more than one type of asset. Once you identify a company with a specific asset, describe the accounting this company uses to allocate the cost of that asset to the periods that benefit from its use.

HITTING THE ROAD

P3   P4

9 Accounting for Current Liabilities

Chapter Preview

KNOWN LIABILITIES

C1 Reporting liabilities

C2 Sales taxes payable

Unearned revenues

P1 Short-term notes

NTK 9-1

PAYROLL LIABILITIES

P2 Employee payroll and deductions

P3 Employer payroll taxes

Multi-period liabilities

NTK 9-2

ESTIMATED LIABILITIES

P4 Reporting for:

Health and pension

Vacation benefits

Bonus plans

Warranty liabilities

NTK 9-3

CONTINGENCIES AND ANALYSIS

C3 Accounting for contingencies:

Probable

Possible

Remote

A1 Times interest earned

NTK 9-4

Learning Objectives

CONCEPTUAL

C1 Describe current and long-term liabilities and their characteristics.

C2 Identify and describe known current liabilities.

C3 Explain how to account for contingent liabilities.

ANALYTICAL

A1 Compute the times interest earned ratio and use it to analyze liabilities.

PROCEDURAL

P1 Prepare entries to account for short-term notes payable.

P2 Compute and record *employee* payroll deductions and liabilities.

P3 Compute and record *employer* payroll expenses and liabilities.

P4 Account for estimated liabilities, including warranties and bonuses.

P5 *Appendix 9A*—Identify and describe the details of payroll reports, records, and procedures.

Sounds Like a Winner!

©Jason Davis/Pandora Media/Getty Images

"Good stuff doesn't come easy"—**TIM WESTERGREN**

OAKLAND, CA—"I was a senior in college," recalls Tim Westergren, "when unbeknownst to me, I decided to become an entrepreneur." Tim was playing in a band and considering ways to discover new music.

"I shared the idea with a former college classmate, Jon Kraft . . . and in a matter of weeks it went from 'we have an idea' to 'we have a business plan and we're pitching it.'" The business Tim and Jon built is now known as **Pandora Media** (**Pandora.com**), an Internet radio that plays music based on the listener's preferences.

Tim and Jon started Pandora with financing help. However, within a year of starting the business, Tim and Jon ran out of money.

"We weren't paying our employees," admits Tim. "About 50 or 55 people worked without getting paid for over two years during that time." To keep the business afloat, Tim and Jon learned about managing current liabilities for payroll, supplies, employee benefits, vacations, training, and taxes.

Tim and Jon insist that effective management of liabilities, especially payroll and employee benefits, is crucial for new businesses. Tim and Jon's ability to juggle their current liabilities enabled them to "hang on" for those crucial first two years.

"Business is an execution game," insists Tim, "not an invention game."

Tim encourages people to start a business doing something they love. "If you're doing it because you love it and because it has meaning for you," proclaims Tim, "then you can't really fail."

Sources: *Pandora website,* January 2019; *Billboard.com,* March 2016; *Fortune,* June 2015; *Washington Post,* February 2015; *GreenBiz,* November 2012

KNOWN LIABILITIES

Characteristics of Liabilities

This section discusses characteristics of liabilities and how liabilities are classified.

Defining Liabilities   A *liability* is a probable future payment of assets or services that a company is presently obligated to make as a result of past transactions or events. This definition includes three elements that are shown in Exhibit 9.1. No liability is reported when one or more of those elements are missing. For example, companies expect to pay wages in future years, but these future payments are *not* liabilities because no past event such as employee work resulted in a present obligation. Instead, liabilities are recorded when employees perform work and earn wages.

C1_____

Describe current and long-term liabilities and their characteristics.

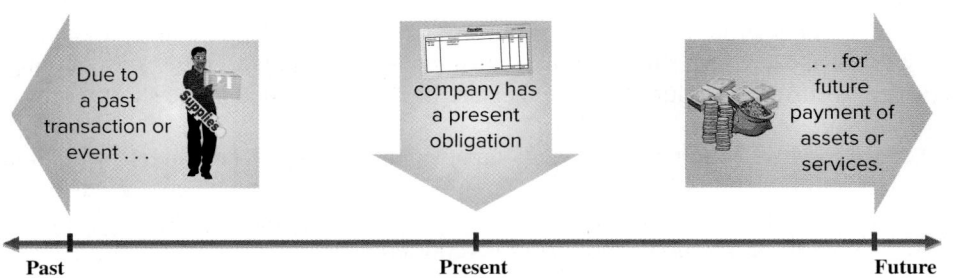

Due to a past transaction or event . . .

company has a present obligation

. . . for future payment of assets or services.

Past   Present   Future

EXHIBIT 9.1

Characteristics of a Liability

Point: Most liability accounts use *payable* or *unearned* in their titles.

Classifying Liabilities   Liabilities are classified as either current or long term.

Current Liabilities   **Current liabilities,** or *short-term liabilities,* **are liabilities due** *within* **one year** (or the company's operating cycle if longer). Most are paid using current assets or by creating other current liabilities. Common examples are accounts payable, short-term notes

Point: For simplicity we assume an operating cycle of one year.

payable, wages payable, warranty liabilities, and taxes payable. Some liabilities do not have a fixed due date but instead are payable on the creditor's demand. These are reported as current liabilities because of the possibility of payment in the near term.

Current liabilities differ across companies because they depend on the type of company operations. For example, **MGM Resorts** reports casino outstanding chip liability. **Harley-Davidson** reports different current liabilities such as warranty, recall, and dealer incentive liabilities. Exhibit 9.2 shows current liabilities as a percentage of total liabilities for selected companies.

EXHIBIT 9.2

Current Liabilities as a Percentage of Total Liabilities

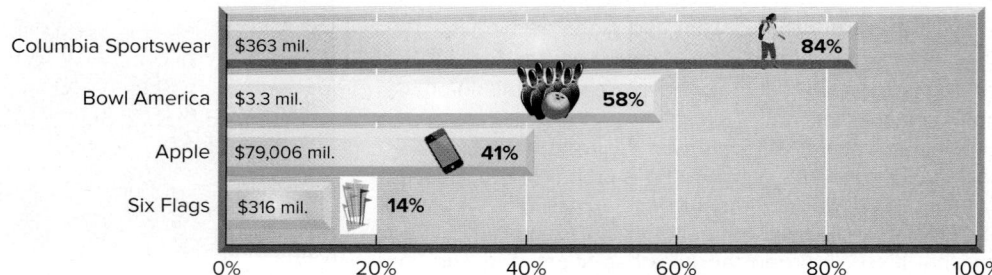

Long-Term Liabilities   **Long-term liabilities are obligations due *after* one year** (or the company's operating cycle if longer). They include long-term notes payable, warranty liabilities, lease liabilities, and bonds payable. For example, **Domino's Pizza** reports long-term liabilities of $2,196 million. A single liability can be divided between the current and noncurrent sections if a company expects to make payments toward it in both the short and long term. Domino's reports long-term debt of $2,149 million and current portion of long-term debt of $39 million. The current portion is reported in current liabilities.

Uncertainty in Liabilities   Accounting for liabilities involves answering three important questions: Whom to pay? When to pay? How much to pay? Answers are usually decided when a liability is incurred. For example, if a company has a $100 account payable to a firm, payable on March 15, the answers are clear. However, answers to one or more of these three questions are uncertain for some liabilities.

Uncertainty in Whom to Pay   Liabilities can involve uncertainty in whom to pay. For example, a company can create a liability with a known amount when issuing a note that is payable to its holder. In this case, a specific amount is payable to the note's holder at a specified date, but the company does not know who the holder is until that date. Despite this uncertainty, the company reports this liability on its balance sheet.

Uncertainty in When to Pay   A company can have an obligation of a specific amount to a known creditor but not know when it must be paid. For example, a law firm can accept fees in advance from a client who plans to use the firm's services in the future. This means that the firm has a liability that it settles by providing services at an unknown future date. Although this uncertainty exists, the law firm's balance sheet must report this liability. These types of obligations are reported as current liabilities because they are likely to be settled in the short term.

Uncertainty in How Much to Pay   A company can be aware of an obligation but not know how much it will be required to pay. For example, a company using electrical power is billed only after the meter has been read. This cost is incurred and the liability created before a bill is received. A liability to the power company is reported as an estimated amount if the balance sheet is prepared before a bill arrives.

Examples of Known Liabilities

C2
_____
Identify and describe known current liabilities.

Known liabilities are measurable obligations arising from agreements, contracts, or laws. Known liabilities include accounts payable, notes payable, payroll obligations, sales taxes, and unearned revenues.

Accounts Payable

Accounts payable, or trade accounts payable, are amounts owed to suppliers for products or services purchased on credit. Accounts payable are a focus of the merchandising chapter.

Sales Taxes Payable

Nearly all states and many cities levy taxes on retail sales. Sales taxes are shown as a percent of selling prices. The seller collects sales taxes from customers when sales occur and sends these collections to the government. Because sellers currently owe these collections to the government, this amount is a current liability. If **Home Depot** sells materials on August 31 for $6,000 cash that are subject to a 5% sales tax, the revenue portion of this transaction is recorded as follows. Later, when Home Depot sends the $300 collected to the government, it debits Sales Taxes Payable and credits Cash.

Aug. 31	Cash...	6,300	
	Sales..		6,000
	Sales Taxes Payable ($6,000 × 0.05)		300
	*Record cash sales and 5% sales tax.**		
	We also Dr. Cost of Sales and Cr. Inventory for cost of sales.		

Assets = Liabilities + Equity
+6,300   +300   +6,000

Unearned Revenues

Unearned revenues, or *deferred revenues,* are amounts received in advance from customers for future products or services. Unearned revenues arise with airline ticket sales, magazine subscriptions, construction projects, hotel reservations, gift card sales, and custom orders. Advance ticket sales for sporting events or concerts are other examples. If **Selena Gomez** sells $5 million in tickets for eight concerts, the entry is

©Dwphotos/Shutterstock

June 30	Cash...	5,000,000	
	Unearned Ticket Revenue.............................		5,000,000
	Record sale of tickets for eight concerts.		

Assets = Liabilities + Equity
+5,000,000   +5,000,000

Unearned Ticket Revenue is reported as a current liability. As each concert is played, 1/8 of the liability is satisfied and 1/8 of the revenue is earned—this entry follows.

Point: To *defer* a revenue means to postpone recording a revenue collected in advance.

Oct. 31	Unearned Ticket Revenue	625,000	
	Ticket Revenue		625,000
	Record concert revenues earned ($5,000,000 × 1/8).		

Assets = Liabilities + Equity
                −625,000   +625,000

Short-Term Notes Payable

A **short-term note payable** is a written promise to pay a specified amount on a stated future date within one year. Notes can be sold or transferred. Most notes payable bear interest. The written documentation with notes is helpful in resolving legal disputes. We describe two transactions that create notes payable.

P1_____

Prepare entries to account for short-term notes payable.

Note Given to Extend Credit Period
A company can replace an account payable with a note payable. A common example is a creditor that requires an interest-bearing note for an overdue account payable. Assume that on August 23, Brady asks to extend its past-due $600 account payable to McGraw. After negotiations, McGraw agrees to accept $100 cash and a 60-day, 12%, $500 note payable to replace the account payable. Brady records the following.

Point: Note requirements: (1) unconditional promise, (2) in writing, (3) specific amount, and (4) stated due date.

Aug. 23	Accounts Payable—McGraw...............................	600	
	Cash		100
	Notes Payable—McGraw.............................		500
	Sent cash and a note for payment on account.		

Assets = Liabilities + Equity
−100   −600
          +500

Point: Excel for accrued interest.

	A	B
1	Principal	$500
2	Rate	12%
3	Issue date	8/23
4	Days	60
5	Accrued interest	◄

=ACCRINTM(B3,B3+B4,B2,B1,2)=$10

Assets = Liabilities + Equity
−510   −500   −10

Signing the note changes Brady's debt from an account payable to a note payable. McGraw prefers the note payable over the account payable because it earns interest and it is written documentation of the debt's existence, term, and amount. When the note comes due, Brady pays the note and interest to McGraw and records this entry.

Oct. 22	Notes Payable—McGraw	500	
	Interest Expense	10	
	Cash..		510
	Paid note with interest ($500 × 12% × 60/360).		

Point: Firms commonly compute interest using a 360-day year, called the *banker's rule.*

Interest expense is computed by multiplying the principal of the note ($500) by the annual interest rate (12%) for the fraction of the year the note is outstanding (60 days/360 days).

Note Given to Borrow from Bank
A bank requires a borrower to sign a note when making a loan. When the note comes due, the borrower repays the note with an amount larger than the amount borrowed. The difference between the amount borrowed and the amount repaid is *interest.* The amount borrowed is called *principal* or *face value* of the note. Assume that a company borrows $2,000 from a bank at 12% annual interest. The loan is made on September 30, 2019, and is due in 60 days. The note says: *"I promise to pay $2,000 plus interest at 12% within 60 days after September 30."* The borrower records its receipt of cash and the new liability with this entry.

Point: A loan is reported as an asset (receivable) on a bank's balance sheet.

Assets = Liabilities + Equity
+2,000   +2,000

Point: Excel for accrued interest.

	A	B
1	Principal	$2,000
2	Rate	12%
3	Issue date	9/30
4	Days	60
5	Accrued interest	◄

=ACCRINTM(B3,B3+B4,B2,B1,2)=$40

Assets = Liabilities + Equity
−2,040   −2,000   −40

Sep. 30	Cash	2,000	
	Notes Payable		2,000
	Borrowed $2,000 cash with a 60-day, 12%, $2,000 note.		

When principal and interest are paid, the borrower records payment with this entry.

Nov. 29	Notes Payable	2,000	
	Interest Expense	40	
	Cash..		2,040
	Paid note with interest ($2,000 × 12% × 60/360).		

When Note Extends over Two Periods
When a note is issued in one period but paid in the next, interest expense is recorded in each period based on the number of days the note extends over each period. Assume a company borrows $2,000 cash on December 16, 2019, at 12% annual interest. This 60-day note matures on February 14, 2020, and the company's fiscal year ends on December 31. This means 15 of the 60 days are in 2019 and 45 of the 60 days are in 2020. Interest for these two periods is:

- 12/16/2019 to 12/31/2019 = 15 days. Interest expense = $2,000 × 12% × 15/360 = $10.
- 01/01/2020 to 02/14/2020 = 45 days. Interest expense = $2,000 × 12% × 45/360 = $30.

The borrower records the 2019 expense with the following adjusting entry.

Assets = Liabilities + Equity
           +10   −10

Dec. 31, 2019	Interest Expense	10	
	Interest Payable		10
	Record accrued interest ($2,000 × 12% × 15/360).		

When this note is paid on February 14, the borrower records 45 days of interest expense in 2020 and removes the balances of the two liability accounts.

Assets = Liabilities + Equity
−2,040   −10   −30
           −2,000

Feb. 14, 2020	Interest Expense*	30	
	Interest Payable.....................................	10	
	Notes Payable	2,000	
	Cash..		2,040
	*Paid note with interest. *$2,000 × 12% × 45/360*		

■ **Decision Insight**

Debt to Pay   Franchisors such as **Pizza Hut** and **Papa John's** use notes to help entrepreneurs acquire their own franchises, including notes to pay for the franchise fee and equipment. Payments on these notes are usually collected monthly and often are secured by the franchisees' assets. For example, a **McDonald's** franchise can cost from under $200,000 to over $2 million, depending on the type selected. ■

Part 1. A retailer sells merchandise for $500 cash on June 30 (cost of merchandise is $300). The retailer collects 7% sales tax. Record the entry for the $500 sale and its applicable sales tax. Also record the entry that shows the taxes collected being sent to the government on July 15.

Part 2. A ticket agency receives $40,000 cash in advance ticket sales for Haim's upcoming four-date tour. Record the advance ticket sales on April 30. Record the revenue earned for the first concert date of May 15, assuming it represents one-fourth of the advance ticket sales.

Part 3. On November 25 of the current year, a company borrows $8,000 cash by signing a 90-day, 5% note payable with a face value of $8,000. (a) Compute the accrued interest payable on December 31 of the current year, (b) prepare the journal entry to record the accrued interest expense at December 31 of the current year, and (c) prepare the journal entry to record payment of the note at maturity.

> **NEED-TO-KNOW** 9-1
>
> Accounting for Known Liabilities
>
> C2   P1
>
> **Point:** *Maturity date* is the day a note's principal and interest are due. *Maturity value* is a note's principal plus interest owed on its maturity date.

Solution—Part 1

June 30	Cash	535	
	Sales		500
	Sales Taxes Payable		35
	Record cash sales and 7% sales tax.		
June 30	Cost of Goods Sold	300	
	Merchandise Inventory.		300
	Record cost of June 30 sales.		
July 15	Sales Taxes Payable.	35	
	Cash.		35
	Record sales taxes sent to govt.		

Solution—Part 2

Apr. 30	Cash	40,000	
	Unearned Ticket Revenue		40,000
	Record sales in advance of concerts.		
May 15	Unearned Ticket Revenue.	10,000	
	Earned Ticket Revenue		10,000
	Record concert revenues earned ($40,000 × 1/4).		

Solution—Part 3

a.

Computation of interest payable at December 31:	
Days from November 25 to December 31	36 days
Accrued interest (5% × $8,000 × 36/360)	<u>$40</u>

b.

Dec. 31	Interest Expense	40	
	Interest Payable		40
	Record accrued interest (5% × $8,000 × 36/360).		

c.

Feb. 23	Interest Expense	60	
	Interest Payable.	40	
	Notes Payable	8,000	
	Cash.		8,100
	Record payment of note plus interest		
	(5% × $8,000 × 90/360 = $100 total interest)		
	(5% × $8,000 × 54/360 = $60 interest expense).		

> **Point:** Accrued interest, 11/25–12/31.
>
> | | A | B |
> |---|---|---|
> | 1 | Principal | $8,000 |
> | 2 | Rate | 5% |
> | 3 | Issue date | 11/25 |
> | 4 | Days | 36 |
> | 5 | Accrued interest | ◄ |
>
> =ACCRINTM(B3,B3+B4,B2,B1,2)=$40
>
> **Point:** Accrued interest, 1/1–2/23.
>
> | | A | B |
> |---|---|---|
> | 1 | Principal | $8,000 |
> | 2 | Rate | 5% |
> | 3 | Issue date | 11/25 |
> | 4 | Days | 54 |
> | 5 | Accrued interest | ◄ |
>
> =ACCRINTM(B3,B3+B4,B2,B1,2)=$60
>
> **Point:** Feb. 23 entry assumes no reversing entry was made.
>
> > **Do More: QS 9-2, QS 9-3, QS 9-4, E 9-2, E 9-3, E 9-4**

PAYROLL LIABILITIES

Payroll liabilities are from salaries and wages, employee benefits, and payroll taxes levied on the employer. For example, **Boston Beer** reports current payroll liabilities of more than $14 million from accrued "employee wages, benefits and reimbursements."

P2

Compute and record *employee* payroll deductions and liabilities.

EMPLOYEE Payroll and Deductions

Gross pay is the total compensation an employee earns including wages, salaries, commissions, bonuses, and any compensation earned before deductions such as taxes. (*Wages* usually refer to payments to employees at an hourly rate. *Salaries* usually refer to payments to employees at a monthly or yearly rate.) **Net pay,** or *take-home pay,* is gross pay minus all deductions. **Payroll deductions,** or *withholdings,* are amounts withheld from an employee's gross pay, either required or voluntary. Required deductions result from laws and include income taxes and Social Security taxes. Voluntary deductions, at an employee's option, include pension and health contributions, health and life insurance premiums, union dues, and donations.

Point: Deductions at some companies, such as those for insurance coverage, are "required" under labor contracts.

Exhibit 9.3 shows typical employee payroll deductions. The employer withholds payroll deductions from employees' pay and sends this money to the designated group or government. The employer records payroll deductions as current liabilities until these amounts are sent. This section covers major payroll deductions.

EXHIBIT 9.3

Payroll Deductions

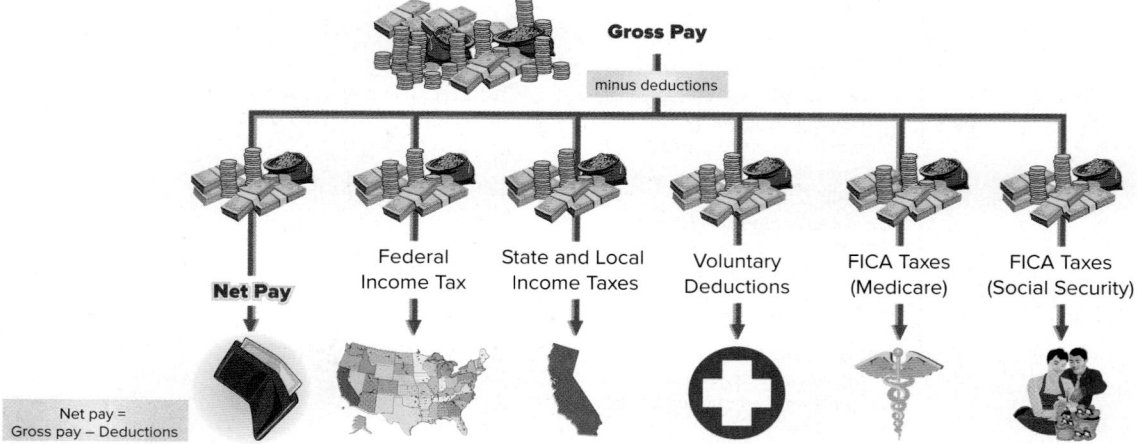

Employee FICA Taxes   Employers withhold **Federal Insurance Contributions Act (FICA) taxes** from employees' pay. Employers separate FICA taxes into two groups.

1. **Social Security taxes**—withholdings to cover retirement, disability, and survivorship.
2. **Medicare taxes**—withholdings to cover medical benefits.

Taxes for Social Security and Medicare are computed separately. For 2018, the amount withheld from each employee's pay for Social Security tax is 6.2% of the first $128,400 the employee earns in the calendar year. The Medicare tax is 1.45% of *all* amounts the employee earns; there is no maximum limit to Medicare tax. A 0.9% *Additional Medicare Tax* is imposed on the high-income employee for pay usually in excess of $200,000 (this additional tax is *not* imposed on the employer, whereas the others are). Until the taxes are sent to the Internal Revenue Service (IRS), they are included in employers' current liabilities. For any changes in rates or earnings levels, check **IRS.gov** or **SSA.gov**.

Point: Sources of U.S. tax receipts:
50%   Personal income tax
35%   FICA and FUTA taxes
10%   Corporate income tax
 5%   Other taxes

Employee Income Tax   Most employers withhold federal income tax from each employee's paycheck. The amount withheld is computed using IRS tables. The amount depends on the employee's income and the number of *withholding allowances* the employee claims. Allowances reduce taxes owed to the government. Employees can claim allowances for themselves and their dependents. Until the government is paid, withholdings are reported as a current liability on the employer's balance sheet.

Employee Voluntary Deductions   Voluntary deduction withholdings come from employee requests, contracts, unions, or other agreements. They include charitable giving, medical and life insurance premiums, pension contributions, and union dues. Until they are paid, voluntary withholdings are reported as part of employers' current liabilities.

Employee Payroll Recording   Employers accrue payroll expenses and liabilities at the end of each pay period. Assume that an employee earns a salary of $2,000 per month. At the end of January, the employer's entry to accrue payroll expenses and liabilities for this employee is

Jan. 31	Salaries Expense	2,000	
	FICA—Social Security Taxes Payable (6.2%)		124
	FICA—Medicare Taxes Payable (1.45%)		29
	Employee Federal Income Taxes Payable*		213
	Employee Medical Insurance Payable*		85
	Employee Union Dues Payable*		25
	Salaries Payable		1,524
	Record accrued payroll for January.		
	*Amounts taken from employer's accounting records.		

Assets = Liabilities + Equity
+124   −2,000
+29
+213
+85
+25
+1,524

Salaries Expense (debit) shows that the employee earns a gross salary of $2,000. The first five payables (credits) show the liabilities the employer owes on behalf of this employee to cover FICA taxes, income taxes, medical insurance, and union dues. The Salaries Payable account (credit) records the $1,524 net pay the employee receives from the $2,000 gross pay earned. The February 1 entry to record cash payment to this employee is

Feb. 1	Salaries Payable.	1,524	
	Cash		1,524
	Record payment of payroll.		

EMPLOYER Payroll Taxes

Employers must pay payroll taxes in addition to those required of employees. Employer taxes include FICA and unemployment taxes.

Employer FICA Tax   Employers must pay FICA taxes on their payroll. For 2018, the employer must pay Social Security tax of 6.2% on the first $128,400 earned by each employee and 1.45% Medicare tax on all earnings of each employee. An employer's tax is credited to the same FICA Taxes Payable accounts used to record the Social Security and Medicare taxes withheld from employees.

Employer Unemployment Taxes   The federal government works with states in a joint federal and state unemployment insurance program. Each state has its own program. These programs provide unemployment benefits to qualified workers.

Federal Unemployment Tax Act (FUTA)   Employers must pay a federal unemployment tax on wages and salaries earned by their employees. For the recent year, employers were required to pay FUTA taxes of as much as 6.0% of the first $7,000 earned by each employee. This federal tax can be reduced by a credit of up to 5.4% for taxes paid to a state program. As a result, the net federal unemployment tax is often 0.6%.

State Unemployment Tax Act (SUTA)   All states fund their unemployment insurance programs by placing a payroll tax on employers. (A few states require employees to make a contribution. In the book's assignments, we assume this tax is only levied on the employer.) In most states, the base rate for SUTA taxes is 5.4% of the first $7,000 earned by each employee (the dollar level varies by state). This base rate is adjusted according to an employer's merit rating.

P3_____

Compute and record *employer* payroll expenses and liabilities.

Point: A self-employed person must pay both the employee and employer FICA taxes.

The state assigns a **merit rating** based on a company's stability in employing workers. A good rating reflects stability in employment and means an employer can pay less than the 5.4% base rate. A low rating means high turnover or seasonal hirings and layoffs.

Recording Employer Payroll Taxes

Employer payroll taxes are an added expense beyond the wages and salaries earned by employees. These taxes are often recorded in an entry separate from the one recording payroll expenses and deductions. Assume that the $2,000 recorded salaries expense from the previous example is earned by an employee whose earnings have not yet reached $5,000 for the year. This means the entire salaries expense for this period is subject to tax because year-to-date pay is under $7,000. Consequently, the FICA portion of the employer's tax is $153, computed by multiplying both the 6.2% and 1.45% by the $2,000 gross pay. Assume that the federal unemployment tax rate is 0.6% and the state unemployment tax rate is 5.4%. This means state unemployment (SUTA) taxes are $108 (5.4% of the $2,000 gross pay) and federal unemployment (FUTA) taxes are $12 (0.6% of $2,000). The entry to record the employer's payroll tax expense and related liabilities is

Assets = Liabilities + Equity
+124   −273
+29
+108
+12

Jan. 31	Payroll Taxes Expense	273	
	FICA—Social Security Taxes Payable (6.2%)		124
	FICA—Medicare Taxes Payable (1.45%)		29
	State Unemployment Taxes Payable		108
	Federal Unemployment Taxes Payable		12
	Record employer payroll taxes.		

Internal Control of Payroll

Internal controls are crucial for payroll because of a high risk of fraud and error. Exhibit 9.4 identifies and explains four key areas of payroll activities that we aim to *separate and monitor*.

EXHIBIT 9.4

Internal Controls in Four Key Areas of Payroll

Employee Hiring	Payroll Preparation	Timekeeping	Payroll Payment

Duty: Authorize, hire, and fire. **Aim:** Keep fake workers off payroll.	**Duty:** Verify tax rates and payroll amounts. **Aim:** Rates updated and amounts accurate.	**Duty:** Track and verify time worked. **Aim:** Paid for time worked only.	**Duty:** Sign and issue prenumbered checks. **Aim:** Checks valid, secured, and correct.

Ethical Risk

Ceridian Connection reports: **8.5%** of fraud is tied to payroll; **$72,000** is the median loss per payroll fraud; and **24 months** is the median time to uncover payroll fraud.

Payroll Fraud   Probably the greatest number of frauds involve payroll. Controls include proper approvals and processes for employee additions, deletions, and pay rate changes. A common fraud is a manager adding a fictitious employee to the payroll and then cashing the fictitious employee's check. A study reports that 42% of employees in operations and service areas witnessed violations of employee wage, overtime, or benefit rules in the past year. Another 33% observed falsifying of time and expense reports (KPMG). ∎

Multi-Period Known Liabilities

Many known liabilities extend over multiple periods. These often include unearned revenues and notes payable. For example, if **Sports Illustrated** sells a three-year digital magazine subscription, it records amounts received for this subscription in an Unearned Subscription Revenues account. Amounts in this account are liabilities, but are they current or long term? They are *both*. The portion of the Unearned Subscription Revenues account that will be fulfilled in the next year is reported as a current liability. The remaining portion is reported as a long-term liability.

The same analysis applies to notes payable. For example, a borrower reports a three-year note payable as a long-term liability in the first two years it is outstanding. In the third year, the borrower reclassifies this note as a current liability because it is due within one year. The **current portion of long-term debt** is that part of long-term debt due within one year. Long-term debt is reported under long-term liabilities, but the *current portion due* is reported under current liabilities. Assume that a $7,500 debt is paid in installments of $1,500 per year for five years. The $1,500 due within the year is reported as a current liability. No journal entry is necessary for this reclassification. Instead, we simply classify the amounts for debt as either current or long term when the balance sheet is prepared.

Point: Some accounting systems make an entry to transfer the current amount due out of Long-Term Debt and into the Current Portion of Long-Term Debt as follows:

Long-Term Debt 1,500
  Current Portion
    of L-T Debt 1,500

■ Decision Ethics

Summer Intern You take a summer job working as a windsurfing instructor. On your first payday, the owner slaps you on the back, gives you full payment in cash, winks, and adds: "No need to pay those high taxes, eh?" What action, if any, do you take? ■ *Answer:* You do not want to be an accomplice to unlawful payroll activities. Not paying federal and state taxes on wages is illegal and unethical. One action is to request payment by check. If this fails, you must consider quitting.

A company's first weekly pay period of the year ends on January 8. Sales employees earned $30,000 and office employees earned $20,000 in salaries. The employees are to have withheld from their salaries FICA Social Security taxes at the rate of 6.2%, FICA Medicare taxes at the rate of 1.45%, $9,000 of federal income taxes, $2,000 of medical insurance deductions, and $1,000 of pension contributions. No employee earned more than $7,000 in the first pay period.

NEED-TO-KNOW 9-2

Payroll Liabilities

P2 P3

Part 1. Compute FICA Social Security taxes payable and FICA Medicare taxes payable. Prepare the journal entry to record the company's January 8 (employee) payroll expenses and liabilities.

Part 2. Prepare the journal entry to record the company's (employer) payroll taxes resulting from the January 8 payroll. Its state unemployment tax rate is 5.4% on the first $7,000 paid to each employee. The federal unemployment tax rate is 0.6%.

Solution—Part 1

Jan. 8	Sales Salaries Expense	30,000	
	Office Salaries Expense	20,000	
	FICA—Social Security Taxes Payable*		3,100
	FICA—Medicare Taxes Payable†		725
	Employee Fed. Income Taxes Payable		9,000
	Employee Med. Insurance Payable . .		2,000
	Employee Pensions Payable		1,000
	Salaries Payable		34,175
	Record payroll for period.		
	*$50,000 × 6.2% = $3,100		
	†$50,000 × 1.45% = $725		

Solution—Part 2

Jan. 8	Payroll Taxes Expense	6,825	
	FICA—Social Security Taxes Payable .		3,100
	FICA—Medicare Taxes Payable		725
	State Unemployment Taxes Payable*		2,700
	Federal Unemployment Taxes Payable†		300
	Record employer payroll taxes.		
	*$50,000 × 5.4% = $2,700		
	†$50,000 × 0.6% = $300		

Do More: QS 9-5, QS 9-6, E 9-5,
E 9-6, E 9-7, E 9-8, E 9-9

ESTIMATED LIABILITIES

An **estimated liability** is a known obligation of an uncertain amount that can be reasonably estimated. Common examples are employee benefits such as pensions, health care, and vacation pay, and warranties offered by a seller.

P4 _____

Account for estimated liabilities, including warranties and bonuses.

Health and Pension Benefits

Many companies provide **employee benefits.** An employer often pays all or part of medical, dental, life, and disability insurance. Many employers also contribute to *pension plans,* which are agreements by employers to provide benefits (payments) to employees after retirement. Many companies also provide medical care and insurance benefits to their retirees. Assume an employer agrees to (1) pay $8,000 for medical insurance and (2) contribute an additional 10% of the employees' $120,000 gross salaries to a retirement program. The entry to record these accrued benefits is

Assets = Liabilities + Equity
      +8,000   −20,000
      +12,000

Dec. 31	Employee Benefits Expense............................	20,000	
	Employee Medical Insurance Payable..............		8,000
	Employee Retirement Program Payable.............		12,000
	Record costs of employee benefits.		

■ Decision Insight

Rest on One's Laurels   **Major League Baseball** was the first pro sport to set up a pension, originally up to $100 per month depending on years played. Many former players now take home six-figure pensions. Cal Ripken Jr.'s pension at age 62 is estimated at $180,000 per year (he played 21 seasons). The same applies to Ichiro Suzuki, who has played 17 seasons—see photo. The requirement is 43 games for a full pension and just one game for full medical benefits for life. ■

©Imac/Alamy Stock Photo

Vacation Benefits

Point: An *accrued expense* is an unpaid expense and is also called an *accrued liability.*

Many employers offer paid vacation benefits, or *paid absences.* Vacation benefits are estimated and expensed in the period when employees earn them. Assume that salaried employees earn 2 weeks' paid vacation per year. The year-end adjusting entry to record $3,200 of accrued vacation benefits follows.

Assets = Liabilities + Equity
      +3,200   −3,200

Dec. 31	Vacation Benefits Expense............................	3,200	
	Vacation Benefits Payable........................		3,200
	Record vacation benefits accrued.		

Vacation Benefits Expense is an operating expense, and Vacation Benefits Payable is a current liability. When an employee takes a one-week vacation, the employer reduces (debits) Vacation Benefits Payable and credits Cash.

Assets = Liabilities + Equity
  −400   −400

Jan. 20	Vacation Benefits Payable............................	400	
	Cash..		400
	Record vacation benefits taken.		

Bonus Plans

Many companies offer bonuses to employees, and many of the bonuses depend on net income. Assume that an employer gives a bonus to its employees based on the company's annual net income (to be equally shared by all). The year-end adjusting entry to record a $10,000 bonus is

Assets = Liabilities + Equity
      +10,000   −10,000

Dec. 31	Employee Bonus Expense............................	10,000	
	Bonus Payable.................................		10,000
	Record expected bonus costs.		

Warranty Liabilities

A **warranty** is a seller's obligation to replace or fix a product (or service) that fails to perform as expected within a specified period. For example, new **Ford** cars are sold with a warranty covering parts for a specified period of time. The seller reports the expected warranty expense in the period

when revenue from the sale of the product or service is reported. The seller reports this warranty liability, even though the existence, amount, payee, and date of future payments are uncertain. This is because warranty costs are probable and the amount can be estimated using past experience.

Assume a dealer sells a car for $16,000 on December 1, 2019, with a one-year or 12,000-mile warranty covering parts. Experience shows that warranty expense is 4% of a car's selling price, or $640 in this case ($16,000 × 4%). The dealer records the estimated expense and liability related to this sale with this entry.

Dec. 1	Warranty Expense	640	
	Estimated Warranty Liability		640
	Record estimated warranty expense.		

Assets = Liabilities + Equity
      +640   −640

This entry alternatively could be made as part of end-of-period adjustments. Either way, the estimated warranty expense is reported on the 2019 income statement and the warranty liability on the 2019 balance sheet. Continuing this example, assume the customer brings the car in for warranty repairs on January 9, 2020. The dealer fixes the car by replacing parts costing $200. The entry to record the repair is

Jan. 9	Estimated Warranty Liability	200	
	Auto Parts Inventory		200
	Record costs of warranty repairs.		

Assets = Liabilities + Equity
−200   −200

This entry reduces the balance of the Estimated Warranty Liability account, but no expense is recorded in 2020 for the repair. Warranty expense was previously recorded in 2019, the year the car was sold with the warranty. Finally, what happens if total warranty expenses are more or less than the estimated 4%, or $640? The answer is that management should monitor actual warranty expenses to see if a 4% rate is accurate. If not, the rate is changed for future periods.

Multi-Period Estimated Liabilities

Estimated liabilities can be both current and long term. For example, pension liabilities to employees are long term to workers who will not retire within the next year. For employees who are retired or will retire within the next year, a portion of pension liabilities is current. Other examples include employee health benefits and warranties.

■ **Decision Insight**

Promises, Promises When we purchase a new laptop at **Best Buy**, a sales clerk commonly asks: *"Do you want the Geek Squad Protection Plan?"* Best Buy earns about a 60% profit margin on such warranty contracts, and those contracts are a large part of its profit—see table (*BusinessWeek*). ■

Warranties as a percent of sales	4%
Warranties as a percent of operating profit....	45%

Part 1. A company's salaried employees earn two weeks' vacation per year. The company estimated and must expense $9,000 of accrued vacation benefits for the year. (a) Prepare the year-end adjusting entry to record accrued vacation benefits. (b) Prepare the entry on May 1 of the next year when an employee takes a one-week vacation and is paid $450 cash for that week.

Part 2. For the current year ended December 31, a company has implemented an employee bonus program based on its net income, which employees share equally. Its bonus expense is $40,000. (a) Prepare the journal entry at December 31 of the current year to record the bonus due. (b) Prepare the journal entry at January 20 of the following year to record payment of that bonus to employees.

Part 3. On June 11 of the current year, a retailer sells a trimmer for $400 with a one-year warranty that covers parts. Warranty expense is estimated at 5% of sales. On March 24 of the next year, the trimmer is brought in for repairs covered under the warranty requiring $15 in materials taken from the Repair Parts Inventory. Prepare the (a) June 11 entry to record the trimmer sale—ignore the cost of sales part of this sales entry—and (b) March 24 entry to record warranty repairs.

NEED-TO-KNOW 9-3

Estimated Liabilities

P4

Solution—Part 1

a.

Dec. 31	Vacation Benefits Expense	9,000	
	Vacation Benefits Payable		9,000
	Record vacation benefits accrued.		

b.

May 1	Vacation Benefits Payable.......	450	
	Cash..................		450
	Record vacation benefits taken.		

Solution—Part 2

a.

Dec. 31	Employee Bonus Expense	40,000	
	Bonus Payable		40,000
	Record expected bonus costs.		

b.

Jan. 20	Bonus Payable	40,000	
	Cash..................		40,000
	Record payment of bonus.		

Solution—Part 3

June 11	Cash	400	
	Sales		400
	Record trimmer sales.		
June 11	Warranty Expense	20	
	Estimated Warranty Liability		20
	Record estimated warranty expense ($400 × 5%).		
Mar. 24	Estimated Warranty Liability	15	
	Repair Parts Inventory		15
	Record cost of warranty repairs.		

Do More: QS 9-7, QS 9-8,
QS 9-9, QS 9-10, E 9-10,
E 9-11, E 9-12, E 9-13

CONTINGENT LIABILITIES

C3_____

Explain how to account for
contingent liabilities.

A **contingent liability** is a potential obligation that depends on a future event arising from a past transaction or event. An example is a pending lawsuit. Here, a past transaction or event leads to a lawsuit whose financial outcome depends on the result of the suit.

Accounting for Contingent Liabilities

Accounting for contingent liabilities depends on the likelihood that a future event will occur and the ability to estimate the future amount owed if this event occurs. Three different possibilities are shown in Exhibit 9.5: record liability with a journal entry, disclose in notes to financial statements, or no disclosure.

EXHIBIT 9.5

Accounting for Contingent
Liabilities

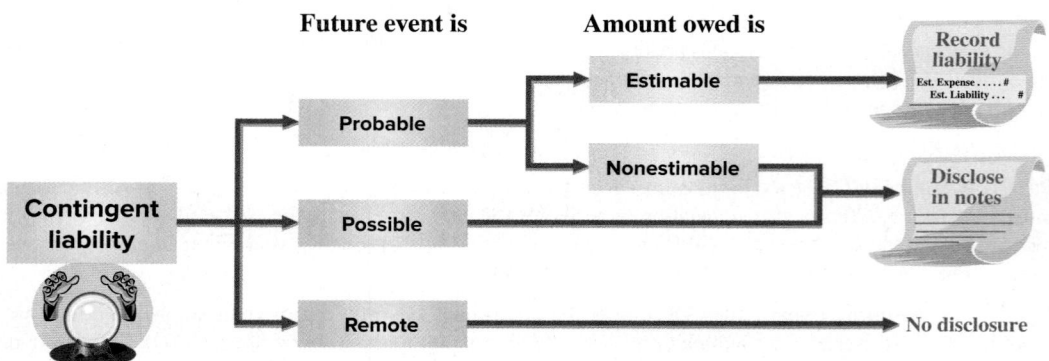

The conditions that determine each of these three possibilities follow.

Point: A contingency is an *if.*
Namely, *if* a future event occurs,
then financial consequences are
likely for the entity.

1. **Record liability.** The future event is *probable* (likely) and the amount owed can be *reasonably estimated.* Examples are warranties, vacation pay, and income taxes.
2. **Disclose in notes.** The future event is *reasonably possible* (could occur).
3. **No disclosure.** The future event is *remote* (unlikely).

Applying Rules of Contingent Liabilities

This section covers common contingent liabilities.

Potential Legal Claims   Many companies are sued or at risk of being sued. The accounting issue is whether the defendant records a liability or discloses a contingent liability in its notes while a lawsuit is outstanding and not yet settled. The answer is that a potential claim is recorded *only* if payment for damages is probable and the amount can be reasonably estimated. If the potential claim cannot be reasonably estimated but is reasonably possible, it is disclosed. For example, **Ford** includes the following note in its annual report: "Various legal actions, proceedings, and claims are pending . . . arising out of alleged defects in our products."

Debt Guarantees   Sometimes a company guarantees the payment of debt owed by a supplier, customer, or another company. The guarantor usually discloses the guarantee in its financial statement notes as a contingent liability. If it is probable that the debtor will default, the guarantor reports the guarantee as a liability. The **Boston Celtics** report a unique guarantee: "Contracts provide for guaranteed payments which must be paid even if the employee [player] is injured or terminated."

Other Contingencies   Other examples of contingencies include environmental damages, possible tax assessments, insurance losses, and government investigations. **Chevron**, for example, reports that it "is subject to loss contingencies . . . related to environmental matters. . . . The amount of additional future costs are not fully determinable." Many of Chevron's contingencies are revealed only in notes.

Uncertainties That Are Not Contingencies

All organizations face uncertainties from future events such as natural disasters and new technologies. These uncertainties are not contingent liabilities because they are future events *not* arising from past transactions. Accordingly, they are not disclosed.

The following legal claims exist for a company. Identify the accounting treatment for each claim as either (a) a liability that is recorded or (b) an item described in notes to its financial statements.

1. The company (defendant) estimates that a pending lawsuit could result in damages of $500,000; it is reasonably possible that the plaintiff will win the case.

2. The company faces a probable loss on a pending lawsuit; the amount is not reasonably estimable.

3. The company estimates environmental damages in a pending case at $900,000 with a high probability of losing the case.

NEED-TO-KNOW 9-4

Contingent Liabilities

C3

Solution

1. (b); reason—is reasonably estimated but not a probable loss.

2. (b); reason—probable loss but cannot be reasonably estimated.

3. (a); reason—can be reasonably estimated and loss is probable.

Do More: QS 9-11, E 9-14

Times Interest Earned Ratio  **Decision Analysis**

Interest expense is often called a *fixed expense* because it usually does not vary due to short-term changes in sales or other operating activities. While fixed expenses can be good when a company is growing, they create risk. The risk is that a company might be unable to pay fixed expenses if sales decline. Consider Diego Co.'s results for 2019 and two possible outcomes for year 2020 in Exhibit 9.6. Expenses excluding interest are expected to remain at 75% of sales. Expenses that change with sales volume are *variable expenses*. Interest expense is fixed at $60 per year.

 A1

Compute the times interest earned ratio and use it to analyze liabilities.

EXHIBIT 9.6

Actual and Projected
Results

$ millions	2019	2020 Projections	
		Sales Increase	Sales Decrease
Sales	$600	$900	$300
Expenses (75% of sales)	450	675	225
Income before interest	150	225	75
Interest expense (fixed)	60	60	60
Net income.....................	$ 90	$165	$ 15

The Sales Increase column of Exhibit 9.6 shows that Diego's net income increases by 83% to $165 if sales increase by 50% to $900. The Sales Decrease column shows that net income decreases by 83% if sales decline by 50%. These results show that the amount of fixed interest expense affects a company's risk of its ability to pay interest. One measure of "ability to pay" is the **times interest earned** ratio in Exhibit 9.7.

EXHIBIT 9.7

Times Interest Earned

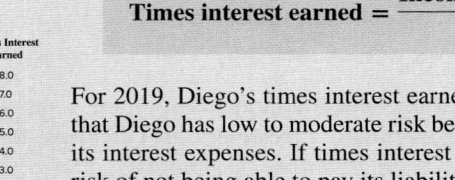

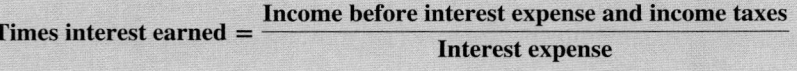

$$\text{Times interest earned} = \frac{\text{Income before interest expense and income taxes}}{\text{Interest expense}}$$

For 2019, Diego's times interest earned is computed as $150/$60, or 2.5 times. This ratio means that Diego has low to moderate risk because its sales must decline sharply before it is unable to pay its interest expenses. If times interest earned falls below around 1.5, a company will likely be at risk of not being able to pay its liabilities.

Decision Maker

Entrepreneur You wish to invest in a franchise for either one of two national chains. Each franchise has an expected annual net income *after* interest and taxes of $100,000. Net income for the first franchise includes a regular fixed interest charge of $200,000. The fixed interest charge for the second franchise is $40,000. Which franchise is riskier to you if sales forecasts are not met? ■   *Answer:* Times interest earned for the first franchise is 1.5 [($100,000 + $200,000)/$200,000], whereas it is 3.5 for the second [($100,000 + $40,000)/$40,000]. This shows the first franchise is more at risk of incurring a loss if its sales decline.

NEED-TO-KNOW 9-5

COMPREHENSIVE

Accounting for Current
Liabilities Including
Warranties, Notes,
Contingencies, Payroll,
and Income Taxes

The following transactions took place at Kern Co. during its recent calendar-year reporting period.

a. In September, Kern sold $140,000 of merchandise covered by a 180-day warranty. Prior experience shows that costs of the warranty equal 5% of sales. Compute September's warranty expense and prepare the adjusting journal entry for the warranty liability as recorded at September 30. Also prepare the journal entry on October 8 to record a $300 cash payment to provide warranty service on an item sold in September.

b. On October 12, Kern replaced an overdue $10,000 account payable by paying $2,500 cash and signing a note for $7,500. The note matures in 90 days and has a 12% interest rate. Prepare the entries recorded on October 12, December 31, and January 10.

c. In late December, Kern is facing a product liability suit filed by an unhappy customer. Kern's lawyer says it will probably suffer a loss from the lawsuit, but the amount is impossible to estimate.

d. Sally Bline works for Kern. For the pay period ended November 30, her gross earnings are $3,000. Bline has $800 deducted for federal income taxes and $200 for state income taxes from each paycheck. Additionally, a $35 premium for health insurance and a $10 donation to United Way are deducted. Bline pays FICA Social Security taxes at a rate of 6.2% and FICA Medicare taxes at a rate of 1.45%. She has not earned enough this year to be exempt from any FICA taxes. Journalize the accrual of salaries expense for Bline by Kern.

e. On November 1, Kern borrows $5,000 cash from a bank in return for a 60-day, 12%, $5,000 note. Record the note's issuance on November 1 and its repayment with interest on December 31.

f.[B] *(Part f covers Appendix 9B.)* Kern has estimated and recorded its quarterly income tax payments. In reviewing its year-end tax adjustments, it identifies an additional $5,000 of income taxes expense that should be recorded. A portion of this additional expense, $1,000, is deferred to future years. Record this year-end income taxes expense adjusting entry.

g. For this calendar year, Kern's net income is $1,000,000, its interest expense is $275,000, and its income taxes expense is $225,000. Compute Kern's times interest earned ratio.

PLANNING THE SOLUTION

- For *a*, compute the warranty expense for September and record it with an estimated liability. Record the October payment as a decrease in the liability.
- For *b*, eliminate the liability for the account payable and create the liability for the note payable. Compute interest expense for the 80 days that the note is outstanding in the current year and record it as a liability. Record the payment of the note, being sure to include the interest for the 10 days in January.
- For *c*, decide whether the company's contingent liability needs to be disclosed or accrued (recorded) according to the two necessary criteria: probable loss and reasonably estimable.
- For *d*, set up payable accounts for all items in Bline's paycheck that require deductions. After all deductions, credit the remaining amount to Salaries Payable.
- For *e*, record the issuance of the note. Compute 60 days' interest due.
- For *f*, determine how much of the income taxes expense is payable in the current year and how much needs to be deferred (see Appendix 9B).
- For *g*, apply and compute times interest earned.

SOLUTION

a. Warranty expense = 5% × $140,000 = $7,000

Sep. 30	Warranty Expense	7,000	
	Estimated Warranty Liability......................		7,000
	Record warranty expense for month.		
Oct. 8	Estimated Warranty Liability	300	
	Cash...		300
	Record cost of warranty service.		

b. Interest expense for current year = 12% × $7,500 × 80/360 = $200
Interest expense for following year = 12% × $7,500 × 10/360 = $25

Oct. 12	Accounts Payable	10,000	
	Notes Payable.................................		7,500
	Cash...		2,500
	Paid $2,500 cash and gave a 90-day, 12% note to extend due date on the account.		
Dec. 31	Interest Expense	200	
	Interest Payable		200
	Accrue interest on note payable.		
Jan. 10	Interest Expense	25	
	Interest Payable....................................	200	
	Notes Payable	7,500	
	Cash...		7,725
	Paid note with interest, including accrued interest payable.		

c. Disclose the pending lawsuit in the financial statement notes. Although the loss is probable, no liability is accrued because the loss cannot be reasonably estimated.

d.

Nov. 30	Salaries Expense	3,000.00	
	FICA—Social Security Taxes Payable (6.2%)		186.00
	FICA—Medicare Taxes Payable (1.45%)		43.50
	Employee Federal Income Taxes Payable		800.00
	Employee State Income Taxes Payable		200.00
	Employee Medical Insurance Payable		35.00
	Employee United Way Payable		10.00
	Salaries Payable................................		1,725.50
	Record Bline's accrued payroll.		

e.

Nov. 1	Cash	5,000	
	Notes Payable...................................		5,000
	Borrowed cash with a 60-day, 12% note.		

When the note and interest are paid 60 days later, Kern Co. records this entry.

Dec. 31	Notes Payable	5,000	
	Interest Expense	100	
	Cash		5,100
	Paid note with interest ($5,000 × 12% × 60/360).		

f.[B]

Dec. 31	Income Taxes Expense	5,000	
	Income Taxes Payable		4,000
	Deferred Income Tax Liability		1,000
	Record added income taxes expense and the *deferred tax liability.*		

g. Times interest earned $= \dfrac{\$1,000,000 + \$275,000 + \$225,000}{\$275,000} = \underline{\underline{5.45 \text{ times}}}$

APPENDIX

9A

Payroll Reports, Records, and Procedures

P5

Identify and describe the details of payroll reports, records, and procedures.

This appendix focuses on payroll accounting reports, records, and procedures.

Payroll Reports   Most employees and employers are required to pay local, state, and federal payroll taxes. Payroll expenses are liabilities to individual employees, to federal and state governments, and to other organizations such as insurance companies. Employers are required to prepare and submit reports explaining how they computed these payments.

Reporting FICA Taxes and Income Taxes   The Federal Insurance Contributions Act (FICA) requires each employer to file an Internal Revenue Service (IRS) **Form 941,** the *Employer's Quarterly Federal Tax Return,* within one month after the end of each calendar quarter. A sample Form 941 is shown in Exhibit 9A.1 for Phoenix Sales & Service, a landscape design company. Accounting information and software are helpful in tracking payroll transactions and reporting the accumulated information on Form 941. Specifically, the employer reports total wages subject to income tax withholding on line 2 of Form 941. (For simplicity, this appendix uses *wages* to refer to both wages and salaries.) The income tax withheld is reported on line 3. The combined amount of employee and employer FICA (Social Security) taxes for Phoenix Sales & Service is reported on line 5a (taxable Social Security wages, $36,599 × 12.4% = $4,538.28). The 12.4% is the sum of the Social Security tax withheld, computed as 6.2% tax withheld from the employee wages for the quarter, plus the 6.2% tax levied on the employer. The combined amount of employee Medicare wages is reported on line 5c. The 2.9% is the sum of 1.45% withheld from employee wages for the quarter plus 1.45% tax levied on the employer. Total FICA taxes are reported on line 5e and are added to the total income taxes withheld of $3,056.47 to yield a total of $8,656.12. For this year, assume that income up to $128,400 is subject to Social Security tax. There is no income limit on amounts subject to Medicare tax. Congress sets rates owed for Social Security tax (and it typically changes each year).

Federal depository banks are authorized to accept deposits of amounts payable to the federal government. Deposit requirements depend on the amount of tax owed. For example, when the sum of FICA taxes plus the employee income taxes is less than $2,500 for a quarter, the taxes can be paid when Form 941 is filed.

Point: Deposits for federal payroll taxes must be made by electronic funds transfer (EFT).

Reporting FUTA Taxes and SUTA Taxes   An employer's federal unemployment taxes (FUTA) are reported on an annual basis by filing an *Annual Federal Unemployment Tax Return,* IRS **Form 940.** It must be mailed on or before January 31 following the end of each tax year. Ten more days are allowed if all required tax deposits are filed on a timely basis and the full amount of tax is paid on or before January 31. FUTA payments are made quarterly to a federal depository bank if the total amount due exceeds $500. If $500 or less

EXHIBIT 9A.1

Form 941

Point: Line 5a shows the matching nature of FICA tax as 6.2% × 2, or 12.4%, which is shown as 0.124.

Point: Auditors rely on the four 941 Forms filed during a year when auditing a company's annual wages and salaries expense account.

Form 941 **Employer's QUARTERLY Federal Tax Return**
Department of the Treasury — Internal Revenue Service

(EIN) Employer identification number 8 6 – 3 2 1 4 5 8 7

Name (not your trade name) Phoenix Sales & Service

Trade name (if any)

Address 1214 Mill Road
Number Street Suite or room number
Phoenix AZ 85621
City State ZIP code

Report for this Quarter ...
(Check one.)
☐ 1: January, February, March
☐ 2: April, May, June
☐ 3: July, August, September
☒ 4: October, November, December

Part 1: Answer these questions for this quarter.

1. Number of employees who received wages, tips, or other compensation for the pay period including: *Mar. 12* (Quarter 1), *June 12* (Quarter 2), *Sept. 12* (Quarter 3), *Dec. 12* (Quarter 4) ... 1 | **2**

2. Wages, tips, and other compensation ... 2 | **36,599.00**

3. Total income tax withheld from wages, tips, and other compensation ... 3 | **3,056.47**

4. If no wages, tips, and other compensation are subject to social security or Medicare tax ... ☐ Check and go to line 6.

5. Taxable social security and Medicare wages and tips:

	Column 1		Column 2
5a Taxable social security wages	36,599.00	× .124 =	4,538.28
5b Taxable social security tips		× .124 =	
5c Taxable Medicare wages & tips	36,599.00	× .029 =	1,061.37
5d Taxable wages & tips subject to Additional Medicare Tax withholding		× 0.009 =	
5e Add Column 2 from lines 5a, 5b, 5c, and 5d		5e	5,599.65

5f Section 3121(q) Notice and Demand–Tax due to unreported tips (see instructions) ... 5f | .

6. Total taxes before adjustments. Add lines 3, 5e, and 5f ... 6 | **8,656.12**

7. Current quarter's adjustment for fractions of cents ... 7 | .

8. Current quarter's adjustment for sick pay ... 8 | .

9. Current quarter's adjustments for tips and group-term like insurance ... 9 | .

10. Total taxes after adjustments. Combine lines 6 through 9 ... 10 | **8,656.12**

11. Qualified small business payroll tax credit for increasing research activities. Attach Form 8974 ... 11 | .

12. Total taxes after adjustments and credits. Subtract line 11 from line 10 ... 12 | **8,656.12**

13. Total deposits for this quarter, including overpayment applied from a prior quarter and overpayments applied from Form 941-X, 941-X (PR), 944-X, or 944-X (SP) filed in the current quarter ... 13 | **8,656.12**

14. Balance due. If line 12 is more than line 13, enter the difference and see instructions ... 14 | **0.00**

15. Overpayment. If line 13 is more than line 12, enter the difference | . Check one: ☐ Apply to next return. ☐ Send a refund.

Part 2: Tell us about your deposit schedule and tax liability for this quarter.

If you are unsure about whether you are a monthly schedule depositor or a semiweekly schedule depositor, see section 11 of Pub. 15.

16. Check one: ☐ Line 12 on this return is less than $2,500 or line 12 (line 10 if the prior quarter was the fourth quarter of last year) on the return for the prior quarter was less than $2,500, and you didn't incur a $100,000 next-day deposit obligation during the current quarter. If line 12 (line 10 if the prior quarter was the fourth quarter of last year) for the prior quarter was less than $2,500 but line 12 on this return is $100,000 or more, you must provide a record of your federal tax liability. If you are a monthly schedule depositor, complete the deposit schedule below; if you are a semiweekly schedule depositor, attach Schedule B (Form 941). Go to Part 3.

☒ You were a monthly schedule depositor for the entire quarter. Enter your tax liability for each month and total liability for the quarter, then go to Part 3.

Tax liability: Month 1 | 3,079.11
Month 2 | 2,049.77
Month 3 | 3,527.24
Total liability for quarter | 8,656.12 | Total must equal line 12.

☐ You were a semiweekly schedule depositor for any part of this quarter. Fill out Schedule B (Form 941), *Report of Tax Liability for Semiweekly Schedule Depositors*, and attach it to Form 941.

Part 3: Tell us about your business. If a question does NOT apply to your business, leave it blank.

17. If your business has closed or you stopped paying wages ... ☐ Check here, and enter the final date you paid wages | / /

18. If you are a seasonal employer and you do not have to file a return for every quarter of the year ... ☐ Check here.

Part 4: May we speak with your third-party designee?

Do you want to allow an employee, a paid tax preparer, or another person to discuss this return with the IRS? See the instructions for details.
☐ Yes. Designee's name and phone number
Select a 5-digit Personal Identification Number (PIN) to use when talking to the IRS. ☐☐☐☐☐
☒ No.

Part 5: Sign here. You MUST complete both pages of Form 941 and SIGN it.

Under penalties of perjury, I declare that I have examined this return, including accompanying schedules and statements, and to the best of my knowledge and belief, it is true, correct, and complete. Declaration of preparer (other than taxpayer) is based on all information of which preparer has any knowledge.

X Sign your name here | Print your name here
Print your title here

Date | / / | Best daytime phone

---

is due, the taxes are remitted annually. Requirements for paying and reporting state unemployment taxes (SUTA) vary depending on the laws of each state. Most states require quarterly payments and reports.

Reporting Wages and Salaries Employers are required to give each employee an annual report of his or her wages subject to FICA and federal income taxes along with the amounts of these taxes withheld. This report is called a *Wage and Tax Statement,* or **Form W-2.** It must be given to employees before January 31 following the year covered by the report. Exhibit 9A.2 shows Form W-2 for one of the

Form W-2 Wage and Tax Statement
Copy 1–For State, City, or Local Tax Department
Department of Treasury—Internal Revenue Service

a Control number AR101 | 22222 | OMB No. 1545-0006

b Employer identification number (EIN) 86-3214587

| 1 Wages, tips, other compensation 4,910.00 | 2 Federal income tax withheld 333.37 |

c Employer's name, address and ZIP code
Phoenix Sales & Service
1214 Mill Road
Phoenix, AZ 85621

3 Social security wages 4,910.00	4 Social security tax withheld 304.42
5 Medicare wages and tips 4,910.00	6 Medicare tax withheld 71.20
7 Social security tips	8 Allocated tips

d Employee's social security number 333-22-9999

| 9 Advance EIC payment | 10 Dependent care benefits |

e Employee's first name and initial Robert J. Last name Austin

| 11 Nonqualified plans | 12a Code |

f Employee's address and ZIP code
18 Roosevelt Blvd., Apt. C
Tempe, AZ 86322

| 13 Statutory employee / Retirement plan / Third-party sick pay | 12b Code |
| 14 Other | 12c Code |

| 15 State AZ Employer's state ID number 13-902319 | 16 State wages, tips, etc. 4,910.00 | 17 State income tax 26.68 | 18 Local wages, tips, etc. | 19 Local income tax | 20 Locality name |

employees at Phoenix Sales & Service. Copies of Form W-2 must be sent to the Social Security Administration, where the amount of the employee's wages subject to FICA taxes and FICA taxes withheld are posted to each employee's Social Security account. These posted amounts become the basis for determining an employee's retirement and survivors' benefits. The Social Security Administration also transmits to the IRS the amount of each employee's wages subject to federal income taxes and the amount of taxes withheld.

Payroll Records
Employers must keep payroll records in addition to reporting and paying taxes. These records usually include a payroll register and an individual earnings report for each employee.

Payroll Register   A **payroll register** usually shows the pay period dates, hours worked, gross pay, deductions, and net pay of each employee for each pay period. Exhibit 9A.3 shows a payroll register for Phoenix Sales & Service. It is organized into nine columns:

Col. A   Employee Identification (ID); Employee name; Social Security number (SS No.); Reference (check number); and Date (date check issued)

Col. B   Pay Type (regular and overtime)

Col. C   Pay Hours (number of hours worked as regular and overtime)

Col. D   Gross Pay (amount of gross pay)

Col. E   FIT (federal income taxes withheld); FUTA (federal unemployment taxes)

Col. F   SIT (state income taxes withheld); SUTA (state unemployment taxes)

Col. G   FICA-SS_EE (Social Security taxes withheld, employee); FICA-SS_ER (Social Security taxes, employer)

Col. H   FICA-Med_EE (Medicare tax withheld, employee); FICA-Med_ER (Medicare tax, employer)

Col. I   Net Pay (gross pay less amounts withheld from employees)

Net pay for each employee is computed as gross pay minus the items on the first line of columns E through H. The employer's payroll tax for each employee is computed as the sum of items on the third line of columns E through H. A payroll register includes all data necessary to record payroll. In some software programs, the entries to record payroll are made in a special *payroll journal.*

EXHIBIT 9A.3

Payroll Register

Point: Gross Pay column shows regular hours worked on the first line multiplied by regular pay rate. Overtime hours multiplied by the overtime premium rate equals overtime pay on the second line. For this company, workers earn 150% of their regular rate for hours in excess of 40 per week.

A	B	C	D	E	F	G	H	I
				Phoenix Sales & Service Payroll Register For Week Ended Jan. 8, 2019				
Employee ID Employee SS No. Refer., Date	Gross Pay			FIT [blank] FUTA	SIT [blank] SUTA	FICA-SS_EE [blank] FICA-SS_ER	FICA-Med_EE [blank] FICA-Med_ER	Net Pay
	Pay Type	Pay Hours	Gross Pay					
AR101 Robert Austin 333-22-9999 9001, 1/8/19	Regular Overtime	40.00 0.00	400.00 0.00 400.00	−28.99 −2.40	−2.32 −10.80	−24.80 −24.80	−5.80 −5.80	338.09
CJ102 Judy Cross 299-11-9201 9002, 1/8/19	Regular Overtime	40.00 1.00	560.00 21.00 581.00	−52.97 −3.49	−4.24 −15.69	−36.02 −36.02	−8.42 −8.42	479.35
DJ103 John Diaz 444-11-9090 9003, 1/8/19	Regular Overtime	40.00 2.00	560.00 42.00 602.00	−48.33 −3.61	−3.87 −16.25	−37.32 −37.32	−8.73 −8.73	503.75
KK104 Kay Keife 909-11-3344 9004, 1/8/19	Regular Overtime	40.00 0.00	560.00 0.00 560.00	−68.57 −3.36	−5.49 −15.12	−34.72 −34.72	−8.12 −8.12	443.10
ML105 Lee Miller 444-56-3211 9005, 1/8/19	Regular Overtime	40.00 0.00	560.00 0.00 560.00	−34.24 −3.36	−2.74 −15.12	−34.72 −34.72	−8.12 −8.12	480.18
SD106 Dale Sears 909-33-1234 9006, 1/8/19	Regular Overtime	40.00 0.00	560.00 0.00 560.00	−68.57 −3.36	−5.49 −15.12	−34.72 −34.72	−8.12 −8.12	443.10
Totals	Regular Overtime	240.00 3.00	3,200.00 63.00 3,263.00	−301.67 −19.58	−24.15 −88.10	−202.30 −202.30	−47.31 −47.31	2,687.57

Payroll Check Payment of payroll is usually done by check or electronic funds transfer. Exhibit 9A.4 shows a *payroll check* for a Phoenix employee. This check includes a detachable *statement of earnings* (at top) showing gross pay, deductions, and net pay.

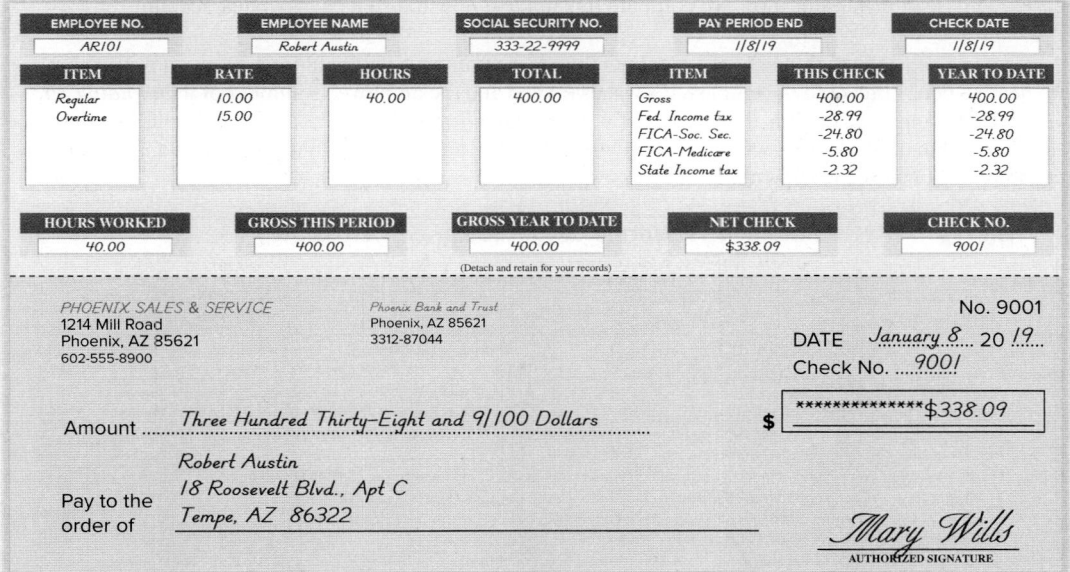

EXHIBIT 9A.4

Check and Statement of Earnings

Employee Earnings Report An **employee earnings report** is a cumulative record of an employee's hours worked, gross earnings, deductions, and net pay. Payroll information on this report is taken from the payroll register. The employee earnings report for R. Austin at Phoenix Sales & Service is shown in Exhibit 9A.5. An employee earnings report accumulates information that can show when an employee's

EXHIBIT 9A.5

Employee Earnings Report

Phoenix Sales & Service							
Employee Earnings Report							
For Month Ended Dec. 31, 2019							
Employee ID **Employee** **SS No.**	**Date** **Reference**	**Gross** **Pay**	**FIT** [blank] **FUTA**	**SIT** [blank] **SUTA**	**FICA-SS_EE** [blank] **FICA-SS_ER**	**FICA-Med_EE** [blank] **FICA-Med_ER**	**Net** **Pay**
Beginning balance for Robert Austin	11/26/19 (balance)	2,910.00	−188.42	−15.08	−180.42	−42.20	2,483.88
			−17.46	−78.57	−180.42	−42.20	
AR101 Robert Austin 333-22-9999	12/03/19 9049	400.00	−28.99	−2.32	−24.80	−5.80	338.09
			−2.40	−10.80	−24.80	−5.80	
AR101 Robert Austin 333-22-9999	12/10/19 9055	400.00	−28.99	−2.32	−24.80	−5.80	338.09
			−2.40	−10.80	−24.80	−5.80	
AR101 Robert Austin 333-22-9999	12/17/19 9061	400.00	−28.99	−2.32	−24.80	−5.80	338.09
			−2.40	−10.80	−24.80	−5.80	
AR101 Robert Austin 333-22-9999	12/24/19 9067	400.00	−28.99	−2.32	−24.80	−5.80	338.09
			−2.40	−10.80	−24.80	−5.80	
AR101 Robert Austin 333-22-9999	12/31/19 9073	400.00	−28.99	−2.32	−24.80	−5.80	338.09
			−2.40	−10.80	−24.80	−5.80	
Total 5-wk month thru 12/31/19		2,000.00	−144.95	−11.60	−124.00	−29.00	1,690.45
			−12.00	−54.00	−124.00	−29.00	
Year-to-date total for Robert Austin	12/31/19 (balance)	4,910.00	−333.37	−26.68	−304.42	−71.20	4,174.33
			−29.46	−132.57	−304.42	−71.20	

Point: Year-end balances agree with W-2.

earnings reach the tax-exempt points for FICA, FUTA, and SUTA taxes. It also gives data an employer needs to prepare Form W-2.

Payroll Procedures
Employers must be able to compute federal income tax for payroll purposes. This section explains how we compute this tax and how to use a payroll bank account.

Computing Federal Income Taxes To compute the amount of taxes withheld from each employee's wages, we need to determine both the employee's wages earned and the employee's number of *withholding allowances.* Each employee records the number of withholding allowances claimed on a withholding allowance certificate, **Form W-4,** filed with the employer. When the number of withholding allowances increases, the amount of income taxes withheld decreases.

Form **W-4**	**Employee's Withholding Allowance Certificate**	OMB No. 1545–0074
Department of the Treasury Internal Revenue Service	▶ Whether you are entitled to claim a certain number of allowances or exemption from withholding is subject to review by the IRS. Your employer may be required to send a copy of this form to the IRS.	20___

1 Your first name and middle initial	Last name	2 Your social security number
Robert J.	Austin	333-22-9999

Home address (number and street or rural route)
18 Roosevelt Blvd., Apt. C

3 ☒ Single ☐ Married ☐ Married, but withhold at higher Single rate.
Note: If married, but legally separated, or spouse is a nonresident alien, check the "Single" box.

City or town, state, and ZIP code
Tempe, AZ 86322

4 If your last name differs from that shown on your social security card,
check here. You must call 1–800–772–1213 for a replacement card. ▶ ☐

5	Total number of allowances you are claiming (from line **H** above **or** from the applicable worksheet on page 2)	5	1
6	Additional amount, if any, you want withheld from each paycheck	6	$

7 I claim exemption from withholding for 20__, and I certify that I meet **both** of the following conditions for exemption.
• Last year I had a right to a refund of **all** federal income tax withheld because I had **no** tax liability, **and**
• This year I expect a refund of **all** federal income tax withheld because I expect to have **no** tax liability.
If you meet both conditions, write "Exempt" here . . . . ▶ | 7

Under penalties of perjury, I declare that I have examined this certificate and, to the best of my knowledge and belief, it is true, correct, and complete.

Employee's signature
(This form is not valid unless you sign it.) ▶ *Robert J. Austin*   Date ▶ *January 1*

8 Employer's name and address (Employer: Complete lines 8 and 10 only if sending to the IRS.)	9 Office code (optional)	10 Employer identification number (EIN)
Phoenix Sales & Service, 1214 Mill Rd, Phoenix, AZ 85621		86-3214587

For Privacy Act and Paperwork Reduction Act Notice, see page 2.   Cat. No. 10220Q   Form **W-4**

Employers often use a **wage bracket withholding table** similar to the one shown in Exhibit 9A.6 to compute the **federal income taxes withheld** from each employee's gross pay. The table in Exhibit 9A.6 is for a single employee paid weekly. Tables also are provided for married employees and for biweekly, semimonthly, and monthly pay periods (most payroll software includes these tables). When using a wage bracket withholding table to compute federal income tax withheld from an employee's gross wages, we need to locate an employee's wage bracket within the first two columns. We then find the amount withheld by looking in the withholding allowance column for that employee.

EXHIBIT 9A.6

Wage Bracket
Withholding Table

SINGLE Persons—WEEKLY Payroll Period												
If the wages are—		And the number of withholding allowances claimed is—										
At least	But less than	0	1	2	3	4	5	6	7	8	9	10
		The amount of income tax to be withheld is—										
$600	$610	$76	$67	$58	$49	$39	$30	$21	$12	$6	$0	$0
610	620	79	69	59	50	41	32	22	13	7	1	0
620	630	81	70	61	52	42	33	24	15	8	2	0
630	640	84	72	62	53	44	35	25	16	9	3	0
640	650	86	73	64	55	45	36	27	18	10	4	0
650	660	89	75	65	56	47	38	28	19	11	5	0
660	670	91	76	67	58	48	39	30	21	12	6	0
670	680	94	78	68	59	50	41	31	22	13	7	1
680	690	96	81	70	61	51	42	33	24	14	8	2
690	700	99	83	71	62	53	44	34	25	16	9	3
700	710	101	86	73	64	54	45	35	27	17	10	4
710	720	104	88	74	65	56	47	37	28	19	11	5
720	730	106	91	76	67	57	48	39	30	20	12	6
730	740	109	93	78	68	59	50	40	31	22	13	7
740	750	111	96	80	70	60	51	42	33	23	14	8

Payroll Bank Account Companies with few employees often pay them with checks drawn on the company's regular bank account. Companies with many employees often use a special **payroll bank account** to pay employees. When this account is used, a company either (1) draws one check for total payroll on the regular bank account and deposits it in the payroll bank account or (2) executes an *electronic funds transfer* to the payroll bank account. Individual payroll checks are then drawn on this payroll bank account. Because only one check for the total payroll is drawn on the regular bank account each payday, use of a special payroll bank account helps with internal control. It also helps in reconciling the regular bank account. When companies use a payroll bank account, they usually include check numbers in the payroll register. The payroll register in Exhibit 9A.3 shows check numbers in column A. For instance, Check No.

9001 is issued to Robert Austin. With this information, the payroll register serves as a supplementary record of wages earned by and paid to employees.

Who Pays What Payroll Taxes and Benefits
We conclude this appendix with the following table identifying who pays which payroll taxes and which common employee benefits such as medical, disability, pension, charitable, and union costs. Who pays which employee benefits, and what portion, is subject to agreements between companies and their workers. Also, self-employed workers must pay both the employer and employee FICA taxes for Social Security and Medicare.

Year-To-Date Pay	Employer Taxes	Employee Taxes
$0 to $7,000	FICA—Medicare FICA—Social Security FUTA SUTA	FICA—Medicare FICA—Social Security State & Federal Income Tax
$7,000 to $128,400	FICA—Medicare FICA—Social Security	FICA—Medicare FICA—Social Security State & Federal Income Tax
Above $128,400	FICA—Medicare	FICA—Medicare State & Federal Income Tax

Employer Payroll Taxes and Costs	Employee Payroll Deductions
• FICA—Social Security taxes	• FICA—Social Security taxes
• FICA—Medicare taxes	• FICA—Medicare taxes
• FUTA (federal unemployment taxes)	• Federal income taxes
• SUTA (state unemployment taxes)	• State and local income taxes
• Share of medical coverage, if any	• Share of medical coverage, if any
• Share of pension coverage, if any	• Share of pension coverage, if any
• Share of other benefits, if any	• Share of other benefits, if any

Point: IRS reports average (effective) income tax rates for categories of income earners:

Top 1%.	24%
Top 5%.	20%
Top 10%	18%
Lower 50%	<2%

Corporate Income Taxes

9B

This appendix covers current liabilities for income taxes of C corporations. Income tax on sole proprietorships, partnerships, S corporations, and LLCs is computed on their owner's tax filings and is not covered here.

Income Tax Liabilities Corporations are subject to income taxes and must estimate their income tax liability when preparing financial statements. Because income tax expense is created by earning income, a liability is incurred when income is earned. This tax must be paid quarterly. Consider a corporation that prepares monthly financial statements. Based on its income in January, this corporation estimates that it owes income taxes of $12,100. The following adjusting entry records this estimate.

Jan. 31	Income Taxes Expense	12,100	
	Income Taxes Payable		12,100
	Accrue January income taxes.		

Assets = Liabilities + Equity
$+12,100 \quad -12,100$

The tax liability is recorded each month until the first quarterly payment is made. If the company's estimated taxes for this first quarter total $30,000, the entry to record its payment is

Apr. 10	Income Taxes Payable	30,000	
	Cash..		30,000
	Paid estimated first-quarter income taxes.		

Assets = Liabilities + Equity
$-30,000 \quad -30,000$

This process of accruing and then paying estimated income taxes continues through the year. When annual financial statements are prepared at year-end, the corporation knows its actual total income and the actual amount of income taxes it must pay. This information allows it to accurately record income taxes expense for the fourth quarter so that the total of the four quarters' expense amounts equals the actual taxes paid to the government.

Deferred Income Tax Liabilities An income tax liability for corporations can arise when the amount of income before taxes that the corporation reports on its income statement is not the same as the amount of income reported on its income tax return. This difference occurs because income tax laws and GAAP measure income differently. Differences between tax laws and GAAP arise because Congress uses tax laws to generate receipts, stimulate the economy, and influence behavior, whereas GAAP is intended to provide financial information useful for business decisions. Also, tax accounting often follows the cash basis, whereas GAAP follows the accrual basis.

Some differences between tax laws and GAAP are temporary. *Temporary differences* arise when the tax return and the income statement report a revenue or expense in different years. As an example, companies are often able to deduct higher amounts of depreciation in the early years of an asset's life and smaller amounts in later years for tax reporting in comparison to GAAP. This means that in the early years, depreciation for tax reporting is often more than depreciation on the income statement. In later years, depreciation for tax reporting is often less than depreciation on the income statement. When temporary differences exist between taxable income on the tax return and the income before taxes on the income statement, corporations compute income taxes expense based on the income reported on the income statement. The result is that income taxes expense reported in the income statement is often different from the amount of income taxes payable to the government. This difference is the **deferred income tax liability.**

Point: For a temporary difference, if GAAP income exceeds taxable income, a deferred tax liability is created. If GAAP income is initially less than taxable income, a deferred tax asset is created.

Assume that in recording its usual quarterly income tax payments, a corporation computes $25,000 of income taxes expense. It also determines that only $21,000 is currently due and $4,000 is deferred to future years (a timing difference). The entry to record this end-of-period adjustment is

Assets = Liabilities + Equity
+21,000   −25,000
+4,000

Dec. 31	Income Taxes Expense	25,000	
	Income Taxes Payable		21,000
	Deferred Income Tax Liability		4,000
	Record tax expense and deferred tax liability.		

The credit to Income Taxes Payable is the amount currently due to be paid. The credit to Deferred Income Tax Liability is tax payments deferred until future years when the temporary difference reverses.

Deferred Income Tax Assets   Temporary differences also can cause a company to pay income taxes *before* they are reported on the income statement. If so, the company reports a *Deferred Income Tax Asset* on its balance sheet.

Summary: Cheat Sheet

KNOWN LIABILITIES

Current liabilities (or short-term liabilities): Liabilities due *within* one year.
Long-term liabilities: Liabilities due *after* one year.

Sales tax collection:

Cash	6,300	
Sales.....................................		6,000
Sales Taxes Payable		300

Unearned revenues (or deferred revenues): Amount received in advance from customers for future products or services; to record cash received in advance.

Cash	5,000,000	
Unearned Revenue		5,000,000

Unearned revenue is earned: To record service or product delivered.

Unearned Revenue........................	625,000	
Revenue............................		625,000

Short-term note payable: A written promise to pay a specified amount on a stated future date within one year.

Note given to replace accounts payable (partial cash paid):

Accounts Payable...........................	600	
Cash....................................		100
Notes Payable		500

Note given to borrow cash:

Cash	2,000	
Notes Payable		2,000

Note and interest paid:

Notes Payable...............................	500	
Interest Expense	10	
Cash.......................................		510

Interest expense incurred but not yet paid:

Interest Expense	10	
Interest Payable		10

Interest formula (year assumed to have 360 days):

$$\text{Principal of the note} \times \text{Annual interest rate} \times \text{Time expressed in fraction of year} = \text{Interest}$$

PAYROLL LIABILITIES

Gross pay: Total compensation an employee earns before deductions such as taxes.
Payroll deductions (or withholdings): Amounts withheld from an employee's gross pay, either required or voluntary.
FICA—Social Security taxes payable: Withholdings to cover retirement, disability, and survivorship. Social Security tax is 6.2% of the first $128,400 the employee earns for the year.

FICA—Medicare taxes payable: Withholdings to cover medical benefits. The Medicare tax is 1.45% of all amounts the employee earns; there is no maximum limit to Medicare tax.

Employee federal income taxes payable: Federal income tax withheld from each employee's paycheck.

Employee voluntary deductions: Voluntary withholdings for things such as union dues, charitable giving, and health insurance.

Employee payroll taxes:

Salaries Expense	2,000	
FICA—Social Security Taxes Payable (6.2%)		124
FICA—Medicare Taxes Payable (1.45%)		29
Employee Federal Income Taxes Payable		213
Employee Medical Insurance Payable		85
Employee Union Dues Payable		25
Salaries Payable		1,524

Payment of salary to employees:

Salaries Payable..............................	1,524	
Cash		1,524

Federal Unemployment Tax Act (FUTA): Employers pay a federal unemployment tax on wages and salaries earned by their employees. FUTA taxes are between 0.6% and 6.0% of the first $7,000 earned by each employee.

State Unemployment Tax Act (SUTA): Employers pay a state unemployment tax on wages and salaries earned by their employees. SUTA taxes are up to 5.4% of the first $7,000 earned by each employee.

Employer payroll taxes expense:

Payroll Taxes Expense	273	
FICA—Social Security Taxes Payable (6.2%)		124
FICA—Medicare Taxes Payable (1.45%)		29
State Unemployment Taxes Payable		108
Federal Unemployment Taxes Payable		12

ESTIMATED LIABILITIES

Health and pension benefits:

Employee Benefits Expense......................	20,000	
Employee Medical Insurance Payable		8,000
Employee Retirement Program Payable		12,000

Accrual of vacation benefits (also called *paid absences*):

Vacation Benefits Expense	3,200	
Vacation Benefits Payable		3,200

Vacation benefits are used:

Vacation Benefits Payable	400	
Cash.....................................		400

Bonus plan accrued:

Employee Bonus Expense	10,000	
Bonus Payable		10,000

Warranty: A seller's obligation to replace or fix a product (or service) that fails to perform as expected within a specified period. Warranty expense is recorded in the period when revenue from the sale of the product or service is reported.

Warranty expense accrued:

Warranty Expense	640	
Estimated Warranty Liability		640

Warranty repairs and replacements:

Estimated Warranty Liability	200	
Auto Parts Inventory		200

CONTINGENCIES AND ANALYSIS

Contingent liability: A potential liability that depends on a future event arising from a past transaction or event. An example is a pending lawsuit.

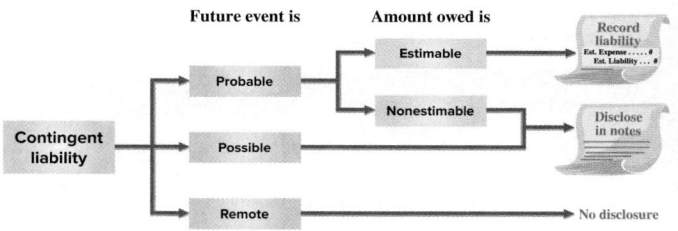

Key Terms

Multiple Choice Quiz

1. On December 1, a company signed a $6,000, 90-day, 5% note payable, with principal plus interest due on March 1 of the following year. What amount of interest expense should be accrued at December 31 on the note?

   a. $300   **c.** $100   **e.** $0

   b. $25   **d.** $75

2. An employee earned $50,000 during the year. FICA tax for Social Security is 6.2% and FICA tax for Medicare is 1.45%. The employer's share of FICA taxes is

   a. $0; employee's pay exceeds FICA limit.

   b. $0; FICA is not an employer tax.

   c. $3,100.

   d. $725.

   e. $3,825.

3. Assume the FUTA tax rate is 0.6% and the SUTA tax rate is 5.4%. Both taxes are applied to the first $7,000 of an employee's pay. What is the total unemployment tax an employer must pay on an employee's annual wages of $40,000?

   a. $2,400

   b. $420

   c. $42

   d. $378

   e. $0; employee's wages exceed the $7,000 maximum.

4. A company sold 10,000 TVs in July and estimates warranty expense for these TVs to be $25,000. During July, 80 TVs were serviced under warranty at a cost of $18,000. The credit balance in the Estimated Warranty Liability account at July 1 was $26,000. What is the company's warranty expense for the month of July?

   a. $51,000   **c.** $25,000   **e.** $18,000

   b. $1,000   **d.** $33,000

5. AXE Co. is the defendant in a lawsuit. AXE reasonably estimates that this pending lawsuit will result in damages of $99,000. It is probable that AXE will lose the case. What should AXE do?

   a. Record a liability   **c.** Have no disclosure

   b. Disclose in notes

ANSWERS TO MULTIPLE CHOICE QUIZ

1. b; $6,000 × 0.05 × 30/360 = $25
2. e; $50,000 × (0.062 + 0.0145) = $3,825
3. b; $7,000 × (0.006 + 0.054) = $420

4. c; $25,000
5. a; Reason—it is reasonably estimated and is a probable loss. AXE would record an estimated legal expense and liability.

$^{A(B)}$ *Superscript letter A or B denotes assignments based on Appendix 9A or 9B.*

🔲 Icon denotes assignments that involve decision making.

Discussion Questions

1. 🔲 What is the difference between a current and a long-term liability?

2. What is an estimated liability?

3. 🔲 What are the three important questions concerning the uncertainty of liabilities?

4. What is the combined amount (in percent) of the employee and employer Social Security tax rate? (Assume wages do not exceed $128,400 per year.)

5. What is the current Medicare tax rate? This rate is applied to what maximum level of salary and wages?

6. Which payroll taxes are the employee's responsibility and which are the employer's responsibility?

7. What determines the amount deducted from an employee's wages for federal income taxes?

8. What is an employer's unemployment merit rating? How are these ratings assigned to employers?

9. 🔲 Why are warranty liabilities usually recognized on the balance sheet as liabilities even when they are uncertain?

10. 🔲 Suppose a company has a facility located where disastrous weather conditions often occur. Should it report a probable loss from a future disaster as a liability on its balance sheet? Explain.

11.^{A} What is a wage bracket withholding table?

12.^{A} What amount of income tax is withheld from the salary of an employee who is single with two withholding allowances and earns $725 per week? What if the employee earns $625 and has no withholding allowances? (Use Exhibit 9A.6.)

13. Refer to **Apple**'s balance sheet in Appendix A. What is the amount of Apple's accounts payable as of September 30, 2017? **APPLE**

14. 🔲 Refer to **Google**'s balance sheet in Appendix A. What "accrued" expenses (liabilities) does Google report at December 31, 2017? **GOOGLE**

15. 🔲 Refer to **Samsung**'s balance sheet in Appendix A. List Samsung's current liabilities as of December 31, 2017. **Samsung**

16. 🔲 Refer to **Samsung**'s recent balance sheet in Appendix A. What current liabilities related to income taxes are on its balance sheet? Explain the meaning of each income tax account identified. **Samsung**

☐ connect

Which of the following items are normally classified as current liabilities for a company that has a one-year operating cycle?

_____ **1.** Portion of long-term note due in 10 months.

_____ **2.** Note payable maturing in 2 years.

_____ **3.** Note payable due in 18 months.

_____ **4.** Accounts payable due in 11 months.

_____ **5.** FICA taxes payable.

_____ **6.** Salaries payable.

QUICK STUDY

QS 9-1
Classifying liabilities
C1

Dextra Computing sells merchandise for $6,000 cash on September 30 (cost of merchandise is $3,900). Dextra collects 5% sales tax. (1) Record the entry for the $6,000 sale and its sales tax. (2) Record the entry that shows Dextra sending the sales tax on this sale to the government on October 15.

QS 9-2
Accounting for sales taxes
C2

Ticketsales, Inc., receives $5,000,000 cash in advance ticket sales for a four-date tour of Bon Jovi. Record the advance ticket sales on October 31. Record the revenue earned for the first concert date of November 5, assuming it represents one-fourth of the advance ticket sales.

QS 9-3
Unearned revenue   **C2**

On November 7, Mura Company borrows $160,000 cash by signing a 90-day, 8%, $160,000 note payable. (1) Compute the accrued interest payable on December 31; (2) prepare the journal entry to record the accrued interest expense at December 31; and (3) prepare the journal entry to record payment of the note at maturity on February 5.

QS 9-4
Interest-bearing note transactions   **P1**

On January 15, the end of the first pay period of the year, North Company's employees earned $35,000 of sales salaries. Withholdings from the employees' salaries include FICA Social Security taxes at the rate of 6.2%, FICA Medicare taxes at the rate of 1.45%, $6,500 of federal income taxes, $772.50 of medical insurance deductions, and $120 of union dues. No employee earned more than $7,000 in this first period. Prepare the journal entry to record North Company's January 15 salaries expense and related liabilities. (Round amounts to cents.)

QS 9-5
Recording employee payroll taxes
P2

Merger Co. has 10 employees, each of whom earns $2,000 per month and has been employed since January 1. FICA Social Security taxes are 6.2% of the first $128,400 paid to each employee, and FICA Medicare taxes are 1.45% of gross pay. FUTA taxes are 0.6% and SUTA taxes are 5.4% of the first $7,000 paid to each employee. Prepare the March 31 journal entry to record the March payroll taxes expense.

QS 9-6
Recording employer payroll taxes   **P3**

Noura Company offers an annual bonus to employees (to be shared equally) if the company meets certain net income goals. Prepare the journal entry to record a $15,000 bonus owed (but not yet paid) to its workers at calendar year-end.

QS 9-7
Accounting for bonuses
P4

Chavez Co.'s salaried employees earn four weeks' vacation per year. Chavez estimated and must expense $8,000 of accrued vacation benefits for the year. (a) Prepare the December 31 year-end adjusting entry for accrued vacation benefits. (b) Prepare the entry on April 1 of the next year when an employee takes a one-week vacation and is paid $500 cash for that week.

QS 9-8
Accounting for vacations
P4

On September 1, Home Store sells a mower (that costs $200) for $500 cash with a one-year warranty that covers parts. Warranty expense is estimated at 8% of sales. On January 24 of the following year, the mower is brought in for repairs covered under the warranty requiring $35 in materials taken from the Repair Parts Inventory. Prepare the September 1 entry to record the mower sale (and cost of sale) and the January 24 entry to record the warranty repairs.

QS 9-9
Recording warranty repairs
P4

Riverrun Co. provides medical care and insurance benefits to its retirees. In the current year, Riverrun agrees to pay $5,500 for medical insurance and contribute an additional $9,000 to a retirement program. Record the entry for these accrued (but unpaid) benefits on December 31.

QS 9-10
Accounting for health and pension benefits   **P4**

Huprey Co. is the defendant in the following legal claims. For each of the following claims, indicate whether Huprey should (a) record a liability, (b) disclose in notes, or (c) have no disclosure.

_____ **1.** Huprey can reasonably estimate that a pending lawsuit will result in damages of $1,250,000. It is probable that Huprey will lose the case.

_____ **2.** It is reasonably possible that Huprey will lose a pending lawsuit. The loss cannot be estimated.

_____ **3.** Huprey is being sued for damages of $2,000,000. It is very unlikely (remote) that Huprey will lose the case.

QS 9-11
Accounting for contingent liabilities
C3

QS 9-12
Times interest earned
A1

Park Company reports interest expense of $145,000 and income before interest expense and income taxes of $1,885,000. (1) Compute its times interest earned. (2) Park's competitor's times interest earned is 4.0. Is Park in a better or worse position than its competitor to make interest payments if the economy turns bad?

QS 9-13^A
Federal income tax withholdings
P5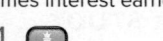

Organic Farmers Co-Op has three employees and pays them weekly. Using the withholding bracket table in Exhibit 9A.6, determine each employee's federal income tax withholding.

1. Maria earns $735 per week and claims three withholding allowances.
2. Jeff earns $607 per week and claims five withholding allowances.
3. Alicia earns $704 per week and does not claim any withholding allowances.

QS 9-14^A
Net pay and tax computations
P5

The payroll records of Speedy Software show the following information about Marsha Gottschalk, an employee, for the weekly pay period ending September 30. Gottschalk is single and claims one allowance. Compute her Social Security tax (6.2%), Medicare tax (1.45%), federal income tax withholding (use the withholding table in Exhibit 9A.6), state income tax (1.0%), and net pay for the current pay period. Round tax amounts to the nearest cent.

Total (gross) earnings for current pay period	$ 740
Cumulative earnings of previous pay periods	$9,700

Check Net pay, $579.99

QS 9-15^B
Recording deferred income tax liability　P4

Sera Corporation has made and recorded its quarterly income tax payments. After a final review of taxes for the year, the company identifies an additional $40,000 of income tax expense that should be recorded. A portion of this additional expense, $6,000, is deferred for payment in future years. Record Sera's year-end adjusting entry for income tax expense.

connect

EXERCISES

Exercise 9-1
Classifying liabilities
C1

The following items appear on the balance sheet of a company with a one-year operating cycle. Identify the proper classification of each item as follows: *C* if it is a current liability, *L* if it is a long-term liability, or *N* if it is not a liability.

_____ **1.** Notes payable (due in 13 to 24 months).
_____ **2.** Notes payable (due in 6 to 11 months).
_____ **3.** Notes payable (mature in five years).
_____ **4.** Current portion of long-term debt.
_____ **5.** Notes payable (due in 120 days).
_____ **6.** FUTA taxes payable.
_____ **7.** Accounts receivable.
_____ **8.** Sales taxes payable.
_____ **9.** Salaries payable.
_____ **10.** Wages payable.

Exercise 9-2
Recording known current liabilities
C2

1. On July 15, Piper Co. sold $10,000 of merchandise (costing $5,000) for cash. The sales tax rate is 4%. On August 1, Piper sent the sales tax collected from the sale to the government. Record entries for the July 15 and August 1 transactions.
2. On November 3, the **Milwaukee Bucks** sold a six-game pack of advance tickets for $300 cash. On November 20, the Bucks played the first game of the six-game pack (this represented one-sixth of the advance ticket sales). Record the entries for the November 3 and November 20 transactions.

Exercise 9-3
Accounting for note payable　P1
Check (2b) Interest expense, $2,200

Sylvestor Systems borrows $110,000 cash on May 15 by signing a 60-day, 12%, $110,000 note.

1. On what date does this note mature?
2. Prepare the entries to record (*a*) issuance of the note and (*b*) payment of the note at maturity.

Exercise 9-4
Interest-bearing notes payable with year-end adjustments　P1
Check (2) $3,000
(3) $1,500

Keesha Co. borrows $200,000 cash on November 1 of the current year by signing a 90-day, 9%, $200,000 note.

1. On what date does this note mature?
2. How much interest expense is recorded in the current year? (Assume a 360-day year.)
3. How much interest expense is recorded in the following year? (Assume a 360-day year.)
4. Prepare journal entries to record (*a*) issuance of the note, (*b*) accrual of interest on December 31, and (*c*) payment of the note at maturity.

BMX Company has one employee. FICA Social Security taxes are 6.2% of the first $128,400 paid to its employee, and FICA Medicare taxes are 1.45% of gross pay. For BMX, its FUTA taxes are 0.6% and SUTA taxes are 5.4% of the first $7,000 paid to its employee. Compute BMX's amounts for each of these four taxes as applied to the employee's gross earnings for September under each of three separate situations (*a*), (*b*), and (*c*). Round amounts to cents.

Exercise 9-5
Computing payroll taxes
P2   P3

	Gross Pay through August 31	Gross Pay for September
a.	$ 6,400	$ 800
b.	2,000	2,100
c.	122,100	8,000

Check   (*a*) FUTA, $3.60; SUTA, $32.40

Using the data in *situation* (*a*) of Exercise 9-5, prepare the employer's September 30 journal entries to record salary expense and its related payroll liabilities for this employee. The employee's federal income taxes withheld by the employer are $80 for this pay period. Round amounts to cents.

Exercise 9-6
Payroll-related journal entries **P2**

Using the data in *situation* (*a*) of Exercise 9-5, prepare the employer's September 30 journal entries to record the *employer's* payroll taxes expense and its related liabilities. Round amounts to cents.

Exercise 9-7
Payroll-related journal entries **P3**

The following monthly data are taken from Ramirez Company at July 31: sales salaries, $200,000; office salaries, $160,000; federal income taxes withheld, $90,000; state income taxes withheld, $20,000; Social Security taxes withheld, $22,320; Medicare taxes withheld, $5,220; medical insurance premiums, $7,000; life insurance premiums, $4,000; union dues deducted, $1,000; and salaries subject to unemployment taxes, $50,000. The employee pays 40% of medical and life insurance premiums.

Prepare journal entries to record (1) accrued payroll, including employee deductions, for July; (2) cash payment of the net payroll (salaries payable) for July; (3) accrued employer payroll taxes, and other related employment expenses, for July—assume that FICA taxes are identical to those on employees and that SUTA taxes are 5.4% and FUTA taxes are 0.6%; and (4) cash payment of all liabilities related to the July payroll.

Exercise 9-8
Recording payroll
P2   P3

Mest Company has nine employees. FICA Social Security taxes are 6.2% of the first $128,400 paid to each employee, and FICA Medicare taxes are 1.45% of gross pay. FUTA taxes are 0.6% and SUTA taxes are 5.4% of the first $7,000 paid to each employee. Cumulative pay for the current year for each of its employees follows.

Exercise 9-9
Computing payroll taxes
P2   P3

Employee	Cumulative Pay	Employee	Cumulative Pay	Employee	Cumulative Pay
Ken S.	$ 6,000	Michelle W.	$143,500	Lori K.	$130,900
Tim V.	40,400	Michael M.	106,900	Kitty O.	36,900
Steve S.	87,000	Zach R.	128,400	John W.	4,000

a. Prepare a table with the following six column headings. Compute the amounts in this table for each employee and then total the numerical columns.

Employee	Cumulative Pay	Pay Subject to FICA Social Security	Pay Subject to FICA Medicare	Pay Subject to FUTA Taxes	Pay Subject to SUTA Taxes

b. For the company, compute each total for FICA Social Security taxes, FICA Medicare taxes, FUTA taxes, and SUTA taxes. *Hint:* Remember to include in those totals any employee share of taxes that the company must collect. Round amounts to cents.

Hitzu Co. sold a copier (that costs $4,800) for $6,000 cash with a two-year parts warranty to a customer on August 16 of Year 1. Hitzu expects warranty costs to be 4% of dollar sales. It records warranty expense with an adjusting entry on December 31. On January 5 of Year 2, the copier requires on-site repairs that are completed the same day. The repairs cost $209 for materials taken from the repair parts inventory. These are the only repairs required in Year 2 for this copier.

1. How much warranty expense does the company report for this copier in Year 1?
2. How much is the estimated warranty liability for this copier as of December 31 of Year 1?
3. How much is the estimated warranty liability for this copier as of December 31 of Year 2?
4. Prepare journal entries to record (*a*) the copier's sale; (*b*) the adjustment to recognize the warranty expense on December 31 of Year 1; and (*c*) the repairs that occur on January 5 of Year 2.

Exercise 9-10
Warranty expense and liability computations and entries
P4
Check   (1) $240

(3) $31

Exercise 9-11
Recording bonuses
P4

For the year ended December 31, Lopez Company implements an employee bonus program based on company net income, which the employees share equally. Lopez's bonus expense is computed as $14,563.

1. Prepare the journal entry at December 31 to record the bonus due the employees.

2. Prepare the later journal entry at January 19 to record payment of the bonus to employees.

Exercise 9-12
Accounting for estimated liabilities
P4

Prepare adjusting entries at December 31 for Maxum Company's year-end financial statements for each of the following separate transactions.

1. Employees earn vacation pay at a rate of one day per month. Maxum estimated and must expense $13,000 of accrued vacation benefits for the year.

2. During December, Maxum Company sold 12,000 units of a product that carries a 60-day warranty. December sales for this product total $460,000. The company expects 10% of the units to need warranty repairs, and it estimates the average repair cost per unit will be $15.

Exercise 9-13
Accounting for health and pension benefits
P4

Vander Co. provides medical care and insurance benefits to its retirees. In the current year, Vander agrees to pay $9,500 for medical insurance and contribute an additional 5% of the employees' $200,000 gross salaries to a retirement program. (1) Record the entry for these accrued (but unpaid) benefits on December 31. (2) Assuming $5,000 of the retirement benefits are not to be paid for five years, how should this amount be reported on the current balance sheet?

Exercise 9-14
Accounting for contingent liabilities
C3

For each separate situation, indicate whether Cruz Company should (*a*) record a liability, (*b*) disclose in notes, or (*c*) have no disclosure.

1. Cruz Company guarantees the $100,000 debt of a supplier. It is not probable that the supplier will default on the debt.

2. A disgruntled employee is suing Cruz Company. Legal advisers believe that the company will likely need to pay damages, but the amount cannot be reasonably estimated.

Exercise 9-15
Preparing a balance sheet
C1   P2   P3

Selected accounts from Lue Co.'s adjusted trial balance for the year ended December 31 follow. Prepare a classified balance sheet.

Total equity	$30,000	Employee federal income taxes payable	$9,000
Equipment	40,000	Federal unemployment taxes payable	200
Salaries payable	34,000	FICA—Medicare taxes payable	725
Accounts receivable	5,100	FICA—Social Security taxes payable	3,100
Cash	50,000	Employee medical insurance payable	2,000
Current portion of long-term debt	4,000	State unemployment taxes payable	1,800
Notes payable (due in 6 years)	10,000	Sales tax payable (due in 2 weeks)	275

Exercise 9-16
Computing and interpreting times interest earned
A1

Check (*b*) 11.0

Use the following information from separate companies *a* through *d* to compute times interest earned. Which company indicates the strongest ability to pay interest expense as it comes due?

	Net Income (Loss)	Interest Expense	Income Taxes
a.	$119,000	$44,000	$35,000
b.	135,000	16,000	25,000
c.	138,000	12,000	30,000
d.	314,000	14,000	50,000

Exercise 9-17ᴮ
Accounting for income taxes   P4

Nishi Corporation prepares financial statements for each month-end. As part of its accounting process, estimated income taxes are accrued each month for 30% of the current month's net income. The income taxes are paid in the first month of each quarter for the amount accrued for the prior quarter. The following information is available for the fourth quarter of the year just ended. When tax computations are completed on January 20 of the following year, Nishi determines that the quarter's Income Taxes Payable account balance should be $28,300 on December 31 of the year just ended (its unadjusted balance is $24,690).

October net income	$28,600	November net income.	$19,100	December net income	$34,600

1. Determine the amount of the accounting adjustment (dated as of December 31) to get the correct ending balance in the Income Taxes Payable account.

2. Prepare journal entries to record (*a*) the December 31 adjustment to the Income Taxes Payable account and (*b*) the later January 20 payment of the fourth-quarter taxes.

Check   (1) $3,610

Lenny Florita, an unmarried employee, works 48 hours in the week ended January 12. His pay rate is $14 per hour, and his wages have deductions for FICA Social Security, FICA Medicare, and federal income taxes. He claims two withholding allowances.

Compute his regular pay, overtime pay (Lenny earns $21 per hour for each hour over 40 per week), and gross pay. Then compute his FICA tax deduction (6.2% for the Social Security portion and 1.45% for the Medicare portion), income tax deduction (use the wage bracket withholding table from Exhibit 9A.6), total deductions, and net pay. Round tax amounts to the nearest cent.

Exercise 9-18ᴬ
Computing gross and net pay
P5

Check   Net pay, $596.30

Stark Company has five employees. Employees paid by the hour earn $10 per hour for the regular 40-hour workweek and $15 per hour beyond the 40 hours per week. Hourly employees are paid every two weeks, but salaried employees are paid monthly on the last biweekly payday of each month. FICA Social Security taxes are 6.2% of the first $128,400 paid to each employee, and FICA Medicare taxes are 1.45% of gross pay. FUTA taxes are 0.6% and SUTA taxes are 5.4% of the first $7,000 paid to each employee. The company has a benefits plan that includes medical insurance, life insurance, and retirement funding for employees. Under this plan, employees must contribute 5% of their gross income as a payroll withholding, which the company matches with *double* the amount. Following is the partially completed payroll register for the biweekly period ending August 31, which is the last payday of August.

Exercise 9-19ᴬ
Preparing payroll register and related entries
P5

Employee	Cumulative Pay (Excludes Current Period)	Current-Period Gross Pay			FIT	FUTA	FICA-SS_EE	FICA-Med_EE	EE-Ben_Plan Withholding	Employee Net Pay (Current Period)
		Pay Type	Pay Hours	Gross Pay	SIT	SUTA	FICA-SS_ER	FICA-Med_ER	ER-Ben_Plan Expense	
Kathleen	$126,600.00	Salary	—	$7,000.00	$2,000.00					
					300.00					
Anthony	6,800.00	Salary	—	500.00	80.00				25.00	
					20.00				50.00	
Nichole	15,100.00	Regular	80		110.00					
		Overtime	8		25.00					
Zoey	6,500.00	Regular	80		100.00					
		Overtime	4		22.00					
Gracie	5,000.00	Regular	74	740.00	90.00					
		Overtime	0	0.00	21.00					
Totals	$160,000.00				2,380.00					
					388.00					

Note: Table abbreviations follow those in Exhibit 9A.3; "Ben_Plan" refers to employee (EE) withholding or the employer (ER) expense for the benefits plan.

a. Complete this payroll register by filling in all cells for the pay period ended August 31. *Hint:* See Exhibit 9A.5 for guidance. Round amounts to cents.

b. Prepare the August 31 journal entry to record the accrued biweekly payroll and related liabilities for deductions.

c. Prepare the August 31 journal entry to record the employer's cash payment of the net payroll of part *b*.

d. Prepare the August 31 journal entry to record the employer's payroll taxes including the contribution to the benefits plan.

e. Prepare the August 31 journal entry to pay all liabilities (except for the net payroll in part *c*) for this biweekly period.

PROBLEM SET A

Problem 9-1A
Short-term notes payable
transactions and entries

P1

Tyrell Co. entered into the following transactions involving short-term liabilities.

Year 1

Apr. 20	Purchased $40,250 of merchandise on credit from Locust, terms n/30.
May 19	Replaced the April 20 account payable to Locust with a 90-day, 10%, $35,000 note payable along with paying $5,250 in cash.
July 8	Borrowed $80,000 cash from NBR Bank by signing a 120-day, 9%, $80,000 note payable.
?	Paid the amount due on the note to Locust at the maturity date.
?	Paid the amount due on the note to NBR Bank at the maturity date.
Nov. 28	Borrowed $42,000 cash from Fargo Bank by signing a 60-day, 8%, $42,000 note payable.
Dec. 31	Recorded an adjusting entry for accrued interest on the note to Fargo Bank.

Year 2

?	Paid the amount due on the note to Fargo Bank at the maturity date.

Required

Check   (2) Locust, $875

(3) $308

(4) $252

1. Determine the maturity date for each of the three notes described.

2. Determine the interest due at maturity for each of the three notes. Assume a 360-day year.

3. Determine the interest expense recorded in the adjusting entry at the end of Year 1.

4. Determine the interest expense recorded in Year 2.

5. Prepare journal entries for all the preceding transactions and events.

Problem 9-2A
Entries for payroll
transactions

P2   P3

On January 8, the end of the first weekly pay period of the year, Regis Company's employees earned $22,760 of office salaries and $65,840 of sales salaries. Withholdings from the employees' salaries include FICA Social Security taxes at the rate of 6.2%, FICA Medicare taxes at the rate of 1.45%, $12,860 of federal income taxes, $1,340 of medical insurance deductions, and $840 of union dues. No employee earned more than $7,000 in this first period.

Required

Check   (1) Cr. Salaries
Payable, $66,782.10

(2) Dr. Payroll Taxes Expense,
$12,093.90

1. Calculate FICA Social Security taxes payable and FICA Medicare taxes payable. Prepare the journal entry to record Regis Company's January 8 *employee* payroll expenses and liabilities. Round amounts to cents.

2. Prepare the journal entry to record Regis's *employer* payroll taxes resulting from the January 8 payroll. Regis's state unemployment tax rate is 5.4% of the first $7,000 paid to each employee. The federal unemployment tax rate is 0.6%. Round amounts to cents.

Problem 9-3A
Payroll expenses,
withholdings, and taxes

P2   P3

Paloma Co. has four employees. FICA Social Security taxes are 6.2% of the first $128,400 paid to each employee, and FICA Medicare taxes are 1.45% of gross pay. Also, for the first $7,000 paid to each employee, the company's FUTA taxes are 0.6% and SUTA taxes are 5.4%. The company is preparing its payroll calculations for the week ended August 25. Payroll records show the following information for the company's four employees.

	A	B	C	D
1		**Gross Pay**	**Current Week**	
2	**Name**	**through Aug. 18**	**Gross Pay**	**Income Tax Withholding**
3	Dali	$127,300	$2,000	$284
4	Trey	127,500	900	145
5	Kiesha	6,900	450	39
6	Chee	1,250	400	30

In addition to gross pay, the company must pay two-thirds of the $60 per employee weekly health insurance; each employee pays the remaining one-third. The company also contributes an extra 8% of each employee's gross pay (at no cost to employees) to a pension fund.

Required

Compute the following for the week ended August 25 (round amounts to the nearest cent):

1. Each employee's FICA withholdings for Social Security.

2. Each employee's FICA withholdings for Medicare.

Check   (3) $176.70

3. Employer's FICA taxes for Social Security.

4. Employer's FICA taxes for Medicare.

5. Employer's FUTA taxes.

6. Employer's SUTA taxes.

7. Each employee's net (take-home) pay.

8. Employer's total payroll-related expense for each employee.

(4) $54.38

(5) $3.00

(7) Total net pay, $2,940.92

On October 29, Lobo Co. began operations by purchasing razors for resale. The razors have a 90-day warranty. When a razor is returned, the company discards it and mails a new one from merchandise inventory to the customer. The company's cost per new razor is $20 and its retail selling price is $75. The company expects warranty costs to equal 8% of dollar sales. The following transactions occurred.

Problem 9-4A
Estimating warranty expense and liability
P4

Nov. 11   Sold 105 razors for $7,875 cash.
    30   Recognized warranty expense related to November sales with an adjusting entry.
Dec. 9   Replaced 15 razors that were returned under the warranty.
    16   Sold 220 razors for $16,500 cash.
    29   Replaced 30 razors that were returned under the warranty.
    31   Recognized warranty expense related to December sales with an adjusting entry.

Jan. 5   Sold 150 razors for $11,250 cash.
    17   Replaced 50 razors that were returned under the warranty.
    31   Recognized warranty expense related to January sales with an adjusting entry.

Required

1. Prepare journal entries to record these transactions and adjustments.

2. How much warranty expense is reported for November and for December?

3. How much warranty expense is reported for January?

4. What is the balance of the Estimated Warranty Liability account as of December 31?

5. What is the balance of the Estimated Warranty Liability account as of January 31?

Check (3) $900

(4) $1,050 Cr.

(5) $950 Cr.

Shown here are condensed income statements for two different companies (assume no income taxes).

Problem 9-5A
Computing and analyzing times interest earned
A1

Miller Company	
Sales	$1,000,000
Variable expenses (80%)	800,000
Income before interest	200,000
Interest expense (fixed)	60,000
Net income	$ 140,000

Weaver Company	
Sales	$1,000,000
Variable expenses (60%)	600,000
Income before interest	400,000
Interest expense (fixed)	260,000
Net income	$ 140,000

Required

1. Compute times interest earned for Miller Company and for Weaver Company.

2. What happens to each company's net income if sales increase by 30%?

3. What happens to each company's net income if sales increase by 50%?

4. What happens to each company's net income if sales decrease by 10%?

5. What happens to each company's net income if sales decrease by 40%?

Check (2) Miller net income, $200,000 (43% increase)

(4) Weaver net income, $100,000 (29% decrease)

Analysis Component

6. Which company would have a greater ability to pay interest expense if sales were to decrease?

Francisco Company has 10 employees, each of whom earns $2,800 per month and is paid on the last day of each month. All 10 have been employed continuously at this amount since January 1. On March 1, the following accounts and balances exist in its general ledger.

Problem 9-6A[A]
Entries for payroll transactions
P5

a. FICA—Social Security Taxes Payable, $3,472; FICA—Medicare Taxes Payable, $812. (The balances of these accounts represent total liabilities for *both* the employer's and employees' FICA taxes for the February payroll only.)

b. Employees' Federal Income Taxes Payable, $4,000 (liability for February only).

c. Federal Unemployment Taxes Payable, $336 (liability for January and February together).

d. State Unemployment Taxes Payable, $3,024 (liability for January and February together).

[continued on next page]

The company had the following payroll transactions.

Mar. 15   Issued check payable to Swift Bank, a federal depository bank authorized to accept employers' payments of FICA taxes and employee income tax withholdings. The $8,284 check is in payment of the February FICA and employee income taxes.

Check   March 31: Salaries
Payable, $21,858

31   Recorded the journal entry for the March salaries payable. Then recorded the cash payment of the March payroll (the company issued checks payable to each employee in payment of the March payroll). The payroll register shows the following summary totals for the March pay period.

	Salaries				Federal	
Office Salaries	Shop Salaries	Gross Pay	FICA Taxes*	Income Taxes	Net Pay
$11,200	$16,800	$28,000	$1,736	$4,000	$21,858
			$ 406		

*FICA taxes are Social Security and Medicare, respectively.

March 31: Dr. Payroll Taxes
Expense, $2,982

31   Recorded the employer's payroll taxes resulting from the March payroll. The company has a state unemployment tax rate of 5.4% on the first $7,000 paid to each employee. The federal rate is 0.6%.

April 15: Cr. Cash, $8,284
(Swift Bank)

Apr. 15   Issued check to Swift Bank in payment of the March FICA and employee income taxes.

15   Issued check to the State Tax Commission for the January, February, and March state unemployment taxes. Filed the check and the first-quarter tax return with the Commission.

30   Issued check payable to Swift Bank in payment of the employer's FUTA taxes for the first quarter of the year.

30   Filed Form 941 with the IRS, reporting the FICA taxes and the employees' federal income tax withholdings for the first quarter.

Required

Prepare journal entries to record these transactions and events.

PROBLEM SET B

Warner Co. entered into the following transactions involving short-term liabilities.

Problem 9-1B
Short-term notes payable transactions and entries

P1

Year 1

Apr. 22   Purchased $5,000 of merchandise on credit from Fox-Pro, terms n/30.

May 23   Replaced the April 22 account payable to Fox-Pro with a 60-day, 15% $4,600 note payable along with paying $400 in cash.

July 15   Borrowed $12,000 cash from Spring Bank by signing a 120-day, 10%, $12,000 note payable.

___?___   Paid the amount due on the note to Fox-Pro at maturity.

___?___   Paid the amount due on the note to Spring Bank at maturity.

Dec. 6   Borrowed $8,000 cash from City Bank by signing a 45-day, 9%, $8,000 note payable.

31   Recorded an adjusting entry for accrued interest on the note to City Bank.

Year 2

___?___   Paid the amount due on the note to City Bank at maturity.

Required

Check   (2) Fox-Pro, $115

(3) $50

(4) $40

1. Determine the maturity date for each of the three notes described.
2. Determine the interest due at maturity for each of the three notes. Assume a 360-day year.
3. Determine the interest expense recorded in the adjusting entry at the end of Year 1.
4. Determine the interest expense recorded in Year 2.
5. Prepare journal entries for all the preceding transactions and events.

Problem 9-2B
Entries for payroll transactions

P2   P3

Tavella Company's first weekly pay period of the year ends on January 8. On that date, Tavella's sales employees earned $34,745, office employees earned $21,225, and delivery employees earned $1,030 in salaries. The employees are to have withheld from their salaries FICA Social Security taxes at the rate of 6.2%, FICA Medicare taxes at the rate of 1.45%, $8,625 of federal income taxes, $1,160 of medical insurance deductions, and $138 of union dues. No employee earned more than $7,000 in the first pay period.

Required

1. Calculate FICA Social Security taxes payable and FICA Medicare taxes payable. Prepare the journal entry to record Tavella Company's January 8 *employee* payroll expenses and liabilities. Round amounts to cents.

2. Prepare the journal entry to record Tavella's *employer* payroll taxes resulting from the January 8 payroll. Tavella's state unemployment tax rate is 5.4% of the first $7,000 paid to each employee. The federal unemployment tax rate is 0.6%. Round amounts to cents.

Check (1) Cr. Salaries Payable, $42,716.50

(2) Dr. Payroll Taxes Expense, $7,780.50

Fishing Guides Co. has four employees. FICA Social Security taxes are 6.2% of the first $128,400 paid to each employee, and FICA Medicare taxes are 1.45% of gross pay. Also, for the first $7,000 paid to each employee, the company's FUTA taxes are 0.6% and SUTA taxes are 5.4%. The company is preparing its payroll calculations for the week ended September 30. Payroll records show the following information for the company's four employees.

Problem 9-3B
Payroll expenses, withholdings, and taxes
P2 P3

	A	B	C	D
1		Gross Pay	Current Week	
2	Name	through Sep. 23	Gross Pay	Income Tax Withholding
3	Ahmed	$126,800	$2,500	$198
4	Carlos	126,885	1,515	182
5	Jun	6,650	475	32
6	Marie	23,700	1,000	68

In addition to gross pay, the company must pay 60% of the $50 per employee weekly health insurance; each employee pays the remaining 40%. The company also contributes an extra 5% of each employee's gross pay (at no cost to employees) to a pension fund.

Required

Compute the following for the week ended September 30 (round amounts to the nearest cent):

1. Each employee's FICA withholdings for Social Security.

2. Each employee's FICA withholdings for Medicare.

3. Employer's FICA taxes for Social Security.

4. Employer's FICA taxes for Medicare.

5. Employer's FUTA taxes.

6. Employer's SUTA taxes.

7. Each employee's net (take-home) pay.

8. Employer's total payroll-related expense for each employee.

Check (3) $284.58

(4) $79.61

(5) $2.10

(7) Total net pay, $4,565.81

On November 10, Lee Co. began operations by purchasing coffee grinders for resale. The grinders have a 60-day warranty. When a grinder is returned, the company discards it and mails a new one from merchandise inventory to the customer. The company's cost per new grinder is $24 and its retail selling price is $50. The company expects warranty costs to equal 10% of dollar sales. The following transactions occurred.

Problem 9-4B
Estimating warranty expense and liability
P4

Nov. 16 Sold 50 grinders for $2,500 cash.
    30 Recognized warranty expense related to November sales with an adjusting entry.
Dec. 12 Replaced six grinders that were returned under the warranty.
    18 Sold 200 grinders for $10,000 cash.
    28 Replaced 17 grinders that were returned under the warranty.
    31 Recognized warranty expense related to December sales with an adjusting entry.

Jan. 7 Sold 40 grinders for $2,000 cash.
    21 Replaced 36 grinders that were returned under the warranty.
    31 Recognized warranty expense related to January sales with an adjusting entry.

Required

1. Prepare journal entries to record these transactions and adjustments.

2. How much warranty expense is reported for November and for December?

3. How much warranty expense is reported for January?

4. What is the balance of the Estimated Warranty Liability account as of December 31?

5. What is the balance of the Estimated Warranty Liability account as of January 31?

Check (3) $200

(4) $698 Cr.

(5) $34 Cr.

Problem 9-5B
Computing and analyzing
times interest earned

A1

Shown here are condensed income statements for two different companies (assume no income taxes).

Ellis Company	
Sales	$240,000
Variable expenses (50%)	120,000
Income before interest.............	120,000
Interest expense (fixed)	90,000
Net income	$ 30,000

Seidel Company	
Sales	$240,000
Variable expenses (75%)	180,000
Income before interest.............	60,000
Interest expense (fixed)	30,000
Net income	$ 30,000

Required

1. Compute times interest earned for Ellis Company and for Seidel Company.
2. What happens to each company's net income if sales increase by 10%?
3. What happens to each company's net income if sales increase by 40%?
4. What happens to each company's net income if sales decrease by 20%?
5. What happens to each company's net income if sales decrease by 50%?

Check (3) Ellis net income, $78,000 (160% increase) (4) Seidel net income, $18,000 (40% decrease)

Analysis Component

6. Which company would have a greater ability to pay interest expense if sales were to decrease?

Problem 9-6B[A]
Entries for payroll
transactions

P5

MLS Company has five employees, each of whom earns $1,600 per month and is paid on the last day of each month. All five have been employed continuously at this amount since January 1. On June 1, the following accounts and balances exist in its general ledger.

a. FICA—Social Security Taxes Payable, $992; FICA—Medicare Taxes Payable, $232. (The balances of these accounts represent total liabilities for *both* the employer's and employees' FICA taxes for the May payroll only.)
b. Employees' Federal Income Taxes Payable, $1,050 (liability for May only).
c. Federal Unemployment Taxes Payable, $66 (liability for April and May together).
d. State Unemployment Taxes Payable, $594 (liability for April and May together).

The company had the following payroll transactions.

June 15 Issued check payable to Security Bank, a federal depository bank authorized to accept employers' payments of FICA taxes and employee income tax withholdings. The $2,274 check is in payment of the May FICA and employee income taxes.

Check June 30: Cr. Salaries Payable, $6,338

30 Recorded the journal entry for the June salaries payable. Then recorded the cash payment of the June payroll (the company issued checks payable to each employee in payment of the June payroll). The payroll register shows the following summary totals for the June pay period.

	Salaries					
Office Salaries	Shop Salaries	Gross Pay	FICA Taxes*	Federal Income Taxes	Net Pay
$3,800	$4,200	$8,000	$496	$1,050	$6,338
			$116		

*FICA taxes are Social Security and Medicare, respectively.

Check June 30: Dr. Payroll Taxes Expense, $612

July 15: Cr. Cash, $2,274 (Security Bank)

30 Recorded the employer's payroll taxes resulting from the June payroll. The company has a state unemployment tax rate of 5.4% on the first $7,000 paid to each employee. The federal rate is 0.6%.
July 15 Issued check payable to Security Bank in payment of the June FICA and employee income taxes.
15 Issued check to the State Tax Commission for the April, May, and June state unemployment taxes. Filed the check and the second-quarter tax return with the State Tax Commission.
31 Issued check payable to Security Bank in payment of the employer's FUTA taxes for the first quarter of the year.
31 Filed Form 941 with the IRS, reporting the FICA taxes and the employees' federal income tax withholdings for the second quarter.

Required

Prepare journal entries to record the transactions and events.

This serial problem began in Chapter 1 and continues through most of the book. If previous chapter segments were not completed, the serial problem can begin at this point.

SERIAL PROBLEM
Business Solutions

C2 P2 P3

SP 9 Review the February 26 and March 25 transactions for **Business Solutions** (SP 4) from Chapter 4.

Feb. 26 The company paid cash to Lyn Addie for eight days' work at $125 per day.

Mar. 25 The company sold merchandise with a $2,002 cost for $2,800 on credit to Wildcat Services, invoice dated March 25.

Required

1. Assume that Lyn Addie is an unmarried employee. Her $1,000 of wages have deductions for FICA Social Security taxes, FICA Medicare taxes, and federal income taxes. Her federal income taxes for this pay period total $159. Compute her net pay for the eight days' work paid on February 26. Round amounts to the nearest cent.

2. Record the journal entry to reflect the payroll payment to Lyn Addie as computed in part 1.

3. Record the journal entry to reflect the (employer) payroll tax expenses for the February 26 payroll payment. Assume Lyn Addie has not met earnings limits for FUTA and SUTA (the FUTA rate is 0.6% and the SUTA rate is 5.4% for the company). Round amounts to the nearest cent.

4. Record the entry(ies) for the merchandise sold on March 25 if a 4% sales tax rate applies.

©Alexander Image/Shutterstock

CP 9 Bug-Off Exterminators provides pest control services and sells extermination products manufactured by other companies. The following six-column table contains the company's unadjusted trial balance as of December 31, 2019.

COMPREHENSIVE PROBLEM

Bug-Off Exterminators
(Review of Chapters 1–9)

December 31, 2019	Unadjusted Trial Balance		Adjustments		Adjusted Trial Balance	
Cash	$ 17,000					
Accounts receivable	4,000					
Allowance for doubtful accounts		$ 828				
Merchandise inventory	11,700					
Trucks	32,000					
Accum. depreciation—Trucks		0				
Equipment	45,000					
Accum. depreciation—Equipment		12,200				
Accounts payable		5,000				
Estimated warranty liability		1,400				
Unearned services revenue		0				
Interest payable		0				
Long-term notes payable		15,000				
Common stock		10,000				
Retained earnings		49,700				
Dividends	10,000					
Extermination services revenue		60,000				
Interest revenue		872				
Sales (of merchandise)		71,026				
Cost of goods sold	46,300					
Depreciation expense—Trucks	0					
Depreciation expense—Equipment	0					
Wages expense	35,000					
Interest expense	0					
Rent expense	9,000					
Bad debts expense	0					
Miscellaneous expense	1,226					
Repairs expense	8,000					
Utilities expense	6,800					
Warranty expense	0					
Totals	$226,026	$226,026				

The following information in *a* through *h* applies to the company at the end of the current year.

a. The bank reconciliation as of December 31, 2019, includes the following facts.

Cash balance per bank	$15,100	Deposit in transit.....................	$2,450
Cash balance per books.............	17,000	Interest earned (on bank account).............	52
Outstanding checks	1,800	Bank service charges (miscellaneous expense)	15

Reported on the bank statement is a canceled check that the company failed to record. (Information from the bank reconciliation allows you to determine the amount of this check, which is a payment on an account payable.)

b. An examination of customers' accounts shows that accounts totaling $679 should be written off as uncollectible. Using an aging of receivables, the company determines that the ending balance of the Allowance for Doubtful Accounts should be $700.

c. A truck is purchased and placed in service on January 1, 2019. Its cost is being depreciated with the straight-line method using the following facts and estimates.

Original cost.......	$32,000	Expected salvage value	$8,000	Useful life (years)	4

d. Two items of equipment (a sprayer and an injector) were purchased and put into service in early January 2017. They are being depreciated with the straight-line method using these facts and estimates.

	Sprayer	Injector
Original cost	$27,000	$18,000
Expected salvage value	$ 3,000	$ 2,500
Useful life (years)	8	5

e. On August 1, 2019, the company is paid $3,840 cash in advance to provide monthly service for an apartment complex for one year. The company began providing the services in August. When the cash was received, the full amount was credited to the Extermination Services Revenue account.

f. The company offers a warranty for the services it sells. The expected cost of providing warranty service is 2.5% of the extermination services revenue of $57,760 for 2019. No warranty expense has been recorded for 2019. All costs of servicing warranties in 2019 were properly debited to the Estimated Warranty Liability account.

g. The $15,000 long-term note is an 8%, five-year, interest-bearing note with interest payable annually on December 31. The note was signed with First National Bank on December 31, 2019.

h. The ending inventory of merchandise is counted and determined to have a cost of $11,700. Bug-Off uses a perpetual inventory system.

Required

1. Use the preceding information to determine amounts for the following items.

Check (1*a*) Reconciled cash bal. $15,750
(1*b*) $551 credit

   a. Correct (reconciled) ending balance of Cash; and the amount of the omitted check.

   b. Adjustment needed to obtain the correct ending balance of the Allowance for Doubtful Accounts.

   c. Depreciation expense for the truck used during year 2019.

   d. Depreciation expense for the two items of equipment used during year 2019.

   e. The adjusted 2019 ending balances of the Extermination Services Revenue and Unearned Services Revenue accounts.

(1*f*) Estimated Warranty Liability, $2,844 Cr.

   f. The adjusted 2019 ending balances of the Warranty Expense and the Estimated Warranty Liability accounts.

   g. The adjusted 2019 ending balances of the Interest Expense and the Interest Payable accounts. (Round amounts to nearest whole dollar.)

(2) Adjusted trial balance totals, $238,207

2. Use the results of part 1 to complete the six-column table by first entering the appropriate adjustments for items *a* through *g* and then completing the Adjusted Trial Balance columns. *Hint:* Item *b* requires two adjustments.

3. Prepare journal entries to record the adjustments entered on the six-column table. Assume Bug-Off's adjusted balance for Merchandise Inventory matches the year-end physical count.

(4) Net income, $9,274; Total assets, $82,771

4. Prepare a single-step income statement, a statement of retained earnings (cash dividends during 2019 were $10,000), and a classified balance sheet.

GL 9-1   General Ledger assignment GL 9-1, based on Problem 9-1A, focuses on transactions related to accounts and notes payable and highlights the impact each transaction has on interest expense, if any. Prepare the journal entries related to accounts and notes payable; the schedules for accounts payable and notes payable are automatically completed using the **General Ledger** tool. Compute both the amount and timing of interest expense for each note. Prepare the subsequent-period journal entries related to accrued interest.

**GENERAL
LEDGER
PROBLEM**

Accounting Analysis

AA 9-1   Use the table below and **Apple**'s financial statements in Appendix A to answer the following.

**COMPANY
ANALYSIS**

A1   P4

APPLE

$ millions	2017	2016	2015
Interest expense.........	$2,323	$1,456	$733

1. Compute times interest earned for each of the three years shown.
2. Is Apple in a good or bad position to pay interest obligations? Assume an industry average of 10.
3. Identify Apple's total accrued expenses in 2017.

AA 9-2   Key figures for **Apple** and **Google** follow.

**COMPARATIVE
ANALYSIS**

A1

**APPLE
GOOGLE**

$ millions	Apple Current Year	Apple One Year Prior	Apple Two Years Prior	Google Current Year	Google One Year Prior	Google Two Years Prior
Net income	$48,351	$45,687	$53,394	$12,662	$19,478	$16,348
Income taxes...........	15,738	15,685	19,121	14,531	4,672	3,303
Interest expense........	2,323	1,456	733	109	124	104

Required

1. Compute times interest earned for the three years' data shown for each company.
2. In the current year, and using times interest earned, which company appears better able to pay interest obligations?
3. In the current year, and using times interest earned, is the company in a good or bad position to pay interest obligations for (*a*) Apple and (*b*) Google? Assume an industry average of 10.

AA 9-3   Comparative figures for **Samsung**, **Apple**, and **Google** follow.

GLOBAL ANALYSIS

A1

**Samsung
APPLE
GOOGLE**

In millions	Samsung Current Year	Samsung Prior Year	Apple Current Year	Apple Prior Year	Google Current Year	Google Prior Year
Net income.....................	₩42,186,747	₩22,726,092	$48,351	$45,687	$12,662	$19,478
Income taxes	14,009,220	7,987,560	15,738	15,685	14,531	4,672
Interest expense	655,402	587,831	2,323	1,456	109	124

Required

1. Compute the times interest earned ratio for the most recent two years for Samsung using the data shown.
2. Is the change in Samsung's times interest earned ratio favorable or unfavorable?
3. In the current year, is Samsung's times interest earned ratio better or worse than the same ratio for (*a*) Apple and (*b*) Google?

Beyond the Numbers

ETHICS CHALLENGE

P4

BTN 9-1 Cameron Bly is a sales manager for an automobile dealership. He earns a bonus each year based on revenue from the number of autos sold in the year less related warranty expenses. Actual warranty expenses have varied over the prior 10 years from a low of 3% of an automobile's selling price to a high of 10%. In the past, Bly has tended to estimate warranty expenses on the high end to be conservative. He must work with the dealership's accountant at year-end to arrive at the warranty expense accrual for cars sold each year.

1. Does the warranty accrual decision create any ethical dilemma for Bly?
2. Because warranty expenses vary, what percent do you think Bly should choose for the current year? Justify your response.

COMMUNICATING IN PRACTICE

C3

BTN 9-2 Dusty Johnson is the accounting and finance manager for a manufacturer. At year-end, he must determine how to account for the company's contingencies. His manager, Tom Pretti, objects to Johnson's proposal to recognize an expense and a liability for warranty service on units of a new product introduced in the fourth quarter. Pretti comments, "There's no way we can estimate this warranty cost. We don't owe anyone anything until a product fails and it is returned. Let's report an expense if and when we do any warranty work."

Required

Prepare a one-page memorandum for Johnson to send to Pretti defending his proposal.

TAKING IT TO THE NET

C1   A1

BTN 9-3 Access the March 1, 2017, filing of the December 31, 2016, annual 10-K report of **McDonald's Corporation** (ticker: MCD), which is available from **SEC.gov**.

Required

1. Identify the current liabilities on McDonald's balance sheet as of December 31, 2016.
2. Use the consolidated statement of income for the year ended December 31, 2016, to compute McDonald's times interest earned ratio. Comment on the result. Assume an industry average of 5.0.

TEAMWORK IN ACTION

C2   P1

BTN 9-4 Assume that your team is in business and you must borrow $6,000 cash for short-term needs. You have been shopping banks for a loan, and you have the following two options.

A. Sign a $6,000, 90-day, 10% interest-bearing note dated June 1.
B. Sign a $6,000, 120-day, 8% interest-bearing note dated June 1.

Required

1. Discuss these two options and determine the better choice. Ensure that all teammates concur with the decision and understand the rationale.
2. Each member of the team is to prepare *one* of the following journal entries.
   a. Option A—at date of issuance.
   b. Option B—at date of issuance.
   c. Option A—at maturity date.
   d. Option B—at maturity date.
3. In rotation, each member is to explain to the team the entry he or she prepared in part 2. Ensure that all team members concur with and understand the entries.
4. Assume that the funds are borrowed on December 1 (instead of June 1) and your business operates on a calendar-year reporting period. Each member of the team is to prepare *one* of the following entries.
   a. Option A—the year-end adjustment.
   b. Option B—the year-end adjustment.
   c. Option A—at maturity date.
   d. Option B—at maturity date.
5. In rotation, each member is to explain to the team the entry he or she prepared in part 4. Ensure that all team members concur with and understand the entries.

BTN 9-5   Review the chapter's opening feature about Tim Westergren and the business he founded, **Pandora**. Assume that he is considering expanding the business to Europe and that the current abbreviated income statement appears as follows.

| PANDORA |
| Income Statement |
| For Year Ended December 31 |

Sales	$1,000,000
Operating expenses (55%)	550,000
Net income	$ 450,000

ENTREPRENEURIAL DECISION

A1

Assume also that the company currently has no interest-bearing debt. If it expands to Europe, it will require a $300,000 loan. The company has found a bank that will loan it the money on a 7% note payable. The company believes that, at least for the first few years, sales in Europe will equal $250,000 and that all expenses at both locations will continue to equal 55% of sales.

Required

1. Prepare an income statement (showing three separate columns for current operations, European, and total) for the company assuming that it borrows the funds and expands to Europe. Annual revenues for current operations are expected to remain at $1,000,000.
2. Compute the company's times interest earned under the expansion assumptions in part 1.
3. Assume sales in Europe are $400,000. Prepare an income statement (with columns for current operations, European, and total) for the company and compute times interest earned.
4. Assume sales in Europe are $100,000. Prepare an income statement (with columns for current operations, European, and total) for the company and compute times interest earned.
5. Comment on your results from parts 1 through 4.

BTN 9-6   Check the Social Security Administration website (SSA.gov) to locate the Social Security office near you. Visit the office to request a personal earnings and estimate form. Fill out the form and mail according to the instructions. You will receive a statement from the Social Security Administration regarding your earnings history and future Social Security benefits you can receive. (Formerly the request could be made online. The online service has been discontinued and is now under review by the Social Security Administration due to security concerns; however, it might once again be available online.) It is good to request an earnings and benefit statement every 5 to 10 years to make sure you have received credit for all wages earned and for which you and your employer have paid taxes into the system.

HITTING THE ROAD

P2

10 Accounting for Long-Term Liabilities

Chapter Preview

BOND BASICS

A1 Bond financing

Bond trading

P1 Par bonds

NTK 10-1

DISCOUNT BONDS

Discount or premium

P2 Bond payments

Amortize discount

Straight-line

NTK 10-2

PREMIUM BONDS

P3 Bond payments

Amortize premium

Straight-line

P4 Bond retirement

NTK 10-3

LONG-TERM NOTES

C1 Recording notes

DEBT ANALYSIS

A2 Debt features

A3 Debt-to-equity

NTK 10-4

Learning Objectives

CONCEPTUAL

C1 Explain the types of notes and prepare entries to account for notes.

C2 *Appendix 10A*—Explain and compute bond pricing.

C3 *Appendix 10C*—Describe accounting for leases and pensions.

ANALYTICAL

A1 Compare bond financing with stock financing.

A2 Assess debt features and their implications.

A3 Compute the debt-to-equity ratio and explain its use.

PROCEDURAL

P1 Record issuance and interest expense for par bonds.

P2 Record issuance and amortization of discount bonds using the straight-line method.

P3 Record issuance and amortization of premium bonds using the straight-line method.

P4 Record the retirement of bonds.

P5 *Appendix 10B*—Compute and record amortization of a bond discount using the effective interest method.

P6 *Appendix 10B*—Compute and record amortization of a bond premium using the effective interest method.

At Face Value

"Believe in your product"—**SCOTT BORBA**

OAKLAND, CA—Joey Shamah, a college student, met Scott Borba at a party. The two men talked at length, but it was not your typical "party" talk. Instead, they discussed the women's cosmetics market!

Scott explains that he saw "all these women with Louis Vuitton purses . . . buying truckloads of lip balms and nail polishes" from 99 cent stores. "There's a major market here," insists Scott.

Joey and Scott agreed to work together to fill this market void by forming **e.l.f. Cosmetics** (**elfCosmetics.com**). "We felt women shouldn't have to skip lunch or not go out for dinner or have other cutbacks to afford makeup," recalls Joey.

As e.l.f. grows, Joey and Scott make decisions on how to finance that growth. Up to now, they have used a mix of long-term debt and equity.

Financing a large part of their business with long-term debt requires that Joey and Scott carefully manage liabilities. This is especially true with long-term financing from sources such as notes and bonds. They also know that retaining more equity in the business helped them personally when e.l.f. issued stock.

©Clemens Bilan/Douglas/Getty Images

Joey and Scott welcome the financial rewards, yet they insist e.l.f. is about making the consumer feel more confident. "The consumer feels better inside" from using e.l.f. products, claims Scott. "There's more of a glimmer."

Sources: *e.l.f. Cosmetics website,* January 2019; *CNN,* January 2006

BASICS OF BONDS

This section explains bonds and reasons for issuing them. Both for-profit and nonprofit companies, as well as governmental units, such as nations, states, cities, and schools, issue bonds.

Bond Financing

Projects that need a lot of money often are financed with bonds. A **bond** is its issuer's written promise to pay the par value of the bond with interest. The **par value of a bond,** or *face value,* is paid at a stated future date called the *maturity date.* Most bonds require the issuer to make semiannual (twice a year) interest payments. Interest is computed by multiplying the par value by the bond's contract rate.

A1

Compare bond financing with stock financing.

Advantages of Bonds   There are three main advantages of bond financing.

1. *Bonds do not affect owner control.* Equity affects ownership in a company, but bonds do not. A person who contributes $1,000 of a company's $10,000 equity financing typically controls one-tenth of the company. A person who owns a $1,000, 11%, 20-year bond has no ownership.

2. *Interest on bonds is tax deductible.* Bond interest payments are tax deductible, but distributions to owners are not. A corporation with no bond financing, $15,000 in pretax income, and a 40% tax rate pays $6,000 ($15,000 × 40%) in taxes. Instead, if it issues bonds and pays $10,000 in bond interest expense, then taxes paid are only $2,000 ([$15,000 − $10,000] × 40%).

3. *Bonds can increase return on equity.* A company that earns a higher return with borrowed funds than it pays in interest on those funds increases its return on equity. This process is called *financial leverage,* or *trading on the equity.*

To demonstrate the third point, consider Magnum Co., which has $1,000 in equity and is planning a $500 expansion ($ millions). Magnum predicts the expansion will increase income by $125 before paying interest. It currently earns $100 per year and has no interest expense. Magnum is considering three plans. Plan A is to not expand. Plan B is to expand and raise $500 from equity financing. Plan C is to expand and issue $500 of bonds that pay 10% annual interest ($50). Exhibit 10.1 shows how these plans affect net income, equity, and return on equity (Net

EXHIBIT 10.1

Financing with Bonds versus Equity

$ millions	Plan A: Do Not Expand	Plan B: Equity Financing	Plan C: Bond Financing
Income before interest expense	$ 100	$ 225	$ 225
Interest expense.	—	—	(50)
Net income	$ 100	$ 225	$ 175
Equity	$1,000	$1,500	$1,000
Return on equity	**10.0%**	**15.0%**	**17.5%**

Example: Compute return on equity for all three plans if Magnum is subject to a 40% income tax. *Answer* ($ mil.):

A = 6.0% ($100[1 − 0.4]/$1,000)

B = 9.0% ($225[1 − 0.4]/$1,500)

C = 10.5% ($175[1 − 0.4]/$1,000)

income/Equity). Magnum earns a higher return on equity under Plan C to issue bonds. Income under Plan C ($175) is smaller than under Plan B ($225), but the return on equity is larger because of less equity investment.

Disadvantages of Bonds   There are two main disadvantages of bond financing.

1. *Bonds can decrease return on equity.* When a company earns a lower return with the borrowed funds than it pays in interest, it decreases return on equity. This is more likely when a company has low income or losses.

Point: There are nearly 5 million individual U.S. bond issues, compared to about 12,000 individual U.S. stocks.

2. *Bonds require payment of both periodic interest and the par value at maturity.* Bond payments are a burden when income and cash flow are low. Equity does not require payments because withdrawals (dividends) are optional.

EXHIBIT 10.2

Bond Certificate

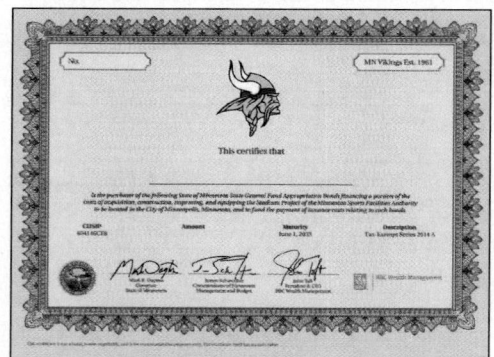

Courtesy of RBC Wealth Management

Bond Issuing

Bond issuances state the number of bonds authorized, their par value, and the contract interest rate. The legal contract between the issuer and the bondholders is called the **bond indenture.** A bondholder may receive a **bond certificate,** which is evidence of the company's debt—see Exhibit 10.2.

Bond Trading

A bond *issue* is the sale of bonds, usually in denominations of $1,000 or $5,000. After bonds are issued, they often are bought and sold among investors, meaning that a bond probably has had many owners before it matures. When bonds are bought and sold, they have a market value (price). Bond market values are shown as a percent of par (face) value. For example, a bond trading at 103½ is bought or sold for 103.5% of par value. A bond trading at 95 is bought or sold at 95% of par value.

Point: A bond with a par value of $1,000 trading at 103½ sells for $1,035 ($1,000 × 1.035).

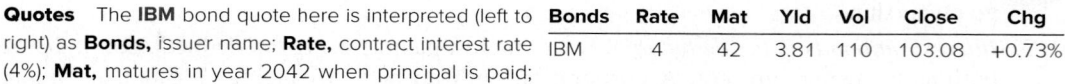

▮ Decision Insight

Quotes   The **IBM** bond quote here is interpreted (left to right) as **Bonds,** issuer name; **Rate,** contract interest rate (4%); **Mat,** matures in year 2042 when principal is paid; **Yld,** yield rate (3.81%) of bond at current price; **Vol,** dollar worth ($110,000) of trades (in 1,000s); **Close,** closing price (103.08) for the day as percentage of par value; **Chg,** change (+0.73%) in closing price from prior day's close. ▪

Bonds	Rate	Mat	Yld	Vol	Close	Chg
IBM	4	42	3.81	110	103.08	+0.73%

PAR BONDS

P1_____

Record issuance and interest expense for par bonds.

Bonds issued at par value are called **par bonds**. Assume **Nike** issues $100,000 of 8%, two-year bonds dated December 31, 2019, that mature on December 31, 2021, and pay interest semiannually each June 30 and December 31. If all bonds are sold at par value, Nike records the sale as follows.

Assets = Liabilities + Equity
+100,000   +100,000

Dec. 31, 2019	Cash	100,000	
	Bonds Payable.		100,000
	Sold bonds at par.		

Nike records the first semiannual interest payment as follows. The same entry is made *every* six months, including at the maturity date.

June 30, 2020	Bond Interest Expense	4,000	
	Cash		4,000
	Paid semiannual interest (8% × $100,000 × 1/2 year).		

Assets = Liabilities + Equity
−4,000   −4,000

When the bonds mature, Nike records its payment of principal as follows.

Dec. 31, 2021	Bonds Payable	100,000	
	Cash		100,000
	Paid bond principal at maturity.		

Assets = Liabilities + Equity
−100,000   −100,000

A company issues 8%, two-year bonds on December 31, 2019, with a par value of $7,000 and semiannual interest payments. On the issue date, the annual market rate for these bonds is 8%, which implies a selling price of $7,000. Prepare journal entries to record (a) the issuance of bonds on December 31, 2019; (b) the first through fourth interest payments on each June 30 and December 31; and (c) the maturity of the bonds on December 31, 2021.

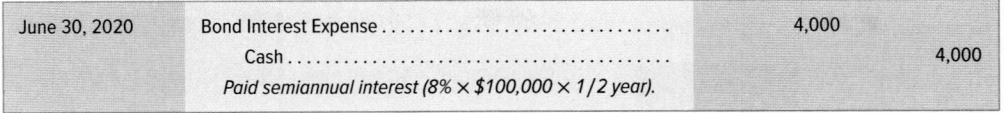

NEED-TO-KNOW 10-1

Recording Par Value Bonds

P1

Solution

a.

Dec. 31, 2019	Cash	7,000	
	Bonds Payable		7,000
	Sold bonds at par.		

b. The following entry is made for each of the four interest payments of June 30 and December 31 for both 2020 and 2021.

2020–2021	Bond Interest Expense	280	
June 30 and	Cash		280
Dec. 31	*Pay semiannual interest ($7,000 × 8% × 1/2).*		

c.

Dec. 31, 2021	Bonds Payable	7,000	
	Cash		7,000
	Record maturity and payment of bonds.		

Do More: QS 10-2, QS 10-3, E 10-2, E 10-3

DISCOUNT BONDS

This section covers bond issuances *below par,* called **discount bonds**.

Bond Discount or Premium

The bond issuer pays the bond interest rate, called the **contract rate** (also called *coupon rate, stated rate,* or *nominal rate*). The annual interest paid is computed by multiplying the bond par value by the contract rate. The contract rate is usually stated on an annual basis, even if interest is paid semiannually. For example, a $1,000, 8% bond paying interest semiannually pays annual interest of $80 (8% × $1,000) in two semiannual payments of $40 each.

The contract rate sets the interest paid in *cash,* which is not necessarily the *bond interest expense* for the issuer. Bond interest expense depends on the bond's market value at issuance. The bond's **market rate** of interest is the rate that borrowers are willing to pay and lenders are willing to accept for a bond and its risk level. As bond risk increases, the market rate increases to compensate bond purchasers.

EXHIBIT 10.3

Relation between Bond Issue Price, Contract Rate, and Market Rate

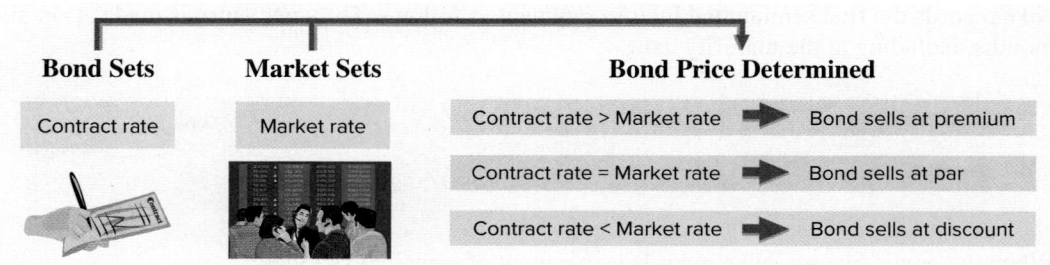

Bond Sets	Market Sets	Bond Price Determined	
Contract rate	Market rate	Contract rate > Market rate ➡	Bond sells at premium
		Contract rate = Market rate ➡	Bond sells at par
		Contract rate < Market rate ➡	Bond sells at discount

When the contract rate and market rate are equal, a bond sells at par value. If they are not equal, it is sold at a *premium* above par value or at a *discount* below par value. Exhibit 10.3 shows the relation between the contract rate, the market rate, and a bond's issue price.

Issuing Bonds at a Discount

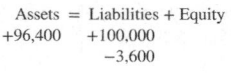

P2

Record issuance and amortization of discount bonds using the straight-line method.

A **discount on bonds payable** occurs when a company issues bonds with a contract rate less than the market rate. This means the issue price is less than par value—the issuer gets less money at issuance than what the issuer must pay back at maturity. Assume **Fila** issues bonds with a $100,000 par value, an 8% annual contract rate (paid semiannually), and a two-year life. These bonds sell at a discount price of 96.400 (meaning 96.400% of par value, or $96,400); we show how to compute bond prices in Appendix 10A.

Cash Payments with Discount Bonds   These bonds require Fila to pay

1. Par value of $100,000 cash at the end of the bonds' two-year life.
2. Semiannual cash interest payments of $4,000 ($100,000 × 8% × 1/2 year).

The pattern of cash receipts and payments for Fila bonds is shown in Exhibit 10.4.

EXHIBIT 10.4

Discount Bond Cash Receipts and Payments

$96,400 rec'd				$100,000	} $116,000 paid
	$4,000	$4,000	$4,000	$4,000	
0	6 mo.	12 mo.	18 mo.	24 mo.	

Recording Issuance of Discount Bonds   When Fila accepts $96,400 cash for its bonds on the issue date of December 31, 2019, it records the sale as follows.

Assets = Liabilities + Equity
+96,400   +100,000
            −3,600

Dec. 31, 2019	Cash	96,400	
	Discount on Bonds Payable	3,600	
	Bonds Payable		100,000
	Sold bonds at a discount on their issue date.		

Point: Book value at issuance always equals the issuer's cash borrowed.

Bonds payable are reported as a long-term liability on Fila's December 31, 2019, balance sheet as in Exhibit 10.5. A discount is subtracted from par value to get the **carrying (book) value of bonds.** Discount on Bonds Payable is a contra liability account.

EXHIBIT 10.5

Balance Sheet Presentation of Bond Discount

Long-term liabilities		
Bonds payable, 8%, due December 31, 2021	$100,000	
Less discount on bonds payable.....................	**3,600**	$96,400 ← Carrying (book) value

Amortizing Discount Bonds   Fila receives $96,400 for its bonds; in return it must pay bondholders $100,000 when the bonds mature in two years (plus four interest payments). Panel A in Exhibit 10.6 shows that the four $4,000 interest payments plus the $3,600 bond discount equals total bond interest expense of $19,600.

The total $19,600 bond interest expense is allocated over the four semiannual periods in the bonds' life, and the bonds' carrying value is updated at each balance sheet date. This is done using

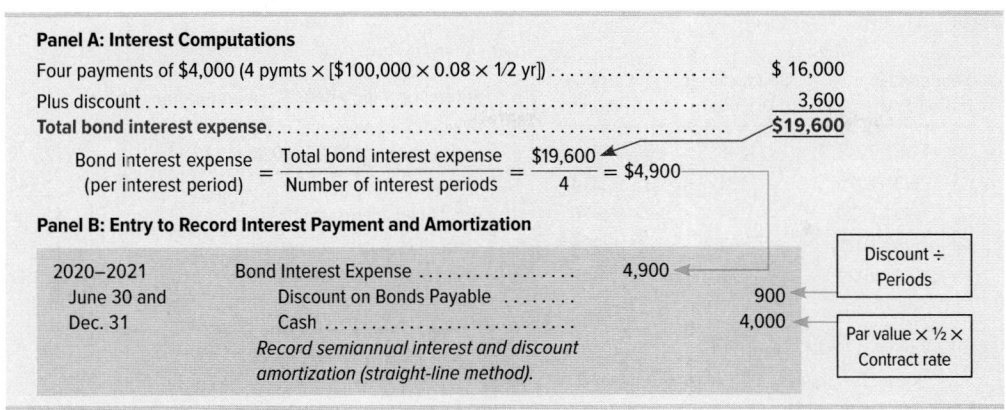

EXHIBIT 10.6

Interest Computation and Entry for Discount Bonds

Panel A: Interest Computations

Four payments of $4,000 (4 pymts × [$100,000 × 0.08 × 1/2 yr]) . . . . $ 16,000

Plus discount   3,600

Total bond interest expense. $19,600

$$\text{Bond interest expense (per interest period)} = \frac{\text{Total bond interest expense}}{\text{Number of interest periods}} = \frac{\$19,600}{4} = \$4,900$$

Panel B: Entry to Record Interest Payment and Amortization

2020–2021	Bond Interest Expense	4,900	
June 30 and	Discount on Bonds Payable		900
Dec. 31	Cash		4,000

Record semiannual interest and discount amortization (straight-line method).

Discount ÷ Periods

Par value × ½ × Contract rate

Bonds Payable

	12/31/2019	100,000
	6/30/2020	—
	12/31/2020	—
	6/30/2021	—
12/31/2021 100,000		
	12/31/2021	0

Discount on Bonds Payable

12/31/2019 3,600		
	6/30/2020	900
	12/31/2020	900
	6/30/2021	900
	12/31/2021	900
	12/31/2021	0

the straight-line method (or the effective interest method in Appendix 10B). Both methods reduce the bond discount to zero over the bond life. This process is called *amortizing a bond discount.*

Straight-Line Method   **Straight-line bond amortization** allocates equal bond interest expense to each interest period. We divide the total bond interest expense of $19,600 by 4 (number of semiannual periods in bonds' life). This gives a bond interest expense of $4,900 per period. Panel B of Exhibit 10.6 shows how the issuer records bond interest expense and updates the bond liability account at the end of *each* of the four semiannual interest periods (June 30, 2020, through December 31, 2021).

Exhibit 10.7 shows the pattern of decreases in the Discount on Bonds Payable account and the pattern of increases in the bonds' carrying value. Three points summarize the discount bonds' straight-line amortization.

Point: Another way to compute bond interest expense: (1) Divide the $3,600 discount by 4 periods to get $900 amortized each period. (2) Add $900 to the $4,000 cash payment to get bond interest expense of $4,900 per period.

EXHIBIT 10.7

Straight-Line Amortization of Bond Discount

Semiannual Period-End	Unamortized Discount*	Carrying Value†
(0) 12/31/2019	$3,600	$ 96,400
(1) 6/30/2020	2,700	97,300
(2) 12/31/2020	1,800	98,200
(3) 6/30/2021	900	99,100
(4) **12/31/2021**	**0**	**100,000**

*Total bond discount of $3,600 less accumulated periodic amortization of $900 per semiannual interest period.

†Bond par value of $100,000 less unamortized discount.

The columns always sum to par value for discount bonds.

1. At issuance, the $96,400 carrying value equals the $100,000 par value minus the $3,600 unamortized discount.

2. During the bonds' life, the (unamortized) discount decreases each period by the $900 amortization ($3,600/4), and carrying value (par value less unamortized discount) increases each period by $900.

3. At maturity, unamortized discount equals zero, and carrying value equals the $100,000 par value that the issuer pays the holder.

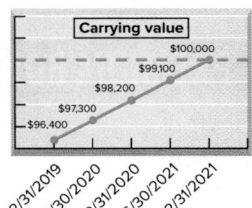

Point: Amortization always gets the carrying value of a bond closer to its par value.

▌ Decision Insight

Ratings Game   Many bond buyers rely on rating services such as **Standard & Poor's**, **Moody's**, and **Fitch** to assess bond risk. These services analyze financial statements and other factors in setting ratings. Standard & Poor's ratings, from best quality to default, are AAA, AA, A, BBB, BB, B, CCC, CC, C, and D. Bonds rated in the A and B range are referred to as *investment grade;* lower-rated bonds are considered riskier. ∎

A company issues 8%, two-year bonds on December 31, 2019, with a par value of $7,000 and semiannual interest payments. On the issue date, the annual market rate for these bonds is 10%, which implies a selling price of 96.46 or $6,752. (a) Prepare an amortization table like Exhibit 10.7 for these bonds; use the straight-line method to amortize the discount. Then prepare journal entries to record (b) the issuance of bonds on December 31, 2019; (c) the first through fourth interest payments on each June 30 and December 31; and (d) the maturity of the bonds on December 31, 2021.

NEED-TO-KNOW 10-2

Recording Discount Bonds

P2

Solution

a.

Semiannual Period-End		Unamortized Discount	Carrying Value
(0)	12/31/2019....	$248	$6,752
(1)	6/30/2020....	186	6,814
(2)	12/31/2020....	124	6,876
(3)	6/30/2021....	62	6,938
(4)	12/31/2021 ...	0	7,000

Interest computations for solutions a, b, and c	
Four interest payments of $280	
(4 pymts × [$7,000 × 0.08 × 1/2 yr])	$1,120
Plus discount	248
Total bond interest expense................	$1,368
Divided by number of periods	÷ 4
Bond interest expense per period...........	$ 342

Point: Straight-line amortization is GAAP when the effect of using it approximates effective interest amortization.

Bonds Payable

	12/31/2019 7,000
	6/30/2020 —
	12/31/2020 —
	6/30/2021 —
12/31/2021 7,000	
12/31/2021 0	

Discount on Bonds Payable

12/31/2019 248	
	6/30/2020 62
	12/31/2020 62
	6/30/2021 62
	12/31/2021 62
12/31/2021 0	

Do More: QS 10-5, QS 10-7, QS 10-8, E 10-4, E 10-5, E 10-6, P 10-1

b.

Dec. 31, 2019	Cash	6,752	
	Discount on Bonds Payable..................................	248	
	Bonds Payable		7,000
	Sold bonds at discount.		

c. The following entry is made for each of the four interest payments on June 30 and December 31 for both 2020 and 2021.

2020–2021	Bond Interest Expense	342	
June 30 and	Discount on Bonds Payable*............................		62
Dec. 31	Cash†		280
	Pay semiannual interest and record amortization.		

*$248/4   †$7,000 × 8% × 1/2

d.

Dec. 31, 2021	Bonds Payable	7,000	
	Cash		7,000
	Record maturity and payment of bonds.		

PREMIUM BONDS

This section covers bond issuances *above par,* called **premium bonds.**

P3

Record issuance and amortization of premium bonds using the straight-line method.

Issuing Bonds at a Premium

When the contract rate is higher than the market rate, the bonds sell at a price higher than par value—the issuer gets more money at issuance than what the issuer must pay back at maturity. The amount by which the bond price exceeds par value is the **premium on bonds.** Assume **Adidas** issues bonds with a $100,000 par value, a 12% annual contract rate, semiannual interest payments, and a two-year life. The Adidas bonds sell at a premium price of 103.600 (meaning 103.600% of par value, or $103,600); we show how to compute bond prices in Appendix 10A.

Point: Contract rate *yields* cash interest payment. **Market** rate *yields* interest expense.

Cash Payments with Premium Bonds   These bonds require Adidas to pay

1. Par value of $100,000 cash at the end of the bonds' two-year life.
2. Semiannual cash interest payments of $6,000 ($100,000 × 12% × 1/2 year).

The pattern of cash receipts and payments for Adidas bonds is shown in Exhibit 10.8.

EXHIBIT 10.8

Premium Bond Cash Receipts and Payments

Recording Issuance of Premium Bonds

When Adidas receives $103,600 cash for its bonds on the issue date of December 31, 2019, it records this as follows.

Dec. 31, 2019	Cash	103,600	
	Premium on Bonds Payable		3,600
	Bonds Payable.................................		100,000
	Sold bonds at a premium on their issue date.		

Assets = Liabilities + Equity
+103,600   +100,000
              +3,600

Bonds payable are reported as a long-term liability on Adidas's December 31, 2019, balance sheet as in Exhibit 10.9. A premium is added to par value to get the carrying (book) value of bonds. Premium on Bonds Payable is an adjunct ("add-on") liability account.

Long-term liabilities		
Bonds payable, 12%, due December 31, 2021.............	$100,000	
Plus premium on bonds payable......................	**3,600**	$103,600

EXHIBIT 10.9

Balance Sheet Presentation of Bond Premium

Amortizing Premium Bonds

Adidas receives $103,600 for its bonds. In return, it pays bondholders $100,000 after two years (plus four interest payments). Panel A of Exhibit 10.10 shows that the four $6,000 interest payments minus the $3,600 bond premium equals total bond interest expense of $20,400. The premium is subtracted because it reduces the issuer's cost. Total bond interest expense is allocated over the four semiannual periods using the straight-line method (or the effective interest method in Appendix 10B).

EXHIBIT 10.10

Interest Computation and Entry for Premium Bonds

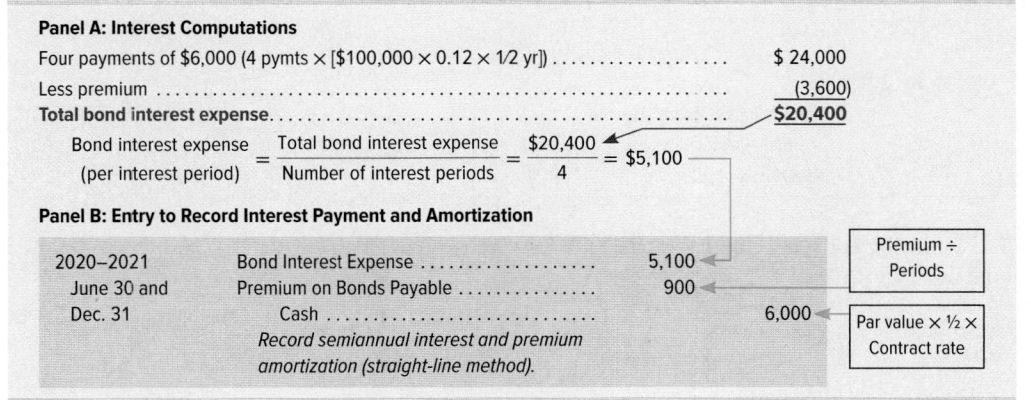

Panel A: Interest Computations

Four payments of $6,000 (4 pymts × [$100,000 × 0.12 × 1/2 yr])	$ 24,000
Less premium	(3,600)
Total bond interest expense.....................................	**$20,400**

$$\frac{\text{Bond interest expense}}{\text{(per interest period)}} = \frac{\text{Total bond interest expense}}{\text{Number of interest periods}} = \frac{\$20,400}{4} = \$5,100$$

Panel B: Entry to Record Interest Payment and Amortization

2020–2021	Bond Interest Expense	5,100	
June 30 and	Premium on Bonds Payable	900	
Dec. 31	Cash		6,000
	Record semiannual interest and premium amortization (straight-line method).		

Premium ÷ Periods

Par value × 1/2 × Contract rate

Bonds Payable

		12/31/2019	100,000
		6/30/2020	—
		12/31/2020	—
		6/30/2021	—
12/31/2021	100,000		
		12/31/2021	0

Premium on Bonds Payable

		12/31/2019	3,600
6/30/2020	900		
12/31/2020	900		
6/30/2021	900		
12/31/2021	900		
		12/31/2021	0

Straight-Line Method

The straight-line method allocates equal bond interest expense to each semiannual interest period. We divide the total bond interest expense of $20,400 by 4 (number of semiannual periods in bonds' life). This gives bond interest expense of $5,100 per period. Panel B of Exhibit 10.10 shows how Adidas records bond interest expense and updates the balance of the bond liability account for *each* semiannual period (June 30, 2020, through December 31, 2021).

Exhibit 10.11 shows the pattern of decreases in the unamortized Premium on Bonds Payable account and

Point: A premium decreases Bond Interest Expense; a discount increases it.

EXHIBIT 10.11

Straight-Line Amortization of Bond Premium

Semiannual Period-End	Unamortized Premium*	Carrying Value†
(0) 12/31/2019	$3,600	$103,600
(1) 6/30/2020	2,700	102,700
(2) 12/31/2020	1,800	101,800
(3) 6/30/2021	900	100,900
(4) 12/31/2021	0	100,000

During the bond life, carrying value is adjusted to par and the amortized premium to zero.

*Total bond premium of $3,600 less accumulated periodic amortization of $900 per semiannual interest period.

†Bond par value of $100,000 plus unamortized premium.

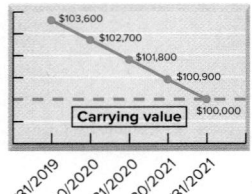

in the bonds' carrying value. Three points summarize straight-line amortization of premium bonds.

1. At issuance, the $103,600 carrying value equals the $100,000 par value plus the $3,600 unamortized premium.
2. During the bonds' life, the (unamortized) premium decreases each period by the $900 amortization ($3,600/4), and carrying value decreases each period by the same $900.
3. At maturity, unamortized premium equals zero, and carrying value equals the $100,000 par value that the issuer pays the holder.

NEED-TO-KNOW 10-3

Recording Premium Bonds

P3

A company issues 8%, two-year bonds on December 31, 2019, with a par value of $7,000 and semiannual interest payments. On the issue date, the annual market rate for these bonds is 6%, which implies a selling price of 103.71 or $7,260. (a) Prepare an amortization table like Exhibit 10.11 for these bonds; use the straight-line method to amortize the premium. Then prepare journal entries to record (b) the issuance of bonds on December 31, 2019; (c) the first through fourth interest payments on each June 30 and December 31; and (d) the maturity of the bonds on December 31, 2021.

Solution

a.

Semiannual Period-End	Unamortized Premium	Carrying Value
(0) 12/31/2019....	$260	$7,260
(1) 6/30/2020....	195	7,195
(2) 12/31/2020....	130	7,130
(3) 6/30/2021....	65	7,065
(4) 12/31/2021....	0	7,000

Interest computations for solutions a, b, and c	
Four interest payments of $280	
(4 pymts × [$7,000 × 0.08 × 1/2 yr])	$1,120
Less premium	260
Total bond interest expense..............	$ 860
Divided by number of periods	÷ 4
Bond interest expense per period........	$ 215

Bonds Payable

12/31/2019	7,000
6/30/2020	—
12/31/2020	—
6/30/2021	—
12/31/2021 7,000	
12/31/2021	**0**

b.

Dec. 31, 2019	Cash.......................................	7,260	
	Premium on Bonds Payable		260
	Bonds Payable		7,000
	Sold bonds at premium.		

Premium on Bonds Payable

		12/31/2019	260
6/30/2020	65		
12/31/2020	65		
6/30/2021	65		
12/31/2021	65		
		12/31/2021	**0**

c. The following entry is made for each of the four interest payments on June 30 and December 31 for both 2020 and 2021.

2020–2021	Bond Interest Expense	215	
June 30 and	Premium on Bonds Payable*	65	
Dec. 31	Cash†		280
	Pay semiannual interest and record amortization.		

*$260/4   †$7,000 × 8% × 1/2

d.

Dec. 31, 2021	Bonds Payable	7,000	
	Cash		7,000
	Record maturity and payment of bonds.		

Do More: QS 10-9, E 10-8, E 10-9, P 10-2, P 10-3

Bond Retirement

P4

Record the retirement of bonds.

This section covers the retirement of bonds.

Bond Retirement at Maturity   The carrying value of bonds at maturity always equals par value. For example, both Exhibits 10.7 (a discount) and 10.11 (a premium) show that the carrying value of bonds at maturity equals par value ($100,000). Retirement of these bonds at maturity, assuming interest is already paid and recorded, is as follows.

Dec. 31, 2021	Bonds Payable....................................	100,000	
	Cash...		100,000
	Record retirement of bonds at maturity.		

Assets   = Liabilities + Equity
−100,000   −100,000

Bond Retirement before Maturity

Issuers sometimes retire some or all of their bonds before maturity. If interest rates decline, an issuer may want to replace high-interest-paying bonds with new low-interest bonds. There are two common ways to retire bonds before maturity.

Point: Bond retirement is also called *bond redemption.*

- **Exercise a call option.** An issuer can reserve the right to retire bonds early by issuing *callable bonds.* This gives the issuer an option to *call* the bonds before they mature by paying the par value plus a *call premium.*
- **Open market purchase.** The issuer can repurchase them from bondholders at current market price.

Whether bonds are called or purchased, the issuer is likely to pay a price different from their carrying value. The issuer records a difference between the bonds' carrying value and the amount paid as a gain or loss. Assume that **Puma** issued callable bonds with a par value of $100,000. The call option requires Puma to pay a call premium of $3,000 to bondholders plus the par value. Next, assume that after the June 30 interest payment, the bonds have a carrying value of $104,500. Then on July 1, Puma calls these bonds and pays $103,000 to bondholders. Puma records a $1,500 gain from the difference between the bonds' carrying value of $104,500 and the retirement price of $103,000 as follows.

July 1	Bonds Payable.....................................	100,000	
	Premium on Bonds Payable	4,500	
	Gain on Bond Retirement........................		1,500
	Cash...		103,000
	Record retirement of bonds before maturity.		

Assets = Liabilities + Equity
−103,000   −100,000   +1,500
−4,500

Convertible Bond

Bond Retirement by Conversion

Holders of *convertible bonds* have the right to convert their bonds to stock. When conversion occurs, the bonds' carrying value is transferred to equity accounts and no gain or loss is recorded. (Convertible bonds are described further in the Decision Analysis section of this chapter.) Assume that on January 1 the $100,000 par value bonds of **Converse**, with a carrying value of $100,000, are converted to 15,000 shares of $2 par value common stock. The entry to record this conversion follows (market prices of the bonds and stock are *not* relevant to this entry).

Jan. 1	Bonds Payable.....................................	100,000	
	Common Stock		30,000
	Paid-In Capital in Excess of Par Value		70,000
	Record retirement of bonds by conversion.		

Assets = Liabilities + Equity
−100,000   +30,000
+70,000

 **Decision Insight**

Junk Bonds   Junk bonds are company bonds with low credit ratings due to a higher likelihood of nonpayment. On the upside, the high risk of junk bonds can yield high returns if the issuer repays its debt. Investors in junk bonds identify and buy bonds with low credit ratings when they believe those bonds will survive and pay their debts. Financial statements are used to identify junk bonds that are better than what their ratings would suggest. ∎

LONG-TERM NOTES PAYABLE

C1

Explain the types of notes and prepare entries to account for notes.

Like bonds, notes are issued in exchange for assets such as cash. Unlike bonds, notes are usually issued to a *single* lender such as a bank. An issuer initially records a note at its selling price—the note's face value minus any discount or plus any premium. Over the note's life, the amount of interest expense allocated to each period is computed by multiplying the market rate (at issuance of the note) by the beginning-of-period note balance. The note's carrying (book) value at any time equals its face value minus any unamortized discount or plus any unamortized premium.

Installment Notes

An **installment note** is a liability requiring a series of payments to the lender. Installment notes are common for franchises and other businesses when lenders and borrowers agree to spread payments over time.

Issuance of Notes   Assume Foghog borrows $60,000 from a bank to purchase equipment. It signs an 8% installment note requiring three annual payments of principal plus interest. Foghog records the note's issuance at January 1, 2019, as follows.

Assets = Liabilities + Equity
+60,000   +60,000

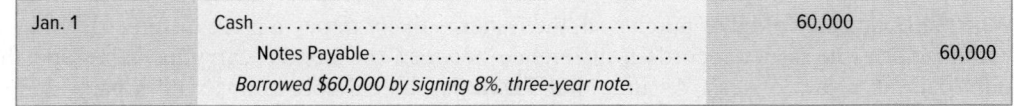

Jan. 1	Cash	60,000	
	Notes Payable..................................		60,000
	Borrowed $60,000 by signing 8%, three-year note.		

Payments of Principal and Interest   Payments on an installment note include accrued interest expense plus part of the amount borrowed (the *principal*). For this section, let's consider an installment note with equal payments. The equal total payments pattern has changing amounts of both interest and principal. Foghog borrows $60,000 by signing a $60,000 note that requires three *equal payments* of $23,282 at each year-end. Exhibit 10.12 shows the pattern of equal total payments and its two parts, interest and principal. Column A shows the note's beginning balance. Column B shows accrued interest at 8% of the beginning note balance. Column C shows the portion that reduces the principal owed, which equals total payment in column D minus interest expense in column B. Column E shows the note's year-end balance.

Years
2019   2020   2021

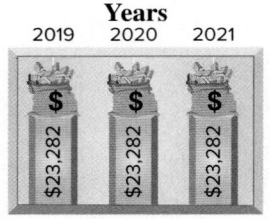

$23,282 $23,282 $23,282

EXHIBIT 10.12

Installment Note:
Equal Total Payments
Amortization Schedule

Point: Installment note payments.

	A	B
1	Rate per period	8%
2	Number of periods	3
3	Loan amount	$60,000
4	Loan payments	◀

=–PMT(B1,B2,B3)=$23,282

Point: Principal portion of note payments.

	A	B
1	Rate per period	8%
2	Number of periods	3
3	Loan amount	$60,000
4		Period	Principal
5	1	◀
6	2	◀
7	3	◀

=–PPMT(B1,A5,B2,B3)=$18,482
=–PPMT(B1,A6,B2,B3)=$19,961
=–PPMT(B1,A7,B2,B3)=$21,557

		Payments			
	(A)	**(B)**	**(C)**	**(D)**	**(E)**
		Debit	*Debit*	*Credit*	
		Interest	**Notes**		**Ending**
	Beginning	**Expense** +	**Payable** =	**Cash**	**Balance**
Period Ending Date	**Balance**	**8% × (A)**	**(D) – (B)**	**(computed)**	**(A) – (C)**
(1) **12/31/2019**	**$60,000**	**$4,800**	**$ 18,482**	**$23,282**	**$41,518**
(2) 12/31/2020	41,518	3,321	19,961	23,282	21,557
(3) 12/31/2021	21,557	1,725	21,557	23,282	0
		$9,846	**$60,000**	**$69,846**	

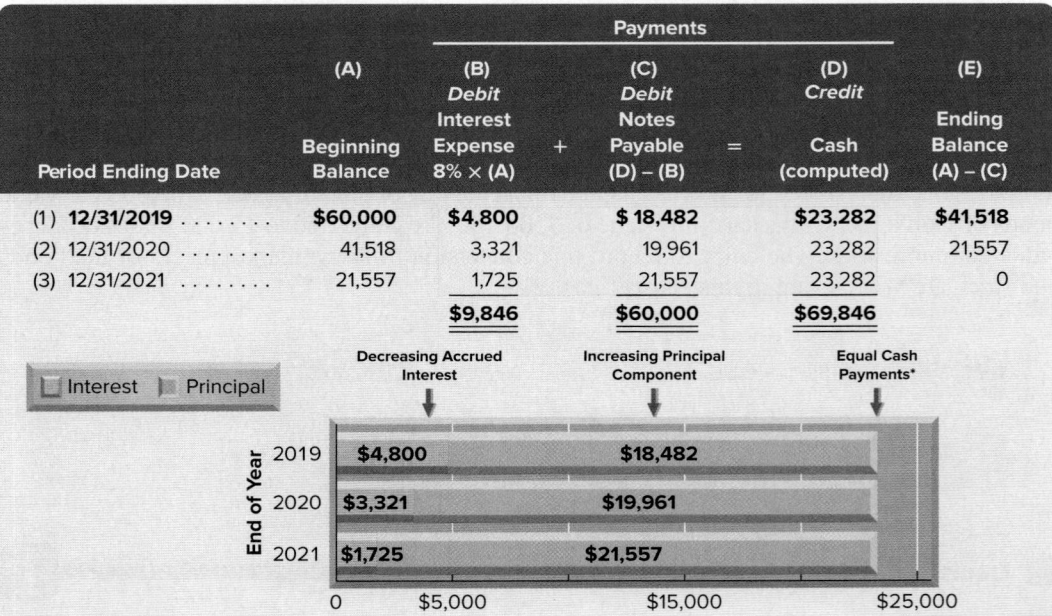

□ Interest ▨ Principal

Decreasing Accrued Interest   Increasing Principal Component   Equal Cash Payments*

End of Year		
2019	$4,800	$18,482
2020	$3,321	$19,961
2021	$1,725	$21,557
	0 $5,000 $15,000 $25,000	

*Table B.3 in Appendix B is used to compute the dollar amount of three payments that equal the initial note balance of $60,000 at 8% interest. We go to Table B.3, row 3, and across to the 8% column, where the present value factor is 2.5771. The dollar amount is then computed by solving the following equation. The amount is computed by dividing $60,000 by 2.5771, yielding $23,282.

Table	Present Value Factor		Dollar Amount		Present Value
B.3	2.5771	×	?	=	$60,000

The three $23,282 cash payments are equal, but accrued interest decreases each year because the principal balance of the note decreases. As the amount of interest decreases each year, the portion of each payment applied to principal increases. This pattern is shown in the lower part of Exhibit 10.12. Foghog uses the amounts in Exhibit 10.12 to record its first two payments (for years 2019 and 2020) as follows. Foghog records a similar entry but with different amounts for the last payment. After three years, the Notes Payable account balance is zero.

Dec. 31, 2019	Interest Expense.	4,800	
	Notes Payable.	18,482	
	Cash		23,282
	Record first installment payment.		

Assets = Liabilities + Equity
−23,282 −18,482 −4,800

Dec. 31, 2020	Interest Expense.	3,321	
	Notes Payable.	19,961	
	Cash		23,282
	Record second installment payment.		

Assets = Liabilities + Equity
−23,282 −19,961 −3,321

Mortgage Notes and Bonds

A **mortgage** is a legal agreement that helps protect a lender if a borrower does not make required payments on notes or bonds. A mortgage gives the lender a right to be paid from the cash proceeds of the sale of a borrower's assets identified in the mortgage. A *mortgage contract* describes the mortgage terms. *Mortgage notes* pledge title to specific assets as security for the note. Mortgage notes are popular in the purchase of homes and plant assets. *Mortgage bonds* are backed by the issuer's assets. Accounting for mortgage notes and bonds is similar to that for unsecured notes and bonds, except that the mortgage agreement must be disclosed. For example, **TIBCO Software** reports that its "mortgage note payable . . . is collateralized by the commercial real property acquired."

Ethical Risk

Lurking Debt   A study reports that 29% of employees in finance and accounting witnessed the falsifying or manipulating of accounting information in the past year. This includes nondisclosure of some long-term liabilities. Another study reports that most people committing fraud (36%) work in the finance function of their firm (KPMG). ■

On January 1, 2019, a company borrows $1,000 cash by signing a four-year, 5% installment note. The note requires four equal payments of $282, consisting of accrued interest and principal on December 31 of each year from 2019 through 2022.

1. Prepare an amortization table for this installment note like the one in Exhibit 10.12.

2. Prepare journal entries to record the loan on January 1, 2019, and the four payments from December 31, 2019, through December 31, 2022.

NEED-TO-KNOW 10-4

Recording Installment Note

C1

Solution

1. Amortization table for loan.

	(A)	Payments			
		(B) **Debit**	(C) **Debit**	(D) **Credit**	(E)
Period Ending Date	**Beginning Balance [Prior (E)]**	**Interest Expense [5% × (A)]** +	**Notes Payable [(D) − (B)]** =	**Cash [computed]**	**Ending Balance [(A) − (C)]**
2019.	$1,000	$ 50	$ 232	$ 282†	$768
2020.	768	38	244	282	524
2021.	524	26	256	282	268
2022.	268	14*	268	282	0
		$128	$1,000	$1,128	

*Adjusted for rounding.   †Amount of each payment = Initial note balance/PV of annuity for 4 periods at 5% (from Table B.3)
= $1,000/3.5460 = $282 (rounded)

Point: An *annuity* is a series of equal payments occurring at equal time intervals.

2.

Jan. 1, 2019	Cash	1,000	
	Notes Payable		1,000
	Borrowed $1,000 by giving a note.		
Dec. 31, 2019	Interest Expense	50	
	Notes Payable	232	
	Cash		282
	Record first installment payment.		
Dec. 31, 2020	Interest Expense	38	
	Notes Payable	244	
	Cash		282
	Record second installment payment.		

Dec. 31, 2021	Interest Expense	26	
	Notes Payable	256	
	Cash		282
	Record third installment payment.		
Dec. 31, 2022	Interest Expense	14	
	Notes Payable	268	
	Cash		282
	Record fourth installment payment.		

> Do More: QS 10-12, E 10-12, E 10-13, P 10-5

Decision Analysis — Debt Features and the Debt-to-Equity Ratio

Features of Bonds and Notes

A2
Assess debt features and their implications.

This section covers features of debt securities.

Secured Debt

Secured or Unsecured   **Secured bonds** (and notes) have specific assets of the issuer pledged (or *mortgaged*) as collateral. If the issuer does not pay its debt, the secured holders can demand that the collateral be sold and the proceeds used to pay the obligation. **Unsecured bonds** (and notes), also called *debentures,* are backed by the issuer's general credit standing and are riskier than secured debt.

Unsecured Debt

Term or Serial   **Term bonds** (and notes) mature on one specified date. **Serial bonds** (and notes) mature at more than one date (often in series) and thus are usually repaid over a number of periods. For instance, $100,000 of serial bonds might mature at the rate of $10,000 each year from 6 to 15 years after they are issued. **Sinking fund bonds** reduce the holder's risk by requiring the issuer to set aside assets to pay debt in a *sinking fund.*

Registered or Bearer   Bonds issued in the names and addresses of their holders are **registered bonds.** The issuer makes bond payments by sending checks (or cash transfers) to registered holders. Bonds payable to whoever holds them (the *bearer*) are called **bearer bonds** or *unregistered bonds*. The holder of a bearer bond is presumed to be its rightful owner. Many bearer bonds are also **coupon bonds.** This term reflects interest coupons that are attached to the bonds. When each coupon matures, the holder presents it to a bank or broker for collection.

Convertible Debt

Callable Debt

Convertible and/or Callable   **Convertible bonds** (and notes) can be exchanged for a fixed number of shares of the issuing corporation's stock. Convertible debt offers holders the potential to profit from increases in stock price. Holders still receive interest while the debt is held and the par value if they hold the debt to maturity. In most cases, the holders decide whether and when to convert debt to stock. **Callable bonds** (and notes) give the issuer the option to retire them at a stated dollar amount before maturity.

Debt-to-Equity Ratio

A3
Compute the debt-to-equity ratio and explain its use.

A company financed mainly with debt is more risky because liabilities must be repaid with interest, whereas equity financing does not. A measure to assess the risk of a company's financing structure is the **debt-to-equity ratio** (see Exhibit 10.13).

EXHIBIT 10.13

Debt-to-Equity Ratio

$$\text{Debt-to-equity} = \frac{\text{Total liabilities}}{\text{Total equity}}$$

The debt-to-equity ratios for **Nike** and **Under Armour** are in Exhibit 10.14. Nike's current-year debt-to-equity ratio is 0.87, meaning that debtholders contributed $0.87 for each $1 contributed by equity holders. This implies a low-risk financing structure for Nike and is similar to its competitors. In comparison, Under Armour's current-year ratio is 0.98. Analysis across the years shows that Nike's debt-to-equity ratio has risen to a riskier level in recent years. In the case of Nike, the increase in debt-to-equity ratio is less concerning as it has historically earned higher returns with this financing than the interest rate it pays. Still, investors and debtholders will continue to monitor Nike's debt-to-equity ratio to be sure it does not reach risky levels.

Company	$ millions	Current Year	1 Year Ago	2 Years Ago
Nike	Total liabilities........................	$10,852	$ 9,138	$ 8,890
	Total equity	$12,407	$12,258	$12,707
	Debt-to-equity.....................	**0.87**	**0.75**	**0.70**
Under Armour	Total liabilities........................	$ 1,988	$ 1,613	$ 1,198
	Total equity	$ 2,019	$ 2,031	$ 1,668
	Debt-to-equity.....................	**0.98**	**0.79**	**0.72**

EXHIBIT 10.14

Analysis using Debt-to-Equity Ratio

■ **Decision Maker**

Bond Investor   You plan to purchase bonds from one of two companies in the same industry that are similar in size and performance. The first company has $350,000 in total liabilities and $1,750,000 in equity. The second company has $1,200,000 in total liabilities and $1,000,000 in equity. Which company's bonds are less risky based on the debt-to-equity ratio? ■   *Answer:* The debt-to-equity ratio for the first company is 0.2 ($350,000/$1,750,000) and for the second is 1.2 ($1,200,000/$1,000,000), suggesting that financing for the second company is riskier than for the first.

Water Sports Company (WSC) patented and successfully test-marketed a new product. To produce and market the new product, WSC needs to raise $800,000 of financing. On January 1, 2019, the company obtained the money in two ways.

a. WSC signed a $400,000, 10% installment note to be repaid with five equal annual installments of $105,519 to be made on December 31 of 2019 through 2023.

b. WSC issued five-year bonds with a par value of $400,000 for $430,881 cash on January 1, 2019. The bonds have a 12% annual contract rate and pay interest on June 30 and December 31. The bonds' annual market rate is 10%.

NEED-TO-KNOW 10-5

COMPREHENSIVE

Accounting for Bonds and Notes—Amortization, Journal Entries, and Disposal

Required

1. For the installment note, (a) prepare an amortization table similar to Exhibit 10.12 and (b) prepare the journal entry for the first payment.

2. For the bonds, (a) prepare the January 1, 2019, journal entry to record their issuance; (b) prepare an amortization table using the straight-line method; (c) prepare the June 30, 2019, journal entry to record the first interest payment; and (d) prepare a journal entry to record retiring the bonds at a $416,000 call price on January 1, 2021.

3.ᴮ Using Appendix 10B, redo parts 2(b), 2(c), and 2(d) assuming the bonds are amortized using the effective interest method.

PLANNING THE SOLUTION

● For the installment note, prepare a table similar to Exhibit 10.12 and use the numbers in the table's first line for the journal entry.

● Record the bonds' issuance. Next, prepare an amortization table like Exhibit 10.11 (and Exhibit 10B.2) and use it to get the numbers for the journal entry. Also use the table to find the carrying value as of the date of the bonds' retirement needed for the journal entry.

SOLUTION

Part 1: Installment Note

a. An amortization table for the long-term note payable follows.

		(a)	(b)		(c)		(d)	(e)
			Debit		**Debit**		**Credit**	
			Interest		**Notes**			**Ending**
		Beginning	**Expense**	**+**	**Payable**	**=**	**Cash**	**Balance**
Annual Period Ending		**Balance**	**10% × (a)**		**(d) − (b)**		**(computed)**	**(a) − (c)**
(1) 12/31/2019		$400,000	$ 40,000		$ 65,519		$105,519*	$334,481
(2) 12/31/2020		334,481	33,448		72,071		105,519	262,410
(3) 12/31/2021		262,410	26,241		79,278		105,519	183,132
(4) 12/31/2022		183,132	18,313		87,206		105,519	95,926
(5) 12/31/2023		95,926	9,593		95,926		105,519	0
			$127,595		$400,000		$527,595	

*Annual payment = Note balance / PV annuity factor = $400,000/3.7908 = $105,519
(The present value annuity factor is for five payments at a rate of 10%.)

b. Journal entry for December 31, 2019, payment.

Dec. 31	Interest Expense	40,000	
	Notes Payable	65,519	
	Cash..		105,519
	Record first installment payment.		

Part 2: Bonds (Straight-Line Amortization)

a. Journal entry for January 1, 2019, issuance.

Jan. 1	Cash...	430,881	
	Premium on Bonds Payable.....................		30,881
	Bonds Payable		400,000
	Sold bonds at a premium.		

Point: Bond issue price equals present value of its future cash payments discounted at bond's market rate.

Cash Flow	Table	Present Value Factor*	Amount	Present Value
Par (maturity) value....	B.1 in App. B (PV of 1)	0.6139	× $400,000 =	$245,560
Interest payments......	B.3 in App. B (PV of annuity)	7.7217	× 24,000 =	185,321
Price of bond				$430,881

*Present value factors are for 10 payments using a semiannual market rate of 5%.

b. The straight-line amortization table for premium bonds follows. The semiannual discount amortization is $3,088, computed as $30,881/10 periods.

Semiannual Period-End	Unamortized Discount	Carrying Value
(0) 1/1/2019	$ 30,881	$ 430,881
(1) 6/30/2019	27,793	427,793
(2) 12/31/2019	24,705	424,705
(3) 6/30/2020	21,617	421,617
(4) 12/31/2020	18,529	418,529
(5) 6/30/2021	15,441	415,441
(6) 12/31/2021	12,353	412,353
(7) 6/30/2022	9,265	409,265
(8) 12/31/2022	6,177	406,177
(9) 6/30/2023	3,089	403,089
(10) 12/31/2023	0*	400,000

*Adjusted for rounding.

c. Journal entry for June 30, 2019, bond payment.

June 30	Bond Interest Expense	20,912	
	Premium on Bonds Payable	3,088	
	Cash.....................................		24,000
	Paid semiannual interest on bonds.		

d. Journal entry for January 1, 2021, bond retirement (use carrying value as of 12/31/2020).

Jan. 1	Bonds Payable......................................	400,000	
	Premium on Bonds Payable	18,529	
	Cash.....................................		416,000
	Gain on Retirement of Bonds.....................		2,529
	Record bond retirement for cash.		

Part 3: Bonds (Effective Interest Amortization)—Using Appendix 10B

b. The effective interest amortization table for premium bonds.

Semiannual Interest Period		(A) Cash Interest Paid 6% × $400,000	(B) Interest Expense 5% × Prior (E)	(C) Premium Amortization (A) – (B)	(D) Unamortized Premium Prior (D) – (C)	(E) Carrying Value $400,000 + (D)
(0)	1/1/2019				$30,881	$430,881
(1)	6/30/2019	$ 24,000	$ 21,544	$ 2,456	28,425	428,425
(2)	12/31/2019	24,000	21,421	2,579	25,846	425,846
(3)	6/30/2020	24,000	21,292	2,708	23,138	423,138
(4)	12/31/2020	24,000	21,157	2,843	20,295	420,295
(5)	6/30/2021	24,000	21,015	2,985	17,310	417,310
(6)	12/31/2021	24,000	20,866	3,134	14,176	414,176
(7)	6/30/2022	24,000	20,709	3,291	10,885	410,885
(8)	12/31/2022	24,000	20,544	3,456	7,429	407,429
(9)	6/30/2023	24,000	20,371	3,629	3,800	403,800
(10)	12/31/2023	24,000	20,200*	3,800	0	400,000
		$240,000	$209,119	$30,881		

*Adjusted for rounding.

> **Point:** Using effective interest, carrying value is also computed as the present value of all remaining payments, discounted using the market rate at issuance.

c. Journal entry for June 30, 2019, bond payment.

June 30	Bond Interest Expense	21,544	
	Premium on Bonds Payable	2,456	
	Cash.....................................		24,000
	Paid semiannual interest on bonds.		

d. Journal entry for January 1, 2021, bond retirement (use carrying value as of 12/31/2020).

Jan. 1	Bonds Payable......................................	400,000	
	Premium on Bonds Payable	20,295	
	Cash.....................................		416,000
	Gain on Retirement of Bonds.....................		4,295
	Record bond retirement for cash.		

Bond Pricing

This section shows how to price the **Fila** discount bond and the **Adidas** premium bond described earlier.

Present Value of Discount Bonds The issue price of bonds is the present value of the bonds' cash payments, discounted at the bonds' market rate. The annual market rate is 10.031% for the Fila bonds. However, for simplicity, we **assume a 10% annual rate** in this appendix. When computing the

C2

Explain and compute bond pricing.

present value of the Fila bonds, we use *semiannual* compounding periods because this is the time between interest payments; the annual market rate of 10% is considered a semiannual rate of 5%. Also, the two-year bond life is viewed as four semiannual periods. The price computation has two parts.

1 Find the present value of the $100,000 par value paid at maturity.

2 Find the present value of the four semiannual payments of $4,000 each; see Exhibit 10.4.

The present values are found using Excel or a calculator (see directions to the side). We also can find present values if the market rate is in *present value tables*. Appendix B at the end of this book shows present value tables and describes their use. Table B.1 in Appendix B is used for the single $100,000 maturity payment, and Table B.3 in Appendix B is used for the $4,000 series of interest payments. The annual market rate is 10%, or 5% semiannually. In this case, we go to Table B.1, row 4, and across to the 5% column to identify the present value factor of 0.8227 for the maturity payment. Next, we go to Table B.3, row 4, and across to the 5% column, where the present value factor is 3.5460 for the interest payments. We compute bond price by multiplying the cash flow payments by their present value factors and adding them—see Exhibit 10A.1.

Point: Excel for bond pricing.

	A	B
1	Annual contract rate	8%
2	Annual market rate	10%
3	Payments within yr	2
4	Years to maturity	2
5	Par (face) value	$100,000
6	Issue price	

=−PV(B2/B3,B3*B4,B5*B1/B3,B5)
=$96,454

EXHIBIT 10A.1

Computing Issue Price for Fila Discount Bonds

Calculator
N = 4   PMT = 4,000
I/Yr = 5   FV = 100,000

PV = 96,454

Cash Flow	Table	Present Value Factor		Amount		Present Value
$100,000 par (maturity) value............	B.1 (PV of 1)	0.8227	×	$100,000	=	$ 82,270
$4,000 interest payments	B.3 (PV of ann.)	3.5460	×	4,000	=	14,184
Price of bond........................	(using a 5% semiannual market rate)					**$96,454**

Present Value of Premium Bonds

We compute the issue price of the Adidas bonds by using the market rate to compute the present value of the bonds' future cash flows. The annual market rate is 9.97% for the Adidas bonds. However, for simplicity, we **assume a 10% annual rate** in this appendix. When computing the present value of these bonds, we again use *semiannual* compounding periods because this is the time between interest payments. The annual 10% market rate is applied as a semiannual rate of 5%, and the two-year bond life is viewed as four semiannual periods. The computation has two parts.

1 Find the present value of the $100,000 par value paid at maturity.

2 Find the present value of the four payments of $6,000 each; see Exhibit 10.8.

These present values are found using Excel or a calculator (see directions to the side). We also can find present value if the market rate is in present value tables. The annual market rate is 10%, or 5% semiannually. In this case, go to Table B.1, row 4, and across to the 5% column, where the present value factor is 0.8227 for the maturity payment. Second, go to Table B.3, row 4, and across to the 5% column, where the present value factor is 3.5460 for the series of interest payments. The bonds' price is computed by multiplying the cash flow payments by their present value factors and adding them—see Exhibit 10A.2.

Point: Excel for bond pricing.

	A	B
1	Annual contract rate	12%
2	Annual market rate	10%
3	Payments within yr	2
4	Years to maturity	2
5	Par (face) value	$100,000
6	Issue price	

=−PV(B2/B3,B3*B4,B5*B1/B3,B5)
=$103,546

EXHIBIT 10A.2

Computing Issue Price for Adidas Premium Bonds

Calculator
N = 4   PMT = 6,000
I/Yr = 5   FV = 100,000

PV = 103,546

Cash Flow	Table	Present Value Factor		Amount		Present Value
$100,000 par (maturity) value............	B.1 (PV of 1)	0.8227	×	$100,000	=	$ 82,270
$6,000 interest payments	B.3 (PV of ann.)	3.5460	×	6,000	=	21,276
Price of bond........................	(using a 5% semiannual market rate)					**$103,546**

Point: Calculator inputs defined:
N   Number of semiannual periods
I/Yr   Market rate per semiannual period
FV   Future (maturity) value
PMT   Payment (interest) per semiannual period
PV   Price (present value)

■ **Decision Insight**

Equivalent Payments Concept   Business decisions involve the time value of money. To help in those decisions, the present value factors can be thought of as *equivalent payments*. For example, using the data in Exhibit 10A.1, one payment of $100,000 scheduled two years from today is the *equivalent* of a 0.8227 payment of $100,000 today (assuming a market with 10% return). Similarly, four semiannual payments of $4,000 over the next two years are the equivalent of 3.5460 payments of $4,000 today (again, assuming a 10% return). ■

Effective Interest Amortization

10B

Effective Interest Amortization of Discount Bonds   The **effective interest method** allocates total bond interest expense over the bonds' life in a way that yields a constant rate of interest. This constant rate of interest is the market rate at the issue date. This means bond interest expense for a period equals the carrying value of the bond at the beginning of that period multiplied by the market rate when issued.

Exhibit 10B.1 shows an effective interest amortization table for **Fila** bonds (as described in Exhibit 10.4). The key difference between the effective interest and straight-line methods is computing bond interest expense. Instead of assigning an equal amount of bond interest expense to each period, the effective interest method assigns a bond interest expense amount that increases over the life of a discount bond. **Both methods allocate the same $19,600 of total bond interest expense over the bonds' life, but in different patterns.** Specifically, the amortization table in Exhibit 10B.1 shows that the balance of the discount (column D) is amortized until it reaches zero. Also, the bonds' carrying value (column E) changes each period until it equals par value at maturity. Compare columns D and E to the columns in Exhibit 10.7 to see the amortization patterns. Total bond interest expense is $19,600, consisting of $16,000 of semiannual cash payments and $3,600 of the original bond discount, the same for both methods.

P5

Compute and record amortization of a bond discount using the effective interest method.

Point: Contract rate determines cash interest paid, but market rate determines the actual interest expense.

EXHIBIT 10B.1

Effective Interest Amortization of Bond Discount

Bonds: $100,000 Par Value, Semiannual Interest Payments, Two-Year Life, 4% Semiannual Contract Rate, 5.0155% Semiannual Market Rate					
Semiannual Interest Period-End	(A) Cash Interest Paid 4% × $100,000	(B) Bond Interest Expense 5.0155% × Prior (E)	(C) Discount Amortization (B) – (A)	(D) Unamortized Discount Prior (D) – (C)	(E) Carrying Value $100,000 – (D)
(0) 12/31/2019				$3,600	$ 96,400
(1) 6/30/2020	$ 4,000	$ 4,835	$ 835	2,765	97,235
(2) 12/31/2020	4,000	4,877	877	1,888	98,112
(3) 6/30/2021	4,000	4,921	921	967	99,033
(4) 12/31/2021	4,000	4,967	967	0	100,000
	$16,000	$19,600	$3,600		

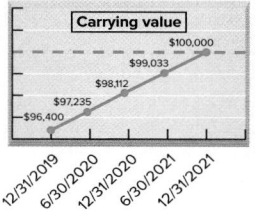

Carrying value

Column (**A**) is the par value ($100,000) multiplied by the semiannual contract rate (4%).
Column (**B**) is the prior period's carrying value multiplied by the semiannual market rate (5.0155%).
Column (**C**) is the difference between interest paid and bond interest expense, or [(B) – (A)].
Column (**D**) is the prior period's unamortized discount less the current period's discount amortization.
Column (**E**) is the par value less unamortized discount, or [$100,000 – (D)].

Except for differences in amounts, journal entries recording the expense and updating the liability balance are the same under the effective interest method and the straight-line method. We use the numbers in Exhibit 10B.1 to record each semiannual entry during the bonds' two-year life (June 30, 2020, through December 31, 2021). The interest payment entry at the end of the first semiannual period is

June 30, 2020	Bond Interest Expense	4,835	
	Discount on Bonds Payable		835
	Cash		4,000
	Record semiannual interest and discount amortization (effective interest method).		

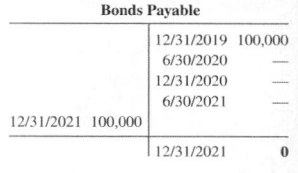

Bonds Payable

		12/31/2019	100,000
		6/30/2020	—
		12/31/2020	—
		6/30/2021	—
12/31/2021	100,000		
		12/31/2021	**0**

Discount on Bonds Payable

12/31/2019	3,600		
		6/30/2020	835
		12/31/2020	877
		6/30/2021	921
		12/31/2021	967
12/31/2021	**0**		

Effective Interest Amortization of Premium Bonds   Exhibit 10B.2 shows the amortization table using the effective interest method for **Adidas** bonds (as described in Exhibit 10.8). Column A lists the semiannual cash payments. Column B shows the amount of bond interest expense, computed as the 4.9851% semiannual market rate at issuance multiplied by the beginning-of-period carrying value. The amount of cash paid in column A is larger than the bond interest expense because the

P6

Compute and record amortization of a bond premium using the effective interest method.

cash payment is based on the higher 6% semiannual contract rate. The excess cash payment over the interest expense reduces the principal. These amounts are shown in column C. Column E shows the carrying value after deducting the amortized premium in column C from the prior period's carrying value. Column D shows the premium's reduction by periodic amortization.

EXHIBIT 10B.2

Effective Interest
Amortization of Bond
Premium

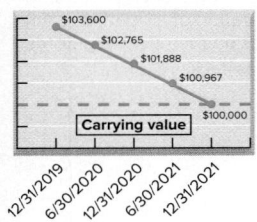

	Bonds: $100,000 Par Value, Semiannual Interest Payments, Two-Year Life, 6% Semiannual Contract Rate, 4.9851% Semiannual Market Rate				
		(A) Cash Interest Paid	(B) Bond Interest Expense	(C) Premium Amortization	(D) Unamortized Premium	(E) Carrying Value
	Semiannual Interest Period-End	6% × $100,000	4.9851% × Prior (E)	(A) − (B)	Prior (D) − (C)	$100,000 + (D)
(0)	**12/31/2019**				**$3,600**	**$103,600**
(1)	**6/30/2020**	**$ 6,000**	**$ 5,165**	**$ 835**	**2,765**	**102,765**
(2)	12/31/2020	6,000	5,123	877	1,888	101,888
(3)	6/30/2021	6,000	5,079	921	967	100,967
(4)	12/31/2021	6,000	5,033	967	0	**100,000**
		$24,000	$20,400	$3,600		

Column (**A**) is the par value ($100,000) multiplied by the semiannual contract rate (6%).
Column (**B**) is the prior period's carrying value multiplied by the semiannual market rate (4.9851%).
Column (**C**) is the difference between interest paid and bond interest expense, or [(A) − (B)].
Column (**D**) is the prior period's unamortized premium less the current period's premium amortization.
Column (**E**) is the par value plus unamortized premium, or [$100,000 + (D)].

Bonds Payable

	12/31/2019	100,000
	6/30/2020	—
	12/31/2020	—
	6/30/2021	—
12/31/2021 100,000		
	12/31/2021	0

Premium on Bonds Payable

		12/31/2019	3,600
6/30/2020	835		
12/31/2020	877		
6/30/2021	921		
12/31/2021	967		
		12/31/2021	0

When the issuer makes the first semiannual interest payment, it records the following. Similar entries with different amounts are recorded at each payment date until the bond matures at the end of 2021. The effective interest method yields decreasing amounts of bond interest expense and increasing amounts of premium amortization over the bonds' life.

June 30, 2020	Bond Interest Expense	5,165	
	Premium on Bonds Payable...........................	835	
	Cash		6,000
	Record semiannual interest and premium *amortization (effective interest method).*		

APPENDIX
10C

Leases and Pensions

C3

Describe accounting for
leases and pensions.

Lease Liabilities

A **lease** is an agreement between a *lessor* (owner) and a *lessee* (renter or tenant) that gives the lessee the right to use the asset for a period of time in return for cash (rent) payments. The financing of leases is a $1 trillion industry. The advantages of lease financing include no up-front, full cash payment and the potential to deduct rental payments from taxable income.

Leases are classified as either finance leases or operating leases. In either case, for noncurrent leases the lessee records a "Right-of-Use Asset" and "Lease Liability" equal to the present value of lease payments. At each period-end, the lessee records financing expense differently depending on whether it's a finance lease or operating lease.

Finance Leases

Finance leases are long-term leases where the lessee receives substantially all remaining benefits of the asset. A *finance lease* meets one or more of five criteria: (1) transfers ownership of lease asset to lessee, (2) has a purchase option that lessee is reasonably certain to exercise, (3) lease term is for major part of the lease asset's remaining economic life, (4) present value of lease payments equals or exceeds substantially all of the lease asset's fair value, or (5) the lease asset is specialized and expected to have no alternative use to lessor at lease-end.

A finance lease is similar to the financing of an asset purchase. Examples include most leases of airplanes, delivery trucks, medical equipment, railcars, and department store buildings. The lessee records the leased item as its own asset along with a lease liability at the start of the lease term; the amount recorded equals the present value of all lease payments.

Lease Start and First Payment   Assume KDI Co. enters into a three-year lease of a building in which it sells sporting equipment. The lease is accounted for as a finance lease, it requires three $21,000 payments (the first at the *beginning* of the lease and the others at December 31 of 2019 and 2020), and the present value of its annual lease payments is $60,000 (implying a 5.086% discount rate). KDI records the asset and liability along with the first-period lease payment as follows. KDI reports the right-of-use lease asset as a long-term asset and the lease liability as a long-term liability. The portion of the lease liability expected to be paid in the next year is reported as a current liability.

Jan. 1, 2019	Right-of-Use Asset......................................	60,000	
	Lease Liability......................................		60,000
	Record right-of-use asset and lease liability.		
Jan. 1, 2019	Lease Liability	21,000	
	Cash...		21,000
	Record beginning-year cash lease payment.		

Lease Asset Amortization   At each year-end, KDI records amortization on the right-of-use asset (assume straight-line amortization, three-year lease term, and no salvage value) as follows.

Dec. 31, 2019	Amortization Expense	20,000	
	Accumulated Amortization—Right-of-Use Asset.........		20,000
	Record amortization on right-of-use asset. ($60,000–$0)/3 yrs		

LEASE

Lease Payment for Liability and Interest   KDI accrues interest expense on the lease liability at each year-end. Interest expense is computed by multiplying the lease liability by the interest rate on the lease. It records interest expense as part of its $21,000 annual lease payment as follows (for its first year).

Dec. 31, 2019	Interest Expense	1,984	
	Lease Liability	19,016	
	Cash...		21,000
	*Record lease payment for interest and lease liability.**		

*Numbers are from a *lease payment schedule* as follows.

	(A)	(B)		(C)		(D)	(E)
		Debit		*Debit*		*Credit*	
		Interest on	+		=		**Ending Balance**
	Beginning Balance	**Lease Liability**		**Lease Liability**		**Cash Lease**	**of Lease Liability**
Date	**of Lease Liability**	**5.086% × (A)**		**(D) – (B)**		**Payment**	**(A) – (C)**
Jan. 1, 2019	**$60,000**	▉▉▉▉▉		**$21,000**		**$21,000**	**$39,000**
Dec 31, 2019	39,000	$1,984		19,016		21,000	19,984
Dec 31, 2020	19,984	1,016		19,984		21,000	0
		$3,000		**$60,000**		**$63,000**	

KDI's entries for the final two years of this lease follow.

Dec. 31, 2020	Amortization Expense...................................	20,000	
	Accumulated Amortization—Right-of-Use Asset		20,000
	Record amortization on right-of-use asset.		
Dec. 31, 2020	Interest Expense.......................................	1,016	
	Lease Liability	19,984	
	Cash		21,000
	Record lease payment for interest and lease liability.		
Dec. 31, 2021	Amortization Expense...................................	20,000	
	Accumulated Amortization—Right-of-Use Asset		20,000
	Record amortization on right-of-use asset.		

Operating Leases   **Operating leases** are long-term leases that do not meet any of the five criteria for finance leases.

Lease Start and Payments   We prepare journal entries using the same *lease payment schedule* shown for the finance lease above. Recall this is a three-year lease that requires three $21,000 payments (the first at the *beginning* of the lease and the others at December 31 of 2019 and 2020), with a present value of its annual lease payments of $60,000 (implying a 5.086% discount rate). All entries under the finance lease apply here, but amounts for amortization entries differ.

Lease Amortization   Total amortization for the lease life is the same for finance and operating leases. The difference is the yearly asset amortization. Those entries follow using the amortization calculated below.

		2019	2020	2021
Dec. 31	Amortization Expense..............................	19,016	19,984	21,000
	Accumulated Amortization—Right-of-Use Asset....	19,016	19,984	21,000
	*Record amortization on right-of-use asset.**			

Point: In the income statement for an operating lease, Amortization Exp. and Interest Exp. are combined as one line item, "Lease Expense." The balance sheet and ledger keep them separate.

	Amortization*	=	Lease Payment	−	Interest on Lease Liability
For 2019 ...	**$19,016**	=	$21,000	−	$1,984
For 2020 ...	**$19,984**	=	$21,000	−	$1,016
For 2021 ...	**$21,000**	=	$21,000	−	$ 0

Short-Term Leases   **Short-term leases** have lease terms of 12 months or less and do not have long-term purchase options. Examples include most car and apartment rental agreements. The lessee records such lease payments as expenses. The lessee does not report the leased item as an asset or a liability (it is the lessor's asset). If **Verizon** leases a kiosk from the mall for $300 per month, its entry follows.

July 4	Rental Expense	300	
	Cash..		300
	Record short-term lease rental payment.		

Pension Liabilities

Point: Fringe benefits are often 40% or more of salaries and wages, and pension benefits make up nearly 15% of fringe benefits.

Pension Liabilities   A **pension plan** is an agreement for the employer to provide benefits (payments) to employees after they retire. Some employers pay the full cost of the pension, and some pay part of the cost. An employer records its payment into a pension plan with a debit to Pension Expense and a credit to Cash. A *plan administrator* invests the payments in pension assets and makes benefit payments to *pension recipients* (retired employees).

Point: Two types of pension plans are (1) *defined benefit plan*—the retirement benefit is defined and the employer estimates the contribution necessary to pay these benefits—and (2) *defined contribution plan*—the pension contribution is defined and the employer and/or employee contribute amounts specified in the pension agreement.

Defined Benefit Plan   *Defined benefit plans* give workers defined future benefits; the employer's contributions vary, depending on assumptions about future pension assets and liabilities. A pension liability is reported when the accumulated benefit obligation is *more than* the plan assets, called an *underfunded plan.* The accumulated benefit obligation is the present value of promised future pension payments to retirees. *Plan assets* refer to the market value of pension assets. A pension asset is reported when the accumulated benefit obligation is *less than* the plan assets, called an *overfunded plan.* An employer reports pension expense when employees earn wages, which is sometimes decades before it pays pension benefits to employees.

Other Postretirement Benefits   *Other postretirement benefits* refer to nonpension benefits such as health care and life insurance benefits. Costs of these benefits are estimated and liabilities accrued when the employees earn them. Many of these benefits are not funded.

Summary: Cheat Sheet

BOND BASICS AND PAR BONDS

Bond advantages: Bonds do not affect owner control, interest on bonds is tax deductible, and bonds can potentially increase return on equity.
Bond disadvantages: Bonds can potentially decrease return on equity and require payments of both periodic interest and the par value at maturity.

Bonds issued at *par value* (called *par bonds*):

Cash	100,000	
Bonds Payable.............................		100,000

Par bonds semiannual interest payment:

Bond Interest Expense..........................	4,000	
Cash....................................		4,000

Maturity of bonds (payment of par): When the bond issuer pays the par value back to the bondholder.

Bonds Payable	100,000	
Cash...................................		100,000

DISCOUNT BONDS

Contract rate: The interest the bond issuer pays in cash.
Market rate: The interest rate that borrowers are willing to pay and lenders are willing to accept.

Contract rate > Market rate ➡	Bond sells at premium
Contract rate = Market rate ➡	Bond sells at par
Contract rate < Market rate ➡	Bond sells at discount

Bond prices: A $1,000 bond with a price of 96.400 is sold for $964.
A $1,000 bond with a price of 103½ is sold for $1,035.
Carrying (book) value of a bond: Equals bond par value plus any premium or minus any discount.
Discount bonds: Bonds issued with a contract rate that is *less* than the market rate.

Issuance of discount bonds:

Cash	96,400	
Discount on Bonds Payable	3,600	
Bonds Payable.		100,000

Reporting of discount bonds:

Long-term liabilities		
Bonds payable, 8%, due December 31, 2021	$100,000	
Less discount on bonds payable.	3,600	$96,400

Amortizing discount bonds (straight-line method):

Panel A: Interest Computations

Four payments of $4,000 (4 pymts × [$100,000 × 0.08 × 1/2 yr])	$ 16,000
Plus discount	3,600
Total bond interest expense.	**$19,600**

$$\text{Bond interest expense (per interest period)} = \frac{\text{Total bond interest expense}}{\text{Number of interest periods}} = \frac{\$19,600}{4} = \$4,900$$

Panel B: Entry to Record Interest Payment and Amortization

2020–2021	Bond Interest Expense	4,900	
June 30 and	Discount on Bonds Payable		900
Dec. 31	Cash		4,000

Discount ÷ Periods
Par value × 1/2 × Contract rate

Straight-line discount bond amortization table:

Semiannual Period-End	Unamortized Discount	Carrying Value
(0) 12/31/2019	$3,600	$ 96,400
(1) 6/30/2020	2,700	97,300
(2) 12/31/2020	1,800	98,200
(3) 6/30/2021	900	99,100
(4) **12/31/2021**	**0**	**100,000**

PREMIUM BONDS

Premium bonds: Bonds issued with a contract rate *higher* than the market rate.

Issuance of premium bonds:

Cash	103,600	
Premium on Bonds Payable		3,600
Bonds Payable.		100,000

Reporting of premium bonds:

Long-term liabilities		
Bonds payable, 12%, due December 31, 2021	$100,000	
Plus premium on bonds payable.	3,600	$103,600

Amortizing premium bonds (straight-line method):

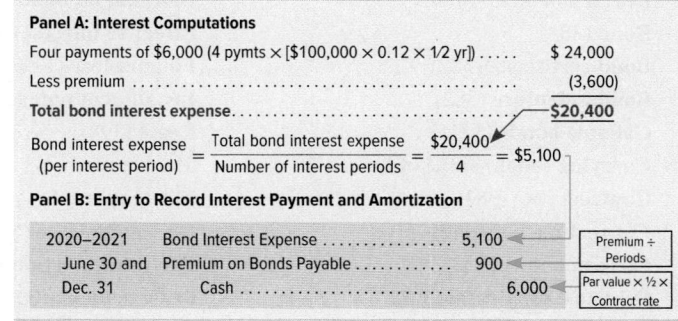

Panel A: Interest Computations

Four payments of $6,000 (4 pymts × [$100,000 × 0.12 × 1/2 yr])	$ 24,000
Less premium	(3,600)
Total bond interest expense.	**$20,400**

$$\text{Bond interest expense (per interest period)} = \frac{\text{Total bond interest expense}}{\text{Number of interest periods}} = \frac{\$20,400}{4} = \$5,100$$

Panel B: Entry to Record Interest Payment and Amortization

2020–2021	Bond Interest Expense	5,100	
June 30 and	Premium on Bonds Payable	900	
Dec. 31	Cash		6,000

Premium ÷ Periods
Par value × 1/2 × Contract rate

Straight-line premium bond amortization table:

Semiannual Period-End	Unamortized Premium	Carrying Value
(0) 12/31/2019	$3,600	$103,600
(1) 6/30/2020	2,700	102,700
(2) 12/31/2020	1,800	101,800
(3) 6/30/2021	900	100,900
(4) **12/31/2021**	**0**	**100,000**

BOND RETIREMENT

Bond retirement by call option: Some bonds give issuers an option to call the bonds before they mature by paying par value plus a call premium. Record a gain if carrying value is *greater* than retirement price (shown here). Record a loss if carrying value is *less* than retirement price.

Bonds Payable	100,000	
Premium on Bonds Payable.	4,500	
Gain on Bond Retirement		1,500
Cash.		103,000

Bond retirement by conversion: Holders of convertible bonds can convert their bonds to stock. No gain or loss is recorded. Bonds are converted to stock at the bonds' carrying value.

Bonds Payable	100,000	
Common Stock		30,000
Paid-In Capital in Excess of Par Value		70,000

LONG-TERM NOTES

Installment note: A liability requiring a series of payments to the lender. Usually issued to a single lender, such as a bank.

Payments of principal and interest payments for note: Payments on an installment note include accrued interest expense plus part of the amount borrowed (the principal).

		Payments			
	(A)	(B) Debit Interest Expense + 8% × (A)	(C) Debit Notes Payable (D) − (B)	(D) Credit Cash (computed)	(E) Ending Balance (A) − (C)
Period Ending Date	Beginning Balance		=		
(1) 12/31/2019	$60,000	$4,800	$ 18,482	$23,282	$41,518
(2) 12/31/2020	41,518	3,321	19,961	23,282	21,557
(3) 12/31/2021	21,557	1,725	21,557	23,282	0
		$9,846	$60,000	$69,846	

Issuance of notes:

Cash	60,000	
Notes Payable.		60,000

Note installment payments:

Dec. 31, 2019	Interest Expense	4,800	
	Notes Payable	18,482	
	Cash		23,282

Dec. 31, 2020	Interest Expense	3,321	
	Notes Payable	19,961	
	Cash		23,282

Key Terms

Bearer bonds (392)
Bond (381)
Bond certificate (382)
Bond indenture (382)
Callable bonds (392)
Carrying (book) value of bonds (384)
Contract rate (383)
Convertible bonds (392)
Coupon bonds (392)
Debt-to-equity ratio (392)

Discount on bonds payable (384)
Effective interest method (397)
Finance lease (398)
Installment note (390)
Lease (398)
Market rate (383)
Mortgage (391)
Operating lease (399)
Par value of a bond (381)
Pension plan (400)

Premium on bonds (386)
Registered bonds (392)
Secured bonds (392)
Serial bonds (392)
Short-term lease (400)
Sinking fund bonds (392)
Straight-line bond amortization (385)
Term bonds (392)
Unsecured bonds (392)

Multiple Choice Quiz

1. A bond traded at 97½ means that
  a. The bond pays 97½% interest.
  b. The bond trades at $975 per $1,000 bond.
  c. The market rate of interest is below the contract rate of interest for the bond.
  d. The bonds can be retired at $975 each.
  e. The bond's interest rate is 2½%.

2. A bondholder that owns a $1,000, 6%, 15-year (term) bond has
  a. The right to receive $1,000 at maturity.
  b. Ownership rights in the bond-issuing entity.
  c. The right to receive $60 per month until maturity.
  d. The right to receive $1,900 at maturity.
  e. The right to receive $600 per year until maturity.

3. A company issues 8%, 20-year bonds with a par value of $500,000. The current market rate for the bonds is 8%. The

amount of interest owed to the bondholders for each semi-annual interest payment is
  a. $40,000.   **c.** $20,000.   **e.** $400,000.
  b. $0.   **d.** $800,000.

4. A company issued five-year, 5% bonds with a par value of $100,000. The company received $95,735 for the bonds. Using the straight-line method, the company's interest expense for the first semiannual interest period is
  a. $2,926.50.   **c.** $2,500.00.   **e.** $9,573.50.
  b. $5,853.00.   **d.** $5,000.00.

5. A company issued eight-year, 5% bonds with a par value of $350,000. The company received proceeds of $373,745. Interest is payable semiannually. The amount of premium amortized for the first semiannual interest period, assuming straight-line bond amortization, is
  a. $2,698.   **c.** $8,750.   **e.** $1,484.
  b. $23,745.   **d.** $9,344.

ANSWERS TO MULTIPLE CHOICE QUIZ

1. b
2. a
3. c; $500,000 × 0.08 × ½ year = $20,000

4. a; Cash interest paid = $100,000 × 5% × ½ year = $2,500
   Discount amortization = ($100,000 − $95,735)/10 periods = $426.50
   Interest expense = $2,500.00 + $426.50 = $2,926.50

5. e; ($373,745 − $350,000)/16 periods = $1,484

A(B,C) Superscript letter A, B, or C denotes assignments based on Appendix 10A, 10B, or 10C.

🚶 Icon denotes assignments that involve decision making.

Discussion Questions

1. What is the main difference between notes payable and bonds payable?

2. What is the main difference between a bond and a share of stock?

3. 🚶 What is the advantage of issuing bonds instead of obtaining financing from the company's owners?

4. What is a bond indenture? What provisions are usually included in it?

5. What are the *contract* rate and the *market* rate for bonds?

6. 🚶 What factors affect the market rates for bonds?

7.B 🚶 Does the straight-line or effective interest method produce an interest expense allocation that yields a constant rate of interest over a bond's life? Explain.

8. Explain the concept of accrued interest on bonds at the end of an accounting period.

9. 🚶 If you know the par value of bonds, the contract rate, and the market rate, how do you compute the bonds' price?

10. What is the issue price of a $2,000 bond sold at 98¼? What is the issue price of a $6,000 bond sold at 101½?

11. Describe the debt-to-equity ratio and explain how creditors and owners use this ratio to evaluate a company's risk.

12. 🚶 What obligation does an entrepreneur (owner) have to investors that purchase bonds to finance the business?

13. Refer to **Apple**'s annual report in Appendix A. Is there any indication that Apple has issued long-term debt? **APPLE**

14. Refer to the statements for **Samsung** in Appendix A. By what amount did Samsung's long-term borrowings increase or decrease in 2017? **Samsung**

15. Refer to the statement of cash flows for **Samsung** in Appendix A. For the year ended December 31, 2017, what was the amount for repayment of long-term borrowings and debentures? **Samsung**

16. Refer to the statements for **Google** in Appendix A. For the year ended December 31, 2017, what was its debt-to-equity ratio? What does this ratio tell us? **GOOGLE**

17.C When can a lease create both an asset and a liability for the lessee?

18.C Compare and contrast a finance lease with an operating lease.

19.C Describe the two basic types of pension plans.

🅼 connect

> *Round dollar amounts to the nearest whole dollar for all assignments in this chapter.*

QUICK STUDY

Identify the following as either an advantage (A) or a disadvantage (D) of bond financing for a company.

_____ **a.** Bonds do not affect owner control.

_____ **b.** A company earns a lower return with borrowed funds than it pays in interest.

_____ **c.** A company earns a higher return with borrowed funds than it pays in interest.

_____ **d.** Bonds require payment of periodic interest.

_____ **e.** Interest on bonds is tax deductible.

_____ **f.** Bonds require payment of par value at maturity.

QS 10-1
Advantages of bond financing
A1

Dunphy Company issued $10,000 of 6%, 10-year bonds at par value on January 1. Interest is paid semiannually each June 30 and December 31. Prepare the entries for (*a*) the issuance of the bonds and (*b*) the first interest payment on June 30.

QS 10-2
Issuing bonds at par   P1

Madrid Company plans to issue 8% bonds with a par value of $4,000,000. The company sells $3,600,000 of the bonds at par on January 1. The remaining $400,000 sells at par on July 1. The bonds pay interest semiannually on June 30 and December 31.

1. Record the entry for the first interest payment on June 30.

2. Record the entry for the July 1 cash sale of bonds.

QS 10-3
Issuing bonds at par

P1

On January 1, Renewable Energy issues bonds that have a $20,000 par value, mature in eight years, and pay 12% interest semiannually on June 30 and December 31.

1. Prepare the journal entry for issuance assuming the bonds are issued at (*a*) 99 and (*b*) 103½.

2. How much interest does the company pay (in cash) to its bondholders every six months if the bonds are sold at par?

QS 10-4
Recording bond issuance and interest

P1   P2   P3 🌐

Enviro Company issues 8%, 10-year bonds with a par value of $250,000 and semiannual interest payments. On the issue date, the annual market rate for these bonds is 10%, which implies a selling price of 87½. Prepare the journal entry for the issuance of the bonds for cash on January 1.

QS 10-5
Journalizing discount bond issuance   P2

QS 10-6
Journalizing premium bond issuance **P3**

Garcia Company issues 10%, 15-year bonds with a par value of $240,000 and semiannual interest payments. On the issue date, the annual market rate for these bonds is 8%, which implies a selling price of 117¼. Prepare the journal entry for the issuance of these bonds for cash on January 1.

QS 10-7
Straight-Line:
Discount bond computations

P2

Enviro Company issues 8%, 10-year bonds with a par value of $250,000 and semiannual interest payments. On the issue date, the annual market rate for these bonds is 10%, which implies a selling price of 87½. The straight-line method is used to allocate interest expense.

1. What are the issuer's cash proceeds from issuance of these bonds?
2. What total amount of bond interest expense will be recognized over the life of these bonds?
3. What is the amount of bond interest expense recorded on the first interest payment date?

QS 10-8
Recording bond issuance and discount amortization

P2

Snap Company issues 10%, five-year bonds, on January 1 of this year, with a par value of $100,000 and semiannual interest payments. Use the following bond amortization table and prepare journal entries to record (*a*) the issuance of bonds on January 1, (*b*) the first interest payment on June 30, and (*c*) the second interest payment on December 31.

Semiannual Period-End	Unamortized Discount	Carrying Value
(0) January 1, issuance	$7,360	$92,640
(1) June 30, first payment	6,624	93,376
(2) December 31, second payment.	5,888	94,112

QS 10-9
Straight-Line: Premium bond computations

P3

Enviro Company issues 8%, 10-year bonds with a par value of $250,000 and semiannual interest payments. On the issue date, the annual market rate for these bonds is 5%, which implies a selling price of 123.375. The straight-line method is used to allocate interest expense.

1. What are the issuer's cash proceeds from issuance of these bonds?
2. What total amount of bond interest expense will be recognized over the life of these bonds?
3. What is the amount of bond interest expense recorded on the first interest payment date?

QS 10-10
Bond retirement by call option **P4**

On July 1, Aloha Co. exercises a call option that requires Aloha to pay $408,000 for its outstanding bonds that have a carrying value of $416,000 and a par value of $400,000. The company exercises the call option after the semiannual interest is paid the day before on June 30. Record the entry to retire the bonds.

QS 10-11
Bond retirement by stock conversion **P4**

On January 1, the $3,000,000 par value bonds of Spitz Company with a carrying value of $3,000,000 are converted to 1,000,000 shares of $1 par value common stock. Record the entry for the conversion of the bonds.

QS 10-12
Issuance and interest for installment note

C1

On January 1, MM Co. borrows $340,000 cash from a bank and in return signs an 8% installment note for five annual payments of $85,155 each.

1. Prepare the journal entry to record issuance of the note.
2. For the first $85,155 annual payment at December 31, what amount goes toward interest expense? What amount goes toward principal reduction of the note?

QS 10-13
Bond features and terminology

A2

Select the description that best fits each term or phrase.

A. Records and tracks the bondholders' names.
B. Is unsecured; backed only by the issuer's credit standing.
C. Has varying maturity dates for amounts owed.
D. The legal contract between the issuer and the bondholders.
E. Can be exchanged for shares of the issuer's stock.
F. Is unregistered; interest is paid to whoever possesses them.
G. Maintains a separate asset account from which bondholders are paid at maturity.
H. Pledges specific assets of the issuer as collateral.

_____ **1.** Registered bond   _____ **5.** Convertible bond
_____ **2.** Serial bond   _____ **6.** Bond indenture
_____ **3.** Secured bond   _____ **7.** Sinking fund bond
_____ **4.** Bearer bond   _____ **8.** Debenture

Compute the debt-to-equity ratio for each of the following companies. Which company appears to have a riskier financing structure?

	Atlanta Company	Spokane Company
Total liabilities	$429,000	$ 549,000
Total equity	572,000	1,830,000

QS 10-14
Debt-to-equity ratio
A3

Compute the selling price of 8%, 10-year bonds with a par value of $250,000 and semiannual interest payments. The annual market rate for these bonds is 10%. Use present value tables B.1 and B.3 in Appendix B.

QS 10-15ᴬ
Computing bond price   C2

Compute the selling price of 10%, 15-year bonds with a par value of $240,000 and semiannual interest payments. The annual market rate for these bonds is 8%. Use present value tables B.1 and B.3 in Appendix B.

QS 10-16ᴬ
Computing bond price   C2

Garcia Company issues 10%, 15-year bonds with a par value of $240,000 and semiannual interest payments. On the issue date, the annual market rate for these bonds is 14%, which implies a selling price of 75¼. The effective interest method is used to allocate interest expense.

1. What are the issuer's cash proceeds from issuance of these bonds?
2. What total amount of bond interest expense will be recognized over the life of these bonds?
3. What amount of bond interest expense is recorded on the first interest payment date?

QS 10-17ᴮ
Effective Interest: Bond discount computations
P5

Garcia Company issues 10%, 15-year bonds with a par value of $240,000 and semiannual interest payments. On the issue date, the annual market rate for these bonds is 8%, which implies a selling price of 117¼. The effective interest method is used to allocate interest expense.

1. What are the issuer's cash proceeds from issuance of these bonds?
2. What total amount of bond interest expense will be recognized over the life of these bonds?
3. What amount of bond interest expense is recorded on the first interest payment date?

QS 10-18ᴮ
Effective Interest: Bond premium computations
P6

Jin Li, an employee of ETrain.com, leases a car at O'Hare Airport for a three-day business trip. The rental cost is $250. Prepare the entry by ETrain.com to record Jin Li's short-term car lease cost.

QS 10-19ᶜ
Recording short-term leases   C3

Algoma, Inc., signs a five-year lease for office equipment with Office Solutions. The present value of the lease payments is $15,499. Prepare the journal entry that Algoma records at the inception of this finance lease.

QS 10-20ᶜ
Recording leases   C3

Mc Graw Hill Education **connect**

No-Toxic-Toys currently has $200,000 of equity and is planning an $80,000 expansion to meet increasing demand for its product. The company currently earns $50,000 in net income, and the expansion will yield $25,000 in additional income before any interest expense.

The company has three options: (1) do not expand, (2) expand and issue $80,000 in debt that requires payments of 8% annual interest, or (3) expand and raise $80,000 from equity financing. For each option, compute (*a*) net income and (*b*) return on equity (Net income ÷ Equity). Ignore any income tax effects.

EXERCISES
Exercise 10-1
Debt versus equity financing
A1

Brussels Enterprises issues bonds at par dated January 1, 2019, that have a $3,400,000 par value, mature in four years, and pay 9% interest semiannually on June 30 and December 31.

1. Record the entry for the issuance of bonds for cash on January 1.
2. Record the entry for the first semiannual interest payment and the second semiannual interest payment.
3. Record the entry for the maturity of the bonds on December 31, 2022 (assume semiannual interest is already recorded).

Exercise 10-2
Recording bond issuance at par, interest payments, and bond maturity
P1

Exercise 10-3
Recording bond issuance and interest
P1

On January 1, Boston Enterprises issues bonds that have a $3,400,000 par value, mature in 20 years, and pay 9% interest semiannually on June 30 and December 31. The bonds are sold at par.

1. How much interest will Boston pay (in cash) to the bondholders every six months?
2. Prepare journal entries to record (a) the issuance of bonds on January 1, (b) the first interest payment on June 30, and (c) the second interest payment on December 31.
3. Prepare the journal entry for issuance assuming the bonds are issued at (a) 98 and (b) 102.

Exercise 10-4
Straight-Line: Amortization of bond discount
P2

Tano Company issues bonds with a par value of $180,000 on January 1, 2019. The bonds' annual contract rate is 8%, and interest is paid semiannually on June 30 and December 31. The bonds mature in three years. The annual market rate at the date of issuance is 10%, and the bonds are sold for $170,862.

1. What is the amount of the discount on these bonds at issuance?
2. How much total bond interest expense will be recognized over the life of these bonds?
3. Prepare a straight-line amortization table like Exhibit 10.7 for these bonds.

Exercise 10-5
Straight-Line:
Recording bond issuance and discount amortization
P2

Paulson Company issues 6%, four-year bonds, on January 1 of this year, with a par value of $200,000 and semiannual interest payments. Use the following bond amortization table and prepare journal entries to record (a) the issuance of bonds on January 1, (b) the first interest payment on June 30, and (c) the second interest payment on December 31.

Semiannual Period-End	Unamortized Discount	Carrying Value
(0) January 1, issuance	$13,466	$186,534
(1) June 30, first payment	11,782	188,218
(2) December 31, second payment . . .	10,098	189,902

Exercise 10-6
Straight-Line:
Recording bond issuance and discount amortization
P2

Dobbs Company issues 5%, two-year bonds, on December 31, 2019, with a par value of $200,000 and semiannual interest payments. Use the following bond amortization table and prepare journal entries to record (a) the issuance of bonds on December 31, 2019; (b) the first through fourth interest payments on each June 30 and December 31; and (c) the maturity of the bonds on December 31, 2021.

Semiannual Period-End	Unamortized Discount	Carrying Value
(0) 12/31/2019	$12,000	$188,000
(1) 6/30/2020	9,000	191,000
(2) 12/31/2020	6,000	194,000
(3) 6/30/2021	3,000	197,000
(4) 12/31/2021	0	200,000

Exercise 10-7
Straight-Line:
Amortization table and bond interest expense
P2

Duval Co. issues four-year bonds with a $100,000 par value on January 1, 2019, at a price of $95,952. The annual contract rate is 7%, and interest is paid semiannually on June 30 and December 31.

1. Prepare a straight-line amortization table like Exhibit 10.7 for these bonds.
2. Prepare journal entries to record the first two interest payments.
3. Prepare the journal entry for maturity of the bonds on December 31, 2022 (assume semiannual interest is already recorded).

Exercise 10-8
Straight-Line:
Recording bond issuance and premium amortization
P3

Wookie Company issues 10%, five-year bonds, on January 1 of this year, with a par value of $200,000 and semiannual interest payments. Use the following bond amortization table and prepare journal entries to record (a) the issuance of bonds on January 1, (b) the first interest payment on June 30, and (c) the second interest payment on December 31.

Semiannual Period-End	Unamortized Premium	Carrying Value
(0) January 1, issuance	$16,222	$216,222
(1) June 30, first payment	14,600	214,600
(2) December 31, second payment . . .	12,978	212,978

Quatro Co. issues bonds dated January 1, 2019, with a par value of $400,000. The bonds' annual contract rate is 13%, and interest is paid semiannually on June 30 and December 31. The bonds mature in three years. The annual market rate at the date of issuance is 12%, and the bonds are sold for $409,850.

1. What is the amount of the premium on these bonds at issuance?

2. How much total bond interest expense will be recognized over the life of these bonds?

3. Prepare a straight-line amortization table like Exhibit 10.11 for these bonds.

Exercise 10-9
Straight-Line:
Amortization of bond premium

P3

Tyrell Company issued callable bonds with a par value of $10,000. The call option requires Tyrell to pay a call premium of $500 plus par (or a total of $10,500) to bondholders to retire the bonds. On July 1, Tyrell exercises the call option. The call option is exercised after the semiannual interest is paid the day before on June 30. Record the entry to retire the bonds under each separate situation.

1. The bonds have a carrying value of $9,000.

2. The bonds have a carrying value of $11,000.

Exercise 10-10
Bond retirement by call option

P4

On January 1, 2019, Shay Company issues $700,000 of 10%, 15-year bonds. The bonds sell for $684,250. Six years later, on January 1, 2025, Shay retires these bonds by buying them on the open market for $731,500. All interest is accounted for and paid through December 31, 2024, the day before the purchase. The straight-line method is used to amortize any bond discount.

1. What is the amount of the discount on the bonds at issuance?

2. How much amortization of the discount is recorded on the bonds for the entire period from January 1, 2019, through December 31, 2024?

3. What is the carrying (book) value of the bonds as of the close of business on December 31, 2024?

4. Prepare the journal entry to record the bond retirement.

Exercise 10-11
Straight-Line: Bond computations, amortization, and bond retirement

P2   P4

On January 1, 2019, Eagle Company borrows $100,000 cash by signing a four-year, 7% installment note. The note requires four equal payments of $29,523, consisting of accrued interest and principal on December 31 of each year from 2019 through 2022. Prepare an amortization table for this installment note like the one in Exhibit 10.12.

Exercise 10-12
Installment note amortization table   **C1**

Use the information in Exercise 10-12 to prepare the journal entries for Eagle to record the note's issuance and each of the four payments.

Exercise 10-13
Installment note entries

C1

Selected accounts from WooHoo Co.'s adjusted trial balance for the year ended December 31 follow. Prepare the liabilities section of its classified balance sheet.

Notes payable (due in 5 years)	$ 3,000	Discount on bonds payable.	$400
Accounts payable.	500	Wages payable.	200
Bonds payable (due in 10 years).	10,000	Interest payable (due in 2 weeks).	100
Machinery.	4,500	Sales tax payable.	50

Exercise 10-14
Reporting liabilities section of balance sheet

C1   P2

Montclair Company is considering a project that will require a $500,000 loan. It presently has total liabilities of $220,000 and total assets of $620,000.

1. Compute Montclair's (a) current debt-to-equity ratio and (b) the debt-to-equity ratio assuming it borrows $500,000 to fund the project.

2. If Montclair borrows the funds, does its financing structure become more or less risky?

Exercise 10-15
Applying debt-to-equity ratio

A3

Bringham Company issues bonds with a par value of $800,000. The bonds mature in 10 years and pay 6% annual interest in semiannual payments. The annual market rate for the bonds is 8%.

1. Compute the price of the bonds as of their issue date.

2. Prepare the journal entry to record the bonds' issuance.

Exercise 10-16[A]
Computing bond interest and price; recording bond issuance   **C2**

Exercise 10-17^A

Computing bond interest and price; recording bond issuance   C2

Citywide Company issues bonds with a par value of $150,000. The bonds mature in five years and pay 10% annual interest in semiannual payments. The annual market rate for the bonds is 8%.

1. Compute the price of the bonds as of their issue date.
2. Prepare the journal entry to record the bonds' issuance.

Exercise 10-18^B

Effective Interest: Amortization of bond discount

P5

Stanford issues bonds dated January 1, 2019, with a par value of $500,000. The bonds' annual contract rate is 9%, and interest is paid semiannually on June 30 and December 31. The bonds mature in three years. The annual market rate at the date of issuance is 12%, and the bonds are sold for $463,140.

1. What is the amount of the discount on these bonds at issuance?
2. How much total bond interest expense will be recognized over the life of these bonds?
3. Prepare an effective interest amortization table like Exhibit 10B.1 for these bonds.

Exercise 10-19^B

Effective Interest: Amortization of bond premium

P6

Quatro Co. issues bonds dated January 1, 2019, with a par value of $400,000. The bonds' annual contract rate is 13%, and interest is paid semiannually on June 30 and December 31. The bonds mature in three years. The annual market rate at the date of issuance is 12%, and the bonds are sold for $409,850.

1. What is the amount of the premium on these bonds at issuance?
2. How much total bond interest expense will be recognized over the life of these bonds?
3. Prepare an effective interest amortization table like Exhibit 10B.2 for these bonds.

Exercise 10-20^C

Identifying finance and operating leases

C3

In each of the following separate cases, indicate whether the company has entered into a finance lease or an operating lease.

_____ 1. The lessor retains title to the asset, and the lease term is 3 years on an asset that has a 10-year useful life.

_____ 2. The title is transferred to the lessee. The lessee can purchase the asset for $1 at the end of the lease, and the lease term is five years. The leased asset has an expected useful life of six years.

_____ 3. The present value of the lease payments is 95% of the leased asset's market value, and the lease term is 90% of the leased asset's useful life.

Exercise 10-21^C

Accounting for finance lease

C3

On January 1, Harbor (lessee) signs a five-year lease for equipment that is accounted for as a finance lease. The lease requires five $10,000 lease payments (the first at the beginning of the lease and the remaining four at December 31 of years 1, 2, 3, and 4), and the present value of the five annual lease payments is $41,000, based on an 11% interest rate.

1. Prepare the January 1 journal entry Harbor records at inception of the lease for any asset or liability.
2. Prepare the January 1 entry Harbor records for the first $10,000 cash lease payment.
3. If the leased asset has a five-year useful life with no salvage value, prepare the December 31 journal entry Harbor records each year for amortization of the leased asset.

Exercise 10-22^C

Analyzing lease purchase options

C3

General Motors advertised three alternatives for a 25-month lease on a new Tahoe: (1) zero dollars down and a lease payment of $1,750 per month for 25 months, (2) $5,000 down and $1,500 per month for 25 months, or (3) $38,500 down and no payments for 25 months. Use the present value Table B.3 in Appendix B to determine which is the best alternative for the customer (assume you have enough cash to accept any alternative and the annual interest rate is 12% compounded monthly).

---

connect

PROBLEM SET A

Hillside issues $4,000,000 of 6%, 15-year bonds dated January 1, 2019, that pay interest semiannually on June 30 and December 31. The bonds are issued at a price of $3,456,448.

Problem 10-1A

Straight-Line: Amortization of bond discount

P2

Check (3) $4,143,552
(4) 12/31/2020 carrying value, $3,528,920

Required

1. Prepare the January 1 journal entry to record the bonds' issuance.
2. For each semiannual period, compute (*a*) the cash payment, (*b*) the straight-line discount amortization, and (*c*) the bond interest expense.
3. Determine the total bond interest expense to be recognized over the bonds' life.
4. Prepare the first two years of a straight-line amortization table like Exhibit 10.7.
5. Prepare the journal entries to record the first two interest payments.

Refer to the bond details in Problem 10-1A, *except* assume that the bonds are issued at a price of $4,895,980.

Required

1. Prepare the January 1 journal entry to record the bonds' issuance.
2. For each semiannual period, compute (*a*) the cash payment, (*b*) the straight-line premium amortization, and (*c*) the bond interest expense.
3. Determine the total bond interest expense to be recognized over the bonds' life.
4. Prepare the first two years of a straight-line amortization table like Exhibit 10.11.
5. Prepare the journal entries to record the first two interest payments.

Problem 10-2A
Straight Line:
Amortization of bond premium

P3

Check   (3) $2,704,020
(4) 12/31/2020 carrying value, $4,776,516

Ellis Company issues 6.5%, five-year bonds dated January 1, 2019, with a $250,000 par value. The bonds pay interest on June 30 and December 31 and are issued at a price of $255,333. The annual market rate is 6% on the issue date.

Required

1. Calculate the total bond interest expense over the bonds' life.
2. Prepare a straight-line amortization table like Exhibit 10.11 for the bonds' life.
3. Prepare the journal entries to record the first two interest payments.

Problem 10-3A
Straight-Line:
Amortization of bond premium

P3

Check   (2) 6/30/2021
carrying value, $252,668

Legacy issues $325,000 of 5%, four-year bonds dated January 1, 2019. that pay interest semiannually on June 30 and December 31. They are issued at $292,181 when the market rate is 8%.

Required

1. Prepare the January 1 journal entry to record the bonds' issuance.
2. Determine the total bond interest expense to be recognized over the bonds' life.
3. Prepare a straight-line amortization table like the one in Exhibit 10.7 for the bonds' first two years.
4. Prepare the journal entries to record the first two interest payments.

Problem 10-4A
Straight-Line:
Amortization of bond discount   **P2**

Check   (2) $97,819

(3) 12/31/2020 carrying value, $308,589

On November 1, 2019, Norwood borrows $200,000 cash from a bank by signing a five-year installment note bearing 8% interest. The note requires equal payments of $50,091 each year on October 31.

Required

1. Complete an amortization table for this installment note similar to the one in Exhibit 10.12.
2. Prepare the journal entries in which Norwood records (*a*) accrued interest as of December 31, 2019 (the end of its annual reporting period), and (*b*) the first annual payment on the note.

Problem 10-5A
Installment notes

C1

Check   (1) 10/31/2023
ending balance, $46,382

At the end of the current year, the following information is available for both Pulaski Company and Scott Company.

	Pulaski Company	Scott Company
Total assets	$860,000	$440,000
Total liabilities	360,000	240,000
Total equity	500,000	200,000

Required

1. Compute the debt-to-equity ratios for both companies.
2. Which company has the riskier financing structure?

Problem 10-6A
Applying the debt-to-equity ratio

A3

Hartford Research issues bonds dated January 1 that pay interest semiannually on June 30 and December 31. The bonds have a $40,000 par value and an annual contract rate of 10%, and they mature in 10 years.

Required

For each separate situation, (*a*) determine the bonds' issue price on January 1 and (*b*) prepare the journal entry to record their issuance.

1. The market rate at the date of issuance is 8%.
2. The market rate at the date of issuance is 10%.
3. The market rate at the date of issuance is 12%.

Problem 10-7A[A]
Computing bond price and recording issuance

C2

Check   (1) Premium, $5,437

(3) Discount, $4,588

Problem 10-8A[B]

Effective Interest:

Amortization of bond discount   **P5**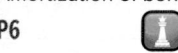

Check   (2) $97,819

(3) 12/31/2020 carrying value, $307,308

Refer to the bond details in Problem 10-4A.

Required

1. Prepare the January 1 journal entry to record the bonds' issuance.
2. Determine the total bond interest expense to be recognized over the bonds' life.
3. Prepare an effective interest amortization table like the one in Exhibit 10B.1 for the bonds' first two years.
4. Prepare the journal entries to record the first two interest payments.

Problem 10-9A[B]

Effective Interest:

Amortization of bond premium   **P6**

Check   (2) 6/30/2021 carrying value, $252,865

Refer to the bond details in Problem 10-3A.

Required

1. Compute the total bond interest expense over the bonds' life.
2. Prepare an effective interest amortization table like the one in Exhibit 10B.2 for the bonds' life.
3. Prepare the journal entries to record the first two interest payments.

Problem 10-10A[B]

Effective Interest:

Amortization of bond

P6

Check   (3) 6/30/2020 carrying value, $182,448

Ike issues $180,000 of 11%, three-year bonds dated January 1, 2019, that pay interest semiannually on June 30 and December 31. They are issued at $184,566 when the market rate is 10%.

Required

1. Prepare the January 1 journal entry to record the bonds' issuance.
2. Determine the total bond interest expense to be recognized over the bonds' life.
3. Prepare an effective interest amortization table like Exhibit 10B.2 for the bonds' first two years.
4. Prepare the journal entries to record the first two interest payments.

Problem 10-11A[C]

Accounting for finance lease

C3

On January 1, Rogers (lessee) signs a three-year lease for machinery that is accounted for as a finance lease. The lease requires three $18,000 lease payments (the first at the beginning of the lease and the remaining two at December 31 of Year 1 and Year 2). The present value of the three annual lease payments is $51,000, using a 6.003% interest rate. The lease payment schedule follows.

	(A)	(B) Debit Interest on	(C) Debit		(D) Credit	(E) Ending Balance
				Payments		
Date	Beginning Balance of Lease Liability	Lease Liability 6.003% × (A)	+ Lease Liability = (D) − (B)		Cash Lease Payment	of Lease Liability (A) − (C)
Jan. 1, Year 1	$51,000	▓▓▓▓	$18,000		$18,000	$33,000
Dec. 31, Year 1. . . .	33,000	$1,981	16,019		18,000	16,981
Dec. 31, Year 2 . . .	16,981	1,019	16,981		18,000	0
		$3,000	**$51,000**		**$54,000**	

Required

1. Prepare the January 1 journal entry at the start of the lease to record any asset or liability.
2. Prepare the January 1 journal entry to record the first $18,000 cash lease payment.
3. Prepare the December 31 journal entry to record straight-line amortization with zero salvage value at the end of (a) Year 1, (b) Year 2, and (c) Year 3.
4. Prepare the December 31 journal entry to record the $18,000 cash lease payment at the end of (a) Year 1 and (b) Year 2.

Problem 10-12A[C]

Accounting for operating lease

C3

Refer to the lease details in Problem 10-11A. Assume that this lease is classified as an operating lease instead of a finance lease.

Required

1. Prepare the January 1 journal entry at the start of the lease to record any asset or liability.
2. Prepare the January 1 journal entry to record the first $18,000 cash lease payment.
3. Prepare the December 31 journal entry to record amortization at the end of (a) Year 1, (b) Year 2, and (c) Year 3.
4. Prepare the December 31 journal entry to record the $18,000 cash lease payment at the end of (a) Year 1 and (b) Year 2.

Romero issues $3,400,000 of 10%, 10-year bonds dated January 1, 2019, that pay interest semiannually on June 30 and December 31. The bonds are issued at a price of $3,010,000.

Required

1. Prepare the January 1 journal entry to record the bonds' issuance.
2. For each semiannual period, compute (*a*) the cash payment, (*b*) the straight-line discount amortization, and (*c*) the bond interest expense.
3. Determine the total bond interest expense to be recognized over the bonds' life.
4. Prepare the first two years of a straight-line amortization table like Exhibit 10.7.
5. Prepare the journal entries to record the first two interest payments.

PROBLEM SET B

Problem 10-1B
Straight-Line: Amortization of bond discount

P2

Check (3) $3,790,000
(4) 6/30/2020 carrying value, $3,068,500

Refer to the bond details in Problem 10-1B, *except* assume that the bonds are issued at a price of $4,192,932.

Required

1. Prepare the January 1 journal entry to record the bonds' issuance.
2. For each semiannual period, compute (*a*) the cash payment, (*b*) the straight-line premium amortization, and (*c*) the bond interest expense.
3. Determine the total bond interest expense to be recognized over the bonds' life.
4. Prepare the first two years of a straight-line amortization table like Exhibit 10.11.
5. Prepare the journal entries to record the first two interest payments.

Problem 10-2B
Straight-Line: Amortization of bond premium

P3

Check (3) $2,607,068
(4) 6/30/2020 carrying value, $4,073,991

Ripkin Company issues 9%, five-year bonds dated January 1, 2019, with a $320,000 par value. The bonds pay interest on June 30 and December 31 and are issued at a price of $332,988. Their annual market rate is 8% on the issue date.

Required

1. Calculate the total bond interest expense over the bonds' life.
2. Prepare a straight-line amortization table like Exhibit 10.11 for the bonds' life.
3. Prepare the journal entries to record the first two interest payments.

Problem 10-3B
Straight-Line: Amortization of bond premium

P3

Check (2) 6/30/2021 carrying value, $326,493

Gomez issues $240,000 of 6%, 15-year bonds dated January 1, 2019, that pay interest semiannually on June 30 and December 31. They are issued at $198,494 when the market rate is 8%.

Required

1. Prepare the January 1 journal entry to record the bonds' issuance.
2. Determine the total bond interest expense to be recognized over the life of the bonds.
3. Prepare a straight-line amortization table like the one in Exhibit 10.7 for the bonds' first two years.
4. Prepare the journal entries to record the first two interest payments.

Analysis Component

5. Assume the market rate at issuance is 4% instead of 8%. Without providing numbers, describe how this change affects the amounts reported on Gomez's financial statements.

Problem 10-4B
Straight-Line: Amortization of bond discount

P2

Check (2) $257,506
(3) 6/30/2020 carrying value, $202,646

On October 1, 2019, Gordon borrows $150,000 cash from a bank by signing a three-year installment note bearing 10% interest. The note requires equal payments of $60,316 each year on September 30.

Required

1. Complete an amortization table for this installment note similar to the one in Exhibit 10.12.
2. Prepare the journal entries to record (*a*) accrued interest as of December 31, 2019 (the end of its annual reporting period), and (*b*) the first annual payment on the note.

Problem 10-5B
Installment notes

C1

Check (1) 9/30/2021 ending balance, $54,836

Problem 10-6B
Applying the debt-to-equity ratio

A3

At the end of the current year, the following information is available for both Atlas Company and Bryan Company.

	Atlas Company	Bryan Company
Total assets	$180,000	$750,000
Total liabilities	80,000	562,500
Total equity	100,000	187,500

Required

1. Compute the debt-to-equity ratios for both companies.

2. Which company has the riskier financing structure?

Problem 10-7B[A]
Computing bond price and recording issuance

C2

Check (1) Premium, $6,948

(3) Discount, $6,326

Flagstaff Systems issues bonds dated January 1 that pay interest semiannually on June 30 and December 31. The bonds have a $90,000 par value and an annual contract rate of 12%, and they mature in five years.

Required

For each separate situation, (a) determine the bonds' issue price on January 1 and (b) prepare the journal entry to record their issuance.

1. The market rate at the date of issuance is 10%.

2. The market rate at the date of issuance is 12%.

3. The market rate at the date of issuance is 14%.

Problem 10-8B[B]
Effective Interest:
Amortization of bond discount   P5

Check (2) $257,506

(3) 6/30/2020 carrying value, $200,803

Refer to the bond details in Problem 10-4B.

Required

1. Prepare the January 1 journal entry to record the bonds' issuance.

2. Determine the total bond interest expense to be recognized over the bonds' life.

3. Prepare an effective interest amortization table like the one in Exhibit 10B.1 for the bonds' first two years.

4. Prepare the journal entries to record the first two interest payments.

Problem 10-9B[B]
Effective Interest:
Amortization of bond premium   P6

Check (2) 6/30/2021 carrying value, $327,136

Refer to the bond details in Problem 10-3B.

Required

1. Compute the total bond interest expense over the bonds' life.

2. Prepare an effective interest amortization table like the one in Exhibit 10B.2 for the bonds' life.

3. Prepare the journal entries to record the first two interest payments.

Problem 10-10B[B]
Effective Interest:
Amortization of bond

P6

Check (3) 6/30/2020 carrying value, $479,202

Valdez issues $450,000 of 13%, four-year bonds dated January 1, 2019, that pay interest semiannually on June 30 and December 31. They are issued at $493,608 when the market rate is 10%.

Required

1. Prepare the January 1 journal entry to record the bonds' issuance.

2. Determine the total bond interest expense to be recognized over the bonds' life.

3. Prepare an effective interest amortization table like the one in Exhibit 10B.2 for the bonds' first two years.

4. Prepare the journal entries to record the first two interest payments.

Analysis Component

5. Assume that the market rate at issuance is 14% instead of 10%. Without presenting numbers, describe how this change affects the amounts reported on Valdez's financial statements.

On January 1, Kwak (lessee) signs a three-year lease for equipment that is accounted for as a finance lease. The lease requires three $14,000 lease payments (the first at the beginning of the lease and the remaining two at December 31 of Year 1 and Year 2). The present value of the three annual lease payments is $39,000, using a 7.9% interest rate. The lease payment schedule follows.

Problem 10-11B^C
Accounting for finance lease
C3

	(A)	(B) Debit Interest on	(C) Debit	(D) Credit	(E) Ending Balance
Date	Beginning Balance of Lease Liability	Lease Liability 7.9% × (A) +	Lease Liability (D) − (B) =	Cash Lease Payment	of Lease Liability (A) − (C)
Jan. 1, Year 1	$39,000	▮▮▮▮▮	$14,000	$14,000	$25,000
Dec. 31, Year 1 ...	25,000	$1,975	12,025	14,000	12,975
Dec. 31, Year 2 ...	12,975	1,025	12,975	14,000	0
		$3,000	$39,000	$42,000	

Required

1. Prepare the January 1 journal entry at the start of the lease to record any asset or liability.
2. Prepare the January 1 journal entry to record the first $14,000 cash lease payment.
3. Prepare the December 31 journal entry to record straight-line amortization with zero salvage value at the end of (*a*) Year 1, (*b*) Year 2, and (*c*) Year 3.
4. Prepare the December 31 journal entry to record the $14,000 cash lease payment at the end of (*a*) Year 1 and (*b*) Year 2.

Refer to the lease details in Problem 10-11B. Assume that this lease is classified as an operating lease instead of a finance lease.

Problem 10-12B^C
Accounting for operating lease
C3

Required

1. Prepare the January 1 journal entry at the start of the lease to record any asset or liability.
2. Prepare the January 1 journal entry to record the first $14,000 cash lease payment.
3. Prepare the December 31 journal entry to record amortization at the end of (*a*) Year 1, (*b*) Year 2, and (*c*) Year 3.
4. Prepare the December 31 journal entry to record the $14,000 cash lease payment at the end of (*a*) Year 1 and (*b*) Year 2.

This serial problem began in Chapter 1 and continues through most of the book. If previous chapter segments were not completed, the serial problem can begin at this point.

SERIAL PROBLEM
Business Solutions
A1 A3

SP 10   Santana Rey has consulted with her local banker and is considering financing an expansion of her business by obtaining a long-term bank loan. Selected account balances at March 31, 2020, for **Business Solutions** follow.

Total assets	$120,268	Total liabilities	$875	Total equity	$119,393

Required

1. The bank has offered a long-term secured note to Business Solutions. The bank's loan procedures require that a client's debt-to-equity ratio not exceed 0.8. As of March 31, 2020, what is the maximum amount that Business Solutions could borrow from this bank?
2. If Business Solutions borrows the maximum amount allowed from the bank, what percentage of assets would be financed (*a*) by debt and (*b*) by equity?
3. What are some factors Santana Rey should consider before borrowing the funds?

©Alexander Image/Shutterstock

Check   (1) $94,639

Accounting Analysis

COMPANY ANALYSIS

A1   A2

APPLE

AA 10-1   Use **Apple**'s financial statements in Appendix A to answer the following.

1. Identify Apple's long-term debt as reported on its balance sheet at (*a*) September 30, 2017, and (*b*) September 24, 2016.
2. Calculate the percentage change in long-term debt from September 24, 2016, to September 30, 2017.
3. If Apple's reported long-term debt continues on the current trend, do we expect total interest expense to increase or decrease?

COMPARATIVE ANALYSIS

A3

APPLE

GOOGLE

AA 10-2   Key figures for **Apple** and **Google** follow.

$ millions	Apple		Google	
	Current Year	Prior Year	Current Year	Prior Year
Total assets	$375,319	$321,686	$197,295	$167,497
Total liabilities	241,272	193,437	44,793	28,461
Total equity	134,047	128,249	152,502	139,036

Required

1. Compute the debt-to-equity ratios for Apple and Google for both the current year and the prior year.
2. Use the ratios from part 1 to determine which company's financing structure is least risky.
3. Is its debt-to-equity ratio more risky or less risky compared to the industry (assumed) average of 0.5 for (*a*) Apple and (*b*) Google?

GLOBAL ANALYSIS

A3

Samsung

APPLE

GOOGLE

AA 10-3   Selected results from **Samsung**, **Apple**, and **Google** follow.

In millions	Samsung		Apple	Google
	Current Year	Prior Year	Current Year	Current Year
Total assets.	₩301,752,090	₩262,174,324	$375,319	$197,295
Total liabilities	87,260,662	69,211,291	241,272	44,793
Total equity.	214,491,428	192,963,033	134,047	152,502

Required

1. Compute Samsung's debt-to-equity ratio for the current year and the prior year.
2. Is Samsung's financing structure more risky or less risky in the current year versus the prior year?
3. In the current year, is Samsung's financing structure more risky or less risky than (*a*) Apple's and (*b*) Google's?

Beyond the Numbers

ETHICS CHALLENGE

C3   A1

BTN 10-1   Traverse County needs a new county government building that would cost $10 million. The politicians feel that voters will not approve a municipal bond issue to fund the building because it would increase taxes. They opt to have a state bank issue $10 million of tax-exempt securities to pay for the building construction. The county then will make yearly lease payments (of principal and interest) to repay the obligation. Unlike conventional municipal bonds, the lease payments are not binding obligations on the county and, therefore, require no voter approval.

Required

1. Do you think the actions of the politicians and the bankers in this situation are ethical?
2. In terms of risk, how do the tax-exempt securities used to pay for the building compare to a conventional municipal bond issued by Traverse County?

COMMUNICATING IN PRACTICE

P3

BTN 10-2   Your business associate mentions that she is considering investing in corporate bonds currently selling at a premium. She says that because the bonds are selling at a premium, they are highly valued and her investment will yield more than the going rate of return for the risk involved. Reply with a memorandum to confirm or correct your associate's interpretation of premium bonds.

BTN 10-3 Access the March 23, 2017, filing of the 10-K report of **Home Depot** for the year ended January 29, 2017, from <u>SEC.gov</u> (ticker: HD). Refer to Home Depot's balance sheet, including its note 4 (on debt).

TAKING IT TO THE NET

A2

Required

1. Identify Home Depot's long-term liabilities and the amounts for those liabilities from Home Depot's balance sheet at January 29, 2017.

2. Review Home Depot's note 4. The note reports that as of January 29, 2017, it had $2.947 billion of "5.875% Senior Notes; due December 16, 2036; interest payable semiannually on June 16 and December 16." These notes have a face value of $3.0 billion and were originally issued at $2.958 billion.

    a. Why would Home Depot issue $3.0 billion of its notes for only $2.958 billion?

    b. How much cash interest must Home Depot pay each June 16 and December 16 on these notes?

BTN 10-4[B] Break into teams and complete the following requirements related to *effective interest* amortization for a premium bond.

TEAMWORK IN ACTION

P5 P6

1. Each team member is to independently prepare a blank table with proper headings for amortization of a bond premium. When all have finished, compare tables and ensure that all are in agreement.

Parts 2 and 3 require use of these facts: On January 1, 2019, McElroy issues $100,000, 9%, five-year bonds at 104.1. The market rate at issuance is 8%. McElroy pays interest semiannually on June 30 and December 31.

2. In rotation, *each* team member must explain how to complete *one* line of the bond amortization table, including all computations for his or her line. All members are to fill in their tables during this process. You need not finish the table; stop after all members have explained a line.

3. In rotation, *each* team member is to identify a separate column of the table and indicate what the final number in that column will be and explain the reasoning.

4. Reach a team consensus as to what the total bond interest expense on this bond issue will be if the bond is not retired before maturity.

5. As a team, prepare a list of similarities and differences between the amortization table just prepared and the amortization table if the bond had been issued at a discount.

Hint: Rotate teams to report on parts 4 and 5. Consider requiring entries for issuance and interest payments.

BTN 10-5 Joey Shamah and Scott Borba are the founders of **e.l.f. Cosmetics**. Assume that the company currently has $250,000 in equity and is considering a $100,000 expansion to meet increased demand. The $100,000 expansion would yield $16,000 in additional annual income before interest expense. Assume that the business currently earns $40,000 annual income before interest expense of $10,000, yielding a return on equity of 12% ($30,000/$250,000). To fund the expansion, the company is considering the issuance of a 10-year, $100,000 note with annual interest payments (the principal due at the end of 10 years).

ENTREPRENEURIAL DECISION

A1

Required

1. Using return on equity as the decision criterion, show computations to support or reject the expansion if interest on the $100,000 note is (*a*) 10%, (*b*) 15%, (*c*) 16%, (*d*) 17%, and (*e*) 20%.

2. What general rule do the results in part 1 illustrate?

BTN 10-6 Visit your city or county library. Ask the librarian to help you locate the most recent financial records of your city or county government. Examine those records.

HITTING THE ROAD

A1

Required

1. Determine the amount of long-term bonds and notes currently outstanding.

2. Read the supporting information to your municipality's financial statements and record

    a. The market interest rate(s) when the bonds and/or notes were issued.

    b. The date(s) when the bonds and/or notes will mature.

    c. Any rating(s) on the bonds and/or notes received from **Moody's Investors Service, Standard & Poor's Ratings Services, Fitch Ratings**, or another rating agency.

---

11 Corporate Reporting and Analysis

Learning Objectives

CONCEPTUAL

C1 Identify characteristics of corporations and their organization.

C2 Explain characteristics of, and distribute dividends between, common and preferred stock.

C3 Explain the items reported in retained earnings.

ANALYTICAL

A1 Compute earnings per share and describe its use.

A2 Compute price-earnings ratio and describe its use in analysis.

A3 Compute dividend yield and explain its use in analysis.

A4 Compute book value and explain its use in analysis.

PROCEDURAL

P1 Record the issuance of corporate stock.

P2 Record transactions involving cash dividends, stock dividends, and stock splits.

P3 Record purchases and sales of treasury stock.

Point of View

"Trust of the consumer is critical"

—JEREMY STOPPELMAN

SAN FRANCISCO—"When I was in business school, I was thinking about doing something entrepreneurial," recalls Jeremy Stoppelman. "I'd always read the little vignettes about how someone started a small business."

"Word of mouth was the best way to find local businesses," explains Jeremy. "If we could find a way to capture that and bring it online, that would be powerful." To turn his idea into a business, Jeremy and his co-founders built **Yelp** (**Yelp.com**). Yelp publishes crowdsourced reviews about local businesses.

In the first few years of business, Jeremy had to make crucial decisions regarding creditor versus equity financing. When **Google** offered to purchase his business, Jeremy had to learn about stock types and ways to finance Yelp.

"I felt like we built this company," recalls Jeremy, "there's no fundamental reason for us to sell." Instead of selling to Google, and armed with knowledge of equity financing, Jeremy raised money from individual investors. Also, instead of paying dividends, he reinvested Yelp income into the company.

©Maria J. Avila/MCT/Newscom

Jeremy has some advice: "Building a great company takes time. If it's not something you're passionate about . . . you're not going to make it."

Sources: *Yelp website,* January 2019; *Yelp Foundation,* January 2018; *Time,* December 2014

CORPORATE FORM OF ORGANIZATION

A **corporation** is an entity that is separate from its owners and has many of the same rights as a person. Owners of corporations are called *stockholders* or *shareholders*. Corporations are separated into two types. A *privately held* (or *closely held*) corporation does not offer its stock for public sale and usually has few stockholders. A *publicly held* corporation offers its stock for public sale and can have thousands of stockholders. *Public sale* means selling and trading stock on an organized stock market.

C1

Identify characteristics of corporations and their organization.

Corporate Advantages

- **Separate legal entity:** A corporation has many of the same rights, duties, and responsibilities as a person. It takes actions through its agents, who are its officers and managers.
- **Limited liability:** Stockholders are not liable for corporate actions or debt.
- **Transferable ownership rights:** Transfer of shares from one stockholder to another has no direct effect on operations except when it causes a change in directors who oversee the corporation.
- **Continuous life:** A corporation's life is indefinite because it is not tied to the physical lives of its owners.
- **No mutual agency for stockholders:** Stockholders, who are not officers and managers, cannot bind the corporation to contracts—called *lack of mutual agency.*
- **Easier capital accumulation:** Buying stock is attractive to investors because of the advantages above, which helps corporations collect large sums of money.

Corporate Disadvantages

- **Government regulation:** A corporation must follow a state's incorporation laws. Proprietorships and partnerships avoid many of these.
- **Corporate taxation:** Corporations pay many of the same taxes as proprietorships and partnerships plus *additional* taxes. The most burdensome are federal and state corporate income taxes that together can take 21% or more of pretax income. Also, corporate income is usually taxed a second time as part of stockholders' personal income when they receive cash dividends. This is called *double taxation.*

■ Decision Insight

Artificial Unintelligence   **Dow Jones** newswire mistakenly published a bogus news story about **Google** acquiring **Apple** for $9 billion. Informed investors were not fooled, as Apple's market value was over $700 billion. However, bots designed to purchase stock of any company rumored of being acquired instantaneously purchased millions of shares of Apple. This event revealed how bots are increasingly impacting our financial markets. ■

Corporate Organization and Management

Incorporation   A corporation is created by getting a charter from a state government. A charter application is signed by the prospective stockholders called *incorporators* or *promoters* and then filed with the state. When the application process is complete and fees paid, the charter is issued and the corporation is formed. Investors then purchase the corporation's stock, meet as stockholders, and elect a board of directors.

Organization Expenses   **Organization expenses** (or *organization costs*) are the costs to start a corporation; they include legal fees, promoters' fees, and payments for a charter. The corporation records (debits) these costs to *Organization Expenses*. Organization costs are expensed as incurred.

EXHIBIT 11.1

Corporate Structure

Corporate governance is the system by which companies are directed and controlled.

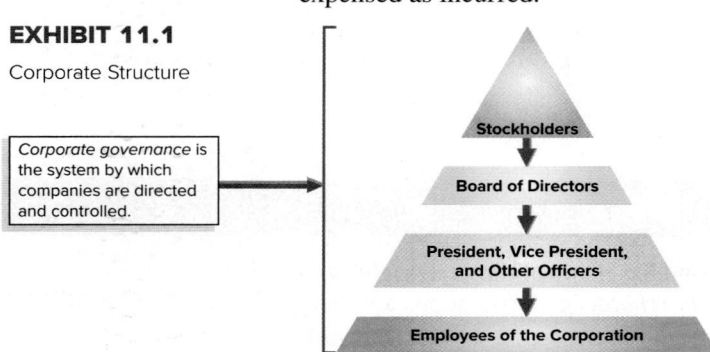

Management   Stockholders control a corporation by electing a *board of directors,* or *directors*. A stockholder usually has one vote for each share of stock owned. This control relation is shown in Exhibit 11.1. Directors are responsible for overseeing corporate activities. A board is in charge of hiring and firing key executives who manage day-to-day operations. A corporation's chief executive officer (CEO) is often its president. Several vice presidents are commonly assigned to specific areas such as finance, production, and marketing.

Point: *Bylaws* are guidelines that govern the corporation.

A corporation usually holds a stockholder meeting at least once a year to elect directors. Stockholders who do not attend stockholders' meetings can give their voting rights to an agent by signing a **proxy,** a document that gives a designated agent the right to vote the stock.

■ Decision Insight

Keep the Faith   Sources for start-up money include (1) "angel" investors such as family, friends, or anyone who believes in a company; (2) employees, investors, and even suppliers; and (3) venture capitalists (investors) who have a record of entrepreneurial success. ■

Corporate Stockholders

Rights of Stockholders   Stockholders have *specific* rights under the corporation's charter and *general* rights under state law. Stockholders also have the right to receive timely financial reports. When a corporation has only one class of stock, it is called **common stock.** State laws vary, but common stockholders usually have the right to

Point: While rare, not all common stock has voting rights; **Google's** C Class shares are nonvoting.

Point: Green Bay Packers are the only nonprofit, community-owned major professional team.

- Vote at stockholders' meetings (or register proxy votes).
- Sell or dispose of their stock.
- Purchase their proportional share of any common stock later issued. This **preemptive right** protects stockholders' proportionate interest. For example, a stockholder who owns 25% of a corporation's stock has the first opportunity to buy 25% of any new stock issued.
- Receive the same dividend, if any, on each common share.
- Share in any assets remaining after creditors and preferred stockholders are paid if the corporation is liquidated. Each common share receives the same amount.

Stock Certificates and Transfer   A corporation sometimes gives a *stock certificate* as proof of share ownership. Exhibit 11.2 shows a stock certificate issued by the **Green Bay Packers**. A certificate shows the company name, stockholder name, number of shares, and other information. Issuance of paper certificates is becoming less common.

Registrar and Transfer Agents   If a corporation's stock is traded on a stock exchange, the corporation has a registrar and a transfer agent. A *registrar* keeps a list of stockholders for stockholder meetings and dividend payments. A *transfer agent* assists with purchases and sales of shares. Registrars and transfer agents are usually large banks or trust companies.

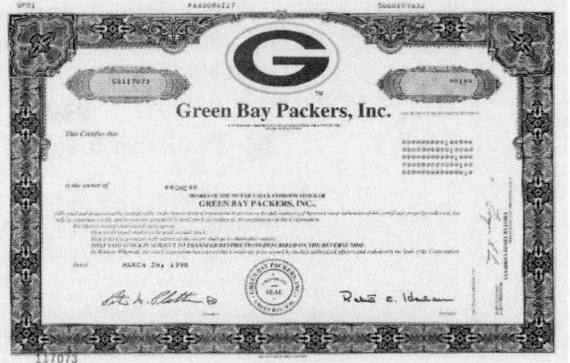

Courtesy of JJW Images

EXHIBIT 11.2

Stock Certificate

Corporate Stock

Capital stock is shares issued to obtain capital (owner financing).

Authorized Stock   **Authorized stock** is the number of shares that a corporation's charter allows it to sell. The number of authorized shares usually exceeds the number of shares issued (and outstanding) by a large amount. *Outstanding stock* is stock held by stockholders. No journal entry is required for stock authorization. A corporation discloses the number of shares authorized in the equity section of its balance sheet or notes. **Apple**'s balance sheet reports 12.6 billion common shares authorized.

Selling (Issuing) Stock   A corporation can sell stock directly or indirectly. To *sell directly,* it offers its stock to buyers. This type of sale is common with privately held corporations. To *sell indirectly,* a corporation pays a brokerage house (investment banker) to sell its stock. Some brokerage houses *underwrite* stock, meaning they buy the stock from the corporation and resell it to investors.

Market Value of Stock   **Market value per share** is the price at which a stock is bought and sold. Expected future income, dividends, growth, and economic factors influence market value. The current market value of previously issued shares does not impact the issuing corporation's stockholders' equity.

Classes of Stock   When all authorized shares have the same rights and characteristics, the stock is called *common stock.* A corporation sometimes issues more than one class of stock, including preferred stock and different classes of common stock. **American Greetings** has two types of common stock: Class A stock has 1 vote per share and Class B stock has 10 votes per share.

Par Value Stock   **Par value stock** is stock that has a **par value,** which is an amount assigned per share by the corporation in its charter. **Monster Worldwide**'s common stock has a par value of $0.001. Other commonly assigned par values are $5, $1 and $0.01. There is no restriction on assigned par value. In many states, the par value of a stock establishes **minimum legal capital,** which is the least amount that the buyers of stock must contribute to the corporation or be at risk to pay creditors at a future date.

No-Par Value Stock   **No-par value stock,** or *no-par stock,* is stock *not* assigned an amount per share by the corporate charter. There is no minimum legal capital with no-par stock.

Stated Value Stock   **Stated value stock** is no-par stock that has an assigned "stated" value per share. Stated value per share is the minimum legal capital per share in this case.

Stockholders' Equity   A corporation's equity is called **stockholders' equity,** or *shareholders' equity.* Exhibit 11.3 shows stockholders' equity consists of (1) paid-in (or contributed) capital and (2) retained

Subcategories of Authorized Stock

Authorized
Authorized & Issued
Authorized, Issued, and Outstanding

Innermost box would show a decline in shares issued if a company buys back its issued stock.

Point: Managers set a low par value when minimum legal capital or state issuance taxes are based on par.

Point: Par, no-par, and stated value do *not* affect the stock's market value.

EXHIBIT 11.3

Equity Composition

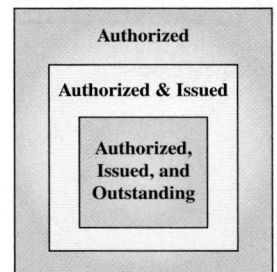

earnings. **Paid-in capital** is the total amount of cash and other assets the corporation receives from its stockholders in exchange for its stock. **Retained earnings** is the cumulative net income (and loss) not distributed as dividends to its stockholders.

■ Decision Insight

Stock Quote   The **AT&T** stock quote is interpreted as (left to right): **Hi,** highest price in past 52 weeks; **Lo,** lowest price in past 52 weeks; **Sym,** company exchange symbol;

52 Weeks									
Hi	**Lo**	**Sym**	**Div**	**Yld %**	**PE**	**Hi**	**Lo**	**Close**	**Net Chg**
42.70	32.55	T	2.00	5.24	7.95	38.31	37.77	37.81	+0.53

Div, dividends paid per share in past year; **Yld %,** dividend divided by closing price; **PE,** stock price per share divided by earnings per share; **Hi,** highest price for the day; **Lo,** lowest price for the day; **Close,** closing price for the day; **Net Chg,** change in closing price from prior day. ■

COMMON STOCK

P1_____

Record the issuance of corporate stock.

Issuance of stock affects paid-in (contributed) capital accounts; retained earnings is unaffected.

Issuing Par Value Stock

Par value stock can be issued at par, at a premium (above par), or at a discount (below par). Cash or other assets are received in exchange for stock.

Issuing Par Value Stock at Par   When common stock is issued at par value, we record both the asset(s) received and the par value stock issued. The entry to record Dillon's issuance of 30,000 shares of $10 par value stock for $300,000 cash on June 5 follows.

Assets = Liabilities + Equity
+300,000   +300,000

June 5	Cash	300,000	
	Common Stock, $10 Par Value*		300,000
	Issued 30,000 shares of $10 par value stock at par.		

*$10 par value × 30,000 shares

Issuing Par Value Stock at a Premium   A **premium on stock** occurs when a corporation sells its stock for more than par (or stated) value. If Dillon issues its $10 par value common stock at $12 per share, its stock is sold at a $2 per share premium. The premium, called **paid-in capital in excess of par value,** is reported as part of equity; it is not revenue and is not listed on the income statement. The entry to issue 30,000 shares of $10 par value stock for $12 per share follows.

Point: Paid-In Capital in Excess of Par Value is also called *Additional Paid-In Capital.*

Assets = Liabilities + Equity
+360,000   +300,000
                            +60,000

June 5	Cash.	360,000	
	Common Stock, $10 Par Value*		300,000
	Paid-In Capital in Excess of Par Value, Common Stock†		60,000
	Sold and issued 30,000 shares of $10 par value common stock at $12 per share.		

*$10 par value × 30,000 shares   †[$12 issue price − $10 par value] × 30,000 shares

Point: The phrase *paid-in capital* is interchangeable with *contributed capital.*

The Paid-In Capital in Excess of Par Value account is added to the par value of the stock in the equity section of the balance sheet, as shown in Exhibit 11.4.

EXHIBIT 11.4

Stockholders' Equity for Stock Issued at a Premium

Common stock—$10 par value; 50,000 shares authorized; 30,000 shares issued and outstanding	$300,000
Paid-in capital in excess of par value, common stock	60,000
Retained earnings*	65,000
Total stockholders' equity.	$425,000

*This is the company's first year of operations, with income of $65,000 and no dividends.

Issuing Par Value Stock at a Discount   A **discount on stock** occurs when it is sold for less than par value. Most states prohibit this. If stock is issued at a discount, the amount by which issue price is less than par is debited to a *Discount on Common Stock* account, a contra to the Common Stock account, and its balance is subtracted from the par value of stock.

Issuing No-Par Value Stock

When no-par stock is issued, the amount the corporation receives is credited to a no-par stock account. The entry to issue 1,000 shares of no-par common stock for $40 cash per share follows.

Oct. 20	Cash	40,000	
	Common Stock, No-Par Value*		40,000
	Issued 1,000 shares of no-par stock at $40 per share.		

*$40 issue price × 1,000 no-par shares

Assets = Liabilities + Equity
+40,000   +40,000

Issuing Stated Value Stock

When stated value stock is issued, the stated value is credited to the stock account. Any amount above the stated value is credited to Paid-In Capital in Excess of Stated Value, which is reported in stockholders' equity. The entry to issue 1,000 shares of no-par common stock having a stated value of $40 per share in return for $50 cash per share follows.

Frequency of Stock Types

Stated 3%
Par 88%
No-par 9%

Oct. 20	Cash	50,000	
	Common Stock, $40 Stated Value*		40,000
	Paid-In Capital in Excess of Stated Value, Common Stock† ...		10,000
	Issued 1,000 shares of $40 per share stated value stock at $50 per share.		

*$40 stated value × 1,000 shares   †[$50 issue price − $40 stated value] × 1,000 shares

Assets = Liabilities + Equity
+50,000   +40,000
                                 +10,000

Issuing Stock for Noncash Assets

A corporation can receive assets other than cash in exchange for its stock. (It also can take liabilities such as a mortgage on property received.) The corporation records the assets received at their market values as of the transaction date. The stock given in exchange is recorded at its par (or stated) value with any excess recorded in the Paid-In Capital in Excess of Par (or Stated) Value account. (If no-par stock is issued, the stock is recorded at the assets' market value.) The entry to record receipt of land valued at $105,000 in return for 4,000 shares of $20 par value common stock is

Point: Stock issued for noncash assets is recorded at the market value of either the stock or the noncash assets, whichever is more determinable.

June 10	Land	105,000	
	Common Stock, $20 Par Value*		80,000
	Paid-In Capital in Excess of Par Value, Common Stock†		25,000
	Exchanged 4,000 shares of $20 par value stock for land.		

*$20 par value × 4,000 shares   †$105,000 asset value − $80,000 par value

Assets = Liabilities + Equity
+105,000   +80,000
                                 +25,000

A corporation sometimes gives shares of its stock to promoters in exchange for their work in organizing the corporation, which it records as organization expenses. The entry to issue 600 shares of $15 par value common stock for $12,000 of organizing work is

June 5	Organization Expenses.................................	12,000	
	Common Stock, $15 Par Value*		9,000
	Paid-In Capital in Excess of Par Value, Common Stock†		3,000
	Gave promoters 600 shares of $15 par value common stock in exchange for their services.		

*$15 par value × 600 shares   †$12,000 services value − $9,000 par value

Assets = Liabilities + Equity
                                 −12,000
                                 +9,000
                                 +3,000

NEED-TO-KNOW 11-1

Recording Stock
Issuance

P1

Prepare journal entries to record the following four separate issuances of stock.

1. Issued 80 shares of $5 par value common stock for $700 cash.

2. Issued 40 shares of no-par common stock to promoters in exchange for their efforts, estimated to be worth $800. The stock has a $1 per share stated value.

3. Issued 40 shares of no-par common stock in exchange for land estimated to be worth $800. The stock has no stated value.

4. Issued 20 shares of no-par common stock with a stated value of $30 per share for $900 cash.

Solution

1.

Cash	700	
Common Stock, $5 Par Value*		400
Paid-In Capital in Excess of Par Value, Common Stock† . .		300
Issued common stock for cash.		

*80 shares × $5 per share = $400   †$700 − $400 = $300

2.

Organization Expenses	800	
Common Stock, $1 Stated Value		40
Paid-In Capital in Excess of Stated Value, Common Stock. . .		760
Issued stock to promoters.		

3.

Land	800	
Common Stock, No-Par Value.		800
Issued stock in exchange for land.		

4.

Cash	900	
Common Stock, $30 Stated Value*.		600
Paid-In Capital in Excess of Stated Value, Common Stock† . .		300
Issued stated value stock for cash.		

*20 shares × $30 stated value = $600   †$900 − $600 = $300

> Do More: QS 11-2, QS 11-3, QS 11-4, QS 11-5, E 11-3,
> E 11-4, E 11-5

DIVIDENDS

P2 _____

Record transactions
involving cash dividends,
stock dividends, and
stock splits.

Point: Amazon has never
declared a cash dividend.

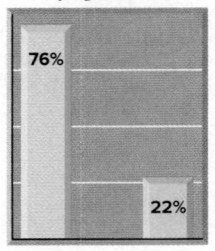

**Percent of Corporations
Paying Dividends**

76% — Cash dividend to common

22% — Cash dividend to preferred

Assets = Liabilities + Equity
  +5,000   −5,000

Cash Dividends

The board of directors decides whether to pay cash dividends. The directors may decide to keep the cash to invest in the corporation's growth, to meet emergencies, or to pay off debt. Alternatively, many corporations pay cash dividends to their stockholders at regular dates.

Accounting for Cash Dividends   Dividend payment has three important dates: declaration, record, and payment. **Date of declaration** is the date the directors vote to declare and pay a dividend. This creates a legal liability of the corporation to its stockholders. **Date of record** is the date for identifying those stockholders to receive dividends. Persons who own stock on the date of record receive dividends. **Date of payment** is the date when the corporation makes payment.

Cash Dividend Dates

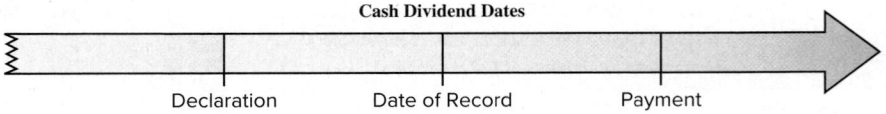

Declaration   Date of Record   Payment

The entry for a January 9 *declaration* of a $1 per share cash dividend by Z-Tech with 5,000 outstanding shares follows. Common Dividend Payable is a current liability.

Date of Declaration—Cash Dividend

Jan. 9	Retained Earnings.	5,000	
	Common Dividend Payable*		5,000
	Declared $1 per common share cash dividend.†		

*$1 per share declared dividend × 5,000 outstanding shares

†To aid learning and show how dividends impact retained earnings, we **debit** (reduce) **Retained Earnings** on the date of declaration in this chapter and all assignments. We normally debit Dividends; then, at period-end, Dividends is closed to Retained Earnings. The effect is the same: Retained earnings is decreased from dividends.

The *date of record* for this dividend is January 22. **No journal entry is made on the date of record.**

The February 1 *date of payment* entry removes the liability and reduces cash.

Date of Payment—Cash Dividend

Feb. 1	Common Dividend Payable	5,000	
	Cash		5,000
	Paid $1 per common share cash dividend.		

Assets = Liabilities + Equity
−5,000   −5,000

Deficits and Cash Dividends   A corporation with a debit (abnormal) balance for Retained Earnings has a **retained earnings deficit,** which occurs when a company has cumulative losses and/or pays more dividends than total earnings from current and prior years. A deficit reduces equity, as shown in Exhibit 11.5. Most states prohibit a corporation with a deficit from paying a cash dividend to protect creditors. Another type of dividend is a **liquidating cash dividend,** or *liquidating dividend,* where a corporation returns a portion of the capital contributed back to stockholders.

Point: The Retained Earnings Deficit account is also called *Accumulated Deficit.*

Common stock—$10 par value, 5,000 shares authorized, issued, and outstanding	$50,000
Retained earnings deficit...	(6,000)
Total stockholders' equity..	$44,000

EXHIBIT 11.5

Stockholders' Equity with a Deficit

Stock Dividends

A **stock dividend,** declared by a corporation's directors, is a distribution of additional shares of its own stock to its stockholders without any payment in return. Stock dividends and cash dividends are different. A stock dividend does not reduce assets and equity but instead transfers a portion of equity from retained earnings to contributed capital.

Reasons for Stock Dividends   Stock dividends are given for at least two reasons. First, stock dividends keep the market price of the stock affordable. When a corporation has a stock dividend, it increases the number of outstanding shares, which lowers the per share stock price. Second, a stock dividend shows management's confidence that the company is doing well and will continue to do well.

Accounting for Stock Dividends   A stock dividend transfers part of retained earnings to contributed capital accounts, called *capitalizing* retained earnings. Accounting for a stock dividend depends on whether it is a small or large stock dividend.

- A **small stock dividend** is a distribution of 25% or less of previously outstanding shares. It is recorded by capitalizing retained earnings for an amount equal to the *market value* of the shares to be distributed.
- A **large stock dividend** is a distribution of more than 25% of previously outstanding shares. It is recorded by capitalizing retained earnings for the *par or stated value* of the stock.

Hint: Five Steps to Record Stock Dividends

Step 1: Identify number of shares outstanding.
Step 2: Identify the stock dividend percentage.
Step 3: Compute number of new shares (step 1 × step 2).
Step 4: Value new shares at market (small stock dividend) *or* par (large stock dividend).
Step 5: Determine debit (reduction) to Retained Earnings (step 3 × step 4).

The equity section of Quest's balance sheet just *before* its declaration of a stock dividend on December 31 follows.

Stockholders' Equity	Before Dividend
Common stock—$10 par value, 15,000 shares authorized, 10,000 shares issued and outstanding......	$100,000
Paid-in capital in excess of par value, common stock	8,000
Retained earnings..	35,000
Total stockholders' equity	$143,000

Small Stock Dividend   Assume that Quest declares a 10% stock dividend on December 31. This stock dividend of 1,000 shares, computed as 10% of its 10,000 outstanding shares, is to be distributed on January 20 to the stockholders of record on January 15. Because the market price of Quest's stock on December 31 is $15 per share, this small stock dividend declaration is recorded as follows.

Date of Declaration—Small Stock Dividend

Assets = Liabilities + Equity
−15,000
+10,000
+ 5,000

Dec. 31	Retained Earnings....................................	15,000	
	Common Stock Dividend Distributable*............		10,000
	Paid-In Capital in Excess of Par Value, Common Stock†		5,000
	Declared a 10% stock dividend of 1,000 shares.		

*10% dividend × 10,000 outstanding shares × $10 par value
†10% dividend × 10,000 outstanding shares × [$15 market price − $10 par value]

The balance sheet changes in three ways when a small stock dividend is declared.

Point: The term *distributable* (not *payable*) is used for stock dividends. A stock dividend is never a liability because it never reduces assets.

Point: The credit to Paid-In Capital in Excess of Par Value is recorded when the stock dividend is declared. This account is not affected when stock is later distributed.

- Common Stock Dividend Distributable, an equity account that exists only until the shares are distributed, increases by $10,000.
- Paid-in capital in excess of par increases by $5,000, which is the amount in excess of par (or stated) value.
- Retained earnings decreases by $15,000, reflecting the increase in both common stock and paid-in capital in excess of par.

The impacts on stockholders' equity from the 10% stock dividend are in Exhibit 11.6.

EXHIBIT 11.6

Stockholders' Equity before, during, and after a Stock Dividend

Stockholders' Equity	Before Dividend	Date of Declaration	Date of Payment	After Dividend
Common stock—$10 par value, 15,000 shares authorized, 10,000 shares issued and outstanding..........	$100,000	$	$+10,000	$110,000
Common stock dividend distributable—1,000 shares...........	0	+10,000	−10,000	0
Paid-in capital in excess of par value, common stock	8,000	+ 5,000		13,000
Retained earnings..	35,000	−15,000		20,000
Total stockholders' equity	$143,000	$ 0	$ 0	$143,000

No entry is made on the date of record for a stock dividend. However, on January 20, the date of payment, Quest distributes the new shares and records the entry below (numbers from the "Payment" column of Exhibit 11.6). The combined effect of these entries is to transfer (or capitalize) $15,000 of retained earnings to paid-in capital accounts (see far right column of Exhibit 11.6). A stock dividend has no effect on the ownership percentage of stockholders.

Point: A stock dividend does not affect total assets or total equity.

Date of Payment—Small Stock Dividend

Assets = Liabilities + Equity
−10,000
+10,000

Jan. 20	Common Stock Dividend Distributable	10,000	
	Common Stock, $10 Par Value....................		10,000
	Record issuance of common stock dividend.		

Large Stock Dividend A corporation capitalizes retained earnings equal to the par or stated value of the newly issued shares for a large stock dividend. Suppose Quest declares a stock dividend of 30% instead of 10% on December 31. Because this dividend is more than 25%, it is a large stock dividend. This means the par value of the 3,000 (10,000 outstanding shares × 30%) dividend shares is capitalized at the date of declaration with the entry below. This transaction decreases retained earnings and increases contributed capital by $30,000.

Date of Declaration—Large Stock Dividend

Assets = Liabilities + Equity
−30,000
+30,000

Dec. 31	Retained Earnings....................................	30,000	
	Common Stock Dividend Distributable*............		30,000
	Declared a 30% stock dividend of 3,000 shares.		

*30% dividend × 10,000 outstanding shares × $10 par value

On the date of payment, the company makes the following entry.

Jan. 15	Common Stock Dividend Distributable	30,000	
	Common Stock, $10 Par Value		30,000

Stock Splits

A **stock split** is the distribution of additional shares to stockholders according to their percent ownership. When a stock split occurs, the corporation "calls in" its outstanding shares and issues more than one new share in exchange for each old share. Splits can be done in any ratio. **Apple** did a 7-for-1 stock split. Stock splits reduce the par or stated value per share. The reasons for stock splits are similar to those for stock dividends, including affordability and management confidence.

Assume CTI has 100,000 outstanding shares of $20 par value common stock with a current market value of $88 per share. A 2-for-1 stock split cuts par value in half as it replaces 100,000 shares of $20 par value stock with 200,000 shares of $10 par value stock. The split does not affect any equity amounts reported on the balance sheet or any individual stockholder's percent ownership. *No journal entry is made.* The only effect on the accounts is a change in the stock account description. After the split, CTI changes its stock account title to *Common Stock, $10 Par Value.* The stock's description on the balance sheet also changes to reflect the additional issued and outstanding shares and the new par value.

Before 5:1 Split: 1 share, $50 par

After 5:1 Split: 5 shares, $10 par

Financial Statement Effects of Dividends and Splits

	Cash Dividend	Small Stock Dividend	Large Stock Dividend	Stock Split
Total assets	Decrease	No change	No change	No change
Total liabilities	No change	No change	No change	No change
Total stockholders' equity	Decrease	No change	No change	No change
Common stock	No change	Increase	Increase	No change
Paid-in capital in excess of par	No change	Increase	No change	No change
Retained earnings	Decrease	Decrease	Decrease	No change

 Decision Maker

Entrepreneur   A company you co-founded and own stock in announces a 50% stock dividend. Has the value of your stock investment increased, decreased, or remained the same? Would it make a difference if it was a 3-for-2 stock split executed in the form of a dividend? ■   *Answer:* The stock dividend does not affect the value of your investment or give you income. However, a stock dividend can reveal positive expectations and also improve a stock's marketability by making it more affordable. The same answer applies to the 3-for-2 stock split.

Point: A reverse stock split is the opposite of a stock split and results in fewer shares. It increases the par or stated value per share.

A company began the current year with the following balances in its stockholders' equity accounts.

NEED-TO-KNOW 11-2

Common stock—$10 par, 500 shares authorized, 200 shares issued and outstanding	$2,000
Paid-in capital in excess of par, common stock	1,000
Retained earnings.	5,000
Total.	$8,000

Recording Dividends

P2

All outstanding common stock was issued for $15 per share when the company was created. Prepare journal entries to account for the following transactions during the current year.

Jan. 10   The board declared a $0.10 cash dividend per share to shareholders of record on January 28.
Feb. 15   Paid the cash dividend declared on January 10.
Mar. 31   Declared a 20% stock dividend when the market value of the stock was $18 per share.
May 1   Distributed the stock dividend declared on March 31.
Dec. 1   Declared a 40% stock dividend when the market value of the stock was $25 per share.
Dec. 31   Distributed the stock dividend declared on December 1.

Solution

Jan. 10	Retained Earnings[a]	20	
	Common Dividend Payable		20
	Declared a $0.10 per share cash dividend.		
	[a]200 outstanding shares × $0.10		
Feb. 15	Common Dividend Payable....................................	20	
	Cash..		20
	Paid $0.10 per share cash dividend.		
Mar. 31	Retained Earnings[b]	720	
	Common Stock Dividend Distributable[c]...................		400
	Paid-In Capital in Excess of Par Value, Common Stock		320
	Declared a small stock dividend of 20%, or		
	40 shares; market value is $18 per share.		
	[b]200 outstanding shares × 20% × $18 market		
	[c]40 new shares × $10 par		
May 1	Common Stock Dividend Distributable.........................	400	
	Common Stock		400
	Distributed 40 shares of common stock.		
Dec. 1	Retained Earnings[d]	960	
	Common Stock Dividend Distributable		960
	Declared a large stock dividend of 40%, or 96 shares		
	(40% × [200 + 40]); par value is $10 per share.		
	[d]240 outstanding shares × 40% × $10 par		
Dec. 31	Common Stock Dividend Distributable.........................	960	
	Common Stock		960
	Distributed 96 shares of common stock.		

Do More: QS 11-6, QS 11-7,
QS 11-8, QS 11-9, QS 11-10,
E 11-6, E 11-7, E 11-8

PREFERRED STOCK

C2

Explain characteristics of, and distribute dividends between, common and preferred stock.

Preferred stock has special rights that give it priority (or senior status) over common stock in one or more areas. Special rights usually include a preference for receiving dividends and assets in liquidation. Preferred stock has the rights of common stock unless the corporate charter excludes them. A common exclusion is the right to vote.

Issuance of Preferred Stock

Preferred stock is recorded in its own separate capital accounts. If Dillon issues 50 shares of $100 par value preferred stock for $6,000 cash, the entry is

Assets = Liabilities + Equity
+6,000   +5,000
                      +1,000

July 1	Cash..	6,000	
	Preferred Stock, $100 Par Value*..................		5,000
	Paid-In Capital in Excess of Par Value, Preferred Stock[†] ..		1,000
	Issued preferred stock for cash.		

*$100 par value × 50 shares   [†]$6,000 cash − [$100 par value × 50 shares]

The equity section of the year-end balance sheet for Dillon, including preferred stock, is in Exhibit 11.7. (The entry for issuing no-par preferred stock is similar to issuing no-par common stock. Also, the entry for issuing preferred stock for noncash assets is similar to that for common stock.)

EXHIBIT 11.7

Stockholders' Equity with Common and Preferred Stock

Stockholders' Equity	
Preferred stock—$100 par value; 1,000 shares authorized; 50 shares issued and outstanding............	$ 5,000
Paid-in capital in excess of par value, preferred stock	1,000
Common stock—$10 par value; 50,000 shares authorized; 30,000 shares issued and outstanding............	300,000
Retained earnings...	65,000
Total stockholders' equity	$371,000

Dividend Preference of Preferred Stock

Preferred stock has preference for dividends, meaning that preferred stockholders are paid their dividends before any dividends are paid to common stockholders. A preference for dividends does *not* guarantee dividends. If the directors do not declare a dividend, neither the preferred nor the common stockholders get dividends.

Cumulative or Noncumulative   Most preferred stock has a cumulative dividend right.

- **Cumulative preferred stock** gives its owners a right to be paid both the current and all prior periods' unpaid dividends before any dividend is paid to common stockholders. When preferred stock is cumulative and the directors either do not declare a dividend to preferred stockholders or declare one that does not cover the total amount of cumulative dividend, the unpaid dividend amount is called **dividend in arrears.** Accumulation of dividends in arrears on cumulative preferred stock does not guarantee they will be paid. Dividend in arrears is not a liability and is usually reported in notes to financial statements.

- **Noncumulative preferred stock** does not have rights to prior periods' unpaid dividends if they were not declared in those prior periods. It does have rights to current-period dividends.

Point: Dividend preference does not mean that preferred stockholders get more dividends than common stockholders.

To show the difference between cumulative and noncumulative preferred stock, assume that a corporation's outstanding stock includes

- 1,000 shares of $100 par, 9% preferred stock—with *potential* dividends of $9,000 per year (1,000 shares × $100 par × 9%).
- 4,000 shares of $50 par value common stock.

During 2018, the first year of operations, the directors declare cash dividends of $5,000. In 2019, they declare cash dividends of $42,000. Exhibit 11.8 shows the allocation of dividends. If the preferred stock is cumulative, the $4,000 in arrears is paid in 2019 before any other dividends are paid—shown in green below. With noncumulative preferred, the preferred stockholders never receive the $4,000 skipped in 2018.

EXHIBIT 11.8

Allocation of Dividends: Cumulative vs. Noncumulative

Preferred Stock Is Cumulative	Preferred	Common
Year 2018	$ 5,000	$ 0
Year 2019		
Step 1: Dividend in arrears	$ 4,000	
Step 2: Current year's preferred dividend	9,000	
Step 3: Remainder to common		$29,000
Totals for year 2019	$13,000	$29,000
Totals for 2018–2019	$18,000	$29,000

Preferred Stock Is Noncumulative	Preferred	Common
Year 2018	$ 5,000	$ 0
Year 2019		
Step 1: Current year's preferred dividend	$ 9,000	
Step 2: Remainder to common		$33,000
Totals for 2018–2019	$14,000	$33,000

Participating or Nonparticipating   Most preferred stock is nonparticipating.

- **Nonparticipating preferred stock** limits dividends each year. Once preferred stockholders receive a stated amount, the common stockholders get any and all additional dividends.
- **Participating preferred stock** allows preferred stockholders to share with common stockholders any dividends paid in excess of the amount stated on the preferred stock. This participation feature applies after common stockholders get dividends equal to the preferred stock's dividend percent.

Reasons for Issuing Preferred Stock

Preferred stock is issued for several reasons. One reason is to raise money without giving up control. We can, for example, raise money by issuing preferred stock with no voting rights.

A second reason is to boost the return earned by common stockholders. Suppose a corporation's organizers expect to earn an annual after-tax income of $22,000 on an investment of $200,000. If they sell $200,000 worth of common stock, the $22,000 income produces an 11%

Frequency of Preferred Stock

No preferred stock 73% Issued preferred stock 27%

return ($22,000/$200,000). If they issue $150,000 of 8% preferred stock to outsiders and $50,000 of common stock to themselves, their own return increases to 20% ([$22,000 − $12,000]/$50,000).

Use of preferred stock to increase return to common stockholders is an example of **financial leverage.** As a general rule, when the dividend rate on preferred stock is less than the rate the corporation earns on its assets, issuing preferred stock increases the rate earned by common stockholders.

Other reasons for issuing preferred stock include its appeal to some investors who believe that the corporation's common stock is too risky or that the expected return on common stock is too low.

■ **Decision Maker**

Concert Organizer Assume that you alter your business strategy from organizing concerts targeted at under 1,000 people to those targeted at between 5,000 and 20,000 people. You also incorporate because of an increased risk of lawsuits and a desire to issue stock for financing. It is important that you control the company for decisions on whom to schedule. What types of stock do you offer? ■ *Answer:* You have two options: (1) different classes of common stock or (2) common and preferred stock. You want to own stock that has all or a majority of voting power. The other class of stock, whether common or preferred, would have limited or no voting rights. In this way, you keep control and are able to raise money.

NEED-TO-KNOW 11-3

Allocating Cash Dividends

C2

A company's outstanding stock consists of 80 shares of *noncumulative* 5% preferred stock with a $5 par value and also 200 shares of common stock with a $1 par value. During its first three years of operation, the corporation declared and paid the following total cash dividends.

2018 total cash dividends $15	2019 total cash dividends.... $5	2020 total cash dividends..... $200

Part 1. Determine the amount of dividends paid each year to each of the two classes of stockholders: preferred and common. Also compute the total dividends paid to each class for the three years combined.

Part 2. Determine the amount of dividends paid each year to each of the two classes of stockholders assuming that the preferred stock is *cumulative.* Also determine the total dividends paid to each class for the three years combined.

Solution—Part 1

	Noncumulative Preferred	Common
2018 ($15 paid)		
Preferred*......................	$15	
Common—remainder............		$ 0
Total for the year	$15	$ 0
2019 ($5 paid)		
Preferred*......................	$ 5	
Common—remainder............		$ 0
Total for the year	$ 5	$ 0
2020 ($200 paid)		
Preferred*......................	$20	
Common—remainder............		$180
Total for the year	$20	$180
2018–2020 (combined $220 paid)		
Total for three years............	$40	$180

*Holders of noncumulative preferred stock are entitled to no more than $20 of dividends in any one year (5% × $5 × 80 shares).

Do More: QS 11-11, QS 11-12, QS 11-13, QS 11-14, E 11-9, E 11-10, E 11-11

Solution—Part 2

	Cumulative Preferred	Common
2018 ($15 paid)		
Preferred*......................	$15	
Common—remainder............		$ 0
Total for the year	$15	$ 0
(Note: $5 in preferred dividends in arrears; [$20 × 1 yr] − $15 paid.)		
2019 ($5 paid)		
Preferred—arrears from 2018......................	$ 5	
Preferred*......................	0	
Common—remainder............		$ 0
Total for the year	$ 5	$ 0
(Note: $20 in preferred dividends in arrears; [$20 × 2 yrs] − $15 paid − $5 paid.)		
2020 ($200 paid)		
Preferred—arrears from 2019......................	$20	
Preferred*......................	20	
Common—remainder............		$160
Total for the year	$40	$160
(Note: $0 in preferred dividends in arrears; [$20 × 3 yrs] − $15 paid − $5 paid − $40 paid.)		
2018–2020 (combined $220 paid)		
Total for three years............	$60	$160

*Holders of cumulative preferred stock are entitled to $20 of dividends declared in any year (5% × $5 × 80 shares) plus any dividends in arrears.

TREASURY STOCK

Corporations buy back their own stock for several reasons: (1) to use their shares to acquire another corporation, (2) to avoid a takeover of the company, (3) to give them to employees as compensation, and (4) to maintain a strong market for their stock or to show confidence in the current price.

A corporation's reacquired shares are called **treasury stock,** which is similar to unissued stock in several ways: (1) neither treasury stock nor unissued stock is an asset, (2) neither receives cash dividends or stock dividends, and (3) neither has voting rights.

P3

Record purchases and sales of treasury stock.

Corporations and Treasury Stock

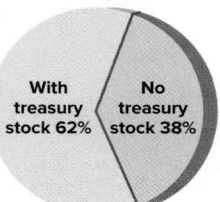

With treasury stock 62%   No treasury stock 38%

Purchasing Treasury Stock

Purchasing treasury stock reduces the corporation's assets and equity by equal amounts. We describe the *cost method* of accounting for treasury stock, which is the most popular method. (The *par value* method is explained in advanced courses.) The simple balance sheet below shows Cyber Inc.'s account balances *before* any treasury stock purchase (Cyber has no liabilities).

Assets		Stockholders' Equity	
Cash..................	$ 30,000	Common stock—$10 par; 10,000 shares authorized, issued, and outstanding................	$100,000
Other assets	95,000	Retained earnings.................................	25,000
Total assets	$125,000	Total stockholders' equity..........................	$125,000

Cyber then purchases 1,000 of its own shares for $11,500. The entry below reduces equity with a debit to the **Treasury Stock account, which is a contra equity account.**

May 1	Treasury Stock, Common*............................	11,500	
	Cash...		11,500
	Purchased 1,000 treasury shares at $11.50 per share.		

*$11.50 cost per share × 1,000 shares

Assets = Liabilities + Equity
−11,500   −11,500

The balance sheet below shows account balances *after* this transaction. The treasury stock purchase reduces Cyber's cash, total assets, and total equity by $11,500 but does not reduce Common Stock or Retained Earnings. The stock description says that 1,000 issued shares are in treasury, leaving only 9,000 shares still outstanding. The description for retained earnings says that it is partly restricted.

Point: A treasury stock purchase is also called a *stock buyback*.

Assets		Stockholders' Equity	
Cash..................	$ 18,500	Common stock—$10 par; 10,000 shares authorized and issued; 1,000 shares in treasury	$100,000
Other assets	95,000	Retained earnings, $11,500 restricted by treasury stock purchase...	25,000
		Less cost of treasury stock.................................	**(11,500)**
Total assets	$113,500	Total stockholders' equity.....................................	$113,500

Reissuing Treasury Stock

Treasury stock can be reissued by selling it at cost, above cost, or below cost.

Selling Treasury Stock at Cost   If treasury stock is reissued at cost, the entry is the reverse of the one made to record the purchase. If on May 21 Cyber reissues 100 of the treasury shares purchased on May 1 at the same $11.50 per share cost, the entry is

Assets = Liabilities + Equity
+1,150   +1,150

May 21	Cash...	1,150	
	Treasury Stock, Common*........................		1,150
	Received $11.50 per share for 100 treasury shares costing $11.50 per share.		

*$11.50 cost per share × 100 shares

Selling Treasury Stock *above* Cost

If treasury stock is sold for more than cost, the amount received in excess of cost is credited to the Paid-In Capital, Treasury Stock account. This account is reported as a separate item in the stockholders' equity section. No "gain" is ever reported from the sale of treasury stock. If Cyber receives $12 cash per share on June 3 for 400 treasury shares costing $11.50 per share, the entry is

Assets = Liabilities + Equity
+4,800   +4,600
                      +200

June 3	Cash...	4,800	
	Treasury Stock, Common*........................		4,600
	Paid-In Capital, Treasury Stock†.................		**200**
	Received $12 per share for 400 treasury shares costing $11.50 per share.		

*$11.50 cost per share × 400 shares   †[$12 issue price − $11.50 cost per share] × 400 shares

Selling Treasury Stock *below* Cost

When treasury stock is sold below cost, the entry depends on whether the Paid-In Capital, Treasury Stock account has a credit balance. If it has a zero balance, the excess of cost over the sales price is debited to Retained Earnings. If the Paid-In Capital, Treasury Stock account has a credit balance, it is debited for the excess of the cost over the selling price but not to exceed the credit balance. When the credit balance is eliminated, any remaining difference between the cost and selling price is debited to Retained Earnings. If Cyber sells its remaining 500 shares of treasury stock at $10 per share on July 10, equity is reduced by $750 (500 shares × $1.50 per share excess of cost over selling price), as shown below. This entry eliminates the $200 credit balance in the Paid-In Capital account created on June 3 and then reduces the Retained Earnings balance by the remaining $550. A company never reports a "loss" from the sale of treasury stock.

Point: Paid-In Capital, Treasury Stock account can have a zero or credit balance but never a debit balance.

Assets = Liabilities + Equity
+5,000   −200
                      −550
                      +5,750

July 10	Cash...	5,000	
	Paid-In Capital, Treasury Stock*	**200**	
	Retained Earnings†	**550**	
	Treasury Stock, Common‡........................		5,750
	Received $10 per share for 500 treasury shares costing $11.50 per share.		

*[$10 issue price − $11.50 cost per share] × 500 shares; not to exceed $200
†For any amount exceeding $200 in Paid-In Capital, Treasury Stock   ‡$11.50 cost per share × 500 shares

---

NEED-TO-KNOW 11-4

Recording Treasury Stock

P3

A company began the current year with the following balances in its stockholders' equity accounts.

Common stock—$10 par, 500 shares authorized, 200 shares issued and outstanding	$2,000
Paid-in capital in excess of par, common stock	1,000
Retained earnings...	5,000
Total...	$8,000

All outstanding common stock was issued for $15 per share when the company was created. Prepare journal entries to account for the following transactions during the current year.

July   1   Purchased 30 shares of treasury stock at $20 per share.
Sep.   1   Sold 20 treasury shares at $26 cash per share.
Dec.   1   Sold the remaining 10 shares of treasury stock at $7 cash per share.

Solution

July 1	Treasury Stock, Common[a]........................	600	
	Cash..		600
	Purchased 30 common shares at $20 per share.		
	[a]30 shares × $20 cost		
Sep. 1	Cash[b]	520	
	Treasury Stock, Common[c]		400
	Paid-In Capital, Treasury Stock		120
	Sold 20 treasury shares at $26 per share.		
	[b]20 shares × $26 reissue price [c]20 shares × $20 cost		
Dec. 1	Cash[d]	70	
	Paid-In Capital, Treasury Stock[e]	120	
	Retained Earnings	10	
	Treasury Stock, Common[f]......................		200
	Sold 10 treasury shares at $7 per share.		
	[d]10 shares × $7 reissue price		
	[e]Not to exceed existing balance [f]10 shares × $20 cost		

Treasury Stock, Common

July 1	600		
		Sep. 1	400
		Dec. 1	200
End. bal.	0		

Do More: QS 11-15, E 11-12

REPORTING OF EQUITY

Statement of Retained Earnings

Retained earnings generally consists of cumulative net income minus any net losses and dividends declared. Retained earnings does *not* mean that a certain amount of cash or other assets is available to pay stockholders. For example, **Abercrombie & Fitch** has $2,474,703 thousand in retained earnings, but only $547,189 thousand in cash.

C3

Explain the items reported in retained earnings.

Restrictions and Appropriations   **Restricted retained earnings** are statutory and contractual restrictions. A common *statutory* (or *legal*) *restriction* is to limit treasury stock purchases to the amount of retained earnings. A common *contractual restriction* is a loan agreement that restricts paying dividends beyond a specified amount of retained earnings. Restrictions are usually described in the notes. **Appropriated retained earnings** is a voluntary transfer of amounts from the Retained Earnings account to the Appropriated Retained Earnings account to inform users of special activities that require funds.

Prior Period Adjustments   **Prior period adjustments** are corrections of material errors in past financial statements. These errors include math errors, improper accounting, and missed facts. Prior period adjustments are reported in the *statement of retained earnings,* net of any income tax effects. Prior period adjustments result in changing the beginning balance of retained earnings for *events occurring prior to the earliest period reported in the current set of financial statements.* Assume that ComUS made an error two years ago in a journal entry for the purchase of land by incorrectly debiting an expense account. When this is discovered in the current year, the statement of retained earnings includes a prior period adjustment, as shown in Exhibit 11.9.

Statement of Retained Earnings	
Retained earnings, Dec. 31, 2018, as previously reported	$4,700
Prior period adjustment	
Cost of land incorrectly expensed (net of $60 of income tax benefit) ...	**200**
Retained earnings, Dec. 31, 2018, as adjusted	4,900
Plus net income	800
Less cash dividends declared	(300)
Retained earnings, Dec. 31, 2019....................................	$5,400

EXHIBIT 11.9

Statement of Retained Earnings with a Prior Period Adjustment

Many items reported in financial statements are based on estimates. Future events reveal that some estimates were inaccurate even when based on the best data available at the time. These inaccuracies are *not* considered errors and are *not* reported as prior period adjustments. Instead, they are **changes in accounting estimates** and are accounted for in current and future periods.

Statement of Stockholders' Equity

A **statement of stockholders' equity** lists the beginning and ending balances of key equity accounts and describes the changes that occur during the period. Exhibit 11.10 shows a condensed statement for **Apple**.

EXHIBIT 11.10

Statement of Stockholders' Equity

APPLE

Statement of Stockholders' Equity $ millions, shares in thousands	Common Stock Shares	Common Stock Amount	Retained Earnings	Other	Total Equity
Beginning balance	5,336,166	$31,251	$96,364	$ 634	$128,249
Net income	—	—	48,351	—	48,351
Issuance of common stock.	36,531	(913)	(581)	—	(1,494)
Repurchase of common stock & other.	(246,496)	5,529	(33,001)	(784)	(28,256)
Cash dividends	—	—	(12,803)	—	(12,803)
Ending balance	5,126,201	$35,867	$98,330	$(150)	$134,047

Ethical Risk

Fake News   Fake information can be used to pump up stock price and cause uninformed investors to buy the stock and drive up its price. After that, those who released fake information dump the stock at an inflated price. When later information reveals that the stock is overvalued, its price declines and investors still holding the stock lose value. This scheme is called *pump 'n dump*. A 15-year-old allegedly made about $1 million in one of the most infamous cases of pump 'n dump. (SEC Release No. 7891) ∎

 **Decision Analysis** ▢▢▢ Earnings per Share, Price-Earnings Ratio, Dividend Yield, and Book Value per Share

Earnings per Share

A1

Compute earnings per share and describe its use.

Earnings per share, also called *EPS* or *net income per share,* is the income earned per share of outstanding common stock. The **basic earnings per share** formula is in Exhibit 11.11. When a company has no preferred stock, then preferred dividends are zero. The weighted-average common shares outstanding is measured over the income reporting period; its computation is explained in advanced courses.

EXHIBIT 11.11

Basic Earnings per Share

$$\text{Basic earnings per share} = \frac{\text{Net income} - \text{Preferred dividends}}{\text{Weighted-average common shares outstanding}}$$

Point: Diluted EPS is another EPS measure covered in advanced courses.

Assume Quantum Co. earns $40,000 net income in 2019 and declares dividends of $7,500 on its noncumulative preferred stock. (If preferred stock is *non*cumulative, preferred dividends are only subtracted if dividends are *declared* in that same period. If preferred stock is cumulative, preferred dividends are subtracted whether declared or not.) Quantum has 5,000 weighted-average common shares outstanding during 2019. Its basic EPS is $6.50, computed as ($40,000 − $7,500) / 5,000 shares.

Price-Earnings Ratio

A2

Compute price-earnings ratio and describe its use in analysis.

A comparison of a company's EPS and its market value per share reveals market expectations. This comparison is made using a **price-earnings (or PE) ratio,** also called *price earnings* or *price to earnings*. Some analysts interpret this ratio as what price the market is willing to pay for a company's current earnings stream. Price-earnings ratios differ across companies that have similar earnings because of either higher or lower expectations of future earnings. The price-earnings ratio is in Exhibit 11.12.

EXHIBIT 11.12

Price-Earnings Ratio

$$\text{Price-earnings ratio} = \frac{\text{Market value (price) per share}}{\text{Earnings per share}}$$

Point: The average PE ratio of stocks in the 1950–2019 period is about 14.

Price-earnings ratios for **Visa** and **Mastercard** follow. Both companies have relatively high PE ratios, showing that investors have high expectations of future earnings for both. Based on Mastercard's higher PE versus Visa, one interpretation is the market is willing to pay more for Mastercard's current earnings stream.

Company	Market Value per Share	Earnings per Share	P/E Ratio
Visa..............	$105.24	$2.80	37.6
Mastercard........	$151.36	$3.67	41.2

■ Decision Maker

Money Manager You plan to invest in one of two companies identified as having identical future prospects. One has a PE of 19 and the other a PE of 25. Which do you invest in? ■ *Answer:* Because one company requires a payment of $19 for each $1 of earnings and the other requires $25, you prefer the stock with a PE of 19; it is a better deal given identical prospects.

Dividend Yield

Investors buy company stock to get a return from either or both cash dividends and stock price increases. Stocks that pay large dividends on a regular basis, called *income stocks,* are attractive to investors who want recurring cash flows from their investments. In contrast, *growth stocks* pay little or no cash dividends but are attractive to investors because of expected stock price increases. One way to help identify whether a stock is an income stock or a growth stock is to analyze its dividend yield. **Dividend yield** is defined in Exhibit 11.13.

$$\text{Dividend yield} = \frac{\text{Annual cash dividends per share}}{\text{Market value per share}}$$

The table below shows recent dividend and stock price data for **Amazon** and **Altria Group** to compute dividend yield. Dividend yield is zero for Amazon, implying it is a growth stock. An investor in Amazon expects increases in stock prices (and eventual cash from the sale of stock). Altria has a dividend yield of 5.0%, implying it is an income stock for which dividends are important in assessing its value.

A3
Compute dividend yield and explain its use in analysis.

EXHIBIT 11.13
Dividend Yield

Point: The *payout ratio* equals cash dividends declared on common stock divided by net income. A low payout ratio suggests that it is retaining earnings for growth.

Company	Cash Dividends per Share	Market Value per Share	Dividend Yield
Amazon	$0.00	$1,603	0.0%
Altria Group	$2.80	$ 56	5.0%

Book Value per Share

Book value per common share, defined in Exhibit 11.14, is the amount of equity applicable to *common* shares on a per share basis. Book value per share is the value per share if a company is liquidated at balance sheet amounts. Book value is also the starting point in many stock valuation models, merger negotiations, price setting for public utilities, and loan contracts. The main limitation in using book value is that the difference between market value and recorded value of assets and liabilities can be large.

$$\text{Book value per common share} = \frac{\text{Stockholders' equity applicable to common shares}}{\text{Number of common shares outstanding}}$$

A4
Compute book value and explain its use in analysis.

EXHIBIT 11.14
Book Value per Common Share

Consider LTD's equity in the table below. At the current date there are two years of preferred dividends in arrears.

Preferred stock—$100 par value, 7% cumulative, 2,000 shares authorized, 1,000 shares issued and outstanding.....	$100,000
Common stock—$25 par value, 12,000 shares authorized, 10,000 shares issued and outstanding...............	250,000
Paid-in capital in excess of par value, common stock	15,000
Retained earnings...	82,000
Total stockholders' equity	$447,000

LTD's book value computations follow. Equity allocated to any preferred shares is removed before the book value of common shares is computed.

Total stockholders' equity		$447,000
Less equity applicable to preferred shares: Par value (1,000 shares × $100)	$100,000	
Dividends in arrears ($100,000 × 7% × 2 years) ...	14,000	(114,000)
Equity applicable to common shares.................................		$333,000
Book value per common share ($333,000/10,000 shares)		**$ 33.30**

NEED-TO-KNOW 11-5

COMPREHENSIVE

Issuance of, and
Dividends to, Common
and Preferred Stock;
Reporting of
Stockholders' Equity

Barton Corporation began operations on January 1, 2018. The following transactions relating to stock-holders' equity occurred in the first two years of the company's operations.

2018

Jan. 1 Authorized the issuance of 2 million shares of $5 par value common stock and 100,000 shares of $100 par value, 10% cumulative preferred stock.
      2 Issued 200,000 shares of common stock for $12 cash per share.
      3 Issued 100,000 shares of common stock in exchange for a building valued at $820,000 and merchandise inventory valued at $380,000.
      4 Paid $10,000 cash to the company's founders for organization activities.
      5 Issued 12,000 shares of preferred stock for $110 cash per share.

2019

June 4 Issued 100,000 shares of common stock for $15 cash per share.

Required

1. Prepare journal entries to record these transactions.

2. Prepare the stockholders' equity section of the balance sheet as of December 31, 2018 and 2019.

3. Prepare a table showing dividend allocations for 2018 and 2019 assuming Barton declares the following cash dividends: 2018, $50,000, and 2019, $300,000.

4. Prepare the January 2, 2018, entry for issuance of 200,000 shares of common stock for $12 cash per share if
   a. Common stock is no-par stock without a stated value.
   b. Common stock is no-par stock with a stated value of $10 per share.

PLANNING THE SOLUTION

● Record journal entries for the transactions for 2018 and 2019.
● Determine the balances for the 2018 and 2019 equity accounts for the balance sheet.
● Prepare the contributed capital portion of the 2018 and 2019 balance sheets.
● Prepare a table similar to Exhibit 11.8 showing dividend allocations for 2018 and 2019.
● Record the issuance of common stock under both specifications of no-par stock.

SOLUTION

1. Journal entries.

Jan. 2, 2018	Cash.	2,400,000	
	Common Stock, $5 Par Value.		1,000,000
	Paid-In Capital in Excess of Par Value, Common Stock. .		1,400,000
	Issued 200,000 shares of common stock.		
Jan. 3, 2018	Building	820,000	
	Merchandise Inventory	380,000	
	Common Stock, $5 Par Value.		500,000
	Paid-In Capital in Excess of Par Value, Common Stock		700,000
	Issued 100,000 shares of common stock.		
Jan. 4, 2018	Organization Expenses	10,000	
	Cash.		10,000
	Paid founders for organization costs.		
Jan. 5, 2018	Cash	1,320,000	
	Preferred Stock, $100 Par Value		1,200,000
	Paid-In Capital in Excess of Par Value, Preferred Stock. . . .		120,000
	Issued 12,000 shares of preferred stock.		
June 4, 2019	Cash	1,500,000	
	Common Stock, $5 Par Value.		500,000
	Paid-In Capital in Excess of Par Value, Common Stock		1,000,000
	Issued 100,000 shares of common stock.		

2. Balance sheet presentations (at December 31 year-end).

Stockholders' Equity	2019	2018
Preferred stock—$100 par value, 10% cumulative, 100,000 shares authorized, 12,000 shares issued and outstanding....................	$1,200,000	$1,200,000
Paid-in capital in excess of par value, preferred stock.........................	120,000	120,000
Total paid-in capital by preferred stockholders...............................	1,320,000	1,320,000
Common stock—$5 par value, 2,000,000 shares authorized, 300,000 shares issued and outstanding in 2018, and 400,000 shares issued and outstanding in 2019............................	2,000,000	1,500,000
Paid-in capital in excess of par value, common stock.........................	3,100,000	2,100,000
Total paid-in capital by common stockholders	5,100,000	3,600,000
Total paid-in capital..	$6,420,000	$4,920,000

3. Dividend allocation table.

	Common	Preferred
2018 ($50,000)		
Preferred—current year (12,000 shares × $10 = $120,000)	$ 0	$ 50,000
Common—remainder (300,000 shares outstanding)	0	0
Total for the year...	$ 0	$ 50,000
2019 ($300,000)		
Preferred—dividend in arrears from 2018 ($120,000 − $50,000)	$ 0	$ 70,000
Preferred—current year	0	120,000
Common—remainder (400,000 shares outstanding)	110,000	0
Total for the year...	$110,000	$190,000

4. Journal entries.

a. For 2018 (no-par stock without a stated value).

Jan. 2	Cash...	2,400,000	
	Common Stock, No-Par Value....................		2,400,000
	Issued 200,000 shares of no-par stock at $12 per share.		

b. For 2018 (no-par stock with a stated value).

Jan. 2	Cash...	2,400,000	
	Common Stock, $10 Stated Value		2,000,000
	Paid-In Capital in Excess of Stated Value, Common Stock .		400,000
	Issued 200,000 shares of $10 stated value common stock at $12 per share.		

Summary: Cheat Sheet

COMMON STOCK

Corporate advantages: Separate legal entity, limited liability, transferable ownership, continuous life, no mutual agency for shareholders, and easier capital accumulation.

Corporate disadvantages: More government regulation and corporate income taxes (double taxation).

Issuing common stock at par value:

Cash	300,000	
Common Stock, $10 Par Value		300,000

Issuing common stock above par: When market value > par value.

Cash	360,000	
Common Stock, $10 Par Value		300,000
Paid-In Capital in Excess of Par Value, Common Stock .		60,000

Issuing no-par common stock:

Cash	40,000	
Common Stock, No-Par Value..................		40,000

Issuing stated value common stock: When market value > stated value.

Cash	50,000	
Common Stock, $40 Stated Value		40,000
Paid-in Capital in Excess of Stated Value, Common Stock		10,000

Issuing common stock for noncash assets:

Land	105,000	
Common Stock, $20 Par Value		80,000
Paid-In Capital in Excess of Par Value, Common Stock		25,000

Issuing common stock in exchange for services:

Organization Expenses	12,000	
Common Stock, $15 Par Value		9,000
Paid-In Capital in Excess of Par Value, Common Stock		3,000

DIVIDENDS

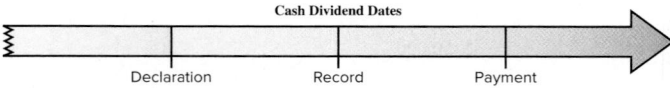

Cash dividend—Date of declaration:

Retained Earnings	5,000	
Common Dividend Payable.....................		5,000

Cash dividend—Date of record: No entry is made.

Cash dividend—Date of payment:

Common Dividend Payable	5,000	
Cash		5,000

Small stock dividend: Distribution of 25% or less of previously outstanding shares. Retained earnings is capitalized for an amount equal to *market value* of shares.

Small stock dividend—Date of declaration:

Retained Earnings	15,000	
Common Stock Dividend Distributable...........		10,000
Paid-In Capital in Excess of Par Value, Common Stock		5,000

Small stock dividend—Date of payment:

Common Stock Dividend Distributable	10,000	
Common Stock, $10 Par Value		10,000

Large stock dividend: Distribution of more than 25% of previously outstanding shares. Retained earnings is capitalized for an amount equal to *par* or *stated value* of shares.

Large stock dividend—Date of declaration:

Retained Earnings	30,000	
Common Stock Dividend Distributable...........		30,000

Large stock dividend—Date of payment:

Common Stock Dividend Distributable	30,000	
Common Stock, $10 Par Value		30,000

Stock split: Distribution of additional shares to stockholders according to percent ownership. It does not affect any equity balances. No journal entry is made. Only effect is a change in stock account description.

PREFERRED STOCK

Issuing preferred stock: When market value > par value.

Cash	6,000	
Preferred Stock, $100 Par Value................		5,000
Paid-In Capital in Excess of Par Value, Preferred Stock		1,000

Cumulative preferred stock: Preferred stockholders are paid both current and all prior periods' unpaid dividends before any dividend is paid to common stockholders.

Dividend in arrears: Unpaid dividends due to cumulative preferred stock.

Noncumulative preferred stock: Does not have rights to prior periods' unpaid dividends, only current-period dividends.

TREASURY STOCK

Treasury stock: Shares reacquired by the company. It reduces equity and does not receive dividends.

Treasury Stock, Common.......................	11,500	
Cash		11,500

Treasury stock in stockholders' equity:

Stockholders' Equity	
Common stock—$10 par; 10,000 shares authorized and issued; 1,000 shares in treasury	$100,000
Retained earnings, $11,500 restricted by treasury stock purchase	25,000
Less cost of treasury stock	**(11,500)**
Total stockholders' equity	$113,500

Selling treasury stock at cost:

Cash	1,150	
Treasury Stock, Common......................		1,150

Selling treasury stock above cost: When sale price > reacquisition price.

Cash	4,800	
Treasury Stock, Common......................		4,600
Paid-In Capital, Treasury Stock		200

Selling treasury stock below cost: When sale price < reacquisition price.

Cash	5,000	
Paid-In Capital, Treasury Stock	200	
Retained Earnings	550	
Treasury Stock, Common......................		5,750

REPORTING AND ANALYSIS

Prior period adjustments: Corrections of material errors in past financial statements. Errors include math errors, improper accounting, and missed facts. Prior period adjustments are reported in statement of retained earnings, net of any income tax effects.

Changes in accounting estimates: Revised estimates that were inaccurate even when based on the best data available at the time. These are not errors and are *not* reported as prior period adjustments. Instead, they are accounted for in current and future periods.

Statement of Retained Earnings	
Retained earnings, Dec. 31, 2018, as previously reported	$4,700
Prior period adjustment	
Cost of land incorrectly expensed (net of $60 of income tax benefit) ...	200
Retained earnings, Dec. 31, 2018, as adjusted	4,900
Plus net income..	800
Less cash dividends declared	(300)
Retained earnings, Dec. 31, 2019..............................	$5,400

Key Terms

Appropriated retained earnings (431)	Earnings per share (EPS) (432)	Preferred stock (426)
Authorized stock (419)	Financial leverage (428)	Premium on stock (420)
Basic earnings per share (432)	Large stock dividend (423)	Price-earnings (PE) ratio (432)
Book value per common share (433)	Liquidating cash dividend (423)	Prior period adjustment (431)
Capital stock (419)	Market value per share (419)	Proxy (418)
Change in an accounting estimate (432)	Minimum legal capital (419)	Restricted retained earnings (431)
Common stock (418)	Noncumulative preferred stock (427)	Retained earnings (420)
Corporation (417)	Nonparticipating preferred stock (427)	Retained earnings deficit (423)
Cumulative preferred stock (427)	No-par value stock (419)	Reverse stock split (425)
Date of declaration (422)	Organization expenses (costs) (418)	Small stock dividend (423)
Date of payment (422)	Paid-in capital (420)	Stated value stock (419)
Date of record (422)	Paid-in capital in excess of par value (420)	Statement of stockholders' equity (432)
Diluted earnings per share (432)	Par value (419)	Stock dividend (423)
Discount on stock (421)	Par value stock (419)	Stock split (425)
Dividend in arrears (427)	Participating preferred stock (427)	Stockholders' equity (419)
Dividend yield (433)	Preemptive right (418)	Treasury stock (429)

Multiple Choice Quiz

1. A corporation issues 6,000 shares of $5 par value common stock for $8 cash per share. The entry to record this transaction includes

  a. A debit to Paid-In Capital in Excess of Par Value for $18,000.

  b. A credit to Common Stock for $48,000.

  c. A credit to Paid-In Capital in Excess of Par Value for $30,000.

  d. A credit to Cash for $48,000.

  e. A credit to Common Stock for $30,000.

2. A company reports net income of $75,000. Its weighted-average common shares outstanding is 19,000. It has no other stock outstanding. Its earnings per share is

  a. $4.69.   **c.** $3.75.   **e.** $4.41.

  b. $3.95.   **d.** $2.08.

3. A company has 5,000 shares of $100 par preferred stock and 50,000 shares of $10 par common stock outstanding. Its total stockholders' equity is $2,000,000. Its book value per common share is

  a. $100.00.   **c.** $40.00.   **e.** $36.36.

  b. $10.00.   **d.** $30.00.

4. A company paid cash dividends of $0.81 per share. Its earnings per share is $6.95 and its market price per share is $45.00. Its dividend yield is

  a. 1.8%.   **c.** 15.4%.   **e.** 8.6%.

  b. 11.7%.   **d.** 55.6%.

5. A company's shares have a market value of $85 per share. Its net income is $3,500,000, and its weighted-average common shares outstanding is 700,000. Its price-earnings ratio is

  a. 5.9.   **c.** 17.0.   **e.** 41.2.

  b. 425.0.   **d.** 10.4.

ANSWERS TO MULTIPLE CHOICE QUIZ

1. e; Entry to record this stock issuance follows.

Cash (6,000 × $8)	48,000
Common Stock (6,000 × $5).	30,000
Paid-In Capital in Excess of Par Value,	
Common Stock.	18,000

2. b; $75,000/19,000 shares = $3.95 per share

3. d; Preferred stock = 5,000 × $100 = $500,000; Book value per share = ($2,000,000 − $500,000)/50,000 shares = $30 per common share

4. a; $0.81/$45.00 = 1.8%

5. c; Earnings per share = $3,500,000/700,000 shares = $5 per share; PE ratio = $85/$5 = 17.0

🔟 Icon denotes assignments that involve decision making.

Discussion Questions

1. What are organization expenses? Provide examples.

2. How are organization expenses reported?

3. 🔟 Who is responsible for overseeing corporate activities?

4. What is the difference between authorized shares and outstanding shares?

5. What is the preemptive right of common stockholders?

6. List the general rights of common stockholders.

7. What is the difference between the market value per share and the par value per share?

8. Identify and explain the importance of the three dates relevant to corporate dividends.

9. Why is the term *liquidating dividend* used to describe cash dividends debited against paid-in capital accounts?

10. 🚺 How does declaring a stock dividend affect the corporation's assets, liabilities, and total equity? What are the effects of the eventual distribution of that stock?

11. 🚺 What is the difference between a stock dividend and a stock split?

12. How does the purchase of treasury stock affect the purchaser's assets and total equity?

13. How are EPS results computed for a corporation with a simple capital structure?

14. How is book value per share computed for a corporation with no preferred stock? What is the main limitation of using book value per share to value a corporation?

15. Refer to **Apple**'s fiscal 2017 balance sheet in Appendix A. How many shares of common **APPLE** stock are authorized? How many shares of common stock are issued and outstanding?

16. 🚺 Refer to the 2017 balance sheet for **Google** in Appendix A. What is the par **GOOGLE** value per share of its preferred stock? Suggest a rationale for the amount of par value it assigned.

17. 🚺 Refer to the financial statements for **Samsung** in Appendix A. How much **Samsung** were its cash payments for treasury stock acquisitions for the year ended December 31, 2017?

🖥 **connect**

QUICK STUDY

Identify which of the following statements are true for the corporate form of organization.

QS 11-1

Characteristics of corporations

C1

_____ **1.** Ownership rights cannot be easily transferred.

_____ **2.** Owners have unlimited liability for corporate debts.

_____ **3.** Capital is more easily accumulated than with most other forms of organization.

_____ **4.** Corporate income that is distributed to shareholders is usually taxed twice.

_____ **5.** It is a separate legal entity.

_____ **6.** It has a limited life.

_____ **7.** Owners are not agents of the corporation.

QS 11-2

Issuance of common stock

P1

Prepare the journal entry to record Zende Company's issuance of 75,000 shares of $5 par value common stock assuming the shares sell for

a. $5 cash per share.   **b.** $6 cash per share.

QS 11-3

Issuance of par and stated value common stock   **P1**

Prepare the journal entry to record Jevonte Company's issuance of 36,000 shares of its common stock assuming the shares have a

a. $2 par value and sell for $18 cash per share.   **b.** $2 stated value and sell for $18 cash per share.

QS 11-4

Issuance of no-par common stock   **P1**

Prepare the journal entry to record Autumn Company's issuance of 63,000 shares of no-par value common stock assuming the shares

a. Sell for $29 cash per share.   **b.** Are exchanged for land valued at $1,827,000.

QS 11-5

Issuance of common stock

P1

Prepare the issuer's journal entry for each of the following separate transactions.

a. On March 1, Atlantic Co. issues 42,500 shares of $4 par value common stock for $297,500 cash.

b. On April 1, OP Co. issues no-par value common stock for $70,000 cash.

c. On April 6, MPG issues 2,000 shares of $25 par value common stock for $45,000 of inventory, $145,000 of machinery, and acceptance of a $94,000 note payable.

QS 11-6

Accounting for cash dividends

P2

Prepare journal entries to record the following transactions for Emerson Corporation.

July 15   Declared a cash dividend payable to common stockholders of $165,000.
Aug. 15   Date of record is August 15 for the cash dividend declared on July 15.
Aug. 31   Paid the dividend declared on July 15.

QS 11-7

Accounting for small stock dividends   **P2**

Epic Inc. has 10,000 shares of $2 par value common stock outstanding. Epic declares a 5% stock dividend on July 1 when the stock's market value is $8 per share. The stock dividend is distributed on July 20. Prepare journal entries for (*a*) declaration and (*b*) distribution of the stock dividend.

The stockholders' equity section of Jun Co.'s balance sheet as of April 1 follows. On April 2, Jun declares and distributes a 10% stock dividend. The stock's per share market value on April 2 is $20 (prior to the dividend). Prepare the stockholders' equity section immediately after the stock dividend is distributed.

QS 11-8
Accounting for small stock dividend
P2

Common stock—$5 par value, 375,000 shares authorized, 200,000 shares issued and outstanding.........	$1,000,000
Paid-in capital in excess of par value, common stock	600,000
Retained earnings...	833,000
Total stockholders' equity	$2,433,000

Belkin Inc. has 100,000 shares of $3 par value common stock outstanding. Belkin declares a 40% stock dividend on March 2 when the stock's market value is $72 per share. Prepare the journal entry for declaration of the stock dividend.

QS 11-9
Accounting for large stock dividends **P2**

Indicate whether each of the following statements regarding dividends is true or false.
_____ **1.** Cash and stock dividends reduce retained earnings.
_____ **2.** Dividends payable is recorded at the time a cash dividend is declared.
_____ **3.** The date of record is the date a cash dividend is paid to stockholders.
_____ **4.** Stock dividends help keep the market price of stock affordable.

QS 11-10
Accounting for dividends
P2

1. Prepare the journal entry to record Tamas Company's issuance of 5,000 shares of $100 par value, 7% cumulative preferred stock for $102 cash per share.
2. Assuming the facts in part 1, if Tamas declares a year-end cash dividend, what is the amount of dividend paid to preferred shareholders? (Assume no dividends in arrears.)

QS 11-11
Preferred stock issuance and dividends **C2**

Stockholders' equity of Ernst Company consists of 80,000 shares of $5 par value, 8% cumulative preferred stock and 250,000 shares of $1 par value common stock. Both classes of stock have been outstanding since the company's inception. Ernst did not declare any dividends in the prior year, but it now declares and pays a $110,000 cash dividend at the current year-end. Determine the amount distributed to each class of stockholders for this two-year-old company.

QS 11-12
Dividend allocation between classes of shareholders **C2**

Green Planet Corp. has 5,000 shares of noncumulative 10% preferred stock with a $2 par value and 17,000 shares of common stock with a $0.01 par value. During its first two years of operation, Green Planet declared and paid the following total cash dividends. Compute the dividends paid *each year* to each of the two classes of stockholders: preferred and common.

QS 11-13
Dividends on noncumulative preferred stock
C2

Year 1 total cash dividends	$800	Year 2 total cash dividends	$1,700

Use the information in QS 11-13 to compute the dividends paid *each year* to each of the two classes of stockholders assuming that the preferred stock is *cumulative*.

QS 11-14
Dividends on cumulative preferred stock **C2**

On May 3, Zirbal Corporation purchased 4,000 shares of its own stock for $36,000 cash. On November 4, Zirbal reissued 850 shares of this treasury stock for $8,500. Prepare the May 3 and November 4 journal entries to record Zirbal's purchase and reissuance of treasury stock.

QS 11-15
Purchase and sale of treasury stock **P3**

Identify whether stockholders' equity would increase (I), decrease (D), or have no effect (NE) as a result of each separate transaction listed below.
_____ **1.** A stock dividend equal to 30% of the previously outstanding shares is declared.
_____ **2.** New shares of common stock are issued for cash.
_____ **3.** Treasury shares of common stock are purchased.
_____ **4.** Cash dividends are paid to shareholders.

QS 11-16
Impacts of stock issuances, dividends, splits, and treasury transactions
P2 **P3**

On December 31, Westworld Inc. has the following equity accounts and balances: Retained Earnings, $45,000; Common Stock, $1,000; Treasury Stock, $2,000; Paid-In Capital in Excess of Par Value, Common Stock, $39,000; Preferred Stock, $7,000; and Paid-In Capital in Excess of Par Value, Preferred Stock, $3,000. Prepare the stockholders' equity section of Westworld's balance sheet.

QS 11-17
Preparing stockholders' equity section
C2 **P1** **P3**

QS 11-18
Accounting for changes in estimates; error adjustments

C3

For each situation, identify whether it is treated as a prior period adjustment or change in accounting estimate.

1. A review of notes payable discovers that three years ago the company reported the entire amount of a payment (principal and interest) on an installment note payable as interest expense. This mistake had a material effect on net income in that year.

2. After using an expected useful life of seven years and no salvage value to depreciate its office equipment over the preceding three years, the company decided early this year that the equipment will last only two more years.

3. Upon reviewing customer contracts, the company realizes it mistakenly reported $150,000 in revenue instead of the actual amount earned of $15,000. This mistake occurred two years ago and had a material effect on financial statements.

QS 11-19
Determining retained earnings balance C3

On January 1, Payson Inc. had a retained earnings balance of $20,000. During the year, Payson reported net income of $30,000 and paid cash dividends of $17,000. Calculate the retained earnings balance at its December 31 year-end.

QS 11-20
Basic earnings per share A1

Murray Company reports net income of $770,000 for the year. It has no preferred stock, and its weighted-average common shares outstanding is 280,000 shares. Compute its basic earnings per share.

QS 11-21
Basic earnings per share A1

Epic Company earned net income of $900,000 this year. There were 400,000 weighted-average common shares outstanding, and preferred shareholders received a $20,000 cash dividend. Compute Epic Company's basic earnings per share.

QS 11-22
Price-earnings ratio

A2

Compute Topp Company's price-earnings ratio if its common stock has a market value of $20.54 per share and its EPS is $3.95. Its key competitor, Lower Deck, has a PE ratio of 9.5. For which company does the market have higher expectations of future performance?

QS 11-23
Dividend yield A3

Foxburo Company expects to pay a $2.34 per share cash dividend this year on its common stock. The current market value of Foxburo stock is $32.50 per share. Compute the expected dividend yield. If a competitor with a dividend yield of 3% is considered an income stock, would we classify Foxburo as a growth or an income stock?

QS 11-24
Book value per common share

A4

The stockholders' equity section of Montel Company's balance sheet follows. No preferred dividends are in arrears at the current date. Determine the book value per share of the common stock.

Preferred stock—5% cumulative, $10 par value, 20,000 shares authorized, issued, and outstanding	$ 200,000
Common stock—$5 par value, 200,000 shares authorized, 150,000 shares issued and outstanding	750,000
Retained earnings	900,000
Total stockholders' equity	$1,850,000

Ⅲ connect

EXERCISES

Exercise 11-1
Characteristics of corporations

C1

Next to each corporate characteristic 1 through 8, enter the letter of the description that best relates to it.

_____ 1. Owner authority and control
_____ 2. Ease of formation
_____ 3. Transferability of ownership
_____ 4. Ability to raise large capital amounts
_____ 5. Duration of life
_____ 6. Owner liability
_____ 7. Legal status
_____ 8. Tax status of income

a. Requires government approval
b. Corporate income is taxed
c. Separate legal entity
d. Readily transferred
e. One vote per share
f. High ability
g. Unlimited
h. Limited

Exercise 11-2
Rights of stockholders

C1

Indicate which activities of Stockton Corporation violated the rights of a stockholder who owned one share of common stock.

1. Did not allow the stockholder to sell the stock to her brother.

2. Rejected the stockholder's request to be put in charge of its retail store.

3. Paid the stockholder a smaller dividend per share than another common stockholder.

4. Rejected the stockholder's request to vote via proxy because she was home sick.

5. In liquidation, paid the common shareholder after all creditors were already paid.

Rodriguez Corporation issues 19,000 shares of its common stock for $152,000 cash on February 20. Prepare journal entries to record this event under each of the following separate situations.

1. The stock has a $2 par value.   **3.** The stock has a $5 stated value.

2. The stock has neither par nor stated value.

Exercise 11-3
Accounting for par, stated, and no-par stock issuances
P1

Prepare journal entries to record each of the following four separate issuances of stock.

1. A corporation issued 4,000 shares of $5 par value common stock for $35,000 cash.

2. A corporation issued 2,000 shares of no-par common stock to its promoters in exchange for their efforts, estimated to be worth $40,000. The stock has a $1 per share stated value.

3. A corporation issued 2,000 shares of no-par common stock to its promoters in exchange for their efforts, estimated to be worth $40,000. The stock has no stated value.

4. A corporation issued 1,000 shares of $50 par value preferred stock for $60,000 cash.

Exercise 11-4
Recording stock issuances
P1

Sudoku Company issues 7,000 shares of $7 par value common stock in exchange for land and a building. The land is valued at $45,000 and the building at $85,000. Prepare the journal entry to record issuance of the stock in exchange for the land and building.

Exercise 11-5
Stock issuance for noncash assets **P1**

On June 30, Sharper Corporation's stockholders' equity section of its balance sheet appears as follows before any stock dividend or split. Sharper declares and immediately distributes a 50% stock dividend. After the distribution is made, (1) prepare the updated stockholders' equity section and (2) compute the number of shares outstanding.

Exercise 11-6
Large stock dividend
P2

Common stock—$10 par value, 50,000 shares issued and outstanding	$ 500,000
Paid-in capital in excess of par value, common stock	200,000
Retained earnings	660,000
Total stockholders' equity	$1,360,000

Refer to the information in Exercise 11-6. Assume that instead of distributing a stock dividend, Sharper did a 3-for-1 stock split. After the split, (1) prepare the updated stockholders' equity section and (2) compute the number of shares outstanding. *Hint:* A 3-for-1 split means that each *old* share is replaced with 3 *new* shares.

Exercise 11-7
Stock split **P2**

The stockholders' equity section of TVX Company on February 4 follows.

Exercise 11-8
Small stock dividend
P2

Common stock—$10 par value, 150,000 shares authorized, 60,000 shares issued and outstanding	$ 600,000
Paid-in capital in excess of par value, common stock	425,000
Retained earnings	550,000
Total stockholders' equity	$1,575,000

On February 5, the directors declare a 20% stock dividend distributable on February 28 to the February 15 stockholders of record. The stock's market value is $40 per share on February 5 before the stock dividend.

1. Prepare entries to record both the dividend declaration and its distribution.

2. Prepare the stockholders' equity section after the stock dividend is distributed. (Assume no other changes to equity.)

Match each description with the characteristic of preferred stock that it best describes.

A. Cumulative   **B.** Noncumulative   **C.** Nonparticipating   **D.** Participating

____ **1.** Receives current and all past dividends before common stockholders receive any dividends.

____ **2.** Receives dividends exceeding the stated rate under certain conditions.

____ **3.** Not entitled to receive dividends in excess of the stated rate.

____ **4.** Loses any dividends that are not declared in the current year.

Exercise 11-9
Identifying characteristics of preferred stock
C2

York's outstanding stock consists of 80,000 shares of *noncumulative* 7.5% preferred stock with a $5 par value and also 200,000 shares of common stock with a $1 par value. During its first four years of operation, the corporation declared and paid the following total cash dividends. Determine the amount of dividends paid each year to each of the two classes of stockholders: preferred and common. Also compute the total dividends paid to each class for the four years combined.

Exercise 11-10
Dividends on common and noncumulative preferred stock
C2

Year 1 total cash dividends	$20,000	Year 3 total cash dividends	$200,000
Year 2 total cash dividends	28,000	Year 4 total cash dividends	350,000

Check 4-year total paid to preferred, $108,000

Exercise 11-11
Dividends on common and cumulative preferred stock

C2

Use the data in Exercise 11-10 to determine the amount of dividends paid each year to each of the two classes of stockholders assuming that the preferred stock is *cumulative*. Also determine the total dividends paid to each class for the four years combined.

Exercise 11-12
Recording and reporting treasury stock transactions

P3

On October 10, the stockholders' equity section of Sherman Systems appears as follows.

Common stock—$10 par value, 72,000 shares authorized, issued, and outstanding......	$ 720,000
Paid-in capital in excess of par value, common stock	216,000
Retained earnings..	864,000
Total stockholders' equity	$1,800,000

1. Prepare journal entries to record the following transactions for Sherman Systems.
   a. Purchased 5,000 shares of its own common stock at $25 per share on October 11.
   b. Sold 1,000 treasury shares on November 1 for $31 cash per share.
   c. Sold all remaining treasury shares on November 25 for $20 cash per share.
2. Prepare the stockholders' equity section after the October 11 treasury stock purchase.

Check (1c) Dr. Retained Earnings, $14,000

Exercise 11-13
Preparing stockholders' equity section

C2   C3   P1   P3

In Draco Corporation's first year of business, the following transactions affected its equity accounts. Prepare the stockholders' equity section of Draco's balance sheet as of December 31.

- Issued 4,000 shares of $2 par value common stock for $18. It authorized 20,000 shares.
- Issued 1,000 shares of 12%, $10 par value preferred stock for $23. It authorized 3,000 shares.
- Reacquired 200 shares of common stock for $30 each.
- Retained earnings is impacted by reported net income of $50,000 and cash dividends of $15,000.

Exercise 11-14
Determining retained earnings balance

C3

Tuscan Inc. had a retained earnings balance of $60,000 at December 31, 2018. During the year, Tuscan had the following selected transactions. Calculate the retained earnings balance at December 31, 2019.

- Reported net income of $100,000.
- Revised an estimate of a machine's salvage value. Depreciation increased by $1,000 per year.
- An error was discovered. Three years ago, a purchase of a building was incorrectly expensed. The effect is understated retained earnings of $12,000 (net of tax benefit).
- Paid cash dividends of $33,000.

Exercise 11-15
Preparing a statement of retained earnings

C3

The following information is from Amos Company for the year ended December 31, 2019. Prepare a statement of retained earnings for Amos Company.

- Retained earnings at December 31, 2018 (before discovery of error), $1,375,000.
- Cash dividends declared and paid during the year, $43,000.
- Two years ago, it forgot to record depreciation expense of $55,500 (net of tax benefit).
- The company earned $126,000 in net income this year.

Exercise 11-16
Earnings per share

A1

Ecker Company reports $2,700,000 of net income and declares $388,020 of cash dividends on its preferred stock for the year. At year-end, the company had 678,000 weighted-average shares of common stock.

1. What amount of net income is available to common stockholders?
2. What is the company's basic EPS?

Check (2) $3.41

Exercise 11-17
Earnings per share

A1

Kelley Company reports $960,000 of net income and declares $120,000 of cash dividends on its preferred stock for the year. At year-end, the company had 400,000 weighted-average shares of common stock.

1. What amount of net income is available to common stockholders?
2. What is the company's basic EPS? Round your answer to the nearest whole cent.

Check (2) $2.10

Compute the price-earnings ratio for each of these four separate companies. For which of these four companies does the market have the lowest expectation of future performance?

Exercise 11-18
Price-earnings ratio
computation and
interpretation

A2

	A	B	C
1	Company	Earnings per Share	Market Value per Share
2	Hilton	$12.00	$176.40
3	SPG	10.00	96.00
4	Hyatt	7.50	93.75
5	Accor	50.00	250.00

Compute the dividend yield for each of these four separate companies. Which company's stock would probably *not* be classified as an income stock?

Exercise 11-19
Dividend yield computation
and interpretation

A3

	A	B	C
1	Company	Annual Cash Dividend per Share	Market Value per Share
2	Etihad	$16.06	$220.00
3	United	13.86	132.00
4	Lingus	3.96	72.00
5	Allied	0.48	80.00

The equity section of Cyril Corporation's balance sheet shows the following.

Exercise 11-20
Book value per share

A4

Preferred stock—6% cumulative, $25 par value, 10,000 shares issued and outstanding.....................	$ 250,000
Common stock—$8 par value, 100,000 shares issued and outstanding	800,000
Retained earnings...	535,000
Total stockholders' equity	$1,585,000

Determine the book value per share of common stock under two separate situations.
1. No preferred dividends are in arrears at the current date.
2. Three years of preferred dividends are in arrears at the current date.

Check (1) Book value of
common, $13.35 per share

Alexander Corporation reports the following components of stockholders' equity at December 31, 2018.

Exercise 11-21
Cash dividends, treasury
stock, and statement of
retained earnings

C3 P2 P3

Common stock—$25 par value, 50,000 shares authorized, 30,000 shares issued and outstanding...........	$ 750,000
Paid-in capital in excess of par value, common stock	50,000
Retained earnings..	340,000
Total stockholders' equity	$1,140,000

During 2019, the following transactions affected its stockholders' equity accounts.

Jan. 2   Purchased 3,000 shares of its own stock at $25 cash per share.
Jan. 7   Directors declared a $1.50 per share cash dividend payable on February 28 to the February 9 stockholders of record.
Feb. 28   Paid the dividend declared on January 7.
July 9   Sold 1,200 of its treasury shares at $30 cash per share.
Aug.27   Sold 1,500 of its treasury shares at $20 cash per share.
Sep. 9   Directors declared a $2 per share cash dividend payable on October 22 to the September 23 stockholders of record.
Oct. 22   Paid the dividend declared on September 9.
Dec. 31   Closed the $52,000 credit balance (from net income) in the Income Summary account to Retained Earnings.

Required

1. Prepare journal entries to record each of these transactions.
2. Prepare a statement of retained earnings for the year ended December 31, 2019.
3. Prepare the stockholders' equity section of the company's balance sheet as of December 31, 2019.

■ connect

PROBLEM SET A

Problem 11-1A
Stockholders' equity
transactions and analysis

P1   A4

Kinkaid Co. was incorporated at the beginning of this year and had a number of transactions. The following journal entries impacted its stockholders' equity during its first year of operations.

a.	Cash	300,000	
	Common Stock, $25 Par Value		250,000
	Paid-In Capital in Excess of Par Value, Common Stock		50,000
b.	Organization Expenses	150,000	
	Common Stock, $25 Par Value		125,000
	Paid-In Capital in Excess of Par Value, Common Stock		25,000
c.	Cash	43,000	
	Accounts Receivable	15,000	
	Building..	81,500	
	Notes Payable		59,500
	Common Stock, $25 Par Value		50,000
	Paid-In Capital in Excess of Par Value, Common Stock		30,000
d.	Cash	120,000	
	Common Stock, $25 Par Value		75,000
	Paid-In Capital in Excess of Par Value, Common Stock		45,000

Required

1. Explain the transaction(s) underlying each journal entry (*a*) through (*d*).
2. How many shares of common stock are outstanding at year-end?
3. What is the total paid-in capital at year-end?
4. What is the book value per share of the common stock at year-end if total paid-in capital plus retained earnings equals $695,000?

Check   (2) 20,000 shares
(3) $650,000

Problem 11-2A
Cash dividends, treasury
stock, and statement of
retained earnings

C3   P2   P3

Kohler Corporation reports the following components of stockholders' equity at December 31, 2018.

Common stock—$10 par value, 100,000 shares authorized, 40,000 shares issued and outstanding..........	$400,000
Paid-in capital in excess of par value, common stock	60,000
Retained earnings...	270,000
Total stockholders' equity	$730,000

During 2019, the following transactions affected its stockholders' equity accounts.

Jan.	2	Purchased 4,000 shares of its own stock at $20 cash per share.
Jan.	5	Directors declared a $2 per share cash dividend payable on February 28 to the February 5 stockholders of record.
Feb.	28	Paid the dividend declared on January 5.
July	6	Sold 1,500 of its treasury shares at $24 cash per share.
Aug.	22	Sold 2,500 of its treasury shares at $17 cash per share.
Sep.	5	Directors declared a $2 per share cash dividend payable on October 28 to the September 25 stockholders of record.
Oct.	28	Paid the dividend declared on September 5.
Dec.	31	Closed the $388,000 credit balance (from net income) in the Income Summary account to Retained Earnings.

Required

1. Prepare journal entries to record each of these transactions.
2. Prepare a statement of retained earnings for the year ended December 31, 2019.
3. Prepare the stockholders' equity section of the company's balance sheet as of December 31, 2019.

Check   (2) Ending retained
earnings, $504,500

At September 30, the end of Beijing Company's third quarter, the following stockholders' equity accounts are reported.

Problem 11-3A
Equity analysis—journal entries and account balances
P2

Common stock, $12 par value.................................	$360,000
Paid-in capital in excess of par value, common stock	90,000
Retained earnings...	320,000

In the fourth quarter, the following entries related to its equity are recorded.

Oct. 2	Retained Earnings..	60,000	
	Common Dividend Payable.............................		60,000
Oct. 25	Common Dividend Payable	60,000	
	Cash		60,000
Oct. 31	Retained Earnings...	75,000	
	Common Stock Dividend Distributable....................		36,000
	Paid-In Capital in Excess of Par Value, Common Stock		39,000
Nov. 5	Common Stock Dividend Distributable	36,000	
	Common Stock, $12 Par Value		36,000
Dec. 1	Memo—Change the title of the Common Stock account to reflect the new par value of $4.		
Dec. 31	Income Summary	210,000	
	Retained Earnings		210,000

Required

1. Explain the transaction(s) underlying each journal entry.
2. Complete the following table showing the equity account balances at each indicated date (take into account the beginning balances from September 30).

	Sep. 30	Oct. 2	Oct. 25	Oct. 31	Nov. 5	Dec. 1	Dec. 31
Common stock	$ 360,000	$____	$____	$____	$____	$____	$____
Common stock dividend distributable	0	____	____	____	____	____	____
Paid-in capital in excess of par, common stock	90,000	____	____	____	____	____	____
Retained earnings	320,000	____	____	____	____	____	____
Total equity	$ 770,000	$____	$____	$____	$____	$____	$____

Check   Total equity: Oct. 2, $710,000; Dec. 31, $920,000

The equity sections for Atticus Group at the beginning of the year (January 1) and end of the year (December 31) follow.

Problem 11-4A
Analyzing changes in stockholders' equity accounts
C3   P2   P3

Stockholders' Equity (January 1)

Common stock—$4 par value, 100,000 shares authorized, 40,000 shares issued and outstanding............	$160,000
Paid-in capital in excess of par value, common stock	120,000
Retained earnings...	320,000
Total stockholders' equity	$600,000

Stockholders' Equity (December 31)

Common stock—$4 par value, 100,000 shares authorized, 47,400 shares issued, 3,000 shares in treasury......	$189,600
Paid-in capital in excess of par value, common stock	179,200
Retained earnings ($30,000 restricted by treasury stock)...	400,000
	768,800
Less cost of treasury stock...	(30,000)
Total stockholders' equity	$738,800

The following transactions and events affected its equity during the year.

Jan.   5   Declared a $0.50 per share cash dividend, date of record January 10.
Mar. 20   Purchased treasury stock for cash.
Apr.   5   Declared a $0.50 per share cash dividend, date of record April 10.
July   5   Declared a $0.50 per share cash dividend, date of record July 10.
July 31   Declared a 20% stock dividend when the stock's market value was $12 per share.
Aug. 14   Issued the stock dividend that was declared on July 31.
Oct.   5   Declared a $0.50 per share cash dividend, date of record October 10.

Required

1. How many common shares are outstanding on each cash dividend date?
2. What is the total dollar amount for each of the four cash dividends?

Check   (3) $88,800

3. What is the amount of retained earnings transferred to paid-in capital accounts (capitalized) for the stock dividend?

(4) $10

4. What is the per share cost of the treasury stock purchased?

(5) $248,000

5. How much net income did the company earn this year?

Problem 11-5A
Computing book values
and dividend allocations

C2   A4

Raphael Corporation's balance sheet shows the following stockholders' equity section.

Preferred stock—5% cumulative, $___ par value, 1,000 shares authorized, issued, and outstanding	$ 50,000
Common stock—$___ par value, 4,000 shares authorized, issued, and outstanding	80,000
Retained earnings.	150,000
Total stockholders' equity	$280,000

Required

1. What are the par values of the corporation's preferred stock and its common stock?
2. If no dividends are in arrears at the current date, what is the book value per share of common stock? Round per share value to the nearest cent.

Check   (3) Book value of
common, $56.25

3. If two years' preferred dividends are in arrears at the current date, what is the book value per share of common stock? Round per share value to the nearest cent.
4. If two years' preferred dividends are in arrears at the current date and the board of directors declares cash dividends of $11,500, what total amount will be paid to the preferred and to the common shareholders?

PROBLEM SET B

Weiss Company was incorporated at the beginning of this year and had a number of transactions. The following journal entries impacted its stockholders' equity during its first year of operations.

Problem 11-1B
Stockholders' equity
transactions and analysis

P1   A4

a.	Cash	120,000	
	Common Stock, $1 Par Value		3,000
	Paid-In Capital in Excess of Par Value, Common Stock		117,000
b.	Organization Expenses	40,000	
	Common Stock, $1 Par Value		1,000
	Paid-In Capital in Excess of Par Value, Common Stock		39,000
c.	Cash	13,300	
	Accounts Receivable	8,000	
	Building.	37,000	
	Notes Payable		18,300
	Common Stock, $1 Par Value		800
	Paid-In Capital in Excess of Par Value, Common Stock		39,200
d.	Cash	60,000	
	Common Stock, $1 Par Value		1,200
	Paid-In Capital in Excess of Par Value, Common Stock		58,800

Required

1. Explain the transaction(s) underlying each journal entry (*a*) through (*d*).

Check   (2) 6,000 shares

2. How many shares of common stock are outstanding at year-end?

3. What is the total paid-in capital at year-end?

4. What is the book value per share of the common stock at year-end if total paid-in capital plus retained earnings equals $283,200?

(3) $260,000

Balthus Corp. reports the following components of stockholders' equity at December 31, 2018.

Common stock—$1 par value, 320,000 shares authorized, 200,000 shares issued and outstanding.	$ 200,000
Paid-in capital in excess of par value, common stock	1,400,000
Retained earnings.	2,160,000
Total stockholders' equity	$3,760,000

It completed the following transactions related to stockholders' equity during 2019.

Jan. 10 Purchased 40,000 shares of its own stock at $12 cash per share.
Mar.   2 Directors declared a $1.50 per share cash dividend payable on March 31 to the March 15 stock-holders of record.
Mar. 31 Paid the dividend declared on March 2.
Nov. 11 Sold 24,000 of its treasury shares at $13 cash per share.
Nov. 25 Sold 16,000 of its treasury shares at $9.50 cash per share.
Dec.   1 Directors declared a $2.50 per share cash dividend payable on January 2 to the December 10 stockholders of record.
Dec. 31 Closed the $1,072,000 credit balance (from net income) in the Income Summary account to Retained Earnings.

Required

1. Prepare journal entries to record each of these transactions.

2. Prepare a statement of retained earnings for the year ended December 31, 2019.

3. Prepare the stockholders' equity section of the company's balance sheet as of December 31, 2019.

Problem 11-2B
Cash dividends, treasury stock, and statement of retained earnings

C3   P2   P3

Check   (2) Ending retained earnings, $2,476,000

At December 31, the end of Chilton Communication's third quarter, the following stockholders' equity accounts are reported.

Common stock, $10 par value.	$ 960,000
Paid-in capital in excess of par value, common stock	384,000
Retained earnings.	1,600,000

In the fourth quarter, the following entries related to its equity are recorded.

Problem 11-3B
Equity analysis—journal entries and account balances

P2

Jan. 17	Retained Earnings.	96,000	
	Common Dividend Payable.		96,000
Feb. 5	Common Dividend Payable	96,000	
	Cash		96,000
Feb. 28	Retained Earnings.	252,000	
	Common Stock Dividend Distributable.		120,000
	Paid-In Capital in Excess of Par Value, Common Stock		132,000
Mar. 14	Common Stock Dividend Distributable	120,000	
	Common Stock, $10 Par Value		120,000
Mar. 25	Memo—Change the title of the Common Stock account to reflect the new par value of $5.		
Mar. 31	Income Summary	720,000	
	Retained Earnings		720,000

Required

1. Explain the transaction(s) underlying each journal entry.
2. Complete the following table showing the equity account balances at each indicated date (take into account the beginning balances from December 31).

	Dec. 31	Jan. 17	Feb. 5	Feb. 28	Mar. 14	Mar. 25	Mar. 31
Common stock	$ 960,000	$_____	$_____	$_____	$_____	$_____	$_____
Common stock dividend distributable	0	_____	_____	_____	_____	_____	_____
Paid-in capital in excess of par, common stock	384,000	_____	_____	_____	_____	_____	_____
Retained earnings	1,600,000	_____	_____	_____	_____	_____	_____
Total equity	$ 2,944,000	$_____	$_____	$_____	$_____	$_____	$_____

Check Total equity: Jan. 17, $2,848,000; Mar. 31, $3,568,000

Problem 11-4B
Analyzing changes in stockholders' equity accounts

C3   P2   P3

The equity sections for Hovo Corp. at the beginning of the year (January 1) and end of the year (December 31) follow.

Stockholders' Equity (January 1)

Common stock—$20 par value, 30,000 shares authorized, 17,000 shares issued and outstanding	$340,000
Paid-in capital in excess of par value, common stock	60,000
Retained earnings...	270,000
Total stockholders' equity	$670,000

Stockholders' Equity (December 31)

Common stock—$20 par value, 30,000 shares authorized, 19,000 shares issued, 1,000 shares in treasury......	$380,000
Paid-in capital in excess of par value, common stock	104,000
Retained earnings ($40,000 restricted by treasury stock)...	295,200
	779,200
Less cost of treasury stock...	(40,000)
Total stockholders' equity	$739,200

The following transactions and events affected its equity during the year.

Feb.	15	Declared a $0.40 per share cash dividend, date of record five days later.
Mar.	2	Purchased treasury stock for cash.
May	15	Declared a $0.40 per share cash dividend, date of record five days later.
Aug.	15	Declared a $0.40 per share cash dividend, date of record five days later.
Oct.	4	Declared a 12.5% stock dividend when the stock's market value is $42 per share.
Oct.	20	Issued the stock dividend that was declared on October 4.
Nov.	15	Declared a $0.40 per share cash dividend, date of record five days later.

Required

1. How many common shares are outstanding on each cash dividend date?
2. What is the total dollar amount for each of the four cash dividends?
3. What is the amount of retained earnings transferred to paid-in capital accounts (capitalized) for the stock dividend?
4. What is the per share cost of the treasury stock purchased?
5. How much net income did the company earn this year?

Check   (3) $84,000

(4) $40

(5) $136,000

Problem 11-5B
Computing book values and dividend allocations

C2   A4

Soltech Company's balance sheet shows the following stockholders' equity section.

Preferred stock—8% cumulative, $___ par value, 1,500 shares authorized, issued, and outstanding	$ 375,000
Common stock—$___ par value, 18,000 shares authorized, issued, and outstanding	900,000
Retained earnings...	1,125,000
Total stockholders' equity	$2,400,000

Required

1. What are the par values of the corporation's preferred stock and its common stock?

2. If no dividends are in arrears at the current date, what is the book value per share of common stock? Round per share value to the nearest cent.

3. If two years' preferred dividends are in arrears at the current date, what is the book value per share of common stock? Round per share value to the nearest cent.

4. If two years' preferred dividends are in arrears at the current date and the board of directors declares cash dividends of $100,000, what total amount will be paid to the preferred and to the common shareholders?

This serial problem began in Chapter 1 and continues through most of the book. If previous chapter segments were not completed, the serial problem can begin at this point.

SERIAL PROBLEM
Business Solutions

P1   C1   C2

SP 11   Santana Rey created **Business Solutions** on October 1, 2019. The company has been successful, and Santana plans to expand her business. She believes that an additional $86,000 is needed and is investigating three funding sources.

a. Santana's sister Cicely is willing to invest $86,000 in the business as a common shareholder. Because Santana currently has about $129,000 invested in the business, Cicely's investment will mean that Santana will maintain about 60% ownership and Cicely will have 40% ownership of Business Solutions.

b. Santana's uncle Marcello is willing to invest $86,000 in the business as a preferred shareholder. Marcello would purchase 860 shares of $100 par value, 7% preferred stock.

c. Santana's banker is willing to lend her $86,000 on a 7%, 10-year note payable. She would make monthly payments of $1,000 per month for 10 years.

Required

1. Prepare the journal entry to reflect the initial $86,000 investment under each of the options (*a*), (*b*), and (*c*).

2. Evaluate the three proposals for expansion, providing the pros and cons of each option.

3. Which option do you recommend Santana adopt? Explain.

©Alexander Image/Shutterstock

The following **General Ledger** assignments highlight the impact, or lack thereof, on financial statements from equity-based transactions.

GL **GENERAL LEDGER PROBLEM**

GL 11-1   General Ledger assignment 11-1 is adapted from Problem 11-2A, including beginning equity balances. Prepare journal entries related to treasury stock, cash dividends, and net income. Then prepare the statement of retained earnings and the stockholders' equity section of the balance sheet.

connect

GL 11-2   General Ledger assignment 11-2 is adapted from Problem 11-4A, including beginning and ending equity balances. Prepare journal entries related to cash dividends and stock dividends. Calculate the number of shares outstanding, the amount of net income, and the amount of retained earnings to be capitalized as a result of the stock dividend, if any.

Accounting Analysis

AA 11-1   Use **Apple's** financial statements in Appendix A to answer the following.

1. How many shares of Apple common stock are issued and outstanding at (*a*) September 30, 2017, and (*b*) September 24, 2016?

2. What is the total amount of cash dividends paid to common stockholders for the years ended (*a*) September 30, 2017, and (*b*) September 24, 2016?

3. Identify basic EPS amounts for fiscal years (*a*) 2017 and (*b*) 2016.

4. Is the change in Apple's EPS from 2016 to 2017 favorable or unfavorable?

5. If Apple buys back outstanding shares from investors, would you expect EPS to increase or decrease from the buyback?

COMPANY ANALYSIS

C2   A1   A4

APPLE

COMPARATIVE ANALYSIS

A1 A2 A3 A4

APPLE

GOOGLE

AA 11-2 Use the following comparative figures for **Apple** and **Google**.

Key Figures	Apple	Google
Net income (in millions)	$ 48,351	$ 12,662
Cash dividends declared per common share	$ 2.40	$ 0.00
Common shares outstanding (in millions)	5,126.201	694.783
Weighted-average common shares outstanding (in millions)	5,217.242	693.049
Market value (price) per share	$ 154.12	$1,046.40
Equity applicable to common shares (in millions)	$ 134,047	$ 152,502

Required

1. Compute the book value per common share for each company using these data.
2. Compute the basic EPS for each company using these data.
3. Compute the dividend yield for each company using these data.
4. Compute the price-earnings ratio for each company using these data.
5. Based on the PE ratio, for which company do investors have greater expectations about future performance?

GLOBAL ANALYSIS

C3 A1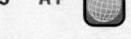

Samsung

AA 11-3 Use the following financial information for **Samsung**.

Net income less dividends available to preferred shares (in millions)	₩ 36,323,611
Number of common shares outstanding (in millions)	119.688
Weighted-average common shares outstanding (in millions)	121.132
Equity applicable to common shares (in millions)	₩214,371,961

Required

1. Compute book value per share for Samsung.
2. Compute earnings per share (EPS) for Samsung.
3. If Samsung buys back outstanding shares from investors, would we expect EPS to increase or decrease from the buyback?

Beyond the Numbers

ETHICS CHALLENGE

C3

BTN 11-1 Harriet Moore is an accountant for New World Pharmaceuticals. Her duties include tracking research and development spending in the new product development division. Over the course of the past six months, Harriet has noticed that a great deal of funds have been spent on a particular project for a new drug. She hears "through the grapevine" that the company is about to patent the drug and expects it to be a major advance in antibiotics. Harriet believes that this new drug will greatly improve company performance and will cause the company's stock to increase in value. Harriet decides to purchase shares of New World in order to benefit from this expected increase.

Required

What are Harriet's ethical responsibilities, if any, with respect to the information she has learned through her duties as an accountant for New World Pharmaceuticals? What are the implications of her planned purchase of New World shares?

COMMUNICATING IN PRACTICE

A1   A2

Hint: Make a slide of each team's memo for a class discussion.

BTN 11-2 Teams are to select an industry, and each team member is to select a different company in that industry. Each team member then is to acquire the selected company's financial statements (or Form 10-K) from the SEC site (**SEC.gov**). Use these data to identify basic EPS. Use the financial press (or **finance.yahoo.com**) to determine the market price of this stock, and then compute the price-earnings ratio. Communicate with teammates via a meeting, e-mail, or telephone to discuss the meaning of this ratio, how companies compare, and the industry norm. The team must prepare a single memorandum reporting the ratio for each company and identifying the team conclusions or consensus of opinion. The memorandum is to be duplicated and distributed to the instructor and teammates.

BTN 11-3 Access the March 1, 2017, filing of the 2016 calendar-year 10-K report of **McDonald's** (ticker: MCD) from **SEC.gov**.

TAKING IT TO THE NET

C1 C3

Required

1. Review McDonald's balance sheet and identify how many classes of stock it has issued.
2. What are the par values, number of authorized shares, and number of issued shares of the classes of stock you identified in part 1?
3. Review its statement of cash flows and identify what total amount of cash it paid in 2016 to purchase treasury stock.
4. What amount did McDonald's pay out in common stock cash dividends for 2016?

BTN 11-4 This activity requires teamwork to reinforce understanding of accounting for treasury stock.

TEAMWORK IN ACTION

P3

1. Write a brief team statement (*a*) generalizing what happens to a corporation's financial position when it engages in a stock buyback and (*b*) identifying reasons why a corporation would engage in this activity.
2. Assume that an entity acquires 100 shares of its $100 par value common stock at a cost of $134 cash per share. Discuss the entry to record this acquisition. Next, assign *each* team member to prepare *one* of the following entries (assume each entry applies to all shares).

   Hint: Instructor must be sure each team accurately completes part 1 before proceeding.

   a. Reissue treasury shares at cost.
   b. Reissue treasury shares at $150 per share.
   c. Reissue treasury shares at $120 per share; assume the paid-in capital account from treasury shares has a $1,500 balance.
   d. Reissue treasury shares at $120 per share; assume the paid-in capital account from treasury shares has a $1,000 balance.
   e. Reissue treasury shares at $120 per share; assume the paid-in capital account from treasury shares has a zero balance.
3. In sequence, each member is to present his/her entry to the team and explain the *similarities* and *differences* between that entry and the previous entry.

BTN 11-5 Assume that **Yelp** decides to launch a new website to market discount bookkeeping services to consumers. This chain, named Aladin, requires $500,000 of start-up capital. The founder contributes $375,000 of personal assets in return for 15,000 shares of common stock, but he must raise another $125,000 in cash. There are two alternative plans for raising the additional cash.

ENTREPRENEURIAL DECISION

C2 P2

- *Plan A* is to sell 3,750 shares of common stock to one or more investors for $125,000 cash.
- *Plan B* is to sell 1,250 shares of cumulative preferred stock to one or more investors for $125,000 cash (this preferred stock would have a $100 par value, have an annual 8% dividend rate, and be issued at par).

1. If the new business is expected to earn $72,000 of after-tax net income in the first year, what rate of return on beginning equity will the founder earn under each alternative plan? Which plan will provide the higher expected return?
2. If the new business is expected to earn $16,800 of after-tax net income in the first year, what rate of return on beginning equity will the founder earn under each alternative plan? Which plan will provide the higher expected return?
3. Analyze and interpret the differences between the results for parts 1 and 2.

BTN 11-6 Review 30 to 60 minutes of financial news programming on television. Take notes on companies that are catching analysts' attention. You might hear reference to over- and undervaluation of firms and to reports about PE ratios, dividend yields, and earnings per share. Be prepared to give a brief description to the class of your observations.

HITTING THE ROAD

A1 A2 A3

12 Reporting Cash Flows

Learning Objectives

CONCEPTUAL

C1 Distinguish between operating, investing, and financing activities, and describe how noncash investing and financing activities are disclosed.

ANALYTICAL

A1 Analyze the statement of cash flows and apply the cash flow on total assets ratio.

PROCEDURAL

P1 Prepare a statement of cash flows.

P2 Compute cash flows from operating activities using the indirect method.

P3 Determine cash flows from both investing and financing activities.

P4 *Appendix 12A*—Illustrate use of a spreadsheet to prepare a statement of cash flows.

P5 *Appendix 12B*—Compute cash flows from operating activities using the direct method.

True Colors

"Work with people who have faith in you"

—BARBARA BRADLEY

FORT WAYNE, IN—"I never saw myself going into business," recalls Barbara Bradley. Until one day, "we were at the airport when we noticed no one was carrying anything colorful or fun. So we decided to start a company to make handbags and luggage for women," exclaims Barbara.

Barbara and her co-founder had no cash, so they borrowed $250 and started "cutting fabric out on a Ping-Pong table," explains Barbara. "We decided to name the company **Vera Bradley** (**VeraBradley.com**) after [my mother]."

As the business grew, Barbara had to manage cash flows. "The first year, we did $10,000 in sales," proclaims Barbara. "Then things got chaotic." While cash flows from operations were good, the business had to expand to meet demand.

"We went to a bank, seeking a $5,000 loan," says Barbara. The loan was a welcome cash inflow that allowed the company to "build its own building!"

Barbara admits that she's "not a great finance [and accounting] person," but she insists that accounting and attention to cash flows are key to running a successful business.

©Robin Marchant/Vera Bradley/Getty Images

Although cash may be king, Barbara insists that "business is all about forming relationships. My father always said, 'In business, you sell yourself first, your company second, and the product third,' and he was right."

Sources: *Vera Bradley website,* January 2019; *Vera Bradley Foundation,* January 2019; *Fortune,* October 2015

BASICS OF CASH FLOW REPORTING

Purpose of the Statement of Cash Flows

The **statement of cash flows** reports cash receipts (inflows) and cash payments (outflows) for a period. Cash flows are separated into operating, investing, and financing activities. The details of sources and uses of cash make this statement useful. The statement of cash flows helps answer

- What explains the change in the cash balance?
- Where does a company spend its cash?
- How does a company receive its cash?
- Why do income and cash flows differ?

Importance of Cash Flows

Information about cash flows influences decisions. Cash flows help users decide whether a company has enough cash to pay its debts. They also help evaluate a company's ability to pursue opportunities. Managers use cash flow information to plan day-to-day operations and make long-term investment decisions.

W. T. Grant Co. is a classic example of the importance of cash flows. Grant reported net income of more than $40 million per year for three consecutive years. At that same time, cash outflow was more than $90 million by the end of that three-year period. Grant soon went bankrupt. Users who relied only on Grant's income numbers were caught off guard.

Measurement of Cash Flows

Cash flows include both *cash* and *cash equivalents*. The statement of cash flows explains the difference between the beginning and ending balances of cash and cash equivalents. We continue to use the phrases *cash flows* and the *statement of cash flows,* but remember that both phrases refer to cash *and* cash equivalents. Because cash and cash equivalents are combined, the statement of cash flows does not report transactions *between* cash and cash equivalents, such as cash paid to purchase cash equivalents and cash received from selling cash equivalents.

A cash equivalent has two criteria: (1) be readily convertible to a known amount of cash and (2) be sufficiently close to its maturity so its market value is unaffected by interest rate changes. **American Express** defines its cash equivalents as including "highly liquid investments with original maturities of 90 days or less."

Cash Equivalents

Classification of Cash Flows

C1 _____

Distinguish between operating, investing, and financing activities, and describe how noncash investing and financing activities are disclosed.

Cash receipts and cash payments are classified in one of three categories: operating, investing, or financing activities. A net cash inflow (source) occurs when the receipts in a category exceed the payments. A net cash outflow (use) occurs when the payments in a category exceed the receipts.

Operating Activities

Operating activities include transactions and events that affect net income. Examples are the production and purchase of inventory, the sale of goods and services to customers, and the expenditures to operate the business. Not all items in income, such as unusual gains and losses, are operating activities (we discuss these exceptions later). Exhibit 12.1 lists common cash inflows and outflows from operating activities.

EXHIBIT 12.1

Cash Flows from Operating Activities

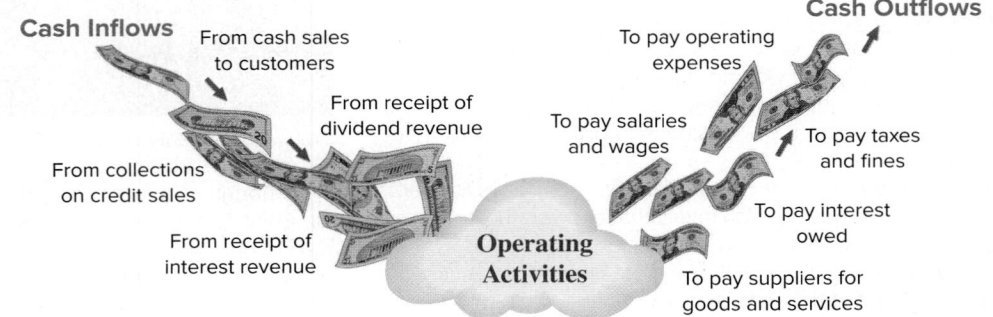

Investing Activities

Point: For simplicity, we assume purchases and sales of equity and debt securities are investing activities.

Investing activities include transactions and events that come from the purchase and sale of long-term assets. They also include (1) the purchase and sale of short-term investments and (2) lending and collecting money for notes receivable. Exhibit 12.2 lists examples of cash flows from investing activities. Cash from collecting the principal on notes is an investing activity. However, collecting interest on notes is an operating activity; also, if a note results from sales to customers, it is an operating activity.

EXHIBIT 12.2

Cash Flows from Investing Activities

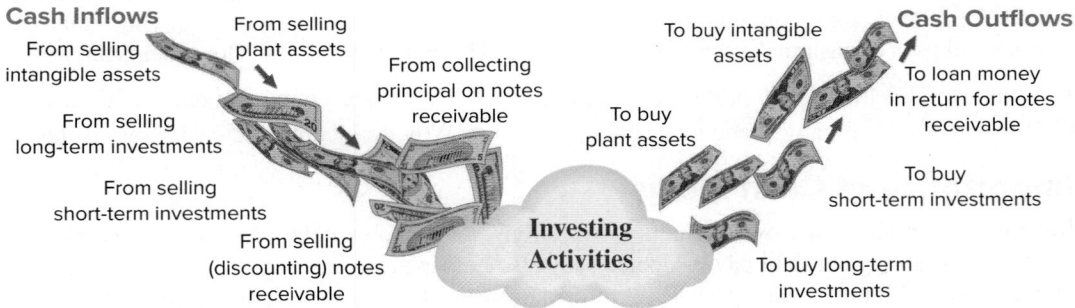

Financing Activities

Financing activities include transactions and events that affect long-term liabilities and equity. Examples are (1) getting cash from issuing debt and repaying debt and (2) receiving cash from or distributing cash to owners. Borrowing and repaying principal on both short- and long-term debt are financing activities. However, payments of interest are operating activities. Exhibit 12.3 lists examples of cash flows from financing activities.

EXHIBIT 12.3

Cash Flows from Financing Activities

Link between Classification of Cash Flows and the Balance Sheet   Operating, investing, and financing activities are loosely linked to different parts of the balance sheet. Operating activities are affected by changes in current assets and current liabilities (and the income statement). Investing activities are affected by changes in long-term assets. Financing activities are affected by changes in long-term liabilities and equity. These links are shown in Exhibit 12.4. Exceptions to these links include (1) current assets *unrelated* to operations—such as short-term notes receivable from noncustomers and from investment securities, which are investing activities, and (2) current liabilities *unrelated* to operations—such as short-term notes payable and dividends payable, which are financing activities.

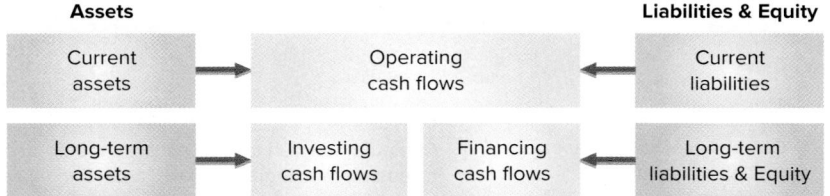

EXHIBIT 12.4

Linkage of Cash Flow Classifications to the Balance Sheet

Noncash Investing and Financing

Some investing and financing activities do not affect cash flows. One example is the purchase of long-term assets using a long-term note payable (loan). This transaction impacts both investing and financing activities but does not impact current-period cash. Such transactions are reported at the bottom of the statement of cash flows or in a note to the statement—Exhibit 12.5 has examples.

● Retirement of debt by issuing equity stock.	● Purchase of long-term assets by issuing a note or bond.
● Conversion of preferred stock to common stock.	● Exchange of noncash assets for other noncash assets.
● Lease of assets in a long-term lease transaction.	● Purchase of noncash assets by issuing equity or debt.

EXHIBIT 12.5

Examples of Noncash Investing and Financing Activities

Format of the Statement of Cash Flows

A statement of cash flows reports cash flows from three activities: operating, investing, and financing. Exhibit 12.6 shows the usual format. The statement shows the net increase or decrease from those activities and ties it into the cash balance. Any noncash investing and financing transactions are disclosed in a note or separate schedule.

P1_____

Prepare a statement of cash flows.

EXHIBIT 12.6

Format of the Statement of Cash Flows

COMPANY NAME
Statement of Cash Flows
For *period* Ended *date*

Cash flows from operating activities		
[Compute operating cash flows using indirect or direct method]		
Net cash provided (used) by operating activities	$ #	
Cash flows from investing activities		
[List of individual inflows and outflows]		
Net cash provided (used) by investing activities	#	
Cash flows from financing activities		
[List of individual inflows and outflows]		
Net cash provided (used) by financing activities	#	
Net increase (decrease) in cash.	$ #	
Cash (and equivalents) balance at prior period-end.	#	
Cash (and equivalents) balance at current period-end	$ #	

Separate schedule or note disclosure of any noncash investing and financing transactions is required.

Point: Positive cash flows for a section are titled net cash "provided by" or "from." Negative cash flows are labeled as net cash "used by" or "for."

Preparing the Statement of Cash Flows

Preparing a statement of cash flows has five steps, shown in Exhibit 12.7. Computing the net increase or net decrease in cash is a simple but crucial computation. It equals the current period's cash balance minus the prior period's cash balance. This is the *bottom-line* figure for the statement of cash flows and is a check on accuracy.

EXHIBIT 12.7

Five Steps in Preparing the Statement of Cash Flows

1 Compute net increase or decrease in cash.

2 Compute net cash from or for operating activities.

3 Compute net cash from or for investing activities.

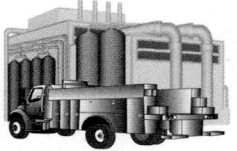

4 Compute net cash from or for financing activities.

5 Compute net cash from all sources; then *prove* it by adding it to beginning cash to get ending cash.

Analyzing the Cash Account

A company's cash receipts and cash payments are recorded in its Cash account. The Cash account is one place to look for information about cash flows. The summarized Cash T-account of Genesis, Inc., is in Exhibit 12.8. Preparing a statement of cash flows requires classifying each cash inflow or outflow as an operating, investing, or financing activity.

EXHIBIT 12.8

Summarized Cash Account

Cash			
Balance, Dec. 31, 2018	12,000		
Receipts from customers	570,000	Payments for inventory	319,000
Receipts from asset sales	2,000	Payments for operating exp.	218,000
Receipts from stock issuance	15,000	Payments for interest	8,000
		Payments for taxes	5,000
		Payments for notes retirement	18,000
		Payments for dividends	14,000
Balance, Dec. 31, 2019	17,000		

Analyzing Noncash Accounts

A second approach to preparing the statement of cash flows analyzes noncash accounts and uses double-entry accounting. Exhibit 12.9 uses the accounting equation to show the relation between the Cash account and the noncash balance sheet accounts. We can explain changes in cash and prepare a statement of cash flows by analyzing changes in liability accounts, equity accounts, and noncash asset accounts (along with income statement accounts).

EXHIBIT 12.9

Relation between Cash and Noncash Accounts

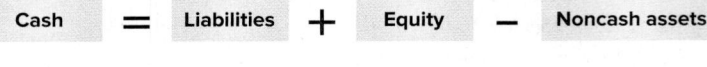

Cash = Liabilities + Equity − Noncash assets

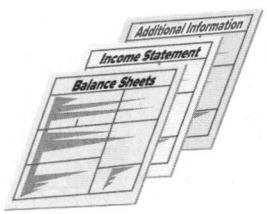

Information to Prepare the Statement

Information to prepare the statement of cash flows comes from three sources: (1) comparative balance sheets, (2) the current income statement, and (3) additional information. Comparative balance sheets are used to compute changes in noncash accounts from the beginning to the end of the period. The current income statement is used to help compute cash flows from operating activities. Additional information includes details that help explain cash flows and noncash activities.

■ **Decision Maker**

Entrepreneur You are considering purchasing a start-up business that recently reported a $110,000 annual net loss and a $225,000 annual net cash inflow. How are these results possible? ■ *Answer:* Several factors can explain an increase in net cash flows when a net loss is reported, including (1) early recognition of expenses relative to revenues generated (such as research and development), (2) cash advances on long-term sales contracts not yet recognized in income, (3) issuances of debt or equity for cash to finance expansion, (4) cash sale of assets, (5) delay of cash payments, and (6) cash prepayment on sales.

Classify each of the following cash flows as operating, investing, or financing activities.

____ **a.** Purchase equipment for cash	____ **g.** Cash paid for utilities
____ **b.** Cash payment of wages	____ **h.** Cash paid to acquire investments
____ **c.** Issuance of stock for cash	____ **i.** Cash paid to retire debt
____ **d.** Receipt of cash dividends from investments	____ **j.** Cash received as interest on investments
____ **e.** Cash collections from customers	____ **k.** Cash received from selling investments
____ **f.** Note payable issued for cash	____ **l.** Cash received from a bank loan

NEED-TO-KNOW 12-1

Classifying Cash Flows

C1   P1 ▶

Solution

a. Investing	**c.** Financing	**e.** Operating	**g.** Operating	**i.** Financing	**k.** Investing
b. Operating	**d.** Operating	**f.** Financing	**h.** Investing	**j.** Operating	**l.** Financing

Do More: QS 12-1, QS 12-2, E 12-1

CASH FLOWS FROM OPERATING

Indirect and Direct Methods of Reporting

Cash flows provided (used) by operating activities are reported using the *direct method* or the *indirect method.* **These two different methods apply only to the operating activities section.**

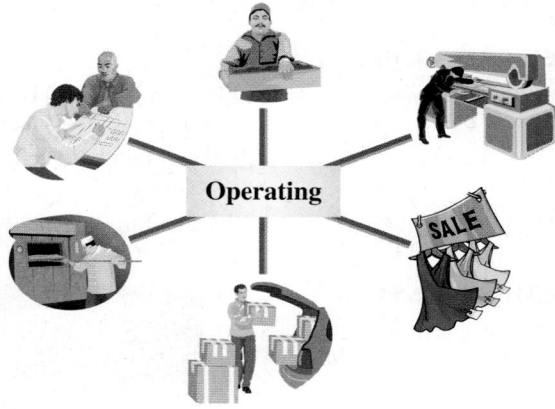

- The **direct method** separately lists operating cash receipts (such as cash received from customers) and operating cash payments (such as cash paid for inventory). The cash payments are then subtracted from cash receipts.

- The **indirect method** reports net income and then adjusts it for items that do not affect cash. It does *not* report individual items of cash inflows and cash outflows from operating activities.

The net cash amount provided by operating activities is *identical* under both the direct and indirect methods. The difference is with the computation and presentation. The indirect method is arguably easier. Nearly all companies report operating cash flows using the indirect method, including **Apple, Google,** and **Samsung** in Appendix A.

Demonstration Data Exhibit 12.10 shows Genesis's income statement and balance sheets. We use this information to prepare a statement of cash flows that explains the $5,000 increase in cash.

Applying the Indirect Method

Net income is computed using accrual accounting. Revenues and expenses rarely match the receipt and payment of cash. The indirect method adjusts net income to get the net cash provided or used by operating activities. We begin with Genesis's income of $38,000 and adjust it

Firms Using Indirect vs. Direct

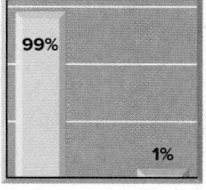

99%

1%

Indirect   Direct

GENESIS Income Statement For Year Ended December 31, 2019		
Sales		$590,000
Cost of goods sold	$300,000	
Wages and other operating expenses.............	216,000	
Interest expense..................	7,000	
Depreciation expense	24,000	(547,000)
		43,000
Other gains (losses)		
Loss on sale of plant assets	(6,000)	
Gain on retirement of notes	16,000	10,000
Income before taxes...............		53,000
Income taxes expense.............		(15,000)
Net income		$ 38,000

Additional information for 2019

a. The accounts payable balances result from inventory purchases.

b. Purchased $60,000 in plant assets by issuing $60,000 of notes payable.

c. Sold plant assets with a book value of $8,000 (original cost of $20,000 and accumulated depreciation of $12,000) for $2,000 cash, yielding a $6,000 loss.

d. Received $15,000 cash from issuing 3,000 shares of common stock.

e. Paid $18,000 cash to retire notes with a $34,000 book value, yielding a $16,000 gain.

f. Declared and paid cash dividends of $14,000.

GENESIS Balance Sheets December 31, 2019 and 2018			
	2019	2018	Change
Assets			
Current assets			
Cash	$ 17,000	$ 12,000	$ 5,000 Increase
Accounts receivable	60,000	40,000	20,000 Increase
Inventory	84,000	70,000	14,000 Increase
Prepaid expenses	6,000	4,000	2,000 Increase
Total current assets	167,000	126,000	
Long-term assets			
Plant assets	250,000	210,000	40,000 Increase
Accumulated depreciation	(60,000)	(48,000)	12,000 Increase
Total assets....................	$357,000	$288,000	
Liabilities			
Current liabilities			
Accounts payable..............	$ 35,000	$ 40,000	$ 5,000 Decrease
Interest payable..............	3,000	4,000	1,000 Decrease
Income taxes payable	22,000	12,000	10,000 Increase
Total current liabilities	60,000	56,000	
Long-term notes payable.........	90,000	64,000	26,000 Increase
Total liabilities..................	150,000	120,000	
Equity			
Common stock, $5 par...........	95,000	80,000	15,000 Increase
Retained earnings	112,000	88,000	24,000 Increase
Total equity.....................	207,000	168,000	
Total liabilities and equity	$357,000	$288,000	

EXHIBIT 12.10

Financial Statements

to get cash provided by operating activities of $20,000—see Exhibit 12.11. There are two types of adjustments: ① Adjustments to income statement items that do not impact cash and ② Adjustments for changes in current assets and current liabilities (linked to operating activities). Nearly all companies group adjustments into these two types, including Apple, Google, and Samsung in Appendix A.

EXHIBIT 12.11

Operating Activities
Section—Indirect Method

GENESIS Statement of Cash Flows—Operating Section under Indirect Method For Year Ended December 31, 2019	
Cash flows from operating activities	
Net income	$ 38,000
Adjustments to reconcile net income to net cash provided by operating activities	
Income statement items not affecting cash	
① Depreciation expense...	24,000
Loss on sale of plant assets	6,000
Gain on retirement of notes	(16,000)
Changes in current assets and liabilities	
Increase in accounts receivable.................................	(20,000)
Increase in inventory..	(14,000)
② Increase in prepaid expenses	(2,000)
Decrease in accounts payable	(5,000)
Decrease in interest payable	(1,000)
Increase in income taxes payable	10,000
Net cash provided by operating activities	**$20,000**

① **Adjustments for Income Statement Items Not Affecting Cash**   Some expenses and losses subtracted from net income were not cash outflows. Examples are depreciation, amortization, depletion, bad debts expense, loss from an asset sale, and loss from retirement of notes payable. The indirect method requires that

> Expenses and losses with no cash outflows are added back to net income.

P2_____

Compute cash flows from operating activities using the indirect method.

These expenses and losses did *not* reduce cash, and adding them back cancels their deductions from net income. Any cash received or paid from a transaction that yields a loss, such as from an asset sale or payoff of a note, is reported under investing or financing activities.

When net income has revenues and gains that are not cash inflows, the indirect method requires that

> Revenues and gains with no cash inflows are subtracted from net income.

Section ① of Exhibit 12.11 shows three adjustments for items that did not impact cash for Genesis.

Point: An income statement reports revenues, gains, expenses, and losses on an accrual basis. The statement of cash flows reports cash received and cash paid for operating, financing, and investing activities.

Depreciation   Depreciation expense is Genesis's only operating item in net income that had no effect on cash flows. We add back the $24,000 depreciation expense to net income because depreciation did not reduce cash.

Loss on Sale of Plant Assets   Genesis reported a $6,000 loss on sale of plant assets that reduced net income but did not affect cash flows. This $6,000 loss is added back to net income because it is not a cash outflow.

Gain on Retirement of Debt   A $16,000 gain on retirement of debt increased net income but did not affect cash flows. This $16,000 gain is subtracted from net income because it was not a cash inflow.

② **Adjustments for Changes in Current Assets and Current Liabilities**   This section covers adjustments for changes in current assets and current liabilities.

Adjustments for Changes in Current Assets

> Decreases in current assets are added to net income.
> Increases in current assets are subtracted from net income.

Adjustments for Changes in Current Liabilities

> Increases in current liabilities are added to net income.
> Decreases in current liabilities are subtracted from net income.

Point: Section ② adjustments.

	Account Increases	Account Decreases
Current assets	Subtract from net income	Add to net income
Current liabilities . . .	Add to net income	Subtract from net income

The lower section of Exhibit 12.11 shows adjustments to the three noncash current assets and three current liabilities for Genesis. We explain each adjustment next.

Accounts Receivable   The $20,000 increase in the current asset of accounts receivable is subtracted from income (showing less cash available). This increase means Genesis collects less cash than is reported in sales. To help see this, we use *account analysis*. This involves setting up a T-account, entering **in black** the balances and entries we know, and computing **in red** the cash receipts or payments. We see cash receipts are $20,000 less than sales, which is why we subtract $20,000 from income in computing the cash flow.

Accounts Receivable			
Bal., Dec. 31, 2018	40,000		
Sales	590,000	Cash receipts = 570,000 ◄	40,000 + 590,000 − 60,000
Bal., Dec. 31, 2019	60,000		

Black numbers are from Exhibit 12.10. Red number is computed.

Inventory			
Bal., Dec. 31, 2018	70,000		
Purchases =	**314,000**	Cost of goods sold	300,000
Bal., Dec. 31, 2019	84,000		

Inventory   The $14,000 increase in inventory is subtracted from income. The T-account shows that purchases are $14,000 more than cost of goods sold. This means that cost of goods sold excludes $14,000 of inventory purchased this year, which is why we subtract $14,000 from income in computing cash flow.

Prepaid Expenses			
Bal., Dec. 31, 2018	4,000		
Cash payments =	**218,000**	Wages and other operating exp.	216,000
Bal., Dec. 31, 2019	6,000		

Prepaid Expenses   The $2,000 increase in prepaid expenses is subtracted from income. The T-account shows that cash paid is $2,000 more than expenses recorded, which is why we subtract $2,000 from income in computing cash flow.

Accounts Payable			
		Bal., Dec. 31, 2018	40,000
Cash payments =	**319,000**	Purchases	314,000
		Bal., Dec. 31, 2019	35,000

Accounts Payable   The $5,000 decrease in accounts payable is subtracted from income. The T-account shows that cash paid is $5,000 more than purchases recorded, which is why we subtract $5,000 from income in computing cash flow.

Interest Payable			
		Bal., Dec. 31, 2018	4,000
Cash paid for interest = **8,000**		Interest expense	7,000
		Bal., Dec. 31, 2019	3,000

Interest Payable   The $1,000 decrease in interest payable is subtracted from income. The T-account shows that cash paid is $1,000 more than interest expense recorded, which is why we subtract $1,000 from income in computing cash flow.

Income Taxes Payable			
		Bal., Dec. 31, 2018	12,000
Cash paid for taxes = **5,000**		Income taxes expense	15,000
		Bal., Dec. 31, 2019	22,000

Income Taxes Payable   The $10,000 increase in income taxes payable is added to income. The T-account shows that cash paid is $10,000 less than tax expense recorded, which is why we add $10,000 to income in computing cash flow.

Summary of Adjustments for Indirect Method

Exhibit 12.12 summarizes the adjustments to net income under the indirect method.

EXHIBIT 12.12

Summary of Adjustments for Operating Activities—Indirect Method

> **Net Income (or Loss)**
> ① Adjustments for operating items not providing or using cash
>   + Noncash expenses and losses
>   *Examples:* Expenses for depreciation, depletion, and amortization; losses from disposal of long-term assets and from retirement of debt
>   − Noncash revenues and gains
>   *Examples:* Gains from disposal of long-term assets and from retirement of debt
> ② Adjustments for changes in current assets and current liabilities
>   + Decrease in noncash current operating asset
>   − Increase in noncash current operating asset
>   + Increase in current operating liability
>   − Decrease in current operating liability
> **Net cash provided (used) by operating activities**

■ Decision Insight

One for the Road   Even though **Tesla** reported net losses and large cash outflows, its market value tripled in five years. Tesla now rivals both **GM** and **Ford** as one of the most valued U.S. automakers. Investors are counting on Tesla's Model 3 to create positive operating cash flows. So far, Tesla has funded its operations with cash inflows from stock and debt issuances. ■

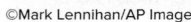
©Mark Lennihan/AP Images

A company's current-year income statement and selected balance sheet data at December 31 of the current and prior years follow. Prepare the operating activities section of the statement of cash flows using the indirect method for the current year.

NEED-TO-KNOW 12-2

Reporting Operating Cash Flows (Indirect)

P2

Income Statement For Current Year Ended December 31	
Sales revenue	$120
Expenses: Cost of goods sold.	50
Depreciation expense.	30
Salaries expense.	17
Interest expense	3
Net income.	$ 20

Selected Balance Sheet Accounts		
At December 31	Current Yr	Prior Yr
Accounts receivable	$12	$10
Inventory	6	9
Accounts payable	7	11
Salaries payable	8	3
Interest payable.	1	0

Solution

Cash Flows from Operating Activities—Indirect Method For Current Year Ended December 31		
Cash flows from operating activities		
Net income.		$20
Adjustments to reconcile net income to net cash provided by operating activities		
Income statement items not affecting cash		
Depreciation expense	$30	
Changes in current assets and current liabilities		
Increase in accounts receivable	(2)	
Decrease in inventory	3	
Decrease in accounts payable.	(4)	
Increase in salaries payable	5	
Increase in interest payable.	1	33
Net cash provided by operating activities		$53

Do More: QS 12-3, QS 12-4, QS 12-5, QS 12-6, QS 12-7, E 12-2, E 12-3, E 12-4, E 12-5, E 12-6, E 12-7

CASH FLOWS FROM INVESTING

To compute cash flows from investing activities, we analyze changes in (1) all long-term asset accounts and (2) any current accounts for notes receivable and investments in securities. **Reporting of investing activities is identical under the direct method and indirect method.**

Three-Step Analysis

To determine cash provided or used by investing activities: (1) identify changes in investing-related accounts, (2) explain these changes using T-accounts and reconstructed entries, and (3) report the cash flow effects.

P3 _____

Determine cash flows from both investing and financing activities.

Analyzing Noncurrent Assets

Genesis both purchased and sold long-term assets during the period. These transactions are investing activities and are analyzed in this section.

Plant Asset Transactions

First Step Analyze Genesis's Plant Assets account and its Accumulated Depreciation account to identify changes in those accounts. Comparative balance sheets in Exhibit 12.10 show a $40,000 increase in plant assets from $210,000 to $250,000 and a $12,000 increase in accumulated depreciation from $48,000 to $60,000.

Point: Investing activities include (1) purchasing and selling long-term assets, (2) lending and collecting on notes receivable, and (3) purchasing and selling short-term investments other than cash equivalents and trading securities.

Second Step   Items *b* and *c* of the additional information in Exhibit 12.10 relate to plant assets. Recall that the Plant Assets account is impacted by both asset purchases and sales; its Accumulated Depreciation account is increased by depreciation and decreased by the removal of accumulated depreciation in asset sales. To explain changes in these accounts and to identify their cash flow effects, we prepare *reconstructed entries, which is our attempt to re-create actual entries made by the preparer.* Item *b* says Genesis purchased plant assets of $60,000 by issuing $60,000 in notes payable. The reconstructed entry is

Reconstruction	Plant Assets...	60,000	
	Notes Payable..		60,000

Item *c* says Genesis sold plant assets costing $20,000 (with $12,000 of accumulated depreciation) for $2,000 cash, resulting in a $6,000 loss. The reconstructed entry is

Reconstruction	Cash..	**2,000**	
	Accumulated Depreciation	12,000	
	Loss on Sale of Plant Assets	6,000	
	Plant Assets...		20,000

We also reconstruct the entry for depreciation from the income statement, which does not impact cash.

Reconstruction	Depreciation Expense	24,000	
	Accumulated Depreciation................................		24,000

The three reconstructed entries are shown in the following T-accounts. This reconstruction analysis is complete in that changes in the long-term asset accounts are entirely explained.

Plant Assets					Accumulated Depreciation—Plant Assets			
Bal., Dec. 31, 2018	210,000						Bal., Dec. 31, 2018	48,000
Purchase	**60,000**	Sale	20,000		Sale	12,000	**Depr. expense**	**24,000**
Bal., Dec. 31, 2019	250,000						Bal., Dec. 31, 2019	60,000

Third Step   Look at the reconstructed entries to identify cash flows. The identified cash flows are reported in the investing section of the statement.

Cash flows from investing activities	
Cash received from sale of plant assets	$2,000

The $60,000 purchase in item *b,* paid for by issuing notes, is a noncash investing and financing activity. It is reported in a note or in a separate schedule to the statement.

Noncash investing and financing activity	
Purchased plant assets with issuance of notes	$60,000

Additional Long-Term Assets   Genesis did not have any additional noncurrent assets (or nonoperating current assets). If such assets do exist, we analyze and report investing cash flows using the same three-step process.

Ethical Risk

Location, Location, Location   Cash flows can be delayed or accelerated at period-end to improve or reduce current-period cash flows. Cash flows also can be misclassified. We know cash outflows under operating activities are viewed as expense payments. However, cash outflows under investing activities are viewed as a sign of growth potential. This requires investors to review where cash flows are reported. ∎

Use the following information to determine this company's cash flows from investing activities.
a. A factory with a book value of $100 and an original cost of $800 was sold at a loss of $10.
b. Paid $70 cash for new equipment.
c. Long-term stock investments were sold for $20 cash, yielding a loss of $4.
d. Sold land costing $175 for $160 cash, yielding a loss of $15.

Solution

Cash flows from investing activities	
Cash received from sale of factory (from *a**—also see margin entry)	$ 90
Cash paid for new equipment (from *b*)	(70)
Cash received from sale of long-term investments (from *c*).	20
Cash received from sale of land (from *d*)	160
Net cash provided by investing activities	$200

*Cash received from sale of factory = Book value − Loss = $100 − $10 = $90.

Reconstruction for part *a*.
Cash **90**
Loss on asset sale   10
   Factory (BV)   100

CASH FLOWS FROM FINANCING

To compute cash flows from financing activities, we analyze changes in all noncurrent liability accounts (including the current portion of any notes and bonds) and equity accounts. These accounts include long-term debt, notes payable, bonds payable, common stock, and retained earnings. **Reporting of financing activities is identical under the direct method and indirect method.**

Three-Step Analysis

To determine cash provided or used by financing activities: (1) identify changes in financing-related accounts, (2) explain these changes using T-accounts and reconstructed entries, and (3) report the cash flow effects.

Analyzing Noncurrent Liabilities

Genesis retired notes payable by paying cash. This is a change in noncurrent liabilities.

Point: Examples of financing activities are (1) receiving cash from issuing debt or repaying amounts borrowed and (2) receiving cash from or distributing cash to owners.

Notes Payable Transactions

First Step   Review comparative balance sheets in Exhibit 12.10, which shows an increase in notes payable from $64,000 to $90,000.

Second Step   Item *e* of the additional information in Exhibit 12.10 reports that notes with a carrying value of $34,000 are retired for $18,000 cash, resulting in a $16,000 gain. The reconstructed entry is

Reconstruction	Notes Payable	34,000	
	Gain on retirement of debt.......................		16,000
	Cash		**18,000**

Item *b* of the additional information reports that Genesis purchased plant assets costing $60,000 by issuing $60,000 in notes payable. This $60,000 increase to notes payable is reported as a noncash investing and financing transaction. The Notes Payable account is explained by these reconstructed entries.

Notes Payable			
		Bal., Dec. 31, 2018	64,000
Retired notes	**34,000**	**Issued notes**	**60,000**
		Bal., Dec. 31, 2019	90,000

Third Step   Report cash paid for the notes retirement in the financing activities section.

Cash flows from financing activities	
Cash paid to retire notes	$(18,000)

Analyzing Equity

Genesis had two equity transactions. The first is the issuance of common stock for cash. The second is the declaration and payment of cash dividends.

Common Stock Transactions

First Step   Review the comparative balance sheets in Exhibit 12.10, which show an increase in common stock from $80,000 to $95,000.

Second Step   Item *d* of the additional information in Exhibit 12.10 reports that 3,000 shares of common stock are issued at par for $5 per share. The reconstructed entry and the complete Common Stock T-account follow.

Reconstruction	Cash	15,000	
	Common Stock		15,000

Common Stock		
	Bal., Dec. 31, 2018	80,000
	Issued stock	**15,000**
	Bal., Dec. 31, 2019	95,000

Third Step   Report cash received from stock issuance in the financing activities section.

Cash flows from financing activities	
Cash received from issuing stock	$15,000

Retained Earnings Transactions

First Step   Review the comparative balance sheets in Exhibit 12.10, which show an increase in retained earnings from $88,000 to $112,000.

Second Step   Item *f* of the additional information in Exhibit 12.10 reports that cash dividends of $14,000 are paid. The reconstructed entry follows.

Reconstruction	Retained Earnings	14,000	
	Cash		14,000

Retained Earnings also is impacted by net income of $38,000. (Net income is covered in operating activities.) The reconstructed Retained Earnings account follows.

Retained Earnings			
		Bal., Dec. 31, 2018	88,000
Cash dividend	**14,000**	**Net income**	**38,000**
		Bal., Dec. 31, 2019	112,000

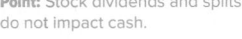

Point: Stock dividends and splits do not impact cash.

Third Step   Report cash paid for dividends in the financing activities section.

Cash flows from financing activities	
Cash paid for dividends	$(14,000)

Proving Cash Balances

The final stage in preparing the statement is to report the beginning and ending cash balances and prove that the *net change in cash* is explained by operating, investing, and financing cash flows. The last three rows of Exhibit 12.13 show that the $5,000 net increase in cash, from $12,000 at the beginning of the period to $17,000 at the end, is reconciled by net cash flows from operating ($20,000 inflow), investing ($2,000 inflow), and financing ($17,000 outflow) activities.

EXHIBIT 12.13

Complete Statement
of Cash Flows—Indirect
Method

GENESIS
Statement of Cash Flows (Indirect Method)
For Year Ended December 31, 2019

Cash flows from operating activities		
Net income		$ 38,000
Adjustments to reconcile net income to net cash provided by operating activities		
Income statement items not affecting cash		
Depreciation expense	24,000	
Loss on sale of plant assets..................................	6,000	
Gain on retirement of notes	(16,000)	
Changes in current assets and liabilities		
Increase in accounts receivable	(20,000)	
Increase in inventory......................................	(14,000)	
Increase in prepaid expenses................................	(2,000)	
Decrease in accounts payable	(5,000)	
Decrease in interest payable................................	(1,000)	
Increase in income taxes payable............................	10,000	
Net cash provided by operating activities......................		$ 20,000
Cash flows from investing activities		
Cash received from sale of plant assets	2,000	
Net cash provided by investing activities		2,000
Cash flows from financing activities		
Cash received from issuing stock	15,000	
Cash paid to retire notes	(18,000)	
Cash paid for dividends	(14,000)	
Net cash used in financing activities		(17,000)
Net increase in cash		$ 5,000
Cash balance at prior year-end		12,000
Cash balance at current year-end		$ 17,000

■ **Decision Maker**

Reporter   Management is in labor contract negotiations and grants you an interview. It highlights a total net cash outflow of $550,000 (which includes net cash outflows of $850,000 for investing activities and $350,000 for financing activities). What is your assessment of this company? ■   *Answer:* An initial reaction from the $550,000 decrease in net cash is not positive. However, closer scrutiny shows a more positive picture. Cash flow from operations is $650,000, computed as [?] − $850,000 − $350,000 = $(550,000).

Use the following information to determine cash flows from financing activities.

a. Issued common stock for $40 cash.

b. Paid $70 cash to retire a note payable at its $70 maturity value.

c. Paid cash dividend of $15.

d. Paid $5 cash to acquire its treasury stock.

NEED-TO-KNOW 12-4

Reporting Financing
Cash Flows

P3

Solution

Cash flows from financing activities	
Cash received from issuance of common stock (from *a*)	$ 40
Cash paid to settle note payable (from *b*).....................	(70)
Cash paid for dividend (from *c*)	(15)
Cash paid to acquire treasury stock (from *d*)	(5)
Net cash used by financing activities	$(50)

Do More: QS 12-14, QS 12-15,
QS 12-16, QS 12-17, E 12-9

SUMMARY USING T-ACCOUNTS

Exhibit 12.14 uses T-accounts to summarize how changes in Genesis's noncash balance sheet accounts affect its cash inflows and outflows (dollar amounts in thousands). The top of the exhibit shows Genesis's Cash T-account, and the lower part shows T-accounts for its remaining balance sheet accounts. We see that the $20,000 net cash provided by operating activities and the $5,000 net increase in cash shown in the Cash T-account agree with the same figures in the statement of cash flows in Exhibit 12.13. We explain Exhibit 12.14 in five parts.

a. Entry (1) records $38 net income on the credit side of the Retained Earnings account and the debit side of the Cash account. This $38 net income in the Cash T-account is adjusted until it reflects the $5 net increase in cash.

b. Entries (2) through (4) add the $24 depreciation and $6 loss on asset sale to net income and subtract the $16 gain on retirement of notes.

c. Entries (5) through (10) adjust net income for changes in current asset and current liability accounts.

EXHIBIT 12.14

Balance Sheet T-Accounts to Explain the Change in Cash ($ thousands)

d. Entry (11) records the noncash investing and financing transaction involving a $60 purchase of assets by issuing $60 of notes.

e. Entries (12) and (13) record the $15 stock issuance and the $14 dividend.

Cash			
(1) Net income	38		
(2) Depreciation	24	(4) Gain on retirement of notes	16
(3) Loss on sale of plant assets	6		
(10) Increase in income taxes payable	10	(5) Increase in accounts receivable	20
		(6) Increase in inventory	14
		(7) Increase in prepaid expense	2
		(8) Decrease in accounts payable	5
		(9) Decrease in interest payable	1
Net cash provided by operating activities [O]	20		
(3) Cash received from sale of plant assets [I]	2	(4) Cash paid to retire notes [F]	18
(12) Cash received from issuing stock [F]	15	(13) Cash paid for dividends [F]	14
Net increase in cash	5		

Info to prepare statement of cash flows

Accounts Receivable		
Beg.	40	
(5)	20	
End.	60	

Inventory		
Beg.	70	
(6)	14	
End.	84	

Prepaid Expenses		
Beg.	4	
(7)	2	
End.	6	

Plant Assets		
Beg.	210	
		(3)	20
(11)	60	
End.	250	

Accumulated Depreciation			
		Beg.	48
(3)	12	(2)	24
		End.	60

Accounts Payable		
		Beg.	40
(8)	5		
		End.	35

Interest Payable		
		Beg.	4
(9)	1		
		End.	3

Income Taxes Payable		
		Beg.	12
		(10)	10
		End.	22

Long-Term Notes Payable		
		Beg.	64
(4)	34		
		(11)	60
		End.	90

Common Stock		
		Beg.	80
		(12)	15
		End.	95

Retained Earnings		
		Beg.	88
		(1)	38
(13)	14		
		End.	112

Analyzing Cash Sources and Uses

Managers review cash flows for business decisions. Creditors evaluate a company's ability to generate enough cash to pay debt. Investors assess cash flows before buying and selling stock.

To effectively evaluate cash flows, we separately analyze investing, financing, and operating activities. Consider data from three different companies in Exhibit 12.15 that operate in the same industry and have been in business for several years. Each company has the same $15,000 net increase in cash, but its sources and uses of cash flows are different. BMX's operating activities provide net cash flows of $90,000, allowing it to purchase plant assets of $48,000 and repay $27,000 of its debt. ATV's operating activities provide $40,000 of cash flows, limiting its purchase of plant assets to $25,000. Trex's $15,000

A1

Analyze the statement of cash flows and apply the cash flow on total assets ratio.

EXHIBIT 12.15

Cash Flows of Competing Companies

$ thousands	BMX	ATV	Trex
Cash provided (used) by operating activities . . .	$90,000	$40,000	$(24,000)
Cash provided (used) by investing activities			
Proceeds from sale of plant assets.			26,000
Purchase of plant assets	(48,000)	(25,000)	
Cash provided (used) by financing activities			
Proceeds from issuance of debt			13,000
Repayment of debt	(27,000)		
Net increase (decrease) in cash	$15,000	$15,000	$ 15,000

net cash increase is due to selling plant assets and incurring additional debt. Its operating activities yield a cash outflow of $24,000. Overall, analysis of cash flows reveals that BMX is more capable of generating future cash flows than is ATV or Trex.

Decision Insight

Free Cash Flows Many investors use cash flows to value company stock. However, cash-based valuation models often yield different stock values due to differences in measurement of cash flows. Most models require cash flows that are "free" for distribution to shareholders. These *free cash flows* are defined as cash flows available to shareholders after operating asset reinvestments and debt payments. A company's growth and financial flexibility depend on adequate free cash flows. ∎

Point: Cash flow from operations
− Capital expenditures
− Debt repayments
= Free cash flows

Cash Flow on Total Assets

Cash flow information can help measure a company's ability to meet its obligations, pay dividends, expand operations, and obtain financing. The **cash flow on total assets** ratio is in Exhibit 12.16.

$$\text{Cash flow on total assets} = \frac{\text{Cash flow from operations}}{\text{Average total assets}}$$

EXHIBIT 12.16

Cash Flow on Total Assets

This ratio measures actual cash flows and is not affected by accounting recognition and measurement. It can help estimate the amount and timing of cash flows from operating activities.

The cash flow on total assets for competitors **Nike** and **Under Armour** are in Exhibit 12.17. In all years, Nike's cash flow on total assets ratio exceeded Under Armour's ratio. This means that Nike did a better job of generating operating cash flows given its assets. However, Nike's cash flow on total assets declined from two years ago, which is not a positive result. At the same time, Under Armour's lower and uneven cash flow on total assets make it difficult to predict the amount and timing of its cash flows.

EXHIBIT 12.17

Cash Flow on Total Assets for Two Competitors

Company	Figure ($ millions)	Current Year	1 Year Ago	2 Years Ago
Nike	Operating cash flows	$ 3,640	$ 3,096	$ 4,680
	Average total assets.	$22,328	$21,497	$20,096
	Cash flow on total assets.	16.3%	14.4%	23.3%
Under Armour	Operating cash flows	$ 234	$ 364	$ 15
	Average total assets.	$ 3,825	$ 3,255	$ 2,479
	Cash flow on total assets.	6.1%	11.2%	0.6%

NEED-TO-KNOW 12-5

COMPREHENSIVE

Preparing Statement of
Cash Flows—Indirect
and Direct Methods

Comparative balance sheets, an income statement, and additional information follow.

UMA COMPANY Balance Sheets December 31, 2019 and 2018		
	2019	**2018**
Assets		
Cash	$ 43,050	$ 23,925
Accounts receivable	34,125	39,825
Inventory	156,000	146,475
Prepaid expenses	3,600	1,650
Total current assets..............	236,775	211,875
Equipment	135,825	146,700
Accum. depreciation—Equipment ...	(61,950)	(47,550)
Total assets	$310,650	$311,025
Liabilities		
Accounts payable	$ 28,800	$ 33,750
Income taxes payable	5,100	4,425
Dividends payable	0	4,500
Total current liabilities............	33,900	42,675
Bonds payable..................	0	37,500
Total liabilities	33,900	80,175
Equity		
Common stock, $10 par	168,750	168,750
Retained earnings	108,000	62,100
Total liabilities and equity	$310,650	$311,025

UMA COMPANY Income Statement For Year Ended December 31, 2019		
Sales		$446,100
Cost of goods sold	$222,300	
Other operating expenses	120,300	
Depreciation expense	25,500	(368,100)
		78,000
Other gains (losses)		
Loss on sale of equipment	3,300	
Loss on retirement of bonds ...	825	(4,125)
Income before taxes		73,875
Income tax expense		(13,725)
Net income		$ 60,150

Additional Information

a. Equipment costing $21,375 with accumulated depreciation of $11,100 is sold for cash.

b. Equipment purchases are for cash.

c. Accumulated Depreciation is affected by depreciation expense and the sale of equipment.

d. The balance of Retained Earnings is affected by dividend declarations and net income.

e. All sales are made on credit.

f. All inventory purchases are on credit.

g. Accounts Payable balances result from inventory purchases.

h. Prepaid expenses relate to "other operating expenses."

Required

1. Prepare a statement of cash flows using the indirect method for year 2019.

2.ᴮ Prepare a statement of cash flows using the direct method for year 2019.

PLANNING THE SOLUTION

- Prepare two blank statements of cash flows with sections for operating, investing, and financing activities using the (1) indirect method format and (2) direct method format.

- Compute the cash paid for equipment and the cash received from the sale of equipment using the additional information provided along with the amount for depreciation expense and the change in the balances of Equipment and Accumulated Depreciation. Use T-accounts to help chart the effects of the sale and purchase of equipment on the balances of the Equipment account and the Accumulated Depreciation account.

- Compute the effect of net income on the change in the Retained Earnings account balance. Assign the difference between the change in retained earnings and the amount of net income to dividends declared. Adjust the dividends declared amount for the change in the Dividends Payable balance.

- Compute cash received from customers, cash paid for inventory, cash paid for other operating expenses, and cash paid for taxes.

- Enter the cash effects of reconstruction entries to the appropriate section(s) of the statement.

- Total each section of the statement, determine the total net change in cash, and add it to the beginning balance to get the ending balance of cash.

SOLUTION

Supporting computations for cash receipts and cash payments.

(1)	Cost of equipment sold*	$ 21,375
	Accumulated depreciation of equipment sold	(11,100)
	Book value of equipment sold......................	10,275
	Loss on sale of equipment.........................	(3,300)
	Cash received from sale of equipment...............	**$ 6,975**
	Cost of equipment sold	$ 21,375
	Less decrease in the Equipment account balance.......	(10,875)
	Cash paid for new equipment......................	**$10,500**
(2)	Loss on retirement of bonds	$ 825
	Carrying value of bonds retired....................	37,500
	Cash paid to retire bonds	**$38,325**

*Supporting T-account analysis for part 1 follows.

Equipment		
Bal., Dec. 31, 2018 146,700		
Cash purchase 10,500	Sale 21,375	
Bal., Dec. 31, 2019 135,825		

Accumulated Depreciation—Equipment		
	Bal., Dec. 31, 2018 47,550	
Sale 11,100	Depr. expense 25,500	
	Bal., Dec. 31, 2019 61,950	

(3)	Net income.................................	$ 60,150
	Less increase in retained earnings	45,900
	Dividends declared	14,250
	Plus decrease in dividends payable	4,500
	Cash paid for dividends.....................	**$ 18,750**
(4)[B]	Sales......................................	$ 446,100
	Add decrease in accounts receivable...........	5,700
	Cash received from customers	**$451,800**
(5)[B]	Cost of goods sold..........................	$ 222,300
	Plus increase in inventory	9,525
	Purchases.................................	231,825
	Plus decrease in accounts payable.............	4,950
	Cash paid for inventory	**$236,775**
(6)[B]	Other operating expenses....................	$ 120,300
	Plus increase in prepaid expenses	1,950
	Cash paid for other operating expenses.........	**$122,250**
(7)[B]	Income tax expense.........................	$ 13,725
	Less increase in income taxes payable..........	(675)
	Cash paid for income taxes	**$ 13,050**

1. Indirect method.

UMA COMPANY
Statement of Cash Flows (Indirect Method)
For Year Ended December 31, 2019

Cash flows from operating activities		
Net income.....................................	$ 60,150	
Adjustments to reconcile net income to net cash provided by operating activities		
Income statement items not affecting cash		
Depreciation expense	25,500	
Loss on sale of plant assets.................	3,300	
Loss on retirement of bonds	825	
Changes in current assets and current liabilities		
Decrease in accounts receivable.............	5,700	
Increase in inventory	(9,525)	
Increase in prepaid expenses	(1,950)	
Decrease in accounts payable...............	(4,950)	
Increase in income taxes payable	675	
Net cash provided by operating activities		$ 79,725
Cash flows from investing activities		
Cash received from sale of equipment.............	6,975	
Cash paid for equipment.......................	(10,500)	
Net cash used in investing activities		(3,525)
Cash flows from financing activities		
Cash paid to retire bonds payable	(38,325)	
Cash paid for dividends........................	(18,750)	
Net cash used in financing activities		(57,075)
Net increase in cash.............................		$ 19,125
Cash balance at prior year-end....................		23,925
Cash balance at current year-end..................		$ 43,050

2.[B] Direct method (Appendix 12B).

UMA COMPANY
Statement of Cash Flows (Direct Method)
For Year Ended December 31, 2019

Cash flows from operating activities		
Cash received from customers.............	$ 451,800	
Cash paid for inventory	(236,775)	
Cash paid for other operating expenses.....	(122,250)	
Cash paid for income taxes	(13,050)	
Net cash provided by operating activities....		$ 79,725
Cash flows from investing activities		
Cash received from sale of equipment	6,975	
Cash paid for equipment	(10,500)	
Net cash used in investing activities		(3,525)
Cash flows from financing activities		
Cash paid to retire bonds payable..........	(38,325)	
Cash paid for dividends	(18,750)	
Net cash used in financing activities		(57,075)
Net increase in cash		$ 19,125
Cash balance at prior year-end		23,925
Cash balance at current year-end		$ 43,050

Spreadsheet Preparation of the Statement of Cash Flows

12A

P4

Illustrate use of a spread-sheet to prepare a statement of cash flows.

This appendix explains how to use a spreadsheet (work sheet) to prepare the statement of cash flows under the indirect method.

Preparing the Indirect Method Spreadsheet   A *spreadsheet*, also called *work sheet,* can help us prepare a statement of cash flows. To demonstrate, we return to the comparative balance sheets and income statement shown in Exhibit 12.10. We use letters *a* through *g* to code changes in accounts, and letters *h* through *m* for additional information, to prepare the statement of cash flows.

  a. Net income is $38,000.

  b. Accounts receivable increase by $20,000.

  c. Inventory increases by $14,000.

  d. Prepaid expenses increase by $2,000.

  e. Accounts payable decrease by $5,000.

  f. Interest payable decreases by $1,000.

  g. Income taxes payable increase by $10,000.

  h. Depreciation expense is $24,000.

  i. Plant assets costing $20,000 with accumulated depreciation of $12,000 are sold for $2,000 cash. This yields a loss on sale of assets of $6,000.

  j. Notes with a book value of $34,000 are retired with a cash payment of $18,000, yielding a $16,000 gain on retirement.

  k. Plant assets costing $60,000 are purchased with an issuance of notes payable for $60,000.

  l. Issued 3,000 shares of common stock for $15,000 cash.

  m. Paid cash dividends of $14,000.

    Exhibit 12A.1 shows the indirect method spreadsheet for Genesis. We enter both beginning and ending balance sheet amounts on the spreadsheet. We also enter information in the Analysis of Changes columns (keyed to the additional information items *a* through *m*) to explain changes in the accounts and determine the cash flows for operating, investing, and financing activities. Information about noncash investing and financing activities is reported near the bottom.

Entering the Analysis of Changes on the Spreadsheet   The following steps are used to complete the spreadsheet after the beginning and ending balances of the balance sheet accounts are entered.

  ① Enter net income as the first item in the statement of cash flows section for computing operating cash inflow (debit) and as a credit to Retained Earnings. **(Entry *a*)**

  ② In the statement of cash flows section, adjustments to net income are entered as debits if they increase cash flows and as credits if they decrease cash flows. Applying this rule, adjust net income for the change in each noncash current asset and current liability account related to operating activities. For each adjustment to net income, the offsetting debit or credit must help reconcile the beginning and ending balances of a current asset or current liability account. **(Entries *b* through *g*)**

  ③ Enter adjustments to net income for income statement items not providing or using cash in the period. For each adjustment, the offsetting debit or credit must help reconcile a noncash balance sheet account. **(Entry *h*)**

  ④ Adjust net income to eliminate any gains or losses from investing and financing activities. Because the cash from a gain must be excluded from operating activities, the gain is entered as a credit in the operating activities section. Losses are entered as debits. For each adjustment, the related debit and/ or credit must help reconcile balance sheet accounts and involve reconstructed entries to show the cash flow from investing or financing activities. **(Entries *i* and *j*)**

  ⑤ After reviewing any unreconciled balance sheet accounts and related information, enter the remaining reconciling entries for investing and financing activities. Examples are purchases of plant assets,

EXHIBIT 12A.1

Spreadsheet for Preparing Statement of Cash Flows—Indirect Method

GENESIS Spreadsheet for Statement of Cash Flows—Indirect Method For Year Ended December 31, 2019	Dec. 31, 2018		Analysis of Changes Debit		Credit	Dec. 31, 2019
Balance Sheet—Debit Bal. Accounts						
Cash	$ 12,000					$ 17,000
Accounts receivable	40,000	(b)	$ 20,000			60,000
Inventory	70,000	(c)	14,000			84,000
Prepaid expenses	4,000	(d)	2,000			6,000
Plant assets	210,000	(k1)	60,000	(i)	$ 20,000	250,000
	$336,000					$417,000
Balance Sheet—Credit Bal. Accounts						
Accumulated depreciation	$ 48,000	(i)	12,000	(h)	24,000	$ 60,000
Accounts payable	40,000	(e)	5,000			35,000
Interest payable	4,000	(f)	1,000			3,000
Income taxes payable	12,000			(g)	10,000	22,000
Notes payable	64,000	(j)	34,000	(k2)	60,000	90,000
Common stock, $5 par value	80,000			(l)	15,000	95,000
Retained earnings	88,000	(m)	14,000	(a)	38,000	112,000
	$336,000					$417,000
Statement of Cash Flows						
Operating activities						
Net income		(a)	38,000			
Increase in accounts receivable				(b)	20,000	
Increase in inventory				(c)	14,000	
Increase in prepaid expenses				(d)	2,000	
Decrease in accounts payable				(e)	5,000	
Decrease in interest payable				(f)	1,000	
Increase in income taxes payable		(g)	10,000			
Depreciation expense		(h)	24,000			
Loss on sale of plant assets		(i)	6,000			
Gain on retirement of notes				(j)	16,000	
Investing activities						
Receipts from sale of plant assets		(i)	2,000			
Financing activities						
Payment to retire notes				(j)	18,000	
Receipts from issuing stock		(l)	15,000			
Payment of cash dividends				(m)	14,000	
Noncash Investing and Financing Activities						
Purchase of plant assets with notes		(k2)	60,000	(k1)	60,000	
			$317,000		$317,000	

issuances of long-term debt, stock issuances, and dividend payments. Some of these may require entries in the noncash investing and financing section of the spreadsheet. (**Entries k through m**)

⑥ Check accuracy by totaling the Analysis of Changes columns and by determining that the change in each balance sheet account has been explained (reconciled).

Because adjustments i, j, and k are more challenging, we show them in the following debit and credit format. These entries are for purposes of our understanding; they are *not* the entries actually made in the journals. Changes in the Cash account are identified as sources or uses of cash.

i.	Cash—Receipt from sale of plant assets **(source of cash)**	2,000	
	Loss from sale of plant assets	6,000	
	Accumulated depreciation	12,000	
	Plant assets		20,000
	Describe sale of plant assets.		
j.	Notes payable	34,000	
	Cash—Payments to retire notes **(use of cash)**		**18,000**
	Gain on retirement of notes		16,000
	Describe retirement of notes.		
k1.	Plant assets	60,000	
	Cash—Purchase of plant assets financed by notes		**60,000**
	Describe purchase of plant assets.		
k2.	Cash—Purchase of plant assets financed by notes	**60,000**	
	Notes payable		60,000
	Issue notes for purchase of assets.		

12B

Direct Method of Reporting Operating Cash Flows

P5

Compute cash flows from operating activities using the direct method.

We compute operating cash flows under the direct method by adjusting accrual-based income statement items to the cash basis as follows.

Revenue or expense	**+ or −**	Adjustments for changes in related balance sheet accounts	**=**	Cash receipts or cash payments

The framework for reporting cash receipts and cash payments for the operating section under the direct method is shown in Exhibit 12B.1.

EXHIBIT 12B.1

Major Classes of Operating Cash Flows

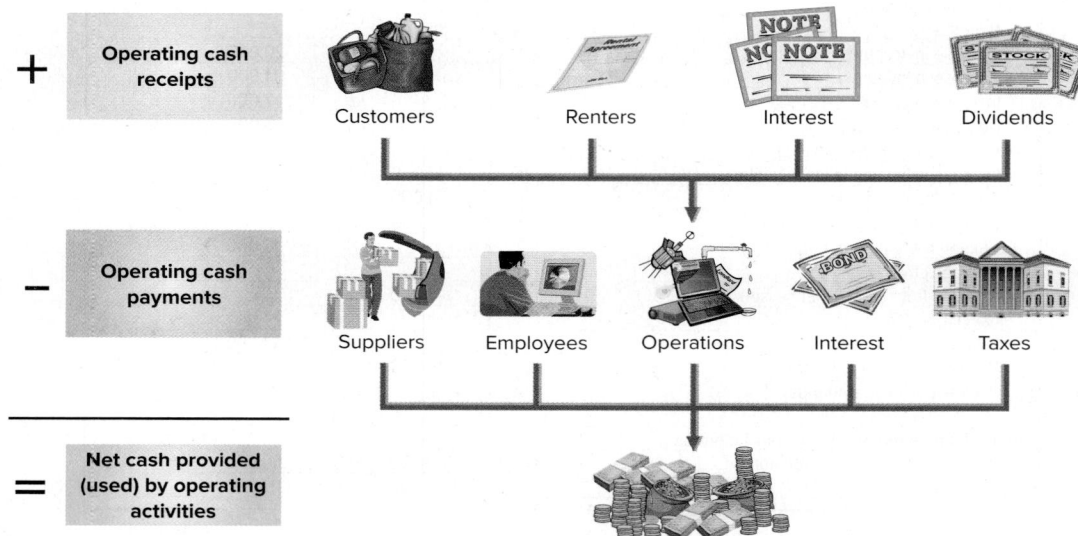

Operating Cash Receipts   The financial statements and additional information reported by Genesis in Exhibit 12.10 show one cash receipt: sales to customers. We start with sales to customers as reported on the income statement and then adjust it to get cash received from customers.

Cash Received from Customers   If all sales are for cash, cash received from customers equals the sales reported on the income statement. When some or all sales are on credit, we must adjust the amount of sales for the change in Accounts Receivable. To help us compute cash receipts, we use a T-account that includes accounts receivable balances for Genesis on December 31, 2018 and 2019. The beginning balance is $40,000 and the ending balance is $60,000. Next, the income statement shows sales of $590,000, which is put on the debit side. We now reconstruct the account to determine the cash receipts from customers are $570,000, computed as $40,000 + $590,000 − [?] = $60,000.

Point: An accounts receivable increase implies that cash received from customers is less than sales (the converse is also true).

Reconstructed Entry

Cash.........	570,000	
Accts Recble....	20,000	
Sales		590,000

Example: If the ending balance of Accounts Receivable is $20,000 (instead of $60,000), what is cash received from customers?
Answer: $610,000

Accounts Receivable			
Bal., Dec. 31, 2018	40,000		
Sales	590,000	**Cash receipts =**	**570,000**
Bal., Dec. 31, 2019	60,000		

Cash receipts also can be computed as sales of $590,000 minus a $20,000 increase in accounts receivable. This computation is in Exhibit 12B.2. Genesis reports the $570,000 cash received from customers as a cash inflow from operating activities.

EXHIBIT 12B.2

Formula to Compute Cash Received from Customers— Direct Method

$$\text{Cash received from customers} = \text{Sales} \quad \begin{array}{l} + \textbf{Decrease in accounts receivable} \\ \text{or} \\ - \textbf{Increase in accounts receivable} \end{array}$$

Other Cash Receipts   Other common cash receipts involve rent, interest, and dividends. We compute cash received from these items by subtracting an increase in their receivable or adding a decrease. For example, if rent receivable increases in the period, cash received from renters is less than rent revenue reported on the income statement. If rent receivable decreases, cash received is more than reported rent revenue. The same applies to interest and dividends.

Operating Cash Payments
The financial statements and additional information for Genesis in Exhibit 12.10 show four operating expenses: cost of goods sold; wages and other operating expenses; interest expense; and taxes expense. We analyze each expense to compute its cash impact.

Cash Paid for Inventory   We compute cash paid for inventory by analyzing both cost of goods sold and inventory. If all inventory purchases are for cash and the balance of Inventory is unchanged, the amount of cash paid for inventory equals cost of goods sold—an uncommon situation. Instead, there normally is some change in the Inventory balance. Also, some or all purchases are often made on credit, which changes the Accounts Payable balance. When the balances of both Inventory and Accounts Payable change, we must adjust the cost of goods sold for changes in both accounts to compute cash paid for inventory. This is a two-step adjustment.

First, we use the change in the account balance of Inventory, along with the cost of goods sold amount, to compute cost of purchases for the period. An increase in inventory means that we bought more than we sold, and we add this inventory increase to cost of goods sold to compute cost of purchases. A decrease in inventory means that we bought less than we sold, and we subtract the inventory decrease from cost of goods sold to compute purchases. We show the *first step* by reconstructing the Inventory account. We determine purchases to be $314,000, computed as cost of goods sold of $300,000 plus the $14,000 increase in inventory.

Inventory			
Bal., Dec. 31, 2018	70,000		
Purchases =	**314,000**	Cost of goods sold	300,000
Bal., Dec. 31, 2019	84,000		

The second step uses the change in the balance of Accounts Payable, and the cost of purchases, to compute cash paid for inventory. A decrease in accounts payable means that we paid for more goods than we acquired this period, and we would add the accounts payable decrease to cost of purchases to compute cash paid for inventory. An increase in accounts payable means that we paid for less than the amount of goods acquired, and we would subtract the accounts payable increase from purchases to compute cash paid for inventory. The *second step* is applied to Genesis by reconstructing its Accounts Payable account to get cash paid of $319,000 (or $40,000 + $314,000 − [?] = $35,000).

Accounts Payable			
		Bal., Dec. 31, 2018	40,000
Cash payments =	319,000	Purchases	**314,000**
		Bal., Dec. 31, 2019	35,000

Reconstructed Entry
COGS 300,000
Inventory 14,000
Accounts Payable . . 5,000
    Cash.   319,000

Alternatively, cash paid for inventory is equal to purchases of $314,000 plus the $5,000 decrease in accounts payable. The $319,000 cash paid for inventory is reported as a cash outflow under operating activities. This two-step adjustment to cost of goods sold to compute cash paid for inventory is in Exhibit 12B.3.

Example: If the ending balances of Inventory and Accounts Payable are $60,000 and $50,000, respectively (instead of $84,000 and $35,000), what is cash paid for inventory? *Answer:* $280,000

EXHIBIT 12B.3

Two Steps to Compute Cash Paid for Inventory— Direct Method

① Purchases = Cost of goods sold $\begin{array}{l} + \textbf{Increase in inventory} \\ \text{or} \\ - \textbf{Decrease in inventory} \end{array}$

② Cash paid for inventory = Purchases $\begin{array}{l} + \textbf{Decrease in accounts payable} \\ \text{or} \\ - \textbf{Increase in accounts payable} \end{array}$

Cash Paid for Wages and Operating Expenses (Excluding Depreciation) The Genesis income statement shows wages and other operating expenses of $216,000 (see Exhibit 12.10). To compute cash paid for wages and other operating expenses, we adjust for any changes in related balance sheet accounts. We begin by looking for any prepaid expenses and accrued liabilities related to wages and other operating expenses in the balance sheets in Exhibit 12.10. The balance sheets show prepaid expenses but no accrued liabilities. Thus, the adjustment is only for the change in prepaid expenses. The adjustment is computed by assuming that all cash paid for wages and other operating expenses is initially debited to Prepaid Expenses. This assumption allows us to reconstruct the Prepaid Expenses account to get cash paid of $218,000.

Point: A decrease in prepaid expenses implies that reported expenses include an amount(s) that did not require a cash outflow in the period.

Reconstructed Entry

Wages & Other Exp.	216,000	
Prepaid Expenses	2,000	
Cash		218,000

Prepaid Expenses				
Bal., Dec. 31, 2018	4,000			
Cash payments =	**218,000**	Wages and other operating exp.	216,000
Bal., Dec. 31, 2019	6,000			

Cash paid also can be calculated as reported expenses of $216,000 plus the $2,000 increase in prepaid expenses. Exhibit 12B.4 summarizes the adjustments to wages (including salaries) and other operating expenses.

EXHIBIT 12B.4

Formula to Compute Cash Paid for Wages and Operating Expenses—Direct Method

$$\text{Cash paid for wages and other operating expenses} = \text{Wages and other operating expenses} \quad \begin{array}{l} \textbf{+ Increase in prepaid expenses} \\ \textit{or} \\ \textbf{– Decrease in prepaid expenses} \end{array} \quad \begin{array}{l} \textbf{+ Decrease in accrued liabilities} \\ \textit{or} \\ \textbf{– Increase in accrued liabilities} \end{array}$$

Cash Paid for Accrued Liabilities The Genesis balance sheet did not report accrued liabilities, but we include them in the formula to explain the adjustment to cash when they do exist. A decrease in accrued liabilities means that we paid cash for more goods or services than received this period, so cash paid is higher than the recorded expense. Alternatively, an increase in accrued liabilities implies that we paid less cash than what was received, so cash paid is less than the recorded expense.

Cash Paid for Interest and Income Taxes Computing operating cash flows for interest and taxes requires adjustments for amounts reported on the income statement for changes in related balance sheet accounts. The Genesis income statement shows interest expense of $7,000 and income taxes expense of $15,000. To compute the cash paid, we adjust interest expense for the change in interest payable and adjust income taxes expense for the change in income taxes payable. These computations involve reconstructing both liability accounts and show cash paid for interest of $8,000 and cash paid for income taxes of $5,000.

Reconstructed Entry

Interest Expense	7,000	
Interest Payable	1,000	
Cash		8,000

Reconstructed Entry

Income Tax Exp.	15,000	
Income Tax Pay.		10,000
Cash		5,000

Interest Payable			
		Bal., Dec. 31, 2018	4,000
Cash paid for interest = 8,000	Interest expense	7,000
		Bal., Dec. 31, 2019	3,000

Income Taxes Payable			
		Bal., Dec. 31, 2018	12,000
Cash paid for taxes = 5,000	Income taxes expense	15,000
		Bal., Dec. 31, 2019	22,000

The formulas to compute these amounts are in Exhibit 12B.5. Both of these cash payments are reported as operating cash outflows.

EXHIBIT 12B.5

Formulas to Compute Cash Paid for Both Interest and Taxes—Direct Method

$$\frac{\text{Cash paid}}{\text{for interest}} = \text{Interest expense} \quad \begin{array}{l} \textbf{+ Decrease in interest payable} \\ \textit{or} \\ \textbf{– Increase in interest payable} \end{array}$$

$$\frac{\text{Cash paid}}{\text{for taxes}} = \text{Income taxes expense} \quad \begin{array}{l} \textbf{+ Decrease in income taxes payable} \\ \textit{or} \\ \textbf{– Increase in income taxes payable} \end{array}$$

Analyzing Additional Expenses, Gains, and Losses Genesis has three more items reported on its income statement: depreciation, loss on sale of assets, and gain on retirement of debt. We consider each for its potential cash effects.

Depreciation Expense Depreciation expense is $24,000. It is often called a *noncash expense* because depreciation has no cash flows. Depreciation expense is *never* reported on a statement of cash flows using the direct method; nor is depletion or amortization expense.

Loss on Sale of Assets Sales of assets frequently result in gains and losses reported as part of net income, but the amount of recorded gain or loss does *not* impact cash. Thus, the loss or gain on a sale of assets is *never* reported on a statement of cash flows using the direct method.

Gain on Retirement of Debt Retirement of debt usually yields a gain or loss reported as part of net income, but that gain or loss does *not* impact cash. Thus, the loss or gain from retirement of debt is *never* reported on a statement of cash flows using the direct method.

Summary of Adjustments for Direct Method Exhibit 12B.6 summarizes common adjustments for net income to yield net cash provided (used) by operating activities under the direct method.

Item	From Income Statement	Adjustments to Obtain Cash Flow Numbers	
Receipts			
From sales	Sales Revenue	+ Decrease in Accounts Receivable − Increase in Accounts Receivable	
From rent	Rent Revenue	+ Decrease in Rent Receivable − Increase in Rent Receivable	
From interest	Interest Revenue	+ Decrease in Interest Receivable − Increase in Interest Receivable	
From dividends	Dividend Revenue	+ Decrease in Dividends Receivable − Increase in Dividends Receivable	
Payments			
To suppliers	Cost of Goods Sold	+ Increase in Inventory − Decrease in Inventory	+ Decrease in Accounts Payable − Increase in Accounts Payable
For operations	Operating Expense	+ Increase in Prepaids − Decrease in Prepaids	+ Decrease in Accrued Liabilities − Increase in Accrued Liabilities
To employees	Wages (Salaries) Expense	+ Decrease in Wages (Salaries) Payable − Increase in Wages (Salaries) Payable	
For interest	Interest Expense	+ Decrease in Interest Payable − Increase in Interest Payable	
For taxes	Income Tax Expense	+ Decrease in Income Tax Payable − Increase in Income Tax Payable	

EXHIBIT 12B.6

Summary of Selected Adjustments for Direct Method

Point: The FASB requires a reconciliation of net income to net cash provided (used) by operating activities when the direct method is used. This reconciliation follows the operating activities section using the indirect method.

Direct Method Format of Operating Activities Section Exhibit 12B.7 shows the Genesis statement of cash flows using the direct method. Operating cash outflows are subtracted from operating cash inflows to get net cash provided (used) by operating activities.

EXHIBIT 12B.7

Statement of Cash Flows—Direct Method

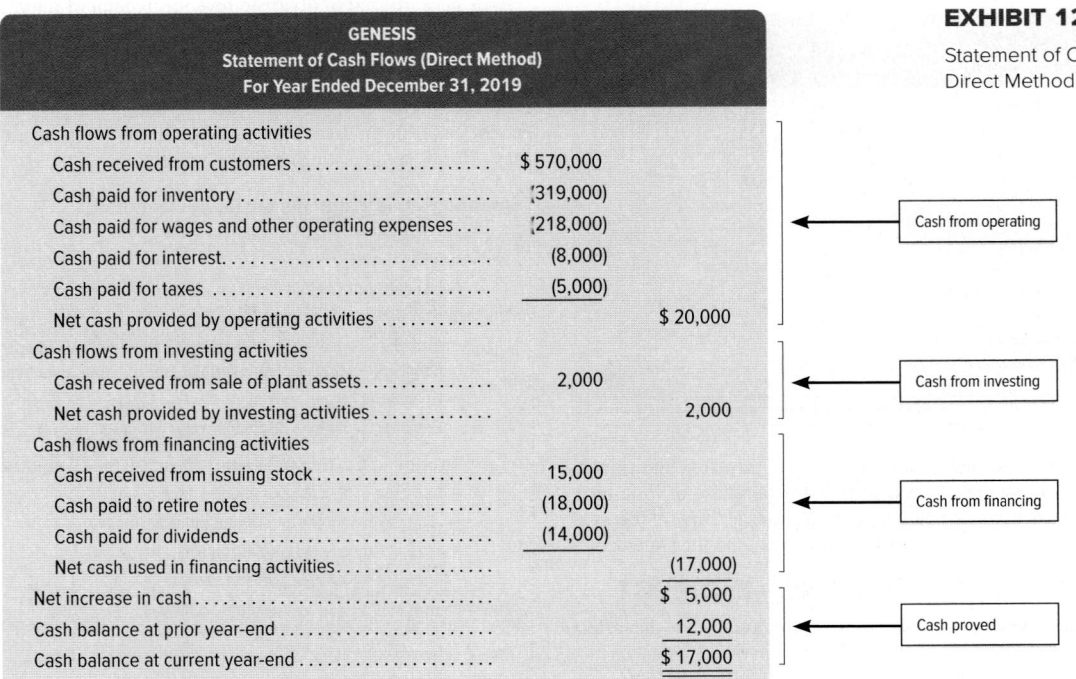

GENESIS Statement of Cash Flows (Direct Method) For Year Ended December 31, 2019		
Cash flows from operating activities		
Cash received from customers	$ 570,000	
Cash paid for inventory	(319,000)	
Cash paid for wages and other operating expenses	(218,000)	
Cash paid for interest.	(8,000)	
Cash paid for taxes	(5,000)	
Net cash provided by operating activities		$ 20,000
Cash flows from investing activities		
Cash received from sale of plant assets	2,000	
Net cash provided by investing activities		2,000
Cash flows from financing activities		
Cash received from issuing stock	15,000	
Cash paid to retire notes	(18,000)	
Cash paid for dividends	(14,000)	
Net cash used in financing activities		(17,000)
Net increase in cash		$ 5,000
Cash balance at prior year-end		12,000
Cash balance at current year-end		$ 17,000

Cash from operating

Cash from investing

Cash from financing

Cash proved

NEED-TO-KNOW 12-6

Reporting Operating
Cash Flows (Direct)

P5

A company's current-year income statement and selected balance sheet data at December 31 of the current and prior years follow. Prepare the operating activities section of the statement of cash flows using the direct method for the current year.

Income Statement For Current Year Ended December 31	
Sales revenue	$120
Expenses: Cost of goods sold.............	50
Depreciation expense..........	30
Salaries expense..............	17
Interest expense..............	3
Net income..........................	$ 20

Selected Balance Sheet Accounts		
At December 31	Current Yr	Prior Yr
Accounts receivable	$12	$10
Inventory	6	9
Accounts payable	7	11
Salaries payable	8	3
Interest payable........	1	0

Solution

Cash Flows from Operating Activities—Direct Method For Current Year Ended December 31	
Cash flows from operating activities*	
Cash received from customers	$118
Cash paid for inventory	(51)
Cash paid for salaries	(12)
Cash paid for interest............................	(2)
Net cash provided by operating activities...............	$53

Do More: QS 12-21, QS 12-22, QS 12-23, QS 12-24, QS 12-25, QS 12-26, QS 12-27, E 12-15, E 12-16, E 12-17, E 12-18, E 12-19

*Supporting computations:
  Cash received from customers = Sales of $120 − Accounts Receivable increase of $2.
  Cash paid for inventory = COGS of $50 − Inventory decrease of $3 + Accounts Payable decrease of $4.
  Cash paid for salaries = Salaries Expense of $17 − Salaries Payable increase of $5.
  Cash paid for interest = Interest Expense of $3 − Interest Payable increase of $1.

Summary: Cheat Sheet

BASICS OF CASH FLOW REPORTING

Format for statement of cash flows:

COMPANY NAME Statement of Cash Flows For *period* Ended *date*	
Cash flows from operating activities	
[Compute operating cash flows using indirect or direct method]	
Net cash provided (used) by operating activities	$ #
Cash flows from investing activities	
[List of individual inflows and outflows]	
Net cash provided (used) by investing activities.......................................	#
Cash flows from financing activities	
[List of individual inflows and outflows]	
Net cash provided (used) by financing activities	#
Net increase (decrease) in cash	$ #
Cash (and equivalents) balance at prior period-end.......................................	#
Cash (and equivalents) balance at current period-end.................................	$ #

Separate schedule or note disclosure of any noncash investing and financing transactions is required.

Noncash investing and financing activities: Some investing and financing activities do not affect cash flows, such as the purchase of long-term assets using a long-term note payable (loan). Such transactions are reported at the bottom of the statement of cash flows or in a note to the statement.

CASH FLOWS FROM OPERATING—INDIRECT

Operating activities: Generally include transactions and events that affect net income.

Operating cash inflow examples: Cash sales to customers, collections on credit sales, receipt of dividend revenue, receipt of interest revenue.

Operating cash outflow examples: Cash to pay salaries and wages, pay operating expenses, pay suppliers for goods and services, pay interest owed, pay taxes and fines.

Indirect method: Reports net income and then adjusts it for items that do not affect cash. Indirect method only affects the presentation of operating cash flows, not investing or financing sections.

Summary of adjustments for *indirect* method:

Net Income (or Loss)
① Adjustments for operating items not providing or using cash
   + Noncash expenses and losses
     Examples: Expenses for depreciation, depletion, and amortization; losses from disposal of long-term assets and from retirement of debt
   − Noncash revenues and gains
     Examples: Gains from disposal of long-term assets and from retirement of debt
② Adjustments for changes in current assets and current liabilities
   + Decrease in noncash current operating asset
   − Increase in noncash current operating asset
   + Increase in current operating liability
   − Decrease in current operating liability
Net cash provided (used) by operating activities

CASH FLOWS FROM INVESTING

Investing activities: Generally include transactions and events that come from the purchase and sale of long-term assets.
Investing cash inflow examples: Cash from selling plant assets, selling intangible assets, selling short-term and long-term investments, selling notes receivable, collecting principal (but *not* interest) on notes receivable.
Investing cash outflow examples: Cash to buy plant assets, buy intangible assets, buy short-term and long-term investments, loan money in return for notes receivable.

Example of investing section format:

Cash flows from investing activities		
Cash received from sale of plant assets	$2,000	
Net cash provided by investing activities		$2,000

CASH FLOWS FROM FINANCING

Financing activities: Generally include transactions and events that affect long-term liabilities and equity.
Financing cash inflow examples: Cash from issuing common and preferred stock, issuing short- and long-term debt (notes payable and bonds payable), reissuing treasury stock.
Financing cash outflow examples: Cash to pay dividends to shareholders, pay off short- and long-term debt (notes payable and bonds payable), purchase treasury stock.

Example of financing section format:

Cash flows from financing activities		
Cash received from issuing stock	$ 15,000	
Cash paid to retire notes	(18,000)	
Cash paid for dividends	(14,000)	
Net cash used in financing activities		$(17,000)

CASH FLOWS FROM OPERATING—DIRECT

Direct method: Separately lists operating cash receipts and operating cash payments. Cash payments are subtracted from cash receipts. Unlike the indirect method, it does not start with net income. This only affects the operating section of the statement of cash flows.

Summary of adjustments for *direct* method:

Item	From Income Statement	Adjustments to Obtain Cash Flow Numbers	
Receipts			
From sales	Sales Revenue	+ Decrease in Accounts Receivable − Increase in Accounts Receivable	
From rent	Rent Revenue	+ Decrease in Rent Receivable − Increase in Rent Receivable	
From interest	Interest Revenue	+ Decrease in Interest Receivable − Increase in Interest Receivable	
From dividends	Dividend Revenue	+ Decrease in Dividends Receivable − Increase in Dividends Receivable	
Payments			
To suppliers	Cost of Goods Sold	+ Increase in Inventory − Decrease in Inventory	+ Decrease in Accounts Payable − Increase in Accounts Payable
For operations	Operating Expense	+ Increase in Prepaids − Decrease in Prepaids	+ Decrease in Accrued Liabilities − Increase in Accrued Liabilities
To employees	Wages (Salaries) Expense	+ Decrease in Wages (Salaries) Payable − Increase in Wages (Salaries) Payable	
For interest	Interest Expense	+ Decrease in Interest Payable − Increase in Interest Payable	
For taxes	Income Tax Expense	+ Decrease in Income Tax Payable − Increase in Income Tax Payable	

Multiple Choice Quiz

1. A company uses the indirect method to determine its cash flows from operating activities. Use the following information to determine its net cash provided or used by operating activities.

Net income	$15,200
Depreciation expense	10,000
Cash payment on note payable	8,000
Gain on sale of land	3,000
Increase in inventory	1,500
Increase in accounts payable.	2,850

  a. $23,550 used by operating activities
  b. $23,550 provided by operating activities
  c. $15,550 provided by operating activities
  d. $42,400 provided by operating activities
  e. $20,850 provided by operating activities

2. A machine with a cost of $175,000 and accumulated depreciation of $94,000 is sold for $87,000 cash. The amount reported as a source of cash under cash flows from investing activities is
  a. $81,000.
  b. $6,000.
  c. $87,000.
  d. $0; this is a financing activity.
  e. $0; this is an operating activity.

3. A company settles a long-term note payable plus interest by paying $68,000 cash toward the principal amount and $5,440 cash for interest. The amount reported as a use of cash under cash flows from financing activities is
  a. $0; this is an investing activity.
  b. $0; this is an operating activity.
  c. $73,440.
  d. $68,000.
  e. $5,440.

4. The following information is available regarding a company's annual salaries and wages. What amount of cash is paid for salaries and wages?

Salaries and wages expense	$255,000
Salaries and wages payable, prior year-end.	8,200
Salaries and wages payable, current year-end.	10,900

a. $252,300   **c.** $255,000   **e.** $235,900
b. $257,700   **d.** $274,100

5. The following information is available for a company. What amount of cash is paid for inventory for the current year?

Cost of goods sold	$545,000
Inventory, prior year-end	105,000
Inventory, current year-end	112,000
Accounts payable, prior year-end	98,500
Accounts payable, current year-end	101,300

a. $545,000   **c.** $540,800   **e.** $549,200
b. $554,800   **d.** $535,200

ANSWERS TO MULTIPLE CHOICE QUIZ

1. b;

Net income	$15,200
Depreciation expense	10,000
Gain on sale of land	(3,000)
Increase in inventory	(1,500)
Increase in accounts payable.	2,850
Net cash provided by operations.	$23,550

2. c; Cash received from sale of machine is reported as an investing activity.

3. d; FASB requires cash interest paid to be reported under operating.

4. a; Cash paid for salaries and wages = $255,000 + $8,200 − $10,900 = $252,300

5. e; Increase in inventory = $112,000 − $105,000 = $7,000
Increase in accounts payable = $101,300 − $98,500 = $2,800
Cash paid for inventory = $545,000 + $7,000 − $2,800 = $549,200

A(B) *Superscript letter A or B denotes assignments based on Appendix 12A or 12B.*

[i] Icon denotes assignments that involve decision making.

Discussion Questions

1. What is the reporting purpose of the statement of cash flows? Identify at least two questions that this statement can answer.

2. What are some investing activities reported on the statement of cash flows?

3. What are some financing activities reported on the statement of cash flows?

4.B Describe the direct method of reporting cash flows from operating activities.

5.B When a statement of cash flows is prepared using the direct method, what are some of the operating cash flows?

6. Describe the indirect method of reporting cash flows from operating activities.

7. Where on the statement of cash flows is the payment of cash dividends reported?

8. [i] Assume that a company purchases land for $1,000,000, paying $400,000 cash and borrowing the remainder with a long-term note payable. How should this transaction be reported on a statement of cash flows?

9. [i] On June 3, a company borrows $200,000 cash by giving its bank a 90-day, interest-bearing note. On the statement of cash flows, where should this be reported?

10. [i] If a company reports positive net income for the year, can it also show a net cash outflow from operating activities? Explain.

11. [i] Is depreciation a source of cash flow?

12. [i] Refer to **Apple**'s statement of cash flows in Appendix A. (*a*) Which method is used to compute its net cash provided by operating activities? (*b*) Its balance sheet shows an increase in accounts receivable from September 24, 2016, to September 30, 2017; why is this increase in accounts receivable subtracted when computing net cash provided by operating activities for the fiscal year ended September 30, 2017?   **APPLE**

13. [i] Refer to **Google**'s statement of cash flows in Appendix A. What are its cash flows from financing activities for the year ended December 31, 2017? List the items and amounts.   **GOOGLE**

14. [i] Refer to **Samsung**'s 2017 statement of cash flows in Appendix A. List its cash flows from operating activities, investing activities, and financing activities.   **Samsung**

15. [i] Refer to **Samsung**'s statement of cash flows in Appendix A. What investing activities result in cash outflows for the year ended December 31, 2017? List items and amounts.   **Samsung**

[Mc Graw Hill] **connect**

QUICK STUDY

QS 12-1

Classifying transactions by activity

C1 [i]

Classify the following cash flows as either operating (O), investing (I), or financing (F) activities.

_____ **1.** Sold stock investments for cash.
_____ **2.** Received cash payments from customers.
_____ **3.** Paid cash for wages and salaries.
_____ **4.** Purchased inventories with cash.
_____ **5.** Paid cash dividends.

_____ **6.** Issued common stock for cash.
_____ **7.** Received cash interest on a note.
_____ **8.** Paid cash interest on outstanding notes.
_____ **9.** Received cash from sale of land.
_____ **10.** Paid cash for property taxes on building.

Label the following headings, line items, and notes with the numbers *1* through *13* according to their sequential order (from top to bottom) for presentation on the statement of cash flows.

____ **a.** "Cash flows from investing activities" title

____ **b.** "For *period* Ended *date*" heading

____ **c.** "Cash flows from operating activities" title

____ **d.** Company name

____ **e.** Schedule or note disclosure of noncash investing and financing transactions

____ **f.** "Statement of Cash Flows" heading

____ **g.** Net increase (decrease) in cash . . . . $

____ **h.** Net cash provided (used) by operating activities . . . . $

____ **i.** Cash (and equivalents) balance at prior period-end . . . . $

____ **j.** Net cash provided (used) by financing activities . . . . $

____ **k.** "Cash flows from financing activities" title

____ **l.** Net cash provided (used) by investing activities. . . . . $

____ **m.** Cash (and equivalents) balance at current period-end . . . . $

QS 12-2
Statement of cash flows

P1

Bryant Co. reports net income of $20,000. For the year, depreciation expense is $7,000 and the company
reports a gain of $3,000 from sale of machinery. It also had a $2,000 loss from retirement of notes.
Compute cash flows from operations using the *indirect* method.

QS 12-3
Indirect: Computing cash
flows from operations   **P2**

Cain Inc. reports net income of $15,000. Its comparative balance sheet shows the following changes: ac-
counts receivable increased $6,000; inventory decreased $8,000; prepaid insurance decreased $1,000;
accounts payable increased $3,000; and taxes payable decreased $2,000. Compute cash flows from operations using the *indirect* method.

QS 12-4
Indirect: Computing cash
flows from operations   **P2**

For each separate company, compute cash flows from operations using the *indirect method.*

	Twix	Dots	Skor
Net income	$ 4,000	$100,000	$72,000
Depreciation expense	30,000	8,000	24,000
Accounts receivable increase (decrease)	40,000	20,000	(4,000)
Inventory increase (decrease)	(20,000)	(10,000)	10,000
Accounts payable increase (decrease)	24,000	(22,000)	14,000
Accrued liabilities increase (decrease)	(44,000)	12,000	(8,000)

QS 12-5
Indirect: Computing cash
flows from operations

P2

Use the following information to determine cash flows from operating activities using the *indirect method.*

QS 12-6
Indirect: Computing cash
from operations   **P2**

MOSS COMPANY		
Income Statement		
For Year Ended December 31, 2019		
Sales		$515,000
Cost of goods sold		331,600
Gross profit		183,400
Operating expenses		
Depreciation expense . . .	$ 36,000	
Other expenses	121,500	157,500
Income before taxes.		25,900
Income taxes expense		7,700
Net income		$ 18,200

MOSS COMPANY		
Selected Balance Sheet Information		
December 31, 2019 and 2018		
	2019	2018
Current assets		
Cash	$84,650	$26,800
Accounts receivable.	25,000	32,000
Inventory.	60,000	54,100
Current liabilities		
Accounts payable.	30,400	25,700
Income taxes payable . . .	2,050	2,200

QS 12-7

Indirect: Computing cash from operations   **P2**

CRUZ, INC.		
Comparative Balance Sheets		
At December 31	**2019**	**2018**
Assets		
Cash.	$ 94,800	$ 24,000
Accounts receivable, net	41,000	51,000
Inventory.	85,800	95,800
Prepaid expenses.	5,400	4,200
Total current assets	227,000	175,000
Furniture	109,000	119,000
Accum. depreciation—Furniture	(17,000)	(9,000)
Total assets.	$319,000	$285,000
Liabilities and Equity		
Accounts payable	$ 15,000	$ 21,000
Wages payable	9,000	5,000
Income taxes payable.	1,400	2,600
Total current liabilities	25,400	28,600
Notes payable (long-term)	29,000	69,000
Total liabilities.	54,400	97,600
Equity		
Common stock, $5 par value	229,000	179,000
Retained earnings.	35,600	8,400
Total liabilities and equity.	$319,000	$285,000

CRUZ, INC.		
Income Statement		
For Year Ended December 31, 2019		
Sales		$488,000
Cost of goods sold		314,000
Gross profit.		174,000
Operating expenses		
Depreciation expense	$37,600	
Other expenses	89,100	126,700
Income before taxes.		47,300
Income taxes expense		17,300
Net income		$ 30,000

Required

Use the *indirect method* to prepare the operating activities section of Cruz's statement of cash flows.

QS 12-8

Computing cash from asset sales

P3

The following information is from Ellerby Company's comparative balance sheets. The current-year income statement reports depreciation expense on furniture of $18,000. During the year, furniture costing $52,500 was sold for its book value. Compute cash received from the sale of furniture.

At December 31	Current Year	Prior Year
Furniture	$132,000	$ 184,500
Accumulated depreciation—Furniture.	(88,700)	(110,700)

QS 12-9

Computing investing cash flows

P3

Indicate the effect each separate transaction has on *investing* cash flows.

a. Sold a truck costing $40,000, with $22,000 of accumulated depreciation, for $8,000 cash. The sale results in a $10,000 loss.

b. Sold a machine costing $10,000, with $8,000 of accumulated depreciation, for $5,000 cash. The sale results in a $3,000 gain.

c. Purchased stock investments for $16,000 cash. The purchaser believes the stock is worth at least $30,000.

QS 12-10

Computing investing cash flows

P3

The plant assets section of the comparative balance sheets of Anders Company is reported below.

ANDERS COMPANY		
Comparative Year-End Balance Sheets		
Plant assets	**2019**	**2018**
Equipment	$ 180,000	$ 270,000
Accumulated depreciation—Equipment	(100,000)	(210,000)
Equipment, net.	$ 80,000	$ 60,000
Buildings.	$ 380,000	$ 400,000
Accumulated depreciation—Buildings	(100,000)	(285,000)
Buildings, net	$ 280,000	$ 115,000

Refer to the balance sheet data above from Anders Company. During 2019, equipment with a book value of $40,000 and an original cost of $210,000 was sold at a loss of $3,000.

1. How much cash did Anders receive from the sale of equipment?

2. How much depreciation expense was recorded on equipment during 2019?

3. What was the cost of new equipment purchased by Anders during 2019?

Refer to the balance sheet data in QS 12-10 from Anders Company. During 2019, a building with a book value of $70,000 and an original cost of $300,000 was sold at a gain of $60,000.

1. How much cash did Anders receive from the sale of the building?

2. How much depreciation expense was recorded on buildings during 2019?

3. What was the cost of buildings purchased by Anders during 2019?

QS 12-11
Computing investing cash flows
P3

Compute cash flows from investing activities using the following company information.

Sale of short-term stock investments	$ 6,000	Cash purchase of used equipment	$5,000
Cash collections from customers.	16,000	Depreciation expense	2,000

QS 12-12
Computing cash flows from investing
P3

Refer to the data in QS 12-7.

Furniture costing $55,000 is sold at its book value in 2019. Acquisitions of furniture total $45,000 cash, on which no depreciation is necessary because it is acquired at year-end. What is the cash inflow from the sale of furniture?

QS 12-13
Computing cash from asset sales P3

Indicate the effect, if any, that each separate transaction has on *financing* cash flows.

a. Notes payable with a carrying value of $15,000 are retired for $16,000 cash, resulting in a $1,000 gain.

b. Paid cash dividends of $11,000 to common stockholders.

c. Acquired $20,000 worth of machinery in exchange for common stock.

QS 12-14
Computing financing cash flows
P3

The following information is from Princeton Company's comparative balance sheets.

At December 31	Current Year	Prior Year
Common stock, $10 par value.	$105,000	$100,000
Paid-in capital in excess of par	567,000	342,000
Retained earnings.	313,500	287,500

The company's net income for the current year ended December 31 was $48,000.

1. Compute the cash received from the sale of its common stock during the current year.

2. Compute the cash paid for dividends during the current year.

QS 12-15
Computing financing cash flows
P3

Compute cash flows from financing activities using the following company information.

Cash received from short-term note payable.	$20,000	Cash dividends paid.	$16,000
Purchase of short-term stock investments	5,000	Interest paid	8,000

QS 12-16
Computing cash flows from financing
P3

Refer to the data in QS 12-7.

1. Assume that all common stock is issued for cash. What amount of cash dividends is paid during 2019?

2. Assume that no additional notes payable are issued in 2019. What cash amount is paid to reduce the notes payable balance in 2019?

QS 12-17
Computing financing cash outflows P3

Use the following information for VPI Co. to prepare a statement of cash flows for the year ended December 31 using the *indirect* method.

Cash balance at prior year-end.	$40,000	Gain on sale of machinery.	$ 2,000
Increase in inventory	5,000	Cash received from sale of machinery	9,500
Depreciation expense	4,000	Increase in accounts payable	1,500
Cash received from issuing stock	8,000	Net income	23,000
Cash paid for dividends	1,000	Decrease in accounts receivable	3,000

QS 12-18
Indirect: Preparing statement of cash flows
P2 P3

QS 12-19

Interpreting disclosures on sources and uses of cash

A1

Financial data from three competitors in the same industry follow.

1. Rank the three companies from high to low on cash from operating activities.
2. Which company has the largest cash outflow for investing activities?
3. Which company has the largest cash inflow from financing activities?
4. Which company has the highest cash flow on total assets ratio?

	Mancala	Yahtzee	Cluedo
Cash provided (used) by operating activities	$ 70,000	$ 60,000	$ (24,000)
Cash provided (used) by investing activities	(28,000)	(34,000)	26,000
Cash provided (used) by financing activities	(6,000)	0	23,000
Net increase (decrease) in cash	$ 36,000	$ 26,000	$ 25,000
Average total assets	$790,000	$625,000	$300,000

QS 12-20^A

Recording entries in a spreadsheet

P4

A company uses a spreadsheet to prepare its statement of cash flows. Indicate whether each of the following items would be recorded in the Debit column or Credit column of the spreadsheet's *statement of cash flows section*.

a. Decrease in accounts payable
b. Payment of cash dividends
c. Increase in accounts receivable

d. Loss on sale of machinery
e. Net income
f. Increase in interest payable

QS 12-21^B

Direct: Computing cash receipts from operations

P5

Russell Co. reports sales revenue of $30,000 and interest revenue of $5,000. Its comparative balance sheet shows that accounts receivable decreased $4,000 and interest receivable increased $1,000. Compute cash provided by operating activities using the *direct* method.

QS 12-22^B

Direct: Computing cash payments to suppliers   P5

Bioware Co. reports cost of goods sold of $42,000. Its comparative balance sheet shows that inventory decreased $7,000 and accounts payable increased $5,000. Compute cash payments to suppliers using the *direct* method.

QS 12-23^B

Direct: Computing cash paid for operations   P5

BTN Inc. reports operating expenses of $27,000. Its comparative balance sheet shows that accrued liabilities decreased $6,000 and prepaid expenses increased $2,000. Compute cash used in operating activities using the *direct* method.

QS 12-24^B

Direct: Computing cash flows

P5

For each separate case, compute the required cash flow information for BioClean.

Case A: Compute cash interest received	
Interest revenue	$5,000
Interest receivable, beginning of year	600
Interest receivable, end of year	1,700

Case B: Compute cash paid for wages	
Wages expense	$9,000
Wages payable, beginning of year	2,200
Wages payable, end of year	1,000

QS 12-25^B

Direct: Computing cash received from customers

P5

Refer to the data in QS 12-7.

1. How much cash is received from sales to customers for year 2019?
2. What is the net increase or decrease in the Cash account for year 2019?

QS 12-26^B

Direct: Computing operating cash outflows

P5

Refer to the data in QS 12-7.

1. How much cash is paid to acquire inventory during year 2019?
2. How much cash is paid for "other expenses" during year 2019? *Hint:* Examine prepaid expenses and wages payable.

QS 12-27^B

Direct: Computing cash from operations   P5

Refer to the data in QS 12-7.

Use the *direct method* to prepare the operating activities section of Cruz's statement of cash flows.

Indicate where each item would appear on a statement of cash flows using the *indirect method* by placing an *x* in the appropriate column.

EXERCISES

Exercise 12-1
Indirect:
Classifying cash flows

C1

	Statement of Cash Flows			Noncash Investing and Financing Activities	Not Reported on Statement or in Notes
	Operating Activities	Investing Activities	Financing Activities		
a. Declared and paid a cash dividend	____	____	____	____	____
b. Recorded depreciation expense	____	____	____	____	____
c. Paid cash to settle long-term note payable . . .	____	____	____	____	____
d. Prepaid expenses increased in the year	____	____	____	____	____
e. Accounts receivable decreased in the year . . .	____	____	____	____	____
f. Purchased land by issuing common stock	____	____	____	____	____
g. Inventory increased in the year	____	____	____	____	____
h. Sold equipment for cash, yielding a loss	____	____	____	____	____
i. Accounts payable decreased in the year	____	____	____	____	____
j. Income taxes payable increased in the year . . .	____	____	____	____	____

Hampton Company reports the following information for its recent calendar year. Prepare the operating activities section of the statement of cash flows using the *indirect method*.

Exercise 12-2
Indirect: Reporting cash flows from operations

P2

Income Statement Data	
Sales.	$160,000
Expenses: Cost of goods sold.	100,000
Salaries expense	24,000
Depreciation expense.	12,000
Net income.	$ 24,000

Selected Year-End Balance Sheet Data	
Accounts receivable increase.	$10,000
Inventory decrease	16,000
Salaries payable increase.	1,000

Arundel Company disclosed the following information for its recent calendar year. Prepare the operating activities section of the statement of cash flows using the *indirect method*.

Exercise 12-3
Indirect: Reporting cash flows from operations

P2

Income Statement Data	
Revenues.	$100,000
Expenses: Salaries expense	84,000
Utilities expense	14,000
Depreciation expense.	14,600
Other expenses	3,400
Net loss	$ (16,000)

Selected Year-End Balance Sheet Data	
Accounts receivable decrease	$24,000
Purchased a machine for cash	10,000
Salaries payable increase.	18,000
Other accrued liabilities decrease	8,000

Using the following income statement and additional year-end information, prepare the operating activities section of the statement of cash flows using the *indirect method*.

Exercise 12-4
Indirect: Cash flows from operating activities

P2

SONAD COMPANY Income Statement For Year Ended December 31		
Sales		$1,828,000
Cost of goods sold		991,000
Gross profit		837,000
Operating expenses		
Salaries expense	$245,535	
Depreciation expense	44,200	
Rent expense	49,600	
Amortization expense—Patents	4,200	
Utilities expense.	18,125	361,660
		475,340
Gain on sale of equipment.		6,200
Net income		$ 481,540

Selected Year-End Balance Sheet Data	
Accounts receivable . .	$30,500 increase
Inventory	25,000 increase
Accounts payable	12,500 decrease
Salaries payable	3,500 decrease

Exercise 12-5
Indirect: Cash flows from operating activities
P2

Fitz Company reports the following information. Use the *indirect method* to prepare the operating activities section of its statement of cash flows for the year ended December 31.

Selected Annual Income Statement Data		Selected Year-End Balance Sheet Data	
Net income	$374,000	Accounts receivable decrease	$17,100
Depreciation expense	44,000	Inventory decrease	42,000
Amortization expense.................	7,200	Prepaid expenses increase.................	4,700
Gain on sale of plant assets............	6,000	Accounts payable decrease	8,200
		Salaries payable increase..................	1,200

Exercise 12-6
Indirect: Cash flows from operating activities
P2

Salud Company reports the following information. Use the *indirect method* to prepare the operating activities section of its statement of cash flows for the year ended December 31.

Selected Annual Income Statement Data		Selected Year-End Balance Sheet Data	
Net income	$400,000	Accounts receivable increase...............	$40,000
Depreciation expense	80,000	Prepaid expenses decrease................	12,000
Gain on sale of machinery	20,000	Accounts payable increase.................	6,000
		Wages payable decrease	2,000

Exercise 12-7
Indirect: Reporting cash flows from operations
P2

Prepare the operating activities section of the statement of cash flows for GreenGarden using the *indirect method*.

Annual Income Statement Data		Selected Year-End Balance Sheet Data	
Sales.....................................	$50,000	Prepaid expenses increase.................	$3,000
Expenses: Cost of goods sold..............	30,000	Inventory increase	500
Wages expense................	10,000	Accounts payable decrease	1,000
Amortization expense	1,500		
Net income..........................	$ 8,500		

Exercise 12-8
Cash flows from investing activities
P3

Use the following information to determine cash flows from investing activities.
 a. Equipment with a book value of $65,300 and an original cost of $133,000 was sold at a loss of $14,000.
 b. Paid $89,000 cash for a new truck.
 c. Sold land costing $154,000 for $198,000 cash, yielding a gain of $44,000.
 d. Stock investments were sold for $60,800 cash, yielding a gain of $4,150.

Exercise 12-9
Cash flows from financing activities
P3

Use the following information to determine cash flows from financing activities.
 a. Net income was $35,000.
 b. Issued common stock for $64,000 cash.
 c. Paid cash dividend of $14,600.
 d. Paid $50,000 cash to settle a note payable at its $50,000 maturity value.
 e. Paid $12,000 cash to acquire its treasury stock.
 f. Purchased equipment for $39,000 cash.

Exercise 12-10
Reconstructed entries
P3

For each of the following separate transactions, (*a*) prepare the reconstructed journal entry and (*b*) identify the effect it has, if any, on the *investing section* or *financing section* of the statement of cash flows.
 1. Sold a building costing $30,000, with $20,000 of accumulated depreciation, for $8,000 cash, resulting in a $2,000 loss.
 2. Acquired machinery worth $10,000 by issuing $10,000 in notes payable.
 3. Issued 1,000 shares of common stock at par for $2 per share.
 4. Notes payable with a carrying value of $40,000 were retired for $47,000 cash, resulting in a $7,000 loss.

The following financial statements and additional information are reported. (1) Prepare a statement of cash flows using the *indirect method* for the year ended June 30, 2019. (2) Compute the company's cash flow on total assets ratio for fiscal year 2019.

Exercise 12-11
Indirect: Preparing statement of cash flows

A1   P2   P3

IKIBAN INC. Income Statement For Year Ended June 30, 2019		
Sales		$678,000
Cost of goods sold		411,000
Gross profit		267,000
Operating expenses		
Depreciation expense	$58,600	
Other expenses	67,000	
Total operating expenses.		125,600
		141,400
Other gains (losses)		
Gain on sale of equipment.		2,000
Income before taxes.		143,400
Income taxes expense		43,890
Net income		$ 99,510

IKIBAN INC. Comparative Balance Sheets		
At June 30	2019	2018
Assets		
Cash.	$ 87,500	$ 44,000
Accounts receivable, net	65,000	51,000
Inventory	63,800	86,500
Prepaid expenses	4,400	5,400
Total current assets	220,700	186,900
Equipment	124,000	115,000
Accum. depreciation—Equipment . . .	(27,000)	(9,000)
Total assets	$317,700	$292,900
Liabilities and Equity		
Accounts payable	$ 25,000	$ 30,000
Wages payable	6,000	15,000
Income taxes payable.	3,400	3,800
Total current liabilities	34,400	48,800
Notes payable (long term)	30,000	60,000
Total liabilities	64,400	108,800
Equity		
Common stock, $5 par value	220,000	160,000
Retained earnings.	33,300	24,100
Total liabilities and equity.	$317,700	$292,900

Additional Information

a. A $30,000 note payable is retired at its $30,000 carrying (book) value in exchange for cash.

b. The only changes affecting retained earnings are net income and cash dividends paid.

c. New equipment is acquired for $57,600 cash.

d. Received cash for the sale of equipment that had cost $48,600, yielding a $2,000 gain.

e. Prepaid Expenses and Wages Payable relate to Other Expenses on the income statement.

f. All purchases and sales of inventory are on credit.

Check (1*b*) Cash paid for dividends, $90,310
(1*d*) Cash received from equip. sale, $10,000

Use the following information to prepare a statement of cash flows for the current year using the *indirect method.*

Exercise 12-12
Indirect: Preparing statement of cash flows

P2   P3

MONTGOMERY INC. Comparative Balance Sheets		
At December 31	Current Year	Prior Year
Assets		
Cash.	$ 30,400	$ 30,550
Accounts receivable, net	10,050	12,150
Inventory	90,100	70,150
Total current assets	130,550	112,850
Equipment	49,900	41,500
Accum. depreciation—Equipment . . .	(22,500)	(15,300)
Total assets	$157,950	$139,050
Liabilities and Equity		
Accounts payable	$ 23,900	$ 25,400
Salaries payable	500	600
Total current liabilities	24,400	26,000
Equity		
Common stock, no par value	110,000	100,000
Retained earnings.	23,550	13,050
Total liabilities and equity.	$157,950	$139,050

MONTGOMERY INC. Income Statement For Current Year Ended December 31		
Sales		$45,575
Cost of goods sold		(18,950)
Gross profit		26,625
Operating expenses		
Depreciation expense	$7,200	
Other expenses	5,550	
Total operating expenses . . .		12,750
Income before taxes		13,875
Income tax expense		3,375
Net income		$10,500

Additional Information on Current-Year Transactions

a. No dividends are declared or paid.

b. Issued additional stock for $10,000 cash.

c. Purchased equipment for cash; no equipment was sold.

Exercise 12-13
Analyzing cash flow on
total assets A1

A company reported average total assets of $1,240,000 in Year 1 and $1,510,000 in Year 2. Its net operating cash flow was $102,920 in Year 1 and $138,920 in Year 2. (1) Calculate its cash flow on total assets ratio for both years. (2) Did its cash flow on total assets improve in Year 2 versus Year 1?

Exercise 12-14ᴬ
Indirect: Cash flows
spreadsheet

P4

Complete the following spreadsheet in preparation of the statement of cash flows. (The statement of cash flows is not required.) Prepare the spreadsheet as in Exhibit 12A.1 under the *indirect method*. Identify the debits and credits in the Analysis of Changes columns with letters that correspond to the following transactions and events *a* through *h*.

a. Net income for the year was $100,000.
b. Dividends of $80,000 cash were declared and paid.
c. The only noncash expense was $70,000 of depreciation.
d. Purchased plant assets for $70,000 cash.

e. Notes payable of $20,000 were issued for $20,000 cash.
f. $70,000 increase in accounts receivable.
g. $20,000 decrease in inventory.
h. $10,000 decrease in accounts payable.

		Analysis of Changes		
SCORETECK CORPORATION **Spreadsheet for Statement of Cash Flows—Indirect Method** **For Year Ended December 31, 2019**	Dec. 31, 2018	Debit	Credit	Dec. 31, 2019
Balance Sheet—Debit Bal. Accounts				
Cash	$ 80,000			$ 60,000
Accounts receivable	120,000			190,000
Inventory	250,000			230,000
Plant assets	600,000			670,000
	$1,050,000			$1,150,000
Balance Sheet—Credit Bal. Accounts				
Accumulated depreciation	$ 100,000			$ 170,000
Accounts payable	150,000			140,000
Notes payable	370,000			390,000
Common stock	200,000			200,000
Retained earnings	230,000			250,000
	$1,050,000			$1,150,000
Statement of Cash Flows				
Operating activities				
Net income				
Increase in accounts receivable				
Decrease in inventory				
Decrease in accounts payable				
Depreciation expense				
Investing activities				
Cash paid to purchase plant assets				
Financing activities				
Cash paid for dividends				
Cash from issuance of notes				

Exercise 12-15ᴮ
Direct: Classifying cash
flows

C1　P5　

Indicate where each item would appear on a statement of cash flows using the *direct method* by placing an *x* in the appropriate column.

	Statement of Cash Flows			Noncash Investing and Financing Activities	Not Reported on Statement or in Notes
	Operating Activities	Investing Activities	Financing Activities		
a. Retired long-term notes payable by 　　issuing common stock	_____	_____	_____	_____	_____
b. Paid cash toward accounts payable . . .	_____	_____	_____	_____	_____
c. Sold inventory for cash	_____	_____	_____	_____	_____
d. Paid cash dividends	_____	_____	_____	_____	_____
e. Accepted note receivable in exchange 　　for plant assets	_____	_____	_____	_____	_____
f. Recorded depreciation expense	_____	_____	_____	_____	_____
g. Paid cash to acquire treasury stock . . .	_____	_____	_____	_____	_____
h. Collected cash from sales	_____	_____	_____	_____	_____
i. Borrowed cash from bank by signing 　　a nine-month note payable	_____	_____	_____	_____	_____
j. Paid cash to purchase a patent	_____	_____	_____	_____	_____

For each of the following separate cases, compute the required cash flow information.

Exercise 12-16ᴮ
Direct: Computing
cash flows

P5

Case X: Compute cash received from customers		**Case Z:** Compute cash paid for inventory	
Sales.	$515,000	Cost of goods sold	$525,000
Accounts receivable, Beginning balance. . . .	27,200	Inventory, Beginning balance	158,600
Accounts receivable, Ending balance	33,600	Accounts payable, Beginning balance . . .	66,700
Case Y: Compute cash paid for rent		Inventory, Ending balance	130,400
Rent expense.	$139,800	Accounts payable, Ending balance	82,000
Rent payable, Beginning balance.	7,800		
Rent payable, Ending balance	6,200		

Refer to the information in Exercise 12-11. Using the *direct method,* prepare the statement of cash flows for the year ended June 30, 2019.

Exercise 12-17ᴮ
Direct: Preparing statement of cash flows   **P5**

Refer to information in Exercise 12-4. Use the *direct method* to prepare the operating activities section of Sonad's statement of cash flows.

Exercise 12-18ᴮ
Direct: Cash flows from operating activities   **P5**

Use the following information about Ferron Company to prepare a complete statement of cash flows (*direct method*) for the current year ended December 31. Use a note disclosure for any noncash investing and financing activities.

Exercise 12-19ᴮ
Direct: Preparing statement of cash flows and supporting note

P5

Cash and cash equivalents, Dec. 31 prior year-end.	$ 40,000	Cash received in exchange for six-month note payable	$ 35,000
Cash and cash equivalents, Dec. 31 current year-end.	148,000	Land purchased by issuing long-term note payable	105,250
Cash received as interest.	3,500	Cash paid for store equipment.	24,750
Cash paid for salaries.	76,500	Cash dividends paid	10,000
Bonds payable retired by issuing common stock (no gain or loss on retirement)	185,500	Cash paid for other expenses.	20,000
		Cash received from customers.	495,000
Cash paid to retire long-term notes payable . . .	100,000	Cash paid for inventory.	254,500
Cash received from sale of equipment	60,250		

The following Cash T-account shows the total debits and total credits to the Cash account of Thomas Corporation for the current year.

1. Prepare a complete statement of cash flows for the current year using the *direct method.*
2. Refer to the statement of cash flows prepared for part 1 to answer the following questions. (*a*) Which section—operating, investing, or financing—shows the largest cash (i) inflow and (ii) outflow? (*b*) What is the largest individual item among the investing cash outflows? (*c*) Are the cash proceeds larger from issuing notes or issuing stock? (*d*) Does the company have a net cash inflow or outflow from borrowing activities?

Exercise 12-20ᴮ
Direct: Preparing statement of cash flows from Cash T-account

P1   P3   P5

Cash			
Balance, Dec. 31, prior year	333,000		
Receipts from customers	5,000,000	Payments for inventory	2,590,000
Receipts from dividends	208,400	Payments for wages	550,000
Receipts from land sale	220,000	Payments for rent	320,000
Receipts from machinery sale	710,000	Payments for interest	218,000
Receipts from issuing stock	1,540,000	Payments for taxes	450,000
Receipts from borrowing	3,600,000	Payments for machinery	2,236,000
		Payments for stock investments	1,260,000
		Payments for note payable	386,000
		Payments for dividends	500,000
		Payments for treasury stock	218,000
Balance, Dec. 31, current year	?		

Mc Graw Hill ■ connect

PROBLEM SET A

Problem 12-1A
Indirect: Computing cash flows from operations

P2

Lansing Company's current-year income statement and selected balance sheet data at December 31 of the current and prior years follow.

LANSING COMPANY Selected Balance Sheet Accounts		
At December 31	**Current Year**	**Prior Year**
Accounts receivable	$5,600	$5,800
Inventory	1,980	1,540
Accounts payable	4,400	4,600
Salaries payable	880	700
Utilities payable	220	160
Prepaid insurance.	260	280
Prepaid rent	220	180

LANSING COMPANY Income Statement For Current Year Ended December 31	
Sales revenue	$97,200
Expenses	
Cost of goods sold	42,000
Depreciation expense.	12,000
Salaries expense.	18,000
Rent expense	9,000
Insurance expense	3,800
Interest expense	3,600
Utilities expense	2,800
Net income.	$ 6,000

Required

Check Cash from operating activities, $17,780

Prepare the operating activities section of the statement of cash flows using the *indirect method* for the current year.

Problem 12-2A[B]
Direct: Computing cash flows from operations

P5

Refer to the information in Problem 12-1A.

Required

Prepare the operating activities section of the statement of cash flows using the *direct method* for the current year.

Problem 12-3A
Indirect: Statement of cash flows

A1   P2   P3

Forten Company's current-year income statement, comparative balance sheets, and additional information follow. For the year, (1) all sales are credit sales, (2) all credits to Accounts Receivable reflect cash receipts from customers, (3) all purchases of inventory are on credit, (4) all debits to Accounts Payable reflect cash payments for inventory, and (5) Other Expenses are paid in advance and are initially debited to Prepaid Expenses.

FORTEN COMPANY Income Statement For Current Year Ended December 31		
Sales		$582,500
Cost of goods sold		285,000
Gross profit		297,500
Operating expenses		
Depreciation expense	$ 20,750	
Other expenses	132,400	153,150
Other gains (losses)		
Loss on sale of equipment.		(5,125)
Income before taxes.		139,225
Income taxes expense		24,250
Net income		$114,975

Additional Information on Current-Year Transactions

a. The loss on the cash sale of equipment was $5,125 (details in *b*).
b. Sold equipment costing $46,875, with accumulated depreciation of $30,125, for $11,625 cash.
c. Purchased equipment costing $96,375 by paying $30,000 cash and signing a long-term note payable for the balance.
d. Borrowed $4,000 cash by signing a short-term note payable.
e. Paid $50,125 cash to reduce the long-term notes payable.
f. Issued 2,500 shares of common stock for $20 cash per share.
g. Declared and paid cash dividends of $50,100.

FORTEN COMPANY Comparative Balance Sheets December 31		
	Current Year	**Prior Year**
Assets		
Cash	$ 49,800	$ 73,500
Accounts receivable	65,810	50,625
Inventory	275,656	251,800
Prepaid expenses	1,250	1,875
Total current assets	392,516	377,800
Equipment	157,500	108,000
Accum. depreciation—Equipment	(36,625)	(46,000)
Total assets	$513,391	$439,800
Liabilities and Equity		
Accounts payable	$ 53,141	$114,675
Short-term notes payable	10,000	6,000
Total current liabilities.	63,141	120,675
Long-term notes payable	65,000	48,750
Total liabilities	128,141	169,425
Equity		
Common stock, $5 par value	162,750	150,250
Paid-in capital in excess of par, common stock . . .	37,500	0
Retained earnings	185,000	120,125
Total liabilities and equity	$513,391	$439,800

Required

1. Prepare a complete statement of cash flows using the *indirect method* for the current year. Disclose any noncash investing and financing activities in a note.

Check Cash from operating activities, $40,900

Analysis Component

2. Analyze and discuss the statement of cash flows prepared in part 1, giving special attention to the wisdom of the cash dividend payment.

Refer to the information reported about Forten Company in Problem 12-3A.

Problem 12-4A[A]
Indirect: Cash flows spreadsheet
P4

Required

Prepare a complete statement of cash flows using a spreadsheet as in Exhibit 12A.1 using the *indirect method*. Identify the debits and credits in the Analysis of Changes columns with letters that correspond to the following list of transactions and events.

a. Net income was $114,975.

b. Accounts receivable increased.

c. Inventory increased.

d. Prepaid expenses decreased.

e. Accounts payable decreased.

f. Depreciation expense was $20,750.

g. Sold equipment costing $46,875, with accumulated depreciation of $30,125, for $11,625 cash. This yielded a loss of $5,125.

h. Purchased equipment costing $96,375 by paying $30,000 cash and **(i.)** by signing a long-term note payable for the balance.

j. Borrowed $4,000 cash by signing a short-term note payable.

k. Paid $50,125 cash to reduce the long-term notes payable.

l. Issued 2,500 shares of common stock for $20 cash per share.

m. Declared and paid cash dividends of $50,100.

Check Analysis of Changes column totals, $600,775

Refer to Forten Company's financial statements and related information in Problem 12-3A.

Problem 12-5A[B]
Direct: Statement of cash flows   **P5**

Required

Prepare a complete statement of cash flows using the *direct method*. Disclose any noncash investing and financing activities in a note.

Check Cash used in financing activities, $(46,225)

Golden Corp.'s current-year income statement, comparative balance sheets, and additional information follow. For the year, (1) all sales are credit sales, (2) all credits to Accounts Receivable reflect cash receipts from customers, (3) all purchases of inventory are on credit, (4) all debits to Accounts Payable reflect cash payments for inventory, (5) Other Expenses are all cash expenses, and (6) any change in Income Taxes Payable reflects the accrual and cash payment of taxes.

Problem 12-6A
Indirect: Statement of cash flows
P2   P3

GOLDEN CORPORATION Comparative Balance Sheets		
At December 31	**Current Year**	**Prior Year**
Assets		
Cash..........................	$ 164,000	$107,000
Accounts receivable	83,000	71,000
Inventory	601,000	526,000
Total current assets..............	848,000	704,000
Equipment.....................	335,000	299,000
Accum. depreciation—Equipment ...	(158,000)	(104,000)
Total assets	$1,025,000	$899,000
Liabilities and Equity		
Accounts payable	$ 87,000	$ 71,000
Income taxes payable.............	28,000	25,000
Total current liabilities............	115,000	96,000
Equity		
Common stock, $2 par value	592,000	568,000
Paid-in capital in excess of par value, common stock......	196,000	160,000
Retained earnings................	122,000	75,000
Total liabilities and equity..........	$1,025,000	$899,000

GOLDEN CORPORATION Income Statement For Current Year Ended December 31		
Sales		$1,792,000
Cost of goods sold		1,086,000
Gross profit		706,000
Operating expenses		
Depreciation expense	$ 54,000	
Other expenses	494,000	548,000
Income before taxes.........		158,000
Income taxes expense		22,000
Net income		$ 136,000

Additional Information on Current-Year Transactions

a. Purchased equipment for $36,000 cash.

b. Issued 12,000 shares of common stock for $5 cash per share.

c. Declared and paid $89,000 in cash dividends.

Required

Prepare a complete statement of cash flows using the *indirect method* for the current year.

Problem 12-7A[A]
Indirect: Cash flows
spreadsheet
P4

Refer to the information reported about Golden Corporation in Problem 12-6A.

Required

Prepare a complete statement of cash flows using a spreadsheet as in Exhibit 12A.1 under the *indirect method*. Identify the debits and credits in the Analysis of Changes columns with letters that correspond to the following list of transactions and events.

a. Net income was $136,000.

b. Accounts receivable increased.

c. Inventory increased.

d. Accounts payable increased.

e. Income taxes payable increased.

f. Depreciation expense was $54,000.

g. Purchased equipment for $36,000 cash.

h. Issued 12,000 shares at $5 cash per share.

i. Declared and paid $89,000 of cash dividends.

Problem 12-8A[B]
Direct: Statement of
cash flows **P5**

Refer to Golden Corporation's financial statements and related information in Problem 12-6A.

Required

Prepare a complete statement of cash flows using the *direct method* for the current year.

PROBLEM SET B

Problem 12-1B
Indirect: Computing cash
flows from operations
P2

Salt Lake Company's current-year income statement and selected balance sheet data at December 31 of the current and prior years follow.

SALT LAKE COMPANY Income Statement For Current Year Ended December 31	
Sales revenue	$156,000
Expenses	
Cost of goods sold	72,000
Depreciation expense	32,000
Salaries expense	20,000
Rent expense	5,000
Insurance expense	2,600
Interest expense	2,400
Utilities expense	2,000
Net income	$ 20,000

SALT LAKE COMPANY Selected Balance Sheet Accounts		
At December 31	**Current Year**	**Prior Year**
Accounts receivable	$3,600	$3,000
Inventory	860	980
Accounts payable	2,400	2,600
Salaries payable	900	600
Utilities payable	200	0
Prepaid insurance	140	180
Prepaid rent	100	200

Required

Prepare the operating activities section of the statement of cash flows using the *indirect method* for the current year.

Problem 12-2B[B]
Direct: Computing cash
flows from operations
P5

Refer to the information in Problem 12-1B.

Required

Prepare the operating activities section of the statement of cash flows using the *direct method* for the current year.

Problem 12-3B
Indirect: Statement of
cash flows
A1   P2   P3

Gazelle Corporation's current-year income statement, comparative balance sheets, and additional information follow. For the year, (1) all sales are credit sales, (2) all credits to Accounts Receivable reflect cash receipts from customers, (3) all purchases of inventory are on credit, (4) all debits to Accounts Payable reflect cash payments for inventory, and (5) Other Expenses are paid in advance and are initially debited to Prepaid Expenses.

GAZELLE CORPORATION Comparative Balance Sheets December 31		
	Current Year	Prior Year
Assets		
Cash..............................	$123,450	$ 61,550
Accounts receivable	77,100	80,750
Inventory	240,600	250,700
Prepaid expenses	15,100	17,000
Total current assets................	456,250	410,000
Equipment	262,250	200,000
Accum. depreciation—Equipment	(110,750)	(95,000)
Total assets	$607,750	$515,000
Liabilities and Equity		
Accounts payable	$ 17,750	$102,000
Short-term notes payable	15,000	10,000
Total current liabilities..............	32,750	112,000
Long-term notes payable	100,000	77,500
Total liabilities	132,750	189,500
Equity		
Common stock, $5 par	215,000	200,000
Paid-in capital in excess		
of par, common stock.............	30,000	0
Retained earnings..................	230,000	125,500
Total liabilities and equity...........	$607,750	$515,000

GAZELLE CORPORATION Income Statement For Current Year Ended December 31		
Sales		$1,185,000
Cost of goods sold		595,000
Gross profit		590,000
Operating expenses		
Depreciation expense	$ 38,600	
Other expenses	362,850	
Total operating expenses.........		401,450
		188,550
Other gains (losses)		
Loss on sale of equipment......		(2,100)
Income before taxes.............		186,450
Income taxes expense		28,350
Net income		$ 158,100

Additional Information on Current-Year Transactions

a. The loss on the cash sale of equipment was $2,100 (details in b).

b. Sold equipment costing $51,000, with accumulated depreciation of $22,850, for $26,050 cash.

c. Purchased equipment costing $113,250 by paying $43,250 cash and signing a long-term note payable for the balance.

d. Borrowed $5,000 cash by signing a short-term note payable.

e. Paid $47,500 cash to reduce the long-term notes payable.

f. Issued 3,000 shares of common stock for $15 cash per share.

g. Declared and paid cash dividends of $53,600.

Required

1. Prepare a complete statement of cash flows using the *indirect method* for the current year. Disclose any noncash investing and financing activities in a note.

Check Cash from operating activities, $130,200

Analysis Component

2. Analyze and discuss the statement of cash flows prepared in part 1, giving special attention to the wisdom of the cash dividend payment.

Refer to the information reported about Gazelle Corporation in Problem 12-3B.

Problem 12-4B[A]
Indirect: Cash flows spreadsheet
P4

Required

Prepare a complete statement of cash flows using a spreadsheet as in Exhibit 12A.1 using the *indirect method*. Identify the debits and credits in the Analysis of Changes columns with letters that correspond to the following list of transactions and events.

a. Net income was $158,100.

b. Accounts receivable decreased.

c. Inventory decreased.

d. Prepaid expenses decreased.

e. Accounts payable decreased.

f. Depreciation expense was $38,600.

g. Sold equipment costing $51,000, with accumulated depreciation of $22,850, for $26,050 cash. This yielded a loss of $2,100.

h. Purchased equipment costing $113,250 by paying $43,250 cash and **(i.)** by signing a long-term note payable for the balance.

j. Borrowed $5,000 cash by signing a short-term note payable.

k. Paid $47,500 cash to reduce the long-term notes payable.

l. Issued 3,000 shares of common stock for $15 cash per share.

m. Declared and paid cash dividends of $53,600.

Check Analysis of Changes column totals, $681,950

Problem 12-5B[B]
Direct: Statement of cash flows   P5

Check   Cash used in financing activities, $(51,100)

Refer to Gazelle Corporation's financial statements and related information in Problem 12-3B.

Required

Prepare a complete statement of cash flows using the *direct method*. Disclose any noncash investing and financing activities in a note.

Problem 12-6B
Indirect: Statement of cash flows

P2   P3

Satu Company's current-year income statement, comparative balance sheets, and additional information follow. For the year, (1) all sales are credit sales, (2) all credits to Accounts Receivable reflect cash receipts from customers, (3) all purchases of inventory are on credit, (4) all debits to Accounts Payable reflect cash payments for inventory, (5) Other Expenses are cash expenses, and (6) any change in Income Taxes Payable reflects the accrual and cash payment of taxes.

SATU COMPANY Comparative Balance Sheets		
At December 31	**Current Year**	**Prior Year**
Assets		
Cash..........................	$ 58,750	$ 28,400
Accounts receivable	20,222	25,860
Total current assets................	78,972	54,260
Inventory	165,667	140,320
Equipment	107,750	77,500
Accum. depreciation—Equipment	(46,700)	(31,000)
Total assets	$305,689	$241,080
Liabilities and Equity		
Accounts payable	$ 20,372	$157,530
Income taxes payable..............	2,100	6,100
Total current liabilities.............	22,472	163,630
Equity		
Common stock, $5 par value	40,000	25,000
Paid-in capital in excess		
of par, common stock.............	68,000	20,000
Retained earnings.................	175,217	32,450
Total liabilities and equity...........	$305,689	$241,080

SATU COMPANY Income Statement For Current Year Ended December 31		
Sales		$750,800
Cost of goods sold		269,200
Gross profit...............		481,600
Operating expenses		
Depreciation expense	$ 15,700	
Other expenses	173,933	189,633
Income before taxes........		291,967
Income taxes expense		89,200
Net income		$202,767

Additional Information on Current-Year Transactions

a. Purchased equipment for $30,250 cash.
b. Issued 3,000 shares of common stock for $21 cash per share.
c. Declared and paid $60,000 of cash dividends.

Check   Cash from operating activities, $57,600

Required

Prepare a complete statement of cash flows using the *indirect method* for the current year.

Problem 12-7B[A]
Indirect: Cash flows spreadsheet

P4

Refer to the information reported about Satu Company in Problem 12-6B.

Required

Prepare a complete statement of cash flows using a spreadsheet as in Exhibit 12A.1 under the *indirect method*. Identify the debits and credits in the Analysis of Changes columns with letters that correspond to the following list of transactions and events.

a. Net income was $202,767.
b. Accounts receivable decreased.
c. Inventory increased.
d. Accounts payable decreased.
e. Income taxes payable decreased.

f. Depreciation expense was $15,700.
g. Purchased equipment for $30,250 cash.
h. Issued 3,000 shares at $21 cash per share.
i. Declared and paid $60,000 of cash dividends.

Check   Analysis of Changes column totals, $543,860

Problem 12-8B[B]
Direct: Statement of cash flows   P5

Check   Cash provided by financing activities, $3,000

Refer to Satu Company's financial statements and related information in Problem 12-6B.

Required

Prepare a complete statement of cash flows using the *direct method* for the current year.

This serial problem began in Chapter 1 and continues through most of the book. If previous chapter segments were not completed, the serial problem can begin at this point.

SP 12   Santana Rey, owner of **Business Solutions**, decides to prepare a statement of cash flows for her business. (Although the serial problem allowed for various ownership changes in earlier chapters, we will prepare the statement of cash flows using the following financial data.)

©Alexander Image/Shutterstock

BUSINESS SOLUTIONS Comparative Balance Sheets December 31, 2019, and March 31, 2020		
	Mar. 31, 2020	**Dec. 31, 2019**
Assets		
Cash	$ 68,057	$48,372
Accounts receivable	22,867	5,668
Inventory	704	0
Computer supplies	2,005	580
Prepaid insurance	1,110	1,665
Prepaid rent	825	825
Total current assets	95,568	57,110
Office equipment	8,000	8,000
Accumulated depreciation—Office equipment	(800)	(400)
Computer equipment	20,000	20,000
Accumulated depreciation—Computer equipment	(2,500)	(1,250)
Total assets	$120,268	$83,460
Liabilities and Equity		
Accounts payable	$ 0	$ 1,100
Wages payable	875	500
Unearned computer service revenue	0	1,500
Total current liabilities	875	3,100
Equity		
Common stock	98,000	73,000
Retained earnings	21,393	7,360
Total liabilities and equity	$120,268	$83,460

BUSINESS SOLUTIONS Income Statement For Three Months Ended March 31, 2020		
Computer services revenue		$25,307
Net sales		18,693
Total revenue		44,000
Cost of goods sold	$14,052	
Depreciation expense—Office equipment	400	
Depreciation expense—Computer equipment	1,250	
Wages expense	3,250	
Insurance expense	555	
Rent expense	2,475	
Computer supplies expense	1,305	
Advertising expense	600	
Mileage expense	320	
Repairs expense—Computer	960	
Total expenses		25,167
Net income		$18,833

Required

Prepare a statement of cash flows for Business Solutions using the *indirect method* for the three months ended March 31, 2020. Recall that owner Santana Rey contributed $25,000 to the business in exchange for additional stock in the first quarter of 2020 and has received $4,800 in cash dividends.

Check   Cash flows used by operations: $(515)

The following **General Ledger** assignments highlight the impact, or lack thereof, on the statement of cash flows from summary journal entries derived from consecutive trial balances. Prepare summary journal entries reflecting changes in consecutive trial balances. Then prepare the statement of cash flows (direct method) from those entries. Finally, prepare the reconciliation to the indirect method for net cash provided (used) by operating activities.

GL 12-1   General Ledger assignment based on Exercise 12-11

GL 12-2   General Ledger assignment based on Problem 12-1

GL 12-3   General Ledger assignment based on Problem 12-6

Accounting Analysis

AA 12-1   Use **Apple's** financial statements in Appendix A to answer the following.

1. Is Apple's statement of cash flows prepared under the direct method or the indirect method?
2. For each fiscal year 2017, 2016, and 2015, identify the amount of cash provided by operating activities and cash paid for dividends.
3. In 2017, did Apple have sufficient cash flows from operations to pay dividends?
4. Did Apple spend more or less cash to repurchase common stock in 2017 versus 2016?

COMPARATIVE ANALYSIS

A1

APPLE

GOOGLE

AA 12-2   Key figures for **Apple** and **Google** follow.

$ millions	Apple			Google		
	Current Year	1 Year Prior	2 Years Prior	Current Year	1 Year Prior	2 Years Prior
Operating cash flows	$ 63,598	$ 65,824	$ 81,266	$ 37,091	$ 36,036	$ 26,572
Total assets	375,319	321,686	290,345	197,295	167,497	147,461

Required

1. Compute the recent two years' cash flow on total assets ratios for Apple and Google.
2. For the current year, which company has the better cash flow on total assets ratio?
3. For the current year, does cash flow on total assets outperform or underperform the industry (assumed) average of 15% for (*a*) Apple and (*b*) Google?

GLOBAL ANALYSIS

C1

Samsung

APPLE

GOOGLE

AA 12-3   Key comparative information for **Samsung**, **Apple**, and **Google** follows.

In millions	Samsung			Apple		Google	
	Current Year	1 Year Prior	2 Years Prior	Current Year	1 Year Prior	Current Year	1 Year Prior
Operating cash flows	₩ 62,162,041	₩ 47,385,644	₩ 40,061,761	$ 63,598	$ 65,824	$ 37,091	$ 36,036
Total assets	301,752,090	262,174,324	242,179,521	375,319	321,686	197,295	167,497

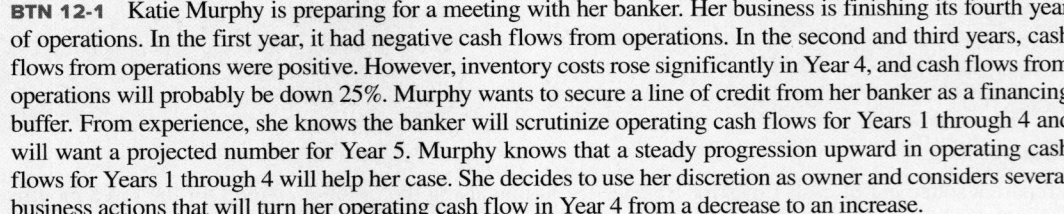

Required

1. Compute the recent two years' cash flow on total assets ratio for Samsung.
2. Is the change in Samsung's cash flow on total assets ratio favorable or unfavorable?
3. For the current year, is Samsung's cash flow on total assets ratio better or worse than (*a*) Apple's and (*b*) Google's?

Beyond the Numbers

ETHICS CHALLENGE

C1 A1

BTN 12-1   Katie Murphy is preparing for a meeting with her banker. Her business is finishing its fourth year of operations. In the first year, it had negative cash flows from operations. In the second and third years, cash flows from operations were positive. However, inventory costs rose significantly in Year 4, and cash flows from operations will probably be down 25%. Murphy wants to secure a line of credit from her banker as a financing buffer. From experience, she knows the banker will scrutinize operating cash flows for Years 1 through 4 and will want a projected number for Year 5. Murphy knows that a steady progression upward in operating cash flows for Years 1 through 4 will help her case. She decides to use her discretion as owner and considers several business actions that will turn her operating cash flow in Year 4 from a decrease to an increase.

Required

1. Identify two business actions Murphy might take to improve cash flows from operations.
2. Comment on the ethics and possible consequences of Murphy's decision to pursue these actions.

COMMUNICATING IN PRACTICE

C1

BTN 12-2   Your friend, Diana Wood, recently completed the second year of her business and just received annual financial statements from her accountant. Wood finds the income statement and balance sheet informative but does not understand the statement of cash flows. She says the first section is especially confusing because it contains a lot of additions and subtractions that do not make sense to her. Wood adds, "The income statement tells me the business is more profitable than last year and that's most important. If I want to know how cash changes, I can look at comparative balance sheets."

Required

Write a half-page memorandum to your friend explaining the purpose of the statement of cash flows. Speculate as to why the first section is so confusing and how it might be rectified.

TAKING IT TO THE NET

A1

BTN 12-3   Access the April 14, 2016, filing of the 10-K report (for year ending December 31, 2015) of **Mendocino Brewing Company, Inc.** (ticker: MENB) at <u>SEC.gov</u>.

Required

1. Does Mendocino Brewing use the direct or indirect method to construct its consolidated statement of cash flows?

2. For the year ended December 31, 2015, what is the largest item in reconciling the net income (or loss) to net cash provided by operating activities?

3. In the recent two years, has the company been more successful in generating operating cash flows or in generating net income? Identify the figures to support the answer.

4. In the year ended December 31, 2015, what was the largest cash outflow for investing activities *and* for financing activities?

5. What item(s) does the company report as supplemental cash flow information?

6. Does the company report any noncash financing activities for 2015? Identify them, if any.

BTN 12-4   Team members are to coordinate and independently answer one question within each of the following three sections. Team members should then report to the team and confirm or correct teammates' answers.

1. Answer *one* of the following questions about the statement of cash flows: (*a*) What are this statement's reporting objectives? (*b*) What two methods are used to prepare it? Identify similarities and differences between them. (*c*) What steps are followed to prepare the statement? (*d*) What types of analyses are often made from this statement's information?

2. Identify and explain the adjustment from net income to obtain cash flows from operating activities using the indirect method for *one* of the following items: (*a*) Noncash operating revenues and expenses. (*b*) Nonoperating gains and losses. (*c*) Increases and decreases in noncash current assets. (*d*) Increases and decreases in current liabilities.

3.^B Identify and explain the formula for computing cash flows from operating activities using the direct method for *one* of the following items: (*a*) Cash receipts from sales to customers. (*b*) Cash paid for inventory. (*c*) Cash paid for wages and operating expenses. (*d*) Cash paid for interest and taxes.

TEAMWORK IN ACTION

C1 A1 P2 P5

Note: For teams of more than four, some pairing within teams is necessary. Use as an in-class activity or as an assignment. If used in class, specify a time limit on each part. Conclude with reports to the entire class, using team rotation. Each team can prepare responses on a transparency.

BTN 12-5   Review the chapter's opener involving **Vera Bradley** and its founder, Barbara Bradley.

Required

1. In a business such as Vera Bradley, monitoring cash flow is always a priority. Explain how cash flow can lag behind net income.

2. What are potential sources of financing for Vera Bradley's future expansion?

ENTREPRENEURIAL DECISION

C1   A1

BTN 12-6   Jenna and Matt Wilder are completing their second year operating Mountain High, a downhill ski area and resort. Mountain High reports a net loss of $(10,000) for its second year, which includes an $85,000 unusual loss from fire. This past year also involved major purchases of plant assets for renovation and expansion, yielding a year-end total asset amount of $800,000. Mountain High's net cash outflow for its second year is $(5,000); a summarized version of its statement of cash flows follows.

ENTREPRENEURIAL DECISION

C1   A1

Net cash flow provided by operating activities	$ 295,000
Net cash flow used by investing activities	(310,000)
Net cash flow provided by financing activities	10,000

Required

Write a one-page memorandum to the Wilders evaluating Mountain High's current performance and assessing its future. Give special emphasis to cash flow data and their interpretation.

BTN 12-7   Visit **The Motley Fool**'s web page on cash flow based valuation (**Fool.com/how-to-invest/how-to-value-stocks-cash-flow-based-valuations.aspx**).

Required

1. How does the Motley Fool define cash flow? What is the reasoning for this definition?

2. Per the Fool's instruction, why do analysts focus on earnings before interest and taxes (EBIT)?

3. Visit other links at this website that interest you such as "How to Read a Balance Sheet," or find out what the "Fool's Ratio" is. Write a half-page report on what you find.

HITTING THE ROAD

C1

---

13 Analysis of Financial Statements

Learning Objectives

CONCEPTUAL

C1 Explain the purpose and identify the building blocks of analysis.

C2 Describe standards for comparisons in analysis.

ANALYTICAL

A1 Summarize and report results of analysis.

A2 *Appendix 13A*—Explain the form and assess the content of a complete income statement.

PROCEDURAL

P1 Explain and apply methods of horizontal analysis.

P2 Describe and apply methods of vertical analysis.

P3 Define and apply ratio analysis.

Numbers Rule

©Jonathan Leibson/AOL/Getty Images

"Expect to win!"—**CARLA HARRIS**

NEW YORK—"I grew up as an only child in a no-nonsense, no-excuses household," recalls Carla Harris. "My parents gave me the sense that I was supposed to do well." Fast-forward and Carla is now vice chair of **Morgan Stanley**'s (**MorganStanley.com**) prized Global Wealth Management division and past-chair of the Morgan Stanley Foundation.

Carla Harris and her colleagues at Morgan Stanley analyze financial statements for profit. One of Morgan Stanley's key tools for analysis is *ModelWare*. ModelWare is a framework to analyze the nuts and bolts of companies' financial statements and then to compare those companies head-to-head. One of its key aims is to provide comparable information that focuses on sustainable performance.

Morgan Stanley uses the accounting numbers in financial statements to produce comparable metrics using techniques such as horizontal and vertical analysis. It also computes financial ratios for analysis and interpretation. Those ratios include return on equity, return on assets, asset turnover, profit margin, price-to-earnings, and many other accounting measures. The focus is to uncover the drivers of profitability and to predict future levels of those drivers.

Carla has experienced much success through analyzing financial statements. As Carla likes to say, "I'm tough and analytical!" She says that people do not take full advantage of information available in financial statements.

Carla plays by the rules and asserts that those with accounting know-how continue to earn profits from financial statement analysis and interpretation. Carla is proud of her success and adds: "Always start from a place of doing the right thing."

Sources: *Morgan Stanley website,* January 2019; *MorganStanleyIQ,* November 2007; *Alumni.HBS.edu/Stories,* September 2006; *Fortune,* August 2013 and March 2016

BASICS OF ANALYSIS

Financial statement analysis applies analytical tools to financial statements and related data for making business decisions.

C1

Explain the purpose and identify the building blocks of analysis.

Purpose of Analysis

Internal users of accounting information manage and operate the company. They include managers, officers, and internal auditors. The purpose of financial statement analysis for internal users is to provide information to improve efficiency and effectiveness.

External users of accounting information are *not* directly involved in running the company. External users use financial statement analysis to pursue their own goals. Shareholders and creditors assess company performance to make investing and lending decisions. A board of directors analyzes financial statements to monitor management's performance. External auditors use financial statements to assess "fair presentation" of financial results.

Point: Financial statement analysis is a topic on the CPA, CMA, CIA, and CFA exams.

The common goal of these users is to evaluate company performance and financial condition. This includes evaluating past and current performance, current financial position, and future performance and risk.

Building Blocks of Analysis

Financial statement analysis focuses on one or more of the four *building blocks* of financial statement analysis. The four building blocks cover different, but interrelated, aspects of financial condition or performance.

- **Liquidity** and **efficiency**—ability to meet short-term obligations and to efficiently generate revenues.
- **Solvency**—ability to meet long-term obligations and generate future revenues.
- **Profitability**—ability to provide financial rewards to attract and retain financing.
- **Market prospects**—ability to generate positive market expectations.

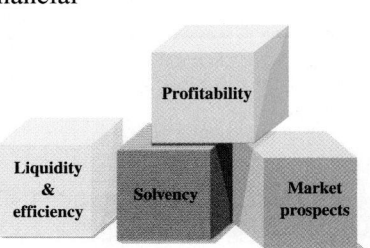

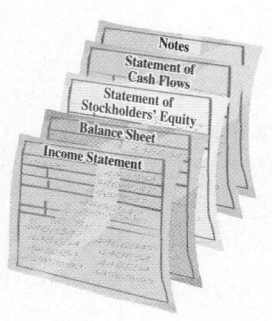

Information for Analysis

Financial analysis uses **general-purpose financial statements** that include the (1) income statement, (2) balance sheet, (3) statement of stockholders' equity (or statement of retained earnings), (4) statement of cash flows, and (5) notes to these statements.

Financial reporting is the communication of financial information useful for making investment, credit, and other business decisions. Financial reporting includes general-purpose financial statements, information from SEC 10-K and other filings, press releases, shareholders' meetings, forecasts, management letters, and auditors' reports.

Management's Discussion and Analysis (MD&A) is one example of useful information outside usual financial statements. **Apple**'s MD&A (available at **Investor.Apple.com** and "Item 7" in the annual report) begins with an overview, followed by critical accounting policies and estimates. It then discusses operating results followed by financial condition (liquidity, capital resources, and cash flows). The final few parts discuss risks. The MD&A is an excellent starting point in understanding a company's business.

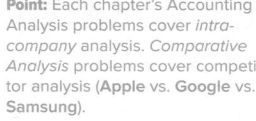

C2

Describe standards for comparisons in analysis.

Standards for Comparisons

When analyzing financial statements, we use the following standards (benchmarks) for comparisons. Benchmarks from a competitor or group of competitors are often best. Intracompany and industry measures are also good. Guidelines can be applied, but only if they seem reasonable given recent experience.

- *Intracompany*—The company's current performance is compared to its prior performance and its relations between financial items. Apple's current net income, for example, can be compared with its prior years' net income and in relation to its revenues or total assets.
- *Competitor*—Competitors provide standards for comparisons. **Coca-Cola**'s profit margin can be compared with **PepsiCo**'s profit margin.
- *Industry*—Industry statistics provide standards of comparisons. **Intel**'s profit margin can be compared with the industry's profit margin.
- *Guidelines (rules of thumb)*—Standards of comparison can develop from experience. Examples are the 2:1 level for the current ratio or 1:1 level for the acid-test ratio.

Point: Each chapter's Accounting Analysis problems cover *intracompany* analysis. *Comparative Analysis* problems cover competitor analysis (**Apple** vs. **Google** vs. **Samsung**).

Tools of Analysis

There are three common tools of financial statement analysis. This chapter describes these analysis tools and how to apply them.

1. **Horizontal analysis**—comparison of financial condition and performance across time.
2. **Vertical analysis**—comparison of financial condition and performance to a base amount.
3. **Ratio analysis**—measurement of key relations between financial statement items.

■ **Decision Insight**

Stock in Trade *Blue chips* are stocks of big, established companies. The phrase comes from poker, where the most valuable chips are blue. *Brokers* execute orders to buy or sell stock. The term comes from wine retailers—individuals who broach (break) wine casks. ■

HORIZONTAL ANALYSIS

P1

Explain and apply methods of horizontal analysis.

Horizontal analysis is the review of financial statement data *across time*. *Horizontal* comes from the left-to-right (or right-to-left) movement of our eyes as we review comparative financial statements across time.

Comparative Statements

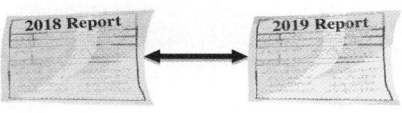

Comparative financial statements show financial amounts in side-by-side columns on a single statement, called a *comparative format*. Using **Apple**'s financial statements, this section explains how to compute dollar changes and percent changes for comparative statements.

Dollar Changes and Percent Changes   Comparing financial statements is often done by analyzing dollar amount changes and percent changes in line items. Both analyses are relevant because small dollar changes can yield large percent changes inconsistent with their importance. A 50% change from a base figure of $100 is less important than a 50% change from a base amount of $100,000. We compute the *dollar change* for a financial statement item as follows.

$$\text{Dollar change} = \text{Analysis period amount} - \text{Base period amount}$$

Analysis period refers to the financial statements under analysis, and *base period* refers to the financial statements used for comparison. The prior year is commonly used as a base period. We compute the *percent change* as follows.

$$\text{Percent change (\%)} = \frac{\text{Analysis period amount} - \text{Base period amount}}{\text{Base period amount}} \times 100$$

We must know a few rules in working with percent changes. Let's look at four separate cases.

- **Cases A and B:** When a negative amount is in one period and a positive amount is in the other, we cannot compute a meaningful percent change.
- **Case C:** When no amount is in the base period, no percent change is computable.
- **Case D:** When a positive amount is in the base period and zero is in the analysis period, the decrease is 100%.

Example: When there is a value in the base period and zero in the analysis period, the decrease is 100%. Why isn't the reverse situation an increase of 100%? *Answer:* A 100% increase of zero is still zero.

	Analysis Period	Base Period	Change Analysis	
Case			Dollar	Percent
A	$ 1,500	$(4,500)	$ 6,000	—
B	(1,000)	2,000	(3,000)	—
C	8,000	—	8,000	—
D	0	10,000	(10,000)	(100%)

Comparative Balance Sheets   Analysis of comparative financial statements begins by focusing on large dollar and percent changes. We then identify the reasons and implications for these changes. We also review small changes when we expected large changes.

Exhibit 13.1 shows comparative balance sheets for **Apple Inc.** (ticker: AAPL). A few items stand out on the asset side. Apple's short-term marketable securities increased by 15.5%, and its long-term marketable securities increased by 14.2%. This combined for a large $31,505 million increase in securities. In response, Apple raised its dividend and announced plans to spend at least $210 billion buying back stock by the end of the next year. Dividends and share repurchase plans are likely to slow Apple's growth of short-term securities. Other notable increases occur with (1) property, plant and equipment, partially related to its new headquarters, and (2) inventories, which had a high percentage increase but relatively small dollar increase.

On Apple's financing side, we see its overall 16.7% increase is driven by a 24.7% increase in liabilities; equity increased only 4.5%. The largest increase is from long-term debt, which increased by $21,780 million, or 28.9%. Much of this increase results from bond offerings by Apple to take advantage of low interest rates. We also see a modest increase of 2.0% ($1,966 million) in retained earnings, which was increased by a strong income of $48,351 million and reduced by cash dividends and stock repurchases.

Comparative Income Statements   Exhibit 13.2 shows Apple's comparative income statements. Apple reports an increase in sales of 6.3%. Cost of sales increased to a greater extent than sales (7.4%), which is not a positive sign. The 10.7% increase in operating expenses is primarily driven by the 15.3% increase in research and development costs, from which management and investors hope to reap future income. While Apple's net income increased just 5.8%, its basic earnings per share increased 11.0%. This is largely due to Apple's share buyback program.

EXHIBIT 13.1

Comparative Balance Sheets

APPLE

APPLE INC. Comparative Year-End Balance Sheets				
$ millions	Current Yr	Prior Yr	Dollar Change	Percent Change
Assets				
Cash and cash equivalents	$ 20,289	$ 20,484	$ (195)	(1.0)%
Short-term marketable securities	53,892	46,671	7,221	15.5
Accounts receivable, net	17,874	15,754	2,120	13.5
Inventories	4,855	2,132	2,723	127.7
Vendor non-trade receivables	17,799	13,545	4,254	31.4
Other current assets...............................	13,936	8,283	5,653	68.2
Total current assets	128,645	106,869	21,776	20.4
Long-term marketable securities.....................	194,714	170,430	24,284	14.2
Property, plant and equipment, net..................	33,783	27,010	6,773	25.1
Goodwill	5,717	5,414	303	5.6
Acquired intangible assets, net	2,298	3,206	(908)	(28.3)
Other non-current assets	10,162	8,757	1,405	16.0
Total assets.....................................	$375,319	$321,686	$53,633	16.7
Liabilities				
Accounts payable	$ 49,049	$ 37,294	$11,755	31.5%
Accrued expenses	25,744	22,027	3,717	16.9
Deferred revenue	7,548	8,080	(532)	(6.6)
Commercial paper	11,977	8,105	3,872	47.8
Current portion of long-term debt...................	6,496	3,500	2,996	85.6
Total current liabilities	100,814	79,006	21,808	27.6
Deferred revenue—non-current.....................	2,836	2,930	(94)	(3.2)
Long-term debt...................................	97,207	75,427	21,780	28.9
Other non-current liabilities	40,415	36,074	4,341	12.0
Total liabilities...................................	241,272	193,437	47,835	24.7
Stockholders' Equity				
Common stock	35,867	31,251	4,616	14.8
Retained earnings.................................	98,330	96,364	1,966	2.0
Accumulated other comprehensive income	(150)	634	(784)	—
Total stockholders' equity	134,047	128,249	5,798	4.5
Total liabilities and stockholders' equity..............	$375,319	$321,686	$53,633	16.7

EXHIBIT 13.2

Comparative Income Statements

APPLE

APPLE INC. Comparative Income Statements				
$ millions, except per share	Current Yr	Prior Yr	Dollar Change	Percent Change
Net sales	$229,234	$215,639	$13,595	6.3%
Cost of sales	141,048	131,376	9,672	7.4
Gross margin.....................................	88,186	84,263	3,923	4.7
Research and development.........................	11,581	10,045	1,536	15.3
Selling, general and administrative..................	15,261	14,194	1,067	7.5
Total operating expenses...........................	26,842	24,239	2,603	10.7
Operating income.................................	61,344	60,024	1,320	2.2
Other income, net.................................	2,745	1,348	1,397	103.6
Income before provision for income taxes	64,089	61,372	2,717	4.4
Provision for income taxes.........................	15,738	15,685	53	0.3
Net income	$ 48,351	$ 45,687	2,664	5.8
Basic earnings per share	$ 9.27	$ 8.35	$ 0.92	11.0
Diluted earnings per share.........................	$ 9.21	$ 8.31	$ 0.90	10.8

Point: Percent change is also computed by dividing the current period by the prior period and then subtracting 1.0.

Trend Analysis

Trend analysis is computing trend percents that show patterns in data across periods. Trend percent is computed as follows.

$$\text{Trend percent (\%)} = \frac{\text{Analysis period amount}}{\text{Base period amount}} \times 100$$

Point: *Index* refers to the comparison of the analysis period to the base period. Percents determined for each period are called *index numbers.*

Trend analysis is shown in Exhibit 13.3 using data from Apple's current and prior financial statements.

$ millions	Current Yr	1 Yr Ago	2 Yrs Ago	3 Yrs Ago	4 Yrs Ago
Net sales...................	$229,234	$215,639	$233,715	$182,795	$170,910
Cost of sales................	141,048	131,376	140,089	112,258	106,606
Operating expenses...........	26,842	24,239	22,396	18,034	15,305

EXHIBIT 13.3

Sales and Expenses

The trend percents—using data from Exhibit 13.3—are shown in Exhibit 13.4. The base period is the number reported four years ago, and the trend percent is computed for each year by dividing that year's amount by the base period amount. For example, the net sales trend percent for the current year is 134.1%, computed as $229,234/$170,910.

Point: Trend analysis expresses a percent of base, not a percent of change.

In trend percent	Current Yr	1 Yr Ago	2 Yrs Ago	3 Yrs Ago	4 Yrs Ago
Net sales...................	134.1%	126.2%	136.7%	107.0%	100.0%
Cost of sales................	132.3	123.2	131.4	105.3	100.0
Operating expenses...........	175.4	158.4	146.3	117.8	100.0

EXHIBIT 13.4

Trend Percents for Sales and Expenses

Exhibit 13.5 shows the trend percents from Exhibit 13.4 in a *line graph,* which helps us see trends and detect changes in direction or magnitude. It shows that the trend line for operating expenses exceeds net sales in each of the years shown. This is not positive for Apple. Apple's net income will suffer if expenses rise faster than sales.

Exhibit 13.6 compares Apple's revenue trend line to those of **Google** and **Samsung**. Google was able to grow revenue in each year relative to the base year. Apple was able to grow revenue overall in the last five years, but at a slower pace than Google. Samsung's revenue was mainly flat.

Trend analysis can show relations between items on different

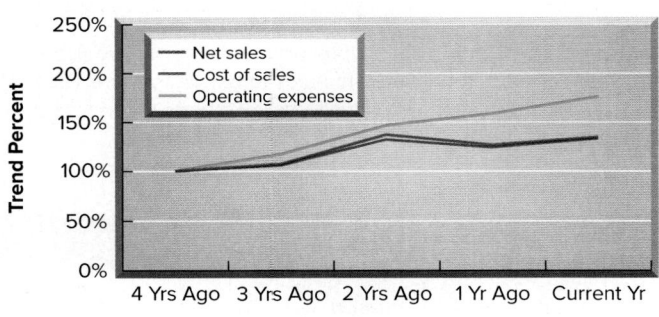

EXHIBIT 13.5

Trend Percent Lines for Apple's Sales and Expenses

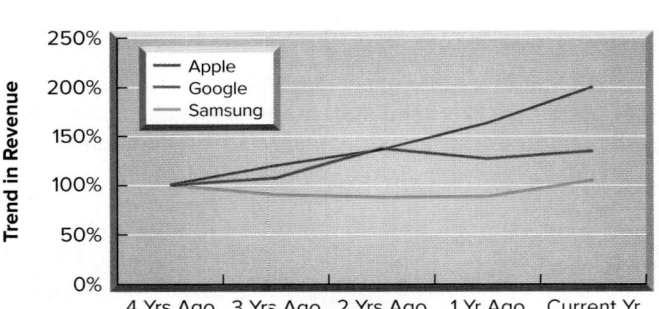

EXHIBIT 13.6

Revenue Trend Percent Lines—Apple, Google, and Samsung

APPLE

GOOGLE

Samsung

EXHIBIT 13.7

Sales and Asset Data for Apple

$ millions	Current Yr	4 Yrs Ago	Change
Net sales	$229,234	$170,910	34.1%
Total assets	375,319	207,000	81.3

financial statements. Exhibit 13.7 compares Apple's net sales and total assets. The increase in total assets (81.3%) has exceeded the increase in net sales (34.1%). Is this result favorable or not? One interpretation is that Apple was *less* efficient in using its assets in the current year versus four years ago.

■ **Decision Maker**

Auditor   Your tests reveal a 3% increase in sales from $200,000 to $206,000 and a 4% decrease in expenses from $190,000 to $182,400. Both changes are within your "reasonableness" criterion of ±5%, and thus you don't pursue additional tests. The audit partner in charge questions your lack of follow-up and mentions the *joint relation* between sales and expenses. What is the partner referring to? ■   *Answer:* Both *individual* accounts (sales and expenses) yield percent changes within the ±5% acceptable range. However, a *joint analysis* shows an increase in sales and a decrease in expenses producing a more than 5% increase in income. This client's profit margin is 11.46% (($206,000 − $182,400)/$206,000) for the current year compared with 5.0% (($200,000 − $190,000)/$200,000) for the prior year—a 129% increase!

NEED-TO-KNOW 13-1

Horizontal Analysis

P1

Compute trend percents for the following accounts using 3 Years Ago as the base year. Indicate whether the trend appears to be favorable or unfavorable for each account.

$ millions	Current Yr	1 Yr Ago	2 Yrs Ago	3 Yrs Ago
Sales	$500	$350	$250	$200
Cost of goods sold	400	175	100	50

Solution

$ millions	Current Yr	1 Yr Ago	2 Yrs Ago	3 Yrs Ago
Sales	250%	175%	125%	100%
	($500/$200)	($350/$200)	($250/$200)	($200/$200)
Cost of goods sold	800%	350%	200%	100%
	($400/$50)	($175/$50)	($100/$50)	($50/$50)

Do More: QS 13-3, QS 13-4, E 13-3

Analysis: The trend in sales is favorable; however, we need more information about economic conditions and competitors' performances to better assess it. Cost of goods sold also is rising (as expected with increasing sales). However, cost of goods sold is rising faster than the increase in sales, which is bad news.

VERTICAL ANALYSIS

P2

Describe and apply methods of vertical analysis.

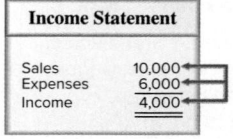

Income Statement	
Sales	10,000
Expenses	6,000
Income	4,000

Point: Numerator and denominator in common-size percent are taken from the same financial statement and from the same period.

Vertical analysis, or *common-size analysis,* is used to evaluate individual financial statement items or a group of items. *Vertical* comes from the up-down [or down-up] movement of our eyes as we review common-size financial statements.

Common-Size Statements

The comparative statements in Exhibits 13.1 and 13.2 show the change in each item over time. **Common-size financial statements** show changes in the relative importance of each financial statement item. All individual amounts in common-size statements are shown in common-size percents. A *common-size percent* is calculated as

$$\text{Common-size percent } (\%) = \frac{\text{Analysis amount}}{\text{Base amount}} \times 100$$

Common-Size Balance Sheets   Common-size statements show each item as a percent of a *base amount,* which for a common-size balance sheet is total assets. The base amount is assigned a value of 100%. (Total liabilities plus equity also equals 100% because this amount equals total assets.) We then compute a common-size percent for each asset, liability, and equity item using total assets as the base amount.

Exhibit 13.8 shows common-size comparative balance sheets for **Apple**. Two results that stand out on both a magnitude and percentage basis include (1) issuance of long-term debt—a 2.5% increase from 23.4% to 25.9%, the largest of any liability, and (2) a 3.8% decrease in retained earnings and 1% decrease in cash and cash equivalents, largely the result of cash dividends and stock buybacks. The absence of other substantial changes in Apple's balance sheet suggests a mature company, but with some lack of focus as evidenced by the large amounts for securities. This buildup in securities is a concern as the return on securities is historically smaller than the return on operating assets.

Point: Common-size statements often are used to compare companies in the same industry.

Common-Size Income Statements   Analysis also involves the use of a common-size income statement. Revenue is the base amount, which is assigned a value of 100%. Each income statement item is shown as a percent of revenue. If we think of the 100% revenue amount

EXHIBIT 13.8

Common-Size Comparative Balance Sheets

APPLE

APPLE INC. Common-Size Comparative Year-End Balance Sheets			Common-Size Percents*	
$ millions	Current Yr	Prior Yr	Current Yr	Prior Yr
Assets				
Cash and cash equivalents	$ 20,289	$ 20,484	5.4%	6.4%
Short-term marketable securities	53,892	46,671	14.4	14.5
Accounts receivable, net	17,874	15,754	4.8	4.9
Inventories	4,855	2,132	1.3	0.7
Vendor non-trade receivables.....................	17,799	13,545	4.7	4.2
Other current assets.............................	13,936	8,283	3.7	2.6
Total current assets	128,645	106,869	34.3	33.2
Long-term marketable securities	194,714	170,430	51.9	53.0
Property, plant and equipment, net	33,783	27,010	9.0	8.4
Goodwill	5,717	5,414	1.5	1.7
Acquired intangible assets, net....................	2,298	3,206	0.6	1.0
Other non-current assets.........................	10,162	8,757	2.7	2.7
Total assets....................................	$375,319	$321,686	100.0%	100.0%
Liabilities				
Accounts payable...............................	$ 49,049	$ 37,294	13.1%	11.6%
Accrued expenses	25,744	22,027	6.9	6.8
Deferred revenue...............................	7,548	8,080	2.0	2.5
Commercial paper	11,977	8,105	3.2	2.5
Current portion of long-term debt..................	6,496	3,500	1.7	1.1
Total current liabilities........................	100,814	79,006	26.9	24.6
Deferred revenue—noncurrent.....................	2,836	2,930	0.8	0.9
Long-term debt.................................	97,207	75,427	25.9	23.4
Other non-current liabilties	40,415	36,074	10.8	11.2
Total liabilities.................................	241,272	193,437	64.3	60.1
Stockholders' Equity				
Common stock..................................	35,867	31,251	9.6	9.7
Retained earnings	98,330	96,364	26.2	30.0
Accumulated other comprehensive income...........	(150)	634	0.0	0.2
Total stockholders' equity	134,047	128,249	35.7	39.9
Total liabilities and stockholders' equity.............	$375,319	$321,686	100.0%	100.0%

*Percents are rounded to tenths and thus may not exactly sum to totals and subtotals.

EXHIBIT 13.9

Common-Size Comparative Income Statements

APPLE

$ millions	Current Yr	Prior Yr	Current Yr	Prior Yr
APPLE INC. Common-Size Comparative Income Statements			Common-Size Percents*	
Net sales	$229,234	$215,639	100.0%	100.0%
Cost of sales	141,048	131,376	61.5	60.9
Gross margin.	88,186	84,263	38.5	39.1
Research and development	11,581	10,045	5.1	4.7
Selling, general and administrative	15,261	14,194	6.7	6.6
Total operating expenses.	26,842	24,239	11.7	11.2
Operating income.	61,344	60,024	26.8	27.8
Other income, net.	2,745	1,348	1.2	0.6
Income before provision for income taxes	64,089	61,372	28.0	28.5
Provision for income taxes.	15,738	15,685	6.9	7.3
Net income	$ 48,351	$ 45,687	21.1%	21.2%

*Percents are rounded to tenths and thus may not exactly sum to totals and subtotals.

as representing one sales dollar, the remaining items show how each revenue dollar is distributed among costs, expenses, and income.

Exhibit 13.9 shows common-size comparative income statements for each dollar of Apple's net sales. The past two years' common-size numbers are similar with two exceptions. One is the increase of 0.4 cents in research and development costs, which can be a positive development if these costs lead to future revenues. Another is the increase in cost of sales of 0.6 cent and increase in selling, general and administrative costs of 0.1 cent. We must monitor the growth in these expenses.

EXHIBIT 13.10

Common-Size Graphic of Income Statement

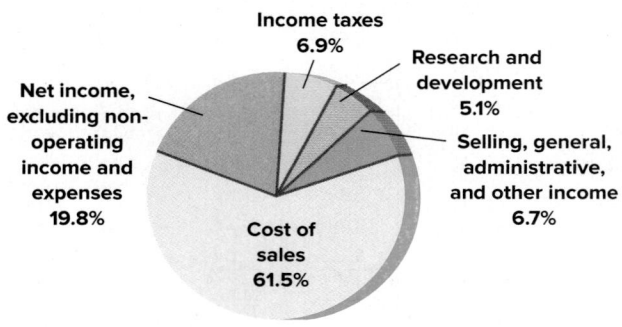

Common-Size Graphics

Exhibit 13.10 is a graphic of Apple's current-year common-size income statement. This pie chart shows the contribution of each cost component of net sales for net income.

Exhibit 13.11 takes data from Apple's *Segments* footnote. The exhibit shows the level of net sales for each of Apple's five operating segments. Its Americas segment generates $96.6 billion net sales, which is roughly 42% of its total sales. Within each bar is that segment's operating income margin (Operating income/Segment net sales). The Americas segment has a 32% operating income margin. This type of graphic can raise questions about the profitability of each segment and lead to discussion of further expansions into more profitable segments. For example, the Japan segment has an operating margin of 46%. A natural question for management is what potential is there to expand sales into the Japan segment and maintain

EXHIBIT 13.11

Sales and Operating Income Margin Breakdown by Segment

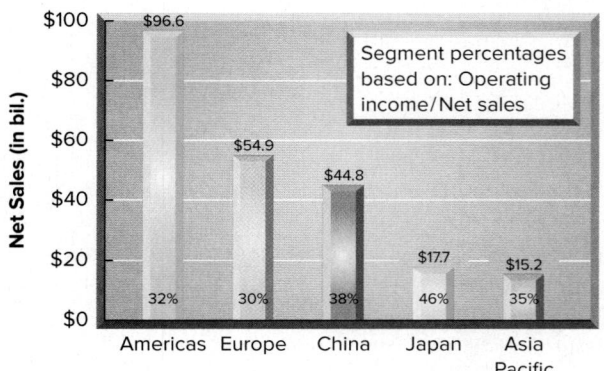

this operating margin? This type of analysis can help determine strategic plans.

Graphics also are used to identify (1) sources of financing, including the distribution among current liabilities, noncurrent liabilities, and equity capital, and (2) focuses of investing activities, including the distribution among current and noncurrent assets. Exhibit 13.12 shows a common-size graphic of Apple's assets, a high percentage of which are in securities, followed by property, plant and equipment.

Common-size financial statements are useful in comparing companies. Exhibit 13.13 shows common-size graphics of Apple, **Google**, and **Samsung** on financing sources. This graphic shows the larger percent of equity financing for Google versus Apple and Samsung. It also shows the larger non-current debt financing of Apple versus Google and Samsung. Comparison of a company's common-size statements with competitors' or industry common-size statistics alerts us to differences in the structure of its financial statements.

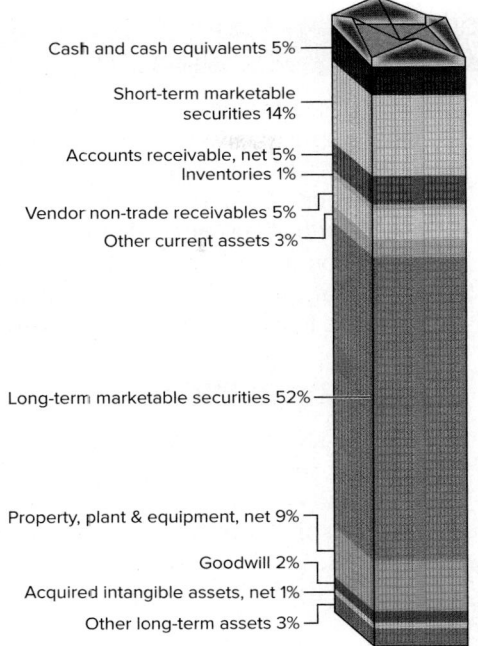

EXHIBIT 13.12

Common-Size Graphic of Asset Components

Cash and cash equivalents 5%
Short-term marketable securities 14%
Accounts receivable, net 5%
Inventories 1%
Vendor non-trade receivables 5%
Other current assets 3%
Long-term marketable securities 52%
Property, plant & equipment, net 9%
Goodwill 2%
Acquired intangible assets, net 1%
Other long-term assets 3%

	Apple	Google	Samsung
▬ Current liabilities	27%	12%	22%
▬ Noncurrent liabilities	37%	11%	7%
▬ Equity	36%	77%	71%

EXHIBIT 13.13

Common-Size Graphic of Financing Sources—Competitor Analysis

APPLE

GOOGLE

Samsung

Ethical Risk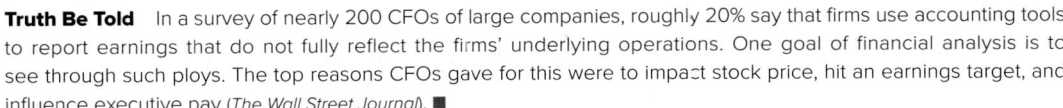

Truth Be Told In a survey of nearly 200 CFOs of large companies, roughly 20% say that firms use accounting tools to report earnings that do not fully reflect the firms' underlying operations. One goal of financial analysis is to see through such ploys. The top reasons CFOs gave for this were to impact stock price, hit an earnings target, and influence executive pay (*The Wall Street Journal*). ■

Express the following comparative income statements in common-size percents and assess whether this company's situation has improved in the current year.

Comparative Income Statements		
For Years Ended December 31	Current Yr	Prior Yr
Sales	$800	$500
Total expenses	560	400
Net income	$240	$100

NEED-TO-KNOW 13-2

Vertical Analysis

P2

Solution

	Current Yr	Prior Yr
Sales	100% ($800/$800)	100% ($500/$500)
Total expenses	70% ($560/$800)	80% ($400/$500)
Net income	30%	20%

Analysis: This company's situation has improved. This is evident from its substantial increase in net income as a percent of sales for the current year (30%) relative to the prior year (20%). Further, the company's sales increased from $500 to $800 (while expenses declined as a percent of sales from 80% to 70%).

Do More: QS 13-5, E 13-4, E 13-5, E 13-6

RATIO ANALYSIS

P3 _____

Define and apply ratio analysis.

Ratios are used to uncover conditions and trends difficult to detect by looking at individual amounts. A ratio shows a relation between two amounts. It can be shown as a percent, rate, or proportion. A change from $100 to $250 can be shown as (1) 150% increase, (2) 2.5 times, or (3) 2.5 to 1 (or 2.5:1). To be useful, a ratio must show an economically important relation. For example, a ratio of cost of goods sold to sales is useful, but a ratio of freight costs to patents is not.

This section covers important financial ratios organized into the four building blocks of financial statement analysis: (1) liquidity and efficiency, (2) solvency, (3) profitability, and (4) market prospects. We use four standards for comparison: intracompany, competitor, industry, and guidelines.

Liquidity and Efficiency

Liquidity is the availability of resources to pay short-term cash requirements. It is affected by the timing of cash inflows and outflows along with prospects for future performance. A lack of liquidity often is linked to lower profitability. To creditors, lack of liquidity can cause delays in collecting payments. *Efficiency* is how productive a company is in using its assets. Inefficient use of assets can cause liquidity problems. This section covers key ratios used to assess liquidity and efficiency.

Working Capital and Current Ratio   The amount of current assets minus current liabilities is called **working capital,** or *net working capital.* A company that runs low on working capital is less likely to pay debts or to continue operating. When evaluating a company's working capital, we look at the dollar amount of current assets minus current liabilities *and* at their ratio. The *current ratio* is defined as follows (see Chapter 3 for additional explanation).

$$\text{Current ratio} = \frac{\text{Current assets}}{\text{Current liabilities}}$$

EXHIBIT 13.14

Apple's Working Capital and Current Ratio

Current ratio
Google = 5.14
Samsung = 2.19
Industry = 2.5

$ millions	Current Yr	Prior Yr
Current assets.............	$128,645	$106,869
Current liabilities...........	100,814	79,006
Working capital............	$ 27,831	$ 27,863
Current ratio		
$128,645/$100,814 =	1.28 to 1	
$106,869/$79,006 =		1.35 to 1

Apple's working capital and current ratio are shown in Exhibit 13.14. Also, **Google**'s (5.14), **Samsung**'s (2.19), and the industry's (2.5) current ratios are shown in the margin. Although its ratio (1.28) is lower than competitors' ratios, Apple is not in danger of defaulting on loan payments. A high current ratio suggests a strong ability to meet current obligations. An excessively high current ratio means that the company has invested too much in current assets compared to current obligations. An excessive investment in current assets is not an efficient use of funds because current assets normally earn a low return on investment (compared with long-term assets).

Many analysts use a guideline of 2:1 (or 1.5:1) for the current ratio. A 2:1 or higher ratio is considered low risk in the short run. Analysis of the current ratio, and many other ratios, must consider type of business, composition of current assets, and turnover rate of current asset components.

- **Business Type**   A service company that grants little or no credit and carries few inventories can probably operate on a current ratio of less than 1:1 if its revenues generate enough cash to pay its current liabilities. On the other hand, a company selling high-priced clothing or furniture requires a higher ratio because of difficulties in judging customer demand and cash receipts.

- **Asset Composition**   The composition of assets is important to assess short-term liquidity. For instance, cash, cash equivalents, and short-term investments are more liquid than accounts and notes receivable. An excessive amount of receivables and inventory weakens a company's ability to pay current liabilities.

- **Turnover Rate**   Asset turnover measures efficiency in using assets. A measure of asset efficiency is revenue generated.

Global: Ratio analysis is unaffected by currency but is affected by differences in accounting principles.

■ **Decision Maker**

Banker   A company requests a one-year, $200,000 loan for expansion. This company's current ratio is 4:1, with current assets of $160,000. Key competitors have a current ratio of 1.9:1. Using this information, do you approve the loan? ■   *Answer:* The loan application is likely approved for at least two reasons. First, the current ratio suggests an ability to meet short-term obligations. Second, current assets of $160,000 and a current ratio of 4:1 imply current liabilities of $40,000 (or one-fourth of current assets) and a working capital excess of $120,000. The working capital is 60% of the loan.

Acid-Test Ratio

Quick assets are cash, short-term investments, and current receivables. These are the most liquid types of current assets. The *acid-test ratio,* also called *quick ratio* and introduced in Chapter 4, evaluates a company's short-term liquidity.

$$\text{Acid-test ratio} = \frac{\text{Cash} + \text{Short-term investments} + \text{Current receivables}}{\text{Current liabilities}}$$

Apple's acid-test ratio is computed in Exhibit 13.15. Apple's acid-test ratio (0.91) is lower than those for Google (4.97), Samsung (1.71), and the 1:1 common guideline for an acceptable acid-test ratio. As with analysis of the current ratio, we must consider other factors. How frequently a company converts its current assets into cash also affects its ability to pay current obligations. This means analysis of short-term liquidity should consider receivables and inventories, which we cover next.

EXHIBIT 13.15

Acid-Test Ratio

$ millions	Current Yr	Prior Yr
Cash and equivalents............	$ 20,289	$20,484
Short-term securities	53,892	46,671
Current receivables	17,874	15,754
Total quick assets...............	$ 92,055	$82,909
Current liabilities................	$100,814	$79,006
Acid-test ratio		
$92,055/$100,814 =	0.91 to 1	
$82,909/$79,006 =		1.05 to 1

Acid-test ratio
Google = 4.97
Samsung = 1.71
Industry = 0.9

Accounts Receivable Turnover

Accounts receivable turnover measures how frequently a company converts its receivables into cash. This ratio is defined as follows (see Chapter 7 for additional explanation). Apple's accounts receivable turnover is computed next to the formula ($ millions). Apple's turnover of 13.6 exceeds Google's 6.8 and Samsung's 9.2 turnover. Accounts receivable turnover is high when accounts receivable are quickly collected. A high turnover is favorable because it means the company does not tie up assets in accounts receivable. However, accounts receivable turnover can be too high; this can occur when credit terms are so restrictive that they decrease sales.

Accounts receivable turnover
Google = 6.8
Samsung = 9.2
Industry = 5.0

$$\frac{\text{Accounts receivable}}{\text{turnover}} = \frac{\text{Net sales}}{\text{Average accounts receivable, net}} = \frac{\$229,234}{(\$15,754 + \$17,874)/2} = 13.6 \text{ times}$$

Inventory Turnover

Inventory turnover measures how long a company holds inventory before selling it. It is defined as follows (see Chapter 5 for additional explanation). Next to the formula we compute Apple's inventory turnover at 40.4. Apple's inventory turnover is higher than Samsung's 6.0 but lower than Google's 89.6. A company with a high turnover requires a smaller investment in inventory than one producing the same sales with a lower turnover. However, high inventory turnover can be bad if inventory is so low that stock-outs occur.

Inventory turnover
Google = 89.6
Samsung = 6.0
Industry = 7.0

$$\text{Inventory turnover} = \frac{\text{Cost of goods sold}}{\text{Average inventory}} = \frac{\$141,048}{(\$2,132 + \$4,855)/2} = 40.4 \text{ times}$$

Days' Sales Uncollected

Days' sales uncollected measures how frequently a company collects accounts receivable and is defined as follows (Chapter 6 provides additional explanation). Apple's days' sales uncollected of 28.5 days is shown next to the formula. Both Google's days' sales uncollected of 60.4 days and Samsung's 48.5 days are more than the 28.5 days for Apple. Days' sales uncollected is more meaningful if we know company credit terms. A rough

©VCG/Getty Images

guideline states that days' sales uncollected should not exceed 1⅓ times the days in its (1) credit period, *if* discounts are not offered, or (2) discount period, *if* favorable discounts are offered.

Days' sales uncollected
Google = 60.4
Samsung = 48.5

$$\text{Days' sales uncollected} = \frac{\text{Accounts receivable, net}}{\text{Net sales}} \times 365 = \frac{\$17{,}874}{\$229{,}234} \times 365 = 28.5 \text{ days}$$

Days' Sales in Inventory

Days' sales in inventory is used to evaluate inventory liquidity. We compute days' sales in inventory as follows (Chapter 5 provides additional explanation). Apple's days' sales in inventory of 12.6 days is shown next to the formula. If the products in Apple's inventory are in demand by customers, this formula estimates that its inventory will be converted into receivables (or cash) in 12.6 days. If all of Apple's sales were credit sales, the conversion of inventory to receivables in 12.6 days *plus* the conversion of receivables to cash in 28.5 days implies that inventory will be converted to cash in about 41.1 days (12.6 + 28.5).

Point: *Average collection period* is estimated by dividing 365 by the accounts receivable turnover ratio. For example, 365 divided by an accounts receivable turnover of 12.6 indicates a 29-day average collection period.

Days' sales in inventory
Google = 6.0
Samsung = 70.5
Industry = 35

$$\text{Days' sales in inventory} = \frac{\text{Ending inventory}}{\text{Cost of goods sold}} \times 365 = \frac{\$4{,}855}{\$141{,}048} \times 365 = 12.6 \text{ days}$$

Total Asset Turnover

Total asset turnover measures a company's ability to use its assets to generate sales and reflects on operating efficiency. The definition of this ratio follows (Chapter 8 offers additional explanation). Apple's total asset turnover of 0.66 is shown next to the formula. Apple's turnover is greater than that for Google (0.61), but not Samsung (0.85).

Total asset turnover
Google = 0.61
Samsung = 0.85
Industry = 1.1

$$\text{Total asset turnover} = \frac{\text{Net sales}}{\text{Average total assets}} = \frac{\$229{,}234}{(\$375{,}319 + \$321{,}686)/2} = 0.66 \text{ times}$$

Solvency

Solvency is a company's ability to meet long-term obligations and generate future revenues. Analysis of solvency is long term and uses broader measures than liquidity. An important part of solvency analysis is a company's capital structure. *Capital structure* is a company's makeup of equity and debt financing. Our analysis here focuses on a company's ability to both meet its obligations and provide security to its creditors *over the long run*.

Debt Ratio and Equity Ratio

One part of solvency analysis is to assess a company's mix of debt and equity financing. The *debt ratio* (described in Chapter 2) shows total liabilities as a percent of total assets. The **equity ratio** shows total equity as a percent of total assets. Apple's debt and equity ratios follow. Apple's ratios reveal more debt than equity. A company is considered less risky if its capital structure (equity plus debt) has more equity. Debt is considered more risky because of its required payments for interest and principal. Stockholders cannot require payment from the company. However, debt can increase income for stockholders if the company earns a higher return than interest paid on the debt.

Point: For analysis purposes, noncontrolling interest is usually included in equity.

Point: Total of debt and equity ratios always equals 100%.

Debt ratio :: Equity ratio
Google = 22.7% :: 77.3%
Samsung = 28.9% :: 71.1%
Industry = 35% :: 65%

$ millions	Current Yr	Ratios	
Total liabilities.....................	$241,272	64.3%	[Debt ratio]
Total equity	134,047	35.7%	[Equity ratio]
Total liabilities and equity...........	$375,319	100.0%	

Debt-to-Equity Ratio

The *debt-to-equity* ratio is another measure of solvency. We compute the ratio as follows (Chapter 10 offers additional explanation). Apple's debt-to-equity ratio of 1.80 is shown next to the formula. Apple's ratio is higher than those of Google (0.29) and Samsung (0.41), and greater than the industry ratio of 0.6. Apple's capital structure has more debt than equity. Debt must be repaid with interest, while equity does not. Debt payments can be burdensome when the industry and/or the economy experience a downturn.

$$\text{Debt-to-equity ratio} = \frac{\text{Total liabilities}}{\text{Total equity}} = \frac{\$241,272}{\$134,047} = 1.80$$

Debt-to-equity
Google = 0.29
Samsung = 0.41
Industry = 0.6

Times Interest Earned   The amount of income before subtracting interest expense and income tax expense is the amount available to pay interest expense. The following *times interest earned* ratio measures a company's ability to pay interest (see Chapter 9 for additional explanation).

$$\text{Times interest earned} = \frac{\text{Income before interest expense and income tax expense}}{\text{Interest expense}}$$

The larger this ratio is, the less risky the company is for creditors. One guideline says that creditors are reasonably safe if the company has a ratio of two or more. Apple's times interest earned ratio of 28.6 follows. It suggests that creditors have little risk of nonrepayment.

$$\frac{\$48,351 + \$2,323 + \$15,738}{\$2,323} = 28.6 \text{ times}$$

Times interest earned
Google = 250.5
Samsung = 86.7

Profitability

Profitability is a company's ability to earn an adequate return. This section covers key profitability measures.

Profit Margin   *Profit margin* measures a company's ability to earn net income from sales (Chapter 3 offers additional explanation). Apple's profit margin of 21.1% is shown next to the formula. To evaluate profit margin, we must consider the industry. For instance, an appliance company might require a profit margin of 15%, whereas a retail supermarket might require a profit margin of 2%. Apple's 21.1% profit margin is better than Google's 11.4%, Samsung's 17.6%, and the industry's 11% margin.

$$\text{Profit margin} = \frac{\text{Net income}}{\text{Net sales}} = \frac{\$48,351}{\$229,234} = 21.1\%$$

Profit margin
Google = 11.4%
Samsung = 17.6%
Industry = 11%

Return on Total Assets   *Return on total assets* is defined as follows. Apple's return on total assets of 13.9% is shown next to the formula. Apple's 13.9% return on total assets is higher than Google's 6.9% and the industry's 8%, but lower than Samsung's 15.0%. We also should evaluate any trend in the return.

$$\text{Return on total assets} = \frac{\text{Net income}}{\text{Average total assets}} = \frac{\$48,351}{(\$375,319 + \$321,686)/2} = 13.9\%$$

Return on total assets
Google = 6.9%
Samsung = 15.0%
Industry = 8%

The relation between profit margin, total asset turnover, and return on total assets follows.

$$\text{Profit margin} \times \text{Total asset turnover} = \text{Return on total assets}$$

$$\frac{\text{Net income}}{\text{Net sales}} \times \frac{\text{Net sales}}{\text{Average total assets}} = \frac{\text{Net income}}{\text{Average total assets}}$$

Both profit margin and total asset turnover affect operating efficiency, as measured by return on total assets. This formula is applied to Apple as follows. This analysis shows that Apple's superior return on assets versus that of Google is driven by its high profit margin and good asset turnover.

$$21.1\% \times 0.66 = 13.9\% \text{ (with rounding)}$$

Google = 11.4% × 0.61 ≈ 6.9%
Samsung = 17.6% × 0.85 ≈ 15.0%
(with rounding)

Return on Common Stockholders' Equity

The most important goal in operating a company is to earn income for its owner(s). *Return on common stockholders' equity* measures a company's ability to earn income for common stockholders and is defined as follows.

$$\textbf{Return on common stockholders' equity} = \frac{\textbf{Net income} - \textbf{Preferred dividends}}{\textbf{Average common stockholders' equity}}$$

Apple's return on common stockholders' equity is computed as follows. The denominator in this computation is the book value of common equity. Dividends on cumulative preferred stock are subtracted from income whether they are declared or are in arrears. If preferred stock is non-cumulative, its dividends are subtracted only if declared. Apple's 36.9% return on common stockholders' equity is superior to Google's 8.7% and Samsung's 20.5%.

Return on common equity
Google = 8.7%
Samsung = 20.5%
Industry = 15%

$$\frac{\$48,351 - \$0}{(\$128,249 + \$134,047)/2} = 36.9\%$$

■ **Decision** Insight

Take It to the Street   *Wall Street* is synonymous with financial markets, but its name comes from the street location of the original New York Stock Exchange. The street's name comes from stockades built by early settlers to protect New York from pirate attacks. ■

Market Prospects

Market measures are useful for analyzing corporations with publicly traded stock. These market measures use stock price, which reflects the market's (public's) expectations for the company. This includes market expectations of both company return and risk.

Point: Low expectations = low PE. High expectations = high PE.

Price-Earnings Ratio

Computation of the *price-earnings ratio* follows (Chapter 11 provides additional explanation). This ratio is used to measure market expectations for future growth. The market price of Apple's common stock at the start of the current fiscal year was $154.12. Using Apple's $9.27 basic earnings per share, we compute its price-earnings ratio as follows. Apple's price-earnings ratio is less than that for Samsung and Google, but it is higher than the industry norm for this period.

PE (year-end)
Google = 57.3
Samsung = 22.9
Industry = 11

$$\textbf{Price-earnings ratio} = \frac{\textbf{Market price per common share}}{\textbf{Earnings per share}} = \frac{\$154.12}{\$9.27} = 16.6$$

Dividend Yield

Dividend yield is used to compare the dividend-paying performance of different companies. We compute dividend yield as follows (Chapter 11 offers additional explanation). Apple's dividend yield of 1.6%, based on its fiscal year-end market price per share of $154.12 and its $2.40 cash dividends per share, is shown next to the formula. Some companies, such as Google, do not pay dividends because they reinvest the cash to grow their businesses in the hope of generating greater future earnings and dividends.

Dividend yield
Google = 0.0%
Samsung = 1.6%

$$\textbf{Dividend yield} = \frac{\textbf{Annual cash dividends per share}}{\textbf{Market price per share}} = \frac{\$2.40}{\$154.12} = 1.6\%$$

■ **Decision** Insight

Bull Session   A *bear market* is a declining market. The phrase comes from bear-skin hunters who sold the skins before the bears were caught. The term *bear* was then used to describe investors who sold shares they did not own in anticipation of a price decline. A *bull market* is a rising market. This phrase comes from the once-popular sport of bear and bull baiting. The term *bull* means the opposite of *bear*. ■

©Partner Media GmbH/Alamy Stock Photo

Summary of Ratios

Exhibit 13.16 summarizes the ratios illustrated in this chapter and throughout the book.

EXHIBIT 13.16

Financial Statement Analysis Ratios

Ratio	Formula	Measure of
Liquidity and Efficiency		
Current ratio	$= \dfrac{\text{Current assets}}{\text{Current liabilities}}$	Short-term debt-paying ability
Acid-test ratio	$= \dfrac{\text{Cash + Short-term investments + Current receivables}}{\text{Current liabilities}}$	Immediate short-term debt-paying ability
Accounts receivable turnover	$= \dfrac{\text{Net sales}}{\text{Average accounts receivable, net}}$	Efficiency of collection
Inventory turnover	$= \dfrac{\text{Cost of goods sold}}{\text{Average inventory}}$	Efficiency of inventory management
Days' sales uncollected	$= \dfrac{\text{Accounts receivable, net}}{\text{Net sales}} \times 365$	Liquidity of receivables
Days' sales in inventory	$= \dfrac{\text{Ending inventory}}{\text{Cost of goods sold}} \times 365$	Liquidity of inventory
Total asset turnover	$= \dfrac{\text{Net sales}}{\text{Average total assets}}$	Efficiency of assets in producing sales
Solvency		
Debt ratio	$= \dfrac{\text{Total liabilities}}{\text{Total assets}}$	Creditor financing and leverage
Equity ratio	$= \dfrac{\text{Total equity}}{\text{Total assets}}$	Owner financing
Debt-to-equity ratio	$= \dfrac{\text{Total liabilities}}{\text{Total equity}}$	Debt versus equity financing
Times interest earned	$= \dfrac{\text{Income before interest expense and income tax expense}}{\text{Interest expense}}$	Protection in meeting interest payments
Profitability		
Profit margin ratio	$= \dfrac{\text{Net income}}{\text{Net sales}}$	Net income in each sales dollar
Gross margin ratio	$= \dfrac{\text{Net sales} - \text{Cost of goods sold}}{\text{Net sales}}$	Gross margin in each sales dollar
Return on total assets	$= \dfrac{\text{Net income}}{\text{Average total assets}}$	Overall profitability of assets
Return on common stockholders' equity	$= \dfrac{\text{Net income} - \text{Preferred dividends}}{\text{Average common stockholders' equity}}$	Profitability of owner investment
Book value per common share	$= \dfrac{\text{Shareholders' equity applicable to common shares}}{\text{Number of common shares outstanding}}$	Liquidation at reported amounts
Basic earnings per share	$= \dfrac{\text{Net income} - \text{Preferred dividends}}{\text{Weighted-average common shares outstanding}}$	Net income per common share
Market Prospects		
Price-earnings ratio	$= \dfrac{\text{Market price per common share}}{\text{Earnings per share}}$	Market value relative to earnings
Dividend yield	$= \dfrac{\text{Annual cash dividends per share}}{\text{Market price per share}}$	Cash return per common share

NEED-TO-KNOW 13-3

Ratio Analysis

P3

For each ratio listed, identify whether the change in ratio value from the prior year to the current year is favorable or unfavorable.

Ratio	Current Yr	Prior Yr	Ratio	Current Yr	Prior Yr
1. Profit margin	6%	8%	4. Accounts receivable turnover.	8.8	9.4
2. Debt ratio.	50%	70%	5. Basic earnings per share	$2.10	$2.00
3. Gross margin	40%	36%	6. Inventory turnover.	3.6	4.0

Solution

Ratio	Current Yr	Prior Yr	Change
1. Profit margin ratio.	6%	8%	Unfavorable
2. Debt ratio.	50%	70%	Favorable
3. Gross margin ratio.	40%	36%	Favorable
4. Accounts receivable turnover.	8.8	9.4	Unfavorable
5. Basic earnings per share	$2.10	$2.00	Favorable
6. Inventory turnover.	3.6	4.0	Unfavorable

Do More: QS 13-6 through QS 13-13, E 13-7, E 13-8, E 13-9, E 13-10, E 13-11, P 13-4

 **Decision Analysis**    **Analysis Reporting**

A1

Summarize and report results of analysis.

A *financial statement analysis report* usually consists of six sections.

1. **Executive summary**—brief analysis of results and conclusions.
2. **Analysis overview**—background on the company, its industry, and the economy.
3. **Evidential matter**—financial statements and information used in the analysis, including ratios, trends, comparisons, and all analytical measures used.
4. **Assumptions**—list of assumptions about a company's industry and economic environment, and other assumptions underlying estimates.
5. **Key factors**—list of favorable and unfavorable factors, both quantitative and qualitative, for company performance; usually organized by areas of analysis.
6. **Inferences**—forecasts, estimates, interpretations, and conclusions of the analysis report.

We must remember that the user dictates relevance, meaning that the analysis report should include a brief table of contents to help readers focus on those areas most relevant to their decisions. Finally, writing is important. Mistakes in grammar and errors of fact compromise the report's credibility.

■ Decision Insight

Short and Sweet   *Short selling* refers to selling stock before you buy it. Here's an example: You borrow 100 shares of **Nike** stock, sell them at $55 each, and receive money from their sale. You then wait. You hope that Nike's stock price falls to, say, $50 each and you can replace the borrowed stock for less than you sold it, reaping a profit of $5 each less any transaction costs. ■

NEED-TO-KNOW 13-4

COMPREHENSIVE

Applying Horizontal, Vertical, and Ratio Analyses

Use the following financial statements of Precision Co. to complete these requirements.

1. Prepare comparative income statements showing the percent increase or decrease for the current year in comparison to the prior year.

2. Prepare common-size comparative balance sheets for both years.

3. Compute the following ratios for the current year and identify each one's building block category for financial statement analysis.

a. Current ratio
b. Acid-test ratio
c. Accounts receivable turnover
d. Days' sales uncollected
e. Inventory turnover
f. Debt ratio

g. Debt-to-equity ratio
h. Times interest earned
i. Profit margin ratio
j. Total asset turnover
k. Return on total assets
l. Return on common stockholders' equity

PRECISION COMPANY Comparative Income Statements		
For Years Ended December 31	Current Yr	Prior Yr
Sales	$2,486,000	$2,075,000
Cost of goods sold	1,523,000	1,222,000
Gross profit	963,000	853,000
Operating expenses		
Advertising expense..................	145,000	100,000
Sales salaries expense...............	240,000	280,000
Office salaries expense	165,000	200,000
Insurance expense..................	100,000	45,000
Supplies expense...................	26,000	35,000
Depreciation expense	85,000	75,000
Miscellaneous expenses	17,000	15,000
Total operating expenses	778,000	750,000
Operating income....................	185,000	103,000
Interest expense.....................	44,000	46,000
Income before taxes..................	141,000	57,000
Income tax expense	47,000	19,000
Net income	$ 94,000	$ 38,000
Earnings per share	$ 0.99	$ 0.40

PRECISION COMPANY Comparative Year-End Balance Sheets		
At December 31	Current Yr	Prior Yr
Assets		
Current assets		
Cash	$ 79,000	$ 42,000
Short-term investments	65,000	96,000
Accounts receivable, net	120,000	100,000
Merchandise inventory	250,000	265,000
Total current assets	514,000	503,000
Plant assets		
Store equipment, net..................	400,000	350,000
Office equipment, net	45,000	50,000
Buildings, net	625,000	675,000
Land	100,000	100,000
Total plant assets	1,170,000	1,175,000
Total assets..........................	$1,684,000	$1,678,000
Liabilities		
Current liabilities		
Accounts payable.....................	$ 164,000	$ 190,000
Short-term notes payable	75,000	90,000
Taxes payable........................	26,000	12,000
Total current liabilities	265,000	292,000
Long-term liabilities		
Notes payable (secured by mortgage on buildings).............	400,000	420,000
Total liabilities........................	665,000	712,000
Stockholders' Equity		
Common stock, $5 par value	475,000	475,000
Retained earnings.....................	544,000	491,000
Total stockholders' equity	1,019,000	966,000
Total liabilities and equity...............	$1,684,000	$1,678,000

PLANNING THE SOLUTION

- Set up a four-column income statement; enter the current-year and prior-year amounts in the first two columns and then enter the dollar change in the third column and the percent change from the prior year in the fourth column.
- Set up a four-column balance sheet; enter the current-year and prior-year year-end amounts in the first two columns and then compute and enter the amount of each item as a percent of total assets.
- Compute the required ratios using the data provided. Use the average of beginning and ending amounts when appropriate (see Exhibit 13.16 for definitions).

SOLUTION

1.

PRECISION COMPANY Comparative Income Statements				
For Years Ended December 31	Current Yr	Prior Yr	Dollar Change	Percent Change
Sales	$2,486,000	$2,075,000	$411,000	19.8%
Cost of goods sold	1,523,000	1,222,000	301,000	24.6
Gross profit	963,000	853,000	110,000	12.9
Operating expenses				
Advertising expense...................	145,000	100,000	45,000	45.0
Sales salaries expense.................	240,000	280,000	(40,000)	(14.3)
Office salaries expense	165,000	200,000	(35,000)	(17.5)
Insurance expense....................	100,000	45,000	55,000	122.2
Supplies expense.....................	26,000	35,000	(9,000)	(25.7)
Depreciation expense	85,000	75,000	10,000	13.3
Miscellaneous expenses	17,000	15,000	2,000	13.3
Total operating expenses	778,000	750,000	28,000	3.7
Operating income.....................	185,000	103,000	82,000	79.6
Interest expense......................	44,000	46,000	(2,000)	(4.3)
Income before taxes..................	141,000	57,000	84,000	147.4
Income tax expense	47,000	19,000	28,000	147.4
Net income	$ 94,000	$ 38,000	$ 56,000	147.4
Earnings per share	$ 0.99	$ 0.40	$ 0.59	147.5

2.

PRECISION COMPANY Common-Size Comparative Year-End Balance Sheets				
			Common-Size Percents	
At December 31	Current Yr	Prior Yr	Current Yr*	Prior Yr*
Assets				
Current assets				
Cash	$ 79,000	$ 42,000	4.7%	2.5%
Short-term investments	65,000	96,000	3.9	5.7
Accounts receivable, net	120,000	100,000	7.1	6.0
Merchandise inventory...............	250,000	265,000	14.8	15.8
Total current assets	514,000	503,000	30.5	30.0
Plant assets				
Store equipment, net	400,000	350,000	23.8	20.9
Office equipment, net................	45,000	50,000	2.7	3.0
Buildings, net	625,000	675,000	37.1	40.2
Land.............................	100,000	100,000	5.9	6.0
Total plant assets	1,170,000	1,175,000	69.5	70.0
Total assets	$1,684,000	$1,678,000	100.0%	100.0%
Liabilities				
Current liabilities				
Accounts payable...................	$ 164,000	$ 190,000	9.7%	11.3%
Short-term notes payable	75,000	90,000	4.5	5.4
Taxes payable......................	26,000	12,000	1.5	0.7
Total current liabilities	265,000	292,000	15.7	17.4
Long-term liabilities				
Notes payable (secured by mortgage on buildings)	400,000	420,000	23.8	25.0
Total liabilities	665,000	712,000	39.5	42.4
Stockholders' Equity				
Common stock, $5 par value	475,000	475,000	28.2	28.3
Retained earnings....................	544,000	491,000	32.3	29.3
Total stockholders' equity..............	1,019,000	966,000	60.5	57.6
Total liabilities and equity..............	$1,684,000	$1,678,000	100.0%	100.0%

*Columns do not always exactly add to 100 due to rounding.

3. Ratios:

a. Current ratio: $514,000/$265,000 = 1.9:1 (liquidity and efficiency)

b. Acid-test ratio: ($79,000 + $65,000 + $120,000)/$265,000 = 1.0:1 (liquidity and efficiency)

c. Average receivables: ($120,000 + $100,000)/2 = $110,000
Accounts receivable turnover: $2,486,000/$110,000 = 22.6 times (liquidity and efficiency)

d. Days' sales uncollected: ($120,000/$2,486,000) × 365 = 17.6 days (liquidity and efficiency)

e. Average inventory: ($250,000 + $265,000)/2 = $257,500
Inventory turnover: $1,523,000/$257,500 = 5.9 times (liquidity and efficiency)

f. Debt ratio: $665,000/$1,684,000 = 39.5% (solvency)

g. Debt-to-equity ratio: $665,000/$1,019,000 = 0.65 (solvency)

h. Times interest earned: $185,000/$44,000 = 4.2 times (solvency)

i. Profit margin ratio: $94,000/$2,486,000 = 3.8% (profitability)

j. Average total assets: ($1,684,000 + $1,678,000)/2 = $1,681,000
Total asset turnover: $2,486,000/$1,681,000 = 1.48 times (liquidity and efficiency)

k. Return on total assets: $94,000/$1,681,000 = 5.6% or 3.8% × 1.48 = 5.6% (profitability)

l. Average total common equity: ($1,019,000 + $966,000)/2 = $992,500
Return on common stockholders' equity: $94,000/$992,500 = 9.5% (profitability)

Sustainable Income

13A

A2

Explain the form and assess the content of a complete income statement.

When a company's activities include income-related events not part of its normal, continuing operations, it must disclose these events. To alert users to these activities, companies separate the income statement into continuing operations, discontinued segments, comprehensive income, and earnings per share. Exhibit 13A.1 shows such an income statement for ComUS. These separations help us measure *sustainable income,* which is the income level most likely to continue into the future. Sustainable income is commonly used in performance measures.

EXHIBIT 13A.1

Income Statement (all-inclusive) for a Corporation

ComUS		
Income Statement		
For Year Ended December 31		
Net sales		$8,478,000
Operating expenses		
Cost of goods sold	$5,950,000	
Depreciation expense	35,000	
Other selling, general, and administrative expenses.	515,000	
Interest expense.	20,000	
① Total operating expenses.		(6,520,000)
Other unusual and/or infrequent gains (losses)		
Loss on plant relocation.		(45,000)
Gain on sale of surplus land.		72,000
Income from continuing operations before taxes		1,985,000
Income tax expense		(595,500)
Income from continuing operations.		1,389,500
Discontinued segment		
② Income from operating Division A (net of $180,000 taxes)	420,000	
Loss on disposal of Division A (net of $66,000 tax benefit)	(154,000)	266,000
Net income		$1,655,500
Earnings per common share (200,000 outstanding shares)		
③ Income from continuing operations		$ 6.95
Discontinued operations		1.33
Net income (basic earnings per share)		$ 8.28

① **Continuing Operations**   Section ① shows revenues, expenses, and income from continuing operations. This information is used to predict future operations, and most view this section as the most important.

Gains and losses that are normal and frequent are reported as part of continuing operations. Gains and losses that are either unusual and/or infrequent are reported as part of continuing operations *but after* the normal revenues and expenses. Items considered unusual and/or infrequent include (1) property taken away by a foreign government, (2) condemning of property, (3) prohibiting use of an asset from a new law, (4) losses and gains from an unusual and infrequent calamity ("act of God"), and (5) financial effects of labor strikes.

Point: FASB no longer allows *extraordinary items.*

② **Discontinued Segments**   A **business segment** is a part of a company that is separated by its products/services or by geographic location. A segment has assets, liabilities, and financial results of operations that can be separated from those of other parts of the company. A gain or loss from selling or closing down a segment is separately reported. Section ② of Exhibit 13A.1 reports both (a) income from operating the discontinued segment before its disposal and (b) the loss from disposing of the segment's net assets. The income tax effects of each are reported separately from the income tax expense in section ①.

③ **Earnings per Share**   Section ③ of Exhibit 13A.1 reports earnings per share for both continuing operations and discontinued segments (when they both exist). Earnings per share is covered in Chapter 11.

Changes in Accounting Principles   Changes in accounting principles require retrospective application to prior periods' financial statements. *Retrospective application* means applying a different accounting principle to prior periods as if that principle had always been used. Retrospective application enhances the consistency of financial information between periods, which improves the usefulness of information, especially with comparative analyses.

 Decision Maker

Small Business Owner You own an orange grove near Jacksonville, Florida. A bad frost destroys about one-half of your oranges. You are currently preparing an income statement for a bank loan. Where on the income statement do you report the loss of oranges? ■ *Answer:* The frost loss is likely unusual, meaning it is reported in the nonrecurring section of continuing operations. Managers would highlight this loss apart from ongoing, normal results so that the bank views it separately from normal operations.

Summary: Cheat Sheet

BASICS OF ANALYSIS

Liquidity and efficiency: Ability to meet short-term obligations and efficiently generate revenues.

Solvency: Ability to meet long-term obligations and generate future revenues.

Profitability: Ability to provide financial rewards to attract and retain financing.

Market prospects: Ability to generate positive market expectations.

General-purpose financial statements: Include the (1) income statement, (2) balance sheet, (3) statement of stockholders' equity (or statement of retained earnings), (4) statement of cash flows, and (5) notes to these statements.

HORIZONTAL ANALYSIS

Comparative financial statements: Show financial amounts in side-by-side columns on a single statement.

Analysis period: The financial statements under analysis.

Base period: The financial statements used for comparison. The prior year is commonly used as a base period.

Dollar change formula:

> **Dollar change = Analysis period amount − Base period amount**

Percent change formula:

$$\text{Percent change (\%)} = \frac{\text{Analysis period amount} - \text{Base period amount}}{\text{Base period amount}} \times 100$$

Apple comparative balance sheet: The prior year is the base period and current year is the analysis period.

$ millions	Current Yr	Prior Yr	Dollar Change	Percent Change
Assets				
Cash and cash equivalents	$20,289	$20,484	$ (195)	(1.0)%
Short-term marketable securities	53,892	46,671	7,221	15.5
Accounts receivable, net	17,874	15,754	2,120	13.5

Trend analysis: Computing trend percents that show patterns in data across periods.

$$\text{Trend percent (\%)} = \frac{\text{Analysis period amount}}{\text{Base period amount}} \times 100$$

Apple trend analysis: 4 years ago is the base period, and each subsequent year is the analysis period.

In trend percent	Current Yr	1 Yr Ago	2 Yrs Ago	3 Yrs Ago	4 Yrs Ago
Net sales................	134.1%	126.2%	136.7%	107.0%	100.0%
Cost of sales.............	132.3	123.2	131.4	105.3	100.0
Operating expenses........	175.4	158.4	146.3	117.8	100.0

VERTICAL ANALYSIS

Common-size financial statements: Show changes in the relative importance of each financial statement item. All individual amounts in common-size statements are shown in common-size percents.

Common-size percent formula:

$$\text{Common-size percent (\%)} = \frac{\text{Analysis amount}}{\text{Base amount}} \times 100$$

Base amount: Comparative balance sheets use total assets, and comparative income statements use net sales.

Apple common-size balance sheet:

$ millions	Current Yr	Prior Yr	Common-Size Percents Current Yr	Common-Size Percents Prior Yr
Goodwill	5,717	5,414	1.5%	1.7%
Acquired intangible assets, net	2,298	3,206	0.6	1.0
Other assets	10,162	8,757	2.7	2.7
Total assets	$375,319	$321,686	100.0	100.0

Apple common-size income statement:

$ millions	Current Yr	Prior Yr	Common-Size Percents Current Yr	Common-Size Percents Prior Yr
Net sales	$229,234	$215,639	100.0%	100.0%
Cost of sales	141,048	131,376	61.5	60.9
Gross margin	88,186	84,263	38.5	39.1

RATIO ANALYSIS AND REPORTING

Ratio	Formula
Liquidity and Efficiency	
Current ratio	$= \dfrac{\text{Current assets}}{\text{Current liabilities}}$
Acid-test ratio	$= \dfrac{\text{Cash + Short-term investments + Current receivables}}{\text{Current liabilities}}$
Accounts receivable turnover	$= \dfrac{\text{Net sales}}{\text{Average accounts receivable, net}}$
Inventory turnover	$= \dfrac{\text{Cost of goods sold}}{\text{Average inventory}}$
Days' sales uncollected	$= \dfrac{\text{Accounts receivable, net}}{\text{Net sales}} \times 365$
Days' sales in inventory	$= \dfrac{\text{Ending inventory}}{\text{Cost of goods sold}} \times 365$
Total asset turnover	$= \dfrac{\text{Net sales}}{\text{Average total assets}}$
Solvency	
Debt ratio	$= \dfrac{\text{Total liabilities}}{\text{Total assets}}$
Equity ratio	$= \dfrac{\text{Total equity}}{\text{Total assets}}$
Debt-to-equity ratio	$= \dfrac{\text{Total liabilities}}{\text{Total equity}}$
Times interest earned	$= \dfrac{\text{Income before interest expense and income tax expense}}{\text{Interest expense}}$
Profitability	
Profit margin ratio	$= \dfrac{\text{Net income}}{\text{Net sales}}$
Gross margin ratio	$= \dfrac{\text{Net sales} - \text{Cost of goods sold}}{\text{Net sales}}$
Return on total assets	$= \dfrac{\text{Net income}}{\text{Average total assets}}$
Return on common stockholders' equity	$= \dfrac{\text{Net income} - \text{Preferred dividends}}{\text{Average common stockholders' equity}}$
Basic earnings per share	$= \dfrac{\text{Net income} - \text{Preferred dividends}}{\text{Weighted-average common shares outstanding}}$
Market Prospects	
Price-earnings ratio	$= \dfrac{\text{Market price per common share}}{\text{Earnings per share}}$
Dividend yield	$= \dfrac{\text{Annual cash dividends per share}}{\text{Market price per share}}$

Key Terms

Business segment (515)

Common-size financial statement (502)

Comparative financial statement (498)

Efficiency (497)

Equity ratio (508)

Financial reporting (498)

Financial statement analysis (497)

General-purpose financial statements (498)

Horizontal analysis (498)

Liquidity (497)

Market prospects (497)

Profitability (497)

Ratio analysis (498)

Solvency (497)

Vertical analysis (498)

Working capital (506)

Multiple Choice Quiz

1. A company's sales in the prior year were $300,000 and in the current year were $351,000. Using the prior year as the base year, the sales trend percent for the current year is

  a. 17%.   **c.** 100%.   **e.** 48%.

  b. 85%.   **d.** 117%.

Use the following information for questions 2 through 5.

ELLA COMPANY			
Balance Sheet			
December 31			
Assets		**Liabilities**	
Cash	$ 86,000	Current liabilities	$124,000
Accounts receivable.	76,000	Long-term liabilities	90,000
Merchandise inventory . .	122,000	**Equity**	
Prepaid insurance	12,000	Common stock	300,000
Long-term investments . .	98,000	Retained earnings	316,000
Plant assets, net.	436,000		
Total assets.	$830,000	Total liabilities and equity . .	$830,000

2. What is Ella Company's current ratio?

  a. 0.69   **d.** 6.69

  b. 1.31   **e.** 2.39

  c. 3.88

3. What is Ella Company's acid-test ratio?

  a. 2.39   **d.** 6.69

  b. 0.69   **e.** 3.88

  c. 1.31

4. What is Ella Company's debt ratio?

  a. 25.78%   **d.** 137.78%

  b. 100.00%   **e.** 34.74%

  c. 74.22%

5. What is Ella Company's equity ratio?

  a. 25.78%   **d.** 74.22%

  b. 100.00%   **e.** 137.78%

  c. 34.74%

ANSWERS TO MULTIPLE CHOICE QUIZ

1. d; ($351,000/$300,000) × 100 = 117%

2. e; ($86,000 + $76,000 + $122,000 + $12,000)/$124,000 = 2.39

3. c; ($86,000 + $76,000)/$124,000 = 1.31

4. a; ($124,000 + $90,000)/$830,000 = 25.78%

5. d; ($300,000 + $316,000)/$830,000 = 74.22%

A   *Superscript letter A denotes assignments based on Appendix 13A.*

🔲 Icon denotes assignments that involve decision making.

Discussion Questions

1. Explain the difference between financial reporting and financial statements.

2. What is the difference between comparative financial statements and common-size comparative statements?

3. Which items are usually assigned a 100% value on (*a*) a common-size balance sheet and (*b*) a common-size income statement?

4. 🔲 What three factors would influence your evaluation as to whether a company's current ratio is good or bad?

5. 🔲 Suggest several reasons why a 2:1 current ratio might not be adequate for a particular company.

6. 🔲 Why is working capital given special attention in the process of analyzing balance sheets?

7. 🔲 What does the number of days' sales uncollected indicate?

8. 🔲 What does a relatively high accounts receivable turnover indicate about a company's short-term liquidity?

9. 🔲 Why is a company's capital structure, as measured by debt and equity ratios, important to financial statement analysts?

10. 🔲 How does inventory turnover provide information about a company's short-term liquidity?

11. 🔲 What ratios would you compute to evaluate management performance?

12. 🔲 Why would a company's return on total assets be different from its return on common stockholders' equity?

13. Where on the income statement does a company report an
unusual gain not expected to occur more often than once
every two years or so?

14. Refer to **Apple**'s financial statements in
Appendix A. Compute its profit margin for the   **APPLE**
years ended September 30, 2017, and September 24, 2016.

15. Refer to **Google**'s financial statements in
Appendix A to compute its equity ratio as   **GOOGLE**
of December 31, 2017, and December 31, 2016.

16. Refer to **Samsung**'s financial statements
in Appendix A. Compute its debt ratio as   **Samsung**
of December 31, 2017, and December 31, 2016.

17. Use **Samsung**'s financial statements in
Appendix A to compute its return on total   **Samsung**
assets for fiscal year ended December 31, 2017.

Ⓜ connect

QUICK STUDY

QS 13-1

Financial reporting

C1

Identify which of the following items are *not* included as part of general-purpose financial statements but
are part of financial reporting.

_____ **a.** Income statement

_____ **b.** Balance sheet

_____ **c.** Shareholders' meetings

_____ **d.** Financial statement notes

_____ **e.** Company news releases

_____ **f.** Statement of cash flows

_____ **g.** Stock price information and analysis

_____ **h.** Statement of shareholders' equity

_____ **i.** Management discussion and analysis of financial
performance

QS 13-2

Standard of comparison

C2

Identify which standard of comparison, (*a*) intracompany, (*b*) competitor, (*c*) industry, or (*d*) guidelines,
best describes each of the following examples.

_____ **1.** Compare **Ford**'s return on assets to **GM**'s return on assets.

_____ **2.** Compare a company's acid-test ratio to the 1:1 rule of thumb.

_____ **3.** Compare **Netflix**'s current-year sales to its prior-year sales.

_____ **4.** Compare **McDonald**'s profit margin to the fast-food industry profit margin.

QS 13-3

Horizontal analysis

P1

Compute the annual dollar changes and percent changes for each of the following accounts.

	Current Yr	Prior Yr
Short-term investments	$374,634	$234,000
Accounts receivable	97,364	101,000
Notes payable	0	88,000

QS 13-4

Trend percents

P1

Use the following information to determine the prior-year and current-year trend percents for net sales
using the prior year as the base year.

$ thousands	Current Yr	Prior Yr
Net sales	$801,810	$453,000
Cost of goods sold	392,887	134,088

QS 13-5

Common-size analysis   **P2**

Refer to the information in QS 13-4. Determine the prior-year and current-year common-size percents for
cost of goods sold using net sales as the base.

QS 13-6

Computing current ratio
and acid-test ratio   **P3**

Pritchett Co. reported the following year-end data: cash of $15,000; short-term investments of $5,000; accounts receivable (current) of $8,000; inventory of $20,000; prepaid (current) assets of $6,000; and total
current liabilities of $20,000. Compute the (*a*) current ratio and (*b*) acid-test ratio. Round to one decimal.

QS 13-7

Computing accounts
receivable turnover and
days' sales uncollected   **P3**

Mifflin Co. reported the following for the current year: net sales of $60,000; cost of goods sold of $38,000;
beginning balance in accounts receivable of $14,000; and ending balance in accounts receivable of $6,000.
Compute (*a*) accounts receivable turnover and (*b*) days' sales uncollected. Round to one decimal. *Hint:*
Recall that accounts receivable turnover uses average accounts receivable and days' sales uncollected uses
the ending balance in accounts receivable.

SCC Co. reported the following for the current year: net sales of $48,000; cost of goods sold of $40,000; beginning balance in inventory of $2,000; and ending balance in inventory of $8,000. Compute (*a*) inventory turnover and (*b*) days' sales in inventory. *Hint:* Recall that inventory turnover uses average inventory and days' sales in inventory uses the ending balance in inventory.

QS 13-8
Computing inventory turnover and days' sales in inventory **P3**

Dundee Co. reported the following for the current year: net sales of $80,000; cost of goods sold of $60,000; beginning balance of total assets of $115,000; and ending balance of total assets of $85,000. Compute total asset turnover. Round to one decimal.

QS 13-9
Computing total asset turnover **P3**

Paddy's Pub reported the following year-end data: income before interest expense and income tax expense of $30,000; cost of goods sold of $17,000; interest expense of $1,500; total assets of $70,000; total liabilities of $20,000; and total equity of $50,000. Compute the (*a*) debt-to-equity ratio and (*b*) times interest earned. Round to one decimal.

QS 13-10
Computing debt-to-equity ratio and times interest earned **P3**

Edison Co. reported the following for the current year: net sales of $80,000; cost of goods sold of $56,000; net income of $16,000; beginning balance of total assets of $60,000; and ending balance of total assets of $68,000. Compute (*a*) profit margin and (*b*) return on total assets.

QS 13-11
Computing profit margin and return on total assets **P3**

Franklin Co. reported the following year-end data: net income of $220,000; annual cash dividends per share of $3; market price per (common) share of $150; and earnings per share of $10. Compute the (*a*) price-earnings ratio and (*b*) dividend yield.

QS 13-12
Computing price-earnings ratio and dividend yield **P3**

For each ratio listed, identify whether the change in ratio value from the prior year to the current year is usually regarded as favorable or unfavorable.

QS 13-13
Ratio interpretation

P3

Ratio	Current Yr	Prior Yr	Ratio	Current Yr	Prior Yr
_____ 1. Profit margin......	9%	8%	_____ 5. Accounts receivable turnover.....	5.5	6.7
_____ 2. Debt ratio........	47%	42%	_____ 6. Basic earnings per share........	$1.25	$1.10
_____ 3. Gross margin	34%	46%	_____ 7. Inventory turnover.............	3.6	3.4
_____ 4. Acid-test ratio.....	1.00	1.15	_____ 8. Dividend yield	2.0%	1.2%

Morgan Company and Parker Company are similar firms operating in the same industry. Write a half-page report comparing Morgan and Parker using the available information. Your discussion should include their ability to meet current obligations and to use current assets efficiently.

QS 13-14
Analyzing short-term financial condition

A1

	Morgan			Parker		
	Current Yr	1 Yr Ago	2 Yrs Ago	Current Yr	1 Yr Ago	2 Yrs Ago
Current ratio	1.7	1.6	2.1	3.2	2.7	1.9
Acid-test ratio	1.0	1.1	1.2	2.8	2.5	1.6
Accounts receivable turnover	30.5	25.2	29.2	16.4	15.2	16.0
Merchandise inventory turnover	24.2	21.9	17.1	14.5	13.0	12.6
Working capital	$70,000	$58,000	$52,000	$131,000	$103,000	$78,000

Team Project: Assume that the two companies apply for a one-year loan from the team. Identify additional information the companies must provide before the team can make a loan decision.

Which of the following gains or losses would Organic Foods account for as unusual and/or infrequent?

a. A hurricane destroys rainwater tanks that result in a loss for Organic Foods.

b. The used vehicle market is weak and Organic Foods is forced to sell its used delivery truck at a loss.

c. Organic Foods owns an organic farm in Venezuela that is seized by the government. The company records a loss.

QS 13-15ᴬ
Identifying unusual and/or infrequent gains or losses

A2

connect

EXERCISES

Exercise 13-1

Building blocks of analysis

C1

Match the ratio to the building block of financial statement analysis to which it best relates.

A. Liquidity and efficiency **B.** Solvency **C.** Profitability **D.** Market prospects

_____ **1.** Equity ratio
_____ **2.** Return on total assets
_____ **3.** Dividend yield
_____ **4.** Book value per common share
_____ **5.** Days' sales in inventory

_____ **6.** Accounts receivable turnover
_____ **7.** Debt-to-equity ratio
_____ **8.** Times interest earned
_____ **9.** Gross margin ratio
_____ **10.** Acid-test ratio

Exercise 13-2

Identifying financial ratios

C2

Identify which of the following six metrics *a* through *f* best completes questions 1 through 3 below.

a. Days' sales uncollected
b. Accounts receivable turnover
c. Working capital

d. Return on total assets
e. Total asset turnover
f. Profit margin

1. Which two ratios are key components in measuring a company's operating efficiency? _____ _____ Which ratio summarizes these two components? _____

2. What measure reflects the difference between current assets and current liabilities? _____

3. Which two short-term liquidity ratios measure how frequently a company collects its accounts? _____ _____

Exercise 13-3

Computing and analyzing trend percents

P1

Compute trend percents for the following accounts using 2015 as the base year. For each of the three accounts, state whether the situation as revealed by the trend percents appears to be favorable or unfavorable.

	2019	2018	2017	2016	2015
Sales	$282,880	$270,800	$252,600	$234,560	$150,000
Cost of goods sold	128,200	122,080	115,280	106,440	67,000
Accounts receivable	18,100	17,300	16,400	15,200	9,000

Exercise 13-4

Computing and interpreting common-size percents

P2

Compute common-size percents for the following comparative income statements (round percents to one decimal). Using the common-size percents, which item is most responsible for the decline in net income?

GOMEZ CORPORATION		
Comparative Income Statements		
For Years Ended December 31	Current Yr	Prior Yr
Sales	$740,000	$625,000
Cost of goods sold	560,300	290,800
Gross profit	179,700	334,200
Operating expenses	128,200	218,500
Net income	$ 51,500	$115,700

Exercise 13-5

Determining income effects from common-size and trend percents

P1   P2

Common-size and trend percents for Roxi Company's sales, cost of goods sold, and expenses follow. Determine whether net income increased, decreased, or remained unchanged in this three-year period.

	Common-Size Percents			Trend Percents		
	Current Yr	1 Yr Ago	2 Yrs Ago	Current Yr	1 Yr Ago	2 Yrs Ago
Sales	100.0%	100.0%	100.0%	105.4%	104.2%	100.0%
Cost of goods sold	63.4	61.9	59.1	113.1	109.1	100.0
Total expenses	15.3	14.8	15.1	106.8	102.1	100.0

Exercise 13-6

Common-size percents

P2

Simon Company's year-end balance sheets follow. (1) Express the balance sheets in common-size percents. Round percents to one decimal. (2) Assuming annual sales have not changed in the last three years, is the change in accounts receivable as a percentage of total assets favorable or unfavorable? (3) Is the change in merchandise inventory as a percentage of total assets favorable or unfavorable?

At December 31	Current Yr	1 Yr Ago	2 Yrs Ago
Assets			
Cash.	$ 31,800	$ 35,625	$ 37,800
Accounts receivable, net	89,500	62,500	50,200
Merchandise inventory.	112,500	82,500	54,000
Prepaid expenses.	10,700	9,375	5,000
Plant assets, net	278,500	255,000	230,500
Total assets	$523,000	$445,000	$377,500
Liabilities and Equity			
Accounts payable	$129,900	$ 75,250	$ 51,250
Long-term notes payable secured by mortgages on plant assets	98,500	101,500	83,500
Common stock, $10 par value.	163,500	163,500	163,500
Retained earnings.	131,100	104,750	79,250
Total liabilities and equity.	$523,000	$445,000	$377,500

Refer to Simon Company's balance sheets in Exercise 13-6. (1) Compute the current ratio for each of the three years. Did the current ratio improve or worsen over the three-year period? (2) Compute the acid-test ratio for each of the three years. Did the acid-test ratio improve or worsen over the three-year period? Round ratios to two decimals.

Exercise 13-7
Analyzing liquidity
P3

Refer to the Simon Company information in Exercise 13-6. The company's income statements for the current year and one year ago follow. Assume that all sales are on credit and then compute (1) days' sales uncollected, (2) accounts receivable turnover, (3) inventory turnover, and (4) days' sales in inventory. For each ratio, determine if it improved or worsened in the current year. Round to one decimal.

Exercise 13-8
Analyzing and interpreting liquidity
P3

For Year Ended December 31		Current Yr		1 Yr Ago
Sales		$673,500		$532,000
Cost of goods sold	$411,225		$345,500	
Other operating expenses	209,550		134,980	
Interest expense.	12,100		13,300	
Income tax expense	9,525		8,845	
Total costs and expenses.		642,400		502,625
Net income		$ 31,100		$ 29,375
Earnings per share		$ 1.90		$ 1.80

Refer to the Simon Company information in Exercises 13-6 and 13-8. For both the current year and one year ago, compute the following ratios: (1) debt ratio and equity ratio—percent rounded to one decimal, (2) debt-to-equity ratio—rounded to two decimals; based on debt-to-equity ratio, does the company have more or less debt in the current year versus one year ago? and (3) times interest earned—rounded to one decimal. Based on times interest earned, is the company more or less risky for creditors in the current year versus one year ago?

Exercise 13-9
Analyzing risk and capital structure
P3

Refer to Simon Company's financial information in Exercises 13-6 and 13-8. For both the current year and one year ago, compute the following ratios: (1) profit margin ratio—percent rounded to one decimal; did profit margin improve or worsen in the current year versus one year ago? (2) total asset turnover—rounded to one decimal, and (3) return on total assets—percent rounded to one decimal. Based on return on total assets, did Simon's operating efficiency improve or worsen in the current year versus one year ago?

Exercise 13-10
Analyzing efficiency and profitability
P3

Refer to Simon Company's financial information in Exercises 13-6 and 13-8. Additional information about the company follows. For both the current year and one year ago, compute the following ratios: (1) return on common stockholders' equity—percent rounded to one decimal, (2) dividend yield—percent rounded to one decimal, and (3) price-earnings ratio on December 31—rounded to one decimal. Assuming Simon's competitor has a price-earnings ratio of 10, which company has higher market expectations for future growth?

Exercise 13-11
Analyzing profitability
P3

Common stock market price, December 31, current year.	$30.00	Annual cash dividends per share in current year	$0.29
Common stock market price, December 31, 1 year ago	28.00	Annual cash dividends per share 1 year ago.	0.24

Exercise 13-12
Computing current ratio and profit margin
P3

Nintendo Company, Ltd., recently reported the following financial information (amounts in millions). Compute Nintendo's current ratio and profit margin. Round to two decimals.

Current assets..........................	$ 9,036	Net sales..............................	$4,464
Total assets...........................	11,477	Net income............................	146
Current liabilities	871		

Exercise 13-13
Analyzing efficiency and profitability
P3

Following are data for BioBeans and GreenKale, which sell organic produce and are of similar size.
1. Compute the profit margin and the return on total assets for both companies.
2. Based on analysis of these two measures, which company is the preferred investment?

	BioBeans	GreenKale
Average total assets...........	$187,500	$150,000
Net sales	75,000	60,000
Net income	15,000	9,000

Exercise 13-14
Reconstructing an income statement with ratios
P3

Following is an incomplete current-year income statement.

Income Statement	
Net sales...	$ (a)
Cost of goods sold	(b)
Selling, general, and administrative expenses..........	7,000
Income tax expense..............................	2,000
Net income	(c)

Determine amounts *a, b,* and *c.* Additional information follows:
- Return on total assets is 16% (average total assets is $68,750).
- Inventory turnover is 5 (average inventory is $6,000).
- Accounts receivable turnover is 8 (average accounts receivable is $6,250).

Exercise 13-15
Analyzing efficiency and financial leverage
A1

Roak Company and Clay Company are similar firms that operate in the same industry. Clay began operations two years ago and Roak started five years ago. In the current year, both companies pay 6% interest on their debt to creditors. The following additional information is available.

	Roak Company			Clay Company		
	Current Yr	1 Yr Ago	2 Yrs Ago	Current Yr	1 Yr Ago	2 Yrs Ago
Total asset turnover	3.1	2.8	3.0	1.7	1.5	1.1
Return on total assets	7.4%	7.0%	6.9%	4.8%	4.5%	3.2%
Profit margin ratio	2.4%	2.5%	2.3%	2.8%	3.0%	2.9%
Sales	$410,000	$380,000	$396,000	$210,000	$170,000	$110,000

Write a half-page report comparing Roak and Clay using the available information. Your analysis should include their ability to use assets efficiently to produce profits. Comment on their success in employing financial leverage in the current year.

Exercise 13-16
Interpreting financial ratios
A1   P3

Refer to the information in Exercise 13-15.
1. Which company has the better (*a*) profit margin, (*b*) asset turnover, and (*c*) return on assets?
2. Which company has the better rate of growth in sales?
3. Did Roak successfully use financial leverage in the current year? Did Clay?

Exercise 13-17ᴬ
Income statement categories
A2

In the current year, Randa Merchandising, Inc., sold its interest in a chain of wholesale outlets, taking the company completely out of the wholesaling business. The company still operates its retail outlets. A listing of the major sections of an income statement follows.
A. Net sales less operating expense section
B. Other unusual and/or infrequent gains (losses)

C. Taxes reported on income (loss) from continuing operations

D. Income (loss) from operating a discontinued segment, or gain (loss) from its disposal

Indicate where each of the following income-related items for this company appears on its current-year income statement by writing the letter of the appropriate section in the blank beside each item.

Section	Item	Debit	Credit
_____	1. Net sales		$2,900,000
_____	2. Gain on state's condemnation of company property		230,000
_____	3. Cost of goods sold	$1,480,000	
_____	4. Income tax expense	217,000	
_____	5. Depreciation expense	232,000	
_____	6. Gain on sale of wholesale business segment, net of tax		775,000
_____	7. Loss from operating wholesale business segment, net of tax . . .	444,000	
_____	8. Loss of assets from meteor strike	640,000	

Use the financial data for Randa Merchandising, Inc., in Exercise 13-17ᴬ to prepare its December 31 year-end income statement. Ignore the earnings per share section.

Exercise 13-18ᴬ
Income statement presentation   A2

Mc Graw Hill Education connect

Selected comparative financial statements of Haroun Company follow.

PROBLEM SET A

Problem 13-1A
Calculating and analyzing trend percents

P1

HAROUN COMPANY Comparative Income Statements For Years Ended December 31							
$ thousands	2019	2018	2017	2016	2015	2014	2013
Sales	$1,694	$1,496	$1,370	$1,264	$1,186	$1,110	$928
Cost of goods sold	1,246	1,032	902	802	752	710	586
Gross profit	448	464	468	462	434	400	342
Operating expenses . . .	330	256	234	170	146	144	118
Net income	$ 118	$ 208	$ 234	$ 292	$ 288	$ 256	$224

HAROUN COMPANY Comparative Year-End Balance Sheets							
At December 31, $ thousands	2019	2018	2017	2016	2015	2014	2013
Assets							
Cash.	$ 58	$ 78	$ 82	$ 84	$ 88	$ 86	$ 89
Accounts receivable, net . . .	490	514	466	360	318	302	216
Merchandise inventory.	1,838	1,364	1,204	1,032	936	810	615
Other current assets.	36	32	14	34	28	28	9
Long-term investments.	0	0	0	146	146	146	146
Plant assets, net	2,020	2,014	1,752	944	978	860	725
Total assets	$4,442	$4,002	$3,518	$2,600	$2,494	$2,232	$1,800
Liabilities and Equity							
Current liabilities.	$1,220	$1,042	$ 718	$ 614	$ 546	$ 522	$ 282
Long-term liabilities	1,294	1,140	1,112	570	580	620	400
Common stock	1,000	1,000	1,000	850	850	650	650
Other paid-in capital.	250	250	250	170	170	150	150
Retained earnings.	678	570	438	396	348	290	318
Total liabilities and equity. . .	$4,442	$4,002	$3,518	$2,600	$2,494	$2,232	$1,800

Required

1. Compute trend percents for all components of both statements using 2013 as the base year. Round percents to one decimal.

Analysis Component

2. Refer to the results from part 1. (*a*) Did sales grow steadily over this period? (*b*) Did net income as a percent of sales grow over the past four years? (*c*) Did inventory increase over this period?

Problem 13-2A

Ratios, common-size statements, and trend percents

P1   P2   P3

Selected comparative financial statements of Korbin Company follow.

KORBIN COMPANY			
Comparative Income Statements			
For Years Ended December 31	2019	2018	2017
Sales	$555,000	$340,000	$278,000
Cost of goods sold	283,500	212,500	153,900
Gross profit	271,500	127,500	124,100
Selling expenses.	102,900	46,920	50,800
Administrative expenses	50,668	29,920	22,800
Total expenses	153,568	76,840	73,600
Income before taxes.	117,932	50,660	50,500
Income tax expense	40,800	10,370	15,670
Net income	$ 77,132	$ 40,290	$ 34,830

KORBIN COMPANY			
Comparative Balance Sheets			
At December 31	2019	2018	2017
Assets			
Current assets.	$ 52,390	$ 37,924	$ 51,748
Long-term investments.	0	500	3,950
Plant assets, net	100,000	96,000	60,000
Total assets	$152,390	$134,424	$115,698
Liabilities and Equity			
Current liabilities.	$ 22,800	$ 19,960	$ 20,300
Common stock	72,000	72,000	60,000
Other paid-in capital.	9,000	9,000	6,000
Retained earnings.	48,590	33,464	29,398
Total liabilities and equity. . . .	$152,390	$134,424	$115,698

Required

1. Compute each year's current ratio. Round ratios to one decimal.

2. Express the income statement data in common-size percents. Round percents to two decimals.

3. Express the balance sheet data in trend percents with 2017 as base year. Round percents to two decimals.

Analysis Component

4. Refer to the results from parts 1, 2, and 3. (*a*) Did cost of goods sold make up a greater portion of sales for the most recent year? (*b*) Did income as a percent of sales improve in the most recent year? (*c*) Did plant assets grow over this period?

Problem 13-3A

Transactions, working capital, and liquidity ratios

P3

Plum Corporation began the month of May with $700,000 of current assets, a current ratio of 2.50:1, and an acid-test ratio of 1.10:1. During the month, it completed the following transactions (the company uses a perpetual inventory system).

May	2	Purchased $50,000 of merchandise inventory on credit.
	8	Sold merchandise inventory that cost $55,000 for $110,000 cash.
	10	Collected $20,000 cash on an account receivable.
	15	Paid $22,000 cash to settle an account payable.
	17	Wrote off a $5,000 bad debt against the Allowance for Doubtful Accounts account.
	22	Declared a $1 per share cash dividend on its 50,000 shares of outstanding common stock.
	26	Paid the dividend declared on May 22.
	27	Borrowed $100,000 cash by giving the bank a 30-day, 10% note.
	28	Borrowed $80,000 cash by signing a long-term secured note.
	29	Used the $180,000 cash proceeds from the notes to buy new machinery.

Required

Prepare a table, similar to the following, showing Plum's (1) current ratio, (2) acid-test ratio, and (3) working capital after each transaction. Round ratios to two decimals.

	A	B	C	D	E	F	G
1	Transaction	Current Assets	Quick Assets	Current Liabilities	Current Ratio	Acid-Test Ratio	Working Capital
3	Beginning	$700,000	—	—	2.50	1.10	—

Selected current year-end financial statements of Cabot Corporation follow. All sales were on credit; selected balance sheet amounts at December 31 of the *prior year* were inventory, $48,900; total assets, $189,400; common stock, $90,000; and retained earnings, $33,748.

Problem 13-4A
Calculating financial statement ratios

P3

CABOT CORPORATION
Balance Sheet
December 31 of Current Year

Assets		Liabilities and Equity	
Cash.	$ 10,000	Accounts payable	$ 17,500
Short-term investments	8,400	Accrued wages payable	3,200
Accounts receivable, net	33,700	Income taxes payable	3,300
Merchandise inventory	32,150	Long-term note payable, secured	
Prepaid expenses	2,650	by mortgage on plant assets	63,400
Plant assets, net	153,300	Common stock	90,000
		Retained earnings	62,800
Total assets	$240,200	Total liabilities and equity	$240,200

CABOT CORPORATION
Income Statement
For Current Year Ended December 31

Sales	$448,600
Cost of goods sold	297,250
Gross profit	151,350
Operating expenses	98,600
Interest expense	4,100
Income before taxes	48,650
Income tax expense	19,598
Net income	$ 29,052

Required

Compute the following: (1) current ratio, (2) acid-test ratio, (3) days' sales uncollected, (4) inventory turnover, (5) days' sales in inventory, (6) debt-to-equity ratio, (7) times interest earned, (8) profit margin ratio, (9) total asset turnover, (10) return on total assets, and (11) return on common stockholders' equity. Round to one decimal place; for part 6, round to two decimals.

Check Acid-test ratio, 2.2 to 1; Inventory turnover, 7.3

Summary information from the financial statements of two companies competing in the same industry follows.

Problem 13-5A
Comparative ratio analysis

P3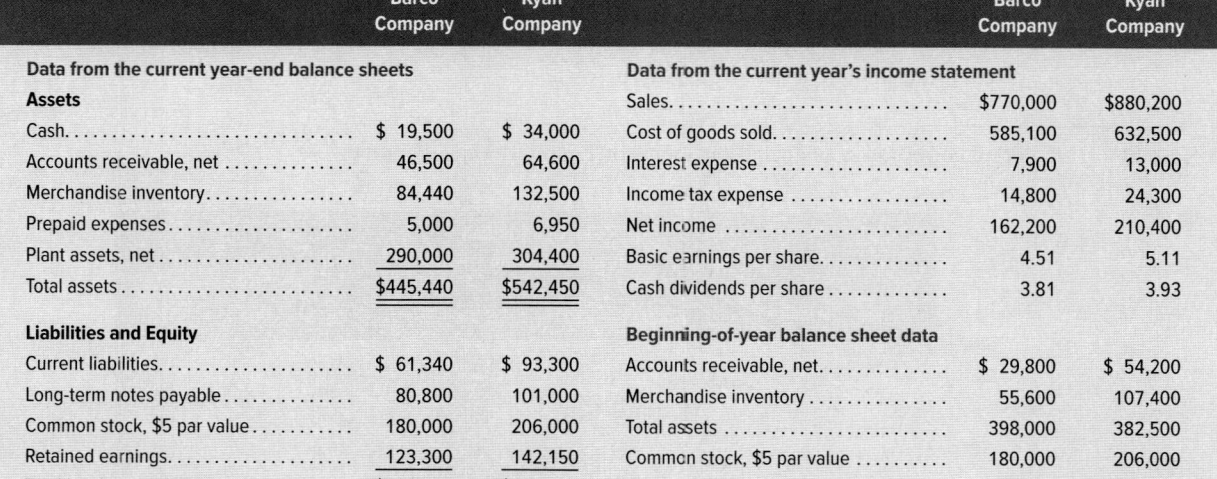

	Barco Company	Kyan Company		Barco Company	Kyan Company
Data from the current year-end balance sheets			**Data from the current year's income statement**		
Assets			Sales	$770,000	$880,200
Cash	$ 19,500	$ 34,000	Cost of goods sold	585,100	632,500
Accounts receivable, net	46,500	64,600	Interest expense	7,900	13,000
Merchandise inventory	84,440	132,500	Income tax expense	14,800	24,300
Prepaid expenses	5,000	6,950	Net income	162,200	210,400
Plant assets, net	290,000	304,400	Basic earnings per share	4.51	5.11
Total assets	$445,440	$542,450	Cash dividends per share	3.81	3.93
Liabilities and Equity			**Beginning-of-year balance sheet data**		
Current liabilities	$ 61,340	$ 93,300	Accounts receivable, net	$ 29,800	$ 54,200
Long-term notes payable	80,800	101,000	Merchandise inventory	55,600	107,400
Common stock, $5 par value	180,000	206,000	Total assets	398,000	382,500
Retained earnings	123,300	142,150	Common stock, $5 par value	180,000	206,000
Total liabilities and equity	$445,440	$542,450	Retained earnings	98,300	93,600

Required

1. For both companies compute the (*a*) current ratio, (*b*) acid-test ratio, (*c*) accounts receivable turnover, (*d*) inventory turnover, (*e*) days' sales in inventory, and (*f*) days' sales uncollected. Round to one decimal place. Identify the company you consider to be the better short-term credit risk and explain why.

2. For both companies compute the (*a*) profit margin ratio, (*b*) total asset turnover, (*c*) return on total assets, and (*d*) return on common stockholders' equity. Assuming that each company's stock can be purchased at $75 per share, compute their (*e*) price-earnings ratios and (*f*) dividend yields. Round to one decimal place. Identify which company's stock you would recommend as the better investment and explain why.

Problem 13-6A[A]
Income statement
computations and format

A2

Selected account balances from the adjusted trial balance for Olinda Corporation as of its calendar year-end December 31 follow.

	Debit	Credit
a. Interest revenue..		$ 14,000
b. Depreciation expense—Equipment..........................	$ 34,000	
c. Loss on sale of equipment................................	25,850	
d. Accounts payable...		44,000
e. Other operating expenses.................................	106,400	
f. Accumulated depreciation—Equipment.....................		71,600
g. Gain from settlement of lawsuit............................		44,000
h. Accumulated depreciation—Buildings		174,500
i. Loss from operating a discontinued segment (pretax)...........	18,250	
j. Gain on insurance recovery of tornado damage		20,000
k. Net sales..		998,000
l. Depreciation expense—Buildings...........................	52,000	
m. Correction of overstatement of prior year's sales (pretax)........	16,000	
n. Gain on sale of discontinued segment's assets (pretax)		34,000
o. Loss from settlement of lawsuit............................	23,250	
p. Income tax expense......................................	?	
q. Cost of goods sold	482,500	

Required

Answer each of the following questions by providing supporting computations.

1. Assume that the company's income tax rate is 30% for all items. Identify the tax effects and after-tax amounts of the three items labeled pretax.

2. Compute the amount of income from continuing operations before income taxes. What is the amount of the income tax expense? What is the amount of income from continuing operations?

3. What is the total amount of after-tax income (loss) associated with the discontinued segment?

4. What is the amount of net income for the year?

PROBLEM SET B

Selected comparative financial statements of Tripoly Company follow.

Problem 13-1B
Calculating and analyzing
trend percents

P1

TRIPOLY COMPANY Comparative Income Statements For Years Ended December 31							
$ thousands	2019	2018	2017	2016	2015	2014	2013
Sales	$560	$610	$630	$680	$740	$770	$860
Cost of goods sold	276	290	294	314	340	350	380
Gross profit	284	320	336	366	400	420	480
Operating expenses	84	104	112	126	140	144	150
Net income	$200	$216	$224	$240	$260	$276	$330

| TRIPOLY COMPANY | | | | | | | |
| Comparative Year-End Balance Sheets | | | | | | | |
At December 31, $ thousands	2019	2018	2017	2016	2015	2014	2013
Assets							
Cash........................	$ 44	$ 46	$ 52	$ 54	$ 60	$ 62	$ 68
Accounts receivable, net	130	136	140	144	150	154	160
Merchandise inventory........	166	172	178	180	186	190	208
Other current assets..........	34	34	36	38	38	40	40
Long-term investments........	36	30	26	110	110	110	110
Plant assets, net	510	514	520	412	420	428	454
Total assets.................	$920	$932	$952	$938	$964	$984	$1,040
Liabilities and Equity							
Current liabilities.............	$148	$156	$186	$190	$210	$260	$ 280
Long-term liabilities	92	120	142	148	194	214	260
Common stock	160	160	160	160	160	160	160
Other paid-in capital..........	70	70	70	70	70	70	70
Retained earnings............	450	426	394	370	330	280	270
Total liabilities and equity......	$920	$932	$952	$938	$964	$984	$1,040

Required

1. Compute trend percents for all components of both statements using 2013 as the base year. Round percents to one decimal.

Check (1) 2019, Total assets trend, 88.5%

Analysis Component

2. Analyze and comment on the financial statements and trend percents from part 1.

Selected comparative financial statement information of Bluegrass Corporation follows.

Problem 13-2B
Ratios, common-size statements, and trend percents

P1   P2   P3

| BLUEGRASS CORPORATION | | | |
| Comparative Year-End Balance Sheets | | | |
At December 31	2019	2018	2017
Assets			
Current assets.................	$ 54,860	$ 32,660	$ 36,300
Long-term investments..........	0	1,700	10,600
Plant assets, net	112,810	113,660	79,000
Total assets..................	$167,670	$148,020	$125,900
Liabilities and Equity			
Current liabilities..............	$ 22,370	$ 19,180	$ 16,500
Common stock	46,500	46,500	37,000
Other paid-in capital............	13,850	13,850	11,300
Retained earnings.............	84,950	68,490	61,100
Total liabilities and equity........	$167,670	$148,020	$125,900

| BLUEGRASS CORPORATION | | | |
| Comparative Income Statements | | | |
For Years Ended December 31	2019	2018	2017
Sales	$198,800	$166,000	$143,800
Cost of goods sold	108,890	86,175	66,200
Gross profit..................	89,910	79,825	77,600
Selling expenses.............	22,680	19,790	18,000
Administrative expenses	16,760	14,610	15,700
Total expenses	39,440	34,400	33,700
Income before taxes..........	50,470	45,425	43,900
Income tax expense	6,050	5,910	5,300
Net income	$ 44,420	$ 39,515	$ 38,600

Required

1. Compute each year's current ratio. Round ratios to one decimal.
2. Express the income statement data in common-size percents. Round percents to two decimals.
3. Express the balance sheet data in trend percents with 2017 as the base year. Round percents to two decimals.

Check (3) 2019, Total assets trend, 133.18%

Analysis Component

4. Comment on any significant relations revealed by the ratios and percents computed.

Problem 13-3B

Transactions, working capital, and liquidity ratios   **P3**

Check   June 3: Current ratio, 2.88; Acid-test ratio, 2.40

June 30: Working capital, $(10,000); Current ratio, 0.97

Koto Corporation began the month of June with $300,000 of current assets, a current ratio of 2.5:1, and an acid-test ratio of 1.4:1. During the month, it completed the following transactions (the company uses a perpetual inventory system).

June   1   Sold merchandise inventory that cost $75,000 for $120,000 cash.
       3   Collected $88,000 cash on an account receivable.
       5   Purchased $150,000 of merchandise inventory on credit.
       7   Borrowed $100,000 cash by giving the bank a 60-day, 10% note.
      10   Borrowed $120,000 cash by signing a long-term secured note.
      12   Purchased machinery for $275,000 cash.
      15   Declared a $1 per share cash dividend on its 80,000 shares of outstanding common stock.
      19   Wrote off a $5,000 bad debt against the Allowance for Doubtful Accounts account.
      22   Paid $12,000 cash to settle an account payable.
      30   Paid the dividend declared on June 15.

Required

Prepare a table, similar to the following, showing the company's (1) current ratio, (2) acid-test ratio, and (3) working capital after each transaction. Round ratios to two decimals.

	A	B	C	D	E	F	G
1		**Current**	**Quick**	**Current**	**Current**	**Acid-Test**	**Working**
2	**Transaction**	**Assets**	**Assets**	**Liabilities**	**Ratio**	**Ratio**	**Capital**
3	Beginning	$300,000	—	—	2.50	1.40	—

Problem 13-4B

Calculating financial statement ratios

P3

Selected current year-end financial statements of Overton Corporation follow. (All sales were on credit; selected balance sheet amounts at December 31 of the *prior year* were inventory, $17,400; total assets, $94,900; common stock, $35,500; and retained earnings, $18,800.)

OVERTON CORPORATION
Income Statement
For Current Year Ended December 31

Sales	$315,500
Cost of goods sold	236,100
Gross profit	79,400
Operating expenses	49,200
Interest expense	2,200
Income before taxes	28,000
Income tax expense	4,200
Net income	$ 23,800

OVERTON CORPORATION
Balance Sheet
December 31 of Current Year

Assets		Liabilities and Equity	
Cash.	$ 6,100	Accounts payable.	$ 11,500
Short-term investments	6,900	Accrued wages payable.	3,300
Accounts receivable, net . . .	15,100	Income taxes payable	2,600
Merchandise inventory.	13,500	Long-term note payable, secured	
Prepaid expenses.	2,000	by mortgage on plant assets. . . .	30,000
Plant assets, net	73,900	Common stock, $5 par value.	35,000
		Retained earnings	35,100
Total assets	$117,500	Total liabilities and equity	$117,500

Required

Check   Acid-test ratio, 1.6 to 1; Inventory turnover, 15.3

Compute the following: (1) current ratio, (2) acid-test ratio, (3) days' sales uncollected, (4) inventory turnover, (5) days' sales in inventory, (6) debt-to-equity ratio, (7) times interest earned, (8) profit margin ratio, (9) total asset turnover, (10) return on total assets, and (11) return on common stockholders' equity. Round to one decimal place; for part 6, round to two decimals.

Problem 13-5B

Comparative ratio analysis   **P3**

Summary information from the financial statements of two companies competing in the same industry follows.

	Fargo Company	Ball Company		Fargo Company	Ball Company
Data from the current year-end balance sheets			**Data from the current year's income statement**		
Assets			Sales..........................	$393,600	$667,500
Cash...............................	$ 20,000	$ 36,500	Cost of goods sold..................	290,600	480,000
Accounts receivable, net	88,700	79,500	Interest expense	5,900	12,300
Merchandise inventory................	86,800	82,000	Income tax expense	5,700	12,300
Prepaid expenses....................	9,700	10,100	Net income	33,850	61,700
Plant assets, net.....................	176,900	252,300	Basic earnings per share.............	1.27	2.19
Total assets........................	$382,100	$460,400			
Liabilities and Equity			**Beginning-of-year balance sheet data**		
Current liabilities....................	$ 90,500	$ 97,000	Accounts receivable, net.............	$ 72,200	$ 73,300
Long-term notes payable..............	93,000	93,300	Merchandise inventory	105,100	80,500
Common stock, $5 par value..........	133,000	141,000	Total assets	383,400	443,000
Retained earnings....................	65,600	129,100	Common stock, $5 par value	133,000	141,000
Total liabilities and equity.............	$382,100	$460,400	Retained earnings..................	49,100	109,700

Required

1. For both companies compute the (a) current ratio, (b) acid-test ratio, (c) accounts receivable turn-over, (d) inventory turnover, (e) days' sales in inventory, and (f) days' sales uncollected. Round to one decimal place. Identify the company you consider to be the better short-term credit risk and explain why.

2. For both companies compute the (a) profit margin ratio, (b) total asset turnover, (c) return on total assets, and (d) return on common stockholders' equity. Assuming that each company paid cash dividends of $1.50 per share and each company's stock can be purchased at $25 per share, compute their (e) price-earnings ratios and (f) dividend yields. Round to one decimal place; for part b, round to two decimals. Identify which company's stock you would recommend as the better investment and explain why.

Check (1) Fargo: Accounts receivable turnover, 4.9; Inventory turnover, 3.0

(2) Ball: Profit margin, 9.2%; PE, 11.4

Selected account balances from the adjusted trial balance for Harbor Corp. as of its calendar year-end December 31 follow.

Problem 13-6B[A]
Income statement computations and format

A2 ▮

	Debit	Credit
a. Accumulated depreciation—Buildings		$ 400,000
b. Interest revenue.......................................		20,000
c. Net sales...		2,640,000
d. Income tax expense.....................................	$?	
e. Loss on hurricane damage	48,000	
f. Accumulated depreciation—Equipment.......................		220,000
g. Other operating expenses..................................	328,000	
h. Depreciation expense—Equipment...........................	100,000	
i. Loss from settlement of lawsuit	36,000	
j. Gain from settlement of lawsuit		68,000
k. Loss on sale of equipment..................................	24,000	
l. Loss from operating a discontinued segment (pretax).............	120,000	
m. Depreciation expense—Buildings.............................	156,000	
n. Correction of overstatement of prior year's expense (pretax)........		48,000
o. Cost of goods sold.......................................	1,040,000	
p. Loss on sale of discontinued segment's assets (pretax)	180,000	
q. Accounts payable..		132,000

Required

Answer each of the following questions by providing supporting computations.

1. Assume that the company's income tax rate is 25% for all items. Identify the tax effects and after-tax amounts of the three items labeled pretax.

2. What is the amount of income from continuing operations before income taxes? What is the amount of income tax expense? What is the amount of income from continuing operations?

Check (3) $(225,000)

(4) $522,000

3. What is the total amount of after-tax income (loss) associated with the discontinued segment?

4. What is the amount of net income for the year?

SERIAL PROBLEM

Business Solutions

P3

©Alexander Image/Shutterstock

This serial problem began in Chapter 1 and continues through most of the book. If previous chapter segments were not completed, the serial problem can begin at this point.

SP 13   Use the following selected data from **Business Solutions**'s income statement for the three months ended March 31, 2020, and from its March 31, 2020, balance sheet to complete the requirements.

Computer services revenue.......	$25,307	Net income.........	$ 18,833	Current liabilities	$ 875
Net sales (of goods)	18,693	Quick assets........	90,924	Total liabilities	875
Total sales and revenue	44,000	Current assets	95,568	Total equity..........	119,393
Cost of goods sold	14,052	Total assets	120,268		

Required

1. Compute the gross margin ratio (both with and without services revenue) and net profit margin ratio (round the percent to one decimal).

2. Compute the current ratio and acid-test ratio (round to one decimal).

3. Compute the debt ratio and equity ratio (round the percent to one decimal).

4. What percent of its assets are current? What percent are long term? Round percents to one decimal.

Accounting Analysis

COMPANY ANALYSIS

A1 P1 P2

APPLE

AA 13-1   Use **Apple**'s financial statements in Appendix A to answer the following.

1. Using fiscal 2015 as the base year, compute trend percents for fiscal years 2015, 2016, and 2017 for net sales, cost of sales, operating income, other income (expense) net, provision for income taxes, and net income. Round percents to one decimal.

2. Compute common-size percents for fiscal years 2016 and 2017 for the following categories of assets: (*a*) total current assets; (*b*) property, plant and equipment, net; and (*c*) goodwill plus acquired intangible assets, net. Round percents to one decimal.

3. Using current assets as a percent of total assets to measure liquidity, did Apple's asset makeup become more liquid or less liquid in 2017?

COMPARATIVE ANALYSIS

C2 P2

APPLE

GOOGLE

AA 13-2   Key figures for **Apple** and **Google** follow.

$ millions	Apple	Google	$ millions	Apple	Google
Cash and equivalents.............	$20,289	$ 10,715	Cost of sales	$141,048	$ 45,583
Accounts receivable, net	17,874	18,336	Revenues.............	229,234	110,855
Inventories	4,855	749	Total assets	375,319	197,295
Retained earnings...............	98,330	113,247			

Required

1. Compute common-size percents for each of the companies using the data provided. Round percents to one decimal.

2. If Google decided to pay a dividend, would retained earnings as a percent of total assets increase or decrease?

3. Which company has a higher gross margin ratio on sales?

AA 13-3 Key figures for **Samsung** follow (in ₩ millions).

GLOBAL ANALYSIS
A1
Samsung

Cash and equivalents...........	₩ 30,545,130	Cost of sales....................	₩129,290,661
Accounts receivable, net	27,695,995	Revenues......................	239,575,376
Inventories	24,983,355	Total assets....................	301,752,090
Retained earnings.............	215,811,200		

Required

1. Compute common-size percents for Samsung using the data provided. Round percents to one decimal.

2. What is Samsung's gross margin ratio on sales?

3. Does Samsung's gross margin ratio outperform or underperform the industry (assumed) average of 25%?

Beyond the Numbers

BTN 13-1 As Beacon Company controller, you are responsible for informing the board of directors about its financial activities. At the board meeting, you present the following information.

ETHICS CHALLENGE
A1

	2019	2018	2017
Sales trend percent	147.0%	135.0%	100.0%
Selling expenses to sales.................	10.1%	14.0%	15.6%
Sales to plant assets ratio	3.8 to 1	3.6 to 1	3.3 to 1
Current ratio	2.9 to 1	2.7 to 1	2.4 to 1
Acid-test ratio	1.1 to 1	1.4 to 1	1.5 to 1
Inventory turnover	7.8 times	9.0 times	10.2 times
Accounts receivable turnover	7.0 times	7.7 times	8.5 times
Total asset turnover	2.9 times	2.9 times	3.3 times
Return on total assets...................	10.4%	11.0%	13.2%
Return on stockholders' equity	10.7%	11.5%	14.1%
Profit margin ratio......................	3.6%	3.8%	4.0%

After the meeting, the company's CEO holds a press conference with analysts in which she mentions the following ratios.

	2019	2018	2017
Sales trend percent	147.0%	135.0%	100.0%
Selling expenses to sales.................	10.1%	14.0%	15.6%
Sales to plant assets ratio	3.8 to 1	3.6 to 1	3.3 to 1
Current ratio	2.9 to 1	2.7 to 1	2.4 to 1

Required

1. Why do you think the CEO decided to report 4 ratios instead of the 11 prepared?

2. Comment on the possible consequences of the CEO's reporting of the ratios selected.

BTN 13-2 Each team is to select a different industry, and each team member is to select a different company in that industry and acquire its financial statements. Use those statements to analyze the company, including at least one ratio from each of the four building blocks of analysis. When necessary, use the financial press to determine the market price of its stock. Communicate with teammates via a meeting, e-mail, or telephone to discuss how different companies compare to each other and to industry norms. The team is to prepare a single one-page memorandum reporting on its analysis and the conclusions reached.

COMMUNICATING IN PRACTICE
A1   P3

TAKING IT TO THE NET

P3

BTN 13-3   Access the February 21, 2017, filing of the December 31, 2016, 10-K report of **The Hershey Company** (ticker: HSY) at <u>SEC.gov</u> and complete the following requirements.

Required

Compute or identify the following profitability ratios of Hershey for its years ending December 31, 2016, *and* December 31, 2015. Interpret its profitability using the results obtained for these two years.

1. Profit margin ratio (round the percent to one decimal).

2. Gross profit ratio (round the percent to one decimal).

3. Return on total assets (round the percent to one decimal). (Total assets at year-end 2014 were $5,622,870 in thousands.)

4. Return on common stockholders' equity (round the percent to one decimal). (Total shareholders' equity at year-end 2014 was $1,519,530 in thousands.)

5. Basic net income per common share (round to the nearest cent).

TEAMWORK IN ACTION

P1   P2   P3

BTN 13-4   A team approach to learning financial statement analysis is often useful.

Required

1. Each team should write a description of horizontal and vertical analysis that all team members agree with and understand. Illustrate each description with an example.

2. *Each* member of the team is to select *one* of the following categories of ratio analysis. Explain what the ratios in that category measure. Choose one ratio from the category selected, present its formula, and explain what it measures.

Hint: Pairing within teams may be necessary for part 2. Use as an in-class activity or as an assignment. Consider presentations to the entire class using team rotation with slides.

    a. Liquidity and efficiency   **c.** Profitability

    b. Solvency   **d.** Market prospects

3. Each team member is to present his or her notes from part 2 to teammates. Team members are to confirm or correct other teammates' presentations.

ENTREPRENEURIAL DECISION

A1   P1   P2   P3

BTN 13-5   Assume that Carla Harris of **Morgan Stanley** (<u>MorganStanley.com</u>) has impressed you with the company's success and its commitment to ethical behavior. You learn of a staff opening at Morgan Stanley and decide to apply for it. Your resume is successfully screened from those received and you advance to the interview process. You learn that the interview consists of analyzing the following financial facts and answering analysis questions below. (The data are taken from a small merchandiser in outdoor recreational equipment.)

	2019	2018	2017
Sales trend percents....................	137.0%	125.0%	100.0%
Selling expenses to sales..................	9.8%	13.7%	15.3%
Sales to plant assets ratio	3.5 to 1	3.3 to 1	3.0 to 1
Current ratio	2.6 to 1	2.4 to 1	2.1 to 1
Acid-test ratio	0.8 to 1	1.1 to 1	1.2 to 1
Merchandise inventory turnover	7.5 times	8.7 times	9.9 times
Accounts receivable turnover	6.7 times	7.4 times	8.2 times
Total asset turnover	2.6 times	2.6 times	3.0 times
Return on total assets.....................	8.8%	9.4%	11.1%
Return on equity.........................	9.75%	11.50%	12.25%
Profit margin ratio.......................	3.3%	3.5%	3.7%

Required

Use these data to answer each of the following questions with explanations.

1. Is it becoming easier for the company to meet its current liabilities on time and to take advantage of any available cash discounts? Explain.

2. Is the company collecting its accounts receivable more rapidly? Explain.

3. Is the company's investment in accounts receivable decreasing? Explain.

4. Is the company's investment in plant assets increasing? Explain.

5. Is the owner's investment becoming more profitable? Explain.

6. Did the dollar amount of selling expenses decrease during the three-year period? Explain.

BTN 13-6   You are to devise an investment strategy to enable you to accumulate $1,000,000 by age 65. Start by making some assumptions about your salary. Next, compute the percent of your salary that you will be able to save each year. If you will receive any lump-sum monies, include those amounts in your calculations. Historically, stocks have delivered average annual returns of around 10%. Given this history, you probably should not assume that you will earn above 10% on the money you invest. It is not necessary to specify exactly what types of assets you will buy for your investments; just assume a rate you expect to earn. Use the future value tables in Appendix B to calculate how your savings will grow. Experiment a bit with your figures to see how much less you have to save if you start at, for example, age 25 versus age 35 or 40. (For this assignment, do not include inflation in your calculations.)

HITTING THE ROAD

C1   P3

14 Managerial Accounting Concepts and Principles

Learning Objectives

CONCEPTUAL

C1 Explain the purpose and nature of, and the role of ethics in, managerial accounting.

C2 Describe accounting concepts useful in classifying costs.

C3 Define product and period costs and explain how they impact financial statements.

C4 Explain how balance sheets and income statements for manufacturing, merchandising, and service companies differ.

C5 Explain manufacturing activities and the flow of manufacturing costs.

C6 Describe trends in managerial accounting.

ANALYTICAL

A1 Assess raw materials inventory management using raw materials inventory turnover and days' sales in raw materials inventory.

PROCEDURAL

P1 Compute cost of goods sold for a manufacturer and for a merchandiser.

P2 Prepare a schedule of cost of goods manufactured and explain its purpose and links to financial statements.

It Grows on Trees

©MoringaConnect

BOSTON—On a college trip to Ghana, students Kwami Williams and Emily Cunningham were struck by the extreme poverty and subsistence farming amid such fertile land and tropical climate. However, one bountiful crop—the moringa tree—caught their eye. Locals call it the "miracle tree" because it grows and spreads so easily.

Moringa leaves are packed with nutrients, and oil from its seeds makes a silky skin moisturizer. Seizing the opportunity, Kwami and Emily started their business, **MoringaConnect** (**MoringaConnect.com**).

"Starting a business in Ghana is not easy," admits Emily. Government corruption and persistent power outages are some of the hurdles. "We had to build trust with local farmers." Now, over 2,000 Ghanaian farmers supply the company with raw materials for its two product lines: True Moringa beauty supplies sold in the United States and Minga Foods powder sold in Ghana.

Kwami and Emily point out that knowing basic managerial principles, cost classifications, and cost flows was crucial to setting up operations. "We manage the whole supply chain," explains Emily. "A good accounting system is needed to monitor costs and operations." Regarding income, Kwami says, "we've provided over $400,000 to farmers." The company also tracks nonfinancial measures like crop yield.

While the global market for moringa is growing, Kwami and Emily remain focused on Ghanaians, advising farmers, buying moringa seeds at a fair price, and employing locals in the company's processing center. Proclaims Emily, "Our purpose is to have an ethical business that improves living and working conditions!"

Sources: *MoringaConnect website,* January 2019; *beautyliestruth.com/blog/truemoringa; bondenavant.com/true-moringa-interview/; mywekustastes.com,* February 11, 2017; *bostonmagazine.com,* June 8, 2016

MANAGERIAL ACCOUNTING BASICS

Managerial accounting provides financial and nonfinancial information to an organization's managers. Managers include, for example, employees in charge of a company's divisions; the heads of marketing, information technology, and human resources; and top-level managers such as the chief executive officer (CEO) and chief financial officer (CFO). This section explains the purpose of managerial accounting (also called *management accounting*) and compares it with financial accounting.

Purpose of Managerial Accounting

The purpose of managerial accounting is to provide useful information to aid in three key managerial tasks.

C1_____
Explain the purpose and nature of, and the role of ethics in, managerial accounting.

- Determining the costs of an organization's products and services.
- Planning future activities.
- Comparing actual results to planned results.

For example, managerial accounting information can help the marketing manager decide whether to advertise on social media such as **Twitter**; it also can help **Google**'s information technology manager decide whether to buy new computers.

The managerial accounting system collects cost information and assigns it to an organization's products and services. Cost information is important for many decisions, such as product pricing, profitability analysis, and whether to make or buy a component. Much of managerial accounting involves gathering information about costs for planning and control decisions.

Planning is the process of setting goals and making plans to achieve them. Companies make long-term strategic plans that usually span a 5- to 10-year horizon. Short-term plans then translate the strategic plan into actions, which are more concrete and consist of better-defined goals. A short-term plan often covers a one-year period that, when translated into monetary terms, is known as a budget.

Point: Costs are important to managers because they impact both the financial position and profitability of a business. Managerial accounting assists in analysis, planning, and control of costs.

Point: Planning involves risk. **Enterprise risk management (ERM)** includes the systems and processes companies use to minimize risks such as data breaches, fraud, and loss of assets.

Control is the process of monitoring planning decisions and evaluating an organization's activities and employees. Feedback provided by the control function allows managers to revise their plans. Managers periodically compare actual results with planned results and take corrective actions to obtain better results. Exhibit 14.1 portrays the important management functions of planning and control and the types of questions they seek to answer.

EXHIBIT 14.1

Planning and Control (including monitoring and feedback)

Planning
- Build a new factory?
- Develop new products?
- Expand into new markets?

Monitoring

Feedback

Control
- Are costs too high?
- Are services profitable?
- Are customers satisfied?

Nature of Managerial Accounting

Managerial accounting differs from financial accounting. We list seven key differences in Exhibit 14.2.

EXHIBIT 14.2

Key Differences between Managerial Accounting and Financial Accounting

"This company's outlook is good. I'll buy its stock."

"This department is doing well. We'll expand its product line."

	Financial Accounting	Managerial Accounting
1. Users and decision makers	External: Investors, creditors, and others outside of the organization's managers	Internal: Managers, employees, and decision makers inside the organization
2. Purpose of information	Help external users make investment, credit, and other decisions	Help managers make planning and control decisions
3. Flexibility of reporting	Structured and often controlled by GAAP	Relatively flexible (no GAAP constraints)
4. Timeliness of information	Often available only after an audit	Available quickly without an audit
5. Time dimension	The past; historical information with some predictions	The future; many projections and estimates, with some historical information
6. Focus of information	The whole organization	An organization's projects, processes, and divisions
7. Nature of information	Monetary information	Mostly monetary; some nonmonetary

Users and Decision Makers Companies report to different groups of decision makers. Financial accounting information is provided primarily to external users including investors, creditors, and regulators. External users do not manage a company's daily activities. Managerial accounting information is provided primarily to internal managers and employees who make and implement decisions about a company's business activities.

Purpose of Information External users of financial accounting information often must decide whether to invest in or lend to a company. Internal decision makers must plan a company's future to take advantage of opportunities or to overcome obstacles. They also try to control activities.

Point: It is desirable to accumulate some information for management reports in a database separate from financial accounting records.

Flexibility of Reporting An extensive set of rules, or GAAP, aims to protect external users from false or misleading information in financial reports. Managers are responsible for preventing and detecting fraudulent activities in their companies, including their financial reports. Managerial accounting does not rely on extensive rules. Instead, companies determine what information they need to make planning and control decisions, and then they decide how that information is best collected and reported.

Timeliness of Information Independent auditors often must *audit* a company's financial statements before providing them to external users. As audits take time to complete, financial reports to outsiders usually are not available until well after the period-end. However, managers can quickly obtain managerial accounting information. External auditors need not review it. Estimates and projections are acceptable. To get information quickly, managers often accept less precision in reports. For example, an early internal report to management could estimate net income for the year between $4.2 and $4.5 million. An audited income statement could later show net income for the year at $4.4 million. The internal report is not precise, but its information can be more useful because it is available earlier.

Point: *Internal auditing* in managerial accounting evaluates information reliability not only inside but outside the company.

Time Dimension   External financial reports deal primarily with results of past activities and current conditions. While some predictions such as service lives and salvage values of plant assets are necessary, financial accounting avoids predictions whenever possible. Managerial accounting regularly includes predictions. One important managerial accounting report is a *budget,* which predicts revenues, expenses, and other items. Making predictions, and evaluating those predictions, are important skills for managers.

EXHIBIT 14.3

Focus of External and Internal Reports

Focus of Information   Companies often organize into divisions and departments, but external investors own shares in or make loans to the entire company. Financial accounting focuses primarily on a company as a whole, as shown in the top part of Exhibit 14.3.

The focus of managerial accounting is different. While the CEO manages the whole company, most other managers are responsible for much smaller sets of activities. These lower-level managers need reports on their specific activities. This information includes the level of success achieved by each individual, product, or department in each division of the whole company, as shown in the bottom part of Exhibit 14.3.

Reports to external users focus on the company as a whole.

Reports to internal users focus on company units and divisions.

Nature of Information   Both financial and managerial accounting systems report monetary information. Managerial accounting systems also report considerable *nonmonetary* information. Common examples of nonmonetary information include customer and employee satisfaction data, percentage of on-time deliveries, product defect rates, energy from renewable sources, and employee diversity.

Fraud and Ethics in Managerial Accounting

Fraud, and the role of ethics in reducing fraud, are important factors in running business operations. Fraud involves the use of one's job for personal gain through the deliberate misuse of the employer's assets. Examples include theft of the employer's cash or other assets, overstating reimbursable expenses, payroll schemes, and financial statement fraud. Three factors must exist for a person to commit fraud: opportunity, financial pressure, and rationalization. This is known as the *fraud triangle.* Fraud affects all business and it is costly: The 2016 *Report to the Nations* from the Association of Certified Fraud Examiners (ACFE) estimates the average U.S. business loses 5% of its annual revenues to fraud.

The most common type of fraud, where employees steal or misuse the employer's resources, results in an average loss of $130,000 per occurrence. For example, in a billing fraud, an employee sets up a bogus supplier. The employee then prepares bills from the supplier and pays these bills from the employer's checking account. The employee cashes the checks sent to the bogus supplier and uses them for his or her own personal benefit. An organization's best chance to minimize fraud is through reducing opportunities for employees to commit fraud.

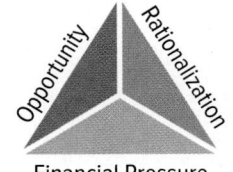

Implications of Fraud for Managerial Accounting   Fraud increases a business's costs and hurts information reliability. Left undetected, inaccurate costs can result in poor pricing decisions, an improper product mix, and faulty performance evaluations. All of these can lead to poor results for the company. Managers rely on a reliable **internal control system** to monitor and control business activities. An internal control system is the policies and procedures managers use to

- Ensure reliable accounting.
- Protect assets.
- Uphold company policies.
- Promote efficient operations.

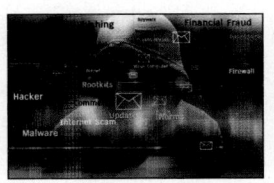

©Joe Prachatree/Shutterstock

Combating fraud requires ethics in accounting. **Ethics** are beliefs that distinguish right from wrong. They are accepted standards of good and bad behavior. Identifying the ethical path can be difficult. The **Institute of Management Accountants (IMA),** the professional association for management accountants, has issued a code of ethics to help accountants solve ethical dilemmas.

Point: The IMA issues the Certified Management Accountant (CMA) and the Certified Financial Manager (CFM) certifications.

Point: The Sarbanes-Oxley Act requires each issuer of securities to disclose whether it has adopted a code of ethics for its senior officers and the content of that code.

The IMA's Statement of Ethical Professional Practice requires that management accountants be competent, maintain confidentiality, act with integrity, and communicate information in a fair and credible manner.

The IMA provides a "road map" for resolving ethical conflicts. It suggests that an employee follow the company's policies on how to resolve such conflicts. If the conflict remains unresolved, an employee should contact the next level of management (such as the immediate supervisor) who is not involved in the ethical conflict.

◼ Decision Ethics

Production Manager   Three friends go to a restaurant. David, a self-employed entrepreneur, says, "I'll pay and deduct it as a business expense." Denise, a salesperson, takes the check and says, "I'll put this on my company's credit card. It won't cost us anything." Derek, a factory manager, says, "I'll use my company's credit card and call it overhead on a cost-plus contract with a client." (*A cost-plus contract means the company receives its costs plus a percent of those costs.*) "That way, my company pays for dinner *and* makes a profit." Who should pay? ◼   *Answer:* All three friends want to pay the bill with someone else's money. To prevent such practices, companies have internal controls. Some entertainment expenses are justifiable and even encouraged. For example, the tax law allows certain deductions for entertainment having a business purpose. Corporate policies sometimes allow and encourage reimbursable spending for social activities, and contracts can include entertainment as allowable costs. Nevertheless, without further details, this bill should be paid from personal accounts.

Career Paths

Managerial accountants are highly regarded and in high demand. Managerial accountants must have strong communication skills, understand how businesses work, and be team players. They must be able to analyze information and think critically, and they are often considered to be important business advisors. Exhibit 14.4 shows estimated annual salaries from recent surveys. Salary variation depends on management level, company size, geographic location, professional designation, experience, and other factors.

EXHIBIT 14.4

Average Annual Salaries for Selected Management Levels

Top-Level Managers	Annual Salary		Senior-Level Managers	Annual Salary		Mid- and Entry-Level Jobs	Annual Salary
Chief financial officer (CFO)	$290,000		Division controller	$130,000		Financial analyst	$85,000
Controller/Treasurer	180,000		General manager	105,000		Senior accountant	85,000
						Staff accountant	60,000

Managerial accounting information is used in many careers.

- **Marketing** staff need sales and cost data to decide which products to promote.
- **Management** needs sales force details to evaluate performance.
- **Entrepreneurs** use costs, budgets, and financial statements to succeed.
- **Nonbusiness majors,** including engineers, health care professionals, and others, increasingly use accounting information as their careers advance.

Point: Employees with the Certified Management Accountant (CMA) or Certified Financial Manager (CFM) certifications typically earn higher salaries than those without.

 **14-1**

Managerial Accounting Basics

C1

Do More: QS 14-1, E 14-1

Following are aspects of accounting information. Classify each as pertaining more to financial accounting or to managerial accounting.

1. Primary users are external
2. Includes more nonmonetary information
3. Focuses more on the future
4. Uses many estimates and projections

5. Controlled by GAAP
6. Used in managers' planning decisions
7. Focuses on the whole organization
8. Not constrained by GAAP

Solution

	Financial	Managerial			Financial	Managerial
1. Primary users are external	X			5. Controlled by GAAP	X	
2. Includes more nonmonetary information		X		6. Used in managers' planning decisions		X
3. Focuses more on the future		X		7. Focuses on the whole organization	X	
4. Uses many estimates and projections		X		8. Not constrained by GAAP		X

MANAGERIAL COST CONCEPTS

Because managers use costs for many different purposes, organizations classify costs in different ways. This section explains three common ways to classify costs and links them to managerial decisions. We illustrate these cost classifications with Rocky Mountain Bikes, a manufacturer of bicycles.

C2

Describe accounting concepts useful in classifying costs.

Types of Cost Classifications

Fixed versus Variable A cost can be classified by how it changes, in total, with changes in the volume of activity.

- **Fixed costs** do not change with changes in the volume of activity (within a range of activity known as an activity's *relevant range*). For example, straight-line depreciation on equipment is a fixed cost.
- **Variable costs** change in proportion to changes in the volume of activity. Sales commissions computed as a percent of sales revenue are variable costs.

Additional examples of fixed and variable costs for a bike manufacturer are provided in Exhibit 14.5. Classifying costs as fixed or variable helps in cost-volume-profit analyses and short-term decision making.

Fixed Cost: Rent for Rocky Mountain Bikes's building is $22,000. It doesn't change with the number of bikes produced.

Variable Cost: Cost of bicycle tires increases by $15 for each bike produced.

EXHIBIT 14.5

Fixed and Variable Costs (in total)

Direct versus Indirect A cost is often traced to a **cost object,** which is a product, process, department, or customer to which costs are assigned.

- **Direct costs** are traceable to a single cost object.
- **Indirect costs** cannot be easily and cost-beneficially traced to a single cost object.

Assuming the cost object is a bicycle, Rocky Mountain Bikes will identify the costs that can be directly traced to bicycles. The direct costs traceable to a bicycle include direct material and direct labor costs used in its production.

What are indirect costs associated with bicycles? One example is the salary of the supervisor. She monitors the production process and other factory activities, but she does not actually make bikes. Thus, her salary cannot be directly traced to bikes. Another example is a maintenance department that provides services to many departments. If the cost object is the bicycle, the wages of the maintenance department employees who clean the factory area are indirect costs. Exhibit 14.6 lists more examples of direct and indirect costs when the cost object is a bicycle.

EXHIBIT 14.6

Direct and Indirect Costs for a Bicycle

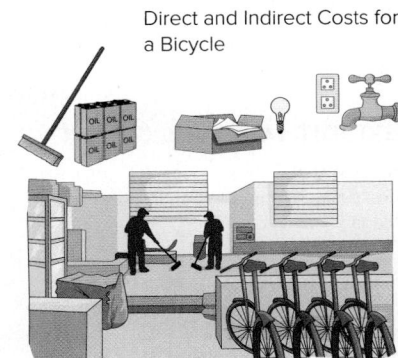

Direct Costs (for bicycle)		Indirect Costs (for bicycle)	
• Tires	• Frames	• Factory accounting	• Factory light and heat
• Seats	• Chains	• Factory administration	• Factory intranet
• Handlebars	• Brakes	• Factory rent	• Insurance on factory
• Cables	• Pedals	• Factory manager's salary	• Factory equipment depreciation*
• Bike maker wages	• Bike maker benefits		

*For all depreciation methods other than units-of-production.

■ Decision Maker

Entrepreneur   You wish to trace as many of your assembly department's direct costs as possible. You can trace 90% of them in an economical manner. To trace the other 10%, you need sophisticated and costly accounting software. Do you buy this software? ■   *Answer:* Tracing all costs directly to cost objects is desirable if it can be economically done. In this case, you can trace 90% of the assembly department's direct costs. It may not be economical to spend more money on new software to trace the final 10% of costs. You need to make a cost-benefit trade-off. If the software offers benefits beyond tracing the remaining 10% of the assembly department's costs, your decision should consider this.

C3 _____

Define product and period costs and explain how they impact financial statements.

Balance sheet → Income stmt.

Income statement

Point: Product costs are either in the income statement as part of cost of goods sold or in the balance sheet as inventory. Period costs appear only on the income statement as operating expenses.

Product versus Period Costs

- **Product costs** are those costs necessary to create a product and consist of: direct materials, direct labor, and factory overhead. Overhead refers to production costs other than direct materials and direct labor. Product costs are capitalized as inventory during and after completion of products; they become cost of goods sold when those products are sold.

- **Period costs** are nonproduction costs and are usually associated more with activities linked to a time period than with completed products. Common examples include salaries of the sales staff, wages of maintenance workers, advertising expenses, and depreciation on office furniture and equipment. Period costs are expensed in the period when incurred either as selling expenses or as general and administrative expenses.

Exhibit 14.7 shows the different effects of product and period costs. Period costs flow directly to the current income statement as expenses. They are not reported as assets. Product costs are first assigned to inventory. Their final treatment depends on when inventory is sold or disposed of. Product costs assigned to finished goods that are sold in year 2019 are reported on the 2019 income statement as cost of goods sold. Product costs assigned to unsold inventory are carried forward on the balance sheet at the end of year 2019. If this inventory is sold in year 2020, product costs assigned to it are reported as cost of goods sold in that year's income statement.

EXHIBIT 14.7

Period and Product Costs in Financial Statements

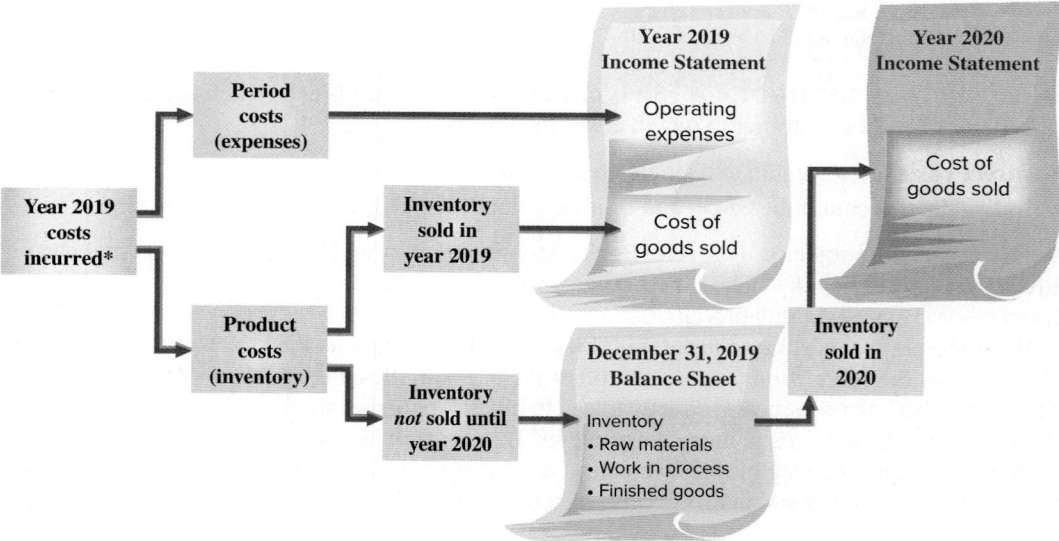

*This diagram excludes costs to acquire assets other than inventory.

Exhibit 14.8 summarizes typical managerial decisions for common cost classifications.

EXHIBIT 14.8

Summary of Cost Classifications and Example Managerial Decisions

Costs Classified As	Example Managerial Decision
Variable or Fixed............	How many units must we sell to break even? What will profit be if we lower selling price? Should we add a new line of business?
Direct or Indirect............	How well did our departments perform?
Product or Period	What is the cost of our inventory? Are selling expenses too high?

Point: Later chapters discuss more ways to classify costs.

Cost Item	Fixed or Variable	Direct or Indirect	Product or Period
Bicycle tires and wheels......................	Variable	Direct	Product
Wages of assembly worker*...................	Variable	Direct	Product
Advertising	Fixed	Indirect	Period
Production manager's salary	Fixed	Indirect	Product
Office depreciation.........................	Fixed	Indirect	Period
Factory depreciation (straight-line)	Fixed	Indirect	Product
Oil and grease applied to gears/chains†	Variable	Indirect	Product
Sales commissions	Variable	Indirect	Period

*In some cases wages can be classified as fixed costs. For example, union contracts might limit an employer's ability to adjust its labor force in response to changes in demand. In this book, unless told otherwise, assume that factory wages are variable costs.
†Oil and grease are indirect costs as it is not practical to track how much of each is applied to each bike.

EXHIBIT 14.9

Examples of Multiple Cost Classifications

Identification of Cost Classifications

Costs can be classified using any one (or combination) of the three different ways described here. Understanding how to classify costs in several different ways enables managers to use cost information for a variety of decisions. Factory rent, for instance, is classified as a *product* cost; it also is *fixed* with respect to the number of units produced, and it is *indirect* with respect to the product. Potential multiple classifications are shown in Exhibit 14.9 when the finished bike is the cost object.

Cost Concepts for Service Companies

Cost concepts also apply to service organizations. For example, consider **Southwest Airlines**, and assume the cost object is a flight. The airline's cost of beverages for passengers is a variable cost based on number of flights. The monthly cost of leasing an aircraft is fixed with respect to number of flights. We can trace a flight crew's salary to a specific flight, whereas we likely cannot trace wages for the ground crew to a specific flight. Classification as product versus period costs is not relevant to service companies because services are not inventoried. Instead, costs incurred by a service firm are expensed in the reporting period when incurred.

Managers in service companies must understand and apply cost concepts. For example, an airline manager must often decide between canceling or rerouting flights. The manager must be able to estimate costs saved by canceling a flight versus rerouting. Knowledge of fixed costs is equally important. We explain more about the cost requirements for these and other managerial decisions throughout this book.

©Justin Sullivan/Getty Images

Service Costs
• Beverages and snacks
• Pilot and copilot salaries
• Attendant salaries
• Fuel and oil costs
• Travel agent fees
• Ground crew salaries

Following are selected costs of a company that manufactures computer chips. Classify each as either a product cost or a period cost. Then classify each of the product costs as direct material, direct labor, or overhead.

1. Plastic boards used to mount chips

2. Advertising costs

3. Factory maintenance workers' salaries

4. Real estate taxes paid on the sales office

5. Real estate taxes paid on the factory

6. Factory supervisor salary

7. Depreciation on factory equipment

8. Assembly worker hourly pay to make chips

NEED-TO-KNOW 14-2

Cost Classification

C2   C3

▶

Solution

	Product Costs			Period Cost
	Direct Material	Direct Labor	Overhead	
1. Plastic boards used to mount chips	X			
2. Advertising costs.........................				X
3. Factory maintenance workers' salaries.......			X	
4. Real estate taxes paid on the sales office				X
5. Real estate taxes paid on the factory.........			X	
6. Factory supervisor salary			X	
7. Depreciation on factory equipment			X	
8. Assembly worker hourly pay to make chips ...		X		

Do More: QS 14-4, QS 14-5, E 14-5

MANAGERIAL REPORTING

Companies with manufacturing activities differ from both merchandising and service companies. The main difference between merchandising and manufacturing companies is that merchandisers buy goods ready for sale while manufacturers produce goods from materials, labor, and equipment.

- **Amazon** is a merchandiser. It buys and sells goods without physically changing them.
- **Adidas** is a manufacturer of shoes, apparel, and accessories. It purchases materials such as leather, cloth, dye, plastic, rubber, glue, and laces and then converts these materials to products.
- **Southwest Airlines** is a service company that transports people and items.
- **Best Buy** is a merchandiser that also provides services via its Geek Squad, showing that some companies pursue multiple activities.

Manufacturing companies like **Dell**, **PepsiCo**, and **Intel** separate their costs into manufacturing and nonmanufacturing costs. We discuss this next.

Typical Manufacturing Costs

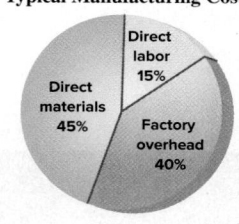

Manufacturing Costs

Direct Materials
Direct materials are tangible components of a finished product. **Direct materials costs** are the expenditures for direct materials that are separately and readily traced through the manufacturing process to finished goods. Examples of direct materials in manufacturing a mountain bike include its tires, seat, frame, pedals, brakes, cables, gears, and handlebars.

Direct Labor
Direct labor refers to employees who physically convert materials to finished product. **Direct labor costs** are the wages and benefits for direct labor that are separately and readily traced through the manufacturing process to finished goods. Examples of direct labor in manufacturing a mountain bike include operators directly involved in converting raw materials into finished products (welding, painting, forming) and assembly workers who attach materials such as tires, seats, pedals, and brakes.

Direct materials
+ Direct labor
+ Overhead
= Total mfg. costs

Factory Overhead
Factory overhead, also called *manufacturing overhead,* consists of all manufacturing costs that are not direct materials or direct labor. **Factory overhead costs** are not separately or readily traced to finished goods. Factory overhead costs are indirect costs that include indirect materials, indirect labor, and other indirect costs not directly traceable to the product.

Point: When overhead costs vary with production, they are called *variable overhead.* When overhead costs don't vary with production, they are called *fixed overhead.*

- **Indirect materials** are components used in manufacturing the product, but they are *not* clearly identified with specific product units. Direct materials are often classified as indirect materials when their costs are low. Examples include screws and nuts used in assembling mountain bikes, and staples and glue used in manufacturing shoes. Applying the *materiality principle,* it is not cost-beneficial to trace costs of each of these materials to individual products.
- **Indirect labor** are workers who assist or supervise in manufacturing the product, but they are *not* clearly identified with specific product units. **Indirect labor costs** refer to the costs of workers who assist in or supervise manufacturing. Examples include costs for employees who maintain and repair manufacturing equipment and salaries of production supervisors. Those workers do not assemble products, though they are indirectly related to production. Overtime premiums paid to direct laborers are also included in overhead because overtime is due to delays, interruptions, or constraints not necessarily identifiable to a specific product or batches of product.
- Indirect other costs include factory utilities (water, gas, electricity), factory rent, depreciation on factory buildings and equipment, factory insurance, property taxes on factory buildings and equipment, and factory accounting and legal services.

Nonmanufacturing Costs

Selling expenses
+ Administrative expenses
= Total nonmfg. costs

Factory overhead does *not* include selling and administrative expenses because they are not incurred in manufacturing products. These expenses are *period costs,* and they are recorded as expenses on the income statement when incurred. For a manufacturing company, such costs are also called *nonmanufacturing costs*. Examples of nonmanufacturing costs follow.

Selling Expenses
- Advertising costs
- Delivery costs
- Salesperson salaries
- Salesperson commissions
- Salesperson travel costs
- Salesperson smartphone costs

Administrative Expenses
- Office accounting
- Office employee wages
- Office rent
- Office equipment depreciation
- Office insurance
- Office manager's salary

EXHIBIT 14.10

Prime and Conversion Costs and Their Makeup

Prime costs =
Direct materials + Direct labor.

Conversion costs =
Direct labor + Factory overhead.

Prime and Conversion Costs

We can classify product costs into prime or conversion costs as in Exhibit 14.10. Direct materials costs and direct labor costs are **prime costs**—costs directly associated with the manufacture of finished goods. Direct labor costs and overhead costs are **conversion costs**—costs incurred in the process of converting raw materials to finished goods. Direct labor costs are considered *both* prime costs and conversion costs.

Costs and the Balance Sheet

Manufacturers have three inventories instead of the single inventory that merchandisers carry. The three inventories are raw materials, work in process, and finished goods.

C4 _____

Explain how balance sheets and income statements for manufacturing, merchandising, and service companies differ.

Raw Materials Inventory   **Raw materials inventory** is the goods a company acquires to use in making products. Companies use raw materials in two ways: directly and indirectly. Raw materials that are possible and practical to trace to a product are called *direct materials;* they are included in raw materials inventory. Raw materials that are either impossible or impractical to trace to a product are classified as indirect materials (such as solder used for welding); they often come from factory supplies or raw materials inventory.

Work in Process Inventory   **Work in process inventory,** also called *goods in process inventory,* consists of products in the process of being manufactured but not yet complete. The amount of work in process inventory depends on the type of production process. Work in process inventory is less for a computer maker such as **Dell** than for an airplane maker such as **Boeing**.

Finished Goods Inventory   **Finished goods inventory** consists of completed products ready for sale. It is similar to merchandise inventory owned by a merchandising company.

Balance Sheets for Manufacturers, Merchandisers, and Servicers   The current assets section of the balance sheet is different for merchandising and service companies as compared to manufacturing companies. A merchandiser reports only merchandise inventory rather than the three types of inventory reported by a manufacturer. A service company's balance sheet does not have any inventory held for sale. Exhibit 14.11 shows the current assets section of the balance sheet for a manufacturer, a merchandiser, and a service company. The manufacturer, Rocky Mountain Bikes, shows three different inventories. The merchandiser, Tele-Mart, shows one inventory, and the service provider, Northeast Air, shows no inventory.

Point: This chapter accounts for indirect materials in Factory Supplies.

Manufacturers often own unique plant assets such as small tools, factory buildings, factory equipment, and patents to manufacture products. Merchandisers and service providers also own plant assets, including buildings, delivery vehicles, and airplanes.

Costs and the Income Statement

The main difference between the income statement of a manufacturer and that of a merchandiser involves the items making up cost of goods sold. In this section, we look at how manufacturers and merchandisers determine and report cost of goods sold.

P1 _____

Compute cost of goods sold for a manufacturer and for a merchandiser.

NORTHEAST AIR (Service Provider) Balance Sheet (partial) December 31, 2019	
Assets	
Current assets	
Cash	$11,000
Accounts receivable, net	30,150
Supplies	350
Prepaid insurance	300
Total current assets	$41,800

TELE-MART (Merchandiser) Balance Sheet (partial) December 31, 2019	
Assets	
Current assets	
Cash	$11,000
Accounts receivable, net	30,150
Merchandise inventory	21,000
Supplies	350
Prepaid insurance	300
Total current assets	$62,800

ROCKY MOUNTAIN BIKES Balance Sheet (partial) December 31, 2019	
Assets	
Current assets	
Cash	$11,000
Accounts receivable, net	30,150
Raw materials inventory	9,000
Work in process inventory	7,500
Finished goods inventory	10,300
Factory supplies	350
Prepaid insurance	300
Total current assets	$68,600

EXHIBIT 14.11

Balance Sheets for Manufacturer, Merchandiser, and Service Provider

Cost of Goods Sold

Exhibit 14.12 compares the components of cost of goods sold for a merchandiser with those for a manufacturer.

- *Merchandisers* add cost of goods purchased to beginning merchandise inventory and then subtract ending merchandise inventory to compute cost of goods sold.
- *Manufacturers* add cost of goods manufactured to beginning finished goods inventory and then subtract ending finished goods inventory to compute cost of goods sold.

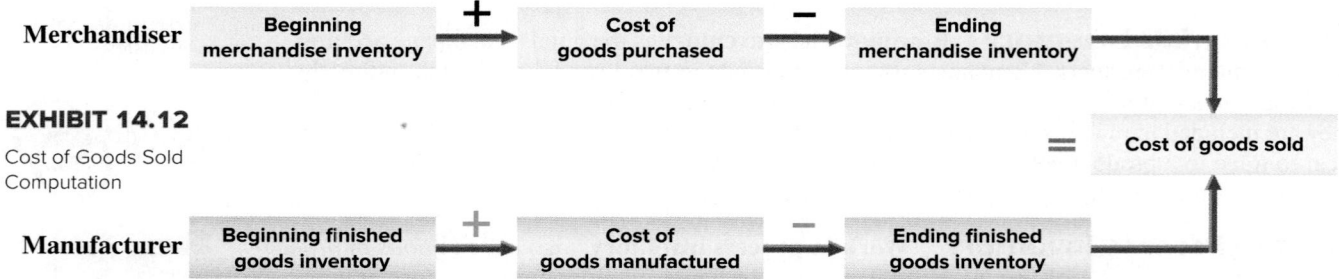

EXHIBIT 14.12

Cost of Goods Sold Computation

In computing cost of goods sold, a merchandiser uses *merchandise* inventory, whereas a manufacturer uses *finished goods* inventory. A manufacturer's inventories of raw materials and work in process are not included in finished goods because they are not available for sale. A manufacturer also shows cost of goods *manufactured* instead of cost of goods *purchased*. A merchandiser's cost of goods purchased is the cost of buying products to be sold. A manufacturer's cost of goods manufactured is the sum of direct materials, direct labor, and factory overhead costs incurred in making products. The Cost of Goods Sold sections for both a merchandiser (Tele-Mart) and a manufacturer (Rocky Mountain Bikes) are shown in Exhibit 14.13. The remaining income statement sections are similar for merchandisers and manufacturers.

EXHIBIT 14.13

Cost of Goods Sold for a Merchandiser and Manufacturer

Merchandising Company (Tele-Mart)		Manufacturing Company (Rocky Mtn. Bikes)	
Cost of goods sold		Cost of goods sold	
Beginning *merchandise* inventory	$ 14,200	**Beginning *finished goods* inventory**.	$ 11,200
Cost of merchandise *purchased*	234,150	**Cost of goods *manufactured***	170,500
Goods available for sale	248,350	Goods available for sale	181,700
Less ending *merchandise* inventory	12,100	**Less ending *finished goods* inventory**	10,300
Cost of goods sold	$236,250	Cost of goods sold	$171,400

*Cost of goods manufactured is in the income statement of Exhibit 14.14.

Costs for a Service Company

Because a service provider does not make or buy inventory to be sold, it does not report cost of goods manufactured or cost of goods sold. Instead, its operating expenses include all of the costs it incurs in providing its service. Southwest Airlines, for example, reports large operating expenses for employee pay and benefits, fuel and oil, and depreciation. Southwest's operating expenses also include selling expenses and general and administrative expenses.

Income Statements for Manufacturers, Merchandisers, and Servicers

Exhibit 14.14 shows the income statement for Rocky Mountain Bikes. Its operating expenses include selling expenses and general and administrative expenses, which include salaries for those business functions as well as depreciation for related equipment. Operating expenses do not include manufacturing costs such as factory workers' wages and depreciation of production equipment and the factory buildings. These manufacturing costs are reported as part of cost of goods manufactured and included in cost of goods sold. This exhibit also shows the income statement for Tele-Mart (merchandiser) and Northeast Air (service provider). Tele-Mart reports *cost of merchandise purchased* instead of cost of goods manufactured. Tele-Mart reports its operating expenses like those of the manufacturing company. The income statement for Northeast Air shows only operating expenses.

EXHIBIT 14.14

Income Statements for Manufacturer, Merchandiser, and Service Provider

ROCKY MOUNTAIN BIKES (Manufacturer)
Income Statement
For Year Ended December 31, 2019

Sales		$310,000
Cost of goods sold		
Finished goods inventory, Dec. 31, 2018	$ 11,200	
Cost of goods manufactured (from Exhibit 14.13)	170,500	
Goods available for sale	181,700	
Less finished goods inventory, Dec. 31, 2019	10,300	
Cost of goods sold		171,400
Gross profit		138,600
Operating expenses		
Selling expenses	38,150	
General and administrative expenses	21,750	
Total operating expenses		59,900
Income before income taxes		78,700
Income tax expense		32,600
Net income		$ 46,100

TELE-MART (Merchandiser)
Income Statement
For Year Ended December 31, 2019

Sales		$345,000
Cost of goods sold		
Merchandise inventory, Dec. 31, 2018	$ 14,200	
Cost of merchandise purchased	234,150	
Goods available for sale	248,350	
Merchandise inventory, Dec. 31, 2019	12,100	
Cost of goods sold		236,250
Gross profit		108,750
Operating expenses		
Selling expenses	43,150	
General and administrative expenses	26,750	
Total operating expenses		69,900
Income before income taxes		38,850
Income tax expense		16,084
Net income		$ 22,766

NORTHEAST AIR (Service Provider)
Income Statement
For Year Ended December 31, 2019

Service revenue		$425,000
Operating expenses		
Salaries and wages	$127,750	
Fuel and oil	159,375	
Maintenance and repairs	29,750	
Rent	42,500	
Depreciation	14,000	
General and admin. expenses	20,000	
Total operating expenses		393,375
Income before income taxes		31,625
Income tax expense		13,100
Net income		$ 18,525

NEED-TO-KNOW 14-3

Costs and Inventories for Different Businesses

C4

Indicate whether the following financial statement items apply to a manufacturer, a merchandiser, or a service provider. Some items apply to more than one type of organization.

_____ **1.** Merchandise inventory
_____ **2.** Finished goods inventory
_____ **3.** Cost of goods sold
_____ **4.** Selling expenses
_____ **5.** Operating expenses
_____ **6.** Cost of goods manufactured
_____ **7.** Supplies inventory
_____ **8.** Raw materials inventory

Solution

	Manufacturer	Merchandiser	Service Provider
1. Merchandise inventory		✓	
2. Finished goods inventory	✓		
3. Cost of goods sold	✓	✓	
4. Selling expenses	✓	✓	✓
5. Operating expenses	✓	✓	✓
6. Cost of goods manufactured	✓		
7. Supplies inventory.	✓	✓	✓
8. Raw materials inventory	✓		

Do More: E 14-7

COST FLOWS AND COST OF GOODS MANUFACTURED

C5

Explain manufacturing activities and the flow of manufacturing costs.

Flow of Manufacturing Activities

For planning and control we must know the flow of manufacturing activities and costs. Exhibit 14.15 shows the flow of manufacturing activities and their cost flows. Looking across the top row, the activities flow consists of _materials activity_ followed by _production activity_ followed by _sales activity_. The boxes below those activities show the costs for each activity and how costs flow across the three activities.

EXHIBIT 14.15

Activities and Cost Flows in Manufacturing

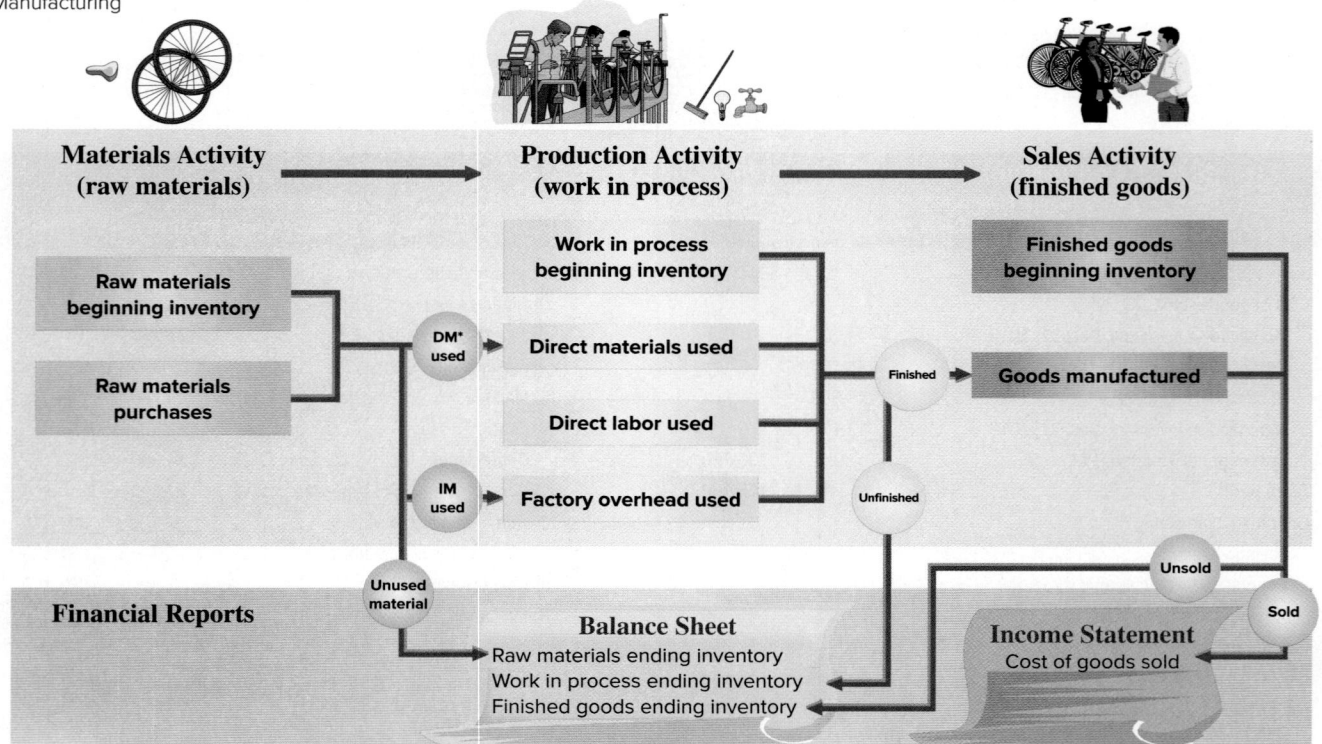

*DM = direct materials, IM = indirect materials.

Materials Activity   The left side of Exhibit 14.15 shows the flow of raw materials. Manufacturers usually start a period with some beginning raw materials inventory left over from the previous period. The company then acquires more raw materials in the current period. Adding these purchases to beginning inventory gives *total raw materials available for use* in production. These raw materials are then either used in production in the current period or remain in raw materials inventory at the end of the period for use in future periods.

Production Activity   The middle section of Exhibit 14.15 describes production activity. The following factors and their costs come together in production.

- Beginning work in process inventory, that is, the costs of partially complete products from the prior period.
- Direct materials, direct labor, and factory overhead incurred in the current period.

The production activity that takes place in the period results in products that are either finished or not finished at the end of the period. The cost of finished products makes up the **cost of goods manufactured** for the current period. The cost of goods manufactured is the total cost of making and finishing products in the period. That amount is included on the income statement in the computation of cost of goods sold, as we showed in Exhibit 14.14. Unfinished products are identified as *ending work in process inventory*. The cost of unfinished products consists of raw materials, direct labor, and factory overhead and is reported on the current period's balance sheet. The costs of both finished goods manufactured and work in process are *product costs*.

Sales Activity   The far right side of Exhibit 14.15 shows what happens to the finished goods: The cost of the beginning inventory of finished goods plus the cost of the newly completed units (goods manufactured) equals *total finished goods available for sale* in the current period. As they are sold, the cost of finished products sold is reported on the income statement as cost of goods sold. The cost of any finished products not sold in the period is reported as a current asset, *finished goods inventory,* on the current period's balance sheet.

Schedule of Cost of Goods Manufactured

Managers of manufacturing firms analyze product costs. Those managers aim to make better decisions about materials, labor, and overhead to reduce the cost of goods manufactured and increase income. A company's manufacturing activities are described in a report called a **schedule of cost of goods manufactured** (also called a *manufacturing statement* or a *statement of cost of goods manufactured*). The schedule of cost of goods manufactured summarizes the types and amounts of costs incurred in the manufacturing process. Exhibit 14.16 shows the schedule of cost of goods manufactured for Rocky Mountain Bikes. The schedule is divided into four parts: *direct materials, direct labor, overhead,* and *computation of cost of goods manufactured.*

P2_____

Prepare a schedule of cost of goods manufactured and explain its purpose and links to financial statements.

① **Compute direct materials used.** Add the beginning raw materials inventory of $8,000 to the current period's purchases of $86,500. This yields $94,500 of total raw materials available for use. A physical count of inventory shows $9,000 of ending raw materials inventory. If $94,500 of materials were available for use and $9,000 of materials remain in inventory, then $85,500 of direct materials were used in the period. (This chapter assumes that only direct materials costs flow through the Raw Materials Inventory account and indirect materials costs are recorded in Factory Supplies.)

② **Compute direct labor costs used.** Rocky Mountain Bikes had total direct labor costs of $60,000 for the period. This amount includes wages, payroll taxes, and fringe benefits.

③ **Compute total factory overhead costs used.** The statement lists each important factory overhead item and its cost. All of these costs are *indirectly* related to manufacturing activities. (Period expenses, such as selling expenses and other costs not related to manufacturing activities, are *not* reported on this statement.) Total factory overhead cost is $30,000. Some companies report only *total* factory overhead on the schedule of cost of goods manufactured and attach a separate schedule listing individual overhead costs.

Raw Materials Inventory		
Beg. bal. 8,000		
Purch. 86,500		
		Mtls. used 85,500
End. bal. 9,000		

Point: Manufacturers sometimes report variable and fixed overhead separately in the schedule of cost of goods manufactured to provide more information to managers about cost behavior.

EXHIBIT 14.16

Schedule of Cost of Goods
Manufactured

ROCKY MOUNTAIN BIKES		
Schedule of Cost of Goods Manufactured		
For Year Ended December 31, 2019		
Direct materials		
Raw materials inventory, Dec. 31, 2018	$ 8,000	
Raw materials purchases	86,500	
Raw materials available for use	94,500	
Less raw materials inventory, Dec. 31, 2019	9,000	
Direct materials used		$ 85,500
Direct labor		60,000
Factory overhead		
Indirect labor	9,000	
Factory supervision	6,000	
Factory utilities	2,600	
Repairs—Factory equipment	2,500	
Property taxes—Factory building	1,900	
Factory supplies used (indirect materials)	600	
Factory insurance expired	1,100	
Depreciation expense—Factory assets	5,500	
Amortization expense—Patents (on factory equipment)	800	
Total factory overhead		30,000
Total manufacturing costs		$175,500
Add work in process inventory, Dec. 31, 2018		2,500
Total cost of work in process		178,000
Less work in process inventory, Dec. 31, 2019		7,500
Cost of goods manufactured		$170,500

The circled numbers ①, ②, ③, ④ appear at the left margin grouping sections of the schedule.

④ **Compute cost of goods manufactured.** Total manufacturing costs for the period are $175,500 ($85,500 + $60,000 + $30,000), the sum of direct materials, direct labor, and overhead costs. This amount is added to beginning work in process inventory, which gives the total work in process during the period of $178,000 ($175,500 + $2,500). A physical count shows $7,500 of work in process inventory remains at the end of the period. We then compute the current period's cost of goods manufactured of $170,500 by taking the $178,000 total work in process and subtracting the $7,500 cost of ending work in process inventory. The cost of goods manufactured amount is also called *net cost of goods manufactured* or *cost of goods completed.*

Work in Process Inventory			
Beg. bal.	2,500		
Mfg. costs	175,500		
		COG Mfg.	170,500
End. bal.	7,500		

Key calculations in the schedule of costs of goods manufactured are summarized as follows.

$$\text{Total manufacturing costs} = \text{Direct materials used} + \text{Direct labor used} + \text{Factory overhead used}$$

$$\text{Cost of goods manufactured} = \text{Total manufacturing costs} + \text{Beginning work in process inventory} - \text{Ending work in process inventory}$$

Using the Schedule of Cost of Goods Manufactured   Management uses the schedule of cost of goods manufactured to plan and control manufacturing activities. To provide timely information for decision making, the schedule is often prepared monthly, weekly, or even daily. In anticipation of release of its much-hyped tablet, **Microsoft** grew its inventory of critical components and its finished goods inventory. The schedule of cost of goods manufactured is rarely published because managers view its information as proprietary and harmful if released to competitors.

Estimating Cost per Unit   Managers use the schedule of cost of goods manufactured to make rough estimates of per unit costs. For example, if Rocky Mountain Bikes makes 1,000 bikes during the year, the average manufacturing cost per unit is $170.50 (computed as $170,500/1,000). Average cost per unit is not always appropriate for managerial decisions. We show in the next two chapters how to compute more reliable unit costs for managerial decisions.

©Vaughn Ridley/Getty Images

Manufacturing Cost Flows across Accounting Reports Cost information is also used to complete financial statements at the end of an accounting period. Exhibit 14.17 summarizes how product costs flow through the accounting system. Direct materials, direct labor, and overhead costs are summarized in the schedule of cost of goods manufactured; then the amount of cost of goods manufactured from that statement is used to compute cost of goods sold on the income statement. Physical counts determine the dollar amounts of ending inventories, and those amounts are included on the end-of-period balance sheet. (*Note:* This exhibit shows only partial reports.)

EXHIBIT 14.17

Manufacturing Cost Flows across Accounting Reports

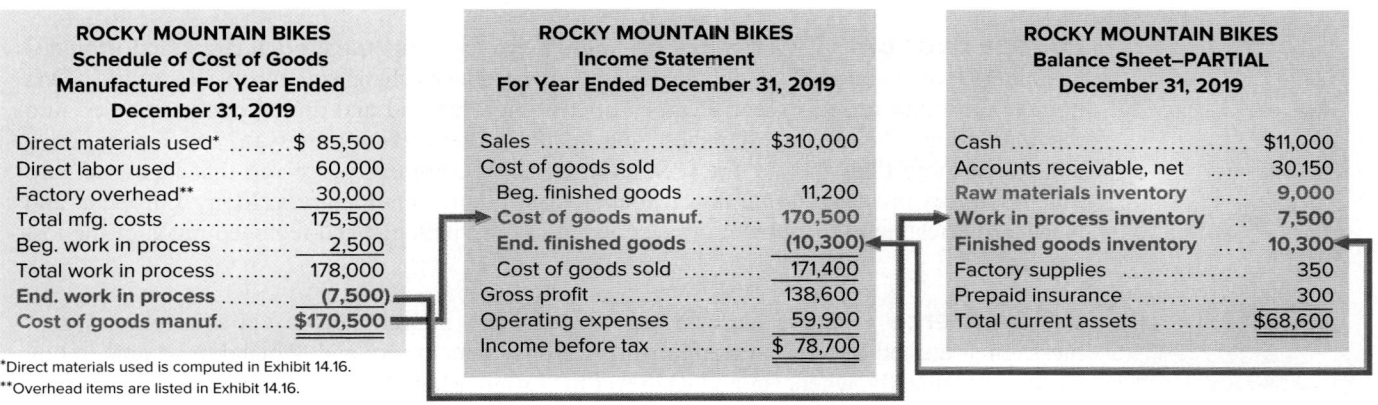

ROCKY MOUNTAIN BIKES
Schedule of Cost of Goods
Manufactured For Year Ended
December 31, 2019

Direct materials used*	$ 85,500
Direct labor used	60,000
Factory overhead**	30,000
Total mfg. costs	175,500
Beg. work in process	2,500
Total work in process	178,000
End. work in process	(7,500)
Cost of goods manuf.	$170,500

*Direct materials used is computed in Exhibit 14.16.
**Overhead items are listed in Exhibit 14.16.

ROCKY MOUNTAIN BIKES
Income Statement
For Year Ended December 31, 2019

Sales		$310,000
Cost of goods sold		
Beg. finished goods	11,200	
Cost of goods manuf.	170,500	
End. finished goods	(10,300)	
Cost of goods sold		171,400
Gross profit		138,600
Operating expenses		59,900
Income before tax		$ 78,700

ROCKY MOUNTAIN BIKES
Balance Sheet–PARTIAL
December 31, 2019

Cash	$11,000
Accounts receivable, net	30,150
Raw materials inventory	9,000
Work in process inventory ..	7,500
Finished goods inventory	10,300
Factory supplies	350
Prepaid insurance	300
Total current assets	$68,600

NEED-TO-KNOW 14-4

Key Cost Measures
P1 P2 C5

Part A: Compute the following three cost amounts using the information below.

_____ **1.** Cost of materials used _____ **2.** Cost of goods manufactured _____ **3.** Cost of goods sold

Beginning raw materials inventory	$15,500	Ending raw materials inventory	$10,600
Beginning work in process inventory	29,000	Ending work in process inventory	44,000
Beginning finished goods inventory	24,000	Ending finished goods inventory	37,400
Raw materials purchased.....................	66,000	Direct labor used.........................	38,000
Total factory overhead used..................	80,000		

Solution

1. $70,900   **2.** $173,900   **3.** $160,500

Raw Materials Inventory			
Begin. inv.	15,500		
Purchases	66,000		
Avail. for use	81,500		
		Matls used	70,900
End. inv.	10,600		

Work in Process Inventory			
Begin. inv.	29,000		
Matls used	70,900		
Labor	38,000		
Overhead	80,000		
Total mfg. costs	217,900		
		Cost of goods manuf.	173,900
End. inv.	44,000		

Finished Goods Inventory			
Begin. inv.	24,000		
Cost of goods manuf.	173,900		
Avail. for sale	197,900		
		Cost of goods sold	160,500
End. inv.	37,400		

Part B: Refer to each of the nine cost items listed above with their dollar amounts and indicate in which section of the schedule of cost of goods manufactured it appears as shown in Exhibit 14.16. Section *1* refers to direct materials; *2* refers to direct labor; *3* refers to factory overhead; and *4* refers to computation of cost of goods manufactured. Write *X* for any item that does not appear on the schedule of cost of goods manufactured.

Solution

__1__	Beginning raw materials inventory	__1__	Ending raw materials inventory
__4__	Beginning work in process inventory	__4__	Ending work in process inventory
__X__	Beginning finished goods inventory	__X__	Ending finished goods inventory
__1__	Raw materials purchased	__2__	Direct labor used
__3__	Total factory overhead used		

Do More: QS 14-8, QS 14-9, QS 14-10, E 14-8, E 14-11

Trends in Managerial Accounting

Tools and techniques of managerial accounting continue to evolve due to changes in the business environment. This section describes some of these changes.

Customer Orientation   There is increased emphasis on *customers* as the most important constituent of a business. Customers expect value for the money they spend to buy products and services. They want the right service (or product) at the right time and the right price. This **customer orientation** means that managers and employees understand the changing needs and wants of customers and align management and operating practices accordingly.

Global Economy   Our *global economy* expands competitive boundaries and provides customers more choices. The global economy also produces changes in business activities. One notable case that reflects these changes in customer demand and global competition is auto manufacturing. The top three Japanese auto manufacturers (**Honda, Nissan,** and **Toyota**) once controlled more than 40% of the U.S. auto market. Customers perceived that Japanese auto manufacturers provided value not available from other manufacturers. Many European and North American auto manufacturers responded to this challenge and regained much of the lost market share.

E-Commerce   People have become increasingly interconnected via smartphones, text messaging, and other electronic applications. Consumers expect and demand to be able to buy items electronically, whenever and wherever they want. Many businesses allow for online transactions. Online sales make up about 8% of total retail sales. Some companies such as **BucketFeet**, a footwear retailer, only sell online to keep costs lower.

Service Economy   Businesses that provide services, such as telecommunications and health care, constitute an ever-growing part of our economy. Many service companies, such as **Uber**, employ part-time workers. This "gig economy" changes companies' cost structures and the nature of competition. In developed economies, service businesses typically account for over 60% of total economic activity.

Lean Principles   Many companies have adopted the **lean business model,** whose goal is to *eliminate waste* while "satisfying the customer" and "providing a positive return" to the company. This is often paired with continuous improvement. **Continuous improvement** rejects the notions of "good enough" or "acceptable" and challenges employees and managers to continuously experiment with new and improved business practices. This has led companies to adopt practices such as total quality management (TQM) and just-in-time (JIT) manufacturing. Continuous improvement underlies both practices; the difference is in the focus.

- **Total quality management** focuses on quality improvement to business activities. Managers and employees seek to uncover waste in business activities, including accounting activities such as payroll and disbursements. To encourage an emphasis on quality, the U.S. Congress established the Malcolm Baldrige National Quality Award (MBNQA). Entrants must conduct a thorough analysis and evaluation of their business using guidelines from the Baldrige committee. **Ritz Carlton Hotel** is a recipient of the Baldrige award in the service category. The company applies a core set of values, collectively called *The Gold Standards,* to improve customer service.

- **Just-in-time manufacturing** is a system that acquires inventory and produces only when needed. An important aspect of JIT is that companies manufacture products only after they receive an order (a *demand-pull* system) and then deliver the customer's requirements on time. This means that processes must be aligned to eliminate delays and inefficiencies including inferior inputs and outputs. Companies also must establish good communications with their suppliers. On the downside, JIT is more susceptible to disruption than traditional systems. As one example, several **General Motors** plants were temporarily shut down due to a strike at a supplier that provided components *just in time* to the assembly division.

Value Chain   The **value chain** refers to the series of activities that add value to a company's products or services. Exhibit 14.18 illustrates a possible value chain for a retail cookie company. Companies can use lean practices across the value chain to increase efficiency and profits.

Acquire raw materials   **Baking**   **Sales**   **Service**

EXHIBIT 14.18

Typical Value Chain (cookie retailer)

How Lean Principles Impact the Value Chain   Adopting lean principles can be challenging because systems and procedures that a company follows must be realigned. Managerial accounting has an important role in providing accurate cost and performance information. Developing such a system is important to measuring the "value" provided to customers. The price that customers pay for acquiring goods and services is a key determinant of value. In turn, the costs a company incurs are key determinants of price.

Corporate Social Responsibility   In addition to maximizing shareholder value, corporations must consider the demands of other stakeholders, including employees, suppliers, and society in general. **Corporate social responsibility (CSR)** is a concept that goes beyond following the law. For example, to reduce its impact on the environment, **Three Twins Ice Cream** uses only cups and spoons made from organic ingredients. **United By Blue**, an apparel and jewelry company, removes one pound of trash from waterways for every product sold. Many companies extend the concept of CSR to include sustainability, which considers future generations when making business decisions.

Point: Companies like **Microsoft**, **Google**, and **Walt Disney**, ranked at the top of large multinational companies in terms of CSR, disclose CSR results on their websites.

Triple Bottom Line   **Triple bottom line** focuses on three measures: financial ("profits"), social ("people"), and environmental ("planet"). Adopting a triple bottom line impacts how businesses report. In response to a growing trend of such reporting, the **Sustainability Accounting Standards Board (SASB)** was established to develop reporting standards for businesses' sustainability activities. Some of the business sectors for which the SASB has developed reporting standards include health care, nonrenewable resources, and renewable resources and alternative energy.

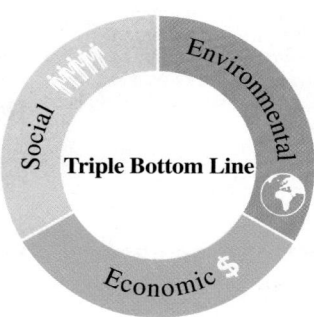

Decision Insight

Balanced Scorecard   The *balanced scorecard* aids continuous improvement by augmenting financial measures with information on the "drivers" (indicators) of future financial performance along four dimensions: **(1)** *financial*—profitability and risk, **(2)** *customer*—value creation and product and service differentiation, **(3)** *internal business processes*—business activities that create customer and owner satisfaction, and **(4)** *learning and growth*—organizational change, innovation, and growth. ∎

 ## SUSTAINABILITY AND ACCOUNTING

In creating sustainability accounting standards, the Sustainability Accounting Standards Board (SASB) has created reporting guidelines. The SASB considers sustainability information as *material* if its disclosure would affect the views of equity investors on a company's financial condition or operating performance.

Material information can vary across industries; for example, while environmental "planet" issues such as air quality, wastewater management, and biodiversity impacts are important for investments in companies in the nonrenewable resources sectors, such issues are likely not as important for investments in banks. In contrast, "people" issues such as diversity and inclusion, fair labor practices, and employee health are considered material for most sectors, particularly those that use considerable direct labor.

©MoringaConnect

MoringaConnect, this chapter's feature company, focuses on sustainability. The company trains and advises Ghanaian farmers in techniques to improve their crop yield. The company's products also do not use synthetic preservatives, and thus are better for consumers.

The company plants moringa trees to ensure sustainability. Emily Cunningham, MoringaConnect co-founder, proclaims that "for every customer order, we plant a tree. We are over half a million trees now and hope to reach one million by the end of the year." This is an example of the triple bottom line in action.

■ Decision Insight

Sustainability Returns A recent study shows the value of investing in material sustainability issues. Companies with good ratings on material sustainability issues perform better than companies with poor ratings. The chart here shows that high sustainability firms have 4% higher stock returns and almost 7% higher return on sales than low sustainability firms. Source: hbswk.hbs.edu/item/corporate-sustainability-first-evidence-on-materiality. ■

High Sustainability Firms vs. Low Sustainability Firms

Stock return +4.05%

Return on sales +6.89%

0% 2% 4% 6% 8% 10%

 **Decision Analysis** Raw Materials Inventory Turnover and Days' Sales in Raw Materials Inventory

A1

Assess raw materials inventory management using raw materials inventory turnover and days' sales in raw materials inventory.

Managerial accounting information helps managers perform analyses that are not readily available to external users of accounting information. Inventory management is one example. Using publicly available financial statements, an external user can compute the *inventory turnover* ratio. However, a managerial accountant can go much further.

Raw Materials Inventory Turnover

A manager can assess how effectively a company manages its *raw materials* inventory by computing the **raw materials inventory turnover** ratio as shown in Exhibit 14.19.

EXHIBIT 14.19

Raw Materials Inventory Turnover

> **Raw materials inventory turnover = Raw materials used/Average raw materials inventory**

This ratio reveals how many times a company turns over (uses in production) its raw materials inventory during a period. Generally, a high ratio of raw materials inventory turnover is preferred, as long as raw materials inventory levels are adequate to meet demand. To illustrate, Rocky Mountain Bikes reports direct (raw) materials used of $85,500 for the year, with a beginning raw materials inventory of $8,000 and an ending raw materials inventory of $9,000 (see Exhibit 14.16). Raw materials inventory turnover for Rocky Mountain Bikes for that year is computed below.

> Raw materials inventory turnover = $85,500/[($8,000 + $9,000)/2] = 10.06 (rounded)

Days' Sales in Raw Materials Inventory

To further assess raw materials inventory management, a manager can measure the adequacy of raw materials inventory to meet production demand. **Days' sales in raw materials inventory** reveals how much raw materials inventory is available in terms of the number of days' sales. It is a measure of how long it takes raw materials to be used in production. It is defined and computed for Rocky Mountain Bikes in Exhibit 14.20.

EXHIBIT 14.20

Days' Sales in Raw Materials Inventory Turnover

> **Days' sales in raw materials inventory = (Ending raw materials inventory/Raw materials used) × 365**
> = $9,000/$85,500 × 365 = 38.4 days (rounded)

This suggests that it will take 38 days for Rocky Mountain Bikes's raw materials inventory to be used in production. Assuming production needs can be met, companies usually prefer a *lower* number of days' sales in raw materials inventory. Just-in-time manufacturing techniques can be useful in lowering days' sales in raw materials inventory; for example, **Dell** keeps less than seven days of production needs in raw materials inventory for most of its computer components.

▪ Decision Maker

CFO Your company regularly reports days' sales in raw materials of 20 days, which is similar to that of competitors. A manager argues that profit can be increased if the company applies just-in-time principles and cuts it down to 2 days. Do you drop it to 2 days? ▪ *Answer:* Cutting days' sales in raw materials to 2 days *might* increase profits. Having less money tied up in inventory is a positive. However, if the company loses customers over out-of-stock inventory or if production is delayed (with costs), then the increase in profit might be outweighed by the increase in costs.

The following account balances and other information are from SUNN Corporation's accounting records for year-end December 31, 2019. Use this information to prepare (1) a table listing factory overhead costs, (2) a schedule of cost of goods manufactured (show only the total factory overhead cost), and (3) an income statement.

NEED-TO-KNOW 14-5

COMPREHENSIVE

Income Statement and COGM Schedule

Advertising expense	$ 85,000	Work in process inventory, Dec. 31, 2018	$	8,000
Amortization expense—Factory patents	16,000	Work in process inventory, Dec. 31, 2019		9,000
Bad debts expense	28,000	Income taxes		53,400
Depreciation expense—Office equipment	37,000	Indirect labor		26,000
Depreciation expense—Factory building	133,000	Interest expense		25,000
Depreciation expense—Factory equipment	78,000	Miscellaneous expense		55,000
Direct labor	250,000	Property taxes on factory equipment		14,000
Factory insurance used up	62,000	Raw materials inventory, Dec. 31, 2018		60,000
Factory supervisor salary	74,000	Raw materials inventory, Dec. 31, 2019		78,000
Factory supplies used (indirect materials)	21,000	Raw materials purchases (direct materials)		313,000
Factory utilities	115,000	Repairs expense—Factory equipment		31,000
Finished goods inventory, Dec. 31, 2018	15,000	Salaries expense		150,000
Finished goods inventory, Dec. 31, 2019	12,500	Sales		1,630,000

PLANNING THE SOLUTION

● Analyze the account balances and select those that are part of factory overhead costs.

● Arrange these costs in a table that lists factory overhead costs for the year.

● Analyze the remaining costs and select those related to production activity for the year; selected costs should include the materials and work in process inventories and direct labor.

● Prepare a schedule of cost of goods manufactured for the year showing the calculation of the cost of direct materials used in production, the cost of direct labor, and the total factory overhead cost. Assume that only direct materials costs flow through the Raw Materials Inventory account. When presenting overhead cost on this statement, report only total overhead cost from the table of overhead costs for the year. Show the costs of beginning and ending work in process inventory to determine cost of goods manufactured.

● Organize the remaining revenue and expense items into the income statement for the year. Combine cost of goods manufactured from the schedule of cost of goods manufactured with the finished goods inventory amounts to compute cost of goods sold for the year.

SOLUTION

SUNN CORPORATION	
Factory Overhead Costs	
For Year Ended December 31, 2019	
Amortization expense—Factory patents	$ 16,000
Depreciation expense—Factory building	133,000
Depreciation expense—Factory equipment	78,000
Factory insurance used up	62,000
Factory supervisor salary	74,000
Factory supplies used (indirect materials).	21,000
Factory utilities	115,000
Indirect labor.	26,000
Property taxes on factory equipment	14,000
Repairs expense—Factory equipment	31,000
Total factory overhead	$570,000

SUNN CORPORATION		
Schedule of Cost of Goods Manufactured		
For Year Ended December 31, 2019		
Direct materials		
Raw materials inventory, Dec. 31, 2018	$ 60,000	
Raw materials purchases	313,000	
Raw materials available for use	373,000	
Less raw materials inventory, Dec. 31, 2019	78,000	
Direct materials used.		295,000
Direct labor		250,000
Factory overhead		570,000
Total manufacturing costs		1,115,000
Add work in process inventory, Dec. 31, 2018		8,000
Total cost of work in process.		1,123,000
Less work in process inventory, Dec. 31, 2019		9,000
Cost of goods manufactured		$1,114,000

Raw Materials Inventory

Beginning	60,000	
Purch.	313,000	
Avail.	373,000	
		Dir. Mtls. Used 295,000
Ending	78,000	

Work in Process Inventory

Beginning	8,000	
Dir. Mtls. Used	295,000	
Dir. Labor	250,000	
FOH	570,000	
	1,123,000	
		COGM 1,114,000
Ending	9,000	

Finished Goods Inventory

Beginning	15,000	
COGM	1,114,000	
Avail.	1,129,000	
		COGS 1,116,500
Ending	12,500	

SUNN CORPORATION		
Income Statement		
For Year Ended December 31, 2019		
Sales		$1,630,000
Cost of goods sold		
Finished goods inventory, Dec. 31, 2018.	$ 15,000	
Cost of goods manufactured	1,114,000	
Goods available for sale	1,129,000	
Less finished goods inventory, Dec. 31, 2019	12,500	
Cost of goods sold		1,116,500
Gross profit		513,500
Operating expenses		
Advertising expense	85,000	
Bad debts expense	28,000	
Depreciation expense—Office equipment	37,000	
Interest expense	25,000	
Miscellaneous expense	55,000	
Salaries expense	150,000	
Total operating expenses		380,000
Income before income taxes		133,500
Income taxes.		53,400
Net income		$ 80,100

Summary: Cheat Sheet

COST CLASSIFICATIONS

Fixed: Costs that do not change as volume changes.
Variable: Costs that change in proportion to volume changes.
Direct: Costs that are traceable to a single cost object.
Indirect: Costs that are not easily traced to a single cost object.
Product (manufacturing) costs: Costs necessary to make a product.
   Direct materials + Direct labor + Overhead.
   Capitalize as inventory until goods are sold.

Period (nonmanufacturing) costs: Costs of nonproduction activities. Expense immediately in period when incurred.

MANUFACTURING COSTS

Direct materials: Materials that are traced to finished goods.
Direct labor: Convert materials to finished goods.
Overhead: Support production, but not separately traced to finished goods. Indirect materials + Indirect labor + Other indirect costs.

FLOW OF MANUFACTURING COSTS

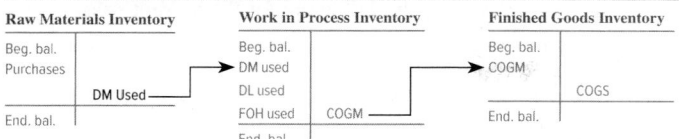

DM = direct materials; DL = direct labor; FOH = factory overhead; COGM = cost of goods manufactured; COGS = cost of goods sold

COSTS AND THE BALANCE SHEET

Manufacturer	
Current assets	
Raw materials inventory	$ 9,000
Work in process inventory	7,500
Finished goods inventory	10,300

Merchandiser	
Current assets	
Merchandise inventory	$21,000

COSTS AND THE INCOME STATEMENT

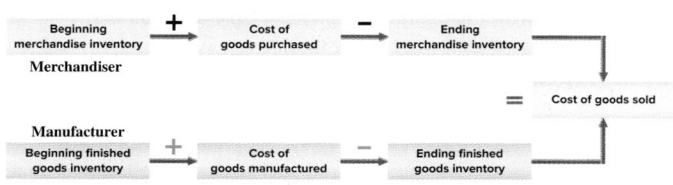

SCHEDULE OF COST OF GOODS MFG.

Schedule of Cost of Goods Manufactured For Year Ended___	
Direct materials used*	$ 85,500
Direct labor used	60,000
Factory overhead**	30,000
Total mfg. costs	175,500
Beg. work in process	2,500
Total work in process	178,000
End. work in process	(7,500)
Cost of goods manuf.	$170,500

*Direct materials used is computed: BI + Purch – EI.
**Overhead items can be listed separately.

RAW MATERIALS INVENTORY MANAGEMENT

RM inventory turnover = Raw materials used/Average RM inventory
Days' sales in RM inventory = (Ending RM inventory/RM used) × 365

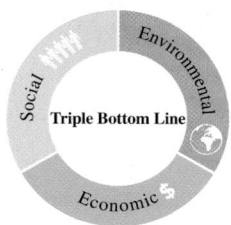 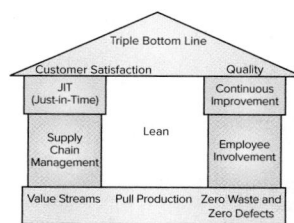

Key Terms

Continuous improvement (550)
Control (536)
Conversion costs (543)
Corporate social responsibility (CSR) (551)
Cost object (539)
Cost of goods manufactured (547)
Customer orientation (550)
Days' sales in raw materials inventory (552)
Direct costs (539)
Direct labor (542)
Direct labor costs (542)
Direct materials (542)
Direct materials costs (542)
Enterprise risk management (ERM) (535)

Ethics (537)
Factory overhead (542)
Factory overhead costs (542)
Finished goods inventory (543)
Fixed cost (539)
Indirect costs (539)
Indirect labor (542)
Indirect labor costs (542)
Indirect materials (542)
Institute of Management Accountants (IMA) (537)
Internal control system (537)
ISO 9000 standards (550)
Just-in-time (JIT) manufacturing (550)
Lean business model (550)
Managerial accounting (535)

Period costs (540)
Planning (535)
Prime costs (543)
Product costs (540)
Raw materials inventory (543)
Raw materials inventory turnover (552)
Sarbanes-Oxley Act (538)
Schedule of cost of goods manufactured (547)
Sustainability Accounting Standards Board (SASB) (551)
Total quality management (TQM) (550)
Triple bottom line (551)
Value chain (551)
Variable cost (539)
Work in process inventory (543)

Multiple Choice Quiz

1. Continuous improvement
  a. Is used to reduce inventory levels.
  b. Is applicable only in service businesses.
  c. Rejects the notion of "good enough."
  d. Is used to reduce ordering costs.
  e. Is applicable only in manufacturing businesses.

2. A direct cost is one that is
  a. Variable with respect to the cost object.
  b. Traceable to the cost object.
  c. Fixed with respect to the cost object.
  d. Allocated to the cost object.
  e. A period cost.

3. Costs that are incurred as part of the manufacturing process, but are not clearly traceable to the specific unit of product or batches of product, are called

  a. Period costs.   **d.** Operating expenses.

  b. Factory overhead.   **e.** Fixed costs.

  c. Variable costs.

4. The three major cost components of manufacturing a product are

  a. Direct materials, direct labor, and factory overhead.

  b. Period costs, product costs, and conversion costs.

  c. Indirect labor, indirect materials, and fixed expenses.

  d. Variable costs, fixed costs, and period costs.

  e. Overhead costs, fixed costs, and direct costs.

5. A company reports the following for the current year.

Finished goods inventory, beginning of year	$6,000
Finished goods inventory, ending of year	3,200
Cost of goods sold	7,500

Its cost of goods manufactured for the current year is

  a. $1,500.   **d.** $2,800.

  b. $1,700.   **e.** $4,700.

  c. $7,500.

ANSWERS TO MULTIPLE CHOICE QUIZ

1. c

2. b

3. b

4. a

5. e; Beginning finished goods + Cost of goods manufactured (COGM) − Ending finished goods = Cost of goods sold

$6,000 + COGM − $3,200 = $7,500

COGM = $\underline{\underline{$4,700}}$

🔲 Icon denotes assignments that involve decision making.

Discussion Questions

1. Describe the managerial accountant's role in business planning, control, and decision making.

2. Distinguish between managerial and financial accounting on

  a. Users and decision makers.   **d.** Time dimension.

  b. Purpose of information.   **e.** Focus of information.

  c. Flexibility of practice.   **f.** Nature of information.

3. 🔲 Identify the usual changes that a company must make when it adopts a customer orientation.

4. Distinguish between direct labor and indirect labor.

5. Distinguish between (*a*) factory overhead and (*b*) selling and administrative overhead.

6. Distinguish between direct material and indirect material.

7. What product cost is both a prime cost and a conversion cost?

8. 🔲 Assume that we tour **Apple**'s factory where it makes iPhones. List three direct costs and three indirect costs that we are likely to see. **APPLE**

9. 🔲 Should we evaluate a production manager's performance on the basis of operating expenses? Why?

10. 🔲 Explain why knowledge of cost behavior is useful in product performance evaluation.

11. Explain why product costs are capitalized but period costs are expensed in the current accounting period.

12. 🔲 Explain how business activities and inventories for a manufacturing company, a merchandising company, and a service company differ.

13. 🔲 Why does managerial accounting often involve working with numerous predictions and estimates?

14. How do an income statement and a balance sheet for a manufacturing company and a merchandising company differ?

15. Besides inventories, what other assets often appear on manufacturers' balance sheets but not on merchandisers' balance sheets?

16. Why does a manufacturing company require three different inventory categories?

17. Manufacturing activities of a company are described in the _____. This schedule summarizes the types and amounts of costs incurred in its manufacturing _____.

18. What are the three categories of manufacturing costs?

19. List several examples of factory overhead.

20. 🔲 List the four components of a schedule of cost of goods manufactured and provide specific examples of each for **Apple**. **APPLE**

21. 🔲 Prepare a proper title for the annual schedule of cost of goods manufactured of **Google**. Does the date match the balance sheet or income statement? Why? **GOOGLE**

22. 🔲 Describe the relations among the income statement, the schedule of cost of goods manufactured, and a detailed listing of factory overhead costs.

23. 🔲 Define and describe two measures to assess raw materials inventory management.

24. 🔲 The triple bottom line includes what three main dimensions?

25. Access **3M Co.**'s annual report (10-K) for the fiscal year ended December 31, 2017, at the SEC's EDGAR database (**SEC.gov**) or its website (**3M.com**). From its balance sheet, identify the titles and amounts of its inventory components.

connect

Identify whether each description most likely applies to managerial (M) or financial (F) accounting.

_____ **1.** Its primary users are company managers.

_____ **2.** Its information is often available only after an audit is complete.

_____ **3.** Its primary focus is on the organization as a whole.

_____ **4.** Its principles and practices are very flexible.

_____ **5.** It focuses mainly on past results.

QUICK STUDY

QS 14-1
Managerial accounting versus financial accounting
C1

A cell phone company offers two different plans. Plan A costs $80 per month for unlimited talk and text. Plan B costs $0.20 per minute plus $0.10 per text message sent. You need to purchase a plan for your teenage sister. Your sister currently uses 1,700 minutes and sends 1,600 texts each month.

1. What is your sister's total cost under each of the two plans?

2. Suppose your sister doubles her monthly usage to 3,400 minutes and sends 3,200 texts. What is your sister's total cost under each of the two plans?

QS 14-2
Fixed and variable costs
C2

Listed below are product costs for production of footballs. Classify each cost as either variable (V) or fixed (F).

_____ **1.** Leather covers for footballs.   _____ **4.** Lace to hold footballs together.

_____ **2.** Machinery depreciation (straight-line).   _____ **5.** Insurance premium on building.

_____ **3.** Wages of assembly workers.   _____ **6.** Factory supervisor salary.

QS 14-3
Fixed and variable costs
C2

Diez Company produces sporting equipment, including leather footballs. Identify each of the following costs as direct (D) or indirect (I). The cost object is a football produced by Diez.

_____ **1.** Electricity used in the production plant.

_____ **2.** Labor used on the football production line.

_____ **3.** Salary of manager who supervises the entire plant.

_____ **4.** Depreciation on equipment used to produce sports equipment.

_____ **5.** Leather used to produce footballs.

QS 14-4
Direct and indirect costs
C2

Identify each of the following costs as either direct materials (DM), direct labor (DL), or factory overhead (FO). The company manufactures tennis balls.

_____ **1.** Rubber used to form the cores.   _____ **4.** Glue used in binding rubber cores to felt covers.

_____ **2.** Factory maintenance.   _____ **5.** Depreciation—Factory equipment.

_____ **3.** Wages paid to assembly workers.   _____ **6.** Cans to package the balls.

QS 14-5
Classifying product costs
C2

Identify each of the following costs as either a product cost (PROD) or a period cost (PER).

_____ **1.** Factory maintenance.   _____ **5.** Rent on factory building.

_____ **2.** Sales commissions.   _____ **6.** Interest expense.

_____ **3.** Depreciation—Factory equipment.   _____ **7.** Office manager salary.

_____ **4.** Depreciation—Office equipment.   _____ **8.** Indirect materials used in making goods.

QS 14-6
Product and period costs
C3

Compute ending work in process inventory for a manufacturer with the following information.

Raw materials purchased...............	$124,800	Total factory overhead	$ 95,700
Direct materials used	74,300	Work in process inventory, beginning of year	26,500
Direct labor used	55,000	Cost of goods manufactured	221,800

QS 14-7
Inventory reporting for manufacturers
C4

Compute the total manufacturing cost for a manufacturer with the following information for the month.

Raw materials purchased...............	$32,400	Salesperson commissions.........................	$6,200
Direct materials used	53,750	Depreciation expense—Factory building...........	3,500
Direct labor used	12,000	Depreciation expense—Delivery equipment	2,200
Factory supervisor salary..............	8,000	Indirect materials................................	1,250

QS 14-8
Manufacturing cost flows
C5

QS 14-9
Cost of goods sold
P1

Compute cost of goods sold using the following information.

Finished goods inventory, beginning	$ 500	Finished goods inventory, ending	$750
Cost of goods manufactured	4,000		

QS 14-10
Cost of goods sold
P1

Compute cost of goods sold using the following information.

Finished goods inventory, beginning............	$345,000	Cost of goods manufactured..............	$918,700
Work in process inventory, beginning	83,500	Finished goods inventory, ending.........	283,600
Work in process inventory, ending..............	72,300		

QS 14-11
Cost of goods
manufactured
P2

Prepare the schedule of cost of goods manufactured for Barton Company using the following information.

Direct materials............................	$190,500	Work in process, beginning..............	$157,600
Direct labor	63,150	Work in process, ending	142,750
Factory overhead costs	24,000		

QS 14-12
Direct materials used
P2

Use the following information to compute the cost of direct materials used for the current year. Assume the Raw Materials Inventory account is used only for direct materials.

	January 1	December 31
Inventories		
Raw materials inventory	$ 6,000	$ 7,500
Work in process inventory	12,000	9,000
Finished goods inventory	8,500	5,500
Activity during current year		
Materials purchased		$123,500
Direct labor.............................		94,000
Factory overhead........................		39,000

QS 14-13
Trends in managerial
accounting
C6

Match each concept with its best description by entering its letter A through E in the blank.

_____ **1.** Just-in-time manufacturing

_____ **2.** Continuous improvement

_____ **3.** Customer orientation

_____ **4.** Total quality management

_____ **5.** Triple bottom line

A. Focuses on quality throughout the production process.

B. Flexible product designs can be modified to accommodate customer choices.

C. Every manager and employee constantly looks for ways to improve company operations.

D. Reports on financial, social, and environmental performance.

E. Inventory is acquired or produced only as needed.

QS 14-14
Direct materials used **C5**

3M Co. reports beginning raw materials inventory of $855 million and ending raw materials inventory of $717 million. If 3M purchased $3,646 million of raw materials during the year, what is the amount of raw materials it used during the year?

QS 14-15
Raw materials inventory
management **A1**

3M Co. reports beginning raw materials inventory of $855 million and ending raw materials inventory of $717 million. Assume 3M purchased $3,646 million of raw materials and used $3,784 million of raw materials during the year. Compute raw materials inventory turnover (round to one decimal) and the number of days' sales in raw materials inventory (round to the nearest day).

QS 14-16
Direct materials used
C5

Nestlé reports beginning raw materials inventory of 3,815 and ending raw materials inventory of 3,499 (both numbers in millions of Swiss francs). If Nestlé purchased 13,860 (in millions) of raw materials during the year, what is the amount of raw materials it used during the year?

QS 14-17
Raw materials inventory
management
A1

Nestlé reports beginning raw materials inventory of 3,815 and ending raw materials inventory of 3,499 (both numbers in millions of Swiss francs). Assume Nestlé purchased 13,860 and used 14,176 (in millions) in raw materials during the year. Compute raw materials inventory turnover (round to one decimal) and the number of days' sales in raw materials inventory (round to the nearest day).

![Mc Graw Hill Education] connect

Indicate in the following chart the most likely source of information for each business decision. Use *M* for managerial accounting information and *F* for financial accounting information.

EXERCISES

Exercise 14-1
Sources of accounting information

C1

Business Decision	Primary Information Source
1. Determine whether to lend to a company.............................	_____
2. Evaluate a purchasing department's performance.......................	_____
3. Report financial performance to board of directors......................	_____
4. Estimate product cost for a new line of shoes...........................	_____
5. Plan the budget for next quarter....................................	_____
6. Measure profitability of an individual store...........................	_____
7. Prepare financial reports according to GAAP..........................	_____
8. Determine location and size for a new plant...........................	_____

Listed here are product costs for the production of soccer balls. Classify each cost (*a*) as either variable (V) or fixed (F) and (*b*) as either direct (D) or indirect (I). What patterns do you see regarding the relation between costs classified in these two ways?

Exercise 14-2
Cost classification

C2

Product Cost	a. Variable or Fixed	b. Direct or Indirect
1. Leather covers for soccer balls......................	_____	_____
2. Annual flat fee paid for office security.................	_____	_____
3. Coolants for machinery.............................	_____	_____
4. Wages of assembly workers.........................	_____	_____
5. Thread to hold leather together......................	_____	_____
6. Taxes on factory..................................	_____	_____
7. Machinery depreciation (straight-line)...............	_____	_____

TechPro offers instructional courses in e-commerce website design. The company holds classes in a building that it owns. Classify each of TechPro's costs below as (*a*) variable (V) or fixed (F) and (*b*) direct (D) or indirect (I). Assume the cost object is an individual class.

Exercise 14-3
Cost classifications for a service provider

C2

<u>**a.**</u> <u>**b.**</u>

____ ____ **1.** Depreciation on classroom building

____ ____ **2.** Monthly Internet connection cost

____ ____ **3.** Instructional manuals for students

<u>**a.**</u> <u>**b.**</u>

____ ____ **4.** Travel expenses for salesperson

____ ____ **5.** Depreciation on computers used for classes

____ ____ **6.** Instructor wage (per class)

Listed below are costs of providing an airline service. Classify each cost as (*a*) either variable (V) or fixed (F) and (*b*) either direct (D) or indirect (I). Consider the cost object to be a flight. Flight attendants and pilots are paid based on hours of flight time.

Exercise 14-4
Cost classifications for a service company

C2

Cost	a. Variable or Fixed	b. Direct or Indirect
1. Advertising......................................	_____	_____
2. Beverages served on planes.......................	_____	_____
3. Regional vice president salary......................	_____	_____
4. Depreciation (straight-line) on ground equipment.......	_____	_____
5. Fuel used in planes...............................	_____	_____
6. Flight attendant wages............................	_____	_____
7. Pilot wages.....................................	_____	_____
8. Aircraft maintenance manager salary.................	_____	_____

Selected costs related to **Apple**'s iPhone are listed below. Classify each cost as either direct materials (DM), direct labor (DL), factory overhead (FO), selling expenses (S), or general and administrative (GA) expenses.

Exercise 14-5
Classifying manufacturing costs

C2

_____ **1.** Display screen

_____ **2.** Assembly-line supervisor salary

_____ **3.** Wages for assembly workers

_____ **4.** Salary of the chief executive officer

_____ **5.** Glue to hold iPhone cases together

_____ **6.** Uniforms provided for each factory worker

_____ **7.** Wages for retail store worker

_____ **8.** Depreciation (straight-line) on robotic equipment used in assembly

Exercise 14-6
Cost classification
C3

Tesla, a vehicle manufacturer, incurs the following costs. (1) Classify each cost as either a product (PROD) or period (PER) cost. If a product cost, identify it as direct materials (DM), direct labor (DL), or factory overhead (FO), and then as a prime (PR) or conversion (CONV) cost. (2) Classify each product cost as either a direct cost (DIR) or an indirect cost (IND) using the product as the cost object.

Cost	Direct or Indirect	Product or Period	If Product Cost, Then: Direct Materials, Direct Labor, or Factory Overhead	If Product Cost, Then: Prime or Conversion
1. Factory electricity	_____	_____	_____	_____
2. Advertising..........................	_____	_____	_____	_____
3. Amortization of patents on factory machine	_____	_____	_____	_____
4. Batteries for electric cars	_____	_____	_____	_____
5. Office supplies used	_____	_____	_____	_____
6. Wages to assembly workers	_____	_____	_____	_____

Exercise 14-7
Balance sheet identification and preparation
C4

Current assets for two different companies at fiscal year-end are listed here. One is a manufacturer, Rayzer Skis Mfg., and the other, Sunrise Foods, is a grocery distribution company.

1. Identify which set of numbers relates to the manufacturer and which to the merchandiser.
2. Prepare the current asset section for each company from this information. Discuss why the current asset section for these two companies is different.

Account	Company 1	Company 2
Cash	$ 7,000	$ 5,000
Raw materials inventory	—	42,000
Merchandise inventory	45,000	—
Work in process inventory	—	30,000
Finished goods inventory	—	50,000
Accounts receivable, net	62,000	75,000
Prepaid expenses	1,500	900

Exercise 14-8
Cost of goods manufactured and cost of goods sold computation
P1   P2

Using the following data from both Garcon Company and Pepper Company for the year ended December 31, 2019, compute (1) the cost of goods manufactured and (2) the cost of goods sold.

	Garcon Co.	Pepper Co.
Beginning finished goods inventory	$ 12,000	$ 16,450
Beginning work in process inventory	14,500	19,950
Beginning raw materials inventory (direct materials) ...	7,250	9,000
Rental cost on factory equipment	27,000	22,750
Direct labor.....................................	19,000	35,000
Ending finished goods inventory	17,650	13,300
Ending work in process inventory	22,000	16,000
Ending raw materials inventory...................	5,300	7,200
Factory utilities.................................	9,000	12,000
Factory supplies used (indirect materials)..........	8,200	3,200
General and administrative expenses	21,000	43,000
Indirect labor....................................	1,250	7,660
Repairs—Factory equipment	4,780	1,500
Raw materials purchases	33,000	52,000
Selling expenses	50,000	46,000
Sales	195,030	290,010
Cash...	20,000	15,700
Factory equipment, net	212,500	115,825
Accounts receivable, net	13,200	19,450

Check   Garcon COGS,
$91,030

Refer to the data in Exercise 14-8. For each company, prepare (1) an income statement and (2) the current assets section of the balance sheet. Ignore income taxes.

Exercise 14-9
Preparing financial statements for a manufacturer C4 P2

Refer to the data in Exercise 14-8. For each company, compute the total (1) prime costs and (2) conversion costs.

Exercise 14-10
Cost classification C2

Compute cost of goods sold for each of these two companies for the year.

Exercise 14-11
Cost of goods sold computation
P1

	A	B	C
1			Precision
2		Unimart	Manufacturing
3	Beginning inventory		
4	Merchandise	$275,000	
5	Finished goods		$450,000
6	Cost of purchases	500,000	
7	Cost of goods manufactured		900,000
8	Ending inventory		
9	Merchandise	115,000	
10	Finished goods		375,000

Check Unimart COGS, $660,000

For each of the following accounts for a manufacturing company, place a ✓ in the appropriate column indicating that it appears on the balance sheet, the income statement, the schedule of cost of goods manufactured, and/or a detailed listing of factory overhead costs. Assume that the income statement shows the calculation of cost of goods sold *and* the schedule of cost of goods manufactured shows only the total amount (not detailed listing) of factory overhead. An account can appear on more than one report.

Exercise 14-12
Components of accounting reports
P2

	A	B	C	D	E
1		Balance	Income	Sched. of Cost	Overhead
2	Account	Sheet	Statement	of Goods Manuf'd	Report
3	Accounts receivable				
4	Beginning finished goods inventory				
5	Computer supplies used (office)				
6	Depreciation expense—Factory building				
7	Depreciation expense—Office building				
8	Wages for assembly workers				
9	Ending work in process inventory				
10	Factory maintenance wages				
11	Property taxes on factory building				
12	Raw materials purchases				
13	Sales				

Given the following selected account balances of Delray Mfg., prepare its schedule of cost of goods manufactured for the current year ended December 31. Include a listing of the individual overhead account balances in this schedule.

Exercise 14-13
Preparing schedule of cost of goods manufactured
P2

Sales	$1,250,000	Repairs—Factory equipment	$ 5,250
Raw materials inventory, beginning	37,000	Rent cost of factory building	57,000
Work in process inventory, beginning	53,900	Advertising expense	94,000
Finished goods inventory, beginning	62,750	General and administrative expenses	129,300
Raw materials purchases	175,600	Raw materials inventory, ending	42,700
Direct labor	225,000	Work in process inventory, ending	41,500
Factory supplies used (indirect materials)	17,840	Finished goods inventory, ending	67,300
Indirect labor	47,000		

Check Cost of goods manufactured, $534,390

Refer to the information in Exercise 14-13 to prepare an income statement for Delray Mfg. (a manufacturer). Assume that its cost of goods manufactured is $534,390.

Exercise 14-14
Income statement preparation P2

Exercise 14-15

Schedule of cost of goods manufactured and cost of goods sold   P1   P2

Beck Manufacturing reports the following information in T-account form for 2019.

1. Prepare the schedule of cost of goods manufactured for the year.

2. Compute cost of goods sold for the year.

Raw Materials Inventory			
Begin. inv.	10,000		
Purchases	45,000		
Avail. for use	55,000		
		DM used	46,500
End. inv.	8,500		

Work in Process Inventory			
Begin. inv.	14,000		
DM used	46,500		
Direct labor	27,500		
Overhead	55,000		
Mfg. costs	143,000		
		Cost of goods manuf.	131,000
End. inv.	12,000		

Finished Goods Inventory			
Begin. inv.	16,000		
Cost of goods manuf.	131,000		
Avail. for sale	147,000		
		Cost of goods sold	129,000
End. inv.	18,000		

Exercise 14-16

Cost flows in manufacturing

C5

The following chart shows how costs flow through a business as a product is manufactured. Not all boxes in the chart show cost amounts. Compute the cost amounts for the boxes that contain question marks.

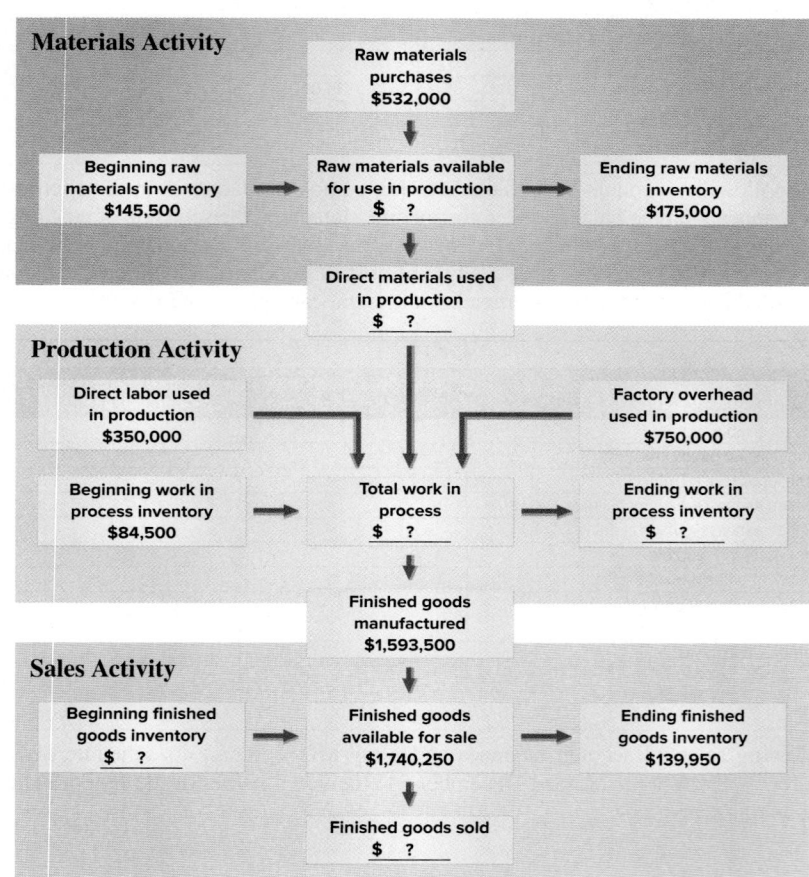

Materials Activity

Raw materials purchases **$532,000**

Beginning raw materials inventory **$145,500** → Raw materials available for use in production **$?** → Ending raw materials inventory **$175,000**

Direct materials used in production **$?**

Production Activity

Direct labor used in production **$350,000**   Factory overhead used in production **$750,000**

Beginning work in process inventory **$84,500** → Total work in process **$?** → Ending work in process inventory **$?**

Finished goods manufactured **$1,593,500**

Sales Activity

Beginning finished goods inventory **$?** → Finished goods available for sale **$1,740,250** → Ending finished goods inventory **$139,950**

Finished goods sold **$?**

Exercise 14-17

Lean business practice

C6

Many fast-food restaurants compete on lean business practices. Match each of the following activities at a fast-food restaurant with one of the three lean business practices *a, b,* or *c* that it strives to achieve. Some activities might relate to more than one lean business practice.

_____ **1.** Courteous employees

_____ **2.** Food produced to order

_____ **3.** Clean tables and floors

_____ **4.** Orders filled within three minutes

_____ **5.** Standardized food-making processes

_____ **6.** New product development

a. Just-in-time (JIT)

b. Continuous improvement (CI)

c. Total quality management (TQM)

In its recent annual report and related *Global Responsibility Report,* **Starbucks** provides information on company performance on several dimensions. Indicate whether the following items best fit into the financial (label your answer "Profit"), social (label your answer "People"), or environmental (label your answer "Planet") aspects of triple bottom line reporting.

Exercise 14-18
Triple bottom line

C6

_____ **1.** Sales revenue totaled $22.4 billion.

_____ **2.** 99% of coffee was purchased from suppliers certified for responsible farming and ethics.

_____ **3.** Reduced water consumption.

_____ **4.** Net income totaled $2.9 billion.

_____ **5.** Increased purchases of energy from renewable sources.

_____ **6.** Stopped working with factories that had poor working conditions.

In its recent annual report and related *Corporate Responsibility Report,* **Hyatt** provides information on company performance on several dimensions. Indicate whether the following items below best fit into the financial (label your answer "Profit"), social (label your answer "People"), or environmental (label your answer "Planet") aspects of triple bottom line reporting.

Exercise 14-19
Triple bottom line

C6

_____ **1.** Sales revenue totaled $4.4 billion.

_____ **2.** Increased women in management positions.

_____ **3.** Invested in career programs in Brazil.

_____ **4.** Operating cash flows totaled $489 million.

_____ **5.** Earned awards for best LGBT workplace.

_____ **6.** Nearly all hotels recycle at least one waste stream.

connect

Listed here are the total costs associated with the production of 1,000 drum sets manufactured by TrueBeat. The drum sets sell for $500 each.

PROBLEM SET A

Problem 14-1A
Cost computation, classification, and analysis

C2 C3

Costs	Variable or Fixed		Product or Period	
	Variable	Fixed	Product	Period
1. Plastic for casing—$17,000	$17,000	____	$17,000	____
2. Wages of assembly workers—$82,000.........................	____	____	____	____
3. Property taxes on factory—$5,000	____	____	____	____
4. Accounting staff salaries—$35,000............................	____	____	____	____
5. Drum stands (1,000 stands purchased)—$26,000.................	____	____	____	____
6. Rent cost of equipment for sales staff—$10,000	____	____	____	____
7. Upper management salaries—$125,000	____	____	____	____
8. Annual flat fee for factory maintenance service—$10,000	____	____	____	____
9. Sales commissions—$15 per unit	____	____	____	____
10. Machinery depreciation, straight-line—$40,000	____	____	____	____

Required

1. Classify each cost and its amount as (*a*) either variable or fixed and (*b*) either product or period. (The first cost is completed as an example.)

2. Compute the manufacturing cost per drum set.

Check   (1) Total variable production cost, $125,000

Analysis Component

3. Assume that 1,200 drum sets are produced in the next year. What do you predict will be the total cost of plastic for the casings and the per unit cost of the plastic for the casings?

4. Assume that 1,200 drum sets are produced in the next year. What do you predict will be the total cost of property taxes and the per unit cost of the property taxes?

Problem 14-2A
Classifying costs
C2   C3

The following calendar year-end information is taken from the December 31, 2019, adjusted trial balance and other records of Leone Company.

Advertising expense	$ 28,750	Miscellaneous production costs	$ 8,425
Depreciation expense—Office equipment	7,250	Office salaries expense	63,000
Depreciation expense—Selling equipment	8,600	Raw materials purchases (direct materials)	925,000
Depreciation expense—Factory equipment	33,550	Rent expense—Office space	22,000
Factory supervision	102,600	Rent expense—Selling space	26,100
Factory supplies used (indirect materials)	7,350	Rent expense—Factory building	76,800
Factory utilities	33,000	Maintenance expense—Factory equipment	35,400
Direct labor	675,480	Sales	4,462,500
Indirect labor	56,875	Sales salaries expense	392,560

Required

1. Classify each cost as either a product or period cost.
2. Classify each product cost as either direct materials, direct labor, or factory overhead.
3. Classify each period cost as either selling expenses or general and administrative expenses.

Problem 14-3A
Schedule of cost of goods manufactured and income statement; inventory analysis
A1   P2

Using the data from Problem 14-2A and the following additional inventory information for Leone Company, complete the requirements below. Assume income tax expense is $233,725 for the year.

Inventories			
Raw materials, December 31, 2018	$166,850	Work in process, December 31, 2019	$ 19,380
Raw materials, December 31, 2019	182,000	Finished goods, December 31, 2018	167,350
Work in process, December 31, 2018	15,700	Finished goods, December 31, 2019	136,490

Required

Check (1) Cost of goods manufactured, $1,935,650

1. Prepare the company's 2019 schedule of cost of goods manufactured.
2. Prepare the company's 2019 income statement that reports separate categories for (*a*) selling expenses and (*b*) general and administrative expenses.

Analysis Component

3. Compute the (*a*) inventory turnover, defined as cost of goods sold divided by average inventory, and (*b*) days' sales in inventory, defined as 365 times ending inventory divided by cost of goods sold, for both its raw materials inventory and its finished goods inventory. (To compute turnover and days' sales in inventory for raw materials, use raw materials used rather than cost of goods sold.) Round answers to one decimal place.

Problem 14-4A
Ending inventory computation and evaluation
C4

Nazaro's Boot Company makes specialty boots for the rodeo circuit. At year-end, the company had (*a*) 300 pairs of boots in finished goods inventory and (*b*) 1,200 heels at a cost of $8 each in raw materials inventory. During the year, the company purchased 35,000 additional heels at $8 each and manufactured 16,600 pairs of boots.

Required

1. Determine the unit and dollar amounts of raw materials inventory in heels at year-end.

Analysis Component

2. Compute the dollar amount of working capital that can be reduced at year-end if the ending heel raw material inventory is cut by half.

Problem 14-5A
Inventory computation and reporting   C4   P1

Shown here are annual financial data taken from two different companies.

	Music World Retail	Wave-Board Manufacturing
Beginning inventory		
Merchandise	$200,000	
Finished goods.....................		$500,000
Cost of purchases.....................	300,000	
Cost of goods manufactured		875,000
Ending inventory		
Merchandise	175,000	
Finished goods.....................		225,000

Required

1. Compute the cost of goods sold section of the income statement for the year for each company.
2. Identify the inventory accounts and describe where each is reported on the income statement and balance sheet for both companies.

Check (1) Wave-Board's cost of goods sold, $1,150,000

Listed here are the total costs associated with the production of 15,000 Blu-ray Discs (BDs) manufactured by Maxwell. The BDs sell for $18 each.

PROBLEM SET B

Problem 14-1B
Cost computation, classification, and analysis

C2 C3

	Variable or Fixed		Product or Period	
Costs	Variable	Fixed	Product	Period
1. Plastic for BDs—$1,500	$1,500	____	$1,500	____
2. Wages of assembly workers—$30,000	____	____	____	____
3. Cost of factory rent—$6,750	____	____	____	____
4. Systems staff salaries—$15,000	____	____	____	____
5. Labeling—$0.25 per BD	____	____	____	____
6. Cost of office equipment rent—$1,050	____	____	____	____
7. Upper management salaries—$120,000	____	____	____	____
8. Annual fixed fee for cleaning service—$4,520	____	____	____	____
9. Sales commissions—$0.50 per BD	____	____	____	____
10. Machinery depreciation, straight-line—$18,000	____	____	____	____

Required

1. Classify each cost and its amount as (*a*) either variable or fixed and (*b*) either product or period. (The first cost is completed as an example.)
2. Compute the manufacturing cost per BD.

Check (2) Total variable production cost, $35,250

Analysis Component

3. Assume that 10,000 BDs are produced in the next year. What do you predict will be the total cost of plastic for the BDs and the per unit cost of the plastic for the BDs? Explain.
4. Assume that 10,000 BDs are produced in the next year. What do you predict will be the total cost of factory rent and the per unit cost of the factory rent? Explain.

The following calendar year-end information is taken from the December 31, 2019, adjusted trial balance and other records of Best Bikes.

Problem 14-2B
Classifying costs

C2 C3

Advertising expense	$ 20,250	Miscellaneous production costs	$ 8,440
Depreciation expense—Office equipment	8,440	Office salaries expense	70,875
Depreciation expense—Selling equipment	10,125	Raw materials purchases (direct materials)	894,375
Depreciation expense—Factory equipment	35,400	Rent expense—Office space	23,625
Factory supervision	121,500	Rent expense—Selling space	27,000
Factory supplies used (indirect materials)	6,060	Rent expense—Factory building	93,500
Factory utilities...........................	37,500	Maintenance expense—Factory equipment	30,375
Direct labor...............................	562,500	Sales.....................................	4,942,625
Indirect labor	59,000	Sales salaries expense	295,300

Required

1. Classify each cost as either a product or period cost.

2. Classify each product cost as either direct materials, direct labor, or factory overhead.

3. Classify each period cost as either selling expenses or general and administrative expenses.

Problem 14-3B
Schedule of cost of goods manufactured and income statement; analysis of inventories

A1   P2

Using the information from Problem 14-2B and the following additional inventory information for Best Bikes, complete the requirements below. Assume income tax expense is $136,700 for the year.

Inventories			
Raw materials, December 31, 2018.........	$40,375	Work in process, December 31, 2019........	$ 14,100
Raw materials, December 31, 2019.........	70,430	Finished goods, December 31, 2018	177,200
Work in process, December 31, 2018	12,500	Finished goods, December 31, 2019	141,750

Required

Check (1) Cost of goods manufactured, $1,816,995

1. Prepare the company's 2019 schedule of cost of goods manufactured.

2. Prepare the company's 2019 income statement that reports separate categories for (*a*) selling expenses and (*b*) general and administrative expenses.

Analysis Component

3. Compute the (*a*) inventory turnover, defined as cost of goods sold divided by average inventory, and (*b*) days' sales in inventory, defined as 365 times ending inventory divided by cost of goods sold, for both its raw materials inventory and its finished goods inventory. (To compute turnover and days' sales in inventory for raw materials, use raw materials used rather than cost of goods sold.) Discuss some possible reasons for differences between these ratios for the two types of inventories. Round answers to one decimal place.

Problem 14-4B
Ending inventory computation and evaluation

C4

Racer's Edge makes specialty skates for the ice skating circuit. At year-end, the company had (*a*) 1,500 skates in finished goods inventory and (*b*) 2,500 blades at a cost of $20 each in raw materials inventory. During the year, Racer's Edge purchased 45,000 additional blades at $20 each and manufactured 20,750 pairs of skates.

Required

1. Determine the unit and dollar amounts of raw materials inventory in blades at year-end.

Analysis Component

2. Write a half-page memorandum to the production manager explaining why a just-in-time inventory system for blades should be considered. Include the amount of working capital that can be reduced at year-end if the ending blade raw materials inventory is cut in half.

Problem 14-5B
Inventory computation and reporting

C4   P1

Shown here are annual financial data taken from two different companies.

	TeeMart (Retail)	Aim Labs (Manufacturing)
Beginning inventory		
Merchandise	$100,000	
Finished goods		$300,000
Cost of purchases....................	250,000	
Cost of goods manufactured		586,000
Ending inventory		
Merchandise	150,000	
Finished goods		200,000

Required

Check (1) TeeMart cost of goods sold, $200,000

1. Compute the cost of goods sold section of the income statement for the year for each company.

2. Write a half-page memorandum to your instructor (*a*) identifying the inventory accounts and (*b*) identifying where each is reported on the income statement and balance sheet for both companies.

This serial problem began in Chapter 1 and continues through most of the book. If previous chapter segments were not completed, the serial problem can begin at this point.

SERIAL PROBLEM
Business Solutions

C2 C4 P1 P2

SP 14 Santana Rey, owner of **Business Solutions**, decides to diversify her business by also manufacturing computer workstation furniture.

Required

1. Classify the following manufacturing costs of Business Solutions as either (*a*) variable (V) or fixed (F) and (*b*) direct (D) or indirect (I).

Manufacturing Costs	a. Variable or Fixed	b. Direct or Indirect
1. Monthly flat fee to clean workshop		
2. Laminate coverings for desktops		
3. Taxes on assembly workshop		
4. Glue to assemble workstation component parts		
5. Wages of desk assembler		
6. Electricity for workshop		
7. Depreciation on manufacturing tools		

©Alexander Image/Shutterstock

2. Prepare a schedule of cost of goods manufactured for Business Solutions for the month ended January 31, 2020. Assume the following manufacturing costs:

Direct materials: $2,200

Factory overhead: $490

Direct labor: $900

Beginning work in process: none (December 31, 2019)

Ending work in process: $540 (January 31, 2020)

Beginning finished goods inventory: none (December 31, 2019)

Ending finished goods inventory: $350 (January 31, 2020)

3. Prepare the cost of goods sold section of a partial income statement for Business Solutions for the month ended January 31, 2020.

Check (3) COGS, $2,700

Accounting Analysis

AA 14-1 Managerial accounting is more than recording, maintaining, and reporting financial results. Managerial accountants must provide managers with both financial and nonfinancial information including estimates, projections, and forecasts. An important estimate for **Apple** is its reserve for warranty claims, and the company must provide shareholders information on this estimate.

COMPANY
ANALYSIS

C1

APPLE

Required

1. Access Apple's annual report in Appendix A and locate "Accrued Warranty and Indemnification" on page A-9 of its notes. What amount of warranty expense did Apple record for 2017?

2. What amount of warranty claims did Apple pay during 2017?

3. What is Apple's accrued warranty liability at the end of 2017?

AA 14-2 Both **Apple** and **Google** (**Alphabet**) invest in research and development. Access each company's 2017 income statement from Appendix A.

COMPARATIVE
ANALYSIS

C2

APPLE
GOOGLE

Required

1. Compute the ratio of research and development expense to net sales for Apple.

2. Compute the ratio of research and development expense to net sales for Google.

3. Which company spent more (as a percentage of net sales) on research and development?

GLOBAL ANALYSIS

C1

Samsung

APPLE

AA 14-3 Samsung's 2017 annual report discloses the warranty information below. Like **Apple**, Samsung offers warranties on its products.

In millions of Korean won	Warranty Liability
Balance at January 1, 2017......................	₩1,747,857
Charged to the statement of profit or loss	2,032,311
Payment	(1,920,926)
Other......................................	152,336
Balance at December 31, 2017.................	₩2,011,578

Required

1. What amount of warranty expense did Samsung record in 2017? What amount of warranty claims did Samsung pay in 2017?

2. Access Apple's report in Appendix A and locate "Accrued Warranty and Indemnification" on page A-9 of its notes. What amount of warranty expense did Apple record during 2017? What amount of warranty claims did Apple pay in 2017?

3. Using answers from parts 1 and 2, which company was more accurate in estimating warranty claims for 2017?

Beyond the Numbers

ETHICS CHALLENGE

C3

BTN 14-1 Assume that you are the managerial accountant at Infostore, a manufacturer of hard drives, CDs, and DVDs. Its reporting year-end is December 31. The chief financial officer is concerned about having enough cash to pay the expected income tax bill because of poor cash flow management. On November 15, the purchasing department purchased excess inventory of CD raw materials in anticipation of rapid growth of this product beginning in January. To decrease the company's tax liability, the chief financial officer tells you to record the purchase of this inventory as part of supplies and expense it in the current year; this would decrease the company's tax liability by increasing expenses.

Required

1. In which account should the purchase of CD raw materials be recorded?

2. How should you respond to this request by the chief financial officer?

COMMUNICATING IN PRACTICE

C6

BTN 14-2 Write a one-page memorandum to a prospective college student about salary expectations for graduates in business. Compare and contrast the expected salaries for accounting (including different subfields such as public, corporate, tax, audit, and so forth), marketing, management, and finance majors. Prepare a graph showing average starting salaries (and those for experienced professionals in those fields if available). To get this information, stop by your school's career services office; libraries also have this information. The website **JobStar.org** (click on "Salary Info") also can get you started.

TAKING IT TO THE NET

C1

BTN 14-3 Managerial accounting professionals follow a code of ethics. As a member of the Institute of Management Accountants, the managerial accountant must comply with standards of ethical conduct.

Required

1. Read the *Statement of Ethical Professional Practice* posted at **IMAnet.org**. (Under "Career Resources" select "Ethics Center," and then select "IMA Statement of Ethical Professional Practice.")

2. What four overarching ethical principles underlie the IMA's statement?

3. Describe the courses of action the IMA recommends in resolving ethical conflicts.

BTN 14-4 The following calendar-year information is taken from the adjusted trial balance and other records of Dahlia Company.

Advertising expense	$ 19,125	Direct labor	$ 650,750
Depreciation expense—Office equipment	8,750	Indirect labor	60,000
Depreciation expense—Selling equipment	10,000	Miscellaneous production costs	8,500
Depreciation expense—Factory equipment	32,500	Office salaries expense	100,875
Factory supervision	122,500	Raw materials purchases (direct materials)	872,500
Factory supplies used (indirect materials)	15,750	Rent expense—Office space	21,125
Factory utilities	36,250	Rent expense—Selling space	25,750
Inventories		Rent expense—Factory building	79,750
Raw materials, beginning	177,500	Maintenance expense—Factory equipment	27,875
Raw materials, ending	168,125	Sales	3,275,000
Work in process, beginning	15,875	Sales discounts	57,500
Work in process, ending	14,000	Sales salaries expense	286,250
Finished goods, beginning	164,375		
Finished goods, ending	129,000		

Required

1. *Each* team member is to be responsible for computing **one** of the following amounts. You are not to duplicate your teammates' work. Get any necessary amounts from teammates. Each member is to explain the computation to the team in preparation for reporting to class.

   a. Direct materials used   **d.** Total cost of work in process

   b. Factory overhead   **e.** Cost of goods manufactured

   c. Total manufacturing costs

2. Check your cost of goods manufactured amount with the instructor. If it is correct, proceed to part 3.

3. *Each* team member is to be responsible for computing **one** of the following amounts. You are not to duplicate your teammates' work. Get any necessary amounts from teammates. Each member is to explain the computation to the team in preparation for reporting to class.

   a. Net sales   **d.** Total operating expenses

   b. Cost of goods sold   **e.** Net income or loss before taxes

   c. Gross profit

BTN 14-5 Kwami Williams and Emily Cunningham of **MoringaConnect** must understand manufacturing costs to effectively operate and succeed as a profitable and efficient business.

Required

1. What are the three main categories of manufacturing costs Kwami and Emily must monitor and control? Provide examples of each.

2. What are four goals of a total quality management process? *Hint:* The goals are listed in a margin "Point." How can MoringaConnect use TQM to improve its business activities?

BTN 14-6 Visit your favorite fast-food restaurant. Observe its business operations.

Required

1. Describe all business activities from the time a customer arrives to the time that customer departs.

2. List all costs you can identify with the separate activities described in part 1.

3. Classify each cost from part 2 as fixed or variable and explain your classification.

15 Job Order Costing and Analysis

Chapter Preview

JOB ORDER COSTING

Cost accounting system

C1 Job order production

Job order vs. process operations

Production activities

Cost flows

C2 Job cost sheet

NTK 15-1

MATERIALS AND LABOR COSTS

P1 Materials cost flows and documents

P2 Labor cost flows and documents

Linking materials and labor with job cost sheet

NTK 15-2, 15-3

OVERHEAD COSTS

P3 Predetermined overhead rate

Applied overhead

Actual overhead

Summary of cost flows

Job cost sheets for decisions

Schedule of cost of goods manufactured

NTK 15-4, 15-5

ADJUSTING OVERHEAD AND SERVICE USES

Overhead account

P4 Underapplied or overapplied overhead

Job order costing for services

A1 Pricing services

NTK 15-6

Learning Objectives

CONCEPTUAL

C1 Describe important features of job order production.

C2 Explain job cost sheets and how they are used in job order costing.

ANALYTICAL

A1 Apply job order costing in pricing services.

PROCEDURAL

P1 Describe and record the flow of materials costs in job order costing.

P2 Describe and record the flow of labor costs in job order costing.

P3 Describe and record the flow of overhead costs in job order costing.

P4 Determine adjustments for overapplied and underapplied factory overhead.

Custom Kid

"You're never too young to be an entrepreneur"
—**BRENNAN AGRANOFF**

©HoopSwagg

PORTLAND, OR—At a high school game, basketball fanatic Brennan Agranoff noticed most players were wearing plain **Nike** elite socks. Why not print custom designs on them, he wondered? Brennan's company, **HoopSwagg** (**hoopswagg.com**), stemmed from that simple question.

Brennan faced several hurdles in getting HoopSwagg off the ground. Only 13 years old at the time, he had no business training, no knowledge of the sock-making process, and no capital. Undaunted, Brennan spent six months learning about business logistics and machinery needs. He then convinced his parents, who "thought the concept was a bit out there," to loan him $3,000. "We checked out his numbers," says mother Maia, "and they made sense." Brennan taught himself computer coding to set up his website and how to use graphic design tools to develop his designs.

Brennan's learning extended to accounting and how to track materials, labor, and overhead costs. Businesses like Brennan's that produce goods to customer order use job order costing to determine the cost of each order. Understanding what customers want, and the costs required, enables Brennan to properly price orders. Rising sales required a new 1,500-square-foot production building that increased overhead costs. Job order costing enables entrepreneurs like Brennan to control these and other types of costs that are often the downfall of start-ups.

From modest beginnings working from his parents' garage, HoopSwagg now processes 70–100 orders per day, generating over $1 million per year in revenue. Brennan recently bought a competitor, increasing his customer base and number of designs. "Get out of your comfort zone and go for it," Brennan advises aspiring young entrepreneurs.

Sources: *HoopSwagg website,* January 2019; *money.cnn.com,* April 20, 2017; *entrepreneur.com,* August 18, 2017; *kgw.com,* April 21, 2017

JOB ORDER COSTING

This section describes a cost accounting system, job order production and costing, and a job cost sheet.

Cost Accounting System

A **cost accounting system** accumulates production costs and assigns them to products and services. Timely information about inventories and costs is used by managers to control costs and set selling prices.

The two basic types of cost accounting systems are *job order costing* and *process costing*. We describe job order costing in this chapter and process costing in the next chapter.

C1

Describe important features of job order production.

Job Order Production

Many companies produce products individually designed to meet the needs of a specific customer. Each customized product is manufactured separately, and its production is called **job order production,** or *job order manufacturing* (also called *customized production,* which is the production of products in response to special orders). Examples of such products or services include special-order machines, a factory building, custom jewelry, wedding invitations, tattoos, and audits by an accounting firm.

The production activities for a customized product represent a **job.** A key feature of job order production is the diversity, often called *heterogeneity,* of the products produced. Each customer order differs from another customer order in some important respect. These differences can be large or small. For example, **Nike** allows custom orders over the Internet, enabling customers to select materials and colors and to personalize their shoes with letters and numbers.

When a job involves producing more than one unit of a custom product, it is called a **job lot.** Products produced as job lots could include benches for a park, imprinted T-shirts for a 10K race, or advertising signs for a chain of stores. Although these orders involve more than one unit, the volume of production is typically low, such as 50 benches, 200 T-shirts, or 100 signs.

Courtesy of JJW Images

Job Order vs. Process Operations

Process operations, also called *process manufacturing* or *process production,* is the mass production of products in a continuous flow of steps. Unlike job order production, where every product differs depending on customer needs, process operations are designed to mass-produce large quantities of identical products. For example, each year **Penn** makes millions of tennis balls and **The Hershey Company** produces over a billion pounds of chocolate.

Exhibit 15.1 lists important features of job order and process operations. Movies made by **Walt Disney** and financial audits done by **KPMG** are examples of job order service operations. Order processing in large mail-order firms like **L.L. Bean** is an example of a process service operation.

EXHIBIT 15.1

Comparing Job Order and Process Operations

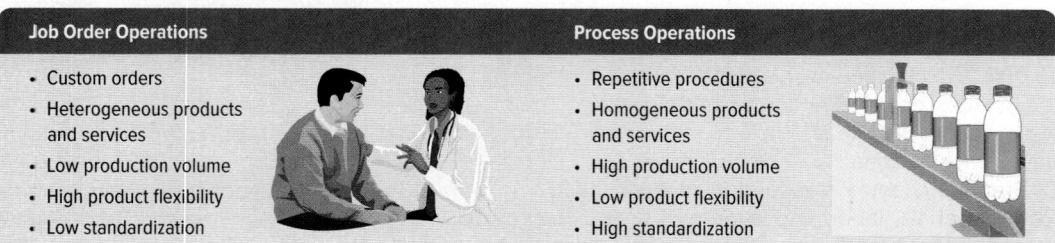

Job Order Operations	Process Operations
• Custom orders	• Repetitive procedures
• Heterogeneous products and services	• Homogeneous products and services
• Low production volume	• High production volume
• High product flexibility	• Low product flexibility
• Low standardization	• High standardization

Production Activities in Job Order Costing

EXHIBIT 15.2

Job Order Production Activities and Cost Flows

An overview of job order production activity and cost flows is shown in Exhibit 15.2. This exhibit shows the March production activity of Road Warriors, which installs entertainment systems and security devices in cars and trucks. The company customizes any vehicle by adding speakers, amplifiers, video systems, alarms, and reinforced exteriors.

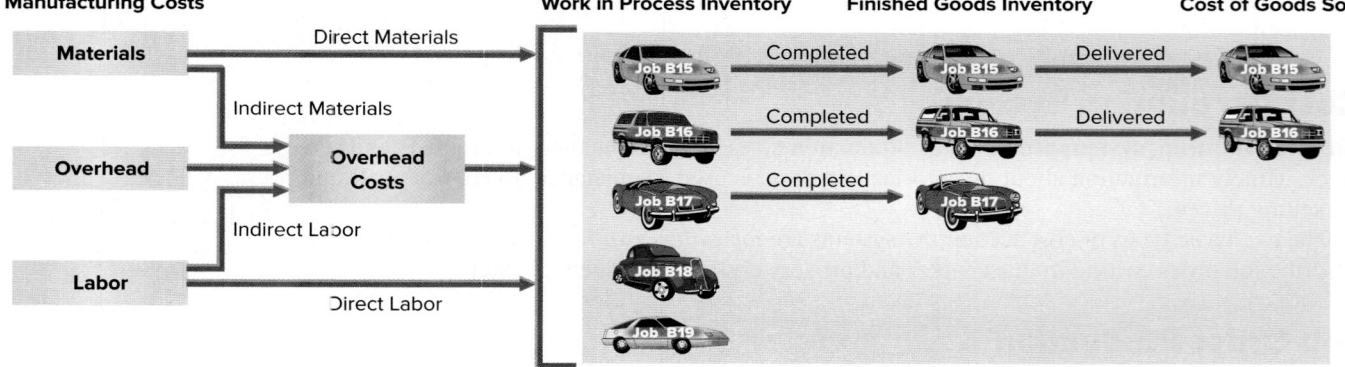

Job order production requires materials, labor, and overhead costs.

- *Direct materials* are used in manufacturing and can be clearly identified with one job.
- *Direct labor* is employee effort on one particular job.
- *Overhead* costs support production of more than one job.

Common overhead items are depreciation on factory buildings and equipment, factory supplies (indirect materials), supervision and maintenance (indirect labor), factory insurance and property taxes, cleaning, and utilities.

Exhibit 15.2 shows that materials, labor, and overhead are added to five jobs started during the month (March). Alarm systems are added to Jobs B15 and B16; Job B17 receives a high-end audio and video entertainment system. Road Warriors completed Jobs B15, B16, and B17 in March and delivered Jobs B15 and B16 to customers. At the end of March, Jobs B18 and B19 remain in work in process inventory and Job B17 is in finished goods inventory.

Decision Insight

Target Costing Many producers determine a **target cost** for their jobs. Target cost is determined as follows: Expected selling price − Desired profit = Target cost. If the projected target cost of the job as determined by job costing is too high, the producer can apply *value engineering,* which is a method of determining ways to reduce job cost until the target cost is met. ∎

Cost Flows

Manufacturing costs flow through inventory accounts (Raw Materials Inventory, Work in Process Inventory, and Finished Goods Inventory) until the related goods are sold. While a job is being produced, its accumulated costs are kept in **Work in Process Inventory.** When a job is finished, its accumulated costs are transferred from Work in Process Inventory to **Finished Goods Inventory.** When a finished job is delivered to a customer, its accumulated costs are transferred from Finished Goods Inventory to Cost of Goods Sold.

These general ledger inventory accounts, however, do not provide enough cost detail for managers of job order operations to plan and control production activities. Managers need to know the costs of each individual job (or job lot). Subsidiary records store this information about the costs for each individual job. The next section describes the use of these subsidiary records and how they relate to general ledger accounts.

Point: Raw Materials Inventory, Work in Process Inventory, Finished Goods Inventory, and Cost of Goods Sold are general ledger accounts.

Job Cost Sheet

A major aim of a **job order costing system** is to determine the cost of producing each job or job lot. In the case of a job lot, the system also computes the cost per unit. The accounting system must include separate records for each job or job lot to accomplish this.

A **job cost sheet** is a cost record maintained for each job. Exhibit 15.3 shows a job cost sheet for Road Warriors. This job cost sheet identifies the customer, the job number, the costs, and key dates. Only product costs are recorded on job cost sheets. Direct materials and direct labor costs incurred on the job are recorded on this sheet. For Job B15, the direct materials and direct labor costs total $600 and $1,000, respectively. *Estimated* overhead costs are included on job cost sheets, through a process we discuss later in the chapter. For Job B15, estimated overhead costs are $1,600, computed as $1,000 of actual direct labor costs × 160%. When each job is complete, the supervisor enters the completion date and signs the sheet. Managers use job cost sheets to monitor costs incurred to date and to predict and control costs for each job.

C2
Explain job cost sheets and how they are used in job order costing.

Point: Documents (electronic and paper) are crucial in a job order system. The job cost sheet is the cornerstone. It aids in grasping concepts of capitalizing product costs and product cost flow.

EXHIBIT 15.3
Job Cost Sheet

Road Warriors, Los Angeles, California							JOB COST SHEET	
Customer's Name	Carroll Connor			Job No.	B15			
Address	1542 High Point Dr.			City & State	Malibu, California			
Job Description	Level 1 Alarm System on Ford Expedition							
Date promised	March 15	Date started	March 3		Date completed	March 11		

Direct Materials			Direct Labor			Overhead		
Date	Requisition	Cost	Date	Time Ticket	Cost	Date	Rate	Cost
3/3/2019	R-4698	$ 100	3/3/2019	L-3393	$ 120	3/11/2019	160% of	$1,600
3/7/2019	R-4705	225	3/4/2019	L-3422	150		Direct	
3/9/2019	R-4725	180	3/5/2019	L-3456	180		Labor	
3/10/2019	R-4777	95	3/8/2019	L-3479	60		Cost	
			3/9/2019	L-3501	90			
			3/10/2019	L-3535	240			
			3/11/2019	L-3559	160			
	Total	$600		Total	$1,000		Total	$1,600

REMARKS: Completed job on March 11, and shipped to customer on March 15. Met all specifications and requirements.	SUMMARY:	
	Materials	$ 600
	Labor	1,000
	Overhead	1,600
Signed: *C. Luther, Supervisor*	Total cost	$3,200

DM (actual)
+ DL (actual)
+ FOH (estimated)
= Total job cost

Linking Job Cost Sheets with General Ledger Accounts Balances in the general ledger accounts equal the sums of costs on job cost sheets as defined in the table below.

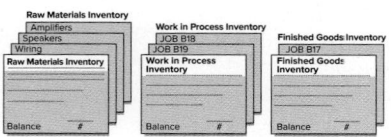

General ledger account	Balance equals sum of costs on job cost sheets for
Work in Process Inventory	All jobs not yet done
Finished Goods Inventory	All jobs complete but not yet sold
Cost of Goods Sold	All jobs sold and delivered during that period

NEED-TO-KNOW 15-1

Job Cost Sheet

C2

A manufacturer's job cost sheet reports direct materials of $1,200 and direct labor of $250 for printing 200 T-shirts for a bikers' reunion. Estimated overhead is computed as 140% of direct labor costs.

1. What is the estimated overhead cost for this job?

2. What is the total cost per T-shirt for this job?

3. What journal entry does the manufacturer make upon completion of this job to transfer costs from work in process to finished goods?

Solution

1. Estimated overhead = $250 \times 140\% = \$350$

2. Cost per T-shirt = Total cost/Total number in job lot = $1,800/200 = $9 per shirt

3.

Finished Goods Inventory	1,800	
Work in Process Inventory....................		1,800
Transfer cost of completed job.		

Do More: QS 15-2, QS 15-15, E 15-2, E 15-3

MATERIALS AND LABOR COSTS

We look at job order costing in more detail, including the source documents for each cost flow.

Materials Cost Flows and Documents

P1

Describe and record the flow of materials costs in job order costing.

Point: Some companies certify certain suppliers based on the quality of their materials. Goods received from these suppliers are not always inspected by the purchaser to save costs.

Continuing our example, assume that Road Warriors begins the month (March) with $1,000 in Raw Materials Inventory and $0 balances in the Work in Process Inventory and Finished Goods Inventory accounts. We begin with analysis of the flow of materials costs in Exhibit 15.4. When materials are first received from suppliers, employees count and inspect them and record the items' quantity and cost on a receiving report. The **receiving report** serves as the *source document* for recording materials received in both a materials ledger card and in the general ledger. In nearly all job order cost systems, **materials ledger cards** (or digital files) are perpetual records that are updated each time materials are purchased and each time materials are issued for use in production.

Materials

EXHIBIT 15.4

Materials Cost Flows

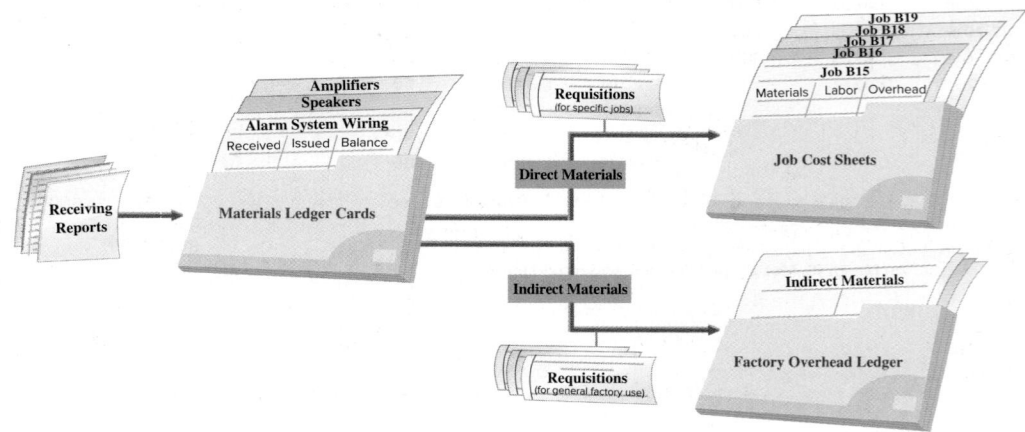

Materials Purchases

Road Warriors bought $2,750 of materials on credit on March 4, 2019. These include both direct and indirect materials. This purchase is recorded below. Each individual materials ledger card is updated to reflect the added materials.

Mar. 4	Raw Materials Inventory	2,750	
	Accounts Payable		2,750
	Record purchase of materials for production.		

Materials Use (Requisitions)

Exhibit 15.4 shows that materials can be requisitioned for use either on a specific job (direct materials) or as overhead (indirect materials). Direct materials include costs, such as alarm system wiring, that are easily traced to individual jobs. Indirect materials include costs, such as those for screws, that are not easily traced to jobs. Direct materials costs flow to job cost sheets. Indirect materials costs flow to the Indirect Materials account in the factory overhead ledger, which is a subsidiary ledger controlled by the Factory Overhead account in the general ledger. The factory overhead ledger includes all of the individual overhead costs.

Exhibit 15.5 shows a materials ledger card for one type of material received and issued by Road Warriors. The card identifies the item as alarm system wiring and shows the item's stock number, its location in the storeroom, information about the maximum and minimum quantities that should be available, and the reorder quantity. For example, two units of alarm system wiring were purchased on March 4, 2019, as evidenced by receiving report C-7117. After this purchase the company has three units of alarm system wiring in inventory.

EXHIBIT 15.5

Materials Ledger Card

MATERIALS LEDGER CARD — Road Warriors, Los Angeles, California

Item	Alarm system wiring	Stock No.	M–347	Location in Storeroom	Bin 137
Maximum quantity	5 units	Minimum quantity	1 unit	Quantity to reorder	2 units

	Received				Issued				Balance		
Date	Receiving Report Number	Units	Unit Price	Total Price	Requi- sition Number	Units	Unit Price	Total Price	Units	Unit Price	Total Price
3/4/2019	C-7117	2	$225	$450					1 3	$225 225	$225 675
3/7/2019					R–4705	1	$225	$225	2	225	450

When materials are needed in production, a production manager prepares a **materials requisition** and sends it to the materials manager. For direct materials, the requisition shows the job number, the type of material, the quantity needed, and the production manager's signature. Exhibit 15.6 shows the materials requisition for alarm system wiring for Job B15. For requisitions of indirect materials, the "Job No." line in the requisition form might read "For General Factory Use."

EXHIBIT 15.6

Materials Requisition

Requisitions often are accumulated by job and recorded in one journal entry. The frequency of entries depends on the job, the industry, and management procedures. In this example, Road Warriors records materials requisitions at the end of each week. Total amounts of materials requisitions follow.

Direct materials—requisitioned for specific jobs	
Job B15	$ 600
Job B16	300
Job B17	500
Job B18	150
Job B19	250
Total direct materials	$1,800
Indirect materials—requisitioned for general factory use	550
Total materials requisitions	$ 2,350

Use of direct materials for the week (including alarm system wiring for Job B15) yields this entry.

Mar. 7	Work in Process Inventory...........	1,800	
	Raw Materials Inventory........		1,800
	Record use of direct materials.		

This entry is posted both to general ledger accounts and to subsidiary records. Exhibit 15.7 shows the postings to general ledger accounts (Work in Process Inventory and Raw Materials Inventory) and to the job cost sheets (subsidiary records). The exhibit shows summary job cost sheets for all five jobs, and it shows a detailed partial job cost sheet (excerpted from Exhibit 15.3) for Job B15.

The Raw Materials Inventory account began the month with $1,000 of beginning inventory; it was increased for the March 4 purchase of $2,750. The $1,800 cost of materials used reduces Raw Materials Inventory and increases Work in Process Inventory. The total amount of direct materials used so far ($1,800) is also reflected in the job cost sheets. Later we show the accounting for indirect materials. At this point, it is important to know that requisitions of indirect materials are not separately recorded on job cost sheets.

EXHIBIT 15.7

Posting Direct Materials Used to the General Ledger and Job Cost Sheets

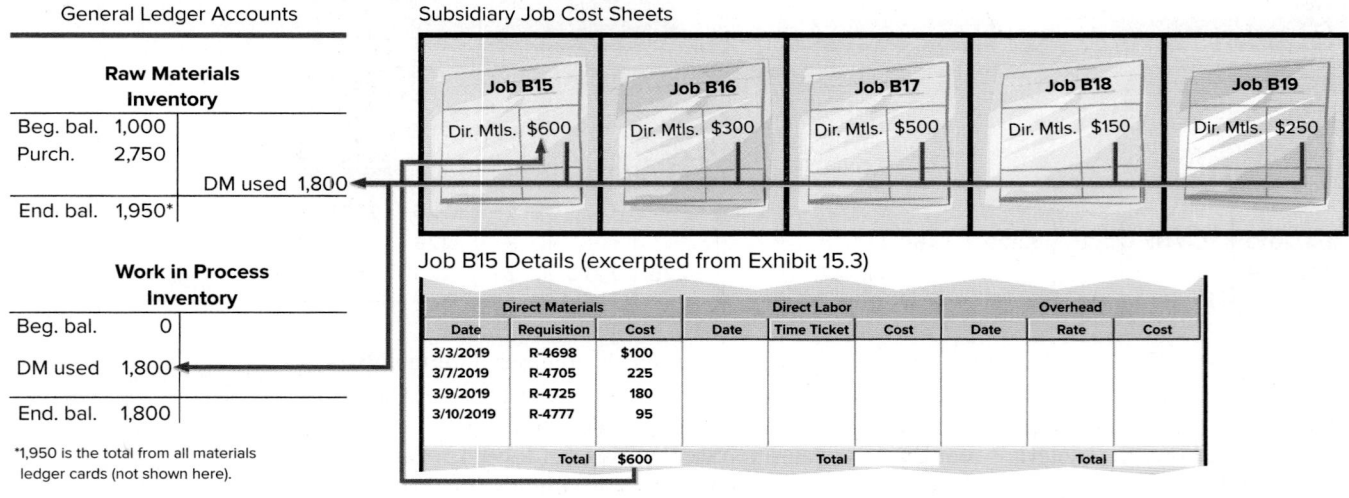

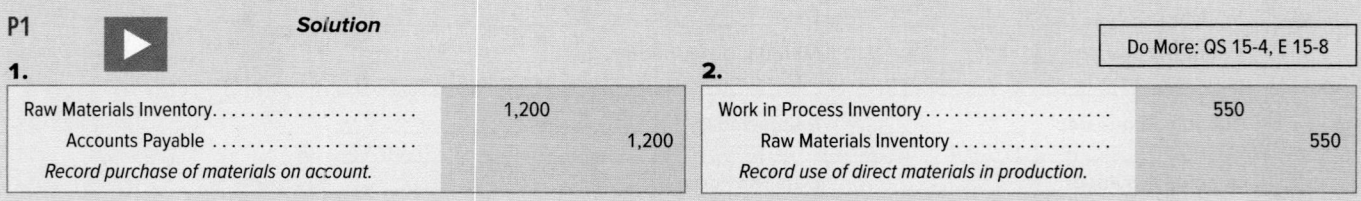

Prepare journal entries to record the following transactions.

1. A manufacturing company purchased $1,200 of materials (on account) for use in production.

2. The company used $200 of direct materials on Job 1 and $350 of direct materials on Job 2.

Recording Direct Materials

P1

Solution

Do More: QS 15-4, E 15-8

1.

Raw Materials Inventory.....................	1,200	
Accounts Payable		1,200
Record purchase of materials on account.		

2.

Work in Process Inventory	550	
Raw Materials Inventory		550
Record use of direct materials in production.		

Labor Cost Flows and Documents

Exhibit 15.8 shows that labor costs are classified as either direct or indirect. Direct labor costs flow to job cost sheets. To assign direct labor costs to individual jobs, companies use **time tickets** to track how each employee's time is used and to record how much time they spent on each job. This process is often automated: Employees swipe electronic identification badges, and a computer system assigns employees' hours worked to individual jobs. An employee who works on several jobs during a day completes separate time tickets for each job. In all cases, supervisors check and approve the accuracy of time tickets.

Indirect labor includes factory costs like supervisor salaries and maintenance worker wages. These costs are not assigned directly to individual jobs. Instead, the company determines the amounts of supervisor salaries from their salary contracts and the amounts of maintenance worker wages from time tickets and classifies those costs as overhead. Indirect labor costs flow to the factory overhead ledger.

P2

Describe and record the flow of labor costs in job order costing.

Labor

Point: Many employee fraud schemes involve payroll, including overstated hours on time tickets.

EXHIBIT 15.8

Labor Cost Flows

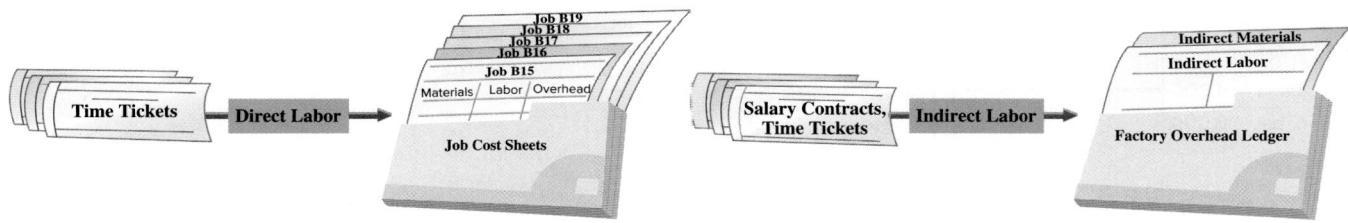

Exhibit 15.9 shows a time ticket reporting the time a Road Warrior employee spent working on Job B15. The employee's supervisor signed the ticket to confirm its accuracy. The hourly rate and total labor cost are recorded after the time ticket is turned in.

EXHIBIT 15.9

Time Ticket

Road Warriors
Los Angeles, California

TIME TICKET No. L–3479 **Date** March 8 **20** 19

Employee Name	Employee Number	Job No.
T. Zeller	3969	B15

TIME AND RATE INFORMATION:

	Start Time	Finish Time	Elapsed Time	Hourly Rate
Remarks	9:00	12:00	3.0	$20

Approved By ...... C. Luther ...... **Total Cost** $60

Time tickets are often accumulated and recorded in one journal entry. The frequency of these entries varies across companies. In this example, Road Warriors journalizes direct labor monthly. During March, Road Warriors's factory payroll costs total $5,300. Of this amount, $4,200 can be traced directly to jobs, and the remaining $1,100 is classified as indirect labor, as shown below.

Direct labor—traceable to specific jobs	
Job B15	$ 1,000
Job B16	800
Job B17	1,100
Job B18	700
Job B19	600
Total direct labor...................	$4,200
Indirect labor—general factory use	1,100
Total labor cost.....................	$ 5,300

This entry records direct labor based on all the direct labor time tickets for the month.

Mar. 31	Work in Process Inventory..........	4,200	
	Factory Wages Payable.........		4,200
	Record direct labor used for the month.		

EXHIBIT 15.10

Posting Direct Labor to General Ledger and Job Cost Sheets

This entry is posted to the general ledger accounts, Work in Process Inventory and Factory Wages Payable (or Cash, if paid), and to individual job cost sheets. Exhibit 15.10 shows these postings. The exhibit shows summary job cost sheets for all five jobs, and it shows a partial job cost sheet (excerpted from Exhibit 15.3) for Job B15.

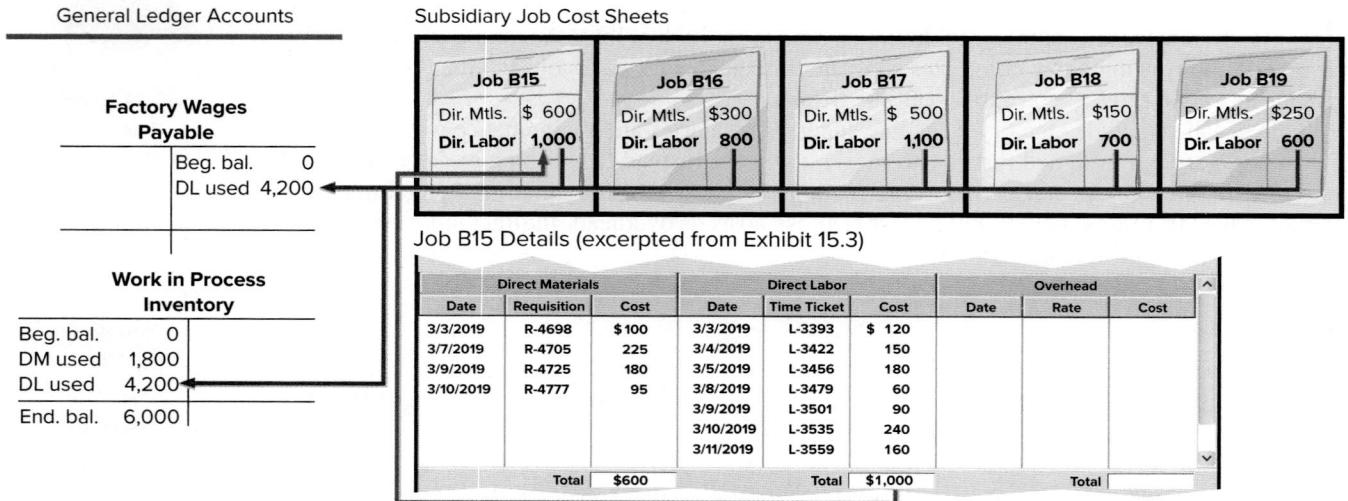

Time tickets are used to determine how much of the monthly direct labor cost ($4,200) to assign to specific jobs. This total matches the amount of direct labor posted to the Work in Process Inventory general ledger account. After this entry is posted, the balance in Work in Process Inventory is $6,000, consisting of $1,800 of direct materials and $4,200 of direct labor. Later we show the accounting for indirect labor, which is not separately recorded on job cost sheets.

 **15-3**

Recording Direct Labor

P2 ▶

Do More: QS 15-5, E 15-9

A manufacturing company used $5,400 of direct labor in production activities in May. Of this amount, $3,100 of direct labor was used on Job A1 and $2,300 of direct labor was used on Job A2. Prepare the journal entry to record direct labor used.

Solution

Work in Process Inventory	5,400	
Factory Wages Payable		5,400
Record direct labor used in production.		

OVERHEAD COSTS

P3 _____

Describe and record the flow of overhead costs in job order costing.

Overhead

Unlike direct materials and direct labor, actual overhead costs are not traced directly to individual jobs. Still, each job's total cost must include *estimated* overhead costs.

Overhead Process   Accounting for overhead costs follows the four-step process shown in Exhibit 15.11. Overhead accounting requires managers to first estimate what total overhead costs will be for the coming period. We cannot wait until the end of a period to apply overhead to jobs because managers' decisions require up-to-date costs. Overhead cost, even if it is not exactly precise, is needed to estimate a job's total costs before its completion. Such estimated costs are useful in setting prices and identifying costs that are out of control. At the end of the year, the company adjusts its estimated overhead to the actual amount of overhead incurred for that year and then considers whether to change its predetermined overhead rate for the next year. We discuss each of these steps.

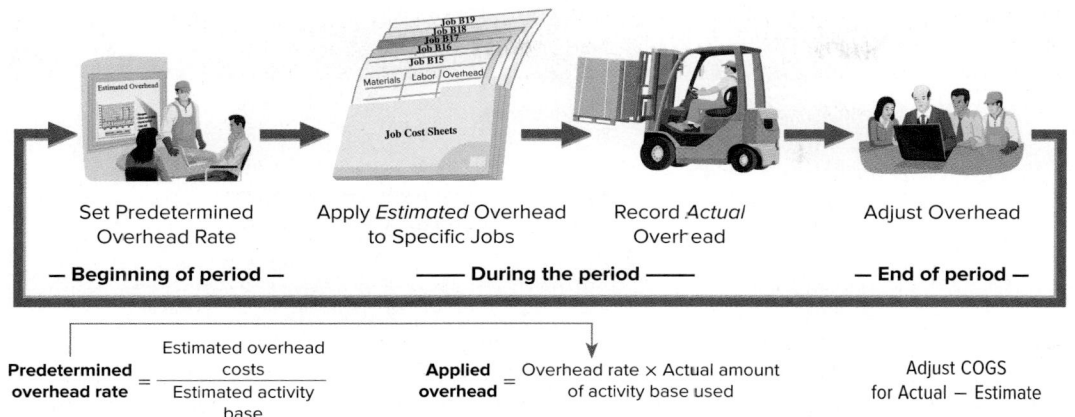

EXHIBIT 15.11

Four-Step Process for Overhead

Set Predetermined Overhead Rate

Estimating overhead in advance requires a **predetermined overhead rate,** also called *predetermined overhead allocation* (or *application*) *rate*. This requires an estimate of total overhead cost and an estimated activity base such as total direct labor cost *before* the start of the period. Exhibit 15.12 shows the formula for computing a predetermined overhead rate (estimates are commonly based on annual amounts). This rate is used during the period to apply estimated overhead to jobs, based on each job's *actual* usage of the activity. Some companies use multiple predetermined overhead rates for different types of products and services.

Point: Predetermined overhead rates can be estimated using mathematical equations, statistical analysis, or professional experience.

$$\text{Predetermined overhead rate} = \frac{\text{Estimated overhead costs}}{\text{Estimated activity base}}$$

EXHIBIT 15.12

Predetermined Overhead Rate Formula

Overhead Activity Base   We apply overhead by linking it to another factor used in production, such as direct labor or machine hours. The factor to which overhead costs are linked is known as the *activity* (or *allocation*) *base*. There should be a "cause and effect" relation between the base and overhead costs. A manager must think carefully about how many and which activity bases to use. This managerial decision influences the accuracy with which overhead costs are applied to individual jobs, which might impact a manager's decisions for pricing or performance evaluation.

Apply Estimated Overhead

Road Warriors applies (also termed *allocates, assigns,* or *charges*) overhead by linking it to direct labor costs using this formula.

Applied overhead = Predetermined overhead rate × Actual amount of activity base used

At the start of the current year, management estimates total direct labor costs of $125,000 and total overhead costs of $200,000. Using these estimates, management computes its predetermined overhead rate as 160% of direct labor cost ($200,000 ÷ $125,000). Earlier we showed that Road Warriors used $4,200 of direct labor in March. We now apply the predetermined overhead rate of 160% to get $6,720 (equal to $4,200 × 1.60) of estimated overhead for March. The entry is

Point: Factory Overhead is a temporary account that is closed to zero at the end of the year.

Mar. 31	Work in Process Inventory............................	6,720	
	Factory Overhead..............................		6,720
	Apply overhead at 160% of direct labor.		

The $6,720 of overhead is then applied to each individual job based on the amount of the activity base that job used (in this example, direct labor). Exhibit 15.13 shows these calculations for March's production activity.

EXHIBIT 15.13

Applying Estimated
Overhead to Specific Jobs*

*160% of direct labor cost

Job	Direct Labor Cost	Predetermined Overhead Rate	Applied Overhead
B15	$1,000	1.6	$1,600
B16	800	1.6	1,280
B17	1,100	1.6	1,760
B18	700	1.6	1,120
B19	600	1.6	960
Total.	$4,200		$6,720

EXHIBIT 15.14

Posting Overhead to
General Ledger and Job
Cost Sheets

After the applied overhead is recorded and the amounts of overhead applied to each job are determined (Exhibit 15.13), postings to general ledger accounts and to individual job cost sheets follow, as in Exhibit 15.14. For all five jobs, summary job cost sheets are presented first, and then a
more detailed partial job cost sheet (excerpted from Exhibit 15.3) is shown for Job B15. (Compare the partial job cost sheet for Job B15 in this exhibit to the complete version in Exhibit 15.3.)

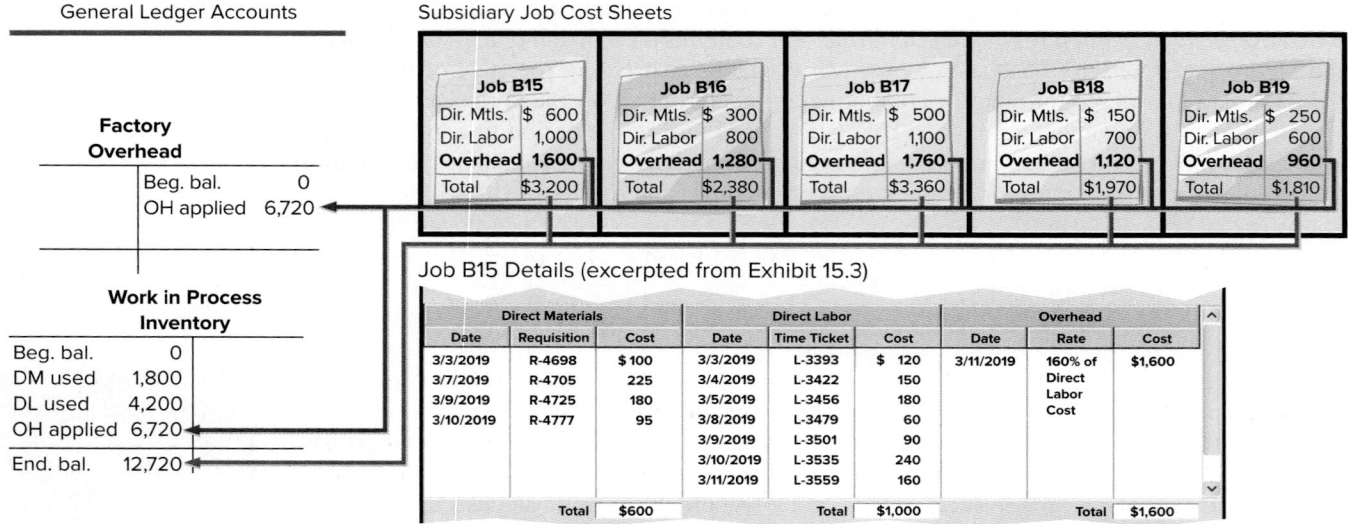

At this point, $6,720 of estimated overhead has been posted to general ledger accounts and to
individual job cost sheets. In addition, the ending balance in the Work in Process Inventory
account ($12,720) equals the sum of the ending balances in the job cost sheets. In the next sec-
tion we discuss how to record *actual* overhead.

NEED-TO-KNOW 15-4

Recording Applied
Overhead

P3

A manufacturing company estimates it will incur $240,000 of overhead costs in the next year. The company
applies overhead using machine hours and estimates it will use 1,600 machine hours in the next year.
During the month of June, the company used 80 machine hours on Job 1 and 70 machine hours on Job 2.

1. Compute the predetermined overhead rate to be used to apply overhead during the year.
2. Determine how much overhead should be applied to Job 1 and to Job 2 for June.
3. Prepare the journal entry to record overhead applied for June.

Solution

1. $240,000/1,600 = $150 per machine hour
2. 80 × $150 = $12,000 applied to Job 1; 70 × $150 = $10,500 applied to Job 2
3.

Work in Process Inventory	22,500	
Factory Overhead		22,500
Record applied overhead.		

Do More: QS 15-6, QS 15-7,
QS 15-8, E 15-10

Record Actual Overhead

We now show the accounting for actual overhead costs. Actual overhead costs are not recorded in job cost sheets. (Recall, allocated overhead costs are recorded on job cost sheets.) Factory overhead includes all factory costs other than direct materials and direct labor. Two major sources of overhead costs are *indirect* materials and *indirect* labor. These costs are recorded from materials requisition forms for indirect materials and from salary contracts or time tickets for indirect labor. Other sources of information on overhead costs include (1) vouchers authorizing payment for factory items such as supplies or utilities and (2) adjusting journal entries for costs such as depreciation on factory assets.

Actual factory overhead costs are recorded with debits to the Factory Overhead general ledger account and with credits to various accounts. While journal entries for different types of overhead costs might be recorded with varying frequency, in our example we assume these entries are made at the end of the month.

Point: Companies also incur *non-manufacturing* costs, such as advertising, salespersons' salaries, and depreciation on assets not used in production. These types of costs are not considered overhead, but instead are treated as period costs and charged directly to the income statement.

Record Indirect Materials Used
During March, Road Warriors incurred $550 of actual indirect materials costs, as supported by materials requisitions. The use of these indirect materials yields the following entry.

Mar. 31	Factory Overhead	550	
	Raw Materials Inventory		550
	Record indirect materials used during the month.		

This entry is posted to the general ledger accounts, Factory Overhead and Raw Materials Inventory, and is posted to Indirect Materials in the subsidiary factory overhead ledger. Unlike the recording of *direct* materials, actual *indirect* materials costs incurred are *not* recorded in Work in Process Inventory and are not posted to job cost sheets.

Record Indirect Labor Used
During March, Road Warriors incurred $1,100 of actual indirect labor costs. These costs might be supported by time tickets for maintenance workers or by salary contracts for production supervisors. The use of this indirect labor yields the following entry.

Mar. 31	Factory Overhead	1,100	
	Factory Wages Payable		1,100
	Record indirect labor used during the month.		

This entry is posted to the general ledger accounts, Factory Overhead and Factory Wages Payable, and is posted to Indirect Labor in the subsidiary factory overhead ledger. Unlike the recording of *direct* labor, actual *indirect* labor costs incurred are *not* recorded in Work in Process Inventory and are not posted to job cost sheets.

Record Other Overhead Costs
During March, Road Warriors incurred $5,270 of actual other overhead costs. These costs could include items such as factory building rent, depreciation on the factory building, factory utilities, and other costs indirectly related to production activities. These costs are recorded with debits to Factory Overhead and credits to other accounts such as Cash, Accounts Payable, Utilities Payable, and Accumulated Depreciation—Factory Equipment. The entry to record Road Warriors's other overhead costs for March follows.

Mar. 31	Factory Overhead	5,270	
	Accumulated Depreciation—Factory Equipment		2,400
	Rent Payable		1,620
	Utilities Payable		250
	Prepaid Insurance		1,000
	Record actual overhead costs for the month.		

Factory Overhead
0	
	550
	1,100
	5,270
	6,920

This entry is posted to the general ledger account, Factory Overhead, and is posted to separate accounts for each of the overhead items in the subsidiary factory overhead ledger. These actual overhead costs are *not* recorded in Work in Process Inventory and are not posted to job cost sheets. Only estimated overhead is recorded in Work in Process Inventory and posted to job cost sheets.

NEED-TO-KNOW 15-5

Recording Actual Overhead

P3

Do More: E 15-6, E 15-10

A manufacturing company used $400 of indirect materials and $2,000 of indirect labor during the month. The company also incurred $1,200 for depreciation on factory equipment, $500 for depreciation on office equipment, and $300 for factory utilities. Prepare the necessary journal entries.

Solution

Factory Overhead...	3,900	
Raw Materials Inventory.................................		400
Factory Wages Payable.................................		2,000
Accumulated Depreciation—Factory Equipment*..............		1,200
Utilities Payable.......................................		300
Record actual overhead costs used in production.		
Depreciation Expense.......................................	500	
Accumulated Depreciation—Office Equipment................		500
Record depreciation on office equipment.		

*Depreciation on office equipment is a period cost and is excluded from factory overhead.

Summary of Cost Flows

EXHIBIT 15.15

Cost Flows and Reports

In this section we summarize the flow of costs. Exhibit 15.15 shows how costs for a manufacturing company flow to its financial statements.

Balance Sheet						Income Statement	
Raw Materials Inventory		**Work in Process Inventory**		**Finished Goods Inventory**			
Beg. bal.		Beg. bal.		Beg. bal.			
Purch.		→DM used	Cost of goods→	→COGM	Cost of goods sold→	→Cost of goods sold............	
Mtls. available		DL used*	manufactured	End. bal.		Selling expenses..............	
	DM used→	OH applied†	(COGM)‡			General and admin. expenses ...	
End. bal.		End. bal.					

*From time tickets.   † Predetermined overhead rate × Actual amount of activity base used.   ‡ Reported on schedule of cost of goods manufactured.

Exhibit 15.15 shows that direct materials used, direct labor used, and factory overhead applied flow through the Work in Process Inventory and Finished Goods Inventory balance sheet accounts. The cost of goods manufactured (COGM) is computed and shown on the schedule of cost of goods manufactured. When goods are sold, their costs are transferred from Finished Goods Inventory on the balance sheet to the income statement as cost of goods sold. For Road Warriors, the journal entries to record the flow of costs from Work in Process Inventory to Finished Goods Inventory, and from Finished Goods Inventory to Cost of Goods Sold, are

Point: Sales revenue is also recorded (see Exhibit 15.17).

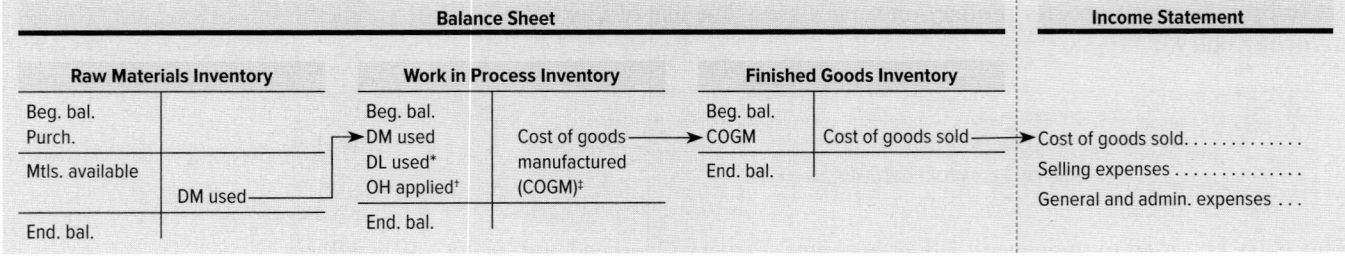

Mar. 31	Finished Goods Inventory..............................	8,940	
	Work in Process Inventory........................		8,940
	Transfer cost of goods manufactured.		
	Cost of Goods Sold	5,580	
	Finished Goods Inventory.........................		5,580
	Record cost of goods sold.		

Period costs (selling expenses and general and administrative expenses) do not impact inventory accounts. As a result, they do not impact cost of goods sold, and they are not reported on the schedule of cost of goods manufactured. They are reported on the income statement as operating expenses.

Fin. Goods Inventory

0	
8,940	
	5,580
3,360	

Cost Flows—Road Warriors

We next show the flow of costs and their reporting for our Road Warriors example. The upper part of Exhibit 15.16 shows the flow of Road Warriors's product costs through general ledger accounts. Arrow lines are numbered to show the flows of costs for March. Each numbered cost flow reflects journal entries made in March. The lower part of Exhibit 15.16 shows summarized job cost sheets at the end of March. The sum of costs assigned to the two jobs in process ($1,970 + $1,810) equals the $3,780 balance in Work in Process Inventory. Costs assigned to the completed Job B17 equal the $3,360 balance in Finished Goods Inventory. These balances in Work in Process Inventory and Finished Goods Inventory are reported on the end-of-period balance sheet. The sum of costs assigned to the sold Jobs B15 and B16 ($3,200 + $2,380) equals the $5,580 balance in Cost of Goods Sold. This amount is reported on the income statement for the period.

EXHIBIT 15.16

Job Order Cost Flows and Ending Job Cost Sheets

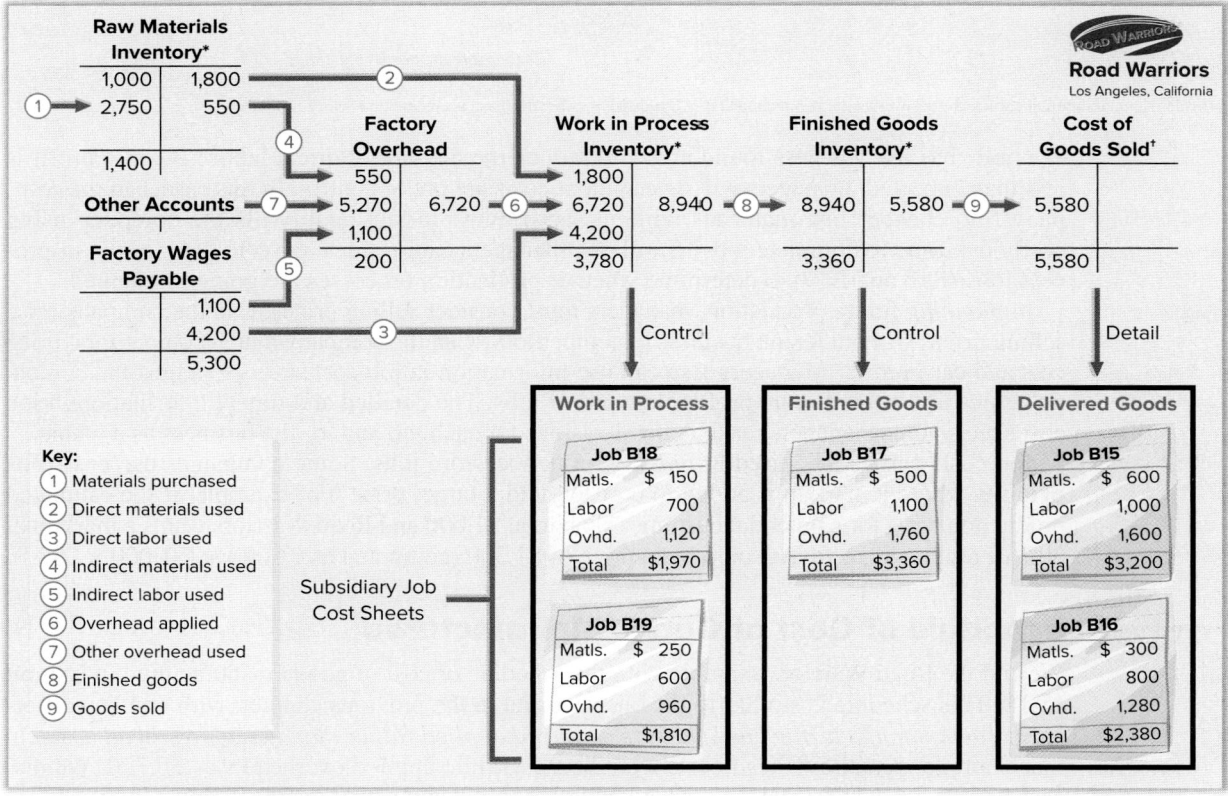

*The ending balances in the inventory accounts are reported on the balance sheet.
†The Cost of Goods Sold balance is reported on the income statement.

Exhibit 15.17 shows the journal entries made in March. Each entry is numbered to link with the arrow lines in Exhibit 15.16. In addition, Exhibit 15.17 concludes with the summary journal entry to record the sales (on account) of Jobs B15 and B16.

Using Job Cost Sheets for Managerial Decisions

Managers' decisions depend on timely information in job cost sheets. In *controlling* operations, managers must assess the profitability of the company's products or services. Road Warriors completed and sold two jobs (B15 and B16) and earned a total gross profit of $2,200 ($7,780 selling price − $5,580 cost of goods sold). If this gross profit is higher than expected, managers will try to determine if there are production efficiencies that can be applied to future jobs. For

Controlling

Sales $7,780
COGS 5,580
Gross profit. . . $2,200

EXHIBIT 15.17

Entries for Job Order Costing*

①	Raw Materials Inventory....................	2,750	
	Accounts Payable		2,750
	Acquired raw materials.		
②	Work in Process Inventory	1,800	
	Raw Materials Inventory		1,800
	Assign costs of direct materials used.		
③	Work in Process Inventory	4,200	
	Factory Wages Payable..................		4,200
	Assign costs of direct labor used.		
④	Factory Overhead..........................	550	
	Raw Materials Inventory		550
	Record use of indirect materials.		
⑤	Factory Overhead..........................	1,100	
	Factory Wages Payable.................		1,100
	Record indirect labor costs.		

⑥	Work in Process Inventory	6,720	
	Factory Overhead		6,720
	Apply overhead at 160% of direct labor.		
⑦	Factory Overhead..........................	5,270	
	Cash (and other accounts)		5,270
	Record factory overhead costs such as insurance, utilities, rent, and depreciation.		
⑧	Finished Goods Inventory	8,940	
	Work in Process Inventory		8,940
	Record completion of Jobs B15, B16, and B17.		
⑨	Cost of Goods Sold........................	5,580	
	Finished Goods Inventory		5,580
	Record cost of goods sold for Jobs B15 and B16.		
⑩	Accounts Receivable	7,780	
	Sales..................................		7,780
	Record sale of Jobs B15 and B16.		

*Exhibit 15.17 provides summary journal entries. *Actual* overhead is debited to Factory Overhead. *Applied* overhead is credited to Factory Overhead.

example, has the business found a way to reduce the amount of direct labor? If gross profit is less than expected, managers will determine if costs are out of control. In this case, can the company find cheaper raw materials without sacrificing product quality? Is the company using costly overtime to complete jobs? Similarly, managers can evaluate costs to date for the in-process jobs (B18 and B19) to determine whether production processes are going as planned.

Planning

In *planning* future production, managers must consider selling prices. Can the company raise selling prices without losing business to competitors? Can the company match competitors' price cuts and earn profit? Managers also can use information in job cost sheets to adjust the company's sales mix toward more profitable types of jobs. The detailed and timely information in job cost sheets helps managers make better decisions for each job and for the business as a whole.

Bidding

Job costs can also be used in *bidding* on new custom jobs. Some companies use **cost-plus pricing,** where a markup is added to cost to yield a target price. For example, if the estimated production costs for a potential customer's job total $1,000 and Road Warriors wants a markup of 30% of production costs, it could bid a price of $1,300 (computed as $1,000 + [$1,000 × 30%]).

Work in Process Inventory

Beg. bal.	0		
DM used	1,800		
DL used	4,200		
OH applied	6,720		
Ttl. mfg. costs	12,720		
		COGM	**8,940**
End. bal.	3,780		

Schedule of Cost of Goods Manufactured

We end the Road Warriors example with the schedule of cost of goods manufactured in Exhibit 15.18. This schedule is similar to the one reported in the previous chapter, with one key difference: *Total manufacturing costs include overhead applied rather than actual overhead costs.* In this example, actual overhead costs were $6,920, while applied overhead was $6,720. We discuss how to account for the difference between applied and actual overhead in the next section.

EXHIBIT 15.18

Schedule of Cost of Goods Manufactured

ROAD WARRIORS Schedule of Cost of Goods Manufactured For the Month of March 2019	
Direct materials used...............................	$ 1,800
Direct labor used	4,200
Factory overhead applied*	6,720
Total manufacturing costs	12,720
Add: Work in process, March 1, 2019.................	0
Total cost of work in process......................	12,720
Less: Work in process, March 31, 2019	3,780
Cost of goods manufactured.......................	$ 8,940

*Actual overhead = $6,920. Overhead is $200 underapplied.

Point: Companies sometimes use more detailed schedules of cost of goods manufactured, as seen in the previous chapter.

ADJUSTING OVERHEAD

Refer to the debits in the Factory Overhead account in Exhibit 15.16 (or Exhibit 15.17). The total cost of actual factory overhead incurred during March is $6,920 ($550 + $5,270 + $1,100). The $6,920 of actual overhead costs does not equal the $6,720 of overhead applied to work in process inventory (see ⑥). This leaves a debit of $200 in the Factory Overhead account. Because it is hard to precisely forecast future costs, actual overhead rarely equals applied overhead. Companies usually wait until the end of the year to adjust the Factory Overhead account for differences between actual and applied overhead. We show how this is done next.

Factory Overhead Account

Exhibit 15.19 shows a Factory Overhead account. The company applies overhead (credits the Factory Overhead account) using a predetermined rate estimated at the beginning of the year. During the year, the company records actual overhead costs with debits to the Factory Overhead account. At year-end we determine whether applied overhead is more or less than actual overhead.

Factory Overhead	
Actual amounts	Applied amounts

EXHIBIT 15.19

Factory Overhead T-account

- When *less* overhead is applied than is actually incurred, the remaining debit balance in the Factory Overhead account is called **underapplied overhead.**
- When *more* overhead is applied than is actually incurred, the resulting credit balance in the Factory Overhead account is called **overapplied overhead.**

When overhead is underapplied, it means that individual jobs have not been charged enough overhead during the year, and cost of goods sold for the year is too low. When overhead is over-applied, it means that jobs have been charged too much overhead during the year, and cost of goods sold is too high. In either case, a journal entry is needed to adjust Factory Overhead and Cost of Goods Sold. Exhibit 15.20 summarizes this entry, assuming the difference between applied and actual overhead is not material.

Example: If we do not adjust for underapplied overhead, will net income be overstated or under-stated? *Answer:* Overstated.

Overhead Costs	Overhead Balance	Overhead Is	Jobs Are	Adjusting Journal Entry Required	
Actual > Applied	Debit	Underapplied	Undercosted	Cost of Goods Sold .... #	
				Factory Overhead	#
Actual < Applied	Credit	Overapplied	Overcosted	Factory Overhead .... #	
				Cost of Goods Sold	#

EXHIBIT 15.20

Adjusting Factory Overhead

Adjust Underapplied or Overapplied Overhead

To illustrate, assume that Road Warriors applied $200,000 of overhead to jobs during 2019, which is the amount of overhead estimated in advance for the year. We further assume that Road Warriors incurred a total of $200,480 of actual overhead costs during 2019. This means, at the end of the year, the Factory Overhead account has a debit balance of $480. This amount is the difference between estimated (applied) and actual overhead costs for the year.

The $480 debit balance reflects manufacturing costs not assigned to jobs. This means the balances in Work in Process Inventory, Finished Goods Inventory, and Cost of Goods Sold do not include all production costs incurred. However, the difference between applied and actual overhead in this case is immaterial, and it is closed to Cost of Goods Sold with the following adjusting entry.

P4

Determine adjustments for overapplied and underapplied factory overhead.

Point: When the underapplied or overapplied overhead is material, the amount is normally allocated to the Cost of Goods Sold, Finished Goods Inventory, and Work in Process Inventory accounts. This process is covered in advanced courses.

Dec. 31	Cost of Goods Sold	480	
	Factory Overhead..............................		480
	Adjust for underapplied overhead costs.		

Factory Overhead	
Actual	$200,480
Applied	200,000
Underapplied.......	$ 480

The $480 debit (increase) to Cost of Goods Sold reduces income by $480. After this entry, the Factory Overhead account has a zero balance. Also, Cost of Goods Sold reflects actual overhead costs for the period. If instead we had overapplied overhead at the end of the period, we would debit Factory Overhead and credit Cost of Goods Sold for the amount.

NEED-TO-KNOW 15-6

Adjusting Overhead

P4

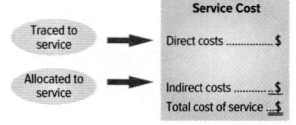

A manufacturing company applied $300,000 of overhead to its jobs during the year. For the independent scenarios below, prepare the journal entry to adjust over- or underapplied overhead. Assume the adjustment amounts are not material.

1. Actual overhead costs incurred during the year equal $305,000.

2. Actual overhead costs incurred during the year equal $298,500.

> Do More: QS 15-11, QS 15-12, E 15-13, E 15-14

Solution

1.

Cost of Goods Sold.............................	5,000	
Factory Overhead		5,000
Close underapplied overhead to Cost of Goods Sold.		

2.

Factory Overhead..............................	1,500	
Cost of Goods Sold		1,500
Close overapplied overhead to Cost of Goods Sold.		

Job Order Costing of Services

Job order costing also applies to service companies. Most service companies meet customers' needs by performing a custom service for a specific customer. Examples include an accountant auditing a client's financial statements, an interior designer remodeling an office, a wedding consultant planning and supervising a reception, and a lawyer defending a client.

Job order costing has some important differences for service firms.

Service Cost

Traced to service ➡ Direct costs .... $

Allocated to service ➡ Indirect costs .... $
Total cost of service ..$

- Most service firms have neither raw materials inventory nor finished goods inventory. They do, however, have inventories of supplies, and they can have work in process inventory. Often these supplies are immaterial and are considered overhead costs.
- Direct labor is often used to apply overhead because service firms do not use direct materials.
- Service firms typically use different account titles, for example **Services in Process Inventory** and **Services Overhead.**

Exhibit 15.21 shows the flow of costs for a service firm called AdWorld, a developer of advertising materials. During the month, AdWorld worked on custom advertising campaigns for clients that wanted ads for three different platforms: mobile devices, television, and radio. In this chapter's Decision Analysis section we show an example of using job order costing to price advertising services for AdWorld.

EXHIBIT 15.21

Flow of Costs for Service Firms

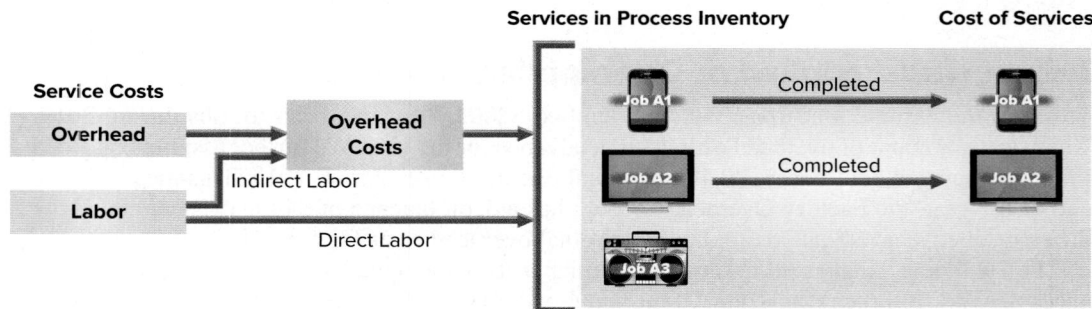

Decision Maker

Management Consultant You control and manage costs for a consulting company. At the end of a recent month, three consulting jobs were completed and two are 60% complete. Each unfinished job is estimated to cost $10,000 and to earn revenue of $12,000. You are unsure how to recognize inventory and record costs and revenues. Do you recognize any inventory? If so, how much? How much revenue is recorded for unfinished jobs this month?
■ *Answer:* Service companies do not recognize work in process inventory or finished goods inventory. For the two jobs that are 60% complete, you could recognize revenues and costs at 60% of the total expected amounts or revenue of $7,200 (0.60 × $12,000) and costs of $6,000 (0.60 × $10,000), yielding net income of $1,200 from each job.

SUSTAINABILITY AND ACCOUNTING

Professional service firms in accounting, consulting, law, and financial services compete for highly talented employees with strong technical skills. In addition, a more diverse workforce is likely to lead to different points of view that arguably can produce even better services and ultimately more profit for the company. Enhancing workforce diversity can also help attract and retain talented people.

Although workforce diversity is typically not recorded on job cost sheets, many companies measure and report it. Along these lines, the Sustainability Accounting Standards Board has developed suggested reporting guidelines for professional service firms. The SASB recommends that companies disclose information on gender and ethnicity for both senior management employees and all other employees.

Consistent with SASB guidelines, the **United States Postal Service (USPS)**, a leading employer of women and minorities, discloses that women comprise roughly 40% and minorities comprise roughly 40% of its overall workforce. Moreover, roughly 21% of USPS's employees are black, 8% Hispanic, and 8% Asian.

HoopSwagg, the focus of this chapter's opening feature, customizes socks for charities and fundraisers. For each pair of Breast Cancer Camo Custom Elite socks sold, the company donates $2 to breast cancer research. For sales of custom-designed socks to honor certain individuals, company founder Brennan Agranoff donates all of the sales to charities of the family's choosing. Brennan notes that "helping others is one of the best things you can do for the world, and you never know what opportunities arise when you work for a greater cause."

©HoopSwagg

Pricing for Services  **Decision Analysis**

A1
Apply job order costing in pricing services.

The chapter described job order costing mainly within a manufacturing setting. However, service providers also use job order costing. Consider AdWorld, an advertising agency that develops web-based ads (and ads for other types of media). Each of its customers has unique requirements, so costs for each individual job must be tracked separately.

AdWorld uses two types of labor: web designers ($65 per hour) and computer staff ($50 per hour). It also incurs overhead costs that it assigns using two different predetermined overhead allocation rates: $125 per designer hour and $96 per staff hour. For each job, AdWorld must estimate the number of designer and staff hours needed. Then, total costs of each job are determined using the procedures in the chapter.

To illustrate, a chip manufacturer requested a quote from AdWorld for an advertising engagement. AdWorld estimates that the job will require 43 designer hours and 61 staff hours, with the following total estimated cost for this job.

Estimated Job Cost—Advertising Services	*AdWorld*	
Direct Labor		
Designers (43 hours × $65)...................	$2,795	
Staff (61 hours × $50)........................	3,050	
Total direct labor.............................		$ 5,845
Overhead		
Designer related (43 hours × $125)..............	5,375	
Staff related (61 hours × $96)...................	5,856	
Total overhead		11,231
Total estimated job cost.......................		$17,076

AdWorld can use this cost information to help determine the price quote for the job (see *Decision Maker*, **Sales Manager**, below).

AdWorld must also consider the market, that is, how much competitors will quote for this job. Competitor information is often unavailable; therefore, AdWorld's managers must use estimates based on their assessment of the competitive environment.

■ **Decision Maker**

Sales Manager   As AdWorld's sales manager, assume that you estimate costs pertaining to a proposed job as $17,076. Your normal pricing policy is to apply a markup of 18% from total costs. However, you learn that three other agencies are likely to bid for the same job, and that their quotes will range from $16,500 to $22,000. What price should you quote? What factors other than cost must you consider? ■   *Answer:* The price based on AdWorld's normal pricing policy is $20,150 ($17,076 × 1.18), which is within the price range offered by competitors. One option is to apply normal pricing policy and quote a price of $20,150. It is, however, useful to assess competitor pricing, especially in terms of service quality and other benefits. Although price is an input customers use to select suppliers, factors such as quality and timeliness (responsiveness) of suppliers are important. Accordingly, the price can reflect such factors.

	Price Quote
Job cost	$17,076
Markup (18%)	3,074
Price	$20,150

NEED-TO-KNOW 15-7

COMPREHENSIVE

Job Costs, Journal
Entries, and Schedule
of Cost of Goods
Manufactured

The following information reflects Walczak Company's job order production activities for May.

Materials and labor		Overhead costs incurred	
Raw materials purchases...........	$16,000	Indirect materials.................	$5,000
Factory payroll cost	15,400	Indirect labor	3,500
		Other factory overhead	9,500

Walczak's predetermined overhead rate is 150% of direct labor cost. Costs are applied to the three jobs worked on during May as follows.

	Job 401	Job 402	Job 403
Work in process inventory, April 30			
Direct materials	$3,600		
Direct labor..........................	1,700		
Applied overhead	2,550		
Costs during May			
Direct materials	3,550	$3,500	$1,400
Direct labor.........................	5,100	6,000	800
Applied overhead....................	?	?	?
Status on May 31	**Finished (sold)**	**Finished (unsold)**	**In process**

Required

1. Determine the total cost for each part *a* through *e*.

  a. The April 30 inventory of jobs in process.

  b. Materials (direct and indirect) used during May.

  c. Labor (direct and indirect) used during May.

  d. Factory overhead incurred and applied during May and the amount of any over- or underapplied overhead on May 31.

  e. The total cost of each job as of May 31, the May 31 inventories of both work in process and finished goods, and the cost of goods sold during May.

2. Prepare summarized journal entries for the month to record each part *a* through *f*.

  a. Materials purchases (on credit), direct materials used in production, direct labor used in production, and overhead applied.

  b. Actual overhead costs, including indirect materials, indirect labor, and other overhead costs.

  c. Transfer of each completed job to the Finished Goods Inventory account.

  d. Cost of goods sold.

  e. The sale (on account) of Job 401 for $35,000.

  f. Removal of any underapplied or overapplied overhead from the Factory Overhead account. (Assume the amount is not material.)

3. Prepare a schedule of cost of goods manufactured for May.

PLANNING THE SOLUTION

● Determine the cost of the April 30 work in process inventory by totaling the materials, labor, and applied overhead costs for Job 401.

● Compute the cost of materials used and labor by totaling the amounts assigned to jobs and to overhead.

● Compute the total overhead incurred by summing the amounts for the three components. Compute the amount of applied overhead by multiplying the total direct labor cost by the predetermined overhead rate. Compute the underapplied or overapplied amount as the difference between the actual cost and the applied cost.

● Determine the total cost charged to each job by adding the costs incurred in April (if any) to the cost of materials, labor, and overhead applied during May.

● Group the costs of the jobs according to their completion status.

● Record the direct materials costs assigned to the three jobs.

● Transfer costs of Jobs 401 and 402 from Work in Process Inventory to Finished Goods.

● Record the costs of Job 401 as cost of goods sold.

● Record the sale (on account) of Job 401 for $35,000.

● On the schedule of cost of goods manufactured, remember to include the beginning and ending work in process inventories and to use applied rather than actual overhead.

SOLUTION

1. Total cost of

a. April 30 inventory of jobs in process (Job 401).

Direct materials.............	$3,600
Direct labor................	1,700
Applied overhead...........	2,550
Total cost..................	$7,850

b. Materials used during May.

Direct materials	
Job 401.....................	$ 3,550
Job 402.....................	3,500
Job 403.....................	1,400
Total direct materials	8,450
Indirect materials	5,000
Total materials used	$13,450

c. Labor used during May.

Direct labor	
Job 401.................	$ 5,100
Job 402.................	6,000
Job 403.................	800
Total direct labor...........	11,900
Indirect labor..............	3,500
Total labor used	$15,400

d. Factory overhead incurred and applied in May.

Actual overhead	
Indirect materials..........................	$ 5,000
Indirect labor	3,500
Other factory overhead	9,500
Total actual overhead.......................	18,000
Overhead applied (150% × $11,900).............	17,850
Underapplied overhead.......................	$ 150

e. Total cost of each job.

	401	**402**	**403**
Work in process, April 30			
Direct materials	$ 3,600		
Direct labor......................	1,700		
Applied overhead*.................	2,550		
Cost incurred in May			
Direct materials (from part b).........	3,550	$ 3,500	$1,400
Direct labor......................	5,100	6,000	800
Applied overhead*.................	7,650	9,000	1,200
Total costs........................	$24,150	$18,500	$3,400

*Equals 150% of that job's direct labor cost.

Total cost of the May 31 inventory of work in process (Job 403) = $3,400
Total cost of the May 31 inventory of finished goods (Job 402) = $18,500
Total cost of goods sold during May (Job 401) = $24,150

2. Journal entries.

a. Record raw materials purchases, direct materials used, direct labor used, and overhead applied.

Raw Materials Inventory	16,000	
Accounts Payable		16,000
Record materials purchases.		
Work in Process Inventory............................	8,450	
Raw Materials Inventory...........................		8,450
Assign direct materials to jobs.		
Work in Process Inventory............................	11,900	
Factory Wages Payable		11,900
Assign direct labor to jobs.		
Work in Process Inventory............................	17,850	
Factory Overhead................................		17,850
Apply overhead to jobs.		

b. Record actual overhead costs.

Factory Overhead		5,000	
Raw Materials Inventory.			5,000
Record indirect materials.			
Factory Overhead		3,500	
Factory Wages Payable			3,500
Record indirect labor.			
Factory Overhead		9,500	
Cash.			9,500
Record other actual factory overhead.			

c. Transfer cost of completed jobs to Finished Goods Inventory.

Finished Goods Inventory		42,650	
Work in Process Inventory			42,650
Record completion of jobs			
($24,150 for Job 401 + $18,500 for Job 402).			

d. Record cost of job sold.

Cost of Goods Sold		24,150	
Finished Goods Inventory.			24,150
Record costs for sale of Job 401.			

e. Record sales for job sold.

Accounts Receivable		35,000	
Sales			35,000
Record sale of Job 401.			

f. Close underapplied overhead to cost of goods sold.

Cost of Goods Sold		150	
Factory Overhead.			150
Assign underapplied overhead to Cost of Goods Sold.			

3.

WALCZAK COMPANY
Schedule of Cost of Goods Manufactured
For Month Ended May 31

Direct materials.	$ 8,450
Direct labor	11,900
Factory overhead applied*.	17,850
Total manufacturing costs	38,200
Add: Work in process, April 30.	7,850
Total cost of work in process	46,050
Less: Work in process, May 31.	3,400
Cost of goods manufactured	$42,650

*Actual overhead = $18,000. Overhead is $150 underapplied.

Summary: Cheat Sheet

JOB ORDER PRODUCTION

Job: Production of a custom product.
Job lot: Producing more than one unit of a custom product.
Job cost sheet: Cost record kept for each job.

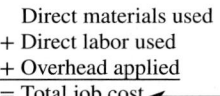

Direct materials used
+ Direct labor used
+ Overhead applied
= Total job cost

→ Total of $ amounts on all job cost sheets = General ledger balances of Work in Process Inventory, Finished Goods Inventory, and COGS.

FLOW OF MANUFACTURING COSTS

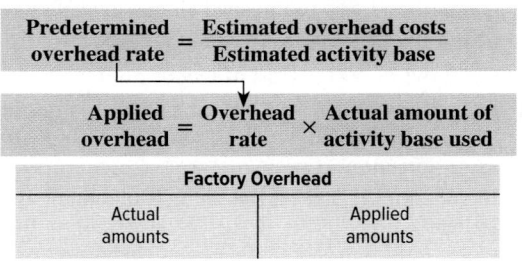

DM = direct materials; DL = direct labor; FOH = factory overhead; COGM = cost of goods manufactured; COGS = cost of goods sold

OVERHEAD

$$\frac{\text{Predetermined}}{\text{overhead rate}} = \frac{\text{Estimated overhead costs}}{\text{Estimated activity base}}$$

$$\frac{\text{Applied}}{\text{overhead}} = \frac{\text{Overhead}}{\text{rate}} \times \frac{\text{Actual amount of}}{\text{activity base used}}$$

Factory Overhead	
Actual amounts	Applied amounts

Adjust overhead and COGS at period-end

Overhead Costs	Factory Overhead Balance	Overhead Is	Adjusting Journal Entry Required	
Actual > Applied	Debit	Underapplied	Cost of Goods Sold........	#
			Factory Overhead	#
Actual < Applied	Credit	Overapplied	Factory Overhead.........	#
			Cost of Goods Sold	#

JOURNAL ENTRIES

Acquire raw materials

Raw Materials Inventory............................	16,000	
Accounts Payable		16,000

Assign costs of *direct* materials used

Work in Process Inventory	8,450	
Raw Materials Inventory		8,450

Assign costs of *direct* labor used

Work in Process Inventory	11,900	
Factory Wages Payable......................		11,900

***Apply* overhead using predetermined rate**

Work in Process Inventory	17,850	
Factory Overhead		17,850

Record use of *indirect* materials

Factory Overhead................................	5,000	
Raw Materials Inventory		5,000

Record *indirect* labor costs

Factory Overhead................................	3,500	
Factory Wages Payable......................		3,500

Record *actual* overhead costs such as insurance, rent, utilities, and depreciation

Factory Overhead................................	9,500	
Cash (and other accounts)		9,500

Record completion of jobs

Finished Goods Inventory	42,650	
Work in Process Inventory....................		42,650

Record cost of goods sold for sold jobs

Cost of Goods Sold................................	24,150	
Finished Goods Inventory....................		24,150

Record sales for sold jobs

Accounts Receivable	35,000	
Sales.....................................		35,000

Assign *underapplied* overhead to cost of goods sold

Cost of Goods Sold................................	150	
Factory Overhead		150

Assign *overapplied* overhead to cost of goods sold

Factory Overhead................................	150	
Cost of Goods Sold...........................		150

Key Terms

Cost accounting system (571)
Cost-plus pricing (584)
Finished Goods Inventory (573)
Job (571)
Job cost sheet (573)
Job lot (571)
Job order costing system (573)

Job order production (571)
Materials ledger card (574)
Materials requisition (575)
Overapplied overhead (585)
Predetermined overhead rate (579)
Process operations (572)
Receiving report (574)

Services in Process Inventory (586)
Services Overhead (586)
Target cost (573)
Time ticket (577)
Underapplied overhead (585)
Work in Process Inventory (573)

Multiple Choice Quiz

1. A company's predetermined overhead rate is 150% of its direct labor costs. How much overhead is applied to a job that requires total direct labor costs of $30,000?

   a. $15,000   **d.** $60,000

   b. $30,000   **e.** $75,000

   c. $45,000

2. A company uses direct labor costs to apply overhead. Its production costs for the period are: direct materials, $45,000; direct labor, $35,000; and overhead applied, $38,500. What is its predetermined overhead rate?

   a. 10%   **d.** 91%

   b. 110%   **e.** 117%

   c. 86%

3. A company's ending inventory of finished goods has a total cost of $10,000 and consists of 500 units. If the overhead applied to these goods is $4,000 and the predetermined overhead rate is 80% of direct labor costs, how much direct materials cost was incurred in producing these 500 units?

   a. $10,000   **d.** $5,000

   b. $6,000   **e.** $1,000

   c. $4,000

4. A company's Work in Process Inventory T-account follows.

Work in Process Inventory			
Beginning balance	9,000		
Direct materials	94,200		
Direct labor	59,200	Cost of goods	
Overhead applied	31,600	manufactured	?
Ending balance	17,800		

The cost of goods manufactured is

   a. $193,000.   **c.** $185,000.   **e.** $176,200.

   b. $211,800.   **d.** $144,600.

5. At the end of its current year, a company learned that its overhead was underapplied by $1,500 and that this amount is not considered material. Based on this information, the company should

   a. Credit the $1,500 to Finished Goods Inventory.

   b. Credit the $1,500 to Cost of Goods Sold.

   c. Debit the $1,500 to Cost of Goods Sold.

   d. Do nothing about the $1,500 because it is not material and it is likely that overhead will be overapplied by the same amount next year.

   e. Include the $1,500 on the income statement as "Other Expense."

ANSWERS TO MULTIPLE CHOICE QUIZ

1. c; $30,000 × 150% = $45,000

2. b; $38,500/$35,000 = 110%

3. e; Direct materials + Direct labor + Overhead = Total cost;
    Direct materials + ($4,000/0.80) + $4,000 = $10,000
    Direct materials = $1,000

4. e; $9,000 + $94,200 + $59,200 + $31,600 − Finished goods
    = $17,800.
    Thus, finished goods = $176,200

5. c

🔲 Icon denotes assignments that involve decision making.

Discussion Questions

1. Why must a company estimate the amount of factory overhead assigned to individual jobs or job lots?

2. 🔲 Some companies use labor cost to apply factory overhead to jobs. Identify another factor (or base) a company might reasonably use to apply overhead costs.

3. 🔲 What information is recorded on a job cost sheet? How do management and employees use job cost sheets?

4. In a job order costing system, what records serve as a subsidiary ledger for Work in Process Inventory? For Finished Goods Inventory?

5. What journal entry is recorded when a materials manager receives a materials requisition and then issues materials (both direct and indirect) for use in the factory?

6. 🔲 How does the materials requisition help safeguard a company's assets?

7. **Google** uses a "time ticket" for some employees. How are time tickets used in job order costing?   **GOOGLE**

8. What events cause debits to be recorded in the Factory Overhead account? What events cause credits to be recorded in the Factory Overhead account?

9. **Google** applies overhead to product costs. What account(s) is(are) used to eliminate overapplied or underapplied overhead from the Factory Overhead account, assuming the amount is not material?   **GOOGLE**

10. 🔲 Assume that **Apple** produces a batch of 1,000 iPhones. Does it account for this as 1,000 individual jobs or as a job lot? Explain (consider costs and benefits).   **APPLE**

11. Why must a company use predetermined overhead rates when using job order costing?

12. 🛈 How would a hospital apply job order costing? Explain.

13. 🛈 **Harley-Davidson** manufactures 30 custom-made, luxury-model motorcycles. Does it account for these motorcycles as 30 individual jobs or as a job lot? Explain.

14. Assume **Sprint** will install and service a server to link all of a customer's employees' smartphones to a centralized company server for an up-front flat price. How can Sprint use a job order costing system?

■ connect

Determine which of the following are most likely to be considered as a job and which as a job lot.

_____ **1.** Hats imprinted with company logo

_____ **2.** Little League trophies

_____ **3.** A handcrafted table

_____ **4.** A 90-foot motor yacht

_____ **5.** Wedding dresses for a chain of stores

_____ **6.** A custom-designed home

QUICK STUDY

QS 15-1

Jobs and job lots   **C1**

Clemens Cars's job cost sheet for Job A40 shows that the cost to add security features to a car was $10,500. The car was delivered to the customer, who paid $14,900 in cash for the added features. What journal entries should Clemens record for the completion and delivery of Job A40?

QS 15-2

Job cost sheets   **C2**

Label each item *a* through *e* below as a feature of either a job order (J) or process (P) operation.

_____ **a.** Heterogeneous products and services

_____ **b.** Routine, repetitive procedures

_____ **c.** Low product flexibility

_____ **d.** Low production volume

_____ **e.** Low product standardization

QS 15-3

Comparing process and job order operations

C1

During the current month, a company that uses job order costing purchases $50,000 in raw materials for cash. It then uses $12,000 of raw materials indirectly as factory supplies and uses $32,000 of raw materials as direct materials. Prepare journal entries to record these three transactions.

QS 15-4

Raw materials
journal entries   **P1**

During the current month, a company that uses job order costing incurred a monthly factory payroll of $180,000. Of this amount, $40,000 is classified as indirect labor and the remainder as direct. Prepare journal entries to record these transactions.

QS 15-5

Labor journal entries   **P2**

A company estimates the following manufacturing costs for the next period: direct labor, $468,000; direct materials, $390,000; and factory overhead, $117,000. Compute its predetermined overhead rate as a percent of (1) direct labor and (2) direct materials. Express your answers as percents, rounded to the nearest whole number.

QS 15-6

Factory overhead rates

P3

At the beginning of the year, a company predicts total overhead costs of $560,000. The company applies overhead using machine hours and estimates it will use 1,400 machine hours during the year. What amount of overhead should be applied to Job 65A if that job uses 13 machine hours during January?

QS 15-7

Applying overhead   **P3**

At the beginning of the year, a company predicts total direct materials costs of $900,000 and total overhead costs of $1,170,000. If the company uses direct materials costs as its activity base to apply overhead, what is the predetermined overhead rate it should use during the year?

QS 15-8

Predetermined
overhead rate   **P3**

On March 1 a dressmaker starts work on three custom-designed wedding dresses. The company uses job order costing and applies overhead to each job (dress) at the rate of 40% of direct materials costs. During the month, the jobs used direct materials as shown below. Compute the amount of overhead applied to each of the three jobs.

QS 15-9

Applying overhead

P3

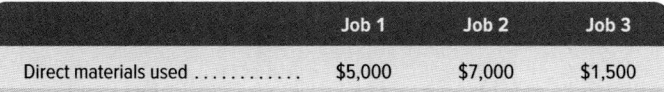

	Job 1	Job 2	Job 3
Direct materials used	$5,000	$7,000	$1,500

QS 15-10
Manufacturing cost flows
P1   P2   P3

Refer to the information in QS 15-9. During the month, the jobs used direct labor as shown below. Jobs 1 and 3 are not finished by the end of March, and Job 2 is finished but not sold by the end of March. (1) Determine the amounts of direct materials, direct labor, and factory overhead applied that would be reported on job cost sheets for each of the three jobs for March. (2) Determine the total dollar amount of Work in Process Inventory at the end of March. (3) Determine the total dollar amount of Finished Goods Inventory at the end of March. Assume the company has no beginning Work in Process or Finished Goods inventories.

	Job 1	Job 2	Job 3
Direct labor used...............	$9,000	$4,000	$3,000

QS 15-11
Entry for over- or
underapplied overhead   **P4**

A company applies overhead at a rate of 150% of direct labor cost. Actual overhead cost for the current period is $950,000, and direct labor cost is $600,000. Prepare the journal entry to close over- or underapplied overhead to Cost of Goods Sold.

QS 15-12
Entry for over- or
underapplied overhead
P4

A company's Factory Overhead account shows total debits of $624,000 and total credits of $646,000 at the end of the year. Prepare the journal entry to close the balance in the Factory Overhead account to Cost of Goods Sold.

QS 15-13
Job order costing
of services   **A1**

An advertising agency is estimating costs for advertising a music festival. The job will require 200 direct labor hours at a cost of $50 per hour. Overhead costs are applied at a rate of $65 per direct labor hour. What is the total estimated cost for this job?

QS 15-14
Job order costing
of services   **A1**

An advertising agency used 65 hours of direct labor in creating advertising for a music festival. Direct labor costs $50 per hour. The agency applies overhead at a rate of $40 per direct labor hour. Prepare journal entries to record the agency's direct labor *and* the applied overhead costs for this job.

QS 15-15
Job cost sheet
C2

EcoSkate makes skateboards from recycled plastic. For a recent job lot of 100 skateboards, the company incurred direct materials costs of $600 and direct labor costs of $200. Overhead is applied using a rate of 150% of direct materials costs. What is the total manufacturing cost of this job lot? What is the cost per skateboard?

EXERCISES

Exercise 15-1
Job order production
C1

Match each of the terms/phrases numbered *1* through *5* with the best definition *a* through *e*.

_____ **1.** Cost accounting system
_____ **2.** Target cost
_____ **3.** Job
_____ **4.** Process operation
_____ **5.** Job order production

a. Production activities for a custom product.
b. Production activities for a special order.
c. A system that records manufacturing costs.
d. The expected selling price of a job minus its desired profit.
e. Mass production in a continuous flow of steps.

Exercise 15-2
Job cost computation
C2

The following information is from the materials requisitions and time tickets for Job 9-1005 completed by Great Bay Boats. The requisitions are identified by code numbers starting with the letter Q, and the time tickets start with W. At the start of the year, management estimated that overhead cost would equal 110% of direct labor cost for each job. Determine the total cost on the job cost sheet for Job 9-1005.

Date	Document	Amount
7/1........................	Q-4698	$1,250
7/1........................	W-3393	600
7/5........................	Q-4725	1,000
7/5........................	W-3479	450
7/10........................	W-3559	300

As of the end of June, the job cost sheets at Racing Wheels, Inc., show the following total costs accumulated on three custom jobs.

Exercise 15-3

Analyzing cost flows

C2

	Job 102	Job 103	Job 104
Direct materials.............	$15,000	$33,000	$27,000
Direct labor................	8,000	14,200	21,000
Overhead applied..........	4,000	7,100	10,500

Job 102 was started in production in May, and the following costs were assigned to it in May: direct materials, $6,000; direct labor, $1,800; and overhead, $900. Jobs 103 and 104 were started in June. Overhead cost is applied with a predetermined rate based on direct labor cost. Jobs 102 and 103 were finished in June, and Job 104 is expected to be finished in July. No raw materials were used indirectly in June. Using this information, answer the following questions. (Assume this company's predetermined overhead rate did not change across these months.)

1. What was the cost of the raw materials requisitioned in June for each of the three jobs?
2. How much direct labor cost was incurred during June for each of the three jobs?
3. What predetermined overhead rate is used during June?
4. How much total cost is transferred to finished goods during June?

Check   (4) $81,300

Starr Company reports the following information for August.

Exercise 15-4

Recording product costs

P1   P2   P3

Raw materials purchased on account	$76,200	Factory wages earned (direct labor) ...	$15,350
Direct materials used in production......	$48,000	Overhead rate.....................	120% of direct labor cost

Prepare journal entries to record the following events.
1. Raw materials purchased.
2. Direct materials used in production.
3. Direct labor used in production.
4. Applied overhead.

Custom Cabinetry has one job in process (Job 120) as of June 30; at that time, its job cost sheet reports direct materials of $6,000, direct labor of $2,800, and applied overhead of $2,240. Custom Cabinetry applies overhead at the rate of 80% of direct labor cost. During July, Job 120 is sold (on account) for $22,000, Job 121 is started and completed, and Job 122 is started and still in process at the end of the month. Custom Cabinetry incurs the following costs during July.

Exercise 15-5

Manufacturing cost flows

P1   P2   P3

July Product Costs	Job 120	Job 121	Job 122	Total
Direct materials.............	$1,000	$6,000	$2,500	$9,500
Direct labor................	2,200	3,700	2,100	8,000
Overhead applied..........	?	?	?	?

1. Prepare journal entries for the following transactions and events a through e in July.
   a. Direct materials used in production.
   b. Direct labor used in production.
   c. Overhead applied.
   d. The sale of Job 120.
   e. Cost of goods sold for Job 120.
2. Compute the July 31 balances of the Work in Process Inventory and the Finished Goods Inventory accounts. (Assume there are no jobs in Finished Goods Inventory as of June 30.)

Using Exhibit 15.17 as a guide, prepare summary journal entries to record the following transactions and events a through g for a company in its first month of operations.
a. Raw materials purchased on account, $90,000.
b. Direct materials used in production, $36,500. Indirect materials used in production, $19,200.
c. Paid cash for factory payroll, $50,000. Of this total, $38,000 is for direct labor and $12,000 is for indirect labor.
d. Paid cash for other actual overhead costs, $11,475.
e. Applied overhead at the rate of 125% of direct labor cost.
f. Transferred cost of jobs completed to finished goods, $56,800.
g. Sold jobs on account for $82,000. The jobs had a cost of $56,800.

Exercise 15-6

Recording events in job order costing

P1   P2   P3   P4

Exercise 15-7

Cost flows in job order costing

P1 P2 P3 P4

The following information is available for Lock-Tite Company, which produces special-order security products and uses a job order costing system.

	April 30	May 31
Inventories		
Raw materials..	$43,000	$ 52,000
Work in process	10,200	21,300
Finished goods..	63,000	35,600
Activities and information for May		
Raw materials purchases (paid with cash)		210,000
Factory payroll (paid with cash).......................		345,000
Factory overhead		
Indirect materials................................		15,000
Indirect labor		80,000
Other overhead costs		120,000
Sales (received in cash)...............................		1,400,000
Predetermined overhead rate based on direct labor cost...............		70%

Compute the following amounts for the month of May.

1. Cost of direct materials used.
2. Cost of direct labor used.

Check   (3) $625,400

3. Cost of goods manufactured.

4. Cost of goods sold. (Do not consider any underapplied or overapplied overhead.)
5. Gross profit.
6. Overapplied or underapplied overhead.

Exercise 15-8

Journal entries for materials

P1

Use information in Exercise 15-7 to prepare journal entries for the following events for the month of May.

1. Raw materials purchases for cash.
2. Direct materials usage.

3. Indirect materials usage.

Exercise 15-9

Journal entries for labor

P2

Use information in Exercise 15-7 to prepare journal entries for the following events for the month of May.

1. Direct labor usage.
2. Indirect labor usage.

3. Total payroll paid in cash.

Exercise 15-10

Journal entries for overhead   P3

Use information in Exercise 15-7 to prepare journal entries for the following events for the month of May.

1. Incurred other overhead costs (record credit to Other Accounts).
2. Applied overhead to work in process.

Exercise 15-11

Overhead rate; costs assigned to jobs

P3

Check   (2) $22,710

Shire Computer's predetermined overhead rate is based on direct labor cost. Management estimates the company will incur $747,500 of overhead costs and $575,000 of direct labor cost for the year. During March, Shire began and completed Job 13-56.

1. What is the predetermined overhead rate for the year?
2. Use the information on the following job cost sheet to determine the total cost of the job.

JOB COST SHEET						
Customer's Name	Keiser Co.			**Job No.**	13-56	
Job Description	5 plasma monitors—61 inch					

	Direct Materials		**Direct Labor**		**Overhead Costs Applied**	
Date	Requisition No.	Amount	Time-Ticket No.	Amount	Rate	Amount
Mar. 8	4-129	$5,000	T-306	$ 700		
Mar. 11	4-142	7,020	T-432	1,250		
Mar. 18	4-167	3,330	T-456	1,250		
Totals						

Lorenzo Company applies overhead to jobs on the basis of direct materials cost. At year-end, the Work in Process Inventory account shows the following.

Exercise 15-12
Analyzing costs assigned to work in process
P3

	A	B	C	D	E
1		Work in Process Inventory—Acct. No. 121			
2	Date	Explanation	Debit	Credit	Balance
3	Dec. 31	Direct materials cost	1,500,000		1,500,000
4	31	Direct labor cost	300,000		1,800,000
5	31	Overhead applied	600,000		2,400,000
6	31	To finished goods		2,350,000	50,000

1. Determine the predetermined overhead rate used (based on direct materials cost).

2. Only one job remained in work in process inventory at December 31. Its direct materials cost is $30,000. How much direct labor cost and overhead cost are assigned to this job?

Refer to information in Exercise 15-7. Prepare the journal entry to close overapplied or underapplied overhead to Cost of Goods Sold.

Exercise 15-13
Adjusting factory overhead   **P4**

Record the journal entry to close over- or underapplied factory overhead to Cost of Goods Sold for each of the two companies below.

Exercise 15-14
Adjusting factory overhead
P4

	Storm Concert Promotions	Valle Home Builders
Actual indirect materials costs............	$22,000	$ 12,500
Actual indirect labor costs	46,000	46,500
Other overhead costs...................	17,000	47,000
Overhead applied......................	88,200	105,200

At the beginning of the year, Custom Mfg. established its predetermined overhead rate by using the following cost predictions: overhead costs, $750,000, and direct materials costs, $625,000. At year-end, the company's records show that actual overhead costs for the year are $830,000. Actual direct materials cost had been assigned to jobs as follows.

Exercise 15-15
Factory overhead computed, applied, and adjusted
P3   P4

Jobs completed and sold.....................	$513,750
Jobs in finished goods inventory..............	102,750
Jobs in work in process inventory.............	68,500
Total actual direct materials cost..............	$685,000

1. Determine the predetermined overhead rate using predicted direct materials costs.

2. Set up a T-account for Factory Overhead and enter the overhead costs incurred and the amounts applied to jobs during the year using the predetermined overhead rate.

3. Determine whether overhead is overapplied or underapplied (and the amount) during the year.

Check   (3) $8,000 underapplied

4. Prepare the adjusting entry to allocate any over- or underapplied overhead to Cost of Goods Sold.

At the beginning of the year, Infodeo established its predetermined overhead rate for movies produced during the year by using the following cost predictions: overhead costs, $1,680,000, and direct labor costs, $480,000. At year-end, the company's records show that actual overhead costs for the year are $1,652,000. Actual direct labor cost had been assigned to jobs as follows.

Exercise 15-16
Factory overhead computed, applied, and adjusted
P3   P4

Movies completed and released	$425,000
Movies still in production	50,000
Total actual direct labor cost	$475,000

1. Determine the predetermined overhead rate for the year.
2. Set up a T-account for overhead and enter the overhead costs incurred and the amounts applied to movies during the year using the predetermined overhead rate.

Check (3) $10,500 overapplied

3. Determine whether overhead is overapplied or underapplied (and the amount) during the year.
4. Prepare the adjusting entry to allocate any over- or underapplied overhead to Cost of Goods Sold.

Exercise 15-17
Overhead rate calculation and allocation
P3

Moonrise Bakery applies factory overhead based on direct labor costs. The company incurred the following costs during the year: direct materials costs, $650,000; direct labor costs, $3,000,000; and factory overhead costs applied, $1,800,000.

1. Determine the company's predetermined overhead rate for the year.
2. Assuming that the company's $71,000 ending Work in Process Inventory account for the year had $20,000 of direct labor costs, determine the inventory's direct materials costs.

Exercise 15-18
Job order costing for services
A1

Hansel Corporation has requested bids from several architects to design its new corporate headquarters. Frey Architects is one of the firms bidding on the job. Frey estimates that the job will require the following direct labor.

	A	B	C
1	**Labor**	**Estimated Hours**	**Hourly Rate**
2	Architects	150	$300
3	Staff	300	75
4	Clerical	500	20

Frey applies overhead to jobs at 175% of direct labor cost. Frey would like to earn at least $80,000 profit on the architectural job. Based on past experience and market research, it estimates that the competition will bid between $285,000 and $350,000 for the job.

Check (1) $213,125

1. What is Frey's estimated cost of the architectural job?
2. If Frey bids a price of $285,000, will it earn its target profit of $80,000?
3. What price would cover Frey's costs and earn the desired target profit?

Exercise 15-19
Job order costing of services
A1

Diaz and Associates incurred the following costs in completing a tax return for a large company. Diaz applies overhead at 50% of direct labor cost.

Labor	Hours Used	Hourly Rate
Partner....................	5	$500
Senior manager	12	200
Staff accountants	100	50

1. Prepare journal entries to record direct labor *and* the overhead applied.
2. Prepare the journal entry to record the cost of services provided. Assume the beginning Services in Process Inventory account has a zero balance.

Exercise 15-20
Direct materials journal entries   **P1**

A recent balance sheet for **Porsche AG** shows beginning raw materials inventory of €83 million and ending raw materials inventory of €85 million. Assume the company purchased raw materials (on account) for €3,108 million during the year. Prepare journal entries to record (*a*) the purchase of raw materials and (*b*) the use of raw materials in production.

---

connect

PROBLEM SET A

Problem 15-1A
Production costs computed and recorded; reports prepared

P1   P2   P3   P4

Marcelino Co.'s March 31 inventory of raw materials is $80,000. Raw materials purchases in April are $500,000, and factory payroll cost in April is $363,000. Overhead costs incurred in April are: indirect materials, $50,000; indirect labor, $23,000; factory rent, $32,000; factory utilities, $19,000; and factory equipment depreciation, $51,000. The predetermined overhead rate is 50% of direct labor cost. Job 306 is sold for $635,000 cash in April. Costs of the three jobs worked on in April follow.

	Job 306	Job 307	Job 308
Balances on March 31			
Direct materials	$ 29,000	$ 35,000	
Direct labor..................	20,000	18,000	
Applied overhead.............	10,000	9,000	
Costs during April			
Direct materials	135,000	220,000	$100,000
Direct labor..................	85,000	150,000	105,000
Applied overhead.............	?	?	?
Status on April 30	Finished (sold)	Finished (unsold)	In process

Required

1. Determine the total of each production cost incurred for April (direct labor, direct materials, and applied overhead) and the total cost assigned to each job (including the balances from March 31).
2. Prepare journal entries for the month of April to record the following.
   a. Materials purchases (on credit).
   b. Direct materials used in production.
   c. Direct labor paid and assigned to Work in Process Inventory.
   d. Indirect labor paid and assigned to Factory Overhead.
   e. Overhead costs applied to Work in Process Inventory.
   f. Actual overhead costs incurred, including indirect materials. (Factory rent and utilities are paid in cash.)
   g. Transfer of Jobs 306 and 307 to Finished Goods Inventory.
   h. Cost of goods sold for Job 306.
   i. Revenue from the sale of Job 306.
   j. Assignment of any underapplied or overapplied overhead to the Cost of Goods Sold account. (The amount is not material.)
3. Prepare a schedule of cost of goods manufactured.
4. Compute gross profit for April. Show how to present the inventories on the April 30 balance sheet.
5. Over- or underapplied overhead is closed to Cost of Goods Sold. Is this adjustment also posted to individual job cost sheets?

Check (2j) $5,000 underapplied

(3) Cost of goods manufactured, $828,500

Bergamo Bay's computer system generated the following trial balance on December 31, 2019. The company's manager knows something is wrong with the trial balance because it does not show any balance for Work in Process Inventory but does show a balance for the Factory Overhead account. In addition, the accrued factory payroll (Factory Wages Payable) has not been recorded.

Problem 15-2A
Source documents, journal entries, overhead, and financial reports

P1 P2 P3 P4

	Debit	Credit
Cash	$170,000	
Accounts receivable	75,000	
Raw materials inventory...............	80,000	
Work in process inventory	0	
Finished goods inventory	15,000	
Prepaid rent	3,000	
Accounts payable		$ 17,000
Notes payable......................		25,000
Common stock		50,000
Retained earnings		271,000
Sales		373,000
Cost of goods sold	218,000	
Factory overhead....................	115,000	
Operating expenses	60,000	
Totals	$736,000	$736,000

After examining various files, the manager identifies the following six source documents that need to be processed to bring the accounting records up to date.

Materials requisition 21-3010: $10,200 direct materials to Job 402	Labor time ticket 6052: $36,000 direct labor to Job 402
Materials requisition 21-3011: $18,600 direct materials to Job 404	Labor time ticket 6053: $23,800 direct labor to Job 404
Materials requisition 21-3012: $5,600 indirect materials	Labor time ticket 6054: $8,200 indirect labor

Jobs 402 and 404 are the only units in process at year-end. The predetermined overhead rate is 200% of direct labor cost.

Required

1. Use information on the six source documents to prepare journal entries to assign the following costs.
   a. Direct materials costs to Work in Process Inventory.
   b. Direct labor costs to Work in Process Inventory.
   c. Overhead costs to Work in Process Inventory.
   d. Indirect materials costs to the Factory Overhead account.
   e. Indirect labor costs to the Factory Overhead account.

Check   (2) $9,200 underapplied overhead

2. Determine the revised balance of the Factory Overhead account after making the entries in part 1. Determine whether there is any under- or overapplied overhead for the year. Prepare the adjusting entry to allocate any over- or underapplied overhead to Cost of Goods Sold, assuming the amount is not material.

(3) T. B. totals, $804,000

3. Prepare a revised trial balance.

(4) Net income, $85,800

4. Prepare an income statement for 2019 and a balance sheet as of December 31, 2019.

5. Assume that the $5,600 on materials requisition 21-3012 should have been direct materials charged to Job 404. Indicate whether this error results in overstated or understated total assets on the balance sheet at December 31, 2019.

Problem 15-3A

Source documents, journal entries, and accounts in job order costing

P1   P2   P3

Widmer Watercraft's predetermined overhead rate is 200% of direct labor. Information on the company's production activities during May follows.

a. Purchased raw materials on credit, $200,000.
b. Materials requisitions record use of the following materials for the month.

Job 136.	$ 48,000
Job 137.	32,000
Job 138.	19,200
Job 139.	22,400
Job 140.	6,400
Total direct materials	128,000
Indirect materials	19,500
Total materials used	$147,500

c. Paid $15,000 cash to a computer consultant to reprogram factory equipment.
d. Time tickets record use of the following labor for the month. These wages were paid in cash.

Job 136	$ 12,000
Job 137	10,500
Job 138	37,500
Job 139	39,000
Job 140	3,000
Total direct labor	102,000
Indirect labor.	24,000
Total	$126,000

e. Applied overhead to Jobs 136, 138, and 139.
f. Transferred Jobs 136, 138, and 139 to Finished Goods.
g. Sold Jobs 136 and 138 on credit at a total price of $525,000.

h. The company incurred the following overhead costs during the month (credit Prepaid Insurance for expired factory insurance).

Depreciation of factory building	$68,000	Expired factory insurance	$10,000
Depreciation of factory equipment	36,500	Accrued property taxes payable	35,000

i. Applied overhead at month-end to the Work in Process Inventory account (Jobs 137 and 140) using the predetermined overhead rate of 200% of direct labor cost.

Required

1. Prepare a job cost sheet for each job worked on during the month. Use the following simplified form.

Job No. _____
Materials........... $_____
Labor............. _____
Overhead .... _____
Total cost .... $_____

2. Prepare journal entries to record the events and transactions *a* through *i*.

3. Set up T-accounts for each of the following general ledger accounts, each of which started the month with a zero balance: Raw Materials Inventory, Work in Process Inventory, Finished Goods Inventory, Factory Overhead, Cost of Goods Sold. Then post the journal entries to these T-accounts and determine the balance of each account.

4. Prepare a report showing the total cost of each job in process and prove that the sum of their costs equals the Work in Process Inventory account balance. Prepare similar reports for Finished Goods Inventory and Cost of Goods Sold.

Check   (2e) Cr. Factory Overhead, $177,000

(4) Finished Goods Inventory, $139,400

At the beginning of the year, Learer Company's manager estimated total direct labor cost assuming 50 persons working an average of 2,000 hours each at an average wage rate of $25 per hour. The manager also estimated the following manufacturing overhead costs for the year.

Problem 15-4A
Overhead allocation and adjustment using a predetermined overhead rate

P3   P4

Indirect labor	$ 319,200
Factory supervision	240,000
Rent on factory building	140,000
Factory utilities	88,000
Factory insurance expired	68,000
Depreciation—Factory equipment	480,000
Repairs expense—Factory equipment	60,000
Factory supplies used	68,800
Miscellaneous production costs	36,000
Total estimated overhead costs	$1,500,000

At year-end, records show the company incurred $1,520,000 of actual overhead costs. It completed and sold five jobs with the following direct labor costs: Job 201, $604,000; Job 202, $563,000; Job 203, $298,000; Job 204, $716,000; and Job 205, $314,000. In addition, Job 206 is in process at the end of the year and had been charged $17,000 for direct labor. No jobs were in process at the beginning of the year. The company's predetermined overhead rate is based on direct labor cost.

Required

1. Determine the following.
   a. Predetermined overhead rate for the year.
   b. Total overhead cost applied to each of the six jobs during the year.
   c. Over- or underapplied overhead at year-end.
2. Assuming that any over- or underapplied overhead is not material, prepare the adjusting entry to allocate any over- or underapplied overhead to Cost of Goods Sold at the end of the year.

Check   (1c) 12,800 underapplied

Problem 15-5A

Production transactions, subsidiary records, and source documents

P1   P2   P3   P4

Sager Company manufactures variations of its product, a technopress, in response to custom orders from its customers. On May 1, the company had no inventories of work in process or finished goods but held the following raw materials.

Material M.....................	200 units @ $250 =	$50,000
Material R	95 units @ 180 =	17,100
Paint	55 units @ 75 =	4,125
Total cost.....................		$71,225

On May 4, the company began working on two technopresses: Job 102 for Worldwide Company and Job 103 for Reuben Company.

Required

Using Exhibit 15.3 as a guide, prepare job cost sheets for Jobs 102 and 103. Using Exhibit 15.5 as a guide, prepare materials ledger cards for Material M, Material R, and paint. Enter the beginning raw materials inventory dollar amounts for each of these materials on their respective ledger cards. Then, follow the instructions in this list of activities.

a. Purchased raw materials on credit and recorded the following information from receiving reports and invoices.

Receiving Report No. 426, Material M, 250 units at $250 each.   Receiving Report No. 427, Material R, 90 units at $180 each.

Instructions: Record these purchases with a single journal entry. Enter the receiving report information on the materials ledger cards.

b. Requisitioned the following raw materials for production.

Requisition No. 35, for Job 102, 135 units of Material M.   Requisition No. 38, for Job 103, 38 units of Material R.
Requisition No. 36, for Job 102, 72 units of Material R.   Requisition No. 39, for 15 units of paint.
Requisition No. 37, for Job 103, 70 units of Material M.

Instructions: Enter amounts for direct materials requisitions on the materials ledger cards and the job cost sheets. Enter the indirect materials amount on the materials ledger card. Do not record a journal entry at this time.

c. Received the following employee time tickets for work in May.

Time tickets Nos. 1 to 10 for direct labor on Job 102, $90,000.
Time tickets Nos. 11 to 30 for direct labor on Job 103, $65,000.
Time tickets Nos. 31 to 36 for equipment repairs, $19,250.

Instructions: Record direct labor from the time tickets on the job cost sheets. Do not record a journal entry at this time.

d. Paid cash for the following items during the month: factory payroll, $174,250, and miscellaneous overhead items, $102,000. Use the time tickets to record the total direct and indirect labor costs.

Instructions: Record these payments with journal entries.

e. Finished Job 102 and transferred it to the warehouse. The company assigns overhead to each job with a predetermined overhead rate equal to 80% of direct labor cost.

Instructions: Enter the applied overhead on the cost sheet for Job 102, fill in the cost summary section of the cost sheet, and then mark the cost sheet "Finished." Prepare a journal entry to record the job's completion and its transfer to Finished Goods.

f. Delivered Job 102 and accepted the customer's promise to pay $400,000 within 30 days.

Instructions: Prepare journal entries to record the sale of Job 102 and the cost of goods sold.

g. Applied overhead cost to Job 103 based on the job's direct labor to date.

Instructions: Enter overhead on the job cost sheet but do not make a journal entry at this time.

Check (*h*) Dr. Work in Process Inventory, $71,050

(*j*) Balance in Factory Overhead, $1,625 Cr., overapplied

h. Recorded the total direct and indirect materials costs as reported on all the requisitions for the month.

Instructions: Prepare a journal entry to record these costs.

i. Recorded the total overhead costs applied to jobs.

Instructions: Prepare a journal entry to record the allocation of these overhead costs.

j. Compute the balance in the Factory Overhead account as of the end of May.

Perez Mfg.'s August 31 inventory of raw materials is $150,000. Raw materials purchases in September are $400,000, and factory payroll cost in September is $232,000. Overhead costs incurred in September are: indirect materials, $30,000; indirect labor, $14,000; factory rent, $20,000; factory utilities, $12,000; and factory equipment depreciation, $30,000. The predetermined overhead rate is 50% of direct labor cost. Job 114 is sold for $380,000 cash in September. Costs for the three jobs worked on in September follow.

PROBLEM SET B

Problem 15-1B
Production costs computed and recorded; reports prepared

P1 P2 P3 P4

	Job 114	Job 115	Job 116
Balances on August 31			
Direct materials	$ 14,000	$ 18,000	
Direct labor.....................	18,000	16,000	
Applied overhead................	9,000	8,000	
Costs during September			
Direct materials	100,000	170,000	$ 80,000
Direct labor.....................	30,000	68,000	120,000
Applied overhead...............	?	?	?
Status on September 30	Finished (sold)	Finished (unsold)	In process

Required

1. Determine the total of each production cost incurred for September (direct labor, direct materials, and applied overhead) and the total cost assigned to each job (including the balances from August 31).

2. Prepare journal entries for the month of September to record the following.

   a. Materials purchases (on credit).
   b. Direct materials used in production.
   c. Direct labor paid and assigned to Work in Process Inventory.
   d. Indirect labor paid and assigned to Factory Overhead.
   e. Overhead costs applied to Work in Process Inventory.
   f. Actual overhead costs incurred, including indirect materials. (Factory rent and utilities are paid in cash.)
   g. Transfer of Jobs 114 and 115 to the Finished Goods Inventory.
   h. Cost of Job 114 in the Cost of Goods Sold account.
   i. Revenue from the sale of Job 114.
   j. Assignment of any underapplied or overapplied overhead to the Cost of Goods Sold account. (The amount is not material.)

3. Prepare a schedule of cost of goods manufactured.

4. Compute gross profit for September. Show how to present the inventories on the September 30 balance sheet.

Check (2*j*) $3,000 overapplied

(3) Cost of goods manufactured, $500,000

Analysis Component

5. The over- or underapplied overhead adjustment is closed to Cost of Goods Sold. Discuss how this adjustment impacts business decision making regarding individual jobs or batches of jobs.

Cavallo Mfg.'s computer system generated the following trial balance on December 31, 2019. The company's manager knows that the trial balance is wrong because it does not show any balance for Work in Process Inventory but does show a balance for the Factory Overhead account. In addition, the accrued factory payroll (Factory Wages Payable) has not been recorded.

Problem 15-2B
Source documents, journal entries, overhead, and financial reports

P1 P2 P3 P4

	Debit	Credit
Cash.........................	$ 64,000	
Accounts receivable	42,000	
Raw materials inventory..............	26,000	
Work in process inventory	0	
Finished goods inventory	9,000	
Prepaid rent	3,000	
Accounts payable		$ 10,500
Notes payable......................		13,500
Common stock		30,000
Retained earnings		87,000
Sales		180,000
Cost of goods sold	105,000	
Factory overhead	27,000	
Operating expenses	45,000	
Totals...........................	$321,000	$321,000

After examining various files, the manager identifies the following six source documents that need to be processed to bring the accounting records up to date.

Materials requisition 94-231: $4,600 direct materials to Job 603	Labor time ticket 765: $5,000 direct labor to Job 603
Materials requisition 94-232: $7,600 direct materials to Job 604	Labor time ticket 766: $8,000 direct labor to Job 604
Materials requisition 94-233: $2,100 indirect materials	Labor time ticket 777: $3,000 indirect labor

Jobs 603 and 604 are the only units in process at year-end. The predetermined overhead rate is 200% of direct labor cost.

Required

1. Use information on the six source documents to prepare journal entries to assign the following costs.

   a. Direct materials costs to Work in Process Inventory.
   b. Direct labor costs to Work in Process Inventory.
   c. Overhead costs to Work in Process Inventory.
   d. Indirect materials costs to the Factory Overhead account.
   e. Indirect labor costs to the Factory Overhead account.

Check (2) $6,100
underapplied overhead

2. Determine the revised balance of the Factory Overhead account after making the entries in part 1. Determine whether there is under- or overapplied overhead for the year. Prepare the adjusting entry to allocate any over- or underapplied overhead to Cost of Goods Sold, assuming the amount is not material.

(3) T. B. totals, $337,000

3. Prepare a revised trial balance.

(4) Net income, $23,900

4. Prepare an income statement for 2019 and a balance sheet as of December 31, 2019.

Analysis Component

5. Assume that the $2,100 indirect materials on materials requisition 94-233 should have been direct materials charged to Job 604. Without providing specific calculations, describe the impact of this error on the income statement for 2019 and the balance sheet at December 31, 2019.

Problem 15-3B
Source documents, journal entries, and accounts in job order costing

P1   P2   P3

Starr Mfg.'s predetermined overhead rate is 200% of direct labor. Information on the company's production activities during September follows.

a. Purchased raw materials on credit, $125,000.
b. Materials requisitions record use of the following materials for the month.

Job 487.	$30,000
Job 488.	20,000
Job 489.	12,000
Job 490.	14,000
Job 491.	4,000
Total direct materials	80,000
Indirect materials	12,000
Total materials used	$92,000

c. Paid $11,000 cash for miscellaneous factory overhead costs.
d. Time tickets record use of the following labor for the month. These wages are paid in cash.

Job 487.	$ 8,000
Job 488.	7,000
Job 489.	25,000
Job 490.	26,000
Job 491.	2,000
Total direct labor.	68,000
Indirect labor.	16,000
Total.	$84,000

e. Applied overhead to Jobs 487, 489, and 490.
f. Transferred Jobs 487, 489, and 490 to Finished Goods.

g. Sold Jobs 487 and 489 on credit for a total price of $340,000.

h. The company incurred the following overhead costs during the month (credit Prepaid Insurance for expired factory insurance).

Depreciation of factory building	$37,000	Expired factory insurance.	$ 7,000
Depreciation of factory equipment	21,000	Accrued property taxes payable	31,000

i. Applied overhead at month-end to the Work in Process Inventory account (Jobs 488 and 491) using the predetermined overhead rate of 200% of direct labor cost.

Required

1. Prepare a job cost sheet for each job worked on in the month. Use the following simplified form.

Job No. _____
Materials. . . . . $ _____
Labor. . . . .   _____
Overhead . . . .   _____
Total cost . . . . $ _____

2. Prepare journal entries to record the events and transactions *a* through *i*.

3. Set up T-accounts for each of the following general ledger accounts, each of which started the month with a zero balance: Raw Materials Inventory, Work in Process Inventory, Finished Goods Inventory, Factory Overhead, Cost of Goods Sold. Then post the journal entries to these T-accounts and determine the balance of each account.

4. Prepare a report showing the total cost of each job in process and prove that the sum of their costs equals the Work in Process Inventory account balance. Prepare similar reports for Finished Goods Inventory and Cost of Goods Sold.

Check   (2*e*) Cr. Factory Overhead, $118,000
(3) Finished Goods Inventory, $92,000 bal.

At the beginning of the year, Pavelka Company's manager estimated next year's total direct labor cost assuming 50 persons working an average of 2,000 hours each at an average wage rate of $15 per hour. The manager also estimated the following manufacturing overhead costs for the year.

Problem 15-4B
Overhead allocation and adjustment using a predetermined overhead rate

P3   P4

Indirect labor	$159,600
Factory supervision	120,000
Rent on factory building	70,000
Factory utilities	44,000
Factory insurance expired	34,000
Depreciation—Factory equipment	240,000
Repairs expense—Factory equipment	30,000
Factory supplies used	34,400
Miscellaneous production costs	18,000
Total estimated overhead costs	$750,000

At year-end, records show the company incurred $725,000 of actual overhead costs. It completed and sold five jobs with the following direct labor costs: Job 625, $354,000; Job 626, $330,000; Job 627, $175,000; Job 628, $420,000; and Job 629, $184,000. In addition, Job 630 is in process at the end of the year and had been charged $10,000 for direct labor. No jobs were in process at the beginning of the year. The company's predetermined overhead rate is based on direct labor cost.

Required

1. Determine the following.

    a. Predetermined overhead rate for the year.

    b. Total overhead cost applied to each of the six jobs during the year.

    c. Over- or underapplied overhead at year-end.

Check   (1*c*) $11,500 overapplied

2. Assuming that any over- or underapplied overhead is not material, prepare the adjusting entry to allocate any over- or underapplied overhead to Cost of Goods Sold at the end of the year.

Problem 15-5B

Production transactions, subsidiary records, and source documents

P1   P2   P3   P4

King Company produces variations of its product, a megatron, in response to custom orders from its customers. On June 1, the company had no inventories of work in process or finished goods but held the following raw materials.

Material M.......................	120 units @ $200 =	$24,000
Material R	80 units @ 160 =	12,800
Paint	44 units @ 72 =	3,168
Total cost.......................		$39,968

On June 3, the company began working on two megatrons: Job 450 for Encinita Company and Job 451 for Fargo, Inc.

Required

Using Exhibit 15.3 as a guide, prepare job cost sheets for Jobs 450 and 451. Using Exhibit 15.5 as a guide, prepare materials ledger cards for Material M, Material R, and paint. Enter the beginning raw materials inventory dollar amounts for each of these materials on their respective ledger cards. Then, follow instructions in this list of activities.

a. Purchased raw materials on credit and recorded the following information from receiving reports and invoices.

> Receiving Report No. 20, Material M, 150 units at $200 each.   Receiving Report No. 21, Material R, 70 units at $160 each.

Instructions: Record these purchases with a single journal entry. Enter the receiving report information on the materials ledger cards.

b. Requisitioned the following raw materials for production.

> Requisition No. 223, for Job 450, 80 units of Material M.   Requisition No. 226, for Job 451, 30 units of Material R.
> Requisition No. 224, for Job 450, 60 units of Material R.   Requisition No. 227, for 12 units of paint.
> Requisition No. 225, for Job 451, 40 units of Material M.

Instructions: Enter amounts for direct materials requisitions on the materials ledger cards and the job cost sheets. Enter the indirect materials amount on the materials ledger card. Do not record a journal entry at this time.

c. Received the following employee time tickets for work in June.

> Time tickets Nos. 1 to 10 for direct labor on Job 450, $40,000.
> Time tickets Nos. 11 to 20 for direct labor on Job 451, $32,000.
> Time tickets Nos. 21 to 24 for equipment repairs, $12,000.

Instructions: Record direct labor from the time tickets on the job cost sheets. Do not record a journal entry at this time.

d. Paid cash for the following items during the month: factory payroll, $84,000, and miscellaneous overhead items, $36,800. Use the time tickets to record the total direct and indirect labor costs.

Instructions: Record these payments with journal entries.

e. Finished Job 450 and transferred it to the warehouse. The company assigns overhead to each job with a predetermined overhead rate equal to 70% of direct labor cost.

Instructions: Enter the applied overhead on the cost sheet for Job 450, fill in the cost summary section of the cost sheet, and then mark the cost sheet "Finished." Prepare a journal entry to record the job's completion and its transfer to Finished Goods.

f. Delivered Job 450 and accepted the customer's promise to pay $290,000 within 30 days.

Instructions: Prepare journal entries to record the sale of Job 450 and the cost of goods sold.

g. Applied overhead cost to Job 451 based on the job's direct labor used to date.

Instructions: Enter overhead on the job cost sheet but do not make a journal entry at this time.

h. Recorded the total direct and indirect materials costs as reported on all the requisitions for the month.

   Instructions: Prepare a journal entry to record these costs.

i. Recorded the total overhead costs applied to jobs.

   Instructions: Prepare a journal entry to record the allocation of these overhead costs.

j. Compute the balance in the Factory Overhead account as of the end of June.

Check   (*h*) Dr. Work in Process Inventory, $38,400

(*j*) Balance in Factory Overhead, $736 Cr., overapplied

This serial problem began in Chapter 1 and continues through most of the book. If previous chapter segments were not completed, the serial problem can begin at this point.

SP 15   The computer workstation furniture manufacturing that Santana Rey started in January is progressing well. As of the end of June, **Business Solutions**'s job cost sheets show the following total costs accumulated on three furniture jobs.

SERIAL PROBLEM
Business Solutions
P1   P2   P3

©Alexander Image/Shutterstock

	Job 602	Job 603	Job 604
Direct materials............	$1,500	$3,300	$2,700
Direct labor...............	800	1,420	2,100
Overhead	400	710	1,050

Job 602 was started in production in May, and these costs were assigned to it in May: direct materials, $600; direct labor, $180; and overhead, $90. Jobs 603 and 604 were started in June. Overhead cost is applied with a predetermined rate based on direct labor costs. Jobs 602 and 603 are finished in June, and Job 604 is expected to be finished in July. No raw materials are used indirectly in June. (Assume this company's predetermined overhead rate did not change over these months.)

Required

1. What is the cost of the raw materials used in June for each of the three jobs and in total?

2. How much total direct labor cost is incurred in June?

3. What predetermined overhead rate is used in June?

4. How much cost is transferred to Finished Goods Inventory in June?

Check   (1) Total materials, $6,900

The **General Ledger** tool in *Connect* automates several of the procedural steps in accounting so that the financial professional can focus on the impacts of each transaction on various reports and performance measures.

GL 15-1   General Ledger assignment GL 15-1, based on Problem 15-1A, focuses on transactions related to job order costing. Prepare summary journal entries to record the cost of jobs and their flow through the manufacturing environment. Then prepare a schedule of cost of goods manufactured and a partial income statement.

GENERAL LEDGER PROBLEM

Accounting Analysis

AA 15-1   Manufacturers and merchandisers can apply just-in-time (JIT) to their inventory management. **Apple** wants to know the impact of a JIT inventory system on operating cash flows. Review Apple's statement of cash flows in Appendix A to answer the following.

FINANCIAL ANALYSIS
P1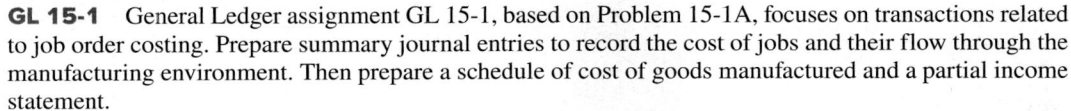

APPLE

Required

1. Identify the impact on operating cash flows (increase or decrease) for changes in inventory levels (increase or decrease) for each of the fiscal years ended September 30, 2017, and September 24, 2016.

2. What impact (increase or decrease) would a JIT inventory system have on Apple's (*a*) inventory and (*b*) operating cash flows?

COMPARATIVE
ANALYSIS

P1

APPLE

GOOGLE

AA 15-2 Apple's and Google's income statements in Appendix A both show increasing sales and cost of sales. The gross margin ratio can be used to analyze how well companies control costs as sales increase.

Required

1. Compute the gross margin ratio for Apple for each of the fiscal years ended September 30, 2017, and September 24, 2016.
2. Compute the gross margin ratio for Google for each of the fiscal years ended December 31, 2017, and December 31, 2016.
3. Which company (Apple, Google, or neither) improved its control of costs during 2017, as reflected in the gross margin ratio?

GLOBAL ANALYSIS

P1

APPLE

Samsung

AA 15-3 Apple and Samsung compete in the global marketplace. Apple's and Samsung's financial statements are in Appendix A.

Required

1. Compute the ratio of inventory to total assets for Apple as of September 30, 2017, and for Samsung as of December 31, 2017. Express your answers as percentages, rounded to two decimal places.
2. Based on the answer to part 1, which company's (Apple's or Samsung's) inventory policy more closely follows a JIT system?

Beyond the Numbers

ETHICS
CHALLENGE

P3

BTN 15-1 Assume that your company sells portable housing to both general contractors and the government. It sells jobs to contractors on a bid basis. A contractor asks for three bids from different manufacturers. The combination of low bid and high quality wins the job. However, jobs sold to the government are bid on a cost-plus basis. This means price is determined by adding all costs plus a profit based on cost at a specified percent, such as 10%. You observe that the amount of overhead applied to government jobs is higher than that applied to contract jobs. These allocations concern you.

Point: Students could compare responses and discuss differences in concerns with allocating overhead.

Required

Write a half-page memo to your company's chief financial officer outlining your concerns with overhead allocation.

COMMUNICATING
IN PRACTICE

C1   C2

BTN 15-2 Assume that you are preparing for a second interview with a manufacturing company. The company is impressed with your credentials, but it has several qualified applicants. You anticipate that in this second interview, you must show what you offer over other candidates. You learn the company is not satisfied with the timeliness of its information and its inventory management. The company manufactures custom-order holiday decorations and display items. To show your abilities, you plan to recommend that the company use a job order accounting system.

Required

In preparation for the interview, prepare notes outlining the following:

1. Your recommendation and why it is suitable for this company.
2. A general description of the documents that the proposed system requires.
3. How the documents in part 2 facilitate the operation of the job order accounting system.

Point: Have students present a mock interview, one assuming the role of the president of the company and the other the applicant.

TAKING IT TO
THE NET

C1

BTN 15-3 Many contractors work on custom jobs that require a job order costing system.

Required

Access the AMSI-Construction Software website (<u>softwareconnect.com/construction/amsi-construction-software/</u>); scroll down and read the section on StarBuilder—Job Cost Accounting. Prepare a one-page memorandum for the CEO of a construction company providing information about the job order costing software this company offers. Would you recommend that the company purchase this software?

BTN 15-4   Consider the activities undertaken by a medical clinic in your area.

Required

1. Is a job order costing system appropriate for the clinic? Explain.

2. Identify as many factors as possible to lead you to conclude that the clinic uses a job order system.

BTN 15-5   Refer to the chapter opener regarding Brennan Agranoff and his company, **HoopSwagg**. All successful businesses track their costs, and it is especially important for start-up businesses to monitor and control costs.

Required

1. Assume that Brennan Agranoff uses a job order costing system. For the basic cost category of direct materials, explain how Brennan's job cost sheet would differ from a job cost sheet for a service company.

2. For the basic cost categories of direct materials, direct labor, and overhead, provide examples of the types of costs that would fall into each category for HoopSwagg.

BTN 15-6   Home builders often use job order costing.

Required

1. You (or your team) are to prepare a job cost sheet for a single-family home under construction. List four items of both direct materials and direct labor. Explain how you think overhead should be applied.

2. Contact a builder and compare your job cost sheet to this builder's job cost sheet. If possible, speak to that company's accountant. Write your findings in a short report.

16 Process Costing and Analysis

Learning Objectives

CONCEPTUAL

C1 Explain process operations and the way they differ from job order operations.

C2 Define and compute equivalent units and explain their use in process costing.

C3 Describe accounting for production activity and preparation of a process cost summary using weighted average.

C4 *Appendix 16A*—Describe accounting for production activity and preparation of a process cost summary using FIFO.

ANALYTICAL

A1 Compare process costing and job order costing.

A2 Explain and illustrate a hybrid costing system.

PROCEDURAL

P1 Record the flow of materials costs in process costing.

P2 Record the flow of labor costs in process costing.

P3 Record the flow of factory overhead costs in process costing.

P4 Record the transfer of goods across departments, to Finished Goods Inventory, and to Cost of Goods Sold.

¡Todos Gritamos por Helado!

"Always room for ice cream"—**SUZY BATLLE**

MIAMI—Suzy Batlle was new to running a business when she started **Azucar Ice Cream Company** (**azucaricecream.com**). But Suzy knew ice cream, having grown up in a family that ate it nearly every night. "We Cuban people love ice cream," exclaims Suzy from her shop in the Little Havana section of Miami. Suzy took classes to learn the ice cream–making process and mastered the legal and permitting process to open her store.

Suzy's recipes use tropical fruits found throughout Central and South America—ruby-red guava, mamey, papaya, and plantains, for example—and stem from an adventurous streak passed down through her family.

"My grandmother traveled extensively," explains Suzy, "and always made ice cream with the new exotic fruits she found. We have Cuban-inspired flavors you won't see anywhere else."

Ice cream is made in a process operation and produced in large volumes. "I'll buy 1,000 pounds of mamey at a time" says Suzy. These perishable raw materials enter a continuous production process that also uses direct labor (Suzy has 14 employees) and overhead (depreciation on processing machines, for example).

©Azucar Ice Cream Company

Each production run yields many gallons of ice cream. Suzy uses a process costing system to determine her production costs per gallon. Suzy credits courses from nearby Miami Dade College with improving her management and accounting skills.

Azucar is flourishing, and Suzy plans to open more stores. Suzy advises, "Work hard and love what you do!"

Sources: *Azucar Ice Cream Company website,* January 2019; *Saveur,* July 7, 2016; *Miami Today,* February 2, 2016; *Mic.com,* November 28, 2016

PROCESS OPERATIONS

Process operations involve the mass production of similar products in a continuous flow of sequential processes. Process operations require a high level of standardization to produce large volumes of products. Thus, process operations use a standardized process to make similar products; job order operations use a customized process to make unique products.

Penn makes tennis balls in a process operation. Tennis balls must be identical in terms of bounce, playability, and durability. This uniformity requires Penn to use a production process that can repeatedly make large volumes of tennis balls to the same specifications. Process operations also extend to services, such as mail sorting in large post offices and order processing in retailers like **Amazon**. Other companies using process operations include:

C1_____
Explain process operations and the way they differ from job order operations.

Company	Product	Company	Product
General Mills.	Cereals	Heinz	Ketchup
Pfizer	Pharmaceuticals	Kar's.	Trail mix
Procter & Gamble.	Household products	Hershey.	Chocolate
Coca-Cola	Soft drinks	Suja	Organic juice

Organization of Process Operations

Each of the above products is made in a series of repetitive *processes,* or steps. Tennis ball production includes the three steps shown in Exhibit 16.1. Understanding such processes is crucial for measuring product costs. Increasingly, process operations use machines and automation to control product quality and reduce manufacturing costs.

In a process operation, each process is a separate *production department, workstation,* or *work center.* Each process applies direct labor, overhead, and, perhaps, direct materials to move the product toward completion. The final process or department in the series finishes the goods and makes them ready for sale.

Courtesy of Ken W. Shaw

EXHIBIT 16.1

Process Operations: Making
Tennis Balls*

* See a virtual tour of a process operation
  at PennRacquet.com/video.html

| Forming rubber cores | → | Gluing felt covers to cores | → | Packaging the tennis balls |

In Exhibit 16.1, the first step in tennis ball production involves cutting rubber into pellets and forming the core of each ball. These rubber cores are passed to the second department, where felt is cut into covers and glued to the rubber cores. The completed tennis balls are then passed to the final department for quality checks and packaging.

A1
Compare process costing
and job order costing.

Comparing Process and Job Order Costing Systems

We use Exhibit 16.2 to discuss similarities and differences in job order and process systems next.

EXHIBIT 16.2

Cost Flows: Comparing
Job Order and Process
Costing Systems

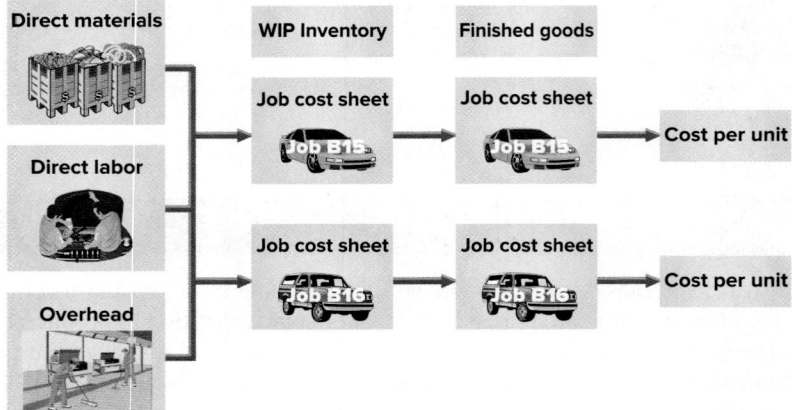

Job Order System

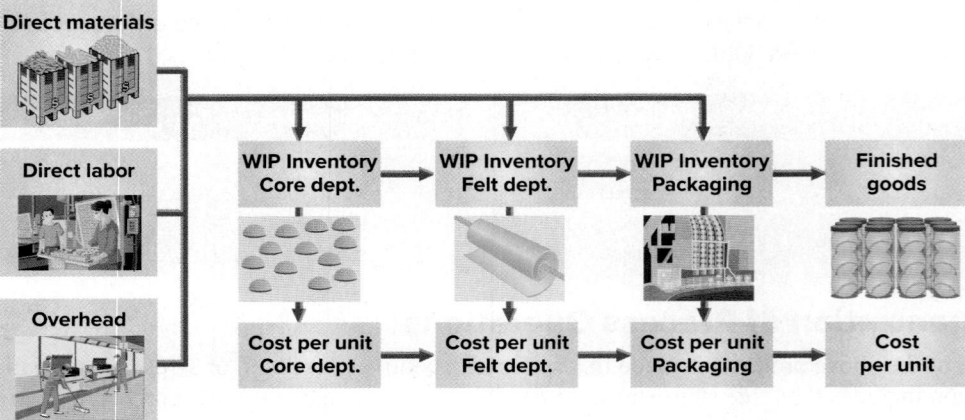

Process System

Job order and process operations share the following features.

- Both use materials, labor, and overhead costs.
- Both aim to compute the cost per unit of product (or service).

Job order and process operations have important differences.

Cost object	In a job order system, the cost object is a job. In a process system, the cost object is the process (or department).
Cost per unit	**Job order costing system** measures cost per unit after completion of a job. **Process costing system** measures unit costs at the end of a period (such as a month) by combining costs per equivalent unit from each department.
Job cost sheets	Only job order systems use job cost sheets.
Work in process inventory	Job order costing systems often use one Work in Process Inventory account. Process costing systems use separate Work in Process Inventory accounts for each process.

Transferring Costs across Departments   In process costing, manufacturing costs are transferred across Work in Process (WIP) Inventory accounts. After production is complete, the completed goods and their accumulated costs are transferred from the Work in Process Inventory account for the final department in the series of processes to the Finished Goods Inventory account.

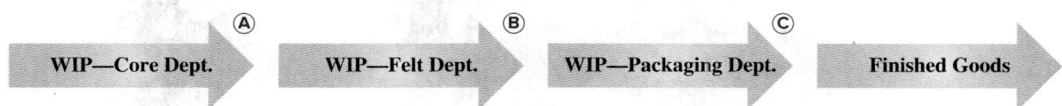

Exhibit 16.3 summarizes the journal entries to capture this flow of manufacturing costs for a tennis ball manufacturer—from Ⓐ, then from Ⓑ, and then from Ⓒ.

EXHIBIT 16.3

Flow of Costs through Separate Work in Process Accounts

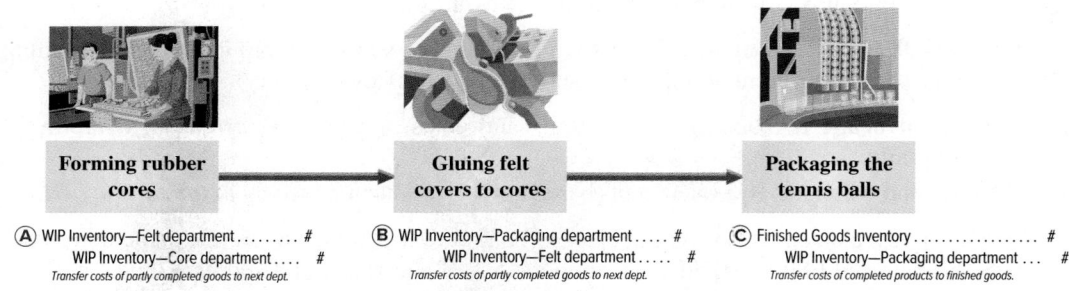

Forming rubber cores	Gluing felt covers to cores	Packaging the tennis balls

Ⓐ WIP Inventory—Felt department . . . . #
     WIP Inventory—Core department . . . . #
Transfer costs of partly completed goods to next dept.
	Ⓑ WIP Inventory—Packaging department . . . . . #
	     WIP Inventory—Felt department . . . . . #
	Transfer costs of partly completed goods to next dept.
		Ⓒ Finished Goods Inventory . . . . #
		     WIP Inventory—Packaging department . . . #
		Transfer costs of completed products to finished goods.

Complete the table with either a *yes* or *no* regarding the attributes of job order and process costing systems.

	Job Order	Process
Uses direct materials, direct labor, and overhead costs	a. _____	e. _____
Uses job cost sheets to accumulate costs	b. _____	f. _____
Typically uses several Work in Process Inventory accounts.	c. _____	g. _____
Yields a cost per unit of product	d. _____	h. _____

NEED-TO-KNOW 16-1

Job Order vs. Process Costing Systems

C1   A1

Do More: QS 16-1, QS 16-2, E 16-1, E 16-2

Solution

a. yes   **b.** yes   **c.** no   **d.** yes   **e.** yes   **f.** no   **g.** yes   **h.** yes

Equivalent Units of Production

Companies with process operations typically end each period with inventories of both finished goods and work in process. For example, a maker of tennis balls ends each period with both completed tennis balls and partially completed tennis balls in inventory. Perhaps only the Core department has completed its work on a batch of tennis balls. How does a process manufacturer measure its production activity when it has some partially completed goods at the end of a period? A key

C2 _____

Define and compute equivalent units and explain their use in process costing.

idea in process costing is **equivalent units of production (EUP),** which is the number of units that *could have been* started and completed given the costs incurred during the period.

EUP is explained as follows: 10,000 tennis balls that are 60% through the production process is *equivalent to* 6,000 (10,000 × 60%) tennis balls that completed the entire production process. This means that the cost to put 10,000 units 60% of the way through the production process is *equivalent to* the cost to put 6,000 units completely through the production process. Knowing the costs of partially completed goods allows us to measure production activity for the period.

EUP for Materials and Conversion Costs

Equivalent units of production for direct materials are often not the same with respect to direct labor and overhead. For example, direct materials, like rubber for tennis ball cores, might enter production entirely at the beginning of a process. In contrast, direct labor and overhead might be used continuously throughout the process. How does a manufacturer account for these timing differences? With equivalent units of production. For example, if all of the direct materials to produce 10,000 units have entered the production process, but those units have received only 20% of their direct labor and overhead costs, equivalent units are computed as:

EUP: Physical unit #s × Complete %		
EUP for direct materials	= 10,000 × 100% =	10,000
EUP for direct labor	= 10,000 × 20% =	2,000
EUP for overhead	= 10,000 × 20% =	2,000

Direct labor and factory overhead are often classified as *conversion costs*—that is, as costs of converting direct materials into finished products. Many businesses with process operations compute **conversion cost per equivalent unit,** which is the combined costs of direct labor and factory overhead per equivalent unit. If direct labor and overhead enter the production process at about the same rate, it is convenient to combine them as conversion costs.

Point: When overhead is applied based on direct labor cost, the percentage of completion for direct labor and overhead will be the same.

Weighted Average versus FIFO

There are two ways to compute equivalent units. These methods make different assumptions about how costs flow.

- **Weighted-average method** combines units and costs *across two periods* in computing equivalent units.
- **FIFO method** computes equivalent units based only on production activity in the *current period*.

The objectives, concepts, and journal entries (but not dollar amounts) are the same under the weighted-average and FIFO methods; the computations of equivalent units differ. While the FIFO method is generally more precise than the weighted-average method, it requires more calculations. Often, the differences between the two methods are small. With a just-in-time inventory system, these different methods yield very similar results because inventories are immaterial. **In this chapter we assume the weighted-average method; we illustrate the FIFO method in Appendix 16A.**

PROCESS COSTING ILLUSTRATION

C3

Describe accounting for production activity and preparation of a process cost summary using weighted average.

We provide a step-by-step illustration of process costing. Each process (or department) in a process operation follows these steps:

1. **Determine the physical flow of units.**
2. **Compute equivalent units of production.**
3. **Compute cost per equivalent unit of production.**
4. **Assign and reconcile costs.**

We show these steps for the first of two sequential processes of a trail mix manufacturer.

Overview of GenX Company's Process Operation

GenX Company produces an organic trail mix called FitMix. Its target customers are active people who are interested in fitness and the environment. GenX sells FitMix to wholesale distributors, who in turn sell it to retailers. FitMix is manufactured in a continuous, two-process operation (Roasting and Blending), shown in Exhibit 16.4.

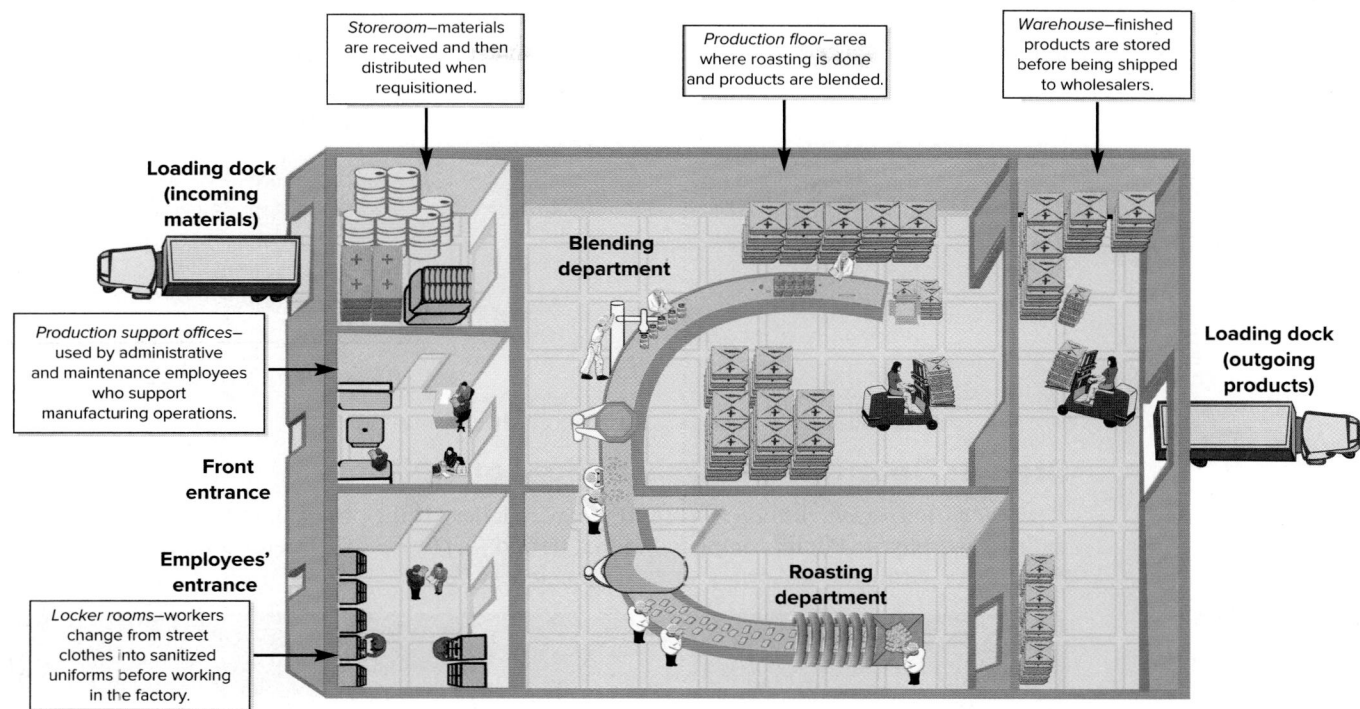

EXHIBIT 16.4

GenX's Process Operation

In the first process (Roasting department), GenX roasts, oils, and salts organically grown peanuts. These peanuts are then passed to the Blending department, the second process. In the Blending department, machines blend organic chocolate pieces and organic dried fruits with the peanuts from the first process. The blended mix is then inspected and packaged for delivery. In both departments, direct materials enter production at the beginning of the process, while conversion costs occur continuously throughout each department's processing.

Pre-Step: Collect Production and Cost Data

Exhibit 16.5 presents production data (in units) for GenX's Roasting department. This exhibit includes the percentage of completion for both materials and conversion; beginning work in process inventory is 100% complete with respect to materials but only 65% complete with respect to conversion. Ending work in process inventory is 100% complete with respect to materials but only 25% complete with respect to conversion. Units completed and transferred to the Blending department are 100% complete with respect to both materials and conversion.

EXHIBIT 16.5

Production Data (in units) for Roasting Department

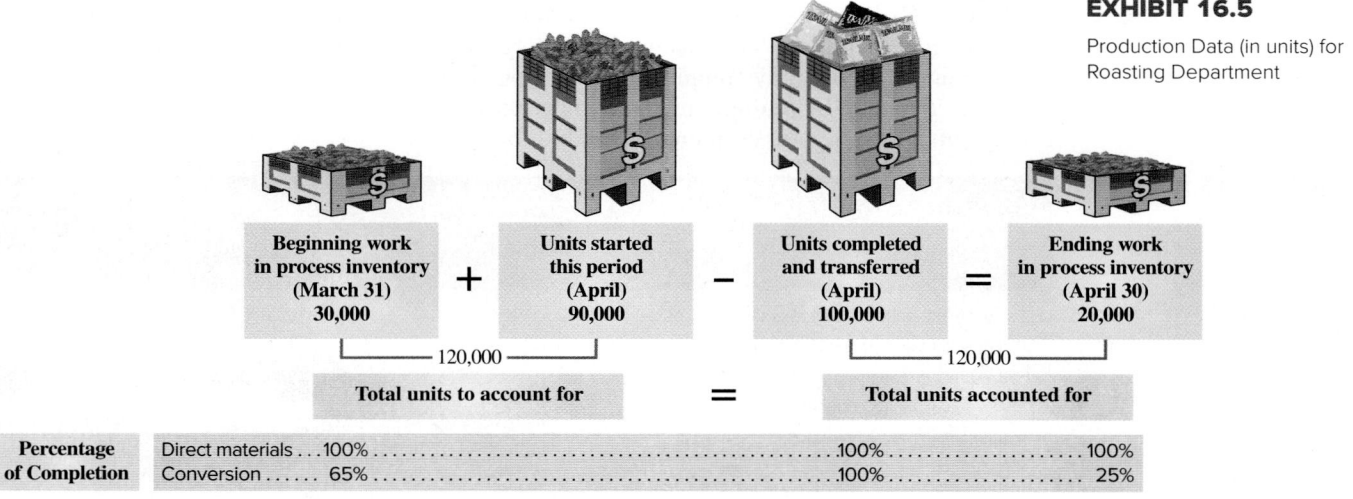

	Beginning work in process inventory (March 31) 30,000	+	Units started this period (April) 90,000	−	Units completed and transferred (April) 100,000	=	Ending work in process inventory (April 30) 20,000

──────── 120,000 ────────

Total units to account for   =   **Total units accounted for**

Percentage of Completion	Direct materials . . . 100% . . . . .100% 100%
	Conversion . . . . . . 65% . . . . .100% 25%

Exhibit 16.6 presents production cost data for GenX's Roasting department. We use the data in Exhibits 16.5 and 16.6 to illustrate the four-step approach to process costing.

EXHIBIT 16.6

Roasting Department
Production Cost Data

GenX—Roasting Department: Production Cost Data (April)		
Beginning work in process inventory (March 31)		
Direct materials costs	$ 81,000	
Conversion costs	108,900	$ 189,900
Costs during the current period (April)		
Direct materials costs	279,000	
Direct labor costs*	171,000	
Factory overhead costs applied (120% of direct labor)*	205,200	655,200
Total production costs		$845,100

*Total conversion costs for the month equal $376,200 (= $171,000 + $205,200).

Step 1: Determine Physical Flow of Units

A *physical flow reconciliation* is a report that reconciles (1) the physical units started in a period with (2) the physical units completed in that period. A physical flow reconciliation for GenX's Roasting department for April is shown in Exhibit 16.7.

EXHIBIT 16.7

Physical Flow Reconciliation

WIP—Roasting (in units)		
Beg. inv.	30,000	
Started	90,000	
To acct. for	120,000	
		100,000 Tr. out
End. inv.	20,000	

GenX—Roasting Department			
Units to Account For		**Units Accounted For**	
Beginning work in process inventory.	30,000 units	Units completed and transferred out.	100,000 units
Units started this period	90,000 units	Ending work in process inventory	20,000 units
Total units to account for	**120,000 units**	Total units accounted for	**120,000 units**

reconciled

Step 2: Compute Equivalent Units of Production

The second step is to compute *equivalent units of production* for direct materials and conversion costs for April. Because direct materials and conversion costs typically enter a process at different rates, departments must compute equivalent units separately for direct materials and conversion costs. Exhibit 16.8 shows the formula to compute equivalent units under the weighted-average method for both direct materials and conversion costs.

EXHIBIT 16.8

Computing EUP—Weighted-
Average Method

Point: We see that under
weighted average, units in beginning work in process are combined with units produced in the
current period to get EU (and
costs per EU). This approach
combines production activity
across two periods.

$$\text{Equivalent units of production (EUP)} = \text{Number of whole units completed and transferred out*} + \text{Number of equivalent units in ending work in process}$$

*Transferred to next department or finished goods inventory.

For GenX's Roasting department, we convert the 120,000 physical units to *equivalent units* based on how each input has been used. The Roasting department fully completed its work on 100,000 units and partially completed its work on 20,000 units (from Exhibit 16.5). Equivalent units are computed by multiplying the number of units accounted for (from step 1) by the percentage of completion for each input—see Exhibit 16.9.

EXHIBIT 16.9

Equivalent Units of
Production—Weighted
Average

GenX—Roasting Department		
Equivalent Units of Production	**Direct Materials**	**Conversion**
Equivalent units completed and transferred out (100,000 × 100%).	100,000 EUP	100,000 EUP
Equivalent units for ending work in process		
Direct materials (20,000 × 100%).	20,000 EUP	
Conversion (20,000 × 25%)		5,000 EUP
Equivalent units of production.	120,000 EUP	105,000 EUP

The first row of Exhibit 16.9 reflects 100,000 completed units transferred out in April. These units have 100% of the materials and conversion required, or 100,000 equivalent units of each input (100,000 × 100%).

Rows two, three, and four refer to the 20,000 partially completed units. For direct materials, the units in ending work in process inventory include all materials required, so there are 20,000 equivalent units (20,000 × 100%) of materials in the unfinished physical units. For conversion, the units in ending work in process inventory include 25% of the conversion required, which implies 5,000 equivalent units of conversion (20,000 × 25%).

The final row reflects the total equivalent units of production, which is whole units of product that could have been manufactured with the amount of inputs used to create some complete and some incomplete units. The amount of inputs used to produce 100,000 complete units and to start 20,000 additional units is equivalent to the amount of direct materials in 120,000 whole units and the amount of conversion in 105,000 whole units.

EUP for Transferred out
+ EUP for WIP
= EUP for Total

©Ken Whitmore/Stone/Getty Images

A department began the month with 8,000 units in work in process inventory. These units were 100% complete with respect to direct materials and 40% complete with respect to conversion.

During the current month, the department started 56,000 units and completed 58,000 units. Ending work in process inventory includes 6,000 units, 80% complete with respect to direct materials and 70% complete with respect to conversion. Use the weighted-average method of process costing to:

1. Compute the department's equivalent units of production for the month for direct materials.
2. Compute the department's equivalent units of production for the month for conversion.

NEED-TO-KNOW 16-2

EUP—Direct Materials and Conversion (Weighted Average)

C2

Solution—see supporting unit computations to the side

1. EUP for materials = 58,000 + (6,000 × 80%) = 62,800 EUP
2. EUP for conversion = 58,000 + (6,000 × 70%) = 62,200 EUP

WIP (in units)			
Beg. inv.	8,000		
Started	56,000		
To acct. for	64,000		
		58,000	Tr. out
End. inv.	6,000		

Do More: QS 16-5, QS 16-10, E 16-4, E 16-8

Step 3: Compute Cost per Equivalent Unit

Under the weighted-average method, computation of EUP does not separate the units in beginning inventory from those started this period. Similarly, the weighted-average method combines the costs of beginning work in process inventory with the costs incurred in the current period. Total cost is then divided by the equivalent units of production (from step 2) to compute the average **cost per equivalent unit.** This is illustrated in Exhibit 16.10. For direct materials, the cost is $3.00 per EUP. For conversion, the cost is $4.62 per EUP.

GenX—Roasting Department		
Cost per Equivalent Unit of Production	Direct Materials	Conversion
Costs of beginning work in process inventory*...............	$ 81,000	$108,900
Costs incurred this period*.............................	279,000	376,200‡
Total costs..	$360,000	$485,100
÷ Equivalent units of production (from step 2)..................	120,000 EUP	105,000 EUP
= Cost per equivalent unit of production......................	$3.00 per EUP†	$4.62 per EUP§

*From Exhibit 16.6   †$360,000 ÷ 120,000 EUP   ‡$171,000 + $205,200, from Exhibit 16.6   §$485,100 ÷ 105,000 EUP

EXHIBIT 16.10

Cost per Equivalent Unit of Production—Weighted Average

$$\text{Cost per EUP} = \frac{\text{Total costs}}{\text{EUP}}$$

Step 4: Assign and Reconcile Costs

The EUP from step 2 and the cost per EUP from step 3 are used in step 4 to assign costs to (a) the 100,000 units that the Roasting department completed and transferred to the Blending department and (b) the 20,000 units that remain in process in the Roasting department. This is illustrated in Exhibit 16.11.

EXHIBIT 16.11

Report of Costs Accounted
For—Weighted Average*

*Equals total production costs from
Exhibit 16.6.

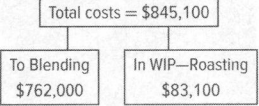

Total costs = $845,100

To Blending	In WIP—Roasting
$762,000	$83,100

GenX—Roasting Department

Cost of units completed and transferred to Blending dept.		
Direct materials (100,000 EUP × $3.00 per EUP)	$300,000	
Conversion (100,000 EUP × $4.62 per EUP)	462,000	
Cost of units completed this period		$762,000
Cost of ending work in process inventory		
Direct materials (20,000 EUP × $3.00 per EUP)	60,000	
Conversion (5,000 EUP × $4.62 per EUP)	23,100	
Cost of ending work in process inventory		83,100
Total costs accounted for		**$845,100***

Cost of Units Completed and Transferred

The 100,000 units completed and transferred to the Blending department required 100,000 EUP of direct materials and 100,000 EUP of conversion. We assign $300,000 (100,000 EUP × $3.00 per EUP) of direct materials cost to those units. We also assign $462,000 (100,000 EUP × $4.62 per EUP) of conversion cost to those units. Total cost of the 100,000 completed and transferred units is $762,000 ($300,000 + $462,000), and the average cost per unit is $7.62 ($762,000 ÷ 100,000 units).

Cost of Units in Ending Work in Process Inventory

There are 20,000 incomplete units in work in process inventory at period-end. For direct materials, those units have 20,000 EUP of material (from step 2) at a cost of $3.00 per EUP (from step 3), which yields the materials cost of work in process inventory of $60,000 (20,000 EUP × $3.00 per EUP). For conversion, the in-process units reflect 5,000 EUP (from step 2). Using the $4.62 conversion cost per EUP (from step 3), we obtain conversion costs for in-process inventory of $23,100 (5,000 EUP × $4.62 per EUP). Total cost of work in process inventory at period-end is $83,100 ($60,000 + $23,100).

20,000 Partially completed units	
Materials	Conversion
20,000 EUP	5,000 EUP

Reconciliation

Management verifies that total costs assigned to units completed and transferred plus the costs of units in process (from Exhibit 16.11) equal the costs incurred by production. Exhibit 16.12 shows the costs incurred by production this period. We then reconcile the *costs accounted for* in Exhibit 16.11 with the *costs to account for* in Exhibit 16.12.

EXHIBIT 16.12

Report of Costs to Account
For—Weighted Average

GenX—Roasting Department

Cost of beginning work in process inventory		
Direct materials.	$ 81,000	
Conversion	108,900	$ 189,900
Cost incurred this period		
Direct materials.	279,000	
Conversion	376,200	655,200
Total costs to account for		**$845,100**

The Roasting department manager is responsible for $845,100 in costs: $189,900 from beginning work in process inventory plus $655,200 of materials and conversion incurred in the period. At period-end, that manager must show where these costs are assigned. The Roasting department manager reports that $83,100 is assigned to units in process and $762,000 is assigned to units completed and transferred out to the Blending department (per Exhibit 16.11). The sum of these amounts equals $845,100. Thus, the total *costs to account for* equal the total *costs accounted for* (minor differences sometimes occur from rounding).

NEED-TO-KNOW 16-3

A department began the month with conversion costs of $65,000 in its beginning work in process inventory. During the current month, the department incurred $55,000 of conversion costs. Equivalent units of production for conversion for the month were 15,000 units. The department completed and transferred 12,000 units to the next department. The department uses the weighted-average method of process costing.

Cost per EUP—
Conversion, with
Transfer

1. Compute the department's cost per equivalent unit for conversion for the month.
2. Compute the department's conversion cost of units transferred to the next department for the month.

C3

Solution

1. ($65,000 + $55,000)/15,000 units = $8.00 per EUP for conversion

2. 12,000 units × $8.00 = $96,000 conversion cost transferred to next department

Do More: QS 16-11, E 16-6

Process Cost Summary

An important managerial accounting report for a process costing system is the **process cost summary** (also called *production report*), which is prepared separately for each process or production department. A process cost summary describes the costs charged to each department, reports the equivalent units of production achieved by each department, and determines the costs assigned to each department's output. It is prepared using a combination of Exhibits 16.7, 16.9, 16.10, 16.11, and 16.12.

Point: The key report in a job order costing system is a job cost sheet, which reports manufacturing costs per job. A process cost summary reports manufacturing costs per equivalent unit of a process or department.

The process cost summary for the Roasting department is shown in Exhibit 16.13. It summarizes the process costing steps.

⬨DATA⬨ Total costs charged to the department, including direct materials and conversion costs incurred, as well as the cost of the beginning work in process inventory.

① Physical flow of units. This reconciles the physical units started with the physical units completed in the period.

② Equivalent units of production for the department. Equivalent units for direct materials and conversion are shown in separate columns.

③ Costs per equivalent unit for direct materials and conversion.

④ Assignment of total costs among units worked on in the period. The $762,000 is the total cost of the 100,000 units transferred out of the Roasting department to the Blending department. The $83,100 is the cost of the 20,000 partially completed units in ending inventory in the Roasting department. The assigned costs are then added to show that the total $845,100 cost charged to the Roasting department is now assigned to the units in step ④.

Using a Process Cost Summary   Process summary reports can be used by managers to:

- **Control costs**—The Roasting department's equivalent costs per unit for April can be compared with prior months. If materials and/or conversion costs have changed a lot, managers should determine why and take corrective action.

Roasting Dept. Costs per EUP		
	April	March
DM	$3.00	$3.10
Conv.	4.62	4.58
Total	$7.62	$7.68

- **Evaluate performance**—GenX's top management can evaluate both the Roasting and Blending department managers based on their control of costs. Often, actual equivalent costs per unit are compared to budgeted amounts.

- **Evaluate process improvements**—Organizations strive to improve their processes. The success of process changes can be evaluated by examining how equivalent costs per unit change after the process improvement.

- **Provide information for financial statements**—The cost of goods sold and ending inventory amounts on process cost summaries are reported on the income statement and balance sheet, respectively.

EXHIBIT 16.13

Process Cost Summary
(Weighted Average)

GenX COMPANY—ROASTING DEPARTMENT
Process Cost Summary (Weighted-Average Method)
For Month Ended April 30

Costs Charged to Production

Costs of beginning work in process

Direct materials		$ 81,000	
Conversion		108,900	$ 189,900

Costs incurred this period

Direct materials		279,000	
Conversion		376,200	655,200
Total costs to account for			$845,100

Unit Information

Units to account for:		Units accounted for:	
Beginning work in process	30,000	Completed and transferred out	100,000
Units started this period	90,000	Ending work in process	20,000
Total units to account for	120,000	Total units accounted for	120,000

Equivalent Units of Production (EUP)	**Direct Materials**	**Conversion**
Units completed and transferred out (100,000 × 100%)	100,000 EUP	100,000 EUP
Units of ending work in process		
Direct materials (20,000 × 100%)	20,000 EUP	
Conversion (20,000 × 25%)		5,000 EUP
Equivalent units of production	120,000 EUP	105,000 EUP

Cost per EUP	**Direct Materials**	**Conversion**
Costs of beginning work in process	$ 81,000	$108,900
Costs incurred this period	279,000	376,200
Total costs	$360,000	$485,100
÷ EUP	120,000 EUP	105,000 EUP
Cost per EUP	$3.00 per EUP	$4.62 per EUP

Cost Assignment and Reconciliation

Costs transferred out (cost of goods manufactured)

Direct materials (100,000 EUP × $3.00 per EUP)		$300,000	
Conversion (100,000 EUP × $4.62 per EUP)		462,000	$ 762,000

Costs of ending work in process

Direct materials (20,000 EUP × $3.00 per EUP)		60,000	
Conversion (5,000 EUP × $4.62 per EUP)		23,100	83,100
Total costs accounted for			$845,100

reconciled

WIP–Roasting (in $)

Beg. inv.	189,900		
Incurred	655,200		
Subtotal	845,100		
		762,000	Tr. out
End. inv.	83,100		

ACCOUNTING FOR PROCESS COSTING

In this section we illustrate the journal entries to account for a process manufacturer. Exhibit 16.14 illustrates the flow of costs for GenX Company's Roasting department. Materials, labor, and overhead costs flow into the manufacturing processes. GenX keeps separate Work in Process Inventory accounts for the Roasting and Blending departments; when goods are packaged and ready for sale, their costs are transferred to the Finished Goods Inventory account.

As in job order costing, a process costing system uses source documents, including *materials requisitions* and *time tickets*. While some companies might combine direct labor and overhead into conversion costs when computing costs per equivalent unit (as we showed), labor and overhead costs are accounted for separately within the company's general ledger accounts. Also, because overhead costs typically cannot be tied to individual processes, but rather benefit all processes or departments, most process operation companies use a single Factory Overhead account to accumulate actual and applied overhead costs.

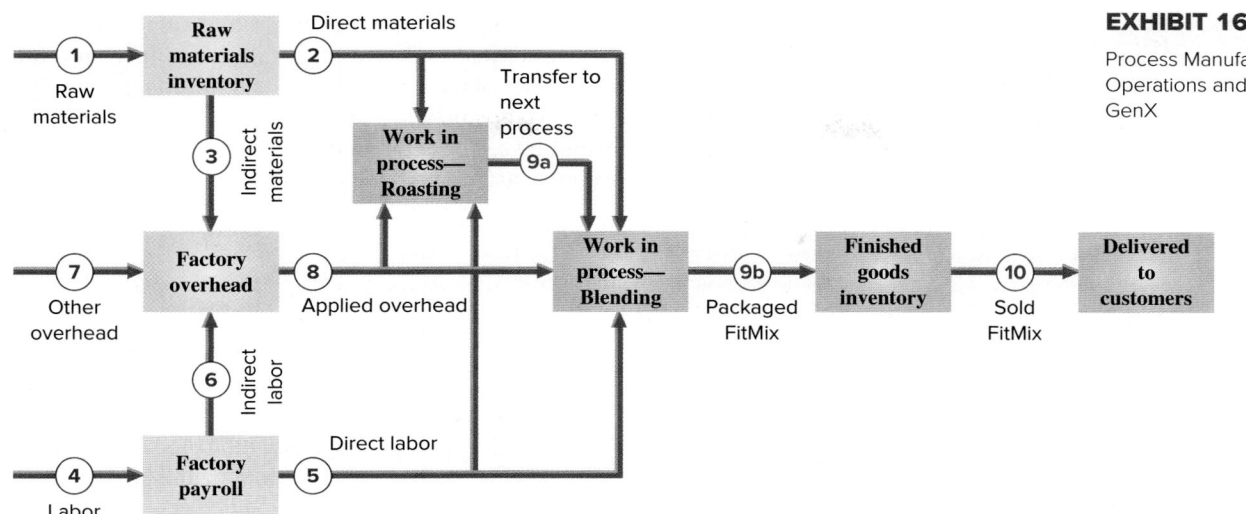

EXHIBIT 16.14

Process Manufacturing Operations and Costs: GenX

As with job order costing, process manufacturers must allocate, or apply, overhead to processes. This requires good *allocation bases.* With increasing automation, companies with process operations use fewer direct labor hours and often use machine hours to allocate overhead.

Sometimes a single allocation base will not provide good overhead allocations. For example, direct labor cost might be a good allocation base for GenX's Roasting department, but not for its Blending department. As a result, a process manufacturer can use different overhead allocation rates for different production departments. However, all applied overhead is credited to a single Factory Overhead account.

Point: Actual overhead is debited to Factory Overhead.

Exhibit 16.15 presents cost data for GenX. Roasting department costs are from Exhibit 16.6. Blending department costs are provided in Exhibit 16.15. We use these data to show the journal entries in a process costing system.

EXHIBIT 16.15

Cost Data—GenX (Weighted Average)

GenX—Cost Data for Month Ending April 30

Raw materials inventory (March 31)	$100,000		Factory payroll for April	
Beginning work in process inventories (March 31)			Direct labor—Roasting	$171,000
Work in process—Roasting	$189,900		Direct labor—Blending	183,160
Work in process—Blending	151,688		Indirect labor.	78,350
Materials purchased (on account)	$400,000		Other actual overhead costs during April	
Materials requisitions during April			Insurance expense—Factory	$ 11,930
Direct materials—Roasting	$279,000		Utilities payable—Factory.	7,945
Direct materials—Blending	102,000		Depreciation expense—Factory equipment . . .	220,650
Indirect materials.	71,250		Other (paid in cash).	21,875

Accounting for Materials Costs

In Exhibit 16.14, arrow line ① reflects the arrival of purchased raw materials at GenX's factory. These materials include organic peanuts, chocolate pieces, dried fruits, oil, salt, and packaging. They also include supplies for the production support office. GenX uses a perpetual inventory system and makes all purchases on credit. The summary entry for receipt of raw materials in April follows (dates in journal entries are omitted because they are summary entries, often reflecting two or more transactions or events).

P1

Record the flow of materials costs in process costing.

①	Raw Materials Inventory.	400,000	
	Accounts Payable		400,000
	Acquired materials on credit for factory use.		

Assets = Liabilities + Equity
+400,000   +400,000

Arrow line ② in Exhibit 16.14 reflects the flow of *direct* materials to production in the Roasting and Blending departments. These direct materials are physically combined into the finished product. The manager of a process usually obtains materials by submitting a *materials requisition* to the materials storeroom manager. The entry to record the use of direct materials by GenX's production departments in April follows. These direct materials costs flow into each department's separate Work in Process Inventory account.

Assets = Liabilities + Equity
+279,000
+102,000
−381,000

②	Work in Process Inventory—Roasting	279,000	
	Work in Process Inventory—Blending	102,000	
	Raw Materials Inventory		381,000
	Assign costs of direct materials used in production.		

In Exhibit 16.14, arrow line ③ reflects the flow of *indirect* materials from the storeroom to factory overhead. These materials are not clearly linked with any specific production process or department but are used to support overall production activity. As these costs cannot be linked directly to either the Roasting or Blending departments, they are recorded in GenX's single Factory Overhead account. The following entry records the cost of indirect materials used by GenX in April.

Example: What types of materials might the flow of arrow line ③ in Exhibit 16.14 reflect? *Answer:* Goggles, gloves, protective clothing, oil, salt, and cleaning supplies.

③	Factory Overhead..................................	71,250	
	Raw Materials Inventory		71,250
	Record indirect materials used in April.		

Accounting for Labor Costs

P2

Record the flow of labor costs in process costing.

Exhibit 16.14 shows GenX's factory payroll costs as reflected in arrow line ④. Exhibit 16.15 shows costs of $171,000 for Roasting department direct labor, $183,160 for Blending department direct labor, and $78,350 for indirect labor. This total payroll of $432,510 is a product cost, and it is assigned to either Work in Process Inventory or Factory Overhead.

Time reports from the production departments and the production support office trigger payroll entries. (For simplicity, we do not separately identify withholdings and additional payroll taxes for employees.) In a process operation, the direct labor of a production department includes all labor used exclusively by that department. This is the case even if labor is not applied to the product itself. If a production department in a process operation, for instance, has a full-time manager and a full-time maintenance worker, their salaries are *direct* labor costs of that process and are not factory overhead.

Arrow line ⑤ in Exhibit 16.14 shows GenX's use of direct labor. The following entry then records direct labor used. These direct labor costs flow into each department's separate Work in Process Inventory account.

Assets = Liabilities + Equity
+171,000   +354,160
+183,160

⑤	Work in Process Inventory—Roasting	171,000	
	Work in Process Inventory—Blending	183,160	
	Factory Wages Payable.........................		354,160
	Record direct labor used in production.		

Point: A department's indirect labor cost might include an allocated portion of wages of a manager who supervises two or more departments. Allocation of costs between departments is discussed in a later chapter.

Arrow line ⑥ in Exhibit 16.14 reflects GenX's indirect labor costs. These employees provide clerical, maintenance, and other services that help production in both the Roasting and Blending departments. For example, they order materials, deliver them to the factory floor, repair equipment, operate and program computers used in production, keep payroll and other production records, clean up, and move goods across departments. The following entry records these indirect labor costs.

⑥	Factory Overhead..................................	78,350	
	Factory Wages Payable.........................		78,350
	Record indirect labor as overhead.		

After GenX posts these entries for direct and indirect labor, the Factory Wages Payable account has a credit balance of $432,510 ($354,160 + $78,350). The entry below shows the payment of this total payroll. After this entry, the Factory Wages Payable account has a zero balance.

	Factory Wages Payable
	354,160 Dir L
	78,350 Ind L
432,510 Pymt	
	0 Bal.

④	Factory Wages Payable	432,510	
	Cash		432,510
	Record factory wages for April.		

Assets = Liabilities + Equity
−432,510   −432,510

Accounting for Factory Overhead

Overhead costs other than indirect materials and indirect labor are reflected by arrow line ⑦ in Exhibit 16.14. These overhead items include the costs of insuring production assets, renting the factory building, using factory utilities, and depreciating factory equipment not directly related to a specific process. The following entry records these other overhead costs for April.

P3

Record the flow of factory overhead costs in process costing.

⑦	Factory Overhead...................................	262,400	
	Prepaid Insurance		11,930
	Utilities Payable...............................		7,945
	Cash		21,875
	Accumulated Depreciation—Factory Equipment......		220,650
	Record other overhead costs incurred in April.		

Applying Overhead to Work in Process   Companies use *predetermined overhead rates* to apply overhead. These rates are estimated at the beginning of a period and used to apply overhead during the period. This allows managers to obtain up-to-date estimates of the costs of their processes during the period. This is important for process costing, where goods are transferred across departments before the entire production process is complete.

Point: The time it takes to process (cycle) products through a process is sometimes used to allocate costs.

Arrow line ⑧ in Exhibit 16.14 reflects the application of factory overhead to the two production departments. Factory overhead is applied to processes by relating overhead cost to another variable such as direct labor hours or machine hours used. In many situations, a single allocation basis such as direct labor hours (or a single rate for the entire plant) fails to provide useful allocations. As a result, management may use different rates for different production departments. In our example, GenX applies overhead using a predetermined rate of 120% of direct labor cost as shown in Exhibit 16.16.

Production Department	Direct Labor Cost	Predetermined Rate	Overhead Applied
Roasting	$171,000	120%	$205,200
Blending	183,160	120	219,792
Total			$424,992

EXHIBIT 16.16

Applying Factory Overhead

GenX records its applied overhead with the following entry.

⑧	Work in Process Inventory—Roasting	205,200	
	Work in Process Inventory—Blending	219,792	
	Factory Overhead		424,992
	Applied overhead costs to production departments at 120% of direct labor cost.		

■ **Decision Ethics**

Budget Officer You are classifying costs of a new processing department as either direct or indirect. This department's manager instructs you to classify most of the costs as indirect so it will be charged a lower amount of overhead (because this department uses less labor, which is the overhead allocation base). This would penalize other departments with higher allocations and cause the ratings of managers in other departments to suffer. What action do you take? ■ *Answer:* By classifying costs as indirect, the manager is passing some of his department's costs to a common overhead pool that other departments will partially absorb. Because overhead costs are allocated on direct labor for this company and the new department has a low direct labor cost, the new department is assigned less overhead. Such action suggests unethical behavior. You must object to such reclassification. If this manager refuses to comply, you must inform someone in a more senior position.

NEED-TO-KNOW 16-4

Overhead Rate and Costs

P1 P2 P3

Tower Mfg. allocates overhead based on machine hours. Tower estimates it will incur $200,000 of total overhead costs and use 10,000 machine hours in the coming year. During February, the Assembly department of Tower Mfg. used 375 machine hours. In addition, Tower incurred actual overhead costs as follows during February: indirect materials, $1,800; indirect labor, $5,700; depreciation on factory equipment, $8,000; and factory utilities, $500.

1. Compute the company's predetermined overhead rate for the year.
2. Prepare journal entries to record (a) overhead applied for the Assembly department for February and (b) actual overhead costs used during February.

Solution

1. Predetermined overhead rate = Estimated overhead costs ÷ Estimated activity base
= $200,000/10,000 machine hours = $20 per machine hour

2a.

Work in Process Inventory—Assembly.	7,500	
Factory Overhead		7,500
Record applied overhead (375 hours × $20 per hour).		

2b.

Factory Overhead	16,000	
Raw Materials Inventory		1,800
Factory Wages Payable.		5,700
Accumulated Depreciation—Factory Equipment		8,000
Utilities Payable.		500
Record actual overhead.		

Do More: QS 16-25, E 16-23

P4 _____

Record the transfer of goods across departments, to Finished Goods Inventory, and to Cost of Goods Sold.

Accounting for Transfers

Transfers across Departments Arrow line ⑨ₐ in Exhibit 16.14 reflects the transfer of partially completed units from the Roasting department to the Blending department. The process cost summary for the Roasting department (Exhibit 16.13) shows that the 100,000 units transferred to the Blending department are assigned a cost of $762,000. The entry to record this transfer follows.

Assets = Liabilities + Equity
+762,000
−762,000

⑨ₐ	Work in Process Inventory—Blending	762,000	
	Work in Process Inventory—Roasting.		762,000
	Record transfer of 100,000 units from		
	Roasting department to Blending department.		

Units and costs *transferred out* of the Roasting department are *transferred into* the Blending department. Exhibit 16.17 shows this transfer using T-accounts for the separate Work in Process Inventory accounts (first in units and then in dollars).

EXHIBIT 16.17

Production and Cost
Activity—Transfer to
Blending Department

Roasting Department—Units			
Beg. inv.	30,000 units		
Started	90,000 units		
Total	120,000 units		
		100,000 units transferred out	
End. inv.	20,000 units		

Blending Department—Units			
Beg. inv.	12,000 units		
Transferred in	100,000 units		
Total	112,000 units		
		97,000 units transferred to Finished Goods	
End. inv.	15,000 units		

WIP Inventory—Roasting Dept. ($)			
Beg. inv.*	189,900		
DM	279,000		
Conv.	376,200		
Total	845,100		
		762,000 Transferred out	
End. inv.	83,100		

WIP Inventory—Blending Dept. ($)			
Beg. inv.†	151,688		
Transferred in	762,000		
DM	102,000		
Conv.	402,952		
Total	1,418,640	1,262,940 Transferred to FG	
End. inv.	155,700		

*$81,000 direct materials + $108,900 conversion

†$91,440 transferred in + $10,000 DM + $50,248 conversion

As Exhibit 16.17 shows, the Blending department began the month with 12,000 units in beginning inventory, with a related cost of $151,688. In computing its production activity and costs, the Blending department must also consider the units and costs transferred in from the Roasting department, as shown in Exhibit 16.17. The 100,000 units transferred in from the Roasting department, and their related costs of $762,000, are added to the Blending department's number of units and separate Work in Process (WIP) Inventory account.

The Blending department adds additional direct materials and conversion costs. The Blending department incurred direct materials costs of $102,000 and conversion costs of $402,952 during the month. (Although not illustrated here, the concepts and methods used in this second department would be similar to those we showed in detail for the first department. The units and costs transferred in are considered separately from the materials and conversion added in the second department. This is shown in advanced courses.)

Accounting for Transfer to Finished Goods
Arrow line ⑨ᵇ in Exhibit 16.14 reflects the transfer of units and their related costs from the Blending department to finished goods inventory. At the end of the month, the Blending department transferred 97,000 completed units, with a related cost of $1,262,940, to finished goods. The entry to record this transfer follows.

⑨ᵇ	Finished Goods Inventory...............................	1,262,940	
	Work in Process Inventory—Blending...............		1,262,940
	Record transfer of completed goods.		

Assets = Liabilities + Equity
+1,262,940
−1,262,940

Accounting for Transfer to Cost of Goods Sold
Arrow line ⑩ reflects the sale of finished goods. Assume that GenX sold 106,000 units of FitMix this period, and that its beginning finished goods inventory was 26,000 units with a cost of $338,520. Also assume that its ending finished goods inventory consists of 20,000 units at a cost of $260,400. Using this information, cost of goods sold is computed as in Exhibit 16.18.

Finished Goods Inventory

Beg. bal.	338,520	
COGM	1,262,940	
Avail.	1,601,460	
		COGS 1,341,060
End. bal.	260,400	

GenX—Cost of Goods Sold	
Beginning finished goods inventory..................	$ 338,520
+ Cost of goods manufactured this period	1,262,940
= Cost of goods available for sale.....................	1,601,460
− Ending finished goods inventory	260,400
= Cost of goods sold	$1,341,060

EXHIBIT 16.18

Cost of Goods Sold

The summary entry to record cost of goods sold for this period follows.

Assets = Liabilities + Equity
−1,341,060   −1,341,060

(10)	Cost of Goods Sold...................................	1,341,060	
	Finished Goods Inventory.........................		1,341,060
	Record cost of goods sold for April.		

Trends in Process Operations

Process Design   Management concerns with production efficiency can lead companies to entirely reorganize production processes. For example, instead of producing different types of computers in a series of departments, a separate work center for each computer type can be established in one department. The process cost system is then changed to account for each work center's costs.

Just-in-Time Production   Companies are increasingly adopting just-in-time techniques. With a just-in-time inventory system, inventory levels can be minimal. If raw materials are not ordered or received until needed, a Raw Materials Inventory account might be unnecessary. Instead, materials cost is immediately debited to the Work in Process Inventory account. Similarly, a Finished Goods Inventory account may not be needed. Instead, cost of finished goods may be immediately debited to the Cost of Goods Sold account.

Robotics and Automation   Companies are increasingly automating their production processes and using robots. Manufacturers use robots on tasks that are hard for humans to perform. This results in reduced direct labor costs and a healthier workforce.

Continuous Processing   In some companies, like **Pepsi Bottling**, materials move continuously through the manufacturing process. In these cases, a **materials consumption report** summarizes the materials used and replaces materials requisitions.

©Natalia Kolesnikova/AFP/Getty Images

Services   Service-based businesses are increasingly prevalent. For routine, standardized services like oil changes and simple tax returns, computing costs based on the process is simpler and more useful than a cost per individual job. More complex service companies use process departments to perform specific tasks for consumers. Hospitals, for example, have radiology and physical therapy facilities, each with special equipment and trained employees. When patients need services, they are processed through departments to receive prescribed care.

Customer Orientation   Focus on customer orientation also leads to improved processes. A manufacturer of control devices improved quality and reduced production time by forming teams to study processes and suggest improvements. An ice cream maker studied customer tastes to develop a more pleasing ice cream texture.

Yield   Many process operations convert large amounts of raw materials into finished goods. In addition to information in process cost summaries, managers often measure **Yield**, which is the amount of *material output* divided by the amount of *material input*. For example, assume a maker of trail mix started 10,000 pounds (units) of peanuts into its production process and ended with finished goods of 9,650 pounds. The Yield is computed as: 9,650/10,000 = 96.5%. Yield might be less than 100% due to lost or stolen peanuts, roasting issues that burned peanuts, or other production problems. When yields are lower than expected, managers usually ask why and then take corrective action.

SUSTAINABILITY AND ACCOUNTING

Food processor **General Mills** needs a steady supply of high-quality corn, oats, and sugarcane. These agricultural inputs face risks due to water scarcity and climate change that could disrupt General Mills's process operations and hurt profits.

Buying from suppliers that follow sustainable principles reduces risk of reputational damage. The Sustainability Accounting Standards Board (SASB) recommends that food processors disclose information on *priority food ingredients* (those that are essential to the company's products), including details on the company's strategies to address strategic risks.

Consistent with SASB guidelines, General Mills disclosed the following information in its recent *Global Responsibility Report*.

General Mills Performance Dashboard (partial)			
Ingredient	Primary Challenges	Target*	Progress
Vanilla	Smallholder farmer incomes, quality of ingredients	100%	45%
Oats	Declining supply due to profitability versus other crops	100	35
Sugarcane	Child and forced labor, working conditions	100	42
Palm oil	Deforestation, indigenous peoples' rights	100	83

*Target and progress amounts are the percent of the ingredient sourced sustainably.
Source: General Mills, *Global Sustainability Report*, 2017.

In addition to making continuous process improvements to reduce materials waste and increase yield, Suzy Batlle, founder of **Azucar Ice Cream Company**, seeks high-quality fresh ingredients. For Suzy, buying from local suppliers provides a sustainable supply chain that benefits her business and the local community.

©Emily Michot/TNS/Newscom

Hybrid Costing System       **Decision Analysis**

Many organizations use a **hybrid costing system** that contains features of both process and job order operations. A recent survey of manufacturers revealed that a majority use hybrid systems (also called **operation costing systems**).

To illustrate, consider a car manufacturer's assembly line. The line resembles a process operation in that the assembly steps for each car are nearly identical. But the specifications of most cars have several important differences. At the **Ford** Mustang plant, each car assembled can be different from the previous car and the next car. This means that the costs of materials (subassemblies or components) for each car can differ. Accordingly, while the conversion costs (direct labor and overhead) can be accounted for using a process costing system, the component costs (direct materials) are accounted for using a job order system (separately for each car or type of car).

A hybrid system of processes requires a *hybrid costing system* to properly cost products or services. In the Ford plant, the assembly costs per car are readily determined using process costing. The costs of additional components then can be added to the assembly costs to determine each car's total cost (as in job order costing). To illustrate, consider the following information for a daily assembly process at Ford.

A2

Explain and illustrate a hybrid costing system.

©David M G/Shutterstock

Assembly Process Costs	
Direct materials	$10.6 million
Conversion costs	$12.0 million
Number of cars assembled	1,000
Costs of three different types of wheels	$240; $330; $480
Costs of three different types of sound systems	$620; $840; $1,360

The assembly process costs $22,600 per car. Depending on the type of wheels and sound system the customer requests, the cost of a car can range from $23,460 to $24,440 (a $980 difference).

Today companies are increasingly trying to standardize processes while attempting to meet individual customer needs. For example, **Lightning Wear** makes custom team uniforms, which are the same except for the team logo and colors added in the final process. **The Planters Company** packages peanuts in different sizes and types of packaging for different retailers. To the extent that differences among individual customers' requests are large, understanding the costs to satisfy those requests is important. Thus, monitoring and controlling both process and job order costs are important.

■ Decision Ethics

Entrepreneur   Your company makes similar products for three different customers. One customer demands 100% quality inspection of products at your location before shipping. The added costs of that inspection are spread across all three customers. If you charge the customer the costs of 100% quality inspection, you could lose that customer and experience a loss. Moreover, your other two customers do not question the amounts they pay. What actions (if any) do you take? ■   *Answer:* By spreading the added quality-related costs across three customers, the price you charge is lower for the customer that demands the 100% quality inspection. You recover much of the added costs from the other two customers. This act likely breaches the trust placed by the other two customers. Your costing system should be changed, and you should consider renegotiating the pricing and/or quality test agreement with this one customer (at the risk of losing this customer).

NEED-TO-KNOW **16-5**

COMPREHENSIVE 1

Weighted-Average
Method

Pennsylvania Company produces a product that passes through two processes: Grinding and Mixing. Information related to its Grinding department manufacturing activities for July follows. The company uses the weighted-average method of process costing.

Grinding Department	
Raw Materials	
Beginning inventory..........................	$100,000
Raw materials purchased on credit............	211,400
Direct materials used........................	(190,000)
Indirect materials used	(51,400)
Ending inventory	$ 70,000
Factory Payroll	
Direct labor incurred	$ 55,500
Indirect labor incurred......................	50,625
Total payroll	$106,125
Factory Overhead	
Indirect materials used	$ 51,400
Indirect labor used.........................	50,625
Other overhead costs.......................	71,725
Total factory overhead incurred	$173,750
Factory Overhead Applied	
Overhead applied (200% of direct labor)	$111,000

Grinding Department	
Beginning work in process inventory (units)	5,000
Percentage completed—Materials..............	100%
Percentage completed—Conversion............	70%
Beginning work in process inventory (costs)	
Direct materials used	$20,000
Direct labor incurred.........................	9,600
Overhead applied (200% of direct labor)	19,200
Total costs of beginning work in process	$48,800
Units started this period	20,000
Units transferred to Mixing this period.............	17,000
Ending work in process inventory (units)	8,000
Percentage completed—Materials..............	100%
Percentage completed—Conversion............	20%

Required

Complete the requirements below for the Grinding department.
1. Prepare a physical flow reconciliation for July.
2. Compute the equivalent units of production in July for direct materials and conversion.
3. Compute the costs per equivalent unit of production in July for direct materials and conversion.
4. Prepare a report of costs accounted for and a report of costs to account for.

PLANNING THE SOLUTION

- Track the physical flow to determine the number of units completed in July.
- Compute the equivalent units of production for direct materials and conversion.

- Compute the costs per equivalent unit of production with respect to direct materials and conversion, and determine the cost per unit for each.
- Compute the total cost of the goods transferred to Mixing by using the equivalent units and unit costs. Determine (a) the cost of the beginning work in process inventory, (b) the materials and conversion costs added to the beginning work in process inventory, and (c) the materials and conversion costs added to the units started and completed in the month.

SOLUTION

1. Physical flow reconciliation.

Units to Account For		Units Accounted For	
Beginning work in process inventory............	5,000 units	Units completed and transferred out......................	17,000 units
Units started this period.........	20,000 units	Ending work in process inventory..........	8,000 units
Total units to account for	**25,000 units**	Total units accounted for	**25,000 units**

reconciled

2. Equivalent units of production (weighted average).

Equivalent Units of Production	Direct Materials	Conversion
Equivalent units completed and transferred out..........	17,000 EUP	17,000 EUP
Equivalent units in ending work in process		
Direct materials (8,000 × 100%).....................	8,000 EUP	
Conversion (8,000 × 20%)		1,600 EUP
Equivalent units of production........................	25,000 EUP	18,600 EUP

3. Costs per equivalent unit of production (weighted average).

Costs per Equivalent Unit of Production	Direct Materials	Conversion
Costs of beginning work in process.................	$ 20,000	$ 28,800
Costs incurred this period	190,000	166,500*
Total costs......................................	$210,000	$195,300
÷ Equivalent units of production (from part 2)	25,000 EUP	18,600 EUP
= Costs per equivalent unit of production	$8.40 per EUP	$10.50 per EUP

*Direct labor of $55,500 + overhead applied of $111,000

4. Reports of costs accounted for and of costs to account for (weighted average).

Report of Costs Accounted For		
Cost of units transferred out (cost of goods manufactured)		
Direct materials ($8.40 per EUP × 17,000 EUP)	$142,800	
Conversion ($10.50 per EUP × 17,000 EUP)	178,500	
Cost of units completed this period		$ 321,300
Cost of ending work in process inventory		
Direct materials ($8.40 per EUP × 8,000 EUP)	67,200	
Conversion ($10.50 per EUP × 1,600 EUP)	16,800	
Cost of ending work in process inventory		84,000
Total costs accounted for		**$405,300**

Report of Costs to Account For		
Cost of beginning work in process inventory		
Direct materials	$ 20,000	
Conversion	28,800	$ 48,800
Cost incurred this period		
Direct materials	190,000	
Conversion	166,500	356,500
Total costs to account for		**$405,300**

reconciled

NEED-TO-KNOW 16-6

COMPREHENSIVE 2

FIFO Method
(Appendix 16A)

Refer to the information in Need-To-Know 16-5. For the Grinding department, complete requirements 1 through 4 using the FIFO method. (Round the cost per equivalent unit of conversion to two decimal places.)

SOLUTION

1. Physical flow reconciliation (FIFO).

Units to Account For		Units Accounted For	
Beginning work in process inventory............	5,000 units	Units completed and transferred out.......................	17,000 units
Units started this period.........	20,000 units	Ending work in process inventory..........	8,000 units
Total units to account for	**25,000 units**	Total units accounted for	**25,000 units**

reconciled

2. Equivalent units of production (FIFO).

Equivalent Units of Production	Direct Materials	Conversion
(a) Equivalent units complete beginning work in process		
Direct materials (5,000 × 0%)................................	0 EUP	
Conversion (5,000 × 30%)		1,500 EUP
(b) Equivalent units started and completed...........................	12,000 EUP	12,000 EUP
(c) Equivalent units in ending work in process		
Direct materials (8,000 × 100%)	8,000 EUP	
Conversion (8,000 × 20%)		1,600 EUP
Equivalent units of production....................................	20,000 EUP	15,100 EUP

3. Costs per equivalent unit of production (FIFO).

Costs per Equivalent Unit of Production	Direct Materials	Conversion
Costs incurred this period	$190,000	$ 166,500*
÷ Equivalent units of production (from part 2)	20,000 EUP	15,100 EUP
= Costs per equivalent unit of production	$9.50 per EUP	$11.03 per EUP†

*Direct labor of $55,500 plus overhead applied of $111,000   †Rounded

4. Reports of costs accounted for and of costs to account for (FIFO).

Report of Costs Accounted For
Cost of units transferred out (cost of goods manufactured)

Cost of beginning work in process inventory		$ 48,800
Cost to complete beginning work in process		
Direct materials ($9.50 per EUP × 0 EUP)	$ 0	
Conversion ($11.03 per EUP × 1,500 EUP)	16,545	16,545
Cost of units started and completed this period		
Direct materials ($9.50 per EUP × 12,000 EUP)	114,000	
Conversion ($11.03 per EUP × 12,000 EUP).................................	132,360	246,360
Total cost of units finished this period		311,705
Cost of ending work in process inventory		
Direct materials ($9.50 per EUP × 8,000 EUP)	76,000	
Conversion ($11.03 per EUP × 1,600 EUP)	17,648	
Total cost of ending work in process inventory		93,648
Total costs accounted for...		**$405,353** ◄
Report of Costs to Account For		
Cost of beginning work in process inventory		
Direct materials	$ 20,000	
Conversion...	28,800	$ 48,800
Costs incurred this period		
Direct materials	190,000	
Conversion...	166,500	356,500
Total costs to account for..		**$405,300** ◄

reconciled (with $53 rounding difference)

Garcia Manufacturing produces a product that passes through a molding process and then through an assembly process. Partial information related to its manufacturing activities for July follows.

NEED-TO-KNOW 16-7

COMPREHENSIVE 3

Journal Entries for
Process Costing

Direct materials

Raw materials purchased on credit	$400,000
Direct materials used—Molding	190,000
Direct materials used—Assembly	88,600

Direct Labor

Direct labor—Molding	$ 42,000
Direct labor—Assembly	55,375

Factory Overhead (Actual costs)

Indirect materials used	$ 51,400
Indirect labor used	50,625
Other overhead costs	71,725
Total factory overhead incurred	$173,750

Factory Overhead Applied

Molding (150% of direct labor)	$ 63,000
Assembly (200% of direct labor)	110,750
Total factory overhead applied	$173,750

Cost Transfers

From Molding to Assembly	$277,200
From Assembly to finished goods	578,400
From finished goods to cost of goods sold	506,100

Required

Prepare summary journal entries to record the transactions and events of July for (a) raw materials purchases, (b) direct materials usage, (c) indirect materials usage, (d) direct labor usage, (e) indirect labor usage, (f) other overhead costs (credit Other Accounts), (g) application of overhead to the two departments, (h) transfer of partially completed goods from Molding to Assembly, (i) transfer of finished goods out of Assembly, and (j) the cost of goods sold.

SOLUTION

Summary journal entries for the transactions and events in July.

a.	Raw Materials Inventory	400,000	
	Accounts Payable		400,000
	Record raw materials purchases.		
b.	Work in Process Inventory—Molding	190,000	
	Work in Process Inventory—Assembly	88,600	
	Raw Materials Inventory		278,600
	Record direct materials usage.		
c.	Factory Overhead	51,400	
	Raw Materials Inventory		51,400
	Record indirect materials usage.		
d.	Work in Process Inventory—Molding	42,000	
	Work in Process Inventory—Assembly	55,375	
	Factory Wages Payable		97,375
	Record direct labor usage.		
e.	Factory Overhead	50,625	
	Factory Wages Payable		50,625
	Record indirect labor usage.		

f.	Factory Overhead	71,725	
	Other Accounts		71,725
	Record other overhead costs.		
g.	Work in Process Inventory—Molding	63,000	
	Work in Process Inventory—Assembly	110,750	
	Factory Overhead		173,750
	Record application of overhead.		
h.	Work in Process Inventory—Assembly	277,200	
	Work in Process Inventory—Molding		277,200
	Record transfer of partially completed goods from Molding to Assembly.		
i.	Finished Goods Inventory	578,400	
	Work in Process Inventory—Assembly		578,400
	Record transfer of finished goods out of Assembly.		
j.	Cost of Goods Sold	506,100	
	Finished Goods Inventory		506,100
	Record cost of goods sold.		

APPENDIX

FIFO Method of Process Costing

16A

C4

Describe accounting for
production activity and
preparation of a process
cost summary using FIFO.

The FIFO method of process costing assigns costs to units assuming a first-in, first-out flow of product. The key difference between the FIFO and weighted-average methods lies in the treatment of beginning work in process inventory. Under the weighted-average method, the number of units and the costs in beginning work in process inventory are combined with production activity in the current period to compute costs per equivalent unit. Thus, the weighted-average method combines production activity across two periods.

The FIFO method, in contrast, focuses on production activity *in the current period only*. The FIFO method assumes that the units that were in process at the beginning of the period are completed during the current period. Thus, under the FIFO method, equivalent units of production are computed as shown in Exhibit 16A.1.

EXHIBIT 16A.1

Computing EUP—FIFO Method

Equivalent units of production (EUP) =	Number of equivalent units needed to complete beginning work in process	+	Number of whole units started, completed, and transferred out*	+	Number of equivalent units in ending work in process

*Transferred to next department or finished goods inventory.

In computing cost per equivalent unit, the FIFO method ignores the cost of beginning work in process inventory. Instead, FIFO uses *only the costs incurred in the current period*, as shown in Exhibit 16A.2.

EXHIBIT 16A.2

Cost per EUP—FIFO Method

$$\text{Cost per EUP (FIFO)} = \frac{\text{Manufacturing costs added during current period}}{\text{Equivalent units of production during current period}}$$

Data We use the data in Exhibit 16A.3 to illustrate the FIFO method for GenX's Roasting department.

EXHIBIT 16A.3

Production Data—Roasting Department (FIFO method)

GenX—Roasting Department: Production Data (April)	
Beginning work in process inventory (March 31)	
Units of product	30,000 units
Percentage of completion—Direct materials	100%
Percentage of completion—Conversion	65%
Direct materials costs.	$ 81,000
Conversion costs	$108,900
Production activity during the current period (April)	
Units started this period.	90,000 units
Units transferred out (completed)	100,000 units
Direct materials costs.	$279,000
Direct labor costs	$171,000
Factory overhead costs applied (120% of direct labor)	$205,200
Ending work in process inventory (April 30)	
Units of product	20,000 units
Percentage of completion—Direct materials	100%
Percentage of completion—Conversion	25%

Exhibit 16A.3 shows selected information from GenX's Roasting department for the month of April. Accounting for a department's activity for a period includes four steps: (1) determine physical flow, (2) compute equivalent units, (3) compute cost per equivalent unit, and (4) determine cost assignment and reconciliation. This appendix describes each of these steps using the FIFO method for process costing.

Step 1: Determine Physical Flow of Units

A *physical flow reconciliation* is a report that reconciles (1) the physical units started in a period with (2) the physical units completed in that period. The physical flow reconciliation for GenX's Roasting department for April is shown in Exhibit 16A.4.

EXHIBIT 16A.4

Physical Flow Reconciliation

GenX—Roasting Department			
Units to Account For		**Units Accounted For**	
Beginning work in process inventory.	30,000 units	Units completed and transferred out.	100,000 units
Units started this period.	90,000 units	Ending work in process inventory	20,000 units
Total units to account for	**120,000 units**	Total units accounted for	**120,000 units**

reconciled

Point: Step 1 is exactly the same under the weighted-average method.

Step 2: Compute Equivalent Units of Production—FIFO

Exhibit 16A.4 shows that the Roasting department completed 100,000 units during the month. The FIFO method assumes that the units in beginning inventory were the first units completed during the month. Thus, FIFO assumes that of the 100,000 completed units, 30,000 consist of units in beginning work in process inventory that were completed during the month. This means that 70,000 (100,000 − 30,000) units were both started and completed during the month. Exhibit 16A.5 shows how units flowed through the Roasting department, assuming FIFO.

Units completed 100,000	−	Units in beginning WIP 30,000	=	Units started and completed 70,000

EXHIBIT 16A.5

FIFO—Flow of Completed Units

In computing equivalent units of production using FIFO, the Roasting department must consider these three distinct groups of units:

- Units in beginning work in process inventory (30,000).
- Units started and completed during the month (70,000).
- Units in ending work in process inventory (20,000).

GenX's Roasting department then computes equivalent units of production under FIFO as shown in Exhibit 16A.6. We compute EUP for each of the three distinct groups of units and sum them to find total EUP.

EXHIBIT 16A.6

Equivalent Units of Production—FIFO

GenX—Roasting Department		
Equivalent Units of Production	**Direct Materials**	**Conversion**
(a) Equivalent units to complete beginning work in process		
Direct materials (30,000 × 0%)	0 EUP	
Conversion (30,000 × 35%)...................................		10,500 EUP
(b) Equivalent units started and completed (70,000 × 100%)*	70,000 EUP	70,000 EUP
(c) Equivalent units in ending work in process		
Direct materials (20,000 × 100%)	20,000 EUP	
Conversion (20,000 × 25%)..................................		5,000 EUP
Equivalent units of production	90,000 EUP	85,500 EUP

*Units completed this period....................	100,000 units
Less units in beginning work in process	30,000 units
Units started and completed this period..........	70,000 units

Point: EUP = Number of physical units × Percent of work completed this period.

EUP for Transferred out
+ EUP for WIP
= EUP for Total

Direct Materials To calculate the equivalent units of production for direct materials, we start with the equivalent units in beginning work in process inventory. We see that beginning work in process inventory was 100% complete with respect to materials; no materials were needed to complete these units. Thus, this group of units required 0 EUP during the month. Next, we consider the units started and completed during the month. In terms of direct materials, the 70,000 units started and completed during the month received 100% of their materials during the month. Thus, EUP for this group is 70,000 units (70,000 × 100%). Finally, we consider the units in ending work in process inventory. The Roasting department started but *did not* complete 20,000 units during the month. This group received all of its materials during the month. Thus, EUP for this group is 20,000 units (20,000 × 100%). The sum of the EUP for these three distinct groups of units is 90,000 (computed as 0 + 70,000 + 20,000), which is the total number of equivalent units of production for direct materials during the month.

Conversion To calculate the equivalent units of production for conversion, we start by determining the percentage of conversion costs needed to complete the beginning work in process inventory. As Exhibit 16A.3 shows, the beginning work in process inventory of 30,000 units was 65% complete with respect to conversion. Thus, this group of units required an additional 35% of conversion costs during the period to complete those units (100% − 65%), or 10,500 EUP (30,000 × 35%). Next, we consider the units started and completed during the month. The units started and completed during the month incurred 100% of their conversion costs during the month. Thus, EUP for this group is 70,000 units (70,000 × 100%). Finally, we consider the units in ending work in process inventory. The ending work in process inventory incurred 25% of its conversion costs (see Exhibit 16A.3) during the month. Thus, EUP for this group is 5,000 units

(20,000 × 25%). The sum of the EUP for these three distinct groups of units is 85,500 (computed as 10,500 + 70,000 + 5,000). Thus, the Roasting department's equivalent units of production for conversion for the month is 85,500 units.

NEED-TO-KNOW 16-8

EUP—Direct Materials and Conversion (FIFO)

C4

Do More: QS 16-14, QS 16-15, E 16-5, E 16-10

A department began the month with 50,000 units in work in process inventory. These units were 90% complete with respect to direct materials and 40% complete with respect to conversion. During the month, the department started 286,000 units; 220,000 of these units were completed during the month. The remaining 66,000 units are in ending work in process inventory, 80% complete with respect to direct materials and 30% complete with respect to conversion. Use the FIFO method of process costing to:

1. Compute the department's equivalent units of production for the month for direct materials.

2. Compute the department's equivalent units of production for the month for conversion.

		Materials		Conversion	
	Units	Current Month %	EUP	Current Month %	EUP
Finish BI	50,000	10%	5,000	60%	30,000
Start & finish	220,000	100%	220,000	100%	220,000
Start EI	66,000	80%	52,800	30%	19,800
			277,800		269,800

Solution—computations to the side show another way to get solutions

1. EUP for materials = (50,000 × 10%) + (220,000 × 100%) + (66,000 × 80%) = 277,800 EUP

2. EUP for conversion = (50,000 × 60%) + (220,000 × 100%) + (66,000 × 30%) = 269,800 EUP

Step 3: Compute Cost per Equivalent Unit—FIFO

To compute cost per equivalent unit, we take the direct materials and conversion costs added in April and divide by the equivalent units of production from step 2. Exhibit 16A.7 illustrates these computations.

EXHIBIT 16A.7

Cost per Equivalent Unit of Production—FIFO

$$\text{Cost per EUP} = \frac{\text{Total costs}}{\text{EUP}}$$

GenX—Roasting Department		
Cost per Equivalent Unit of Production	Direct Materials	Conversion
Costs incurred this period (from Exhibit 16A.3)	$279,000	$376,200
÷ Equivalent units of production (from step 2)	90,000 EUP	85,500 EUP
Cost per equivalent unit of production.	$3.10 per EUP	$4.40 per EUP

It is essential to compute costs per equivalent unit for *each* input because production inputs are added at different times in the process. The FIFO method computes the cost per equivalent unit based solely on this period's EUP and costs (unlike the weighted-average method, which adds in the costs of the beginning work in process inventory).

NEED-TO-KNOW 16-9

Cost per EUP—Direct Materials and Conversion (FIFO)

C4

Do More: QS 16-15, E 16-7

A department started the month with beginning work in process inventory of $130,000 ($90,000 for direct materials and $40,000 for conversion). During the month, the department incurred additional direct materials costs of $700,000 and conversion costs of $500,000. Assume that equivalent units for the month were computed as 250,000 for materials and 200,000 for conversion.

1. Compute the department's cost per equivalent unit of production for the month for direct materials.

2. Compute the department's cost per equivalent unit of production for the month for conversion.

Solution

1. Cost per EUP of materials = $700,000/250,000 = $2.80

2. Cost per EUP of conversion = $500,000/200,000 = $2.50

Step 4: Assign and Reconcile Costs

The equivalent units determined in step 2 and the cost per equivalent unit computed in step 3 are both used to assign costs (1) to units that the production department completed and transferred to the Blending department and (2) to units that remain in process at period-end.

As it did in computing equivalent units in step 2, the Roasting department now must compute costs for three distinct groups of units:

- Costs to complete the beginning work in process inventory.
- Costs to complete the units started and completed during the month.
- Costs of ending work in process inventory.

From the first section of Exhibit 16A.8, the cost of units completed in April includes the $189,900 cost carried over from March for work already applied to the 30,000 units that make up beginning work in process inventory, plus the $46,200 incurred in April to complete those units. The next section includes the $525,000 of cost assigned to the 70,000 units started and completed this period. Thus, the total cost of goods manufactured in April is $761,100.

EXHIBIT 16A.8

Report of Costs Accounted For—FIFO

GenX—Roasting Department		
Cost of beginning work in process inventory		$ 189,900
Cost to complete beginning work in process		
Direct materials ($3.10 per EUP × 0 EUP).	$ 0	
Conversion ($4.40 per EUP × 10,500 EUP)	46,200	46,200
Cost of units started and completed this period		
Direct materials ($3.10 per EUP × 70,000 EUP).	217,000	
Conversion ($4.40 per EUP × 70,000 EUP)	308,000	525,000
Total cost of units finished and transferred out this period		761,100
Cost of ending work in process inventory		
Direct materials ($3.10 per EUP × 20,000 EUP).	62,000	
Conversion ($4.40 per EUP × 5,000 EUP)	22,000	
Total cost of ending work in process inventory		84,000
Total costs accounted for		**$845,100**

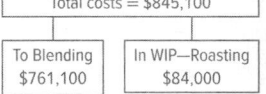

Total costs = $845,100

| To Blending $761,100 | In WIP—Roasting $84,000 |

The computation for cost of ending work in process inventory is in the final section of Exhibit 16A.8. That cost of $84,000 ($62,000 + $22,000) also is the ending balance for the Work in Process Inventory—Roasting account.

The Roasting department manager verifies that the total costs assigned to units transferred out and units still in process equal the total costs incurred by production. We reconcile the costs accounted for (in Exhibit 16A.8) to the costs that production was charged for as shown in Exhibit 16A.9.

EXHIBIT 16A.9

Report of Costs to Account For—FIFO

Cost of beginning work in process inventory		
Direct materials	$ 81,000	
Conversion	108,900	$ 189,900
Costs incurred this period		
Direct materials	279,000	
Conversion	376,200	655,200
Total costs to account for		**$845,100**

The Roasting department production manager is responsible for $845,100 in costs: $189,900 that had been assigned to the department's work in process inventory as of April 1 plus $655,200 of costs the department incurred in April. At period-end, the manager must identify where those costs were assigned. The production manager can report that $761,100 of cost was assigned to units completed in April and $84,000 was assigned to units still in process at period-end.

Process Cost Summary

The final report is the process cost summary, which summarizes key information from previous exhibits. Reasons for the summary are to (1) help managers control and monitor costs, (2) help upper management assess department manager performance, and (3) provide cost information for financial reporting. The process cost summary, using FIFO, for GenX's Roasting department is in Exhibit 16A.10. It summarizes the process costing steps.

⬙ DATA   Total costs charged to the department, including direct materials and conversion costs incurred, as well as the cost of the beginning work in process inventory.

① Physical flow of units. This reconciles the physical units started with the physical units completed in the period.

② Equivalent units of production for the department. Equivalent units for direct materials and conversion are shown in separate columns.

③ Costs per equivalent unit for direct materials and conversion.

④ Assignment of total costs among units worked on in the period.

EXHIBIT 16A.10

Process Cost Summary (FIFO)

GenX COMPANY— ROASTING DEPARTMENT
Process Cost Summary (FIFO Method)
For Month Ended April 30

DATA

Costs charged to production		
Costs of beginning work in process inventory		
Direct materials	$ 81,000	
Conversion	108,900	$ 189,900
Costs incurred this period		
Direct materials	279,000	
Conversion	376,200	655,200
Total costs to account for		$845,100

1

Unit information			
Units to account for		Units accounted for	
Beginning work in process	30,000	Transferred out	100,000
Units started this period	90,000	Ending work in process	20,000
Total units to account for	120,000	Total units accounted for	120,000

2

Equivalent units of production	**Direct Materials**	**Conversion**
Equivalent units to complete beginning work in process		
Direct materials (30,000 × 0%)	0 EUP	
Conversion (30,000 × 35%)		10,500 EUP
Equivalent units started and completed	70,000 EUP	70,000 EUP
Equivalent units in ending work in process		
Direct materials (20,000 × 100%)	20,000 EUP	
Conversion (20,000 × 25%)		5,000 EUP
Equivalent units of production	90,000 EUP	85,500 EUP

3

Cost per equivalent unit of production	**Direct Materials**	**Conversion**
Costs incurred this period	$279,000	$376,200
÷ Equivalent units of production	90,000 EUP	85,500 EUP
Cost per equivalent unit of production	$3.10 per EUP	$4.40 per EUP

4

Cost assignment and reconciliation		
(cost of units completed and transferred out)		
Cost of beginning work in process		$ 189,900
Cost to complete beginning work in process		
Direct materials ($3.10 per EUP × 0 EUP)	$ 0	
Conversion ($4.40 per EUP × 10,500 EUP)	46,200	46,200
Cost of units started and completed this period		
Direct materials ($3.10 per EUP × 70,000 EUP)	217,000	
Conversion ($4.40 per EUP × 70,000 EUP)	308,000	525,000
Total cost of units finished this period		761,100
Cost of ending work in process		
Direct materials ($3.10 per EUP × 20,000 EUP)	62,000	
Conversion ($4.40 per EUP × 5,000 EUP)	22,000	
Total cost of ending work in process		84,000
Total costs accounted for		$845,100

reconciled

WIP—Roasting (in $)

Beg. Inv.	189,900	
Incurred	655,200	
Subtotal	845,100	761,100 Tr. out
End. Inv.	84,000	

Decision Maker

Cost Manager As cost manager for an electronics manufacturer, you apply a process costing system using FIFO. Your company plans to adopt a just-in-time system and eliminate inventories. What is the impact of using FIFO (versus the weighted-average method) given these plans? ■ *Answer:* Differences between the FIFO and weighted-average methods are greatest when large work in process inventories exist and when costs fluctuate. The method used if inventories are eliminated does not matter; both produce identical costs.

Summary: Cheat Sheet

Process operation: Mass production of similar products in a flow of sequential processes.
Conversion costs: Direct labor + Applied overhead.

FLOW OF COSTS

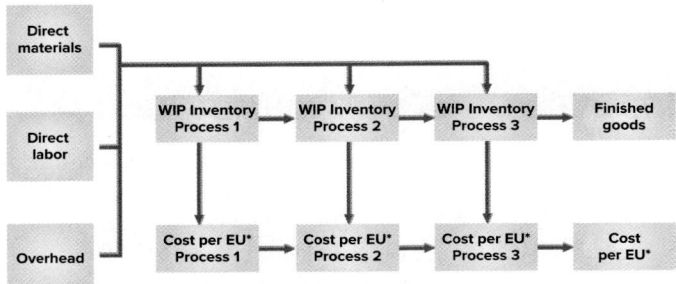

*EU = equivalent unit

PHYSICAL FLOW OF UNITS

Units to Account For		Units Accounted For	
Beginning work in process inventory	30,000 units	Units completed and transferred out...............	100,000 units
Units started this period	90,000 units	Ending work in process inventory...	20,000 units
Total units to account for....	**120,000 units**	Total units accounted for	**120,000 units**

reconciled

EQUIVALENT UNITS OF PRODUCTION (EUP)

EUP: Number of units that could have been started and completed given the costs incurred. Compute separately for direct materials and conversion costs.
Weighted-average: Combines units and costs across *two periods* in computing EUP.

Weighted-average (WA) computations:

$$\text{Equivalent units of production (EUP)} = \text{Number of whole units completed and transferred out*} + \text{Number of equivalent units in ending work in process}$$

*Transferred to next department or finished goods inventory.

$$\text{Cost per EUP (WA)} = \frac{\text{Costs of beginning WIP} + \text{Costs incurred this period}}{\text{Equivalent units of production}}$$

FIFO: Based on *current-period* production activity.
FIFO computations:

$$\text{Equivalent units of production (EUP)} = \text{Number of equivalent units needed to complete beginning work in process} + \text{Number of whole units started, completed, and transferred out*} + \text{Number of equivalent units in ending work in process}$$

*Transferred to next department or finished goods inventory.

$$\text{Cost per EUP (FIFO)} = \frac{\text{Manufacturing costs added during current period}}{\text{Equivalent units of production during current period}}$$

ASSIGN COSTS

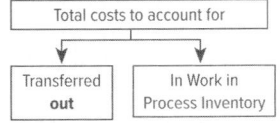

JOURNAL ENTRIES

Acquire raw materials:

Raw Materials Inventory.........................	16,000	
Accounts Payable............................		16,000

Assign costs of *direct* materials used:

Work in Process Inventory—Process 1	279,000	
Work in Process Inventory—Process 2	102,000	
Raw Materials Inventory		381,000

Assign costs of *direct* labor used:

Work in Process Inventory—Process 1	171,000	
Work in Process Inventory—Process 2	183,160	
Factory Wages Payable.......................		354,160

Apply overhead using predetermined rate:

Work in Process Inventory—Process 1	205,200	
Work in Process Inventory—Process 2	219,792	
Factory Overhead		424,992

Record use of *indirect* materials:

Factory Overhead................................	5,000	
Raw Materials Inventory		5,000

Record *indirect* labor costs:

Factory Overhead................................	3,500	
Factory Wages Payable........................		3,500

Record *actual* overhead costs such as insurance, rent, utilities, and depreciation:

Factory Overhead................................	9,500	
Cash (and other accounts).....................		9,500

Record transfer of costs to next department:

Work in Process Inventory—Process 2	762,000	
Work in Process Inventory—Process 1		762,000

Record transfer of costs to finished goods:

Finished Goods Inventory	1,262,940	
Work in Process Inventory—Process 2		1,262,940

Record cost of goods sold for sold jobs:

Cost of Goods Sold...............................	24,150	
Finished Goods Inventory		24,150

Record sales for sold jobs:

Accounts Receivable	35,000	
Sales.......................................		35,000

Assign *underapplied* overhead to cost of goods sold:

Cost of Goods Sold...............................	150	
Factory Overhead		150

Assign *overapplied* overhead to cost of goods sold:

Factory Overhead................................	150	
Cost of Goods Sold		150

Key Terms

Conversion cost per equivalent unit (614)	Hybrid costing system (627)	Process cost summary (619)
Equivalent units of production (EUP) (614)	Job order costing system (613)	Process costing system (613)
	Materials consumption report (626)	Process operations (611)
FIFO method (614)	Operation costing system (627)	Weighted-average method (614)

Multiple Choice Quiz

1. Equivalent units of production are equal to
   a. Physical units that were completed this period from all effort being applied to them.
   b. The number of units introduced into the process this period.
   c. The number of finished units actually completed this period.
   d. The number of units that could have been started and completed given the cost incurred.
   e. The number of units in the process at the end of the period.

2. Recording the cost of raw materials purchased for use in a process costing system includes a
   a. Credit to Raw Materials Inventory.
   b. Debit to Work in Process Inventory.
   c. Debit to Factory Overhead.
   d. Credit to Factory Overhead.
   e. Debit to Raw Materials Inventory.

3. The Cutting department started the month with a beginning work in process inventory of $20,000. During the month, it was assigned the following costs: direct materials, $152,000; direct labor, $45,000; and overhead applied at the rate of 40% of direct labor cost. Inventory with a cost of $218,000 was transferred to the next department. The ending balance of Work in Process Inventory—Cutting is
   a. $330,000.   c. $220,000.   e. $118,000.
   b. $17,000.   d. $112,000.

4. A process's beginning work in process inventory consists of 10,000 units that are 20% complete with respect to conversion costs. A total of 40,000 units are completed this period. There are 15,000 units in work in process, one-third complete for conversion, at period-end. The equivalent units of production (EUP) with respect to conversion at period-end, assuming the weighted-average method, are
   a. 45,000 EUP.   c. 5,000 EUP.   e. 43,000 EUP.
   b. 40,000 EUP.   d. 37,000 EUP.

5. Assume the same information as in question 4. Also assume that beginning work in process had $6,000 in conversion cost and that $84,000 in conversion is added during this period. What is the cost per EUP for conversion?
   a. $0.50 per EUP   c. $2.00 per EUP   e. $2.25 per EUP
   b. $1.87 per EUP   d. $2.10 per EUP

ANSWERS TO MULTIPLE CHOICE QUIZ

1. d
2. e
3. b; $20,000 + $152,000 + $45,000 + $18,000 − $218,000 = $17,000

4. a; 40,000 + (15,000 × 1/3) = 45,000 EUP
5. c; ($6,000 + $84,000) ÷ 45,000 EUP = $2 per EUP

[A] *Superscript letter A denotes assignments based on Appendix 16A.*

🅸 Icon denotes assignments that involve decision making.

Discussion Questions

1. 🅸 What is the main factor for a company in choosing between job order costing and process costing systems? Give two likely applications of each system.

2. The focus in a job order costing system is the job or batch. Identify the main focus in process costing.

3. 🅸 Can services be delivered by means of process operations? Support your answer with an example.

4. Are the journal entries that match cost flows to product flows in process costing primarily the same or much different than those in job order costing? Explain.

5. Identify the control document for materials flow when a materials requisition slip is not used.

6. 🅸 Explain in simple terms the notion of equivalent units of production (EUP). Why is it necessary to use EUP in process costing?

7. 🅸 What are the two main inventory methods used in process costing? What are the differences between these methods?

8. 🅸 Why is it possible for direct labor in process operations to include the labor of employees who do not work directly on products or services?

9. Direct labor costs flow through what accounts in a company's process cost system?

10. At the end of a period, what balance should remain in the Factory Overhead account?

11. ⬛ Is it possible to have under- or overapplied overhead costs in a process costing system? Explain.

12. Explain why equivalent units of production for both direct labor and overhead can be the same as, and why they can be different from, equivalent units for direct materials.

13. List the four steps in accounting for production activity in a reporting period (for process operations).

14. Companies such as **Apple** commonly prepare a process cost summary. What purposes does a process cost summary serve? **APPLE**

15. ⬛ Are there situations where **Google** can use process costing? Identify at least one and explain it. **GOOGLE**

16. ⬛ **Samsung** produces digital televisions with a multiple-process production line. Identify and list some of its production processing steps and departments. **Samsung**

17. ⬛ **General Mills** needs a steady supply of ingredients for processing. What are some risks the company faces regarding its ingredients?

18. ⬛ How could a company manager use a process cost summary to determine if a program to reduce water usage is successful?

19. Explain a hybrid costing system. Identify a product or service operation that might be suited to a hybrid costing system.

---

connect

For each of the following products and services, indicate whether it is more likely produced in a process operation (P) or in a job order operation (J).

_____ **1.** Tennis courts _____ **3.** Audit of financial statements _____ **5.** Vanilla ice cream

_____ **2.** Organic juice _____ **4.** Luxury yachts _____ **6.** Tennis balls

QUICK STUDY

QS 16-1
Process vs. job order operations **C1**

Label each statement below as either true (T) or false (F).

_____ **1.** The cost per equivalent unit is computed as the total costs of a process divided by the number of equivalent units passing through that process.

_____ **2.** Service companies are not able to use process costing.

_____ **3.** Costs per job are computed in both job order and process costing systems.

_____ **4.** Job order and process operations both combine materials, labor, and overhead in producing products or services.

QS 16-2
Process vs. job order costing
A1

For each of the following products and services, indicate whether it is more likely produced in a process operation (P) or a job order operation (J).

_____ **1.** Beach toys _____ **4.** Wedding reception _____ **7.** Tattoos

_____ **2.** Concrete swimming pool _____ **5.** Custom suits _____ **8.** Guitar picks

_____ **3.** iPhones _____ **6.** Juice _____ **9.** Solar panels

QS 16-3
Process vs. job order operations
C1

Prepare a physical flow reconciliation with the information below.

Blending Process	Units of Product	Percent of Conversion
Beginning work in process............	150,000	80%
Goods started......................	310,000	100
Goods completed....................	340,000	100
Ending work in process	120,000	25

QS 16-4
Physical flow reconciliation
C2

Refer to QS 16-4. Compute the total equivalent units of production for conversion using the weighted-average method.

QS 16-5
Weighted average:
Computing equivalent units of production **C2**

Refer to QS 16-4. Compute the total equivalent units of production for conversion using the FIFO method.

QS 16-6[A]
FIFO: Computing equivalent units **C4**

QS 16-7
Weighted average:
Cost per EUP   **C3**

A production department's beginning inventory cost includes $394,900 of conversion costs. This department incurs an additional $907,500 in conversion costs in the month of March. Equivalent units of production for conversion total 740,000 for March. Calculate the cost per equivalent unit of conversion using the weighted-average method.

QS 16-8
Weighted average:
Computing equivalent units of production   **C2**

The following refers to units processed by an ice cream maker in July. Compute the total equivalent units of production for conversion for July using the weighted-average method.

	Gallons of Product	Percent of Conversion
Beginning work in process	320,000	25%
Goods started	620,000	100
Goods completed	680,000	100
Ending work in process	260,000	75

QS 16-9[A]
FIFO: Computing equivalent units   **C4**

Refer to QS 16-8 and compute the total equivalent units of production for conversion for July using the FIFO method.

QS 16-10
Weighted average:
Equivalent units of production   **C2**

The following information applies to QS 16-10 through QS 16-17.

Carlberg Company has two manufacturing departments, Assembly and Painting. The Assembly department started 10,000 units during November. The following production activity unit and cost information refers to the Assembly department's November production activities.

Assembly Department	Units	Percent of Direct Materials	Percent of Conversion
Beginning work in process	2,000	60%	40%
Units transferred out	9,000	100	100
Ending work in process	3,000	80	30

Beginning work in process inventory—Assembly dept.	$1,581 (consists of $996 for direct materials and $585 for conversion)

Costs added during the month:	
Direct materials	$10,404
Conversion	$12,285

Required

Calculate the Assembly department's equivalent units of production for materials and for conversion for November. Use the weighted-average method.

QS 16-11
Weighted average:
Cost per EUP   **C3**

Refer to the information in QS 16-10. Calculate the Assembly department's cost per equivalent unit of production for materials and for conversion for November. Use the weighted-average method.

QS 16-12
Weighted average:
Assigning costs to output
C3

Refer to the information in QS 16-10. Assign costs to the Assembly department's output—specifically, the units transferred out to the Painting department and the units that remain in process in the Assembly department at month-end. Use the weighted-average method.

QS 16-13
Weighted average: Journal entry to transfer costs   **P4**

Refer to the information in QS 16-10. Prepare the November 30 journal entry to record the transfer of costs from the Assembly department to the Painting department. Use the weighted-average method.

QS 16-14[A]
FIFO: Equivalent units of production   **C4**

Refer to the information in QS 16-10. Calculate the Assembly department's equivalent units of production for materials and for conversion for November. Use the FIFO method.

Refer to the information in QS 16-10. Calculate the Assembly department's cost per equivalent unit of production for materials and for conversion for November. Use the FIFO method.

QS 16-15ᴬ
FIFO: Cost per EUP **C4**

Refer to the information in QS 16-10. Assign costs to the Assembly department's output—specifically, the units transferred out to the Painting department and the units that remain in process in the Assembly department at month-end. Use the FIFO method.

QS 16-16ᴬ
FIFO: Assigning costs to output **C4**

Refer to the information in QS 16-10. Prepare the November 30 journal entry to record the transfer of costs from the Assembly department to the Painting department. Use the FIFO method.

QS 16-17ᴬ
FIFO: Journal entry to transfer costs **P4**

Zia Co. makes flowerpots from recycled plastic in two departments, Molding and Packaging. At the beginning of the month, the Molding department has 2,000 units in inventory, 70% complete as to materials. During the month, the Molding department started 18,000 units. At the end of the month, the Molding department had 3,000 units in ending inventory, 80% complete as to materials. Units completed in the Molding department are transferred into the Packaging department.
  Cost information for the Molding department for the month follows.

QS 16-18
Weighted average: Computing equivalent units and cost per EUP (direct materials)

C2 C3

Beginning work in process inventory (direct materials)	$ 1,200
Direct materials added during the month	27,900

Using the weighted-average method, compute the Molding department's (a) equivalent units of production for materials and (b) cost per equivalent unit of production for materials for the month. (Round to two decimal places.)

Refer to information in QS 16-18. Using the weighted-average method, assign direct materials costs to the Molding department's output—specifically, the units transferred out to the Packaging department and the units that remain in process in the Molding department at month-end.

QS 16-19
Weighted average: Assigning costs to output

C3

Azule Co. manufactures in two sequential processes, Cutting and Binding. The two departments report the information below for a recent month. Determine the ending balances in the Work in Process Inventory accounts of each department.

QS 16-20
Transfer of costs; ending WIP balances **C3**

	Cutting	Binding
Beginning work in process		
Transferred in from Cutting dept.		$ 1,200
Direct materials	$ 845	1,926
Conversion	2,600	3,300

	Cutting	Binding
Costs added during March		
Direct materials	$ 8,240	$ 6,356
Conversion	11,100	18,575
Transferred in from Cutting dept. . .		15,685
Transferred to finished goods		30,000

BOGO Inc. has two sequential processing departments, Roasting and Mixing. At the beginning of the month, the Roasting department had 2,000 units in inventory, 70% complete as to materials. During the month, the Roasting department started 18,000 units. At the end of the month, the Roasting department had 3,000 units in ending inventory, 80% complete as to materials.
  Cost information for the Roasting department for the month follows.

QS 16-21ᴬ
FIFO: Computing equivalent units and cost per EUP (direct materials)

C4

Beginning work in process inventory (direct materials)	$ 2,170
Direct materials added during the month	27,900

Using the FIFO method, compute the Roasting department's (a) equivalent units of production for materials and (b) cost per equivalent unit of production for materials for the month.

QS 16-22 [A]
FIFO: Assigning costs to output **C4**

Refer to QS 16-21. Using the FIFO method, assign direct materials costs to the Roasting department's output—specifically, the units transferred out to the Mixing department and the units that remain in process in the Roasting department at month-end.

QS 16-23
Recording costs of materials **P1**

Hotwax makes surfboard wax in two sequential processes. This period, Hotwax purchased on account $62,000 in raw materials. Its Mixing department requisitioned $50,000 of direct materials for use in production. Prepare journal entries to record its (1) purchase of raw materials and (2) requisition of direct materials.

QS 16-24
Recording costs of labor

P2

Prepare journal entries to record the following production activities for Hotwax.

1. Incurred $75,000 of direct labor in its Mixing department and $50,000 of direct labor in its Shaping department (credit Factory Wages Payable).
2. Incurred indirect labor of $10,000 (credit Factory Wages Payable).
3. Total factory payroll of $135,000 was paid in cash.

QS 16-25
Recording costs of factory overhead

P1 P3

Prepare journal entries to record the following production activities for Hotwax.

1. Requisitioned $9,000 of indirect materials for use in production of surfboard wax.
2. Incurred $156,000 overhead costs (credit Other Accounts).
3. Applied overhead at the rate of 140% of direct labor costs. Direct labor costs were $75,000 in the Mixing department and $50,000 in the Shaping department.

QS 16-26
Recording transfer of costs to finished goods **P4**

Hotwax completed products costing $275,000 and transferred them to finished goods. Prepare the journal entry to record the transfer of units from Shaping to finished goods inventory.

EXERCISES

Exercise 16-1
Process vs. job order operations **C1**

For each of the following products and services, indicate whether it is more likely produced in a process operation (P) or in a job order operation (J).

____ **1.** Beach towels   ____ **4.** Headphones   ____ **7.** Cut flower arrangements
____ **2.** Bolts and nuts   ____ **5.** Designed patio   ____ **8.** House paints
____ **3.** Lawn chairs   ____ **6.** Door hardware   ____ **9.** Concrete swimming pools

Exercise 16-2
Comparing process and job order operations

C1

Identify each of the following features as applying more to job order operations (J), process operations (P), or both job order and process operations (B).

____ **1.** Cost object is a process.   ____ **4.** Uses indirect costs.
____ **2.** Measures unit costs only at period-end.   ____ **5.** Uses only one Work in Process account.
____ **3.** Transfers costs between Work in Process   ____ **6.** Uses materials, labor, and overhead costs.
       Inventory accounts.

Exercise 16-3
Terminology in process costing

C1 A1

Match each of the following items A through G with the best numbered description of its purpose.

A. Factory Overhead account   **E.** Raw Materials Inventory account
B. Process cost summary   **F.** Materials requisition
C. Equivalent units of production   **G.** Finished Goods Inventory account
D. Work in Process Inventory accounts

_____ **1.** Notifies the materials manager to send materials to a production department.
_____ **2.** Holds indirect costs until assigned to production.
_____ **3.** Hold production costs until products are transferred from production to finished goods (or another department).
_____ **4.** Standardizes partially completed units into equivalent completed units.
_____ **5.** Holds costs of finished products until sold to customers.
_____ **6.** Describes the activity and output of a production department for a period.
_____ **7.** Holds costs of materials until they are used in production or as factory overhead.

A production department in a process manufacturing system completed its work on 80,000 units of product and transferred them to the next department during a recent period. Of these units, 24,000 were in process at the beginning of the period. The other 56,000 units were started and completed during the period. At period-end, 16,000 units were in process. Compute the production department's equivalent units of production for direct materials under each of three separate assumptions using the weighted-average method:

Exercise 16-4
Weighted average:
Computing equivalent units
C2

1. All direct materials are added to products when processing begins.
2. Beginning inventory is 40% complete as to materials and conversion costs. Ending inventory is 75% complete as to materials and conversion costs.
3. Beginning inventory is 60% complete as to materials and 40% complete as to conversion costs. Ending inventory is 30% complete as to materials and 60% complete as to conversion costs.

Refer to the information in Exercise 16-4 and complete the requirements for each of the three separate assumptions using the FIFO method for process costing.

Exercise 16-5ᴬ
FIFO: Computing equivalent units   C4

Fields Company has two manufacturing departments, Forming and Painting. The company uses the weighted-average method of process costing. At the beginning of the month, the Forming department has 25,000 units in inventory, 60% complete as to materials and 40% complete as to conversion costs. The beginning inventory cost of $60,100 consisted of $44,800 of direct materials costs and $15,300 of conversion costs.

During the month, the Forming department started 300,000 units. At the end of the month, the Forming department had 30,000 units in ending inventory, 80% complete as to materials and 30% complete as to conversion. Units completed in the Forming department are transferred to the Painting department.

Cost information for the Forming department follows.

Exercise 16-6
Weighted average:
Cost per EUP and costs assigned to output
C3

Beginning work in process inventory	$ 60,100
Direct materials added during the month	1,231,200
Conversion added during the month.	896,700

1. Calculate the equivalent units of production for the Forming department.
2. Calculate the costs per equivalent unit of production for the Forming department.
3. Using the weighted-average method, assign costs to the Forming department's output—specifically, its units transferred to Painting and its ending work in process inventory.

Refer to the information in Exercise 16-6. Assume that Fields uses the FIFO method of process costing.
1. Calculate the equivalent units of production for the Forming department.
2. Calculate the costs per equivalent unit of production for the Forming department.

Exercise 16-7ᴬ
FIFO: Costs per EUP
C4

During April, the first production department of a process manufacturing system completed its work on 300,000 units of a product and transferred them to the next department. Of these transferred units, 60,000 were in process in the production department at the beginning of April and 240,000 were started and completed in April. April's beginning inventory units were 60% complete with respect to materials and 40% complete with respect to conversion. At the end of April, 82,000 additional units were in process in the production department and were 80% complete with respect to materials and 30% complete with respect to conversion. Compute the number of equivalent units with respect to both materials used and conversion used in the first production department for April using the weighted-average method.

Exercise 16-8
Weighted average:
Computing equivalent units of production
C2

The production department described in Exercise 16-8 had $850,368 of direct materials and $649,296 of conversion costs charged to it during April. Also, its April beginning inventory of $167,066 consists of $118,472 of direct materials cost and $48,594 of conversion costs.
1. Compute the direct materials cost per equivalent unit for April.
2. Compute the conversion cost per equivalent unit for April.
3. Using the weighted-average method, assign April's costs to the department's output—specifically, its units transferred to the next department and its ending work in process inventory.

Exercise 16-9
Weighted average:
Costs assigned to output and inventories
C2

Exercise 16-10^A
FIFO: Computing
equivalent units of
production C4

Refer to the information in Exercise 16-8 to compute the number of equivalent units with respect to both materials and conversion costs in the production department for April using the FIFO method.

Exercise 16-11^A
FIFO: Costs assigned to
output C4   P4

Refer to the information in Exercise 16-9 and complete its parts 1, 2, and 3 using the FIFO method.

Exercise 16-12
Weighted average:
Completing a process cost
summary C3

The following partially completed process cost summary describes the July production activities of the Molding department at Ashad Company. Its production output is sent to the next department. All direct materials are added to products when processing begins. Beginning work in process inventory is 20% complete with respect to conversion. Prepare its process cost summary using the weighted-average method.

Equivalent Units of Production	Direct Materials	Conversion	Units	
Units transferred out	32,000 EUP	32,000 EUP	Units in beginning work in process (all completed during July)	2,000
Units of ending work in process	2,500 EUP	1,500 EUP	Units started this period	32,500
Equivalent units of production	34,500 EUP	33,500 EUP	Units completed and transferred out	32,000
			Units in ending work in process	2,500
Costs per EUP	Direct Materials	Conversion		
Costs of beginning work in process. . . .	$ 18,550	$ 2,280		
Costs incurred this period	357,500	188,670		
Total costs.	$376,050	$190,950		

Exercise 16-13^A
FIFO: Completing a
process cost summary
C3   C4

Refer to the information in Exercise 16-12. Prepare a process cost summary using the FIFO method. (Round cost per equivalent unit calculations to two decimal places.)

Exercise 16-14
Production cost flow
and measurement;
journal entries
P4

Pro-Weave manufactures stadium blankets by passing the products through a Weaving department and a Sewing department. The following information is available regarding its June inventories.

	Beginning Inventory	Ending Inventory
Raw materials inventory.	$ 120,000	$ 185,000
Work in process inventory—Weaving	300,000	330,000
Work in process inventory—Sewing	570,000	700,000
Finished goods inventory.	1,266,000	1,206,000

The following additional information describes the company's manufacturing activities for June.

Raw materials purchases (on credit)	$ 500,000	Labor used	
Factory payroll cost (paid in cash)	3,060,000	Direct—Weaving.	$1,200,000
Other factory overhead cost (Other Accounts credited)	156,000	Direct—Sewing.	360,000
Materials used		Indirect	1,500,000
Direct—Weaving.	$ 240,000	Overhead rates as a percent of direct labor	
Direct—Sewing.	75,000	Weaving	80%
Indirect	120,000	Sewing	150%
		Sales (on credit)	$4,000,000

Required

1. Compute the (*a*) cost of products transferred from Weaving to Sewing, (*b*) cost of products transferred from Sewing to finished goods, and (*c*) cost of goods sold.
2. Prepare journal entries dated June 30 to record (*a*) goods transferred from Weaving to Sewing, (*b*) goods transferred from Sewing to finished goods, (*c*) sale of finished goods, and (*d*) cost of goods sold.

Check   (1c) Cost of goods sold, $3,275,000

Refer to the information in Exercise 16-14. Prepare journal entries dated June 30 to record (*a*) raw materials purchases, (*b*) direct materials usage, (*c*) indirect materials usage, (*d*) direct labor usage, (*e*) indirect labor usage, (*f*) other overhead costs, (*g*) overhead applied, and (*h*) payment of total payroll costs.

Exercise 16-15
Recording product costs

P1   P2   P3

Elliott Company produces large quantities of a standardized product. The following information is available for the first process in its production activities for March.

Exercise 16-16
Weighted average:
Process cost summary   **C3**

Units		Costs		
Beginning work in process inventory...........	2,000	Beginning work in process inventory		
Started	20,000	Direct materials.....................	$2,500	
Ending work in process inventory.............	5,000	Conversion.........................	6,360	$ 8,860
		Direct materials added		168,000
Status of ending work in process inventory		Direct labor added....................		199,850
Materials—Percent complete...............	100%	Overhead applied (140% of direct labor) . . .		279,790
Conversion—Percent complete	35%	Total costs to account for		$656,500
		Ending work in process inventory........		$ 84,110

Prepare a process cost summary report for this process using the weighted-average method.

Check   Cost per equivalent unit: conversion, $25.92

Oslo Company produces large quantities of a standardized product. The following information is available for the first process in its production activities for May.

Exercise 16-17
Weighted average:
Process cost summary   **C3**

Units		Costs		
Beginning work in process inventory	4,000	Beginning work in process inventory		
Started.....................................	12,000	Direct materials.....................	$2,880	
Ending work in process inventory	3,000	Conversion.........................	5,358	$ 8,238
		Direct materials added		197,120
Status of ending work in process inventory		Direct labor added....................		123,680
Materials—Percent complete	100%	Overhead applied (90% of direct labor) . . .		111,312
Conversion—Percent complete.............	25%	Total costs to account for		$440,350
		Ending work in process inventory........		$ 50,610

Prepare a process cost summary report for this process using the weighted-average method.

Check   Cost per equivalent unit: materials, $12.50

RSTN Co. produces its product through two sequential processing departments. Direct materials and conversion are added to the product evenly throughout each process.

During October, the first process finished and transferred 150,000 units of its product to the second process. Of these units, 30,000 were in process at the beginning of the month and 120,000 were started and completed during the month. The beginning work in process inventory was 30% complete. At the end of the month, the work in process inventory consisted of 20,000 units that were 80% complete.

Compute the number of equivalent units of production for the first process for October using the FIFO method.

Exercise 16-18ᴬ
FIFO: Equivalent units

C4   P4

The flowchart below shows the August production activity of the Punching and Bending departments of Wire Box Company. Use the amounts shown on the flowchart to compute the missing numbers identified by question marks.

Exercise 16-19
Production cost flows

P1   P2   P3   P4

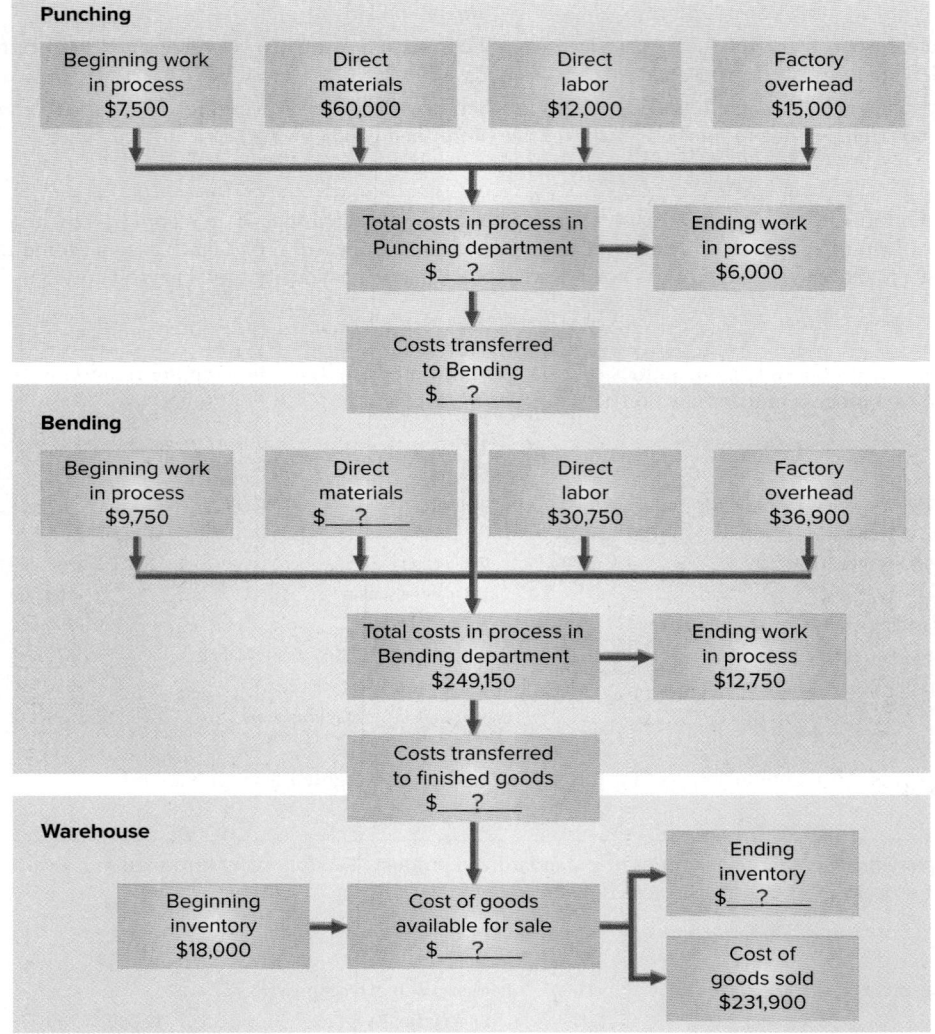

Exercise 16-20

Weighted average:

Process cost summary

C3

Hi-Test Company uses the weighted-average method of process costing to assign production costs to its products. Information for the company's first production process for September follows. Assume that all materials are added at the beginning of this production process, and that conversion costs are added uniformly throughout the process.

Work in process inventory, September 1 (2,000 units, 100% complete with respect to direct materials, 80% complete with respect to direct labor and overhead; consists of $45,000 of direct materials cost and $56,320 conversion cost).....................................	$101,320
Costs incurred in September	
Direct materials	$375,000
Conversion	$341,000
Work in process inventory, September 30 (7,000 units, 100% complete with respect to direct materials, 40% complete with respect to conversion)	$?
Units started in September	28,000
Units completed and transferred to finished goods inventory..........................	23,000

Compute each of the following using the weighted-average method of process costing.

1. The number of equivalent units for materials for the month.

2. The number of equivalent units for conversion for the month.

3. The cost per equivalent unit of materials for the month.

4. The cost per equivalent unit for conversion for the month.

5. The total cost of goods transferred out.

6. The total cost of ending work in process inventory.

Prepare journal entries to record the following production activities.

1. Purchased $80,000 of raw materials on credit.
2. Used $42,000 of direct materials in the Roasting department.
3. Used $22,500 of indirect materials in production.

Exercise 16-21
Recording costs of materials
P1

Prepare journal entries to record the following production activities.

1. Incurred $42,000 of direct labor in the Roasting department and $33,000 of direct labor in the Blending department (credit Factory Wages Payable).
2. Incurred $20,000 of indirect labor in production (credit Factory Wages Payable).
3. Paid factory payroll of $95,000.

Exercise 16-22
Recording costs of labor
P2

Prepare journal entries to record the following production activities.

1. Paid overhead costs (other than indirect materials and indirect labor) of $38,750.
2. Applied overhead at 110% of direct labor costs. Direct labor costs were $42,000 in the Roasting department and $33,000 in the Blending department.

Exercise 16-23
Recording overhead costs
P3

Prepare journal entries to record the following production activities.

1. Transferred completed goods from the Assembly department to finished goods inventory. The goods cost $135,600.
2. Sold $315,000 of goods on credit. Their cost is $175,000.

Exercise 16-24
Recording cost of completed goods
P4

Re-Tire produces bagged mulch made from recycled tires. Production involves shredding tires and bagging the pieces in the Bagging department. All direct materials enter in the Shredding process. The following describes production operations for October.

Exercise 16-25
Recording cost flows in a process cost system
P1 P2 P3 P4

	A	B
1		
2	Direct materials used (Shredding)	$ 522,000
3	Direct labor used (20% in Shredding; 80% in Bagging)	$ 130,000
4	Predetermined overhead rate (based on direct labor)	175%
5	Transferred to Bagging	$ 595,000
6	Transferred from Bagging to finished goods	$ 580,000

The company's revenue for the month totaled $950,000 from credit sales, and its cost of goods sold for the month is $540,000. Prepare summary journal entries dated October 31 to record its October production activities for (1) direct materials usage, (2) direct labor incurred, (3) overhead applied, (4) goods transfer from Shredding to Bagging, (5) goods transfer from Bagging to finished goods, (6) credit sales, and (7) cost of goods sold.

Check (3) Cr. Factory Overhead, $227,500

The following journal entries are recorded in Kiesha Co.'s process costing system. Kiesha produces apparel and accessories. Overhead is applied to production based on direct labor cost for the period. Prepare a brief explanation (including any overhead rates applied) for each journal entry *a* through *k*.

Exercise 16-26
Interpretation of journal entries in process costing
P1 P2 P3 P4

a.	Raw Materials Inventory..................	52,000	
	Accounts Payable		52,000
b.	Work in Process Inventory...............	42,000	
	Raw Materials Inventory.............		42,000
c.	Work in Process Inventory...............	32,000	
	Factory Wages Payable..............		32,000
d.	Factory Overhead......................	6,000	
	Factory Wages Payable..............		6,000
e.	Factory Overhead.....................	12,000	
	Cash..............................		12,000
f.	Factory Overhead......................	10,000	
	Raw Materials Inventory.............		10,000

g.	Factory Wages Payable	38,000	
	Cash.............................		38,000
h.	Work in Process Inventory...............	33,600	
	Factory Overhead		33,600
i.	Finished Goods Inventory	88,000	
	Work in Process Inventory		88,000
j.	Accounts Receivable	250,000	
	Sales.............................		250,000
k.	Cost of Goods Sold.....................	100,000	
	Finished Goods Inventory............		100,000

PROBLEM SET A

Problem 16-1A
Production cost flow
and measurement;
journal entries

P1 P2 P3 P4

Sierra Company manufactures soccer balls in two sequential processes: Cutting and Stitching. All direct materials enter production at the beginning of the cutting process. The following information is available regarding its May inventories.

	Beginning Inventory	Ending Inventory
Raw materials inventory..............	$ 6,000	$ 9,250
Work in process inventory—Cutting	43,500	51,500
Work in process inventory—Stitching	63,300	60,500
Finished goods inventory..............	20,100	8,250

The following additional information describes the company's production activities for May.

Direct Materials		**Factory Overhead (actual costs)**	
Raw materials purchased on credit.....	$ 25,000	Indirect materials used	$ 6,000
Direct materials used—Cutting	21,750	Indirect labor used............	55,000
Direct materials used—Stitching	0	Other overhead costs	47,000
Direct Labor		**Factory Overhead Rates**	
Direct labor—Cutting	$ 15,600	Cutting	150% of direct materials used
Direct labor—Stitching	62,400	Stitching	120% of direct labor used
Total factory payroll paid (in cash)......	133,000	Sales.....................	$256,000

Required

Check (1c) Cost of goods sold, $213,905

1. Compute the amount of (*a*) production costs transferred from Cutting to Stitching, (*b*) production costs transferred from Stitching to finished goods, and (*c*) cost of goods sold.

2. Prepare summary journal entries dated May 31 to record the following May activities: (*a*) raw materials purchases, (*b*) direct materials usage, (*c*) indirect materials usage, (*d*) direct labor costs incurred, (*e*) indirect labor costs incurred, (*f*) payment of factory payroll, (*g*) other overhead costs (credit Other Accounts), (*h*) overhead applied, (*i*) goods transferred from Cutting to Stitching, (*j*) goods transferred from Stitching to finished goods, (*k*) cost of goods sold, and (*l*) sales.

Problem 16-2A
Weighted average:
Cost per equivalent unit;
costs assigned to products

C2 C3

Victory Company uses weighted-average process costing to account for its production costs. The company has two production processes. Conversion cost is added evenly throughout each process. Direct materials are added at the beginning of the first process. Additional information for the first process follows.

During November, the first process transferred 700,000 units of product to the second process. At the end of November, work in process inventory consists of 180,000 units that are 30% complete with respect to conversion. Beginning work in process inventory had $420,000 of direct materials and $139,000 of conversion cost. The direct material cost added in November is $2,220,000, and the conversion cost added is $3,254,000. Beginning work in process consisted of 60,000 units that were 100% complete with respect to direct materials and 80% complete with respect to conversion. Of the units completed, 60,000 were from beginning work in process and 640,000 units were started and completed during the period.

Required

For the first process:

1. Determine the equivalent units of production with respect to (*a*) direct materials and (*b*) conversion.

Check (2) Conversion cost per equivalent unit, $4.50
(3b) $783,000

2. Compute both the direct material cost and the conversion cost per equivalent unit.

3. Compute the direct material cost and the conversion cost assigned to (*a*) units completed and transferred out and (*b*) ending work in process inventory.

Problem 16-3A
Weighted average:
Process cost summary;
equivalent units

C2 C3 P4

Fast Co. produces its product through two processing departments: Cutting and Assembly. Direct materials are added at the start of production in the Cutting department, and conversion costs are added evenly throughout each process. The company uses monthly reporting periods for its weighted-average process costing system. The Work in Process Inventory—Cutting account has a balance of $84,300 as of October 1, which consists of $17,100 of direct materials and $67,200 of conversion costs.

During the month, the Cutting department incurred the following costs.

Direct materials...........	$144,400	Conversion	$862,400

At the beginning of the month, 30,000 units were in process in the Cutting department. During October, the Cutting department started 140,000 units and transferred 150,000 units to the Assembly department. At the end of the month, the Cutting department's work in process inventory consisted of 20,000 units that were 80% complete with respect to conversion costs.

Required

1. Prepare the Cutting department's process cost summary for October using the weighted-average method.

2. Prepare the journal entry dated October 31 to transfer the cost of the partially completed units to Assembly.

Check   (1) Costs transferred out, $982,500

Tamar Co. manufactures a single product in two departments: Forming and Assembly. All direct materials are added at the beginning of the forming process. Conversion costs are added evenly throughout each process. During May, the Forming department started 21,600 units and completed and transferred 22,200 units of product to the Assembly department. The Forming department's 3,000 units of beginning work in process consisted of $19,800 of direct materials and $221,940 of conversion costs. It has 2,400 units (100% complete with respect to direct materials and 80% complete with respect to conversion) in process at month-end. During the month, $496,800 of direct materials costs and $2,165,940 of conversion costs were charged to the Forming department.

Problem 16-4A
Weighted average: Process cost summary, equivalent units, cost estimates

C2   C3   P4

Required

1. Prepare the Forming department's process cost summary for May using the weighted-average method.

2. Prepare the journal entry dated May 31 to transfer the cost of units to Assembly.

Check   (1) EUP for conversion, 24,120
(2) Cost transferred out, $2,664,000

Analysis Component

3. The costing process depends on numerous estimates.

a. Identify two major estimates that determine the cost per equivalent unit.

b. Assume management compensation is based on maintaining low inventory amounts. Is management more likely to overestimate or understimate the percentage complete?

Refer to the data in Problem 16-4A. Assume that Tamar uses the FIFO method to account for its process costing system. The following additional information is available for the Forming department:

- Beginning work in process consisted of 3,000 units that were 100% complete with respect to direct materials and 40% complete with respect to conversion.
- Of the 22,200 units transferred out, 3,000 were from beginning work in process. The remaining 19,200 were units started and completed during May.

Problem 16-5A^A
FIFO: Process cost summary; equivalent units; cost estimates

C3   C4   P4

Required

1. Prepare the Forming department's process cost summary for May using FIFO.

2. Prepare the journal entry dated May 31 to transfer the cost of units to Assembly.

Check   (1) EUP for conversion, 22,920
(2) Cost transferred out, $2,667,840

QualCo manufactures a single product in two departments: Cutting and Assembly. During May, the Cutting department completed a number of units of a product and transferred them to Assembly. Of these transferred units, 37,500 were in process in the Cutting department at the beginning of May and 150,000 were started and completed in May. May's Cutting department beginning inventory units were 60% complete with respect to materials and 40% complete with respect to conversion. At the end of May, 51,250 additional units were in process in the Cutting department and were 60% complete with respect to materials and 20% complete with respect to conversion. The Cutting department had $505,035 of direct materials and $396,568 of conversion cost charged to it during May. Its beginning inventory included $74,075 of direct materials cost and $28,493 of conversion cost.

Problem 16-6A^A
FIFO: Costs per equivalent unit; costs assigned to products

C2   C4

1. Compute the number of units transferred to Assembly.

2. Compute the number of equivalent units with respect to both materials used and conversion used in the Cutting department for May using the FIFO method.

3. Compute the direct materials cost and the conversion cost per equivalent unit for the Cutting department.

4. Using the FIFO method, assign the Cutting department's May costs to the units transferred out and assign costs to its ending work in process inventory.

Check   (2) EUP for materials, 195,750

Problem 16-7A[A]

FIFO: Process cost summary, equivalent units, cost estimates

C2 C3 C4 P4

Dengo Co. makes a trail mix in two departments: Roasting and Blending. Direct materials are added at the beginning of each process, and conversion costs are added evenly throughout each process. The company uses the FIFO method of process costing. During October, the Roasting department completed and transferred 22,200 units to the Blending department. Of the units completed, 3,000 were from beginning inventory and the remaining 19,200 were started and completed during the month. Beginning work in process was 100% complete with respect to direct materials and 40% complete with respect to conversion. The company has 2,400 units (100% complete with respect to direct materials and 80% complete with respect to conversion) in process at month-end. Information on the Roasting department's costs of beginning work in process inventory and costs added during the month follows.

Cost	Direct Materials	Conversion
Beginning work in process inventory	$ 9,900	$ 110,970
Added during the month	248,400	1,082,970

Required

Check (1) EUP for conversion, 22,920
(2) Cost transferred out to Blending, $1,333,920

1. Prepare the Roasting department's process cost summary for October using the FIFO method.

2. Prepare the journal entry dated October 31 to transfer the cost of completed units to the Blending department.

Analysis Component

3. The company provides incentives to department managers by paying monthly bonuses based on their success in controlling costs per equivalent unit of production. Assume that a production department underestimates the percentage of completion for units in ending inventory with the result that its equivalent units of production for October are understated. Will this error increase or decrease the October bonuses paid?

PROBLEM SET B

Problem 16-1B

Production cost flow and measurement; journal entries

P1 P2 P3 P4

Ho Chee I.C. makes ice cream in two sequential processes: Mixing and Blending. Direct materials enter production at the beginning of each process. The following information is available regarding its March inventories.

	Beginning Inventory	Ending Inventory
Raw materials inventory................	$ 72,000	$110,000
Work in process inventory—Mixing	156,000	250,000
Work in process inventory—Blending	160,000	198,000
Finished goods inventory..............	80,200	60,250

The following additional information describes the company's production activities for March.

Direct Materials		**Factory Overhead (actual costs)**	
Raw materials purchased on credit......	$212,000	Indirect materials used........................	$41,200
Direct materials used—Mixing..........	174,000	Indirect labor used	69,500
Direct materials used—Blending........	44,000	Other overhead costs..........................	64,660
Direct Labor		**Factory Overhead Rates**	
Direct labor—Mixing..................	$ 52,500	Mixing	75% of direct materials used
Direct labor—Blending...............	74,680	Blending	60% of direct labor used
Total factory payroll paid (in cash).......	196,680	Sales........................	$490,000

Required

Check (1c) Cost of goods sold, $408,438

1. Compute the amount of (*a*) production costs transferred from Mixing to Blending, (*b*) production costs transferred from Blending to finished goods, and (*c*) cost of goods sold.

2. Prepare journal entries dated March 31 to record the following March activities: (*a*) raw materials purchases, (*b*) direct materials usage, (*c*) indirect materials usage, (*d*) direct labor costs, (*e*) indirect labor costs, (*f*) payment of factory payroll, (*g*) other overhead costs (credit Other Accounts), (*h*) overhead applied, (*i*) goods transferred from Mixing to Blending, (*j*) goods transferred from Blending to finished goods, (*k*) cost of goods sold, and (*l*) sales.

Abraham Company uses process costing to account for its production costs. The company has two production processes. Conversion is added evenly throughout each process. Direct materials are added at the beginning of the first process. Additional information for the first process follows.

During September, the first process transferred 80,000 units of product to the next process. Beginning work in process consisted of 2,000 units that were 100% complete with respect to direct materials and 85% complete with respect to conversion. Of the units completed, 2,000 were from beginning work in process and 78,000 units were started and completed during the period. Beginning work in process had $58,000 of direct materials and $86,400 of conversion cost. At the end of September, the work in process inventory consists of 8,000 units that are 25% complete with respect to conversion. The direct materials cost added in September is $712,000, and conversion cost added is $1,980,000. The company uses the weighted-average method.

Required

For the first process:

1. Determine the equivalent units of production with respect to (*a*) conversion and (*b*) direct materials.
2. Compute both the conversion cost and the direct materials cost per equivalent unit.
3. Compute both conversion cost and direct materials cost assigned to (*a*) units completed and transferred out and (*b*) ending work in process inventory.

Analysis Component

4. Assume that an error is made in determining the percentage of completion for units in ending inventory in the first process. Instead of being 25% complete with respect to conversion, they are actually 75% complete. Write a one-page memo to the plant manager describing how this error affects its September financial statements.

> **Problem 16-2B**
> **Weighted average:**
> Cost per equivalent unit;
> costs assigned to products
>
> C2   C3
>
> **Check**   (2) Conversion cost
> per equivalent unit, $25.20
> (3*b*) $120,400

Brun Company produces its product through two processing departments: Mixing and Baking. Direct materials are added at the beginning of the mixing process. Conversion costs are added evenly. The company uses monthly reporting periods for its weighted-average process costing. The Work in Process Inventory—Mixing account had a balance of $21,300 on November 1, which consisted of $6,800 of direct materials and $14,500 of conversion costs.

During the month, the Mixing department incurred the following costs.

Direct materials............	$116,400	Conversion	$1,067,000

At the beginning of the month, 7,500 units were in process in the Mixing department. During November, the Mixing department started 104,500 units and transferred 100,000 units of its product to Baking. At the end of the month, the Mixing department's work in process inventory consisted of 12,000 units that were 100% complete with respect to direct materials and 25% complete with respect to conversion.

Required

1. Prepare the Mixing department's process cost summary for November using the weighted-average method.
2. Prepare the journal entry dated November 30 to transfer the cost of the completed units to Baking.

> **Problem 16-3B**
> **Weighted average:**
> Process cost summary;
> equivalent units
>
> C2   C3   P4
>
> **Check**   (1) Cost transferred
> out, $1,160,000

Switch Co. manufactures a single product in two departments: Cutting and Assembly. Direct labor and overhead are added evenly throughout each process. Direct materials are added at the beginning of the cutting process. During January, the Cutting department started 250,000 units and completed and transferred 220,000 units of product to the Assembly department. The Cutting department's 10,000 units of beginning work in process consisted of $7,500 of direct materials and $49,850 of conversion. In process in the Cutting department at month-end are 40,000 units (50% complete with respect to direct materials and 30% complete with respect to conversion). During the month, the Cutting department used direct materials of $112,500 in production and incurred conversion costs of $616,000.

Required

1. Prepare the Cutting department's process cost summary for January using the weighted-average method.
2. Prepare the journal entry dated January 31 to transfer the cost of units from Cutting to Assembly.

Analysis Component

3. The cost accounting process depends on several estimates.
   a. Identify two major estimates that affect the cost per equivalent unit.
   b. In what direction might you anticipate a bias from management for each estimate in part 3a (assume that management compensation is based on maintaining low inventory amounts)? Explain your answer.

> **Problem 16-4B**
> **Weighted average:**
> Process cost summary;
> equivalent units;
> cost estimates
>
> C2   C3   P4
>
> **Check**   (1) EUP for
> conversion, 232,000
> (2) Cost transferred out,
> $741,400

Problem 16-5B[A]
FIFO: Process cost summary; equivalent units; cost estimates

C3 C4 P4

Refer to the information in Problem 16-4B. Assume that Switch uses the FIFO method to account for its process costing system. The following additional information is available for the Cutting department.

- Beginning work in process consists of 10,000 units that were 75% complete with respect to direct materials and 60% complete with respect to conversion.
- Of the 220,000 units transferred out, 10,000 were from beginning work in process; the remaining 210,000 were units started and completed during January.

Check (1) Conversion EUP, 226,000

(2) Cost transferred out, $743,554

Required

1. Prepare the Cutting department's process cost summary for January using FIFO. Round cost per EUP to three decimal places.
2. Prepare the journal entry dated January 31 to transfer the cost of units to Assembly.

Problem 16-6B[A]
FIFO: Costs per equivalent unit; costs assigned to products

C2 C4

Harson Co. manufactures a single product in two departments: Forming and Assembly. During May, the Forming department completed a number of units of a product and transferred them to Assembly. Of these transferred units, 62,500 were in process in the Forming department at the beginning of May and 175,000 were started and completed in May. May's Forming department beginning inventory units were 40% complete with respect to materials and 80% complete with respect to conversion. At the end of May, 76,250 additional units were in process in the Forming department and were 80% complete with respect to materials and 20% complete with respect to conversion. The Forming department had $683,750 of direct materials and $446,050 of conversion cost charged to it during May. Its beginning inventory included $99,075 of direct materials cost and $53,493 of conversion cost.

1. Compute the number of units transferred to Assembly.

Check (2) EUP for materials, 273,500

2. Compute the number of equivalent units with respect to both materials used and conversion used in the Forming department for May using the FIFO method.
3. Compute the direct materials cost and the conversion cost per equivalent unit for the Forming department.
4. Using the FIFO method, assign the Forming department's May costs to the units transferred out and assign costs to its ending work in process inventory.

Problem 16-7B[A]
FIFO: Process cost summary, equivalent units, cost estimates

C2 C3 C4 P4

Belda Co. makes organic juice in two departments: Cutting and Blending. Direct materials are added at the beginning of each process, and conversion costs are added evenly throughout each process. The company uses the FIFO method of process costing. During March, the Cutting department completed and transferred 220,000 units to the Blending department. Of the units completed, 10,000 were from beginning inventory and the remaining 210,000 were started and completed during the month. Beginning work in process was 75% complete with respect to direct materials and 60% complete with respect to conversion. The company has 40,000 units (50% complete with respect to direct materials and 30% complete with respect to conversion) in process at month-end. Information on the Cutting department's costs of beginning work in process inventory and costs added during the month follows.

Cost	Direct Materials	Conversion
Beginning work in process inventory	$ 16,800	$ 97,720
Added during the month	223,200	1,233,960

Check (1) EUP for conversion, 226,000
(2) Cost transferred out, $1,486,960

Required

1. Prepare the Cutting department's process cost summary for March using the FIFO method.
2. Prepare the journal entry dated March 31 to transfer the cost of completed units to the Blending department.

Analysis Component

3. The company provides incentives to department managers by paying monthly bonuses based on their success in controlling costs per equivalent unit of production. Assume that a production department overestimates the percentage of completion for units in ending inventory with the result that its equivalent units of production for March are overstated. What impact does this error have on the March bonuses paid to the managers of the production department? What impact, if any, does this error have on these managers' April bonuses?

This serial problem began in Chapter 1 and continues through most of the book. If previous chapter segments were not completed, the serial problem can begin at this point.

SP 16 The computer workstation furniture manufacturing that Santana Rey started for **Business Solutions** is progressing well. Santana uses a job order costing system to account for the production costs of this product line. Santana is wondering whether process costing might be a better method for her to keep track of and monitor her production costs.

Required

1. What are the features that distinguish job order costing from process costing?
2. Should Santana continue to use job order costing or switch to process costing for her workstation furniture manufacturing? Explain.

SERIAL PROBLEM
Business Solutions

C1   A1

©Alexander Image/Shutterstock

CP 16   Major League Bat Company manufactures baseball bats. In addition to its work in process inventories, the company maintains inventories of raw materials and finished goods. It uses raw materials as direct materials in production and as indirect materials. Its factory payroll costs include direct labor for production and indirect labor. All materials are added at the beginning of the process, and conversion costs are applied uniformly throughout the production process.

COMPREHENSIVE PROBLEM

Major League Bat Company

Weighted average:
Review of
Chapters 14 and 16

Required

You are to maintain records and produce measures of inventories to reflect the July events of this company. Set up the following general ledger accounts and enter the June 30 balances: Raw Materials Inventory, $25,000; Work in Process Inventory, $8,135 ($2,660 of direct materials and $5,475 of conversion); Finished Goods Inventory, $110,000; Sales, $0; Cost of Goods Sold, $0; Factory Wages Payable, $0; and Factory Overhead, $0.

1. Prepare journal entries to record the following July transactions and events.
    a. Purchased raw materials for $125,000 cash (the company uses a perpetual inventory system).
    b. Used raw materials as follows: direct materials, $52,440; and indirect materials, $10,000.
    c. Recorded factory wages payable costs as follows: direct labor, $202,250; and indirect labor, $25,000.
    d. Paid factory payroll cost of $227,250 with cash (ignore taxes).
    e. Incurred additional factory overhead costs of $80,000 paid in cash.
    f. Applied factory overhead to production at 50% of direct labor costs.
2. Information about the July inventories follows. Use this information with that from part 1 to prepare a process cost summary, assuming the weighted-average method is used.

Check   (1*f*) Cr. Factory Overhead, $101,125

(2) EUP for conversion, 14,200

Units		Beginning inventory			Ending inventory		
Beginning inventory.....	5,000 units	Materials—Percent complete	100%		Materials—Percent complete	100%	
Started	14,000 units	Conversion—Percent complete.....	75%		Conversion—Percent complete.....	40%	
Ending inventory	8,000 units						

3. Using the results from part 2 and the available information, make computations and prepare journal entries to record the following:
    g. Total costs transferred to finished goods for July (label this entry *g*).
    h. Sale of finished goods costing $265,700 for $625,000 in cash (label this entry *h*).
4. Post entries from parts 1 and 3 to the ledger accounts set up at the beginning of the problem.
5. Compute the amount of gross profit from the sales in July. *Hint:* Add any underapplied overhead to, or deduct any overapplied overhead from, the cost of goods sold. Ignore the corresponding journal entry.

(3*g*) $271,150

The **General Ledger** tool in Connect automates several of the procedural steps in accounting so that the financial professional can focus on the impacts of each transaction on various reports and performance measures.

GL 16-1   General Ledger assignment GL 16-1, based on Problem 16-1A, focuses on transactions related to process costing. Prepare summary journal entries to record the cost of units manufactured and their flow through the manufacturing environment. Then prepare a schedule of cost of goods manufactured and a partial income statement.

GENERAL LEDGER PROBLEM

Accounting Analysis

COMPANY
ANALYSIS

C2

APPLE

AA 16-1   **Apple** has entered into contracts that require the future purchase of goods or services ("unconditional purchase obligations"). At year-end 2017, Apple reports the following for these future payments.

$ millions	2018	2019	2020	2021	2022
Future payments.........	$1,798	$2,675	$1,626	$1,296	$1,268

Required

1. As of year-end 2017, what was the total dollar amount (in millions) of Apple's future payments for unconditional purchase obligations?
2. As of year-end 2017, compute the ratio of the total dollar amount of Apple's future payments for unconditional purchase obligations divided by Apple's total liabilities. (Obtain total liabilities from Apple's balance sheet as of September 30, 2017, in Appendix A.)
3. Is the ratio computed in part 2 greater than or less than the ratio of accounts payable divided by total liabilities as of year-end 2017? (Obtain accounts payable from Apple's balance sheet as of September 30, 2017, in Appendix A.)

COMPARATIVE
ANALYSIS

C1

APPLE

GOOGLE

AA 16-2   **Apple** and **Google** work to maintain high-quality and low-cost operations. One ratio routinely computed for this assessment is the cost of goods sold divided by total expenses. A decline in this ratio can mean that the company is spending too much on selling and administrative activities. An increase in this ratio beyond a reasonable level can mean that the company is not spending enough on selling activities. (Assume for this analysis that total expenses equal the cost of goods sold plus total operating expenses.)

Required

1. For Apple and Google, refer to Appendix A and compute the ratios of cost of goods sold to total expenses for fiscal years 2017 and 2016. Record answers as percents, rounded to one decimal.
2. Based on answers to part 1, which company had a greater percentage reduction in selling and administrative expenses in 2017?

GLOBAL ANALYSIS

C1

Samsung

APPLE

GOOGLE

AA 16-3   **Samsung, Apple,** and **Google** are competitors in the global marketplace. Selected data for Samsung follow.

Korean won in billions	2017	2016
Cost of goods sold	₩129,291	₩120,278
Operating expenses	56,640	52,348
Total expenses	₩185,931	₩172,626

Required

1. Review the discussion of the importance of the cost of goods sold divided by total expenses ratio in AA 16-2. Compute the cost of goods sold to total expenses ratio for Samsung for the two years of data provided. Record answers as percents, rounded to one decimal.
2. Which company (Apple, Google, or Samsung) has the highest ratio of cost of goods sold to total expenses for 2017? (AA 16-2 part 1 must be completed to answer this requirement.)

Beyond the Numbers

ETHICS
CHALLENGE

P1

BTN 16-1   Many accounting and accounting-related professionals are skilled in financial analysis, but most are not skilled in manufacturing. This is especially the case for process manufacturing environments (for example, a bottling plant or chemical factory). To provide professional accounting and financial services, one must understand the industry, product, and processes. We have an ethical responsibility to develop this understanding before offering services to clients in these areas.

Required

Write a one-page action plan, in memorandum format, discussing how you would obtain an understanding of key business processes of a company that hires you to provide financial services. The memorandum should specify an industry, a product, and one selected process and should draw on at least one reference, such as a professional journal or industry magazine.

BTN 16-2 You hire a new assistant production manager whose prior experience is with a company that produced goods to order. Your company engages in continuous production of homogeneous products that go through various production processes. Your new assistant e-mails you questioning some cost classifications on an internal report—specifically why the costs of some materials that do not actually become part of the finished product, including some labor costs not directly associated with producing the product, are classified as direct costs. Respond to this concern via memorandum.

COMMUNICATING IN PRACTICE

C1 A1 P1 P2

BTN 16-3 Many companies use technology to help them improve processes. One example of such a tool is robotic process automation. Access **deloitte.com/us/en/pages/operations/articles/a-guide-to-robotic-process-automation-and-intelligent-automation.html** and read the information displayed.

TAKING IT TO THE NET

C1

Required

What processes are robotic process automation (RPA) tools most useful for? Explain how RPA tools work and list their proposed benefits.

BTN 16-4 The purpose of this team activity is to ensure that each team member understands process operations and the related accounting entries. Find the activities and flows identified in Exhibit 16.14 with numbers ① through ⑩. Pick a member of the team to start by describing activity number ① in this exhibit, then verbalizing the related journal entry, and describing how the amounts in the entry are computed. The other members of the team are to agree or disagree; discussion is to continue until all members express understanding. Rotate to the next numbered activity and next team member until all activities and entries have been discussed. If at any point a team member is uncertain about an answer, the team member may pass and get back in the rotation when he or she can contribute to the team's discussion.

TEAMWORK IN ACTION

C1 P1 P2 P3 P4

BTN 16-5 This chapter's opener featured Suzy Batlle and her company **Azucar Ice Cream Company**.

Required

1. Suzy tries to buy raw materials just-in-time for their use in production. How does holding raw materials inventories increase costs? If the items are not used in production, how can they impact profits? Explain.
2. How can companies like Suzy's use *yield* to improve their production processes?
3. Suppose Azucar Ice Cream decides to allow customers to make their own unique ice cream flavors. Why might the company then use a hybrid costing system?

ENTREPRENEURIAL DECISION

C3 A2

BTN 16-6 In process costing, the process is analyzed first, and then a unit measure is computed in the form of equivalent units for direct materials, conversion (direct labor and overhead), and both types of costs combined. The same analysis applies to both manufacturing and service processes.

HITTING THE ROAD

C2

Required

Visit your local **U.S. Postal Service** office. Look into the back room, and you will see several ongoing processes. Select one process, such as sorting, and list the costs associated with this process. Your list should include materials, labor, and overhead; be specific. Classify each cost as fixed or variable. At the bottom of your list, outline how overhead should be assigned to your identified process. The following format (with an example) is suggested.

| | | Conversion | | | |
Cost Description	Direct Material	Direct Labor	Overhead	Variable Cost	Fixed Cost
Manual sorting		X		X	
:					

Overhead allocation suggestions:

Point: The class can compare and discuss the different processes studied and the answers provided.

Design elements: Lightbulb: ©Chuhail/Getty Images; Blue globe: ©nidwlw/Getty Images and ©Dizzle52/Getty Images; Chess piece: ©Andrei Simonenko/Getty Images and ©Dizzle52/Getty Images; Mouse: ©Siede Preis/Getty Images; Global View globe: ©McGraw-Hill Education and ©Dizzle52/Getty Images; Sustainability: ©McGraw-Hill Education and ©Dizzle52/Getty Images

17 Activity-Based Costing and Analysis

Learning Objectives

CONCEPTUAL

C1 Distinguish between the plantwide overhead rate method, the departmental overhead rate method, and the activity-based costing method.

C2 Explain cost flows for activity-based costing.

C3 Describe the four types of activities that cause overhead costs.

ANALYTICAL

A1 Identify and assess advantages and disadvantages of the plantwide overhead and departmental overhead rate methods.

A2 Identify and assess advantages and disadvantages of activity-based costing.

PROCEDURAL

P1 Allocate overhead costs to products using the plantwide overhead rate method.

P2 Allocate overhead costs to products using the departmental overhead rate method.

P3 Allocate overhead costs to products using activity-based costing.

Brewing Profits

"Believe in yourself . . . success will come"

—SARAH TAYLOR BRIGHAM

CHARLOTTE, NC—Sarah Taylor Brigham and Justin Brigham's dream was to run their own brewery. With little more than optimism, determination, and a willingness to work hard, the duo started **Sycamore Brewing** (**sycamorebrew.com**). "We had no idea what we were getting into!" laughs Sarah. The Brighams did much of the construction work needed to transform an auto garage into a brewery, and Justin spent several sleepless nights getting the brewhouse working.

"Our goal was to brew 100 different beers in our first year," says Justin. To do that, Justin had to convert his recipes designed for a 5-gallon brewing system into 500-gallon batches. Justin uses only top-quality ingredients and monitors the activities in his brewing process to control costs. Sarah and Justin know that how they control and allocate overhead costs is crucial for product pricing and product mix decisions. Overhead costs, including brewery maintenance, supervision, and cleanup, must be allocated to products. In small businesses with few product lines, a *single plantwide overhead rate* is often sufficient.

Sycamore Brewing has had over 200% annual growth since its inception. As businesses grow and offer more diverse product

©Sycamore Brewing

lines, more detailed costing techniques are often needed. *Activity-based costing* is useful when different product lines use different amounts of the activities that drive overhead costs.

Sycamore's recipe is working. The company has over 50 employees and a new automated production facility, and recently began selling its beer in grocery stores. Sarah advises aspiring young entrepreneurs to "focus on your passion." "I'm so fired up for Sycamore's next chapter!" she says.

Sources: *Sycamore Brewing website,* January 2019; *CharlotteFive.com,* October 12, 2017; *The Charlotte Observer,* October 22, 2015; *CharlotteAgenda.com,* October 19, 2016

ASSIGNING OVERHEAD COSTS

Product pricing, product mix decisions, and cost control depend on accurate product cost information. Product cost consists of direct materials, direct labor, and overhead (indirect costs). Because direct materials and direct labor can be traced to units of output, assigning these costs to products is usually straightforward. Overhead costs, however, are not directly related to production and cannot be traced to units of product like direct materials and direct labor can. We use an allocation system to assign overhead costs such as utilities and factory maintenance. This chapter shows three methods of overhead allocation: (1) the single plantwide overhead rate method, (2) the departmental overhead rate method, and (3) the activity-based costing method.

C1

Distinguish between the plantwide overhead rate method, the departmental overhead rate method, and the activity-based costing method.

Point: Evidence suggests overhead costs have steadily increased while direct labor costs have steadily decreased as a percentage of total manufacturing costs over recent decades. This puts greater importance on accurate cost allocations.

Alternative Methods of Overhead Allocation

Exhibit 17.1 summarizes some key features of the three alternative methods.

- The *plantwide overhead rate method* and the *departmental overhead rate method* use volume-based measures such as direct labor hours or machine hours to allocate overhead costs to products. The plantwide method uses a single rate for allocating overhead costs, and the departmental rate method uses at least two rates. The departmental method arguably provides more accurate cost allocations than the plantwide method.

- *Activity-based costing* focuses on activities (not just volume) and their costs. Rates based on these activities are used to assign overhead to products in proportion to the amount of activity required to produce them. Activity-based costing typically uses more overhead allocation rates than the plantwide and departmental methods.

EXHIBIT 17.1

Overhead Cost Allocation Methods

Allocation Method	Number of Overhead Rates	Overhead Allocation Rates Based on
Plantwide rate..................	One rate	Volume-based measures such as direct labor hours or machine hours
Departmental rate	Two or more rates	Volume-based measures such as direct labor hours or machine hours
Activity-based costing	At least two (but often many) rates	Activities that drive costs, such as number of batches of product produced

Plantwide Overhead Rate Method

The first method of allocating overhead costs to products is the *single plantwide overhead rate method,* or simply the *plantwide overhead rate method.*

Cost Flows under Plantwide Overhead Rate Method
For the plantwide overhead rate method, the target of the cost assignment, or **cost object,** is the unit of product—see Exhibit 17.2. The overhead rate is determined using a volume-related measure such as direct labor hours or machine hours, both of which are readily available in most manufacturing settings. In some industries, overhead costs are closely related to these volume-related measures. If so, it is logical to use this method to assign overhead costs to products.

EXHIBIT 17.2

Plantwide Overhead Rate Method

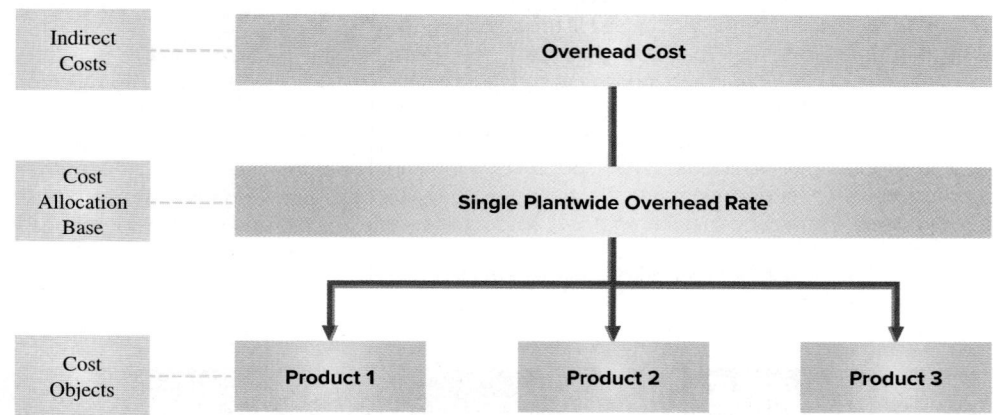

Applying the Plantwide Overhead Rate Method
Under the single plantwide overhead rate method, total budgeted overhead costs are divided by the chosen allocation base, such as total direct labor hours, to arrive at a single plantwide overhead rate. This rate then is applied to assign overhead costs to all products based on their *actual* usage of the allocation base.

To illustrate, consider KartCo, a go-kart manufacturer that produces both standard and custom go-karts for amusement parks. The standard go-kart is a basic model sold mainly to amusement parks that service county and state fairs. Custom go-karts are produced for theme parks that want unique go-karts to fit specific themes.

Assume that KartCo applies the plantwide overhead rate method and uses direct labor hours (DLH) as its overhead allocation base. KartCo's budgeted DLH information for the coming year is in Exhibit 17.3.

EXHIBIT 17.3

KartCo's Budgeted Direct Labor Hours

	Number of Units		Direct Labor Hours per Unit		Total Direct Labor Hours
Standard go-kart........	5,000	×	15	=	75,000
Custom go-kart.........	1,000	×	25	=	25,000
Total.................					100,000

KartCo's budgeted overhead cost information for the coming year is in Exhibit 17.4. Its overhead cost consists of indirect labor and factory utilities.

EXHIBIT 17.4

KartCo's Budgeted Overhead Cost

Overhead Item	Budgeted Cost
Indirect labor cost...........................	$4,000,000
Factory utilities	800,000
Total budgeted overhead cost	$4,800,000

The single plantwide overhead rate for KartCo is computed as

$$
\begin{aligned}
\text{Plantwide overhead rate} &= \text{Total budgeted overhead cost} \div \text{Total budgeted direct labor hours} \\
&= \$4,800,000 \div 100,000\ \text{DLH} \\
&= \$48\ \text{per DLH}
\end{aligned}
$$

This plantwide overhead rate is then used to allocate overhead cost to products based on the number of direct labor hours required to produce each unit as follows.

Overhead allocated to each product unit = Plantwide overhead rate × DLH per unit

KartCo allocates overhead cost to its two products as follows (on a per unit basis).

Overhead Cost per Unit Using the Plantwide Rate Method
Standard go-kart. . . . . . . $48 per DLH × 15 DLH per unit = $ 720 per unit
Custom go-kart. . . . . $48 per DLH × 25 DLH per unit = $1,200 per unit

Exhibit 17.5 summarizes the plantwide overhead method for KartCo.

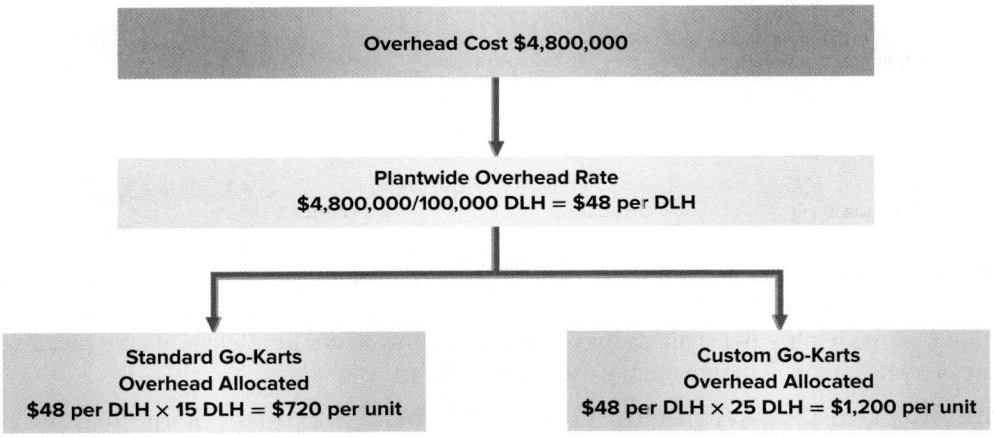

EXHIBIT 17.5

Plantwide Method—KartCo

KartCo uses these per unit overhead costs, and per unit direct materials and direct labor costs from other records, to compute product cost per unit as follows.

Product Cost per Unit Using the Plantwide Rate Method				
	Direct Materials	Direct Labor	Overhead	Product Cost per Unit
Standard go-kart	$400 +	$350 +	$ 720 =	$1,470
Custom go-kart.	600 +	500 +	1,200 =	2,300

KartCo sells its standard model go-karts for $2,000 and its custom go-karts for $3,500. A recent report from its marketing staff indicates that competitors are selling go-karts like Kart-Co's standard model for $1,200. KartCo management is concerned that selling at this lower price would result in a loss of $270 ($1,200 − $1,470) on each standard go-kart sold.

Interestingly, KartCo has been swamped with orders for its custom go-kart and cannot meet demand. Accordingly, management is considering dropping the standard model and concentrating on the custom model. Yet management recognizes that its pricing decisions are influenced by its cost allocations. Before making any strategic decisions, management asks its cost analysts to further review KartCo's overhead allocation. The cost analysts first consider the departmental overhead rate method.

Departmental Overhead Rate Method

P2
_____

Allocate overhead costs to products using the departmental overhead rate method.

Many companies have several departments that produce various products using different amounts of overhead. Under such circumstances, a single plantwide overhead rate can produce cost assignments that do not reflect the cost to manufacture products. Multiple overhead rates can result in better overhead cost allocations and improve management decisions.

Cost Flows under Departmental Overhead Rate Method   The _departmental overhead rate method_ uses a different overhead rate for each production department. This is usually done through a four-step process (see Exhibit 17.6):

1 Assign overhead costs to departmental _cost pools._

2 Select an allocation base for each department.

3 Compute overhead allocation rates for each department.

4 Use departmental overhead rates to assign overhead costs to cost objects (products).

EXHIBIT 17.6

Departmental Overhead Rate Method

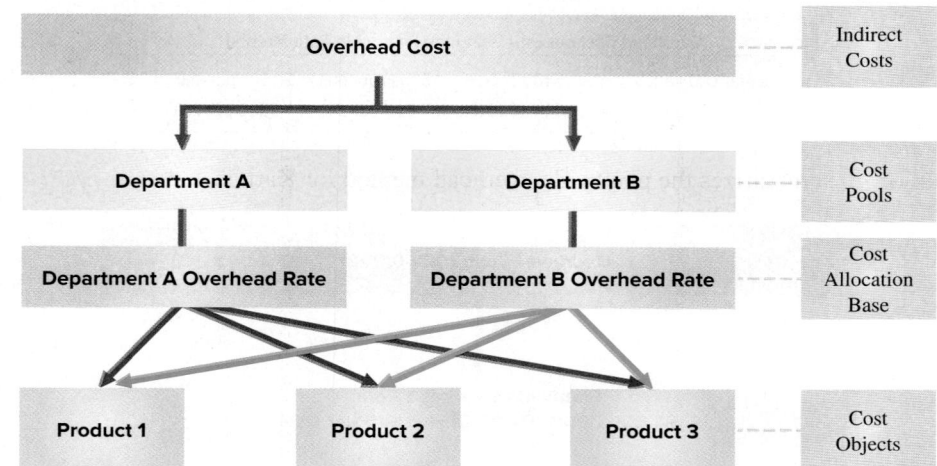

The departmental overhead method uses several departments and several overhead rates. This allows each department to have its own overhead rate and its own allocation base. For example, an Assembly department may use direct labor hours to allocate its overhead cost, whereas a Machining department may use machine hours as its base.

Applying the Departmental Overhead Rate Method   KartCo has two production departments, the Machining department and the Assembly department.

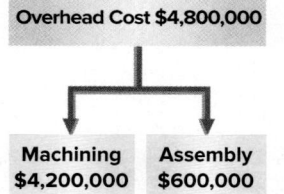

1 The first step requires that KartCo assign its $4,800,000 overhead cost to its two production departments. KartCo determines that $4,200,000 of overhead costs is traceable to its Machining department and the remaining $600,000 is traceable to its Assembly department.

2 The second step requires each department to determine an allocation base. For KartCo, the Machining department uses machine hours (MH) to allocate its overhead; the Assembly department uses direct labor hours (DLH) to allocate its overhead. The budgeted information for KartCo's Machining and Assembly departments is shown below.

	Number of Units	Machining Department		Assembly Department	
		Hours per Unit	Total Hours	Hours per Unit	Total Hours
Standard go-kart........	5,000	10 MH per unit	50,000 MH	5 DLH per unit	25,000 DLH
Custom go-kart.........	1,000	20 MH per unit	20,000 MH	5 DLH per unit	5,000 DLH
Totals................			70,000 MH		30,000 DLH

3 In step three, each department computes its own overhead rate using this formula.

$$\text{Departmental overhead rate} = \frac{\text{Total budgeted departmental overhead cost}}{\text{Total amount of departmental allocation base}}$$

KartCo's departmental overhead rates are computed as follows.

$$\text{Machining department overhead rate} = \frac{\$4,200,000}{70,000 \text{ MH}} = \$60 \text{ per MH}$$

$$\text{Assembly department overhead rate} = \frac{\$600,000}{30,000 \text{ DLH}} = \$20 \text{ per DLH}$$

4 Step four applies overhead costs to each product using departmental overhead rates. Because each standard go-kart requires 10 MH from the Machining department and five DLH from the Assembly department, the overhead cost allocated to each standard go-kart is $600 from the Machining department (10 MH × $60 per MH) and $100 from the Assembly department (5 DLH × $20 per DLH). The same procedure is applied for its custom go-kart. Exhibit 17.7 summarizes KartCo's overhead allocation per go-kart using the departmental method.

		Standard Go-Kart		Custom Go-Kart	
Department	**Departmental Overhead Rate**	**Hours per Unit**	**Overhead Allocated**	**Hours per Unit**	**Overhead Allocated**
Machining	$60 per MH	10 MH per unit	$600	20 MH per unit	$1,200
Assembly...........	$20 per DLH	5 DLH per unit	100	5 DLH per unit	100
Totals.............			$700		$1,300

EXHIBIT 17.7

Overhead Allocation Using Departmental Overhead Rates

Departmental versus Plantwide Overhead Rate Methods

Allocated overhead costs vary depending upon the allocation methods used. Exhibit 17.8 summarizes and compares the allocated overhead costs for standard and custom go-karts under the single plantwide overhead rate and the departmental overhead rate methods.

The overhead cost allocated to each standard go-kart *decreased* from $720 under the plantwide overhead rate method to $700 under the departmental overhead rate method, whereas overhead cost allocated to each custom go-kart *increased* from $1,200 to $1,300. These differences occur because the custom go-kart requires more hours in the Machining department (20 MH) than the standard go-kart requires (10 MH).

Point: Total budgeted overhead costs are the same under both the plantwide and departmental rate methods.

Overhead per Unit Using:	Standard Go-Kart	Custom Go-Kart
Plantwide overhead rate method	$720	$1,200
Departmental overhead rate method	700	1,300

EXHIBIT 17.8

Comparison of Plantwide Overhead Rate and Departmental Overhead Rate Methods

For KartCo, using the departmental overhead rate method yields the following total product cost per unit.

Product Cost per Unit Using Departmental Rate Method				
	Direct Materials	Direct Labor	Overhead	Product Cost per Unit
Standard go-kart	$400 +	$350 +	$ 700 =	$1,450
Custom go-kart	600 +	500 +	1,300 =	2,400

The total product costs per unit under the departmental overhead rate method differ from those under the plantwide overhead rate method. Compared to the plantwide overhead rate method, the departmental overhead rate method usually results in more accurate overhead allocations. When cost analysts are able to logically trace overhead costs to different cost allocation bases, costing accuracy is improved. These cost data imply that KartCo cannot make a profit on its standard go-kart if it meets competitors' $1,200 price, as it would lose $250 (computed as $1,200 − $1,450) per go-kart.

Assessing Plantwide and Departmental Overhead Rate Methods

The plantwide and departmental overhead rate methods have three key advantages: (1) They are based on readily available information, like direct labor hours. (2) They are easy to implement. (3) They are consistent with GAAP and can be used for external reporting. Both suffer from an important disadvantage, in that overhead costs are frequently too complex to be explained by only one factor like direct labor hours or machine hours.

Plantwide Overhead Rate Method   The usefulness of the single plantwide overhead rate depends on two assumptions: (1) overhead costs change with the allocation base (such as direct labor hours) and (2) all products use overhead costs in the same proportions.

For companies with many different products or those with products that use overhead costs in very different ways, the assumptions of the single plantwide rate are not reasonable. Most of KartCo's overhead is related to machining, and a custom go-kart uses more machine hours than does a standard go-kart. When overhead costs, like machinery depreciation, bear little relation to direct labor hours used, allocating overhead cost using a single plantwide overhead rate based on direct labor hours can distort product cost and lead to poor managerial decisions. Despite such shortcomings, some companies continue to use the plantwide method for its simplicity.

©Radharc Images/Alamy Stock Photo

Departmental Overhead Rate Method   The departmental overhead rate method assumes that (1) different products are similar in volume, complexity, and batch size and (2) departmental overhead costs are directly proportional to the department allocation base (such as direct labor hours and machine hours for KartCo).

When products differ in batch size and complexity, they usually consume different amounts of overhead costs. This is likely the case for KartCo with its high-volume standard model and its low-volume custom model built to customer specifications. However, the departmental overhead rate method can distort product costs. Because the departmental overhead rate method still allocates overhead costs based on measures closely related to production volume, it fails to accurately assign many overhead costs, like machine depreciation or utility costs, that are not driven by production volume.

 Decision Ethics ━━━━━━━━━━━━━━━━━━━━━━━━━

Department Manager   Three department managers hire a consulting firm for advice on increasing departmental effectiveness and efficiency. The consulting firm spends 50% of its efforts on department A and 25% on each of the other two departments. The manager for department A suggests that the three departments equally share the consulting fee. As a manager of one of the other two departments, do you believe equal sharing is fair? ■   *Answer:* When dividing a bill, common sense suggests fairness. That is, if one department consumes more services than another, we attempt to share the bill in proportion to consumption. Equally dividing the bill among the number of departments is fair if each consumed equal services. This same notion applies in assigning costs to products and services. For example, dividing overhead costs by the number of units is fair if all products consumed overhead in equal proportion.

NEED-TO-KNOW 17-1

Plantwide and Departmental Rate Methods

P1   P2

A manufacturer reports the following budgeted data for its two production departments.

	Machining	Assembly
Manufacturing overhead costs	$600,000	$300,000
Machine hours to be used (MH)...............	20,000	0
Direct labor hours to be used (DLH)	20,000	5,000

1. What is the company's single plantwide overhead rate based on direct labor hours?

2. What are the company's departmental overhead rates if the Machining department assigns overhead based on machine hours and the Assembly department assigns overhead based on direct labor hours?

3. Using the departmental overhead rates from part 2, how much overhead should be assigned to a job that uses 16 machine hours in the Machining department and 5 direct labor hours in the Assembly department?

Solution

1. Plantwide overhead rate $= \dfrac{\$600{,}000 + \$300{,}000}{20{,}000 \text{ DLH} + 5{,}000 \text{ DLH}} = \dfrac{\$900{,}000}{25{,}000 \text{ DLH}} = \$36$ per direct labor hour

2. Machining department rate $= \dfrac{\$600{,}000}{20{,}000 \text{ MH}} = \$30$ per machine hour

   Assembly department rate $= \dfrac{\$300{,}000}{5{,}000 \text{ DLH}} = \$60$ per direct labor hour

3. Overhead assigned to job $= (16 \text{ MH} \times \$30 \text{ per MH}) + (5 \text{ DLH} \times \$60 \text{ per DLH}) = \$780$

> Do More: QS 17-9, QS 17-10, QS 17-11, E 17-3

ACTIVITY-BASED COSTING

Activity-based costing (ABC) attempts to more accurately assign overhead costs by focusing on *activities*. Unlike the plantwide rate method, ABC uses more than a single rate. Unlike the departmental rate method, ABC focuses on activities rather than departments. We illustrate the activity-based costing method of assigning overhead costs.

Steps in Activity-Based Costing

The basic principle underlying activity-based costing is that an **activity,** which is a task, operation, or procedure, is what causes costs to be incurred. For example:

C2

Explain cost flows for activity-based costing.

- Cutting raw materials consumes labor and machine hours.
- Storing products consumes employee time for driving a forklift, electricity to power the forklift, and wear and tear on the forklift.
- Training employees drives costs such as fees or salaries paid to trainers and the training supplies required.

All of an organization's activities use resources. An **activity cost pool** is a collection of costs that are related to the same activity. For example, handling raw materials requires several activities, including wages of receiving department employees, wages of forklift employees who move materials, and depreciation on forklifts. These activities can be grouped into a single cost pool because they are all caused by the amount of materials moved.

There are four steps to the ABC method (see Exhibit 17.9):

©Carl Lyttle/The Image Bank/Getty Images

1. Identify activities and the overhead costs they cause.
2. Trace overhead costs to activity cost pools.
3. Compute overhead allocation rates for each activity.
4. Use the activity overhead rates to assign overhead costs to cost objects (products).

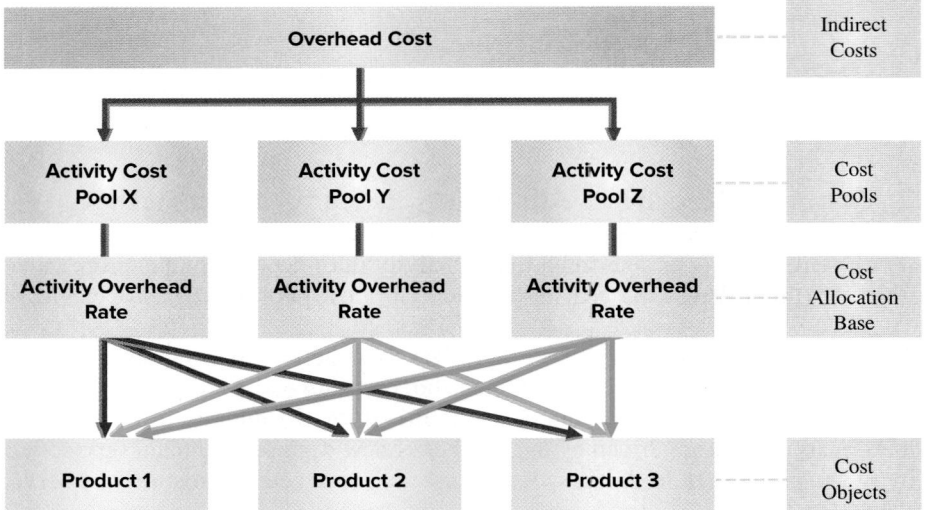

EXHIBIT 17.9

Activity-Based Costing Method

Applying Activity-Based Costing

Step 1: Identify Activities and the Overhead Costs They Cause

P3

Allocate overhead costs to products using activity-based costing.

Step 1 in applying ABC is to identify activities and the costs they cause. KartCo has total overhead costs of $4,800,000, consisting of $4,000,000 in indirect labor costs and $800,000 in factory utilities costs. After reviewing activities with production employees, KartCo identifies the activities and their costs shown in Exhibit 17.10.

EXHIBIT 17.10

KartCo Overhead Cost Details

Activity	Indirect Labor	Factory Utilities	Total Overhead
Machine setup	$ 700,000	—	$ 700,000
Machine repair	1,300,000	—	1,300,000
Factory maintenance	800,000	—	800,000
Engineer salaries	1,200,000	—	1,200,000
Assembly line power	—	$600,000	600,000
Heating and lighting	—	200,000	200,000
Totals	$4,000,000	$800,000	$4,800,000

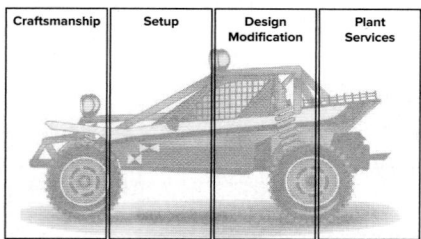

| Craftsmanship | Setup | Design Modification | Plant Services |

Step 2: Trace Overhead Costs to Activity Cost Pools

Step 2 in applying ABC is to assign activities and their overhead costs to activity cost pools. KartCo management assigns its overhead costs to four activity cost pools: craftsmanship, setup, design modification, and plant services (see Exhibit 17.11). To assign costs to activity cost pools, management looks for costs that are caused by similar activities.

Exhibit 17.11 shows that $600,000 of overhead costs are assigned to the craftsmanship cost pool; $2,000,000 to the setup cost pool; $1,200,000 to the design modification cost pool; and $1,000,000 to the plant services cost pool. The use of cost pools reduces the potential number of overhead rates from six (one for each of its six activities) to four (one for each activity cost pool).

EXHIBIT 17.11

Assigning Overhead to Activity Cost Pools

Activity Cost Pools		Activity Cost	Pool Cost
Craftsmanship:	Assembly line power	$ 600,000	$ 600,000
Setup:	Machine setup	700,000	
	Machine repair	1,300,000	2,000,000
Design modification:	Engineer salaries	1,200,000	1,200,000
Plant services:	Factory maintenance	800,000	
	Heating and lighting	200,000	1,000,000
Total overhead cost			$4,800,000

Step 3: Compute Overhead Allocation Rates for Each Activity

Step 3 is to compute **activity overhead (cost pool) rates** used to assign overhead costs to final cost objects such as products. Proper determination of activity rates depends on (1) proper identification of the factor that drives the cost in each activity cost pool and (2) proper measures of activities.

The factor that drives cost, or **activity cost driver,** is an activity that causes costs in the pool to be incurred. For KartCo's overhead, craftsmanship costs are mainly driven by the direct labor hours used to assemble products; setup costs are driven by the number of batches produced; design modification costs are driven by the number of new designs; and plant services costs are driven by the square feet of building space occupied. These activity cost drivers serve as the allocation base for each activity cost pool. KartCo then determines an expected activity level for each activity cost pool, as shown below.

Activity Cost Pools	Activity Driver (# of)	Expected Activity Level
Craftsmanship.................	Direct labor hours	30,000 DLH
Setup........................	Batches	200 batches
Design modification	Designs	10 design modifications
Plant services	Square feet	20,000 square feet

In general, cost pool activity rates are computed as follows.

Cost pool activity rate = Overhead costs assigned to pool ÷ Expected activity level

For KartCo, the activity rate for the craftsmanship cost pool is computed as follows.

Craftsmanship cost pool activity rate = $600,000 ÷ 30,000 DLH = $20 per DLH

The activity rate computations for KartCo are summarized in Exhibit 17.12.

Activity Cost Pools	Activity Driver	Overhead Costs Assigned to Pool	÷	Expected Activity Level	=	Activity Rate
Craftsmanship	Direct labor hours	$ 600,000		30,000 DLH		$20 per DLH
Setup	Batches	2,000,000		200 batches		$10,000 per batch
Design modification	Number of designs	1,200,000		10 designs		$120,000 per design
Plant services	Square feet	1,000,000		20,000 sq. ft.		$50 per sq. ft.

EXHIBIT 17.12

Activity Rates for KartCo

Step 4: Assign Overhead Costs to Cost Objects   Step 4 is to assign overhead costs in each activity cost pool to cost objects using activity rates. To do this, overhead costs are allocated to products based on the *actual* levels of activities used.

For KartCo, overhead costs in each pool are allocated to the standard go-karts and the custom go-karts using the activity rates from Exhibit 17.12. The actual activities used by each product line and the overhead costs allocated to standard and custom go-karts under ABC for KartCo are summarized in Exhibit 17.13. To illustrate, of the $600,000 of overhead costs in the craftsmanship cost pool, $500,000 is allocated to standard go-karts as follows.

Overhead from craftsmanship pool allocated to standard go-kart	**=**	**Activities consumed**	**×**	**Activity rate**
	=	25,000 DLH	×	$20 per DLH
	=	$500,000		

Standard go-karts used 25,000 direct labor hours, and the activity rate for craftsmanship is $20 per direct labor hour. Multiplying the number of direct labor hours by the activity rate yields the craftsmanship costs assigned to standard go-karts ($500,000). Custom go-karts consumed 5,000 direct labor hours, so we assign $100,000 (5,000 DLH × $20 per DLH) of craftsmanship costs to that product line. We similarly allocate overhead costs of setup, design modification, and plant services pools to each type of go-kart.

KartCo assigned no design modification costs to standard go-karts because standard go-karts are sold as "off-the-shelf" items. Using ABC, a total of $1,500,000 of overhead costs is allocated to standard go-karts and a total of $3,300,000 is allocated to custom go-karts. While the

Point: In ABC, overhead is allocated based on the actual level of activities used, multiplied by a predetermined activity rate for each cost pool.

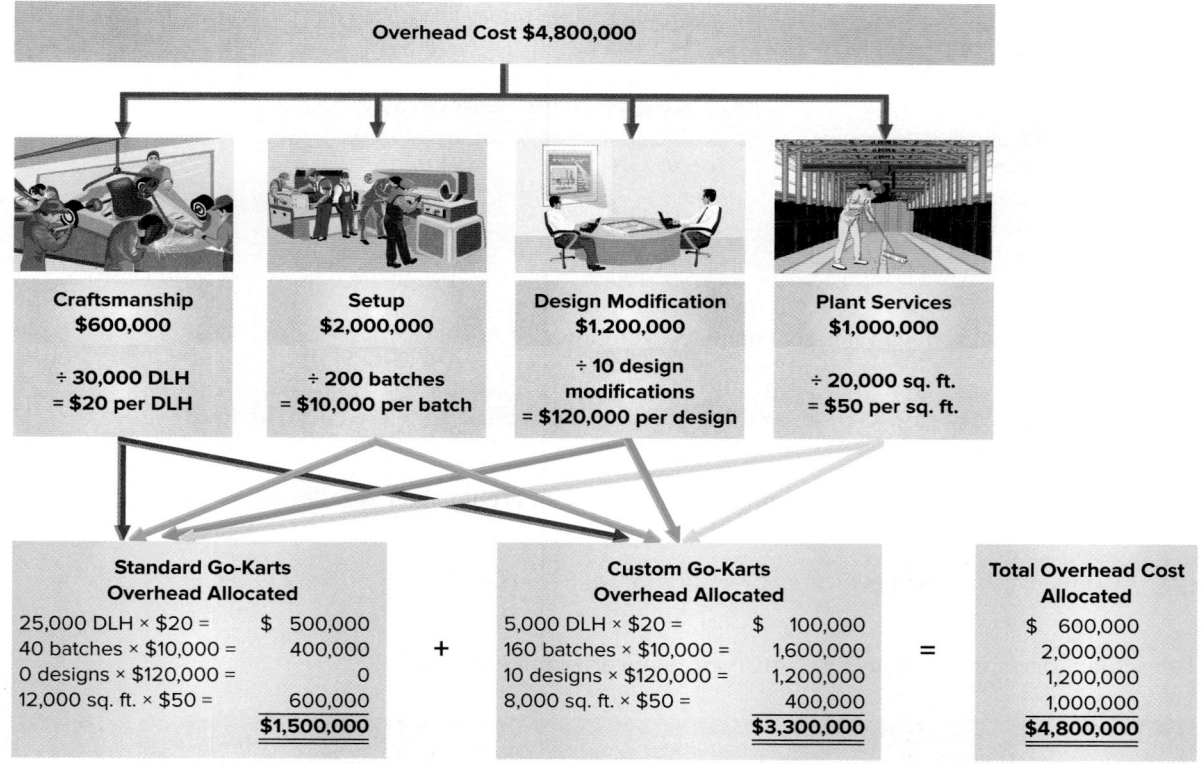

EXHIBIT 17.13

Overhead Allocated
to Go-Karts for KartCo

$4,800,000 total overhead cost allocated is the same as under the plantwide and departmental rate methods, the amounts allocated to the two product lines differ.

Overhead cost per unit is computed by dividing total overhead cost allocated to each product line by the number of product units. KartCo's overhead cost per unit for its standard and custom go-karts is computed and shown in Exhibit 17.14.

EXHIBIT 17.14

Overhead Cost per Unit for
Go-Karts Using ABC

	(A) Total Overhead Cost Allocated	(B) Units Produced	(A ÷ B) Overhead Cost per Unit
Standard go-kart	$1,500,000	5,000 units	$ 300 per unit
Custom go-kart	3,300,000	1,000 units	3,300 per unit

Total product cost per unit for KartCo using ABC for its two products follows.

	Direct Materials		Direct Labor		Overhead		Product Cost per Unit
Standard go-kart	$400	+	$350	+	$ 300	=	$1,050
Custom go-kart	600	+	500	+	3,300	=	4,400

Point: Accurately assigning costs to products is key to setting many product prices. If product costs are inaccurate and result in prices that are too low, the company loses money on each item sold. Likewise, if product prices are improperly set too high, the company loses business to competitors. ABC can be used to more accurately set prices.

Assuming that ABC more accurately assigns costs, KartCo's management now sees how its competitors can sell their standard models at $1,200 and why KartCo is flooded with orders for custom go-karts. Specifically, if the cost to produce a standard go-kart is $1,050, as shown above (and not $1,470 as computed using the plantwide rate or $1,450 as computed using departmental rates), a profit of $150 ($1,200 − $1,050) occurs on each standard unit sold at the competitive $1,200 market price. Further, selling its custom go-kart at $3,500 is a mistake because KartCo loses $900 ($3,500 − $4,400) on each custom go-kart sold. KartCo has under-priced its custom go-kart relative to its production costs and competitors' prices, which explains why the company has more custom orders than it can supply.

Exhibit 17.15 summarizes KartCo's overhead allocation per go-kart under the plantwide rate method, departmental rate method, and ABC. Overhead cost allocated to standard go-karts is

EXHIBIT 17.15

Comparison of Overhead
Allocations by Method

| Overhead Cost | Overhead Cost per Go-Kart | |
Allocation Method	Standard Go-Kart	Custom Go-Kart
Plantwide method............................	$720	$1,200
Departmental method	700	1,300
Activity-based costing	300	3,300

much less under ABC than under either of the volume-based costing methods. One reason for this difference is the large design modification costs that were spread over all go-karts under both the plantwide rate and the departmental rate methods even though standard go-karts require no design modification. When ABC is used, overhead costs commonly shift from standardized, high-volume products to low-volume, customized specialty products that consume more resources.

Differences between ABC and Multiple Departmental Rates   Using ABC differs from using multiple departmental rates in how overhead cost pools are identified and in how overhead cost in each pool is allocated. When using multiple departmental rates, each *department* is a cost pool, and overhead cost allocated to each department is assigned to products using a volume-based factor (such as direct labor hours or machine hours). This assumes that overhead costs in each department are directly proportional to the volume-based factor.

ABC, on the other hand, recognizes that overhead costs are more complex. For example, purchasing costs might make up one activity cost pool, spanning more than one department and being driven by a single cost driver (number of invoices). ABC emphasizes *activities* and costs of carrying out these activities. Therefore, ABC arguably better reflects the complex nature of overhead costs and how these costs are used in making products.

■ **Decision Maker**

Entrepreneur   You own a start-up pharmaceutical company. You assign overhead to products based on machine hours in the packaging area. Profits are slim due to increased competition. One of your larger overhead costs is $10,000 for cleaning and sterilization that occurs each time the packaging system is converted from one product to another. Can you reduce cleaning and sterilizing costs by reducing the number of units produced? If not, what should you do to control these overhead costs? ■   *Answer:* Cleaning and sterilizing costs are not directly related to the volume of product manufactured. Thus, changing the number of units produced does not necessarily reduce these costs. Costs of cleaning and sterilizing are related to changing from one product line to another. The way to control those costs is to control the number of times the packaging system has to be changed for a different product line. Thus, efficient product scheduling would help reduce those overhead costs and improve profitability.

A manufacturer makes two types of snowmobiles, Basic and Deluxe, and reports the following data to be used in applying activity-based costing. The company budgets production of 6,000 Basic snowmobiles and 2,000 Deluxe snowmobiles.

NEED-TO-KNOW 17-2

Activity-Based Costing

P3

Activity Cost Pool	Activity Cost Driver	Cost Assigned to Pool	Basic	Deluxe
Machine setup	Number of setups	$ 150,000	200 setups	300 setups
Materials handling	Number of parts	250,000	10 parts per unit	20 parts per unit
Machine depreciation	Machine hours (MH)	720,000	1 MH per unit	1.5 MH per unit
Total.................		$1,120,000		

1. Compute overhead activity rates for each activity cost pool using ABC.

2. Compute the total amount of overhead cost to be allocated to each of the company's product lines using ABC.

3. Compute the overhead cost per unit for each product line using ABC.

Solution

1. Machine setup activity rate $= \dfrac{\$150,000}{200 + 300} = \$300$ per machine setup

Materials handling activity rate $= \dfrac{\$250,000}{60,000 + 40,000*} = \$2.50$ per part

*(6,000 units × 10 parts per unit for Basic, 2,000 units × 20 parts per unit for Deluxe)

Machine depreciation activity rate $= \dfrac{\$720,000}{6,000 + 3,000^\dagger} = \$80$ per machine hour

†(6,000 units × 1 MH per unit for Basic, 2,000 units × 1.5 MH per unit for Deluxe)

2.

Activity Cost Pool	Activity Pool Rate	Basic		Deluxe	
Machine setup	$300 per setup	$300 × 200 =	$ 60,000	$300 × 300 =	$ 90,000
Materials handling	$2.50 per part	$2.50 × 6,000 × 10 =	150,000	$2.50 × 2,000 × 20 =	100,000
Machine depreciation..	$80 per MH	$80 × 6,000 × 1 =	480,000	$80 × 2,000 × 1.5 =	240,000
Totals..............			$690,000		$430,000

Do More: QS 17-13, QS 17-14, QS 17-15, E 17-4, E 17-14, E 17-15

3. Basic snowmobile overhead cost per unit $= \dfrac{\$690,000}{6,000} = \$115$ per unit

Deluxe snowmobile overhead cost per unit $= \dfrac{\$430,000}{2,000} = \$215$ per unit

Assessing Activity-Based Costing

A2

Identify and assess advantages and disadvantages of activity-based costing.

While activity-based costing can improve the accuracy of overhead cost allocations to products, it too has limitations. This section describes the major advantages and disadvantages of activity-based costing.

Advantages of Activity-Based Costing

More Effective Overhead Cost Control   KartCo's design modifications were costly. ABC can be used to identify activities that can benefit from process improvement by focusing on activities instead of focusing only on direct labor or machine hours. For KartCo, identification of large design modification costs would allow managers to work on ways to improve this process.

Better Production and Pricing Decisions   As in the KartCo example, ABC can provide more accurate overhead cost allocation. This is because ABC uses more cost pools and activity rates than other methods. More accurate costs allow managers to focus production activities on more profitable products and to set selling prices above product cost.

Additional Uses   ABC has uses beyond determining product costs. For example, ABC can be used to

©Paul Gilham/Getty Images

- Allocate the selling and administrative costs expensed by GAAP to activities; such costs can include marketing costs, order processing costs, and order return costs. Analyzing these activities and their costs can lead to cost reductions.
- Determine the profitability of various market segments or customers. Accurately assigning the costs of shipping, advertising, and customer service might reveal that some customers or segments should not be pursued. ABC provides better customer profitability information by including all the costs consumed to serve a customer. Many companies use ABC techniques for these analyses, even if they don't use ABC in determining overall product costs.

Disadvantages of Activity-Based Costing

Point: ABC is not acceptable under GAAP for external financial reporting.

Costs to Implement and Maintain ABC   Designing and implementing an ABC system is costly. For ABC to be effective, a thorough analysis of cost activities must be performed and appropriate cost pools must be determined. Collecting and analyzing cost data is expensive, and so is maintaining an ABC system. While technology, such as bar coding, has made it possible for many companies to use ABC, it is still too costly for some.

Some Product Cost Distortion Remains   Even with ABC, product costs can be distorted because

- Some costs cannot be readily classified into ABC cost pools.
- Some cost drivers may not have a strong cause-effect relation with the costs in some pools.

Uncertainty with Decisions Remains   Managers must interpret ABC data with caution in making decisions. In the KartCo case, given the huge design modification costs for custom go-karts determined under ABC, a manager might be tempted to decline some custom go-kart orders to save overhead costs. However, in the short run, some or all of the design modification costs cannot be saved even if some custom go-kart orders are rejected. Managers must examine carefully the controllability of costs before making decisions.

ACTIVITY-BASED MANAGEMENT

Activity Levels and Cost Management

Activities causing overhead costs can be separated into four levels: (1) **unit-level activities,** (2) **batch-level activities,** (3) **product-level activities,** and (4) **facility-level activities.** These four activities are described as follows.

C3

Describe the four types of activities that cause overhead costs.

Activity Levels

Unit-level activities are performed on each product unit. For example, the Machining department needs electricity to power the machinery to produce each unit of product. Unit-level costs tend to change with the number of units produced.

Craftsmanship

Setup

Batch-level activities are performed only on each batch or group of units. For example, machine setup is needed only for each batch regardless of the units in that batch, and customer order processing must be performed for each order regardless of the number of units ordered. Batch-level costs do not vary with the number of units, but instead vary with the number of batches.

Design Modification

Product-level activities are performed on each product line and are not affected by either the numbers of units or batches. For example, product design is needed only for each product line. Product-level costs do not vary with the number of units or batches produced.

Plant Services

Facility-level activities are performed to sustain facility capacity as a whole and are not caused by any specific product. For example, rent and factory maintenance costs are incurred no matter what is being produced. Facility-level costs do not vary with what is manufactured, the number of batches produced, or the output quantity.

In the KartCo example, the craftsmanship pool reflects unit-level costs, the setup pool reflects batch-level costs, the design modification pool reflects product-level costs, and plant services reflect facility-level costs. Exhibit 17.16 shows additional examples of activities commonly found within each of the four activity levels. This list also includes common activity drivers.

Understanding the four levels of overhead costs is a first step toward controlling costs. **Activity-based management (ABM)** is an outgrowth of ABC that uses the link between activities and costs for better management.

EXHIBIT 17.16

Examples of Activities
by Activity Level

Activity Level	Examples of Activity	Activity Driver (Measure)
Unit level	Cutting parts	Machine hours
	Assembling components	Direct labor hours
	Printing checks	Number of checks
Batch level	Calibrating machines	Number of batches
	Receiving shipments	Number of orders
	Sampling product quality	Number of lots produced
	Recycling hazardous waste	Tons recycled
Product level	Designing modifications	Change requests
	Organizing production	Engineering hours
	Controlling inventory	Parts per product
Facility level	Cleaning workplace	Square feet of floors*
	Providing electricity	Kilowatt hours*
	Providing personnel support	Number of employees*
	Reducing greenhouse gas emissions	Tons of CO_2

*Facility-level costs are not traceable to individual product lines, batches, or units. They are normally assigned to units
using a unit-level driver such as direct labor hours or machine hours even though they are caused by another activity.

Activity-based management can be useful in distinguishing **value-added activities,** which
add value to a product, from *non-value-added activities,* which do not. KartCo's value-added
activities include machining, assembly, and the costs of engineering design changes. Its non-
value-added activity is machine repair. ABM aids in cost control by reducing how much of an
activity is performed.

■ Decision Insight

The ABCs of Decisions   Business managers must make long-
term strategic decisions, day-to-day operating decisions, and decisions on the type of financing the business needs. Survey
evidence suggests that managers find ABC more useful in making
strategic, operating, and financing decisions than non-ABC methods. Managers using ABC also felt better able to apply activity-
based management. ■

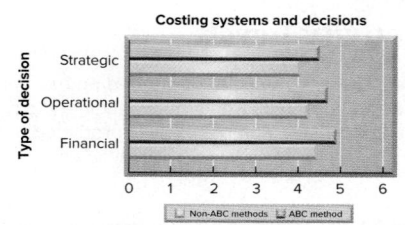

Average response: 0=Not useful, 6=Extremely useful
Source: Stratton et al., *Management Accounting Quarterly,* 2009.

Costs of Quality

A focus on the costs of activities, via ABC and ABM, lends itself to assessments of the **costs of
quality.** These costs refer to costs resulting from manufacturing defective products or providing
services that do not meet customer expectations.

Exhibit 17.17 summarizes the typical costs of quality. These costs can be summarized in a
cost of quality report, which lists the costs of quality activities by category. A focus on activities and quality costs can lead to higher quality and lower costs.

EXHIBIT 17.17

Types and Reporting
of Quality Costs

Costs of Good Quality

Prevention costs

Appraisal costs

Costs of Poor Quality

Internal failure costs

External failure costs

Cost of Quality Report	
Quality Activity	Cost
Prevention	
Training.....................	$ 22,000
Appraisal	
Inspecting materials...........	37,500
Testing finished goods..........	14,200
Internal failure	
Rework......................	8,250
Scrap.......................	11,750
External failure	
Warranty claims..............	45,700
Total cost of quality..............	$139,400

Costs of Good Quality   Prevention and appraisal costs are incurred before a good or service is provided to a customer. The purpose of these costs is to reduce the chance the customer is provided a defective good or service. These are the costs of trying to ensure that only good-quality items are produced.

Point: Prevention and appraisal costs are usually considered value-added costs, while internal and external costs are considered non-value-added costs.

- *Prevention* activities focus on quality training and improvement programs to ensure quality is built into the product or service.
- *Appraisal* activities include the costs of inspections to ensure that materials and supplies meet specifications and inspections of finished goods.

Costs of Poor Quality   Internal and external failure costs are the costs of making poor-quality items.

- *Internal failure costs* are incurred after a company has manufactured a defective product but before that product has been delivered to a customer. Internal failure costs include the costs of reworking products, reinspecting reworked products, and scrap.
- *External failure costs* are incurred after a customer has been provided a defective product or service. Examples of this type of cost include costs of warranty repairs and costs of recalling products. This category also includes lost profits due to dissatisfied customers buying from other companies.

Lean Manufacturing

Focusing on activities is common in *lean manufacturing,* which strives to eliminate waste while satisfying customers. Lean manufacturers produce to customer orders (a "pull" system) rather than to forecasted demand (a "push" system). Common features of lean manufacturing include

- Just-in-time (JIT) inventory systems to reduce the costs of moving and storing inventory. With JIT, raw materials are put into production after a customer order, and the finished goods are delivered soon after completion. This reduces the costs of storing and moving inventory.
- Cellular manufacturing, where products are made by teams of employees in small workstations ("cells"). Producing an entire product in one cell allows manufacturers to reduce machine setup times, produce in smaller batches, and meet customer orders more quickly.
- Building quality into products by focusing on the costs of good quality. Lean manufacturers do not have time to rework defective products and usually are not able to meet customer orders from inventory.

Many lean manufacturers embrace **lean accounting,** which typically includes

- Lean thinking to eliminate waste in the accounting process.
- Alternative performance measures, like the percentage of products made without defects and the percentage of on-time deliveries.
- Simplified product costing. With JIT, most of the product costs during a period will be included in cost of goods sold rather than in inventory. Instead of transferring costs across inventory accounts during a period, a **backflush costing** system measures the costs of inventory only at the end of the period. Costs of unfinished products are "flushed out" of Cost of Goods Sold and transferred to inventory accounts.

ABC for Service Providers

Although we've shown how to use ABC in a manufacturing setting, ABC also applies to service providers. The only requirements for ABC are the existence of costs and demand for reliable cost information. Shipping companies like **FedEx** and **UPS** use ABC to track the activities and costs involved with delivering packages. **Southwest Airlines** uses ABC to allocate costs to its passenger and ticketing cost pools. **First Tennessee National Corporation**, a bank, applied ABC and found that 30% of its certificate of deposit (CD) customers provided nearly 90% of its profits from CDs. Further, 30% of the bank's CD customers were actually losing money for the bank. The bank's management used ABC to correct the problem and increase profits.

Laboratories performing medical tests, accounting and law offices, and advertising agencies are other examples of service firms that can benefit from ABC. (Refer to this chapter's Decision Analysis for an example of applying ABC to assess customer profitability and this chapter's Comprehensive Need-to-Know for an example of applying ABC to a law firm.)

In applying ABC, service companies must classify costs by activity levels. Exhibit 17.18 shows typical activities within the four activity levels (unit, batch, service, and facility) for three service providers.

EXHIBIT 17.18

Examples of Activities for Service Providers

Activity Level	Sports Arena	Hotel	Online Education
Unit Level	Sell a ticket to a fan	Check in a guest	Register a student
Batch Level	Hire vendors and security for a game	Prepare buffet, receive supply shipments	Deliver an online course
Service Level	Schedule a season of games	Schedule personnel	Create a new course
Facility Level	Clean the arena, provide utilities, update the website	Clean rooms, maintain pool	Maintain course sites, control course data

©Gallo Images/Getty Images; ©Jade LLC/Blend Images; ©Prasit Rodphan/Shutterstock

 NEED-TO-KNOW 17-3

Activities Causing Overhead Costs

C3 ▶

Do More: QS 17-4, QS 17-5, E 17-1, E 17-2

Identify the activity levels of each of the following overhead activities as unit level (U), batch level (B), product or service level (P or S), or facility level (F).

_____ **1.** Cutting steel for go-kart frames
_____ **2.** Receiving shipments of tires
_____ **3.** Using electricity for equipment
_____ **4.** Modifying custom go-kart design
_____ **5.** Selling an airline ticket

_____ **6.** Painting go-karts
_____ **7.** Setting up machines for production
_____ **8.** Recycling hazardous waste
_____ **9.** Reducing water usage
_____ **10.** Creating a new online course

Solution

1. U **2.** B **3.** F **4.** P **5.** U **6.** U **7.** B **8.** B **9.** F **10.** S

 **SUSTAINABILITY AND ACCOUNTING**

Analyzing activities leads many companies to study **supply chain management,** which involves the coordination and control of goods, services, and information as they move from suppliers to consumers. A recent study by **Accenture** estimates that supply chains account for 50%–70% of total expenses and greenhouse gas emissions for most manufacturing companies. More effective supply chains can benefit the bottom line and the environment.

Walmart, in conjunction with The Sustainability Consortium™, developed an index to assess its suppliers' policies and programs related to sustainability. Companies with high scores on the index are identified as Sustainability Leaders on Walmart's website, enabling customers to readily identify and perhaps buy from companies committed to sustainable practices. Walmart, in conjunction with its suppliers, is meeting its goal of eliminating 20 million metric tons of greenhouse gases from its supply chain.

 Sarah Taylor Brigham and Justin Brigham, owners of **Sycamore Brewing,** this chapter's feature company, try to buy local ingredients whenever possible. "We want to contribute in a meaningful way to our community," says Justin. The company also impacts the people aspect of the triple bottom line by keeping production local and hiring from the Charlotte area.

©Sycamore Brewing

Customer Profitability  **Decision Analysis**

Are all customers equal? To answer this, let's return to KartCo and assume that costs of providing customer support (such as delivery, installation, and warranty work) are related to the distance a technician must travel to provide services. Also assume that, as a result of applying activity-based costing, KartCo plans to sell its standard go-kart for $1,200 per unit. If the annual cost of customer services is expected to be $250,000 and the distance traveled by technicians is 100,000 miles annually, KartCo would want to link the cost of customer services with individual customers to make efficient marketing decisions.

Using these data, an activity rate of $2.50 per mile ($250,000/100,000 miles) is computed for assigning customer service costs to individual customers. KartCo would compute a typical **customer profitability report** for one of its customers, Six Flags, as follows.

Customer Profitability Report—Six Flags		
Sales (10 standard go-karts × $1,200).		$12,000
Less: Product costs		
Direct materials (10 go-karts × $400 per go-kart)	$4,000	
Direct labor (10 go-karts × $350 per go-kart).	3,500	
Overhead (10 go-karts × $300 per go-kart, Exhibit 17.14)	3,000	10,500
Product profit margin		1,500
Less: Customer service costs (200 miles × $2.50 per mile)		500
Customer profit margin		$ 1,000

Analysis indicates that a total profit margin of $1,000 is generated from this customer. KartCo's management can see that if this customer requires service technicians to travel more than 600 miles ($1,500 ÷ $2.50 per mile), the sale of 10 standard go-karts to this customer would be unprofitable. ABC encourages management to consider all resources consumed to serve a customer, not just manufacturing costs that are the focus of traditional costing methods.

Silver Law Firm provides litigation and mediation services to a variety of clients. Attorneys keep track of the time they spend on each case, which is used to charge fees to clients at a rate of $300 per hour. A management advisor commented that activity-based costing might prove useful in evaluating the costs of its legal services, and the firm has decided to evaluate its fee structure by comparing ABC to its alternative cost allocations. The following data relate to a typical month at the firm. During a typical month, the firm handles seven mediation cases and three litigation cases.

NEED-TO-KNOW 17-4

COMPREHENSIVE

Overhead Allocation for a Service Provider

	Activity Driver	Total Amount	Consumption by Service Type		Activity Cost
			Litigation	Mediation	
Providing legal advice	Billable hours	200	75	125	$30,000
Overhead costs					
Internal support departments					
Preparing documents	Documents	30	16	14	$ 4,000
Occupying office space	Billable hours	200	75	125	1,200
Heating and lighting of office	Billable hours	200	75	125	350
External support departments					
Registering court documents	Documents	30	16	14	1,250
Retaining consultants					
(investigators, psychiatrists)	Court dates	6	5	1	10,000
Using contract services					
(couriers, security guards)	Court dates	6	5	1	5,000
Total overhead costs.					$21,800

Required

1. Determine the cost of providing legal services to each type of case using activity-based costing (ABC).

2. Determine the cost of each type of case using a single plantwide rate for nonattorney costs based on billable hours.

3. Determine the cost of each type of case using multiple departmental overhead rates for the internal support department (based on number of documents) and external support department (based on billable hours).

4. Compare and discuss the costs assigned under each method for management decisions.

PLANNING THE SOLUTION

- Compute pool rates and assign costs to cases using ABC.
- Compute costs for the cases using the volume-based methods and discuss differences between these costs and the costs computed using ABC.

SOLUTION

1. We need to set up activity pools and compute pool rates for ABC. All activities except "occupying office space" and "heating and lighting" are unit-level activities (meaning they are traceable to the individual cases handled by the law firm). "Preparing documents" and "registering documents" are both driven by the number of documents associated with each case. We can therefore combine these activities and their costs into a single pool, which we call "clerical support." Similarly, "retaining consultants" and "using services" are related to the number of times the attorneys must go to court (court dates). We combine these activities and their costs into another activity cost pool labeled "litigation support." The costs associated with occupying office space and the heating and lighting are facility-level activities and are not traceable to individual cases, yet they are costs that must be covered by fees charged to clients. We assign these costs using a convenient base—in this example we use the number of billable hours, which attorneys record for each client. Providing legal advice is the direct labor for a law firm.

Activity Cost Pools	Activity Cost	Pool Cost	Activity Driver	Pool Rate (Pool Cost ÷ Activity Driver)
Providing legal advice	$30,000	$30,000	200 billable hours	$150 per billable hour
Clerical support				
Preparing documents	4,000			
Registering documents	1,250	5,250	30 documents	$175 per document
Litigation support				
Retaining consultants	10,000			
Using services	5,000	15,000	6 court dates	$2,500 per court date
Facility costs				
Occupying office space	1,200			
Heating and lighting	350	1,550	200 billable hours	$7.75 per billable hour

We next determine the cost of providing each type of legal service as shown in the following table. Specifically, the pool rates from above are used to assign costs to each type of service provided by the law firm. Because litigation consumed 75 billable hours of attorney time, we assign $11,250 (75 billable hours × $150 per billable hour) of the cost of providing legal advice to this type of case. Mediation required 125 hours of attorney time, so $18,750 (125 billable hours × $150 per billable hour) of the cost to provide legal advice is assigned to mediation cases. Clerical support costs $175 per document, so the costs associated with activities in this cost pool are assigned to litigation cases (16 documents × $175 per document = $2,800) and mediation cases (14 documents × $175 per document = $2,450). The costs of activities in the litigation support and the facility cost pools are similarly assigned to the two case types.

We compute the total cost of litigation ($27,131.25) and mediation ($24,668.75) and divide these totals by the number of cases of each type to determine the average cost of each case type: $9,044 for litigation and $3,524 for mediation. This analysis shows that charging clients $300 per billable hour without regard to the type of case results in litigation clients being charged less than the cost to provide that service ($7,500 versus $9,044).

Activity Cost Pools	Pool Rate	Litigation		Mediation	
Providing legal advice	$150 per billable hour	75 hours	$11,250.00	125 hours	$18,750.00
Clerical support	$175 per document	16 docs	2,800.00	14 docs	2,450.00
Litigation support	$2,500 per court date	5 court dates	12,500.00	1 court date	2,500.00
Facility costs	$7.75 per billable hour	75 hours	581.25	125 hours	968.75
Total cost			$27,131.25		$24,668.75
÷ Number of cases			3 cases		7 cases
Average cost per case			**$9,044**		**$3,524**
Average fee per case			**$7,500***		**$5,357**†

*(75 billable hours × $300 per hour) ÷ 3 cases   †(125 billable hours × $300 per hour) ÷ 7 cases

2. The cost of each type of case using a single plantwide rate for nonattorney costs (that is, all costs except for those related to providing legal advice) based on billable hours is as follows.

> Total overhead cost/Total billable hours = $21,800/200 billable hours = $109 per hour

We then determine the cost of providing each type of legal service as follows.

			Litigation		Mediation	
Providing legal advice	$150 per billable hour	75 hours	$11,250	125 hours	$18,750
Overhead (from part 2)	$109 per billable hour	75 hours	8,175	125 hours	13,625
Total cost			$19,425		$32,375
÷ Number of cases			3 cases		7 cases
Average cost per case			**$6,475**		**$4,625**
Average fee per case (from part 1)			**$7,500**		**$5,357**

3. The cost of each type of case using multiple departmental overhead rates for the internal support department (based on number of documents) and external support department (based on billable hours) is determined as follows.

	Departmental Cost	Base	Departmental Rate (Departmental Cost ÷ Base)
Internal support department			
Preparing documents	$ 4,000		
Occupying office space	1,200		
Heating and lighting of office	350	$5,550	30 documents	$185 per document
External support department			
Registering documents	1,250		
Retaining consultants	10,000		
Using contract services	5,000	$16,250	200 billable hours	$81.25 per hour

The departmental overhead rates computed above are used to assign overhead costs to the two types of legal services. For the internal support department, we use the overhead rate of $185 per document to assign $2,960 ($185 × 16 documents) to litigation and $2,590 ($185 × 14 documents) to mediation. For the external support department, we use the overhead rate of $81.25 per hour to assign $6,093.75 ($81.25 × 75 hours) to litigation and $10,156.25 ($81.25 × 125 hours) to mediation. As shown below, the resulting average costs of litigation cases and mediation cases are $6,768 and $4,499, respectively. Using this method of cost assignment, it *appears* that the fee of $300 per billable hour is adequate to cover costs associated with each case.

			Litigation		Mediation	
Attorney fees	$150 per billable hour	75 hours	$11,250.00	125 hours	$18,750.00
Internal support	$185 per document	16 documents	2,960.00	14 documents	2,590.00
External support	$81.25 per hour	75 hours	6,093.75	125 hours	10,156.25
Total cost			$20,303.75		$31,496.25
÷ Number of cases			3 cases		7 cases
Average cost per case			**$6,768**		**$4,499**
Average fee per case (from part 1)			**$7,500**		**$5,357**

4. A comparison and discussion of the costs assigned under each method follows.

| | Method of Assigning Overhead Costs | | |
Average Cost per Case	Activity-Based Costing	Plantwide Overhead Rate	Departmental Overhead Rates
Litigation cases....................	$9,044	$6,475	$6,768
Mediation cases	3,524	4,625	4,499

The departmental and plantwide overhead rate methods assign overhead with volume-related measures (billable hours and document filings). Litigation cases *appear* profitable under these methods. ABC, however, focuses on activities that drive costs. A large part of overhead costs was for consultants and contract services, which were unrelated to the number of cases but related to the type of cases consuming those resources. Using ABC, the costs shift from the high-volume cases (mediation) to the low-volume cases (litigation). Using ABC, the fees charged to litigate cases is insufficient (average revenue of $7,500 versus average cost of $9,044). The law firm is charging too little for the complex cases that require litigation.

Summary: Cheat Sheet

ASSIGNING OVERHEAD COSTS

Plantwide rate method: Uses one overhead rate.

$$\text{Overhead rate} = \frac{\text{Total budgeted overhead cost}}{\text{Total budgeted amount of allocation base}}$$

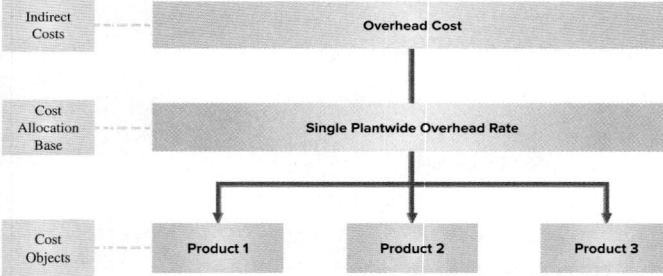

Departmental overhead rate method: Uses different overhead rates for each department.

$$\text{Departmental overhead rate} = \frac{\text{Total budgeted departmental overhead cost}}{\text{Total amount of departmental allocation base}}$$

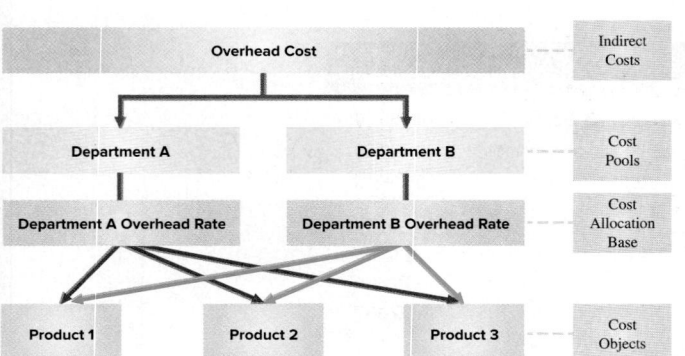

ACTIVITY-BASED COSTING

Activity cost pool: Collection of costs that are related to the same activity.
Activity cost driver: Activity that causes costs in the pool to be incurred.

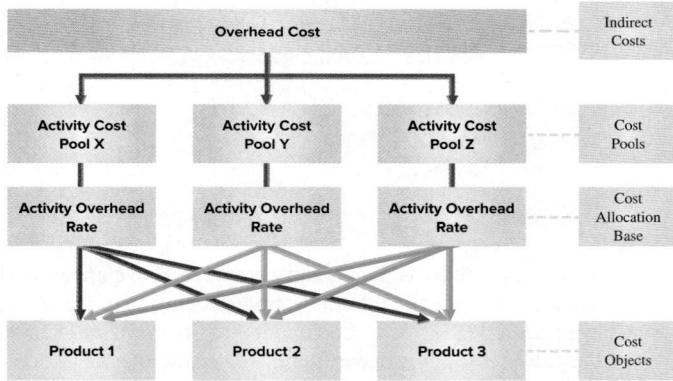

Four Steps of ABC costing:
1. Identify activities and the costs they cause.
2. Trace overhead costs to activity cost pools.
3. Compute overhead rates for each activity.

> Cost pool activity rate = Overhead costs assigned to pool ÷ Expected activity level

4. Use activity overhead rates to assign overhead costs to cost objects.

$$\frac{\text{Overhead}}{\text{allocated}} = \frac{\text{Activities}}{\text{consumed}} \times \frac{\text{Activity}}{\text{rate}}$$

ACTIVITY LEVELS

Unit—performed on each unit.
Batch—performed on batches or groups of units.
Product—performed on each product line.
Facility—performed to sustain facility capacity.

COSTS OF QUALITY

Prevention—Training and quality improvement ⎫ [Good quality]
Appraisal—Inspections ⎭
Internal failure—Rework and scrap
External failure—Warranty claims, recalls, ⎫ [Poor quality]
       dissatisfied customers ⎭

Key Terms

Activity (663)
Activity-based costing (ABC) (663)
Activity-based management (ABM) (669)
Activity cost driver (664)
Activity cost pool (663)
Activity overhead (cost pool) rate (664)

Backflush costing (671)
Batch-level activities (669)
Cost object (658)
Cost of quality report (670)
Costs of quality (670)
Facility-level activities (669)

Lean accounting (671)
Product-level activities (669)
Supply chain management (672)
Unit-level activities (669)
Value-added activities (670)

Multiple Choice Quiz

1. In comparison to a traditional cost system, and when there are batch-level or product-level costs, an activity-based costing system usually shifts costs from
  a. Low-volume to high-volume products.
  b. High-volume to low-volume products.
  c. Standardized to specialized products.
  d. Specialized to standardized products.

2. Which of the following statements is true?
  a. An activity-based costing system is generally easier to implement and maintain than a traditional costing system.
  b. Activity-based management eliminates waste by allocating costs to products that waste resources.
  c. Activity-based costing uses a single rate to allocate overhead.
  d. Activity rates in activity-based costing are computed by dividing costs from the first-stage allocations by the activity measure for each activity cost pool.

3. All of the following are examples of batch-level activities except
  a. Purchase order processing.
  b. Setting up equipment.
  c. Clerical activity associated with processing purchase orders to produce an order for a standard product.
  d. Employee recreational facilities.

4. A company has two products: A and B. It uses activity-based costing and prepares the following analysis showing budgeted cost and activity for each of its three activity cost pools.

Activity Cost Pool	Budgeted Overhead Cost	Budgeted Activity Product A	Budgeted Activity Product B	Total
Activity 1	$ 80,000	200	800	1,000
Activity 2	58,400	1,000	500	1,500
Activity 3	360,000	600	5,400	6,000

The annual production and sales level of Product A is 18,188 units, and the annual production and sales level of Product B is 31,652 units. The approximate overhead cost per unit of Product B under activity-based costing is
  a. $2.02.   **c.** $12.87.
  b. $5.00.   **d.** $22.40.

5. A company uses activity-based costing to determine the costs of its two products: A and B. The budgeted cost and activity for each of the company's three activity cost pools follow.

Activity Cost Pool	Budgeted Cost	Budgeted Activity Product A	Budgeted Activity Product B	Total
Activity 1	$19,800	800	300	1,100
Activity 2	16,000	2,200	1,800	4,000
Activity 3	14,000	400	300	700

The activity rate under the activity-based costing method for Activity 3 is
  a. $4.00.   **c.** $18.00.
  b. $8.59.   **d.** $20.00.

ANSWERS TO MULTIPLE CHOICE QUIZ

1. b; Under traditional costing methods, overhead costs are allocated to products on the basis of some measure of volume such as direct labor hours or machine hours. This results in much of the overhead cost being allocated to high-volume products. In contrast, under activity-based costing, some overhead costs are allocated on the basis of batch-level or product-level activities. This change in allocation bases results in shifting overhead costs from high-volume products to low-volume products.

2. d; Generally, an activity-based costing system is more difficult to implement and maintain than a traditional costing system (thus answer **a** is false). Instead of eliminating waste by allocating costs to products that waste resources, activity-based management is a management approach that focuses on managing activities as a means of eliminating waste and reducing delays and defects (thus answer **b** is false). Instead of using a single allocation base (such as direct labor hours), activity-based costing uses a number of allocation bases for assigning costs to products (thus answer **c** is false). Answer **d** is true.

3. d; Batch-level activities are activities that are performed each time a batch of goods is handled or processed, regardless of how many units are in a batch. Further, the amount of resources consumed depends on the number of batches rather than on the number of units in the batch. Worker recreational facilities relate to the organization as a whole rather than to specific batches and, as such, are not considered to be batch level. On the other hand, purchase order processing, setting up equipment, and the clerical activities described are activities that are performed each time a batch of goods is handled or processed, and, as such, are batch-level activities.

4. c;

Activity Cost Pools	(A) Activity Rate (Budgeted overhead cost ÷ Budgeted activity)	(B) Actual Activity	(A × B) Overhead Cost Applied to Production
Activity 1.....	($80,000 ÷ 1,000) = $80.00	800	$ 64,000
Activity 2.....	($58,400 ÷ 1,500) = $38.93*	500	19,465
Activity 3.....	($360,000 ÷ 6,000) = $60.00	5,400	324,000
Total overhead cost for Product B			$407,465
Number of units produced...............................			÷ 31,652
Overhead cost per unit of Product B			$ 12.87*

*Rounded

5. d; The activity rate for Activity 3 is determined as follows:

$$\text{Budgeted cost} \div \text{Budgeted activity} = \text{Activity rate}$$
$$\$14,000 \quad \div \quad 700 \quad = \quad \$20$$

🔲 Icon denotes assignments that involve decision making.

Discussion Questions

1. Why are overhead costs allocated to products and not traced to products as direct materials and direct labor are?

2. What are three common methods of assigning overhead costs to a product?

3. Why are direct labor hours and machine hours commonly used as the bases for overhead allocation?

4. What are the advantages of using a single plantwide overhead rate?

5. The usefulness of a single plantwide overhead rate is based on two assumptions. What are those assumptions?

6. What is a cost object?

7. 🔲 Explain why a single plantwide overhead rate can distort the cost of a particular product.

8. 🔲 Why are multiple departmental overhead rates more accurate for product costing than a single plantwide overhead rate?

9. In what way are departmental overhead rates similar to a single plantwide overhead rate? How are they different?

10. Why is overhead allocation under ABC usually more accurate than either the plantwide overhead allocation method or the departmental overhead allocation method?

11. 🔲 **Google** reports costs in financial state-ments. If plantwide overhead rates are allowed for reporting costs to external users, why might a company choose to use a more complicated and more expensive method for assigning overhead costs to products? **GOOGLE**

12. What is the first step in applying activity-based costing?

13. What is an activity cost driver?

14. **Apple**'s production requires activities. What are value-added activities? **APPLE**

15. What are the four activity levels associated with activity-based costing? Define each.

16. 🔲 **Samsung** is a manufacturer. "Activity-based costing is only useful for manufacturing companies." Is this a true statement? Explain. **Samsung**

17. 🔲 **Apple** must assign overhead costs to its products. Activity-based costing is generally considered more accurate than other methods of assigning overhead. If this is so, why don't all manufacturing companies use it? **APPLE**

18. **Toyota** embraces lean techniques, including lean accounting. What are the key components of lean accounting?

📊 **connect**

QUICK STUDY

QS 17-1
Overhead cost allocation methods

C1

In the blank next to each of the following terms, place the letter *A* through *D* that corresponds to the description of that term. Some letters are used more than once.

_____ **1.** Activity-based costing

_____ **2.** Plantwide overhead rate method

_____ **3.** Departmental overhead rate method

A. Uses more than one rate to allocate overhead costs to products.

B. Uses only volume-based measures such as direct labor hours to allocate overhead costs to products.

C. Typically uses the most overhead allocation rates.

D. Focuses on the costs of carrying out activities.

1. Which costing method assumes all products use overhead costs in the same proportions?

    a. Activity-based costing   **c.** Departmental overhead rate method

    b. Plantwide overhead rate method   **d.** All cost allocation methods

2. Which of the following would usually *not* be used in computing plantwide overhead rates?

    a. Direct labor hours   **c.** Direct labor dollars

    b. Number of quality inspections   **d.** Machine hours

3. With ABC, overhead costs should be traced to which cost object first?

    a. Units of product   **c.** Activities

    b. Departments   **d.** Product batches

QS 17-2

Cost allocation methods

C1

In the blank next to the following terms, place the letter *A* through *D* that corresponds to the best description of that term.

    _____ **1.** Activity   **A.** Measurement associated with an activity.

    _____ **2.** Activity driver   **B.** A group of costs that have the same activity drivers.

    _____ **3.** Cost object   **C.** Anything to which costs will be assigned.

    _____ **4.** Cost pool   **D.** A task that causes a cost to be incurred.

QS 17-3

Costing terminology

C2

Classify each of the following activities as unit level (U), batch level (B), product level (P), or facility level (F) for a manufacturer of organic juices.

    _____ **1.** Cutting fruit   _____ **4.** Receiving fruit shipments

    _____ **2.** Developing new types of juice   _____ **5.** Cleaning blending machines

    _____ **3.** Blending fruit into juice   _____ **6.** Reducing water usage

QS 17-4

Identifying activity levels

C3

Classify each of the following activities as unit level (U), batch level (B), product level (P), or facility level (F) for a manufacturer of trail mix.

    _____ **1.** Roasting peanuts   _____ **4.** Providing utilities for factory

    _____ **2.** Cleaning roasting machines   _____ **5.** Calibrating mixing machines

    _____ **3.** Sampling product quality   _____ **6.** Reducing electricity usage

QS 17-5

Identifying activity levels

C3

Which of the following are advantages of the plantwide and departmental overhead rate methods? Indicate advantages with an **A** and disadvantages with a **D**.

    _____ **1.** They are based on readily available information.

    _____ **2.** They can be used for external financial reporting.

    _____ **3.** Overhead costs are too complex to be explained by only one factor.

    _____ **4.** They violate GAAP.

    _____ **5.** They are easy to implement.

QS 17-6

Advantages of plantwide and departmental rate methods

A1

---

1. If management wants the most accurate product cost, which of the following costing methods should be used?

    a. Volume-based costing using departmental overhead rates

    b. Volume-based costing using a plantwide overhead rate

    c. Normal costing using a plantwide overhead rate

    d. Activity-based costing

2. Which costing method tends to overstate the cost of high-volume products?

    a. Traditional volume-based costing   **c.** Job order costing

    b. Activity-based costing   **d.** Differential costing

3. Disadvantages of activity-based costing include

    a. It is not acceptable under GAAP   **c.** It can be used in activity-based
        for external reporting.   management.

    b. It can be costly to implement.   **d.** Both a. and b.

QS 17-7

Multiple choice overhead questions

A2

QS 17-8
Costs of quality
A2

A list of activities that generate quality costs is provided below. For each activity, indicate whether it relates to a prevention (P), appraisal (A), internal failure (I), or external failure (E) activity.

_____ **1.** Inspecting raw materials

_____ **2.** Training workers in quality techniques

_____ **3.** Collecting data on a manufacturing process

_____ **4.** Overtime labor to rework products

_____ **5.** Cost of additional materials to rework a product

_____ **6.** Inspecting finished goods inventory

_____ **7.** Scrapping defective goods

_____ **8.** Lost sales due to customer dissatisfaction

QS 17-9
Plantwide rate method
P1

A manufacturer uses machine hours to assign overhead costs to products. Budgeted information for the next year follows. Compute the plantwide overhead rate for the next year based on machine hours.

Budgeted factory overhead costs	$544,000
Budgeted machine hours.	6,400

QS 17-10
Computing plantwide overhead rates
P1

Rafner Manufacturing identified the following budgeted data in its two production departments.

	Assembly	Finishing
Manufacturing overhead costs	$1,200,000	$600,000
Direct labor hours.	12,000 DLH	20,000 DLH
Machine hours	6,000 MH	16,000 MH

1. What is the company's single plantwide overhead rate based on direct labor hours?

2. What is the company's single plantwide overhead rate based on machine hours? (Round your answer to two decimal places.)

QS 17-11
Computing departmental overhead rates **P2**

Refer to the information in QS 17-10. What is the company's Assembly department overhead rate using direct labor hours?

QS 17-12
Computing departmental overhead rates **P2**

Refer to the information in QS 17-10. What is the company's Finishing department overhead rate using machine hours?

QS 17-13
Computing activity rates
P3

A manufacturer uses activity-based costing to assign overhead costs to products. Budgeted cost information for selected activities for next year follows. Form two cost pools and compute activity rates for each of the cost pools.

Activity	Expected Cost	Cost Driver	Expected Usage of Cost Driver
Purchasing	$135,000	Purchase orders	4,500 purchase orders
Cleaning factory	32,000	Square feet	5,000 square feet
Providing utilities	65,000	Square feet	5,000 square feet

---

QS 17-14
Assigning service costs using ABC
P3

Aziz Company sells two types of products, basic and deluxe. The company provides technical support for users of its products at an expected cost of $250,000 per year. The company expects to process 10,000 customer service calls per year.

1. Determine the company's cost of technical support per customer service call.

2. During the month of January, Aziz received 550 calls for customer service on its deluxe model and 250 calls for customer service on its basic model. Assign technical support costs to each model using activity-based costing (ABC).

A company uses activity-based costing to determine the costs of its three products: A, B, and C. The budgeted cost and cost driver activity for each of the company's three activity cost pools follow. Compute the activity rates for each of the company's three activities.

QS 17-15
Computing activity rates
P3

Activity Cost Pools	Budgeted Cost	Budgeted Activity of Cost Driver		
		Product A	Product B	Product C
Activity 1	$140,000	20,000	9,000	6,000
Activity 2	$ 90,000	8,000	15,000	7,000
Activity 3	$ 82,000	1,625	1,000	2,500

A manufacturer uses activity-based costing to assign overhead costs to products. In the coming year, it expects to incur $825,000 of costs to dispose of 3,300 tons of hazardous waste.

1. Compute the company's cost of hazardous waste disposal per ton.

2. During the year, the company disposes of 5 tons of hazardous waste in the completion of Job 125. Assign hazardous waste disposal cost to Job 125 using activity-based costing.

QS 17-16
Activity-based costing

P3

connect

Identify each of the following activities as unit level (U), batch level (B), product level (P), or facility level (F) to indicate the way each is incurred with respect to production.

_____ **1.** Paying real estate taxes on the factory building
_____ **2.** Attaching labels to collars of shirts
_____ **3.** Redesigning a bicycle seat
_____ **4.** Cleaning the Assembly department

_____ **5.** Polishing gold wedding rings
_____ **6.** Mixing bread dough in a commercial bakery
_____ **7.** Sampling cookies to determine quality
_____ **8.** Recycling hazardous waste
_____ **9.** Reducing greenhouse gas emissions

EXERCISES

Exercise 17-1
Identifying activity levels

C3

Following are activities in providing medical services at Healthsmart Clinic.

A. Registering patients
B. Cleaning beds
C. Stocking examination rooms
D. Washing linens

E. Ordering medical equipment
F. Heating the clinic
G. Providing security services
H. Filling prescriptions

Classify each activity as unit level (U), batch level (B), service level (S), or facility level (F).

Exercise 17-2
Classifying activities

C3

Xie Company identified the following activities, costs, and activity drivers for this year. The company manufactures two types of go-karts: deluxe and basic.

Exercise 17-3
Computing plantwide overhead rates

P1

Activity	Expected Costs	Expected Activity
Handling materials	$625,000	100,000 parts
Inspecting product	900,000	1,500 batches
Processing purchase orders.	105,000	700 orders
Paying suppliers	175,000	500 invoices
Insuring the factory.	300,000	40,000 square feet
Designing packaging	75,000	2 models

Required

1. Compute a single plantwide overhead rate for the year, assuming that the company assigns overhead based on 125,000 budgeted direct labor hours.

2. In January of this year, the deluxe model required 2,500 direct labor hours and the basic model required 6,000 direct labor hours. Assign overhead costs to each model using the single plantwide overhead rate.

Refer to the information in Exercise 17-3. Compute the activity rate for each activity, assuming the company uses activity-based costing.

Exercise 17-4
Computing overhead rates
under ABC   **P3**

Exercise 17-5
Assigning costs using ABC
P3

Refer to the information in Exercise 17-3. Assume that the following information is available for the company's two products for the first quarter of this year.

	Deluxe Model	Basic Model
Production volume	10,000 units	30,000 units
Parts required	20,000 parts	30,000 parts
Batches made	250 batches	100 batches
Purchase orders	50 orders	20 orders
Invoices	50 invoices	10 invoices
Space occupied	10,000 square feet	7,000 square feet
Models.	1 model	1 model

Required

Compute activity rates for each activity and assign overhead costs to each product model using activity-based costing (ABC). What is the overhead cost per unit of each model?

Exercise 17-6
Plantwide overhead rate
P1

Textra Plastics produces parts for a variety of small machine manufacturers. Most products go through two operations, molding and trimming, before they are ready for packaging. Expected costs and activities for the Molding department and for the Trimming department for this year follow.

	Molding	Trimming
Direct labor hours	52,000 DLH	48,000 DLH
Machine hours	30,500 MH	3,600 MH
Overhead costs.	$730,000	$590,000

Data for two special-order parts to be manufactured by the company in this year follow.

	Part A27C	Part X82B
Number of units	9,800 units	54,500 units
Machine hours: Molding	5,100 MH	1,020 MH
Trimming	2,600 MH	650 MH
Direct labor hours: Molding	5,500 DLH	2,150 DLH
Trimming	700 DLH	3,500 DLH

Required

1. Compute the plantwide overhead rate using direct labor hours as the base.
2. Determine the overhead cost assigned to each product line using the plantwide rate computed in requirement 1.

Exercise 17-7
Departmental overhead rates
P2

Refer to the information in Exercise 17-6.

Required

1. Compute a departmental overhead rate for the Molding department based on machine hours and a department overhead rate for the Trimming department based on direct labor hours.
2. Determine the total overhead cost assigned to each product line using the departmental overhead rates from requirement 2.
3. Determine the overhead cost per unit for each product line using the departmental rate.

Exercise 17-8
Using the plantwide overhead rate to assess prices   **P1**

Way Cool produces two different models of air conditioners. The company produces the mechanical systems in its Components department. The mechanical systems are combined with the housing assembly in its Finishing department. The activities, costs, and drivers associated with these two manufacturing processes and the production support process follow.

Process	Activity	Overhead Cost	Driver	Quantity
Components	Changeover	$ 500,000	Number of batches	800
	Machining	279,000	Machine hours	6,000
	Setups	225,000	Number of setups	120
		$1,004,000		
Finishing	Welding	$ 180,300	Welding hours	3,000
	Inspecting	210,000	Number of inspections	700
	Rework	75,000	Rework orders	300
		$ 465,300		
Support	Purchasing	$ 135,000	Purchase orders	450
	Providing space	32,000	Number of units	5,000
	Providing utilities	65,000	Number of units	5,000
		$ 232,000		

Additional production information concerning its two product lines follows.

	Model 145	Model 212
Units produced	1,500	3,500
Welding hours	800	2,200
Batches	400	400
Number of inspections	400	300
Machine hours	1,800	4,200
Setups	60	60
Rework orders	160	140
Purchase orders	300	150

Required

1. Using a plantwide overhead rate based on machine hours, compute the overhead cost per unit for each product line.
2. Determine the total cost per unit for each product line if the direct labor and direct materials costs per unit are $250 for Model 145 and $180 for Model 212.
3. If the market price for Model 145 is $820 and the market price for Model 212 is $480, determine the profit or loss per unit for each model.

Check   (3) Model 212, $(40.26) per unit loss

Refer to the information in Exercise 17-8 to answer the following requirements.

Required

1. Determine departmental overhead rates and compute the overhead cost per unit for each product line. Base your overhead assignment for the Components department on machine hours. Use welding hours to assign overhead costs to the Finishing department. Assign costs to the Support department based on number of purchase orders.
2. Determine the total cost per unit for each product line if the direct labor and direct materials costs per unit are $250 for Model 145 and $180 for Model 212.
3. If the market price for Model 145 is $820 and the market price for Model 212 is $480, determine the profit or loss per unit for each model.

Exercise 17-9
Using departmental overhead rates to assess prices

P2

Check   (3) Model 212, $(20.38) per unit loss

Laval produces lamps and home lighting fixtures. Its most popular product is a brushed aluminum desk lamp. This lamp is made from components shaped in the Fabricating department and assembled in the Assembly department. Information related to the 35,000 desk lamps produced annually follows.

Direct materials.	$280,000
Direct labor: Fabricating department (7,000 DLH × $20 per DLH)	$140,000
Assembly department (16,000 DLH × $29 per DLH)	$464,000
Machine hours: Fabricating department	15,040 MH
Assembly department	21,000 MH

Exercise 17-10
Assigning overhead costs using the plantwide rate and departmental rate methods

P1   P2

Expected overhead cost and related data for the two production departments follow.

	Fabricating	Assembly
Direct labor hours..	75,000 DLH	125,000 DLH
Machine hours	80,000 MH	62,500 MH
Overhead cost...	$300,000	$200,000

Required

Check   (2) $26.90 per unit

1. Determine the plantwide overhead rate for Laval using direct labor hours as a base.
2. Determine the total manufacturing cost per unit for the aluminum desk lamp using the plantwide overhead rate.
3. Compute departmental overhead rates based on machine hours in the Fabricating department and direct labor hours in the Assembly department.

(4) $27.60 per unit

4. Use departmental overhead rates from requirement 3 to determine the total manufacturing cost per unit for the aluminum desk lamps.

Exercise 17-11

Using ABC to assess prices

P3

Refer to the information in Exercise 17-8 to answer the following requirements.

Required

1. Using ABC, compute the overhead cost per unit for each product line.
2. Determine the total cost per unit for each product line if the direct labor and direct materials costs per unit are $250 for Model 145 and $180 for Model 212.

Check   (3) Model 212,
$34.88 per unit profit

3. If the market price for Model 145 is $820 and the market price for Model 212 is $480, determine the profit or loss per unit for each model.

Exercise 17-12

Using ABC for strategic decisions

P1   P3

Consider the following data for two products of Gitano Manufacturing.

	Overhead Cost	Product A	Product B
Number of units produced.....................		10,000 units	2,000 units
Direct labor cost (@ $24 per DLH)..............		0.20 DLH per unit	0.25 DLH per unit
Direct materials cost		$2 per unit	$3 per unit
Activity: Machine setup	$121,000		
Materials handling	48,000		
Quality control inspections.............	80,000		
	$249,000		

Required

1. Using direct labor hours as the basis for assigning overhead costs, determine the total production cost per unit for each product line.

Check   (2) Product B,
$26.10 per unit profit

2. If the market price for Product A is $20 and the market price for Product B is $60, determine the profit or loss per unit for each product. Comment on the results.
3. Consider the following additional information about these two product lines. If ABC is used for assigning overhead costs to products, what is the cost per unit for Product A and for Product B?

	Product A	Product B
Number of setups required for production	10 setups	12 setups
Number of parts required...........................	1 part/unit	3 parts/unit
Inspection hours required	40 hours	210 hours

(4) Product B, $(24.60) per
unit loss

4. Determine the profit or loss per unit for each product. Should this information influence company strategy (yes or no)?

Smythe Co. makes furniture. The following data are taken from its production plans for the year.

Direct labor costs	$5,870,000
Hazardous waste disposal costs	630,000

Exercise 17-13
Comparing costs under
ABC to traditional
plantwide overhead rate

P1 P3

	Chairs	Tables
Expected production	211,000 units	17,000 units
Direct labor hours required	254,000 DLH	16,400 DLH
Hazardous waste disposed	200 pounds	800 pounds

Required

1. Determine the hazardous waste disposal cost per unit for chairs and for tables if costs are assigned using a single plantwide overhead rate based on direct labor hours.
2. Determine hazardous waste disposal costs per unit for chairs and for tables if costs are assigned based on the number of pounds disposed of.

Check (2) Tables, $29.65 per unit

The following is taken from Ronda Co.'s internal records of its factory with two production departments. The cost driver for indirect labor and supplies is direct labor costs, and the cost driver for the remaining overhead items is number of hours of machine use. Compute the total amount of overhead cost allocated to Department 1 using activity-based costing.

Exercise 17-14
Activity-based costing and
overhead cost allocation

P3

	Direct Labor	Machine Use Hours
Department 1	$18,800	2,000
Department 2	13,200	1,200
Totals	$32,000	3,200
Factory overhead costs		
Rent and utilities	$12,200	
Indirect labor	5,400	
General office expense	4,000	
Depreciation—Equipment	3,000	
Supplies	2,600	
Total factory overhead	$27,200	

Check Dept. 1 allocation, $16,700

A company has two products: standard and deluxe. The company expects to produce 36,375 standard units and 62,240 deluxe units. It uses activity-based costing and has prepared the following analysis showing budgeted cost and cost driver activity for each of its three activity cost pools.

Exercise 17-15
Activity-based costing rates
and allocations

P3

		Budgeted Activity of Cost Driver	
Activity Cost Pool	Budgeted Cost	Standard	Deluxe
Activity 1	$93,000	2,500	5,250
Activity 2	$92,000	4,500	5,500
Activity 3	$87,000	3,000	2,800

Required

1. Compute overhead rates for each of the three activities.
2. What is the expected overhead cost per unit for the standard units?
3. What is the expected overhead cost per unit for the deluxe units?

Exercise 17-16
Using ABC in a service company
P3

Cardiff and Delp is an architectural firm that provides services for residential construction projects. The following data pertain to a recent reporting period.

	Activities	Costs
Design department: Client consultation	1,500 contact hours	$270,000
Drawings.............................	2,000 design hours	115,000
Modeling	40,000 square feet	30,000
Project management department: Supervision	600 days	$120,000
Billing	8 jobs	10,000
Collections	8 jobs	12,000

Required

Check (2) $150,200

1. Using ABC, compute the firm's activity overhead rates. Form activity cost pools where appropriate.
2. Assign costs to a 9,200-square-foot job that requires 450 contact hours, 340 design hours, and 200 days to complete.

Exercise 17-17
Activity-based costing
P3

Glassworks Inc. produces two types of glass shelving, rounded edge and squared edge, on the same production line. For the current period, the company reports the following data.

	Rounded Edge	Squared Edge	Total
Direct materials	$19,000	$ 43,200	$ 62,200
Direct labor.............................	12,200	23,800	36,000
Overhead (300% of direct labor cost)	36,600	71,400	108,000
Total cost.....................	$67,800	$138,400	$206,200
Quantity produced	10,500 ft.	14,100 ft.	
Average cost per ft. (rounded)................	$ 6.46	$ 9.82	

Glassworks's controller wishes to apply activity-based costing (ABC) to allocate the $108,000 of overhead costs incurred by the two product lines to see whether cost per foot would change markedly from that reported above. She has collected the following information.

Overhead Cost Category (Activity Cost Pool)	Cost
Supervision	$ 5,400
Depreciation of machinery...	56,600
Assembly line preparation	46,000
Total overhead	$108,000

She also has collected the following information about the cost drivers for each category (cost pool) and the amount of each driver used by the two product lines.

Overhead Cost Category (Activity Cost Pool)	Driver	Usage		
		Rounded Edge	Squared Edge	Total
Supervision	Direct labor cost ($)	$12,200	$23,800	$36,000
Depreciation of machinery	Machine hours	500 hours	1,500 hours	2,000 hours
Assembly line preparation	Setups (number)	40 times	210 times	250 times

Required

Check (2) Rounded edge, $5.19; Squared edge, $10.76

1. Assign these three overhead cost pools to each of the two products using ABC.
2. Determine average cost per foot for each of the two products using ABC.

Surgery Center is an outpatient surgical clinic that was profitable for many years, but Medicare has cut its reimbursements by as much as 40%. As a result, the clinic wants to better understand its costs. It decides to prepare an activity-based cost analysis, including an estimate of the average cost of both general surgery and orthopedic surgery. The clinic's three activity cost pools and their cost drivers follow.

Exercise 17-18
Activity-based costing
P3

Activity Cost Pool	Cost	Cost Driver	Driver Quantity
Professional salaries..................	$1,600,000	Professional hours	10,000
Patient services and supplies	27,000	Number of patients	600
Building cost	150,000	Square feet	1,500

The two main surgical units and their related data follow.

Service	Hours	Square Feet*	Patients
General surgery	2,500	600	400
Orthopedic surgery......................	7,500	900	200

*Orthopedic surgery requires more space for patients, supplies, and equipment.

Required

1. Compute the cost per cost driver for each of the three activity cost pools.

2. Use the results from part 1 to allocate costs to both the General surgery and the Orthopedic surgery units. Compute total cost and average cost per patient for both the General surgery and the Orthopedic surgery units.

Check   (2) Average cost of General (Orthopedic) surgery, $1,195 ($6,495) per patient

connect

The following data are for the two products produced by Tadros Company.

PROBLEM SET A

Problem 17-1A
Comparing costs using ABC with the plantwide overhead rate
A1   A2   P1   P3

	Product A	Product B
Direct materials....................	$15 per unit	$24 per unit
Direct labor hours..................	0.3 DLH per unit	1.6 DLH per unit
Machine hours	0.1 MH per unit	1.2 MH per unit
Batches..........................	125 batches	225 batches
Volume	10,000 units	2,000 units
Engineering modifications	12 modifications	58 modifications
Number of customers..............	500 customers	400 customers
Market price	$30 per unit	$120 per unit

The company's direct labor rate is $20 per direct labor hour (DLH). Additional information follows.

	Costs	Driver
Indirect manufacturing		
Engineering support	$24,500	Engineering modifications
Electricity	34,000	Machine hours
Setup costs	52,500	Batches
Nonmanufacturing		
Customer service.............	81,000	Number of customers

Required

1. Compute the manufacturing cost per unit using the plantwide overhead rate based on direct labor hours. What is the gross profit per unit?

2. How much gross profit is generated by each customer of Product A using the plantwide overhead rate? How much gross profit is generated by each customer of Product B using the plantwide overhead rate?

3. What is the cost of providing customer service to each customer?

4. Determine the manufacturing cost per unit of each product line using ABC. What is the gross profit per unit?

5. How much gross profit is generated by each customer of Product A using ABC? How much gross profit is generated by each customer of Product B using ABC? Is the gross profit per customer adequate? Is the gross profit per customer for each of these products greater than the cost of providing customer service?

Check   (1) Product A, $26.37 per unit cost

(3) Product A, $24.30 per unit cost

Problem 17-2A
Assessing impacts of using a plantwide overhead rate versus ABC

A1   A2

Xylon Company manufactures custom-made furniture for its local market and produces a line of home furnishings sold in retail stores across the country. The company uses traditional volume-based methods of assigning direct materials and direct labor to its product lines. Overhead has always been assigned by using a plantwide overhead rate based on direct labor hours. In the past few years, management has seen its line of retail products continue to sell at high volumes, but competition has forced it to lower prices on these items. The prices are declining to a level close to its cost of production.

Meanwhile, its custom-made furniture is in high demand, and customers have commented on its favorable (lower) prices compared to its competitors. Management is considering dropping its line of retail products and devoting all of its resources to custom-made furniture.

Required

1. What reasons could explain why competitors are forcing the company to lower prices on its high-volume retail products?

2. Why do you believe the company charges less for custom-order products than its competitors?

3. Does a company's costing method have any effect on its pricing decisions? Explain.

4. Aside from the differences in volume of output, what production differences do you believe exist between making custom-order furniture and mass-market furnishings?

5. What information might the company obtain from using ABC that it might not obtain using volume-based costing methods?

Problem 17-3A
Applying activity-based costing

C3   A1   A2   P1   P3

Craft Pro Machining produces machine tools for the construction industry. The following details about overhead costs were taken from its company records.

Production Activity	Indirect Labor	Indirect Materials	Other Overhead
Grinding..............	$320,000		
Polishing.............		$135,000	
Product modification	600,000		
Providing power			$255,000
System calibration	500,000		

Additional information on the drivers for its production activities follows.

Grinding..	13,000 machine hours
Polishing...	13,000 machine hours
Product modification	1,500 engineering hours
Providing power	17,000 direct labor hours
System calibration	400 batches

Required

1. Classify each activity as unit level, batch level, product level, or facility level.

2. Compute the activity overhead rates using ABC. Combine the grinding and polishing activities into a single cost pool.

3. Determine overhead costs to assign to the following jobs using ABC.

	Job 3175	Job 4286
Number of units	200 units	2,500 units
Machine hours	550 MH	5,500 MH
Engineering hours	26 eng. hours	32 eng. hours
Batches	30 batches	90 batches
Direct labor hours	500 DLH	4,375 DLH

Check (4) Job 3175, $373.25 per unit

4. What is the overhead cost per unit for Job 3175? What is the overhead cost per unit for Job 4286?

5. If the company uses a plantwide overhead rate based on direct labor hours, what is the overhead cost for each unit of Job 3175? Of Job 4286?

6. Compare the overhead costs per unit computed in requirements 4 and 5 for each job. Which method more accurately assigns overhead costs?

Bright Day Company produces two beverages, Hi-Voltage and EasySlim. Data about these products follow.

	Hi-Voltage	EasySlim
Production volume	12,500 bottles	180,000 bottles
Liquid materials	1,400 gallons	37,000 gallons
Dry materials	620 pounds	12,000 pounds
Bottles...	12,500 bottles	180,000 bottles
Labels	3 labels per bottle	1 label per bottle
Machine setups	500 setups	300 setups
Machine hours	200 MH	3,750 MH

Problem 17-4A
Evaluating product line
costs and prices using ABC

P3

Additional data from its two production departments follow.

Department	Driver	Cost
Mixing department: Liquid materials...................	Gallons	$ 2,304
Dry materials	Pounds	6,941
Utilities.........................	Machine hours	1,422
Bottling department: Bottles	Units	$77,000
Labeling........................	Labels per bottle	6,525
Machine setup...................	Setups	20,000

Required

1. Determine the cost of each product line using ABC.
2. What is the cost per bottle of Hi-Voltage? What is the cost per bottle of EasySlim? *Hint:* Your answer should draw on the total cost for each product line computed in requirement 1.
3. If Hi-Voltage sells for $3.75 per bottle, how much profit does the company earn per bottle of Hi-Voltage that it sells?
4. What is the minimum price that the company should set per bottle of EasySlim?

Check (3) $2.22 profit per bottle

Sara's Salsa Company produces its condiments in two types: Extra Fine for restaurant customers and Family Style for home use. Salsa is prepared in Department 1 and packaged in Department 2. The activities, overhead costs, and drivers associated with these two manufacturing processes and the company's production support activities follow.

Problem 17-5A
Pricing analysis with ABC
and a plantwide overhead
rate

A1 A2 P1 P3

Process	Activity	Overhead Cost	Driver	Quantity
Department 1	Mixing	$ 4,500	Machine hours	1,500
	Cooking	11,250	Machine hours	1,500
	Product testing	112,500	Batches	600
		$128,250		
Department 2	Machine calibration	$250,000	Production runs	400
	Labeling	12,000	Cases of output	120,000
	Defects	6,000	Cases of output	120,000
		$268,000		
Support	Recipe formulation	$ 90,000	Focus groups	45
	Heat, lights, and water	27,000	Machine hours	1,500
	Materials handling	65,000	Container types	8
		$182,000		

Additional production information about its two product lines follows.

	Extra Fine	Family Style
Units produced	20,000 cases	100,000 cases
Batches	200 batches	400 batches
Machine hours	500 MH	1,000 MH
Focus groups	30 groups	15 groups
Container types.	5 containers	3 containers
Production runs.	200 runs	200 runs

Required

1. Using a plantwide overhead rate based on cases, compute the overhead cost that is assigned to each case of Extra Fine Salsa and each case of Family Style Salsa.

Check (2) Cost per case: Extra Fine, $10.82; Family Style, $9.82

2. Using the plantwide overhead rate, determine the total cost per case for the two products if the direct materials and direct labor cost is $6 per case of Extra Fine and $5 per case of Family Style.

3. If the market price of Extra Fine Salsa is $18 per case and the market price of Family Style Salsa is $9 per case, determine the gross profit per case for each product. Do both products have positive gross profits?

(4) Cost per case: Extra Fine, $20.02; Family Style, $7.98

4. Using ABC, compute the total cost per case for each product type if the direct labor and direct materials cost is $6 per case of Extra Fine and $5 per case of Family Style.

5. If the market price is $18 per case of Extra Fine and $9 per case of Family Style, determine the gross profit per case for each product. Using ABC, is Extra Fine Salsa profitable?

PROBLEM SET B

Wade Company makes two distinct products, with the following information available for each.

Problem 17-1B
Comparing costs using ABC with the plantwide overhead rate

A1   A2   P1   P3

	Standard	Deluxe
Direct materials	$4 per unit	$8 per unit
Direct labor hours	4 DLH per unit	5 DLH per unit
Machine hours	3 MH per unit	3 MH per unit
Batches	175 batches	75 batches
Volume	40,000 units	10,000 units
Engineering modifications	50 modifications	25 modifications
Number of customers.	1,000 customers	1,000 customers
Market price	$92 per unit	$125 per unit

The company's direct labor rate is $20 per direct labor hour (DLH). Additional information follows.

	Costs	Driver
Indirect manufacturing		
Engineering support	$ 56,250	Engineering modifications
Electricity	112,500	Machine hours
Setup costs.	41,250	Batches
Nonmanufacturing		
Customer service	250,000	Number of customers

Required

Check (1) Gross profit per unit: Standard, $3.80; Deluxe, $12.80

1. Compute the manufacturing cost per unit using the plantwide overhead rate based on machine hours. What is the gross profit per unit?

2. How much gross profit is generated by each customer of the standard product using the plantwide overhead rate? How much gross profit is generated by each customer of the deluxe product using the plantwide overhead rate? What is the cost of providing customer service to each customer? What information is provided by this comparison?

(3) Gross profit per unit: Standard, $4.09; Deluxe, $11.64

3. Determine the manufacturing cost per unit of each product line using ABC. What is the gross profit per unit?

4. How much gross profit is generated by each customer of the standard product using ABC? How much gross profit is generated by each customer of the deluxe product using ABC? Is the gross profit per customer adequate?

5. Which method of product costing gives better information to managers of this company? Explain.

Midwest Paper produces cardboard boxes. The boxes require designing, cutting, and printing. (The boxes are shipped flat, and customers fold them as necessary.) Midwest has a reputation for providing high-quality products and excellent service to customers, who are major U.S. manufacturers. Costs are assigned to products based on the number of machine hours required to produce them.

Three years ago, a new marketing executive was hired. She suggested the company offer custom design and manufacturing services to small specialty manufacturers. These customers required boxes for their products and were eager to have Midwest as a supplier. Within one year, Midwest found that it was so busy with orders from small customers, it had trouble supplying boxes to all its customers on a timely basis. Large, long-time customers began to complain about slow service, and several took their business elsewhere. Within another 18 months, Midwest was in financial distress with a backlog of orders to be filled.

Problem 17-2B
Assessing impacts of using a plantwide overhead rate versus ABC

A1   A2

Required

1. What do you believe are the major costs of making boxes? How are those costs related to the volume of boxes produced?

2. How did Midwest's new customers differ from its previous customers?

3. Would the unit cost to produce a box for new customers be different from the unit cost to produce a box for its previous customers? Explain.

4. Could Midwest's fate have been different if it had used ABC for determining the cost of its boxes?

5. What information would have been available with ABC that might have been overlooked using a traditional volume-based costing method?

Ryan Foods produces gourmet gift baskets that it distributes online as well as from its small retail store. The following details about overhead costs are taken from its records.

Problem 17-3B
Applying activity-based costing

C3   A1   A2   P1   P3

Production Activity	Indirect Labor	Indirect Materials	Other Overhead
Wrapping..........................	$300,000	$200,000	
Assembling........................	400,000		
Product design	180,000		
Quality inspection	100,000		
Cooking..........................	150,000	120,000	

Additional information on the drivers for its production activities follows.

Wrapping...	100,000 units
Assembling...	20,000 direct labor hours
Product design	3,000 design hours
Quality inspection	20,000 direct labor hours
Cooking...	1,000 batches

Required

1. Classify each activity as unit level, batch level, product level, or facility level.

2. Compute the activity overhead rates using ABC. Combine the assembling and quality inspection activities into a single cost pool.

3. Determine the overhead costs to assign to the following jobs using ABC.

	Holiday Basket	Executive Basket
Number of units	8,000 units	1,000 units
Direct labor hours.......................................	2,000 DLH	500 DLH
Design hours..	40 design hours	40 design hours
Batches	80 batches	200 batches

[continued on next page]

[continued from previous page]

4. What is the overhead cost per unit for the Holiday Basket? What is the overhead cost per unit for the Executive Basket?

5. If the company used a plantwide overhead rate based on direct labor hours, what would be the overhead cost for each Holiday Basket unit? What would be the overhead cost for each Executive Basket unit if a single plantwide overhead rate were used?

6. Compare the costs per unit computed in requirements 4 and 5 for each job. Which cost assignment method provides the most accurate cost? Explain.

Problem 17-4B
Evaluating product line costs and prices using ABC

P3

Mathwerks produces two electronic, handheld educational games: *Fun with Fractions* and *Count Calculus*. Data on these products follow.

	Fun with Fractions	Count Calculus
Production volume	150,000 units	10,000 units
Components	450,000 parts	100,000 parts
Direct labor hours	15,000 DLH	2,000 DLH
Packaging materials	150,000 boxes	10,000 boxes
Shipping cartons	100 units per carton	25 units per carton
Machine setups	52 setups	52 setups
Machine hours	5,000 MH	2,000 MH

Additional data from its two production departments follow.

Department		Driver	Cost
Assembly department:	Component cost	Parts	$495,000
	Assembly labor	Direct labor hours	244,800
	Maintenance	Machine hours	100,800
Wrapping department:	Packaging materials	Boxes	$460,800
	Shipping	Cartons	27,360
	Machine setup	Setups	187,200

Required

1. Using ABC, determine the cost of each product line.

2. What is the cost per unit of *Fun with Fractions?* What is the cost per unit of *Count Calculus?*

3. If *Count Calculus* sells for $59.95 per unit, how much profit does the company earn per unit of *Count Calculus* sold?

4. What is the minimum price that the company should set per unit of *Fun with Fractions?* Explain.

Problem 17-5B
Pricing analysis with ABC and a plantwide overhead rate

A1   A2   P1   P3

Tent Pro produces two lines of tents sold to outdoor enthusiasts. The tents are cut to specifications in Department A. In Department B, the tents are sewn and folded. The activities, costs, and drivers associated with these two manufacturing processes and the company's production support activities follow.

Process	Activity	Overhead Cost	Driver	Quantity
Department A	Pattern alignment	$ 64,400	Batches	560
	Cutting	50,430	Machine hours	12,300
	Moving product	100,800	Moves	2,400
		$215,630		
Department B	Sewing	$327,600	Direct labor hours	4,200
	Inspecting	24,000	Inspections	600
	Folding	47,880	Units	22,800
		$399,480		
Support	Design	$280,000	Modification orders	280
	Providing space	51,600	Square feet	8,600
	Materials handling	184,000	Square yards	920,000
		$515,600		

Additional production information on the two lines of tents follows.

	Pup Tent	Pop-up Tent
Units produced.................	15,200 units	7,600 units
Moves........................	800 moves	1,600 moves
Batches......................	140 batches	420 batches
Number of inspections...........	240 inspections	360 inspections
Machine hours	7,000 MH	5,300 MH
Direct labor hours..............	2,600 DLH	1,600 DLH
Modification orders	70 modification orders	210 modification orders
Space occupied	4,300 square feet	4,300 square feet
Material required	450,000 square yards	470,000 square yards

Required

1. Using a plantwide overhead rate based on direct labor hours, compute the overhead cost that is assigned to each pup tent and each pop-up tent.
2. Using the plantwide overhead rate, determine the total cost per unit for the two products if the direct materials and direct labor cost is $25 per pup tent and $32 per pop-up tent.
3. If the market price of the pup tent is $65 and the market price of the pop-up tent is $200, determine the gross profit per unit for each tent. What might management conclude about the pup tent?
4. Using ABC, compute the total cost per unit for each tent if the direct labor and direct materials cost is $25 per pup tent and $32 per pop-up tent.

Check (4) Pup tent, $58.46 per unit cost

5. If the market price is $65 per pup tent and $200 per pop-up tent, determine the gross profit per unit for each tent. Comment on the results.
6. Would your pricing analysis be improved if the company used, instead of ABC, departmental rates determined using machine hours in Department A and direct labor hours in Department B? Explain.

This serial problem began in Chapter 1 and continues through most of the book. If previous chapter segments were not completed, the serial problem can begin at this point.

SERIAL PROBLEM
Business Solutions
P3

SP 17   After reading an article about activity-based costing in a trade journal for the furniture industry, Santana Rey wondered if it was time to critically analyze overhead costs at **Business Solutions**. In a recent month, Santana found that setup costs, inspection costs, and utility costs made up most of its overhead. Additional information about overhead follows.

Activity	Cost	Driver
Setting up machines.............	$20,000	25 batches
Inspecting components	$ 7,500	5,000 parts
Providing utilities	$10,000	5,000 machine hours

©Alexander Image/Shutterstock

Overhead has been applied to output at a rate of 50% of direct labor costs. The following data pertain to Job 615.

Direct materials...............................	$2,500
Direct labor...................................	$3,500
Batches......................................	2 batches
Number of parts	400 parts
Machine hours	600 machine hours

Required

1. Classify each of its three overhead activities as unit level, batch level, product level, or facility level.
2. What is the total cost of Job 615 if Business Solutions applies overhead at 50% of direct labor cost?
3. What is the total cost of Job 615 if Business Solutions uses activity-based costing?
4. Which approach to assigning overhead gives a better representation of the costs incurred to produce Job 615? Explain.

Accounting Analysis

COMPANY ANALYSIS

P3

APPLE

AA 17-1 **Apple** reports the following net sales (in $ millions) by product line in its fiscal-year 2017 annual report.

Product line	2017 Sales	2016 Sales
iPhone	$141,319	$136,700
iPad	19,222	20,628
Mac	25,850	22,831
Services	29,980	24,348
Other	12,863	11,132

Required

1. If Apple assigns overhead costs to product lines based on sales, which product line would be assigned the highest amount of overhead costs for 2017?
2. If Apple assigns overhead costs to product lines based on sales, which product line would be assigned the lowest amount of overhead costs for 2017?
3. Which of Apple's product lines had the largest percentage increase in sales from 2016 to 2017?

COMPARATIVE ANALYSIS

P3

APPLE

GOOGLE

AA 17-2 The ratio of costs to revenues can indicate opportunities for activity-based costing to increase efficiency and reduce costs. Refer to **Apple**'s and **Google**'s 2017 income statements in Appendix A to answer the following.

Required

1. For Apple, compute the ratio of costs (titled as cost of sales plus operating expenses) to net sales for 2017.
2. For Google, compute the ratio of costs (titled as total costs and expenses) to revenues for 2017.
3. Which company has the higher ratio of costs to revenues for 2017?

GLOBAL ANALYSIS

P3

Samsung

AA 17-3 The ratio of costs to revenues can indicate opportunities for activity-based costing to increase efficiency and reduce costs. Refer to **Samsung**'s financial statements in Appendix A to answer the following.

Required

1. Compute the ratio of costs (titled as cost of sales plus selling and administrative expenses) to revenue for 2017.
2. Compute the ratio of costs (titled as cost of sales plus selling and administrative expenses) to revenue for 2016.
3. Was Samsung's ratio of costs to revenues higher in 2017 or 2016?

Beyond the Numbers

ETHICS CHALLENGE

C3   A2

BTN 17-1 In conducting interviews and observing factory operations to implement an activity-based costing system, you determine that several activities are unnecessary or redundant. For example, warehouse personnel were inspecting purchased components as they were received at the loading dock. Later that day, the components were inspected again on the shop floor before being installed in the final product. Both of these activities caused costs to be incurred but were not adding value to the product. If you include this observation in your report, one or more employees who perform inspections will likely lose their jobs.

Required

1. As a plant employee, what is your responsibility to report your findings to superiors?
2. Should you attempt to determine if the redundancy is justified? Explain.
3. What is your responsibility to the employees whose jobs will likely be lost because of your report?
4. What facts should you consider before making your decision to report or not?

BTN 17-2 The chief executive officer (CEO) of your company recently returned from a luncheon meeting where activity-based costing was presented and discussed. Though her background is not in accounting, she has worked for the company for 15 years and is thoroughly familiar with its operations. Her impression of the presentation about ABC was that it was just another way of dividing up total overhead cost and that the total would still be the same "no matter how you sliced it."

Required

Write a memorandum to the CEO, no more than one page, explaining how ABC is different from traditional volume-based costing methods. Also identify its advantages and disadvantages vis-à-vis traditional methods. Be sure it is written to be understandable to someone who is not an accountant.

COMMUNICATING IN PRACTICE
A2

BTN 17-3 Accounting professionals who work for private companies often obtain the Certified Management Accountant (CMA) designation to indicate their proficiency in several business areas in addition to managerial accounting. The CMA examination is administered by the Institute of Management Accountants (IMA).

Required

Go to the IMA website (**IMAnet.org**) and determine which parts of the CMA exam likely cover activity-based costing. A person planning to become a CMA should take what college coursework?

TAKING IT TO THE NET
A2

BTN 17-4 Observe the operations at your favorite fast-food restaurant.

Required

1. How many people does it take to fill a typical order of a sandwich, beverage, and one side order?
2. Describe the activities involved in its food service process.
3. What costs are related to each activity identified in requirement 2?

TEAMWORK IN ACTION
C2   C3

BTN 17-5 **Sycamore Brewing** brews many varieties of beer. Company founders Sarah Taylor Brigham and Justin Brigham know that financial success depends on cost control as well as revenue generation.

Required

1. If Sycamore Brewing wanted to expand its product line to include whiskey, what activities would it need to perform that are not required for its current product lines?
2. Related to part 1, should the additional overhead costs related to new product lines be shared by existing product lines? Explain your reasoning.

ENTREPRENEURIAL DECISION
C3

BTN 17-6 Visit and observe the processes of three different fast-food restaurants—these visits can be done as individuals or as teams. The objective of activity-based costing is to accurately assign costs to products and to improve operational efficiency.

Required

1. Individuals (or teams) can be assigned to each of three different fast-food establishments. Make a list of the activities required to process an order of a sandwich, beverage, and one side order at each restaurant. Record the time required for each process, from placing the order to receiving the completed order.
2. What activities do the three establishments have in common? What activities are different across the establishments?
3. Is the number of activities related to the time required to process an order? Is the number of activities related to the price charged to customers? Explain both.
4. Make recommendations for improving the processes you observe. Would your recommendations increase or decrease the cost of operations?

HITTING THE ROAD
C2   C3

---

18 Cost Behavior and Cost-Volume-Profit Analysis

Learning Objectives

CONCEPTUAL

C1 Describe different types of cost behavior in relation to production and sales volume.

C2 Describe several applications of cost-volume-profit analysis.

ANALYTICAL

A1 Compute the contribution margin and describe what it reveals about a company's cost structure.

A2 Analyze changes in sales using the degree of operating leverage.

PROCEDURAL

P1 Determine cost estimates using the scatter diagram, high-low, and regression methods of estimating costs.

P2 Compute the break-even point for a single-product company.

P3 Interpret a CVP chart and graph costs and sales for a single-product company.

P4 Compute the break-even point for a multiproduct company.

P5 *Appendix 18B*—Compute unit cost and income under both absorption and variable costing.

Profitabili-Tea

"Sell it, don't tell it"—**NAILAH ELLIS-BROWN**

DETROIT, MI—Nailah Ellis-Brown's great-grandfather immigrated to the United States from Jamaica in the early 1900s with, among other possessions, a prized family recipe for hibiscus tea. Nailah recalls her great-grandfather's command: "This recipe is to be sold, not told." This is exactly what her company, **Ellis Island Tropical Tea** (**Ellisislandtea.com**), does today.

Nailah started small, making tea in her mother's basement and selling it out of the trunk of her car. "Everything from day one has been trial and error," Nailah recalls.

In addition to production, packaging, and distribution, Nailah must measure and control costs. Concepts of fixed and variable costs, and how to control them to break even and make profits, are critical for her start-up. "Because our sales volume was low," explains Nailah, "we had to set our price too high to cover costs."

With a corrected lower selling price, Nailah recently landed distribution contracts with several major airports and **Sam's Club**. This will increase sales and enable her company to recover its fixed costs.

To meet higher expected sales volume, Nailah needed a new production facility, which increased fixed costs. Understanding relations between costs, volume, and profit, called *CVP analysis,* helps guide her decisions. Further, contribution margin income statements and CVP analysis help her predict the effects of different selling prices and costs on profits.

©Ellis Infinity, LLC

Nailah advises entrepreneurs to find a niche and be persistent. "Ours is the only Jamaican sweet tea on the market . . . quitting is not an option."

Sources: *Ellisislandtea website,* January 2019; *Blackenterprise.com,* January 4, 2016; *ModelDmedia.com,* October 10, 2016; *MSNBC.com* video interview, June 9, 2017; *Youtube.com* video, youtube.com/watch?v=dSWVMVZoLL4

IDENTIFYING COST BEHAVIOR

Planning a company's future activities is crucial to successful management. Managers use **cost-volume-profit (CVP) analysis** to predict how changes in costs and sales levels affect profit. CVP analysis requires four inputs, as shown in Exhibit 18.1.

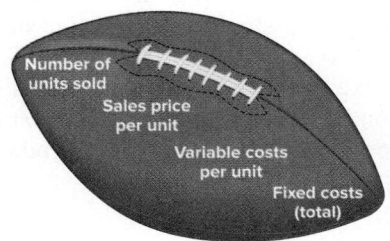

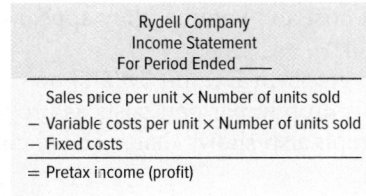

Rydell Company
Income Statement
For Period Ended ____

Sales price per unit × Number of units sold
− Variable costs per unit × Number of units sold
− Fixed costs

= Pretax income (profit)

EXHIBIT 18.1

Inputs for CVP Analysis

Using these four inputs, managers apply CVP analysis to answer questions such as:

- How many units must we sell to break even?
- How much will income increase if we install a new machine to reduce labor costs?
- What is the change in income if selling prices decline and sales volume increases?
- How will income change if we change the sales mix of our products or services?
- What sales volume is needed to earn a target income?

This chapter uses Rydell, a football manufacturer, to explain CVP analysis. We first review cost classifications like fixed and variable costs, and then we show methods for measuring these costs.

The concept of *relevant range* is important to classifying costs for CVP analysis. The **relevant range of operations** is the normal operating range for a business. Except for unusually good or bad times, management plans for operations within a range of volume neither close to zero nor at maximum capacity. The relevant range excludes extremely high or low operating levels that are unlikely to occur. CVP analysis requires management to classify costs as either *fixed* or *variable* with respect to production or sales volume, within the relevant range of operations.

Describe different types of cost behavior in relation to production and sales volume.

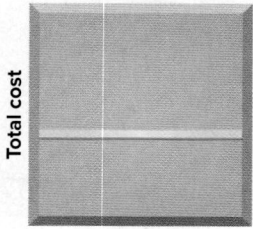

Fixed Costs

Fixed costs do not change when the volume of activity changes (within a relevant range). For example, $32,000 in monthly rent paid for a factory building remains the same whether the factory operates with a single eight-hour shift or around the clock with three shifts. This means that rent cost is the same each month at any level of output from zero to the plant's full productive capacity.

Though the *total* amount of fixed cost does not change as volume changes, fixed cost *per unit* of output decreases as volume increases. For instance, if 200 units are produced when monthly rent is $32,000, the average rent cost per unit is $160 (computed as $32,000/200 units). When production increases to 1,000 units per month, the average rent cost per unit decreases to $32 (computed as $32,000/1,000 units).

Variable Costs

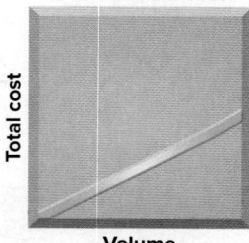

Variable costs change in proportion to changes in volume of activity. Direct materials cost is one example of a variable cost. If one unit of product requires materials costing $20, total materials costs are $200 when 10 units are manufactured, $400 for 20 units, and so on. While the *total* amount of variable cost changes with the level of production, variable cost *per unit* remains constant as volume changes.

Graphing Fixed <u>and</u> Variable Costs against Volume

When production volume and costs are graphed, units of product are usually plotted on the *horizontal axis* and dollars of cost are plotted on the *vertical axis*. The upper graph in Exhibit 18.2 shows the relation between total fixed costs and volume, and the relation between total variable costs and volume. Total fixed costs of $32,000 remain the same at all production levels up to the company's monthly capacity of 2,000 units. Total variable costs increase by $20 per unit for each additional unit produced. When variable costs are plotted on a graph of cost and volume, they appear as an upward-sloping straight line starting at the zero cost level.

Point: Fixed costs stay constant in total but decrease per unit as more units are produced. Variable costs vary in total but are fixed per unit as production changes.

The lower graph in Exhibit 18.2 shows that fixed costs *per unit* decrease as production increases. This drop in per unit costs as production increases is known as *economies of scale*. This lower graph also shows that variable costs per unit remain constant as production levels change.

Mixed Costs

Are all costs either fixed or variable? No. **Mixed costs** include both fixed and variable cost components. For example, compensation for sales representatives often includes a fixed monthly salary and a variable commission based on sales. Utilities can also be considered a mixed cost; even if no units are produced, it is not likely a manufacturing plant will use no electricity or water. Like a fixed cost, a mixed cost is greater than zero when volume is zero; but unlike a fixed cost, it increases steadily in proportion to increases in volume.

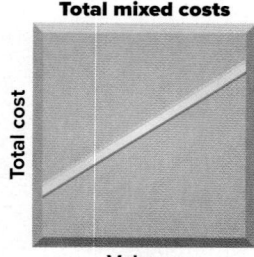

Graphing Mixed Costs against Volume   The total cost line in the top graph in Exhibit 18.2 starts on the vertical axis at the $32,000 fixed cost point. At the zero volume level, total cost equals the fixed costs. As the volume of activity increases, the total cost line increases at an

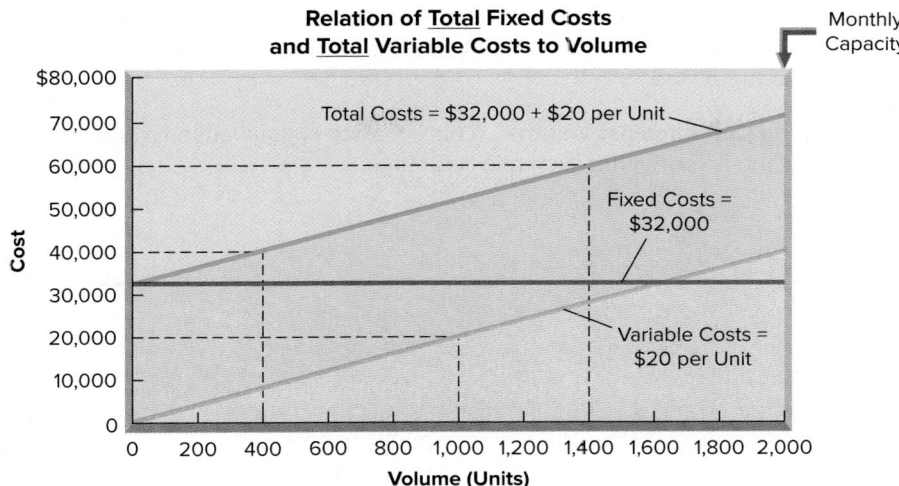

EXHIBIT 18.2

Relations of Total and Per Unit Costs to Volume

Units Produced	Total Fixed Costs	Total Variable Costs
0	$32,000	$ 0
200	32,000	4,000
400	32,000	8,000
⋮	⋮	⋮
1,800	32,000	36,000
2,000	32,000	40,000

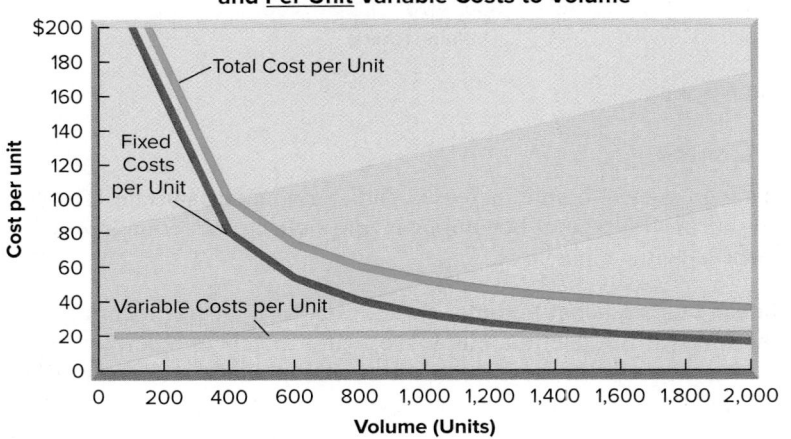

Units Produced	Per Unit Fixed Costs	Per Unit Variable Costs
1	$32,000	$20
200	160	20
400	80	20
⋮	⋮	⋮
2,000	16	20

amount equal to the variable cost per unit. This total cost line is a "mixed cost"—and it is highest when the volume of activity is at 2,000 units (the end point of the relevant range). In CVP analysis, mixed costs should be separated into fixed and variable components. The fixed component is added to other fixed costs, and the variable component is added to other variable costs. We show how to separate costs later in this chapter.

Below are examples of fixed, variable, and mixed costs for a manufacturer of footballs.

Fixed Costs	Variable Costs	Mixed Costs
• Rent	• Direct materials	• Electricity
• Depreciation*	• Direct labor	• Water
• Property taxes	• Shipping	• Sales rep (salary plus commission)
• Supervisor salaries	• Packaging	• Natural gas
• Office salaries	• Indirect materials	• Maintenance

*Computed using a method other than units-of-production depreciation.

Step-wise Costs

A **step-wise cost** (or *stair-step cost*) reflects a step pattern in costs. Salaries of production supervisors are fixed within a *relevant range* of the current production volume. However, if production volume expands greatly (for example, with the addition of another shift), more supervisors must be hired. This means that the total cost for supervisory salaries steps up by a lump-sum amount. Similarly, if production volume takes another large step up, supervisory salaries will increase by another lump sum.

Graphing Step-Wise Costs against Volume   This behavior is graphed in Exhibit 18.3. See how the step-wise cost line is flat within each relevant range.

EXHIBIT 18.3

Step-wise and
Curvilinear Costs

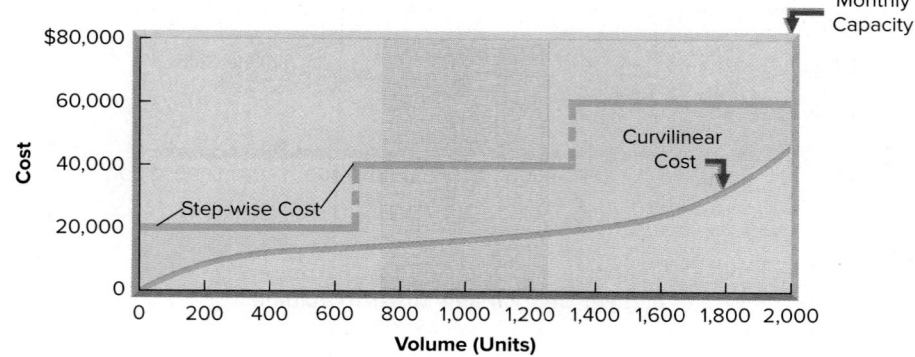

Curvilinear Costs

Curvilinear costs increase as volume increases, but at a nonconstant rate. The curved line in Exhibit 18.3 shows a curvilinear cost beginning at zero (when production is zero) and increasing at different rates as volume increases.

Graphing Curvilinear Costs against Volume   One example of a curvilinear cost is total direct labor cost. At low levels of production, employees can specialize in certain tasks. This efficiency results in a flatter slope in the curvilinear cost graph at lower levels of production in Exhibit 18.3. At some point, adding more employees creates inefficiencies (they get in each other's way or do not have special skills). This inefficiency is reflected in a steeper slope at higher levels of production in the curvilinear cost graph in Exhibit 18.3.

In CVP analysis, step-wise costs are usually treated as either fixed *or* variable costs. Curvilinear costs are typically treated as variable costs, and thus remain constant per unit. These treatments involve manager judgment and depend on the width of the relevant range and the expected volume.

NEED-TO-KNOW 18-1

Classifying Costs

C1

Determine whether each of the following is best described as a fixed, variable, mixed, step-wise, or curvilinear cost as the number of product units changes.

	Type of Cost		Type of Cost
Rubber used to manufacture tennis balls . .	**a.** _____	Supervisory salaries	**d.** _____
Depreciation (straight-line method).	**b.** _____	A salesperson's commission is 7% for sales of up to	
Electricity usage	**c.** _____	$100,000 and 10% of sales for sales above $100,000. . . .	**e.** _____

Solution

a. variable   **b.** fixed   **c.** mixed   **d.** fixed*   **e.** curvilinear

Do More: QS 18-1, QS 18-2,
E 18-1, E 18-2, E 18-3

*If more shifts are added, then supervisory salaries behave like a step-wise cost with respect to the number of shifts.

MEASURING COST BEHAVIOR

Identifying and measuring cost behavior require analysis and judgment. A key part of this process is to classify costs as either fixed or variable, which often requires analysis of past cost behavior. A goal of classifying costs is to develop a *cost equation*. The cost equation expresses total costs as a function of total fixed costs plus variable cost per unit. Three methods are commonly used:

- **Scatter diagram**
- **High-low method**
- **Regression**

P1

Determine cost estimates using the scatter diagram, high-low, and regression methods of estimating costs.

Each method is explained using the unit and cost data shown in Exhibit 18.4, which are from a start-up company that uses units produced as the activity base in estimating cost behavior.

Month	Units Produced	Total Cost	Month	Units Produced	Total Cost
January	27,500	$21,500	July	30,000	$23,500
February	22,500	20,500	August	52,500	28,500
March	25,000	25,000	September	37,500	26,000
April	35,000	21,500	October	62,500	29,000
May	47,500	25,500	November	67,500	31,000
June	17,500	18,500	December	57,500	26,000

EXHIBIT 18.4

Data for Estimating Cost Behavior

Scatter Diagram

A **scatter diagram** is a graph of unit volume and cost data. Units are plotted on the horizontal axis and costs are plotted on the vertical axis. Each point on a scatter diagram reflects the cost and number of units for a prior period. In Exhibit 18.5, the prior 12 months' costs and units are graphed. Each point reflects total costs incurred and units produced in that month. For instance, the point labeled March shows units produced of 25,000 and costs of $25,000. Appendix 18A shows how to create a scatter diagram using Excel.

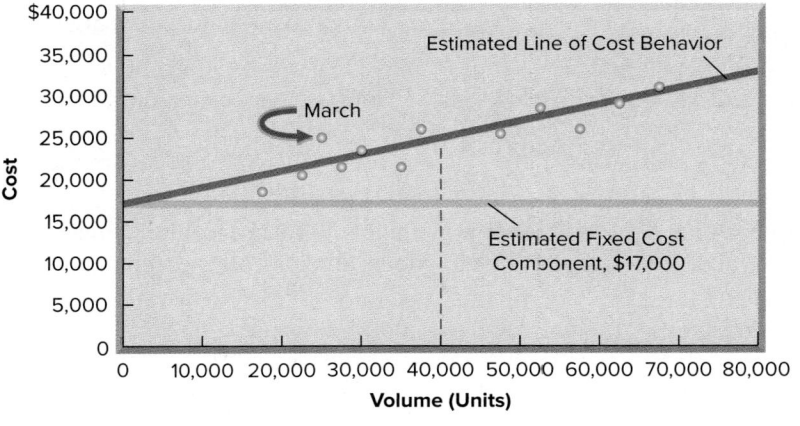

EXHIBIT 18.5

Scatter Diagram

The scatter diagram is useful for identifying extreme data points ("outliers") and for visually classifying costs. Outliers might be due to data errors, which must be corrected before computing variable and fixed costs. If there is no obvious visual relation between costs and the selected activity base, management should consider whether there is a better activity base. The scatter diagram in Exhibit 18.5 suggests there are no outliers in these data and that total costs increase with the number of units produced. Appendix 18A shows how to use a scatter diagram to estimate fixed and variable costs.

The **estimated line of cost behavior** is drawn on a scatter diagram to reflect the relation between cost and unit volume. This line best visually "fits" the points in a scatter diagram. Fitting this line is done with spreadsheet software, as we illustrate in Appendix 18A. The line in Exhibit 18.5 reflects a mixed cost. We next discuss two approaches to estimating the fixed and variable cost components of this mixed cost.

Point: Outliers are points that are far from the line of best fit.

High-Low Method

The **high-low method** uses just two points to estimate the cost equation: the highest and lowest *volume* levels. The high-low method follows three steps.

Step 1: Identify the highest and lowest volume levels. These might not be the highest or lowest levels of *costs*.

Step 2: Compute the slope (variable cost per unit) using the high and low volume levels.

Step 3: Compute the total fixed costs by computing the total variable cost at either the high or low volume level, and then subtracting that amount from the total cost at that volume level.

We illustrate the high-low method next.

Step 1: In our case, the lowest number of units is 17,500 and the highest is 67,500. The costs corresponding to these unit volumes are $18,500 and $31,000, respectively (see the data in Exhibit 18.4).

Step 2: The variable cost per unit is calculated using a simple formula: change in cost divided by the change in units. Using the data from the high and low unit volumes, this results in a *slope,* or estimated variable cost per unit, of $0.25 as computed in Exhibit 18.6.

EXHIBIT 18.6

Variable Cost per Unit—
High-Low Method

$$\frac{\text{Change in cost}}{\text{Change in units}} = \frac{\$31,000 - \$18,500}{67,500 - 17,500} = \frac{\$12,500}{50,000} = \$0.25 \text{ per unit}$$

Step 3: To estimate the fixed cost for the high-low method, we know that total cost equals fixed cost plus variable cost per unit times the number of units. Then we pick either the high or low volume point to determine the fixed cost. This computation is shown in Exhibit 18.7—where we use the high point (67,500 units) in determining the fixed cost of $14,125. (Use of the low volume point yields the same fixed cost estimate.)

EXHIBIT 18.7

Determining Fixed Costs—
High-Low Method

> **Total cost = Fixed cost + (Variable cost per unit × Units)**
>
> $31,000 = Fixed cost + ($0.25 per unit × 67,500 units)
>
> $31,000 = Fixed cost + $16,875
>
> $14,125 = Fixed cost

Example: Using information from Exhibit 18.7, what is the amount of fixed cost at the low level of volume? *Answer:* $14,125, computed as $18,500 − ($0.25 × 17,500 units).

Thus, the cost equation from the high-low method is **$14,125 plus $0.25 per unit produced**. A weakness of the high-low method is that it ignores all data points except the highest and lowest volume levels.

Regression

Least-squares regression, or simply *regression,* is a statistical method for identifying cost behavior. We use the cost equation estimated from this method but leave the computational details for advanced courses. Computations for least-squares regression are readily done using most spreadsheet programs or calculators. We illustrate this using Excel in Appendix 18A. Using least-squares regression, the cost equation for the data presented in Exhibit 18.4 is **$16,688 plus $0.20 per unit produced**; that is, the fixed cost is estimated as $16,688 and the variable cost at $0.20 per unit.

Comparing Cost Estimation Methods

Different cost estimation methods result in different estimates of fixed and variable costs, as summarized in Exhibit 18.8. Estimates from the high-low method use only two sets of values corresponding to the lowest and highest unit volumes. Sometimes these two activity levels do not reflect the more usual conditions likely to recur. Estimates from least-squares regression use a statistical technique and all available data points.

Estimation Method	Fixed Cost	Variable Cost
High-low	$14,125	$0.25 per unit
Regression	16,688	0.20 per unit

EXHIBIT 18.8

Comparison of Cost
Estimation Methods

These methods use *past data.* Thus, cost estimates resulting from these methods are only as good as the data used. Managers must establish that the data are reliable. If the data are reliable, the use of more data points, as in the regression method, should yield more accurate estimates than the high-low method. However, the high-low method is easier to apply and thus might be useful for obtaining a quick cost equation estimate.

Using the information below, apply the high-low method to determine the *cost equation* (total fixed costs plus variable costs per unit).

NEED-TO-KNOW 18-2

High-Low Method

P1

Volume	Units Produced	Total Cost
Highest	4,000	$17,000
Lowest.............	1,600	9,800

Solution

The variable cost per unit is computed as: [$17,000 − $9,800]/[4,000 units − 1,600 units] = $3 per unit. Total fixed costs using the lowest activity level are computed from the following equation: $9,800 = Fixed costs + ($3 × 1,600 units); thus, fixed costs = $5,000. This implies the cost equation is **$5,000 plus $3 per unit produced.** We can prove the accuracy of this cost equation at either the highest or lowest point shown here.

Highest point:
Total cost = $5,000 + ($3 per unit × 4,000 units)
       = $5,000 + $12,000
       = $17,000

Lowest point:
Total cost = $5,000 + ($3 per unit × 1,600 units)
       = $5,000 + $4,800
       = $9,800

Do More: QS 18-3, E 18-6

CONTRIBUTION MARGIN AND BREAK-EVEN ANALYSIS

This section explains *contribution margin,* a key measure in CVP analysis. We also discuss break-even analysis, an important special case of CVP analysis.

Contribution Margin and Its Measures

After classifying costs as fixed or variable, we can compute **contribution margin,** which equals total sales minus total variable costs. Contribution margin contributes to covering fixed costs and generating profits. **Contribution margin per unit,** or *unit contribution margin,* is the amount by which a product's unit selling price exceeds its variable cost per unit. Exhibit 18.9 shows the formula for contribution margin per unit.

A1

Compute the contribution margin and describe what it reveals about a company's cost structure.

$$\text{Contribution margin per unit} = \text{Selling price per unit} - \text{Total variable cost per unit}$$

EXHIBIT 18.9

Contribution Margin
per Unit

Contribution margin ratio is the percent of a unit's selling price that exceeds total unit variable cost. It is interpreted as the percent of each sales dollar that remains after deducting the unit variable cost. Exhibit 18.10 shows the formula for contribution margin ratio.

$$\text{Contribution margin ratio} = \frac{\text{Contribution margin per unit}}{\text{Selling price per unit}}$$

EXHIBIT 18.10

Contribution Margin Ratio

To illustrate contribution margin, consider Rydell, which sells footballs for $100 each and incurs variable costs of $70 per football sold. Its fixed costs are $24,000 per month with monthly capacity of 1,800 units (footballs). Rydell's contribution margin per unit is $30, and its contribution ratio is 30%, computed as follows.

Selling price per unit.	$100
Variable cost per unit	70
Contribution margin per unit	$ 30
Contribution margin ratio ($30/$100)	30%

©Darren Greenwood/Design Pics

At a selling price of $100 per football, Rydell covers its per unit variable costs and makes $30 per unit to contribute to fixed costs and profit. Rydell's contribution margin ratio is 30%, computed as $30/$100. A contribution margin ratio of 30% implies that for each $1 in sales, Rydell has $0.30 that contributes to fixed cost and profit. Next we show how to use these contribution margin measures in break-even analysis.

■ Decision Maker

Sales Manager   You can accept only one of two customer orders due to limited capacity. The first order is for 100 units with a contribution margin ratio of 60% and a selling price of $1,000 per unit. The second order is for 500 units with a contribution margin ratio of 20% and a selling price of $800 per unit. Incremental fixed costs are the same for both orders. Which order do you accept? ■   *Answer:* You must compute the *total* contribution margin for each order. Total contribution margin is $60,000 ($600 per unit × 100 units) and $80,000 ($160 per unit × 500 units) for the two orders, respectively. The second order provides the largest return in absolute dollars and is the order you would accept. Another factor to consider in your selection is the potential for a long-term relationship with these customers including repeat sales and growth.

Break-Even Point

P2

Compute the break-even point for a single-product company.

The **break-even point** is the sales level at which total sales equal total costs and a company neither earns a profit nor incurs a loss. Break-even applies to nearly all organizations, activities, and events. A key concern when launching a project is whether it will break even—that is, whether sales will at least cover total costs. The break-even point can be expressed in either units or dollars of sales. To illustrate break-even analysis, let's again look at Rydell, which sells footballs for $100 per unit and incurs $70 of variable costs per unit sold. Its fixed costs are $24,000 per month. Three different methods are used to find the break-even point.

- **Formula method**
- **Contribution margin income statement**
- **Cost-volume-profit chart**

Point: Selling prices and variable costs are usually expressed in per unit amounts. Fixed costs are usually expressed in total amounts.

Formula Method   We compute the break-even point using the formula in Exhibit 18.11. This formula uses the contribution margin per unit (calculated above), which for Rydell is $30 ($100 − $70). The break-even sales volume in units follows.

EXHIBIT 18.11

Formula for Computing Break-Even Sales (in Units)

$$\text{Break-even point in units} = \frac{\text{Fixed costs}}{\text{Contribution margin per unit}}$$
$$= \$24,000/\$30$$
$$= 800 \text{ units per month}$$

Point: Even if a company operates at a level above its break-even point, management may decide to stop operating because it is not earning a reasonable return on investment.

If Rydell sells 800 units, its profit will be zero. Profit increases or decreases by $30 for every unit sold above or below that break-even point; for example, if Rydell sells 801 units, profit will equal $30. We also can calculate the break-even point in dollars. Also called *break-even sales dollars,* it uses the contribution margin ratio to determine the required sales dollars needed for the company to break even. Exhibit 18.12 shows the formula and Rydell's break-even point in dollars.

$$\text{Break-even point in dollars} = \frac{\text{Fixed costs}}{\text{Contribution margin ratio}}$$

$$= \$24,000/30\%$$

$$= \$24,000/0.30$$

$$= \$80,000 \text{ of monthly sales}$$

EXHIBIT 18.12

Formula for Computing Break-Even Sales (in Dollars)

Contribution Margin Income Statement Method

The center of Exhibit 18.13 shows the general format of a *contribution margin income statement*. It differs in format from a traditional income statement in two ways. First, it separately classifies costs and expenses as variable or fixed. A traditional income statement classifies costs as product or period. Second, it reports contribution margin (Sales − Variable costs). A traditional income statement reports gross profit (Sales − Cost of sales), as shown at the left of Exhibit 18.13.

EXHIBIT 18.13

Contribution Margin Income Statement for Break-Even Sales

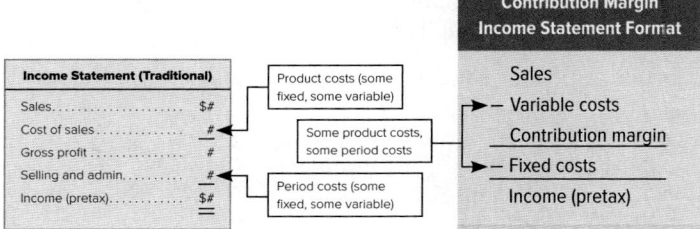

Contribution Margin Income Statement Format	Contribution Margin Income Statement (at Break-Even) For Month Ended January 31, 2019	
Sales	Sales (800 units at $100 each)	$80,000
Variable costs	Variable costs (800 units at $70 each)	56,000
Contribution margin	Contribution margin (800 units at $30 each) ...	24,000
Fixed costs	Fixed costs	24,000
Income (pretax)	Income (pretax)...........................	$ 0

The right side of Exhibit 18.13 uses this format to find the break-even point for Rydell. To use this method, set income equal to zero and work up the income statement to find sales. At the break-even point, Rydell's contribution margin must exactly equal its fixed costs of $24,000. For Rydell's contribution margin to equal $24,000, it must sell 800 units ($24,000/$30). The resulting contribution margin income statement shows that the $80,000 revenue from sales of 800 units exactly equals the sum of variable and fixed costs.

Hudson Co. predicts fixed costs of $400,000 for 2019. Its one product sells for $170 per unit, and it incurs variable costs of $150 per unit. The company predicts total sales of 25,000 units for 2019.

1. Compute the contribution margin per unit.
2. Compute the break-even point (in units) using the formula method.
3. Prepare a contribution margin income statement at the break-even point.

Solution

1. Contribution margin per unit
   = $170 − $150 = $20
2. Break-even point = $400,000/$20
   = 20,000 units

3.

Contribution Margin Income Statement (at Break-Even) For Year Ended December 31, 2019	
Sales (20,000 units at $170 each)............	$3,400,000
Variable costs (20,000 units at $150 each)	3,000,000
Contribution margin (20,000 units at $20 each) ..	400,000
Fixed costs	400,000
Income (pretax)...........................	$ 0

 NEED-TO-KNOW 18-3

Contribution Margin and Break-Even Point

A1   P2

Do More: QS 18-5, QS 18-6, QS 18-10, E 18-8, E 18-9, E 18-16

P3_____

Interpret a CVP chart and graph costs and sales for a single-product company.

Cost-Volume-Profit Chart

A third way to find the break-even point is to examine a **cost-volume-profit (CVP) chart** (*break-even chart*). Exhibit 18.14 shows Rydell's CVP chart. In a CVP chart, the horizontal axis is the number of units produced and sold, and the vertical axis is dollars of sales and costs. The lines in the chart show both sales and costs at different output levels.

A CVP chart shows two key lines.

Point: CVP analysis is often based on *sales volume,* using either units sold or dollar sales. Other output measures, such as the number of units produced, also can be used.

① **Total costs.** This line starts at the fixed costs level on the vertical axis ($24,000 for Rydell). The slope of this line is the variable cost per unit ($70 per unit for Rydell).

② **Total sales.** This line starts at zero on the vertical axis (zero units and zero dollars of sales). The slope of this line equals the selling price per unit ($100 per unit for Rydell). This line must not extend beyond the company's productive capacity.

The CVP chart provides several key observations.

1. **Break-even point,** where the total cost line and total sales line intersect—at 800 units, or $80,000, for Rydell.

2. **Profit or loss expected,** measured as the vertical distance between the sales line and the total cost line at any level of units sold (a loss is to the left of the break-even point, a profit is to the right). As the number of units sold increases, the loss area decreases and the profit area increases.

Example: In Exhibit 18.14, the sales line intersects the cost line at 800 units. At what point would the two lines intersect if selling price is increased to $120 per unit? *Answer:* $24,000/($120 − $70) = 480 units

3. **Maximum productive capacity,** which is 1,800 units (the last point on the CVP chart). At this point Rydell expects sales of $180,000 and its largest profit.

We show how to prepare a CVP chart in Appendix 18C.

EXHIBIT 18.14

Cost-Volume-Profit Chart

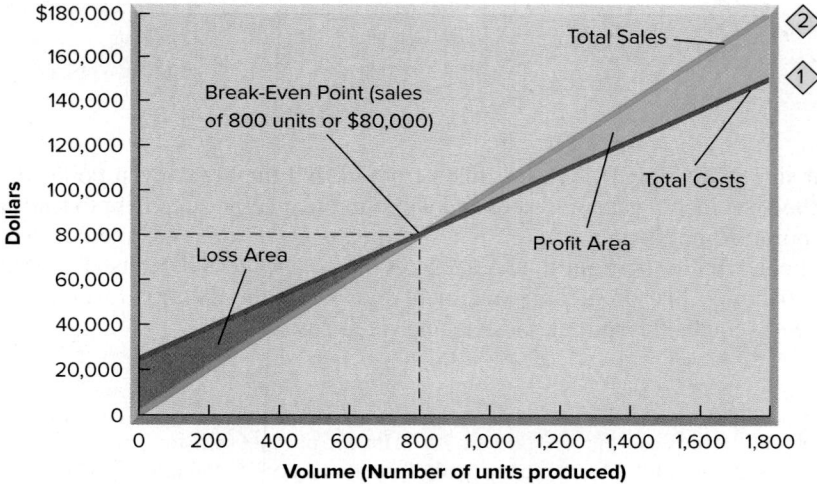

Changes in Estimates

CVP analysis uses estimates, and knowing how changes in those estimates impact break-even is useful. For example, a manager might form three estimates for each of the inputs of break-even: optimistic, most likely, and pessimistic. Then ranges of break-even points in units can be computed using any of the three methods shown above. To illustrate, assume Rydell's managers provide the estimates in Exhibit 18.15.

EXHIBIT 18.15

Alternative Estimates for Break-Even Analysis

	Selling Price per Unit	Variable Cost per Unit	Total Fixed Costs
Optimistic............	$105	$68	$21,000
Most likely	100	70	24,000
Pessimistic...........	95	72	27,000

If, for example, Rydell's managers believe they can raise the selling price of a football to $105, without any change in unit variable or total fixed costs, then the revised contribution margin per football is $35 ($105 − $70), and the revised break-even in units follows in Exhibit 18.16.

$$\text{Revised break-even point in units} = \frac{\$24,000}{\$35} = 686 \text{ units (rounded)}$$

EXHIBIT 18.16

Revised Break-Even in Units

Repeating this calculation using each of the other eight separate estimates above (keeping other estimates unchanged from their original amounts), and graphing the results, yields the three graphs in Exhibit 18.17.

EXHIBIT 18.17

Break-Even Points for Alternative Estimates

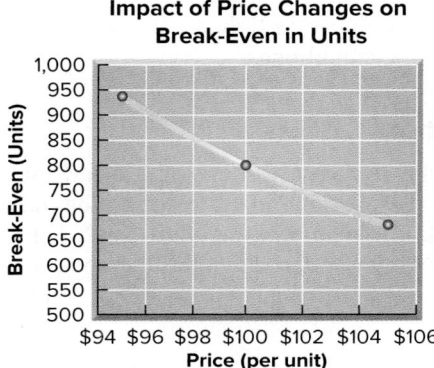

(A)

Impact of Price Changes on Break-Even in Units

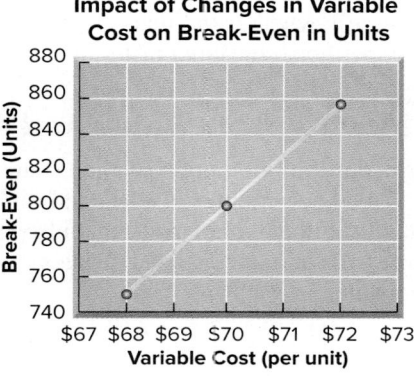

(B)

Impact of Changes in Variable Cost on Break-Even in Units

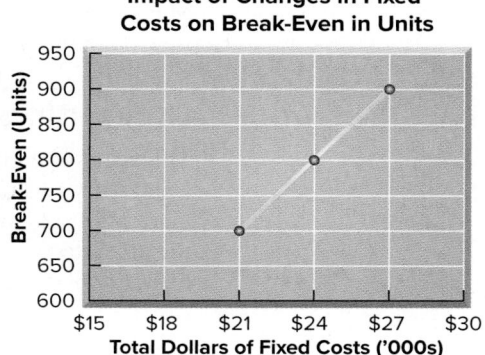

(C)

Impact of Changes in Fixed Costs on Break-Even in Units

These graphs show how changes in selling prices, variable costs, and fixed costs impact break-even. When selling prices can be increased without impacting unit variable costs or total fixed costs, break-even decreases (graph A). When competition reduces selling prices and the company cannot reduce costs, break-even increases (graph A). Increases in either variable (graph B) or fixed costs (graph C), if they cannot be passed on to customers via higher selling prices, will increase break-even. If costs can be reduced and selling prices held constant, the break-even point decreases.

Point: This analysis changed only one estimate at a time; managers can examine how combinations of changes in estimates impact break-even.

■ **Decision Ethics**

Supervisor Your team is conducting a CVP analysis for a new product. Different sales projections have different incomes. One member suggests picking numbers yielding favorable income because any estimate is "as good as any other." Another member suggests dropping unfavorable data points for cost estimation. What do you do? ■ *Answer:* Your dilemma is whether to go along with the suggestions to "manage" the numbers to make the project look like it will achieve sufficient profits. You should not follow these suggestions. People will be affected negatively if you manage the predicted numbers and the project eventually is unprofitable. Moreover, if it does fail, an investigation would likely reveal that data in the proposal were "fixed" to make the project look good. One way to deal with this dilemma is to prepare several analyses showing results under different assumptions and then let senior management make the decision.

©Caiaimage/Glow Images

APPLYING COST-VOLUME-PROFIT ANALYSIS

Managers consider many strategies in planning business operations. Cost-volume-profit analysis is useful in evaluating the likely effects of these strategies.

Margin of Safety

All companies desire results in excess of break-even. The excess of expected sales over the break-even sales level is called **margin of safety,** the amount that sales can drop before the company incurs a loss. It often is expressed in dollars or as a percent of the expected sales level.

C2

Describe several applications of cost-volume-profit analysis.

To illustrate, Rydell's break-even point in dollars is $80,000. If its expected sales are $100,000, the margin of safety is $20,000 ($100,000 − $80,000). As a percent, the margin of safety is 20% of expected sales, as shown in Exhibit 18.18.

EXHIBIT 18.18

Computing Margin of Safety (in Percent)

$$\text{Margin of safety (in percent)} = \frac{\text{Expected sales} - \text{Break-even sales}}{\text{Expected sales}}$$

$$= \frac{\$100,000 - \$80,000}{\$100,000}$$

$$= \$20,000/\$100,000$$

$$= 20\%$$

Management must assess whether the margin of safety is adequate in light of factors such as sales variability, competition, consumer tastes, and economic conditions.

Computing Income from Sales and Costs

Managers often use contribution margin income statements to forecast future sales or income. Exhibit 18.19 shows the key variables in CVP analysis—sales, variable costs, contribution margin, and fixed costs—and their relations to income (pretax). To answer the question "What is the predicted income from a predicted level of sales?" we work our way down this income statement to compute income.

EXHIBIT 18.19

Income Relations in CVP Analysis

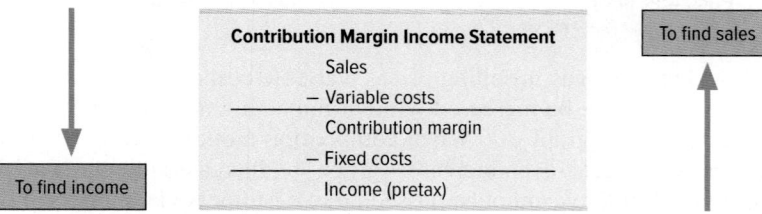

Point: 1,500 units of sales is 700 units above Rydell's break-even point. Income can also be computed as 700 units × $30 contribution margin per unit.

To illustrate, assume Rydell's management expects to sell 1,500 units in January 2019. What is the amount of income if this sales level is achieved? We first compute dollar sales, and then use the format in Exhibit 18.19 to compute Rydell's expected income in Exhibit 18.20. This $21,000 income amount can also be computed as (Units sold × Contribution margin per unit) − Fixed costs, or (1,500 × $30) − $24,000. The $21,000 income is pretax.

EXHIBIT 18.20

Computing Expected Pretax Income from Expected Sales

Contribution Margin Income Statement (Pretax) For Month Ended January 31, 2019	
Sales (1,500 units at $100 each)	$150,000
Variable costs (1,500 units at $70 each)	105,000
Contribution margin (1,500 units at $30 each)	45,000
Fixed costs	24,000
Income (pretax)	$ 21,000

Computing After-Tax Income   To find the amount of *after-tax* income from selling 1,500 units, management uses the tax rate. Assume that the tax rate is 25%. Then we can prepare a projected after-tax income statement, shown in Exhibit 18.21. After-tax income can also be computed as Pretax income × (1 − Tax rate).

EXHIBIT 18.21

Computing Expected
After-Tax Income from
Expected Sales

Contribution Margin Income Statement (After-Tax) For Month Ended January 31, 2019	
Sales (1,500 units at $100 each)	$150,000
Variable costs (1,500 units at $70 each)	105,000
Contribution margin (1,500 units at $30 each)	45,000
Fixed costs	24,000
Pretax income	21,000
Income taxes ($21,000 × 25%)	5,250
Net income (after tax)	$ 15,750

EXHIBIT 18.21

Computing Expected
After-Tax Income from
Expected Sales

Point: Pretax income
= $15,750/(1 − 0.25), or $21,000.

Management then assesses whether this income is an adequate return on assets invested. Management will also consider whether sales and income can be increased by changing prices or reducing costs. CVP analysis is good for addressing these kinds of "what-if" questions.

"How many units must we sell to earn $50,000?"

Computing Sales for a Target Income

Many companies' annual plans are based on income targets (sometimes called *budgets*). Rydell's goal for this year is to increase income by 10% over the prior year. CVP analysis helps to determine the sales level needed to achieve the target income. Planning for the year is then based on this level.

We use the formula in Exhibit 18.22 to compute sales for a target income (pretax). To illustrate, Rydell has monthly fixed costs of $24,000 and a 30% contribution margin ratio. Assume that it sets a target monthly income of $12,000. Using the formula in Exhibit 18.22, we find that Rydell needs $120,000 of sales to produce a $12,000 pretax target income.

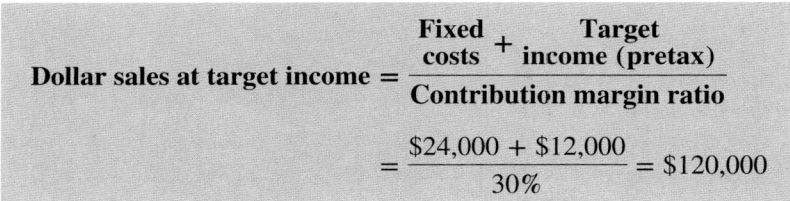

$$\text{Dollar sales at target income} = \frac{\text{Fixed costs} + \text{Target income (pretax)}}{\text{Contribution margin ratio}}$$

$$= \frac{\$24,000 + \$12,000}{30\%} = \$120,000$$

EXHIBIT 18.22

Computing Sales (Dollars)
for a Target Income

Alternatively, we can compute *unit sales* instead of dollar sales. To do this, use *contribution margin per unit*. Exhibit 18.23 illustrates this for Rydell. The two computations in Exhibits 18.22 and 18.23 are equivalent because sales of 1,200 units at $100 sales price per unit equal $120,000 of sales.

Point: Break-even is a special case of the formulas in Exhibits 18.22 and 18.23; simply set target income to $0, and the formulas reduce to those in Exhibits 18.11 and 18.12.

EXHIBIT 18.23

Computing Sales (Units) for
a Target Income

$$\text{Unit sales at target income} = \frac{\text{Fixed costs} + \text{Target income (pretax)}}{\text{Contribution margin per unit}}$$

$$= \frac{\$24,000 + \$12,000}{\$30} = 1,200 \text{ units}$$

We can also use the contribution margin income statement approach to compute sales for a target income in two steps.

Step 1: Insert the fixed costs ($24,000) and the target profit level ($12,000) into a contribution margin income statement, as shown in Exhibit 18.24. To cover its fixed costs of $24,000 and yield target income of $12,000, Rydell must generate a contribution margin of $36,000 (computed as $24,000 plus $12,000).

Step 2: Enter $36,000 in the contribution margin row as step 2. With a contribution margin ratio of 30%, sales must be $120,000, computed as $36,000/0.30, to yield a contribution margin of $36,000. We enter $120,000 in the sales row of the contribution margin income statement and solve for variable costs of $84,000 (computed as $120,000 − $36,000). At a selling price of $100 per unit, Rydell must sell 1,200 units ($120,000/$100) to earn a target income of $12,000.

EXHIBIT 18.24

Using the Contribution Margin Income Statement to Find Target Sales

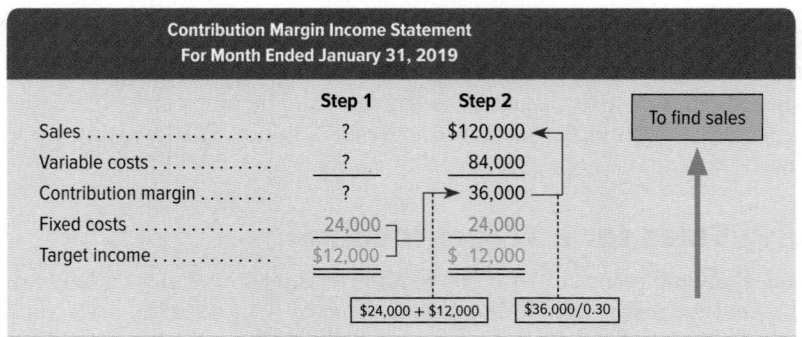

NEED-TO-KNOW 18-4

Contribution Margin, Target Income, and Margin of Safety

A1   C2

Do More: QS 18-9, QS 18-11, QS 18-13, E 18-12, E 18-17

A manufacturer predicts fixed costs of $502,000 for the next year. Its one product sells for $180 per unit, and it incurs variable costs of $126 per unit. Its target (pretax) income is $200,000.

1. Compute the contribution margin ratio.

2. Compute the dollar sales needed to yield the target income.

3. Compute the unit sales needed to yield the target income.

4. Assume break-even sales of 9,296 units. Compute the margin of safety (in dollars) if the company expects to sell 10,000 units.

Solution

1. Contribution margin ratio = [$180 − $126]/$180 = 30%

2. Dollar sales at target income = [$502,000 + $200,000]/0.30 = $2,340,000

3. Unit sales at target income = [$502,000 + $200,000]/[$180 − $126] = 13,000 units

4. Margin of safety = (10,000 × $180) − (9,296 × $180) = $126,720

©Dave Hogan for One Love Manchester/Getty Images

■ **Decision Insight** ━━━━━━━━━━━━━━━━━━━━

Mic Drop   Concert promotion is a risky and low-margin business. A recent Ariana Grande tour grossed nearly $70 million in ticket revenue. How much went to the promoter? After paying taxes, fixed costs of each venue (venue staff, electricity, security, insurance), and Ariana's share of ticket revenues, the promoter might have about $9 million to apply against its own fixed costs. **Live Nation**, Ariana's promoter, recently posted a small profit after several successive years of not breaking even. ■

Evaluating Strategies

Earlier we showed how changing one of the estimates in a CVP analysis impacts break-even. We can also examine strategies that impact several estimates in the CVP analysis. For instance, we might want to know what happens to income if we automate a currently manual process. We can use *sensitivity analysis* to predict income if we can describe how these changes affect a company's fixed costs, variable costs, selling price, and volume. CVP analyses based on different estimates can be useful to management in planning business strategy. We provide some examples.

Buy a Productive Asset A new machine would increase monthly fixed costs from $24,000 to $30,000 and decrease variable costs by $10 per unit (from $70 per unit to $60 per unit). Rydell's break-even point in dollars is currently $80,000. How would the new machine affect Rydell's break-even point in dollars? If Rydell maintains its selling price of $100 per unit, its contribution margin per unit will increase to $40—computed as $100 per unit minus the (new) variable costs of $60 per unit. With this new machine, the revised contribution margin ratio per unit is 40% (computed as $40/$100). Rydell's revised break-even point in dollars would be $75,000, as computed in Exhibit 18.25. The new machine would lower Rydell's break-even point by $5,000, or 50 units, per month. The revised margin of safety increases to 25%, computed as ($100,000 − $75,000)/$100,000.

EXHIBIT 18.25
Revised Break-Even

$$\text{Revised break-even point in dollars} = \frac{\text{Revised fixed costs}}{\text{Revised contribution margin ratio}} = \frac{\$30,000}{40\%} = \$75,000$$

Increase Advertising Expense Instead of buying a new machine, Rydell's advertising manager suggests increasing advertising. She believes that an increase of $3,000 in the monthly advertising budget will increase sales by $25,000 per month (at a selling price of $100 per unit). The contribution margin will continue to be $30 per unit. Exhibit 18.8 showed the company's margin of safety was 20% when Rydell's expected sales level was $100,000. With the advertising campaign, Rydell's revised break-even point in dollars is $90,000, as computed in Exhibit 18.26.

EXHIBIT 18.26
Revised Break-Even (in Dollars)

$$\text{Revised break-even point in dollars} = \frac{\text{Revised fixed costs}}{\text{Revised contribution margin ratio}} = \frac{\$27,000}{30\%} = \$90,000$$

The revised margin of safety is computed in Exhibit 18.27. Without considering other factors, the advertising campaign would increase Rydell's margin of safety from 20% to 28%.

EXHIBIT 18.27
Revised Margin of Safety (in Percent)

$$\text{Revised margin of safety (in percent)} = \frac{\text{Expected sales} - \text{Break-even sales}}{\text{Expected sales}} = \frac{\$125,000 - \$90,000}{\$125,000} = 28\%$$

Sales Mix and Break-Even

Many companies sell multiple products or services, and we can modify CVP analysis for these cases. An important assumption in a multiproduct setting is that *the sales mix of different products is known and remains constant* during the planning period. **Sales mix** is the ratio (proportion) of the sales volumes for the various products. For instance, if a company normally sells 10,000 footballs, 5,000 softballs, and 4,000 basketballs per month, its sales mix can be expressed as 10:5:4 for footballs, softballs, and basketballs.

When companies sell more than one product or service, we estimate the break-even point by using a **composite unit,** which summarizes the sales mix and contribution margins of each product. Multiproduct CVP analysis treats this composite unit as a single product. To illustrate, let's look at Hair-Today, a styling salon that offers three cuts: basic, ultra, and budget in the ratio of 4 basic cuts to 2 ultra cuts to 1 budget cut (expressed as 4:2:1). Management wants to estimate its break-even point for next year. Unit selling prices for these three cuts are basic, $20;

P4
Compute the break-even point for a multiproduct company.

©Sergey Novikov/Shutterstock

ultra, $32; and budget, $16. Unit variable costs for these three cuts are basic, $13; ultra, $18; and budget, $8. Using the 4:2:1 sales mix, the selling price and variable costs of a composite unit of the three products are computed as follows.

Selling price per composite unit		Variable costs per composite unit	
4 units of basic @ $20 per unit..............	$ 80	4 units of basic @ $13 per unit..............	$52
2 units of ultra @ $32 per unit	64	2 units of ultra @ $18 per unit	36
1 unit of budget @ $16 per unit............	16	1 unit of budget @ $8 per unit..............	8
Selling price of a composite unit...........	**$160**	Variable costs of a composite unit...........	**$96**

We compute the contribution margin for a *composite unit* using essentially the same formula used earlier (see Exhibit 18.9), as shown in Exhibit 18.28.

EXHIBIT 18.28

Contribution Margin per Composite Unit

$$\begin{array}{ccc} \textbf{Contribution margin} & = & \textbf{Selling price} & - & \textbf{Variable cost} \\ \textbf{per composite unit} & & \textbf{per composite unit} & & \textbf{per composite unit} \\ \$64 & = & \$160 & - & \$96 \end{array}$$

Assuming Hair-Today's fixed costs are $192,000 per year, we compute its break-even point in composite units in Exhibit 18.29.

EXHIBIT 18.29

Break-Even Point in Composite Units

$$\textbf{Break-even point in composite units} = \frac{\textbf{Fixed costs}}{\textbf{Contribution margin per composite unit}}$$
$$= \frac{\$192,000}{\$64} = 3,000 \text{ composite units}$$

Point: The break-even point in dollars for Exhibit 18.29 is $192,000/($64/$160) = $480,000.

This computation implies that Hair-Today breaks even when it sells 3,000 *composite* units. Each composite unit represents seven haircuts. To determine how many units of each product it must sell to break even, we use the expected sales mix of 4:2:1 and multiply the number of units of each product in the composite by 3,000, as follows.

Basic:	4 × 3,000..........	12,000 units
Ultra:	2 × 3,000..........	6,000 units
Budget:	1 × 3,000..........	3,000 units
	7 × 3,000..........	21,000 units

Exhibit 18.30 verifies that with this sales mix and unit sales computed above, Hair-Today would break even.

EXHIBIT 18.30

Multiproduct Break-Even Income

	Basic	Ultra	Budget	Total
Contribution margin				
Basic (12,000 @ $7)..............	$84,000			
Ultra (6,000 @ $14)..............		$84,000		
Budget (3,000 @ $8).............			$24,000	
Total contribution margin.........				$192,000
Fixed costs				192,000
Net income				$ 0

Point: Enterprise resource planning (ERP) systems can quickly generate multiproduct break-even analyses.

If the sales mix changes, the break-even point will likely change. For example, if Hair-Today sells more ultra cuts and fewer basic cuts, its break-even point will decrease. We can vary the sales mix to see what happens under alternative strategies.

For companies that sell many different products, multiproduct break-even computations can become hard. **Amazon**, for example, sells over 200 million different products. In such cases,

managers can group these products into departments (such as clothing, sporting goods, music) and compute department contribution margins. The department contribution margins and the sales mix can be used as we illustrate in this section.

■ Decision **Maker**

Entrepreneur   CVP analysis indicates that your start-up will break even with the current sales mix and price levels. You have a target income in mind. What analysis might you perform to assess the likelihood of achieving this income?

■   *Answer:* First compute the level of sales to achieve the desired net income. Then conduct sensitivity analysis by varying the price, sales mix, and cost estimates to assess the possibility of reaching the target sales level. For instance, you might have to pursue aggressive marketing strategies to push the high-margin products, you might have to cut prices to increase sales and profits, or another strategy might emerge.

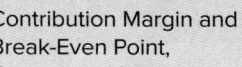

The sales mix of a company's two products, X and Y, is 2:1. Unit variable costs for both products are $2, and unit selling prices are $5 for X and $4 for Y. The company has $640,000 of fixed costs.

1. What is the contribution margin per composite unit?

2. What is the break-even point in composite units?

3. How many units of X and how many units of Y will be sold at the break-even point?

NEED-TO-KNOW **18-5**

Contribution Margin and Break-Even Point, Composite Units

P4

Solution

1.

Selling price of a composite unit		Variable costs of a composite unit	
2 units of X @ $5 per unit....................	$10	2 units of X @ $2 per unit....................	$4
1 unit of Y @ $4 per unit.....................	4	1 unit of Y @ $2 per unit....................	2
Selling price of a composite unit	$14	Variable costs of a composite unit	$6

Therefore, the contribution margin per composite unit is $8.

2. The break-even point in composite units = $640,000/$8 = 80,000 units.

3. At break-even, the company will sell 160,000 units (80,000 × 2) of X and 80,000 units of Y (80,000 × 1).

Do More: QS 18-14, E 18-22, E 18-23

Assumptions in Cost-Volume-Profit Analysis

CVP analysis relies on several assumptions:

● Costs can be classified as variable or fixed.
● Costs are linear within the relevant range.
● All units produced are sold (inventory levels do not change).
● Sales mix is constant.

If costs and sales differ from these assumptions, the results of CVP analysis can be less useful. Managers understand that CVP analysis gives approximate answers to questions and enables them to make rough estimates about the future.

 ## SUSTAINABILITY AND ACCOUNTING

Manufacturers try to increase the sustainability of their materials and packaging. **Nike** recently reengineered its shoeboxes to use 30% less material. These lighter shoeboxes can be shipped in cartons that are 20% lighter. Nike also now uses recycled polyester in much of its clothing. The company estimates it has reused the equivalent of over 2 billion plastic bottles in recent years.

These and other sustainability initiatives impact both variable and fixed costs and CVP analysis. Consider Rydell, the football manufacturer illustrated in this chapter. Rydell expects to sell 1,500 footballs per month, at a price of $100 per unit. Variable costs are $70 per unit and monthly fixed costs are $24,000. Rydell is considering using some recycled materials. This would add $1,160 in fixed costs per month and reduce variable costs by \$4 per unit. Management wants to know how this initiative would impact the company's break-even point, margin of safety, and forecasted income. Relevant calculations follow.

Before Initiative

Break-even	800 units
Margin of safety	20%
Forecasted income	\$21,000

©Ellis Infinity, LLC

$$\text{Revised break-even point in units} = \frac{\text{Revised fixed costs}}{\text{Revised contribution margin}} = \frac{\$25,160}{\$34} = 740 \text{ units}$$

$$\text{Revised margin of safety} = \frac{\text{Expected sales} - \text{Break-even sales}}{\text{Expected sales}} = \frac{\$150,000 - \$74,000}{\$150,000} = 50.7\%$$

$$\text{Revised forecasted income} = (\text{Units sold} \times \text{Contribution margin per unit}) - \text{Fixed costs}$$

$$= (1{,}500 \times \$34) - \$25{,}160 = \$25{,}840$$

Nailah Ellis-Brown, founder of this chapter's featured company, **Ellis Island Tropical Tea**, focuses on the "people" aspect of the triple bottom line. For her, that means doing what she can to help the people of Detroit recover from the hardships caused by the decline of the auto industry. "My passion is for [Michigan] natives," exclaims Nailah, "many of whom happen to be black."

Decision Analysis    Degree of Operating Leverage

A2

Analyze changes in sales using the degree of operating leverage.

CVP analysis is especially useful when management wishes to predict outcomes of alternative strategies. These strategies can involve changes in selling prices, fixed costs, variable costs, sales volume, and product mix. Managers are interested in seeing the effects of changes in some or all of these factors.

Managers try to get maximum benefits from their fixed costs. Managers want to use 100% of their capacity so that fixed costs are spread over the largest number of units. This would decrease fixed cost per unit and increase income. The extent, or relative size, of fixed costs in the total cost structure is known as **operating leverage.** Companies having a higher proportion of fixed costs in their total cost structure have higher operating leverage. An example is a company that automates its processes instead of using direct labor, increasing its fixed costs and lowering its variable costs.

A useful managerial measure to assess the effect of changes in the level of sales on income is the **degree of operating leverage (DOL),** calculated as shown in Exhibit 18.31.

EXHIBIT 18.31

Degree of Operating Leverage

> **DOL = Total contribution margin (in dollars)/Pretax income**

To illustrate, assume Rydell Company sells 1,200 footballs. At this sales level, its contribution margin (in dollars) and pretax income are computed as

Rydell Company	
Sales (1,200 × \$100).................	\$120,000
Variable costs (1,200 × \$70)...........	84,000
Contribution margin..................	36,000
Fixed costs	24,000
Income (pretax)......................	**\$ 12,000**

Rydell's degree of operating leverage (DOL) is then computed as shown in Exhibit 18.32.

EXHIBIT 18.32

Rydell's Degree of Operating Leverage

> **DOL = Total contribution margin (in dollars)/Pretax income**
> DOL = \$36,000/\$12,000 = 3.0

We then can use DOL to predict the effect of changes in the level of sales on pretax income. For example, if Rydell expects sales can either increase or decrease by 10%, and these changes would be within Rydell's relevant range, we can compute the change in pretax income using DOL, as shown in Exhibit 18.33.

EXHIBIT 18.33

Impact of Change in Sales on Income

> **Change in income (%) = DOL × Change in sales (%)**
> = 3.0 × 10% = 30%

Thus, if Rydell's sales *increase* by 10%, its income will increase by $3,600 (computed as $12,000 × 30%), to $15,600. If, instead, Rydell's sales decrease by 10%, its net income will decrease by $3,600, to $8,400. We can prove these results with contribution margin income statements, as shown below.

	Current	Sales Increase by 10%	Sales Decrease by 10%
Sales..........................	$120,000	$132,000	$108,000
Variable costs	84,000	92,400	75,600
Contribution margin	$ 36,000	$ 39,600	$ 32,400
Fixed costs......................	24,000	24,000	24,000
Target (pretax) income	$ 12,000	$ 15,600	$ 8,400

Sport Caps Co. manufactures and sells caps for different sporting events. The fixed costs of operating the company are $150,000 per month, and variable costs are $5 per cap. The caps are sold for $8 per unit. The production capacity is 100,000 caps per month.

NEED-TO-KNOW 18-6

COMPREHENSIVE

Break-Even, CVP Chart, and Sales for Target Income

Required

1. Use the formulas in the chapter to compute the following:
  a. Contribution margin per cap.
  b. Break-even point in terms of the number of caps produced and sold.
  c. Amount of income at 30,000 caps sold per month (ignore taxes).
  d. Amount of income at 85,000 caps sold per month (ignore taxes).
  e. Number of caps to be produced and sold to provide $60,000 of income (pretax).
2. Draw a CVP chart for the company, showing cap output on the horizontal axis. Identify (a) the break-even point and (b) the amount of pretax income when the level of cap production is 70,000.
3. Use the formulas in the chapter to compute the
  a. Contribution margin ratio.
  b. Break-even point in terms of sales dollars.
  c. Amount of income at $250,000 of sales per month (ignore taxes).
  d. Amount of income at $600,000 of sales per month (ignore taxes).
  e. Dollars of sales needed to provide $60,000 of pretax income.

PLANNING THE SOLUTION

- Identify the formulas in the chapter for the required items expressed in units and solve them using the data given in the problem.
- Draw a CVP chart that reflects the facts in the problem. The horizontal axis should plot the volume in units up to 100,000, and the vertical axis should plot the total dollars up to $800,000. Plot the total cost line as upward sloping, starting at the fixed cost level ($150,000) on the vertical axis and increasing until it reaches $650,000 at the maximum volume of 100,000 units. Verify that the break-even point (where the two lines cross) equals the amount you computed in part 1.
- Identify the formulas in the chapter for the required items expressed in dollars and solve them using the data given in the problem.

SOLUTION

1. a. Contribution margin per cap $= $ Selling price per unit $-$ Variable cost per unit
$= \$8 - \$5 = \underline{\underline{\$3}}$

b. Break-even point in caps $= \dfrac{\text{Fixed costs}}{\text{Contribution margin per cap}} = \dfrac{\$150,000}{\$3} = \underline{\underline{50,000 \text{ caps}}}$

c. Income at 30,000 caps sold = (Units × Contribution margin per unit) − Fixed costs
= (30,000 × \$3) − \$150,000 = \$(60,000) loss

d. Income at 85,000 caps sold = (Units × Contribution margin per unit) − Fixed costs
= (85,000 × \$3) − \$150,000 = \$105,000 profit

e. Units needed for \$60,000 income $= \dfrac{\text{Fixed costs} + \text{Target income}}{\text{Contribution margin per cap}}$

$= \dfrac{\$150,000 + \$60,000}{\$3} = 70,000 \text{ caps}$

2. CVP chart.

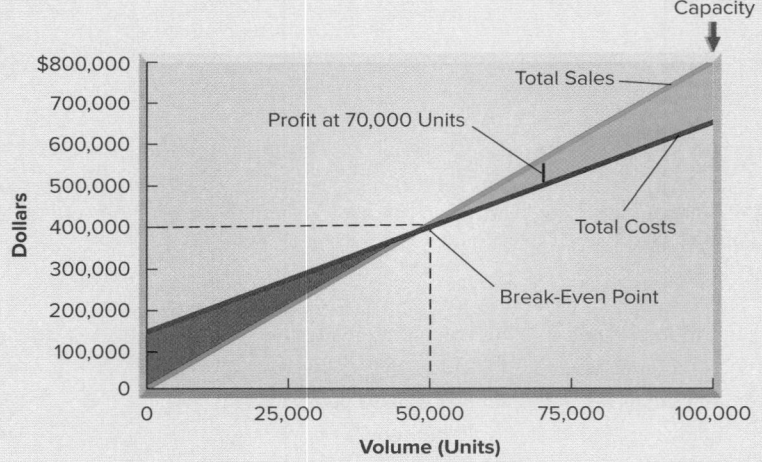

3. a. Contribution margin ratio $= \dfrac{\text{Contribution margin per unit}}{\text{Selling price per unit}} = \dfrac{\$3}{\$8} = 0.375 \text{ or } 37.5\%$

b. Break-even point in dollars $= \dfrac{\text{Fixed costs}}{\text{Contribution margin ratio}} = \dfrac{\$150,000}{37.5\%} = \$400,000$

c. Income at sales of \$250,000 = (Sales × Contribution margin ratio) − Fixed costs
= (\$250,000 × 37.5%) − \$150,000 = \$(56,250) loss

d. Income at sales of \$600,000 = (Sales × Contribution margin ratio) − Fixed costs
= (\$600,000 × 37.5%) − \$150,000 = \$75,000 income

e. Dollars of sales to yield
\$60,000 pretax income $= \dfrac{\text{Fixed costs} + \text{Target pretax income}}{\text{Contribution margin ratio}}$

$= \dfrac{\$150,000 + \$60,000}{37.5\%} = \$560,000$

APPENDIX

18A   Using Excel for Cost Estimation

Microsoft Excel® and other spreadsheet software can be used to perform least-squares regressions to identify cost behavior. In Excel, the INTERCEPT and SLOPE functions are used. The following screen shot reports the data from Exhibit 18.4 in cells Al through C13 and shows the cell contents to find the intercept (cell B15) and slope (cell B16). Cell B15 uses Excel to find the intercept from a least-squares regression of total cost (shown as C2:C13 in cell B15) on units produced (shown as B2:B13 in cell B15). Spreadsheet software is useful in understanding cost behavior when many data points (such as monthly total costs and units produced) are available.

Excel can also be used to create scatter diagrams such as that in Exhibit 18.5. In contrast to visually drawing a line that "fits" the data, Excel more precisely fits the line. To draw a scatter diagram with a line of fit, follow these steps:

1. Highlight the data cells you wish to diagram; in this example, start from cell C13 and highlight through cell B2.

2. Then select "Insert" and "Scatter" from the drop-down menus. Selecting the chart type in the upper left corner of the choices under "Scatter" will produce a diagram that looks like that in Exhibit 18.5, without a line of fit.

3. To add a line of fit (also called a trend line), select "Design," "Add Chart Element," "Trendline," and "Linear" from the drop-down menus. This will produce a diagram that looks like that in Exhibit 18.5, including the line of fit.

	A	B	C
1	**Month**	**Units Produced**	**Total Cost**
2	January	27,500	$21,500
3	February	22,500	20,500
4	March	25,000	25,000
5	April	35,000	21,500
6	May	47,500	25,500
7	June	17,500	18,500
8	July	30,000	23,500
9	August	52,500	28,500
10	September	37,500	26,000
11	October	62,500	29,000
12	November	67,500	31,000
13	December	57,500	26,000
14			**Result**
15	**Intercept**	=INTERCEPT(C2:C13, B2:B13)	$16,688.24
16	**Slope**	=SLOPE(C2:C13, B2:B13)	$ 0.1995

The line drawn in Exhibit 18.5 intersects the vertical axis at approximately $17,000, which represents an estimate of fixed costs. To compute an estimated variable cost per unit, select any two levels of output and compute a slope as in the high-low method. Using 0 and 25,000 units as the two activity points, the slope is

Point: The intercept function solves for total fixed costs. The slope function solves for the variable cost per unit.

$$\frac{\text{Change in cost}}{\text{Change in units}} = \frac{\$25,000 - \$17,000}{25,000 - 0} = \frac{\$8,000}{25,000} = \$0.32 \text{ per unit}$$

Variable cost is $0.32 per unit. Thus, the cost equation that management will use to estimate costs for different unit levels is **$17,000 plus $0.32 per unit produced**.

APPENDIX

Variable Costing and Performance Reporting

18B

This chapter showed the usefulness of *contribution margin,* or selling price minus variable costs, in CVP analysis. The contribution margin income statement introduced in this chapter is also known as a **variable costing income statement.** In **variable costing,** only costs that change in total with changes in production levels are included in product costs. These costs include direct materials, direct labor, and *variable* overhead costs. Thus, under variable costing, *fixed* overhead costs are excluded from product costs and instead are expensed in the period incurred. As we showed in this chapter, a variable costing approach can be useful in many managerial analyses and decisions.

The variable costing method is not allowed, however, for external financial reporting. Instead, GAAP requires **absorption costing.** Under absorption costing, product costs include direct materials, direct labor, *and all overhead,* both variable and fixed. Thus, under absorption costing, fixed overhead costs are expensed when the goods are sold. Managers can use variable costing information for internal decision making, but they must use absorption costing for external reporting purposes.

P5

Compute unit cost and income under both absorption and variable costing.

Computing Unit Cost
To illustrate the difference between absorption costing and variable costing, let's consider the product cost data in Exhibit 18B.1 from IceAge, a skate manufacturer.

Direct materials cost.	$4 per unit	Overhead cost (per year)	
Direct labor cost	$8 per unit	Variable overhead cost	$180,000
Expected units produced	60,000 units	Fixed overhead cost.	600,000
		Total overhead cost	$780,000

EXHIBIT 18B.1

Summary Product Cost Data

Using the product cost data, Exhibit 18B.2 shows the product cost per unit computations for both absorption and variable costing. These computations are shown both in a tabular format (left side of exhibit) and a visual format (right side of exhibit). For absorption costing, the product cost per unit is $25, which consists of $4 in direct materials, $8 in direct labor, $3 in variable overhead ($180,000/60,000 units), and $10 in fixed overhead ($600,000/60,000 units).

For variable costing, the product cost per unit is $15, which consists of $4 in direct materials, $8 in direct labor, and $3 in variable overhead. Fixed overhead costs of $600,000 are treated as a period cost and are recorded as expense in the period incurred. *The difference between the two costing methods is the exclusion of fixed overhead from product costs for variable costing.*

EXHIBIT 18B.2

Unit Cost Computation

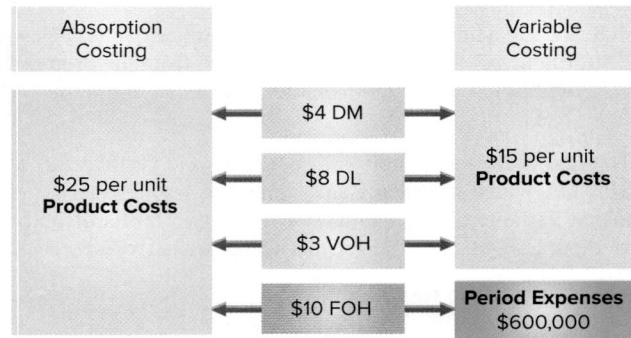

Product Cost per Unit	Absorption Costing	Variable Costing
Direct materials............	$ 4	$ 4
Direct labor...............	8	8
Overhead costs		
Variable overhead	3	3
Fixed overhead	10	—
Total product cost per unit ...	$25	$15

NEED-TO-KNOW 18-7

Computing Product Cost per Unit

P5

A manufacturer reports the following data.

Direct materials cost...............	$6 per unit	Variable overhead	$220,000 per year
Direct labor cost	$14 per unit	Fixed overhead.............	$680,000 per year
Expected units produced	20,000 units		

1. Compute the total product cost per unit under absorption costing.
2. Compute the total product cost per unit under variable costing.

Solution

Per Unit Costs	(1) Absorption Costing	(2) Variable Costing
Direct materials.............................	$ 6	$ 6
Direct labor.................................	14	14
Variable overhead ($220,000/20,000)	11	11
Fixed overhead ($680,000/20,000)*	34	—
Total product cost per unit.....................	$65	$31

*Not included in product costs under variable costing.

Do More: QS 18-17, QS 18-18, QS 18-19, QS 18-20, E 18-26

Income Reporting

The prior section showed how the different treatment of fixed overhead costs leads to different product costs per unit under absorption and variable costing. This section shows the implications of this difference for income reporting.

To illustrate the income reporting implications, we return to IceAge Company. Below are the manufacturing cost data for IceAge as well as additional data on selling and administrative expenses. Assume that IceAge began year 2019 with no units in inventory. During 2019, IceAge produced 60,000 units and sold 40,000 units at $40 each, leaving 20,000 units in ending inventory.

Using the information above, we prepare income statements for IceAge both under absorption costing and under variable costing. Under variable costing, expenses are grouped according to cost behavior—variable or fixed, and production or nonproduction. Under the traditional format of absorption costing, expenses are grouped by function but not separated into variable and fixed components.

Units Produced Exceed Units Sold   Exhibit 18B.3 shows absorption costing and variable costing income statements. In 2019, 60,000 units were produced, but only 40,000 units were sold, which means 20,000 units remain in ending inventory.

ICEAGE COMPANY Income Statement (Absorption Costing) For Year Ended December 31, 2019	
Sales* (40,000 × $40).................	$1,600,000
Cost of goods sold (40,000 × $25†).......	1,000,000
Gross margin	600,000
Selling and administrative expenses [$200,000 + (40,000 × $2)]	280,000
Net income...........................	$ 320,000

*Units produced equal 60,000; units sold equal 40,000.
†$4 DM + $8 DL + $3 VOH + $10 FOH.
‡$4 DM + $8 DL + $3 VOH.

ICEAGE COMPANY Income Statement (Variable Costing) For Year Ended December 31, 2019		
Sales* (40,000 × $40)...........		$1,600,000
Variable expenses		
Variable production costs (40,000 × $15‡)	$600,000	
Variable selling and administrative expenses (40,000 × $2).....	80,000	680,000
Contribution margin............		920,000
Fixed expenses		
Fixed overhead	600,000	
Fixed selling and administrative expense......	200,000	800,000
Net income....................		$ 120,000

EXHIBIT 18B.3

Income under Absorption or Variable Costing

The income statements reveal that for 2019, income is $320,000 under absorption costing. Under variable costing, income is $120,000, which is $200,000 less than under absorption costing. This $200,000 difference is due to the different treatment of fixed overhead under the two costing methods. Because variable costing expenses fixed manufacturing overhead (FOH) based on the number of units produced (60,000 × $10), and absorption costing expenses FOH based on the number of units sold (40,000 × $10), net income is lower under variable costing by $200,000 (20,000 units × $10).

Under variable costing, the entire $600,000 fixed overhead cost is treated as an expense in computing 2019 income. Under absorption costing, the fixed overhead cost is allocated to each unit of product at the rate of $10 per unit (from Exhibit 18B.2). When production exceeds sales by 20,000 units (60,000 versus 40,000), the $200,000 ($10 × 20,000 units) of fixed overhead cost allocated to these 20,000 units is included in the cost of ending inventory. This means that $200,000 of fixed overhead cost incurred in 2019 is not expensed until future years under absorption costing, when it is reported in cost of goods sold as those products are sold. Consequently, income for 2019 under absorption costing is $200,000 higher than income under variable costing. Even though sales (of 40,000 units) and the number of units produced (totaling 60,000) are the same under both costing methods, net income differs greatly due to the treatment of fixed overhead.

©Toshifumi Kitamura/AFP/Getty Images

Converting Income under Variable Costing to Income under Absorption Costing   In 2019, IceAge produced 20,000 more units than it sold. Those 20,000 units remaining in ending inventory will be sold in future years. When those units are sold, the $200,000 of fixed overhead costs attached to them will be expensed, resulting in lower income under the absorption costing method. This leads to a simple way to convert income under variable costing to income under absorption costing:

$$\text{Income under absorption costing} = \text{Income under variable costing} + \text{Fixed overhead cost in ending inventory} - \text{Fixed overhead cost in beginning inventory}$$

For example, assume IceAge produces 60,000 units and sells 80,000 units in 2020, and reports income under variable costing of $1,040,000. Income under absorption costing is then computed as

$$\text{Income under absorption costing} = \$1,040,000 + \$0 - \$200,000 = \$840,000$$

Differences in income between variable and absorption costing are summarized below.

Production		Sales	Income under
60,000 pairs	>	40,000 pairs	Absorption costing > Variable costing $320,000 > $120,000
	>		**2019**
60,000 pairs	<	80,000 pairs	Absorption costing < Variable costing $840,000 < $1,040,000
	<		**2020**

APPENDIX

18C

Preparing a CVP Chart

	A	B	C
1	**Units**	**Sales**	**Total Cost**
2	200	$ 20,000	$ 38,000
3	400	40,000	52,000
4	600	60,000	66,000
5	800	80,000	80,000
6	1,000	100,000	94,000
7	1,200	120,000	108,000
8	1,400	140,000	122,000
9	1,600	160,000	136,000
10	1,800	180,000	150,000

Here are the data to prepare a CVP chart in Excel for Rydell.
To draw a CVP chart as shown in Exhibit 18.14, follow these steps.

1. Highlight cells containing the data to graph, in this case B2:C10.
2. Select Insert>Charts>All Charts>Line, then select the first of the line chart choices.

These steps produce the chart in Exhibit 18.14, but without the formatting and labeling.

Summary: Cheat Sheet

COST BEHAVIOR

Fixed costs: Do not change in total as volume changes.

Variable costs: Change proportionately with volume.

Mixed costs: Include both fixed and variable components.

Step-wise costs: Step pattern, but fixed within each relevant range.

Relevant range: Normal operating range; neither near zero nor maximum.

MEASURING COST BEHAVIOR

Cost equation: Fixed costs + Variable cost per unit

High-low method: Estimates a cost equation using high and low *activity*.

$$\frac{\text{Variable cost}}{\text{per unit}} = \frac{\text{High cost} - \text{Low cost}}{\text{High volume} - \text{Low volume}}$$

Fixed costs in total = Total cost − (Variable cost per unit × # of units)

Regression method: Statistical method using all data.

CONTRIBUTION MARGIN

$$\frac{\text{Contribution margin}}{\text{per unit}} = \text{Selling price per unit} - \text{Total variable cost per unit}$$

$$\text{Contribution margin ratio} = \frac{\text{Contribution margin per unit}}{\text{Selling price per unit}}$$

Contribution Margin Income Statement Format

Sales
− Variable costs
Contribution margin
− Fixed costs
Income (pretax)

BREAK-EVEN POINT

$$\text{Break-even point in units} = \frac{\text{Fixed costs}}{\text{Contribution margin per unit}}$$

$$\text{Break-even point in dollars} = \frac{\text{Fixed costs}}{\text{Contribution margin ratio}}$$

APPLYING CVP

Margin of safety: Amount that sales can drop before company incurs a loss.

$$\text{Margin of safety (in percent)} = \frac{\text{Expected sales} - \text{Break-even sales}}{\text{Expected sales}}$$

$$\text{Dollar sales at target income} = \frac{\text{Fixed costs} + \text{Target income (pretax)}}{\text{Contribution margin ratio}}$$

$$\text{Unit sales at target income} = \frac{\text{Fixed costs} + \text{Target income (pretax)}}{\text{Contribution margin per unit}}$$

SALES MIX

Sales mix: Ratio of sales volumes for various products.

Price (or variable) cost per composite unit:

$$\begin{aligned}
&\text{\# product } 1 \times \text{\$ per unit of product 1} \\
+\ &\text{\# product } 2 \times \text{\$ per unit of product 2} \\
+\ &\text{\# product } 3 \times \text{\$ per unit of product 3} \\
\hline
=\ &\text{Price (or variable) cost per composite unit}
\end{aligned}$$

$$\frac{\text{Contribution margin}}{\text{per composite unit}} = \frac{\text{Selling price}}{\text{per composite unit}} - \frac{\text{Variable cost}}{\text{per composite unit}}$$

$$\frac{\text{Break-even point in}}{\text{composite units}} = \frac{\text{Fixed costs}}{\text{Contribution margin per composite unit}}$$

OPERATING LEVERAGE

Operating leverage (DOL): Degree of fixed costs in the cost structure. More fixed costs *means* More leverage.

$$\text{DOL} = \text{Total contribution margin (in dollars)}/\text{Pretax income}$$

$$\text{Change in income (\%)} = \text{DOL} \times \text{Change in sales (\%)}$$

VARIABLE COSTING

$$\frac{\text{Income under}}{\text{absorption costing}} = \frac{\text{Income under}}{\text{variable costing}} + \frac{\text{Fixed overhead cost}}{\text{in ending inventory}} - \frac{\text{Fixed overhead cost}}{\text{in beginning inventory}}$$

Key Terms

Absorption costing (707)

Break-even point (704)

Composite unit (711)

Contribution margin (703)

Contribution margin per unit (703)

Contribution margin ratio (703)

Cost-volume-profit (CVP) analysis (697)

Cost-volume-profit (CVP) chart (706)

Curvilinear cost (700)

Degree of operating leverage (DOL) (714)

Estimated line of cost behavior (701)

High-low method (702)

Least-squares regression (702)

Margin of safety (707)

Mixed cost (698)

Operating leverage (714)

Relevant range of operations (698)

Sales mix (711)

Scatter diagram (701)

Step-wise cost (699)

Variable costing (717)

Variable costing income statement (717)

Multiple Choice Quiz

1. A company's only product sells for $150 per unit. Its variable costs per unit are $100, and its fixed costs total $75,000. What is its contribution margin per unit?

a. $50   c. $100   e. $25

b. $250   d. $150

2. Using information from question 1, what is the company's contribution margin ratio?

a. 66⅔%   c. 50%   e. 33⅓%

b. 100%   d. 0%

3. Using information from question 1, what is the company's break-even point in units?

a. 500 units   c. 1,500 units   e. 1,000 units

b. 750 units   d. 3,000 units

4. A company's forecasted sales are $300,000 and its sales at break-even are $180,000. Its margin of safety in dollars is

a. $180,000.   c. $480,000.   e. $300,000.

b. $120,000.   d. $60,000.

5. A product sells for $400 per unit and its variable costs per unit are $260. The company's fixed costs are $840,000. If the company desires $70,000 pretax income, what is the required dollar sales?

a. $2,400,000   c. $2,600,000   e. $1,400,000

b. $200,000   d. $2,275,000

ANSWERS TO MULTIPLE CHOICE QUIZ

1. a; $150 − $100 = $50
2. e; ($150 − $100)/$150 = 33⅓%
3. c; $75,000/$50 CM per unit = 1,500 units

4. b; $300,000 − $180,000 = $120,000
5. c; Contribution margin ratio = ($400 − $260)/$400 = 0.35
   Targeted sales = ($840,000 + $70,000)/0.35 = $2,600,000

A,B,C *Superscript letter A, B, or C denotes assignments based on Appendix 18A, 18B, or 18C.*

🔲 Icon denotes assignments that involve decision making.

Discussion Questions

1. What is a variable cost? Identify two variable costs.
2. 🔲 When output volume increases, do variable costs per unit increase, decrease, or stay the same within the relevant range of activity? Explain.
3. 🔲 When output volume increases, do fixed costs per unit increase, decrease, or stay the same within the relevant range of activity? Explain.
4. 🔲 How is cost-volume-profit analysis useful?
5. How do step-wise costs and curvilinear costs differ?
6. Describe the contribution margin ratio in layperson's terms.
7. Define and explain the *contribution margin ratio.*
8. Define and describe *contribution margin per unit.*
9. In performing CVP analysis for a manufacturing company, what simplifying assumption is usually made about the volume of production and the volume of sales?
10. What two arguments tend to justify classifying all costs as either fixed or variable even though individual costs might not behave exactly as classified?
11. 🔲 How does assuming that operating activity occurs within a relevant range affect cost-volume-profit analysis?
12. List three methods to measure cost behavior.
13. How is a scatter diagram used to identify and measure the behavior of a company's costs?
14. In cost-volume-profit analysis, what is the estimated profit at the break-even point?
15. 🔲 Assume that a straight line on a CVP chart intersects the vertical axis at the level of fixed costs and has a positive slope that rises with each additional unit of volume by the amount of the variable costs per unit. What does this line represent?
16. **Google** has both fixed and variable costs. Why are fixed costs depicted as a horizontal line on a CVP chart? **GOOGLE**
17. 🔲 Each of two similar companies has sales of $20,000 and total costs of $15,000 for a month. Company A's total costs include $10,000 of variable costs and $5,000 of fixed costs. If Company B's total costs include $4,000 of variable costs and $11,000 of fixed costs, which company will enjoy more profit if sales double?
18. _____ of _____ reflects expected sales in excess of the level of break-even sales.
19. 🔲 **Apple** produces tablet computers. Identify some of the variable and fixed product costs associated with that production. *Hint:* Limit costs to product costs. **APPLE**
20. 🔲 Should **Apple** use single-product or multi-product break-even analysis? Explain. **APPLE**
21. 🔲 **Samsung** is thinking of expanding sales of its most popular smartphone model by 65%. Should we expect its variable and fixed costs for this model to stay within the relevant range? Explain. **Samsung**
22.ᴮ **Google** uses variable costing for several business decisions. How can variable costing income be converted to absorption costing income? **GOOGLE**

🔲 **connect**

QUICK STUDY

QS 18-1

Cost behavior identification

C1

Excel:
Enter data
Select:
Insert
Charts
All Charts
Line

Listed here are four series of separate costs measured at various volume levels. Examine each series and identify whether it is best described as a fixed, variable, step-wise, or curvilinear cost. *Hint:* It can help to graph each cost series.

Volume (Units)	Series 1	Series 2	Series 3	Series 4
0	$ 0	$450	$ 800	$100
100	800	450	800	105
200	1,600	450	800	120
300	2,400	450	1,600	145
400	3,200	450	1,600	190
500	4,000	450	2,400	250
600	4,800	450	2,400	320

Determine whether each of the following is best described as a fixed, variable, or mixed cost with respect to product units.

_____ **1.** Rubber used to manufacture athletic shoes.   _____ **5.** Factory supervisor's salary.

_____ **2.** Maintenance of factory machinery.   _____ **6.** Taxes on factory building.

_____ **3.** Packaging expense.   _____ **7.** Depreciation expense of warehouse.

_____ **4.** Wages of an assembly-line worker paid
on the basis of acceptable units produced.

QS 18-2
Cost behavior identification
C1

The following information is available for a company's maintenance cost over the last seven months. Using the high-low method, estimate both the fixed and variable components of its maintenance cost.

QS 18-3
Cost behavior estimation—
high-low method
P1

Month	Units Produced	Maintenance Cost
June...............	90	$5,450
July	180	6,900
August.............	120	5,100
September	150	6,000
October............	210	6,900
November...........	240	8,100
December	60	3,600

This scatter diagram reflects past units produced and their corresponding maintenance costs.

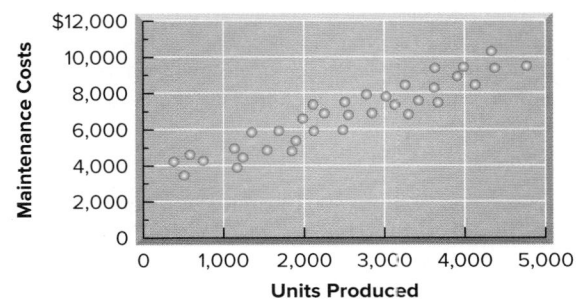

QS 18-4
Interpreting a scatter
diagram
P1

1. Review the scatter diagram and classify these costs as either fixed, variable, or mixed.

2. If 3,000 units are produced, are maintenance costs expected to be greater than $6,000?

Compute the contribution margin ratio using the following data: sales, $5,000; total variable cost, $3,000.

QS 18-5
Contribution margin
ratio **A1**

SBD Phone Company sells its waterproof phone case for $90 per unit. Fixed costs total $162,000, and variable costs are $36 per unit. Determine the (1) contribution margin per unit and (2) break-even point in units.

QS 18-6
Contribution margin per
unit and break-even units
P2

SBD Phone Company sells its waterproof phone case for $90 per unit. Fixed costs total $162,000, and variable costs are $36 per unit. How will the break-even point in units change in response to each of the following independent changes in selling price per unit, variable cost per unit, or total fixed costs? Use **I** for increase and **D** for decrease. (It is not necessary to compute new break-even points.)

QS 18-7
Assumptions in CVP
analysis
C2

Change	Break-Even in Units will:	Change	Break-Even in Units will:
1. Total fixed costs to $190,000	_____	4. Variable costs to $67 per unit	_____
2. Variable costs to $34 per unit	_____	5. Total fixed costs to $150,000	_____
3. Selling price per unit to $80	_____	6. Selling price per unit to $120	_____

QS 18-8 Contribution margin ratio and break-even dollars **P2**	SBD Phone Company sells its waterproof phone case for $90 per unit. Fixed costs total $162,000, and variable costs are $36 per unit. Determine the (1) contribution margin ratio and (2) break-even point in dollars.
QS 18-9 CVP analysis and target income **C2**	SBD Phone Company sells its waterproof phone case for $90 per unit. Fixed costs total $162,000, and variable costs are $36 per unit. Compute the units of product that must be sold to earn pretax income of $200,000. (Round to the nearest whole unit.)
QS 18-10 Computing break-even **P2**	Zhao Co. has fixed costs of $354,000. Its single product sells for $175 per unit, and variable costs are $116 per unit. Determine the break-even point in units.
QS 18-11 Margin of safety **C2**	Zhao Co. has fixed costs of $354,000. Its single product sells for $175 per unit, and variable costs are $116 per unit. If the company expects sales of 10,000 units, compute its margin of safety (a) in dollars and (b) as a percent of expected sales.
QS 18-12 Contribution margin income statement **P2**	Zhao Co. has fixed costs of $354,000. Its single product sells for $175 per unit, and variable costs are $116 per unit. The company expects sales of 10,000 units. Prepare a contribution margin income statement for the year ended December 31, 2019.
QS 18-13 Target income **C2**	Zhao Co. has fixed costs of $354,000. Its single product sells for $175 per unit, and variable costs are $116 per unit. Compute the level of sales in units needed to produce a target (pretax) income of $118,000.
QS 18-14 Sales mix and break-even **P4**	US-Mobile manufactures and sells two products, tablet computers and smartphones, in the ratio of 5:3. Fixed costs are $105,000, and the contribution margin per composite unit is $125. What number of each type of product is sold at the break-even point?
QS 18-15[C] CVP chart **P3**	Corme Company expects sales of $34 million (400,000 units). The company's total fixed costs are $17.5 million and its variable costs are $35 per unit. Prepare a CVP chart from this information.
QS 18-16 Operating leverage analysis **A2**	Singh Co. reports a contribution margin of $960,000 and fixed costs of $720,000. (1) Compute the company's degree of operating leverage. (2) If sales increase by 15%, what amount of income will Singh Co. expect?
QS 18-17[B] Computing unit cost under absorption costing **P5**	Vijay Company reports the following information regarding its production costs. Compute its product cost per unit under absorption costing.

Direct materials.	$10 per unit	Overhead costs for the year	
Direct labor	$20 per unit	Variable overhead	$10 per unit
Units produced	20,000 units	Fixed overhead.	$160,000

QS 18-18[B] Computing unit cost under variable costing **P5**	Refer to Vijay Company's data in QS 18-17. Compute its product cost per unit under variable costing.
QS 18-19[B] Variable costing income statement **P5**	Aces Inc., a manufacturer of tennis rackets, began operations this year. The company produced 6,000 rackets and sold 4,900. Each racket was sold at a price of $90. Fixed overhead costs are $78,000, and fixed selling and administrative costs are $65,200. The company also reports the following per unit costs for the year. Prepare an income statement under variable costing.

Variable production costs.	$25
Variable selling and administrative expenses.	2

Aces Inc., a manufacturer of tennis rackets, began operations this year. The company produced 6,000 rackets and sold 4,900. Each racket was sold at a price of $90. Fixed overhead costs are $78,000, and fixed selling and administrative costs are $65,200. The company also reports the following per unit costs for the year. Prepare an income statement under absorption costing.

QS 18-20ᴮ
Absorption costing income statement
P5

Variable production costs.	$25
Variable selling and administrative expenses.	2

A recent income statement for **BMW** reports the following (in € millions). Assume 75% of the cost of sales and 75% of the selling and administrative costs are variable costs, and the remaining 25% of each is fixed. Compute the contribution margin (in € millions). (Round computations using percentages to the nearest whole euro.)

QS 18-21
Contribution margin
A1

Sales	€92,175
Cost of sales	74,043
Selling and administrative expenses.	8,633

≡ connect

Following are five graphs representing various cost behaviors. (1) Identify whether the cost behavior in each graph is mixed, step-wise, fixed, variable, or curvilinear. (2) Identify the graph (by number) that best illustrates each cost behavior: (*a*) Factory policy requires one supervisor for every 30 factory workers; (*b*) real estate taxes on factory; (*c*) electricity charge that includes the standard monthly charge plus a charge for each kilowatt hour; (*d*) commissions to salespersons; and (*e*) costs of hourly paid workers that provide substantial gains in efficiency when a few workers are added but gradually smaller gains in efficiency when more workers are added.

EXERCISES

Exercise 18-1
Cost behavior in graphs
C1

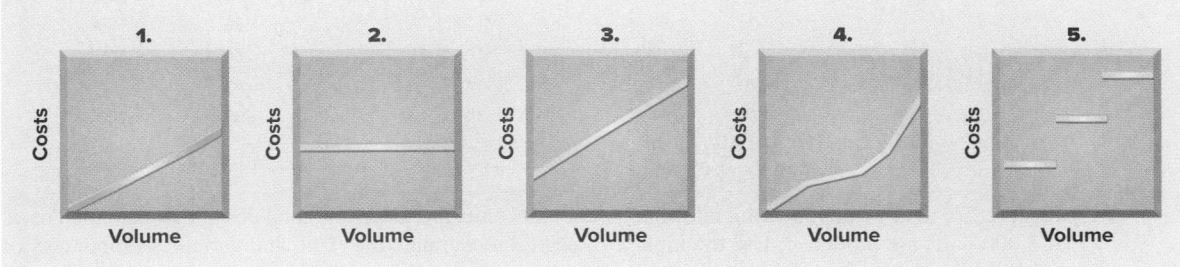

The left column lists several cost classifications. The right column presents short definitions of those costs. In the blank space beside each of the numbers in the right column, write the letter of the cost best described by the definition.

Exercise 18-2
Cost behavior defined
C1

A. Total cost

B. Mixed cost

C. Variable cost

D. Curvilinear cost

E. Step-wise cost

F. Fixed cost

_____ **1.** This cost is the combined amount of all the other costs.

_____ **2.** This cost remains constant over a limited range of volume; when it reaches the end of its limited range, it changes by a lump sum and remains at that level until it exceeds another limited range.

_____ **3.** This cost has a component that remains the same over all volume levels and another component that increases in direct proportion to increases in volume.

_____ **4.** This cost increases when volume increases, but the increase is not constant for each unit produced.

_____ **5.** This cost remains constant over all volume levels within the productive capacity for the planning period.

_____ **6.** This cost increases in direct proportion to increases in volume; its amount is constant for each unit produced.

Exercise 18-3

Cost behavior identification

C1

Excel:
Enter data
Select:
Insert
Charts
All Charts
Line

Following are five series of costs A through E measured at various volume levels. Identify each series as either fixed, variable, mixed, step-wise, or curvilinear.

	A	B	C	D	E	F
	Volume (Units)	Series A	Series B	Series C	Series D	Series E
1	0	$ 0	$2,500	$ 0	$1,000	$5,000
2	400	3,600	3,100	6,000	1,000	5,000
3	800	7,200	3,700	6,600	2,000	5,000
4	1,200	10,800	4,300	7,200	2,000	5,000
5	1,600	14,400	4,900	8,200	3,000	5,000
6	2,000	18,000	5,500	9,600	3,000	5,000
7	2,400	21,600	6,100	13,500	4,000	5,000

Exercise 18-4[A]

Measurement of cost behavior using a scatter diagram

P1

A company reports the following information about its unit sales and its cost of sales. Each unit sells for $500. Use these data to prepare a scatter diagram. Draw an estimated line of cost behavior and determine whether the cost appears to be variable, fixed, or mixed.

Period	Unit Sales	Cost of Sales	Period	Unit Sales	Cost of Sales
1	22,500	$15,150	4	11,250	$ 8,250
2	17,250	11,250	5	13,500	9,000
3	15,750	10,500	6	18,750	14,250

Exercise 18-5[A]

Scatter diagram and measurement of cost behavior

P1

Use the following information about unit sales and total cost of sales to prepare a scatter diagram. Draw a cost line that reflects the behavior displayed by this cost. Determine whether the cost is variable, step-wise, fixed, mixed, or curvilinear.

Period	Unit Sales	Cost of Sales	Period	Unit Sales	Cost of Sales
1	760	$590	9	580	$390
2	800	560	10	320	240
3	200	230	11	240	230
4	400	400	12	720	550
5	480	390	13	280	260
6	620	550	14	440	410
7	680	590	15	380	260
8	540	430			

Exercise 18-6

Cost behavior estimation—scatter diagram and high-low

P1

Felix & Co. reports the following information about its units produced and total costs. Estimate total costs if 3,000 units are produced. Use the high-low method to estimate the fixed and variable components of total costs.

Period	Units Produced	Total Costs	Period	Units Produced	Total Costs
1	0	$2,500	6	2,000	$5,500
2	400	3,100	7	2,400	6,100
3	800	3,700	8	2,800	6,700
4	1,200	4,300	9	3,200	7,300
5	1,600	4,900	10	3,600	7,900

Exercise 18-7[A]

Measurement of cost behavior using regression   P1

Refer to the information from Exercise 18-6. Use spreadsheet software to use ordinary least-squares regression to estimate the cost equation, including fixed and variable cost amounts.

Exercise 18-8

Contribution margin

A1

A jeans maker is designing a new line of jeans called Slims. The jeans will sell for $205 per pair and cost $164 per pair in variable costs to make.

1. Compute the contribution margin per pair.

2. Compute the contribution margin ratio.

3. Describe what the contribution margin ratio reveals about this new jeans line.

Blanchard Company manufactures a single product that sells for $180 per unit and whose total variable costs are $135 per unit. The company's annual fixed costs are $562,500. Use this information to compute the company's (*a*) contribution margin, (*b*) contribution margin ratio, (*c*) break-even point in units, and (*d*) break-even point in dollars of sales.

Exercise 18-9
Contribution margin and break-even   **P2**

Blanchard Company manufactures a single product that sells for S180 per unit and whose total variable costs are $135 per unit. The company's annual fixed costs are $562,500. Prepare a CVP chart for the company.

Exercise 18-10^c
CVP chart   **P3**

Blanchard Company manufactures a single product that sells for $180 per unit and whose total variable costs are $135 per unit. The company's annual fixed costs are $562,500.

1. Prepare a contribution margin income statement for Blanchard Company showing sales, variable costs, and fixed costs at the break-even point.
2. If the company's fixed costs increase by $135,000, what amount of sales (in dollars) is needed to break even?

Exercise 18-11
Income reporting and break-even analysis
P2

Blanchard Company manufactures a single product that sells for $180 per unit and whose total variable costs are $135 per unit. The company's annual fixed costs are $562,500. Management targets an annual pretax income of $1,012,500. Assume that fixed costs remain at $562,500. Compute the (1) unit sales to earn the target income and (2) dollar sales to earn the target income.

Exercise 18-12
Computing sales to achieve target income   **C2**

Blanchard Company manufactures a single product that sells for $180 per unit and whose total variable costs are $135 per unit. The company's annual fixed costs are $562,500. The sales manager predicts that annual sales of the company's product will soon reach 40,000 units and its price will increase to $200 per unit. According to the production manager, variable costs are expected to increase to $140 per unit, but fixed costs will remain at $562,500. The income tax rate is 20%. What amounts of pretax and after-tax income can the company expect to earn from these predicted changes? *Hint:* Prepare a forecasted contribution margin income statement as in Exhibit 18.21.

Exercise 18-13
Forecasted income statement
C2

Bloom Company management predicts that it will incur fixed costs of $160,000 and earn pretax income of $164,000 in the next period. Its expected contribution margin ratio is 25%. Use this information to compute the amounts of (1) total dollar sales and (2) total variable costs.

Exercise 18-14
Predicting sales and variable costs using contribution margin   **C2**

Harrison Co. expects to sell 200,000 units of its product next year, which would generate total sales of $17 million. Management predicts that pretax net income for next year will be $1,250,000 and that the contribution margin per unit will be $25. Use this information to compute next year's total expected (*a*) variable costs and (*b*) fixed costs.

Exercise 18-15
Computing variable and fixed costs   **C2**

Hudson Co. reports the contribution margin income statement for 2019 below. Using this information, compute Hudson Co.'s (1) break-even point in units and (2) break-even point in sales dollars.

Exercise 18-16
Break-even
P2

Contribution Margin Income Statement	
For Year Ended December 31, 2019	
Sales (9,600 units at $225 each).....................	$2,160,000
Variable costs (9,600 units at $180 each)............	1,728,000
Contribution margin	432,000
Fixed costs	324,000
Pretax income......................................	$ 108,000

Refer to the information in Exercise 18-16.

1. Assume Hudson Co. has a target pretax income of $162,000 for 2020. What amount of sales (in dollars) is needed to produce this target income?
2. If Hudson achieves its target pretax income for 2020, what is its margin of safety (in percent)? (Round to one decimal place.)

Exercise 18-17
Target income and margin of safety (in dollars)
C2

Exercise 18-18
Evaluating strategies
C2

Refer to the information in Exercise 18-16. Assume the company is considering investing in a new machine that will increase its fixed costs by $40,500 per year and decrease its variable costs by $9 per unit. Prepare a forecasted contribution margin income statement for 2020 assuming the company purchases this machine.

Exercise 18-19
Evaluating strategies   **C2**

Refer to the information in Exercise 18-16. If the company raises its selling price to $240 per unit, compute its (1) contribution margin per unit, (2) contribution margin ratio, (3) break-even point in units, and (4) break-even point in sales dollars.

Exercise 18-20
Evaluating strategies   **C2**

Refer to the information in Exercise 18-16. The marketing manager believes that increasing advertising costs by $81,000 in 2020 will increase the company's sales volume to 11,000 units. Prepare a forecasted contribution margin income statement for 2020 assuming the company incurs the additional advertising costs.

Exercise 18-21
Predicting unit and dollar
sales   **C2**

Nombre Company management predicts $390,000 of variable costs, $430,000 of fixed costs, and a pretax income of $155,000 in the next period. Management also predicts that the contribution margin per unit will be $9. Use this information to compute the (1) total expected dollar sales for next period and (2) number of units expected to be sold next period.

Exercise 18-22
CVP analysis using
composite units
P4

Handy Home sells windows and doors in the ratio of 8:2 (windows:doors). The selling price of each window is $200 and of each door is $500. The variable cost of a window is $125 and of a door is $350. Fixed costs are $900,000. Use this information to determine the (1) selling price per composite unit, (2) variable costs per composite unit, (3) break-even point in composite units, and (4) number of units of each product that will be sold at the break-even point.

Exercise 18-23
CVP analysis using
composite units
P4

R&R Tax Service offers tax and consulting services to individuals and small businesses. Data for fees and costs of three types of tax returns follow. R&R provides services in the ratio of 5:3:2 (easy, moderate, business). Fixed costs total $18,000 for the tax season. Use this information to determine the (1) selling price per composite unit, (2) variable costs per composite unit, (3) break-even point in composite units, and (4) number of units of each product that will be sold at the break-even point.

Type of Return	Fee Charged	Variable Cost per Return
Easy (Form 1040EZ).............	$ 50	$ 30
Moderate (Form 1040)	125	75
Business	275	100

Exercise 18-24
Operating leverage
computed and applied
A2

Company A is a manufacturer with sales of $6,000,000 and a 60% contribution margin. Its fixed costs equal $2,600,000. Company B is a consulting firm with service revenues of $4,500,000 and a 25% contribution margin. Its fixed costs equal $375,000. Compute the degree of operating leverage (DOL) for each company. Which company benefits more from a 20% increase in sales?

Exercise 18-25
Degree of operating
leverage
A2

Refer to the information in Exercise 18-16.

1. Compute the company's degree of operating leverage for 2019.
2. If sales decrease by 5% in 2020, what will be the company's pretax income?
3. Assume sales for 2020 decrease by 5%. Prepare a contribution margin income statement for 2020.

Exercise 18-26B
Computing absorption
costing income
P5

A manufacturer reports the information below for three recent years. Compute income for each of the three years using absorption costing.

	Year 1	Year 2	Year 3
Variable costing income	$110,000	$114,400	$118,950
Beginning finished goods inventory (units)	0	1,200	700
Ending finished goods inventory (units)	1,200	700	800
Fixed manufacturing overhead per unit	$2.50	$2.50	$2.50

Use the amounts shown on the contribution margin income statements below to compute the missing amounts denoted by letters *a* through *n*.

Exercise 18-27
Contribution margin
income statement

A1

	Company A		Company B	
Number of units sold	*a*		1,975	
	Total	**Per unit**	**Total**	**Per unit**
Sales	$208,000	$65	*h*	*i*
Variable costs	150,400	*b*	$39,500	*j*
Contribution margin	*c*	*d*	43,450	*k*
Fixed costs	*e*	*f*	19,750	*l*
Net income	$ 46,400	*g*	*m*	*n*

⧉ connect

The following costs result from the production and sale of 1,000 drum sets manufactured by Tight Drums Company for the year ended December 31, 2019. The drum sets sell for $500 each. The company has a 25% income tax rate.

PROBLEM SET A

Problem 18-1A
Contribution margin
income statement and
contribution margin ratio

A1

Variable production costs		Fixed manufacturing costs	
Plastic for casing	$17,000	Taxes on factory	$ 5,000
Wages of assembly workers	82,000	Factory maintenance	10,000
Drum stands..........................	26,000	Factory machinery depreciation	40,000
Variable selling costs		Fixed selling and administrative costs	
Sales commissions.....................	15,000	Lease of equipment for sales staff.........	10,000
		Accounting staff salaries	35,000
		Administrative management salaries.......	125,000

Required

1. Prepare a contribution margin income statement for the year.

2. Compute its contribution margin per unit and its contribution margin ratio.

Check (1) Net income, $101,250

Analysis Component

3. For each dollar of sales, how much is left to cover fixed costs and contribute to operating income?

Alden Co.'s monthly unit sales and total cost data for its operating activities of the past year follow. Management wants to use these data to predict future fixed and variable costs.

Problem 18-2A
Cost behavior estimation—
high-low

P1

Month	Units Sold	Total Cost	Month	Units Sold	Total Cost
1	320,000	$160,000	7	340,000	$220,000
2	160,000	100,000	8	280,000	160,000
3	280,000	220,000	9	80,000	64,000
4	200,000	100,000	10	160,000	140,000
5	300,000	230,000	11	100,000	100,000
6	200,000	120,000	12	110,000	80,000

Required

1. Estimate both the variable costs per unit and the total monthly fixed costs using the high-low method.

2. Use the results from part 1 to predict future total costs when sales volume is (*a*) 200,000 units and (*b*) 300,000 units.

Problem 18-3A

Break-even analysis

P2   P3

Praveen Co. manufactures and markets a number of rope products. Management is considering the future of Product XT, a special rope for hang gliding, that has not been as profitable as planned. Since Product XT is manufactured and marketed independently of the other products, its total costs can be precisely measured. Next year's plans call for a $200 selling price per 100 yards of XT rope. Its fixed costs for the year are expected to be $270,000, up to a maximum capacity of 700,000 yards of rope. Forecasted variable costs are $140 per 100 yards of XT rope.

Required

Check (1a) Break-even sales, 4,500 units

1. Estimate Product XT's break-even point in terms of (*a*) sales units and (*b*) sales dollars.
2. Prepare a contribution margin income statement showing sales, variable costs, and fixed costs for Product XT at the break-even point.

Problem 18-4A

Break-even analysis; income targeting and forecasting

C2   A1   P2

Astro Co. sold 20,000 units of its only product and incurred a $50,000 loss (ignoring taxes) for the current year, as shown here. During a planning session for year 2020's activities, the production manager notes that variable costs can be reduced 50% by installing a machine that automates several operations. To obtain these savings, the company must increase its annual fixed costs by $200,000. The maximum output capacity of the company is 40,000 units per year.

Contribution Margin Income Statement	
For Year Ended December 31, 2019	
Sales	$1,000,000
Variable costs	800,000
Contribution margin	200,000
Fixed costs	250,000
Net loss	$ (50,000)

Required

1. Compute the break-even point in dollar sales for 2019.
2. Compute the predicted break-even point in dollar sales for 2020 assuming the machine is installed and there is no change in the unit selling price.

Check (3) Net income, $150,000

(4) Required sales, $1,083,333 or 21,667 units (both rounded)

3. Prepare a forecasted contribution margin income statement for 2020 that shows the expected results with the machine installed. Assume that the unit selling price and the number of units sold will not change, and no income taxes will be due.
4. Compute the sales level required in both dollars and units to earn $200,000 of target pretax income in 2020 with the machine installed and no change in unit sales price. Round answers to whole dollars and whole units.
5. Prepare a forecasted contribution margin income statement that shows the results at the sales level computed in part 4. Assume no income taxes will be due.

Problem 18-5A

Break-even analysis, different cost structures, and income calculations

C2   A1   P4

Henna Co. produces and sells two products, T and O. It manufactures these products in separate factories and markets them through different channels. They have no shared costs. This year, the company sold 50,000 units of each product. Sales and costs for each product follow.

	Product T	Product O
Sales	$2,000,000	$2,000,000
Variable costs	1,600,000	250,000
Contribution margin	400,000	1,750,000
Fixed costs	125,000	1,475,000
Income before taxes...............	275,000	275,000
Income taxes (32% rate)............	88,000	88,000
Net income	$ 187,000	$ 187,000

Required

1. Compute the break-even point in dollar sales for each product. (Round the answer to whole dollars.)

2. Assume that the company expects sales of each product to decline to 30,000 units next year with no change in unit selling price. Prepare forecasted financial results for next year following the format of the contribution margin income statement as just shown with columns for each of the two products (assume a 32% tax rate). Also, assume that any loss before taxes yields a 32% tax benefit.

3. Assume that the company expects sales of each product to increase to 60,000 units next year with no change in unit selling price. Prepare forecasted financial results for next year following the format of the contribution margin income statement shown with columns for each of the two products (assume a 32% tax rate).

Check   (2) After-tax income: T, $78,200; O, $(289,000)

(3) After-tax income: T, $241,400; O, $425,000

Analysis Component

4. If sales greatly decrease, which product would experience a greater decrease in net income?

This year Burchard Company sold 40,000 units of its only product for $25 per unit. Manufacturing and selling the product required $200,000 of fixed manufacturing costs and $325,000 of fixed selling and administrative costs. Its per unit variable costs follow.

Problem 18-6A
Analysis of price, cost, and volume changes for contribution margin and net income

A1   P2

Material......................................	$8.00	Variable overhead costs..................	$1.00
Direct labor (paid on the basis of completed units)	5.00	Variable selling and administrative costs	0.50

Next year the company will use a new material, which will reduce material costs by 50% and direct labor costs by 60% and will not affect product quality or marketability. Management is considering an increase in the unit selling price to reduce the number of units sold because the factory's output is nearing its annual output capacity of 45,000 units. Two plans are being considered. Under plan 1, the company will keep the selling price at the current level and sell the same volume as last year. This plan will increase income because of the reduced costs from using the new material. Under plan 2, the company will increase the selling price by 20%. This plan will decrease unit sales volume by 10%. Under both plans, the total fixed costs and the variable costs per unit for overhead and for selling and administrative costs will remain the same.

Required

1. Compute the break-even point in dollar sales for (*a*) plan 1 and (*b*) plan 2.

2. Prepare a forecasted contribution margin income statement with two columns showing the expected results of plan 1 and plan 2. The statements should report sales, total variable costs, contribution margin, total fixed costs, income before taxes, income taxes (30% rate), and net income.

Check   (1) Break-even: Plan 1, $750,000; Plan 2, $700,000

(2) Net income: Plan 1, $122,500; Plan 2, $199,500

Patriot Co. manufactures and sells three products: red, white, and blue. Their unit selling prices are red, $20; white, $35; and blue, $65. The per unit variable costs to manufacture and sell these products are red, $12; white, $22; and blue, $50. Their sales mix is reflected in a ratio of 5:4:2 (red:white:blue). Annual fixed costs shared by all three products are $250,000. One type of raw material has been used to manufacture all three products. The company has developed a new material of equal quality for less cost. The new material would reduce variable costs per unit as follows: red, by $6; white, by $12; and blue, by $10. However, the new material requires new equipment, which will increase annual fixed costs by $50,000. (Round answers to whole composite units.)

Problem 18-7A
Break-even analysis with composite units

P4

Required

1. If the company continues to use the old material, determine its break-even point in both sales units and sales dollars of each individual product.

2. If the company uses the new material, determine its new break-even point in both sales units and sales dollars of each individual product.

Check   (1) Old plan break-even, 2,050 composite units (rounded)

PROBLEM SET B

Problem 18-1B

Contribution margin income statement and contribution margin ratio

A1

The following costs result from the production and sale of 12,000 CD sets manufactured by Gilmore Company for the year ended December 31, 2019. The CD sets sell for $18 each. The company has a 25% income tax rate.

Variable manufacturing costs		Fixed manufacturing costs	
Plastic for CD sets	$ 1,500	Rent on factory	$ 6,750
Wages of assembly workers	30,000	Factory cleaning service.................	4,520
Labeling	3,000	Factory machinery depreciation	20,000
Variable selling costs		Fixed selling and administrative costs	
Sales commissions.....................	6,000	Lease of office equipment	1,050
		Systems staff salaries...................	15,000
		Administrative management salaries.......	120,000

Required

Check   (1) Net income, $6,135

1. Prepare a contribution margin income statement for the year.
2. Compute its contribution margin per unit and its contribution margin ratio.

Analysis Component

3. Interpret the contribution margin and contribution margin ratio from part 2.

Problem 18-2B

Cost behavior estimation—high-low

P1

Sun Co.'s monthly unit sales and total cost data for its operating activities of the past year follow. Management wants to use these data to predict future fixed and variable costs. (Dollar and unit amounts are in thousands.)

Month	Units Sold	Total Cost	Month	Units Sold	Total Cost
1	195	$ 97	7	145	$ 93
2	125	87	8	185	105
3	105	73	9	135	85
4	155	89	10	85	58
5	95	81	11	175	95
6	215	110	12	115	79

Required

1. Estimate both the variable costs per unit and the total monthly fixed costs using the high-low method.
2. Use the results from part 1 to predict future total costs when sales volume is (*a*) 100 units and (*b*) 170 units.

Problem 18-3B

Break-even analysis

P2   P3

Hip-Hop Co. manufactures and markets several products. Management is considering the future of one product, electronic keyboards, that has not been as profitable as planned. Since this product is manufactured and marketed independently of the other products, its total costs can be precisely measured. Next year's plans call for a $350 selling price per unit. The fixed costs for the year are expected to be $42,000, up to a maximum capacity of 700 units. Forecasted variable costs are $210 per unit.

Required

Check   (1) Break-even sales, 300 units

1. Estimate the keyboards' break-even point in terms of (*a*) sales units and (*b*) sales dollars.
2. Prepare a contribution margin income statement showing sales, variable costs, and fixed costs for keyboards at the break-even point.
3. Prepare a CVP chart for keyboards like that in Exhibit 18.14. Use 700 keyboards as the maximum number of sales units on the horizontal axis of the graph and $250,000 as the maximum dollar amount on the vertical axis.

Rivera Co. sold 20,000 units of its only product and incurred a $50,000 loss (ignoring taxes) for the current year, as shown here. During a planning session for year 2020's activities, the production manager notes that variable costs can be reduced 50% by installing a machine that automates several operations. To obtain these savings, the company must increase its annual fixed costs by $150,000. The maximum output capacity of the company is 40,000 units per year.

Problem 18-4B
Break-even analysis; income targeting and forecasting

C2 A1 P2

Contribution Margin Income Statement For Year Ended December 31, 2019	
Sales	$750,000
Variable costs	600,000
Contribution margin	150,000
Fixed costs	200,000
Net loss	$ (50,000)

Required

1. Compute the break-even point in dollar sales for 2019.
2. Compute the predicted break-even point in dollar sales for 2020 assuming the machine is installed and no change occurs in the unit selling price. (Round the change in variable costs to a whole number.)
3. Prepare a forecasted contribution margin income statement for 2020 that shows the expected results with the machine installed. Assume that the unit selling price and the number of units sold will not change, and no income taxes will be due.

Check (3) Net income, $100,000

4. Compute the sales level required in both dollars and units to earn $200,000 of target pretax income in 2020 with the machine installed and no change in unit sales price. (Round answers to whole dollars and whole units.)

(4) Required sales, $916,667 or 24,445 units (both rounded)

5. Prepare a forecasted contribution margin income statement that shows the results at the sales level computed in part 4. Assume no income taxes will be due.

Stam Co. produces and sells two products, BB and TT. It manufactures these products in separate factories and markets them through different channels. They have no shared costs. This year, the company sold 50,000 units of each product. Sales and costs for each product follow.

Problem 18-5B
Break-even analysis, different cost structures, and income calculations

C2 A1 P4

	Product BB	Product TT
Sales	$800,000	$800,000
Variable costs	560,000	100,000
Contribution margin	240,000	700,000
Fixed costs	100,000	560,000
Income before taxes.	140,000	140,000
Income taxes (32% rate).	44,800	44,800
Net income	$ 95,200	$ 95,200

Required

1. Compute the break-even point in dollar sales for each product. (Round the answer to the next whole dollar.)
2. Assume that the company expects sales of each product to decline to 33,000 units next year with no change in the unit selling price. Prepare forecasted financial results for next year following the format of the contribution margin income statement as shown here with columns for each of the two products (assume a 32% tax rate and that any loss before taxes yields a 32% tax benefit).

Check (2) After-tax income: BB, $39,712; TT, $(66,640)

3. Assume that the company expects sales of each product to increase to 64,000 units next year with no change in the unit selling prices. Prepare forecasted financial results for next year following the format of the contribution margin income statement as shown here with columns for each of the two products (assume a 32% tax rate).

(3) After-tax income: BB, $140,896; TT, $228,480

Analysis Component

4. If sales greatly increase, which product would experience a greater increase in profit? Explain.
5. Describe some factors that might have created the different cost structures for these two products.

Problem 18-6B

Analysis of price, cost, and volume changes for contribution margin and net income

A1   P2

This year Best Company earned a disappointing 5.6% after-tax return on sales (net income/sales) from marketing 100,000 units of its only product. The company buys its product in bulk and repackages it for resale at the price of $20 per unit. Best incurred the following costs this year.

Total variable unit costs	$800,000	Fixed costs	$950,000
Total variable packaging costs.	$100,000	Income tax rate.	25%

The marketing manager claims that next year's results will be the same as this year's unless some changes are made. The manager predicts the company can increase the number of units sold by 80% if it reduces the selling price by 20% and upgrades the packaging. This change would increase variable packaging costs by 20%. Increased sales would allow the company to take advantage of a 25% quantity purchase discount on the cost of the bulk product. Neither the packaging change nor the volume discount would affect fixed costs, which provide an annual output capacity of 200,000 units.

Required

Check (1*b*) Break-even sales for new strategy, $1,727,273 (rounded)
(2) Net income: Existing strategy, $112,500; new strategy, $475,500

1. Compute the break-even point in dollar sales under the (*a*) existing business strategy and (*b*) new strategy that alters both unit selling price and variable costs. (Round answers to the next whole dollar.)

2. Prepare a forecasted contribution margin income statement with two columns showing the expected results of (*a*) the existing strategy and (*b*) changing to the new strategy. The statements should report sales, total variable costs (unit and packaging), contribution margin, fixed costs, income before taxes, income taxes, and net income. Also determine the after-tax return on sales for these two strategies.

Problem 18-7B

Break-even analysis with composite units

P4

Milano Co. manufactures and sells three products: product 1, product 2, and product 3. Their unit selling prices are product 1, $40; product 2, $30; and product 3, $20. The per unit variable costs to manufacture and sell these products are product 1, $30; product 2, $15; and product 3, $8. Their sales mix is reflected in a ratio of 6:4:2. Annual fixed costs shared by all three products are $270,000. One type of raw material has been used to manufacture products 1 and 2. The company has developed a new material of equal quality for less cost. The new material would reduce variable costs per unit as follows: product 1 by $10 and product 2 by $5. However, the new material requires new equipment, which will increase annual fixed costs by $50,000.

Required

Check (1) Old plan break-even, 1,875 composite units

1. If the company continues to use the old material, determine its break-even point in both sales units and sales dollars of each individual product.

2. If the company uses the new material, determine its new break-even point in both sales units and sales dollars of each individual product. (Round to the next whole unit.)

Analysis Component

3. What insight does this analysis offer management for long-term planning?

SERIAL PROBLEM

Business Solutions   P4

©Alexander Image/Shutterstock

Check (3) 60 composite units

This serial problem began in Chapter 1 and continues through most of the book. If previous chapter segments were not completed, the serial problem can begin at this point.

SP 18   **Business Solutions** sells upscale modular desk units and office chairs in the ratio of 3:2 (desk unit:chair). The selling prices are $1,250 per desk unit and $500 per chair. The variable costs are $750 per desk unit and $250 per chair. Fixed costs are $120,000.

Required

1. Compute the selling price per composite unit.

2. Compute the variable costs per composite unit.

3. Compute the break-even point in composite units.

4. Compute the number of units of each product that would be sold at the break-even point.

Accounting Analysis

AA 18-1 **Apple** offers extended service contracts that provide repair coverage for its products. Assume Apple charges $160 to repair an iPhone screen and $400 for other repairs. Services are provided in a ratio of 2 screens to 1 other repair (2:1). Variable costs are 40% of selling price for iPhone screen repairs and 48% of selling price for other repairs. Assume fixed costs are $2 billion per year for the repair services department.

COMPANY ANALYSIS

P2

APPLE

Required

1. Compute the selling price per composite unit for Apple's repair services.
2. Compute the variable cost per composite unit for Apple's repair services.
3. How many composite units must Apple's repair services department sell each year to break even?
4. At the break-even level, how many screen repairs and other repairs will Apple complete each year?

AA 18-2 Both **Apple** and **Google** sell electronic devices, and each of these companies has a different product mix. Assume the following data are available for both companies.

COMPARATIVE ANALYSIS

A2   P2

APPLE
GOOGLE

	Apple	Google
Average selling price per unit sold	$550 per unit	$470 per unit
Average variable cost per unit sold	$250 per unit	$270 per unit
Total fixed costs ($ millions)	$36,000	$10,000

Required

1. Compute each company's break-even point in unit sales. (Each company sells many devices at many different selling prices, and each has its own variable costs. This assignment assumes an *average* selling price per unit and an *average* cost per item.)
2. If unit sales were to decline, which company would experience the larger decline in operating profit?

AA 18-3 Both **Samsung** and **Apple** sell smartphones. Assume the following data are available for a popular smartphone model of each company.

GLOBAL ANALYSIS

A1

APPLE
Samsung

	Samsung	Apple
Selling price per unit........................	$720	$650
Variable cost per unit	288	221

Required

1. Compute the contribution margin ratio for each model.
2. Based on contribution margin ratio, which company's smartphone sales contribute more to covering fixed costs?

Beyond the Numbers

BTN 18-1 Labor costs of an auto repair mechanic are seldom based on actual hours worked. Instead, this labor cost is based on an industry average of time estimated to complete a repair job. This means a customer can pay, for example, $120 for two hours of work on a car when the actual time worked was only one hour. Many experienced mechanics can complete repair jobs faster than the industry average. Assume that you are asked to complete such a survey for a repair center. The survey calls for objective input, and many questions require detailed cost data and analysis. The mechanics and owners know you have the survey and encourage you to complete it in a way that increases the average billable hours for repair work.

ETHICS CHALLENGE

C1

Required

Write a one-page memorandum to the mechanics and owners that describes the direct labor analysis you will undertake in completing this survey.

COMMUNICATING IN PRACTICE

C2

BTN 18-2 Several important assumptions underlie CVP analysis. Assumptions often help simplify and focus our analysis of sales and costs. A common application of CVP analysis is as a tool to forecast sales, costs, and income.

Required

Assume that you are actively searching for a job. Prepare a half-page report identifying (1) three assumptions relating to your expected revenue (salary) and (2) three assumptions relating to your expected costs for the first year of your new job. Be prepared to discuss your assumptions in class.

TAKING IT TO THE NET

C1

BTN 18-3 Access and review the entrepreneurial information at **Bizfilings** (<u>bizfilings.com</u>). Search for *New Business Cash Needs Checklist* and review the resulting material.

Required

Write a half-page report that describes the information and resources available to help the owner of a start-up business control and monitor its cash flows and costs.

TEAMWORK IN ACTION

C2

BTN 18-4 A local movie theater owner explains to you that ticket sales on weekends and evenings are strong, but attendance during the weekdays, Monday through Thursday, is poor. The owner proposes to offer a contract to the local grade school to show educational materials at the theater for a set charge per student during school hours. The owner asks your help to prepare a CVP analysis listing the cost and sales projections for the proposal. The owner must propose to the school's administration a charge per child. At a minimum, the charge per child needs to be sufficient for the theater to break even.

Required

Your team is to prepare two separate lists of questions that enable you to complete a reliable CVP analysis of this situation. One list is to be answered by the school's administration, the other by the owner of the movie theater.

ENTREPRENEURIAL DECISION

C1 A1

BTN 18-5 **Ellis Island Tropical Tea**, launched by entrepreneur Nailah Ellis-Brown as described in this chapter's opener, makes Jamaican sweet tea from all-natural ingredients.

Required

1. Identify at least two fixed costs that do not change regardless of how much tea Nailah's company sells.
2. Ellis Island Tropical Tea is growing. How could overly optimistic sales estimates hurt Nailah's business?
3. Explain how cost-volume-profit analysis can help Nailah manage her company.

HITTING THE ROAD

P4

BTN 18-6 Multiproduct break-even analysis is often viewed differently when actually applied in practice. You are to visit a local fast-food restaurant and count the number of items on the menu. To apply multiproduct break-even analysis to the restaurant, similar menu items must often be fit into groups. A reasonable approach is to classify menu items into approximately five groups. We then estimate average selling price and average variable cost to compute average contribution margin. (*Hint:* For fast-food restaurants, the highest contribution margin is with its beverages, at about 90%.)

Required

1. Prepare a one-year multiproduct break-even analysis for the restaurant you visit. Begin by establishing groups. Next, estimate each group's volume and contribution margin. These estimates are necessary to compute each group's contribution margin. Assume that annual fixed costs in total are $500,000 per year. (*Hint:* You must develop your own estimates on volume and contribution margin for each group to obtain the break-even point and sales.)

2. Prepare a one-page report on the results of your analysis. Comment on the volume of sales necessary to break even at a fast-food restaurant.

19 Variable Costing and Analysis

Learning Objectives

CONCEPTUAL

C1 Describe how absorption costing can result in overproduction.

ANALYTICAL

A1 Use variable costing in pricing special orders.

PROCEDURAL

P1 Compute unit cost under both absorption and variable costing.

P2 Prepare and analyze an income statement using absorption costing and using variable costing.

P3 Convert income under variable costing to the absorption cost basis.

P4 Determine product selling price based on absorption costing.

Ray of Light

"Make your dream reality"—**SHAY DOYON**

©Lantern Inn

LACONIA, NH—Lifelong Northeasterners David and Shay Doyon were looking for a change. "I always had a dream and passion of owning an inn," recalls Shay. "I love the cozy, quaint feeling that emanates from a country inn." After a stay at the **Lantern Inn B&B** (**lanterninnbb.com**), they bought it.

David and Shay faced challenges in making their dream a reality. "We are first-time operators of a bed and breakfast," explains David. The couple used accounting concepts to develop their business plan and set up an accounting system to measure, track, and report on profits and cash flows.

David and Shay's understanding of variable and fixed costs allows them to compute the break-even number of rooms they must rent to cover fixed costs. David and Shay set their prices to cover their costs using a market analysis of going rates in the area. This approach is common in competitive industries like hospitality.

The owners also provide special offers to veterans and parties who wish to rent the entire inn. In these cases, the owners focus on variable costs and *incremental* fixed costs.

Shay advises aspiring entrepreneurs to "pursue your dream and work hard!" David adds: "An understanding of accounting helps in starting and running your business."

Sources: *Lantern Inn B&B website,* January 2019; correspondence with David Doyon, March 2018

INTRODUCING VARIABLE COSTING AND ABSORPTION COSTING

This chapter illustrates and compares two costing methods.

- **Variable costing,** where direct materials, direct labor, and *variable* overhead costs are included in product costs. This method is useful for many managerial decisions, but it cannot be used for external financial reporting.
- **Absorption costing,** where direct materials, direct labor, and both *variable* and *fixed* overhead costs are included in product costs. This method is required for external financial reporting under U.S. GAAP, but it can result in misleading product cost information and poor managerial decisions.

Exhibit 19.1 compares the absorption and variable costing methods. Both methods include direct materials, direct labor, and variable overhead in product costs. The key difference between the methods lies in their treatment of *fixed* overhead costs—such costs are included in product costs under absorption costing but included in period expenses under variable costing. Product costs are included in inventory until the goods are sold, at which time they are included in cost of goods sold. Period expenses are reported as expenses immediately in the period in which they are incurred.

Point: Under variable costing, fixed overhead is expensed at the time the units are produced. Under absorption costing, fixed overhead is expensed at the time the units are sold (as a component of cost of goods sold).

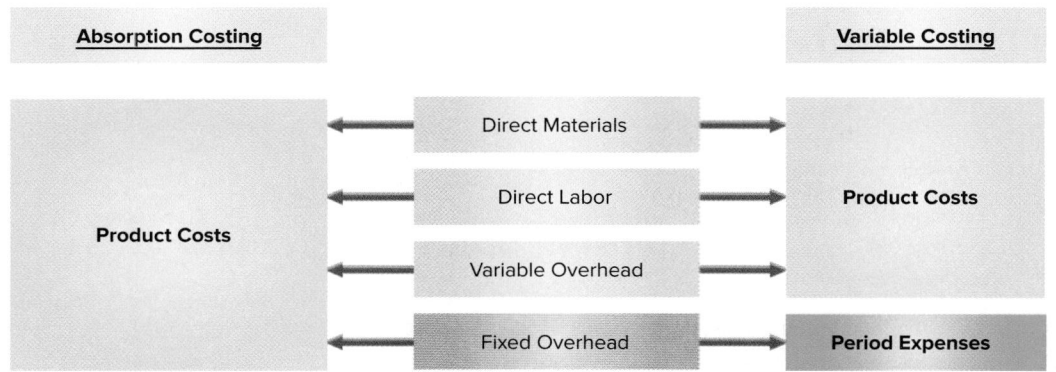

EXHIBIT 19.1

Absorption Costing versus Variable Costing

Exhibit 19.1 helps us understand when the absorption and variable costing methods will yield different income amounts. Differences in income resulting from the alternative costing methods will be *small* when

- Fixed overhead is a small percentage of total manufacturing costs.
- Inventory levels are low. As more companies adopt lean techniques, including just-in-time manufacturing, inventory levels fall. Lower inventory levels reduce income differences between absorption and variable costing.
- Inventory turnover is rapid. The more quickly inventory turns over, the more product costs are included in cost of goods sold relative to the product costs that remain in inventory.
- The period of analysis is long. Different costing methods might yield very different income numbers over a quarter or year, but these differences will decrease as income is compared over longer periods.

P1 _____

Compute unit cost under both absorption and variable costing.

Computing Unit Product Cost

To illustrate the difference between absorption costing and variable costing, consider the product cost data in Exhibit 19.2 from IceAge, a skate manufacturer.

EXHIBIT 19.2

Summary Product Cost Data

Direct materials	$4 per unit	Variable overhead	$3 per unit
Direct labor	$8 per unit	Fixed overhead	$600,000 per year
Expected units produced (per year)..........	60,000 units		

©Karl Weatherly/Corbis/Getty Images

Using these product cost data, Exhibit 19.3 shows the product cost per unit computations for both absorption and variable costing. These computations are shown both in a visual format and a tabular format.

- For absorption costing, the product cost per unit is $25, which consists of $4 in direct materials, $8 in direct labor, $3 in variable overhead, and $10 in fixed overhead ($600,000/60,000 units).
- For variable costing, the product cost per unit is $15, which consists of $4 in direct materials, $8 in direct labor, and $3 in variable overhead. Fixed overhead costs of $600,000 are treated as a period cost and are recorded as expense in the period incurred. **The difference between the two costing methods is the exclusion of fixed overhead from product costs for variable costing.**

EXHIBIT 19.3

Unit Cost Computation

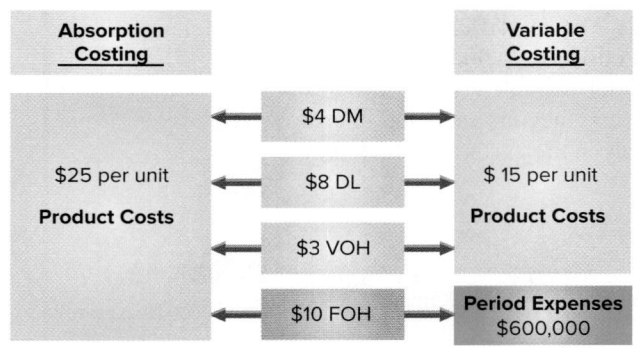

	Product Cost per Unit	
	Absorption Costing	Variable Costing
Direct materials......................	$ 4	$ 4
Direct labor.........................	8	8
Overhead costs		
Variable overhead	3	3
Fixed overhead...................	10	—
Total product cost per unit.............	$25	$15

NEED-TO-KNOW **19-1**

Computing Product Cost per Unit

P1

A manufacturer reports the following data.

Direct materials cost	$6 per unit	Variable overhead	$11 per unit
Direct labor cost	$14 per unit	Fixed overhead	$680,000 per year
Expected units produced	20,000 units		

1. Compute the total product cost per unit under absorption costing.
2. Compute the total product cost per unit under variable costing.

Solution

Per Unit Costs	(1) Absorption Costing	(2) Variable Costing
Direct materials	$ 6	$ 6
Direct labor	14	14
Variable overhead	11	11
Fixed overhead ($680,000/20,000)*	34	—
Total product cost per unit	$65	$31

*Not included in product costs under variable costing.

Do More: QS 19-1, QS 19-2, E 19-1, E 19-2

INCOME REPORTING IMPLICATIONS

The different treatment of fixed overhead costs leads to different product costs per unit under absorption and variable costing. This section shows how this impacts income reporting.

Below are data for IceAge Company. Assume IceAge's variable costs per unit are constant and its annual fixed costs do not change during the three-year period 2017 through 2019.

P2

Prepare and analyze an income statement using absorption costing and using variable costing.

Manufacturing Costs		Selling and Administrative Expenses	
Direct materials	$4 per unit	Variable.......................	$2 per unit
Direct labor	$8 per unit	Fixed	$200,000 per year
Variable overhead	$3 per unit		
Fixed overhead.................	$600,000 per year		

Sales and production information for IceAge follows. Its sales price was a constant $40 per unit over this time period. Units produced equal those sold for 2017, exceed those sold for 2018, and are less than those sold for 2019. IceAge began 2017 with no units in beginning inventory.

	Units Produced	Units Sold	Units in Ending Inventory
2017	60,000	60,000	0
2018	60,000	40,000	20,000
2019	60,000	80,000	0

We prepare income statements for IceAge under absorption costing and under variable costing. We consider three different cases: when units produced are equal to, exceed, or are less than units sold. **In general, income differs between the costing methods when inventory levels change.** Inventory levels change when units produced do not equal units sold.

Units Produced Equal Units Sold

Exhibit 19.4 presents the 2017 income statement for both costing methods (2018 and 2019 statements will follow). The income statement under variable costing (on the right) is a **contribution margin income statement.** Contribution margin is the excess of sales over variable costs. This margin contributes to covering all fixed costs and earning income. In the absorption costing income statement, expenses are not separated into variable and fixed components.

Production	=	Sales	Income under
60,000 pairs	=	60,000 pairs	Absorption costing = Variable costing
			$580,000 = $580,000

2017

Exhibit 19.4 reveals that **reported income is identical under absorption costing and variable costing when the number of units produced equals the number of units sold.** Because variable costing expenses the same amount

EXHIBIT 19.4

Income for 2017—Quantity Produced Equals Quantity Sold*

Point: Contribution margin (Sales − Variable expenses) is different from gross margin (Sales − Cost of sales).

ICEAGE COMPANY Income Statement (Absorption Costing) For Year Ended December 31, 2017		
Sales* (60,000 × $40)		$2,400,000
Cost of goods sold (60,000 × $25‡).		1,500,000
Gross margin		900,000
Selling and administrative expenses [$200,000 + (60,000 × $2)].		320,000
Net income		**$ 580,000**

*Units produced equal 60,000; units sold equal 60,000.
†($4 DM + $8 DL + $3 VOH + $10 FOH)
‡($4 DM + $8 DL + $3 VOH)

> A performance report that excludes fixed expenses and net income is a *contribution margin report*. Its bottom line is contribution margin.

ICEAGE COMPANY Income Statement (Variable Costing) For Year Ended December 31, 2017		
Sales* (60,000 × $40)		$2,400,000
Variable expenses		
Variable production costs (60,000 × $15‡)	$900,000	
Variable selling and administrative expenses (60,000 × $2).	120,000	1,020,000
Contribution margin.		1,380,000
Fixed expenses		
Fixed overhead	600,000	
Fixed selling and administrative expenses	200,000	800,000
Net income		**$ 580,000**

Point: Contribution margin income statements prepared under variable costing are useful in performing cost-volume-profit analyses.

of fixed overhead cost ($600,000) that absorption costing includes in cost of goods sold ($600,000 = 60,000 units × $10 fixed overhead per unit), net income is the same under either method when units produced equal units sold.

Exhibit 19.5 reorganizes the information from Exhibit 19.4 to show the assignment of costs to different expenses and assets under both absorption costing and variable costing. In this year, there are no units in ending inventory, so the finished goods inventory is $0 under both methods. When units produced equal units sold, there is no difference in *total* expenses reported on the income statement. Yet, there is a difference in what categories receive those costs. Absorption costing assigns $1,500,000 to cost of goods sold compared to $900,000 for variable costing. The $600,000 difference is a period cost for variable costing.

EXHIBIT 19.5

Production Cost Assignment for 2017

Absorption Costing	For Year 2017	
Beginning finished goods inventory	$	0
Cost of goods manufactured		
Direct materials	$240,000	
Direct labor.	480,000	
Variable manufacturing overhead.	180,000	
Fixed manufacturing overhead	600,000	1,500,000
Cost of goods available for sale		1,500,000
Less: Ending finished goods inventory		0
Cost of goods sold		$1,500,000

Variable Costing	For Year 2017	
Beginning finished goods inventory	$	0
Cost of goods manufactured		
Direct materials	$240,000	
Direct labor.	480,000	
Variable manufacturing overhead.	180,000	
Fixed manufacturing overhead	0	900,000
Cost of goods available for sale		900,000
Less: Ending finished goods inventory		0
Cost of goods sold		900,000
Period costs		
Fixed manufacturing overhead		600,000
Total expenses		$1,500,000

Income statement

Balance sheet

(Absorption) FG Inventory			
Beg.	0		
COGM	1,500,000		
		1,500,000	COGS
End.	0		

Balance sheet   Income statement

(Variable) FG Inventory			
Beg.	0		
COGM	900,000		
		900,000	COGS
End.	0		

 **Decision Insight**

Manufacturing Margin   Some managers compute **manufacturing margin** (also called *production margin*), which is sales less variable production costs. Some managers also require that internal income statements show this amount to highlight the impact of variable product costs on income. The contribution margin section of IceAge's variable costing income statement would appear as here (compare this to Exhibit 19.4).

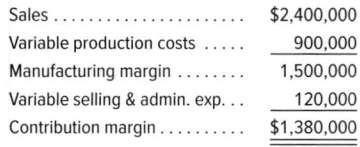

Sales	$2,400,000
Variable production costs	900,000
Manufacturing margin	1,500,000
Variable selling & admin. exp. . .	120,000
Contribution margin	$1,380,000 ∎

Units Produced Exceed Units Sold

Production	>	Sales		Income under
60,000 pairs	>	40,000 pairs		Absorption costing > Variable costing $320,000 > $120,000
	>			**2018**

Exhibit 19.6 shows absorption costing and variable costing income statements for 2018. In 2018, 60,000 units were produced, which is the same as in 2017. However, only 40,000 units were sold, which means 20,000 units remain in ending inventory.

For 2018, income is $320,000 under absorption costing. Under variable costing income is $120,000. The cause of this $200,000 income difference is the different treatment of fixed overhead. Because variable costing expenses the $600,000 of fixed manufacturing overhead (FOH) as a period cost, and absorption costing expenses FOH based on the number of units sold (40,000 × $10), net income is lower under variable costing by $200,000 (20,000 units × $10).

EXHIBIT 19.6

Income for 2018—Quantity Produced Exceeds Quantity Sold

ICEAGE COMPANY
Income Statement (Absorption Costing)
For Year Ended December 31, 2018

Sales* (40,000 × $40)................	$1,600,000
Cost of goods sold (40,000 × $25†).......	1,000,000
Gross margin	600,000
Selling and administrative expenses [$200,000 + (40,000 × $2)]	280,000
Net income	**$ 320,000**

*Units produced equal 60,000; units sold equal 40,000.
†($4 DM + $8 DL + $3 VOH + $10 FOH)
‡($4 DM + $8 DL + $3 VOH)

ICEAGE COMPANY
Income Statement (Variable Costing)
For Year Ended December 31, 2018

Sales* (40,000 × $40)...........		$1,600,000
Variable expenses		
Variable production costs (40,000 × $15‡)	$600,000	
Variable selling and administrative expenses (40,000 × $2)......	80,000	680,000
Contribution margin.............		920,000
Fixed expenses		
Fixed overhead	600,000	
Fixed selling and administrative expenses......	200,000	800,000
Net income		**$ 120,000**

Exhibit 19.7 reorganizes the information from Exhibit 19.6 to show the assignment of costs to different expenses and assets under both absorption costing and variable costing. When units produced exceed units sold, there is a difference in total expenses. Under absorption costing, cost of goods sold of $1,000,000 is $200,000 lower than the total expenses ($1,200,000) under variable costing. As a result, income (and ending finished goods inventory) under absorption costing is $200,000 greater than under variable costing because of the fixed overhead cost included in ending

EXHIBIT 19.7

Production Cost Assignment for 2018

Absorption Costing		For Year 2018
Beginning finished goods inventory		$ 0
Cost of goods manufactured		
Direct materials	$240,000	
Direct labor.........................	480,000	
Variable manufacturing overhead........	180,000	
Fixed manufacturing overhead	600,000	1,500,000
Cost of goods available for sale		1,500,000
Less: Ending finished goods inventory		500,000*
Cost of goods sold		$1,000,000

*20,000 units × $25 per unit
†20,000 units × $15 per unit

Variable Costing		For Year 2018
Beginning finished goods inventory		$ 0
Cost of goods manufactured		
Direct materials	$240,000	
Direct labor.........................	480,000	
Variable manufacturing overhead........	180,000	
Fixed manufacturing overhead	0	900,000
Cost of goods available for sale		900,000
Less: Ending finished goods inventory		300,000†
Cost of goods sold		600,000
Period costs		
Fixed manufacturing overhead		600,000
Total expenses		$1,200,000

Income statement

Balance sheet

(Absorption) FG Inventory			
Beg.	0		
COGM	1,500,000		
		1,000,000	COGS
End.	500,000		

(Variable) FG Inventory			
Beg.	0		
COGM	900,000		
		600,000	COGS
End.	300,000		

Income statement

Balance sheet

inventory (asset) under absorption costing. This $200,000 of fixed overhead cost will be reported in cost of goods sold in future years (under absorption costing) as those products are sold.

Production	<	Sales
60,000 pairs	<	80,000 pairs

Income under
Absorption costing < Variable costing
$840,000 < $1,040,000

2019

Units Produced Are Less Than Units Sold

Exhibit 19.8 shows absorption costing and variable costing income statements for 2019. In 2019, IceAge produced 60,000 units and sold 80,000 units. Thus, IceAge produced 20,000 units fewer than it sold. This means IceAge sold all that it produced during the period, and it sold all of its beginning finished goods inventory. IceAge's income is $840,000 under absorption costing, but it is $1,040,000 under variable costing.

EXHIBIT 19.8

Income for 2019—Quantity Produced Is Less Than Quantity Sold

ICEAGE COMPANY
Income Statement (Absorption Costing)
For Year Ended December 31, 2019

Sales* (80,000 × $40).................	$3,200,000
Cost of goods sold (80,000 × $25†)	2,000,000
Gross margin	1,200,000
Selling and administrative expenses	
[$200,000 + (80,000 × $2)]	360,000
Net income	**$ 840,000**

*Units produced equal 60,000; units sold equal 80,000.
†($4 DM + $8 DL + $3 VOH + $10 FOH)
‡($4 DM + $8 DL + $3 VOH)

ICEAGE COMPANY
Income Statement (Variable Costing)
For Year Ended December 31, 2019

Sales* (80,000 × $40)...........		$ 3,200,000
Variable expenses		
Variable production costs		
(80,000 × $15‡)	$1,200,000	
Variable selling and administrative		
expenses (80,000 × $2)	160,000	1,360,000
Contribution margin..............		1,840,000
Fixed expenses		
Fixed overhead	600,000	
Fixed selling and administrative		
expenses..................	200,000	800,000
Net income		**$1,040,000**

This $200,000 income difference is due to the treatment of fixed overhead (FOH). Beginning inventory in 2019 under absorption costing included $200,000 of fixed overhead cost incurred in 2018, which is assigned to cost of goods sold in 2019 under absorption costing. Because absorption costing expenses FOH based on the number of units sold (80,000), net income is higher under variable costing by $200,000 (20,000 units × $10).

Exhibit 19.9 reorganizes the information from Exhibit 19.8 to show the assignment of costs to different expenses and assets under both absorption costing and variable costing. When quantity produced is less than quantity sold, there is a difference in total costs assigned.

EXHIBIT 19.9

Production Cost Assignment for 2019

Absorption Costing		For Year 2019
Beginning finished goods inventory		$ 500,000*
Cost of goods manufactured		
Direct materials	$240,000	
Direct labor.........................	480,000	
Variable manufacturing overhead.........	180,000	
Fixed manufacturing overhead	600,000	1,500,000
Cost of goods available for sale		2,000,000
Less: Ending finished goods inventory		0
Cost of goods sold		$2,000,000

*20,000 units × $25 per unit
†20,000 units × $15 per unit

Income statement

Balance sheet

Variable Costing		For Year 2019
Beginning finished goods inventory		$ 300,000†
Cost of goods manufactured		
Direct materials	$240,000	
Direct labor.........................	480,000	
Variable manufacturing overhead.........	180,000	
Fixed manufacturing overhead	0	900,000
Cost of goods available for sale		1,200,000
Less: Ending finished goods inventory		0
Cost of goods sold		1,200,000
Period costs		
Fixed manufacturing overhead		600,000
Total expenses		$1,800,000

Income statement

Balance sheet

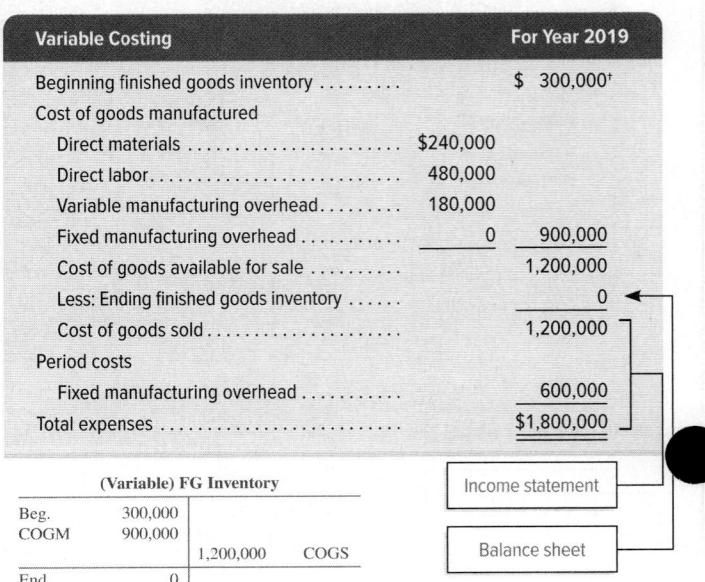

(Absorption) FG Inventory			
Beg.	500,000		
COGM	1,500,000		
		2,000,000	COGS
End.	0		

(Variable) FG Inventory			
Beg.	300,000		
COGM	900,000		
		1,200,000	COGS
End.	0		

Specifically, beginning inventory in 2019 under absorption costing was $500,000 (20,000 units × $25), whereas it was only $300,000 (20,000 units × $15) under variable costing. Consequently, when that inventory is sold in 2019, that $200,000 difference in inventory is included in cost of goods sold under absorption costing. Thus, the 2019 income under absorption costing is $200,000 less than the income under variable costing.

Summarizing Income Reporting

IceAge's income reported under both variable costing and absorption costing for the years 2017 through 2019 is summarized in Exhibit 19.10. Total income is $1,740,000 for this time period for *both* methods. Further, **income under absorption costing and income under variable costing differ whenever the quantity produced and the quantity sold differ.** These differences in income are due to the different timing with which fixed overhead costs are reported in income under the two methods. Specifically, *income under absorption costing is higher when more units are produced than are sold and is lower when fewer units are produced than are sold.*

FG Inventory	Income Effect
No change	No difference
Increases	Absorption > Variable
Decreases	Variable > Absorption

	Units Produced	Units Sold	Income under Absorption Costing	Income under Variable Costing	Income Differences
2017	60,000	60,000	$ 580,000	$ 580,000	$ 0
2018	60,000	40,000	320,000	120,000	200,000
2019	60,000	80,000	840,000	1,040,000	(200,000)
Totals	180,000	180,000	$1,740,000	$1,740,000	$ 0

EXHIBIT 19.10

Summary of Income Reporting

For IceAge, the total number of units produced over 2017–2019 exactly equals the number of units sold over that period. This means that the difference between absorption costing income and variable costing income for the *total* three-year period is zero. In reality, production and sales quantities rarely exactly equal each other over such a short period of time. We normally see differences in income for these two methods extending over several years.

Point: In our illustration the company produces the same number of units (60,000) each year. We provide an example with varying yearly production levels in **Need-to-Know 19-4** at the end of the chapter.

ZBest Mfg. reports the following data for 2019.

Direct materials cost.........	$6 per unit	Units produced	20,000 units
Direct labor cost	$11 per unit	Units sold	14,000 units
Variable overhead cost	$3 per unit	Variable selling and administrative expenses	$2 per unit
Fixed overhead	$680,000 per year	Fixed selling and administrative expenses	$112,000 per year
Sales price...............	$80 per unit		

NEED-TO-KNOW 19-2

Computing Income under Absorption and Variable Costing

P2

1. Prepare an income statement for 2019 under absorption costing.
2. Prepare an income statement for 2019 under variable costing.

Solution

ZBEST MFG. Income Statement (Absorption Costing) For Year Ended December 31, 2019	
Sales (14,000 × $80)...................	$1,120,000
Cost of goods sold (14,000 × $54*).......	756,000
Gross margin	364,000
Selling and admin. expenses [$112,000 + (14,000 × $2)]..........	140,000
Net income..........................	$ 224,000

*$6 DM + $11 DL + $3 VOH + $34 FOH ($680,000/20,000)
†$6 DM + $11 DL + $3 VOH
‡14,000 × $2 per unit

The difference in income between the two methods ($204,000) can be computed as the 6,000 units added to ending inventory × $34 FOH per unit.

ZBEST MFG. Income Statement (Variable Costing) For Year Ended December 31, 2019		
Sales (14,000 × $80).............		$1,120,000
Variable expenses		
Variable production costs (14,000 × $20†)	$280,000	
Variable selling and admin. expenses‡	28,000	308,000
Contribution margin.............		812,000
Fixed expenses		
Fixed overhead	680,000	
Fixed selling and admin. expenses	112,000	792,000
Net income..........		$ 20,000

Do More: QS 19-3, QS 19-4, E 19-3, E 19-4, E 19-5

Converting Income under Variable Costing to Absorption Costing

P3

Convert income under variable costing to the absorption cost basis.

Companies can use variable costing for *internal* reporting and business decisions, but they must use absorption costing for *external* reporting and tax reporting. For companies concerned about maintaining two costing systems, we can readily convert reports under variable costing to those using absorption costing.

Income under variable costing is restated to that under absorption costing by adding the fixed overhead cost in ending inventory and subtracting the fixed overhead cost in beginning inventory. Exhibit 19.11 shows the formula for this calculation.

EXHIBIT 19.11

Formula to Convert Variable Costing Income to Absorption Costing

| Income under absorption costing | = | Income under variable costing | + | Fixed overhead cost in ending inventory* | − | Fixed overhead cost in beginning inventory* |

*Under absorption costing.

Exhibit 19.12 shows the computations of absorption costing income. To restate variable costing income to absorption costing income for 2018, add back the **fixed overhead cost deferred in** (ending) **inventory.** To restate variable costing income to absorption costing income for 2019, deduct the **fixed overhead cost recognized from** (beginning) **inventory,** which was incurred in 2018 but expensed in the 2019 cost of goods sold when the inventory was sold.

EXHIBIT 19.12

Converting Variable Costing Income to Absorption Costing Income

	2017	2018	2019
Variable costing income (Exhibit 19.10)	$580,000	$120,000	$1,040,000
Add: Fixed overhead cost deferred in ending inventory (20,000 × $10)	0	200,000	0
Less: Fixed overhead cost recognized from beginning inventory (20,000 × $10)	0	0	(200,000)
Absorption costing income	$580,000	$320,000	$ 840,000

COMPARING VARIABLE COSTING AND ABSORPTION COSTING

This section compares the roles of absorption and variable costing in the following decisions.

- **Planning production**
- **Setting prices**
- **Controlling costs**
- **Cost-volume-profit analysis**

Planning Production

C1

Describe how absorption costing can result in overproduction.

Many companies link manager bonuses to income computed under absorption costing because this is how income is reported to shareholders (per GAAP). This can lead some managers to produce excess inventory, as we show next.

To illustrate how a reward system can lead to overproduction under absorption costing, let's use IceAge's 2017 data with one change: its manager decides to produce 100,000 units instead of 60,000. Because only 60,000 units are sold, the 40,000 units of excess production will be stored in ending finished goods inventory.

The left side of Exhibit 19.13 shows the product cost per unit under absorption costing when 60,000 units are produced (same as Exhibit 19.3). The right side shows product cost per unit when 100,000 units are produced.

Total product cost *per unit* is $4 less when 100,000 units are produced. This is because the company is spreading the $600,000 fixed overhead cost over 40,000 more units when 100,000 units are produced than when 60,000 units are produced.

Absorption Costing When 60,000 Units Are Produced		Absorption Costing When 100,000 Units Are Produced	
	Per Unit		Per Unit
Direct materials	$ 4	Direct materials	$ 4
Direct labor	8	Direct labor	8
Variable overhead	3	Variable overhead	3
Total variable	15	Total variable	15
Fixed overhead ($600,000/60,000 units)	10	Fixed overhead ($600,000/100,000 units)	6
Total product cost	**$25**	**Total product cost**	**$21**

The $4 per unit difference in product cost impacts income reporting. Exhibit 19.14 presents the 2017 income statement under absorption costing for the two alternative production levels.

ICEAGE COMPANY
Income Statement (Absorption Costing)
For Year Ended December 31, 2017
[60,000 Units Produced; 60,000 Units Sold]

Sales (60,000 × $40)		$2,400,000
Cost of goods sold (60,000 × $25)		1,500,000
Gross margin		900,000
Selling and administrative expenses		
Variable (60,000 × $2)	$120,000	
Fixed.	200,000	320,000
Net income		**$ 580,000**

ICEAGE COMPANY
Income Statement (Absorption Costing)
For Year Ended December 31, 2017
[100,000 Units Produced; 60,000 Units Sold]

Sales (60,000 × $40)		$2,400,000
Cost of goods sold (60,000 × $21)		1,260,000
Gross margin		1,140,000
Selling and administrative expenses		
Variable (60,000 × $2)	$120,000	
Fixed.	200,000	320,000
Net income		**$ 820,000**

Common sense suggests that because the company's variable cost per unit, total fixed costs, and sales are identical in both cases, merely producing more units and creating excess ending inventory should not increase income. Yet, income under absorption costing is $240,000 greater if IceAge produces 40,000 more units than necessary and builds up ending inventory. The reason is that $240,000 of fixed overhead (40,000 units × $6) is assigned to ending inventory instead of being expensed as cost of goods sold in 2017. This shows that under absorption costing, a manager can increase income just by producing more and disregarding whether the excess units can be sold or not. This incentive problem encourages inventory buildup, which leads to increased costs in storage, financing, and obsolescence. If the excess inventory is never sold, it will be disposed of at a loss.

The manager incentive problem is avoided when income is measured using variable costing. To illustrate, Exhibit 19.15 reports income under variable costing for the same production levels used in Exhibit 19.14. This demonstrates that managers cannot increase income under variable costing by merely increasing production without increasing sales.

Reported income under variable costing is not affected by production level changes because *all* fixed production costs are expensed in the year when incurred. Under variable costing, companies increase income by selling more units, not by producing excess inventory.

■ Decision Ethics

Production Manager   Your company produces and sells MP3 players. Due to competition, your company projects sales to be 35% less than last year. The CEO is concerned that top executives won't receive bonuses because of the expected sales decrease. The controller suggests that if the company produces as many units as last year, reported income might achieve the level for bonuses to be paid. Should your company produce excess inventory to maintain income? What ethical issues arise? ■   *Answer:* Under absorption costing, fixed overhead costs are spread over all units produced. Thus, fixed cost for each unit will be lower if more units are produced. This means the company can increase income by producing excess units even if sales remain constant. But excess inventory leads to increased financing cost and obsolescence. Also, producing excess inventory to meet income levels for bonuses harms company owners and is unethical. You must discuss this with the appropriate managers.

EXHIBIT 19.15

Income under Variable
Costing for Different
Production Levels

ICEAGE COMPANY Income Statement (Variable Costing) For Year Ended December 31, 2017 [60,000 Units Produced; 60,000 Units Sold]		
Sales (60,000 × $40)		$2,400,000
Variable expenses		
Variable production costs (60,000 × $15)	$900,000	

Variable selling and
    administrative expenses
    (60,000 × $2) . . . .
	120,000	1,020,000

Contribution margin.		1,380,000
Fixed expenses		
Fixed overhead	600,000	

Fixed selling and
    administrative
    expenses . . . .
	200,000	800,000

Net income		**$ 580,000**

ICEAGE COMPANY Income Statement (Variable Costing) For Year Ended December 31, 2017 [100,000 Units Produced; 60,000 Units Sold]		
Sales (60,000 × $40).		$2,400,000
Variable expenses		
Variable production costs (60,000 × $15)	$900,000	

Variable selling and
    administrative expenses
    (60,000 × $2) . . . .
	120,000	1,020,000

Contribution margin.		1,380,000
Fixed expenses		
Fixed overhead	600,000	

Fixed selling and
    administrative
    expenses . . . .
	200,000	800,000

Net income		**$ 580,000**

Setting Prices

P4

Determine product selling
price based on absorption
costing.

Over the long run, prices must be high enough to cover all costs, including variable costs and fixed costs, and still provide an acceptable return to owners. For this purpose, *absorption* cost information is useful because it reflects the full costs that sales must exceed for the company to be profitable. We can use a three-step process to determine product selling prices.

Step 1: Determine the product cost per unit using absorption costing.

Step 2: Determine the target *markup* on product cost per unit.

Step 3: Add the target markup to the product cost to find the target selling price.

To illustrate, consider IceAge. Under absorption costing, its product cost is $25 per unit (from Exhibit 19.3). IceAge's management must then determine a target markup on this product cost. This target markup could be based on industry averages, prices that have been charged in the past, or other information. In addition, this markup must be set high enough to cover selling and administrative expenses (both variable and fixed) that are excluded from product costs. Assume IceAge targets a markup of 60% of absorption cost. With that information, the company computes a target selling price as in Exhibit 19.16.

EXHIBIT 19.16

Determining Selling Price
with Absorption Costing

Step 1	Absorption cost per unit (from Exhibit 19.3)	$25
Step 2	Target markup per unit ($25 × 60%)	15
Step 3	Target selling price per unit	$40

IceAge can use this target selling price as a starting point in setting prices. Management must also consider the level of competition in its industry and customer preferences. If customers are not willing to pay $40 per unit, IceAge must either lower its target markup or find ways to reduce its costs.

While absorption cost information is useful in setting long-run prices, it can lead to misleading decisions in analyzing special orders. We show how variable cost information can be used to analyze special-order decisions in the Decision Analysis at the end of the chapter.

Controlling Costs

An effective management practice is to hold managers responsible only for their **controllable costs.** A cost is controllable if a manager can determine or greatly affect the amount incurred.

Uncontrollable costs are not within the manager's influence. In general, variable production costs and fixed production costs are controlled at different levels of management.

- Variable production costs, like direct materials and direct labor, are controlled by the production supervisor.
- Fixed costs related to production capacity, like depreciation, are controlled by higher-level managers who make decisions to change factory size or add new machines.

Income statements that separately report variable and fixed costs, as is done in the **contribution format** used in variable costing, are more useful for controlling costs. Because absorption costing does not separate variable from fixed costs, it is less useful in evaluating the effectiveness of cost control by different levels of managers.

■ **Decision Maker**

Internal Auditor   Your company uses absorption costing. Management is disappointed because its external auditors are requiring it to write off an inventory amount because it exceeds what the company could reasonably sell in the foreseeable future. Why would management produce more than it sells? Why would management be disappointed about the write-off? ■   *Answer:* If bonuses are tied to income, managers have incentives to increase income for personal gain. If absorption costing is used to determine income, management can reduce current-period expenses (and raise income) with overproduction, which shifts fixed production costs to future periods. This decision fails to consider whether there is a viable market for all units that are produced. If there is not, an auditor can conclude that the inventory does not have "future economic value" and pressure management to write it off. Such a write-off reduces income by the cost of the excess inventory.

CVP Analysis

The previous chapter discussed cost-volume-profit (CVP) analysis for making managerial decisions. If the income statement is prepared under variable costing and presented in the contribution format, the data for CVP analysis are readily available.

Using the variable costing income statement from the left side of Exhibit 19.15, IceAge computes its break-even point as follows.

$$\text{Break-even (in units)} = \frac{\text{Fixed costs}}{\text{Contribution margin per unit}} = \frac{\$800,000}{\$23^*} = 34,783 \text{ (rounded)}$$

*Total contribution margin/Units produced = $1,380,000/60,000

If the income statement is prepared under absorption costing, the data needed for CVP analysis are not readily available. Thus, we must reclassify cost data in order to conduct CVP analysis if absorption costing is used.

Variable Costing for Service Firms

Variable costing also applies to service companies. Because service companies do not produce inventory, the differences in income from absorption and variable costing shown for a manufacturer do not apply. Still, a focus on variable costs can be useful in managerial decisions for service firms. One example is a hotel receiving an offer to reserve a large block of rooms at a discounted price. Another example is "special-order" pricing for airlines when they sell tickets shortly before a flight at deeply discounted prices. If the discounted price exceeds variable costs, such sales increase contribution margin and net income.

For example, BlueSky provides charter airline services. Its variable costing income for 2019 is shown in Exhibit 19.17. Based on an activity level of 120 flights (60% of its capacity), BlueSky's variable cost per flight is $30,000, computed as $3,600,000/120. BlueSky's normal price is $50,000 per flight. A community group has offered BlueSky $35,000 to fly its members to Washington, D.C. In making its decision, BlueSky should *ignore allocated fixed costs*. If fixed costs will not increase from accepting this charter flight, the company's expected contribution margin from the special offer is

Revenue from charter flight	$35,000
Variable costs of charter flight	30,000
Contribution margin of charter flight	$ 5,000

EXHIBIT 19.17

Variable Costing Income
Statement for Service
Provider

Income Statement (Variable Costing) For Year Ended December 31, 2019		
Revenue (120 flights)		$6,000,000
Variable expenses		
Wages, salaries, and benefits	$1,920,000	
Fuel and oil	1,080,000	
Food and beverages	600,000	3,600,000
Contribution margin		2,400,000
Fixed expenses		
Depreciation	300,000	
Rentals	420,000	720,000
Operating income		$1,680,000

BlueSky should accept the charter-flight offer, as it provides a contribution margin of $5,000. An incorrect analysis based on absorption costing might lead management to reject the offer.

 **NEED-TO-KNOW 19-3**

Setting Prices

P4

Do More: QS 19-17, E 19-11

Part 1. A manufacturer's absorption cost per unit is $60. Compute the target selling price per unit if a 30% markup is targeted.

Solution

Absorption cost per unit	$60
Target markup per unit ($60 × 30%)	18
Target selling price per unit	$78

Considering Special
Offers

A1

Part 2. A hotel rents its 200 luxury suites at a rate of $500 per night per suite. The hotel's cost per night per suite is $400, consisting of

Variable costs	$160
Fixed costs (allocated)	240
Total cost per night per suite	$400

The hotel's manager has received an offer to reserve a block of 40 suites for $250 per suite per night during the hotel's off-season, when it has many available suites. Determine whether the offer should be accepted or rejected.

Solution

Do More: QS 19-18, E 19-13,
E 19-14, E 19-15

The allocated fixed costs should be ignored. Because the offer price of $250 per suite is greater than the variable costs of $160 per suite, the offer should be accepted.

 # SUSTAINABILITY AND ACCOUNTING

This chapter showed alternative ways to compute income. When businesses consider the effects of their operations on the environment, more ways to measure income emerge.

For example, **PUMA**, a maker of athletic shoes and apparel, developed an **environmental profit and loss (EP&L) account,** also called *EP&L report,* which is a listing in monetary terms of the impact on human welfare from PUMA's business activities. In this report, profit is the monetary value of activities that benefit the environment and loss is the monetary value of activities that harm the environment. While many companies measure and attempt to reduce their water usage, carbon emissions, and waste, PUMA takes the next step by putting environmental impacts into monetary terms.

Exhibit 19.18 shows one form of an EP&L report for PUMA. In this year, PUMA reported no profits from activities that benefited the environment, but it did report losses (costs) of several activities that harmed the environment.

Environmental Profit and Loss (in € millions)		
Environmental profits		€ 0
Environmental losses		
Water use.	€47	
Carbon emissions	47	
Land use	37	
Air pollution	11	
Waste	3	145
Net environmental loss		€145

EXHIBIT 19.18

Environmental Profit and Loss Report

Putting environmental impacts into monetary terms enables companies to better grasp the effects of their activities. PUMA's €145 million net environmental loss from Exhibit 19.18, although not included in computing GAAP net income, was over 70% of net income for that year. In addition, over 85% of the company's environmental costs are from suppliers and processors at early stages of the company's supply chain, and roughly 66% of its environmental costs are from its footwear division. The EP&L report enables managers to develop strategies that are likely to have the greatest impact in reducing environmental costs.

Lantern Inn B&B, this chapter's opening company, advocates the importance of small, local businesses for sustainable communities. David Doyon, co-owner of Lantern Inn, agrees that "small businesses are the largest employer nationally, and local business have less environmental impact." "We buy locally," explains co-owner Shay Doyon, thus reducing transportation costs, habitat loss, and pollution.

©Lantern Inn

Pricing Special Orders    **Decision Analysis**

A1

Use variable costing in pricing special orders.

Over the long run, prices must cover all fixed and variable costs. Over the short run, however, fixed production costs such as the cost to maintain plant capacity do not change with changes in production levels. With excess capacity, increases in production levels would increase variable production costs, but not fixed costs. This implies that while managers try to maintain the long-run price on existing orders, which covers all production costs, managers should accept special orders *provided the special-order price exceeds variable cost.*

To illustrate, let's return to the data of IceAge Company. Recall that its variable production cost per unit is $15 and its total production cost per unit is $25 (at a production level of 60,000 units). Assume that it receives a special order for 1,000 pairs of skates at an offer price of $22 per pair from a foreign skating school. This special order will not affect IceAge's regular sales, and its plant has excess capacity to fill the order.

Point: Total cost per unit is computed under absorption costing.

Using absorption costing information, cost is $25 per unit and the special-order price is $22 per unit. These data might suggest that management should reject the order as it would lose $3,000, computed as 1,000 units at $3 loss per pair ($22 − $25).

However, closer analysis suggests that this order should be accepted. The $22 order price exceeds the $15 *variable* cost of the product. Specifically, Exhibit 19.19 reveals that the incremental revenue from accepting the order is $22,000 (1,000 units at $22 per unit), whereas the incremental production cost of the order is $15,000 (1,000 units at $15 per unit) and the incremental variable selling and administrative cost is $2,000 (1,000 units at $2 per unit). Thus, both contribution margin and net income would increase by $5,000 from accepting the order. Variable costing reveals this profitable opportunity, while absorption costing hides it.

Point: Use of relevant costs in special-order and other managerial decisions is covered more extensively in a later chapter.

Reject Special Order		Accept Special Order	
Incremental sales	$0	Incremental sales (1,000 × $22)	$22,000
Incremental costs	0	Incremental costs	
		Variable production cost (1,000 × $15)	15,000
		Variable selling and admin. expense (1,000 × $2)	2,000
Incremental income	$0	Incremental income	$ 5,000

EXHIBIT 19.19

Computing Incremental Income for a Special Order

The reason for increased income from accepting the special order lies in the different behavior of variable and fixed production costs. If the order is rejected, only variable costs are saved. Fixed costs, however, do not change in the short run regardless of rejecting or accepting this order. Because incremental revenue from the order exceeds incremental costs (only variable costs in this case), accepting the special order increases company income.

Point: Fixed overhead costs won't increase when these additional units are sold because the company already has excess capacity.

NEED-TO-KNOW 19-4

COMPREHENSIVE

Variable and Absorption
Costing

Navaroli Company began operations on January 5, 2018. Cost and sales information for its first two calendar years of operations are summarized below.

Manufacturing costs		Production and sales data	
Direct materials	$80 per unit	Units produced, 2018	200,000 units
Direct labor.........................	$120 per unit	Units sold, 2018	140,000 units
Factory overhead costs		Units in ending inventory, 2018.......	60,000 units
Variable overhead	$30 per unit	Units produced, 2019	80,000 units
Fixed overhead (per year)...........	$14,000,000	Units sold, 2019	140,000 units
Nonmanufacturing costs		Units in ending inventory, 2019.......	0 units
Variable selling and administrative.......	$10 per unit	Sales price per unit.................	$600 per unit
Fixed selling and administrative	$ 8,000,000		

Required

1. Prepare an income statement for the company for 2018 under absorption costing.
2. Prepare an income statement for the company for 2018 under variable costing.
3. Explain the source(s) of the difference in reported income for 2018 under the two costing methods.
4. Prepare an income statement for the company for 2019 under absorption costing.
5. Prepare an income statement for the company for 2019 under variable costing.
6. Prepare a schedule to convert variable costing income to absorption costing income for each of the years 2018 and 2019. Use the format in Exhibit 19.12.

PLANNING THE SOLUTION

- Set up a table to compute the product cost per unit under the two costing methods (refer to Exhibit 19.3).
- Prepare income statements under the two costing methods (refer to Exhibit 19.6).
- Consider differences in the treatment of fixed overhead costs for the income statement to answer requirements 3 and 6.

SOLUTION

Before the income statement for 2018 is prepared, unit costs for 2018 are computed under the two costing methods as follows.

Product Cost per Unit	Absorption Costing	Variable Costing
Direct materials........................	$ 80	$ 80
Direct labor	120	120
Overhead		
Variable overhead....................	30	30
Fixed overhead*	70	—
Total product cost per unit	$300	$230

*Fixed overhead per unit = $14,000,000 ÷ 200,000 units = $70 per unit.

1. Absorption costing income statement for 2018.

Income Statement (Absorption Costing) For Year Ended December 31, 2018	
Sales (140,000 × $600)	$84,000,000
Cost of goods sold (140,000 × $300)	42,000,000
Gross margin	42,000,000
Selling and administrative expenses ($1,400,000 + $8,000,000)	9,400,000
Net income	$32,600,000

2. Variable costing income statement for 2018.

Income Statement (Variable Costing) For Year Ended December 31, 2018		
Sales (140,000 × $600)		$84,000,000
Variable expenses		
Variable production costs (140,000 × $230)..............	$32,200,000	
Variable selling and administrative costs	1,400,000	33,600,000
Contribution margin		50,400,000
Fixed expenses		
Fixed overhead.......................................	14,000,000	
Fixed selling and administrative	8,000,000	22,000,000
Net income		$28,400,000

3. Income under absorption costing is $4,200,000 more than that under variable costing even though sales are identical for each. This difference is due to the different treatment of fixed overhead cost. Under variable costing, the entire $14,000,000 of fixed overhead is expensed on the 2018 income statement. However, under absorption costing, $70 of fixed overhead cost is allocated to each of the 200,000 units produced. Because there were 60,000 units unsold at year-end, $4,200,000 (60,000 units × $70 per unit) of fixed overhead cost allocated to these units will be carried on its balance sheet in ending inventory. Consequently, reported income under absorption costing is $4,200,000 higher than variable costing income for the current period.

Before the income statement for 2019 is prepared, product cost per unit in 2019 is computed under the two costing methods as follows.

Product Cost per Unit	Absorption Costing	Variable Costing
Direct materials	$ 80	$ 80
Direct labor	120	120
Overhead		
Variable overhead.....................	30	30
Fixed overhead*	175	
Total product cost per unit	$405	$230

*Fixed overhead per unit = $14,000,000/80,000 units = $175 per unit.

4. Absorption costing income statement for 2019.

Income Statement (Absorption Costing) For Year Ended December 31, 2019		
Sales (140,000 × $600)......................................		$84,000,000
Cost of goods sold		
From beginning inventory (60,000 × $300).............................	$18,000,000	
Produced during the year (80,000 × $405)	32,400,000	50,400,000
Gross margin...		33,600,000
Selling and administrative expenses ($1,400,000 + $8,000,000)...............		9,400,000
Net income		$24,200,000

5. Variable costing income statement for 2019.

Income Statement (Variable Costing) For Year Ended December 31, 2019		
Sales (140,000 × $600)		$84,000,000
Variable expenses		
Variable product costs (140,000 × $230)................	$32,200,000	
Variable selling and administrative costs	1,400,000	33,600,000
Contribution margin		50,400,000
Fixed expenses		
Fixed overhead.......................................	14,000,000	
Fixed selling and administrative	8,000,000	22,000,000
Net income		$28,400,000

6. Conversion of variable costing income to absorption costing income.

	2018	2019
Variable costing income.....................................	$28,400,000	$28,400,000
Add: Fixed overhead cost deferred in ending inventory (60,000 × $70)...................	4,200,000	0
Less: Fixed overhead cost recognized from beginning inventory (60,000 × $70).............	0	(4,200,000)
Absorption costing income	$32,600,000	$24,200,000

Point: Total income over the two years equals $56,800,000 under both costing methods. This is because the total number of units produced over these two years equals the total number of units sold over these two years.

Summary: Cheat Sheet

ABSORPTION AND VARIABLE COSTING

Absorption costing: Fixed overhead part of product costs.
Variable costing: Fixed overhead part of period expenses.

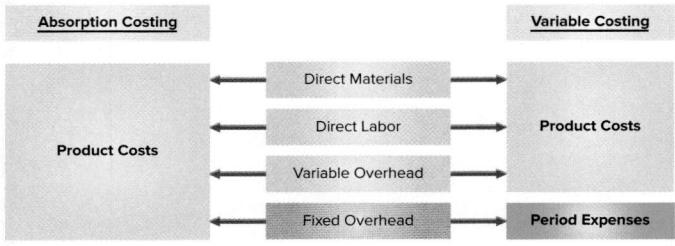

INCOME REPORTING

General rule—When inventory levels *change:* Absorption costing income ≠ Variable costing income.
- Production = Sales → Inventory unchanged
  Absorption income = Variable income   **See Exhibit 19.4**
- Production > Sales → Inventory increases
  Absorption income > Variable income   **See Exhibit 19.6**
- Production < Sales → Inventory decreases
  Absorption income < Variable income   **See Exhibit 19.8**

CONVERT INCOME: VARIABLE TO ABSORPTION

$$\begin{array}{c} \text{Income under} \\ \text{absorption costing} \end{array} = \begin{array}{c} \text{Income under} \\ \text{variable costing} \end{array} + \begin{array}{c} \text{Fixed overhead cost} \\ \text{in ending inventory*} \end{array} - \begin{array}{c} \text{Fixed overhead cost} \\ \text{in beginning inventory*} \end{array}$$

*Under absorption costing.

SETTING PRICE WITH ABSORPTION COSTING

$$\begin{array}{c} \text{Target} \\ \text{price} \end{array} = \begin{array}{c} \text{Absorption cost} \\ \text{per unit} \end{array} + \begin{array}{c} \text{Target markup} \\ \text{per unit} \end{array}$$

INCOME STATEMENT FORMATS

Income Statement (Absorption Costing)	
Sales.......................................	$#
Cost of goods sold	#
Gross margin	#
Selling and administrative expenses.....	#
Net income	$#

Income Statement (Variable Costing)		
Sales.......................................		$#
Variable expenses		
Variable production costs.............	$#	
Variable selling and administrative expenses	#	#
Contribution margin....................		#
Fixed expenses		
Fixed overhead	#	
Fixed selling and administrative expenses	#	#
Net income		$#

Formats Applied:
Absorption costing required for external reporting under GAAP.
Variable costing useful for planning production, controlling costs, CVP analysis, and analyzing special orders.

SPECIAL ORDER

ACCEPT if: Price > Variable costs + Incremental fixed costs.

Key Terms

Absorption costing (also called **full costing**) (739)

Contribution format (749)

Contribution margin income statement (741)

Controllable costs (748)

Environmental profit and loss (EP&L) account (750)

Fixed overhead cost deferred in inventory (746)

Fixed overhead cost recognized from inventory (746)

Manufacturing margin (742)

Uncontrollable costs (749)

Variable costing (also called **direct** or **marginal costing**) (739)

Multiple Choice Quiz

Answer questions 1 and 2 using the following data.

Units produced	1,000
Variable costs	
Direct materials	$3 per unit
Direct labor.	$5 per unit
Variable overhead	$3 per unit
Variable selling and administrative	$1 per unit
Fixed overhead.	$3,000 total
Fixed selling and administrative	$1,000 total

1. Product cost per unit under absorption costing is

   a. $11.   **c.** $14.   **e.** $16.

   b. $12.   **d.** $15.

2. Product cost per unit under variable costing is

   a. $11.   **c.** $14.   **e.** $16.

   b. $12.   **d.** $15.

3. Under variable costing, which costs are included in product cost?

   a. All variable product costs, including direct materials, direct labor, and variable overhead.

   b. All variable and fixed allocations of product costs, including direct materials, direct labor, and both variable and fixed overhead.

   c. All variable product costs except for variable overhead.

   d. All variable and fixed allocations of product costs, except for both variable and fixed overhead.

4. The difference between product cost per unit under absorption costing as compared to that under variable costing is

   a. Direct materials and direct labor.

   b. Fixed and variable portions of overhead.

   c. Fixed overhead only.

   d. Variable overhead only.

5. When production exceeds sales, which of the following is true?

   a. No change occurs to inventories for either absorption costing or variable costing methods.

   b. Use of absorption costing produces a higher net income than the use of variable costing.

   c. Use of absorption costing produces a lower net income than the use of variable costing.

   d. Use of absorption costing causes inventory value to decrease more than it would through the use of variable costing.

ANSWERS TO MULTIPLE CHOICE QUIZ

1. c; $14, computed as $3 + $5 + $3 + ($3,000/1,000 units).

2. a; $11, computed as $3 + $5 + $3 (consisting of all variable product costs).

3. a

4. c

5. b

🛇 Icon denotes assignments that involve decision making.

Discussion Questions

1. What costs are normally included in product costs under variable costing?

2. What costs are normally included in product costs under absorption costing?

3. 🛇 When units produced exceed units sold for a reporting period, would income under variable costing be greater than, equal to, or less than income under absorption costing? Explain.

4. Describe how the following items are computed: (*a*) gross margin and (*b*) contribution margin.

5. 🛇 How can absorption costing lead to incorrect short-run pricing decisions?

6. What conditions must exist to achieve accurate short-run pricing decisions using variable costing?

7. 🛇 Describe the usefulness of variable costing for controlling company costs.

8. 🔲 Describe how use of absorption costing in determining income can lead to overproduction and a buildup of inventory. Explain how variable costing can avoid this same problem.

9. What are the major limitations of variable costing?

10. **Google** uses variable costing for several **GOOGLE** business decisions. How can variable costing income statements be converted to absorption costing?

11. 🔲 Explain how contribution margin analysis is useful for managerial decisions and performance evaluations.

12. 🔲 **Samsung**'s managers rely on reports of variable costs. How can variable costing **Samsung**

reports prepared using the contribution margin format help managers in computing break-even volume in units?

13. 🔲 Assume that **Apple** has received a special order from a retailer for 1,000 specially **APPLE** outfitted iPads. This is a one-time order, which will not require any additional capacity or fixed costs. What should Apple consider when determining a selling price for these iPads?

14. 🔲 How can **Samsung** use variable costing to help better understand its operations and to make better pricing decisions? **Samsung**

Mc Graw Hill **connect**

QUICK STUDY

QS 19-1
Computing unit cost under absorption costing
P1

Vijay Company reports the following information regarding its production costs. Compute its product cost per unit under absorption costing.

Direct materials...........................	$10 per unit
Direct labor..............................	$20 per unit
Variable overhead	$10 per unit
Fixed overhead	$160,000 (per year)
Units produced	20,000 units

QS 19-2
Computing unit cost under variable costing P1

Refer to Vijay Company's data in QS 19-1. Compute its product cost per unit under variable costing.

QS 19-3
Variable costing income statement
P2

Aces Inc., a manufacturer of tennis rackets, began operations this year. The company produced 6,000 rackets and sold 4,900. Each racket was sold at a price of $90. Fixed overhead costs are $78,000, and fixed selling and administrative costs are $65,200. The company also reports the following per unit variable costs for the year. Prepare an income statement under variable costing.

Variable product costs	$25.00
Variable selling and administrative expenses............	2.00

QS 19-4
Absorption costing income statement
P2

Aces Inc., a manufacturer of tennis rackets, began operations this year. The company produced 6,000 rackets and sold 4,900. Each racket was sold at a price of $90. Fixed overhead costs are $78,000, and fixed selling and administrative costs are $65,200. The company also reports the following per unit variable costs for the year. Prepare an income statement under absorption costing.

Variable product costs	$25.00
Variable selling and administrative expenses............	2.00

QS 19-5
Absorption costing and gross margin
P2

Ramort Company reports the following cost data for its single product. The company regularly sells 20,000 units of its product at a price of $60 per unit. Compute gross margin under absorption costing.

Direct materials..	$10 per unit
Direct labor	$12 per unit
Overhead costs: Variable	$3 per unit
Fixed	$40,000 (per year)
Selling and administrative costs: Variable...............................	$2 per unit
Fixed	$65,200 (per year)
Normal production level (in units)	20,000 units

Refer to the information about Ramort Company in QS 19-5. If Ramort doubles its production to 40,000 units while sales remain at the current 20,000-unit level, by how much would the company's gross margin increase or decrease under absorption costing?

QS 19-6
Absorption costing and gross margin **P2**

Refer to the information about Ramort Company in QS 19-5. Compute contribution margin under variable costing.

QS 19-7
Variable costing and contribution margin **P2**

Refer to the information about Ramort Company in QS 19-5. If Ramort doubles its production to 40,000 units while sales remain at the current 20,000-unit level, would the company's contribution margin increase or decrease under variable costing?

QS 19-8
Variable costing and contribution margin **P2**

D'Souza Company sold 10,000 units of its product at a price of $80 per unit. Total variable cost is $50 per unit, consisting of $40 in variable production cost and $10 in variable selling and administrative cost. Compute the manufacturing (production) margin for the company under variable costing.

QS 19-9
Computing manufacturing margin **P2**

D'Souza Company sold 10,000 units of its product at a price of $80 per unit. Total variable cost is $50 per unit, consisting of $40 in variable production cost and $10 in variable selling and administrative cost. Compute the contribution margin.

QS 19-10
Computing contribution margin **P2**

Diaz Company reports the following variable costing income statement for its single product. This company's sales totaled 50,000 units, but its production was 80,000 units. It had no beginning finished goods inventory for the current period.

QS 19-11
Converting variable costing income to absorption costing

P3

Income Statement (Variable Costing)	
Sales (50,000 units × $60 per unit)	$3,000,000
Variable expenses	
Variable manufacturing expense (50,000 units × $28 per unit)	1,400,000
Variable selling and admin. expense (50,000 units × $5 per unit)	250,000
Total variable expenses.	1,650,000
Contribution margin.	1,350,000
Fixed expenses	
Fixed overhead	320,000
Fixed selling and administrative expenses	160,000
Total fixed expenses	480,000
Net income	$ 870,000

1. Convert this company's variable costing income statement to an absorption costing income statement.
2. Fill in the blanks: The dollar difference in variable costing income and absorption costing income = _____ units × _____ fixed overhead per unit.

Ming Company had net income of $772,200 based on variable costing. Beginning and ending inventories were 7,800 units and 5,200 units, respectively. Assume the fixed overhead per unit was $3.00 for both the beginning and ending inventory. What is net income under absorption costing?

QS 19-12
Converting variable costing income to absorption costing income **P3**

Mortech had net income of $250,000 based on variable costing. Beginning and ending inventories were 50,000 units and 48,000 units, respectively. Assume the fixed overhead per unit was $0.75 for both the beginning and ending inventory. What is net income under absorption costing?

QS 19-13
Converting variable costing income to absorption costing income **P3**

Hong Co. had net income of $386,100 under variable costing. Beginning and ending inventories were 2,600 units and 3,900 units, respectively. Fixed overhead cost was $4.00 per unit for both the beginning and ending inventory. What is net income under absorption costing?

QS 19-14
Converting variable costing income to absorption costing income **P3**

QS 19-15

Converting variable costing income to absorption costing income   **P3**

E-Com had net income of $130,000 under variable costing. Beginning and ending inventories were 1,200 units and 4,900 units, respectively. Fixed overhead cost was $2.50 per unit for both the beginning and ending inventory. What is net income under absorption costing?

QS 19-16

Absorption costing and overproduction

C1

Under absorption costing, a company had the following per unit costs when 10,000 units were produced.

Direct labor	$ 2
Direct materials	3
Variable overhead	4
Total variable cost	9
Fixed overhead ($50,000/10,000 units)	5
Total product cost per unit	$14

1. Compute the company's total product cost per unit under absorption costing if 12,500 units had been produced.

2. Fill in the blank with *increase* or *decrease*: If production is greater than sales, cost of goods sold under absorption costing will _____.

QS 19-17

Absorption costing and product pricing

P4

A manufacturer reports the following information on its product. Compute the target selling price per unit under absorption costing.

Direct materials cost	$50 per unit	Fixed overhead cost	$2 per unit
Direct labor cost	$12 per unit	Target markup	40%
Variable overhead cost	$6 per unit		

QS 19-18

Special-order pricing

A1

Li Company produces a product that sells for $84 per unit. A customer contacts Li and offers to purchase 2,000 units of its product at a price of $68 per unit. Variable production costs with this order would be $30 per unit, and variable selling expenses would be $18 per unit. Assume that this special order would not require any additional fixed costs and that Li has sufficient capacity to produce the product without affecting regular sales. Should Li accept this special order?

QS 19-19

Sustainability and product costing   **P1**

Refer to the information in QS 19-16. The company sells its product for $50 per unit. Due to new regulations, the company must now incur $2 per unit of hazardous waste disposal costs and $8,500 per year of fixed hazardous waste disposal costs. Compute the contribution margin per unit, including hazardous waste disposal costs.

QS 19-20

Sustainability and product costing   **P1**

Refer to the information in QS 19-16. The company sells its product for $50 per unit. Due to new regulations, the company must now incur $2 per unit of hazardous waste disposal costs and $8,500 per year of fixed hazardous waste disposal costs. Compute the company's break-even point (in units), including hazardous waste disposal costs.

---

connect

EXERCISES

Exercise 19-1

Computing unit and inventory costs under absorption costing

P1

Trio Company reports the following information for the current year, which is its first year of operations.

Direct materials	$15 per unit
Direct labor	$16 per unit
Variable overhead	$ 4 per unit
Fixed overhead	$160,000 per year
Units produced this year	20,000 units
Units sold this year	14,000 units
Ending finished goods inventory in units	6,000 units

1. Compute the product cost per unit using absorption costing.
2. Determine the cost of ending finished goods inventory using absorption costing.
3. Determine the cost of goods sold using absorption costing.

Check   (1) Absorption cost per unit, $43

Refer to the information in Exercise 19-1. Assume instead that Trio Company uses variable costing.
1. Compute the product cost per unit using variable costing.
2. Determine the cost of ending finished goods inventory using variable costing.
3. Determine the cost of goods sold using variable costing.

Exercise 19-2
Computing unit and inventory costs under variable costing   **P1**

Check   (1) Variable cost per unit, $35

Sims Company, a manufacturer of tablet computers, began operations on January 1, 2019. Its cost and sales information for this year follows.

Exercise 19-3
Income reporting under absorption costing and variable costing

P2

Manufacturing costs	
Direct materials	$40 per unit
Direct labor..................................	$60 per unit
Overhead costs	
Variable	$30 per unit
Fixed	$7,000,000 (per year)
Selling and administrative costs for the year	
Variable.....................................	$770,000
Fixed	$4,250,000
Production and sales for the year	
Units produced.............................	100,000 units
Units sold	70,000 units
Sales price per unit	$350 per unit

1. Prepare an income statement for the year using variable costing.
2. Prepare an income statement for the year using absorption costing.

Check   (1) Variable costing income, $3,380,000

Kenzi Kayaking, a manufacturer of kayaks, began operations this year. During this first year, the company produced 1,050 kayaks and sold 800 at a price of $1,050 each. At this first year-end, the company reported the following income statement information using absorption costing.

Exercise 19-4
Variable costing income statement

P2

Sales (800 × $1,050).....................................	$840,000
Cost of goods sold (800 × $500)	400,000
Gross margin...	440,000
Selling and administrative expenses	230,000
Net income	$210,000

Additional Information

a. Product cost per kayak totals $500, which consists of $400 in variable production cost and $100 in fixed production cost—the latter amount is based on $105,000 of fixed production costs allocated to the 1,050 kayaks produced.
b. The $230,000 in selling and administrative expenses consists of $75,000 that is variable and $155,000 that is fixed.

Required

1. Prepare an income statement for the current year under variable costing.
2. Fill in the blanks: The dollar difference in variable costing income and absorption costing income = _____ units × _____ fixed overhead per unit.

Exercise 19-5

Absorption costing and variable costing income statements

P2

Rey Company's single product sells at a price of $216 per unit. Data for its single product for its first year of operations follow. Prepare an income statement for the year assuming (*a*) absorption costing and (*b*) variable costing.

Direct materials..	$20 per unit
Direct labor...	$28 per unit
Overhead costs: Variable	$6 per unit
Fixed	$160,000 per year
Selling and administrative expenses: Variable	$18 per unit
Fixed	$200,000 per year
Units produced (and sold)	20,000 units

---

Exercise 19-6

Absorption costing income statement

P2

Hayek Bikes prepares the income statement under variable costing for its managerial reports, and it prepares the income statement under absorption costing for external reporting. For its first month of operations, 375 bikes were produced and 225 were sold; this left 150 bikes in ending inventory. The income statement information under variable costing follows.

Sales (225 × $1,600)...	$360,000
Variable product cost (225 × $625)	140,625
Variable selling and administrative expenses (225 × $65)	14,625
Contribution margin...	204,750
Fixed overhead cost	56,250
Fixed selling and administrative expenses	75,000
Net income	$ 73,500

1. Prepare this company's income statement for its first month of operations under absorption costing.
2. Fill in the blanks: The dollar difference in variable costing income and absorption costing income = _____ units × _____ fixed overhead per unit.

Exercise 19-7

Income reporting under absorption costing and variable costing

P2

Oak Mart, a producer of solid oak tables, reports the following data from its second year of business.

Sales price per unit..................	$320 per unit	Manufacturing costs this year		
Units produced this year	115,000 units	Direct materials	$40 per unit
Units sold this year..................	118,000 units	Direct labor..........................	$62 per unit
Units in beginning-year inventory	3,000 units	Overhead costs this year	
Beginning inventory costs		Variable overhead..................	$3,220,000
Variable (3,000 units × $135).......	$405,000	Fixed overhead	$7,400,000
Fixed (3,000 units × $80)	240,000	Selling and administrative costs this year	
Total	$645,000	Variable	$1,416,000
		Fixed	$4,600,000

1. Prepare the current-year income statement for the company using variable costing.
2. Prepare the current-year income statement for the company using absorption costing.

Check (2) Absorption costing income, $8,749,000

3. Fill in the blanks: The dollar difference in variable costing income and absorption costing income = _____ units × _____ fixed overhead per unit.

Exercise 19-8

Contribution margin format income statement

P2

Polarix is a retailer of ATVs (all-terrain vehicles) and accessories. An income statement for its Consumer ATV department for the current year follows. ATVs sell for $3,800 each. Variable selling expenses are $270 per ATV. The remaining selling expenses are fixed. Administrative expenses are 40% variable and 60% fixed. The company does not manufacture its own ATVs; it purchases them from a supplier for $1,830 each.

Income Statement—Consumer ATV Department		
For Year Ended December 31		
Sales		$646,000
Cost of goods sold		311,100
Gross margin		334,900
Operating expenses: Selling expenses	$135,000	
Administrative expenses	59,500	194,500
Net income		$140,400

1. Prepare an income statement for the current year using the contribution margin format.
2. For each ATV sold during this year, what is the contribution toward covering fixed expenses and earning income?

Check (2) $1,560

Cool Sky reports the following costing data on its product for its first year of operations. During this first year, the company produced 44,000 units and sold 36,000 units at a price of $140 per unit.

Exercise 19-9
Income statement under absorption costing and variable costing
P1   P2

Manufacturing costs	
Direct materials per unit	$60
Direct labor per unit	$22
Variable overhead per unit	$8
Fixed overhead for the year	$528,000
Selling and administrative costs	
Variable selling and administrative cost per unit	$11
Fixed selling and administrative cost per year	$105,000

1. Assume the company uses absorption costing.
  a. Determine its product cost per unit.
  b. Prepare its income statement for the year under absorption costing.
2. Assume the company uses variable costing.
  a. Determine its product cost per unit.
  b. Prepare its income statement for the year under variable costing.

Check   (1a) Absorption cost per unit, $102

(2a) Variable cost per unit, $90

A manufacturer reports the information below for three recent years. Compute income for each of the three years using absorption costing.

Exercise 19-10
Computing absorption costing income
P3

	Year 1	Year 2	Year 3
Variable costing income	$110,000	$114,400	$118,950
Beginning finished goods inventory (units)	0	1,200	700
Ending finished goods inventory (units)	1,200	700	800
Fixed manufacturing overhead per unit	$2.50	$2.50	$2.50

Sirhuds Inc., a maker of smartwatches, reports the information below on its product. The company uses absorption costing and has a target markup of 40% of absorption cost per unit. Compute the target selling price per unit under absorption costing.

Exercise 19-11
Absorption costing and product pricing
P4

Direct materials cost	$100 per unit	Variable selling and administrative expenses	$3 per unit
Direct labor cost	$30 per unit	Fixed selling and administrative expenses	$120,000 per year
Variable overhead cost	$8 per unit	Expected production (and sales)	50,000 units per year
Fixed overhead cost	$600,000 per year		

Exercise 19-12
Absorption costing and overproduction
C1

Jacquie Inc. reports the following annual cost data for its single product.

Normal production and sales level	60,000 units	Direct labor	$6.50 per unit
Sales price...........................	$56.00 per unit	Variable overhead..........	$11.00 per unit
Direct materials.....................	$9.00 per unit	Fixed overhead	$720,000 in total

If Jacquie increases its production to 80,000 units, while sales remain at the current 60,000-unit level, by how much would the company's gross margin increase or decrease under absorption costing? Assume the company has idle capacity to double current production.

Exercise 19-13
Analyzing variable cost for a special order
A1

Grand Garden is a hotel with 150 suites. Its regular suite rate is $250 per night per suite. The hotel's cost per night is $140 per suite and consists of the following.

Variable cost.............................	$ 30
Fixed cost	110
Total cost per night per suite.................	$140

The hotel manager receives an offer to hold the local Bikers' Club annual meeting at the hotel in March, which is the hotel's low season with an occupancy rate of under 50%. The Bikers' Club would reserve 50 suites for three nights if the hotel could offer a 50% discount, or a rate of $125 per night. The hotel manager is inclined to reject the offer because the cost per suite per night is $140. Prepare an analysis of this offer for the hotel manager. Should the offer from the Bikers' Club be accepted or rejected? What is the contribution margin from accepting the offer?

Exercise 19-14
Analyzing variable cost for a special order
A1

Empire Plaza Hotel is a hotel with 400 rooms. Its regular room rate is $300 per night per room. The hotel's cost is $165 per night per room and consists of the following.

Variable cost.............................	$ 40
Fixed cost	125
Total cost per night per room................	$165

The hotel manager receives an offer to hold the Junior States of America (JSA) convention at the hotel in February, which is the hotel's low season with an occupancy rate of under 45%. JSA would reserve 100 rooms for four nights if the hotel could offer a 50% discount, or a rate of $150 per night. The hotel manager is inclined to reject the offer because the cost per room per night is $165. Should the offer from JSA be accepted or rejected? What is the contribution margin from accepting the offer?

Exercise 19-15
Analyzing variable cost for a special order
A1

MidCoast Airlines provides charter airplane services. In October of this year, the company is operating at 60% of its capacity when it receives a bid from the local community college. The college is organizing a Washington, D.C., trip for its international student group. The college budgeted only $30,000 for round-trip airfare. MidCoast Airlines normally charges between $50,000 and $60,000 for such service. MidCoast determines its cost for the round-trip flight to Washington to be $44,000, which consists of the following.

Variable cost...........................	$15,000
Fixed cost (allocated)	29,000
Total cost.............................	$44,000

Although the manager at MidCoast supports the college's educational efforts, she cannot justify accepting the $30,000 bid for the trip given the projected $14,000 loss. Still, she decides to consult with you, an independent financial consultant. Should the airline accept the bid from the college? What is the contribution margin from accepting the offer?

A recent annual report for **Nike** reports the following operating income for its United States and China geographic segments.

Exercise 19-16
Analyzing income growth

P2

$ millions	2017	2016
United States	$3,875	$3,763
China..	1,507	1,372

Required

1. Is operating income growing faster in the United States or in the China segment?
2. Is the difference in operating income growth due to the use of different costing methods (absorption or variable costing) in the two geographic segments?

Mc Graw Hill Education connect

Dowell Company produces a single product. Its income statements under absorption costing for its first two years of operation follow.

PROBLEM SET A

Problem 19-1A
Variable costing income statement and conversion to absorption costing income (two consecutive years)

P2   P3

	2018	2019
Sales ($46 per unit)...	$920,000	$1,840,000
Cost of goods sold ($31 per unit)	620,000	1,240,000
Gross margin	300,000	600,000
Selling and administrative expenses	290,000	340,000
Net income..	$ 10,000	$ 260,000

Additional Information

a. Sales and production data for these first two years follow.

	2018	2019
Units produced..	30,000	30,000
Units sold..	20,000	40,000

b. Variable cost per unit and total fixed costs are unchanged during 2018 and 2019. The company's $31 per unit product cost consists of the following.

Direct materials...	$ 5
Direct labor...	9
Variable overhead	7
Fixed overhead ($300,000/30,000 units)	10
Total product cost per unit...................................	$31

c. Selling and administrative expenses consist of the following.

	2018	2019
Variable selling and administrative expenses ($2.50 per unit)	$ 50,000	$100,000
Fixed selling and administrative expenses.......................	240,000	240,000
Total selling and administrative expenses......................	$290,000	$340,000

Required

1. Prepare income statements for the company for each of its first two years under variable costing.
2. Prepare a table as in Exhibit 19.12 to convert variable costing income to absorption costing income for both 2018 and 2019.

Check (1) 2018 net loss, $(90,000)

Problem 19-2A

Variable costing income statement and conversion to absorption costing income

P2 P3

Trez Company began operations this year. During this first year, the company produced 100,000 units and sold 80,000 units. The absorption costing income statement for this year follows.

Sales (80,000 units × $50 per unit)		$4,000,000
Cost of goods sold		
Beginning inventory	$ 0	
Cost of goods manufactured (100,000 units × $30 per unit)	3,000,000	
Cost of goods available for sale	3,000,000	
Ending inventory (20,000 × $30)	600,000	
Cost of goods sold		2,400,000
Gross margin		1,600,000
Selling and administrative expenses		530,000
Net income		$1,070,000

Additional Information

a. Selling and administrative expenses consist of $350,000 in annual fixed expenses and $2.25 per unit in variable selling and administrative expenses.

b. The company's product cost of $30 per unit is computed as follows.

Direct materials	$5 per unit	Variable overhead	$2 per unit
Direct labor	$14 per unit	Fixed overhead ($900,000/100,000 units)	$9 per unit

Required

1. Prepare an income statement for the company under variable costing.

2. Fill in the blanks: The dollar difference in variable costing income and absorption costing income = _____ units × _____ fixed overhead per unit.

Problem 19-3A

Income reporting, absorption costing, and managerial ethics

C1 P2

Blazer Chemical produces and sells an ice-melting granular used on roadways and sidewalks in winter. It annually produces and sells about 100 tons of its granular. In its nine-year history, the company has never reported a net loss. However, because of this year's unusually mild winter, projected demand for its product is only 60 tons. Based on its predicted production and sales of 60 tons, the company projects the following income statement (under absorption costing).

Sales (60 tons at $21,000 per ton)	$1,260,000
Cost of goods sold (60 tons at $16,000 per ton)	960,000
Gross margin	300,000
Selling and administrative expenses	318,600
Net loss	$ (18,600)

Its product cost information follows and consists mainly of fixed cost because of its automated production process requiring expensive equipment.

Variable direct labor and material costs per ton	$ 3,500
Fixed cost per ton ($750,000 ÷ 60 tons)	12,500
Total product cost per ton	$16,000

Selling and administrative expenses consist of variable selling and administrative expenses of $310 per ton and fixed selling and administrative expenses of $300,000 per year. The company's president is concerned about the adverse reaction from its creditors and shareholders if the projected net loss is reported. The operations manager mentions that because the company has large storage capacity, it can report a net income by keeping its production at the usual 100-ton level even though it expects to sell only 60 tons. The president is puzzled by the suggestion that the company can report income by producing more without increasing sales.

Required

1. Prepare an income statement (using absorption costing) based on production of 100 tons and sales of 60 tons.

2. By how much does net income increase by producing 100 tons and storing 40 tons in inventory?

Azule Company produces a single product. Its income statements under absorption costing for its first two years of operation follow.

PROBLEM SET B

	2018	2019
Sales ($35 per unit).	$1,925,000	$2,275,000
Cost of goods sold ($26 per unit)	1,430,000	1,690,000
Gross margin.	495,000	585,000
Selling and administrative expenses	465,000	495,000
Net income	$ 30,000	$ 90,000

Problem 19-1B
Variable costing income statement and conversion to absorption costing income (two consecutive years)

P2   P3

Additional Information

a. Sales and production data for these first two years follow.

	2018	2019
Units produced.	60,000	60,000
Units sold	55,000	65,000

b. Its variable cost per unit and total fixed costs are unchanged during 2018 and 2019. Its $26 per unit product cost consists of the following.

Direct materials.	$ 4
Direct labor	6
Variable overhead	8
Fixed overhead ($480,000/60,000 units)	8
Total product cost per unit	$26

c. Its selling and administrative expenses consist of the following.

	2018	2019
Variable selling and administrative expenses ($3 per unit)	$165,000	$195,000
Fixed selling and administrative expenses	300,000	300,000
Total selling and administrative expenses.	$465,000	$495,000

Required

1. Prepare this company's income statements under variable costing for each of its first two years.

2. Explain any difference between the absorption costing income and the variable costing income for these two years.

Check   (1) 2018 net loss, $(10,000)

E'Lonte Company began operations this year. During this first year, the company produced 300,000 units and sold 250,000 units. Its income statement under absorption costing for this year follows.

Problem 19-2B
Variable costing income statement and conversion to absorption costing income

P2   P3

Sales (250,000 units × $18 per unit).		$4,500,000
Cost of goods sold		
Beginning inventory	$ 0	
Cost of goods manufactured (300,000 units × $7.50 per unit).	2,250,000	
Cost of goods available for sale.	2,250,000	
Ending inventory (50,000 × $7.50)	375,000	
Cost of goods sold		1,875,000
Gross margin		2,625,000
Selling and administrative expenses		2,200,000
Net income.		$ 425,000

Additional Information

a. Selling and administrative expenses consist of $1,200,000 in annual fixed expenses and $4 per unit in variable selling and administrative expenses.

b. The company's product cost of $7.50 per unit is computed as follows.

Direct materials.............	$2.00 per unit	Variable overhead............................	$1.60 per unit
Direct labor................	$2.40 per unit	Fixed overhead ($450,000/300,000 units)........	$1.50 per unit

Required

1. Prepare the company's income statement under variable costing.

2. Explain any difference between the company's income under variable costing (from part 1) and the income reported above.

Problem 19-3B
Income reporting, absorption costing, and managerial ethics

C1   P2

Chem-Melt produces and sells an ice-melting granular used on roadways and sidewalks in winter. The company annually produces and sells about 300,000 pounds of its granular. In its 10-year history, the company has never reported a net loss. Because of this year's unusually mild winter, projected demand for its product is only 250,000 pounds. Based on its predicted production and sales of 250,000 pounds, the company projects the following income statement under absorption costing.

Sales (250,000 lbs. at $8 per lb.).......................................	$2,000,000
Cost of goods sold (250,000 lbs. at $6.80 per lb.).........................	1,700,000
Gross margin..	300,000
Selling and administrative expenses.....................................	450,000
Net loss...	$ (150,000)

Its product cost information follows and consists mainly of fixed production cost because of its automated production process requiring expensive equipment.

Variable direct labor and materials costs per pound	$2.00
Fixed production cost per pound ($1,200,000/250,000 lbs.)	4.80
Total product cost per pound...	$6.80

The company's selling and administrative expenses are all fixed. The president is concerned about the adverse reaction from its creditors and shareholders if the projected net loss is reported. The controller suggests that because the company has large storage capacity, it can report a net income by keeping its production at the usual 300,000-pound level even though it expects to sell only 250,000 pounds. The president is puzzled by the suggestion that the company can report a profit by producing more without increasing sales.

Required

1. Can the company report a net income by increasing production to 300,000 pounds and storing the excess production in inventory? Prepare an income statement (using absorption costing) based on production of 300,000 pounds and sales of 250,000 pounds.

2. Should the company produce 300,000 pounds given that projected demand is 250,000 pounds? Explain, and also refer to any ethical implications of such a managerial decision.

SERIAL PROBLEM
Business Solutions

P2   P3

This serial problem began in Chapter 1 and continues through most of the book. If previous chapter segments were not completed, the serial problem can begin at this point.

SP 19   Santana Rey expects sales of **Business Solutions**'s line of computer workstation furniture to equal 300 workstations (at a sales price of $3,000 each) for 2019. The workstations' manufacturing costs include the following.

| Direct materials............ | $800 per unit | Variable overhead .... | $100 per unit |
| Direct labor............... | $400 per unit | Fixed overhead........... | $24,000 per year |

The selling expenses related to these workstations follow.

| Variable selling expenses.... | $50 per unit | Fixed selling expenses...... | $4,000 per year |

Santana is considering how many workstations to produce in 2019. She is confident that she will be able to sell any workstations in her 2019 ending inventory during 2020. However, Santana does not want to overproduce as she does not have sufficient storage space for many more workstations.

©Alexander Image/Shutterstock

Required

For parts 1 and 2, assume 300 workstations are sold.

1. Compute Business Solutions's absorption costing income assuming
   a. 300 workstations are produced.
   b. 320 workstations are produced.
2. Compute Business Solutions's variable costing income assuming
   a. 300 workstations are produced.
   b. 320 workstations are produced.
3. For parts 1 and 2, which costing method, absorption or variable, yields the higher net income when 320 workstations are produced and 300 are sold?

Accounting Analysis

AA 19-1   Review **Apple**'s income statement in Appendix A for the year ending September 30, 2017, and identify its net income for 2017.

1. Is Apple's net income prepared using absorption costing or variable costing?
2. Review Apple's balance sheet data in Appendix A as of September 30, 2017, and September 24, 2016. What amounts (in $ millions) does Apple report for inventory at each of these balance sheet dates?
3. Assume Apple's fixed overhead costs equal 10% of the total reported inventory cost at each of these two balance sheet dates. Compute Apple's 2017 net income under variable costing. *Hint:* Refer to Exhibit 19.11.

COMPANY ANALYSIS
P2
APPLE

AA 19-2   **Apple**'s and **Google**'s ending inventory amounts (in $ millions) are shown below:

	Apple		Google	
	2017	2016	2017	2016
Ending inventory...........	$4,855	$2,132	$749	$268

COMPARATIVE ANALYSIS
P2
APPLE
GOOGLE

Required

1. Assume Apple uses variable costing for some of its internal reports. For 2017, would net income based on variable costing be higher, lower, or no different from net income based on absorption costing?
2. Assume Google uses variable costing for some of its internal reports. For 2017, would net income based on variable costing be higher, lower, or no different from net income based on absorption costing?
3. Assume both companies are considering implementing just-in-time (JIT) inventory systems. After implementing JIT systems, would differences in income between absorption costing and variable costing be more likely to increase or to decrease?

GLOBAL ANALYSIS

P3

Samsung

AA 19-3   Review **Samsung**'s income statement in Appendix A for the year ending December, 31 2017, and identify its net income for 2017.

1. Review Samsung's balance sheet data in Appendix A as of December 31, 2017, and December 31, 2016. What amounts (in ₩ millions) does Samsung report for inventory at each of these balance sheet dates?
2. Assume Samsung uses absorption costing for financial reporting and its fixed overhead costs equal 10% of the total reported inventory cost at each of these two balance sheet dates. Compute Samsung's 2017 net income under variable costing. *Hint:* Refer to Exhibit 19.11.

Beyond the Numbers

ETHICS CHALLENGE

C1

BTN 19-1   FDP Company produces a variety of home security products. Gary Price, the company's president, is concerned with the fourth-quarter market demand for the company's products. Unless something is done in the last two months of the year, the company is likely to miss its earnings expectation of Wall Street analysts. Price still remembers when FDP's earnings were below analysts' expectation by two cents a share three years ago and the company's share price fell 19% the day earnings were announced. In a recent meeting, Price told his top management that something must be done quickly. One proposal by the marketing vice president was to give a deep discount to the company's major customers to increase the company's sales in the fourth quarter. The company controller pointed out that while the discount could increase sales, it may not help the bottom line; to the contrary, it could lower income. The controller said, "Since we have enough storage capacity, we might simply increase our production in the fourth quarter to increase our reported profit."

Required

1. Gary Price is not sure how the increase in production without a corresponding increase in sales could help boost the company's income. Explain to Price how reported income varies with respect to production level.
2. Is there an ethical concern in this situation? If so, which parties are affected? Explain.

COMMUNICATING IN PRACTICE

P3

BTN 19-2   Mertz Chemical has three divisions. Its consumer product division faces strong competition from companies overseas. During its recent teleconference, Ryan Peterson, the consumer product division manager, reported that his division's sales for the current year were below its break-even point. However, when the division's annual reports were received, Billie Mertz, the company president, was surprised that the consumer product division actually reported a profit of $264,000. How could this be possible?

Required

Assume that you work in the corporate controller's office. Write a half-page memorandum to the president explaining how the division can report income even if its sales are below the break-even point.

TAKING IT TO THE NET

P2

BTN 19-3   This chapter discussed the variable costing method and how to use variable costing information to make various business decisions. We also can find several websites on variable costing and its business applications.

Required

1. Review the website of **Value Based Management** at **ValueBasedManagement.net**. Identify and read the page on the topic of variable costing (**valuebasedmanagement.net/methodsvariablecosting.html**).
2. What other phrases are used in practice for *variable costing?*
3. According to this website, what are the consequences of variable costing for profit calculation?

TEAMWORK IN ACTION

P4

BTN 19-4   This chapter identified several decision contexts in which managers use product cost information.

Required

Break into teams and identify at least one specific decision context in which absorption costing information is more relevant than variable costing information and at least one decision context in which variable costing information is more relevant than absorption costing. Be prepared to discuss your answers in class.

BTN 19-5 **Lantern Inn** is a bed and breakfast operated by Shay and David Doyon.

Required

Shay and David use variable costing to make business decisions. If Shay and David used absorption costing, would we expect the company's income to be more than, less than, or about the same as its income measured under variable costing? Explain.

ENTREPRENEURIAL DECISION

P3

BTN 19-6 Visit a local hotel and observe its daily operating activities. The costs associated with some of its activities are variable while others are fixed with respect to occupancy levels.

Required

1. List costs that are likely variable for the hotel.
2. List costs that are likely fixed for the hotel.
3. Using your lists from parts 1 and 2, which type of costs (fixed or variable) is likely to be larger (in dollars)?
4. Based on your observations and the answers to parts 1 through 3, explain why many hotels offer discounts as high as 50% or more during their low occupancy season.

HITTING THE ROAD

A1

20 Master Budgets and Performance Planning

Chapter Preview

BUDGET PROCESS AND ADMINISTRATION

C1 Budgeting process

Benefits of budgeting

Human behavior

Reporting and timing

Master budget components

NTK 20-1

OPERATING BUDGETS

P1 Prepare operating budgets, including

Sales

Production

Direct materials

Direct labor

Overhead

Selling expenses

General expenses

NTK 20-2, 20-3, 20-4

INVESTING AND FINANCING BUDGETS

Capital expenditures budget

P2 Cash budget

NTK 20-5

BUDGETED FINANCIAL STATEMENTS

P3 Budgeted income statement

Budgeted balance sheet

Master budget

Service companies

A1 Activity-based budgeting

P4 *Appendix:* Merchandiser budgeting

NTK 20-6, 20-8

Learning Objectives

CONCEPTUAL

C1 Describe the benefits of budgeting.

ANALYTICAL

A1 Analyze expense planning using activity-based budgeting.

PROCEDURAL

P1 Prepare the operating budgets of a master budget—for a manufacturing company.

P2 Prepare a cash budget—for a manufacturing company.

P3 Prepare budgeted financial statements.

P4 *Appendix 20A*—Prepare each component of a master budget—for a merchandising company.

Crushing It

"We make juice from misfits"—**ANNA YANG**

WASHINGTON, DC—Billions of pounds of edible food—from discarded fruits and vegetables from retailers to scraps of pre-cut goods from food processors—are wasted each year. Seizing a delicious opportunity, college students Anna Yang and Phil Wong started by repurposing these unwanted raw materials into cold-pressed juices.

Starting with a borrowed blender and a few discarded peaches, Anna and Phil's vision to reduce waste turned into a company, **Misfit Juicery** (**Misfitjuicery.com**). "We had never started a company," admits Phil. "We were complete amateurs, selling juice out of mason jars."

Misfit obtains ingredients from local farmers, national food distributors, and fresh-cut producers. "We attack the issue all along the supply chain," explains Anna. Their supply chain strategy requires them to budget the cost of their fruit and vegetable purchases. They must also track costs of storing these perishable raw materials. Anna and Phil also budget for direct labor costs of several full- and part-time employees.

In explaining budgets, Anna says "our company changes on a day-to-day basis." Rapid change and many unknowns make sales forecasts difficult. Anna knows that a good sales forecast is the cornerstone of a good budget. She also explains that all companies set budgets—manufacturers budget costs of direct materials, direct labor, and overhead, and service firms focus on direct labor budgets.

©Misfit Juicery

Misfit's blend is working. It recently expanded into new markets and products, added flavors, and moved into a larger production site. Anna proclaims, "We want to be THE food brand that squeezes inefficiencies from the supply chain."

Sources: *Misfit Juicery website,* January 2019; *DC Inno,* October 18, 2016; *ABC News* interview, July 24, 2017; *Bevnet,* April 15, 2016; *Vogue,* October 26, 2016

BUDGET PROCESS AND ADMINISTRATION

Budgeting Process

Managers must ensure that activities of employees and departments contribute to meeting the company's overall goals. This requires coordination and budgeting. **Budgeting,** the process of planning future business actions and expressing them as formal plans, helps to achieve this coordination.

C1

Describe the benefits of budgeting.

A **budget** is a formal statement of a company's plans, expressed in monetary terms. Unlike long-term *strategic plans,* budgets typically cover shorter periods such as a month, quarter, or year. Budgets are useful in controlling operations. The **budgetary control** process, shown in Exhibit 20.1, refers to management's use of budgets to see that planned objectives are met.

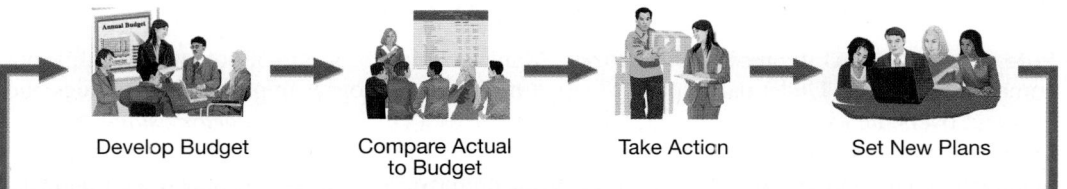

Develop Budget → Compare Actual to Budget → Take Action → Set New Plans

EXHIBIT 20.1

Process of Budgetary Control

The budgetary control process involves at least four steps: (1) develop the budget from planned objectives, (2) compare actual results to budgeted amounts and analyze differences, (3) take corrective and strategic actions, and (4) establish new objectives and a new budget.

In this chapter we focus on the first step in the budgetary control process, developing a budget. In the next chapter we show how managers compare budgeted and actual amounts to guide corrective actions and make new plans.

Benefits of Budgeting

Budgets benefit the key managerial functions of planning and controlling.

- **Plan**   A budget focuses on the future opportunities and threats to the organization. This focus on the future is important because the daily pressures of operating an organization can divert management's attention from planning. Budgeting makes managers devote time to *plan* for the future.

- **Control**   The *control* function requires management to evaluate (benchmark) operations against some norm. Since budgeted performance considers important company, industry, and economic factors, a comparison of actual to budgeted performance provides an effective monitoring and control system. This comparison assists management in identifying problems and taking corrective actions if necessary.

- **Coordinate**   Budgeting helps to *coordinate* activities so that all employees and departments understand and work toward the company's overall goals.

- **Communicate**   Written budgets effectively *communicate* management's specific action plans to all employees. When plans are not written down, conversations can lead to uncertainty and confusion among employees.

- **Motivate**   Budgets can be used to *motivate* employees. Budgeted performance levels can provide goals for employees to attain or even exceed. Many companies provide incentives, like cash bonuses, for employee performance that meets or exceeds budget goals.

■ Decision Insight

Budget Bonus   Budgets are important in determining managers' pay. A recent survey shows that 82% of large companies tie managers' bonus payments to beating budget goals. For these companies, bonus payments are frequently more than 20% of total manager pay. ■

Budgeting and Human Behavior

Budgets provide standards for evaluating performance and can affect employee attitudes. Budgeted levels of performance must be realistic to avoid discouraging employees. Employees who will be evaluated should help prepare the budget to increase their commitment to it. For example, the sales department should be involved in developing sales estimates, while the production department should prepare its initial expense budget. This *bottom-up* process is usually more useful than a *top-down* approach in which top management passes down the budget without input. Performance evaluations must allow the affected employees to explain the reasons for apparent performance deficiencies, rather than assigning blame.

Budgeting has three important guidelines.

1. Employees affected by a budget should help prepare it (*participatory budgeting*).
2. Goals reflected in a budget should be challenging but attainable.
3. Evaluations offer opportunities to explain differences between actual and budgeted amounts.

Budgeting can be a positive motivating force when the guidelines are followed.

Example: Assume a company's sales force receives a bonus when sales exceed the budgeted amount. How would this arrangement affect the participatory sales forecasts? *Answer:* Sales reps may understate their budgeted sales.

Potential Negative Outcomes of Budgeting   Managers must be aware of potential negative outcomes of budgeting. Under participatory budgeting, some employees might understate sales budgets and overstate expense budgets to allow themselves a cushion, or *budgetary slack,* to aid in meeting targets. Sometimes, pressure to meet budgeted results leads employees to engage in unethical behavior or commit fraud. Finally, some employees might always spend their budgeted amounts, even on unnecessary items, to ensure their budgets aren't reduced for the next period.

©Cultura RF/Getty Images

■ Decision Insight

Budget Strategy   Most companies allocate dollars based on budgets submitted by department managers. These managers verify the numbers and monitor the budget. Managers must remember, however, that a budget is judged by its success in helping achieve the company's mission. One analogy is that a hiker must know the route to properly plan a hike and monitor hiking progress. ■

Budget Reporting and Timing

The budget period usually coincides with the company's fiscal year. To provide specific guidance to help control operations, the annual budget usually is separated into quarterly or monthly budgets. These short-term budgets allow management to periodically evaluate performance and take corrective action.

The time required to prepare a budget can vary a lot. Large, complex organizations usually take longer to prepare their budgets than do smaller ones. This is because of the effort required to coordinate the different units (departments) within large organizations.

Many companies apply **continuous budgeting** by preparing **rolling budgets.** In continuous budgeting, a company continually revises its budgets as time passes. In a rolling budget, a company revises its entire set of budgets by adding a new quarterly budget to replace the quarter that just elapsed. Thus, at any point in time, monthly or quarterly budgets are available for the next 12 months or four quarters. The rolling budget below shows rolling budgets prepared at the end of two consecutive periods. The first set (at top) is prepared in December 2018 and covers the four calendar quarters of 2019. In March 2019, the company prepares another rolling budget for the next four quarters through March 2020. This same process is repeated every three months. As a result, management is continuously planning ahead.

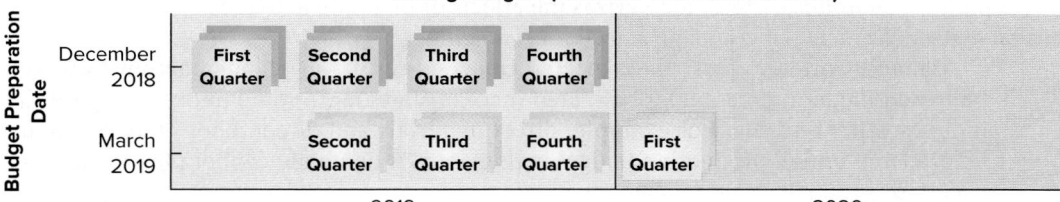

Rolling Budgets (Calendar Years and Quarters)

Decision Insight

Budget Needs Many companies use **zero-based budgeting,** which requires all expenses to be justified for each new budget. Rather than using last period's budgeted or actual amounts to determine this period's budgets, managers instead analyze each activity in the organization to see if it is necessary. Managers then budget for only those necessary activities. Made-from-scratch budgets can be useful in identifying waste and reducing costs. ■

Label each item below with a "**B**" if it describes a benefit of budgeting or a "**Not B**" if it describes a potential negative outcome of budgeting.

_____ **1.** Budgets provide goals for employees to work toward.

_____ **2.** Written budgets help communicate plans to all employees.

_____ **3.** Some employees might understate sales targets in budgets.

_____ **4.** A budget forces managers to spend time planning for the future.

_____ **5.** Some employees might always spend budgeted amounts.

_____ **6.** With rolling budgets, managers can continuously plan ahead.

NEED-TO-KNOW 20-1

Budgeting Benefits

C1

Solution

1. B   **2.** B   **3.** Not B   **4.** B   **5.** Not B   **6.** B

Do More: QS 20-1, QS 20-2

Master Budget Components

A **master budget** is a formal, comprehensive plan for a company's future. It contains several individual budgets that are linked together to form a coordinated plan. Exhibit 20.2 summarizes the master budgeting process. The master budgeting process typically begins with the sales budget and ends with a cash budget and budgeted financial statements. The master budget includes individual budgets for sales, production (or purchases), various expenses, capital expenditures, and cash.

EXHIBIT 20.2

Master Budget Process
for a Manufacturer

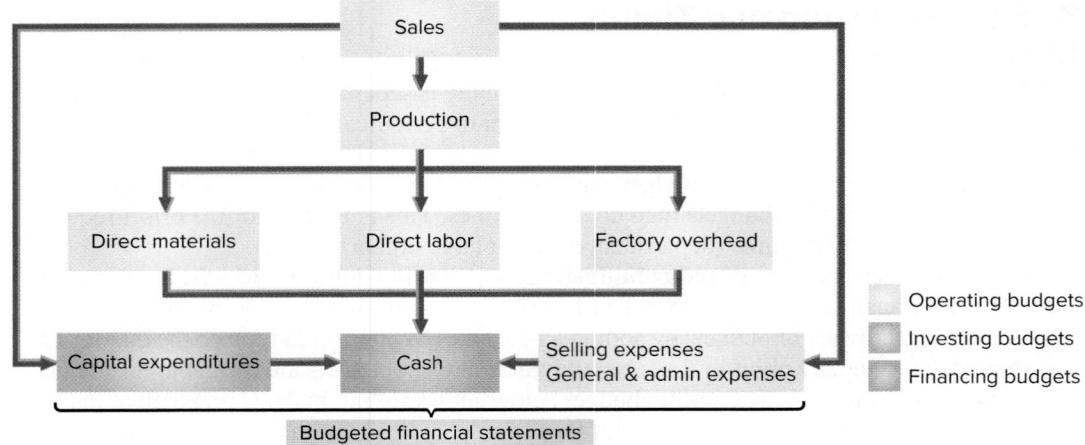

The number and types of budgets included in a master budget depend on the company's size and complexity. A manufacturer's master budget should include, at a minimum, several *operating* budgets (shown in yellow in Exhibit 20.2), a capital expenditures budget, and a cash budget. The capital expenditures budget summarizes the effects of *investing* activities on cash. The cash budget helps determine the company's need for *financing*.

Point: Merchandisers prepare *merchandise purchase* budgets instead of the production and manufacturing budgets in Exhibit 20.2.

Managers often express the expected financial results of planned activities with a budgeted balance sheet and a budgeted income statement. Some budgets require the input of other budgets. For example, direct materials and direct labor budgets cannot be prepared until a production budget is prepared. A company cannot plan its production until it prepares a sales budget.

The rest of this chapter explains how **Toronto Sticks Company (TSC)**, a manufacturer of youth hockey sticks, prepares its budgets. Its master budget includes operating, capital expenditures, and cash budgets for each month in each quarter. It also includes a budgeted income statement for each quarter and a budgeted balance sheet as of the last day of each quarter. We show how TSC prepares budgets for October, November, and December 2019. Exhibit 20.3 presents TSC's balance sheet at the start of this budgeting period, which we refer to in preparing the component budgets.

Courtesy of JJW Images

EXHIBIT 20.3

Balance Sheet prior to the
Budgeting Period

TORONTO STICKS COMPANY					
Balance Sheet					
September 30, 2019					
Assets			**Liabilities and Equity**		
Cash		$ 20,000	Liabilities		
Accounts receivable		25,200	Accounts payable	$ 7,060	
Raw materials inventory (178 pounds @ $20) ...		3,560	Income taxes payable (due 10/31/2019)	20,000	
Finished goods inventory (1,010 units @ $17) ..		17,170	Note payable	10,000	$ 37,060
Equipment*	$200,000		Stockholders' equity		
Less: Accumulated depreciation	36,000	164,000	Common stock	150,000	
			Retained earnings	42,870	192,870
Total assets		$229,930	Total liabilities and equity		$229,930

*Equipment is depreciated on a straight-line basis over 10 years (salvage value is $20,000).

OPERATING BUDGETS

P1

Prepare the operating budgets of a master budget—for a manufacturing company.

This section explains TSC's preparation of operating budgets. Its operating budgets consist of the sales budget, production and manufacturing budgets, selling expense budget, and general and administrative expense budget. (*Note:* The preparation of merchandising budgets is described in this chapter's appendix.)

Sales Budget

The first step in preparing the master budget is the **sales budget,** which shows the planned sales units and the expected dollars from these sales. The sales budget is the starting point in the budgeting process because plans for most departments are linked to sales.

The sales budget comes from a careful analysis of forecasted economic and market conditions, business capacity, and advertising plans. To illustrate, in September 2019, TSC sold 700 hockey sticks at $60 per unit. After considering sales predictions and market conditions, TSC prepares its sales budget for the next three months (see Exhibit 20.4). The sales budget in Exhibit 20.4 includes forecasts of both unit sales and unit prices. Some sales budgets are expressed only in total sales dollars, but most are more detailed and can include budgets for many different products, regions, departments, and sales representatives.

	A	B	C	D	E
1		TORONTO STICKS COMPANY			
2		Sales Budget			
3		October 2019–December 2019			
4		October	November	December	Totals
5	Budgeted sales (units)	1,000	800	1,400	3,200
6	Selling price per unit	× $ 60	× $ 60	× $ 60	× $ 60
7	Total budgeted sales (dollars)	$60,000	$48,000	$84,000	$192,000

EXHIBIT 20.4

Sales Budget

Operating Budgets

Sales
Production
Direct materials
Direct labor
Factory overhead
Selling expenses
General & administrative

■ **Decision Maker**

Entrepreneur You run a start-up that manufactures designer clothes. Business is seasonal, and fashions and designs quickly change. How do you prepare reliable annual sales budgets? ■ *Answer:* You face two issues. First, because fashions and designs frequently change, you cannot rely on previous budgets. You must carefully analyze the market to understand what designs are in vogue. This will help you plan the product mix and estimate demand. The second issue is the budgeting period. An annual sales budget may be unreliable because tastes can quickly change. Your might prepare monthly and quarterly sales budgets that you continuously monitor and revise.

Production Budget

A manufacturer prepares a **production budget,** which shows the number of units to be produced in a period. The production budget is based on the budgeted unit sales from the sales budget, along with inventory considerations. Manufacturers often determine a certain amount of **safety stock,** a quantity of inventory that provides protection against lost sales caused by unfulfilled demands from customers or delays in shipments from suppliers. Exhibit 20.5 shows how to compute the production required for a period. **A production budget does not show costs; it is always expressed in units of product.**

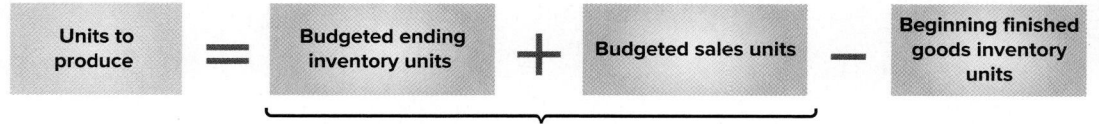

Required units for the period

EXHIBIT 20.5

Computing Production Requirements

After assessing the cost of keeping inventory along with the risk and cost of inventory shortages, TSC decides that the number of units in its finished goods inventory at each month-end should equal 90% of next month's predicted sales. For example, inventory at the end of October should equal 90% of budgeted November sales, and so on. This information, along with knowledge of 1,010 units in inventory at September 30 (see Exhibit 20.3), allows the company to prepare the production budget shown in Exhibit 20.6. The actual number of units of ending inventory at September 30 is not consistent with TSC's policy. This is common, as sales forecasts are uncertain and production can sometimes be disrupted.

Use three steps to complete the production budget.

1. Compute budgeted ending inventory based on the company's inventory policy.
2. Add budgeted sales (from the sales budget).
3. Subtract beginning inventory.

Units of Finished Goods Inventory

Beg. inv.	#		
Required prod. units	#	Sales	#
End. inv.	#		

Example: Under a JIT system, how will sales in units differ from the number of units to produce? *Answer:* The two amounts are similar because future inventory should be near zero.

	A	B	C	D
1	**TORONTO STICKS COMPANY**			
2	**Production Budget**			
3	**October 2019–December 2019**			
4		**October**	**November**	**December**
5	Next month's budgeted sales (units) from sales budget*	800	1,400	900
6	Ratio of inventory to future sales	× 90%	× 90%	× 90%
7	Budgeted ending inventory (units)	720	1,260	810
8	Add: Budgeted sales (units)	1,000	800	1,400
9	Required units of available production	1,720	2,060	2,210
10	Deduct: Beginning inventory (units)	1,010†	720	1,260
11	Units to produce	710	1,340	950

*From sales budget (Exhibit 20.4); January budgeted sales of 900 units from next quarter's sales budget.
†October's beginning inventory (1,010 units) is inconsistent with company policy.

Steps

Budgeted ending inventory
+ Budgeted sales
− Beginning inventory
= Units to produce

The result is the required units to be produced for the period. The number of units to be produced provides the basis for *manufacturing budgets* for the production costs of those units—direct materials, direct labor, and overhead.

Decision Insight

Point: Accurate estimates of future sales are crucial in a JIT system.

Just-in-Time   Managers of *just-in-time* (JIT) inventory systems use sales budgets for short periods (often as few as one or two days) to order just enough merchandise or materials to satisfy the immediate sales demand. This keeps the amount of inventory to a minimum (or zero in an ideal situation). A JIT system minimizes the costs of maintaining inventory, but it is practical only if customers are content to order in advance or if managers can accurately determine short-term sales demand. Suppliers also must be able and willing to ship small quantities regularly and promptly. ■

 **20-2**

Production Budget

P1

A manufacturing company predicts sales of 220 units for May and 250 units for June. The company wants each month's ending inventory to equal 30% of next month's predicted unit sales. Beginning inventory for May is 66 units. Compute the company's budgeted production in units for May.

Solution

Production Budget (May)	Units
Budgeted ending inventory for May (250 × 30%)	75
Plus: Budgeted sales for May.	220
Required units of available production	295
Less: Beginning inventory	(66)
Total units to be produced during May	229

Do More: QS 20-12, QS 20-16, QS 20-17, E 20-3, E 20-10, E 20-11

Direct Materials Budget

The **direct materials budget** shows the budgeted costs for direct materials that must be purchased to satisfy the budgeted production for the period. Whereas the production budget shows *units* to be produced, the direct materials budget translates the units to be produced into budgeted *costs*. (The same is true for the other two manufacturing budgets that we will discuss below—the direct labor budget and the factory overhead budget).

A direct materials budget requires the following inputs.

©Juanmonino/E+/Getty Images

1 Number of units to produce (from the production budget).

2 Materials requirements per unit—How many units (pounds, gallons, etc.) of direct materials go into each unit of finished product?

3 Budgeted ending inventory (in units) of direct materials—As with finished goods, most companies maintain a safety stock of materials to ensure that production can continue.

4 Beginning inventory (in units) of direct materials.

5 Cost per unit of direct materials.

Materials (in pounds) to purchase are computed as follows.

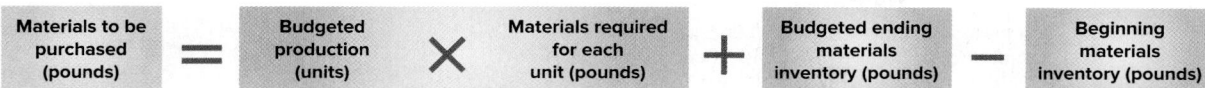

| Materials to be purchased (pounds) | = | Budgeted production (units) | × | Materials required for each unit (pounds) | + | Budgeted ending materials inventory (pounds) | − | Beginning materials inventory (pounds) |

Exhibit 20.7 shows the direct materials budget for TSC.

1 This budget begins with the budgeted production from the production budget.

2 Next, TSC needs to know the amount of direct materials needed for each of the units to be produced—in this case, half a pound (0.5) of wood. With these two inputs we can compute the amount of direct materials needed for production. For example, to produce 710 hockey sticks in October, TSC will need 355 pounds of wood (710 units × 0.5 lbs. = 355 lbs.).

3 TSC wants a safety stock of direct materials in inventory at the end of each month to complete 50% of the budgeted units to be produced in the next month. Because TSC expects to produce 1,340 units in November, requiring 670 pounds of materials, it needs ending inventory of direct materials of 335 pounds (50% × 670) in inventory at the end of October. TSC's total direct materials requirement for October is therefore 690 pounds (355 + 335).

4 TSC already has 178 pounds of direct materials in its beginning inventory (refer to Exhibit 20.3). TSC deducts this amount from the total materials requirements for the month. For October, the calculation is 690 pounds − 178 pounds = 512 pounds of direct materials to be purchased in October.

5 The direct materials budget next translates the *pounds* of direct materials to be purchased into budgeted *costs*. TSC estimates that the cost of direct materials will be $20 per pound over the quarter. At $20 per pound, purchasing 512 pounds of direct materials for October production will cost $10,240 (computed as $20 × 512). Similar calculations yield the cost of direct materials purchases for November ($11,450) and December ($9,700). (For December, assume the budgeted ending inventory of direct materials, based on January's production requirements, is 247.5 pounds.)

If the company expects direct materials costs to change in the future, it can easily include changes in the direct materials budget. For example, if the price of wood jumps to $25 per pound in December—say, because a long-term contract with the supplier was about to expire—TSC could simply change December's material price per pound in the direct materials budget.

Point: Most hockey sticks are composites of several raw materials, including wood, fiberglass, and graphite. We focus on one raw material for simplicity.

Units of Direct Materials

Beg. inv.	
Direct materials to purchase	Direct materials required for prod.
End. inv.	

	A	B	C	D
1	TORONTO STICKS COMPANY			
2	Direct Materials Budget			
3	October 2019–December 2019			
4		October	November	December
1 5	Budgeted production units*	710	1,340	950
2 6	Materials requirements per unit	× 0.5	× 0.5	× 0.5
7	Materials needed for production (pounds)	355	×50% 670	×50% 475
3 8	Add: Budgeted ending inventory (pounds)	335	237.5	247.5†
9	Total materials requirements (pounds)	690	907.5	722.5
4 10	Deduct: Beginning inventory (pounds)	(178)	(335)	(237.5)
11	Materials to be purchased (pounds)	512	572.5	485.0
12				
5 13	Material price per pound	$ 20	$ 20	$ 20
14	Total cost of direct materials purchases	$10,240	$11,450	$9,700

EXHIBIT 20.7

Direct Materials Budget

Materials needed for production
+ Budgeted ending mtls. inventory
− Beginning mtls. inventory
= Materials to be purchased

*From production budget (Exhibit 20.6).

†Computed from January 2020 production requirements, assumed to be 990 units. 990 units × 0.5 lbs. per unit × 50% safety stock = 247.5 lbs.

Direct Labor Budget

The **direct labor budget** shows the budgeted costs for direct labor that will be needed to satisfy the budgeted production for the period. Because there is no "inventory" of labor, the direct labor budget is easier to prepare than the direct materials budget.

A direct labor budget requires the following inputs.

1 Number of units to produce (from the production budget).

2 Labor requirements per unit—direct labor hours for each unit of finished product.

3 Cost per direct labor hour.

©Monkey Business Images/ Shutterstock

Budgeted amount of direct labor cost is computed as follows.

Budgeted direct labor cost (dollars)	=	Budgeted production (units)	×	Direct labor required per unit (hours)	×	Direct labor cost per hour (dollars)

TSC's direct labor budget is shown in Exhibit 20.8.
1 The budgeted production units are from the production budget.
2 Fifteen minutes of labor time (a quarter of an hour) are required to produce one unit. Compute budgeted direct labor hours by multiplying the budgeted production for each month by one-quarter (0.25) of an hour.
3 Labor is paid $12 per hour. Compute the total cost of direct labor by multiplying budgeted labor hours by the labor rate of $12 per hour.

Estimated changes in direct labor costs can be easily included in the budgeting process. Companies thus can ensure the right amount of direct labor for periods in which production is expected to change or to take into account expected changes in direct labor rates.

EXHIBIT 20.8

Direct Labor Budget

		A	B	C	D
	1	TORONTO STICKS COMPANY			
	2	Direct Labor Budget			
	3	October 2019–December 2019			
	4		October	November	December
1	5	Budgeted production (units)*	710	1,340	950
2	6	Direct labor requirements per unit (hours)	× 0.25	× 0.25	× 0.25
	7	Total direct labor hours needed	177.5	335	237.5
	8				
3	9	Direct labor rate (per hour)	$ 12	$ 12	$ 12
	10	Total cost of direct labor	$2,130	$4,020	$2,850

*From production budget (Exhibit 20.6).

NEED-TO-KNOW 20-3

Direct Materials and Direct Labor Budgets

P1

A manufacturing company budgets production of 800 units during June and 900 units during July. Each unit of finished goods requires 2 pounds of direct materials, at a cost of $8 per pound. The company maintains an inventory of direct materials equal to 10% of next month's budgeted production. Beginning direct materials inventory for June is 160 pounds. Each finished unit requires 1 hour of direct labor at the rate of $14 per hour. Compute the budgeted (a) cost of direct materials purchases for June and (b) direct labor cost for June.

Solution

a.

Direct Materials Budget (June)	
Budgeted production (units)	800
Materials requirements per unit (lbs.)	× 2
Materials needed for production (lbs.)	1,600
Add: Budgeted ending inventory (lbs.)	180*
Total materials requirements (lbs.).	1,780
Less: Beginning inventory (lbs.).	(160)
Materials to be purchased (lbs.).	1,620
Material price per pound	$ 8
Total cost of direct materials purchases	$12,960

*900 units × 2 lbs. per unit × 10% = 180 lbs.

b.

Direct Labor Budget (June)	
Budgeted production (units)	800
Labor requirements per unit (hours)	× 1
Total direct labor hours needed.	800
Labor rate (per hour)	$ 14
Direct labor cost (June)	$11,200

> **Do More:** QS 20-7, QS 20-8, QS 20-13, QS 20-14, E 20-4, E 20-5, E 20-8

Factory Overhead Budget

The **factory overhead budget** shows the budgeted costs for factory overhead that will be needed to complete the budgeted production for the period. TSC's factory overhead budget is shown in Exhibit 20.9. TSC separates variable and fixed overhead costs in its overhead budget, as do many companies.

EXHIBIT 20.9

Factory Overhead Budget

	A	B	C	D
1	**TORONTO STICKS COMPANY**			
2	**Factory Overhead Budget**			
3	**October 2019–December 2019**			
4		**October**	**November**	**December**
5	Budgeted production (units)*	710	1,340	950
6	Variable factory overhead rate	× $ 2.50	× $ 2.50	× $ 2.50
7	Budgeted variable overhead	1,775	3,350	2,375
8	Budgeted fixed overhead	1,500	1,500	1,500
9	Budgeted total overhead	$3,275	$4,850	$3,875

*From production budget (Exhibit 20.6).

Separating variable and fixed overhead costs enables companies to more closely estimate changes in overhead costs as production volume varies. TSC assigns the variable portion of overhead using a predetermined overhead rate of $2.50 per unit of production. This rate might be based on inputs such as direct materials costs, machine hours, direct labor hours, or other activity measures.

Point: Companies can use scatter diagrams, the high-low method, or regression analysis to classify overhead costs as fixed or variable.

TSC's fixed overhead consists entirely of depreciation on manufacturing equipment. From Exhibit 20.3, this is computed as $18,000 per year [($200,000 – $20,000)/10 years], or $1,500 per month ($18,000/12 months). This fixed overhead cost stays constant at $1,500 per month.

The budget in Exhibit 20.9 is in condensed form; most overhead budgets are more detailed, listing each overhead cost item. Overhead budgets also commonly include supervisor salaries, indirect materials, indirect labor, utilities, and maintenance of manufacturing equipment. We explain these more detailed overhead budgets in the next chapter.

Product Cost per Unit   With the three manufacturing budgets (direct materials, direct labor, and factory overhead), we compute TSC's budgeted **product cost per unit**. This amount is then used to prepare the:

- **Cost of goods sold budget,** which budgets the total manufacturing costs for the period.
- Budgeted income statement, which summarizes the expected income from budgeted activities.

For budgeting purposes, TSC assumes it will normally produce 3,000 units of product each quarter, yielding fixed overhead of $1.50 per unit (computed as $4,500/3,000). TSC's other product costs are all variable. Exhibit 20.10 summarizes the product cost per unit calculation. We use this total product cost per unit as a simplified budgeted cost of goods sold.

EXHIBIT 20.10

Product Cost per Unit

Product Cost	Per Unit
Direct materials (½ pound of materials × $20 per pound of materials)	$10.00
Direct labor (0.25 hours of direct labor × $12 per hour of direct labor)	3.00
Variable overhead (from predetermined overhead rate)	2.50
Fixed overhead ($4,500 total fixed overhead per quarter/3,000 units of expected production per quarter)	1.50
Total product cost per unit*	$17.00

*Computed at the normal production level of 3,000 units per quarter. (Cost of goods sold budgets also can consider changing product costs, changing inventory levels, and different inventory cost flow assumptions. These issues are covered in advanced courses.)

Selling Expense Budget

The **selling expense budget** is an estimate of the types and amounts of selling expenses expected during the budget period. It is usually prepared by the vice president of marketing or a sales manager. Budgeted selling expenses are based on the sales budget, plus a fixed amount of sales manager salaries.

TSC's selling expense budget is in Exhibit 20.11. The firm's selling expenses consist of commissions paid to sales personnel and a $2,000 monthly salary paid to the sales manager. Sales commissions equal 10% of total sales and are paid in the month sales occur. Sales commissions

Cost of Goods Sold Budget

Budgeted sales units	#
× Product cost per unit	$
= Budgeted COGS	$

EXHIBIT 20.11

Selling Expense Budget

	A	B	C	D	E
1	TORONTO STICKS COMPANY				
2	Selling Expense Budget				
3	October 2019–December 2019				
4		October	November	December	Totals
5	Budgeted sales*	$60,000	$48,000	$84,000	$192,000
6	Sales commission %	× 10%	× 10%	× 10%	× 10%
7	Sales commissions	6,000	4,800	8,400	19,200
8	Salary for sales manager	2,000	2,000	2,000	6,000
9	Total selling expenses	$ 8,000	$ 6,800	$ 10,400	$ 25,200

*From sales budget (Exhibit 20.4).

Example: If TSC expects a 12% sales commission will result in budgeted sales of $220,000 for the quarter, what is the total amount of selling expenses for the quarter? *Answer:* $32,400.

vary with sales volume, but the sales manager's salary is fixed. Other common selling expenses include advertising, delivery expenses, and marketing expenses.

General and Administrative Expense Budget

The **general and administrative expense budget** plans the predicted operating expenses not included in the selling expenses or manufacturing budgets. The office manager responsible for general administration often is responsible for preparing the general and administrative expense budget.

Exhibit 20.12 shows TSC's general and administrative expense budget. It includes salaries of $54,000 per year, or $4,500 per month (paid each month when they are earned). Insurance, taxes, and depreciation on nonmanufacturing assets are other common examples of general and administrative expenses.

Point: Some companies combine selling and general administrative expenses into a single budget.

EXHIBIT 20.12

General and Administrative Expense Budget

	A	B	C	D	E
1	TORONTO STICKS COMPANY				
2	General and Administrative Expense Budget				
3	October 2019–December 2019				
4		October	November	December	Totals
5	Administrative salaries	$4,500	$4,500	$4,500	$13,500
6	Total general and administrative expenses	$4,500	$4,500	$4,500	$13,500

Example: In Exhibit 20.12, how would a rental agreement of $5,000 per month plus 1% of sales affect the general and administrative expense budget? (Budgeted sales are in Exhibit 20.4.) *Answer: Rent expense:* Oct. = $5,600; Nov. = $5,480; Dec. = $5,840; Total = $16,920; *Revised total general and administrative expenses:* Oct. = $10,100; Nov. = $9,980; Dec. = $10,340; Total = $30,420.

■ **Decision Insight**

No Biz Like Snow Biz Ski resorts' costs of making snow are in the millions of dollars for equipment alone. Snowmaking involves spraying droplets of water into the air, causing them to freeze and come down as snow. Making snow can cost more than $2,000 an hour. Snowmaking accounts for 40–50 percent of the budgeted costs for many ski resorts. ■

©Gail Shotlander/Getty Images

NEED-TO-KNOW 20-4

Selling and General and Administrative Expense Budgets

P1

Do More: QS 20-5, QS 20-11

A manufacturing company budgets sales of $70,000 during July. It pays sales commissions of 5% of sales and also pays a sales manager a salary of $3,000 per month. Other monthly costs include depreciation on office equipment ($500), insurance expense ($200), advertising ($1,000), and an office manager salary of $2,500 per month. Compute the total (a) budgeted selling expense and (b) budgeted general and administrative expense for July.

Solution

a. Total budgeted selling expense = ($70,000 × 5%) + $3,000 + $1,000 = $7,500

b. Total budgeted general and administrative expense = $500 + $200 + $2,500 = $3,200

INVESTING AND FINANCING BUDGETS

Information from operating budgets is useful in preparing the capital expenditures budget—a key part of investing budgets.

Capital Expenditures Budget

The **capital expenditures budget** shows dollar amounts estimated to be spent to purchase additional plant assets and any cash expected to be received from plant asset disposals. The capital expenditures budget shows the company's expected *investing* activities in plant assets. It is usually prepared after the operating budgets. Because a company's plant assets determine its productive capacity, this budget is affected by long-range plans for the business. The process of preparing other budgets can reveal that the company requires more (or less) plant assets.

TSC does not anticipate disposal of any plant assets through December, but it does plan to buy additional equipment for $25,000 cash near the end of December. This is the only budgeted capital expenditure from October through December. Thus, no separate budget is shown. TSC's December 2019 cash budget will reflect this $25,000 planned expenditure.

> **Investing Budgets**
> Capital expenditures

Cash Budget

A **cash budget** shows expected cash inflows and outflows during the budget period. Managing cash flows is vital for a firm's success. Most companies set an amount of cash they require for operations. The cash budget is important because it helps the company meet this cash balance goal. If the cash budget indicates a potential cash shortfall, the company can prearrange loans to meet its obligations. If the cash budget indicates a potential cash windfall, the company can plan to pay off prior loans or make other investments. Exhibit 20.13 shows the general formula for the cash budget.

> **P2**
> Prepare a cash budget—for a manufacturing company.

EXHIBIT 20.13

General Formula for Cash Budget

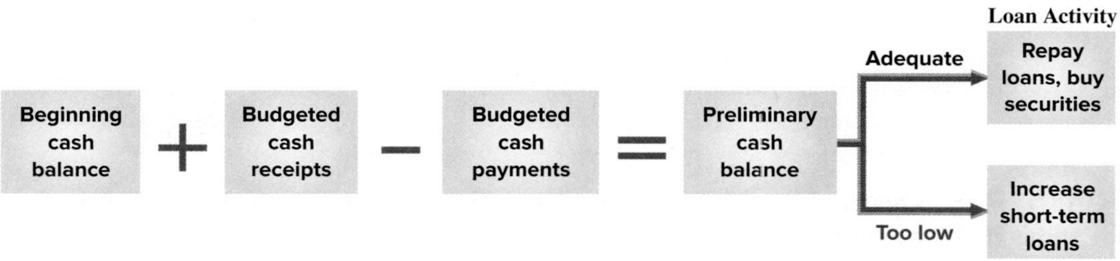

When preparing a cash budget, add budgeted cash receipts to the beginning cash balance and subtract budgeted cash payments. If the preliminary cash balance is too low, additional cash requirements appear in the budget as planned increases from short-term loans. If the preliminary cash balance exceeds the balance the company wants to maintain, the excess is used to repay loans (if any) or to acquire short-term investments.

Information for preparing the cash budget is taken mainly from the operating and capital expenditures budgets. Preparing the cash budget typically requires the preparation of other supporting schedules; we show the first of these, a schedule of cash receipts from sales, next.

> **Financing Budgets**
> Cash budgets

Cash Receipts from Sales
Managers use the sales budget and knowledge about how frequently customers pay on credit sales to budget monthly cash receipts. To illustrate, Exhibit 20.14 presents TSC's schedule of budgeted cash receipts.

We begin with TSC's budgeted sales (Exhibit 20.4). Analysis of past sales indicates that 40% of the firm's sales are for cash. The remaining 60% are credit sales; these customers are expected to pay in full in the month following the sales. We now can compute the budgeted cash receipts from customers, as shown in Exhibit 20.14. October's budgeted cash receipts consist of $24,000 from expected October cash sales ($60,000 × 40%) plus the anticipated collection of $25,200 of accounts receivable from the end of September.

> **Point:** Budgeted cash collections can be impacted by transaction fees for credit or debit cards. Companies like **Visa** and **American Express** charge different credit card fees, and banks charge fees to use debit cards.

EXHIBIT 20.14

Computing Budgeted Cash Receipts from Sales

	A	B	C	D	E
1		**TORONTO STICKS COMPANY**			
2		**Schedule of Cash Receipts from Sales**			
3		**October 2019–December 2019**			
4		**September**	**October**	**November**	**December**
5	Sales*	$42,000	$60,000	$48,000	$84,000
6	Less: Ending accounts receivable (60%)	25,200†	36,000	28,800	50,400
7	Cash receipts from				
8	Cash sales (40% of sales)		24,000	19,200	33,600
9	Collections of prior month's receivables		25,200	36,000	28,800
10	Total cash receipts		$49,200	$55,200	$62,400

*From sales budget (Exhibit 20.4).

†Accounts receivable balance from September 30 balance sheet (Exhibit 20.3).

Alternative Collection Timing   The schedule above can be modified for alternative collection timing and/or uncollectible accounts. For example, if TSC collects 80% of credit sales in the first month after sale, 20% of credit sales in the second month after sale, and all other assumptions are unchanged, budgeted cash receipts for December follow.

December budgeted cash receipts with alternative collection timing	
Cash receipts from December cash sales	$ 33,600
Collections of November's receivables ($48,000 × 60% × 80%)	23,040
Collections of October's receivables ($60,000 × 60% × 20%)	7,200
Total cash receipts	**$63,840**

Uncollectible Accounts   Some companies consider uncollectible accounts in their cash budgets. To do so, multiply credit sales by (1 − % of uncollectible receivables). For example, if in addition to the alternative collection timing above TSC estimates that 5% of all credit sales will not be collected, it computes its December cash receipts as follows.

December budgeted cash receipts with alternative collection timing and uncollectible accounts	
Cash receipts from December cash sales	$ 33,600
Collections of November's receivables ($48,000 × 95% × 60% × 80%)	21,888
Collections of October's receivables ($60,000 × 95% × 60% × 20%)	6,840
Total cash receipts	**$62,328**

Cash Payments for Materials   Managers use the beginning balance sheet (Exhibit 20.3) and the direct materials budget (Exhibit 20.7) to help prepare a schedule of cash payments for materials. Managers also must know *how* TSC purchases direct materials (pay cash or on account) and, for credit purchases, how quickly TSC pays. TSC's materials purchases are entirely on account. It makes full payment during the month following its purchases. Using this information, the schedule of cash payments for materials is shown in Exhibit 20.15.

EXHIBIT 20.15

Computing Cash Payments for Materials Purchases

	A	B	C	D
1		**TORONTO STICKS COMPANY**		
2		**Schedule of Cash Payments for Direct Materials**		
3		**October 2019–December 2019**		
4		**October**	**November**	**December**
5	Materials purchases*	$10,240	$11,450	$ 9,700
6	Cash payments for			
7	Current month purchases (0%)	0	0	0
8	Prior month purchases (100%)	7,060†	10,240	11,450
9	Total cash payments for direct materials	$ 7,060	$10,240	$11,450

*From direct materials budget (Exhibit 20.7).

†Accounts Payable balance from September 30 balance sheet (Exhibit 20.3).

The schedule above can be modified for alternative payment timing. For example, if TSC paid for 20% of its purchases in the month of purchase and paid the remaining 80% of a month's purchases in the following month, its cash payments in December would equal $11,100, computed as (20% × $9,700) plus (80% × $11,450).

Preparing the Cash Budget   The cash budget summarizes many other budgets in terms of their effects on cash. To prepare the cash budget, TSC's managers use the budgets and other schedules listed below.

1. Cash receipts from sales (Exhibit 20.14).
2. Cash payments for direct materials (Exhibit 20.15).
3. Cash payments for direct labor (Exhibit 20.8).
4. Cash payments for overhead (Exhibit 20.9).
5. Cash payments for selling expenses (Exhibit 20.11).
6. Cash payments for general and administrative expenses (Exhibit 20.12).

The *fixed overhead* assigned to depreciation in the factory overhead budget (Exhibit 20.9) does not require a cash payment. Therefore, it is not included in the cash budget. Other types of fixed overhead—such as payments for property taxes and insurance—*are* included if they require cash payments.

Additional information is typically needed to prepare the cash budget. For TSC, this additional information includes

1. Income taxes payable: $20,000, from the beginning balance sheet in Exhibit 20.3.
2. Expected dividend payments: TSC plans to pay $3,000 of cash dividends in the second month of each quarter.
3. Loan activity: TSC wants to maintain a minimum cash balance of $20,000 at each month-end. This is important, as it helps ensure TSC maintains enough cash to pay its bills as they come due. If TSC borrows cash, it must pay interest at the rate of 1% per month.

Exhibit 20.16 shows the full cash budget for TSC. The company begins October with $20,000 in cash. To this is added $49,200 in expected cash receipts from customers (from Exhibit 20.14). We next subtract expected cash payments for direct materials, direct labor, overhead, selling expenses, and general and administrative expenses. Income taxes of $20,000 were due as of the end of September 30, 2019, and payable in October. We next discuss TSC's loan activity, including any interest payments.

EXHIBIT 20.16

Cash Budget

	A	B	C	D
1	TORONTO STICKS COMPANY			
2	Cash Budget			
3	October 2019–December 2019			
4		October	November	December
5	Beginning cash balance	$20,000	$20,000	$38,881
6	Add: Cash receipts from customers (Exhibit 20.14)	49,200	55,200	62,400
7	Total cash available	69,200	75,200	101,281
8	Less: Cash payments for			
9	Direct materials (Exhibit 20.15)	7,060	10,240	11,450
10	Direct labor (Exhibit 20.8)	2,130	4,020	2,850
11	Variable overhead (Exhibit 20.9)	1,775	3,350	2,375
12	Sales commissions (Exhibit 20.11)	6,000	4,800	8,400
13	Sales salaries (Exhibit 20.11)	2,000	2,000	2,000
14	General and administrative expenses (Exhibit 20.12)	4,500	4,500	4,500
15	Income taxes payable (Exhibit 20.3)	20,000		
16	Dividends		3,000	
17	Interest on bank loan			
18	October ($10,000 × 1%)*	100		
19	November ($4,365 × 1%)†		44	
20	Purchase of equipment			25,000
21	Total cash payments	43,565	31,954	56,575
22	Preliminary cash balance	$25,635	$43,246	$44,706
23	Loan activity			
24	Additional loan from bank			
25	Repayment of loan to bank	5,635	4,365	
26	Ending cash balance	$20,000	$38,881	$44,706
27	Loan balance, end of month‡	$ 4,365	$ 0	$ 0

Cash			
Oct. 1	20,000		
Receipts	49,200		
		43,565	Payments
Prelim. bal.	25,635		
		5,635	Repay loan
Oct. 31	20,000		

*Beginning loan balance (note payable) from Exhibit 20.3.   †Rounded to the nearest dollar.
‡Beginning loan balance + New loans – Loan repayments. For October: $10,000 – $5,635 = $4,365.

Loan Activity   TSC's bank promises additional loans at each month-end, if necessary, so that the company keeps a minimum cash balance of $20,000. If the cash balance exceeds $20,000 at month-end, TSC uses the excess to repay loans (if any) or buy short-term investments. If the cash balance is less than $20,000 at month-end, the bank loans TSC the difference.

Monthly interest on bank loans is computed as:

$$\text{Cash paid for interest} = \text{Monthly interest rate (\%)} \times \text{Beginning loan balance}$$

Using TSC's interest rate of 1% per month, budgeted cash payments for interest follow.

Budgeted cash payments for interest	Interest Rate	Beginning Loan Balance	Interest Cost
October...............................	1%	$10,000	$100
November..............................	1	4,365	44
December..............................	1	0	0

Exhibit 20.16 shows that the October 31 cash balance increases to $25,635 (before any loan-related activity). This amount is more than the $20,000 minimum. Thus, TSC will use the excess cash of $5,635 (computed as $25,635 − $20,000) to pay off a portion of its loan. At the end of November, TSC's preliminary cash balance is sufficient to pay off its remaining loan balance.

Had TSC's preliminary cash balance been below the $20,000 minimum in any month, TSC would have increased its loan from the bank so that the ending cash balance was $20,000. We show an example of this situation in **Need-to-Know 20-7** at the end of this chapter.

Note Payable

Repay		10,000	Sep. 30
Repay	5,635		
		4,365	Oct. 31
Repay	4,365		
		0	Nov. 30

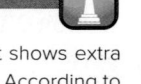

■ **Decision Insight**

Cash Cushion   Why do some companies maintain a minimum cash balance even when the budget shows extra cash is not needed? For example, **Apple**'s cash and short-term investments balance is over $70 billion. According to Apple's CEO, Tim Cook, the cushion provides "flexibility and security," important in navigating uncertain economic times. A cash cushion enables companies to jump on new ventures or acquisitions that may present themselves. The **Boston Red Sox** keep a cash cushion for its trades involving players with "cash considerations." ■

©Adam Glanzman/Getty Images

NEED-TO-KNOW 20-5

Cash Budget

P2

Part 1

Diaz Co. predicts sales of $80,000 for January and $90,000 for February. Seventy percent of Diaz's sales are for cash, and the remaining 30% are credit sales. All credit sales are collected in the month after sale. January's beginning accounts receivable balance is $20,000. Compute budgeted cash receipts for January and February.

Solution

Budgeted Cash Receipts	January	February
Sales	$80,000	$90,000
Less: Ending accounts receivable (30%)..................	24,000 ┐	27,000
Cash receipts from		
Cash sales (70% of sales)	56,000	63,000
Collections of prior month's receivables...............	20,000 └→	24,000
Total cash receipts	$76,000	$87,000

Do More: QS 20-6, QS 20-10,
QS 20-19, E 20-18

Part 2

Use the following information to prepare a cash budget for the month ended January 31 for Garcia Company. The company requires a minimum $30,000 cash balance at the end of each month. Any preliminary cash balance above $30,000 is used to repay loans (if any). Garcia has a $2,000 loan outstanding at the beginning of January.

  a. January 1 cash balance, $30,000

  b. Cash receipts from sales, $132,000

  c. Budgeted cash payments for materials, $63,500

  d. Budgeted cash payments for labor, $33,400

  e. Other budgeted cash expenses,* $8,200

  f. Cash repayment of bank loan, $2,000

*Including loan interest for January.

Solution

Cash Budget For Month Ended January 31		
Beginning cash balance	$ 30,000	
Add: Cash receipts from sales	132,000	
Total cash available		$162,000
Less: Cash payments for		
Direct materials	63,500	
Direct labor	33,400	
Other cash expenses	8,200	
Total cash payments		105,100
Preliminary cash balance.		$ 56,900
Loan activity:		
Repayment of loan to bank		2,000
Ending cash balance.		$ 54,900
Loan balance, end of month		$ 0

> **Do More:** QS 20-24, E 20-17, E 20-21, E 20-22

BUDGETED FINANCIAL STATEMENTS

One of the final steps in the budgeting process is summarizing the financial statement effects. We next illustrate TSC's budgeted income statement and budgeted balance sheet.

P3

Prepare budgeted financial statements.

Budgeted Income Statement

The **budgeted income statement** shows predicted amounts of sales and expenses for the budget period. It summarizes the predicted income effects of the budgeted activities. Information to prepare a budgeted income statement is primarily taken from already-prepared budgets. The volume of information summarized in the budgeted income statement is so large for some companies that they often use spreadsheets to accumulate the budgeted transactions and classify them by their effects on income.

We condense TSC's budgeted income statement and show it in Exhibit 20.17. All information in this exhibit is taken from the component budgets we've examined in this chapter. Also, we now can predict the amount of income tax expense for the quarter, computed as 40% of the budgeted pretax income. For TSC, these taxes are not payable until January 31, 2020. Thus, these taxes are not shown on the October–December 2019 cash budget in Exhibit 20.16, but they are included on the December 31, 2019, balance sheet (shown next).

> **Budgeted Financial Statements**
> Income statement
> Balance sheet

> **Point:** Lenders often require potential borrowers to provide cash budgets, budgeted income statements, and budgeted balance sheets, as well as data on past performance.

EXHIBIT 20.17

Budgeted Income Statement

TORONTO STICKS COMPANY Budgeted Income Statement For Three Months Ended December 31, 2019		
Sales (Exhibit 20.4, 3,200 units @ $60)		$192,000
Cost of goods sold (3,200 units @ $17)*		54,400
Gross profit		137,600
Operating expenses		
Sales commissions (Exhibit 20.11)	$19,200	
Sales salaries (Exhibit 20.11)	6,000	
Administrative salaries (Exhibit 20.12)	13,500	
Interest expense (Exhibit 20.16)	144	38,844
Income before income taxes		98,756
Income tax expense ($98,756 × 40%)†		39,502
Net income		$ 59,254

*$17 product cost per unit from Exhibit 20.10.   †Rounded to the nearest dollar.

Budgeted Balance Sheet

The final step in preparing the master budget is summarizing the company's predicted financial position. The **budgeted balance sheet** shows predicted amounts for the company's assets, liabilities, and equity as of the end of the budget period. TSC's budgeted balance sheet in Exhibit 20.18 is prepared using information from the other budgets. The sources of amounts are reported in the notes to the budgeted balance sheet.

EXHIBIT 20.18

Budgeted Balance Sheet

Retained Earnings

		42,870	Sep. 30
		59,254	Net income
Dividends	3,000		
		99,124	Dec. 31

TORONTO STICKS COMPANY					
Budgeted Balance Sheet					
December 31, 2019					
Assets			**Liabilities and Equity**		
Cash[a]		$ 44,706	Liabilities		
Accounts receivable[b]		50,400	Accounts payable[g]	$ 9,700	
Raw materials inventory[c]		4,950	Income taxes payable[h] . . .	39,502	$ 49,202
Finished goods inventory[d]		13,770	Stockholders' equity		
Equipment[e]	$225,000		Common stock[i]	150,000	
Less: Accumulated depreciation[f] . . .	40,500	184,500	Retained earnings[j]	99,124	249,124
Total assets		$298,326	Total liabilities and equity. . . .		$298,326

[a] Ending balance for December from the cash budget (in Exhibit 20.16).
[b] 60% of $84,000 sales budgeted for December from the sales budget (in Exhibit 20.4).
[c] 247.5 pounds of raw materials in budgeted ending inventory at the budgeted cost of $20 per pound (direct materials budget, Exhibit 20.7).
[d] 810 units in budgeted finished goods inventory (Exhibit 20.6) at the budgeted cost of $17 per unit (Exhibit 20.10).
[e] September 30 balance of $200,000 from the beginning balance sheet in Exhibit 20.3 plus $25,000 cost of new equipment from the cash budget in Exhibit 20.16.
[f] September 30 balance of $36,000 from the beginning balance sheet in Exhibit 20.3 plus $4,500 depreciation expense from the factory overhead budget in Exhibit 20.9.
[g] Budgeted cost of materials purchases for December from Exhibit 20.7, to be paid in January.
[h] Income tax expense from the budgeted income statement for the fourth quarter in Exhibit 20.17, to be paid in January.
[i] Unchanged from the beginning balance sheet in Exhibit 20.3.
[j] September 30 balance of $42,870 from the beginning balance sheet in Exhibit 20.3 plus budgeted net income of $59,254 from the budgeted income statement in Exhibit 20.17 minus budgeted cash dividends of $3,000 from the cash budget in Exhibit 20.16.

Using the Master Budget

Managers use the master budget in several ways.

- *Sensitivity analysis*—Technologies like Excel and enterprise resource planning (ERP) systems enable managers to quickly get alternative master budgets under different assumptions, allowing them to better plan for and adapt to changing conditions.

  - *Planning*—Any stage in the master budgeting process might show results that require new plans. For example, an early version of the cash budget might show too little cash unless payments are reduced. A budgeted income statement might show income below its target, or a budgeted balance sheet might show too much debt from planned equipment purchases. Management can change its plans to aim for better results.
  - *Controlling*—Managers compare actual results to budgeted results. Differences between actual and budgeted results are called *variances*. Managers examine variances to identify areas to improve and take corrective action.

Budgeting for Service Companies

Service providers also use master budgets; however, because they do not manufacture goods and hold no inventory, they typically need fewer operating budgets than manufacturers do. Exhibit 20.19 shows the master budget process for a service provider.

Exhibit 20.19 shows that service providers *do not prepare production, direct materials, or factory overhead budgets.* In addition, because many services such as accounting, banking, and

EXHIBIT 20.19

Master Budget Process
for a Service Company

```
                        ┌──────────────────┐
                        │      Sales       │
                        └──────────────────┘
                                 │
                                 ▼
                        ┌──────────────────┐
                        │   Direct labor   │
                        └──────────────────┘
                                 │
                                 ▼
┌──────────────────┐    ┌──────────────────┐    ┌──────────────────────┐
│Capital expenditures│──▶│      Cash       │◀───│  Selling expenses    │
└──────────────────┘    └──────────────────┘    │General & admin expenses│
                                                 └──────────────────────┘
        └──────────────────┬────────────────────┘
              Budgeted financial statements
```

☐ Operating budgets
☐ Investing budgets
☐ Financing budgets

landscaping are labor-intensive, the direct labor budget is important. If an accounting firm greatly underestimates the hours needed to complete an audit, it might charge too low a price. If the accounting firm greatly overestimates the hours needed, it might bid too high a price (and lose jobs) or incur excessive labor costs. Either way, the firm's profits can suffer if its direct labor budget is unrealistic.

SUSTAINABILITY AND ACCOUNTING

Budgets translate an organization's strategic goals into dollar terms. When deciding on strategic goals, managers must consider their effects on budgets. **Johnson & Johnson**, a large manufacturer of pharmaceuticals, medical devices, and consumer health products, sets goals for both profits and sustainable practices. A recent company sustainability report discusses several sustainability goals and strategies, including some shown in Exhibit 20.20.

EXHIBIT 20.20

Sustainability Goals
and Strategies

Sustainability Goal	Strategy to Achieve Goal
Reduce waste by 10%.	Purchase pulping machine to grind and recycle packaging.
Reduce CO_2 emissions by 20%.	Purchase hybrid vehicles.
Reduce water usage by 10%.	Update plumbing, install water recovery systems, employee training.

Several of the company's strategies involve asset purchases that will impact the capital expenditures budget. Additional employee training will impact the overhead budget. By reducing waste, increasing recycling, and reducing water usage, the company hopes to reduce some of the costs reflected in the direct materials and overhead budgets. Company managers periodically evaluate performance with respect to these goals and make any necessary adjustments to budgets.

Misfit Juicery, this chapter's feature company, "is a company fighting food waste with juice," according to co-founder Phil Wong. The company's focus on repurposing "misfits" extends to its labor force, which includes chronically underemployed groups like the homeless. "Yes, we make delicious juice," says co-founder Anna Yang, "but our mission is to fix waste!"

©Misfit Juicery

Activity-Based Budgeting      **Decision Analysis**

Activity-based budgeting (ABB) is a budget system based on expected *activities*. Knowledge of expected activities and their levels for the budget period enables management to plan for resources required to perform the activities.

Exhibit 20.21 contrasts a traditional budget with an activity-based budget for a company's accounting department. With a traditional budget, management often makes across-the-board budget cuts or increases. For example, management might decide that each of the line items in the traditional budget must be cut by 5%. This might not be a good strategic decision.

ABB requires management to list activities performed by, say, the accounting department, such as auditing, tax reporting, financial reporting, and cost accounting. By focusing on the relation between activities and costs, management can attempt to reduce costs by eliminating non-value-added activities.

A1
_____

Analyze expense planning using activity-based budgeting.

EXHIBIT 20.21

Activity-Based Budgeting versus Traditional Budgeting (for an accounting department)

Traditional Budget		Activity-Based Budget	
Salaries	$152,000	Auditing	$ 58,000
Supplies.	22,000	Tax reporting	71,000
Depreciation	36,000	Financial reporting.	63,000
Utilities	14,000	Cost accounting	32,000
Total.	$224,000	Total	$224,000

■ **Decision Maker**

Environmental Manager You hold the new position of Sustainability Manager for a chemical company. You are asked to develop a budget for your job and identify job responsibilities. How do you proceed? ■ *Answer:* You are unlikely to have data on this new position to use in preparing your budget. In this situation, you can use activity-based budgeting. This requires developing a list of activities to conduct, the resources required to perform these activities, and the expenses associated with these resources. You should challenge yourself to be absolutely certain that the listed activities are necessary and that the listed resources are required.

NEED-TO-KNOW 20-6

COMPREHENSIVE 1

Master Budget— Manufacturer

Payne Company's management asks you to prepare its master budget using the following information. The budget is to cover the months of April, May, and June of 2019.

PAYNE COMPANY
Balance Sheet
March 31, 2019

Assets			Liabilities and Equity		
Cash	$ 50,000		Accounts payable	$ 63,818	
Accounts receivable	175,000		Short-term notes payable	12,000	
Raw materials inventory	30,798*		Total current liabilities		$ 75,818
Finished goods inventory	96,600†		Long-term note payable		200,000
Total current assets		$352,398	Total liabilities		275,818
Equipment	480,000		Common stock	435,000	
Less: Accumulated depreciation	(90,000)		Retained earnings	31,580	
Equipment, net		390,000	Total stockholders' equity		466,580
Total assets		$742,398	Total liabilities and equity		$742,398

*2,425 pounds @ $12.70 per pound, rounded to nearest whole dollar.   †8,400 units @ $11.50 per unit.

Additional Information

a. Sales for March total 10,000 units. Expected sales (in units) are 10,500 (April), 9,500 (May), 10,000 (June), and 10,500 (July). The product's selling price is $25 per unit.

b. Company policy calls for a given month's ending finished goods inventory to equal 80% of the next month's expected unit sales. The March 31 finished goods inventory is 8,400 units, which complies with the policy. The product's manufacturing cost is $11.50 per unit, including per unit costs of $6.35 for materials (0.5 lbs. at $12.70 per lb.), $3.75 for direct labor (0.25 hour × $15 direct labor rate per hour), $0.90 for variable overhead, and $0.50 for fixed overhead. Fixed overhead consists entirely of $5,000 of monthly depreciation expense. Company policy also calls for a given month's ending raw materials inventory to equal 50% of next month's expected materials needed for production. The March 31 inventory is 2,425 units of materials, which complies with the policy. The company expects to have 2,100 units of materials inventory on June 30.

c. Sales representatives' commissions are 12% of sales and are paid in the month of the sales. The sales manager's monthly salary will be $3,500 in April and $4,000 per month thereafter.

d. Monthly general and administrative expenses include $8,000 administrative salaries and 0.9% monthly interest on the long-term note payable.

e. The company expects 30% of sales to be for cash and the remaining 70% on credit. Receivables are collected in full in the month following the sale (none are collected in the month of the sale).

f. All direct materials purchases are on credit, and no payables arise from any other transactions. One month's purchases are fully paid in the next month. Materials cost $12.70 per pound.

g. The minimum ending cash balance for all months is $50,000. If necessary, the company borrows enough cash using a short-term note to reach the minimum. Short-term notes require an interest payment of 1% at each month-end (before any repayment). If the ending cash balance exceeds the minimum, the excess will be applied to repaying the short-term notes payable balance.

h. Dividends of $100,000 are to be declared and paid in May.

i. No cash payments for income taxes are to be made during the second calendar quarter. Income taxes will be assessed at 35% in the quarter.

j. Equipment purchases of $55,000 are scheduled for June.

Required

Prepare the following budgets and other financial information as required.

1. Sales budget, including budgeted sales for July.
2. Production budget.
3. Direct materials budget. Round costs of materials purchases to the nearest dollar.
4. Direct labor budget.
5. Factory overhead budget.
6. Selling expense budget.
7. General and administrative expense budget.

8. Expected cash receipts from customers and the expected June 30 balance of accounts receivable.
9. Expected cash payments for purchases and the expected June 30 balance of accounts payable.
10. Cash budget.
11. Budgeted income statement, budgeted statement of retained earnings, and budgeted balance sheet.

SOLUTION

1.

	A	B	C	D	E
1	**Sales Budget**	**April**	**May**	**June**	**Quarter**
2	Projected unit sales	10,500	9,500	10,000	
3	Selling price per unit	× $ 25	× $ 25	× $ 25	
4	Projected sales	$262,500	$237,500	$250,000	$750,000

2.

	A	B	C	D	E
1	**Production Budget**	**April**	**May**	**June**	**Quarter**
2	Next period's unit sales (part I)	9,500	10,000	10,500	
3	Ending inventory percent	× 80 %	× 80 %	× 80 %	
4	Desired ending inventory	7,600	8,000	8,400	
5	Current period's unit sales (part I)	10,500	9,500	10,000	
6	Required units of available production	18,100	17,500	18,400	
7	Less: Beginning inventory	8,400	7,600	8,000	
8	Total units to be produced	9,700	9,900	10,400	30,000

3.

	A	B	C	D
1	**Direct Materials Budget**	**April**	**May**	**June**
2	Budgeted production (units) (part 2)	9,700	9,900	10,400
3	Materials requirements per unit (pounds)	× 0.5	× 0.5	× 0.5
4	Materials needed for production (pounds)	4,850	4,950	5,200
5	Add: Budgeted ending inventory (pounds)	2,475	2,600	2,100
6	Total material requirements (pounds)	7,325	7,550	7,300
7	Deduct: Beginning inventory (pounds)	2,425	2,475	2,600
8	Materials to be purchased (pounds)	4,900	5,075	4,700
9				
10	Materials price per pound	$ 12.70	$ 12.70	$ 12.70
11	Total cost of direct materials purchases	$62,230	$64,453*	$59,690

*Rounded to nearest dollar.

4.

	A	B	C	D
1	**Direct Labor Budget**	**April**	**May**	**June**
2	Budgeted production (units) (part 2)	9,700	9,900	10,400
3	Labor requirements per unit (hours)	× 0.25	× 0.25	× 0.25
4	Total labor hours needed	2,425	2,475	2,600
5				
6	Labor rate (per hour)	$ 15	$ 15	$ 15
7	Total direct labor cost	$36,375	$37,125	$39,000

5.

	A	B	C	D
1	**Factory Overhead Budget**	**April**	**May**	**June**
2	Budgeted production (units) (part 2)	9,700	9,900	10,400
3	Variable factory overhead rate	× $ 0.90	× $ 0.90	× $ 0.90
4	Budgeted variable overhead	8,730	8,910	9,360
5	Budgeted fixed overhead	5,000	5,000	5,000
6	Budgeted total overhead	$13,730	$13,910	$14,360

6.

	A	B	C	D	E
1	**Selling Expense Budget**	**April**	**May**	**June**	**Quarter**
2	Budgeted sales (part 1)	$262,500	$237,500	$250,000	$750,000
3	Commission %	× 12 %	× 12 %	× 12 %	× 12 %
4	Sales commissions	31,500	28,500	30,000	90,000
5	Manager's salary	3,500	4,000	4,000	11,500
6	Budgeted selling expenses	$ 35,000	$ 32,500	$ 34,000	$101,500

7.

	A	B	C	D	E
1	**General and Administrative Expense Budget**	**April**	**May**	**June**	**Quarter**
2	Administrative salaries	$8,000	$8,000	$8,000	$24,000
3	Interest on long-term note				
4	payable (0.9% × $200,000)	1,800	1,800	1,800	5,400
5	Budgeted general and administrative expenses	$9,800	$9,800	$9,800	$29,400

8.

	A	B	C	D	E
1	**Schedule of Cash Receipts**	**April**	**May**	**June**	**Quarter**
2	Budgeted sales (part 1)	$262,500	$237,500	$250,000	
3	Ending accounts receivable (70%)	$ 183,750	$ 166,250	$ 175,000	
4	Cash receipts				
5	Cash sales (30% of budgeted sales)	$ 78,750	$ 71,250	$ 75,000	$225,000
6	Collections of prior month's receivables	175,000*	183,750	166,250	525,000
7	Total cash to be collected	$ 253,750	$ 255,000	$ 241,250	$750,000

*Accounts Receivable balance from March 31 balance sheet.

9.

	A	B	C	D	E
1	**Schedule of Cash Payments for Materials**	**April**	**May**	**June**	**Quarter**
2	Cash payments (equal to prior month's				
3	materials purchases)	$63,818*	$62,230	$64,453	$190,501
4	Expected June 30 balance of accounts				
5	payable (June purchases)			$59,690	

*Accounts Payable balance from March 31 balance sheet.

10.

	A	B	C	D
1	**Cash Budget**	**April**	**May**	**June**
2	Beginning cash balance	$ 50,000	$137,907	$142,342
3	**Add:** Cash receipts from customers (part 8)	253,750	255,000	241,250
4	Total cash available	303,750	392,907	383,592
5	**Less:** Cash payments for			
6	Direct materials (part 9)	63,818	62,230	64,453
7	Direct labor (part 4)	36,375	37,125	39,000
8	Variable overhead (part 5)	8,730	8,910	9,360
9	Sales commissions (part 6)	31,500	28,500	30,000
10	Salaries			
11	Sales (part 6)	3,500	4,000	4,000
12	Administrative (part 7)	8,000	8,000	8,000
13	Dividends		100,000	
14	Interest on long-term note (part 7)	1,800	1,800	1,800
15	Interest on bank loan			
16	October ($12,000 × 1%)	120		
17	Purchase of equipment			55,000
18	Total cash payments	153,843	250,565	211,613
19	**Loan activity:** Preliminary cash balance	$149,907	$142,342	$171,979
20	Additional loan from bank			
21	Repayment of loan to bank	12,000	0	0
22	Ending cash balance	$137,907	$142,342	$ 171,979
23	Loan balance, end of month	$ 0	$ 0	$ 0

11.

PAYNE COMPANY
Budgeted Income Statement
For Quarter Ended June 30, 2019

Sales (part 1)		$750,000
Cost of goods sold (30,000 units @ $11.50)		345,000
Gross profit		405,000
Operating expenses		
Sales commissions (part 6)	$90,000	
Sales salaries (part 6)	11,500	
Administrative salaries (part 7)	24,000	
Interest on long-term note (part 7)	5,400	
Interest on short-term notes (part 10)	120	
Total operating expenses		131,020
Income before income taxes		273,980
Income taxes ($273,980 × 35%)		95,893
Net income		$178,087

PAYNE COMPANY
Budgeted Statement of Retained Earnings
For Quarter Ended June 30, 2019

Retained earnings, March 31, 2019	$ 31,580
Net income	178,087
	209,667
Less: Cash dividends (part 10)	100,000
Retained earnings, June 30, 2019	$109,667

PAYNE COMPANY
Budgeted Balance Sheet
June 30, 2019

Assets

Cash (part 10)	$171,979	
Accounts receivable (part 8)	175,000	
Raw materials inventory (2,100 pounds @ $12.70)*	26,671	
Finished goods inventory (8,400 units @ $11.50)	96,600	
Total current assets		$470,250
Equipment (Mar. 31 bal. plus purchase)	535,000	
Less: Accumulated depreciation		
(Mar. 31 bal. plus depreciation expense)	105,000	430,000
Total assets		$900,250

Liabilities and Equity

Accounts payable (part 9)	$ 59,690	
Income taxes payable	95,893	
Total current liabilities		$155,583
Long-term note payable (Mar. 31 bal.)		200,000
Total liabilities		355,583
Common stock (Mar. 31 bal.)	435,000	
Retained earnings	109,667	
Total stockholders' equity		544,667
Total liabilities and equity		$900,250

*Plus $1 rounding difference.

Wild Wood Company's management asks you to prepare its master budget using the following information. The budget is to cover the months of April, May, and June of 2019. Wild Wood is a merchandiser.

NEED-TO-KNOW 20-7

COMPREHENSIVE 2

Master Budget—
Merchandiser

WILD WOOD COMPANY
Balance Sheet
March 31, 2019

Assets

Cash	$ 50,000
Accounts receivable	175,000
Merchandise inventory (8,400 units × $15)	126,000
Total current assets	351,000
Equipment	480,000
Less: Accumulated depreciation	(90,000)
Equipment, net	390,000
Total assets	$741,000

Liabilities and Equity

Accounts payable	$156,000
Short-term notes payable	12,000
Total current liabilities	168,000
Long-term note payable	200,000
Total liabilities	368,000
Common stock	235,000
Retained earnings	138,000
Total stockholders' equity	373,000
Total liabilities and equity	$741,000

Additional Information

a. Sales for March total 10,000 units. Each month's sales are expected to exceed the prior month's results by 5%. The product's selling price is $25 per unit.

b. Company policy calls for a given month's ending inventory to equal 80% of the next month's expected unit sales. The March 31 inventory is 8,400 units, which complies with the policy. The purchase price is $15 per unit.

c. Sales representatives' commissions are 12.5% of sales and are paid in the month of the sales. The sales manager's monthly salary will be $3,500 in April and $4,000 per month thereafter.

d. Monthly general and administrative expenses include $8,000 administrative salaries, $5,000 depreciation, and 0.9% monthly interest on the long-term note payable.

e. The company expects 30% of sales to be for cash and the remaining 70% on credit. Receivables are collected in full in the month following the sale (none are collected in the month of the sale).

f. All merchandise purchases are on credit, and no payables arise from any other transactions. One month's purchases are fully paid in the next month.

g. The minimum ending cash balance for all months is $50,000. If necessary, the company borrows enough cash using a short-term note to reach the minimum. Short-term notes require an interest payment of 1% at each month-end (before any repayment). If the ending cash balance exceeds the minimum, the excess will be applied to repaying the short-term notes payable balance.

h. Dividends of $100,000 are to be declared and paid in May.

i. No cash payments for income taxes are to be made during the second calendar quarter. Income taxes will be assessed at 35% in the quarter.

j. Equipment purchases of $55,000 are scheduled for June.

Required

Prepare the following budgets and other financial information as required.

1. Sales budget, including budgeted sales for July.

2. Purchases budget.

3. Selling expense budget.

4. General and administrative expense budget.

5. Expected cash receipts from customers and the expected June 30 balance of accounts receivable.

6. Expected cash payments for purchases and the expected June 30 balance of accounts payable.

7. Cash budget.

8. Budgeted income statement, budgeted statement of retained earnings, and budgeted balance sheet.

PLANNING THE SOLUTION

- The sales budget shows expected sales for each month in the quarter. Start by multiplying March sales by 105% and then do the same for the remaining months. July's sales are needed for the purchases budget. To complete the budget, multiply the expected unit sales by the selling price of $25 per unit.

- Use these results and the 80% inventory policy to budget the size of ending inventory for April, May, and June. Add the budgeted sales to these numbers and subtract the actual or expected beginning inventory for each month. The result is the number of units to be purchased each month. Multiply these numbers by the per unit cost of $15. Find the budgeted cost of goods sold by multiplying the unit sales in each month by the $15 cost per unit. Compute the cost of the June 30 ending inventory by multiplying the expected units available at that date by the $15 cost per unit.

- The selling expense budget has only two items. Find the amount of the sales representatives' commissions by multiplying the expected dollar sales in each month by the 12.5% commission rate. Then include the sales manager's salary of $3,500 in April and $4,000 in May and June.

- The general and administrative expense budget should show three items. Administrative salaries are fixed at $8,000 per month, and depreciation is $5,000 per month. Budget the monthly interest expense on the long-term note by multiplying its $200,000 balance by the 0.9% monthly interest rate.

- Determine the amounts of cash sales in each month by multiplying the budgeted sales by 30%. Add to this amount the credit sales of the prior month (computed as 70% of prior month's sales). April's cash receipts from collecting receivables equals the March 31 balance of $175,000. The expected June 30 accounts receivable balance equals 70% of June's total budgeted sales.

- Determine expected cash payments on accounts payable for each month by making them equal to the merchandise purchases in the prior month. The payments for April equal the March 31 balance of accounts payable shown on the beginning balance sheet. The June 30 balance of accounts payable equals merchandise purchases for June.

- Prepare the cash budget by combining the given information and the amounts of cash receipts and cash payments on account that you computed. Complete the cash budget for each month by either borrowing enough to raise the preliminary balance to the minimum or paying off short-term debt as much as the balance allows without falling below the minimum. Show the ending balance of the short-term note in the budget.

- Prepare the budgeted income statement by combining the budgeted items for all three months. Determine the income before income taxes and multiply it by the 35% rate to find the quarter's income tax expense.

- The budgeted statement of retained earnings should show the March 31 balance plus the quarter's net income minus the quarter's dividends.
- The budgeted balance sheet includes updated balances for all items that appear in the beginning balance sheet and an additional liability for unpaid income taxes. Amounts for all asset, liability, and equity accounts can be found either in the budgets, in other calculations, or by adding amounts found there to the beginning balances.

SOLUTION

1.

	A	B	C	D	E
1	**Calculation of Unit Sales**	**April**	**May**	**June**	**July**
2	Prior period's unit sales	10,000	10,500	11,025	11,576
3	Plus 5% growth*	500	525	551	579
4	Projected unit sales	10,500	11,025	11,576	12,155

*Rounded to nearest whole unit.

	A	B	C	D	E
1	**Sales Budget**	**April**	**May**	**June**	**Quarter**
2	Projected unit sales	10,500	11,025	11,576	
3	Selling price per unit	×$ 25	×$ 25	×$ 25	
4	Projected sales	$262,500	$275,625	$289,400	$827,525

2.

	A	B	C	D	E
1	**Purchases Budget**	**April**	**May**	**June**	**Quarter**
2	Next period's unit sales (part 1)	11,025	11,576	12,155	
3	Ending inventory percent	× 80%	× 80%	× 80%	
4	Desired ending inventory (units)	8,820	9,261	9,724	
5	**Add:** Current period's unit sales (part 1)	10,500	11,025	11,576	
6	Units to be available	19,320	20,286	21,300	
7	**Less:** Beginning inventory (units)	8,400	8,820	9,261	
8	Units to be purchased	10,920	11,466	12,039	
9	Budgeted cost per unit	×$ 15	×$ 15	×$ 15	
10	Budgeted purchases	$163,800	$171,990	$180,585	$516,375

3.

	A	B	C	D	E
1	**Selling Expense Budget**	**April**	**May**	**June**	**Quarter**
2	Budgeted sales (part 1)	$262,500	$275,625	$289,400	$827,525
3	Commission %	× 12.5%	× 12.5%	× 12.5%	× 12.5%
4	Sales commissions*	32,813	34,453	36,175	103,441
5	Manager's salary	3,500	4,000	4,000	11,500
6	Budgeted selling expenses*	$ 36,313	$ 38,453	$ 40,175	$ 114,941

*Rounded to the nearest dollar.

4.

	A	B	C	D	E
1	**General and Administrative Expense Budget**	**April**	**May**	**June**	**Quarter**
2	Administrative salaries	$ 8,000	$ 8,000	$ 8,000	$24,000
3	Depreciation	5,000	5,000	5,000	15,000
4	Interest on long-term note payable (0.9% × $200,000)	1,800	1,800	1,800	5,400
5	Budgeted expenses	$14,800	$14,800	$14,800	$44,400

5.

	A	B	C	D	E
1	**Schedule of Cash Receipts from Sales**	**April**	**May**	**June**	**Quarter**
2	Budgeted sales (part 1)	$262,500	$275,625	$289,400	
3	Ending accounts receivable (70% of sales)	$ 183,750	$192,938	$202,580	
4	Cash receipts				
5	Cash sales (30% of budgeted sales)	$ 78,750	$ 82,687	$ 86,820	$248,257
6	Collections of prior month's receivables	175,000*	183,750	192,938	551,688
7	Total cash to be collected	$253,750	$266,437	$ 279,758	$799,945

*March 31 Accounts Receivable balance (from balance sheet).

6.

	A	B	C	D	E
1	**Schedule of Cash Payments to Suppliers**	**April**	**May**	**June**	**Quarter**
2	Cash payments (equal to prior month's				
3	purchases)	$156,000*	$163,800	$171,990	$491,790
4	Expected June 30 balance of accounts				
5	payable (part 2, June purchases)			$180,585	

*March 31 Accounts Payable balance (from balance sheet).

7.

	A	B	C	D
1	**Cash Budget**	**April**	**May**	**June**
2	Beginning cash balance	$ 50,000	$ 89,517	$ 50,000
3	Add: Cash receipts (part 5)	253,750	266,437	279,758
4	Total cash available	303,750	355,954	329,758
5	Less: Cash payments for			
6	Merchandise (part 6)	156,000	163,800	171,990
7	Sales commissions (part 3)	32,813	34,453	36,175
8	Salaries			
9	Sales (part 3)	3,500	4,000	4,000
10	Administrative (part 4)	8,000	8,000	8,000
11	Interest on long-term note (part 4)	1,800	1,800	1,800
12	Dividends		100,000	
13	Equipment purchase			55,000
14	Interest on short-term notes			
15	April ($12,000 × 1%)	120		
16	June ($6,099 × 1%)			61
17	Total cash payments	202,233	312,053	277,026
18	Preliminary balance	101,517	43,901	52,732
19	Loan activity			
20	Additional loan		6,099	
21	Loan repayment	(12,000)		(2,732)
22	Ending cash balance	$ 89,517	$ 50,000	$ 50,000
23	Ending short-term notes payable balance	$ 0	$ 6,099	$ 3,367

8.

WILD WOOD COMPANY
Budgeted Income Statement
For Quarter Ended June 30, 2019

Sales (part 1)	$827,525
Cost of goods sold*	496,515
Gross profit	331,010

Operating expenses

Sales commissions (part 3)	$103,441
Sales salaries (part 3)	11,500
Administrative salaries (part 4)	24,000
Depreciation (part 4)	15,000
Interest on long-term note (part 4)	5,400
Interest on short-term note (part 7)	181
Total operating expenses	159,522
Income before income taxes	171,488
Income taxes (35%)	60,021
Net income	$111,467

*33,101 units sold @ $15 per unit.

WILD WOOD COMPANY
Budgeted Statement of Retained Earnings
For Quarter Ended June 30, 2019

Beginning retained earnings (Mar. 31 bal.)	$138,000
Net income	111,467
	249,467
Less: Cash dividends (part 7)	100,000
Ending retained earnings	$149,467

WILD WOOD COMPANY
Budgeted Balance Sheet
June 30, 2019

Assets

Cash (part 7)	$ 50,000	
Accounts receivable (part 5)	202,580	
Inventory (9,724 units @ $15 each)	145,860	
Total current assets		$398,440
Equipment (Mar. 31 bal. plus purchase)	535,000	
Less: Accumulated depreciation		
(Mar. 31 bal. plus depreciation expense)	105,000	430,000
Total assets		$828,440

Liabilities and Equity

Accounts payable (part 6)	$180,585	
Short-term notes payable (part 7)	3,367	
Income taxes payable	60,021	
Total current liabilities		$243,973
Long-term note payable (Mar. 31 bal.)		200,000
Total liabilities		443,973
Common stock (Mar. 31 bal.)	235,000	
Retained earnings	149,467	
Total stockholders' equity		384,467
Total liabilities and equity		$828,440

Merchandise Purchases Budget 20A

P4

Prepare each component of a master budget—for a merchandising company.

Exhibit 20A.1 shows the master budget sequence for a merchandiser. Unlike a manufacturing company, a merchandiser must prepare a merchandise purchases budget rather than a production budget. In addition, a merchandiser does not prepare direct materials, direct labor, or factory overhead budgets. In this appendix we show the merchandise purchases budget for Hockey Den (HD), a retailer of hockey sticks.

EXHIBIT 20A.1

Master Budget Sequence—Merchandiser

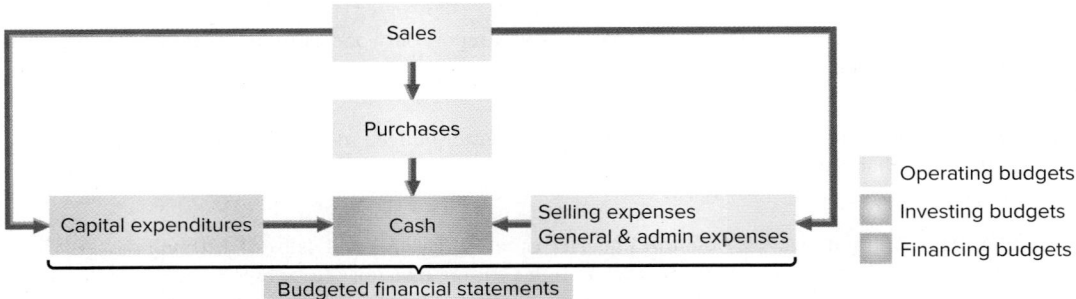

Operating budgets
Investing budgets
Financing budgets

Preparing the Merchandise Purchases Budget A merchandiser usually expresses a **merchandise purchases budget** in both units and dollars. Exhibit 20A.2 shows the general layout for this budget in equation form. If this formula is expressed in units and only one product is involved, we can compute the number of dollars of inventory to be purchased for the budget by multiplying the units to be purchased by the cost per unit.

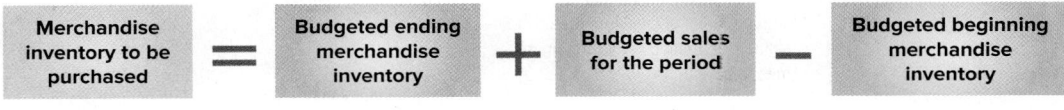

EXHIBIT 20A.2

General Formula for Merchandise Purchases Budget

A merchandise purchases budget requires the following inputs.

1 Sales budget (in units).   **2** Budgeted ending inventory (in units).   **3** Cost per unit.

1 Toronto Sticks Company is an exclusive supplier of hockey sticks to HD, meaning that the companies use the same budgeted sales figures in preparing budgets. Thus, HD predicts unit sales as follows: October, 1,000; November, 800; December, 1,400; and January, 900.

2 After considering the costs of keeping inventory and inventory shortages, HD set a policy that ending inventory (in units) should equal 90% of next month's predicted sales. For example, inventory at the end of October should equal 90% of November's budgeted sales.

3 Finally, HD expects the per unit purchase cost of $60 to remain unchanged through the budgeting period. This information, along with knowledge of 1,010 units in inventory at September 30 (given), allows the company to prepare the merchandise purchases budget shown in Exhibit 20A.3.

EXHIBIT 20A.3

Merchandise Purchases Budget

		A	B	C	D
	1		HOCKEY DEN		
	2		Merchandise Purchases Budget		
	3		October 2019–December 2019		
	4		October	November	December
1	5	Next month's budgeted sales (units)	800	1,400	900
	6	Ratio of inventory to future sales	× 90 %	× 90 %	× 90 %
2	7	Budgeted ending inventory (units)	720	1,260	810
	8	Add: Budgeted sales (units)	1,000	800	1,400
	9	Required units of available merchandise	1,720	2,060	2,210
	10	Deduct: Beginning inventory (units)	1,010*	720	1,260
	11	Total units to be purchased	710	1,340	950
	12				
3	13	Budgeted cost per unit	$ 60	$ 60	$ 60
	14	Budgeted cost of merchandise purchases	$42,600	$80,400	$57,000

Units to Purchase

  Budgeted ending inventory
+ Budgeted sales
− Beginning inventory
= Units to be purchased

*Does not comply with company policy.

The first three lines of HD's merchandise purchases budget determine the required ending inventories (in units). Budgeted unit sales are then added to the desired ending inventory to give the required units of available merchandise. We then subtract beginning inventory to determine the budgeted number of units to be purchased. The last line is the budgeted cost of the purchases, computed by multiplying the number of units to be purchased by the predicted cost per unit.

Other Master Budget Differences—Merchandiser vs. Manufacturer   In addition to preparing a purchases budget instead of production, direct materials, direct labor, and overhead budgets, other key differences in master budgets for merchandisers include:

- Depreciation expense is included in the general and administrative expense budget of the merchandiser. For the manufacturer, depreciation on manufacturing assets is included in the factory overhead budget and treated as a product cost.
- The budgeted balance sheet for the merchandiser will report only one asset for inventory. The balance sheet for the manufacturer will typically report three inventory assets: raw materials, work in process, and finished goods.

See **Need-to-Know 20-7** for illustration of a complete master budget, including budgeted financial statements, for a merchandising company.

NEED-TO-KNOW 20-8

Merchandise
Purchases Budget

P4

Do More: QS 20-28, QS 20-29,
QS 20-30, E 20-24

In preparing monthly budgets for the third quarter, a company budgeted sales of 120 units for July and 140 units for August. Management wants each month's ending inventory to be 60% of next month's sales. The June 30 inventory consists of 72 units. How many units should be purchased in July?

Solution

Merchandise Purchases Budget	July
Next month's budgeted sales (units)...............	140
Ratio of inventory to future sales....................	× 60%
Budgeted ending inventory (units).................	84
Add: Budgeted sales (units).......................	+120
Required units of available merchandise	204
Deduct: Beginning inventory (units)	− 72
Units to be purchased	132

Summary: Cheat Sheet

BUDGET PROCESS

Budget: Statement of plans, in monetary terms.

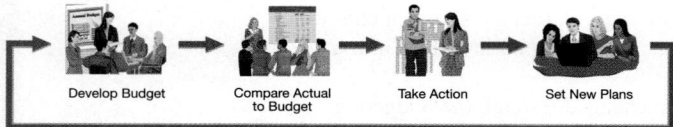

Develop Budget → Compare Actual to Budget → Take Action → Set New Plans

BUDGETING BENEFITS

Plan, control, coordinate, communicate, and motivate.

MASTER BUDGET COMPONENTS

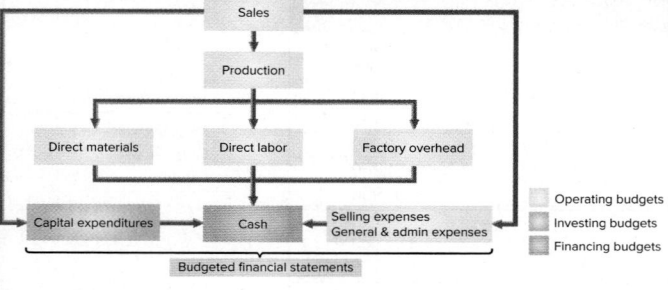

Budgeted sales $ = Budgeted sales in units × Selling price per unit

PRODUCTION BUDGET

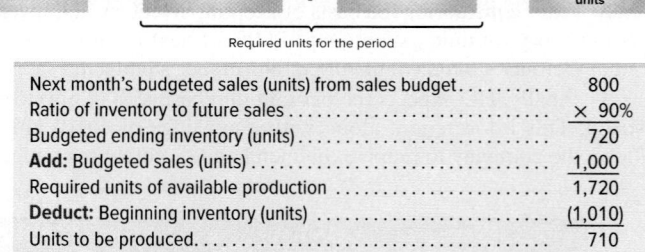

Next month's budgeted sales (units) from sales budget..........	800
Ratio of inventory to future sales	× 90%
Budgeted ending inventory (units)..........................	720
Add: Budgeted sales (units)	1,000
Required units of available production	1,720
Deduct: Beginning inventory (units)	(1,010)
Units to be produced..	710

DIRECT MATERIALS BUDGET

Budgeted production units................................	710
Materials requirements per unit...........................	× 0.5
Materials needed for production (pounds)..................	355
Add: Budgeted ending inventory (pounds)	335
Total materials requirements (pounds).....................	690
Deduct: Beginning inventory (pounds)	(178)
Materials to be purchased (pounds).......................	512
Material price per pound.................................	$ 20
Total cost of direct materials purchases...................	$10,240

DIRECT LABOR BUDGET

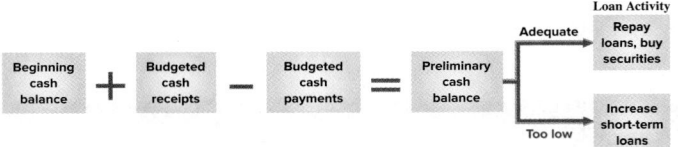

| Budgeted direct labor cost (dollars) | = | Budgeted production (units) | × | Direct labor required per unit (hours) | × | Direct labor cost per hour (dollars) |

Budgeted production (units).............................	710
Direct labor requirements per unit (hours)....................	× 0.25
Total direct labor hours needed	177.5
Direct labor rate (per hour).............................	$ 12
Total cost of direct labor	$2,130

OVERHEAD BUDGET

Budgeted production (units).............................	710
Variable factory overhead rate............................	× $ 2.50
Budgeted variable overhead	$1,775
Budgeted fixed overhead	$1,500
Budgeted total overhead	$3,275

Cash Budget

Beginning cash balance	$20,000
Add: Cash receipts from customers	49,200
Total cash available	69,200
Less: Cash payments for	
Direct materials	$ 7,060
Direct labor	2,130
Overhead	1,775
Selling and general admin. expenses	12,500
Income taxes payable	20,000
Dividends	0
Interest on bank loan	100
Purchase of equipment	0
Total cash payments	43,565
Preliminary cash balance	$25,635
Loan activity	
Additional loan or repayment of loan	(5,635)
Ending cash balance	$20,000

CASH BUDGET

| Beginning cash balance | + | Budgeted cash receipts | − | Budgeted cash payments | = | Preliminary cash balance | | **Adequate** → Loan Activity Repay loans, buy securities |
| | | | | | | | | **Too low** → Increase short-term loans |

MERCHANDISE PURCHASES BUDGET

| Merchandise inventory to be purchased | = | Budgeted ending merchandise inventory | + | Budgeted sales for the period | − | Budgeted beginning merchandise inventory |

Key Terms

Activity-based budgeting (ABB) (781)
Budget (771)
Budgetary control (771)
Budgeted balance sheet (786)
Budgeted income statement (785)
Budgeting (771)
Capital expenditures budget (781)
Cash budget (781)

Continuous budgeting (773)
Cost of goods sold budget (779)
Direct labor budget (777)
Direct materials budget (776)
Factory overhead budget (778)
General and administrative expense budget (780)
Master budget (773)

Merchandise purchases budget (795)
Production budget (775)
Rolling budget (773)
Safety stock (775)
Sales budget (775)
Selling expense budget (779)
Zero-based budgeting (773)

Multiple Choice Quiz

1. A plan that reports the units of merchandise to be produced by a manufacturing company during the budget period is called a
  a. Capital expenditures budget.
  b. Cash budget.
  c. Production budget.
  d. Manufacturing budget.
  e. Sales budget.

2.ᴬ A hardware store has budgeted sales of $36,000 for its power tool department in July. Management wants to have $7,000 in power tool inventory at the end of July. Its beginning inventory of power tools is expected to be $6,000. What is the budgeted dollar amount of merchandise purchases?
  a. $36,000
  b. $43,000
  c. $42,000
  d. $35,000
  e. $37,000

3. A store has the following budgeted sales for the next three months.

	July	August	September
Budgeted sales	$180,000	$220,000	$240,000

Cash sales are 25% of total sales and all credit sales are expected to be collected in the month following the sale. The total amount of cash expected to be received from customers in September is
  a. $240,000.
  b. $225,000.
  c. $60,000.
  d. $165,000.
  e. $220,000.

4. A plan that shows the expected cash inflows and cash outflows during the budget period, including receipts from loans needed to maintain a minimum cash balance and repayments of such loans, is called

    a. A rolling budget.   **d.** A cash budget.

    b. An income statement.   **e.** An operating budget.

    c. A balance sheet.

5. The following sales are predicted for a company's next four months.

	April	May	June	July
Unit sales	480	560	600	480

Each month's ending inventory of finished goods should be 30% of the next month's sales. The budgeted production of units for May is

    a. 572 units.   **c.** 548 units.   **e.** 180 units.

    b. 560 units.   **d.** 600 units.

ANSWERS TO MULTIPLE CHOICE QUIZ

1. c

2. e; Budgeted purchases = \$36,000 + \$7,000 − \$6,000 = \$37,000

3. b; Cash collected = 25% of September sales + 75% of August sales = (0.25 × \$240,000) + (0.75 × \$220,000) = \$225,000

4. d

5. a; 560 units + (0.30 × 600 units) − (0.30 × 560 units) = 572 units

---

^A ^ *Superscript letter A denotes assignments based on Appendix 20A, which relates to budgets for merchandising companies.*

🔲 Icon denotes assignments that involve decision making.

Discussion Questions

1. 🔲 Identify at least three benefits of budgeting in helping managers plan and control a business.

2. How does a budget benefit management in its control function?

3. 🔲 What is the benefit of continuous budgeting?

4. Identify three usual time horizons for short-term planning and budgets.

5. 🔲 Why should each department participate in preparing its own budget?

6. 🔲 How does budgeting help management coordinate and plan business activities?

7. 🔲 Why is the sales budget so important to the budgeting process?

8. What is a selling expense budget? What is a capital expenditures budget?

9. Identify at least two potential negative outcomes of budgeting.

10. **Google** prepares a cash budget. What is a **GOOGLE** cash budget? Why must operating budgets and the capital expenditures budget be prepared before the cash budget?

11. **Apple** regularly uses budgets. What is the difference between a production budget and a **APPLE** manufacturing budget?

12. 🔲 Would a manager of an **Apple** retail store participate more in budgeting than a manager at **APPLE** the corporate offices? Explain.

13. 🔲 Does the manager of a **Samsung** distribution center participate in long-term **Samsung** budgeting? Explain.

14. 🔲 Assume that **Samsung**'s consumer electronics division is charged with preparing a master budget. Identify the participants—for example, the sales manager for the sales budget—and describe the information each person provides in preparing the master budget.

15. 🔲 **Coca-Cola** recently redesigned its bottle to reduce its use of glass, thus lowering its bottle's weight and CO_2 emissions. Which budgets in the company's master budget will this redesign impact?

16. Activity-based budgeting is a budget system based on *expected activities*. Describe activity-based budgeting, and explain its preparation of budgets. How does activity-based budgeting differ from traditional budgeting?

≡ connect·

QUICK STUDY

QS 20-1

Budget motivation

C1

For each of the following items 1 through 5, indicate *yes* if the item is an important budgeting guideline or *no* if it is not.

_____ **1.** Employees should have the opportunity to explain differences from budgeted amounts.

_____ **2.** Budgets should include budgetary slack.

_____ **3.** Employees impacted by a budget should be consulted when it is prepared.

_____ **4.** Goals in a budget should be set low so targets can be reached.

_____ **5.** Budgetary goals should be attainable.

For each of the following items 1 through 6, indicate *yes* if it describes a potential benefit of budgeting or *no* if it describes a potential negative outcome of budgeting.

_____ **1.** Budgets help coordinate activities across departments.

_____ **2.** Budgets are useful in assigning blame for unexpected results.

_____ **3.** A budget forces managers to spend time planning for the future.

_____ **4.** Some employees might overstate expenses in budgets.

_____ **5.** Budgets can lead to excessive pressure to meet budgeted results.

_____ **6.** Budgets can provide incentives for good performance.

QS 20-2
Budgeting benefits
C1

Zahn Co. predicts sales of 220 units in May and 240 units in June. Each month's ending inventory should be 25% of the next month's sales. The April 30 ending finished goods inventory is 55 units. Compute budgeted production (in units) for May.

QS 20-3
Production budget   **P1**

Grace manufactures and sells miniature digital cameras for $250 each. 1,000 units were sold in May, and management forecasts 4% growth in unit sales each month. Determine (*a*) the number of units of camera sales and (*b*) the dollar amount of camera sales for the month of June.

QS 20-4
Sales budget   **P1**

Zilly Co. predicts sales of $400,000 for June. Zilly pays a sales manager a monthly salary of $6,000 and a commission of 8% of that month's sales dollars. Prepare a selling expense budget for the month of June.

QS 20-5
Selling expense budget   **P1**

Liza's predicts sales of $40,000 for May and $52,000 for June. Assume 60% of Liza's sales are for cash. The remaining 40% are credit sales; credit customers pay in the month following the sale. Compute the budgeted cash receipts for June.

QS 20-6
Cash budget   **P2**

Zortek Corp. budgets production of 400 units in January and 200 units in February. Each finished unit requires five pounds of raw material Z, which costs $2 per pound. Each month's ending inventory of raw materials should be 40% of the following month's budgeted production. The January 1 raw materials inventory has 130 pounds of Z. Prepare a direct materials budget for January.

QS 20-7
Manufacturing: Direct materials budget   **P1**

Tora Co. plans to produce 1,020 units in July. Each unit requires two hours of direct labor. The direct labor rate is $20 per hour. Prepare a direct labor budget for July.

QS 20-8
Manufacturing:
Direct labor budget   **P1**

Scora, Inc., is preparing its master budget for the quarter ending March 31. It sells a single product for $50 per unit. Budgeted sales for the next three months follow. Prepare a sales budget for the months of January, February, and March.

QS 20-9
Sales budget
P1

	January	February	March
Sales in units	1,200	2,000	1,600

X-Tel budgets sales of $60,000 for April, $100,000 for May, and $80,000 for June. In addition, sales are 40% cash and 60% on credit. All credit sales are collected in the month following the sale. The April 1 balance in accounts receivable is $15,000. Prepare a schedule of budgeted cash receipts for April, May, and June.

QS 20-10
Cash receipts budget   **P2**

X-Tel budgets sales of $60,000 for April, $100,000 for May, and $80,000 for June. In addition, sales commissions are 10% of sales dollars and the company pays a sales manager a salary of $6,000 per month. Sales commissions and salaries are paid in the month incurred. Prepare a selling expense budget for April, May, and June.

QS 20-11
Selling expense budget
P1

Champ, Inc., predicts the following sales in units for the coming two months. Each month's ending inventory of finished units should be 60% of the next month's sales. The April 30 finished goods inventory is 108 units. Compute budgeted production (in units) for May.

QS 20-12
Manufacturing:
Production budget
P1

	May	June
Sales in units	180	200

QS 20-13
Manufacturing:
Direct materials budget
P1

Miami Solar manufactures solar panels for industrial use. The company budgets production of 5,000 units (solar panels) in July and 5,300 units in August. Each unit requires 3 pounds of direct materials, which cost $6 per pound. The company's policy is to maintain direct materials inventory equal to 30% of the next month's direct materials requirement. As of June 30, the company has 4,500 pounds of direct materials in inventory, which complies with the policy. Prepare a direct materials budget for July.

QS 20-14
Manufacturing:
Direct labor budget   **P1**

Miami Solar budgets production of 5,000 solar panels in July. Each unit requires 4 hours of direct labor at a rate of $16 per hour. Prepare a direct labor budget for July.

QS 20-15
Manufacturing: Factory
overhead budget   **P1**

Miami Solar budgets production of 5,300 solar panels for August. Each unit requires 4 hours of direct labor at a rate of $16 per hour. Variable factory overhead is budgeted to be 70% of direct labor cost, and fixed factory overhead is $180,000 per month. Prepare a factory overhead budget for August.

QS 20-16
Manufacturing:
Production budget
P1

Atlantic Surf manufactures surfboards. The company's sales budget for the next three months is shown below. In addition, company policy is to maintain finished goods inventory equal (in units) to 40% of the next month's unit sales. As of June 30, the company has 1,600 finished surfboards in inventory, which complies with the policy. Prepare a production budget for the months of July and August.

	July	August	September
Sales in units..........	4,000	6,500	3,500

QS 20-17
Manufacturing:
Production budget
P1

Forrest Company manufactures phone chargers and has a JIT policy that ending inventory should equal 10% of the next month's estimated unit sales. It estimates that October's actual ending inventory will consist of 40,000 units. November and December sales are estimated to be 400,000 and 350,000 units, respectively. Compute the number of units to be produced in November.

QS 20-18
Manufacturing: Factory
overhead budget   **P1**

Hockey Pro budgets production of 3,900 hockey pucks during May. The company assigns variable overhead at the rate of $1.50 per unit. Fixed overhead equals $46,000 per month. Prepare a factory overhead budget for May.

QS 20-19
Cash receipts   **P2**

Music World reports the following sales forecast: August, $150,000; and September, $170,000. Cash sales are normally 40% of total sales and all credit sales are expected to be collected in the month following the date of sale. Prepare a schedule of cash receipts for September.

QS 20-20
Cash receipts, with
uncollectible accounts
P2

The Guitar Shoppe reports the following sales forecast: August, $150,000; and September, $170,000. Cash sales are normally 40% of total sales, 55% of credit sales are collected in the month following sale, and the remaining 5% of credit sales are written off as uncollectible. Prepare a schedule of cash receipts for September.

QS 20-21
Cash receipts, with
uncollectible accounts   **P2**

Wells Company reports the following sales forecast: September, $55,000; October, $66,000; and November, $80,000. All sales are on account. Collections of credit sales are received as follows: 25% in the month of sale, 60% in the first month after sale, and 10% in the second month after sale. 5% of all credit sales are written off as uncollectible. Prepare a schedule of cash receipts for November.

QS 20-22
Computing budgeted
accounts receivable
P2

Kingston anticipates total sales for June and July of $420,000 and $398,000, respectively. Cash sales are normally 60% of total sales. Of the credit sales, 20% are collected in the same month as the sale, 70% are collected during the first month after the sale, and the remaining 10% are collected in the second month after the sale. Determine the amount of accounts receivable reported on the company's budgeted balance sheet as of July 31.

QS 20-23
Budgeted loan activity
P2

Santos Co. is preparing a cash budget for February. The company has $20,000 cash at the beginning of February and anticipates $75,000 in cash receipts and $100,250 in cash payments during February. What amount, if any, must the company borrow during February to maintain a $5,000 cash balance? The company has no loans outstanding on February 1.

Use the following information to prepare a cash budget for the month ended on March 31 for Gado Company. The budget should show expected cash receipts and cash payments for the month of March and the balance expected on March 31.

a. Beginning cash balance on March 1, $72,000.

b. Cash receipts from sales, $300,000.

c. Budgeted cash payments for direct materials, $140,000.

d. Budgeted cash payments for direct labor, $80,000.

e. Other budgeted cash expenses, $45,000.

f. Cash repayment of bank loan, $20,000.

QS 20-24
Manufacturing:
Cash budget
P2

Following are selected accounts for a manufacturing company. For each account, indicate whether it will appear on a budgeted income statement (BIS) or a budgeted balance sheet (BBS). If an item will not appear on either budgeted financial statement, label it NA.

Sales	_____	Interest expense on loan payable	_____
Office salaries expense	_____	Cash dividends paid	_____
Accumulated depreciation	_____	Bank loan owed	_____
Amortization expense.	_____	Cost of goods sold	_____

QS 20-25
Budgeted financial statements
P3

Garda purchased $600,000 of merchandise in August and expects to purchase $720,000 in September. Merchandise purchases are paid as follows: 25% in the month of purchase and 75% in the following month. Compute cash payments for merchandise for September.

QS 20-26[A]
Merchandising:
Cash payments for merchandise P4

Torres Co. forecasts merchandise purchases of $15,800 in January, $18,600 in February, and $20,200 in March; 40% of purchases are paid in the month of purchase and 60% are paid in the following month. At December 31 of the prior year, the balance of accounts payable (for December purchases) is $22,000. Prepare a schedule of cash payments for merchandise for each of the months of January, February, and March.

QS 20-27[A]
Merchandising:
Cash payments for merchandise P4

Raider-X Company forecasts sales of 18,000 units for April. Beginning inventory is 3,000 units. The desired ending inventory is 30% higher than the beginning inventory. How many units should Raider-X purchase in April?

QS 20-28[A]
Merchandising:
Computing purchases P4

Lexi Company forecasts unit sales of 1,040,000 in April, 1,220,000 in May, 980,000 in June, and 1,020,000 in July. Beginning inventory on April 1 is 280,000 units, and the company wants to have 30% of next month's sales in inventory at the end of each month. Prepare a merchandise purchases budget for the months of April, May, and June.

QS 20-29[A]
Merchandising:
Computing purchases P4

Montel Company's July sales budget calls for sales of $600,000. The store expects to begin July with $50,000 of inventory and to end the month with $40,000 of inventory. Gross margin is typically 40% of sales. Determine the budgeted cost of merchandise purchases for July.

QS 20-30[A]
Merchandising:
Purchases budget P4

Royal Philips Electronics of the Netherlands reports sales of €24.5 billion for a recent year. Assume that the company expects sales growth of 3% for the next year. Also assume that selling expenses are typically 20% of sales, while general and administrative expenses are 4% of sales.

1. Compute budgeted sales for the next year.

2. Assume budgeted sales for next year are €25 billion, and then compute budgeted selling expenses and budgeted general and administrative expenses for the next year.

QS 20-31
Operating budgets
P1

■ connect

MM Co. predicts sales of $30,000 for May. MM Co. pays a sales manager a monthly salary of $3,000 plus a commission of 6% of sales dollars. MM's production manager recently found a way to reduce the amount of packaging MM uses. As a result, MM's product will receive better placement on store shelves and thus May sales are predicted to increase by 8%. In addition, MM's shipping costs are predicted to decrease from 4% of sales to 3% of sales. Compute (1) budgeted sales and (2) budgeted selling expenses for May assuming MM switches to this more sustainable packaging.

EXERCISES

Exercise 20-1
Sustainability and selling expense budget P1

Exercise 20-2
Budget definitions
C1

Match the definitions 1 through 8 with the term or phrase *a* through *h*.

a. Budget
b. Top-down budgeting
c. Participatory budgeting
d. Cash budget

e. Master budget
f. Budgetary slack
g. Sales budget
h. Budgeted income statement

_____ **1.** Shows expected cash inflows and outflows and helps determine financing needs.
_____ **2.** A plan showing units to be sold; the usual starting point in the master budget process.
_____ **3.** A report that shows predicted revenues and expenses for a budgeting period.
_____ **4.** A formal statement of future plans, usually expressed in monetary terms.
_____ **5.** Approach in which top management passes down a budget without employee input.
_____ **6.** A budgetary cushion used to meet performance targets.
_____ **7.** A comprehensive business plan that includes operating, investing, and financing budgets.
_____ **8.** Employees affected by a budget help in preparing it.

Exercise 20-3
Manufacturing:
Production budget
P1

Ruiz Co. provides the following sales forecast for the next four months.

	April	May	June	July
Sales (units)...........	500	580	540	620

The company wants to end each month with ending finished goods inventory equal to 25% of next month's forecasted sales. Finished goods inventory on April 1 is 190 units. Prepare a production budget for the months of April, May, and June.

Exercise 20-4
Manufacturing: Direct materials budget
P1

Zira Co. reports the following production budget for the next four months.

	April	May	June	July
Production (units)......	455	570	560	540

Each finished unit requires five pounds of raw materials, and the company wants to end each month with raw materials inventory equal to 30% of next month's production needs. Beginning raw materials inventory for April was 663 pounds. Assume direct materials cost $4 per pound. Prepare a direct materials budget for April, May, and June.

Exercise 20-5
Manufacturing: Direct labor budget   P1

The production budget for Manner Company shows units to be produced as follows: July, 620; August, 680; and September, 540. Each unit produced requires two hours of direct labor. The direct labor rate is currently $20 per hour but is predicted to be $21 per hour in September. Prepare a direct labor budget for the months July, August, and September.

Exercise 20-6
Manufacturing: Direct materials budget
P1

Rida, Inc., a manufacturer in a seasonal industry, is preparing its direct materials budget for the second quarter. It plans production of 240,000 units in the second quarter and 52,500 units in the third quarter. Raw material inventory is 43,200 pounds at the beginning of the second quarter. Other information follows. Prepare a direct materials budget for the second quarter.

Direct materials............	Each unit requires 0.60 pounds of raw material, priced at $175 per pound. The company plans to end each quarter with an ending inventory of materials equal to 30% of next quarter's budgeted materials requirements.

Exercise 20-7
Manufacturing: Direct labor and factory overhead budgets
P1

Addison Co. budgets production of 2,400 units during the second quarter. In addition, information on its direct labor and its variable and fixed overhead is shown below. For the second quarter, prepare (1) a direct labor budget and (2) a factory overhead budget.

Direct labor...	Each finished unit requires 4 direct labor hours, at a cost of $20 per hour.	Variable overhead...	Applied at the rate of $11 per direct labor hour.
		Fixed overhead	Budgeted at $450,000 per quarter.

Ramos Co. provides the following sales forecast and production budget for the next four months.

	April	May	June	July
Sales (units)......................	500	580	530	600
Budgeted production (units)	442	570	544	540

The company plans for finished goods inventory of 120 units at the end of June. In addition, each finished unit requires 5 pounds of direct materials, and the company wants to end each month with direct materials inventory equal to 30% of next month's production needs. Beginning direct materials inventory for April was 663 pounds. Direct materials cost $2 per pound. Each finished unit requires 0.50 hours of direct labor at the rate of $16 per hour. The company budgets variable overhead at the rate of $20 per direct labor hour and budgets fixed overhead of $8,000 per month. Prepare a direct materials budget for April, May, and June.

Exercise 20-8
Manufacturing: Direct materials budget
P1

Refer to Exercise 20-8. Prepare (1) a direct labor budget and (2) a factory overhead budget for April, May, and June.

Exercise 20-9
Manufacturing:
Direct labor and factory overhead budgets   **P1**

Blue Wave Co. predicts the following unit sales for the coming four months: September, 4,000 units; October, 5,000 units; November, 7,000 units; and December, 7,600 units. The company's policy is to maintain finished goods inventory equal to 60% of the next month's sales. At the end of August, the company had 2,400 finished units on hand. Prepare a production budget for each of the months of September, October, and November.

Exercise 20-10
Manufacturing:
Production budget   **P1**

Tyler Co. predicts the following unit sales for the next four months: April, 3,000 units; May, 4,000 units; June, 6,000 units; and July, 2,000 units. The company's policy is to maintain finished goods inventory equal to 30% of the next month's sales. At the end of March, the company had 900 finished units on hand. Prepare a production budget for each of the months of April, May, and June.

Exercise 20-11
Manufacturing:
Production budget
P1

Electro Company manufactures an innovative automobile transmission for electric cars. Management predicts that ending finished goods inventory for the first quarter will be 90,000 units. The following unit sales of the transmissions are expected during the rest of the year: second quarter, 450,000 units; third quarter, 525,000 units; and fourth quarter, 475,000 units. Company policy calls for the ending finished goods inventory of a quarter to equal 20% of the next quarter's budgeted sales. Prepare a production budget for both the second and third quarters that shows the number of transmissions to manufacture.

Exercise 20-12
Manufacturing: Preparing production budgets (for two periods)   **P1**
Check   Second-quarter production, 465,000 units

Electro Company budgets production of 450,000 transmissions in the second quarter and 520,000 transmissions in the third quarter. Each transmission requires 0.80 pounds of a key raw material. The company aims to end each quarter with an ending inventory of direct materials equal to 20% of next quarter's budgeted materials requirements. Beginning inventory of this raw material is 72,000 pounds. Direct materials cost $1.70 per pound. Prepare a direct materials budget for the second quarter.

Exercise 20-13
Manufacturing: Direct materials budget   **P1**

Branson Belts makes handcrafted belts. The company budgets production of 4,500 belts during the second quarter. Each belt requires 4 direct labor hours, at a cost of $17 per hour. Prepare a direct labor budget for the second quarter.

Exercise 20-14
Manufacturing: Direct labor budget   **P1**

MCO Leather manufactures leather purses. Each purse requires 2 pounds of direct materials at a cost of $4 per pound and 0.8 direct labor hours at a rate of $16 per hour. Variable manufacturing overhead is charged at a rate of $2 per direct labor hour. Fixed manufacturing overhead is $10,000 per month. The company's policy is to end each month with direct materials inventory equal to 40% of the next month's materials requirement. At the end of August the company had 3,680 pounds of direct materials in inventory. The company's production budget reports the following. Prepare budgets for September and October for (1) direct materials, (2) direct labor, and (3) factory overhead.

Exercise 20-15
Manufacturing: Direct materials, direct labor, and overhead budgets
P1

Production Budget	September	October	November
Units to be produced	4,600	6,200	5,800

Exercise 20-16
Manufacturing: Direct materials, direct labor, and overhead budgets
P1

Ornamental Sculptures Mfg. manufactures garden sculptures. Each sculpture requires 8 pounds of direct materials at a cost of $3 per pound and 0.5 direct labor hours at a rate of $18 per hour. Variable manufacturing overhead is charged at a rate of $3 per direct labor hour. Fixed manufacturing overhead is $4,000 per month. The company's policy is to maintain direct materials inventory equal to 20% of the next month's materials requirement. At the end of February the company had 5,280 pounds of direct materials in inventory. The company's production budget reports the following. Prepare budgets for March and April for (1) direct materials, (2) direct labor, and (3) factory overhead.

Production Budget	March	April	May
Units to be produced	3,300	4,600	4,800

Exercise 20-17
Preparation of cash budgets (for three periods)
P2

Kayak Co. budgeted the following cash receipts (excluding cash receipts from loans received) and cash payments (excluding cash payments for loan principal and interest payments) for the first three months of next year.

	Cash Receipts	Cash Payments
January	$525,000	$475,000
February	400,000	350,000
March	450,000	525,000

According to a credit agreement with its bank, Kayak requires a minimum cash balance of $30,000 at each month-end. In return, the bank has agreed that the company can borrow up to $150,000 at a monthly interest rate of 1%, paid on the last day of each month. The interest is computed based on the beginning balance of the loan for the month. The company repays loan principal with any cash in excess of $30,000 on the last day of each month. The company has a cash balance of $30,000 and a loan balance of $60,000 at January 1. Prepare monthly cash budgets for January, February, and March.

Exercise 20-18
Budgeted cash receipts
P2

Jasper Company has sales on account and for cash. Specifically, 70% of its sales are on account and 30% are for cash. Credit sales are collected in full in the month following the sale. The company forecasts sales of $525,000 for April, $535,000 for May, and $560,000 for June. The beginning balance of accounts receivable is $400,000 on April 1. Prepare a schedule of budgeted cash receipts for April, May, and June.

Exercise 20-19
Budgeted cash payments
P2

Zisk Co. purchases raw materials on account. Budgeted purchase amounts are April, $80,000; May, $110,000; and June, $120,000. Payments are made as follows: 70% in the month of purchase and 30% in the month after purchase. The March 31 balance of accounts payable is $22,000. Prepare a schedule of budgeted cash payments for April, May, and June.

Exercise 20-20
Cash budget
P2

Karim Corp. requires a minimum $8,000 cash balance. Loans taken to meet this requirement cost 1% interest per month (paid monthly). Any excess cash is used to repay loans at month-end. The cash balance on July 1 is $8,400, and the company has no outstanding loans. Forecasted cash receipts (other than for loans received) and forecasted cash payments (other than for loan or interest payments) follow. Prepare a cash budget for July, August, and September. (Round interest payments to the nearest whole dollar.)

	July	August	September
Cash receipts	$20,000	$26,000	$40,000
Cash payments	28,000	30,000	22,000

Exercise 20-21
Cash budget
P2

Foyert Corp. requires a minimum $30,000 cash balance. Loans taken to meet this requirement cost 1% interest per month (paid monthly). Any excess cash is used to repay loans at month-end. The cash balance on October 1 is $30,000, and the company has an outstanding loan of $10,000. Forecasted cash receipts (other than for loans received) and forecasted cash payments (other than for loan or interest payments) follow. Prepare a cash budget for October, November, and December. (Round interest payments to the nearest whole dollar.)

	October	November	December
Cash receipts	$110,000	$80,000	$100,000
Cash payments	120,000	75,000	80,000

Use the following information to prepare the September cash budget for PTO Co. The following information relates to expected cash receipts and cash payments for the month ended September 30.

a. Beginning cash balance, September 1, $40,000.

b. Budgeted cash receipts from sales in September, $255,000.

c. Raw materials are purchased on account. Purchase amounts are August (actual), $80,000; and September (budgeted), $110,000. Payments for direct materials are made as follows: 65% in the month of purchase and 35% in the month following purchase.

d. Budgeted cash payments for direct labor in September, $40,000.

e. Budgeted depreciation expense for September, $4,000.

f. Other cash expenses budgeted for September, $60,000.

g. Accrued income taxes payable in September, $10,000.

h. Bank loan interest payable in September, $1,000.

Exercise 20-22
Manufacturing: Cash budget
P2

Mike's Motors Corp. manufactures motors for dirt bikes. The company requires a minimum $30,000 cash balance at each month-end. If necessary, the company borrows to meet this requirement at a cost of 2% interest per month (paid at the end of each month). Any cash balance above $30,000 at month-end is used to repay loans. The cash balance on July 1 is $34,000, and the company has no outstanding loans at that time. Forecasted cash receipts and forecasted cash payments (other than for loan activity) are as follows. Prepare a cash budget for July, August, and September.

	Cash Receipts	Cash Payments
July	$ 85,000	$113,000
August.....................	111,000	99,900
September	150,000	127,400

Exercise 20-23
Manufacturing: Cash budget
P2

Walker Company prepares monthly budgets. The current budget plans for a September ending merchandise inventory of 30,000 units. Company policy is to end each month with merchandise inventory equal to 15% of budgeted sales for the following month. Budgeted sales and merchandise purchases for the next three months follow. The company budgets sales of 200,000 units in October.

Prepare the merchandise purchases budgets for the months of July, August, and September.

	Sales (Units)	Purchases (Units)
July	180,000	200,250
August..............	315,000	308,250
September	270,000	259,500

Exercise 20-24[A]
Merchandising:
Preparation of purchases budgets (for three periods)
P4

Use the following information to prepare the July cash budget for Acco Co. It should show expected cash receipts and cash payments for the month and the cash balance expected on July 31.

a. Beginning cash balance on July 1: $50,000.

b. Cash receipts from sales: 30% is collected in the month of sale, 50% in the next month, and 20% in the second month after sale (uncollectible accounts are negligible and can be ignored). Sales amounts are May (actual), $1,720,000; June (actual), $1,200,000; and July (budgeted), $1,400,000.

c. Payments on merchandise purchases: 60% in the month of purchase and 40% in the month following purchase. Purchases amounts are: June (actual), $700,000; and July (budgeted), $750,000.

d. Budgeted cash payments for salaries in July: $275,000.

e. Budgeted depreciation expense for July: $36,000.

f. Other cash expenses budgeted for July: $200,000.

g. Accrued income taxes due in July: $80,000.

h. Bank loan interest paid in July: $6,600.

Exercise 20-25[A]
Merchandising:
Preparing a cash budget
P4

Check   Ending cash balance, $122,400

Use the information in Exercise 20-25 and the following additional information to prepare a budgeted income statement for the month of July and a budgeted balance sheet for July 31.

a. Cost of goods sold is 55% of sales.

b. Inventory at the end of June is $80,000 and at the end of July is $60,000.

c. Salaries payable on June 30 are $50,000 and are expected to be $60,000 on July 31.

[continued on next page]

Exercise 20-26[A]
Merchandising: Preparing a budgeted income statement and balance sheet
P4

d. The equipment account balance is $1,600,000 on July 31. On June 30, the accumulated depreciation on equipment is $280,000.

e. The $6,600 cash payment of interest represents the 1% monthly expense on a bank loan of $660,000.

f. Income taxes payable on July 31 are $30,720, and the income tax rate is 30%.

g. The only other balance sheet accounts are Common Stock, with a balance of $600,000 on June 30; and Retained Earnings, with a balance of $964,000 on June 30.

Check Net income, $71,680; Total assets, $2,686,400

Exercise 20-27^A

Merchandising: Computing budgeted cash payments for purchases **P4**

Check Budgeted purchases: August, $194,400; October, $157,200

Hardy Company's cost of goods sold is consistently 60% of sales. The company plans ending merchandise inventory for each month equal to 20% of the next month's budgeted cost of goods sold. All merchandise is purchased on credit, and 50% of the purchases made during a month is paid for in that month. Another 35% is paid for during the first month after purchase, and the remaining 15% is paid for during the second month after purchase. Expected sales are August (actual), $325,000; September (actual), $320,000; October (estimated), $250,000; and November (estimated), $310,000. Compute October's expected cash payments for purchases.

Exercise 20-28^A

Merchandising: Computing budgeted purchases and cost of goods sold

P4

Check June purchases, $1,540,000; June cost of goods sold, $1,390,000

Ahmed Company purchases all merchandise on credit. It recently budgeted the month-end accounts payable balances and merchandise inventory balances below. Cash payments on accounts payable during each month are expected to be May, $1,600,000; June, $1,490,000; July, $1,425,000; and August, $1,495,000. Use the available information to compute the budgeted amounts of (1) merchandise purchases for June, July, and August and (2) cost of goods sold for June, July, and August.

	Accounts Payable	Merchandise Inventory
May 31	$150,000	$250,000
June 30	200,000	400,000
July 31	235,000	300,000
August 31	195,000	330,000

Exercise 20-29^A

Merchandising: Computing budgeted accounts payable and purchases—sales forecast in dollars

P4

Check July purchases, $236,600; Sep. payments on accts. pay., $214,235

Big Sound, a merchandising company specializing in home computer speakers, budgets its monthly cost of goods sold to equal 70% of sales. Its inventory policy calls for ending inventory at the end of each month to equal 20% of the next month's budgeted cost of goods sold. All purchases are on credit, and 25% of the purchases in a month is paid for in the same month. Another 60% is paid for during the first month after purchase, and the remaining 15% is paid for in the second month after purchase. The following sales budgets are set: July, $350,000; August, $290,000; September, $320,000; October, $275,000; and November, $265,000.

Compute the following: (1) budgeted merchandise purchases for July, August, September, and October; (2) budgeted payments on accounts payable for September and October; and (3) budgeted ending balances of accounts payable for September and October. *Hint:* For part 1, refer to Exhibits 20A.2 and 20A.3 for guidance, but note that budgeted sales are in dollars for this assignment.

Exercise 20-30^A

Merchandising: Budgeted cash payments

P4

Hector Company reports the following sales and purchases data. Payments for purchases are made in the month after purchase. Selling expenses are 10% of sales, administrative expenses are 8% of sales, and both are paid in the month of sale. Rent expense of $7,400 is paid monthly. Depreciation expense is $2,300 per month. Prepare a schedule of budgeted cash payments for August and September.

	July	August	September
Sales	$50,000	$72,000	$66,000
Purchases	14,400	19,200	21,600

Exercise 20-31^A

Merchandising: Cash budget

P4

Castor, Inc., is preparing its master budget for the quarter ended June 30. Budgeted sales and cash payments for merchandise for the next three months follow.

Budgeted	April	May	June
Sales	$32,000	$40,000	$24,000
Cash payments for merchandise	20,200	16,800	17,200

Sales are 50% cash and 50% on credit. All credit sales are collected in the month following the sale. The March 31 balance sheet includes balances of $12,000 in cash, $12,000 in accounts receivable, $11,000 in accounts payable, and a $2,000 balance in loans payable. A minimum cash balance of $12,000 is required. Loans are obtained at the end of any month when a cash shortage occurs. Interest is 1% per month based on the beginning-of-the-month loan balance and is paid at each month-end. If an excess balance of cash exists, loans are repaid at the end of the month. Operating expenses are paid in the month incurred and include sales commissions (10% of sales), shipping (2% of sales), office salaries ($5,000 per month), and rent ($3,000 per month). Prepare a cash budget for each of the months of April, May, and June (round all dollar amounts to the nearest whole dollar).

Kelsey is preparing its master budget for the quarter ended September 30. Budgeted sales and cash payments for merchandise for the next three months follow.

Exercise 20-32^A
Merchandising: Cash budget
P4

Budgeted	July	August	September
Sales	$64,000	$80,000	$48,000
Cash payments for merchandise	40,400	33,600	34,400

Sales are 20% cash and 80% on credit. All credit sales are collected in the month following the sale. The June 30 balance sheet includes balances of $15,000 in cash; $45,000 in accounts receivable; $4,500 in accounts payable; and a $5,000 balance in loans payable. A minimum cash balance of $15,000 is required. Loans are obtained at the end of any month when a cash shortage occurs. Interest is 1% per month based on the beginning-of-the-month loan balance and is paid at each month-end. If an excess balance of cash exists, loans are repaid at the end of the month. Operating expenses are paid in the month incurred and consist of sales commissions (10% of sales), office salaries ($4,000 per month), and rent ($6,500 per month). (1) Prepare a cash receipts budget for July, August, and September. (2) Prepare a cash budget for each of the months of July, August, and September. (Round all dollar amounts to the nearest whole dollar.)

The following information is available for Zetrov Company.

a. The cash budget for March shows an ending bank loan of $10,000 and an ending cash balance of $50,000.

b. The sales budget for March indicates sales of $140,000. Accounts receivable are expected to be 70% of the current-month sales.

c. The merchandise purchases budget indicates that $89,000 in merchandise will be purchased on account in March. Purchases on account are paid 100% in the month following the purchase. Ending inventory for March is predicted to be 600 units at a cost of $35 each.

d. The budgeted income statement for March shows net income of $48,000. Depreciation expense of $1,000 and S26,000 in income tax expense were used in computing net income for March. Accrued taxes will be paid in April.

e. The balance sheet for February shows equipment of $84,000 with accumulated depreciation of $46,000, common stock of $25,000, and ending retained earnings of $8,000. There are no changes budgeted in the Equipment or Common Stock accounts.

Prepare a budgeted balance sheet at the end of March.

Exercise 20-33^A
Merchandising: Budgeted balance sheet
P3

Fortune, Inc., is preparing its master budget for the first quarter. The company sells a single product at a price of $25 per unit. Sales (in units) are forecasted at 45,000 for January, 55,000 for February, and 50,000 for March. Cost of goods sold is $14 per unit. Other expense information for the first quarter follows. Prepare a budgeted income statement for this first quarter. (Round expense amounts to the nearest dollar.)

Exercise 20-34
Budgeted income statement
P3

Commissions	8% of sales dollars	Rent	$14,000 per month
Advertising	15% of sales dollars	Office salaries	$75,000 per month
Interest	5% annually on a $250,000 note payable	Depreciation.........	$40,000 per month
Tax rate	30%		

Render Co. CPA is preparing activity-based budgets for 2019. The partners expect the firm to generate billable hours for the year as follows.

Exercise 20-35
Activity-based budgeting
A1

Data entry	2,200 hours	Tax.................	4,300 hours
Auditing.............	4,800 hours	Consulting.........	750 hours

The company pays $15 per hour to data-entry clerks, $30 per hour to audit personnel, $40 per hour to tax personnel, and $50 per hour to consulting personnel. Prepare a schedule of budgeted labor costs for 2019 using activity-based budgeting.

PROBLEM SET A

Problem 20-1A

Manufacturing:

Preparing production and manufacturing budgets

P1

Check   (1) Units manuf., 148,500

Black Diamond Company produces snow skis. Each ski requires 2 pounds of carbon fiber. The company's management predicts that 5,000 skis and 6,000 pounds of carbon fiber will be in inventory on June 30 of the current year and that 150,000 skis will be sold during the next (third) quarter. A set of two skis sells for $300. Management wants to end the third quarter with 3,500 skis and 4,000 pounds of carbon fiber in inventory. Carbon fiber can be purchased for $15 per pound. Each ski requires 0.5 hours of direct labor at $20 per hour. Variable overhead is applied at the rate of $8 per direct labor hour. The company budgets fixed overhead of $1,782,000 for the quarter.

Required

1. Prepare the third-quarter production budget for skis.
2. Prepare the third-quarter direct materials (carbon fiber) budget; include the dollar cost of purchases.
3. Prepare the direct labor budget for the third quarter.
4. Prepare the factory overhead budget for the third quarter.

Problem 20-2A

Manufacturing:

Cash budget

P2

Built-Tight is preparing its master budget for the quarter ended September 30. Budgeted sales and cash payments for product costs for the quarter follow.

	A	B	C	D
1		July	August	September
2	Budgeted sales	$64,000	$80,000	$48,000
3	Budgeted cash payments for			
4	Direct materials	16,160	13,440	13,760
5	Direct labor	4,040	3,360	3,440
6	Factory overhead	20,200	16,800	17,200

Sales are 20% cash and 80% on credit. All credit sales are collected in the month following the sale. The June 30 balance sheet includes balances of $15,000 in cash; $45,000 in accounts receivable; $4,500 in accounts payable; and a $5,000 balance in loans payable. A minimum cash balance of $15,000 is required. Loans are obtained at the end of any month when a cash shortage occurs. Interest is 1% per month based on the beginning-of-the-month loan balance and is paid at each month-end. If an excess balance of cash exists, loans are repaid at the end of the month. Operating expenses are paid in the month incurred and consist of sales commissions (10% of sales), office salaries ($4,000 per month), and rent ($6,500 per month).

1. Prepare a cash receipts budget for July, August, and September.
2. Prepare a cash budget for each of the months of July, August, and September. (Round amounts to the dollar.)

Problem 20-3A

Manufacturing:

Preparation and analysis of budgeted income statements

P3

Merline Manufacturing makes its product for $75 per unit and sells it for $150 per unit. The sales staff receives a 10% commission on the sale of each unit. Its December income statement follows.

MERLINE MANUFACTURING
Income Statement
For Month Ended December 31, 2019

Sales	$2,250,000
Cost of goods sold	1,125,000
Gross profit	1,125,000
Operating expenses	
Sales commissions (10%)	225,000
Advertising	250,000
Store rent	30,000
Administrative salaries	45,000
Depreciation—Office equipment	50,000
Other expenses	10,000
Total expenses	610,000
Net income	$ 515,000

Management expects December's results to be repeated in January, February, and March of 2020 without any changes in strategy. Management, however, has an alternative plan. It believes that unit sales will increase at a rate of 10% *each* month for the next three months (beginning with January) if the item's selling price is reduced to $125 per unit and advertising expenses are increased by 15% and remain at that level for all three months. The cost of its product will remain at $75 per unit, the sales staff will continue to earn a 10% commission, and the remaining expenses will stay the same.

Required

1. Prepare budgeted income statements for each of the months of January, February, and March that show the expected results from implementing the proposed changes. Use a three-column format, with one column for each month.

Check   (1) Budgeted net income: January, $196,250

Analysis Component

2. Is net income for March expected to increase with the proposed strategy changes?

The management of Zigby Manufacturing prepared the following estimated balance sheet for March 2019.

Problem 20-4A
Manufacturing:
Preparation of a complete master budget

P1   P2   P3

ZIGBY MANUFACTURING			
Estimated Balance Sheet			
March 31, 2019			
Assets		**Liabilities and Equity**	
Cash	$ 40,000	Accounts payable	$ 200,500
Accounts receivable	342,248	Short-term notes payable	12,000
Raw materials inventory	98,500	Total current liabilities	212,500
Finished goods inventory	325,540	Long-term note payable	500,000
Total current assets	806,288	Total liabilities	712,500
Equipment	600,000	Common stock	335,000
Accumulated depreciation.............	(150,000)	Retained earnings	208,788
Equipment, net......................	450,000	Total stockholders' equity	543,788
Total assets........................	$1,256,288	Total liabilities and equity	$1,256,288

To prepare a master budget for April, May, and June of 2019, management gathers the following information.

a. Sales for March total 20,500 units. Forecasted sales in units are as follows: April, 20,500; May, 19,500; June, 20,000; and July, 20,500. Sales of 240,000 units are forecasted for the entire year. The product's selling price is $23.85 per unit and its total product cost is $19.85 per unit.

b. Company policy calls for a given month's ending raw materials inventory to equal 50% of the next month's materials requirements. The March 31 raw materials inventory is 4,925 units, which complies with the policy. The expected June 30 ending raw materials inventory is 4,000 units. Raw materials cost $20 per unit. Each finished unit requires 0.50 units of raw materials.

c. Company policy calls for a given month's ending finished goods inventory to equal 80% of the next month's expected unit sales. The March 31 finished goods inventory is 16,400 units, which complies with the policy.

d. Each finished unit requires 0.50 hours of direct labor at a rate of $15 per hour.

e. Overhead is allocated based on direct labor hours. The predetermined variable overhead rate is $2.70 per direct labor hour. Depreciation of $20,000 per month is treated as fixed factory overhead.

f. Sales representatives' commissions are 8% of sales and are paid in the month of the sales. The sales manager's monthly salary is $3,000.

g. Monthly general and administrative expenses include $12,000 administrative salaries and 0.9% monthly interest on the long-term note payable.

h. The company expects 30% of sales to be for cash and the remaining 70% on credit. Receivables are collected in full in the month following the sale (none are collected in the month of the sale).

i. All raw materials purchases are on credit, and no payables arise from any other transactions. One month's raw materials purchases are fully paid in the next month.

j. The minimum ending cash balance for all months is $40,000. If necessary, the company borrows enough cash using a short-term note to reach the minimum. Short-term notes require an interest payment of 1% at each month-end (before any repayment). If the ending cash balance exceeds the minimum, the excess will be applied to repaying the short-term notes payable balance.

k. Dividends of $10,000 are to be declared and paid in May.

l. No cash payments for income taxes are to be made during the second calendar quarter. Income tax will be assessed at 35% in the quarter and paid in the third calendar quarter.

m. Equipment purchases of $130,000 are budgeted for the last day of June.

[continued on next page]

Required

Prepare the following budgets and other financial information as required. All budgets and other financial information should be prepared for the second calendar quarter, except as otherwise noted below. Round calculations up to the nearest whole dollar, except for the amount of cash sales, which should be rounded down to the nearest whole dollar.

1. Sales budget.
2. Production budget.
3. Raw materials budget.
4. Direct labor budget.
5. Factory overhead budget.
6. Selling expense budget.
7. General and administrative expense budget.
8. Cash budget.
9. Budgeted income statement for the entire second quarter (not for each month separately).
10. Budgeted balance sheet as of the end of the second calendar quarter.

Problem 20-5A[A]

Merchandising:
Preparation and analysis of purchases budgets

P4

Keggler's Supply is a merchandiser of three different products. The company's February 28 inventories are footwear, 20,000 units; sports equipment, 80,000 units; and apparel, 50,000 units. Management believes each of these inventories is too high. As a result, a new policy dictates that ending inventory in any month should equal 30% of the expected unit sales for the following month. Expected sales in units for March, April, May, and June follow.

	Budgeted Sales in Units			
	March	April	May	June
Footwear..................	15,000	25,000	32,000	35,000
Sports equipment	70,000	90,000	95,000	90,000
Apparel	40,000	38,000	37,000	25,000

Required

Prepare a merchandise purchases budget (in units) for each product for each of the months of March, April, and May.

Problem 20-6A[A]

Merchandising:
Preparation of cash budgets (for three periods)

P4

During the last week of August, Oneida Company's owner approaches the bank for a $100,000 loan to be made on September 2 and repaid on November 30 with annual interest of 12%, for an interest cost of $3,000. The owner plans to increase the store's inventory by $80,000 during September and needs the loan to pay for inventory acquisitions. The bank's loan officer needs more information about Oneida's ability to repay the loan and asks the owner to forecast the store's November 30 cash position. On September 1, Oneida is expected to have a $5,000 cash balance, $159,100 of net accounts receivable, and $125,000 of accounts payable. Its budgeted sales, merchandise purchases, and various cash payments for the next three months follow.

	A	B	C	D
1	**Budgeted Figures***	**September**	**October**	**November**
2	Sales	$250,000	$375,000	$400,000
3	Merchandise purchases	240,000	225,000	200,000
4	Cash payments			
5	Payroll	20,000	22,000	24,000
6	Rent	10,000	10,000	10,000
7	Other cash expenses	35,000	30,000	20,000
8	Repayment of bank loan			100,000
9	Interest on the bank loan			3,000

*Operations began in August; August sales were $215,000 and purchases were $125,000.

The budgeted September merchandise purchases include the inventory increase. All sales are on account. The company predicts that 25% of credit sales is collected in the month of the sale, 45% in the month following the sale, 20% in the second month, 9% in the third, and the remainder is uncollectible. Applying these percents to the August credit sales, for example, shows that $96,750 of the $215,000 will be collected in September, $43,000 in October, and $19,350 in November. All merchandise is purchased on credit; 80% of the balance is paid in the month following a purchase, and the remaining 20% is paid in the second month. For example, of the $125,000 August purchases, $100,000 will be paid in September and $25,000 in October.

Required

Prepare a cash budget for September, October, and November. Show supporting calculations as needed.

Check   Budgeted cash balance: September, $99,250

Aztec Company sells its product for $180 per unit. Its actual and budgeted sales follow.

	Units	Dollars
April (actual)	4,000	$ 720,000
May (actual).................	2,000	360,000
June (budgeted)	6,000	1,080,000
July (budgeted).............	5,000	900,000
August (budgeted)	3,800	684,000

All sales are on credit. Recent experience shows that 20% of credit sales is collected in the month of the sale, 50% in the month after the sale, 28% in the second month after the sale, and 2% proves to be uncollectible. The product's purchase price is $110 per unit. 60% of purchases made in a month is paid in that month and the other 40% is paid in the next month. The company has a policy to maintain an ending monthly inventory of 20% of the next month's unit sales plus a safety stock of 100 units. The April 30 and May 31 actual inventory levels are consistent with this policy. Selling and administrative expenses for the year are $1,320,000 and are paid evenly throughout the year in cash. The company's minimum cash balance at month-end is $100,000. This minimum is maintained, if necessary, by borrowing cash from the bank. If the balance exceeds $100,000, the company repays as much of the loan as it can without going below the minimum. This type of loan carries an annual 12% interest rate. On May 31, the loan balance is $25,000, and the company's cash balance is $100,000. (Round amounts to the nearest dollar.)

Required

1. Prepare a schedule that shows the computation of cash collections of its credit sales (accounts receivable) in each of the months of June and July.
2. Prepare a schedule that shows the computation of budgeted ending inventories (in units) for April, May, June, and July.
3. Prepare the merchandise purchases budget for May, June, and July. Report calculations in units and then show the dollar amount of purchases for each month.
4. Prepare a schedule showing the computation of cash payments for product purchases for June and July.
5. Prepare a cash budget for June and July, including any loan activity and interest expense. Compute the loan balance at the end of each month.

Problem 20-7A[A]
Merchandising:
Preparation and analysis of cash budgets with supporting inventory and purchases budgets

P4

Check   (1) Cash collections: June, $597,600; July, $820,800

(3) Budgeted purchases: May, $308,000; June, $638,000

(5) Budgeted ending loan balance: June, $43,650; July, $0

Near the end of 2019, the management of Dimsdale Sports Co., a merchandising company, prepared the following estimated balance sheet for December 31, 2019.

Problem 20-8A[A]
Merchandising:
Preparation of a complete master budget   **P4**

DIMSDALE SPORTS COMPANY					
Estimated Balance Sheet					
December 31, 2019					
Assets			**Liabilities and Equity**		
Cash	$ 36,000		Accounts payable	$360,000	
Accounts receivable	525,000		Bank loan payable	15,000	
Inventory	150,000		Taxes payable (due 3/15/2020) ...	90,000	
Total current assets		$ 711,000	Total liabilities		$ 465,000
Equipment	540,000		Common stock	472,500	
Less: Accumulated depreciation ...	67,500		Retained earnings	246,000	
Equipment, net...............		472,500	Total stockholders' equity		718,500
Total assets		$1,183,500	Total liabilities and equity		$1,183,500

To prepare a master budget for January, February, and March of 2020, management gathers the following information.

a. The company's single product is purchased for $30 per unit and resold for $55 per unit. The expected inventory level of 5,000 units on December 31, 2019, is more than management's desired level, which is 20% of the next month's expected sales (in units). Expected sales are January, 7,000 units; February, 9,000 units; March, 11,000 units; and April, 10,000 units.

b. Cash sales and credit sales represent 25% and 75%, respectively, of total sales. Of the credit sales, 60% is collected in the first month after the month of sale and 40% in the second month after the month of sale. For the December 31, 2019, accounts receivable balance, $125,000 is collected in January 2020 and the remaining $400,000 is collected in February 2020.

c. Merchandise purchases are paid for as follows: 20% in the first month after the month of purchase and 80% in the second month after the month of purchase. For the December 31, 2019, accounts payable balance, $80,000 is paid in January 2020 and the remaining $280,000 is paid in February 2020.

d. Sales commissions equal to 20% of sales are paid each month. Sales salaries (excluding commissions) are $60,000 per year.

e. General and administrative salaries are $144,000 per year. Maintenance expense equals $2,000 per month and is paid in cash.

f. Equipment reported in the December 31, 2019, balance sheet was purchased in January 2019. It is being depreciated over eight years under the straight-line method with no salvage value. The following amounts for new equipment purchases are planned in the coming quarter: January, $36,000; February, $96,000; and March, $28,800. This equipment will be depreciated under the straight-line method over eight years with no salvage value. A full month's depreciation is taken for the month in which equipment is purchased.

g. The company plans to buy land at the end of March at a cost of $150,000, which will be paid with cash on the last day of the month.

h. The company has a working arrangement with its bank to obtain additional loans as needed. The interest rate is 12% per year, and interest is paid at each month-end based on the beginning balance. Partial or full payments on these loans can be made on the last day of the month. The company has agreed to maintain a minimum ending cash balance of $25,000 at the end of each month.

i. The income tax rate for the company is 40%. Income taxes on the first quarter's income will not be paid until April 15.

Required

Prepare a master budget for each of the first three months of 2020; include the following component budgets (show supporting calculations as needed, and round amounts to the nearest dollar).

1. Monthly sales budgets (showing both budgeted unit sales and dollar sales).

2. Monthly merchandise purchases budgets.

3. Monthly selling expense budgets.

4. Monthly general and administrative expense budgets.

5. Monthly capital expenditures budgets.

6. Monthly cash budgets.

7. Budgeted income statement for the entire first quarter (not for each month).

8. Budgeted balance sheet as of March 31, 2020.

Check (2) Budgeted purchases: January, $114,000; February, $282,000
(3) Budgeted selling expenses: January, $82,000; February, $104,000
(6) Ending cash bal.: January, $30,100; February, $210,300
(8) Budgeted total assets at March 31, $1,568,650

PROBLEM SET B

Problem 20-1B
Manufacturing:
Preparing production and manufacturing budgets

P1

Check (1) Units manuf., 248,000

NSA Company produces baseball bats. Each bat requires 3 pounds of aluminum alloy. Management predicts that 8,000 bats and 15,000 pounds of aluminum alloy will be in inventory on March 31 of the current year and that 250,000 bats will be sold during this year's second quarter. Bats sell for $80 each. Management wants to end the second quarter with 6,000 finished bats and 12,000 pounds of aluminum alloy in inventory. Aluminum alloy can be purchased for $4 per pound. Each bat requires 0.5 hours of direct labor at $18 per hour. Variable overhead is applied at the rate of $12 per direct labor hour. The company budgets fixed overhead of $1,776,000 for the quarter.

Required

1. Prepare the second-quarter production budget for bats.

2. Prepare the second-quarter direct materials (aluminum alloy) budget; include the dollar cost of purchases.

[continued on next page]

3. Prepare the direct labor budget for the second quarter.

4. Prepare the factory overhead budget for the second quarter.

A1 Manufacturing is preparing its master budget for the quarter ended September 30. Budgeted sales and cash payments for product costs for the quarter follow.

Problem 20-2B
Manufacturing:
Cash budget

P2

	A	B	C	D
1		July	August	September
2	Budgeted sales	$63,400	$80,600	$48,600
3	Budgeted cash payments for			
4	Direct materials	12,480	9,900	10,140
5	Direct labor	10,400	8,250	8,450
6	Factory overhead	18,720	14,850	15,210

Sales are 20% cash and 80% on credit. All credit sales are collected in the month following the sale. The June 30 balance sheet includes balances of $12,900 in cash; $47,000 in accounts receivable; $5,100 in accounts payable; and a $2,600 balance in loans payable. A minimum cash balance of $12,600 is required. Loans are obtained at the end of any month when a cash shortage occurs. Interest is 1% per month based on the beginning-of-the-month loan balance and is paid at each month-end. If an excess balance of cash exists, loans are repaid at the end of the month. Operating expenses are paid in the month incurred and consist of sales commissions (10% of sales), office salaries ($4,600 per month), and rent ($7,100 per month).

1. Prepare a cash receipts budget for July, August, and September.

2. Prepare a cash budget for each of the months of July, August, and September. (Round amounts to the dollar.)

HCS MFG. makes its product for $60 per unit and sells it for $130 per unit. The sales staff receives a commission of 10% of dollar sales. Its June income statement follows.

Problem 20-3B
Manufacturing:
Preparation and analysis of budgeted income statements

P3

HCS MFG.	
Income Statement	
For Month Ended June 30, 2019	
Sales	$1,300,000
Cost of goods sold	600,000
Gross profit	700,000
Operating expenses	
Sales commissions (10%)	130,000
Advertising	200,000
Store rent	24,000
Administrative salaries	40,000
Depreciation—Office equipment	50,000
Other expenses	12,000
Total expenses	456,000
Net income	$ 244,000

Management expects June's results to be repeated in July, August, and September without any changes in strategy. Management, however, has another plan. It believes that unit sales will increase at a rate of 10% *each* month for the next three months (beginning with July) if the item's selling price is reduced to $115 per unit and advertising expenses are increased by 25% and remain at that level for all three months. The cost of its product will remain at $60 per unit, the sales staff will continue to earn a 10% commission, and the remaining expenses will stay the same.

Required

1. Prepare budgeted income statements for each of the months of July, August, and September that show the expected results from implementing the proposed changes. Use a three-column format, with one column for each month.

Check Budgeted net income: July, $102,500

Analysis Component

2. Use the budgeted income statements from part 1 to recommend whether management should implement the proposed plan. Explain.

Problem 20-4B
Manufacturing:
Preparation of a complete
master budget

P1   P2   P3

The management of Nabar Manufacturing prepared the following estimated balance sheet for June 2019.

NABAR MANUFACTURING				
Estimated Balance Sheet				
June 30, 2019				
Assets			**Liabilities and Equity**	
Cash	$ 40,000		Accounts payable	$ 51,400
Accounts receivable	249,900		Income taxes payable	10,000
Raw materials inventory	35,000		Short-term notes payable	24,000
Finished goods inventory	241,080		Total current liabilities	85,400
Total current assets	565,980		Long-term note payable	300,000
Equipment	720,000		Total liabilities	385,400
Accumulated depreciation	(240,000)		Common stock	600,000
Equipment, net	480,000		Retained earnings	60,580
			Total stockholders' equity	660,580
Total assets	$1,045,980		Total liabilities and equity	$1,045,980

To prepare a master budget for July, August, and September of 2019, management gathers the following information.

a. Sales were 20,000 units in June. Forecasted sales in units are as follows: July, 21,000; August, 19,000; September, 20,000; and October, 24,000. The product's selling price is $17 per unit and its total product cost is $14.35 per unit.

b. Company policy calls for a given month's ending finished goods inventory to equal 70% of the next month's expected unit sales. The June 30 finished goods inventory is 16,800 units, which does not comply with the policy.

c. Company policy calls for a given month's ending raw materials inventory to equal 20% of the next month's materials requirements. The June 30 raw materials inventory is 4,375 units (which also fails to meet the policy). The budgeted September 30 raw materials inventory is 1,980 units. Raw materials cost $8 per unit. Each finished unit requires 0.50 units of raw materials.

d. Each finished unit requires 0.50 hours of direct labor at a rate of $16 per hour.

e. Overhead is allocated based on direct labor hours. The predetermined variable overhead rate is $2.70 per direct labor hour. Depreciation of $20,000 per month is treated as fixed factory overhead.

f. Monthly general and administrative expenses include $9,000 administrative salaries and 0.9% monthly interest on the long-term note payable.

g. Sales representatives' commissions are 10% of sales and are paid in the month of the sales. The sales manager's monthly salary is $3,500.

h. The company expects 30% of sales to be for cash and the remaining 70% on credit. Receivables are collected in full in the month following the sale (none are collected in the month of the sale).

i. All raw materials purchases are on credit, and no payables arise from any other transactions. One month's raw materials purchases are fully paid in the next month.

j. Dividends of $20,000 are to be declared and paid in August.

k. Income taxes payable at June 30 will be paid in July. Income tax expense will be assessed at 35% in the quarter and paid in October.

l. Equipment purchases of $100,000 are budgeted for the last day of September.

m. The minimum ending cash balance for all months is $40,000. If necessary, the company borrows enough cash using a short-term note to reach the minimum. Short-term notes require an interest payment of 1% at each month-end (before any repayment). If the ending cash balance exceeds the minimum, the excess will be applied to repaying the short-term notes payable balance.

Required

Prepare the following budgets and other financial information as required. All budgets and other financial information should be prepared for the third calendar quarter, except as otherwise noted below. Round calculations to the nearest whole dollar.

Check   (2) Units to produce:
July, 17,500; August, 19,700
(3) Cost of raw materials
purchases: July, $50,760
(5) Total overhead cost:
August, $46,595
(8) Ending cash balance: July,
$96,835; August, $141,180
(10) Budgeted total assets:
Sep. 30, $1,054,920

1. Sales budget.
2. Production budget.
3. Raw materials budget.
4. Direct labor budget.
5. Factory overhead budget.
6. Selling expense budget.

7. General and administrative expense budget.
8. Cash budget.
9. Budgeted income statement for the entire quarter (not for each month separately).
10. Budgeted balance sheet as of September 30, 2019.

H20 Sports is a merchandiser of three different products. The company's March 31 inventories are water skis, 40,000 units; tow ropes, 90,000 units; and life jackets, 150,000 units. Management believes inventory levels are too high for all three products. As a result, a new policy dictates that ending inventory in any month should equal 10% of the expected unit sales for the following month. Expected sales in units for April, May, June, and July follow.

Problem 20-5B[A]
Merchandising:
Preparation and analysis of purchases budgets

P4

	Budgeted Sales in Units			
	April	May	June	July
Water skis	70,000	90,000	130,000	100,000
Tow ropes	100,000	90,000	110,000	100,000
Life jackets	160,000	190,000	200,000	120,000

Required

1. Prepare a merchandise purchases budget (in units) for each product for each of the months of April, May, and June.

Analysis Component

2. What business conditions might lead to inventory levels becoming too high?

Check   (1) April budgeted purchases: Water skis, 39,000; Tow ropes, 19,000; Life jackets, 29,000

During the last week of March, Sony Stereo's owner approaches the bank for an $80,000 loan to be made on April 1 and repaid on June 30 with annual interest of 12%, for an interest cost of $2,400. The owner plans to increase the store's inventory by $60,000 in April and needs the loan to pay for inventory acquisitions. The bank's loan officer needs more information about Sony Stereo's ability to repay the loan and asks the owner to forecast the store's June 30 cash position. On April 1, Sony Stereo is expected to have a $3,000 cash balance, $135,000 of accounts receivable, and $100,000 of accounts payable. Its budgeted sales, merchandise purchases, and various cash payments for the next three months follow.

Problem 20-6B[A]
Merchandising:
Preparation of cash budgets (for three periods)

P4

	A	B	C	D
1	Budgeted Figures*	April	May	June
2	Sales	$220,000	$300,000	$380,000
3	Merchandise purchases	210,000	180,000	220,000
4	Cash payments			
5	Payroll	16,000	17,000	18,000
6	Rent	6,000	6,000	6,000
7	Other cash expenses	64,000	8,000	7,000
8	Repayment of bank loan			80,000
9	Interest on bank loan			2,400

*Operations began in March; March sales were $180,000 and purchases were $100,000.

The budgeted April merchandise purchases include the inventory increase. All sales are on account. The company predicts that 25% of credit sales is collected in the month of the sale, 45% in the month following the sale, 20% in the second month, 9% in the third, and the remainder is uncollectible. Applying these percents to the March credit sales, for example, shows that $81,000 of the $180,000 will be collected in April, $36,000 in May, and $16,200 in June. All merchandise is purchased on credit; 80% of the balance is paid in the month following a purchase, and the remaining 20% is paid in the second month. For example, of the $100,000 March purchases, $80,000 will be paid in April and $20,000 in May.

Required

Prepare a cash budget for April, May, and June. Show supporting calculations as needed.

Check   Budgeted cash balance: April, $53,000

Connick Company sells its product for $22 per unit. Its actual and budgeted sales follow.

Problem 20-7B[A]
Merchandising:
Preparation and analysis of cash budgets with supporting inventory and purchases budgets

P4

	Units	Dollars
January (actual)	18,000	$396,000
February (actual)	22,500	495,000
March (budgeted)	19,000	418,000
April (budgeted)	18,750	412,500
May (budgeted)	21,000	462,000

All sales are on credit. Recent experience shows that 40% of credit sales is collected in the month of the sale, 35% in the month after the sale, 23% in the second month after the sale, and 2% proves to be uncollectible. The product's purchase price is $12 per unit. Of purchases made in a month, 30% is paid in that month and the other 70% is paid in the next month. The company has a policy to maintain an ending monthly inventory of 20% of the next month's unit sales plus a safety stock of 100 units. The January 31 and February 28 actual inventory levels are consistent with this policy. Selling and administrative expenses for the year are $1,920,000 and are paid evenly throughout the year in cash. The company's minimum cash balance for month-end is $50,000. This minimum is maintained, if necessary, by borrowing cash from the bank. If the balance exceeds $50,000, the company repays as much of the loan as it can without going below the minimum. This type of loan carries an annual 12% interest rate. At February 28, the loan balance is $12,000, and the company's cash balance is $50,000.

Required

Check (1) Cash collections:
March, $431,530;
April, $425,150

1. Prepare a schedule that shows the computation of cash collections of its credit sales (accounts receivable) in each of the months of March and April.

2. Prepare a schedule showing the computations of budgeted ending inventories (in units) for January, February, March, and April.

(3) Budgeted purchases:
February, $261,600;
March, $227,400

3. Prepare the merchandise purchases budget for February, March, and April. Report calculations in units and then show the dollar amount of purchases for each month.

4. Prepare a schedule showing the computation of cash payments on product purchases for March and April.

(5) Ending cash balance:
March, $58,070; April, $94,920

5. Prepare a cash budget for March and April, including any loan activity and interest expense. Compute the loan balance at the end of each month.

Analysis Component

6. Refer to your answer to part 5. The cash budget indicates whether the company must borrow additional funds at the end of March. Suggest some reasons that knowing the loan needs in advance would be helpful to management.

Problem 20-8B[A]

Merchandising: Preparation of a complete master budget

P4

Near the end of 2019, the management of Isle Corp., a merchandising company, prepared the following estimated balance sheet for December 31, 2019.

ISLE CORPORATION
Estimated Balance Sheet
December 31, 2019

Assets			Liabilities and Equity		
Cash	$ 36,000		Accounts payable	$360,000	
Accounts receivable	525,000		Bank loan payable	15,000	
Inventory	150,000		Taxes payable (due 3/15/2020)	90,000	
Total current assets		$ 711,000	Total liabilities		$ 465,000
Equipment	540,000		Common stock	472,500	
Less: Accumulated depreciation	67,500		Retained earnings	246,000	
Equipment, net...............		472,500	Total stockholders' equity		718,500
Total assets		$1,183,500	Total liabilities and equity		$1,183,500

To prepare a master budget for January, February, and March of 2020, management gathers the following information.

a. The company's single product is purchased for $30 per unit and resold for $45 per unit. The expected inventory level of 5,000 units on December 31, 2019, is more than management's desired level for 2020, which is 25% of the next month's expected sales (in units). Expected sales are January, 6,000 units; February, 8,000 units; March, 10,000 units; and April, 9,000 units.

b. Cash sales and credit sales represent 25% and 75%, respectively, of total sales. Of the credit sales, 60% is collected in the first month after the month of sale and 40% in the second month after the month of sale. For the $525,000 accounts receivable balance at December 31, 2019, $315,000 is collected in January 2020 and the remaining $210,000 is collected in February 2020.

c. Merchandise purchases are paid for as follows: 20% in the first month after the month of purchase and 80% in the second month after the month of purchase. For the $360,000 accounts payable balance at December 31, 2019, $72,000 is paid in January 2020 and the remaining $288,000 is paid in February 2020.

d. Sales commissions equal to 20% of sales dollars are paid each month. Sales salaries (excluding commissions) are $90,000 per year.

e. General and administrative salaries are $144,000 per year. Maintenance expense equals $3,000 per month and is paid in cash.

f. Equipment reported in the December 31, 2019, balance sheet was purchased in January 2019. It is being depreciated over eight years under the straight-line method with no salvage value. The following amounts for new equipment purchases are planned in the coming quarter: January, $72,000; February, $96,000; and March, $28,800. This equipment will be depreciated using the straight-line method over eight years with no salvage value. A full month's depreciation is taken for the month in which equipment is purchased.

g. The company plans to buy land at the end of March at a cost of $150,000, which will be paid with cash on the last day of the month.

h. The company has a contract with its bank to obtain additional loans as needed. The interest rate is 12% per year, and interest is paid at each month-end based on the beginning balance. Partial or full payments on these loans are made on the last day of the month. The company has agreed to maintain a minimum ending cash balance of $36,000 at the end of each month.

i. The income tax rate for the company is 40%. Income taxes on the first quarter's income will not be paid until April 15.

Required

Prepare a master budget for each of the first three months of 2020; include the following component budgets (show supporting calculations as needed, and round amounts to the nearest dollar).

1. Monthly sales budgets (showing both budgeted unit sales and dollar sales).

2. Monthly merchandise purchases budgets.

3. Monthly selling expense budgets.

4. Monthly general and administrative expense budgets.

5. Monthly capital expenditures budgets.

6. Monthly cash budgets.

7. Budgeted income statement for the entire first quarter (not for each month).

8. Budgeted balance sheet as of March 31, 2020.

Check   (2) Budgeted purchases: January, $90,000; February, $255,000
(3) Budgeted selling expenses: January, $61,500; February, $79,500
(6) Ending cash bal.: January, $182,850; February, $107,850
(8) Budgeted total assets at March 31, $1,346,875

This serial problem began in Chapter 1 and continues through most of the book. If previous chapter segments were not completed, the serial problem can begin at this point.

SERIAL PROBLEM
Business Solutions

P3

©Alexander Image/Shutterstock

SP 20   Santana Rey expects second-quarter 2020 sales of **Business Solutions**'s line of computer furniture to be the same as the first quarter's sales (reported below) without any changes in strategy. Monthly sales averaged 40 desk units (sales price of $1,250) and 20 chairs (sales price of $500).

BUSINESS SOLUTIONS—Computer Furniture Segment Segment Income Statement* For Quarter Ended March 31, 2020	
Sales[†]	$180,000
Cost of goods sold[‡]	115,000
Gross profit	65,000
Expenses	
Sales commissions (10%)	18,000
Advertising expenses	9,000
Other fixed expenses	18,000
Total expenses	45,000
Net income	$ 20,000

*Reflects revenue and expense activity only related to the computer furniture segment.
[†] Revenue: (120 desks × $1,250) + (60 chairs × $500) = $150,000 + $30,000 = $180,000.
[‡] Cost of goods sold: (120 desks × $750) + (60 chairs × $250) + $10,000 = $115,000.

Santana Rey believes that sales will increase each month for the next three months (April, 48 desks, 32 chairs; May, 52 desks, 35 chairs; June, 56 desks, 38 chairs) *if* selling prices are reduced to $1,150 for desks and $450 for chairs and advertising expenses are increased by 10% and remain at that level for all three months. The products' variable cost will remain at $750 for desks and $250 for chairs. The sales staff will continue to earn a 10% commission, the fixed manufacturing costs per month will remain at $10,000, and other fixed expenses will remain at $6,000 per month.

Required

Check (1) Budgeted income (loss): April, $(660); May, $945

1. Prepare budgeted income statements for the computer furniture segment for each of the months of April, May, and June that show the expected results from implementing the proposed changes. Use a three-column format, with one column for each month.

2. Use the budgeted income statements from part 1 to recommend whether Santana Rey should implement the proposed changes.

Accounting Analysis

COMPANY ANALYSIS

P3

APPLE

AA 20-1 Financial statements often serve as a starting point in formulating budgets. Review **Apple**'s financial statements in Appendix A to determine its cash paid for acquisitions of property, plant, and equipment.

Required

1. Which financial statement reports the amount of cash paid for acquisitions of property, plant, and equipment? In which section (operating, investing, or financing) of this statement is the information reported?

2. Indicate the amount of cash paid for acquisitions of property and equipment in the year ended September 30, 2017.

COMPARATIVE ANALYSIS

P1

APPLE

GOOGLE

AA 20-2 Companies often budget selling expenses and general and administrative expenses (SGA) as a percentage of expected sales.

Required

1. For both **Apple** and **Google**, list sales (in dollars) and *total* selling expenses and general and administrative expenses (in dollars) for the 2017 and 2016 fiscal years. Use the financial statements in Appendix A.

2. Compute each company's ratio of *total* selling expenses and general and administrative expenses to sales for the 2017 and 2016 fiscal years.

3. Which company (Apple or Google) spends more, as a percent of sales, on selling, general, and administrative expenses?

GLOBAL ANALYSIS

P2

Samsung

APPLE

AA 20-3 Access **Samsung**'s and **Apple**'s income statements (in Appendix A) for fiscal year 2017. The ratio of investments in property, plant, and equipment to sales can be used to assess how much a company is investing to maintain and expand its productive capacity.

Required

1. Compute Samsung's ratio of investments in property, plant, and equipment to sales for 2017.

2. Compute Apple's ratio of investments in property, plant, and equipment to sales for fiscal 2017.

3. Drawing on the answers to parts 1 and 2, which company (Samsung or Apple) invested more (as a percent of sales) in property, plant, and equipment?

4. Assume Samsung forecasts total sales of 24,000,000 for 2018 and plans to invest 18% of 2018 forecasted sales in property, plant, and equipment. What amount will Samsung budget for investments in property, plant, and equipment for 2018? Forecasts and budgets are all in millions of Korean won.

Beyond the Numbers

ETHICS CHALLENGE

C1

BTN 20-1 The budget process and budgets themselves can impact management actions, both positively and negatively. For instance, a common practice among not-for-profit organizations and government agencies is for management to spend any amounts remaining in a budget at the end of the budget period, a practice often called "use it or lose it." The view is that if a department manager does not spend the budgeted amount, top management will reduce next year's budget by the amount not spent. To avoid losing budget dollars, department managers often spend all budgeted amounts regardless of the value added to products or services. All of us pay for the costs associated with this budget system.

Required

Write a half-page report to a local not-for-profit organization or government agency offering a solution to the "use it or lose it" budgeting problem.

BTN 20-2   The sales budget is usually the first and most crucial of the component budgets in a master budget because all other budgets usually rely on it for planning purposes.

COMMUNICATING IN PRACTICE

C1

Required

Assume that your company's sales staff provides information on expected sales and selling prices for items making up the sales budget. Prepare a one-page memorandum to your supervisor outlining concerns with the sales staff's input in the sales budget when its compensation is at least partly tied to these budgets. More generally, explain the importance of assessing any potential bias in information provided to the budget process.

BTN 20-3   Certified Management Accountants must understand budgeting. Access the **Institute of Management Accountants** website (**imanet.org**), click on the "CMA Certification" tab, and select "Taking the Exam." Scroll down and select "Review the Most Recent Content Specifications Outline."

TAKING IT TO THE NET

C1

Required

1. List the budgeting methodologies that are covered on the CMA exam.
2. List the types of budgets ("annual profit plans") covered on the CMA exam.

BTN 20-4   Your team is to prepare a budget report outlining the costs of attending college (full-time) for the next two semesters (30 hours) or three quarters (45 hours). This budget's focus is solely on attending college; do not include personal items in the team's budget. Your budget must include tuition, books, supplies, club fees, food, housing, and all costs associated with travel to and from college. This budgeting exercise is similar to the initial phase in activity-based budgeting. Include a list of any assumptions you use in completing the budget. Be prepared to present your budget in class.

TEAMWORK IN ACTION

A1

BTN 20-5   **Misfit Juicery** sells juice made from misshapen and scrap fruit and vegetables. Co-founders Anna Yang and Phil Wong stress the importance of planning and budgeting for business success.

ENTREPRENEURIAL DECISION

C1

Required

1. How can budgeting help Anna and Phil efficiently develop and operate their business?
2. Anna and Phil hope to expand their business. How can a budget be useful in expanding a business's operations?

BTN 20-6   To help understand the factors impacting a sales budget, you are to visit three businesses with the same ownership or franchise membership. Record the selling prices of two identical products at each location, such as regular and premium gas sold at gas stations. You are likely to find a difference in prices for at least one of the three locations you visit.

HITTING THE ROAD

P1

Required

1. Identify at least three external factors that must be considered when setting the sales budget. *Note:* There is a difference between internal and external factors that impact the sales budget.
2. What factors might explain any differences identified in the prices of the businesses you visited?

---

21 Flexible Budgets and Standard Costs

Chapter Preview

FIXED AND FLEXIBLE BUDGETS

Fixed budget reports

Evaluation focus

P1 Flexible budget reports

NTK 21-1

STANDARD COSTING

C1 Standard costs

Setting standard costs

P2 Cost variance analysis

NTK 21-2

MATERIALS AND LABOR VARIANCES

Price variance

Quantity variance

P3 Materials variances

Labor variances

NTK 21-3, 21-4

OVERHEAD STANDARDS AND VARIANCES

Flexible overhead budget

Standard overhead rate

P4 Overhead variances

Analyzing

A1 Sales variances

NTK 21-5

Learning Objectives

CONCEPTUAL

C1 Define *standard costs* and explain how standard cost information is useful for management by exception.

ANALYTICAL

A1 Analyze changes in sales from expected amounts.

PROCEDURAL

P1 Prepare a flexible budget and interpret a flexible budget performance report.

P2 Compute the total cost variance.

P3 Compute materials and labor variances.

P4 Compute overhead controllable and volume variances.

P5 *Appendix 21A*—Compute overhead spending and efficiency variances.

P6 *Appendix 21A*—Prepare journal entries for standard costs and account for price and quantity variances.

Up and Away

"Take the risk!"—**JEN RUBIO**

New York—"The idea for Away came about when I was traveling and my suitcase broke," recalls Jen Rubio. "I called my most well-traveled friends and none of them could recommend a decent option to replace it, so my co-founder Steph Korey and I decided to look into why that was, and whether or not we could fix it." Their company, **Away** (**AwayTravel.com**), has seen its sales for luggage soar.

"We interviewed hundreds of travelers to find out more about how they actually traveled," explains Steph. "We asked them to tell us what bothered them most about the experience and then designed luggage with thoughtful features so that we could solve problems travelers face."

"We obsessed over every detail," says Jen. "We set incredibly high standards." Away uses only quality materials—"best in the world" wheels and zippers, and a lightweight but strong shell. Jen and Steph also determined how long it takes to make each bag in developing labor and overhead standards.

"We keep costs for the customer low with our direct-to-consumer model," explains Steph. Away focuses on *variances* between actual and expected costs. Manufacturers like Away use standard costs to set budgets and control costs.

Away has already sold more than 300,000 suitcases. When production booms, budgets can become outdated. *Flexible*

©Away

budgets, which reflect budgeted costs at different production levels, are then used to analyze results and control costs.

Although budgeting, standard costs, and variances are crucial, Jen and Steph tell entrepreneurs to be passionate and "take thoughtful risks."

Sources: *Away website,* January 2019; *Money.cnn.com,* October 24, 2017; *Createcultivate.com,* January 23, 2017; *Travelandleisure.com,* March 9, 2017; *Fastcodesign.com,* September 11, 2017

FIXED AND FLEXIBLE BUDGETS

Managers use budgets to control operations and see that planned objectives are met. **Budget reports** compare budgeted results to actual results. Budget reports are progress reports, or *report cards,* on management's performance in achieving planned objectives. These reports can be prepared at any time and for any period. Three common periods for a budget report are a month, quarter, and year.

Point: Budget reports are often used to determine bonuses of managers.

From the previous chapter, a *master budget* is based on a predicted level of activity, such as sales volume, for the budget period. In preparing a master budget, two alternative approaches can be used: *fixed budgeting* or *flexible budgeting.*

- A **fixed budget,** also called a *static budget,* is based on a single predicted amount of sales or other activity measure.
- A **flexible budget,** also called a *variable budget,* is based on several different amounts of sales or other activity measure.

Exhibit 21.1 shows fixed and flexible budgets for a guitar manufacturer.

Fixed Budget (One activity level)	
Sales (in units)............	100
Sales (in dollars)...........	$80,000
Costs..................	56,000
Net income..............	$24,000

Flexible Budget (Several activity levels)			
Sales (in units)............	100	120	140
Sales (in dollars).........	$80,000	$96,000	$112,000
Costs..................	56,000	67,200	78,400
Net income..............	$24,000	$28,800	$ 33,600

EXHIBIT 21.1

Fixed versus Flexible Budgets (condensed)

Exhibit 21.1 shows that the guitar maker forecasts $24,000 of net income if it sells 100 guitars. Only if exactly 100 guitars are sold will the fixed budget be useful in evaluating how well the company controlled costs. A flexible budget can be prepared for any sales level (three are shown in Exhibit 21.1). It is more useful when the actual number of units sold differs from the predicted level of unit sales.

We next look at fixed budget reports. Knowing the limitations of such reports helps us see the benefits of flexible budgets.

Fixed Budget Reports

One use of a budget is to compare actual results with planned activities. Information for this analysis is often presented in a *performance report* that shows budgeted amounts, actual amounts, and **variances** (differences between budgeted and actual amounts). In a fixed budget, the master budget is based on a *single prediction* for sales volume, and the budgeted amount for each cost essentially assumes this specific (or *fixed*) amount of sales will occur.

We illustrate fixed budget performance reports with SolCel, which manufactures portable solar cell phone chargers and related supplies. For January 2019, SolCel based its fixed budget on a prediction of 10,000 (composite) units of sales; costs also were budgeted based on 10,000 composite units of sales.

Fixed Budget Performance Report   Exhibit 21.2 shows a **fixed budget performance report,** a report that compares actual results with the results expected under a fixed budget. SolCel's actual sales for the period were 12,000 composite units. In addition, SolCel produced 12,000 composite units during the period (meaning its inventory level did not change). The final column in the performance report shows the differences (variances) between the budgeted and actual dollar amounts for each budget item.

EXHIBIT 21.2

Fixed Budget Performance Report

SOLCEL Fixed Budget Performance Report For Month Ended January 31, 2019	Fixed Budget	Actual Results	Variances*
Sales (in units).....................	**10,000**	**12,000**	
Sales (in dollars)	$100,000	$125,000	$25,000 F
Cost of goods sold			
Direct materials	10,000	13,000	3,000 U
Direct labor.....................	15,000	20,000	5,000 U
Overhead			
Factory supplies.....................	2,000	2,100	100 U
Utilities.....................	3,000	4,000	1,000 U
Depreciation—Machinery	8,000	8,000	0
Supervisory salaries.....................	11,000	11,000	0
Selling expenses			
Sales commissions.....................	9,000	10,800	1,800 U
Shipping expenses.....................	4,000	4,300	300 U
General and administrative expenses			
Office supplies	5,000	5,200	200 U
Insurance expenses.....................	1,000	1,200	200 U
Depreciation—Office equipment.....................	7,000	7,000	0
Administrative salaries.....................	13,000	13,000	0
Total expenses	88,000	99,600	11,600 U
Income from operations.....................	$ 12,000	$ 25,400	$13,400 F

*F = Favorable variance; U = Unfavorable variance.

This type of performance report designates differences between budgeted and actual results as *variances*. We use the letters *F* and *U* to describe variances, with meanings as follows:

F = Favorable variance   When compared to budget, the actual cost or revenue contributes to a *higher* income. That is, actual revenue is higher than budgeted revenue, or actual cost is lower than budgeted cost.

U = Unfavorable variance   When compared to budget, the actual cost or revenue contributes to a *lower* income; actual revenue is lower than budgeted revenue, or actual cost is higher than budgeted cost.

Example: How is it that the favorable sales variance in Exhibit 21.2 is linked with so many unfavorable cost and expense variances? *Answer:* Costs have increased with the increase in sales.

Budget Reports for Evaluation

Managers use budget reports to monitor and control operations. From the report in Exhibit 21.2, SolCel's management might ask:

- Why is actual income from operations $13,400 higher than budgeted?
- Is manufacturing using too much direct material?
- Is manufacturing using too much direct labor?
- Why are sales commissions higher than budgeted?
- Why are so many of the variances unfavorable?

The performance report in Exhibit 21.2 will not be very useful in answering these types of questions because it is not based on an "apples to apples" comparison. That is, the budgeted dollar amounts are based on 10,000 units of sales, but the actual dollar amounts are based on 12,000 units of sales. Clearly, the costs to make 12,000 units will be greater than the costs to make 10,000 units, so it is no surprise that SolCel's total expense variance is unfavorable. In addition, the costs in Exhibit 21.2 with the highest unfavorable variances (direct materials, direct labor, and sales commissions) are typically considered *variable* costs, which increase directly with sales activity. In general, the *fixed* budget performance report is not useful in analyzing performance when actual sales differ from predicted sales. In the next section, we show how a *flexible* budget can be more useful in analyzing performance.

Point: The fixed budget report can be useful in evaluating the sales manager's performance because it shows both budgeted and actual sales, as seen in this chapter's Decision Analysis.

 Decision Insight

Cruise Control Budget reporting and evaluation are used at service providers such as **Royal Caribbean Cruises**, **Carnival Cruise Line**, and **Norwegian Cruise Line**. These service providers regularly prepare performance plans and budget requests for their fleets of cruise ships, which describe performance goals, measure outcomes, and analyze variances. ∎

©Melanie Stetson Freeman/The Christian Science Monitor/Getty Images

Flexible Budget Reports

To address limitations with the fixed budget performance report due to its lack of adjustment to changes in sales volume, management can use a flexible budget. A flexible budget is useful both before and after the period's activities are complete.

P1

Prepare a flexible budget and interpret a flexible budget performance report.

Purpose of Flexible Budgets

- A flexible budget prepared **before** the period is often based on several levels of activity. Budgets for those different levels can provide a "what-if" look at operations. The different levels often include both a best-case and worst-case scenario. This allows management to make adjustments to avoid or lessen the effects of the worst-case scenario.
- A flexible budget prepared **after** the period helps management evaluate past performance. It is especially useful for such an evaluation because it reflects budgeted revenues and costs based on the *actual* level of activity. The flexible budget gives an "apples to apples" comparison because the budgeted activity level is the same as the actual activity level. With a flexible budget, comparisons of actual results with budgeted performance are likely to reveal the real causes of any differences. Such information can help managers focus attention on real problem areas and implement corrective actions.

Preparation of Flexible Budgets   To prepare a flexible budget, follow these steps:

1. Identify the activity level, such as units produced or sold.
2. Identify costs and classify them as fixed or variable within the relevant range of activity.
3. Compute budgeted *sales* (Sales price per unit × Number of units of activity). Then subtract the sum of budgeted *variable costs* (Variable cost per unit × Number of units of activity) plus budgeted *fixed* costs.

EXHIBIT 21.3

Flexible Budgets (prepared
before the period)

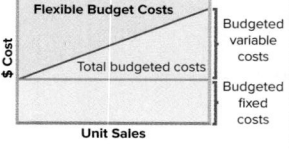

SOLCEL Flexible Budgets	Flexible Budget		Flexible Budget for Unit Sales of		
For Month Ended January 31, 2019	Variable Amount per Unit	Total Fixed Cost	10,000	12,000	14,000
Sales	$10.00		$100,000	$120,000	$140,000
Variable costs					
Direct materials	1.00		10,000	12,000	14,000
Direct labor.	1.50		15,000	18,000	21,000
Factory supplies	0.20		2,000	2,400	2,800
Utilities	0.30		3,000	3,600	4,200
Sales commissions.	0.90		9,000	10,800	12,600
Shipping expenses.	0.40		4,000	4,800	5,600
Office supplies	0.50		5,000	6,000	7,000
Total variable costs	4.80		48,000	57,600	67,200
Contribution margin	$ 5.20		$ 52,000	$ 62,400	$ 72,800
Fixed costs					
Depreciation—Machinery		$ 8,000	8,000	8,000	8,000
Supervisory salaries.		11,000	11,000	11,000	11,000
Insurance expense.		1,000	1,000	1,000	1,000
Depreciation—Office equipment.		7,000	7,000	7,000	7,000
Administrative salaries.		13,000	13,000	13,000	13,000
Total fixed costs		$40,000	40,000	40,000	40,000
Income from operations.			$ 12,000	$ 22,400	$ 32,800

Point: The total amount of a variable cost changes in direct proportion to a change in activity level. The total amount of a fixed cost remains unchanged regardless of changes in the level of activity within a relevant (normal) operating range.

Point: The usefulness of a flexible budget depends on valid classification of variable and fixed costs. Some costs are mixed and must be analyzed to determine their variable and fixed portions.

Example: Using Exhibit 21.3, what is the budgeted income from operations for unit sales of (a) 11,000 and (b) 13,000? *Answers:* $17,200 for unit sales of 11,000; $27,600 for unit sales of 13,000.

In a flexible budget, we express each variable cost in one of two ways: either as (1) a constant dollar amount per unit of sales or as (2) a constant percentage of a sales dollar. In the case of a fixed cost, we express its budgeted amount as the total amount expected to occur at any sales volume within the relevant range.

Exhibit 21.3 shows a set of flexible budgets for SolCel for January 2019.

1 SolCel's management decides that the number of units sold is the relevant activity level. (For SolCel, the number of units sold equals the number of units produced.) For purposes of preparing the flexible budget, management decides it wants budgets at three different activity levels: 10,000 units, 12,000 units, and 14,000 units.

2 SolCel's management classifies its costs as variable (seven items listed under the "Variable costs" heading) or fixed (five costs listed under the "Fixed costs" heading). These classifications result from management's investigation of each expense using techniques such as the high-low or regression methods we showed in a previous chapter. Variable and fixed expense categories are *not* the same for every company, and we must avoid drawing conclusions from specific cases.

3 SolCel next computes budgeted sales and variable costs. At the three different activity levels, sales are budgeted to equal $100,000 (computed as $10 × 10,000), $120,000 (computed as $10 × 12,000), and $140,000 (computed as $10 × 14,000), respectively. Likewise, budgeted direct labor equals $15,000 (computed as $1.50 × 10,000) if 10,000 units are sold and $21,000 (computed as $1.50 × 14,000) if 14,000 units are sold. SolCel then lists each of the fixed costs in total.

The flexible budgets in Exhibit 21.3 follow a *contribution margin format*—beginning with sales followed by variable costs and then fixed costs. The amounts in the first Flexible Budget column are the same as those in the fixed budget report in Exhibit 21.2, as both budgets are based on 10,000 units. As budgeted activity levels increase to 12,000 and 14,000 units, total variable costs increase but total fixed costs stay unchanged.

A flexible budget like that in Exhibit 21.3 can be useful to management in planning operations. In addition, as we will show next, a flexible budget prepared after period-end is particularly useful in analyzing performance when the actual activity level differs from that predicted by a fixed budget.

Point: Flexible budgeting allows a budget to be prepared at any *actual* output level. Performance reports are then prepared comparing the flexible budget to actual revenues and costs.

Formula for Total Budgeted Costs   For approximate "what-if" analyses, compute total budgeted costs at any activity level with this flexible budget formula.

> **Total budgeted costs = Total fixed costs + (Total variable cost per unit × Units of activity level)**

Using this formula, management can compute total budgeted costs for any number of activity levels, and then, at the end of the period, compare actual costs to budgeted costs at any activity level. For example, if 11,250 units are actually produced and sold, total budgeted costs are:

$$\$94{,}000 = \$40{,}000 + (\$4.80 \times 11{,}250)$$

Flexible Budget Performance Report   SolCel's actual sales volume for January was 12,000 units. This sales volume is 2,000 units more than the 10,000 units originally predicted in the fixed budget. So, when management evaluates SolCel's performance, it needs a flexible budget report showing actual and budgeted dollar amounts at 12,000 units.

A **flexible budget performance report** compares actual performance and budgeted performance based on actual sales volume (or other activity level). This report directs management's attention to those costs or revenues that differ substantially from budgeted amounts. In SolCel's case, we prepare this report after January's sales volume is known to be 12,000 units. Exhibit 21.4 shows SolCel's flexible budget performance report for January.

EXHIBIT 21.4

Flexible Budget Performance Report (prepared after the period)

SOLCEL Flexible Budget Performance Report For Month Ended January 31, 2019	Flexible Budget (12,000 units)	Actual Results (12,000 units)	Variances*
Sales.	$120,000	$125,000	$5,000 F
Variable costs			
Direct materials.	12,000	13,000	1,000 U
Direct labor	18,000	20,000	2,000 U
Factory supplies	2,400	2,100	300 F
Utilities.	3,600	4,000	400 U
Sales commissions	10,800	10,800	0
Shipping expenses	4,800	4,300	500 F
Office supplies	6,000	5,200	800 F
Total variable costs.	57,600	59,400	1,800 U
Contribution margin	62,400	65,600	3,200 F
Fixed costs			
Depreciation—Machinery.	8,000	8,000	0
Supervisory salaries	11,000	11,000	0
Insurance expense	1,000	1,200	200 U
Depreciation—Office equipment	7,000	7,000	0
Administrative salaries	13,000	13,000	0
Total fixed costs	40,000	40,200	200 U
Income from operations.	$ 22,400	$ 25,400	$3,000 F

*F = Favorable variance; U = Unfavorable variance.

Point: Total budgeted costs = $97,600, computed as $40,000 + ($4.80 × 12,000).

Analyzing Variances

Management uses this report to investigate variances and evaluate SolCel's performance. Quite often management will focus on large variances. This report shows a $5,000 favorable variance in total dollar sales. Because actual and budgeted volumes are both 12,000 units, the $5,000 favorable sales variance must have resulted from a higher-than-expected selling price. Management would like to determine if the conditions that resulted in higher selling prices are likely to continue.

The other variances in Exhibit 21.4 also direct management's attention to areas where corrective actions can help control SolCel's operations. For example, both the direct materials and direct labor variances are relatively large and unfavorable. On the other hand, relatively large favorable variances are observed for shipping expenses and office supplies. Management will try to determine the causes for these variances, both favorable and unfavorable, and make changes to SolCel's operations if needed.

In addition to analyzing variances using a flexible budget performance report, management can also take a more detailed approach based on a *standard cost* system. We illustrate this next.

■ Decision Maker

Entrepreneur The head of the strategic consulting division of your financial services firm complains to you about the unfavorable variances on the division's performance reports. "We worked on more consulting assignments than planned. It's not surprising our costs are higher than expected. To top it off, this report characterizes our work as *poor!*" How do you respond? ■ *Answer:* From the complaints, this performance report appears to compare actual results with a fixed budget. This comparison is useful in determining whether the amount of work actually performed was more or less than planned, but it is not useful in determining whether the division was more or less efficient than planned. If the division worked on more assignments than expected, some costs will certainly increase. Therefore, you should prepare a flexible budget using the actual number of consulting assignments and then compare actual performance to the flexible budget.

NEED-TO-KNOW 21-1

Flexible Budget

P1

A manufacturing company reports the following fixed budget and actual results for the past year. The fixed budget assumes a selling price of $40 per unit. The fixed budget is based on 20,000 units of sales, and the actual results are based on 24,000 units of sales. Prepare a flexible budget performance report for the past year. Label variances as favorable (F) or unfavorable (U).

	Fixed Budget (20,000 units)	Actual Results (24,000 units)
Sales	$800,000	$972,000
Variable costs*	160,000	240,000
Fixed costs	500,000	490,000

*Budgeted variable cost per unit = $160,000/20,000 = $8.00.

Solution

Flexible Budget Performance Report			
	Flexible Budget (24,000 units)	Actual Results (24,000 units)	Variances
Sales	$960,000*	$972,000	$12,000 F
Variable costs	192,000†	240,000	48,000 U
Contribution margin	768,000	732,000	36,000 U
Fixed costs	500,000	490,000	10,000 F
Income from operations....	$268,000	$242,000	$26,000 U

*24,000 × $40   †24,000 × $8

Do More: QS 21-1, QS 21-2, QS 21-3, QS 21-4, E 21-3, E 21-4, E 21-5, E 21-6

STANDARD COSTING

We next show how *standard costs* can be used in a flexible budgeting system to enable management to better understand the reasons for variances.

C1_____

Define *standard costs* and explain how standard cost information is useful for management by exception.

Standard Costs

Standard costs are preset costs for delivering a product or service under normal conditions. These costs are established by personnel, engineering, and accounting studies using past experiences. Manufacturing companies usually use standard costing for direct materials, direct labor, and overhead costs.

When actual costs vary from standard costs, management identifies potential problems and takes corrective actions. **Management by exception** means that managers focus attention on the most significant differences between actual costs and standard costs. Management by exception is most useful when directed at controllable revenues and costs.

Standard costs are often used in preparing budgets because they are the anticipated costs under normal conditions. For example, if the standard direct materials cost is $2.00 per unit and expected production is 50,000 units, the total budgeted direct materials cost is $100,000. Terms such as *standard materials cost, standard labor cost,* and *standard overhead cost* are often used to refer to amounts budgeted for direct materials, direct labor, and overhead.

Standard costs can also help control *nonmanufacturing* costs. Companies providing services can also use standard costs. For example, while quality medical service is paramount, efficiency in providing that service is also important in controlling medical costs. The use of budgeting and standard costing is touted as an effective means to control and monitor medical costs, especially overhead.

Setting Standard Costs

Managerial accountants, engineers, personnel administrators, purchasing managers, and production managers work together to set standard costs. To identify standards for direct labor costs, we can conduct time and motion studies for each labor operation in the process of providing a product or service. From these studies, management can learn the best way to perform the operation and then set the standard labor time required for the operation under normal conditions. Similarly, standards for direct materials are set by studying the quantity, grade, and cost of each material used. Overhead standards are set by considering the resources needed to support production activities. Standards should be challenging but attainable and should acknowledge machine breakdowns, material waste, and idle time. Regardless of the care used in setting standard costs and in revising them as conditions change, actual costs frequently differ from standard costs.

Example: What factors might be considered when deciding whether to revise standard costs? *Answer:* Changes in the processes and/or resources needed to carry out the processes.

■ **Decision Insight**

Cruis'n Standards   The **Tesla** Model S consists of hundreds of parts for which engineers set standards. Various types of labor are also involved in its production, including machining, assembly, painting, and welding, and standards are set for each. Actual results are periodically compared with standards to assess performance. ■

To illustrate the setting of standard costs, we consider wooden baseball bats manufactured by ProBat. Its engineers have determined that manufacturing one bat requires 0.90 kilograms (kg) of high-grade wood. They also expect some loss of material as part of the process because of inefficiencies and waste. This results in adding an *allowance* of 0.10 kg, making the standard requirement 1.0 kg of wood for each bat.

The 0.90-kg portion is called an *ideal standard;* it is the quantity of material required if the process is 100% efficient without any loss or waste. Reality suggests that some loss of material usually occurs with any process. The standard of 1.0 kg is known as the *practical standard,* the quantity of material required under normal application of the process. The standard direct labor rate should include allowances for employee breaks, cleanup, and machine downtime. Most companies use practical rather than ideal standards.

Point: Companies promoting continuous improvement strive to achieve ideal standards by eliminating inefficiencies and waste.

ProBat needs to develop standard costs for direct materials, direct labor, and overhead. For direct materials and direct labor, ProBat must develop standard quantities and standard prices. For overhead, ProBat must consider the activities that drive overhead costs. ProBat's standard costs are:

Direct materials   High-grade wood is purchased at a standard price of $25 per kg. The purchasing department sets this price as the expected price for the budget period. To determine this price, the purchasing department considers factors such as the quality of materials, economic conditions, supply factors (shortages and excesses), and available discounts.

Direct labor   Two hours of labor time are required to manufacture a bat. The direct labor rate is $20 per hour. This rate includes wages, taxes, and fringe benefits. When wage rates differ across employees due to seniority or skill level, the standard direct labor rate is based on the expected mix of workers.

Overhead   ProBat assigns overhead at the rate of $10 per direct labor hour.

The standard costs of direct materials, direct labor, and overhead for one bat are shown in Exhibit 21.5 in a *standard cost card*. These standard cost amounts are then used to prepare manufacturing budgets for a budgeted level of production.

STANDARD COST CARD			
Production Factor	**Standard Quantity per Unit**	**Standard Cost per Unit**	**Total Standard Cost**
Direct materials (wood)	**1 kg**	**$25 per kg**	**$25**
Direct labor	**2 hours**	**$20 per hour**	40
Overhead	**2 labor hours**	**$10 per hour**	20
		Total	**$85**

Cost Variance Analysis

Companies analyze differences between actual costs and standard costs to assess performance. A **cost variance,** also simply called a *variance,* is the difference between actual and standard costs. Cost variances can be favorable (F) or unfavorable (U).

- If actual cost is less than standard cost, the variance is favorable (F).
- If actual costs are greater than standard costs, the variance is unfavorable (U).[1]

Exhibit 21.6 shows the flow of events in **variance analysis:** (1) preparing a standard cost performance report, (2) computing and analyzing variances, (3) identifying questions and their answers, and (4) taking corrective and strategic actions (if needed). These variance analysis steps are interrelated and are frequently applied in good organizations.

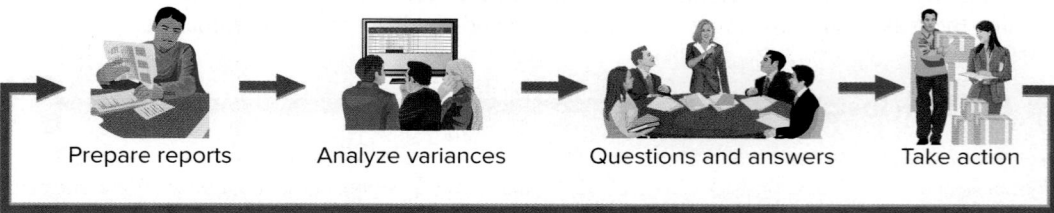

Prepare reports   Analyze variances   Questions and answers   Take action

Cost Variance Computation   Exhibit 21.7 shows a general formula for computing any cost variance (CV).

$$\underbrace{\underset{AQ \times AP}{\textbf{Actual Cost (AC)}} \quad - \quad \underset{SQ \times SP}{\textbf{Standard Cost (SC)}}}_{\textbf{Cost Variance (CV)}}$$

*AQ is actual quantity; AP is actual price; SP is standard price; SQ is standard quantity allowed for actual output.

---

[1]Short-term favorable variances can sometimes lead to long-term unfavorable variances. For instance, if management spends less than the budgeted amount on maintenance or insurance, the performance report would show a favorable short-term variance. Cutting these expenses can lead to major losses in the long run if machinery wears out prematurely or insurance coverage proves inadequate.

Actual quantity (AQ) is the actual amount of material or labor used to manufacture the actual quantity of output for the period. Standard quantity (SQ) is the standard amount of input for the actual quantity of output for the period. Actual price (AP) is the actual amount paid to acquire the actual direct material or direct labor used for the period. SP is the standard price.

We show how to compute the total cost variance for G-Max, a manufacturer of golf equipment and accessories. G-Max set the following standard costs per unit for one of its specialty clubheads.

Standard	
Direct materials..............	0.5 lb. per unit @ $20 per lb.
Direct labor	1 hour per unit @ $16 per hour
Overhead	$2 per direct labor hour

During May, G-Max actually produced 3,500 clubheads at a total manufacturing cost of $101,550. Budgeted costs, which equal the standard costs per unit multiplied by the number of units actually produced, are computed below.

Budgeted Cost	
Direct materials...........	$0.5 \times 3,500 \times \$20 = \$35,000$
Direct labor	$1 \times 3,500 \times \$16 = \ 56,000$
Overhead	$1 \times 3,500 \times \$2 \ \ = \ \ \underline{\ 7,000}$
Total budgeted cost	$98,000

G-Max then computes the total cost variance as follows.

Budgeted (standard) cost.....................	$ 98,000
Actual cost...............................	101,550
Total cost variance	$ 3,550 U

Budgeted and actual costs are based on the actual number of units produced (3,500). To make 3,500 clubheads, G-Max should have used 1,750 pounds (0.5 lb. per unit × 3,500 units) of direct materials and 3,500 direct labor hours (1 hour per unit × 3,500 units). Multiplying these standard quantities by their standard unit costs and summing yields the total budgeted cost ($98,000). As G-Max's actual cost to produce 3,500 units ($101,500) is more than the budgeted cost to produce 3,500 units ($98,000), the total cost variance is unfavorable ($3,550). Next we show how to use more detailed variances to determine the causes of G-Max's unfavorable total cost variance.

Point: In this example overhead is allocated based on direct labor hours.

A manufacturer reports the following standard cost card. For June, the company made 1,200 units and incurred actual total manufacturing costs of $135,850. Compute the standard cost per unit and the total cost variance. Label the variance as favorable (F) or unfavorable (U).

NEED-TO-KNOW 21-2

Cost Variances

P2

Production Factor	Standard
Direct materials...........	2 lbs. per unit @ $25 per lb.
Direct labor	1.5 hours per unit @ $18 per hour
Overhead	$24 per direct labor hour

Solution

Standard cost per unit = $(2 \times \$25) + (1.5 \times \$18) + (1.5 \times \$24) = \$113$
Total cost variance = $135,850 − $135,600 = $250 U

Budgeted Cost	
Direct materials...........	$2 \times 1,200 \times \$25 = \$ \ 60,000$
Direct labor..............	$1.5 \times 1,200 \times \$18 = \ \ 32,400$
Overhead	$1.5 \times 1,200 \times \$24 = \ \underline{\ 43,200}$
Total budgeted cost	$135,600

Do More: QS 21-6, E 21-8

MATERIALS AND LABOR VARIANCES

Two main factors cause materials and labor variances:

1. **Price variance.** A difference between actual *price* per unit of input and standard price per unit of input results in a **price** (or rate) **variance.**
2. **Quantity variance.** A difference between actual *quantity* of input used and standard quantity of input that should have been used results in a **quantity** (or usage or efficiency) **variance.**

Isolating these price and quantity factors in a cost variance leads to the formulas in Exhibit 21.8.

EXHIBIT 21.8

Price Variance and Quantity Variance Formulas

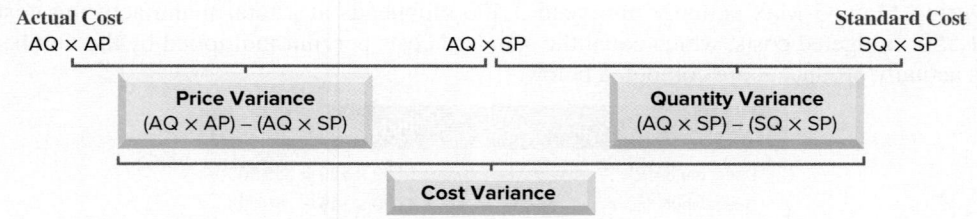

The model in Exhibit 21.8 separates total cost variances for materials or labor into separate price and quantity variances, which is useful in analyzing performance. Exhibit 21.8 illustrates three important rules in computing these variances:

Point: Detailed overhead variances are computed differently, as we show later in this chapter.

1. In computing a price variance, the quantity (actual) is held constant.
2. In computing a quantity variance, the price (standard) is held constant.
3. Cost variance, or total variance, is the sum of price and quantity variances.

Managers sometimes find it useful to use an alternative (but equivalent) computation for the price and quantity variances, as shown in Exhibit 21.9.

EXHIBIT 21.9

Alternative Price Variance and Quantity Variance Formulas

Price Variance (PV) = [**Actual Price** (AP) − **Standard Price** (SP)] × **Actual Quantity** (AQ)

Quantity Variance (QV) = [**Actual Quantity** (AQ) − **Standard Quantity** (SQ)] × **Standard Price** (SP)

The results from applying the formulas in Exhibits 21.8 and 21.9 are identical.

Materials Variances

P3

Compute materials and labor variances.

©Kristjan Maack/Getty Images/ Nordic Photos

G-Max produced 3,500 units in May. In producing 3,500 units, it actually used 1,800 pounds of direct materials (titanium) at a cost of $21 per pound. It should have used 1,750 pounds of direct materials (3,500 × 0.5 lb. per unit). This amount of 1,750 pounds is the standard quantity of direct materials that should have been used to produce 3,500 units. This information allows us to compute both actual and standard direct materials costs for G-Max's 3,500 units and its total direct materials cost variance as follows.

Direct Materials	Quantity	Price per Unit	Cost
Actual quantity and cost	1,800 lbs. ×	$21 per lb.	= $37,800
Standard quantity and cost	1,750 lbs.* ×	$20 per lb.	= 35,000
Direct materials cost variance			= $ 2,800 U

*Standard quantity = 3,500 units × 0.5 lb. per unit.

To better isolate the causes of this $2,800 unfavorable total direct materials cost variance, the materials price and quantity variances are computed and shown in Exhibit 21.10.

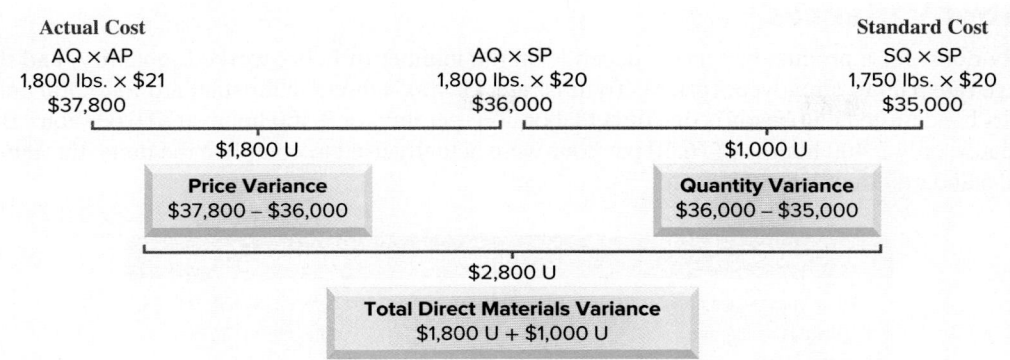

EXHIBIT 21.10

Materials Price and
Quantity Variances*

*AQ is actual quantity; AP is actual price; SP is standard price; SQ is standard quantity allowed for actual output.

Point: The direct materials price variance can also be computed as ($21 − $20) × 18,000 = $1,800. The direct materials quantity variance can also be computed as (1,800 − 1,750) × $20 = $1,000.

We now can see the two components of the $2,800 unfavorable direct materials cost variance: The $1,800 unfavorable price variance results from paying $1 more per pound than the standard price, computed as 1,800 lbs. × $1. G-Max also used 50 pounds more of materials than the standard quantity (1,800 actual pounds − 1,750 standard pounds). The $1,000 unfavorable quantity variance is computed as [(1,800 actual lbs. − 1,750 standard lbs.) × $20 standard price per lb.]. Detailed price and quantity variances allow management to ask the responsible individuals for explanations and take corrective actions.

DM Price	DM Qty.
$1,800 U	$1,000 U

| DM Var. $2,800 U | |

Evaluating Materials Variances   The purchasing department is responsible for the price paid for materials. The purchasing manager must explain why a price higher than standard was paid. The purchasing manager might have negotiated poor prices, or purchased higher-quality materials.

The production department is responsible for the quantity of material used. The production manager must explain why the process used more than the standard amount of materials. Perhaps poorly trained workers used excess amounts of materials.

Variance analysis presents challenges. For instance, the production department could have used more than the standard amount of material because the materials' quality did not meet specifications and led to excessive waste. In this case, the purchasing manager must explain why inferior materials were acquired. However, if analysis shows that waste was due to inefficiencies, not poor-quality material, the production manager must explain what happened.

A manufacturing company reports the following for one of its products. Compute the direct materials (a) price variance and (b) quantity variance and classify each as favorable or unfavorable.

NEED-TO-KNOW 21-3

Direct Materials Price
and Quantity Variances

P3

Direct materials standard..........	8 pounds @ $6 per pound
Actual direct materials used........	83,000 pounds @ $5.80 per pound
Actual finished units produced	10,000

Solution

a. Price variance = (Actual quantity × Actual price) − (Actual quantity × Standard price)
= (83,000 × $5.80) − (83,000 × $6) = $16,600 Favorable

b. Quantity variance = (Actual quantity × Standard price) − (Standard quantity* × Standard price)
= (83,000 × $6) − (80,000 × $6) = $18,000 Unfavorable

*Standard quantity = 10,000 units × 8 standard pounds per unit = 80,000 pounds.

Do More: QS 21-8, E 21-9,
E 21-13

Labor Variances

Labor cost for a product or service depends on the number of hours worked (quantity) and the wage rate paid to employees (price). To illustrate, G-Max's direct labor standard for 3,500 units of its handcrafted clubheads is one direct labor hour per unit, or 3,500 hours at $16 per hour. But because only 3,400 hours at $16.50 per hour were actually used to complete the units, the actual and standard direct labor costs are

Direct Labor	Quantity	Rate per Hour	Cost
Actual quantity and cost..........	3,400 hrs. × $16.50 per hr.	= $56,100
Standard quantity and cost	3,500 hrs.* × $16.00 per hr.	= 56,000
Direct labor cost variance		= $ 100 U

*Standard quantity = 3,500 units × 1 standard direct labor hour per unit.

Actual direct labor cost is merely $100 over the standard; that small difference might suggest no immediate concern. A closer look, however, might suggest problems. The direct labor cost variance can be divided into price and quantity variances, which are usually called *rate* and *efficiency* variances. Computing both the labor rate and efficiency variances reveals a more precise picture, as shown in Exhibit 21.11.

EXHIBIT 21.11

Labor Rate and Efficiency Variances*

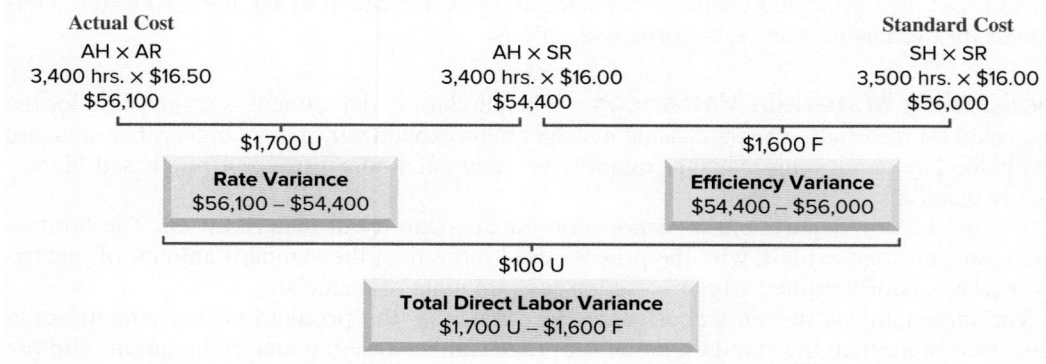

Point: The direct labor efficiency variance can also be computed as $(3,400 − 3,500) × $16 = $1,600$. The direct labor rate variance can also be computed as $($16.50 − $16) × 3,400 = $1,700$.

*Here, we use hours (H) for quantity (Q) and the wage rate (R) for price (P). Thus: AH is actual direct labor hours; AR is actual wage rate; SH is standard direct labor hours allowed for actual output; SR is standard wage rate.

Example: Compute the rate variance and the efficiency variance for Exhibit 21.11 if 3,700 actual hours are used at an actual price of $15.50 per hour. *Answer:* $1,700 favorable labor rate variance and $3,200 unfavorable labor efficiency variance.

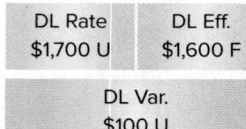

DL Rate	DL Eff.
$1,700 U	$1,600 F

DL Var.	
$100 U	

Evaluating Labor Variances   Exhibit 21.11 shows that the $100 total unfavorable labor cost variance results from a $1,600 favorable efficiency variance and a $1,700 unfavorable rate variance. To produce 3,500 units, G-Max should use 3,500 direct labor hours (3,500 units × 1 direct labor hour per unit). The favorable efficiency variance results from using 100 fewer direct labor hours (3,400 actual DLH − 3,500 standard DLH) than standard for the units produced. The unfavorable rate variance results from paying a wage rate that is $0.50 per hour higher ($16.50 actual rate − $16.00 standard rate) than standard. The personnel administrator or the production manager needs to explain why the wage rate is higher than expected. The production manager should explain how the labor hours were reduced. If this experience can be repeated and transferred to other departments, more savings are possible.

One possible explanation of these labor rate and efficiency variances is the use of workers with different skill levels. If so, management must discuss the implications with the production manager who assigns workers to tasks. This might show that higher-skilled workers were used. As a result, fewer labor hours might be required for the work, but the wage rate paid these workers is higher than standard because of their greater skills. This higher-than-standard labor cost might require an adjustment of the standard labor rates, or the use of more lower-skilled workers.

Other explanations for direct labor variances are possible. Lower-quality materials, poor employee training or supervision, equipment breakdowns, and idle workers due to reduced demand for the company's products could lead to unfavorable direct labor efficiency variances.

Production Manager   A manufacturing variance report for June shows a large unfavorable labor efficiency (quantity) variance. What factors do you investigate to identify its possible causes? ■   *Answer:* An unfavorable labor efficiency variance occurs because more labor hours than standard were used during the period. Possible reasons for this include (1) materials quality could be poor, resulting in more labor consumption due to rework; (2) unplanned interruptions (strike, breakdowns, accidents) could have occurred during the period; and (3) a different labor mix might have occurred for a strategic reason such as to expedite orders. This new labor mix could have consisted of a larger proportion of untrained labor, which resulted in more labor hours.

©Sollina Images/Blend Images

The following information is available for a manufacturer. Compute the direct labor rate and efficiency variances and label them as favorable (F) or unfavorable (U).

NEED-TO-KNOW 21-4

Direct Labor Rate and Efficiency Variances

P3

Actual direct labor cost (6,250 hours @ $13.10 per hour)...	$81,875	Actual production (units) ...... 2,500 units
Standard direct labor hours per unit	2.0 hours	Budgeted production (units) ... 3,000 units
Standard direct labor rate per hour..................	$13.00	

Solution

Rate variance   = ($13.10 − $13.00) × 6,250 = $625 U
Efficiency variance = (6,250 − 5,000) × $13.00 = $16,250 U
Total standard hours = 2,500 × 2.0 = 5,000

Do More: QS 21-11, E 21-10, E 21-16

OVERHEAD STANDARDS AND VARIANCES

In previous chapters we showed how companies use *predetermined overhead rates* to allocate overhead costs to products or services. In a standard costing system, this allocation is done using the *standard* amount of the overhead allocation base, such as standard labor hours or standard machine hours. We now show how to use standard costs to develop flexible overhead budgets.

Flexible Overhead Budgets

Standard overhead costs are the overhead amounts expected to occur at a certain activity level. Overhead includes fixed costs and variable costs. This requires management to classify overhead costs as fixed or variable (within a relevant range) and to develop a flexible budget for overhead costs.

To illustrate, the first two number columns of Exhibit 21.12 show the overhead cost structure to develop G-Max's flexible overhead budgets for May 2019. At the beginning of the year, G-Max predicted variable overhead costs of $1.00 per unit (clubhead), comprised of $0.40 per unit for indirect labor, $0.30 per unit for indirect materials, $0.20 per unit for power and lights, and $0.10 per unit for factory maintenance. In addition, G-Max predicts monthly fixed overhead of $4,000.

With these variable and fixed overhead cost amounts, G-Max can prepare flexible overhead budgets at various capacity levels (four rightmost number columns in Exhibit 21.12). At its maximum capacity (100% column), G-Max could produce 5,000 clubheads. At 70% of maximum capacity, G-Max could produce 3,500 (computed as 5,000 × 70%) clubheads. Recall that total variable costs will increase as production activity increases, but total fixed costs will not change as production activity changes. At 70% capacity, variable overhead costs are budgeted at $3,500 (3,500 × $1.00), while at 100% capacity, variable overhead costs are budgeted at $5,000 (5,000 × $1.00). At all capacity levels within the relevant range, fixed overhead costs are budgeted at $4,000 per month.

Standard Overhead Rate

To apply standard overhead costs to products or services, management establishes the standard overhead cost rate, using the three-step process below.

Step 1: Determine an Allocation Base   The allocation base is a measure of input that is related to overhead costs. Examples can include direct labor hours or machine hours. We

Point: With increased automation, machine hours are frequently used in applying overhead instead of labor hours.

©Fuse/Getty Images

EXHIBIT 21.12

Flexible Overhead Budgets

G-MAX Flexible Overhead Budgets Flexible Budget						
For Month Ended May 31, 2019	Variable Amount per Unit	Total Fixed Cost	Flexible Budget at Capacity Level of			
			70%	80%	90%	100%
Production (in units)	1 unit		3,500	4,000	4,500	5,000
Factory overhead						
Variable costs						
Indirect labor	$0.40/unit		$1,400	$1,600	$1,800	$2,000
Indirect materials.	0.30/unit		1,050	1,200	1,350	1,500
Power and lights	0.20/unit		700	800	900	1,000
Maintenance	0.10/unit		350	400	450	500
Total variable overhead costs	$1.00/unit		3,500	4,000	4,500	5,000
Fixed costs (per month)						
Building rent.		$1,000	1,000	1,000	1,000	1,000
Depreciation—Machinery		1,200	1,200	1,200	1,200	1,200
Supervisory salaries		1,800	1,800	1,800	1,800	1,800
Total fixed overhead costs		$4,000	4,000	4,000	4,000	4,000
Total factory overhead			$7,500	$8,000	$8,500	$9,000
Standard direct labor hours (1 DL hr./unit)			3,500 hrs.	4,000 hrs.	4,500 hrs.	5,000 hrs.
Predetermined overhead rate per standard direct labor hour.				$ 2.00		

assume that G-Max uses direct labor hours as an allocation base, and it has a standard of one direct labor hour per finished unit.

Step 2: Choose a Predicted Activity Level   The predicted activity level is rarely set at 100% of capacity. Difficulties in scheduling work, equipment breakdowns, and insufficient product demand typically cause the activity level to be less than full capacity. Also, good long-run management practices usually call for some excess plant capacity to allow for special opportunities and demand changes. G-Max managers predicted an 80% activity level for May, or a production volume of 4,000 clubheads.

Step 3: Compute the Standard Overhead Rate   At the predicted activity level of 4,000 units, the flexible budget in Exhibit 21.12 predicts total overhead of $8,000. At this activity level of 4,000 units, G-Max's standard direct labor hours are 4,000 hours (4,000 units × 1 direct labor hour per unit). G-Max's standard overhead rate is then computed as:

$$\text{Standard overhead rate} = \frac{\text{Total overhead cost at predicted activity level}}{\text{Total direct labor hours at predicted activity level}}$$

$$= \frac{\$8,000}{4,000} = \$2 \text{ per direct labor hour}$$

This standard overhead rate is used in computing overhead cost variances, as we show next, and in recording journal entries in a standard cost system, which we show in the appendix to this chapter.

©ColorBlind Images/Blend Images

■ **Decision Insight** ━━━━━━━━━━━━━━━━━━━━

Measuring Up   In the spirit of continuous improvement, competitors compare their processes and performance standards against benchmarks established by industry leaders. Companies that use **benchmarking** include **Jiffy Lube, All Tune and Lube,** and **SpeeDee Oil Change and Auto Service.** ■

Computing Overhead Cost Variances

P4 _____

Compute overhead controllable and volume variances.

In a standard costing system, overhead is applied with the formula in Exhibit 21.13.

EXHIBIT 21.13

Applying Standard Overhead Cost

$$\begin{array}{ccccc}
\text{Standard overhead} \\ \text{applied}
\end{array} = \begin{array}{c}\text{Actual} \\ \text{production}\end{array} \times \begin{array}{c}\text{Standard amount of} \\ \text{allocation base}\end{array} \times \begin{array}{c}\text{Standard overhead rate} \\ \text{(at predicted activity level)}\end{array}$$

The standard overhead applied is based on the standard amount of the allocation base that *should have been used,* based on the actual production. This standard activity amount is then multiplied by the predetermined standard overhead rate (at the predicted activity level). For G-Max for May, standard overhead applied is computed as:

$$\text{Standard overhead applied} = 3{,}500 \text{ units} \times 1 \text{ DLH per unit} \times \$2.00 \text{ per DLH} = \$7{,}000$$

G-Max produced 3,500 units during the month, which should have used 3,500 direct labor hours. At G-Max's predicted capacity level of 80%, the standard overhead rate was $2.00 per direct labor hour. The standard overhead applied is $7,000, as computed above.

Actual overhead incurred might differ from the standard overhead applied for the period, and management again will use *variance analysis.* The difference between the standard amount of overhead cost applied and the total actual overhead incurred is the **overhead cost variance** (total overhead variance), shown in Exhibit 21.14.

EXHIBIT 21.14

Overhead Cost Variance

$$\begin{array}{c}\text{Overhead cost} \\ \text{variance}\end{array} = \begin{array}{c}\text{Actual overhead} \\ \text{incurred}\end{array} - \begin{array}{c}\text{Standard overhead} \\ \text{applied}\end{array}$$

To illustrate, G-Max's actual overhead cost incurred in the month (found in other cost reports) is $7,650. Using the formula in Exhibit 21.14, G-Max's total overhead variance is $650, computed as:

Total Overhead Variance	
Actual total overhead (given)	$7,650
Standard overhead applied (3,500 units × 1 DLH per unit × $2.00 per DLH)	7,000
Total overhead variance	$ 650 U

This variance is unfavorable: G-Max's actual overhead was higher than the standard amount.

Overhead Controllable and Volume Variances

To help identify factors causing the total overhead cost variance, managers compute *overhead volume* and *overhead controllable variances,* as illustrated in Exhibit 21.15. The results are useful for taking strategic actions to improve company performance.

EXHIBIT 21.15

Framework for Understanding Total Overhead Variance

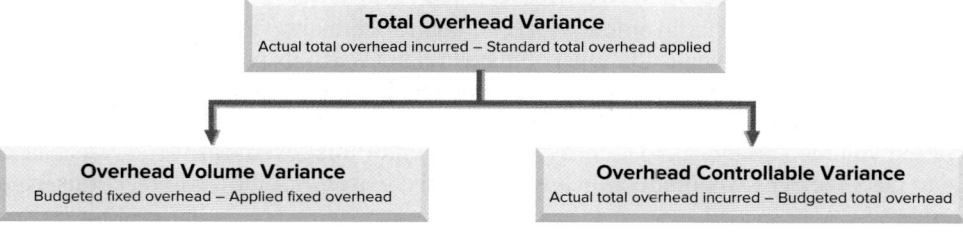

A **volume variance** occurs when the company operates at a different capacity level than was predicted. G-Max predicted it would manufacture 4,000 units, but it only manufactured 3,500 units. The volume variance is usually considered outside the control of the production manager, as it depends mainly on customer demand for the company's products.

The volume variance is based solely on *fixed* overhead. Recall that G-Max's standard *fixed* overhead rate at the predicted capacity level of 4,000 units was $1 per direct labor hour. The overhead volume variance is computed as:

Overhead Volume Variance	
Budgeted fixed overhead (at predicted capacity)	$4,000
Applied fixed overhead (3,500 units × 1 DLH per unit × $1.00 per DLH)	3,500
Volume variance	$ 500 U

The volume variance is unfavorable because G-Max made 500 fewer units than it expected. With a total overhead variance of $650 (unfavorable) and a volume variance of $500 (unfavorable), the controllable overhead variance is computed as:

> **Controllable variance = Total overhead variance − Overhead volume variance**
> $150 U = $650 − $500

More formally, the **controllable variance** is the difference between the actual overhead costs incurred and the budgeted overhead costs for the standard hours that should have been used for actual production. Controllable variance is the portion of total overhead variance that is considered to be under management's control. Because G-Max only produced 3,500 units during the month, we need to compare *actual* overhead costs to make 3,500 units to the *budgeted* cost to make 3,500 units. Budgeted total overhead cost to make 3,500 units is computed as:

Budgeted Total Overhead Cost	
Budgeted variable overhead cost (3,500 units × 1 DLH per unit × $1 VOH* rate per DLH)	$3,500
Budgeted fixed overhead cost	4,000
Budgeted total overhead cost	$7,500

*VOH is variable overhead.

Controllable variance is then computed as:

Overhead Controllable Variance	
Actual total overhead (given)	$7,650
Budgeted total overhead (from above)	7,500
Controllable variance	$ 150 U

Analyzing Overhead Controllable and Volume Variances   How should management interpret the unfavorable overhead controllable and volume variances? An unfavorable volume variance means that the company did not reach its predicted operating level. In this case, 80% of manufacturing capacity was budgeted, but only 70% was used. Management needs to know why the actual level of production differs from the expected level. The main purpose of the volume variance is to identify what portion of total overhead variance is caused by failing to meet the expected production level. Often the reasons for failing to meet this expected production level are due to factors, such as customer demand, that are beyond employees' control. This information permits management to focus on explanations for the controllable variance, as we discuss next.

Controllable	Volume
$150 U	$500 U

Ovhd. Var $650 U

Overhead Variance Reports

To help management isolate the reasons for the $150 unfavorable overhead controllable variance, an *overhead variance report* can be prepared. An overhead variance report shows specific overhead costs and how they differ from budgeted amounts. Exhibit 21.16 shows G-Max's overhead variance report for May. The detailed listing of individual overhead costs reveals the following sources of the $150 unfavorable overhead controllable variance: (1) Fixed overhead costs and variable factory maintenance costs were incurred as expected. (2) Costs for indirect labor and power and lights were higher than expected. (3) Indirect materials cost was less than expected. Management can use the variance overhead report to identify individual overhead costs to investigate.

Appendix 21A describes an expanded analysis of overhead variances.

EXHIBIT 21.16

Overhead Variance Report

G-MAX
Overhead Variance Report
For Month Ended May 31, 2019

Production Level

Expected...	80% of capacity (4,000 units)
Actual	70% of capacity (3,500 units)

Overhead Controllable Variance	Flexible Budget	Actual Results	Variances*
Variable overhead costs			
Indirect labor	$1,400	$1,525	$125 U
Indirect materials.............................	1,050	1,025	25 F
Power and lights	700	750	50 U
Maintenance..................................	350	350	0
Total variable overhead costs	3,500	3,650	150 U
Fixed overhead costs			
Building rent..................................	1,000	1,000	0
Depreciation—Machinery	1,200	1,200	0
Supervisory salaries..........................	1,800	1,800	0
Total fixed overhead costs....................	4,000	4,000	0
Total overhead costs	$7,500	$7,650	$150 U

Overhead Volume Variance

Budgeted fixed overhead (4,000 DLH × $1.00).........	$4,000
Fixed overhead applied (3,500 DLH × $1.00)	$3,500
Volume variance...................................	$ 500 U

Total overhead variance = $650 unfavorable

Point: Both the flexible budget and actual results are based on 3,500 units produced.

*F = Favorable variance; U = Unfavorable variance.

A manufacturing company uses standard costs and reports the information below for January. The company uses machine hours to apply overhead, and the standard is two machine hours per finished unit. Compute the total overhead cost variance, overhead controllable variance, and overhead volume variance for January. Indicate whether each variance is favorable or unfavorable.

NEED-TO-KNOW 21-5

Overhead Variances

P4

Predicted activity level...............	1,500 units
Variable overhead rate budgeted	$2.50 per machine hour
Fixed overhead budgeted	$6,000 per month ($2.00 per machine hour at predicted activity level)
Actual activity level..................	1,800 units
Actual overhead costs	$15,800

Solution

Do More: QS 21-13, QS 21-14, QS 21-15, E 21-17, E 21-19, E 21-20

Total overhead cost variance	
Actual total overhead cost (given)..	$15,800
Standard overhead applied (1,800 × 2 × $4.50).........................	16,200
Total overhead variance..	$ 400 F

Overhead controllable variance	
Actual total overhead cost (given).....................	$15,800
Budgeted total overhead (1,800 × 2 × $2.50) + $6,000 ..	15,000
Overhead controllable variance......................	$ 800 U

Overhead volume variance	
Budgeted fixed overhead................	$ 6,000
Applied fixed overhead (1,800 × 2 × $2) ..	7,200
Overhead volume variance	$1,200 F

Summary of Variances Exhibit 21.17 summarizes the manufacturing variances for G-Max.

EXHIBIT 21.17

Variance Summary

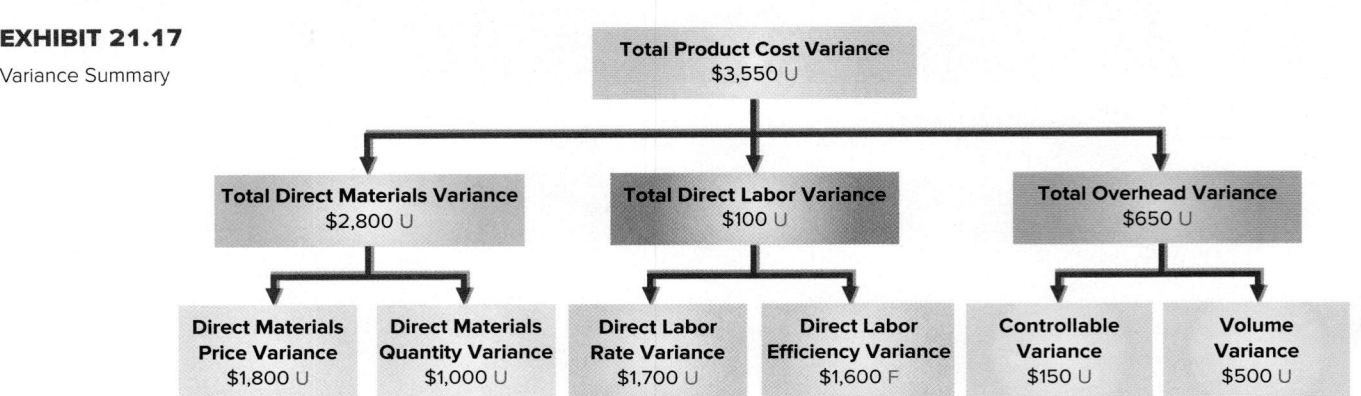

Standard Costing—Management Considerations

Companies must consider many factors, both positive and negative, in deciding whether and how to use standard costing systems. Below we summarize some of these factors.

Standard Costing Considerations	
Positives	**Negatives**
Provides benchmarks for management by exception.	Standards are costly to develop and keep up-to-date.
Motivates employees to work toward goals.	Variances are not timely for adapting to rapidly changing business conditions.
Useful in the budgeting process.	
Isolates reasons for good or bad performance.	Employees might not try for continuous improvement.

SUSTAINABILITY AND ACCOUNTING

As more companies report on their sustainability efforts, organizations provide structure for these reports. One group, the **International Integrated Reporting Council** (IIRC), is a global group of regulators, investors, and accountants that develops methods for integrated reporting. **Integrated reporting** is designed to concisely report how an organization's strategy, performance, sustainability efforts, and governance lead to value creation.

Intel, a maker of computer chips, follows many of the IIRC's recommendations. In its integrated report, Intel notes it links executive pay, in part, to corporate responsibility metrics. For example, 50% of top management's annual cash bonus is based on meeting operating performance targets, including those for corporate responsibility and environmental sustainability. Recertly, Intel's top five managers were paid nearly $10 million for meeting performance targets. By linking executive pay to sustainability targets, Intel motivates managers to integrate sustainability initiatives with their efforts to make financial profits and increase firm value.

Away, this chapter's feature company, has teamed with **charity: water** to increase access to clean water. The company donates $30 to charity: water each time an item from its special line of carry-on bags is sold. Although initiatives like these reduce Away's financial profits, the founders stress the importance of "planet and people" in defining success.

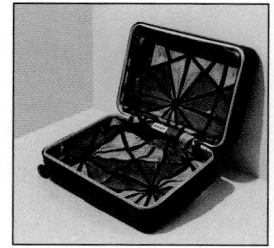

©Away

Sales Variances  **Decision Analysis**

Variance analysis can also be applied to sales. The budgeted amount of unit sales is the predicted activity level, and the budgeted selling price is treated as a "standard" price. To illustrate, consider the following sales data from G-Max for two of its golf products, Excel golf balls and Big Bert drivers.

A1

Analyze changes in sales from expected amounts.

	Budgeted	Actual
Sales of Excel golf balls (units)...............	1,000 units	1,100 units
Sales price per Excel golf ball	$10	$10.50
Sales of Big Bert drivers (units)	150 units	140 units
Sales price per Big Bert driver..............	$200	$190

The *sales price variance* and the *sales volume variance* are as shown in Exhibit 21.18. The sales price variance measures the impact of the actual sales price differing from the expected price. The sales volume variance measures the impact of operating at a different capacity level than predicted by the fixed budget. The total sales price variance is $850 unfavorable, and the total sales volume variance is $1,000 unfavorable. However, further analysis of these total sales variances reveals that both the sales price and sales volume variances for Excel golf balls are favorable, while both variances are unfavorable for the Big Bert driver.

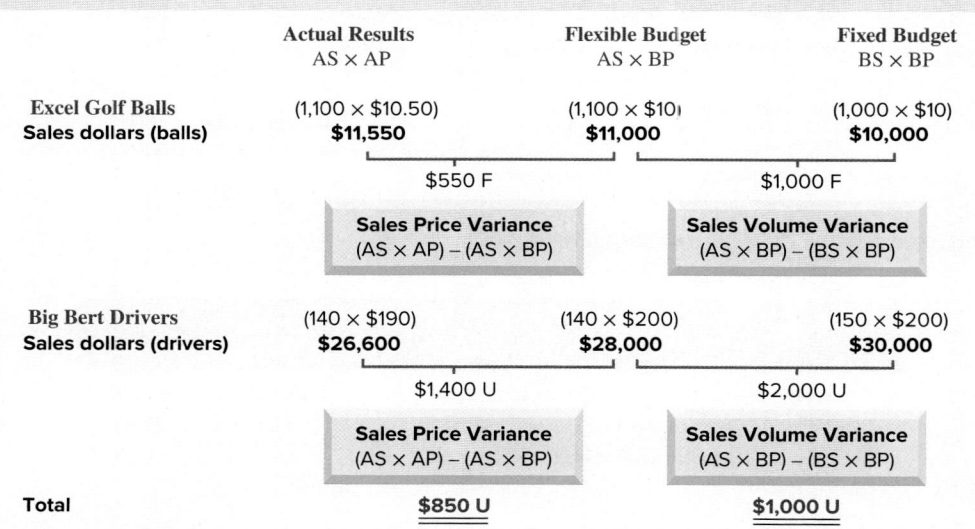

EXHIBIT 21.18

Computing Sales Variances*

*AS = actual sales units; AP = actual sales price; BP = budgeted sales price; BS = budgeted sales units (fixed budget).

Managers use sales variances for planning and control purposes. G-Max sold 90 combined total units (both balls and drivers) more than budgeted, yet its total sales price and sales volume variances are unfavorable. The unfavorable sales price variance is due mainly to a decrease in the selling price of Big Bert drivers by $10 per unit. Management must assess whether this price decrease will continue. Likewise, the unfavorable sales volume variance is due to G-Max selling fewer Big Bert drivers (140) than were budgeted (150). Management must assess whether this decreased demand for Big Bert drivers will persist.

Overall, management can use the detailed sales variances to examine what caused the company to sell more golf balls and fewer drivers. Managers can also use this information to evaluate and even reward salespeople. Extra compensation is paid to salespeople who contribute to a higher profit margin.

Decision Maker

Sales Manager   The current performance report reveals a large favorable sales volume variance but an unfavorable sales price variance. You did not expect a large increase in sales volume. What steps do you take to analyze this situation? ■   *Answer:* The unfavorable sales price variance suggests that actual prices were lower than budgeted prices. As the sales manager, you want to know the reasons for a lower-than-expected price. Perhaps your salespeople lowered the price of certain products by offering quantity discounts. You then might want to know what prompted them to offer the quantity discounts (perhaps competitors were offering discounts). You want to determine if the increased sales volume is due mainly to discounted prices or other factors (such as advertising).

NEED-TO-KNOW 21-6

COMPREHENSIVE

Flexible Budgets and Variance Analysis

Pacific Company provides the following information about its budgeted and actual results for June 2019. Although the expected June volume was 25,000 units produced and sold, the company actually produced and sold 27,000 units, as detailed here.

	Budget (25,000 units)	Actual (27,000 units)
Selling price	$5.00 per unit	$141,210
Variable costs (per unit)		
Direct materials	1.24 per unit	$30,800
Direct labor.................................	1.50 per unit	37,800
Factory supplies*	0.25 per unit	9,990
Utilities*	0.50 per unit	16,200
Selling costs	0.40 per unit	9,180
Fixed costs (per month)		
Depreciation—Machinery*....................	$3,750	$3,710
Depreciation—Factory building*..............	2,500	2,500
General liability insurance....................	1,200	1,250
Property taxes on office equipment	500	485
Other administrative expense.................	750	900

*Indicates factory overhead item; $0.75 per unit or $3 per direct labor hour for variable overhead, and $0.25 per unit or $1 per direct labor hour for fixed overhead.

Standard costs based on expected output of 25,000 units.

	Standard Quantity	Total Cost
Direct materials, 4 oz. per unit @ $0.31 per oz..................	100,000 oz.	$31,000
Direct labor, 0.25 hr. per unit @ $6.00 per hr....................	6,250 hrs.	37,500
Overhead, 6,250 standard hours × $4.00 per DLH...............		25,000

Actual costs incurred to produce 27,000 units.

	Actual Quantity	Total Cost
Direct materials, 110,000 oz. @ $0.28 per oz....................	110,000 oz.	$30,800
Direct labor, 5,400 hrs. @ $7.00 per hr.	5,400 hrs.	37,800
Overhead ($9,990 + $16,200 + $3,710 + $2,500)		32,400

Required

1. Prepare June flexible budgets showing expected sales, costs, and net income assuming 20,000, 25,000, and 30,000 units of output produced and sold.

2. Prepare a flexible budget performance report that compares actual results with the amounts budgeted if the actual volume of 27,000 units had been expected.

3. Apply variance analysis for direct materials and direct labor.

4. Compute the total overhead variance and the overhead controllable and overhead volume variances.

5. Compute spending and efficiency variances for overhead. (Refer to Appendix 21A.)

6. Prepare journal entries to record standard costs, and price and quantity variances, for direct materials, direct labor, and factory overhead. (Refer to Appendix 21A.)

PLANNING THE SOLUTION

- Prepare a table showing the expected results at the three specified levels of output. Compute the variable costs by multiplying the per unit variable costs by the expected volumes. Include fixed costs at the given amounts. Combine the amounts in the table to show total variable costs, contribution margin, total fixed costs, and income from operations.

- Prepare a table showing the actual results and the amounts that should be incurred at 27,000 units. Show any differences in the third column and label them with an *F* for favorable if they increase income or a *U* for unfavorable if they decrease income.

- Using the chapter's format, compute these total variances and the individual variances requested:
    - Total materials variance (including the direct materials quantity variance and the direct materials price variance).
    - Total direct labor variance (including the direct labor efficiency variance and rate variance).
    - Total overhead variance (including both controllable and volume overhead variances and their component variances). Variable overhead is applied at the rate of $3.00 per direct labor hour. Fixed overhead is applied at the rate of $1.00 per direct labor hour.

SOLUTION

1.

	Flexible Budgets				
	Flexible Budget				
	Variable	Total	Flexible Budget for Unit Sales of		
	Amount	Fixed			
For Month Ended June 30, 2019	per Unit	Cost	20,000	25,000	30,000
Sales	$5.00		$100,000	$125,000	$150,000
Variable costs					
Direct materials	1.24		24,800	31,000	37,200
Direct labor..........................	1.50		30,000	37,500	45,000
Factory supplies......................	0.25		5,000	6,250	7,500
Utilities	0.50		10,000	12,500	15,000
Selling costs	0.40		8,000	10,000	12,000
Total variable costs	3.89		77,800	97,250	116,700
Contribution margin	$1.11		22,200	27,750	33,300
Fixed costs					
Depreciation—Machinery		$3,750	3,750	3,750	3,750
Depreciation—Factory building..........		2,500	2,500	2,500	2,500
General liability insurance..............		1,200	1,200	1,200	1,200
Property taxes on office equipment		500	500	500	500
Other administrative expense............		750	750	750	750
Total fixed costs		$8,700	8,700	8,700	8,700
Income from operations.................			$ 13,500	$ 19,050	$ 24,600

2.

Flexible Budget Performance Report			
For Month Ended June 30, 2019	Flexible Budget	Actual Results	Variance†
Sales (27,000 units)	$135,000	$141,210	$6,210 F
Variable costs			
Direct materials	33,480	30,800	2,680 F
Direct labor.	40,500	37,800	2,700 F
Factory supplies*	6,750	9,990	3,240 U
Utilities*	13,500	16,200	2,700 U
Selling costs	10,800	9,180	1,620 F
Total variable costs	105,030	103,970	1,060 F
Contribution margin	29,970	37,240	7,270 F
Fixed costs			
Depreciation—Machinery*	3,750	3,710	40 F
Depreciation—Factory building*	2,500	2,500	0
General liability insurance	1,200	1,250	50 U
Property taxes on office equipment	500	485	15 F
Other administrative expense	750	900	150 U
Total fixed costs	8,700	8,845	145 U
Income from operations	$ 21,270	$ 28,395	$7,125 F

*Indicates factory overhead item.   †F = Favorable variance; U = Unfavorable variance.

3. Variance analysis of materials and labor costs.

Direct materials cost variances

Actual cost (110,000 oz. @ $0.28)	$30,800
Standard cost (108,000 oz. @ $0.31)	33,480
Direct materials cost variance	$ 2,680 F

Price and quantity variances (based on formulas in Exhibit 21.10):

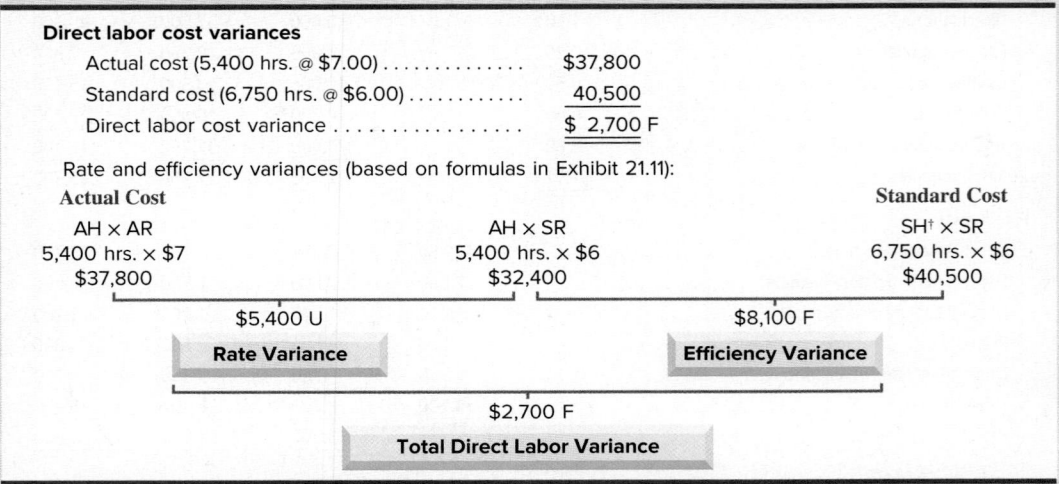

Actual Cost		**Standard Cost**
AQ × AP	AQ × SP	SQ* × SP
110,000 oz. × $0.28	110,000 oz. × $0.31	108,000 oz. × $0.31
$30,800	$34,100	$33,480

$3,300 F — **Price Variance**

$620 U — **Quantity Variance**

$2,680 F — **Total Direct Materials Variance**

*SQ = 27,000 actual units of output × 4 oz. standard quantity per unit.

Direct labor cost variances

Actual cost (5,400 hrs. @ $7.00)	$37,800
Standard cost (6,750 hrs. @ $6.00)	40,500
Direct labor cost variance	$ 2,700 F

Rate and efficiency variances (based on formulas in Exhibit 21.11):

Actual Cost		**Standard Cost**
AH × AR	AH × SR	SH† × SR
5,400 hrs. × $7	5,400 hrs. × $6	6,750 hrs. × $6
$37,800	$32,400	$40,500

$5,400 U — **Rate Variance**

$8,100 F — **Efficiency Variance**

$2,700 F — **Total Direct Labor Variance**

†SH = 27,000 actual units of output × 0.25 standard DLH per unit.

4. Total, controllable, and volume variances for overhead.

Total overhead cost variance	
Total overhead cost incurred (given)	$32,400
Total overhead applied (27,000 units × 0.25 DLH per unit × $4 per DLH)	27,000
Overhead cost variance	$ 5,400 U
Controllable variance	
Total overhead cost incurred (given)	$32,400
Budgeted overhead (from flexible budget for 27,000 units)	26,500
Controllable variance	$ 5,900 U
Volume variance	
Budgeted fixed overhead (at predicted capacity)	$ 6,250
Applied fixed overhead (6,750 standard DLH × $1.00 fixed overhead rate per DLH)	6,750
Volume variance	$ 500 F

5. Variable overhead spending variance, variable overhead efficiency variance, fixed overhead spending variance, and fixed overhead volume variance. (See Appendix 21A.)

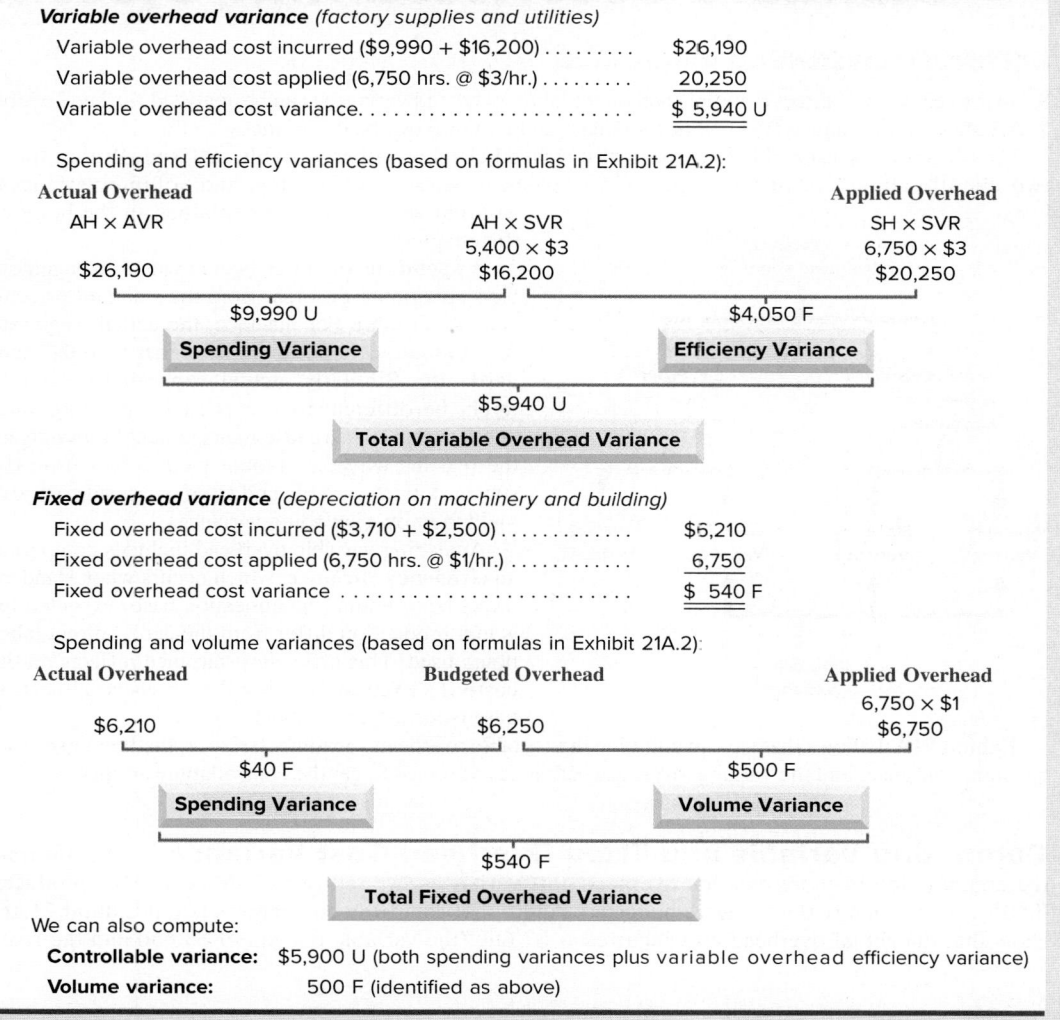

Variable overhead variance (factory supplies and utilities)

Variable overhead cost incurred ($9,990 + $16,200)	$26,190
Variable overhead cost applied (6,750 hrs. @ $3/hr.)	20,250
Variable overhead cost variance.	$ 5,940 U

Spending and efficiency variances (based on formulas in Exhibit 21A.2):

Actual Overhead		**Applied Overhead**
AH × AVR	AH × SVR	SH × SVR
	5,400 × $3	6,750 × $3
$26,190	$16,200	$20,250

$9,990 U — **Spending Variance**

$4,050 F — **Efficiency Variance**

$5,940 U — **Total Variable Overhead Variance**

Fixed overhead variance (depreciation on machinery and building)

Fixed overhead cost incurred ($3,710 + $2,500)	$6,210
Fixed overhead cost applied (6,750 hrs. @ $1/hr.)	6,750
Fixed overhead cost variance	$ 540 F

Spending and volume variances (based on formulas in Exhibit 21A.2):

Actual Overhead	**Budgeted Overhead**	**Applied Overhead**
		6,750 × $1
$6,210	$6,250	$6,750

$40 F — **Spending Variance**

$500 F — **Volume Variance**

$540 F — **Total Fixed Overhead Variance**

We can also compute:

Controllable variance: $5,900 U (both spending variances plus variable overhead efficiency variance)

Volume variance: 500 F (identified as above)

6. Journal entries under a standard cost system. (Refer to Appendix 21A.)

Work in Process Inventory	33,480	
Direct Materials Quantity Variance	620	
Direct Materials Price Variance		3,300
Raw Materials Inventory		30,800
Work in Process Inventory	40,500	
Direct Labor Rate Variance	5,400	
Direct Labor Efficiency Variance		8,100
Factory Wages Payable		37,800

Work in Process Inventory*	27,000	
Variable Overhead Spending Variance	9,990	
Variable Overhead Efficiency Variance. . .		4,050
Fixed Overhead Spending Variance		40
Fixed Overhead Volume Variance		500
Factory Overhead†		32,400

*Overhead applied = 6,750 standard DLH × $4 per DLH.
†Overhead incurred = $9,990 + $16,200 + $3,710 + $2,500.

21A

Expanded Overhead Variances and Standard Cost Accounting System

P5

Compute overhead spending and efficiency variances.

EXPANDED OVERHEAD VARIANCES

Similar to analysis of direct materials and direct labor, overhead variances can be analyzed further. Exhibit 21A.1 shows an expanded framework for understanding these overhead variances.

This framework uses classifications of overhead costs as either variable or fixed. Within those two classifications are further types of variances—spending, efficiency, and volume variances. Volume variances were explained in the body of the chapter.

A **spending variance** occurs when management pays an amount different from the standard price to acquire an item. For instance, the actual wage rate paid to indirect labor might be higher than the standard rate. Similarly, actual supervisory salaries might be different than expected. Spending variances such as these cause management to investigate the reasons why the amount paid differs from the standard. Both variable and fixed overhead costs can yield their own spending variances.

Analyzing variable overhead includes computing an **efficiency variance,** which occurs when standard direct labor hours (the allocation base) expected for actual production differ from the actual direct labor hours used. This efficiency variance reflects on the cost-effectiveness in using the overhead allocation base (such as direct labor).

EXHIBIT 21A.1

Expanded Framework for Total Overhead Variance

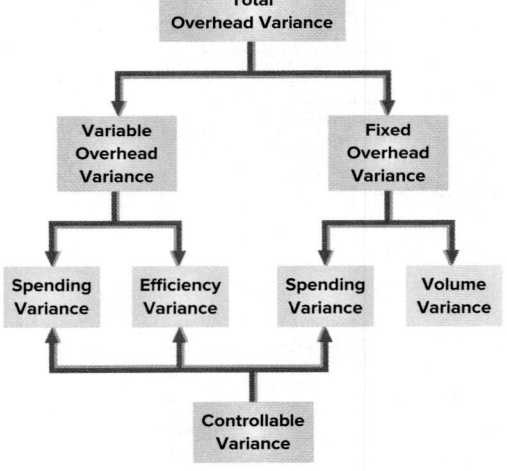

Exhibit 21A.1 shows that we can combine the variable overhead spending variance, the fixed overhead spending variance, and the variable overhead efficiency variance to get the controllable variance.

Computing Variable and Fixed Overhead Cost Variances
To illustrate the computation of more detailed overhead cost variances, we return to G-Max. G-Max produced 3,500 units when 4,000 units were budgeted. Additional data from cost reports (from Exhibit 21.16) show that the actual overhead cost incurred is $7,650 (the variable portion of $3,650 and the fixed

portion of $4,000). From Exhibit 21.12, each unit requires one hour of direct labor, variable overhead is applied at a rate of $1.00 per direct labor hour, and the predetermined fixed overhead rate is $1.00 per direct labor hour. With this information, we compute overhead variances for both variable and fixed overhead as follows.

Variable Overhead Variance	
Actual variable overhead (given)	$ 3,650
Applied variable overhead (3,500 units × 1 standard DLH × $1.00 VOH rate per DLH) . . .	3,500
Variable overhead variance	$ 150 U

Fixed Overhead Variance	
Actual fixed overhead (given)	$ 4,000
Applied fixed overhead (3,500 units × 1 standard DLH × $1.00 FOH rate per DLH)	3,500
Fixed overhead variance	$ 500 U

Management should seek to determine the causes of these unfavorable variances and take corrective action. To help better isolate the causes of these variances, more detailed overhead variances can be used, as we show next.

Expanded Overhead Variance Formulas
Exhibit 21A.2 shows formulas to use in computing detailed overhead variances.

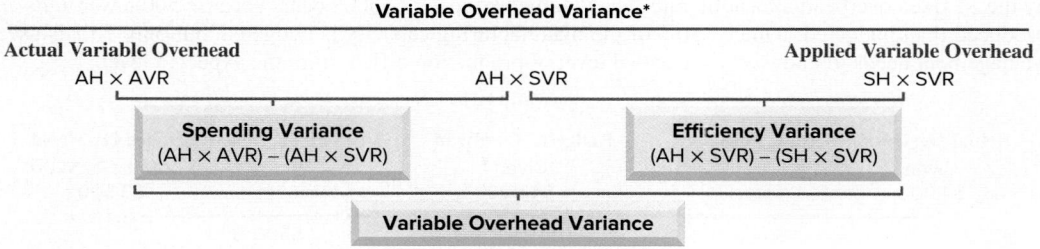

*AH = actual direct labor hours; AVR = actual variable overhead rate; SH = standard direct labor hours; SVR = standard variable overhead rate.

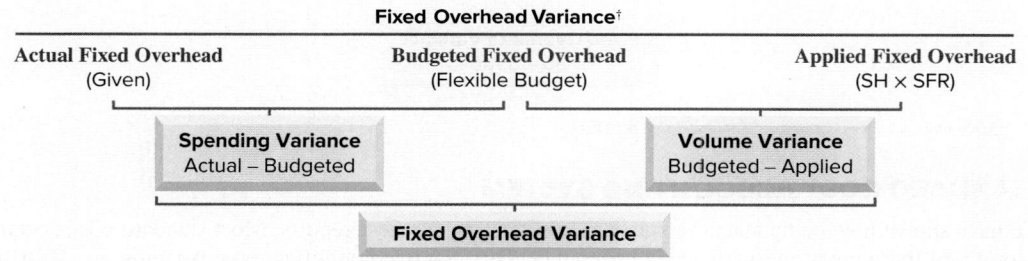

†SH = standard direct labor hours; SFR = standard fixed overhead rate.

Variable Overhead Cost Variances
Using these formulas, Exhibit 21A.3 offers insight into the causes of G-Max's $150 unfavorable variable overhead cost variance. G-Max applies overhead based on direct labor hours. It used 3,400 direct labor hours to produce 3,500 units. This compares favorably to the standard requirement of 3,500 direct labor hours at one labor hour per unit. At a standard variable overhead rate of $1.00 per direct labor hour, this should have resulted in variable overhead costs of $3,400 (middle column of Exhibit 21A.3).

EXHIBIT 21A.3

Computing Variable
Overhead Cost Variances

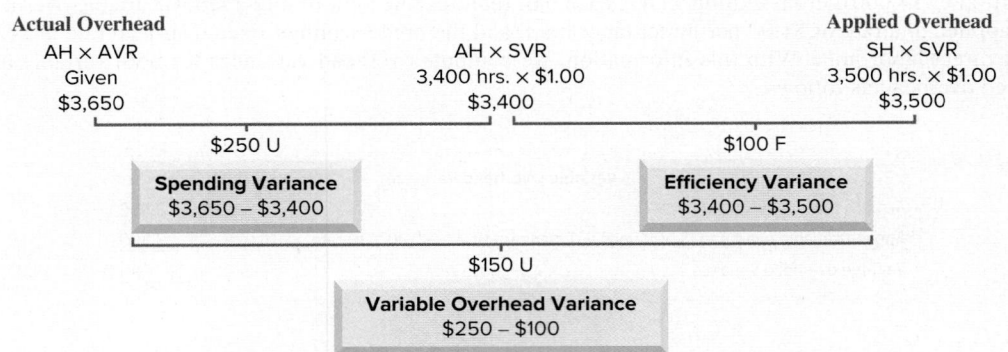

G-Max's cost records, however, report actual variable overhead of $3,650, or $250 higher than expected. This means G-Max has an unfavorable variable overhead spending variance of $250 ($3,650 − $3,400). On the other hand, G-Max used 100 fewer labor hours than expected to make 3,500 units, and its actual variable overhead is lower than its applied variable overhead. Thus, G-Max has a favorable variable overhead efficiency variance of $100 ($3,400 − $3,500).

Fixed Overhead Cost Variances

Exhibit 21A.4 provides insight into the causes of G-Max's $500 unfavorable fixed overhead variance. G-Max reports that it incurred $4,000 in actual fixed overhead; this amount equals the budgeted fixed overhead for May at the expected production level of 4,000 units (see Exhibit 21.12). Thus, the fixed overhead spending variance is zero, suggesting good control of fixed overhead costs. G-Max's budgeted fixed overhead application rate is $1 per hour ($4,000/4,000 direct labor hours), but the actual production level is only 3,500 units.

With this information, we compute the fixed overhead volume variance shown in Exhibit 21A.4. The applied fixed overhead is computed by multiplying 3,500 standard hours allowed for the actual production by the $1 fixed overhead allocation rate. The volume variance of $500 occurs because 500 fewer units are produced than budgeted; namely, 80% of the manufacturing capacity is budgeted, but only 70% is used. Management needs to know why the actual level of production differs from the expected level.

EXHIBIT 21A.4

Computing Fixed Overhead
Cost Variances

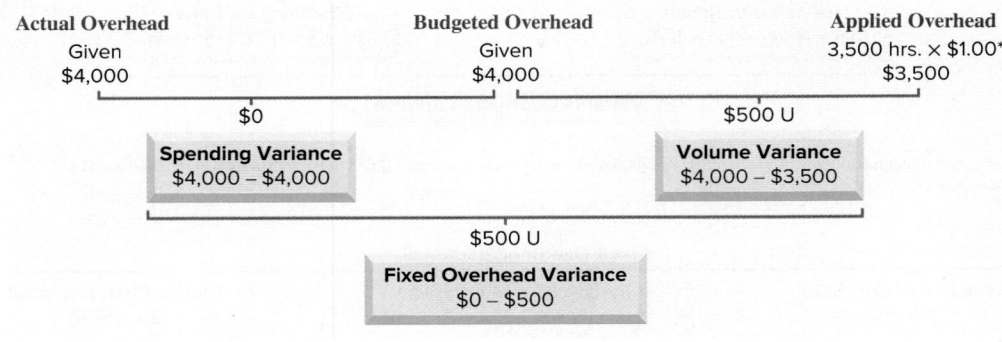

*3,500 units × 1 DLH per unit × $1.00 FOH rate per DLH.

STANDARD COST ACCOUNTING SYSTEM

P6

Prepare journal entries for
standard costs and account
for price and quantity
variances.

We have shown how companies use standard costs in management reports. Most standard cost systems also record these costs and variances in accounts. This practice simplifies recordkeeping and helps in preparing reports. Although we do not need knowledge of standard cost accounting practices to understand standard costs and their use, we must know how to interpret the accounts in which standard costs and variances are recorded. The entries in this section briefly illustrate the important aspects of this process for G-Max's standard costs and variances for May.

The first of these entries records standard materials cost incurred in May in the Work in Process Inventory account. This part of the entry is similar to the usual accounting entry, but the amount of the debit equals the standard cost ($35,000) instead of the actual cost ($37,800). This entry credits Raw Materials Inventory for actual cost. The difference between standard and actual direct materials costs is recorded with debits to two separate materials variance accounts (recall Exhibit 21.10). Both the materials price and quantity variances are recorded as debits because they reflect additional costs higher than the standard cost (if actual costs are less than the standard, they are recorded as credits). This treatment (debit) reflects their unfavorable effect because they represent higher costs and lower income.

May 31	Work in Process Inventory (standard cost)...............	35,000	
	Direct Materials Price Variance*	**1,800**	
	Direct Materials Quantity Variance....................	**1,000**	
	Raw Materials Inventory (actual cost)...............		37,800
	Record standard cost of direct materials used		
	and record materials variances.		

*Many companies record the materials price variance when materials are purchased. For simplicity, we record both the materials price and quantity variances when materials are issued to production.

The second entry debits Work in Process Inventory for the standard labor cost of the goods manufactured during May ($56,000). Actual labor cost ($56,100) is recorded with a credit to the Factory Wages Payable account. The difference between standard and actual labor costs is explained by two variances (see Exhibit 21.11). The direct labor rate variance is unfavorable and is debited to that account. The direct labor efficiency variance is favorable and that account is credited. The direct labor efficiency variance is favorable because it represents a lower cost and a higher net income.

May 31	Work in Process Inventory (standard cost)...............	56,000	
	Direct Labor Rate Variance..........................	**1,700**	
	Direct Labor Efficiency Variance..................		1,600
	Factory Wages Payable (actual cost)...............		56,100
	Record standard cost of direct labor used and		
	record labor variances.		

The entry to assign standard predetermined overhead to the cost of goods manufactured must debit the $7,000 predetermined amount to the Work in Process Inventory account. Actual overhead costs of $7,650 were debited to Factory Overhead during the period (entries not shown here). Thus, when Factory Overhead is applied to Work in Process Inventory, the actual amount is credited to the Factory Overhead account. To account for the difference between actual and standard overhead costs, the entry includes a $250 debit to the Variable Overhead Spending Variance, a $100 credit to the Variable Overhead Efficiency Variance, and a $500 debit to the Volume Variance (recall Exhibits 21A.3 and 21A.4). (An alternative [simpler] approach is to record the difference with a $150 debit to the Controllable Variance account and a $500 debit to the Volume Variance account.)

May 31	Work in Process Inventory............................	7,000	
	Volume Variance	**500**	
	Variable Overhead Spending Variance.................	**250**	
	Variable Overhead Efficiency Variance		100
	Factory Overhead..............................		7,650
	Apply overhead at standard rate of $2 per standard direct		
	labor hour (3,500 hours) and record overhead variances.		

The balances of these different variance accounts accumulate until the end of the accounting period. As a result, the unfavorable variances of some months can offset the favorable variances of other months.

These ending variance account balances, which reflect results of the period's various transactions and events, are closed at period-end. If the amounts are *immaterial,* they are added to or subtracted from the balance of the Cost of Goods Sold account. This process is similar to that shown in the job order costing chapter for eliminating an underapplied or overapplied balance in the Factory Overhead account. (*Note:* These variance balances, which represent differences between actual and standard costs, must be added to or subtracted from the materials, labor, and overhead costs recorded. In this way, the recorded costs equal the actual costs incurred in the period; a company must use actual costs in external financial statements prepared in accordance with generally accepted accounting principles.)

Point: If variances are material, they can be allocated between Work in Process Inventory, Finished Goods Inventory, and Cost of Goods Sold. This closing process is explained in advanced courses.

Standard Costing Income Statement
In addition to the reports discussed in this chapter, management can use a **standard costing income statement** to summarize company performance for a period. This income statement reports sales and cost of goods sold at their *standard* amounts, and then

lists the individual sales and cost variances to compute gross profit at actual cost. Exhibit 21A.5 provides an example. Unfavorable variances are *added* to cost of goods sold at standard cost; favorable variances are *subtracted* from cost of goods sold at standard cost.

EXHIBIT 21A.5

Standard Costing Income Statement

Standard Costing Income Statement For Year Ended December 31, 2019		
Sales revenue (at standard)		•••••
Sales price variance.	•••	
Sales volume variance	•••	•••
Sales revenue (actual)		•••••
Cost of goods sold (at standard)		•••••
Manufacturing cost variances		
Direct materials price variance	•••	
Direct materials quantity variance.	•••	
Direct labor rate variance	•••	
Direct labor efficiency variance.	•••	
Variable overhead spending variance	•••	
Variable overhead efficiency variance	•••	
Fixed overhead spending variance.	•••	
Fixed overhead volume variance	•••	
Total manufacturing cost variances	•••	
Cost of goods sold (actual).		•••••
Gross profit	••••	
Selling expenses.	•••	
General and administrative expenses.	•••	
Income from operations.	•••••	

> Add unfavorable variances; subtract favorable variances.

NEED-TO-KNOW 21-7

Recording Variances

P6

Prepare the journal entry to record these direct materials variances.

Direct materials cost actually incurred.	$73,200
Direct materials quantity variance	3,800 F
Direct materials price variance.	1,300 U

Solution

Work in Process Inventory.	75,700	
Direct Materials Price Variance	1,300	
Direct Materials Quantity Variance.		3,800
Raw Materials Inventory.		73,200

Do More: QS 21-17, E 21-14

Summary: Cheat Sheet

STANDARD COSTING

Standard cost: Preset cost for a product or service.

Management by exception: When managers focus on significant differences between actual costs and standard costs.

Cost variance: Actual cost − Standard cost
          Actual cost < Standard cost → Favorable
          Actual cost > Standard cost → Unfavorable

Price variance: $(AQ \times AP) - (AQ \times SP)$

Quantity variance: $(AQ \times SP) - (SQ \times SP)$
  AQ = actual quantity, AP = actual price,
  SQ = standard quantity, SP = standard price

FIXED AND FLEXIBLE BUDGETS

Fixed budget: Based on a single activity level.

Flexible budget: Based on several activity levels.

Variance: If difference between budgeted and actual amounts is:
        Favorable → Leads to higher income.
        Unfavorable → Leads to lower income.

Total budgeted costs = Total fixed costs + (Total variable cost per unit × Units of activity level)

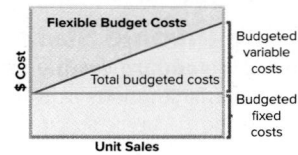

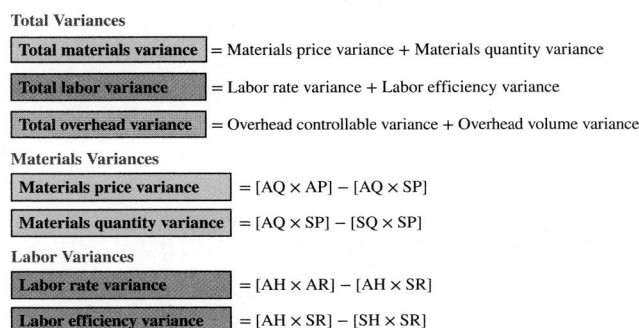

STANDARD COST VARIANCES

Total Variances

Total materials variance = Materials price variance + Materials quantity variance

Total labor variance = Labor rate variance + Labor efficiency variance

Total overhead variance = Overhead controllable variance + Overhead volume variance

Materials Variances

Materials price variance = [AQ × AP] − [AQ × SP]

Materials quantity variance = [AQ × SP] − [SQ × SP]

Labor Variances

Labor rate variance = [AH × AR] − [AH × SR]

Labor efficiency variance = [AH × SR] − [SH × SR]

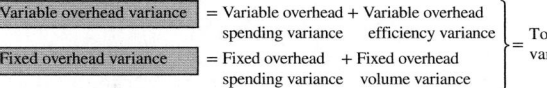

Overhead controllable variance = Actual total overhead − Budgeted total overhead

Overhead volume variance = Budgeted fixed overhead − Applied fixed overhead

Detailed Overhead Variances (Appendix 21A)

Variable overhead variance = Variable overhead + Variable overhead spending variance efficiency variance

Fixed overhead variance = Fixed overhead + Fixed overhead spending variance volume variance

} = Total overhead variance

Variable overhead spending variance = [AH × AVR] − [AH × SVR]

Variable overhead efficiency variance = [AH × SVR] − [SH × SVR]

Fixed overhead spending variance = Actual fixed overhead − Budgeted fixed overhead

where AQ is Actual Quantity of materials; AP is Actual Price of materials; AH is Actual Hours of labor; AR is Actual Rate of wages; AVR is Actual Variable Rate of overhead; SQ is Standard Quantity of materials; SP is Standard Price of materials; SH is Standard Hours of labor; SR is Standard Rate of wages; SVR is Standard Variable Rate of overhead.

Sales Variances

Sales price variance = [AS × AP] − [AS × BP]

Sales volume variance = [AS × BP] − [BS × BP]

where AS = Actual Sales units; AP = Actual sales Price; BP = Budgeted sales Price; BS = Budgeted Sales units (fixed budget).

Key Terms

Benchmarking (834)

Budget report (821)

Controllable variance (836)

Cost variance (828)

Efficiency variance (844)

Favorable variance (822)

Fixed budget (821)

Fixed budget performance report (822)

Flexible budget (821)

Flexible budget performance report (825)

Integrated reporting (838)

International Integrated Reporting Council (838)

Management by exception (827)

Overhead cost variance (835)

Price variance (830)

Quantity variance (830)

Spending variance (844)

Standard costing income statement (847)

Standard costs (827)

Unfavorable variance (822)

Variance (822)

Variance analysis (828)

Volume variance (836)

Multiple Choice Quiz

1. A company predicts its production and sales will be 24,000 units. At that level of activity, its fixed costs are budgeted at $300,000, and its variable costs are budgeted at $246,000. If its activity level declines to 20,000 units, what will be its budgeted fixed costs and its variable costs?
   a. Fixed, $300,000; variable, $246,000
   b. Fixed, $250,000; variable, $205,000
   c. Fixed, $300,000; variable, $205,000
   d. Fixed, $250,000; variable, $246,000
   e. Fixed, $300,000; variable, $300,000

2. Using the following information about a single-product company, compute its total actual cost of direct materials used.
   • Direct materials standard cost: 5 lbs. × $2 per lb. = $10.
   • Total direct materials cost variance: $15,000 unfavorable.
   • Actual direct materials used: 300,000 lbs.
   • Actual units produced: 60,000 units.

   a. $585,000   c. $300,000   e. $615,000
   b. $600,000   d. $315,000

3. A company uses four hours of direct labor to produce a product unit. The standard direct labor cost is $20 per hour. This period the company produced 20,000 units and used 84,160 hours of direct labor at a total cost of $1,599,040. What is its labor rate variance for the period?
   a. $83,200 F   c. $84,160 F   e. $960 F
   b. $84,160 U   d. $83,200 U

4. A company's standard for a unit of its single product is $6 per unit in variable overhead (4 hours × $1.50 per hour). Actual data for the period show variable overhead costs of $150,000 and production of 24,000 units. Its total variable overhead cost variance is
   a. $6,000 F.   c. $114,000 U.   e. $0.
   b. $6,000 U.   d. $114,000 F.

5. A company's standard for a unit of its single product is $4 per unit in fixed overhead ($24,000 total/6,000 units budgeted). Actual data for the period show total actual fixed overhead of $24,100 and production of 4,800 units. Its volume variance is

a. $4,800 U.   **c.** $100 U.   **e.** $4,900 U.

b. $4,800 F.   **d.** $100 F.

ANSWERS TO MULTIPLE CHOICE QUIZ

1. c; Fixed costs remain at $300,000; Variable costs = ($246,000/24,000 units) × 20,000 units = $205,000

2. e; Budgeted direct materials + Unfavorable variance = Actual cost of direct materials used; or 60,000 units × $10 per unit = $600,000 + $15,000 U = $615,000

3. c; (AH × AR) − (AH × SR) = $1,599,040 − (84,160 hours × $20 per hour) = $84,160 F

4. b; Actual variable overhead − Variable overhead applied to production = Variable overhead cost variance; or $150,000 − (96,000 hours × $1.50 per hour) = $6,000 U

5. a; Budgeted fixed overhead − Fixed overhead applied to production = Volume variance; or $24,000 − (4,800 units × $4 per unit) = $4,800 U

[A] *Superscript letter A denotes assignments based on Appendix 21A.*

🔲 Icon denotes assignments that involve decision making.

Discussion Questions

1. 🔲 What limits the usefulness to managers of fixed budget performance reports?

2. 🔲 Identify the main purpose of a flexible budget for managers.

3. Prepare a flexible budget performance report title (in proper form) for Spalding Company for calendar-year 2019. Why is a proper title important for this or any report?

4. 🔲 What type of analysis does a flexible budget performance report help management perform?

5. In what sense can a variable cost be considered constant?

6. 🔲 What department is usually responsible for a direct labor rate variance? What department is usually responsible for a direct labor efficiency variance? Explain.

7. What is a price variance? What is a quantity variance?

8. 🔲 What is the purpose of using standard costs?

9. **Google** monitors its fixed overhead. In an analysis of fixed overhead cost variances, **GOOGLE** what is the volume variance?

10. What is the predetermined standard overhead rate? How is it computed?

11. In general, variance analysis is said to provide information about _____ and _____ variances.

12. 🔲 **Samsung** monitors its overhead. In an analysis of overhead cost variances, **Samsung** what is the controllable variance and what causes it?

13. What are the relations among standard costs, flexible budgets, variance analysis, and management by exception?

14. 🔲 How can the manager of advertising sales at **Google** use flexible budgets to enhance performance? **GOOGLE**

15. 🔲 Is it possible for a retail store such as **APPLE** **Apple** to use variances in analyzing its operating performance? Explain.

16. 🔲 Assume that **Samsung** is budgeted to operate at 80% of capacity but actually **Samsung** operates at 75% of capacity. What effect will the 5% deviation have on its controllable variance? Its volume variance?

17. List at least two positive and two negative features of standard costing systems.

18. Describe the concept of *management by exception* and explain how standard costs help managers apply this concept to control costs.

🔲 **connect**

QUICK STUDY

QS 21-1

Flexible budget performance report

P1

Beech Company produced and sold 105,000 units of its product in May. For the level of production achieved in May, the budgeted amounts were: sales, $1,300,000; variable costs, $750,000; and fixed costs, $300,000. The following actual financial results are available for May. Prepare a flexible budget performance report for May.

	Actual
Sales (105,000 units)	$1,275,000
Variable costs	712,500
Fixed costs	300,000

QS 21-2

Flexible budget   **P1**

Based on predicted production of 24,000 units, a company anticipates $300,000 of fixed costs and $246,000 of variable costs. If the company actually produces 20,000 units, what are the flexible budget amounts of fixed and variable costs?

Brodrick Company expects to produce 20,000 units for the year ending December 31. A flexible budget for 20,000 units of production reflects sales of $400,000; variable costs of $80,000; and fixed costs of $150,000. If the company instead expects to produce and sell 26,000 units for the year, calculate the expected level of income from operations.

QS 21-3
Flexible budget
P1

Refer to information in QS 21-3. Assume that actual sales for the year are $480,000 (26,000 units), actual variable costs for the year are $112,000, and actual fixed costs for the year are $145,000. Prepare a flexible budget performance report for the year.

QS 21-4
Flexible budget
performance report **P1**

BatCo makes metal baseball bats. Each bat requires 1 kg of aluminum at $18 per kg and 0.25 direct labor hours at $20 per hour. Overhead is assigned at the rate of $40 per direct labor hour. What amounts would appear on a standard cost card for BatCo?

QS 21-5
Standard cost card **P2**

Refer to information in QS 21-5. Assume the actual cost to manufacture one metal bat is $40. Compute the cost variance and classify it as favorable or unfavorable.

QS 21-6
Cost variances **P2**

Tercer reports the following for one of its products. Compute the total direct materials cost variance and classify it as favorable or unfavorable.

QS 21-7
Materials variances
P3

Direct materials standard (4 lbs. @ $2 per lb.)	$8 per finished unit
Actual finished units produced	60,000 units
Actual cost of direct materials used	$540,000

Tercer reports the following for one of its products. Compute the direct materials price and quantity variances and classify each as favorable or unfavorable.

QS 21-8
Materials variances
P3

Direct materials standard (4 lbs. @ $2 per lb.) . . .	$8 per finished unit	Actual finished units produced	60,000 units
Actual direct materials used	300,000 lbs.	Actual cost of direct materials used . . .	$540,000

For the current period, Kayenta Company's manufacturing operations yield a $4,000 unfavorable direct materials price variance. The actual price per pound of material is $78; the standard price is $77.50 per pound. How many pounds of material were used in the current period?

QS 21-9
Materials cost variances **P3**

Juan Company's output for the current period was assigned a $150,000 standard direct materials cost. The direct materials variances included a $12,000 favorable price variance and a $2,000 favorable quantity variance. What is the actual total direct materials cost for the current period?

QS 21-10
Materials cost variances **P3**

The following information describes a company's direct labor usage in a recent period. Compute the direct labor rate and efficiency variances for the period and classify each as favorable or unfavorable.

QS 21-11
Direct labor variances
P3

Actual direct labor hours used.	65,000	Standard direct labor rate per hour.	$14
Actual direct labor rate per hour	$15	Standard direct labor hours for units produced	67,000

Frontera Company's output for the current period results in a $20,000 unfavorable direct labor rate variance and a $10,000 unfavorable direct labor efficiency variance. Production for the current period was assigned a $400,000 standard direct labor cost. What is the actual total direct labor cost for the current period?

QS 21-12
Labor cost variances **P3**

Fogel Co. expects to produce 116,000 units for the year. The company's flexible budget for 116,000 units of production shows variable overhead costs of $162,400 and fixed overhead costs of $124,000. For the year, the company incurred actual overhead costs of $262,800 while producing 110,000 units. Compute the controllable overhead variance and classify it as favorable or unfavorable.

QS 21-13
Controllable overhead
variance **P4**

QS 21-14
Controllable overhead variance
P4

AirPro Corp. reports the following for November. Compute the total overhead variance and controllable overhead variance for November and classify each as favorable or unfavorable.

Actual total factory overhead incurred	$28,175
Standard factory overhead:	
Variable overhead	$3.10 per unit produced
Fixed overhead ($12,000/12,000 predicted units to be produced)	$1 per unit
Predicted units to produce......................................	12,000 units
Actual units produced..	9,800 units

QS 21-15
Volume variance   **P4**

Refer to the information in QS 21-14. Compute the overhead volume variance for November and classify it as favorable or unfavorable.

QS 21-16
Overhead cost variances
P4

Alvarez Company's output for the current period yields a $20,000 favorable overhead volume variance and a $60,400 unfavorable overhead controllable variance. Standard overhead applied to production for the period is $225,000. What is the actual total overhead cost incurred for the period?

QS 21-17^A
Preparing overhead entries
P6

Refer to the information in QS 21-16. Alvarez records standard costs in its accounts. Prepare the journal entry to charge overhead costs to the Work in Process Inventory account and to record any variances.

QS 21-18^A
Total variable overhead cost variance
P5

Mosaic Company applies overhead using machine hours and reports the following information. Compute the total variable overhead cost variance and classify it as favorable or unfavorable.

Actual machine hours used	4,700 hours
Standard machine hours (for actual production).............................	5,000 hours
Actual variable overhead rate per hour.....................................	$4.15
Standard variable overhead rate per hour	$4.00

QS 21-19^A
Overhead spending and efficiency variances   **P5**

Refer to the information from QS 21-18. Compute the variable overhead spending variance and the variable overhead efficiency variance and classify each as favorable or unfavorable.

QS 21-20
Computing sales price and volume variances   **A1**

Farad, Inc., specializes in selling used trucks. During the month, Farad sold 50 trucks at an average price of $9,000 each. The budget for the month was to sell 45 trucks at an average price of $9,500 each. Compute the dealership's sales price variance and sales volume variance for the month and classify each as favorable or unfavorable.

QS 21-21
Sales variances   **A1**

In a recent year, **BMW** sold 182,158 of its 1 Series cars. Assume the company expected to sell 191,158 of these cars during the year. Also assume the budgeted sales price for each car was $30,000 and the actual sales price for each car was $30,200. Compute the sales price variance and the sales volume variance.

QS 21-22
Sustainability and standard costs
P1

MM Co. uses corrugated cardboard to ship its product to customers. Management believes it has found a more efficient way to package its products and use less cardboard. This new approach will reduce shipping costs from $10.00 per shipment to $9.25 per shipment. (1) If the company forecasts 1,200 shipments this year, what amount of total direct materials costs would appear on the shipping department's flexible budget? (2) How much is this sustainability improvement predicted to save in direct materials costs for this coming year?

HH Co. uses corrugated cardboard to ship its product to customers. Currently, the company's returns department incurs annual overhead costs of $72,000 and forecasts 2,000 returns per year. Management believes it has found a better way to package its products. As a result, the company expects to reduce the number of shipments that are returned due to damage by 5%. In addition, the initiative is expected to reduce the department's annual overhead by $12,000. Compute the returns department's standard overhead rate per return (*a*) before the sustainability improvement and (*b*) after the sustainability improvement. Round to the nearest cent.

QS 21-23
Sustainability and standard overhead rate

P4

Match the terms *a* through *d* with their correct definition 1 through 4.

a. Standard cost card
b. Management by exception
c. Standard cost
d. Ideal standard

_____ **1.** Quantity of input required if a production process is 100% efficient.
_____ **2.** Managing by focusing on large differences from standard costs.
_____ **3.** Record that accumulates standard cost information.
_____ **4.** Preset cost for delivering a product or service under normal conditions.

QS 21-24
Standard costs

C1

---

connect

Resset Co. provides the following results of April's operations: *F* indicates favorable and *U* indicates unfavorable. In applying management by exception, the company investigates all variances of $400 or more. Which variances will the company investigate?

Direct materials price variance	$ 300 F	Direct labor efficiency variance	$2,200 F
Direct materials quantity variance	3,000 U	Controllable overhead variance	400 U
Direct labor rate variance	100 U	Fixed overhead volume variance	500 F

EXERCISES

Exercise 21-1
Management by exception
C1

JPAK manufactures and sells mountain bikes. It operates eight hours a day, five days a week. Using this information, classify each of the following costs as fixed or variable with respect to the number of bikes made.

_____ **a.** Bike frames
_____ **b.** Screws for assembly
_____ **c.** Direct labor
_____ **d.** Taxes on property
_____ **e.** Bike tires
_____ **f.** Gas used for heating
_____ **g.** Office supplies
_____ **h.** Depreciation on tools
_____ **i.** Management salaries

Exercise 21-2
Classifying costs as fixed or variable
P1

Tempo Company's fixed budget (based on sales of 7,000 units) for the first quarter reveals the following. Compute (1) the total variable cost per unit, (2) total fixed costs, (3) income from operations for sales volume of 6,000 units, and (4) income from operations for sales volume of 8,000 units.

	Fixed Budget	
Sales (7,000 units × $400 per unit)		$2,800,000
Cost of goods sold		
Direct materials	$280,000	
Direct labor	490,000	
Production supplies	175,000	
Plant manager salary	65,000	1,010,000
Gross profit		1,790,000
Selling expenses		
Sales commissions	140,000	
Packaging	154,000	
Advertising	125,000	419,000
Administrative expenses		
Administrative salaries	85,000	
Depreciation—Office equip.	35,000	
Insurance	20,000	
Office rent	36,000	176,000
Income from operations		$1,195,000

Exercise 21-3
Preparing flexible budgets
P1

Check   Income (at 6,000 units), $972,000

Exercise 21-4

Preparing a flexible budget performance report **P1**

Check Sales variance, $21,000 F

Xion Co. budgets a selling price of $80 per unit, variable costs of $35 per unit, and total fixed costs of $270,000. During June, the company produced and sold 10,800 units and incurred actual variable costs of $351,000 and actual fixed costs of $285,000. Actual sales for June were $885,000. Prepare a flexible budget report showing variances between budgeted and actual results. List variable and fixed expenses separately.

Exercise 21-5

Preparing a flexible budget performance report

P1

Check Income variance, $4,000 F

Bay City Company's fixed budget performance report for July follows. The $647,500 budgeted total expenses include $487,500 variable expenses and $160,000 fixed expenses. Actual expenses include $158,000 fixed expenses. Prepare a flexible budget performance report that shows any variances between budgeted results and actual results. List fixed and variable expenses separately.

	Fixed Budget	Actual Results	Variances
Sales (in units)	7,500	7,200	
Sales (in dollars)	$750,000	$737,000	$13,000 U
Total expenses	647,500	641,000	6,500 F
Income from operations	$102,500	$ 96,000	$ 6,500 U

Exercise 21-6

Preparing a flexible budget report

P1

Lewis Co. reports the following results for May. Prepare a flexible budget report showing variances between budgeted and actual results. List variable and fixed expenses separately, and indicate variances as favorable (F) or unfavorable (U).

	Budgeted	Actual
Sales	$300 per unit	$435,000
Variable expenses	$120 per unit	$172,000
Fixed expenses (total)	$125,000	$122,000
Units produced and sold	1,200	1,400

Exercise 21-7

Standard unit cost; cost variances

P2

A manufactured product has the following information for August.

	Standard	Actual
Direct materials.................	2 lbs. per unit @ $2.50 per lb.	
Direct labor	0.5 hours per unit @ $16 per hour	
Overhead	$12 per direct labor hour	
Units manufactured		12,000
Total manufacturing costs		$225,400

Compute the (1) standard cost per unit, (2) total budgeted cost for production in August, and (3) total cost variance for August. Indicate whether the cost variance is favorable or unfavorable.

Exercise 21-8

Standard unit cost; total cost variance

P2

A manufactured product has the following information for June.

	Standard	Actual
Direct materials.................	6 lbs. @ $8 per lb.	48,500 lbs. @ $8.10 per lb.
Direct labor	2 hrs. @ $16 per hr.	15,700 hrs. @ $16.50 per hr.
Overhead	2 hrs. @ $12 per hr.	$198,000
Units manufactured		8,000

Compute the (1) standard cost per unit and (2) total cost variance for June. Indicate whether the cost variance is favorable or unfavorable.

Exercise 21-9

Direct materials variances **P3**

Refer to the information in Exercise 21-8 and compute the (1) direct materials price and (2) direct materials quantity variances. Indicate whether each variance is favorable or unfavorable.

Exercise 21-10

Direct labor variances **P3**

Refer to the information in Exercise 21-8 and compute the (1) direct labor rate and (2) direct labor efficiency variances. Indicate whether each variance is favorable or unfavorable.

Hutto Corp. has set the following standard direct materials and direct labor costs per unit for the product it manufactures.

| Direct materials (15 lbs. @ $4 per lb.) .... | $60 | Direct labor (3 hrs. @ $15 per hr.) .... | $45 |

During May the company incurred the following actual costs to produce 9,000 units.

| Direct materials (138,000 lbs. @ $3.75 per lb.).... | $517,500 | Direct labor (31,000 hrs. @ $15.10 per hr.).... | $468,100 |

Compute the (1) direct materials price and quantity variances and (2) direct labor rate and efficiency variances. Indicate whether each variance is favorable or unfavorable.

Exercise 21-11
Direct materials and direct labor variances
P3

Reed Corp. has set the following standard direct materials and direct labor costs per unit for the product it manufactures.

| Direct materials (10 lbs. @ $3 per lb.) .... | $30 | Direct labor (2 hrs. @ $12 per hr.) .... | $24 |

During June the company incurred the following actual costs to produce 9,000 units.

| Direct materials (92,000 lbs. @ $2.95 per lb.)..... | $271,400 | Direct labor (18,800 hrs. @ $12.05 per hr.).... | $226,540 |

Compute the (1) direct materials price and quantity variances and (2) direct labor rate and efficiency variances. Indicate whether each variance is favorable or unfavorable.

Exercise 21-12
Direct materials and direct labor variances
P3

Hart Company made 3,000 bookshelves using 22,000 board feet of wood costing $266,200. The company's direct materials standards for one bookshelf are 8 board feet of wood at $12 per board foot.

1. Compute the direct materials price and quantity variances and classify each as favorable or unfavorable.
2. Hart applies management by exception by investigating direct materials variances of more than 5% of actual direct materials costs. Which direct materials variances will Hart investigate further?

Exercise 21-13
Computing and interpreting materials variances   **P3**

Check   Price variance, $2,200 U

Refer to Exercise 21-13. Hart Company uses a standard costing system.

1. Prepare the journal entry to charge direct materials costs to Work in Process Inventory and record the materials variances.
2. Assume that Hart's materials variances are the only variances accumulated in the accounting period and that they are immaterial. Prepare the adjusting journal entry to close the variance accounts at period-end.

Exercise 21-14[A]
Recording and closing materials variances

P6

Check   (2) Cr. to Cost of Goods Sold, $21,800

The following describes production activities of Mercer Manufacturing for the year.

Actual direct materials used	16,000 lbs. at $4.05 per lb.
Actual direct labor used	5,545 hours for a total of $105,355
Actual units produced	30,000

Budgeted standards for each unit produced are 0.50 pound of direct material at $4.00 per pound and 10 minutes of direct labor at $20 per hour.

1. Compute the direct materials price and quantity variances and classify each as favorable or unfavorable.
2. Compute the direct labor rate and efficiency variances and classify each as favorable or unfavorable.

Exercise 21-15
Direct materials and direct labor variances
P3

Javonte Co. set standards of 3 hours of direct labor per unit of product and $15 per hour for the labor rate. During October, the company uses 16,250 hours of direct labor at a $247,000 total cost to produce 5,600 units of product. In November, the company uses 22,000 hours of direct labor at a $335,500 total cost to produce 6,000 units of product.

1. Compute the direct labor rate variance, the direct labor efficiency variance, and the total direct labor cost variance for each of these two months. Classify each variance as favorable or unfavorable.
2. Javonte investigates variances of more than 5% of actual direct labor cost. Which direct labor variances will the company investigate further?

Exercise 21-16
Computing and interpreting labor variances   **P3**

Check   (1) October rate variance, $3,250 U

Exercise 21-17

Computing total variable and fixed overhead variances

P4

Sedona Company set the following standard costs for one unit of its product for this year.

Direct material (20 lbs. @ $2.50 per lb.)	$ 50
Direct labor (10 hrs. @ $22.00 per hr.)	220
Variable overhead (10 hrs. @ $4.00 per hr.)	40
Fixed overhead (10 hrs. @ $1.60 per hr.)	16
Total standard cost	$326

The $5.60 ($4.00 + $1.60) total overhead rate per direct labor hour is based on an expected operating level equal to 75% of the factory's capacity of 50,000 units per month. The following monthly flexible budget information is also available.

	Operating Levels (% of capacity)		
Flexible Budget	**70%**	**75%**	**80%**
Budgeted output (units)	35,000	37,500	40,000
Budgeted labor (standard hours)	350,000	375,000	400,000
Budgeted overhead (dollars)			
Variable overhead	$ 1,400,000	$1,500,000	$ 1,600,000
Fixed overhead	600,000	600,000	600,000
Total overhead	$2,000,000	$2,100,000	$2,200,000

During the current month, the company operated at 70% of capacity, employees worked 340,000 hours, and the following actual overhead costs were incurred.

Variable overhead costs	$1,375,000
Fixed overhead costs	628,600
Total overhead costs	$2,003,600

1. Compute the predetermined overhead application rate per hour for total overhead, variable overhead, and fixed overhead.

2. Compute the total variable and total fixed overhead variances and classify each as favorable or unfavorable.

Exercise 21-18[A]

Detailed overhead variances **P5**

Check (1) Variable overhead: Spending, $15,000 U

Refer to the information from Exercise 21-17. Compute the following.

1. Variable overhead spending and efficiency variances.

2. Fixed overhead spending and volume variances.

3. Controllable variance.

Exercise 21-19

Computing total overhead rate and total overhead variance

P4

World Company expects to operate at 80% of its productive capacity of 50,000 units per month. At this planned level, the company expects to use 25,000 standard hours of direct labor. Overhead is allocated to products using a predetermined standard rate of 0.625 direct labor hour per unit. At the 80% capacity level, the total budgeted cost includes $50,000 fixed overhead cost and $275,000 variable overhead cost. In the current month, the company incurred $305,000 actual overhead and 22,000 actual labor hours while producing 35,000 units.

1. Compute the predetermined standard overhead rate for total overhead.

2. Compute the total overhead variance.

Exercise 21-20

Computing volume and controllable overhead variances **P4**

Refer to the information from Exercise 21-19. Compute the (1) overhead volume variance and (2) overhead controllable variance and classify each as favorable or unfavorable.

James Corp. applies overhead on the basis of direct labor hours. For the month of May, the company planned production of 8,000 units (80% of its production capacity of 10,000 units) and prepared the following overhead budget.

Exercise 21-21
Overhead controllable and volume variances; overhead variance report

P4

Overhead Budget	80% Operating Level
Production in units	8,000
Standard direct labor hours	24,000
Budgeted overhead	
Variable overhead costs	
Indirect materials................	$15,000
Indirect labor	24,000
Power.........................	6,000
Maintenance	3,000
Total variable costs	48,000
Fixed overhead costs	
Rent of factory building	15,000
Depreciation—Machinery	10,000
Supervisory salaries	19,400
Total fixed costs	44,400
Total overhead costs	$92,400

During May, the company operated at 90% capacity (9,000 units) and incurred the following actual overhead costs.

Overhead costs (actual)	
Indirect materials	$15,000
Indirect labor	26,500
Power	6,750
Maintenance	4,000
Rent of factory building	15,000
Depreciation—Machinery	10,000
Supervisory salaries	22,000
Total actual overhead costs	$99,250

1. Compute the overhead controllable variance and classify it as favorable or unfavorable.
2. Compute the overhead volume variance and classify it as favorable or unfavorable.
3. Prepare an overhead variance report at the actual activity level of 9,000 units.

Blaze Corp. applies overhead on the basis of direct labor hours. For the month of March, the company planned production of 8,000 units (80% of its production capacity of 10,000 units) and prepared the following budget.

Exercise 21-22
Overhead controllable and volume variances; overhead variance report

P4

Overhead Budget	80% Operating Level
Production in units	8,000
Standard direct labor hours	32,000
Budgeted overhead	
Variable overhead costs	
Indirect materials................	$10,000
Indirect labor	16,000
Power.........................	4,000
Maintenance	2,000
Total variable costs	32,000
Fixed overhead costs	
Rent of factory building...........	12,000
Depreciation—Machinery	20,000
Taxes and insurance	2,400
Supervisory salaries	13,600
Total fixed costs.................	48,000
Total overhead costs	$80,000

During March, the company operated at 90% capacity (9,000 units), and it incurred the following actual overhead costs.

Overhead costs (actual)	
Indirect materials..............................	$10,000
Indirect labor	16,000
Power	4,500
Maintenance...................................	3,000
Rent of factory building	12,000
Depreciation—Machinery	19,200
Taxes and insurance...........................	3,000
Supervisory salaries...........................	14,000
Total actual overhead costs	$81,700

1. Compute the overhead controllable variance.

2. Compute the overhead volume variance.

3. Prepare an overhead variance report at the actual activity level of 9,000 units.

Exercise 21-23
Computing sales variances
A1

Comp Wiz sells computers. During May, it sold 350 computers at a $1,200 average price each. The May fixed budget included sales of 365 computers at an average price of $1,100 each.

1. Compute the sales price variance and classify it as favorable or unfavorable.

2. Compute the sales volume variance and classify it as favorable or unfavorable.

■ connect

PROBLEM SET A

Problem 21-1A
Preparing and analyzing
a flexible budget
A1   P1

Phoenix Company's 2019 master budget included the following fixed budget report. It is based on an expected production and sales volume of 15,000 units.

Fixed Budget Report For Year Ended December 31, 2019		
Sales		$3,000,000
Cost of goods sold		
Direct materials	$975,000	
Direct labor...	225,000	
Machinery repairs (variable cost)	60,000	
Depreciation—Plant equipment (straight-line)	300,000	
Utilities ($45,000 is variable)	195,000	
Plant management salaries	200,000	1,955,000
Gross profit		1,045,000
Selling expenses		
Packaging..	75,000	
Shipping	105,000	
Sales salary (fixed annual amount)	250,000	430,000
General and administrative expenses		
Advertising expense	125,000	
Salaries..	241,000	
Entertainment expense	90,000	456,000
Income from operations		$ 159,000

Required

1. Classify all items listed in the fixed budget as variable or fixed. Also determine their amounts per unit or their amounts for the year, as appropriate.

2. Prepare flexible budgets (see Exhibit 21.3) for the company at sales volumes of 14,000 and 16,000 units.

3. The company's business conditions are improving. One possible result is a sales volume of 18,000 units. The company president is confident that this volume is within the relevant range of existing capacity. How much would operating income increase over the budgeted amount of $159,000 if this level is reached without increasing capacity?

4. An unfavorable change in business is remotely possible; in this case, production and sales volume for the year could fall to 12,000 units. How much income (or loss) from operations would occur if sales volume falls to this level?

Check (2) Budgeted income at 16,000 units, $260,000

(4) Potential operating loss, $(144,000)

Refer to the information in Problem 21-1A. Phoenix Company's actual income statement follows.

Problem 21-2A
Preparing and analyzing a flexible budget performance report
A1   P1   P2

Statement of Income from Operations For Year Ended December 31, 2019		
Sales (18,000 units)		$3,648,000
Cost of goods sold		
Direct materials	$1,185,000	
Direct labor.	278,000	
Machinery repairs (variable cost)	63,000	
Depreciation—Plant equipment	300,000	
Utilities (fixed cost is $147,500)	200,500	
Plant management salaries.	210,000	2,236,500
Gross profit		1,411,500
Selling expenses		
Packaging.	87,500	
Shipping	118,500	
Sales salary (annual)	268,000	474,000
General and administrative expenses		
Advertising expense	132,000	
Salaries.	241,000	
Entertainment expense	93,500	466,500
Income from operations		$ 471,000

Required

1. Prepare a flexible budget performance report for 2019.

2. Compute both the (*a*) sales variance and (*b*) direct materials cost variance.

Check (1) Variances: Fixed costs, $36,000 U; Income, $9,000 F

Antuan Company set the following standard costs for one unit of its product.

Problem 21-3A
Flexible budget preparation; computation of materials, labor, and overhead variances; and overhead variance report
P1   P2   P3   P4

Direct materials (6 lbs. @ $5 per lb.)	$ 30
Direct labor (2 hrs. @ $17 per hr.)	34
Overhead (2 hrs. @ $18.50 per hr.)	37
Total standard cost	$101

The predetermined overhead rate ($18.50 per direct labor hour) is based on an expected volume of 75% of the factory's capacity of 20,000 units per month. Following are the company's budgeted overhead costs per month at the 75% capacity level.

Overhead Budget (75% Capacity)		
Variable overhead costs		
Indirect materials	$ 45,000	
Indirect labor	180,000	
Power	45,000	
Repairs and maintenance	90,000	
Total variable overhead costs		$360,000
Fixed overhead costs		
Depreciation—Building	24,000	
Depreciation—Machinery	80,000	
Taxes and insurance	12,000	
Supervision	79,000	
Total fixed overhead costs		195,000
Total overhead costs		$555,000

The company incurred the following actual costs when it operated at 75% of capacity in October.

Direct materials (91,000 lbs. @ $5.10 per lb.)		$ 464,100
Direct labor (30,500 hrs. @ $17.25 per hr.)		526,125
Overhead costs		
Indirect materials	$ 44,250	
Indirect labor	177,750	
Power	43,000	
Repairs and maintenance	96,000	
Depreciation—Building	24,000	
Depreciation—Machinery	75,000	
Taxes and insurance	11,500	
Supervision	89,000	560,500
Total costs		$1,550,725

Required

1. Examine the monthly overhead budget to (*a*) determine the costs per unit for each variable overhead item and its total per unit costs and (*b*) identify the total fixed costs per month.

Check   (2) Budgeted total overhead at 13,000 units, $507,000
(3) Materials variances: Price, $9,100 U; Quantity, $5,000 U
(4) Labor variances: Rate, $7,625 U; Efficiency, $8,500 U

2. Prepare flexible overhead budgets (as in Exhibit 21.12) for October showing the amounts of each variable and fixed cost at the 65%, 75%, and 85% capacity levels.

3. Compute the direct materials cost variance, including its price and quantity variances.

4. Compute the direct labor cost variance, including its rate and efficiency variances.

5. Prepare a detailed overhead variance report (as in Exhibit 21.16) that shows the variances for individual items of overhead.

Problem 21-4A
Computing materials, labor, and overhead variances

P3   P4

Trico Company set the following standard unit costs for its single product.

Direct materials (30 lbs. @ $4 per lb.)	$120
Direct labor (5 hrs. @ $14 per hr.)	70
Factory overhead—Variable (5 hrs. @ $8 per hr.)	40
Factory overhead—Fixed (5 hrs. @ $10 per hr.)	50
Total standard cost	$280

The predetermined overhead rate is based on a planned operating volume of 80% of the productive capacity of 60,000 units per quarter. The following flexible budget information is available.

	Operating Levels		
	70%	80%	90%
Production in units	42,000	48,000	54,000
Standard direct labor hours	210,000	240,000	270,000
Budgeted overhead			
Fixed factory overhead	$2,400,000	$2,400,000	$2,400,000
Variable factory overhead	$1,680,000	$1,920,000	$2,160,000

During the current quarter, the company operated at 90% of capacity and produced 54,000 units of product; actual direct labor totaled 265,000 hours. Units produced were assigned the following standard costs.

Direct materials (1,620,000 lbs. @ $4 per lb.)	$ 6,480,000
Direct labor (270,000 hrs. @ $14 per hr.)	3,780,000
Factory overhead (270,000 hrs. @ $18 per hr.)	4,860,000
Total standard cost..	$15,120,000

Actual costs incurred during the current quarter follow.

Direct materials (1,615,000 lbs. @ $4.10 per lb.)	$ 6,621,500
Direct labor (265,000 hrs. @ $13.75 per hr.)	3,643,750
Fixed factory overhead costs	2,350,000
Variable factory overhead costs	2,200,000
Total actual costs	$14,815,250

Required

1. Compute the direct materials cost variance, including its price and quantity variances.
2. Compute the direct labor cost variance, including its rate and efficiency variances.
3. Compute the overhead controllable and volume variances.

Check (1) Materials variances: Price, $161,500 U; Quantity, $20,000 F
(2) Labor variances: Rate, $66,250 F; Efficiency, $70,000 F

Refer to the information in Problem 21-4A.

Required

Compute these variances: (*a*) variable overhead spending and efficiency, (*b*) fixed overhead spending and volume, and (*c*) total overhead controllable.

Problem 21-5A^A [rendered as] **Problem 21-5A[A]**
Expanded overhead variances
P5

Boss Company's standard cost accounting system recorded this information from its December operations.

Standard direct materials cost..	$100,000
Direct materials quantity variance (unfavorable)	3,000
Direct materials price variance (favorable)............................	500
Actual direct labor cost..	90,000
Direct labor efficiency variance (favorable)	7,000
Direct labor rate variance (unfavorable).............................	1,200
Actual overhead cost	375,000
Volume variance (unfavorable)	12,000
Controllable variance (unfavorable)	9,000

Problem 21-6A[A]
Recording and analyzing materials, labor, and overhead variances

C1   P6

Required

1. Prepare December 31 journal entries to record the company's costs and variances for the month. (Do not prepare the journal entry to close the variances.)

Check (1) Dr. Work in Process Inventory (for overhead), $354,000

Analysis Component

2. If management investigates all variances above $5,000, which variances will management investigate?

PROBLEM SET B

Problem 21-1B
Preparing and analyzing
a flexible budget

A1   P1

Tohono Company's 2019 master budget included the following fixed budget report. It is based on an expected production and sales volume of 20,000 units.

Fixed Budget Report For Year Ended December 31, 2019		
Sales		$3,000,000
Cost of goods sold		
Direct materials	$1,200,000	
Direct labor..	260,000	
Machinery repairs (variable cost)	57,000	
Depreciation—Machinery (straight-line)	250,000	
Utilities (25% is variable cost)	200,000	
Plant manager salaries	140,000	2,107,000
Gross profit		893,000
Selling expenses		
Packaging..	80,000	
Shipping	116,000	
Sales salary (fixed annual amount)	160,000	356,000
General and administrative expenses		
Advertising	81,000	
Salaries..	241,000	
Entertainment expense	90,000	412,000
Income from operations............................		$ 125,000

Required

1. Classify all items listed in the fixed budget as variable or fixed. Also determine their amounts per unit or their amounts for the year, as appropriate.

Check   (2) Budgeted income at 24,000 units, $372,400

2. Prepare flexible budgets (see Exhibit 21.3) for the company at sales volumes of 18,000 and 24,000 units.

3. The company's business conditions are improving. One possible result is a sales volume of 28,000 units. The company president is confident that this volume is within the relevant range of existing capacity. How much would operating income increase over the budgeted amount of $125,000 if this level is reached without increasing capacity?

(4) Potential operating loss, $(246,100)

4. An unfavorable change in business is remotely possible; in this case, production and sales volume for the year could fall to 14,000 units. How much income (or loss) from operations would occur if sales volume falls to this level?

Problem 21-2B
Preparing and analyzing
a flexible budget
performance report

A1   P1   P2

Refer to the information in Problem 21-1B. Tohono Company's actual income statement follows.

Statement of Income from Operations For Year Ended December 31, 2019		
Sales (24,000 units)		$3,648,000
Cost of goods sold		
Direct materials	$1,400,000	
Direct labor................................	360,000	
Machinery repairs (variable cost)	60,000	
Depreciation—Machinery	250,000	
Utilities (variable cost, $64,000)..............	218,000	
Plant manager salaries	155,000	2,443,000
Gross profit		1,205,000
Selling expenses		
Packaging.................................	90,000	
Shipping	124,000	
Sales salary (annual)	162,000	376,000
General and administrative expenses		
Advertising expense	104,000	
Salaries	232,000	
Entertainment expense	100,000	436,000
Income from operations		$ 393,000

Required

1. Prepare a flexible budget performance report for 2019.

Analysis Component

2. Compute and interpret both the (*a*) sales variance and (*b*) direct materials cost variance.

Check (1) Variances: Fixed costs, $45,000 U; Income, $20,600 F

Suncoast Company set the following standard costs for one unit of its product.

Direct materials (4.5 lbs. @ $6 per lb.)	$27
Direct labor (1.5 hrs. @ $12 per hr.)	18
Overhead (1.5 hrs. @ $16 per hr.)	24
Total standard cost	$69

Problem 21-3B
Flexible budget preparation; computation of materials, labor, and overhead variances; and overhead variance report

P1   P2   P3   P4

The predetermined overhead rate ($16.00 per direct labor hour) is based on an expected volume of 75% of the factory's capacity of 20,000 units per month. Following are the company's budgeted overhead costs per month at the 75% capacity level.

Overhead Budget (75% Capacity)		
Variable overhead costs		
Indirect materials	$22,500	
Indirect labor	90,000	
Power	22,500	
Repairs and maintenance	45,000	
Total variable overhead costs		$180,000
Fixed overhead costs		
Depreciation—Building	24,000	
Depreciation—Machinery	72,000	
Taxes and insurance	18,000	
Supervision	66,000	
Total fixed overhead costs		180,000
Total overhead costs		$360,000

The company incurred the following actual costs when it operated at 75% of capacity in December.

Direct materials (69,000 lbs. @ $6.10 per lb.)		$ 420,900
Direct labor (22,800 hrs. @ $12.30 per hr.)		280,440
Overhead costs		
Indirect materials	$21,600	
Indirect labor	82,260	
Power	23,100	
Repairs and maintenance	46,800	
Depreciation—Building	24,000	
Depreciation—Machinery	75,000	
Taxes and insurance	16,500	
Supervision	66,000	355,260
Total costs		$1,056,600

Required

1. Examine the monthly overhead budget to (*a*) determine the costs per unit for each variable overhead item and its total per unit costs and (*b*) identify the total fixed costs per month.

2. Prepare flexible overhead budgets (as in Exhibit 21.12) for December showing the amounts of each variable and fixed cost at the 65%, 75%, and 85% capacity levels.

3. Compute the direct materials cost variance, including its price and quantity variances.

[continued on next page]

Check (2) Budgeted total overhead at 17,000 units, $384,000
(3) Materials variances: Price, $6,900 U; Quantity, $9,000 U

(4) Labor variances: Rate,
$6,840 U; Efficiency, $3,600 U

4. Compute the direct labor cost variance, including its rate and efficiency variances.

5. Prepare a detailed overhead variance report (as in Exhibit 21.16) that shows the variances for individual items of overhead.

Problem 21-4B
Computing materials,
labor, and overhead
variances

P3   P4

Kryll Company set the following standard unit costs for its single product.

Direct materials (25 lbs. @ $4 per lb.)	$100
Direct labor (6 hrs. @ $8 per hr.)	48
Factory overhead—Variable (6 hrs. @ $5 per hr.)	30
Factory overhead—Fixed (6 hrs. @ $7 per hr.)	42
Total standard cost	$220

The predetermined overhead rate is based on a planned operating volume of 80% of the productive capacity of 60,000 units per quarter. The following flexible budget information is available.

	Operating Levels		
	70%	80%	90%
Production in units	42,000	48,000	54,000
Standard direct labor hours	252,000	288,000	324,000
Budgeted overhead			
Fixed factory overhead	$2,016,000	$2,016,000	$2,016,000
Variable factory overhead	1,260,000	1,440,000	1,620,000

During the current quarter, the company operated at 70% of capacity and produced 42,000 units of product; direct labor hours worked were 250,000. Units produced were assigned the following standard costs.

Direct materials (1,050,000 lbs. @ $4 per lb.)	$4,200,000
Direct labor (252,000 hrs. @ $8 per hr.)	2,016,000
Factory overhead (252,000 hrs. @ $12 per hr.)	3,024,000
Total standard cost	$9,240,000

Actual costs incurred during the current quarter follow.

Direct materials (1,000,000 lbs. @ $4.25 per lb.)	$4,250,000
Direct labor (250,000 hrs. @ $7.75 per hr.)	1,937,500
Fixed factory overhead costs	1,960,000
Variable factory overhead costs	1,200,000
Total actual costs	$9,347,500

Check   (1) Materials
variances: Price, $250,000 U;
Quantity, $200,000 F
(2) Labor variances: Rate,
$62,500 F; Efficiency,
$16,000 F

Required

1. Compute the direct materials cost variance, including its price and quantity variances.

2. Compute the direct labor cost variance, including its rate and efficiency variances.

3. Compute the total overhead controllable and volume variances.

Problem 21-5B[A]
Expanded overhead
variances

P5

Refer to the information in Problem 21-4B.

Required

Compute these variances: (*a*) variable overhead spending and efficiency, (*b*) fixed overhead spending and volume, and (*c*) total overhead controllable.

Kenya Company's standard cost accounting system recorded this information from its June operations.

Standard direct materials cost...	$130,000
Direct materials quantity variance (favorable)	5,000
Direct materials price variance (favorable)................................	1,500
Actual direct labor cost..	65,000
Direct labor efficiency variance (favorable)	3,000
Direct labor rate variance (unfavorable)...................................	500
Actual overhead cost	250,000
Volume variance (unfavorable)..	12,000
Controllable variance (unfavorable)	8,000

Problem 21-6B[A]
Recording and analyzing materials, labor, and overhead variances

C1   P6

Required

1. Prepare journal entries dated June 30 to record the company's costs and variances for the month. (Do not prepare the journal entry to close the variances.)

Analysis Component

2. Identify the variances that would attract the attention of a manager who uses management by exception. Describe what action(s) the manager should consider.

Check   (1) Dr. Work in Process Inventory (for overhead), $230,000

This serial problem began in Chapter 1 and continues through most of the book. If previous chapter segments were not completed, the serial problem can begin at this point.

SP 21   Business Solutions's second-quarter 2020 fixed budget performance report for its computer furniture operations follows. The $156,000 budgeted expenses include $108,000 in variable expenses for desks and $18,000 in variable expenses for chairs, as well as $30,000 fixed expenses. The actual expenses include $31,000 fixed expenses. Prepare a flexible budget performance report that shows any variances between budgeted results and actual results. List fixed and variable expenses separately.

SERIAL PROBLEM
Business Solutions

P1

	Fixed Budget	Actual Results	Variances
Desk sales (in units)	144	150	
Chair sales (in units)	72	80	
Desk sales......................	$180,000	$186,000	$6,000 F
Chair sales.......................	36,000	41,200	5,200 F
Total expenses	156,000	163,880	7,880 U
Income from operations...........	$ 60,000	$ 63,320	$3,320 F

©Alexander Image/Shutterstock

Check   Variances: Fixed expenses, $1,000 U

Accounting Analysis

AA 21-1   Flexible budgets and standard costs emphasize the importance of a similar unit of measure for meaningful analysis. When **Apple** compiles GAAP financial reports, it applies the same unit of measurement, U.S. dollars, for most measures of business operations. One issue is how to adjust account values for its subsidiaries that compile financial reports in currencies other than the U.S. dollar. Apple's annual report says: "The Company translates the assets and liabilities of its non-U.S. dollar functional currency subsidiaries into U.S. dollars using exchange rates in effect at the end of each period. Revenue and expenses for these subsidiaries are translated using rates that approximate those in effect during the period. Gains and losses from these translations are recognized in foreign currency translation included in AOCI in shareholders' equity."

COMPANY ANALYSIS

C1

APPLE

Required

1. In which financial statement does Apple report the gains and losses from foreign currency translation for subsidiaries that do not use the U.S. dollar as their functional currency?

[continued on next page]

2. Translating financial statements requires the use of a *currency exchange rate*. For each of the following financial statement items, indicate the exchange rate the company would apply to translate into U.S. dollars. Enter "CR" (current rate in effect at the balance sheet date) or "Avg" (the average rate in effect during the period).

   a. Cash

   b. Sales revenue

   c. Property, plant and equipment

COMPARATIVE ANALYSIS

A1

APPLE

GOOGLE

AA 21-2   The usefulness of budgets, variances, and related analyses often depends on the accuracy of management's estimates of future sales activity.

Required

1. Identify and enter the 2016 and 2017 sales (in $ millions) into a table for **Apple** and **Google** using their financial statements in Appendix A.

2. Assume that at the end of 2016 we estimate Apple's 2017 sales will increase by 5% from its 2016 sales. What is Apple's 2017 estimated sales?

3. Assume that at the end of 2016 we estimate Google's 2017 sales will increase by 20% from its 2016 sales. What is Google's 2017 estimated sales?

4. Using answers to parts 2 and 3, which company's estimated 2017 sales is closer to its actual 2017 sales?

GLOBAL ANALYSIS

A1

Samsung

AA 21-3   Access **Samsung**'s financial statements in Appendix A.

Required

1. Identify and enter the 2016 and 2017 sales (in ₩ millions) into a table for Samsung.

2. Assume that at the end of 2016 we estimate Samsung's 2017 sales will increase by 20% from its 2016 sales. What is Samsung's 2017 estimated sales?

3. Are the estimated 2017 sales from part 2 higher or lower than Samsung's actual 2017 sales?

Beyond the Numbers

ETHICS CHALLENGE

C1

BTN 21-1   Setting materials, labor, and overhead standards is challenging. If standards are set too low, companies might purchase inferior products and employees might not work to their full potential. If standards are set too high, companies could be unable to offer a quality product at a profitable price and employees could be overworked. The ethical challenge is to set a high but reasonable standard. Assume that as a manager you are asked to set the standard materials price and quantity for the new 1,000 CKB Mega-Max chip, a technically advanced product. To properly set the price and quantity standards, you assemble a team of specialists to provide input.

Required

Identify four types of specialists that you would assemble to provide information to help set the materials price and quantity standards. Briefly explain why you chose each individual.

COMMUNICATING IN PRACTICE

P6

BTN 21-2   The reason we use the words *favorable* and *unfavorable* when evaluating variances is made clear when we look at the closing of accounts. To see this, consider that (1) all variance accounts are closed at the end of each period (temporary accounts), (2) a favorable variance is always a credit balance, and (3) an unfavorable variance is always a debit balance. Write a half-page memorandum to your instructor with three parts that answer the following three requirements. (Assume that variance accounts are closed to Cost of Goods Sold.)

Required

1. Does Cost of Goods Sold increase or decrease when closing a favorable variance? Does gross margin increase or decrease when a favorable variance is closed to Cost of Goods Sold? Explain.

2. Does Cost of Goods Sold increase or decrease when closing an unfavorable variance? Does gross margin increase or decrease when an unfavorable variance is closed to Cost of Goods Sold? Explain.

3. Explain the meaning of a favorable variance and an unfavorable variance.

BTN 21-3 Access **iSixSigma**'s website (**iSixSigma.com**) to search for and read information about the purpose and use of *benchmarking* to complete the following requirements. *Hint:* Look in the "Methodology" link.

TAKING IT TO THE NET

C1

Required

1. Write a one-paragraph explanation (in layperson's terms) of benchmarking.

2. How does standard costing relate to benchmarking?

BTN 21-4 Many service industries link labor rate and time (quantity) standards with their processes. One example is the standard time to board an aircraft. The reason time plays such an important role in the service industry is that it is viewed as a competitive advantage: best service in the shortest amount of time. Although the labor rate component is difficult to observe, the time component of a service delivery standard is often readily apparent—for example, "Lunch will be served in less than five minutes, or it is free."

TEAMWORK IN ACTION

C1

Required

Break into teams and select two service industries for your analysis. Identify and describe all the time elements each industry uses to create a competitive advantage.

BTN 21-5 **Away**, as discussed in the chapter opener, uses a costing system with standard costs for direct materials, direct labor, and overhead costs. Two comments frequently are mentioned in relation to standard costing and variance analysis: "Variances are not explanations" and "Management's goal is not to minimize variances."

ENTREPRENEURIAL DECISION

C1

Required

Write a short memo (no more than one page) to Jen Rubio and Steph Korey, Away's co-founders, interpreting these two comments in the context of their luggage business.

BTN 21-6 Training employees to use standard amounts of materials in production is common. Typically, large companies invest in this training but small organizations do not. One can observe these different practices in a trip to two different pizza businesses. Visit both a local pizza business and a national pizza chain business and then complete the following.

HITTING THE ROAD

C1

Required

1. Observe and record the number of raw material items used to make a typical cheese pizza. Also observe how the person making the pizza applies each item when preparing the pizza.

2. Record any differences in how items are applied between the two businesses.

3. Estimate which business is more profitable from your observations. Explain.

---

22 Performance Measurement and Responsibility Accounting

Learning Objectives

CONCEPTUAL

C1 Distinguish between direct and indirect expenses and identify bases for allocating indirect expenses to departments.

C2 Explain transfer pricing and methods to set transfer prices.

C3 *Appendix 22C—*Describe allocation of joint costs across products.

ANALYTICAL

A1 Analyze investment centers using return on investment and residual income.

A2 Analyze investment centers using profit margin and investment turnover.

A3 Analyze investment centers using the balanced scorecard.

A4 Compute the number of days in the cash conversion cycle.

PROCEDURAL

P1 Prepare a responsibility accounting report using controllable costs.

P2 Allocate indirect expenses to departments.

P3 Prepare departmental income statements and contribution reports.

Drink Up!

"It takes courage to dream big"—**GALEN WELSCH**

COLORADO SPRINGS, CO—Millions of people do not have access to safe drinking water. Seeking to help remedy this crisis, father-son duo Randy and Galen Welsch started **Jibu** (**Jibuco.com**). Jibu gives African entrepreneurs training and resources to start their own water supply businesses. In turn, Jibu's franchisees provide their communities with safe drinking water and jobs.

Instead of drilling, owners draw water from nearby sources and use solar-powered equipment to clean it. "There's nothing more important than safe drinking water," explains Randy. "Our model produces water that people can actually afford . . . [and] we harness the spirit of local owners." Randy asserts that "by making profits, their businesses are more sustainable than relying on donations to provide water."

Randy and Galen rely on accounting to help run the business. "To break even," says Galen, "a franchisee must sell about 1,000 liters of water per day. Pricing is critical. If owners sell at our prescribed price, they should be cash-flow positive in about three months." Randy and Galen rely on income statements from each franchisee to monitor performance. Entrepreneurs must understand return on investment (ROI) and residual income, along with cost concepts such as direct and indirect expenses, to grow their businesses.

©Jibu

From an idea sparked by Galen's Peace Corps trip to Africa, Jibu is flourishing. The company has over two hundred franchise locations, has provided over five hundred jobs, and has sold over 30 million liters of drinking water. "Build the plane as you fly it," Galen advises. "Success comes from many failures."

Sources: *Jibu website,* January 2019; *Colorado Springs Business Journal,* December 31, 2015; *EY Citizen Today,* December 2015; *Forbes.com,* August 24, 2017

RESPONSIBILITY ACCOUNTING

Performance Evaluation

Many large companies are easier to manage if they are divided into smaller units, called *divisions, segments,* or *departments.* For example, **LinkedIn** organizes its operations around three geographic segments: North America, Europe, and Asia-Pacific. **Callaway Golf** organizes its operations around two product lines, golf balls and golf clubs, while **Kraft Heinz** organizes its operations both geographically and around several product lines. In these **decentralized organizations,** decisions are made by unit managers rather than by top management. Top management then evaluates the performance of unit managers.

In **responsibility accounting,** unit managers are evaluated only on things they can control. Methods of performance evaluation vary for cost centers, profit centers, and investment centers.

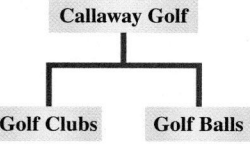

Point: Responsibility accounting does not place blame. Instead, it is used to identify opportunities to improve performance.

- A **cost center** incurs costs without directly generating revenues. The manufacturing departments of a manufacturer are cost centers. Also, its service departments, such as accounting, advertising, and purchasing, are cost centers. Kraft Heinz's Dover, Delaware, manufacturing plant is a cost center. *Cost center managers are evaluated on their success in controlling actual costs* compared to budgeted costs.

- A **profit center** generates revenues and incurs costs. Product lines are often evaluated as profit centers. Kraft Heinz's beverage and condiment product lines are profit centers. *Profit center managers are evaluated on their success in generating income.* A profit center manager would not have the authority to make major investing decisions, such as the decision to build a new manufacturing plant.

- An **investment center** generates revenues and incurs costs, and its manager is also responsible for the investments made in its operating assets. Kraft Heinz's chief operating officer for U.S. operations has the authority to make decisions such as building a new manufacturing plant. *Investment center managers are evaluated on their use of investment center assets to generate income.*

This chapter describes ways to measure performance for these three types of responsibility centers.

P1

Prepare a responsibility accounting report using controllable costs.

Controllable versus Uncontrollable Costs

We often evaluate a manager's performance using responsibility accounting reports that describe a department's activities in terms of whether a cost is controllable.

- **Controllable costs** are those for which a manager has the power to determine or at least significantly affect the amount incurred.
- **Uncontrollable costs** are not within the manager's control or influence.

Point: *Cost* refers to a monetary outlay to acquire some resource that has a future benefit. *Expense* usually refers to an expired cost.

For example, department managers often have little or no control over depreciation expense because they cannot affect the amount of equipment assigned to their departments. Also, department managers rarely control their own salaries. However, they can control or influence items such as the cost of supplies used in their department. When evaluating managers' performance, we should use data reflecting their departments' outputs along with their controllable costs and expenses.

A responsibility accounting system recognizes that control over costs and expenses belongs to several levels of management. We illustrate this in the partial organization chart in Exhibit 22.1. The lines in this chart connecting the managerial positions reflect channels of authority. For example, the three department managers (beverage, food, and service) in this company are responsible for controllable costs incurred in their departments. These department managers report to the vice president (VP) of the West region, who has overall control of the department costs. Similarly, the costs of the West region are reported to and controlled by the executive vice president (EVP) of U.S. operations, who in turn reports to the president, and, ultimately, the board of directors.

Responsibility Accounting for Cost Centers

A **responsibility accounting performance report** lists actual expenses that a manager is responsible for and their budgeted amounts. Management's analysis of differences between

EXHIBIT 22.1

Responsibility Accounting Chart (partial)

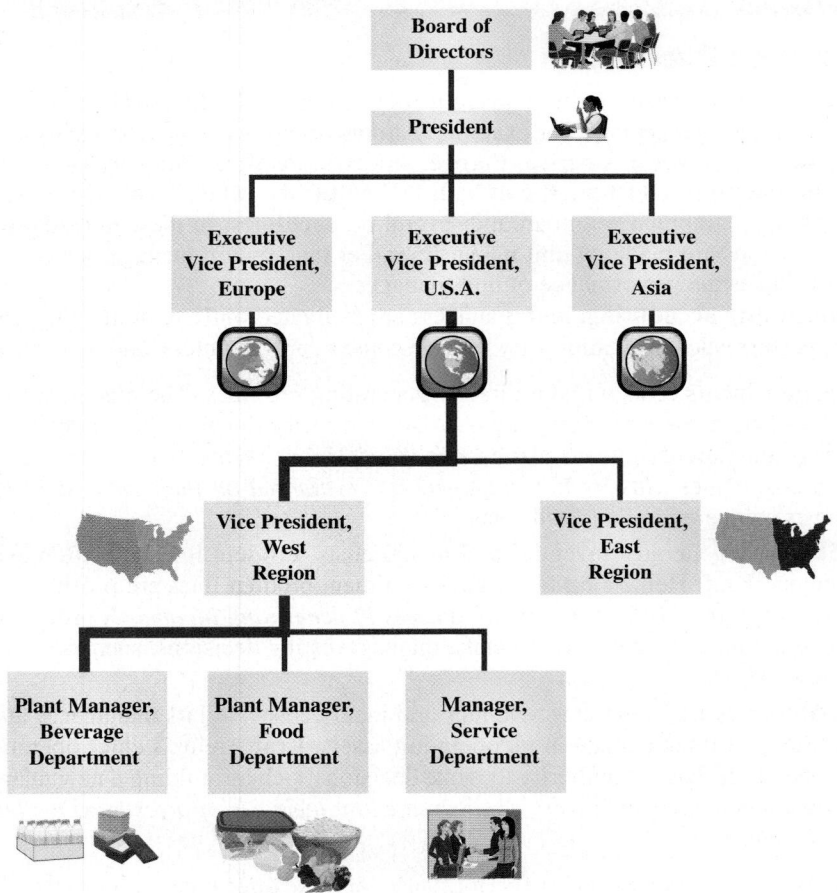

EXHIBIT 22.2

Responsibility Accounting
Performance Reports

Executive Vice President, U.S. Operations

Controllable Costs	For July Budgeted Amount	Actual Amount	Over (Under) Budget
Salaries, VPs	$ 80,000	$ 80,000	$ 0
Quality control costs	21,000	22,400	1,400
Office costs	29,000	28,800	(700)
West region	**276,700**	**279,500**	**2,800** ◄
East region	390,000	380,600	(9,400)
Totals	$797,200	$ 791,300	$(5,900)

Vice President, West Region

Controllable Costs	For July Budgeted Amount	Actual Amount	Over (Under) Budget
Salaries, department managers	$ 75,000	$ 76,500	$ 1,500
Depreciation	10,600	10,600	0
Insurance	6,800	6,300	(500)
Beverage department	**79,600**	**79,900**	**300**
Food department	61,500	64,200	2,700
Service department	43,200	42,000	(1,200)
Totals	$276,700	$279,500	$ 2,800

Plant Manager, Beverage Department

Controllable Costs	For July Budgeted Amount	Actual Amount	Over (Under) Budget
Direct materials	$ 51,600	$ 52,500	$ 900
Direct labor	20,000	19,600	(400)
Overhead	8,000	7,800	(200)
Totals	$ 79,600	$ 79,900	$ 300

budgeted and actual amounts often results in corrective or strategic managerial actions. Upper-level management uses performance reports to evaluate the effectiveness of lower-level managers in keeping costs within budgeted amounts.

Exhibit 22.2 shows summarized performance reports for the three management levels identified in Exhibit 22.1. The Beverage department is a **cost center**, and its manager is responsible for controlling costs. Costs under the control of the Beverage department plant manager are totaled and included among the controllable costs of the VP of the West region. Costs under the control of this VP are totaled and included among the controllable costs of the EVP of U.S. operations. In this way, responsibility accounting reports provide relevant information for each management level. (If the VP and EVP are responsible for more than just costs, the responsibility accounting system is expanded, as we show later in this chapter.)

The number of controllable costs reported varies across management levels. At lower levels, managers have limited responsibility and fewer controllable costs. Responsibility and control broaden for higher-level managers; their reports span a wider range of costs. However, reports to higher-level managers usually are summarized because (1) lower-level managers are often responsible for detailed costs and (2) detailed reports can obscure the broader issues facing top managers of an organization.

Point: Responsibility accounting typically uses *flexible* budgets.

Point: Responsibility accounting divides a company into subunits, or *responsibility centers.*

Below are Rios Co.'s annual budgeted and actual costs for the Western region's manufacturing plant. The plant has two operating departments: Motorcycle and ATV. The plant manager is responsible for all of the plant's costs (other than her own salary). Each operating department has a manager who is responsible for that department's direct materials, direct labor, and overhead costs. Prepare responsibility accounting reports like those in Exhibit 22.2 for (1) the plant manager and (2) each operating department manager.

 NEED-TO-KNOW 22-1

Responsibility
Accounting

P1

	Budgeted Amount		Actual Amount	
	Motorcycle	ATV	Motorcycle	ATV
Direct materials..........	$ 97,000	$138,000	$ 98,500	$133,800
Direct labor..............	52,000	105,000	56,100	101,300
Dept. mgr. salary..........	60,000	56,000	60,000	56,000
Rent and utilities..........	9,000	12,000	8,400	10,900
Overhead	45,000	81,000	47,000	78,000
Totals..................	$263,000	$392,000	$270,000	$380,000

Solution   1.

Responsibility Accounting Performance Report Plant Manager, Western Region			
	Budgeted	Actual	Over (Under) Budget
Dept. mgr. salaries	$116,000	$116,000	$ 0
Rent and utilities..........	21,000	19,300	(1,700)
Motorcycle dept.*	194,000	201,600	7,600
ATV dept.†	324,000	313,100	(10,900)
Totals..................	$655,000	$650,000	$ (5,000)

*Costs are from Motorcycle responsibility report, solution 2a.
†Costs are from ATV responsibility report, solution 2b.

2a.

Responsibility Accounting Performance Report Department Manager, Motorcycle Department			
	Budgeted	Actual	Over (Under) Budget
Direct materials...........	$ 97,000	$ 98,500	$1,500
Direct labor..............	52,000	56,100	4,100
Overhead	45,000	47,000	2,000
Totals..................	$194,000	$201,600	$7,600

2b.

Responsibility Accounting Performance Report Department Manager, ATV Department			
	Budgeted	Actual	Over (Under) Budget
Direct materials...........	$138,000	$133,800	$ (4,200)
Direct labor..............	105,000	101,300	(3,700)
Overhead	81,000	78,000	(3,000)
Totals..................	$324,000	$313,100	$(10,900)

Do More: QS 22-3, E 22-1,
E 22-2, P 22-1

PROFIT CENTERS

When departments are organized as profit centers, responsibility accounting focuses on how well each department controlled costs *and* generated revenues. This leads to **departmental income statements** as a common way to report profit center performance. When computing departmental profits, we confront two accounting challenges that involve allocating expenses.

1. How to allocate *indirect expenses* such as rent and utilities, which benefit several departments.
2. How to allocate *service department expenses* such as payroll or purchasing, which perform services that benefit several departments.

We explain these allocations and profit center income reporting.

Direct and Indirect Expenses

Direct expenses are costs readily traced to a department because they are incurred for that department's sole benefit. They are not allocated across departments. For example, the salary of an employee who works in only one department is a direct expense of that one department. Direct expenses are often, but not always, controllable costs.

Indirect expenses are costs incurred for the joint benefit of more than one department; they cannot be readily traced to only one department. For example, if two or more departments share a single building, all enjoy the benefits of the expenses for rent, heat, and light. Likewise, the *operating departments* that perform an organization's main functions, for example, manufacturing and selling, benefit from the work of *service departments*. Service departments, like payroll and human resource management, do not generate revenues, but their support is crucial for the operating departments' success.

Expense Allocations

General Model Indirect and service department expenses are allocated across departments that benefit from them. Ideally, we allocate these expenses by using a cause-effect relation. Often such cause-effect relations are hard to identify. When we cannot identify cause-effect relations, we allocate each indirect or service department expense based on *approximating* the relative benefit each department receives. Exhibit 22.3 summarizes the general model for cost allocation.

> **Allocated cost = Total cost to allocate × Percentage of allocation base used**

Allocating Indirect Expenses Allocation bases vary across departments and organizations. No standard rule for the "best" allocation bases exists. Managers must use judgment in developing allocation bases because employee morale can suffer if allocations are perceived as unfair. Exhibit 22.4 shows some commonly used bases for allocating indirect expenses.

Indirect Expense	Common Allocation Bases
Wages and salaries	Relative amount of hours worked in each department
Rent	Square feet of space occupied
Utilities	Square feet of space occupied
Advertising	Percentage of total sales
Depreciation	Hours of depreciable asset used

More complicated allocation schemes are possible. For example, some locations in a retail store (ground floor near the entrance, for example) are more valuable than others. Departments with better locations can be allocated more cost. Advertising campaigns can be analyzed to see the amount of advertising devoted to each department, or utilities costs can be allocated based on machine hours used in each department. Management must determine whether these more accurate cost allocations justify the effort and expense to compute them.

©Ariel Skelley/Blend Images

Allocating Service Department Expenses To generate revenues, operating departments require services provided by departments such as personnel, payroll, and purchasing. Such service departments are typically evaluated as *cost centers* because they do not produce revenues. A departmental accounting system can accumulate and report costs incurred by each service department for this purpose. The system then allocates a service department's expenses to operating departments that benefit from them. Exhibit 22.5 shows some commonly used bases for allocating service department expenses to operating departments.

Service Department	Common Allocation Bases
Office expenses	Number of employees or sales in each department
Personnel expenses	Number of employees in each department
Payroll expenses	Number of employees in each department
Purchasing costs	Dollar amounts of purchases or number of purchase orders processed
Maintenance expenses	Square feet of floor space occupied

Illustration of Cost Allocation   We illustrate the general approach to allocating costs by looking at cleaning services for a retail store (an indirect cost). An outside company cleans the retail store for a total cost of $800 per month. Management allocates this cost across the store's three departments based on floor space (in square feet) that each department occupies. Exhibit 22.6 shows this allocation.

EXHIBIT 22.6

Cost Allocation

Department	Department Square Feet	Percent of Total Square Feet	Cost Allocated to Department
Jewelry	2,400	60% (2,400 sq ft/4,000 sq ft)	$480
Watch Repair	600	15 (600 sq ft/4,000 sq ft)	120
China and Silver	1,000	25 (1,000 sq ft/4,000 sq ft)	200
Totals	4,000	100%	$800

The total cost to allocate is $800. Since the Jewelry department occupies 60% of the store's total floor space (2,400 square feet/4,000 square feet), it is allocated 60% of the total cleaning cost. This allocated cost of $480 is computed as $800 × 60%. When the allocation process is complete, these and other allocated costs are deducted in computing the net income for each department. The calculations are similar for other allocation bases and for service department costs.

NEED-TO-KNOW 22-2

Cost Allocations

P2

Allocate a retailer's purchasing department's costs of $20,000 to its operating departments using each department's percentage of total purchase orders.

Department	Number of Purchase Orders
Clothing................	250
Health Care.............	450
Sporting Goods..........	300
Total...................	1,000

Solution

Department		
Clothing................	$20,000 × 25% =	$ 5,000
Health Care.............	20,000 × 45% =	9,000
Sporting Goods..........	20,000 × 30% =	6,000
Total...................		$20,000

Do More: QS 22-4, QS 22-5, QS 22-6, E 22-3, E 22-4, E 22-5

Departmental Income Statements

Departmental income is computed using the formula in Exhibit 22.7.

EXHIBIT 22.7

Departmental Income

$$\text{Departmental income} = \text{Department sales} - \text{Department direct expenses} - \text{Allocated indirect expenses} - \text{Allocated service department expenses}$$

P3

Prepare departmental income statements and contribution reports.

We prepare departmental income statements using **A-1 Hardware** and its five departments. Two of them (general office and purchasing) are service departments, and the other three (Hardware, Housewares, and Appliances) are operating departments. Since the service departments do not generate sales, we do not prepare departmental income statements for them. Instead, we allocate their expenses to operating departments.

Preparing departmental income statements involves four steps.

Step ①: Accumulating revenues, direct expenses, and indirect expenses by department.
Step ②: Allocating indirect expenses across both service and operating departments.
Step ③: Allocating service department expenses to operating departments.
Step ④: Preparing departmental income statements.

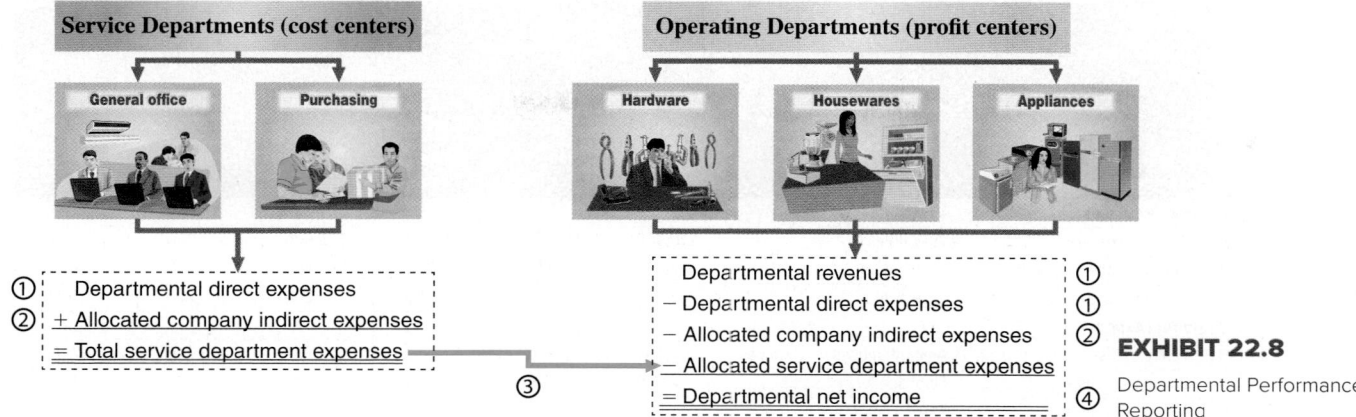

EXHIBIT 22.8

Departmental Performance
Reporting

Exhibit 22.8 summarizes these steps in preparing departmental performance reports for cost centers and profit centers (links to the steps are coded with circled numbers *1* through *4*). A-1 Hardware's service departments (general office and purchasing) are cost centers, so their performance is based on how well they control their direct department expenses. The company's operating departments (Hardware, Housewares, and Appliances) are **profit centers**, and their performance is based on how well they generate departmental net income.

Point: Operating departments generate revenues. Service departments do not.

Point: We sometimes allocate service department costs across other service departments before allocating them to operating departments. This "step-wise" process is covered in advanced courses.

Apply Step 1:   We first collect the necessary data from general company and departmental accounts. Exhibit 22.9 shows these data.

EXHIBIT 22.9

Cost Data

For Year Ended December 31, 2019	Expense Account Bal.	Service Departments		Operating Departments		
		General Office	Purchasing	Hardware	Housewares	Appliances
Sales...................................		$ 0	$ 0	$119,500	$71,700	$47,800
Direct expenses						
Cost of goods sold.................	$ 147,800	0	0	73,800	43,800	30,200
Salaries.................................	51,900	13,300	8,200	15,600	7,000	7,800
Depreciation—Equip...............	1,500	500	300	400	100	200
Supplies.................................	900	200	100	300	200	100
Indirect expenses						
Rent	12,000					
Utilities..................................	2,400					
Advertising............................	1,000					
Insurance...............................	2,500					
Total expenses.....................	**$220,000**					

A-1 HARDWARE
Revenues and Expenses

Exhibit 22.9 shows the direct and indirect expenses by department. Each department uses payroll records, fixed asset and depreciation records, and supplies requisitions to determine the amounts of its expenses for salaries, depreciation, and supplies. The total amount for each of these direct expenses is entered in the Expense Account Balance column. That column also lists the amount of each indirect expense.

Point: Sales and cost of goods sold data are from operating department records.

Apply Step 2:   Using the general model, A-1 Hardware allocates indirect costs. We show this with the *departmental expense allocation spreadsheet* in Exhibit 22.10. After selecting allocation bases, indirect expenses are recorded in company accounts and allocated to both operating and service departments. **Detailed calculations for indirect expense allocations, which follow the general model of cost allocation, are in Appendix 22A** (see Exhibits 22A.1 thru 22A.6).

	A-1 HARDWARE Departmental Expense Allocations						
				Allocation of Expenses to Departments			
For Year Ended December 31, 2019	**Allocation Base**	**Expense Account Bal.**	**General Office Dept.**	**Purchasing Dept.**	**Hardware Dept.**	**Housewares Dept.**	**Appliances Dept.**
Direct expenses							
Salaries expense..................	(see note *a*)	$51,900	$13,300	$8,200	$15,600	$ 7,000	$ 7,800
Depreciation—Equipment......	(see note *a*)	1,500	500	300	400	100	200
Supplies expense..................	(see note *a*)	900	200	100	300	200	100
Indirect expenses							
Rent expense......	Amount and value of space...	12,000	600	600	4,860	3,240	2,700
Utilities expense...................	Floor space...........................	2,400	300	300	810	540	450
Advertising expense.............	Sales.....................................	1,000			500	300	200
Insurance expense................	Value of insured assets.........	2,500	400	200	900	600	400
Total department expenses.......		72,200	15,300	9,700	23,370	11,980	11,850
Service department expenses							
General office department.....	Sales.....................................		(15,300)		7,650	4,590	3,060
Purchasing department..........	Purchase orders...................			(9,700)	3,880	2,630	3,190
Total expenses allocated to operating departments...		$72,200	$ 0	$ 0	$34,900	$19,200	$18,100

*a*The allocation base is not relevant as direct expenses are *not* allocated.

EXHIBIT 22.10

Departmental Expense
Allocation Spreadsheet

Apply Step 3:   We then allocate service department expenses to operating departments. Service department expenses typically are not allocated to other service departments. After service department costs are allocated, no expenses remain in the service departments, as shown in row 21 of Exhibit 22.10. **Detailed calculations for service department expense allocations, which follow the general model of cost allocation, are in Appendix 22A (see Exhibits 22A.7 and 22A.8).**

Apply Step 4:   The departmental expense allocation spreadsheet is now used to prepare departmental performance reports. The general office and purchasing departments are cost centers, and their managers are evaluated on their control of costs.

Exhibit 22.11 shows income statements for the three operating departments. This exhibit uses the spreadsheet (in Exhibit 22.10) for its operating expenses; information on sales and cost of goods sold comes from departmental records.

EXHIBIT 22.11

Departmental Income
Statements (operating
departments)

A-1 HARDWARE Departmental Income Statements				
For Year Ended December 31, 2019	**Hardware Department**	**Housewares Department**	**Appliances Department**	**Combined**
Sales	$119,500	$71,700	$47,800	$239,000
Cost of goods sold	73,800	43,800	30,200	147,800
Gross profit	45,700	27,900	17,600	91,200
Operating expenses				
Salaries expense	15,600	7,000	7,800	30,400
Depreciation expense—Equipment.............	400	100	200	700
Supplies expense..........................	300	200	100	600
Rent expense	4,860	3,240	2,700	10,800
Utilities expense............................	810	540	450	1,800
Advertising expense.......................	500	300	200	1,000
Insurance expense..........................	900	600	400	1,900
Share of general office expenses	7,650	4,590	3,060	15,300
Share of purchasing expenses	3,880	2,630	3,190	9,700
Total operating expenses	34,900	19,200	18,100	72,200
Operating income (loss)....................	**$ 10,800**	**$ 8,700**	**$ (500)**	**$ 19,000**

Direct expenses — Salaries expense, Depreciation expense—Equipment, Supplies expense

Allocated indirect expenses — Rent expense, Utilities expense, Advertising expense, Insurance expense

Allocated service department expenses — Share of general office expenses, Share of purchasing expenses

Higher-level managers use departmental income statements to determine which of a company's departments are most profitable. After considering all costs, the Hardware department is most profitable. The company might attempt to expand its Hardware department.

Departmental Contribution to Overhead

Exhibit 22.11 shows that the Appliances department reported an operating loss of $(500). Should this department be eliminated? We must be careful when indirect expenses are a large portion of total expenses and when weaknesses in assumptions and decisions in allocating indirect expenses can greatly affect income. Also, operating department managers might have no control over the level of service department services they use. In these and other cases, we might better evaluate profit center performance using the **departmental contribution to overhead,** a measure of the amount of sales less *direct* expenses. A department's contribution is said to be "to overhead" because of the practice of considering all indirect expenses as overhead. Thus, the excess of a department's sales over direct expenses is a contribution toward at least a portion of total overhead.

The upper half of Exhibit 22.12 shows a departmental contribution to overhead as part of an expanded income statement. Departmental contribution to overhead, because it focuses on the direct expenses that are under the profit center manager's control, is often a better way to assess that manager's performance.

EXHIBIT 22.12

Departmental Contribution to Overhead

A-1 HARDWARE Income Statement Showing Departmental Contribution to Overhead				
For Year Ended December 31, 2019	Hardware Department	Housewares Department	Appliances Department	Combined
Sales	$119,500	$ 71,700	$47,800	$239,000
Cost of goods sold	73,800	43,800	30,200	147,800
Gross profit	45,700	27,900	17,600	91,200
Direct expenses				
Salaries expense	15,600	7,000	7,800	30,400
Depreciation expense—Equipment.	400	100	200	700
Supplies expense.	300	200	100	600
Total direct expenses.	16,300	7,300	8,100	31,700
Departmental contributions to overhead	**$ 29,400**	**$20,600**	**$ 9,500**	**$ 59,500**
Indirect expenses				
Rent expense				10,800
Utilities expense.				1,800
Advertising expense.				1,000
Insurance expense.				1,900
General office department expense				15,300
Purchasing department expense				9,700
Total indirect expenses				40,500
Operating income.				**$ 19,000**

Point: Operating income is the same in Exhibits 22.11 and 22.12. The method of reporting indirect expenses in Exhibit 22.12 does not change income but does identify each operating department's contribution to overhead.

Exhibit 22.12 shows a $9,500 positive contribution to overhead for the Appliances department. If this department were eliminated, the company would be worse off. Further, the Appliance department's manager is better evaluated using this $9,500 than on the department's operating loss of $(500). The company also compares each department's contribution to overhead to budgeted amounts to assess each department's performance.

Behavioral Aspects of Departmental Performance Reports An organization must consider potential effects on employee behavior from departmental income statements and contribution to overhead reports. These include:

- Indirect expenses are typically uncontrollable costs for department managers. Thus, departmental contribution to overhead might be a better way to evaluate department manager performance. Including uncontrollable costs in performance evaluation is inconsistent with responsibility accounting and can reduce manager morale.

- Alternatively, including indirect expenses in the department manager's performance evaluation can lead the manager to be more careful in using service departments, which can reduce the organization's costs.
- Some companies allocate *budgeted* service department costs rather than actual service costs. In this way, operating departments are not held responsible for excessive costs from service departments, and service departments are more likely to control their costs.

INVESTMENT CENTERS

We describe both financial and nonfinancial measures of investment center performance.

A1

Analyze investment centers using return on investment and residual income.

Return-on-Investment and Residual Income

Investment center managers are typically evaluated using performance measures that combine income and assets. These measures include:

- return on investment
- profit margin
- residual income
- investment turnover

To illustrate, let's consider ZTel Company, which operates two divisions as **investment centers**: LCD and S-Phone. The LCD division manufactures liquid crystal display (LCD) touch-screen monitors and sells them for use in computers, cellular phones, and other products. The S-Phone division sells smartphones. Exhibit 22.13 shows current-year income and assets for the divisions.

EXHIBIT 22.13

Investment Center Income and Assets

	LCD Division	S-Phone Division
Investment center income	$ 526,500	$ 417,600
Investment center average invested assets	2,500,000	1,850,000

Investment Center Return on Investment   One measure to evaluate division performance is the investment center **return on investment (ROI),** also called *return on assets* (ROA). This measure is computed as follows.

$$\text{Return on investment} = \frac{\text{Investment center income}}{\text{Investment center average invested assets}}$$

The return on investment for the LCD division is 21% (rounded), computed as $526,500/$2,500,000. The S-Phone division's return on investment is 23% (rounded), computed as $417,600/$1,850,000. ZTel's management can use ROI as part of its performance evaluation for its investment center managers. For example, actual ROI can be compared to targeted ROI or to the ROI for similar departments at competing businesses.

Investment Center Residual Income   Another way to evaluate division performance is to compute investment center **residual income,** which is computed as follows.

$$\text{Residual income} = \frac{\text{Investment center}}{\text{income}} - \frac{\text{Target investment center}}{\text{income}}$$

Assume ZTel's top management sets target income at 8% of investment center assets. For an investment center, this target percentage is typically the cost of obtaining financing. Applying this formula using data from Exhibit 22.13 yields the residual income for ZTel's divisions in Exhibit 22.14.

	LCD Division	S-Phone Division
Investment center income	$526,500	$417,600
Less target investment center income: $2,500,000 × 8%.	200,000	
$1,850,000 × 8%.		148,000
Investment center residual income	$326,500	$269,600

EXHIBIT 22.14

Investment Center
Residual Income

Residual income is usually expressed in dollars. The LCD division produced more dollars of residual income than the S-Phone division. ZTel's management can use residual income, along with ROI, to evaluate investment center manager performance.

Using residual income to evaluate division performance encourages division managers to accept all opportunities that return more than the target income, thus increasing company value. For example, the S-Phone division might (mistakenly) not want to accept a new customer that will provide a 15% return on investment because that will reduce the S-Phone division's overall return on investment (23%, as shown above). However, the S-Phone division *should* accept this opportunity because the new customer would increase residual income by providing income above the target income of 8% of invested assets.

The Media division of a company reports income of $600,000, average invested assets of $7,500,000, and a target income of 6% of average invested assets. Compute the division's (a) return on investment and (b) residual income.

Solution

a. $600,000/$7,500,000 = 8%
b. $600,000 − ($7,500,000 × 6%) = $150,000

NEED-TO-KNOW 22-3

Return on Investment and Residual Income

A1

Do More: QS 22-9, QS 22-10, E 22-9, E 22-10

Measurement Issues   Evaluations of investment center performance using return on investment and residual income can be affected by how a company answers these questions:

1. How do you compute *average* invested assets? It is common to compute the average by adding the year's beginning amount of invested assets to the year's ending amount of invested assets and dividing that sum by 2. Averages based on monthly or quarterly asset amounts are also acceptable. Seasonal variations in invested assets, if any, impact this average.

2. How do you measure invested assets? It is common to measure invested assets using their *net* book values. For example, depreciable assets would be measured at their cost minus accumulated depreciation. As net book value declines over a depreciable asset's useful life, the result is that return on investment and residual income would increase over that asset's life. This might cause managers not to invest in new assets. In addition, in measuring invested assets, companies commonly exclude assets that are not used in generating investment center income, such as land held for resale.

3. How do you measure investment center income? It is common to exclude both interest expense and tax expense from investment center income. Interest expense reflects a company's financing decisions, and tax expense is typically considered outside the control of an investment center manager. Excluding interest and taxes in these calculations enables more meaningful comparisons of return on investment and residual income across investment centers and companies.

Point: *Economic Value Added* (EVA®), developed and trademarked by Stern, Stewart, and Co., addresses issues in computing residual income. This method uses a variety of adjustments to compute income, assets, and the target rate.

■ **Decision Insight**

In the Money   Executive pay is often linked to performance measures. Bonus payments are often based on exceeding a target return on investment or certain balanced scorecard indicators. Stock awards, such as stock options and restricted stock, reward executives when their company's stock price rises. The goal of bonus plans and stock awards is to encourage executives to make decisions that increase company performance and value. ■

Investment Center Profit Margin and Investment Turnover

A2
Analyze investment centers using profit margin and investment turnover.

We can further examine investment center (division) performance by splitting return on investment into two measures—profit margin and investment turnover—as follows.

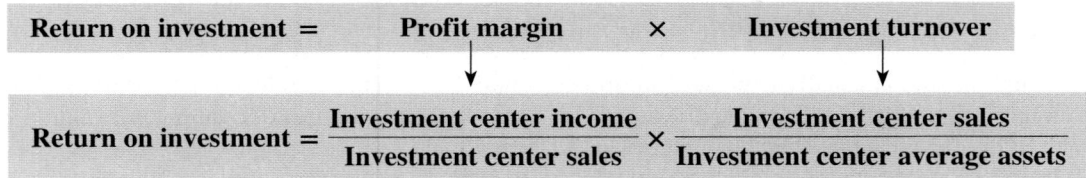

$$\text{Return on investment} = \text{Profit margin} \times \text{Investment turnover}$$

$$\text{Return on investment} = \frac{\text{Investment center income}}{\text{Investment center sales}} \times \frac{\text{Investment center sales}}{\text{Investment center average assets}}$$

- **Profit margin** measures the income earned per dollar of sales. It equals investment center income divided by investment center sales. In analyzing investment center performance, we typically use a measure of income *before* tax.
- **Investment turnover** measures how efficiently an investment center generates sales from its invested assets. It equals investment center sales divided by investment center average assets.

Point: This partitioning of return on investment is sometimes called *DuPont analysis.*

Profit margin is expressed as a percent, while investment turnover is interpreted as the number of times assets were converted into sales. Higher profit margin and higher investment turnover indicate better performance.

To illustrate, consider **Walt Disney Co.**, which reports in Exhibit 22.15 results for two of its operating divisions: Media Networks and Parks and Resorts.

EXHIBIT 22.15

Walt Disney Division Sales, Income, and Assets

$ millions	Media Networks	Parks and Resorts
Sales	$23,510	$18,415
Income	6,902	3,774
Average invested assets	32,591	28,884

Profit margin and investment turnover for these two divisions are computed and shown in Exhibit 22.16.

EXHIBIT 22.16

Walt Disney Division Profit Margin and Investment Turnover

$ millions		Media Networks	Parks and Resorts
Profit margin:	$6,902/$23,510	29.36%	
	$3,774/$18,415		20.49%
Investment turnover:	$23,510/$32,591	0.72	
	$18,415/$28,884		0.64
Return on investment:	29.36% × 0.72	21.14%	
	20.49% × 0.64		13.11%

Disney's Media Networks division makes 29.36 cents of profit for every dollar of sales, while its Parks and Resorts division makes 20.49 cents of profit per dollar of sales. The Media Networks division (0.72 investment turnover) is slightly more efficient than the Parks and Resorts division (0.64 investment turnover) in using assets. Top management can use profit margin and investment turnover to evaluate the performance of division managers. The measures can also aid management when considering further investment in its divisions. Because of both a much higher profit margin and higher investment turnover, the Media Networks division's return on investment (21.14%) is much greater than that of the Parks and Resorts division (13.11%).

Decision Maker

Division Manager You manage a division in a highly competitive industry. You will receive a cash bonus if your division achieves an ROI above 12%. Your division's profit margin is 7%, equal to the industry average, and your division's investment turnover is 1.5. How can you increase your chance of receiving the bonus? ■ *Answer:* Your division's ROI is 10.5% (7% × 1.5). In a competitive industry, it is difficult to increase profit margins by raising prices. Your division might be better able to control costs than increase profit margin. You might increase advertising to increase sales without increasing invested assets. Investment turnover and ROI increase if the advertising attracts customers.

A division reports sales of $50,000, income of $2,000, and average invested assets of $10,000. Compute the division's (a) profit margin, (b) investment turnover, and (c) return on investment.

Solution

a. $2,000/$50,000 = 4%   **b.** $50,000/$10,000 = 5.0   **c.** $2,000/$10,000 = 20%

NEED-TO-KNOW 22-4

Margin, Turnover, and Return on Investment

A2

Do More: QS 22-12, E 22-11, E 22-12

NONFINANCIAL PERFORMANCE EVALUATION MEASURES

Evaluating performance solely on financial measures has limitations. For example, some investment center managers might forgo profitable opportunities to keep their return on investment high. Also, residual income is less useful when comparing investment centers of different size. And, both return on investment and residual income can encourage managers to focus too heavily on short-term financial goals.

In response to these limitations, companies consider *nonfinancial* measures. A delivery company such as **FedEx** might track the percentage of on-time deliveries. The percentage of defective tennis balls manufactured can be used to assess performance of **Penn**'s production managers. **Walmart**'s credit card screens commonly ask customers at checkout whether the cashier was friendly or the store was clean. **Coca-Cola** measures its water usage as part of an effort to enhance the sustainability of its production process. This kind of information can help division managers run their divisions and help top management evaluate division manager performance. A popular measure that includes nonfinancial indicators is the balanced scorecard.

Balanced Scorecard

The **balanced scorecard** is a system of performance measures, including nonfinancial measures, used to assess company and division manager performance. The balanced scorecard requires managers to think of their company from four perspectives.

A3
Analyze investment centers using the balanced scorecard.

1. **Customer:** What do customers think of us?
2. **Internal Processes:** Which operations are crucial to customer needs?
3. **Innovation/Learning:** How can we improve?
4. **Financial:** What do our owners think of us?

The balanced scorecard collects information on several *key performance indicators* (KPIs) within each of the four perspectives. These key indicators vary across companies. Exhibit 22.17 lists common performance indicators used in the balanced scorecard.

After selecting key performance indicators, companies collect data on each indicator and compare actual amounts to target (goal) amounts to assess performance. For example, a company might have a goal of filling 98% of customer orders within two hours. Balanced scorecard reports are often presented in graphs or tables that can be updated frequently. Such timely information aids division managers in their decisions and can be used by top management to evaluate division manager performance.

Point: One survey indicates that nearly 60% of global companies use some form of balanced scorecard.

EXHIBIT 22.17

Balanced Scorecard
Performance Indicators

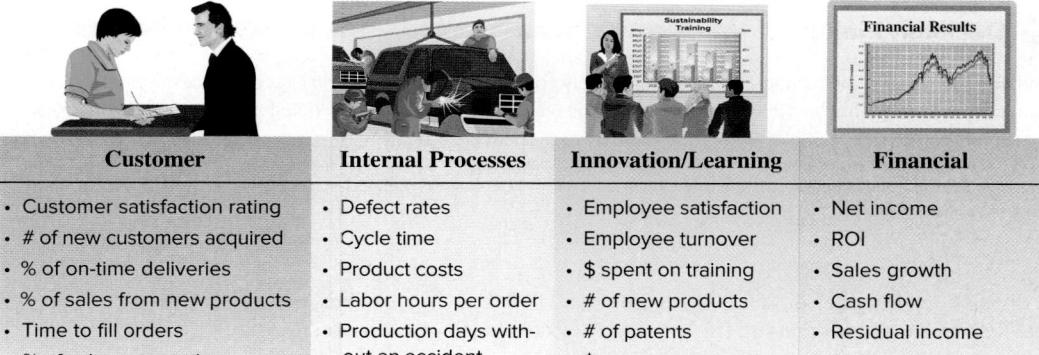

Customer	Internal Processes	Innovation/Learning	Financial
• Customer satisfaction rating • # of new customers acquired • % of on-time deliveries • % of sales from new products • Time to fill orders • % of sales returned	• Defect rates • Cycle time • Product costs • Labor hours per order • Production days without an accident	• Employee satisfaction • Employee turnover • $ spent on training • # of new products • # of patents • $ spent on research	• Net income • ROI • Sales growth • Cash flow • Residual income • Stock price

Exhibit 22.18 is an example of balanced scorecard reporting on the customer perspective for an Internet retailer. This scorecard reports that the retailer is getting 62% of its potential customers successfully through the purchasing process and that 2.2% of all orders are returned. The *color* of the circles in the Trend column reveals whether the company is exceeding its goal (green), roughly meeting the goal (gray), or not meeting the goal (red). The *direction* of the arrows reveals any trend in performance: An upward arrow indicates improvement, a downward arrow indicates declining performance, and an arrow pointing sideways indicates no change.

A review of this balanced scorecard suggests the retailer is meeting or exceeding its goals on orders returned and customer satisfaction. Further, purchasing success and customer satisfaction are improving. The company has received more customer complaints than was hoped for; *however,* the number of customer complaints is declining. A manager would combine this information with similar information from the other three performance indicators (internal processes, innovation and learning, and financial perspectives) to get an overall view of division performance.

EXHIBIT 22.18

Balanced Scorecard
Reporting: Internet Retailer

KPI: Customer Perspective	Actual	Goal	Trend
Potential customers purchasing	62%	80%	● ↑
Orders returned	2.2%	2%	● ↔
Customer satisfaction rating	9.5 of 10.0	9.5	● ↑
Number of customer complaints	142	100	● ↓

■ **Decision Maker**

CEO As CEO, your best-performing division, based on ROI, reported a large decrease in employee satisfaction. Should you investigate reasons for employee dissatisfaction or ignore it because financial performance is superb? ■ *Answer:* You should investigate. Lower employee satisfaction can lead to increased employee turnover and lower customer satisfaction, both of which can have serious financial costs to the company.

NEED-TO-KNOW 22-5

Balanced Scorecard

A3

Do More: QS 22-13, QS 22-14,
E 22-16, E 22-17

Classify each of the performance measures below into the most likely balanced scorecard perspective to which it relates: customer (**C**), internal processes (**P**), innovation and growth (**I**), or financial (**F**).

1. On-time delivery rate
2. Accident-free days
3. Sustainability training workshops held
4. Defective products made

5. Residual income
6. Patents applied for
7. Sales returns
8. Customer complaints

Solution

1. C **2.** P **3.** I **4.** P **5.** F **6.** I **7.** C **8.** C

Transfer Pricing

Divisions in decentralized companies sometimes do business with one another. For example, a separate division of **Harley-Davidson** manufactures the plastic and fiberglass parts used in the company's motorcycles. **Anheuser-Busch InBev**'s metal container division makes cans used in its brewing operations and also sells cans to soft-drink companies. A division of **Prince** produces strings used in tennis rackets made by Prince and other manufacturers.

The price used to record transfers of goods across divisions of the same company is called the **transfer price.** Transfer prices can be used in cost, profit, and investment centers.

In decentralized organizations, division managers have input on or decide transfer prices. Since these transfers are not with customers outside the company, the transfer price has no direct impact on the *company's* overall profits. However, transfer prices can impact *division* performance evaluations and, if set incorrectly, lead to bad decisions.

Transfer prices are set using one of three approaches.

1. Cost (such as variable manufacturing cost per unit)
2. Market price
3. Negotiated price

To illustrate the impact of alternative transfer prices on divisional profits, consider ZTel, a Smartphone manufacturer. ZTel's LCD division makes touch-screen monitors that are used in ZTel's Smartphone division or sold to outside customers. LCD's variable manufacturing cost is $40 per monitor, and the market price is $80 per monitor. There are two extreme positions one can take for the transfer price.

- **Low Transfer Price** The *Smartphone division manager* wants to pay a *low* transfer price. The transfer price cannot be less than $40 per monitor, as any lower price would cause the LCD manager to lose money on each monitor sold.
- **High Transfer Price** The *LCD division manager* wants to receive a *high* transfer price. The transfer price cannot be more than $80 per monitor, as the Smartphone division manager will not pay more than the market price.

This means the transfer price must be between $40 and $80 per monitor, and a negotiated price somewhere between these two extremes is reasonable. Appendix 22B expands on transfer pricing and details on the three approaches.

SUSTAINABILITY AND ACCOUNTING

This chapter focused on performance measurement and reporting. Companies report on their sustainability performance in a variety of ways. One approach integrates sustainability metrics in the four balanced scorecard perspectives (customer, internal process, innovation and learning, and financial). Many key performance indicators address the internal process and innovation and learning perspectives. For example, **General Mills** reports on its environmental targets and progress in its annual corporate sustainability report. Exhibit 22.19 captures how this information might appear as part of a balanced scorecard report.

Some companies can report the direct effects on profits from a focus on sustainability. For example, **Target** recently started a *Made to Matter* department. To be sold in this department, brands must focus on consumer wellness and be committed to social responsibility. Target's *Made to Matter* department reported sales of over $1 billion in a recent year.

Jibu, this chapter's feature company, prioritizes "impact maximization." Co-founder Galen Welsch believes that a socially driven business model can "solve the world's problems, like lack of water, and transform lives. Profits are a means to an end. They enable us to attract great owners who can provide workers with reliable incomes. All while selling a product that is critical to life at a fair price."

©Jibu

EXHIBIT 22.19

Balanced Scorecard—
Sustainability

KPI: Internal Process Perspective	Actual Reduction	Target Reduction	Trend
Emissions	23%	20%	🔘 ⬆
Energy usage	10	20	⚫ ⬆
Solid waste	38	50	⚫ ⬆
Fuel	25	35	⚫ ⬆

 Decision Analysis  Cash Conversion Cycle

A4

Compute the number of days in the cash conversion cycle.

Effectively managing working capital is important for businesses to survive and profit. For example, lean manufacturers try to reduce the time from paying for raw materials from suppliers (cash outflow) to collecting on credit sales from customers (cash inflow). As we show in other chapters, ratios based on accounts receivable, accounts payable, and inventory are used to evaluate performance on each of these separate working capital dimensions. These ratios can be combined to summarize how effectively a company manages its working capital. The **cash conversion cycle,** or *cash-to-cash cycle,* measures the average time it takes to convert cash outflows into cash inflows from customers. It is defined in Exhibit 22.20.

EXHIBIT 22.20

Cash Conversion Cycle

$$\text{Cash conversion cycle} = \frac{\text{Days' sales in}}{\text{accounts receivable}} + \frac{\text{Days' sales in}}{\text{inventory}} - \frac{\text{Days' payable}}{\text{outstanding}}$$

Formulas for Components of the Cash Conversion Cycle

Days' sales in accounts receivable	$= \dfrac{\text{Accounts receivable, net}}{\text{Net sales}} \times 365$
Days' sales in inventory	$= \dfrac{\text{Inventory}}{\text{Cost of goods sold}} \times 365$
Days' payable outstanding (or *Days' sales in accounts payable*)	$= \dfrac{\text{Accounts payable}}{\text{Cost of goods sold}} \times 365$

Exhibit 22.21 shows these calculations for **General Mills**, a food processor.

EXHIBIT 22.21

General Mills Cash Conversion Cycle

$ millions		2017	2016
Accounts receivable, net, end of year		$ 1,430	$ 1,361
Net sales.		$15,620	$16,563
1	**Days' sales in accounts receivable**	**33 days**	**30 days**
Inventory, end of year		$ 1,484	$ 1,414
Cost of goods sold.		$10,056	$10,734
2	**Days' sales in inventory**	**54 days**	**48 days**
Accounts payable, end of year		$ 2,120	$ 2,047
Cost of goods sold.		$10,056	$10,734
3	**Days' payable outstanding. . . . .**	**77 days**	**70 days**
	Cash conversion cycle (1) + (2) − (3).	**10 days**	**8 days**

General Mills's cash conversion cycle is 8 days in 2016 and 10 days in 2017. This is low and indicates General Mills efficiently manages its cash. For comparison, the American Productivity and Quality Center (APQC), a benchmarking company, reports an average cash conversion cycle of 45 days for the companies it studies. The most efficient companies report cash conversion cycles of 30 days or less, while the least efficient take over 80 days to convert cash outflows to suppliers to cash inflows from customers.

If a company's cash conversion cycle is too long, it risks missing good investment opportunities. Companies can consider the following actions to speed up the cash conversion cycle.

- Offering customers fewer days to pay.
- Offering customers discounts for prompt payment.
- Adopting lean principles to reduce inventory levels.
- Negotiating longer times to pay suppliers.

Management requests departmental income statements for Gamer's Haven, a computer store that has five departments. Three are operating departments (Hardware, Software, and Repairs) and two are service departments (general office and purchasing).

NEED-TO-KNOW 22-6

COMPREHENSIVE

Departmental Cost Allocations and Income Statements

	General Office	Purchasing	Hardware	Software	Repairs
Sales	—	—	$960,000	$600,000	$840,000
Cost of goods sold	—	—	500,000	300,000	200,000
Direct expenses					
Payroll	$60,000	$45,000	80,000	25,000	325,000
Depreciation	6,000	7,200	33,000	4,200	9,600
Supplies	15,000	10,000	10,000	2,000	25,000

The departments incur several indirect expenses. To prepare departmental income statements, the indirect expenses must be allocated across the five departments. Then the expenses of the two service departments must be allocated to the three operating departments. Total cost amounts and the allocation bases for each indirect expense follow.

Indirect Expense	Total Cost	Allocation Basis
Rent.	$150,000	Square footage occupied
Utilities	50,000	Square footage occupied
Advertising	125,000	Dollars of sales
Insurance	30,000	Value of assets insured
Service departments		
General office.	?	Number of employees
Purchasing	?	Dollars of cost of goods sold

The following additional information is needed for indirect expense allocations.

Department	Square Feet	Sales	Insured Assets	Employees	Cost of Goods Sold
General office	500		$ 60,000		
Purchasing	500		72,000		
Hardware	4,000	$ 960,000	330,000	5	$ 500,000
Software	3,000	600,000	42,000	5	300,000
Repairs	2,000	840,000	96,000	10	200,000
Totals.	10,000	$2,400,000	$600,000	20	$1,000,000

Required

1. Prepare a departmental expense allocation spreadsheet for Gamer's Haven.

2. Prepare a departmental income statement reporting net income for each operating department and for all operating departments combined.

PLANNING THE SOLUTION

- Set up and complete four tables to allocate the indirect expenses—one each for rent, utilities, advertising, and insurance.
- Allocate the departments' indirect expenses using a spreadsheet like the one in Exhibit 22.10. Enter the given amounts of the direct expenses for each department. Then enter the allocated amounts of the indirect expenses that you computed.
- Complete two tables for allocating the general office and purchasing department costs to the three operating departments. Enter these amounts on the spreadsheet and determine the total expenses allocated to the three operating departments.
- Prepare departmental income statements like the one in Exhibit 22.11. Show sales, cost of goods sold, gross profit, individual expenses, and net income for each of the three operating departments and for the combined company.

SOLUTION

Allocations of the four indirect expenses across the five departments.

Rent	Square Feet	Percent of Total	Allocated Cost
General office	500	5.0%	$ 7,500
Purchasing	500	5.0	7,500
Hardware	4,000	40.0	60,000
Software	3,000	30.0	45,000
Repairs	2,000	20.0	30,000
Totals	10,000	100.0%	$150,000

Utilities	Square Feet	Percent of Total	Allocated Cost
General office	500	5.0%	$ 2,500
Purchasing	500	5.0	2,500
Hardware	4,000	40.0	20,000
Software	3,000	30.0	15,000
Repairs	2,000	20.0	10,000
Totals	10,000	100.0%	$50,000

Advertising	Sales Dollars	Percent of Total	Allocated Cost
Hardware	$ 960,000	40.0%	$ 50,000
Software	600,000	25.0	31,250
Repairs	840,000	35.0	43,750
Totals	$2,400,000	100.0%	$125,000

Insurance	Assets Insured	Percent of Total	Allocated Cost
General office	$ 60,000	10.0%	$ 3,000
Purchasing	72,000	12.0	3,600
Hardware	330,000	55.0	16,500
Software	42,000	7.0	2,100
Repairs	96,000	16.0	4,800
Totals	$600,000	100.0%	$30,000

1. Allocations of service department expenses to the three operating departments.

General Office Allocations to	Employees	Percent of Total	Allocated Cost
Hardware	5	25.0%	$23,500
Software	5	25.0	23,500
Repairs	10	50.0	47,000
Totals	20	100.0%	$94,000

Purchasing Allocations to	Cost of Goods Sold	Percent of Total	Allocated Cost
Hardware	$ 500,000	50.0%	$37,900
Software	300,000	30.0	22,740
Repairs	200,000	20.0	15,160
Totals	$1,000,000	100.0%	$75,800

GAMER'S HAVEN
Departmental Expense Allocations

For Year Ended December 31, 2019	Allocation Base	Expense Account Balance	General Office Dept.	Purchasing Dept.	Hardware Dept.	Software Dept.	Repairs Dept.
Direct Expenses							
Payroll		$ 535,000	$ 60,000	$ 45,000	$ 80,000	$ 25,000	$ 325,000
Depreciation		60,000	6,000	7,200	33,000	4,200	9,600
Supplies		62,000	15,000	10,000	10,000	2,000	25,000
Indirect Expenses							
Rent	Square ft.	150,000	7,500	7,500	60,000	45,000	30,000
Utilities	Square ft.	50,000	2,500	2,500	20,000	15,000	10,000
Advertising	Sales	125,000	—	—	50,000	31,250	43,750
Insurance	Assets	30,000	3,000	3,600	16,500	2,100	4,800
Total expenses		1,012,000	94,000	75,800	269,500	124,550	448,150
Service Department Expenses							
General office	Employees		(94,000)		23,500	23,500	47,000
Purchasing	Goods sold			(75,800)	37,900	22,740	15,160
Total expenses allocated to operating departments		$1,012,000	$ 0	$ 0	$330,900	$170,790	$510,310

2. Departmental income statements.

GAMER'S HAVEN Departmental Income Statements				
For Year Ended December 31, 2019	Hardware	Software	Repairs	Combined
Sales	$ 960,000	$ 600,000	$ 840,000	$2,400,000
Cost of goods sold	500,000	300,000	200,000	1,000,000
Gross profit.....................	460,000	300,000	640,000	1,400,000
Expenses				
Payroll........................	80,000	25,000	325,000	430,000
Depreciation...................	33,000	4,200	9,600	46,800
Supplies	10,000	2,000	25,000	37,000
Rent..........................	60,000	45,000	30,000	135,000
Utilities	20,000	15,000	10,000	45,000
Advertising	50,000	31,250	43,750	125,000
Insurance	16,500	2,100	4,800	23,400
Share of general office	23,500	23,500	47,000	94,000
Share of purchasing.............	37,900	22,740	15,160	75,800
Total expenses	330,900	170,790	510,310	1,012,000
Operating income...............	**$129,100**	**$129,210**	**$129,690**	**$ 388,000**

Cost Allocations

22A

In this appendix we use our general model of cost allocation (see Exhibit 22.3) to show how the cost allocations in Exhibits 22.10 and 22.11 are computed. A-1 Hardware's departments use the allocation bases in Exhibit 22A.1: square feet of floor space, dollar value of insured assets, sales dollars, and number of purchase orders.

EXHIBIT 22A.1

Departments' Allocation Bases

Department	Floor Space (square feet)	Value of Insured Assets ($)	Sales ($)	Number of Purchase Orders*
General office	1,500	$ 38,000		—
Purchasing.............	1,500	19,000		—
Hardware..............	4,050	85,500	$119,500	394
Housewares...........	2,700	57,000	71,700	267
Appliances............	2,250	38,000	47,800	324
Total.................	12,000	$237,500	$239,000	985

*Purchasing department tracks purchase orders by department.

For each cost allocation that follows, we use the general formula here from Exhibit 22.3 to allocate indirect and service department costs.

> **Allocated cost = Total cost to allocate × Percentage of allocation base used**

From Exhibit 22.9, the company has these four indirect costs to allocate.

Rent expense.............	$12,000	Advertising expense	$1,000
Utilities expense	2,400	Insurance expense	2,500

Allocation of Rent The two service departments (General office and Purchasing) occupy 25% of the total space (3,000 sq. feet/12,000 sq. feet). However, they are located near the back of the building, which is of lower value than space near the front that is occupied by operating departments. Management estimates that space near the back accounts for $1,200 (10%) of the total rent expense of $12,000. Exhibit 22A.2 shows how we allocate the $1,200 rent expense between these two service departments in proportion to their square footage.

EXHIBIT 22A.2

Allocating Indirect (Rent) Expense to Service Departments

Department	Square Feet	Percent of Total	Allocated Cost*
General office	1,500	50.0%	$ 600
Purchasing	1,500	50.0	600
Totals................	3,000	100.0%	$1,200

*See row 13 of departmental expense allocation spreadsheet (Exhibit 22.10).

We then have the remaining amount of $10,800 ($12,000 − $1,200) of rent expense to allocate to the three operating departments, as shown in Exhibit 22A.3.

EXHIBIT 22A.3

Allocating Indirect (Rent) Expense to Operating Departments

Department	Square Feet	Percent of Total	Allocated Cost*
Hardware	4,050	45.0%	$ 4,860
Housewares	2,700	30.0	3,240
Appliances	2,250	25.0	2,700
Totals................	9,000	100.0%	$10,800

*See row 13 of departmental expense allocation spreadsheet (Exhibit 22.10).

Allocation of Utilities We next allocate the $2,400 of utilities expense to all departments based on square footage occupied, as shown in Exhibit 22A.4.

EXHIBIT 22A.4

Allocating Indirect (Utilities) Expense to All Departments

Department	Square Feet	Percent of Total	Allocated Cost*
General office	1,500	12.50%	$ 300
Purchasing	1,500	12.50	300
Hardware	4,050	33.75	810
Housewares	2,700	22.50	540
Appliances	2,250	18.75	450
Totals..................	12,000	100.00%	$2,400

*See row 14 of departmental expense allocation spreadsheet (Exhibit 22.10).

Allocation of Advertising Exhibit 22A.5 shows the allocation of $1,000 of advertising expense to the three operating departments on the basis of sales dollars. We exclude the service departments from this allocation because they do not generate sales.

EXHIBIT 22A.5

Allocating Indirect (Advertising) Expense to Operating Departments

Department	Sales	Percent of Total	Allocated Cost*
Hardware	$119,500	50.0%	$ 500
Housewares	71,700	30.0	300
Appliances	47,800	20.0	200
Totals..................	$239,000	100.0%	$1,000

*See row 15 of departmental expense allocation spreadsheet (Exhibit 22.10).

Allocation of Insurance We allocate the $2,500 of insurance expense to each service and operating department, as shown in Exhibit 22A.6.

EXHIBIT 22A.6

Allocating Indirect (Insurance) Expense to All Departments

Department	Value of Insured Assets	Percent of Total	Allocated Cost*
General office	$ 38,000	16.0%	$ 400
Purchasing	19,000	8.0	200
Hardware	85,500	36.0	900
Housewares	57,000	24.0	600
Appliances	38,000	16.0	400
Total...................	$237,500	100.0%	$2,500

*See row 16 of departmental expense allocation spreadsheet (Exhibit 22.10).

Allocation of Service Department Expenses Next we allocate the total expenses of the two service departments to the three operating departments. Exhibit 22A.7 shows the allocation of total General office expenses ($15,300) to operating departments. This amount of $15,300 includes the $14,000 of direct service department expenses, plus $1,300 of indirect expenses that were allocated to the General office department.

Department	Sales	Percent of Total	Allocated Cost*
Hardware	$119,500	50.0%	$ 7,650
Housewares	71,700	30.0	4,590
Appliances	47,800	20.0	3,060
Total	$239,000	100.0%	$15,300

EXHIBIT 22A.7

Allocating Service Department (General Office) Expenses to Operating Departments

*See row 19 of departmental expense allocation spreadsheet (Exhibit 22.10).

Exhibit 22A.8 shows the allocation of total Purchasing department expenses ($9,700) to operating departments. This amount of $9,700 includes $8,600 of direct expenses plus $1,100 of indirect expenses that were allocated to the Purchasing department.

Department	Number of Purchase Orders	Percent of Total	Allocated Cost*
Hardware	394	40.00%	$3,880
Housewares	267	27.11	2,630
Appliances	324	32.89	3,190
Total	985	100.00%	$9,700

EXHIBIT 22A.8

Allocating Service Department (Purchasing) Expenses to Operating Departments

*See row 20 of departmental expense allocation spreadsheet (Exhibit 22.10).

APPENDIX

Transfer Pricing

22B

In this appendix we show how to determine transfer prices and discuss issues in transfer pricing.

Alternative Transfer Prices   The top portion of Exhibit 22B.1 reports data on the LCD division of ZTel. That division manufactures liquid crystal display (LCD) touch-screen monitors for use in ZTel's S-Phone division's smartphones. The monitors can also be used in other products. The LCD division can sell its monitors to the S-Phone division as well as to buyers other than S-Phone. Likewise, the S-Phone division can purchase monitors from suppliers other than LCD.

| Production capacity | 100,000 units | Variable manufacturing costs per unit | $40 |
| Selling price per unit to outside customers | $80 | Fixed manufacturing costs | $2,000,000 |

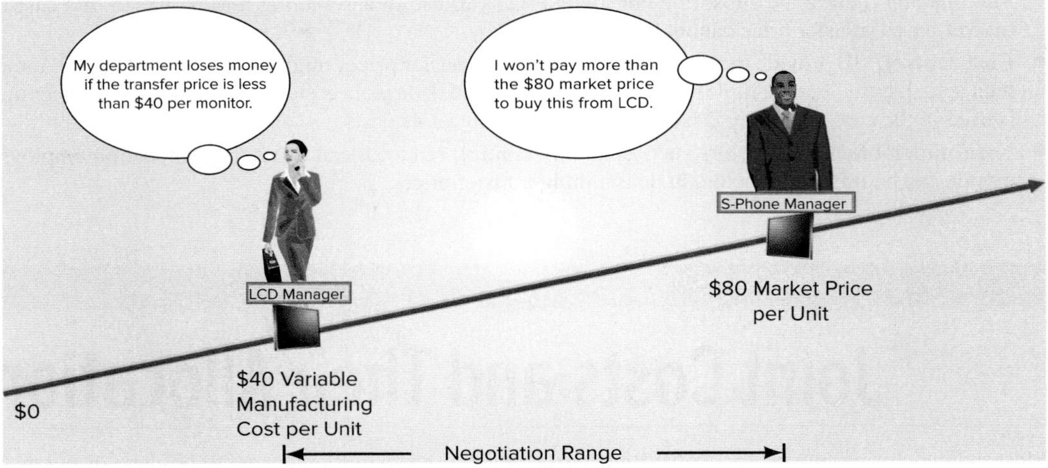

EXHIBIT 22B.1

LCD Division Manufacturing Information—Monitors

The bottom portion of Exhibit 22B.1 reveals the range of transfer prices for transfers of monitors from LCD to S-Phone. The transfer price can reasonably range from $40 (the variable manufacturing cost per unit) to $80 (the cost of buying the monitor from an outside supplier).

- The LCD manager wants to report a divisional profit. Thus, this manager will not accept a transfer price less than $40; a price less than $40 would cause the division to lose money on each monitor transferred. The LCD manager will consider transfer prices of only $40 or more.

- The S-Phone division manager also wants to report a divisional profit. Thus, this manager will not pay more than $80 per monitor because similar monitors can be bought from outside suppliers at that price. The S-Phone manager will consider transfer prices of only $80 or less.

As any transfer price between $40 and $80 per monitor is possible, how does ZTel determine the transfer price? The answer depends in part on whether the LCD division has excess capacity to manufacture monitors.

No Excess Capacity If the LCD division can sell every monitor it produces (100,000 units) at a market price of $80 per monitor, LCD managers would not accept any transfer price less than $80 per monitor. This is a **market-based transfer price**—one based on the market price of the good or service being transferred. Any transfer price less than $80 would cause the LCD division managers to incur an unnecessary *opportunity cost* that would lower the division's income and hurt its managers' performance evaluation.

Typically, a division operating at full capacity will sell to external customers rather than sell internally. Still, the market-based transfer price of $80 can be considered the maximum possible transfer price when there is excess capacity, which is the case we consider next.

Excess Capacity Assume the LCD division is producing only 80,000 units. Because LCD has $2,000,000 of fixed manufacturing costs, both the LCD division and the top management of ZTel prefer that the S-Phone division purchases its monitors from LCD. For example, if S-Phone purchases its monitors from an outside supplier at the market price of $80 each, LCD manufactures no units. Then, LCD reports a division loss equal to its fixed costs, and ZTel overall reports a lower net income. With excess capacity, LCD should accept any transfer price of $40 per unit or greater, and S-Phone should purchase monitors from LCD. This will allow LCD to recover some (or all) of its fixed costs and increase ZTel's overall profits.

For example, if a transfer price of $50 per monitor is used, the S-Phone manager is pleased to buy from LCD because that price is below the market price of $80. For each monitor transferred from LCD to S-Phone at $50, the LCD division receives a *contribution margin* of $10 (computed as $50 transfer price less $40 variable cost) to contribute toward recovering its fixed costs. This form of transfer pricing is called **cost-based transfer pricing.** Under this approach, the transfer price might be based on variable costs, total costs, or variable costs plus a markup.

With excess capacity, division managers will often negotiate a transfer price that lies between the variable cost per unit and the market price per unit. In this case, the **negotiated transfer price** and resulting departmental performance reports reflect, in part, the negotiating skills of the respective division managers. This might not be best for overall company performance. Determining the transfer price under excess capacity is complex and is covered in advanced courses.

Additional Issues in Transfer Pricing Several additional issues arise in determining transfer prices.

- **No market price exists.** Sometimes there is no market price for the product being transferred. The product might be a key component that requires additional conversion costs at the next stage and is not easily replicated by an outside company. For example, there is no market for a console for a **Nissan** Maxima and there is no substitute console Nissan can use in assembling a Maxima. In this case, a market-based transfer price cannot be used.
- **Cost control.** To provide incentives for cost control, transfer prices might be based on standard, rather than actual, costs. For example, if a transfer price of actual variable costs plus a markup of $20 per unit is used in the case above, LCD has no incentive to control its costs.
- **Nonfinancial factors.** Factors such as quality control, reduced lead times, and impact on employee morale can be important factors in determining transfer prices.

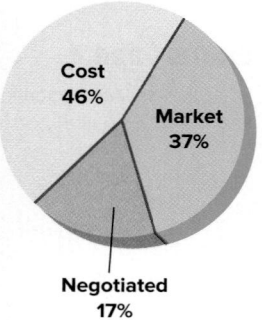

Transfer Pricing Approaches Used by Companies

Cost 46%
Market 37%
Negotiated 17%

APPENDIX

22C Joint Costs and Their Allocation

C3

Describe allocation of joint costs across products.

Most manufacturing processes involve **joint costs,** which refer to costs incurred to produce or purchase two or more products at the same time. For example, a sawmill company incurs joint costs when it buys logs that it cuts into lumber, as shown in Exhibit 22C.1. The joint costs include the logs (raw material) and their being cut (conversion) into boards classified as Clear, Select, No. 1 Common, No. 2 Common, No. 3 Common, and other types of lumber and by-products. After the logs are cut into boards, any further processing costs on the boards are not joint costs.

When a joint cost is incurred, a question arises as to whether to allocate it to different products resulting from it. The answer is that when management wishes to estimate the costs of individual products, joint costs are included and must be allocated to these joint products. However, when management needs information to help decide whether to sell a product at a certain point in the production process or to process it further, the joint costs are ignored. (We study this sell-or-process-further decision in a later chapter.)

Financial statements prepared according to GAAP must assign joint costs to products. To do this, management must decide how to allocate joint costs across products benefiting from these costs. If some products are sold and others remain in inventory, allocating joint costs involves assigning costs to both cost of goods sold and ending inventory.

The two usual methods to allocate joint costs are the (1) *physical basis* and (2) *value basis.* The physical basis typically involves allocating a joint cost using physical characteristics such as the ratio of pounds, cubic feet, or gallons of each joint product to the total pounds, cubic feet, or gallons of all joint products flowing from the cost. This method is not preferred because the resulting cost allocations do not reflect the relative market values the joint cost generates. The preferred approach is the value basis, which allocates a joint cost in proportion to the sales value of the output produced by the process at the "split-off point"; see Exhibit 22C.1. The split-off point is the point at which separate products can be identified.

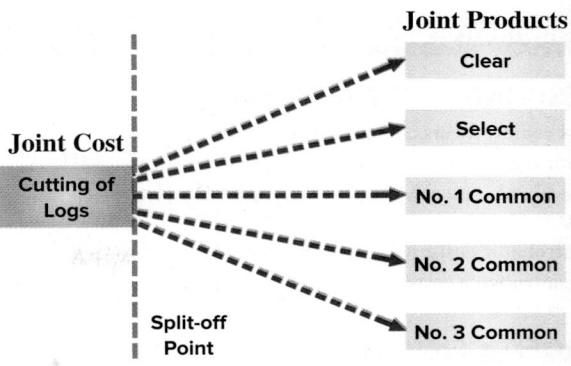

EXHIBIT 22C.1

Joint Products from Logs

Physical Basis Allocation of Joint Costs   To illustrate the physical basis of allocating a joint cost, we consider a sawmill that bought logs for $30,000. When cut, these logs produce 100,000 board feet of lumber in the grades and amounts shown in Exhibit 22C.2. The logs produce 20,000 board feet of No. 3 Common lumber, which is 20% of the total. With physical allocation, the No. 3 Common lumber is assigned 20% of the $30,000 cost of the logs, or $6,000 ($30,000 × 20%). Because this low-grade lumber sells for $4,000, this allocation gives a $2,000 loss from its production and sale. The physical basis for allocating joint costs does not reflect the extra value flowing into some products or the inferior value flowing into others. That is, the portion of a log that produces Clear- and Select-grade lumber is worth more than the portion used to produce the three grades of common lumber, but the physical basis fails to reflect this.

EXHIBIT 22C.2

Allocating Joint Costs on a Physical Basis

Grade of Lumber	Board Feet Produced	Percent of Total	Allocated Cost	Sales Value	Gross Profit
Clear and Select	10,000	10.0%	$ 3,000	$12,000	$ 9,000
No. 1 Common	30,000	30.0	9,000	18,000	9,000
No. 2 Common	40,000	40.0	12,000	16,000	4,000
No. 3 Common	20,000	20.0	6,000	4,000	(2,000)
Totals	100,000	100.0%	$30,000	$50,000	$20,000

Value Basis Allocation of Joint Costs   Exhibit 22C.3 illustrates the value basis method of allocation. It determines the percents of the total costs allocated to each grade by the ratio of each grade's sales value at the split-off point to the total sales value of $50,000 (sales value is the unit selling price multiplied by the number of units produced). The Clear and Select lumber grades receive 24% of the total cost ($12,000/$50,000) instead of the 10% portion using a physical basis. The No. 3 Common lumber receives only 8% of the total cost, or $2,400, which is much less than the $6,000 assigned to it using the physical basis.

EXHIBIT 22C.3

Allocating Joint Costs on a Value Basis

Grade of Lumber	Sales Value	Percent of Total	Allocated Cost	Gross Profit
Clear and Select	$12,000	24.0%	$ 7,200	$ 4,800
No. 1 Common	18,000	36.0	10,800	7,200
No. 2 Common	16,000	32.0	9,600	6,400
No. 3 Common	4,000	8.0	2,400	1,600
Totals	$50,000	100.0%	$30,000	$20,000

An outcome of value basis allocation is that *each* grade produces exactly the same 40% gross profit at the split-off point. This 40% rate equals the gross profit rate from selling all the lumber made from the $30,000 logs for a combined price of $50,000. It is this closer matching of cost and revenues that makes the value basis allocation of joint costs the preferred method.

Example: Refer to Exhibit 22C.3. If the sales value of Clear and Select lumber is changed to $10,000, what is the revised ratio of the market value of No. 1 Common to the total? *Answer:* $18,000/$48,000 = 37.5%

Summary: Cheat Sheet

RESPONSIBILITY ACCOUNTING

Cost center: Incurs costs; generates no revenues.

Profit center: Generates revenues and incurs costs.

Investment center: Manager is responsible for investments, revenues, and costs.

Controllable costs: Manager can determine or influence.

Uncontrollable costs: Not within the manager's control or influence.

PROFIT CENTERS

Direct expenses: Can be readily traced to departments; *not* allocated.

Indirect expenses: Incurred for joint benefit of more than one department; *must be* allocated.

General model of cost allocation

Allocated cost = Total cost to allocate × Percentage of allocation base used

Departmental income statement

$$\text{Departmental income} = \text{Department sales} - \text{Department direct expenses} - \text{Allocated indirect expenses} - \text{Allocated service department expenses}$$

Departmental contribution to overhead

Department sales − Direct expenses

INVESTMENT CENTERS

$$\text{Return on investment} = \frac{\text{Investment center income}}{\text{Investment center average invested assets}}$$

$$\text{Residual income} = \text{Investment center income} - \text{Target investment center income}$$

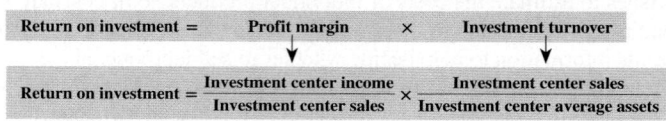

$$\text{Return on investment} = \text{Profit margin} \times \text{Investment turnover}$$

$$\text{Return on investment} = \frac{\text{Investment center income}}{\text{Investment center sales}} \times \frac{\text{Investment center sales}}{\text{Investment center average assets}}$$

BALANCED SCORECARD

System of performance measures.

Customers: What do they think of us?

Internal processes: Which are crucial to customer needs?

Innovation/learning: How can we improve?

Financial: What do owners think of us?

TRANSFER PRICING

Price set on transfers of goods across divisions.

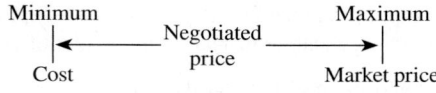

CASH CONVERSION CYCLE

Measures efficiency of cash management.

$$\frac{\text{Days' sales in}}{\text{Accounts Receivable}} + \frac{\text{Days' sales in}}{\text{Inventory}} - \frac{\text{Days' payable}}{\text{outstanding}}$$

$$\text{Days' sales in accounts receivable} = \frac{\text{Accounts receivable, net}}{\text{Net sales}} \times 365$$

$$\text{Days' sales in inventory} = \frac{\text{Inventory}}{\text{Cost of goods sold}} \times 365$$

$$\text{Days' payable outstanding (or } \textit{Days' sales in accounts payable}) = \frac{\text{Accounts payable}}{\text{Cost of goods sold}} \times 365$$

Key Terms

Balanced scorecard (881)

Cash conversion cycle (884)

Controllable costs (870)

Cost-based transfer pricing (890)

Cost center (869)

Decentralized organization (869)

Departmental contribution to overhead (877)

Departmental income statements (872)

Direct expenses (872)

Indirect expenses (873)

Investment center (869)

Investment turnover (880)

Joint cost (890)

Market-based transfer price (890)

Negotiated transfer price (890)

Profit center (869)

Profit margin (880)

Residual income (878)

Responsibility accounting (869)

Responsibility accounting performance report (870)

Return on investment (ROI) (878)

Transfer price (883)

Uncontrollable costs (870)

Multiple Choice Quiz

1. A retailer has three departments—Housewares, Appliances, and Clothing—and buys advertising that benefits all departments. Advertising expense is $150,000 for the year, and departmental sales for the year follow: Housewares, $356,250; Appliances, $641,250; and Clothing, $427,500.

How much advertising expense is allocated to Appliances if allocation is based on departmental sales?

a. $37,500   **c.** $45,000   **e.** $641,250

b. $67,500   **d.** $150,000

2. Indirect expenses
  a. Cannot be readily traced to one department.
  b. Are allocated to departments based on the relative benefit each department receives.
  c. Are the same as uncontrollable expenses.
  d. *a*, *b*, and *c* above are all true.
  e. *a* and *b* above are true.

3. A division reports the information below. What is the division's investment turnover?

Sales	$500,000
Income.	75,000
Average assets	200,000

  a. 37.5%   **c.** 2.5   **e.** 4
  b. 15   **d.** 2.67

4. A company operates three retail departments X, Y, and Z as profit centers. Which department has the largest dollar amount of departmental contribution to overhead, and what is the dollar amount contributed?

Department	Sales	Cost of Goods Sold	Direct Expenses	Allocated Indirect Expenses
X	$500,000	$350,000	$50,000	$40,000
Y	200,000	75,000	20,000	50,000
Z	350,000	150,000	75,000	10,000

  a. Department Y, $55,000   **d.** Department Z, $200,000
  b. Department Z, $125,000   **e.** Department X, $60,000
  c. Department X, $500,000

5. Using the data in question 4, Department X's contribution to overhead as a percentage of sales is
  a. 20%.   **c.** 12%.   **e.** 32%.
  b. 30%.   **d.** 48%.

ANSWERS TO MULTIPLE CHOICE QUIZ

1. b; [$641,250/($356,250 + $641,250 + $427,500)] × $150,000 = $67,500

2. d

3. c; $500,000/200,000 = 2.5

4. b;

	Dept. X	Dept. Y	Dept. Z
Sales.	$500,000	$200,000	$350,000
Cost of goods sold	350,000	75,000	150,000
Gross profit.	150,000	125,000	200,000
Direct expenses	50,000	20,000	75,000
Departmental contribution to overhead . . .	$100,000	$105,000	$125,000

5. a; $100,000/$500,000 = 20%

A,B,C *Superscript letter A, B, or C denotes assignments based on Appendix 22A, 22B, or 22C.*

[I] Icon denotes assignments that involve decision making.

Discussion Questions

1. Why are many companies divided into departments?

2. What is the difference between operating departments and service departments?

3. [I] What are controllable costs?

4. _____ costs are not within the manager's control or influence.

5. [I] In responsibility accounting, why are reports to higher-level managers usually summarized?

6. [I] How are decisions made in decentralized organizations?

7. [I] Is it possible to evaluate a cost center's profitability? Explain.

8. What is the difference between direct and indirect expenses?

9. [I] Suggest a reasonable basis for allocating each of the following indirect expenses to departments: (*a*) salary of a supervisor who manages several departments, (*b*) rent, (*c*) heat, (*d*) electricity for lighting, (*e*) janitorial services, (*f*) advertising, (*g*) expired insurance on equipment, and (*h*) property taxes on equipment.

10. **Samsung** has many departments. How is a department's contribution to overhead **Samsung** measured?

11. [I] **Google** aims to give its managers **GOOGLE** timely cost reports. In responsibility accounting, who receives timely cost reports and specific cost information? Explain.

12. What is a transfer price? What are the three main approaches to setting transfer prices?

13.[B] Under what conditions is a market-based transfer price most likely to be used?

14.[C] What is a joint cost? How are joint costs usually allocated among the products produced from them?

15. Each **Apple** retail store has several departments. Why is it useful for its management to **APPLE** (*a*) collect accounting information about each department and (*b*) treat each department as a profit center?

16. **Apple** delivers its products to locations around the world. List three controllable and **APPLE** three uncontrollable costs for its delivery department.

17. Define and describe the *cash conversion cycle* and identify its three components.

18. Can management of a company such as **Samsung** use the cash conversion cycle as a useful measure of performance? Explain. **Samsung**

---

connect

QUICK STUDY

QS 22-1

Allocation and measurement terms

C1

In each blank next to the following terms, place the identifying letter of its best description.

_____ **1.** Cost center

_____ **2.** Profit center

_____ **3.** Responsibility accounting system

_____ **4.** Service department

_____ **5.** Indirect expenses

_____ **6.** Controllable costs

A. Incurs costs without directly yielding revenues.

B. Provides information used to evaluate the performance of a department.

C. Does not directly manufacture products but contributes to profitability of the entire company.

D. Costs incurred for the joint benefit of more than one department.

E. Costs that a manager has the ability to affect.

F. Incurs costs and also generates revenues.

QS 22-2

Basis for cost allocation

C1

In each blank next to the following types of indirect expenses and service department expenses, place the identifying letter of the best allocation basis to use to distribute it to the departments indicated.

_____ **1.** Computer service expenses of production scheduling for operating departments.

_____ **2.** General office department expenses of the operating departments.

_____ **3.** Maintenance department expenses of the operating departments.

_____ **4.** Electric utility expenses of all departments.

A. Relative number of employees.

B. Proportion of total time in each department for maintenance.

C. Proportion of floor space occupied by each department.

D. Proportion of total processing time for each operating department.

QS 22-3

Responsibility accounting report

P1

Jose Ruiz manages a car dealer's service department. His department is organized as a cost center. Costs for a recent quarter are shown below. List the costs that would appear on a responsibility accounting report for the service department.

Cost of parts	$22,400	Shop supplies	$1,200
Mechanics' wages	14,300	Utilities (allocated)	800
Manager's salary.	8,000	Administrative costs (allocated).	2,200
Building depreciation (allocated).	4,500		

QS 22-4

Allocating costs to departments

P2

Macee Department Store has three departments, and it conducts advertising campaigns that benefit all departments. Advertising costs are $100,000 this year, and departmental sales for this year follow. How much advertising cost is allocated to each department if the allocation is based on departmental sales?

Department	Sales
1	$220,000
2	400,000
3	180,000

QS 22-5

Allocating costs to departments   **P2**

Mervon Company has two operating departments: Mixing and Bottling. Mixing has 300 employees and Bottling has 200 employees. Indirect factory costs include administrative costs of $160,000. Administrative costs are allocated to operating departments based on the number of workers. Determine the administrative costs allocated to each operating department.

Mervon Company has two operating departments: Mixing and Bottling. Mixing occupies 22,000 square feet. Bottling occupies 18,000 square feet. Indirect factory costs include maintenance costs of $200,000. If maintenance costs are allocated to operating departments based on square footage occupied, determine the amount of maintenance costs allocated to each operating department.

QS 22-6
Allocating costs to
departments   **P2**

A retailer pays $130,000 rent each year for its two-story building. The space in this building is occupied by five departments as specified here.

QS 22-7
Rent expense allocated
to departments

P2

Department	Square feet occupied
Jewelry	1,440 (first-floor)
Cosmetics	3,360 (first-floor)
Housewares	2,016 (second-floor)
Tools	960 (second-floor)
Shoes	1,824 (second-floor)

The company allocates 65% of total rent expense to the first floor and 35% to the second floor, and then allocates rent expense for each floor to the departments occupying that floor on the basis of space occupied. Determine the rent expense to be allocated to each department.

Check   Allocated to Jewe ry
dept., $25,350

Use the information in the following table to compute each department's contribution to overhead (both in dollars and as a percent). Which department contributes the largest dollar amount to total overhead? Which contributes the highest percent (as a percent of sales)? Round percents to one decimal.

QS 22-8
Departmental contribution
to overhead

P3

	Dept. A	Dept. B	Dept. C
Sales	$53,000	$180,000	$84,000
Cost of goods sold	34,185	103,700	49,560
Gross profit	18,815	76,300	34,440
Total direct expenses	3,660	37,060	7,386
Contribution to overhead	$	$	$
Contribution percent (of sales)	%	%	%

Compute return on investment for each of the divisions below (each is an investment center). Which division performed the best, based on return on investment?

QS 22-9
Computing return
on investment

A1

Investment Center	Net Income	Average Assets	Return on Investment
Cameras and camcorders	$4,500,000	$20,000,000	%
Phones and communications	1,500,000	12,500,000	
Computers and accessories	800,000	10,000,000	

Refer to the information in QS 22-9. Assume a target income of 12% of average invested assets. Compute residual income for each division.

QS 22-10
Computing residual
income   **A1**

Fill in the blanks in the schedule below for two separate investment centers A and B. Round answers to the nearest whole percent.

QS 22-11
Performance measures

A1   **A2**

Investment Center	A	B
Sales	$	$10,400,000
Income	$ 352,000	$
Average invested assets	$1,400,000	$
Profit margin	8.0%	%
Investment turnover		1.5
Return on investment	%	12.0%

QS 22-12

Computing profit margin and investment turnover **A2**

A company's shipping division (an investment center) has sales of $2,420,000, net income of $516,000, and average invested assets of $2,250,000. Compute the division's profit margin and investment turnover.

QS 22-13

Performance measures—balanced scorecard

A3

Classify each of the performance measures below into the most likely balanced scorecard perspective it relates to. Label your answers using *C* (customer), *P* (internal process), *I* (innovation and growth), or *F* (financial).

_____ **1.** Customer wait time

_____ **2.** Number of days of employee absences

_____ **3.** Profit margin

_____ **4.** Number of new products introduced

_____ **5.** Employee sustainability training sessions attended

_____ **6.** Length of time raw materials are in inventory

_____ **7.** Customer satisfaction index

_____ **8.** Gallons of water reused

QS 22-14

Performance measures—balanced scorecard

A3

Walt Disney reports the following information for its two Parks and Resorts divisions.

	U.S.		International	
	Current Year	Prior Year	Current Year	Prior Year
Hotel occupancy rates	87%	83%	79%	78%

Assume Walt Disney uses a balanced scorecard and sets a target of 85% occupancy in its resorts.
(1) Which division(s) exceeded the occupancy target during the current year?
(2) Which division(s) improved its occupancy performance during the current year?

QS 22-15

Cash conversion cycle and efficiency

A4

(1) Use the information below to compute the number of days in the cash conversion cycle for each company. (2) Which company is more effective at managing cash?

	Spartan Co.	Chen Co.
Days' sales in accounts receivable	32	45
Days' sales in inventory	20	24
Days' payable outstanding	27	32

QS 22-16^B

Determining transfer prices without excess capacity

C2

The Windshield division of Fast Car Co. makes windshields for use in Fast Car's Assembly division. The Windshield division incurs variable costs of $200 per windshield and has capacity to make 500,000 windshields per year. The market price is $450 per windshield. The Windshield division incurs total fixed costs of $3,000,000 per year. If the Windshield division is operating at full capacity, what transfer price should be used on transfers between the Windshield and Assembly divisions?

QS 22-17^B

Determining transfer prices with excess capacity

C2

The Windshield division of Fast Car Co. makes windshields for use in Fast Car's Assembly division. The Windshield division incurs variable costs of $200 per windshield and has capacity to make 500,000 windshields per year. The market price is $450 per windshield. The Windshield division incurs total fixed costs of $3,000,000 per year. If the Windshield division has excess capacity, what is the range of possible transfer prices that could be used on transfers between the Windshield and Assembly divisions?

QS 22-18^C

Joint cost allocation

C3

A company purchases a 10,020-square-foot commercial building for $325,000 and spends an additional $50,000 to divide the space into two separate rental units and prepare it for rent. Unit A, which has the desirable location on the corner and contains 3,340 square feet, will be rented for $1.00 per square foot. Unit B contains 6,680 square feet and will be rented for $0.75 per square foot. How much of the joint cost should be assigned to Unit B using the value basis of allocation?

For a recent year **L'Oréal** reported operating profit of €3,385 (in millions) for its cosmetics division. Total assets were €12,888 (in millions) at the beginning of the year and €13,099 (in millions) at the end of the year. Compute return on investment for the year. State your answer as a percent, rounded to two decimals.

QS 22-19
Return on investment

A1

connect

Arctica manufactures snowmobiles and ATVs. These products are made in different departments, and each department has its own manager. Each responsibility performance report only includes those costs that the particular department manager can control: raw materials, wages, supplies used, and equipment depreciation. Using the data below, prepare a responsibility accounting report for the Snowmobile department.

EXERCISES

Exercise 22-1
Responsibility accounting report—cost center

P1

	Budget			Actual		
	Snowmobile	ATV	Combined	Snowmobile	ATV	Combined
Raw materials	$19,500	$27,500	$ 47,000	$ 19,420	$28,820	$ 48,240
Employee wages	10,400	20,500	30,900	10,660	21,240	31,900
Dept. manager salary	4,300	5,200	9,500	4,400	4,400	8,800
Supplies used	3,300	900	4,200	3,170	920	4,090
Depreciation—Equip.	6,000	12,500	18,500	6,000	12,500	18,500
Utilities	360	540	900	330	500	830
Rent	5,700	6,300	12,000	5,300	6,300	11,600
Totals	**$49,560**	**$73,440**	**$123,000**	**$49,280**	**$74,680**	**$123,960**

Refer to the information in Exercise 22-1 and prepare a responsibility accounting report for the ATV department.

Exercise 22-2
Responsibility accounting report—cost center   **P1**

The following is a partially completed lower section of a departmental expense allocation spreadsheet for Cozy Bookstore. It reports the total amounts of direct and indirect expenses allocated to its five departments. Complete the spreadsheet by allocating the expenses of the two service departments (advertising and purchasing) to the three operating departments.

Exercise 22-3
Service department expenses allocated to operating departments   **P2**

			Allocation of Expenses to Departments				
Allocation Base	Expense Account Bal.	Advertising Dept.	Purchasing Dept.	Books Dept.	Magazines Dept.	Newspapers Dept.
Total department expenses..........	$698,000	$24,000	$34,000	$425,000	$90,000	$125,000
Service department expenses						
Advertising department............. Sales		?		?	?	?
Purchasing department.............Purch. orders			?	?	?	?
Total expenses allocated to operating departments...............	?	$ 0	$ 0	?	?	?

Advertising and purchasing department expenses are allocated to operating departments on the basis of dollar sales and purchase orders, respectively. Information about the allocation bases for the three operating departments follows.

Department	Sales	Purchase Orders
Books	$495,000	516
Magazines.....................	198,000	360
Newspapers	207,000	324
Total.........................	$900,000	1,200

Check   Total expenses allocated to Books dept., $452,820

Exercise 22-4

Indirect payroll expense allocated to departments

P2

Jessica Porter works in both the Jewelry department and the Cosmetics department of a retail store. She assists customers in both departments and arranges and stocks merchandise in both departments. The store allocates her $30,000 annual wages between the two departments based on the time worked in the two departments in each two-week pay period. On average, Jessica reports the following hours and activities spent in the two departments. Allocate Jessica's annual wages between the two departments.

Activities	Hours
Selling in Jewelry department	51
Arranging and stocking merchandise in Jewelry department	6
Selling in Cosmetics department	12
Arranging and stocking merchandise in Cosmetics department	7
Idle time spent waiting for a customer to enter one of the departments	4

Check Assign $7,500 to Cosmetics

Exercise 22-5

Departmental expense allocations

P2

Woh Che Co. has four departments: Materials, Personnel, Manufacturing, and Packaging. In a recent month, the four departments incurred three shared indirect expenses. The amounts of these indirect expenses and the bases used to allocate them follow.

Indirect Expense	Cost	Allocation Base
Supervision	$ 82,500	Number of employees
Utilities	50,000	Square feet occupied
Insurance	22,500	Value of assets in use
Total	$155,000	

Departmental data for the company's recent reporting period follow.

Department	Employees	Square Feet	Asset Values
Materials	27	25,000	$ 6,000
Personnel	9	5,000	1,200
Manufacturing	63	55,000	37,800
Packaging	51	15,000	15,000
Total	150	100,000	$60,000

Check (2) Total of $29,600 assigned to Materials dept.

1. Use this information to allocate each of the three indirect expenses across the four departments.
2. Prepare a summary table that reports the indirect expenses assigned to each of the four departments.

Exercise 22-6

Departmental expense allocation spreadsheet

P2

Marathon Running Shop has two service departments (advertising and administrative) and two operating departments (Shoes and Clothing). The table that follows shows the direct expenses incurred and square footage occupied by all four departments, as well as total sales for the two operating departments for the year 2019.

Department	Direct Expenses	Square Feet	Sales
Advertising	$ 18,000	1,120	—
Administrative	25,000	1,400	—
Shoes	103,000	7,140	$273,000
Clothing	15,000	4,340	77,000

Check Total expenses allocated to Shoes dept., $177,472

The advertising department developed and distributed 120 advertisements during the year. Of these, 90 promoted shoes and 30 promoted clothing. Utilities expense of $64,000 is an indirect expense to all departments. Prepare a departmental expense allocation spreadsheet for Marathon Running Shop. The spreadsheet should assign (1) direct expenses to each of the four departments, (2) the $64,000 of utilities expense to the four departments on the basis of floor space occupied, (3) the advertising department's expenses to the two operating departments on the basis of the number of ads placed that promoted a department's products, and (4) the administrative department's expenses to the two operating departments based on the amount of sales. Provide supporting computations for the expense allocations.

Below are departmental income statements for a guitar manufacturer. The manufacturer is considering eliminating its Electric Guitar department since it has a net loss. The company classifies advertising, rent, and utilities expenses as indirect.

Exercise 22-7
Departmental contribution report
P3

Departmental Income Statements		
For Year Ended December 31, 2019	Acoustic	Electric
Sales.....................................	$112,500	$105,500
Cost of goods sold........................	55,675	66,750
Gross profit..............................	56,825	38,750
Operating expenses		
Advertising expense	8,075	6,250
Depreciation expense—Equipment	10,150	9,000
Salaries expense.........................	17,300	13,500
Supplies expense	2,030	1,700
Rent expense............................	6,105	5,950
Utilities expense	3,045	2,550
Total operating expenses	46,705	38,950
Net income (loss).......................	$ 10,120	$ (200)

1. Prepare a departmental contribution report that shows each department's contribution to overhead.
2. Based on contribution to overhead, should the Electric Guitar department be eliminated?

Jansen Company reports the following for its Ski department for the year 2019. All of its costs are direct, except as noted.

Exercise 22-8
Departmental income statement and contribution to overhead
P3

Sales	$605,000	Utilities	$14,000 ($3,000 is indirect)
Cost of goods sold	425,000	Depreciation	42,000 ($10,000 is indirect)
Salaries	112,000 ($15,000 is indirect)	Office expenses	20,000 (all indirect)

Prepare a (1) departmental income statement for 2019 and (2) departmental contribution to overhead report for 2019. (3) Based on these two performance reports, should Jansen eliminate the Ski department?

You must prepare a return on investment analysis for the regional manager of Fast & Great Burgers. This growing chain is trying to decide which outlet of two alternatives to open. The first location (A) requires a $1,000,000 investment and is expected to yield annual net income of $160,000. The second location (B) requires a $600,000 investment and is expected to yield annual net income of $108,000. Compute the return on investment for each Fast & Great Burgers alternative. Using return on investment as your only criterion, which location (A or B) should the company open? (The chain currently generates an 18% return on total assets.)

Exercise 22-9
Investment center analysis
A1

Megamart, a retailer of consumer goods, provides the following information on two of its departments (each considered an investment center).

Exercise 22-10
Computing return on investment and residual income; investing decision
A1

Investment Center	Sales	Income	Average Invested Assets
Electronics....................	$40,000,000	$2,880,000	$16,000,000
Sporting Goods...............	20,000,000	2,040,000	12,000,000

1. Compute return on investment for each department. Using return on investment, which department is most efficient at using assets to generate returns for the company?
2. Assume a target income level of 12% of average invested assets. Compute residual income for each department. Which department generated the most residual income for the company?
3. Assume the Electronics department is presented with a new investment opportunity that will yield a 15% return on investment. Should the new investment opportunity be accepted?

Exercise 22-11
Computing margin and
turnover; department
efficiency   A2

Refer to information in Exercise 22-10. Compute profit margin and investment turnover for each department. (1) Which department generates the most net income per dollar of sales? (2) Which department is most efficient at generating sales from average invested assets?

Exercise 22-12
Return on investment

A1   A2

A food manufacturer reports the following for two of its divisions for a recent year.

$ millions	Beverage Division	Cheese Division
Invested assets, beginning	$2,662	$4,455
Invested assets, ending	2,593	4,400
Sales	2,681	3,925
Operating income.................	349	634

For each division, compute (1) return on investment, (2) profit margin, and (3) investment turnover for the year. Round answers to two decimals.

Exercise 22-13
Residual income   A1

Refer to the information in Exercise 22-12. Assume that each of the company's divisions has a required rate of return of 7%. Compute residual income for each division.

Exercise 22-14
Profit margin

A2

Apple Inc. reports the following for three of its geographic segments for a recent year.

$ millions	Americas	Europe	China
Operating income...................	$30,684	$16,514	$17,032
Sales	96,600	54,938	44,764

Compute profit margin for each division. Express answers as percentages, rounded to one decimal.

Exercise 22-15
Return on investment

A1   A2

ZNet Co. is a web-based retail company. The company reports the following for the past year.

Sales	$5,000,000	Operating income	$1,000,000	Average invested assets ...	$12,500,000

The company's CEO believes that sales for next year will increase by 20% and both profit margin (%) and the level of average invested assets will be the same as for the past year.

1. Compute return on investment for the past year.
2. Compute profit margin for the past year.
3. If the CEO's forecast is correct, what will return on investment equal for next year?
4. If the CEO's forecast is correct, what will investment turnover equal for next year?

Exercise 22-16
Performance measures—
balanced scorecard

A3

USA Airlines uses the following performance measures. Classify each of the performance measures below into the most likely balanced scorecard perspective it relates to. Label your answers using C (customer), P (internal process), I (innovation and growth), or F (financial).

_____ **1.** Cash flow from operations
_____ **2.** Number of reports of mishandled or lost baggage
_____ **3.** Percentage of on-time departures
_____ **4.** On-time flight percentage
_____ **5.** Percentage of ground crew trained
_____ **6.** Return on investment
_____ **7.** Market value

_____ **8.** Accidents or safety incidents per mile flown
_____ **9.** Customer complaints
_____ **10.** Flight attendant training sessions attended
_____ **11.** Time airplane is on ground between flights
_____ **12.** Airplane miles per gallon of fuel
_____ **13.** Revenue per seat
_____ **14.** Cost of leasing airplanes

Midwest Mfg. uses a balanced scorecard as part of its performance evaluation. The company wants to include information on its sustainability efforts in its balanced scorecard. For each of the sustainability items below, indicate the most likely balanced scorecard perspective it relates to. Label your answers using *C* (customer), *P* (internal process), *I* (innovation and learning), or *F* (financial).

_____ **1.** CO_2 emissions
_____ **2.** Number of solar panels installed
_____ **3.** Gallons of water used
_____ **4.** Customer surveys of company's sustainability reputation
_____ **5.** Pounds of recyclable packaging used

_____ **6.** Pounds of trash diverted from landfill
_____ **7.** Dollar sales of green products
_____ **8.** Number of sustainability training workshops held
_____ **9.** Cubic feet of natural gas used
_____ **10.** Patents for green products applied for

Exercise 22-17
Sustainability and the balanced scorecard
A3

---

(1) Use the information below to compute the number of days in the cash conversion cycle for each year. Round calculations to the nearest whole day. (2) Did the company manage cash more effectively in the current year?

	Current Year	Prior Year
Accounts payable, end of year.	$ 4,603	$ 8,548
Accounts receivable, net, end of year.	18,685	15,726
Inventory, end of year.	6,904	6,055
Net sales	220,000	205,000
Cost of goods sold	140,000	130,000

Exercise 22-18
Cash conversion cycle
A4

Use the information below to compute the number of days in the cash conversion cycle for **Apple** ($ millions). Round calculations to the nearest whole day.

Accounts payable, end of year.	$49,049	Inventory, end of year	$ 4,855
Accounts receivable, net, end of year.	17,874	Net sales	229,234
		Cost of goods sold	141,048

Exercise 22-19
Cash conversion cycle
A4

The Trailer division of Baxter Bicycles makes bike trailers that attach to bicycles and can carry children or cargo. The trailers have a retail price of $200 each. Each trailer incurs $80 of variable manufacturing costs. The Trailer division has capacity for 40,000 trailers per year and incurs fixed costs of $1,000,000 per year.

1. Assume the Assembly division of Baxter Bicycles wants to buy 15,000 trailers per year from the Trailer division. If the Trailer division can sell all of the trailers it manufactures to outside customers, what price should be used on transfers between Baxter Bicycles's divisions? Explain.

2. Assume the Trailer division currently only sells 20,000 Trailers to outside customers, and the Assembly division wants to buy 15,000 trailers per year from the Trailer division. What is the range of acceptable prices that could be used on transfers between Baxter Bicycles's divisions? Explain.

Exercise 22-20ᴮ
Determining transfer prices
C2

Heart & Home Properties is developing a subdivision that includes 600 home lots. The 450 lots in the Canyon section are below a ridge and do not have views of the neighboring canyons and hills; the 150 lots in the Hilltop section offer unobstructed views. The expected selling price for each Canyon lot is $55,000 and for each Hilltop lot is $110,000. The developer acquired the land for $4,000,000 and spent another $3,500,000 on street and utilities improvements. Assign the joint land and improvement costs to the lots using the value basis of allocation and determine the average cost per lot.

Exercise 22-21ᶜ
Assigning joint real estate costs   C3

Check   Total Hilltop cost, $3,000,000

Pirate Seafood Company purchases lobsters and processes them into tails and flakes. It sells the lobster tails for $21 per pound and the flakes for $14 per pound. On average, 100 pounds of lobster are processed into 52 pounds of tails and 22 pounds of flakes, with 26 pounds of waste. Assume that the company purchased 2,400 pounds of lobster for $4.50 per pound and processed the lobsters with an additional labor cost of $1,800. No materials or labor costs are assigned to the waste. If 1,096 pounds of tails and 324 pounds of flakes are sold, what is (1) the allocated cost of the sold items and (2) the allocated cost of the ending inventory? The company allocates joint costs on a value basis.

Exercise 22-22ᶜ
Assigning joint product costs   C3

Check   (2) Inventory cost, $2,268

Exercise 22-23
Profit margin and
investment turnover

A2

L'Oréal reports the following for a recent year for the major divisions in its cosmetics branch.

€ millions	Sales	Income	Total Assets End of Year	Total Assets Beginning of Year
Professional products............	€ 2,717	€ 552	€ 2,624	€ 2,516
Consumer products	9,530	1,765	5,994	5,496
Luxury products	4,507	791	3,651	4,059
Active cosmetics................	1,386	278	830	817
Total.........................	€18,140	€3,386	€13,099	€12,888

1. Compute profit margin for each division. State your answers as percents, rounded to two decimal places. Which L'Oréal division has the highest profit margin?

2. Compute investment turnover for each division. Round your answers to two decimal places. Which L'Oréal division has the best investment turnover?

connect

PROBLEM SET A

Problem 22-1A
Responsibility accounting
performance reports;
controllable and budgeted
costs

P1

Billie Whitehorse, the plant manager of Travel Free's Indiana plant, is responsible for all of that plant's costs other than her own salary. The plant has two operating departments and one service department. The Camper and Trailer operating departments manufacture different products and have their own managers. The office department, which Whitehorse also manages, provides services equally to the two operating departments. A budget is prepared for each operating department and the office department.

The company's responsibility accounting system must assemble information to present budgeted and actual costs in performance reports for each operating department manager and the plant manager. Each performance report includes only those costs that a particular operating department manager can control: raw materials, wages, supplies used, and equipment depreciation. The plant manager is responsible for the department managers' salaries, utilities, building rent, office salaries other than her own, and other office costs plus all costs controlled by the two operating department managers. The annual departmental budgets and actual costs for the two operating departments follow.

	Budget			Actual		
	Campers	Trailers	Combined	Campers	Trailers	Combined
Raw materials	$195,000	$275,000	$ 470,000	$194,200	$273,200	$ 467,400
Employee wages	104,000	205,000	309,000	106,600	206,400	313,000
Dept. manager salary...........	43,000	52,000	95,000	44,000	53,500	97,500
Supplies used	33,000	90,000	123,000	31,700	91,600	123,300
Depreciation—Equip.	60,000	125,000	185,000	60,000	125,000	185,000
Utilities	3,600	5,400	9,000	3,300	5,000	8,300
Building rent	5,700	9,300	15,000	5,300	8,700	14,000
Office department costs........	68,750	68,750	137,500	67,550	67,550	135,100
Totals......................	$513,050	$830,450	$1,343,500	$512,650	$830,950	$1,343,600

The office department's annual budget and its actual costs follow.

	Budget	Actual
Plant manager salary	$ 80,000	$ 82,000
Other office salaries............	32,500	30,100
Other office costs	25,000	23,000
Totals.......................	$137,500	$135,100

Required

1. Prepare responsibility accounting performance reports like those in Exhibit 22.2 that list costs controlled by the following.

   a. Manager of the Camper department.   **c.** Manager of the Indiana plant.

   b. Manager of the Trailer department.

In each report, include the budgeted and actual costs and show the amount that each actual cost is over or under the budgeted amount.

Analysis Component

2. Did the plant manager or the operating department managers better manage costs?

National Bank has several departments that occupy both floors of a two-story building. The departmental accounting system has a single account, Building Occupancy Cost, in its ledger. The types and amounts of occupancy costs recorded in this account for the current period follow.

Depreciation—Building..................	$18,000
Interest—Building mortgage	27,000
Taxes—Building and land..............	9,000
Gas (heating) expense	3,000
Lighting expense	3,000
Maintenance expense	6,000
Total occupancy cost	$66,000

The building has 4,000 square feet on each floor. In prior periods, the accounting manager merely divided the $66,000 occupancy cost by 8,000 square feet to find an average cost of $8.25 per square foot and then charged each department a building occupancy cost equal to this rate times the number of square feet that it occupied.

Diane Linder manages a first-floor department that occupies 1,000 square feet, and Juan Chiro manages a second-floor department that occupies 1,800 square feet of floor space. In discussing the departmental reports, the second-floor manager questions whether using the same rate per square foot for all departments makes sense because the first-floor space is more valuable. This manager also references a recent real estate study of average local rental costs for similar space that shows first-floor space worth $30 per square foot and second-floor space worth $20 per square foot (excluding costs for heating, lighting, and maintenance).

Required

1. Allocate occupancy costs to the Linder and Chiro departments using the current allocation method.
2. Allocate the depreciation, interest, and taxes occupancy costs to the Linder and Chiro departments in proportion to the relative market values of the floor space. Allocate the heating, lighting, and maintenance costs to the Linder and Chiro departments in proportion to the square feet occupied (ignoring floor space market values).
3. Which allocation method (1 or 2) produces the lowest allocated occupancy cost for a manager of a second-floor department?

Problem 22-2A
Allocation of building occupancy costs to departments

P2

Check (1) Total allocated to Linder and Chiro, $23,100
(2) Total occupancy cost to Linder, $9,600

Williams Company began operations in January 2019 with two operating (selling) departments and one service (office) department. Its departmental income statements follow.

Problem 22-3A
Departmental income statements; forecasts

P3

Departmental Income Statements			
For Year Ended December 31, 2019	Clock	Mirror	Combined
Sales	$130,000	$55,000	$185,000
Cost of goods sold	63,700	34,100	97,800
Gross profit................................	66,300	20,900	87,200
Direct expenses			
Sales salaries	20,000	7,000	27,000
Advertising	1,200	500	1,700
Store supplies used	900	400	1,300
Depreciation—Equipment	1,500	300	1,800
Total direct expenses.....................	23,600	8,200	31,800
Allocated expenses			
Rent expense	7,020	3,780	10,800
Utilities expense.........................	2,600	1,400	4,000
Share of office department expenses............	10,500	4,500	15,000
Total allocated expenses....................	20,120	9,680	29,800
Total expenses	43,720	17,880	61,600
Net income	$ 22,580	$ 3,020	$ 25,600

Williams plans to open a third department in January 2020 that will sell paintings. Management predicts that the new department will generate $50,000 in sales with a 55% gross profit margin and will require the following direct expenses: sales salaries, $8,000; advertising, $800; store supplies, $500; and equipment depreciation, $200. It will fit the new department into the current rented space by taking some square footage from the other two departments. When opened, the new Painting department will fill one-fifth of the space presently used by the Clock department and one-fourth used by the Mirror department.

Management does not predict any increase in utilities costs, which are allocated to the departments in proportion to occupied space (or rent expense). The company allocates office department expenses to the operating departments in proportion to their sales. It expects the Painting department to increase total office department expenses by $7,000. Since the Painting department will bring new customers into the store, management expects sales in both the Clock and Mirror departments to increase by 8%. No changes for those departments' gross profit percents or their direct expenses are expected except for store supplies used, which will increase in proportion to sales.

Required

Prepare departmental income statements that show the company's predicted results of operations for calendar-year 2020 for the three operating (selling) departments and their combined totals. (Round percents to the nearest one-tenth and dollar amounts to the nearest whole dollar.)

Problem 22-4A
Departmental contribution to income

P3

Vortex Company operates a retail store with two departments. Information about those departments follows.

	Department A	Department B
Sales	$800,000	$450,000
Cost of goods sold	497,000	291,000
Direct expenses: Salaries..........	125,000	88,000
Insurance	20,000	10,000
Utilities	24,000	14,000
Depreciation.......	21,000	12,000
Maintenance.......	7,000	5,000

The company also incurred the following indirect costs.

Salaries	$36,000	Depreciation	$15,000
Insurance	6,000	Office expenses	50,000

Indirect costs are allocated as follows: salaries on the basis of sales; insurance and depreciation on the basis of square footage; and office expenses on the basis of number of employees. Additional information about the departments follows.

Department	Square Footage	Number of Employees
A	28,000	75
B	12,000	50

Required

1. For each department, determine the departmental contribution to overhead and the departmental net income.

2. Should Department B be eliminated?

Problem 22-5A^C
Allocation of joint costs

C3

Georgia Orchards produced a good crop of peaches this year. After preparing the following income statement, the company is concerned about the net loss on its No. 3 peaches.

Income Statement				
For Year Ended December 31, 2019	**No. 1**	**No. 2**	**No. 3**	**Combined**
Sales (by grade)				
No. 1: 300,000 lbs. @ $1.50/lb	$450,000			
No. 2: 300,000 lbs. @ $1.00/lb		$300,000		
No. 3: 750,000 lbs. @ $0.25/lb			$ 187,500	
Total sales				$937,500
Costs				
Tree pruning and care @ $0.30/lb	90,000	90,000	225,000	405,000
Picking, sorting, and grading @ $0.15/lb	45,000	45,000	112,500	202,500
Delivery costs	15,000	15,000	37,500	67,500
Total costs	150,000	150,000	375,000	675,000
Net income (loss)	$300,000	$150,000	$(187,500)	$262,500

In preparing this statement, the company allocated joint costs among the grades on a physical basis as an equal amount per pound. The company's delivery cost records show that $30,000 of the $67,500 relates to crating the No. 1 and No. 2 peaches and hauling them to the buyer. The remaining $37,500 of delivery costs is for crating the No. 3 peaches and hauling them to the cannery.

Required

1. Prepare reports showing cost allocations on a sales value basis to the three grades of peaches. Separate the delivery costs into the amounts directly identifiable with each grade. Then allocate any shared delivery costs on the basis of the relative sales value of each grade. (Round percents to the nearest one-tenth and dollar amounts to the nearest whole dollar.)

2. Using answers to part 1, prepare an income statement using the joint costs allocated on a sales value basis.

Analysis Component

3. Do delivery costs fit the definition of a joint cost?

Check (1) $129,600 tree pruning and care costs allocated to No. 2

(2) Net income from No. 1 & No. 2 peaches, $140,400 & $93,600

Britney Brown, the plant manager of LMN Co.'s Chicago plant, is responsible for all of that plant's costs other than her own salary. The plant has two operating departments and one service department. The Refrigerator and Dishwasher operating departments manufacture different products and have their own managers. The office department, which Brown also manages, provides services equally to the two operating departments. A monthly budget is prepared for each operating department and the office department.

The company's responsibility accounting system must assemble information to present budgeted and actual costs in performance reports for each operating department manager and the plant manager. Each performance report includes only those costs that a particular operating department manager can control: raw materials, wages, supplies used, and equipment depreciation. The plant manager is responsible for the department managers' salaries, utilities, building rent, office salaries other than her own, and other office costs plus all costs controlled by the two operating department managers. The April departmental budgets and actual costs for the two operating departments follow.

PROBLEM SET B

Problem 22-1B
Responsibility accounting performance reports; controllable and budgeted costs

P1

	Budget			Actual		
	Refrigerators	**Dishwashers**	**Combined**	**Refrigerators**	**Dishwashers**	**Combined**
Raw materials	$400,000	$200,000	$ 600,000	$385,000	$202,000	$ 587,000
Employee wages	170,000	80,000	250,000	174,700	81,500	256,200
Dept. manager salary	55,000	49,000	104,000	55,000	46,500	101,500
Supplies used	15,000	9,000	24,000	14,000	9,700	23,700
Depreciation—Equip.	53,000	37,000	90,000	53,000	37,000	90,000
Utilities	30,000	18,000	48,000	34,500	20,700	55,200
Building rent	63,000	17,000	80,000	65,800	16,500	82,300
Office department costs . . .	70,500	70,500	141,000	75,000	75,000	150,000
Totals	$856,500	$480,500	$1,337,000	$857,000	$488,900	$1,345,900

The office department's budget and its actual costs for April follow.

	Budget	Actual
Plant manager salary	$ 80,000	$ 85,000
Other office salaries	40,000	35,200
Other office costs	21,000	29,800
Totals	$141,000	$150,000

Required

1. Prepare responsibility accounting performance reports like those in Exhibit 22.2 that list costs controlled by the following.

   a. Manager of the Refrigerator department.

   b. Manager of the Dishwasher department.

   c. Manager of the Chicago plant.

   In each report, include the budgeted and actual costs for the month and show the amount by which each actual cost is over or under the budgeted amount.

Analysis Component

2. Did the plant manager or the operating department managers better manage costs?

Check   (1a) $11,300 total under budget

(1c) Chicago plant controllable costs, $3,900 total over budget

---

Problem 22-2B
Allocation of building occupancy costs to departments

P2

Harmon's has several departments that occupy all floors of a two-story building that includes a basement floor. Harmon rented this building under a long-term lease negotiated when rental rates were low. The departmental accounting system has a single account, Building Occupancy Cost, in its ledger. The types and amounts of occupancy costs recorded in this account for the current period follow.

Building rent	$400,000
Lighting expense	25,000
Cleaning expense	40,000
Total occupancy cost	$465,000

The building has 7,500 square feet on each of the upper two floors but only 5,000 square feet in the basement. In prior periods, the accounting manager merely divided the $465,000 occupancy cost by 20,000 square feet to find an average cost of $23.25 per square foot and then charged each department a building occupancy cost equal to this rate times the number of square feet that it occupies.

Jordan Style manages a department that occupies 2,000 square feet of basement floor space. In discussing the departmental reports with other managers, she questions whether using the same rate per square foot for all departments makes sense because different floor space has different values. Style checked a recent real estate report of average local rental costs for similar space that shows first-floor space worth $40 per square foot, second-floor space worth $20 per square foot, and basement space worth $10 per square foot (excluding costs for lighting and cleaning).

Required

Check   (1) Total costs allocated to Style's dept., $46,500

(2) Total occupancy cost to Style, $22,500

1. Allocate occupancy costs to Style's department using the current allocation method.

2. Allocate the building rent cost to Style's department in proportion to the relative market value of the floor space. Allocate to Style's department the lighting and cleaning costs in proportion to the square feet occupied (ignoring floor space market values). Then, compute the total occupancy cost allocated to Style's department.

3. Which allocation method (1 or 2) produces the lowest allocated occupancy cost for a manager of a basement department?

Bonanza Entertainment began operations in January 2019 with two operating (selling) departments and one service (office) department. Its departmental income statements follow.

Problem 22-3B
Departmental income
statements; forecasts

P3

Departmental Income Statements			
For Year Ended December 31, 2019	Movies	Video Games	Combined
Sales	$600,000	$200,000	$800,000
Cost of goods sold	420,000	154,000	574,000
Gross profit.....	180,000	46,000	226,000
Direct expenses			
Sales salaries	37,000	15,000	52,000
Advertising	12,500	6,000	18,500
Store supplies used	4,000	1,000	5,000
Depreciation—Equipment	4,500	3,000	7,500
Total direct expenses.....	58,000	25,000	83,000
Allocated expenses			
Rent expense	41,000	9,000	50,000
Utilities expense.....	7,380	1,620	9,000
Share of office department expenses.....	56,250	18,750	75,000
Total allocated expenses.....	104,630	29,370	134,000
Total expenses	162,630	54,370	217,000
Net income (loss)	$ 17,370	$ (8,370)	$ 9,000

The company plans to open a third department in January 2020 that will sell compact discs. Management predicts that the new department will generate $300,000 in sales with a 35% gross profit margin and will require the following direct expenses: sales salaries, $18,000; advertising, $10,000; store supplies, $2,000; and equipment depreciation, $1,200. The company will fit the new department into the current rented space by taking some square footage from the other two departments. When opened, the new Compact Disc department will fill one-fourth of the space presently used by the Movie department and one-third of the space used by the Video Game department.

Management does not predict any increase in utilities costs, which are allocated to the departments in proportion to occupied space (or rent expense). The company allocates office department expenses to the operating departments in proportion to their sales. It expects the Compact Disc department to increase total office department expenses by $10,000. Since the Compact Disc department will bring new customers into the store, management expects sales in both the Movie and Video Game departments to increase by 8%. No changes for those departments' gross profit percents or for their direct expenses are expected except for store supplies used, which will increase in proportion to sales.

Required

Prepare departmental income statements that show the company's predicted results of operations for cal-endar-year 2020 for the three operating (selling) departments and their combined totals. (Round percents to the nearest one-tenth and dollar amounts to the nearest whole dollar.)

Check   2020 forecasted
Movies net income (sales),
$52,450 ($648,000)

Sadar Company operates a store with two departments: Guitar and Piano. Information about those departments follows.

Problem 22-4B
Departmental contribution
to income

P3

	Guitar Department	Piano Department
Sales	$370,500	$279,500
Cost of goods sold	320,000	175,000
Direct expenses: Salaries.....	35,000	25,000
Maintenance...	12,000	10,000
Utilities	5,000	4,500
Insurance	4,200	3,700

The company also incurred the following indirect costs.

| Advertising | $15,000 | Salaries | $27,000 | Office expenses | $3,200 |

Indirect costs are allocated as follows: advertising on the basis of sales; salaries on the basis of number of employees; and office expenses on the basis of square footage. Additional information about the departments follows.

Department	Square Footage	Number of Employees
Guitar...	5,000	3
Piano...	3,000	2

Required

Check (1) Piano dept. net income, $42,850

1. For each department, determine the departmental contribution to overhead and the departmental net income.
2. Should the Guitar department be eliminated? Explain.

Problem 22-5B^C

Allocation of joint costs

C3

Rita and Rick Redding own and operate a tomato grove. After preparing the following income statement, Rita and Rick are concerned about the loss on the No. 3 tomatoes.

Income Statement				
For Year Ended December 31, 2019	**No. 1**	**No. 2**	**No. 3**	**Combined**
Sales (by grade)				
No. 1: 500,000 lbs. @ $1.80/lb...	$900,000			
No. 2: 400,000 lbs. @ $1.25/lb...		$500,000		
No. 3: 100,000 lbs. @ $0.40/lb...			$ 40,000	
Total sales...				$1,440,000
Costs				
Land preparation, seeding, and cultivating @ $0.70/lb...	350,000	280,000	70,000	700,000
Harvesting, sorting, and grading @ $0.04/lb...	20,000	16,000	4,000	40,000
Delivery costs...	10,000	7,000	3,000	20,000
Total costs...	380,000	303,000	77,000	760,000
Net income (loss)...	$520,000	$197,000	$(37,000)	$ 680,000

In preparing this statement, Rita and Rick allocated joint costs among the grades on a physical basis as an equal amount per pound. Also, their delivery cost records show that $17,000 of the $20,000 relates to crating the No. 1 and No. 2 tomatoes and hauling them to the buyer. The remaining $3,000 of delivery costs is for crating the No. 3 tomatoes and hauling them to the cannery.

Required

Check (1) $1,120 harvesting, sorting, and grading costs allocated to No. 3

1. Prepare reports showing cost allocations on a sales value basis to the three grades of tomatoes. Separate the delivery costs into the amounts directly identifiable with each grade. Then allocate any shared delivery costs on the basis of the relative sales value of each grade. (Round percents to the nearest one-tenth and dollar amounts to the nearest whole dollar.)

(2) Net income from No. 1 & No. 2 tomatoes, $426,569 & $237,151

2. Using answers to part 1, prepare an income statement using the joint costs allocated on a sales value basis.

Analysis Component

3. Do delivery costs fit the definition of a joint cost?

This serial problem began in Chapter 1 and continues through most of the book. If previous chapter segments were not completed, the serial problem can begin at this point.

SP 22 Santana Rey's two departments, Computer Consulting Services and Computer Workstation Furniture Manufacturing, have each been profitable for **Business Solutions**. Santana has heard of the cash conversion cycle and wants to use it as another performance measure for the workstation manufacturing department. Data below are for the most recent two quarters.

	1st Quarter	2nd Quarter
Days' sales in accounts receivable	19 days	21 days
Days' sales in inventory	25 days	24 days
Days' payable outstanding.	31 days	28 days

Required

1. Compute the cash conversion cycle for the first quarter.
2. Compute the cash conversion cycle for the second quarter.
3. Did the cash conversion cycle increase or decrease from the first to the second quarter?

©Alexander Image/Shutterstock

Accounting Analysis

AA 22-1 Review **Apple**'s financial statements in Appendix A and identify its (*a*) total assets as of September 30, 2017, and September 24, 2016, and (*b*) operating income for the year ended September 30, 2017.

Required

1. Assume Apple's target income is 12% of average assets. Compute Apple's residual income for fiscal 2017 using operating income.
2. Compute Apple's return on investment (in percent) for fiscal 2017 using operating income. Round to two decimals.

AA 22-2 **Apple** and **Google** compete in several product categories. Sales, income, and asset information are provided for fiscal year 2017 for each company below.

$ millions	Apple	Google
Sales	$229,234	$110,855
Net income	48,351	12,662
Invested assets, beginning of year	321,686	167,497
Invested assets, end of year	375,319	197,295

Required

1. Compute profit margin for each company.
2. Compute investment turnover for each company.
3. Refer to answers for parts 1 and 2. Which company performed better?

AA 22-3 Review **Samsung**'s financial statements in Appendix A and identify its (*a*) total assets as of December 31, 2017, and December 31, 2016, and (*b*) operating profit for the year ended December 31, 2017.

Required

1. Assume Samsung's target income is 12% of average assets. Compute Samsung's residual income for 2017 using operating profit (in millions of Korean won).

[continued on next page]

2. Compute Samsung's return on investment (in percent) for 2017 using operating profit. Round to two decimals.

3. Compute **Apple**'s return on investment (in percent) for fiscal 2017 using operating income (from Appendix A). Round to two decimals.

4. Using the answers for parts 2 and 3, which company (Samsung or Apple) had the higher return on investment?

Beyond the Numbers

ETHICS CHALLENGE

P3

BTN 22-1 Super Security Co. offers a range of security services for athletes and entertainers. Each type of service is considered within a separate department. Marc Pincus, the overall manager, is compensated partly on the basis of departmental performance by staying within the quarterly cost budget. He often revises operations to make sure departments stay within budget. Says Pincus, "I will not go over budget even if it means slightly compromising the level and quality of service. These are minor compromises that don't significantly affect my clients, at least in the short term."

Required

1. Is there an ethical concern in this situation? If so, which parties are affected? Explain.

2. Can Pincus take action to eliminate or reduce any ethical concerns? Explain.

3. What is Super Security's ethical responsibility in offering professional services?

COMMUNICATING IN PRACTICE

P2

BTN 22-2 Improvement Station is a national home improvement chain with more than 100 stores throughout the country. The manager of each store receives a salary plus a bonus equal to a percent of the store's net income for the reporting period. The following net income calculation is on the Denver store manager's performance report for the recent monthly period.

Sales	$2,500,000
Cost of goods sold	800,000
Wages expense	500,000
Utilities expense	200,000
Home office expense	75,000
Net income	$ 925,000
Manager's bonus (0.5%)	$ 4,625

In previous periods, the bonus had also been 0.5%, but the performance report had not included any charges for the home office expense, which is now assigned to each store as a percent of its sales.

Required

Assume that you are the national office manager. Write a half-page memorandum to your store managers explaining why home office expense is in the new performance report.

TAKING IT TO THE NET

P2

BTN 22-3 This chapter described and used spreadsheets to prepare various managerial reports (see Exhibit 22.10). You can download from websites various tutorials showing how spreadsheets are used in managerial accounting and other business applications.

Required

1. Link to the website **Lacher.com**. Select "Table of Contents" under "Microsoft Excel Examples." Identify and list three tutorials for review.

2. Describe in a half-page memorandum to your instructor how the applications described in each tutorial are helpful in business and managerial decision making.

BTN 22-4   **Apple** and **Samsung** compete across the world in several markets.

Required

1. Design a three-tier responsibility accounting organizational chart assuming that you have available internal information for both companies. Use Exhibit 22.1 as an example. The goal of this assignment is to design a reporting framework for the companies; numbers are not required. Limit your reporting framework to sales activity only.

2. Explain why it is important to have similar performance reports when comparing performance within a company (and across different companies). Be specific in your response.

TEAMWORK IN ACTION

P1

APPLE

Samsung

BTN 22-5   Randy and Galen Welsch's company **Jibu** provides African franchisees with training and resources to sell drinking water.

Required

1. How can Jibu use departmental (franchisee) income statements to assist in understanding and controlling operations?

2. Are departmental income statements always the best measure of a department's performance? Explain.

ENTREPRENEURIAL DECISION

P3

BTN 22-6   Visit a local movie theater and check out both its concession area and its viewing areas. The manager of a theater must confront questions such as

- How much return do we earn on concessions?
- What types of movies generate the greatest sales?
- What types of movies generate the greatest net income?

Required

Assume that you are the new accounting manager for a 16-screen movie theater. You are to set up a responsibility accounting reporting framework for the theater.

1. Recommend how to segment the different departments of a movie theater for responsibility reporting.

2. Propose an expense allocation system for heat, rent, insurance, and maintenance costs of the theater.

HITTING THE ROAD

C1   P1

23

Relevant Costing for Managerial Decisions

Chapter Preview

DECISIONS AND INFORMATION

Managerial decisions

C1 Relevant costs and benefits

NTK 23-1

PRODUCTION DECISIONS

P1 Make or buy

P2 Sell or process

P3 Sales mix

NTK 23-2, 23-3, 23-4

CAPACITY DECISIONS

P4 Segment elimination

P5 Keep or replace

NTK 23-5

PRICING DECISIONS

P6 Normal pricing

P7 Special offer

A1 Time and materials

NTK 23-6

Learning Objectives

CONCEPTUAL

C1 Describe the importance of relevant costs for short-term decisions.

ANALYTICAL

A1 Determine service selling price using time and materials pricing.

PROCEDURAL

P1 Evaluate make or buy decisions.

P2 Evaluate sell or process further decisions.

P3 Determine sales mix with constrained resources.

P4 Evaluate segment elimination decisions.

P5 Evaluate keep or replace decisions.

P6 Determine product selling price using cost data.

P7 Evaluate special offer decisions.

Green Is Good

©Solugen

"We're green chemists"—**Sean Hunt**

PHILADELPHIA—Hydrogen peroxide is used in many common household products, including toothpastes and cleaners, yet the traditional process to produce it is energy-intensive and hazardous. Completing their advanced studies, Gaurab Chakrabarti and Sean Hunt discovered a simple process to convert plant starches into hydrogen peroxide. "Not only does our process reduce manufacturing waste," says Gaurab, "it creates a pure product that is clean and safe." Sean calls their company, **Solugen** (**Solugentech.com**), a "green chemistry" company.

Avoiding the gases, chemicals, and cancer-causing agents used by traditional manufacturers, Solugen uses few inputs: air, water, proprietary enzymes, and plant material. "Not only is our process emissions-free, it actually reduces CO_2 levels," says Sean.

The duo's main product, Bioperoxide, has many possible applications. As Solugen's production process is about 10 times cheaper than the traditional process, consumer product manufacturers might buy hydrogen peroxide from Solugen rather than making their own.

While Gaurab and Sean started by selling Bioperoxide as a cleaner for hot tubs and pools, their company now also processes Bioperoxide further into its Ode to Clean branded cleaning products. These make or buy, sell or process further, and other short-term decisions depend on incremental costs and revenues of the alternative courses of action, as this chapter shows.

Sources: *Solugen website*, January 2019; *Ag Funder News*, October 24, 2017; *PR Newswire*, October 24, 2017; *Forbes.com*, October 24, 2017

DECISIONS AND INFORMATION

This chapter focuses on the use of accounting information to make several important managerial decisions. Most of these involve short-term decisions. This differs from methods used for longer-term managerial decisions described in the next chapter and in several other chapters of this text.

Decision Making

Managerial decision making involves five steps: (1) Define the decision task, (2) identify alternative courses of action, (3) collect relevant information and evaluate each alternative, (4) select the preferred course of action, and (5) analyze and assess decisions made. These five steps are illustrated in Exhibit 23.1.

Define task and goal → Identify alternative actions → Collect relevant information → Select course of action → Analyze and assess decision

EXHIBIT 23.1

Managerial Decision Making

Both managerial and financial accounting information play important roles in most management decisions. The accounting system provides primarily *financial* information such as performance reports and budget analyses for decision making. *Nonfinancial* information is also important and includes environmental effects, political sensitivities, and social responsibility.

Relevant Costs and Benefits

C1

Describe the importance of relevant costs for short-term decisions.

In making short-term decisions, managers focus on the relevant benefits and the relevant costs.

- **Incremental costs,** or *differential costs,* are the relevant costs in making decisions. These are the additional costs incurred if a company pursues a certain course of action.

- **Incremental revenues,** the additional revenue generated by selecting a certain course of action over another, are the key rewards from that action.

Three types of costs are important in our discussion of relevant costs: sunk costs, out-of-pocket costs, and opportunity costs.

"Sunk costs are not relevant to my decision."

"I must consider out-of-pocket and opportunity costs."

- *Sunk cost* arises from a past decision and cannot be avoided or changed; it is irrelevant to future decisions. An example is the cost of computer equipment previously purchased by a company. This cost is not relevant to the decision of whether to replace the computer equipment. Likewise, depreciation of the original cost of plant (and intangible) assets is a sunk cost. Most of a company's allocated costs, including fixed overhead items such as depreciation and administrative expenses, are sunk costs.

- *Out-of-pocket cost* requires a future outlay of cash and is relevant for current and future decisions. These costs are usually the direct result of management's decisions. For instance, future purchases of computer equipment involve out-of-pocket costs. The cost of future computer purchases is relevant to the decision of whether to replace the computer equipment.

- *Opportunity cost* is the potential benefit lost by taking a specific action when two or more alternative choices are available. An example is a student giving up wages from a job to attend summer school. The forgone wages should be considered as part of the total cost of attending summer school. Companies continually choose between alternative courses of action. For instance, a company making standardized products might be approached by a customer to supply a special (nonstandard) product. A decision to accept or reject the special order must consider not only the profit to be made from the special order but also the profit given up by devoting time and resources to this order instead of pursuing an alternative project. The profit given up is an opportunity cost. Consideration of opportunity costs is important. Although opportunity costs are not entered in accounting records, they are relevant to many managerial decisions.

We show how to apply relevant costs and benefits to analyze common managerial decisions. We also discuss some qualitative factors, not easily expressed in terms of costs and benefits, that managers must consider.

NEED-TO-KNOW 23-1

Relevant Costs

C1

Do More: QS 23-4

Match each of the terms below with its definition.

_____ **1.** Sunk cost
_____ **2.** Out-of-pocket cost
_____ **3.** Opportunity cost
_____ **4.** Incremental cost
_____ **5.** Incremental revenue

a. Additional costs incurred from a course of action
b. Additional revenue from a course of action
c. A future outlay of cash
d. Potential benefit lost from taking a course of action
e. A cost that arises from a past decision and cannot be changed

Solution

1. e **2.** c **3.** d **4.** a **5.** b

PRODUCTION DECISIONS

Managers experience many different scenarios that require analyzing alternative actions and making decisions. We describe several different decision scenarios next. We set these tasks in the context of FasTrac, an exercise supplies and equipment manufacturer. For each decision, we assume FasTrac is operating at 80% of its full capacity. *We treat each of these decision tasks as separate from each other.*

Make or Buy

P1⎯⎯⎯⎯⎯

Evaluate make or buy decisions.

The decision to make or buy a component is common. **Apple** buys the component parts for its electronic products, but it could consider making these components in its own manufacturing facilities. The process of buying goods or services from an external supplier is called **outsourcing.** This decision depends on incremental costs. We use FasTrac to illustrate.

FasTrac currently buys Part 417, a component of the main product it sells, for $1.20 per unit. With excess productive capacity, management is considering making Part 417 instead of buying it. Making Part 417 would incur variable costs of $0.45 for direct materials and $0.50 for direct labor. FasTrac's normal predetermined overhead rate is 100% of direct labor cost. If management *incorrectly* relies on this historical overhead rate, it would mistakenly believe that the cost to make the component part is $1.45 per unit ($0.45 + $0.50 + $0.50) and conclude the company is better off buying the part at $1.20 per unit. This analysis is flawed, however, because it uses the historical predetermined overhead rate.

Only *incremental* overhead costs are relevant to this decision. Incremental overhead costs of making the part might include, for example, additional power for operating machines, extra supplies, added cleanup costs, materials handling, and quality control. Assume that management computes an *incremental overhead rate* of $0.20 per unit if it makes the part. We can then prepare a per unit analysis, using relevant costs, as shown in Exhibit 23.2.

$ per unit	Make	Buy
Direct materials	$0.45	—
Direct labor	0.50	—
Overhead costs (using incremental rate)	0.20	—
Purchase price	—	$1.20
Total cost per unit	$1.15	$1.20

EXHIBIT 23.2

Make or Buy Analysis Using Relevant Costs

Exhibit 23.2 shows that the relevant cost to make Part 417 is $1.15. It is cheaper to make the part than to buy it. If incremental overhead costs are less than $0.25 per unit, the total cost to make the part will be less than the purchase price of $1.20 per unit.

Decision rule: If the incremental cost to make is less than the cost to buy, make the product.

Additional Factors   While it is cheaper to make Part 417, FasTrac must also consider several nonfinancial factors. These factors might include product quality, timeliness of delivery (especially in a just-in-time setting), reactions of customers and suppliers, and other intangibles like employee morale and workload. It must also consider whether making the part requires incremental fixed costs to expand plant capacity. When these additional factors are considered, small unit cost differences might not matter.

▐ Decision Insight ━━━━━━━━━━━━━━━━━━━━━━━━━━━━━━━━━

Make or Buy IT   Companies apply make or buy decisions to their services. Many now outsource their information technology activities. Information technology companies provide infrastructure and services to enable businesses to focus on their key activities. It is argued that outsourcing saves money and streamlines operations, and without the headaches. ∎

A company currently pays $5 per unit to buy a key part for a product it manufactures. It can make the part for $1.50 per unit for direct materials and $2.50 per unit for direct labor. The company normally allocates overhead costs at the rate of 50% of direct labor. Incremental overhead costs to make this part are $0.75 per unit. Should the company make or buy the part?

Solution

$ per unit	Make	Buy
Direct materials.	$1.50	—
Direct labor	2.50	—
Overhead (incremental)	0.75	—
Cost to buy the part	—	$5.00
Total cost per unit	$4.75	$5.00

The company should **make the part** because the cost to make it is less than the cost to buy it.

Sell or Process Further

Some companies must decide whether to sell partially completed products as is or to process them further for sale as other products. For example, a peanut grower could sell its peanut harvest as is, or it could process peanuts into other products such as peanut butter, trail mix, and candy. The decision depends on the incremental costs and benefits of further processing.

To illustrate, suppose FasTrac has 40,000 units of partially finished Product Q. It has already spent $30,000 to manufacture these 40,000 units. FasTrac can sell the 40,000 units to another manufacturer as raw material for $50,000. Alternatively, it can process them further and produce finished Products X, Y, and Z. Processing the units further will cost an additional $80,000 and will yield total revenues of $150,000. FasTrac must decide whether the added revenues from selling finished Products X, Y, and Z exceed the costs of finishing them.

Exhibit 23.3 presents the analysis.

EXHIBIT 23.3

Sell or Process Further Analysis

	Sell as Product Q	Process Further into Products X, Y, and Z
Incremental revenue.	$50,000	$150,000
Incremental cost	—	(80,000)
Incremental income.	$50,000	$ 70,000

The incremental income from processing further ($70,000) is greater than the incremental income ($50,000) from selling Product Q as is. Therefore, FasTrac should process further and earn an additional $20,000 of income ($70,000 − $50,000). The $30,000 of previously incurred manufacturing costs are *excluded* from the analysis. These costs are sunk, and they are not relevant to the decision. The incremental revenue from selling Product Q as is ($50,000) is properly included. It is the opportunity cost associated with processing further. The incremental income from processing further is $20,000. **Decision rule:** Select the alternative with the higher incremental income.

For each of the two independent scenarios below, determine whether the company should sell the partially completed product as is or process it further into other saleable products.

1. $10,000 of manufacturing costs have been incurred to produce Product Alpha. Alpha can be sold as is for $30,000 or processed further into two separate products. The further processing will cost $15,000, and the resulting products can be sold for total revenues of $60,000.

2. $5,000 of manufacturing costs have been incurred to produce Product Delta. Delta can be sold as is for $150,000 or processed further into two separate products. The further processing will cost $75,000, and the resulting products can be sold for total revenues of $200,000.

Solution

1.

Alpha	Sell As Is	Process Further
Incremental revenue	$30,000	$60,000
Incremental cost..............	—	(15,000)
Incremental income	$30,000	$45,000

Alpha should be **processed further;** doing so will yield an extra $15,000 ($45,000 − $30,000) of income.

2.

Delta	Sell As Is	Process Further
Incremental revenue	$150,000	$200,000
Incremental cost	—	(75,000)
Incremental income	$150,000	$125,000

Delta should be **sold as is;** doing so will yield an extra $25,000 ($150,000 − $125,000) of income.

Do More: QS 23-8, QS 23-9, E 23-3

Scrap or Rework
A variation of the sell or process decision is the scrap or rework decision. Manufacturing processes sometimes yield defective products. Managers must decide whether to scrap or rework these products in process.

Assume that FasTrac has 10,000 defective units of a product that have already cost $1 per unit to manufacture. These units can be sold as is (as scrap) for $0.40 each, or they can be reworked for $0.80 per unit and then sold for their full price of $1.50 each. Should FasTrac sell the units as scrap or rework them?

The $1 per unit manufacturing cost already incurred is a sunk cost and is irrelevant. The $0.40 selling price as scrap is the opportunity cost of reworking. Our analysis is reflected in Exhibit 23.4. FasTrac should rework the units and obtain the higher incremental income.

$ per unit	Scrap	Rework
Sale of scrapped/reworked units..............	$0.40	$ 1.50
Less out-of-pocket costs to rework defects		(0.80)
Incremental income (per unit)...............	$0.40	$ 0.70

EXHIBIT 23.4

Scrap or Rework Analysis

Sales Mix Selection When Resources Are Constrained

When a company sells a mix of products, some are more profitable than others. Management concentrates sales efforts on more profitable products. If production facilities or other factors are limited, producing more of one product usually requires producing less of others. In this case, management must identify the most profitable combination, or *sales mix,* of products. To identify the best sales mix, management focuses on the *contribution margin per unit of scarce resource.*

To illustrate, assume FasTrac makes and sells two products, A and B. The same machines are used to produce both products. A and B have the following selling prices and variable costs per unit.

$ per unit	Product A	Product B
Selling price	$5.00	$7.50
Variable costs	3.50	5.50

P3

Determine sales mix with constrained resources.

FasTrac has an existing capacity of 100,000 machine hours per year. In addition, Product A uses 1 machine hour per unit while Product B uses 2 machine hours per unit. With limited resources, FasTrac should focus its productive capacity on the product that yields the highest contribution margin *per machine hour,* until market demand for that product is satisfied. Exhibit 23.5 shows the relevant analysis.

EXHIBIT 23.5

Sales Mix Analysis

	Product A	Product B
Selling price per unit..........................	$5.00	$7.50
Variable costs per unit	(3.50)	(5.50)
Contribution margin per unit (i)	$1.50	$2.00
Machine hours per unit (ii)	1 hr.	2 hrs.
Contribution margin per machine hour (i) ÷ (ii)	$1.50	$1.00

Exhibit 23.5 shows that although Product B has a higher contribution margin per *unit,* Product A has a higher contribution margin per *machine hour*. In this case, FasTrac should produce as much of Product A as possible, up to the market demand. For example, if the market will buy all of Product A that FasTrac can produce, FasTrac should produce 100,000 units of Product A and none of Product B. This sales mix would yield a contribution margin of $150,000 per year, the maximum the company could make subject to its resource constraint.

Point: With such high demand, management should consider expanding its productive capacity.

Point: A strategy designed to reduce the impact of constraints or bottlenecks on production is called the *theory of constraints.*

If demand for Product A is limited—say, to 80,000 units—FasTrac will begin by producing those 80,000 units. This production level would leave 20,000 machine hours to devote to production of Product B. FasTrac would use these remaining machine hours to produce 10,000 units (20,000 machine hours/2 machine hours per unit) of Product B. This sales mix would yield the contribution margin shown in Exhibit 23.6.

EXHIBIT 23.6

Contribution Margin from Sales Mix with Resource Constraint

Sales Mix	Contribution Margin	Machine Hours Used
Product A (80,000 × $1.50 per unit)......	$120,000	80,000
Product B (10,000 × $2.00 per unit)......	20,000	20,000
Total................................	$140,000	100,000

Example: Increasing capacity adds fixed costs. To evaluate such strategies, subtract these incremental fixed costs from contribution margin at the optimal sales mix.

With limited demand for Product A, the optimal sales mix yields a contribution margin of $140,000, the best the company can do subject to its resource constraint and market demand. **Decision rule:** If demand for products is limited, produce the most profitable product (per unit of scarce resource) up to the point of total demand (or the capacity constraint). Use remaining capacity to produce the next most profitable product.

©Purestock/SuperStock

■ **Decision Insight**

Fashion Mix Companies such as **Gap**, **TJX Companies**, **Urban Outfitters**, and **American Eagle** must continuously monitor and manage the sales mix of their product lists. Selling their products worldwide further complicates their decision process. The contribution margin of each product is crucial to their product mix strategies. ■

NEED-TO-KNOW 23-4

Sales Mix with Constrained Resources

P3 ▶

A company produces two products, Gamma and Omega. Gamma sells for $10 per unit and Omega sells for $12.50 per unit. Variable costs are $7 per unit of Gamma and $8 per unit of Omega. The company has a capacity of 5,000 machine hours per month. Gamma uses 1 machine hour per unit and Omega uses 3 machine hours per unit.

1. Compute the contribution margin per machine hour for each product.
2. Assume demand for Gamma is limited to 3,800 units per month. How many units of Gamma and Omega should the company produce, and what will be the total contribution margin from this sales mix?

Solution

1.

	Gamma	Omega
Selling price per unit....................................	$10.00	$12.50
Variable costs per unit	(7.00)	(8.00)
Contribution margin per unit (i)	$ 3.00	$ 4.50
Machine hours per unit (ii)	1 hr.	3 hrs.
Contribution margin per machine hour [(i) ÷ (ii)]	$ 3.00	$ 1.50

2. The company will begin by producing Gamma to meet the market demand of 3,800 units. This production level will consume 3,800 machine hours, leaving 1,200 machine hours to produce Omega. With 1,200 machine hours, the company can produce 400 units (1,200 machine hours/3 machine hours per unit) of Omega. The total contribution margin from this sales mix is

Gamma	3,800 units × $3.00 per unit = $ 11,400
Omega.	400 units × $4.50 per unit = 1,800
Total contribution margin	**$13,200**

Do More: QS 23-11, E 23-6, E 23-7

CAPACITY DECISIONS

Segment Elimination

P4

Evaluate segment elimination decisions.

When a segment, division, or store is performing poorly, management must consider eliminating it. As we showed in a previous chapter, determining a segment's *contribution to overhead* is an important first step in this analysis. Segments with revenues less than direct costs are candidates for elimination. However, contribution to overhead is not sufficient for this decision. We must further classify the segment's expenses as avoidable or unavoidable.

- **Avoidable expenses** are amounts the company would not incur if it eliminated the segment.
- **Unavoidable expenses** are amounts that would continue even if the segment was eliminated.

To illustrate, FasTrac is considering eliminating its Treadmill division, which reported a $500 operating loss for the recent year, as shown in Exhibit 23.7. Exhibit 23.7 shows the Treadmill division contributes $9,700 to recovery of overhead costs. The next step is to classify the division's costs as either avoidable or unavoidable. Variable costs, such as cost of goods sold and wages expense, are avoidable. In addition, some of the division's indirect expenses are avoidable; for example, if the Treadmill division were eliminated, FasTrac could reduce its overall advertising expense by $400 and its overall insurance expense by $300. In addition, FasTrac could avoid office department expenses of $2,200 and purchasing expenses of $1,000 if the Treadmill division were eliminated. These *avoidable* expenses would not be allocated to other divisions of the company; rather, these expenses would be eliminated. *Unavoidable* expenses, however, would be reallocated to other divisions if the Treadmill division were eliminated.

Example: How can insurance be classified as either avoidable or unavoidable? *Answer:* It depends on whether the assets insured can be removed and the premiums canceled.

FasTrac can avoid a total of $41,800 of expenses if it eliminates the Treadmill division. However, because this division's sales are $47,800, eliminating the division would reduce FasTrac's income by $6,000 ($47,800 − $41,800). Based on this analysis, FasTrac should not eliminate its Treadmill division. **Decision rule:** A segment is a candidate for elimination if its revenues are less than its avoidable expenses.

EXHIBIT 23.7

Classification of Segment Operating Expenses for Analysis

Treadmill Division	Total	Avoidable Expenses	Unavoidable Expenses
Sales.	$47,800		
Cost of goods sold.	30,000	$30,000	
Gross profit	17,800		
Direct expenses			
Wages expense.	7,900	7,900	
Depreciation expense—Equipment	200		$ 200
Total direct expenses	8,100		
Departmental contribution to overhead.	$ 9,700		
Indirect expenses			
Rent and utilities expense	3,150		3,150
Advertising expense	400	400	
Insurance expense	400	300	100
Share of office department expenses	3,060	2,200	860
Share of purchasing department expenses.	3,190	1,000	2,190
Total indirect expenses.	10,200		
Operating income (loss)	$ (500)		
Total avoidable expenses		$41,800	
Total unavoidable expenses			$6,500

Point: Analysis is summarized as:

Sales	$ 47,800
Avoidable expenses	(41,800)
Reduction in income	$ 6,000

Because sales > avoidable expenses, do *not* eliminate division.

Additional Factors   When considering elimination of a segment, we must assess its impact on other segments. A segment could be unprofitable on its own, but it might still contribute to other segments' revenues and profits. It is possible then to continue a segment even when its revenues are less than its avoidable expenses. Similarly, a profitable segment might be discontinued if its space, assets, or staff can be more profitably used by expanding existing segments or by creating new ones. Our decision to keep or eliminate a segment requires a more complex analysis than simply looking at a segment's performance report.

Example: Give an example of a segment that a company might profitably use to attract customers even though it might incur a loss. *Answer:* Warranty and post-sales services.

NEED-TO-KNOW 23-5

Segment Elimination

P4

A bike maker is considering eliminating its Tandem Bike division because it operates at a loss of $6,000 per year. Division sales for the year total $40,000, and the company reports the costs for this division as shown below. Should the Tandem Bike division be eliminated?

	Avoidable Expenses	Unavoidable Expenses
Cost of goods sold	$30,000	$ —
Direct expenses	8,000	—
Indirect expenses	2,500	3,000
Service department costs.	250	2,250
Total.	$40,750	$5,250

Solution

Total avoidable costs of $40,750 are greater than the division's sales of $40,000, suggesting the division **should be eliminated.** Other factors might be relevant since the shortfall in sales ($750) is low. For example, are tandem bike sales expected to increase in the future? Does the sale of tandem bikes generate sales of other types of products?

Do More: QS 23-12, QS 23-13, E 23-8

P5 _____

Evaluate keep or replace decisions.

Keep or Replace Equipment

Businesses periodically must decide whether to keep using equipment or replace it. Advances in technology typically mean newer equipment can operate more efficiently and at lower cost than older equipment. If the reduction in *variable* manufacturing costs with the new equipment is greater than its net purchase price, the equipment should be replaced. In this setting, the net purchase price of the equipment is its total cost minus any trade-in allowance or cash receipt for the old equipment.

For example, FasTrac has a piece of manufacturing equipment with a book value (cost minus accumulated depreciation) of $20,000 and a remaining useful life of four years. At the end of four years the equipment will have a salvage value of zero. The market value of the equipment is currently $25,000.

FasTrac can purchase a new machine for $100,000 and receive $25,000 in return for trading in its old machine. The new machine will reduce FasTrac's variable manufacturing costs by $18,000 per year over the four-year life of the new machine. FasTrac's incremental analysis is shown in Exhibit 23.8.

EXHIBIT 23.8

Keep or Replace Analysis

	Increase or (Decrease) in Income
Cost to buy new machine.	$(100,000)
Cash received to trade in old machine	25,000
Reduction in variable manufacturing costs ($18,000 × 4 years).	72,000
Total increase (decrease) in income	$ (3,000)

Exhibit 23.8 shows that FasTrac should not replace the old equipment with this newer version as it will decrease income by $3,000. The book value of the old equipment ($20,000) is not relevant to this analysis. Book value is a sunk cost, and it cannot be changed regardless of whether FasTrac keeps or replaces this equipment. **Decision rule:** If the reduction in variable manufacturing cost is greater than the net cost to buy the new machine, the machine should be replaced. The analysis above ignores the time value of money. We consider this in the next chapter.

PRICING DECISIONS

Normal Pricing

Managers consider several factors in setting normal selling prices.

- Target profit: Owners expect a return on their investment (ROI), for example an ROI of 12%.
- Customer demand: How much will customers pay, and how will they respond to price increases?
- Competition: Markets for some products are very competitive, and companies are **price-takers,** unable to control prices, and simply sell at the market price.
- Differentiation: Companies with unique products or well-known brands can be **price-setters,** having more control in setting prices.
- Product life cycles: Many products have relatively short life cycles before they are replaced with new models. These life cycles and expected upgrades can influence pricing.

Normal product selling prices must be set high enough to cover all costs and provide an acceptable return to owners. We consider several pricing approaches using cost data next.

Cost-Plus Methods   *Cost-plus* methods are common when companies are price-setters. Management adds a **markup** to cost to reach a target price. We first describe the **total cost method,** where management sets price equal to the product's total costs plus a desired profit on the product. This is a three-step process:

1. Determine total cost per unit.

> **Total costs =** **Product (direct materials, direct labor, and overhead) costs** **+** **Selling and administrative costs**

> **Total cost per unit = Total costs ÷ Total units expected to be produced and sold**

2. Determine the dollar markup per unit.

> **Markup per unit = Total cost per unit × Markup percentage**

3. Determine selling price per unit.

> **Selling price per unit = Total cost per unit + Markup per unit**

To illustrate, consider MpPro, a company that produces MP3 players. The company desires a 20% markup on the total cost of this product. It expects to produce and sell 10,000 players. The following additional information is available:

Variable costs (per unit)		Fixed costs (total)	
Product costs	$44	Overhead	$140,000
Selling and administrative costs	6	Selling and administrative costs	60,000

We apply the three-step total cost method to determine price.

1. Total costs = Product costs + Selling and administrative costs
   = [($44 × 10,000 units) + $140,000] + [($6 × 10,000 units) + $60,000]
   = $700,000

   Total cost per unit = Total costs/Total units expected to be produced and sold
   = $700,000/10,000
   = $70

2. Markup per unit = Total cost per unit × Markup percentage
   = $70 × 20%
   = $14

3. Selling price per unit = Total cost per unit + Markup per unit
   = $70 + $14
   = $84

P6

Determine product selling price using cost data.

Companies often use cost-plus pricing as a starting point in determining selling prices. Many factors determine price, including consumer preferences and competition.

Target Costing   When competition is high, companies might be price-takers and have little control in setting prices. In such cases **target costing** can be useful. Target cost is defined as

$$\text{Target cost} = \text{Expected selling price} - \text{Desired profit}$$

If the target cost is too high, lean techniques can be used to determine whether the cost can be reduced enough that the desired profit can be made. For example, if the market price for MP3 players is $80 each and MpPro still wants to make a profit of $14 per unit, it must find a way to reduce its total cost per unit to $66 (computed as $80 price − $14 desired profit).

Sometimes companies compute the desired markup percentage using a target return on investment. For example, if MpPro targets a 14% return on invested assets of $1,000,000, its target profit is $140,000. This equals $14 per unit if 10,000 units are sold, as in this example. The markup percentage is then $14/$70 = 20%.

Variable Cost Method   In addition to the total cost approach of the cost-plus methods, one alternative is to base price on variable cost. Because variable cost is less than total cost, companies that use this method must increase the markup percentage to ensure that the selling price covers all costs. For the **variable cost method,** the markup percentage to variable cost is determined as

$$\frac{\text{Markup percentage}}{\text{to variable cost}} = \frac{\text{Target profit} + \text{Fixed overhead costs} + \text{Fixed selling and administrative costs}}{\text{Total variable cost}}$$

For MpPro, the markup percentage, using the variable cost approach, is computed as

$$\frac{\text{Markup percentage}}{\text{to variable cost}} = \frac{\$140,000 + \$140,000 + \$60,000}{[(\$44 + \$6) \times 10,000]} = 68\%$$

With this markup percentage and total variable cost per unit of $50 (from $44 + $6), the selling price is computed as

$$\text{Selling price} = \$50 + (\$50 \times 68\%) = \$84$$

Other Pricing Methods   Increased global competition and technological advances have led to other pricing methods.

- **Value-based pricing**   By focusing on what customers value, this approach determines the maximum amount customers will pay without reducing demand. **Starbucks** uses research and customer analysis in setting value-based prices.
- **Auction-based pricing**   Rather than forcing sellers to set prices, this approach uses potential buyers' bid prices. **Priceline** uses electronic auctions to sell hotel rooms and airline flights.
- **Dynamic pricing** (*surge pricing*)   This strategy uses prices that vary depending on changing market conditions or customer demand. **Uber**'s fares are higher during peak travel times and popular events.

©Spaxiax/Shutterstock

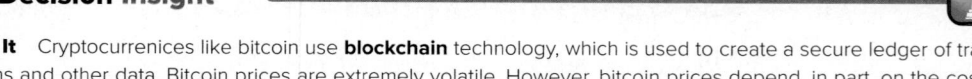

■ **Decision Insight**

Mine It   Cryptocurrenices like bitcoin use **blockchain** technology, which is used to create a secure ledger of transactions and other data. Bitcoin prices are extremely volatile. However, bitcoin prices depend, in part, on the cost to mine bitcoin (electricity and computers). Some estimate a cost of about $4,000 per bitcoin, with the cost rising as more bitcoins are mined. ■

Companies sometimes receive special offers at prices lower than their normal selling prices. We show how to evaluate these special offers by focusing on incremental revenues and incremental expenses next.

Special Offers

FasTrac produces and sells approximately 100,000 units of product annually. Its per unit and annual total sales and costs are shown in the contribution margin income statement in Exhibit 23.9. Its normal selling price is $10.00 per unit, and each unit sold generates $1.00 per unit of operating income.

P7_____

Evaluate special offer decisions.

EXHIBIT 23.9

Selected Operating Income Data

FasTrac Contribution Margin Income Statement For Year Ended December 31, 2019		
	Per Unit	**Annual Total**
Sales (100,000 units)	$10.00	$1,000,000
Variable costs		
Direct materials	(3.50)	(350,000)
Direct labor	(2.20)	(220,000)
Variable overhead	(0.50)	(50,000)
Selling expenses	(1.40)	(140,000)
Contribution margin	2.40	240,000
Fixed costs		
Fixed overhead	(0.60)	(60,000)
Administrative expenses	(0.80)	(80,000)
Operating income	$ 1.00	$ 100,000

A current customer wants to buy more units and export them to another country. This buyer offers to buy 10,000 units of the product at $8.50 per unit. The offer price is below the normal price of $10.00 per unit, but this sale would be several times larger than any single previous sale and it would use idle capacity. Because the units will be exported, this new business will not affect current domestic sales.

Management needs to know whether accepting the offer will increase income. If management relies incorrectly on per unit historical costs, it would mistakenly reject the sale because the selling price ($8.50) per unit is less than the total historical costs per unit ($9.00).

FasTrac must analyze the costs of this potential new business differently. The $9.00 historical cost per unit is not necessarily the incremental cost of this special order. The following information regarding the order is available:

- The variable manufacturing costs to produce this order will be the same as for FasTrac's normal business—$3.50 per unit for direct materials, $2.20 per unit for direct labor, and $0.50 per unit for variable overhead.
- Selling expenses for this order will be $0.20 per unit, which is less than the selling expenses of FasTrac's normal business.
- Fixed overhead expenses will not change regardless of whether this order is accepted. They are not relevant to the decision.
- This order will incur *incremental* administrative expenses of $1,000 for clerical work. These are additional fixed costs due to this order.

We use this incremental cost information to determine whether FasTrac should accept this new business. The analysis of relevant benefits and costs in Exhibit 23.10 suggests that the additional business should be accepted. **The incremental revenue ($8.50 per unit) exceeds the incremental cost ($6.50 per unit), and the order would yield $20,000 of additional operating income.** More generally, FasTrac would increase its income with any price that exceeds $6.50 per unit ($65,000 incremental cost/10,000 additional units). The key point is that *management must not blindly use historical costs, especially allocated overhead costs.* Instead, management must focus on the incremental costs to be incurred if the additional business is accepted.

EXHIBIT 23.10

Analysis of Special Offer Using Relevant Costs

FasTrac Contribution Margin Income Statement (for special offer) For Year Ended December 31, 2019		
	Per Unit*	**Annual Total**
Sales (10,000 units)......................	$ 8.50	$ 85,000
Variable costs		
Direct materials.......................	(3.50)	(35,000)
Direct labor	(2.20)	(22,000)
Variable overhead....................	(0.50)	(5,000)
Selling expenses	(0.20)	(2,000)
Contribution margin.....................	2.10	21,000
Fixed costs		
Fixed overhead	—	—
Administrative expenses...............	(0.10)	(1,000)
Operating income (incremental)...........	$ 2.00	$ 20,000

*Total cost per unit = $3.50 + $2.20 + $0.50 + $0.20 + $0.10 = $6.50.

Point: Ignore allocated overhead costs. The analysis in Exhibit 23.10 uses only *incremental* fixed overhead costs.

Additional Factors   An analysis of the incremental costs pertaining to the additional volume is always relevant for this type of decision. We must be careful when the additional volume approaches or exceeds the factory's existing available capacity. If the additional volume requires the company to expand its capacity by obtaining more equipment, more space, or more personnel, the incremental costs could quickly exceed the incremental revenue.

Example: Exhibit 23.10 uses quantitative information. Suggest some qualitative factors to be considered when deciding whether to accept this project. *Answer:* (1) Impact on relationships with other customers and (2) improved relationship with customer buying additional units.

Another cautionary note is the effect on existing sales. All new units of the extra business will be sold outside FasTrac's normal domestic sales channels. If accepting additional business would cause existing sales to decline, this information must be included in our analysis. The contribution margin lost from a decline in sales is an opportunity cost. The company must also consider whether this customer is really a one-time customer. If not, can the company continue to offer this low price in the long run?

 Decision Maker

Partner   You are a partner in a small accounting firm that specializes in keeping the books and preparing taxes for clients. A local restaurant is interested in obtaining these services from your firm. Identify factors that are relevant in deciding whether to accept the engagement. ■ *Answer:* You should identify the differences between existing clients and this potential client. A key difference is that the restaurant business has additional inventory components (groceries, vegetables, meats) and is likely to have a higher proportion of depreciable assets. These differences imply that the partner must spend more hours auditing the records and understanding the business, regulations, and standards that pertain. Such differences suggest that the partner must use a different "formula" for quoting a price to this potential client vis-à-vis current clients.

NEED-TO-KNOW 23-6

Special Order

P7

A company receives a special order for 200 units that requires stamping the buyer's name on each unit, yielding an additional fixed cost of $400. Without the order, the company operates at 75% of capacity and produces 7,500 units of product at the costs below. The company's normal selling price is $22 per unit.

Direct materials..	$37,500
Direct labor...	60,000
Overhead (30% variable)	20,000
Selling expenses (60% variable)	25,000

The requested sales price for the special order is $18 per unit. The special order will not affect normal unit sales and will not increase fixed overhead or fixed selling expenses. Variable selling expenses on the special order are reduced to one-half the normal amount. Should the company accept the special order?

Solution

Incremental variable costs per unit for this order of 200 units are computed as follows.

Direct materials ($37,500/7,500).	$ 5.00
Direct labor ($60,000/7,500)	8.00
Variable overhead [(0.30 × $20,000)/7,500]	0.80
Variable selling expenses [(0.60 × $25,000 × 0.5)/7,500]	1.00
Total incremental variable costs per unit.	$14.80

The contribution margin from the special order is $640, computed as [($18.00 − $14.80) × 200]. This will cover the incremental fixed costs of $400 and yield incremental income of $240. **The offer should be accepted.**

> Do More: QS 23-15, E 23-13, E 23-14

SUSTAINABILITY AND ACCOUNTING

Managers consider sustainability issues in many of the decisions discussed in this chapter. Companies that buy rather than make components must consider the labor and safety practices of their suppliers. **Apple** requires its suppliers to comply with its *Supplier Code of Conduct* (**https://images.apple.com/supplier-responsibility/pdf/Apple-Supplier-Code-of-Conduct-January.pdf**). This code details Apple's requirements with respect to anti-discrimination, anti-harassment, prevention of involuntary labor and human trafficking, and other issues.

For example, workers are allowed to work no more than 60 hours per week, with a required day of rest every seven days. A real-time work-hour tracking system and frequent reporting enable Apple to assess compliance with the code. In a recent report, Apple noted 97% compliance with its workweek requirement.

For sustainability of direct materials, "we use what's local," says Gaurab Chakrabarti, co-founder of **Solugen**, in describing the raw materials for his company's plant-based hydrogen peroxide production process. "Sugar, plant starch, you can feed anything into it," says co-founder Sean Hunt. Instead of using costly petroleum, the duo's process uses local plants that are in high supply—cane sugar in India and beet sugar in Chile, for example. This is good for the planet and Solugen's bottom line.

©Solugen

Time and Materials Pricing  **Decision Analysis**

It is common to price services using **time and materials pricing.** With this method, companies set a price for labor and a price for materials, and each includes a charge for overhead costs and a desired profit margin. Auto mechanics, construction companies, electricians, and accounting and law firms commonly use time and materials pricing.

Time and materials pricing follows these steps.

A1_____

Determine service selling price using time and materials pricing.

1 Compute the rate (in $) per hour of direct labor. This rate includes a charge for other (non-materials related) overhead costs plus a desired profit margin.
2 Compute the **materials markup** (%), which includes the overhead costs related to buying, storing, and handling materials, plus a desired profit margin on the materials' cost.
3 Estimate the number of direct labor hours (DLH) and the total direct materials cost for the service.
4 Using steps 1, 2, and 3, compute the price for the service.

We illustrate time and materials pricing using the following estimates for Erin Builders.

Direct labor rate, including fringe benefits	$40 per DLH
Annual direct labor hours.	3,600 hours
Annual direct materials purchases	$600,000
Annual overhead costs:	
Materials purchasing, handling, and storage.	$18,000
Non-materials related overhead (depreciation, insurance, taxes, rent)	$36,000
Target profit margin (on both labor and materials).	22%

1 The rate per hour of direct labor is computed as

Direct labor rate per hour.	$40
Non-materials related overhead per hour ($36,000/3,600)	+10
Total hourly conversion cost	50
Profit margin (22% × $50)	+11
Rate per hour of direct labor	$61

2 The materials markup per dollar of material cost is computed as

Materials purchasing, handling, and storage ($18,000/$600,000).	3%
Profit margin	+22%
Materials markup	25%

3 The job is estimated to use 300 direct labor hours and $14,000 of direct materials.

4 Erin uses time and materials pricing to set the $35,800 price for the job as we see in Exhibit 23.11.

EXHIBIT 23.11

Time and Materials Pricing

ERIN BUILDERS	
Time and Materials Price Quote to Install Deck and Porch	
Direct labor (300 hours @ $61 per DLH)	$18,300
Direct materials cost.	14,000
Materials markup ($14,000 × 25%)	3,500
Time and materials price	**$35,800**

NEED-TO-KNOW **23-7**

COMPREHENSIVE

Manager Decisions

Determine the appropriate action in each of the following managerial decision situations.

1. Packer Company is operating at 80% of its manufacturing capacity of 100,000 product units per year. A chain store has offered to buy an additional 10,000 units at $22 each and sell them to customers so as not to compete with Packer Company. The following data are available. In producing 10,000 additional units, fixed overhead costs would remain at their current level, but incremental variable overhead costs of $3 per unit would be incurred. Should the company accept or reject this order?

Costs at 80% Capacity	Per Unit	Total
Direct materials.	$ 8.00	$ 640,000
Direct labor	7.00	560,000
Overhead (fixed and variable)	12.50	1,000,000
Totals.	$27.50	$2,200,000

2. Green Company uses Part JR3 in manufacturing its products. It has always purchased this part from a supplier for $40 each. It recently upgraded its own manufacturing capabilities and has enough excess capacity (including trained workers) to begin manufacturing Part JR3 instead of buying it. The company prepares the following cost projections of making the part, assuming that overhead is allocated to the part at the normal predetermined rate of 200% of direct labor cost. The required volume of output to produce the part will not require any incremental fixed overhead. Incremental variable overhead cost will be $17 per unit. Should the company make or buy this part?

Direct materials.	$11
Direct labor	15
Overhead (fixed and variable) (200% of direct labor).	30
Total.	$56

3. Gold Company's manufacturing process causes a relatively large number of defective parts to be produced. The defective parts can be (a) sold for scrap, (b) melted to recover the recycled metal for reuse, or (c) reworked to be good units. Reworking defective parts reduces the output of other good units because no excess capacity exists. Each reworked unit means that one new unit cannot be produced. The following information reflects 500 defective parts currently available. Should the company melt the parts, sell them as scrap, or rework them?

Proceeds of selling as scrap	$2,500
Additional cost of melting down defective parts	400
Cost of purchases avoided by using recycled metal from defects	4,800
Cost to rework 500 defective parts	
Direct materials	0
Direct labor	1,500
Incremental overhead	1,750
Cost to produce 500 new parts	
Direct materials	6,000
Direct labor	5,000
Incremental overhead	3,200
Selling price per good unit	40

PLANNING THE SOLUTION

- Determine whether Packer Company should accept the additional business by finding the incremental costs of materials, labor, and overhead that will be incurred if the order is accepted. Omit fixed costs that the order will not increase. If the incremental revenue exceeds the incremental cost, accept the order.
- Determine whether Green Company should make or buy the component by finding the incremental cost of making each unit. If the incremental cost exceeds the purchase price, the component should be purchased. If the incremental cost is less than the purchase price, make the component.
- Determine whether Gold Company should sell the defective parts, melt them down and recycle the metal, or rework them. To compare the three choices, examine all costs incurred and benefits received from the alternatives in working with the 500 defective units versus the production of 500 new units. For the scrapping alternative, include the costs of producing 500 new units and subtract the $2,500 proceeds from selling the old ones. For the melting alternative, include the costs of melting the defective units, add the net cost of new materials in excess over those obtained from recycling, and add the direct labor and overhead costs. For the reworking alternative, add the costs of direct labor and incremental overhead. Select the alternative that has the lowest cost. The cost assigned to the 500 defective units is sunk and not relevant in choosing among the three alternatives.

SOLUTION

1. This decision involves accepting additional business. Since current unit costs are $27.50, it appears initially as if the offer to sell for $22 should be rejected, but the $27.50 cost includes fixed costs. When the analysis includes only *incremental* costs, the per unit cost is as shown in the following table. The offer should be accepted because it will produce $4 of additional profit per unit (computed as $22 price less $18 incremental cost), which yields a total profit of $40,000 for the 10,000 additional units.

Direct materials	$ 8.00
Direct labor	7.00
Variable overhead (given)	3.00
Total incremental cost	$18.00

2. For this make or buy decision, the analysis must include only incremental overhead per unit ($30 − $17). When only the $17 incremental overhead is included, the relevant unit cost of manufacturing the part is shown in the following table. It would be better to continue buying the part for $40 instead of making it for $43.

Direct materials	$11.00
Direct labor	15.00
Variable overhead	17.00
Total incremental cost	$43.00

3. The goal of this scrap or rework decision is to identify the alternative that produces the greatest net benefit to the company. To compare the alternatives, we determine the net cost of obtaining 500 marketable units as follows. Analysis shows that the incremental cost of 500 marketable parts is smallest if the defects are reworked.

Incremental Cost to Produce 500 Marketable Units	Sell As Is	Melt and Recycle	Rework Units
Direct materials			
New materials	$ 6,000	$6,000	
Recycled metal materials..........................		(4,800)	
Net materials cost		1,200	
Melting costs		400	
Total direct materials cost	6,000	1,600	
Direct labor.....................................	5,000	5,000	$1,500
Incremental overhead	3,200	3,200	1,750
Cost to produce 500 marketable units	14,200	9,800	3,250
Less proceeds of selling defects as scrap..............	(2,500)		
Opportunity costs*			5,800
Incremental cost.................................	$11,700	$9,800	$9,050

*The $5,800 opportunity cost is the lost contribution margin from not being able to produce and sell 500 units because of reworking, computed as ($40 − [$14,200/500 units]) × 500 units.

Summary: Cheat Sheet

Incremental costs: Additional costs incurred from a course of action.

Incremental revenues: Additional revenues from a course of action.

Sunk cost: From a past decision and cannot be changed.

Out-of-pocket cost: Future outlay of cash.

Opportunity cost: Potential benefit lost by taking an action when alternatives exist.

PRODUCTION DECISIONS

Make or buy

If, Incremental cost to make > Cost to buy → then, Make

Sell or process

If, Revenues from processing − Processing costs > Sale price → then, Process

Sales mix Produce as much of the product with the highest contribution margin per unit of scarce resource, up to customer demand. Then produce the other product until capacity is used up.

CAPACITY DECISIONS

Segment

Eliminate if, Revenues < Avoidable expenses

Equipment

Replace if, Reduction in variable mfg. costs > Net cost of new machine

PRICING DECISIONS

Normal Price must cover all costs plus provide a profit.

Cost-plus   **Price = Cost + Markup**

where Markup per unit = Cost per unit × Markup %

Target costing

Target cost = Expected selling price − Desired profit

Special offer

If, Incremental revenue > Incremental cost → then, Accept

Service Use time and materials pricing.

Both labor and materials prices include charges for overhead *and* a desired profit margin.

Time and Materials Price Quote

Labor: Rate per hour of direct labor × Direct labor hours

Materials: Direct materials cost × (1 + Markup %),
where Markup % = Materials overhead % + Profit %

A charge for overhead and a desired profit margin are included in the Rate per hour of direct labor and in the materials Markup %.

Key Terms

Multiple Choice Quiz

1. A company inadvertently produced 3,000 defective MP3 players. The players cost $12 each to produce. A recycler offers to purchase the defective players as they are for $8 each. The production manager reports that the defects can be corrected for $10 each, enabling them to be sold at their regular market price of $19 each. The company should
   a. Correct the defect and sell them at the regular price.
   b. Sell the players to the recycler for $8 each.
   c. Sell 2,000 to the recycler and repair the rest.
   d. Sell 1,000 to the recycler and repair the rest.
   e. Throw the players away.

2. A company's productive capacity is limited to 480,000 machine hours. Product X requires 10 machine hours to produce; Product Y requires 2 machine hours to produce. Product X sells for $32 per unit and has variable costs of $12 per unit; Product Y sells for $24 per unit and has variable costs of $10 per unit. Assuming that the company can sell as many of either product as it produces, it should
   a. Produce X and Y in the ratio of 57% X and 43% Y.
   b. Produce X and Y in the ratio of 83% X and 17% Y.
   c. Produce equal amounts of Product X and Product Y.
   d. Produce only Product X.
   e. Produce only Product Y.

3. A company receives a special one-time order for 3,000 units of its product at $15 per unit. The company has excess capacity and it currently produces and sells the units at $20 each to its regular customers. Production costs are $13.50 per unit, which includes $9 of variable costs. To produce the special order, the company must incur additional fixed costs of $5,000. Should the company accept the special order?
   a. Yes, because incremental revenue exceeds incremental costs.
   b. No, because incremental costs exceed incremental revenue.
   c. No, because the units are being sold for $5 less than the regular price.
   d. Yes, because incremental costs exceed incremental revenue.
   e. No, because incremental costs exceed $15 per unit when total costs are considered.

4. A cost that cannot be changed because it arises from a past decision and is irrelevant to future decisions is
   a. An uncontrollable cost.   d. An opportunity cost.
   b. An out-of-pocket cost.   e. An incremental cost.
   c. A sunk cost.

5. The potential benefit of one alternative that is lost by choosing another is known as
   a. An alternative cost.   d. An opportunity cost.
   b. A sunk cost.   e. An out-of-pocket cost.
   c. A differential cost.

ANSWERS TO MULTIPLE CHOICE QUIZ

1. a; Reworking provides incremental revenue of $11 per unit ($19 − $8); it costs $10 to rework them. The company is better off by $1 per unit when it reworks these products and sells them at the regular price.

2. e; Product X has a $2 contribution margin per machine hour [($32 − $12)/10 MH]; Product Y has a $7 contribution margin per machine hour [($24 − $10)/2 MH]. It should produce as much of Product Y as possible.

3. a; Total revenue from the special order = 3,000 units × $15 per unit = $45,000; and Total costs for the special order = (3,000 units × $9 per unit) + $5,000 = $32,000. Net income from the special order = $45,000 − $32,000 = $13,000. Thus, it should accept the order.

4. c

5. d

🔲 Icon denotes assignments that involve decision making.

Discussion Questions

1. 🔲 Identify the five steps involved in the managerial decision-making process.

2. Is nonfinancial information ever useful in managerial decision making?

3. What is a relevant cost? Identify the two types of relevant costs.

4. 🔲 What are incremental revenues?

5. 🔲 Identify some qualitative factors that should be considered when making managerial decisions.

6. **Google** has many types of costs. What is an out-of-pocket cost? What is an opportunity **GOOGLE** cost? Are opportunity costs recorded in the accounting records?

7. 🔲 **Samsung** must confront sunk costs. Why are sunk costs irrelevant in decid- **Samsung** ing whether to sell a product in its present condition or to make it into a new product through additional processing?

8. 🔲 Identify the incremental costs incurred by **APPLE** **Apple** for shipping one additional iPod from a warehouse to a retail store along with the store's normal order of 75 iPods.

9. 📖 **Apple** is considering eliminating one of its stores in a large U.S. city. What are some **APPLE** factors that it should consider in making this decision?

10. 📖 Assume that **Samsung** manufactures and sells 60,000 units of a product at **Samsung** $11,000 per unit in domestic markets. It costs $6,000 per

unit to manufacture ($4,000 variable cost per unit, $2,000 fixed cost per unit). Can you describe a situation in which the company is willing to sell an additional 8,000 units of the product in an international market at $5,000 per unit?

11. Explain how a price-setter differs from a price-taker.

12. What is time and materials pricing?

■ **connect**

QUICK STUDY

QS 23-1
Identifying relevant costs

C1

Helix Company has been approached by a new customer to provide 2,000 units of its regular product at a special price of $6 per unit. The regular selling price of the product is $8 per unit. Helix is operating at 75% of its capacity of 10,000 units. Identify whether the following costs are relevant to Helix's decision as to whether to accept the order at the special selling price. No additional fixed manufacturing overhead will be incurred because of this order. The only additional selling expense on this order will be a $0.50 per unit shipping cost. There will be no additional administrative expenses because of this order. Place an X in the appropriate column to identify whether the cost is relevant or irrelevant to accepting this order.

Item	Relevant	Not Relevant
a. Selling price of $6.00 per unit	_____	_____
b. Direct materials cost of $1.00 per unit	_____	_____
c. Direct labor of $2.00 per unit	_____	_____
d. Variable manufacturing overhead of $1.50 per unit	_____	_____
e. Fixed manufacturing overhead of $0.75 per unit	_____	_____
f. Regular selling expenses of $1.25 per unit	_____	_____
g. Additional selling expenses of $0.50 per unit	_____	_____
h. Administrative expenses of $0.60 per unit	_____	_____

QS 23-2
Special offer   **P7**

Refer to the data in QS 23-1. Based on financial considerations alone, should Helix accept this order at the special price?

QS 23-3
Identifying relevant costs

C1

Zycon has produced 10,000 units of partially finished Product A. These units cost $15,000 to produce, and they can be sold to another manufacturer for $20,000. Instead, Zycon can process the units further and produce finished Products X, Y, and Z. Processing further will cost an additional $22,000 and will yield total revenues of $35,000. Place an X in the appropriate column to identify whether the item is relevant or irrelevant to the sell or process further decision.

Item	Relevant	Not Relevant
a. $15,000 cost already incurred to produce	_____	_____
b. $20,000 selling price	_____	_____
c. $22,000 additional processing costs	_____	_____
d. $35,000 revenues from processing	_____	_____

QS 23-4
Relevant costs

C1

Label each of the following statements as either true ("T") or false ("F").

_____ **1.** Relevant costs are also known as unavoidable costs.

_____ **2.** Incremental costs are also known as differential costs.

_____ **3.** An out-of-pocket cost requires a current and/or future outlay of cash.

_____ **4.** An opportunity cost is the potential benefit that is lost by taking a specific action when two or more alternative choices are available.

_____ **5.** A sunk cost will change with a future course of action.

QS 23-5
Sell or process

P2

Garcia Company has 10,000 units of its product that were produced last year at a total cost of $150,000. The units were damaged in a rainstorm because the warehouse where they were stored developed a leak in the roof. Garcia can sell the units as is for $2 each or it can repair the units at a total cost of $18,000 and then sell them for $5 each. Should Garcia sell the units as is or repair them and then sell them?

Kando Company incurs a $9 per unit cost for Product A, which it currently manufactures and sells for $13.50 per unit. Instead of manufacturing and selling this product, the company can purchase it for $5 per unit and sell it for $12 per unit. If it does so, unit sales would remain unchanged and $5 of the $9 per unit costs of Product A would be eliminated. Should the company continue to manufacture Product A or purchase it for resale?

QS 23-6
Make or buy
P1

Xia Co. currently buys a component part for $5 per unit. Xia believes that making the part would require $2.25 per unit of direct materials and $1.00 per unit of direct labor. Xia allocates overhead using a predetermined overhead rate of 200% of direct labor cost. Xia estimates an incremental overhead rate of $0.75 per unit to make the part. Should Xia make or buy the part?

QS 23-7
Make or buy
P1

Holmes Company produces a product that can be either sold as is or processed further. Holmes has already spent $50,000 to produce 1,250 units that can be sold now for $67,500 to another manufacturer. Alternatively, Holmes can process the units further at an incremental cost of $250 per unit. If Holmes processes further, the units can be sold for $375 each. Should Holmes sell the product now or process it further?

QS 23-8
Sell or process further
P2

A company has already incurred $5,000 of costs in producing 6,000 units of Product XY. Product XY can be sold as is for $15 per unit. Instead, the company could incur further processing costs of $8 per unit and sell the resulting product for $21 per unit. Should the company sell Product XY as is or process it further?

QS 23-9
Sell or process further   **P2**

Signal mistakenly produced 1,000 defective cell phones. The phones cost $60 each to produce. A salvage company will buy the defective phones as they are for $30 each. It would cost Signal $80 per phone to rework the phones. If the phones are reworked, Signal could sell them for $120 each. Signal has excess capacity. Should Signal scrap or rework the phones?

QS 23-10
Scrap or rework
P2

Excel Memory Company can sell all units of computer memory X and Y that it can produce, but it has limited production capacity. It can produce two units of X per hour *or* three units of Y per hour, and it has 4,000 production hours available. Contribution margin is $5 for Product X and $4 for Product Y. What is the most profitable sales mix for this company?

QS 23-11
Selection of sales mix
P3

A guitar manufacturer is considering eliminating its Electric Guitar division because its $76,000 expenses are higher than its $72,000 sales. The company reports the following expenses for this division. Should the division be eliminated?

QS 23-12
Segment elimination
P4

	Avoidable Expenses	Unavoidable Expenses
Cost of goods sold	$56,000	
Direct expenses	9,250	$1,250
Indirect expenses	470	1,600
Service department costs	6,000	1,430

A division of a large company reports the information shown below for a recent year. Variable costs and direct fixed costs are avoidable, and 40% of the indirect fixed costs are avoidable. Based on this information, should the division be eliminated?

QS 23-13
Segment elimination
P4

Sales	$200,000
Variable costs	145,000
Fixed costs	
Direct	30,000
Indirect	50,000
Operating loss	$ (25,000)

Rory Company has a machine with a book value of $75,000 and a remaining five-year useful life. A new machine is available at a cost of $112,500, and Rory can also receive $60,000 for trading in its old machine. The new machine will reduce variable manufacturing costs by $13,000 per year over its five-year useful life. Should the machine be replaced?

QS 23-14
Keep or replace
P5

QS 23-15
Special offer
P7

Radar Company sells bikes for $300 each. The company currently sells 3,750 bikes per year and could make as many as 5,000 bikes per year. The bikes cost $225 each to make: $150 in variable costs per bike and $75 of fixed costs per bike. Radar received an offer from a potential customer who wants to buy 750 bikes for $250 each. Incremental fixed costs to make this order are $50,000. No other costs will change if this order is accepted. Compute Radar's additional income (ignore taxes) if it accepts this order.

QS 23-16
Product pricing using total cost P6

Garcia Co. sells snowboards. Each snowboard requires direct materials of $100, direct labor of $30, and variable overhead of $45. The company expects fixed overhead costs of $635,000 and fixed selling and administrative costs of $115,000 for the next year. It expects to produce and sell 10,000 snowboards in the next year. What will be the selling price per unit if Garcia uses a markup of 15% of total cost?

QS 23-17
Product pricing using total cost P6

José Ruiz wants to start a company that makes snowboards. Competitors sell a similar snowboard for $240 each. José believes he can produce a snowboard for a total cost of $200 per unit, and he plans a 25% markup on his total cost. Compute José's planned selling price. Can José compete with his planned selling price?

QS 23-18
Product pricing using variable costs
P6

GoSnow sells snowboards. Each snowboard requires direct materials of $110, direct labor of $35, and variable overhead of $45. The company expects fixed overhead costs of $265,000 and fixed selling and administrative costs of $211,000 for the next year. The company has a target profit of $200,000. It expects to produce and sell 10,000 snowboards in the next year. Compute the selling price using the variable cost method.

QS 23-19
Target costing P6

Raju is a price-taker in a competitive product market. The current market price is $80 per unit, and Raju's desired profit is 20% of market price. Using target costing, what is the highest Raju's costs can be?

QS 23-20
Time and materials pricing A1

Meng uses time and materials pricing. Its rate per hour of direct labor is $55. Its materials markup is 30%. What price should Meng quote for a job that will take 80 direct labor hours and use $3,800 of direct materials?

QS 23-21
Time and materials pricing
A1

Cheng Co. reports the following information for the coming year. Determine its (*a*) rate per hour of direct labor (in $) and (*b*) materials markup (in %).

Direct labor rate, including fringe benefits	$50 per DLH
Annual direct labor hours	3,800 hours
Annual direct materials purchases	$560,000
Annual overhead costs:	
Materials purchasing, handling, and storage	$39,200
Non-materials related overhead	$114,000
Target profit margin (on both labor and materials)	30%

Mc Graw Hill connect

EXERCISES

Exercise 23-1
Make or buy
P1

Gilberto Company currently manufactures 65,000 units per year of one of its crucial parts. Variable costs are $1.95 per unit, fixed costs related to making this part are $75,000 per year, and allocated fixed costs are $62,000 per year. Allocated fixed costs are unavoidable whether the company makes or buys the part. Gilberto is considering buying the part from a supplier for a quoted price of $3.25 per unit guaranteed for a three-year period. Should the company continue to manufacture the part, or should it buy the part from the outside supplier?

Exercise 23-2
Make or buy
P1

Gelb Company currently manufactures 40,000 units per year of a key component for its manufacturing process. Variable costs are $1.95 per unit, fixed costs related to making this component are $65,000 per year, and allocated fixed costs are $58,500 per year. The allocated fixed costs are unavoidable whether the company makes or buys this component. The company is considering buying this component from a supplier for $3.50 per unit. Should it continue to manufacture the component, or should it buy this component from the outside supplier?

Exercise 23-3
Sell or process further
P2

Cobe Company has already manufactured 28,000 units of Product A at a cost of $28 per unit. The 28,000 units can be sold at this stage for $700,000. Alternatively, the units can be processed further at a $420,000 total additional cost and be converted into 5,600 units of Product B and 11,200 units of Product C. Per unit selling price for Product B is $105 and for Product C is $70. Should the 28,000 units of Product A be processed further or not?

A company must decide between scrapping or reworking units that do not pass inspection. The company has 22,000 defective units that cost $6 per unit to manufacture. The units can be sold as is for $2.00 each, or they can be reworked for $4.50 each and then sold for the full price of $8.50 each. If the units are sold as is, the company will be able to build 22,000 replacement units at a cost of $6 each and sell them at the full price of $8.50 each. (1) What is the incremental income from selling the units as scrap? (2) What is the incremental income from reworking and selling the units? (3) Should the company sell the units as scrap or rework them?

Exercise 23-4
Scrap or rework
P2

Varto Company has 7,000 units of its sole product in inventory that it produced last year at a cost of $22 each. This year's model is superior to last year's, and the 7,000 units cannot be sold at last year's regular selling price of $35 each. Varto has two alternatives for these items: (1) They can be sold to a wholesaler for $8 each or (2) they can be processed further at a cost of $125,000 and then sold for $25 each. Should Varto sell the products as is or process further and then sell them?

Exercise 23-5
Sell or process further
P2

Colt Company owns a machine that can produce two specialized products. Production time for Product TLX is two units per hour and for Product MTV is five units per hour. The machine's capacity is 2,750 hours per year. Both products are sold to a single customer who has agreed to buy all of the company's output up to a maximum of 4,700 units of Product TLX and 2,500 units of Product MTV. Selling prices and variable costs per unit to produce the products follow. Determine (1) the company's most profitable sales mix and (2) the contribution margin that results from that sales mix.

Exercise 23-6
Sales mix determination and analysis
P3

$ per unit	Product TLX	Product MTV
Selling price per unit	$15.00	$9.50
Variable costs per unit	4.80	5.50

Check (2) $55,940

Childress Company produces three products, K1, S5, and G9. Each product uses the same type of direct material. K1 uses 4 pounds of the material, S5 uses 3 pounds of the material, and G9 uses 6 pounds of the material. Demand for all products is strong, but only 50,000 pounds of material are available. Information about the selling price per unit and variable cost per unit of each product follows. Orders for which product should be produced and filled first, then second, and then third?

Exercise 23-7
Sales mix
P3

$ per unit	K1	S5	G9
Selling price	$160	$112	$210
Variable costs	96	85	144

Check K1 contribution margin per pound, $16

Marinette Company makes several products, including canoes. The company has been experiencing losses from its canoe segment and is considering dropping that product line. The following information is available regarding its canoe segment. Should management discontinue the manufacturing of canoes?

Exercise 23-8
Income analysis of eliminating departments
P4

Income Statement—Canoe Segment		
Sales		$2,000,000
Variable costs		
Direct materials	$450,000	
Direct labor....................................	500,000	
Variable overhead	300,000	
Variable selling and administrative..................	200,000	
Total variable costs............................		1,450,000
Contribution margin		550,000
Fixed costs		
Direct	375,000	
Indirect	300,000	
Total fixed costs		675,000
Net income		$ (125,000)

Check Income impact if canoe segment dropped, $(175,000)

Exercise 23-9
Analyzing income effects
from eliminating
departments

P4

Suresh Co. expects its five departments to yield the following income for next year.

	Dept. M	Dept. N	Dept. O	Dept. P	Dept. T	Total
Sales	$63,000	$35,000	$56,000	$42,000	$28,000	$224,000
Expenses						
Avoidable	9,800	36,400	22,400	14,000	37,800	120,400
Unavoidable	51,800	12,600	4,200	29,400	9,800	107,800
Total expenses	61,600	49,000	26,600	43,400	47,600	228,200
Net income (loss)	$ 1,400	$(14,000)	$29,400	$ (1,400)	$(19,600)	$ (4,200)

Recompute and prepare the departmental income statements (including a combined total column) for the company under each of the following separate scenarios: Management (1) eliminates departments with expected net losses and (2) eliminates departments with sales dollars that are less than avoidable expenses.

Exercise 23-10
Keep or replace

P5

Xinhong Company is considering replacing one of its manufacturing machines. The machine has a book value of $45,000 and a remaining useful life of five years, at which time its salvage value will be zero. It has a current market value of $52,000. Variable manufacturing costs are $36,000 per year for this machine. Information on two alternative replacement machines follows. Should Xinhong keep or replace its manufacturing machine? If the machine should be replaced, which alternative new machine should Xinhong purchase?

	Alternative A	Alternative B
Cost.....................................	$115,000	$125,000
Variable manufacturing costs per year	19,000	15,000

Exercise 23-11
Product pricing using
total costs

P6

Steeze Co. makes snowboards and uses the total cost approach in setting product prices. Its costs for producing 10,000 units follow. The company targets a profit of $300,000 on this product.

Variable Costs per Unit		Fixed Costs (in total)	
Direct materials...........................	$100	Overhead.............................	$470,000
Direct labor	25	Selling	105,000
Overhead...............................	20	Administrative	325,000
Selling	5		

1. Compute the total cost per unit.
2. Compute the markup percentage on total cost.
3. Compute the product's selling price using the total cost method.

Exercise 23-12
Product pricing using
variable costs

P6

Rios Co. makes drones and uses the variable cost approach in setting product prices. Its costs for producing 20,000 units follow. The company targets a profit of $300,000 on this product.

Variable Costs per Unit		Fixed Costs (in total)	
Direct materials...........................	$70	Overhead.............................	$670,000
Direct labor	40	Selling	305,000
Overhead...............................	25	Administrative	285,000
Selling	15		

1. Compute the variable cost per unit.
2. Compute the markup percentage on variable cost.
3. Compute the product's selling price using the variable cost method.

Farrow Co. expects to sell 150,000 units of its product in the next period with the following results.

Exercise 23-13
Special offer

P7

Sales (150,000 units)	$2,250,000
Costs and expenses	
Direct materials	300,000
Direct labor	600,000
Overhead	150,000
Selling expenses	225,000
Administrative expenses	385,500
Total costs and expenses	1,660,500
Net income	$ 589,500

The company has an opportunity to sell 15,000 additional units at $12 per unit. The additional sales would not affect its current expected sales. Direct materials and labor costs per unit would be the same for the additional units as they are for the regular units. However, the additional volume would create the following incremental costs: (1) total overhead would increase by 15% and (2) administrative expenses would increase by $64,500. Prepare an analysis to determine whether the company should accept or reject the offer to sell additional units at the reduced price of $12 per unit.

Check   Income increase, $3,000

Goshford Company produces a single product and has capacity to produce 100,000 units per month. Costs to produce its current sales of 80,000 units follow. The regular selling price of the product is $100 per unit. Management is approached by a new customer who wants to purchase 20,000 units of the product for $75 per unit. If the order is accepted, there will be no additional fixed manufacturing overhead and no additional fixed selling and administrative expenses. The customer is not in the company's regular selling territory, so there will be a $5 per unit shipping expense in addition to the regular variable selling and administrative expenses. Determine whether management should accept or reject the new business.

Exercise 23-14
Special offer

P7

	Per Unit	Costs at 80,000 Units
Direct materials	$12.50	$1,000,000
Direct labor	15.00	1,200,000
Variable manufacturing overhead	10.00	800,000
Fixed manufacturing overhead	17.50	1,400,000
Variable selling and administrative expenses	14.00	1,120,000
Fixed selling and administrative expenses	13.00	1,040,000
Totals	$82.00	$6,560,000

HH Auto Repair reports the following information for the coming year.

Exercise 23-15
Time and materials pricing

A1

Direct labor rate, including fringe benefits	$36 per DLH
Annual direct labor hours	10,000 hours
Annual direct materials (parts) purchases	$2,000,000
Annual overhead costs:	
Materials purchasing, handling, and storage	$360,000
Non-materials related overhead (depreciation, insurance, taxes, rent)	$170,000
Target profit margin (on both labor and materials)	32%

1. Compute the rate per hour of direct labor (in $).
2. Compute the materials markup (in %).
3. What price should the company quote for a job requiring four direct labor hours and $580 in parts?

≡ connect·

Jones Products manufactures and sells to wholesalers approximately 400,000 packages per year of underwater markers at $6 per package. Annual costs for the production and sale of this quantity are shown in the table.

Direct materials.	$ 576,000
Direct labor	144,000
Overhead	320,000
Selling expenses.	150,000
Administrative expenses	100,000
Total costs and expenses	$1,290,000

A new wholesaler has offered to buy 50,000 packages for $5.20 each. These markers would be marketed under the wholesaler's name and would not affect Jones Products's sales through its normal channels. A study of the costs of this additional business reveals the following:

- Direct materials costs are 100% variable.
- Per unit direct labor costs for the additional units would be 50% higher than normal because their production would require overtime pay at 1½ times the usual labor rate.
- Twenty-five percent of normal annual overhead costs are fixed at any production level from 350,000 to 500,000 units. The remaining 75% of annual overhead costs are variable with volume.
- Accepting the new business would involve no additional selling expenses.
- Accepting the new business would increase administrative expenses by a $5,000 fixed amount.

Required

Prepare a three-column comparative income statement that shows the following:

Check   Operating income:

(1) $1,110,000

(2) $126,000

1. Annual operating income without the special order (column 1).
2. Annual operating income received from the new business only (column 2).
3. Combined annual operating income from normal business and the new business (column 3).

Problem 23-2A
Analyzing income effects
of additional business

P7

Calla Company produces skateboards that sell for $50 per unit. The company currently has the capacity to produce 90,000 skateboards per year but is selling 80,000 skateboards per year. Annual costs for 80,000 skateboards follow.

Direct materials.	$ 800,000
Direct labor	640,000
Overhead	960,000
Selling expenses.	560,000
Administrative expenses	480,000
Total costs and expenses	$3,440,000

A new retail store has offered to buy 10,000 of its skateboards for $45 per unit. The store is in a different market from Calla's regular customers and would not affect regular sales. A study of its costs in anticipation of this additional business reveals the following:

- Direct materials and direct labor are 100% variable.
- Thirty percent of overhead is fixed at any production level from 80,000 units to 90,000 units; the remaining 70% of annual overhead costs are variable with respect to volume.
- Selling expenses are 60% variable with respect to number of units sold, and the other 40% of selling expenses are fixed.
- There will be an additional $2 per unit selling expense for this order.
- Administrative expenses would increase by a $1,000 fixed amount.

Required

1. Prepare a three-column comparative income statement that reports the following:
   a. Annual income without the special order.
   b. Annual income from the special order.
   c. Combined annual income from normal business and the new business.
2. Should Calla accept this order?

Check   (1*b*) Added income from order, $123,000

Haver Company currently produces component RX5 for one of its products. The current cost per unit to manufacture the required 50,000 units of RX5 follows.

Problem 23-3A
Make or buy

P1

Direct materials.	$ 5.00
Direct labor	8.00
Overhead	9.00
Total cost per unit	$22.00

Direct materials and direct labor are 100% variable. Overhead is 80% fixed. An outside supplier has offered to supply the 50,000 units of RX5 for $18.00 per unit.

Required

1. Determine the total incremental cost of making 50,000 units of RX5.
2. Determine the total incremental cost of buying 50,000 units of RX5.
3. Should the company make or buy RX5?

Check   (1) Incremental cost to make RX5, $740,000

Harold Manufacturing produces denim clothing. This year, it produced 5,000 denim jackets at a manufacturing cost of $45 each. These jackets were damaged in the warehouse during storage. Management investigated the matter and identified three alternatives for these jackets.

1. Jackets can be sold as is to a secondhand clothing shop for $6 each.
2. Jackets can be disassembled at a cost of $32,000 and sold to a recycler for $12 each.
3. Jackets can be reworked and turned into good jackets. However, with the damage, management estimates it will be able to assemble the good parts of the 5,000 jackets into only 3,000 jackets. The remaining pieces of fabric will be discarded. The cost of reworking the jackets will be $102,000, but the jackets can then be sold for their regular price of $45 each.

Problem 23-4A
Sell or process

P2

Required

Which alternative should Harold choose? Show analysis for each alternative.

Check   Incremental income for alternative 2, $28,000

Edgerron Company is able to produce two products, G and B, with the same machine in its factory. The following information is available.

Problem 23-5A
Analyzing sales mix strategies

P3

	Product G	Product B
Selling price per unit.	$120	$160
Variable costs per unit	40	90
Contribution margin per unit	$ 80	$ 70
Machine hours to produce 1 unit.	0.4 hour	1.0 hours
Maximum unit sales per month	600 units	200 units

The company presently operates the machine for a single eight-hour shift for 22 working days each month. Management is thinking about operating the machine for two shifts, which will increase its productivity by another eight hours per day for 22 days per month. This change would require $15,000 additional fixed costs per month.

Required

1. Determine the contribution margin per machine hour that each product generates.

2. How many units of Product G and Product B should the company produce if it continues to operate with only one shift? How much total contribution margin does this mix produce each month?

3. If the company adds another shift, how many units of Product G and Product B should it produce? How much total incremental income would this mix produce each month? Should the company add the new shift?

4. Suppose the company determines that it can increase Product G's maximum sales to 700 units per month by spending $12,000 per month in marketing efforts. Should the company pursue this strategy and the double shift? Compute total incremental income.

Problem 23-6A
Analyzing possible
elimination of a department

P4

Elegant Decor Company's management is trying to decide whether to eliminate Department 200, which has produced losses or low profits for several years. The company's departmental income statements show the following.

Departmental Income Statements			
For Year Ended December 31, 2019	Dept. 100	Dept. 200	Combined
Sales	$436,000	$290,000	$726,000
Cost of goods sold	262,000	207,000	469,000
Gross profit	174,000	83,000	257,000
Operating expenses			
Direct expenses			
Advertising..............................	17,000	12,000	29,000
Store supplies used......................	4,000	3,800	7,800
Depreciation—Store equipment	5,000	3,300	8,300
Total direct expenses....................	26,000	19,100	45,100
Allocated expenses			
Sales salaries	65,000	39,000	104,000
Rent expense.............................	9,440	4,720	14,160
Bad debts expense	9,900	8,100	18,000
Office salary	18,720	12,480	31,200
Insurance expense	2,000	1,100	3,100
Miscellaneous office expenses	2,400	1,600	4,000
Total allocated expenses.................	107,460	67,000	174,460
Total expenses	133,460	86,100	219,560
Net income (loss)	$ 40,540	$ (3,100)	$ 37,440

In analyzing whether to eliminate Department 200, management considers the following:

a. The company has one office worker who earns $600 per week, or $31,200 per year, and four sales-clerks who each earns $500 per week, or $26,000 per year for each salesclerk.

b. The full salaries of two salesclerks are charged to Department 100. The full salary of one salesclerk is charged to Department 200. The salary of the fourth clerk, who works half-time in both departments, is divided evenly between the two departments.

c. Eliminating Department 200 would avoid the sales salaries and the office salary currently allocated to it. However, management prefers another plan. Two salesclerks have indicated that they will be quit-ting soon. Management believes that their work can be done by the other two clerks if the one office worker works in sales half-time. Eliminating Department 200 will allow this shift of duties. If this change is implemented, half the office worker's salary would be reported as sales salaries and half would be reported as office salary.

d. The store building is rented under a long-term lease that cannot be changed. Therefore, Department 100 will use the space and equipment currently used by Department 200.

e. Closing Department 200 will eliminate its expenses for advertising, bad debts, and store supplies; 70% of the insurance expense allocated to it to cover its merchandise inventory; and 25% of the miscellaneous office expenses presently allocated to it.

Required

1. Prepare a three-column report that lists items and amounts for (*a*) the company's total expenses (including cost of goods sold)—in column 1, (*b*) the expenses that would be eliminated by closing Department 200—in column 2, and (*c*) the expenses that will continue—in column 3.

2. Prepare a forecasted annual income statement for the company reflecting the elimination of Department 200 assuming that it will not affect Department 100's sales and gross profit. The statement should reflect the reassignment of the office worker to one-half time as a salesclerk.

3. Should Department 200 be eliminated?

Check (1) Total expenses: (*a*) $688,560, (*b*) $284,070

(2) Forecasted net income without Department 200, $31,510

Windmire Company manufactures and sells to local wholesalers approximately 300,000 units per month at a sales price of $4 per unit. Monthly costs for the production and sale of this quantity follow.

PROBLEM SET B

Problem 23-1B
Analyzing income effects of additional business

P7

Direct materials.	$384,000
Direct labor	96,000
Overhead	288,000
Selling expenses.	120,000
Administrative expenses	80,000
Total costs and expenses.	$968,000

A new out-of-state distributor has offered to buy 50,000 units next month for $3.44 each. These units would be marketed in other states and would not affect Windmire's sales through its normal channels. A study of the costs of this new business reveals the following:

- Direct materials costs are 100% variable.
- Per unit direct labor costs for the additional units would be 50% higher than normal because their production would require overtime pay at 1½ times their normal rate to meet the distributor's deadline.
- Twenty-five percent of normal annual overhead costs are fixed at any production level from 250,000 to 400,000 units. The remaining 75% of annual overhead costs are variable with volume.
- Accepting the new business would involve no additional selling expenses.
- Accepting the new business would increase administrative expenses by a $4,000 fixed amount.

Required

Prepare a three-column comparative income statement that shows the following:

1. Monthly operating income without the special order (column 1).
2. Monthly operating income received from the new business only (column 2).
3. Combined monthly operating income from normal business and the new business (column 3).

Check Operating income: (1) $232,000, (2) $44,000

Mervin Company produces circuit boards that sell for $8 per unit. It currently has capacity to produce 600,000 circuit boards per year but is selling 550,000 boards per year. Annual costs for the 550,000 circuit boards follow.

Problem 23-2B
Analyzing income effects of additional business

P7

Direct materials.	$ 825,000
Direct labor	1,100,000
Overhead	1,375,000
Selling expenses.	275,000
Administrative expenses	550,000
Total costs and expenses.	$4,125,000

An overseas customer has offered to buy 50,000 circuit boards for $6 per unit. The customer is in a different market from Mervin's regular customers and would not affect regular sales. A study of its costs in anticipation of this additional business reveals the following:

- Direct materials and direct labor are 100% variable.
- Twenty percent of overhead is fixed at any production level from 550,000 units to 600,000 units; the remaining 80% of annual overhead costs are variable with respect to volume.
- Selling expenses are 40% variable with respect to number of units sold, and the other 60% of selling expenses are fixed.
- There will be an additional $0.20 per unit selling expense for this order.
- Administrative expenses would increase by a $700 fixed amount.

Required

1. Prepare a three-column comparative income statement that reports the following:
   a. Annual income without the special order.
   b. Annual income from the special order.
   c. Combined annual income from normal business and the new business.
2. Should management accept the order?

Analysis Component

3. What nonfinancial factors should Mervin consider? Explain.
4. Assume that the new customer wants to buy 100,000 units instead of 50,000 units—it will only buy 100,000 units or none and will not take a partial order. Without any computations, how does this change your answer in part 2?

Check (1b) Additional income from order, $4,300

Problem 23-3B
Make or buy
P1

Alto Company currently produces component TH1 for one of its products. The current cost per unit to manufacture its required 400,000 units of TH1 follows.

Direct materials	$1.20
Direct labor	1.50
Overhead	6.00
Total cost per unit	$8.70

Direct materials and direct labor are 100% variable. Overhead is 75% fixed. An outside supplier has offered to supply the 400,000 units of TH1 for $4 per unit.

Required

1. Determine whether management should make or buy the TH1.

Check (1) Incremental cost to make TH1, $1,680,000

Analysis Component

2. What factors besides cost must management consider when deciding whether to make or buy TH1?

Problem 23-4B
Sell or process
P2

Micron Manufacturing produces electronic equipment. This year, it produced 7,500 oscilloscopes at a manufacturing cost of $300 each. These oscilloscopes were damaged in the warehouse during storage and, while usable, cannot be sold at their regular selling price of $500 each. Management has investigated the matter and has identified three alternatives for these oscilloscopes.

1. They can be sold as is to a wholesaler for $75 each.
2. They can be disassembled at a cost of $400,000 and the parts sold to a recycler for $130 each.
3. They can be reworked and turned into good units. The cost of reworking the units will be $3,200,000, after which the units can be sold at their regular price of $500 each.

Required

Check Incremental income for alternative 2, $575,000

Which alternative should management pursue? Show analysis for each alternative.

Sung Company is able to produce two products, R and T, with the same machine in its factory. The following information is available.

Problem 23-5B
Analyzing sales mix strategies

P3

	Product R	Product T
Selling price per unit	$60	$80
Variable costs per unit	20	45
Contribution margin per unit	$40	$35
Machine hours to produce 1 unit........................	0.4 hour	1.0 hours
Maximum unit sales per month	550 units	175 units

The company presently operates the machine for a single eight-hour shift for 22 working days each month. Management is thinking about operating the machine for two shifts, which will increase its productivity by another eight hours per day for 22 days per month. This change would require $3,250 additional fixed costs per month.

Required

1. Determine the contribution margin per machine hour that each product generates.
2. How many units of Product R and Product T should the company produce if it continues to operate with only one shift? How much total contribution margin does this mix produce each month?
3. If the company adds another shift, how many units of Product R and Product T should it produce? How much total incremental income would this mix produce each month? Should the company add the new shift?
4. Suppose the company determines that it can increase Product R's maximum sales to 675 units per month by spending $4,500 per month in marketing efforts. Should the company pursue this strategy and the double shift? Compute incremental income.

Check Units of Product R:
(2) 440
(3) 550

Esme Company's management is trying to decide whether to eliminate Department Z, which has produced low profits or losses for several years. The company's departmental income statements show the following.

Problem 23-6B
Analyzing possible elimination of a department

P4

Departmental Income Statements			
For Year Ended December 31, 2019	Dept. A	Dept. Z	Combined
Sales	$700,000	$175,000	$875,000
Cost of goods sold	461,300	125,100	586,400
Gross profit.................................	238,700	49,900	288,600
Operating expenses			
Direct expenses			
Advertising..............................	27,000	3,000	30,000
Store supplies used......................	5,600	1,400	7,000
Depreciation—Store equipment	14,000	7,000	21,000
Total direct expenses	46,600	11,400	58,000
Allocated expenses			
Sales salaries	70,200	23,400	93,600
Rent expense...........................	22,080	5,520	27,600
Bad debts expense	21,000	4,000	25,000
Office salary	20,800	5,200	26,000
Insurance expense	4,200	1,400	5,600
Miscellaneous office expenses	1,700	2,500	4,200
Total allocated expenses...................	139,980	42,020	182,000
Total expenses	186,580	53,420	240,000
Net income (loss)	$ 52,120	$ (3,520)	$ 48,600

In analyzing whether to eliminate Department Z, management considers the following items:

a. The company has one office worker who earns $500 per week, or $26,000 per year, and four sales-clerks who each earns $450 per week, or $23,400 per year for each salesclerk.

b. The full salaries of three salesclerks are charged to Department A. The full salary of one salesclerk is charged to Department Z.

c. Eliminating Department Z would avoid the sales salaries and the office salary currently allocated to it. However, management prefers another plan. Two salesclerks have indicated that they will be quitting soon. Management believes that their work can be done by the two remaining clerks if the one office worker works in sales half-time. Eliminating Department Z will allow this shift of duties. If this change is implemented, half the office worker's salary would be reported as sales salaries and half would be reported as office salary.

d. The store building is rented under a long-term lease that cannot be changed. Therefore, Department A will use the space and equipment currently used by Department Z.

e. Closing Department Z will eliminate its expenses for advertising, bad debts, and store supplies; 65% of the insurance expense allocated to it to cover its merchandise inventory; and 30% of the miscellaneous office expenses presently allocated to it.

Required

Check   (1) Total expenses:
(*a*) $826,400, (*b*) $181,960

(2) Forecasted net income
without Department Z,
$55,560

1. Prepare a three-column report that lists items and amounts for (*a*) the company's total expenses (including cost of goods sold)—in column 1, (*b*) the expenses that would be eliminated by closing Department Z—in column 2, and (*c*) the expenses that will continue—in column 3.

2. Prepare a forecasted annual income statement for the company reflecting the elimination of Department Z assuming that it will not affect Department A's sales and gross profit. The statement should reflect the reassignment of the office worker to one-half time as a salesclerk.

Analysis Component

3. Reconcile the company's combined net income with the forecasted net income assuming that Department Z is eliminated (list both items and amounts). Analyze the reconciliation and explain why you think the department should or should not be eliminated.

SERIAL PROBLEM
Business Solutions

P3

©Alexander Image/Shutterstock

This serial problem began in Chapter 1 and continues through most of the book. If previous chapter segments were not completed, the serial problem can begin at this point.

SP 23 Santana Rey has found that **Business Solutions**'s line of computer desks and chairs has become popular, and she is finding it hard to keep up with demand. She knows that she cannot fill all of her orders for both items, so she decides she must determine the optimal sales mix given the resources she has available. Information about the desks and chairs follows.

	Desks	Chairs
Selling price per unit..........................	$1,125	$375
Variable costs per unit	500	200
Contribution margin per unit	$ 625	$175
Direct labor hours per unit	5 hours	4 hours
Expected demand for next quarter	175 desks	50 chairs

Santana has determined that she only has 1,015 direct labor hours available for the next quarter and wants to optimize her contribution margin given the limited number of direct labor hours available.

Required

Determine the optimal sales mix and the contribution margin the business will earn at that sales mix.

Accounting Analysis

AA 23-1 Assume **Apple** is designing a new smartphone. Each unit of this new phone is expected to require $230 of direct materials, $10 of direct labor, $20 of variable overhead, and $20 of variable selling and administrative costs.

COMPANY ANALYSIS

P6

APPLE

Required

1. If Apple uses the variable cost method to set selling prices and plans a markup of 200% of variable costs, what is the expected selling price per unit of this new phone?

2. Assume that Apple is a "price-taker" and the market sales price for this type of phone is $800 per unit. Compute Apple's target cost if the company desires a profit of 60% of sales price.

AA 23-2 **Apple** and **Google** sell a variety of products. Some products are more profitable than others. Teams of employees in each company make advertising, investment, and product mix decisions. Assume a typical ad costs $800,000 and that the average product for both Apple and Google sells for $400 per unit and generates a contribution margin of 20%.

COMPARATIVE ANALYSIS

P6

APPLE

GOOGLE

Required

1. Estimate how many additional products this ad must sell to justify its cost.

2. If instead Google targets its advertising toward products with contribution margins of 25% or higher, and all other information is unchanged, estimate how many additional products this ad must sell to justify its cost.

AA 23-3 Assume **Samsung** is designing a new smartphone. Each unit of this new phone is expected to require $285 of direct materials, $10 of direct labor, $30 of variable overhead, $5 of variable selling and administrative costs, and $20 of fixed selling and administrative costs.

GLOBAL ANALYSIS

P6

Samsung

Required

1. If Samsung uses the variable cost method to set selling prices and plans a markup of 250% of variable costs, what is the expected selling price per unit of this new phone?

2. If instead Samsung uses the total cost method to set selling prices and plans a markup of 220% of total costs, what is the expected selling price per unit of this new phone?

Beyond the Numbers

BTN 23-1 Bert Asiago, a salesperson for Convertco, received an order from a potential new customer for 50,000 units of Convertco's single product at a price $25 below its regular selling price of $65. Asiago knows that Convertco has the capacity to produce this order without affecting regular sales. He has spoken to Convertco's controller, Bia Morgan, who has informed Asiago that at the $40 selling price, Convertco will not be covering its variable costs of $42 for the product, and she recommends the order not be accepted. Asiago knows that variable costs include his sales commission of $4 per unit. If he accepts a $2 per unit commission, the sale will produce a contribution margin of zero. Asiago is eager to get the new customer because he believes that this could lead to the new customer becoming a regular customer.

ETHICS CHALLENGE

P7

Required

1. Determine the contribution margin per unit on the order as determined by the controller.

2. Determine the contribution margin per unit on the order as determined by Asiago if he takes the lower commission.

3. Do you recommend Convertco accept the special order? What factors must management consider?

COMMUNICATING IN PRACTICE

C1

BTN 23-2 Assume that you work for Greeble's Sporting Goods, and your manager requests that you outline the pros and cons of discontinuing its Golf department. That department appears to be generating losses, and your manager believes that discontinuing it will increase overall store profits.

Required

Prepare a memorandum to your manager outlining what management should consider when trying to decide whether to discontinue its Golf department.

TAKING IT TO THE NET

P1

BTN 23-3 Many companies must determine whether to internally produce their component parts or to outsource them. Further, some companies now outsource key components or business processes to international providers. Access the website **SourcingMag.com** and review the available information on business process outsourcing (search for "What is Business Process Outsourcing?").

Required

1. According to this website, what is business process outsourcing?
2. What types of processes are commonly outsourced, according to this website?

TEAMWORK IN ACTION

C1

BTN 23-4 Break into teams and identify costs that an airline such as **Delta Air Lines** would incur on a flight from Green Bay to Minneapolis. (1) Identify the individual costs as variable or fixed. (2) Assume that Delta is trying to decide whether to drop this flight because it seems to be unprofitable. Determine which costs are likely to be saved if the flight is dropped. Set up your answer in the following format.

Cost	Variable or Fixed	Cost Saved If Flight Is Dropped	Rationale

ENTREPRENEURIAL DECISION

P3

BTN 23-5 Suppose Gaurab Chakrabarti and Sean Hunt's company, **Solugen**, makes peroxide-based cleaners in different strengths. The founders must decide on the best sales mix. Assume the company has a capacity of 400 hours of processing time available each month and it makes two types of cleaners, Deluxe and Premium. Information on these products follows.

	Deluxe	Premium
Selling price per unit......................	$70	$90
Variable costs per unit	$40	$50
Processing time per unit	1 hour	2 hours

Required

1. Assume the markets for both types of cleaners are unlimited. How many Deluxe cleaners and how many Premium cleaners should the company make each month? Explain. How much total contribution margin does this mix produce each month?

2. Assume the market for the Deluxe model is limited to 60 per month, with no market limit for the Premium model. How many Deluxe cleaners and how many Premium cleaners should the company make each month? Explain. How much total contribution margin does this mix produce each month?

BTN 23-6 Restaurants often add and remove menu items. Visit a restaurant and identify a new food item. Make a list of costs that the restaurant must consider when deciding whether to add that new item. Also, make a list of nonfinancial factors that the restaurant must consider when adding that item.

HITTING THE ROAD

C1

24 Capital Budgeting and Investment Analysis

Learning Objectives

ANALYTICAL

A1 Analyze a capital investment project using break-even time.

PROCEDURAL

P1 Compute payback period and describe its use.

P2 Compute accounting rate of return and explain its use.

P3 Compute net present value and describe its use.

P4 Compute internal rate of return and explain its use.

Hi, Robot!

©Fellow Robots

"How may I help you?"—**ROBOT**

BURLINGAME, CA—Many companies use robots in their operations. Manufacturers have robots perform repetitive tasks that can cause injuries if done by human workers. This allows humans to focus on more value-added work. **Fellow Robots** (**fellowrobots.com**) extends this concept to retailers. The company manufactures robots that perform inventory tasks for retailers—locating inventory, notifying management of out of stocks, checking prices, and ensuring products are in the proper locations on the shelves.

As CEO Marco Mascorro notes, these "social" robots can also guide customers to products in the store and recommend items based on what the customer is shopping for. "These robots don't just do things for us," says Marco, "they do things with us." The company's robots use artificial intelligence (AI) to "continually learn from [their] interactions with humans," says Marco, and retail employees use data analytics techniques to better manage the customer experience.

Businesses considering robots must consider whether the future benefits—increased revenues, lower costs, and increased customer satisfaction—outweigh the costs of purchasing robots and training workers. The methods shown in this chapter, such as payback period, net present value analysis, and internal rates of return, can be used to make good investment decisions.

Sources: *Fellow Robots website*, January 2019; *CNBC.com*, March 26, 2015; *CNBC.com*, August 30, 2016; *Robophil.com*, April 25, 2016

CAPITAL BUDGETING

Capital budgeting is the process of analyzing alternative long-term investments and deciding which assets to acquire or sell. Common examples of capital budgeting decisions include buying a machine or a building or acquiring an entire company. An objective for these decisions is to earn a satisfactory return on investment.

Capital Budgeting Process

Exhibit 24.1 summarizes the capital budgeting process.

EXHIBIT 24.1

Capital Budgeting Process

The process begins when department or plant managers submit proposals for new investments in property, plant, and equipment. A capital budget committee, usually consisting of members with accounting and finance expertise, evaluates the proposals and forms recommendations for approval or rejection. Finally, the board of directors approves the capital expenditures for the year.

Capital budgeting decisions require careful analysis because they are usually the most difficult and risky decisions that managers make. These decisions are difficult because they require predicting events that will not occur until well into the future. A capital budgeting decision is risky because

- The outcome is uncertain.
- Large amounts of money are usually involved.
- The investment involves a long-term commitment.
- The decision could be difficult or impossible to reverse, no matter how poor it turns out to be.

Risk is especially high for investments in technology due to innovations and uncertainty.

Capital Investment Cash Flows

Managers use several methods to evaluate capital budgeting decisions. Nearly all of these methods involve predicting future cash inflows and cash outflows of proposed investments, assessing the risk of and returns on those cash flows, and then choosing which investments to make. Exhibit 24.2 summarizes cash outflows (−) and cash inflows (+) over the life of a typical capital expenditure for a depreciable asset.

EXHIBIT 24.2

Capital Investment
Cash Flows

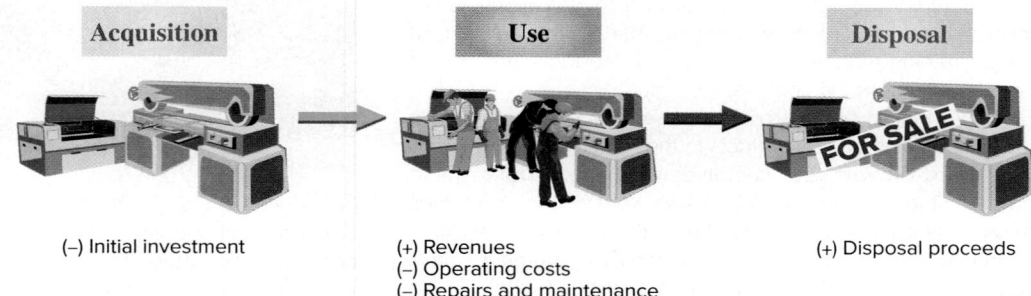

Acquisition	Use	Disposal
(−) Initial investment	(+) Revenues (−) Operating costs (−) Repairs and maintenance	(+) Disposal proceeds

The investment begins with an initial cash outflow to acquire the asset. Over the asset's life it generates cash inflows from revenues. The asset also creates cash outflows for operating costs, repairs, and maintenance. Finally, the asset is disposed of, and its salvage value can provide another cash inflow.

Management often restates future cash flows in terms of their present value. This approach applies the time value of money: *A dollar today is worth more than a dollar tomorrow.* Similarly, a dollar tomorrow is worth less than a dollar today. Restating future cash flows in terms of their present value is called *discounting.* The time value of money is important when evaluating capital investments, but managers sometimes use methods that ignore it.

METHODS NOT USING TIME VALUE OF MONEY

All investments, whether they involve the purchase of a machine or another long-term asset, are expected to produce net cash flows. *Net cash flow* is cash inflows minus cash outflows. Sometimes managers perform simple analyses of the financial feasibility of an investment's net cash flow without using the time value of money. This section explains two common methods in this category: (1) payback period and (2) accounting rate of return.

Payback Period

An investment's **payback period (PBP)** is the expected amount of time to recover the initial investment amount. Managers prefer investing in assets with shorter payback periods to reduce the risk of an unprofitable investment over the long run. Acquiring assets with short payback periods reduces a company's risk from potentially inaccurate long-term predictions of future cash flows.

P1

Compute payback period and describe its use.

Payback Period with Even Cash Flows

To illustrate payback period for an investment with even cash flows, we look at data from FasTrac, a manufacturer of exercise equipment and supplies. (*Even cash flows* are cash flows that are the same amount each year; *uneven cash flows* are cash flows that are not all equal in amount.) FasTrac is considering several different capital investments, one of which is to purchase a machine to use in manufacturing a new product. The machine has the following features.

Cost of machine	$16,000	Expected sales per year	1,000 units
Useful life	8 years	Product selling price per unit	$30
Salvage value	$0		

EXHIBIT 24.3

Cash Flow Analysis

Cash Flow Analysis—Machinery Investment	Expected Net Income	Expected Net Cash Flow
Annual sales of new product (1,000 × $30)	$30,000	$30,000
Less annual expenses		
Materials, labor, and overhead (except depreciation)	15,500	15,500
Depreciation—Machinery	2,000	
Additional selling and administrative expenses	9,500	9,500
Annual pretax income.	3,000	
Less income taxes (30% of pretax income)	900	900
Annual net income	$ 2,100	
Annual net cash flow		$ 4,100

Exhibit 24.3 shows the expected annual net income and expected annual net cash flow for this asset over its expected useful life.

The amount of net cash flow from the machinery is computed by subtracting expected cash outflows from expected cash inflows. The Expected Net Cash Flow column of Exhibit 24.3 excludes all noncash revenues and expenses. Because depreciation does not impact cash flows, it is excluded. Alternatively, managers can adjust the projected net income for revenue and expense items that do not affect cash flows. For FasTrac, this means taking the $2,100 net income and adding back the $2,000 depreciation, to yield $4,100 of net cash flow.

Point: The payback method uses cash flows, not net income.

The formula for computing the payback period of an investment that produces even net cash flows is in Exhibit 24.4.

EXHIBIT 24.4

Payback Period Formula with Even Cash Flows

$$\text{Payback period} = \frac{\text{Cost of investment}}{\text{Annual net cash flow}}$$

The payback period reflects the amount of time for the investment to generate enough net cash flow to return (or pay back) the cash initially invested to purchase it. FasTrac's payback period for this machine is just under four years.

$$\text{Payback period} = \frac{\$16,000}{\$4,100} = 3.9 \text{ years } \text{(rounded)}$$

The initial investment is fully recovered in 3.9 years, or just before reaching the halfway point of this machine's useful life of eight years.

Companies prefer short payback periods to increase return and reduce risk. The more quickly a company receives cash, the sooner it is available for other uses and the less time it is at risk of loss. A shorter payback period also improves the company's ability to respond to unanticipated changes and lowers its risk of having to keep an unprofitable investment.

Point: Excel for payback.

	A	B
1	Investment	$16,000
2	Cash flow	$4,100
3	Payback period	

=B1/B2 = 3.9

Decision Insight

e-Payback   Health care providers use electronic systems to improve their operations. With *e-charting*, doctors' orders and notes are saved electronically. Such systems allow for more personalized care plans, more efficient staffing, and reduced costs. Investments in such systems are evaluated on the basis of payback periods and other financial measures. ■

©JGI/Tom Grill/Blend Images LLC

Payback Period with Uneven Cash Flows   What happens if the net cash flows are uneven? In this case, the payback period is computed using the *cumulative total of net cash flows*. The word *cumulative* refers to the addition of each period's net cash flows as we progress through time. To illustrate, consider data for another investment that FasTrac is considering. This machine is predicted to generate uneven net cash flows over the next eight years. The relevant data and payback period computation are shown in Exhibit 24.5.

EXHIBIT 24.5

Payback Period Calculation with Uneven Cash Flows

Period*	Expected Net Cash Flows	Cumulative Net Cash Flows
Year 0	$(16,000)	$(16,000)
Year 1	3,000	(13,000)
Year 2	4,000	(9,000)
Year 3	4,000	(5,000)
Year 4	4,000	**(1,000)** ⎫
Year 5	**5,000**	**4,000** ⎬
Year 6	3,000	7,000 ⎭
Year 7	2,000	9,000
Year 8	2,000	11,000
Payback period = 4 years + $1,000/$5,000 of Year 5 = 4.2 years		

Payback occurs between Years 4 and 5.

Example: Find the payback period in Exhibit 24.5 if net cash flows for the first 4 years are:
Year 1 = $6,000; Year 2 = $5,000; Year 3 = $4,000; Year 4 = $3,000.
Answer: 3.33 years

*All cash inflows and outflows occur uniformly within each year 1 through 8.

Year 0 refers to the date of initial investment at which the $16,000 cash outflow occurs to acquire the machinery. By the end of Year 1, the cumulative net cash flow is $(13,000), computed as the $(16,000) initial cash outflow plus Year 1's $3,000 cash inflow. This process continues throughout the asset's life. The cumulative net cash flow amount changes from negative to positive in Year 5. Specifically, at the end of Year 4, the cumulative net cash flow is $(1,000). As soon as FasTrac receives net cash inflow of $1,000 during the fifth year, it has fully recovered the $16,000 initial investment. If we assume that cash flows are received uniformly *within* each year, receipt of the $1,000 occurs about one-fifth (0.20) of the way through the fifth year. This is computed as $1,000 divided by Year 5's total net cash flow of $5,000, or 0.20. This yields a payback period of 4.2 years, computed as 4 years plus 0.20 of Year 5.

Point: 4.2 years is 4 years + (0.20 × 12 months) = 4 years + 2.4 months.

Evaluating Payback Period   Payback period has two strengths.

● It uses cash flows, not income.
● It is easy to use.

Payback period has three main weaknesses.

● It does not reflect differences in the *timing* of net cash flows within the payback period.
● It ignores *all* cash flows after the point where an investment's costs are fully recovered.
● It ignores the time value of money.

To illustrate, if FasTrac had another investment with predicted cash inflows of $9,000, $3,000, $2,000, $1,800, and $1,000 in its first 5 years, its payback period would also be 4.2 years. However, this alternative is more desirable because it returns cash more quickly. In addition, an investment with a 3-year payback period that stops producing cash after 4 years is likely not as good as an alternative with a 5-year payback period that generates net cash flows for 15 years. Because of these limitations, payback period should never be the only consideration in capital budgeting decisions.

NEED-TO-KNOW 24-1

Payback Period

P1

A company is considering purchasing equipment costing $75,000. Future annual net cash flows from this equipment are $30,000, $25,000, $15,000, $10,000, and $5,000. Cash flows occur uniformly within each year. What is this investment's payback period?

Solution

Period	Expected Net Cash Flows	Cumulative Net Cash Flows
Year 0	$(75,000)	$(75,000)
Year 1	30,000	(45,000)
Year 2	25,000	(20,000)
Year 3	15,000	(5,000) ⎫
Year 4	10,000	5,000 ⎬
Year 5	5,000	10,000 ⎭
Payback period = 3.5 years, computed as 3 + $5,000/$10,000		

Payback occurs between Years 3 and 4.

Do More: QS 24-1, QS 24-5, E 24-1, E 24-3, E 24-5

Accounting Rate of Return

The **accounting rate of return (ARR)** is the percentage accounting return on annual average investment. It is called an "accounting" return because it is based on net income, rather than on cash flows. It is computed by dividing a project's after-tax net income by the average amount invested in it. To illustrate, we return to FasTrac's $16,000 machinery investment described in Exhibit 24.3. We first compute (1) the after-tax net income and (2) the average amount invested. The $2,100 after-tax net income is from Exhibit 24.3.

If a company uses straight-line depreciation, we find the average amount invested by using the formula in Exhibit 24.6. Because FasTrac uses straight-line depreciation, its average amount invested for the eight years equals the sum of the book value at the beginning of the asset's investment period ($16,000) and the book value at the end of its investment period ($0), divided by 2, as shown in Exhibit 24.6.

P2

Compute accounting rate of return and explain its use.

Point: Amount invested includes all costs that must be incurred to get the asset in its location and ready for use.

EXHIBIT 24.6

Computing Average Amount Invested under Straight-Line Depreciation

$$\text{Annual average investment} = \frac{\text{Beginning book value} + \text{Ending book value}}{2}$$
$$\text{(straight-line case only)}$$
$$= \frac{\$16,000 + \$0}{2} = \$8,000$$

If an investment has a salvage value, the average amount invested when using straight-line depreciation is computed as (Beginning book value + Salvage value)/2.

If a company uses a depreciation method other than straight-line, for example, MACRS for tax purposes, the calculation of average book value is more complicated. In this case, the book value of the asset is computed for *each year* of its life. The general formula for the annual average investment is shown in Exhibit 24.7.

EXHIBIT 24.7

General Formula for Average Amount Invested

$$\text{Annual average investment} = \frac{\text{Sum of individual years' average book values}}{\text{Number of years of the planned investment}}$$
$$\text{(general case)}$$

Once we determine the annual after-tax net income and the annual average amount invested, FasTrac's accounting rate of return is computed as shown in Exhibit 24.8.

EXHIBIT 24.8

Accounting Rate of Return Formula

$$\text{Accounting rate of return} = \frac{\text{Annual after-tax net income}}{\text{Annual average investment}}$$
$$= \frac{\$2,100}{\$8,000} = 26.25\%$$

Point: Excel for ARR.

	A	B
1	Beg. book value	$16,000
2	End. book value	$0
3	Net income	$2,100
4	Acctg rate of return	◀

=B3/((B1+B2)/2) = 26.25%

FasTrac management must decide whether a 26.25% accounting rate of return is satisfactory. To make this decision, we must consider the investment's risk. We cannot say an investment with a 26.25% return is preferred over one with a lower return unless we consider any differences in risk. When comparing investments with similar lives and risk, a company will prefer the investment with the higher accounting rate of return.

Evaluating Accounting Rate of Return   The accounting rate of return has three weaknesses.

- It ignores the time value of money.
- It focuses on income, not cash flows.
- If income (and thus the accounting rate of return) varies from year to year, the project might appear desirable in some years and not in others.

Because of these limitations, the accounting rate of return should never be the only consideration in capital budgeting decisions.

NEED-TO-KNOW 24-2

Accounting Rate of Return

P2

Do More: QS 24-6, QS 24-7, E 24-7, E 24-8

The following data relate to a company's decision on whether to purchase a machine. The company uses straight-line depreciation. What is the machine's accounting rate of return?

Cost.	$180,000
Salvage value	15,000
Annual after-tax net income.	40,000

Solution

Annual average investment = ($180,000 + $15,000)/2 = $97,500
Accounting rate of return   = $40,000/$97,500 = 41% (rounded)

METHODS USING TIME VALUE OF MONEY

Methods Using Time Value of Money

P3

Compute net present value and describe its use.

Point: The assumption of end-of-year cash flows simplifies computations and is common in practice.

This section describes two capital budgeting methods that use the time value of money: (1) net present value and (2) internal rate of return. These methods require an understanding of the concept of present value—see Appendix B. This chapter's assignments that use time value of money can be solved using tables in Appendix B, Excel, or a financial calculator.

Net Present Value

Net present value analysis applies the time value of money to future cash inflows and cash outflows so management can evaluate a project's benefits and costs at one point in time. Specifically, **net present value (NPV)** is computed by discounting the future net cash flows from the investment at the project's required rate of return and then subtracting the initial amount invested. A company's required rate of return, often called its **hurdle rate,** is typically its **cost of capital,** which is an average of the rate the company must pay to its lenders and investors.

To illustrate, let's return to FasTrac's proposed machinery purchase described in Exhibit 24.3. Does this machine provide a satisfactory return while recovering the amount invested? Recall that the machine requires a $16,000 investment and is expected to provide $4,100 annual net cash inflows for the next eight years. If we assume that net cash inflows from this machine are received at each year-end and that FasTrac requires a 12% annual return, net present value can be computed as in Exhibit 24.9. (The initial investment occurs at the beginning of Year 0.)

EXHIBIT 24.9

Net Present Value Calculation with Equal Cash Flows

	Net Cash Flows*	Present Value of 1 at 12%†	Present Value of Net Cash Flows
Year 1	$ 4,100	0.8929	$ 3,661
Year 2	4,100	0.7972	3,269
Year 3	4,100	0.7118	2,918
Year 4	4,100	0.6355	2,606
Year 5	4,100	0.5674	2,326
Year 6	4,100	0.5066	2,077
Year 7	4,100	0.4523	1,854
Year 8	4,100	0.4039	1,656
Totals.	$32,800		20,367
Initial investment			(16,000)
Net present value			$ 4,367

Discounted future net cash flows
− Initial investment
= Net present value

Example: What is the net present value in Exhibit 24.9 if a 10% return is applied? *Answer:* $5,873

*Net cash flows occur at the end of each year.
†Present value of 1 factors are taken from Table B.1 in Appendix B.

The first number column of Exhibit 24.9 shows annual net cash flows. Present value of 1 factors, also called *discount factors,* are shown in the second column. Taken from Table B.1 in Appendix B, they assume that net cash flows are received at each year-end. *(To simplify present value computations and for assignment material at the end of this chapter, we assume that net cash flows are received at year-end.)* Annual net cash flows from Exhibit 24.9 are multiplied by the discount factors to give present values of annual net cash flows in the far-right column. These annual amounts are summed to yield total present value of net cash flows of $20,367.

The last three lines of Exhibit 24.9 show the NPV computations. The asset's $16,000 initial cost is deducted from the $20,367 total present value of all future net cash flows to give this asset's NPV of $4,367. This means the present value of this machine's future net cash flows exceeds the initial $16,000 investment by $4,367. FasTrac should invest in this machine. **Rule:** If NPV > 0, invest.

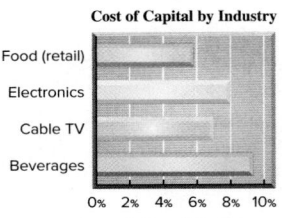

Source: Damodaran, Aswath, "Damodaran Online," http://pages.stern.nyu.edu/~adamodar/

Point: Cost of capital computation is covered in advanced courses.

Net Present Value Decision Rule The decision rule in applying NPV is as follows: When an asset's expected future cash flows yield a *positive* net present value when discounted at the required rate of return, the asset should be acquired. This decision rule is reflected in the graphic below. When comparing several investment opportunities of similar cost and risk, we prefer the one with the highest positive net present value.

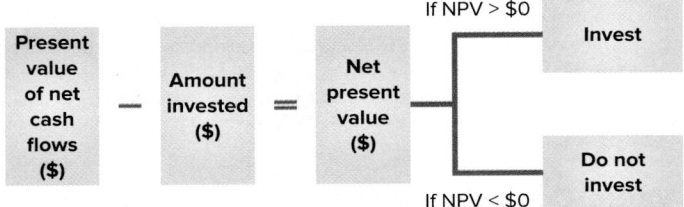

Simplifying Computations—Annuity The computations in Exhibit 24.9 use separate present value of 1 factors for each of the eight years. Each year's net cash flow is multiplied by its present value of 1 factor to determine its present value; these are then added to give the asset's total present value. This computation can be simplified if annual net cash flows are equal in amount. A series of cash flows of equal dollar amount is called an **annuity.** In this case we use Table B.3, which gives the present value of 1 to be received for a number of periods. To determine the present value of these eight annual receipts discounted at 12%, go down the 12% column of Table B.3 to the factor on the eighth line. This cumulative discount factor, also known as an *annuity* factor, is 4.9676. We then compute the $20,367 present value for these eight annual $4,100 receipts, computed as 4.9676 × $4,100. These calculations are summarized below.

Example: Why does the net present value of an investment increase when a lower discount rate is used? *Answer:* The present value of net cash flows increases.

Point: Excel for NPV.

	A	B
1	Investment	$16,000
2	Cash flow	$4,100
3	Periods	8
4	Interest rate	12%
5	Net present value	◄

=PV(B4,B3,−B2)−B1 = $4,367

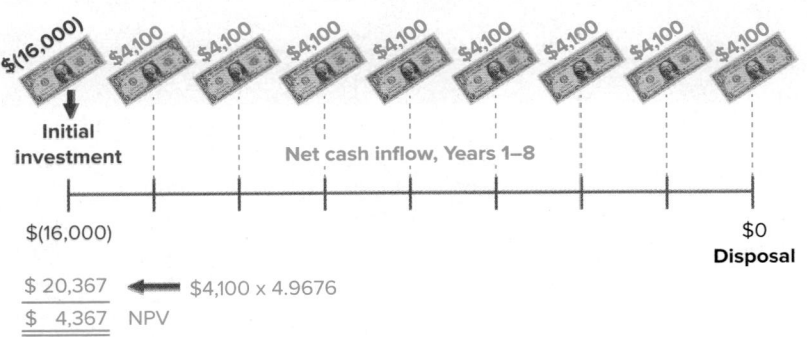

$ 20,367 ◄—— $4,100 × 4.9676
$ 4,367 NPV

Simplifying Computations—Calculator or Excel Another way to simplify present value calculations, whether net cash flows are equal in amount or not, is to use a calculator with compound interest functions or a spreadsheet program. Whatever procedure you use, it is important to understand the concepts behind these computations.

With a financial calculator:
N   8
I/Y   12
PMT   4100
CPT   PV
Multiply answer ($−20,367) by −1 since the company is receiving cash, and subtract initial investment ($16,000) to yield NPV of $4,367.

Cash Savings from Automation NPV analysis also can be used to decide whether to automate a production process. Increased automation from the use of robotics and *computer numerical control* (CNC) machines can yield cash savings from reduced direct labor costs. For example, an eyewear manufacturer is considering investing in an $8 million automated manufacturing system. If the investment is made, the company can reduce its direct labor costs by $1.5 million in each year of the 10-year useful life of the system. All other costs and revenues are expected to be unchanged. The NPV analysis, using a 10% discount rate and assuming the system has no salvage value, follows. The NPV is positive. The present value of the cash savings from reduced direct labor costs exceeds the cost of the automated manufacturing system. The company should automate its production process.

	Net Cash Savings	Present Value of an Annuity at 10%	Present Value of Net Cash Flows
Years 1–10	$1,500,000	6.1446	$ 9,216,900
Initial investment			(8,000,000)
Net present value			$ 1,216,900

■ Decision Ethics

Systems Manager   Management adopts a policy requiring purchases above $5,000 to be submitted with cash flow projections for capital budget approval. As systems manager, you want to upgrade your computers at a $25,000 cost. You consider submitting several orders each under $5,000 to avoid the approval process. You believe the computers will increase profits and wish to avoid a delay. What do you do? ■   *Answer:* Your dilemma is whether to abide by rules designed to prevent abuse or to bend them to acquire an investment that you believe will benefit the firm. You should not pursue the latter action because breaking up the order into small components is dishonest and there are consequences. Develop a proposal for the entire package and then do all you can to expedite its processing, particularly by pointing out its benefits.

Net Present Value Complications   The following factors can complicate NPV analysis. We discuss each of them.

- Unequal cash flows
- Salvage value
- Accelerated depreciation

- Inflation
- Comparing positive NPV projects
- Capital rationing

Uneven Cash Flows   Net present value analysis can also be used when net cash flows are uneven (unequal). To illustrate, assume that FasTrac can choose only one capital investment from among Projects A, B, and C. Each project requires the same $12,000 initial investment. Future net cash flows for each project are shown in the first three number columns of Exhibit 24.10.

EXHIBIT 24.10

Net Present Value Calculation with Uneven Cash Flows

	Net Cash Flows			Present Value of 1 at 10%	Present Value of Net Cash Flows		
	A	B	C		A	B	C
Year 1	$ 5,000	$ 8,000	$ 1,000	0.9091	$ 4,546	$ 7,273	$ 909
Year 2	5,000	5,000	5,000	0.8264	4,132	4,132	4,132
Year 3	5,000	2,000	9,000	0.7513	3,757	1,503	6,762
Totals	$15,000	$15,000	$15,000		12,435	12,908	11,803
Initial investment					(12,000)	(12,000)	(12,000)
Net present value					$ 435	$ 908	$ (197)

Example: If 12% is the required return in Exhibit 24.10, which project is preferred? *Answer:* Project B. Net present values are: A = $10; B = $553; C = $(715).

Example: Will the rankings of Projects A, B, and C change with the use of different discount rates, assuming the same rate is used for all projects? *Answer:* No; only the NPV amounts will change.

The three projects in Exhibit 24.10 have the same expected total net cash flows of $15,000. Project A is expected to produce equal amounts of $5,000 each year. Project B is expected to produce a larger amount in the first year. Project C is expected to produce a larger amount in the third year. The fourth column of Exhibit 24.10 shows the present value of 1 factors from Table B.1 assuming a 10% required return.

Computations in the three rightmost columns show that Project A has a $435 positive NPV. Project B has the largest NPV of $908 because it brings in cash more quickly. Project C has a $(197) *negative* NPV because its larger cash inflows are delayed. Projects with higher cash flows in earlier years generally yield higher net present values. If FasTrac requires a 10% return, it should reject Project C because its NPV implies a return *under* 10%. If only one project can be accepted, Project B appears best because it yields the highest NPV.

Salvage Value   FasTrac predicted the $16,000 machine to have zero salvage value at the end of its useful life. In many cases, assets are expected to have nonzero salvage values. If so, this amount is an additional net cash inflow expected to be received at the end of the final year of the asset's life. All other computations remain the same. For example, the net present value of the $16,000 investment that yields $4,100 of net cash flows for eight years is $4,367, as shown in Exhibit 24.9. If that machine is expected to have a $1,500 salvage value at the end of its eight-year life, the present value of this salvage amount is $606 (computed as $1,500 × 0.4039). The net present value of the machine, including the present value of its expected salvage amount, is $4,973 (computed as $4,367 + $606).

Point: Excel for PV of salvage value.

	A	B
1	Salvage value	$1,500
2	Useful life	8
3	Interest rate	12%
4	Present value	◄

=PV(B3,B2,0,−B1) = $606

Accelerated Depreciation   Depreciation methods can affect net present value analysis. Accelerated depreciation is commonly used for income tax purposes. Accelerated depreciation produces larger depreciation deductions in the early years of an asset's life and smaller deductions in later years. This pattern results in smaller income tax payments in early years and larger tax payments in later years. Using accelerated depreciation for tax reporting increases the NPV of an asset's cash flows because it produces larger net cash inflows in the early years of the asset's life. Using accelerated depreciation for tax reporting always makes an investment more desirable because early cash flows are more valuable than later ones.

Point: Salvage values and the use of accelerated depreciation increase the NPV.

Point: Tax savings from depreciation is called *depreciation tax shield.*

Inflation   Large price-level increases should be considered in NPV analyses. Discount rates should already include inflation forecasts. Net cash flows can be adjusted for inflation by using *future value* computations. For example, if the expected net cash inflow in Year 1 is $4,100 and 5% inflation is expected, then the expected net cash inflow in Year 2 is $4,305, computed as $4,100 × 1.05 (1.05 is the future value of $1 [Table B.2] for 1 period with a 5% rate).

Comparing Positive NPV Projects   When considering several projects of similar investment amounts and risk levels, we can compare the different projects' NPVs and rank them on the dollar amounts of their NPVs. However, if the amount invested differs substantially across projects, this is of limited value for comparison purposes. One way to compare projects, especially when a company cannot fund all positive net present value projects, is to use the **profitability index,** which is computed as

Example: When is it appropriate to use different discount rates for different projects? *Answer:* When risk levels are different.

$$\text{Profitability index} = \frac{\textbf{Present value of net cash flows}}{\textbf{Initial investment}}$$

Exhibit 24.11 illustrates computation of the profitability index for three potential research and development (R&D) investments. A profitability index less than 1 indicates an investment with a *negative* net present value. Investment 3 shows an index of 0.9, meaning a negative NPV. This means we can drop Investment 3 from consideration. Both Investments 1 and 2 have profitability indexes greater than 1; thus, they have positive net present values. Investment 1's NPV equals $150,000 (computed as $900,000 − $750,000); Investment 2's NPV equals $125,000 (computed as $375,000 − $250,000). Ideally, the company would accept all positive NPV projects, but if forced to choose, it should select the project with the higher profitability index. Thus, Investment 2 is ranked ahead of Investment 1 based on its higher profitability index. Investment 2 returns $1.50 NPV per dollar invested, whereas Investment 1 returns only $1.20 NPV per dollar invested. **Rule:** Invest in the project with the highest profitability index.

EXHIBIT 24.11

Profitability Index

	R&D Investment		
	1	**2**	**3**
Present value of net cash flows (a)	$900,000	$375,000	$270,000
Amount invested (b)	750,000	250,000	300,000
Profitability index (a)/(b)	**1.2**	**1.5**	**0.9**

Capital Rationing   Some firms face **capital rationing,** or financing constraints that limit them from accepting all positive NPV projects. This can be in two forms, hard rationing and soft rationing.

- *Hard rationing* is imposed by external forces, such as debt covenants that restrict the firm's ability to borrow more money.
- *Soft rationing* is internally imposed by management and the board of directors. For example, management might place spending limits on certain employees or departments until they show they can make good decisions.

Whether due to hard or soft capital rationing, the profitability index can be used to select the best of several competing projects.

NEED-TO-KNOW 24-3

Net Present Value

P3

A company is considering two potential projects. Each project requires a $20,000 initial investment and is expected to generate end-of-year annual cash flows as shown below. Assuming a discount rate of 10%, compute the net present value of each project.

	Net Cash Inflows			
	Year 1	Year 2	Year 3	Total
Project A	$12,000	$8,500	$ 4,000	$24,500
Project B	4,500	8,500	13,000	26,000

Solution

Net present values are computed as follows.

		Project A		Project B	
Year	Present Value of 1 at 10%	Net Cash Flows	Present Value of Net Cash Flows	Net Cash Flows	Present Value of Net Cash Flows
1	0.9091	$12,000	$ 10,909	$ 4,500	$ 4,091
2	0.8264	8,500	7,024	8,500	7,024
3	0.7513	4,000	3,005	13,000	9,767
Totals		$24,500	$ 20,938	$26,000	$ 20,882
Initial investment			(20,000)		(20,000)
Net present value			$ 938		$ 882

Do More: QS 24-2, QS 24-8, QS 24-9, QS 24-11, E 24-2, E 24-6, E 24-9

Internal Rate of Return

P4 _____

Compute internal rate of return and explain its use.

Project A Net Cash Flows

Investment . . . . $(12,000)
Annuity, Yrs 1-3 . . .   5,000
Hurdle rate = 10%

Point: Excel for IRR.

	A	B
1	Investment	−$12,000
2	Cash flow Year 1	5,000
3	Cash flow Year 2	5,000
4	Cash flow Year 3	5,000
5	Internal rate of return	◀
	=IRR(B1:B4) = 12.04%	

Another way to evaluate capital investments is to use the **internal rate of return (IRR),** which equals the discount rate that yields an NPV of zero for an investment. If we compute the total present value of a project's net cash flows using the IRR as the discount rate, and then subtract the initial investment from this total present value, we will get a zero NPV.

We use the data for FasTrac's Project A from Exhibit 24.10 to compute its IRR. Below is the two-step process for computing IRR with even cash flows.

Step 1: **Compute the present value factor for the investment project.**

$$\text{Present value factor} = \frac{\text{Amount invested}}{\text{Annual net cash flows}} = \frac{\$12,000}{\$5,000} = 2.4000$$

Step 2: **Identify the discount rate (IRR) yielding the present value factor.**
Search Table B.3 for a present value factor of 2.4000 in the 3-year row (equaling the 3-year project duration). The 12% discount rate yields a present value factor of 2.4018. This implies that the IRR is approximately 12%.

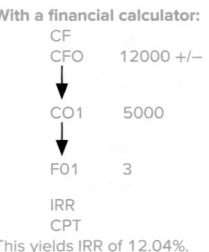

When cash flows are equal, as with Project A, we compute the present value factor by dividing the initial investment by its annual net cash flows. We then use an annuity table to determine the discount rate equal to this present value factor. For FasTrac's Project A, we look across the 3-period row of Table B.3 and find that the discount rate corresponding to the present value factor of 2.4000 roughly equals the 2.4018 value for the 12% rate. This row of Table B.3 is reproduced here.

Present Value of an Annuity of 1 for Three Periods					
	Discount Rate				
Periods	1%	5%	10%	12%	15%
3	2.9410	2.7232	2.4869	**2.4018**	2.2832

The 12% rate is the project's IRR. Because this project's IRR is greater than the hurdle rate of 10%, it should be accepted. **Rule:** If IRR > hurdle rate, invest.

Uneven Cash Flows   If net cash flows are uneven, it is best to use either a calculator or spreadsheet software to compute IRR. We show the use of Excel in this chapter's appendix.

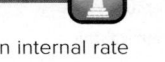

■ Decision Insight

Manager Pay and IRR   A survey reported that 41% of top managers would reject a project with an internal rate of return *above* the cost of capital *if* the project would cause the firm to miss its earnings forecast. The roles of benchmarks and manager compensation plans must be considered in capital budgeting decisions. ■

Use of Internal Rate of Return   To use the IRR to evaluate a project, compare it to a predetermined *hurdle rate,* which is a minimum acceptable rate of return. The decision rule using IRR is applied as follows.

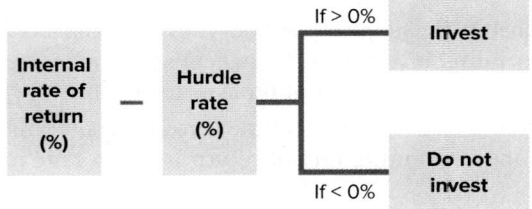

If the IRR is higher than the hurdle rate, the investment should be made. If the IRR is less than the hurdle rate, do not invest.

Comparing Projects Using IRR   Multiple projects are often ranked by the extent to which their IRR exceeds the hurdle rate. IRR can be used to compare projects with different amounts invested because the IRR is expressed as a percent rather than as a dollar value in NPV.

■ Decision Maker

Entrepreneur   You are developing a new product and you use a 12% discount rate to compute its NPV. Your banker, from whom you hope to obtain a loan, expresses concern that your discount rate is too low. How do you respond? ■   *Answer:* The banker is probably concerned because new products are risky and therefore should be evaluated using a higher rate of return. You should conduct a thorough technical analysis and obtain detailed market data and information about any similar products. These factors might support the use of a lower return. You must convince yourself that the risk level is consistent with the discount rate used. You should also be confident that your company has the capacity and the resources to handle the new product.

NEED-TO-KNOW 24-4

Internal Rate of Return

P4

Do More: QS 24-3, QS 24-13, E 24-14

A machine costing $58,880 is expected to generate net cash flows of $8,000 for each of the next 10 years.
1. Compute the machine's internal rate of return (IRR).
2. If a company's hurdle rate is 6.5%, use IRR to determine whether the company should purchase this machine.

Solution

1. PV factor = Amount invested/Net cash flows = $58,880/$8,000 = 7.36. Scanning the "Periods equal 10" row in Table B.3 for a present value factor near 7.36 indicates the IRR is 6%.
2. The machine should <u>not</u> be purchased because its IRR (6%) is less than the company's hurdle rate (6.5%).

Comparison of Capital Budgeting Methods

EXHIBIT 24.12

Comparing Capital Budgeting Methods

We explained four methods that managers use to evaluate capital investment projects. How do these methods compare with each other? Exhibit 24.12 addresses that question. Neither the payback period nor the accounting rate of return considers the time value of money. Both the net present value and the internal rate of return do.

	Payback Period	Accounting Rate of Return	Net Present Value	Internal Rate of Return
Measurement basis	• Cash flows	• Accrual income	• Cash flows	• Cash flows
Measurement unit	• Years	• Percent	• Dollars	• Percent
Strengths	• Easy to understand	• Easy to understand	• Reflects time value of money	• Reflects time value of money
	• Allows comparison of projects	• Allows comparison of projects	• Reflects varying risks over project's life	• Allows comparisons of dissimilar projects
Limitations	• Ignores time value of money	• Ignores time value of money	• Difficult to compare dissimilar projects	• Ignores varying risks over life of project
	• Ignores cash flows after payback period	• Ignores annual rates over life of project		

- Payback period is probably the simplest method. It gives managers an estimate of how soon they will recover their initial investment. Managers sometimes use this method when they have limited cash to invest and a number of projects to choose from.
- Accounting rate of return yields a percent measure computed using accrual income instead of cash flows. The accounting rate of return is an average rate for the entire investment period.
- Net present value considers all estimated net cash flows for the project's expected life. It can be applied to even and uneven cash flows and can reflect changes in the level of risk over a project's life. Because NPV yields a dollar measure, comparing projects of unequal sizes is more difficult. The profitability index, based on each project's net present value, can be used in this case.
- Internal rate of return considers all cash flows from a project. It is readily computed when the cash flows are even but requires some trial and error or use of a financial calculator or computer when cash flows are uneven. Because the IRR is a percent measure, it is readily used to compare projects with different investment amounts. However, IRR does not reflect changes in risk over a project's life.

Postaudit

Companies should evaluate the outcomes of capital budgeting decisions. A **postaudit** is an evaluation of a project's actual results versus its projected results. The same method used to support the capital budgeting decision should be used in the postaudit. For example, if an NPV analysis was used to make an investment decision, NPV analysis should be used to evaluate that investment decision. Instead of forecasted cash flows, the postaudit uses *actual* cash flows (for periods that have passed) and *revised* future cash flows. Benefits of a postaudit include

- Managers will likely be more careful in the investment proposals they submit.
- Poor investments can be identified earlier and management can change its investments.

For example, FasTrac's machinery purchase in Exhibit 24.9 was expected to generate future cash flows of $4,100 per year for eight years and an NPV of $4,367. Assume the machinery only generates $3,000 of actual net cash flows in both Years 1 and 2, and FasTrac expects net cash flows of $3,000 per year for the next six years. The present value of this investment is now only $14,902.80 (computed as $3,000 × 4.9676), and the machinery's NPV is now −$1,097.20 (computed as $14,902.80 − $16,000). Based on this postaudit, FasTrac might sell the machinery and invest in a different project.

Point: 4.9676 is the present value of ordinary annuity factor for 8 periods at 12%.

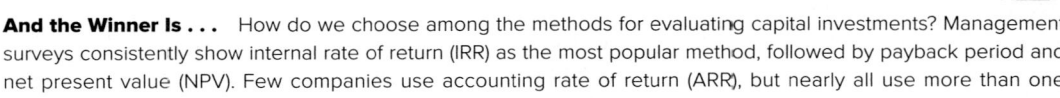

■ Decision Insight

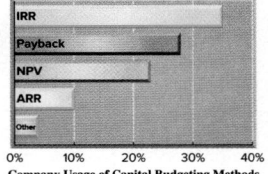

And the Winner Is . . . How do we choose among the methods for evaluating capital investments? Management surveys consistently show internal rate of return (IRR) as the most popular method, followed by payback period and net present value (NPV). Few companies use accounting rate of return (ARR), but nearly all use more than one method. ■

Company Usage of Capital Budgeting Methods

 ## SUSTAINABILITY AND ACCOUNTING

Net present value calculations extend to investments in sustainable energy sources like solar power. To illustrate, consider a potential investment of $11,000 in a solar panel system in Phoenix. The system is expected to last for 30 years and require $100 of maintenance costs per year. The typical home uses 14,000 kilowatt hours (kWh) of electricity per year, at a cost of $0.12 per kilowatt hour. According to the **National Renewable Energy Laboratory (pvwatts.nrel.gov)**, a typical solar panel system in Phoenix could supply 8,642 kilowatt hours (kWh) of electricity per year. The net present value of a potential investment in a solar panel system, using a 6% discount rate, is computed in Exhibit 24.13. The NPV is $1,898, indicating the investment should be accepted.

Electricity cost savings (8,642 kWh × $0.12)	$ 1,037
Annual maintenance costs	(100)
Net annual cash inflows	$ 937
Present value of net cash inflows ($937 × 13.7648*)	$12,898
Initial investment	(11,000)
Net present value	**$ 1,898**

EXHIBIT 24.13

NPV of Solar Investment

*From Table B.3: 30 periods, 6%

Predicting the future benefits of solar panel installations in terms of reduced energy costs, however, is challenging for several reasons. First, the amount of solar energy that can be produced depends on geographic location, with locations nearer the equator typically better. Second, south-facing roofs are better able to capture solar energy than other orientations. Third, cost savings from solar energy require predictions of the future costs of other sources of power, which can be volatile. These factors must be considered when performing a net present value calculation on a potential investment in solar power.

Fellow Robots, this chapter's feature company, makes "social" robots that handle simple inventory-related tasks, allowing retail employees to focus on the activities that add value to customers. This not only increases profits, but also increases employee satisfaction, which can increase morale and decrease turnover.

©Fellow Robots

Decision Analysis    Break-Even Time

A1

Analyze a capital
investment project using
break-even time.

The first section of this chapter explained several methods to evaluate capital investments. Break-even time of an investment project is a variation of the payback period method that overcomes the limitation of not using the time value of money. **Break-even time (BET)** is a time-based measure used to evaluate a capital investment's acceptability. Its computation yields a measure of expected time, reflecting the time period until the *present value* of the net cash flows from an investment equals the initial cost of the investment. In basic terms, break-even time is computed by restating future cash flows in terms of present values and then determining the payback period using these present values.

To illustrate, we return to the FasTrac case involving a $16,000 investment in machinery. The annual net cash flows from this investment are projected at $4,100 for eight years. Exhibit 24.14 shows the computation of break-even time for this investment decision.

EXHIBIT 24.14

Break-Even Time Analysis*

Year	Cash Flows	Present Value of 1 at 10%	Present Value of Cash Flows	Cumulative Present Value of Cash Flows
0...........	$(16,000)	1.0000	$(16,000)	$(16,000)
1...........	4,100	0.9091	3,727	(12,273)
2...........	4,100	0.8264	3,388	(8,885)
3...........	4,100	0.7513	3,080	(5,805)
4...........	4,100	0.6830	2,800	(3,005)
5...........	4,100	0.6209	2,546	(459)
6...........	4,100	0.5645	2,314	1,855
7...........	4,100	0.5132	2,104	3,959
8...........	4,100	0.4665	1,913	5,872

Break-even time → between (459) and 1,855

*The time of analysis is the start of Year 1 (same as end of Year 0). All cash flows occur at the end of each year.

The rightmost column of this exhibit shows that break-even time is between 5 and 6 years, or about 5.2 years—also see margin graph (where the line crosses the zero point). This is the time the project takes to break even after considering the time value of money (recall that the payback period computed without considering the time value of money was 3.9 years). We interpret this as cash flows earned after 5.2 years contribute to a positive net present value that, in this case, eventually amounts to $5,872.

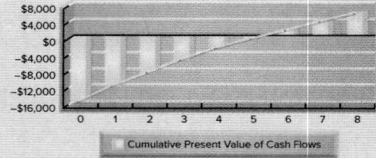

Break-even time is a useful measure for managers because it identifies the point in time when they can expect the cash flows to begin to yield net positive returns. Managers expect a positive net present value from an investment if break-even time is less than the investment's estimated life. The method allows managers to compare and rank alternative investments, giving the project with the shortest break-even time the highest rank.

◼ Decision Maker

Investment Manager   Management asks you, the investment manager, to evaluate three alternative investments. Investment recovery time is crucial because cash is scarce. The time value of money is also important. Which capital budgeting method(s) do you use to assess the investments? ◼   *Answer:* You should use break-even time because both the time value of money and recovery time are important. The break-even time method is superior because it accounts for the time value of money, which is an important consideration in this decision.

NEED-TO-KNOW **24-5**

COMPREHENSIVE

Evaluating Investments

White Company can invest in one of two projects, TD1 or TD2. Each project requires an initial investment of $101,250 and produces the year-end cash inflows shown in the following table.

	Net Cash Flows	
	TD1	TD2
Year 1	$ 20,000	$ 40,000
Year 2	30,000	40,000
Year 3	70,000	40,000
Totals..........	$120,000	$120,000

Required

1. Compute the payback period for both projects. Which project has the shortest payback period?
2. Assume that the company requires a 10% return from its investments. Compute the net present value of each project.
3. Drawing on your answers to parts 1 and 2, determine which project, if any, should be chosen.
4. Compute the internal rate of return for Project TD2. Based on its internal rate of return, should Project TD2 be chosen?

PLANNING THE SOLUTION

- Compute the payback period for the series of unequal cash flows (Project TD1) and for the series of equal cash flows (Project TD2).
- Compute White Company's net present value of each investment using a 10% discount rate.
- Use the payback and net present value rules to determine which project, if any, should be selected.
- Compute the internal rate of return for the series of equal cash flows (Project TD2) and determine whether that internal rate of return is greater than the company's 10% discount rate.

SOLUTION

1. The payback period for a project with a series of equal cash flows is computed as follows.

$$\text{Payback period} = \frac{\text{Cost of investment}}{\text{Annual net cash flow}}$$

For Project TD2, the payback period equals 2.53 (rounded), computed as $101,250/$40,000. This means that the company expects to recover its investment in Project TD2 after approximately two and one-half years of its three-year life.

Next, determining the payback period for a series of unequal cash flows (as in Project TD1) requires us to compute the cumulative net cash flows from the project at the end of each year. Assuming the cash outflow for Project TD1 occurs at the end of Year 0 and cash inflows occur continuously over Years 1, 2, and 3, the payback period calculation follows.

TD1:

Period	Expected Net Cash Flows	Cumulative Net Cash Flows
0	$(101,250)	$(101,250)
1	20,000	(81,250)
2	30,000	(51,250)
3	70,000	18,750

The cumulative net cash flow for Project TD1 changes from negative to positive in Year 3. As cash flows are received continuously, the point at which the company has recovered its investment into Year 3 is 0.73 (rounded), computed as $51,250/$70,000. This means that the payback period for TD1 is 2.73 years, computed as 2 years plus 0.73 of Year 3.

2. **TD1:**

	Net Cash Flows	Present Value of 1 at 10%	Present Value of Net Cash Flows
Year 1	$ 20,000	0.9091	$ 18,182
Year 2	30,000	0.8264	24,792
Year 3	70,000	0.7513	52,591
Totals........................	$120,000		95,565
Amount invested.............			(101,250)
Net present value			$ (5,685)

TD2:

	Net Cash Flows	Present Value of 1 at 10%	Present Value of Net Cash Flows
Year 1	$ 40,000	0.9091	$ 36,364
Year 2	40,000	0.8264	33,056
Year 3	40,000	0.7513	30,052
Totals........................	$120,000		99,472
Amount invested.............			(101,250)
Net present value			$ (1,778)

3. White Company should not invest in either project. Both are expected to yield a negative net present value, and it should invest only in positive net present value projects. Although the company expects to recover its investment from both projects before the end of these projects' useful lives, the projects are not acceptable after considering the time value of money.

4. To compute Project TD2's internal rate of return, we first compute a present value factor as follows.

$$\text{Present value factor} = \frac{\text{Amount invested}}{\text{Net cash flow}} = \$101{,}250/\$40{,}000 = 2.5313 \text{ (rounded)}$$

Then, we search Table B.3 for the discount rate that corresponds to the present value factor of 2.5313 for three periods. From Table B.3, this discount rate is 9%. Project TD2's internal rate of return of 9% is below this company's hurdle rate of 10%. Thus, Project TD2 should *not* be chosen.

APPENDIX

24A Using Excel to Compute Net Present Value and Internal Rate of Return

Computing present values and internal rates of return for projects with uneven cash flows is tedious and error prone. These calculations can be performed simply and accurately by using functions built into Excel. Many calculators and other types of spreadsheet software can perform them too. To illustrate, consider FasTrac, a company that is considering investing in a new machine with the expected cash flows shown in the following spreadsheet. Cash outflows are entered as negative numbers, and cash inflows are entered as positive numbers. Assume FasTrac requires a 12% annual return, entered as 0.12 in cell C1.

	A	B	C
1	Annual discount rate		0.12
2	Initial investment, made at beginning of period 1		−16000
3	Annual cash flows received at end of period:		
4		1	3000
5		2	4000
6		3	4000
7		4	4000
8		5	5000
9		6	3000
10		7	2000
11		8	2000
12			
13			=NPV(C1,C4:C11)+C2
14			
15			=IRR(C2:C11)

To compute the net present value of this project, the following is entered into cell C13:

=NPV(C1,C4:C11)+C2

This instructs Excel to use its NPV function to compute the present value of the cash flows in cells C4 through C11, using the discount rate in cell C1, and then add the amount of the (negative) initial investment. For this stream of cash flows and a discount rate of 12%, the net present value is $1,326.03.

To compute the internal rate of return for this project, the following is entered into cell C15:

=IRR(C2:C11)

This instructs Excel to use its IRR function to compute the internal rate of return of the cash flows in cells C2 through C11. By default, Excel starts with a guess of 10%, and then uses trial and error to find the IRR. The IRR equals 14.47% for this project.

Summary: Cheat Sheet

NON–PRESENT VALUE METHODS

Payback period: Expected time to recover initial investment.
With even cash flows:

$$\text{Payback period} = \frac{\text{Cost of investment}}{\text{Annual net cash flow}}$$

With uneven cash flows: Determine when cumulative cash flows change from negative to positive.

Excel for payback.

	A	B
1	Investment	$16,000
2	Cash flow	$4,100
3	Payback period	←

=B1/B2 = 3.9

Accounting rate of return: Percentage accounting return on annual average investment.

$$\text{Accounting rate of return} = \frac{\text{Annual after-tax net income}}{\text{Annual average investment}}$$

$$\text{Annual average investment} = \frac{\text{Beginning book value} + \text{Ending book value}}{2}$$
(straight-line case only)

Excel for ARR.

	A	B
1	Beg. book value	$16,000
2	End. book value	$0
3	Net income	$2,100
4	Acctg rate of return	←

=B3/((B1+B2)/2) = 26.25%

PRESENT VALUE METHODS

Annuity: Series of cash flows of equal dollar amounts.
Net present value (NPV):
Discounted future cash flows − Initial amount invested.
Cost of capital (*hurdle rate*): Required rate of return on a potential investment.

Net present value decision rule:

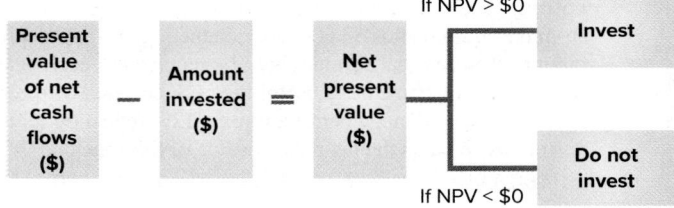

Excel for NPV.

	A	B
1	Investment	$16,000
2	Cash flow	$4,100
3	Periods	8
4	Interest rate	12%
5	Net present value	←

=PV(B4,B3,−B2)−B1 = $4,367

$$\text{Profitability index} = \frac{\text{Present value of net cash flows}}{\text{Initial investment}}$$

Internal rate of return (IRR):
Discount rate that yields NPV of zero for an investment.

Internal rate of return decision rule:

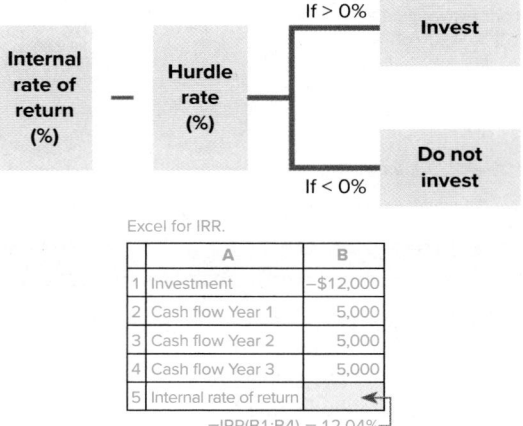

Excel for IRR.

	A	B
1	Investment	−$12,000
2	Cash flow Year 1	5,000
3	Cash flow Year 2	5,000
4	Cash flow Year 3	5,000
5	Internal rate of return	←

=IRR(B1:B4) = 12.04%

Break-even time: Payback period using discounted cash flows.

Key Terms

Accounting rate of return (ARR) (951)	**Capital rationing** (956)	**Net present value (NPV)** (952)
Annuity (953)	**Cost of capital** (952)	**Payback period (PBP)** (948)
Break-even time (BET) (960)	**Hurdle rate** (952)	**Postaudit** (958)
Capital budgeting (947)	**Internal rate of return (IRR)** (956)	**Profitability index** (955)

Multiple Choice Quiz

1. The minimum acceptable rate of return for an investment decision is called the

   a. Hurdle rate of return.
   b. Payback rate of return.
   c. Internal rate of return.
   d. Average rate of return.
   e. Break-even rate of return.

2. A company is considering the purchase of new equipment costing $90,000. The projected after-tax annual net income from the equipment is $3,600, after deducting $30,000 depreciation. Assume that revenue is to be received at each year-end, and the machine has a useful life of three years with zero salvage value. Management requires a 12% return on its investments. What is the net present value of this machine?

   a. $60,444
   b. $80,700
   c. $(88,560)
   d. $90,000
   e. $(9,300)

3. A disadvantage of using the payback period to compare investment alternatives is that it

   a. Ignores cash flows beyond the payback period.
   b. Cannot be used to compare alternatives with different initial investments.
   c. Cannot be used when cash flows are not uniform.
   d. Involves the time value of money.
   e. Cannot be used if a company records depreciation.

4. A company is considering the purchase of equipment for $270,000. Projected annual cash inflow from this equipment is $61,200 per year. The payback period is

   a. 0.2 years.
   b. 5.0 years.
   c. 4.4 years.
   d. 2.3 years.
   e. 3.9 years.

5. A company buys a machine for $180,000 that has an expected life of nine years and no salvage value. The company expects an annual net income (after taxes of 30%) of $8,550. What is the accounting rate of return?

   a. 4.75%
   b. 42.75%
   c. 2.85%
   d. 9.50%
   e. 6.65%

ANSWERS TO MULTIPLE CHOICE QUIZ

1. a
2. e;

	Net Cash Flow	Present Value of an Annuity of 1 at 12%	Present Value of Cash Flows
Years 1–3	$3,600 + $30,000	2.4018	$ 80,700
Amount invested			(90,000)
Net present value			$ (9,300)

3. a
4. c; Payback = $270,000/$61,200 per year = 4.4 years
5. d; Accounting rate of return = $8,550/[($180,000 + $0)/2] = 9.5%

---

^A *Superscript letter A denotes assignments based on Appendix 24A.*

[I] Icon denotes assignments that involve decision making.

Discussion Questions

1. Capital budgeting decisions require careful analysis because they are generally the most _____ and _____ decisions that management faces.

2. What is capital budgeting?

3. [I] Identify four reasons that capital budgeting decisions are risky.

4. Identify two disadvantages of using the payback period for comparing investments.

5. [I] Why is an investment more attractive to management if it has a shorter payback period?

6. What is the average amount invested in a machine during its predicted five-year life if it costs $200,000 and has a $20,000 salvage value? Assume that net income is received evenly throughout each year and straight-line depreciation is used.

7. If the present value of the expected net cash flows from a machine, discounted at 10%, exceeds the amount to be invested, what can you say about the investment's expected rate of return? What can you say about the expected rate of return if the present value of the net cash flows, discounted at 10%, is less than the investment amount?

8. Why is the present value of $100 that you expect to receive one year from today worth less than $100 received today? What is the present value of $100 that you expect to receive one year from today, discounted at 12%?

9. [I] If a potential investment's internal rate of return is above the company's hurdle rate, should the investment be made?

10. 🔲 **Google** managers must select deprecia- **GOOGLE** tion methods. Why does the use of the ac- celerated depreciation method (instead of straight-line) for income tax reporting increase an investment's value?

11. **Samsung** management is planning to in- **Samsung** vest in a new companywide computerized inventory tracking system. What makes this potential in- vestment risky?

12. **Google** management is planning to acquire **GOOGLE** new equipment to manufacture tablet

computers. What are some of the costs and benefits that would be included in Google's analysis?

13. 🔲 **Apple** is considering expanding a store. **APPLE** Identify three methods management can use to evaluate whether to expand.

14. What is a postaudit? What are its potential benefits?

15. Discuss the advantages of break-even time over the payback period. List two conditions under which payback period and break-even time are similar.

▣ connect ───────────────────────────────────────

Park Co. is considering an investment that requires immediate payment of $27,000 and provides expected cash inflows of $9,000 annually for four years. What is the investment's payback period?

QUICK STUDY
QS 24-1
Payback period **P1**

Park Co. is considering an investment that requires immediate payment of $27,000 and provides expected cash inflows of $9,000 annually for four years. If Park Co. requires a 10% return on its investments, what is the net present value of this investment? (Round your calculations to the nearest dollar.)

QS 24-2
Net present value **P3**

Park Co. is considering an investment that requires immediate payment of $27,000 and provides expected cash inflows of $9,000 annually for four years. Assume Park Co. requires a 10% return on its investments. Based on its internal rate of return, should Park Co. make the investment?

QS 24-3
Internal rate of return **P4**

Howard Co. is considering two alternative investments. The payback period is 3.5 years for Investment A and 4 years for Investment B.

1. If management relies on the payback period, which investment is preferred?

2. Will an investment with a shorter payback period always be chosen over an investment with a longer payback period?

QS 24-4
Analyzing payback periods
P1

Project A requires a $280,000 initial investment for new machinery with a five-year life and a salvage value of $30,000. The company uses straight-line depreciation. Project A is expected to yield annual net income of $20,000 per year for the next five years. Compute Project A's payback period.

QS 24-5
Payback period **P1**

Project A requires a $280,000 initial investment for new machinery with a five-year life and a salvage value of $30,000. The company uses straight-line depreciation. Project A is expected to yield annual net income of $20,000 per year for the next five years. Compute Project A's accounting rate of return. Express your answer as a percentage, rounded to two decimal places.

QS 24-6
Accounting rate of return
P2

Peng Company is considering an investment expected to generate an average net income after taxes of $1,950 for three years. The investment costs $45,000 and has an estimated $6,000 salvage value. Compute the accounting rate of return for this investment; assume the company uses straight-line depreciation. Express your answer as a percentage, rounded to two decimal places.

QS 24-7
Compute accounting rate of return **P2**

Peng Company is considering an investment expected to generate an average net income after taxes of $1,950 for three years. The investment costs $45,000 and has an estimated $6,000 salvage value. Assume Peng requires a 15% return on its investments. Compute the net present value of this investment. (Round each present value calculation to the nearest dollar.)

QS 24-8
Net present value
P3

If Quail Company invests $50,000 today, it can expect to receive $10,000 at the end of each year for the next seven years, plus an extra $6,000 at the end of the seventh year. What is the net present value of this investment assuming a required 10% return on investments? (Round present value calculations to the near- est dollar.)

QS 24-9
Compute net present value
P3

QS 24-10
Profitability index
P3

Yokam Company is considering two alternative projects. Project 1 requires an initial investment of $400,000 and has a present value of cash flows of $1,100,000. Project 2 requires an initial investment of $4 million and has a present value of cash flows of $6 million. Compute the profitability index for each project. Based on the profitability index, which project should the company prefer? Explain.

QS 24-11
Net present value
P3

Following is information on an investment considered by Hudson Co. The investment has zero salvage value. The company requires a 12% return from its investments. Compute this investment's net present value.

	Investment A1
Initial investment	$(200,000)
Expected net cash flows: Year 1	100,000
Year 2	90,000
Year 3	75,000

QS 24-12
Net present value, with
salvage value   **P3**

Refer to the information in QS 24-11 and instead assume the investment has a salvage value of $20,000. Compute the investment's net present value.

QS 24-13
Internal rate of return   **P4**

A company is considering investing in a new machine that requires a cash payment of $47,947 today. The machine will generate annual cash flows of $21,000 for the next three years. What is the internal rate of return if the company buys this machine?

QS 24-14
Net present value
P3

A company is considering investing in a new machine that requires a cash payment of $47,947 today. The machine will generate annual cash flows of $21,000 for the next three years. Assume the company uses an 8% discount rate. Compute the net present value of this investment. (Round your answer to the nearest dollar.)

QS 24-15
Net present value
P3

A company is investing in a solar panel system to reduce its electricity costs. The system requires a cash payment of $125,374.60 today. The system is expected to generate net cash flows of $13,000 per year for the next 35 years. The investment has zero salvage value. The company requires an 8% return on its investments. Compute the net present value of this investment.

QS 24-16
Internal rate of return
P4

A company is investing in a solar panel system to reduce its electricity costs. The system requires a cash payment of $125,374.60 today. The system is expected to generate net cash flows of $13,000 per year for the next 35 years. The investment has zero salvage value. Compute the internal rate of return on this investment.

QS 24-17
Compute break-even time
A1

Heels, a shoe manufacturer, is evaluating the costs and benefits of new equipment that would custom fit each pair of athletic shoes. The customer would have his or her foot scanned by digital computer equipment; this information would be used to cut the raw materials to provide the customer a perfect fit. The new equipment costs $90,000 and is expected to generate an additional $35,000 in cash flows for five years. A bank will make a $90,000 loan to the company at a 10% interest rate for this equipment's purchase. Use the following table to determine the break-even time for this equipment. (Round the present value of cash flows to the nearest dollar.)

Year	Cash Flows*	Present Value of 1 at 10%	Present Value of Cash Flows	Cumulative Present Value of Cash Flows
0	$(90,000)	1.0000	_____	_____
1	35,000	0.9091	_____	_____
2	35,000	0.8264	_____	_____
3	35,000	0.7513	_____	_____
4	35,000	0.6830	_____	_____
5	35,000	0.6209	_____	_____

*All cash flows occur at year-end.

Siemens AG invests €80 million to build a manufacturing plant to build wind turbines. The company predicts net cash flows of €16 million per year for the next eight years. Assume the company requires an 8% rate of return from its investments.

1. What is the payback period of this investment?
2. What is the net present value of this investment?

QS 24-18
Capital budgeting methods
P1   P3

 connect ────────────────────────────────

Beyer Company is considering the purchase of an asset for $180,000. It is expected to produce the following net cash flows. The cash flows occur evenly within each year. Compute the payback period for this investment (round years to two decimals).

	Year 1	Year 2	Year 3	Year 4	Year 5	Total
Net cash flows	$60,000	$40,000	$70,000	$125,000	$35,000	$330,000

EXERCISES

Exercise 24-1
Payback period computation; uneven cash flows   P1

Refer to the information in Exercise 24-1 and assume that Beyer requires a 10% return on its investments. Compute the net present value of this investment. (Round to the nearest dollar.) Should Beyer accept the investment?

Exercise 24-2
Net present value   P3

A machine can be purchased for $150,000 and used for five years, yielding the following net incomes. In projecting net incomes, straight-line depreciation is applied using a five-year life and zero salvage value. Compute the machine's payback period (ignore taxes). (Round the payback period to three decimals.)

	Year 1	Year 2	Year 3	Year 4	Year 5
Net income	$10,000	$25,000	$50,000	$37,500	$100,000

Exercise 24-3
Payback period computation; straight-line depreciation
P1

Refer to the information in Exercise 24-3 and assume instead that double-declining depreciation is applied. Compute the machine's payback period (ignore taxes). (Round the payback period to three decimals.)

Exercise 24-4
Payback period; accelerated depreciation   P1

Compute the payback period for each of these two separate investments (round the payback period to two decimals).

a. A new operating system for an existing machine is expected to cost $520,000 and have a useful life of six years. The system yields an incremental after-tax income of $150,000 each year after deducting its straight-line depreciation. The predicted salvage value of the system is $10,000.

b. A machine costs $380,000, has a $20,000 salvage value, is expected to last eight years, and will generate an after-tax income of $60,000 per year after straight-line depreciation.

Exercise 24-5
Payback period computation; even cash flows
P1

Refer to the information in Exercise 24-5. Assume the company requires a 10% rate of return on its investments. Compute the net present value of each potential investment. (Round to the nearest dollar.)

Exercise 24-6
Net present value   P3

A machine costs $700,000 and is expected to yield an after-tax net income of $52,000 each year. Management predicts this machine has a 10-year service life and a $100,000 salvage value, and it uses straight-line depreciation. Compute this machine's accounting rate of return.

Exercise 24-7
Accounting rate of return
P2

Exercise 24-8

Payback period and accounting rate of return on investment

P1   P2

B2B Co. is considering the purchase of equipment that would allow the company to add a new product to its line. The equipment is expected to cost $360,000 with a 12-year life and no salvage value. It will be depreciated on a straight-line basis. The company expects to sell 144,000 units of the equipment's product each year. The expected annual income related to this equipment follows. Compute the (1) payback period and (2) accounting rate of return for this equipment.

Sales	$225,000
Costs	
Materials, labor, and overhead (except depreciation on new equipment)	120,000
Depreciation on new equipment.	30,000
Selling and administrative expenses.	22,500
Total costs and expenses.	172,500
Pretax income.	52,500
Income taxes (30%)	15,750
Net income	$ 36,750

Check (1) 5.39 years, (2) 20.42%

Exercise 24-9

Computing net present value **P3**

After evaluating the risk of the investment described in Exercise 24-8, B2B Co. concludes that it must earn at least an 8% return on this investment. Compute the net present value of this investment. (Round the net present value to the nearest dollar.)

Exercise 24-10

NPV and profitability index

P3

Following is information on two alternative investments being considered by Jolee Company. The company requires a 10% return from its investments.

	Project A	Project B
Initial investment	$(160,000)	$(105,000)
Expected net cash flows: Year 1	40,000	32,000
Year 2	56,000	50,000
Year 3	80,295	66,000
Year 4	90,400	72,000
Year 5	65,000	24,000

For each alternative project, compute the (*a*) net present value and (*b*) profitability index. (Round your answers in part *b* to two decimal places.) If the company can only select one project, which should it choose?

Exercise 24-11

Net present value, profitability index

P3

Following is information on two alternative investments being considered by Tiger Co. The company requires a 4% return from its investments.

	Project X1	Project X2
Initial investment	$(80,000)	$(120,000)
Expected net cash flows: Year 1	25,000	60,000
Year 2	35,500	50,000
Year 3	60,500	40,000

Compute each project's (*a*) net present value and (*b*) profitability index. (Round present value calculations to the nearest dollar and round the profitability index to two decimal places.) If the company can choose only one project, which should it choose?

Exercise 24-12

Net present value, profitability index **P3**

Refer to the information in Exercise 24-11 and instead assume the company requires a 12% return on its investments. Compute each project's (*a*) net present value and (*b*) profitability index. (Round present value calculations to the nearest dollar.) Express the profitability index as a percentage (rounded to two decimal places). If the company can choose only one project, which should it choose?

Refer to the information in Exercise 24-11. Create an Excel spreadsheet to compute the internal rate of return for each of the projects. Based on internal rate of return, determine whether the company should accept either of the two projects.

Exercise 24-13[A]
Internal rate of return **P4**

Phoenix Company can invest in each of three cheese-making projects: C1, C2, and C3. Each project requires an initial investment of $228,000 and would yield the following annual cash flows.

Exercise 24-14
Computing and interpreting net present value and internal rate of return

P3 **P4**

	C1	C2	C3
Year 1	$ 12,000	$ 96,000	$180,000
Year 2	108,000	96,000	60,000
Year 3	168,000	96,000	48,000
Totals..........................	$288,000	$288,000	$288,000

1. Assuming that the company requires a 12% return from its investments, use net present value to determine which projects, if any, should be acquired.

2. Using the answer from part 1, is the internal rate of return higher or lower than 12% for Project C2?

OptiLux is considering investing in an automated manufacturing system. The system requires an initial investment of $4 million, has a 20-year life, and will have zero salvage value. If the system is implemented, the company will save $500,000 per year in direct labor costs. The company requires a 10% return from its investments.

Exercise 24-15
NPV and IRR for automation investment

P3 **P4**

1. Compute the proposed investment's net present value.

2. Using your answer from part 1, is the investment's internal rate of return higher or lower than 10%?

Refer to the information in Exercise 24-15. Create an Excel spreadsheet to compute the internal rate of return for the proposed investment. Round the percentage return to two decimals.

Exercise 24-16[A]
IRR for automation investment **P4**

Refer to the information in Exercise 24-10. Create an Excel spreadsheet to compute the internal rate of return for each of the projects. Round the percentage return to two decimals.

Exercise 24-17[A]
Using Excel to compute IRR **P4**

This chapter explained two methods to evaluate investments using recovery time, the payback period and break-even time (BET). Refer to QS 24-17 and compute the recovery time for both the payback period and break-even time.

Exercise 24-18
Comparing payback and BET **A1** **P1**

---

connect

Factor Company is planning to add a new product to its line. To manufacture this product, the company needs to buy a new machine at a $480,000 cost with an expected four-year life and a $20,000 salvage value. All sales are for cash, and all costs are out-of-pocket, except for depreciation on the new machine. Additional information includes the following.

PROBLEM SET A

Problem 24-1A
Computing payback period, accounting rate of return, and net present value

P1 **P2** **P3**

Expected annual sales of new product	$1,840,000
Expected annual costs of new product	
Direct materials	480,000
Direct labor...	672,000
Overhead (excluding straight-line depreciation on new machine)	336,000
Selling and administrative expenses......................................	160,000
Income taxes	30%

Required

1. Compute straight-line depreciation for each year of this new machine's life. (Round depreciation amounts to the nearest dollar.)
2. Determine expected net income and net cash flow for each year of this machine's life. (Round answers to the nearest dollar.)
3. Compute this machine's payback period, assuming that cash flows occur evenly throughout each year. (Round the payback period to two decimals.)
4. Compute this machine's accounting rate of return, assuming that income is earned evenly throughout each year. (Round the percentage return to two decimals.)
5. Compute the net present value for this machine using a discount rate of 7% and assuming that cash flows occur at each year-end. *Hint:* Salvage value is a cash inflow at the end of the asset's life. Round the net present value to the nearest dollar.

Check   (4) 21.56%

(5) $107,356

Problem 24-2A

Analyzing and computing payback period, accounting rate of return, and net present value

P1   P2   P3

Most Company has an opportunity to invest in one of two new projects. Project Y requires a $350,000 investment for new machinery with a four-year life and no salvage value. Project Z requires a $350,000 investment for new machinery with a three-year life and no salvage value. The two projects yield the following predicted annual results. The company uses straight-line depreciation, and cash flows occur evenly throughout each year.

	Project Y	Project Z
Sales	$350,000	$280,000
Expenses		
Direct materials	49,000	35,000
Direct labor	70,000	42,000
Overhead including depreciation	126,000	126,000
Selling and administrative expenses	25,000	25,000
Total expenses	270,000	228,000
Pretax income	80,000	52,000
Income taxes (30%)	24,000	15,600
Net income	$ 56,000	$ 36,400

Required

Check   For Project Y:
(2) 2.44 years, (3) 32%

(4) $125,286

1. Compute each project's annual expected net cash flows. (Round the net cash flows to the nearest dollar.)
2. Determine each project's payback period. (Round the payback period to two decimals.)
3. Compute each project's accounting rate of return. (Round the percentage return to one decimal.)
4. Determine each project's net present value using 8% as the discount rate. For part 4 only, assume that cash flows occur at each year-end. (Round the net present value to the nearest dollar.)

Problem 24-3A

Computing cash flows and net present values with alternative depreciation methods

P3

Manning Corporation is considering a new project requiring a $90,000 investment in test equipment with no salvage value. The project would produce $66,000 of pretax income before depreciation at the end of each of the next six years. The company's income tax rate is 40%. In compiling its tax return and computing its income tax payments, the company can choose between the two alternative depreciation schedules shown in the table.

	Straight-Line Depreciation	MACRS Depreciation*
Year 1	$ 9,000	$18,000
Year 2	18,000	28,800
Year 3	18,000	17,280
Year 4	18,000	10,368
Year 5	18,000	10,368
Year 6	9,000	5,184
Totals	$90,000	$90,000

*The modified accelerated cost recovery system (MACRS) for depreciation is discussed in Chapter 8.

Required

1. Prepare a five-column table that reports amounts (assuming use of straight-line depreciation) for each of the following for each of the six years: (*a*) pretax income before depreciation, (*b*) straight-line depreciation expense, (*c*) taxable income, (*d*) income taxes, and (*e*) net cash flow. Net cash flow equals the amount of income before depreciation minus the income taxes. (Round answers to the nearest dollar.)

2. Prepare a five-column table that reports amounts (assuming use cf MACRS depreciation) for each of the following for each of the six years: (*a*) pretax income before depreciation, (*b*) MACRS depreciation expense, (*c*) taxable income, (*d*) income taxes, and (*e*) net cash flow. Net cash flow equals the income amount before depreciation minus the income taxes. (Round answers to the nearest dollar.)

3. Compute the net present value of the investment if straight-line depreciation is used. Use 10% as the discount rate. (Round the net present value to the nearest dollar.)

4. Compute the net present value of the investment if MACRS depreciation is used. Use 10% as the discount rate. (Round the net present value to the nearest dollar.)

Check   Net present value:
(3) $108,518

(4) $110,303

Analysis Component

5. Which depreciation method (straight-line or MACRS) results in a higher net present value?

Interstate Manufacturing is considering either replacing one of its old machines with a new machine or having the old machine overhauled. Information about the two alternatives follows. Management requires a 10% rate of return on its investments.

Problem 24-4A
Computing net present value of alternate investments

P3

Alternative 1: Keep the old machine and have it overhauled. If the old machine is overhauled, it will be kept for another five years and then sold for its salvage value.

Cost of old machine.................................	$112,000
Cost of overhaul......................................	150,000
Annual expected revenues generated	95,000
Annual cash operating costs after overhaul.............	42,000
Salvage value of old machine in 5 years	15,000

Alternative 2: Sell the old machine and buy a new one. The new machine is more efficient and will yield substantial operating cost savings with more product being produced and sold.

Cost of new machine.............................	$300,000
Salvage value of old machine now	29,000
Annual expected revenues generated	100,000
Annual cash operating costs......................	32,000
Salvage value of new machine in 5 years	20,000

Required

1. Determine the net present value of alternative 1.
2. Determine the net present value of alternative 2.
3. Which alternative do you recommend that management select?

Sentinel Company is considering an investment in technology to improve its operations. The investment will require an initial outlay of $250,000 and will yield the following expected cash flows. Management requires a 10% return on investments.

Problem 24-5A
Payback period, break-even time, and net present value

P1   A1

	Period 1	Period 2	Period 3	Period 4	Period 5
Cash flow	$47,000	$52,000	$75,000	$94,000	$125,000

Required

1. Determine the payback period for this investment. (Round the answer to one decimal.)
2. Determine the break-even time for this investment. (Round the answer to one decimal.)
3. Determine the net present value for this investment.

Analysis Component

4. Should management invest in this project?

Problem 24-6A
Payback period,
break-even time,
and net present value

A1   P1

Lenitnes Company is considering an investment in technology to improve its operations. The investment will require an initial outlay of $250,000 and will yield the following expected cash flows. Management requires a 10% return on its investments.

	Period 1	Period 2	Period 3	Period 4	Period 5
Cash flow.	$125,000	$94,000	$75,000	$52,000	$47,000

Required

1. Determine the payback period for this investment. (Round the answer to one decimal.)
2. Determine the break-even time for this investment. (Round the answer to one decimal.)
3. Determine the net present value for this investment.

Analysis Component

4. Should management invest in this project?

PROBLEM SET B

Problem 24-1B
Computing payback period,
accounting rate of return,
and net present value

P1   P2   P3

Cortino Company is planning to add a new product to its line. To manufacture this product, the company needs to buy a new machine at a $300,000 cost with an expected four-year life and a $20,000 salvage value. All sales are for cash and all costs are out-of-pocket, except for depreciation on the new machine. Additional information includes the following.

Expected annual sales of new product	$1,150,000
Expected annual costs of new product	
Direct materials	300,000
Direct labor.	420,000
Overhead (excluding straight-line depreciation on new machine)	210,000
Selling and administrative expenses.	100,000
Income taxes	30%

Required

1. Compute straight-line depreciation for each year of this new machine's life. (Round depreciation amounts to the nearest dollar.)
2. Determine expected net income and net cash flow for each year of this machine's life. (Round answers to the nearest dollar.)
3. Compute this machine's payback period, assuming that cash flows occur evenly throughout each year. (Round the payback period to two decimals.)

4. Compute this machine's accounting rate of return, assuming that income is earned evenly throughout each year. (Round the percentage return to two decimals.)

5. Compute the net present value for this machine using a discount rate of 7% and assuming that cash flows occur at each year-end. *Hint:* Salvage value is a cash inflow at the end of the asset's life.

Aikman Company has an opportunity to invest in one of two projects. Project A requires a $240,000 investment for new machinery with a four-year life and no salvage value. Project B also requires a $240,000 investment for new machinery with a three-year life and no salvage value. The two projects yield the following predicted annual results. The company uses straight-line depreciation, and cash flows occur evenly throughout each year.

Problem 24-2B

Analyzing and computing payback period, accounting rate of return, and net present value

P1 P2 P3

	Project A	Project B
Sales	$250,000	$200,000
Expenses		
Direct materials	35,000	25,000
Direct labor.	50,000	30,000
Overhead including depreciation	90,000	90,000
Selling and administrative expenses.	18,000	18,000
Total expenses	193,000	163,000
Pretax income.	57,000	37,000
Income taxes (30%)	17,100	11,100
Net income	$ 39,900	$ 25,900

Required

1. Compute each project's annual expected net cash flows. (Round net cash flows to the nearest dollar.)
2. Determine each project's payback period. (Round the payback period to two decimals.)
3. Compute each project's accounting rate of return. (Round the percentage return to one decimal.)
4. Determine each project's net present value using 8% as the discount rate. For part 4 only, assume that cash flows occur at each year-end. (Round net present values to the nearest dollar.)

Check For Project A:
(2) 2.4 years
(3) 33.3%
(4) $90,879

Analysis Component

5. Identify the project you would recommend to management and explain your choice.

Grossman Corporation is considering a new project requiring a $30,000 investment in an asset having no salvage value. The project would produce $12,000 of pretax income before depreciation at the end of each of the next six years. The company's income tax rate is 40%. In compiling its tax return and computing its income tax payments, the company can choose between two alternative depreciation schedules as shown in the table.

Problem 24-3B

Computating cash flows and net present values with alternative depreciation methods

P3

	Straight-Line Depreciation	MACRS Depreciation*
Year 1	$ 3,000	$ 6,000
Year 2	6,000	9,600
Year 3	6,000	5,760
Year 4	6,000	3,456
Year 5	6,000	3,456
Year 6	3,000	1,728
Totals.	$30,000	$30,000

*The modified accelerated cost recovery system (MACRS) for depreciation is discussed in Chapter 8.

Required

1. Prepare a five-column table that reports amounts (assuming use of straight-line depreciation) for each of the following items for each of the six years: (*a*) pretax income before depreciation, (*b*) straight-line depreciation expense, (*c*) taxable income, (*d*) income taxes, and (*e*) net cash flow. Net cash flow equals the amount of income before depreciation minus the income taxes. (Round answers to the nearest dollar.)
2. Prepare a five-column table that reports amounts (assuming use of MACRS depreciation) for each of the following items for each of the six years: (*a*) pretax income before depreciation, (*b*) MACRS depreciation expense, (*c*) taxable income, (*d*) income taxes, and (*e*) net cash flow. Net cash flow equals the amount of income before depreciation minus the income taxes. (Round answers to the nearest dollar.)

3. Compute the net present value of the investment if straight-line depreciation is used. Use 10% as the discount rate. (Round the net present value to the nearest dollar.)

4. Compute the net present value of the investment if MACRS depreciation is used. Use 10% as the discount rate. (Round the net present value to the nearest dollar.)

Analysis Component

5. Explain why the MACRS depreciation method increases the net present value of this project.

Problem 24-4B
Computing net present value of alternate investments

P3

Archer Foods has a freezer that is in need of repair and is considering whether to replace the old freezer with a new freezer or have the old freezer extensively repaired. Information about the two alternatives follows. Management requires a 10% rate of return on its investments.

Alternative 1: Keep the old freezer and have it repaired. If the old freezer is repaired, it will be kept for another eight years and then sold for its salvage value.

Cost of old freezer	$75,000
Cost of repair	50,000
Annual expected revenues generated	63,000
Annual cash operating costs after repair	55,000
Salvage value of old freezer in 8 years.	3,000

Alternative 2: Sell the old freezer and buy a new one. The new freezer is larger than the old one and will allow the company to expand its product offerings, thereby generating more revenues. Also, it is more energy efficient and will yield substantial operating cost savings.

Cost of new freezer	$150,000
Salvage value of old freezer now	5,000
Annual expected revenues generated	68,000
Annual cash operating costs	30,000
Salvage value of new freezer in 8 years.	8,000

Required

1. Determine the net present value of alternative 1.

2. Determine the net present value of alternative 2.

3. Which alternative do you recommend that management select? Explain.

Problem 24-5B
Payback period, break-even time, and net present value

P1   A1

Aster Company is considering an investment in technology to improve its operations. The investment will require an initial outlay of $800,000 and yield the following expected cash flows. Management requires investments to have a payback period of two years, and it requires a 10% return on its investments.

	Period 1	Period 2	Period 3	Period 4
Cash flow	$300,000	$350,000	$400,000	$450,000

Required

1. Determine the payback period for this investment.

2. Determine the break-even time for this investment.

3. Determine the net present value for this investment.

Analysis Component

4. Should management invest in this project? Explain.

Retsa Company is considering an investment in technology to improve its operations. The investment will require an initial outlay of $800,000 and will yield the following expected cash flows. Management requires investments to have a payback period of two years, and it requires a 10% return on its investments.

Problem 24-6B

Payback period, break-even time, and net present value

P1   A1

	Period 1	Period 2	Period 3	Period 4
Cash flow.................	$450,000	$400,000	$350,000	$300,000

Required

1. Determine the payback period for this investment. (Round the answer to one decimal.)

2. Determine the break-even time for this investment. (Round the answer to one decimal.)

3. Determine the net present value for this investment.

Check   (1) Payback period, 1.9 years

Analysis Component

4. Should management invest in this project? Explain.

5. Compare your answers for parts 1 through 4 with those for Problem 24-5B. What are the causes of the differences in results and your conclusions?

This serial problem began in Chapter 1 and continues through most of the book. If previous chapter segments were not completed, the serial problem can begin at this point.

SP 24   Santana Rey is considering the purchase of equipment for **Business Solutions** that would allow the company to add a new product to its computer furniture line. The equipment is expected to cost $300,000 and to have a six-year life and no salvage value. It will be depreciated on a straight-line basis. Business Solutions expects to sell 100 units of the equipment's product each year. The expected annual income related to this equipment follows.

SERIAL PROBLEM

Business Solutions

P1   P2

Sales	$375,000
Costs	
Materials, labor, and overhead (except depreciation)	200,000
Depreciation on new equipment............................	50,000
Selling and administrative expenses.........................	37,500
Total costs and expenses.....................................	287,500
Pretax income..	87,500
Income taxes (30%)	26,250
Net income	$ 61,250

©Alexander Image/Shutterstock

Required

Compute the (1) payback period and (2) accounting rate of return for this equipment. Report ARR in percent, rounded to one decimal.

Accounting Analysis

AA 24-1   Assume **Apple** invested $2.12 billion to expand its manufacturing capacity. Assume that these assets have a 10-year life and that Apple requires a 10% internal rate of return on these assets.

COMPANY ANALYSIS

P3

APPLE

Required

1. What is the amount of annual cash flows that Apple must earn from these projects to have a 10% internal rate of return? *Hint:* Identify the 10-period, 10% factor from the present value of an annuity table, and then divide $2.12 billion by this factor to get the annual cash flows necessary.

[continued on next page]

[continued from previous page]

2. Access Apple's financial statements for the fiscal year ended September 30, 2017, from Appendix A.

    a. Determine the amount that Apple invested in capital assets for 2017. *Hint:* Refer to the statement of cash flows.

    b. Did Apple invest more in capital assets or in marketable securities for 2017?

COMPARATIVE ANALYSIS

P3

GOOGLE

APPLE

AA 24-2   Assume that **Google** invests $2.42 billion in capital assets. Assume that these assets have a seven-year life and that management requires a 15% internal rate of return on those projects.

Required

1. What is the amount of annual cash flows that Google must earn from those expenditures to achieve a 15% internal rate of return? *Hint:* Identify the seven-period, 15% factor from the present value of an annuity table and then divide $2.42 billion by the factor to get the annual cash flows required.

2. Refer to the financial statements in Appendix A. Identify the amount that Google invested in capital assets for the year ended December 31, 2017.

3. Refer to AA 24-1, part 2a. Did Google or **Apple** invest more in capital assets for 2017?

GLOBAL ANALYSIS

P3

Samsung

AA 24-3   Refer to **Samsung**'s statement of cash flows in Appendix A for the year ended December 31, 2017.

Required

1. What amount (in millions of Korean won) did Samsung spend to acquire property, plant, and equipment during 2017?

2. Assume the investment in part 1 is expected to generate annual net cash flows of 7,000,000 (in millions of Korean won) per year for the next 10 years. Compute the net present value of the investment using a discount rate of 9%.

Beyond the Numbers

ETHICS CHALLENGE

P3

BTN 24-1   A consultant commented that "too often the numbers look good but feel bad." This comment often stems from *estimation error* common to capital budgeting proposals that relate to future cash flows. Three reasons for this error often exist. First, reliably predicting cash flows several years into the future is very difficult. Second, the present value of cash flows many years into the future (say, beyond 10 years) is often very small. Third, personal biases and expectations can influence present value computations.

Required

1. Compute the present value of $100 to be received in 10 years assuming a 12% discount rate.

2. Why is understanding the three reasons mentioned for estimation error important when evaluating investment projects? Link this response to your answer for part 1.

COMMUNICATING IN PRACTICE

P1   P2   P3   P4

BTN 24-2   Payback period, accounting rate of return, net present value, and internal rate of return are common methods to evaluate capital investment opportunities. Assume that your manager asks you to identify the measurement basis and unit that each method offers and to list the advantages and disadvantages of each method. Present your response in memorandum format of less than one page.

TAKING IT TO THE NET

P1   P3

BTN 24-3   Capital budgeting is an important topic, and there are websites designed to help people understand the methods available. Access **TeachMeFinance.com**'s capital budgeting web page (**teachmefinance.com/capitalbudgeting.html**). This web page contains an example of a capital budgeting case involving a $15,000 initial cash outflow.

Required

Compute the payback period and the net present value (assuming a 10% required rate of return) of the following investment—assume that its cash flows occur at year-end. Compared to the example case at the website, the larger cash inflows in the example below occur in the later years of the project's life. Is this investment acceptable based on the application of these two capital budgeting methods? Explain.

	Period 0	Period 1	Period 2	Period 3	Period 4	Period 5
Cash flow..............	$(15,000)	$1,000	$2,000	$3,000	$6,000	$7,000

BTN 24-4   Break into teams and identify four reasons that an international airline such as **Southwest** or **Delta** would invest in a project when an analysis using both payback period and net present value indicates it to be a poor investment. (*Hint:* Think about qualitative factors.) Provide an example of an investment project that supports your answer.

TEAMWORK IN ACTION

P1   P3

BTN 24-5   Read the chapter opener about Marco Mascorro and his company, **Fellow Robots**. Suppose Marco's business continues to grow, and he builds a massive new manufacturing facility and warehousing center to make the business more efficient and reduce costs.

ENTREPRENEURIAL DECISION

P1 P2 P3 P4

Required

1. What are some of the management tools that Marco can use to evaluate whether the new manufacturing facility and warehousing center will be a good investment?
2. What information does Marco need to use the tools that you identified in your answer to part 1?
3. What are some of the advantages and disadvantages of each tool identified in your answer to part 1?

BTN 24-6   Visit or call a local auto dealership and inquire about leasing a car. Ask about the down payment and the required monthly payments. You will likely find the salesperson does not discuss the cost to purchase this car but focuses on the affordability of the monthly payments. This chapter gives you the tools to compute the cost of this car using the lease payment schedule in present dollars and to estimate the profit from leasing for an auto dealership.

HITTING THE ROAD

P3

Required

1. Compare the cost of leasing the car to buying it in present dollars using the information from the dealership you contact. (Assume you will make a final payment at the end of the lease and then own the car.)
2. Is it more costly to lease or buy the car? Support your answer with computations.

Financial Statement Information

This appendix includes financial information for (1) **Apple**, (2) **Google**, and (3) **Samsung**. Apple states that it designs, manufactures, and markets mobile communication and media devices, personal computers, and portable digital music players, and sells a variety of related software, services, peripherals, networking solutions, and third-party digital content and applications; it competes with both Google and Samsung in the United States and globally. The information in this appendix is taken from annual 10-K reports (or annual report for Samsung) filed with the SEC or other regulatory agency. An **annual report** is a summary of a company's financial results for the year along with its current financial condition and future plans. This report is directed to external users of financial information, but it also affects the actions and decisions of internal users.

A company often uses an annual report to showcase itself and its products. Many annual reports include photos, diagrams, and illustrations related to the company. The primary objective of annual reports, however, is the financial section, which communicates much information about a company, with most data drawn from the accounting information system. The content of a typical annual report's financial section follows.

- Letter to Shareholders
- Financial History and Highlights
- Quantitative and Qualitative Disclosures about Risk Factors
- Management Discussion and Analysis
- Management's Report on Financial Statements and on Internal Controls
- Report of Independent Accountants (Auditor's Report) and on Internal Controls
- Financial Statements
- Notes to Financial Statements
- Directors, Officers, and Corporate Governance
- Executive Compensation
- Accounting Fees and Services

This appendix provides the financial statements for Apple (plus selected notes), Google, and Samsung. The appendix is organized as follows:

- **Apple A-2** through **A-9**
- **Google A-10** through **A-13**
- **Samsung A-14** through **A-17**

APPLE
GOOGLE
Samsung

Many assignments at the end of each chapter refer to information in this appendix. We encourage readers to spend time with these assignments; they are especially useful in showing the relevance and diversity of accounting and reporting.

Special note: The SEC maintains the EDGAR (**E**lectronic **D**ata **G**athering, **A**nalysis, and **R**etrieval) database at **SEC.gov** for U.S. filers. The **Form 10-K** is the annual report form for most companies. It provides electronically accessible information. The **Form 10-KSB** is the annual report form filed by small businesses. It requires slightly less information than the Form 10-K. One of these forms must be filed within 90 days after the company's fiscal year-end. (Forms 10-K405, 10-KT, 10-KT405, and 10-KSB405 are slight variations of the usual form due to certain regulations or rules.)

Apple Inc.
CONSOLIDATED BALANCE SHEETS
(In millions, except number of shares which are reflected in thousands and par value)

	September 30, 2017	September 24, 2016
ASSETS		
Current assets		
Cash and cash equivalents	$ 20,289	$ 20,484
Short-term marketable securities	53,892	46,671
Accounts receivable, less allowances of $58 and $53, respectively	17,874	15,754
Inventories	4,855	2,132
Vendor non-trade receivables	17,799	13,545
Other current assets	13,936	8,283
Total current assets	128,645	106,869
Long-term marketable securities	194,714	170,430
Property, plant and equipment, net	33,783	27,010
Goodwill	5,717	5,414
Acquired intangible assets, net	2,298	3,206
Other non-current assets	10,162	8,757
Total assets	$ 375,319	$ 321,686
LIABILITIES AND SHAREHOLDERS' EQUITY		
Current liabilities		
Accounts payable	$ 49,049	$ 37,294
Accrued expenses	25,744	22,027
Deferred revenue	7,548	8,080
Commercial paper	11,977	8,105
Current portion of long-term debt	6,496	3,500
Total current liabilities	100,814	79,006
Deferred revenue, non-current	2,836	2,930
Long-term debt	97,207	75,427
Other non-current liabilities	40,415	36,074
Total liabilities	241,272	193,437
Commitments and contingencies		
Shareholders' equity		
Common stock and additional paid-in capital, $0.00001 par value: 12,600,000 shares authorized; 5,126,201 and 5,336,166 shares issued and outstanding, respectively	35,867	31,251
Retained earnings	98,330	96,364
Accumulated other comprehensive income (loss)	(150)	634
Total shareholders' equity	134,047	128,249
Total liabilities and shareholders' equity	$ 375,319	$ 321,686

See accompanying Notes to Consolidated Financial Statements.

Apple Inc.
CONSOLIDATED STATEMENTS OF OPERATIONS
(In millions, except number of shares which are reflected in thousands and per share amounts)

Years ended	September 30, 2017	September 24, 2016	September 26, 2015
Net sales	$ 229,234	$ 215,639	$ 233,715
Cost of sales	141,048	131,376	140,089
Gross margin	88,186	84,263	93,626
Operating expenses			
Research and development	11,581	10,045	8,067
Selling, general and administrative	15,261	14,194	14,329
Total operating expenses	26,842	24,239	22,396
Operating income	61,344	60,024	71,230
Other income (expense), net	2,745	1,348	1,285
Income before provision for income taxes	64,089	61,372	72,515
Provision for income taxes	15,738	15,685	19,121
Net income	$ 48,351	$ 45,687	$ 53,394
Earnings per share:			
Basic	$ 9.27	$ 8.35	$ 9.28
Diluted	$ 9.21	$ 8.31	$ 9.22
Shares used in computing earnings per share:			
Basic	5,217,242	5,470,820	5,753,421
Diluted	5,251,692	5,500,281	5,793,069
Cash dividends declared per share	$ 2.40	$ 2.18	$ 1.98

See accompanying Notes to Consolidated Financial Statements.

Apple Inc.
CONSOLIDATED STATEMENTS OF COMPREHENSIVE INCOME
(In millions)

Years ended	September 30, 2017	September 24, 2016	September 26, 2015
Net income	$ 48,351	$ 45,687	$ 53,394
Other comprehensive income (loss):			
Change in foreign currency translation, net of tax effects of $(77), $8 and $201, respectively	224	75	(411)
Change in unrealized gains/losses on derivative instruments:			
Change in fair value of derivatives, net of tax benefit (expense) of $(478), $(7) and $(441), respectively	1,315	7	2,905
Adjustment for net (gains) losses realized and included in net income, net of tax expense (benefit) of $475, $131 and $630, respectively	(1,477)	(741)	(3,497)
Total change in unrealized gains/losses on derivative instruments, net of tax	(162)	(734)	(592)
Change in unrealized gains/losses on marketable securities:			
Change in fair value of marketable securities, net of tax benefit (expense) of $425, $(863) and $264, respectively	(782)	1,582	(483)
Adjustment for net (gains) losses realized and included in net income, net of tax expense (benefit) of $35, $(31), and $(32), respectively	(64)	56	59
Total change in unrealized gains/losses on marketable securities, net of tax	(846)	1,638	(424)
Total other comprehensive income (loss)	(784)	979	(1,427)
Total comprehensive income	$ 47,567	$ 46,666	$ 51,967

See accompanying Notes to Consolidated Financial Statements.

APPLE

Apple Inc.
CONSOLIDATED STATEMENTS OF SHAREHOLDERS' EQUITY
(In millions, except number of shares which are reflected in thousands)

	Common Stock and Additional Paid-In Capital		Retained Earnings	Accumulated Other Comprehensive Income (Loss)	Total Shareholders' Equity
	Shares	Amount			
Balances as of September 27, 2014	5,866,161	$ 23,313	$ 87,152	$ 1,082	$ 111,547
Net income	—	—	53,394	—	53,394
Other comprehensive income (loss)	—	—	—	(1,427)	(1,427)
Dividends and dividend equivalents declared	—	—	(11,627)	—	(11,627)
Repurchase of common stock	(325,032)	—	(36,026)	—	(36,026)
Share-based compensation	—	3,586	—	—	3,586
Common stock issued, net of shares withheld for employee taxes	37,624	(231)	(609)	—	(840)
Tax benefit from equity awards, including transfer pricing adjustments	—	748	—	—	748
Balances as of September 26, 2015	5,578,753	$ 27,416	$ 92,284	$ (345)	$ 119,355
Net income	—	—	45,687	—	45,687
Other comprehensive income (loss)	—	—	—	979	979
Dividends and dividend equivalents declared	—	—	(12,188)	—	(12,188)
Repurchase of common stock	(279,609)	—	(29,000)	—	(29,000)
Share-based compensation	—	4,262	—	—	4,262
Common stock issued, net of shares withheld for employee taxes	37,022	(806)	(419)	—	(1,225)
Tax benefit from equity awards, including transfer pricing adjustments	—	379	—	—	379
Balances as of September 24, 2016	5,336,166	$ 31,251	$ 96,364	$ 634	$ 128,249
Net income	—	—	48,351	—	48,351
Other comprehensive income (loss)	—	—	—	(784)	(784)
Dividends and dividend equivalents declared	—	—	(12,803)	—	(12,803)
Repurchase of common stock	(246,496)	—	(33,001)	—	(33,001)
Share-based compensation	—	4,909	—	—	4,909
Common stock issued, net of shares withheld for employee taxes	36,531	(913)	(581)	—	(1,494)
Tax benefit from equity awards, including transfer pricing adjustments	—	620	—	—	620
Balances as of September 30, 2017	5,126,201	$ 35,867	$ 98,330	$ (150)	$ 134,047

See accompanying Notes to Consolidated Financial Statements.

Apple Inc.
CONSOLIDATED STATEMENTS OF CASH FLOWS
(In millions)

Years ended	September 30, 2017	September 24, 2016	September 26, 2015
Cash and cash equivalents, beginning of the year	$ 20,484	$ 21,120	$ 13,844
Operating activities:			
Net income	48,351	45,687	53,394
Adjustments to reconcile net income to cash generated by operating activities:			
Depreciation and amortization	10,157	10,505	11,257
Share-based compensation expense	4,840	4,210	3,586
Deferred income tax expense	5,966	4,938	1,382
Other	(166)	486	385
Changes in operating assets and liabilities:			
Accounts receivable, net	(2,093)	527	417
Inventories	(2,723)	217	(238)
Vendor non-trade receivables	(4,254)	(51)	(3,735)
Other current and non-current assets	(5,318)	1,055	(283)
Accounts payable	9,618	1,837	5,001
Deferred revenue	(626)	(1,554)	1,042
Other current and non-current liabilities	(154)	(2,033)	9,058
Cash generated by operating activities	63,598	65,824	81,266
Investing activities:			
Purchases of marketable securities	(159,486)	(142,428)	(166,402)
Proceeds from maturities of marketable securities	31,775	21,258	14,538
Proceeds from sales of marketable securities	94,564	90,536	107,447
Payments made in connection with business acquisitions, net	(329)	(297)	(343)
Payments for acquisition of property, plant and equipment	(12,451)	(12,734)	(11,247)
Payments for acquisition of intangible assets	(344)	(814)	(241)
Payments for strategic investments, net	(395)	(1,388)	—
Other	220	(110)	(26)
Cash used in investing activities	(46,446)	(45,977)	(56,274)
Financing activities:			
Proceeds from issuance of common stock	555	495	543
Excess tax benefits from equity awards	627	407	749
Payments for taxes related to net share settlement of equity awards	(1,874)	(1,570)	(1,499)
Payments for dividends and dividend equivalents	(12,769)	(12,150)	(11,561)
Repurchases of common stock	(32,900)	(29,722)	(35,253)
Proceeds from issuance of term debt, net	28,662	24,954	27,114
Repayments of term debt	(3,500)	(2,500)	—
Change in commercial paper, net	3,852	(397)	2,191
Cash used in financing activities	(17,347)	(20,483)	(17,716)
Increase (decrease) in cash and cash equivalents	(195)	(636)	7,276
Cash and cash equivalents, end of the year	$ 20,289	$ 20,484	$ 21,120
Supplemental cash flow disclosure:			
Cash paid for income taxes, net	$ 11,591	$ 10,444	$ 13,252
Cash paid for interest	$ 2,092	$ 1,316	$ 514

See accompanying Notes to Consolidated Financial Statements.

APPLE

APPLE INC.
SELECTED NOTES TO CONSOLIDATED FINANCIAL STATEMENTS

Basis of Presentation and Preparation

In the opinion of the Company's management, the consolidated financial statements reflect all adjustments, which are normal and recurring in nature, necessary for fair financial statement presentation.

The Company's fiscal year is the 52 or 53-week period that ends on the last Saturday of September. The Company's fiscal year 2017 included 53 weeks and ended on September 30, 2017. A 14th week was included in the first fiscal quarter of 2017, as is done every five or six years, to realign the Company's fiscal quarters with calendar quarters. The Company's fiscal years 2016 and 2015 ended on September 24, 2016 and September 26, 2015, respectively, and spanned 52 weeks each. Unless otherwise stated, references to particular years, quarters, months and periods refer to the Company's fiscal years ended in September and the associated quarters, months and periods of those fiscal years.

Revenue Recognition

Net sales consist primarily of revenue from the sale of hardware, software, digital content and applications, accessories, and service and support contracts. The Company recognizes revenue when persuasive evidence of an arrangement exists, delivery has occurred, the sales price is fixed or determinable and collection is probable. Product is considered delivered to the customer once it has been shipped and title, risk of loss and rewards of ownership have been transferred. For most of the Company's product sales, these criteria are met at the time the product is shipped. For online sales to individuals, for some sales to education customers in the U.S., and for certain other sales, the Company defers revenue until the customer receives the product because the Company retains a portion of the risk of loss on these sales during transit. For payment terms in excess of the Company's standard payment terms, revenue is recognized as payments become due unless the Company has positive evidence that the sales price is fixed or determinable, such as a successful history of collection, without concession, on comparable arrangements. The Company recognizes revenue from the sale of hardware products, software bundled with hardware that is essential to the functionality of the hardware and third-party digital content sold on the iTunes Store in accordance with general revenue recognition accounting guidance. The Company recognizes revenue in accordance with industry-specific software accounting guidance for the following types of sales transactions: (i) standalone sales of software products, (ii) sales of software upgrades and (iii) sales of software bundled with hardware not essential to the functionality of the hardware.

For the sale of most third-party products, the Company recognizes revenue based on the gross amount billed to customers because the Company establishes its own pricing for such products, retains related inventory risk for physical products, is the primary obligor to the customer and assumes the credit risk for amounts billed to its customers. For third-party applications sold through the App Store and Mac App Store and certain digital content sold through the iTunes Store, the Company does not determine the selling price of the products and is not the primary obligor to the customer. Therefore, the Company accounts for such sales on a net basis by recognizing in net sales only the commission it retains from each sale. The portion of the gross amount billed to customers that is remitted by the Company to third-party app developers and certain digital content owners is not reflected in the Company's Consolidated Statements of Operations.

The Company records deferred revenue when it receives payments in advance of the delivery of products or the performance of services. This includes amounts that have been deferred for unspecified and specified software upgrade rights and non-software services that are attached to hardware and software products. The Company sells gift cards redeemable at its retail and online stores, and also sells gift cards redeemable on iTunes Store, App Store, Mac App Store, TV App Store and iBooks Store for the purchase of digital content and software. The Company records deferred revenue upon the sale of the card, which is relieved upon redemption of the card by the customer. Revenue from AppleCare service and support contracts is deferred and recognized over the service coverage periods. AppleCare service and support contracts typically include extended phone support, repair services, web-based support resources and diagnostic tools offered under the Company's standard limited warranty.

The Company records reductions to revenue for estimated commitments related to price protection and other customer incentive programs. For transactions involving price protection, the Company recognizes revenue net of the estimated amount to be refunded. For the Company's other customer incentive programs, the estimated cost of these programs is recognized at the later of the date at which the Company has sold the product or the date at which the program is offered. The Company also records reductions to revenue for expected future product returns based on the Company's historical experience. Revenue is recorded net of taxes collected from customers that are remitted to governmental authorities, with the collected taxes recorded as current liabilities until remitted to the relevant government authority.

For multi-element arrangements that include hardware products containing software essential to the hardware product's functionality, undelivered software elements that relate to the hardware product's essential software, and undelivered non-software services, the Company allocates revenue to all deliverables based on their relative selling prices.

For sales of qualifying versions of iPhone, iPad, iPod touch, Mac, Apple Watch and Apple TV, the Company has

Apple Inc. Notes—continued

indicated it may from time to time provide future unspecified software upgrades to the device's essential software and/or non-software services free of charge. The Company has identified up to three deliverables regularly included in arrangements involving the sale of these devices. The Company allocates revenue between these deliverables using the relative selling price method. Revenue allocated to the delivered hardware and the related essential software is recognized at the time of sale, provided the other conditions for revenue recognition have been met. Revenue allocated to the embedded unspecified software upgrade rights and the non-software services is deferred and recognized on a straight-line basis over the estimated period the software upgrades and non-software services are expected to be provided. Cost of sales related to delivered hardware and related essential software, including estimated warranty costs, are recognized at the time of sale. Costs incurred to provide non-software services are recognized as cost of sales as incurred, and engineering and sales and marketing costs are recognized as operating expenses as incurred.

Shipping Costs

Amounts billed to customers related to shipping and handling are classified as revenue, and the Company's shipping and handling costs are classified as cost of sales.

Warranty Costs

The Company generally provides for the estimated cost of hardware and software warranties in the period the related revenue is recognized. The Company assesses the adequacy of its accrued warranty liabilities and adjusts the amounts as necessary based on actual experience and changes in future estimates.

Software Development Costs

Research and development ("R&D") costs are expensed as incurred. Development costs of computer software to be sold, leased, or otherwise marketed are subject to capitalization beginning when a product's technological feasibility has been established and ending when a product is available for general release to customers. In most instances, the Company's products are released soon after technological feasibility has been established and as a result software development costs were expensed as incurred.

Advertising Costs

Advertising costs are expensed as incurred and included in selling, general and administrative expenses.

Other Income and Expense

$ millions	2017	2016	2015
Interest and dividend income	$ 5,201	$ 3,999	$2,921
Interest expense	(2,323)	(1,456)	(733)
Other expense, net	(133)	(1,195)	(903)
Total other income (expense), net	$ 2,745	$ 1,348	$1,285

Earnings Per Share

Basic earnings per share is computed by dividing income available to common shareholders by the weighted-average number of shares of common stock outstanding during the period. Diluted earnings per share is computed by dividing income available to common shareholders by the weighted-average number of shares of common stock outstanding during the period increased to include the number of additional shares of common stock that would have been outstanding if the potentially dilutive securities had been issued.

Cash Equivalents and Marketable Securities

All highly liquid investments with maturities of three months or less at the date of purchase are classified as cash equivalents. The Company's marketable debt and equity securities have been classified and accounted for as available-for-sale. Management determines the appropriate classification of its investments at the time of purchase and reevaluates the classifications at each balance sheet date. The Company classifies its marketable debt securities as either short-term or long-term based on each instrument's underlying contractual maturity date. Marketable debt securities with maturities of 12 months or less are classified as short-term and marketable debt securities with maturities greater than 12 months are classified as long-term. Marketable equity securities, including mutual funds, are classified as either short-term or long-term based on the nature of each security and its availability for use in current operations. The Company's marketable debt and equity securities are carried at fair value, with unrealized gains and losses, net of taxes, reported as a component of accumulated other comprehensive income/(loss) ("AOCI") in shareholders' equity, with the exception of unrealized losses believed to be other-than-temporary which are reported in earnings in the current period. The cost of securities sold is based upon the specific identification method.

Accounts Receivable (Trade Receivables)

The Company has considerable trade receivables outstanding with its third-party cellular network carriers, wholesalers, retailers, value-added resellers, small and mid-sized businesses and education, enterprise and government customers.

As of September 30, 2017, the Company had two customers that individually represented 10% or more of total trade receivables, each of which accounted for 10%. As of September 24, 2016, the Company had one customer that represented 10% or more of total trade receivables, which accounted for 10%. The Company's cellular network carriers accounted for 59% and 63% of trade receivables as of September 30, 2017 and September 24, 2016, respectively.

Allowance for Doubtful Accounts

The Company records its allowance for doubtful accounts based upon its assessment of various factors, including

Apple Inc. Notes—continued

historical experience, age of the accounts receivable balances, credit quality of the Company's customers, current economic conditions and other factors that may affect the customers' abilities to pay.

Inventories

Inventories are stated at the lower of cost, computed using the first-in, first-out method, and net realizable value. Any adjustments to reduce the cost of inventories to their net realizable value are recognized in earnings in the current period.

Property, Plant and Equipment

Property, plant and equipment are stated at cost. Depreciation is computed by use of the straight-line method over the estimated useful lives of the assets, which for buildings is the lesser of 30 years or the remaining life of the underlying building; between one and five years for machinery and equipment, including product tooling and manufacturing process equipment; and the shorter of lease term or useful life for leasehold improvements. The Company capitalizes eligible costs to acquire or develop internal-use software that are incurred subsequent to the preliminary project stage. Capitalized costs related to internal-use software are amortized using the straight-line method over the estimated useful lives of the assets, which range from three to five years. Depreciation and amortization expense on property and equipment was $8.2 billion, $8.3 billion and $9.2 billion during 2017, 2016 and 2015, respectively.

Property, Plant and Equipment, Net

($ millions)	2017	2016
Land and buildings	$ 13,587	$ 10,185
Machinery, equipment and internal-use software	54,210	44,543
Leasehold improvements	7,279	6,517
Gross property, plant and equipment	75,076	61,245
Accumulated depreciation and amortization	(41,293)	(34,235)
Total property, plant and equipment, net	$ 33,783	$ 27,010

Long-Lived Assets Including Goodwill and Other Acquired Intangible Assets

The Company reviews property, plant and equipment, inventory component prepayments and identifiable intangibles, excluding goodwill and intangible assets with indefinite useful lives, for impairment. Long-lived assets are reviewed for impairment whenever events or changes in circumstances indicate the carrying amount of an asset may not be recoverable. Recoverability of these assets is measured by comparison of their carrying amounts to future undiscounted cash flows the assets are expected to generate. If property, plant and equipment, inventory component prepayments and certain identifiable intangibles are considered to be impaired, the impairment to be recognized equals the amount by which the carrying value of the asset exceeds its fair value.

The Company does not amortize goodwill and intangible assets with indefinite useful lives; rather, such assets are required to be tested for impairment at least annually or sooner if events or changes in circumstances indicate that the assets may be impaired. The Company performs its goodwill and intangible asset impairment tests in the fourth quarter of each year. The Company did not recognize any impairment charges related to goodwill or indefinite lived intangible assets during 2017, 2016 and 2015. For purposes of testing goodwill for impairment, the Company established reporting units based on its current reporting structure. Goodwill has been allocated to these reporting units to the extent it relates to each reporting unit. In 2017 and 2016, the Company's goodwill was primarily allocated to the Americas and Europe reporting units.

The Company amortizes its intangible assets with definite useful lives over their estimated useful lives and reviews these assets for impairment. The Company typically amortizes its acquired intangible assets with definite useful lives over periods from three to seven years.

Acquired Intangible Assets

The Company's acquired intangible assets with definite useful lives primarily consist of patents and licenses. The following table summarizes the components of acquired intangible asset balances as of September 30, 2017. Amortization expense related to acquired intangible assets was $1.2 billion in 2017.

$ millions	Gross Carrying Amount	Accumulated Amortization	Net Carrying Amount
Definite-lived and amortizable acquired intangible assets	$ 7,507	$ (5,309)	$ 2,198
Indefinite-lived and non-amortizable acquired intangible assets	100	—	100
Total acquired intangible assets	$ 7,607	$ (5,309)	$ 2,298

Fair Value Measurements

The Company applies fair value accounting for all financial assets and liabilities and non-financial assets and liabilities that are recognized or disclosed at fair value in the financial statements on a recurring basis. The Company defines fair value as the price that would be received from selling an asset or paid to transfer a liability in an orderly transaction between market participants at the measurement date. When determining the fair value measurements for assets and liabilities that are required to be recorded at fair value, the Company considers the principal or most advantageous market in which the Company would transact and the market-based risk measurements or assumptions that market participants would use to price the asset or liability, such as risks inherent in valuation techniques, transfer restrictions and credit risk. Fair value is estimated by applying the following hierarchy,

Apple Inc. Notes—continued

which prioritizes the inputs used to measure fair value into three levels and bases the categorization within the hierarchy upon the lowest level of input that is available and significant to the fair value measurement:

Level 1—Quoted prices in active markets for identical assets or liabilities.
Level 2—Observable inputs other than quoted prices in active markets for identical assets and liabilities, quoted prices for identical or similar assets or liabilities in inactive markets, or other inputs that are observable or can be corroborated by observable market data for substantially the full term of the assets or liabilities.
Level 3—Inputs that are generally unobservable and typically reflect management's estimate of assumptions that market participants would use in pricing the asset or liability.

The Company's valuation techniques used to measure the fair value of money market funds and certain marketable equity securities were derived from quoted prices in active markets for identical assets or liabilities. The valuation techniques used to measure the fair value of the Company's debt instruments and all other financial instruments, all of which have counterparties with high credit ratings, were valued based on quoted market prices or model-driven valuations using significant inputs derived from or corroborated by observable market data.

In accordance with the fair value accounting requirements, companies may choose to measure eligible financial instruments and certain other items at fair value. The Company has not elected the fair value option for any eligible financial instruments.

Accrued Warranty and Indemnification

The following table shows changes in the Company's accrued warranties and related costs for 2017 and 2016:

$ millions	2017	2016
Beginning accrued warranty and related costs	$ 3,702	$ 4,780
Cost of warranty claims	(4,322)	(4,663)
Accruals for product warranty	4,454	3,585
Ending accrued warranty and related costs	$ 3,834	$ 3,702

Term Debt

As of September 30, 2017, the Company had outstanding floating- and fixed-rate notes with varying maturities for an aggregate principal amount of $104.0 billion (collectively the "Notes"). The Notes are senior unsecured obligations, and interest is payable in arrears.

The Company recognized $2.2 billion, $1.4 billion and $722 million of interest expense on its term debt for 2017, 2016 and 2015, respectively.

As of September 30, 2017 and September 24, 2016, the fair value of the Company's Notes, based on Level 2 inputs, was $106.1 billion and $81.7 billion, respectively.

Dividends

The Company declared and paid cash dividends per share during the periods presented as follows:

	2017		2016	
	Dividends Per Share	Amount (in millions)	Dividends Per Share	Amount (in millions)
Fourth quarter	$ 0.63	$ 3,252	$ 0.57	$ 3,071
Third quarter	0.63	3,281	0.57	3,117
Second quarter	0.57	2,988	0.52	2,879
First quarter	0.57	3,042	0.52	2,898
Total cash dividends declared and paid	$ 2.40	$ 12,563	$ 2.18	$ 11,965

Segment Information and Geographic Data

Net sales by product (mil.)	2017	2016	2015
iPhone	$141,319	$136,700	$155,041
iPad	19,222	20,628	23,227
Mac	25,850	22,831	25,471
Services	29,980	24,348	19,909
Other Products	12,863	11,132	10,067
Total net sales	$229,234	$215,639	$233,715

Reportable segment (mil.)	2017	2016	2015
Americas:			
Net sales	$96,600	$ 86,613	$ 93,864
Operating income	$30,684	$ 28,172	$ 31,186
Europe:			
Net sales	$54,938	$ 49,952	$ 50,337
Operating income	$16,514	$ 15,348	$ 16,527
Greater China:			
Net sales	$44,764	$ 48,492	$ 58,715
Operating income	$17,032	$ 18,835	$ 23,002
Japan:			
Net sales	$17,733	$ 16,928	$ 15,706
Operating income	$ 8,097	$ 7,165	$ 7,617
Rest of Asia Pacific:			
Net sales	$15,199	$ 13,654	$ 15,093
Operating income	$ 5,304	$ 4,781	$ 5,518

A reconciliation of the Company's segment operating income to the Consolidated Statements of Operations for 2017, 2016 and 2015 is as follows:

$ millions	2017	2016	2015
Segment operating income	$ 77,631	$ 74,301	$83,850
Research and development expense	(11,581)	(10,045)	(8,067)
Other corporate expenses, net	(4,706)	(4,232)	(4,553)
Total operating income	$ 61,344	$ 60,024	$71,230

Google Inc. (Alphabet Inc.)[a]
CONSOLIDATED BALANCE SHEETS
(In millions, except share and par value amounts which are reflected in thousands,
and par value per share amounts)

	As of December 31, 2016	As of December 31, 2017
Assets		
Current assets		
Cash and cash equivalents	$ 12,918	$ 10,715
Marketable securities	73,415	91,156
Total cash, cash equivalents, and marketable securities	86,333	101,871
Accounts receivable, net of allowance of $467 and $674	14,137	18,336
Income taxes receivable, net	95	369
Inventory	268	749
Other current assets	4,575	2,983
Total current assets	105,408	124,308
Non-marketable investments	5,878	7,813
Deferred income taxes	383	680
Property and equipment, net	34,234	42,383
Intangible assets, net	3,307	2,692
Goodwill	16,468	16,747
Other non-current assets	1,819	2,672
Total assets	$ 167,497	$ 197,295
Liabilities and Stockholders' Equity		
Current liabilities		
Accounts payable	$ 2,041	$ 3,137
Accrued compensation and benefits	3,976	4,581
Accrued expenses and other current liabilities	6,144	10,177
Accrued revenue share	2,942	3,975
Deferred revenue	1,099	1,432
Income taxes payable, net	554	881
Total current liabilities	16,756	24,183
Long-term debt	3,935	3,969
Deferred revenue, non-current	202	340
Income taxes payable, non-current	4,677	12,812
Deferred income taxes	226	430
Other long-term liabilities	2,665	3,059
Total liabilities	28,461	44,793
Commitments and contingencies		
Stockholders' equity:		
Convertible preferred stock, $0.001 par value per share, 100,000 shares authorized; no shares issued and outstanding	0	0
Class A and Class B common stock, and Class C capital stock and additional paid-in capital, $0.001 par value per share: 15,000,000 shares authorized (Class A 9,000,000, Class B 3,000,000, Class C 3,000,000); 691,293 (Class A 296,992, Class B 47,437, Class C 346,864) and 694,783 (Class A 298,470, Class B 46,972, Class C 349,341) shares issued and outstanding	36,307	40,247
Accumulated other comprehensive loss	(2,402)	(992)
Retained earnings	105,131	113,247
Total stockholders' equity	139,036	152,502
Total liabilities and stockholders' equity	$ 167,497	$ 197,295

[a]Google is part of Alphabet, but we loosely refer to Alphabet as "Google" because of its global familiarity and that Google provides 99% of Alphabet's $110,855 billion in revenues.

See accompanying notes.

Google Inc. (Alphabet Inc.)[a]
CONSOLIDATED STATEMENTS OF INCOME
(In millions)

Year Ended December 31	2015	2016	2017
Revenues	$ 74,989	$ 90,272	$ 110,855
Costs and expenses			
Cost of revenues	28,164	35,138	45,583
Research and development	12,282	13,948	16,625
Sales and marketing	9,047	10,485	12,893
General and administrative	6,136	6,985	6,872
European Commission fine	0	0	2,736
Total costs and expenses	55,629	66,556	84,709
Income from operations	19,360	23,716	26,146
Other income (expense), net	291	434	1,047
Income before income taxes	19,651	24,150	27,193
Provision for income taxes	3,303	4,672	14,531
Net income	$ 16,348	$ 19,478	$ 12,662
Less: Adjustment Payment to Class C capital stockholders	522	0	0
Net income available to all stockholders	$ 15,826	$ 19,478	$ 12,662

[a]Google is part of Alphabet, but we loosely refer to Alphabet as "Google" because of its global familiarity and that Google provides 99% of Alphabet's $110,855 billion in revenues.

See accompanying notes.

Google Inc. (Alphabet Inc.)[a]
CONSOLIDATED STATEMENTS OF COMPREHENSIVE INCOME
(In millions)

Year Ended December 31	2015	2016	2017
Net income	$ 16,348	$ 19,478	$ 12,662
Other comprehensive income (loss):			
Change in foreign currency translation adjustment	(1,067)	(599)	1,543
Available-for-sale investments:			
Change in net unrealized gains (losses)	(715)	(314)	307
Less: reclassification adjustment for net (gains) losses included in net income	208	221	105
Net change (net of tax effect of $29, $0, and $0)	(507)	(93)	412
Cash flow hedges:			
Change in net unrealized gains (losses)	676	515	(638)
Less: reclassification adjustment for net (gains) losses included in net income	(1,003)	(351)	93
Net change (net of tax effect of $115, $64, and $247)	(327)	164	(545)
Other comprehensive income (loss)	(1,901)	(528)	1,410
Comprehensive income	$ 14,447	$ 18,950	$ 14,072

[a]Google is part of Alphabet, but we loosely refer to Alphabet as "Google" because of its global familiarity and that Google provides 99% of Alphabet's $110,855 billion in revenues.

See accompanying notes.

GOOGLE

Google Inc. (Alphabet Inc.)[a]
CONSOLIDATED STATEMENTS OF STOCKHOLDERS' EQUITY
(In millions, except share amounts which are reflected in thousands)

	Class A and Class B Common Stock, Class C Capital Stock and Additional Paid-In Capital		Accumulated Other Comprehensive Income (Loss)	Retained Earnings	Total Stockholders' Equity
	Shares	Amount			
Balance as of December 31, 2014	680,172	$ 28,767	$ 27	$ 75,066	$ 103,860
Common and capital stock issued	8,714	664	0	0	664
Stock-based compensation expense	0	5,151	0	0	5,151
Stock-based compensation tax benefits	0	815	0	0	815
Tax withholding related to vesting of restricted stock units	0	(2,779)	0	0	(2,779)
Repurchases of capital stock	(2,391)	(111)	0	(1,669)	(1,780)
Adjustment Payment to Class C capital stockholders	853	475	0	(522)	(47)
Net income	0	0	0	16,348	16,348
Other comprehensive loss	0	0	(1,901)	0	(1,901)
Balance as of December 31, 2015	687,348	32,982	(1,874)	89,223	120,331
Cumulative effect of accounting change	0	180	0	(133)	47
Common and capital stock issued	9,106	298	0	0	298
Stock-based compensation expense	0	6,700	0	0	6,700
Tax withholding related to vesting of restricted stock units	0	(3,597)	0	0	(3,597)
Repurchases of capital stock	(5,161)	(256)	0	(3,437)	(3,693)
Net income	0	0	0	19,478	19,478
Other comprehensive loss	0	0	(528)	0	(528)
Balance as of December 31, 2016	691,293	36,307	(2,402)	105,131	139,036
Cumulative effect of accounting change	0	0	0	(15)	(15)
Common and capital stock issued	8,652	212	0	0	212
Stock-based compensation expense	0	7,694	0	0	7,694
Tax withholding related to vesting of restricted stock units	0	(4,373)	0	0	(4,373)
Repurchases of capital stock	(5,162)	(315)	0	(4,531)	(4,846)
Sale of subsidiary shares	0	722	0	0	722
Net income	0	0	0	12,662	12,662
Other comprehensive loss	0	0	1,410	0	1,410
Balance as of December 31, 2017	694,783	$ 40,247	$ (992)	$ 113,247	$ 152,502

[a]Google is part of Alphabet, but we loosely refer to Alphabet as "Google" because of its global familiarity and that Google provides 99% of Alphabet's $110,855 billion in revenues.

See accompanying notes.

GOOGLE

Google Inc. (Alphabet Inc.)[a]
CONSOLIDATED STATEMENTS OF CASH FLOWS
(In millions)

Year Ended December 31	2015	2016	2017
Operating activities			
Net income	$ 16,348	$ 19,478	$ 12,662
Adjustments:			
Depreciation and impairment of property and equipment	4,132	5,267	6,103
Amortization and impairment of intangible assets	931	877	812
Stock-based compensation expense	5,203	6,703	7,679
Deferred income taxes	(179)	(38)	258
Loss on marketable and non-marketable investments, net	334	275	194
Other	212	174	137
Changes in assets and liabilities, net of effects of acquisitions:			
Accounts receivable	(2,094)	(2,578)	(3,768)
Income taxes, net	(179)	3,125	8,211
Other assets	(318)	312	(2,164)
Accounts payable	203	110	731
Accrued expenses and other liabilities	1,597	1,515	4,891
Accrued revenue share	339	593	955
Deferred revenue	43	223	390
Net cash provided by operating activities	26,572	36,036	37,091
Investing activities			
Purchases of property and equipment	(9,950)	(10,212)	(13,184)
Proceeds from disposals of property and equipment	35	240	99
Purchases of marketable securities	(74,368)	(84,509)	(92,195)
Maturities and sales of marketable securities	62,905	66,895	73,959
Purchases of non-marketable investments	(2,326)	(1,109)	(1,745)
Maturities and sales of non-marketable investments	154	494	533
Cash collateral related to securities lending	(350)	(2,428)	0
Investments in reverse repurchase agreements	425	450	0
Acquisitions, net of cash acquired, and purchases of intangible assets	(236)	(986)	(287)
Proceeds from collection of notes receivable	0	0	1,419
Net cash used in investing activities	(23,711)	(31,165)	(31,401)
Financing activities			
Net payments related to stock-based award activities	(2,375)	(3,304)	(4,166)
Adjustment Payment to Class C capital stockholders	(47)	0	0
Repurchases of capital stock	(1,780)	(3,693)	(4,846)
Proceeds from issuance of debt, net of costs	13,705	8,729	4,291
Repayments of debt	(13,728)	(10,064)	(4,377)
Proceeds from sale of subsidiary shares	0	0	800
Net cash used in financing activities	(4,225)	(8,332)	(8,298)
Effect of exchange rate changes on cash and cash equivalents	(434)	(170)	405
Net decrease in cash and cash equivalents	(1,798)	(3,631)	(2,203)
Cash and cash equivalents at beginning of period	18,347	16,549	12,918
Cash and cash equivalents at end of period	$ 16,549	$ 12,918	$ 10,715
Supplemental disclosures of cash flow information			
Cash paid for taxes, net of refunds	$ 3,651	$ 1,643	$ 6,191
Cash paid for interest, net of amounts capitalized	$ 96	$ 84	$ 84

[a]Google is part of Alphabet, but we loosely refer to Alphabet as "Google" because of its
global familiarity and that Google provides 99% of Alphabet's $110,855 billion in revenues.

See accompanying notes.

Samsung Electronics Co., Ltd. and Subsidiaries
CONSOLIDATED STATEMENTS OF FINANCIAL POSITION

(In millions of Korean won)	December 31, 2017	December 31, 2016
Assets	KRW	KRW
Current assets		
Cash and cash equivalents	30,545,130	32,111,442
Short-term financial instruments	49,447,696	52,432,411
Short-term available-for-sale financial assets	3,191,375	3,638,460
Trade receivables	27,695,995	24,279,211
Non-trade receivables	4,108,961	3,521,197
Advance payments	1,753,673	1,439,938
Prepaid expenses	3,835,219	3,502,083
Inventories	24,983,355	18,353,503
Other current assets	1,421,060	1,315,653
Assets held-for-sale	—	835,806
Total current assets	**146,982,464**	**141,429,704**
Non-current assets		
Long-term available-for-sale financial assets	7,752,180	6,804,276
Held-to-maturity financial assets	106,751	—
Investment in associates and joint ventures	6,802,351	5,837,884
Property, plant and equipment	111,665,648	91,473,041
Intangible assets	14,760,483	5,344,020
Long-term prepaid expenses	3,434,375	3,834,831
Net defined benefit assets	825,892	557,091
Deferred income tax assets	5,061,687	5,321,450
Other non-current assets	4,360,259	1,572,027
Total assets	**301,752,090**	**262,174,324**
Liabilities and Equity		
Current liabilities		
Trade payables	9,083,907	6,485,039
Short-term borrowings	15,767,619	12,746,789
Other payables	13,899,633	11,525,910
Advances received	1,249,174	1,358,878
Withholdings	793,582	685,028
Accrued expenses	13,996,273	12,527,300
Income tax payable	7,408,348	2,837,353
Current portion of long-term liabilities	278,619	1,232,817
Provisions	4,294,820	4,597,417
Other current liabilities	403,139	351,176
Liabilities held-for-sale	—	356,388
Total current liabilities	**67,175,114**	**54,704,095**
Non-current liabilities		
Debentures	953,361	58,542
Long-term borrowings	1,814,446	1,244,238
Long-term other payables	2,043,729	3,317,054
Net defined benefit liabilities	389,922	173,656
Deferred income tax liabilities	11,710,781	7,293,514
Provisions	464,324	358,126
Other non-current liabilities	2,708,985	2,062,066
Total liabilities	**87,260,662**	**69,211,291**
Equity attributable to owners of the parent		
Preference shares	119,467	119,467
Ordinary shares	778,047	778,047
Share premium	4,403,893	4,403,893
Retained earnings	215,811,200	193,086,317
Other components of equity	(13,899,191)	(11,934,586)
Accumulated other comprehensive income attributable to assets held for-sale	—	(28,810)
	207,213,416	**186,424,328**
Non-controlling interests	7,278,012	6,538,705
Total equity	**214,491,428**	**192,963,033**
Total liabilities and equity	**301,752,090**	**262,174,324**

The above consolidated statement of financial position should be read in conjunction with the accompanying notes.

Samsung Electronics Co., Ltd. and Subsidiaries
CONSOLIDATED STATEMENTS OF PROFIT OR LOSS

For the year ended December 31	2017	2016
(In millions of Korean won)	KRW	KRW
Revenue	239,575,376	201,866,745
Cost of sales	129,290,661	120,277,715
Gross profit	**110,284,715**	**81,589,030**
Selling and administrative expenses	56,639,677	52,348,358
Operating profit	**53,645,038**	**29,240,672**
Other non-operating income	3,010,657	3,238,261
Other non-operating expense	1,419,648	2,463,814
Share of profit of associates and joint ventures	201,442	19,501
Financial income	9,737,391	11,385,645
Financial expense	8,978,913	10,706,613
Profit before income tax	**56,195,967**	**30,713,652**
Income tax expense	14,009,220	7,987,560
Profit for the period	**42,186,747**	**22,726,092**
Profit attributable to owners of the parent	41,344,569	22,415,655
Profit attributable to non-controlling interests	842,178	310,437
Earnings per share		
—Basic	299,868	157,967
—Diluted	299,868	157,967

The above consolidated statement of financial position should be read in conjunction with the accompanying notes.

Samsung Electronics Co., Ltd. and Subsidiaries
CONSOLIDATED STATEMENTS OF COMPREHENSIVE INCOME

For the year ended December 31	2017	2016
(In millions of Korean won)	KRW	KRW
Profit for the period	42,186,747	22,726,092
Other comprehensive income (loss)		
Items not to be reclassified to profit or loss subsequently:		
Remeasurement of net defined benefit liabilities, net of tax	414,247	963,602
Shares of other comprehensive income (loss) of associates and joint ventures, net of tax	(6,347)	50,438
Items to be reclassified to profit or loss subsequently:		
Changes in value of available-for-sale financial assets, net of tax	511,207	(23,839)
Share of other comprehensive income (loss) of associates and joint ventures, net of tax	(49,256)	(130,337)
Foreign currency translation, net of tax	(6,334,987)	1,131,536
Gain (loss) on valuation of derivatives	(37,121)	—
Other comprehensive income (loss) for the period, net of tax	**(5,502,257)**	**1,991,400**
Total comprehensive income for the period	**36,684,490**	**24,717,492**
Comprehensive income attributable to:		
Owners of the parent	35,887,505	24,310,814
Non-controlling interests	796,985	406,678

The above consolidated statement of financial position should be read in conjunction with the accompanying notes.

Samsung Electronics Co., Ltd. and Subsidiaries
CONSOLIDATED STATEMENTS OF CHANGES IN EQUITY

In millions of Korean won	Preference shares	Ordinary shares	Share premium	Retained earnings	Other Components of equity	Accumulated other comprehensive income attributable to assets held-for-sale	Equity attributable to owners of the parent	Non controlling interests	Total
Balance as at January 1, 2016	119,467	778,047	4,403,893	185,132,014	(17,580,451)	23,797	172,876,767	6,183,038	179,059,805
Profit for the period	—	—	—	22,415,655	—	—	22,415,655	310,437	22,726,092
Changes in value of available-for-sale financial assets, net of tax	—	—	—	—	(87,706)	(23,797)	(111,503)	87,664	(23,839)
Share of other comprehensive income (loss) of associates and joint ventures, net of tax	—	—	—	—	(80,146)	212	(79,934)	35	(79,899)
Foreign currency translation, net of tax	—	—	—	—	1,160,316	—	1,160,316	(28,780)	1,131,536
Remeasurement of net defined benefit liabilities, net of tax	—	—	—	—	926,280	—	926,280	37,322	963,602
Classified as held-for-sale	—	—	—	—	29,022	(29,022)	—	—	—
Total comprehensive income (loss)	—	—	—	22,415,655	1,947,766	(52,607)	24,310,814	406,678	24,717,492
Dividends	—	—	—	(3,061,361)	—	—	(3,061,361)	(65,161)	(3,126,522)
Capital transaction under common control	—	—	—	—	(37)	—	(37)	12,272	12,235
Changes in consolidated entities	—	—	—	—	—	—	—	1,790	1,790
Acquisition of treasury stock	—	—	—	—	(7,707,938)	—	(7,707,938)	—	(7,707,938)
Retirement of treasury stock	—	—	—	(11,399,991)	11,399,991	—	—	—	—
Others	—	—	—	—	6,083	—	6,083	88	6,171
Total transactions with owners	—	—	—	(14,461,352)	3,698,099	—	(10,763,253)	(51,011)	(10,814,264)
Balance as at December 31, 2016	119,467	778,047	4,403,893	193,086,317	(11,934,586)	(28,810)	186,424,328	6,538,705	192,963,033
Profit for the period	—	—	—	41,344,569	—	—	41,344,569	842,178	42,186,747
Changes in value of available-for-sale financial assets, net of tax	—	—	—	—	489,150	—	489,150	22,057	511,207
Share of other comprehensive income (loss) of associates and joint ventures, net of tax	—	—	—	—	(54,300)	—	(54,300)	(1,303)	(55,603)
Foreign currency translation, net of tax	—	—	—	—	(6,289,926)	28,810	(6,261,116)	(73,871)	(6,334,987)
Remeasurement of net defined benefit liabilities, net of tax	—	—	—	—	406,323	—	406,323	7,924	414,247
Gain (loss) on valuation of derivatives	—	—	—	—	(37,121)	—	(37,121)	—	(37,121)
Total comprehensive income (loss)	—	—	—	41,344,569	(5,485,874)	28,810	35,887,505	796,985	36,684,490
Dividends	—	—	—	(6,747,123)	—	—	(6,747,123)	(64,277)	(6,811,400)
Capital transaction under common control	—	—	—	—	(2,992)	—	(2,992)	15,114	12,122
Changes in consolidated entities	—	—	—	—	(2,699)	—	(2,699)	(9,352)	(12,051)
Acquisition of treasury stock	—	—	—	—	(8,350,424)	—	(8,350,424)	—	(8,350,424)
Retirement of treasury stock	—	—	—	(11,872,563)	11,872,563	—	—	—	—
Others	—	—	—	—	4,821	—	4,821	837	5,658
Total transactions with owners	—	—	—	(18,619,686)	3,521,269	—	(15,098,417)	(57,678)	(15,156,095)
Balance as at December 31, 2017	119,467	778,047	4,403,893	215,811,200	(13,899,191)	—	207,213,416	7,278,012	214,491,428

The above consolidated statement of financial position should be read in conjunction with the accompanying notes.

Samsung Electronics Co., Ltd. and Subsidiaries
CONSOLIDATED STATEMENTS OF CASH FLOWS

For the year ended December 31	2017	2016
(In millions of Korean won)	KRW	KRW
Cash flows from operating activities		
Profit for the period	42,186,747	22,726,092
Adjustments	36,211,232	30,754,471
Changes in assets and liabilities arising from operating activities	(10,620,547)	(1,180,953)
Cash generated from operations	67,777,432	52,299,610
Interest received	1,581,117	1,405,085
Interest paid	(542,715)	(443,838)
Dividends received	173,305	256,851
Income tax paid	(6,827,098)	(6,132,064)
Net cash inflow from operating activities	**62,162,041**	**47,385,644**
Cash flows from investing activities		
Net decrease (increase) in short-term financial instruments	387,627	(6,780,610)
Disposal of short-term available-for-sale financial assets	499,856	3,010,003
Acquisition of short-term available-for-sale financial assets	—	(2,129,551)
Disposal of long-term financial instruments	1,750,221	789,862
Acquisition of long-term financial instruments	(1,079,355)	(1,741,547)
Disposal of long-term available-for-sale financial assets	191,826	2,010,356
Acquisition of long-term available-for-sale financial assets	(358,497)	(1,498,148)
Acquisition of held-to-maturity financial assets	(106,751)	—
Disposal of investment in associates and joint ventures	355,926	2,280,203
Acquisition of investment in associates and joint ventures	(25,293)	(84,306)
Disposal of property, plant and equipment	308,354	270,874
Acquisition of property, plant and equipment	(42,792,234)	(24,142,973)
Disposal of intangible assets	733	6,944
Acquisition of intangible assets	(983,740)	(1,047,668)
Cash outflow from business combinations	(8,754,268)	(622,050)
Cash inflow from business transfers	1,248,834	—
Others	(28,455)	19,936
Net cash outflow from investing activities	**(49,385,216)**	**(29,658,675)**
Cash flows from financing activities		
Net increase in short-term borrowings	2,730,676	1,351,037
Acquisition of treasury stock	(8,350,424)	(7,707,938)
Proceeds from long-term borrowings and debentures	998,311	1,041,743
Repayment of long-term borrowings and debentures	(1,140,803)	(252,846)
Dividends paid	(6,804,297)	(3,114,742)
Net increase in non-controlling interests	5,670	13,232
Net cash outflow from financing activities	**(12,560,867)**	**(8,669,514)**
Effect of exchange rate changes on cash and cash equivalents	(1,782,270)	417,243
Net (decrease) increase in cash and cash equivalents	**(1,566,312)**	**9,474,698**
Cash and cash equivalents		
Beginning of the period	**32,111,442**	**22,636,744**
End of the period	**30,545,130**	**32,111,442**

The above consolidated statements of cash flows should be read in conjunction with the accompanying notes.

B Time Value of Money

Learning Objectives

CONCEPTUAL

C1 Describe the earning of interest and the concepts of present and future values.

PROCEDURAL

P1 Apply present value concepts to a single amount by using interest tables.

P2 Apply future value concepts to a single amount by using interest tables.

P3 Apply present value concepts to an annuity by using interest tables.

P4 Apply future value concepts to an annuity by using interest tables.

PRESENT AND FUTURE VALUE CONCEPTS

The old saying "Time is money" means that as time passes, the values of assets and liabilities change. This change is due to *interest,* which is a borrower's payment to the owner of an asset for its use. The most common example of interest is a savings account. Cash in the account earns interest paid by the financial institution. An example of a liability is a car loan. As we carry the balance of the loan, we accumulate interest costs on it. We must ultimately repay this loan with interest.

    Present and future value computations enable us to measure or estimate the interest component of holding assets or liabilities over time. The present value computation is used to compute the value of future-day assets *today.* The future value computation is used to compute the value of present-day assets *at a future date.* The first section focuses on the present value of a single amount. The second section focuses on the future value of a single amount. Then both the present and future values of a series of amounts (called an *annuity*) are defined and explained.

C1_____

Describe the earning of interest and the concepts of present and future values.

■ **Decision Insight** ═══

What's Five Million Worth? Robert Miles, a maintenance worker, purchased a scratch-off ticket that won him a $5 million jackpot. The $5 million payout was offered to Miles as a $250,000 annuity for 20 years **or** as a lump-sum payment of $3,210,000, which is about $2,124,378 after taxes. ■

PRESENT VALUE OF A SINGLE AMOUNT

Graph of PV of a Single Amount   We graphically express the present value, called p, of a single future amount, called f, that is received or paid at a future date in Exhibit B.1.

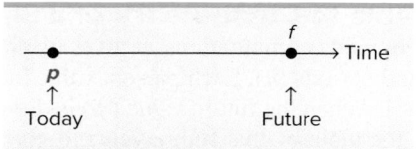

EXHIBIT B.1

Present Value of a Single Amount Diagram

Formula of PV of a Single Amount   The formula to compute the present value of a single amount is shown in Exhibit B.2, where p = present value (PV); f = future value (FV); i = rate of interest per period; and n = number of periods. (Interest is also called the *discount,* and interest rate is also called the *discount rate.*)

$$p = \frac{f}{(1+i)^n}$$

P1_____

Apply present value concepts to a single amount by using interest tables.

EXHIBIT B.2

Present Value of a Single Amount Formula

Illustration of PV of a Single Amount for One Period   To illustrate present value concepts, assume that we need $220 one period from today. We want to know how much we must invest now, for one period, at an interest rate of 10% to provide for this $220. For this illustration, the p, or present value, is the unknown amount—the specifics are shown graphically as follows.

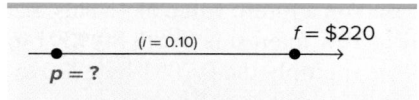

Conceptually, we know p must be less than $220. This is clear from the answer to: Would we rather have $220 today or $220 at some future date? If we had $220 today, we could invest it and see it grow to something more than $220 in the future. Therefore, we would prefer the $220 today. This means that if we were promised $220 in the future, we would take less than $220 today. But how much less? To answer that question, we compute an estimate of the present value of the $220 to be received one period from now using the formula in Exhibit B.2 as follows.

$$p = \frac{f}{(1 + i)^n} = \frac{\$220}{(1 + 0.10)^1} = \$200$$

We interpret this result to say that given an interest rate of 10%, we are indifferent between $200 today or $220 at the end of one period.

Illustration of PV of a Single Amount for Multiple Periods   We can use this formula to compute the present value for *any number of periods*. To illustrate, consider a payment of $242 at the end of two periods at 10% interest. The present value of this $242 to be received two periods from now is computed as follows.

$$p = \frac{f}{(1 + i)^n} = \frac{\$242}{(1 + 0.10)^2} = \$200$$

I will pay your allowance at the end of the month. Do you want to wait or receive its present value today?

Together, these results tell us we are indifferent between $200 today, or $220 one period from today, or $242 two periods from today given a 10% interest rate per period.

The number of periods (n) in the present value formula does not have to be expressed in years. Any period of time such as a day, a month, a quarter, or a year can be used. Whatever period is used, the interest rate (i) must be compounded for the same period. This means that if a situation expresses n in months and i equals 12% per year, then i is transformed into interest earned per month (or 1%). In this case, interest is said to be *compounded monthly*. For example, the present value of $1 when n is 12 months and i is 12% compounded monthly follows.

$$p = \frac{1}{(1 + 0.01)^{12}} = \$0.8874$$

Using Present Value Table to Compute PV of a Single Amount   A present value table helps us with present value computations. It gives us present values (factors) for a variety of both interest rates (i) and periods (n). Each present value in a present value table assumes that the future value (f) equals 1. When the future value (f) is different from 1, we simply multiply the present value (p) from the table by that future value to give us the estimate. The formula used to construct a table of present values for a single future amount of 1 is shown in Exhibit B.3.

EXHIBIT B.3

Present Value of 1 Formula

$$p = \frac{1}{(1 + i)^n}$$

This formula is identical to that in Exhibit B.2 except that f equals 1. Table B.1 at the end of this appendix is such a present value table. It is often called a **present value of 1 table**. A present value table has three factors: p, i, and n. Knowing two of these three factors allows us to compute the third. (A fourth is f, but, as already explained, we need only multiply the 1 used in the formula by f.) To illustrate the use of a present value table, consider three cases.

Case 1   **Solve for p when knowing i and n.** To show how we use a present value table, let's look again at how we estimate the present value of $220 (the f value) at the end of one period ($n = 1$) where the interest rate (i) is 10%. To solve this case, we go to the present value table (Table B.1) and look in the row for one period and in the column for 10% interest. Here we find a present value (p) of 0.9091 based on a future value of 1. This means, for instance, that $1 to be received one period from today at 10% interest is worth $0.9091 today. Because the future value in this case is not $1 but $220, we multiply the 0.9091 by $220 to get an answer of $200.

Case 2   **Solve for n when knowing p and i.** To illustrate, assume a $100,000 future value ($f$) that is worth $13,000 today ($p$) using an interest rate of 12% (i) but where n is unknown. In particular, we want to know how many periods (n) there are between the present value and the future value. To put this in context, it would fit a situation in which we want to retire with $100,000 but currently have only $13,000 that is earning a 12% return and we are unable to save additional money. How long will it be before we can retire? To answer this, we go to Table B.1 and look in the 12% interest column. Here we find a column of present values (*p*) based on a future value of 1. To use the present value table for this solution, we must divide $13,000 (*p*) by $100,000 (*f*), which equals 0.1300. This is necessary because *a present value table defines* f *equal to 1, and* p *as a fraction of 1.* We look for a value nearest to 0.1300 (*p*), which we find in the row for 18 periods (*n*). This means that the present value of $100,000 at the end of 18 periods at 12% interest is $13,000; alternatively stated, we must work 18 more years.

Case 3   Solve for *i* when knowing *p* and *n*. In this case, we have, say, a $120,000 future value (*f*) worth $60,000 today (*p*) when there are nine periods (*n*) between the present and future values, but the interest rate is unknown. As an example, suppose we want to retire with $120,000 in nine years, but we have only $60,000 and we are unable to save additional money. What interest rate must we earn to retire with $120,000 in nine years? To answer this, we go to the present value table (Table B.1) and look in the row for nine periods. To use the present value table, we must divide $60,000 (*p*) by $120,000 (*f*), which equals 0.5000. Recall that this step is necessary because a present value table defines *f* equal to 1 and *p* as a fraction of 1. We look for a value in the row for nine periods that is nearest to 0.5000 (*p*), which we find in the column for 8% interest (*i*). This means that the present value of $120,000 at the end of nine periods at 8% interest is $60,000 or, in our example, we must earn 8% annual interest to retire in nine years.

A company is considering an investment expected to yield $70,000 after six years. If this company demands an 8% return, how much is it willing to pay for this investment today?

NEED-TO-KNOW B-1

Present Value of a Single Amount

Solution

Today's value = $70,000 × 0.6302 = $44,114 (using PV factor from Table B.1, *i* = 8%, *n* = 6)

P1

FUTURE VALUE OF A SINGLE AMOUNT

Formula of FV of a Single Amount   We must modify the formula for the present value of a single amount to obtain the formula for the future value of a single amount. In particular, we multiply both sides of the equation in Exhibit B.2 by $(1 + i)^n$ to get the result shown in Exhibit B.4.

$$f = p \times (1 + i)^n$$

P2

Apply future value concepts to a single amount by using interest tables.

EXHIBIT B.4

Future Value of a Single Amount Formula

Illustration of FV of a Single Amount for One Period   The future value (*f*) is defined in terms of *p*, *i*, and *n*. We can use this formula to determine that $200 (*p*) invested for one period (*n*) at an interest rate of 10% (*i*) yields a future value of $220 as follows.

$$
\begin{aligned}
f &= p \times (1 + i)^n \\
&= \$200 \times (1 + 0.10)^1 \\
&= \$220
\end{aligned}
$$

Illustration of FV of a Single Amount for Multiple Periods   This formula can be used to compute the future value of an amount for *any number of periods* into the future. To illustrate, assume that $200 is invested for three periods at 10%. The future value of this $200 is $266.20, computed as follows.

$$
\begin{aligned}
f &= p \times (1 + i)^n \\
&= \$200 \times (1 + 0.10)^3 \\
&= \$200 \times 1.3310 \\
&= \$266.20
\end{aligned}
$$

Point: The FV factor in Table B.2 when *n* = 3 and *i* = 10% is 1.3310.

Point: Excel for FV.

	A	B
1	Present value	$200
2	Periods	3
3	Period int. rate	10%
4	Future value	

=−FV(B3,B2,0,B1) = $266.20

Using Future Value Table to Compute FV of a Single Amount   A future value table makes it easier for us to compute future values (*f*) for many different combinations of interest rates (*i*) and time periods (*n*). Each future value in a future value table assumes the present value (*p*) is 1. If the future amount is something other than 1, we multiply our answer by that amount. The formula used to construct a table of future values (factors) for a single amount of 1 is in Exhibit B.5.

EXHIBIT B.5

Future Value of 1 Formula

$$f = (1 + i)^n$$

Table B.2 at the end of this appendix shows a table of future values for a current amount of 1. This type of table is called a **future value of 1 table**.

There are some important relations between Tables B.1 and B.2. In Table B.2, for the row where $n = 0$, the future value is 1 for each interest rate. This is because no interest is earned when time does not pass. We also see that Tables B.1 and B.2 report the same information but in a different manner. In particular, one table is simply the *reciprocal* of the other. To illustrate this inverse relation, let's say we invest $100 for a period of five years at 12% per year. How much do we expect to have after five years? We can answer this question using Table B.2 by finding the future value (f) of 1, for five periods from now, compounded at 12%. From that table we find $f = 1.7623$. If we start with $100, the amount it accumulates to after five years is $176.23 ($100 × 1.7623). We can alternatively use Table B.1. Here we find that the present value (p) of 1, discounted five periods at 12%, is 0.5674. Recall the inverse relation between present value and future value. This means that $p = 1/f$ (or equivalently, $f = 1/p$). We can compute the future value of $100 invested for five periods at 12% as follows: $f = \$100 \times (1/0.5674) = \$176.24$ (which equals the $176.23 just computed, except for a 1 cent rounding difference).

Point:
1/PV factor = FV factor.
1/FV factor = PV factor.

Point: The FV factor when $n = 2$ and $i = 10\%$, is 1.2100. Its reciprocal, 0.8264, is the PV factor when $n = 2$ and $i = 10\%$.

A future value table has three factors: f, i, and n. Knowing two of these three factors allows us to compute the third. To illustrate, consider three possible cases.

Case 1   Solve for f when knowing i and n. Our preceding example fits this case. We found that $100 invested for five periods at 12% interest accumulates to $176.24.

Case 2   Solve for n when knowing f and i. In this case, we have, say, $2,000 ($p$) and we want to know how many periods (n) it will take to accumulate to $3,000 ($f$) at 7% interest ($i$). To answer this, we go to the future value table (Table B.2) and look in the 7% interest column. Here we find a column of future values (f) based on a present value of 1. To use a future value table, we must divide $3,000 ($f$) by $2,000 ($p$), which equals 1.500. This is necessary because *a future value table defines* p *equal to 1, and* f *as a multiple of 1.* We look for a value nearest to 1.50 (f), which we find in the row for six periods (n). This means that $2,000 invested for six periods at 7% interest accumulates to $3,000.

Case 3   Solve for i when knowing f and n. In this case, we have, say, $2,001 ($p$), and in nine years ($n$) we want to have $4,000 ($f$). What rate of interest must we earn to accomplish this? To answer that, we go to Table B.2 and search in the row for nine periods. To use a future value table, we must divide $4,000 ($f$) by $2,001 ($p$), which equals 1.9990. Recall that this is necessary because a future value table defines p equal to 1 and f as a multiple of 1. We look for a value nearest to 1.9990 (f), which we find in the column for 8% interest (i). This means that $2,001 invested for nine periods at 8% interest accumulates to $4,000.

■ **Decision Maker**

Entrepreneur   You are a retailer planning a sale on a security system that requires no payments for two years. At the end of two years, buyers must pay the full amount. The system's suggested retail price is $4,100, but you are willing to sell it today for $3,000 cash. What is your sale price if payment will not occur for two years and the market interest rate is 10%? ■   *Answer:* This is a present value question. The interest rate (10%) and present value ($3,000) are known, but the payment required two years later is unknown. The two-year-later price of $3,630 is computed as $3,000 × 1.10 × 1.10. The $3,630 two years from today is equivalent to $3,000 today.

 **B-2**

Future Value of a Single Amount

P2

Assume that you win a $150,000 cash sweepstakes today. You decide to deposit this cash in an account earning 8% annual interest, and you plan to quit your job when the account equals $555,000. How many years will it be before you can quit working?

Solution

Future value factor = $555,000/$150,000 = 3.7000

Searching for 3.7 in the 8% column of Table B.2 shows you cannot quit working for 17 years if your deposit earns 8% interest.

PRESENT VALUE OF AN ANNUITY

Graph of PV of an Annuity   An *annuity* is a series of equal payments occurring at equal intervals. One example is a series of three annual payments of $100 each. An *ordinary annuity* is defined as equal end-of-period payments at equal intervals. An ordinary annuity of $100 for three periods and its present value (*p*) are illustrated in Exhibit B.6.

P3

Apply present value concepts to an annuity by using interest tables.

EXHIBIT B.6

Present Value of an Ordinary Annuity Diagram

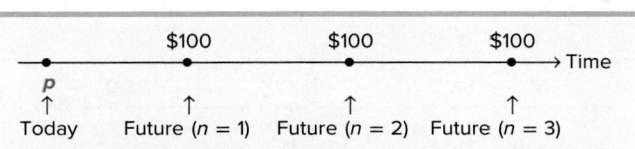

Formula and Illustration of PV of an Annuity   One way to compute the present value of an ordinary annuity is to find the present value of each payment using our present value formula from Exhibit B.3. We then add each of the three present values. To illustrate, let's look at three $100 payments at the end of each of the next three periods with an interest rate of 15%. Our present value computations are

$$p = \frac{\$100}{(1 + 0.15)^1} + \frac{\$100}{(1 + 0.15)^2} + \frac{\$100}{(1 + 0.15)^3} = \$228.32$$

Using Present Value Table to Compute PV of an Annuity   This computation is identical to computing the present value of each payment (from Table B.1) and taking their sum or, alternatively, adding the values from Table B.1 for each of the three payments and multiplying their sum by the $100 annuity payment.

A more direct way is to use a present value of annuity table. Table B.3 at the end of this appendix is one such table. This table is called a **present value of an annuity of 1 table**. If we look at Table B.3 where *n* = 3 and *i* = 15%, we see the present value is 2.2832. This means that the present value of an annuity of 1 for three periods, with a 15% interest rate, equals 2.2832.

A present value of an annuity formula is used to construct Table B.3. It also can be constructed by adding the amounts in a present value of 1 table. To illustrate, we use Tables B.1 and B.3 to confirm this relation for the prior example.

From Table B.1		From Table B.3	
i = 15%, *n* = 1	0.8696		
i = 15%, *n* = 2	0.7561		
i = 15%, *n* = 3	0.6575		
Total.	2.2832	*i* = 15%, *n* = 3	2.2832

Point: Excel for PV annuity.

	A	B
1	Payment	$100
2	Periods	3
3	Period int. rate	15%
4	Present value	

=−PV(B3,B2,B1) = $228.32

We also can use business calculators or spreadsheet programs to find the present value of an annuity.

■ Decision Insight

Count Your Blessings   "I don't have good luck—I'm blessed," proclaimed Andrew "Jack" Whittaker, a sewage treatment contractor, after winning the largest ever undivided jackpot in a U.S. lottery. Whittaker had to choose between $315 million in 30 annual installments or $170 million in one lump sum ($112 million after-tax). ■

A company is considering an investment that would produce payments of $10,000 every six months for three years. The first payment would be received in six months. If this company requires an 8% annual return, what is the maximum amount it is willing to pay for this investment today?

NEED-TO-KNOW **B-3**

Present Value of an Annuity

P3

Solution

Maximum paid = $10,000 × 5.2421 = $52,421 (using PV of annuity factor from Table B.3, *i* = 4%, *n* = 6)

FUTURE VALUE OF AN ANNUITY

P4 _____

Apply future value concepts to an annuity by using interest tables.

Graph of FV of an Annuity
The future value of an *ordinary annuity* is the accumulated value of each annuity payment with interest as of the date of the final payment. To illustrate, let's consider the earlier annuity of three annual payments of $100. Exhibit B.7 shows the point in time for the future value (f). The first payment is made two periods prior to the point when future value is determined, and the final payment occurs on the future value date.

EXHIBIT B.7

Future Value of an Ordinary Annuity Diagram

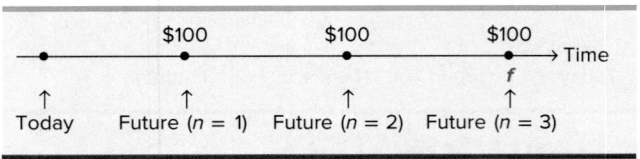

Point: An ordinary annuity is a series of equal cash flows, with the payment at the *end* of each period.

Formula and Illustration of FV of an Annuity
One way to compute the future value of an annuity is to use the formula to find the future value of *each* payment and add them. If we assume an interest rate of 15%, our calculation is

$$f = \$100 \times (1 + 0.15)^2 + \$100 \times (1 + 0.15)^1 + \$100 \times (1 + 0.15)^0 = \$347.25$$

This is identical to using Table B.2 and summing the future values of each payment, or adding the future values of the three payments of 1 and multiplying the sum by $100.

Using Future Value Table to Compute FV of an Annuity
A more direct way is to use a table showing future values of annuities. Such a table is called a **future value of an annuity of 1 table**. Table B.4 at the end of this appendix is one such table. Note that in Table B.4 when $n = 1$, the future values equal 1 ($f = 1$) for all rates of interest. This is because such an annuity consists of only one payment, and the future value is determined on the date of that payment—no time passes between the payment and its future value. The future value of an annuity formula is used to construct Table B.4. We also can construct it by adding the amounts from a future value of 1 table. To illustrate, we use Tables B.2 and B.4 to confirm this relation for the prior example.

Point: Excel for FV annuity.

	A	B
1	Payment	$100
2	Periods	3
3	Period int. rate	15%
4	Future value	

=−FV(B3,B2,B1) = $347.25

From Table B.2		From Table B.4	
$i = 15\%, n = 0$	1.0000		
$i = 15\%, n = 1$	1.1500		
$i = 15\%, n = 2$	1.3225		
Total..................	3.4725	$i = 15\%, n = 3$	3.4725

Note that the future value in Table B.2 is 1.0000 when $n = 0$, but the future value in Table B.4 is 1.0000 when $n = 1$. Is this a contradiction? No. When $n = 0$ in Table B.2, the future value is determined on the date when a single payment occurs. This means that no interest is earned because no time has passed, and the future value equals the payment. Table B.4 describes annuities with equal payments occurring at the end of each period. When $n = 1$, the annuity has one payment, and its future value equals 1 on the date of its final and only payment. Again, no time passes between the payment and its future value date.

NEED-TO-KNOW B-4

Future Value of an Annuity

P4

A company invests $45,000 per year for five years at 12% annual interest. Compute the value of this annuity investment at the end of five years.

Solution

Future value = $45,000 × 6.3528 = <u>$285,876</u> (using FV of annuity factor from Table B.4, $i = 12\%, n = 5$)

Summary: Cheat Sheet

PV OF A SINGLE AMOUNT

$$p = \frac{f}{(1+i)^n}$$

where p = present value (PV); f = future value (FV); i = rate of interest per period; and n = number of periods. Excel follows:

Point: Excel for PV.

	A	B
1	Future value	$242
2	Periods	2
3	Period int. rate	10%
4	Present value	

=−PV(B3,B2,0,B1) = $200

PV OF AN ANNUITY

$$p = f \times \left[1 - \frac{1}{(1+i)^n}\right]/i$$

where p = present value (PV); f = future value (FV); i = rate of interest per period; and n = number of periods. Excel follows:

Point: Excel for PV annuity.

	A	B
1	Payment	$100
2	Periods	3
3	Period int. rate	15%
4	Present value	

=−PV(B3,B2,B1) = $228.32

FV OF A SINGLE AMOUNT

$$f = p \times (1+i)^n$$

where p = present value (PV); f = future value (FV); i = rate of interest per period; and n = number of periods. Excel follows:

Point: Excel for FV.

	A	B
1	Present value	$200
2	Periods	3
3	Period int. rate	10%
4	Future value	

=−FV(B3,B2,0,B1) = $266.20

FV OF AN ANNUITY

$$f = p \times [(1+i)^n - 1]/i$$

where p = present value (PV); f = future value (FV); i = rate of interest per period; and n = number of periods. Excel follows:

Point: Excel for FV annuity.

	A	B
1	Payment	$100
2	Periods	3
3	Period int. rate	15%
4	Future value	

=−FV(B3,B2,B1) = $347.25

connect

Assume that you must estimate what the future value will be two years from today using the *future value of 1 table* (Table B.2). Which interest rate column *and* number-of-periods row do you use when working with the following rates?

1. 12% annual rate, compounded annually
2. 6% annual rate, compounded semiannually
3. 8% annual rate, compounded quarterly
4. 12% annual rate, compounded monthly (the answer for number-of-periods in part 4 is not shown in Table B.2)

QUICK STUDY

QS B-1
Identifying interest rates in tables
C1

Ken Francis is offered the possibility of investing $2,745 today; in return, he would receive $10,000 after 15 years. What is the annual rate of interest for this investment? (Use Table B.1.)

QS B-2
Interest rate on an investment   **P1**

Megan Brink is offered the possibility of investing $6,651 today at 6% interest per year in a desire to accumulate $10,000. How many years must Brink wait to accumulate $10,000? (Use Table B.1.)

QS B-3
Number of periods of an investment   **P1**

Flaherty is considering an investment that, if paid for immediately, is expected to return $140,000 five years from now. If Flaherty demands a 9% return, how much is she willing to pay for this investment?

QS B-4
Present value of an amount   **P1**

CII, Inc., invests $630,000 in a project expected to earn a 12% annual rate of return. The earnings will be reinvested in the project each year until the entire investment is liquidated 10 years later. What will the cash proceeds be when the project is liquidated?

QS B-5
Future value of an amount   **P2**

Beene Distributing is considering a project that will return $150,000 annually at the end of each year for the next six years. If Beene demands an annual return of 7% and pays for the project immediately, how much is it willing to pay for the project?

QS B-6
Present value of an annuity   **P3**

Claire Fitch is planning to begin an individual retirement program in which she will invest $1,500 at the end of each year. Fitch plans to retire after making 30 annual investments in the program earning a return of 10%. What is the value of the program on the date of the last payment (30 years from the present)?

QS B-7
Future value of an annuity   **P4**

EXERCISES

Exercise B-1
Present value of an amount **P1**

Mike Derr Company expects to earn 10% per year on an investment that will pay $606,773 six years from now. Use Table B.1 to compute the present value of this investment. (Round the amount to the nearest dollar.)

Exercise B-2
Present value of an amount **P1**

On January 1, a company agrees to pay $20,000 in three years. If the annual interest rate is 10%, determine how much cash the company can borrow with this agreement.

Exercise B-3
Number of periods of an investment **P2**

Tom Thompson expects to invest $10,000 at 12% and, at the end of a certain period, receive $96,463. How many years will it be before Thompson receives the payment? (Use Table B.2.)

Exercise B-4
Interest rate on an investment **P2**

Bill Padley expects to invest $10,000 for 25 years, after which he wants to receive $108,347. What rate of interest must Padley earn? (Use Table B.2.)

Exercise B-5
Future value of an amount **P2**

Mark Welsch deposits $7,200 in an account that earns interest at an annual rate of 8%, compounded quarterly. The $7,200 plus earned interest must remain in the account 10 years before it can be withdrawn. How much money will be in the account at the end of 10 years?

Exercise B-6
Future value of an amount **P2**

Catten, Inc., invests $163,170 today earning 7% per year for nine years. Use Table B.2 to compute the future value of the investment nine years from now. (Round the amount to the nearest dollar.)

Exercise B-7
Interest rate on an investment **P3**

Jones expects an immediate investment of $57,466 to return $10,000 annually for eight years, with the first payment to be received one year from now. What rate of interest must Jones earn? (Use Table B.3.)

Exercise B-8
Number of periods of an investment **P3**

Keith Riggins expects an investment of $82,014 to return $10,000 annually for several years. If Riggins earns a return of 10%, how many annual payments will he receive? (Use Table B.3.)

Exercise B-9
Present value of an annuity **P3**

Dave Krug finances a new automobile by paying $6,500 cash and agreeing to make 40 monthly payments of $500 each, the first payment to be made one month after the purchase. The loan bears interest at an annual rate of 12%. What is the cost of the automobile?

Exercise B-10
Present values of annuities **P3**

C&H Ski Club recently borrowed money and agreed to pay it back with a series of six annual payments of $5,000 each. C&H subsequently borrows more money and agrees to pay it back with a series of four annual payments of $7,500 each. The annual interest rate for both loans is 6%.

1. Use Table B.1 to find the present value of these two separate annuities. (Round amounts to the nearest dollar.)
2. Use Table B.3 to find the present value of these two separate annuities. (Round amounts to the nearest dollar.)

Exercise B-11
Present value with semiannual compounding
C1 P3

Otto Co. borrows money on April 30, 2019, by promising to make four payments of $13,000 each on November 1, 2019; May 1, 2020; November 1, 2020; and May 1, 2021.

1. How much money is Otto able to borrow if the interest rate is 8%, compounded semiannually?
2. How much money is Otto able to borrow if the interest rate is 12%, compounded semiannually?
3. How much money is Otto able to borrow if the interest rate is 16%, compounded semiannually?

Exercise B-12
Present value of bonds
P1 P3

Spiller Corp. plans to issue 10%, 15-year, $500,000 par value bonds payable that pay interest semiannually on June 30 and December 31. The bonds are dated December 31, 2019, and are issued on that date. If the market rate of interest for the bonds is 8% on the date of issue, what will be the total cash proceeds from the bond issue?

Compute the amount that can be borrowed under each of the following circumstances:

1. A promise to repay $90,000 seven years from now at an interest rate of 6%.

2. An agreement made on February 1, 2019, to make three separate payments of $20,000 on February 1 of 2020, 2021, and 2022. The annual interest rate is 10%.

Exercise B-13
Present value of an amount and of an annuity
P1 P3

Algoe expects to invest $1,000 annually for 40 years to yield an accumulated value of $154,762 on the date of the last investment. For this to occur, what rate of interest must Algoe earn? (Use Table B.4.)

Exercise B-14
Interest rate on an investment **P4**

Steffi Derr expects to invest $10,000 annually that will earn 8%. How many annual investments must Derr make to accumulate $303,243 on the date of the last investment? (Use Table B.4.)

Exercise B-15
Number of periods of an investment **P4**

Kelly Malone plans to have $50 withheld from her monthly paycheck and deposited in a savings account that earns 12% annually, compounded monthly. If Malone continues with her plan for two and one-half years, how much will be accumulated in the account on the date of the last deposit?

Exercise B-16
Future value of an annuity **P4**

Starr Company decides to establish a fund that it will use 10 years from now to replace an aging production facility. The company will make a $100,000 initial contribution to the fund and plans to make quarterly contributions of $50,000 beginning in three months. The fund earns 12%, compounded quarterly. What will be the value of the fund 10 years from now?

Exercise B-17
Future value of an amount plus an annuity
P2   P4

---

a. How much would you have to deposit today if you wanted to have $60,000 in four years? Annual interest rate is 9%.

b. Assume that you are saving up for a trip around the world when you graduate in two years. If you can earn 8% on your investments, how much would you have to deposit today to have $15,000 when you graduate?

c. Would you rather have $463 now or $1,000 ten years from now? Assume that you can earn 9% on your investments.

d. Assume that a college parking sticker today costs $90. If the cost of parking is increasing at the rate of 5% per year, how much will the college parking sticker cost in eight years?

e. Assume that the average price of a new home is $158,500. If the cost of a new home is increasing at a rate of 10% per year, how much will a new home cost in eight years?

f. An investment will pay you $10,000 in 10 years *and* it also will pay you $400 at the end of *each* of the next 10 years (Years 1 through 10). If the annual interest rate is 6%, how much would you be willing to pay today for this type of investment?

g. A college student is reported in the newspaper as having won $10,000,000 in the Kansas State Lottery. However, as is often the custom with lotteries, she does *not* actually receive the entire $10 million now. Instead she will receive $500,000 at the end of the year for *each* of the next 20 years. If the annual interest rate is 6%, what is the present value (today's amount) that she won? (Ignore taxes.)

Exercise B-18
Practical applications of the time value of money
P1   P2   P3   P4

For each of the following situations, identify (1) the case as either (*a*) a present or a future value and (*b*) a single amount or an annuity, (2) the table you would use in your computations (but do not solve the problem), and (3) the interest rate and time periods you would use.

a. You need to accumulate $10,000 for a trip you wish to take in four years. You are able to earn 8% compounded semiannually on your savings. You plan to make only one deposit and let the money accumulate for four years. How would you determine the amount of the one-time deposit?

b. Assume the same facts as in part (*a*) except that you will make semiannual deposits to your savings account.

c. You want to retire after working 40 years with savings in excess of $1,000,000. You expect to save $4,000 a year for 40 years and earn an annual rate of interest of 8%. Will you be able to retire with more than $1,000,000 in 40 years? Explain.

d. A sweepstakes agency names you a grand prize winner. You can take $225,000 immediately or elect to receive annual installments of $30,000 for 20 years. You can earn 10% annually on any investments you make. Which prize do you choose to receive?

Exercise B-19
Using present and future value tables
C1   P1   P2   P3   P4

Design elements: Lightbulb: ©Chuhail/Getty Images; Blue globe: ©nidwlw/Getty Images and ©Dizzle52/Getty Images; Chess piece: ©Andrei Simonenko/Getty Images and ©Dizzle52/Getty Images; Mouse: ©Siede Preis/Getty Images; Global View globe: ©McGraw-Hill Education and ©Dizzle52/Getty Images; Sustainability: ©McGraw-Hill Education and ©Dizzle52/Getty Images

TABLE B.1*

Present Value of 1

$$p = 1/(1 + i)^n$$

Periods	1%	2%	3%	4%	5%	6%	7%	8%	9%	10%	12%	15%	Periods
1	0.9901	0.9804	0.9709	0.9615	0.9524	0.9434	0.9346	0.9259	0.9174	0.9091	0.8929	0.8696	1
2	0.9803	0.9612	0.9426	0.9246	0.9070	0.8900	0.8734	0.8573	0.8417	0.8264	0.7972	0.7561	2
3	0.9706	0.9423	0.9151	0.8890	0.8638	0.8396	0.8163	0.7938	0.7722	0.7513	0.7118	0.6575	3
4	0.9610	0.9238	0.8885	0.8548	0.8227	0.7921	0.7629	0.7350	0.7084	0.6830	0.6355	0.5718	4
5	0.9515	0.9057	0.8626	0.8219	0.7835	0.7473	0.7130	0.6806	0.6499	0.6209	0.5674	0.4972	5
6	0.9420	0.8880	0.8375	0.7903	0.7462	0.7050	0.6663	0.6302	0.5963	0.5645	0.5066	0.4323	6
7	0.9327	0.8706	0.8131	0.7599	0.7107	0.6651	0.6227	0.5835	0.5470	0.5132	0.4523	0.3759	7
8	0.9235	0.8535	0.7894	0.7307	0.6768	0.6274	0.5820	0.5403	0.5019	0.4665	0.4039	0.3269	8
9	0.9143	0.8368	0.7664	0.7026	0.6446	0.5919	0.5439	0.5002	0.4604	0.4241	0.3606	0.2843	9
10	0.9053	0.8203	0.7441	0.6756	0.6139	0.5584	0.5083	0.4632	0.4224	0.3855	0.3220	0.2472	10
11	0.8963	0.8043	0.7224	0.6496	0.5847	0.5268	0.4751	0.4289	0.3875	0.3505	0.2875	0.2149	11
12	0.8874	0.7885	0.7014	0.6246	0.5568	0.4970	0.4440	0.3971	0.3555	0.3186	0.2567	0.1869	12
13	0.8787	0.7730	0.6810	0.6006	0.5303	0.4688	0.4150	0.3677	0.3262	0.2897	0.2292	0.1625	13
14	0.8700	0.7579	0.6611	0.5775	0.5051	0.4423	0.3878	0.3405	0.2992	0.2633	0.2046	0.1413	14
15	0.8613	0.7430	0.6419	0.5553	0.4810	0.4173	0.3624	0.3152	0.2745	0.2394	0.1827	0.1229	15
16	0.8528	0.7284	0.6232	0.5339	0.4581	0.3936	0.3387	0.2919	0.2519	0.2176	0.1631	0.1069	16
17	0.8444	0.7142	0.6050	0.5134	0.4363	0.3714	0.3166	0.2703	0.2311	0.1978	0.1456	0.0929	17
18	0.8360	0.7002	0.5874	0.4936	0.4155	0.3503	0.2959	0.2502	0.2120	0.1799	0.1300	0.0808	18
19	0.8277	0.6864	0.5703	0.4746	0.3957	0.3305	0.2765	0.2317	0.1945	0.1635	0.1161	0.0703	19
20	0.8195	0.6730	0.5537	0.4564	0.3769	0.3118	0.2584	0.2145	0.1784	0.1486	0.1037	0.0611	20
25	0.7798	0.6095	0.4776	0.3751	0.2953	0.2330	0.1842	0.1460	0.1160	0.0923	0.0588	0.0304	25
30	0.7419	0.5521	0.4120	0.3083	0.2314	0.1741	0.1314	0.0994	0.0754	0.0573	0.0334	0.0151	30
35	0.7059	0.5000	0.3554	0.2534	0.1813	0.1301	0.0937	0.0676	0.0490	0.0356	0.0189	0.0075	35
40	0.6717	0.4529	0.3066	0.2083	0.1420	0.0972	0.0668	0.0460	0.0318	0.0221	0.0107	0.0037	40

*Used to compute the present value of a known future amount. For example: How much would you need to invest today at 10% compounded semiannually to accumulate $5,000 in 6 years from today? Using the factors of $n = 12$ and $i = 5$% (12 semiannual periods and a semiannual rate of 5%), the factor is 0.5568. You would need to invest $2,784 today ($5,000 × 0.5568).

TABLE B.2†

Future Value of 1

$$f = (1 + i)^n$$

Periods	1%	2%	3%	4%	5%	6%	7%	8%	9%	10%	12%	15%	Periods
0	1.0000	1.0000	1.0000	1.0000	1.0000	1.0000	1.0000	1.0000	1.0000	1.0000	1.0000	1.0000	0
1	1.0100	1.0200	1.0300	1.0400	1.0500	1.0600	1.0700	1.0800	1.0900	1.1000	1.1200	1.1500	1
2	1.0201	1.0404	1.0609	1.0816	1.1025	1.1236	1.1449	1.1664	1.1881	1.2100	1.2544	1.3225	2
3	1.0303	1.0612	1.0927	1.1249	1.1576	1.1910	1.2250	1.2597	1.2950	1.3310	1.4049	1.5209	3
4	1.0406	1.0824	1.1255	1.1699	1.2155	1.2625	1.3108	1.3605	1.4116	1.4641	1.5735	1.7490	4
5	1.0510	1.1041	1.1593	1.2167	1.2763	1.3382	1.4026	1.4693	1.5386	1.6105	1.7623	2.0114	5
6	1.0615	1.1262	1.1941	1.2653	1.3401	1.4185	1.5007	1.5869	1.6771	1.7716	1.9738	2.3131	6
7	1.0721	1.1487	1.2299	1.3159	1.4071	1.5036	1.6058	1.7138	1.8280	1.9487	2.2107	2.6600	7
8	1.0829	1.1717	1.2668	1.3686	1.4775	1.5938	1.7182	1.8509	1.9926	2.1436	2.4760	3.0590	8
9	1.0937	1.1951	1.3048	1.4233	1.5513	1.6895	1.8385	1.9990	2.1719	2.3579	2.7731	3.5179	9
10	1.1046	1.2190	1.3439	1.4802	1.6289	1.7908	1.9672	2.1589	2.3674	2.5937	3.1058	4.0456	10
11	1.1157	1.2434	1.3842	1.5395	1.7103	1.8983	2.1049	2.3316	2.5804	2.8531	3.4785	4.6524	11
12	1.1268	1.2682	1.4258	1.6010	1.7959	2.0122	2.2522	2.5182	2.8127	3.1384	3.8960	5.3503	12
13	1.1381	1.2936	1.4685	1.6651	1.8856	2.1329	2.4098	2.7196	3.0658	3.4523	4.3635	6.1528	13
14	1.1495	1.3195	1.5126	1.7317	1.9799	2.2609	2.5785	2.9372	3.3417	3.7975	4.8871	7.0757	14
15	1.1610	1.3459	1.5580	1.8009	2.0789	2.3966	2.7590	3.1722	3.6425	4.1772	5.4736	8.1371	15
16	1.1726	1.3728	1.6047	1.8730	2.1829	2.5404	2.9522	3.4259	3.9703	4.5950	6.1304	9.3576	16
17	1.1843	1.4002	1.6528	1.9479	2.2920	2.6928	3.1588	3.7000	4.3276	5.0545	6.8660	10.7613	17
18	1.1961	1.4282	1.7024	2.0258	2.4066	2.8543	3.3799	3.9960	4.7171	5.5599	7.6900	12.3755	18
19	1.2081	1.4568	1.7535	2.1068	2.5270	3.0256	3.6165	4.3157	5.1417	6.1159	8.6128	14.2318	19
20	1.2202	1.4859	1.8061	2.1911	2.6533	3.2071	3.8697	4.6610	5.6044	6.7275	9.6463	16.3665	20
25	1.2824	1.6406	2.0938	2.6658	3.3864	4.2919	5.4274	6.8485	8.6231	10.8347	17.0001	32.9190	25
30	1.3478	1.8114	2.4273	3.2434	4.3219	5.7435	7.6123	10.0627	13.2677	17.4494	29.9599	66.2118	30
35	1.4166	1.9999	2.8139	3.9461	5.5160	7.6861	10.6766	14.7853	20.4140	28.1024	52.7996	133.1755	35
40	1.4889	2.2080	3.2620	4.8010	7.0400	10.2857	14.9745	21.7245	31.4094	45.2593	93.0510	267.8635	40

†Used to compute the future value of a known present amount. For example: What is the accumulated value of $3,000 invested today at 8% compounded quarterly for 5 years? Using the factors of $n = 20$ and $i = 2$% (20 quarterly periods and a quarterly interest rate of 2%), the factor is 1.4859. The accumulated value is $4,457.70 ($3,000 × 1.4859).

$$p = \left[1 - \frac{1}{(1+i)^n}\right]/i$$

TABLE B.3‡

Present Value of an Annuity of 1

Periods	1%	2%	3%	4%	5%	6%	7%	8%	9%	10%	12%	15%	Periods
1	0.9901	0.9804	0.9709	0.9615	0.9524	0.9434	0.9346	0.9259	0.9174	0.9091	0.8929	0.8696	1
2	1.9704	1.9416	1.9135	1.8861	1.8594	1.8334	1.8080	1.7833	1.7591	1.7355	1.6901	1.6257	2
3	2.9410	2.8839	2.8286	2.7751	2.7232	2.6730	2.6243	2.5771	2.5313	2.4869	2.4018	2.2832	3
4	3.9020	3.8077	3.7171	3.6299	3.5460	3.4651	3.3872	3.3121	3.2397	3.1699	3.0373	2.8550	4
5	4.8534	4.7135	4.5797	4.4518	4.3295	4.2124	4.1002	3.9927	3.8897	3.7908	3.6048	3.3522	5
6	5.7955	5.6014	5.4172	5.2421	5.0757	4.9173	4.7665	4.6229	4.4859	4.3553	4.1114	3.7845	6
7	6.7282	6.4720	6.2303	6.0021	5.7864	5.5824	5.3893	5.2064	5.0330	4.8684	4.5638	4.1604	7
8	7.6517	7.3255	7.0197	6.7327	6.4632	6.2098	5.9713	5.7466	5.5348	5.3349	4.9676	4.4873	8
9	8.5660	8.1622	7.7861	7.4353	7.1078	6.8017	6.5152	6.2469	5.9952	5.7590	5.3282	4.7716	9
10	9.4713	8.9826	8.5302	8.1109	7.7217	7.3601	7.0236	6.7101	6.4177	6.1446	5.6502	5.0188	10
11	10.3676	9.7868	9.2526	8.7605	8.3064	7.8869	7.4987	7.1390	6.8052	6.4951	5.9377	5.2337	11
12	11.2551	10.5753	9.9540	9.3851	8.8633	8.3838	7.9427	7.5361	7.1607	6.8137	6.1944	5.4206	12
13	12.1337	11.3484	10.6350	9.9856	9.3936	8.8527	8.3577	7.9038	7.4869	7.1034	6.4235	5.5831	13
14	13.0037	12.1062	11.2961	10.5631	9.8986	9.2950	8.7455	8.2442	7.7862	7.3667	6.6282	5.7245	14
15	13.8651	12.8493	11.9379	11.1184	10.3797	9.7122	9.1079	8.5595	8.0607	7.6061	6.8109	5.8474	15
16	14.7179	13.5777	12.5611	11.6523	10.8378	10.1059	9.4466	8.8514	8.3126	7.8237	6.9740	5.9542	16
17	15.5623	14.2919	13.1661	12.1657	11.2741	10.4773	9.7632	9.1216	8.5436	8.0216	7.1196	6.0472	17
18	16.3983	14.9920	13.7535	12.6593	11.6896	10.8276	10.0591	9.3719	8.7556	8.2014	7.2497	6.1280	18
19	17.2260	15.6785	14.3238	13.1339	12.0853	11.1581	10.3356	9.6036	8.9501	8.3649	7.3658	6.1982	19
20	18.0456	16.3514	14.8775	13.5903	12.4622	11.4699	10.5940	9.8181	9.1285	8.5136	7.4694	6.2593	20
25	22.0232	19.5235	17.4131	15.6221	14.0939	12.7834	11.6536	10.6748	9.8226	9.0770	7.8431	6.4641	25
30	25.8077	22.3965	19.6004	17.2920	15.3725	13.7648	12.4090	11.2578	10.2737	9.4269	8.0552	6.5660	30
35	29.4086	24.9986	21.4872	18.6646	16.3742	14.4982	12.9477	11.6546	10.5668	9.6442	8.1755	6.6166	35
40	32.8347	27.3555	23.1148	19.7928	17.1591	15.0463	13.3317	11.9246	10.7574	9.7791	8.2438	6.6418	40

‡Used to calculate the present value of a series of equal payments made at the end of each period. For example: What is the present value of $2,000 per year for 10 years assuming an annual interest rate of 9%? For ($n = 10$, $i = 9\%$), the PV factor is 6.4177. $2,000 per year for 10 years is the equivalent of $12,835 today ($2,000 × 6.4177).

TABLE B.4§

Future Value of an Annuity of 1

$$f = [(1+i)^n - 1]/i$$

Periods	1%	2%	3%	4%	5%	6%	7%	8%	9%	10%	12%	15%	Periods
1	1.0000	1.0000	1.0000	1.0000	1.0000	1.0000	1.0000	1.0000	1.0000	1.0000	1.0000	1.0000	1
2	2.0100	2.0200	2.0300	2.0400	2.0500	2.0600	2.0700	2.0800	2.0900	2.1000	2.1200	2.1500	2
3	3.0301	3.0604	3.0909	3.1216	3.1525	3.1836	3.2149	3.2464	3.2781	3.3100	3.3744	3.4725	3
4	4.0604	4.1216	4.1836	4.2465	4.3101	4.3746	4.4399	4.5061	4.5731	4.6410	4.7793	4.9934	4
5	5.1010	5.2040	5.3091	5.4163	5.5256	5.6371	5.7507	5.8666	5.9847	6.1051	6.3528	6.7424	5
6	6.1520	6.3081	6.4684	6.6330	6.8019	6.9753	7.1533	7.3359	7.5233	7.7156	8.1152	8.7537	6
7	7.2135	7.4343	7.6625	7.8983	8.1420	8.3938	8.6540	8.9228	9.2004	9.4872	10.0890	11.0668	7
8	8.2857	8.5830	8.8923	9.2142	9.5491	9.8975	10.2598	10.6366	11.0285	11.4359	12.2997	13.7268	8
9	9.3685	9.7546	10.1591	10.5828	11.0266	11.4913	11.9780	12.4876	13.0210	13.5795	14.7757	16.7858	9
10	10.4622	10.9497	11.4639	12.0061	12.5779	13.1808	13.8164	14.4866	15.1929	15.9374	17.5487	20.3037	10
11	11.5668	12.1687	12.8078	13.4864	14.2068	14.9716	15.7836	16.6455	17.5603	18.5312	20.6546	24.3493	11
12	12.6825	13.4121	14.1920	15.0258	15.9171	16.8699	17.8885	18.9771	20.1407	21.3843	24.1331	29.0017	12
13	13.8093	14.6803	15.6178	16.6268	17.7130	18.8821	20.1406	21.4953	22.9534	24.5227	28.0291	34.3519	13
14	14.9474	15.9739	17.0863	18.2919	19.5986	21.0151	22.5505	24.2149	26.0192	27.9750	32.3926	40.5047	14
15	16.0969	17.2934	18.5989	20.0236	21.5786	23.2760	25.1290	27.1521	29.3609	31.7725	37.2797	47.5804	15
16	17.2579	18.6393	20.1569	21.8245	23.6575	25.6725	27.8881	30.3243	33.0034	35.9497	42.7533	55.7175	16
17	18.4304	20.0121	21.7616	23.6975	25.8404	28.2129	30.8402	33.7502	36.9737	40.5447	48.8837	65.0751	17
18	19.6147	21.4123	23.4144	25.6454	28.1324	30.9057	33.9990	37.4502	41.3013	45.5992	55.7497	75.8364	18
19	20.8109	22.8406	25.1169	27.6712	30.5390	33.7600	37.3790	41.4463	46.0185	51.1591	63.4397	88.2118	19
20	22.0190	24.2974	26.8704	29.7781	33.0660	36.7856	40.9955	45.7620	51.1601	57.2750	72.0524	102.4436	20
25	28.2432	32.0303	36.4593	41.6459	47.7271	54.8645	63.2490	73.1059	84.7009	98.3471	133.3339	212.7930	25
30	34.7849	40.5681	47.5754	56.0849	66.4388	79.0582	94.4608	113.2832	136.3075	164.4940	241.3327	434.7451	30
35	41.6603	49.9945	60.4621	73.6522	90.3203	111.4348	138.2369	172.3168	215.7108	271.0244	431.6635	881.1702	35
40	48.8864	60.4020	75.4013	95.0255	120.7998	154.7620	199.6351	259.0565	337.8824	442.5926	767.0914	1,779.0903	40

§Used to calculate the future value of a series of equal payments made at the end of each period. For example: What is the future value of $4,000 per year for 6 years assuming an annual interest rate of 8%? For ($n = 6$, $i = 8\%$), the FV factor is 7.3359. $4,000 per year for 6 years accumulates to $29,343.60 ($4,000 × 7.3359).

C Investments

Learning Objectives

CONCEPTUAL

C1 Distinguish between debt and equity securities and between short-term and long-term investments.

C2 Describe how to report equity securities with controlling influence.

ANALYTICAL

A1 Compute and analyze the components of return on total assets.

PROCEDURAL

P1 Account for debt securities as trading.

P2 Account for debt securities as held-to-maturity.

P3 Account for debt securities as available-for-sale.

P4 Account for equity securities with insignificant influence.

P5 Account for equity securities with significant influence.

BASICS OF INVESTMENTS

In prior chapters we covered the reporting of both equity (common and preferred stock) and debt (bonds and notes) from the seller's (also called *issuer* or *investee*) standpoint. **This appendix covers the reporting of both equity and debt from the buyer's (or *investor*) standpoint.**

C1

Distinguish between debt and equity securities and between short-term and long-term investments.

Purposes and Types of Investments

Companies make investments for at least three reasons. (1) Companies invest their *extra cash* to earn more income. (2) Some entities, such as mutual funds and pension funds, are set up to earn income from investments. (3) Companies make investments for strategic reasons such as investments in competitors, suppliers, and customers. Exhibit C.1 shows short-term (ST) and long-term (LT) investments as a percent of total assets for several companies.

EXHIBIT C.1

Investments of Selected Companies

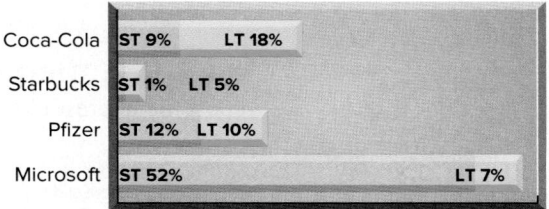

Coca-Cola ST 9% LT 18%
Starbucks ST 1% LT 5%
Pfizer ST 12% LT 10%
Microsoft ST 52% LT 7%

Percent of total assets

Short-Term Investments **Short-term investments,** or *marketable securities,* are investments that (1) management intends to convert to cash within one year or the operating cycle, whichever is longer, and (2) are readily convertible to cash. These investments usually mature between 3 and 12 months. Cash equivalents are not short-term investments because they usually mature within 3 months. Short-term investments are current assets.

Long-Term Investments **Long-term investments** are investments that are not readily convertible to cash or are not intended to be converted into cash in the short term. Long-term investments also include funds designated for a special purpose, such as investments in land or other assets not used in operations. Long-term investments are noncurrent assets.

Debt Securities versus Equity Securities Investments in securities include both debt and equity securities. *Debt securities* reflect a creditor relation such as investments in notes, bonds, and certificates of deposit; they are issued by governments, companies, and individuals. *Equity securities* reflect an owner relation such as investments in shares of stock issued by companies.

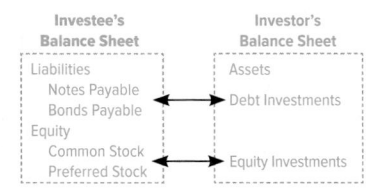

Investee's Balance Sheet — Investor's Balance Sheet

Liabilities
  Notes Payable
  Bonds Payable ↔ Debt Investments — Assets
Equity
  Common Stock
  Preferred Stock ↔ Equity Investments

Classification and Reporting

Accounting for investments in securities depends on three factors: (1) security type, either debt or equity; (2) the company's intent to hold the security either short term or long term; and (3) the investor's percentage of ownership in the other company's (investee's) equity securities. Exhibit C.2 identifies six classes of securities using these three factors.

EXHIBIT C.2

Investments in Securities

Debt Investments			Equity Investments		
Held-to-Maturity	**Trading**	**Available-for-Sale**	**Insignificant Influence**	**Significant Influence**	**Controlling Influence**
Debt securities intended to be held until maturity	Debt securities that are actively traded	Debt securities that are not HTM or Trading	Equity securities with insignificant influence	Equity securities with significant influence	Equity securities with controlling influence

Debt Investments

Debt Investments—Basics

This section covers the purchase, sale, and any interest received for **debt investments** (also called *debt securities*).

©Scott Olson/Getty Images

Recording Acquisition Debt investments are recorded at cost when purchased. Assume that Ling Co. paid $30,000 on July 1, 2019, to buy Dell's 7%, two-year bonds payable with a $30,000 par value. The bonds pay interest semiannually on December 31 and June 30. The entry to record this purchase follows.

	July 1, 2019	Debt Investments	30,000	
Assets = Liabilities + Equity +30,000 −30,000		Cash		30,000
		Purchased bonds as debt investments.		

Recording Interest　Interest revenue for debt investments is recorded when earned. On December 31, 2019, Ling records cash receipt of interest as follows. The $1,050 interest earned from July 1 to December 31 is computed as Principal × Annual rate × Fraction of year.

	Dec. 31, 2019	Cash	1,050	
Assets = Liabilities + Equity +1,050　　　　　+1,050		Interest Revenue		1,050
		Record interest earned ($30,000 × 7% × 6/12).		

Reporting Debt Investments　Ling's financial statements at December 31, 2019, report the interest revenue and the investment as shown in Exhibit C.3.

EXHIBIT C.3

Financial Statement
Presentation of Debt
Investments

On the income statement for year 2019:		On the December 31, 2019, balance sheet:	
Interest revenue.................	$ 1,050	Debt investments...................	$30,000

Maturity　When bonds mature, we record the proceeds (assuming interest was already recorded).

	July 1, 2021	Cash	30,000	
Assets = Liabilities + Equity +30,000 −30,000		Debt Investments		30,000
		Received cash from matured bonds.		

Point: It is common to add the security name to the account title to track as a subsidiary ledger. For example, the Debt Investments account can be titled Debt Investments (Dell).

The cost of a debt security can be either higher or lower than its maturity value. When the investment is long term, the difference between cost and maturity value is amortized as an adjustment to interest revenue over the remaining life of the security. We assume for simplicity that the cost of a long-term debt security equals its maturity value for all assignments.

DEBT INVESTMENTS—TRADING

P1

Account for debt securities as trading.

Trading securities are *debt* investments that the company actively buys and sells for profit. **Trading securities are *always* current assets.**

　The portfolio of trading securities is reported at fair value; this requires a "fair value adjustment" from the cost of the portfolio. A *portfolio* is a group of securities. **Any unrealized gain (or loss) from a change in the fair value of the portfolio of trading securities is reported on the income statement.**

Recording Fair Value　TechCom's portfolio of trading securities had a total cost of $11,500 and a fair value of $13,000 on December 31, 2019, the first year it held trading securities. The difference between the $11,500 cost and the $13,000 fair value is a $1,500 gain. It is an **unrealized gain** because it is not yet confirmed by actual sales of securities. The fair value adjustment for trading securities is recorded with an adjusting entry at the end of each period to equal the difference between the portfolio's cost and its fair value. TechCom records this gain as follows.

Point: Fair Value Adj. is a balance sheet account with either a debit balance (Fair value > Cost) or credit balance (Fair value < Cost).

	Dec. 31, 2019	Fair Value Adjustment—Trading........................	1,500	
Assets = Liabilities + Equity +1,500　　　　　+1,500		Unrealized Gain—Income		1,500
		Record unrealized gain in trading securities.		

This adjustment is computed using our three-step adjusting process.

Step 1:	Determine what unadjusted balance equals: Fair Value Adj.–Trading = $0. ◄
Step 2:	Determine what adjusted balance should equal: Fair Value Adj.–Trading = $1,500 Dr.
	Explanation: $13,000 fair value > $11,500 cost; thus Fair Value Adj.–Trading requires a $1,500 debit to be at fair value.
Step 3:	Record the $1,500 adjusting entry to get from step 1 to step 2.
	Explanation: This means a $1,500 debit to Fair Value Adj.–Trading and a $1,500 credit to Unrealized Gain–Income.

> Unadj. bal. is rarely $0; it is $0 here because it's the first year.

Example: If TechCom's trading securities have a cost of $14,800 and a fair value of $16,100 at Dec. 31, 2020, its adjusting entry is

Unreal. Loss—Income... 200
  Fair Value Adj.—Trading   200

This is computed as:
$1,500 Beg. Dr. bal. + $200 Cr.
= $1,300 End. Dr. bal.

Reporting Fair Value   The **unrealized gain (or loss)** is reported in the Other Revenues and Gains (or Expenses and Losses) section on the income statement. Unrealized Gain—Income (or Unrealized Loss—Income) is a *temporary* account that is closed to Income Summary at the end of each period. Fair Value Adjustment—Trading is a *permanent* asset account that adjusts the reported value of the trading securities portfolio from its prior-period fair value to the current period fair value. The total cost of the trading securities portfolio is maintained in one account, and the fair value adjustment is recorded in a separate account. For example, TechCom's investment in trading securities is reported in current assets as follows.

Current Assets		
Debt investments—Trading (at cost)	$11,500	
Fair value adjustment—Trading.	1,500	
Debt investments—Trading (at fair value).		$13,000
or simply		
Debt investments—Trading (at fair value; cost is $11,500)		$13,000

Debt Investments–Trading

1/1/2019	0	
Purch.	11,500	
12/31/2019	11,500	

Fair Value Adj.–Trading

1/1/2019	0	
Adj.	**1,500**	
12/31/2019	1,500	

Selling Trading Securities   When individual trading securities are sold, the difference between the net proceeds (sale price minus fees) and the cost of the individual trading securities sold is recorded as a gain or a loss. **Any prior-period fair value adjustment to the portfolio is *not* used to compute the gain or loss from the sale of individual trading securities.** This is because the balance in the Fair Value Adjustment account is for the entire portfolio, not individual securities. If TechCom sold some of its trading securities that had cost $100 for $120 cash on January 9, 2020, it records the following.

Jan. 9, 2020	Cash	120	
	Debt Investments—Trading.		100
	Gain on Sale of Debt Investments.		20
	Sold trading securities costing $100 for $120 cash.		

Assets = Liabilities + Equity
+120   +20
−100

A gain is reported in the Other Revenues and Gains section on the income statement, and a loss is reported in Other Expenses and Losses. When the period-end fair value adjustment for the portfolio of trading securities is computed, it excludes the cost and fair value of any securities sold.

Point: This is a *realized* $20 gain—realized by actual sale.

Berkshire Co. purchases debt investments in trading securities at a cost of $130 on July 1. (This is its first and only purchase of trading securities.) On December 30, Berkshire received $1 of interest from its trading securities. At year-end December 31, the trading securities had a fair value of $140.

a. Prepare the July 1 purchase entry of trading securities.

b. Prepare the December 30 entry for receipt of cash interest.

c. Prepare the December 31 year-end adjusting entry for the trading securities' portfolio.

NEED-TO-KNOW C-1

Trading Securities

P1

d. Explain how each account in entry *c* is reported in financial statements.

e. Prepare the January 3 entry when a portion of its trading securities (that had cost $33) is sold for $36.

Solution

a.

July 1	Debt Investments—Trading.........................	130	
	Cash..		130
	Record purchase of trading securities.		

b.

Dec. 30	Cash	1	
	Interest Revenue............................		1
	Record interest received on trading securities.		

c.

Fair Value Adj.–Trading	
Unadj. bal. 0	
Adj. 10	
Dec. 31 10	

Dec. 31	Fair Value Adjustment—Trading	10	
	Unrealized Gain—Income.....................		10
	Record unrealized gain in fair value of trading securities.		

d. **(i)** The $10 debit in the Fair Value Adjustment—Trading account is an adjunct asset account in the balance sheet. It increases the $130 balance of the Debt Investments—Trading account to its $140 fair value.

    (ii) The $10 credit for Unrealized Gain is reported in the Other Revenues and Gains section of the income statement.

e.

Jan. 3	Cash	36	
	Gain on Sale of Debt Investments		3
	Debt Investments—Trading		33
	Record sale of trading securities.		

Do More: QS C-3, QS C-4, QS C-5, E C-2, P C-1

DEBT INVESTMENTS—HELD-TO-MATURITY

P2

Account for debt securities as held-to-maturity.

Held-to-maturity (HTM) securities are *debt* securities a company intends and is able to hold until maturity. They are reported in current assets if their maturity dates are within one year or the operating cycle, whichever is longer. Otherwise, they are classified as long-term investments.

The cost of a debt security can be either higher or lower than its maturity value. When the investment is long term, the difference between cost and maturity value is amortized over the remaining life of the security. We assume for simplicity that the cost of a long-term HTM debt security equals its maturity value for all assignments.

Recording Acquisition and Interest   All HTM securities are recorded at cost when purchased, and interest revenue is recorded when earned—see earlier "basic" entries.

Reporting HTM Securities at Cost   The portfolio of HTM securities is usually reported at (amortized) cost, which is explained in advanced courses. **There is *no* fair value adjustment to the portfolio of HTM securities—neither to short-term nor long-term portfolios.**

Prepare journal entries to record the following transactions involving short-term debt investments.

a. On May 15, paid $100 cash to purchase Muni's 120-day short-term debt securities ($100 principal), dated May 15, that pay 6% interest (categorized as held-to-maturity securities).

b. On September 13, received a check from Muni in payment of the principal and 120 days' interest on the debt securities purchased in transaction *a*.

NEED-TO-KNOW C-2

Held-to-Maturity
Securities

P2

Solution

a.

May 15	Debt Investments—HTM	100	
	Cash..		100
	Purchased 120-day, 6% debt securities.		

b.

Sep. 13	Cash	102	
	Debt Investments—HTM		100
	Interest Revenue................................		2
	Collect $100 principal plus interest of $100 × 6% × 120/360.		

Do More: QS C-6, E C-3

DEBT INVESTMENTS—AVAILABLE-FOR-SALE

Available-for-sale (AFS) securities are *debt* investments not classified as trading or held-to-maturity securities. If the intent is to sell AFS securities within the longer of one year or the operating cycle, they are classified as short-term investments. Otherwise, they are classified as long-term investments.

Companies adjust the cost of the portfolio of AFS securities for changes in fair value. This is done with a fair value adjustment to its portfolio cost. **Any unrealized gain or loss for the portfolio of AFS securities is *not* reported on the income statement. It is reported in the equity section of the balance sheet** (as part of *comprehensive income,* covered later).

P3_____

Account for debt securities as available-for-sale.

Recording Fair Value   Assume that Mitsu Co. had no prior investments in available-for-sale securities other than those purchased in the current period. Exhibit C.4 shows the cost and fair value of the portfolio of investments on December 31, 2019, the end of its reporting period.

	Cost	Fair Value	Unrealized Gain (Loss)
Apple bonds	$30,000	$29,050	$ (950)
Intex notes	43,000	45,500	2,500
Total...............	$73,000	$74,550	$1,550

EXHIBIT C.4

Cost and Fair Value of Available-for-Sale Securities

Example: If fair value in Exhibit C.4 is $70,000 (instead of $74,550), what entry is made? *Answer:* Unreal. Loss—Equity . . . 3,000
  Fair Value Adj.—AFS . .   3,000

The year-end adjusting entry to record the fair value of the portfolio of investments follows.

Dec. 31, 2019	Fair Value Adjustment—Available-for-Sale	1,550	
	Unrealized Gain—Equity		1,550
	Record adjustment to fair value of AFS securities.		

Assets = Liabilities + Equity
+1,550   +1,550

Point: Unrealized Loss—Equity and Unrealized Gain—Equity are *permanent* (balance sheet) equity accounts.

Reporting Fair Value

Exhibit C.5 shows the December 31, 2019, balance sheet—it assumes these investments are long term, but they also can be short term. It is also common to combine the cost of investments with the balance in the Fair Value Adjustment account and report the net as a single amount.

EXHIBIT C.5

Balance Sheet Presentation of Available-for-Sale Securities

Debt Investments–AFS

1/1/2019	0
Purch.	73,000
12/31/2019	73,000

Fair Value Adj.–AFS

1/1/2019	0
Adj.	**1,550**
12/31/2019	1,550

Reconciled

Assets

Debt investments—Available-for-sale (at cost)............................	$73,000
Fair value adjustment—Available-for-sale................................	1,550
Debt investments—Available-for-sale (at fair value)......................	$74,550
or simply	
Debt investments—Available-for-sale (at fair value; cost is $73,000)........	$74,550

Equity

Add unrealized gain on available-for-sale securities*...................	$ 1,550

*Included under Accumulated Other Comprehensive Income.

Point: Income is increased by selling AFS securities with unrealized gains; income is reduced by selling those with unrealized losses.

Reporting for Next Year

Let's extend this example and assume that at the end of its next year, December 31, 2020, Mitsu's portfolio of long-term AFS securities has an $81,000 cost and an $82,000 fair value. The year-end adjustment is computed using our three-step adjusting process.

Point: Fair Value Adj.—AFS is a permanent account, shown as a deduction or addition to the investment account.

Step 1:	Determine what unadjusted balance equals: Fair Value Adj.–AFS = $1,550 Dr. (from Exhibit C.5).	
Step 2:	Determine what adjusted balance should equal: Fair Value Adj.–AFS = $1,000 Dr.	
	Explanation: $82,000 fair value > $81,000 cost; thus Fair Value Adj.–AFS must have a $1,000 Dr. bal. so securities are at fair value.	
Step 3:	Record the $550 adjusting entry to get from step 1 to step 2.	
	Explanation: This implies a $550 credit to Fair Value Adj.–AFS (and a $550 debit to Unrealized Gain).	

It records the year-end adjustment to fair value as follows.

Assets = Liabilities + Equity
−550   −550

Dec. 31, 2020	Unrealized Gain—Equity..............................	**550**	
	Fair Value Adjustment—Available-for-Sale		**550**
	Record adjustment to fair value of AFS securities.		

The effects of the 2019 and 2020 securities transactions are shown in the following T-accounts.

Example: If cost is $83,000 and fair value is $82,000 at Dec. 31, 2020, it records the following adjustment:
Unreal. Gain—Equity 1,550
Unreal. Loss—Equity 1,000
   Fair Value Adj.—AFS   2,550

Unrealized Gain—Equity

		Bal. 12/31/19	1,550
Adj. 12/31/20	550		
		Bal. 12/31/20	1,000

Fair Value Adjustment—Available-for-Sale

Bal. 12/31/19	1,550		
		Adj. 12/31/20	550
Bal. 12/31/20	1,000		

Selling AFS Securities

Accounting for the sale of individual AFS securities is identical to accounting for the sale of trading securities. When individual AFS securities are sold, the difference between the cost of the individual securities sold and the net proceeds (sale price less fees) is recorded as a gain or loss on sale of debt investments.

 **NEED-TO-KNOW C-3**

Available-for-Sale Securities

P3

Gard Company completes the following transactions related to its short-term debt investments.

May 8   Purchased FedEx notes as a short-term investment in available-for-sale securities for $12,975.
Sep. 2   Sold part of its investment in FedEx notes for $4,475, which had cost $4,325.
Oct. 2   Purchased Ajay bonds for $25,600 as a short-term investment in available-for-sale securities.

Required

1. Prepare journal entries for the transactions.
2. Prepare a year-end adjusting journal entry as of December 31 if the fair values of the debt securities held by Gard are $9,600 for FedEx and $22,000 for Ajay. (This year is the first year Gard Company acquired short-term debt investments.)

Solution

1.

May 8	Debt Investments—AFS	12,975	
	Cash..		12,975
	Purchased FedEx notes.		
Sep. 2	Cash	4,475	
	Gain on Sale of Debt Investment		150
	Debt Investments—AFS		4,325
	Sold a portion of its FedEx notes.		
Oct. 2	Debt Investments—AFS	25,600	
	Cash..		25,600
	Purchased Ajay bonds.		

2. Computation of unrealized gain or loss, along with the adjusting entry, follows.

Debt Investments in Available-for-Sale Securities	Total Cost	Total Fair Value	Unrealized Gain (Loss)
FedEx...........................	$ 8,650*	$ 9,600	
Ajay	25,600	22,000	
Totals...........................	$34,250	$31,600	$(2,650)

*$12,975 − $4,325

Dec. 31	Unrealized Loss—Equity	2,650	
	Fair Value Adjustment—Available-for-Sale		2,650
	Record unrealized loss in fair value of ST AFS portfolio.		

Debt Investments–AFS

Jan. 1	0		
May 8	12,975		
		Sep. 2	4,325
Oct. 2	25,600		
Dec. 31 bal.	34,250		

Fair Value Adj.–AFS

Jan. 1	0		
		Dec. 31 adj.	**2,650**
		Dec. 31 bal.	2,650

Do More: QS C-7, QS C-8, QS C-9, QS C-10, E C-4, E C-5, E C-6

Equity Investments

This section covers **equity investments** (also called *equity securities*). Exhibit C.6 summarizes the accounting for equity investments based on an investor's ownership in the stock. We cover each of these three cases.

Insignificant Influence	Significant Influence	Controlling	
Fair value method (under 20%)	**Equity method** (20% to 50%)	**Consolidation method** (more than 50%)	

0%   20%   50%   100%

Investor's percent ownership of a company's stock

EXHIBIT C.6

Accounting for Equity Investments by Percent of Ownership

EQUITY INVESTMENTS—INSIGNIFICANT INFLUENCE, UNDER 20%

When an investor has insignificant influence over another company, presumably when it owns less than 20% of voting stock, the stock investment is reported at fair value. Stock investments are classified as short or long term based on managers' intent and the stock's marketability. Any cash dividends are recorded as dividend revenue.

P4 _____

Account for equity securities with insignificant influence.

Recording Acquisition

Equity investments are recorded at cost when acquired, including any commissions and brokerage fees paid. Assume ITI purchases 100 shares of Lynx common stock for $7,000 on October 10, 2019. After the purchase, ITI has insignificant influence over Lynx. It records this purchase as follows.

Assets = Liabilities + Equity
+7,000
−7,000

Oct. 10	Stock Investments	7,000	
	Cash		7,000
	Purchased 100 shares of Lynx.		

Recording Dividends

If ITI receives $10 in dividends on November 1 from its stock investment, it records the following.

Assets = Liabilities + Equity
+10   +10

Nov. 1	Cash	10	
	Dividend Revenue		10
	Record dividend received on stock investments.		

Recording Fair Value

The stock investments portfolio is reported at fair value; this requires a "fair value adjustment" from cost of the portfolio. **Any unrealized gain (or loss) from a change in the fair value of this portfolio of stock investments is reported on the income statement.**

Assume ITI's portfolio of stock investments with insignificant influence has a total cost of $7,000 and a fair value of $9,000 on December 31, 2019, the first year it held these securities. The difference between the $7,000 cost and the $9,000 fair value is a $2,000 **unrealized gain.** The fair value adjustment is recorded at the end of each period to equal the difference between the portfolio's cost and its fair value. ITI records this gain as follows.

Assets = Liabilities + Equity
+2,000   +2,000

Dec. 31	Fair Value Adjustment—Stock	2,000	
	Unrealized Gain—Income		2,000
	Record unrealized gain in stock investments.		

This adjustment is computed using our three-step adjusting process.

Unadj. bal. is rarely $0; it is $0 here because it's the first year.

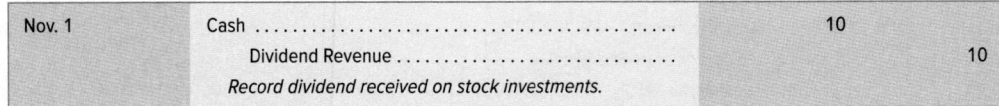

Step 1:	Determine what unadjusted balance equals: Fair Value Adj.–Stock = $0.
Step 2:	Determine what adjusted balance should equal: Fair Value Adj.–Stock = $2,000 Dr.
	Explanation: $9,000 fair value > $7,000 cost; thus Fair Value Adj.–Stock requires a $2,000 debit to be at fair value.
Step 3:	Record the $2,000 adjusting entry to get from step 1 to step 2.
	Explanation: This means a $2,000 debit to Fair Value Adj.–Stock and a $2,000 credit to Unrealized Gain–Income.

Example: If cost is $10,000 and fair value is $8,500 at Dec. 31, 2020, it records the following adjustment:
Unreal. Loss—Income 3,500
    Fair Value Adj.—Stock   3,500

The FVA—Stock Cr. is computed as: $2,000 Beg. Dr. bal. + **$3,500 Cr.** = $1,500 End. Cr. bal.

Reporting Fair Value

The **unrealized gain (or loss)** is reported in the Other Revenues and Gains (or Expenses and Losses) section on the income statement. Unrealized Gain (or Loss)—Income is a *temporary* account that is closed to Income Summary at the end of each period. Fair Value Adjustment—Stock is a *permanent* asset account that adjusts the reported value of the stock investments portfolio from its prior-period fair value to the current-period fair value. The total cost of the portfolio is kept in one account, and the fair value adjustment is kept in a separate account. ITI's stock investment is reported in its assets.

Stock Investments

1/1/2019	0	
Purch.	7,000	
12/31/2019	7,000	

Fair Value Adj.–Stock

1/1/2019	0	
Adj.	**2,000**	
12/31/2019	2,000	

Assets

Stock investments (at cost)	$7,000	
Fair value adjustment—Stock	2,000	
Stock investments (at fair value)		$9,000

or simply

Stock investments (at fair value; cost is $7,000)		$9,000

Selling Stock Investments   When individual stock investments are sold, the difference between the net proceeds (sale price minus fees) and the cost of the individual stocks that are sold is recorded as a gain or a loss. **Any prior-period fair value adjustment to the portfolio is *not* used to compute the gain or loss from the sale of individual stocks.** This is because the balance in the Fair Value Adjustment account is for the entire portfolio, not individual stocks. If ITI sold some of its stock investments that had cost $500 for $800 cash on March 9, 2020, it records the following. A gain is reported in the Other Revenues and Gains section on the income statement and a loss is reported in Other Expenses and Losses.

Mar. 9	Cash	800	
	Stock Investments		500
	Gain on Sale of Stock Investments		300
	Sold stock investments costing $500 for $800 cash.		

Assets = Liabilities + Equity
+800   +300
−500

Derr Co. purchases stock investments (with insignificant influence) at a cost of $250 on December 15. This is its first and only purchase of such securities. On December 28, Derr received a $15 cash dividend from the stock investments. At year-end December 31, the stock investments had a fair value of $200.

a. Prepare the December 15 purchase entry for stock investments.

b. Prepare the December 28 receipt of cash dividends entry.

c. Prepare the December 31 year-end adjusting entry for the stock investments' portfolio.

d. Explain how each account in entry *c* is reported in financial statements.

e. Prepare the January 3 entry when a portion of its stock investments (that had cost $37) is sold for $40.

NEED-TO-KNOW C-4

Stock Investments with Insignificant Influence (<20%)

P4   ▶

Solution

a.

Dec. 15	Stock Investments	250	
	Cash.		250
	Record purchase of stock investments.		

b.

Dec. 28	Cash	15	
	Dividend Revenue.		15
	Record dividend received on stock investments.		

c.

Dec. 31	Unrealized Loss—Income	50	
	Fair Value Adjustment—Stock		50
	Record unrealized loss in stock investments.		

Fair Value Adj.–Stock

Unadj. bal.	0		
		Adj.	50
		Dec. 31	50

d. (i) The $50 credit in the Fair Value Adjustment—Stock account is a contra asset account in the balance sheet. It decreases the $250 balance of the Stock Investments account to its $200 fair value.

(ii) The $50 debit for Unrealized Loss is reported in the Other Expenses and Losses section of the income statement.

e.

Jan. 3	Cash	40	
	Gain on Sale of Stock Investments		3
	Stock Investments.		37
	Record sale of stock investments.		

Do More: QS C-11, QS C-12, QS C-13, E C-7, E C-8, E C-9, E C-10

EQUITY INVESTMENTS—SIGNIFICANT INFLUENCE, 20% TO 50%

A long-term investment classified as **equity securities with significant influence** means that the investor has significant influence over the investee. An investor that owns between 20% and 50% of a company's voting stock usually has significant influence. The **equity method** is used for long-term investments in equity securities with significant influence, which is explained in this section.

P5

Account for equity securities with significant influence.

Recording Acquisition

Long-term investments in equity securities with significant influence are recorded at cost when acquired. Micron Co. records the purchase of 3,000 shares (30%) of Star Co. common stock at a total cost of $70,000 on January 1, 2019, as follows.

Assets = Liabilities + Equity
+70,000
−70,000

Jan. 1	Equity Method Investments	70,000	
	Cash		70,000
	Record purchase of 3,000 Star shares.		

Recording Share of Earnings

When the investee reports its earnings, the investor records its share of those earnings in its investment account. Assume that Star reports net income of $20,000 for 2019. Micron records its 30% share of those earnings—see entry below. The debit increases Micron's equity in Star. The credit is 30% of Star's net income. Earnings from Equity Method Investments is a *temporary* account (closed to Income Summary at each period-end) and is reported on the investor's (Micron's) income statement. If the investee incurs a net loss instead of net income, the investor records its share of the loss and reduces (credits) its investments account.

Assets = Liabilities + Equity
+6,000   +6,000

Dec. 31	Equity Method Investments	6,000	
	Earnings from Equity Method Investments...........		6,000
	Record 30% equity in investee's $20,000 earnings.		

Recording Share of Dividends

Cash dividends received by an investor from an investee under the equity method are accounted for as a conversion of one asset to another. Dividends reduce the Equity Method Investments account. Assume Star pays a total of $10,000 in cash dividends on its common stock. Micron records its 30% share of these dividends received on January 9, 2020, as follows.

Assets = Liabilities + Equity
+3,000
−3,000

Jan. 9	Cash	3,000	
	Equity Method Investments		3,000
	Record 30% share of $10,000 dividend paid by Star.		

Reporting Investments with Significant Influence

The book value of investments under the equity method equals the cost of investments *plus* the investor's share of net income or loss and *minus* its share of dividends. **The Equity Method Investments account is not adjusted to fair value.** After Micron records these transactions, its Equity Method Investments account appears as in Exhibit C.7. Micron's account balance on January 9, 2020, for its investment in Star is $73,000. This is the investment's cost *plus* Micron's share of Star's earnings *minus* Micron's share of Star's cash dividends.

EXHIBIT C.7

Investment in Star Common Stock (ledger T-account)

Equity Method Investments				
1/1/2019 Investment acquisition	70,000			
12/31/2019 Share of earnings	6,000			
12/31/2019 Balance	76,000			
		1/9/2020 Share of dividend	3,000	
1/9/2020 Balance	73,000			

Selling Investments with Significant Influence

When equity method investments are sold, the gain or loss is computed by comparing proceeds from the sale with the book value of the investments on the sale date. If Micron sells all of its Star stock for $80,000 on January 10, 2020, it records the sale as follows.

Assets = Liabilities + Equity
+80,000   +7,000
−73,000

Jan. 10	Cash	80,000	
	Equity Method Investments		73,000
	Gain on Sale of Stock Investments................		7,000
	Sold 3,000 shares of stock for $80,000.		

Prepare entries to record the following transactions of Garcia Company.

2019

Jan. 1   Purchased 400 shares of Lopez Co. common stock for $3,000 cash. Lopez has 1,000 shares of common stock outstanding, and its policies will be significantly influenced by Garcia.
Aug. 1   Lopez declared and paid a cash dividend of $2 per share.
Dec. 31   Lopez reported net income for the year of $2,500.

2020

Aug. 1   Lopez declared and paid a cash dividend of $2.25 per share.
Dec. 31   Lopez reported net income for the year of $2,750.

2021

Jan. 1   Garcia sold 100 shares of Lopez for $1,300 cash.

Solution

Jan. 1, 2019	Equity Method Investments	3,000	
	Cash.		3,000
	Record purchase of investment. *		

*Garcia's investment is 40% of Lopez's stock (400/1,000). Garcia uses the equity method.

Aug. 1, 2019	Cash	800	
	Equity Method Investments		800
	Record receipt of cash dividend (400 × $2).		
Dec. 31, 2019	Equity Method Investments	1,000	
	Earnings from Equity Method Investments		1,000
	Record equity in investee earnings ($2,500 × 40%).		

Aug. 1, 2020	Cash	900	
	Equity Method Investments		900
	Record receipt of cash dividend (400 × $2.25).		
Dec. 31, 2020	Equity Method Investments	1,100	
	Earnings from Equity Method Investments		1,100
	Record equity in investee earnings ($2,750 × 40%).		

Jan. 1, 2021	Cash	1,300	
	Gain on Sale of Stock Investments		450
	Equity Method Investments*		850
	Record sale of investment.		

*Book value (Lopez stock) at 1/1/2021.

Original cost.	$3,000
Less 2019 dividends.	(800)
Plus share of 2019 earnings	1,000
Less 2020 dividends.	(900)
Plus share of 2020 earnings	1,100
Book value at date of sale.	$3,400
Book value of shares sold ($3,400 × [100/400])	$ 850

Do More: QS C-15, E C-12,
E C-13, E C-14

EQUITY INVESTMENTS—CONTROLLING INFLUENCE, MORE THAN 50%

A long-term investment classified as **equity securities with controlling influence** means that the investor has a controlling influence over the investee. An investor who owns more than 50% of a company's voting stock has control over the investee. This investor can dominate all other shareholders in electing the corporation's board of directors and has control over the investee's management.

C2

Describe how to report equity securities with controlling influence.

©Tim Greenway/Portland Press
Herald/Getty Images

The *consolidation method* is used for long-term investments in equity securities with controlling influence. The investor reports *consolidated financial statements* when owning such securities. The controlling investor is called the **parent** and the investee is called the **subsidiary.** Many companies are parents with subsidiaries. **Amazon** is the parent of Whole Foods Market, Zappos, and other subsidiaries. When a company operates as a parent with subsidiaries, each entity maintains separate accounting records.

Consolidated financial statements show the financial statements of all entities under the parent's control, including all subsidiaries. These statements are prepared as if the business were organized as one entity. The individual assets and liabilities of the parent and its subsidiaries are combined on one balance sheet. Their revenues and expenses also are combined on one income statement, and their cash flows are combined on one statement of cash flows. Preparing consolidated financial statements is covered in advanced courses.

Accounting Summary for Debt and Equity Investments

Exhibit C.8 summarizes accounting for debt and equity investments.

EXHIBIT C.8

Accounting for Investments in Securities

Classification	Investments Account Reported at
Short-Term Investment in Securities	
Debt Investments—Held-to-Maturity...................	Cost (without any discount or premium amortization)
Debt Investments—Trading...........................	**Fair value** (with fair value adjustment to income)
Debt Investments—Available-for-Sale..................	**Fair value** (with fair value adjustment to equity)
Stock Investments—insignificant influence	**Fair value** (with fair value adjustment to income)
Long-Term Investment in Securities	
Debt Investments—Held-to-Maturity	Cost (with any discount or premium amortized)
Debt Investments—Available-for-Sale	**Fair value** (with fair value adjustment to equity)
Stock Investments—insignificant influence	**Fair value** (with fair value adjustment to income)
Equity Method Investments—significant influence	Equity method (no fair value adjustment)
Consolidated Investments—controlling influence	Consolidation method (no fair value adjustment)

Computing and Reporting Comprehensive Income   **Comprehensive income** is all changes in equity during a period except those from owners' investments and dividends. Specifically, comprehensive income is computed by adding *other comprehensive income* to or subtracting it from net income.

Statement of Comprehensive Income	
Net income..	$ #
Other comprehensive income	#
Comprehensive income	$ #

Frequently consists of:
Change in value of available-for-sale investment, net of tax
Change in foreign currency translation adjustment
Change in cash flow hedges, net of tax

Other comprehensive income includes **unrealized** gains and losses on available-for-sale securities, foreign currency translation adjustments, and other adjustments. (*Accumulated other comprehensive income* is the cumulative impact for all periods of *other comprehensive income*.) Comprehensive income is reported in financial statements in one of two ways.

1. On a separate *statement of comprehensive income* that follows the income statement.
2. On the lower section of the income statement (as a single continuous *statement of income and comprehensive income*).

Option 1 is most common. **Google**, for example, reports a statement of comprehensive income following its income statement (see Appendix A).

GOOGLE

Components of Return on Total Assets ⬜⬜⬜ **Decision Analysis**

A company's **return on total assets** (or *return on assets*) is used to assess financial performance. The return on total assets can be separated into two components, profit margin and total asset turnover, for additional analyses. Exhibit C.9 shows how these two components determine return on total assets.

A1

Compute and analyze the components of return on total assets.

EXHIBIT C.9

Components of Return on Total Assets

$$\text{Return on total assets} = \text{Profit margin} \times \text{Total asset turnover}$$

$$\frac{\text{Net income}}{\text{Average total assets}} = \frac{\text{Net income}}{\text{Net sales}} \times \frac{\text{Net sales}}{\text{Average total assets}}$$

Profit margin reflects the percent of net income in each dollar of net sales. Total asset turnover reflects a company's ability to produce net sales from total assets. All companies want a high return on total assets. By considering these two components, we can often discover strengths and weaknesses not revealed by return on total assets alone. This improves our ability to assess future performance and company strategy.

Costco's return on total assets and its components are in Exhibit C.10.

EXHIBIT C.10

Components of Return on Total Assets for Two Competitors

| | Costco | | | | Walmart |
Year	Return on Total Assets	=	Profit Margin	× Total Asset Turnover	Return on Total Assets
Current Year	7.8%	=	2.1%	× 3.7	7.2%
1 Year Ago	7.2%	=	2.0%	× 3.6	7.5%
2 Years Ago	7.0%	=	2.0%	× 3.5	8.4%

Costco's return on total assets improved over the three-year period. This increase is driven by both an increase in profit margin and in total asset turnover. Costco increased its return on total assets during a time when other retailers like **Walmart** have struggled. To continue this trend, Costco's management must increase net income while keeping total asset turnover steady or at least at a level where it does not decrease return on total assets.

■ Decision Maker ━━━━━━━━━━━━━━━

Retailer You are an owner of a retail store. The store's recent annual performance reveals (industry norms in parentheses) return on total assets = 11% (11.2%); profit margin = 4.4% (3.5%); anc total asset turnover = 2.5 (3.2). What does your analysis reveal? ■ *Answer:* The store's 11% return on assets is similar to the 11.2% industry norm. However, the store's 4.4% profit margin is much higher than the 3.5% norm, but the 2.5 asset turnover is much lower than the 3.2 norm. The poor turnover suggests that this store is less efficient in using assets. It must focus on increasing sales or reducing assets.

The following transactions relate to Brown Company's long-term investments. Brown did not own any long-term investments prior to these transactions. Show (1) the necessary journal entries and (2) the relevant portions of each year's balance sheet and income statement that reflect these transactions for both years.

NEED-TO-KNOW C-6

COMPREHENSIVE

Accounting for Equity Securities with Insignificant Influence and for Equity Securities with Significant Influence

2019

Sep. 9 Purchased 1,000 shares of Packard common stock for $80,000 cash. These shares represent 30% of Packard's outstanding shares.

Oct. 2 Purchased 2,000 shares of AT&T common stock for $60,000 cash as a long-term investment. These shares represent less than a 1% ownership in AT&T.

  17 Purchased as a long-term investment 1,000 shares of Apple common stock for $40,000 cash. These shares are less than 1% of Apple's outstanding shares.

Nov. 1 Received $5,000 cash dividend from Packard.

  30 Received $3,000 cash dividend from AT&T.

Dec. 15 Received $1,400 cash dividend from Apple.

  31 Packard's net income for this year is $70,000.

[continued on next page]

31   Fair values for the investments in equity securities are Packard, $84,000; AT&T, $48,000; and Apple, $45,000.

31   For preparing financial statements, note the following post-closing account balances: Common Stock, $500,000, and Retained Earnings, $350,000.

2020

Jan.   1   Sold all of the Packard shares for $108,000 cash.

May 30   Received $3,100 cash dividend from AT&T.

June 15   Received $1,600 cash dividend from Apple.

Aug. 17   Sold all of the AT&T stock for $52,000 cash.

19   Purchased 2,000 shares of Coca-Cola common stock for $50,000 cash as a long-term investment. The stock represents less than a 5% ownership in Coca-Cola.

Dec. 15   Received $1,800 cash dividend from Apple.

31   Fair values of the investments in equity securities are Apple, $39,000, and Coca-Cola, $48,000.

31   For preparing financial statements, note the following post-closing account balances: Common Stock, $500,000, and Retained Earnings, $410,000.

PLANNING THE SOLUTION

- Account for the investment in Packard under the equity method.
- Account for the investments in AT&T, Apple, and Coca-Cola as stock investments with insignificant influence.
- Prepare the information for the two years' balance sheets by including the relevant asset and equity accounts, and the two years' income statements by identifying the relevant revenues, earnings, gains, and losses.

SOLUTION

1. Journal entries for 2019.

Sep. 9	Equity Method Investments	80,000	
	Cash..		80,000
	Acquired 1,000 shares, a 30% equity in Packard.		
Oct. 2	Stock Investments	60,000	
	Cash..		60,000
	Acquired 2,000 shares of AT&T.		
Oct. 17	Stock Investments	40,000	
	Cash..		40,000
	Acquired 1,000 shares of Apple.		
Nov. 1	Cash	5,000	
	Equity Method Investments		5,000
	Received dividend from Packard.		
Nov. 30	Cash	3,000	
	Dividend Revenue..............................		3,000
	Received dividend from AT&T.		
Dec. 15	Cash	1,400	
	Dividend Revenue..............................		1,400
	Received dividend from Apple.		
Dec. 31	Equity Method Investments	21,000	
	Earnings from Equity Method Investments		21,000
	Record 30% share of Packard's earnings of $70,000.		
Dec. 31	Unrealized Loss—Income	7,000	
	Fair Value Adjustment—Stock*...................		7,000
	Record change in fair value of stock investments.		

*Fair value adjustment computations.

Stock Investments

12/31/2018	0		
10/2/2019	60,000		
10/17/2019	40,000		
12/31/2019	100,000		

Fair Value Adj.–Stock

12/31/2018 0			
		Adj.	**7,000**
		12/31/2019	7,000

	Cost	Fair Value	Unrealized Gain (Loss)
AT&T	$ 60,000	$48,000	$(12,000)
Apple	40,000	45,000	5,000
Total	$100,000	$93,000	$ (7,000)

Required balance of the Fair Value Adjustment—Stock account (credit) .... $(7,000)

Existing balance.................. 0

Necessary adjustment (credit) .... $(7,000)

2. The December 31, 2019, selected balance sheet items follow.

Assets—Long-term investments	
Stock investments (at fair value; cost is $100,000) . . .	$ 93,000
Equity method investments	96,000
Total long-term investments	$189,000

The relevant income statement items for the year ended December 31, 2019, follow.

Dividend revenue	$ 4,400
Unrealized loss—Income	(7,000)
Earnings from equity method investments	21,000

1. Journal entries for 2020.

Jan. 1	Cash	108,000	
	Equity Method Investments		96,000
	Gain on Sale of Stock Investments		12,000
	Sold 1,000 shares of Packard for cash.		
May 30	Cash	3,100	
	Dividend Revenue		3,100
	Received dividend from AT&T.		
June 15	Cash	1,600	
	Dividend Revenue		1,600
	Received dividend from Apple.		
Aug. 17	Cash	52,000	
	Loss on Sale of Stock Investments	8,000	
	Stock Investments		60,000
	Sold 2,000 shares of AT&T for cash.		
Aug. 19	Stock Investments	50,000	
	Cash		50,000
	Acquired 2,000 shares of Coca-Cola.		
Dec. 15	Cash	1,800	
	Dividend Revenue		1,800
	Received dividend from Apple.		
Dec. 31	Fair Value Adjustment—Stock*	4,000	
	Unrealized Gain—Income		4,000
	Record change in fair value of stock investments.		

Packard cost at Jan. 1 is $80,000
− $5,000 + $21,000 = $96,000.

Stock Investments

12/31/2019	100,000		
		8/17/2020	60,000
8/19/2020	50,000		
12/31/2020	90,000		

Fair Value Adj.–Stock

		12/31/2019	7,000
Adj.	**4,000**		
		12/31/2020	3,000

*Fair value adjustment computations.

	Cost	Fair Value	Unrealized Gain (Loss)
Apple	$40,000	$39,000	$(1,000)
Coca-Cola	50,000	48,000	(2,000)
Total	$90,000	$87,000	$(3,000)

Required balance of the Fair Value Adjustment—Stock account (credit)	$(3,000)
Existing balance (credit)	(7,000)
Necessary adjustment (debit)	$ 4,000

2. The December 31, 2020, balance sheet items follow.

Assets—Long-term investments	
Stock investments (at fair value; cost is $90,000)	$87,000

The relevant income statement items for the year ended December 31, 2020, follow.

Dividend revenue	$ 6,500
Unrealized gain—Income	4,000
Gain on sale of stock investments	12,000
Loss on sale of stock investments	(8,000)

Summary: Cheat Sheet

BASICS OF INVESTMENTS

Short-term investments: Investments that (1) management intends to convert to cash within one year and (2) are readily convertible to cash. Short-term investments are current assets.
Long-term investments: Investments that are not going to be converted into cash in the short term. Long-term investments are noncurrent assets.
Debt securities: Reflect a creditor relation and include notes and bonds.
Equity securities: Reflect an owner relation and include stock.

DEBT INVESTMENTS

Acquiring debt investments:

Debt Investments	30,000	
Cash		30,000

Interest earned and received:

Cash	1,050	
Interest Revenue		1,050

Unrealized gain (or loss): A gain (or loss) not yet confirmed by actual sales of securities.
TRADING SECURITIES:
Debt investments that are actively bought and sold for profit. Trading securities are *always* current assets.

Fair value adjustment—Trading securities: Reflects gain (shown here) or loss.

Fair Value Adjustment—Trading.	1,500	
Unrealized Gain—Income.		1,500

Reporting fair value—Trading securities: An unrealized gain (or loss) from a change in the fair value of the portfolio of trading securities is reported on the income statement under Other Revenues and Gains (or Expenses and Losses). Fair Value Adjustment—Trading is an asset account that adjusts the trading securities portfolio to fair value.

Current Assets		
Debt investments—Trading (at cost)	$11,500	
Fair value adjustment—Trading.	1,500	
Debt investments—Trading (at fair value).		$13,000

Selling trading securities: When sale price > cost, record a gain (shown here). When sale price < cost, record a loss. A gain (or loss) is reported in Other Revenues and Gains (or Expenses and Losses) section on the income statement.

Cash	120	
Debt Investments—Trading.		100
Gain on Sale of Debt Investments		20

HELD-TO-MATURITY (HTM) SECURITIES:
Debt investments that are held until maturity. They are current assets if their maturity is *within* one year and are long-term investments if their maturity is *over* one year. They are *not* reported at fair value.

Receipt of principal and interest—HTM:

Cash	102	
Debt Investments—HTM		100
Interest Revenue		2

AVAILABLE-FOR-SALE (AFS) SECURITIES:
Debt investments not classified as trading or held-to-maturity. They are current assets if they are to be sold *within* one year and long-term investments if they are to be sold *beyond* one year.

Fair value adjustment—AFS securities: Reflects gain (shown here) or loss.

Fair Value Adjustment—Available-for-Sale	1,550	
Unrealized Gain—Equity		1,550

Reporting fair value—AFS securities: An unrealized gain (or loss) from a change in the fair value of the portfolio of AFS securities is reported in the equity section of the balance sheet (as part of comprehensive income). Fair Value Adjustment—AFS is an asset account that adjusts the AFS securities portfolio to fair value.

Assets		
Debt investments—Available-for-sale (at cost)	$73,000	
Fair value adjustment—Available-for-sale.	1,550	
Debt investments—Available-for-sale (at fair value). . . .		$74,550

Selling AFS securities: Identical to selling trading securities.

EQUITY INVESTMENTS

Stock investments (insignificant influence): When a company owns less than 20% of voting stock of another company, it has insignificant influence. Can be classified as short or long term.

Acquiring stock investments (insignificant influence):

Stock Investments	7,000	
Cash		7,000

Dividends received from stock investment (insignificant influence):

Cash	10	
Dividend Revenue		10

Fair value adjustment—Stock (insignificant influence): Reflects gain (shown here) or loss.

Fair Value Adjustment—Stock	2,000	
Unrealized Gain—Income		2,000

Reporting fair value adjustment from stock (insignificant influence): An unrealized gain (or loss) from a change in the fair value of the portfolio of stock investments is reported on the income statement under Other Revenues and Gains (or Expenses and Losses). Fair Value Adjustment—Stock is an asset account that adjusts the stock investments portfolio to fair value.

Assets		
Stock investments (at cost)	$7,000	
Fair value adjustment—Stock	2,000	
Stock investments (at fair value)		$9,000

Selling stock investments: When sale price > cost, record a gain (shown here). When sale price < cost, record a loss. A gain (or loss) is reported in Other Revenues and Gains (or Expenses and Losses) section on the income statement.

Cash	800	
Stock Investments		500
Gain on Sale of Stock Investments		300

Equity method investments: When a company owns between 20% and 50% of voting stock of another company, it has significant influence. Classified as long term.

Acquiring equity method investments:

| Equity Method Investments . . . . | 70,000 | |
| Cash . . . . | | 70,000 |

Recording share of earnings (equity method): Calculated as percentage of ownership times net income of investee.

| Equity Method Investments . . . . | 6,000 | |
| Earnings from Equity Method Investments . . . . . . | | 6,000 |

Recording share of dividends (equity method): Calculated as percentage of ownership times total dividends paid by investee.

| Cash . . . . | 3,000 | |
| Equity Method Investments . . . . | | 3,000 |

Reporting equity method investments: Equity method investments are not adjusted to fair value. Instead, the account is increased by investee net income and decreased by investee dividends.

Equity Method Investments	
1/1/2019 Investment acquisition 70,000	
12/31/2019 Share of earnings 6,000	
12/31/2019 Balance 76,000	
	1/9/2020 Share of dividend 3,000
1/9/2020 Balance 73,000	

Selling equity method investments: When sale price > book value, record a gain (shown here). When sale price < book value, record a loss.

Cash	80,000	
Equity Method Investments		73,000
Gain on Sale of Stock Investments		7,000

Equity securities with controlling influence: When an investor owns more than 50% of a company's voting stock, it has control over the investee and the *consolidation method* is used. The controlling investor is called the **parent,** and the investee is called the **subsidiary.**

REPORTING AND ANALYSIS

Classification	Investments Account Reported at
Short-Term Investment in Securities	
Debt Investments—Held-to-Maturity	Cost (without any discount or premium amortization)
Debt Investments—Trading	**Fair value** (with fair value adjustment to income)
Debt Investments—Available-for-Sale	**Fair value** (with fair value adjustment to equity)
Stock Investments—insignificant influence	**Fair value** (with fair value adjustment to income)
Long-Term Investment in Securities	
Debt Investments—Held-to-Maturity	Cost (with any discount or premium amortized)
Debt Investments—Available-for-Sale	**Fair value** (with fair value adjustment to equity)
Stock Investments—insignificant influence	**Fair value** (with fair value adjustment to income)
Equity Method Investments—significant influence . . .	Equity method (no fair value adjustment)
Consolidated Investments—controlling influence . . .	Consolidation method (no fair value adjustment)

Key Terms

Available-for-sale (AFS) securities (C-5)	**Fair Value Adjustment** (C-2)	**Short-term investments** (C-1)
Comprehensive income (C-12)	**Held-to-maturity (HTM) securities** (C-4)	**Subsidiary** (C-12)
Consolidated financial statements (C-12)	**Long-term investments** (C-1)	**Total asset turnover** (C-13)
Equity method (C-9)	**Other comprehensive income** (C-12)	**Trading securities** (C-2)
Equity securities with controlling influence (C-11)	**Parent** (C-12)	**Unrealized gain (loss)** (C-3, C-8)
Equity securities with significant influence (C-9)	**Profit margin** (C-13)	
	Return on total assets (C-13)	

Multiple Choice Quiz

1. A company purchased $30,000 of 5% bonds for investment purposes on May 1. The bonds pay interest on February 1 and August 1. The amount of interest revenue accrued at December 31 (the company's year-end) is
   - **a.** $1,500.
   - **b.** $1,375.
   - **c.** $1,000.
   - **d.** $625.
   - **e.** $300.

2. This period, Amadeus Co. purchased its only available-for-sale investment in the notes of Bach Co. for $83,000. The period-end fair value of these notes is $84,500. Amadeus records a
   - **a.** Credit to Unrealized Gain—Equity for $1,500.
   - **b.** Debit to Unrealized Loss—Equity for $1,500.
   - **c.** Debit to Investment Revenue for $1,500.
   - **d.** Credit to Fair Value Adjustment—Available-for-Sale for $3,500.
   - **e.** Credit to Cash for $1,500.

3. Mozart Co. owns 35% of Melody Inc. Melody pays $50,000 in cash dividends to its shareholders for the period. Mozart's entry to record the Melody dividend includes a
   - **a.** Credit to Investment Revenue for $50,000.
   - **b.** Credit to Equity Method Investments for $17,500.
   - **c.** Credit to Cash for $17,500.
   - **d.** Debit to Equity Method Investments for $17,500.
   - **e.** Debit to Cash for $50,000.

4. A company has net income of $300,000, net sales of $2,500,000, and total assets of $2,000,000. Its return on total assets equals

  a. 6.7%.   **c.** 8.3%.   **e.** 15.0%.

  b. 12.0%.   **d.** 80.0%.

5. A company had net income of $80,000, net sales of $600,000, and total assets of $400,000. Its profit margin and total asset turnover are

	Profit Margin	Total Asset Turnover
a.	1.5%	13.3
b.	13.3%	1.5
c.	13.3%	0.7
d.	7.0%	13.3
e.	10.0%	26.7

ANSWERS TO MULTIPLE CHOICE QUIZ

1. d; $30,000 × 5% × 5/12 = $625

2. a; Unrealized gain = $84,500 − $83,000 = $1,500

3. b; $50,000 × 35% = $17,500

4. e; $300,000/$2,000,000 = 15%

5. b; Profit margin = $80,000/$600,000 = 13.3%
      Total asset turnover = $600,000/$400,000 = 1.5

🔲 Icon denotes assignments that involve decision making.

Discussion Questions

1. Under what two conditions should investments be classified as current assets?

2. 🔲 On a balance sheet, what valuation must be reported for short-term debt investments in trading securities?

3. If a stock investment with insignificant influence costs $10,000 and is sold for $12,000, how should the difference between these two amounts be recorded?

4. Identify the three classes of debt investments and the three classes of equity investments.

5. Under what conditions should investments be classified as current assets? As long-term assets?

6. For investments in available-for-sale debt securities, how are unrealized (holding) gains and losses reported?

7. If a company purchases its only long-term investments in available-for-sale debt securities this period and their fair value is below cost at the balance sheet date, what entry is required to recognize this unrealized loss?

8. On a balance sheet, what valuation must be reported for debt securities classified as available-for-sale?

9. Under what circumstances are long-term investments in debt securities reported at cost and adjusted for amortization of any difference between cost and maturity value?

10. In accounting for investments in equity securities, when should the equity method be used?

11. Under what circumstances does a company prepare consolidated financial statements?

12. 🔲 Refer to **Apple**'s statement of comprehensive income in Appendix A. What is the amount **APPLE** of *change in foreign currency translation, net of tax effects,* for the year ended September 30, 2017? Is this change an unrealized gain or an unrealized loss?

13. Refer to **Google**'s statement of comprehensive income in Appendix A. What was the **GOOGLE** amount of its 2017 *change in net unrealized gains (losses)* for its AFS investments?

14. 🔲 Refer to the income statement of **Samsung** in Appendix A. How can you **Samsung** tell that it uses the consolidated method of accounting?

🔲🟥 **connect**

QUICK STUDY

QS C-1

Distinguishing between short- and long-term investments

C1

Which of the following statements are true of long-term investments?

_____ **a.** They can be considered cash equivalents.

_____ **b.** They can include assets not used in operations, such as investments in land.

_____ **c.** They generally include investments that will mature in 3 to 12 months.

_____ **d.** They are reported with noncurrent assets on the balance sheet.

_____ **e.** They are always easily sold and therefore qualify as being marketable.

_____ **f.** They can include bonds and stocks not intended to be sold in the near future.

QS C-2

Distinguishing between debt and equity securities

C1

Identify investments as an investment in either debt (D) securities or equity (E) securities.

_____ **a.** U.S. Treasury bonds   _____ **e.** IBM corporate notes   _____ **i.** Chicago municipal bonds

_____ **b.** Google stock   _____ **f.** German government bonds   _____ **j.** Apple stock

_____ **c.** Certificate of deposit   _____ **g.** Amazon stock   _____ **k.** David Bowie bonds

_____ **d.** Apple bonds   _____ **h.** Costco corporate notes   _____ **l.** Facebook stock

Prepare Hertog Company's journal entries to record the following transactions for the current year.

May 7   Purchases Kraft bonds as a short-term investment in trading securities at a cost of $10,300.
June 6   Sells its entire investment in Kraft bonds for $11,050 cash.

QS C-3
Accounting for debt investments classified as trading   **P1**

Kitty Company began operations in the current year and acquired short-term debt investments in trading securities. The year-end cost and fair values for its portfolio of these debt investments follow. Prepare the journal entry to record the December 31 year-end fair value adjustment for these debt securities.

QS C-4
Fair value adjustment to a portfolio of trading securities

P1

Trading Securities	Cost	Fair Value
Tesla bonds	$12,000	$ 9,000
Nike bonds	20,000	21,000
Ford bonds	5,000	4,000

Refer to the information in QS C-4. (1) After the fair value adjustment is made, prepare the assets section of Kitty Company's December 31 classified balance sheet. (2) In which income statement section is the unrealized gain (or loss) on the portfolio of trading securities reported?

QS C-5
Reporting trading securities on financial statements   **P1**

Prepare Garzon Company's journal entries to record the following transactions for the current year.

Jan. 1   Purchases 6% bonds (as a held-to-maturity investment) issued by PBS at a cost of $40,000, which is the par value.
July 1   Receives first semiannual payment of interest from PBS bonds.
Dec. 31   Receives a check from PBS in payment of principal ($40,000) and the second semiannual payment of interest.

QS C-6
Accounting for debt investments classified as held-to-maturity

P2

Journ Co. purchased short-term investments in available-for-sale debt securities at a cost of $50,000 cash on November 25. At December 31, these securities had a fair value of $47,000. This is the first and only time the company has purchased such securities.

1. Prepare the November 25 entry to record the purchase of debt securities.
2. Prepare the December 31 year-end adjusting entry for the securities' portfolio.
3. Prepare the April 6 entry when Journ sells 10% of these securities ($5,000 cost) for $6,000 cash.

QS C-7
Accounting for available-for-sale debt securities

P3

During the current year, Reed Consulting acquired long-term available-for-sale debt securities on July 1 at a $70,000 cost. At its December 31 year-end, these securities had a fair value of $58,000. This is the first and only time the company purchased such securities.

1. Prepare the July 1 entry to record the purchase of these debt securities.
2. Prepare the year-end adjusting entry related to these securities.

QS C-8
Recording fair value adjustment for available-for-sale debt securities

P3

On December 31, Reggit Company held the following short-term investments in its portfolio of available-for-sale debt securities. Reggit had no short-term investments in its prior accounting periods. Prepare the December 31 adjusting entry to report these investments at fair value.

QS C-9
Adjusting available-for-sale debt securities to fair value

P3

Available-for-Sale Securities	Cost	Fair Value
Verrizano Corporation bonds......................	$89,600	$91,600
Preble Corporation notes.........................	70,600	62,900
Lucerne Company bonds..........................	86,500	83,100

Check   Unrealized loss, $9,100

Refer to the information in QS C-9. (1) After the fair value adjustment is made, prepare the assets section of Reggit Company's December 31 classified balance sheet. (2) Is the unrealized gain (or loss) on the portfolio of available-for-sale securities reported on the income statement?

QS C-10
Reporting available-for-sale securities on financial statements   **P3**

Prepare Riley Company's journal entries to record the following transactions for the current year.

Apr. 18   Purchases 300 common shares of XLT Co. as a short-term investment at a cost of $42 per share. With this stock investment, Riley has an insignificant influence over XLT.
May 30   Receives $1 per share from XLT in dividends.

QS C-11
Accounting for stock investments   **P4**

QS C-12 Adjusting stock investments to fair value **P4**	Prepare Tiker Company's journal entries to record the following transactions and the adjusting entry to record the fair value of the stock investments portfolio. This is the first and only time the company purchased such securities. May 9 Purchases 200 shares of Higo stock as a short-term investment at a cost of $30 per share. Tiker has insignificant influence over Higo. June 2 Sells 20 shares of its investment in Higo stock ($600 cost) at $33 per share. Dec. 31 The closing market price (fair value) of the Higo stock is $23 per share.
QS C-13 Reporting stock investments with insignificant influence **P4**	On May 20, Montero Co. paid $150,000 to acquire 30 shares (4%) of ORD Corp. as a long-term investment. On August 5, Montero sold one-tenth of the ORD shares for $18,000. **1.** Prepare entries to record both (*a*) the acquisition and (*b*) the sale of these shares. **2.** Should this stock investment be reported at fair value or at cost on the balance sheet?
QS C-14 Financial statement presentation of investments **C1 P1 P2 P3 P4**	Indicate where each of the following items is reported on financial statements. Choose from the following categories: (*a*) current assets, (*b*) long-term investments, (*c*) current liabilities, (*d*) long-term liabilities, (*e*) other revenues and gains, (*f*) other expenses and losses, and (*g*) equity. _____ **1.** Trading securities _____ **2.** Unrealized gain on available-for-sale securities _____ **3.** Held-to-maturity securities (due in 15 years) _____ **4.** Unrealized gain on trading securities _____ **5.** Fair value adjustment—Trading
QS C-15 Equity method transactions **P5**	Rowan Co. purchases 100 common shares (40%) of JBI Corp. as a long-term investment for $500,000 cash on July 1. JBI paid $5,000 in total cash dividends on November 1 and reported net income of $100,000 for the year. Prepare Rowan's entries to record (1) the purchase of JBI shares, (2) the receipt of its share of JBI dividends, and (3) the December 31 year-end adjustment for its share of JBI net income.
QS C-16 Equity securities with controlling influence **C2**	Accenture purchases 55% of the voting common stock of JBL. After the purchase, Accenture has a controlling influence over JBL. (1) Which method does Accenture use to account for its investment in JBL? (2) What type of financial statements does Accenture prepare after the acquisition?
QS C-17 Return on total assets **A1**	Fivio Co. reports the following information. (1) Compute return on total assets for the current year and for 1 year ago. (2) Is Fivio more efficient or less efficient in using total assets to produce income in the current year versus 1 year ago?

	A	B	C	D
1		**Current Year**	**1 Year Ago**	**2 Years Ago**
2	Total assets, December 31	$770,000	$340,000	$210,000
3	Net income	55,500	38,400	30,200

QS C-18 Component return on total assets **A1**	The return on total assets is the focus of analysts, creditors, and other users of financial statements. **1.** How is the return on total assets computed? **2.** What does this important ratio reflect? **3.** Return on total assets can be separated into two important components. Write the formula to separate the return on total assets into its two basic components. **4.** Explain how these components of the return on total assets are helpful to financial statement users for business decisions.

■ connect·

EXERCISES **Exercise C-1** Debt and equity securities and short- and long-term investments **C1**	Complete the following descriptions by filling in the blanks using the terms or phrases *a* through *g*. **a.** not intended **b.** not readily **c.** cash **d.** operating cycle **e.** one year **f.** owner **g.** creditor **1.** Debt securities reflect a(n) _____ relation such as with investments in notes and bonds. **2.** Equity securities reflect a(n) _____ relation such as with investments in shares of stock. **3.** Short-term investments are securities that (1) management intends to convert to cash within _____ _____ or the _____ _____, whichever is longer, and (2) are readily convertible to _____. **4.** Long-term investments in securities are defined as those securities that are _____ _____ convertible to cash or are _____ _____ to be converted into cash in the short term.

Brooks Co. purchases debt investments as trading securities at a cost of $66,000 on December 27. This is its first and only purchase of such securities. At December 31, these securities had a fair value of $72,000.

1. Prepare the December 27 entry for the purchase of debt investments.
2. Prepare the December 31 year-end fair value adjusting entry for the trading securities' portfolio.
3. Prepare the January 3 entry when Brooks sells a portion of its trading securities (costing $3,000) for $4,000 cash.

Exercise C-2
Accounting for debt investments classified as trading **P1**

Check   (3) Gain, $1,000

Prepare Natura Co.'s journal entries to record the following transactions involving its short-term investments in held-to-maturity debt securities, all of which occurred during the current year.

a. On June 15, paid $1,000 cash to purchase Remed's 90-day short-term debt securities ($1,000 principal), dated June 15, that pay 10% interest.
b. On September 16, received a check from Remed in payment of the principal and 90 days' interest on the debt securities purchased in part *a*.

Exercise C-3
Accounting for held-to-maturity debt securities
P2

Prepare Krum Co.'s journal entries to record the following transactions involving its short-term investments in available-for-sale debt securities, all of which occurred during the current year.

a. On August 1, paid $50,000 cash to purchase Houtte's 9%, six-month debt securities ($50,000 principal), dated August 1.
b. On October 30, received a check from Houtte for 90 days' interest on the debt securities in part *a*.

Exercise C-4
Accounting for available-for-sale debt securities
P3

On December 31, Lujack Co. held the following short-term available-for-sale securities. Lujack had no short-term investments prior to the current period. Prepare the December 31 year-end adjusting entry to record the fair value adjustment for these debt securities.

Available-for-Sale Securities	Cost	Fair Value
Nintendo Co. notes.............................	$44,450	$48,900
Atlantic bonds.....................................	49,000	47,000
Kellogg Co. notes	25,000	23,200
McDonald's Corp. bonds	46,300	44,800

Exercise C-5
Fair value adjustment to available-for-sale debt securities
P3

Ticker Services began operations in Year 1 and holds long-term investments in available-for-sale debt securities. The year-end cost and fair values for its portfolio of these investments follow. Prepare journal entries to record each year-end fair value adjustment for these securities.

Portfolio of Available-for-Sale Securities	Cost	Fair Value
December 31, Year 1	$13,000	$15,000
December 31, Year 2	20,000	25,000
December 31, Year 3	23,000	29,000
December 31, Year 4	16,500	19,000

Exercise C-6
Multiyear fair value adjustments to available-for-sale debt securities
P3

Prepare journal entries to record the following transactions involving the short-term stock investments of Duke Co., all of which occurred during the current year.

a. On March 22, purchased 1,000 shares of RPI Company stock at $10 per share. Duke's stock investment results in it having an insignificant influence over RPI.
b. On July 1, received a $1 per share cash dividend on the RPI stock purchased in part *a*.
c. On October 8, sold 50 shares of RPI stock for $15 per share.

Exercise C-7
Accounting for stock investments with insignificant influence
P4

Check   (c) Dr. Cash $750

On December 31, Mars Co. had the following portfolio of stock investments with insignificant influence. Mars had no stock investments in prior periods. Prepare the December 31 adjusting entry to report these investments at fair value.

Stock Investments	Cost	Fair Value
Apple stock	$ 6,000	$ 8,000
Chipotle stock	4,000	1,500
Under Armour stock................................	12,000	14,000

Exercise C-8
Fair value adjustment to stock investments with insignificant influence **P4**

Exercise C-9

Reporting stock
investments on financial
statements   **P4**

Refer to the information in Exercise C-8. (1) After the fair value adjustment is made, prepare the assets section of Mars Co.'s December 31 classified balance sheet. Assume Mars plans to sell its trading securities within the next six months. (2) In which income statement section is the unrealized gain (or loss) on the portfolio of stock investments reported?

Exercise C-10

Transactions and fair value
adjustments for stock
investments with
insignificant influence

P4

Check Dec. 31: Dr. Fair
Value Adjustment—Stock,
$4,400

Carlsville Company began operations in the current year and had no prior stock investments. The following transactions are from its short-term stock investments with insignificant influence. Prepare journal entries to record these transactions. On December 31, prepare the adjusting entry to record the fair value adjustment for the portfolio of stock investments.

July 22	Purchased 1,600 shares of Hunt Corp. at $30 per share.
Sep. 5	Received a $2 cash dividend for each share of Hunt Corp.
Sep. 27	Purchased 3,400 shares of HCA at $34 per share.
Oct. 3	Sold 1,600 shares of Hunt at $25 per share.
Oct. 30	Purchased 1,200 shares of Black & Decker at $50 per share.
Dec. 17	Received a $3 cash dividend for each share of Black & Decker.
Dec. 31	Fair value of the short-term stock investments is $180,000.

Exercise C-11

Transactions in held-to-
maturity, trading, and stock
investments

P1 P2 P4

Prepare journal entries to record the following transactions involving both the short-term and long-term investments of Cancun Corp., all of which occurred during the current year.

a. On February 15, paid $160,000 cash to purchase GMI's 90-day short-term notes at par, which are dated February 15 and pay 10% interest (classified as held-to-maturity).

b. On March 22, bought 700 shares of Fran Inc. common stock at $51 cash per share. Cancun's stock investment results in it having an insignificant influence over Fran.

c. On May 15, received a check from GMI in payment of the principal *and* 90 days' interest on the notes purchased in part *a*.

d. On July 30, paid $100,000 cash to purchase MP Inc.'s 8%, six-month notes at par, dated July 30 (classified as trading securities).

e. On September 1, received a $1 per share cash dividend on the Fran Inc. common stock purchased in part *b*.

f. On October 8, sold 30 shares of Fran Inc. common stock for $54 cash per share.

g. On October 30, received a check from MP Inc. for three months' interest on the notes purchased in part *d*.

Exercise C-12

Accounting for equity
method investments

P5

Prepare journal entries to record the following transactions and events of Kodax Company.

Year 1

Jan. 2	Purchased 30,000 shares of Grecco Co. common stock for $411,000 cash. Grecco has 90,000 shares of common stock outstanding, and its activities will be significantly influenced by Kodax.
Sep. 1	Grecco declared and paid a cash dividend of $1.50 per share.
Dec. 31	Grecco announced that net income for the year is $486,900.

Year 2

June 1	Grecco declared and paid a cash dividend of $2.10 per share.
Dec. 31	Grecco announced that net income for the year is $702,750.
Dec. 31	Kodax sold 3,000 shares of Grecco for $71,000 cash.

Exercise C-13

Classifying investments in
securities; recording fair
values

C1 P2 P3 P4 P5

The following information shows Carperk Company's individual investments in securities during its current year, along with the December 31 fair values.

a. Investment in Brava Company bonds: $420,500 cost; $457,000 fair value. Carperk intends to hold these bonds until they mature in 5 years.

b. Investment in Baybridge common stock: 29,500 shares; $362,450 cost; $391,375 fair value. Carperk owns 32% of Baybridge's voting stock and has a significant influence over Baybridge.

c. Investment in Duffa bonds: $165,500 cost; $178,000 fair value. This investment is not readily marketable and is not classified as held-to-maturity or trading.

d. Investment in Newton notes: $90,300 cost; $88,625 fair value. Newton notes are not readily market-able and are not classified as held-to-maturity or trading.

e. Investment in Farmers common stock: 16,300 shares; $100,860 cost; $111,210 fair value. This stock is marketable, and Carperk intends to sell it within the year. This stock investment results in Carperk having an insignificant influence over Farmers.

Required

1. Identify whether each investment *a* through *e* should be classified as a short-term or long-term invest-ment. For each investment, indicate in which of the six investment classifications listed in Exhibit C.2 it should be placed.

2. Prepare a journal entry dated December 31 to record the fair value adjustment for the portfolio of available-for-sale debt securities. Carperk had no available-for-sale debt securities prior to this year.

Check   (2) Unrealized gain, $10,825

Selected accounts from GermX Co.'s adjusted trial balance for the year ended December 31 follow. Prepare the assets section of a classified balance sheet. *Hint:* Fair Value Adjustment—Trading *increases* trading securities; Fair Value Adjustment—Stock *decreases* stock investments.

Exercise C-14
Prepare assets section of balance sheet

C1   P1   P2   P3   P4   P5

Trading securities (at cost)	$ 5,000	Cash	$10,000
Short-term stock investments (at cost)	23,000	Fair value adjustment—Stock	(1,000)
Equity method investments	70,000	Accounts receivable	2,000
Held-to-maturity securities (long-term)	13,000	Fair value adjustment—Trading	500

Wixi Co. has the following equity investments in FSN, DELL, and ATI. (1) Which of these companies are subsidiaries of Wixi? (2) How are individual assets and liabilities of a parent and its subsidiary(ies) re-ported on a balance sheet?

FSN stock: Wixi owns 70% of the voting common stock and has controlling influence.

DELL stock: Wixi owns 5% of the voting common stock and has insignificant influence.

ATI stock: Wixi owns 30% of the voting common stock and has significant influence.

Exercise C-15
Equity securities with controlling influence

C2

Use the following information of Prescrip Co. to prepare a calendar year-end statement of comprehensive income.

Exercise C-16
Preparing a statement of comprehensive income

C2

Total comprehensive income (final total)	$ 9,400	Other comprehensive income (subtotal)	$ (600)
Net income	10,000	Change in foreign currency translation	1,400
Change in value of available-for-sale securities	(2,000)		

Following are financial data for **Nike** and **Under Armour**. (1) Compute return on total assets for the current year for (*a*) Nike and (*b*) Under Armour. (2) Compute both profit margin and total asset turnover for the current year for (*a*) Nike and (*b*) Under Armour. (3) Which company more efficiently used its assets in the current year?

Exercise C-17
Return on total assets

A1

	Nike		Under Armour	
$ millions	Current Year	1 Year Prior	Current Year	1 Year Prior
Net income	$ 3,760	$ 3,273	$ 257	$ 233
Net sales	32,376	30,601	4,825	3,963
Total assets	21,396	21,597	3,644	2,866

■ connect

Kirkland Company had no trading debt securities prior to this year. It had the following transactions this year involving trading debt securities.

Aug. 2 Purchased Verizon bonds for $10,000.
Sep. 7 Purchased Apple bonds for $35,000.
      12 Purchased Mastercard bonds for $20,000.
Oct. 21 Sold some of its Verizon bonds that had cost $2,000 for $2,100 cash.
      23 Sold some of its Apple bonds that had cost $15,000 for $15,400 cash.
Nov. 1 Purchased Walmart bonds for $40,000.
Dec. 10 Sold all of its Mastercard bonds for $18,000 cash.

PROBLEM SET A

Problem C-1A
Recording and adjusting trading debt securities

P1

Required

1. Prepare journal entries to record these transactions.
2. Prepare a table to compare the year-end cost and fair values of its trading debt securities. Year-end fair values: Verizon, $8,500; Apple, $22,000; and Walmart, $39,000.
3. Prepare the adjusting entry to record the year-end fair value adjustment for the portfolio of trading debt securities.

Problem C-2A

Recording, adjusting, and reporting available-for-sale debt securities

P3

Mead Inc. began operations in Year 1. Following is a series of transactions and events involving its long-term debt investments in available-for-sale securities.

Year 1

Jan.	20	Purchased Johnson & Johnson bonds for $20,500.
Feb.	9	Purchased Sony notes for $55,440.
June	12	Purchased Mattel bonds for $40,500.
Dec.	31	Fair values for debt in the portfolio are Johnson & Johnson, $21,500; Sony, $52,500; and Mattel, $46,350.

Year 2

Apr.	15	Sold all of the Johnson & Johnson bonds for $23,500.
July	5	Sold all of the Mattel bonds for $35,850.
July	22	Purchased Sara Lee notes for $13,500.
Aug.	19	Purchased Kodak bonds for $15,300.
Dec.	31	Fair values for debt in the portfolio are Kodak, $17,325; Sara Lee, $12,000; and Sony, $60,000.

Year 3

Feb.	27	Purchased Microsoft bonds for $160,800.
June	21	Sold all of the Sony notes for $57,600.
June	30	Purchased Black & Decker bonds for $50,400.
Aug.	3	Sold all of the Sara Lee notes for $9,750.
Nov.	1	Sold all of the Kodak bonds for $20,475.
Dec.	31	Fair values for debt in the portfolio are Black & Decker, $54,600, and Microsoft, $158,600.

Required

1. Prepare journal entries to record these transactions and the year-end fair value adjustments to the portfolio of long-term available-for-sale debt securities.

Check (2b) Fair Value Adj. bal.: 12/31/Year 1, $3,910 Dr.; 12/31/Year 2, $5,085 Dr.

  (3b) Unrealized Gain at 12/31/Year 3, $2,000

2. Prepare a table that summarizes the (a) total cost, (b) total fair value adjustment, and (c) total fair value of the portfolio of long-term available-for-sale debt securities at each year-end.
3. Prepare a table that summarizes (a) the realized gains and losses and (b) the unrealized gains or losses for the portfolio of long-term available-for-sale debt securities at each year-end.

Problem C-3A

Debt investments in available-for-sale securities; unrealized and realized gains and losses

P3

Stoll Co.'s long-term available-for-sale portfolio at the *start* of this year consists of the following.

Available-for-Sale Securities	Cost	Fair Value
Company A bonds	$535,300	$490,000
Company B notes	159,380	154,000
Company C bonds	662,750	640,940

Stoll enters into the following transactions involving its available-for-sale debt securities this year.

Jan.	29	Sold one-half of the Company B notes for $79,200.
July	6	Purchased Company X bonds for $126,600.
Nov.	13	Purchased Company Z notes for $267,900.
Dec.	9	Sold all of the Company A bonds for $515,000.

The fair values at December 31 are B, $81,000; C, $610,000; X, $118,000; and Z, $278,000.

Required

1. Prepare journal entries to record these transactions, including the December 31 adjusting entry to record the fair value adjustment for the long-term investments in available-for-sale securities.

2. Determine the amount Stoll reports on its December 31 balance sheet for its long-term investments in available-for-sale securities.

3. What amount of gains or losses on transactions relating to long-term investments in available-for-sale debt securities does Stoll report on its income statement for this year?

Check (1) Dec 31: Cr. Unrealized Loss— Equity, $22,550

Rose Company had no short-term investments prior to this year. It had the following transactions this year involving short-term stock investments with insignificant influence.

Apr.	16	Purchased 3,500 shares of Gem Co. stock at $24 per share.
July	7	Purchased 2,000 shares of PepsiCo stock at $49 per share.
	20	Purchased 1,000 shares of Xerox stock at $16 per share.
Aug.	15	Received a $1.00 per share cash dividend on the Gem Co. stock.
	28	Sold 2,000 shares of Gem Co. stock at $30 per share.
Oct.	1	Received a $2.50 per share cash dividend on the PepsiCo shares.
Dec.	15	Received a $1.00 per share cash dividend on the remaining Gem Co. shares.
	31	Received a $1.50 per share cash dividend on the PepsiCo shares.

Problem C-4A
Recording, adjusting, and reporting stock investments with insignificant influence

P4 🎖️

Required

1. Prepare journal entries to record the preceding transactions and events.

2. Prepare a table to compare the year-end cost and fair values of Rose's short-term stock investments. The year-end fair values per share are Gem Co., $26; PepsiCo, $46; and Xerox, $13.

3. Prepare an adjusting entry to record the year-end fair value adjustment for the portfolio of short-term stock investments.

Check (2) Cost = $150,000

(3) Dr. Unrealized Loss— Income, $6,000

Analysis Component

4. Explain the balance sheet presentation of the fair value adjustment for Rose's short-term investments.

5. How do these short-term stock investments affect Rose's (*a*) income statement for this year and (*b*) the equity section of its balance sheet at this year-end?

Selk Steel Co., which began operations in Year 1, had the following transactions and events in its long-term investments.

Year 1

Jan.	5	Selk purchased 60,000 shares (20% of total) of Kildaire's common stock for $1,560,000.
Oct.	23	Kildaire declared and paid a cash dividend of $3.20 per share.
Dec.	31	Kildaire's net income for the year is $1,164,000, and the fair value of its stock at December 31 is $30.00 per share.

Year 2

Oct.	15	Kildaire declared and paid a cash dividend of $2.60 per share.
Dec.	31	Kildaire's net income for the year is $1,476,000, and the fair value of its stock at December 31 is $32.00 per share.

Year 3

Jan.	2	Selk sold 3% (equal to 1,800 shares) of its investment in Kildaire for $54,200 cash.

Problem C-5A
Accounting for long-term investments in stock with significant influence

P5

Required

Prepare journal entries to record these transactions and events for Selk. Assume that Selk has a significant influence over Kildaire with its 20% share of stock.

Refer to the transactions in Problem C-5A. Assume that although Selk owns 20% of Kildaire's outstanding stock, circumstances indicate that it does *not* have a significant influence over the investee.

Required

Prepare journal entries to record the preceding transactions and events for Selk.

Problem C-6A
Accounting for long-term investments in stock without significant influence

P4

PROBLEM SET B

Problem C-1B
Recording and adjusting trading debt securities

P1

Ancore Company had no trading debt securities prior to this year. It had the following transactions this year involving trading debt securities.

July	28	Purchased Target bonds for $30,000.
Aug.	17	Purchased Kroger bonds for $105,000.
	26	Purchased Ford bonds for $60,000.
Sep.	5	Sold some of its Target bonds that had cost $6,000 for $6,300 cash.
	8	Sold some of its Kroger bonds that had cost $45,000 for $46,200 cash.
Oct.	12	Purchased Marshall bonds for $120,000.
Nov.	28	Sold all of its Ford bonds for $54,000 cash.

Required

1. Prepare journal entries to record these transactions.

2. Prepare a table to compare the year-end cost and fair values of Ancore's trading debt securities. Year-end fair values: Target, $25,500; Kroger, $66,000; and Marshall, $117,000.

3. Prepare the adjusting entry to record the year-end fair value adjustment for the portfolio of trading debt securities.

Problem C-2B
Recording, adjusting, and reporting available-for-sale debt securities

P3

Paris Inc. began operations in Year 1. Following is a series of transactions and events involving its long-term debt investments in available-for-sale securities.

Year 1

Mar.	10	Purchased Apple bonds for $30,600.
Apr.	7	Purchased Ford notes for $56,250.
Sep.	1	Purchased Polaroid bonds for $28,200.
Dec.	31	Fair values for debt in the portfolio are Apple, $33,000; Ford, $54,600; and Polaroid, $29,400.

Year 2

Apr.	26	Sold all of the Ford notes for $51,250.
June	2	Purchased Duracell bonds for $34,650.
June	14	Purchased Sears notes for $25,200.
Nov.	27	Sold all of the Polaroid bonds for $30,600.
Dec.	31	Fair values for debt in the portfolio are Apple, $31,000; Duracell, $32,400; and Sears, $27,600.

Year 3

Jan.	28	Purchased Coca-Cola bonds for $40,000.
Aug.	22	Sold all of the Apple bonds for $25,800.
Sep.	3	Purchased Motorola notes for $84,000.
Oct.	9	Sold all of the Sears notes for $28,800.
Oct.	31	Sold all of the Duracell bonds for $27,000.
Dec.	31	Fair values for debt in the portfolio are Coca-Cola, $48,000, and Motorola, $82,000.

Required

1. Prepare journal entries to record these transactions and events and any year-end fair value adjustments to the portfolio of long-term available-for-sale debt securities.

Check (2b) Fair Value Adj. bal.: 12/31/Year 1, $1,950 Dr.; 12/31/Year 2, $550 Dr.

(3b) Unrealized Gain at 12/31/Year 3, $6,000

2. Prepare a table that summarizes the (a) total cost, (b) total fair value adjustment, and (c) total fair value for the portfolio of long-term available-for-sale debt securities at each year-end.

3. Prepare a table that summarizes (a) the realized gains and losses and (b) the unrealized gains or losses for the portfolio of long-term available-for-sale debt securities at each year-end.

Problem C-3B
Debt investments in available-for-sale securities; unrealized and realized gains and losses

P3

Troy's long-term available-for-sale portfolio at the *start* of this year consists of the following.

Available-for-Sale Securities	Cost	Fair Value
Company R bonds	$559,125	$580,440
Company S notes	308,380	293,250
Company T bonds.....................................	147,295	151,800

Troy enters into the following transactions involving its available-for-sale debt securities this year.

Jan. 13   Sold one-fourth of the Company S notes for $72,250.
Apr.   5   Purchased Company V bonds for $133,875.
Sep.   2   Sold all of the Company T bonds for $156,750.
Oct. 30   Purchased Company X notes for $48,750.

The fair values at December 31 are R, $568,125; S, $234,345; V, $134,940; and X, $45,625.

Required

1. Prepare journal entries to record these transactions, including any necessary December 31 adjusting entry to record the fair value adjustment of the long-term investments in available-for-sale securities.

2. Determine the amount Troy reports on its December 31 balance sheet for its long-term investments in available-for-sale securities.

3. What amount of gains or losses on transactions relating to long-term investments in available-for-sale securities does Troy report on its income statement for this year?

Check (1) Dec. 31: Cr. Fair Value Adj—AFS, $690

Slip Systems had no short-term investments prior to this year. It had the following transactions this year involving short-term stock investments with insignificant influence.

Feb.   6   Purchased 3,400 shares of Nokia stock at $41 per share.
Apr.   7   Purchased 1,200 shares of Dell stock at $39 per share.
June   2   Purchased 2,500 shares of Merck stock at $72 per share.
       30   Received a $1.00 per share cash dividend on the Nokia shares.
Aug. 11   Sold 850 shares of Nokia stock at $46 per share.
       24   Received a $0.10 per share cash dividend on the Dell shares.
Nov.   9   Received a $1.50 per share cash dividend on the remaining Nokia shares.
Dec. 18   Received a $0.15 per share cash dividend on the Dell shares.

Problem C-4B
Recording, adjusting, and reporting stock investments with insignificant influence

P4

Required

1. Prepare journal entries to record the preceding transactions and events.

2. Prepare a table to compare the year-end cost and fair values of the short-term stock investments. The year-end fair values per share are Nokia, $40; Dell, $41; and Merck, $59.

3. Prepare an adjusting entry, if necessary, to record the year-end fair value adjustment for the portfolio of short-term stock investments.

Check (2) Cost = $331,350

(3) Dr. Unrealized Loss—Income, $32,650

Analysis Component

4. Explain the balance sheet presentation of the fair value adjustment to Slip's short-term investments.

5. How do these short-term stock investments affect (*a*) its income statement this year and (*b*) the equity section of its balance sheet at this year-end?

Brinkley Company, which began operations in Year 1, had the following transactions and events in its long-term investments.

Year 1

Jan.   5   Brinkley purchased 20,000 shares (25% of total) of Bloch's common stock for $200,500.
Aug.   1   Bloch declared and paid a cash dividend of $1.05 per share.
Dec. 31   Bloch's net income for the year is $82,000, and the fair value of its stock is $11.90 per share.

Year 2

Aug.   1   Bloch declared and paid a cash dividend of $1.35 per share.
Dec. 31   Bloch's net income for the year is $78,000, and the fair value of its stock is $13.65 per share.

Year 3

Jan.   8   Brinkley sold 5% (equal to 1,000 shares) of its investment in Bloch for $12,025 cash.

Problem C-5B
Accounting for long-term investments in stock with significant influence

P5

Required

Prepare journal entries to record these transactions and events for Brinkley. Assume that Brinkley has a significant influence over Bloch with its 25% share.

Problem C-6B
Accounting for long-term investments in stock without significant influence
P4

Refer to the transactions in Problem C-5B. Assume that although Brinkley owns 25% of Bloch's outstanding stock, circumstances indicate that it does *not* have a significant influence over the investee.

Required

Prepare journal entries to record these transactions and events for Brinkley.

SERIAL PROBLEM
Business Solutions
P1

©Alexander Image/Shutterstock

This serial problem began in Chapter 1 and continues through most of the book. If previous chapter segments were not completed, the serial problem can begin at this point.

SP C   While reviewing the March 31, 2020, balance sheet of **Business Solutions,** Santana Rey notes that the business has built a large cash balance of $68,057. Its most recent bank money market statement shows that the funds are earning an annualized return of 0.75%. S. Rey decides to make several investments with the desire to earn a higher return on the idle cash balance. Accordingly, in April 2020, Business Solutions makes the following investments in trading securities.

Apr. 16   Purchases Johnson & Johnson bonds for $10,000.
Apr. 30   Purchases Starbucks notes for $4,400.

On June 30, 2020, the fair value of the Johnson & Johnson bonds is $12,000 and the Starbucks notes is $3,800.

Required

1. Prepare journal entries to record the April purchases of trading securities by Business Solutions.
2. On June 30, 2020, prepare the adjusting entry to record any necessary fair value adjustment to its portfolio of trading securities.

GENERAL LEDGER PROBLEM

The following **General Ledger** assignments focus on the account for investments in available-for-sale securities and equity method investments.

GL C-1   General Ledger assignment C-1 is adapted from Problem C-4A. Prepare journal entries related to short-term investments in available-for-sale securities, including the adjustment to fair value, if necessary.

GL C-2   General Ledger assignment C-2 is adapted from Problem C-3A. Prepare journal entries related to long-term investments transactions and the related realized and unrealized gains.

Accounting Analysis

COMPANY ANALYSIS
A1  **APPLE**

AA C-1   Use **Apple's** financial statements in Appendix A to answer the following.
1. Compute Apple's return on total assets for the years ended September 30, 2017, and September 24, 2016.
2. Is the change in Apple's return on total assets from part 1 favorable or unfavorable?
3. Recently, Apple acquired 100% of Beats Electronics (Beats by Dre) for $3 billion. Will Apple account for Beats using the equity method or consolidation?

AA C-2   Key figures for **Apple** and **Google** follow.

$ millions	Apple			Google		
	Current Year	1 Year Prior	2 Years Prior	Current Year	1 Year Prior	2 Years Prior
Net income	$ 48,351	$ 45,687	$ 53,394	$ 12,662	$ 19,478	$ 16,348
Net sales	229,234	215,639	233,715	110,855	90,272	74,989
Total assets	375,319	321,686	290,345	197,295	167,497	147,461

Required

1. Compute return on total assets for Apple and Google for the two most recent years.
2. Which of these two companies has the better return on total assets for the current year?
3. Compute both profit margin and total asset turnover for Apple and Google for the most recent year.

AA C-3   Following are selected data from **Samsung**, **Apple**, and **Google**.

In millions	Samsung			Apple		Google	
	Current Year	One Year Prior	Two Years Prior	Current Year	Prior Year	Current Year	Prior Year
Net income	₩ 42,186,747	₩ 22,726,092	₩ 19,060,144	$ 48,351	$ 45,687	$ 12,662	$ 19,478
Net sales	239,575,376	201,866,745	200,653,482	229,234	215,639	110,855	90,272
Total assets	301,752,090	262,174,324	242,179,521	375,319	321,686	197,295	167,497

Required

1. Compute Samsung's return on total assets for the two most recent years.
2. For the current year, is Samsung's return on total assets better or worse than (a) Apple's and (b) Google's?
3. For the current year, compute Samsung's profit margin.
4. For the current year, compute Samsung's total asset turnover.

Beyond the Numbers

BTN C-1   Kasey Hartman is the controller for Wholemart Company, which has numerous long-term investments in debt securities. Wholemart's investments are mainly in five-year bonds. Hartman is preparing its year-end financial statements. In accounting for long-term debt securities, she knows that each long-term investment must be designated as a held-to-maturity or an available-for-sale security. Interest rates rose sharply this past year, causing the portfolio's fair value to substantially decline. The company does not intend to hold the bonds for the entire five years. Hartman also earns a bonus each year, which is computed as a percent of net income.

Required

1. Will Hartman's bonus depend in any way on the classification of the debt securities? Explain.
2. What criteria must Hartman use to classify the securities as held-to-maturity or available-for-sale?
3. Is there likely any company oversight of Hartman's classification of the securities? Explain.

BTN C-2   Assume that you are Jolee Company's accountant. Company owner Mary Jolee has reviewed the 2019 financial statements you prepared and questions the $6,000 loss reported on the sale of its investment in Kemper Co. common stock. Jolee acquired 50,000 shares of Kemper's common stock on December 31, 2017, at a cost of $500,000. This stock purchase represented a 40% interest in Kemper. The 2018 income statement reported that earnings from all investments were $126,000. On January 3, 2019, Jolee Company sold the Kemper stock for $575,000. Kemper did not pay any dividends during 2018 but reported a net income of $202,500 for that year. Mary Jolee believes that because the Kemper stock purchase price was $500,000 and was sold for $575,000, the 2019 income statement should report a $75,000 gain on the sale.

Required

Draft a half-page memorandum to Mary Jolee explaining why the $6,000 loss on sale of Kemper stock is correctly reported.

TAKING IT TO THE NET

P1 P2 P3 P4

BTN C-3 Access the July 28, 2016, 10-K filing (for year-end June 30, 2016) of **Microsoft** (ticker: MSFT) at **SEC.gov**. Review its note 4, "Investments."

Required

1. How does the "cost-basis" total amount for its investments as of June 30, 2016, compare to the prior year-end amount?
2. Identify at least eight types of investments held by Microsoft as of June 30, 2016.
3. What were Microsoft's unrealized gains and its unrealized losses from its investments for 2016?
4. Was the cost or fair value ("recorded basis") of the investments higher as of June 30, 2016?

TEAMWORK IN ACTION

C2 P1 P2 P3 P4

BTN C-4 Each team member is to become an expert on a specific classification of long-term investments. This expertise will be used to facilitate other teammates' understanding of the concepts and procedures relevant to the classification chosen.

1. Each team member must select an area for expertise by choosing one of the following classifications of long-term investments.
   a. Held-to-maturity debt securities
   b. Available-for-sale debt securities
   c. Equity securities with significant influence
   d. Equity securities with controlling influence
2. Learning teams are to disperse and expert teams are to be formed. Expert teams are made up of those who select the same area of expertise. The instructor will identify the location where each expert team will meet.
3. Expert teams will collaborate to develop a presentation based on the following requirements. Students must write the presentation in a format they can show to their learning teams in part 4.

   Requirements for Expert Presentation

   a. Write a transaction for the acquisition of this type of investment security. The transaction description is to include all necessary data to reflect the chosen classification.
   b. Prepare the journal entry to record the acquisition.

      [*Note:* The expert team on equity securities with controlling influence will substitute requirements (*d*) and (*e*) with a discussion of the reporting of these investments.]

   c. Identify information necessary to complete the end-of-period adjustment for this investment.
   d. Assuming that this is the only investment owned, prepare any necessary year-end entries.
   e. Present the relevant balance sheet section(s).
4. Re-form learning teams. In rotation, experts are to present to their teams the presentations they developed in part 3. Experts are to encourage and respond to questions.

ENTREPRENEURIAL DECISION

P4

BTN C-5 Assume that **Echoing Green** makes an investment in **Sustain Inc.,** a sustainability consulting firm. The company purchases 200 shares of Sustain stock for $15,000 cash plus a broker's fee of $500 cash. Sustain has 500 shares of common stock outstanding, and Echoing Green will be able to significantly influence its policies.

Required

1. Prepare the journal entry to record the investment in Sustain on January 1.
2. Sustain declares and pays a dividend of $1,000. Prepare the journal entry to record Echoing Green's receipt of its share of the dividend on July 1.
3. Sustain reports net income of $5,000. Prepare the journal entry to record Echoing Green's share of those earnings on December 31.

HITTING THE ROAD

C2

BTN C-6 Review financial news sources such as **Yahoo! Finance** (**finance.yahoo.com**) and **Google Finance** (**google.com/finance**). Identify a company that has recently purchased 50% or more of another company's outstanding shares and will report consolidated financial statements.

Required

1. Identify whether the acquired company is a supplier, customer, competitor, or unrelated company relative to the purchasing company.
2. What does the purchasing company hope to accomplish with the investment? What is its strategy?

D Lean Principles and Accounting

Learning Objectives

CONCEPTUAL

C1 Describe lean principles.

ANALYTICAL

A1 Compute cycle time and cycle efficiency, and explain their importance to production management.

A2 Compute days' sales in work in process inventory.

A3 Compute days' payable outstanding.

PROCEDURAL

P1 Record product costs using lean accounting.

LEAN BUSINESS MODEL

C1 _____

Describe lean principles.

Competition forces businesses to improve. One approach is to adopt the **lean business model,** whose goal is to use fewer resources while still satisfying customers. Exhibit D.1 shows key aspects of the lean business model. At the top are overall strategies aimed to eliminate waste in processes and meet customer needs. In the middle are lean business practices such as continuous improvement, just-in-time inventory systems, supply chain management, and total quality management. These practices aim to cut waste in spending and increase quality and productivity. Businesses that produce better quality products and services with lower costs are more successful. At the base of this model are key principles. While all types of businesses can apply lean principles, we focus on manufacturers.

EXHIBIT D.1

Lean Business Model

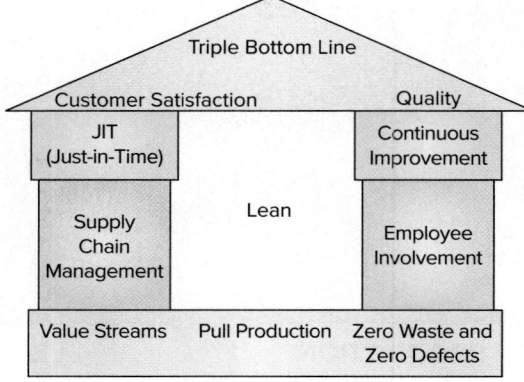

Lean Principles

Following are the three key principles of the lean business model.

> **Value streams** > **Pull production** > **Zero waste and zero defects**

Value Streams   Lean businesses aim to provide customers what they want, and when they want it. Customers increasingly want customized products, so manufacturers must be able to produce quickly and without waste. Rather than build standard products in a long assembly line, lean manufacturers use smaller **value streams.** Value streams consist of all the activities needed to create customer value. For example, a food processor might have separate value streams for its trail mix, energy bars, and energy drinks. All of the processes for each product type occur in one value stream. A trail mix value stream is shown in Exhibit D.2.

EXHIBIT D.2

Trail Mix Value Stream

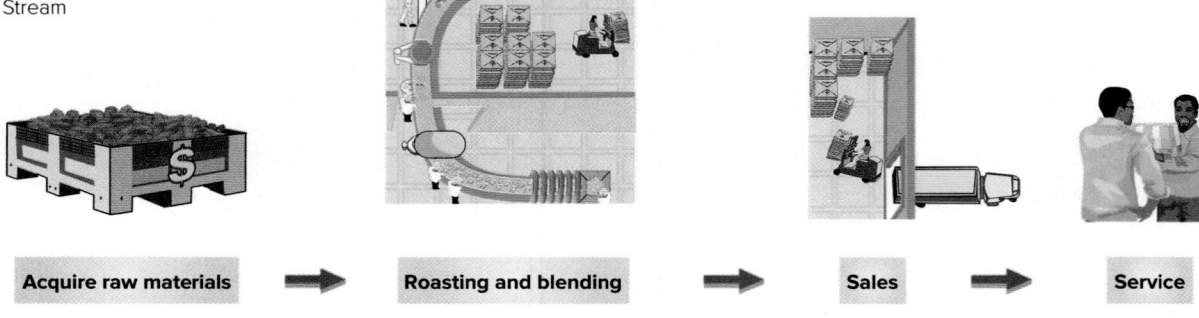

| Acquire raw materials | → | Roasting and blending | → | Sales | → | Service |

Pull Production   Lean manufacturing differs from traditional manufacturing. Lean businesses use **pull production,** where production begins with a customer order. Goods are "pulled" through the manufacturing process "just-in-time" and delivered to the customer after completion.

Traditional manufacturing uses **push production,** where goods are produced before a customer order and based on sales forecasts. Goods are "pushed" into inventory and wait for a customer order.

Exhibit D.3 shows push production compared with pull production.

Push (Traditional) Production

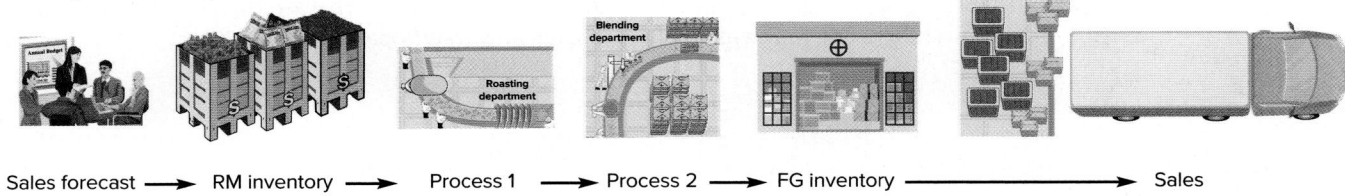

Sales forecast ⟶ RM inventory ⟶ Process 1 ⟶ Process 2 ⟶ FG inventory ⟶ Sales

Pull (Lean) Production

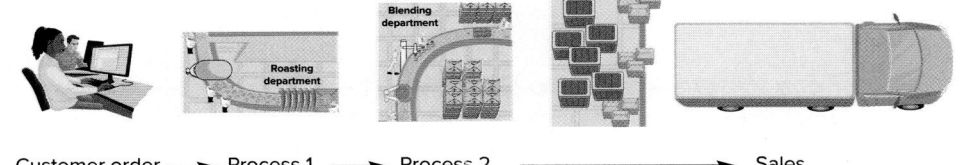

Customer order ⟶ Process 1 ⟶ Process 2 ⟶ Sales

EXHIBIT D.3

Push Production Compared with Pull Production

Push production has several challenges that include the following.

- Inaccurate sales forecasts can cause too many goods to be produced. This increases storage costs and risk of obsolescence (decrease in value).
- Inaccurate sales forecasts can cause not enough goods to be produced. This creates stock-outs and lost sales.
- **Batch sizes** (*lot sizes*), which are the number of units produced after a machine setup, are high. This makes it hard to produce customized products. Large batch sizes can also produce more defects before the issue is identified and production is stopped.

To address these issues, many turn to pull production. Pull production follows a lean strategy which includes a focus on reducing (1) cycle time, (2) setup time, and (3) inventory levels.

Cycle Time   Cycle time (CT) is the total time a production process takes, starting from putting raw materials into production to completing a finished good. This can be in minutes, such as with fast-food restaurants, or weeks, such as with jet engines. Lean businesses reduce cycle time by producing in smaller batch sizes and making goods to customer order. Smaller batch sizes reduce time because goods spend less time waiting for other goods to finish in the production cycle. Customers get the goods they want more quickly.

Lean businesses focus on improving the following components to reduce cycle time.

- *Process time*—Time spent working on and producing the product. Lean companies reduce process time by simplifying the production process and by excluding unwanted product features. } **Value-added**
- *Inspection time*—Time spent inspecting raw materials received, work in process in production, and finished goods before shipment. Lean companies emphasize quality materials and processes to reduce inspection time.
- *Move time*—Time spent moving materials and inventory, and employee time spent moving around the production area. Lean businesses reduce move time by strategically placing tools and machinery in the production area. } **Non-value-added**
- *Wait time*—Time an order sits before or between production processes. Lean businesses reduce wait time by avoiding raw material order delays, production bottlenecks, and poor production scheduling.

Of the four parts of cycle time, only process time is a **value-added time** activity that adds value to the customer. Inspection, move, and wait time are **non-value-added time** activities because they do not add value to customers.

Setup Time   **Setup time** is the amount of time to prepare a process for production; for example, preparing the roasting process to make trail mix. Setup time includes time spent starting and calibrating machines. Lean companies want quick setups so they can reduce cycle time when producing goods to customer order in smaller batch sizes.

Inventory Levels   Lean businesses believe holding inventory is wasteful and instead use *just-in-time* inventory. The following table compares how traditional and lean manufacturers manage inventory.

Inventory	Traditional Approach	Lean (Just-in-Time) Approach
Raw materials	Bought to hold in inventory; enters production based on sales forecast.	Bought after a customer order; enters production immediately after receipt.
Work in process	Larger; not a priority to reduce.	Reduced as cycle times get faster.
Finished goods	Held in inventory until sold.	Delivered to customers after goods are finished.

Zero Waste and Zero Defects   Lean businesses aim for zero waste and zero defects. Employees of lean businesses are empowered to stop production if they see something wrong. Defective goods are not passed on to the next process. Instead, the source of the problem is identified and corrected before production resumes. Fewer defects lead to lower scrap and rework costs, fewer warranty claims, and increased customer satisfaction.

Lean Production Example

Nike implemented a lean approach to its clothes manufacturing in several countries. Clothes manufacturing requires sewing, ironing, and packing processes. Exhibit D.4 compares Nike's traditional approach to its new lean approach. Several benefits and cost savings are identified.

EXHIBIT D.4

Lean Production at Nike

	Traditional Approach	Lean Approach	Benefits from Lean Approach
Production layout	Sewing, ironing, and packing processes are physically separated.	All processes in the apparel value stream are located together.	Reduced move time of both employees and inventory.
Production starts with	Sales forecast.	Customer order.	Less inventory.
Quality control	End-of-line quality inspection.	Each employee inspects her own output before passing it to the next step.	Fewer defects.
Supervision	One supervisor for each process.	One supervisor for the entire value stream.	Reduced overhead costs.

Source: Distelhorst, Greg; Hainmueller, Jens; and Locke, Richard M. *Does Lean Improve Labor Standards? Management and Social Performance in the Nike Supply Chain,* August 29, 2015.

Lean Processes for Service Businesses

©Mihajlo Maricic/Alamy Stock Photo

Lean principles also apply to retailers and service businesses. **Amazon** applied lean principles when it changed its fulfillment process to use machines for repetitive, low-value-added steps and human employees for high-value, complex work. As a result, the number of defects (incorrect order fulfillments) was reduced. Amazon also applies lean principles to customer service. Employees are empowered to make quick decisions to satisfy customers. If customers call about a defective product, employees can "stop the line" by removing the product from Amazon's website until the source of the defect is resolved. This lean approach reduced the number of defective products sold and increased customer satisfaction.

Taco Bell applies lean principles to food service. By focusing on customer value, management determined "We are in the business of feeding people, not making food." As a result, the company changed from food *processing* to food *assembly*. Ingredients are preprocessed in off-site facilities and shipped just-in-time to restaurants. Employees then assemble ingredients to suit customer orders. With a lean approach, inventory levels fell, quality and customer satisfaction increased, and costs decreased.

Supply Chain Management

Supply chain management or *logistics* is the control of materials, information, and finances as they move between suppliers, manufacturers, and customers. Lean businesses use supply chain management to ensure raw materials arrive just-in-time for production and customers receive their orders on schedule.

All types of businesses must manage their supply chains. **Nike** outsources all of its production, and it uses review programs to make sure its suppliers follow ethical practices while supplying quality goods. **Taco Bell**'s just-in-time preprocessed food deliveries require close coordination and information sharing with its suppliers.

One measure of success in supply chain management is in the demand for its services. A materials handling industry report forecasts over 1.4 million openings for logistics jobs in supply chain management. These include jobs for data analysts, marketers, human resource managers, and fulfillment center employees. Average annual salaries of around $100,000 are common for supply chain managers.

Point: The Council of Supply Chain Professionals (**cscmp.org**) offers more information.

Part A For each item, identify whether it best applies to lean businesses (L) or traditional businesses (T).

_____ **1.** Production begins with a sales forecast.	_____ **4.** Processes are located together.
_____ **2.** Only finished goods are inspected for quality.	_____ **5.** Uses push production.
_____ **3.** Uses pull production.	_____ **6.** Produces in small lot sizes.

NEED-TO-KNOW D-1

Lean Production

C1 ▶

Solution

1. T   **2.** T   **3.** L   **4.** L   **5.** T   **6.** L

Part B Identify which of the statements below are true (T) or false (F). Lean businesses aim to:

_____ **1.** Reduce inventory levels.	_____ **4.** Produce many defective products.
_____ **2.** Increase profits.	_____ **5.** Reduce wait time.
_____ **3.** Produce in large lot sizes.	_____ **6.** Reduce inspection time.

Solution

1. T   **2.** T   **3.** F   **4.** F   **5.** T   **6.** T

Do More: QS D-1, QS D-2, E D-1

PRODUCTION PERFORMANCE

Cycle Time and Cycle Efficiency

Lean businesses use many nonfinancial measures to evaluate the performance of their production processes. It is important for lean businesses to reduce the time it takes to produce products and to improve efficiency. Cycle time (CT), as covered earlier, is the time it takes to produce a good or provide a service. It is more specifically defined in Exhibit D.5.

A1 _____

Compute cycle time and cycle efficiency, and explain their importance to production management.

Cycle time = Process time + Inspection time + Move time + Wait time

EXHIBIT D.5

Cycle Time

As explained, process time is the only activity that adds value to the customer (*value-added activity*). Inspection, move, and wait times do not add value to customers (*non-value-added activities*).

Lean businesses try to reduce non-value-added time to improve **cycle efficiency (CE).** Cycle efficiency, defined in Exhibit D.6, measures the amount of cycle time spent on value-added activities. A CE of 1 means a value stream's time is spent entirely on value-added activities. If the CE is low, too much time is being spent on non-value-added activities and the production process should be reviewed with an aim to eliminate waste.

EXHIBIT D.6

Cycle Efficiency

$$\text{Cycle efficiency} = \frac{\text{Value-added time}}{\text{Cycle time}}$$

To illustrate, assume that Rocky Mountain Bikes receives and produces an order for 500 mountain bikes. Assume that it took the following times to produce this order.

 Process time... 1.8 days

 Inspection time... 0.5 days

 Move time... 0.7 days

 Wait time... 3.0 days

In this case, cycle time is 6.0 days (1.8 + 0.5 + 0.7 + 3.0 days). Cycle efficiency is computed as

$$\text{Cycle efficiency} = \frac{1.8 \text{ days}}{6.0 \text{ days}} = 0.30, \text{ or } 30\%$$

Time Type	Days	%
Value-added	1.8	30%
Non-value-added	4.2	70
Total	6.0	100%

This means that Rocky Mountain Bikes's value-added time (its process time, or time spent working on the product) is 30%. The other 70% of time is spent on non-value-added activities. The 30% CE for Rocky Mountain Bikes is low. Employees and managers try to reduce time spent on non-value-added activities.

Days' Sales in Work in Process Inventory

A2

Compute days' sales in work in process inventory.

Lean businesses aim to reduce inventory. They typically do not have a separate Raw Materials Inventory account and hold few finished goods. This means the Work in Process Inventory account can be used to measure production efficiency. Work in process inventory reflects delay in getting products to customers, which lean businesses consider wasteful. Getting products to customers sooner by reducing work in process inventory can increase customer satisfaction. To measure production efficiency, we can use **days' sales in work in process inventory,** defined in Exhibit D.7 and usually rounded to the nearest whole day.

EXHIBIT D.7

Days' Sales in Work in Process Inventory

$$\text{Days' sales in work in process inventory} = \frac{\text{Work in process inventory}}{\text{Cost of goods sold}} \times 365$$

Axis Co., a computer maker, reports work in process inventory of $503 and cost of goods sold of $45,829. Axis computes its days' sales in work in process inventory as follows.

$$\frac{\$503}{\$45,829} \times 365 = 4 \text{ days}$$

Lower days' sales in work in process inventory means the company is completing its production cycle more quickly. Adopting a lean model should result in a smaller number of days' sales in work in process inventory.

NEED-TO-KNOW **D-2**

Part 1

The following information is for an order of Aero Guitars produced by Tyler Co. Compute cycle time and cycle efficiency.

Process time . . .	8 days	Inspection time . . .	0.2 days	Move time . . .	0.4 days	Wait time	1.4 days

Cycle Time and Cycle Efficiency

A1

Solution

Cycle time   = Process time + Inspection time + Move time + Wait time
               = 8 + 0.2 + 0.4 + 1.4 = <u>10 days</u>

Cycle efficiency = Value-added time / Cycle time
                    = 8/10 = <u>80%</u> → 80% of the company's time is spent on value-added activities.
                        Only process time is considered value-added time.

Do More: QS D-9, QS D-10, E D-6, E D-7, E D-8, E D-9

Part 2

Use the following information to compute days' sales in work in process inventory.

Work in process inventory	$2,053	Cost of goods sold	$46,828

Days' Sales in Work in Process Inventory

A2

Solution

Days' sales in work in process inventory = ($2,053/$46,828) × 365 = <u>16 days</u>

Do More: QS D-11, E D-10, E D-11

LEAN ACCOUNTING

Key Accounts

Lean businesses usually have fewer transactions to record and use fewer accounts. The key accounts in lean accounting follow.

P1

Record product costs using lean accounting.

- **Work in Process Inventory** Lean businesses put raw materials immediately into production, so a separate Raw Materials Inventory account is not used. Raw materials purchases are recorded in Work in Process Inventory.

- **Conversion Costs** Direct labor, indirect labor, and overhead costs are recorded in this account. In lean businesses, employees work within individual value streams and they do both direct and indirect labor tasks. For example, employees in a trail mix value stream might do roasting, blending, packaging, and cleaning duties. Therefore, all of these costs are accumulated in the Conversion Costs account.

Point: Work in Process Inventory is also called Raw and In Process Inventory.

Work in Process Inventory			
Raw mtls.	#		
Conversion	#	To COGS	#

Conversion Costs

In lean accounting, *estimated* conversion costs are applied to work in process. For example, if a business budgets for $10,000,000 of conversion costs and 4,000 production hours in a value stream, the **conversion cost rate** is computed as follows.

$$\textbf{Conversion cost rate} = \frac{\textbf{Budgeted conversion costs}}{\textbf{Budgeted production hours}} = \frac{\$10,000,000}{4,000 \text{ hours*}} = \$2,500 \text{ per production hour}$$

*Two 8-hour shifts per day × 250 factory days per year.

This rate can be expressed in terms of units of product. For example, if 5 products can be made each hour, the conversion cost rate is $500 per unit ($2,500/5 units).

Point: Conversion Costs is a temporary account.

Actual and applied (budgeted) conversion costs often differ in an accounting period. Applied conversion costs are based on estimates made at the beginning of the period. Actual conversion costs can differ from estimates because of events such as wage rate changes or utility cost changes. Accounting for such differences is covered in advanced courses.

Accounting Entries

Point: Variations of lean accounting exist. Some use "backflush" accounting, where entries are delayed until goods are finished or sold. Other methods are in advanced courses.

Solshine manufactures solar panels. Each solar panel requires $40 of raw materials and $160 of conversion costs. The company produced and sold 200 solar panels for $480 each this period. Actual conversion costs equaled applied conversion costs. The relevant journal entries follow.

①	Work in Process Inventory	8,000			④	Accounts Receivable	96,000	
	Accounts Payable		8,000			Sales		96,000
	Acquired raw materials on credit (200 units × $40).					*Record sales on credit (200 units × $480).*		
②	Work in Process Inventory	32,000			⑤	Cost of Goods Sold	40,000	
	Conversion Costs		32,000			Work in Process Inventory		40,000
	Apply conversion costs to production (200 units × $160).					*Record cost of goods sold (200 × $200).*		
③	Conversion Costs	32,000						
	Various Accounts		32,000					
	Record actual conversion costs (given).							

Conversion Costs

Actual	#	Applied	#

Conversion Costs

	32,000
32,000	
	0

Work in Process Inventory

8,000	
32,000	40,000
0	

Entry ① records materials purchased ($40 per panel × 200 panels to produce = $8,000) as Work in Process Inventory. Separate raw materials inventory accounts are not used.

Entry ② applies conversion costs ($160 per panel × 200 panels to produce = $32,000) to Work in Process Inventory. This applied conversion cost is based on a predetermined budgeted amount of conversion costs.

Entry ③ records actual conversion costs to produce 200 solar panels. This amount includes the actual costs of direct labor, indirect labor, and other overhead costs. The various credit accounts in this journal entry would include Salaries Payable, Wages Payable, Utilities Payable, Accumulated Depreciation—Manufacturing Equipment, and others.

Entry ④ records the sale of goods on account (200 panels sold × $480 sales price per panel = $96,000).

Point: A traditional manufacturer would first transfer finished product costs to Finished Goods Inventory.

Entry ⑤ records the related cost of 200 panels sold (200 × $200 = $40,000). Because lean businesses make goods to order, finished product costs are immediately recorded in Cost of Goods Sold.

When Finished Goods Inventory Remains

Lean businesses sometimes end an accounting period with finished but unsold goods. If instead of selling 200 panels, assume Solshine sold 185 panels and had 15 panels left in inventory. It records journal entries ①, ②, and ③ as above; but it records entries ④ and ⑤ as follows. Finished Goods Inventory is increased for the cost of goods *not* sold (15 units × $200). Cost of goods sold is computed as 185 units sold × $200 = $37,000.

④	Accounts Receivable	88,800			⑤	Finished Goods Inventory	3,000	
	Sales		88,800			Cost of Goods Sold	37,000	
	Record sales on credit (185 units × $480 selling price).					Work in Process Inventory		40,000
						Record inventory and cost of goods sold.		

A lean business incurs $45 in raw materials costs and $75 in conversion costs to produce an office chair. Each chair is sold for $170. In the current period, the business produced 500 units and sold 470 units. Prepare the necessary journal entries following lean accounting. Assume actual conversion costs equal applied conversion costs.

NEED-TO-KNOW D-3

Lean Accounting Entries

P1

Solution

Work in Process Inventory....................	22,500	
Accounts Payable........................		22,500
Acquired raw materials on credit ($45 × 500).		
Work in Process Inventory....................	37,500	
Conversion Costs........................		37,500
Apply conversion costs to production ($75 × 500).		
Conversion Costs............................	37,500	
Various Accounts........................		37,500
Record actual conversion costs.		

Accounts Receivable...........................	79,900	
Sales		79,900
Sold on credit ($170 × 470).		
Finished Goods Inventory......................	3,600	
Cost of Goods Sold...........................	56,400	
Work in Process Inventory................		60,000
Record ending inventory ($120 × 30) and cost of goods sold ($120 × 470).		

Do More: QS D-3, QS D-4, QS D-5, QS D-6, E D-2, E D-3, E D-4

SUSTAINABILITY AND ACCOUNTING

Nike implemented lean processes and achieved increased productivity, lower inventory levels, lower defect rates, and faster production. These improvements benefited the "profit" aspect of the triple bottom line, but lean processes can have other triple bottom line benefits. Nike saw major improvements in compliance with labor rules. This means that, with lean principles, Nike both increased profits and working conditions for employees ("people") in its supply chain.

Lean businesses also try to reduce waste. **Apple**'s *Environmental Responsibility Report* shows a focus on the "planet" aspect of the triple bottom line. Apple strives for a **closed-loop supply chain,** where products are built using only renewable resources or recycled material, as shown in Exhibit D.8.

To achieve its goal, Apple works with its suppliers to use 100% recycled tin in the main part of its iPhone. It also has programs to encourage customers to recycle old devices. Robots disassemble more than 2.5 million iPhones per year to reclaim materials.

©Petovarga/Shutterstock

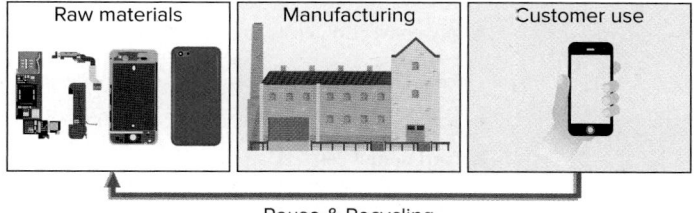

Raw materials   Manufacturing   Customer use

Reuse & Recycling

EXHIBIT D.8

Closed-Loop Supply Chain

Days' Payable Outstanding   ☐☐☐   **Decision Analysis**

Companies that buy on credit monitor how long they take to pay creditors. This is particularly important for lean businesses because they usually have long-term contracts with important suppliers. Taking too long to pay could harm important partnerships. Paying too soon, however, means the company has less cash

A3

Compute days' payable outstanding.

available for other needs. **Days' payable outstanding,** defined in Exhibit D.9, is a measure of how long, on average, a company takes to pay its creditors and is usually rounded to the nearest whole day.

EXHIBIT D.9

Days' Payable Outstanding

$$\text{Days' payable outstanding} = \frac{\text{Accounts payable}}{\text{Cost of goods sold}} \times 365$$

Under Armour	2016
Accounts payable	$ 410
Cost of goods sold	$2,585
Days' payable	58 days

Nike's days' payable outstanding is shown in Exhibit D.10. Its days' payable outstanding is roughly 39 days [($2,048/$19,038) × 365] in 2017. This decreased from the two prior years. A company's days' payable outstanding can be compared to its typical credit terms and to its industry competitors. **Under Armour's** days' payable outstanding was 75 at the end of 2017. A company with 30 days to pay and a days' payable outstanding of 12 days should consider paying its creditors later. On the other hand, a company with 30 days to pay and a days' payable outstanding of 55 days risks hurting its partnerships with key suppliers.

EXHIBIT D.10

Days' Payable Outstanding for Two Competitors

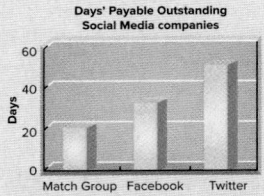
Days' Payable Outstanding Social Media companies

Company	$ millions	2017	2016	2015
Nike	Accounts payable, end of year	$ 2,048	$ 2,191	$ 2,131
	Cost of goods sold	$19,038	$17,405	$16,534
	Days' payable outstanding	39 days	46 days	47 days
Under Armour	Days' payable outstanding	75 days	58 days	36 days

Days' payable outstanding varies across industries and across companies within an industry. **Yum Brands's** (a restaurant operator) days' payable outstanding has been over 100 days in recent years. **Pandora Media Group** (a music streaming company) has about 6 days' payable outstanding.

Summary: Cheat Sheet

LEAN BUSINESS MODEL

Goal: Use fewer resources while satisfying customers.
Key Principles: Value streams :: Pull production :: Zero waste & Zero defects
Value streams: Activities that create customer value.
Pull production: Production starts with customer order.
Push production: Production begins with sales forecast.

PRODUCTION PERFORMANCE

Time Components
Process time   } **Value-added**
Inspection time ⎫
Move time   ⎬ **Non-value-added**
Wait time   ⎭

Setup time: Time to prepare a process for production.

Cycle time = Process time + Inspection time + Move time + Wait time

$$\text{Cycle efficiency} = \frac{\text{Value-added time}}{\text{Cycle time}}$$

$$\text{Days' sales in WIP} = \frac{\text{Work in process inventory}}{\text{Cost of goods sold}} \times 365$$

LEAN ACCOUNTING

$$\text{Conversion cost rate} = \frac{\text{Budgeted conversion costs}}{\text{Budgeted production hours}}$$

Entries for Materials and Conversion Costs
No separate Raw Materials Inventory account.

Acquire raw materials on credit:

| Work in Process Inventory .... | 8,000 | |
| Accounts Payable............................... | | 8,000 |

Apply conversion costs to production:

| Work in Process Inventory (Conversion cost rate × Units of activity)... | 32,000 | |
| Conversion Costs............................... | | 32,000 |

Record actual conversion costs:

| Conversion Costs .... | 32,000 | |
| Various Costs (Wages Payable, Acc. Dep.-Mfg. Eq., etc) .... | | 32,000 |

$$\text{Days' Payable Outstanding} = \frac{\text{Accounts payable}}{\text{Cost of goods sold}} \times 365$$

Key Terms

Batch size (lot size) (D-3)

Closed-loop supply chain (D-9)

Conversion cost rate (D-7)

Cycle efficiency (CE) (D-6)

Cycle time (CT) (D-3)

Days' payable outstanding (D-10)

Days' sales in work in process inventory (D-6)
Lean business model (D-2)
Non-valued-added time (D-4)

Pull production (D-3)
Push production (D-3)
Setup time (D-4)

Supply chain management (D-5)
Value-added time (D-4)
Value stream (D-2)

Discussion Questions

1. What are the three key principles of the lean business model?

2. How does *push* production differ from *pull* production?

3. What are three common problems with push production?

4. Define *supply chain management.*

5. **Apple** wants a closed-loop supply chain. **APPLE** Define a closed-loop supply chain and discuss methods the company uses to meet its goal.

6. Can management of a retail company like **Amazon** use lean techniques? Explain.

7. Define *setup time* and provide some examples of tasks that are included in setup time.

8. Why do lean accounting systems not use separate Raw Materials Inventory accounts?

9. Do lean accounting systems use Finished Goods Inventory accounts? Explain.

10. Define and describe *cycle time* and identify the components of cycle time.

11. Explain the difference between *value-added time* and *non-value-added time.*

12. Define and describe *cycle efficiency.*

13. Can management of a company like **Samsung** use cycle time and cycle efficiency as useful measures of performance? Explain.

▪ connect

Identify each of the following as applying more to lean (L) or to traditional (T) businesses.

_____ **1.** Production begins with sales forecasts.

_____ **2.** Uses "pull" production.

_____ **3.** Aims for zero defects.

_____ **4.** Uses large batch sizes.

_____ **5.** Quality is controlled at each process.

_____ **6.** Uses just-in-time inventory systems.

QUICK STUDY

QS D-1
Lean business model **C1**

Identify each of the following as applying more to lean (L) or to traditional (T) businesses.

_____ **1.** Production begins with a customer order. _____ **5.** Uses small batch sizes.

_____ **2.** Reducing defects is *not* a priority. _____ **6.** Quality control is only at product completion.

_____ **3.** Inventory levels are lower. _____ **7.** Cycle times are shorter.

_____ **4.** Wait times are high. _____ **8.** Move times are high.

QS D-2
Lean business model
C1

Use lean accounting to prepare the journal entry to record the purchase of $28,000 of raw materials on credit.

QS D-3
Lean accounting for materials **P1**

Use lean accounting to prepare journal entries for the following transactions.

1. Applied $43,600 of conversion costs to production.

2. Incurred actual conversion costs of $43,600. *Hint:* Credit "Various Accounts."

QS D-4
Lean accounting for conversion costs **P1**

Use lean accounting to prepare journal entries for the following transactions.

1. Sold $16,800 of goods on credit.

2. Recorded cost of goods sold of $11,760.

QS D-5
Lean accounting for cost of goods sold **P1**

Use lean accounting to prepare journal entries for the following transactions.

1. Sold $33,250 of goods for cash.

2. Recorded cost of goods sold of $23,250, and finished goods inventory of $1,860.

QS D-6
Lean accounting for COGS and inventory **P1**

A manufacturer estimates annual conversion costs of $1,207,500 and plans production of 2,100 hours. Compute the conversion cost rate per hour.

QS D-7
Conversion cost rate **P1**

QS D-8
Conversion cost rate

P1

A manufacturer estimates annual conversion costs of $1,000,000 and plans production of 1,600 hours to make 12,800 units. The company can produce 8 units per hour.

1. Compute the conversion cost rate per hour.

2. Prepare the journal entry to apply conversion costs to an order of 520 units.

QS D-9
Cycle time and cycle efficiency

A1

Compute (*a*) manufacturing cycle time and (*b*) manufacturing cycle efficiency using the following information from a manufacturing company.

Process time.........................	15.0 minutes	Move time.........................	6.4 minutes
Inspection time......................	2.0 minutes	Wait time..........................	36.6 minutes

---

QS D-10
Cycle time and cycle efficiency

A1

Compute (*a*) cycle time, (*b*) value-added time, (*c*) non-value-added time, and (*d*) cycle efficiency using the following information for a manufacturer.

Process time.........................	2.10 days	Move time.........................	0.75 days
Inspection time......................	0.50 days	Wait time..........................	0.15 days

---

QS D-11
Days' sales in work in process inventory   **A2**

A company reports ending work in process inventory of $770 and cost of goods sold of $23,404. Compute days' sales in work in process inventory. Round the answer to the nearest whole day.

QS D-12
Days' payable outstanding

A3

A company reports ending accounts payable of $2,055 and cost of goods sold of $18,300. Compute days' payable outstanding. Round the answer to the nearest whole day.

QS D-13
Days' payable outstanding

A3

Samsung

Samsung reports accounts payable of ₩9,569,549 (in millions) and cost of goods sold of ₩28,155,597 (in millions) for a recent year. Compute days' payable outstanding. Round the answer to the nearest whole day.

Mc
Graw
Hill **connect**

EXERCISES

Exercise D-1
Lean business model

C1

Identify each of the following production processes as lean (L) or traditional (T).

_____ **1.** The process produces standard goods, with no option for customization. Production begins with the quarterly sales forecast, and finished goods are stored until sold.

_____ **2.** The process uses push production. Large batch sizes are used, and inspection occurs only when goods are completed.

_____ **3.** The process uses value streams to meet the demand for customized products. The value streams depend on quality materials, and employees are empowered to "stop the line" if defects are detected.

_____ **4.** The production process begins when a customer makes an order. Raw materials are delivered just-in-time for the process to begin. Little inventory and raw materials are held.

Exercise D-2
Lean accounting

P1

Use lean accounting to prepare journal entries for the following transactions.

1. Purchased $22,500 of raw materials on credit.

2. Applied conversion costs of $67,500.

3. Incurred actual conversion costs of $67,500. *Hint:* Credit "Various Accounts."

4. Sold $120,000 of goods on credit.

5. Recorded cost of goods sold of $90,000.

Exercise D-3
Lean accounting

P1

Robo-Pool manufactures robotic pool vacuums. Each unit requires $225 of raw materials and $375 of conversion costs and is sold for $700. During a recent month, the company produced and sold 120 units. Prepare journal entries to record each of the following.

1. Purchase of raw materials on credit.   **3.** Sold 120 units on credit.

2. Applied conversion costs to production.   **4.** Record cost of goods sold.

Robo-Pool manufactures robotic pool vacuums. Each unit requires $225 of raw materials and $375 of conversion costs and is sold for $700. During a recent month the company produced 120 units and sold 100 units. Prepare journal entries to record each of the following.

1. Purchase of raw materials on credit.   **3.** Sold 100 units on credit.
2. Applied conversion costs to production.   **4.** Record ending inventory and cost of goods sold.

Exercise D-4
Lean accounting
P1

Dyzor is a lean manufacturer of wireless sound systems. Its wireless speaker value stream budgets $270,000 of conversion costs and 500 production hours for the next quarter. The company can produce three speaker systems per production hour. Each unit requires materials costs of $44. Assume the company produces and sells 400 units in the next month at a price of $320 each. Prepare journal entries to record each of the following.

1. Purchase of raw materials on credit.   **3.** Sold 400 units on credit.
2. Applied conversion costs to production.   **4.** Record cost of goods sold.

Exercise D-5
Lean accounting
P1

Oakwood Company produces maple bookcases. The following information is available for the production of a recent order of 500 bookcases.

Process time	6.0 days	Move time	3.2 days
Inspection time	0.8 days	Wait time	5.0 days

1. Compute the company's manufacturing cycle time.
2. Compute the company's manufacturing cycle efficiency.
3. Management believes it can reduce move time by 1.2 days and wait time by 2.8 days by adopting lean manufacturing techniques. Compute the company's cycle efficiency assuming the company's predictions are correct.

Exercise D-6
Cycle time and cycle efficiency
A1

Best Ink produces printers for personal computers. The following information is available for production of a recent order of 500 printers.

Process time	16.0 hours	Move time	9.0 hours
Inspection time	3.5 hours	Wait time	21.5 hours

1. Compute the company's manufacturing cycle time.
2. Compute the company's manufacturing cycle efficiency.
3. Assume the company wishes to increase its manufacturing cycle efficiency to 0.80. If process time is unchanged, what is the maximum number of hours of non-value-added time the company can have and meet this goal?

Exercise D-7
Cycle time and cycle efficiency
A1

A manufacturer makes T-shirts in several processes. Information on the components of cycle time follow. Compute (*a*) value-added time, (*b*) inspection time, (*c*) move time, (*d*) wait time, and (*e*) cycle time.

Cutting and sewing processing	18 min.	Wait time before moving	4 min.
Wait time before moving	6 min.	Moving shirts to packaging	2 min.
Moving shirts to ironing	8 min.	Packaging T-shirts	10 min.
Ironing T-shirts	8 min.	Quality inspection	12 min.

Exercise D-8
Cycle time
A1

Management of a T-shirt manufacturer believes if the company applies lean principles, then cycle efficiency can be improved. The following are estimated completion times for different activities in the manufacturing process. Compute cycle efficiency for the (*a*) traditional approach and (*b*) lean approach.

Activity	Traditional	Lean	Activity	Traditional	Lean
Cutting and sewing processing	18 min.	18 min.	Wait time before moving	8 min.	2 min.
Wait time before moving	6 min.	3 min.	Moving shirts to packaging	6 min.	1 min.
Moving shirts to ironing	8 min.	4 min.	Packaging T-shirts	10 min.	10 min.
Ironing T-shirts	8 min.	8 min.	Quality inspection	16 min.	4 min.

Exercise D-9
Cycle efficiency
A1

Exercise D-10
Days' sales in work
in process inventory

A2

Use the information below for a soda maker to answer the requirements.

	Current Year	Prior Year
Work in process at year-end	$ 81,000	$ 94,000
Cost of goods sold for the year	1,967,000	1,800,000

1. Compute days' sales in work in process inventory for the current year. Round to the nearest day.
2. Compute days' sales in work in process inventory for the prior year. Round to the nearest day.
3. Did days' sales in work in process inventory increase or decrease from the prior year?

Exercise D-11
Days' sales in work
in process inventory

A2

Use the information below for **Tesla** to answer the requirements.

$ thousands	Current Year
Work in process at year-end	$ 233,476
Cost of goods sold for the year	4,453,776

1. Compute days' sales in work in process inventory for the current year. Round to the nearest day.
2. If the company's work in process inventory were 5% lower, by how many days would days' sales in work in process inventory be reduced? Round to the nearest day.
3. If the company's cost of goods sold were 12% higher, by how many days would days' sales in work in process inventory be reduced? Round to the nearest day.

Exercise D-12
Days' payable outstanding

A3

Use the information below for **Netflix** to answer the requirements.

$ thousands	Current Year	Prior Year
Accounts payable at year-end	$ 312,842	$ 253,491
Cost of goods sold for the year	6,029,901	4,591,476

1. Compute days' payable outstanding for the current year. Round to the nearest day.
2. Compute days' payable outstanding for the prior year. Round to the nearest day.
3. Did days' payable outstanding increase or decrease from the prior year?

Exercise D-13
Days' payable outstanding

A3

Use the information below to answer the requirements.

$ millions	Current Year
Accounts payable at year-end	$ 1,931
Cost of goods sold for the year	28,164

1. Compute days' payable outstanding for the current year. Round to the nearest day.
2. If the company's accounts payable were 8% lower, by how many days would days' payable outstanding be reduced? Round to the nearest day.
3. If the company's accounts payable were 8% higher, by how many days would days' payable outstanding be increased? Round to the nearest day.

Exercise D-14
Lean business model
and sustainability

C1

APPLE

Apple uses lean principles to reduce waste and use fewer resources. The data below are from its recent *Environmental Responsibility Report*.

Key Performance Indicator	Current Year	Prior Year
% of energy from renewable sources	96	93
Recycled waste (millions of pounds)	28.2	19.6

1. Did Apple's percent (%) of energy used from renewable sources increase or decrease in the current year?
2. How much more waste (in millions of pounds) did Apple recycle in the current year relative to the prior year?

connect

Robo-Lawn is a lean manufacturer of robotic lawn mowers. Each mower requires $250 of raw materials. Estimated conversion costs to produce 2,000 units in the next year are $300,000. During a recent quarter, the company produced 600 mowers and sold 580 mowers. Each mower is sold for $1,000.

Required

1. Compute the conversion cost rate per mower.
2. Prepare journal entries to record (*a*) purchase of raw materials on credit, (*b*) applied conversion costs to production, (*c*) sale of mowers on credit, and (*d*) cost of goods sold and finished goods inventory.

PROBLEMS

Problem D-1
Lean accounting

P1

Auto-Motion is a lean manufacturer of self-driving wheelchairs. The company budgets $680,000 of conversion costs and 2,000 production hours for the next year. Each wheelchair requires 25 production hours and materials costs of $4,300. The company started and completed 75 wheelchairs during the year and sold 68. Each wheelchair is sold for $15,000. Actual conversion costs equal applied conversion costs.

Required

1. Prepare journal entries to record (*a*) the purchase of raw materials on credit to produce 80 units, (*b*) applied conversion costs to the production of 75 units, (*c*) actual conversion costs of $637,500 (credit "Various Accounts"), (*d*) sale of 68 units on credit, and (*e*) ending inventory and cost of goods sold.
2. Compute the ending balances of Work in Process Inventory, Finished Goods Inventory, and Conversion Costs. Assume each of these inventory accounts began the year with a balance of zero.

Problem D-2
Lean accounting

P1

Ruiz Foods makes energy bars using a traditional manufacturing process. Raw materials are stored in inventory and then moved into production. Work in process inventory is moved across the company's three separate departments. The information below (in the Traditional column) is available for a recent order. If the company adopts lean manufacturing, management believes both move time and wait time can be reduced, as shown in the Lean column.

Problem D-3
Cycle time and cycle efficiency

A1

Activity	Traditional	Lean
Process time	24 hours	24 hours
Inspection time	4 hours	4 hours
Move time	6 hours	3 hours
Wait time	2 hours	1 hour

Required

1. Compute the total amount of non-value-added time under the traditional manufacturing process.
2. Compute cycle efficiency under the traditional manufacturing process. Round to two decimals.
3. Compute the total amount of non-value-added time under the proposed lean manufacturing process.
4. Compute cycle efficiency under the proposed lean manufacturing process. Round to two decimals.
5. Would the proposed lean approach improve cycle efficiency?

Index

Chart of Accounts

Following is a typical chart of accounts, which is used in several assignments. Each company has its own unique set of accounts and numbering system.
*An asterisk denotes a contra account.

Assets

Current Assets

101 Cash
102 Petty cash
103 Cash equivalents
104 Short-term investments
105 Fair value adjustment–_____ (ST)
106 Accounts receivable
107 Allowance for doubtful accounts*
108 Allowance for sales discounts*
109 Interest receivable
110 Rent receivable
111 Notes receivable
112 Legal fees receivable
119 Merchandise inventory (or Inventory)
120 _____ inventory
121 Inventory returns estimated
124 Office supplies
125 Store supplies
126 _____ supplies
128 Prepaid insurance
129 Prepaid interest
131 Prepaid rent
132 Raw materials inventory
133 Work in process inventory, _____
134 Work in process inventory, _____
135 Finished goods inventory
136 Debt investments–Trading (ST)
137 Debt investments–Held-to-maturity (ST)
138 Debt investments–Available-for-sale (ST)
139 Stock investments (ST)

Long-Term Investments

141 Long-term investments
142 Fair value adjustment–_____ (LT)
144 Investment in _____
145 Bond sinking fund
146 Debt investments–Held-to-maturity (LT)
147 Debt investments–Available-for-sale (LT)
148 Stock investments (LT)
149 Equity method investments

Plant Assets

151 Automobiles
152 Accumulated depreciation–Automobiles*
153 Trucks
154 Accumulated depreciation–Trucks*
155 Boats
156 Accumulated depreciation–Boats*
157 Professional library
158 Accumulated depreciation–Professional library*
159 Law library
160 Accumulated depreciation–Law library*

161 Furniture
162 Accumulated depreciation–Furniture*
163 Office equipment
164 Accumulated depreciation–Office equipment*
165 Store equipment
166 Accumulated depreciation–Store equipment*
167 _____ equipment
168 Accumulated depreciation–_____ equipment*
169 Machinery
170 Accumulated depreciation–Machinery*
173 Building _____
174 Accumulated depreciation–Building _____*
175 Building _____
176 Accumulated depreciation–Building _____*
179 Land improvements _____
180 Accumulated depreciation–Land improvements _____*
181 Land improvements _____
182 Accumulated depreciation–Land improvements _____*
183 Land

Natural Resources

185 Mineral deposit
186 Accumulated depletion–Mineral deposit*

Intangible Assets

191 Patents
192 Leasehold
193 Franchise
194 Copyrights
195 Leasehold improvements
196 Licenses
197 Right-of-use asset
198 Accumulated amortization–_____*
199 Goodwill

Liabilities

Current Liabilities

201 Accounts payable
202 Insurance payable
203 Interest payable
204 Legal fees payable
207 Office salaries payable
208 Rent payable
209 Salaries payable
210 Wages payable
211 Accrued payroll payable
212 Factory wages payable

214 Estimated warranty liability
215 Income taxes payable
216 Common dividend payable
217 Preferred dividend payable
218 State unemployment taxes payable
219 Employee federal income taxes payable
221 Employee medical insurance payable
222 Employee retirement program payable
223 Employee union dues payable
224 Federal unemployment taxes payable
225 FICA taxes payable
226 Estimated vacation pay liability
227 Sales refund payable
229 Current portion of long-term debt

Unearned Revenues

230 Unearned consulting fees
231 Unearned legal fees
232 Unearned property management fees
233 Unearned _____ fees
234 Unearned _____ fees
235 Unearned janitorial revenue
236 Unearned _____ revenue
238 Unearned rent

Notes Payable

240 Short-term notes payable
241 Discount on short-term notes payable*
244 Current portion of long-term notes payable
245 Notes payable
251 Long-term notes payable
252 Discount on long-term notes payable*

Long-Term Liabilities

253 Lease liability
255 Bonds payable
256 Discount on bonds payable*
257 Premium on bonds payable
258 Deferred income tax liability

Equity

Owner's Equity

301 _____, Capital
302 _____, Withdrawals
303 _____, Capital
304 _____, Withdrawals
305 _____, Capital
306 _____, Withdrawals

Paid-In Capital

307 Common stock, $ _____ par value
308 Common stock, no-par value
309 Common stock, $ _____ stated value
310 Common stock dividend distributable

311 Paid-in capital in excess of par value, Common stock
312 Paid-in capital in excess of stated value, No-par common stock
313 Paid-in capital from retirement of common stock
314 Paid-in capital, Treasury stock
315 Preferred stock
316 Paid-in capital in excess of par value, Preferred stock

Retained Earnings

318 Retained earnings
319 Cash dividends (or Dividends)
320 Stock dividends

Other Equity Accounts

321 Treasury stock, Common*
322 Unrealized gain–Equity
323 Unrealized loss–Equity

Revenues

401 _____ fees earned
402 _____ fees earned
403 _____ revenues
404 Revenues
405 Commissions earned
406 Rent revenue (or Rent earned)
407 Dividends revenue (or Dividends earned)
408 Earnings from investment in _____
409 Interest revenue (or Interest earned)
410 Sinking fund earnings
413 Sales
414 Sales returns and allowances*
415 Sales discounts*
420 Earnings from equity method investments

Cost of Sales

Cost of Goods Sold

502 Cost of goods sold
505 Purchases
506 Purchases returns and allowances*
507 Purchases discounts*
508 Transportation-in

Manufacturing

520 Raw materials purchases
521 Freight-in on raw materials
530 Direct labor
540 Factory overhead
541 Indirect materials
542 Indirect labor
543 Factory insurance expired
544 Factory supervision
545 Factory supplies used
546 Factory utilities
547 Miscellaneous production costs
548 Property taxes on factory building
549 Property taxes on factory equipment
550 Rent on factory building
551 Repairs, factory equipment
552 Small tools written off
560 Depreciation of factory equipment

561 Depreciation of factory building
570 Conversion costs

Standard Cost Variances

580 Direct material quantity variance
581 Direct material price variance
582 Direct labor quantity variance
583 Direct labor price variance
584 Factory overhead volume variance
585 Factory overhead controllable variance

Expenses

Amortization, Depletion, and Depreciation

601 Amortization expense–_____
602 Amortization expense–_____
603 Depletion expense–_____
604 Depreciation expense–Boats
605 Depreciation expense–Automobiles
606 Depreciation expense–Building _____
607 Depreciation expense–Building _____
608 Depreciation expense–Land improvements _____
609 Depreciation expense–Land improvements _____
610 Depreciation expense–Law library
611 Depreciation expense–Trucks
612 Depreciation expense–_____ equipment
613 Depreciation expense–_____ equipment
614 Depreciation expense–_____
615 Depreciation expense–_____

Employee-Related Expenses

620 Office salaries expense
621 Sales salaries expense
622 Salaries expense
623 _____ wages expense
624 Employee benefits expense
625 Payroll taxes expense

Financial Expenses

630 Cash over and short
631 Discounts lost
632 Factoring fee expense
633 Interest expense

Insurance Expenses

635 Insurance expense–Delivery equipment
636 Insurance expense–Office equipment
637 Insurance expense–_____

Rental Expenses

640 Rent (or Rental) expense
641 Rent expense–Office space
642 Rent expense–Selling space
643 Press rental expense
644 Truck rental expense
645 _____ rental expense

Supplies Expenses

650 Office supplies expense
651 Store supplies expense

652 _____ supplies expense
653 _____ supplies expense

Miscellaneous Expenses

655 Advertising expense
656 Bad debts expense
657 Blueprinting expense
658 Boat expense
659 Collection expense
661 Concessions expense
662 Credit card expense
663 Delivery expense
664 Dumping expense
667 Equipment expense
668 Food and drinks expense
671 Gas and oil expense
672 General and administrative expense
673 Janitorial expense
674 Legal fees expense
676 Mileage expense
677 Miscellaneous expenses
678 Mower and tools expense
679 Operating expense
680 Organization expense
681 Permits expense
682 Postage expense
683 Property taxes expense
684 Repairs expense–_____
685 Repairs expense–_____
687 Selling expense
688 Telephone expense
689 Travel and entertainment expense
690 Utilities expense
691 Warranty expense
692 _____ expense
695 Income tax expense

Gains and Losses

701 Gain on retirement of bonds
702 Gain on sale of machinery
703 Gain on sale of investments
704 Gain on sale of trucks
705 Gain on _____
706 Foreign exchange gain or loss
801 Loss on disposal of machinery
802 Loss on exchange of equipment
803 Loss on exchange of _____
804 Loss on sale of notes
805 Loss on retirement of bonds
806 Loss on sale of investments
807 Loss on sale of machinery
808 Loss on _____
809 Unrealized gain–Income
810 Unrealized loss–Income
811 Impairment gain
812 Impairment loss
815 Gain on sale of debt investments
816 Loss on sale of debt investments
817 Gain on sale of stock investments
818 Loss on sale of stock investments

Clearing Accounts

901 Income summary
902 Manufacturing summary

BRIEF REVIEW: MANAGERIAL ANALYSES AND REPORTS

① Cost Types
Variable costs: Total cost changes in proportion to volume of activity.
Fixed costs: Total cost does not change in proportion to volume of activity.
Mixed costs: Cost consists of both a variable and a fixed element.

② Product Costs
Direct materials: Raw materials costs directly linked to finished product.
Direct labor: Employee costs directly linked to finished product.
Overhead: Production costs indirectly linked to finished product.

③ Costing Systems
Job order costing: Costs assigned to each unique unit or batch of units.
Process costing: Costs assigned to similar products that are mass-produced in a continuous manner.

④ Costing Ratios
Contribution margin ratio = (Net sales − Variable costs)/Net sales
Predetermined overhead rate = Estimated overhead costs/Estimated activity base
Break-even point in units = Total fixed costs/Contribution margin per unit

⑤ Planning and Control Metrics
Cost variance = Actual cost − Standard (budgeted) cost
Sales (revenue) variance = Actual sales − Standard (budgeted) sales

⑥ Capital Budgeting
Payback period = Time expected to recover investment cost
Accounting rate of return = Expected annual net income/Average annual investment
Net present value (NPV) = Present value of future cash flows − Investment cost
NPV rule: 1. Compute net present value (NPV in $).
          2. If NPV > 0, then accept project; If NPV < 0, then reject project.
Internal rate 1. Compute internal rate of return (IRR in %).
of return rule: 2. If IRR > hurdle rate, accept project; If IRR < hurdle rate, reject project.

⑦ Costing Terminology
Relevant range: Organization's normal range of operating activity.
Direct cost: Cost incurred for the benefit of one cost object.
Indirect cost: Cost incurred for the benefit of more than one cost object.
Product cost: Cost that is necessary and integral to finished products.
Period cost: Cost identified more with a time period than with finished products.
Overhead cost: Cost not separately or directly traceable to a cost object.
Relevant cost: Cost that is pertinent to a decision.
Opportunity cost: Benefit lost by choosing an action from two or more alternatives.
Sunk cost: Cost already incurred that cannot be avoided or changed.
Standard cost: Cost computed using standard price and standard quantity.
Budget: Formal statement of an organization's future plans.
Break-even point: Sales level at which an organization earns zero profit.
Incremental cost: Cost incurred only if the organization undertakes a certain action.
Transfer price: Price on transaction between divisions within a company.

⑧ Standard Cost Variances

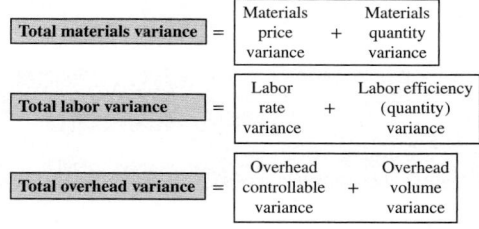

Total materials variance = Materials price variance + Materials quantity variance

Total labor variance = Labor rate variance + Labor efficiency (quantity) variance

Total overhead variance = Overhead controllable variance + Overhead volume variance

Overhead controllable variance = Actual total overhead − Budgeted total overhead
Overhead volume variance = Budgeted fixed overhead − Applied fixed overhead
Variable overhead variance = Variable overhead spending variance + Variable overhead efficiency variance ⎫
Fixed overhead variance = Fixed overhead spending variance + Fixed overhead volume variance ⎬ = Total overhead variance

Materials price variance = [AQ × AP] − [AQ × SP]
Materials quantity variance = [AQ × SP] − [SQ × SP]
Labor rate variance = [AH × AR] − [AH × SR]
Labor efficiency (quantity) variance = [AH × SR] − [SH × SR]

Variable overhead spending variance = [AH × AVR] − [AH × SVR]
Variable overhead efficiency variance = [AH × SVR] − [SH × SVR]
Fixed overhead spending variance = Actual fixed overhead − Budgeted fixed overhead

where AQ is Actual Quantity of materials; AP is Actual Price of materials; AH is Actual Hours of labor; AR is Actual Rate of wages; AVR is Actual Variable Rate of overhead; SQ is Standard Quantity of materials; SP is Standard Price of materials; SH is Standard Hours of labor; SR is Standard Rate of wages; SVR is Standard Variable Rate of overhead.

⑨ Sales Variances

Sales price variance = [AS × AP] − [AS × BP]
Sales volume variance = [AS × BP] − [BS × BP]

where AS = Actual Sales units; AP = Actual sales Price; BP = Budgeted sales Price; BS = Budgeted Sales units (fixed budget).

Schedule of Cost of Goods Manufactured
For *period* Ended *date*

Direct materials		
Raw materials inventory, Beginning	$	#
Raw materials purchases.		#
Raw materials available for use		#
Less raw materials inventory, Ending		(#)
Direct materials used		#
Direct labor.		#
Overhead costs (applied).		#
Total manufacturing costs		#
Add work in process inventory, Beginning		#
Total cost of work in process		#
Less work in process inventory, Ending		(#)
Cost of goods manufactured	$	#

Contribution Margin Income Statement
For *period* Ended *date*

Net sales (revenues).	$	#
Total variable costs.		#
Contribution margin		#
Total fixed costs		#
Net income (pretax)	$	#

Flexible Budget
For *period* Ended *date*

	Flexible Budget		Flexible Budget for Unit Sales of #
	Variable Amount per Unit	Fixed Cost	
Sales (revenues)	$ #		$ #
Variable costs			
Examples: Direct materials, Direct labor,			
Other variable costs	#		#
Total variable costs	#		#
Contribution margin	$ #		#
Fixed costs			
Examples: Depreciation, Property taxes, Manager		$ #	#
salaries, Administrative salaries		#	#
Total fixed costs		$ #	#
Income from operations			$ #

Total flexible budget costs = Total fixed costs + (Total variable costs per unit × Units of activity level)

Budget variance* = Budget amount − Actual amount
  *Applies to both flexible and fixed budgets. *F* = Favorable variance; *U* = Unfavorable variance.

Activity-Based Costing Steps
① Identify activities and the overhead costs they cause.
② Trace overhead costs to activity cost pools.
③ Compute overhead allocation rates for each activity.
④ Use rates to assign overhead costs to cost objects.

Cost pool activity rate = Overhead costs assigned to pool ÷ Expected activity level

Variable and Absorption Costing

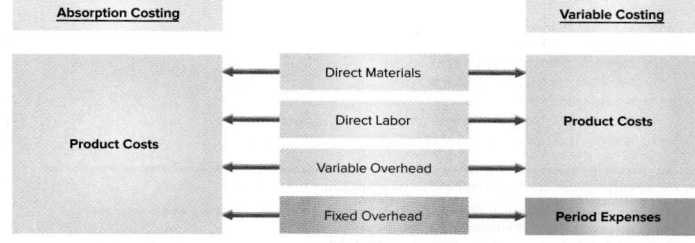

Absorption costing includes fixed overhead in product costs.
Variable costing includes fixed overhead in period expenses.

Master Budget Sequence

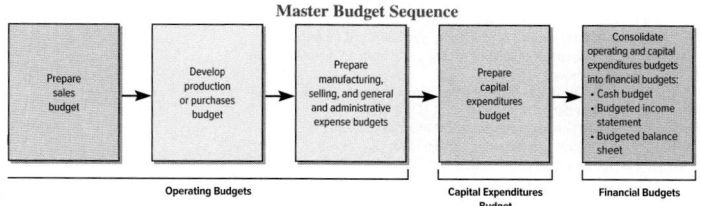

BRIEF REVIEW: FINANCIAL REPORTS AND TABLES

Income Statement*
For *period* Ended *date*

Net sales (revenues)	$	#
Cost of goods sold (cost of sales)		#
Gross margin (gross profit)		#
Operating expenses		
Examples: depreciation, salaries, wages, rent, utilities,	$ #	
interest, amortization, advertising, insurance,	#	
taxes, selling, general and administrative	#	
Total operating expenses		#
Nonoperating gains and losses (unusual and/or infrequent)		#
Net income (net profit or earnings)		$ #

*A typical chart of accounts is at the end of the book and classifies all accounts by financial statement categories.

Balance Sheet
Date

ASSETS

Current assets

Examples: cash, cash equivalents, short-term investments,	$	#
accounts receivable, current portion of notes receivable,		#
inventory, inventory returns estimated, prepaid expenses		#
Total current assets	$	#

Long-term investments

Examples: investment in stock, investment in bonds,		#
land for expansion		#
Total long-term investments		#

Plant assets

Examples: equipment, machinery, buildings, land		#
Total plant assets, net of depreciation		#

Intangible assets

Examples: patent, trademark, copyright, license, right-of-use, goodwill		#
Total intangible assets, net of amortization		#
Total assets		$ #

LIABILITIES AND EQUITY

Current liabilities

Examples: accounts payable, wages payable, salaries payable,	$	#
current notes payable, taxes payable, interest payable,		#
unearned revenues, current portion of debt, sales refund payable		#
Total current liabilities	$	#

Long-term liabilities

Examples: notes payable, bonds payable, lease liability		#
Total long-term liabilities		#
Total liabilities		#

Equity

Common stock		#
Paid-in capital in excess of par (or stated value)		#
Retained earnings		#
Less treasury stock		(#)
Total equity		#
Total liabilities and equity		$ #

Statement of Cash Flows
For *period* Ended *date*

Cash flows from operating activities		
[Prepared using the indirect (see below)† or direct method]		
Net cash provided (used) by operating activities	$	#
Cash flows from investing activities		
[List of individual investing inflows and outflows]		
Net cash provided (used) by investing activities		#
Cash flows from financing activities		
[List of individual financing inflows and outflows]		
Net cash provided (used) by financing activities		#
Net increase (decrease) in cash	$	#
Cash (and equivalents) balance at beginning of period		#
Cash (and equivalents) balance at end of period		$ #

Attach separate schedule or note disclosure of "Noncash investing and financing transactions."

†Indirect Method: Cash Flows from Operating Activities

Cash flows from operating activities		
Net income	$	#
Adjustments for operating items not providing or using cash		
+Noncash expenses and losses	$ #	
Examples: Expenses for depreciation, depletion, and amortization; losses from disposal of long-term assets and from retirement of debt		
−Noncash revenues and gains	#	
Examples: Gains from disposal of long-term assets and from retirement of debt		
Adjustments for changes in current assets and current liabilities		
+Decrease in noncash current operating asset	#	
−Increase in noncash current operating asset	#	
+Increase in current operating liability	#	
−Decrease in current operating liability	#	
Net cash provided (used) by operating activities		$ #

Statement of Retained Earnings
For *period* Ended *date*

Retained earnings, beginning	$	#
Add: Net income		#
		#
Less: Dividends declared		#
Net loss (if exists)		#
Retained earnings, ending		$ #

Statement of Stockholders' Equity†
For *period* Ended *date*

	Common Stock	Capital in Excess of Par	Retained Earnings	Treasury Stock	Total
Balances, beginning	$ #	$ #	$ #	$ #	$ #
Net income					
Cash dividends					
Stock issuance					
Treasury stock purchase					
Treasury stock reissuance					
Other					
Balances, ending	$ #	$ #	$ #	$ #	$ #

† Additional columns and account titles commonly include number of shares, preferred stock, unrealized gains and losses on available-for-sale securities, foreign currency translation, and comprehensive income.

Premium Bond Amortization (Straight-Line) Table*

Semiannual Period-End	Unamortized Bond Premium†	Bond Carrying Value‡
Bond life-start	$ #	$ #
....		
Bond life-end	0	par

*Bond carrying value is adjusted downward to par and its amortized premium downward to zero over the bond life (note: carrying value less unamortized bond premium equals par).
†Equals total bond premium less its accumulated amortization.
‡Equals bond par value plus its unamortized bond premium.

Discount Bond Amortization (Straight-Line) Table*

Semiannual Period-End	Unamortized Bond Discount†	Bond Carrying Value‡
Bond life-start	$ #	$ #
....		
Bond life-end	0	par

*Bond carrying value is adjusted upward to par and its amortized discount downward to zero over the bond life (note: unamortized bond discount plus carrying value equals par).
†Equals total bond discount less its accumulated amortization.
‡Equals bond par value less its unamortized bond discount.

Effective Interest Amortization Table for Bonds with Semiannual Interest Payment

Semiannual Interest Period-End	Cash Interest Paid[A]	Bond Interest Expense[B]	Discount or Premium Amortization[C]	Unamortized Discount or Premium[D]	Carrying Value[E]
#	#	#	#	#	#

[A]Par value multiplied by the semiannual contract rate.
[B]Prior period's carrying value multiplied by the semiannual market rate.
[C]The difference between interest paid and bond interest expense.
[D]Prior period's unamortized discount or premium less the current period's discount or premium amortization.
[E]Par value less unamortized discount or plus unamortized premium.

Installment Notes Payment Table

Period Ending Date	Beginning Balance	*Debit* Interest Expense	+	*Debit* Notes Payable	=	*Credit* Cash	Ending Balance
#	#	#		#		#	#

Bank Reconciliation
Date

Bank statement balance	$#	Book balance		$#
Add: Deposits in transit	#	Add: Interest earned & unrecorded cash receipts		#
Bank errors understating the balance	#	Book errors understating the balance		#
Less: Outstanding checks	#	Less: Bank fees & NSF checks		#
Bank errors overstating the balance	#	Book errors overstating the balance		#
Adjusted bank balance	$#	**Adjusted book balance**		$#

Balances are equal (reconciled)

BRIEF REVIEW: SELECTED TRANSACTIONS AND RELATIONS

① Merchandising Transactions Summary—Perpetual Inventory System

	Merchandising Transactions	Merchandising Entries	Dr.	Cr.
Purchases	Purchasing merchandise for resale.	Merchandise Inventory	#	
		Cash or Accounts Payable		#
	Paying freight costs on purchases; FOB shipping point.	Merchandise Inventory	#	
		Cash		#
	Paying within discount period.	Accounts Payable	#	
		Merchandise Inventory................		#
		Cash		#
	Paying outside discount period.	Accounts Payable	#	
		Cash		#
	Recording purchases returns or allowances.	Cash or Accounts Payable..............	#	
		Merchandise Inventory................		#
Sales	Selling merchandise.	Cash or Accounts Receivable	#	
		Sales		#
		Cost of Goods Sold	#	
		Merchandise Inventory................		#
	Receiving payment within discount period.	Cash	#	
		Sales Discounts	#	
		Accounts Receivable		#
	Receiving payment outside discount period.	Cash	#	
		Accounts Receivable		#
	Receiving sales returns of nondefective inventory.	Sales Returns and Allowances	#	
		Cash or Accounts Receivable		#
		Merchandise Inventory	#	
		Cost of Goods Sold		#
	Recognizing sales allowances.	Sales Returns and Allowances	#	
		Cash or Accounts Receivable		#
	Paying freight costs on sales; FOB destination.	Delivery Expense.......................	#	
		Cash		#

	Merchandising Events	Adjusting and Closing Entries	Dr.	Cr.
Adjusting	Adjustment for shrinkage (occurs when recorded amount larger than physical inventory).	Cost of Goods Sold	#	
		Merchandise Inventory................		#
	Period-end adjustment for expected sales discounts.*	Sales Discounts....................	#	
		Allowance for Sales Discounts.........		#
	Period-end adjustment for expected returns—both revenue side and cost side.*	Sales Returns and Allowances	#	
		Sales Refund Payable.............		#
		Inventory Returns Estimated................	#	
		Cost of Goods Sold		#
Closing	Closing temporary accounts with credit balances.	Sales	#	
		Income Summary		#
	Closing temporary accounts with debit balances.	Income Summary	#	
		Sales Returns and Allowances..........		#
		Sales Discounts.....................		#
		Cost of Goods Sold		#
		Delivery Expense		#
		"Other Expenses"....................		#

*Period-end adjustments depend on unadjusted balances, which can reverse the debit and credit in the adjusting entries shown; the entries in gray are covered in Appendix 4B.

⑥ Stock Transactions Summary

	Stock Transactions	Stock Entries	Dr.	Cr.
Issue Common Stock	Issue par value common stock at par (par stock recorded at par).	Cash...........................	#	
		Common Stock....................		#
	Issue par value common stock at premium (par stock recorded at par).	Cash...........................	#	
		Common Stock....................		#
		Paid-In Capital in Excess of Par Value, Common Stock		#
	Issue no-par value common stock (no-par stock recorded at amount received).	Cash...........................	#	
		Common Stock....................		#
	Issue stated value common stock at stated value (stated stock recorded at stated value).	Cash...........................	#	
		Common Stock		#
	Issue stated value common stock at premium (stated stock recorded at stated value).	Cash...........................	#	
		Common Stock		#
		Paid-In Capital in Excess of Stated Value, Common Stock		#
Issue Preferred Stock	Issue par value preferred stock at par (par stock recorded at par).	Cash...........................	#	
		Preferred Stock		#
	Issue par value preferred stock at premium (par stock recorded at par).	Cash...........................	#	
		Preferred Stock		#
		Paid-In Capital in Excess of Par Value, Preferred Stock		#
Reacquire Common Stock	Reacquire its own common stock (treasury stock recorded at cost).	Treasury Stock, Common	#	
		Cash.............................		#
Reissue Common Stock	Reissue its treasury stock at cost (treasury stock removed at cost).	Cash.............................	#	
		Treasury Stock, Common		#
	Reissue its treasury stock above cost (treasury stock removed at cost).	Cash.............................	#	
		Treasury Stock, Common		#
		Paid-In Capital, Treasury..........		#
	Reissue its treasury stock below cost (treasury stock removed at cost; if paid-in capital is insufficient to cover amount below cost, retained earnings is debited for remainder).	Cash.............................	#	
		Paid-In Capital, Treasury............	#	
		Retained Earnings (if necessary)	#	
		Treasury Stock, Common		#

② Merchandising Cash Flows

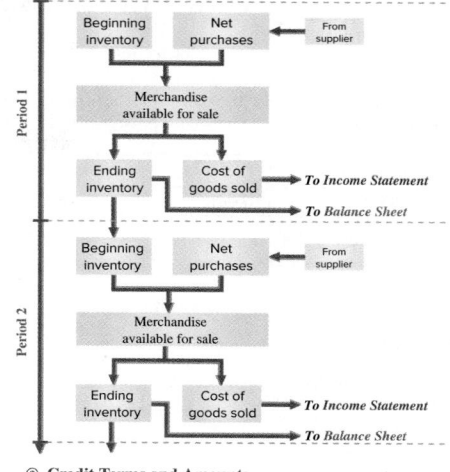

③ Credit Terms and Amounts

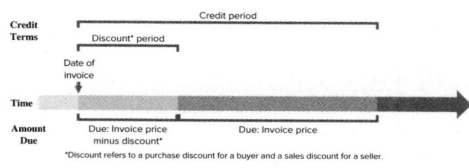

*Discount refers to a purchase discount for a buyer and a sales discount for a seller.

④ Bad Debts Estimation

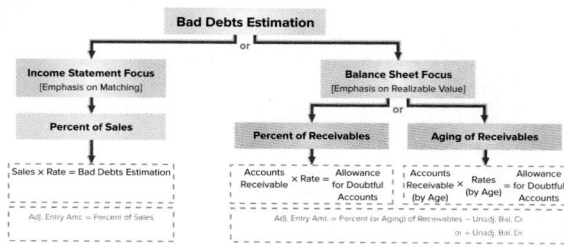

⑤ Bond Valuation

Bond Sets · **Market Sets** · **Bond Price Determined**

Contract rate

Market rate

Contract rate > Market rate ➡ Bond sells at premium

Contract rate = Market rate ➡ Bond sells at par

Contract rate < Market rate ➡ Bond sells at discount

⑦ Financial Statement Effects of Dividends and Splits

	Cash Dividend	Small Stock Dividend	Large Stock Dividend	Stock Split
Total assets	Decrease	No change	No change	No change
Total liabilities	No change	No change	No change	No change
Total stockholders' equity	Decrease	No change	No change	No change
Common stock		Increase	Increase	No change
Paid-in capital in excess of par	No change	Increase	No change	No change
Retained earnings	Decrease	Decrease	Decrease	No change

⑧ A Rose by Any Other Name

The same financial statement sometimes receives different titles. Following are some of the more common aliases.*

Balance Sheet	Statement of Financial Position Statement of Financial Condition
Income Statement	Statement of Income Operating Statement Statement of Operations Statement of Operating Activity Earnings Statement Statement of Earnings Profit and Loss (P&L) Statement
Statement of Cash Flows	Statement of Cash Flow Cash Flows Statement Statement of Changes in Cash Position Statement of Changes in Financial Position
Statement of Stockholders' Equity	Statement of Shareholders' Equity Statement of Changes in Shareholders' Equity Statement of Stockholders' Equity and Comprehensive Income Statement of Changes in Owner's Equity Statement of Changes in Owner's Capital Statement of Changes in Capital Accounts

*The term **Consolidated** often precedes or follows these statement titles to reflect the combination of different entities, such as a parent company and its subsidiaries.

FUNDAMENTALS

① Accounting Equation

Assets	=	Liabilities	+	Equity

Debit for increases ↑	Credit for decreases ↓	Debit for decreases ↓	Credit for increases ↑	Debit for decreases ↓	Credit for increases ↑

Contributed Capital* + Retained Earnings

Common Stock	− Dividends	+ Revenues	− Expenses

Dr. for decreases	Cr. for increases ↑	Dr. for increases ↑	Cr. for decreases	Dr. for decreases	Cr. for increases ↑	Dr. for increases ↑	Cr. for decreases

▉ Indicates normal balance.
*Includes common stock and any preferred stock.

② Accounting Cycle

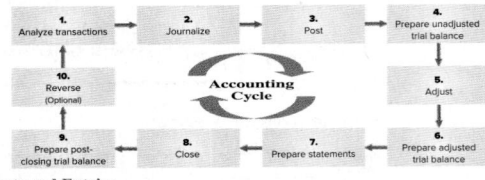

1. Analyze transactions
2. Journalize
3. Post
4. Prepare unadjusted trial balance
5. Adjust
6. Prepare adjusted trial balance
7. Prepare statements
8. Close
9. Prepare post-closing trial balance
10. Reverse (Optional)

Accounting Cycle

③ Adjustments and Entries

Type	Adjusting Entry	
Prepaid Expenses	Dr. Expense	Cr. Asset*
Unearned Revenues	Dr. Liability	Cr. Revenue
Accrued Expenses	Dr. Expense	Cr. Liability
Accrued Revenues	Dr. Asset	Cr. Revenue

*For depreciation, credit Accumulated Depreciation (contra asset).

④ Four-Step Closing Process

1. Transfer revenue and gain account balances to Income Summary.
2. Transfer expense and loss account balances to Income Summary.
3. Transfer Income Summary balance to Retained Earnings.
4. Transfer Dividends balance to Retained Earnings.

⑤ Accounting Concepts

Characteristics	Assumptions	Principles	Constraints
Relevance	Business entity	Measurement	Cost-benefit
Faithful representation	Going concern	Revenue recognition	*Materiality*
	Monetary unit	Expense recognition	*Industry practice*
	Time period	Full disclosure	*Conservatism*

⑥ Ownership of Inventory

Shipping Terms	Ownership Transfers at	Goods in Transit Owned by	Transportation Costs Paid by
FOB shipping point	Shipping point	Buyer	**Buyer** Merchandise Inventory . . . # Cash . . . . #
FOB destination	Destination	Seller	**Seller** Delivery Expense . . . . # Cash . . . . #

⑦ Inventory Costing Methods

- Specific identification (SI)
- First-in, first-out (FIFO)
- Weighted-average (WA)
- Last-in, first-out (LIFO)

⑧ Depreciation and Depletion

Straight-line: $\dfrac{\text{Cost} - \text{Salvage value}}{\text{Useful life in periods}}$

Units-of-production: $\dfrac{\text{Cost} - \text{Salvage value}}{\text{Useful life in units}} \times \text{Units produced in current period}$

Declining-balance: Rate* × Beginning-of-period book value
*Rate is often double the straight-line rate, or 2 × (1/Useful life)

Depletion: $\dfrac{\text{Cost} - \text{Salvage value}}{\text{Total capacity in units}} \times \text{Units extracted in current period}$

⑨ Interest Computation

Interest = Principal (face) × Rate × Time

⑩ Accounting for Investment Securities

Classification	Investments Account Reported at
Short-Term Investment in Securities	
Debt Investments—Held-to-Maturity	Cost (without any discount or premium amortization)
Debt Investments—Trading	**Fair value** (with fair value adjustment to income)
Debt Investments—Available-for-Sale	**Fair value** (with fair value adjustment to equity)
Stock Investments—insignificant influence	**Fair value** (with fair value adjustment to income)
Long-Term Investment in Securities	
Debt Investments—Held-to-Maturity	Cost (with any discount or premium amortization)
Debt Investments—Available-for-Sale	**Fair value** (with fair value adjustment to equity)
Stock Investments—insignificant influence	**Fair value** (with fair value adjustment to income)
Equity Method Investments—significant influence	Equity method (no fair value adjustment)
Consolidated Investments—controlling influence	Consolidation method (no fair value adjustment)

ANALYSES

① Liquidity and Efficiency

Current ratio $= \dfrac{\text{Current assets}}{\text{Current liabilities}}$ pp. 108 & 506

Working capital = Current assets − Current liabilities   p. 506

Acid-test ratio $= \dfrac{\text{Cash} + \text{Short-term investments} + \text{Current receivables}}{\text{Current liabilities}}$ pp. 159 & 507

Accounts receivable turnover $= \dfrac{\text{Net sales}}{\text{Average accounts receivable, net}}$ pp. 285 & 507

Inventory turnover $= \dfrac{\text{Cost of goods sold}}{\text{Average inventory}}$ pp. 203 & 507

Days' sales uncollected $= \dfrac{\text{Accounts receivable, net}}{\text{Net sales}} \times 365^{*}$ pp. 250 & 508

Days' sales in inventory $= \dfrac{\text{Ending inventory}}{\text{Cost of goods sold}} \times 365^{*}$ pp. 203 & 508

Days' payable outstanding (or Days' sales in payables) $= \dfrac{\text{Accounts payable}}{\text{Cost of goods sold}} \times 365^{*}$ p. 884

Cash conversion cycle $= \dfrac{\text{Days' sales}}{\text{uncollected}} + \dfrac{\text{Days' sales}}{\text{in inventory}} - \dfrac{\text{Days' payable}}{\text{outstanding}}$ p. 884

Total asset turnover $= \dfrac{\text{Net sales}}{\text{Average total assets}}$ pp. 320 & 508

Plant asset useful life $= \dfrac{\text{Plant asset cost}}{\text{Depreciation expense}}$

Plant asset age $= \dfrac{\text{Accumulated depreciation}}{\text{Depreciation expense}}$

*360 days is also commonly used.

② Solvency

Debt ratio $= \dfrac{\text{Total liabilities}}{\text{Total assets}}$ Equity ratio $= \dfrac{\text{Total equity}}{\text{Total assets}}$ p. 62

Debt-to-equity $= \dfrac{\text{Total liabilities}}{\text{Total equity}}$ pp. 392 & 509

Times interest earned $= \dfrac{\text{Income before interest expense and income taxes}}{\text{Interest expense}}$ pp. 354 & 509

③ Profitability

Profit margin ratio $= \dfrac{\text{Net income}}{\text{Net sales}}$ pp. 108 & 509

Gross margin ratio $= \dfrac{\text{Net sales} - \text{Cost of goods sold}}{\text{Net sales}}$ p. 159

Return on total assets $= \dfrac{\text{Net income}}{\text{Average total assets}}$ pp. 18 & 509

$= \text{Profit margin ratio} \times \text{Total asset turnover}$ p. C-13

Return on common stockholders' equity $= \dfrac{\text{Net income} - \text{Preferred dividends}}{\text{Average common stockholders' equity}}$ p. 510

Book value per common share $= \dfrac{\text{Stockholders' equity applicable to common shares}}{\text{Number of common shares outstanding}}$ p. 433

Basic earnings per share $= \dfrac{\text{Net income} - \text{Preferred dividends}}{\text{Weighted-average common shares outstanding}}$ p. 432

Cash flow on total assets $= \dfrac{\text{Cash flow from operations}}{\text{Average total assets}}$ p. 467

Payout ratio $= \dfrac{\text{Cash dividends declared on common stock}}{\text{Net income}}$ p. 433

④ Market

Price-earnings ratio $= \dfrac{\text{Market price per share}}{\text{Earnings per share}}$ pp. 432 & 510

Dividend yield $= \dfrac{\text{Annual cash dividends per share}}{\text{Market price per share}}$ pp. 433 & 510

Residual income = Net income − Target net income   p. 878